A NEW HISTORY OF PHOTOGRAPHY

CONTRIBUTORS:
Pierre Albert, Stuart Alexander, Hubertus von Amelunxen,
Sylvie Aubenas, Anne Cartier-Bresson, Peter Bunnell,
Françoise Ducros, Gilles Feyel, Michel Frizot, Jean-Claude Gautrand,
Thomas Michael Gunther, Anne Hammond, Andreas Haus,
Françoise Heilbrun, Ian Jeffrey, Thilo Koenig, Yves Michaud,
Chihiro Minato, Molly Nesbit, Elvire Perego, John Pultz,
Shelley Rice, Pierre-Marc Richard, Fred Ritchin, Jean Sagne,
Timm Starl, Pierre Vaisse, Mike Weaver, Colin Westerbeck.

Claire Bustarret, Anne Lilensztein,
Joël Petitjean, Patrick Roegiers.

BIBLIOGRAPHY: Fred and Elizabeth Pajerski.

CONCEPT AND CHOICE OF ILLUSTRATIONS: Michel Frizot.

DESIGN AND LAYOUT: Jérôme Faucheux.

PICTURE RESEARCH: Elvire Perego.
PRODUCTION COORDINATOR: Maryse Hubert.
PHOTOGRAPHIC WORK: Sylvain Pelly, Hervé Jézéquel.

EDITORIAL PRODUCTION: Éditions Adam Biro.

TRANSLATION FROM FRENCH: Susan Bennett, Liz Clegg, John Crook, Caroline Higgitt.
TRANSLATION FROM GERMAN: Helen Atkins.
EDITOR OF THE ENGLISH LANGUAGE EDITION: Colin Harding.
PROJECT MANAGERS: Stephan Küffner and Bettina Kaufmann.
TYPESETTING: Goodfellow & Egan.
PRODUCTION MANAGER: Detlev Schaper.
ASSISTANT: Nicola Leurs.
PRINTING AND BINDING: Amilcare Pizzi, Milan.
Printed in Italy
ISBN 3-8290-1328-0

10 9 8 7 6 5 4 3 2 1

A NEW HISTORY OF PHOTOGRAPHY

EDITED BY MICHEL FRIZOT

KÖNEMANN

ACKNOWLEDGMENTS

This project would not have been possible without the Arts Commission of the Centre National du Livre, whose strong interest in photography has given new life to an often neglected field of creation. I wish to thank the people who were in charge of putting together this collection for their valuable judgement and concerted efforts, in particular Jean Gattégno and Michel Richard. My thanks also go to two publishers, Adam Biro and Bordas, who have in turn undertaken this courageous venture in the field of photographic documentation with is surprisingly still somewhat disorganised. I would also especially like to thank Adam Biro, Philippe Fournier-Bourdier, Nathalie Michel, Brigitte Videcoq, Maryse Hubert, Muriel Chalandre, the translators Jeanne Bouniort, Denis-Armand Canal, Valérie Morlot, Christian Martin Diebold, Rose-Marie Makino-Fayolle, and the proofreaders Gérard Haller, François Raymond, and Dominique Lahaussois.

The elegant and attractive design in which this collection of texts and images is presented today would not have been possible without the close collaboration of Jérôme Faucheux, whose constant dedication was indispensable for achieving visual clarity while maintaining full respect for the works of art. I am similarly grateful to Lisa Faucheux and Erwan Gauthier.

I owe special thanks to all the lenders, collectors and institutions, the staff in charge of reproduction (in particular at the International Museum of Photography at George Eastman House, Rochester, the Harry Ransom Humanities Research Center/University of Texas, Austin, the J. Paul Getty Museum, Malibu, the Royal Photographic Society, Bath, the Musée d'Orsay, Paris, the Bibliothèque Nationale, Paris, and the Société Française de Photographie, Paris), as well as to all the individuals who have helped us to find particular information or images, or who showed patience and understanding in circumstances at times difficult.

My personal gratitude goes to all the people who lent support to this project, which could not have been realised without their friendship, presence and kindness, or their conversation and advice: Hubertus von Ameluxen, Stuart Alexander, Martine d'Astier, Hélène Baltrusaitis, Raymond Bellour, Françoise Bonnefoy, Roxane Debuisson, Robert Delpire, Françoise Ducros, Guy Duhoux, Anne-Laure Frizot, Julien Frizot, Anne Hammond, André Jammes, Maurice Lecomte, Pietro Morelli, Dominique Païni, Eugenia Parry Janis, Valérie Morlot, Elvire Perego, Shelley Rice, Pierre-Marc Richard, Benoît Rivero, and Mike Weaver. I would particularly like to thank Daniel and Mireille Raimboux for their unstinting hospitality, as well as Eric Poitevin and Patou Diez, Balthus the cat and his feline court in Mangiennes.

I am grateful to all the contributors who have agreed to participate in writing this book, and who took interest in the project in spite of the drawbacks and inconveniences involved in producing a collective work.

I would also like to express my gratitude for the indispensable encouragement offered by André Jammes and Eugenia Parry Janis, whose example has shown me that the history of photography derives primarily from the pleasure of seeing and directly communicating with original works, whether they are acknowledged works of art or amateur creations. I also thank my students who, perhaps unawares, have helped me to develop my understanding of photography.

Finally, I would like to dedicate this book to the memory of two friends who are no longer with us, but whose rigorous judgement has nourished this research from afar: Jurgis Baltrusaitis, who taught us how to read images and the complexity of meanings; and Edouard Doerr, who inspired us to unearth the traces of former know-how in the very surface of images.

Michel Frizot

NOTE

The titles, subtitles and introductory texts of each chapter are by the general editor. The captions give the name of the photographer where this is known, the title featured on the original prints or the title indicated by the lender or, failing this, a straightforward description, the date (as precise as possible), and the location of the original image. Photographic credits are indicated at the end of the volume.

All illustrations reproduced in this work are protected by copyright. The publishers gratefully acknowledge permission to reproduce illustrations on the pages indicated by the bodies listed on page 776. The compilers and publishers have taken pains to locate all copyright owners. In certain cases, they have been unsuccessful. Claims of right should be addressed to the publishers.

FOREWORD

The inspiration for this volume was an observation by the Commission for Arts of the Centre National du Livre, part of the French Ministry of Culture, that there was no book produced in France dealing with the history of photography and quite independent of volumes commissioned in other countries in recent decades – an omission all the more regrettable because 1989 was the official 150th anniversary of photography. The options considered to rectify this state of affairs took account of the few existing works, and the proposals which were submitted to the Commission were based on the most recent studies which over the past ten years had led to a new awareness of photography, its role in society, and its historical evolution.

This book is not an anthology of the lives of the great photographers, nor a collection of the best contemporary photographs, nor a sounding-board for recognized celebrities. It is a book conceived as such – both in its images and its text – and readable at two levels: a collection of images chosen to illustrate visual continuity and changes while demonstrating the relevance of the author's viewpoint, combined with texts providing historical and analytical information with which the reader may confront their own knowledge, for greater understanding.

Consequently, the illustrations were not chosen to "represent" such and such a photographer, nor as a summary of their "style" (even supposing that the notion of style in photography is as valid as it may be in painting). It would be fruitless to undertake a statistical study of the illustrations or to consider what has been omitted. Sometimes this resulted from refusals on the part of photographers or their financial demands. Within the limits set by the editor and those who commissioned the work, for whose generosity we are indeed grateful, we have tried to render justice to all, to pure art forms as well as to the spontaneity of popular practice. Photography is only the fragile product of a black box pointed more or less in the right direction, and held more or less steady. The individual working the apparatus varies greatly in their level of skill.

In the end, it is more important for us to know why people take photographs (well or badly) than to show how to take good photographs. This book is an exploration of a type of image which can, at the same time, be considered exotic despite its familiarity, be suspected of taking away part of one's soul, be the bearer of a memory, arouse mental images, and provoke desire or repulsion. It is by referring to this ambiguity of photographs, their centrifugal dynamic rather than their classification into categories, that we chose the images for each chapter. This was not, in any case, a question of finding "illustrations" to support the text, but of "photo-mechanical reproductions of photographs" which were as close as possible to the original images, even if they could claim to replace the originals only by an effort of the imagination.

As for the general scheme which guided the commissioning of texts and the selection of subjects, three levels of presentation emerged: chapters, which generally deal with a specific period, social practice, contextual analysis or a purely "photographic" concept popular during a particular period; dossiers, which at regular intervals provide an "enlarged" view of a particular theme, by means of a greater number of images which explore that theme in detail; and boxes, which dwell more fully on particular historical questions, influential innovations or aesthetic turning-points. The chapters set the chronological and intellectual framework and provide the historical and aesthetic analysis, renewing perspectives in a way commensurate with the growth of our knowledge of photography. The dossiers provide a cross-section of the real corpus of photography by partially reconstructing a series of images or by bringing a selection of images together. The boxes provide precise scientific information, articulate historic moments or bring out the role of an important figure in photography or the appearance of a new technique. It is in this clearly presented interplay that we hope to have done justice both to the attractive nature of each photograph and to the constant coherence of the medium.

CONTENTS

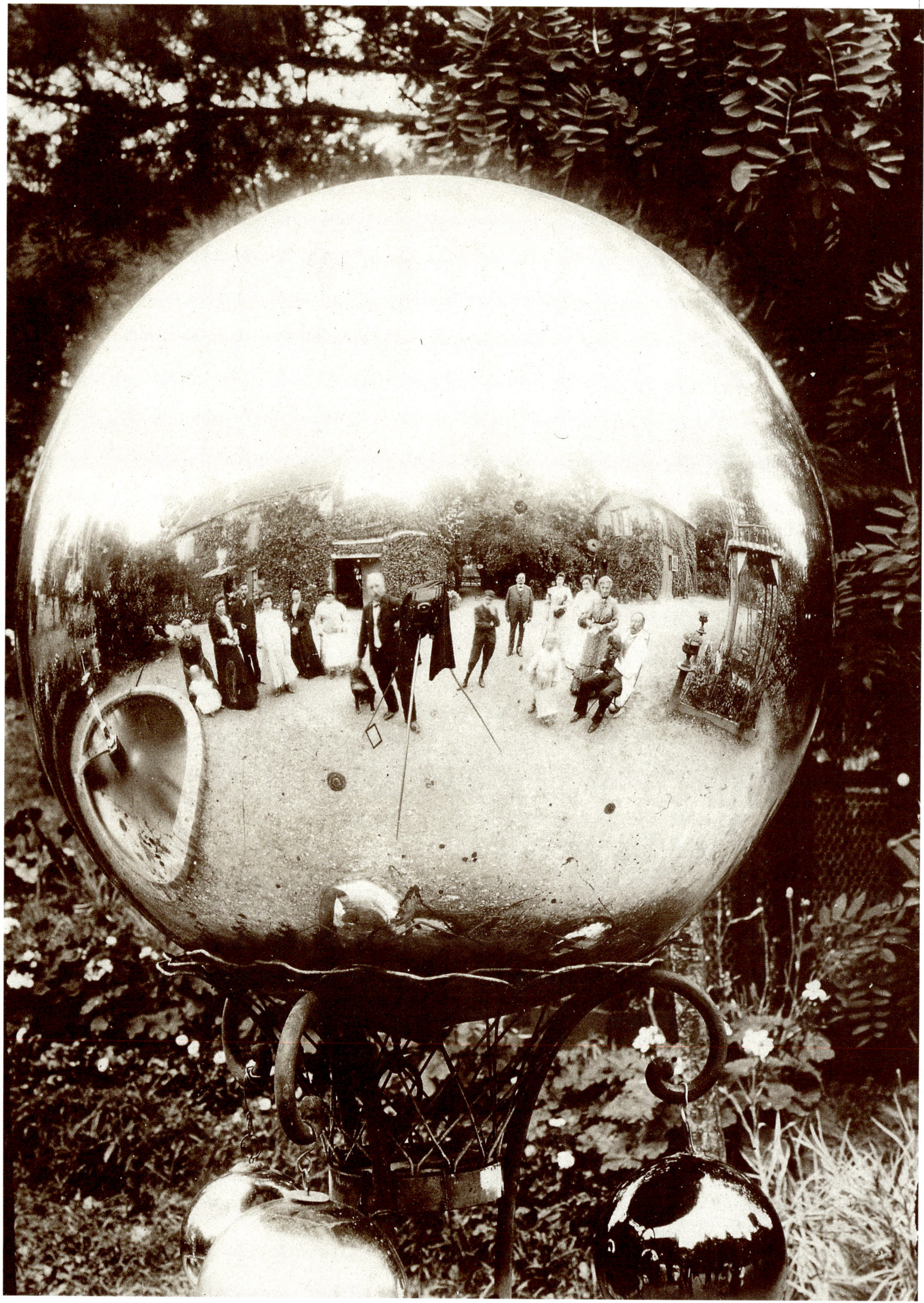

INTRODUCTION

The age of light

Michel Frizot

At the very beginning of the novel *Bouvard et Pécuchet*, Flaubert, describing Bouvard's apartment, observes that on the chest of drawers, "flanking the looking-glass, were daguerreotypes portraying his friends". A little further on in the story Bouvard receives from the notary a letter informing him of the inheritance which will decide the destiny of the two accomplices. According to Flaubert, "it was January 20, 1839"; the notary's letter was dated January 14, 1839.[1]

It was precisely one week earlier, on January 7, that the French Academy of Sciences first became aware of a completely new process which was given the name of daguerreotype. Yet at that date not a single portrait had been produced by the process, which was not sensitive enough for this application. The presence of daguerreotypes in the bedroom of someone like Bouvard would be historically plausible only from the end of the 1840s. Although they were commoner at the time that Flaubert was writing his novel (1874), they would still be much more appropriate in a bourgeois home than in that of a minor civil servant.

Flaubert was by no means ignorant of photographic techniques (during his trip to Egypt in 1849–1851 he was accompanied by his friend Maxime Du Camp, who, equipped with his camera, produced numerous paper negatives there). For want, no doubt, of precise documentation Flaubert simply did not possess a particularly clear idea of the place of the daguerreotype in history, in the period during which his literary creation lived.

In some ways, undertaking a history of photography today is rather like being a writer: seeking out information, collecting images, and writing a kind of adventure story – the life of photographs – creating reality while avoiding historical blunders, putting images in their proper place, and relocating the world of people like Bouvard and Pécuchet *around* images.

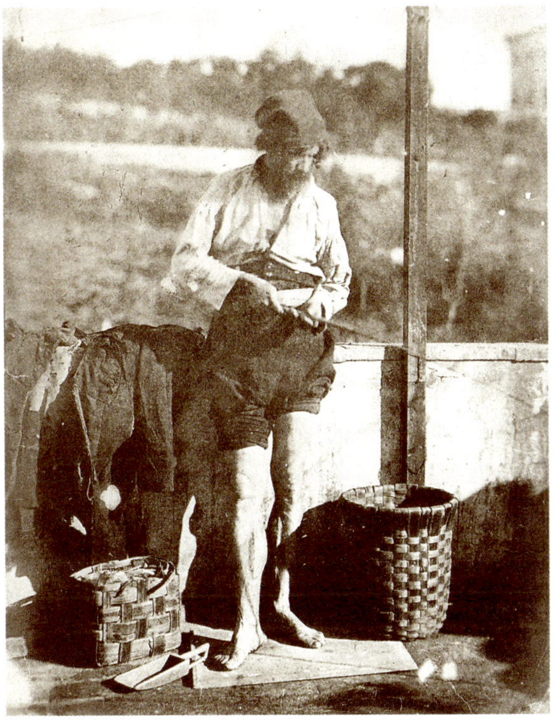

GIACOMO CANEVA, (attributed), ***Fisherman, Southern Italy,*** from a paper negative, 1850s, private collection.

History and historiography

◀ ANONYMOUS AMATEUR, circa 1910, private collection.

The difficulty of writing a history of photography derives in the first place from the supremacy of the model in the history of art, specifically in the history of painting, a model about which one does not always know what to expect, but already used – and by renowned figures – to justify its hierarchical value. This omnipresent reference point inevitably raises the difficult question of the relationship of photography to art, a debate which has raged from the mid-nineteenth century. Their relations were marked by rivalry, denunciation, and anathema, without any real respite and without any forum in which constructive discussion could take place.

Photographs, being monochrome images on paper, were from the outset perceived as graphical documents akin to drawings, lithographs, and

1. G. Flaubert, *Bouvard et Pécuchet*, Paris, Gallimard, 1979, p. 57 and pp. 62–63.

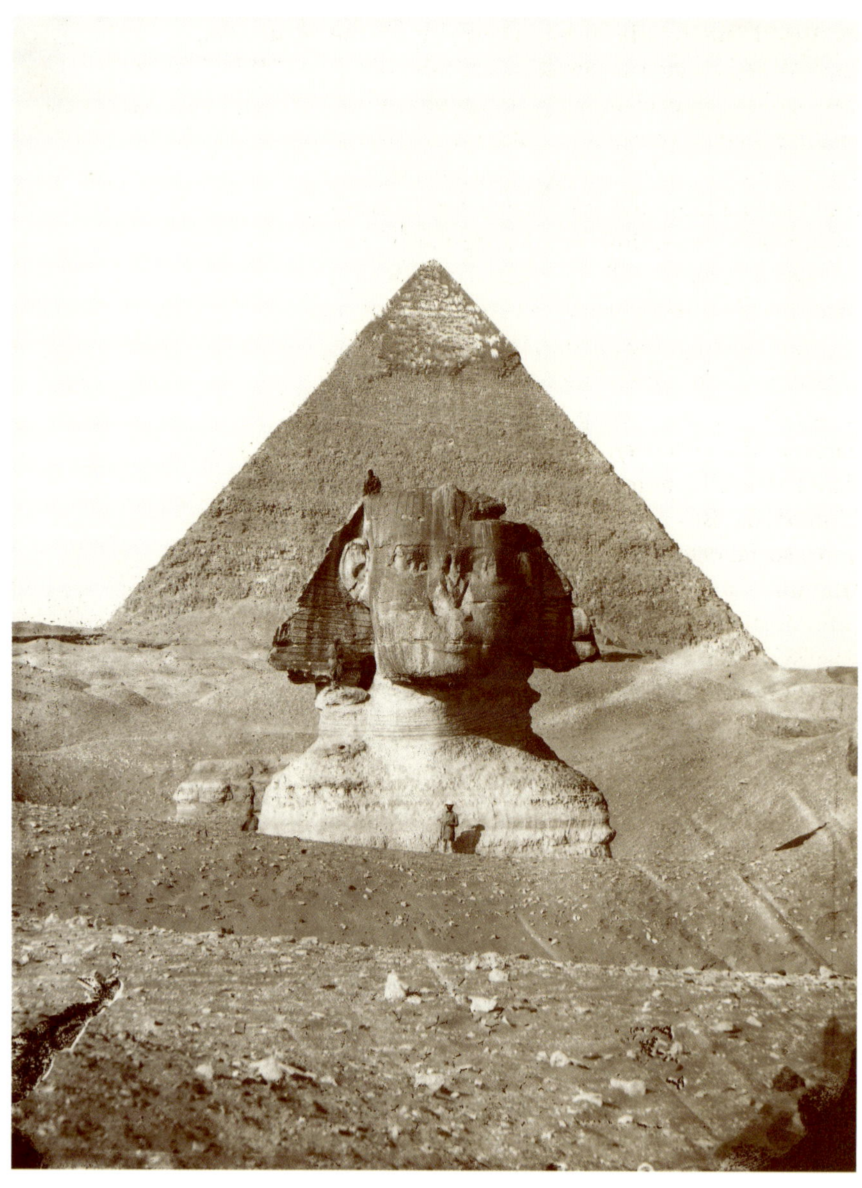

AYMARD DE BANVILLE, *Giza: Sphinx and Pyramid of Khephren*, 1863.

engravings, a categorization reinforced by the illustrative use made of them. But this put photography merely in the role of an artistic accessory, "the humble servant of the arts", as Baudelaire called it in his critique of the 1859 Salon. Fortunately, photographs remained on the sidelines, as much because of their method of production and usage as their significance as images. The history of photography may therefore be traced by assuming this difference, and recognizing that this process has an ontological significance. While the history of painting was an analysis of the variables of formal or iconographical codes, the history of photography has had to invent for itself reasons for existence which are not merely a vague way of capturing the world in images.

For while a photograph is certainly a document, and an historical one at that – in which the date and current peculiarities form, as it were, a water-mark – it is also a fragment of general history. For one hundred and fifty years, history has been influenced – with increasing speed towards the present day – by photography, which "wishes to be present in history, and in official history just as much as in the most secret history, in collective history as much as that of the individual".[2] History from the point of view of photography is, in a manner of speaking, that kind of discursive way in which one introduces photographic documents, linking one to the next, explaining the inner variability of photographic images, while recognizing an evolutionary aspect to this material which allows us to make history. The very study of the history of painting is only possible thanks to photography. It would be inappropriate to try, on the other hand, to force photography into the strait-jacket of schemata devised for other arts (and which are sometimes contested or altered).

The difficulties of working out a structure suitable for this history of photography are all too obvious in previous studies – the presence of the model of the history of art, with its almost biological evolutionary periods of genesis, vocation, maturity, and decadence, the duality of the medium between craft techniques, and an art of communication connected with language. Until the 1930s, the notion of technical evolution prevailed.[3] The first attempt at bringing criteria together was that of Beaumont Newhall (on the occasion of an exhibition to commemorate the centenary of the invention of photography). He constructed a global view of images, their techniques, and the external influences which motivated them.[4] But the framework established by Newhall was applicable only to photographic categories regarded as artistic, or aspiring to be so. What is more, it confirmed the museum-type recognition of "photography-as-art". It fell to Raymond Lécuyer[5] to attempt, in 1945, to show the irrevocable link between technique and the meaning of images. The effect was to recognize that photography had achieved an immediate maturity, contemporary with its invention. Next, came the history of photography by A. and H. Gernsheim,[6] which restricted itself to the period 1839–1914 and included a rich documentary apparatus – partly due to Josef-Maria Eder. For a long time, this meant that writers in English on the subject maintained pole position. More recently, Naomi Rosenblum[7] attempted something which had become difficult – to present the development of photography from a single viewpoint, centered on the notion of constant technical progress and ending up with the omnipresent reference point of photojournalism, capturing the moment. The multi-authored book edited by André Rouillé and Jean-Claude Lemagny[8] had the legitimate ambition of treating photography in

2. H. Damisch, "A partir de la photographie", preface to R. Krauss, *Le Photographique: Pour une théorie des écarts*, Paris, Macula, 1990, p. 10.

3. J. M. Eder, *Geschichte der Photographie*, Halle, Knapp, 3rd. ed., 1905; Eng. trans., *History of Photography*, New York, Columbia University Press, 1945; repr., New York, Dover, 1978.

4. *Photography 1839–1937: A Short Critical History*, New York, Museum of Modern Art, 1937, reissued as *The History of Photography from 1839 to the Present Day*, New York, 1949.

5. R. Lécuyer, *Histoire de la photographie*, Paris, Baschet, 1945.

6. H. and A. Gernsheim, *The History of Photography, from the Earliest Use of the Camera Obscura to the Beginning of the Modern Era*, London, New York, Oxford University Press, 1955.

7. N. Rosenblum, *A World History of Photography*, New York, Abbeville Press, 1984.

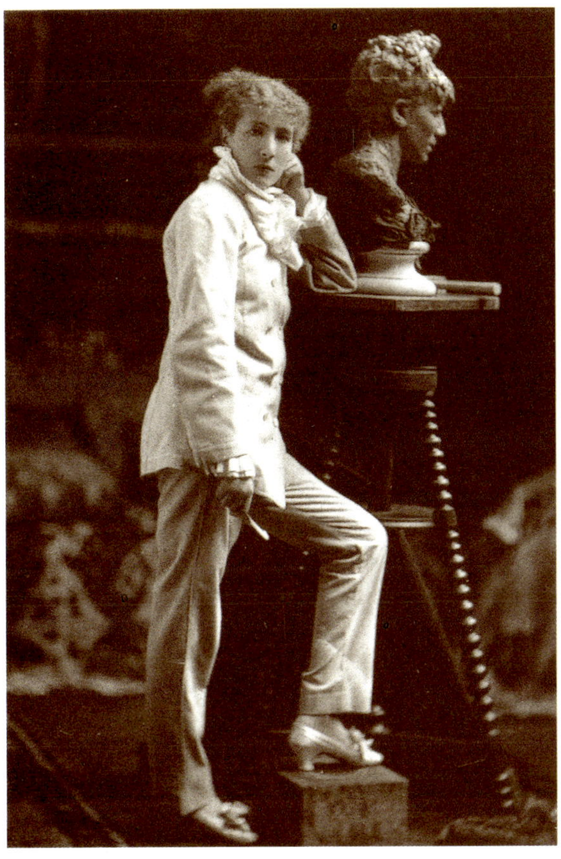

◀ MÉLANDRI,
Sarah Bernhardt,
1876,
private collection.

history from the viewpoint of social evolution, but the project was marred by the restricted amount of space available.

From these too few general works, it emerges that photographic history cannot be a chronological continuum arbitrarily attached to the medium and its technique. It can result only from taking into account that which is peculiar to photography – its serial nature, its temporal quality, its viewpoint (in the sense of the place from where the view is taken), and the degree to which each image departs from what is regarded as the norm in a given period (what has been called "photographic").

Photography

Not only the works quoted but numerous studies in specialist magazines[9] show how it is in photography itself that the methods and means by which it may be evaluated are to be found. By examining all forms of photography in its history innovations will become apparent to us.

Firstly, we need to define what we mean by "photography". Above all, it is an ensemble of highly disparate images which possess in common the fact that they were created by the action of light on a sensitive surface. For some, photography is an objective view of the world, a means of producing a record. For others, the vision is totally subjective, and the photographer an artist who reaches agreement with reality and appropriates it to themselves in order to reveal it all the better. We have tried to break down this dichotomy between image and art in order to emphasize the variety of practice and intentional usages which underlie photographic production. It should not be forgotten that images have a destination which determines in advance their form, their size, and their quality, a destination which is often objective, and to which the historian must refer more openly: the archive, the artist's folder, the family album, the frame on the mantelpiece, the art book, the newspaper, the advertising hoarding, the cemetery. We have therefore considered that all photographs are subject to the action of "fields" – influences, affinities, reference points, social determinants, conventions of interpretation – not only to technological determinism. Most people use photography to obtain an image with someone or something in mind – a person, a use or function – an aim which may or may not be fulfilled. The history of photography can open itself up more widely only by considering private photographic practice as much as use by the media, the former being the real reflection of photographic reality even if it has not yet reached museums and galleries.

In consequence, photography will not be judged by what it "represents". In comparison with painting, which may be likened to an icon, photography reveals to us a sense of the fortuitous, the image-making possibilities of everything that occurs optically. It appears to us like the carrier of an epiphany-like message, modest but tenacious, anodyne but essential. After all, photography is really nothing more than a detector of photons, those particles which signal to our eyes the innumerable events of the universe.

NAYA Studio,
Pigeon Shooting at the Hotel Excelsior, Venice Lido,
circa 1900.
▼

8. *Histoire de la Photographie*, ed. André Rouillé and Jean-Claude Lemagny, Paris, Bordas, 1986.

9. *Fotogeschichte* (from 1981), *History of Photography* (from 1977), *Photographies* (1983–1985), *Prestige de la photographie* (1977–1980), *La Recherche photographique* (1986–1997), *Études Photographiques* (from 1996).

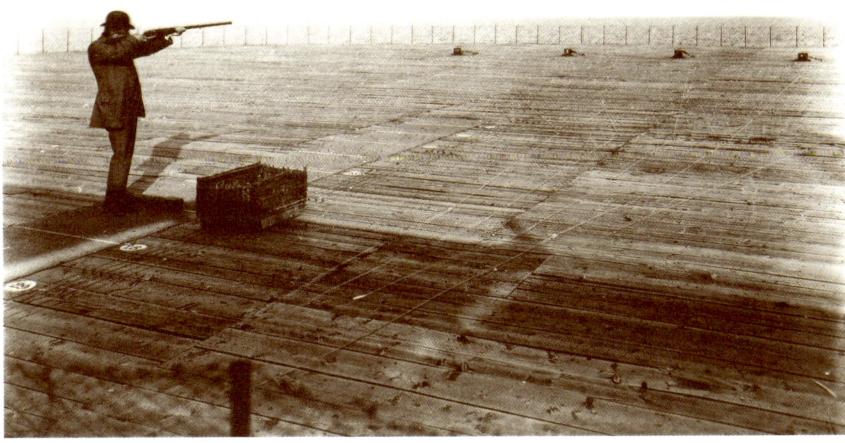

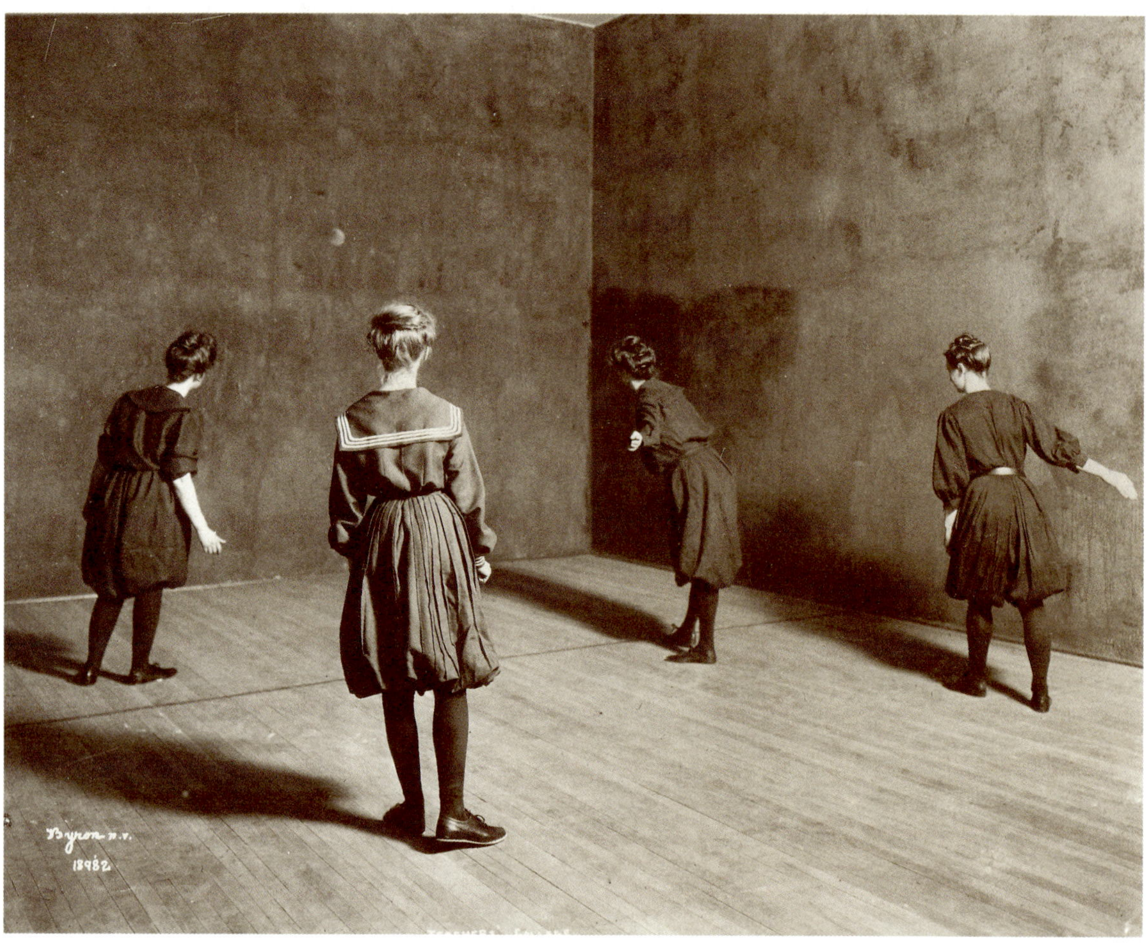

JOSEPH BYRON, *Handball, Teachers' College, New York,* 1904, Museum of the City of New York.

Towards a history of photographs

The history of photography is sometimes attacked by critics who suspect it of perpetuating an aesthetic doctrine that seeks to subject the present to rules based on the model of the past.

For this reason, our aim is to undertake a history of photographs considered as working objects in their own time, over the century and a half since photography first made its appearance. This approach cannot be neatly summed up as a demonstration of an evolutionary sequence. It demands instead an archaeological approach to the subject, by identifying the strata and establishing a typology of the language of photography and the implications and interaction of these aspects at any given moment. It is a question of "accepting only to deal with a multitude of separate events", as Foucault put it.[10] This type of history does not consist simply of recognizing the sequence of stratified layers. Rather, it is the relationship between a certain number of circumstances which defines the archeological artifact which constitutes a photograph, those circumstances which brought it into being and which led to its burial – only to be "read" afresh when it has been brought to the surface again, which itself endows it with an unexpected new aura. A history of photographs is an examination of a combination of factors, the short-term reasons for the creation of the images and their eventual fate.

Since a historical study is always something of a gamble on what the very notion of history will be in the future, we have favored the content of the photographs rather than the actual history of photography. In this book each author defends what seems to us a valid historical point of view with regard to each defined subject, to the extent that the photographer and the spectator are placed face to face within their different historic perspectives. The integrity of the entire work, transcending obvious differences in the authors' viewpoints, lies in the choice of illustrations. These have been selected not on the basis of some theoretical aesthetic standpoint, but because, in our view, they best represent the wide variety of photographic images. The aim of the selection process is to show how the whole of society is actively or passively involved in, or through, photography. It remains to be seen how these "modes of being" operate within everyday life for photography spread with the rapidity first of engravings, then of portfolios, and finally of books, magazines, and printing in general. It is the end-product of these means of communication.

Wishing to consider photography as a broad, unsorted whole, we have been careful not to recreate obsolete categories. In order to justify

10. M. Foucault, *The Archaeology of Knowledge and the Discourse on Knowledge*, trans. A. M. Sheridan Smith, New York, Pantheon, 1972.

11. *Ibid.* p. 10.

their place in a corpus which some would like to be homogeneous, the definition of the various fields of photography has often been stretched to absurd limits: scientific photography, *reportage*, current affairs, fashion, advertising , art – categories which demonstrate a tacit lack of acceptance of these fields grafted onto the primary art form. By probing beneath these often simplistic categories, whose function is mainly one of professional convenience, we have sought out the essential inner core of photographic unity within which they all form part of "photography", that broad, disparate ensemble which includes both artistic creation and routine work, which manifests itself in the photographic studio, the family album, the advertisement, the tourist view, the exotic image. All these are autonomous units with their own internal history, bound together more or less tightly and unfurling at varying speeds. For the historical development of these categories has taken place at different rates, running down "a gentle historical slope",[11] so that the evolution of photography is marked by phases of sudden extinction, rapid spurts or disconcerting periods of stability.

Our final objective, beyond the necessary chronology of techniques and use, is firstly the history of functions – what was expected of the images under discussion – the history of optical science and of the spaces crossed (and invented) by photography. Then, the history of the meaning of photographs each time its function was renewed. Our aim, too, is to make some inroad into neglected sectors (social, popular, family, media photography), to ask why a photograph should exist at all, knowing that we cannot avoid from the outset all pre-existing schemata. Getting out of a strictly historic narrative and the restrictions imposed by the *a priori* limitations of the field of photography is not an easy matter for participants in a multi-authored collection. If this work still carries, despite our best efforts, the marks of former categories, nevertheless it should be possibly to discover within it different criteria for reading, ways of access to another type of photography which had scarcely been given breathing-space, thus recreating the visual foundation of modern society, and stressing photography's role as one of the most visible indices of the quest for modernity.

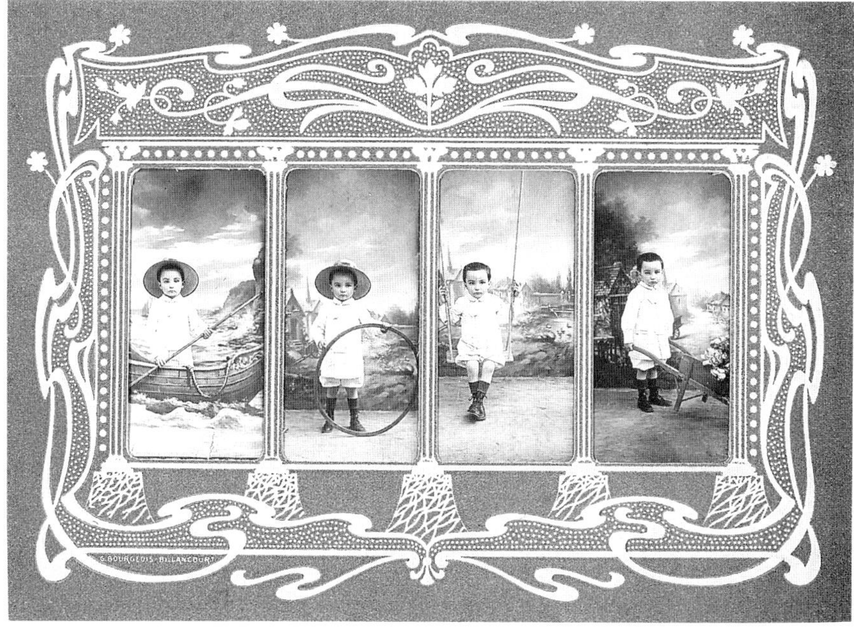

G. Bourgeois Studio,
Raymond,
1906,
private collection.

Pierre Dubreuil,
The Aviator,
circa 1929–1933.
Museum voor Fotografie,
Antwerp.

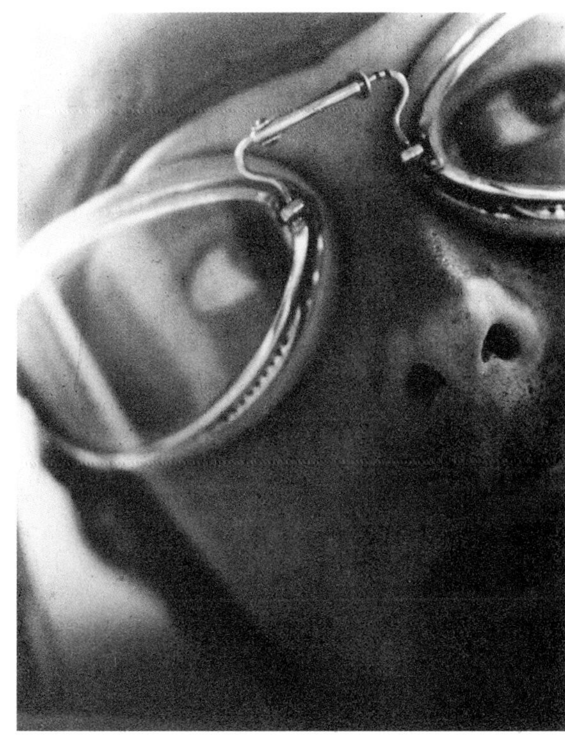

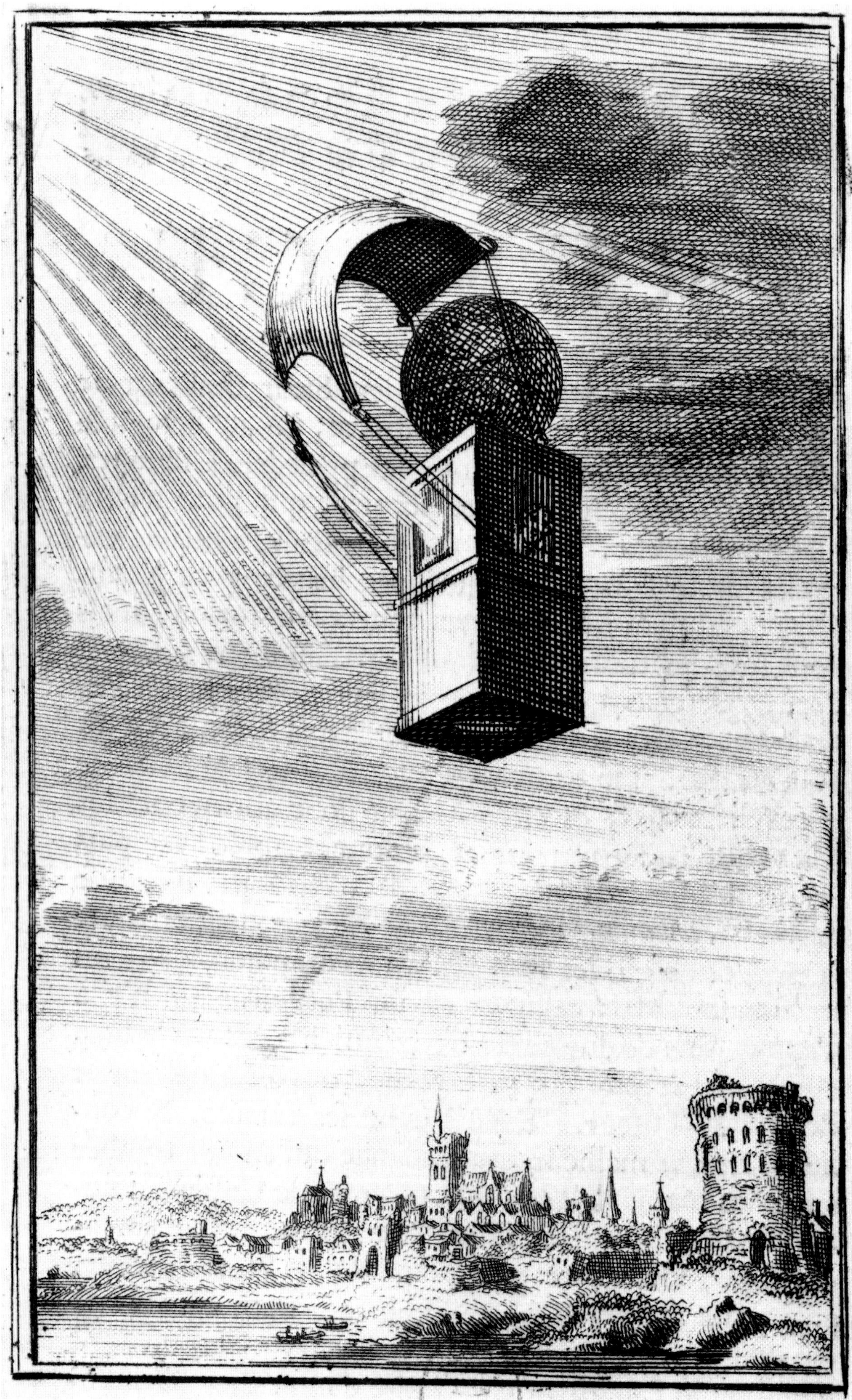

LIGHT MACHINES 1

On the threshold of invention

Michel Frizot

Can we imagine, today, how the idea of photography could have evolved at the beginning of the nineteenth century – when we consider that only a few minds were even able to understand the basic principle, and even they had no idea of its potential? In the small enclosed contemporary world of scientists and natural philosophers, the most common and popularly understood idea was that of the machine – the place where energy might be transformed and transmitted. It was to this concept that the action of light would have to be adapted. The Frenchman Nicéphore Niépce was to be the first to conceive and realize such a "light machine" for producing images.

Officially at least, photography was invented in 1839. It was in this year that "photography" was made public – or at least a particular photographic process (actually the daguerreotype), followed immediately by very different techniques (those of W. H. Fox Talbot and H. Bayard) and by controversy over the exact role of Nicéphore Niépce, who had died in 1833.

What, then, had happened before 1839 which allowed this technique to appear, succeed, and place itself "on the market"? Photography today has very little to do with the "photography" invented in 1839, or a little before. The question of the antecedents of a practice which has become both commercially successful and popular is more philosophical than might first appear. It is not simply a question of research for its own sake, seeking in the past those once famous forgotten people who might have been the first to have such and such an idea, some tentative experiment which today would be regarded as a decisive moment in a carefully planned evolutionary sequence leading inevitably towards a hypothetical goal which would be called "photography". It is, rather, a question of seeing how a technological concept could germinate without appearing totally idealistic, how a "technical object" was conceived before it was realized, "a conditioning of the present by the future, by what doesn't yet exist."[1] Before an inventive imagination can be set working on the gestation of a technical process, it must first take into account:

– A fund of empirical knowledge acquired over centuries, sometimes gathered by chance, which permits the construction of a technical hypothesis, and, little by little, makes possible the concept and its realization.

– A mental attitude which foresees what the future process can and must be – aiming intentionally at creating almost instant natural images, together with a desire to reach that promised land, now perceived as being nearly at hand and attainable through experimentation.

Such a method of proceeding should not necessarily be viewed or presented in the context of "precursors". Constant research into earlier and earlier achievements should not disguise our ignorance of the real chances of success of adopting such a methodical approach. From the extant sources it would seem that before 1839 only Nicéphore Niépce had any wish to be an inventor in the field of the mechanical image, to be the creator of a new industry.

The time of machines

The fundamental question is *Why* photography? Historians of science might reply: for reasons very similar to those which produced the steam engine, the flying machine or the telephone. Art historians or students of the media, on the other hand, would put forward reasons analogous to those which motivated oil painting or printing in the fifteenth century. Standing at the junction of science and art, photography, as it would exist in its mature form in the 1850s is impossible to

◀ ***Flying machine powered by the sun,***
engraving from *Œuvres diverses de Monsieur Cyrano de Bergerac,*
Amsterdam, 1699,
Bibliothèque Nationale, Paris.

1. G. Simondon, *Du mode d'existence des objets techniques*, Paris, Aubier, 1958; reprinted 1989.

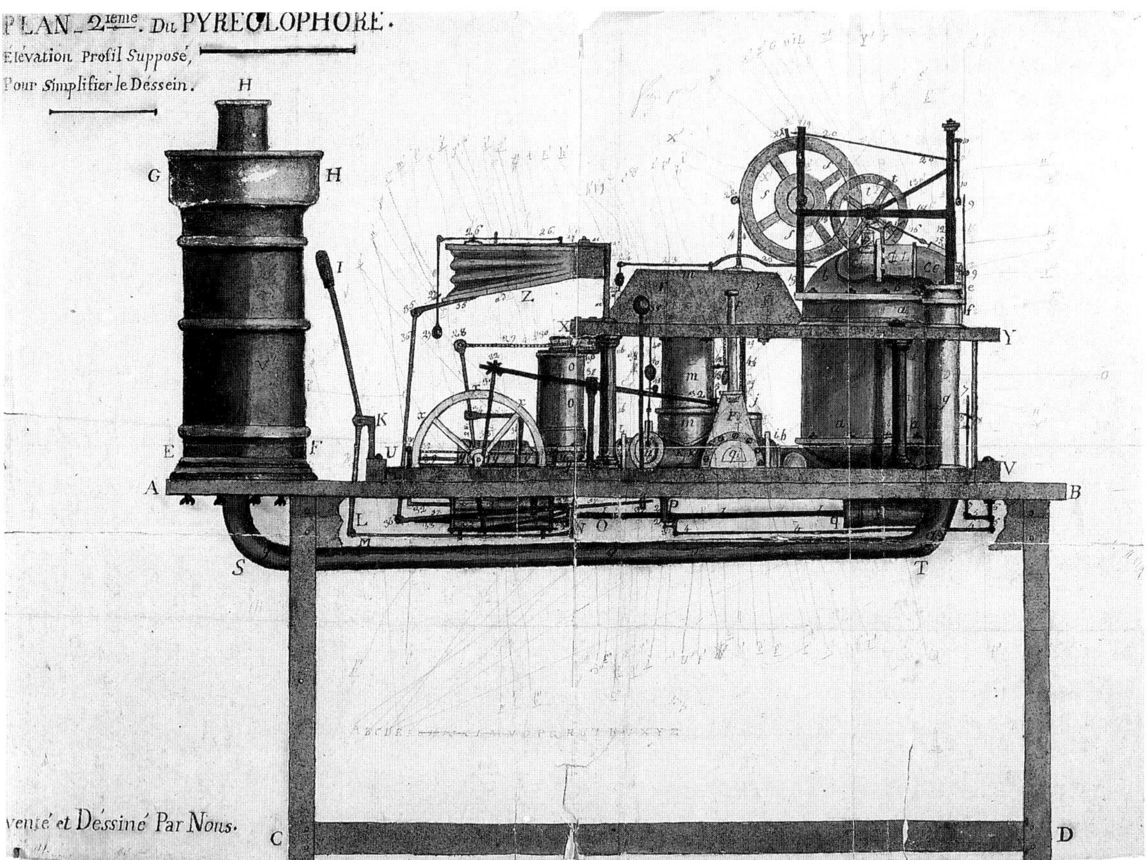

Nicéphore and Claude Niépce, ***Working drawing for the pyréolophore,*** plate forming part of the patent, 1807, Institut national de la Propriété Industrielle, Paris.

classify. It is an invention outside the norm, which is determined – depending whether one considers the technical side (the camera) or the finished product (the image) – by several definitions, each of which is keen to prove its pedigree, its legitimate lineage in the annals of both the arts and the sciences.

More than a century and a half later, it is tempting to assimilate photography within the totality of nineteenth-century inventions by considering it as a "machine", a term which was indeed applied to it in numerous writings around 1839 (people spoke of the daguerreotype as *la machine Daguerre*). In more precise terms, a piece of photographic apparatus, ancient or modern, light or heavy, is a transformation machine which takes in luminous energy in order to produce an image, fixed and stable with its gradation of black and white. From a more modern viewpoint, the photographic process could also be defined as the utilization of an automatic machine for transmitting information, a recording apparatus along the same lines as the gramophone, invented a few decades later. The birth of photography implies a kind of Copernican revolution in the science of optics, recognizing the action of "the luminous fluid". Thus, nature was no longer inert, subject merely to observation – it acted, as though by remote control, on certain sensitive substances.

The earliest definition of what photography would become (in a sense, its research program) was provided by Nicéphore Niépce in 1829, following the death of his brother Claude the previous year: "heliography consisted of *spontaneously* reproducing the image received in the *camera obscura* by the action of light, with all the gradations from black to white".[2] This corresponds pretty well with the definition of a machine; it was just a question of controlling physical or chemical change caused by light. Furthermore, when, in 1816, Nicéphore Niépce spoke of such research to his brother Claude, they had already been very busy for several years perfecting a "machine" which they had baptized the "pyréolophore":[3] a combustion engine powered by vegetable (lycopodium) or mineral (coal or asphalt) matter intended to propel boats, in competition with the steam engines already installed in some ships. The concept of the machine controlled all technical research, especially at craft level. In a letter to Claude in which he dealt with their current business, Nicéphore spoke of "our latest machine"[4] with reference to their research on photography (which did not yet have a special name). The optician Chevalier also wrote to him concerning "the machines which he usually builds", referring by this term to the *camera obscura*. The pyréolophore, which was the subject of a patent signed by the Emperor in 1807, was not a provincial amusement but a real invention which in itself would have been enough to count them among professional "engi-

2. P. Jay, *Niépce: genèse d'une invention*, Chalon-sur-Saône, 1988, p. 280, and *Nicéphore Niépce: lettres et documents*, Photo Poche, no. 8, Paris, Centre National de la Photographie, 1983.

3. Letter dated April 22, 1816, in *J. N. Niépce: lettres 1816–1817*, Rouen, Pavillon de la Photographie, 1973, p. 16. The "Montgolfière" hot-air balloon in 1783 was called an "aerostatic machine".

4. Letter dated July 11, 1817, *ibid.*, pp. 170–172. Niépce still spoke of a "machine" with regard to Wollaston's "camera lucida" (letter, July 27, 1818) or "machines of this sort" for the *camera obscura* (letter, July 18, 1827). Things which exploded, such as bombs, were also called "machines" (e.g. the "machine" used in Fieschi's assassination attempt on King Louis-Philippe in 1835).

neers" were it not for the fact that they had to put off perfecting it for ten years. In the same year they also submitted to Lazare Carnot a scheme for a hydrostatic pump to replace an earlier machine at Marly, and in 1811 they embarked with enthusiasm on the cultivation of woad. Talbot himself often worked on the idea of machines – motors, mills, applications involving trains – and he took out several patents for "obtaining motive energy". It will be recalled, furthermore, that in the seventeenth century the moveable installations designed by Torelli or Bérain for the theatre were entitled "machines": changeable scenery, *deus ex machina*, special effects and clouds.

Drawing machines

We have seen that via Niépce's initial research, photography maintained a relationship with scientific machines. However, it was also linked with machines used by artists, "drawing machines" which used optical devices to follow the outline of a face or a landscape by projecting it onto a flat surface, rather than drawing it by eye. A development of the apparatus that Leonardo da Vinci and Dürer had already described, the drawing machines of Dubreuil (in *La Perspective practique*, 1663) or Christopher Wren (1669) consisted of semi-transparent paper attached to a frame through which the landscape to be drawn was viewed through a fixed eyepiece. By the end of the eighteenth century profiling machines had been developed based on the concept of a silhouette produced by the projection of light (sun or lantern), the profile being subsequently reduced mechanically (using the "pantograph" invented in 1743). The "silhouette", a cut-price type of portrait, maliciously named after one of Louis XV's financial controllers in 1759, formed the basis for the practice of physiognomy extolled by the Swiss scientist Lavater. In his *Physiognomische Fragmente* (Zürich, 1775–1778),[5] he sought to define personal character by the study of individual features, "to determine the link between the interior and the exterior", a pseudo-science of observing "what does not present itself" to the eye. The influence of silhouettes on subsequent photographic portraiture has been much exaggerated. However, it should be noted that Lavater's work includes an engraving of "a faithful and convenient machine for taking silhouettes" by the projection of light. Another "drawing machine" (a pantograph coupled with a translucent window like that of Dürer) was put forward by Gilles-Louis Chrétien as part of his invention, the "physionotrace" – a profile, to which anatomical annotations had been added, was scaled down by a horizontal pantograph. While the silhouette was cut out of black paper or some other material and mounted on a white or gold background, the physionotrace was engraved on copper, allowing numerous copies to be produced in ink. Towards 1830 there appeared the "Gavard machine" or "diagraphe", and Boucher's "coordonographe".[6]

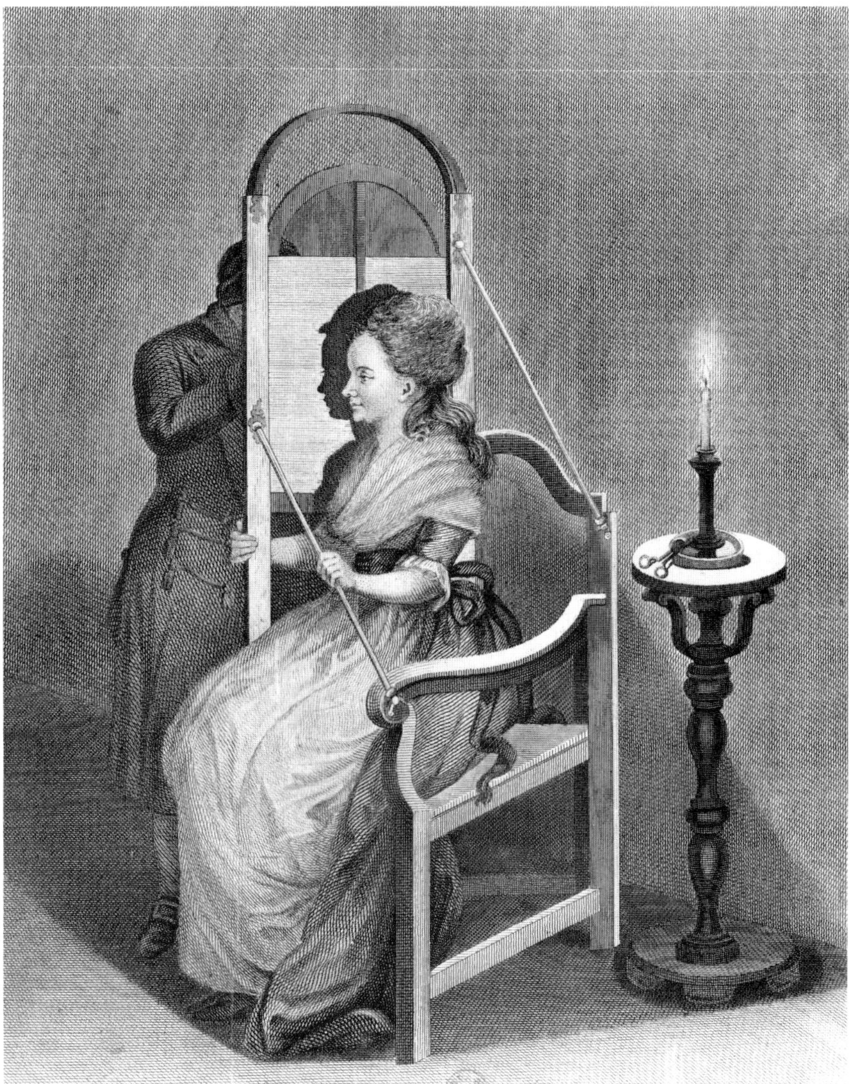

"A Faithful and Convenient Machine for Taking Silhouettes",
after J. K. Lavater, *Essai sur la physiognomonie*,
The Hague, 1781–1803,
Bibliothèque Nationale,
Paris.

It is in this context of the mechanization of drawing that the development of the *camera obscura* in the eighteenth century must be understood. This was the determining force for the birth of photography whose very core and mechanism it provided – the machine for transforming energy. The *camera obscura* concentrates, by means of a lens, the rays of light transmitted by a distant object and projects, onto the surface opposite this lens, an upside-down image of the scene (even this simplified description is nevertheless too scientific for the time of its invention, when it was regarded in terms of magic). This apparatus – whose fundamental principles have persisted until the present day – was freely available at the beginning of the nineteenth century. It was at one and the same time an object of curiosity, a scientific instrument, and a piece of drawing

5. J. K. Lavater, *Physiognomische Fragmente zur Beförderung der Menschenkenntnis und Menschenliebe*, Leipzig and Winterthur, 1775–1778; Engl. ed. J. K. Lavater, *Essays on Physiognomy, designed to promote the Knowledge and Love of Mankind*, ed. by Thomas Holloway, 3 vols., London, 1789–1798.

6. H. Buddemeier, *Panorama, Diorama, Photographie*, Munich, Fink, 1970, pp. 194–196.

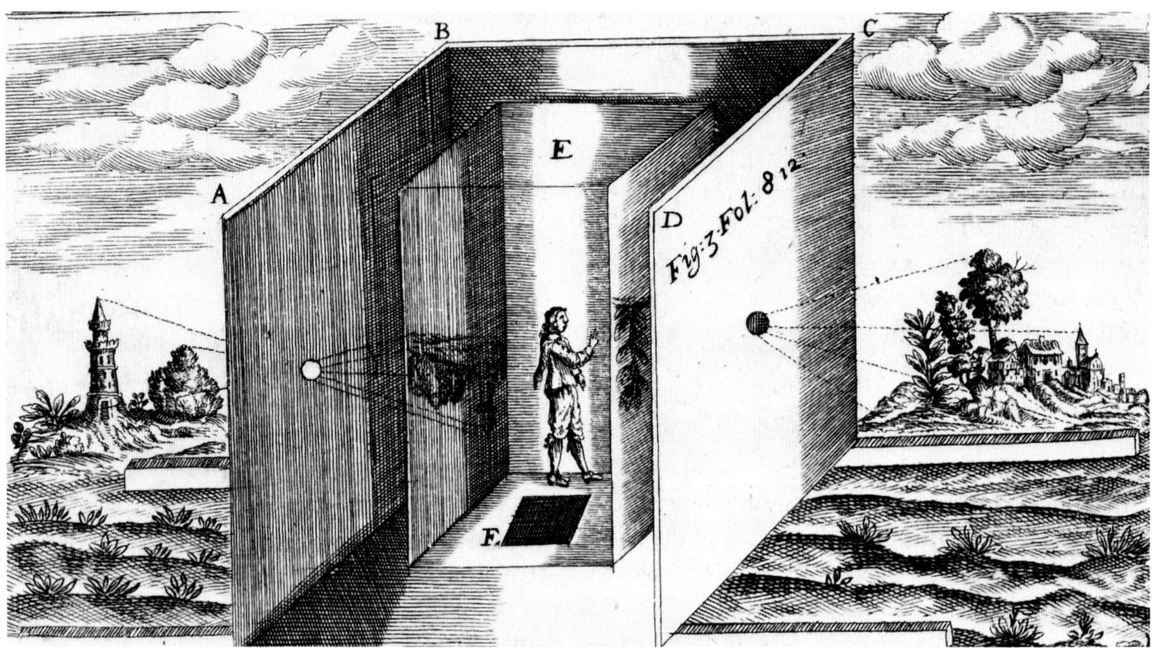

***Principle of the* camera obscura,**
after A. Kircher,
Ars magna lucis et umbrae,
Amsterdam, 1671,
Biblioteca Nacional, Madrid.

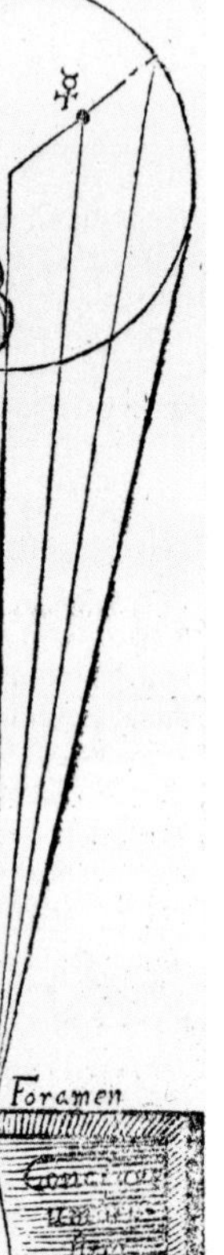

***Observing an eclipse through a* camera obscura,**
after J. Kepler, *Phaenomenon singulare [...],*
1609,
Biblioteca Nacional, Madrid.

equipment for travelers (Talbot used one in his tour of Italy in 1833).

The evolution of the *camera obscura* can be traced from antiquity. Originally the *camera* was indeed an actual room, totally enclosed, with a hole in one wall which, by the effect of diffraction of the light coming through it, produced an image of the scene outside on the opposite wall. The first recorded reference is by Aristotle, in the fourth century B.C., concerning the observation of eclipses. It recurs in Alhazen (Ibn al Haitham, eleventh century) and Roger Bacon (thirteenth century), and then in the manuscripts of Leonardo da Vinci (which had long been unpublished and, therefore, unknown).[7] Finally, it is described in the *Magia naturalis* of Giovanni Battista Della Porta (Naples, 1553),[8] the forefather of modern photography. It appears that it was Barbaro who, in 1568, introduced the lens in order to improve image sharpness (Della Porta incorporated it in his 1588 edition), which turned the *camera obscura* into an optical instrument, reflecting the Renaissance interest in perspective. These *camera obscura* were still actual rooms which the observer had to enter to contemplate the image produced.

It was not until the seventeenth century that the *camera obscura* became a portable instrument. The first representation of this apparatus, which probably measured a foot square, occurs in Zahn's *Oculus artificialis.*[9] This clearly shows a lens in a metal tube and an internal mirror to turn the image the right way round in the horizontal plane. The famous work of Kircher, *Ars magna lucis,* contains, in the 1671 edition,[10] a similar design. This could be used for copying landscapes onto oiled (thus transparent) paper placed on the glass screen which acted as the receiving wall of the *camera.* As a device used by magicians and charlatans to create "apparitions", the *camera obscura* became quite common in the seventeenth and eighteenth centuries. However, it was also used widely by scientists such as Huygens and Kepler[11] as well as by painters (Canaletto, among others).

Luminous magic

The invention of photography has often been described as the inevitable merging of optics (the *camera obscura*) and chemistry (the light-sensitivity of certain substances). However, observations on these two aspects coexisted for a century or two without any idea of bringing them together. The goal had to be clearly defined before the means of achieving it were discerned and (sometimes in vain) adopted. In order to understand the first fumbling attempts at invention we have to go back in our imagination to the uncertainty and mystery of the age, the confusion of a period still pervaded with the notion of "natural magic", which paid little heed to physico-chemical matters.

Around 1800, a knowledge of chemistry depended on numerous scattered observations, many of which could have been very productive, but which could lead to nothing without imagination and method. Nevertheless, the photosensitivity of silver salts was known as long ago as the thirteenth century when Albertus Magnus noted that light turned them black. However, only serious experimentation could increase knowledge of this phenomenon. Schulze described his experiments in an essay written in 1727, which remained unpublished.[12] He made words appear by sticking a stencil onto a flask containing chalk soaked in silver nitrate. The work of Scheele, who took up and completed these observations in 1777, became better known, as was that of Jean Senebier,[13] who studied photochemical changes in numerous types of wood and resin (sandarac and guaiacum, which Niépce mentions) and plant extracts. The most decisive (though ultimately unsuccessful) pre-photographic experiments were those carried out by Thomas Wedgwood who, with Humphrey Davy, published in 1802 *An Account of a Method [...]*.[14] Wedgwood copied silhouettes or drawings on glass by placing them in bright light onto material (paper or pale-colored leather) soaked in silver nitrate. These "drawings", however, could only be kept in the dark, as the salts continued darkening in the light. Wedgwood tried to obtain comparable images in a *camera obscura*, but was unsuccessful. Even in their wildest dreams, none of these experimenters could have had any inkling of the future development of photography.

In 1819 a well-known British scientist, Sir John Herschel, discovered sodium hyposulphite and its silver chloride dissolving properties. It was not until twenty years later, in 1839, with the competition among inventors to lay claim to primacy in the discovery of photography, that Herschel passed on to his friend Fox Talbot this straightforward method of "fixing" the residual salts, that is, producing actual photography.

It seems that it was in 1816 that Nicéphore Niépce carried out his first experiments on light, at a time when his work on the pyréolophore appears to have reached its peak, but when financial problems were becoming more and more pressing. Claude Niépce, then living in Paris, was conscious of Britain's technical pre-eminence and moved to London in August 1817. He sent increasingly optimistic reports, whilst also incurring new debts in the perfection of "the machine" until Nicéphore, alarmed by his exultation, traveled to be at his sick brother's bedside and only then discovered the extent of his dementia and the folly of the discoveries he had claimed. Claude died in February 1828.

During the period 1816–1828 Nicéphore was buoyed up by his hopes for another invention, another "machine", whose evolving concept derived from the practice of lithography (invented in Munich in 1796 by Senefelder). This invention would, he hoped, make up for his earlier failures and provide him with some financial benefit.

Heliography

Senefelder's lithographic technique was soon practiced in Burgundy by the Niépce brothers (1813–1815), but without success. Nevertheless, it was this pioneering technique for the production and distribution of images which determined the attraction of the *camera obscura* for Nicéphore Niépce. In essence, this involved obtaining, on a locally obtained lithographic stone placed in the *camera*, the direct impression of a "view", capable of being transformed, after a minimum number of operations, into an inked and printed image. Sometimes Niépce injected gases to speed up the reactions in the *camera*, as if it was a combustion chamber similar to that used in the pyréolophore. Even if the base materials and procedures varied, there was one constant aspect of his research which initiated the concept of photography from 1816. Its developmental stages are well known. A clear understanding of the ultimate goal was quickly arrived at, although the results did not follow as quickly (see box). After about twelve years of intermittent research, Nicéphore Niépce obtained some qualified success – images on pewter – one of which is preserved to this day. He showed these to British scientists during his long stay in London at the end of 1827, in the hope of making some money out of his process. These demonstrations, however, were not spectacular enough to arouse support and enthusiasm, as the daguerreotype would later.

Heliography, as Niépce described it in 1829 in his *Notice sur l'héliographie*, may be divided into two different methods:

– Copying, by the action of light, existing images (engravings) which had been made transparent by means of varnish. The light-sensitive intermediary was bitumen of Judea. This procedure formed the basis of later techniques (particularly photogravure).

– Copying "viewpoints" in the *camera obscura*, that is, obtaining images directly from nature (often taken from a bedroom window), in black and white and with true tonal values (a "positive") by means of differential changes in the solubility of bitumen of Judea. This was the

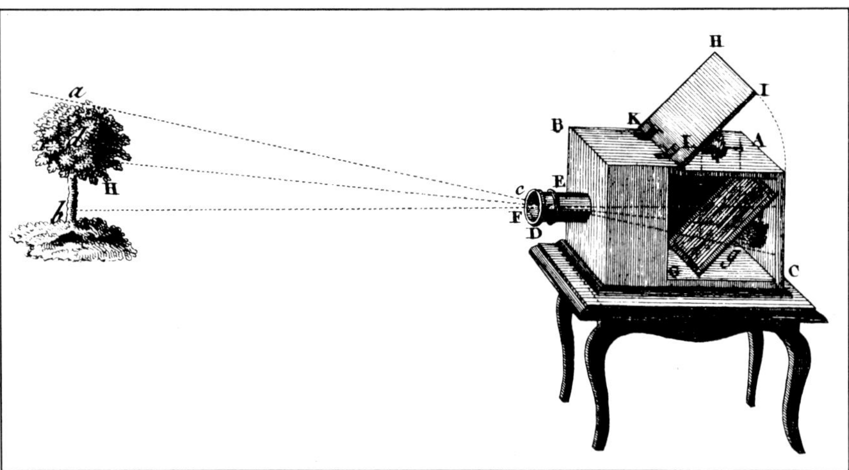

Portable* camera obscura *for drawing from nature,
from Brisson's *Physique*, Paris, 1781, private collection.

7. *Codex Atlanticus*, vol. D, fol. 8, Milan, Biblioteca Ambrosiana.

8. G. B. Della Porta, *Magia naturalis*, Naples, 1553; Antwerp, 1561 (*La magie naturelle qui est les secrets et miracles de nature*, Rouen, T. Daré, 1612).

9. J. Zahn, *Oculus artificialis telediοptricus*, Würzburg, 1685–1686.

10. A. Kircher, *Ars Magna lucis et umbrae*, Amsterdam, 1671; 1st edition, Rome, 1646.

11. S. Alpers, *The Art of Describing: Dutch Art in the Seventeenth Century*, Chicago, University of Chicago Press, 1983; J. Hammond, *The Camera Obscura: A Chronicle*, Bristol, A. Hilger, 1981.

12. J. M. Eder, *Geschichte der Photographie*, 3rd edition, Vienna, 1905; New York, Dover, 1978; J. H. Schultze, "Scotophorus pro phosphorus inventus [...]", in *Acta physicomedica Acad. Caesareae*, Nuremberg, 1727.

13. J. Senebier, *Mémoires physico-chimiques sur l'influence de la lumière solaire pour modifier les êtres des trois règnes de la nature*, Geneva, 1782.

14. T. Wedgwood and H. Davy, "An Account of a Method of Copying Paintings upon Glass and of Making Profiles by the Agency of Light upon Nitrate of Silver", in *Journal of the Royal Institution*, London, 1802, no. 1, p. 170.

15. H. Gernsheim, "The 150th Anniversary of Photography", in *History of Photography*, January 1977, pp. 3–8.

Joseph Nicéphore Niépce
From alchemy to the work of light

Nicéphore Niépce's training was not that of a scientist, but that of an occasionally self-taught provincial who drew his knowledge from books and journals, and his energy from indefatigable experimentation. During their various mechanical works, the two brothers, Claude and Nicéphore, were in contact with scholars, businessmen (e.g. the Jouffroy d'Abbans firm which built steamships), the Society for the Encouragement of National Industry, and even Lazare Carnot. However, the language and general conception of their work on physico-chemical phenomena was still imbued with the alchemical notions which preceded the development of modern chemistry in the nineteenth century. Niépce often seems to "try out" processes and substances without following any logic other than the hope of a significant improvement, while freely confessing his ignorance of the subtleties of optics. For example, he found hints in Klaproth's *Dictionnaire de Chimie* (the design of the *camera obscura* was illustrated in Abbé Nollet's *Leçons de physique expérimentale)*, in Guyot's *Nouvelles Récréations*, and in Brisson's *Physique*, all commonly available works. Niépce's great merit was to adhere stubbornly to a key idea – producing multiple copies of images by a method derived from engraving (on metal) or lithography (on stone), using a matrix prepared *directly* by the action of light. From this sprang his two research objectives:

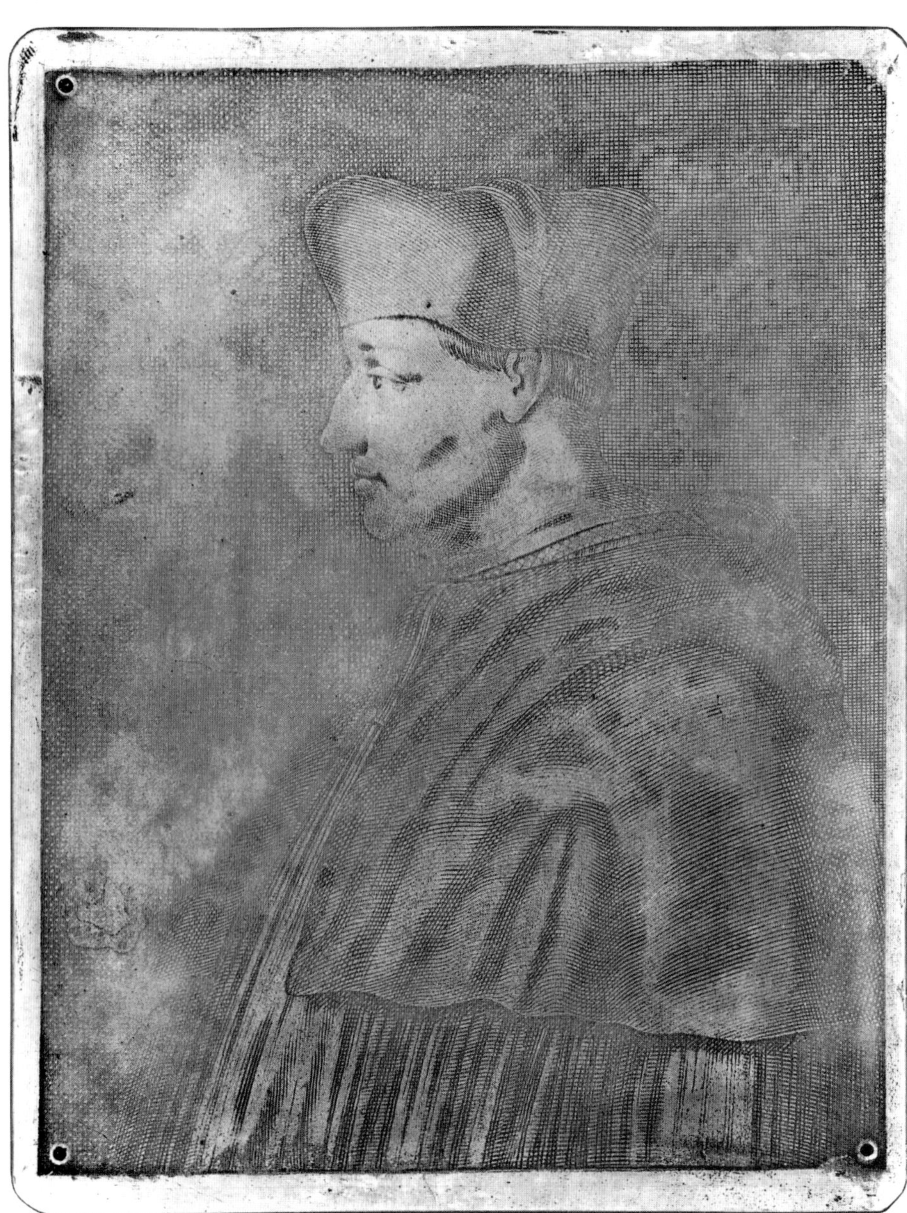

Nicéphore Niépce,
Cardinal d'Amboise,
heliograph on pewter plate (reproduction of a print), 1826, Musée Nicéphore Niépce, Chalon-sur-Saône.

1. The reproduction of already existing engravings, which his process would provide with a lucrative means of distribution.

2. Obtaining direct images of nature in a *camera obscura*, with the same objective of producing multiple copies as engraved plates. Until his death in 1833 Niépce sought to etch his printing plates, a stubbornness which his associate Daguerre criticized. These two methods based on the action of light were brought together in 1829 under the name "heliography".

Research into the first category went ahead quite quickly from 1822. A print made translucent by means of varnish or oil was placed on a supporting medium – glass, then stone, copper, and, finally, pewter (1826) – covered in a light-sensitive substance (usually bitumen of Judea), which the action of light rendered insoluble in lavender oil. The exposed metal areas of the plate, corresponding to the lines of the original, were then etched using acid. From 1827 onwards, Niépce enlisted the help of the Paris engraver Lemaître.

Examples of both pewter plates and original prints survive, reproducing commercial engravings of well-known paintings: *Cardinal d'Amboise*, a landscape by Claude Lorraine, the *Holy Family* after Raphael, etc. This process provided the model for "photo-mechanical" research (the reproduction of photographs by printing), later carried out by Niépce de Saint-Victor and Poitevin.

The second research objective (which employed the *camera obscura*) started in 1816, using silver chloride on paper – a process which was considered a failure (Niépce was not able to conceive the notion of a reversible "negative"). From 1816 to 1820, he undertook numerous trials on paper, stone, and metal with guaiacum resin, phosphorus, Dippel oil, injecting hydrogen, carbon dioxide or acidic vapour into the *camera obscura*. In 1826–1827, he mainly used bitumen of Judea on pewter, as, it seems, for the *View from the Window* at the estate of Le Gras, near Chalon-sur-Saône, which Niépce left to his British spokesman, Bauer, and which was rediscovered in 1952.

The year 1829 saw the introduction of a silver-coated copper plate on which bitumen of Judea and iodine were combined (to produce the blackening of the light parts of the image, in collaboration with Daguerre). However, heliographs taken from nature still required exposure times ranging from half an hour to several hours. Silver-plated copper was the support used for the daguerreotype process which Louis-Jacques Mandé Daguerre perfected between 1833 and 1837, when he exploited the light-sensitivity of silver iodide.

Michel Frizot

technique used for the view of Niépce's estate, Le Gras, rediscovered in 1952. This view from the window at Saint-Loup de Varennes (a pewter plate undoubtedly dating from 1826–1827) is in the Gernsheim Collection at the University of Texas, Austin.[15]

In 1829, however, the Niépces' indistinct images could not really be viewed as a complete success. It was at this point that the great Daguerre arrived – theatrical scenic artist, director of the Paris diorama, and the only researcher capable of achieving success after Niépce's death in methods which were marked by obstinacy and indecision. The first contact between the two men dated from January 25, 1826, following an indiscreet remark by the optician Chevalier, Niépce's supplier. Daguerre, whom Niépce met in Paris on his way to London, made a strong impression on the provincial scientist, who, following his London failures, detected in him the possibility of unhoped-for assistance in overcoming numerous obstacles – including his imperfect mastery of optics. A contract was signed on December 14, 1829, sealing their partnership. Niépce "gave up his invention" to the partnership, and Daguerre "brought in a new combination of the *camera obscura*".

Each worked independently, but it is certain that Niépce was stubbornly resolved to perfect "his" bitumen of Judea method, while Daguerre, wanting to modify the procedure and materials used, aimed to reduce the exposure time (which was still about one hour) and obtain a definitive image, not just an intermediary stage in a final engraving process. The research of both men led to the successful use of silvered copper plates (silver-plated, whose first use must be accredited to Niépce) when, following numerous experiments, a chemical was introduced which proved decisive for Daguerre's method – iodine. Niépce died suddenly, on July 5, 1833, at his estate of Le Gras, which features in the first "photographed" image to survive, without having substantially modified his process.

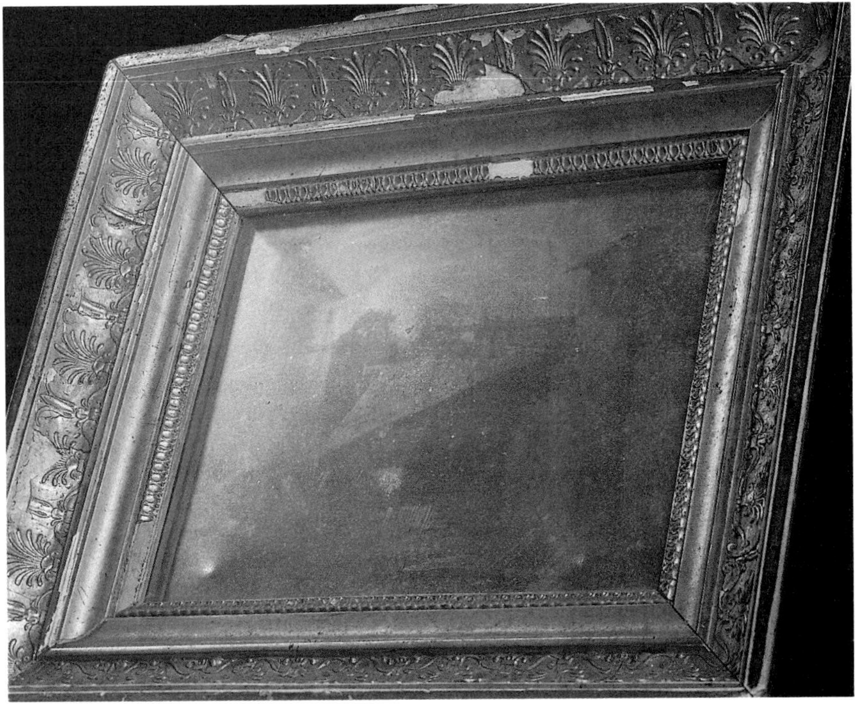

Oblique view of NICÉPHORE NIÉPCE'S original heliograph (see below), presented to the University of Texas, Austin.

At the time of Niépce's death, the concept of photography had reached maturity. However, there was still no practicable or commercially viable process. It is not impossible that during the same period other researchers had obtained equally encouraging results. In 1833, a French technician isolated in Brazil, Hercule Florence, is said – according to his private diary – to have used the action of light on paper treated with silver nitrate to "print" labels and ornamental devices which had been scratched onto a glass plate blackened with soot.[16] We also know that, from 1835, Talbot carried out experiments on the sensitivity of silver salts, and obtained in the *camera obscura* a negative of a bay window. However, he attached no further importance to this, absorbed as he was by his unceasing scholarly research.[17]

Although the "photographic" problem was potentially resolved, as would be shown by future events, the invention, in a form which would be of practical use, did not yet exist. The mechanism of the light machine was not yet perfected, yet Daguerre, who was highly skilled in theatre machinery, was now in a potentially successful position. The engraver Lemaître fully understood that Daguerre was capable of combining machinery and light when he wrote about him to Niépce: "I believe him to possess a rare intelligence in everything to do with machines and the effects of light."[18]

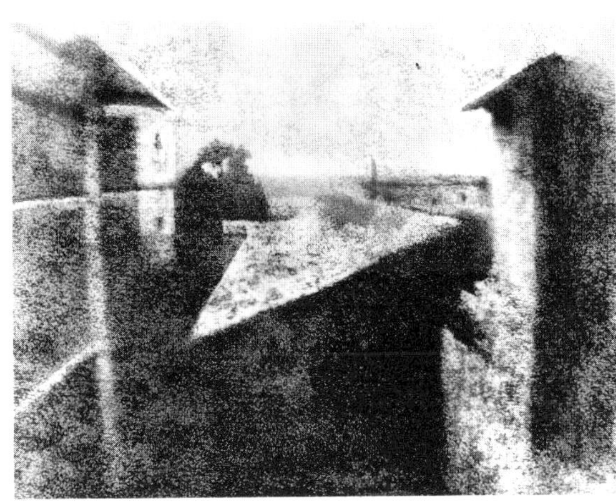

◀ NICÉPHORE NIÉPCE, ***View from the Window at Le Gras,*** modern reproduction (enhanced contrast) taken from the original heliograph, 1826–1827, University of Texas, Austin.

16. See B. Kossoy, *Hercule Florence, 1833: a descoberta isolada de fotografia no Brasil,* 2nd edn., Saõ Paulo, Duas Cidades, 1980, and *Les multiples inventions de la photographie,* Paris, Mission du Patrimoine Photographique, 1989, pp. 73–78.

17. G. Buckland, *Fox Talbot and the Invention of Photography,* Boston, Godine, 1980, p. 30.

18. Kravetz, *Dokumentii po istorii izobretenia fotografii,* Moscow and Leningrad, 1949, p. 193. At the 1851 Great Exhibition in London photography would feature in the "Machinery" section in the class entitled "Philosophical Instruments".

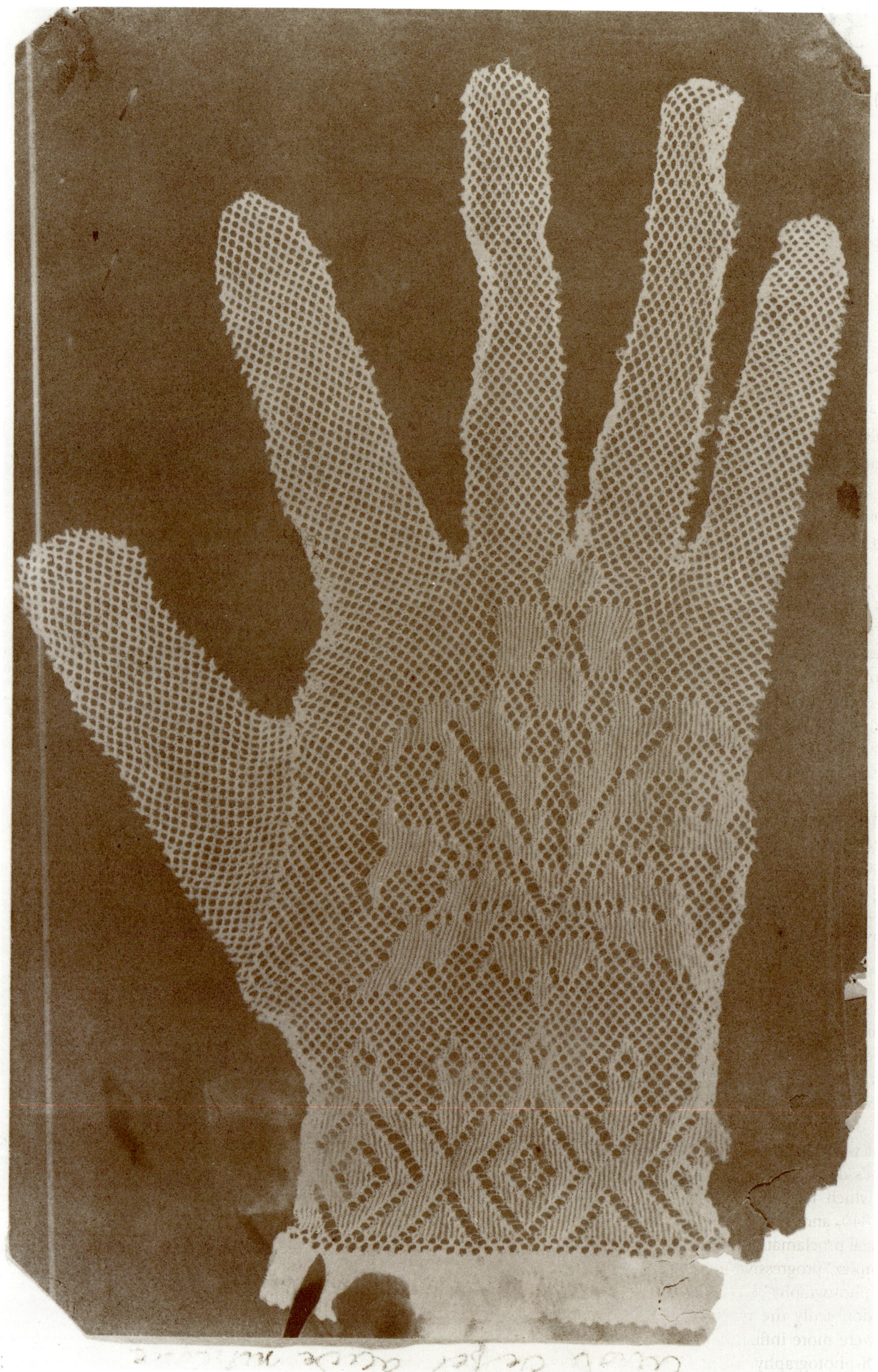

1839–1840 2

Photographic developments

Michel Frizot

Photography was not invented by one person. Nor was it the result of a single inspired moment of genius. Economic, political, and social circumstances counted just as much as scientific criteria, lucky observations, and the intuition of a few clever men. During a period of two critical years (1839–1840) photography took a decisive path, whose success and survival – which were not achieved straight off – determined its technical future and its fields of application. At the end of 1840, the general principles of "photography", which would be based on the concept of the "negative", had scarcely been sketched out.

It was on August 19, 1839, in the Institut de France, that the brand-new technique of the daguerreotype was revealed to the world and the birth of photography was proclaimed. The Institut's session was official, accompanied by speeches, and destined to be recognized as an historic date. Daguerre himself, the inventor honored that great day, was unable to utter a word, and is said to have asked François Arago to read the technical communication he had prepared. Even on that day, photography could not escape the official protocol which regulated who was allowed to speak and was dominated by the imposing figure of Arago.[1]

The meanderings of history

In fact, everything took place outside this historic place and date. Details of the nature of the daguerreotype image had been known for several months, following indiscretions by members of the three-man commission entrusted with studying the discovery.[2] However solemn the actual event, it was only a part of the evolution of an inventor's dream, one among many noteworthy events which took place during the two years 1839–1840, and which contributed, as much as the official proclamation of the daguerreotype, to the complex, progressive invention of what was called "photography".[3] While the daguerreotype was undoubtedly the revelation of 1839, other events were more influential in determining the future of photography. To provide further milestones: January 31, 1839 was an important date in photographic history, the day when W. H. Fox Talbot (already well known to Jean-Baptiste Biot, one of the members of the French Commission on the daguerreotype) read before the Royal Society in London a paper which he had hastily put together in order to prove that he was the pioneer "in the art of photogenic drawing, or the process whereby natural objects can trace themselves, without the help of the artist's pencil".

This, too, was photography, six months before it was officially recognized. Also earlier than the official date was an event which took place on May 20, 1839, when an unknown man, Hippolyte Bayard, met Arago – Daguerre's fervent supporter – and showed him some "direct positives" which he had been producing in a *camera obscura* since March 20. Equally historic were the final days of September 1840, when Talbot discovered the "latent image" and perfected the technique of the calotype, which embodied the principle of negative/positive on which almost the whole of the history of photography is based. Important, too, was June 24, 1839, when Bayard tried to attract attention by staging the very first photographic exhibition, at a charity fête.

Should one moment be allowed to represent the sudden appearance of a complex and varied technique, when it was constantly improved, diversified, and renewed? It is difficult today to pronounce on the reality of this so-called "invention" of photography when the technical notions of that age are so different from our modern

◄ Hippolyte Bayard,
Lace Glove,
1840s,
photogenic drawing,
John Paul Getty Museum,
Malibu.
The original print is a cyanotype and is thus blue in color.

1. The custom in the French academies was that communications by non-members were read by an academician.

2. Arago, Biot, and von Humboldt; two letters from the last are extant on this subject: see R. Recht, *La Lettre de Humboldt,* Paris, Christian Bourgois, 1989. There also exists a letter from S. Morse, dated March 9, 1839: *ibid.*, p. 34, n. 3.

3. *1839, La photographie révélée,* Paris, Centre National de la Photographie et Archives Nationales, 1989, and B. Newhall, *Latent Image: The Discovery of Photography,* New York, Doubleday, 1967.

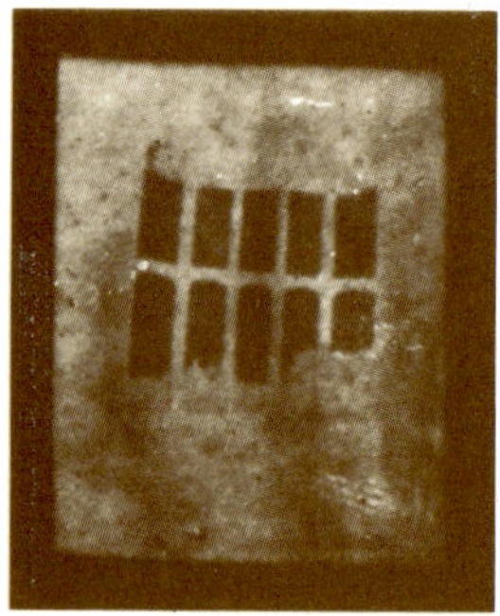

William Henry Fox Talbot, *Latticed Window*, negative, August 1835, Fox Talbot Museum, Lacock Abbey.

concepts. In order to assess these two historic years, let us try to reconstruct the chronology of small discoveries from publications, personal journals, and official communications. In this way it is possible to follow, step by step, the meanderings of the inventive mind, the wanderings, and the false trails which are the continual fate of ideas, whether technological or not.

Three figures dominate the years 1839–1840, contributing, with varying degrees of success, to the perfection of photographic techniques: Louis-Jacques-Mandé Daguerre, William Henry Fox Talbot, and Hippolyte Bayard. Others may have played a seminal role, not forgetting the guiding hand of Nicéphore Niépce, who died in 1833, and who so influenced Daguerre. These three did not all "go into photography" at the same date and with the same stubborn determination for it is certain that these men, of unequal scientific capabilities, did not know exactly what they were seeking. All that they had in common was their goal – the chemical fixing of images produced by the rays of the sun, in particular those formed in the *camera obscura*. Daguerre had been carrying out research since 1826, when he made contact with Niépce, whose experiments went back to 1816. It is now certain that Talbot started experimenting in this field in 1834: in August 1835, he obtained a "negative" of a window, of very small format, measuring just over an inch square, without continuing his experiments until he received Arago's first official communication on the daguerreotype in January 1839. As for Bayard, it appears that it was the leaks of 1838,[4] or Arago's actual announcement, which encouraged him to take his chance. At present, however, we are unable to know what his previous projects or ambitions may have been.

Daguerre's secret

Following Niépce's death on July 5, 1833, Daguerre remained in charge of the contract which he had signed on December 14, 1829, sharing it with Nicéphore's heir, Isidore Niépce, who, although not active, continued to follow the path chosen by his father. Daguerre was a Parisian, a painter "of talent" who specialized in theatrical sets and the panoramas which were so fashionable at that time. He had achieved a certain renown since 1822 with his diorama, where illusionist spectacles were staged using lighting effects combined with huge paintings. His success led him to open an establishment in London and won him the Légion d'Honneur. Furthermore, his drawing skills made him appreciate the advantages of the *camera obscura*. At the time of Niépce's death, the joint research, to which Daguerre brought his "perfecting of the *chambre noire*", appeared to be progressing on the basis of the partnership contract and Niepce's "notice on heliography", a technique to obtain, by means of the *camera obscura*, metal engraving plates suitable for almost unlimited reproductions of "views". In Nicéphore Niépce's opinion the best sensitive substance was bitumen of Judea. Daguerre regarded this as far too slow, without apparently being able to suggest a more effective substance, despite the use of heat, gases, and even liquids in his *camera obscura*. In 1831, Daguerre seems to have taken a more individual path, mentioning "trials with iodine" he had undertaken and "a great sensitivity to the impressions of light when it comes into contact with polished silver".[5]

The ingenious process of the daguerreotype gradually became formulated around the use of iodine on a silver plate. Niépce had already mentioned iodine in his *Notice* "in order to blacken the [pewter] plate". Daguerre used it as a sensitizing agent for silver and obtained "results" in three minutes (Niépce was still using exposures of several hours), "inverted" images (negatives) which he was unable to fix. Until 1833, the two men seem to have kept to their own personal research, communicating mainly by letter (Daguerre in Paris, Niépce in Chalon-sur-Saône). Everything changed with Nicéphore Niépce's death, and from then on Daguerre seemed to follow two parallel courses: the research initiated by Niépce, and his own personal experiments, which were taking a different path. In September, Daguerre formulated the idea of an image "produced promptly" but invisible (later called "latent"). He continued his research with iodine, which he could not share with Isidore Niépce, entirely absorbed in pursuing his father's theories. In 1835, he suddenly proposed to Isidore

Hubert, *Daguerreotype*, presented at the Academy of Sciences on October 29, 1839, Société Française de Photographie, Paris. ▼

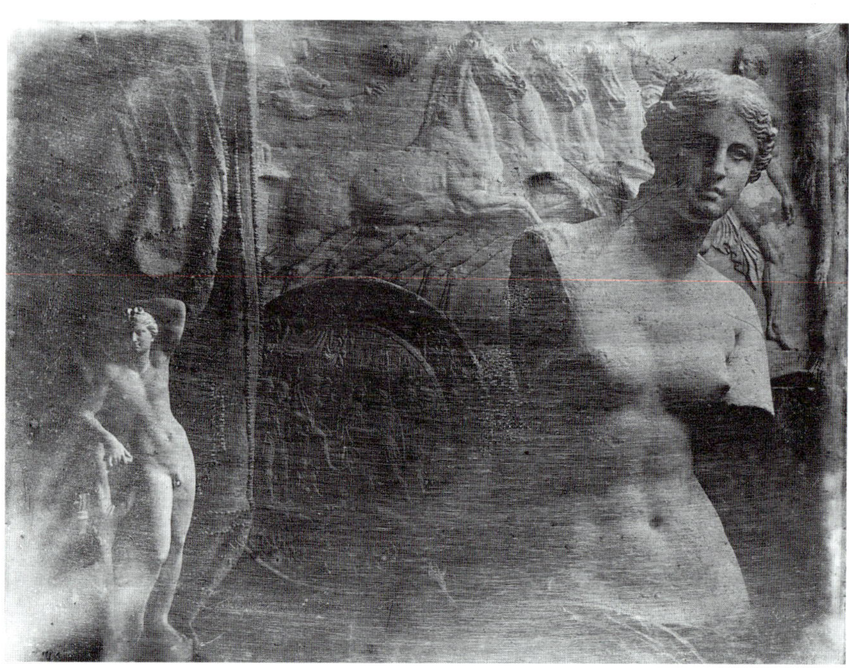

4. Bayard counted Grévedon among his friends, showing him his work on March 22, 1839. Grévedon, a lithographic engraver, had sketched Daguerre's portrait as early as February 1837 (letter from Daguerre to Isidore Niépce dated February 28, 1837).

5. Letters from Daguerre to Niépce dated April 10, 1831 and May 21, 1831, published in Kravetz, *Dokumentii po istorii izobretenia fotografii*, Moscow and Leningrad, 1949.

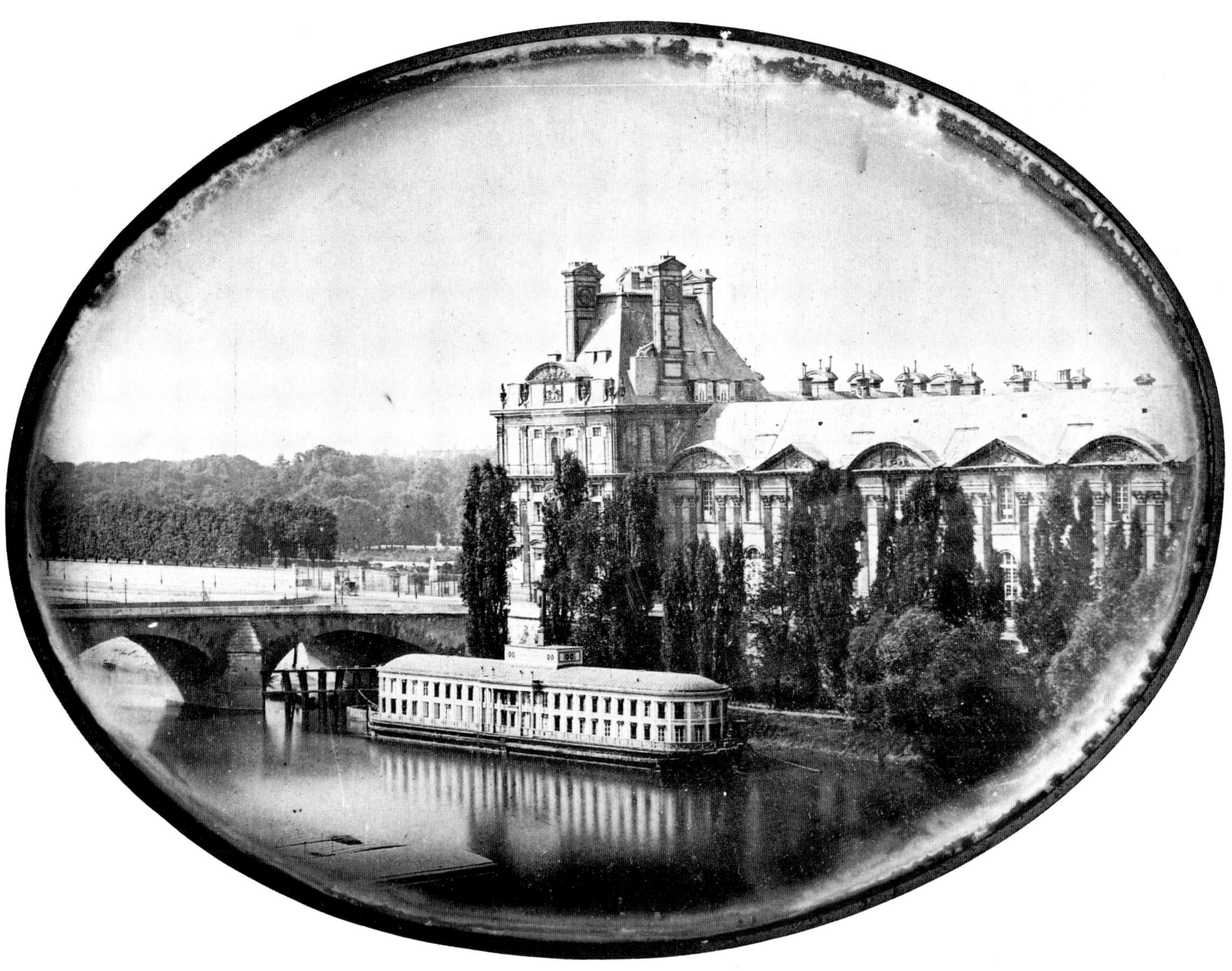

LOUIS-JACQUES-MANDÉ DAGUERRE,
The Louvre from the Left Bank of the Seine,
daguerreotype, 1839,
Musée National des Techniques,
C.N.A.M., Paris.

that an additional clause be added to the contract (May 9, 1835) whereby "M. Daguerre having [...] recognized the possibility of obtaining a more advantageous result in terms of speed, with the help of a process which he has discovered", priority in the discovery was to be accorded to Daguerre himself. By August 1835, he was confident enough to be more precise: "I have achieved the main thing, that is to say, to re-establish the light areas in their true nature and to arrest everything in a durable manner". Having reversed the tonal values of the captured image, Daguerre seems likely to have fully exploited his discovery at this date, using the properties of mercury vapor, which revealed the image by selectively affecting those parts of the surface of the plate which had been exposed to light.

All that was required was "a wash to eliminate the first material" (iodine). This problem, however (which would not have impeded a scientist like Talbot), was still unresolved in February 1837, by which time Daguerre was obtaining images in "seven to ten minutes". He was, nevertheless, determined to get rid of every trace of the iodine which formed part of his "secret" (we now know that a common salt solution would have done the trick). In June 1837, Isidore Niépce came to Paris to sign a "definitive contract" whereby he had to recognize that "M. Daguerre [...] has introduced me to a process of which he is the inventor". This contract mentions two processes: Nicéphore Niépce's, which had scarcely changed, and the process which Daguerre had perfected on his own, and which he baptized (April 28, 1838) the "daguerreotype". After an abortive attempt at obtaining shareholders, Daguerre, who had made contacts at the court of Louis-Philippe, was granted that Arago should announce the result of his work, without divulging its details, to the Academy of Sciences (January 7, 1839). He envisaged "getting the government to buy this discovery". After a fire at the diorama on March 8, 1839, it was agreed that a life annuity of 4,000 francs should be granted to each of the signatories of the contract (Isidore Niépce and Daguerre), linked in addition to a bonus of 2,000 francs to Daguerre for "the secrets of the diorama".

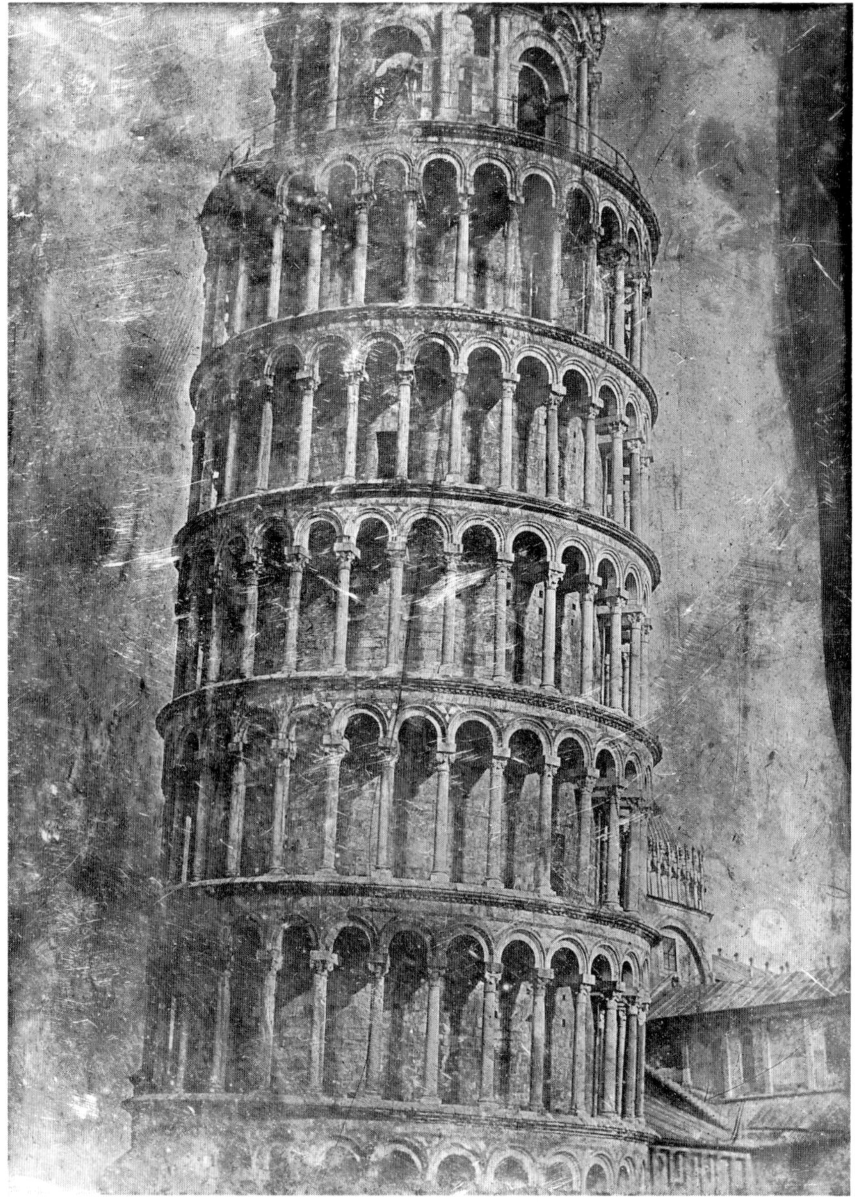

▲ ANONYMOUS,
The Leaning Tower of Pisa,
daguerréotype, undated,
Bibliothèque Nationale, Paris.

LOUIS-JACQUES-MANDÉ DAGUERRE,
Fossils and Shells,
daguerreotype, 1839,
Musée National des Techniques,
▼ C.N.A.M., Paris.

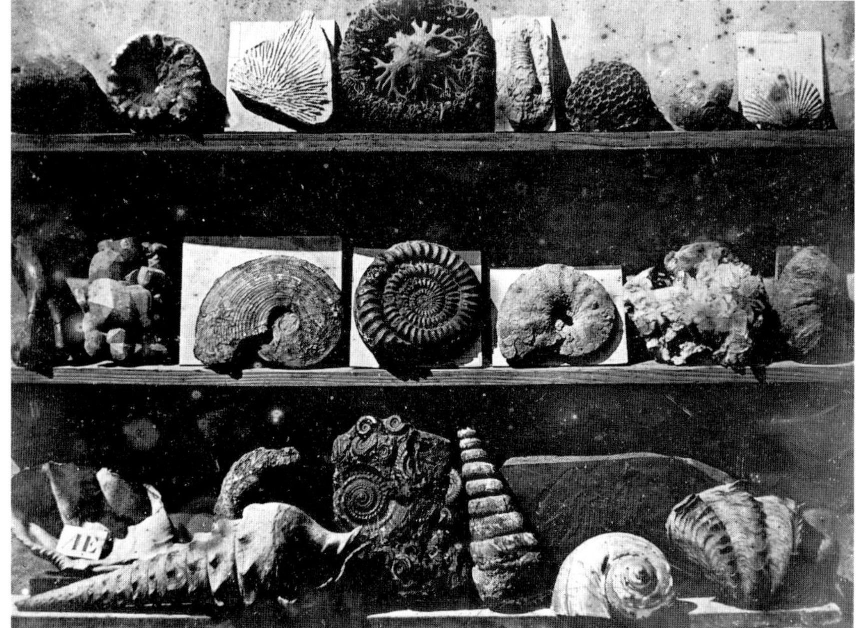

Daguerre was implicitly recognized as the father of the "daguerreotype" process, even though quarrels subsequently developed over the role of Niépce senior. Arago submitted a report to the Chambre des Députés on July 3, 1839, and Gay-Lussac did the same at the Chambre des Pairs on July 30. The process was unveiled and "given to the world" on August 19, 1839 (even though Daguerre had taken out a patent in England on August 14 which excluded the principal rival nation from this generous French donation). The "Arago event" of that day claimed photography for the service of humanity,[6] a force for social progress: "France nobly endows the whole world with a discovery which can contribute so much to the progress of the arts and sciences." Arago, who had already played down Bayard's role, would later lend his weight to refute Talbot's claims by emphasizing that another "compatriot", Niépce, had obtained a successful result before him.

Marc Antoine Gaudin, one of the first "daguerreotypists", present at this famous session of the Academy, described the fever which gripped the first amateur photographers. "Soon the crowd surrounded a newly initiated member. He told us that it involved iodine and mercury, without giving further details. Finally the session closed and the secret was out [...]. A few days later [...] each of us wanted to copy the view from our windows. Fortunate indeed was the man who on the first attempt obtained a silhouette of roofs against the sky: he went into ecstasies over chimney-pots." A brochure was immediately published which went into several French editions in 1839 alone as well as numerous foreign-language editions. The daguerreotype (see following chapter) was a reliable process, despite its undeniably complex manipulations, demanding extreme care in preparation. After a few months of fine-tuning it was accessible to all, and the results were judged to be astonishing.

Today, we know about fifteen daguerreotypes, dating from 1839, attributed to Daguerre, including a triptych offered to Arago (now in Perpignan museum), and another given to the king of Bavaria (destroyed), mainly still-lifes with arrangements of statuettes, views of Paris, and collections of fossils and shells.

Fox Talbot's determination

After his first experiments in 1834–1835 (successful, although he did not realize it at the time) Talbot undertook other scholarly work, for his background was completely different from that of Daguerre. A specialist in classical languages and mathematics, he was in contact with some of the best minds in science, literature, philology, archeology, etc. It was only in January 1839, when news of Arago's communication was published, that he realized his lack of foresight. Possessing only limited information as to the nature of Daguerre's work, he had (wrongly) imagined that it was closer to his own research, and he set about proving his anteriority. From the January 25, he displayed photogenic drawings (a process used from 1834) at the Royal Institution, and he read a paper on the subject to the Royal Society on January 31.[7]

All the "drawings" which he displayed employed the same principle. A flat object, such as a piece of lace, grass, a flower or foliage, was placed on a sheet of paper soaked in silver nitrate or chloride and placed in sunlight for ten to thirty minutes. Areas unprotected from the sun's rays went black, while the paper beneath the object remained white. The main problem was how to prevent the whole image darkening whilst one was actually looking at it – the question of "fixing" the image, dissolving the residual salts which had not been reduced to black metallic silver. At first, Talbot used seasalt (sodium chloride) and potassium iodide. Soon, however (February 1, 1839), his friend Herschel gave him the idea of using sodium hyposulphate as a fixer (still in use today). It should be mentioned that in the context of contemporary research one element of the invention today judged crucial (the use of hypo) was never patented and was freely distributed. In Paris, Biot received this information directly and openly from Talbot, and presumably passed it to Daguerre who immediately used this method for fixing his images.

Talbot obtained three different types of image with inversed tonal values, in which dark tones corresponded to the "light" or transparent parts of an object. Firstly, his photogenic drawings, silhouettes – white on a dark background – of the actual subject, appearing precise, cut out, and detailed. Secondly, his images using the solar microscope, enlargements of very small objects lit by sunlight, fascinating because they were difficult to draw, even under a microscope. Finally, his images produced by the *camera obscura*, obtained in what he called his "mouse-traps", which "produced a bit of magic: natural magic". With these, said Talbot, one could "copy the portrait of a distant object, the façade of a building".[8] Talbot also saw that one could reverse negative images, either by taking them again or by making them transparent and printing them in order to "bring back the shadows and light areas to their original values" (on February 28, 1839, in a letter to Talbot, Herschel first proposed the word *photograph*).

Because full details of the daguerreotype had not yet been divulged, there were reckoned to be

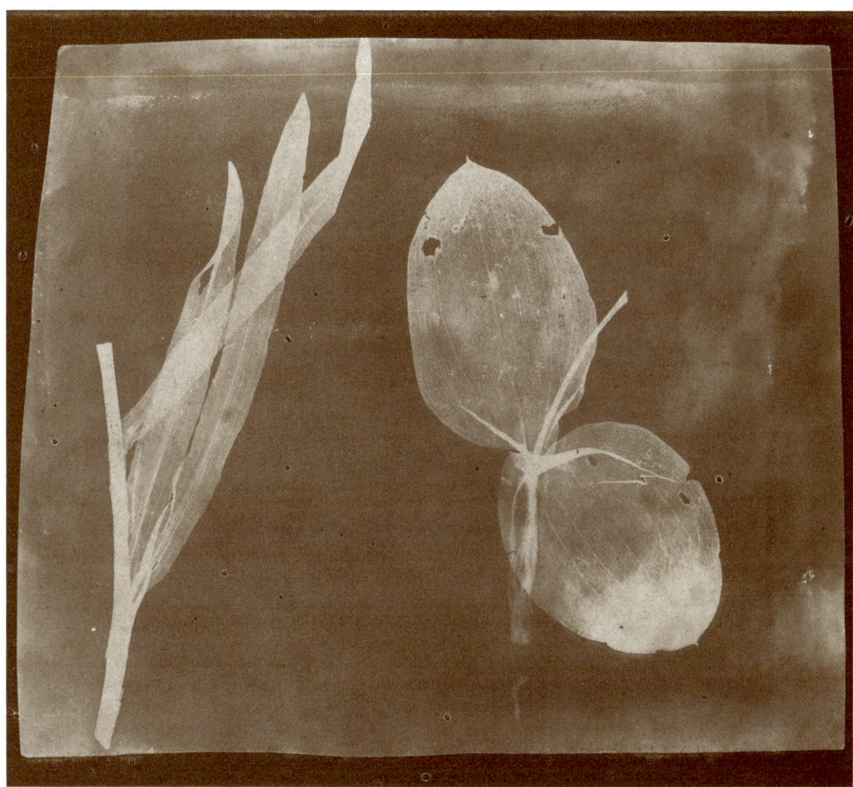

William Henry Fox Talbot, *Orchid Leaves,* April 1839, photogenic drawing, John Paul Getty Museum, Malibu.

similarities between the two processes. Talbot did not want people to accuse him of plagiarism, and he did not as yet know that daguerreotypes were made on metal plates.[9] Thanks to his ensuing correspondence with Biot, Talbot realized that his process and Daguerre's had nothing in common, either in technique or appearance (a shiny metal plate compared with matte paper). Daguerre prepared, in February, to set forth a process on paper in order to goad Talbot into action; he had not yet communicated anything of his method! In this war of uncertainty, and despite Talbot's rapid improvements, it is clear that from April 1839 "M. Daguerre's images far surpass those which are produced over here [in Britain]."[10]

It was already known, however, that the daguerreotype had one major drawback: it allowed only a single copy to be made, and successive copies could not be produced. This was to be the trump card of the English process. However, when visiting Paris, Herschel could not conceal his admiration for daguerreotype images, which he judged "miraculous" for their precision and tonal detail, their "soft, faithful gradation of light and shade, which far surpasses all painting", and their very short exposure time (three minutes in sunlight).[11] Nevertheless, Talbot exhibited 95 photogenic drawings at a meeting of the British Association in Birmingham, a complete presentation of the possibilities offered by his invention – impressions of plants in white on a dark background, copies of engravings, lithographs, and drawings (re-inverted by a second operation so that they appeared in black on a white back-

6. A. Jammes, "L'événement Arago", in *1839, la photographie révélée, cit.*, pp. 23–24.

7. G. Buckland, *Fox Talbot and the Invention of Photography*, Boston, D. R. Codine, 1980; H. J. P. Arnold, *W. H. Fox Talbot, Pioneer of Photography and Man of Science*, London, H. Benham, 1977; H. von Amelunxen, *Die Aufgehobene Zeit*, Berlin, Nishen, 1988.

8. *Literary Gazette*, February 2, 1839.

9. The information was published in the *Athenaeum*, April 6, 1839.

10. *Ibid.*

11. Letter to Talbot dated May 9, 1839. It is quite unambiguous: "excuse this exultation", Herschel apologizes.

The daguerreotype, total impression of reality

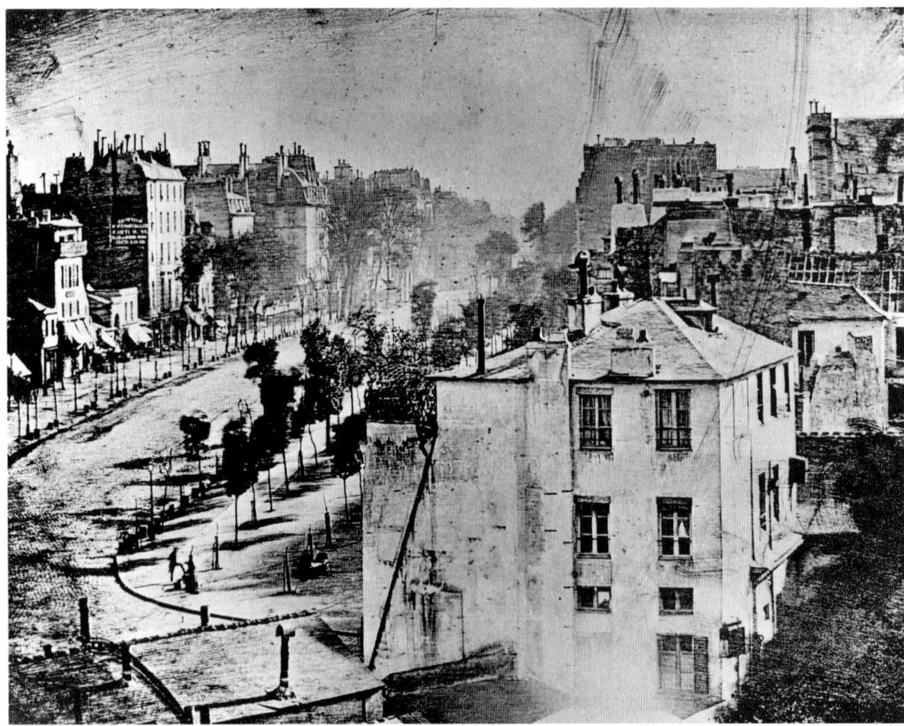

L. J. M. Daguerre,
View of the Boulevard du Temple,
daguerreotype, Paris, 1839, Stadtmuseum, Munich.

Very few people would have been allowed to look at a daguerreotype before the official announcement in August 1839. Among them, the American painter and physician, Samuel F. B. Morse – who invented the electric telegraph – had the privilege of a meeting with Daguerre on March 7, 1839. Shortly afterwards, he told his family about his visit, describing the new object he had been able to admire, a daguerreotype, with its "metallic surface" and having "the appearance of an aquatint engraving" (uncolored).

Niépce, then Daguerre, had adopted the habit of working by pointing their *camera obscura* out of a window. Thus, it was a view of the Boulevard du Temple, taken from his apartment next to the Diorama that Daguerre showed to Morse (he later gave it to King Ludwig I of Bavaria).

Morse was particularly enthusiastic about the detail of the "drawing". "You cannot imagine how exquisite is the fine detail portrayed. No painting or engraving could ever hope to touch it. For example, when looking over a street one might notice a distant advertisement hoarding and be aware of the existence of lines or letters, without being able to read these tiny signs with the naked eye. With the help of a hand-lens, pointed at this detail, each letter became perfectly and clearly visible, and it was the same thing for the tiny cracks on the walls of buildings or the pavements of the streets."

Above all, Morse realized that the length of the exposure, which at this time was several minutes, would not allow passers-by or the traffic on the boulevard to appear, their movement being too rapid to leave an impression on the sensitive surface. "Moving objects leave no impression. The boulevard, though constantly crossed by a flood of pedestrians and carriages, appeared completely deserted, apart from a person who was having his boots polished. His feet must, of course, have remained immobile for a certain time, one of them being placed on the boot-black's box, the other on the ground."

Another renowned scientist, Alexander von Humboldt, who took part in the commission charged with judging the importance of Daguerre's discovery (with Biot and Arago), also wrote two letters on the subject, one of them to C. G. Carus, a scientist and philosopher. He too was struck by the extreme precision of the image, in which not even the least significant detail was omitted, as though the process possessed the power to "represent" everything. "One could see in the image that in one skylight – and what a trifle – a pane had been broken, and mended using gummed paper." He too noticed the fortuitous presence of people who had remained almost motionless: "In the middle of the river were horses and men fishing, with their shadows projected in the most precise manner, for being a great distance away their slight movements scarcely spoiled things, thanks to the small angle involved."

These expressions of amazement reflect the visual novelty that photography introduced into a world of images created "by hand" and subject to rules which would soon appear artificial compared with this ability to record everything automatically without any manual or mental judgement.

Michel Frizot

ground), views taken by means of the *camera obscura*, in particular interior and exterior views of his residence at Lacock Abbey, and enlargements, up to 400 times natural size, obtained via the solar microscope. The collection demonstrated the scientific interest of his research.

Nevertheless, from September 14, 1839, demonstrations of the daguerreotype were held in London. Discussions moved from technical considerations to become an argument about perceived injustices between the two industrial neighbors. Talbot, who acquired apparatus for making daguerreotypes, admitted that his images lacked the formal perfection of the daguerreotype. However, he insisted, justly, that the English method was better for duplicating images, which must recommend it for the publication of works including photographs. It was on this basis that the future of photography (and the decline of the daguerreotype) would be established.

Bayard's disappointment

Meanwhile, Biot told Talbot about the experiments with photography on paper made by a certain Bayard, to encourage Talbot to perfect "a fast paper-based procedure for travelers".[12] It is not clear how this civil servant at the Ministry of Finance, a friend of painters and engravers (Ziegler, Gavarni, Bertall) but lacking any

12. Letter dated November 10, 1839. An English journal, the *Art Union*, mentioned Bayard's "drawings" on paper on October 15, 1839.

scientific training, became interested in images produced in the *camera obscura*. Only his research notebook (at the Société Française de Photographie, Paris) allows us to suppose that he worked to a tight time-scale, with the "first trials" beginning on February 1, 1839, soon after he received the details of the daguerreotype. Indeed, the details given in the notebook leave no doubt about the sequence of events: "March 20, obtained direct images via the *camera obscura*. 22 inst., showed samples to M. Grévedon and M. Saint. One needs about an hour. April 6, half an hour or 35 minutes. May 13, M. Biot. May 20, M. Arago. 10 June, half an hour for statues and 20 minutes for landscapes." On June 24, 1839, Bayard displayed a frame containing 30 prints of architectural views and still-lifes on the occasion of a charity fête for victims of the Martinique earthquake. Two newspapers reported it, referring to "a different process from M. Daguerre's".[13]

In the political and journalistic context of the announcement of the daguerreotype, Bayard would have found it hard to generate interest in his process, which appeared less spectacular. His paper images looked very similar to drawings, with their smooth appearance, subtle tonal changes, deep blacks, and grainy texture (that of the paper and the irregularities of its impregnation by the chemicals). Above all, they were unique, rather than being able to be produced as multiple copies. The appearance of the daguerreotype, on the other hand, is very different, being on metal and distinguished by its extreme precision (the artistic character of the one was, perhaps excessively, compared with the scientific character of the other).

Rejected by Arago – the official umpire – and receiving little support from Biot, Bayard had no alternative but to turn to the Academy of Fine Arts (who also played a role in the acceptance of the daguerreotype, despite the supremacy of the Academy of Sciences.).[14] Being forced to follow this path created competition, albeit prejudicial and false, between the "scientific" daguerreotype and the "artistic" paper print. Bayard displayed "a view of Paris which brings together all the conditions of perfection as regards accuracy of perspective and the picturesque effect", and photographs of statues, his favorite subject, combining whiteness, luminosity of modeling, effects of matter, and immobility with references to the art of the past. However, the process remained slow. The report mentions exposure times of half an hour, and "one would wish rather more sharpness of detail, less indecision or softness in the outline".

Despite their very different methods of production, Bayard's images combine the advantages and disadvantages of Talbot's photogenic drawings. They were slow to make, but had the appearance of a drawing; they lacked precision but were simple to produce; they were easy to store and economical in the materials used (Talbot included an analogous process in his patent of 1841). As for the actual method, Bayard did not release it until February 24, 1840, when he revealed before the Academy of Sciences how "writing paper prepared according to Mr. Talbot's method is soaked for a few seconds in a solution of potassium iodide. Then, applying this paper to a slate, it is placed at the back of a *camera obscura*. When the image has formed, the paper is washed in a solution of sodium hyposulfite." The distinctive factor of Bayard's process was that it produced a direct positive image in which the action

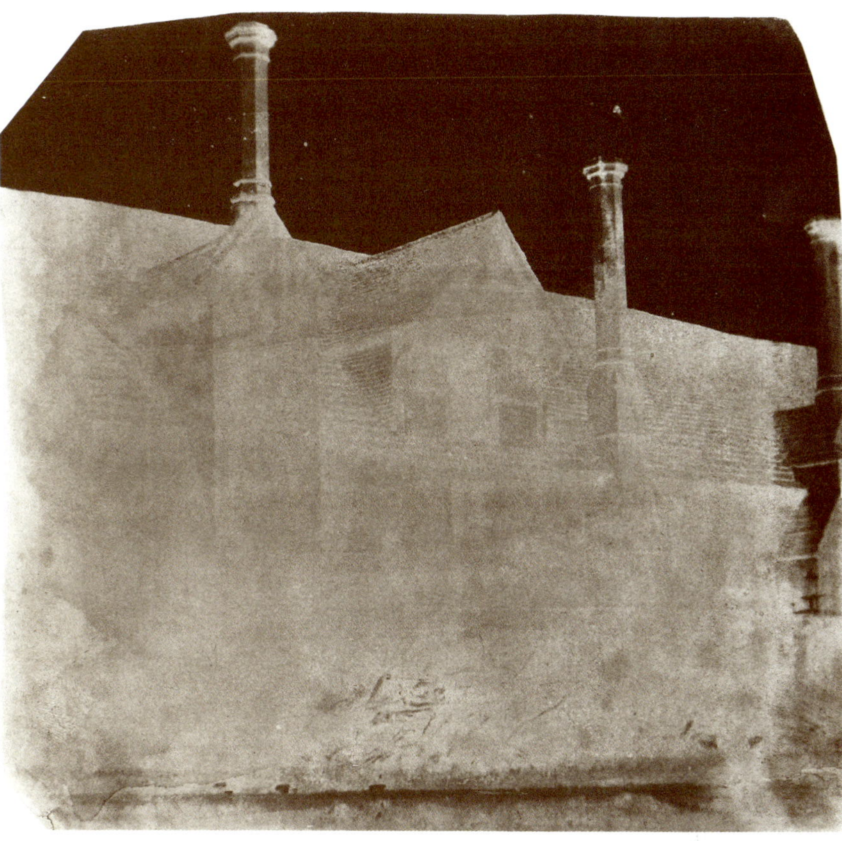

WILLIAM HENRY FOX TALBOT,
Roofs of Lacock Abbey,
paper negative,
June 1840,
Fox Talbot Museum,
Lacock.

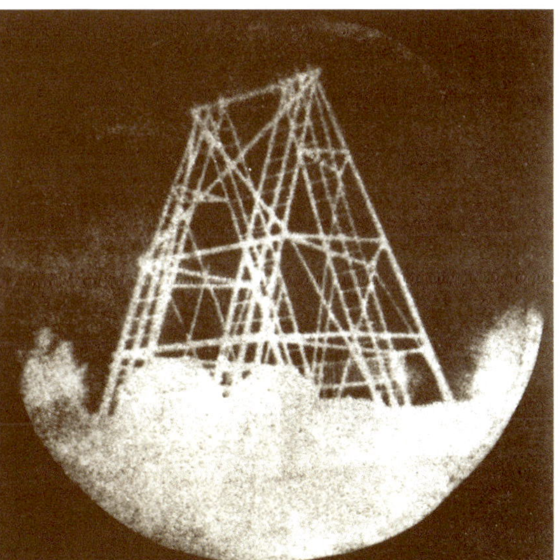

JOHN HERSCHEL,
W. Herschel's Telescope at Slough,
November 1839,
paper negative,
Oxford Museum
of the History of Science.

13. *Le Moniteur*, July 22, 1839; *Le Constitutionnel*, August 3, 1839. J.-C. Gautrand and M. Frizot, *Hippolyte Bayard: naissance de l'image photographique*, Amiens, Trois Cailloux, 1986.

14. Session of the Royal Academy of Fine Arts, "Report on the drawings produced by M. Bayard's process", by R. Rochette, November 2, 1839.

Le Noyé [Self-portrait as a drowned man] by Hippolyte Bayard

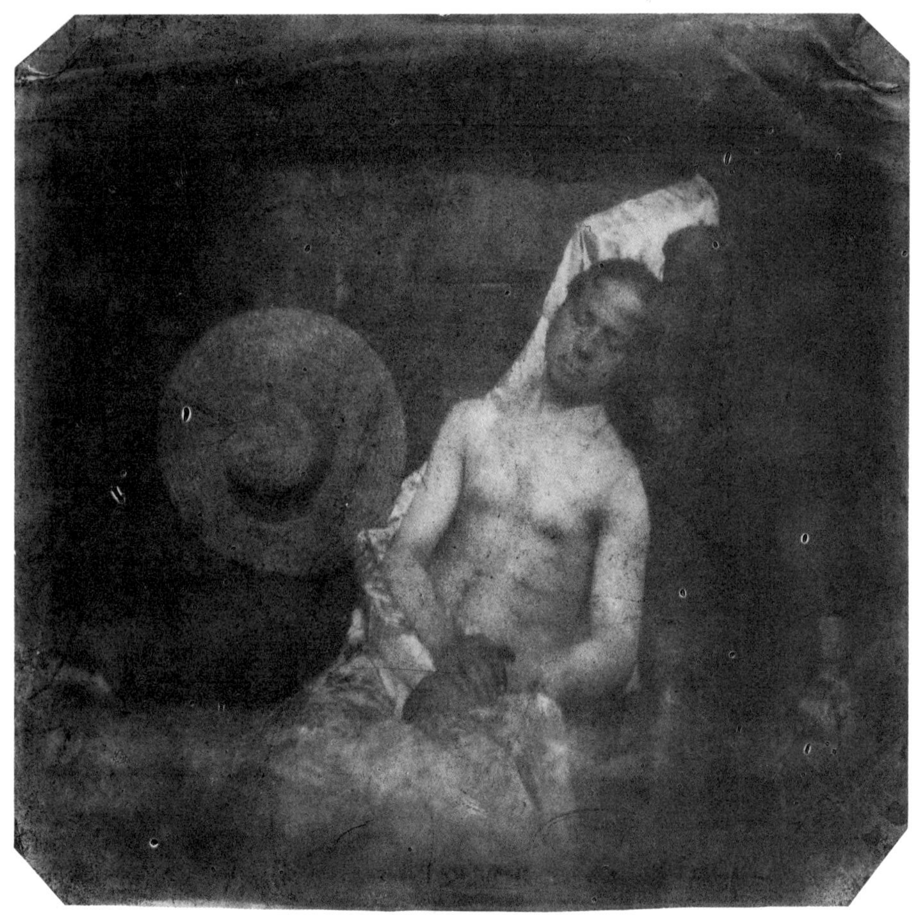

Hippolyte Bayard, *Self-portrait as a Drowned Man,* *October 1840, direct positive print, Société Française de Photographie, Paris.*

On October 18, 1840, Hippolyte Bayard put his signature to a strange piece of text, written on the back of an equally strange photograph. It showed a man who was stripped to the waist, wrapped in a sheet, and sitting on a sort of bench, apparently asleep. Two objects appear next to him: a vase and a straw hat. The text adds further information about the subject of the photograph and about how it should be interpreted: "The corpse of the gentleman which you see on the other side is that of M. Bayard, the inventor of the pro-cess whose marvelous results you have just seen or which you are going to see. As far as I know, this ingenious and indefatigable researcher has been busy perfecting his invention for about three years."

"The Academy, the king, and all those who have seen his drawings, which he himself considered imperfect, have admired them as you are admiring them at this moment. This has honored him greatly and has earned him not a penny. The government, which had given far too much to M. Daguerre, said it could not do anything for M. Bayard, and the poor man drowned himself."

"O, the fleeting nature of human things! Artists, scientists, and newspapers have been concerned with him for a long time, and now that he has been exposed at the morgue for several days, nobody has yet recognized him or asked for him. Ladies and gentlemen, let us pass on to other things, for fear your sense of smell may be affected, for the head and the hands of the gentleman are beginning to rot, as you can see."

The scene is thus to be interpreted as the corpse of a drowned man at the morgue, the inventor of a photographic process – Bayard himself – unrecognized by society (government, scientists, newspapers). The man who had invented the direct positive process in 1839 complains, a year later, that people had preferred Daguerre to him and that his only recourse is suicide.

A diatribe against the uncertainties of politics and industry, this image is, therefore, primarily a work of denunciation, of resignation, of disappointment. It is the representation of the melancholy of the solitary artist. It is also the very first fictional photograph, the illustration of a story in which visible clues are to be interpreted with respect to a key, a "caption".

To give credence to this reading, Bayard exploits fully the veracity of the photograph, insisting, for example, on the decomposition of the head and the hand (a summer tan, reinforced by the lack of sensitivity of silver salts to brown or red colors). Bayard also relies on another specific characteristic of the photographic process: the need for a long exposure – as long as several minutes in full sunshine – which excluded the possibility of portraiture (at this date it was still difficult to take portraits using the daguerreotype process) and allowed scarcely anything other than deathbed portraits or posing with closed eyes. The subject evoked by Bayard (the drowned man) thus stems from the very nature of photography.

When we know that Bayard made three exposures (by his direct positive process, each giving only a single, unique image) and that he was accompanied by a statuette of a woman bathing, at his feet (scarcely visible in this version), a vase, and the hat – all three of which appear in many of his photographic compositions, like fetish objects – it is clear that Bayard wanted to create a personal and symbolic "œuvre". He enriched the recurrent theme of the self-portrait of the artist with the double proof of the success of his process (by means of which the image which "you are admiring [...] this moment" was produced) and the ingratitude of destiny towards an "ingenious and indefatigable researcher".

Michel Frizot

of light produced white silver iodide on a darkened paper.

A little later, at the start of 1841, when replying to Talbot who had let him know how his work on the calotype process was proceeding, Bayard demanded that a sealed envelope which he had deposited at the Academy of Sciences on November 8, 1839 be opened. Inside were notes in which he clearly described a paper process employing iodine and mercury vapor in order to develop a latent image, and produce a negative.

In spite of a further mention by the Academy of Fine Arts in November 1840 (when the exposure time had been reduced to 20 minutes), Bayard's process would never succeed as a real "photographer's tool", challenged as it was by the mimetic magic of the daguerreotype and Talbot's new proposals (the calotype), which Bayard was not slow in using. By opting for the rival process, it would be impossible for him to carry on promoting his own process. Photography had wandered off one of its potential paths (obtaining an image without a negative and without development) – a path which would be rediscovered only with the Polaroid process.

Up until this time, Bayard had embarked on numerous experiments with the direct positive process, producing hundreds of images showing arrangements of statues, busts, and reliefs carefully set up in symmetrical arrangements occupying all the available space, an obsessive quest for the best visual proof of his technical success. Sometimes photographing himself beside his disdainful plaster models, Bayard wished to show that his method was not applicable only to human beings – here was living proof of the absence of trickery. His *Self-portrait as a Drowned Man* made in October 1840, the first "fictional" photograph, accompanied by a lament against the fate which had made people prefer Daguerre's process to his own, is without doubt one of the last manifestations of a process which was destined to be forgotten.

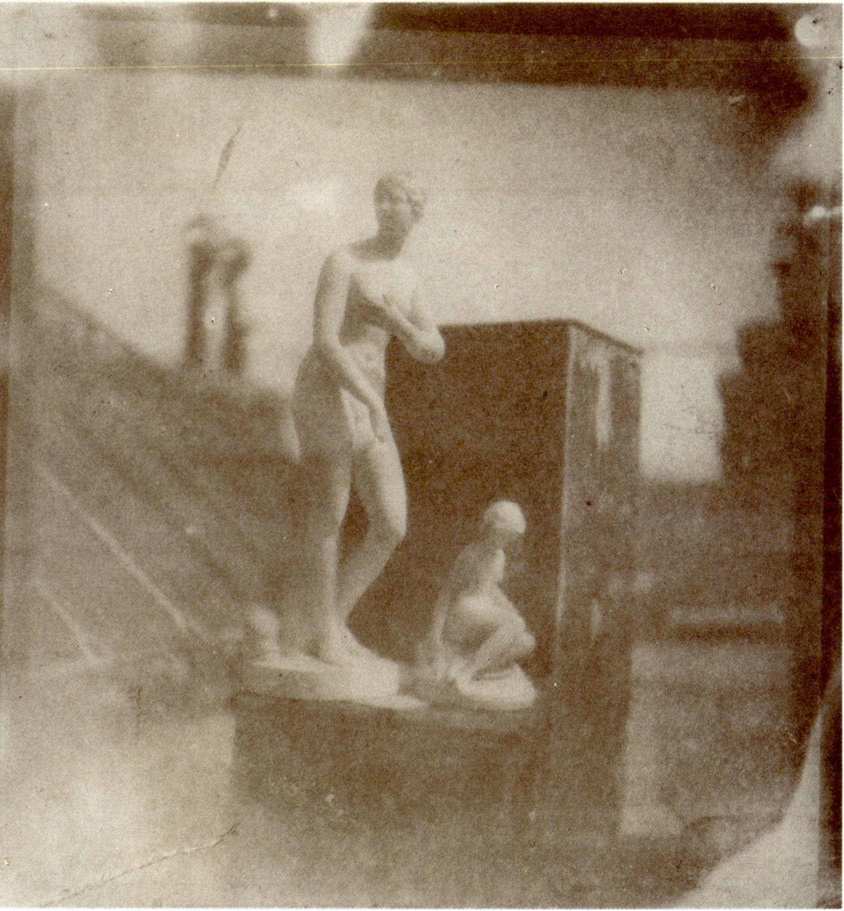

Hippolyte Bayard,
Two Statues Photographed on Roof-tops,
direct positive print,
1839,
Société Française
de Photographie, Paris.

Long live the calotype!

Bayard's disappointment at the end of 1840 would not affect Talbot, who had just succeeded with a "second invention" in the field of photography. Rivalries continued. When Daguerre announced in January 1841 (probably exaggerating) that he had reduced exposure times to one or two seconds Talbot decided to make public his research of September–October 1840,[15] and his discovery of a process to which he had given the name "calotype". While reducing exposure time to a few minutes (at best, even ten seconds) the calotype process, which produced a paper negative, used the concept of the "latent image" (also in Daguerre's process). The negative had, furthermore, the advantage of being able to be stored after being exposed and developed later. This discovery (the separation of the exposure and the physical appearance of the negative image) was the basis of all subsequent photography, whatever the support material. It gave a second wind to Talbot's experiments, which was subsequently applied to virtually all subject matter, a challenge to the supposed advantages of the daguerreotype.

For practical purposes, only two processes remained in use in 1841 (insomuch as Bayard would soon give up his ambitions): Daguerre's, which was completely operational and which would soon spread into every portrait studio, and Talbot's, whose future was still uncertain but which would play an ever important role during the following years thanks to its ingenuity and its indisputable advantages.

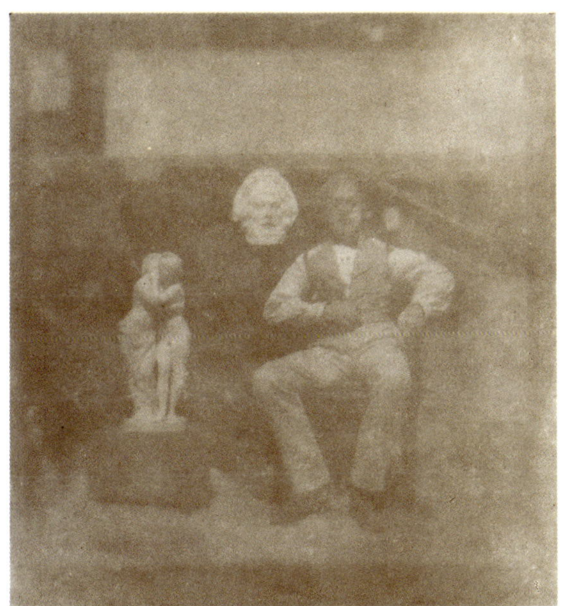

◀ Hippolyte Bayard,
Self-portrait,
1839-1840,
direct positive print,
Société Française
de Photographie, Paris.

15. *Comptes rendus des séances de l'Académie des sciences*, 24 February 1840, p. 337.

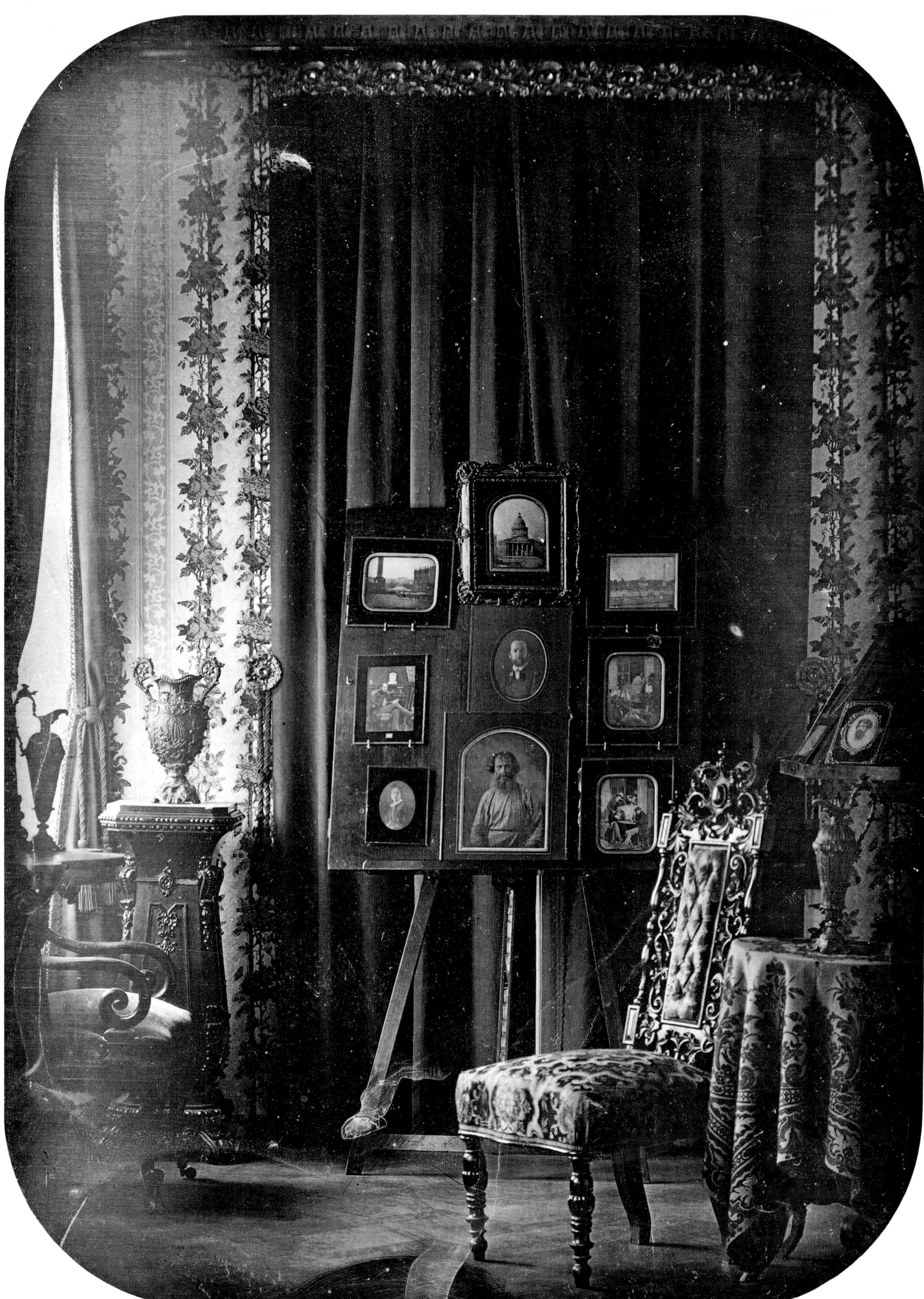

A NEW WORLD OF PICTURES 3

The use and spread of the daguerreotype process

Timm Starl

In 1839, the daguerreotype would suddenly offer an incredibly precise and effective image of the world as it had never before been seen. When portraiture became technically feasible, the spread of daguerreotypes, each a unique and expensive object, was subject to market forces and at first was restricted to towns and the well-off middle classes. Improvements in the process would soon lead to the opening of numerous studios, encouraging a whole network of traveling photographers. The world in all its aspects – people's role in society, inaccessible places, phenomena invisible to the naked eye – seemed destined to be preserved in a museum of images, an inventory of curiosities; but this would quickly be overtaken by innovations which made duplication on paper possible.

In 1815, the German author E. T. A. Hoffmann wrote his story *The Sandman*, which tells of a student's love for a life-size doll. From his window, Nathanaël watches Olympia in the house opposite. Seen through his small telescope, she appears to him to be a living being. This story is one of a collection of "night pieces" – "piece" here signifying a painting or picture – of which the first part was published in 1816.[1] The same year also saw the first attempts by J. N. Niépce to fix images obtained using the *camera obscura*.

In 1822, *My Cousin's Corner Window* appeared. A writer, confined to his room by illness and sinking into melancholia because of a failure of his creative powers, watches from his study all the coming and goings in the marketplace below. Sometimes simply looking out, sometimes observing through a telescope, he gazes upon "the most varied scenes of life among the townspeople", trying to form connections between individuals and making conjectures about their lives. To the man at the window the world becomes a picture and "the art of looking" brings him renewed courage and hope. The author of the story,[2] Hoffmann, died in 1822. This was the year when Niépce's experimenting brought successful results – he managed to produce the first light-resistant pictures, even though they were only copies of copperplate engravings.

Only two years later Niépce was able to preserve permanently the view from his brother's window at Le Gras. The imaginative sketches of the writer now had, so to speak, a material counterpart. From now on, the nineteenth century's way of seeing was to be shaped by ever more sophisticated devices producing pictures which, taken together, embodied a particular world-view. The eye, registering and ordering, arranging and delimiting, created a panorama which seemed to suggest that everything that could be depicted was also amenable to calculation and to domination. To those living at the time of the Industrial Revolution, the camera was at the same time both a guarantor and an expression of progress. It also became an indispensable piece of equipment with which to track down and record all phenomena, as accurately and as comprehensively as possible. Pictures of oneself and of the world demonstrated that it was possible to share in every new achievement.

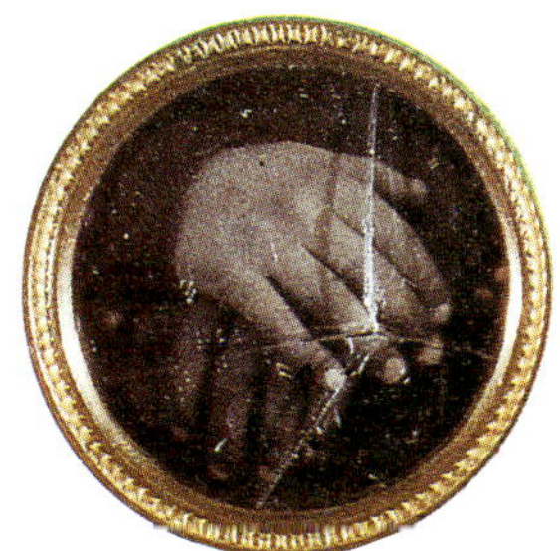

Albert S. Southworth and Josiah J. Hawes, (attributed), ***Button with inlaid daguerreotype,*** circa 1847, George R. Rinhart Collection.

◀ J.-B. L. Gros, ***The Salon,*** daguerreotype, circa 1844–1856, private collection.

Enthusiasm (1839)

Daguerre's invention of 1839 was indeed hailed by many in the kind of terms that might be used by a mechanical engineer. The physicist and chemist J. L. Gay-Lussac, describing the *View of a Landscape and Every Object* to the Chambre des Pairs (Upper House of Parliament), spoke of "mathematical precision". For commentators in the daily and weekly press, too, precision was the chief criterion by which the invention was

1. See *Der Automaten-Mensch: E. T. A. Hoffmanns Erzählung vom "Sandmann": Mit Bildern aus Alltag und Wahnsinn.* Berlin, Klaus Wagenbach, 1976, pp. 58–92.

2. E. T. A. Hoffmann, "Des Vetters Eckfenster", in Hoffmann, *Werke in einem Band,* Dortmund, Harenberg Kommunikation, 1982, pp. 548–576.

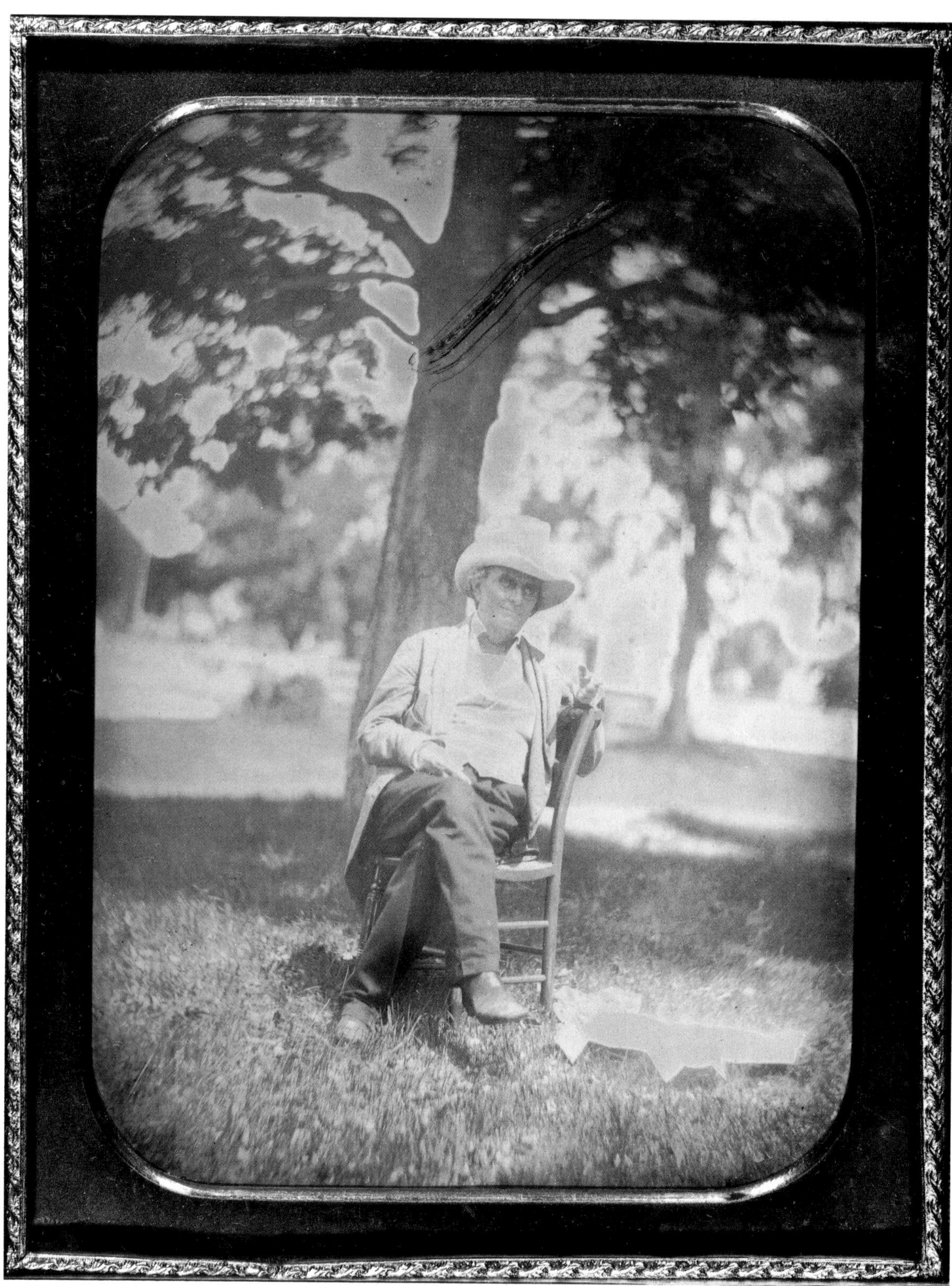

ANONYMOUS,
Daniel Webster on his Massachusetts Estate,
daguerreotype,
circa 1848,
International Museum of Photography,
George Eastman House,
Rochester.

judged. This is because only the sharpness of the image and the wealth of detail it contained could give the viewer the sense of seeing something that had really existed. People picked out every detail with astonished delight, since this proved the authenticity of the reproduction: "By the assistance of a powerful lens, which magnified fifty times, applied to the delineation, every letter was clearly and distinctly legible, and so also were the minutest breaks and lines in the walls of the buildings", reported S. F. B. Morse, the American inventor of the electric telegraph, writing from Paris to New York about the new invention on March 9, 1839.[3]

This need for confirmation of the real world was, naturally, most marked in those countries or regions where daily life was most affected by change. The demand for pictures would naturally be greatest where it was already most apparent that only a small minority could acquire the new products. This applied, above all, to countries where industrialization and capitalist methods of production and distribution of goods were most highly developed. It was almost inevitable, there-

3. Quoted from Beaumont Newhall, *History of Photography*, revised and enlarged edition, London, Secker and Warburg 1986, p. 16. The letter was printed in the New York *Observer* on April 19, 1839.

fore, that photography should have been invented in Britain and the daguerreotype process in France. Later it would become clear that it was the discovery made in Britain, then the greatest industrial nation, that was the more significant of the two, especially as it brought with it the possibility of a division of labor in the production of photographic prints.

However, it seems equally appropriate that the triumphal progress of daguerreotyping, with its unique (because non-copiable) pictures, should have started out from Paris, at that time the cultural center of the world. The great advantage of these pictures was that they were able to satisfy people's wish for an exact representation of a subject more completely than the images on paper. At first this is one of the main reasons why they were more popular.

While the spread of the daguerreotype process was to some extent determined by the different levels of technical development and economic prosperity in particular countries and regions, the speed with which, once the news of the invention became known, individuals began to make their own practical experiments, seems to suggest that such pictures had been long-awaited. For even before Daguerre's instructions had been translated or cameras and chemicals from Paris were available, experiments were being made in many different places using homemade apparatus and hastily prepared mixtures of chemicals. Within a few weeks of the process being made public by Arago on August 19, 1839, aspects of the invention were being reinvented or adapted. M.-A. Gaudin, unwilling to rely on a Paris optician to supply him

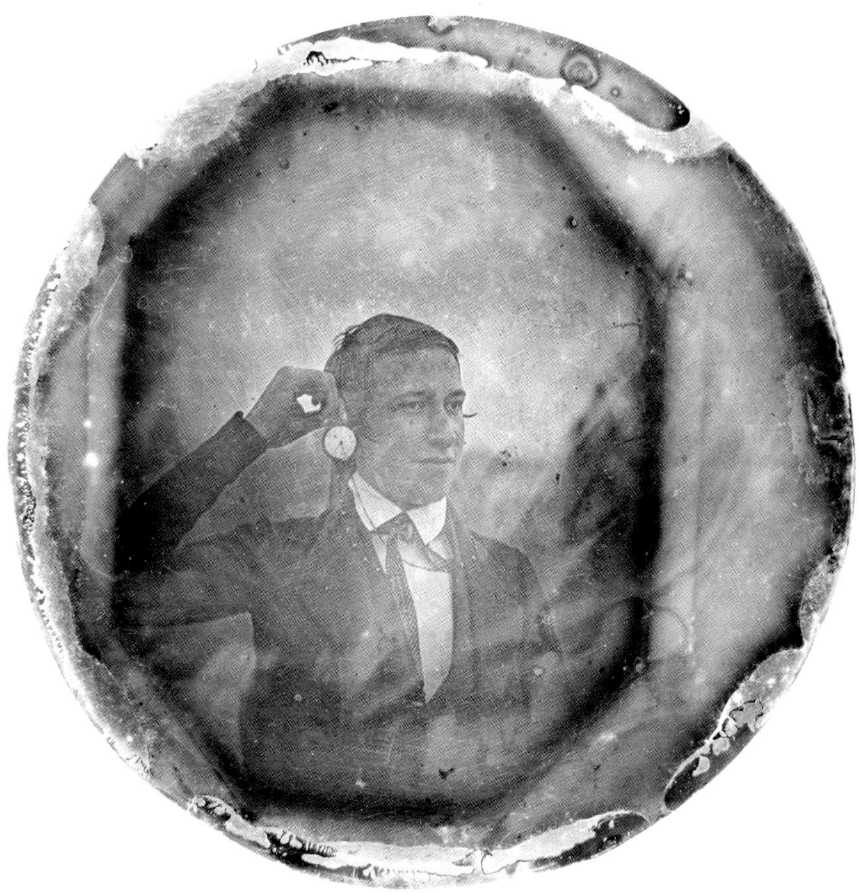

Henri Ziegler,
Portrait of Gaspar Ziegler at Mulhouse,
daguerreotype, 1841,
Musée Historique de Mulhouse.

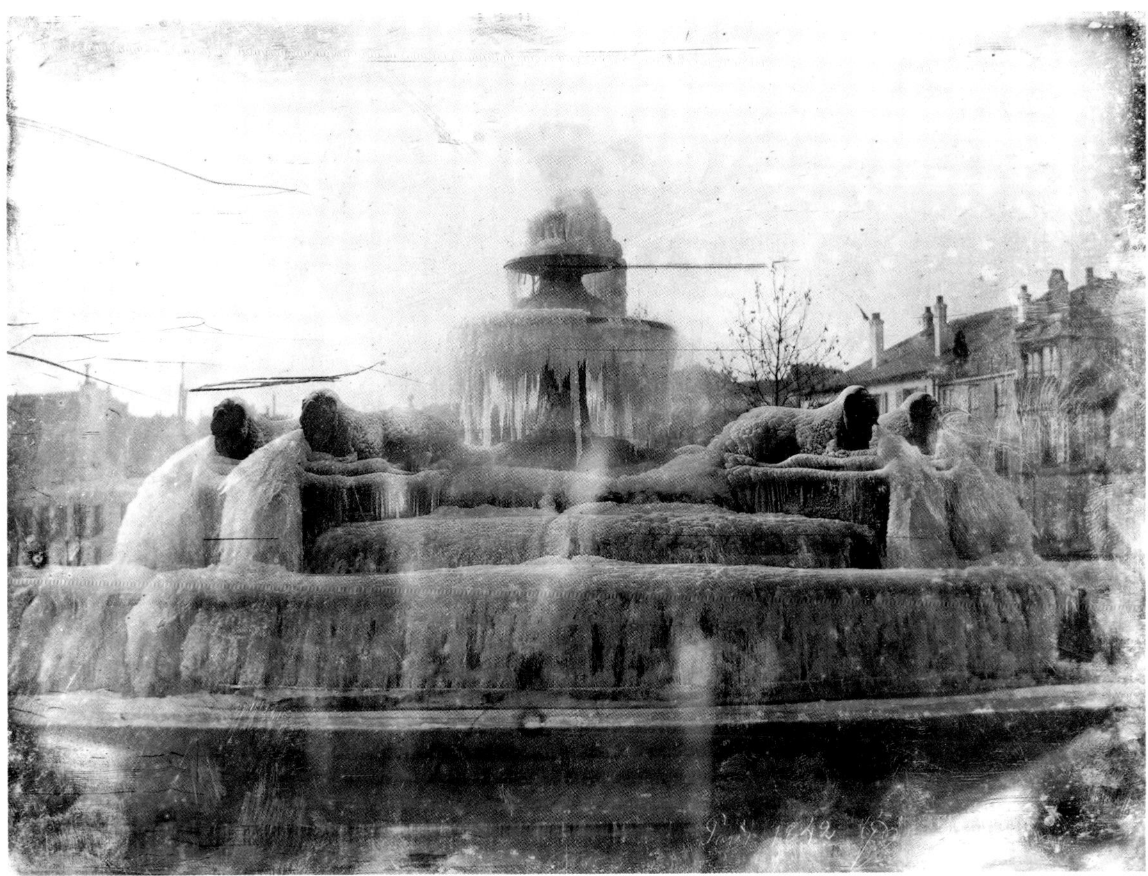

Joseph-Philibert Girault de Prangey,
Frozen Water in the Fountain at the Château d'Eau,
Paris, daguerreotype, 1842,
Bibliothèque Nationale, Paris.

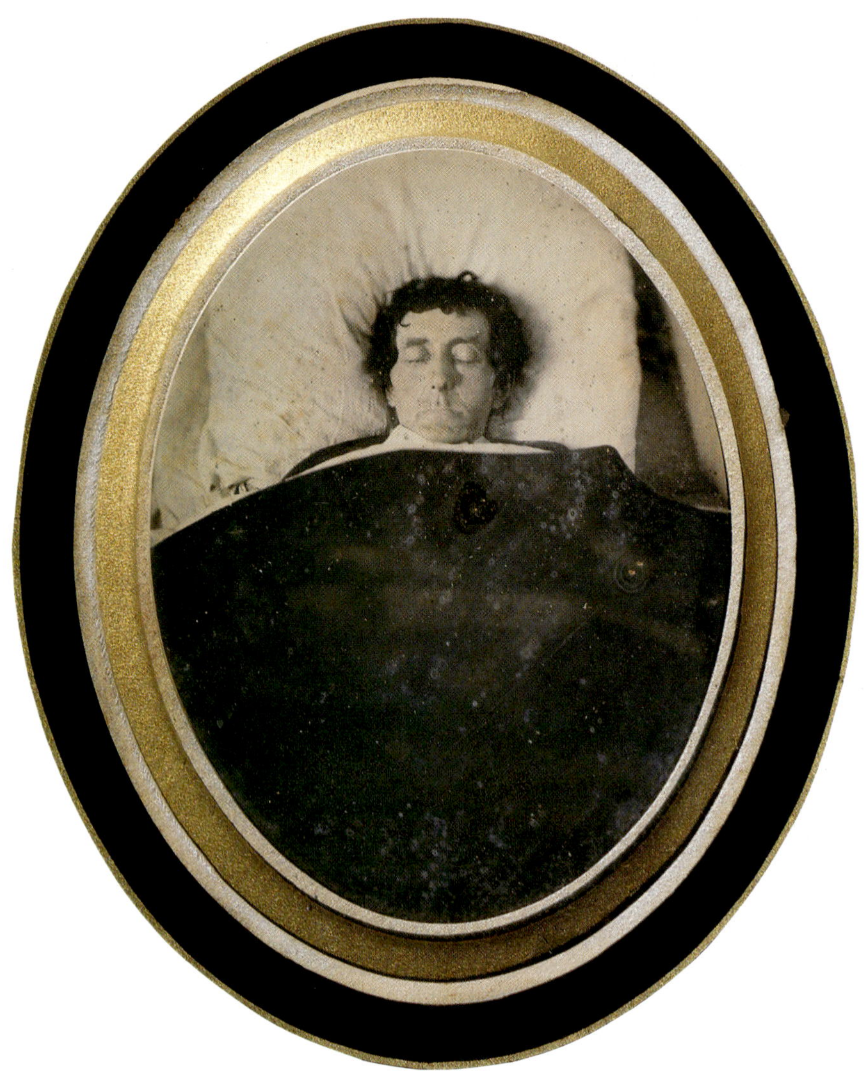

D.-F. Millet, *Posthumous portrait,* colored daguerreotype, circa 1854–1860, Bibliothèque Nationale, Paris.

with a suitable *camera obscura,* instead began on 20 August to experiment with an "appareil [...] composé, d'une lentille ordinaire de trois pouces de foyer, adaptée à un étui de carton" [a camera [...] made up of an ordinary lens with a focal length of three inches, fitted into a cardboard box].[4] The first pictures made in Berlin were produced on September 16 by the optician T. Durffel using a camera which he had made himself.[5] In New York, A. S. Wolcott and J. Johnson finally succeeded in producing a portrait on October 6, using a small camera, without a lens but with a mirror, which they had constructed that day.[6]

When experiments were successful, the results were at once put on public view, after first being announced in the local press. Usually they were displayed in the windows or glass cases of opticians, art dealers or booksellers. In the countries of southern Europe, on the other hand, it was sometimes the experiments themselves that were announced in advance and carried out on a suitable public square in the town. In this way the citizens of Florence, Turin, and Trieste, or of Barcelona, actually witnessed the making of the first daguerreotype in their native city. In Warsaw it was in the city hall, between October 13 and November 2, that daguerreotypes were exhibited. At first, only an anonymous example from Paris and then another from Berlin were on view, but, finally, the first successful examples produced in Poland were added to the display.[7] The daguerreotype was also admitted to centers of serious scientific study. The pictures made on October 2 by A. von Ettingshausen at Johannisberg Castle were displayed on November 22 in the physics lecture theatre of the University of Vienna.[8] One might say that the places most strongly associated with daguerreotypes in 1839 and 1840 were the street, the shop, and the laboratory.

Because plates were still not very light-sensitive and lenses not very fast, bright daylight was one of the chief preconditions for the success of a picture. For this reason, most experiments were conducted in the open air, if possible in sunshine or at around midday, and certainly not in very cloudy weather or at twilight. To escape from the press of spectators and to be able to make the necessary preparations undisturbed, a daguerreotypist would often place the camera on a window-ledge or on the balcony of a flat on an upper story of a building. This is why many of the early pictures show views across roofs or down onto a street, like the two by Daguerre of the Boulevard du Temple. These were the best-known pictures of 1839: every Paris correspondent, whether he had seen them with his own eyes or could only follow descriptions given by others, gave an account of the sensational new process using these two pictures as examples and pointing out the innumerable details that could be picked out in them. The general fascination may have been heightened by the fact that, for the first time, the image of a human being had been captured, a man who had been having his shoes cleaned and had therefore stood still for a long time, while vehicles and passers-by had moved, as it were, out of the picture.

However, pictures taken from above were also part of a new vision. An elevated vantage point was chosen in order to widen the horizon and to make a record of everything that was in front of the camera – whether it was clearly visible, discernible only on close inspection or had entered the field of vision merely by chance. The camera registered everything with equal clarity, capturing everything in its entirety, both foreground objects and those further back, the sublime and the ephemeral. At the same time, by choosing the city as their subject, these pioneers were indicating that they were at the center of public life, at the point from which all progress emanated, at the hub of modernity.

Pictures of this kind were soon on sale to the public. In the autumn of 1839 they were available

4. M. A. Gaudin, *Traité pratique de Photographie*, Paris, 1844, pp. 5–7.

5. See Baier, *Quellendarstellungen zur Geschichte der Fotografie*, Munich, Schirmer/Mosel, 1977, p. 485. Baier quotes reports of September 16, 1839 which appeared on the following day in the *Vossische Zeitung* and in the *Spernesche Zeitung*.

6. See F. and M. Rinhart, *The American Daguerreotype*, Athens, Georgia, University of Georgia Press, 1981, p. 27.

7. See Julius Garztecki, "Early Photography in Eastern Europe: Poland", in *History of Photography*, no. 1, 1979, pp. 39–62, esp. p. 41.

8. W. Neite, in *"In unnachahmlicher Treue": Photographie im 19. Jahrhundert — ihre Geschichte in den deutschsprachigen Ländern*, Cologne, 1979, pp. 27–41, esp. p. 38.

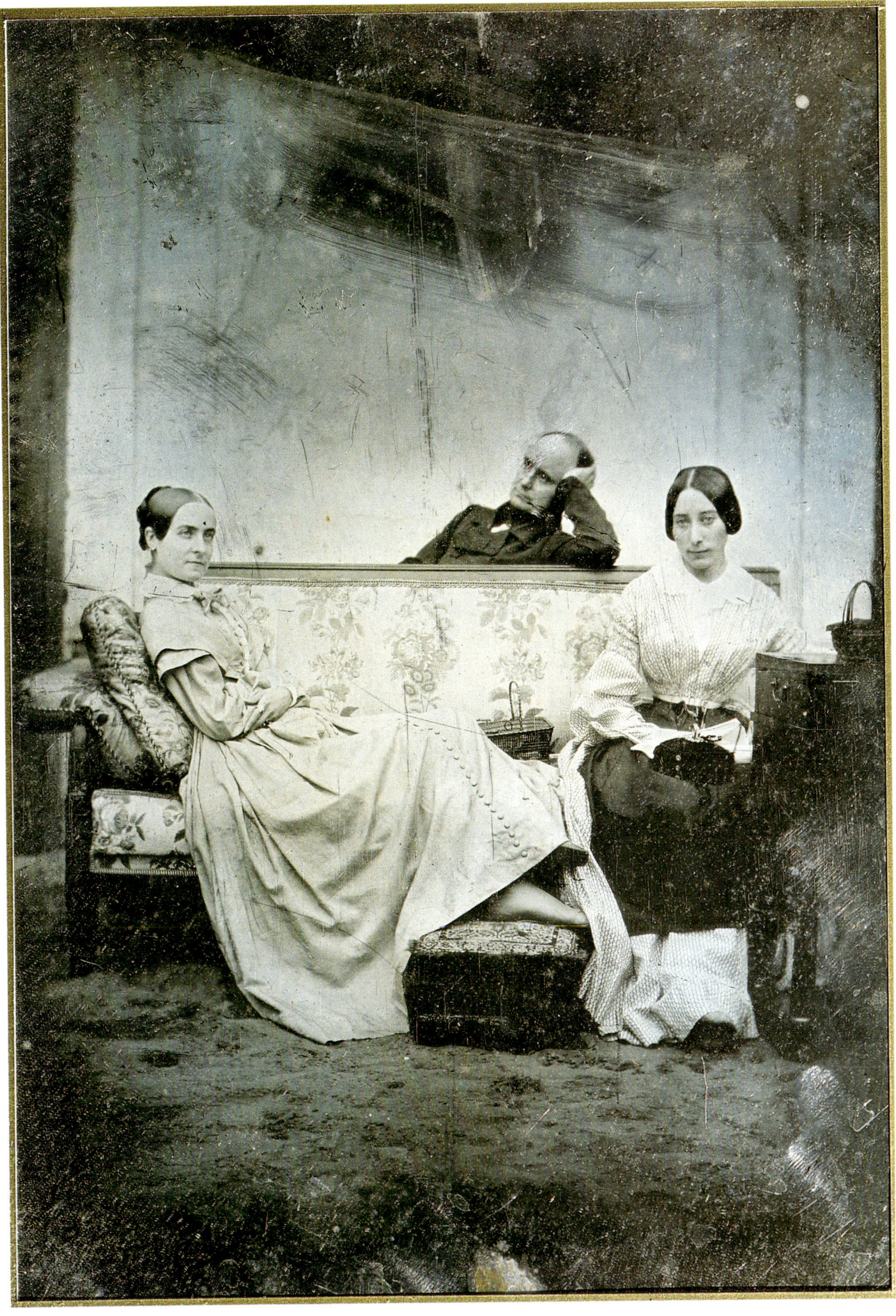

Anonymous,
Group with Mme E. Bertin,
daguerreotype,
circa 1845–1850,
Bibliothèque Nationale,
Paris.

in many major European cities and also in New York. True, the extremely high prices ruled out at least 95 per cent of the population as potential buyers, but they attracted businessmen who were interested in any new source of profit. Some tried to defeat the competition by themselves venturing into the production of daguerreotypes and offering these at lower prices than those imported from France.[9] Others, lacking the knowledge of optics or of chemistry necessary to experiment for themselves, looked for partners who could supply this expertise.

Businessmen and manufacturers frequently formed partnerships with scientists and engineers. They would then collaborate in working on improvements and trying to exploit the results

9. See M. Dost, *Die Daguerreotype in Berlin 1839–1860: Ein Beitrag zur Geschichte der photographischen Kunst*, Berlin, R. Bredow, 1922, reprinted in *The Daguerreotype in Germany: Three Accounts*, ed. R. Sobieszek, New York, Arno Press, 1979.

The Daguerreotype

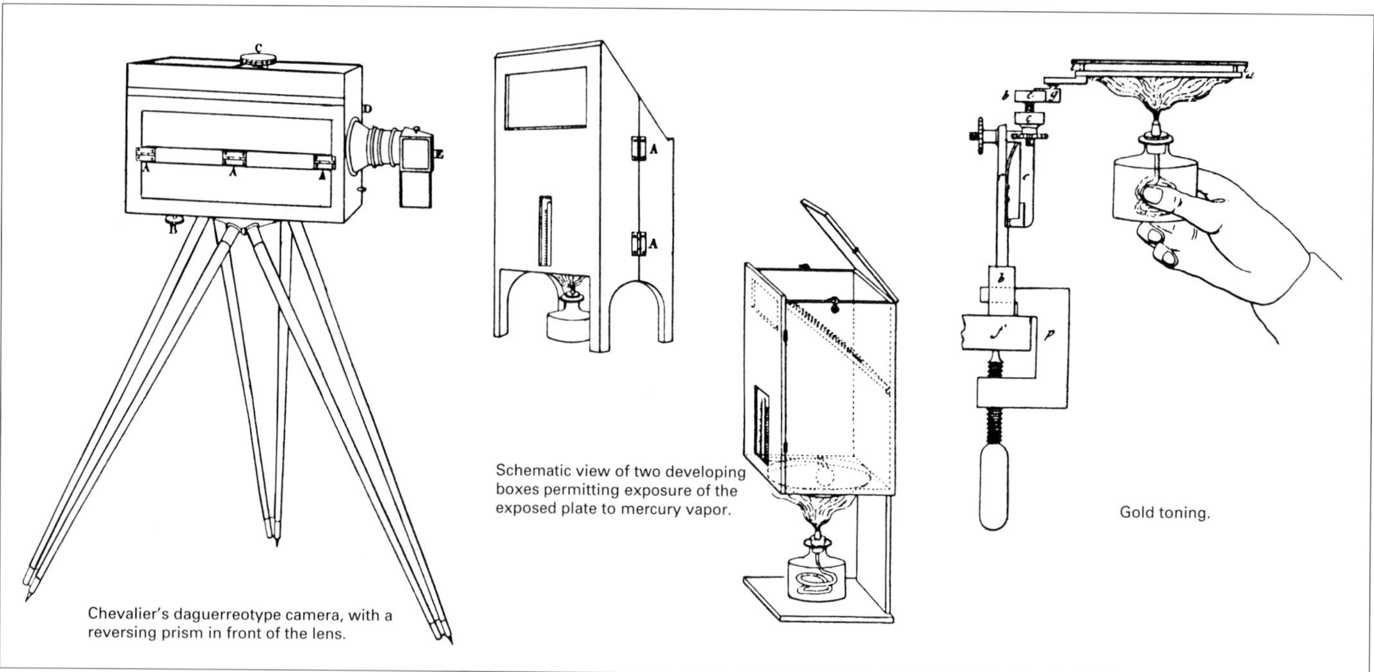

Chevalier's daguerreotype camera, with a reversing prism in front of the lens.

Schematic view of two developing boxes permitting exposure of the exposed plate to mercury vapor.

Gold toning.

Apparatus for producing daguerreotypes, after E. de Valicourt.

As soon as Daguerre's process was made known, crowds of people besieged the shops of the Susse Brothers and of Alphonse Giroux, who had obtained the contract to market the first cameras.

Expensive (400 francs) and heavy (about a hundredweight), these ingeniously constructed cameras contained all the apparatus which was necessary to obtain a daguerreotype: iodine and mercury boxes, camera body, etc. They were provided with a 12-inch f14 lens. The shutter consisted of a copper flap operated by a knurled wheel.

The photographic plate was made of copper, thinly plated on one side with the purest silver, a standard format of 6.5 x 9 inches. Its preparation demanded several careful operations:

1. Having been sprinkled with pumice, the plate was buffed with a soft cotton rag lightly soaked in olive oil. Then it was cleaned with dilute nitric acid and dried over a spirit burner.

2. The plate, fixed on a backing board, was then placed face down inside a box containing iodine crystals. It was left there for 5 to 30 minutes, until the iodine vapor gave it a golden-yellow color which indicated that the sensitization process was complete. This part of the process could be controlled in a dim light.

3. Within a period of an hour, in total darkness, the plate was placed in the camera, and the exposure was made: this varied from 3 to 30 minutes.

4. Still in total darkness, the plate was then placed face down in another box, made of wood and equipped with slots holding it at an angle of 45 degrees over a small cup containing mercury, which was heated to 60 degrees Celsius by means of a spirit lamp beneath it. The mercury vapor condensed on the plate, but only on those parts which had been exposed to the light.

Thus the latent image gradually appeared; a stage which could be controlled through a panel of yellow glass in one side of the box. When the temperature had gone down to 45 degrees, after two or three minutes, the operation was complete.

5. The image was then fixed by immersing the plate in a solution of sea salt or sodium thiosulfate ("hyposulfite of sodium"), which Herschel had discovered in 1819.

6. Finally, the plate was thoroughly washed in warm distilled water.

7. Greater permanence could be given to the image by toning it with gold chloride, an innovation discovered by Fizeau.

Obviously this process included a certain number of difficulties and was more or less subject to chance, as Daguerre would soon describe in his famous booklet, published in no fewer than 26 editions in six languages.

Many aspects of Daguerre's equipment would rapidly be improved. For example, the optical system was refined with the perfectioning of Chevalier's system of combination lenses in 1840 and Petzval's objective, a faster lens of f3.4. The chemistry was improved when Claudel discovered a way of speeding up the process in 1840, and, above all, when Fizeau discovered how to reduce the exposure by a factor of 15 by using bromine in place of iodine. Thus the exposure was reduced from several minutes to a few seconds.

Jean-Claude Gautrand

commercially. It was not, therefore, primarily artists who popularized the daguerreotype. Rather, publishers and physicists, printers and chemists, opticians and mathematicians, businessmen and precision engineers applied the process, developed it further, and extended its distribution.

This alliance between economics and science – always the motive force behind industrial progress in the nineteenth century – was also the determining factor governing the fortunes of the daguerreotype, promoting or at times holding back its expansion as commercial considerations dictated.

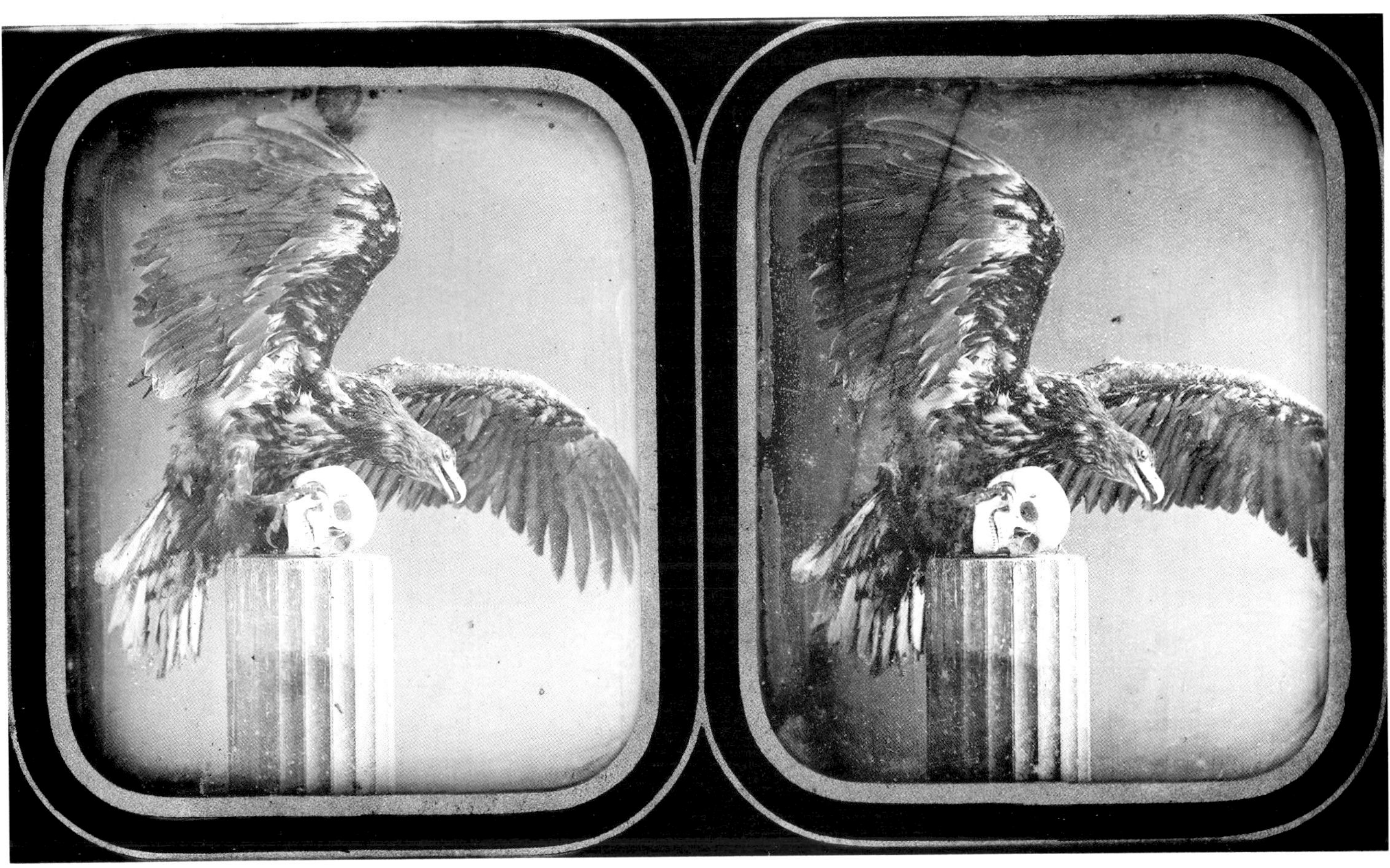

Jules Duboscq,
Still-life,
daguerreotype,
stereoscopic pair,
circa 1855,
International Museum of Photography,
George Eastman House,
Rochester.

Improvements (1839–1842)

How rapidly a combination of inventiveness and business sense can lead to success can be seen in the collaboration of Wolcott and Johnson, partners in a New York manufactory which produced and distributed optical instruments and other equipment involving precision engineering. After their initial successes in early October 1839, the two continued to work on improving their mirror camera. This not only had the advantage of reproducing the view the right way round but also avoided the loss of light which occurred with the usual lenses. In addition, the concave mirror focused the light, so that far more light reached the plate. With the exposure time thus reduced, the making of portraits became a practical proposition, although the construction of the camera permitted only a small format of, at most, five square centimeters.

Early in March 1840 Wolcott, with Johnson as a partner, opened a portrait studio in New York, the first anywhere in the world. On March 15 they moved to other premises and installed a lighting system by which two mirrors reflected light from outside onto the subject. On May 8 Wolcott patented the camera, which was to have a major influence on the early spread of the daguerreotype in the United States and Britain. The idea of using a mirror instead of a lens, which tended to swallow up light had, in fact, first been put forward in Scotland in April 1839, but had not been followed up. The deficiencies of Daguerre's process were thus being addressed very early on, indicating a desire to make it suitable for use by a larger number of people as quickly as possible.

It frequently happened that identical or similar ideas cropped up in towns that were far apart, and were developed further without the inventors knowing of each other's work. This simultaneity shows that the invention of the daguerreotype was in line with the current state of scientific thinking and that its further development was determined by the requirements of its potential users – whether behind or in front of the camera. Almost all the significant inventions relating to the daguerreotype between 1839 and 1841 were arrived at independently by several different people. Which one of them first became publicly known was often a matter of pure chance.

The main goal was to reduce exposure times, which, in the autumn of 1839, were usually – depending on the time of day and weather conditions – somewhere between five and 30 minutes. Many experiments were made with all kinds of chemicals and combinations of chemicals in order to increase the sensitivity of the plates, until, finally, three people, in England and in Austria, achieved significant improvements. As early as September 1839, the Viennese civil

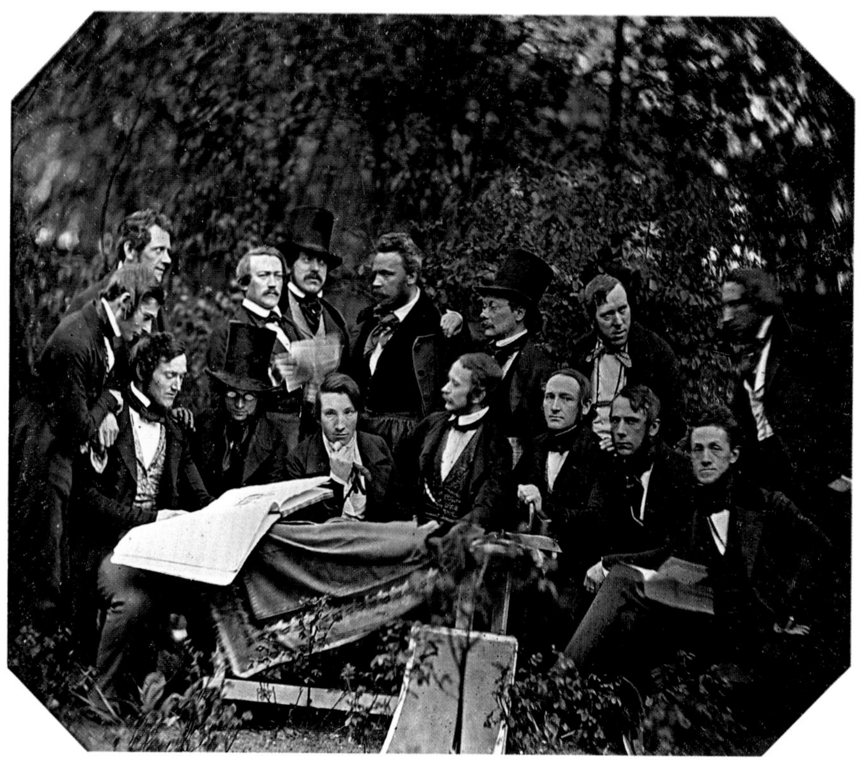

C. F. STELZNER, *The Hamburg Artists' Association,* daguerreotype, May 1843, Museum für Kunst und Gewerbe, Hamburg. ▼

servant F. Kratochwila started to treat iodised plates, "smoking" them with bromine and chlorine, but he did not report on this in writing until January 19, 1840. J. F. Goddard, a lecturer on optics at the Adelaide Gallery in London, recognized the advantages of iodine bromide in October 1839 and mentioned the favorable results achieved with this substance in a letter to the *Literary Gazette* published on December 12. Finally, in May 1841, A. F. J Claudet, who had been working with the daguerreotype process since August 1839 and who was to become one of Britain's leading portraitists, discovered a compound of iodine which also increased the light sensitivity of the plates. He reported on this in the following month.[10] Although Claudet's discovery was made comparatively late, it was taken up and used, for not every improvement came to the knowledge of the other experimenters and practitioners of daguerreotyping.

In October 1839, F. K. A. Himly, a lecturer in physics and chemistry at the Royal University of Göttingen, recognized the possibility of making daguerreotypes more durable by treating them with salts of gold or platinum while applying heat.[11] This made the plate less sensitive to physical contact, so that the lightest touch would not immediately leave marks, as was the case with the pictures produced by Daguerre's method. This "toning" also gave the pictures a more pleasing colour and largely prevented the oxidation of the layer of silver. Although this process, which was demonstrated in the same month (October 1839) and published in December, was shown to be practical, it was never widely used: instead, the gold toning method put forward on August 10, 1840 by the Parisian L. A. H. Fizeau was immediately adopted both in France and elsewhere. Shortly before that, on June 19, 1840, a Moscow paper had reported that A. F. Grekov was applying a gold coating to the plates by electrochemical means.[12]

Among the most frequently mentioned drawbacks of the daguerreotype process was the fact that each image was unique. One of the first photographers in Rome, Suscipj, tried to overcome this problem by using a twin-lens camera, halving the exposed plate and so obtaining two almost identical pictures.[13] In his London studio R. Beard set up several cameras and was therefore able to take a number of portraits of the same person, as was J. B. Isenring, who built a pyramid of six cameras, and who, in late May 1841, claimed in advertisements in Stuttgart to be able to produce daguerreotypes "in an unbelievably short time".[14] Although such arrangements might go some way towards satisfying the desire for identical portraits, the needs of publishing demanded that much larger numbers be produced. The single image needed to be copied, which meant that it needed to be printable.

Here again, a number of interested individuals applied themselves to the problem. In the spring of 1840, quite independently of one another, two doctors, A. Donné, director of the Paris Charité, and J. Berres, professor of anatomy in Vienna, developed an etching process for daguerreotype plates which allowed multiple copies to be made using intaglio printing. In April, Berres presented some successful etchings and he published an account of his "Phototypie" a few days later. It was not until a month later that Donne patented the detailed instructions for his method, which he finally published on June 15, 1840. Neither process was widely adopted, mainly because making the printing plates was an elaborate and expensive business. For the great majority of illustrated books and folio volumes, lithographs which had been made from daguerreotypes were generally preferred.

In the matter of shorter exposure times the decisive breakthrough was finally achieved by the mathematician J. Petzval, a Hungarian teaching at Vienna University, who calculated the necessary specifications for a fast lens. He finally developed a lens combination with a speed sixteen times that of the best lenses produced by the Paris opticians. In May 1840, the librarian A. Martin made the first experiments in portraiture, and by November the lenses were available for purchase, produced by the optical firm of P. W. F. Voigtlander. The metal camera designed early in 1841 by Petzval, and also made by Voigtlander,

10. On the improvements made by Kratochwila, Goddard, and Claudet, see J. M. Eder and E. Kuchinka, *Die Daguerreotypie und die Anfänge der Negativphotographie auf Papier und Glas (Talbotypie und Niepçotypie),* Halle, W. Knapp, 1927, reprinted Aachen, H. L. Haupt, 1977.

11. See L. Hoerner, *Hannover in frühen Photographien, 1840–1910,* Munich, Schirmer/Mosel, 1979, pp. 19–22.

12. See S. Morozov, "Early Photography in Eastern Europe: Russia", in *History of Photography,* no. 1, 1977, pp. 327–347.

13. See *Rom in frühen Photographien 1846–1878 aus römischen und dönischen Sammlungen,* trans. G. Asmus, Munich, Schirmer/Mosel, 1988, p. 33.

14. J. W. Siener, *Von der maskierten Schlittenfahrt zum Hof Photographen: Die Photographie und Stuttgart 1839–1900,* Stuttgart and Bad Canstatt, Edition Cantz, 1989, p. 49.

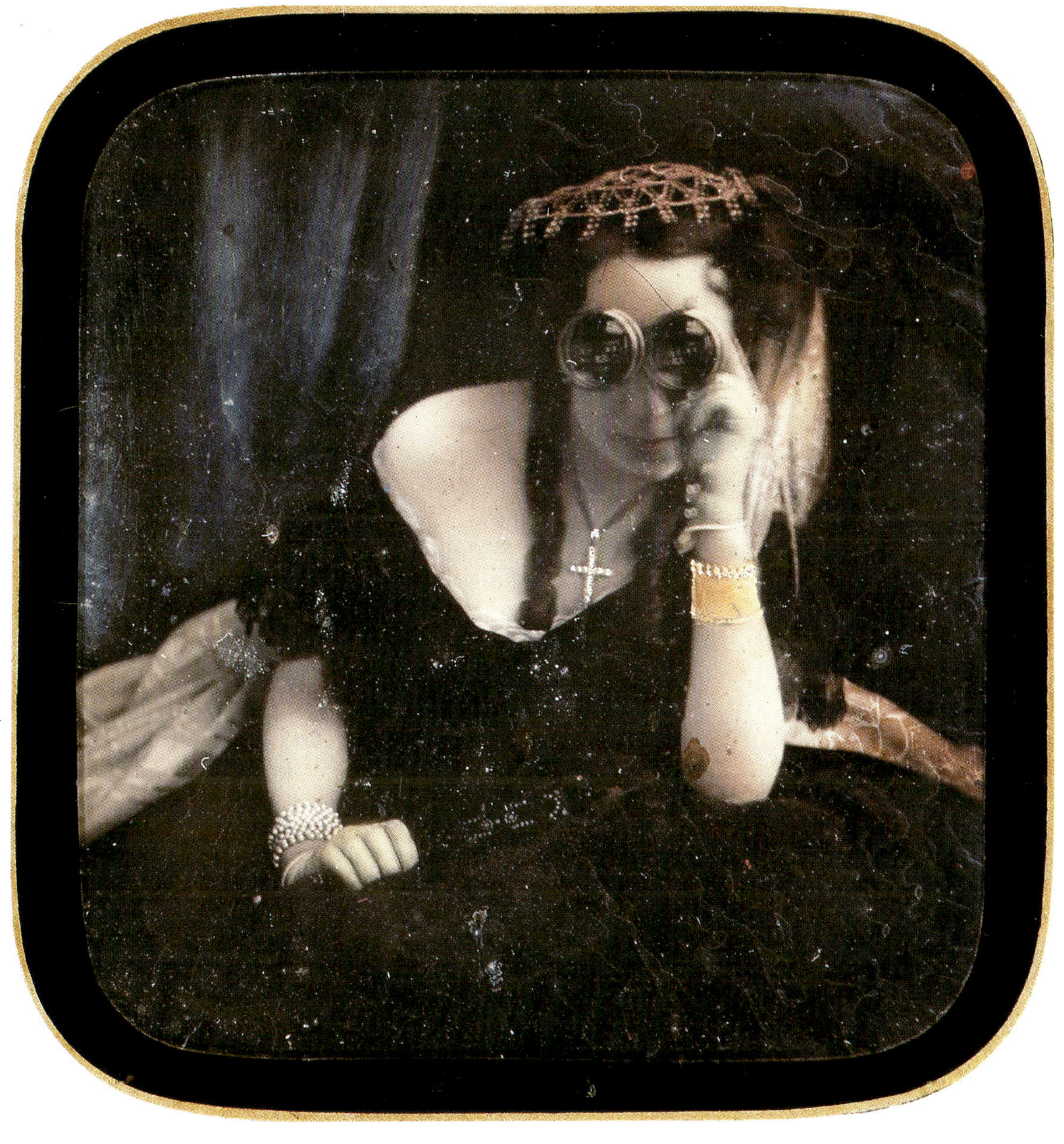

Anonymous,
Untitled,
colored daguerreotype,
1850s,
Uwe Scheid Collection.

which produced circular pictures of 9cm diameter, gained only limited popularity – higher sales were achieved with a wooden camera which produced daguerreotypes measuring 5.7 x 7.6 or 7.6 x 10.2 cm. In March of that year the officer Gottfried von Dreger traveled to Paris, informed Arago, who acclaimed Petzval's invention, and daguerreotyped the French royal couple.[15]

Daguerreotyping and studios (1841–1853)

Once it was possible to produce a portrait in less than a minute, the daguerreotype became commercially viable on a large scale. A phase of expansion began with the opening of portrait studios. In less than two years, in March 1841 the first "one-second pictures" were produced, taken by the Natterer brothers of public events in Vienna. In April 1841, Morse successfully used the same exposure time of only one second to produce a portrait. In the following years exposure times, which depended on the equipment and materials used, the plate size, and light conditions, were usually considerably higher than this – about 15 to 25 seconds for a portrait. However, this did not deter anyone who wanted a picture of themselves and their family. People's sense of time was, after all, still formed by an environment that was only minimally industrialized. Travel on the roads was by horse-drawn carriage, and in 1843 a journey from Berlin to Paris by train and fast mailcoach could not be completed, even with the most favorable connections, in less than 80 hours.

In any case, the majority of portraitists' customers belonged to that prosperous section of the population which had ample time at its disposal. For the price of a portrait was considerable – in Berlin, in 1844, a 1/4 plate daguerreo-

15. See Eder, *Geschichte der Photographie,* Halle, W. Knapp, 1932, vol. 1, pp. 382–421.

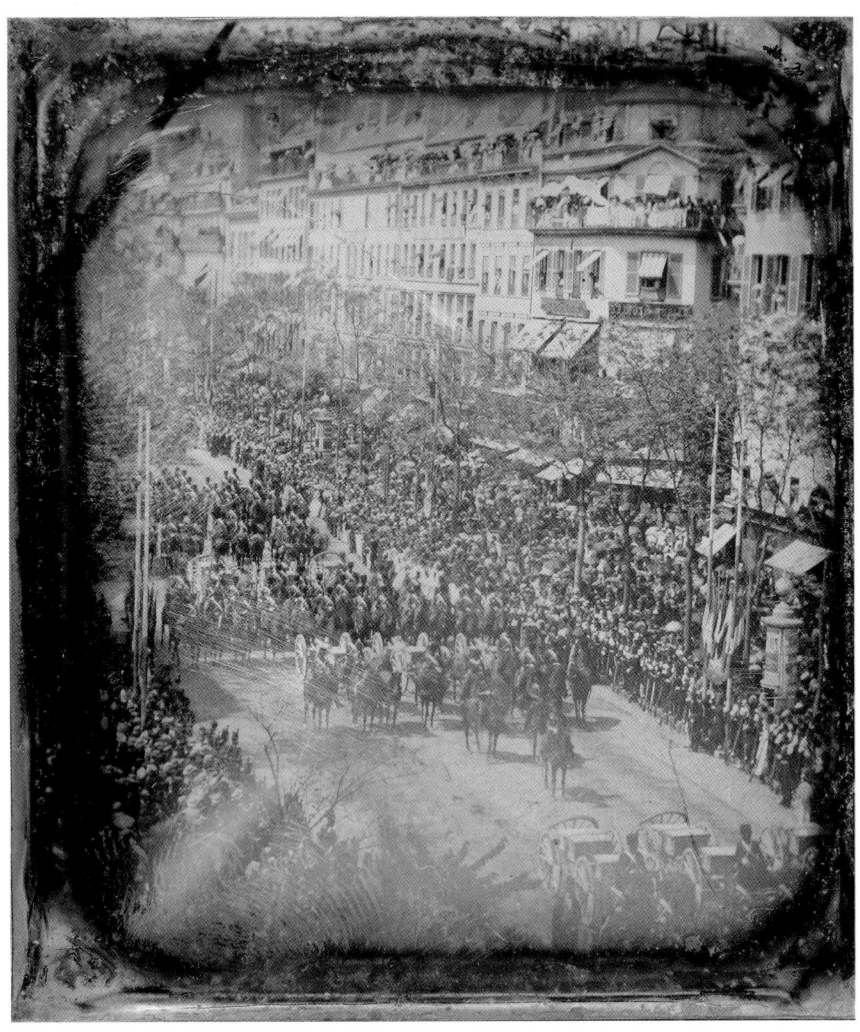

ANONYMOUS, *Return of the Troops from Italy*, daguerreotype, Paris, 1859, International Museum of Photography, George Eastman House, Rochester.

type generally cost two thalers, which was roughly equivalent to the wages (rarely sufficient to live on) earned by a Berlin carpenter in 1845 for two weeks' work.[16] Essentially, the only people who could afford a daguerreotype were those who had property or fairly high incomes – the aspiring middle classes, which in countries like Britain, France, and the German states were increasingly becoming part of the dominant class, at least in terms of economic power. Such people had often attained prosperity and status only in the present generation, while their origins frequently lay in the obscurity of poverty. Seeing themselves as the avant-garde of the business world, they were ready to embrace the most up-to-date means of obtaining pictures. It provided them with portraits to immortalize them and to found, as it were, a history of their own.

What they wanted was a portrait which would display all their newly acquired refinement and dignity and also the status they occupied in the social hierarchy. Very soon after the first studios opened, it became the norm for them to be furnished as a domestic interior, so that the sitter could show off both the material means and the education they possessed. A painted background, expensive-looking furniture, and various accessories, almost always including a book, formed the setting in which the sitter took up their pose. They might have been averse to having their head clamped in position, for this ensured that they would not be caught by the camera in an unguarded moment but that their posture and expression would remain wholly under their control.[17] In any case, these aids were already regularly used by portrait and miniature painters, whose sittings, moreover, lasted considerably longer. A physionotrace portrait – the technique most widely used in portraiture at that time – was not to be had in half a minute. And so, finally, one acquired a valued item, valued all the more because its uniqueness satisfied the claim to individuality which was characteristic of the new middle class.

Both this personal note and the uniqueness of the portrait were heightened when parts of it were highlighted by hand-coloring, a practice already begun by Isenring at St. Gallen early in 1841.[18] The size of the plate, too, was also a sign of what one could afford. Pictures were often of a size which could be produced as part of a whole plate.[19] Though at first, because of the relatively long exposure times, small formats were the norm, from the middle of the 1840s the 1/4 plate became the most common format. For protection against damage the exposed plate would be placed behind glass, given a passe-partout frame, and usually placed in a case with a lid. The often elaborate style and the materials used for these cases indicate, once again, that they contained an object of value. The pictures of oneself and one's family gradually built up to form a picture gallery to compensate for the lack of distinguished ancestry. If a close relative of whom no picture existed died unexpectedly, the deceased could be daguerreotyped – such portraits were part of the daily business of local or itinerant photographers.

The wish for self-portrayal on the part of a successful section of middle-class society was the reason for the massive spread of the daguerreotype. That this happened more rapidly in North America was, perhaps, due in part to the early successes of inventors in New York and Philadelphia, but still more to the fact that, compared to Europe, America had a far shorter tradition of portraiture. The advent of the daguerreotype coincided with the exploration and cultivation of large areas of the country which were being opened up by the railways. The pictures were thus also seen as documents of an era of great national importance. They accompanied the pioneers on their exploratory journeys, and bore witness to their achievements. Furthermore, manufacturers of cameras and accessories were becoming increasingly independent of imports

16. Numerous examples of prices up to 1845 are given by Dost, *cit.*, pp. 67–84 and 88–91; the lowest charge is always 1 1/2 thalers. Cameras cost between 29 and 144 thalers in 1844.

17. In 1842 it was feared that "since it is possible to produce portraits in 1 second, even in parts of a second", someone might be caught by the camera "while in the grip of emotion". Quoted from D. Hoffmann and U. Wocklage, "Die daguerreotypisierten Männer der Paulskirche", and in B. von Dewitz, R. Matz (eds.), *Silber und Salz*, Cologne and Heidelberg, Braus, 1989, pp. 404–437.

18. Isenring is believed to have been the first to color daguerreotypes; the fact that he did this was mentioned in a newspaper report on March 15, 1840.

19. The whole plate measured 16.5 x 21.5 cm; the division of it into 1/2, 1/4, 1/6, 1/8, etc. determined the sizes of the smaller plates.

from Europe,[20] and the studios' customers were often less interested in an opulent background than in technical quality.[21] For this reason, too, portraits were comparatively cheap. In New York, in 1846, a portrait – no doubt in a small format – could be had for only a dollar, including a leather case or a frame.

Competition also brought down the price. The number of registered professional daguerreotypists and studios that we know of rose rapidly in many places. In New York, where a population of over 300,000 in 1840 had risen to over 500,000 ten years later, there were 16 studios in 1846 and 59 in 1850; by the following year there were already 71 and in 1853 over 100.[22]

In Britain, the development followed quite a different course, although Wolcott and Johnson's camera had found its way to London as early as February 1840. Shortly before his invention was made public, Daguerre had applied for a patent which was granted on August 14, 1839. Beard took over the patent on the American camera, and had it tested by J. F. Goddard. After Goddard had also made improvements to the sensitivity of the plates, Beard opened the first studio in Britain on March 23, 1841 and on July 23 took out a licence on Daguerre's process, but not on the Parisian camera. Apart from Claudet, who had already taken out a licence on Daguerre's patent in March 1840, no one in Britain or the Colonies could now make daguerreotypes without obtaining a licence from Beard. Beard's charges were extremely high, so that while he made good profits and in the course of time opened eight provincial branches, the number of licence-holders remained extremely small. When, in May 1843, Claudet introduced Petzval's lens, Beard was obliged to give up the patent on Wolcott's camera. Protracted court cases between him and his clients finally brought his career to an end in the late 1840s. The excessively rigorous application of patent rights meant that in Britain daguerreotyping was to have only a marginal existence.[23]

Beard, who had started out as a coal merchant, took up daguerreotyping because it promised good profits. In this motivation he was no different from his contemporaries, who came from many different walks of life and in some cases continued to practice their old occupations because the new trade did not always earn them enough to live on. If one looks at the training and former occupations of those who interested themselves in photography, the whole gamut of professions is represented, though "artists" alone make up a good fifth of the number, and "technicians" over a tenth. Among the amateurs, especially the earliest experimenters, physicists, chemists, and other scientists predominate. However, there were also many opticians and precision engineers who tried out the process so as to be able to show expertise when selling the cameras and photographic materials. Around three-quarters of all daguerreotypists came from

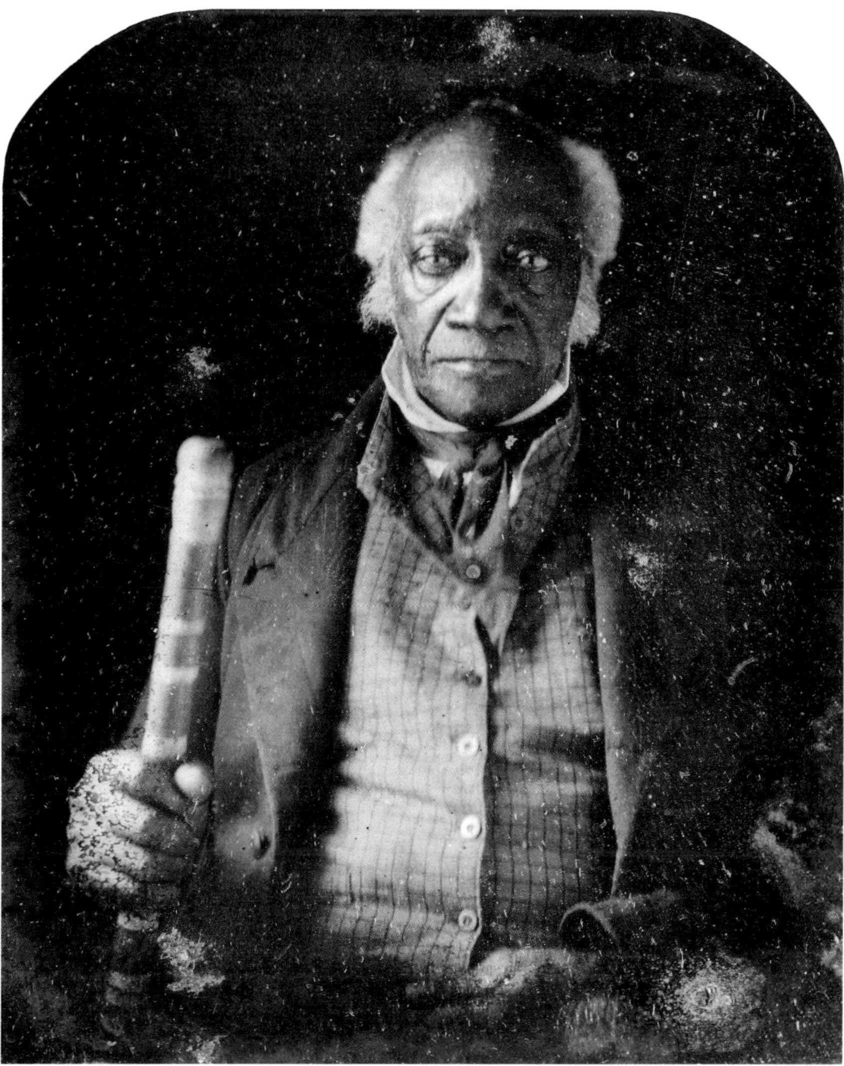

ANONYMOUS,
Caesar, the Last Negro Slave Owned in New York State.
daguerreotype,
1851,
New York
Historical Society.

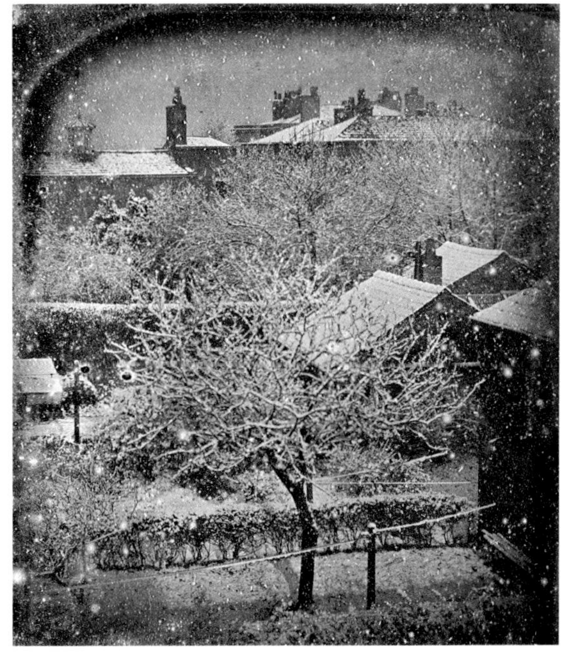

◀ ANONYMOUS,
Snow in Liverpool or Manchester,
undated daguerreotype,
University of Texas,
Austin.

20. Rinhart, *op. cit.*, pp. 357–369.

21. R. Taft, *Photography and the American Scene: A Social History, 1839–1889*, New York, Dover, 1964, p. 70.

22. See Rinhart, *op. cit.*, p. 96.

23. See A. F. Gill, "Wolcott's Camera in England and the Bromine-Iodine Process", in *History of Photography*, no. 1, 1977, pp. 215–220, and B. V. and P. H. Heathcote, "Richard Beard: an Ingenious and Enterprising Patentee", in *History of Photography*, no. 3, 1979, pp. 313–329.

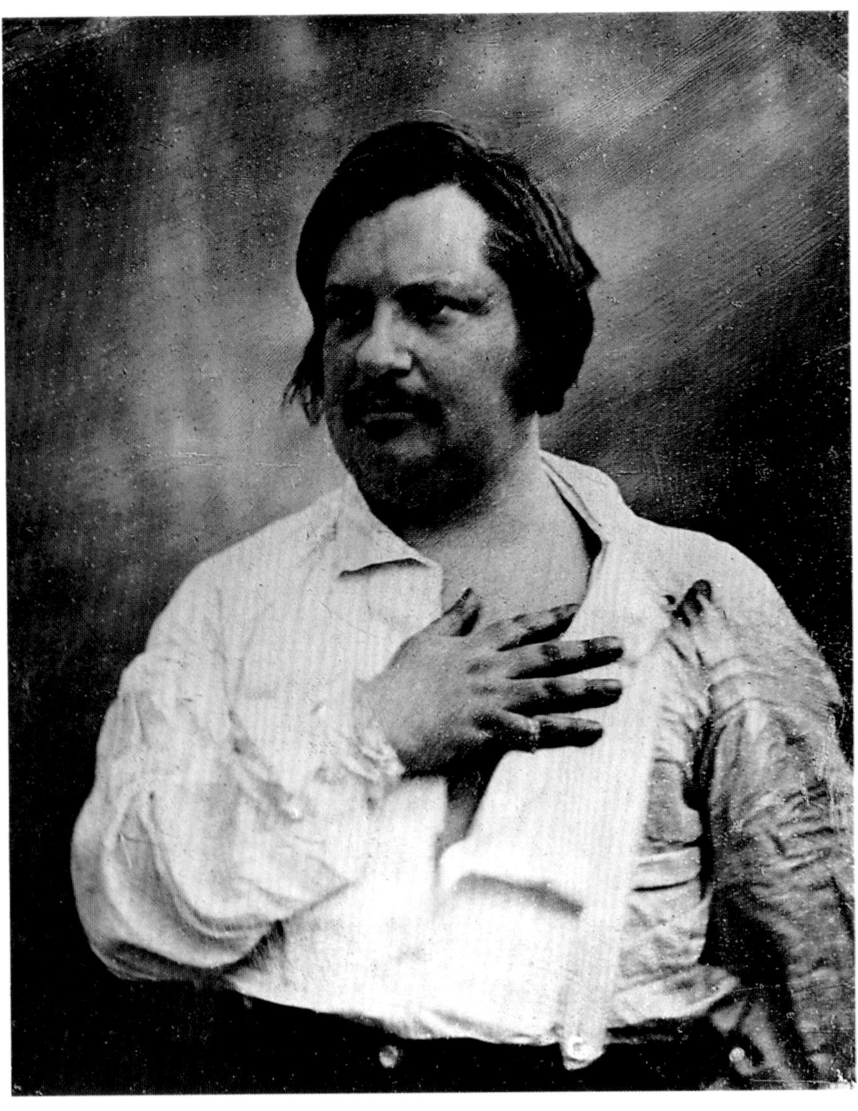

Louis-Auguste Bisson, ***Portrait of Honoré de Balzac***, daguerreotype, 1842, Maison de Balzac, Paris.

unrelated professions. In the great majority of cases it was not a very young man who opened a studio, traveled with a camera or tried his hand at daguerreotyping as a hobby or out of scientific curiosity. The "typical" daguerreotypist was a man in his mid-thirties with a professional training and experience, who had artistic leanings or at least some technical knowledge.[24]

When an individual decided to open a studio, he would generally put an announcement in the newspaper and continue to place advertisements as and when the level of competition or the state of his order book made it advisable. These advertisements would emphasize his particular merits – for instance, if he had been a pupil of a famous daguerreotypist or if he also worked as a portrait painter. They would also give the location and opening hours of the studio, and boast of what he had to offer: how the rooms in the studio were furnished, the fact of being unaffected by the weather, short waiting times, a sliding scale of prices for individual and group portraits, charges made only for successful pictures, acceptance of commissions to reproduce pictures, willingness to take daguerreotypes elsewhere than in the studio, for instance in the client's home. Some owners of studios also mention the number of portraits they had produced to date. These vary widely. In the second half of the 1840s a prospering business in a major city might produce about 5,000 pictures annually, while a daguerreotypist in a smaller town would make no more than half that number.[25] For Basle we have the claim by E. Wick that in about 18 years he had produced 35–40,000 daguerreotypes.

The demand for portraits was catered for in urban areas by studios. The countryside was served by itinerant daguerreotypists, who would set up their equipment at inns or in the back rooms of well-known local shops, announcing their arrival in the regional newspaper or by handbills. If possible, they would time their visits to coincide with markets, festivals linked to shooting competitions or similar events. They preferred to avoid areas where a photographer was already permanently settled, and often offered other services besides portraiture or gave demonstrations of microscopes, various machines or other items of interest. Particular regions would be favored according to the time of year. In winter, because of the poor light, many daguerreotypists from northern parts of the United States would migrate southwards. Similarly, in the summer, North German photographers would often go to the island of Norderney, because of the many summer visitors to the bathing resorts there. Local variations in regulations led to a preference for certain regions, for instance, the Netherlands, where, in contrast to the German states, no license needed to be obtained and there were no official restrictions on where or when a daguerreotypist might ply his trade.

Wherever these itinerant daguerreotypists appeared, while the pictures themselves might often be a novelty, the way in which they were offered was not. For there was a long tradition of traveling tradesmen and salesmen, and country people were used to seeing them. If business went well in a particular town, one of the travelers might sometimes stay for longer, or for good, setting up a studio there. Equally, the venture might come to an end at the first place visited, because the pictures were only mediocre and there were no customers. After itinerant daguerreotypists first made their appearance in the fall of 1839, the new technique became known relatively quickly in medium-sized towns and then in smaller places. The daguerreotypists often covered tremendous distances. For instance, H. Weninger, starting out from Vienna, visited Hamburg in 1841, Copenhagen, Göteborg, Odense, and Flensburg in 1842, went from there to Schleswig, and on to Kiel, Aarhus, Aalborg, and

24. T. Starl, "Überwiegend Künstler? Zur beruflichen Herkunft von Daguerreotypisten", in *Fotogeschichte*, no. 11, 1991, pp. 39–44.

25. J. Buerger, *French Daguerreotypes* (International Museum of Photography, Rochester), Chicago and London, University of Chicago, 1989, pp. 201–212.

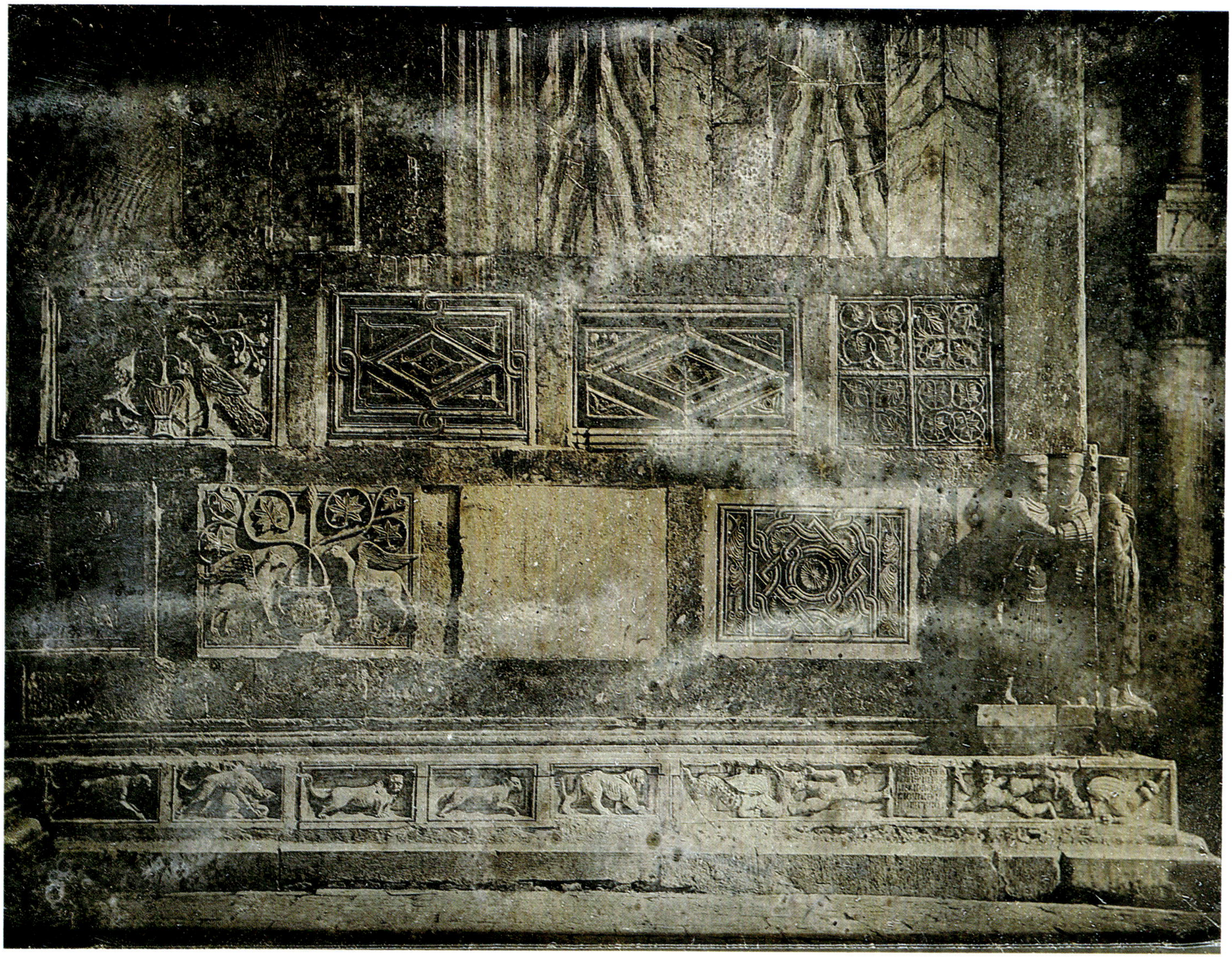

Copenhagen in 1843, and finally traveled via Stockholm and Helsinki to St. Petersburg, where, together with his brother, he was soon counted among the leading portraitists.[26]

There were also itinerant daguerreotypists who would offer pictures, taken by themselves or by others, for sale, or let people pay to see them. The Swiss Isenring was one of the first to earn money in this way. As early as December 6, 1839 at St. Gallen he was charging an entrance fee if people wished to see his work. From August 13 to 27, 1840 he exhibited 47 daguerreotypes of his own, including 39 portraits, first in his home town, then, in the following month, in Zurich, in October in Munich, then in Augsburg and Vienna and, finally, in Stuttgart.[27] Sellers of daguerreotyping equipment and materials who wanted to lure the public into their premises operated in a similar way, though only in a single place. Both pictures and photographic apparatus were also shown at trade and industrial exhibitions, documenting the progress made in the production and use of the new technology. At the "Trade Exhibition of the German Customs Union" held in the Berlin Arsenal from August 15 to October 13, 1844, four daguerreotypists and the same number of manufacturers of cameras or other equipment were represented at any given time.[28]

The far greater attention paid to the daguerreotype process in France was evident at the "Exposition des Produits de L'Industrie Française" held in Paris in 1844, where about 1,000 pictures were exhibited, including works by

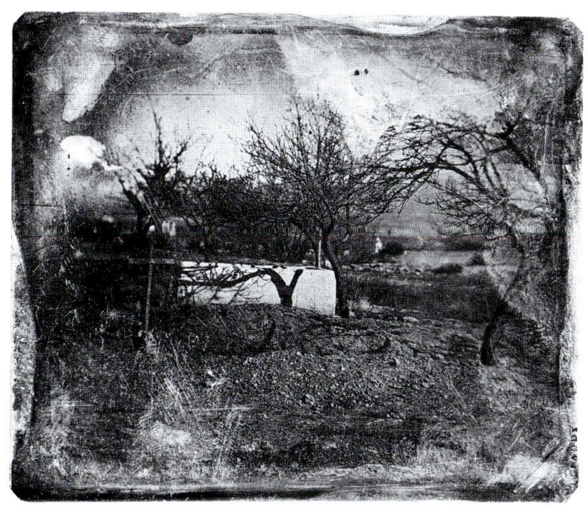

ANONYMOUS,
Venice,
St. Mark's Basilica, Venice, detail of south wall,
daguerreotype,
Ruskin Collection,
Ruskin Galleries,
Bembridge School,
Isle of Wight.

◀ ANONYMOUS,
Burial Place of Henry Clay's Son in Mexico,
daguerreotype,
circa 1847,
Amon Carter Museum of Western Art, Fort Worth.

26. U. Steen, "Die Anfänge der Photographie in Schleswig-Holstein (1839–1848)", in *Nordelbingen: Beiträge zur Kunst und Kulturgeschichte*, no. 55, 1987, pp. 101–150.

27. E. Stenger, *Die beginnende Photographie im Spiegel von Tageszeitungen und Tagebüchern*, Würzburg, Konrad Triltsch, 1943, pp. 25–37.

28. See Dost, *op. cit.*, pp. 84–88.

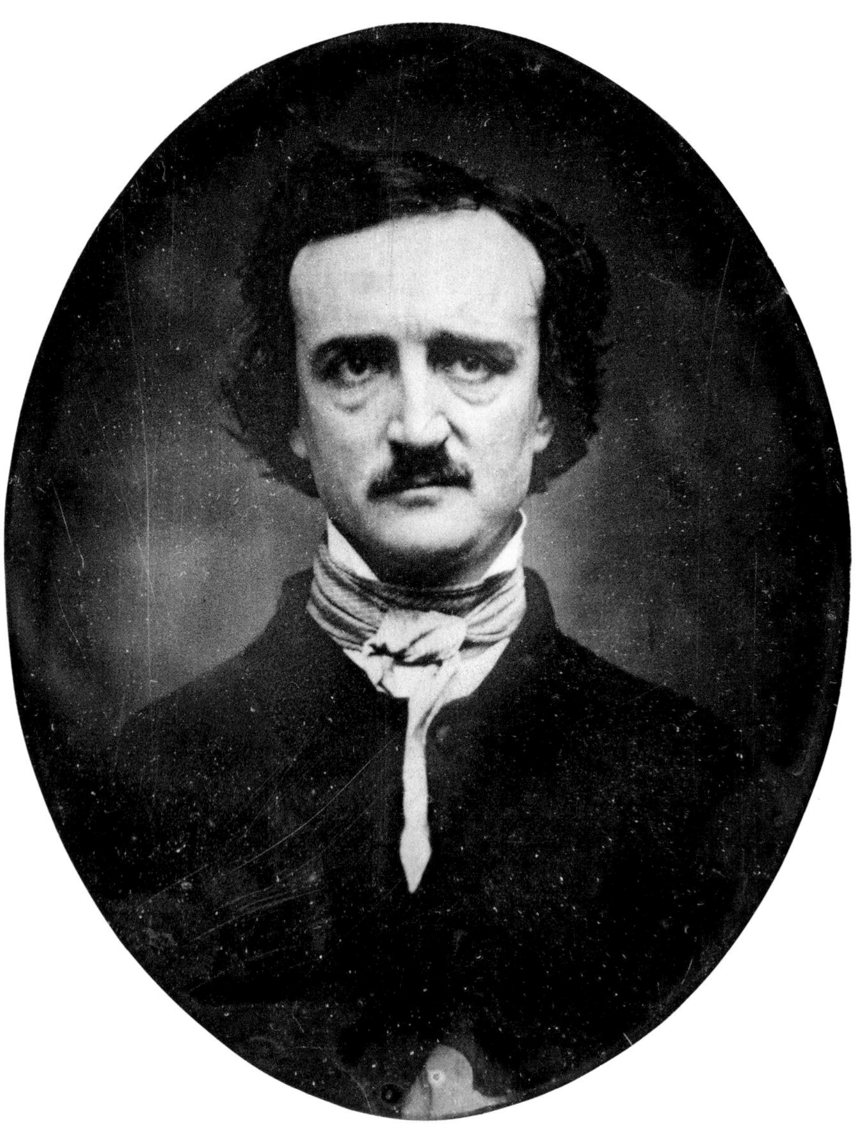

HARRY N. AND EDWARD H. MANCHESTER, *Edgar Allen Poe*, daguerreotype, 1848, American Antiquarian Society, Worcester.

the best-known French and foreign representatives. This was probably the largest display of daguerreotypes ever presented in Europe, for the Great Exhibition of 1851 in London had only about 700 exhibits in the field of daguerreotypy and photography. There, almost all the major awards were won by Americans. The stereoscopic daguerreotype alone caused a great stir, but, apart from that, just as much interest was shown in prints on paper.

In North America the calotype did not become particularly widespread, and, because of the size of the country, the daguerreotype process was slow to reach the remoter regions. The process of expansion therefore took longer, and the "American International Exhibition" which opened on July 14, 1853 in New York marked the highest point reached by the daguerreotype process with regard to its spread and public visibility in that part of the world. Although the majority of the 4,685 exhibitors came from abroad, in the "Photographic Section", with one exception, only American photographers and firms were represented.[29]

The subjects (1839–1853)

At the New York exhibition, as at the others, the portrait predominated. Yet alongside the portraits of the president, famous artists, and unknown contemporaries, the visitor could find a whole range of applications, ranging from the illustration of "Shakespeare's 'Seven Ages'" by the Meade Brothers and other genre scenes to the panorama of Cincinnati made up of six large plates daguerreotyped by Newport, and from pictures of the Moon by the Bostonian J. A. Whipple to views of the Niagara Falls.[30] Every conceivable subject seemed to be included in this array, a diversity which reflected the encyclopedic approach common among daguerreotypists. This world of images was not governed by the traditional creative possibilities of artistic composition. Instead, the empirical capacities of the process – which in this one respect was far superior to all other arts – influenced the way it was used. The camera was set to work as though there were a need to compile a catalogue of all possible phenomena.

Such a purpose can clearly be seen, for instance, in the many attempts at producing topographical surveys. As early as 1841, Suscipj created a panorama of Rome made up of eight daguerreotypes, and, in 1845, F. Martens in Paris constructed, and successfully used, a camera with an angle of vision of over 150 degrees.[31] However, because of the difficulty of handling the cylindrical plate, Marten's design did not gain wide acceptance. W. Shew had to use ten plates for a view of San Francisco made in 1852.[32] These efforts to produce comprehensive documentary images reflect the prevailing idea that only the study of visible things made it possible to compare them and so gain insight into the connections between all events or processes of the past and present.

With almost scientific meticulousness, journeys, objects, and events were pictorially recorded. In 1850–1851, J. W. Jones brought back over 1,500 pictures from the Rocky Mountains and the Missouri plains. In September 1845, the German A. Schaefer took more than 50 pictures of the reliefs in the temple complex of Borobudur in the Dutch East Indies. He intended, however, that the project should last for four or five years and result in a collection of 4,000 to 5,000 plates.[33] Starting in 1842, the Paris portraitist and friend of Daguerre, J.-B. Sabatier-Blot, took pictures of his daughter over a period of years.[34]

At times of great social, economic, technical, and urban change there is a heightened awareness of the past and of what is passing, and pictures are a way of preserving it. In this way daguerreotyping to some extent took on the role of a

29. See Rinhart, *op. cit.*, pp. 121 ff.

30. *Ibid.*, pp. 125–128.

31. See Baier, *op. cit.*, p. 287; J. E. Buerger, *op. cit.*, p. 46, and *Paris et le daguerréotype*, Musée Carnavalet, exhibition catalogue, Paris, 1989, pp. 246–247.

32. P. E. Palmquist, "The Daguerreotype in San Francisco", in *History of Photography*, no. 4, 1980, pp. 207–238, esp. pp. 218 ff.

33. See H. J. Moeshart, "Daguerreotypieren in der Tropensonne: Adolf Schaefer in Niederländisch-Indien (1844–1849)", in *Silber und Salz*, pp. 458–479.

34. See Buerger, *op. cit.*, p. 53.

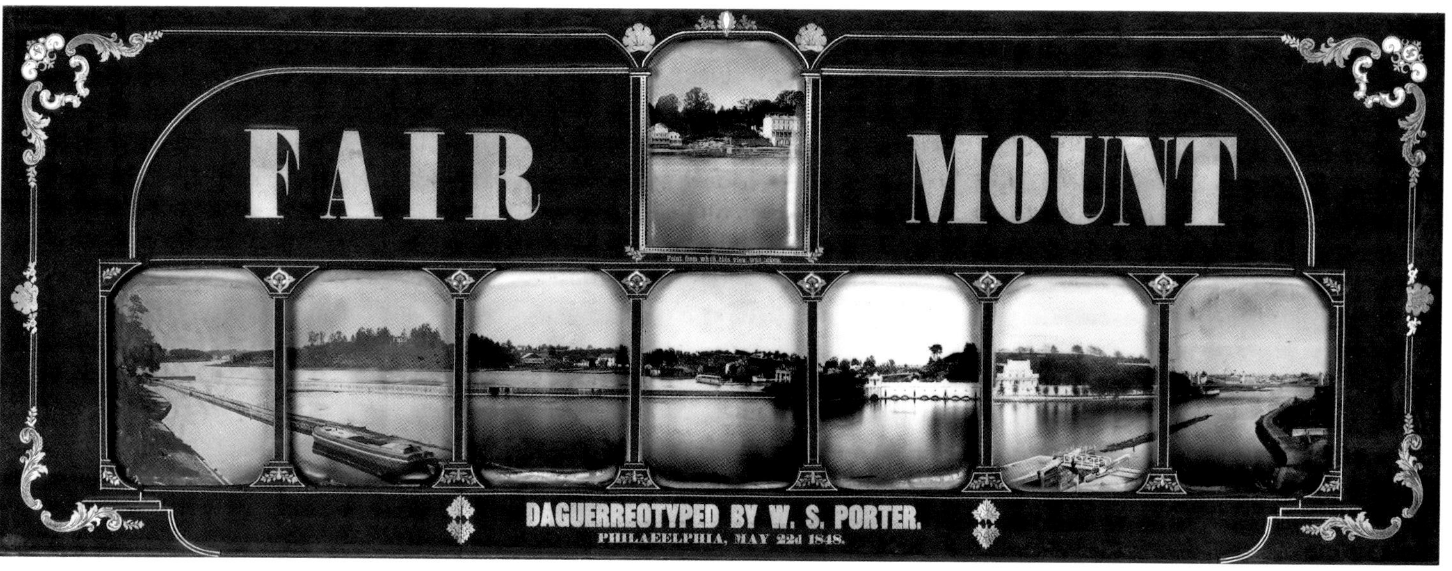

museum. Single daguerreotypes, however, were unsuited to the purpose of showing the world thus discovered to the greatest possible number of people. In most large-scale projects, daguerreotypes were intended to be used only as the model for other techniques which could be duplicated. When, in the autumn of 1839, N. M. Lerebours commissioned a number of people to take pictures of the main "sights" of the eastern and southern Mediterranean countries and of some European cities, only a selection was intended to be published. Out of about 1,200 views, only 110 actually appeared, as lithographs, in two series between 1840 and 1843. In 1841, the Bisson brothers started work on the reproduction as daguerreotypes of 200 portraits of natives of New Zealand and elsewhere taken with the aid of physionotypes by Dr. Dumoutier during a world tour in 1840. They then converted them into lithographs. The Société Ethnologique de Paris was founded in the same year. Four years later, its first president, Serres, proposed that a "photographic museum" of human races be assembled.[35]

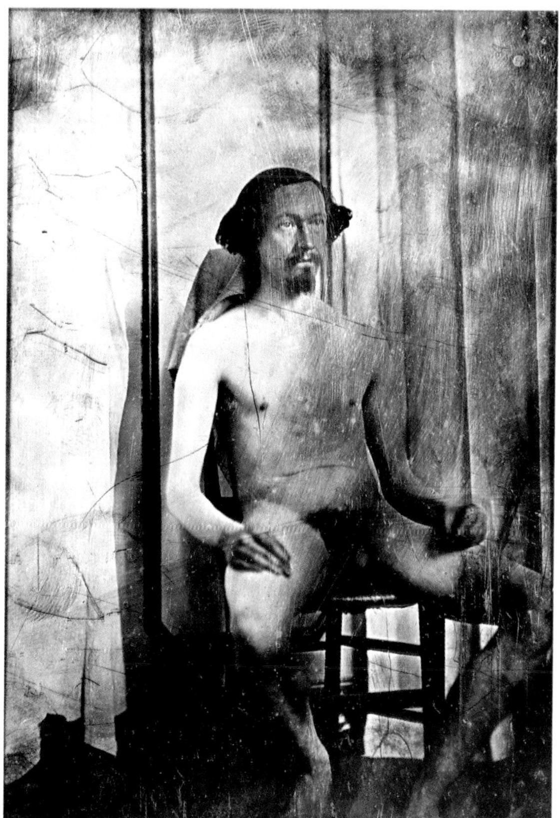

The interest of the public, as opposed to that of scientists, focused more on prominent people. Politicians were accorded a whole gallery of their own. All 900 members of the Paris Chamber of Deputies and Senate were to have their pictures taken by Bisson from 1841 onwards. Over 100 American Senators were daguerreotyped by E. Anthony in 1844, and the parliamentarians of the first German Assembly of 1848–1849 in Frankfurt found pictorial chroniclers in Biow and others. In all three cases the portraits were published in the form of lithographs.

It was also Biow who recorded, in about 50 pictures, the catastrophic fire which raged in Hamburg during March 5–8, 1842, but his images of the ruins give only a retrospective view of the consequences of the event.[36] In 1853, however, G. N. Barnard was on the spot in time to capture the burning grain silos at Oswego, New York. The wish to make all phenomena visible also extended to those things that could not be seen by the naked eye – a momentary movement or objects that could be discerned only through the telescope or microscope. Even before 1839 Daguerre had succeeded in making a microphotograph of the "spinnerets of a spider". On January 3 he showed A. von Humboldt what the latter called a "portrait of Luna". The pictures taken on April 2, 1845 by Fizeau and J. B. L. Foucault show the sun and sunspots.

In fact, there was no subject that escaped the daguerreotypists' cameras. They took pictures of

William Southgate Porter, *Fair Mount,* panorama made up of 8 daguerreotypes, 1848, International Museum of Photography, George Eastman House, Rochester.

◄ Anonymous, undated daguerreotype, Bibliothèque Nationale, Paris.

35. See H. Krech, "Lichtbilder vom Menschen: Vom Typenbild zur anthropologischen Photographie", in *Fotogeschichte,* no. 4, 1984, pp. 3–15, esp. pp. 8–10.

36. W. Weimar, *Die Daguerreotypie in Hamburg, 1839–1860: Ein Beitrag zur Geschichte der Photographie,* Hamburg, O. Meissner, 1915, pp. 15–18.

Paris in the Daguerreotype

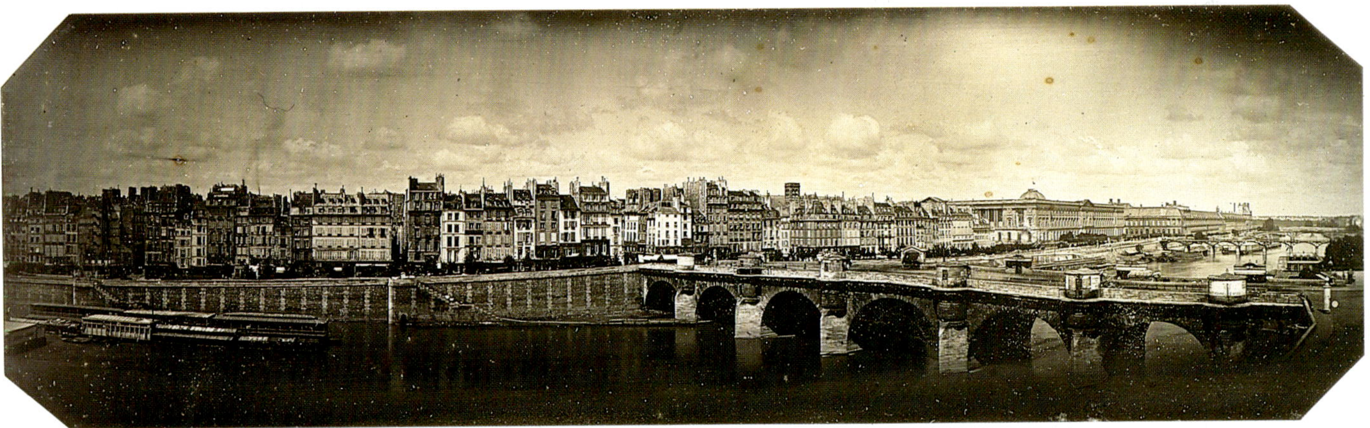

ANONYMOUS (attributed to Lerebours),
Pont-Neuf, the Louvre, and Quai de la Mégisserie,
panoramic daguerreotype (reverse view),
circa 1845–1850,
Musée Carnavalet, Paris.

Paris is the city which was daguerreotyped most: it was where the process was invented, and also the most typical of towns at that time, being already over-populated (around 1 million inhabitants) but still contained within its original limits. Yet at the beginning the process was unsuitable for capturing that unceasing din of individuals and horse-drawn vehicles which characterized Paris. And so, as was demonstrated by an exhibition at the Musée Carnavalet in 1989,[1] photography was motivated by other considerations: it was not yet a question of that hankering after the past caused by the major destruction of the Haussmann era, nor a desire to retain an image of things that were going to disappear.

In around 1839, the spirit of the age concerned rather the convergence of arts and sciences, techniques, and aesthetics, including the research into mechanical perspective which Daguerre undertook for his diorama. The daguerreotype was undoubtedly the new representation of a spectacle which showed the creations of God in facsimile, "of a perfection [...] equal to Nature herself" as the chemist Gay-Lussac said. Those who took these views formulated through images the very character of their town.

Well before Haussmann decided how to do this in a more concrete manner, they formed a global perspective of urban space. And to achieve this they chose viewpoints (an expression already used by Niépce to designate his attempts at capturing landscape) by turning to the decorated squares of public buildings.

The principal monuments of the town, private town palaces, and a few notable sites such as the new railway stations and the pavilions of the great exhibitions form the repertoire of the majority of daguerreotypists which have come down to us. In this matter, the daguerreotypists conformed to the hierarchy of acceptable urban subjects which painters and engravers had established. But the absolute novelty is in the complete fidelity to nature, without manual intervention, and also without syntax (W. Ivins) which such images immediately achieved. They favorized visual sensitivity to the reality of ancient architecture (in particular, Gothic), and a scientific approach to art – the images being virtually direct and not manipulated. One must not forget that the daguerreotype – a mirror of nature – transported the real image of the subject into places where it could previously have been known only through engravings.

Travel souvenirs (mostly lithographs of monuments) did not escape the truth of the daguerreotype: between 1840 and 1844 114 such views were published in the form of lithographs produced from daguerreotypes, under the title *Excursions dagueréennes.* Objects had lost their unique situation in space and in a given cultural tradition; they traveled, so to speak, without losing any of the intrinsic qualities linked to their origins.

But with their daguerreotype a new way of capturing the space of the town had also been gained, which no longer gave a privileged place to the square or the monument. The Place de la Concorde, for example, no longer appears central and near, but in the background of the view of the Seine and of the bridge, the Obelisk and the church of the Madeleine being diminished by the distant view which confines them to the horizon under an immense sky. The image, with its fragmentary, asymmetrical framing, thus shows the monuments in the visibly infinite setting of an town which has developed piecemeal, and of which they form but a small part. Here the entire web of the urban environment is drawn, including its modest buildings, its shops, and its signs, which have no pretensions and yet suddenly feature on a par with the most prestigious groups of buildings, without any possibiity of being airbrushed out.

One should add that many daguerreotypists were amateurs who had received no training in the rules of composition and thus were subject to no constraints, thus unwittingly breaking with artistic traditions; they simply went where there was enough light or something interesting.

A large number of dageuerreotypes (notably those of Jules Itier or Fizeau) show the roofs of Paris and the extent of the town seen from the top floor of a building. As one of the earliest daguerreotypists, M.-A. Gaudin, recalled, everyone wanted to take the view from their window; by doing this, they created a new interpretation of the town, one which paid more attention to roofs and chimney-stacks than to the monuments which arose in the distance. Panoramic views are the most spectacular representations of this, sometimes taken from the workshops of Lerebours (a lens maker) on the Pont-Neuf, the central point of the various perspectives on the banks of the Seine.

Often it was the river which organized the composition, providing a dynamic vision of the landscape in opposition to the static, symmetrical, and eternal interpretation. The panoramic daguerreotypes of Friedrich von Martens have a magical presence, such as the view of Pont-Neuf taken from the Île de la Cité, where the town appears as a single entity, like an unrolled parchment, unfurling its internal relations as a living social organism (which shortly afterwards would be reorganized by Haussmann).

Thanks to the publicity which Daguerre gave to his process, such images of a town which was admired but known above all through engravings – and thus in a somewhat imaginary way – were distributed throughout the whole of Europe, reaching royal courts and exhibitions. In them, Paris could be appreciated in its reality, magnified by the microscopic impression which the previously unknown precision of the daguerreotype could provide.

Shelley Rice

1. *Paris et le daguerréotype,* exhibition catalogue, Musée Carnavalet, Paris-Musées. 1989.

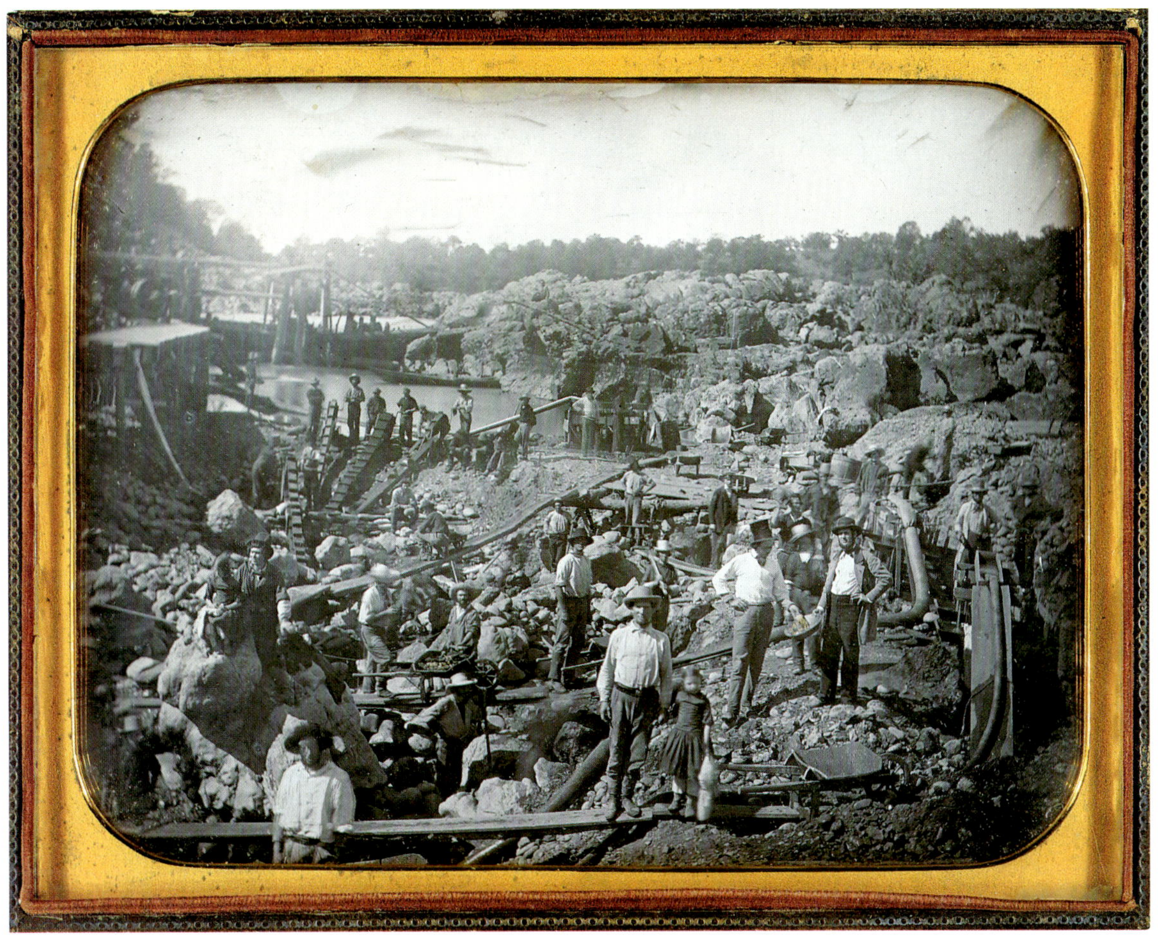

GEORGE H. JOHNSON,
Miners near Sacramento,
daguerreotype,
circa 1852,
Matthew R. Isenburg
Collection.

domestic scenes and of actors posing in costume in the studio, and captured the appearance of street traders as well as architectural details; they searched out stranded ships and frequented the halls of international exhibitions, they turned their gaze upon snow-covered mountains and on rural idylls, they arranged still-lifes and nude studies – the latter usually stereoscopic and colored, and distributed with no indication of their provenance. In the whole cosmos, whatever the eye could see provided subject matter for the daguerreotype.

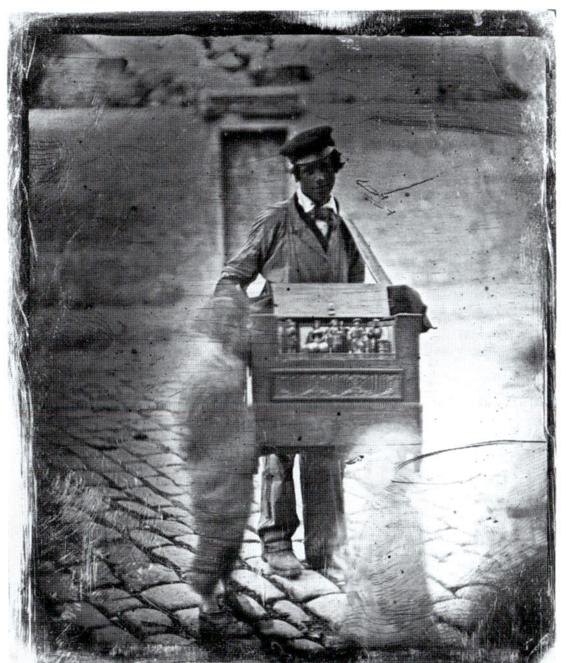

◄ "CROMER'S AMATEUR",
Organ-grinder,
daguerreotype,
circa 1848,
International Museum of
Photography, George
Eastman House, Rochester.

The decline of the non-reproducible image

To conquer the world with a new vision is not, however, the domain of daguerreotyping alone but the aim of all photographic techniques. Accordingly, despite differences of emphasis – linked to the size, nature, and ease of handling of the surface bearing the image – the makers of calotypes adopted the same themes and subjects. No prior rights attached even to portraiture, except where patents limited the use of a particular process. Thus, in Frankfurt am Main, on December 17, 1844, E. Tanner, a Londoner and pupil of Talbot, advertised that he produced "portraits on paper". Only two months later the first studio announced that it too could supply such portraits, and by the end of 1845, all five daguerreotypists in the city had mastered the calotype process. Frankfurt became the center of this technique in Germany, even though daguerreotyping was still carried out alongside it until the mid-1850s.[37]

This was by no means an isolated case of photographers being skilled in the use of both

37. E. Mayer-Wegelin, *Frühe Photographie in Frankfurt am Main, 1839–1870,* exhibition catalogue, Historisches Museum Frankfurt, Munich, Schirmer-Mosel, 1982, pp. 22–27.

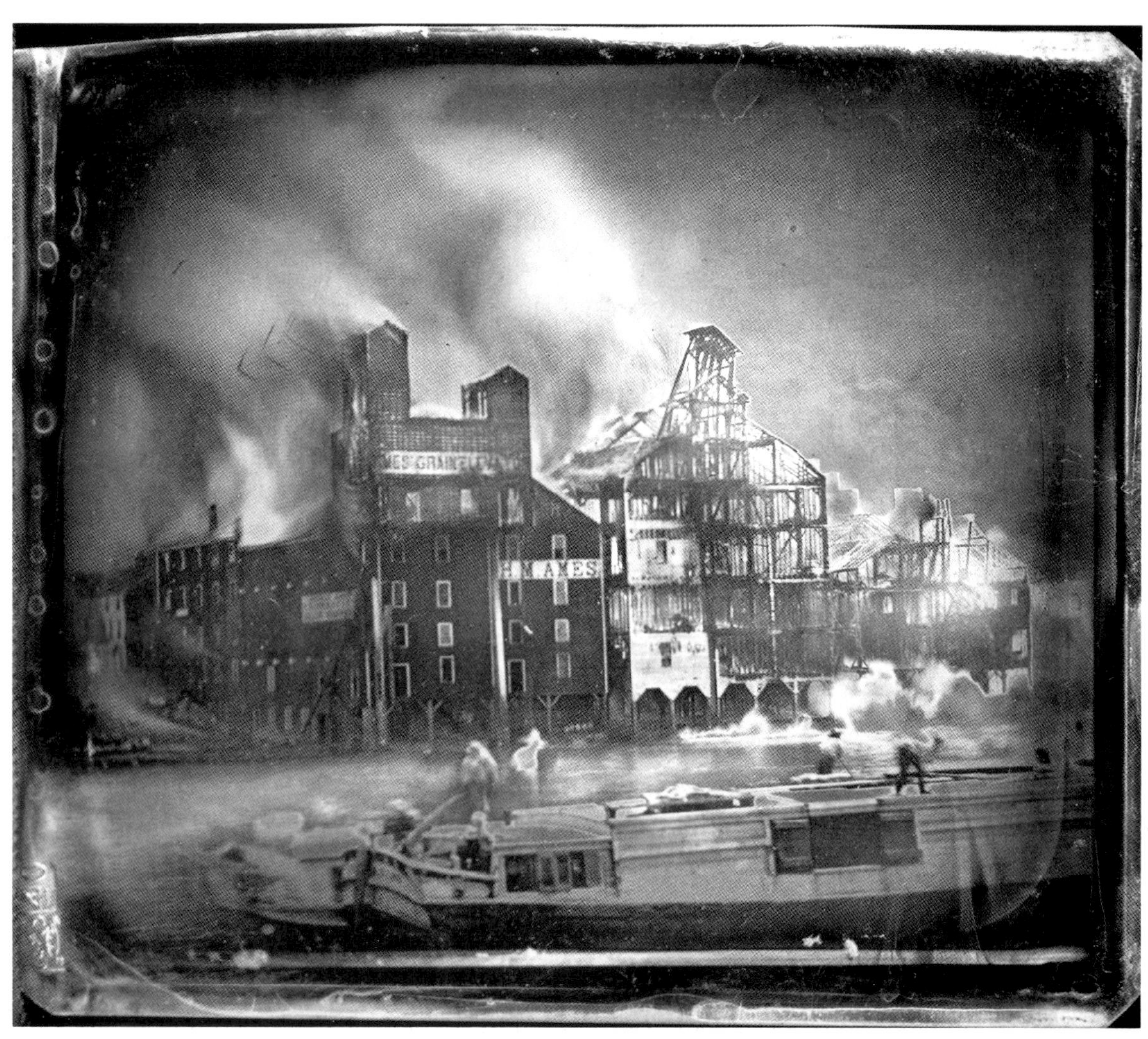

George N. Barnard, *Burning Mills, Oswego*, daguerreotype, July 5, 1853, International Museum of Photography, George Eastman House, Rochester.

techniques. Sometimes they even used both processes to complement each other, exploiting the advantages of each. In 1842, Beard bought a licence for calotyping from Talbot in order to produce enlargements or multiple copies of small daguerreotypes. The first photographs of warfare in Europe were daguerreotypes taken by Lecchi during the siege of Rome in 1849 and then reproduced as calotypes. The expedition which M. Perry led to China and Japan in 1853 took cameras both for daguerreotyping and for calotyping.

When, in the early 1850s, the wet-collodion process was introduced, the daguerreotype held its own at first. In North America it still enjoyed some popularity in the 1860s and it was still being used on the fifth continent even in the early 1870s.[38] It was only when the size of prints on paper became standardized (this applied first to stereoscopic pictures, then from the second half of the 1850s onwards to photographs in carte-de-visite format) that production of some of the materials by industrial methods became possible. This – together with the division of labour in the studios, the operator being responsible for the negative and the copyist for the prints – led to photographs on paper becoming considerably cheaper. Above all, however, there was the massive demand for pictures, which the daguerreotype had awakened but could not satisfy. The less well-off sections of the middle class also wanted their likenesses to be captured for posterity and included in the gallery of famous contemporaries, relatives, and friends.

The uniqueness of the daguerreotype was its special feature – and its greatest drawback. As far as faithful reproduction of the subject was concerned, photography on paper did not represent an advance. However, the daguerreotype process, still very much a craft, was an anachronism in the age of the Industrial Revolution. It was fostering the use of images by an elite few at a time when photography was already attracting the attention of the many. People longed for a picture of themselves. The daguerreotype process could satisfy some of them, but it placed each portrait on the pedestal of incomparability. It was only with the large-scale representation of contemporaries by the photographic print that the private portrait truly evolved into a picture of society. Just as Hoffmann's prescient narratives could not attain significance until the texts were published, so in the history of photography the daguerreotype process was, one might say, the handwritten manuscript.

38. See H. Knight, "Alfred Charles Barker (1819–1873): A Lonely Genius", in *History of Photography*, no. 2, 1978, pp. 123–133; Barker was still daguerreotyping in New Zealand in 1872.

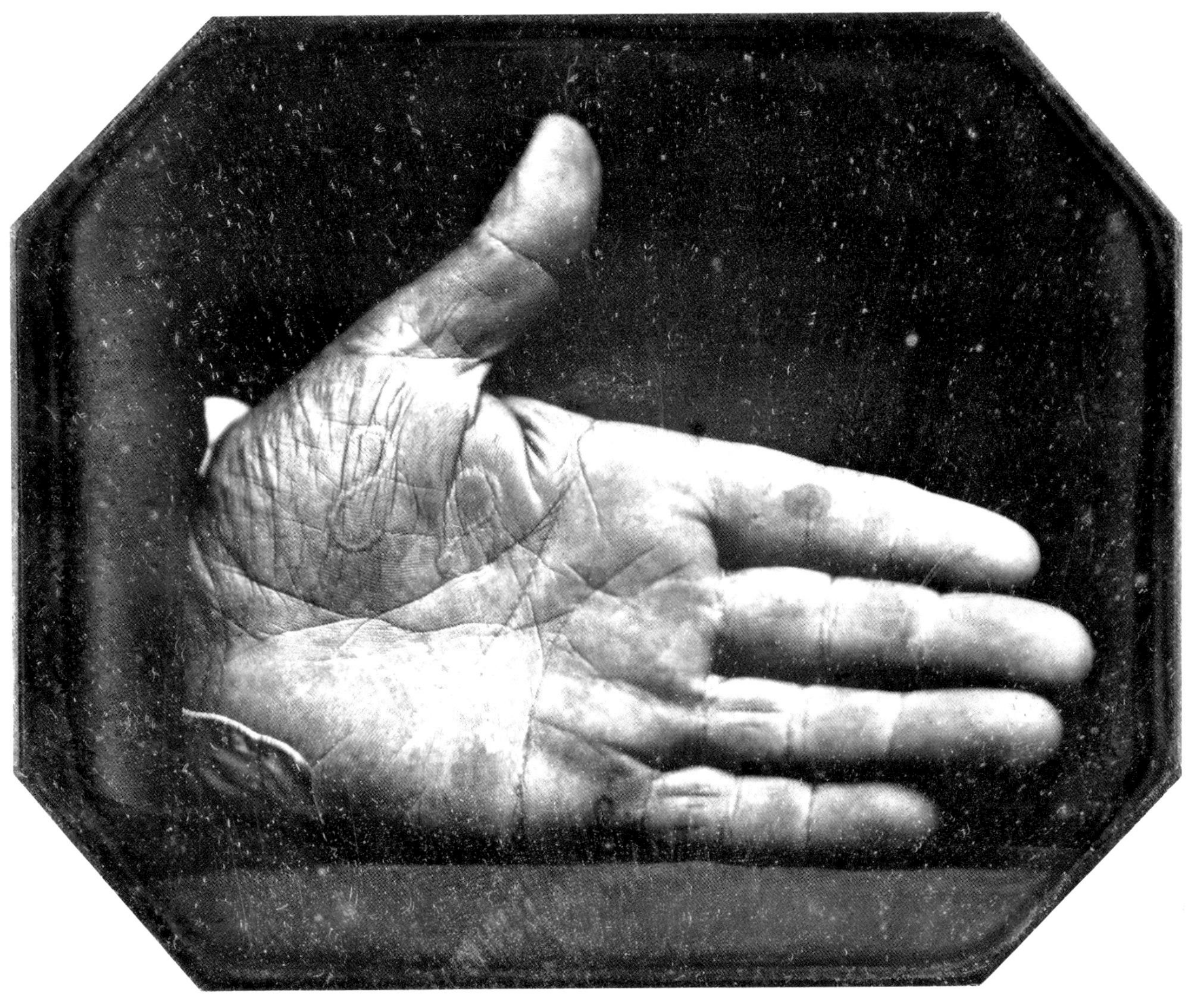

Daguerreotypes

The mirror of nature

"Scientific rather than documentary" is the description which best characterizes the daguerreotype. To complement the account given in the previous chapter, this section provides an idea of the extraordinarily varied nature of daguerreotypes, which in their day went far beyond being mere photographic illustrations. It was the precise nature of the process, its fidelity, its unusual presence, which was noted by all commentators, starting with Arago when he presented the invention in 1839. Before regarding it as a means by which ordinary people could produce pictures or obtain portraits, he envisaged first and foremost its advantages for the scientific community. French and English daguerreotypists in particular showed themselves keen to appropriate this technique in a scientific way. In the daguerreotype there is an optical emphasis, an objective insistance resulting from the way the image is framed and the fact it uses instruments comparable to the microscope; the daguerreotype seems concentrated on a limited visual field and to absorb it by saturating its restricted area of vision.

Many of the first daguerreotypists preferred to take arrangements rather than still-lifes: collections of objects akin to cabinets of curiosities, displaying various qualities of light and texture, as are implied by the words of Daguerre's collaborator, Hubert (1840): "crystals, glass vases filled with water or colored liquids [...] bronze or silver *objets d'art*, objects that were red or black, glazed or polished, such as Etruscan vases". Foucault's views through the microscope, pictures of sunspots by Fizeau and Foucault (1845), and Dubosc's images of optical instruments (displayed in London in 1851) and his quartz crystals (shown in Paris, 1855) bear witness to an experimental method which records and builds up data before drawing conclusions. Topography, monuments, plants, sculpture, and archeology, all played a part in forming the varied international jigsaw puzzle of "industrial products" which was brought together for the first time in London in 1851 (the Great Exhibition itself featured in daguerreotypes). In London too the stereoscopic process was unveiled, which particularly used daguerreotypes (Claudet was the best-known exponent). The way the images were mounted in the stereoscope lent itself especially well to the refinement of hand-colored academic nude portraits. Though rarely signed, they were the speciality of Belloc, Braquehais, and Gouin. A frivolous, even pornographic, character was apparent in these images from the outset.

The realism of the genre scene—a new form of pictorial composition—found an echo in the photographic process. Baron Humbert de Molard, one of the founders, made members of his family or his servants pose in scenes from rural life, himself posing on his sick-bed (1848) or transforming his steward into a prisoner in chains.

Thus the daguerreotype appeared as one of those rare moments when art and science come together, an image laboratory, an event in the history of representation which, until it was superseded by other techniques, appears to have produced a flourish of visual novelties which are still little known today.

Michel Frizot

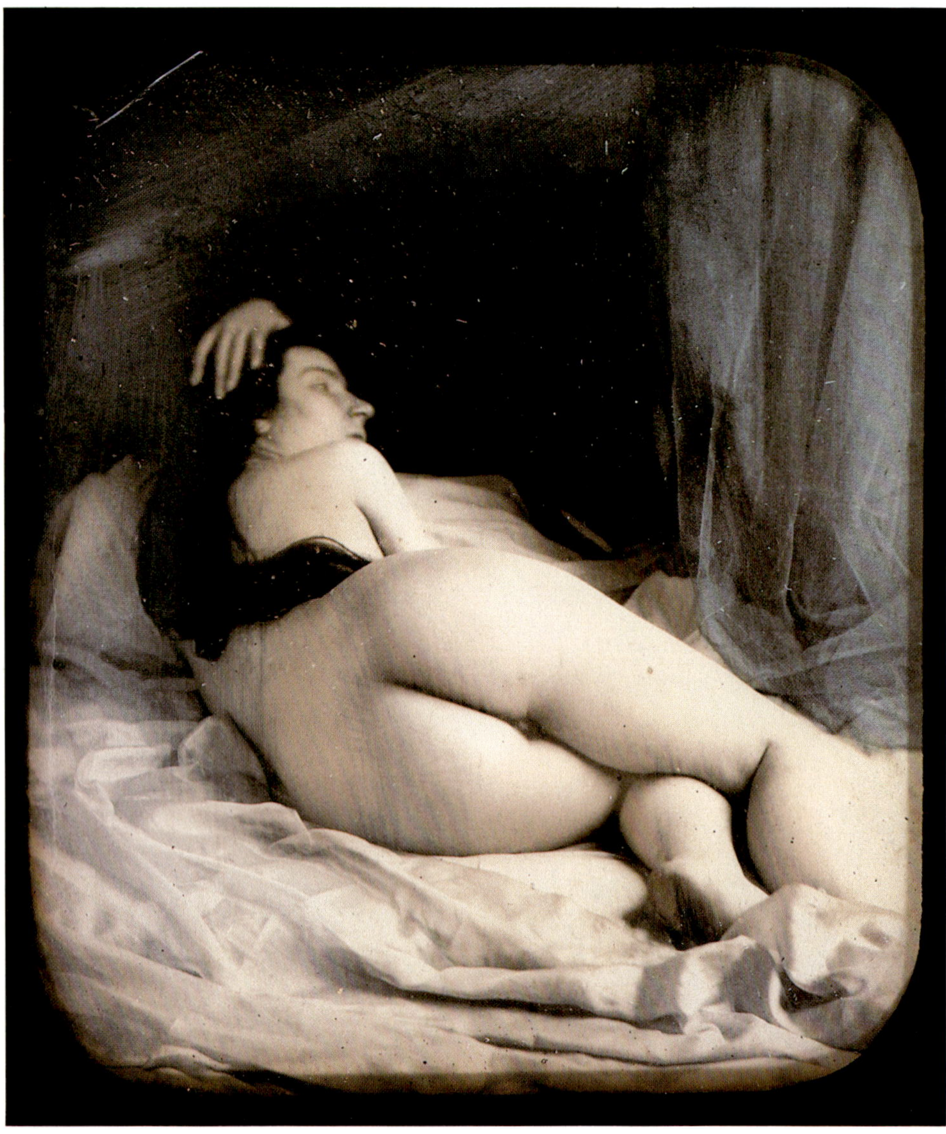

Anonymous,
Nude,
daguerreotype from a stereoscopic pair,
circa 1850,
Stefan Richter Collection.

Anonymous,
Nude,
daguerreotype from a
stereoscopic pair,
circa 1850,
Uwe Scheid Collection.

Previous page:
Albert S. Southworth and Josiah J. Hawes,
Brand on the Hand of Captain J. W. Walker,
daguerreotype, 1845, Massachusetts Historical Society, Boston.

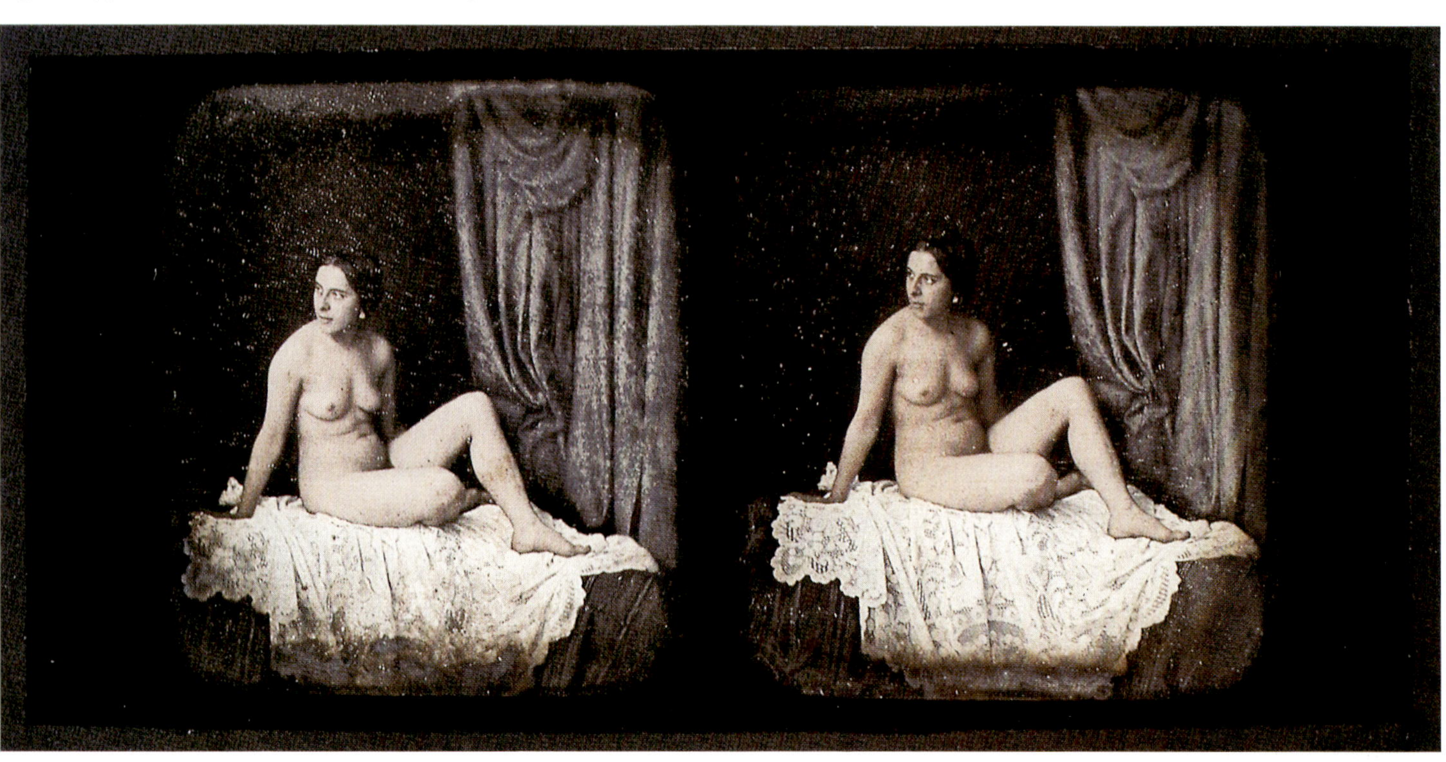

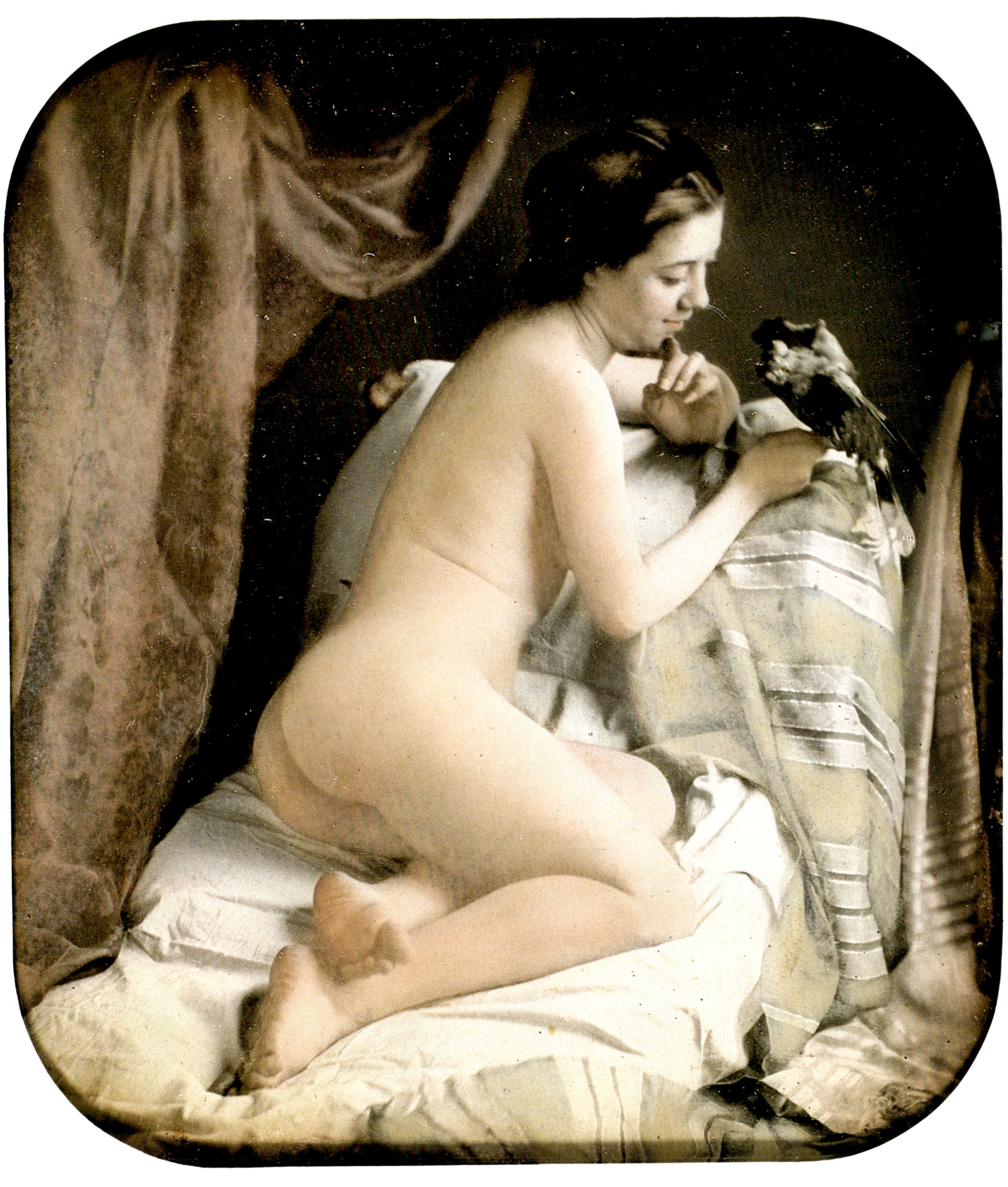

Anonymous,
Nude,
daguerreotype from a stereoscopic pair,
circa 1850,
Stefan Richter Collection.

◀ Anonymous,
Nude,
stereoscopic pair of daguerreotypes,
circa 1850,
Uwe Scheid Collection.

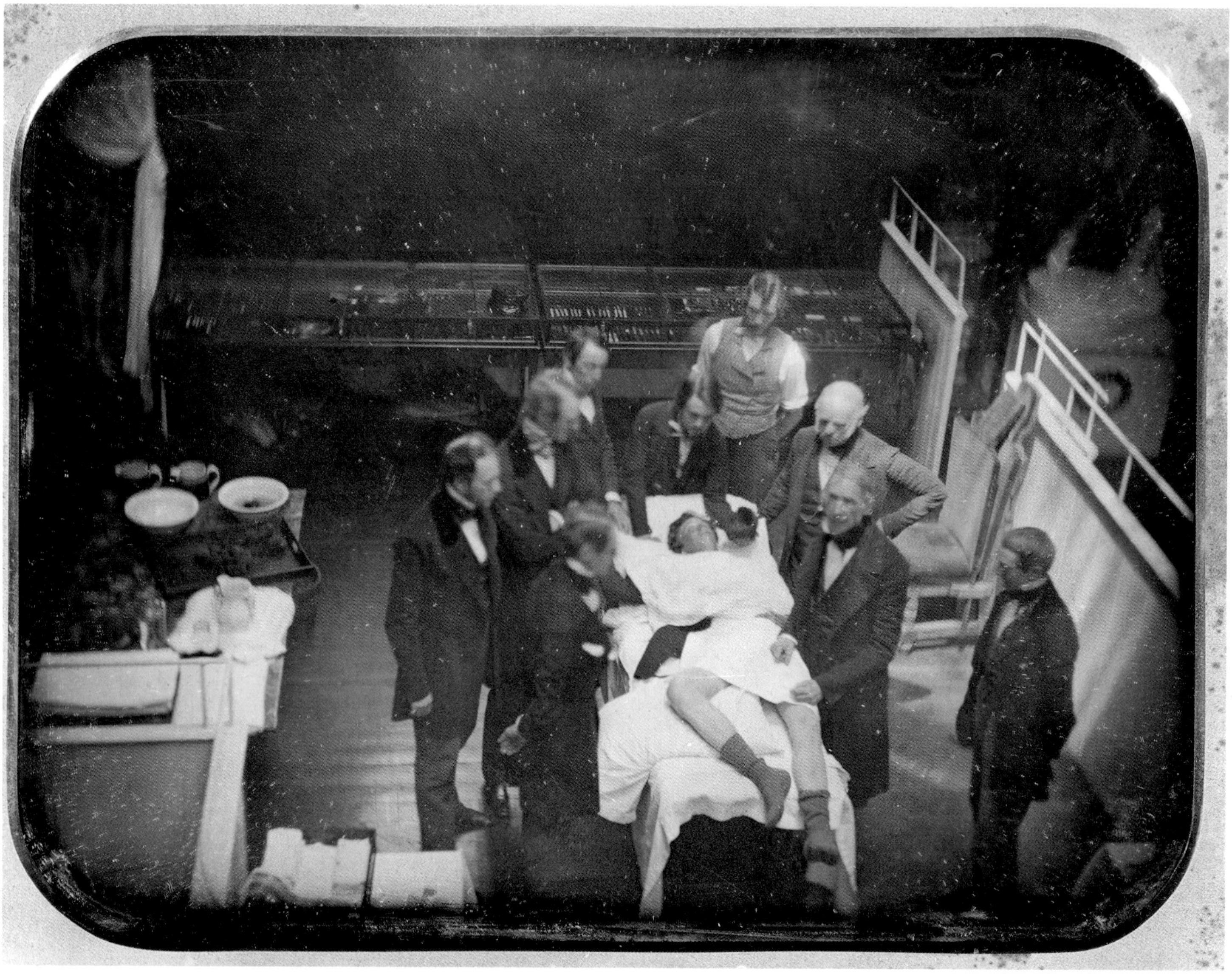

ANONYMOUS,
The First Operation under Anaesthetic, Using Ether, 1846,
rephotographed circa 1847,
daguerreotype,
John Paul Getty Museum,
Malibu.

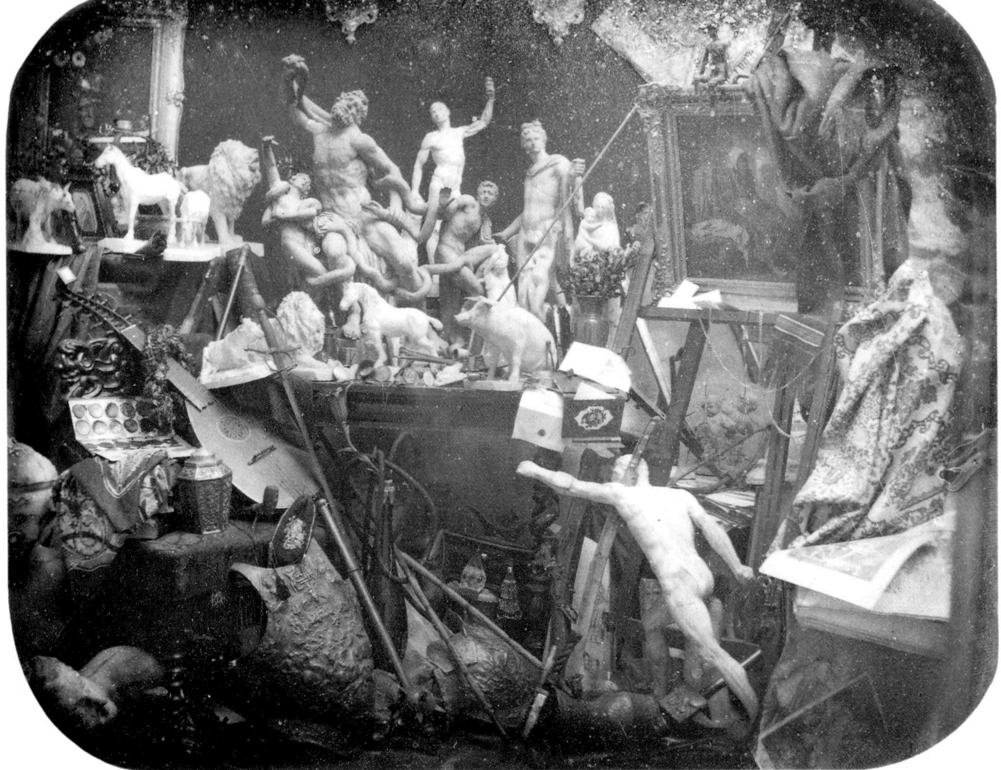

CHARLES WINTER,
Artist's Studio,
circa 1850,
daguerreotype,
Musée de Strasbourg.

Robert Cornelius,
Self-portrait as an Experimental Chemist,
daguerreotype,
December 1843,
International Museum of Photography, George Eastman House, Rochester.

Léon Foucalt,
Bunch of Grapes,
daguerreotype,
1844,
Société Française de Photographie.

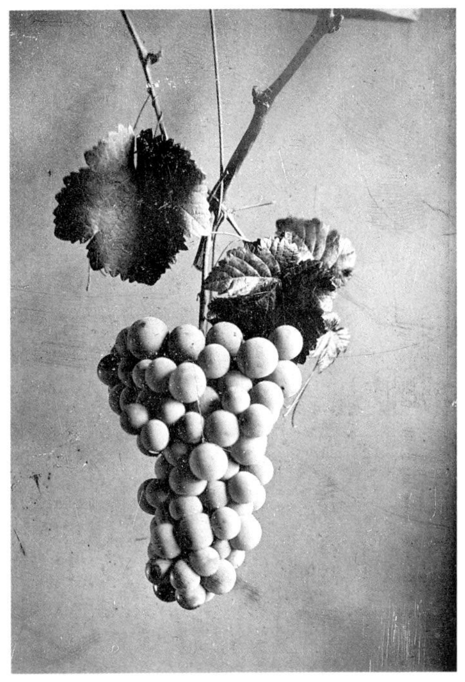

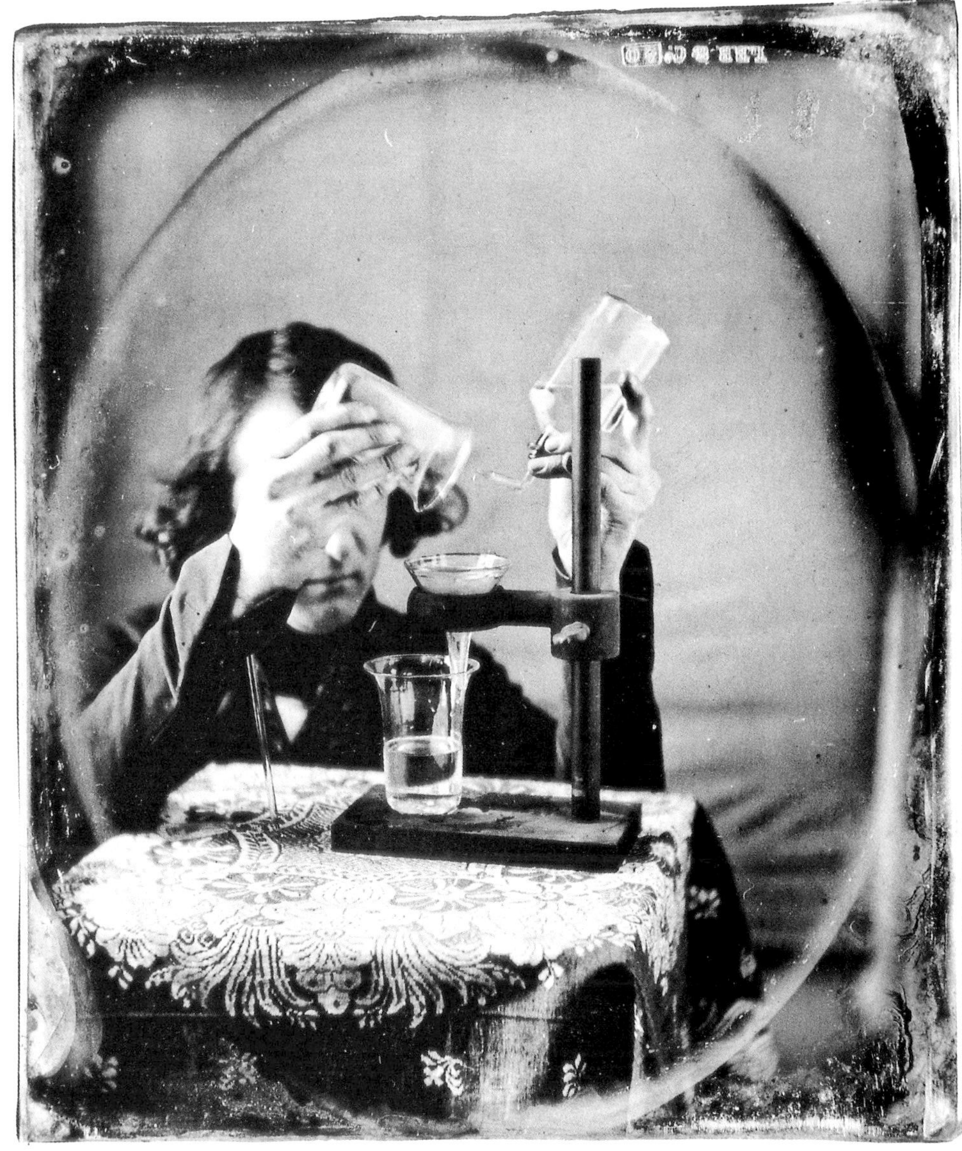

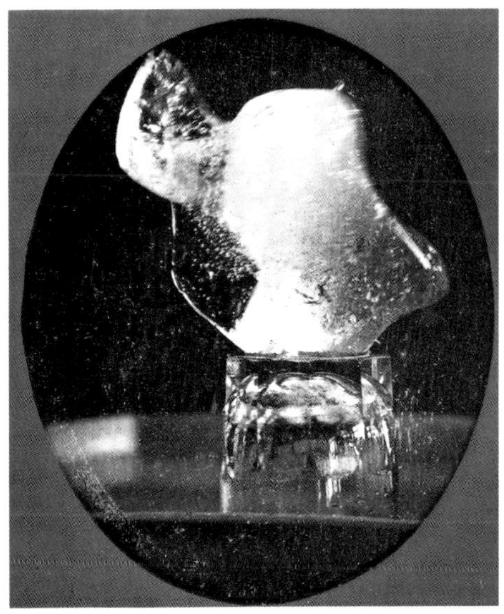

Jules Dubosq,
Rock Crystal on a Glass,
circa 1855, International Museum of Photography, George Eastman House, Rochester.

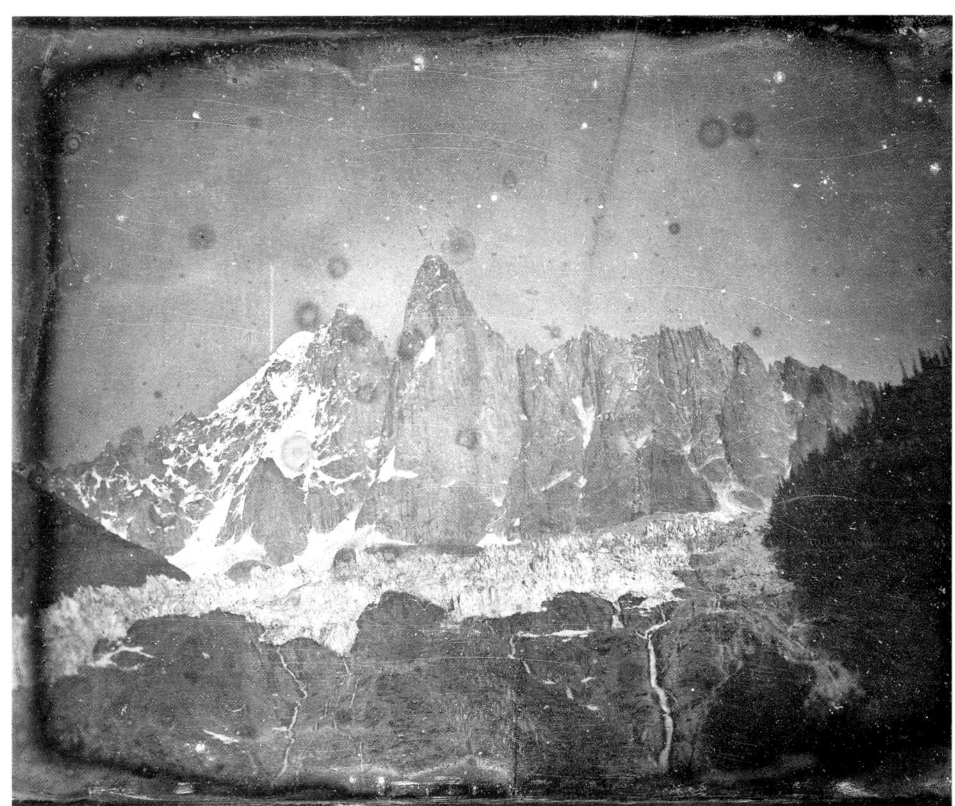

Frederic Crawley,
Mont-Blanc, Chamonix,
(Ruskin Collection), daguerreotype, 1854,
Ruskin Galleries, Isle of Wight.

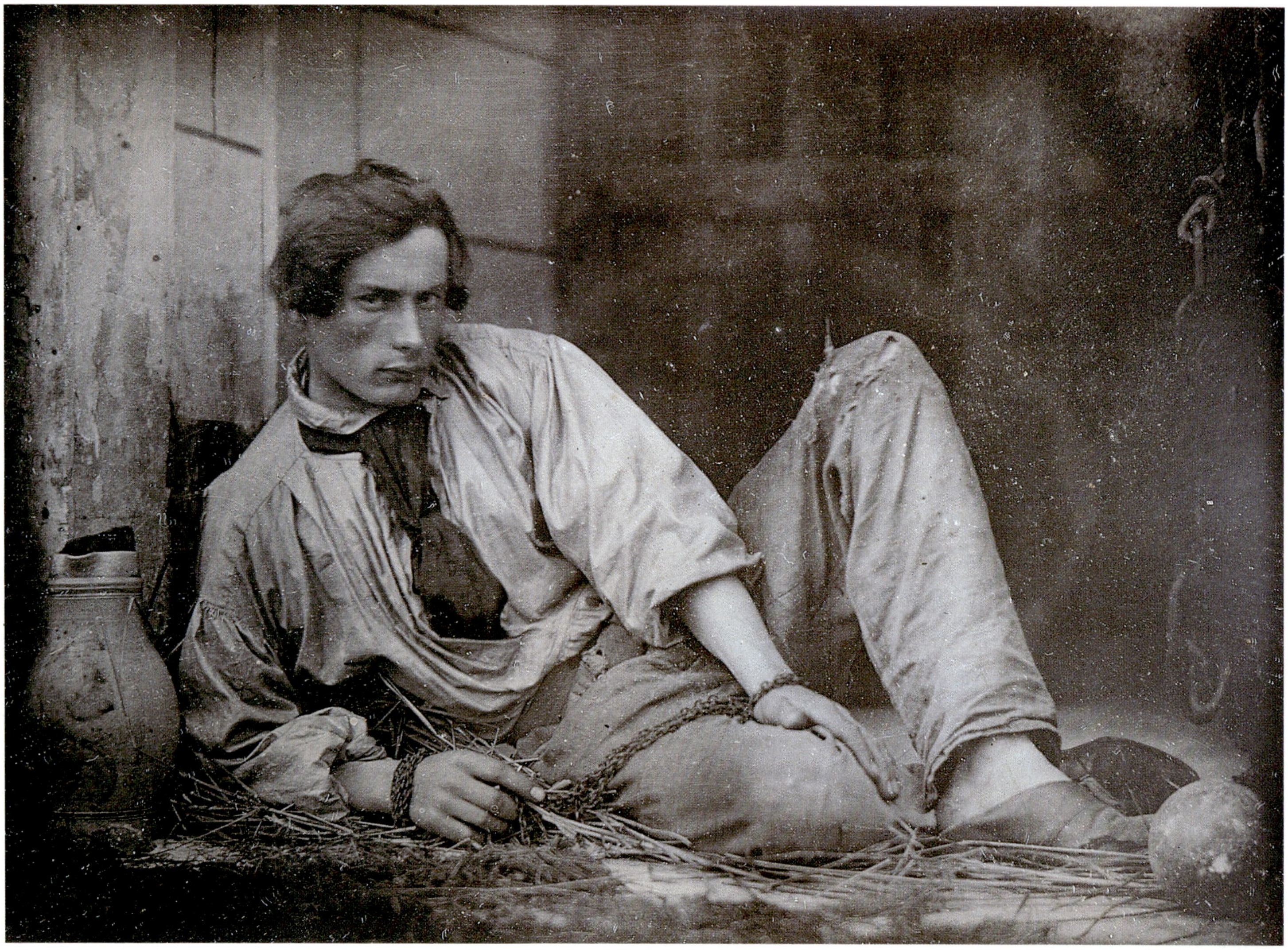

LOUIS-ADOLPHE HUMBERT DE MOLARD,
The Prisoner,
daguerreotype,
circa 1848,
Musée d'Orsay, Paris.

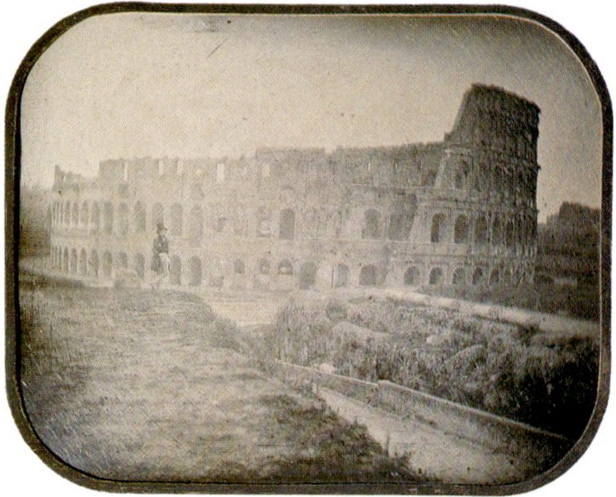

ANONYMOUS,
The Coliseum, Rome,
daguerreotype, 1851,
Bibliothèque Nationale, Paris.

BARON J-B. LOUIS GROS, ▶
Great Exhibition at the Crystal Palace, London,
daguerreotype, 1851,
Bibliothèque Nationale, Paris.

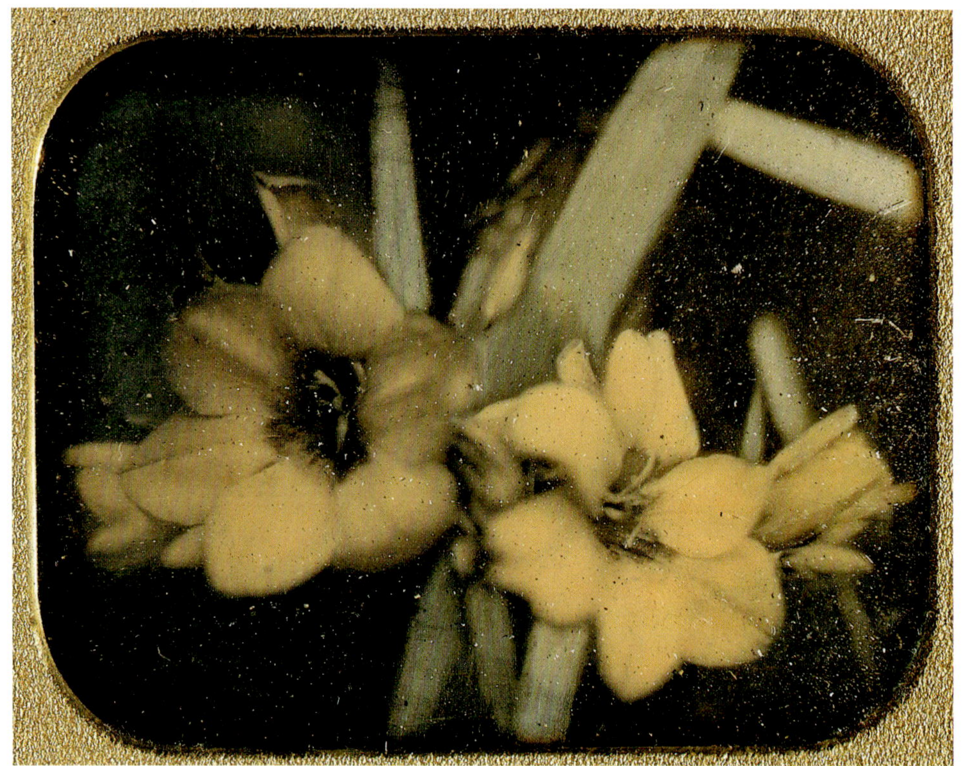

ALBERT S. SOUTHWORTH AND JOSIAH J. HAWES,
Flowers,
daguerreotype,
circa 1852,
private collection.

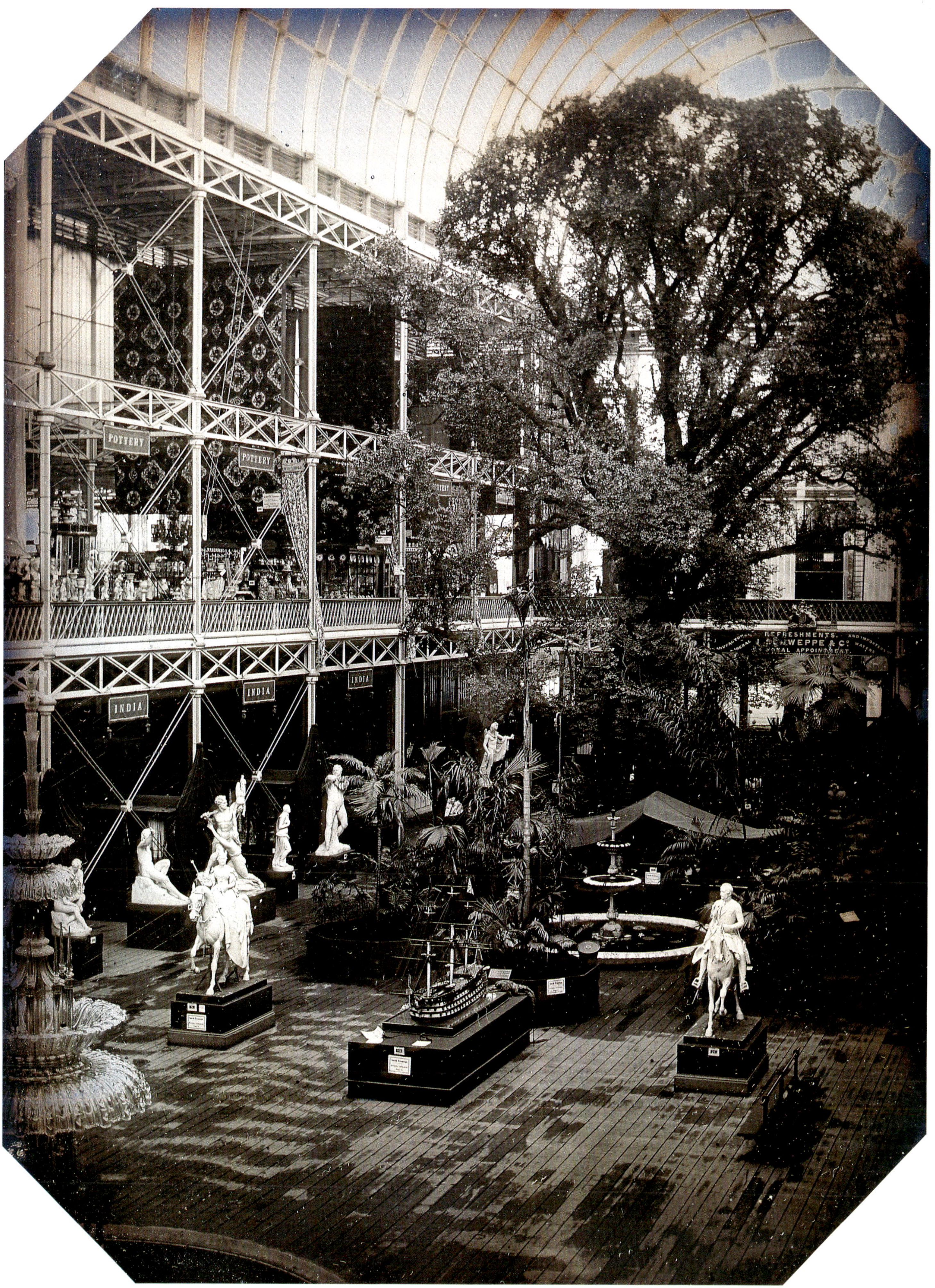
POTTERY
POTTERY
INDIA
INDIA
REFRESHMENTS.
AND IMPORTERS
WATERS

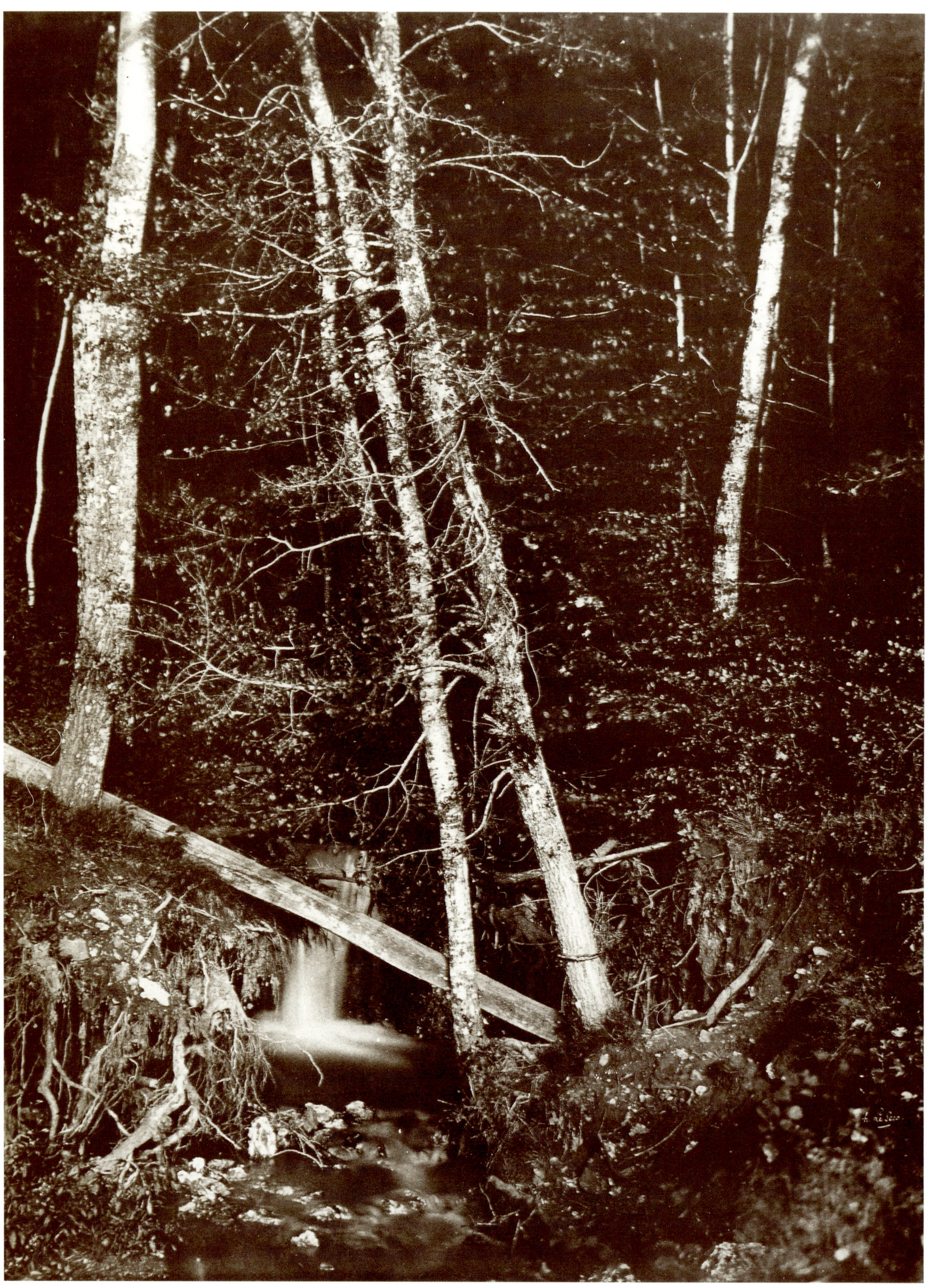

AUTOMATED DRAWING

4

The truthfulness of the calotype

Michel Frizot

Photography – in the generally accepted sense of the term – only really began with the invention by Talbot of the calotype, a process which combined the concepts of the paper negative and the latent image. The photographic process, based on long exposure times of at least a few seconds, was perceived by the operator as a slow deposit of light on a surface; the graphic result was comparable to a monochrome drawing, with a grainy and rather hazy appearance. The calotype process, for the most part practiced in Britain and France before 1855, was characterized by its ambiguous relationship with the pictorial arts (painting, lithography, drawing), which often provided it with a model. However, in practice, photography was also affirming its independence through its unique ability to record shapes without omitting any detail.

The year 1839 had been significant for developments in the field of photography: the daguerreotype, Talbot's photogenic drawing, and Bayard's direct positive process. However, these processes, already the subject of experimentation for several years, had finally evolved somewhat hastily; Talbot, in semi-ignorance of what Daguerre was doing, wanted to affirm the priority of his claim. In his view this was assured by the scientific work he had begun in 1834. The spirit of competition provoked by the need to pursue research in several directions would be beneficial for future discoveries. In the climate of 1839 Talbot began increasingly to consider the originality of his process (on paper, rather than on a metal plate) and its drawbacks (slowness, lack of success in the *camera obscura*, reversal of tonal values, etc.), which at that time meant that the daguerreotype remained unrivaled.

It would be over-hasty to regard the daguerreotype as a process without a future. One must recognize that for around fifteen years in Europe (much longer in the United States and other countries) the daguerreotype was an accomplished process, giving complete satisfaction for many different applications. Whilst it was subject to improvements, these continued to conform to Daguerre's original principles (including ways of transferring the image to paper by impression using oil-based inks).

Photography in 1840

The fact that in a few years an alternative photographic process appeared we owe to Talbot's strategy and to certain aspects of his research. This process was similar to the daguerreotype (taking a picture by the impression of light) but at the same time very different in its procedure and final appearance. It attracted the support of experimenters and was to redefine the very notion of photography, to the point of stimulating other research, but was eventually to disappear in favor of these advances, just as the daguerreotype had done. Between 1850 and 1855 the practice and trade of photography were shared, as it were, between the daguerreotype and the "talbotype", the former being used mainly for professional portraiture, the latter for landscapes and amateur photography.

Talbot's "photogenic drawing" process, which he had worked on since his return from Italy in 1834, experimented with once more in January 1839, and improved in 1839–1840, formed the basis for his future work, as, little by little, details of the daguerreotype reached him. Photogenic drawings were images formed by the action of light on sensitized paper – in other words, silhouettes on a dark background which appeared "negative". The process could take place in a *camera obscura*, but produced, of course, what we

◀ Henri Le Secq, *Forest Stream* circa 1853, Bibliothèque des Arts Décoratifs, Paris.

should call a negative. In theory, this image was reversible by exposing a second sheet of photosensitive paper placed beneath it. However, Talbot's negatives were insufficiently dense in the shadows to allow good positive prints to be produced (one negative survives, from August 1835, which shows a lattice window, in which Talbot was delighted to be able to distinguish the individual panes of glass. Apparently, however, this was taken no further.) It was at this stage, in 1835, that, discouraged perhaps, Talbot abandoned his photographic work in order to devote himself to mathematics and classical languages. Then, at the end of 1838, rumors of a French invention reached him.

At the beginning of 1839 the question of priority over Daguerre provided the impetus for research, intended to demonstrate the originality of the principles established by Talbot. In March he investigated the possibility of adding gallic acid (which John Herschel had suggested) to silver nitrate.[1] He also began studying how to transfer from the negative to the positive in order to return to "the original disposition" of the image (in August 1839, before a meeting of the British Association in Birmingham, he referred to "a *transfer* or reversed image"). The method was sufficiently efficacious for Talbot's process to be considered superior to the French one, notably in its "capability of multiplication of copies, and therefore of publishing a work with photographic plates";[2] It was practicable enough, too, for Biot to encourage Talbot to provide a more sensitive

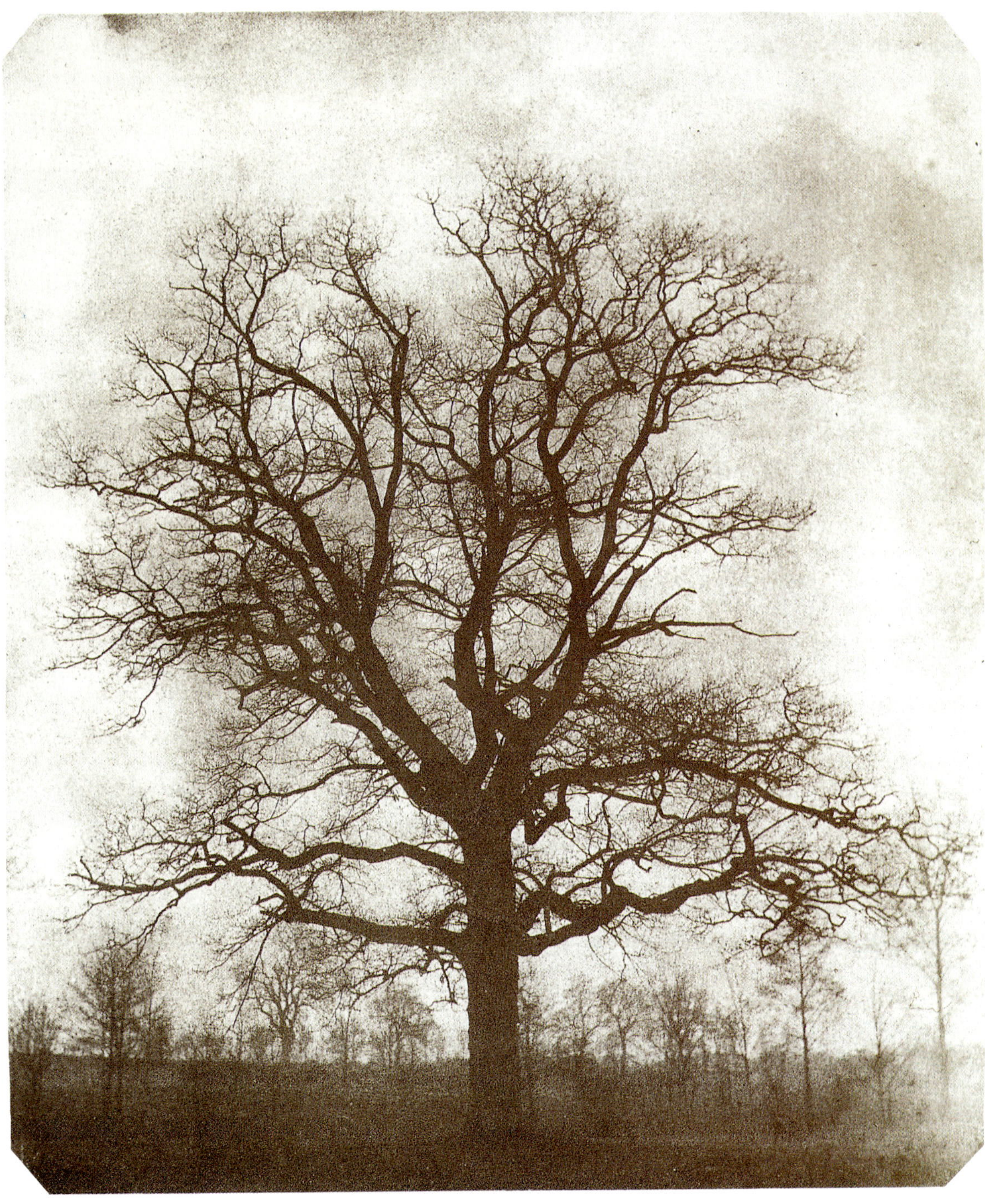

William H. Fox Talbot, ***Tree,*** circa 1842, Fox Talbot Museum, Lacock Abbey.

1. For a chronology of Talbot's work, see G. Buckland, *Fox Talbot and the Invention of Photography,* Boston, D. R. Godine, 1980.

2. Letter from Talbot to Herschel, December 7, 1839.

paper process intended for travelers and artists, "the rapidity of the operation being a condition of success".[3]

The revelation of the calotype

In September 1840 Talbot discovered, by chance, a process "to which [he] gave the name of calotype" (from the Greek *kalos*: beautiful, good, useful). His laboratory notebook records the progress of the discovery, from September 20 to October 11, 1840. Exposures of one hour were suddenly reduced to a few minutes or seconds; the image support was paper prepared with silver nitrate, acetic acid, and gallic acid. An image did not appear during the exposure in the *camera obscura*, but the silver salts, on which the light had worked for a very short time, were darkened at a later stage during "development" in gallic acid, which speeded up the reaction. Apart from the ease of obtaining a negative which could subsequently be used to produce as many positive images as one liked, the value of the process lay above all in the other characteristic linked to the use of an accelerating agent (gallic acid) – the concept of the latent image.[4] This separated the two operations of taking a photograph and making the negative visible. Today this remains fundamental to the photographic process. Through Biot, the Academy of Sciences in Paris was informed of this discovery, news of which was beginning to spread: "No impression may be seen, not even the slightest beginning of the picture. And yet the picture already exists there in all its perfection, but in a perfectly invisible state. By simple procedures, which I shall later disclose, the picture is made to appear as if by magic. It really is the most marvelous thing you could ever see."[5] Talbot immediately took a few portraits (his wife Constance on October 6, 1840; Amélina Petit, on October 13, 1840; a servant standing near a coach, October 14, in 3 minutes), and he photographed an elm tree using an exposure time of one minute.

An English patent was taken out for the calotype (Calotype Photographic Process) on 8 February 1841 (the very same day when, in the feverish quest to prove priority, Bayard made a communication to the French Academy of Sciences on a similar process), and it was patented in France on August 20, 1841. The text specifically mentions gallic acid, development, fixing, and application to portraiture, but, curiously, does not protect the one feature which, in our view, makes the calotype so original: the intermediary function of the negative. A second patent, taken out on June 1, 1843, gave a more detailed account of the procedure and introduced some improvements. These were designed to make the negative more transparent for printing and to produce "photographs" which could be included in publications, something which Talbot would shortly achieve with his *Pencil of Nature* begun in 1843 (a patent was taken out in the United States in 1847 and subsequently taken up by the Langenheim brothers). The successive operations required for the production of a calotype were as follows (patent no. 8842):

1. Brush a solution of silver nitrate on to a sheet of paper. Leave it to dry, then apply a solution of potassium iodide. This paper can be kept for a long time and is not particularly light sensitive.
2. To use, coat the iodized paper, in darkness, with a mixture of silver nitrate, gallic acid, and acetic acid. This makes the paper very light-sensitive.
3. This "calotype paper" is placed in the *camera obscura*, in the focusing plane of the lens which has been properly adjusted, and the exposure made.
4. The exposed paper, on which no image is visible, is treated in the laboratory with a further coating of gallo-nitrate of silver, which makes the image appear in a few minutes.
5. Finally, the image is fixed in a solution of hypo, then washed in water and dried.

The procedure for printing a positive from the negative is worth describing in detail, since it would in future form the basis of most photography. Prints were made on salted paper – paper soaked in a solution of sodium chloride (common salt) then coated (using a brush) with silver nitrate solution and dried. The negative is placed in direct contact with this "positive" paper in a

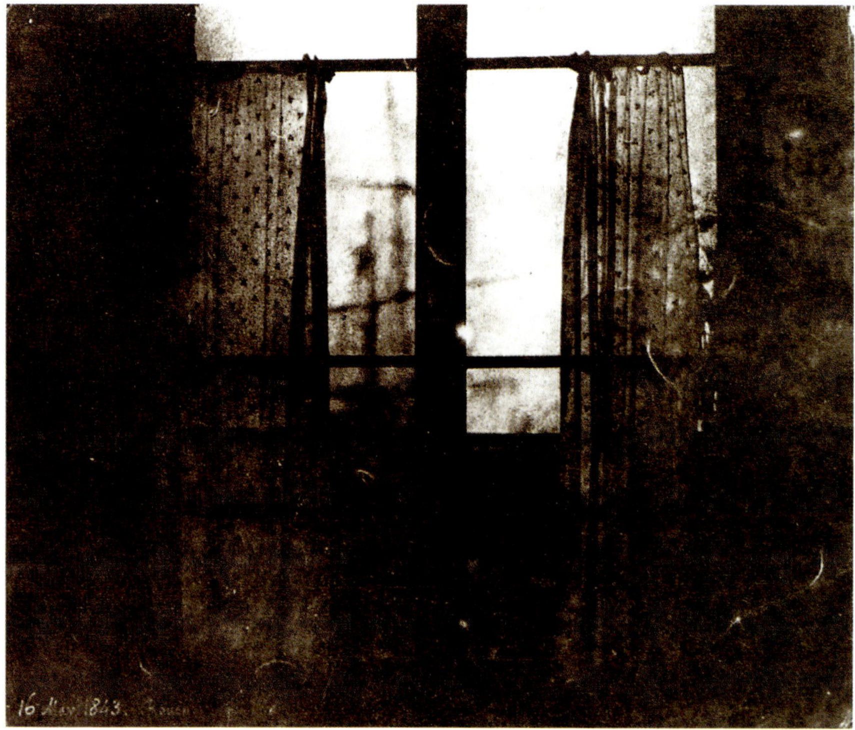

WILLIAM H. FOX TALBOT, ***Rouen, May 16, 1843,*** National Museum of Photography, Film and Television, Bradford.

3. Letter from Biot to Talbot, November 10, 1839.

4. The term appeared on September 23, 1840.

5. Academy of Sciences, Paris, February 1, 1841.

The Pencil of Nature

The Pencil of Nature, the first work illustrated with photographs, was intended to publicize the merits of calotype as a means of "illustration" in the broadest sense. The publisher was W. H. Fox Talbot who used it to promulgate his own process. He brought the work out in six parts, each containing between three and seven photographs, between June 29, 1844 and April 23, 1846. The *Athenaeum* review complained about the long gaps between parts and their exorbitant price compared to other techniques (engravings, lithographs): "all this proves that the effort required to take a photograph is too great for it to ever become a generally useful means of illustration".

Talbot wrote a commentary for each of the 24 images explaining the necessary way to "decode" the particular subject. His introduction underlines that photography was a complete innovation, far closer to lithography or drawing than the daguerreotype. "The plates shown in this work have been produced solely by the action of light, without any help from the artist's hand. The images are produced by the sun and not, as some people think, by copying engravings."

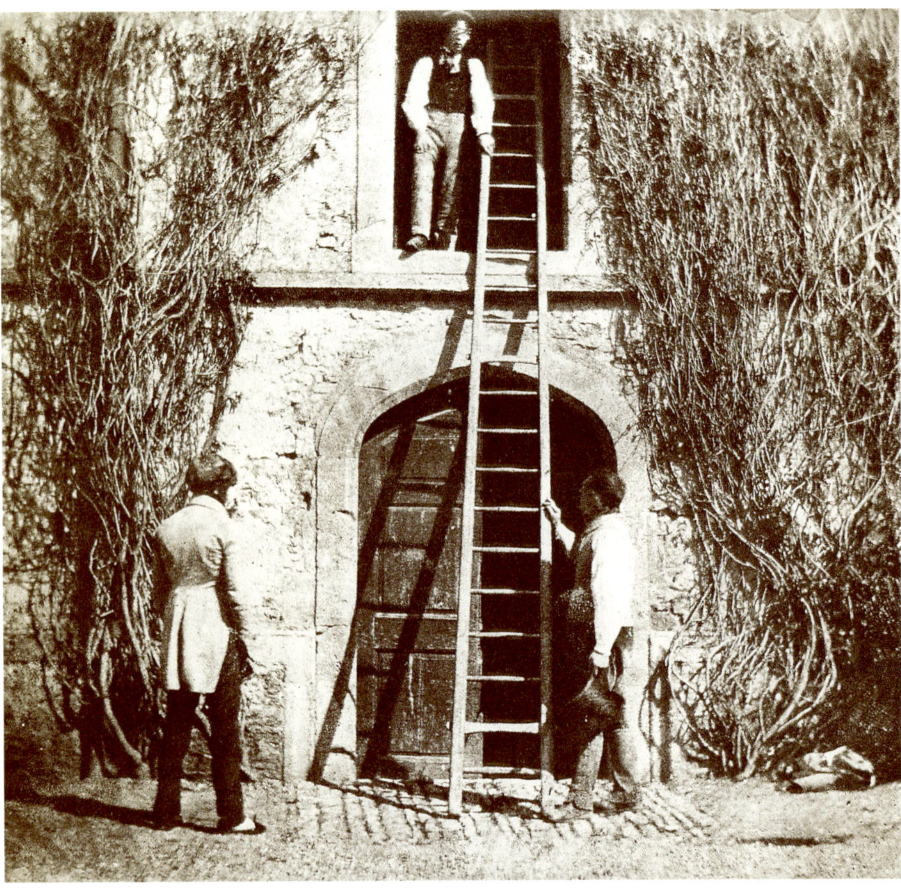

William H. Fox Talbot,
The Ladder,
1843,
plate XIV of *The Pencil of Nature.*

The commentaries elucidate the way in which the photographs were conceived. They set out Talbot's personal vision while forestalling misconceptions. Describing a view of the Parisian boulevards, he noted that "the instrument chronicles whatever it sees, and certainly would delineate a chimney-pot or a chimney-sweep with the same impartiality as it would the Apollo of Belvedere". The idea behind *The Pencil of Nature* was to provide a sampler for the merits of calotype. The book contains shots of porcelain objects (capturing the state of things in a given moment), glassware (delicately transparent luminous effects), a manuscript, copies of both lithographs and engravings, a photogenic drawing of tree foliage and another of lace. There are also two versions of the bust of Patroclus, illustrating that photography could be of service to artists.

A Scene in a Library (pl. VIII) is a close-up of a library bookcase containing a selection of books which can be interpreted as a list of Talbot's interests. In his commentary to this plate, Talbot touches on the possibility of taking photographs in the dark, using ultra-violet light. *The Haystack* (pl. X) is just that: a haystack with a ladder leaning against it. The accompanying commentary discusses photography's ability to capture a completely accurate image down to the smallest blade of straw and to deliver clear compositions including light and shade. "A multitude of minute details which add to the truth and reality of representation, but which no artist would take the trouble to copy faithfully from nature." *The Open Door* (pl. X) is a composition in the Dutch style that Talbot describes as a rapid sketch of something encountered, a half-glimpsed arrangement that engendered "picturesque" thoughts, feelings, and associations.

Finally, Talbot used the only image containing people, *The Ladder* (pl. XIV), to demonstrate the calotype's potential use in portraiture (even though here the figures are shot from a little way off). He makes an astonishing comment that gives us an insight into how his contemporaries must have felt about the new medium: "groups of figures take no longer time to obtain than single figures would require, since the camera depicts them all at once, however numerous they may be". Unquestionably, this gives us the true measure of just how modern photography was.

Michel Frizot

printing frame, and exposed to the sun for about half an hour or longer, until a satisfactory image appears. The exposure time is judged by inspecting the color of the positive image. The print is then fixed with hypo, thoroughly washed, and dried.

Use and distribution

From August 1841, the miniaturist Henry Collen, who had bought a license from Talbot, had used the calotype process to take portraits, in direct competition with the daguerreotype which, despite the fact that multiple copies could not be made, gave more detailed and attractive results. Talbot spoke of applying his process to architectural and landscape work during his travels. Following Collen, Antoine F. J. Claudet unsuccessfully attempted, in 1844, to popularize the calotype for portraiture. His experiment was taken up again on Talbot's behalf by Nikolaas Henneman in 1847, in a studio he opened in

Regent Street, London. This studio also sold photographic prints, particularly the French views which Talbot had taken in 1843. Thus, little by little, a new process established itself – very different from the daguerreotype, promoted by a scholar of the highest caliber, W. H. Fox Talbot, and aiming at other objectives than those of the rival French process. Although the first "calotypists" also attempted portraiture, the advantages of the calotype were primarily its reproducibility (the possibility of an unlimited number of prints), the materials used (an image on paper, very close to engravings or drawings), and an imprecise, rather blurred appearance (which could be regarded as a defect when compared to the precision of the daguerreotype). Thus around 1843 two very different techniques were available which produced images of very different appearance and application.

While the daguerreotype process became a practical procedure which itinerant practitioners adopted with enthusiasm, the calotype, a slower process, demanding more care and more subject to variations (and expensive), seemed destined to be thought of as a process for making "fine images" to be stored in cabinets of curiosities, just as one might keep an ancient engraving, away from light.

To this must be added the obligatory payment of a fee, imposed in all countries, to Talbot by each person who used his patented process. By contrast, people could use the daguerreotype without charge, since it had been "given to the world". This would restrict the distribution of the calotype, even among those who perceived its undoubted advantages. In 1843 Talbot set up a photographic printing establishment at Reading (managed by his assistants Nikolaas Henneman and Thomas Malone), the aim of which was to facilitate the production of large numbers of prints from negatives. Licenses were delivered for the use of the calotype, and prints for commercial distribution were produced on demand. Talbot published, as a form of advertisement for the calotype process, *The Pencil of Nature*,[6] the first book to be illustrated with pasted-in photographs, containing examples of all the subjects which an enthusiast might possibly take an interest in. The interest of the work is not only historical, but also aesthetic, for it allows us to reconstruct contemporary perceptions of the photograph in its context (i.e. compared with other types of images produced at the same time) and to understand its meaning (the visual and mental implications of the automatic nature of the process) and its ambiguities. For a public, albeit limited, which could not conceive of images other than those made by the hand of man, calotypes "resembled" a sepia wash, lithograph, or mezzotint engraving; the title *The Pencil of Nature* emphasized the lack of human intervention and the way nature "represented itself" (see

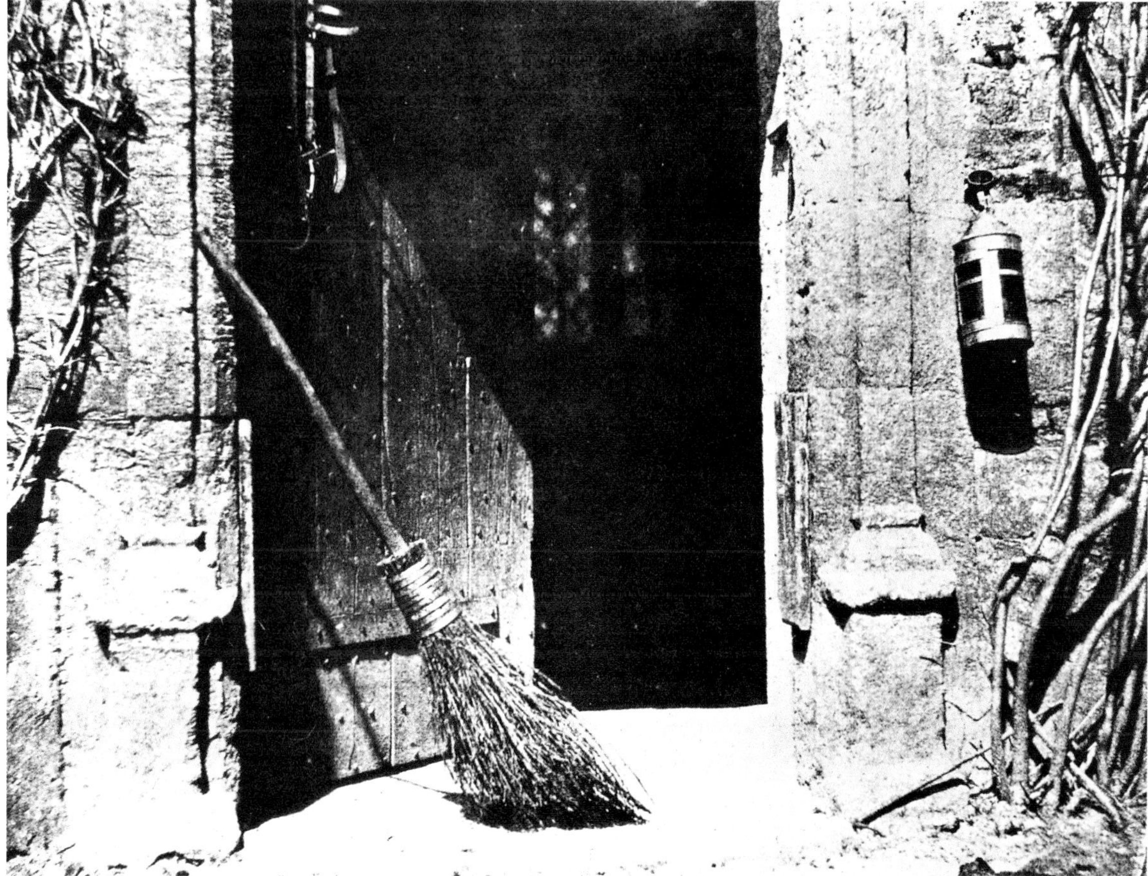

William H. Fox Talbot,
The Open Door,
1843,
plate VI of *The Pencil of Nature*.

6. *The Pencil of Nature*, London, Longman, Brown, Green, and Longmans, 1844–1846; reprinted New York, H. P. Kraus Jr., 1989.

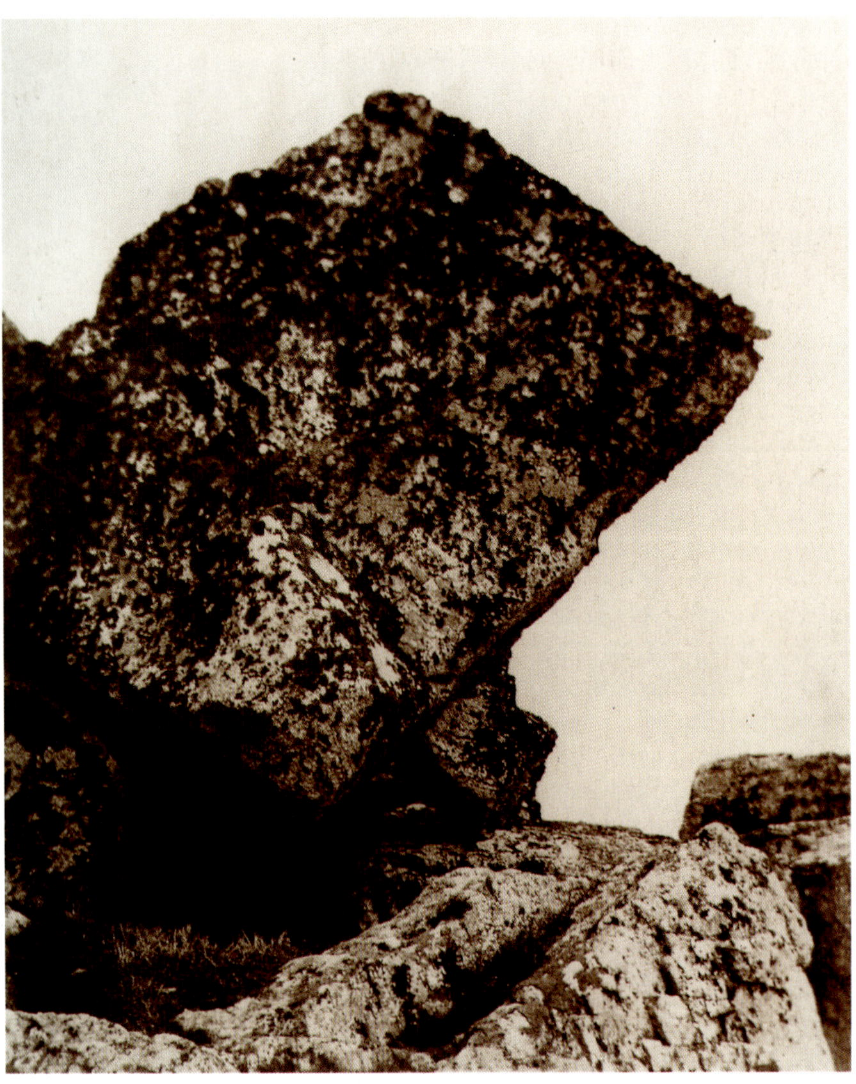

JOHN DILLWYN LLEWELYN, *Granite Boulders, Cornwall,* October 11, 1852.

box, p. 62). Next at Reading were published Talbot's *Sun Pictures of Scotland* (1845, 23 photographs), showing the sites on a tour in the footsteps of Sir Walter Scott, and *Annals of the Artists of Spain*, by Sir W. Stirling (66 calotypes, 1848).

British practitioners

During the years 1843–1847, however, the calotype achieved only partial success, limited as it was by technical constraints and Talbot's patent restrictions. Calotypists were drawn from a circle close to the inventor – prominent people, scientists, and artists, rather than commercial practitioners. The first important users of the process were two Scotsmen, David O. Hill and Robert Adamson in Edinburgh.[7] Adamson, who was introduced to the calotype through the influence of his brother and David Brewster of St. Andrew's University, is said to have opened a portrait studio in 1843 (encouraged by Talbot, who had not taken out a patent for Scotland). It seems that it was following a meeting in Edinburgh of the Church of Scotland, then splitting from its English counterpart, that the painter Hill contacted Adamson with a view to taking portraits for a great commemorative painting of the event. Their collaboration, in which they shared technical and artistic responsibilities, was to last until Adamson's premature death in January 1848, much longer than they had foreseen. Individuals or groups posed in the open air (the process was slow, and required the subjects to remain completely still for one or two minutes in full daylight), in a natural setting embellished with curtains, tables, flowers, and other "props". Hill and Adamson, (who signed their photographs jointly as "executed by R. Adamson under the artistic direction of D. O. Hill"), did not limit themselves to simple portraits. They dreamed up compositions, going into villages to photograph fishermen or photographing masons working on the Scott Monument. From the outset, Hill and Adamson created a distinctive photographic style, thus demonstrating that in expert hands the process could achieve perfection. Unlike other artists, they did not see themselves as social observers, restricting themselves to a picturesque approach, often agreed in advance. In four years, these pioneers of location photography produced at least 3,000 photographs, some of which were published as albums or sold as individual prints.

During the 1840s calotypes were given the poetic name of Sun Pictures. The first group of practitioners emerged from the immediate social and family circle of Talbot: his cousins John Dillwyn Llewelyn and Calvert Richard Jones, who both made a specialty of views of Welsh ports, seaside subjects, and moored boats, were later joined by Nevil Story-Maskelyne, Llewelyn's son-in-law.[8] Jones undertook a family journey to the Mediterranean, hoping to make the best use of the calotype in a sunny climate (Malta, Naples, Rome, 1845–1846), and set about providing images for the studio and print shop in Regent Street. In Italy he met another member of the family, Kit Talbot.[9] Jones photographed famous monuments (such as the Coliseum), boats in harbor, and general views, and on his return specialized in producing prints tinted with watercolors. Negotiations with Talbot aiming for closer collaboration came to nothing.

The Rev. G. W. Bridges had learned Talbot's process from Henneman in 1845, also with a view to using it during a Mediterranean trip. He used the calotype process for seven years, until 1852. In 1846 he met the Rev. Calvert Jones and Kit Talbot. They traveled together to Rome, Pompeii, and Naples. Bridges, who continued on his own through Greece, Egypt, and the Holy Land (a nineteenth-century Grand Tour), claimed to have taken 1,700 negatives, many of which were printed in the Reading Establishment. Despite his plans for several illustrated publications, only *Palestine As It Is* appeared, in 1858.

7. S. Stevenson, *D. O. Hill and R. Adamson: Catalogue of their Calotypes taken between 1843 and 1847 [...]*, Edinburgh, National Galleries of Scotland, 1981.

8. *Llewelyn, Maskelyne, Talbot: a Family Circle* (Sun Pictures, Catalogue 2), New York, H.P. Kraus Jr., 1986.

9. R. Lassam and M. Gray, *The Romantic Era: C. R. Jones, G. W. Bridges, W. R. Baker*, Florence, Alinari, 1988; L. Schaaf, *The Reverend Calvert Jones* (Sun Pictures, Catalogue 5), New York, H. P. Kraus Jr., 1990.

In 1847 the Calotype Club was formed (renamed the Photographic Club in 1848), around Robert Hunt, Peter Fry, Joseph Cundall, Hugh Owen, Hugh Diamond, and William Newton. This created a certain amount of competition as regards the calotype process – partly to rival French developments in the technique, where it enjoyed its greatest popularity in the late 1840s. Benjamin Brecknell Turner assiduously photographed the English countryside and rural working life in large format from 1849 to 1862 (by which date calotypists appeared rather old-fashioned); his participation in an exhibition at the Society of Arts in 1852 caused much comment. John Shaw Smith, of Cork, undertook a tour of Europe and the Middle East in 1852. A doctor, Thomas Keith, who had been introduced to the calotype by Hill and who became technically very proficient, photographed Edinburgh between 1851 and 1856, recording the appearance of the city. Occasionally, he would also revisit Hill and Adamson's subjects, adopting a different style.[10]

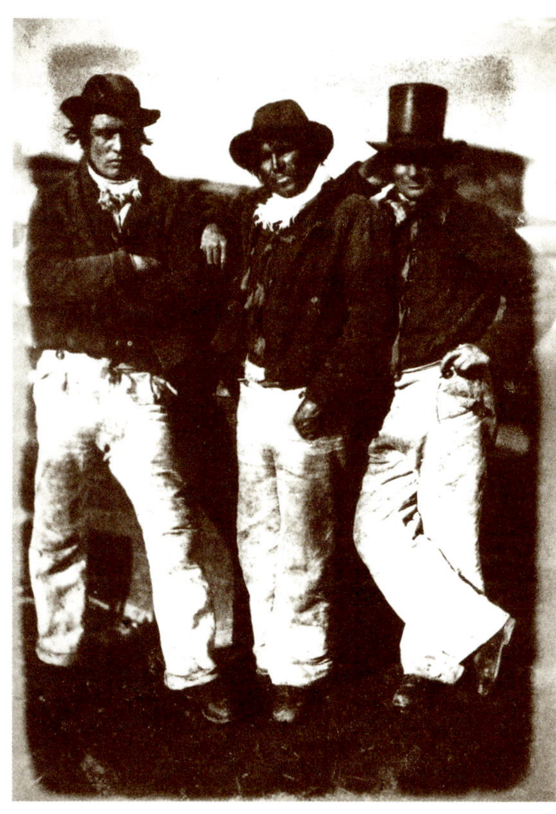

David O. Hill and Robert Adamson,
Newhaven Fishermen,
June 1845,
Victoria and Albert Museum, London.

A number of events would led to the gradual demise of the talbotype (Talbot's calotype in the strict sense of the patent description). In 1851, at the Great Exhibition in London, where it was possible to view 700 photographs from six countries (including many daguerreotypes), everyone could compare a range of techniques and their respective qualities. In the same year, Scott Archer published details of his collodion on glass process. For the *Report of the Juries* Henneman produced 20,000 prints made from the Ferrier brothers' glass negatives and Hugh Owen's calotypes. During the winter of 1851–1852 Roger Fenton, who had been a pupil of the painter Delaroche in 1841–1843, at the same time as Le Secq, Le Gray, and Nègre, made his way to Paris. His aim was to discover more about the creation of the Heliographic Society, from which

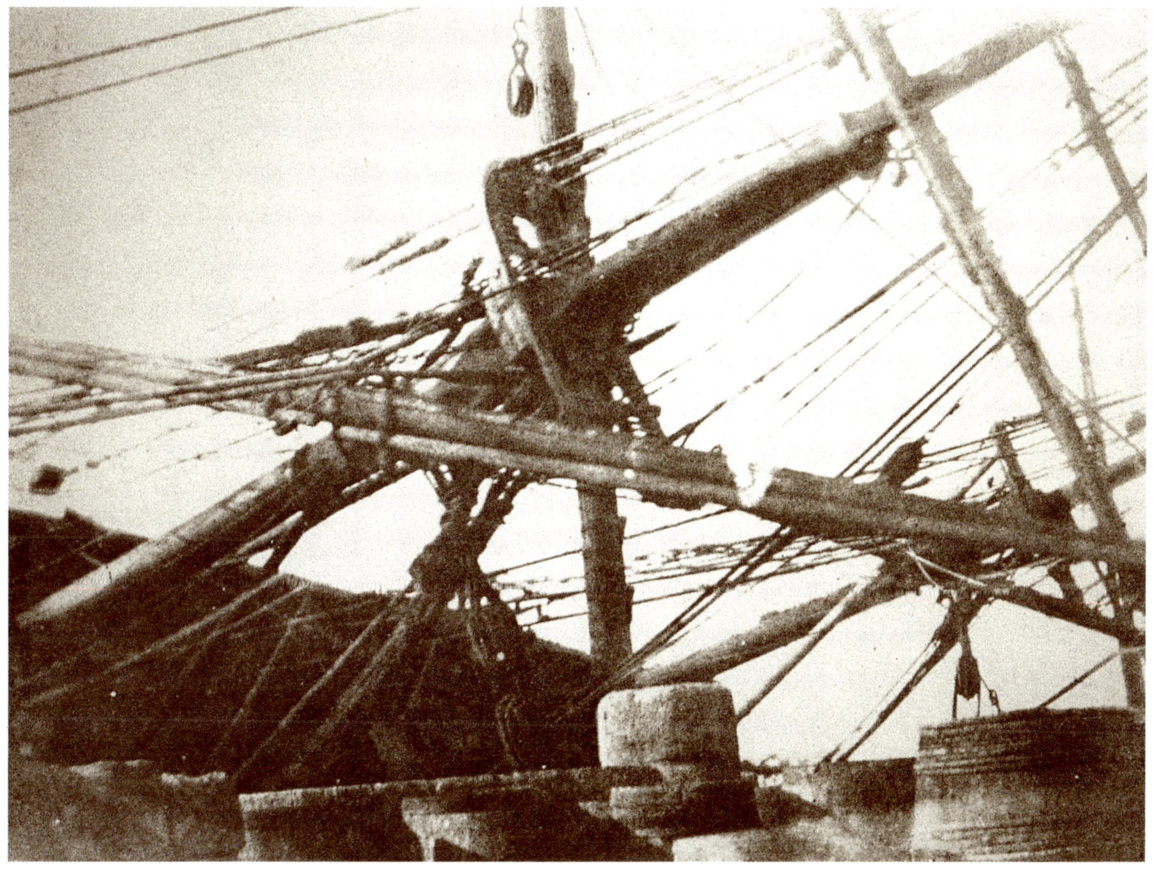

Calvert Richard Jones,
The Brig "Palacea", Malta,
1845–1846.

10. J. Hannavy, *Thomas Keith's Scotland: The Work of a Victorian Amateur Photographer, 1852–1857*, Edinburgh, Canongate, 1981.

The Heliographic Mission

The Heliographic Mission was created by the French Administration for Fine Arts in 1851, on the advice of the Historical Monuments Commission, by the sub-commission for photography "charged with reaching an understanding with artists on the itineraries which they should follow" (February 28, 1851). The idea was to send photographers into various parts of France to photograph historic buildings – mainly using the calotype process, which had certain practical advantages over daguerreotypes. This official mission was apparently the result of a joint initiative by Baron Taylor and the Comte de Laborde. Baron Taylor was a member of the Commission and already the photographer for the *Voyages pittoresques dans l'ancienne France* of Prosper Mérimée (Inspector-General of the Historical Monuments Commission since 1834). The Comte de Laborde, a curator at the Louvre and responsible for the sub-commission, was an advocate of photography at a time when all architectural recording was done by drawing. The role played by Francis Wey, president of the Society for Men of Letters, author, serial-writer, member of the Heliographic Society, and editor of the photographic magazine *La Lumière*, is harder to determine.

The Mission established the importance of photography (then often still referred to by Niépce's term, "heliography") as a medium for representing architecture and automatically recording the "state" of an historic building. For Francis Wey, "a mediocre heliograph is always preferable, both in its finish and its detail, to the most accomplished engraving" (*La Lumière*, February 9, 1851). Five photographers, among the most renowned of their day for their technical skill – Hippolyte Bayard, Édouard Baldus, Henri Le Secq, Gustave Le Gray, and Mestral – were taken on. Each was given an itinerary, with a list of buildings to photograph (and perhaps more detailed instructions, now lost). The usual process used for obtaining the photographic negative was the calotype, invented by Talbot and improved or modified by Blanquart-Evrard (from 1847) and Le Gray (dry waxed paper negative process, published in 1850). A large number of fairly similar processes to the calotype existed at the beginning of the decade, at a time when glass negatives using albumen or collodion were already beginning to appear. Only Bayard, who nevertheless had used Talbot's method from a very early date, used albumen glass-type negatives for his Mission work. The itineraries were as follows: Fontainebleau, Burgundy, the Lyonnais, and Dauphiné as far as Provence for Baldus; Normandy for Bayard; Champagne, Lorraine, and Alsace for Le Secq; Orléans, the Loire Valley, Poitou, Charente, Limousin, and Angoumois for Le Gray; Charente, Languedoc, the Auvergne, Nevers, and Bourges for Mestral.

The Mission concentrated mainly on medieval buildings "on which restoration work was in progress or planned" (P. Néagu), but which today are not always considered as the most important. Approximately 300 paper negatives survive in the Archives Photographiques (deposited at the Musée d'Orsay); Bayard's negatives do not appear to have survived.

While the circumstances surrounding the setting up of the Heliographic Mission were important for the future of both the calotype process in particular and photography in general, the negatives brought back did not receive the welcome they deserved. As Francis Wey noted, angrily, the administration simply "locked them away in a drawer" without publishing them. Though positive prints were produced (some survive), the reports of the architects of the Historical Monuments Commission make no reference to these photographs, and numerous drawings continued to be made in relation to work carried out on the restoration of these buildings.

The challenge was to find a cheap means of producing and distributing photographic prints. In 1851, this ambition remained out of reach for technical reasons. However, it is not known why no attempt was made subsequently, though in 1851 there was a good deal of activity in the calotype's favor: the formation of the Heliographic Society, the planned "printing works" (linked with the Society), and the effective creation of such an enterprise by Blanquart-Evrard (himself skeptical about whether the Mission's monuments project would be successful).

It was not until the 1870s that the administration of the Historical Monuments Commission would commission the photographer Mieusement with a huge and more systematic project covering most of the historic buildings in the whole of France (his negatives are also kept at the Archives Photographiques). The Mission had been the first official attempt at recognizing some of photography's advantages – recording information, preservation of an object, and faithfulness of recording – at a period when Romantic nostalgia was beginning to tune into the message of the "ancients".

Michel Frizot

Édouard-Denis Baldus,
The Walls of Avignon,
1851, Archives Photographiques, Paris.

the Photographic Society would evolve in 1853, and of which Talbot refused the presidency. What is more, Fenton had introduced dry waxed paper negatives (an improvement due to Le Gray). He himself experimented with the technique during his trip to Russia in the summer of 1852; Philip H. Delamotte used it for his views of the Crystal Palace, as did William R. Baker (after 1855) in Florence, Venice, and Como and A. and E. Backhouse in Nice (1854).[11]

11. R. R. Bretell, *Paper and Light: The Calotype in France and Great Britain, 1839–1870*, Boston, D. R. Godine, 1984.

France adapts the calotype

Until 1846, the calotype, which was encountering difficulties in Britain, was relatively unknown in France. In Paris, only Hippolyte Bayard seems to have practiced it seriously – with some personal modifications which were noted by the Rev. Calvert Jones in 1845, having abandoned his own process, the direct positive, which the French authorities had rejected, or at least ignored. Most probably, Hippolyte Bayard played a key role in the propagation of the calotype process during the 1840s. Paradoxically, just when he was smarting with envy at the double glory of Daguerre and Talbot, he adopted both the daguerreotype and the paper negative – the latter probably in 1842.[12] The Corpus Christi processions in the Rue des Batignolles (1842) must have been taken with a two-second exposure. Bayard took many photographs of Paris buildings, including the famous Montmartre windmills, particularly during 1847. His garden scenes, self-portraits, and groups reveal aptitude for the "photographic" treatment of the subject, which culminated with *Le Tombereau* [The Dust-cart], *La Colonnade de la Madeleine, Le Moulin de la Lage,* and *Les Barricades dans la Rue Royale* (1848). His compositions of garden tools, in particular, departed completely from conventional picturesque practice and followed the innovative trend that Bayard had already displayed with his *Self-portrait as a Drowned Man* (1840).

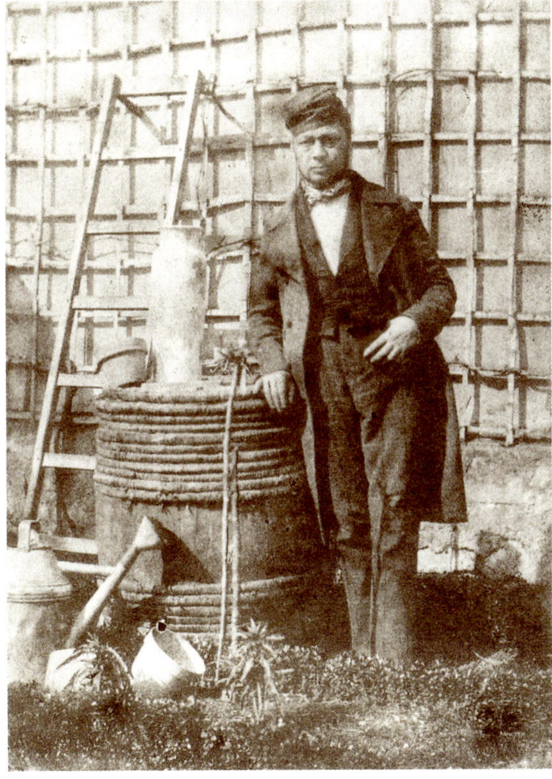

HIPPOLYTE BAYARD, ***Self-portrait,*** circa 1847, Société Française de Photographie, Paris.

Another early calotypist, Louis-Adolphe Humbert de Molard, produced accomplished calotypes in

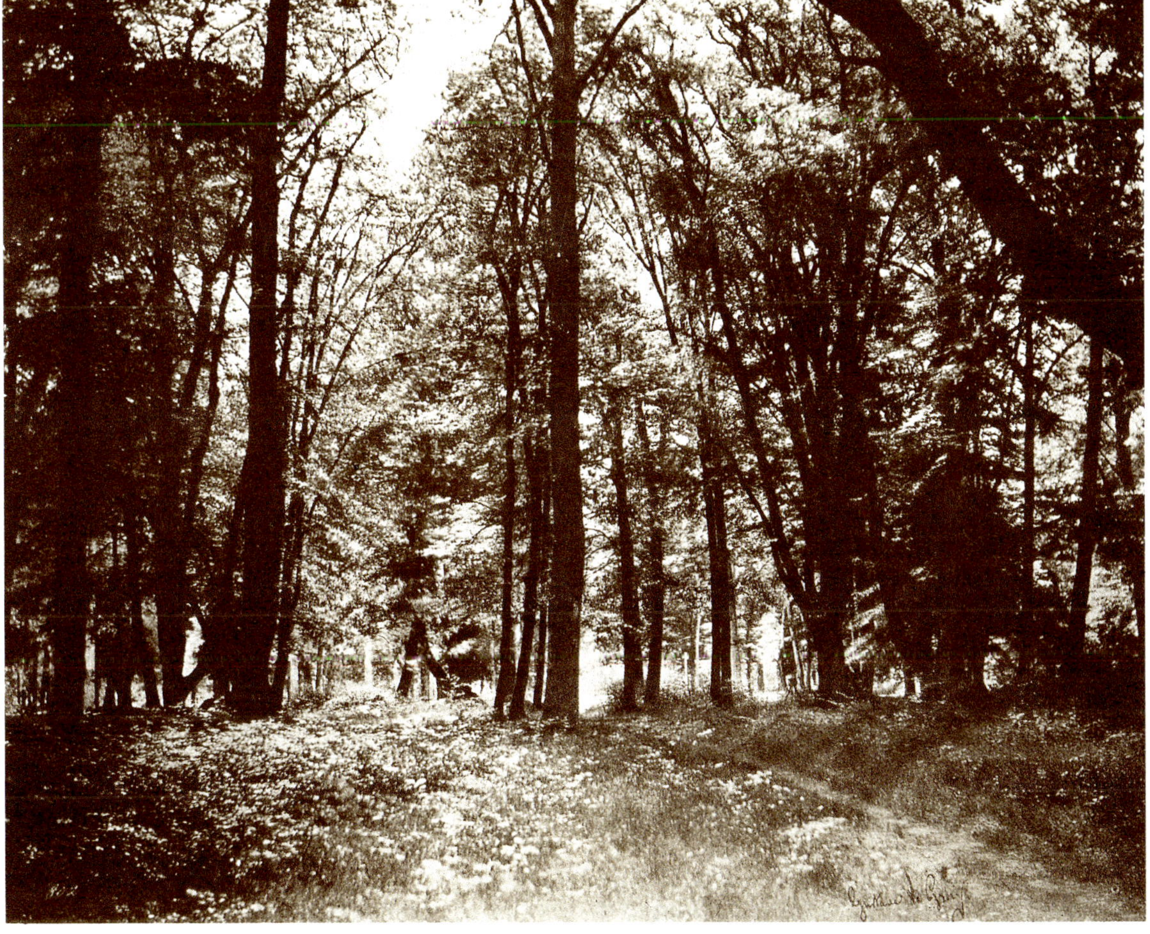

GUSTAVE LE GRAY, ***Le Bas-Bréau, Forest of Fontainebleau,*** circa 1853, John Paul Getty Museum, Malibu.

12. M. Frizot and J.-C. Gautrand, *Hippolyte Bayard: naissance de l'image photographique,* Amiens, Trois Cailloux, 1986.

1846–1848; he composed, with varying degrees of success, tableaux depicting day-to-day occupations and rustic labor, re-enacted by his family – a gamekeeper, farmers (shelling beans, bleeding the pig), wash-day, preparing for the hunt, a game of cards – and recorded local scenes (a Normandy manor, a garden shed) in a style close to Bayard's.[13]

However, it was Louis-Désiré Blanquart-Evrard, a Lille draper keen on chemistry, who systematically experimented with improving the calotype process. He worked independently, without any contact with the inventor of the process, Talbot. (English calotypists, on the other hand, were inclined to follow Talbot's advice.) Modifications of the English process appeared: A. Guillot-Saguez, a physician, published his method for taking photographs on paper in September 1847 (Paris, V. Masson). While retaining the basic principle – negative-positive, latent image – the process underwent important modifications, in particular concerning the way in which the various solutions were applied to the paper support. Instead of applying them with a brush, which produced irregularities, Blanquart-Evrard floated the paper on the surface of the solution in order to impregnate the surface evenly (a technique which Bayard also used). Furthermore, French paper did not have the same texture as English; it was thinner, less grainy, made from a more coherent pulp, and more suitable for capturing the subtleties of light and shade. Finally, Blanquart-Evrard completely separated the stage of applying silver salts from that of developing the latent image (using gallic acid).

Without quoting Talbot (presumably to avoid legal action for counterfeiting) he published his process in 1847.[14] The still damp sensitized paper was exposed for 10 to 20 seconds in sunny weather. A positive print on salted paper was made from the negative by contact printing, in sunlight, using a printing frame. Blanquart-Evrard noted the important place that "this branch of photography" ought to occupy: "To provide the man of the world with living memories of his peregrinations and faithful images of the objects of his affection, scientists with exact reproductions of mechanical subjects, anatomy, and natural history, and historians, archeologists and artists with picturesque views general and detailed studies of the great works of art of antiquity and the Middle Ages, the rare drawings of which are shared by only a small number of people."

This program does not differ from that of Talbot (or of Daguerre, as presented by Arago in 1839). However, Blanquart-Evrard's technical specifications were precise, simplified, and fixed for standardized industrial application. The care which he introduced into the washing process would prevent the prints from fading rapidly, as often happened to those made by Talbot.[15] He envisaged "carrying out photography on simple paper, a certain and easy method for people who are less accomplished in manipulating chemicals", and sending photographers out with pre-prepared paper (for the negative) which would be ready to be sensitized and exposed. Positive prints would be made after their return.

The idea of the "photographic printing-house" (an establishment which would undertake the production of large numbers of positive prints) arose in 1851 from the work of the new Heliographic Society (which brought together calotypists and other people who wanted to participate in the promotion of the new medium) and the Heliographic Mission (see box). The problem was essentially economic. A new method for producing positive prints (adopting the principle of revealing the latent image by means of a developer, in the same way as for the negative) was published by Blanquart-Evrard in April 1851. It allowed the production of "200 to 300 prints per day" from a single negative.[16] Blanquart-Evrard opened his photographic printing-house at Loos-lès-Lille in the summer

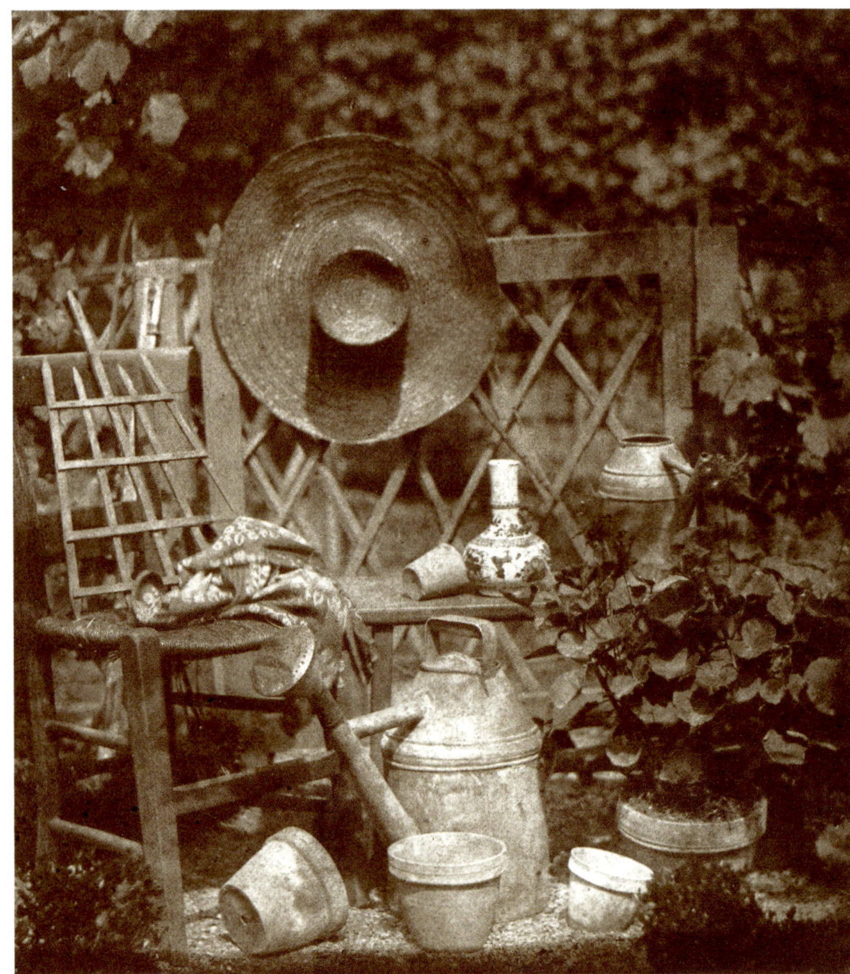

Hippolyte Bayard,
In the Garden,
circa 1842,
Société Française
de Photographie, Paris.
▼

13. G. Gimon, "Humbert de Molard (1800–1847)", in *Prestige de la photographie*, no. 5, pp. 67–95, and no. 7, pp. 6–35.

14. "Procédés employés pour obtenir les épreuves de photographie sur papier", in *Comptes rendus de l'Académie des sciences*, January 27, 1847, communication read by Arago.

15. It was Chevalier who made known the process in *Recueils de mémoires et procédés nouveaux [...]*, Paris, 1847.

16. L. D. Blanquart-Evrard, *Manuel de photographie sur papier*, Paris, Librairie Encyclopédique Roret, 1851.

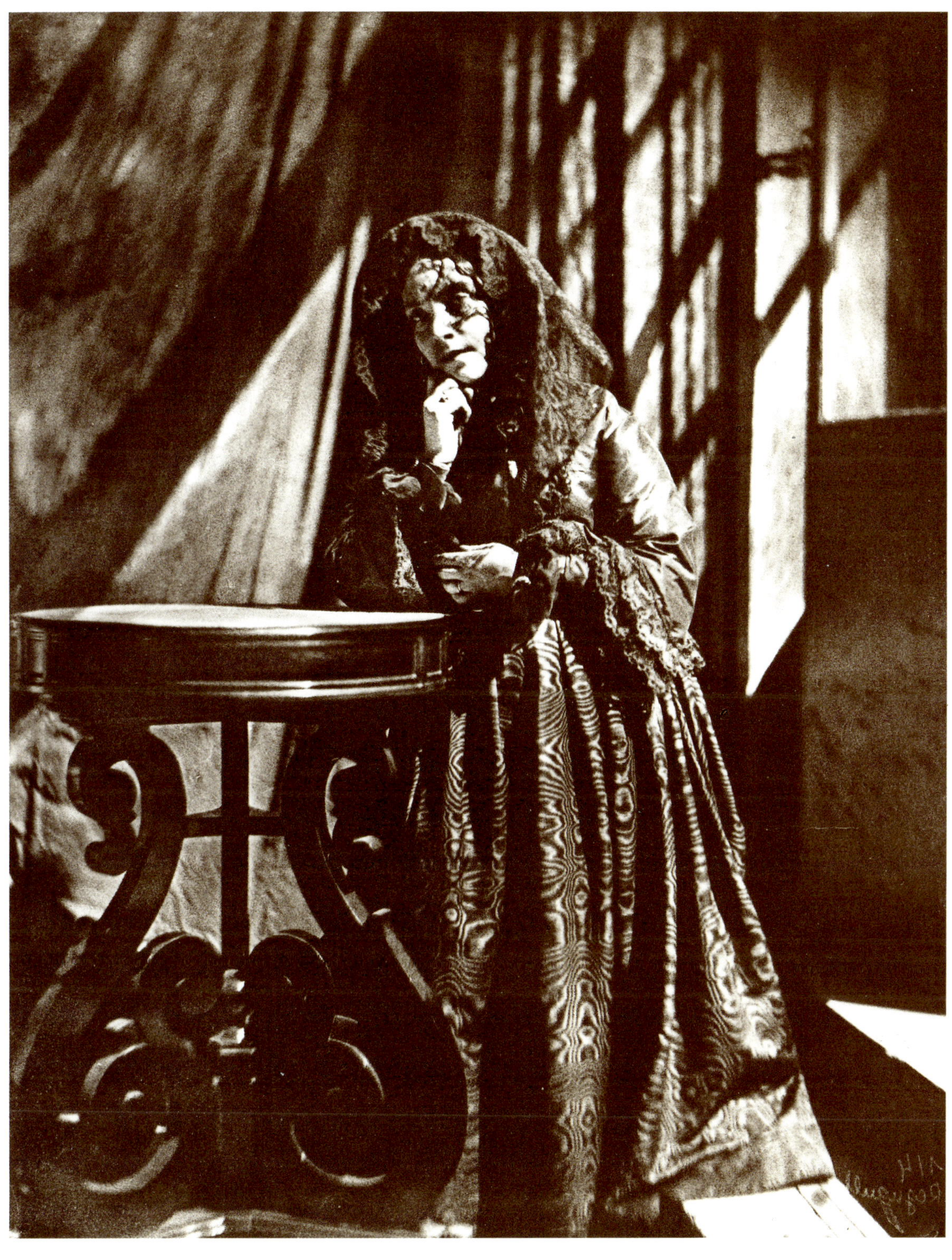

Victor Regnault,
Portrait of Madame Regnault,
circa 1852,
Société Française
de Photographie, Paris.

of 1851, and the first deliveries of the *Album photographique de l'artiste et de l'amateur* were made in September. The establishment was responsible for printing and selling prints, the negative remaining the "artistic property" of the photographer.

The dry waxed paper negative process

A great master of photography on paper appeared at this time – Gustave le Gray,[17] son of a Paris landlord, painter, and pupil of Delaroche. Having spent time in Rome until 1847, he began to experiment with the process after his return (it is likely that he already had a practical knowledge of daguerreotypes, glass negatives, and collodion negatives, of which he was one of the first users). He won an award at the Exhibition of the Products of Industry in 1848, and set up a workshop at the Porte de Clichy to the north of Paris. He perfected a type of paper which absorbed chemicals more uniformly and possessed enhanced sensitivity – waxed paper, prepared by soaking it in melted beeswax, the surplus absorbed by a hot iron. The pre-sensitized paper (using silver salts) was used dry in the *camera obscura* (hence the name – dry waxed paper). A possible delay of several days, even weeks, between

17. E. Parry Janis, *The Photography of Gustave Le Gray*, Chicago, Art Institute and University of Chicago, 1987.

18. *Traité pratique de photographie sur papier et sur verre*, Paris, Germer Baillière, 1850; a *Nouveau Traité* was published in 1851, 1852, and 1854.

Calotypist circles

The calotype was a difficult artistic process, often subject to chance, whose effects could be modified during printing, and which did not enjoy great commercial success. The technique spread thanks to personal contacts and exchanges between practitioners, a process which was facilitated in the 1850s by photographic exhibitions.

The creation in Paris in 1851 of the Heliographic Society, the first gathering of amateur photographers (mostly calotypists), was a particular response to this need to share information about an uncertain technique, to share methods and tips, and discuss recent improvements. Under the presidency of Baron Gros, the main participants were Bayard, Durieu, Baldus, Le Gray, Le Secq, Regnault, and Vigier, but the Society also included non-photographers such as Delacroix, Champfleury, and Wey. In 1854 the Heliographic Society gave way to the Société Française de Photographie; this "secession" may be related to the change in technique from paper to glass negatives and the need for better organization of meetings, which remained informal and friendly. Certain calotypists (notably Le Secq) would give up photography around 1855 rather than adopt a new technique which was considered more mechanical and less artistic. This attachment could only strengthen the resolve of the group formed by the first calotypists.

La Lumière, the magazine published by the Heliographic Society, served as a rallying point, publishing articles about the work produced by its members, the Salons, and current projects, often under the leadership of Ernest Lacan and Francis Wey.

If the first users had to be content with Talbot's process, it was the methods of Blanquart-Evrard (1847) and Le Gray (dry waxed paper, 1851) which provoked considerable development of the calotype, particularly in France, where British patents did not apply. It is likely that in the 1840s Hippolyte Bayard was one of the very few French calotypists – together with Humbert de Molard – who also used the daguerreotype process.

However, around 1850 circles began to form of people who encouraged each other by exchanges of prints and methods. Through their varied content, the albums put together by A. de Brébisson (Musée d'Orsay), Bayard (J. Paul Getty Museum), Jeuffrain, and Regnault (Société Française de Photographie) bear witness to this community of ideas and friendship. De Brébisson in Falaise in Normandy, a skilful calotype worker from 1848 (he changed fairly quickly to albumen/glass negatives), knew, for example, Humbert de Molard, Bayard, Ferdinand Tillard (from Bayeux), and Edmond Bacot (from Rouen); the latter, who appeared in around 1850, taught the calotype process to Charles Hugo, son of Victor Hugo, who was in exile in Jersey. Bacot's fine views of Rouen Cathedral and the church of Saint-Maclou are, furthermore, studies of shadows in the Hugo style, rather than simple photographic documents. In 1853, Victor Hugo supported the publication of a book on Jersey illustrated with photographs. This project, however, never got beyond the planning stage. It is therefore possible to speak of a regional circle centered in Normandy, within which each person worked on several projects.

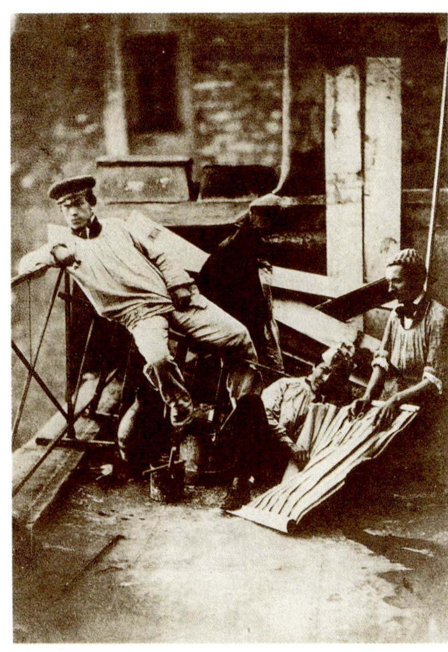

Felix J. Moulin,
Decorators
calotype, circa 1855, Y. Christ collection.

In Britain, the calotype process was formally organized around Talbot, either through direct collaborators (Henneman) or with the close circle of practitioners who had become friends, all of whom exchanged information and prints. They included Revs. George Bridges and Calvert Jones (who both traveled to Italy specifically to try out the calotype process) – Jones met Bayard in Paris in 1845 – and John Dillwyn Llewelyn, Talbot's Welsh cousin. William Baker also traveled in northern Italy after 1855. In 1847 the Calotype Club was formed, whose members included Robert Hunt, Roger Fenton, Hugh Diamond, Frederick Scott Archer, William Newton, and Hugh Owen. The albums exchanged regularly during the 1850s by members of the Photographic Exchange Club, containing collections of their prints, are typical of this group practice. In Edinburgh, where a club had also been formed, in 1843, Thomas Keith was trained by Hill and threw himself passionately into calotyping from 1851 to 1856.

A little group had also formed in the neighborhood of Chalon-sur-Saône, in Burgundy, where Nicéphore Niépce had officiated, consisting of Petiot-Groffier, mayor of the town (who accompanied his master Baldus to the Auvergne in 1854), and Édouard Loydreau, archeologist and mayor of Chagny.

Another group formed at the Sèvres works around Victor Regnault, a physician who had become director of the company in 1852. It included among others Louis Robert, head of the painting workshop, E. Béranger, and J. Diéterle. Another group, thought to meet at the Caffè Greco in Rome, appeared around 1850, and included G. Caneva, Count Flachéron, Eugène Constant, and Alfred Normand, to whom one might also add Alphonse Davanne and Thomas Sutton, who participated briefly. Flachéron had taken calotypes of the sites of antiquity since 1848; Normand arrived as a scholar of the Villa Medici (another focus of interest for photography) in 1847, and continued his work during a trip to Greece and as far as Constantinople in 1851. It was at the Villa Medici that he also met Du Camp and Flaubert, just returned from Egypt in 1851 with several hundred paper negatives. Eugène Piot, who published his *Italie monumentale* in 1851 (125 calotype prints), may also have been linked with this group.

The great photographic exhibitions would also provide an opportunity for such links to be developed, such as those held at the Society of Arts in London in 1852, and those of the Société Française de Photographie from 1855 onwards, as well as the great celebrations of photography at the universal exhibitions (London, 1851 and Paris, 1855).

The activities of "photographic printing workshops" also formed part of this exchange of ideas. In France, these followed Talbot's example at Reading. Here, the works of numerous calotypists were brought together and could be compared: Blanquart-Evrard's in the first instance (see the following dossier), but also Fonteny. Furthermore, printing workshops in the usual sense of the word (using photo-mechanical processes), usually producing lithographs, run by Poitevin, then Lemercier, distributed the work of calotypists, and brought together photographs by Berthier, Cuvelier, Teynard, and Aguado to reproduce them as photolithographs.

The calotype, both an artistic and a craft technique, was continuously being modified. It developed through a series of improvements and through exchanges between its adherents, who cultivated a taste for chemistry and an interest in artistic creation. Dependent on manual interventions which were sometimes a matter of chance, the calotype process coped with the limited possibilities for reproduction and distribution. Its use was restricted to elitist circles of friends rather than being adopted for commercial and popular production.

Michel Frizot

the preparation of the paper and its use made the process much more flexible. Le Gray's treatise explaining the process appeared in June 1850.[18] Not only an unparalleled inventor and technician whose prints were unrivaled, he was also a teacher who trained his friend Le Secq (and, through him, Charles Nègre), Adrien Tournachon (Nadar's brother), Count Aguado, and the Delessert cousins. He gave lessons to Maxime Du Camp in 1849 in preparation for his forthcoming Egyptian trip (however, his failure there with waxed paper encouraged Du Camp to use Blanquart-Evrard's process). Le Gray was acknowledged as the great photographic artist of the early 1850s, when rivalry between photography and painting was at its height and the debate about photography's legitimacy as "art" called for direct comparison.

After 1849, Le Gray worked for several years on views of trees and undergrowth in the forest of Fontainebleau, a series which he continued using glass negatives. The large size of these images and the perfection of his prints indicate their almost experimental character. Their theme was typical of pre-Impressionist naturalism. However, no other photographer could hope to treat the subject with such subtlety, so great were the possible pitfalls. Le Gray set the criteria for a whole genre. These criteria owed little to painting, beyond perhaps a superficial comparison with images which totally lack the same philosophy and visual response.

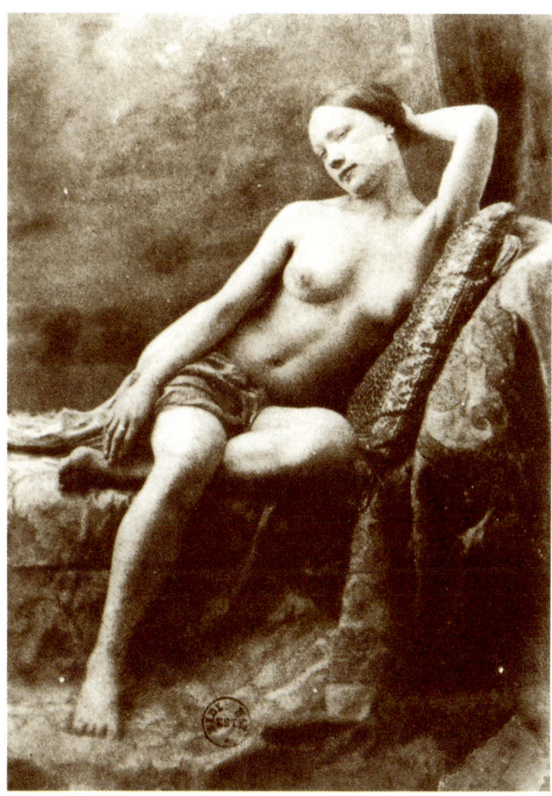

EUGÈNE DURIEU,
Nude Study,
1853–1854,
from Delacroix Album,
Bibliothèque Nationale,
Paris.

Photographic artists

The photographic events of 1851 (photographic printing, the creation of the Heliographic Society) stimulated a resurgence of activity in France, mainly in the calotype. They heralded a veritable

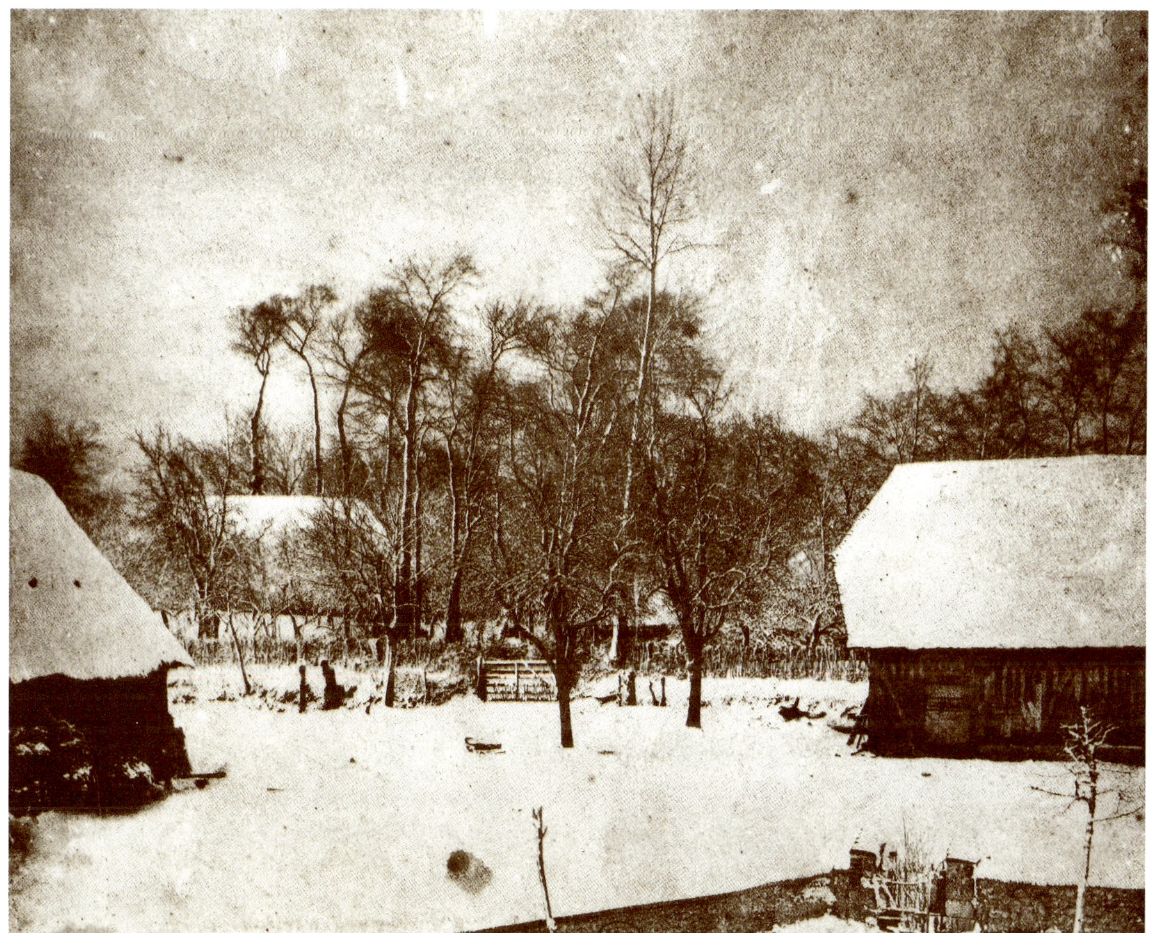

LOUIS-ADOLPHE HUMBERT DE MOLARD,
Snowy Landscape,
circa 1850,
Musée d'Orsay, Paris.

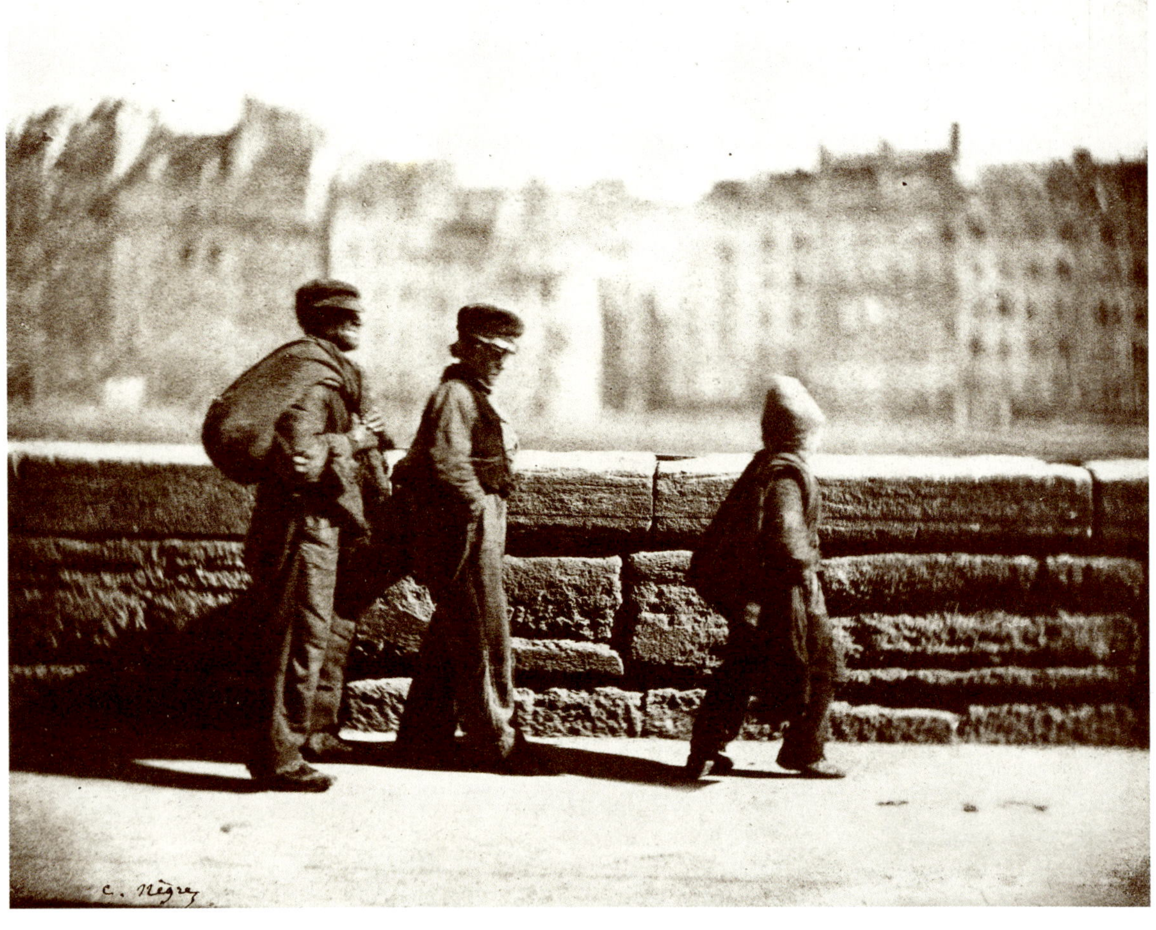

Charles Nègre,
Chimney-sweeps Walking, Paris,
1851–1852,
National Gallery of Canada, Ottawa.

Charles Nègre,
Market near the Hôtel de Ville, Paris,
1851–1852,
private collection.
▼

19. A. Jammes and E. Parry Janis, *The Art of the French Calotype*, Princeton University, 1983.

20. Eugène de Valicourt, *Nouveau Manuel complet de photographie sur métal, sur papier et sur verre*, Paris, Roret, 1851.

French "school" in the tradition of Bayard and Humbert de Molard[19] not without influence in other countries – Italy, Germany, even Britain, where new processes were appearing at the same time that Talbot's process was being abandoned. The manuals written by each inventor, pamphlets published at the author's expense, derivative accounts, all describe a great number of techniques and variations which today often appear quite incongruous.[20]

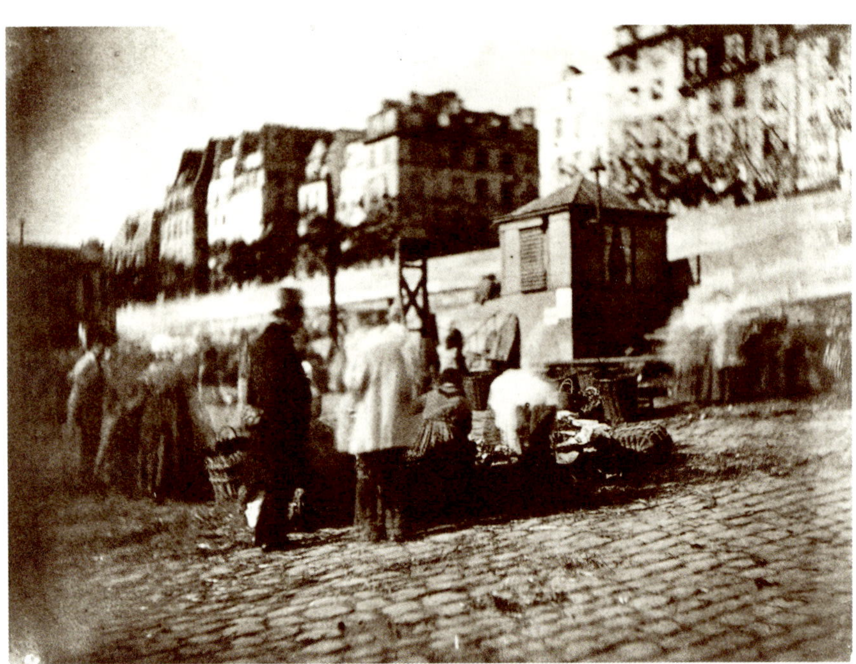

The Heliographic Mission, instituted by the French Historical Monuments Commission, provided a forum for debates on the choice and specific contribution of this modern recording medium – a technique still considered suspect. It also had the effect of spurring on photography, providing a testing-ground and, at last, allowing its advocates to conduct a practical exercise on a large scale throughout the whole country. It involved drawing up an inventory of the principal historic buildings by sending five photographers on an exploratory mission, following a precise itinerary. The best practitioners of the time were chosen: Bayard, Baldus, Le Secq, Le Gray, and Mestral, all using paper negatives (except Bayard, who had adopted glass). The results were disappointing. This was not due to the work accomplished, but rather to the difficulty in obtaining reasonably priced prints and in distributing the images. Nevertheless, some of the key personalities in early photography made their appearance as a result of this enterprise. At the same time as a code of practice for the recording of historic monuments was being worked out, they were able to develop their own distinctive styles.

Édouard-Denis Baldus, of Prussian origin (which would arouse some suspicion about him), moved to France in 1839 in order to improve his painting. He learned photography in 1848 and soon dedicated himself to this new art rather than to the fine arts (his workshop employed about ten men in 1856). In 1849 he undertook a photographic tour in the south of France (notably Montmajour), which made him ideally placed to participate in the Heliographic Mission in 1851. Once again he found himself photographing Provence, passing via Burgundy and the Rhône valley. In all, he produced about a hundred views. On his own initiative, Baldus planned a series, the "Towns of France". This does not seem to have followed any preconceived order (the South of France, Paris, Mont-Saint-Michel, Chartres, Orléans). His trips to the Dauphiné region and the Auvergne (1854) provided the opportunity for obtaining views of landscapes, historic buildings, rocks, fine perspectives, and a variety of natural elements. He specialized in such subjects and was praised by his peers: "[he has] the secret of wide perspectives and distant horizons. His lens takes in spaces which the eye can scarcely measure."[21] In 1855 he produced an album of fifty plates on the northern French railway (Chemin de Fer du Nord), a commission hurriedly put together on the occasion of a visit by Queen Victoria. In 1856, following a commission from the Ministry of the Interior, Baldus produced around thirty paper negatives (measuring up to 16 x 20 in., some of which formed a panorama by means of montage) recording the damage caused by the flooding of the Rhône in the region of Avignon and Tarascon. After about 1855 he increasingly used collodion glass negatives.

Charles Nègre, also a painter, who worked closely for a time with Le Secq, took photography in a spirit which showed greater respect for the pictorial traditions of the Salon – composition, imaginary tableaux, and the artist's and the engraver's skill: "where science ends, art begins: when the chemist has prepared the paper sheet, the artist directs the lens and, by means of those three guiding lights which he must unceasingly follow in the study of nature – observation, sentiment, and reasoning power – he reproduces effects which make us dream, simple motifs which move us, and sites whose strong powerful outlines astonish and startle us [...] The most perfect artist is the one who chooses out of nature with the greatest taste. Before it was reproducing nature, now it is choosing within nature";[22] a creed which someone like Le Gray could not dispute, and which Baldus had illustrated in 1848 with his astonishing, Ingres-like, studio nudes.

His *Chimney-sweeps* of 1851–1852 were much praised for the realism of their pose, which contrasted strongly with the conventions of drawing. Critics compared the picture to Rembrandt and Murillo, "whose painting is summed up in this scene".[23] For the first time, contemporaries had the sense of being present at a sudden arresting of motion, of seeing movement frozen by the camera – in what would later be called an "instantaneous photograph" (he continued this line of research in the summer of 1853 using collodion negatives which were a little faster). His *Ragman, Market Scenes* (c. 1850) – which he turned into a painting with the same quest for vivacity – and *Hurdy-gurdy Player*, despite its lengthy exposure, all have the same intention of evoking the natural motion of life by imperceptible movements and the lightness of a "vaporous" outline (E. Lacan). After 1852, when the widespread distribution of photographs had become fashionable, Nègre envisaged publishing a series of photographs of the South of France, with prints also sold separately.

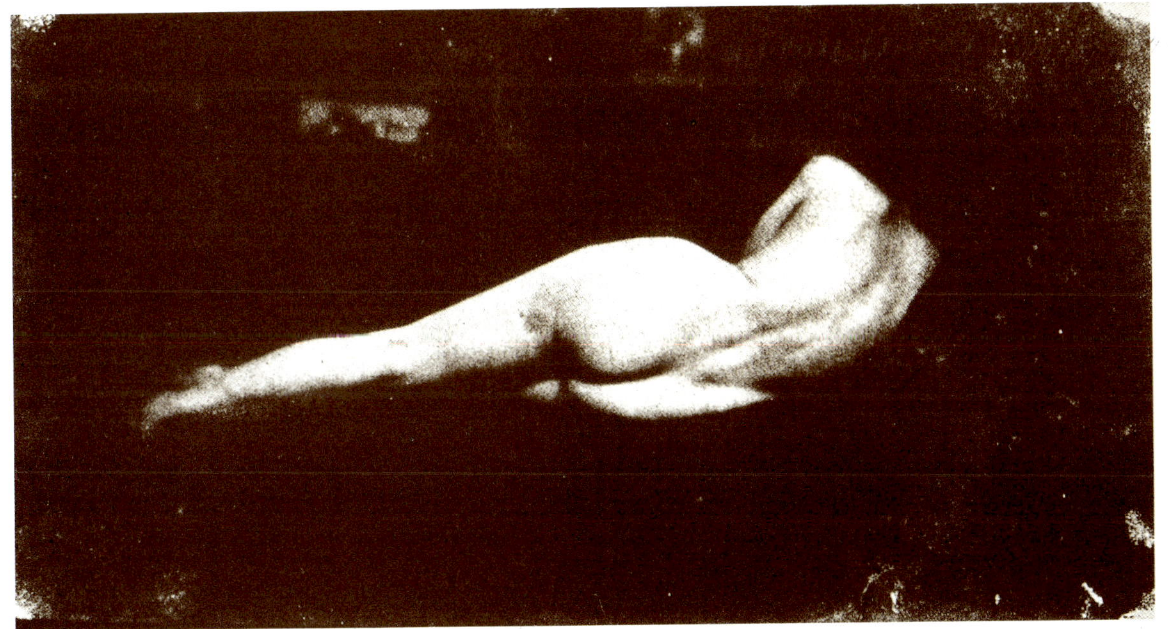

CHARLES NÈGRE,
Nude Study,
circa 1848,
Musée Ingres, Montauban.

21. E. Lacan, *Esquisses photographiques*, 1856, pp. 26-32, quoted by P. Néagu and F. Heilbrun, "Baldus: paysages, architectures", in *Photographies*, no. 1, 1983, pp. 56–77.

22. C. Nègre, *La Lumière*, May 15, 1851, p. 56, quoted in F. Heilbrun, *Charles Nègre, photographe*, Paris, RMN, 1980; see also J. Borcoman, *Charles Nègre, 1820–1880*, National Gallery of Canada, Ottawa, 1976.

23. *La Lumière*, May 29, 1852.

24. E. Parry-Janis, *Henry Le Secq, photographe de 1850 à 1860*, Paris, Flammarion, 1986.

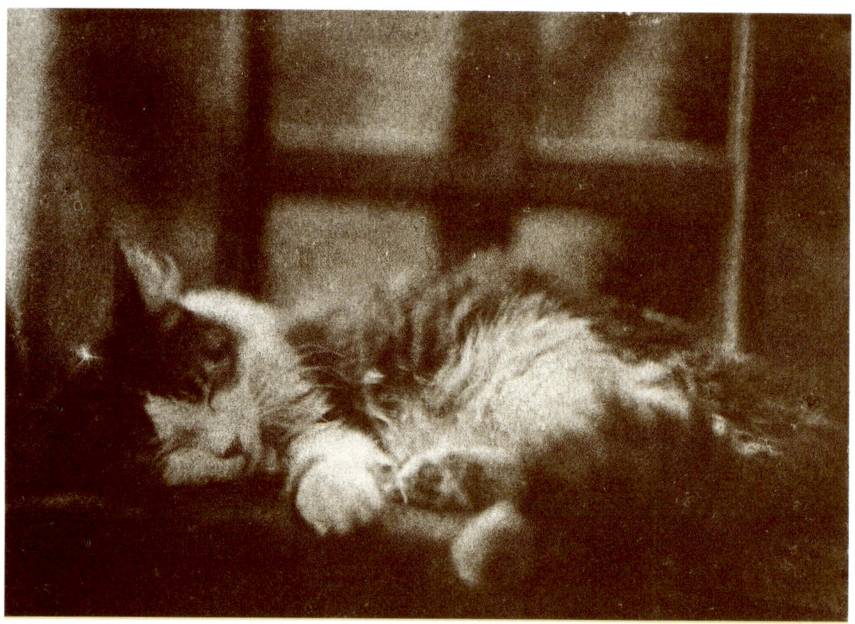

Auguste Vacquerie,
Minette the Cat, Jersey,
1853,
Musée d'Orsay,
Paris.

The work of Henri Le Secq, who trained as a painter, is now better known thanks to the recent discovery of several important prints.[24] In his work, more than in that of anyone else, the variety of genres and pictorial effects which can be obtained from the paper negative is apparent: the series taken for the city hall official, Berger in 1852–1853 showing demolition work in Paris, portraits, Gothic architecture in Paris, Strasbourg, Chartres, and Amiens, picturesque rural scenes, foliage and sculpture and painting. Le Secq's imaginary world owes much to Victor Hugo and Charles Méryon. He transforms nature into a sinister apparition, a strange chaos, relying more on shadows and hollows than on the presence of matter. Notre-Dame de Paris, near to his l'Île Saint-Louis home, where Le Secq and Nègre photographed each other, acted as a magnet, a survival from uncertain times, menacing and the town's supernatural guardian. If most of his still-lifes remain traditional in their composition, a certain surreal element seems to prevail when the subject is restricted to dried herrings suspended on a nail. *Fantasies,* the title of one of his collections, describes very well this state of mind, always on tenterhooks, living the photographic collecting process like some mysterious sub-plot, interpreting the most static subjects (statues from the cathedral portals at Chartres or Amiens) as mythical figures which appeared from the mists of time. His roadside scenes (Montmirail) and views of quarries are among the most visionary and enigmatic images.

With the demise of paper negatives, Le Secq gave up photography in 1856. However, he still worried about the permanence of his earlier prints, as though he was aware of having accomplished in them a pictorial work which could not be separated from his creative technique and whose sense would be provided by practical deontology. The calotype was clearly recognized as an artistic medium, that is to say, a means of producing images possessing artistic qualities.

Henri Le Secq,
Public Baths, Paris,
circa 1852–1853,
Bibliothèque des Arts
Décoratifs, Paris.

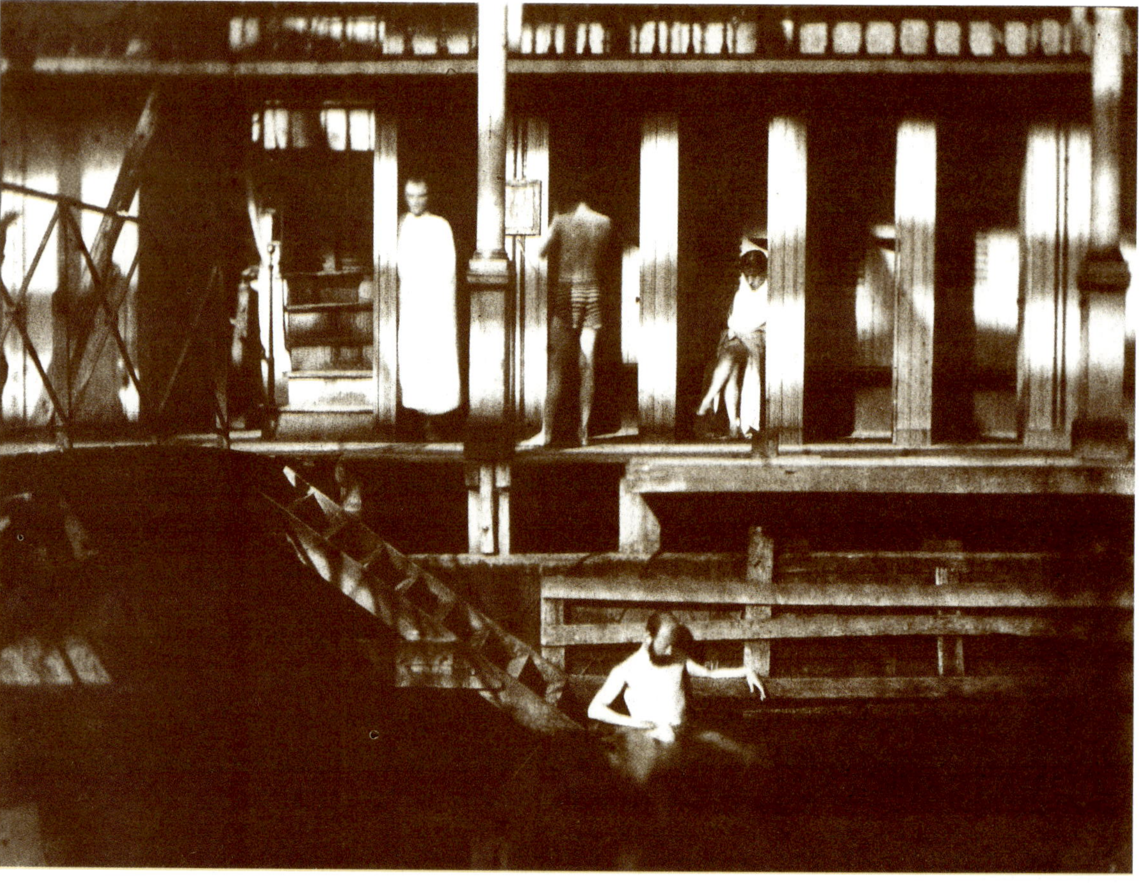

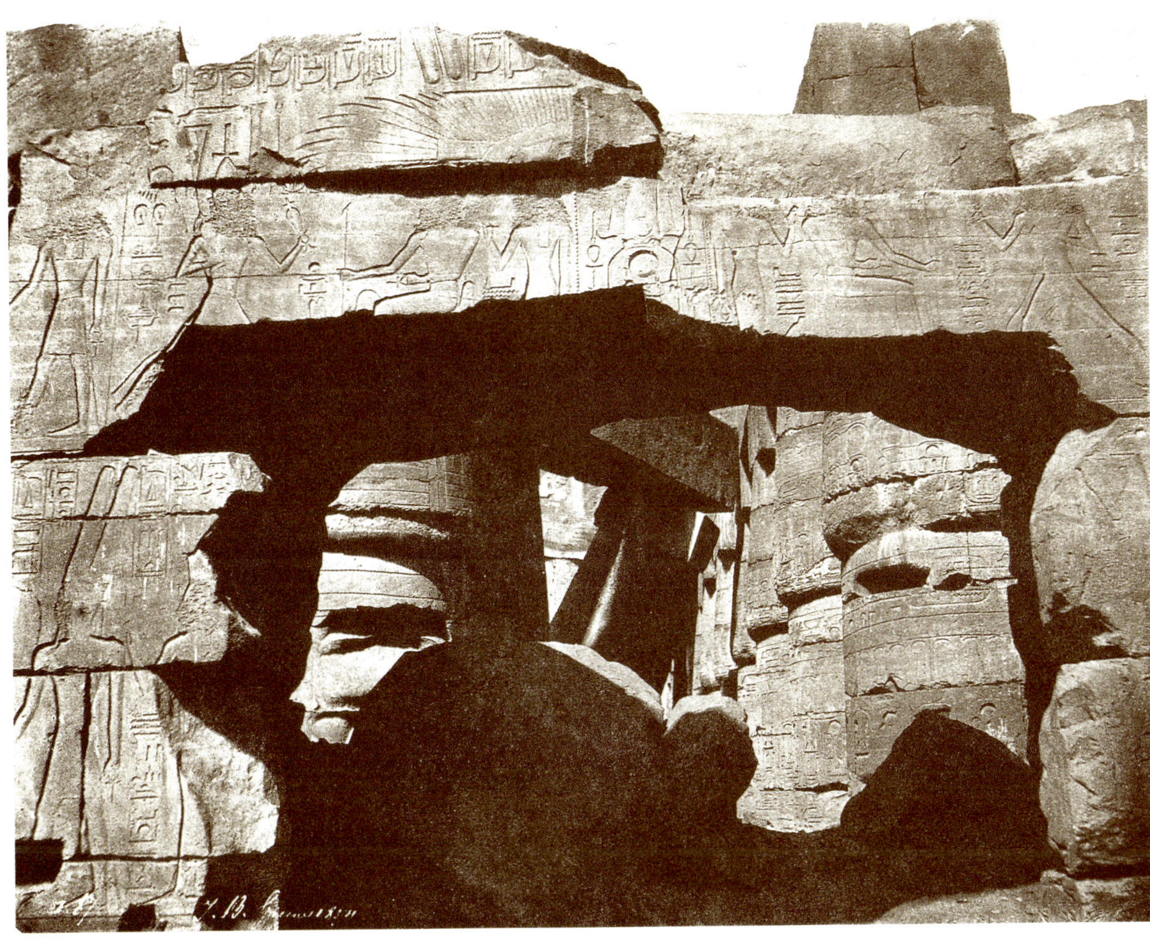

JOHN B. GREENE,
Entrance to the Hypostyle Hall at Karnak,
1854,
Musée d'Orsay, Paris.

Eugène Durieu, director of the Administration des Cultes [religion], was an advocate of the paper negative for recording historical monuments, though critical of it in other respects. He produced pictures of artists' models, naked or clothed, Arab slave-girls, Italian characters, and theatrical-style studies – one of his albums (now in the Bibliothèque Nationale) belonged to Delacroix, who had no qualms about copying its prints in pencil. Photographs, being "studies" in the sense used by painters, that is, attempts at rendering light, were for Delacroix "an intermediary charged with initiating us more deeply into the secrets of nature [...] a copy, in some ways false by dint of being exact."[25]

It was around such characters (Durieu, Delacroix, Wey, Lacan, Périer) that a whole critical theory developed, expounding the difference between photography and the pictorial arts while drawing together arguments for a renewal which would certainly be provoked by the explosion in photography during the 1860s, unforeseen at that time. A definition of "photography as art" appeared, based on the need for the photographer to make a personal choice (far from the supposed purely mechanical nature of the process) concerning the unity of the image, obtained in a single exposure, and the avoidance of superfluous detail, aims that the calotype process favored.

The motives of the artist, the traveler, the recorder, and the dilettante content with producing flattering results became mingled: Eugène Cuvelier photographed the landscapes of Fontainebleau and Barbizon among the painters who were beginning to frequent these places; Alphonse Davanne, also a chemist, produced grandiose views of the park of Versailles; Count Olympe Aguado was an amateur who produced "tree portraits". L. A. de Brébisson, Gustave de Beaucorps, Ferdinand Tillard (in Normandy), and Édouard Delessert (Sardinia, 1855) "heliographed" their region as if to create visual typologies – capturing the essence of a landscape via rays of light. Vicomte Vigier, skilled in both the dry waxed paper technique and the original calotype as a result of his Anglophilia, traveled around the Pyrenees (*Album des Pyrénées*, published by Blanquart-Evrard in 1853) and the Dauphiné region, renowned for his subtle effects and sense of atmosphere. Shortly afterwards, Aimé Civiale devoted himself to studies of the Pyrenees (1857–1858) and the Alps (1859–1868), continuing to use paper negatives.

The huge success enjoyed by Charles Marville in the 1860s has somewhat eclipsed his work in the previous decade, when he brought back a complete album for Blanquart-Evrard (*Bords du Rhin* [Along the Rhine]) and when he reconsidered

25. J. Sagne, *Delacroix et la photographie*, Paris, Herscher, 1982.

The journey to Egypt

Following Champollion's Egyptian expedition in 1829, the insatiable "need for images" invoked by Romantic travelers to the East changed direction. The documentary function of photography found a new embodiment, within French academic institutions, in the mythology of Egypt, birthplace of civilization and emblem of the conquest of knowledge.

Numerous travelers would undertake, with the support of official missions, the systematic photographic exploration of the Nile valley, "in order to provide documents for science". However, such an application demanded manageable equipment, a reliable process, and, above all, the possibility of duplication. The rare daguerreotypes brought back from Egypt by Vernet and Goupil-Fesquet from 1839, afterwards by Itier, bear witness to the difficulties encountered, just as much as Nerval's disappointments at Cairo.

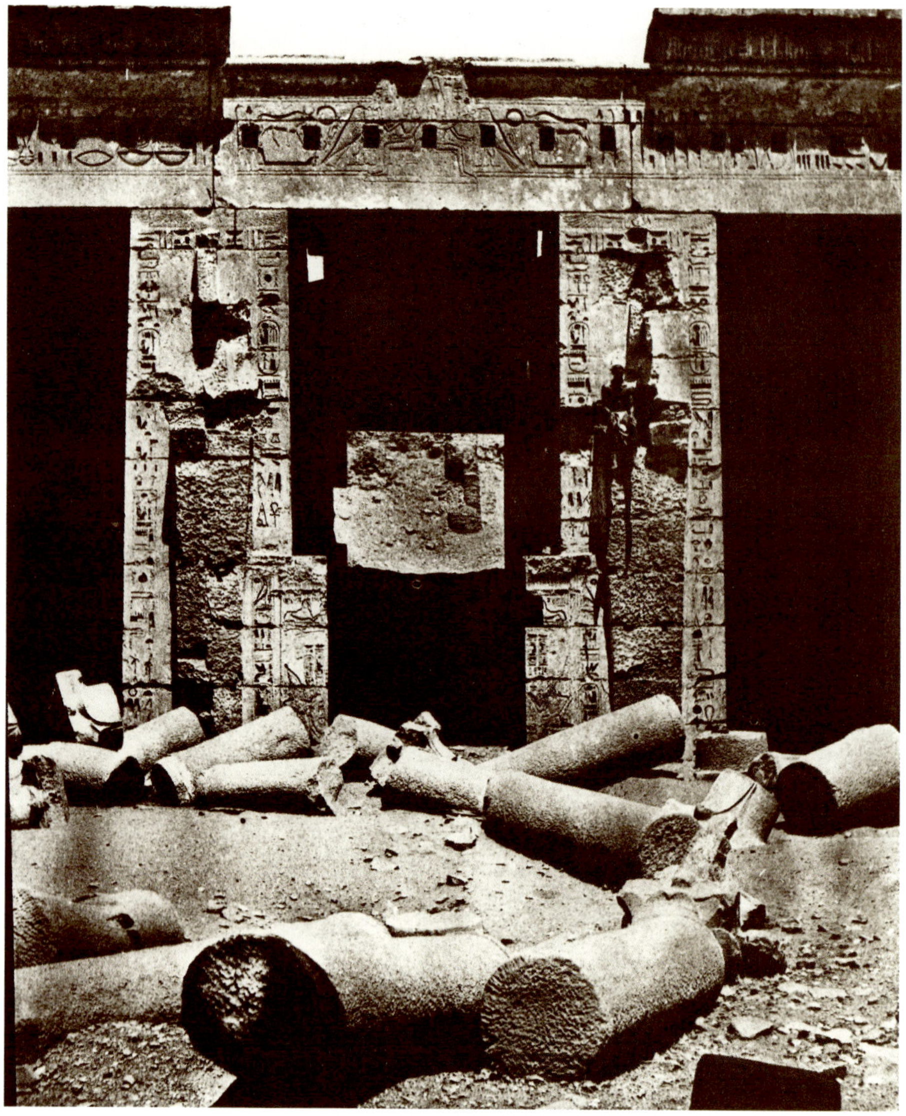

Maxime du Camp,
Pylons of Rameses' Palace, Medinet-Habu, 1850, Bibliothèque Nationale, Paris.

With the appearance of Talbot's calotype process (himself an Egyptologist), photographic expeditions multiplied during the 1850s. Numerous calotypists – French (Du Camp, Teynard, Trémaux, De Clercq, Salzmann), British (Bridges, Wheelhouse, Smith, Graham), and even German (Lorent) – chose to photograph the eastern Mediterranean and, in first place, Egypt. The attraction of the exotic mingled with a taste for archeological description and the re-creation of the past.

The archeological sites and monuments were photographed following an unchanging itinerary imposed by the very course of the Nile, between Nubia – desert country, with oases in the idyllic countryside of Philae – and Cairo, an Islamic town influenced by the West. Following Champollion's itinerary, Du Camp, accompanied by Flaubert, went quickly up the Nile as far as Wadi Halfa, then came down it again between March and June 1850, stopping methodically in order to photograph each temple, whether famous or not, from Abu Simbel to Luxor, without forgetting the cataracts at Philae or the charm of Fayyum. Ancient monuments took precedence over landscapes, while the close-ups of hieroglyphics, intended for members of the Academy, scarcely allowed the personal feelings of the traveler to show through.

Following the same journey, Teynard, whose graphic sensitivity was much more expressive, set about complementing archeological subjects with scenes from daily life – streets and squares, shops and gardens, villages and palm-groves.

These picturesque and modern aspects also attracted the attention of Bartholdi who accompanied the painter Gérôme into Upper Egypt in 1855, and of Devéria, who practiced the art of the calotype as a sideline during his work for Mariette at Memphis.

Because of the long exposure times required by calotypes, the sites almost always appear to be deserted, and therefore more suitable as illustrations of an imaginary journey into timeless antiquity. The indistinct quality of distant scenes provided by the paper negative helped create a special aesthetic – found especially in John B. Greene – to which artists and writers were sensitive, as with Gautier, who wrote *Roman de la momie*.

But travel to Egypt was becoming banal, and photographic output soon passed from the hands of businessmen/travelers, such as the Englishman Frith, into those of professionals living on the spot, like Beato and Bonfils, who would exclusively use collodion. Photographers like Méhédin (in 1859) or Cammas (in 1861) appear like rather out-of-date amateurs with their calotypes, while De Clercq gave pride of place during his eastern travels to less frequented sites in Syria, dealing with Egypt in about fifty pictures.

Without going so far as to replace engraved plates in scholarly works from the outset, the collections of views brought back by calotypists, published in albums accompanied by text, enjoyed real success with the educated public. Visually, the viewer's contact with the object pictured assumed an intensity and a verisimilitude which far surpassed the engraved and painted illustrations which were the current norm. The 10 x 8 inch prints created by Blanquart-Evrard or Fonteny for the publishers Gide and Goupil inaugurated deluxe photographic publishing. These sumptuous photographic volumes, produced in limited editions, played their part in the evolution of a taste for historical realism, while providing the illustrators of popular magazines with a source of new escapist imagery. This imagery, both exotic and antiquarian, responded to the slogan of the *Tour du monde*: "armchair traveling".

Claire Bustarret

ancient monuments by placing them in a nostalgic context (overgrown with vegetation, covered in snow). He provided Blanquart-Evrard with more than 100 views, scattered through the albums *Mélanges photographiques, Paris*, etc.

Many non-professional photographers (lacking a studio and a marketing structure) found in their pursuit of photography a chance of working at the interface of art and science. Victor Regnault, for example, a chemist, director of the Sèvres porcelain factory in 1852, and President of the Academy of Sciences, had shown an interest in Blanquart-Evrard's work since 1847. He appears to have wanted to try out all subjects without preconceptions.[26] He photographed his children in a natural, relaxed way, as well as his colleagues at the Collège de France (in the open air, posing with laboratory instruments), showing a great mastery of the interplay of light and the composition of a scene, and using the effects of different textiles (e.g. his portrait of Mme Regnault). Some of his studies of laboratory instruments are more like still-lifes than scientific documents. Using a large format, he photographed the Sèvres factory, the nearby banks of the Seine, and the park of Saint-Cloud without worrying about including the visible signs of technological "progress" – chimneys and smoke – just as, later, the Impressionists would also do. The picturesque approach which turns around the subject was about to be succeeded by a modernist vision which took the transformation of the landscape into account: an effect of snow need no longer be emphasized by the presence of a dead tree. On the other hand, Louis-Rémi Robert, head of the painting workshop at Sèvres, shows an interest in composition, objects, the setting down of elements on the paper, and the invention of astonishing subject-matter (especially in his still-lifes).

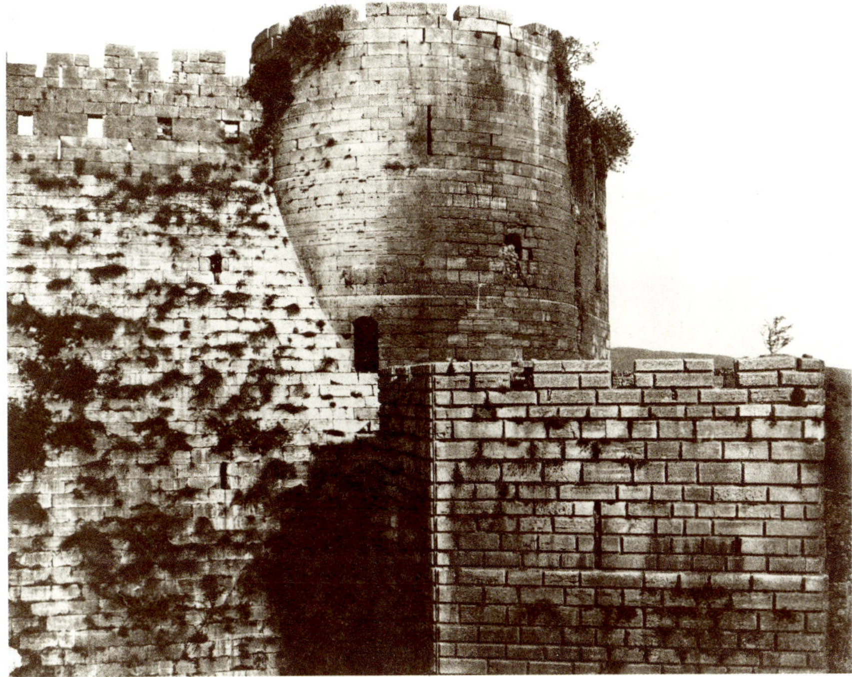

Louis de Clercq,
Castle of Kalaat-el-Hosn, Syria,
1859–1860,
private collection.

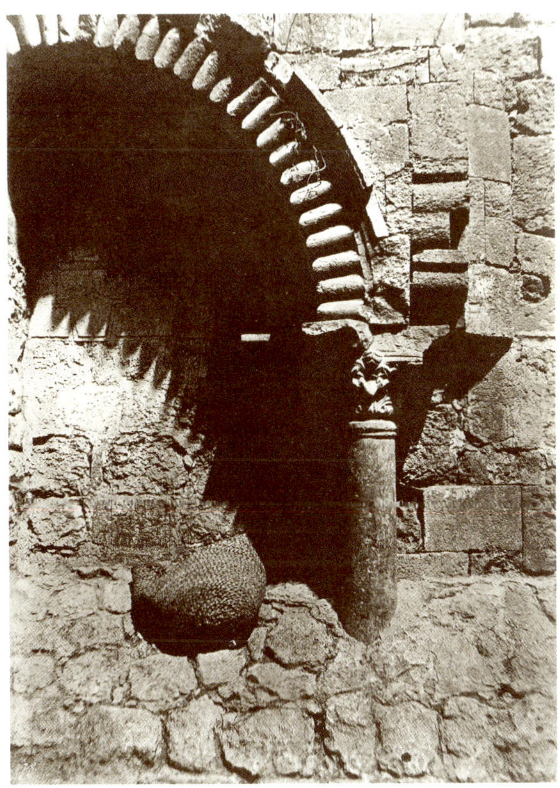

◄ Auguste Salzmann,
Western Portal of the Church of the Holy Sepulchre, Jerusalem,
1854,
private collection.

Archeology

Archeology, which was not yet a scientific discipline, was nevertheless at the interface of art (the archeological object, the monument) and technique (collecting artifacts, the documentary record). Photography as an analytical tool made its appearance at the end of the 1840s: Théodule Devéria would be in charge with Mariette at Memphis for a few years (1855–1860); Louis De Clercq, an archeologist working in Syria with the Comte de Vogüé, brought back *Voyage en Orient, 1859–1860: villes, monuments et vues pittoresques*, more than 200 views in six albums of Syria, Palestine, Egypt, and Spain, in a bold and simple compositional style.

Just as Arago had predicted, archeology was one of the main applications of photography during its infancy. Not because the calotype suited its objectives perfectly, but because it was far superior to all other kinds of archeological recording. From the outset there existed a balance between the conservation and interpretation of the past – a balance reflected in the qualities of archeology and paper negative photography. In Egypt, Devéria (at Memphis), Teynard, and De Clercq (see box), but also travelers in Italy or the producers of images, in their own way gave a further boost to archeology through photography. Although it was still viewed with suspicion by scholars, it became common practice on the ground, with the German Jakob Lorent in Venice

26. *Victor Regnault (1810–1876): œuvre photographique*, Paris, Musée des Arts Décoratifs, 1979.

The ring of truth

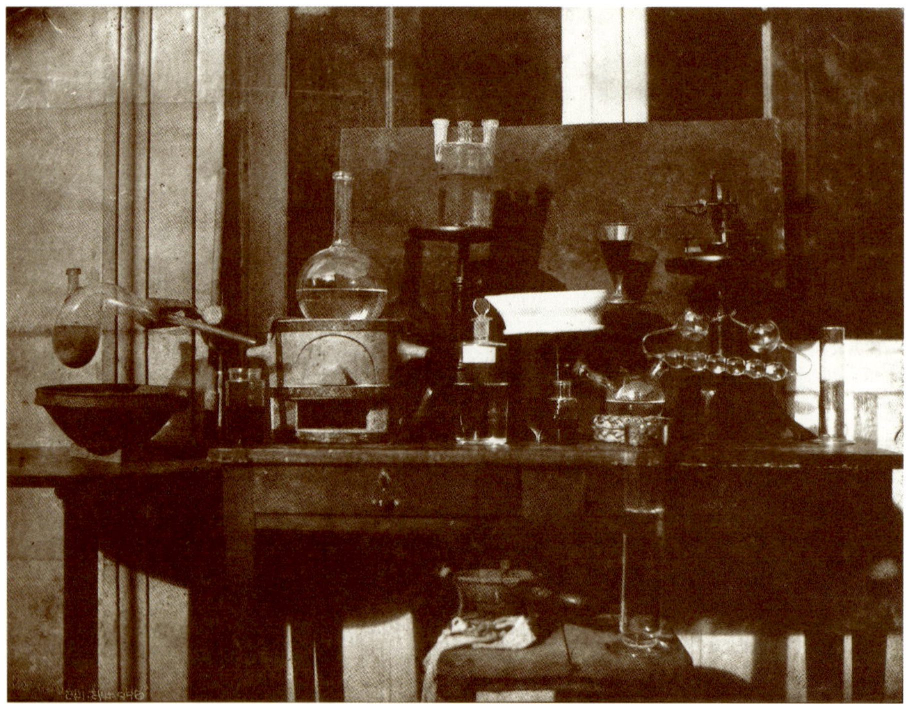

Victor Regnault,
Laboratory Equipment, Collège de France, Paris,
circa 1852, Société Française de Photographie, Paris

The calotype was, above all, a new and "modern" process for the protagonists of 1845–1855. However, while the production of images could take place only with reference to paintings and illustrations, it is no less certain that the possibilities suddenly offered by such a medium called for a reconsideration of aesthetics (understanding by that term the intentions determining the setting up of a particular course of action, the subliminal messages which show through a work of art as if in a watermark). Calotypists, among the first users of a photographic process, seem to have evolved a language for the direct capture of reality, a photographic syntax acquired as a result of the length of the exposure required and the care taken in composition using a ground-glass screen, in operating a process which is closer to stratigraphical recording than the skill of the draftsman, to which all users turn their thoughts. And yet the calotype was conceived as a form of "drawing by light", with unimaginable probity that forgot no element of detail, from the smallest branch to the smallest pebble, however indiscernible or superfluous.

Insofar as it was the first process based on the concept of the negative and positive, the calotype required great attention in these two successive stages. The nature of the negative image (composition, contrast) plays just as decisive a role as the final positive print. The first difficulty was in obtaining a good tonal range in the negative, with an adequate exposure time, enhancing this at the printing stage. Next, the variations in the method used for printing are important, for they give the print its distinctive quality – similar to an engraving, drawing or lithograph – perhaps simply photographic, according to the tonality chosen. The "tone" (a word which frequently crops up) was the result of deliberate choice. The techniques of toning, the addition of various chemicals – which Blanquart-Evrard called "the demands of the art", and which sometimes prevented long-term conservation – gave color tones ranging through wine-dregs, violet, gray-green, brick-red, and even blue, for cyanotypes. Up to six different toning processes are known for a single image by Le Secq, that great master of the calotype between 1851 and 1855.

These conscientious practices, however, always accompany and reinforce a personal inclination to conceive images without equivalents – realistic transpositions of an insistent imaginary world, or even impressions of mental states which could at last be visualized. Le Secq's views of quarries, his collection of small stunted pale trees in the undergrowth, and his Paris architectural images haunted by reminiscences of a disturbing Gothic element – as also occur with his friend Méryon – cannot be considered simply as a skilful consistency of transformations or an escape from the "great art" of painting. Although photography emerged from a pre-existing image world, it did not slavishly follow its edicts, particularly when the operator was conscious of the potential of his equipment. While Le Secq sought the effects of shadow, Le Gray, on the other hand, captured the trembling instability of light which filtered through leaves. While Shaw or Newton perceived ghosts in front of the bare Burnham beeches, Regnault lingered over the majesty of the park at Saint-Cloud, producing contact prints more than 16 inches across (which meant producing a negative of the same dimensions).

Above all, what strikes one about calotypes is a certain crudity of vision, which seems to want to adhere to the truth of the subject, dispensing with any adornments. An ox's head on a table by Louis Robert, a dust-cart in the street by Bayard, a tree-trunk by Marville, the Crystal Palace by B. B. Turner, a Russian log cabin by Fenton, a hand by Charles Hugo – all these are not necessarily picturesque motifs, but true photographs, works produced by light.

Their existence remains, even now, astonishing for anyone who understands that they were produced by a process which has little or nothing in common with the automatic functions of modern cameras. The subtle spirit of the calotype, a quasi-supernatural image composed of contrasts and appearances), combined with skill in the eye of the photographer and raw, untamed objectivity, may still be discerned in the ring of truth through which it strives to demonstrate its different character.

Michel Frizot

in 1853, or Léon Gérard (more romantic in his approach) in Nuremberg, Bamberg, and Switzerland in 1857. The natural outcome was the album or the book. Eugène Piot had produced his *Italie monumentale* in June 1851, shortly before Blanquart-Evrard but with similar ambitions. Flachéron, in assiduously photographing the Roman forum, acted as an archeologist, for he minutely observed the changes that had occurred over the centuries. A number of photographs, now mainly regarded as examples of the picturesque, serve two functions, combining the ideal of the beauty associated with ancient artifacts with the desire to convey as precisely as possible a large amount of information. Men such as Alfred Normand, architect and winner of the Prix de

Rome, thus combined a passion for ruins with a structural understanding of Roman architecture, the influence of which would be felt in architecture at the end of the century. Paul Jeuffrain, a naval officer, was more concerned with the picturesque aspects of Italian streets than the gravity of Pompeii (1852).[27]

One has only to compare the three huge volumes of prints produced by the Blanquart-Evrard photographic printing workshop to understand to what extent the *camera obscura* leaves the field open to a personal vision,[28] without imposing obligations. Melancholy, the sense of ruin and the inevitable, a desire to understand, and curiosity about another life are combined, sometimes seeming to challenge the apparent objectivity of photographic recording. Maxime Du Camp set off in 1849 in Flaubert's company, not with purely archeological motives, but tempted by the exotic associations of ancient history. He brought back, at the end of 1851, more than 200 paper negative photographs, of which 125 would be published by Blanquart-Evrard under the title *Égypte, Nubie, Palestine et Syrie: dessins photographiques recueillis pendant les années 1849, 1850 et 1851 [...] par Maxime Du Camp*. For him, the camera was "a precision instrument to bring back images which will allow me to reconstitute things exactly". The "exact faithfulness", the recording of ancient monuments "in their tiniest details, while also retaining the general aspect of the whole structure", immediately established photography as the rival of engravers and lithographers. The tourist or the scholar no longer had to view a plan or elevation drawn up according to artistic rules. They could confront the monument in miniature, a representation so realistic that they could almost reach out and touch it.

In 1856 the same publishers (Gide et Baudry) produced a collection of 174 plates, also printed by Blanquart-Evrard. The work of Auguste Salzmann, these were entitled *Jérusalem, époques judaïque, romaine, chrétienne, arabe: explorations photographiques*. More detached than those of Du Camp and less of a romanticized impression of past grandeur, Salzmann's views – for a scientific mission by the Ministry of Public Instruction – were taken in Jerusalem to corroborate or refute the historical theories of Ferdinand de Saulcy.[29] In this case photography fulfilled its role of total conformity to a rigorous recording process, helping the viewer to understand how things were without any subjective intermediary and without that medium – drawing – which disguised reality by pencil lines or illusions of perspective and encouraged the viewer to see it with certain preconceptions. The absence of plastic effects, that arrangement of reality as seen from a single viewpoint, makes these photographs particularly effective.

The photographs taken in Egypt by John B. Greene, on the other hand, are continuously astonishing and varied, since one has the impression that the monument at which he pointed his camera was not his primary interest. An archeologist, the son of an American banker living in Paris, Greene traveled in Upper Egypt and Nubia in 1853 (when he was 21) and 1854 and in North Africa in 1855. He died in Egypt in 1856. Greene provides topographical, architectural, and pictorial information within an artistic vision of the site, exploiting effects of light and shade. Egyptian obelisks, hieroglyphics, and statues still submerged in the sand all seem to emerge out of nothing, as if from the shadows, allowing themselves to be overcome – and seen at last – by the sun. A selection from his 200 paper negatives was published in 1854 by Blanquart-Evrard, *Le Nil: monuments, paysages, explorations photographiques*. Only a very small number of copies were produced, so that one can scarcely talk of an edition. Greene's premature death contributed to the small number of his images published.

PAUL JEUFFRAIN,
Grocery, Naples,
1852,
Société Française
de Photographie, Paris.
▼

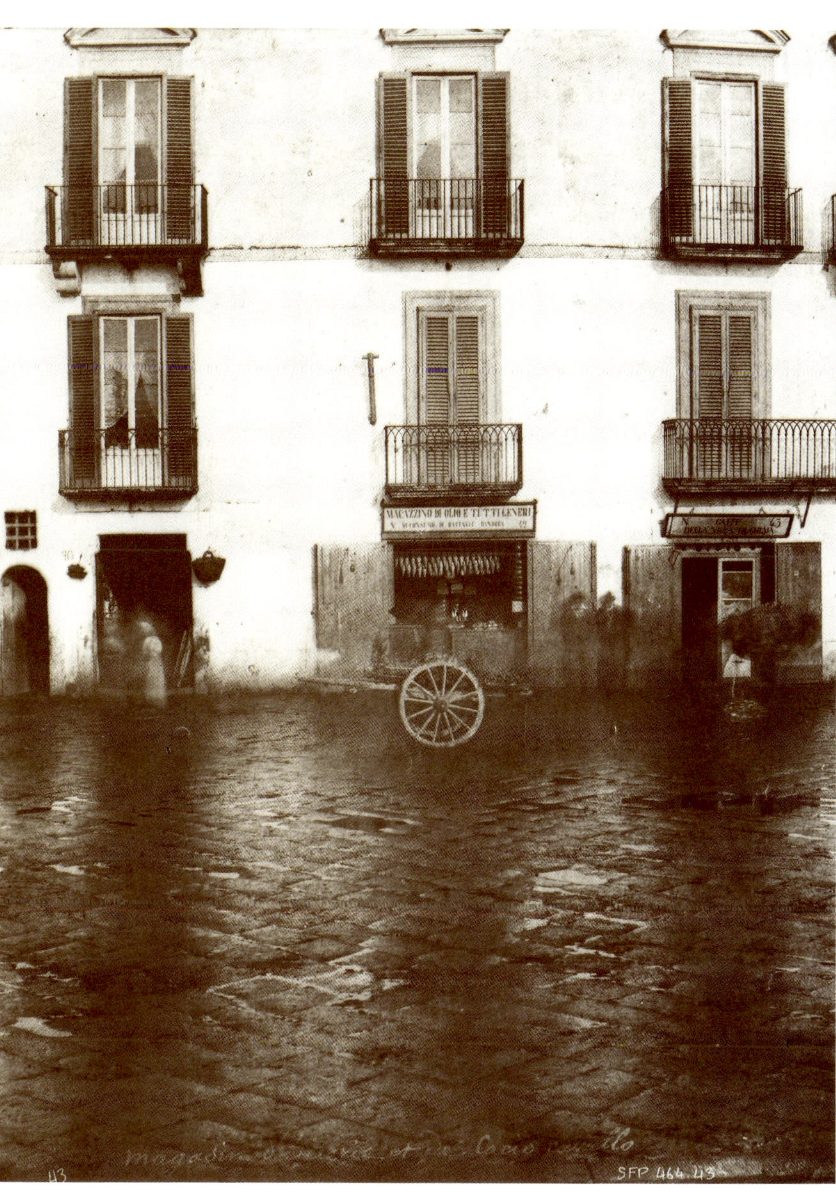

27. *I calotipi della Società Francese di Fotografia, 1840–1860*, Venice, Marsilio, 1981.

28. I. Jammes, *Blanquart-Evrard et les origines de l'édition photographique française: catalogue raisonné des albums édités, 1851–1855*, Geneva, Droz, 1981.

29. *F. de Saulcy et la Terre sainte*, Paris, RMN, 1982.

30. B. Jammes, "John B. Greene; an American Calotypist", in *History of Photography*, no. 4, 1981.

Blanquart-Evrard's photographic printing workshop

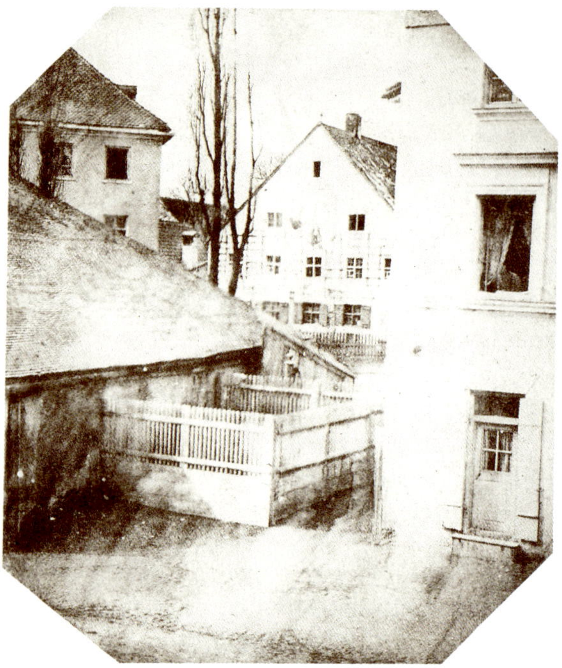

Alois Löcherer, ▶ *Backyard,* circa 1845, Höhere Graphische Bundes-Lehr und Versuchsanstalt, Vienna.

Blanquart-Evrard played a fundamental role in the calotype. In his own day he promoted the process through his need for negatives to supply printing workshop. It is because of him that so many images are preserved today and the names of so many photographers known which would otherwise be lost.

What is more, all of this enormous output has not yet been tracked down. Many photographs are still awaiting identification and attribution – 24 volumes, containing more than 550 photographs.

Blanquart-Evrard published and sold his original salted-paper prints mounted individually on card and titled, with an indication that they came from his workshop, or brought together in unbound "albums" issued in parts, the custom in publishing at that time. The way he divided up the photographs was not predetermined but was mainly a response to commercial pressures, reflecting the way in which negatives were provided by various travelers, some of them amateurs, whose work varied greatly widely in quality.

The *Album photographique de l'artiste et de l'amateur,* which appeared first, contains examples of many different types of subject, ranging from an Indian temple (Alexis de Lagrange), by way of a fragment of the Parthenon and a painting by Van Eyck, to a cedar of Lebanon. The majority of his output consisted of architectural and sculptural monuments: *L'Art religieux: architecture et sculpture* (mostly Marville for the architecture, Bayard and Renard for painting, 1853–1854), *La Belgique* (Desplanques, 1854), *Les Bords du Rhin* (Marville, 1853), *Bruxelles photographique* (Guillaume Claine), *Mélanges photographiques* (paintings and views of Paris by Marville, and of Venice by Walther, 1851–1853), *Monuments de Paris* (Fortier), *Paris photographique* (Marville and Le Secq and anonymous photographers, 1851–1853), *Recueil photographique: souvenirs photographiques* (Bayard, Fortier, and Marville, 1853).

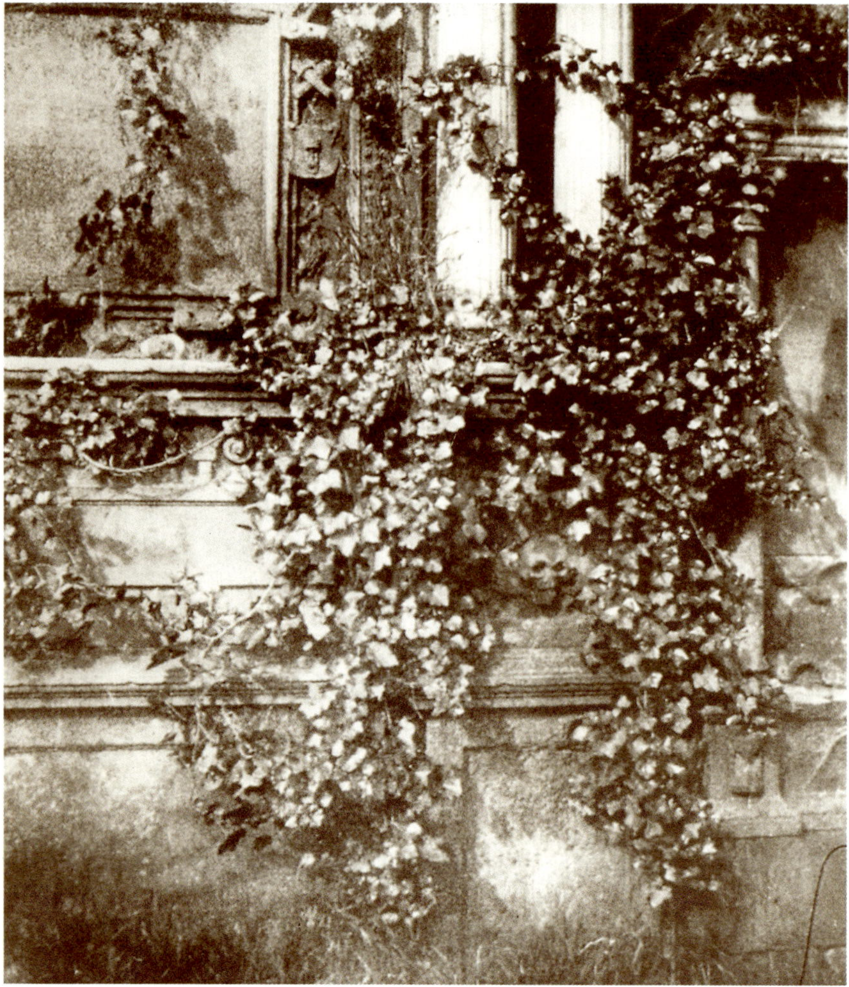

Thomas Keith, *Ivy on a Tomb, Greyfriars Cemetery, Edinburgh,* 1851–1865, City Libraries, Edinburgh.

Certain monograph albums (the work of a single photographer) seem to be complete: *Paysages de Flandres* and *Souvenir de Jersey* (Thomas Sutton), *Souvenirs de Versailles* (Louis Robert), and *Souvenirs des Pyrénées* (John Stewart). Given contemporary interest in an idealized "imaginary museum" of all the arts, the inevitable collections of reproductions are found, such as *L'art contemporain* (on the 1853 Salon, by Bayard and Renard, 1854).

The most creative images were undoubtedly those which gave the photographer the greatest freedom of choice in their subject, even if the prints were then grouped together under the title "studies" (see the following dossier).

The printing works closed, quite suddenly, in 1855 through commercial failure and because of the new competition of photo-lithographic printing and photogravure on copper or steel plates. Through these methods photography would enter the era of reproduction and photomechanical processes, which led eventually to the illustrated press.

The photographic diaspora

Unlike the modern photographer, the calotypist did not work spontaneously. His technique demanded patience. Due to lack of interest in these works for more than a century, many photographs have been lost. Fortunately, however, thanks to the large number of copies made, images have survived: Marville photographing the banks of the Rhine, Louis Robert's poetic vision of Versailles, Fenton's travels in Russia, and Le Gray's trip with Dumas to Palermo at the time of the events of 1860.

Certain photographers whose intention was to produce images to be sold in shops were quite specialized: Louis d'Olivier and Julien Vallou de Villeneuve, for example, specialized in studies of naked artists' models. The latter also produced studies of drapery, clothed models, and human "types" (servant, monk, Algerian woman, peasant, etc.), which were published by Lemercier in 1853.

As already noted, after 1850 photography in France enjoyed a period of growth for several years thanks to the commercial distribution of photographs. Many photographers who achieved fame around 1860 had first worked with the calotype. They continued its "grand manner" style thanks to the use of large-format negatives and a breadth of composition, even though they moved to glass negatives.

Technical considerations are not always paramount in regard to changes in a photographic aesthetic. Fortunately, the photographer's vision owes more to their ability to circumvent any technical constraints. With the majority of calotypists, their use of a cumbersome and slow process does not permit us to consider them simply as "primitives" – the calotype process was an accomplished craft form and the years when it was in use should certainly not be considered as merely a trial period.

Enthusiasts in Britain,[31] where the calotype originated, remained close to Talbot, forming circles of kinship and mutual exchange of information (see box). However, their work was not distributed to any large extent after the semi-failure of *The Pencil of Nature*. The debate concerning Scott Archer's use of glass negatives, about 1853, led both to an initial decline of the calotype and to the setting up in London of the Photographic Society, which tended to support the new technique of collodion glass negatives.

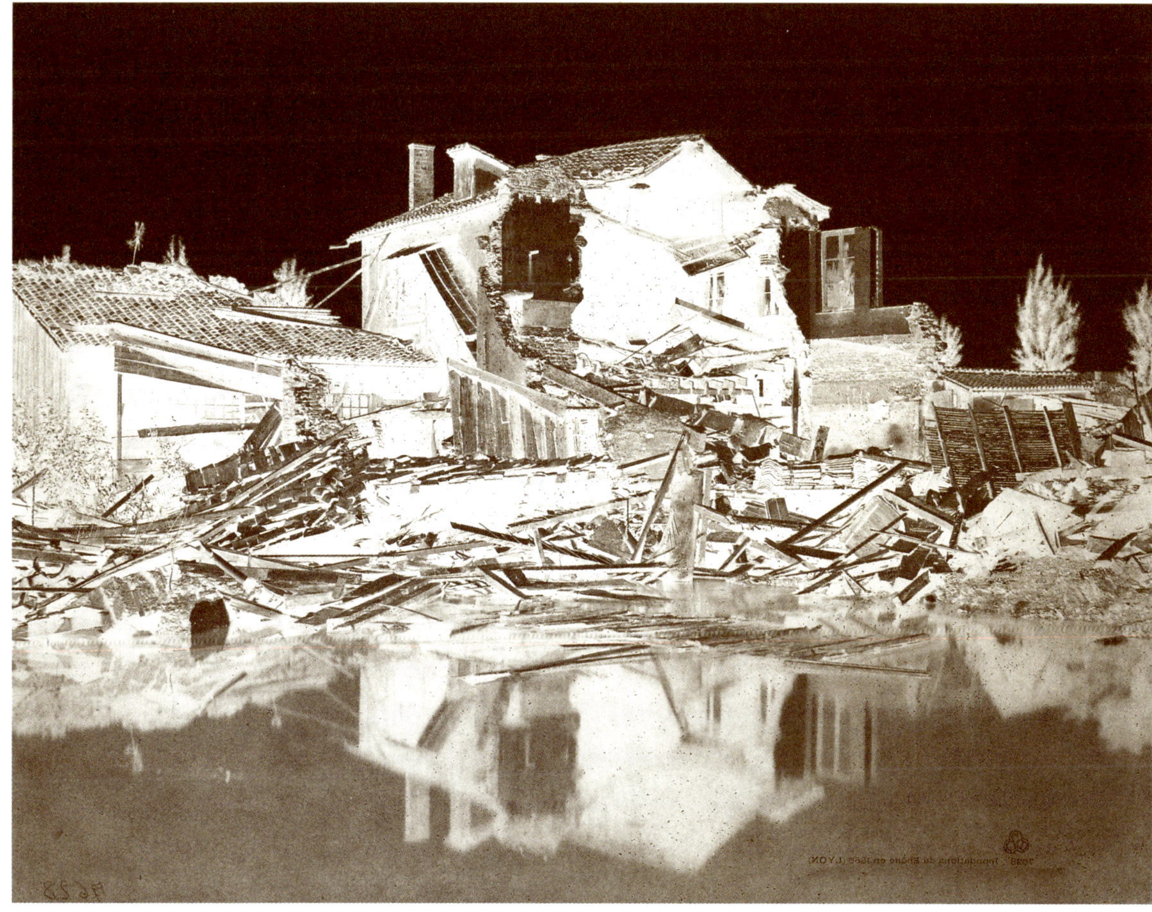

Édouard-Denis Baldus, *Floods at Lyons,* paper negative, 1856, Musée d'Orsay, Paris.

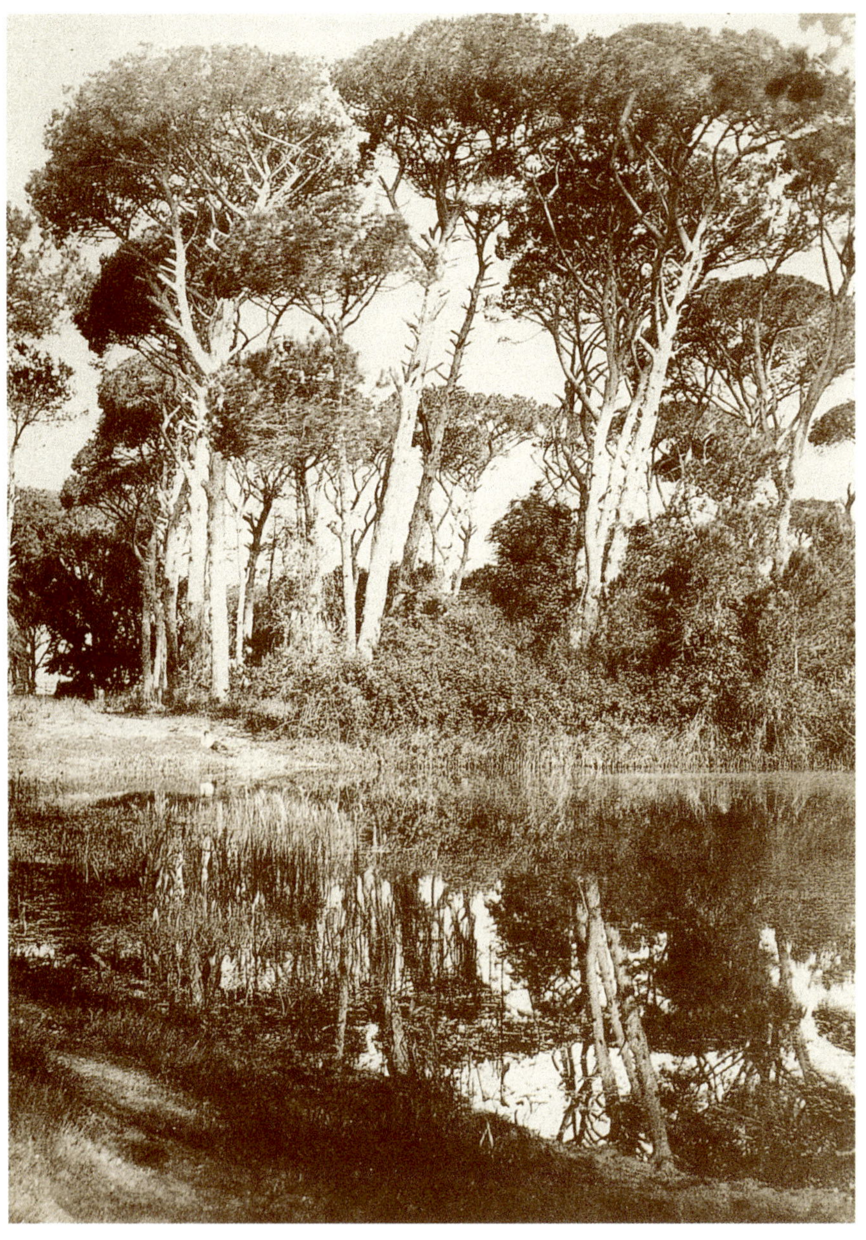

GIACOMO CANEVA, *Pinegrove, Castel Fusano,* circa 1855, Piero Becchetti collection.

The British abroad also formed a significant group, particularly in India. Sometimes these photographers adopted French processes. As photographer to the British mission at Ava (Burma), Linnaeus Tripe used the calotype process from 1855.[32] His views were published in 1857 at Bangalore. He worked in Madras from 1856 to 1860. Tripe distinguished himself with calotypes showing imposing architectural façades. John Murray who worked as a military doctor in Agra, India exhibited his views in London in 1857 (a portfolio was published in 1859 entitled *Picturesque Views of the Northwestern Provinces of India*).

John Shaw Smith, a skilful exponent of Blanquart-Evrard's process, traveled in the Holy Land and Egypt in 1850–1852. Weelhouse was in the Mediterranean in 1850.

E. K. Tenison, probably of English origin, worked in Spain in 1853, Charles Clifford settled in Madrid in 1852, the court photographer of Isabella II. His *Voyage en Espagne*, which the critic Lacan described as "in the French spirit", was published in Paris in 1856. His large-format shots (up to 24 inches wide), his astonishing oblique views, and his interplay of light and shade are among the most beautiful effects achieved by the calotype process.

In other European countries, professional photographers appeared in any numbers only after the arrival of the collodion process. However we should mention, in Germany, Aloïs Löcherer (especially his views of the preliminary work on the Bavaria statue) as well as Ludwig Belitski (photographs of the Minutoli collection at Legnica).[33]

In Italy, Giacomo Caneva was author of a *Practical Treatise* in 1855. His collection would be taken up by Ludovico Tuminello, who produced large-format views of the Italian countryside. His work surpassed that of all his colleagues, such as Simelli or Brezolin,[34] few though they were, who were attracted by this process.[34]

The calotype (by which we include all paper negative processes) was not yet the process dreamed of by the new "heliographers" and was destined to become virtually extinct after a golden age of five or six years. Nevertheless, this period formed a period of grace for photography: an entirely perfected technique, distributed in numerous countries and opening up frontiers of communication, knowledge and aesthetic pleasure. Eminently suitable for personal interpretation, the calotype defined an image quality and a mode of existence for photography inextricably linked with the technical conditions of its production.

The symbolic value of the *camera obscura*, the obligatory use of an intermediary negative, the delay in appreciation caused by the fact that an image was left in the latent state, and the possibilities of intervention as work progressed, all comprised a craft – requiring a period of apprenticeship – combining the mysteries of technology (optics and chemistry) and the creative impulse of art. In many respects, the history of photography reflects this fine balance between art and technique.

31. R. R. Bretell, *op. cit.*

32. J. Dewan and M. M. Sutnik, *Linnaeus Tripe: Photographer of British India, 1854–1870*, Toronto, Museum of Fine Arts, 1986.

33. B. von Dewitz and R. Matz, *Silber und Salz: Zur Frühzeit der Photographie im deutschen Sprachraum 1839–1860*, Cologne and Heidelberg, Braus, 1989.

34. P. Becchetti, *Giacomo Caneva e la Scuola Fotografica Romana (1847–1855)*, Florence, Alinari, 1989.

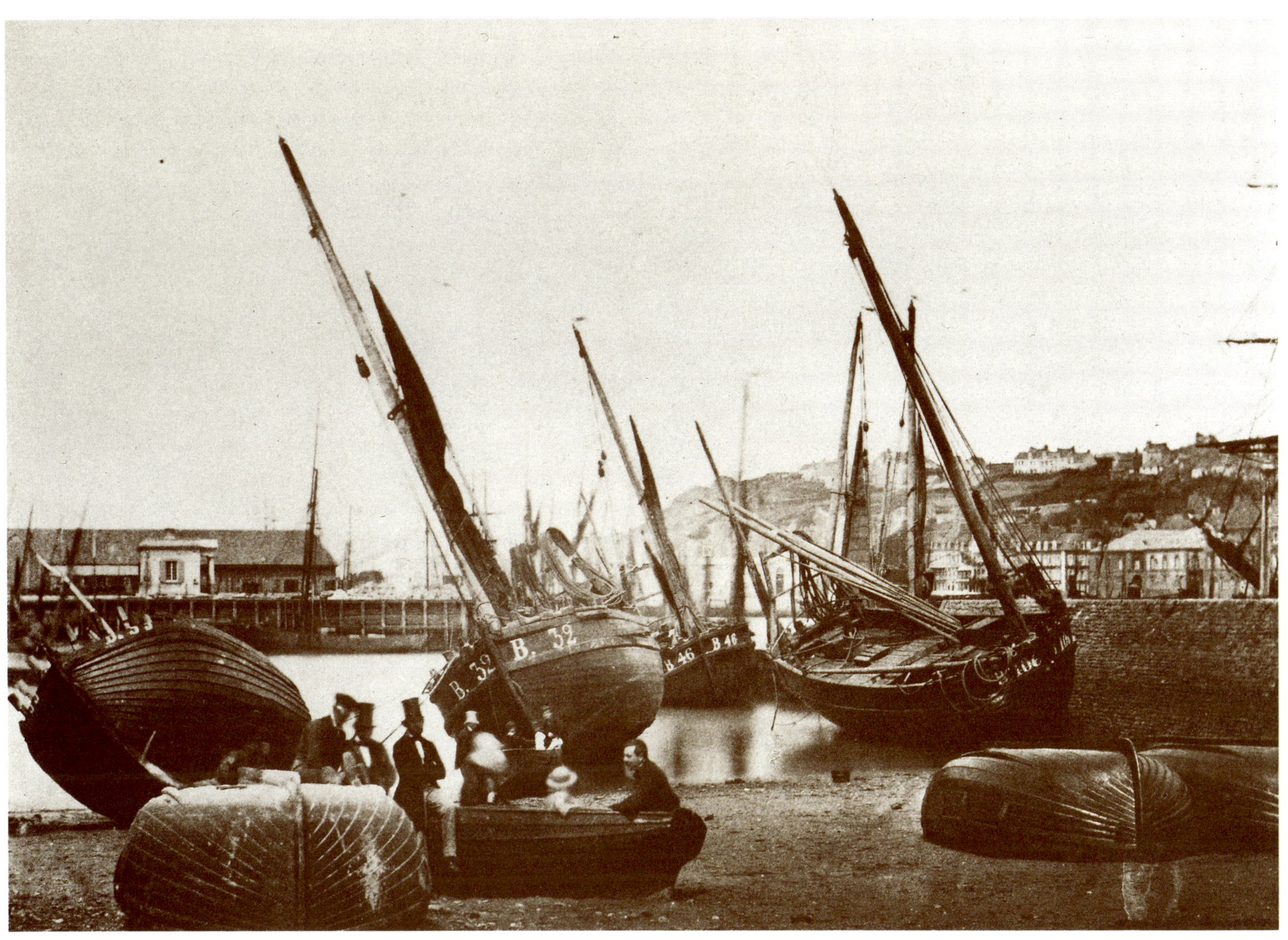

Blanquart-Evrard, photographic publisher

Over the past decade or two the technique of the calotype has been reconsidered, after long neglect; but the photographs produced by this method are still debated. Often judged too "primitive", they visibly break the rules imposed by modern photography, such as those of sharpness or rapidity of execution. Whether they liked it or not, calotypists had to resolve fundamental aesthetic questions – to which critical writing in around 1850 bears witness – and invent a type of image onto which later photographic developments would be grafted.

The majority of Blanquart-Evrard's output, fortunately preserved, provides an unrivaled collection, of both what might have interested his customers and what was considered "photographable", taking the serious technical constraints into account. One only has to compare this "block" of imagery from the mid-nineteenth century with other coherent contemporary collections, such as the steel engravings which art magazines printed in abundance, to see that photography had in a few years created its own operative logic, system of signs, principles of reading, and relationship with reality. Of course all this was based on the graphic languages then in force, but the debate focuses on departures from the norm, on the displacement of the senses wrought by photographic automaticity, which replaced the manual dexterity of the painter, and on the symbolic transference process which the direct, optical rapport with that which the camera has really "seen" cannot be avoided.

We have brought together here a few of the most original – the most resolutely photographic – of the images published by Blanquart-Evrard, who chose negatives from the output of friends, amateurs, and professionals, and edited the prints into thematic portfolios. The photographs chosen here belong to three innovative albums: *Études photographiques, Études et paysages, Keepsake photographique*, The term *études* (studies) refers to the practice of painters, to whom these views after nature are in theory addressed. But even when the photographer has become subservient to the painter, this does not lead to servile imitation of naturalistic and conventional works. The photographer creates a new type of image, whose pictorial equivalents, whether drawn or engraved, may be found only superficially. The studies of trees by Marville or Benecke, the anonymous rural views in fact precede a number of artists of the Barbizon school, Loydreau's snow or frost effects precede Impressionism, and the rural scenes with people are more realistic than painting of the Realist school, which had only recently appeared in Paris; Benecke's *Lofia, A Cairo Woman* owes nothing to orientalism, but invents the science of "ethnophotography". Regnault's "still-life" disturbs the very nature of still-life: the atmosphere of the image and the arrangement of objects and farm produce, like the natural quality of the surrounding space, contradict all those artificial combinations which would have made it a composition based on the rules. After the strangeness of the daguerrian mirror, photography here teaches a new lesson about things, and provides a practical guide to the art of seeing properly.

Michel Frizot

All the photographs in this dossier form part of albums of prints published by Blanquart-Evrard, and come from the Bibliothèque Municipale in Lille.

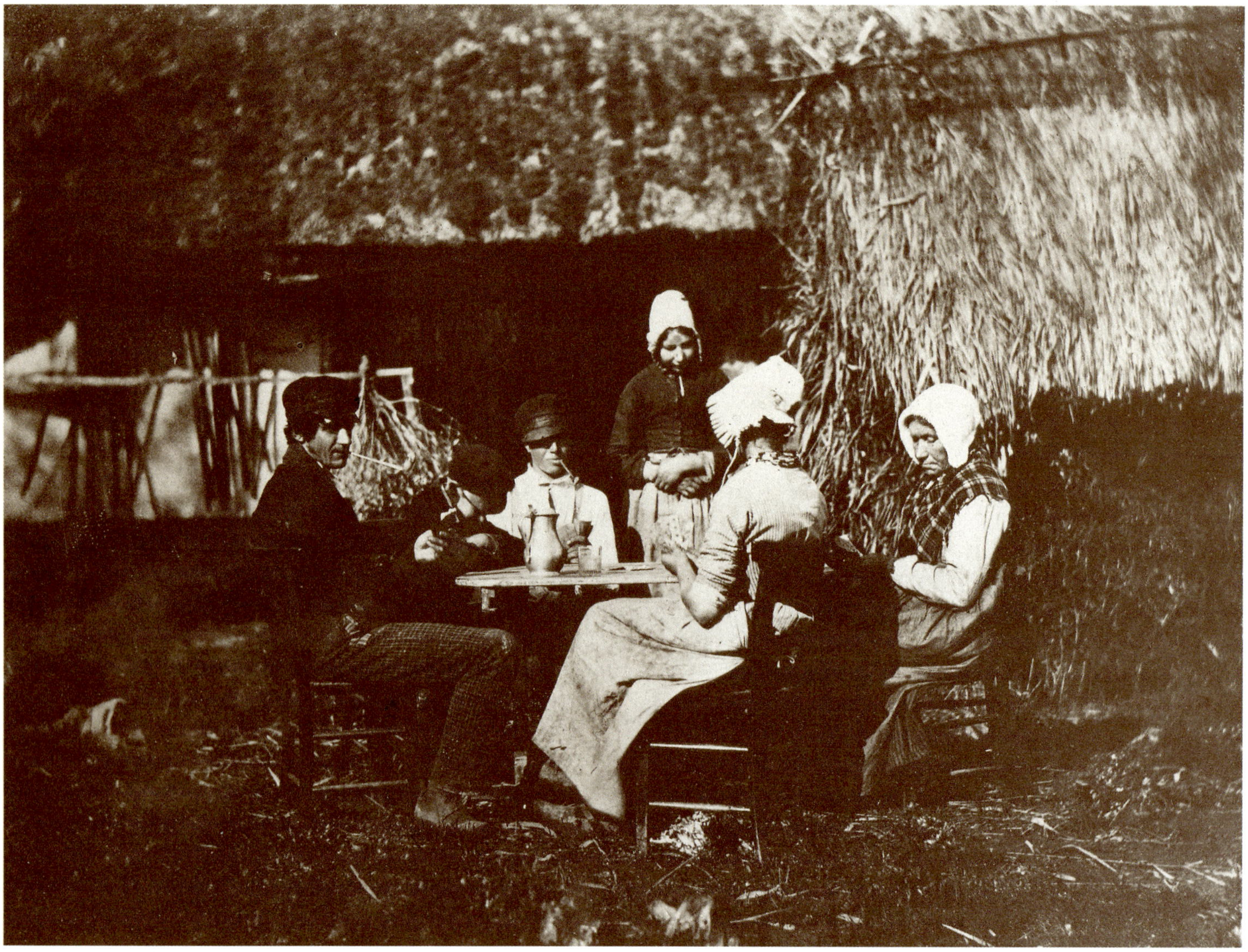

ANONYMOUS,
Peasant Family Playing Cards,
Études photographiques,
1st series, no. 31, 1853.

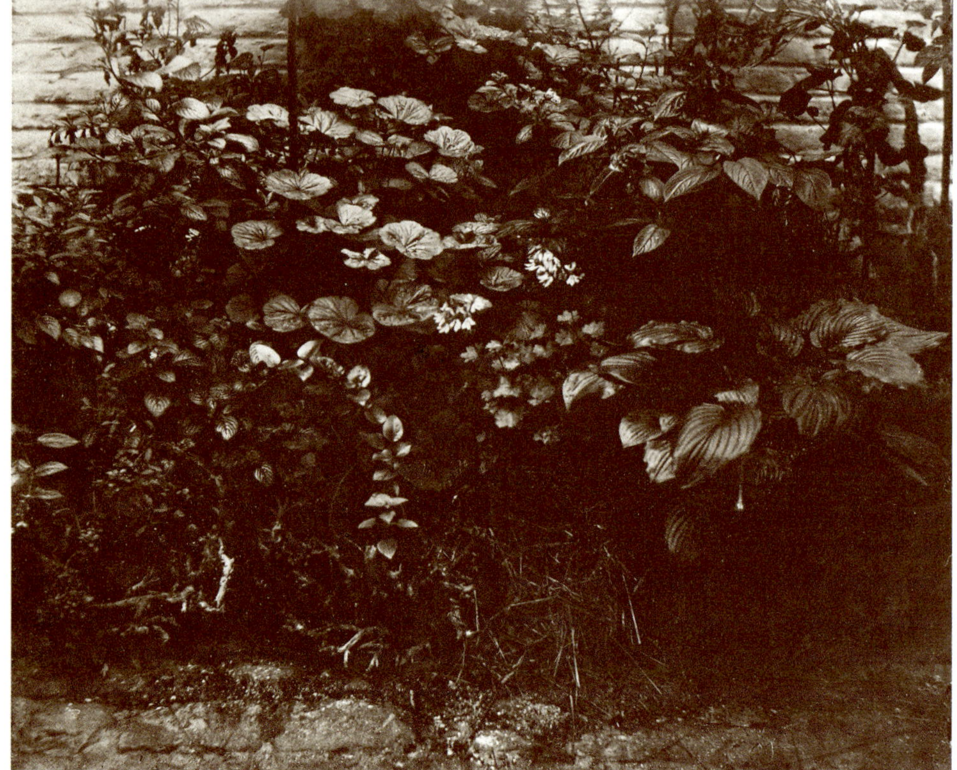

ANONYMOUS,
Flowers and Foliage,
Études photographiques,
1st series, no. 23, 1853.

VICTOR REGNAULT, ►
(attributed),
Still-life on Trestles,
Études photographiques,
1st series, no. 17, 1853.

◄◄ Preceding page:
ANONYMOUS,
The Port of Boulogne,
Keepsake photographique,
circa 1853, plate X.

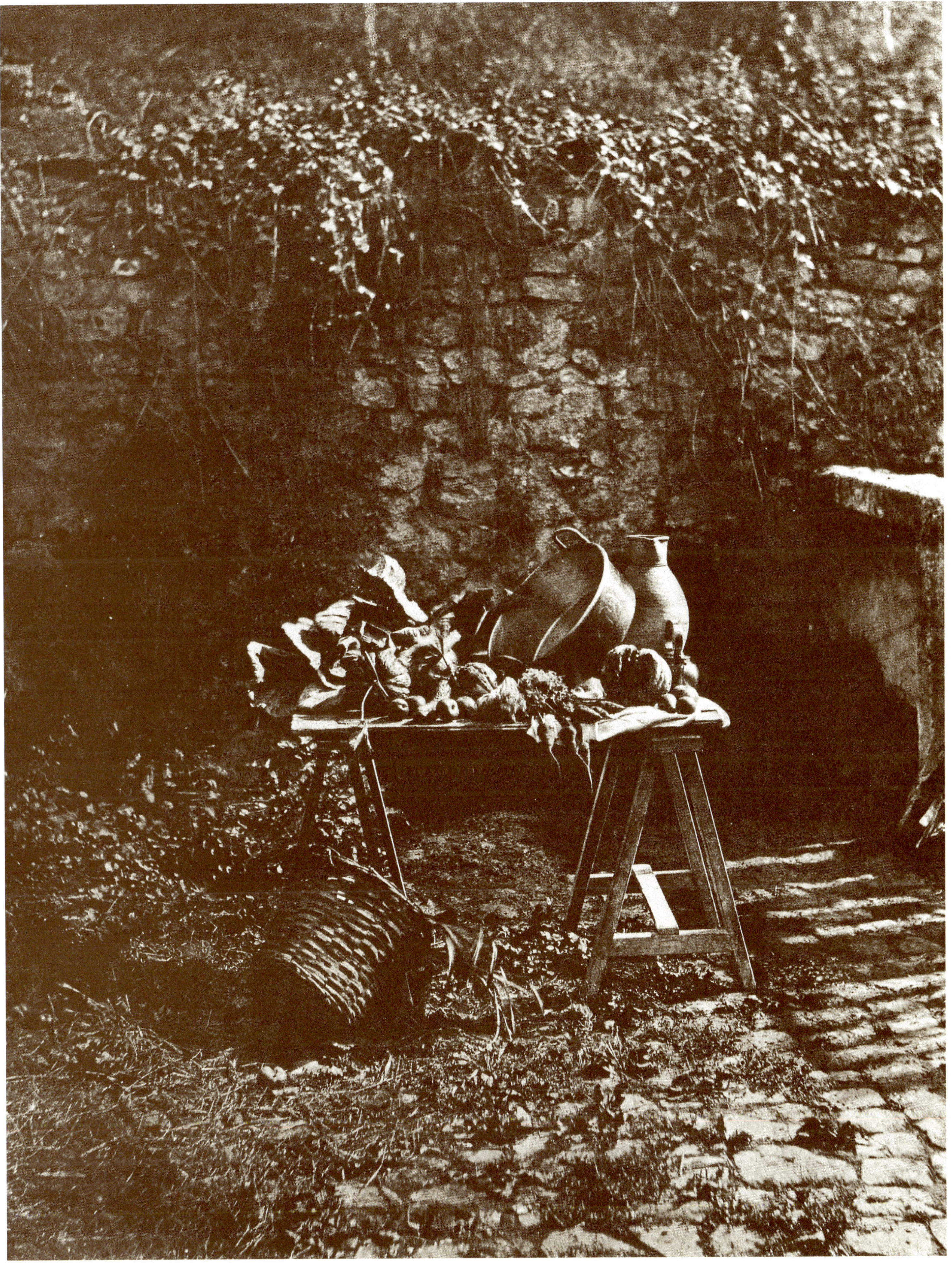

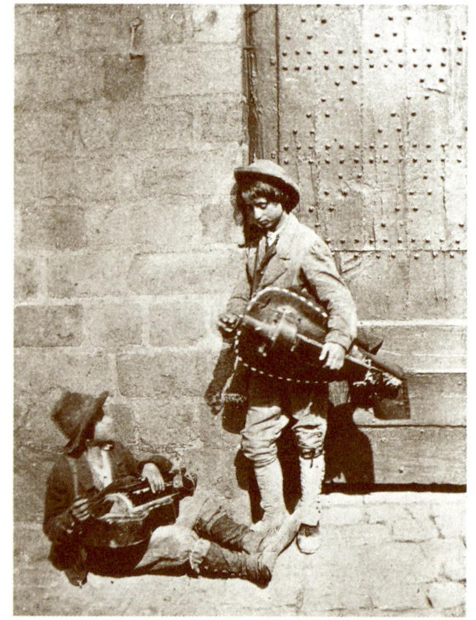

ANONYMOUS,
Fiddle Players,
Études photographiques,
1st series, no. 58, 1853.

ANONYMOUS,
Young Man Mounting a Donkey,
Études photographiques,
1st series, no. 27, 1853.

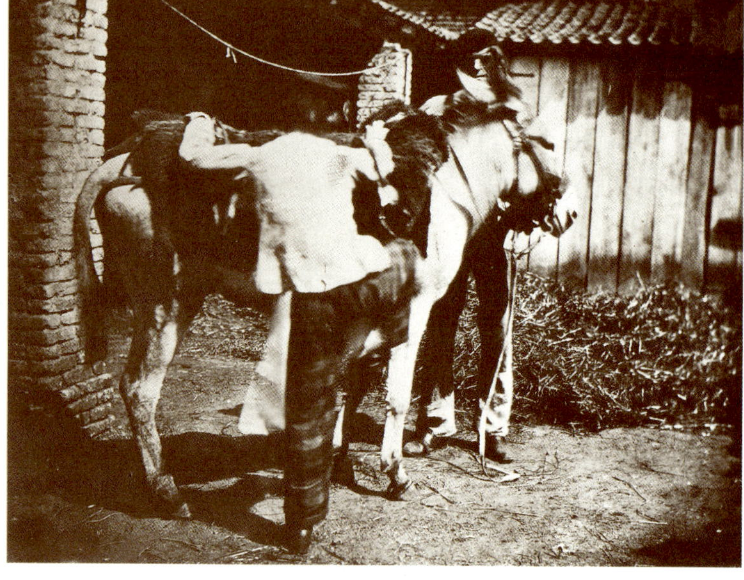

ANONYMOUS,
Street Scene,
Études photographiques,
1st series, no. 24, 1853.

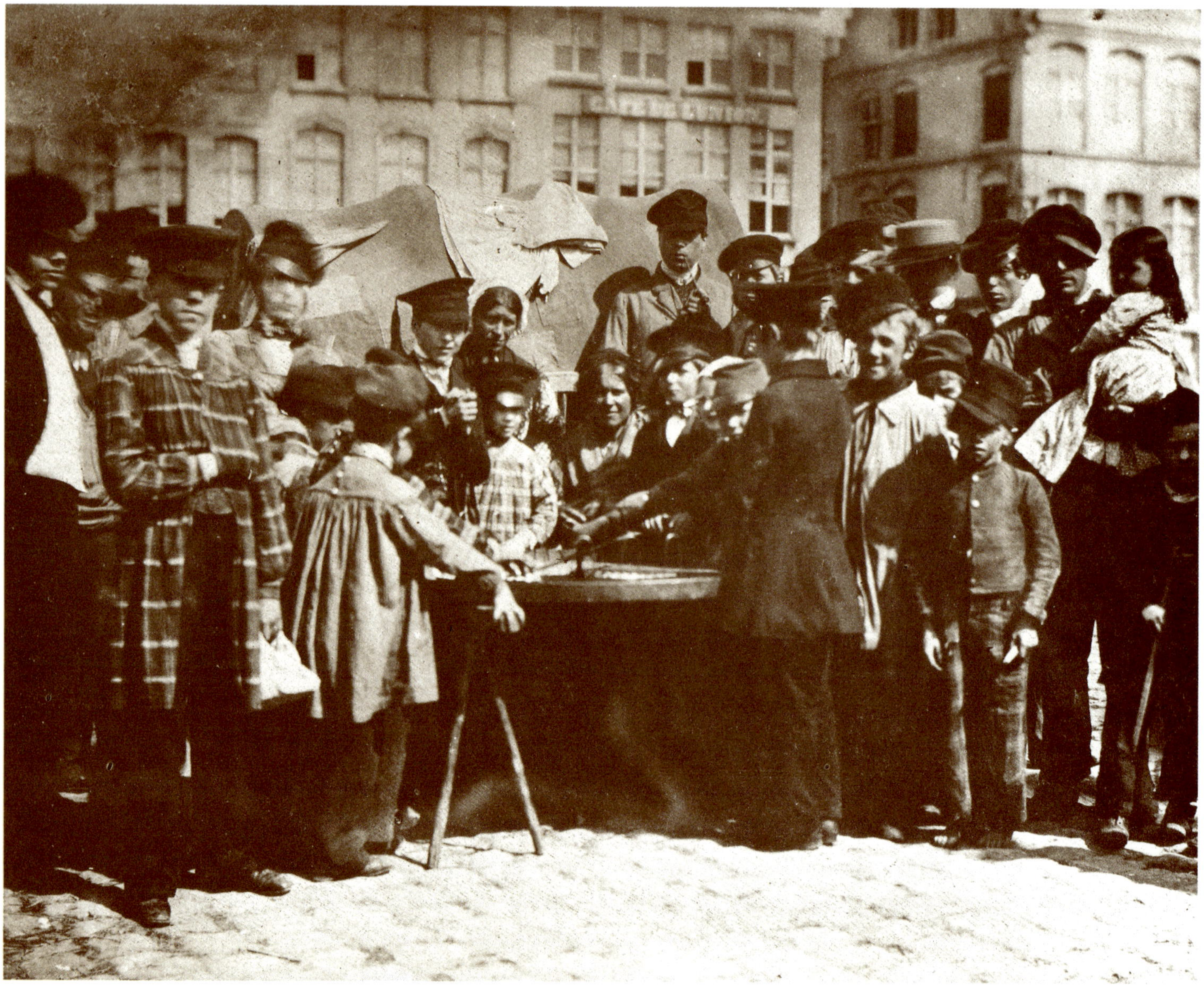

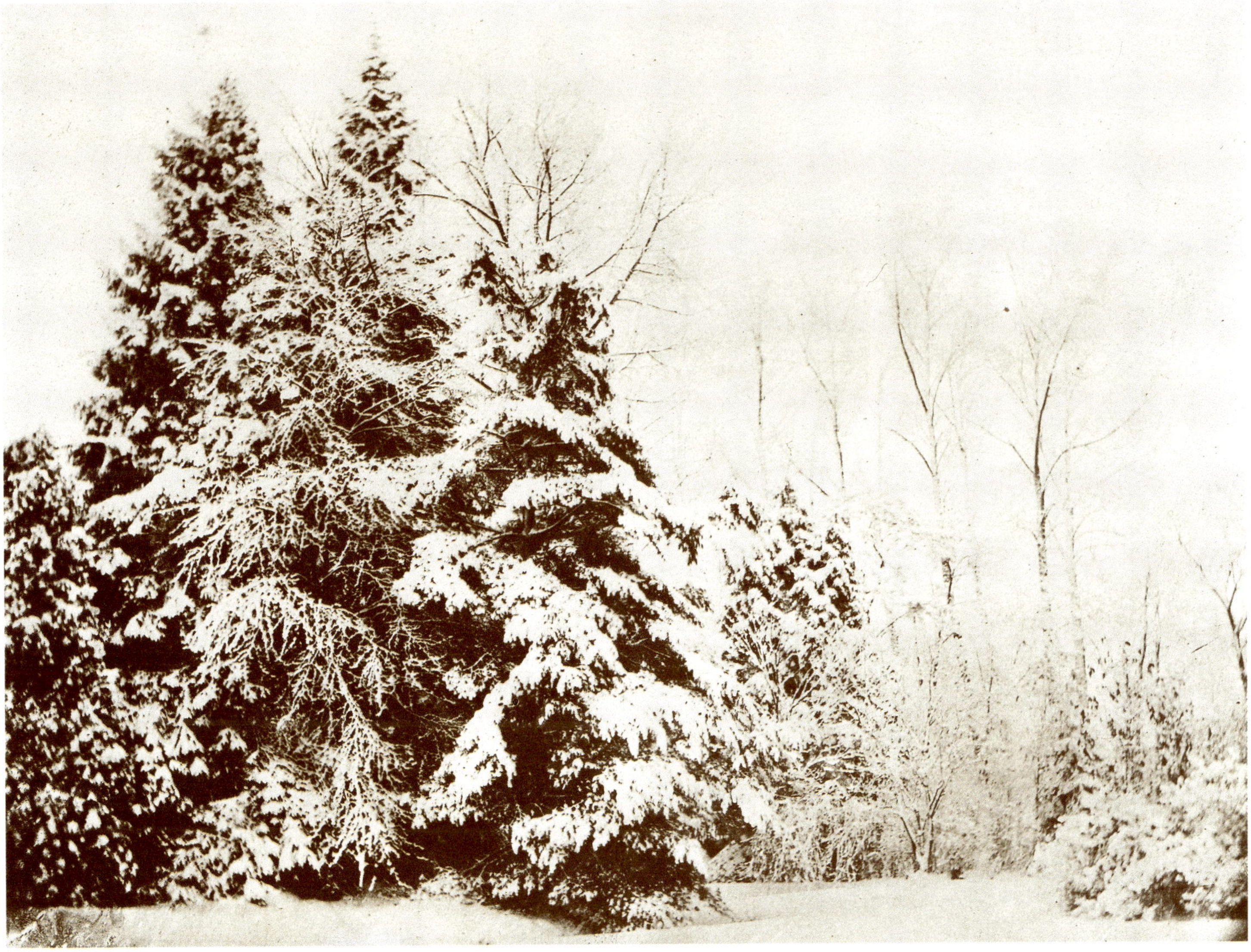

ANONYMOUS,
Landscape with Fir Trees in the Snow,
Études photographiques,
1st series, no. 46, 1853.

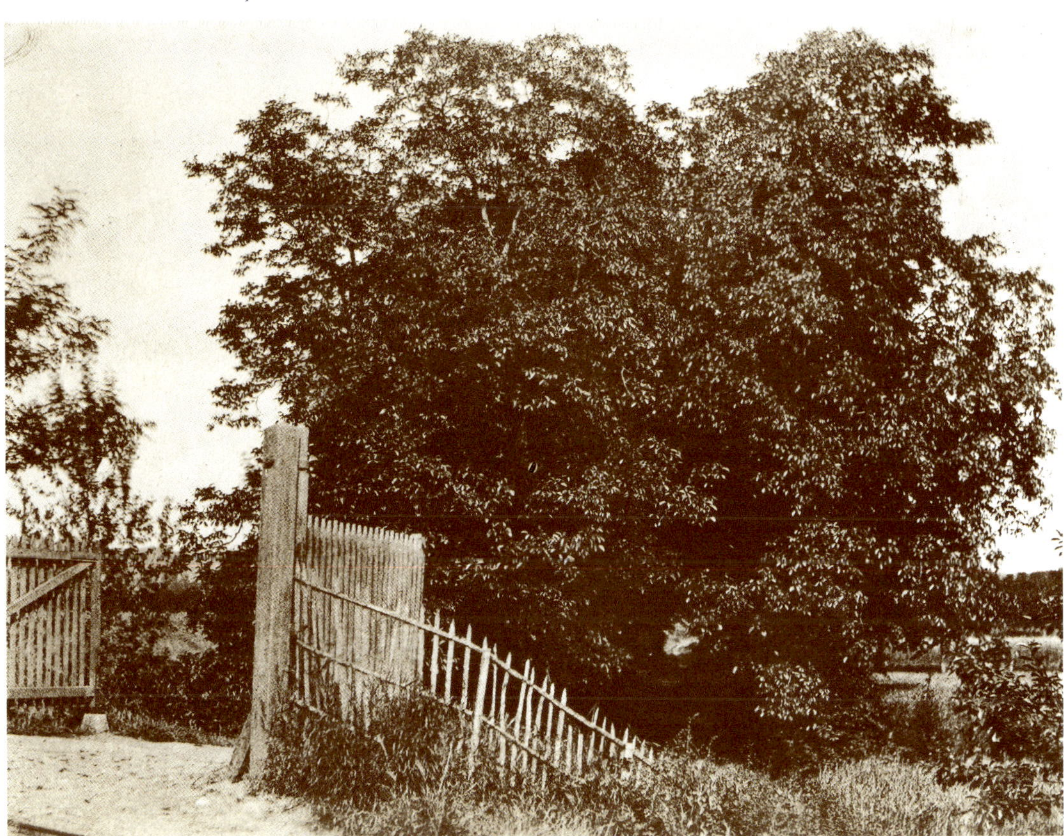

CHARLES MARVILLE,
The Open Gate,
Études photographiques,
1st series, no. 19, 1853.

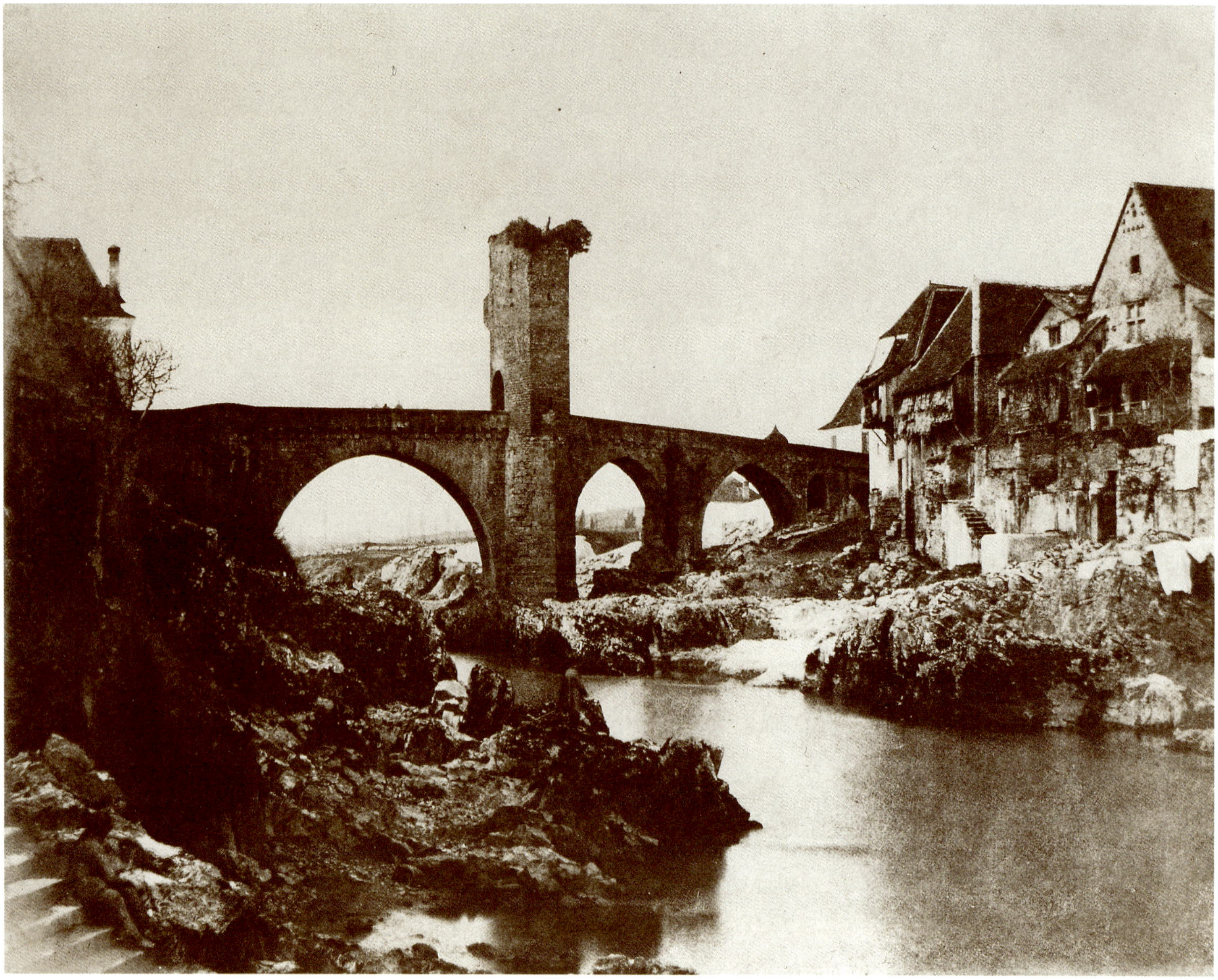

JOHN STEWART,
The Bridge at Orthez,
Souvenirs photographiques,
1853, plate LIX.

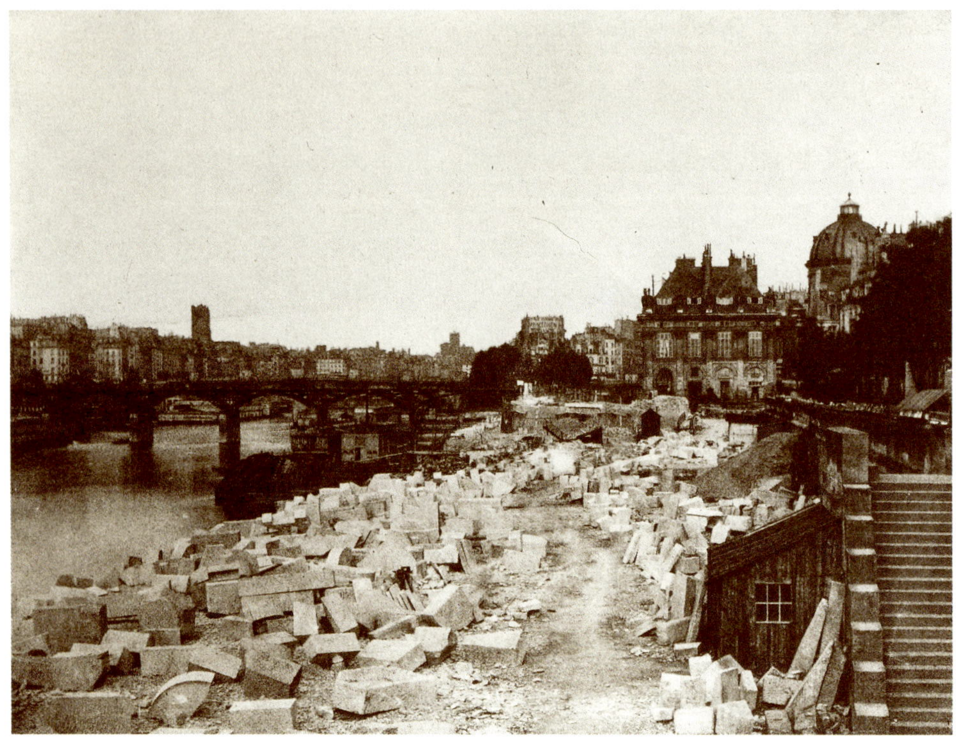

CHARLES MARVILLE,
(attributed),
View from the Pont des Arts, Paris,
Mélanges photographiques,
1851.

E. BENECKE, ►
Lofia, A Cairo Woman,
Études photographiques,
1st series, 1853, plate LIV.

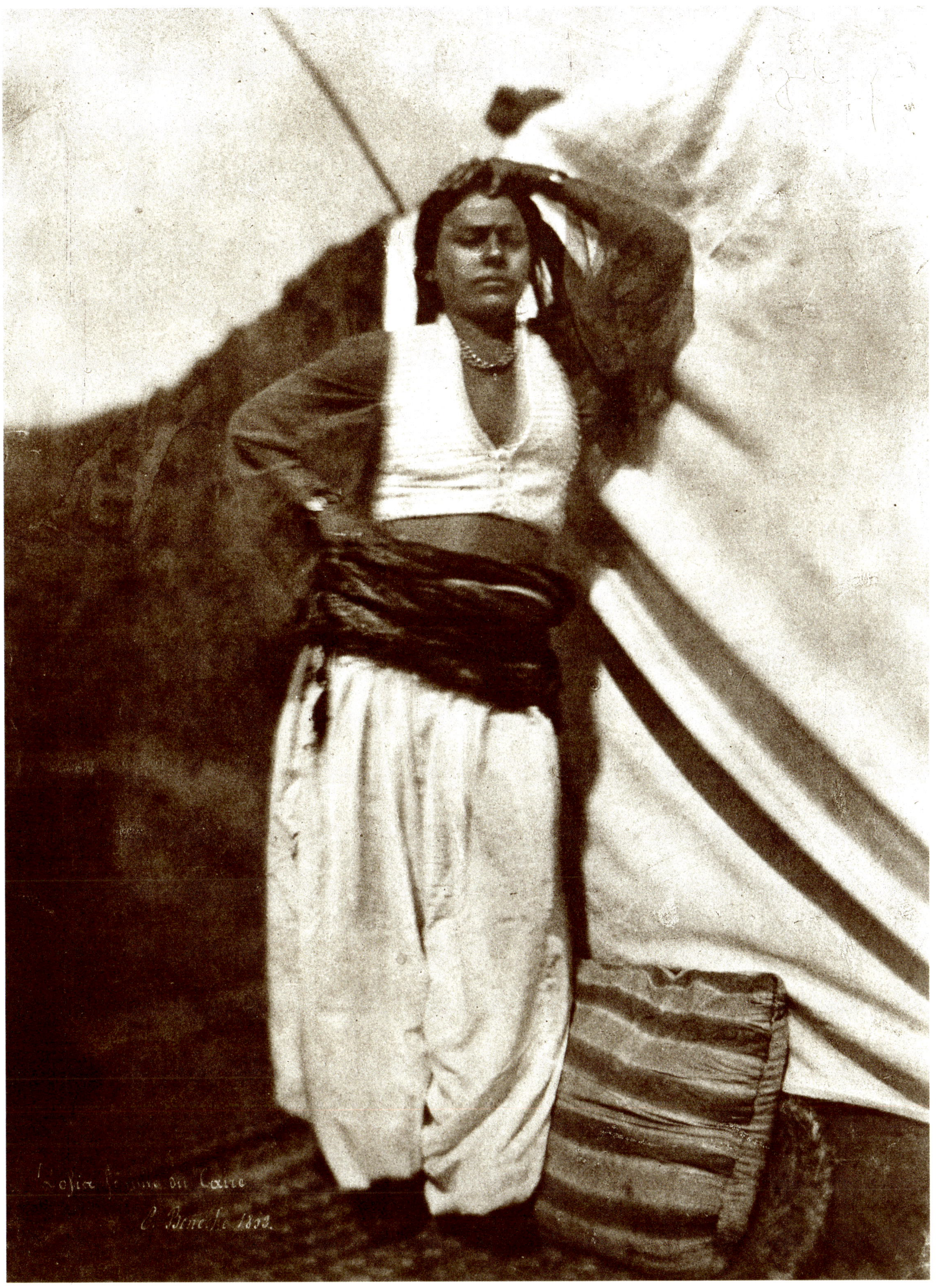
Kesia femme du Caire
E. Benecke

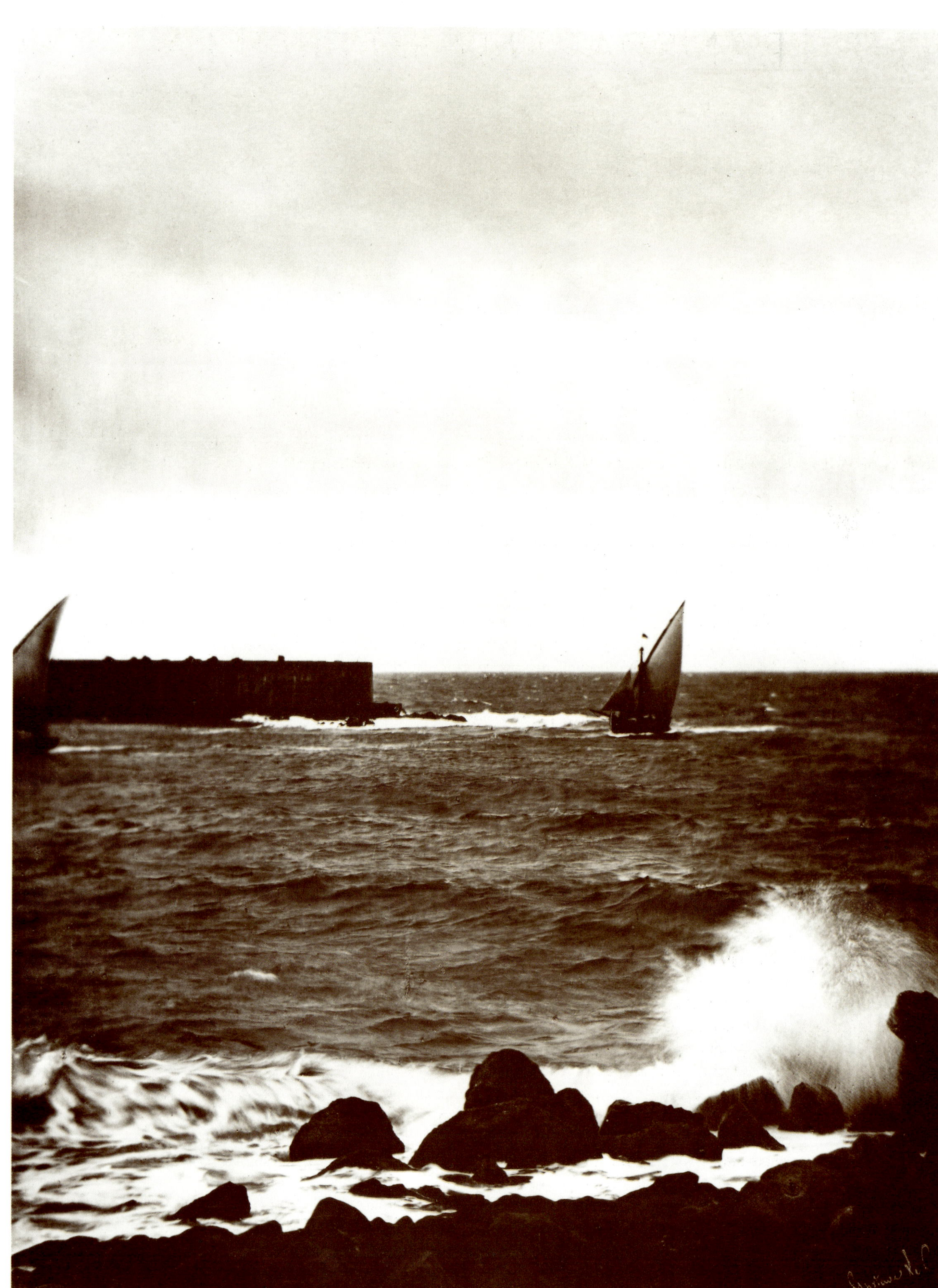

THE TRANSPARENT MEDIUM 5

From industrial product to the Salon des Beaux-Arts

Michel Frizot

The very process by which a picture is made influences the world the image inhabits as well as its content and meaning. For this reason, it has never been easy to change photographic production techniques. The advent of the glass negative brought a fresh appreciation of the subject and new ways of tapping into reality. Many new processes appeared in the 1850s. Photographic manuals were packed with recipes and variations which opened the way to individual adaptations. But one thing did not change - there were still ongoing experiments into the light-sensitivity of photographic materials. "Copying from nature" acquired a degree of precision that considerably enhanced the effectiveness of photography.

Unlike the histories of other media used in art, photography has gone through a number of phases or stages, each corresponding roughly to a development in technique or the way in which images are produced. Although photography is constantly undergoing new developments, the broad aesthetic conventions that they engender never last very long. Between 1840 and 1855 the daguerreotype and the calotype provided two very different conceptions of natural images derived from the *camera obscura*. Neither process, however, was a commercial success. This was due mainly to the circumstances of the times, such as the continuing high cost of the techniques involved. Consequently, the cost of these images was such that, on the whole, they were only for the affluent. Because the calotype process required so much manipulation, Blanquart-Evrard's attempts at standardization were not sufficient to boost production and push down prices. Indeed, most technical advances in photography were aimed at controlling and reducing the time needed for the various phases of the process.

As early as 1839, the advantages of the calotype over the daguerreotype – a unique image on metal – had become apparent. It was clear, however, that other techniques were needed to speed up and simplify the negative/positive process. The younger cousin of Nicéphore Niépce, Abel Niépce de Saint-Victor, a soldier by profession, decided to use glass plates as a support. The technical solution he came up with consisted of binding silver salts to the non-absorbent surface by means of a permeable and adhesive coating. He experimented first with starch and then diluted egg white (albumen). The dried plate was then sensitized by immersing it in a solution of acidified silver nitrate which soaked into the albumen coating. This albumen-on-glass process[1] produced "remarkably pure and detailed images" but was nevertheless slower than the calotype. In 1851, Blanquart-Evrard published a paper on it, spreading the idea more widely. Le Gray also published a paper referring to the subject in 1850.[2] The process was very much in the public eye. Fox Talbot even tried to patent it in his own name in December 1849 and again in June 1851. Positives were printed both on the traditional salted paper and on a paper lightly coated with albumen introduced by Blanquart-Evrard in 1850.[3]

But in the same period the Englishman Scott Archer was experimenting with a more sensitive process, still using glass plates, which was to be the standard method in photography for several decades. It also opened up totally new aesthetic possibilities. In 1849, Scott Archer started coating his plates with collodion (a product already available from chemist's shops, consisting of nitrocellulose – guncotton – dissolved in alcohol and ether). This was then sensitized by immersing it in a solution of silver nitrate. The exposure had to be made while the plate was still wet.

◄ Gustave Le Gray, *Wave Breaking, Sète*, circa 1856–1859, Bibliothèque Nationale, Paris.

1. *Comptes rendus de l'Académie de Sciences*, October 25, 1847 and June 12, 1848.

2. L.-A. de Brébisson added honey which reduced exposure to "a few seconds" for portraits and views.

3. *Comptes rendus de l'Académie de Sciences*, May 27, 1850.

Collodion

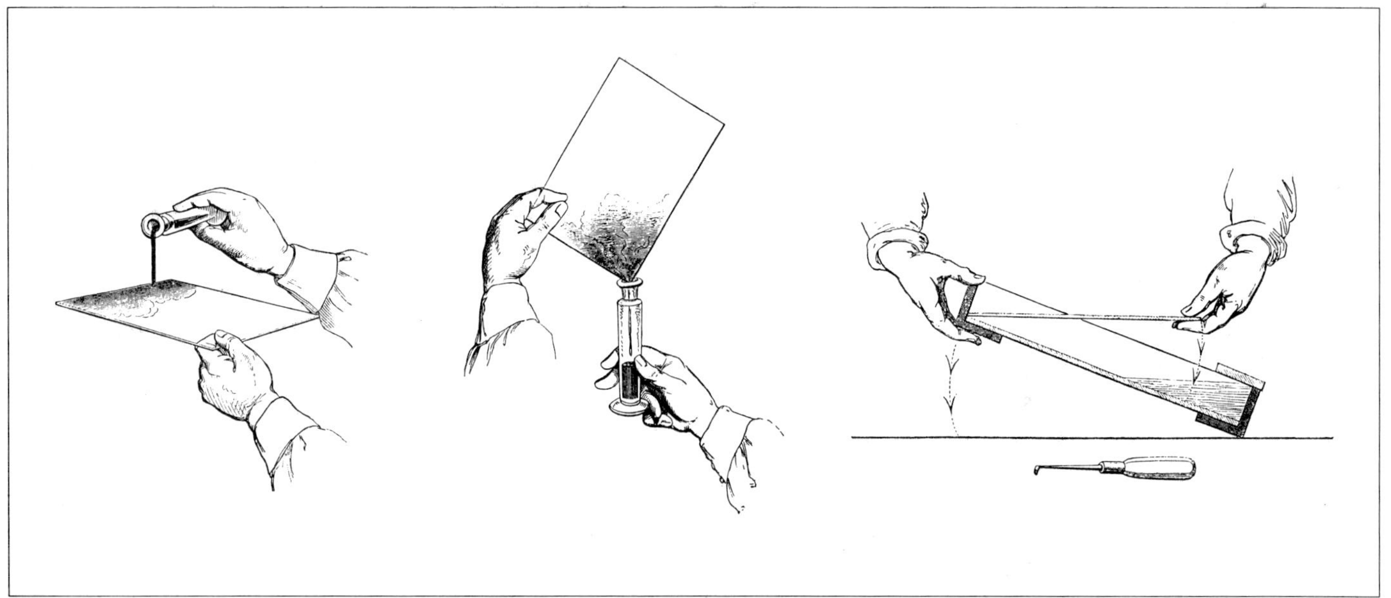

When Niépce de Saint-Victor developed the glass plate coated with albumen (1847) it did not appear to be sensitive enough. Even worse, after paper-negatives, the plates seemed tricky to prepare. In about 1849, to get round these difficulties, Gustave Le Gray suggested using collodion. However, it was an Englishman, Scott Archer (1813–1857), who, in 1851, was to come up with a practical method which was to supersede all others. This was the wet-collodion process.

Guncotton, a powerful explosive, (invented in 1846 and made by soaking cotton cellulose in nitric acid), was dissolved in a solution of ether and alcohol. The result was a syrupy emulsion which adhered to glass. With the addition of potassium or ammonium iodide this then became "photographic collodion". Each photographer would prepare it in his own way, carrying out a series of highly intricate steps as quickly as possible.

The glass plate is washed in a mixture of pumice and alcohol. The iodized collodion is poured over the plate, which the photographer tilts carefully in each direction to ensure a completely even coating. A certain amount of manual dexterity is needed for this, as is a degree of muscular strength when handling large-format plates.

The plate is left to dry in yellow light for a short while. Using a rod, it is then immersed in a bath of 12 parts water to one part silver nitrate. As soon as the plate takes on a creamy-white color (after about three minutes), it must be drained and partially dried. While still wet, it is inserted into a special plate holder inside the camera and exposed for a few seconds.

Once the exposure has been made, the photographer develops the plate by pouring a solution of ferrous sulphate or pyrogallic acid over it. The plate is washed and the image fixed using sodium thiosulphate (commonly known as hypo) or potassium cyanide. It is then dried and given a protective coating of varnish. A positive proof is then obtained by making a contact print on paper which has been sensitized with silver chloride.

Fast exposure gave good contrast and subtleties of tonality. The process offered the public fair-quality portraits at a reasonable price. On the other hand, the number of steps involved in the process meant that the equipment was heavy and bulky, making outdoor photography troublesome.

The use of collodion on a glass negative also led to a spin-off known as the ambrotype (another of Scott Archer's inventions) and to the ferrotype or tintype, which was patented by Hannibal L. Smith in the United States in 1856. These variants were extensively used in portraiture.

Jean-Claude Gautrand

Under good conditions, exposure times could be shortened to as little as one second. The use of collodion, or the wet-plate process, was not patented and from 1851 the method spread.[4] In the same year, Blanquart-Evrard set up his "photographic printing press" in Lille, turning out mass-produced original photographs from paper negatives until the business went bankrupt in 1855.

The glass negative resolved a number of problems that had beset photography from its early years. It substantially reduced exposure times – opening the way to portraiture. Detail was captured far better and there was greater nuance of light and shade.

There was much debate at the time about the aesthetic advantages of the calotype process. Its slightly blurred and grainy effect was considered to possess a more "pictorial" quality (in other words it was closer to the look and feel of a drawing). The new technique drew on and improved the main strengths of the daguerreotype – accuracy, sharpness, clear outlines, life-like quality. These have practically become synonymous with "true" photography, or at least its academic study.

Despite this, the glass negative still fell short of the absolute ideal that photographers of the day were seeking. To begin with, it was not easy to get a uniform coating of collodion onto the plate.

4. "On the Use of Collodion in Photography", in *The Chemist*, no. 2, March 1851, p. 257.

Even then, it had to be sensitized immediately. Traveling photographers had to carry around chemicals, water, and accessories, not to mention the glass plates themselves. Paradoxically, unlike Le Gray's dry-waxed paper process, the new process was moving away from reducing the amount of materials required and separating the steps involved (preparing the sensitized support and making the exposure). At this time, only contact prints were made since the technique of negative enlargement had not yet been introduced. Nevertheless, in the 1850s there was a passion for bigger prints (frequently 30 x 40 cm or more) which, of course, meant that the negative itself had to be large. Clearly, this did not make transport or handling any easier.[5]

However, at the start of the 1850s, a number of factors came together which boosted the popularity of the glass negative, to the detriment of its paper counterpart. It was clear at once that much was at stake, as was illustrated by a famous trial held in London (1854). Talbot held the calotype patent. He sued a photographer called Laroche (a pseudonym used by Silvester) for using the collodion process. Laroche was backed by the liberal and progressive lobby, including Roger Fenton.[6] Talbot laid claim to Scott Archer's method on the basis that it employed the general negative/positive principle, as well as developing and printing, which were already part of the calotype process. He ignored fundamental differences in the materials used. Even though the (lay) judge appeared alienated by the technical arguments, he ruled against Talbot and dismissed the suit. Scott Archer's process was therefore recognized as autonomous and "different" enough to slip through Talbot's grasp. In Britain at least, the future of photography was decided in that courtroom since developments for years to come might have been fettered by patents, just as had happened to the calotype in the past. The basic principle of photography as a free enterprise (since it had indeed been "given to the world" in the form of the daguerreotype in 1839) did not, then, become a legal reality until 1854.

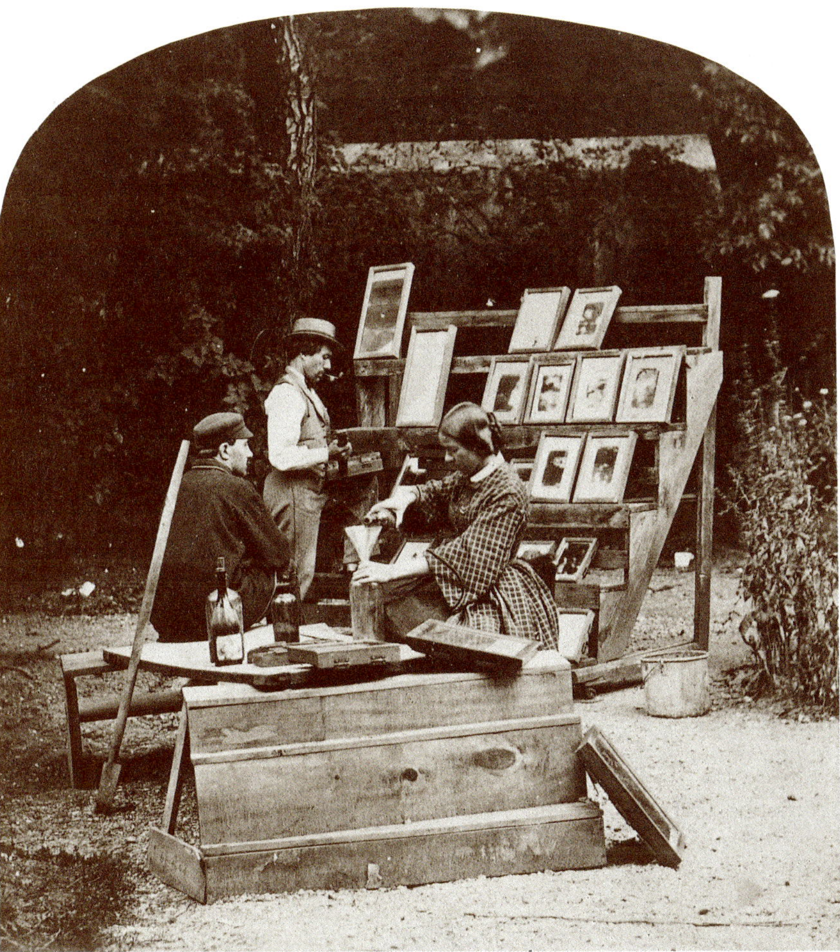

Printing photographic proofs in the open air
(from glass-negatives, contacts in a printing frame), image from a stereoscopic, circa 1860, private collection.

Other things then occurred which were to establish photography in its own right, something its practitioners had been attempting for some years. It was, however, the new glass negative technique that benefited most from the change, especially in view of the rapid decline of the calotype.

Photography gains recognition

At the Bibliothèque Nationale in Paris, the establishment in 1851 of the obligatory legal deposit of photographs, because of their similarity to prints, set the seal of legitimacy on photography, putting it on a similar footing to its rivals (painting, printing, engraving). At the same time, it also afforded copyright protection and rights for all photographs sold. In 1851, the Société Héliographique was founded in Paris, to be replaced in 1854 by the Société Française de Photographie. Similarly, a Photographic Society was set up in London in 1853. They both encouraged the spread of a practice which in France and

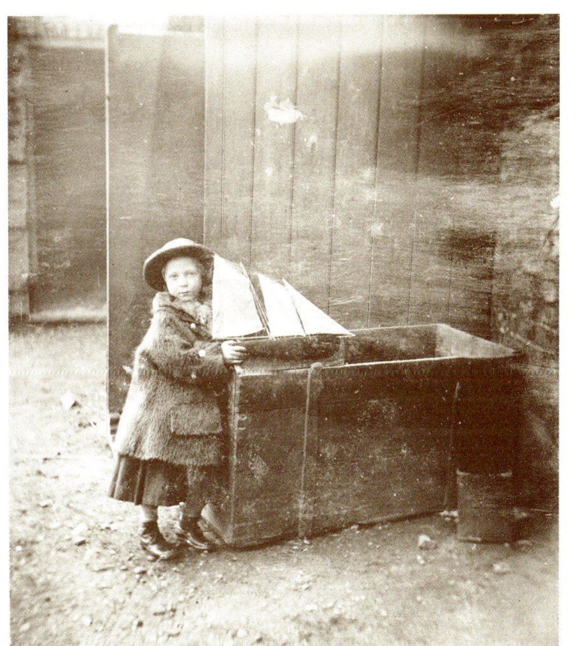

◀ J. B. Dancer,
Portrait of One of His Children,
ambrotype,
circa 1857,
University of Texas, Austin.

5. The Bisson brothers shot to fame when they submitted a view measuring 122 x 77 cm (*Pavillon de l'Horloge, the Louvre*) to the French Academy of Science on June 25, 1855.

6. H. J. P. Arnold, *W. H. Fox Talbot: Pioneer of Photography and Man of Science*, London, Hutchinson Benham, 1977, pp. 199 ff.

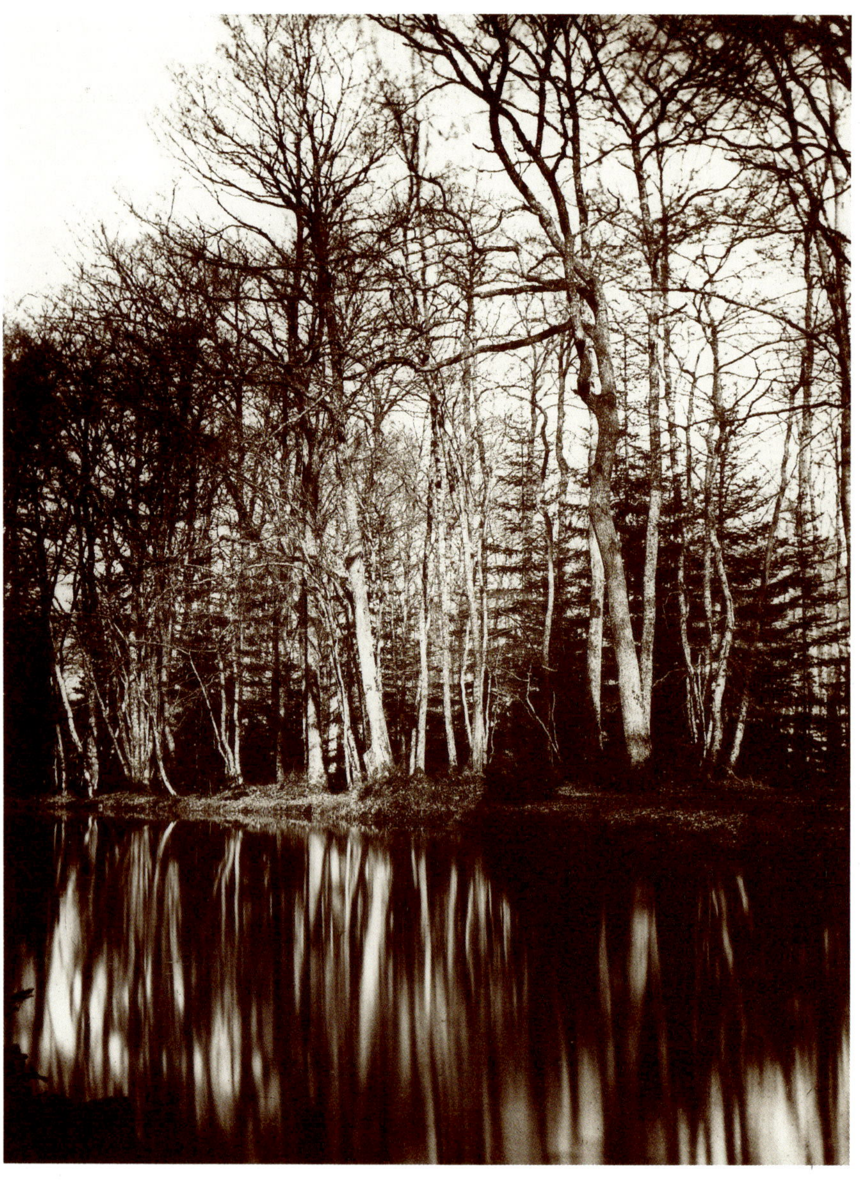

LOUIS-ALPHONSE DE BRÉBISSON, *Study of Trees and Reflections,* circa 1855, Archives Photographiques, Paris.

Britain was moving out of a fairly private phase into the public domain. It was during this transition that glass became the most common negative support (in North America the daguerreotype lasted far longer).[7] A number of magazines started to appear in connection with the fledgling associations (*La Lumière, Bulletin de la Société Française de Photographie, Journal of the Photographic Society*). These, and countless other works and manuals,[8] popularized different techniques. They were not simply setting out to play at chemistry, but were aimed at better adapting techniques to the subject and circumstances of a given exposure.

At this time, photography was still very much a craft – slightly shrouded in secrecy, perhaps, but open to improvements or suggestions, an area where anyone could impose their own personal stamp on the creation of images that were deemed to be "mechanical". For instance, the collodion on glass negative was quickly adapted to suit "while-you-wait" portraiture, especially by traveling photographers. The negative was bleached and mounted on a black background, thus appearing as a positive image. This was the ambrotype which was often confused – deliberately or not – with the daguerreotype, whose clients it gradually stole. The ferrotypes (or tintypes) produced by traveling photographers worked on a similar principle: a thin negative was laid down directly on a tin support coated in black paint.

During the 1850s several factors worked in photography's favor. One was the stable political situation and economic prosperity enjoyed by both France and Britain (Victoria had been crowned in 1837; Napoleon III became Emperor in 1852). Other factors at play in these countries were their constitutions, exploitation of colonial empires, and the frenzied pace of industrial and technological development and the spread of manufactured goods. There were also the attempts to rationalize town and city planning (especially in Paris). Broad avenues were built, transport improved, and street lighting and sewerage introduced, after which everything was enhanced by fountains and open vistas. This complex infrastructure improved the comfort of city-dwellers. Photography was considered a modern "invention" – along with battleships, diving suits, Volta's battery, electrical machines, the telegraph, and anesthetics.[9] As such, it played its part in the onward march of technical progress and "civilization".

The very status of photography (this term was adopted once and for all during the 1850s) was shifting. This was due both to the attitude taken by the authorities and the choices made by the public. Together, they boosted the institutional and commercial importance of photography. For the first time, it was included in art exhibitions. Countless technical shows charting the progress of materials used and illustrating the appearance of new products and processes prove how much photography was growing in popularity. We can see that photography had gained a foothold in the upper echelons of industrial and artistic production. Photographers knew that the social status of their "art" depended upon it being accepted among the fine arts rather than industrial arts and crafts. The Great Exhibition of 1851 was staged in London to show industrial products from all nations. Photography was included in the class of "Philosophical Instruments" in the "Machines" section.

Relations between photography and fine art were not improved by the 1855 Exposition Universelle held in Paris. "Despite all efforts, photography was firmly kept out of the inner sanctum, the pavilion on Avenue Montaigne" (where paintings, sculpture and engravings were housed, in other words the Salon).[10] It found itself relegated to the other exhibition site, the

7. Daguerre's death in 1853 passed almost unnoticed, even among "photographic" circles.

8. E. de Valicourt, *Nouveau Manuel complet de photographie sur métal, sur papier et sur verre*, Paris, Roret, 1862.

9. L. Figuier, *Les Merveilles de la science, ou description populaire des inventions modernes*, Paris, Furne, Jouvet et Cie, 4 vols, 1867–1870.

10. L. Figuier, *La Photographie au Salon de 1859*, Paris, Hachette, 1860, p. 2.

11. *Ibid.*

Industry Pavilion on the Champs-Elysées. It was not until 1859 that photographers were (almost) satisfied. The Salon des Beaux-Arts itself was housed inside the Industry Pavilion and "the Museum Commissioners settled for a compromise: they placed the photography section right next to the exhibition of paintings and engravings, but made separate entrances for the two. In other words, they spelled out the distinction."[11] The photographic display was organized by the Société Française de Photographie, which had already mounted its own shows in the Rue Drouot gallery in 1855, and in Le Gray's gallery at 35 Boulevard des Capucines in 1857. Nevertheless, it had still not quite succeeded in gaining the acceptance it wanted for the new artistic medium.

The transparent image

Did the use of glass plates create its own aesthetic? The new type of negative support certainly contributed to substantial changes in the way photography was approached. These were not limited to the process itself or to the practices and customs of the practitioners involved. What also came into play was the mental attitude with which the photographer approached reality, how he conceived what could and had to be done to obtain an image. In effect, the "philosophy" of the calotype had more or less turned paper negatives into an obstacle since they received an impression in light, fixed it, and absorbed it to make an image that was intuitively understood as a semi-opaque print. On the contrary, the "new" photography on glass introduced (unknown to those involved) transparency into the medium.

This transparency was as much in the material sense as in any subjective meaning. In terms of image, what appeared on the glass-negative was a thin light brown-yellow transparent coating of collodion carrying the image. At the same time, the support used in printing (albumen paper) was thinner and less grainy since the albumen made it glossy and shiny. By about 1855, the photographic print – by then commonly known as a "photograph" – produced from a glass negative was really a new, fairly standardized "object", a far cry from the matte finish of the salted-paper print and its colored variants (green-blue as well as red) at the heart of the photographic virtuosity of people like Le Secq or Le Gray.

Disdéri,
Marbles,
1853,
Bibliothèque Nationale, Paris.

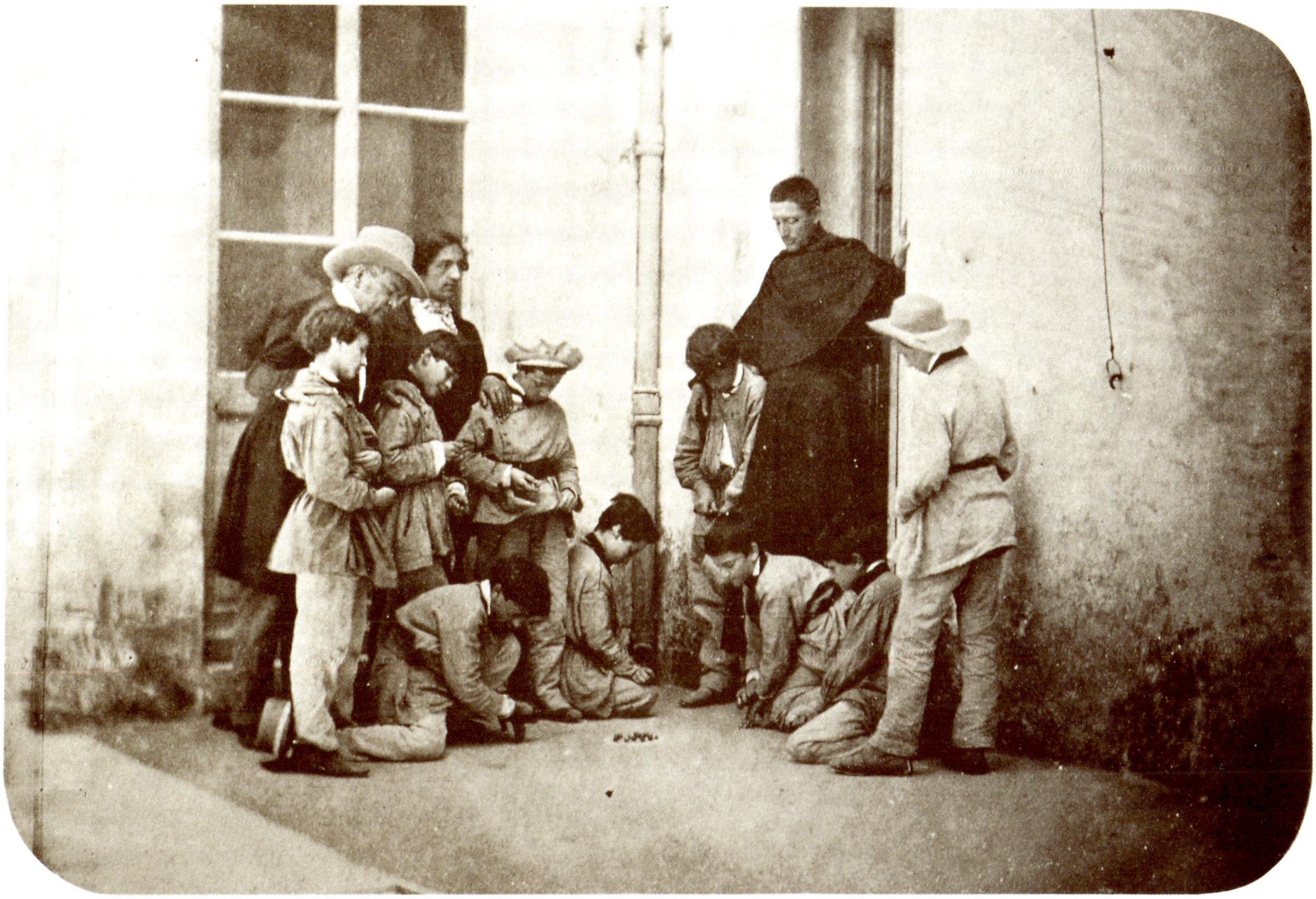

Photographic societies

The growing interest in photography led the Baron de Montfort to set up the Société Héliographique [Heliographic Society] in January 1851. The association, formed for "purely artistic and scientific" purposes, was made up of "men dedicated to the study and practice of the art and science [of photography]". The Society's first president was Baron Gros, who was flanked by Hippolyte Bayard, Becquerel, Niépce de Saint-Victor, Durieu, and Ziegler. Among the first members were Le Gray, Le Secq, the scholar Regnault, the optician Chevalier, the painter Delacroix, and the critic Francis Wey. One of the first things the Society did was to launch a journal, *La Lumière*, to make a major contribution to the success and propagation of photography.

In Britain, the first exhibition dedicated exclusively to photography was opened on December 22, 1852 at the Royal Society of Art. This, in turn, gave birth, in January 1853, to the Photographic Society of London, later to become the Royal Photographic Society (R.P.S.), whose headquarters are now in Bath.

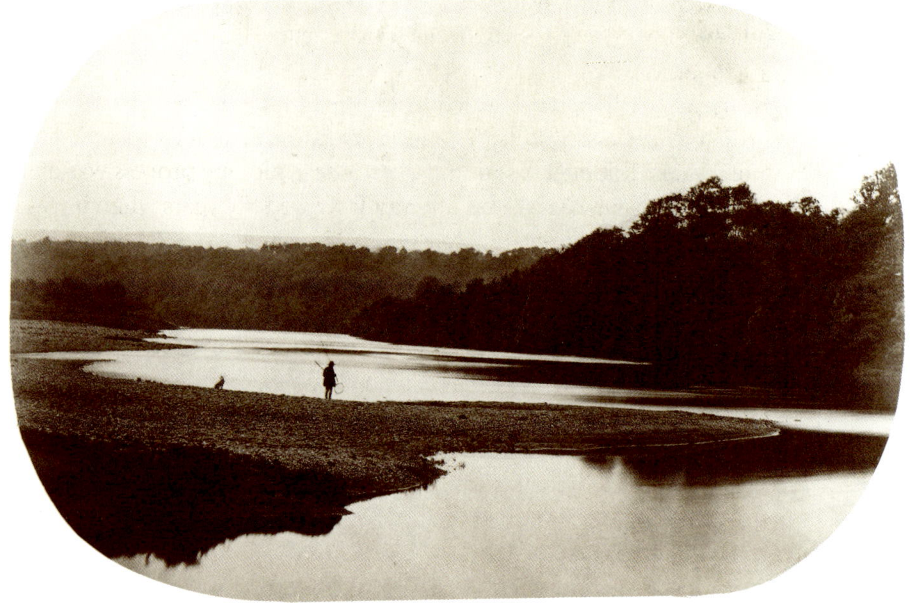

Roger Fenton,
Down the Ribble near Ribchester,
1858–1859, Royal Photographic Society, Bath.

The first honorary secretary of the Society was Roger Fenton, who went to Paris to see how the Heliographic Society worked.

On November 15, 1854, the Société Héliographique became the Société Française de Photographie [French Photographic Society] or S.F.P. Its first president, Victor Regnault, a member of the French Academy of Science and a director of the Sèvres factory. published an independent bulletin and staged exhibitions. The first exhibition was held in 1855 at the Society's headquarters (11 Rue Drouot). It covered the early days of photography and became the foundation of a collection whose importance following continued to grow over the years.

In Austria the first society was formed in 1861 and the following year the Photographic Society of Philadelphia was established in the United States.

The S.F.P. was a place where discoveries and technical improvements were unveiled. It also collected works by the pioneers of photography. It fought to have photography included in the Exposition des Beaux-Arts (1859). It was also a forum where papers were read. We should mention Dagron's paper (1864) on microphotography, L. Ducos du Hauron and Charles Cros (1869) on three-color images, and others on Lumière's cinematography (1895).

Toward 1895, the two societies (the S.F.P. and the R.P.S.) were thrown into disarray when the Pictorialists broke away. After the Second World War, however, they both played an important role in the rediscovery of early photography and its history. This, however, has given rise to conservation problems similar to those encountered by museums. They publicize their heritage through exhibitions and publications.

Among others, Roger Fenton and Alvin Langdon Coburn left legacies to the R.P.S. Hippolyte Bayard and Demachy did the same for the S.F.P. This makes their collections a true reflection of the spontaneous nature of the associations. They are custodians of a more "private" history of the medium as well as of its public heritage.

Jean-Claude Gautrand

The new photographic images were a dark reddish-brown (sepia). They were more detailed – more an accurate replica of reality than a graphic interpretation of it. The subject appeared refined, as though viewed through (or on) a transparent surface, the only visible difference being that the photograph was monochrome. At the same time, photography lost the pictorial attractiveness of the calotype, where the materials used gave an effect similar to drawing (incidentally, the term "drawing" was still widely used for photographs around 1850).

The new medium no longer modified the structure of what one saw. Nor was there any longer a need for the interpretation or transformation which had made photography so close to pictorial "art". Now the eye could read even the tiniest detail and varying nuances of shade were faithfully transcribed. This gave photography its independence and its own identity. It affirmed its difference and no longer traded on appearances rivaling the fine arts. Nonetheless, for many years to come, photography would still be reproached for its scientific nature, its objective virtues, its ability to automatically register the constant changes of light as well as for the exact way it portrayed the forms it captured. By around 1855, the glass negative had been adopted practically everywhere. This then became the hallmark of photography. The resulting image was sometimes rather stark but it provided an imprint of reality. It captured the light emitted by objects, surfaces, and textures without interpreting it. It gave a degree of realism that the eye cannot attain in nature.

The immediacy of nature

Just as modernist ideas flourished in Europe and North America in the 1920s, to some extent we can speak of a "new look" that came in with the glass-negative technique and began to spread from 1853 onwards. As the way in which photographs were taken became freer and less restrictive, so the subjects too became more fluent and less constrained. Many photographers, and not just the lesser known ones, abandoned the calotype for collodion on glass. In France, these included Charles Nègre, Gustave Le Gray, the Bisson brothers, and Disdéri.[12] Others, however, declined to switch to a process which robbed them of the specifically pictorial qualities of the calotype, and preferred to give up photography altogether (Henri Le Secq stands out among them). Throughout Europe – Britain, Germany, Italy, Spain – and soon after in Brazil, Mexico and so on, the photographic profession boomed.

The expansion happened along two main lines: on the one hand there was the studio photographer, tied to one locality where his customers visited him; on the other, there was the traveling photographer, careful to provide the world with real, non-interpretative images of things (see the following chapters). It was not uncommon, however, for the same person to alternate between the two types of activity, all the more so since the by now universally used wet-plate process was supplemented by the "dry plate" variation whose only drawback was that it needed a

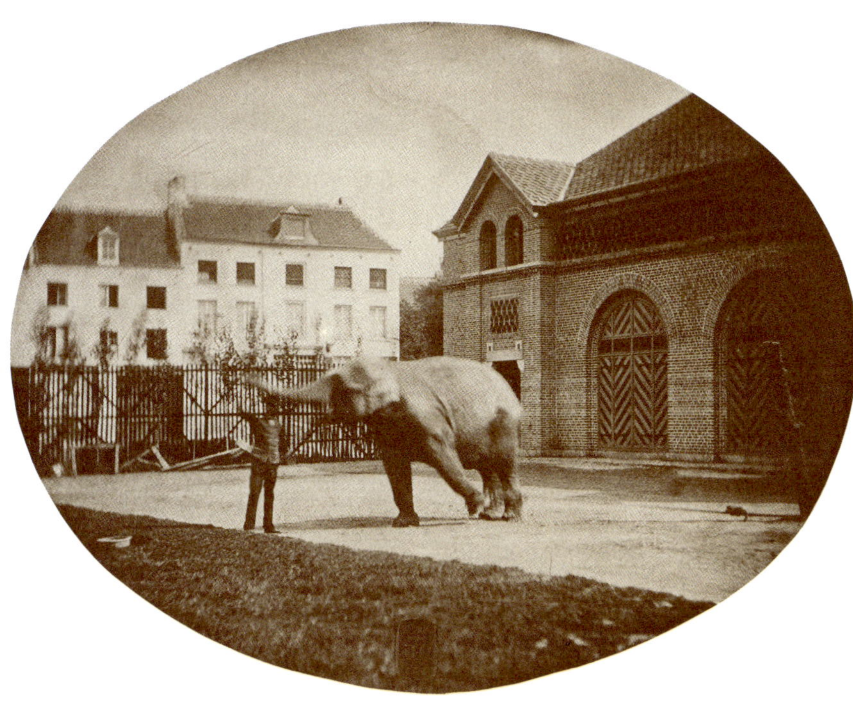

L. P. T. Dubois de Néhaut,
Miss Betzy the Elephant,
Brussels Zoo, 1854,
Museum voor Fotografie,
Antwerp.

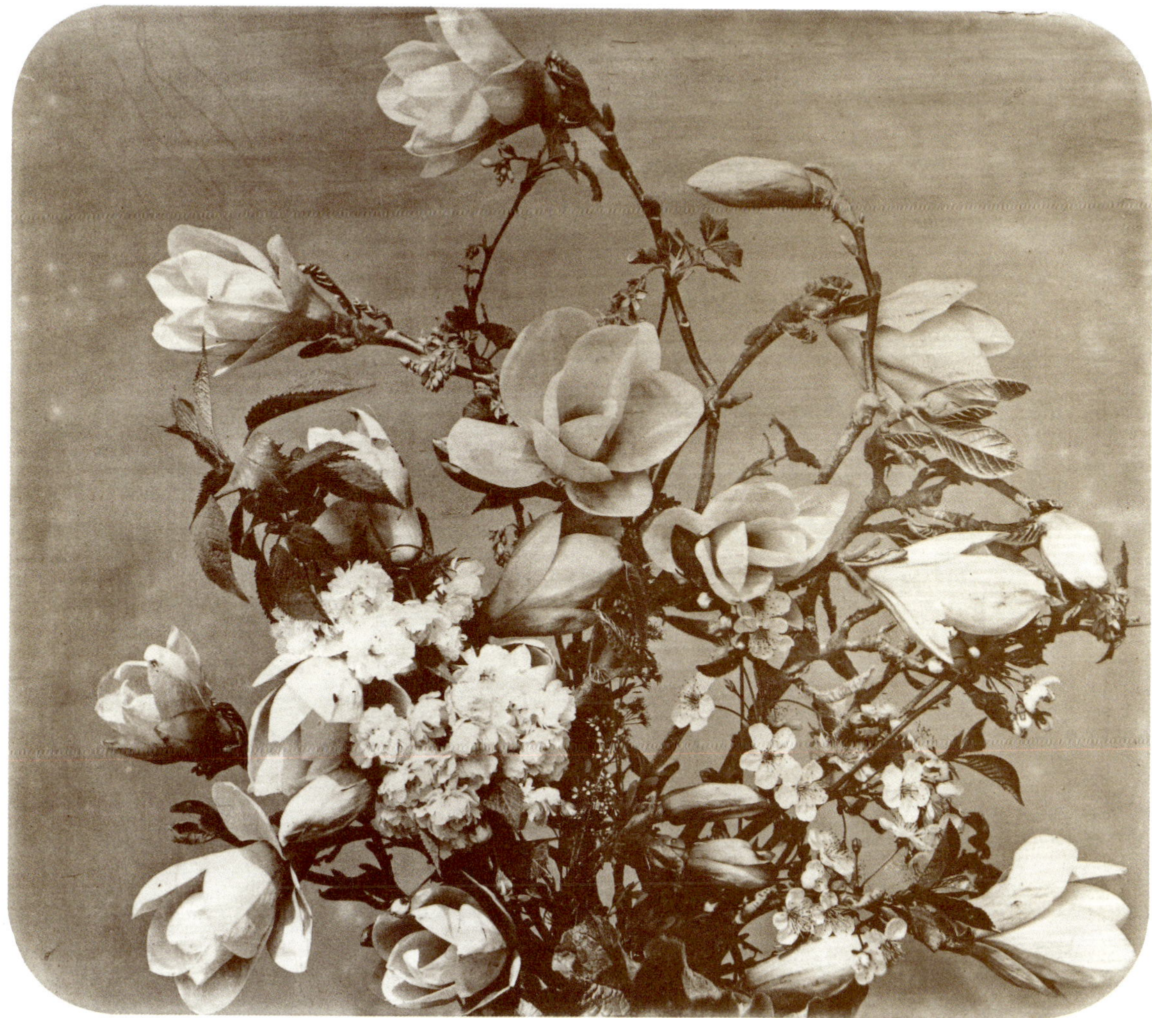

Adolphe Braun,
Flower Study,
circa 1854–1855,
Bibliothèque de la Ville,
Colmar.

12. As well as A. Davanne, C. Marville, L.-A. Humbert de Molard, and L.-A. de Brébisson, who wrote the *Traité complet de photographie sur collodion*, 1855.

The cliché-verre

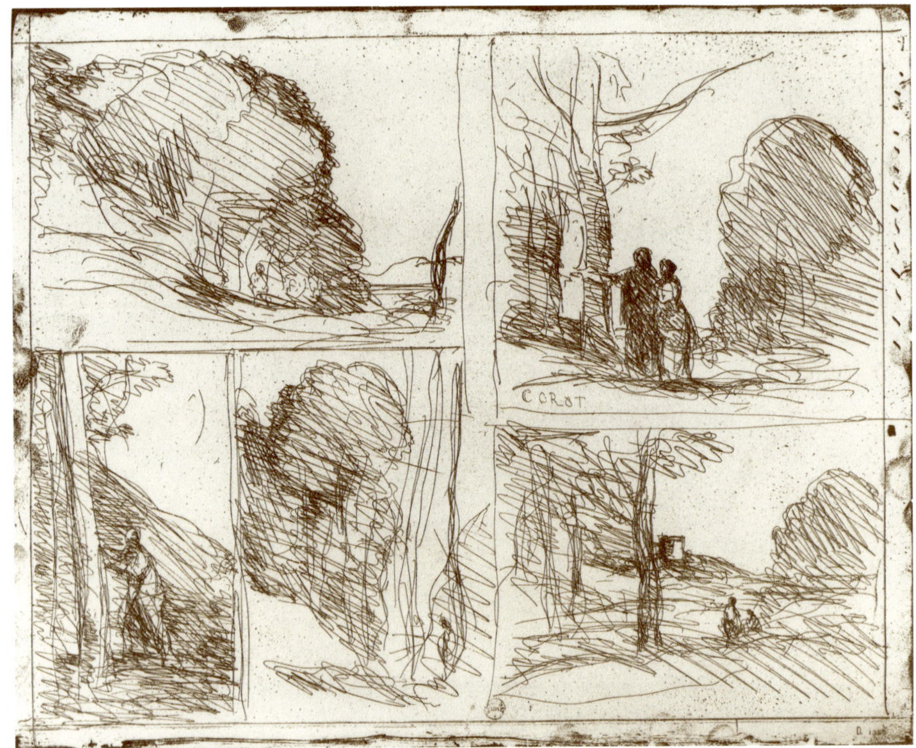

Camille Corot, *Five Landscapes,* cliché-verre, 1856, Bibliothèque Nationale, Paris.

The invention of the cliché-verre, like that of most photo-mechanical processes, came about when photographic techniques were melded with traditional ways of reproducing images. This allowed a photographic print to be made from a drawing done directly onto the support normally used for the negative.

The concept is simple. A glass plate is covered with a light but opaque coating. A black surface is placed underneath the plate then, using a stylus, the artist draws on the plate. The lines of the drawing immediately stand out in black against the light background. This also provides a good idea of what the finished image will look like. The plate is then treated like an ordinary photographic negative. Multiple positive prints of the original drawing can be made on photographic paper. The result is similar to etching but allows a greater fluidity of line.

Talbot, Fielding, Barthélemy Pont, and Hunt all claimed to have invented it. In January 1856, Eugène Cuvelier, a painter and photographer from Arras, revealed that the method had been used since 1853 by a group of artists which had gathered around Constant Dutilleux. The best-known figure in the group was Corot. From 1855 onwards, clichés-verre were produced mainly in France, by the Arras group and later also at Barbizon. The main practitioners were Corot, Millet, Daubigny, and Théodore Rousseau. Landscapes, undergrowth, and bucolic and rustic scenes were the main sources of inspiration. They were, indeed, very suited to the rapidity of stylus drawing.

The success of the cliché-verre among art-lovers was very minor. It had neither the unique character of the drawing nor the pedigree of an engraving. These hybrid images failed to attract any interest at the time they were produced (roughly from 1853 to 1875). It was not until after the First World War that art historians even gave them a mention.

Invented by photographers but made by artists during a period distinguished by intense research, the cliché-verre seemed neither to challenge the artist's talents nor to match the modern triumphs of photography. Perhaps it added nothing of worth. Nevertheless, it remains an object of curiosity on the sidelines of the debate about the advent of photography and in an area where little was at stake.

"Hand-drawn, light-printed" was the happy expression coined by Elisabeth Glassman[1] to describe the cliché-verre. It was an illustration of the climate of a time when old and new image-making techniques melded and were reciprocally enriched. Very often there was no real future for them, although the cliché-verre has enjoyed a revival in the last decade.

Sylvie Aubenas

1. Elisabeth Glassman and Marilyn F. Symmes, *Cliché-Verre: Hand-Drawn, Light-Painted: A Survey of the Medium from 1839 to the Present,* Detroit Institute of Arts, 1980.

longer exposure time (several minutes). This did not matter, however, if you were photographing buildings, still-lifes, etc. It was not long (Macpherson, Rome, 1856) before dry plate methods were perfected, using tannin, albumen or gelatin with a ready-to-use emulsion based on silver bromide. This was first sold by Bolton and Sayce in 1864. In 1867, the Liverpool Dry Plate and Photographic Company launched ready-prepared dry plates.

If we were to try to describe the new photographic images that emerged from the wet-collodion process, the most suitable epithets would be "from nature" or "from life" as well as the much used "studies from nature". This description is most frequently associated with nudes (Vallou de Villeneuve, Louis d'Olivier, Paul Berthier, Voland) and studies (Bilordeaux, Bolotte) and less often with views of places (Charles Soulier). From now on, anything that was mobile, anything that moved too much to be captured with the lengthy calotype exposure, anything that cried out to be captured in a natural manner, became a potential subject for photography. Henceforth, it was open to experiments of all kinds in an attempt to capture the fleeting moment.[13]

Although we cannot dogmatically assume that the trend was completely reversed, we must nevertheless acknowledge that the stilted poses which so often typified the calotypes that Blanquart-Evrard published now gave way to a feeling of freedom. The new photographs conveyed the impression of being in the presence of their subjects. For their part, the subjects no longer turned their back on the camera or looked

13. A. Bertsch, who wrote *Notice sur l'emploi du collodion* (1852), perfected the process to such an extent that in 1855 he suggested views could be taken in 1/4 of a second.

away from it. On the contrary, they acknowledged the presence of the photographer by looking straight into his lens.

Charles Nègre was among the first to adopt collodion-glass (roughly in the summer of 1853) while he was shooting "life" studies – busy scenes of everyday life on the streets. His problem was getting a readable, tangible image. His subjects did not know they were being photographed and moved too quickly (like those in his market scenes shot in 1850–1852). He had used a special optical system to shoot paper-negatives for his series *Chimneysweeps Walking*; late 1851 – early 1852. This was hailed as "instantaneous" photography and was greeted by critical acclaim. However, it was clearly still troubled by the artifice demanded by exposure times and the natural quality that walking has in real time. The two remained resolutely incompatible so long as exposure times could not be reduced. During 1853, Charles Nègre produced *The Stonemason* and *The Roofer*, two studies from nature on which he used the same optical technique combined with the increased sensitivity of collodion. "M. Nègre was not content with the beautiful results he got from paper photography but wanted to do as much with collodion. As with a painter, the rapidity of this process gave him the means of shooting groups and attitudes as they occur. He was thus able to immortalize them in precious little sketches," wrote Ernest Lacan. The critic then went on to hazard a technical point: "The rapidity is such that a portrait is taken in three seconds. In other words, it is practically instantaneous."[14] Indeed, the roofer is aware of what is going on and is not at all inhibited by it. He smiles as he looks at the photographer, giving us a glimpse of his mobile features, like *Pipers* which followed, or *Navvies Resting*.

At about the same time, Adolphe Braun, a fabric designer and newcomer to photography, put together "a collection of studies intended for artists using flowers in decorative motifs" (300 plates). Working in Dornach, near Mulhouse, his collection was aimed principally at designers employed by the local mills. It contained photo-

GUSTAVE LE GRAY, *The Sun at Zenith in Normandy*, 1856–1859.
▼

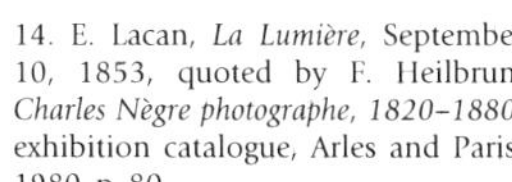
14. E. Lacan, *La Lumière*, September 10, 1853, quoted by F. Heilbrun, *Charles Nègre photographe, 1820–1880*, exhibition catalogue, Arles and Paris, 1980, p. 80.

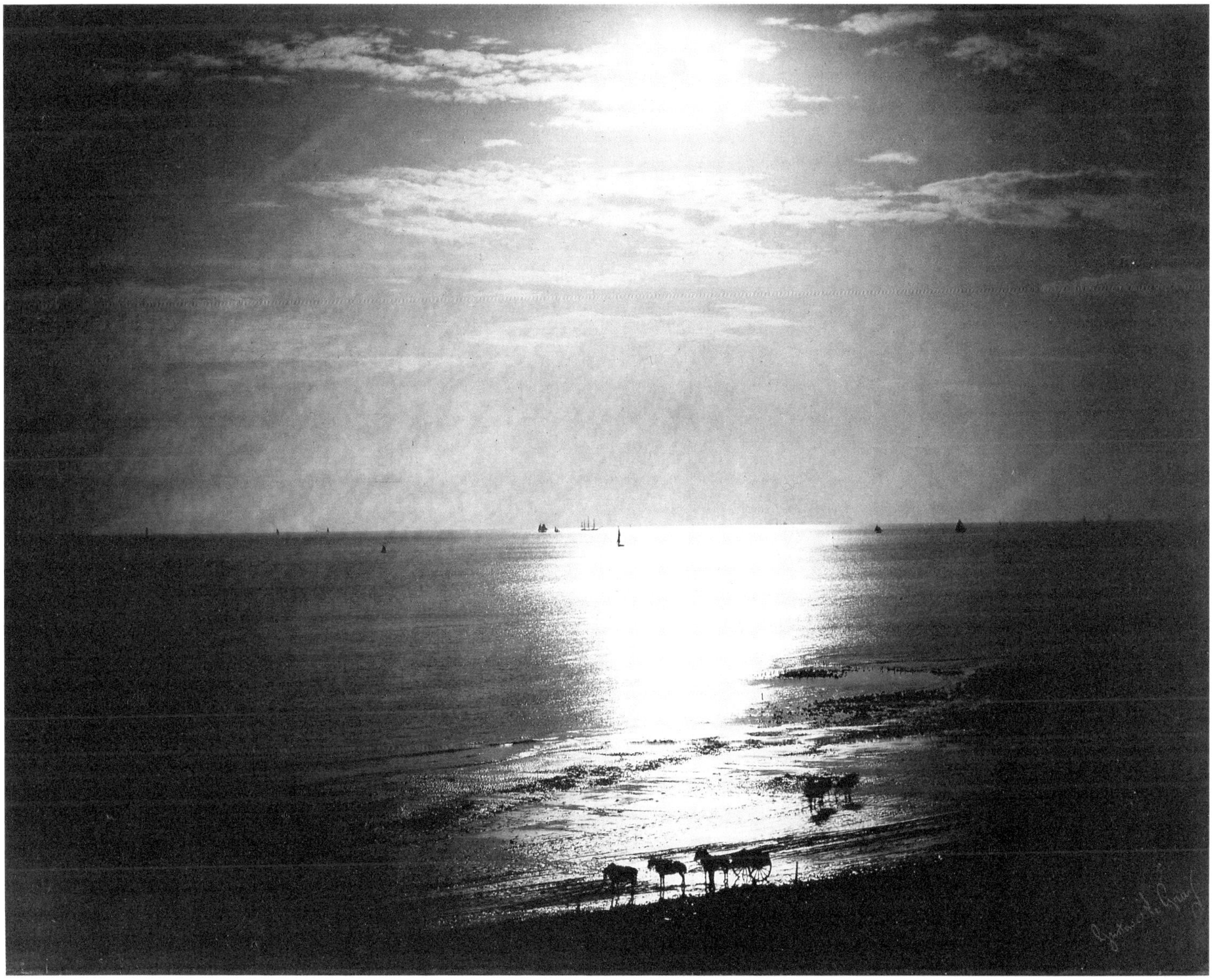

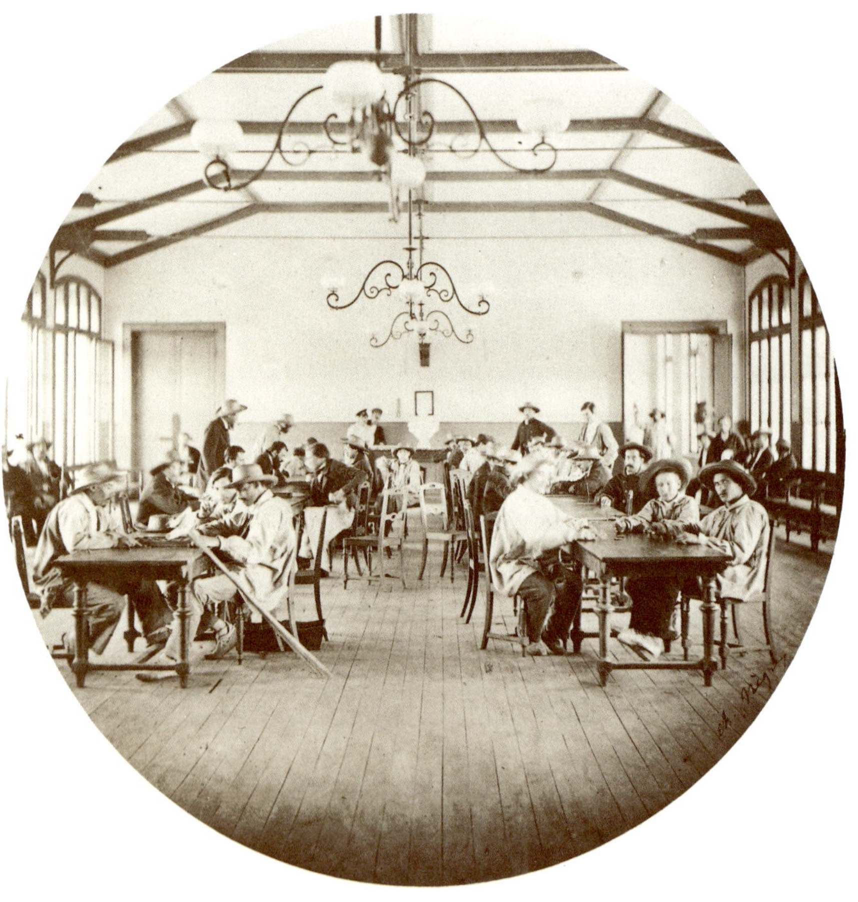

Charles Nègre, ***Vincennes Asylum, Canteen,*** 1859, Bibliothèque Nationale, Paris.

graphic "designs" of a variety of floral arrangements and natural flowers. It was much admired at the 1855 Exposition Universelle where it won a gold medal. It was considered both an adjunct to the applied arts (a trend which was boosted by a new method of teaching drawing) and the product of the art and sensibility of Braun himself. Even though the subjects were unquestionably static, people admired the sensuality of the textures, the softness of tones, which hinted at the missing color, and the play of reflections and of shiny or matte surfaces. "It is no longer just black and white as photographs were until not so long ago. M. Braun's photographs contain varying degrees of light and shade from the most vigorous tone right through to the lightest nuance. The most delicate objects, the finest things are portrayed with sharpness, purity, and mathematical accuracy that was never previously encountered in art."[15]

For his part, in December 1856 Gustave Le Gray was given an enthusiastic welcome in London (then in Paris in 1857) when he exhibited his "marine" studies. These were studies of the shoreline aimed at conveying something close to the presence of natural elements. This concept lent exceptional authority to the new process. In his large-format images (roughly 30 x 40 cm) Le Gray gave the impression of an instantaneity which can suddenly capture the impetuous movement of the waves or of boats passing by (*Wave Breaking*, 1856–59). He combined this with accurate and virtuoso images of backlit skies heavy with clouds or, in some of the calmer photographs, of the sky at sunset. All this was enhanced by simultaneous effects which photographers had never before achieved or even dreamed of. "Sailing ships in motion, the swell of the sea, clouds floating in the air, and the sun itself with its long rays of glory are all reproduced and fixed, instantly and simultaneously, with no sleight of hand, no tricks. This time, the boundaries of the possible have been attained. We are not at all surprised that these enchanting pictures have caused such a stir."[16] Despite Le Gray's protestations to the contrary, however, it has recently been established beyond all doubt that he obtained simultaneity in his prints by using two separate negatives – one for the sea, the other for the sky. These were then cleverly superimposed in the final print. They could also be swapped around to create a variety of images. This new technique enabled photographers to both "import" skies (for example, F. M. Lyte, C. Silvy, C. Soulier) and shoot studies of clouds showing the ephemeral effects which are generally so difficult to capture (for example, C. Marville, 1857, E. Colliau, C. Macaire).[17]

The passion for studies from nature was induced by "instantaneous photography" – a strictly relative term, meaning about one second in the case of the wet-plate process. However, some photographers continued to shoot compositions of real-life scenes. Among them were F.-J. Moulin (*Painters in a Building, Hunter, Workers' Household*, 1853), Disdéri (*Marbles, Plowmen Eating, The Washerwoman, Physics*, 1853)[18] or Taupenot (*A Game of Boules*, 1855), as well as images of the usual transient *pifferari* (local characters captured for their picturesque qualities), and Louis d'Olivier's or Voland's nudes. There was also a great deal of interest in animals: "My animal subjects [...] groups of horses, dogs, peacocks, sheep, ducks, etc." (Disdéri, 1857). In Britain, the Count de Montizon photographed a sleeping hippopotamus at the zoo while Dilwyn Llewelyn took pictures of cranes.

Adrien Tournachon (younger brother of Nadar) owed his technique to Le Gray – and may have passed it on to his elder brother who used it so successfully. In 1856, Adrien took a series of photographs of prize cattle at the agricultural fair which were used to produce lithographs.[19] Chevalier Dubois de Néhaut was working in Brussels in 1854 when he also shot some brief moments: a square during the September holidays, a train traveling into the sunset, an elephant in the zoo (which needed 12 attempts). He also photographed public holidays in July 1856.[20] In

15. Report published by Mulhouse Industrial Association, quoted by A. Rouillé, *La Photographie en France: textes et controverses, une anthologie*, 1816–1871, Paris, Macula, 1989, p. 199.

16. *Revue photographique*, February 5, 1857.

17. B. Marbot, *Quand passent les nuages*, Paris, Bibliothèque Nationale, 1988.

18. Author of *Manuel pratique de photographie sur collodion instantané* (Nîmes, 1853), he recommended reducing exposure time to two seconds: see A. McCauley, "A. E. Disdéri", in *Prestige de la photographie*, no. 5, November 1978, pp. 4-47, and *A. A. E. Disdéri and the Carte de Visite Portrait Photography*, New Haven and London, Yale University Press, 1985.

19. Baudement, *Les Races bovines au Councours universel agricole de Paris, en 1856: études zootechniques*, Paris, Imprimerie Impériale, 1861.

20. S. F. Joseph and T. Schwilden, *Le Chevalier L. P. T. Dubois de Néhaut: sa vie et son œuvre*, Antwerp, Crédit Communal, 1987.

1859, Charles Nègre again achieved one of the greatest successes of "real-life" photography with a series of plates taken in the Vincennes asylum. Despite being obliged to work in badly lit rooms and to have recourse to posed compositions – however briefly they were held – he managed to convey a sense of what life was like inside the asylum. This was emphasized by the way perspectives were staggered and light graded, giving an effect very close to what the eye sees.

After 1855, many people with an interest in photography set about making use of the glass negative's qualities for artistic or commercial ends. Indeed, it is not really possible to separate the two. It was at about this time that the idea of there being different "branches of photography" first appeared. As we shall see, these branches produced results as varied as they were unexpected, even though with hindsight we are lulled into the false belief that they were always obvious.

The contribution made by the collodion glass-negative, which remained in use for nearly 30 years (until about 1880), concerned the very nature of the photographic image. It gave the impression of being there as a spectator, looking directly at the subject and actually holding the little viewfinder and framing the entire image, the whole picture, within a proscribed, flat surface. The effects of light, the lively nature of the groups, and the apparently instant nature of the photographic record all combined to give an impression of a palpable reality that was constantly evolving.[21]

This was emphasized still further by the contemporary craze for the stereoscope. This invention could have been designed to be used by a peeping Tom, forcing the viewer's gaze to savor a thousand details in every scene, view or object in a way never before experienced. The viewer's eye was forced to become sharper and, because there was plenty of time to observe properly, it could linger in almost scientific inspection.

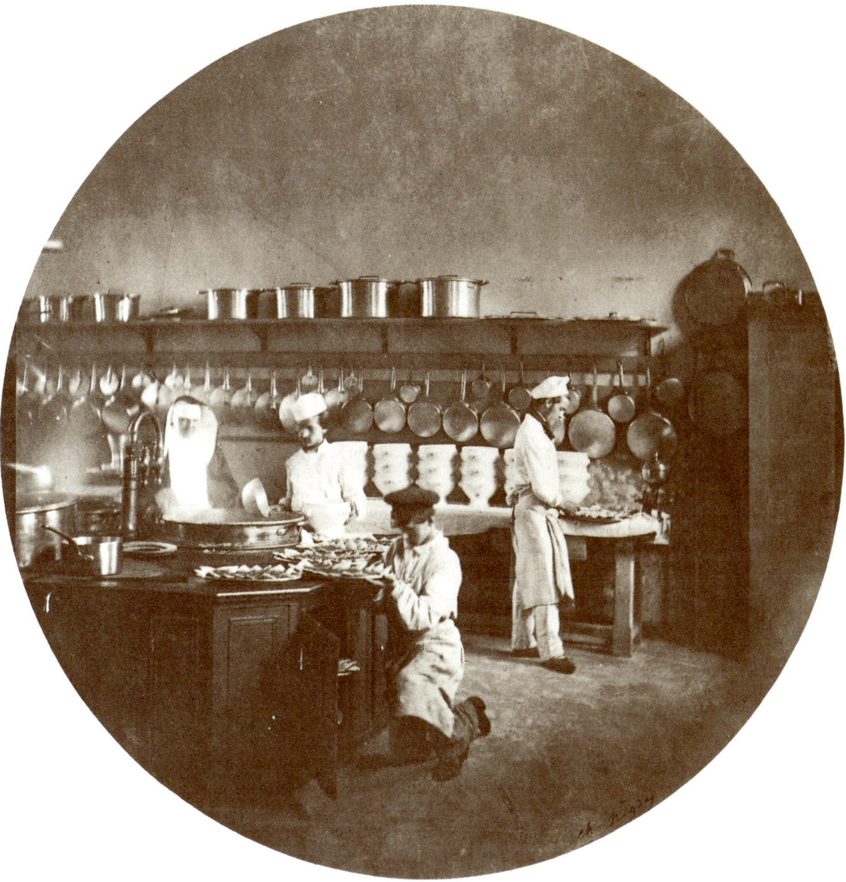

Charles Nègre, *Vincennes Asylum, the Kitchens,* 1859, Bibliothèque Nationale, Paris.

During the 1850s, photography underwent a major change. Its end-product was no longer considered industrial but had found its place among the fine arts of the Salon des Beaux-Arts. It accomplished this despite people's misgivings and without making any demeaning concessions to an aesthetic that was foreign to it. On the contrary, its position – slightly on the margin of things – allowed its status as a separate medium to remain intact. Photography may well have been criticized and it was often despised, but it also enjoyed a greater degree of freedom in which to act and propagate its message. Photographers tackled themes that were specifically photographic. They produced images which more often than not owed their graphic qualities and symbolic meaning solely to the use of the camera.

Thanks to its original function of providing an instant, transparent version of reality, photography was to shape the way we both represent and see things. As for lessons, it was to give (even to illustration) far more than it ever received. It very soon became ubiquitous. Painters, architects, engravers, and illustrators used it for their sketches; publishers and military strategists used it as part of their preparatory work; it provided a record of events in schools, towns, and entire nations. The photograph became the way we saw things, playing a decisive role. Even if it was still not properly praised in artistic circles, it was indirectly recognized by them.

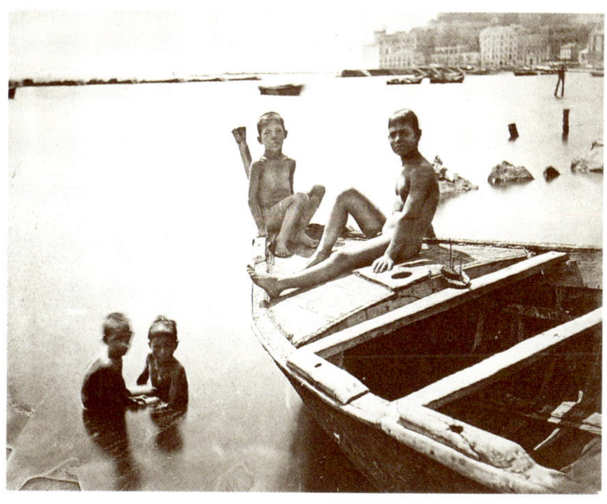

◀ C. Naya, (attributed), *Children Bathing,* circa 1860, private collection.

21. L. Figuier, *op. cit.* p. 59.

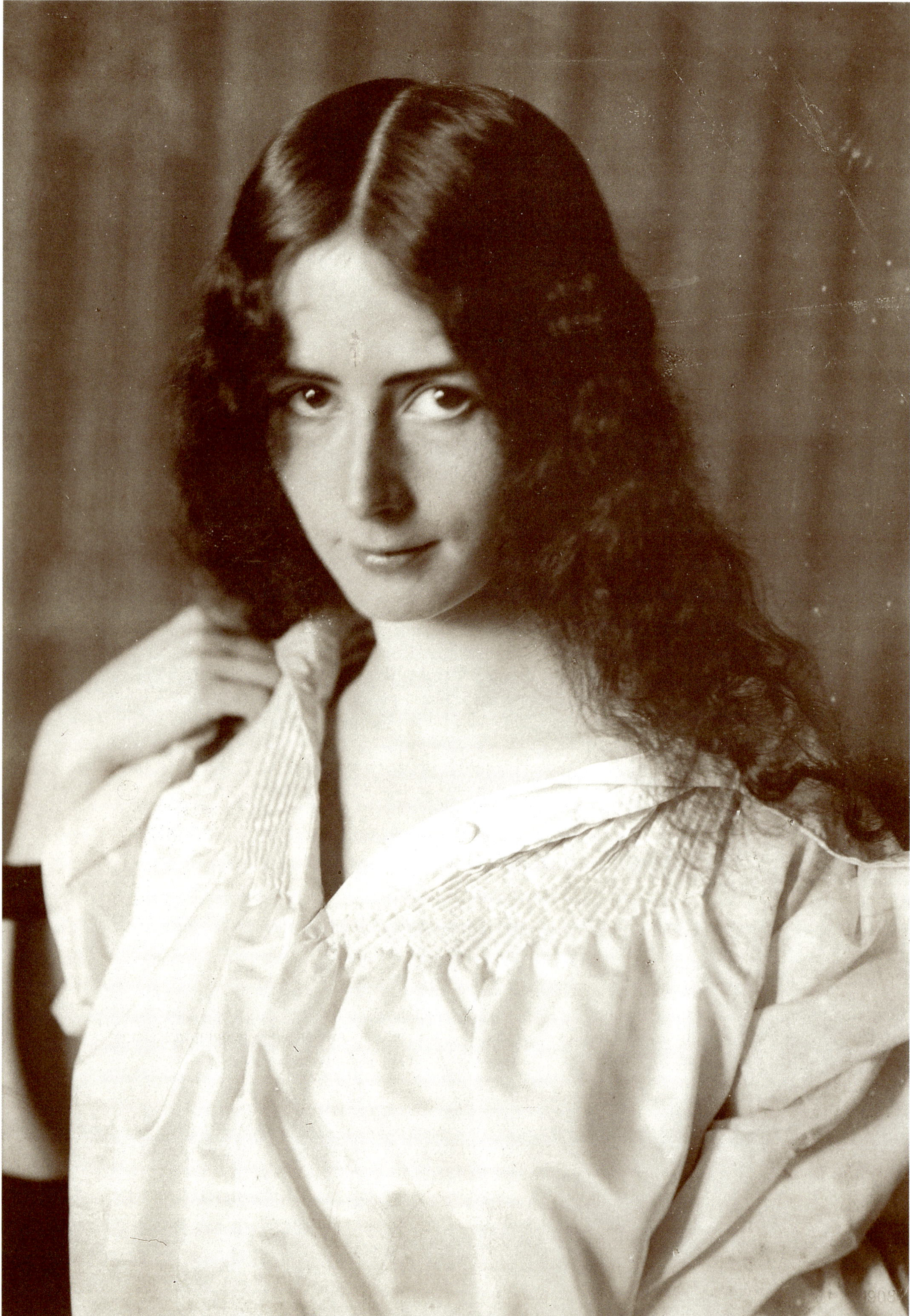

ALL KINDS OF PORTRAITS 6

The photographer's studio

Jean Sagne

During the 1850s, a completely new place where fashionable people congregated seemed to appear out of nowhere. This was the photographer's studio. It combined the attractions of a stroll along the boulevard with a visit to the theater. At the same time, the price, quality, and standard of a personal portrait were changing constantly. This meant that the narcissistic pleasures of possessing an image of oneself could be enjoyed by an ever wider public, just at a time when kings and princes were busy making sure everyone had pictures of them in an attempt to convey a sense of both authority and social stability.

In Paris around 1860 the entertainment district known as "the street of crime" (Boulevard du Temple and Boulevard Saint-Martin) was pushing further to the west. This area had been given its name because of the concentration of theaters which all served up a constant diet of melodrama. Alongside the theaters, another type of establishment was emerging – "the temple of photography" – whose close ties with the theater have never been properly understood. Night and day, theaters and photographic studios worked on the same principles and used the same tricks. However, what went on in the photographic studios of Disdéri, Mayer & Pierson, and, later, Nadar could well be described as bodily violence. It is no coincidence that studios were popularly referred to as "torture chambers". In 1839, when the daguerreotype first appeared, those few people who wanted their portraits taken had no qualms about sitting stock-still under the midday sun for up to a quarter of an hour. The images captured reveal the faces of true martyrs. By the time of Napoleon III's Second Empire, however, the number of people visiting the photographer had increased considerably. For a few seconds they were subjected to a process of petrifaction that was still an indispensable part of the photographer's art. Complete immobility was secured by the use of a number of accessories – including the head-supports that humorists depicted as instruments of torture. The resulting portraits were like deathmasks. The theater, too, frequently required actors to play dead. "Don't move!",[1] cried one forgetful photographer whom Abel Faivre cast in a morgue. Perhaps it is not just by chance that deathbed photography was so popular during the nineteenth century. Like those of a number of daguerreotypists, and even Nadar, Millet's advertisements offer home visits to take posthumous portraits.[2]

Photographers soon moved to premises on the boulevards. Their grandiose establishments vied with one another in ostentatious displays of wealth. The move, however, merely followed trends of the day. New building had already tempted historic names, including banks such as Crédit Lyonnais, theaters like the Vaudeville, and restaurants such as the Café Riche or the Grand Hôtel, to move in alongside the Chinese Baths, the Maison Dorée, Tortoni, and the Café Anglais. The area around the Palais-Royal had been the fashionable place to be seen during the splendors of the July Monarchy but over the years it had gradually gone out of fashion. The geographic shift of the city's nerve center did not spare photography which was going through major upheavals of another kind. The early daguerreotype portrait studios – run by people such as Chevalier, Legros, Sabatier, and Vaillat – had been concentrated in the Palais-Royal district. Their glass walls and roofs were very often tinted blue.[3]

In terms of production, however, daguerreotype studios struggled to produce more than a few thousand plates a year. The limitations inherent in the process (single plates which could not be

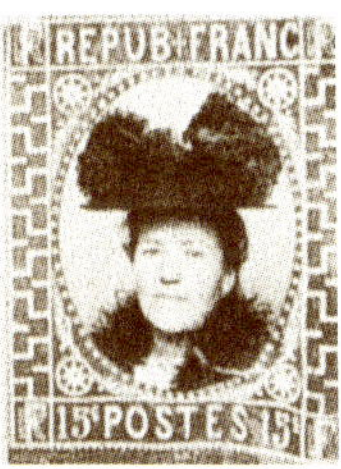

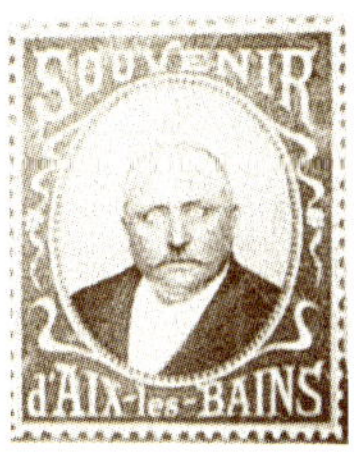

Photographic portraits using a postage-stamp format,
circa 1900,
private collection.

◀ Anton Blomberg,
Portrait of Cléo de Mérode,
1903,
France Debuisson Collection.

1. Disdéri was responsible for this formula which became the butt of so many jokes the humorists made about photography.

2. Many nineteenth-century celebrities, including Victor Hugo, Napoleon III, the Curé d'Ars (by C. Dolard), Maximilian I, and even Bernadette Soubirou, were photographed after death.

3. Like all the early techniques, daguerreotype plates were particularly sensitive to blue light. For this reason, blue-tinted glass was used to reduce exposure times.

At the photographer's studio

A heavy camera mounted on a tripod stood ready for the photographer. An armchair bristling with headrests awaited the sitter. Whatever the size of the studio, this layout never varied. The photographer, his head buried under a black focusing cloth, would face a client who was clamped into a dignified pose, as if they wanted to prove right the jibes by humorists from Daumier to Dubout. For over a century, the roles of photographer and sitter were thus fixed in the popular imagination. The photographer's workroom, at the heart of the whole studio, resembled a theatrical set erected in the middle of the props department. Around the sitter, white screens were used to model the light, channeled in through a series of curtains after entering through a large window. The studio was a self-contained capsule where all notions of time and space disappeared.

Within the photographer's studio as a whole, the workroom marked the frontier between two separate worlds. On the one hand there was the reception area which drew clients into the labyrinth, gradually stripping away contact with the real world and immersing them in a virtual world. The other side was the complete opposite. The world where portraits were created was filled with every conceivable contraption to conjure up illusions and weave deceptions. It was a world of shadow where the plates were prepared and developed, a dull blue-green universe, a variation on hell made dangerous by the toxic materials used. Before posing for the camera, clients would be shown to a room where mirrors were provided for them to check their hair. On the other side of the partition, assistants would be busy coating a glass plate with collodion before slipping it into the plate holder. These assistants worked in cramped conditions breathing in ether and alcohol vapors not properly extracted by the primitive ventilation systems. Meanwhile, comfortably seated in armchairs in the reception area, customers would leaf through albums littering the tables and compare notes on the celebrities they contained, admire works of art on the walls or puzzle over oddities displayed in glass cabinets.

The studios were places where contrasts were starkly black and white. They concealed sleights of hand and wizardry delivered with a whiff of sulphur. The commercial imperatives were based on flatter and human vanity. These came face to face with the tough laws of economics. History was to prove that the studios' existence was as precarious as the fragile glass walls that encased them and behind which the master photographers did their work.

Jean Sagne

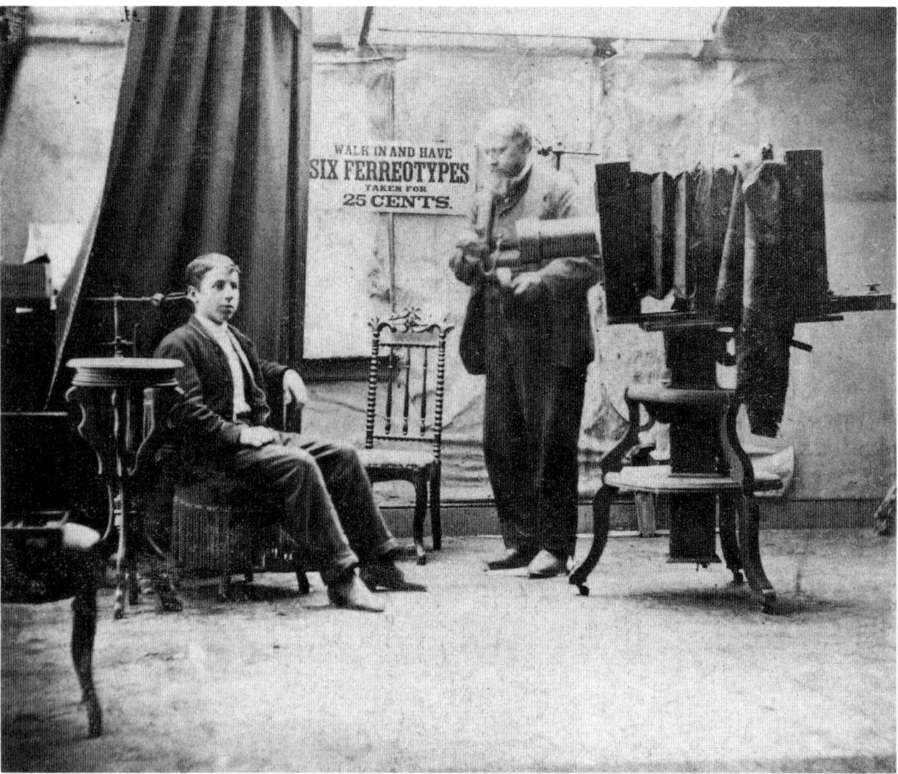

Anonymous, *Tintype studio,*
circa 1900, I.M.P. George Eastman House, Rochester.

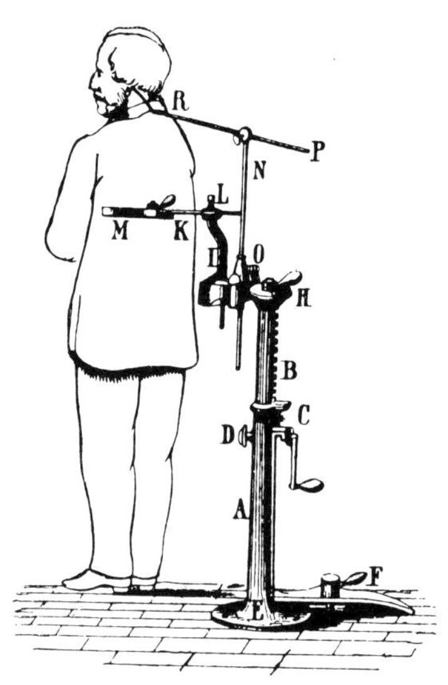

Head and body-rest dating from the 1850s. The rest was designed to keep the sitter still during the portrait session.

reproduced plus the length of time and amount of detail called for by each step in the process) made it impossible even to contemplate an infinite proliferation of photographic images. Apart from this, early photographic portrait studios, which tended to employ one or two assistants, were organized along the same lines as craft workshops. One of the innovations of the wet-collodion process, the glass negative, finally opened the way for an increase in both number and quality.[4]

It also meant that production could expand to an almost industrial scale. The metamorphosis that was sweeping through the studios at this time was, therefore, just a reflection of technological change. By exploiting fully the way the production of images could be broken down into individual steps, it became feasible to increase the number of portraits taken and reduce their price. The ratio between the two was crucial. Nadar, who was shortly to set up shop on the Boulevard

4. See previous chapter.

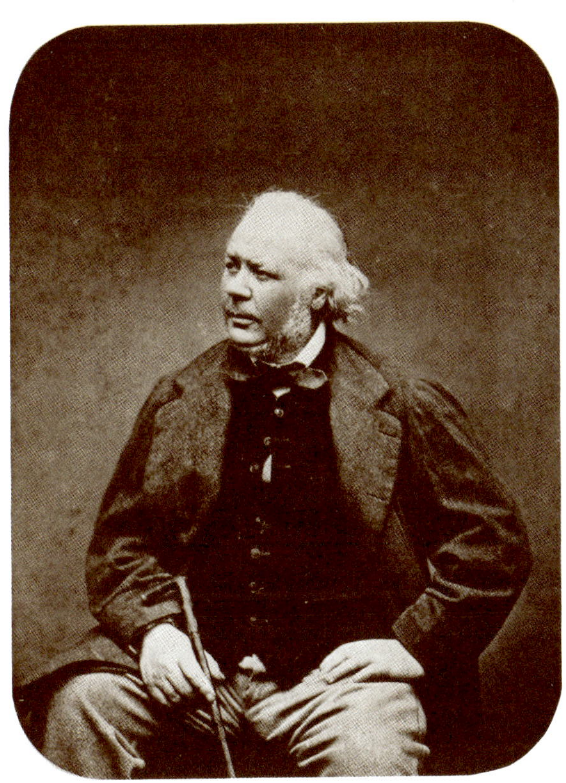

◀ **Étienne Carjat,**
Portrait of Honoré Daumier,
circa 1864,
private collection.

des Capucines, was very aware of these changes. "The ineffable Legros, a colorful man who always wore a brocade smoking jacket, galvanized the glory days at Palais-Royal. His faithful provincial following could not bring itself to stop loving him. He cleverly managed to die at the same time as it did."[5]

Somehow the old-fashioned charm of the Palais-Royal arcades managed to keep its hold over people traveling to Paris to have their photograph taken. But fashionable studios, favored by well-heeled Parisians, moved out to the boulevards further north. Some measure of the changes that were taking place can also be seen in the increase in the number of studios, which mushroomed in France and abroad. In London, there were 12 in 1851, 66 in 1855, 155 in 1857, and 200 in 1860.[6] By this date, 33,000 people in Paris alone were, directly or indirectly, earning their living from photography. As the Palais-Royal district lost its stranglehold, studios spread out to the furthest-flung parts of town, such as Ménilmontant or Belleville. Seven photographic studios opened along the Boulevard des Italiens, including one belonging to Nadar's brother, Adrien Tournachon. He moved into number 17, together with a mediocre tenor and a number of actors.[7]

Disdéri took over two floors at number 8, which belonged to the famous Robert Houdin. In 1896, it was here that Méliès' first films would be shown (Lumière's first projections took place at the Grand Café, 14 Boulevard des Capuchines). Photography and cinema flirted with theater folk, magicians, and conjurers. When Tournachon's studio opened in June 1854 it was described as "the biggest in Paris". In terms of luxury, his premises rivaled those of Kilburn, Claudet, and Hennemann in London. In London photographers were moving into fashionable areas. No fewer than sixty studios opened in Regent Street. Back in Paris, Mayer and Pierson, who had formed themselves into a company in 1855, set up business at 5 Boulevard des Capucines. Three years later, their advertisements boasted that they were "photographers to His Majesty the Emperor and to His Majesty the King of Württemberg". In the same year, when he was still in Rue Saint-Lazare, Nadar was listed in Bottin – the Paris *Who's Who* – as "member of the Literary Society; editor of a photographic collection of contemporary figures, sovereigns, statesmen, churchmen, soldiers, philosophers, men of letters, and artists". Nadar the caricaturist was converted to photography at the time he got the idea for his *Pantheon*, a lithographic work which featured the celebrities of the day.

The heyday of the portrait

The craze for portraits of figures from the worlds of politics, literature, and the arts was so great

Mayer & Pierson,
The Imperial Prince,
circa 1859,
Archives of the Haut-Rhin Department.
▼

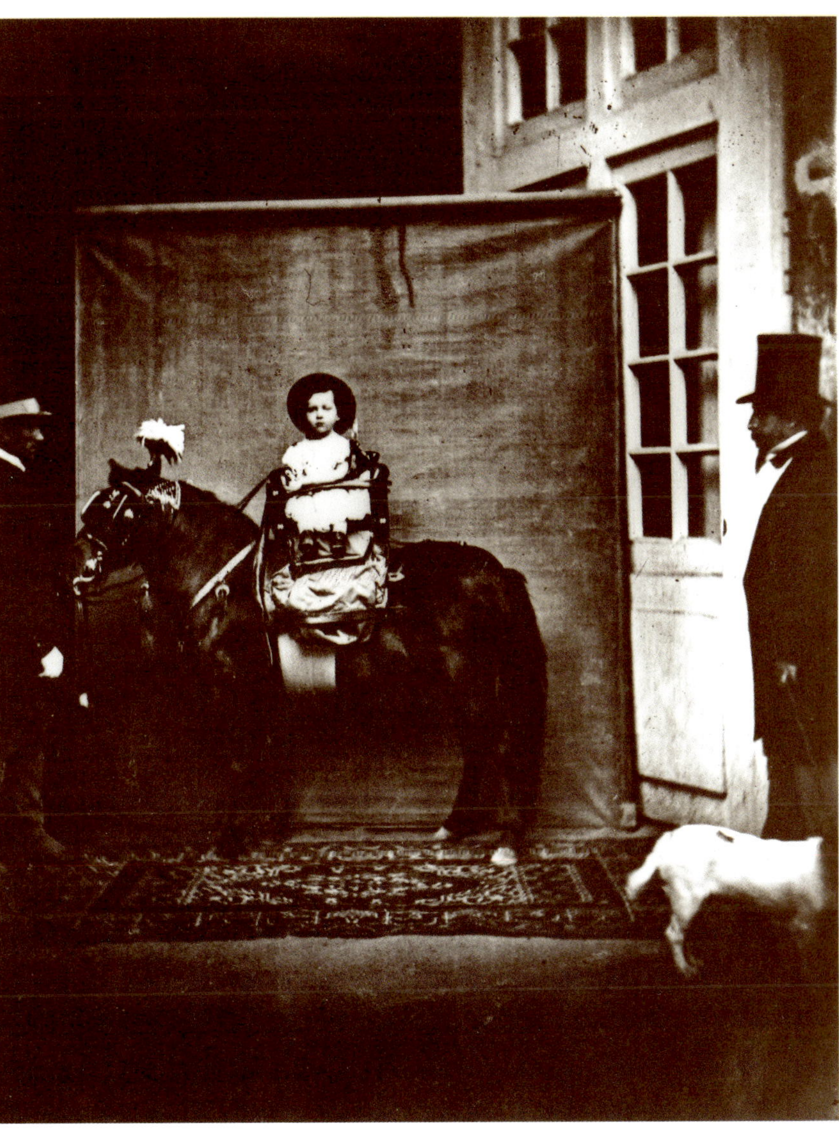

5. Nadar, *Quand j'étais photographe*, Paris, Flammarion, 1900, p. 192.

6. H. and A. Gernsheim, *History of Photography*, New York, McGraw-Hill, 1969, p. 234.

7. The group also included Zacharie, Schobloch, Mulnier, Numa Blanc, and Duchenne de Boulogne, who went on to carry out experiments into facial expression by stimulating the muscles of the face.

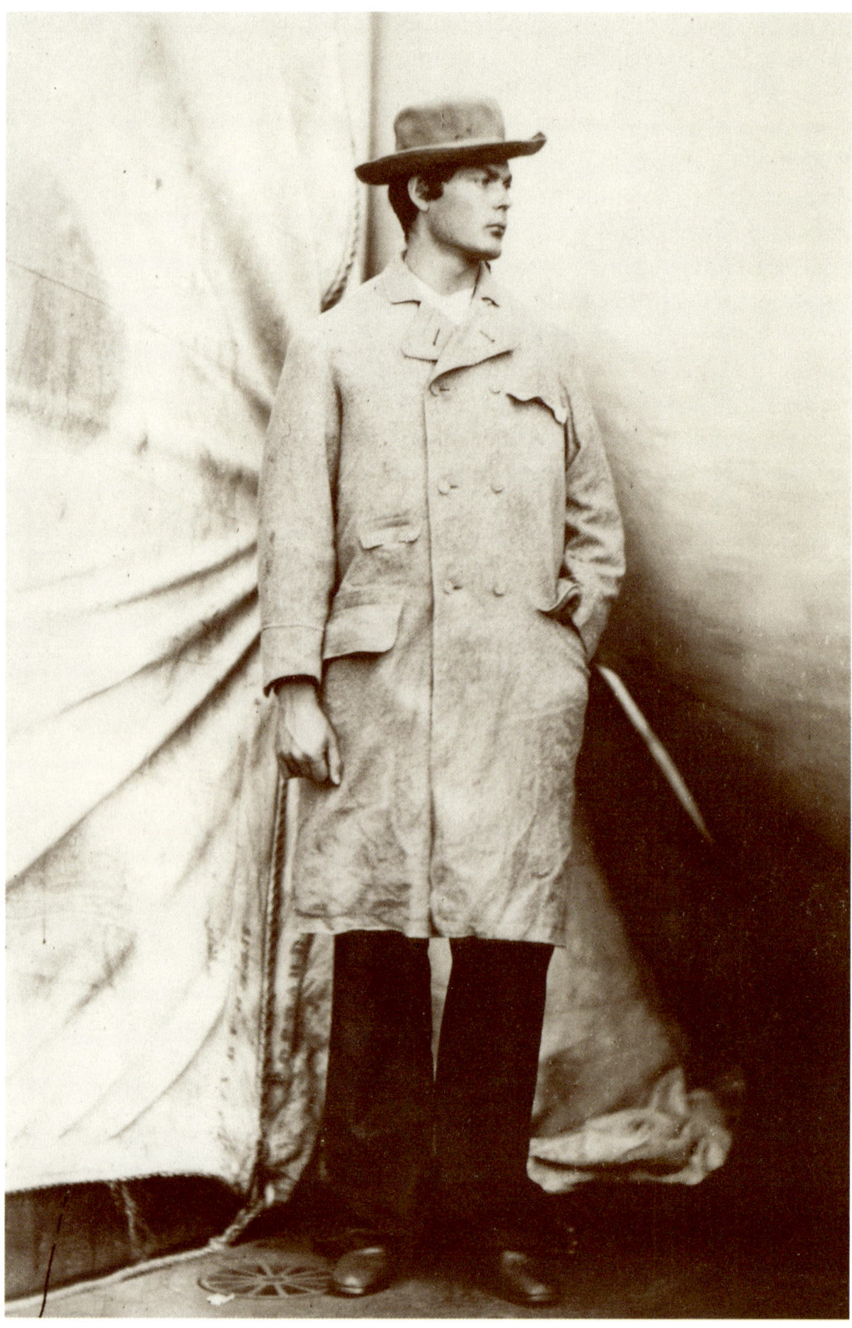

Alexander Gardner, ***Portrait of Lewis Payne, Conspirator against Lincoln,*** 1865, International Museum of Photography, George Eastman House, Rochester.

that their sale soon became one of the driving forces behind the way studios operated. Sales were handled through book stores and stationers. Photography thus supplanted engraving and lithography as the most common means by which famous people's faces became known. It also offered far greater opportunity. Barbey d'Aurevilly sounded off against the profusion of "mug shots", a trend he thought appalling. "What intelligent and charming fame photography brings! Shop-window celebrity. More often than not you get a lousy name under a lousy face, badly reproduced by a lousy process. What a blessing! It's music to the ears of self-love!" He goes on to ask, "What wind of posthumous self-conceit blew such madness into their heads?"[8] But the frenzied fad for portraits had attractions for everyone. Well-known people thought that portraits would boost their prestige. Photographers watched business increase. Famous people were subjected to pressure to get them in front of the camera.[9]

Nadar was at the center of republican opposition to the régime. Sporting a red tunic, he welcomed Proudhon, Daumier, Baudelaire, and Courbet to his premises in Rue Saint-Lazare. Disdéri and Mayer & Pierson were visited by a host of people who between them embodied imperial power. Even the Emperor himself regularly turned up. He commissioned a photograph of his son, the Imperial Prince, on a pony. Quite by accident, the Emperor's profile was captured on the right side of the negative. Deputies and ambassadors posed with dignified demeanor. These portraits were exhibited in display windows at the entrance to photographers' studios. These displays never failed to attract a crowd, especially when they included photos of stars from the popular theater, operetta or vaudeville, revealing their legs or in provocative poses.

In *La Curée,* Émile Zola writes about this proliferation of actress's portraits. He describes how popular they were. "[Maxime] carried portraits of actresses in every pocket. He even had one in his cigarette case. From time to time he cleared them all out and moved the ladies into an album which he left lying around the drawing room and which was already full of portraits of Renée's friends."

For very little cost, it was now possible to acquire a collection of likenesses of the famous (or infamous). The brisk sale of such portraits became a stampede as members of the public started flocking to the photographer's studio themselves. On the Boulevard des Capucines, Gustave Le Gray and the Bisson brothers opened shops on either side of a photo-sculpture studio. The Bisson brothers' premises, financed by Dolfus, from Mulhouse, was frequented by the intelligentsia, who came to admire the beautiful views of Paris. Delacroix, Baudelaire, and Gautier were among the visitors. By now, anyone who was anyone in the world of Paris photography could be found on the Boulevard des Italiens or the Boulevard des Capucines. In New York, the great studios belonging to Gurney, Lawrence, and Brady were all on Broadway. Whatever city they were in, photographers always indulged in huge, lavishly decorated premises to impress their clients. The walls and tables were covered with images of famous people who were already customers of the studio.

Such was the passion for photography that its impact on public life became considerable. One of Mathew Brady's portraits of Abraham Lincoln was taken the night before his speech at the Cooper Union (February 22, 1860). Several

8. Barbey d'Aurevilly, "Le portrait photographique", in *Le Nain jaune,* January 3, 1867.

9. A number of unauthorized portraits appeared which led to laws being introduced regulating artistic ownership over photographs and the individual's right to their own image.

hundred thousand copies were printed, which were used in the President's re-election campaign.[10]

The Frenchman Antoine Claudet went into business in London. Thanks to the quality of the photos he produced, he was given a royal warrant. In 1851 he commissioned Charles Barry, architect of the Houses of Parliament, to build him one of the most luxurious of all the "temples of photography" in Regent Street.

Up to this time, the circulation of any photograph published had been restricted since prints had to be made from calotype paper negatives. Luxury photographic prints and albums had been the province of rich amateurs or painters. Now photographs could spread to a far wider public. The Alinari brothers in Florence opened a studio in 1854. They styled themselves "photographic publishers" and played a major role in creating the rich iconography that surrounded Garibaldi. His portrait was made by photographers the length and breadth of Italy: Bernieri in Turin, Monnier in Naples, Bettini in Livorno, Trainini in Brescia. After he was wounded at Aspromonte in 1862, the hero was photographed in his hospital bed, his leg in plaster. Dr. Moreau-Nélaton takes his pulse and gives his verdict: amputation is not necessary.[11]

Photography reacted to current events by turning out portraits of people in the news. This meant that the emotional impact of the news itself was boosted. After the dramatic events in Mexico, Disdéri published portraits of Maximilian and photographs of the execution squad, the clothes riddled with bullet holes, and even the Emperor's corpse in its coffin, all taken on the spot by Aubert.

Towards the middle of the nineteenth century, in France and elsewhere, industrial growth gave rise to a new social class hungry for recognition. Photography offered a rapid and cheap process that perfectly fitted its ambitions. At the 1855 Paris exhibition, Adrien Tournachon exhibited a series of Pierrots (the mime artist Deburau Jr.). Hanfstaengl from Munich exhibited the first retouched photographs. This exhibition was to prove a turning point for the photographic profession.

By the end of the decade, studios had grown even larger and were becoming prosperous businesses, big enough to attract investors. Disdéri's first-floor studio dedicated one room to nothing but sales. In another, all they did was frame portraits. The Comte de Briges was the financial backer of Le Gray's studio, while Louis le Prévost, a banker from the firm Charles Laffitte & Blount, did the same for Adrien Tournachon. When Nadar moved into the Boulevard des Capucines it was to an iron and glass building, a true "crystal palace". The new studio was financed by a company which included Philippon, publisher of *Charivari*, *Lefranc*, *Hérald de Page*, and *Mollevault*. Nadar became creditor to the Péreire brothers, who had already got into some publishing scrapes,[12] and the photographic business venture run by the sculptor Adam-Salomon.

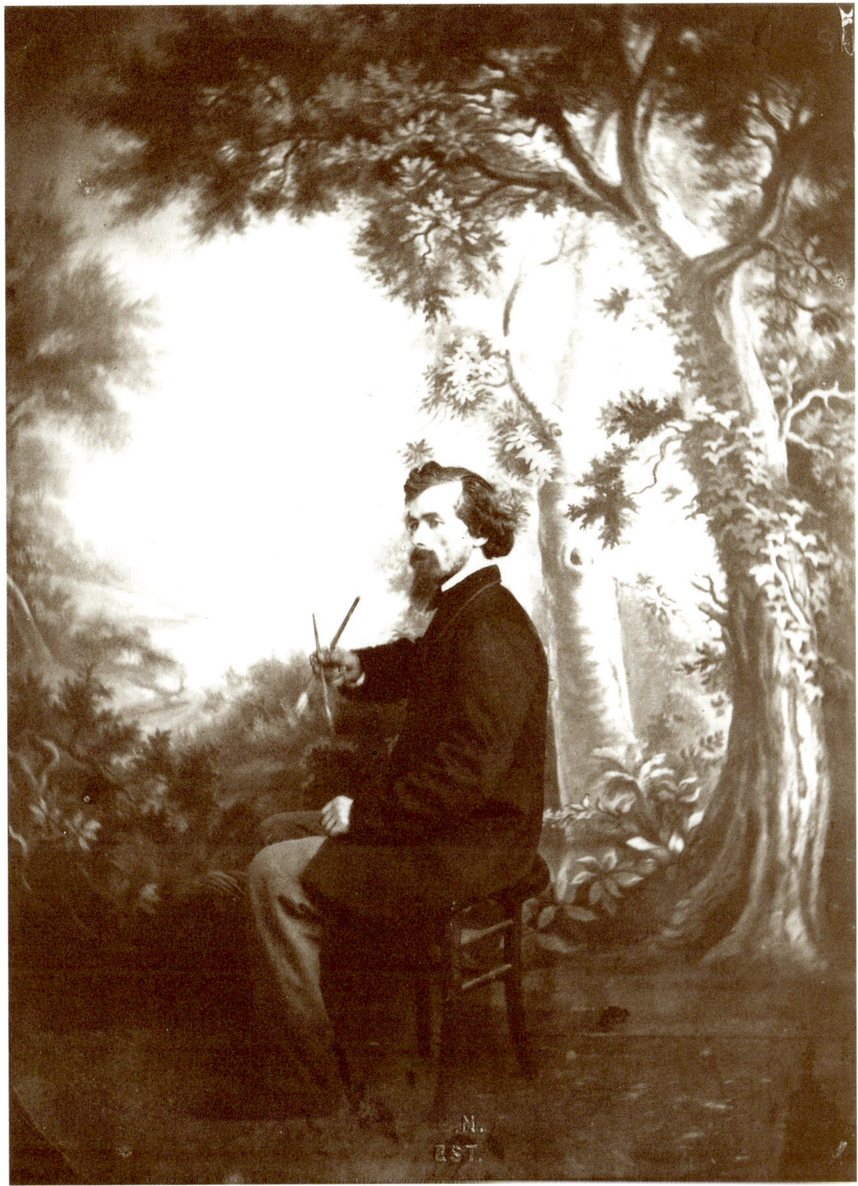

Anonymous,
Studio portrait,
circa 1870,
Bibliothèque Nationale,
Paris.

The commercial imperatives imposed by the growth in customers required photographers to come up with studio space and money to match. Nadar criticized the methods employed by his colleagues and neighbors, Mayer & Pierson, to comply with market conditions limiting portraits to a single format. This, according to Nadar, "takes no account of framing a shot in the way that best suits the sitter. Nor does it allow for facial expression, nor indeed the various ways in which light falls on the scene. Instead, they make every client sit in exactly the same place and shoot a single gray and drab plate. In short, it's slapdash."[13]

Paradoxically, it was just when production started to become fully industrialized that

10. R. Taft, *Photography and the American Scene*, p. 194.

11. W. Settimelli, *Garibaldi: l'Album fotografico*, Florence, Alinari, 1982.

12. V. R. Greaves, *Nadar*, Paris, Flammarion, 1980, p. 147.

13. Nadar, *op. cit.*, p. 197.

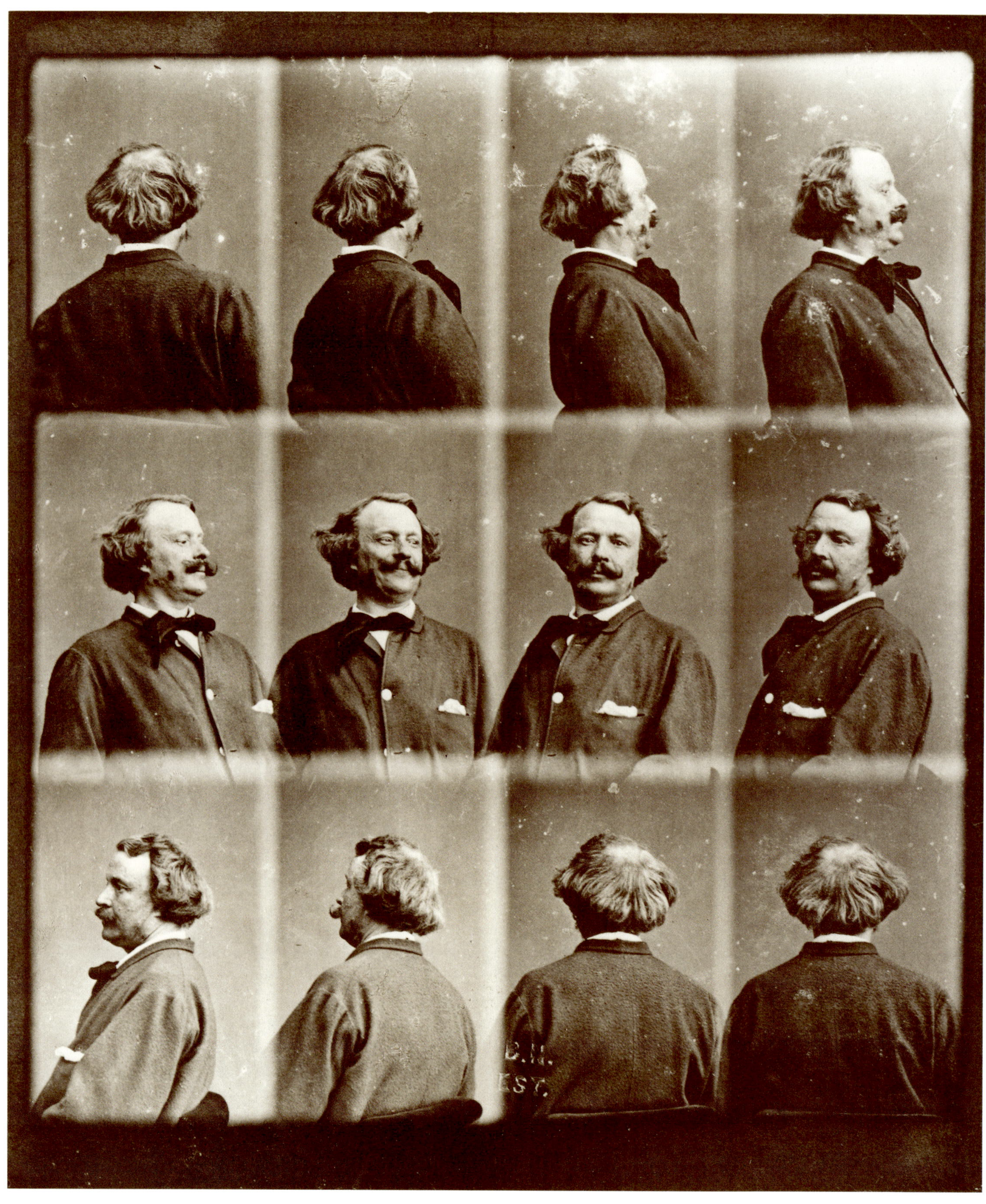

NADAR,
"Revolving" Self-portrait,
circa 1865,
Bibliothèque Nationale,
Paris.

photographers began to get an often exaggerated notion of their artistic worth. Their pretensions were, however, no more than a strategy to boost the status of their profession in the eyes of the public. Nadar, also a draughtsman, humorist, journalist, and novelist, poked fun at the attempts made by photographers to force their way into the international exhibitions and into the Salon des Beaux-Arts. He summed up the pretensions of a whole class of makeshift photographers. "Thus it is that all and sundry, those who've gone down in the world and those who were never even in it, have now set up as photographers. Be they scholars or tenors who've lost their voice, they all style themselves 'artistic'. Second-rate painters and failed sculptors are a dime a dozen." In 1854, when Nadar had opened his first studio in Rue Saint-Lazare, he too had sought the patronage of an artistic elite and had been blessed by the support of no less a figure than Delacroix. Lazergues and Dallemagne got their clients to pose inside richly carved frames hung with drapery swags, an echo of ceremonial portraiture. Mayer & Pierson specialized in hand-colored portraits even though the critic Ernest Lacan protested that this devalued photography. Adam-Salomon was noted for his sophisticated research into backlighting, seeking effects like a Rembrandt painting. He also took a keen interest in the science of composition and was able to persuade Lamartine to revise his negative opinion about photography.[14]

All these efforts attempted to make the most of what could now be done with glass negatives. They also happened to coincide with commercial requirements and mass production. Daumier's sketch *Nadar Elevating Photography to an Art Form* is certainly funny. The caricaturist was among the most virulent in his attacks on the pretensions of the new medium. His drawing shows his friend with his head in the clouds, in a balloon.[15]

A BAS LA PHOTHOGRAPHIE (1) !!!

TEXTE ET DESSINS PAR MARCELIN.

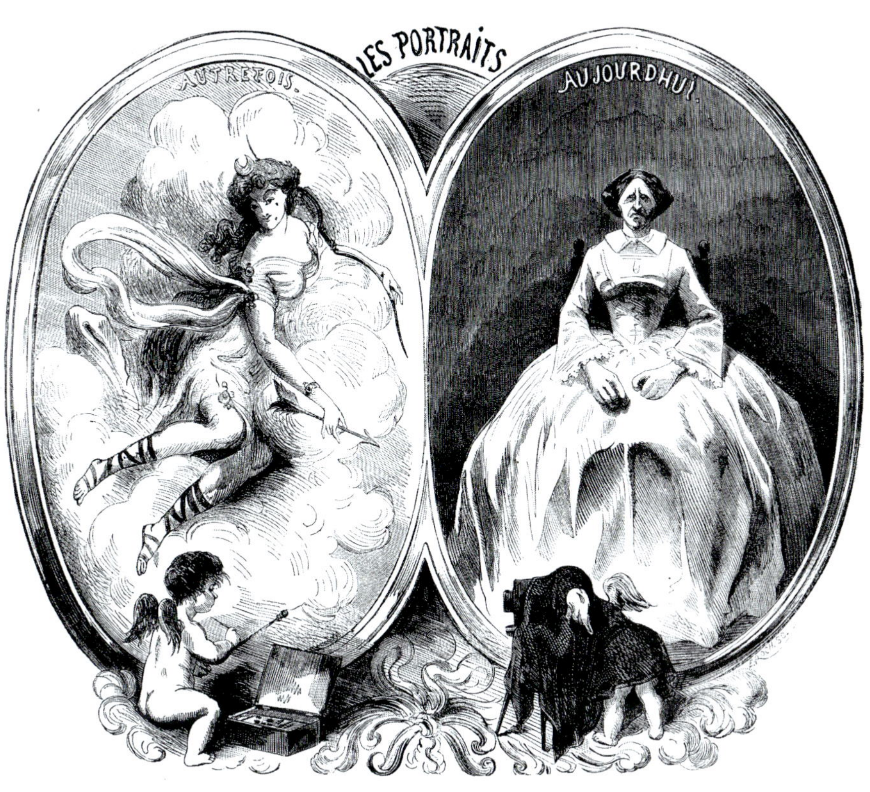

MARCELIN, **Portraits of Yesteryear and Today,** *Journal amusant,* September 6, 1856.

Many painters discovered that photography could provide them with a livelihood. Artists who converted to photography included the cartoonist Bertall, who had illustrated *La Comédie Humaine* and also produced satirical sketches. Similarly, Louis de Lucy and Berne-Bellecourt moved from painting to photography. In Rome, photographic studios were opened by Altobelli, Danesi, and Mario de Maria. In Hamburg, Ferdinand Stelzner, a miniaturist who had been a pupil of Isabey, went into business with Hermann Biow, who had opened a "heliographic studio" as early as 1841. They were so successful that they traveled to Dresden, Berlin, and Frankfurt to take portraits of celebrities such as Alexander von Humboldt. Biow's ambition, modeled on Brady's project in the United States, was "a national gallery of photographic portraits".[16]

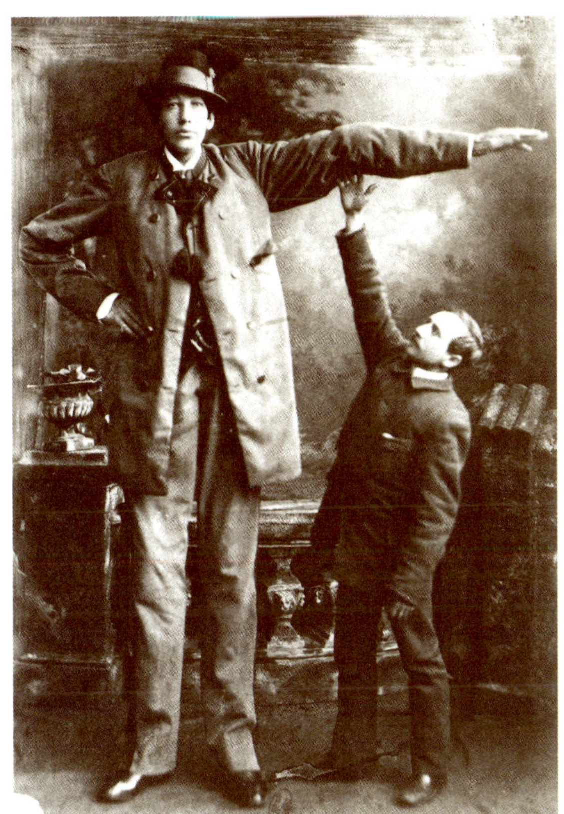

◀ ANONYMOUS, **Tyrolean Giant,** circa 1870, Bibliothèque Nationale, Paris.

Carte-de-visite portraits

The boom of 1860 which led to such an extraordinary growth in the number of studios would never have happened if the only factor at work was existing market demand. In fact, a new photographic format was on offer, the carte de visite. Disdéri had come up with a brand new type of portrait. It was the same size as a calling card and showed the subject standing up, leaning against a truncated column or sitting on a balustrade, hat in hand or reading a newspaper. In 1853, he filed a patent to protect his rights to any

14. After having written that "this hazardous invention will never be an art", Lamartine later wrote that the photographer "works with the sun".

15. Daumier's sketch appeared in May 1862 in *Le Boulevard*, a periodical published by Carjat who was also a caricaturist and photographer. Nadar had begun experimenting with taking photographs from a balloon in 1857, but without success. In 1858 (or 1868 according to some researchers), he managed to get 12 views of the Bois de Boulogne, the Avenue des Ternes, and Batignolles.

16. H. and A. Gernsheim, *op. cit.*, p. 159

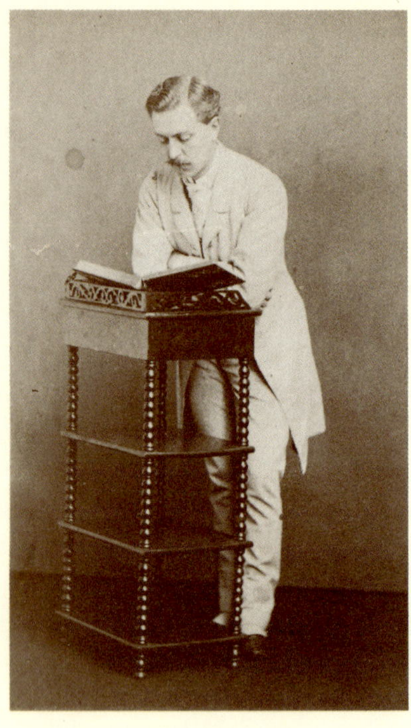
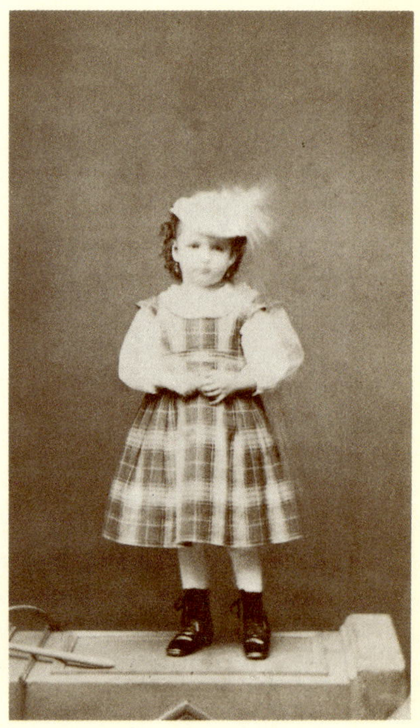
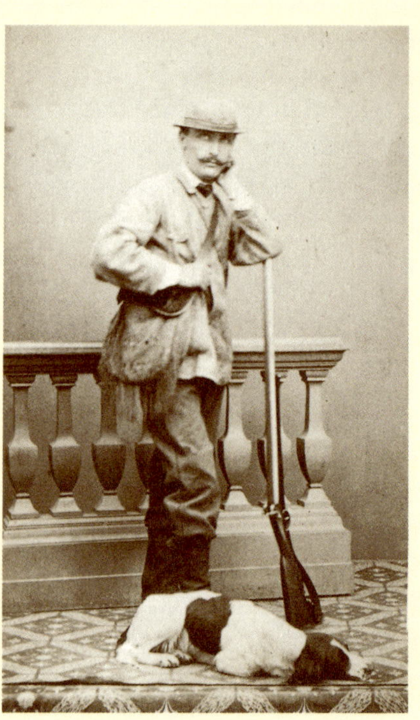

Cartes-de-visite portraits by BARON & MITKIEWICZ, Brussels, ANONYMOUS, France, and VIANE, Besançon, 1860s, private collection.

innovations derived from the "multiple slide frame", a device which allowed him to make a number of different negatives on the same glass plate. He filed another patent claim on November 27, 1854 over the photographic calling card or carte de visite. Thanks to technical innovations, the price per portrait fell dramatically. For much less than it cost to have one large-format print, Disdéri could offer a dozen carte-de-visite portraits which could be swiftly handed out to family and friends. By 1859–1860, these tiny portraits filled every photographer's window.[17]

The fad that Disdéri unleashed by redefining how a portrait could be used was not welcomed by every photographer. Abraham Bogardus, an American photographer, poked fun at the tiny format, little realizing how many he was soon going to turn out himself. An implacable logic was at work. Photographers could either conform to the new rules of the market or go under. This was how Nadar explained Le Gray's failure: his colleague was unable to submit to the laws of industrialized production. Le Gray was an artist who had chosen photography as his personal means of expression. All he could see in the small format was vulgarity. He handed his business over to Alophe, a painter and lithographer who illustrated novels, and instead went off to Cairo to teach drawing.

The daguerreotype had borrowed many of its ideas on composition from painted portraits. Its place had been within the bosom of the family. Daguerreotypes had been hung, almost like religious relics, on the wainscoted walls of the bourgeoisie. The aesthetic framework Disdéri used for the small format was the same as a painted portrait. Studios were filled with props and accessories (drapery swags, balustrades, columns, *trompe-l'œil* moldings) which symbolized the power of the middle classes. Anyone who aspired to belong to the elite, or to marry into it, could now slip into this mold. Taking a portrait, however, was not without violence. The body had to be contorted to assume the desired demeanour. Expressions had to be coaxed and manipulated to guarantee success.

With the carte de visite, photography slid out of frames on the wall and into albums on the table. Nothing short of "family museums" where collective memories were garnered, they shed light on a whole network of relationships. In the case of the highest echelons of society they have provided us with complete political or cultural blueprints. According to Walter Benjamin,[18] these heavy, hardback volumes tended to be placed on ornamental tables in the coldest corners of the house. They contained images of the nearest and dearest, distant relatives, close friends, and famous people. Portraits were often mixed together haphazardly.

The carte de visite speeded up the leveling out of society's values by making one part of it look like the next. Photography arrived at the right moment to highlight the overriding desire for uniformity. It penetrated every layer of society as effectively as the wearing of mourning or the fashion for crinolines. This dulling down of

17. On July 23, 1859 Nadar wrote in his "Revue trimestrielle" for the *Journal amusant* about the "invasion of the new cartes de visite".

18. W. Benjamin, "Kleine Geschichte der Photographie", in W. Benjamin, *Das Kunstwerk im Zeitalter seiner technischen Reproduzierbarkeit*, Frankfurt am Main, 1979, p. 54.

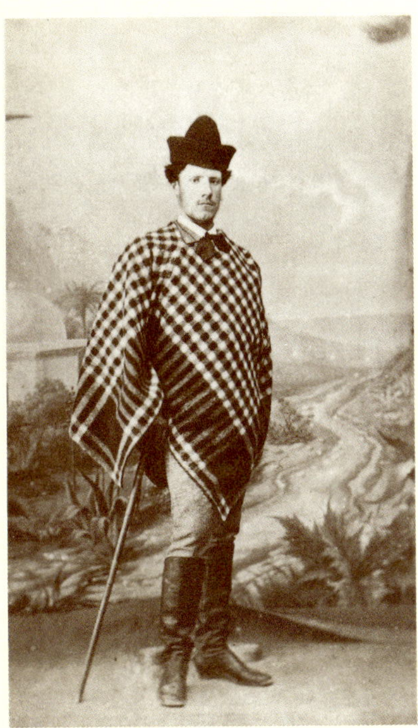

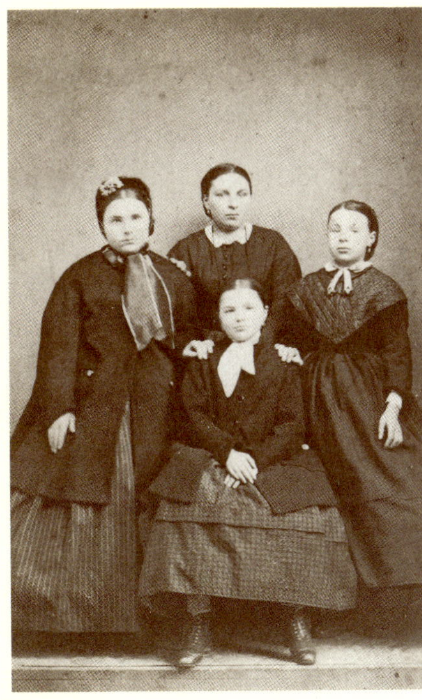

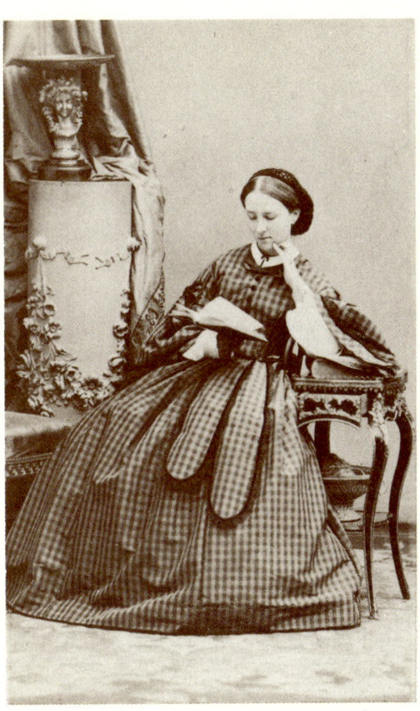

Carte-de-visite portraits by ALARY & GEISER, Algiers, SEYWERT, Sainte-Marie aux Mines, and DISDÉRI, Paris, 1860s, private collection.

distinctive features did not pass without irritating a number of painters and writers. Flaubert, Gautier, Barbey d'Aurevilly, and, later on, Loti all shared the same sense of loss. For them, industrialized society had plunged the world into mourning and photography confirmed, indeed trivialized, the phenomenon.

When Baudelaire wrote his virulent pamphlet about the 1859 Salon, he pointed an accusing finger at daguerreotype portraits, condemning them as "trivial images on metal". It would appear, however, that it was really the carte de visite which had sparked his belated, but categorical, stand on the matter. "From this moment on, society, like a solitary Narcissus, dashed headlong to contemplate its trivial image on metal. Folly and extraordinary fanaticism gripped these new sun-worshippers."[19]

He lashes out at "an obscene society", by which he means that mass of individuals in search of an "identity" – the anonymous masses of the industrial age. Edmond de Goncourt, also deeply attached to the values of the ancien régime, regretted the passing of picture galleries full of ancestors. In 1867, Barbey d'Aurevilly, writing in *Le Nain jaune*, questioned why people were so anxious to see themselves in photographers' windows. To him, the proliferation of portraits seemed the mark of "a decadent race gone soft". He believed that the phenomenon should be condemned and said that "no plague of real frogs or true toads could equal the horror of these photographs of human frogs and toads".[20]

Death-mask-like portraits, stony stillness, and poses perfect in their rigidity lay at the heart of the attacks by the humorists. Marcelin wrote an article for the *Journal amusant* entitled "À bas la photographie" [Down with Photography]. He waxed indignant over the fate awaiting the great men of the day whose characters and presence were diminished by photography. Delacroix, when viewed through this great leveling process, appeared little more than "a ticket clerk" while Ingres looked like "a constipated grocer".[21]

Caricaturists also attacked photography, poking fun at the conventional and stereotypical poses used for cartes de visite. A set of conventions had rapidly grown up which juxtaposed austere and dignified demeanour with luxurious décor. These conventions swept across the world. In 1862, Augusto De Azevedo opened a studio in São Paolo. He was in contact with Liébert in Paris who kept him informed about new techniques. De Azevedo followed Disdéri's ideas to the letter when it came to installing the backgrounds for his pictures.[22]

Things were no different in the provinces. Only a handful of photographers left their mark on photographs, which would otherwise be distinguished by excessive monotony. Charles Winter, a Strasbourg-based photographer, took portraits of his children and of the Comte de Pourtalès which are not devoid of interest. More often than not, however, both his regular customers and actors passing through town were photographed in the conventional manner for their carte-de-visite portraits. Photographers were reduced to mechanical operatives who did little more than "shoot" in a slapdash fashion anyone who

19. C. Baudelaire, "Le public moderne et la photographie", in *Œuvres complètes*, Paris, Gallimard, 1977.

20. Barbey d'Aurevilly, *op. cit.*

21. *Journal amusant*, September 6, 1856.

22. B. Kossoy, "Militao Agusto de Azevedo of Brazil", in *History of Photography*, January 1980, pp. 9–17.

Composite *cartes*

On April 23, 1863, Disdéri filed a patent application to protect his rights over what he called the "mosaic", a composite carte de visite, a photomontage of portraits of different people. This type of composition was only ever produced in this small format. It came in the wake of the unflagging craze for celebrity portraits. Images were multiplied, pasted together, and reproduced on a single carte. The photographic king of the Boulevard des Italiens had the idea of thematically assembling images of people from one social group or another. A few days before his patent was granted, he had filed a copyright claim for cartes grouping together different dancers from the Opéra and the Théâtre Italien as well as groups of French generals and admirals and even the royal family. Since all of these celebrities had already been to him for portraits, it was an easy task to group them together thematically and offer a composite image to a wider public. By multiplying the numbers, he reduced the unit price. Generally he included no more than 20 or so portraits, arranged in medallion form and showing each person's name.

One of Disdéri's more original photomontages shows only the legs of dancers from the Opéra. At other times he blocked out the background and arranged heads together at an angle, pasting the images in tightly until he was able to compose large groups which conveyed the feeling of a pulsating crowd. Disdéri used this formula for his cartes of soldiers and actors, even of the Pope and his prelates. One carte could contain up to 1,000 portraits, each no bigger than a pinhead.

These composite cartes were great advertisements for photographers since they could be used as a sampler of their work. Pierre Petit did a photomontage of lawyers from the Paris Bar and Terruel the clergy, while composite cartes by Franck showed the crowned heads of Europe. But the most original use for photomontage came from the theater, with portraits of all the leading actors and actresses in a play together on one carte. These unusual pocket programs then went on sale. This was the method that Disdéri chose when he created cartes for shows such as *Diavolina*, *Diable à Quatre*, and *Gracissa* while in Amiens, Courieux used the same method for *Rigoletto* and *Le Bossu*.

Jean Sagne

Disdéri, *Legs at the Opera; Famous Frenchmen,*
composite cartes (photomontages),
circa 1864, private collection.

Nadar, ▶
Charles Baudelaire,
circa 1854
(single print not in circulation at the time),
Musée d'Orsay, Paris.

walked through the studio door. Even Nadar, from 1855 onwards responsible for an amazing series of large-format portraits of the literary figures of his day, was doomed to the tyranny of the carte de visite. His premises on the Boulevard des Capucines were housed on the upper floors of a building dominated by a luminous sign carrying his signature in red letters. Nevertheless, this studio turned out thousands of tiny banal portraits distinguished only by his majestic initial *N*.

The carte de visite offered little scope for individuality. Even though the principle of multiple negatives should have encouraged a variety of poses – and indeed a few of the more adventurous photographers, such as Cabanès, actually took advantage of this – it led to a uniformity that exactly reflected society's wishes. Those who wanted to break the mold also had to smash a dominant way of thinking. Sitting astride chairs, lounging with their legs on a table, perched cross-legged on top of a column, their portraits taken from behind – these were the poses adopted by those trying to shun uniformity, to reclaim their own image, to redefine their own identity.

A number of people who defied the conventions of their day have left us images of themselves which form nothing short of a manifesto. Decked out in costumes borrowed from civilizations labeled primitive by Western industrial society, they set their face against mass production. They shun conventional stiff dark suits. Instead they appear in Arab burnous, loincloths or kimonos brought back from their travels in front of backdrops showing deserts or tropical forests. Gautier, Loti, and Savorgnan de Brazza were photographed in all manner of costumes. For them, it was a way of standing out from the crowd.

If adopting a certain style of dress was a way of distinguishing identity, it was also a sign that a less clear-cut form of experimentation was going on. The studio became a place where people could play with identity. Every photographic session

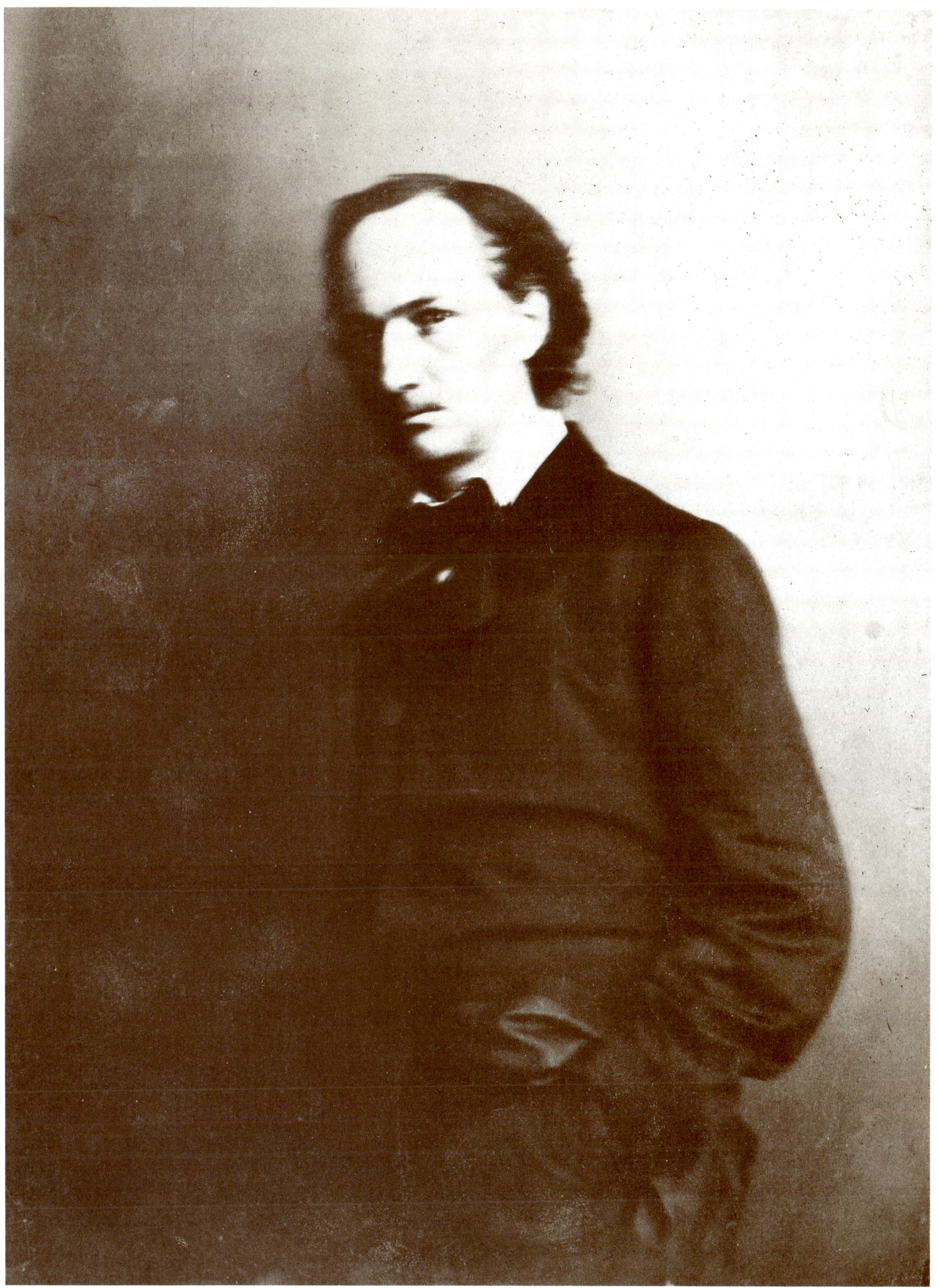

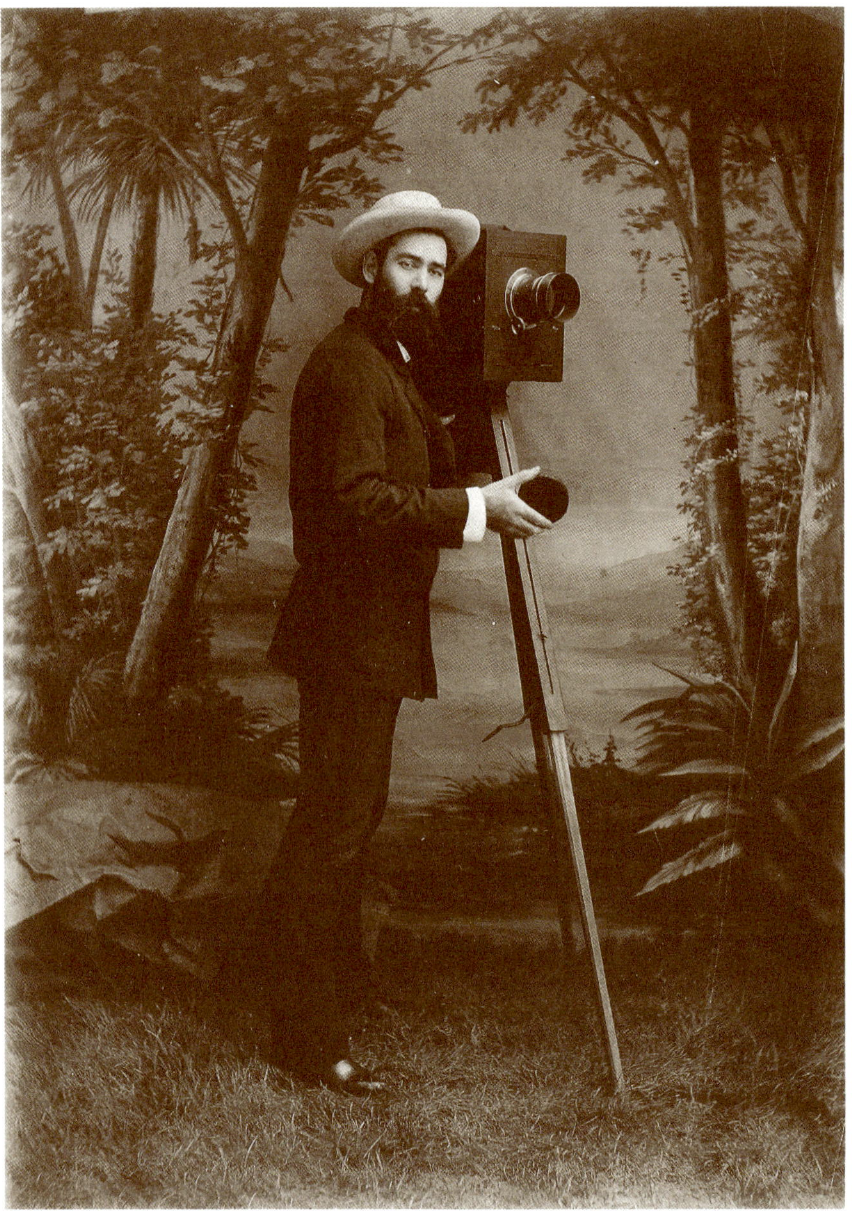

SULLY
(photographer in Pointe-à-Pitre),
Self-portrait,
circa 1870,
private collection.

produced a proof of at least one of the sitter's possible images. In the numerous portraits the Countess of Castiglione had taken of herself, the attitudes she strikes are countless clues to her obsessional character. At Mayer & Pierson, she agreed to pose in the most unexpected stances and was willing to slip into the most extraordinary outfits. Driven by her narcissism, she had her own image reflected in a mirror, or her own face framed in an oval frame. In front of the camera, she uncovered her legs and arms with a lack of reserve which in its time could not have been countenanced anywhere but in the photographer's studio.[23]

In another vein, Lewis Carroll used photography as a way of giving his fantasy free rein. In his studio at Christ Church, Oxford, he persuaded young girls of his acquaintance to dress up for him. In this way he pushed the games he regularly played with them even further. Photography readily lent itself to such intentions since undressing was a requirement. Thus intimacy grew. Ensnared in the trap of his own desires, Carroll was gradually drawn to taking nude portraits of his models. He himself destroyed these images and none survives today.[24]

The photographer: the individual within society

There came a time when the man behind the camera was almost overwhelmed by what he was doing. He had to submit to the conformist tyranny of his clients and renege on his own creative spirit. It was precisely at this time that he started to behave and dress in the most extravagant fashion, to try and claw back some of his old prestige. Disdéri may have been a slave to his work, but he always donned a rainbow-colored tunic and riding boots. We can see him in the little sketches Cham did for *Charivari*. He stands with his shoulders back and head held high – even his beard seems to point aggressively. Pierre Petit, with his long hair and flowing beard, posed next to a giant. Nadar always sported a red tunic as a symbol of his radical leanings. In one photograph, we see him in a balloon. In another he is dressed in costume from the days of Louis XIV and wearing the same wig that George Sand wore for the portrait he took of her. The photographer had to be surprising in appearance. He had to give himself artistic airs because otherwise his social standing did not amount to much. Take the example of Harmand, a traveling photographer who worked on Boulevard Sébastopol and always wore leather gaiters. His dress "rustled with fantasy; his Olympian hair style was fashioned to flop carelessly beneath his Calabrian hat".[25]

The photographer became "the great creator", almost a demiurge. The signature of a famous photographer in the corner of a tiny portrait was a mark of distinction, perhaps the only thing that could distinguish it from a host of identical images. His signature, that minuscule inscription, encapsulated the photographer's power to bestow an "identity" on his subject. Goncourt noted that photographers' rise in status, their admission to the circles that mattered, was marked by the fact that they became regular customers (along with stockbrokers and racegoers) at Peters, a restaurant at the height of fashion.[26]

Disdéri was the prototype of the new celebrity photographer who set out to conquer the boulevards. Following a number of failed enterprises in lingerie, he went into the theater. In 1848, he was working as a photographer in Brest where he managed to come to the attention of the authorities for his revolutionary sympathies during the insurrections that year. Opportunism brought

23. P. Tyl, "Mayer & Pierson", in *Prestige de la photographie*, no. 7, pp. 36-63.

24. H. Gernsheim, *Lewis Carroll Photographer*, New York, Dover, 1962; P. Rogiers, *Le visage regardé ou Lewis Carroll dessinateur et photographe*, Paris, Créatis, 1982.

25. Méphis, *La Lumière*, February 18, 1860.

26. E. and J. de Goncourt, *Le Journal*, Paris, February 9, 1867, Laffont, 1989.

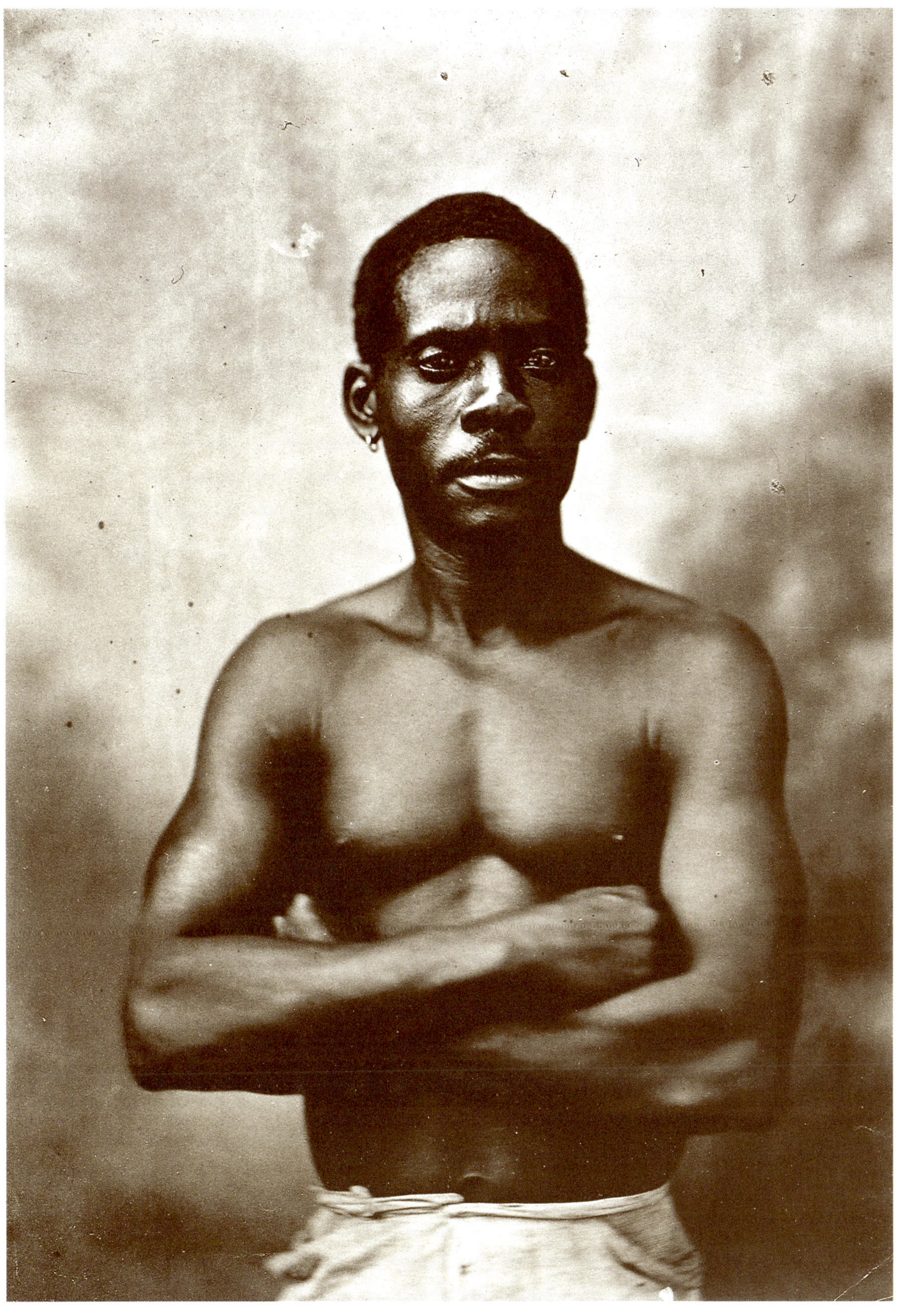

SULLY,
Portrait of a Man,
circa 1870,
private collection.

him back to the cause of empire. In 1856, he wrote a dedication in his album on Versailles to "their Imperial Majesties the Emperor Napoleon III and the Empress Eugénie, a gift inspired by the deepest respect felt by their most humble and obedient servant and subject". Nadar wrote in his memoirs that when the Emperor, Napoleon III, at the head of his troops, was setting off for the Italian campaign and heading out of Paris down the boulevard, he stopped off at Disdéri's to have his photograph taken. Nadar's success was thus assured. We now know that Nadar made all this up.[27] It is, nevertheless, indicative of the role played by portraits of the Emperor which were circulating at the time as cartes de visite.

27. A. MacCauley, *A. A. E. Disdéri and the Carte de Visite Portrait Photograph*, Yale University Press, 1985.

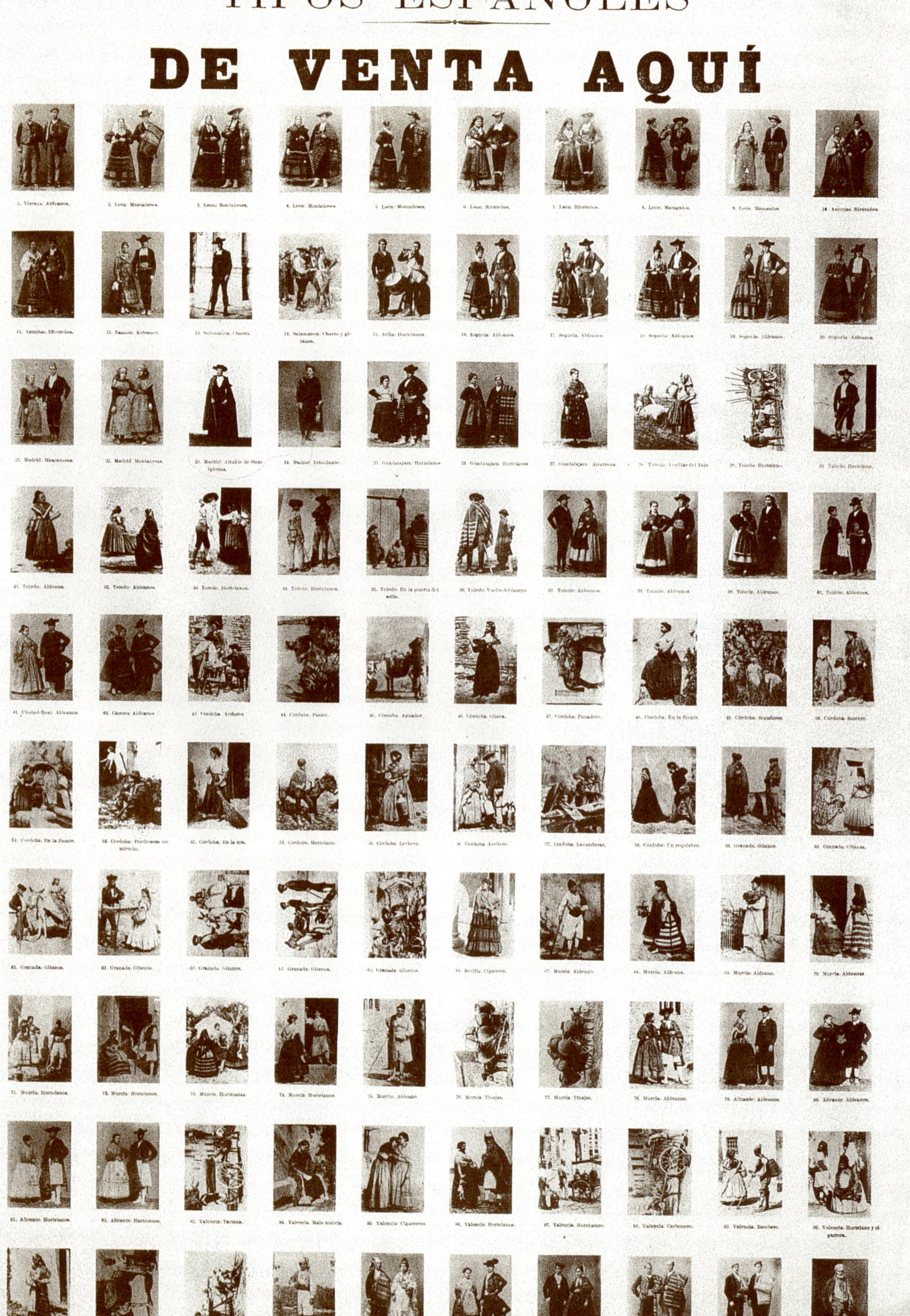
CASA DE LAURENT, TURCO, 18, MADRID
TIPOS ESPAÑOLES
DE VENTA AQUÍ

To a great extent, photography only reinforced the phenomenon of conformity that was already at work within the fabric of society. This is why we can understand both Disdéri and Napoleon III. The photographer was driven by commercial ambition. The Emperor had his eye on the political climate. The success of the carte de visite was clinched in France when the Emperor and his family had theirs taken (the same thing happened with the ruling families in every other country). Ludwig Angerer, who, along with Monckhoven and Rabending, introduced the carte de visite to Vienna, sold countless portraits of the Austrian emperor and empress. The same formula worked for Lewitzky in St. Petersburg, Georg Hansen in Copenhagen, Haase in Berlin, and Josef Albert in Munich.[28] In India, Deen Dayal was official photographer to the Nizam of Hyderabad and worked under exceptionally favorable conditions. Over the course of 25 years he compiled an invaluable record of life at the Nizam's court.[29] In Britain, in August 1860, Mayall published a series of carte-de-visite portraits of the royal family taken on May 17 and July 1. Queen Victoria was enthusiastic about photography and had over a hundred albums in which she collected portraits from every foreign court.

Since anyone could have their portrait taken in the same format and against the same background as the head of state, king or emperor, a direct relationship was established between those in power and their subjects. Napoleon III, who had been the butt of vicious caricatures, found that he could use photography to suit his own purposes to alter his public image. More than anything else, it allowed him to shift from an authority figure to one that people cared about. He cultivated the appearance of a middle-class fellow that people could identify with. He assumed the guise of emperor-cum-president just as Louis-Philippe had tried to be a citizen-king.

The proliferation of cartes de visite might lead one to think that portraiture had been democratized. But this was an illusion. In fact, only rarely does one find pictures of peasants, workers or craftsmen in this small format. And they generally turn out to be actors photographed in costume – chambermaids, water-carriers, and so on. The calling card itself was aristocratic in origin. The idea of a version on glossy paper came from Aguado and Delessert, two aristocratic members of the Société Française de Photographie. The cards were a means of drawing social distinctions.

The way in which studios, the so-called "temples of photography", were structured and organized played a key part in this process. The luxury of the studio surroundings made it almost impossible for people of modest means to go there, simply because it made them feel uncomfortable. A hierarchy emerged between various establishments in accordance with the kind of public they catered to. On the same boulevard you would find grand photographic studios and stalls set up by street photographers amid a throng of other fairground attractions. There is no doubt that between the two of them they covered the social spectrum.

People patronizing a traveling photographer who had set up his stall on the pavement did not choose him simply because he was cheaper. Indeed, traveling photographers were just as expensive, sometimes more expensive, than the major studios. The difference was that they were catering to a public that wanted portraits for a totally different purpose. The improvised photographer's tent appears to have attracted "a clientele mainly recruited from soldiers and nursemaids". It proved a remarkably resilient trade and has survived to this day in Mediterranean countries. What were these people expecting when their image circulated in their own social sphere? Special processes were developed to

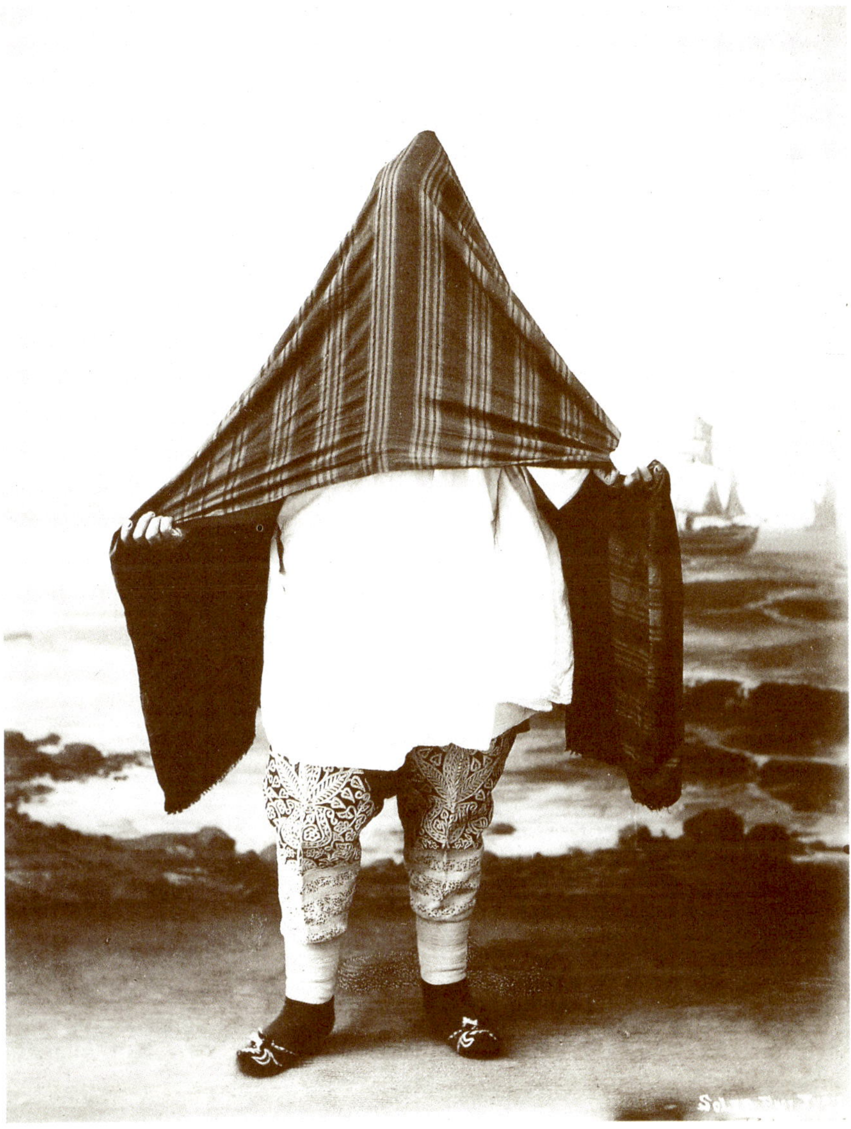

SOLER,
A Local,
Tunis, circa 1890,
private collection.

◄ J. LAURENT,
Advertisement for Spanish Portraits,
circa 1870,
Biblioteca Nacional,
Madrid.

28. H. Gernsheim, *A Concise History of Photography*, London, Thames & Hudson, 1965, p. 118.

29. C. Worswick, *Princely India: Photographs by Raja Lala Deen Dayal, 1884–1910*, New York, A. A. Knopf, 1980.

30. R. Lécuyer, *Histoire de la photographie*, Paris, Baschet, 1945, p. 107.

Nadar's studio

In 1853 Nadar moved to 113 Rue Saint-Lazare and bought his first photographic equipment. This was about the time that he had his idea for the *Pantheon*. Countless writers, including Gautier and de Banville, sat for him. His first prints date from when the photographic studio opened, in 1854. The Goncourt brothers, Gérard de Nerval, and Marceline Desbordes-Valmore all had their portraits taken in the garden with its thick shrubbery. At the bottom of the garden, a sloping-roofed summer house doubled as Nadar's laboratory. Here he welcomed the "Republic of Letters", leaving us many penetrating and incisive portraits of the intelligentsia of the day.

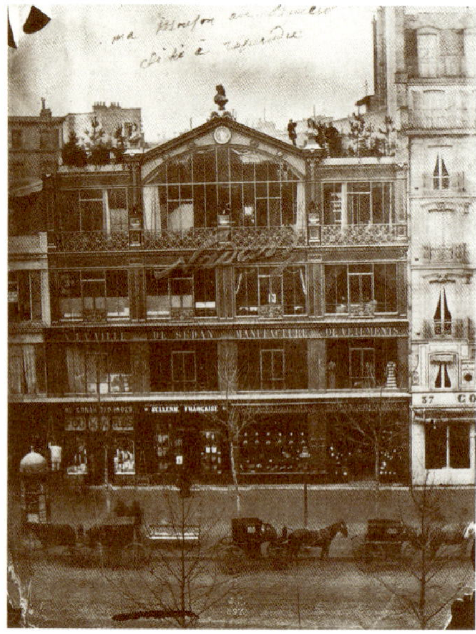

In 1861, in the wake of Disdéri's success, Nadar put a new business plan into operation. He fitted out luxurious premises at 35 Boulevard des Capucines, the same building that had housed Le Gray and the Bisson brothers. His signature had previously appeared in gigantic letters on a blank wall near 113 Rue Saint-Lazare – his Great Wall of China. Now it shone out in red, illuminated by gas lamps. There was a gallery on the ground floor and two richly decorated parlors on the first floor, reached by a highly elaborate staircase. A sheet of water ran over the window, cascading over rocks surrounded by huge pillars set among a riot of green plants. There was no doubt that Nadar's was one of the most eye-catching studios in Paris.

By the end of the Franco-Prussian War and the Paris Commune, Nadar was ruined. He decided to move to new, more modest premises at 51 Rue d'Anjou which he hoped would attract the local aristocratic clientele. A white cashmere jacket replaced his red tunic. The old republican hated change. When he fell out with his son Paul over selling Eastman cameras in the shop he decided to quit photography.

However, the number of clients fell dramatically, a number of people failed to pay their bills, and Nadar was forced to open a new studio in Marseilles. Thanks to the support of assistants who were fully conversant with the new techniques, and the introduction of fresh commercial formulas, business remained buoyant for some time. But Nadar had grown tired of it all and sold out to Fred Boissonas, a dynamic photographer from Geneva who went on to open a whole chain of branches.

Before Nadar died, in 1910, he saw his dream come true. Men flew machines that were heavier than air. As far as photography was concerned, his career of over half a century was groundbreaking. With astonishing clarity he showed the way that portrait studios would need to follow.

Jean Sagne

NADAR,
Nadar's Studio, Boulevard des Capucines, Paris,
1860s, Bibliothèque Nationale, Paris.

meet the needs of this trade, among them the "ambrotype" and "ferrotype" (or "tintype"), which meant that the photograph could be delivered to the customer after only a minimum waiting time. In both cases, the photographer used bleached collodion negatives on a black background. For the ambrotype, a glass support was used with dark paper placed behind it to produce a positive image. The ferrotype process used a tin plate that had been specially coated with black paint.

JOHN THOMAS,
Lloyd George,
circa 1880,
National Library
of Wales, Aberystwyth.

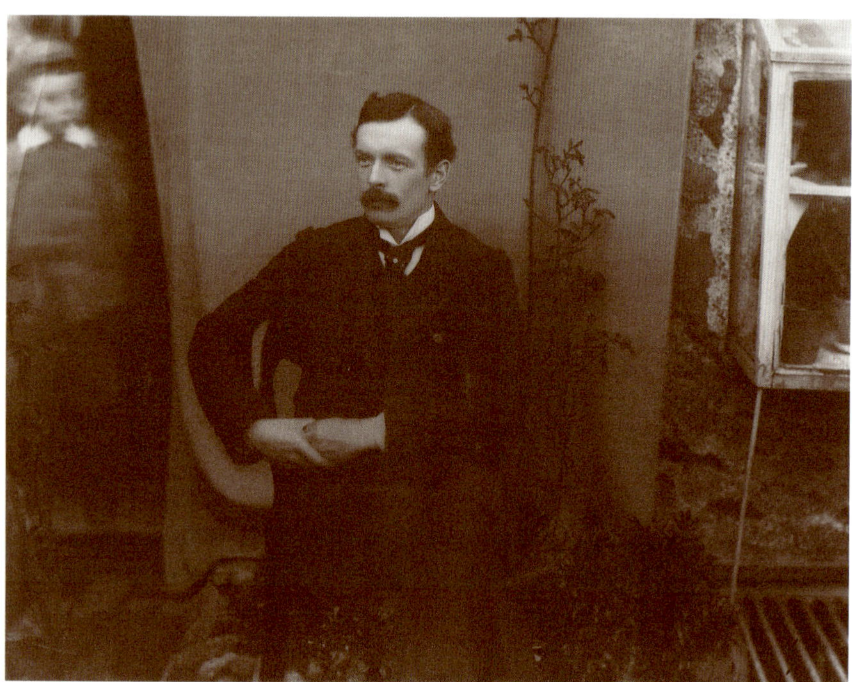

As soon as it made its first public appearance, photography became one of the attractions at fairs, just one curiosity among a host of monsters, physical phenomena, and exotica. Fairground photographers would travel to the big events, the Foire de Trône, the Fête de Neuilly or Montmartre. The public, decked out in their Sunday best, would have their photographs taken for one franc. Sometimes photographers would rig up a tent as a makeshift studio, but they usually worked in the open air. Watching people having their portraits taken became one of the fairground attractions which had the crowds laughing and jeering. Photographers themselves were also something worth watching. Some were real performance artists. For example, Charavay, using the stage name of "The Masked Man", took photographs of top wrestlers.[30]

Among early photographers was the Swiss engraver Jean-Baptiste Isenring. He ordered one of Daguerre's cameras from Giroux in 1839 and experimented by taking photographs of his family and friends. He then set off for Germany, ending up in Munich where he set up his make-

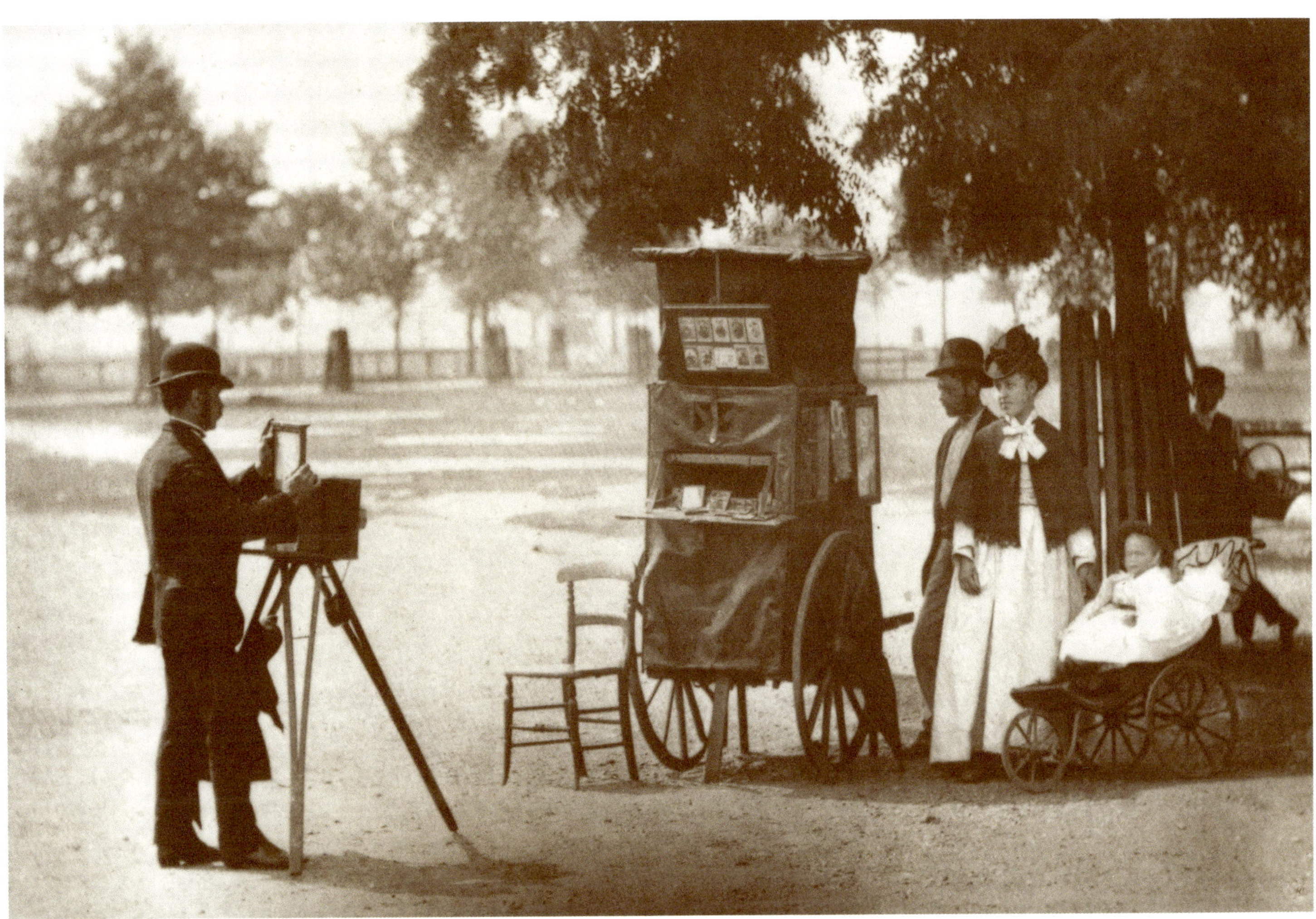

John Thomson,
Traveling Photographer,
Clapham Common,
circa 1876,
Royal Photographic Society,
Bath.

shift studio in Maximiliansplatz and became one of the city's attractions.[31]

The photographic ritual

Photography's origins placed it in the same sphere as magic and illusion. Daguerre had perfected Niépce's invention but he was also responsible for the diorama, an immense panorama on which light played cleverly to give the impression of the different times of day. The atmosphere created by so many photographers had its roots in these early magical beginnings. When you went to visit Nadar, you would be greeted by a crocodile hanging from the ceiling while skins of wild animals covered the walls. In New York, Sarony also had a crocodile. The entrance to Lafosse's studio in Manchester was full of helmets and suits of armor. Anson Clark's waiting room housed a mineral collection, various bits of machinery, pictures of pagan gods, shells, and a selection of eggs. Andrew Van Alstin returned from a world trip with a huge number of stuffed birds which he kept in his drawing room. Nugent's premises on Place de la Bourse in Paris housed a museum of Indian artifacts.[32]

From the humblest traveling stall to the most luxurious studio, the same strategies were deployed. Photography, which made the same form of representation common throughout the world, became part of a movement experienced by cultures the world over. It also encouraged every type of escapism. From one establishment to the next, photography revealed the path along which clients could move from the secular world they inhabited to the sacred world of representation – without even realizing it.

The room in which the photograph was taken was almost exactly like the props department of any theater. There was no logic as to how the balustrades and columns were arranged on oriental rugs or parquet floors, jumbled together alongside a variety of chairs and tables of every style. Heavy drapery swags opened onto painted backcloths showing snow-capped mountains, undergrowth or the view of a port. It was unusual for a portrait to be taken in an everyday setting. Outdoor shots were practically unheard of and someone like Camille Silvy, who took his aristocratic clients' portraits in a studio decorated to look like a Paris apartment, was the exception, not the rule. In nearly every studio, space was stage-managed, filled with props and accessories.

The work produced by Napoléon Sarony in New York is a perfect example of this type of stage-managed setting showing a whole range of

31. H. Loetscher, *et al.*, *Photography in Switzerland: 1840 to Today*, Teufen, Niggli, 1974.

32. For complete information on the interior decor of studios, see H. B. Pritchard, *The Studios of Europe*, London, Piper and Carter, 1882.

The photograph album

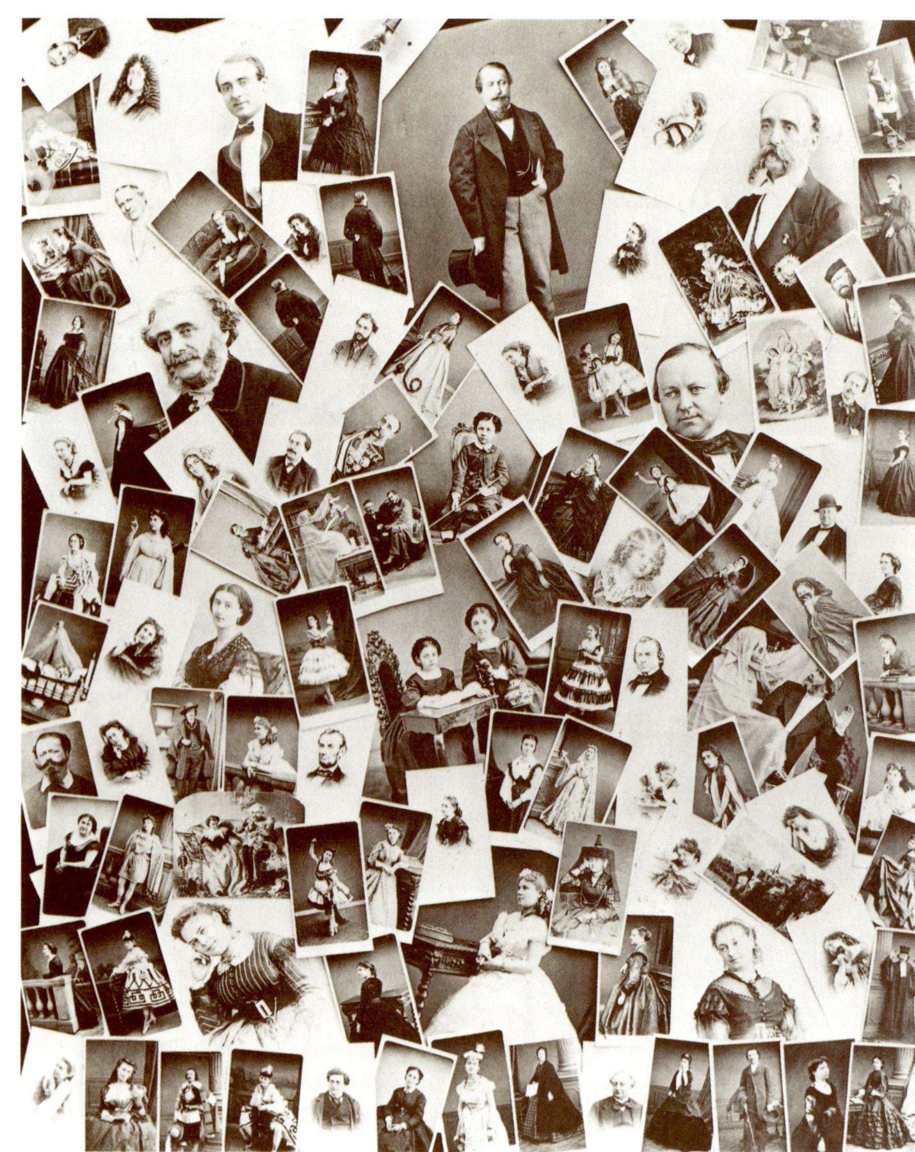

In France, on February 18, 1860, Marcelin wrote a piece for the *Journal amusant* about the appearance of albums for carte-de-visite portraits. He dubbed them "new family museums". As soon as cartes de visite started being mass-produced they spread like wildfire. This made the introduction of albums, "truly portable museums", inevitable. Albums, already used by autograph collectors, were soon used for photography. Very soon, every middle-class family would own at least one. Scattered family members were placed in its pages and classified into new-found unity. At a time when economic development seemed to endanger the fabric of society and the structure of the family, the album was seen as a method of ensuring cohesion, a symbolic object which safeguarded emotional attachments and social relationships. It was also a place to note political and artistic preferences. Arguments raged over the way pictures should be classified. The inclusion of some faces was bound to give rise to comment. In *La Curée*, Zola describes the place the album held in everyday life: "When it rained or when they were bored, the album became the center of conversation. Then they spent hours debating Ecrevisse's hair, Madame de Meinhold's double chin, Lauwerens' eyes, Blanche Muller's neck, the Countess's slightly crooked nose or little Sylvia's mouth, famed for its heavy lips." Cartes were slotted into place in the thick card pages. The heavy leather-bound volume was held together with ornamental clasps and sometimes doubled as a musical box.

Jean Sagne

ANONYMOUS, *Composite photograph using cartes de visites, album cards, etc.,*
circa 1880, private collection.

geographical locations. The Egyptian mummy placed in the entrance hall to the studio prepared the client for the wildest journey. As they moved from room to room, clients might encounter Chinese parasols, Russian sleighs or Turkish tapestries.[33]

To a lesser extent, local photographers also came up with similar diversions, although romantic backdrops with ruined castles may have sounded an incongruous note. In the novel *Gigi*, Colette described the props that cluttered up M. Armand's studio: a Gothic chair for the sitter, "a wickerwork alcove with a stuffed dog, and a couple of shrimping nets that the children in sailor's outfits liked so much".[34]

In the provinces, recently discovered records show that establishments such as those of the "bridge-photographer" in Saint-Etienne turned out work every bit as good as the big-name studios. Indeed, they often demonstrate an exceptionally fresh take on the world of ordinary people, exploited or discarded in the rush for economic advancement. The people who came to have their pictures taken by the bridge-photographer were laborers or Polish and Spanish immigrants. Their faces look weary as they pose in front of misty or rustic backdrops.[35]

From 1880 onwards, photographers started to follow the crowds as they left town for spas and seaside resorts. Hikers were persuaded to pose for portraits in their hiking boots, knapsacks on their backs. Photographers convinced bathers in striped bathing costumes to have their pictures taken in front of painted backdrops showing swelling seas or a port. It was not long before photographers started to comb the beaches in search of groups of holiday-makers building sandcastles they would immortalize. After the

33. R. Taft, *op. cit.*, p. 342.

34. Colette, *Gigi*, Paris, Le Fleuron, 1949.

35. *Le Photographe des ponts: cérémonie du portrait*, with introduction by M. Muller and P.-Y. Perrier, Saint-Etienne, Le Hénaff, 1983.

collapse of his business in 1875, the renowned Disdéri ended up working as a photographer in Nice.[36] For a while, his studio at 15 Promenade des Anglais continued to siphon off the richest clientele. Then Disdéri was forced to move to a less fashionable address and within ten years the man who had once run one of the grandest studios in Paris had fallen right to the bottom of the photographic heap. He died in 1889 at the Hôpital Sainte-Anne, an institute for "the destitute, drunks, and mentally ill".

Matthew Brady paid for about twenty photographers to cover the American Civil War from mobile studios rigged up in wagons. The response he had reckoned on from front-line soldiers was not forthcoming and he ended up with huge debts. One of his best photographers, Alexander Gardner, left him in 1862 to set up his own studio in Washington. Toward the end of the century, increasing competition between rival photographers pushed some into the schoolyard,

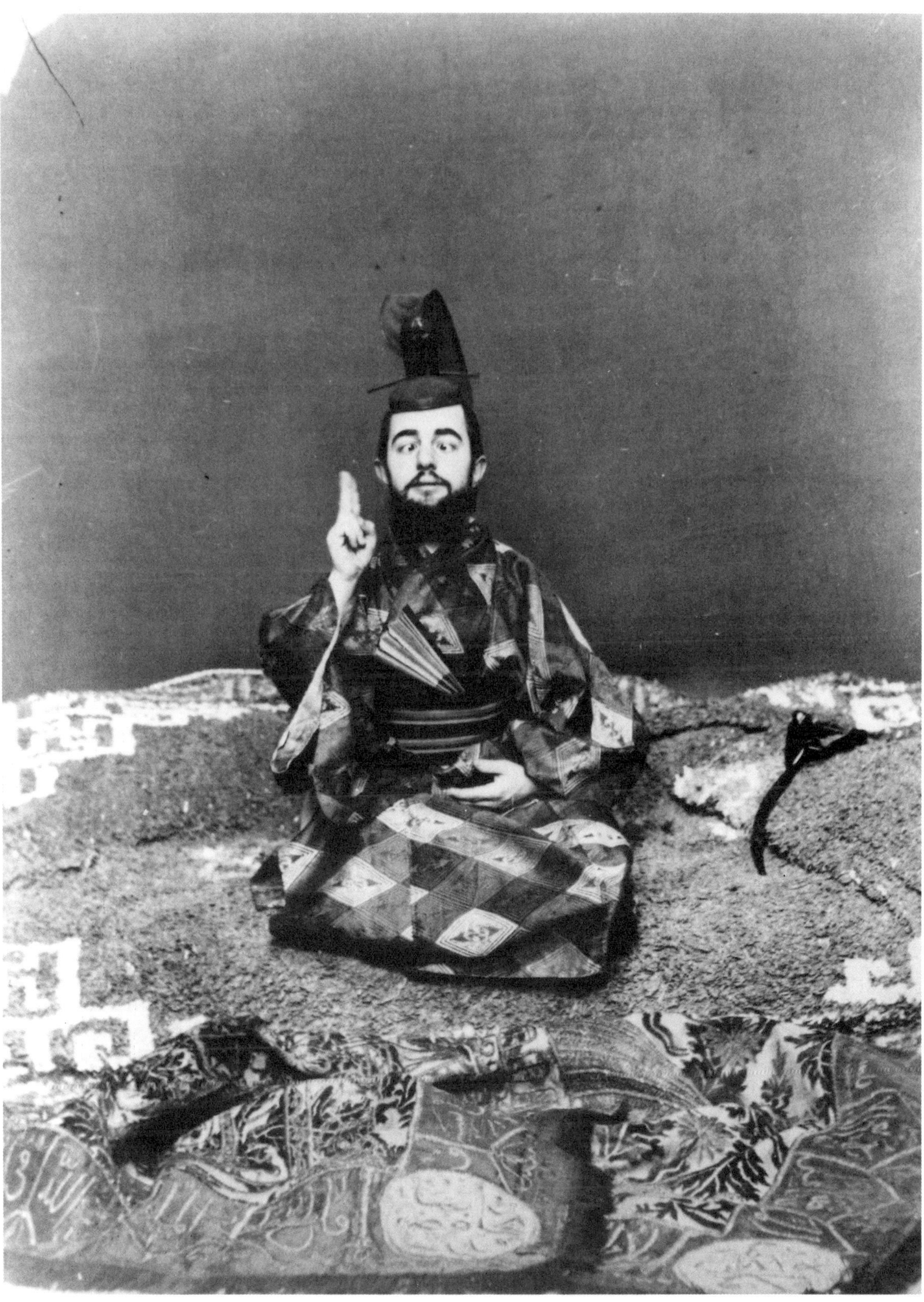

Anonymous, ***Henri de Toulouse-Lautrec in a Japanese Costume,*** circa 1892, Musée Toulouse-Lautrec, Albi.

36. See. A. MacCauley, "Disdéri", in *Prestige de la photographie*, no. 5, pp. 4–47.

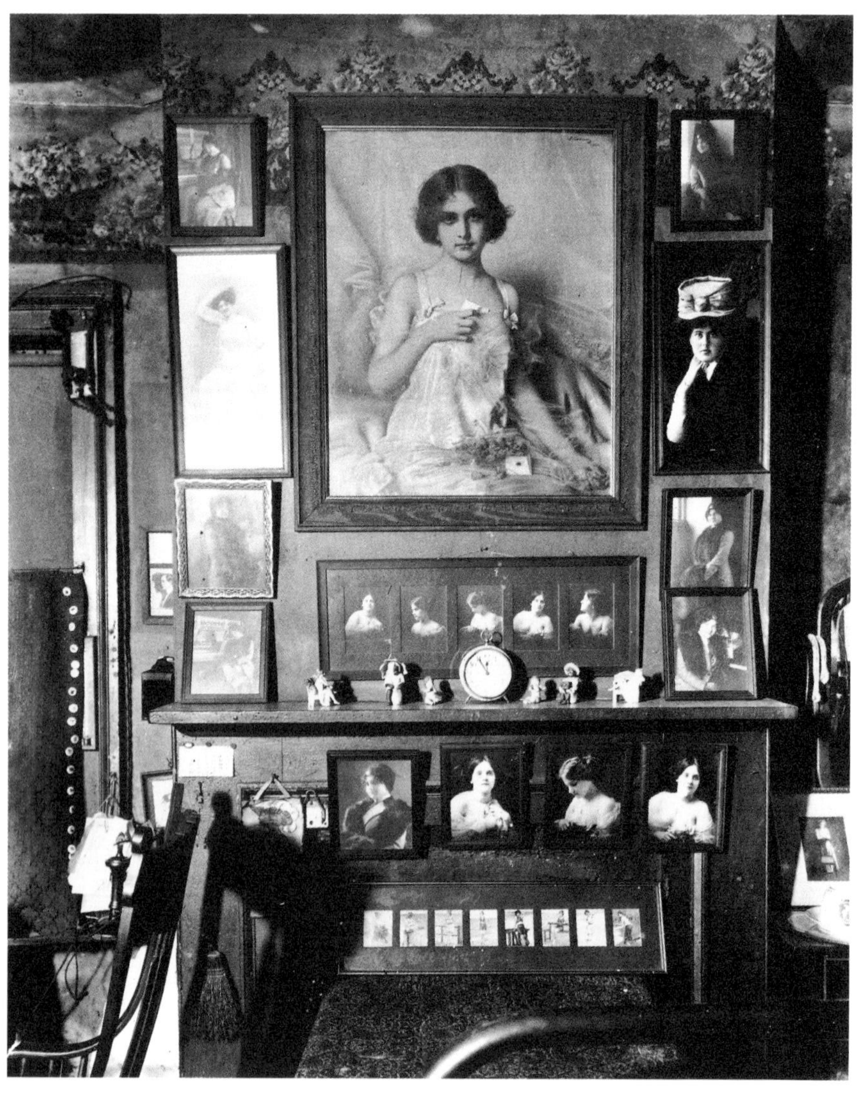

E. J. Bellocq, *Interior with Photographic Portraits,* circa 1911-1913.

where they took group pictures, or to the villages, lining up groups of "ordinary people". This type of group portrait captured a fleeting moment and gave it the chance to survive. Soldiers in dormitories or families gathered for a wedding were lined up in front of the camera.

After 1880, the increased sensitivity of dry plates using the gelatine-silver bromide emulsions gave fresh impetus to this type of outdoor work. A portrait photographer no longer had to wait for clients to come to him. Alphonse Deriaz, Niépce de Saint-Victor's assistant, stranded in Switzerland at the outbreak of the Franco-Prussian War in 1870, switched to photographing people at work – laborers, chimneysweeps, and navvies. He went wherever there was a festivity or public holiday. His son, Armand, who took over the studio in Morges, photographed soldiers or peasants.[37] The negatives were printed onto postcards and sent to friends. His lens captured a café owner with his family posing in front of the shop window, a group of touring cyclists, a brass band in a remote village.

In 1874 Antoine Lumière started a second business in Lyons, parallel with his main studio. Called *Photographie japonaise* and open only on Sundays, it specialized in tintype portraits for the mass market. Auguste and Louis Lumière, still children, helped out. Antoine introduced a true innovation – a system of electric lights which allowed him to work at night. He then set about manufacturing gelatine-bromide plates and ended up with a business of world renown.[38]

This period was one in which photography evolved rapidly. Paul Nadar, who had taken over the new studio in Rue d'Anjou from his father, had begun to market Eastman cameras (George Eastman was the founder of Kodak). Soon, as well as the carte de visite, other, larger formats such as cabinet, boudoir, and imperial became available. Thanks to new printing papers, their appearance became much shinier, with backgrounds in hazy, soft gradation. Gold, copper or iron toning was used which allowed red or green-tinted prints to be made on bromide paper.

A few of the great Paris studios, such as Reutlinger's, did survive. It had been opened in 1850 by Charles Reutlinger at 33 Boulevard Saint-Martin. It then moved into more up-market premises at 112 Rue de Richelieu to be nearer the big-name studios. Like Paul Nadar, Pirou, Waléry, and Manuel, it specialized in portraits of actors in general but actresses in particular.[39] A number of publishing houses, such as Tresse at the Palais-Royal which produced *Foyers et coulisses* about Paris theatrical life also specialized along these lines. By the end of the century, photomechanical processes made portraits of actresses in provocative poses available in magazines or as postcards.

This opened up new commercial avenues for the large studios. Prints of stars such as Liane de Pougy, Gaby Deslys, Meyan or Suzanne Duvernoir wearing flimsy garments sold like hot cakes. Competition, already fierce during the Second Empire, became still stiffer. The theater kept many photographers in business. No other method of enticing private customers in front of the camera could compete with stars such as Sarah Bernhardt or Cécile Sorel.

The last surviving temple of photography was the Harcourt studio, which established its reputation in exactly this way. Between the two world wars a whole galaxy of film stars came here to be photographed. The fate of the portrait studios was dependent upon outside money – which, in turn, liked the idea of being involved with celebrities.

Photography had been desperate to be taken as seriously as painting. What actually occurred was a revelation of how much it owed to theatrical production and show business. When we examine how the big photographic studios worked, it is clear that had the desire to limit the scope of photography to the purely aesthetic been implemented, it would have meant closing off all kinds of avenues which were only just beginning to open up.

37. C.-H. Favrod, *La famille Deriaz,* Zurich, Stemmle, 1988.

38. G. Borgé, "Les Lumière", in *Prestige de la photographie,* no. 8, pp. 100–141.

39. J.-P. Bourgeron, *Les Reutlinger photographes à Paris,* Paris, J.-P. Bourgeron, 1977.

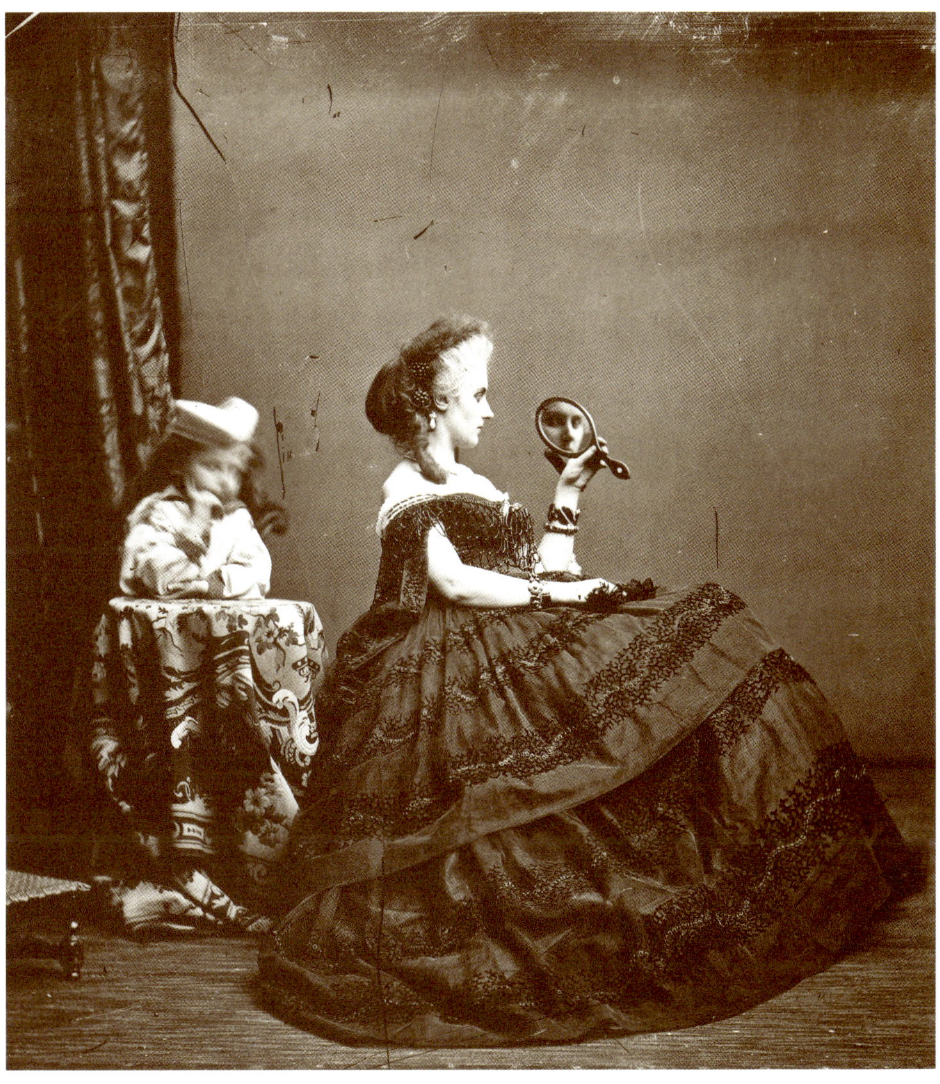

Distinguished personages

From the end of the 1850s, interest in portraiture spread wider and wider. At the same time, far more photographs were in circulation thanks to affordable prices. Both factors undoubtedly contributed to the advent of one of the stereotypes of the modern era – our fascination with the appearance of well-known people. Our interest is not just limited to their faces but includes their bodies too. And when it comes to stars or really famous people, our level of curiosity is even greater.

It all began around 1855 when printing and engraving started to make regular use of photographic records (*Gallery of Illustrious Americans*, by Brady, 1850, *Histoire des artistes vivants*, by Théophile Silvestre in 1853, *Panthéon des illustrations française au XIXe siècle*, by Victor Frond, 1869). From then on, every portrait appearing in the illustrated press was engraved from a photograph supplied by one of the big studios. *Pantheon Nadar* (1854) was inspired by the idea of putting together a series of "mug shots" and producing something along the lines of the "ancestral portrait gallery" which was so dear to every aristocratic heart.

Countless photographers latched onto the concept and published series of prints. Some focused on particular social categories and many were accompanied by biographical notes. Examples include Adolphe Dallemagne's *Galerie des artistes contemporains* (circa 1866), Auguste Lacroix's *Galerie photographique et biographique des sauveteurs* (1860), Pierre Petit's *Galerie des hommes du jour* (1861), Adolphe-Eugène Disdéri's *Galerie des contemporains* (1862), Dornac's *Nos contemporains chez eux* (1889), Barraud's *Men and Women of the day* (1888–1889), and Eugène Pirou's *Nos actrices chez elles* (1896). This fashion culminated in the appearance of *Galerie contemporaine, littéraire, artistique* published by L. Baschet in two series (1876–1880 and 1881–1884). It included Woodburytypes by Goupil which had been taken from original negatives by Nadar, Carjat, and Adam-Salomon.

No country escaped the desire to get to know its political leaders, royal family, fashionable people, authors, philosophers, and artists. Actresses, singers, and ladies of the *demi-monde* were also photographed. Everyone went along with the narcissistic game of portraiture. You could buy portraits in bulk or as a one-off from souvenir shops and sales counters on the boulevards. The Imperial Prince, Queen Victoria, and President Lincoln were quickly ousted by Sarah Bernhardt. Cartes de visite were soon superseded by cabinet-sized photographs. These larger-format pictures were tremendously popular with collectors.

The nineteenth century was also the age of methodical classification. Finding one's own image included in this or that category gave a cachet that was the height of social recognition.

It is still difficult to assess the social impact of the new visual framework which accompanied other forms of democratization (novels, serials, art). Furthermore, it is hard to judge how far the public was manipulated with regard not just to politics (the image of power) but also culture (photographs of George Sand, Baudelaire, and Colette, for instance). The writer Alexandre Dumas positively encouraged the circulation of pictures taken of him in tender poses with his young mistress.

This inclination toward what could be considered photographic fetishes could also be found in the strictly private photographs Lewis Carroll took of young girls. Similarly, the Countess of Castiglione, at the court of Napoleon III, used photography to her own ends. Her behavior underlined her natural inclination to emphasize appearances. She was a lifelong, almost obsessive, collector of photographs of herself (by Pierson) in evocative poses.

Michel Frizot

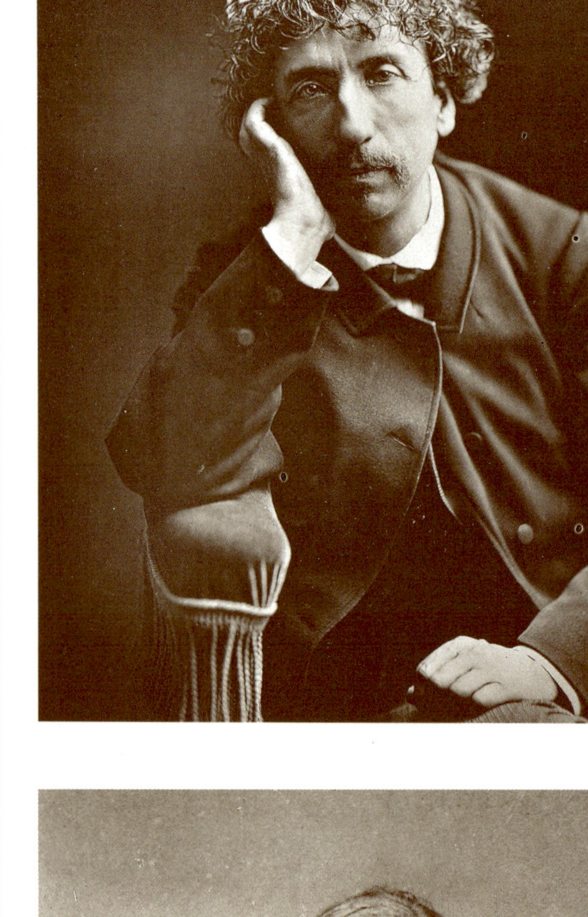

ADAM-SALOMON,
Charles Garnier,
circa 1865,
from *Galerie Contemporaine,*
private collection.

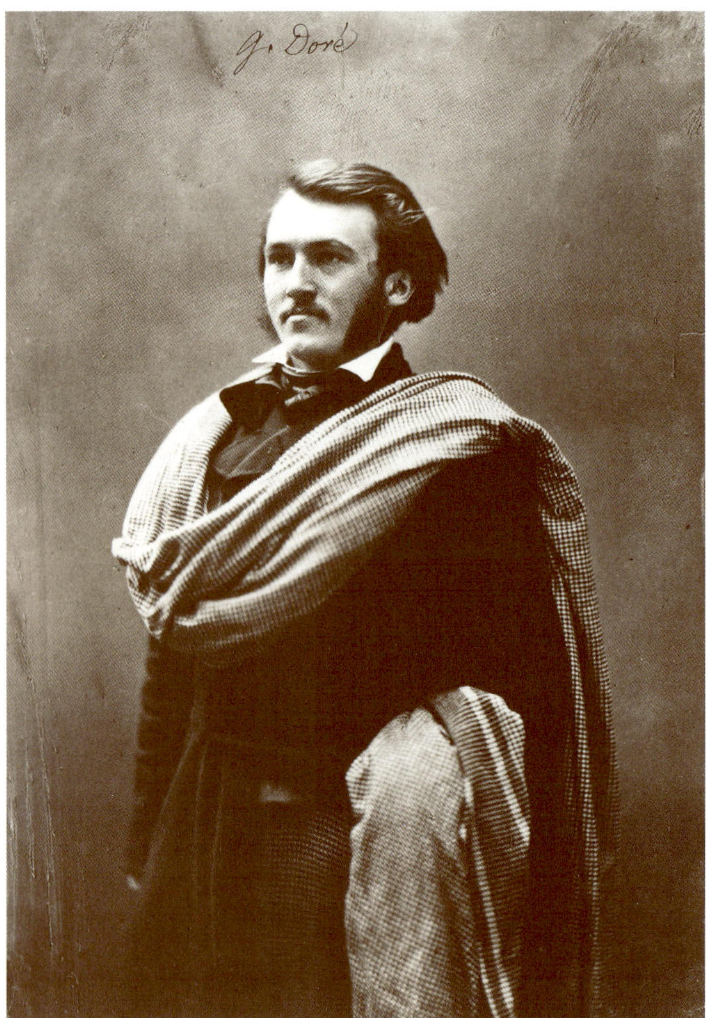

NADAR,
Portrait of Gustave Doré,
circa 1855–1865,
private collection.

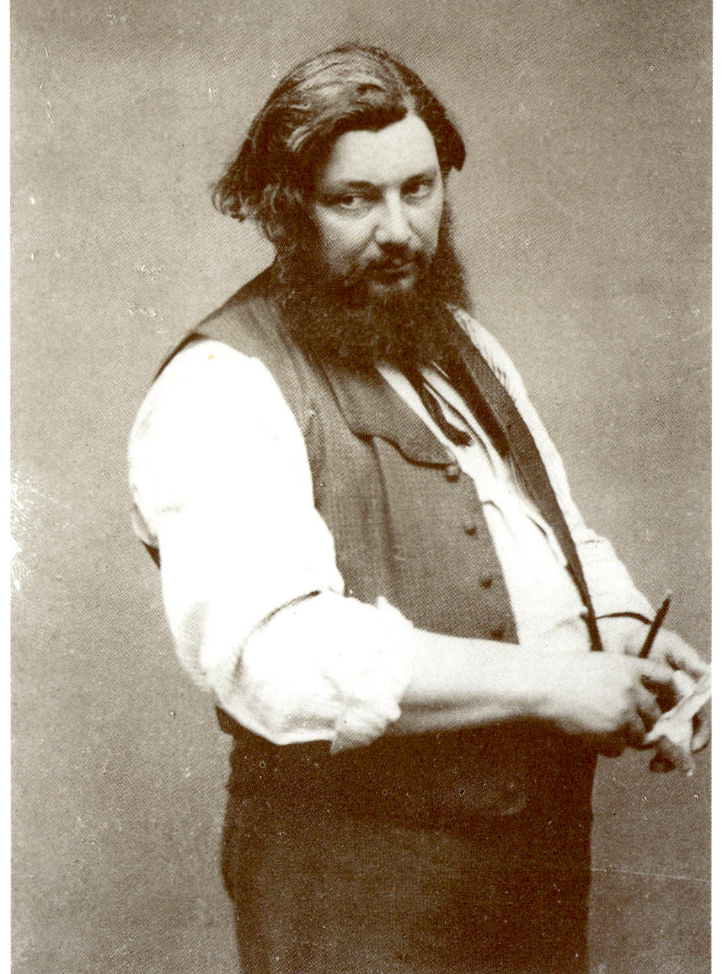

NADAR,
Gustave Courbet,
circa 1865,
Archives Photographiques, Paris.

◀◀ On the previous page:
LOUIS PIERSON,
Countess Castiglione and Her Son,
circa 1864,
Musée Unterlinden, Colmar/ Archives of the Haut-Rhin Department.

On the facing page: ▶▶
HERBERT BARRAUD,
Alfred Tennyson,
from *Men and Women of the Day,*
1888–1889.

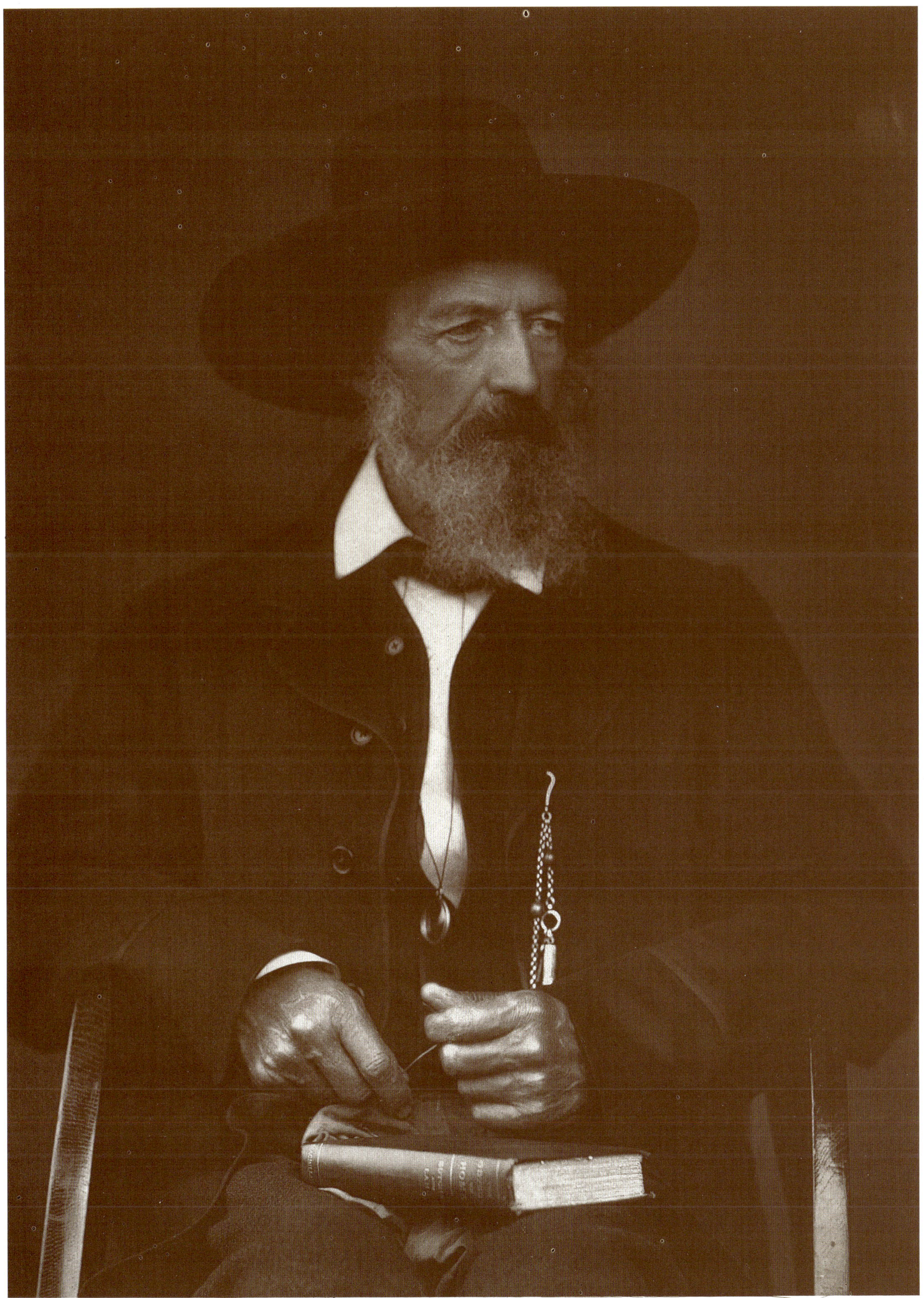

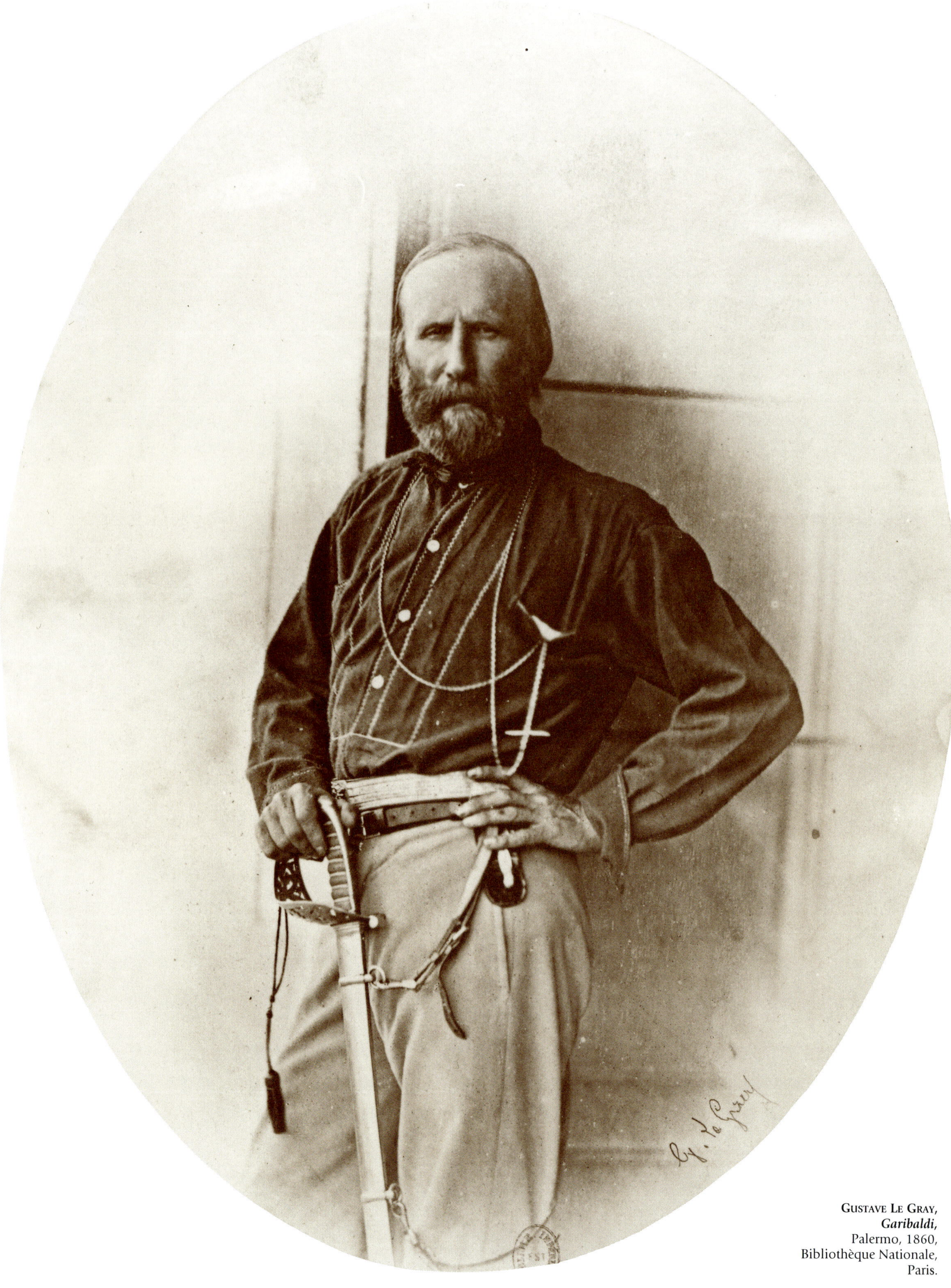

Gustave Le Gray,
Garibaldi,
Palermo, 1860,
Bibliothèque Nationale,
Paris.

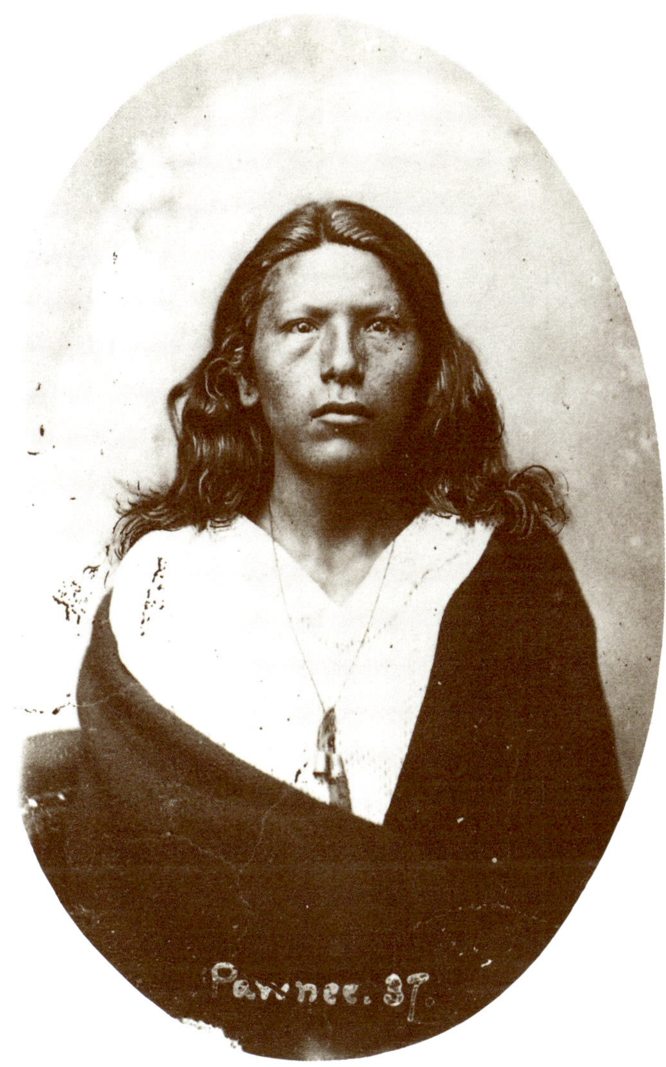

William H. Jackson,
Crow Eyes, Pawnee,
1862,
Amon Carter Museum of
Western Art,
Fort Worth.

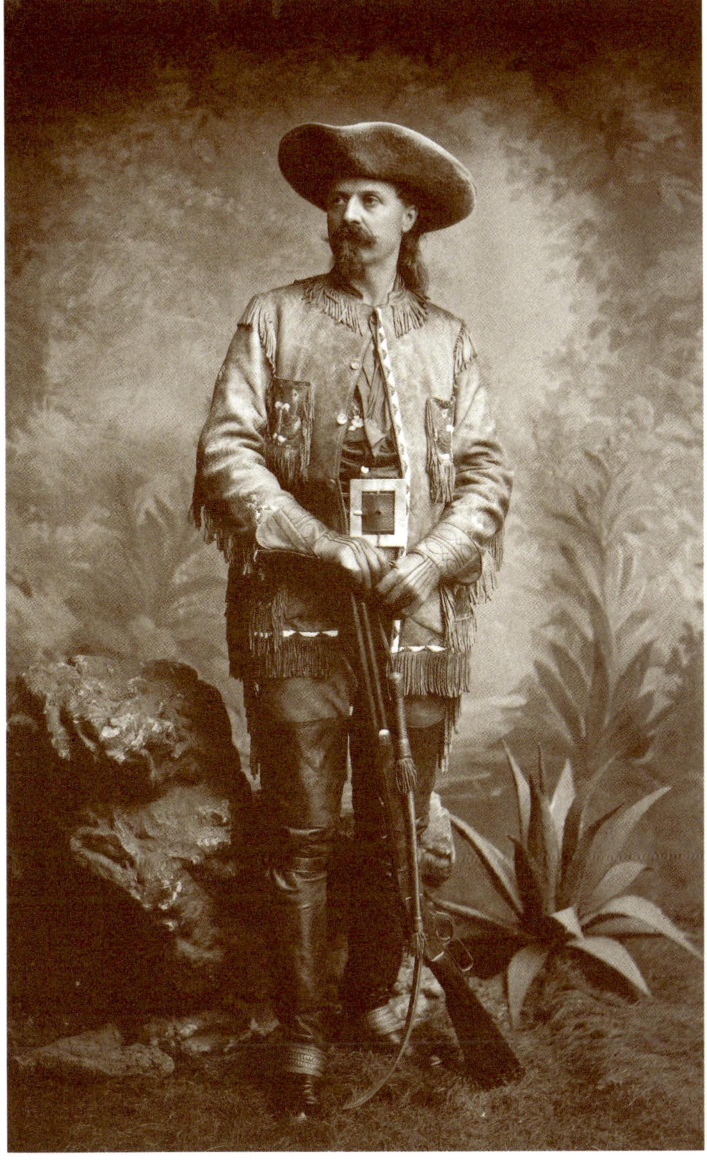

Elliot & Fry,
Colonel Cody, Known as Buffalo Bill,
1892,
Royal Archives,
Windsor Castle.

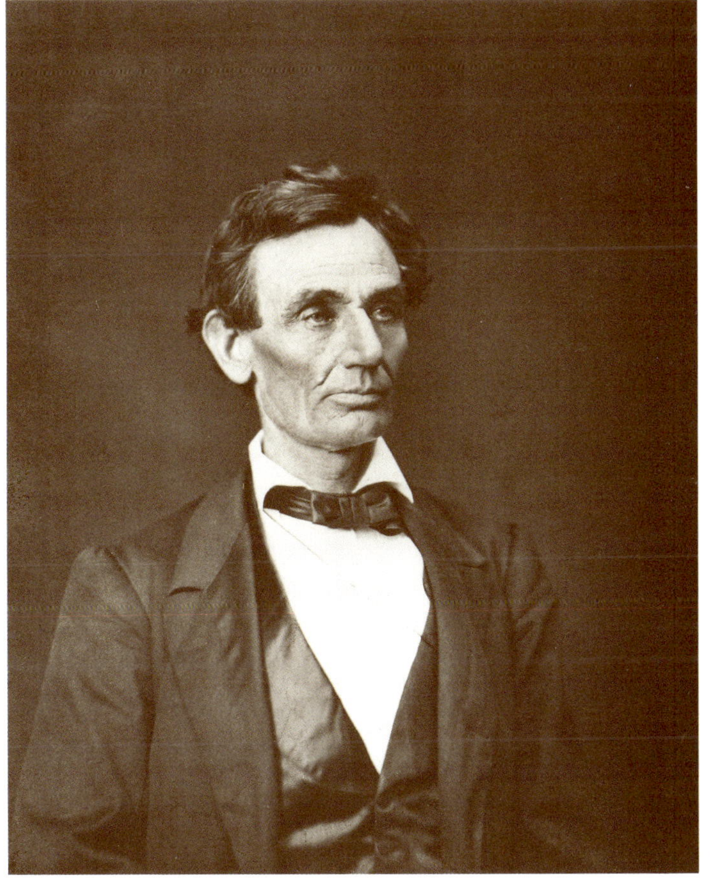

Alexander Hesler,
Portrait of Abraham Lincoln in Chicago,
1860,
Chicago Historical
Society.

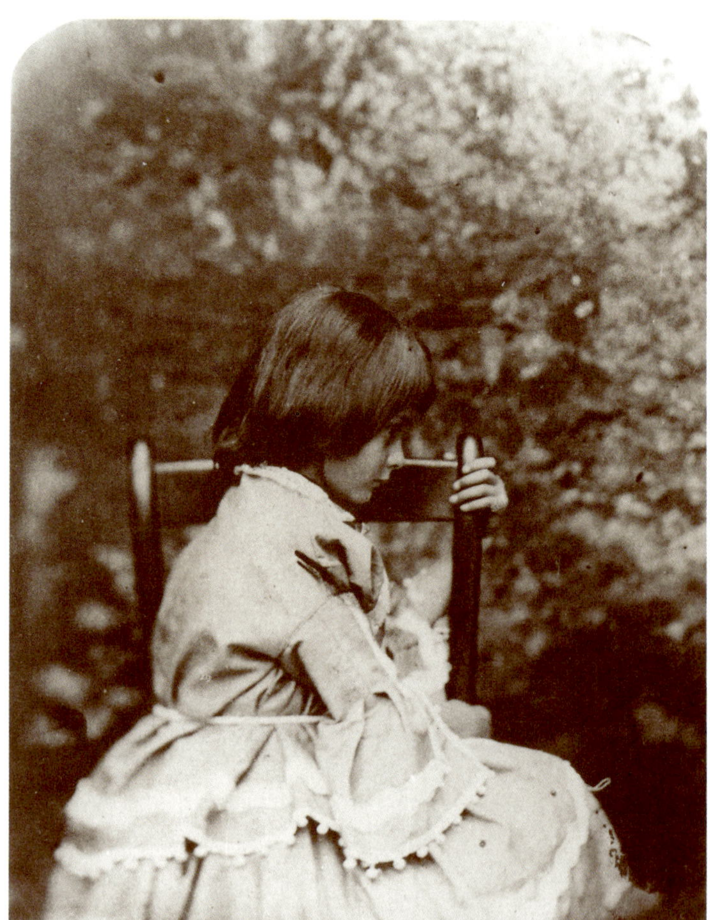

Lewis Carroll,
Alice Liddell,
circa 1860,
Parrish Collection,
Princeton University
Library.

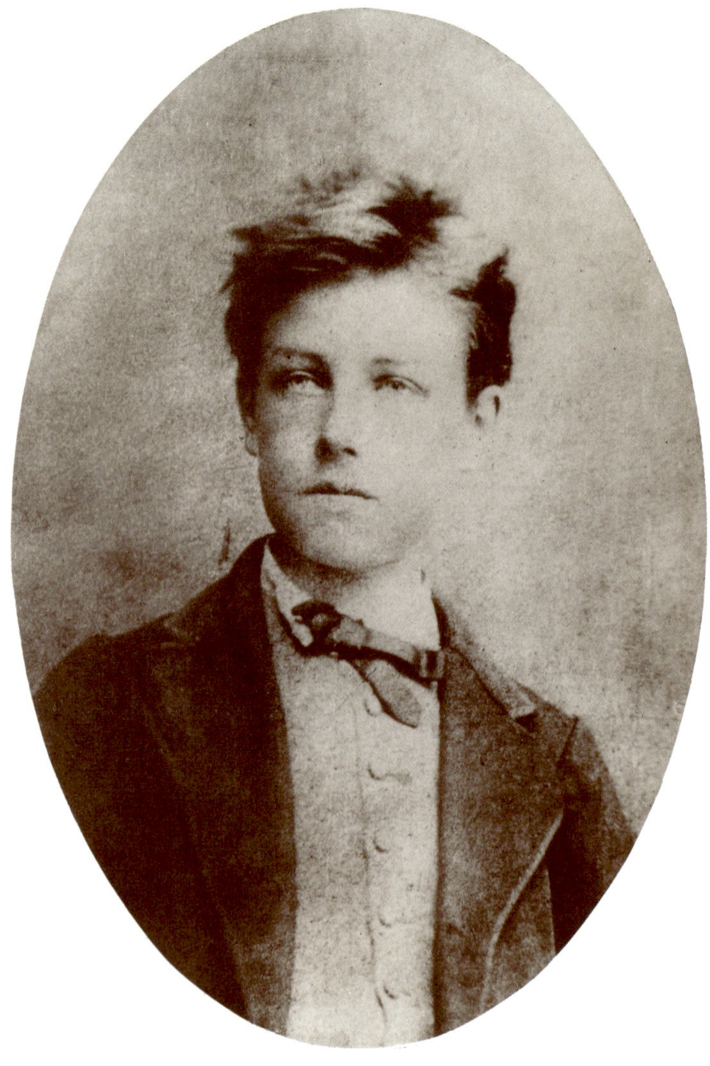

Étienne Carjat
(attributed),
Arthur Rimbaud,
1872,
Raymond Gid collection.

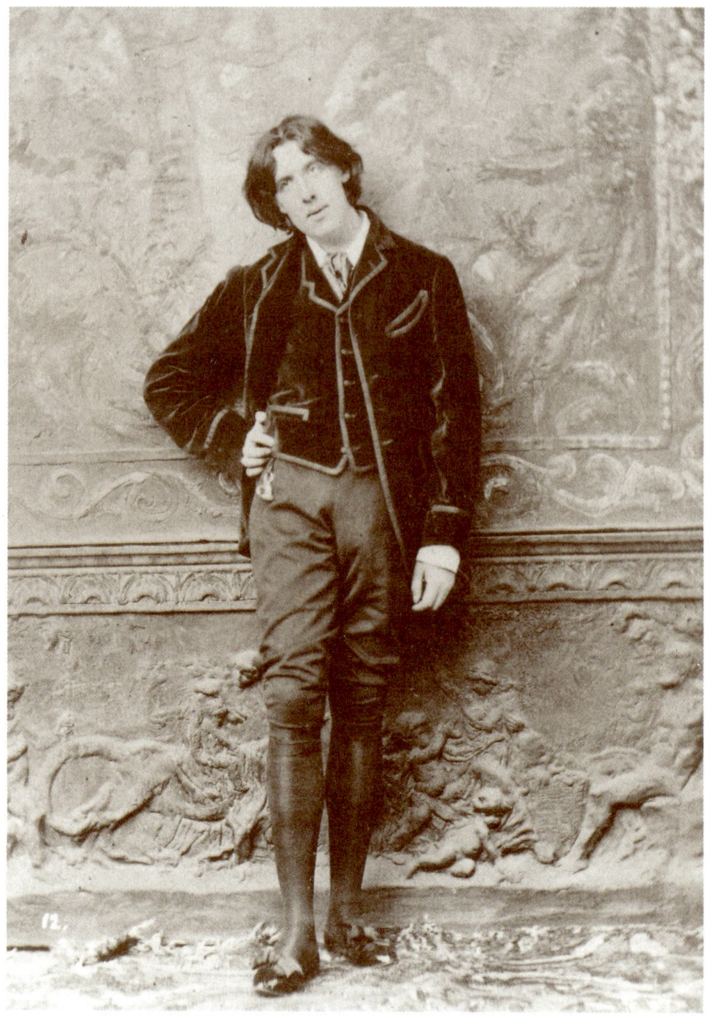

Sarony,
Oscar Wilde,
1882,
International Museum of
Photography,
George Eastman House, Rochester.

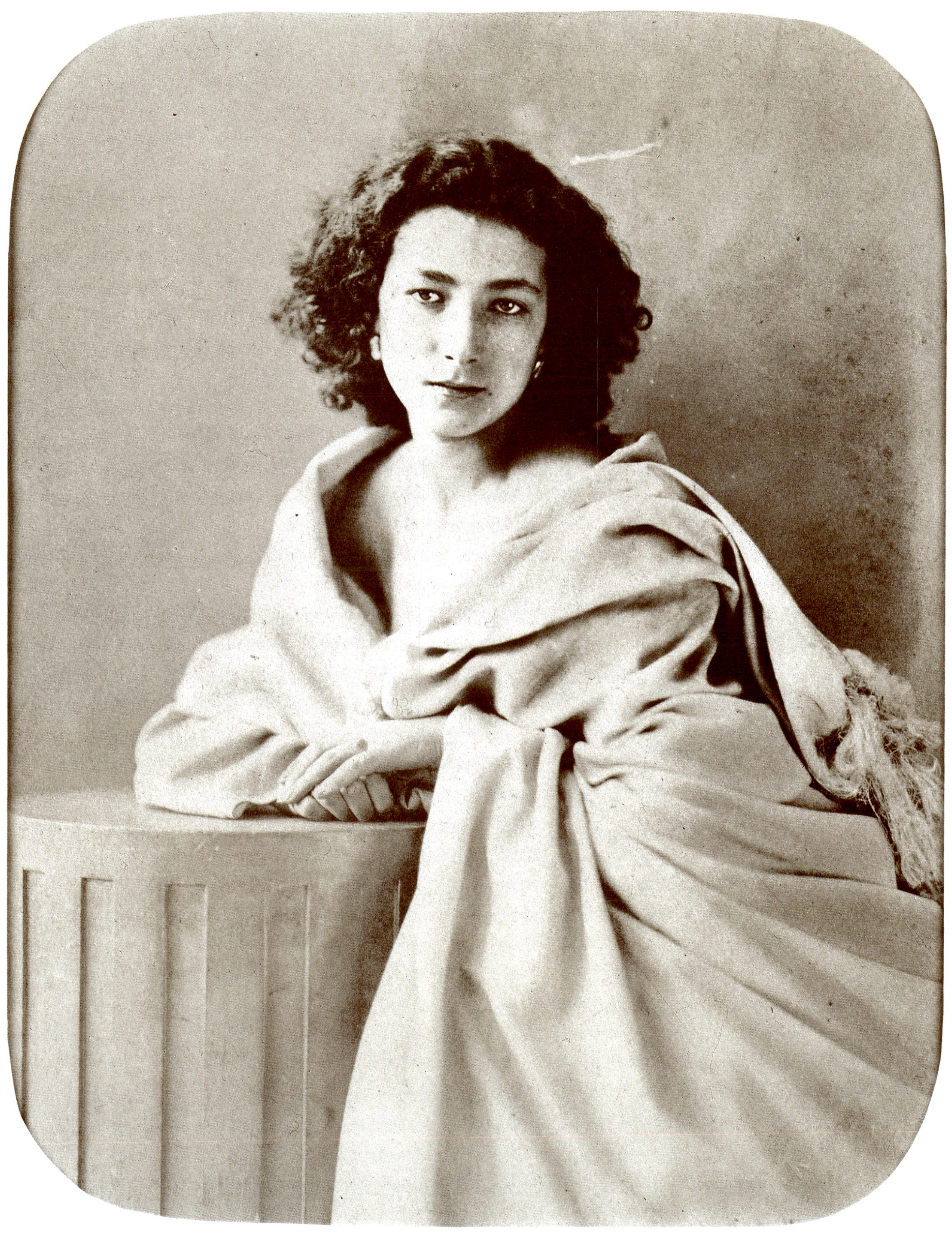

NADAR,
Sarah Bernhardt,
circa 1860,
Musée d'Orsay, Paris.

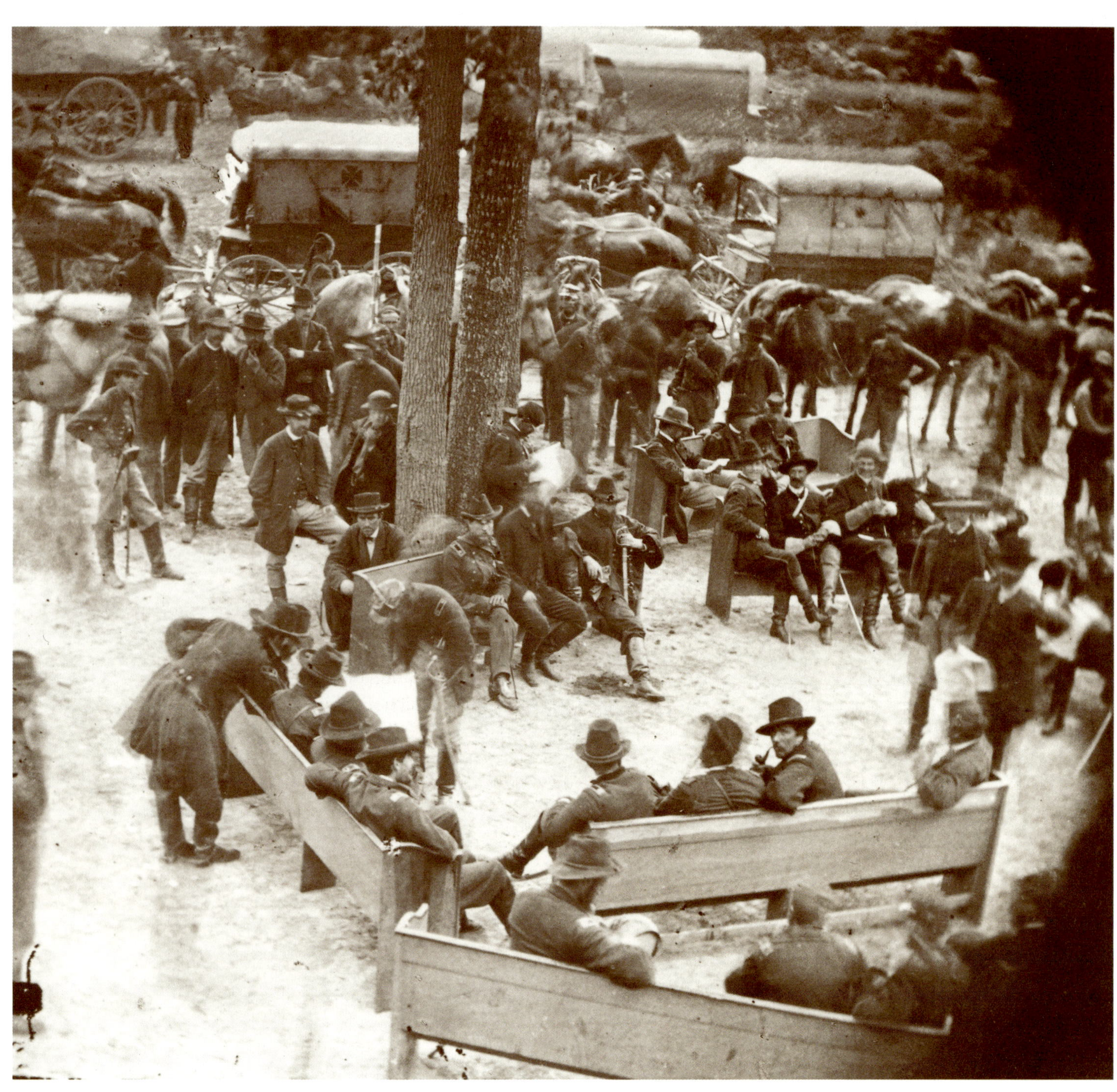

Timothy O'Sullivan,
General Grant and His General Staff
(American Civil War),
1864,
Library of Congress,
Washington.

THE CENTURY'S MEMORIAL 7

Photography and the recording of history

Hubertus von Amelunxen

The modernity of photography is clear in its relationship with "the news", the unexpected, current affairs, and contemporary life, and in the way the time-lag between an event and its record became shorter until the photographer was the direct eyewitness of events. But everyone had their own view about what aspect of an event provided an image, what characterized the emotional center of a conflict, what allowed war to be denounced. As soon as it was possible to participate visually in the very birth of history, the photographer indirectly passed a moral judgement on the event, which sometimes ran counter to what political powers and society would like.

"No journal, I declare", wrote Baudelaire, "no written record, no book could express so well this great epic of the Crimean War, in all its distressing detail and sinister breadth. The eye moves from the banks of the Danube to the shores of the Bosporus, from Cape Kerson to the plain of Balaclava or the fields of Inkerman, and on to the English, French, Turkish, and Piedmontese encampments, from the streets of Constantinople to the hospitals and to a variety of solemn religious and military ceremonies."[1] Time and distance melt away as the picture transports the viewer to the very scene of the event and promises direct, danger-free, involvement in what they see. Already in 1855, Ernest Lacan, in *Le Moniteur Universel*, had described a photographic album of distant scenes as a "magical journey" for the viewer, "in which his thought needs only to form a wish for his eye to be satisfied".[2]

When Baudelaire described his visual journey it was not photographs that he was looking at but the pen-and-ink drawings and watercolors of Constantin Guys, the artist whose work he had singled out as exemplifying his own idea of modernism – *Le peintre de la vie moderne*. The views drawn by Guys, who was at Balaclava and other Crimean War locations, for the *Illustrated London News* were, said Baudelaire, "living and surprising images, traced from life itself". Baudelaire had already used the word "traced" in 1857, to describe Henri Monnier's *Scènes populaires*, comparing them to the "cruel and amazing charm of the daguerreotype".[3] Here, the ambivalence of modernism becomes apparent. Photography is the representation of that ambivalence, which lies in the depiction of that which cannot be represented, in the linking of the ephemeral – the momentary – and the eternal, which transcends time.

The historic event and modernity

The nineteenth century witnessed the emergence of the media which would document it. More than any previous century, it took enormous pains to provide a record of itself for posterity. Although in the first third of the century lithography and the momentous advances made in publishing and in printing had made it possible to illustrate everyday life as it happened, it was photography which was to create the century's true memorial. Even if, today, one may have justifiable doubts as to the objective, documentary status of photography, it does, nevertheless, represent unmistakably a past which has been bequeathed as a legacy to the twentieth century. Early reactions to photography often included expressions of regret that the invention had come so late. Thus, as early as July 3, 1839, Arago was already writing in his *Rapport sur le Daguerreotype* of "the immense benefit that could have been derived, during the expedition to Egypt, from such an exact and rapid means of reproduction". While there could be no doubts about the faith-

1. C. Baudelaire, "The Painter of Modern Life", in *Baudelaire: Selected Writings on Art and Literature*, trans. with an introduction by P. E. Charvet, London, Penguin Books, 1992, p. 410.

2. E. Lacan, "De la Photographie", in *Le Moniteur Universel*, no. 12, January 12, 1844, p. 44.

3. C. Baudelaire, "Some French Caricaturists", in *The Painter of Modern Life*, trans. by J. Mayne, London, Phaidon Press, 1964, p. 180.

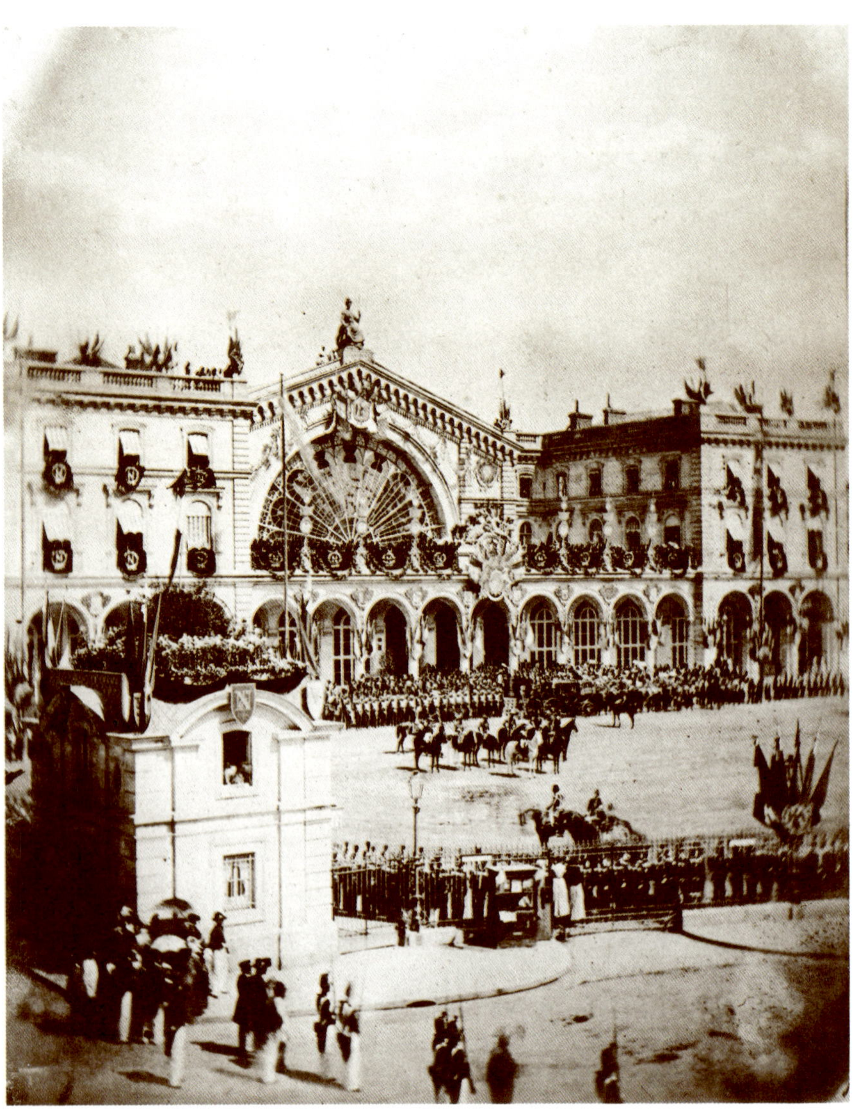

Disdéri,
Queen Victoria Arriving at the Gare de l'Est, Paris,
August 18, 1855,
Musée de l'Armée, Paris.

fulness and precision of the photographic image, it was too early, however, to speak of the process being "rapid". Only after the improvements which followed in the choice of materials, light-sensitivity of plates, construction of cameras, and design of lenses was it possible to photograph moving objects. Exposure time, determined by a combination of physical and chemical factors, became the decisive criterion as to the truthfulness of the image.

Before we can discuss news photography during the nineteenth century, we must first define what we mean by news. Any such definition is clearly problematic. Unlike the historiography of the nineteenth century, which aimed to give an "objective" account of those events which were considered to be historically significant, photography offers us the opportunity of studying the significance of an event with reference to the historical document itself. The newsworthy event – for example, the burning grain silos at Oswego in America, daguerreotyped by George N. Barnard (1853), or the great flooding of the Rhône (1856), photographed by Baldus – is the taking of the photograph. Each photograph acts as a silent witness and itself bears witness. The viewer has to form their own opinion as to its character and importance. An event can be said to be "historic" only when it can be placed in a chronological narrative of "before" and "after". This has been well expressed by Panofsky: "Lightning that strikes on a particular day at a particular place is, despite its uniqueness, not an 'historic' event so long as it does not, for instance, set fire to a cathedral, or kill an important person, and so become involved in particular contexts of meaning."[4] In theatrical terms the event is seen as the last act of a tragedy. Historiography could describe an event only with the benefit of hindsight – retrospectively.

In the history of representation, no medium had ever been able to reduce the time between an event occurring and its being recorded to the same extent as photography. Only after the invention of photography could anyone conceive of a medium in which reproduction was actually simultaneous with the event itself. With photography, "the blue flower in the land of technology", as Walter Benjamin once called it, a medium was born which possessed that "essential quality of the present" which Baudelaire demanded of art.

Early photographs are as significant in their own right, as part of cultural history, as the events that they recorded. In 1841, for example, the Natterer brothers caused a sensation with two daguerreotypes, so-called *Sekundenbilder* [pictures made in a second], of a procession which took place in Vienna, probably to mark the hundredth anniversary of the birth of Joseph II. The fact that these daguerreotypes rendered details of the procession fairly clearly – that, for the first time, it was possible to freeze and photograph movement – was sensational.[5] Another example is a calotype by Hippolyte Bayard which shows the Corpus Christi procession in Rue des Batignolles in 1842. Taken with an exposure time of two seconds, it conveys a suggestion of movement. The 46 daguerreotypes which the Hamburg photographer and graphic artist Hermann Biow (1804–1850) made of the ruins and devastation following the great Hamburg fire of May 1842 are often regarded as the first "disaster pictures". Reports of the time paid tribute to Biow's achievement, asserting that "since Daguerre made his invention this is probably the first time that it has found an application of such historic importance".[6] It is through being reproduced that an event acquires an historic significance. Nevertheless, photography takes on the character of an epilogue; it concludes history.

Many "historic" events of the nineteenth century are regarded as such only because they

4. E. Panofsky, "Zum Problem der historischen Zeit" (1927), in Panofsky, *Aufsätze zu Grundfragen der Kunstwissenschaft*, Berlin, Volker Spiess GmbH, 1985, p. 81.

5. See Hans Frank, *Vom Zauber alter Licht-Bilder: Frühe Photographie in Österreich, 1840–1860*, Vienna-Munich-Zurich-New York, Molden-Edition, 1981, and *Geschichte der Fotografie in Österreich*, vol. 1, Bad Ischl, Verein zur Erarbeitung der Geschichte der Fotografie in Österreich, 1983, p. 61.

6. See E. Kaufhold in *Silber und Salz: Zur Frühzeit der Photographie im deutschen Sprachraum 1839–1860*, ed. Bodo von Dewitz and Reinhard Matz, Cologne and Heidelberg, Edition Braus, 1989, pp. 352–403.

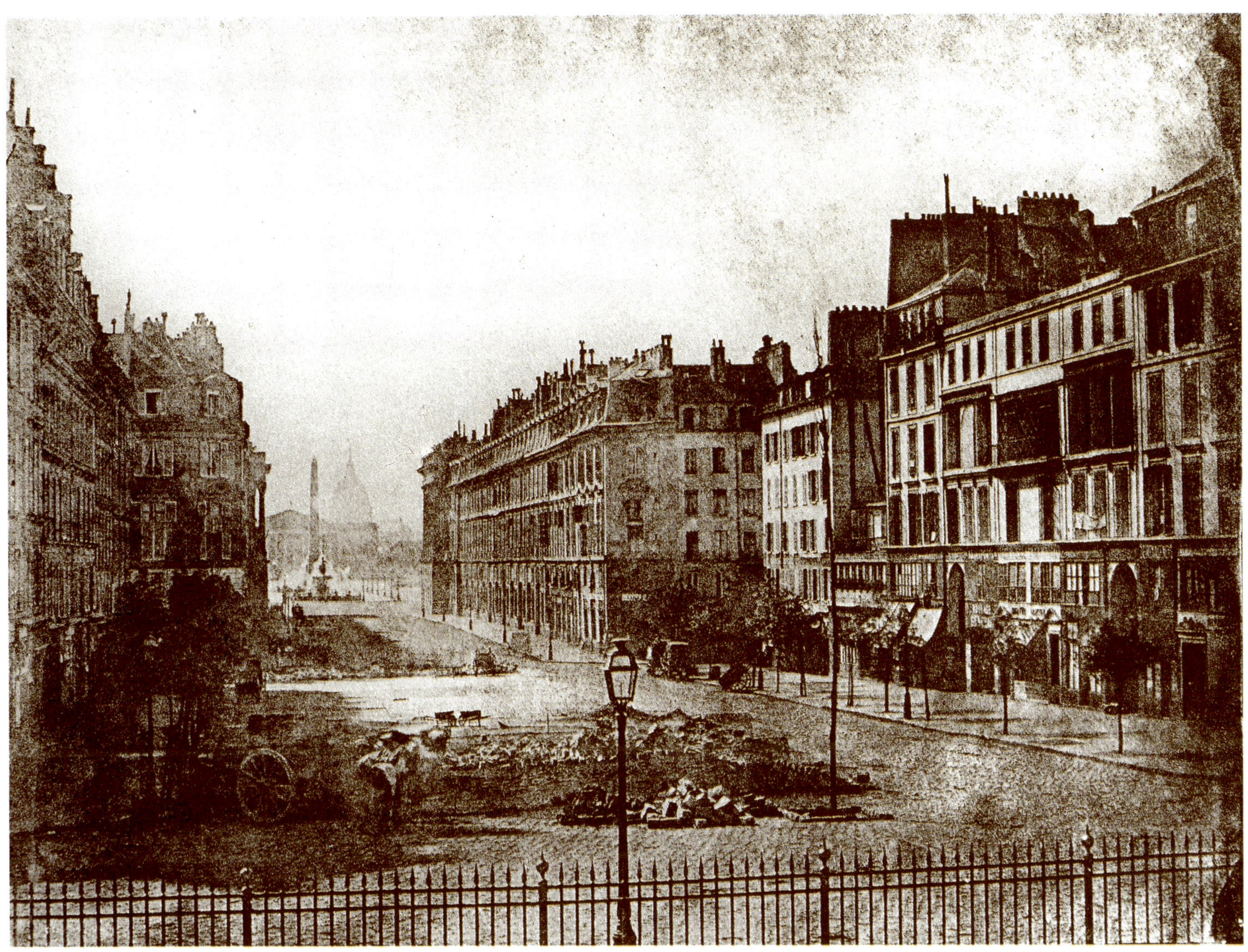

Hippolyte Bayard,
Remains of Barricades in Rue Royale,
1848.
Société Française de Photographie, Paris.

appeared sensational to contemporaries. Today they would often be seen as relatively trivial news items. The Great Exhibition at the Crystal Palace, opened by Queen Victoria on May 1, 1851, marked the beginning of a new age. Claude-Marie Ferrier, Charles Soulier, and Hugh Owen photographed both the opening and the exhibition itself. Talbot's former assistant, Nicolaas Henneman, was commissioned to print the photographs for a splendid three-volume catalogue. The equally lavish reopening by the queen after the Crystal Palace was moved to Sydenham, on June 19, 1854, and the welcoming reception for Emperor Napoleon III and Empress Eugenie in April 1855 were daguerreotyped by, among others, Philip Henry Delamotte.[7] The difficulty of making such a pictorial record can be appreciated (the firm of Negretti & Zambra had a monopoly on photography at the Crystal Palace).

The elusive conflict

The earliest photographs of war date from the time of the Mexican-American War. The "Texan War" broke out in 1846, after Texas had declared itself independent of Mexico in 1845 and had been incorporated into the Union of the United States. In 1848, after losing the war, Mexico was obliged to cede almost half of its territory to the United States. We know that during the war an American daguerreotypist, Charles J. Betts, was with the American army in Veracruz. An advertisement of April 1847 announced that for two weeks Betts would, on request, visit homes "to take miniatures of the dead and wounded". No outdoor photographs by him are known.[8] Of more than 60 anonymous daguerreotypes of the Texan War which survive, many were taken around Saltillo. They show buildings, views of streets, and troop movements, but the majority are portraits of American officers. These daguerreotype portraits have a symbolic quality which goes beyond mere likeness – they represent the embodiment of patriotism. Almost certainly, however, more daguerreotypes were carried to the war than were made on the spot. Like the painted miniature, photographs were kept as keepsakes. There are no known daguerreotypes showing the actual fighting – the battles of Veracruz or Resaca de la Palma – although, with an exposure time of

7. See H. von Amelunxen, *Die aufgehobene Zeit: Die Erfindung der Photographie durch William Henry Fox Talbot*, Berlin, Dirk Nishen 1988, pp. 54 ff.

8. See M. A. Sandweiss, R. Stewart, and B. W. Huseman, *Eyewitness to War: Prints and Daguerreotypes of the Mexican War, 1846–1848*, Amon Carter Museum, Smithsonian Institution Press, Washington, 1989, p. 51.

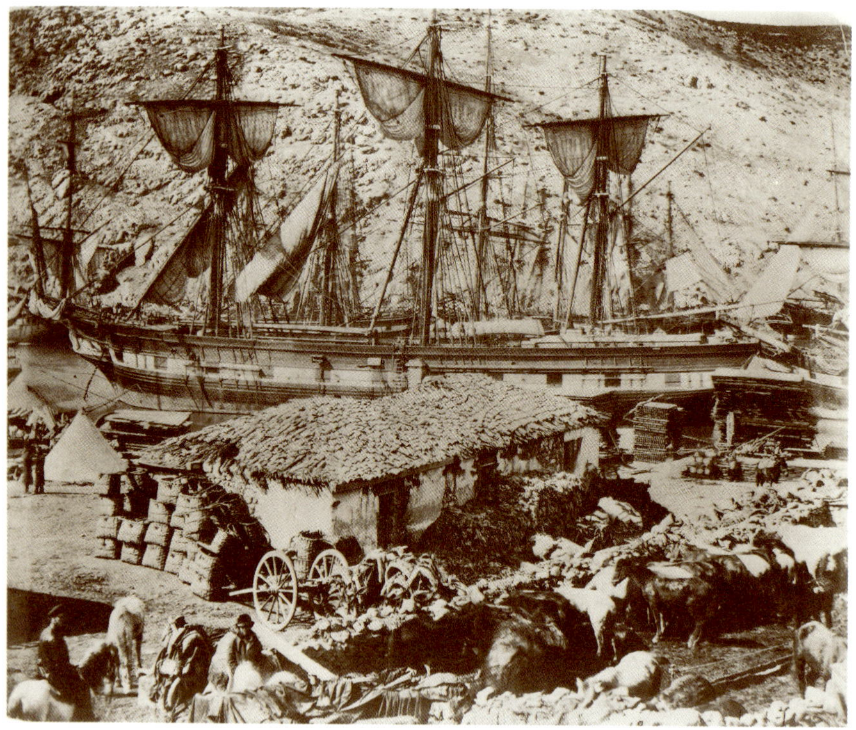

Roger Fenton,
The Harbour of Balaclava,
1855.
Library of Congress, Washington.

one to three seconds, such pictures would have been perfectly possible. In contrast to the Crimean War and, to some extent, the American Civil War, no photographic documentation of the war was officially commissioned, nor is it known whether newspaper illustrations were ever made from daguerreotypes. Later, however, a satirical "war report" described the possibility of falsification by means of the daguerreotype. Given the then unlimited faith in the authenticity of photographs, faking was an easy matter.

The most popular forms of pictorial media at the time were lithographs and so-called "transparencies". The latter were pictures of battles painted on large waxed linen cloths. Incorporating all kinds of patriotic symbolism, they were exhibited in United States cities as a kind of war reportage. Like Daguerre's diorama, they were exhibited illuminated by up to 1,200 candles, and the event would be the occasion for a kind of popular festival. Most of these pictures caught fire and suffered the same tragic fate as did so many Mexican villages.

In general, although some were publicly exhibited, the daguerreotype was not accessible to a wide public, nor could it pander to war fever by using symbolism and metaphor.[9] Objects can be arranged and photographed in a certain setting to convey an idea that goes beyond their mere physical presence; as we know, the angle from which a photograph is taken has symbolic value. A photograph can, therefore, by stylistic means, suggest a meaning transcending the mere reporting of what took place. However, it is precisely this stylistic element which replaces the axiomatic authenticity of the picture with a fictional construction. One can, for example, compare the photographs of the barricades of the 1848 Revolution taken by Hippolyte Bayard with an astonishing picture taken in the same year by an anonymous photog-

Roger Fenton,
The Valley of the Shadow of Death,
Crimea, 1855.
University of Texas, Austin.

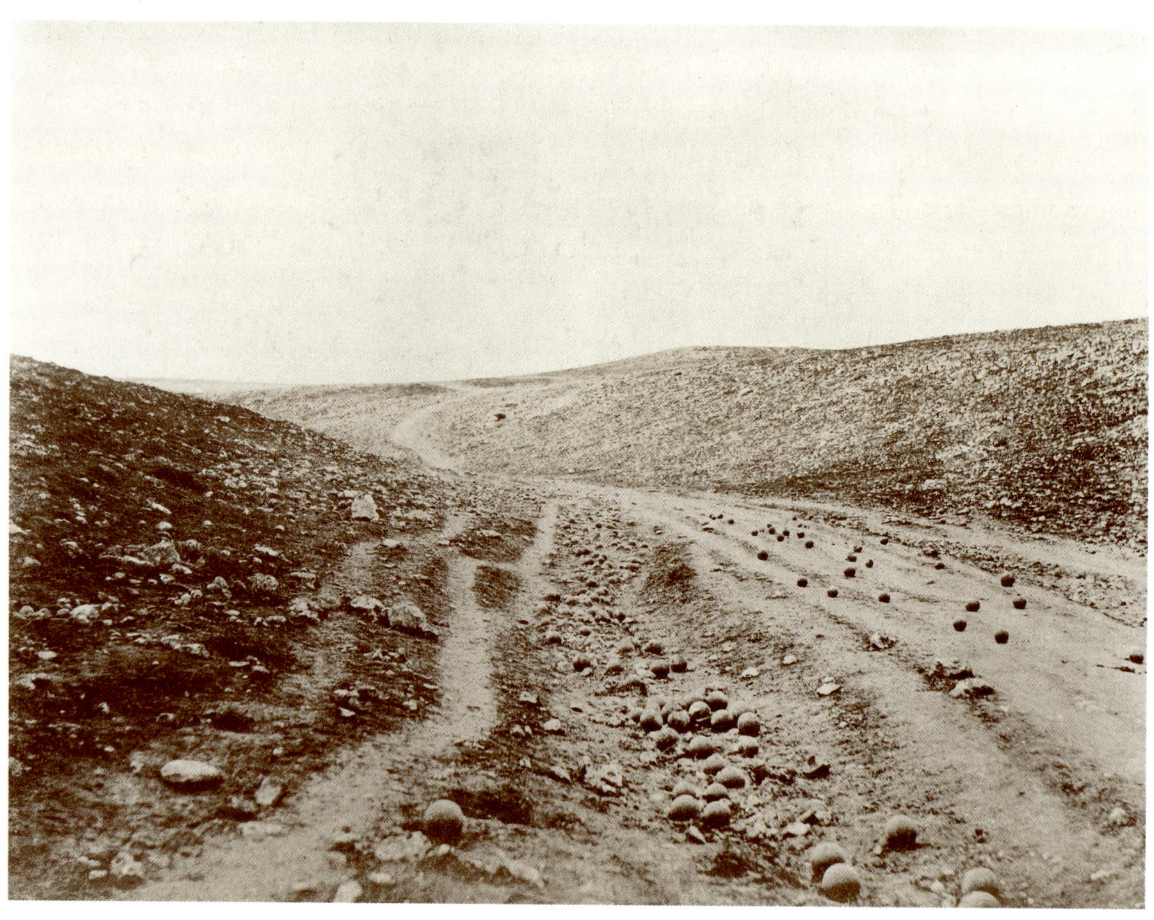

9. See G.W. Kendall, *The War Between the United States and Mexico Illustrated,* New York, D. Appleton & Co., 1851.

10. See E. Parry Janis, *The Photography of Gustave Le Gray,* Illinois and London, Art Institute of Chicago and University of Chicago Press, 1987.

11. See *Fotogeschichte (Photographie als historisches Dokument)*, no. 15, Frankfurt am Main, 1986.

12. See I. Zannier, "Die Anfänge der italienischen Fotografie", in *Fotogeschichte,* no. 25, 1987, pp. 17–29.

13. We do not know of the survival of any of these albums today. See É. Lacan, *Esquisses Photographiques à propos de l'Exposition Universelle et de la Guerre d'Orient,* Paris, 1856, pp. 155 ff.

14. See C. Savulescu, "The First War Photographic Reportage", in *Image,* no. 16, 1973, pp. 13–16, and "Early photography in Eastern Europe: Romania", in *History of Photography,* no. 1, 1977. pp. 63–77.

rapher. While Bayard's picture shows a street with what remains of the barricades, the anonymous picture shows an isolated heap of stones, most probably paving-stones, piled up as though to form a wall. The allegorical significance of this photograph lies in the conscious fragmentation and the allusion – which can be understood only through a knowledge of the historical context – to the revolutionary events. It is precisely the absence of a representational context such as that given in Bayard's photograph that makes this picture of stones, heaped up and blocking any view, into an abstraction.

While Bayard's photograph shows a precise moment in time, and the symbolic character of the anonymous photograph renders it timeless, a further example by the photographer Thibaut suggests a chronological narrative. His two daguerreotypes of Rue Saint-Maur show the barricades on June 25, 1848 and, again, on the following day – before and after they were stormed by the National Guard. The invisible event, the storming of the barricades, is caught in the temporal tension between the two images. In photographs taken by Gustave Le Gray of the rising led by Garibaldi in Palermo in 1860 the barricades are abandoned, the empty view of the Strada di Toledo symbolises hope, and the camera is in the line of fire.[10]

However, when we speak of photographs of historical events we usually mean pictures in which the historical occurrences themselves are recorded – representations, not abstractions.[11] In the case of war photography, the difficulty of making such images is obvious. Since the time of Herodotus, war, as a bringer of territorial, political, and social change, has been seen as the most significant kind of historical event.

Drawing or photography

The daguerreotypes of the Mexican-American war were not taken for any official purpose. It was during the Crimean War that for the first time pictorial reporting was co-ordinated by governments and also by publishers, though in 1849 S. Lecchi from Lombardy had photographed fighting between French and republican troops in Rome.[12] On July 2, 1853, Tsar Nicholas of Russia sent 40,000 troops into the Danubian principalities. In October, Turkey declared war on Russia, and in March 1854 France and Britain formed an alliance with Turkey.

The earliest photographs are those taken by the Romanian painter and photographer, Carol Szathmari. As early as April 1854, Szathmari, who had not been officially commissioned but was aware of the propaganda value of war photographs, photographed the Cossacks under the leadership of the Russian, Prince Gorchakov, and the Turkish camp.[13] In these calotypes the war is represented only by uniforms and encampments – there is no sign of the extent of the destruction. Of more than 300 photographs by Szathmari, few have survived. It is only from contemporary reports that we know that he also took at least one photograph of a battle. As early as February 1855, Szathmari tried to sell an album of his pictures (in the form of lithographs) commercially, but without success. The decisive battles around Sebastopol in September 1855, "where", as Ernest Lacan wrote, "the conflict moved to a different setting, and evolved into the Crimean War", were not photographed.[14]

In June 1854, the photographer Richard Nicklin, who had been sent out by the British War

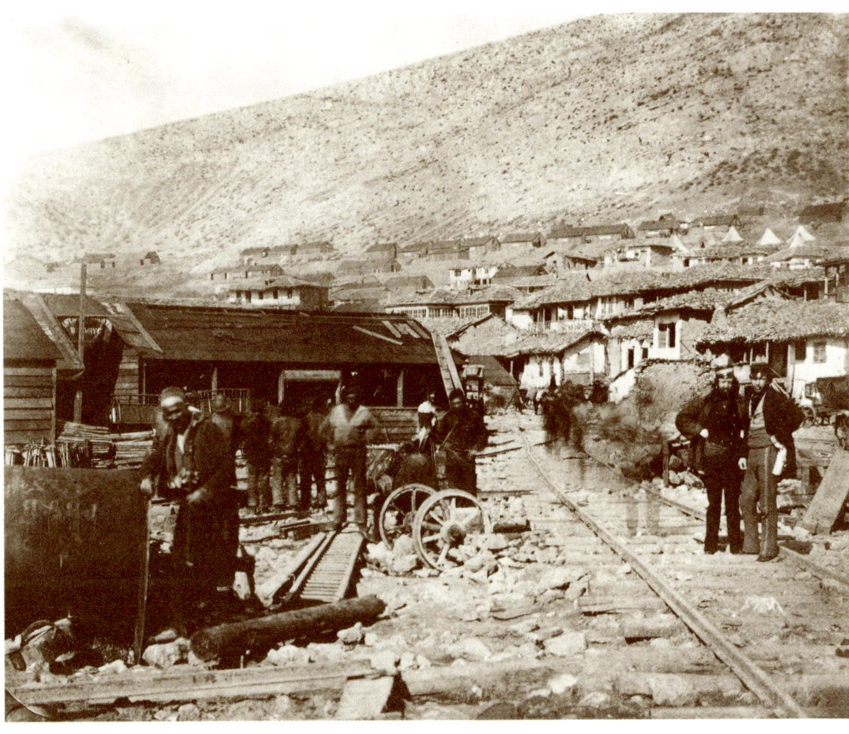

ROGER FENTON,
Railroad Running through the Town of Balaclava,
Crimea, 1855,
private collection.

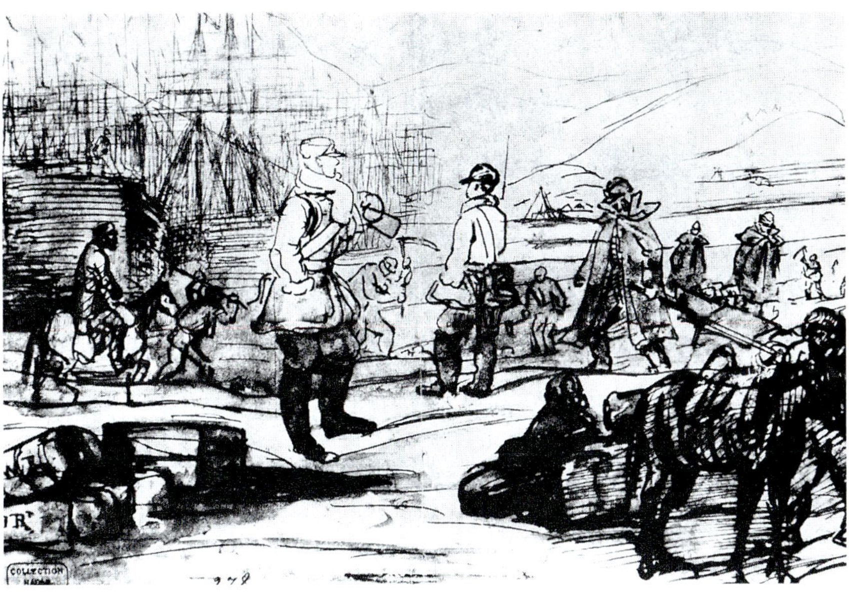

CONSTANTIN GUYS,
Sketch of the Crimean War,
1855
(former Nadar collection).

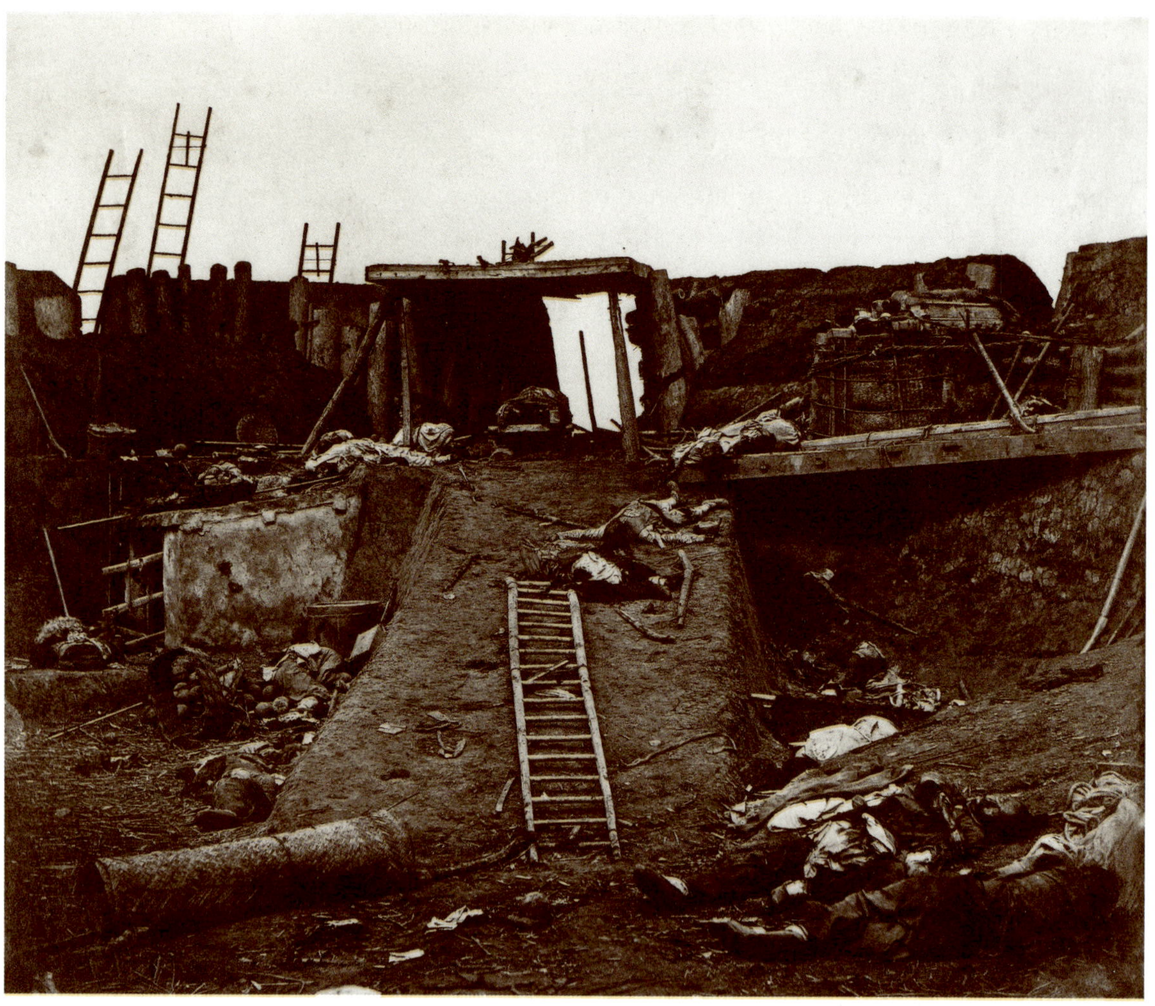

FELICE BEATO, *The Capture of Fort Taku,* China, 1860, International Museum of Photography, George Eastman House, Rochester.

Office to take photographs for documentary purposes, arrived at Varna with two assistants. On the return voyage their ship sank off Balaclava. Of two other photographers also commissioned by the War Office, Brandon and Dawson, all that is known is that their photographs were inadequately fixed and every single one faded. That Roger Fenton's photographs are now regarded as the outstanding visual record of the Crimean War is due largely to his seven-month period of preparation for his expedition as a war photographer.[15]

Public opinion in Victorian England was divided because of descriptions, especially those by William Howard Russell in the *Times,* of the horrors of the battlefield and of the hunger, epidemics, and inadequate medical care to which four out of five of soldiers succumbed. Not least in order to keep in check the euphoria unleashed in Britain by Queen Victoria's declaration of war on Russia, Russell telegraphed reports to the *Times* which were hardly calculated to fan the flames of patriotism. On November 14, 1854, he telegraphed: "At ten minutes past eleven our Light Cavalry Brigade advanced [...] At the distance of 1,200 yards the whole line of the enemy belched forth, from thirty iron mouths, a flood of smoke and flame. Their flight was marked by instant gaps in our ranks, by dead men and horses, by steeds flying wounded or riderless across the plain [...] At thirty-five minutes past eleven not a British soldier, except the dead and the dying, was left in front of those bloody Muscovite guns." The perceived authenticity of this report was heightened by the medium through which it came – telegraphy. The speed of communication reinforced the credibility of the eyewitness account.

There was a great demand from the public for images of the war. The *Illustrated London News* published engravings of events in the Crimea each week, and commissioned drawings from two artists, Goodall and Constantin Guys, while a third, William Simpson, made drawings for the publishing firm of Colnaghi. There is no doubt that, even at that time, written narratives of events took second place to visual depictions – Russell's reports were now merely an exception, standing on the threshold between narrative and news. The production of photographic "news" was fostered by commercial interests. Fenton was commissioned by the publishers and printsellers, Thomas Agnew & Sons. On the subject of his "competitors" he wrote to his publisher, "I see no drawings here that deserve to be bought [...] Simpson merely makes pencil drawings on the spot and colors them at home. The only French artist I have seen does the same."[16]

15. Only a few pictures by other photographers of the Crimean War have survived. Others who should be mentioned are Durand-Brager, Lassimone, Ludwig Angerer, and the Scottish doctors John Kirk and William Robertson. See J. Lawson, "Dr John Kirk and Dr William Robertson: Photographers in the Crimea", in *History of Photography,* no. 12, July-September 1988. pp. 227–242.

16. See P. Duflo, *Constantin Guys: Fou de dessin, grand reporter, 1802–1892,* Paris, Éditions Arnaud Seydoux, 1988, p. 334; *Roger Fenton, Photographer of the 1850s,* with text by Valerie Lloyd, London, Yale University Press, 1988; Lawrence James, *Crimea 1854–1856: The War with Russia from Contemporary Photographs,* Oxfordshire, Hayes Kennedy, 1981.

In January 1854, the *Practical Mechanics Journal* demanded that instead of the "dimly allusive information, which alone the conventional works of the painter can convey", photography should be used for information about the war, "to obtain undeniably accurate representations of the realities of war and its contingent scenery, its struggles, its failures and triumphs". The difference between the techniques of the various media for recording events was, from now on, the decisive criterion for quality, that is to say, for the authenticity of the event. The act of picture-making was to be judged by the time taken for its execution, that is, the exposure time. This, and later the speed of its transposition into another medium, print, determined its value.

The theater of war

In preparation for his journey, on which he set out, together with his two assistants, Marcus Sparling and Williams, on February 20, 1855, on board the *Hecla*, Fenton practiced in Yorkshire, carrying out photography in the sort of conditions which awaited him in the Crimea. He fitted out a photographic van with five cameras, 700 glass plates in three different formats, laboratory materials, and a bed. Szathmari had used the comparatively slow salted-paper process, but Fenton opted for the fastest method then available – the collodion process. He was able to take photographs which he regarded as "almost instantaneous" with exposure times of between three and twenty seconds, according to light conditions. The majority of his photographs are portraits, either of the commanders (Lord Raglan, Marshal Pélissier, Omar Pasha), or of the officers and men. Instead of battles, the dead and wounded, the field hospitals, and the devastation wrought at Sebastopol, he photographed the unloading of military equipment in the harbor, encampments, soldiers resting, and graves. His aim was to produce tasteful views of picturesque scenes, as required by Queen Victoria, rather than to convey an accurate impression of war. His famous photograph *The Valley of the Shadow of Death* (1855) shows cannonballs strewn around a path after battle. Only the title gives the photograph its mood. It conveys a sense of gloom rather than reflecting the full horror of war. It is not unlike the wide-angle photographs taken in 1857 by Gustave Le Gray of military manoeuvres at Châlons, in which soldiers are posed on the broad expanse of the landscape to represent both themselves and the enemy.[17]

A British officer, Captain Cuninghame, wrote in a letter home of his astonishment at the peaceful images of the war that appeared in the *Illustrated London News*: "The pictures in the *Illustrated* of the charge of our Cavalry, and indeed of all fights, must be drawn in London; they are as unlike reality as possible [...] Everything seems to be carried out in the quietest and most gentlemanlike manner, very little smoke, no dust and very little noise, just pop, pop, bang, pop, pop, pop, bang, bang, pop, and that is all."[18] The documentary character of photography lay in its supposed truthfulness based on the technology used, not in the scenes represented. The medium had not yet achieved such a decisive change in perception as to enable the photographer or the viewer to break free from a time-honored pictorial aesthetic. This is revealed by a remark made by Fenton about Goodall's pencil drawings for the *Illustrated London News*. Fenton wrote to his publisher, William Agnew, on April 9, 1855: "The drawings of his which are appearing in the newspapers seem to astonish everyone by their complete lack of resemblance to reality, and it is

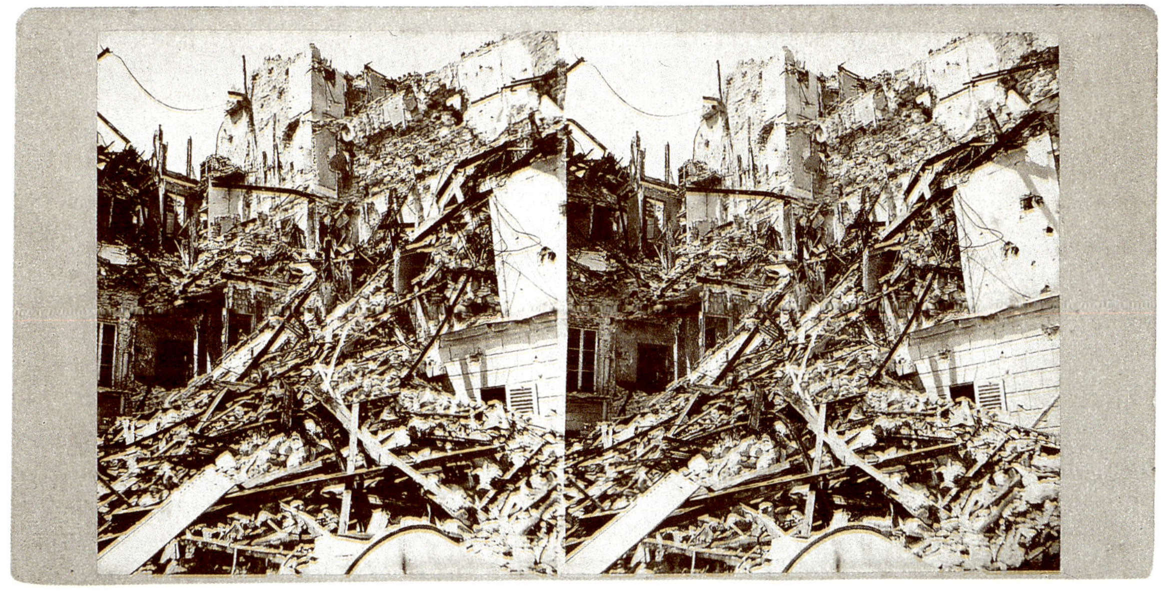

ANONYMOUS,
Buildings Destroyed at Auteuil during the Commune,
May 1871,
stereoscopic pair,
private collection.

17. See E. Parry Janis, *The Photography of Gustave Le Gray*, pp. 85–100.

18. Quotation from L. James, *Crimea, 1854–1856*, p. 11.

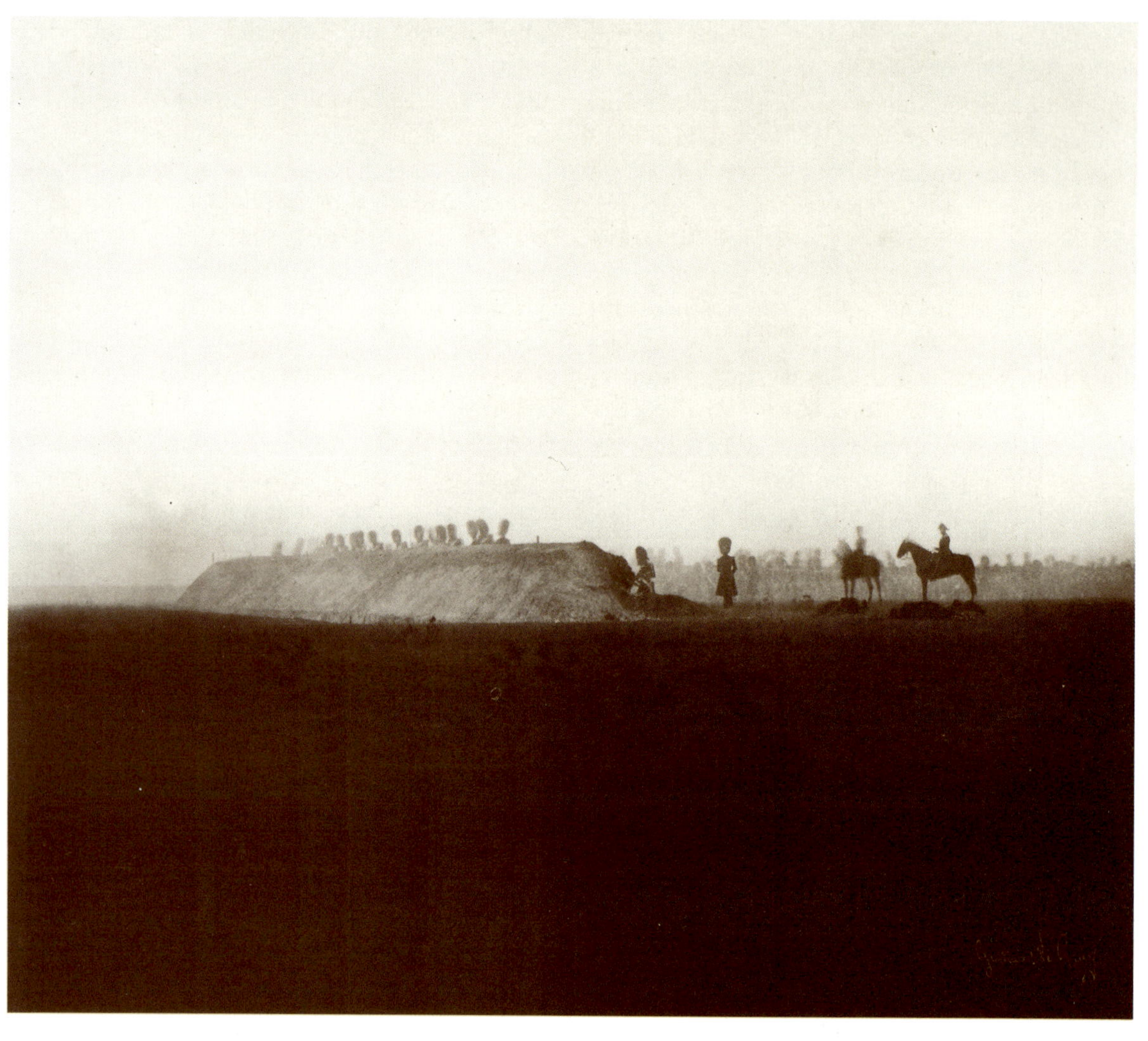

GUSTAVE LE GRAY,
Exercises at Châlons Military Camp,
1857, private collection.

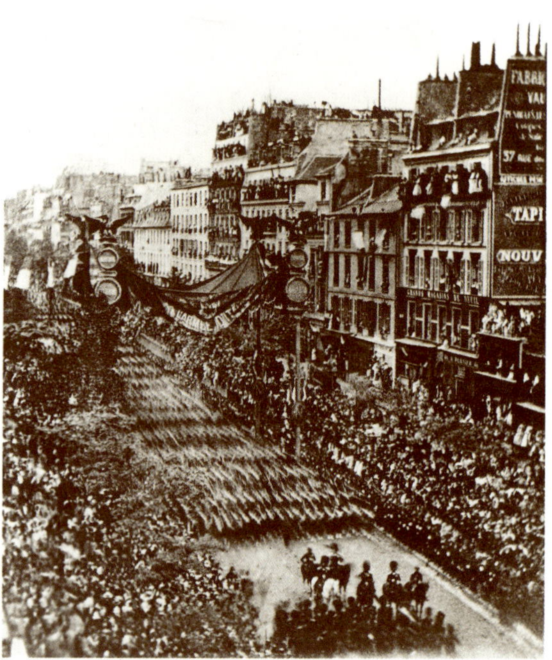

ANONYMOUS,
French Army Returning from Italy,
1859,
Roger-Viollet Collection,
Paris.

not surprising that this should be so, for as you will see from the enclosed prints the sites of events here have not a trace of the kind of artistic effect that could be successfully reproduced by a quick sketch, consisting rather of wide expanses of open country covered with innumerable details." Fenton's description suggests that he himself tried in his photography to move from mere representation to expressiveness.

Photography has often been criticized for exchanging resemblance for identicalness. In 1841, Rodolphe Töpffer was already complaining that the daguerreotype offered "the image of the visible instead of a sign of the invisible". For the picture to be identical would mean that the object had no significance beyond itself. Identicalness, Topffer said, is the indirect and therefore verifiable product of the daguerreotype process, whereas resemblance is the freely expressive sign of something other than the image. Truthfulness, then, is to be found not in the identical picture but in the picture which gives a resemblance. This traditional distinction shows the dilemma of photography, which was not permitted to depict what it could depict, but was unable to depict what people demanded of it. Only the type of war

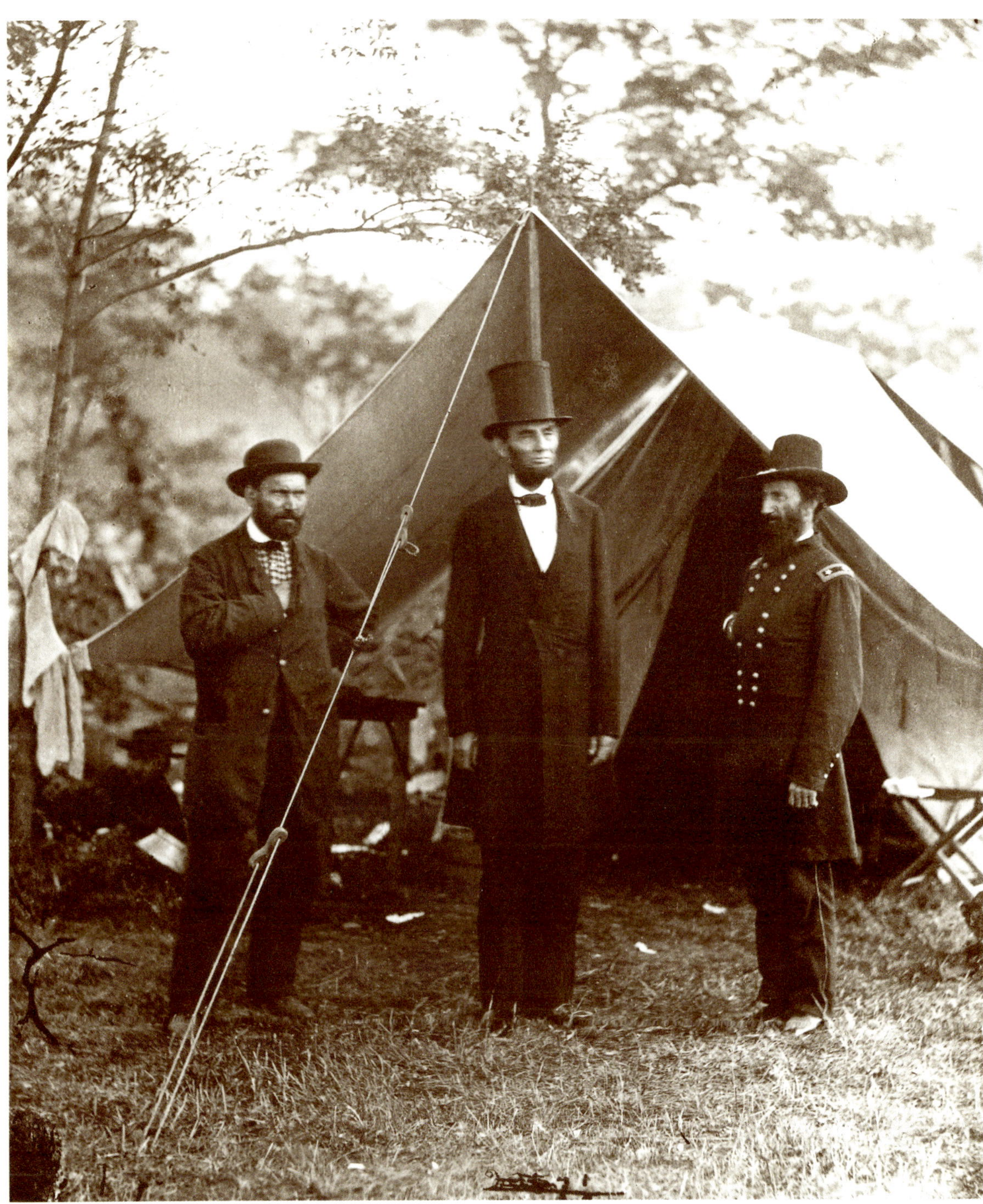

ALEXANDER GARDNER, *President Lincoln on the Battlefield of Antietam,* October 2, 1862, John Paul Getty Museum, Malibu.

photography which then still lay in the future would show that the "artistic effect" referred to by Fenton can be achieved equally well photographing by a battery of cannons or a mountain of corpses, by powder-smoke or a camp. In photography, identicalness, resemblance, and truthfulness would, from now on, have relevance only as different interpretations of representation; the distinction between false and true representation is applicable only where photography is perceived to be a medium of information.

When, in relation to Goodall's drawings, Fenton speaks of "a lack of resemblance to reality", he is, in effect, defining reality itself as representation – reality created by photography. War photographs have been compared by Ernst Jünger to fossils, which offer only "the raw material for contemplation" and need to be supplemented by "imagination".[19]

The French officer and panorama painter, the inventor of the military panorama, Jean-Charles Langlois, had, together with his assistant Léon-Eugene Mehédin, been commissioned by the French War Ministry to take photographs in 1855 and 1856 for a panorama of the victorious battle of Sebastopol, exhibited in Paris in 1860. Langlois was, for the first time, using photography as a rapid medium, not least to satisfy the shareholders in his specially founded limited company. However, the intense cold and the unfavorable light conditions in December 1855 brought him close to despair. He wrote to his wife on December 20, 1855, "One has to keep coming back to that terrible word,

19. E. Jünger (ed.), *Das Antlitz des Weltkrieges: Fronterlebnisse deutscher Soldaten*, Berlin, Neufeld & Henius Verlag, 1930, p. 10.

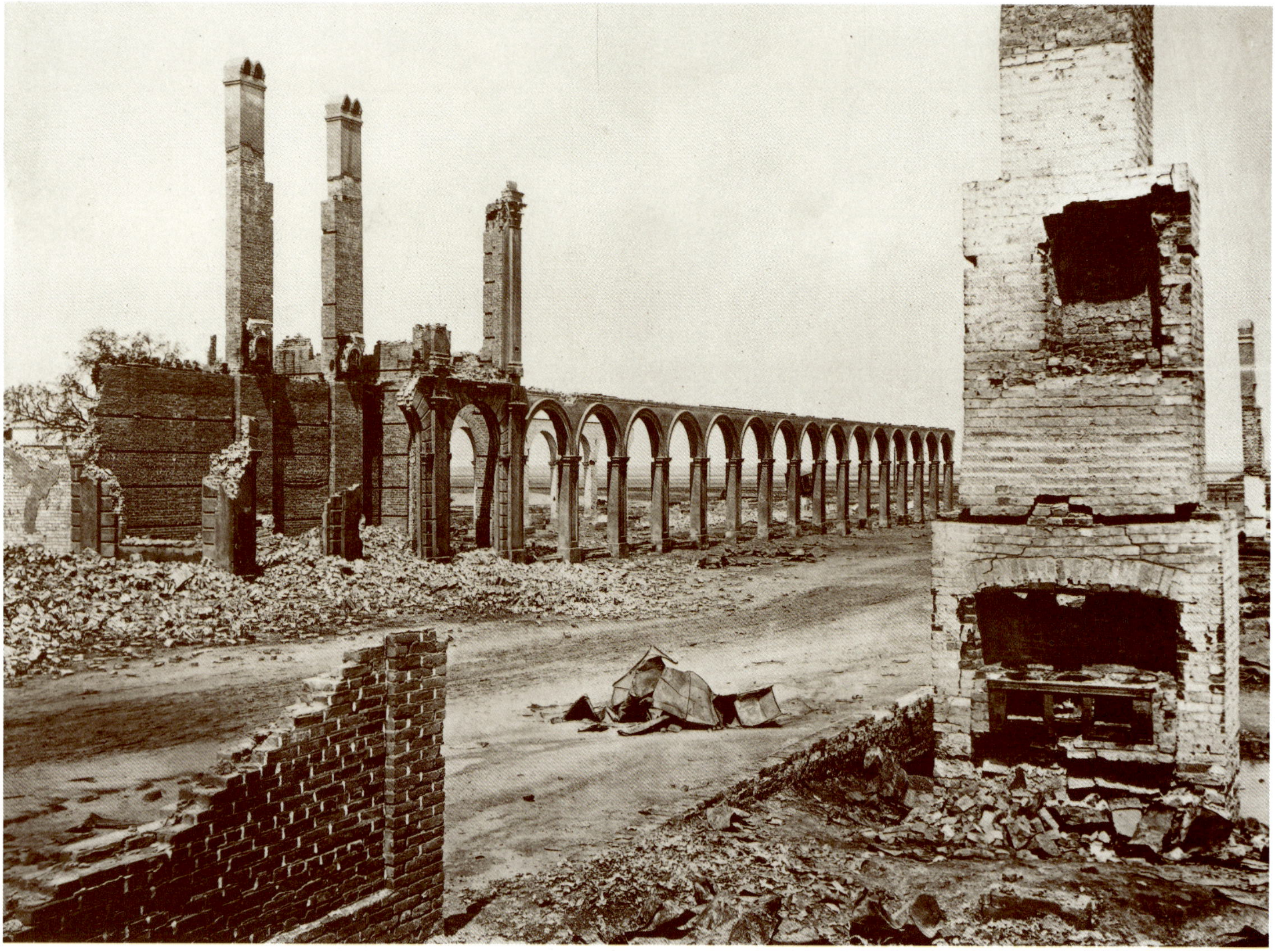

GEORGE N. BARNARD,
Ruins of the Railroad Depot, Charleston,
1865,
International Museum of Photography,
George Eastman House, Rochester.

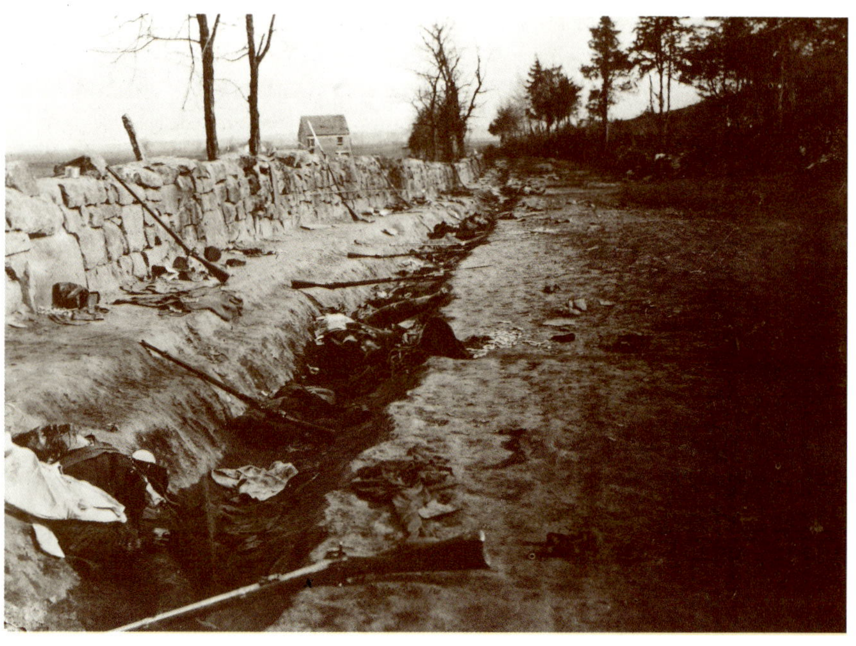

patience, when time presses." The supposedly instantaneous medium of photography had to submit to the passing of time in the form of light: "exposure times of several hours".[20]

Another British photographer of the Crimean War was James Robertson. Already well known for his work in Greece, he was living in Constantinople when the allied troops arrived there in April 1854. In June 1855 he traveled to the Crimea together with his assistant, a photographer of equal importance, the Venetian and naturalized British subject, Felice Antonio Beato. Perhaps Robertson knew that Roger Fenton – after making preparations to photograph the attack on Sebastopol on June 18 (which, contrary to all expectations, ended in failure) – had sold his photographic van and, having contracted cholera, had left Balaclava on June 26 to return home. Like Fenton's, Robertson's photographs show no military action as such, but the pictures that he took around Malakoff and Sebastopol after the city's capture on September 8 reveal a different approach. Rather than the wide expanses apparently untouched by war, that we see in Fenton's photographs, Robertson shows

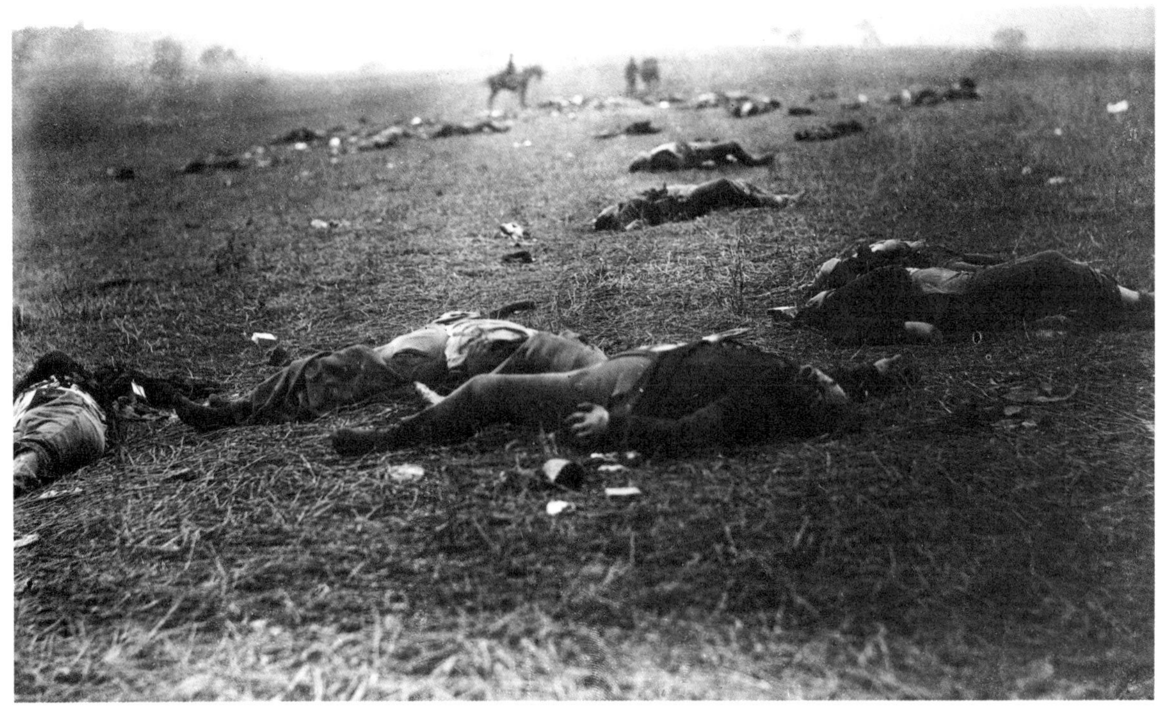

TIMOTHY O'SULLIVAN, *The Battlefield at Gettysburg* (American Civil War), July 1863, New York Public Library.

buildings destroyed by artillery (which he could now photograph without any danger), the craters and the trenches of siege warfare, and the bomb-proof shelters of the Russian generals – visible signs of destruction. His pictures convey a strong impression of the catastrophic damage suffered by villages and towns and give at least a suggestion of the massive loss of life. Robertson's photographs (made by the albumen glass plate process) are far closer than Fenton's to later photographs taken during the American Civil War, the Franco-Prussian War, and the Paris Commune. Robertson still refrains from showing corpses. However, pictures taken by other photographers only a few years later show dead bodies as well as shattered buildings.

Photographs by James Robertson and Felice Beato of British colonial wars have also survived. To free themselves from British control, Hindus and Muslims of the East India Company mutinied in 1857 and, in Delhi, proclaimed the Mogul Bahadur Shah II the Emperor of India. After bloody battles the mutiny was finally suppressed and India became a part of the British Empire. Photographs show Indians executed by hanging (1857) and the ruins of the Secundra Bagh at Lucknow, scattered with the remains of Indians killed in the fighting (1858). Robertson remained in India, but, in 1859, Beato, whom the *Times* dubbed "a knight of the camera", joined the British military expedition to China, to cover the events of the Opium War. At Tientsin, on August 21, 1860, he took several photographs shortly after the bloody storming of the Taku forts. Bodies lay scattered within the fortress, and Beato took photographs from various angles. An eye-witness reported: "I walked round the ramparts on the West side. They were thickly strewn with dead – in the North-West angle thirteen were lying in one group round a gun. Signor Beato was there in great excitement, characterising the group as 'beautiful' and begging that it might not be interfered with until perpetuated by his photographic apparatus, which was done a few minutes afterwards."[21] The historical event, unlike the horrors surrounding it, is stylized into a picturesque composition. The eye of the photographer is thus able to document violence and, at the same time, hide the reality of war behind the cloak of pictorial composition – "artistic effect". Photography, as a pictorial epilogue, depicted the empty stage where the drama had taken place.

◄ ANDREW JOSEPH RUSSELL, *Stone Wall, Rear of Fredericksburg,* (American Civil War), May 3, 1863, Library of Congress, Washington.

The eye of history

In an essay written in 1859, the American essayist and doctor Oliver Wendell Holmes refers to the fundamental shift from substance to form

20. See A. Rouillé, "Un combat photographique en Crimée", in *La Recherche Photographique* [La guerre], no. 6, June 1989, pp. 13–21. See also *Crimée, 1854–1856: premiers reportages de guerre*, Paris, Musée de l'Armée, 1994.

21. D. F. Rennie, *British Arms in North China and Japan*, Shanghai 1863, p. 112, quoted by H. Gernsheim in *The Rise of Photography, 1850–1880: The Age of Collodion*, London, Thames and Hudson, 1988, p. 100. See also *Felice Beato in Japan*, Heidelberg, Braus, 1991.

Manet's *Execution of Emperor Maximilian*

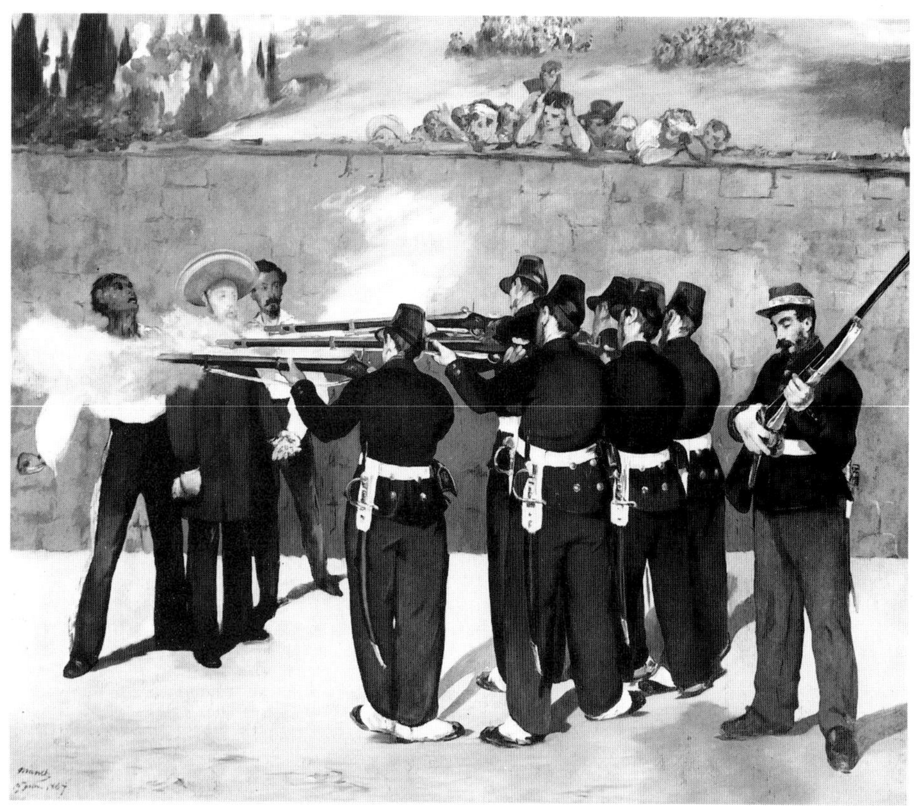

Édouard Manet,
Execution of Emperor Maximilian,
circa 1868–1869, Städtische Kunsthalle, Mannheim.

Manet's famous painting, *Execution of Emperor Maximilian*, precursor of abstract art, may be considered as the first attempt in painting which, while being aware of the competition of the photograph as an historical record, went beyond what photography could provide in order to formulate a new pictorial aesthetic. *The Execution of Maximilian* is "unique in its type", wrote the art critic Théodore Duret; this painting is "the only one which provides a painted scene which has not been witnessed".

The Emperor Maximilian was executed by firing-squad by the Juarist government in Mexico on June 19, 1867. Manet began his first version of the painting, the so-called "Boston painting", shortly afterwards, and this was followed by one lithograph and four paintings. Both the genesis and the conception of the work were closely linked to the new phenomenon of photography.

What could now be the nature of a historical painting in the tradition of David or Goya after photography had gained the upper hand in documentary recording? Manet himself always seemed critical of this genre. "To undertake an historical painting from contemporary accounts", he is supposed to have said during a discussion with the painter Henri Detouche, "is like trying to base someone's description on the details given in his passport." We know today that Manet carefully collected information concerning the soldiers' uniforms, as well as eyewitness accounts, images from the illustrated press, and photographs. Immediately after the execution the soldiers and their officer had their photographs taken. The photographer was most probably François Aubert, who is know to us from a whole series of images: portraits of the Mexican officers, Maximilian's waistcoat and shirt, his body in a coffin, the burial site near Querétaro.

On the one hand, Manet had recourse to photographs as documents which would assure him of the truthfulness of the historic event – the "passport description" – on the other, he invited French soldiers to pose for him in his studio in Rue Guyot. The reconstruction of the event thus came to be a stage setting of the execution as a tableau. His painting was considered a still-life with "lead soldiers"; and he was accused of being impassive or indifferent. The analyses of Sandblad and Fried have underlined the subtlety of Manet's pictorial technique, which aimed at going beyond photographic representation by showing movement contained within total immobility.

Thus, the "execution" should be understood in all senses of the word: the putting to death of the Emperor, supplemented by Aubert's photos; the "execution" by Manet, who required four attempts before arriving at the final painting, which he signed with his name, giving it the date of the unique, real execution: "Manet, June 19, 1867".

Hubertus von Amelunxen

brought about by photography – "this greatest of human triumphs over earthly conditions" – especially by stereoscopic photography, which, next to the *carte de visite*, was now the main commercial product of photography. "The time is perhaps at hand when a flash of light, as sudden and brief as that of the lightning which shows a whirling wheel standing stock-still, shall preserve the very instant of the shock of contact of the mighty armies that are even now gathering."[22] Holmes had, as early as 1859, worked out a philosophy of photography that was extraordinarily farsighted. With photography, said Holmes, form was from now on separated from matter: "Give us a few negatives of a thing worth seeing, taken from different points of view, and that is all we want of it. Pull it down or burn it up, if you please." According to Democritus' theory of perception, in which the nineteenth century showed a renewed interest and to which Holmes refers, the fine membrane-like images which emanate from things – the eidolon – have no real existence and so disappear if the object from which they emanate disappears; the photographic negative, on the other hand, can survive when the original object is lost. An inversion of simulation has taken place and the age of immateriality is at hand. There is only one Colosseum, one Pantheon, but there are billions of possible negatives; matter may be immovable and costly, but form is cheap, transportable, and potentially ubiquitous. "We have got the fruit of creation now, and need not trouble ourselves with the core." The fields of perception of the future will

22. O. W. Holmes, "The Stereoscope and the Stereograph", in *Atlantic Monthly*, no. 3, June 1859, pp. 747–748 (reprinted in B. Newhall, *Photography: Essays and Images*, New York, 1980, pp. 53–61).

have to orient themselves by the archives of the present. Holmes therefore recommends setting up a library of stereographs encompassing the whole world, in which people and buildings, battlefields, and the idylls of nature would all be included. Historic events would from henceforth be no more than the originals necessary for their reproduction and mass availability. This library would become the sanctuary of history, uniting non-synchronous events in the synchronicity of reproduction.

The expectation voiced by Holmes was all too understandable: "The next European war will send us stereographs of battles".[23] At that time the Franco-Sardinian alliance was fighting the Austrians in support of Italian unification, and Holmes mentions stereographs of the battles of Magenta and Melegnano. "Here are the encampments of Napoleon's army in the recent campaign. This is the battlefield of Magenta with its trampled grass and splintered trees, and the fragments of soldiers' accoutrements lying about [...] Look away, young maiden or tender child, for this is what war leaves after it."[24] Holmes is probably describing the stereographs made by the Ferrier brothers and Charles Soulier, and also by Berady, all of whom accompanied Napoleon III's campaign against Austria. According to another contemporary report, these photographs showed corpses that were horribly disfigured.[25] Holmes's theory of immateriality points far beyond his own century. Just a few years before the First World War, the American historian Henry Wysham Lanier, in the foreword to his ten-volume *Photographic History of the Civil War*, wrote that the American Civil War is the only major conflict in world history that can "really" be illustrated "with a pictorial record which is indisputably authentic, vividly illuminating, and the final evidence in any question of detail".[26]

We owe the first "picture book" of war to the initiative of Mathew B. Brady, at that time the most famous photographer in the USA. In 1839, he had visited Daguerre, together with Samuel B. Morse, and he opened his first portrait studio in New York in 1844. Tom Maloney was to confirm Holmes's prediction when he wrote in 1944 that not only are Brady's pictures the indispensable source for the study of the American Civil War, but "they *are* the Civil War"; photography no longer merely documents but "is the eye that rules the battle in the making as well as the battle in being".[27]

Brady photographed the war from the Union side. If Balzac still saw himself as the secretary and stenographer of his era, Brady – marking the shift from writing to the visual medium – was able to call himself "the eye of history". In June

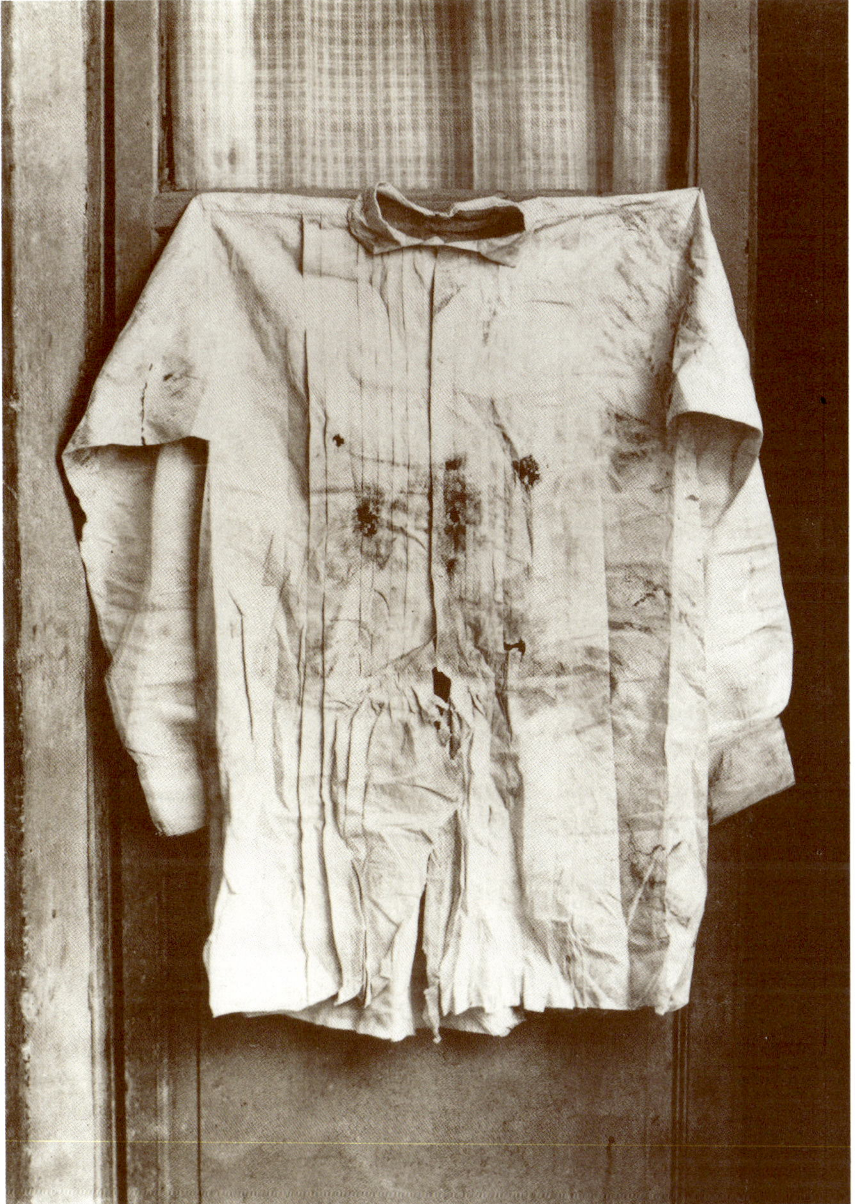

François Aubert, ***Emperor Maximilian's Shirt After his Execution,*** 1867, S. Kakou Collection.

1861, the American Photographical Society resolved to enter into talks with the War Department with a view to obtaining official sanction for photographers to move about between the front lines as military photographic reporters. In September of that year the Society's president, John W. Draper, reported that these efforts had been unsuccessful. Despite this, Brady had already equipped himself with two "photographic wagons" for the first major battle, that of Bull Run, Virginia, on July 21, 1861. Although the War Department showed little interest, Brady obtained the necessary papers and carried out his "reporting" together with a newspaper editor and an artist. While the equipment of other photographers fell into the hands of the Confederates as "spoils of war", Brady's photographs were hailed as those of a "veteran". "Brady never misrepresents", it was said, contrasting him with the newspaper reports. Between January and April 1862, Brady trained more than ten photographers. The best-known, besides Alexander Gardner, were T.

23. On Holmes's theory of immateriality, see H. von Amelunxen, "Einbruch in die Transzendenz", in E. Decker, P. Weibel (eds.), *Das Verschwinden der Ferne. Telekommunikation und Kunst,* Cologne, DuMont, 1990, pp. 307–316.

24. O. W. Holmes, "Sun-Painting and Sun-Sculpture", in *Atlantic Monthly,* no. 8, July 1861, p. 27.

25. See *La Lumière,* September 10, 1859.

26. F. Trevelyan Miller (ed.), *The Photographic History of the Civil War,* New York, 1911, vol. I, p. 30.

27. T. Maloney (ed.), *The USA at War: U.S. Camera 1945,* New York, Duell Sloan & Pearce, 1945, pp. 8–9.

O'Sullivan, George N. Barnard, and George Cook; they were then sent to the various scenes of conflict. In the four years of that destructive war – the first modern war in terms of the media and military technology – over 8,000 photographs were taken. A study has revealed that the Army of the Potomac issued passes to a total of 300 photographers. Brady had 35 separate operational centers with sometimes more than twenty photographers whose work he co-ordinated.

Photographic wagons moving around between the fronts were often mistaken for ammunition wagons. Both Confederate and Union troops called the black wagon the "Whatizzit-wagon", unsure what kind of mortal danger might threaten from the vehicle. Fleeing soldiers, it was said, mistook it for the steam-driven machine-gun that had just been developed by Gatling in 1861, which could fire up to 500 shots a minute, "and immediately took to their heels when they got within its focus!" At all events, continues the contemporary report, "it is certain that they did not get away from Brady as easily as they did from the enemy".[28] There are few photographs showing actual fighting. Brady and his photographers were present at all the great battles (Fredericksburg and Antietam in 1862, Gettysburg in 1863, Petersburg in 1864), but almost all their photographs show these places before or after the devastation wrought by the battle. Minute examination of photographs taken at Gettysburg has shown that some of the pictures were posed – some retrospectively, even years later – and some of Brady's assistants had to play the part of dead soldiers, with the result that they sometimes reappear as corpses in several different places.[29] The photographs, some of them distributed by Brady as stereographs, showed both the machinery of killing and the disfigured victims on both sides with unprecedented directness. In October 1862, Brady exhibited some of his photographs of the battle of Antietam. A report in the *New York Times* commented: "Mr. Brady has done something to bring home to us the terrible reality and earnestness of war. If he has not brought bodies and laid them in our door-yards and along the streets, he has done something very like it. At the door of his gallery hangs a little placard, 'The dead at Antietam' [...] These pictures have a terrible distinctness. By the aid of the magnifying-glass, the very features of the slain may be distinguished."[30]

The photographic equipment used by Brady may be seen as the first instance of the parallel development of vision, weapons, and the media that has been familiar to us ever since the First World War. "It is the same intelligence", wrote Ernst Jünger, looking back to the First World War, "which even from a great distance can manage to target an opponent precisely, to the second and to the meter, with its weapons of destruction, and which also strives to record that great historical event down to the smallest detail [...] Side by side with the muzzles of rifles and artillery, lenses were trained day after day on the field of battle [...]"[31] The qualitative difference in war photography may be shown by a comparison between Fenton's photograph of the valley of death, already mentioned, and a picture by Timothy O'Sullivan. *Gardner's Photographic Sketch Book of the War*, published in two volumes in 1866, and illustrated with one hundred photographs includes O'Sullivan's photograph of the Gettysburg battlefield of 1863. Unlike Fenton's picture, this shows the bodies of soldiers, lying scattered and distorted. Alexander Gardner – it was as a member of his team that O'Sullivan took his photographs – wrote about this picture, symbolically entitled *The Harvest of Death*: "Such a picture conveys a useful moral: it shows the blank horror and reality of war, in opposition to its pageantry. Here are the dreadful details! Let them aid in preventing such another calamity falling upon the nation."[32] Whether this photograph was, perhaps, posed is of secondary importance. Its effect derives from the theatricality of the horror, from its being placed on public view.

Commercial exploitation

It was only during the Paris Commune that the commercialization and systematic exploitation of war photography began. From the Franco-Prussian War only isolated photographs and albums, mainly of carte-de-visite photographs belonging to French or Prussian officers, are known to have survived. However, the signifi-

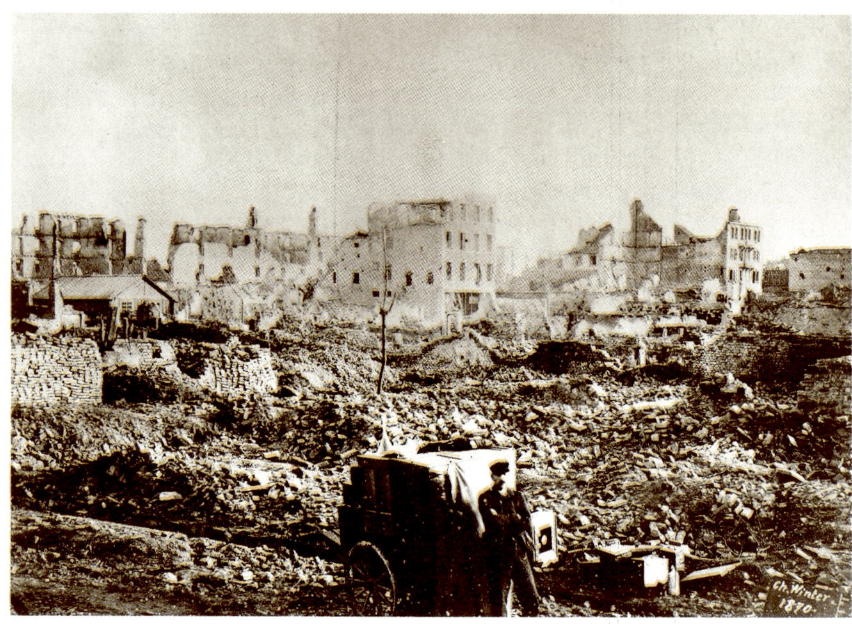

Charles Winter, ***Photographer's Wagon in the Pierre District During the Siege of Strasbourg,*** 1870, Musée de Strasbourg. ▼

28. Quoted from R. Taft, *Photography and the American Scene: A Social History 1839–1889*, 2nd ed, New York 1964, p. 228. On Brady see also Roy Meredith, *Mr. Lincoln's Camera Man: Mathew B. Brady*, New York, Scribner, 1946.

29. See W. A. Frassanito, *Gettysburg: A Journey in Time*, New York, Scribner, 1975; idem, *Antietam: The Photographic Legacy of America's Bloodiest Day*, New York, Scribner, 1978.

30. Quoted from Beaumont Newhall, *The History of Photography*, revised and enlarged edition, London, Martin Secker & Warburg, 1986, pp. 91 ff.

31. E. Jünger, *Antlitz des 1. Weltkrieges*, p. 10.

32. Quoted from F. Farlin (ed.), *The Indelible Image: Photographs of War – 1846 to the Present*, New York, H. N. Abrams, 1985, p. 46. See also J. Lewinski, *The Camera at War: A History of War Photography from 1848 to the Present Day*, London, W. H. Allen & Co. Ltd., 1978, R. Fabian and H. C. Adam, *Bilder vom Krieg: 130 Jahre Kriegsfotografie – eine Anklage*, Hamburg, Stern-Buch, 1983, and A. Barret, *Die ersten Photoreporter 1848–1914*, Frankfurt am Main, W. Krüger, 1978.

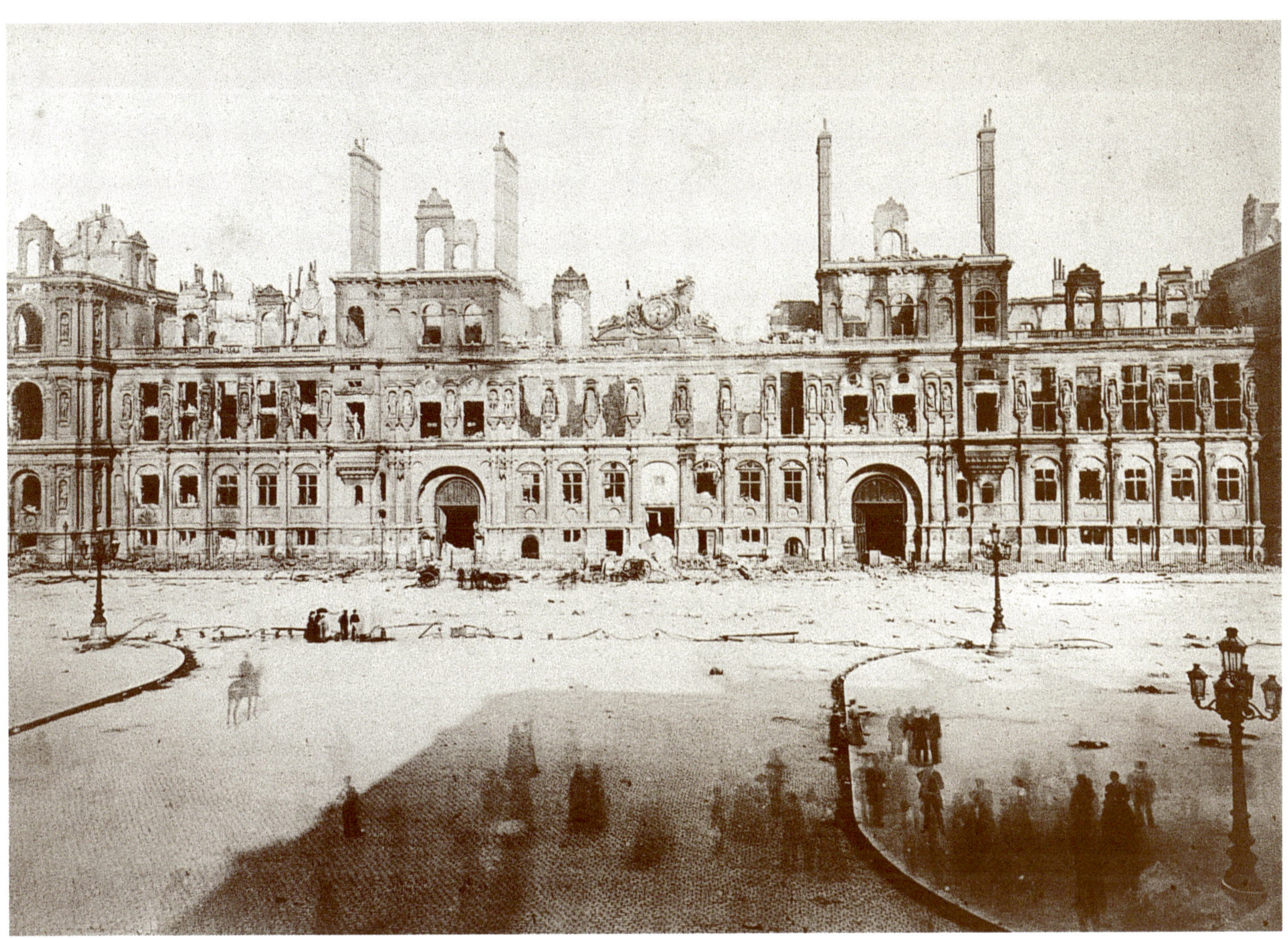

Alphonse Liébert,
Place de l'Hôtel de Ville, Paris, After the Fire,
May 1871,
private collection.

cance of photography for the conduct of war was now recognized. Disdéri, who taught photography to the French army, had pointed out its value in 1862 in his book *L'Art de la Photographie*. Photography extended the vision of commanding officers, who were now able to survey the battlefield in photographs, detached from reality. "What is very important," wrote Disdéri, " is that there should be a large number of photographers, who should be present everywhere at all times, spread out along the whole battle-line or besieging force, ready to record uninterruptedly everything that is of interest in the scenes that strike the eye."

Whereas photographs by Brady, Gardner, and O'Sullivan achieved only limited distribution, photography during the Commune played a more important role than ever before. Newspapers such as *L'Illustration* and *Le Monde illlustré* used engravings made from photographs to illustrate highly topical events. Drawings receded into the background, and photography had the field to itself – apart from the deliberately non-realistic cartoon, the one form of visual representation which interpreted events critically.[33] Whether one should speak here of photographic reportage is questionable however, for most of those who saw the illustrated reports had witnessed the events themselves, so that one might say that the event was closer to them than its reproductions were. The photographic reporter suffered the disadvantage of being "a photographer in his own country".[34] Of the events themselves – the defense and the storming of the barricades, the bloody week, starting on May 21, in which between 20,000 and 30,000 communards were killed, the countless executions – no photographs survive, or only faked photomontages. The photographer Eugène Appert had, with official permission from the Thiers government, taken photographs of captured communards and of executions carried out by both sides, which he used to make montages. For the series *Crimes de la Commune*, heads were cut out of pictures, added to bodies obtained by photographing people in costume acting as models, and fitted into a specially constructed setting. The picture created in this way was rephotographed and sold as a genuine image. Events were reconstructed and faked for propaganda purposes. In these "photographs", as Armand Dayot remarked, looking back in 1901, historical truth was sacrificed to the picturesque. Photographs by Disdéri, Alphonse-J. Liébert, B. Braquehais, and A. Collard show

33. See J. A. Leith, "The War of Images surrounding the Commune", in J. A. Leith (ed.), *Images of the Commune – Images de la Commune*, Montreal and London, McGill and Queen's University Press, 1978, pp. 101–151.

34. See C. Lapostolle, "La Commune; De la barricade à la ruine", in *La Recherche photographique*, no. 6, June 1989, pp. 21–29.

The Paris Commune

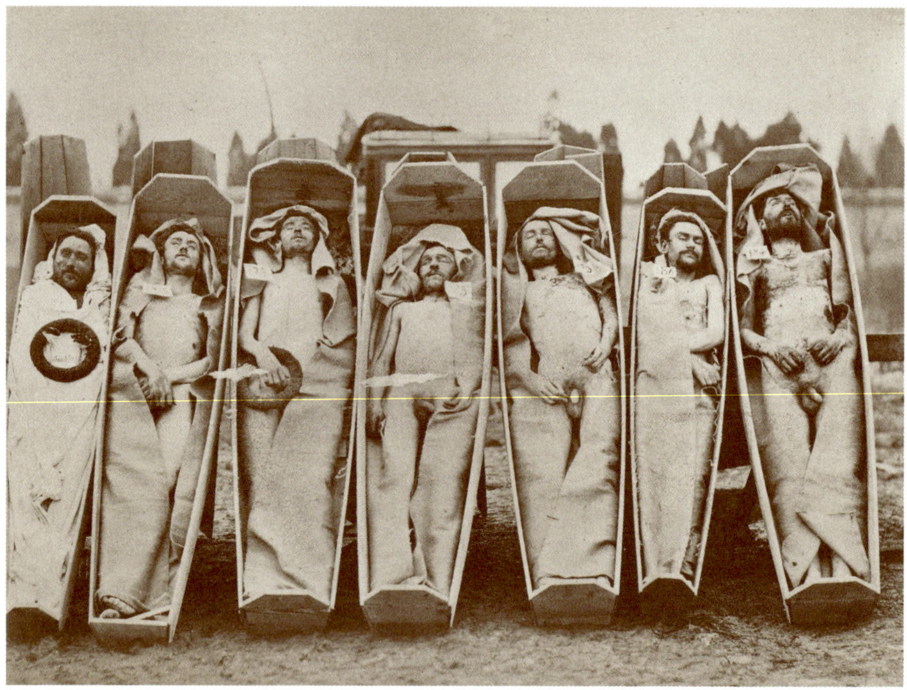

Anonymous (Attributed to Disdéri),
Paris Commune: Bodies of Insurgents,
1871, University of Texas, Austin.

The uprising of the Paris Commune began on March 18, 1871. Thiers took refuge at Versailles; Paris underwent a second siege. During the "bloody week", May 21–28, the people of Versailles crushed the Commune. Massive repression began. For those who had not been present at the drama, and who were not to visit the ruins, photography brought things closer. Very quickly "the shop windows of printsellers disappeared under a fantastic quantity of photographic postcards" (Maxime du Camp, *Les Convulsions de Paris*). Cartes de Visite, rudimentary albums, photo-series in an edition of a few hundred copies, engravings "after photographs", and subsequent photogravures spread a certain image of the Commune.

Thanks to its (supposed) objectivity, photography would be a means of propaganda which generally denounced the reprisals against the communards. From 1871 "collections" of demolished buildings were published: the Hôtel de Ville, the Tuileries, etc. Numerous Paris photographers such as Andrieu, Franck, Langerock, Liébert, Petit, and Wulff wandered around Paris during the events. For technical reasons (the exposure time) or because of possible risks, Paris seems deserted in their images; only a few people who remained still appear and fires are evoked only by crude touching-up of prints in paint (Taupin, Ferrier, and Lecadre). All seems in ruins, blamed only on the communards.

"Grandiose, strange, picturesque" ruin was sometimes the pretext for an aesthetic approach. Liébert published a collection of 100 views of "Ruins of Paris" (the siege of 1870 and the Commune of 1871), which later appeared as postcards. As for the events, they often escaped being truly shown: "historical photography" (a photographic version of the genre of history painting), reproduced engravings (Betsellère, Leroy, Quinet) or resorted to tricks of photomontage (Appert, Vauvray, Daubiance). For his *Crimes of the Commune* the "painter-photographer" Appert made people pose in the original settings. The images produced aim at reproducing the truth, but are often tendentious (Raudnitz's *Sacking of the Hôtel Thiers.*)

The other images may, to a varying extent, be considered as "identification" images. Firstly individual portraits are involved (mostly communards). These were sought after as they allow the public to see the "faces of the guilty men" (Appert was still publishing them in 1878), and they were sometimes used for caricatures. Even communards in prison were often able to use their portraits, "palpable memories of the time when they were someone" (Maxime du Camp), which they gave away and signed.

Collective portraits were taken at symbolic places, such as the barricades or the overturned Vendôme column (Braquehais). The communards enthusiastically posed, miming the action on the spot, and took part eagerly in the re-enactment of their "successful part".

But while censorship attempted to regulate photographs which might hinder the "re-establishment of public order" (sales were controlled), portraits of the communards made repression easier, and the police assembled large filing cabinets of photographs. There were albums which allowed fugitives to be sought out, useful in ports or on frontiers, or files on communards who were exiled, in prison, or executed – all kept up to date. Each portrait was accompanied by handwritten details (marital status, physical appearance, role during the Commune, etc). Many of them were by Appert, who systematically photographed people held in the Versailles prisons. It is known that group portraits were also used: a famous example is an image of the overturned Vendôme column, in which Courbet has been identified. He was wrongly accused of having taken part in its destruction.

The conditions under which photographs were used did not allow them to serve to their best advantage. But "the experiment was not useless, and it was [from] this moment that a photographic studio was set up in the police station" (Maxime Du Camp).

As for authentic pictures of those killed during the bloody week, they are rare: a portrait of the dead Dombrowski by Darlot, and two images of the corpses of shot communards, one taken in the hospital and the other, attributed to Disdéri, an exceptionally explicit one, of numbered corpses placed in coffins.

Joël Petitjean

communard barricades and ruins – though often one cannot distinguish between the effects of the Commune and of the Prussian occupation of Paris – and central, very visual, events such as the fall of the victory column on Place Vendôme. Of the last-mentioned picture alone, 50,000 copies in carte-de-visite format were sold to Britain in the year 1871.[35] Photographs like the one by Disdéri of dead communards lined up in coffins and numbered had now become a part of the historic spectacle of war.

It is well-known that photography, which had been used since the 1860s as a means of identifying criminals, was the undoing of many communards. Frontier police were provided with portraits of wanted communards – up to 4,000

35. On this and on the role of photography in propaganda after the Commune see the excellent study by D. E. English, *Political Use of Photography in the Third French Republic, 1871–1914*, Ann Arbor, Michigan, UMI Press, 1984, pp. 21–81.

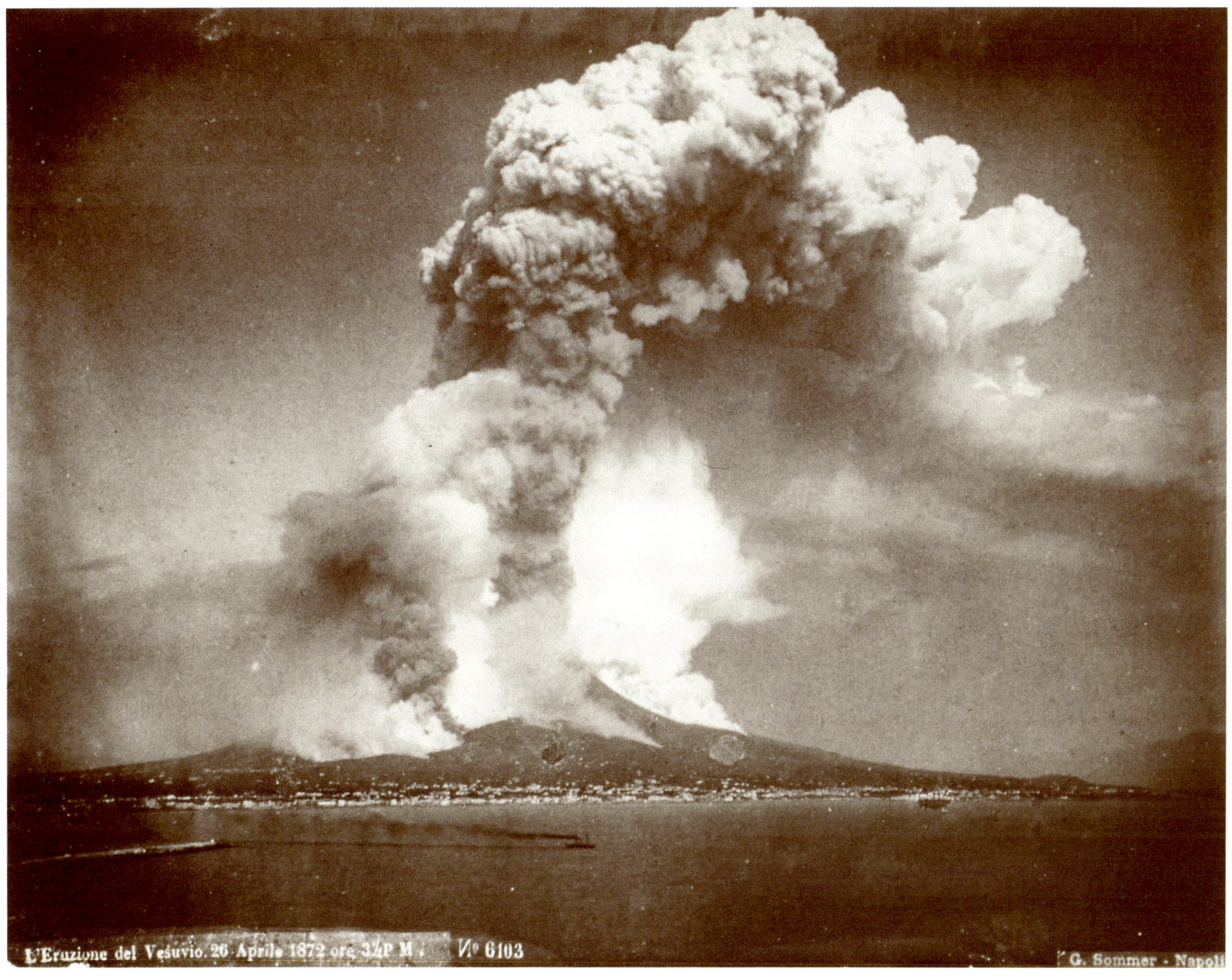

GIORGIO SOMMER,
Eruption of Mount Vesuvius,
April 26, 1872,
private collection.

carte-de-visite copies of each one. With the Commune, photography became a weapon of investigation in the logistics of war. The supposedly objective photographic documentation of war became the ornament of nationalism. As a weapon, it now found a place in the arsenals of warfare.

An article in the *Magasin pittoresque* of 1872 on the history of war – it calculated that 40 million people died in wars in the nineteenth century – closes with the words: "With the heads of all the victims one could build a vault of heaven with the same perspective as the one that we see [...] That sky of severed heads has been produced and is maintained by the spirit of conquest, by antipathies and dissensions between nations. O reason! O justice! O goodness! When will your kingdom come?"[36]

Ten years earlier, Disdéri had ended his chapter on the usefulness of photography to the army with the exhortation, "En avant!"

36. *Magasin Pittoresque*, 40th year, 1872, p. 323.

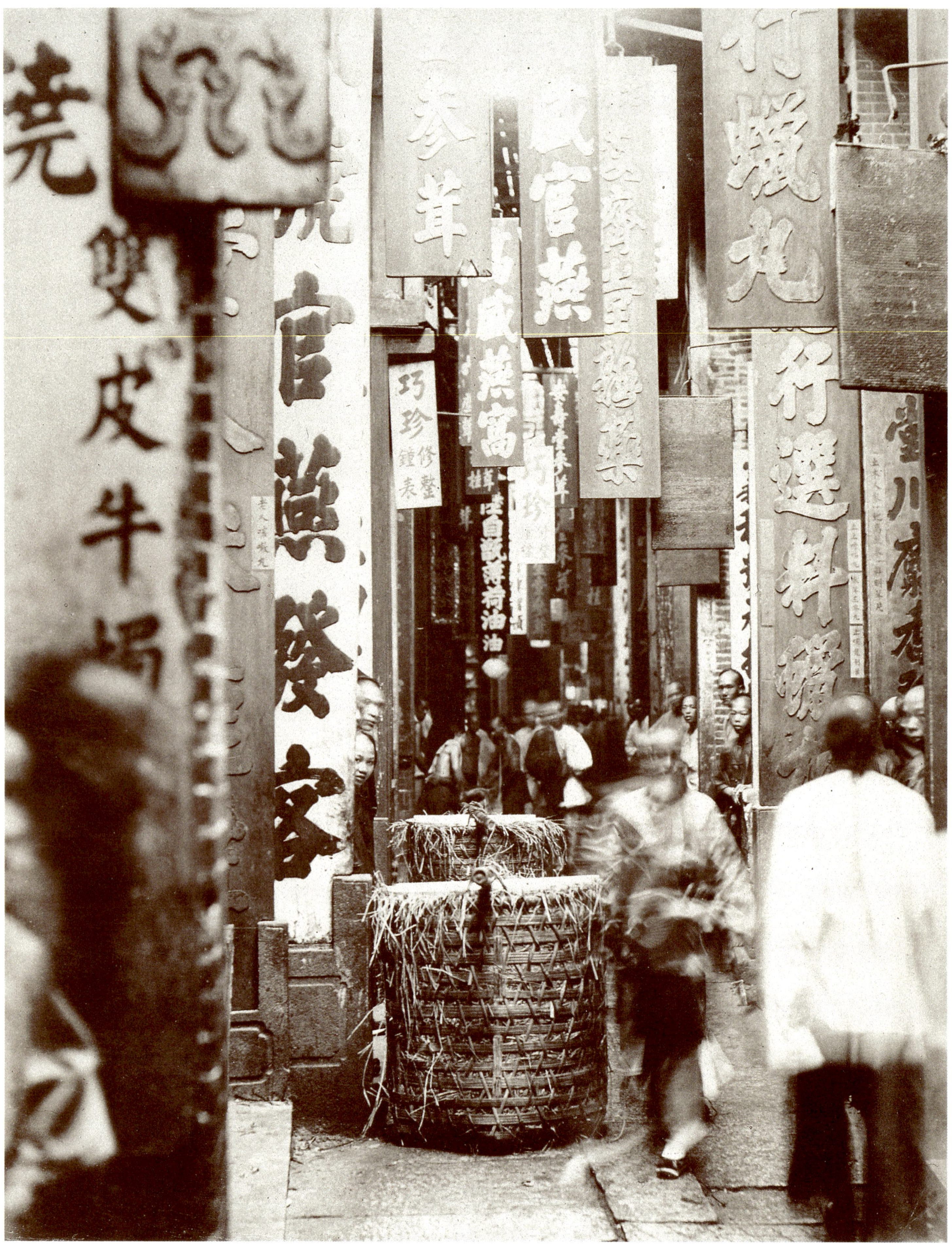

参茸
官燕
蠟丸
巧珍
修整
鐘表
燕窩
自製薄荷油
雙皮牛

AROUND THE WORLD

8

Explorers, travelers, and tourists

Françoise Heilbrun

The hallmark of the second half of the nineteenth century was a taste for discoveries of every kind, particularly for new peoples, nations, places, and landscapes. This "need to know" was reinforced by the lure of the exotic, a prevailing taste for the picturesque, colonial expansion, and the growth of tourism. It was also fueled by countless magazines which were illustrated increasingly "with photographs". Systematic journeys of photographic exploration, the fact that studios sprang up in towns which had become stopping places for tourists, and the advent of photographic publishers and distributors, all combined to make the world a more mobile, less enclosed place. The acceptance of the world's diversity also brought with it economic risks, social misgivings, and power struggles. These were particularly visible in the international exhibitions held toward the end of the century.

In the minds of sociologists, the invention of photography is often linked to the emergence of the middle classes. However, it can equally well be seen as a corollary to the systematic attempt to explore the world begun by the Encyclopedists. As early as 1840, topographical daguerreotypists claimed lineage from the scientist Alexander von Humboldt, who was indeed interested in photography. As the knowledge of discoveries spread, the public's enthusiasm and curiosity grew. With this came a taste for the picturesque and a growing thirst for knowledge.

During the 1850s, and especially after photographic societies were established in France and Britain, this form of exploration started to develop along more organized lines. At the same time, the conditions of photographic production were about to change. Photographers, all too aware that the practice of their "art" did not afford them a living, set up their own firms and aimed no longer at publishing luxury prints, but at broadening the market for photography. On the other hand, from 1860 onwards, public bodies, the navy, the army, and a variety of national record offices took over the role of royal patronage and became the major commissioners of photography. Railroad building projects of the 1850s also gave the whole process fresh impetus and opened the way for even more far-reaching discoveries of the world.

The traveler's horizons

Topographical exploration melded landscape with historic architecture, most notably in the work of Hippolyte Bayard, Gustave Le Gray, Henri Le Secq, and Edouard Baldus. All had taken part in the Heliographic Mission of 1851 and later undertook geographical expeditions of their own. Added to this, other photographers were interested in industrial buildings and regional facial types, first highlighted in 1852 by Charles Nègre in the south of France. This gave rise to a real, albeit rather quaint, inquiry into social and ethnographic types. Gradually, ethnographic photography, architectural photography, and nature (flora and fauna) photography became specializations, a trend which gathered momentum after 1880. Until then they had been more an expression of the geographical and geological attitudes of the explorers themselves than a reflection of whether they were working on a scientific or military mission, or of amateur or professional status.

The quest to document the world in no way diminished aesthetic considerations – as can be seen from landscapes of India or the American West. These photographs reveal scientific intentions despite their "conquering" aims. Photographers were always careful to please their public and to anticipate its taste. Initially, even

◀ A. Fong, (attributed), *Street in Canton*, circa 1870, private collection.

Photographic exhibitions

Photographic exhibitions flourished during the nineteenth century in a disordered and haphazard fashion. This was a direct reflection of the burgeoning vitality of the times and of a totally new form of social instinct. An exhibition dedicated to the work of a single photographer was still unusual. What was very common, on the other hand, was the group exhibition where large numbers of pictures were amassed alphabetically into anthologies or into encyclopedic combinations. Very often, photographs were used as specimens, displayed alongside artifacts and the products of nature, industry, and commerce. This meant that people's perception of photography was ambiguous, falling as it did between art and science and torn as it was between commercial imperatives, technological prowess, and the artistic high ground.

In particular, before every major exhibition it was necessary to enter negotiations about the nature of the space that would be allocated to photography. In the Paris Exhibition of 1855, for instance, photography was relegated to a place among the products of industry, whereas in the 1859 show the 148 photographic exhibitors were located near to the Salon des Beaux-Arts. In 1855, the Société Française de Photographie held the first of its biennial exhibitions at its own headquarters (11 Rue Drouot); the second, in 1857, was hosted at the photographer Gustave Le Gray's premises on Boulevard des Capucines. This was a retrospective exhibition covering "works by French and foreign artists and amateurs as well as equipment and products for all branches of photographic art". There was also a historical section (heliography on pewter by Niépce).

Photography was granted access to the sanctuary of fine art more quickly in the provinces. Nantes was very much a pioneer in this respect. A series of exhibitions in the museum and library (1842, 1843, 1851, 1854, 1858, 1861, 1875, 1881) displayed, side by side, paintings, sculptures, drawings, and "artistic photography" by living artists, including Martens, Nègre, and Richebourg.

Elvire Perego

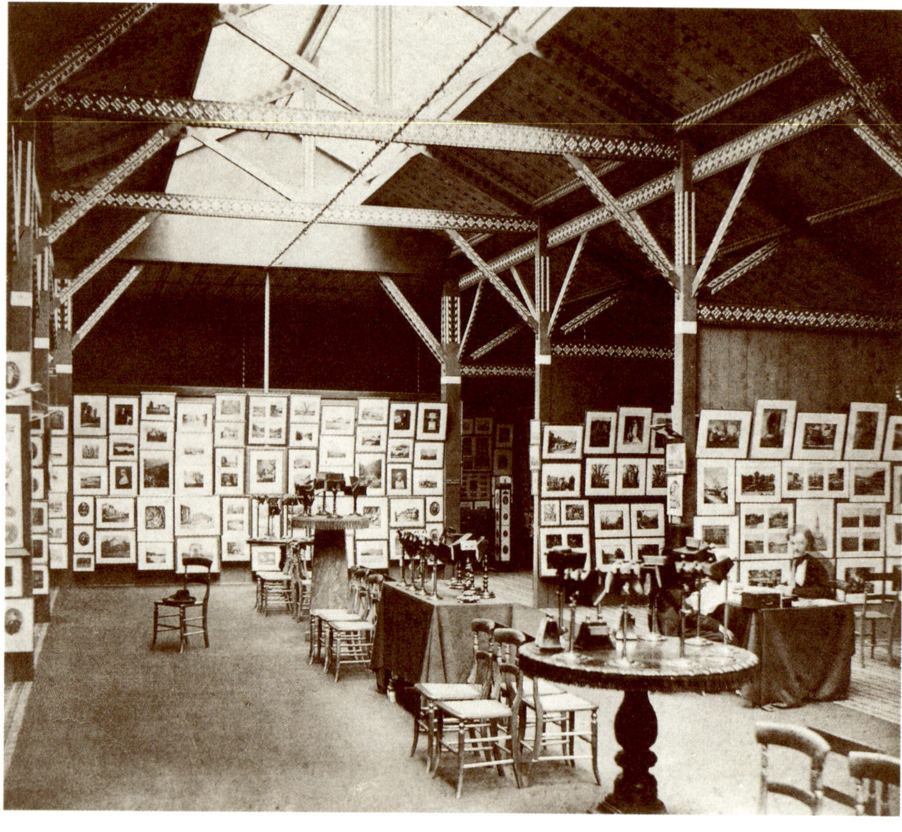

Anonymous,
London Photographic Society, Annual Exhibition,
1858, Victoria & Albert Museum, London.

didactic compositions had a fresh approach. This can be seen in the work of G. W. Wilson, or in the Alinari brothers' early prints, between 1860 and 1870. All too quickly, however, success spelled banality. These images contained as much visual knowledge of the world's geography as was possible. At the same time, it is legitimate to ask if they may not have lulled the public into believing that the photographic eye was necessarily neutral and bland.

Topographical views evolved in much the same way in different countries. First came the great "primitives" of the 1850s: Roger Fenton in Britain, Gustave Le Gray in France, Robert Macpherson in Italy, Francis Frith in the Middle East. During the 1860s, a number, such as the Bisson brothers, Edouard Baldus, Charles Nègre, and Francis Frith, adapted their work for commercial production since they were not lucky enough (unlike Charles Marville or Charles Clifford) to be financed by the state or a sovereign. Soon, new people appeared. Some, such as Commander Miot, Ferrez, O'Sullivan, Murray, and Weed, obtained government commissions. Others – Valentine, Bedford, Alinari, Naya or Beato – were prepared to go into business on their own. A few fortunate amateurs such as Lorent survived, as did a number of entrepreneurs such as Charnay or Samuel Bourne. The international commercial circuit (see box) meant that different production categories and different formats could be mixed.

The technical industrialization of photography during the 1860s meant that, by about 1875, albumen prints had become standard, to be superseded, in turn, in the 1890s, by gelatin-bromide prints. From 1855, many (Baldus, Nègre, Fenton, Le Secq, Davanne) tried to overcome the problem of the non-permanence of photographic prints by using the photogravure

1. See F. Heilbrun in *L'Impressionisme et le Paysage française*, Paris, Grand Palais, 1984, Los Angeles, City Museum of Art, 1984, pp. 371–389.

2. M. Daniel, "Edouard Baldus: Les albums du Chemin de fer du Nord", in *La Recherche photographique*, no. 8, February 1990, pp. 83–89.

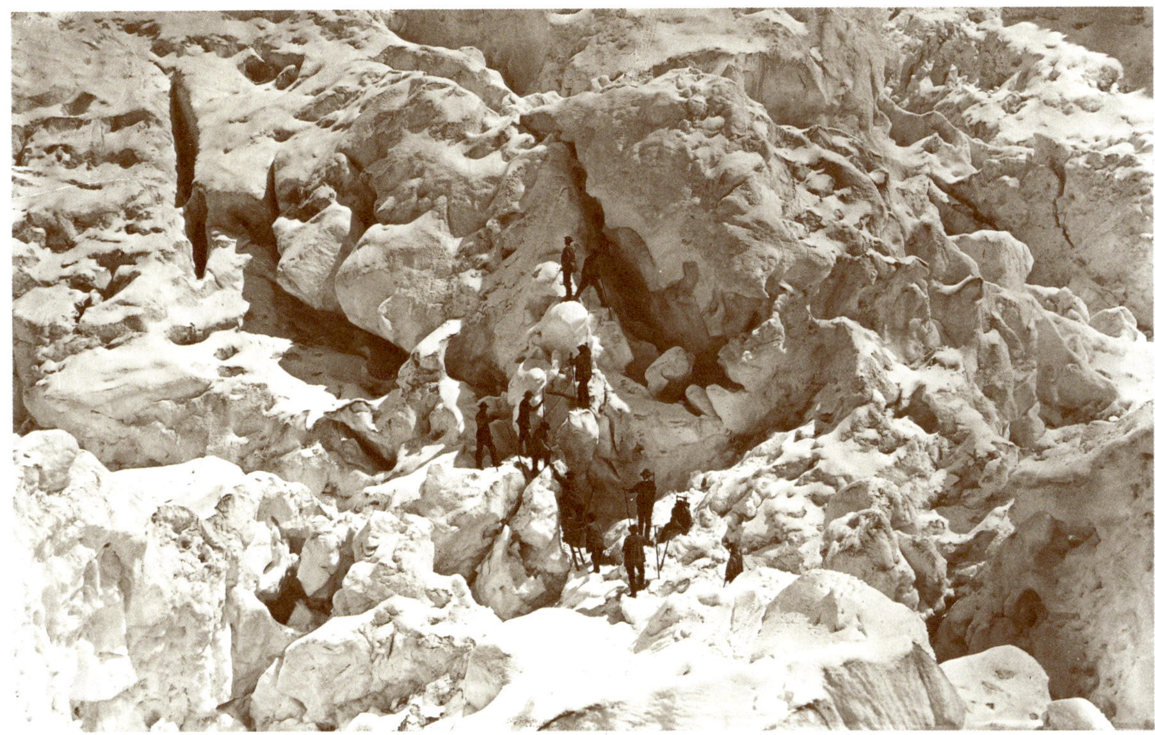

Bisson Frères,
Ascent of Mont Blanc,
1862,
Société Française
de Photographie, Paris.

process. *Calle e Canali di Venezia* (1891–1892), a heliotype published by Ongania, is the last example. However, it was only when the half-tone process was invented that the way was finally open for the sale of truly permanent images. From the 1890s, this was the most popular process for postcards. Finally, after instantaneous exposures (the snapshot) had been mastered in the 1880s, there was a proliferation of animated scenes, snaps of people walking or on the beach, and port scenes.

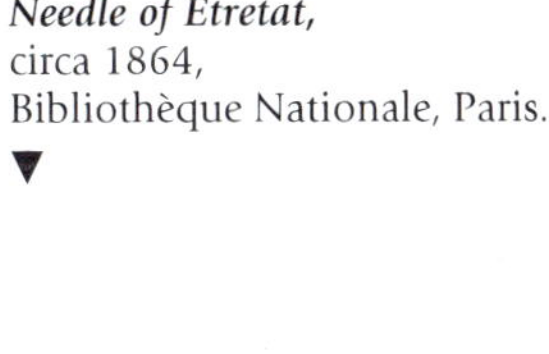

Louis-Alphonse Davanne,
Needle of Étretat,
circa 1864,
Bibliothèque Nationale, Paris.
▼

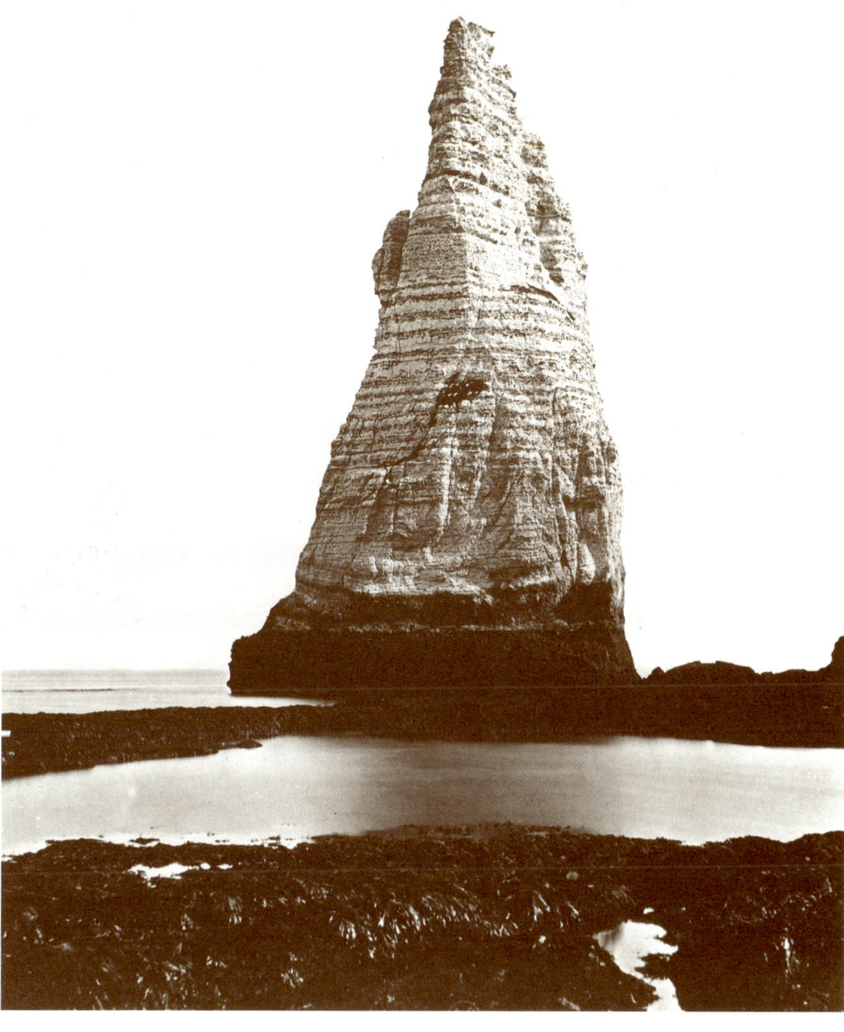

Images of France

A number of calotypists were quickly won over by the glass negative, among them Le Gray, who used it for a (second) series of pictures of the Forest of Fontainebleau (1855), and Baldus, who photographed the waterfalls in the Dauphiné region (1854). Their work established models of method and balance which were part of the pre-Impressionist and Impressionist[1] fashion for the outdoors. When Queen Victoria traveled by train from Boulogne to Paris (1855),[2] Baldus celebrated the modernity of the French landscape – changed for the Chemin de Fer du Nord railroad. Not only did he create a truly separate genre, but he also provided it with its very best examples, later imitated by photographers employed by the École des Ponts et Chaussées. Not many people would have been able to show, as Baldus did, the way in which the new architecture fitted into the landscape (railroad, viaducts, and bridges) and complement these images with far more "picturesque" views of nature spared by the machine.

The spread of topographical views

In the nineteenth century photographers generally made prints from negatives themselves. Then, so that they could market their prints as cheaply as possible, they sometimes sold their negatives to the state on a subscription basis (Piot in 1850; Baldus and Nègre in 1852). From 1851, first Blanquart-Evrard and then Lachevardière came up with the idea of establishing a "photographic printing works". In London Frith was already working in this way by 1851. Photographers bought up negative libraries or negotiated publishing agreements with other photographers. In France, Moulin published Fenton's views of the Crimea and Martens handled work by Colonel Langlois and Méhédin while Furne and Tournier produced Miot's Newfoundland photographs. In 1853, Cundall published Robertson's views of Constantinople (the prints, made at the Photographic Institution in London, belonged to a number of photographers). This practice led to a number of law suits when the publisher "omitted" to mention the author of the original negative.

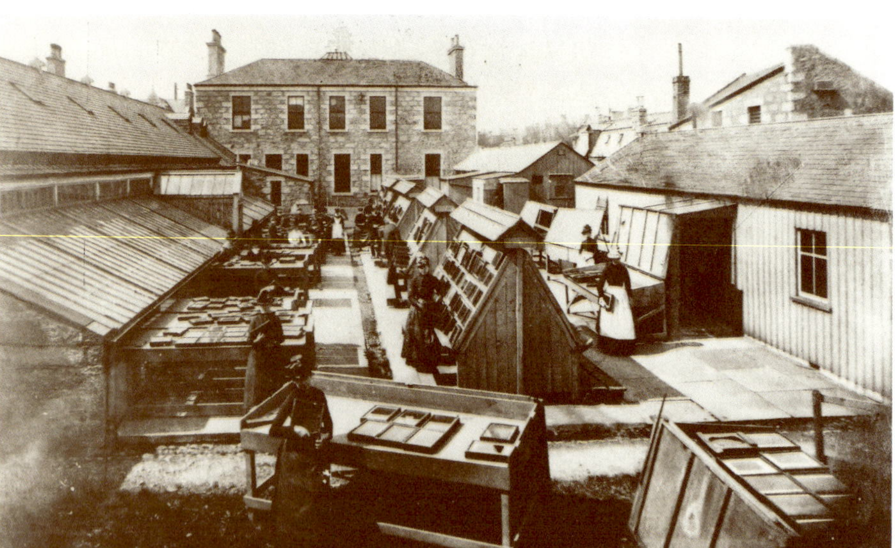

George Washington Wilson, ***Photographic Print Studio of Saint-Swithin,*** circa 1900, Aberdeen Art Gallery.

Sales were handled either through the printer-photographer or, more often, through publishers, booksellers or printsellers such as E. Gambart or Marion & Co in Britain. It was Gambart who looked after the London publication of Teynard's album and was the distributor for Robertson's album *Jerusalem*, published in Leipzig. As early as 1862, Clifford had hoped Marion would act as the publisher for his views of Spain, a project halted by his untimely death. Marion handled the distribution of G. W. Wilson's views throughout Europe and the world. In 1856 and 1857, James Virtue looked after sales of Francis Frith's large views of Egypt.

A number of publishers specialized in stereoscopic views, among them Negretti and Zambra in London, Ferrier and Clouzard in Paris, Edward Anthony in New York, Thomas Houseworth in San Francisco, and George Leuzinger – who started off as a lithographer and trained Marc Ferrez (1860) – in Brazil.

Topographical collections were as easy to come by then as postcards are today, on sale in shops, on passenger boats, in stations and hotels. The British Consul in Jerusalem reported that in 1864 Robertson used a local banker as a middleman to publish albums on the Holy Land which he then sold to the best hotels, thus breaching his exclusive contract with the photographer Diness.

Apart from exhibitions and sales organized through photographic societies, photographers could also find outlets in a large number of periodicals which reproduced their negatives as woodcuts. In Madrid, Clifford and Laurent were generally commissioned by *Museo Nacional, La Crónica* or *Museo Universal*. During the 1860s illustrations "from a photograph" were published by *Le Monde illustré*, and *Le Tour du monde* (founded in 1860) in Paris and by the *Illustrated London News* in London, although the original photographer rarely got a mention.

Françoise Heilbrun

See S. Rochard, "La photographie et la presse illustrée sous le second Empire", in *Histoire de l'art*, no. 13/14, pp. 47–54.

Other "new" genres sprang up. Leading the way were seascapes which included studies of sky. The prototypes were by Le Gray (Mediterranean Coast and Normandy, 1856–1857) enormously successful and a blueprint for other photographers with an eye for the picturesque (G. W. Wilson, J. Valentine). In his unrivaled series of twenty or so views, Le Gray attempted to capture the way light moves over the ocean, rather than showing any particular locality.

Glacier photography was the next novelty. In France it was a completely new theme, for until then it had been overlooked by painters.[3] The Bisson brothers, two outstanding Paris photographers, started exploring Savoy from 1859, producing large negatives (as big as 70 x 100 cm). In 1860, they published a collection of photographs dedicated to the Emperor and Empress and entitled *Haute-Savoie: le Mont-Blanc et ses glaciers*. In 1861 and 1862, Auguste Rosalie Bisson photographed Mont Blanc and Monte Rosa with a panoramic camera, returning in 1869. From 1870, their prints were sold by Émile Placet.

During the 1860s Adolphe Braun (1812–1877) concentrated on mountains. He took imposing views – probably by his assistant Jean-Claude Marmand – of the glaciers in Savoy and Northern Italy (sometimes using panoramic techniques). In 1869, Charles Soulier did the same with a series of views of the Alps. His links with publishers (Clouzard, Ferrier, and then Léon & Lévy) meant that he produced many stereoscopic views. Aimé Civiale photographed the Pyrenees (1859), concentrating on the structure and formation of geological strata since he was

3. F. Guichon, *La Montagne, photographies de 1845 à 1914*, Paris, 1984.

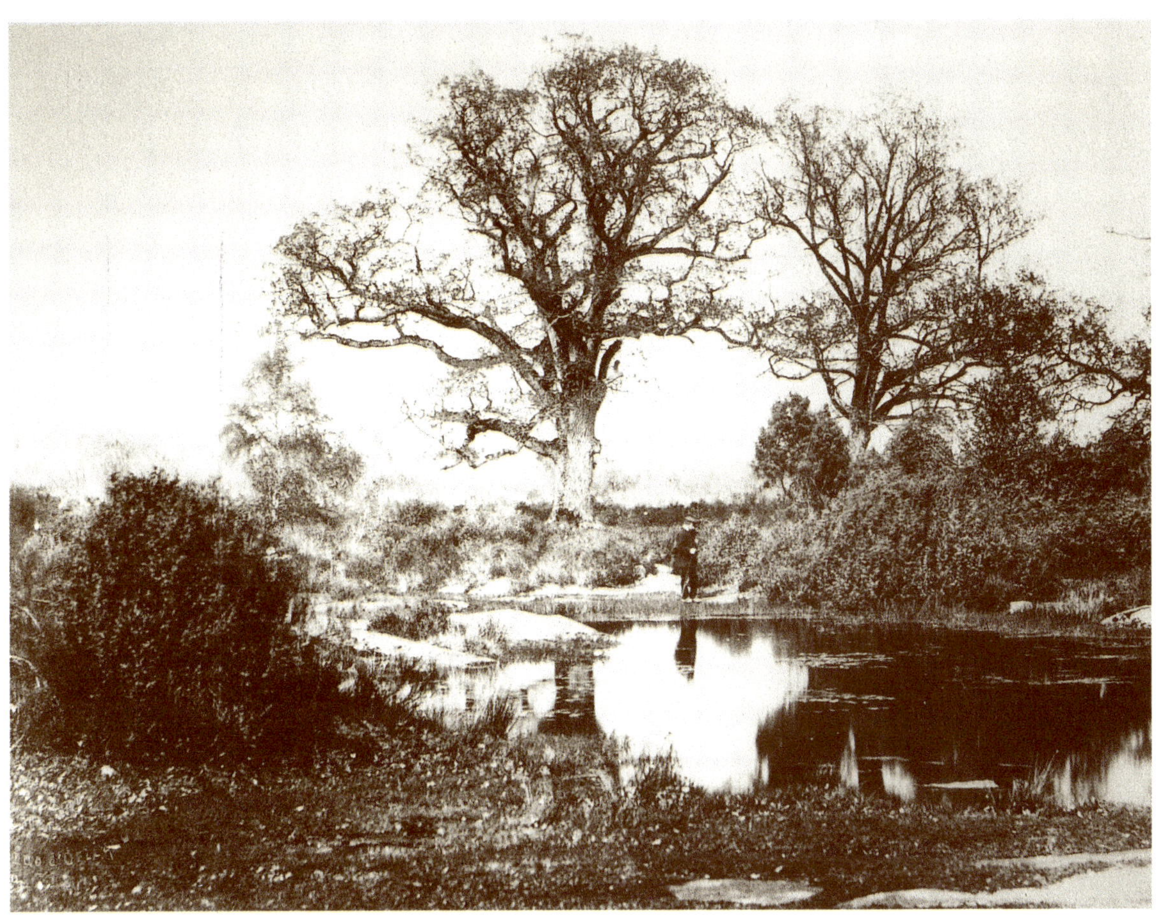

CHARLES FAMIN, ***Dagneau Pond, Fontainebleau Forest,*** circa 1870, Bibliothèque Nationale, Paris.

working as a geologist. This was even more apparent when the photographer shot 600 views and 41 panoramas of the Alps from the Dauphiné to the Tyrol (1868).

Another topographical genre grew up around middle-class pastimes. People at leisure were photographed in the outskirts of Paris or in recently developed seaside resorts. Photographers recorded the localities, their infrastructure, and the people there. Between 1855 and 1857, Olympe Aguado, an amateur photographer close to the Emperor, was the leading exponent of this genre. In the 1860s, Alphonse Davanne published series of photographs of Tréport, Dieppe, Trouville, and Le Havre. There were also a large number of stereoscopic views in circulation. Their subjects were photographed again in the 1890s using a larger format (21 x 27 cm) (Neurdein, Léon & Lévy picture library bought by Roger Viollet in the twentieth century).

By about 1860, every region had its favorite photographers. In the Pyrenees, with its fashionable mountain resorts where people came to take the waters, the most sought-after photographer was an Englishman, Farnam Maxwell Lyte (1828–1906), based in Bagnère-de-Bigorre. After him came Pacault, L. Lafon, and Lamazouère. However, none of them ever matched the beauty of the prints of the Pyrenees (1853) caught by a great amateur, Viscount Joseph Vigier. Brittany was the fiefdom of Furne the Younger (*Vues des côtes de Bretagne* then *Vues, Monuments, Estuaires de la Bretagne* from 1857 onwards). After Bayard and Davanne, Normandy was photographed by Edmond Bacot, a republican with links to the family of Victor Hugo, then exiled in Jersey. In about 1853, Hugo's work inspired Bacot to take wonderful views of the Gothic architecture in Rouen.[4] But all too quickly the quality of the views declined. Speaking of the 1867 Exposition Universelle, Davanne deplored the passing of amateur photographers capable of visualizing a landscape as an artist does. He also lamented the passing of the paper negative which encouraged artistic work. On the other side of the Alps, in Mulhouse, Adolphe Braun specialized in the topography of Alsace (his stereoscopic views were advertised in *La Lumière* in 1857). Before long, his father, his brother Charles, and his son Gaston (who was to take over from him) were crossing Alsace, Savoy, Holland, and Hungary, bringing back stylish large-format views which were published as albums. By 1870, the firm was expanding rapidly, owning a branch in Paris and specializing in the reproduction of works of art.

Photographers who stand out in Provence are Edouard Baldus, Charles Nègre, and Dominique Roman from Arles. In 1856 and 1857, Baldus brought a truly epic style to the way he reported the flooding of the River Rhône at Lyons, and Avignon. In 1859, he published a collection of photographs to commemorate the extension of

4. See F. Heilbrun, "Un album de primitifs de la photographie française", in *Revue du Louvre*, no. 1, 1980, and B. Chéreau, J. Py, J. Bergeret, *E. Bacot, A. de Brébisson. A. Humbert de Molard: Trois photographes en basse Normandie au XIXe siècle*, Caen, 1989. See also J.-J. Henry, *Photographie, les débuts en Normandie*, Le Havre, 1989.

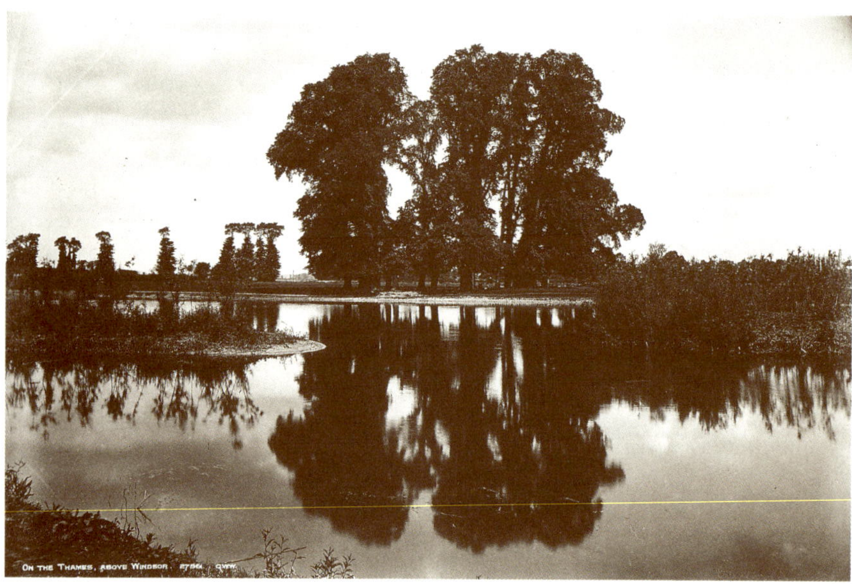

George Washington Wilson, *On The Thames, Above Windsor,* circa 1880, private collection.

the Paris-Lyons railroad to the Mediterranean. The album, large-format and as skilful as his photographs of the floods, illustrated the places the railroad went through from the port of La Ciotat to the Moine rock. At the time,[5] Baldus had a Paris studio employing eleven people. Later on, he turned out better-quality prints but these were average-sized and rather uniform in nature. As for Charles Nègre,[6] he had returned home to the south of France. He produced countless views of Cannes and Nice for the tourist trade; these lacked the poetry evident in his earlier work.

Alongside truly topographical photographs, there were also the "Studies from nature" so dear to the calotypists. These supplied the market for prints aimed at "artists and amateurs". Louis Robert and Alphonse de Brébisson continued this genre through the 1860s. Until at least 1858, the painter André Giroux (1801–1879) had been exhibiting and selling heavily retouched landscapes, notable for their turbulent skies. Another inspired amateur, closely connected to Barbizon's circle of painters, was Eugène Cuvelier (1837–1909). He remained faithful to the calotype and explored the Forest of Fontainebleau where sand dunes and rocks created an almost lunar landscape.[7] Between 1870 and 1880, Fontainebleau attracted tourists, artists, and photographers, including Charles Famin, who took views of the forest and rustic scenes with figures and animals, and Achille Quinet, close to Famin. From about 1870 publishers, such as Taupin, Ziegler & Cie, and Giraudon started selling collections of studies from nature: plants, undergrowth, animals, people working the land. Alongside these commercial offerings, amateurs like the lawyer Paul Delondre, Alphonse Jeanrenaud or Arthur Taylor exhibited large-scale landscapes to the end of the 1870s. This type of view culminated in an album about the Bois de Boulogne (1858) by Charles Marville, appointed official photographer to the city of Paris. From 1866 the French Geographic Society, founded in 1826, started playing an active role, collecting photographs and organizing lectures.

Occasionally, foreign expeditions were sponsored by the French government. F. J. Moulin, a

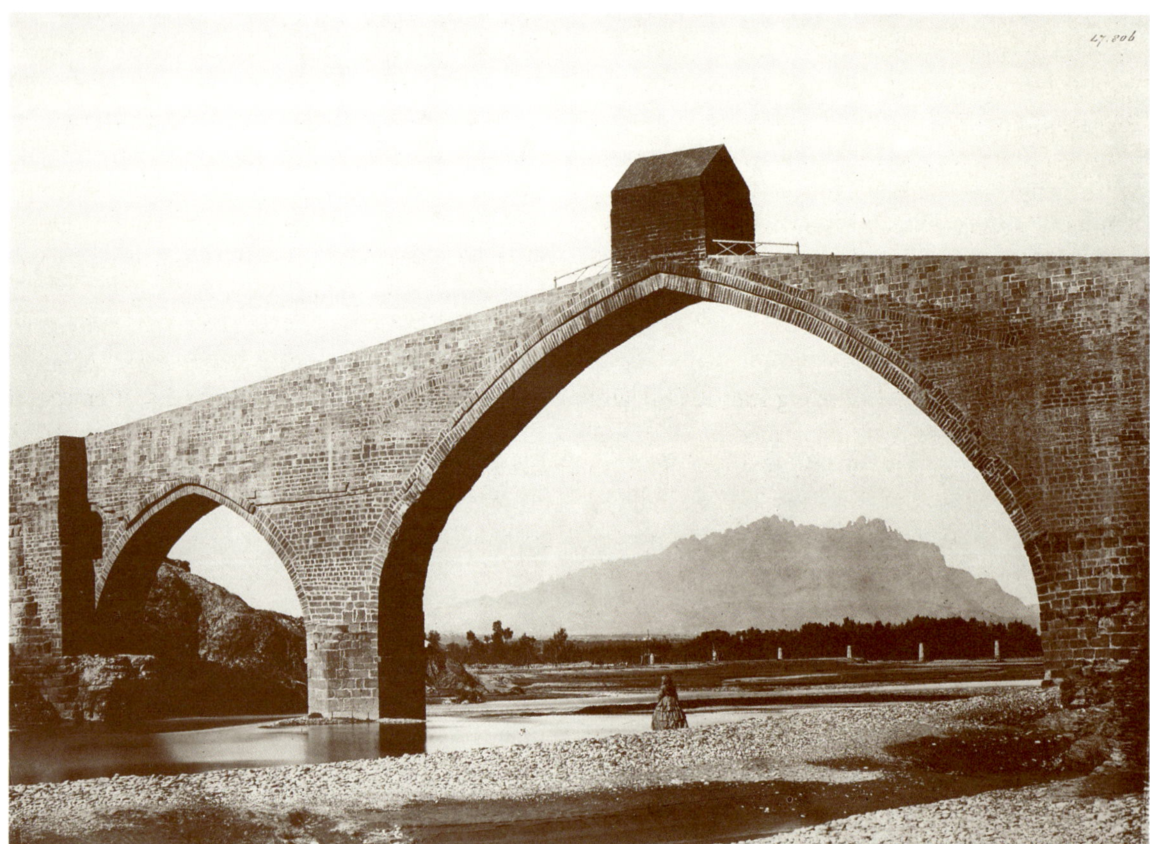

Charles Clifford, *Devil's Bridge at Martorell, Spain,* circa 1858.

5. F. Heilbrun and P. Néagu, *Photographies*, no. 1, 1983, pp. 56–77.

6. F. Heilbrun, *Charles Nègre (1820–1880)*, Paris, 1980, note 65, pp. 32–34.

7. With regard to Cuvelier and Famin, see D. Challe and B. Marbot, *Les Photographes de Barbizon: La forêt de Fontainebleau*, Paris, 1991; *Eugène Cuvelier*, Stuttgart, Cantz, 1996.

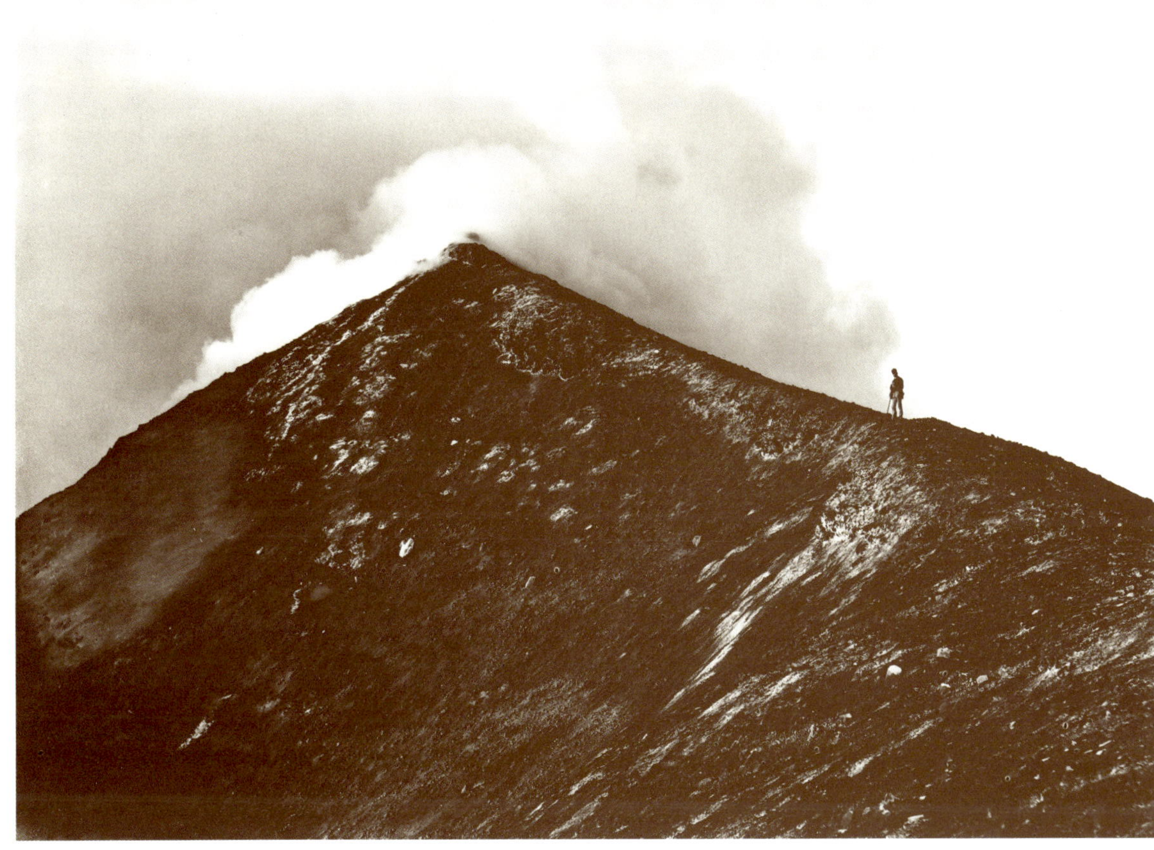

VITTORIO SELLA,
Mount Etna, Eastern End of the Great Crater,
1888,
Istituto di Fotografia Alpina Vittorio Sella, Biella.

photographer-publisher who specialized in nudes and genre photographs, left for Algeria in 1858 with the backing of the French Minister for War. He brought back three series of albums on the regions around Algiers, Oran, and Constantine. These were dedicated to the Emperor and contained panoramic shots of ports as well as numerous studies of natives, posed in groups in indoor settings. Thanks to Gabriel de Rumine, a Russian noble who accompanied the Grand Duke Constantin on his journey to the Mediterranean, there is an admirable series of views of Nice, Naples, Palermo, Pompeii, Monreale, Athens, Jerusalem, etc.

The picturesque in Britain

In Britain in the 1850s, following Talbot, Hill, and Adamson in the 1840s, the role model was Roger Fenton (1819–1869). However, he was to give up photography in 1862.[8] His photojournalistic coverage of Russia (calotype, 1852) and the Crimean War (collodion on glass, 1854) proved that the urge to record did not prevent the creation of truly lyrical compositions. At home, Fenton played an active role in compiling a photographic inventory of important localities, churches, and abbeys. Taste was for Gothic revival architecture, and the Church encouraged photography in order to highlight its religious patrimony. In particular, this was done through the Architectural Photographic Association and the Antiquarian Photographic Club, established in 1854. Often the places photographed by Fenton had already been explored by watercolor artists such as William Gilpin. Indeed, the Photographic Society sometimes held exhibitions at the Society of Watercolourists. From 1857 to 1861, about 40 of Fenton's prints, mainly topographical views, were included in these exhibitions. In 1857, they included views of Scotland, Newcastle, Berwick, and Yorkshire. In 1858, they were of North Wales, in 1859 they were mainly photographs of abbeys, and in 1860 of Lancashire and Oxford. Fenton exhibited large contact prints made from wet-collodion glass negatives, printed first on salted paper then on albumen paper. His technique was always perfect but his style varied from naturalism, admired by contemporaries for its attention to fine detail and the perfection of atmospheric perspective (Wales), to noble severity (architectural views). He sometimes introduced figures among the ruins. His scenes are characterised by effects of light, as in his photographs of Rievaulx (1854) and Furness (1860) abbeys. This gave his work the allegorical significance of a *memento mori*. Some of his later landscapes such as the park at Harewood House (1860) reached the twin pinnacles of simplicity and perfect craftsmanship. The son of a wealthy family, Fenton was not averse to selling his work. Indeed his large prints were very expensive. Neither did he have any objection to

8. J. Hannavy, *Roger Fenton of Crimble Hall*, London, 1975, and V. Lloyd, *Roger Fenton, Photographer of the 1850s*, London, Hayward Gallery, 1988.

Fratelli Alinari, Florence

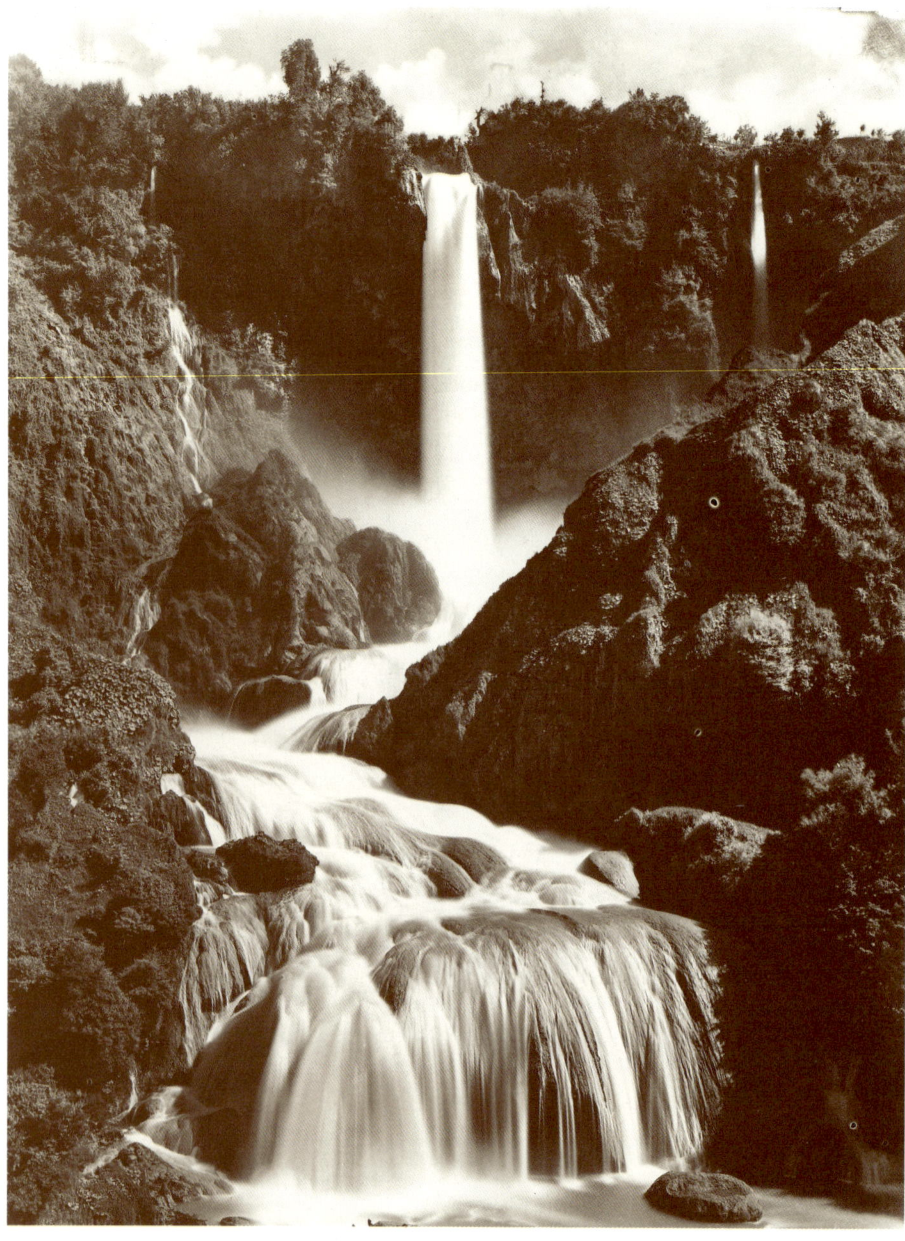

Alinari, *Cascate delle Marmore,* Terni, circa 1860.

The Alinari studios, founded in Florence in 1852 and in business until nearly 1920, were started by Leopoldo Alinari and taken over on his death in 1865 by his brothers Giuseppe, the technical brain, and Romualdo, the business brain. Fratelli Alinari specialized in reproductions of works of art. They rapidly made an international name for themselves and were leaders in the photographic industry thanks to their contacts with major museums and art historians such as Ruskin or Berenson. In 1881, they were the first to photograph the Piero della Francesca frescos in Arezzo. The firm's artistic inventory was balanced by its topographical work. They spread from Florence to Tuscany and soon through Italy.

The glory years of Fratelli Alinari came at the end of the century when the firm was run by Vittorio. Passionate about landscapes, between 1890 and 1900 he photographed Genoa, Turin, Piedmont, Valle d'Aosta, the Alps, and Sicily. He then went on to Sardinia and finally covered all the places mentioned in Dante (1920) as well as taking snapshots of popular scenes.

Alinari's didactic and sometimes rather severe style worked wonders for views of shops, hotels, banks, hospitals, and modern factories, either privately commissioned or part of encyclopedic series. All too few examples of the large 30 x 40 cm prints from the 1850–1860 period survive. The same goes for views of localities, buildings, and landscapes, undoubtedly the best of their production.

In about 1930, when the picture library was sold, it comprised 70,000 itemized negatives. Like Braun's picture store in Mulhouse, the distribution of Alinari photographs in France was handled by Giraudon. The photographic archive (15 Largo Fratelli Alinari) today includes pictures from the stores of other photographers who were competitors (Anderson, Brogi, Villani).

Françoise Heilbrun

stereoscopic views, taking twenty to illustrate J. B. Davidson's *The Conway in Stereoscope* (London, Lovell Rive, 1860).

From 1856, Fenton published permanent prints (using Pretsch's "photo-galvanographic" process), sold in binders or albums entitled *Photographic Art Treasures.* His results were violently criticized by Thomas Sutton, himself published by Blanquart-Evrard. Sutton, nevertheless, paid homage to Fenton: "It is not possible to take the art of photography further (within the current technical limitations)."[9] Finally, Fenton worked on illustrations for a book by William and Mary Howitt, *Ruined Abbeys and Castles of Great Britain* (1862), to which Cundall, Bedford, Sedgfield, and Wilson contributed.

Around 1860, photographers who had started as amateurs and artists established commercial firms. Francis Frith (1822–1898), who bought a large proportion of Fenton's picture library in 1862, emphasized the effort required to successfully take a single view. His photographic business in Reigate became the biggest in Britain and by the time of his death had branches all over the world. George Washington Wilson (1823–1893) from Aberdeen was also successful. In the *British Journal of Photography* (1864), he gave his definition of the picturesque:[10] a simple viewpoint that the traveler

9. T. Sutton, *Photographic Notes,* 1856, vol. I, p. 235. See H. Gernsheim, *The Rise of Photography, 1850–1880: The Age of Collodion,* New York, 1988, p. 121 and note 9, p. 273.

10. R. Taylor, *George Washington Wilson, Artist and Photographer, 1823–1893,* Aberdeen University, 1981.

or amateur would easily find for themselves; a convergence point toward which the eye is drawn imperceptibly by a gradation of tones and a dark foreground; a harmony of all the parts, in a closed composition which does not arouse unsatisfied curiosity. Wilson tried to combine artistic quality with high-volume production (400 prints a day, up to 55,000 prints in 1864)[11] by imitating Fenton's landscapes and Le Gray's seascapes. He also specialized in sunsets and mists. He illustrated an encyclopedia of picturesque Scottish localities and never stopped exhibiting. His main concern, however, was distribution and output. His assistants traveled through France, Switzerland, Spain, and Gibraltar, even Morocco. James Valentine (1815–1880), from Dundee, was Wilson's great rival. Francis Bedford (1816–1894), who modeled himself on Frith, or Ross and Thompson, who set up their own business, never equaled Wilson's success. In the shadow of these professionals were amateurs such as Alfred Pumphrey,[12] Victor Prout, author of *The Thames from London to Oxford in Forty Photographs*, and James Mudd (1864 Sheffield floods).

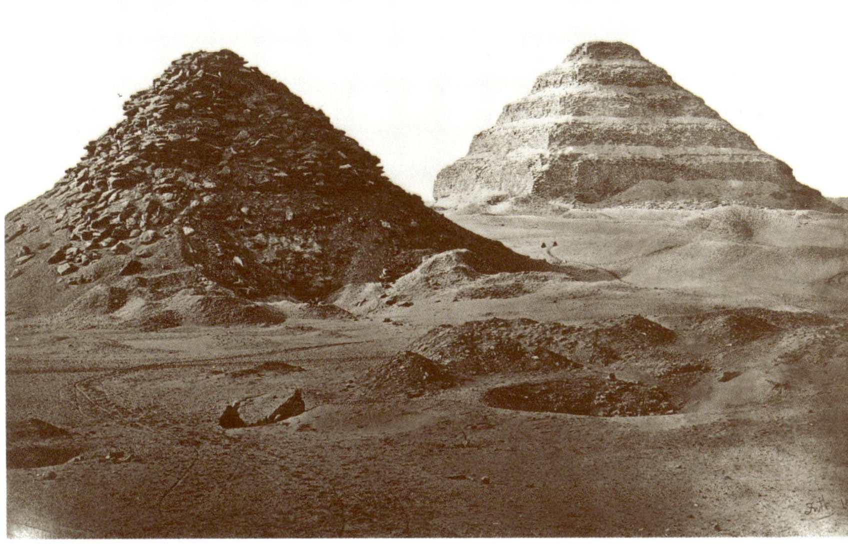

Francis Frith, ***Sakkarah Pyramids from the North-East,*** circa 1858, International Museum of Photography, George Eastman House, Rochester.

European tourism

During the first half of the nineteenth century, Italy continued to be the obligatory reference point for artists. It is hardly surprising then that from the end of the 1840s, Rome emerged as a center for amateur photographers. The first was Giacomo Caneva (about 1813–1865), a wonderful calotypist from Padua[13] who provided views of the Roman Campagna for a whole host of French artists who stayed at the Villa Medici (his picture library was bought and distributed by Ludovico Tuminello). Tommaso Cuccioni, another

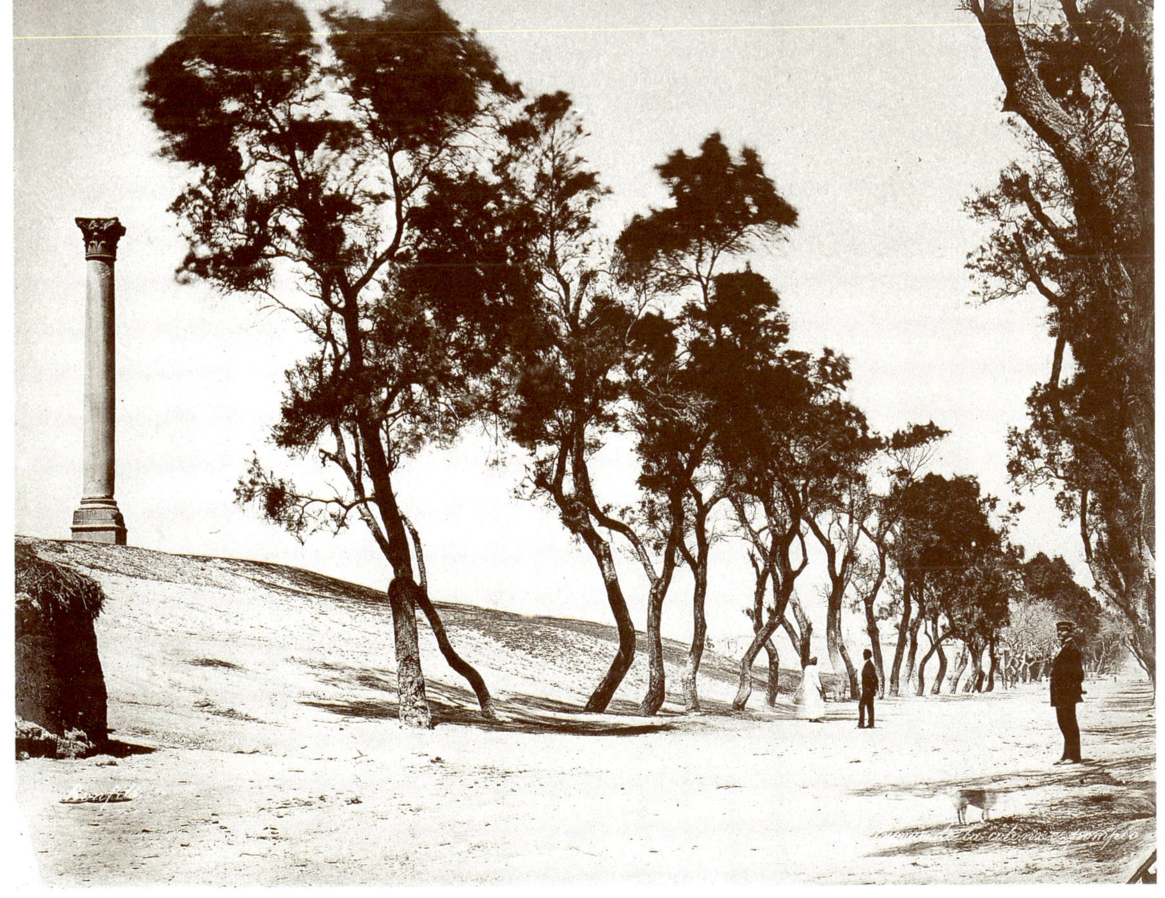

Bonfils, ***Avenue at Pompey's Column, Alexandria,*** circa 1890, private collection.

11. In 1877, Wilson & Co.'s studio in Saint Swithin's House produced 800 prints a day. They had 45,000 negatives in the picture library and 2,500 different subjects on sale at any one time.

12. See R. Flukinger, *The Formative Decades: Photography in Great Britain, 1839–1920*, Austin, University of Texas, 1985.

13. See P. Becchetti, *Regione Lazio: Giacomo Caneva e la Scuola fotografica romana, 1847–1855*, Florence, 1989.

The traveler's paraphernalia

From the beginning of the 1840s, scholars with enough curiosity and money, like Baron Gros or Girault de Prangey, set a fashion for long expeditions – sometimes as far as the Middle East – on which they would take darkrooms, silver-coated metal plates, and chemicals. As early as 1849, Maxime du Camp, traveling with Flaubert to Egypt, wrote: "Learning how to take a photograph is not too hard, but transporting all the equipment you need on the back of a mule, camel or man is really hard work". It was all the worse because the equipment was heavy. When Moulin went on a photographic expedition to Algeria in 1856, his baggage weighed 1,100 kilos!

After the wet-plate process appeared in the 1850s, things became even more difficult. Collodion plates had to be exposed while still wet – and, therefore, prepared in situ – and developed immediately after the exposure had been made. This meant that traveling photographers had to carry a whole laboratory around with them. In addition to the darkroom and its accessories, there was a folding tent which, once pitched, provided the total darkness in which the photographer could process the plates. They also carried a wooden box which doubled as a table. This contained a dozen or so flasks of chemicals, a supply of clean plates, basins and glasses, distilled water, plate-holders, a tripod, and, of course, the camera itself which alone could weigh a dozen kilos.

Josef Albert,
Photographer at Hohenschwangau,
1857, Stadtmuseum, Munich.
On the right is a portable cabin used to prepare the plates.

Early in 1855, Roger Fenton arrived in the Crimea, with a wine merchant's wagon he had converted into a traveling darkroom. It was equipped with five cameras, 700 glass plates, several crates of chemicals, basins, and two water tanks. He went back and forth across the battle fields in torrid heat. "When the wagon door is closed, long before the plate is ready my face is running with sweat [...] I can scarcely put my hands into the developing bath because it's so hot [...]" In 1861, Mathew Brady and his team were to encounter the same problems when they covered the battlefields of the American Civil War. Brady's wagon even suffered a direct hit from a cannonball.

But it was not only the early war photographers who were zealous and intrepid characters. The mountain photographer Aimé Civiale's baggage weighed 250 kilos and had to be carried in backpacks across seracs and crevasses at temperatures of –6 to –8°C. In 1859, Bisson Jr. wanted to be the first to climb Mont Blanc: "When you have to carry with you a whole cargo of delicate equipment, flasks, and basins [...] you have to hire sufficient men and then the difficulties assume colossal proportions or become plain insurmountable [...]" He made another, this time successful, attempt in 1861, when he was accompanied by a caravan of 25 guides and porters.

When he made his first journey across the American West in 1861, Watkins had not only a wagon-cum-darkroom but also a dozen pack mules carrying his equipment. "The camera was a heavy enough load to carry to the top of rocks, but that proved nothing in comparison with the chemicals and boxes of plates – which in turn seemed as light as a feather next to what seemed like a portable organ but was in fact the darkroom [...]" wrote F. S. Dellenbaugh in 1871. Since enlargements were not common practice at the time, most photographers carried with them different cameras for different formats. Even in the Rocky Mountains, Jackson carried 50 x 60 cm plates.

Working with such large cameras was exhausting. For instance, it took Jackson three days and three climbs up a rocky peak before he took his first negative. On the first day, the wind was too strong. On the second day the bath of silver nitrate solution spilt. On the third day, finally, "everything went wonderfully well and a good negative was procured at the first attempt". The same luck was not enjoyed by the two photographers who visited Kanab Canyon and did not managed to bring a single negative back: "the bath of silver nitrate solution was unusable and the pack horse carrying the equipment fell off a rock, crushing the camera that was strapped to the outside of its load".

Jean-Claude Gautrand

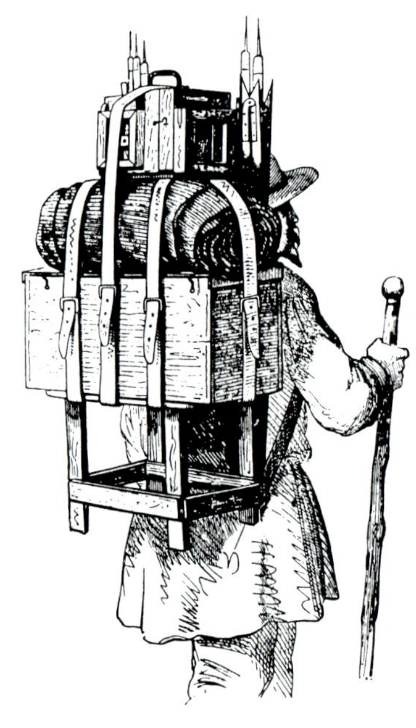

The Photographer on Tour,
Le Magasin Pittoresque, 1863.

talented Roman topographer, worked with glass negatives, as did his colleagues Gioacchino Altobelli and Mollins. Tuminello had to leave Rome between 1852 and 1858 because of his republican beliefs. Together with Pietro Dovizielli (1804–1885),[14] Pietro Poppi, and Federico Faruffini, he left countless studies of nature, with and without figures, taken in Lazio and Emilia. These went on sale between 1860 and 1880. Gustavo Eugenio Chauffourier (1845–1919) moved from Palermo to Rome about 1871 and provided views of the region's official buildings. The Scot Robert Macpherson (1811–1872) also lived in Rome for a while, painting for ten years before taking up photography. An exceptional artist, he mastered the wet-plate process and sold large-format *vedute* to tourists (Rome and its surroundings, Orvieto, Spoleto, Perugia, and Assisi). His views of architecture or of sculpture, his beautifully composed landscapes, such as the famous *Ruins of Tivoli*, and his close-up studies, such as the astonishing *Cloaca Maxima*, brought a fresh vision, noted in the *Art Journal* as early as 1862. Macpherson left valuable notes: "For a distant landscape with good light [...] a five-minute exposure is sufficient. For objects in the background, you need 10 to 20 minutes, and for some of the sculpture galleries in the Vatican, where the light is poor, two hours are often required, and in one or two cases, two days of exposure were needed to get a decent negative."[15] In 1853, James Anderson, a British watercolor artist and rival of Macpherson, set up a firm (trading until 1960) which specialized in the ruins of ancient Rome.[16]

Every major Italian city – or famous locality – had its contingent of accredited photographers. Once they had acquired a firm footing, they spread out across the country and abroad. Naples-based Giorgio Sommer, originally from Frankfurt, was known for the photographs of Etna he took between 1860 and 1880. The Fratelli Alinari were masters of Florence (see box). Their studio was able to take advantage of the economic and demographic growth of the city. Giacomo Brogi's Tuscan dynasty, unable to compete with Alinari, avoided their territory, the topographical genre, and concentrated on the area's artistic heritage. In Venice, the family studio established by Carlo Naya (1816–1882) grew enormously[17] and turned out large-format architectural views, impressively composed. On a par with Naya was Carlo Ponti, another great publisher – if not the creator – of topographical views of Venice. From 1870, Naya and one of his assistants, Tommaso Filippi, diversified into local-color scenes of Chioggia, Capri, and the Abruzzi region.

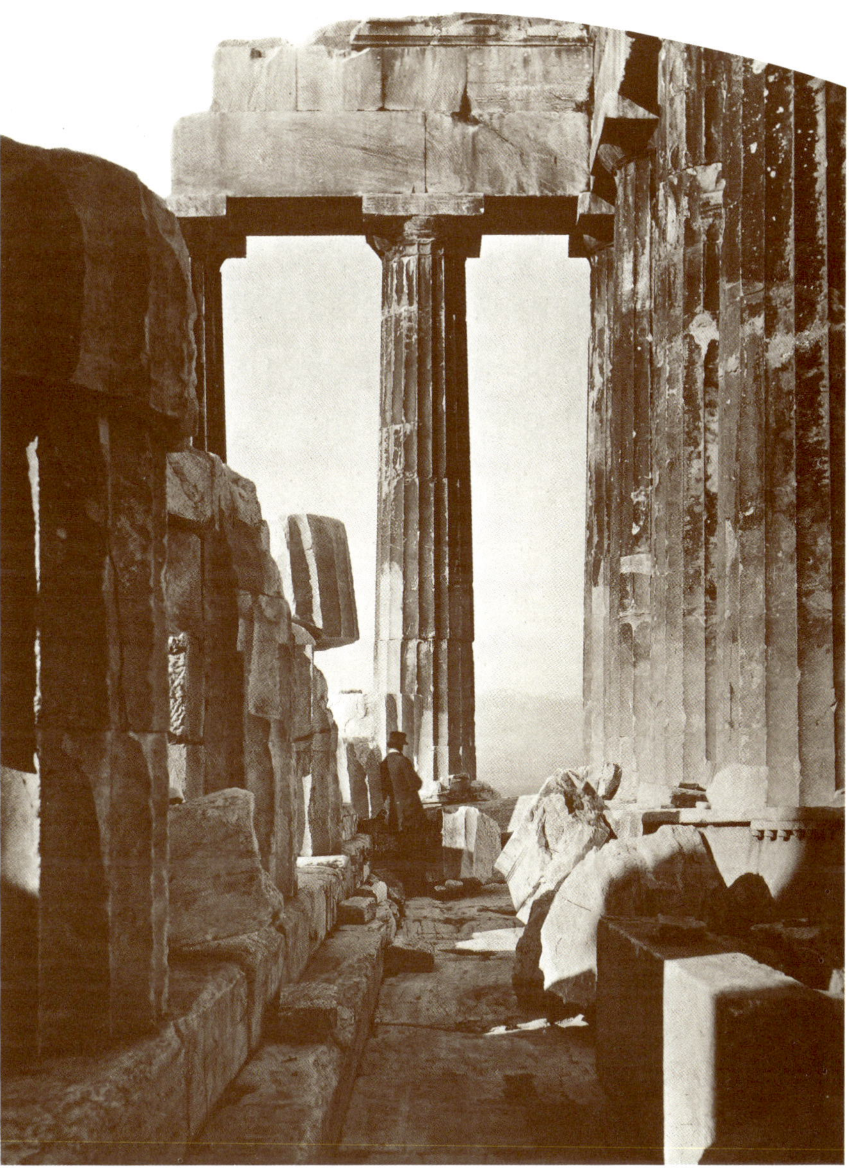

William J. Stillmann, ***Portico of the Parthenon, Athens,*** 1869, J. Paul Getty Museum, Malibu.

One of the rare amateur photographers with great artistic skill still at work into the 1880s was Dr. Jakob August Lorent (1810–1884), from Mannheim. Between 1855 and 1864, after he had inherited a substantial fortune, he took large views of Italy, Venice in particular, using paper negatives which gave a characteristic brown-red color. His work was extremely successful in Germany. In Spain, the topographical genre was pursued by Clifford and Laurent. Clifford, a British photographer in the service of Queen Isabella II, accompanied her when she toured the provinces and took photographs of gardens, architecture, and interiors.[18] He also photographed the art collections in royal residences and local people. The 400 views he exhibited at the 1859 Salon de la photographie in Paris[19] were well received.

Starting as Clifford's assistant in 1858, Jean Laurent worked under very different conditions. Living in Madrid from 1857 to 1880, he photographed royal residences, treasures of architecture

14. See I. Zannier, *Storia della fotografia italiana*, Rome, 1988.

15. H. Gernsheim, *op. cit.*, p. 132.

16. H. Gernheim, "James Anderson, 1813–1877", in *Fotografia*, no. 6, 1986, pp. 17–24.

17. I. Zannier, *Venise, collection Naya*, Venice, 1981.

18. L. Fontanella, *La Historia de la fotografía en España de sus orígenes hasta 1900*, Madrid, Biblioteca Nacional, 1982, pp. 126–129.

19. *Ibid.*

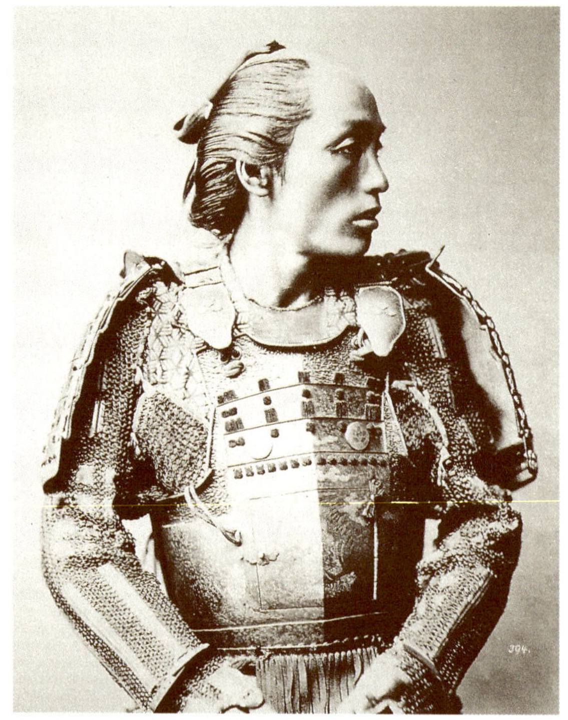

BEATO'S STUDIO, *Samurai in Chainmail and Armor*, circa 1865, Bibliothèque Nationale, Paris.

and sculpture, and paintings and armor. He also shot engineering projects.[20] However, he never overlooked everyday subjects, rearranging and regrouping scenes into series – costumes, physical types, workshops – such as the *Relic-seller* or *Soup Kitchen in Cordoba* (his picture library of 20,000 negatives was increased to 50,000 by his successors). After 1880, Laurent worked with Martinez Sanchez, who specialized in photographs of public works.

The fashion for topographical views linked to tourism or geographical exploration never seemed to inspire German photographers. Between 1850 and 1880, they concentrated on technique. About the only work known is the *Album der Sächsischen Schweiz* (1853) by Hermann Krone, a well-known portrait photographer who also published views of Dresden. In 1867 and 1879, J. A. Lorent published works on the medieval architecture of Wurttemberg and Neckar, but these images (collodion glass) do not possess the outstanding quality of his views of Venice. On the other hand, a Frenchman, Léon Gérard, an amateur calotypist and traveler, was responsible for fine views of Bamberg, Augsburg, Nuremberg, and the surrounding area (1857). Apart from the countless views taken by overseas photographers working for Frith or Braun, local photographers occasionally produced topographical views, for example, the views of Munich and Ludwig II's castles by Josef Albert or Victor Angerer's work in Vienna. Primarily, however, it was the banks of the Rhine, celebrated in Romantic fiction, that attracted illustrators and photographers, such as Marville (1852). The first publication of the London-based Architectural

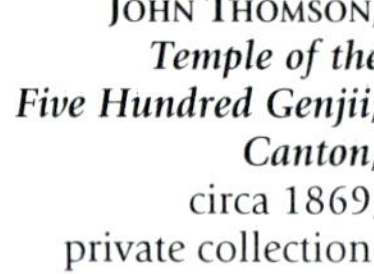

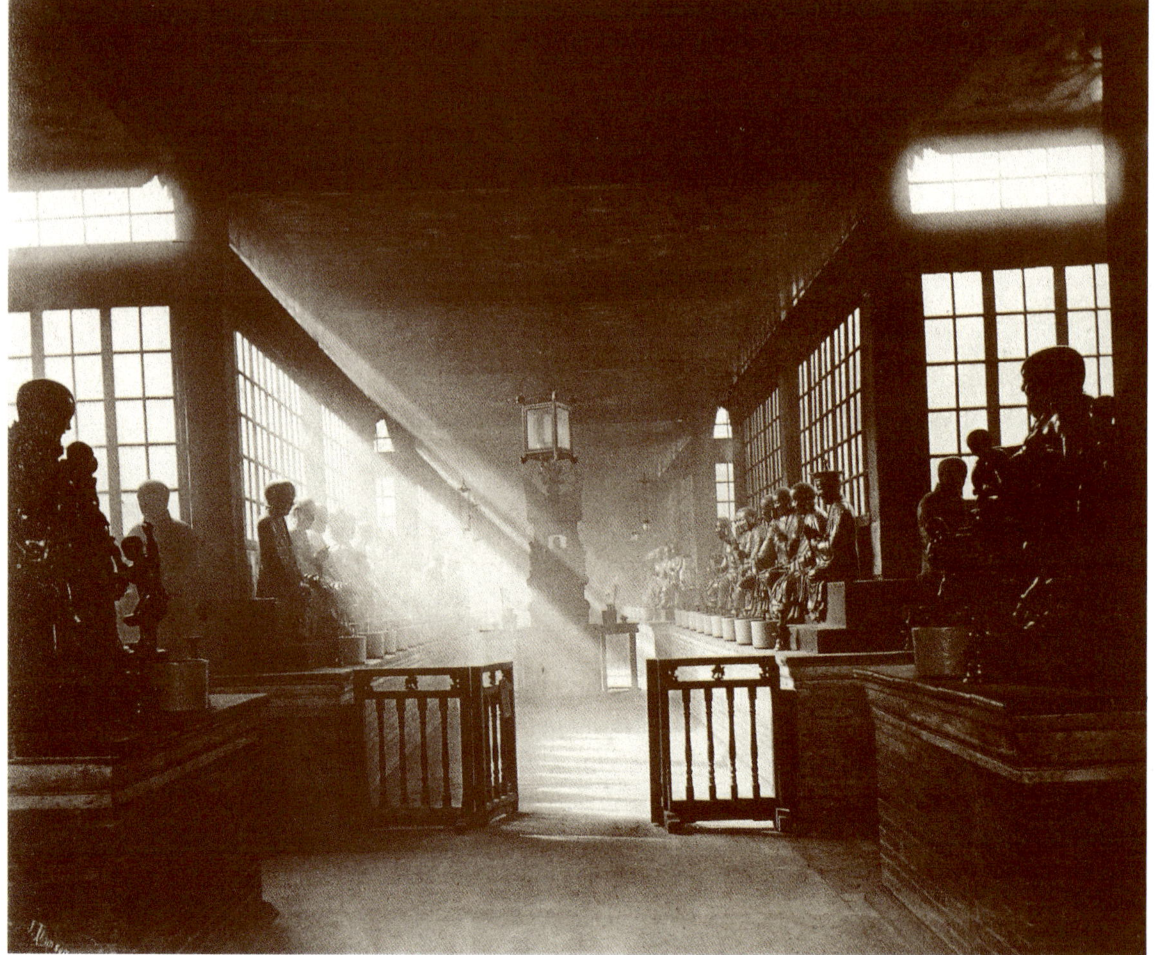

JOHN THOMSON, *Temple of the Five Hundred Genjii, Canton*, circa 1869, private collection.

Photographic Society was *Rambles in the Rhine Province* (1868), notable for its plates by Cundall.

The old world of the Mediterranean

From the end of the eighteenth century, the Middle East exerted an irresistible attraction over European scholars and artists. They, in turn, passed their enthusiasm onto daguerreotypists and calotypists such as Du Camp, Green, De Clercq, John Shaw Smith, Teynard, and Devéria.[21] On his first trip to Egypt, Nubia, Palestine, and Syria in 1856, Francis Frith took a great number of views in different formats using collodion on glass. He set out again in 1857 (Syria and Palestine) and in 1859 (Egypt), getting just beyond the fifth cataract of the Nile. He published the resulting prints as *Egypt, Sinai, Jerusalem* (1861, 73 x 53 cm plates) and *The Queen Bible* (1862) (170 copies). His fellow countryman, Francis Bedford, already known for his topographical views of Britain, published *Tour in the East* (London, 1872, 172 plates), a record of his travels with the Prince of Wales.

It was in Egypt that the first resident photographic studios were opened, initially run by foreigners such as Antonio Beato (circa 1825–1903), brother of Felice Beato, who opened studios in Cairo in 1862 and in Luxor in 1872. W. Hammerschmidt, from Berlin, arrived in Cairo in 1860 and set about taking animated scenes. Désiré Ermé covered the construction of the Suez Canal. Contemporary Egypt was represented in the 155 large plates entitled *Egypte et Nubie* that Émile Béchard exhibited in Paris in 1878. Like Naya, Béchard was successful with his studio photographs of physical types for the tourist market. His namesake, Henri Béchard, made his reputation by large-format street scenes. An Armenian photographer called Lékégian also worked extensively in Egypt between 1860 and 1890. Honoré d'Albert, the Duc de Luynes, was a keen archeologist. In 1865 he toured the Dead Sea with the photographer Louis Vignes. His posthumous work *Le Voyage d'exploration à la mer morte, à Pétra et sur la rive gauche du Jourdan* was published between 1871 and 1877 using Vignes's negatives, wonderfully translated into photo-engravings by Charles Nègre.

In 1865, the British set up a fund for the exploration of Palestine. A mission was sent to Jerusalem and in 1869 another to Sinai. The Scot James Graham[22] was among the most remarkable of these photographer-missionaries to the Holy Land (from 1853 to 1857). An Austrian, O. von Ostheim, owned a photographic studio in Jerusalem and followed the travels of the Comte de Chambord, a keen collector of photographs, from Jericho to the Dead Sea. Syria and Lebanon attracted fewer photographers. Graham worked there, as did Ostheim, but above all the area was covered by an amateur from Marseilles, Henry Sauvaire, French consul in Beirut, Damascus, Jerusalem, and then Alexandria. Baron Victor Nau de Champlouis exhibited his views of Lebanon (1860) and Algeria (1867) in Paris and London. The Italian Tancredi Dumas learned his craft in Milan under Fratelli Alinari. He opened a studio in Beirut in 1867. Between 1875 and 1877 he worked for the American mission exploring Palestine. However, the most famous family studio, opening in Beirut in 1867 but active throughout the Middle East, belonged to Félix Bonfils (1831–1855), from Alès. His son Adrien took over from him during the 1880s and his widow in turn took over the running of the studio about 1900.[23]

In 1872 and 1877, Félix Bonfils went to Athens to photograph monuments. However, there is no doubt that Constantinople-based James Robertson (1800–1881), a former colleague of Beato, produced the best pictures of Greece. He

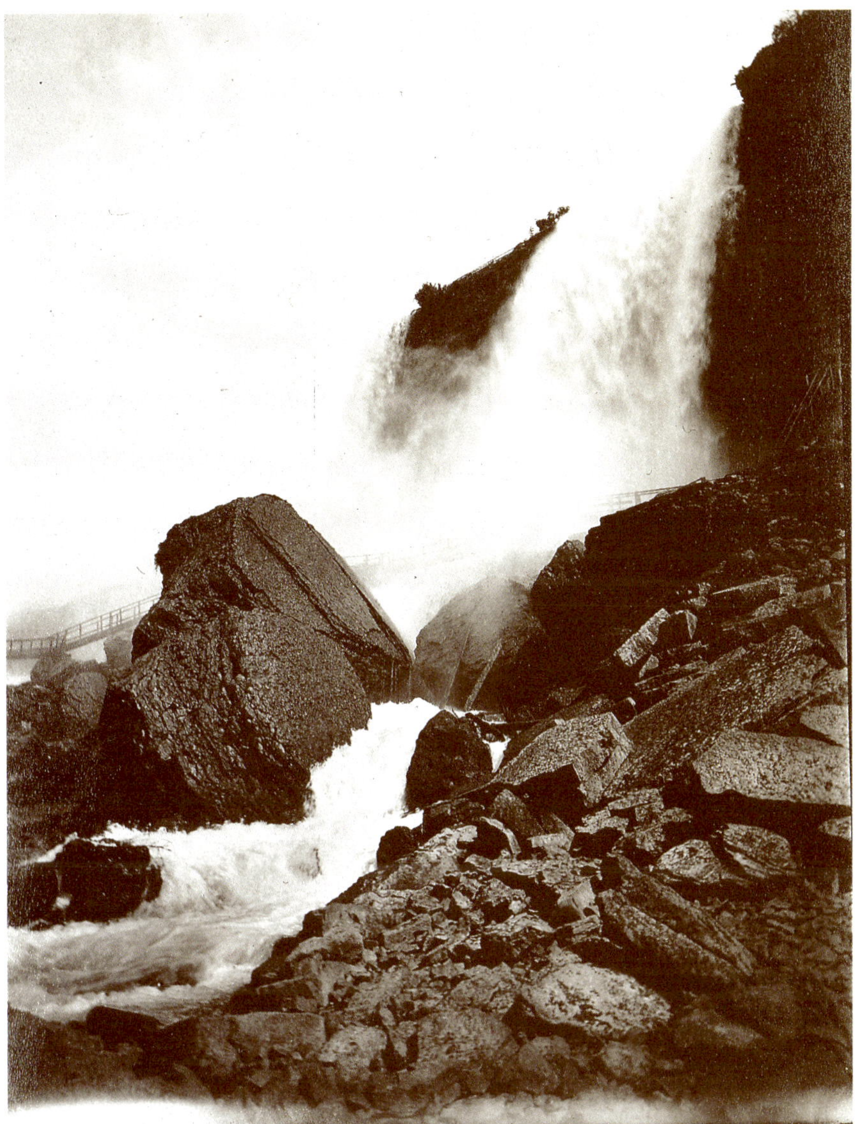

GEORGE BARKER, *Niagara Falls,* 1888, private collection.

20. *Ibid.*, p. 137.

21. N. Perez, *Focus East*, Jerusalem, 1988.

22. See B. Lazard, "The Photographs of James Graham in the Middle East", in *The Photohistorian Supplement*, no. 89, summer 1990.

23. See C. S. Gavin, *The Image of the East from the Photographs by Bonfils*, Chicago, University Press, 1982.

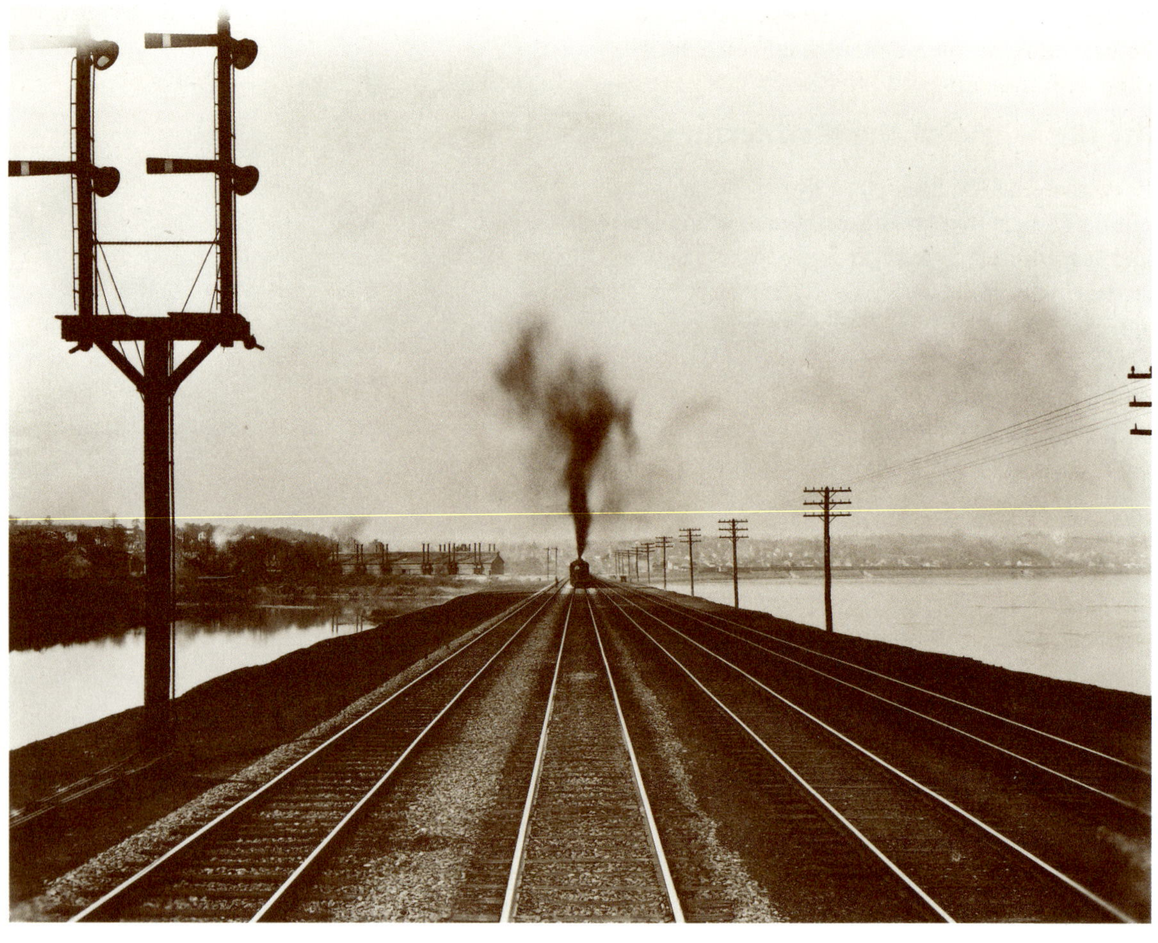

WILLIAM H. RAU, *New Railroad, Duncannon, Pennsylvania,* circa 1890–1900, J. Paul Getty Museum, Malibu.

approached the country from the picturesque angle and spent a lot of time on studies of Athenian monuments and localities (1854). His pictures were always animated with figures. He also photographed Egine (Kemaliye) and Corinth, then, in 1856–1857, Smyrna, and, of course, Constantinople itself, in 1857.[24] The American diplomat William J. Stillmann revolutionized the way the temples of the Acropolis were viewed with *The Acropolis of Athens Illustrated Picturesquely and Architecturally in Photography* (London, 1870). The Greek photographer Dimitrios Konstantinou, who opened a studio in 1857, copied Robertson's effects. Petros Moraites and Philippos Margaritis, who worked in Athens from 1853, were highly thought of locally and abroad.[25] Pascal Sebah settled in Constantinople in 1870. His prolific production is an illustration of the low quality of photography at the end of the century. Finally, the Zangaki brothers, two Greeks, worked all round the Mediterranean, in Egypt in particular.

The lure of the forbidden East

The British were careful about how they used photography in India during the 1850s. It was put to political and economic ends, documenting the country's topography and way of life, just as the East India Company had in the eighteenth century used engravings.[26] Between 1857 and 1875, work forged ahead under a new Viceroy, Lord Canning, backed up by the India Office in London. This meant that topographical photography remained of the highest quality and photographers enjoyed high social status, with the rank of officer or civil engineer.

The first significant topographers to specialize in the architecture or landscape of the subcontinent were Captains Tripe, Biggs, Pigou, Lyon, and Murray. They all sold prints and, on the whole, found it easier to work with waxed-paper negatives. In 1855, Linnaeus Tripe (1822–1902) was sent on a mission to the court at Ava in Burma. With the assistance of the Photographic Society in Madras, he published 300 views of Burma, including many religious sanctuaries. Later on, toward 1870, when he was using the collodion process, he took views of Burmese vegetation patently aimed at the commercial market.[27] The government in Bombay gave Captain Biggs, soon replaced by H. W. Pigou and then A. C. Neill, the task of photographing ancient sculptures and inscriptions in the west of India, especially Beejapoor and Ahmdadabad. In 1866, their prints were published as albums (*Architecture in Dharwar and Mysore, Architecture at Beejapoor*). Finally, in 1853, an army doctor, John

24. A. and H. K. Henisch, "James Robertson and Constantinople: A Chronology", in *History of Photography*, no. XIV, January 1990, pp. 22–33.

25. G. Edwards, A. X. Xanthakis *et al.*, *Athens 1839–1900: A Photographic Record*, Athens, Beanki Museum, 1985; A. Ehrenkranz (ed.), *Poetic Localities: Photographs of the Adirondacks, Crete, Athens, Italy and Cambridge by William J. Stillmann*, New York 1988; G. Edwards, "Photographs of Greece in the Musée d'Orsay's Album of the Duc de Chartres", in *History of Photography*, no. XIV, April 1990, pp. 165–179.

26. C. Worswick, *The Last Empire: Photography in British India*, New York, 1976.

27. U. Desaï, *Captain Linnaeus Tripe, 1822–1902: Photographs in India and Burma in the 1850s*, London, 1977.

Murray (1809–1898), took views of Allahabad, Benares, Kanpur, and Delhi, distributed by the School of Industrial Art in Delhi and by the London-based publisher J. Hogarth. Very often the composition was inspired by drawings by Thomas and William Daniell in *Oriental Scenery* (1795). The government appointed Captain E. D. Lyon to photograph ancient religious monuments. He developed a system of reflectors which made it easy to light the long corridors typical of Indian architecture. His work met with great success in London in 1869. John Burke illustrated H. H. Cole's work *Illustrations of Ancient Buildings in Kashmir* (1869). Captain Melville Clarke published his views shot in Northern India, right up to the Tibetan frontier, *From Simla through Ladac and Kashmir*. From 1870, in all large Indian cities, especially Bombay, there was a booming trade in *vedute*, archeological views, physical types, and genre photographs aimed at the tourist trade. Native photographers contributed to this boom, the most important being Lala Deen Dayal (1844–1910). Views of roads and railroads under construction, jute manufacturers or teak factories were used to illustrate the *Encyclopaedia Britannica*.

Among the principal firms are Johnston & Hoffman, Burke, Saché, J. A. Rust – one of the first to take photographs in the foothills of the Himalayas – and Bourne & Shepherd. This last firm was set up in Agra in 1862 by Arthur Robertson and Charles Shepherd, but it was thanks to Samuel Bourne (1834–1912), who landed in Calcutta in 1863, that it was to grow in importance. Bourne[28] was without question the most original and noteworthy of the three. Shepherd, with whom he opened a studio in Simla and a branch in Calcutta, took charge of the printing and business side. Bourne made his mark with three Himalayan expeditions in 1864, 1865, and 1866 with a whole army of coolies. They faced extreme heat and cold but did not hesitate to wait for days for the best light for a view. Bourne excelled at views of glaciers, mountainous panoramas, lines of trees, details of vegetation and so on. In France, Goupil worked on a project compiling 160 photographs that Louis Rousselet took in 1868.[29]

It was the disastrous opium wars that opened China up to European (Anglo-French) trade. By 1840, the British had invaded Macao and, after its first defeat, China was forced to cede Hong Kong to the invaders. From 1860, the coastal towns from Amoy to Shanghai were opened to traders, soldiers, consuls, merchants, and photographers. Felice Beato (1830–1906), an Italian photographer who had adopted British nationality and one of James Robertson's assistants, was among the first photographers to work in China. More or less officially attached to the British army during

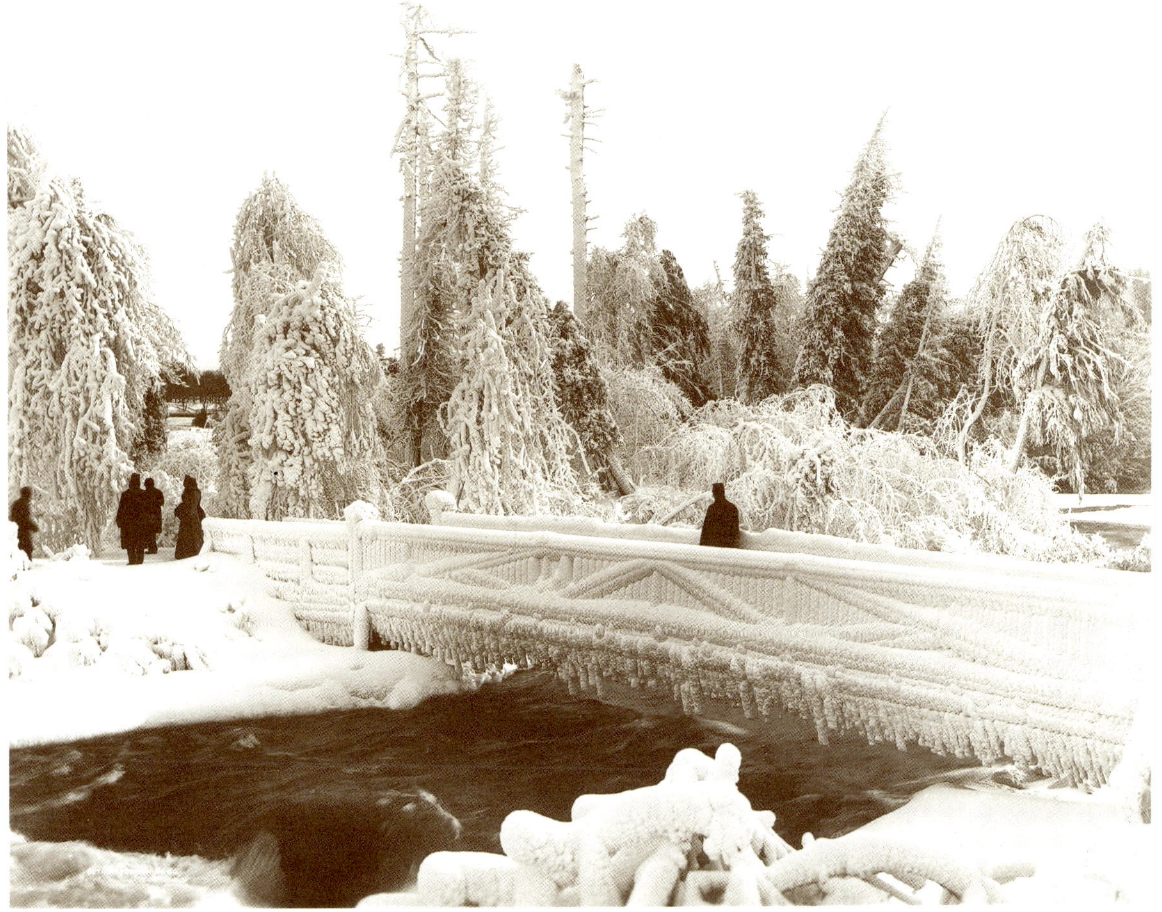

William H. Jackson,
Luna Island,
Niagara Falls,
circa 1890,
private collection.

28. On Bourne, apart from Worswick, *op. cit.*, see in particular P. F. Heathcote, "Samuel Bourne of Nottingham", in *History of Photography*, no. 6. April 1982, pp. 99–112.

29. The images, produced as woodcuts, ended up as illustrations for *L'Inde des Rajahs*, Hachette, 1875. See B. Marbot *et al.*, *L'Inde, photographies de Louis Rousselet, 1865–1868*, Bordeaux, Musée Goupil, 1992.

the Second Opium War (1858–1860), he had a talent for visualizing military situations and produced multiple panoramas of British army positions in Hong Kong at the time the Taku forts were taken. Beato also explored Canton (1860) and Peking, where he photographed the famous Summer Palace built by Jesuits in the seventeenth century and destroyed by Lord Elgin.[30]

Other photographers working in China for foreign publication[31] at this time include Antoine Fauchery, whose photographic work has not survived, and Paul Champion, who exhibited in Paris in 1867. From 1860 onwards, a Hong Kong firm working under a variety of different names exercised what amounted to a monopoly in China. In 1877 it owned more than 10,000 negatives, taken by as many as eleven photographers, mostly British.

Apart from Miller, highly thought of as a studio specialist in genre photography, a Scot, John Thomson (1837–1921), deserves mention. He traveled through Malaysia and Indochina, opening a studio in Singapore in 1865. From there, he went on to Cambodia, where in 1867 he published *The Antiquities of Cambodia.*[32] He then passed through Hong Kong and on to China in 1872, traveling over 5,000 miles, mainly along the Yangtze Jiang, as far as Peking. Upon his return to Britain he published *Illustrations of China and its People* (1877–1878), a work centered around the social aspects of the country, with commentaries for each illustration, a method later used by photojournalists on illustrated magazines. An ethnographic and journalistic turn of mind, impeccable technique, original vision, and an

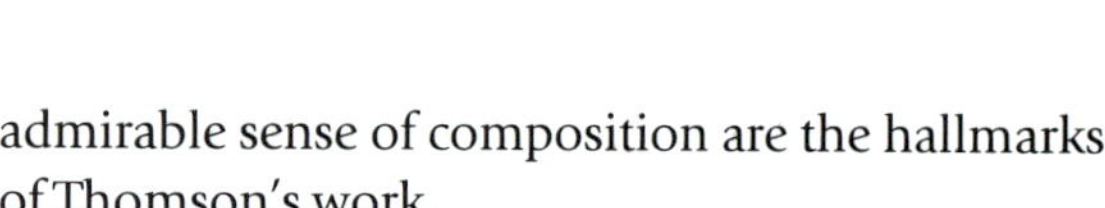

admirable sense of composition are the hallmarks of Thomson's work.

Japan's closure to the outside world meant that photography did not reach there until 1854.[33] Even then, foreigners were not allowed to work in Japan until 1859. In 1859, a Norwegian view-photographer, writing in the *Photographic News*, recorded the admiration and astonishment expressed by the Japanese on first seeing his photographs. He also noted their total lack of understanding of perspective. It was foreigners who produced commercial topographical views of Japan, mainly for Westerners. They could not work in absolute safety until 1868 when Emperor Mutsuhito supported opening up his country and modernization. Felice Beato,[34] the first and most notable of topographical photographers to visit Japan, in 1868 published two albums of 100 prints (21 x 29 cm) entitled *Photographic Views of Japan* and *Native Types of Japan*, a human and picturesque images. Beato drew inspiration from the famous woodcuts of the popular *ukiyoe* tradition. He showed everyday life among the middle classes and craftsmen, posed in stylized groups in their workshops. The manner was at once harmonious and theatrical. His prints were hand-colored in watercolors by Japanese artists. In this way, he managed to please the local public and foreigners who all collected his albums, frequently in ornate lacquer bindings, like Japanese artifacts. Arriving in Japan in

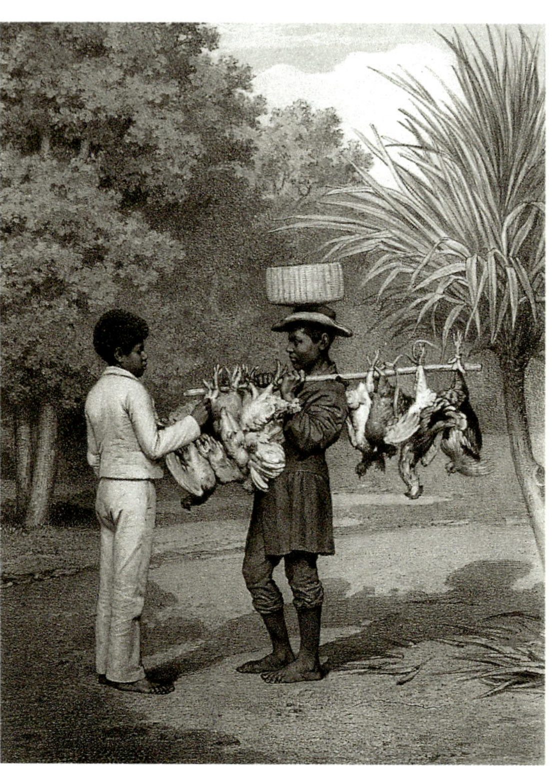

Poultry-Seller at La Roca, lithograph from a photograph by **Victor Frond**, from *Brasil Pittoresco,* 1861, private collection.

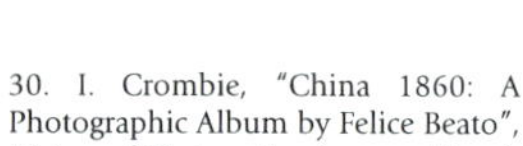

30. I. Crombie, "China 1860: A Photographic Album by Felice Beato", *History of Photography*, January–March 1987, pp. 25–35.

31. B. Marbot and R. Viénet, *Notes sur quelques photographes de la Chine au XIXe siècle*, Paris, Centre de Publications, Asie Orientale, 1979, p. 17.

32. R. Fabian and H. C. Adam, *Masters of Early Travel Photography*, London, 1983; S. White, *John Thomson, Life and Photographs*, London, Thames and Hudson, 1985.

33. C. Worswick, *Japan, Photographs, 1854–1905*, New York, 1979.

34. I. Zannier and P. Constantini, *Verso Oriente: Fotografie di Antonio e Felice Beato*, Florence, 1986.

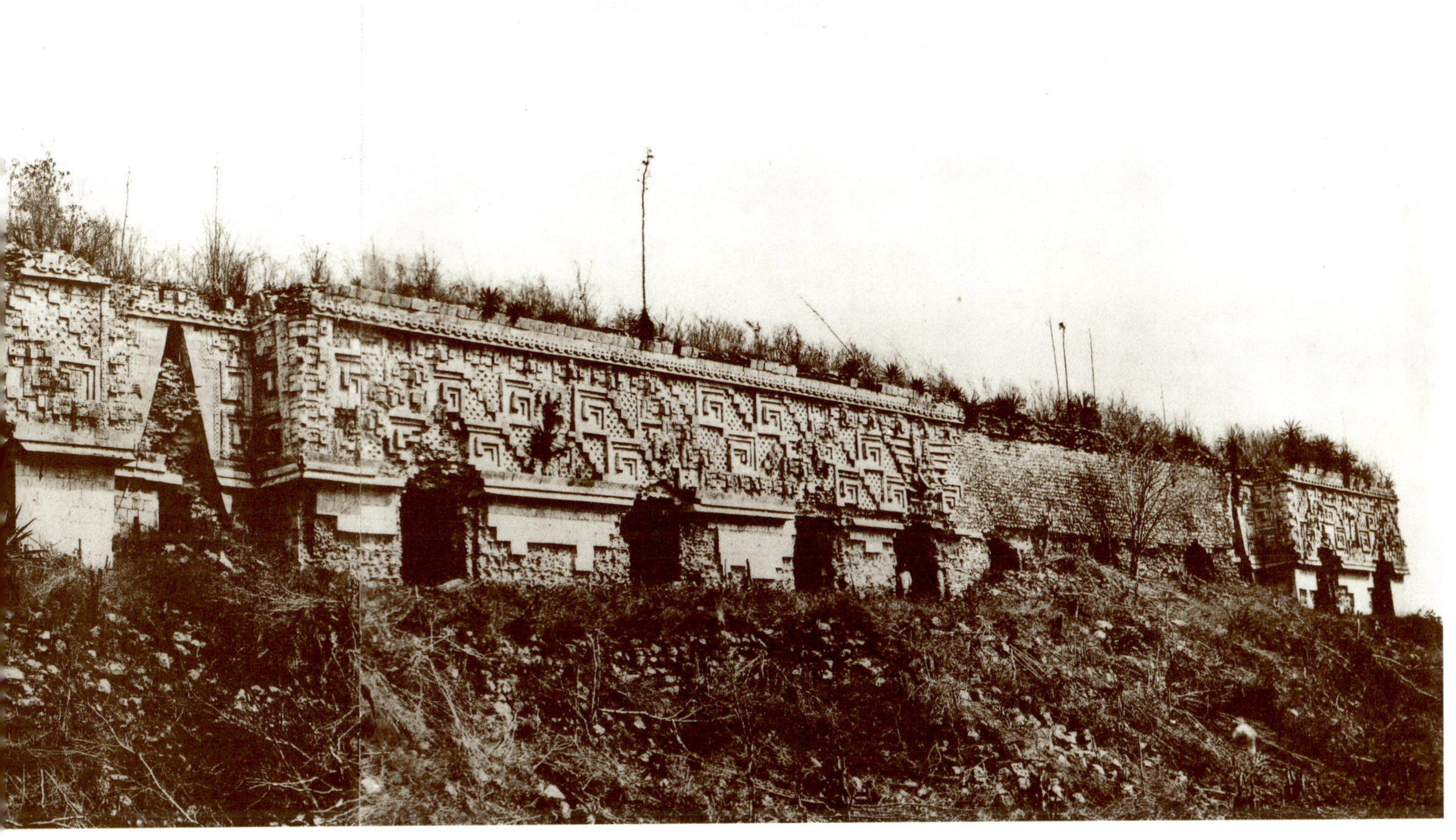

Désiré Charnay,
Façade of the Governor's Palace in Uxmal, Mexico,
1860,
Bibliothèque des Arts Décoratifs, Paris.

1863, Beato had opened a studio in Yokohama by 1865. In 1877, he sold out to a rival, the Austrian baron R. von Stillfried. In 1884, the studio was bought by a Japanese, Kusakabe Kimbei. By the 1880s, the image of Japan thus created in Europe (powerless Samurais, for example) was already out of date. Photography was not far behind the country itself in its quest for modernity.

The discovery of the Americas

From the 1850s a thriving photographic business based on stereoscopic landscapes began to build up in the eastern United States, especially Philadelphia. George N. Barnard (1819–1902) was commissioned by the firm of Anthony to produce a series of stereoscopes of Cuba (1860) and Niagara Falls (1862). He was sent to cover the defeat of the Confederate Army in Virginia. The album Barnard put together in 1866 to commemorate General Sherman's campaign consisted mainly of majestic compositions of localities, often photographed after battle.

But the discovery of the Western landscape was due to Carleton E. Watkins (1828–1916) who in 1851 went to live in San Francisco. In 1861, he traveled up the Yosemite Valley, discovered in 1856, using large plates to capture the romantic and sublime mood of the magnificent virgin territory. He returned in 1866 with a geological expedition organized by Congress, and accompanied by the painter William Keith.[35] Timothy O'Sullivan (1840–1882) was chosen by Clarence King to travel with him from 1867 to 1869 on a journey of exploration along the 40th parallel, between the Sierra Nevada and the Rocky Mountains, financed by the Department of War. From 1871 to 1873 O'Sullivan was engaged on another geological expedition to the west of the 100° meridian. The expedition, led by G. M. Wheeler, went into Death Valley. Although he was not known by the wider public in his own day, O'Sullivan was the first to understand how to bring out the stark beauty and telluric power of these desert and hostile places.[36] Andrew Joseph Russell (1830–1902) had the same talent. He initially went West in 1867 for Union Pacific to document the laying of the Omaha to Utah railroad. He ended up traveling with King's Utah expedition for three years.

Eadweard Muybridge (1830–1904), originally from Britain, knew California well and wanted to set up in competition with Watkins. In 1867 and 1872 he shot fifty or so rule-breaking plates of the Yosemite Valley, obtaining dramatic chiaroscuro effects, sometimes from giddy viewpoints. His photographs were more stylized and pictorial that Watkins's thanks to a number of tricks: masks to frame his shots and separate negatives for clouds and ground. For a long time, William H. Jackson was one of the most famous photogra-

35. P. E. Palmquist, *Carleton E. Watkins, Photographer of the American West*, Albuquerque, University of New Mexico Press, 1983.

36. J. Snyder, *American Frontiers: The Photographs of Timothy H. O'Sullivan, 1867–1874*, Millerton, Aperture, 1981.

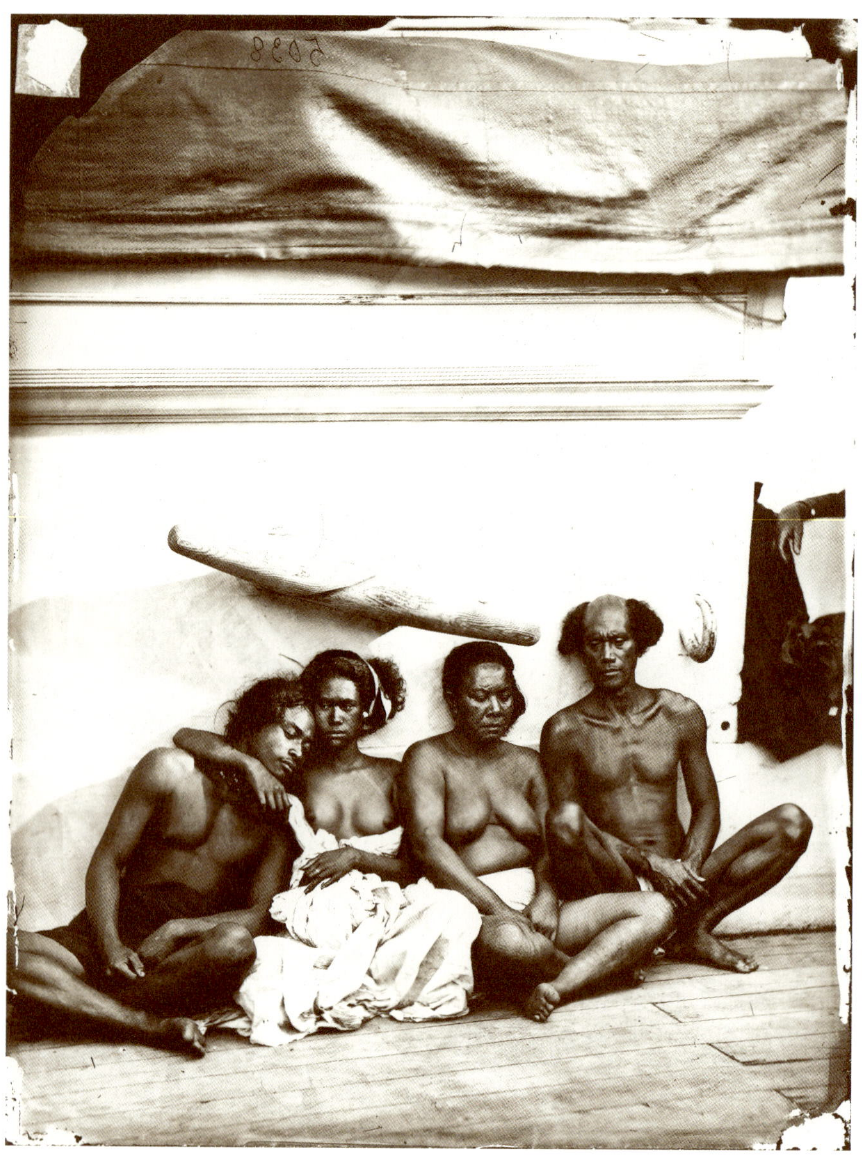

PAUL-EMILE MIOT,
The Royal Family of Vahitao, Marquesas Islands,
1869–1870,
Musée de l'Homme, Paris.

phers in the West. In 1867, he opened a studio in Omaha, and followed the building of the Union Pacific railroad. Between 1870 and 1873 he was a member of a geological and geographical expedition led by F. V. Hayden (Wyoming and Colorado). It is to him that we owe the grandiose views of geysers and hot springs in Wyoming and studies of Indians living in caves at Chelley Canyon (1875) and the Hopis in their *pueblos.*[37] In the West, the tradition of a series of large-format photos about railroads or natural beauty was to continue to the end of the century. Outstanding photographers in this tradition include W. H. Rau (1855–1920) from Philadelphia or G. Barker, the author of a famous album on Niagara Falls around 1888. There was also the more ethnographic work of Vroman and Curtis.

In Brazil,[38] paradoxically, landscape photography aimed at tourists grew far more rapidly. Photography boomed during the reign of Dom Pedro II, passionate about the medium. Augusto Stahl worked in Recife from 1853 and in Rio de Janeiro from 1859. Victor Frond, a Frenchman who moved to Rio about 1857, also kept very busy. He ran a traveling studio and visited the furthest reaches of the empire before returning to France in 1865. All that remains of his work is a beautiful album of lithographs from photographs, *Brasil pittoresco* (1859–1861). R. H. Klumb worked in the imperial botanical gardens of Petropolis. In 1868, the German Augusto Riedel accompanied the Duke of Saxony on a voyage to Minas Gerais. Around 1865, A. Frish became one of the rare explorers to have traveled the length of the Amazon, bringing back photographs of aboriginal Indians. Marc Ferrez,[39] the outstanding Brazilian photographer of the nineteenth century due to the quality and diversity of his views, had a thriving career in Rio from 1863. Thanks to him we can see the construction of railroads and highways, Botocudo Indians (1877), ports, seascapes, and the small population of black slaves freed by Dom Pedro II in 1865.

Désiré Charnay (1828–1915), the epitome of an explorer, went in search of ancient Mayan cities, funded by the Ministry of Public Education. He set off from Veracruz in November 1857 with 1,800 kilos of baggage. He returned to Mexico City in 1860 and published one album (25 plates) in Mexico and another in Paris (*Cités et ruines américaines;* 49 plates in two volumes, Paris, Gide, 1862–1863). This expensive work was welcomed with rapturous critical acclaim at exhibitions in London (1862) and Paris (1863). A cheaper supplement was brought out in 1864.[40] Charnay went on a second expedition, to Madagascar in 1863. He photographed landscapes, trees, and physical types, naked and in brightly colored costumes. He went on to explore Chile and Argentina (1875), Java (1878), and Australia (1878–1879), returning with plates, objects, and highly colored tales.

Paul-Emile Miot (1827–1900), who originally came from the Antilles, joined the French navy in 1847. A draughtsman and hydrographer, in 1857 he set up a photographic laboratory at the Ministry and recorded his missions at sea: Newfoundland (1857–1859), Senegal, Peru, Chile, and Oceania (1869–1871),[41] Tahiti, and the Marquesas Islands. He photographed the boat, crew, landscapes, and native peoples, houses, and way of life.

What is striking is the human understanding and sympathy with which Miot approached his subjects (especially young King Vahitao and his family on the Marquesas Islands) some thirty years before Gauguin arrived in the region – a symbolic image of the role played by photography in the days before it was looking solely for objectivity and when it still played a part in the wonders of discovery.

37. P. Hales, *Willliam Henry Jackson and the Transformation of the American Landscape,* Philadelphia, Temple University Press, 1988; W. J. Naef, *Era of Exploration: The Rise of Landscape Photography in the American West, 1860–1885,* Buffalo, Fine Arts Academy, 1975.

38 G. Ferrez and W. J. Naef, *Pioneer Photographers in Brazil (1840–1920),* New York, 1976; G. Ferrez, *A Fotografia no Brasil, 1840–1900,* Rio de Janeiro, 1985; P. Vasquez, *Dom Pedro II e a Fotografia no Brasil,* Rio de Janeiro, Index, 1985.

39. G. Ferrez, *O Rio Antigo do fotografo Marc Ferrez,* São Paulo, Ex Libris, 1984.

40. K. F. Davis, *Désiré Charnay, Expeditionary Photographer,* Albuquerque, 1981.

41. Miot's negatives are in Vincennes, in the Ministère de la Marine's records. See P. O'Reilly, *Les Photographes à Tahiti et leurs œuvres, 1842–1962,* Paris, 1969, and J.-P. Castelain and Y. Leroy, *Images de Saint-Pierre-et-Miquelon,* Le Havre, 1990.

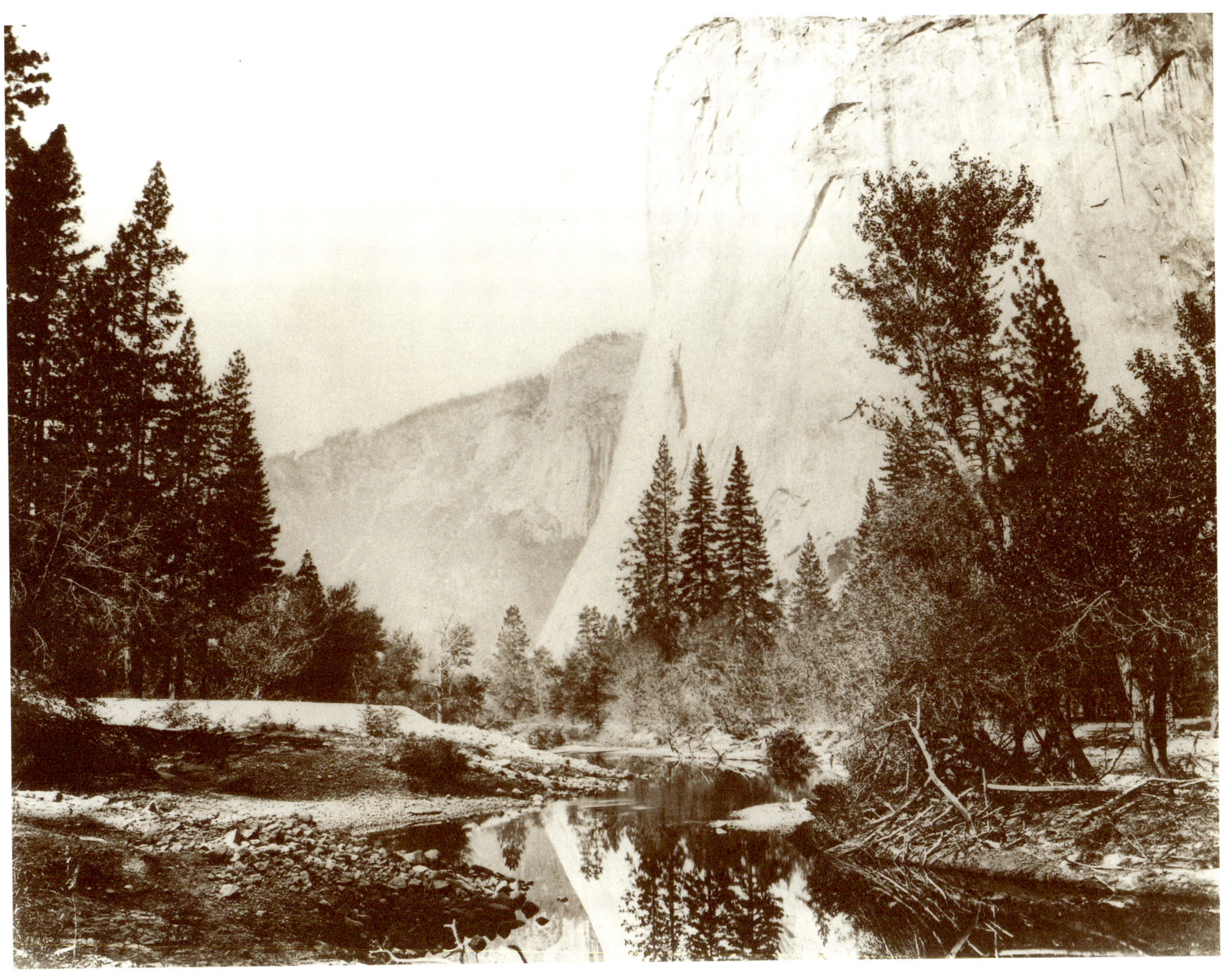

The American West

This portfolio is drawn from the work of the major figures of the heroic era of the 1860s and 1870s working in the western regions of the United States, such as William Henry Jackson, Timothy O'Sullivan, Andrew J. Russell, William Bell, Carleton E. Watkins, and Eadweard Muybridge. Many of these photographers had already covered the Civil War, an excellent training ground for working in adverse conditions. After the war, both the government and private enterprise sought to know more about the West and to exploit its vast unexplored regions. The first transcontinental railroad lines were built which opened the territory to a variety of activities including logging, mining, farming, and even tourism. Venturesome photographers soon found work recording and interpreting the landscape for this myriad of needs.

Different branches of the federal government financed topographical expeditions that included artists and photographers on their teams of scientists and cartographers. The character of their images is affected as much by the particular terrain and their own personality and technique as it is by the interests of the members of the survey parties. Expedition leaders such as Clarence King and Ferdinand V. Hayden were charismatic and cultivated men who passed on their scientific ideas and religious convictions to the men who worked with them. It has been suggested that Timothy O'Sullivan made some photographs in such a way as to exaggerate the sudden and violent forces required to create certain geological formations. This may have been to support theories of geological "catastrophism" popular among some scientific circles at the time. This forced the "evidence" to fit with the biblical explanation of creation and countered Darwin's theory of evolution. Acclaimed landscape painters such as Sanford Gifford and Thomas Moran were invited to accompany survey parties. By all accounts, the painters and photographers shared ideas about compositio- n and reciprocally influenced each other's work.

Landscape photography was a reasonably profitable business that reached an international audience. The photographers chose large plate cameras, sometimes as large as 20 by 24 inches, in order to have large detailed prints that they would include in such promotional affairs as the Exposition Universelle in Paris in 1867. They also made stereoscopic views to feed the ravenous appetite for images and for vicarious adventure.

American western landscape photographs had both widespread and specific effects on society. W. H. Jackson's view of the Mount of the Holy Cross (a gigantic cruciform of snow on the side of a rocky mountain peak) struck a romantic chord among the public at large and even inspired Alfred Tennyson to write a poem about it. Jackson's photographs of the natural wonders of Yellowstone positively influenced legislation to create the first National Park in 1872. But by the 1880s, photography and travel had become easier and the needs of the country had shifted. This initial flourishing of American landscape photography had passed. Later generations, from Ansel Adams to Mark Klett, have been profoundly influenced by the work of these intrepid pioneers.

Stuart Alexander

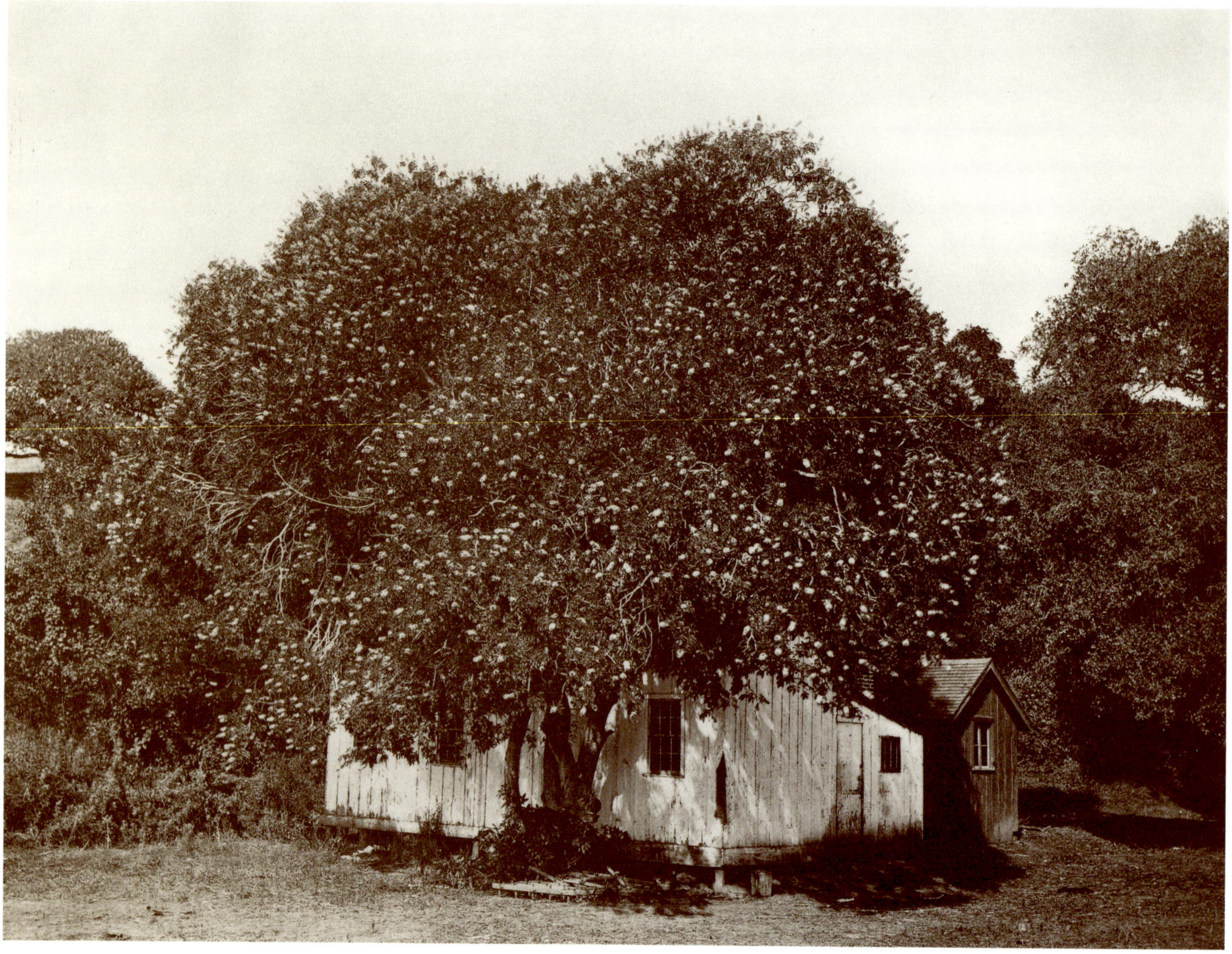

◀◀ previous page:
EADWEARD J. MUYBRIDGE,
El Capitan, Yosemite Valley,
1872,
University of California, Los Angeles.

CARLETON E. WATKINS,
Cala Buckeye Tree, California,
circa 1870,
Centre Canadien d'Architecture, Montreal.

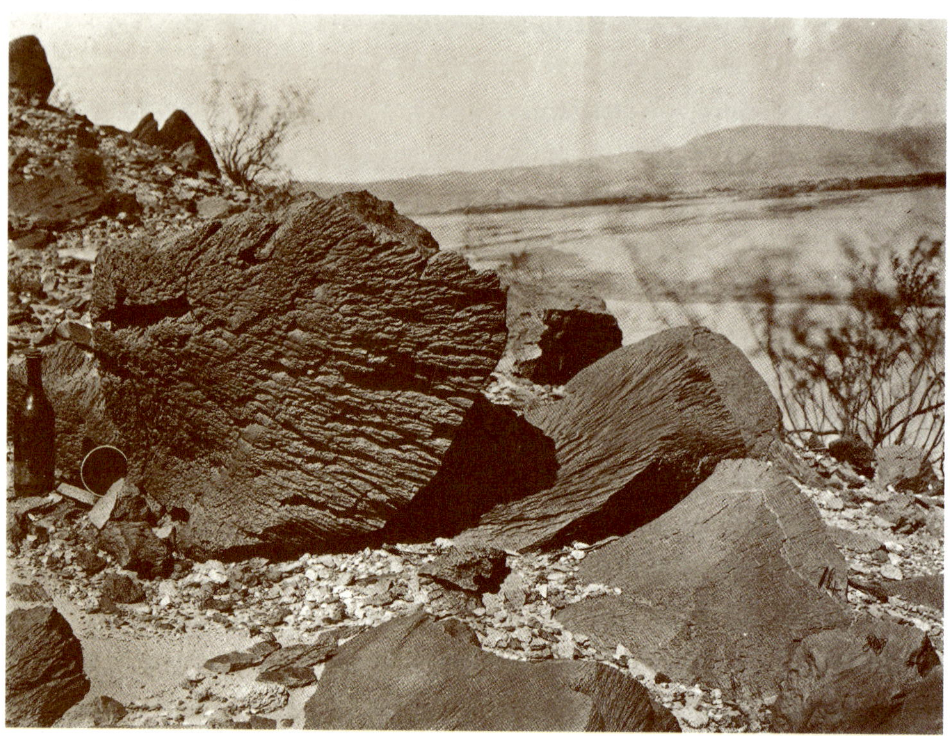

TIMOTHY O'SULLIVAN,
Rocks Carved by Drifting Sand, Arizona,
1871,
Denver Art Museum.

CARLETON E. WATKINS, ▶
Turn Redwoods, Palo Alto, California,
circa 1870,
Fraenkel Gallery, San Francisco.

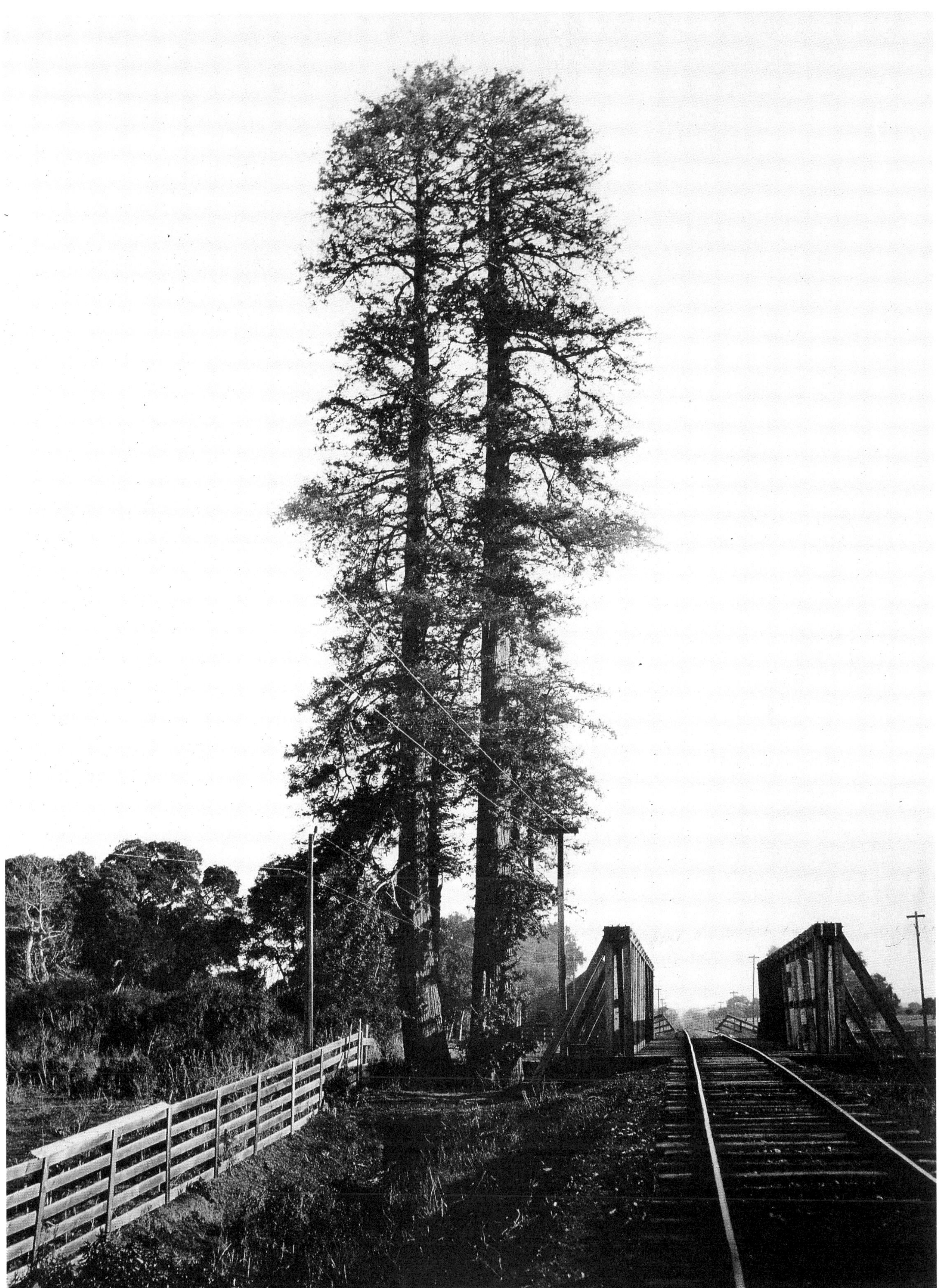

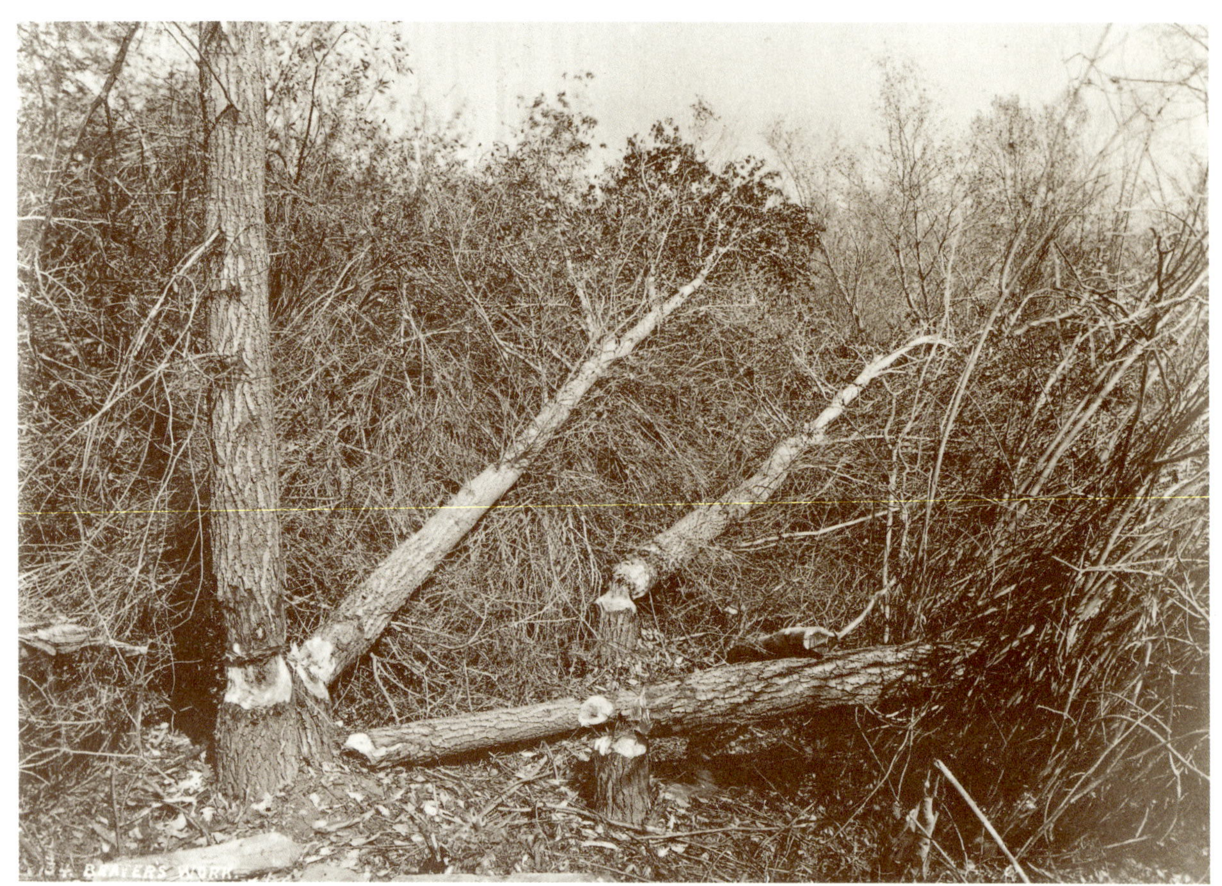

William H. Jackson, *Beavers' Work,* 1870, Academy of Natural Sciences, Philadelphia.

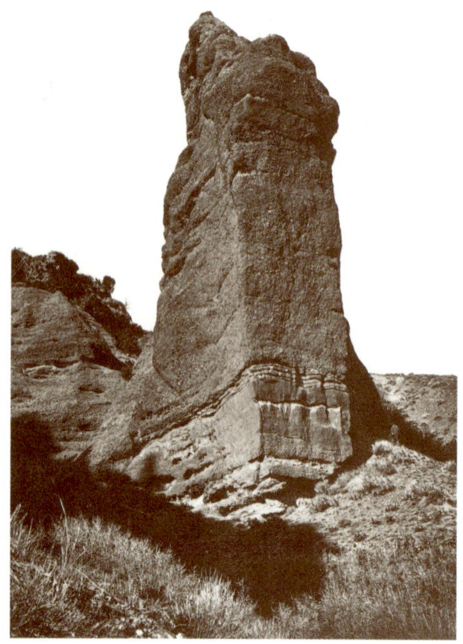

Andrew J. Russell, *Monument Rock, Echo Canyon,* 1867–1868, Fraenkel Gallery, San Francisco.

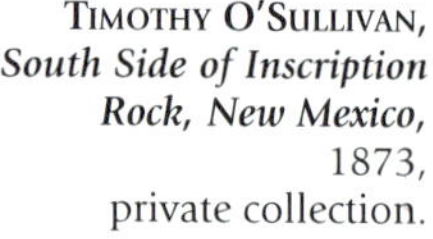

Timothy O'Sullivan, *South Side of Inscription Rock, New Mexico,* 1873, private collection.

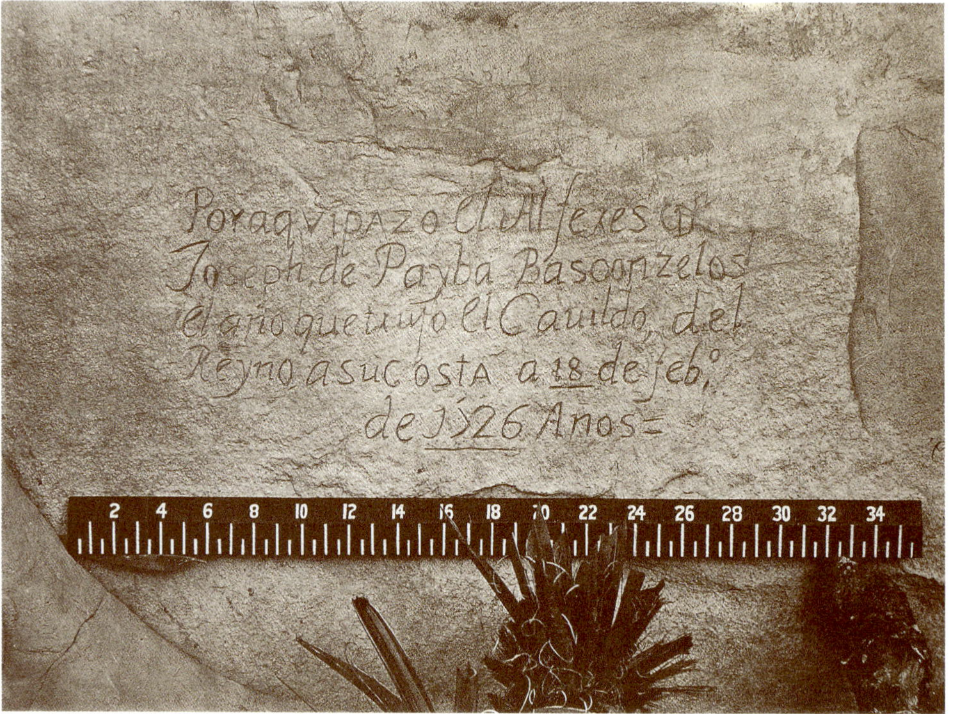

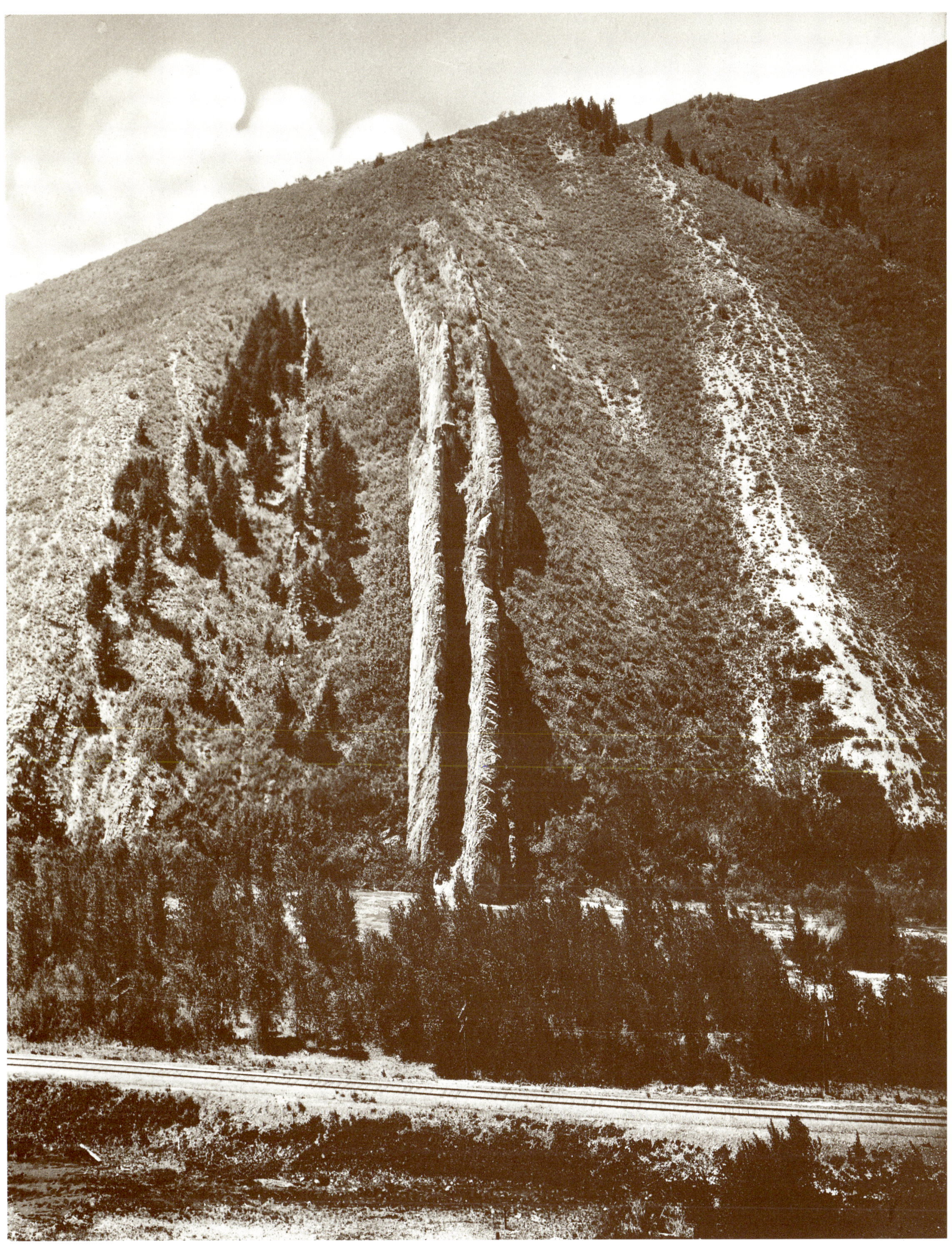

William H. Jackson,
Devil's Slide, Weber Canyon, Utah,
circa 1913, Amon Carter Museum of Western Art, Fort Worth.

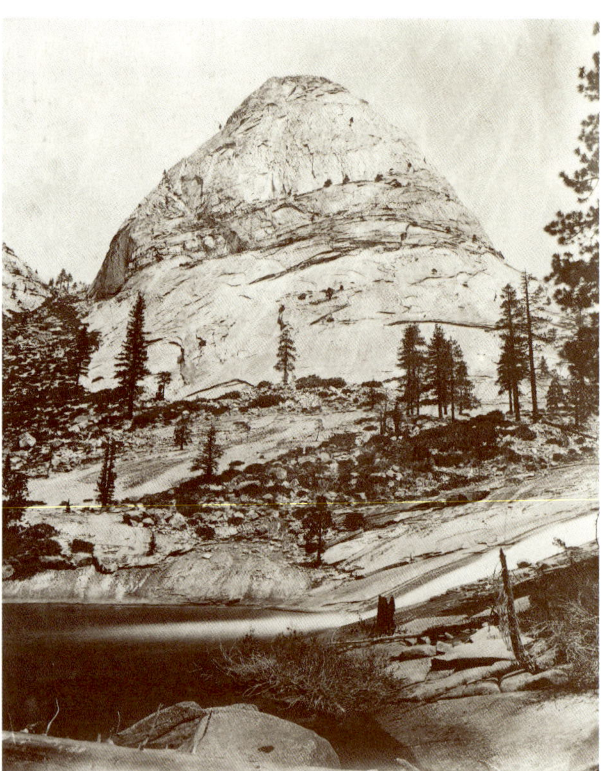

CHARLES L. WEED,
Sugar Loaf,
Little Yosemite Valley,
1864–1865,
New York Public Library.

CARLETON E. WATKINS,
The Three Brothers,
Yosemite Valley,
1865–1866,
Fraenkel Gallery,
San Francisco.

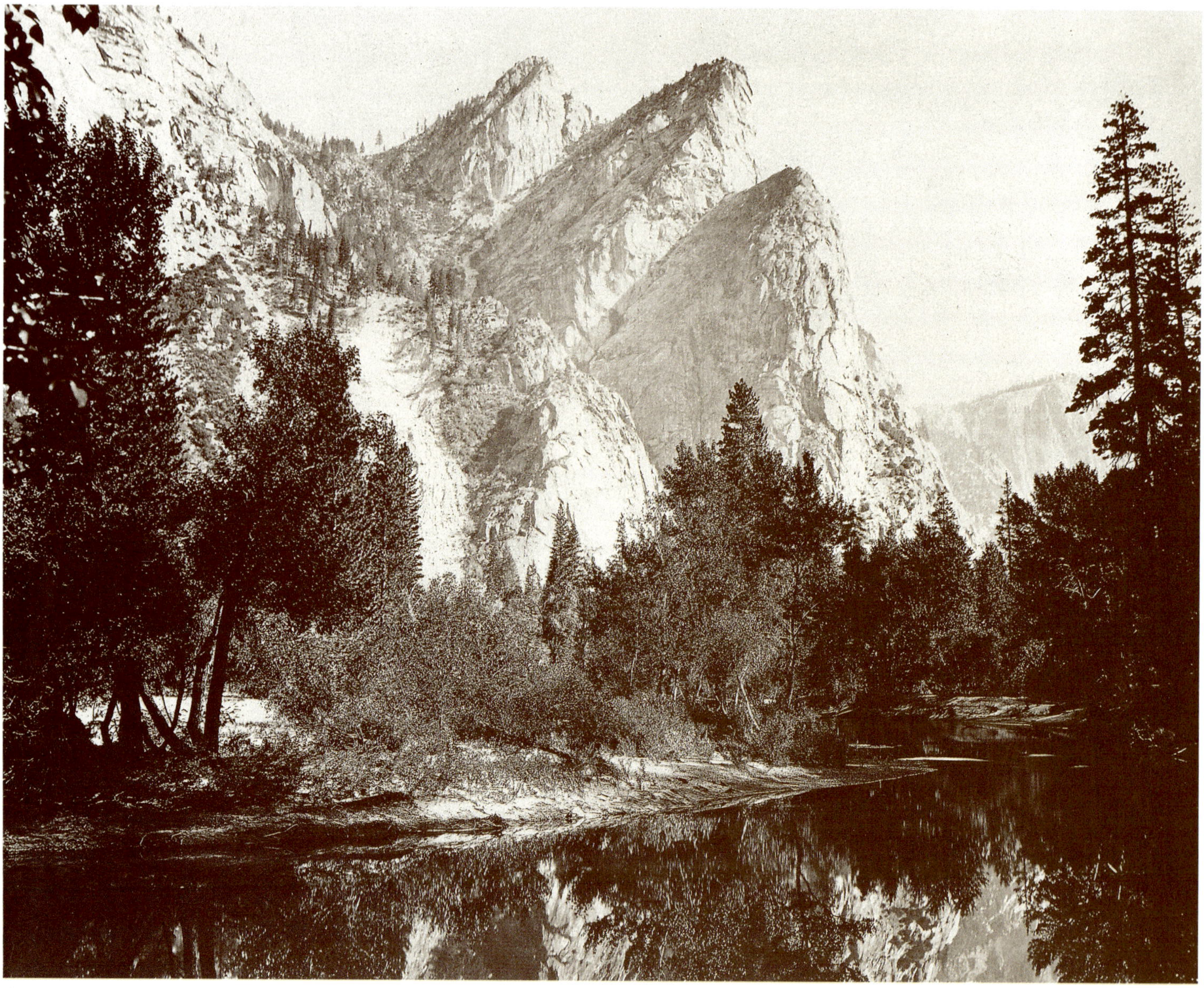

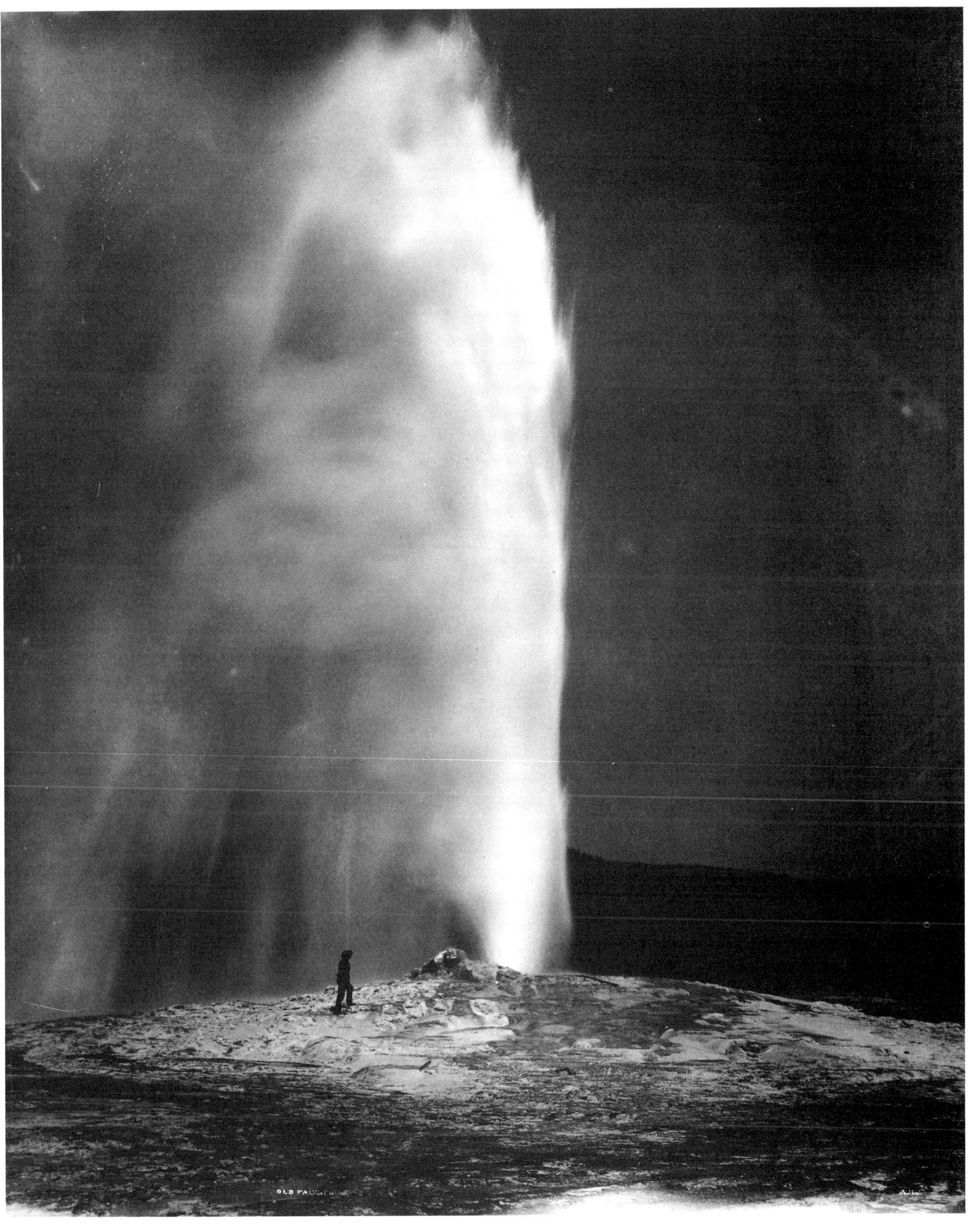

WILLIAM H. JACKSON,
Old Faithful Geyser, Yellowstone, Wyoming,
circa 1870,
J. Paul Getty Museum, Malibu.

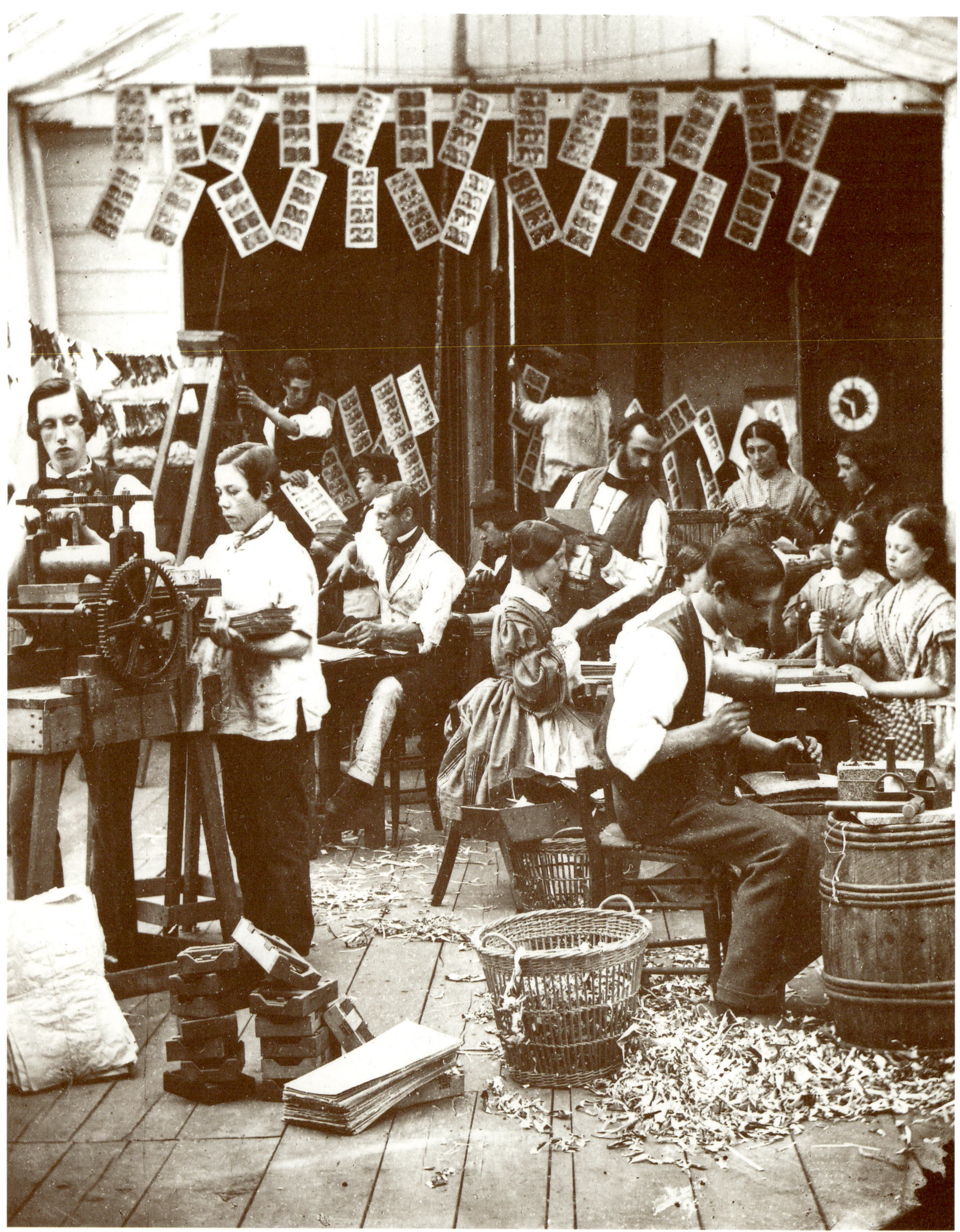

LIFE IN THREE DIMENSIONS 9

The charms of stereoscopy

Pierre-Marc Richard

Theories which compared lenses to the human eye led to the invention of stereoscopy – a simple device for taking pictures (with two lenses) and for viewing them (with two eye-pieces) thereby creating an illusion of depth. The stereoscope became a feature of middle-class drawing rooms during the Second Empire, and went on enlivening long evenings and family reunions until the end of the century. Stereoscopy opened people's minds to a fuller, more accurate knowledge of the world, making it seem predestined to systematic coverage by photography. Once established, stereoscopic photography began to create a comprehensive pictorial catalogue of society and our planet, comparable to a detailed topographical survey.

Following a paper on the "physiology of vision", presented by Charles Wheatstone to the Royal Society in London in 1838, there appeared an optical instrument called a "stereoscope", the purpose of which was to unite and superimpose two images, drawn from different viewpoints, thus reconstituting an illusion of depth. The stereoscope is based on the principle of human vision, whereby each eye transmits a slightly different image to the brain, according to the position of the eyes. The brain combines these two images so that we perceive them as one image `in relief'. The phenomenon of binocular vision, which allows the perception of depth, was mentioned in antiquity by Euclid and Galen, then taken up again by Leonardo da Vinci (in the Milan manuscript) in 1484.[1] It is also discussed by the Italian natural philosopher Della Porta in 1594, and by François Aguillon (Aguilonius) in his treatise on optics published in Antwerp in 1613. In 1844, Sir David Brewster, the inventor of the kaleidoscope, who was also in contact with Talbot, Hill, Adamson, and others, first had the idea of applying it to photography. He tried in vain to interest the opticians of London and Birmingham in his first models. On a visit to Paris in 1850, he made the acquaintance, through Abbé Moigno, of the optician-photographer Jules Duboscq, who then mass-produced the instrument with the aid of his father-in-law J. B. F. Soleil. The following year, on the occasion of the Great Exhibition in London, Sir David Brewster demonstrated the instrument to Queen Victoria, and Jules Duboscq presented her with an example, together with some "very beautiful prints". "A short time later, thousands of eyes were bent avidly over the holes in the stereoscope, which were like skylights onto infinity." (Charles Baudelaire, 1859)

The specific technology of the new invention was to bring important changes to the way photographs were taken. It also affected both the photographer's vision and the public's way of seeing, relating to their perception of relief and depth. It was to influence the whole way of reading images and evaluating their content.

The technique of double vision

The stereoscopic effect is produced by two slightly dissimilar photographs, taken from viewpoints 10 to 20 centimeters apart. The illusion of depth does not appear without the addition of a binocular viewing device. Stereoscope in hand, the spectator is cut off from the world in their own silent little theater, in front of a stage that reconstitutes the dimensions of the real world. To us, a hundred years later, the relief effect obtained in this way seems exaggerated – like the reassembled planes of a cardboard stage-set. We see it as out of proportion because of the image-culture we live in, and we cannot imagine the way it gripped the

◄ A. Gaudin, *Workshop producing stereoscopic photographs,* circa 1860, Roger-Viollet collection.

1. Noted for the first time by Venturi in 1797 (G. Potonniée, *Cent Ans de Photographie, 1839–1939*, Paris, 1940).

Wendt Brother,
High Water on the Hudson,
1902, stereoscopic view,
J. Paul Getty Museum,
Malibu.

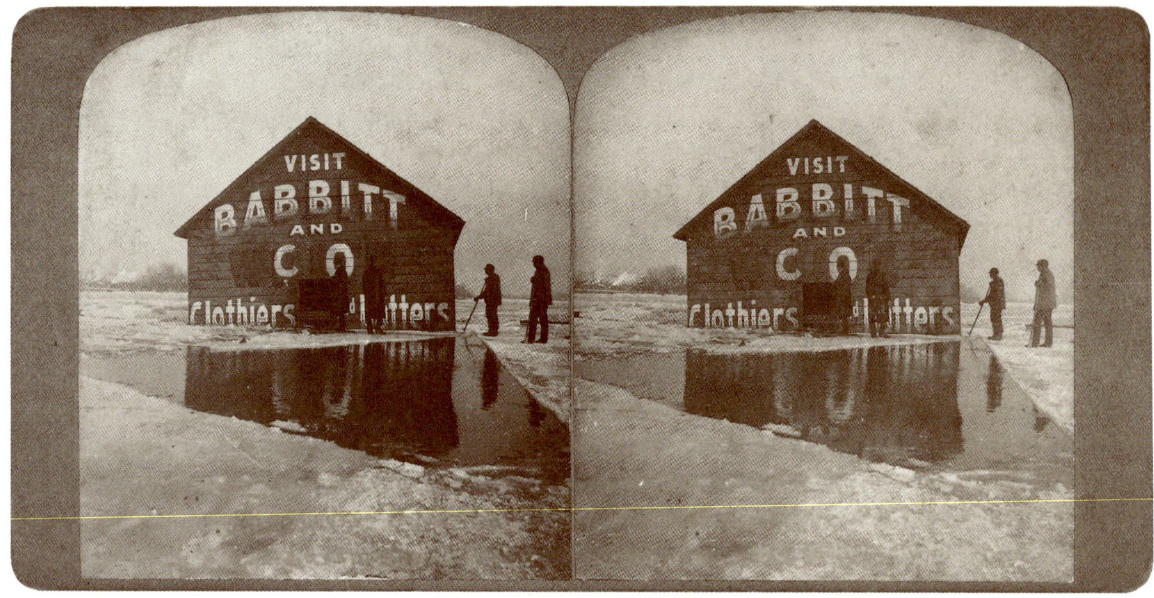

Charles Bierstadt,
Niagara Falls
circa 1873, print from a pair
of stereoscopic pictures,
private collection.
▼

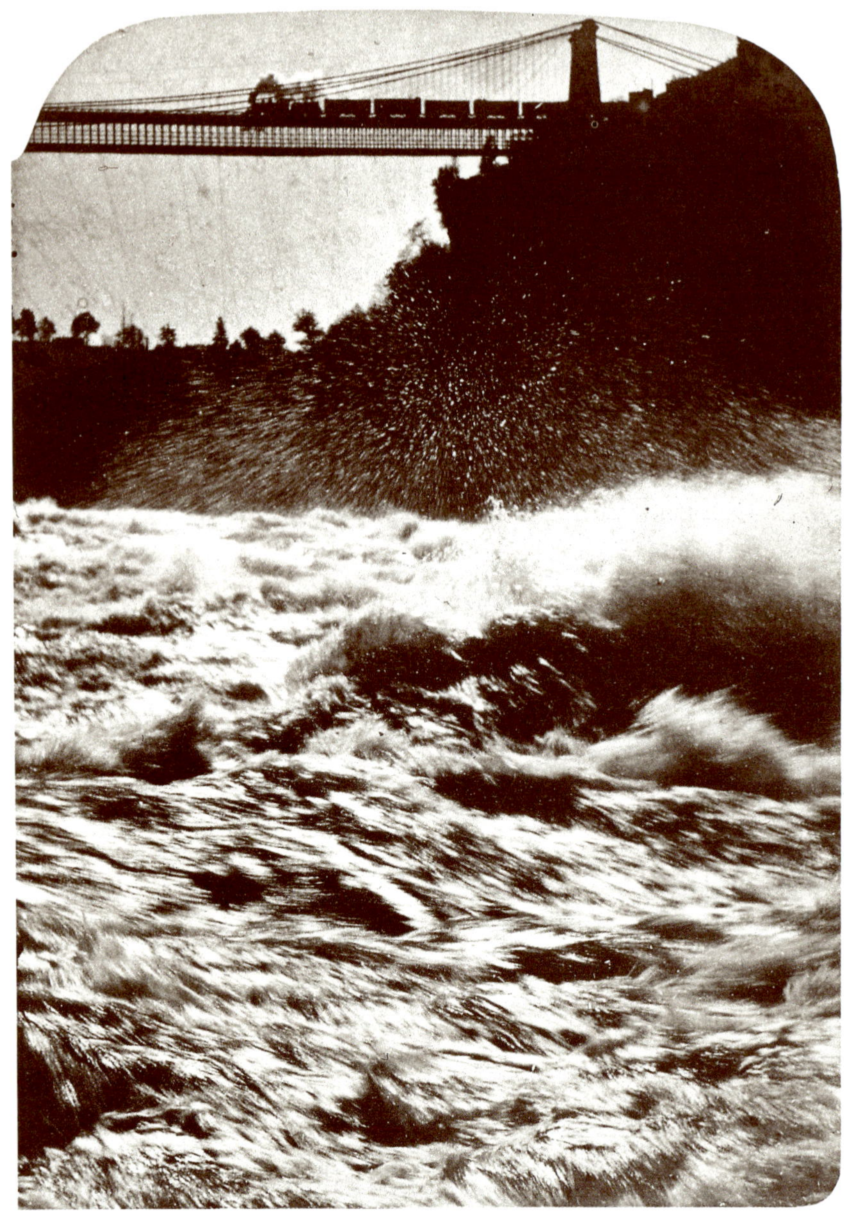

spectator of yesterday. But the fascination lives on. Modern man, despite being saturated with images, still finds something surprising and magical in the procedure, as Abbé Moigno said (*Cosmos*, 1855): "It is quite impossible to imagine, without having experienced it, what impression is produced on one's feelings by seeing things in relief in such a striking and natural way." The sensation it gives one of looking into the image as if through binoculars is still extraordinary.

Despite the absence of contemporary eyewitness descriptions of the workshop-production of stereoscopic views, the stages are known from a photograph (stereoscopic, reproduced at the beginning of this chapter). On the floor are the contact printing frames in which sensitized paper is exposed to the sun under collodion glass negatives; the prints are drying by the window, attached to a length of string; in the front of the picture a worker is stamping out the images with the aid of a mallet; the waste-basket is overflowing with the trimmings; a woman and two girls are sticking the pairs of views, four at a time, onto ready-cut sheets of colored cardboard which are drying at ceiling-level; after the four views have been through the roller-press, the man seated at the back is separating them with a trimmer.

An English traveler[2] describes the difficulties that a photographer might encounter. Sometimes he had to wait several days for favorable weather-conditions. Then, after setting up his tent near the scene he wished to photograph (someone had to stand guard over the tent to protect the equipment from the inquisitive), he had to persuade some people to pose for him so as to give scale to the picture. Several exposures would be needed before he was certain he had a good negative. With exposure times that could sometimes be very long, unwanted people sometimes appeared in the picture. Finally, one had to contend with the muddled insistence of people who wanted to see their picture at once. Stereoscopic photography was beset by all the difficulties and pitfalls

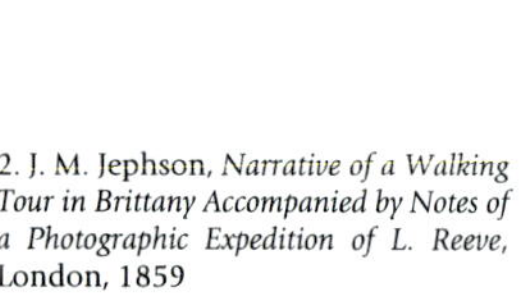

2. J. M. Jephson, *Narrative of a Walking Tour in Brittany Accompanied by Notes of a Photographic Expedition of L. Reeve*, London, 1859

3. "I am a trader, and in my spare time I play the violin, model statues, collect antiques, and practice photography. I want to enrich the world with a stereoscopic China which will all go into one pocket." Legrand (Shanghai), quoted by Sir E. Broomely, *L'Illustration*, 9 November, 1861.

associated with expedition photography, but it remained much easier than using a large-format plate camera.

Stereoscopic cameras were cheaper, lighter, and less cumbersome to use which made them the first choice of camera for amateurs, offering freedom of use without complications or constraints. Travelers could envisage taking such a camera on remote expeditions. At first, however, photographers for the most part excitedly photographed family, friends, and surroundings. When they later began to explore the commercial possibilities of stereography, the first images they published were these early attempts, which bear witness to spontaneous enjoyment without concern for profitability. However, it was the commercial exploitation of stereoscopic views that resulted in stereoscopy's growth in popularity. It adopted all the photographic processes known as they evolved during the period 1850-1870, notably daguerreotypes, ambrotypes, paper negatives and glass negatives treated with albumen or collodion, salted paper prints, albumen prints, and transparent positives on glass treated with collodion or albumen, including Poitevins' carbon-printing process. Some of these views were colored, with a greater or lesser degree of finesse. The most spectacular were transparencies made of very fine paper with watercolor applied to the back of the photographic image (either directly or on transparent paper). These offered a succession of effects: day, night, fire, illumination (miniature versions of the "polyrama panoptique", Daguerre's diorama). Most stereoscopic views were produced in a standard format (approximately 17.5 x 8.5 cm).

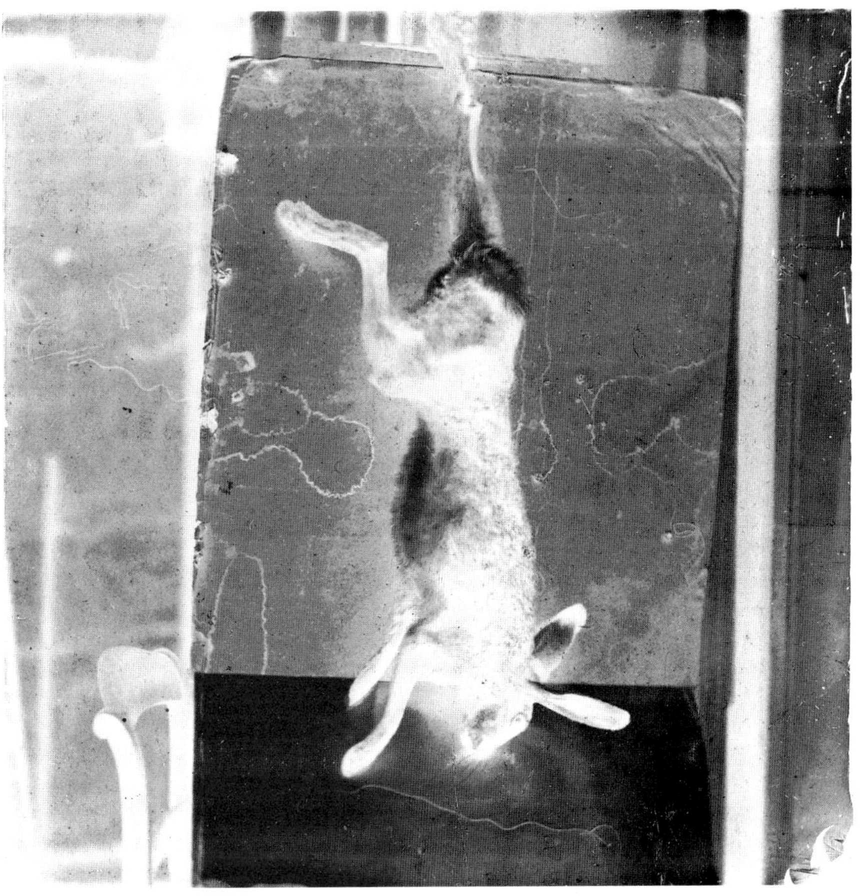

Alphonse Poitevin,
The Hare,
glass negative of a stereoscopic pair,
circa 1860,
P.M. Richard collection.

A survey of society

As early as the 1850s, stereoscopy was tackling everything from anecdotal scenes to a geographical and sociological survey of our planet.[3] In the binocular universe, at once so intimate and so alive, the amateur made the world his own. *By the Fireside* (as the collection of sets issued by Alphonse Ninet was entitled), one could view the

Anonymous,
Porte Saint-Martin, Paris
circa 1865,
stereoscopic view,
Debuisson collection.
▼

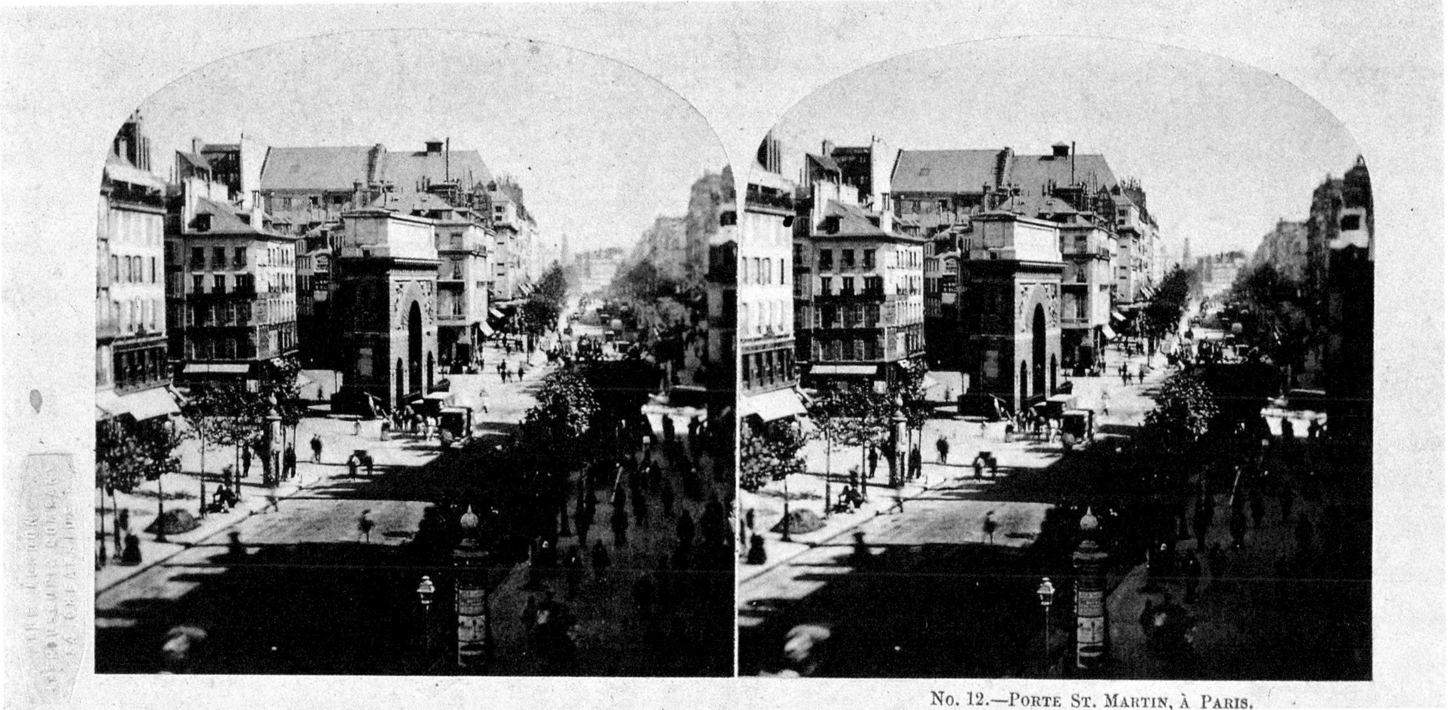

Stereoscopy

The optical impression of seeing things in relief is due to the mechanism of bi-focal vision. Each of our eyes acts as an independent *camera obscura*, with its own optical axis. When we look at something, the two axes converge on that object. Because of the distance between them, each eye receives a slightly different image. Synthesized by the brain, these two images combine to convey an impression of depth. This phenomenon was demonstrated in 1838 by the Englishman, Charles Wheatstone, who made a binocular apparatus which produced a picture in relief from two flat images. This apparatus, christened "the stereoscope" consisted of a frame with, at each end, two drawings of the same object, as seen by either eye. These drawings were positioned facing one another on either side of two mirrors which were set at an angle of 90 degrees. To obtain the best illusion of depth, the user viewed the drawings through two openings placed 65 mm apart in front of the mirrors.

Sir David Brewster, a Scot with a passion for photography, combined photography with the stereoscope in 1844. Brewster invented a new form of stereoscope which superimposed images by refraction rather than reflection. This apparatus was first made commercially available in 1850 by the Paris opticians Soleil and Duboscq, and was displayed the following year at the Great Exhibition in London. Its success was immediate. "Thousands of eyes were bent avidly over the holes in the stereoscope, which were like skylights onto infinity", as Baudelaire testified in 1859.

The equipment of the first "stereoscopists" consisted of a tripod and a level board which allowed the photographer to use either a single camera that one moved between exposures to take two successive images, or two separate cameras fixed at an appropriate distance apart. Numerous improvements swiftly appeared. In

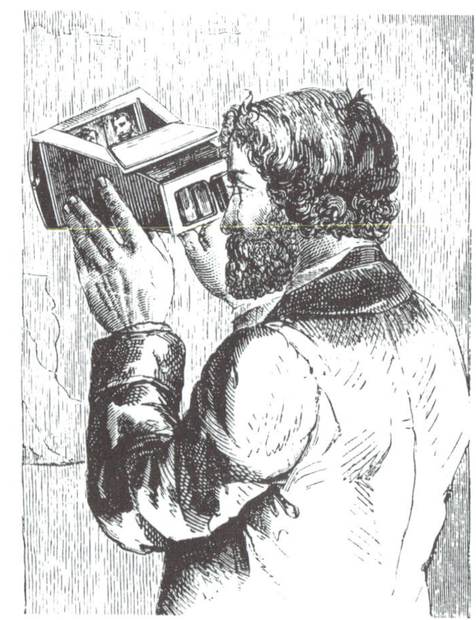

How to use the stereoscope.

some later models the camera had two compartments and remained fixed while the lens, mounted on a sliding panel, moved from one to the other. Other models consisted of twin cameras mounted on the same support. In 1860, Bertsch invented an automatic binocular camera whose two lenses, positioned 65 mm apart, could be uncapped and capped simultaneously by means of a connecting rod. By the time gelatin-bromide dry-plates appeared, this was the standard design adopted by the most noted manufacturers of the numerous stereoscopic cameras then available: Mackenstein, Belliéni, Gaumont, Joux, Bazin, Sigriste, and, above all, Jules Richard. His "Vérascope" (1894) or the "Glyphoscope" (reversible stereoscopic binoculars) were the first real small-format cameras, using plates measuring 45 x 107 mm which permitted the user "after having taken the photograph to see the print enlarged to true size in natural relief [...]. One experiences on the retina an absolute illusion of reality...."

Prints were made by contact-printing. The two halves of each stereoscopic pair had to be reversed in order to restore the correct three-dimensional image. This was done either on the negative or during printing, before the pictures were stuck to cardboard.

To see a picture in relief, you looked through a viewer fitted with two lenses. There was the box type (like Brewster's or Duboscq's), which could be held up by a handle or placed on a stand, or there was the free-standing version, often made of mahogany and sometimes in the form of a column containing several dozen views on a rack. The "Taxiphote" was a turn-of-the-century piece of furniture containing glass stereoscopic views. These were stored in the lower part and raised up to be viewed in sequence by means of an internal mechanism. The stereoscope was a feature of most middle-class drawing rooms during the Second Empire and the *Belle Époque*.

Jean-Claude Gautrand

Théâtres of Paris (Bloch) and *Pradier's Sculptures* (de Soye) without leaving home, visit Peru or Russia (A. Bertrand), or China (H. Voland). Stereoscopy also contributed to the idea of bringing back an event in pictures. You could experience the earthquake in Italy (A. Bernoud) or the great flood of the Loire in 1856 (Ferrier), follow the Italian campaign (Bénédict), frequent all the imperial residences without needing to be presented at court (Furne, Grau, Gentil, and Speisser) or attend the Emperor's wedding at Notre-Dame (1852) or the christening of his son (1856, Richbourg).

The most prolific producers in France were Andrieux (seaside towns and ports), A. Bertrand (Imperial palaces, snapshots of Paris, Switzerland, Peru, Russia, Savoy, the Pyrenees, and the banks of the Rhine), Block (*Devilry, The Life of Christ, The Gospel in Pictures, Our High-society*

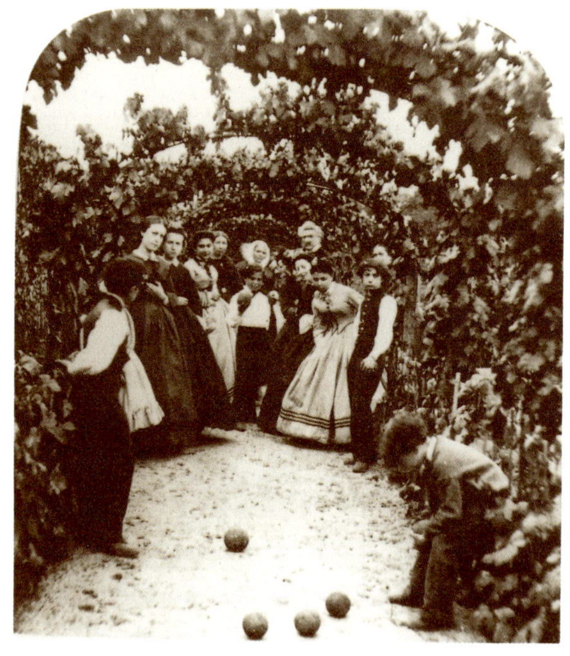

RAUDNITZ, ► *A Game of Boules,* print from a stereoscopic pair, Bibliothèque Nationale, Paris.

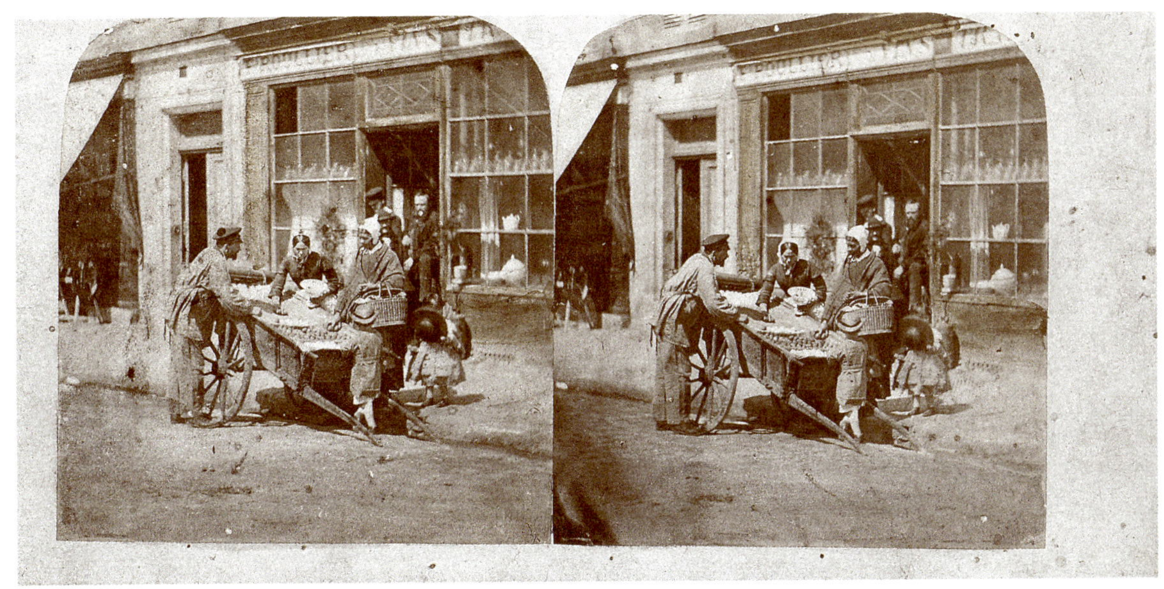

ANONYMOUS,
Egg-seller,
about 1860,
stereoscopic view,
private collection.

Ladies, works of Pradier, theaters of Paris), A. Braun (views of Alsace, Switzerland, Savoy, Belgium), Clouzard and Soulier (views of Germany, the banks of the Rhine, Switzerland), J. Delplanque (Paris, Le Havre, maritime snaps), J. Duboscq (England, Scotland, Paris), Ferrier and son (more than 10,000 views), Franck de Villecholes (Spain and Germany), Furne and Tournier (more than 60 series and 2000 views published in 5 years), Gaudin (romantic scenes from England, Germany, and Paris), J. Jouvin (Paris, the South of France, the 1855 Exhibition), H. Jouvin (Paris, churches of Paris), Moulin (Paris, nudes, fantasies, Algeria), D'Olivier (nudes, Paris), Plaut (the Pyrenees, Paris, Egypt, Mexico), Quéval (Paris and views of the whole of France), Viret (rural scenes), and Voland (views of China).

From the beginning, production was widespread throughout France, and expanded quickly. There was international trade, then exchange clubs, first with Britain, as early as 1851, then with Germany, Italy, and all of Europe and as far as the New World. In Britain, among the most noteworthy producers were William England, chief photographer of the London Stereoscopic Company (several thousand views between 1854 and 1860), Negretti and Zambra, J. Elliott and C.E. Elliott, William M. Grundy, George Washington Wilson, Francis Bedford, Francis Frith, and Roger Fenton. In the United States, there were numerous producers, right from stereoscopy's beginnings (by 1864, 10,000 different views in one year). Among those famous for their large output were the Langenheim brothers, Carleton E. Watkins, Eadweard J. Muybridge, William H. Jackson, J. K. Hillers, John P. Soule, and William Notman of Canada. Stereoscopic photography enjoyed great popularity and many photographers practiced both conventional photography in various formats and stereoscopy at the same time.[4] There was not a part of Europe, nor subsequently the rest of the accessible world, that was not covered by this pictorial survey, carried out either by local photographers or by travelers, going off on their own initiative or commissioned by one of the big distributors. Famous practitioners of the photographer's art also tried stereoscopy: É. Baldus, L. and A. Bisson, Humbert de Molard, and C. Nègre. In 1860 Gustave Le Gray invented a device for taking four stereoscopic views on the same plate. There is evidence that stereoscopic views were

HIPPOLYTE JOUVIN,
Children Playing with a Hoop
1860s,
print from a
stereoscopic pair,
Bibliothèque Nationale,
Paris.

4. W. C. Darrah, *The World of Stereographs*, Gettysburg, W. C. Darrah, 1977.

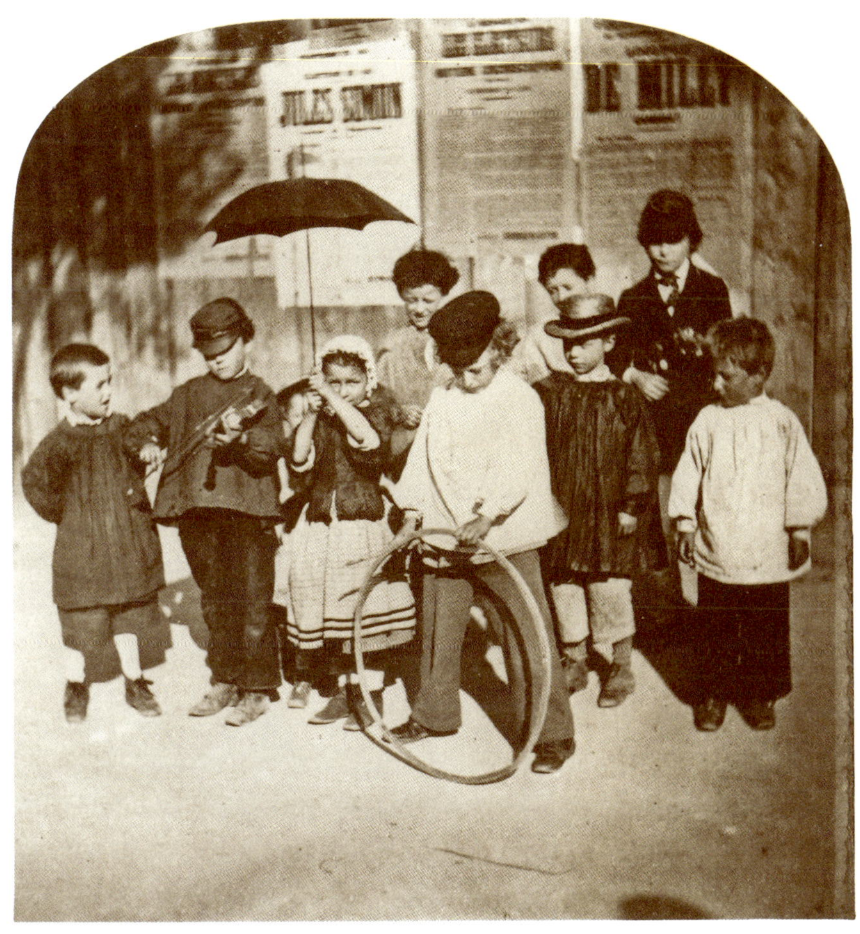

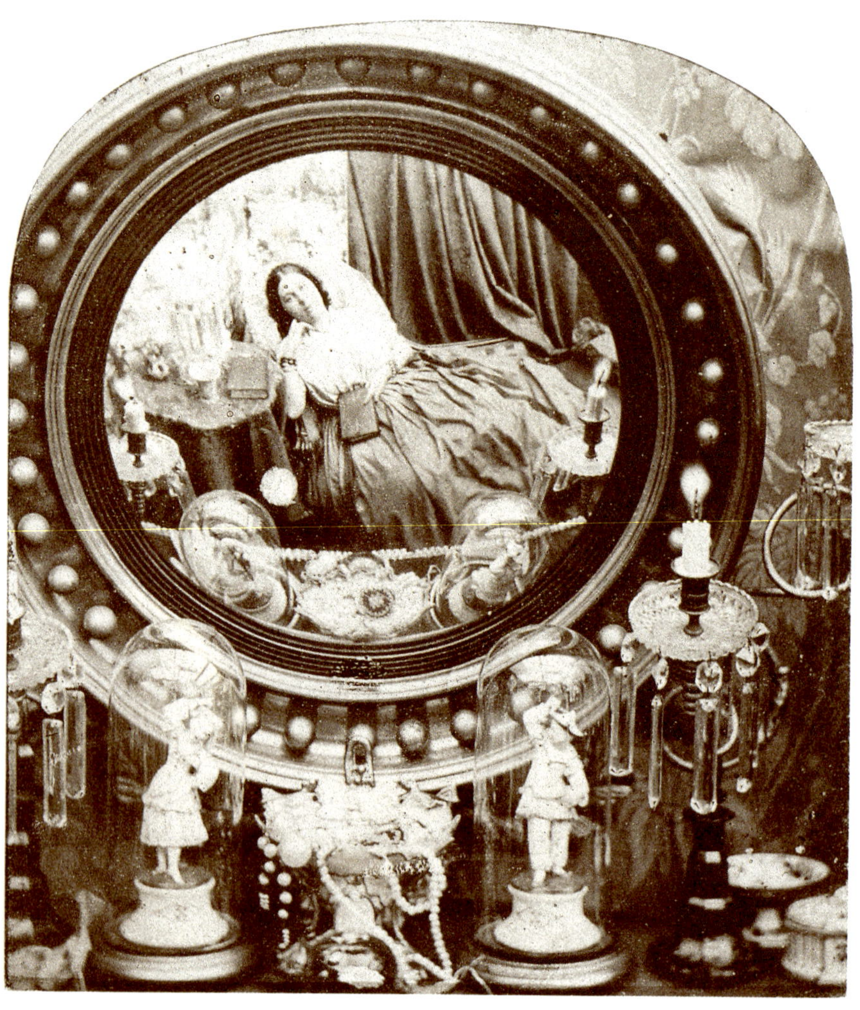

▲
J. Elliot, *"Pretty reflection"*, print from a stereoscopic pair, about 1860, private coll.

also taken by A. Bilordeaux, A. de Brébisson, D. Charnay, A. Davanne, A. Disderi, E. Burieu, C. Famin, M. Lyte, A. Quinet, G. de Rumine, and A. Tournachon.

Even the military were not immune to the craving: they expected the process to give a "perfectly exact description of the relief of the battlefield" (*Cosmos*, March 1854). Nor were surgeons, who saw an immediate application for it on the dissecting-table (clinic of the School of Medicine, 1857); it was used for the infinitely small (A. Moitessier) and for astronomy (Warren de la Rue). It was stereoscopy that dared for the first time to show dead soldiers on the battlefield, during the Italian campaign, took viewers to Victor Hugo's home (Edmond Bacot), to the South Sea Islands, and to the barricades of the Commune (Jules Quéval).

With the "moving" stereoscopic view (patented by Furne) there was a premonition of the cinema in that it exploited the phenomenon of persistence of vision (you shut each eye in turn to see the character come to life); all the inventor did was exploit a "defect" of early stereoscopy where the two views were not taken simultaneously but successively (a single lens sliding from one compartment in the camera to the other). There are old slides where you can see a cab in front of the Hôtel de Cluny drawn by a black horse in one picture which is "replaced" in the other by a white one, or two people sitting by the fountain in the Square Louvois with the clock showing 10.20 on one picture, and ten minutes later on the other (the people have gone to sleep!)

In the field of pornography, stereoscopy found an outlet in the shape of pocket-sized views which could be handed on under one's coat. The roles were often taken by the same models who

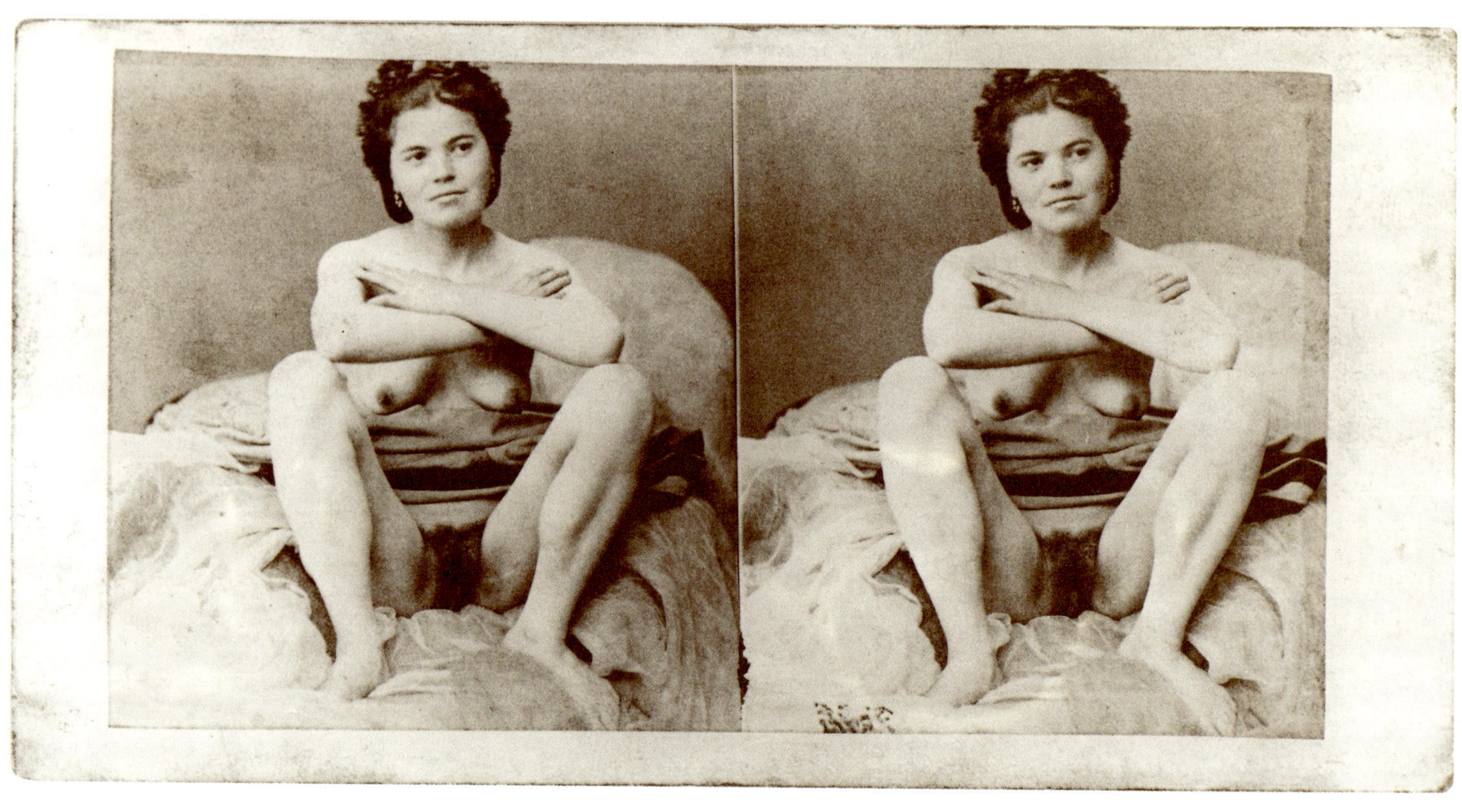

posed for one studio after another. This type of subject lent itself to fraud: some productions were confiscated, others pirated. Some photographers were even tried and went to jail (Malacrida, an optician, and Moulin, a daguerreotypist, were sentenced for obscenity at the Seine Assize Court). The law saw this voyeurism as morally deviant, and took it seriously, though today it often raises a smile: Camille d'Olivier's stereoscopic views were "prohibited for exhibition but authorized for sale on condition they are not viewed in relief" (copyright note). Some specialists in stereoscopic nudes did, however, dare to sign their name: Auguste Belloc, Bruno Braquehais, Eugène Durieu, Félix Moulin, Louis Camille d'Olivier, Henri Plaut, and Ambroise Richebourg. Though these nudes were in part circulated clandestinely, most were sold in arcade bookshops or opticians, even pharmacies. Views sold by itinerant dealers bear the stamp M.I., Ministry of the Interior (decree of August 2, 1862).

The distribution network

A chain of users, collectors, and dealers created a worldwide network of visual communication. Stereoscopic views circulated particularly freely and penetrated all kinds of markets thanks to distribution on a truly phenomenal scale and at a minimal price, all of which made them the type of photograph most frequently viewed at home in the second half of Napoleon III's reign. In the first years when it was commercially available, stereoscopy was dependent on the daguerreotype, and was still rare and expensive. Duboscq and Soleil's idea of producing multiple prints by making aquatints from daguerreotypes was a failure, doubtless because photography was not yet really established. Charles Nègre and Poitevin certainly had the same end in view when they made trial prints utilizing the extraordinary sharpness produced by albumen on glass. It must be said that in 1856 Ferrier was selling views on glass for six francs each, the same price as Blanquart-Evrard was charging for a plate of average size (24 x 30 cm).[5] In 1859, Henri Plaut quoted his retailers a price of 12 francs a dozen for his views.[6] After the mid-1860s, competition brought about a decrease not only in price but also in print-quality, presentation, and color. Enterprising manufacturers no longer dared to finance distant journeys or elaborate scenes for fear of pirate copying. Landscape views on paper were divided and reused as cartes de visite for albums. Transparent views on glass were cut in two to make lantern slides.

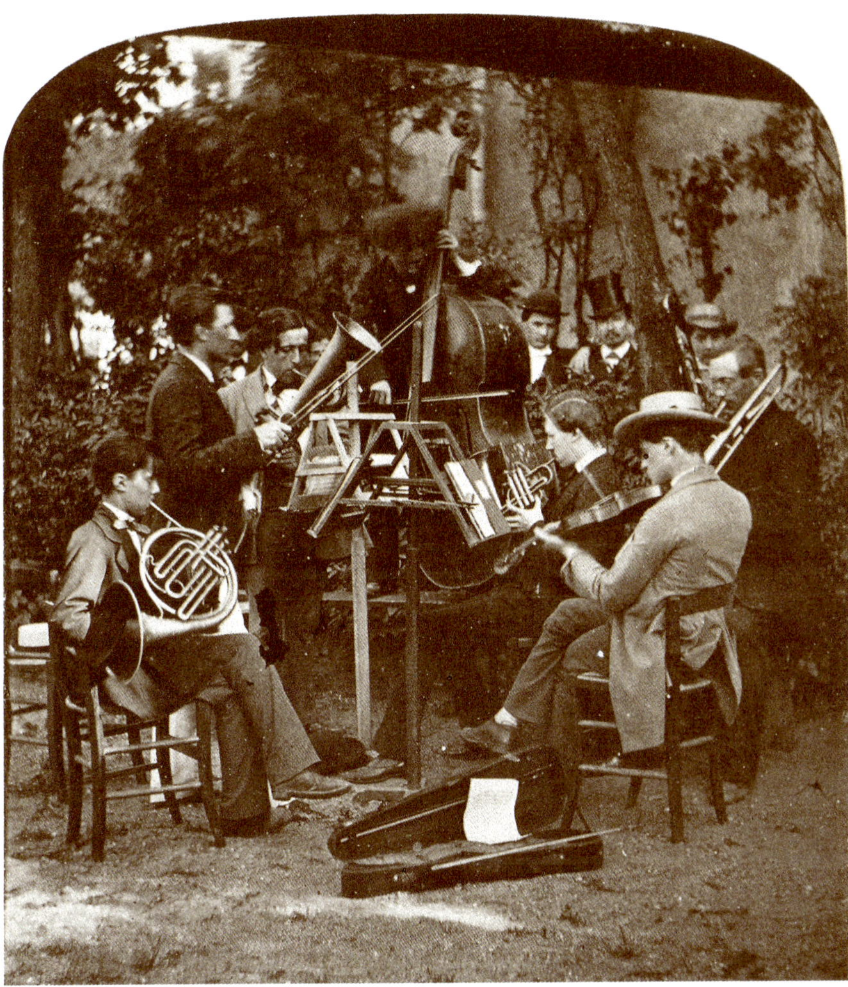

ANONYMOUS,
Outdoor Concert
1860s,
print from a stereoscopic pair,
private collection.

◄ ANONYMOUS,
Untitled
1860s,
stereoscopic view,
Bibliothèque Nationale,
Paris.

The profits were such that a regular trade in pirate copying was set up. Everyone took the precaution of depositing two copies of their latest productions at the Bibliothèque Nationale to protect their work. Unfortunately the copyright register[7] was not reliable. Some people got their employees to deposit their views, who then signed their own name, others registered negatives as their own that they had bought.[8]

For instance, the stylistic differences between the *Paris* series attributed at the time of deposit in 1868 to H. Jouvin and his famous series *Snapshots of Paris* (copyright 1865) are so great that they cannot be attributed to the same maker; the former are, however, very close to those which had been deposited by Jules Deplanque (1865). The buying up of stocks of photographs, the printing of transparencies and pirate copies are not the only things that make attribution difficult. Some photographers who traveled abroad improved their profits by selling doubles or variants of their negatives when they got home, using the others themselves. Finally, numerous were the publishers, investors, and so-called photographers who "forgot" to mention the names of those who took the pictures. The judgment in the action by Mayer and Pierson against Herlich and Vust stated, "Any employee

5. The same year J. Couppier was selling views on glass for 4 to 5.50 francs; Furne and Tournier sold views on paper for 2 to 3 francs in 1857.

6. Colored on paper, 17 francs a dozen; transparent on paper, 12 francs a dozen, black on glass, 36 francs a dozen; and colored on glass, 48 francs a dozen.

7. It was only from 1851 that photographers took part in the copyright system.

8. Advertisement by A. Belloc: "We buy all stereoscopic negatives". For instance, in 1857 Gaudin presented the copyright office with views of Paris that Fronti had deposited the same year.

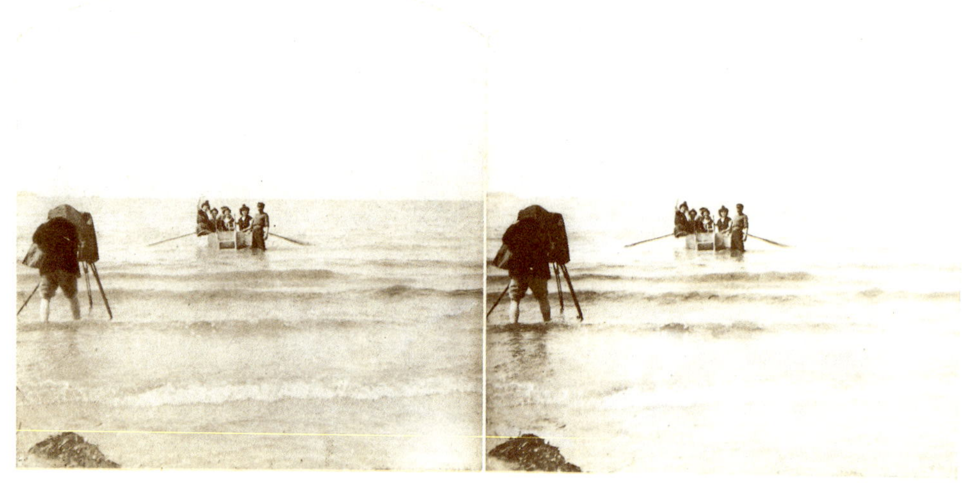

ANONYMOUS,
Seaside Photographer
stereoscopic view,
circa 1900,
private collection

ANONYMOUS,
Gare de Strasbourg, Paris,
stereoscopic view,
circa 1865,
Debuisson collection.

or artist working for a commercial company cannot claim the right to conserve his individuality in the work in which he took part"; this judgment applied, among others, to stereoscopy. The attribution of works to their real author, which was already confusing at the time, is all the more awkward today in that one has to sort through the names – printed, on a label, or handwritten – on the back of the cards, to know who is a photographer, publisher or owner-collector.

The innumerable stereoscopic views that were produced are a mine of information, so far little used, for the ethnologist, the sociologist, and the historian of photography. Within this confused outpouring the historian can find things he has sought in vain in other forms of photography: a clue, a hypothesis, even a proof. The discovery of "great images"among these miniature pictures, important works produced for private pleasure or never distributed, suggests a broader historical and aesthetic view of photography, since it is in stereoscopic form that a quantity of documentary evidence is conserved: fragments of albums by photographers known only by name, a review of an exhibition or a single picture. This extraordinary mosaic tells us about travels, friendships, faces; it constitutes a veritable archeological memory of that epoch.

Stereoscopy prefigured the future development of the photographic image, and fell victim to the

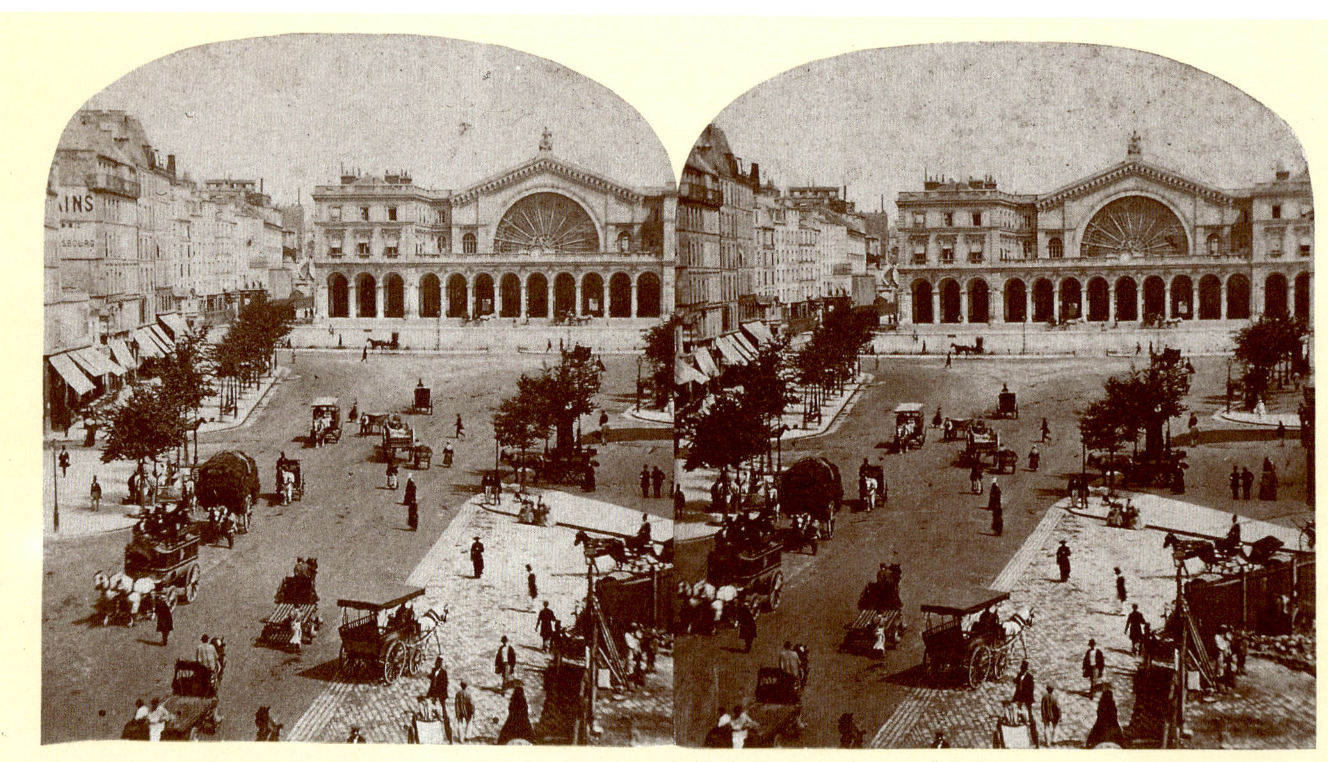

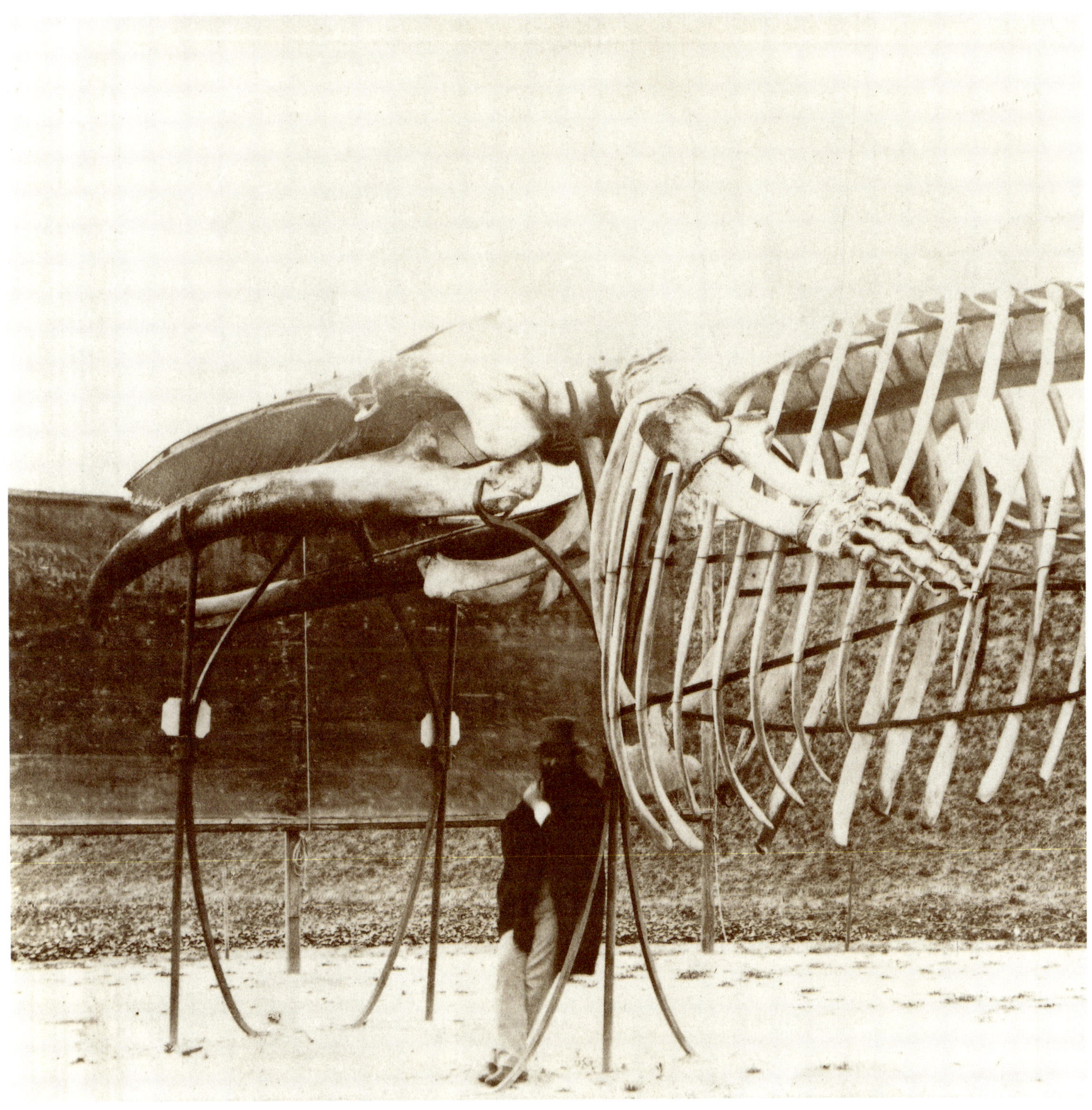

very ideas it exploited. The profuse and detailed inventory of the earth's riches that had been its ambition was overtaken at the end of the century by the next fashion in popular photography – the postcard. The hegemony of cinema and television would soon make twentieth-century man forget the third dimension of his vision, and 3-D cinema never took off. The decline in artistic and technical quality continued until 1900, though the American publishers Underwood and Underwood and the Keystone View Company recaptured an international public with the quality and variety of their productions. Stereoscopy retained its popularity for longer in the USA, but the success of these series was eclipsed by the formidable tide of postcards from the turn of the century and people finally lost interest in stereoscopic images. Stereoscopic photographs were for collecting, for viewing on Sunday afternoons, for an intimate social circle. They gave way to images which were accompanied by written messages, allowing people to communicate – to talk about their village or events in their lives. Stereoscopy had, after a fashion, inaugurated and enlarged this taste for description.

Capt. Charlois,
Skeleton of a Whale,
print from a
stereoscopic pair,
circa 1865,
P.M. Richard collection.

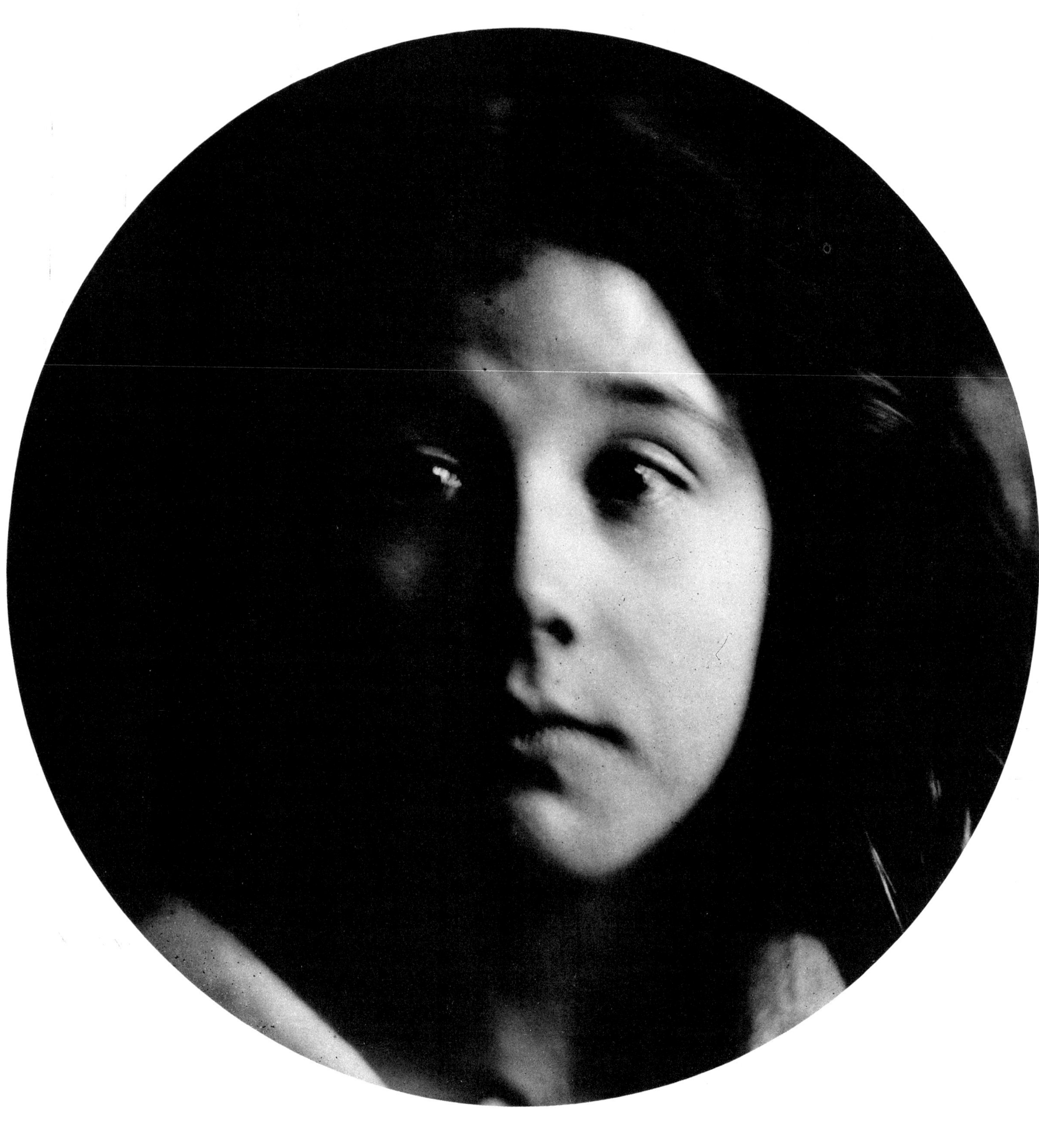

Julia Margaret Cameron,
Head of a Child,
1866.

ARTISTIC ASPIRATIONS 10

The lure of fine art

Mike Weaver

From the moment photography was invented, photographers strove to be recognized as artists. However, the very notions of art and the fine arts depend on the milieu in which one is operating and on the public for whom the "works of art" are intended. It was in Victorian Britain, in the aesthetic climate of the Pre-Raphaelite movement (a rediscovery of the Italian Renaissance), that the artistic current developed that tended to mythological references and the imitation of the accepted canons of painting using means which were specifically photographic.

The aspiration of photography to achieve the status of fine art occurred during a period of growing art-historical consciousness throughout Europe. The international exhibitions of the 1850s and 1860s were, in part, a reflection of the competition between the imperial nations for commercial dominance, but they also signaled a bourgeois interest in improving taste in art. In Britain, a great survey of paintings in private and public collections was undertaken by the German art historian Gustave Waagen, whose findings were published in 1854.

Furthermore, the first generation of photographers to possess a reliable photographic process, such as Roger Fenton and Charles Nègre, assumed from the beginning that their work would take its place in the history of graphic art. In the hierarchical world of art history, however, graphic art (engraving, etching, and lithography) was a relatively lowly art, a skill practiced more by artisans than artists, and the desire to be recognized as an artist-photographer was keenly felt by some practitioners. In Britain, the patronage of Prince Albert undoubtedly created in some photographers an ambition and a pride which was excessive – indeed, overweening.

It is a common enough recurrence in the history of photography that whenever the medium has been considered essentially mechanical, or has achieved great success in the realist mode, there spring up those who become more pretentiously artistic than simply creative within the limits of the medium. The Great Exhibition in London, which the photographer Julia Margaret Cameron attended in 1862, saw photography still classified with scientific instruments. It is not surprising that certain photographers resented this slur on their creativity as potential artists.

Emulating pictures

Roger Fenton (1819–1869) at the British Museum and C. Thurston Thompson at the new South Kensington Museum were both serving the public and producing a considerable income by copying photographically works of fine and applied art. In 1858–1859 the Art Union of London selected work by these and other photographers for free distribution, doing its patriotic duty towards the industrialization of taste. But whereas Francis Bedford photographed throughout the 1850s to create a "museographic" survey of the *objets d'art* at the great exhibitions, in order to make lithographs, Fenton actually combined these objects with flowers to make still-life photographs which transcended the museum function – he made works of art.

In *Still-life with Mirror and Chalice* Fenton took as his precedent the eighteenth-century still-life style of Alexandre-François Desportes, who also showed reflections of objects in mirrors.[1] But whereas Desportes did this primarily as an exercise in virtuoso realism, as a High Victorian Fenton was concerned with the symbolic as well as the aesthetic aspect of such images. The chalice next to the Ceres figure holding up ears of wheat

1. For example, A. F. Desportes, *Silver, Peaches, and Game-birds*, c. 1739, National Museum, Stockholm.

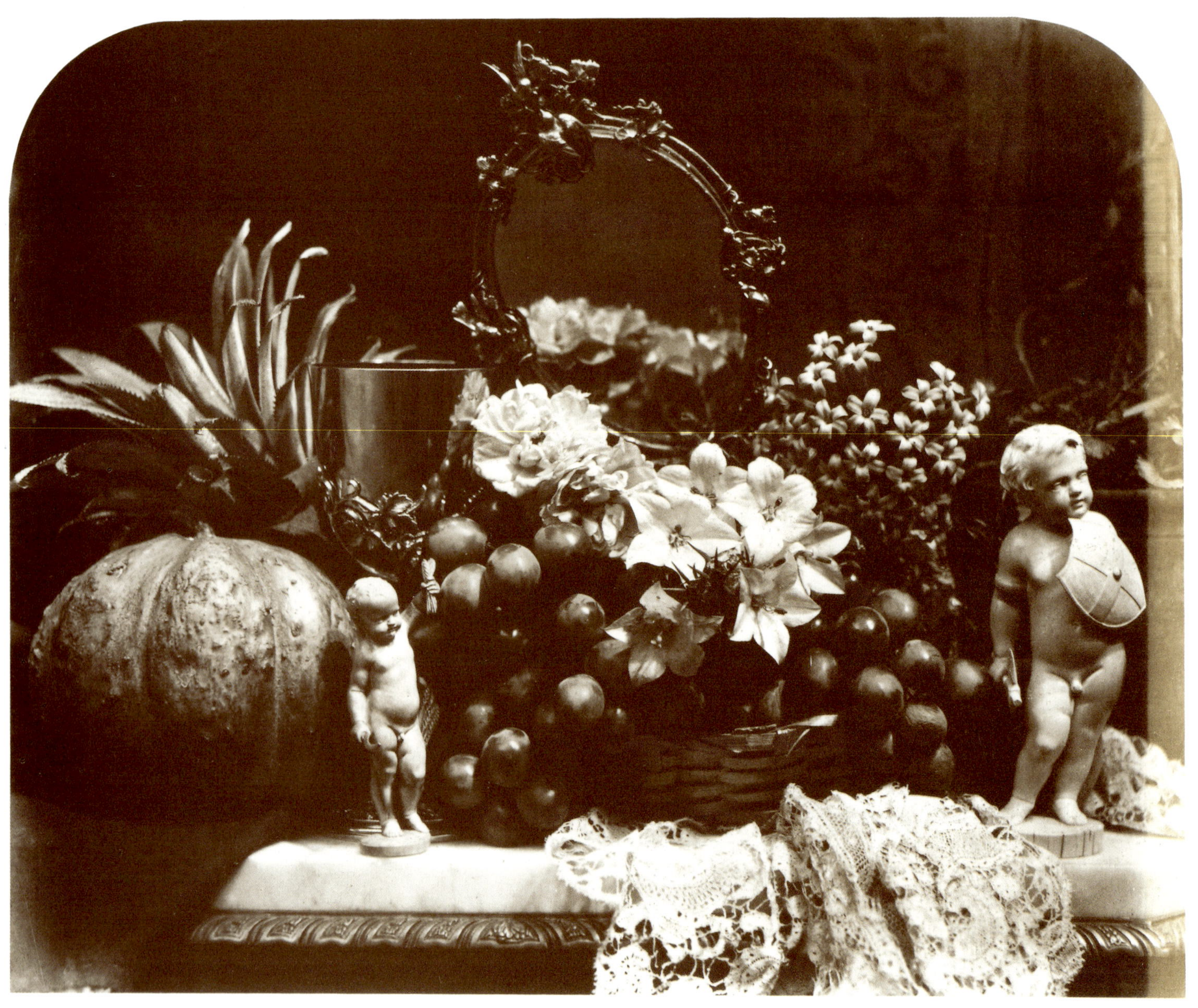

Roger Fenton,
Still-life,
circa 1858,
Royal Photographic Society,
Bath.

situates the picture as Christianized classical, an image in which pagan wine and bread are given a Eucharistic overtone. Protruding between lilies, emblematic of Christian purity and faith, is a wicked-looking thorn, unexpectedly taking the place usually given to a rose in such a composition – sin thus replacing love. The highly ornate mirror reflects a lace-like image, but the presence of this thorn suggests a world of torn illusions.

Fenton's kind of picture-making, ambitious and subtle as it was, drew upon Flemish and French pictorial traditions, but this practice was not confined to him alone. In France, in the 1850s, Bilordeaux also made compositions of an allegorical character, referring to the vanities, and to the cabinet of curiosities. Boitouzet and Carey were successful at the salons with their still-lifes, as was Braun with his game subjects. Like their work, the contributions by Charles Aubry, made later around 1864, are often studies from nature rather than fully fledged painterly photographs, just as the academic female nudes by Braquehais tend to keep somewhat close company with suits of armor and plaster Venuses. In Dresden, Hermann Krone made less contrived arrangements of scientific instruments and equipment in the early days of the wet-collodion process. But on the continent of Europe in general, photography tended to keep to its own specific field of realism, hardly ever asserting the claims to high art that someone with the talented background of Adam-Salomon might make.

Similarly, while Thompson copied photographically Thomas Couture's *Les Romains de la décadence* at the Exposition Universelle in Paris in 1855, Oscar Gustave Rejlander (1813–1875) made his own version of a potentially orgiastic scene for the Manchester Art Treasures Exhibition of 1857. *The Two Ways of Life*, Rejlander's combination photograph, composed from a large number of separate negatives, was designed as a competition picture, and dedicated to British artists. Rejlander wrote that the principal reasons which motivated him in its production were as follows: "Firstly, it was to be competitive with what might be expected from abroad. Secondly, I wished to show to artists how useful photography might be as an aid to their art, not only in details, but in preparing what may be regarded as a most perfect sketch of their composition, thereby enabling them to judge of effect, before proceeding to the elaboration of their finished work. Thirdly, to show the plasticity of photography. I sought to bring in figures draped and nude, some clear and rounded in the light, others transparent in the shade, and to prove that you are not, by my way of proceeding, confined to one plane, but may place figures and objects at any distances, as clear and distinct as they relatively ought to be."[2]

Rejlander's earlier career as a painter is the best clue to his hopes for photography as a fine art. Born in Sweden, he made a living in Rome in the 1830s copying Old Master paintings, and making lithographs.[3] Having married an Englishwoman, he came to England and exhibited in 1848, for the first time, a painting at the Royal Academy of Arts. Thus, his remark that he wanted to recommend photography to artists as an aid to composition came from experience and from the heart.

However, he made two great mistakes. Firstly, he did not realize that artists would conceal their use of this aid, and, secondly, he was not to know that artists would prefer literal records to work from rather than photographs with a certain creative expression of their own. If he had been willing to present photography as a medium which simply imitated nature accurately all would have been well, but he could not resist the desire to express the ideas of an artist himself.

Not that everyone noticed at once that he was interpreting his subject matter. Indeed, his famous pupil Julia Margaret Cameron's own work was also acquired in great quantity by the South Kensington Museum as an aid to composition without regard to her capacity to express ideas. But Rejlander, like Cameron after him, believed that it was the thought expressed, and not the particular medium, which made an object a work of art. Art was a means of making such thought visible.

The poses and gestures which he derived from his extensive study of Old Masters provided scenes for his own dramatic moments, but his study of facial expression carried his work into a realm of psychological interpretation quite beyond the bounds of the usual pictorial aid. He acknowledged his debt to Charles Lebrun's *Expressions des passions de l'âme* (1667) and later in life made a set of photographs for Charles Darwin's *Expressions of the Emotions in Man and Animals* (1872). His own evident ability as an actor who had analyzed the meaning of facial expression for himself made him a photographer of remarkable psychological penetration. His photograph *Salome* may be in the manner of Guido Reni but Salome's facial expression combines a subtle blend of knowingness and innocence which makes the picture a profound examination of the state of her soul at a particular moment in her life.

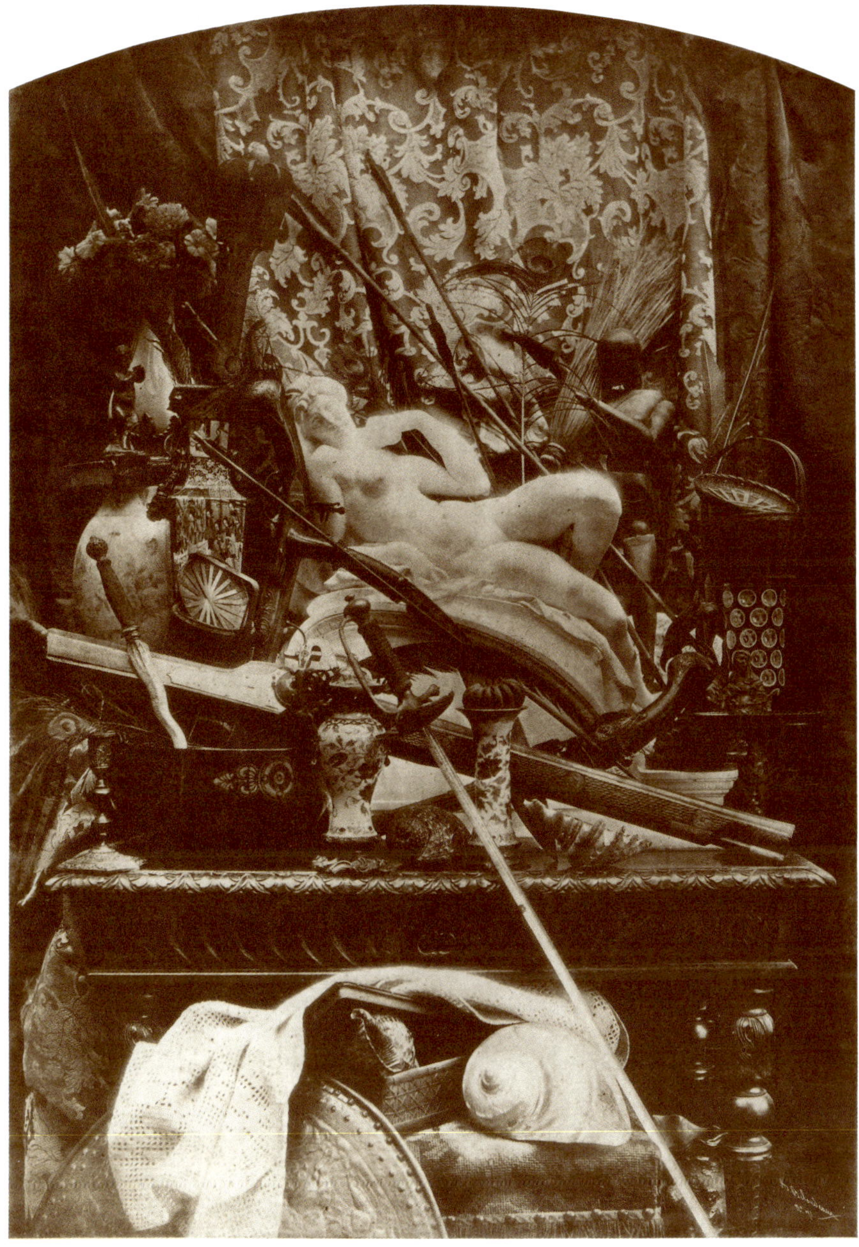

ADOLPHE BILORDEAUX, *Still-life*, circa 1859, International Museum of Photography, George Eastman House, Rochester.

Artistic effects

In 1857, H. P. Robinson (1830–1901) followed Rejlander's lead with studies of facial expression, but, regrettably, without Rejlander's outstanding firsthand knowledge and experience. The virtue of Rejlander's girl with a jug, as we can tell from the expression in her eyes, will last only

2. O. G. Rejlander, "Photographic Composition" in *Photographic Journal* (21 April 1858), p. 191.

3. See S. Spencer, *O. G. Rejlander: Photography as Art*, Ann Arbor, UMI Research Press, Michigan 1985.

O. G. Rejlander, *The Two Ways of Life*

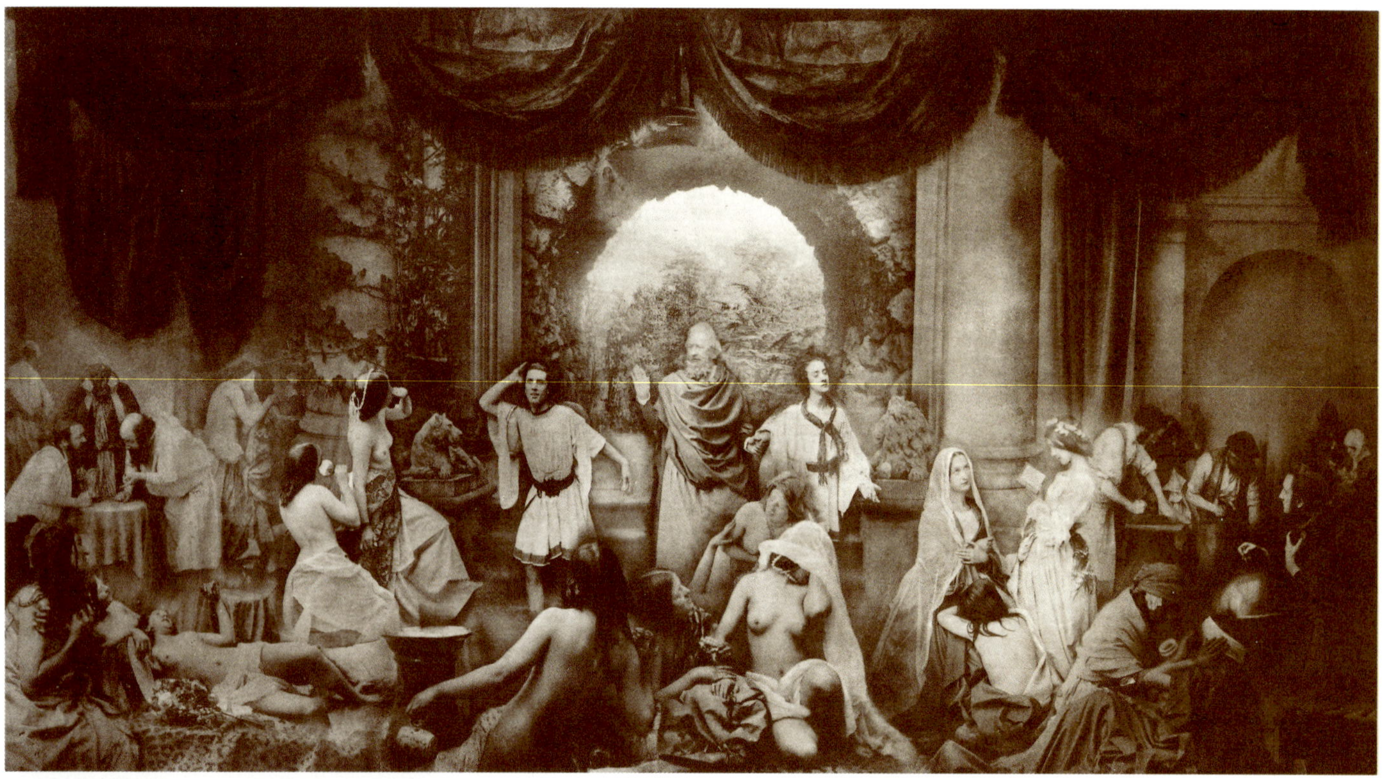

OSCAR G. REJLANDER,
The Two Ways of Life,
1857, Royal Society, Bath.

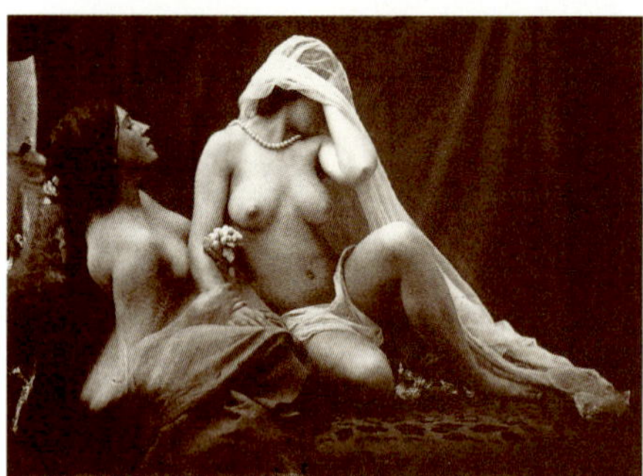

OSCAR G. REJLANDER,
Nude Study for The Two Ways of Life,
1857, Royal Society, Bath.

In 1857, Oscar Rejlander advertised in the photographic press copies of a combination print entitled *The Two Ways of Life*. The largest version, shown at the Manchester Art Treasures Exhibition where Queen Victoria bought a print for Prince Albert, was 31 x 16 inches. Rejlander had made the picture in about six weeks using a method of combination printing employing some thirty negatives. This technique allowed the artist to conceive a picture in separate parts, photograph each part individually, and then combine them all on one piece of paper – except that in the case of *The Two Ways of Life* the image was so large Rejlander had to join two pieces of paper together. He prepared a negative for each part of the picture by painting out with black varnish those portions of the negative which he did not want in the final picture. He then exposed his sensitized printing paper under each negative in succession. With rudimentary equipment this must have required great skill. When the paper had been exposed to all thirty negatives it was toned and fixed like any other albumen print.

This allegorical subject shows a father leading two sons through an arch which symbolizes the boundary between city and country. One youth chooses to follow the path of Religion, Mercy, and Industry, the other will inhabit a world of Idlers, Gamblers, and Bacchantes. The veiled nude in the foreground, possibly representing a penitent Magdalene, gave the picture its subtitle, *Hope in Repentance*. But, as we can see from one of the original studies for the picture, the moral tone of *The Two Ways of Life* is a good deal more ambiguous. The picture caused viewers to call it both indelicate and indecent.

Mike Weaver

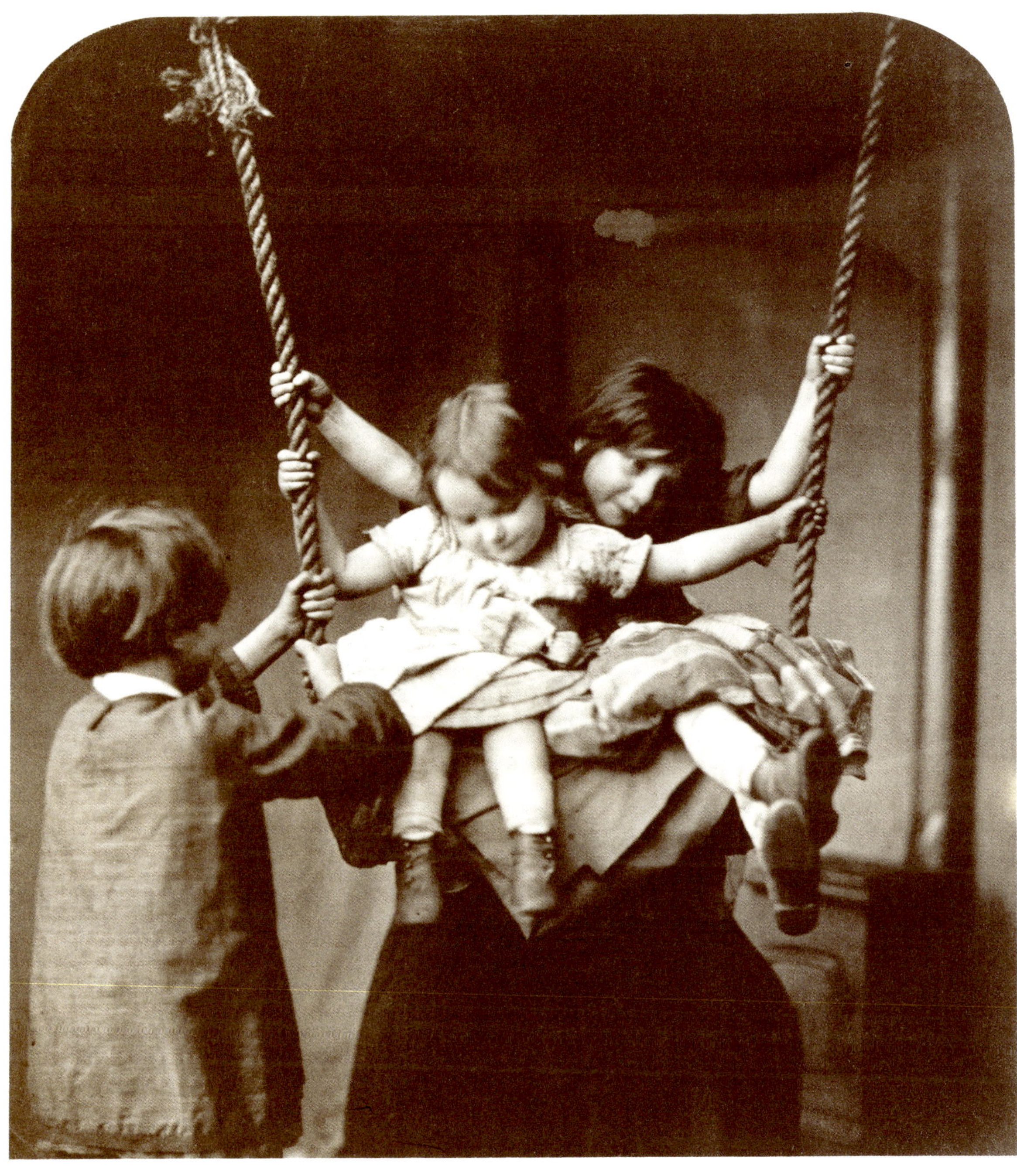

OSCAR G. REJLANDER, *Children on a Swing*, circa 1860, University of Texas, Austin.

as long as temptation does not cross her way, whereas Robinson's many girls with jugs will, we feel, never even be put to the test. Of course, the major difference between Rejlander and Robinson is that Rejlander's world is very much that of the sinful city whereas Robinson's is usually that of an Arcadian countryside. The background of *The Two Ways of Life* shows gamblers on the one side, and people engaged in productive work on the other. This contrast derives from a tradition of subject-pictures (genre) found in British painting from William Hogarth through to George Morland, depicting idleness and industry. Rejlander's interest in genre work, several rungs lower down on the artistic ladder than his art studies, was extensive. He became as committed to the depiction of the urban unemployed as Robinson was to the bucolic "peasant".

His photograph depicting an unemployed carpenter, whose Christian fortitude (marked by the inclusion on the wall of a Rejlander photograph of Mary at the foot of the Cross) is not in doubt, is entitled *Hard Times,* after Dickens. It contrasts starkly with the carpenter busily planing wood in the background of *The Two Ways of Life.*

The two major categories of Victorian art were dramas from domestic life and literary illustration. By the 1860s, Dickens believed that these two categories had become one. He described the usual scenes: "Two or three people seated round a table, partaking of a meal; a couple of young fellows chatting over their wine; a lady showing a

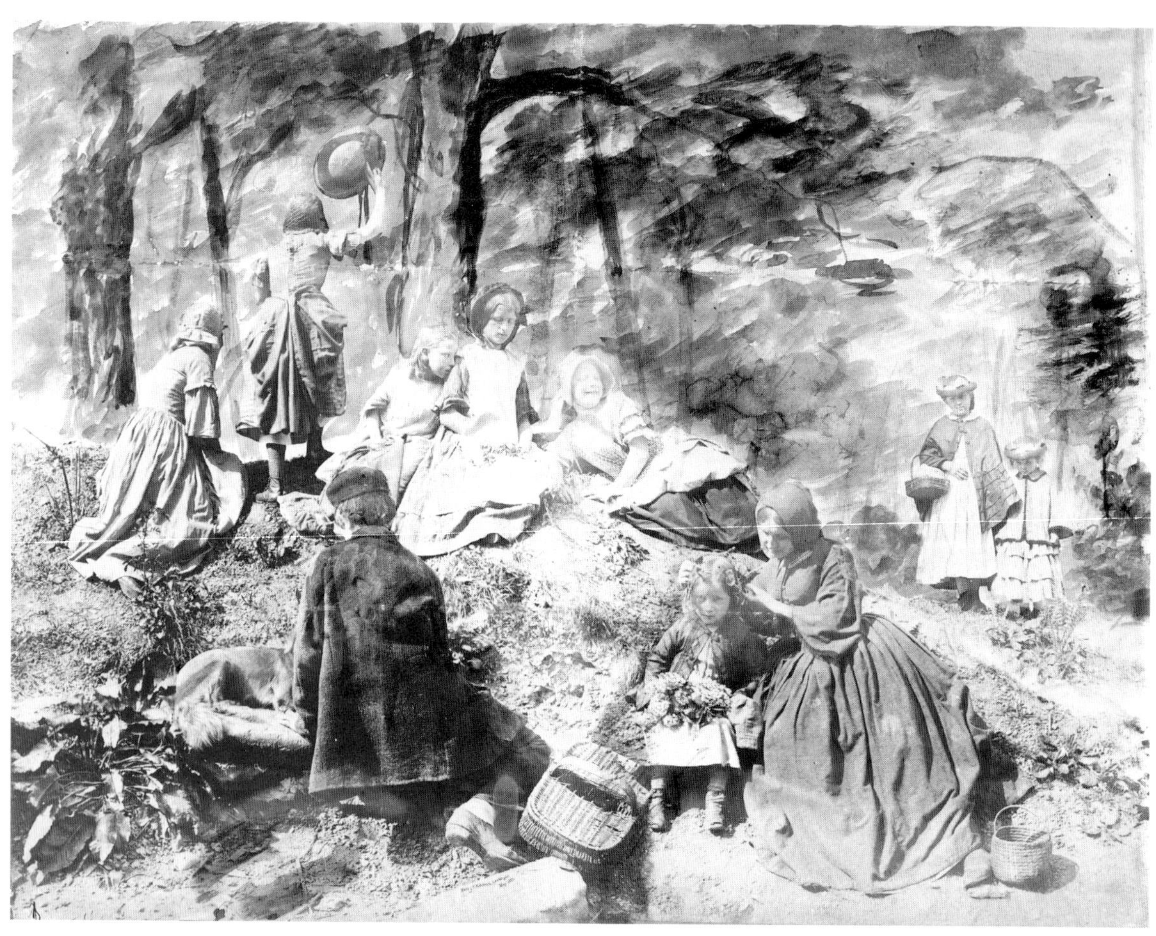

HENRY PEACH ROBINSON, ***Photo sketch,*** (photography with watercolor) for *A Holiday in the Wood,* 1860, University of Texas, Austin.

picture-book to her little girl; lovers in pairs, without end; single figures, also without end; young ladies reading love-letters, or overwhelmed with some piece of ill news just received."[4]

Charles Baudelaire, appraising the British school at the Exposition Universelle (1855), also noted the predilection for intimate glimpses of home. The emphasis on contemporary subjects went back to the peasant paintings of Sir David Wilkie and middle-class scenes of William Mulready, both of whom were admired by Robinson.[5] In the 1850s and 1860s, these already socially critical themes were made even more subversive by allowing the viewer to derive from them a more or less tragic conception of life.

Robinson's *A Cottage Home*, a combination print made from three negatives, evokes feelings of anxiety and misery in the context of household labor. The dog in the foreground suggests exhaustion rather than contentment. Childhood, motherhood, and grandmotherhood are just different stages in a life of total tedium and drudgery.

The most celebrated of Robinson's photographs, *Fading Away*, is said to have as its subject death by tuberculosis, but this intimate glimpse of domestic life may, perhaps, have for its theme a moral as much as a physical disease. This photograph was shown by Robinson the same year that Augustus Egg exhibited at the Royal Academy his three-part painting *Past and Present*[6] which portrayed how a woman's adultery led her to abandon her children and to descend into a life of prostitution. Robinson's photograph, this time composed of five negatives, may allude to a less obvious theme of morbid sexuality. The clue lies in another photograph, based upon the same motif of the dying girl but with a Shakespearean quotation for its title: "She never told her love / But let concealment, like a worm i' the bud, / Feed on her damask cheek." This quotation, from *Twelfth Night* (Act II, Scene 4, lines 112 ff.), refers to Viola's description of unrequited love. The woman pines away from the green and yellow melancholy of unsatisfied love in a patriarchal society which does not allow her to declare her true feelings.

In Robinson's *Fading Away*, the man with his back turned away from the girl allows the viewer to identify him equally as father, husband or lover. He evokes a feeling of repression and guilt in his grief. The fallen flowers and the dying sunset suggest not just death but also sin. The woman evokes in us the disturbing feeling that undeclared love may be the guilty passion eating her from within.

Robinson, who was active in photography for half a century, did not make so unsentimental a picture of such subtle horror again. His later use of the theme of youth and age, the cycle of life

4. C. Dickens, "Book Illustration", in *All the Year Round*, no. 17 (August 10, 1867), p. 151.

5. See M. F. Harker, *Henry Peach Robinson: Master of Photographic Art*, Oxford, Basil Blackwell, 1988.

6. Tate Gallery, London.

made popular by Thomas Faed in genre painting, was masterly in execution, but comparatively conventional in feeling. Dickens said that when it came to genre all too often the extraordinary technical effort and manual skill which went into the making of illustrations was not demanded by the subject at hand. In *Fading Away* it was indeed justified, in Robinson's later composite pictures it was probably not.

If *The Two Ways of Life* was made by Rejlander to put Britain on the international competitive map, *Fading Away* was intended to revive business in Robinson's professional studio which, in 1858, was already failing after it had opened the previous year. Robinson had learned to make composite prints under Rejlander's instruction in London before opening his own studio in Leamington. The composite photograph was an annual exhibition picture which was designed to drum up business.

Robinson succeeded in producing a series of such pictures over the next few years, thus becoming the leading member of the photographic establishment. He was on the council of what later became the Royal Photographic Society for thirty years, until, in 1892, he became a founder member of the Linked Ring. His influential book *Pictorial Effect in Photography* (1869), which went into many editions and was translated into French and German, emphasized how much could be done by photographers to mix the real and the artificial to pictorial effect. Stressing skill and effect rather than emotional intensity and meaning, Robinson ended his life as a founder of an "ism" known only to photography – Pictorialism, the self-conscious making of pictures according to the principles of painting.

Julia Margaret Cameron

Typically, it was the artisan photographer like Robinson who accused Rejlander and Cameron of slovenliness of execution and of failing to produce blemish-free prints. In doing so, however, technically painstaking practitioners misunderstood their intentions as artists. Lewis Carroll, for instance, never understood why Julia Margaret Cameron (1815–1879) wanted not sharp but differential focus. What she was seeking, of course, was Rejlander's sense of "plasticity", a modeled effect which created an expression of feeling rather than a depiction of fact. She was benefiting from Rejlander's art studies to achieve the high drama of Old Master paintings. Long before she took up photography seriously in 1863, Cameron had presented albums and gift books to her many friends. In 1859, she gave one to the Marquis of Lansdowne

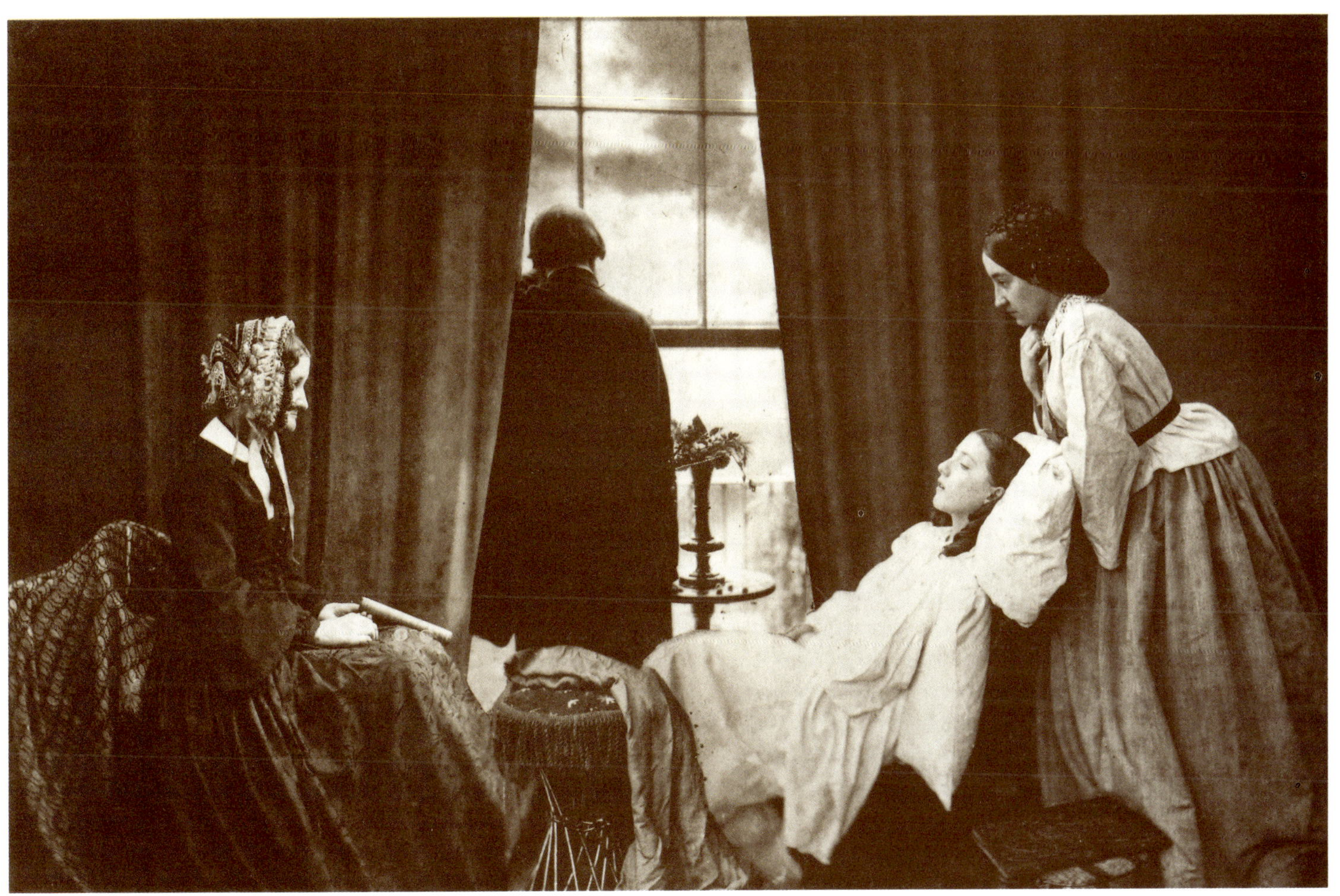

Henry Peach Robinson, *Fading Away*, 1858, Royal Photographic Society, Bath.

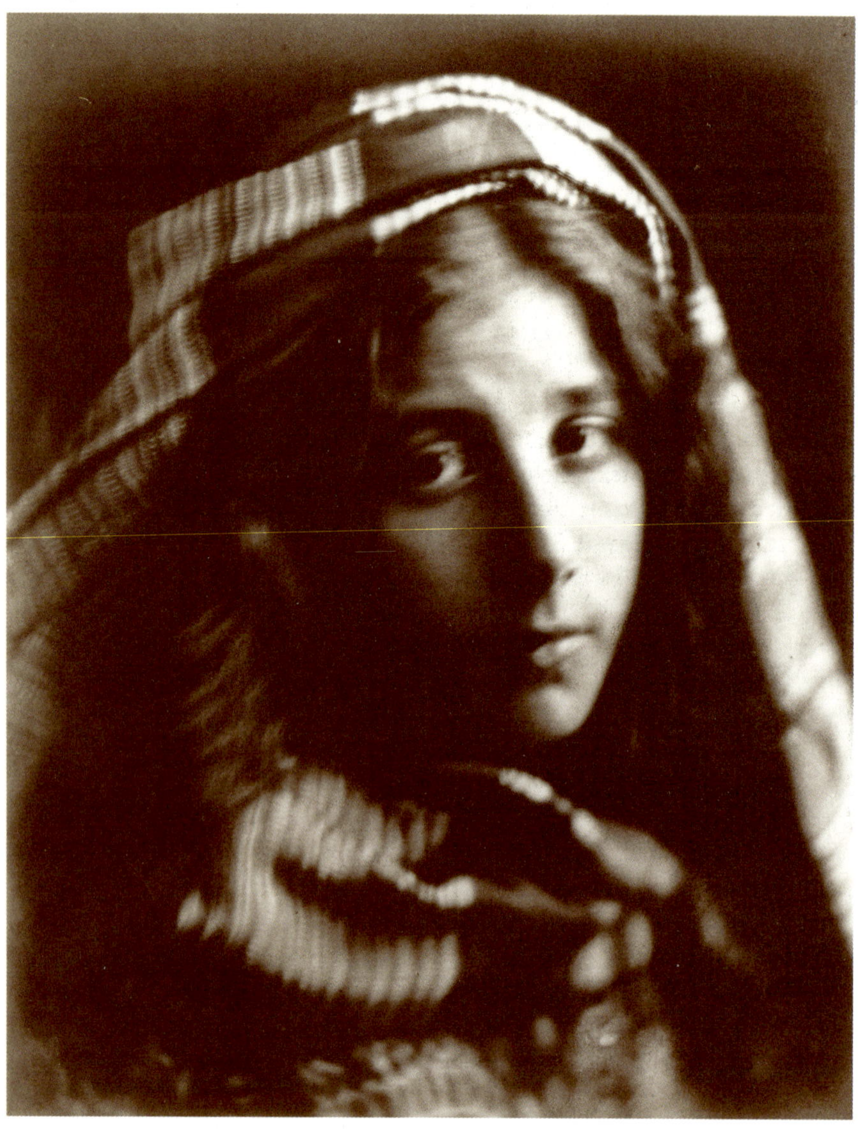

JULIA MARGARET CAMERON,
A Study of the Cenci,
1868,
Maison Victor Hugo, Paris.

which consisted mainly of photographs by Rejlander.

In 1863, Rejlander came to the Isle of Wight to photograph her neighbor Tennyson and it seems likely that she learned her basic technique from him then, when he made genre subjects involving her family and servants. Also on the Isle of Wight was C. Jabez Hughes, who had written on art photography in terms which exactly matched Cameron's intentions: "When deep and earnest minds, seeking to express their ideas of Moral and Religious Beauty, employ High Art Photography, then may we be proud of our glorious art, and of having aided in its elevation."[7]

Secure in her religious beliefs as a High Church Anglican, Cameron thought that religious art was far from dead and could be revived in photography – if only she could strike the right chord. To the Victorian, "art" was technique, "fine art" was expressive but not necessarily ethical, and "high art" was Christian. It was a moral duty for Cameron, therefore, to show people in the light of their potential immortality. John Henry Newman wrote: "Even our friends around are invested with unearthly brightness – no longer imperfect men, but beings taken into Divine favor, stamped with His seal, and in training for future happiness."[8] This reference to stamping with a seal reflected the typological aesthetic of the Victorian period: divine meaning was inherent in every event, and links with the next world were detectable in every person.

For instance, Cameron's *The Return: After Three Days* conflates several episodes in the life of Christ: his youthful disputation with the doctors in the Temple, the presence of the three Marys at his entombment, and his appearance to the same three women at the Resurrection. The focus of the pictures falls on the boy Christ. The flowers, which are out of focus, suggest rather than represent his passion. Flesh and Spirit are thus united in this typological aesthetic.

Cameron, born in Calcutta, was married to Art in the person of a husband who had written a treatise on the sublime and beautiful, and to Science in the person of Sir John Herschel, who had discovered the photographic use of hypo and sent her Talbotypes as early as 1841. In 1848, she returned to Britain with her husband to raise their six children, to read Tennyson and Carlyle, to go to art exhibitions, and to befriend G. F. Watts, the Symbolist painter.

Moral she may have been, puritanical she was not. She acknowledged her husband's recognition (in his treatise) that there are certain qualities in the human figure that arouse sexual desire, although her translation of Gottfried Bürger's *Leonora* (1847) suggests she believed that the will of God should exercise some control over it.[9] Bürger's poem, also translated by Dante Gabriel Rossetti, is about a maiden, who, unreconciled to God's will, receives Death into her arms in the guise of her absent lover. It is a Gothic version of the type of impenitent Magdalene whom Cameron portrayed in the guise of Goethe's Gretchen, Tennyson's May Queen, and Shakespeare's Ophelia.

But in Cameron's time, the penitent Magdalene was considered to be highly privileged, insofar as she was the last to leave Christ on the cross, and the very first to see him in the garden of the Resurrection. Cameron merges her with *The Angel at the Tomb*, a single figure who combines both carnal and heavenly love to become a woman charged with bringing believers to the faith.

The fact that Cameron used the same model in a similar pose in *The Kiss of Peace*, where she has the task of comforting the young Virgin in a scene evoking the subject of the Visitation, confirms her desire to connect the flesh with the spirit in a way which was to an extent subversive of conventional doctrine.

7. C. Jabez Hughes, "Art Photography", in *Photographic News*, no. 7 (February 15, 1861), p. 60.

8. Cited in G. B. Tennyson, *Victorian Devotional Poetry*, London, Harvard University Press, 1981, p. 41.

9. For Cameron's translation, see M. Weaver, *Julia Margaret Cameron 1815–1879*, London, Herbert Press, 1984.

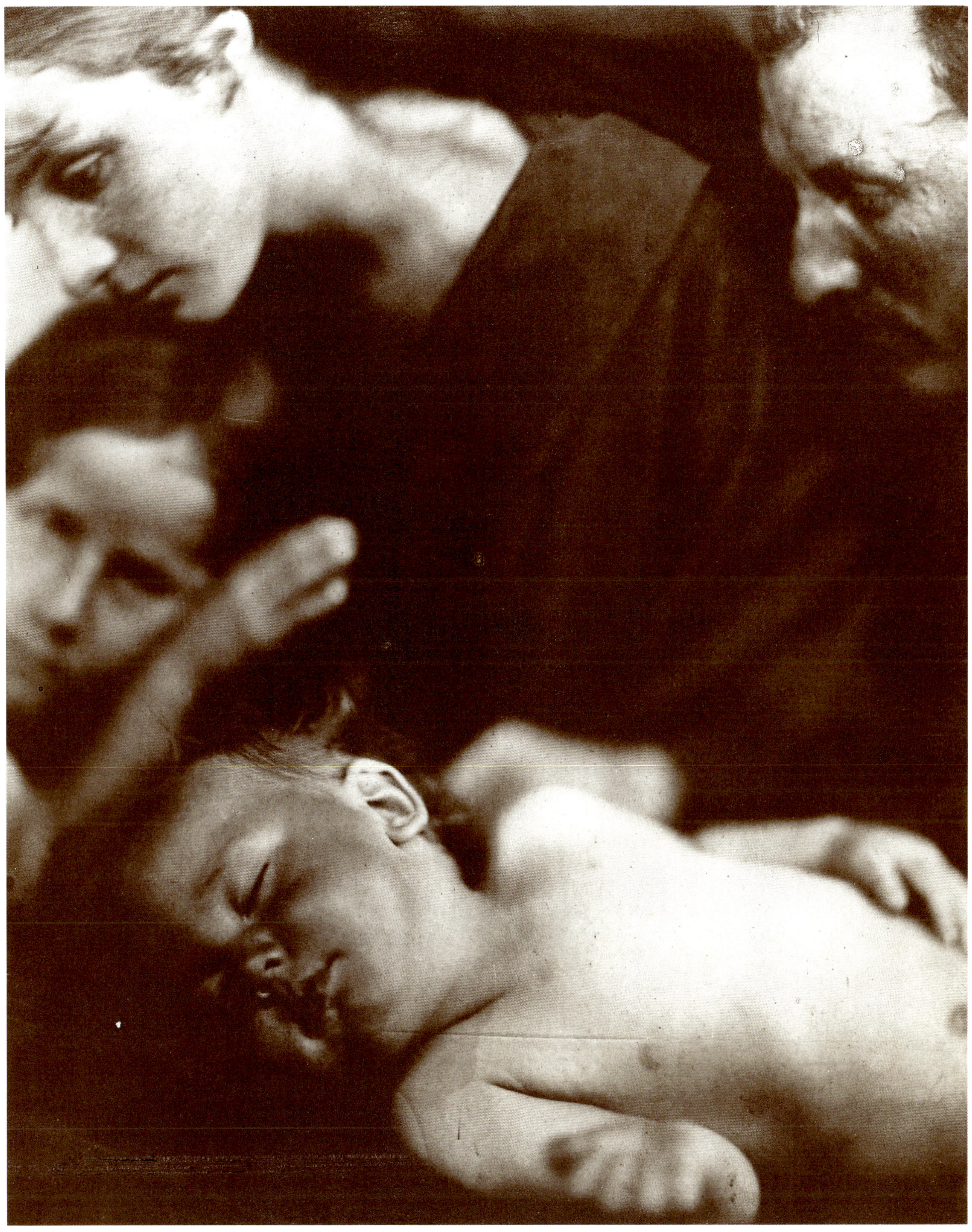

Julia Margaret Cameron,
Prayer and Praise,
1865,
John Paul Getty Museum,
Malibu.

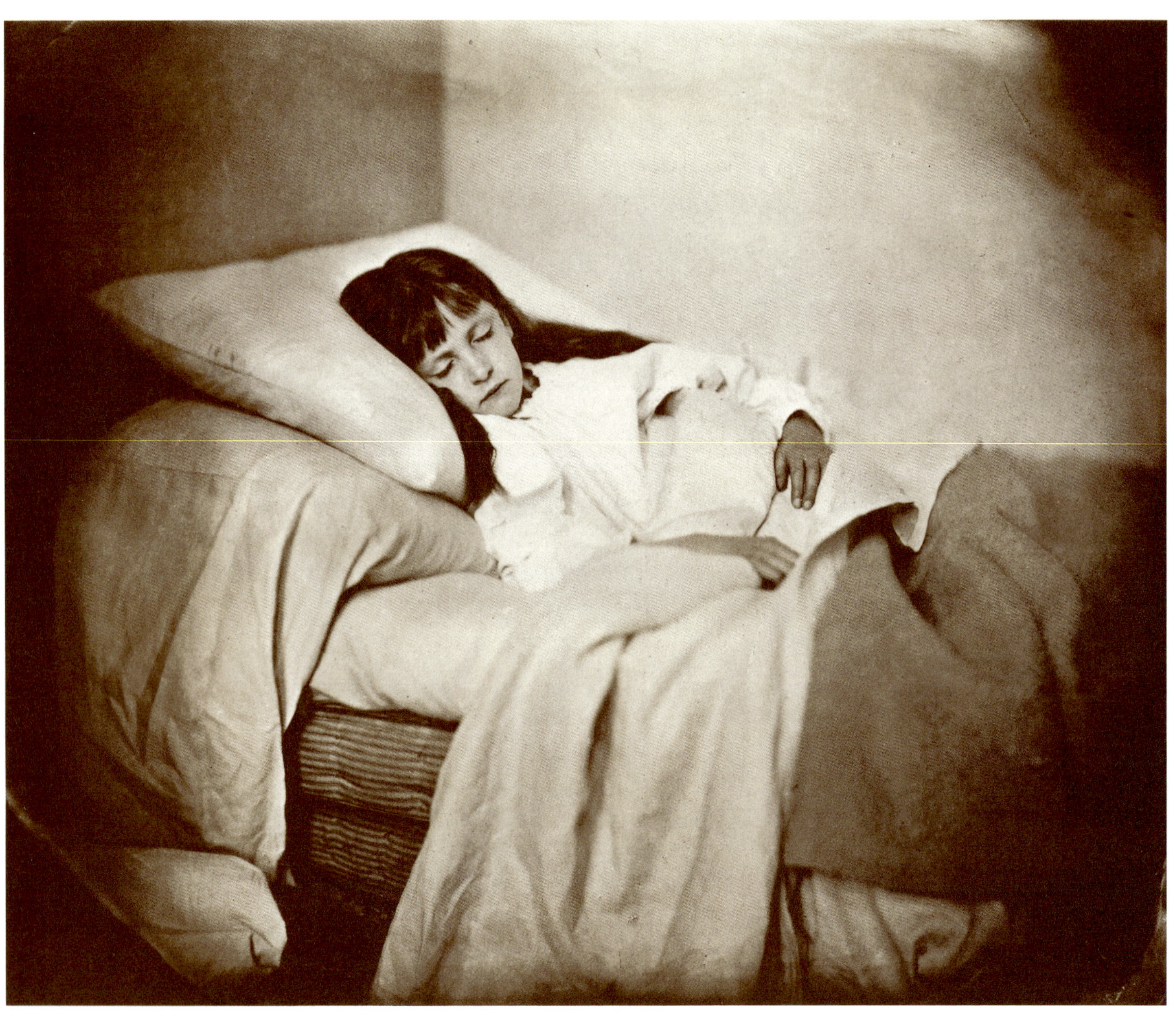

LEWIS CARROLL,
Xie Kitchin Asleep,
1873,
University of Texas, Austin.

It was this boldness of interpretation and confidence in treating a difficult subject which made Cameron not merely derivative as an artist. She created a style in which she could work out her cultural conflicts visually, and so offer imaginative solutions to moral and religious questions.

Her most dangerous venture into the realm of Christian psychology is found in her portrait of a man of Mediterranean type with lowered eyes and several days' growth of beard. Feelings of mental pain rather than physical suffering are expressed in the downcast eyes which suggest an interior state of resentment as well as resignation. It comes as a surprise to discover that this image, with its startling resemblance to Domenico Fetti's painting of the face of Christ with lowered eyes,[10] is entitled *Iago: Study from an Italian*; it seems to depict an *Ecce Homo* or Man of Sorrows. The absence of a bloody crown of thorns does nothing to divert us from this profound typological impression. But in giving her photograph a Shakespearean title Cameron opted for artistic discretion and theological reserve. Such an image in paint would have been troubling enough to an age which preferred Christ meek and mild, even in his suffering, but to portray him at such a moment of emotional intensity in such an ambiguous way was sheer heresy – the smashing of a shibboleth. To do it in the most incarnational of all mediums, photography, was to break the ultimate taboo of depicting the Messiah naturalistically.

Yet her title revealed as much as it concealed. Iago and Othello are as indissolubly linked as complementary figures, as Christ and Judas – the Judas who grimly fulfilled Christ's destiny, and so earned, perhaps, a place in the Christian mystery comparable with that of Mary Magdalene.

Between 1870 and 75, Cameron sent twenty-eight of her photographs to Victor Hugo. Among them were two of the three or more art studies she

10. National Gallery of Art, Washington.

11. *Hommage de Julia Margaret Cameron à Victor Hugo*, Paris, Maison de Victor Hugo, 1980, p. 19.

12. J. M. Bruson, *ibid.*

made of the story of Beatrice Cenci who committed incest with her father, conspired with her mother to kill him, and was martyred for both "crimes". Derived though the theme was from a painting attributed in her time to Guido Reni, Cameron's versions far excel the original in psychological insight and artistic treatment. As Jean-Marie Bruson has commented: "In the midst of the flowing mass of hair and drapery, the still child-like face, skillfully modeled by the softest of lights and bathed in dreamlike soft-focus, seems to quiver with pent-up emotion, marvelously expressing the distress of the young girl weighed down by destiny."[11] This compassionate – even sympathetic – attitude towards those who commit sin is one which appealed to the Symbolists later in the century.

Cameron's was a luminous and visionary art of photography, pursued against the positivistic tendency of the day. She rejected the meticulously observed and highly defined detail of the artisan photographers, yet there was nothing eccentric or amateur in her approach. The financial plight of her family at the time when she began to work at her photography was so acute that it must have taken an incredible act of will to launch herself into a field where few women had a place. Her astonishing energy and boldness carried her through all difficulties, even if she did not make the living she had hoped for. When she returned to the East in 1875, to die in Ceylon in 1879, it was because her family was utterly penniless. This remarkable woman, with enough Indian blood on the French side of the family and enough of an education in France to make her different from the ordinary Englishwoman, was a radical conservative like Rejlander, who also came from an unconventional origin. They both believed in the Old Masters but, in Cameron's case especially, they managed to transform art studies into pictures completely expressive in their own right.

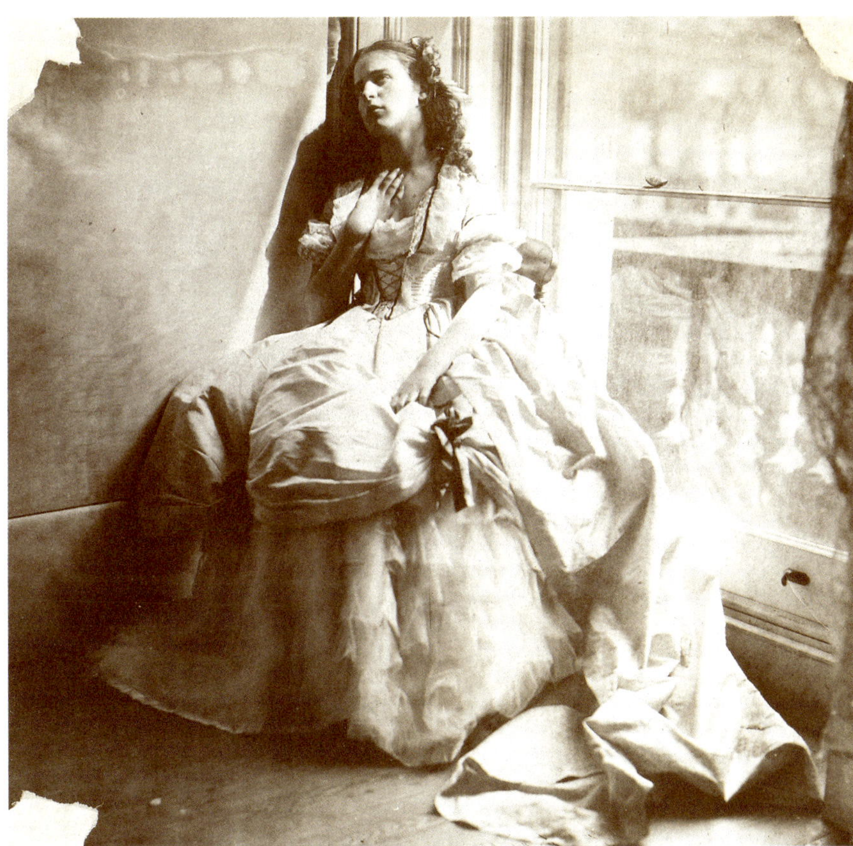

Lady Clementina Hawarden,
Study,
circa 1863,
Victoria and Albert Museum, London.

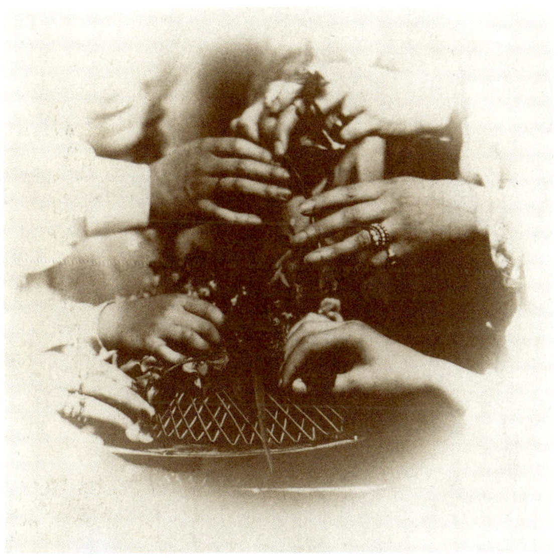

◀ Nevil Story-Maskelyne,
Hands,
circa 1855,
Hans P. Kraus Jr. Collection.

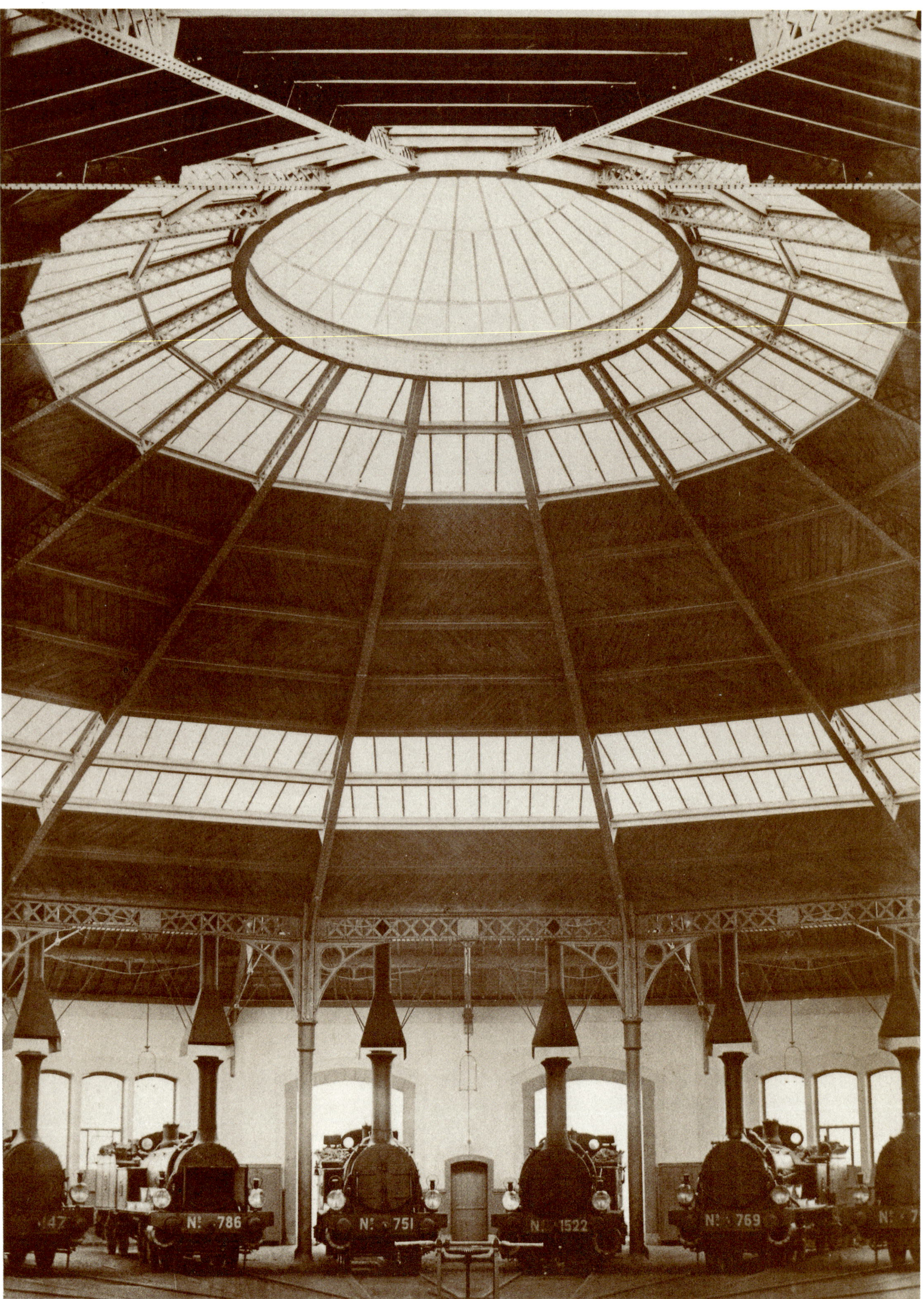
N° 786
N° 751
N° 1522
N° 769

THE URBAN MACHINE

11

Architecture and industry

Elvire Perego

In Renaissance Italy, as in antiquity, the words *machine* and *edifice* meant the same thing. In fact, *edifice* was often applied to a war-machine or hydraulic apparatus, the framework of which looked like a building, whereas *machine* was also used for architectural works – for example, Milan Cathedral or Brunelleschi's dome in Florence Cathedral.[1] This observation opens our eyes to the all-powerful nature of technology, the mechanistic principle within those intellectual creations, machines, and constructions. It also provides an intriguing point of departure for research into the two-fold influence of mechanization in the nineteenth century, via what lies behind the photographic lens – the *camera obscura*.

"The invention of photography has produced a revolution in art quite as great as that which the invention of railways has produced in industry."[2] Such was the opinion of one contemporary, the painter Alfred Stevens, who, even at that time (1886), was able to grasp and put into context, through metaphor and aphorism, the still unconscious relationship between technology and sensibility.

It might be argued that this was simply a case of coincidence, but in fact it was a genuine case of two methodologies running in parallel – a "synchronicity" converging in a creative process which evolved almost in secret. Indeed, during the nineteenth century, the feelings aroused by technological progress only rarely found symbolic expression in official art. In the world of artistic representation, it fell to a parallel medium, the still marginal one of photography, to call attention to the products of industry and of architecture in metal. Between the two, the first fruits of our modern culture, we find a deep-lying relationship, a partnership which laid the foundations for a decisive optical revolution which allowed us to understand a new concept of space.

The photographer, therefore, played the role, readily attributed to artists, of mediator between the outside world (that is, the new fields of perception) and contemporary society. Photographers very different from one other but all engaged in genuinely inquiring and inventive work gradually opened the way, unseen by the public and outside academic circles, to new ways of seeing.

Some bodies of work are striking for their sense of space and the aesthetic they derived from it. Some, frequently of astonishing visionary quality, were the work of artists who were under-valued at the time, or even until quite recently anonymous and forgotten.

◀ August Collard, *Locomotive Shed of the Bourbonnais Railway,* Nevers, circa 1860, International Museum of Photography, George Eastman House, Rochester.

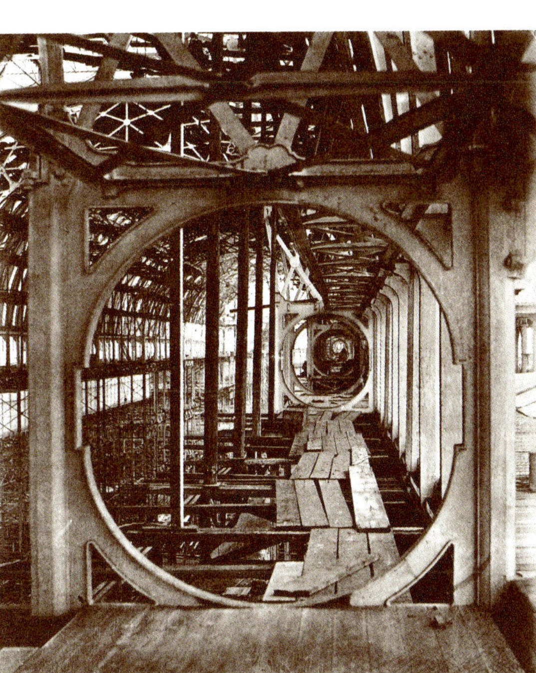

Philip Henry Delamotte, *Interior of the Crystal Palace,* 1853–1854, Metropolitan Museum of Art, New York.

1. C. Pedretti, *Léonard de Vinci Architecte,* Paris, Electa Moniteur, 1983, p. 309.

2. A. Stevens, *Impressions sur la Peinture,* Paris, 1886, p. 32.

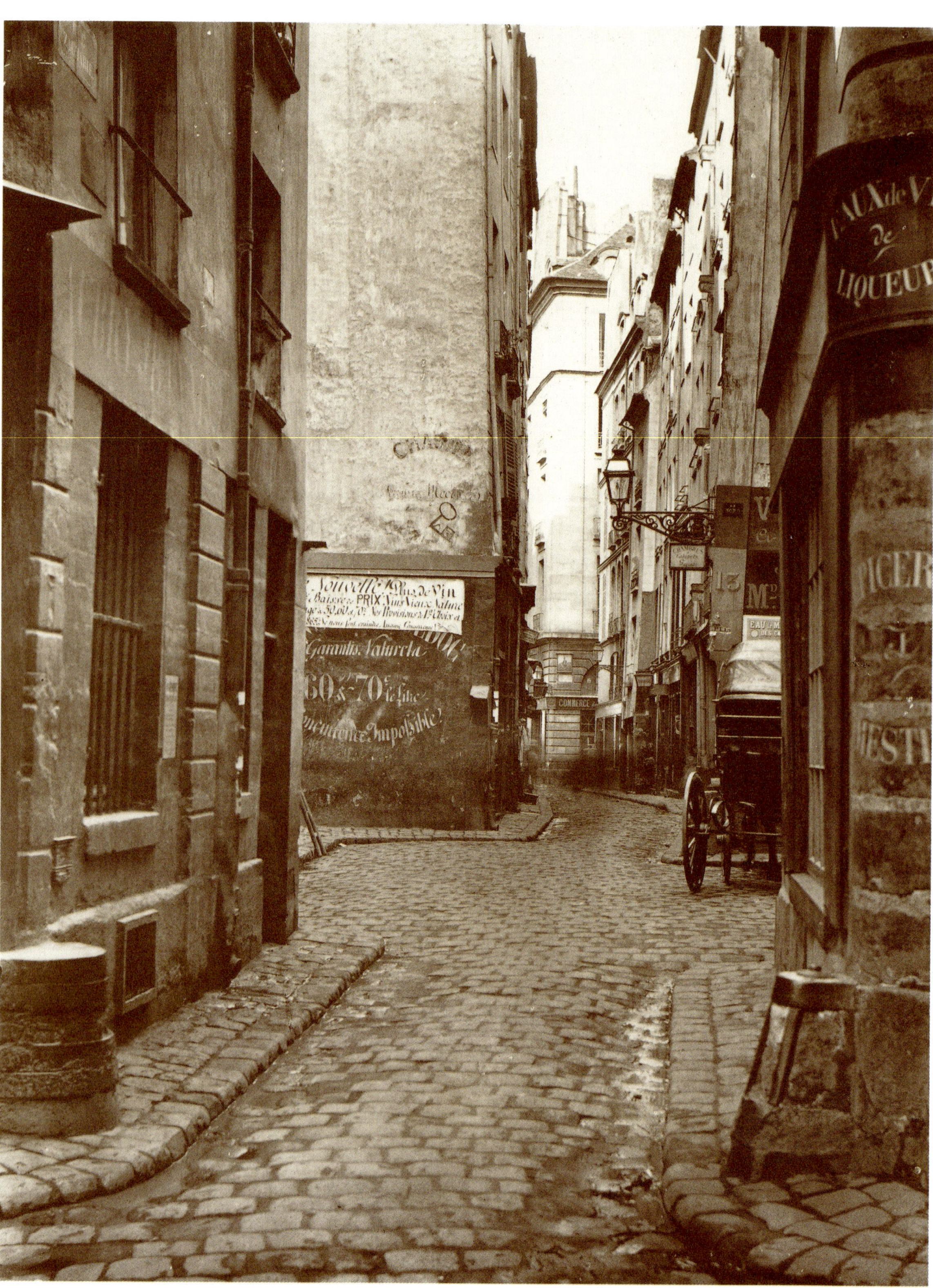

CHARLES MARVILLE, *Rue Zacharie, from Rue Saint-Séverin,* Paris, 1860s.

This new generation of photographers (Delamotte, Marville, Baldus, Collard, the Bisson brothers, Delmaet and Durandelle) came on the scene in the years 1850–1890. They got to know the professional circuits for public and private commissions, and also new construction materials and methods. They combined the two, and from this alliance was born what we call modern art – long before the works of fine art conceived by avant-garde artists around 1910. The artistic imagination in this way gained access to new horizons.

The metamorphoses of the city

Chronologically, the transformation of Paris, "the capital of the nineteenth century",[3] happened at the height of railway mania. Between 1850 and 1870, Paris suddenly became the archetypal Great City of the second half of the nineteenth century, the metropolis of the industrial age. In no other city at this time did the upheavals produced by industrial development manifest themselves with such force. Haussmann was the man of the Second Empire. His first

3. W. Benjamin, *Das Passagen-Werk* (= Gesammelte Schriften, Vol. V.1), Frankfurt am Main, 1982, pp. 45-59.

principle was "to disencumber large buildings, palaces and barracks in such a way as to make them more pleasing to the eye and afford easier access on days of celebration and a simplified defense in time of riot."[4] His second principle was the improvement of sanitary conditions in the city by systematically demolishing the filthy medieval alleyways which were breeding grounds of infectious disease. Thanks to photography, which "had turned itself into the permanent adjunct of History",[5] Haussmann took up the ideas of his time to their fullest extent, writing to the Emperor in 1865: "Under my administration the city has assumed the task of remaining constantly in touch with every effort of the contemporary mind. The history of the capital remains still to be made."[6] In 1865 this was his aim when he set up the *Travaux historiques* – a municipal commission composed of councillors and experts, who appointed the photographer Charles Marville to take "before and after" pictures recording the transformation of the city which Haussmann was going to turn into "the most splendid and salubrious of European capitals."[7]

People who admire Marville's work today share the view expressed by Nadar [8] that the quintessence of that work is the body of photographs produced for the bureaucrats of his day. Marville is the only person of that time to have left to the municipality such a large and important body of photographs: around 900 plates, in a format slightly smaller than 30 x 40 cm, mostly collodion, conserved today almost in their entirety at the Bibliothèque Historique de la Ville de Paris. These undated photographs were taken over a period of at least twenty years, from 1858 to 1878, the probable date of the photographer's death. Marville often got in just before the demolition-men. Thanks to his work, many aspects of the old Paris and the new city in the making were recorded for posterity. Marville explored both the geographical aspect of the enterprise and its topographical impact. From the construction of the Grandes Halles – Baltard's "umbrellas" – to the destruction of the little streets in front of the Hôtel de Ville, from the eruption of the Place du Châtelet and the Opéra de Paris to the creation of the Bois de Boulogne and green spaces like the Parc Montsouris and the Buttes-Chaumont, from the opening up of the twelve avenues that radiate out from the Étoile to the gutting of the Île de la Cité and the Latin Quarter, Marville's images are full of meaning for the sociology of the Great City. This determination to capture and record the metamorphoses of the city evinces support for a hitherto unrivalled scheme of urban renewal. It also testifies to a political intent, promoting the greater glory of the Second Empire.

With the full-scale emergence of the modern city, there arose the idea of a perfect match between the city and the photographic style with which it was documented, a style totally dedicated to the "cult of the axis" as the ordering principle of urbanism and thus of the formal structure of the photographic approach. Marville enumerates, highlights, "crystallizes" the checker-board layout of the streets, the roadways often bisected

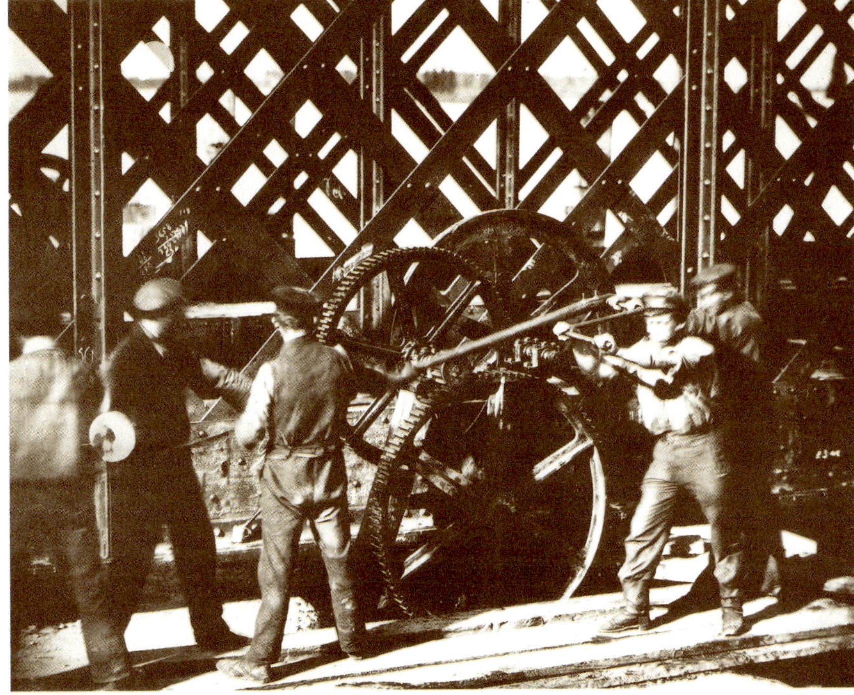

Charles Winter,
Construction of the Railway Bridge over the Rhine,
1860,
Cabinet des Estampes,
Musées de Strasbourg

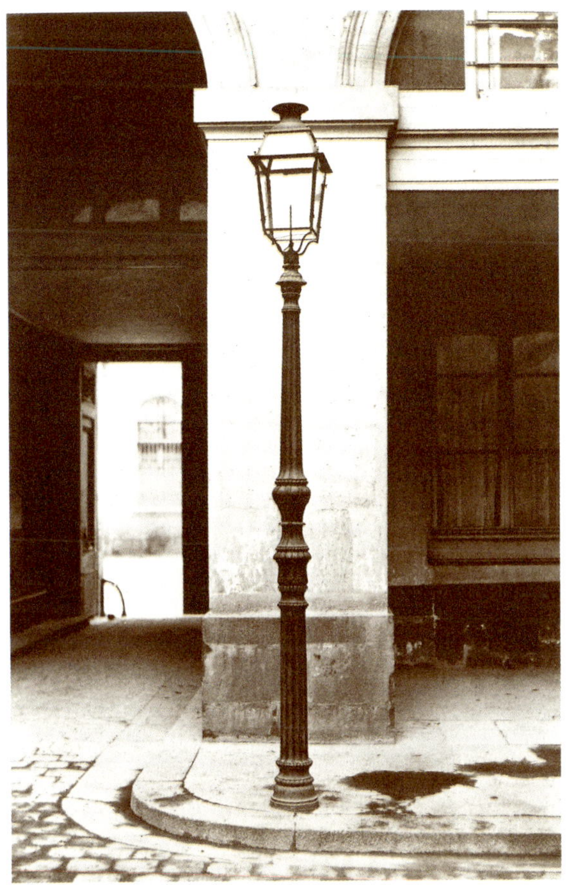

◀ Charles Marville,
Lamppost in the Palais-Royal area,
1860s,
Bibliothèque Administrative de la Ville de Paris.

4. See G.-E. Haussmann, *Mémoires*, Paris, 1890–1893. This policy is summed up in E.-M. Bouillat, *Georges-Eugene Haussmann*, Paris, 1901, pp. 8–9. Quoted by S. Giedion in *Space, Time, and Architecture*, Harvard University Press, 1941, p. 648.

5. In *La Lumière*, 21 June 1856, p. 97.

6. Quoted by M. de Thézy, *Charles Marville, Photographe de Paris de 1851 à 1879*, exhibition catalogue. Bibliothèque Historique de la Ville de Paris, 21 November 1980–31 January 1981, p. 18.

7. Napoleon III, letter, quoted by L. M. Tisserand, in *Introduction à l'Histoire Générale de Paris*, Paris, Imprimerie Impériale, 1866, p.13.

8. Nadar, *Quand J'étais Photographe*, Paris, Flammarion, 1899, p.209; repr., New York, Arno Press, 1979.

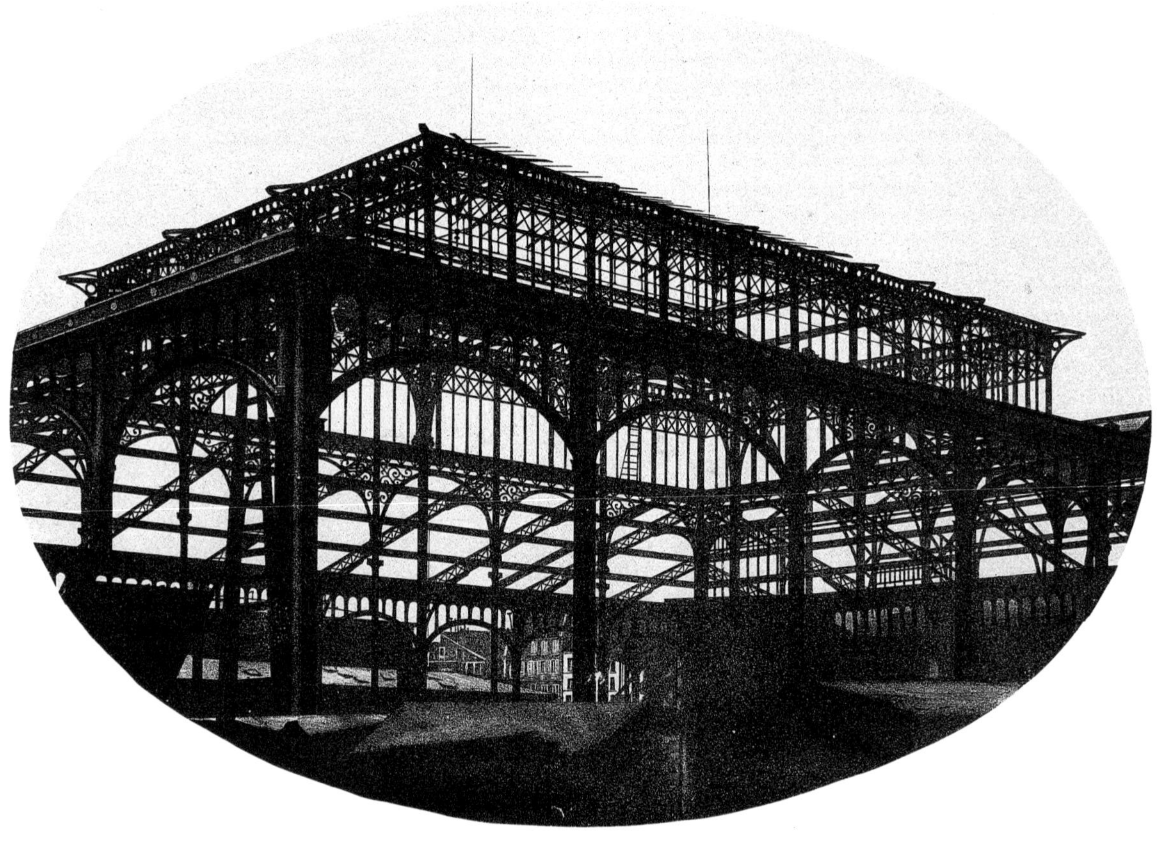

Les Halles, Paris, photolithograph produced by the POITEVIN process, 1857, plate from *Revue Générale de l'Architecture et des Travaux Publics.*

down the middle by a drain. He links all these disparate segments which intercut one another in an alternating pattern of displacement to the side and static central framing: a monumental accentuation of angles which, as Marie de Thézy, one of the most perceptive students of his work, has pointed out, recalls an upside-down version of the letter "L" in ornate lithographic printing.[9] His topographical investigations went ever further, beyond the modeling of vertical and rectangular planes, to the point where the slightest unevenness or slope at the sides of a street or a crossroads is made meaningful.

And yet, despite being described in their time as "administrative views",[10] these unpretentious photographs, with their great economy of means and their austere forms, conjure up before our eyes what Benjamin called "the malaise and the aura" of the romantic Paris of cheap popular fiction, haunted by the literary specters of novelists and poets, from Balzac to Ponson du Terrail. Marville had, for Paris, as Dickens had for London, "in the most serious and time-honored sense *the key of the street* [...] His earth was the paving-stones, his stars were the lamps of the street".[11] Well before Atget, the Futurists, and the Surrealists, Marville was able to find – perhaps unknowingly, by a methodical, analytic approach – an urban poetry. Behind its obsessive exactness, behind its illustrative vision, the city constituted a system of signs: "This intoxication with latent memories which accompanies the flaneur around the town (and is not the photographer the flaneur par excellence?) feeds not only on what is perceptible to sight, but on simple knowledge and inert data, which it transforms into lived experience."[12] The layout of the city, its topographical slippage, roads that move, names that move, crossroads, boundary-stones, doorways, "pavement architecture", flagstones, gas lamps, signs, fronts of buildings, fountains, urinals, inscriptions, door-plates, black lettering, numbers of apartment-blocks, "this kind of optical and phonetic image of the city", might correspond to that "phenomenon of being in a spatial box of tricks [...] where the mystery resides in always being in an equivocal situation, in double and triple reflections of barely glimpsed reflections (images within images), forms which are going to exist or will exist according to the mind of the observer. Suggestive, but more, because these things actually appear."[13] The power of the image turns a tour of the city into a revelation of the secret meaning of objects, of the communal subconscious of beings and things, which reinforces the mental experience of the past, not only through the surface of things, but as an interiorized relationship, an internal evocation. One becomes aware of the historic atmosphere with which the city is impregnated; one becomes familiar, by mutual interaction, with the spirit of place, with the details and the stylistic traces of an age gone by.

9. M. de Thézy, "Marville et la Naissance du Paris d'Haussmann", in *Actes du Colloque Atget*, Collège de France, 14–15 June 1985, special number of the review *Photographies*, March 1986, pp. 46–51.

10. *Bulletin de la Société française de Photographie*, 1875, p.269.

11. G. K. Chesterton, *Dickens* (Lives of Famous Men no. 9), quoted by W. Benjamin, *op. cit.*, p.455.

12. W. Benjamin, *op. cit.*, p. 525.

13. O. Redon, quoted by Raymond Escholier, "Artiste", in *Arts et Métiers Graphiques*, 11 June 1935, no. 47, p. 7, quoted by W. Benjamin, *op.cit.*, p. 447.

The constructors

Thanks to photography, the century of the machine cult gave rise to a modern poetry of the city: a veritable introductory course in ways of seeing. If modernity, in the sense in which Baudelaire understood it, consisted of "drawing the eternal from the transitory",[14] the result, for a new generation of photographers who could be called the "constructors", was to open up poetry to the forms created by a technological civilization. Although the word *modernity*, meaning the characteristic of being modern, appears in Balzac in 1823, before being coined in the accepted sense by Baudelaire, and the word *modernism*, in the sense of a particular taste (usually judged to be excessive) appears in Huysmans on the occasion of the 1879 Salon, the adjective *modern* is much older, according to the philosopher Hans Robert Jauss, who has traced its history, pointing out that *modernus*, which is derived from the word *modo* in low Latin, meaning "now, just now, recently", designates not that which is new, but that which is present, current, contemporary with the speaker.[15]

In the nineteenth century, engineering constructions – pavilions at exhibitions, bridges, stations, factories, department stores – allowed tendencies which had only a latent existence in the architecture of the period to find expression through the most contemporary, the most truly modern artistic medium, photography. In studying the developing relationship between photography and architecture, we see motifs emerging which were the springboard for a renewal in artistic creation upon which our modernity is based.

The year 1851, a turning-point in more than one respect in the history of photography, saw the

Joseph Albert,
Glaspalast, Munich
after 1861,
Stadtmuseum, Munich.
▼

14. C. Baudelaire, "The Painter of Modern Life", in *Baudelaire: Selected Writings on Art and Literature*, trans. with an introduction by P. E. Charvet, London, Penguin Books, 1992, p. 410.

15. See, on this subject, H. R. Jauss, *Toward an Aesthetic of Reception*, introduction by Paul de Man, translated from the German by Timothy Bahti, Brighton, Harvester Press, 1982, and A. Compagnon, *Les Cinq Paradoxes de la Modernité*, Paris, Éd. du Seuil, 1990.

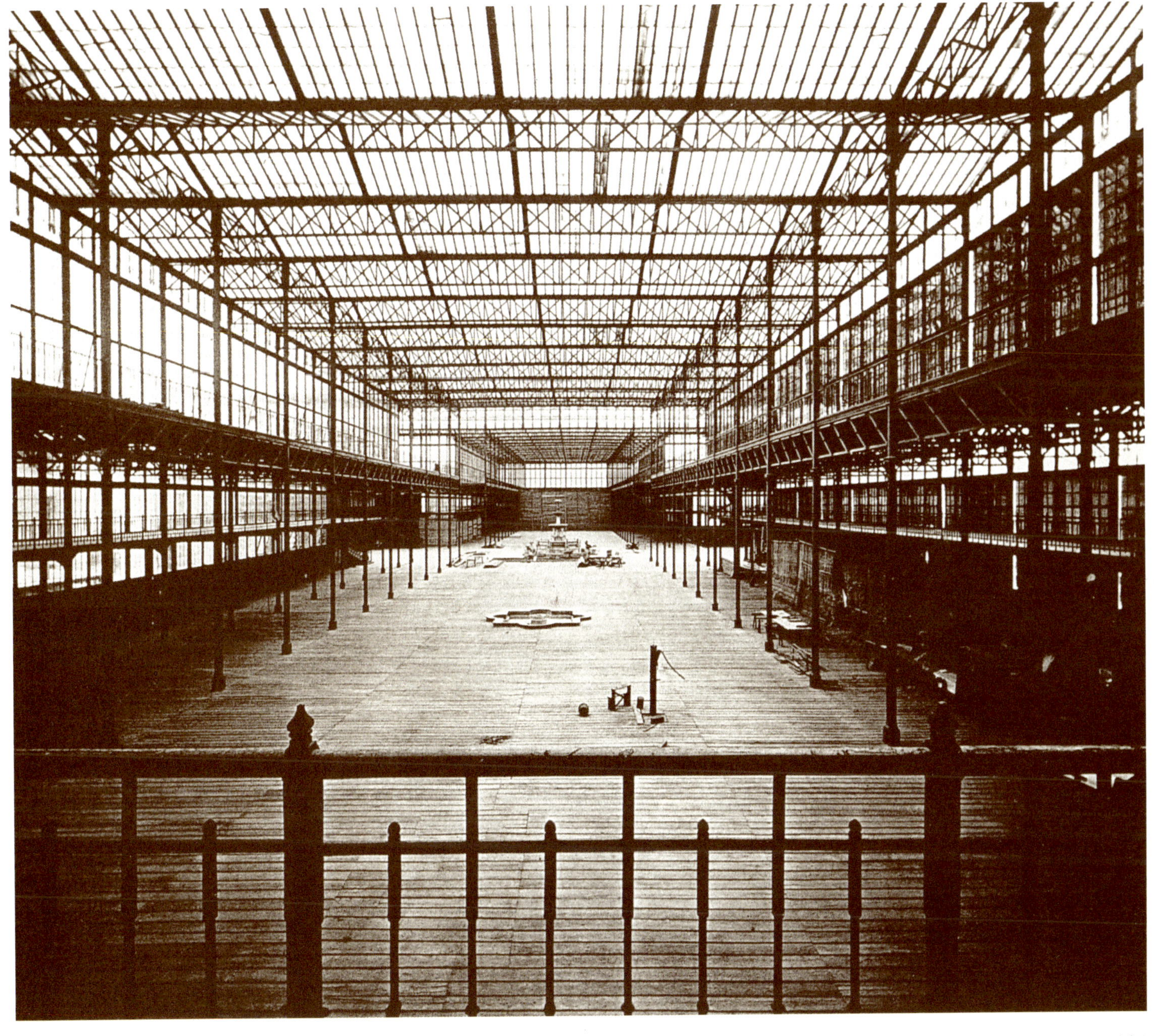

The vogue for international exhibitions

The first exhibition described as *industrial* dates only from the eighteenth century, in Prague in 1791. It gave François de Neufchâteau, Minister of the Interior under the Directory, the idea of creating "an annual public exhibition of the fruits of French industry" (ministerial circular of 7 Fructidor, Year Six) to stimulate competition among French industrialists in order to "strike the most deadly blow to British industry". It was economic rivalry with Britain that pushed France to play a decisive role in the expansion of exhibitions – regional, national or international, particularly during the second half of the nineteenth century.

From 1855 to 1900, five universal exhibitions linking the fine arts and industry took place one after the other in Paris, in the area round the Champ-de-Mars, though it was actually the city of London which saw the inauguration, in 1851, of the first of these new "world fairs". As the historian Madeleine Reberioux proves, France was the "uncontested leader of the exhibitionary phenomenon". These great exhibitions resulted from a laissez-faire economic concept: free-exchange, free circulation, and improvement of production and profit, thanks to free competition, in a spirit of Saint-Simon positivism.

From this point of view, the advantage of these protean manifestations was incontestable, as they gave the widest possible publicity to the technological transformations that were taking place. The concentration in one place of all the discoveries of the century attracted a vast cosmopolitan crowd of visitors. The highly effective system of awards and the extremely detailed reports published by the administrative boards of the various organizing countries show that people were fully aware of their importance.

Exhibitors rivaled one another in the boldness of their concepts in all areas, particularly that of architecture. "A new, ephemeral city, hidden within the other", as Paul Morand wrote. Universal exhibitions were frequently sited in capital cities: London (1851, 1862, 1871, 1874), Paris (1855, 1867, 1878, 1889, 1900), Vienna (1873), Sydney (1879), Amsterdam, (1883), Brussels (1888, 1897, 1910). Other cities, too, were also keen to enhance their status by attracting international crowds: Philadelphia (1876), Melbourne (1880), Antwerp (1885), Barcelona (1888), Chicago (1893), St. Louis (1904), Liège (1905), Milan (1906), and San Francisco (1915).

The history of the nineteenth-century exhibitions merges with that of construction using iron and steel. The fact that people were obliged to put up both main exhibition buildings and national pavilions – which were intended only for temporary use – in record time, favored the experimental use of iron and numerous other building materials. Some of these edifices were grandiose, like Paxton's Crystal Palace or Dutert and Contamine's Galerie des Machines, others were more picturesque and eccentric (the search for novelty provoked the temptation to indulge in exotic, pastiche, kitsch, and eye-catching effects). Most of them have now disappeared. Architects with temperaments as different as Le Play, Krantz, Eiffel, Pavillée, Garnier, Sullivan, Norman Shaw, Redgrave, Saarinen, Ruprich-Robert, Sédille, Lavirotte, Sauvage, Bouwens, Lecoeur, Granet, Laloux, Mewes, Girault, and Umbdenstock willingly lent their talents to this short-term "exhibition architecture".

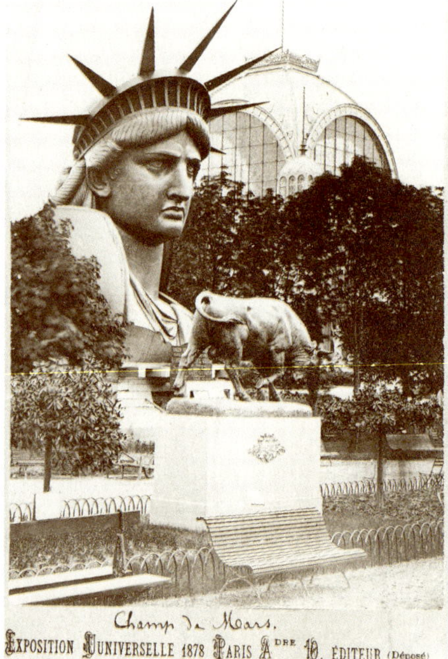

Pierre Petit,
Paris International Exhibition,
1878.

A great deal of photographic work bears witness to this privileged moment when architecture was so closely linked to industrial development. Among others, we might note Baron Gros, P. H. Delamotte (Crystal Palace, 1851–1855), C. Thurston Thompson and R. J. Bingham (Paris, 1855), the Bisson brothers and Pierre Petit (Paris, 1867, 1878, 1889), Sir Charles Dilke (London 1862), Josef Albert and Voigtlander (Vienna, 1873), Durandelle and Chevojon (Paris, 1889), and C. D. Arnold (Chicago, 1893).

We must not forget the hundreds of amateur snapshots taken by the writer Émile Zola (Paris 1900), who talked about a battle of the exhibitions raging in the nineteenth century, the "neurosis of the great bazaars", and the "symphony of exhibitions"; stating in his writings that "to show is the crucial issue".[1] Flaubert, for his part, noted in his *Dictionnaire des Idées Reçues*: "Exhibition: subject of frenzy in the nineteenth century".

Elvire Perego

1. Philippe Hamon, *Expositions, Littérature et Architecture au dix-neuvième Siècle*, Paris, José Corti, 1989.

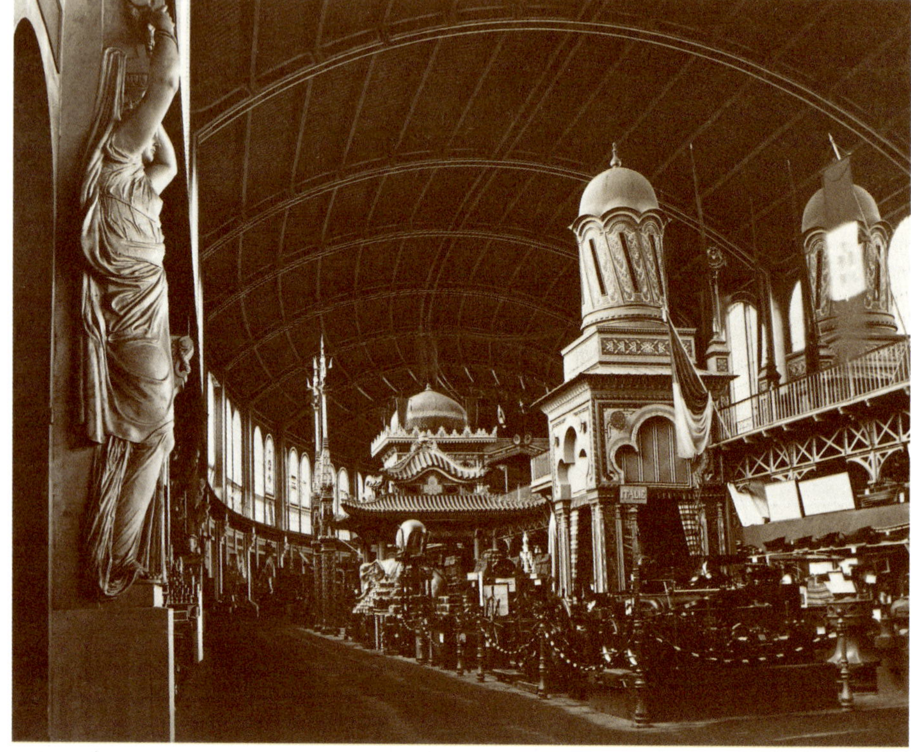

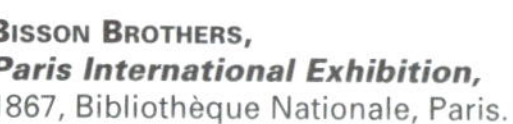

Bisson Brothers,
Paris International Exhibition,
1867, Bibliothèque Nationale, Paris.

first commission from an official source in France: the Heliographic Mission ordered by the Commission des Monuments Historiques. Photographers Le Gray, Mestral, Baldus, Le Secq and Bayard were commissioned to produce a record of the most important historic monuments all around the country. From this point on, the "photographic view" became the center of a complex network of sensations, memories, knowledge, a visual thesaurus of anything that might excite human curiosity. The didactic point of view at first joined, and then gradually replaced, the act of simple contemplation and the evocation of the past with its architectural heritage, a heritage endowed with all the qualities of beauty, durability, prestige, serenity of location, and symbolic force. The vestiges of older times were confronted by the hum of industrial and commercial activity.

The first example was an album published in 1855 in Britain – the cradle of the industrial revolution – by Philip Henry Delamotte, devoted to the rebuilding of the Crystal Palace at Sydenham, and considered to be the most complete album of its kind. Lothar Bucher, who was living in London at the time, and who later became Bismarck's right-hand man at the foreign office, described his impression of the Crystal Palace: "We see a delicate network of lines without any clue to judge their distance from the eye or the real size. The side walls are too far apart to be embraced in a single glance. Instead of moving from the wall at one end to that at the other, the eye sweeps along an unending perspective which fades into the horizon. We cannot tell if this structure towers a hundred or a thousand feet above us, or whether the roof is flat or built up from a succession of ridges, for there is no play of shadows to enable our optic nerves to gauge the measurements. If we let our gaze travel downwards it encounters blue-painted lattice girders. At first these occur only at wide intervals, then they range closer and closer together until they are interrupted by a dazzling band of light – the transept – which dissolves into a distant background where all materiality is blended into the atmosphere[...] It is sober economy of language if I call the spectacle incomparable and fairy-like. It is a midsummer night's dream seen in the clear light of midday."[16]

The Crystal Palace translated an unheard-of concept of construction into physical form. Its maker, the landscape-gardener Joseph Paxton, who was more used to dealing with landscape than with machines, gave it a frame of cast and wrought iron, assembled with the greatest precision on the stepped-roof principle. It was also the first building in glass, wood, and iron "of such romantic beauty that reproductions of it were soon hanging on cottage walls in remote German villages".[17] Philip Henry Delamotte's album was the starting point for a new style, a revolution in architectural photography. It shows that already at this time it was realized that what was needed was not so much to enclose space but to liberate it. These structures contributed to the lightening effect that was to take hold of architecture in general. A new emotion arose, in keeping with the brightness of this sculptured space, the harmony created by the magical effects of those "impossible fluids" light and space.[18]

In the second half of the century, optical analysis attained a previously unknown degree of precision. The visual complexity of architecture invited the photographer to take both a panoramic and a perpendicular sweep. A full understanding of the architecture necessitated a study of the vertical, and the photographer's spellbound gaze reeled under its vertiginous transparency. Iron and glass were the two materials whose conjuncture led the architects of the nineteenth century towards new solutions. The

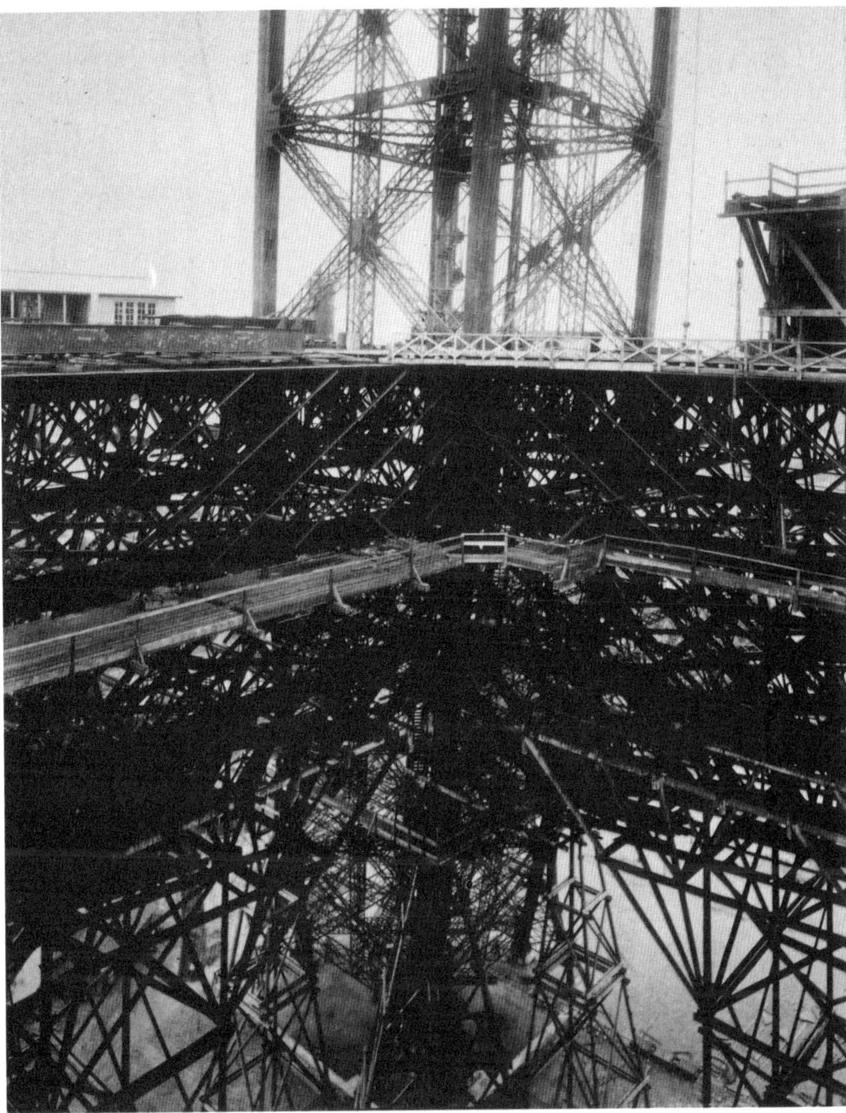

Durandelle and Chevojon,
Construction of the Eiffel Tower,
1888,
Musée d'Orsay,
Paris.

16. L. Bucher, *Kulturhistorische Skizzen aus der Industrieausstellung aller Völker,* Frankfurt, 1851, p. 174, quoted by S. Giedion, *op. cit.* pp. 251–252.

17. *Ibid.*

18. Architect Boileau in *Encyclopédie d'Architecture,* 1887–1888, p. 57.

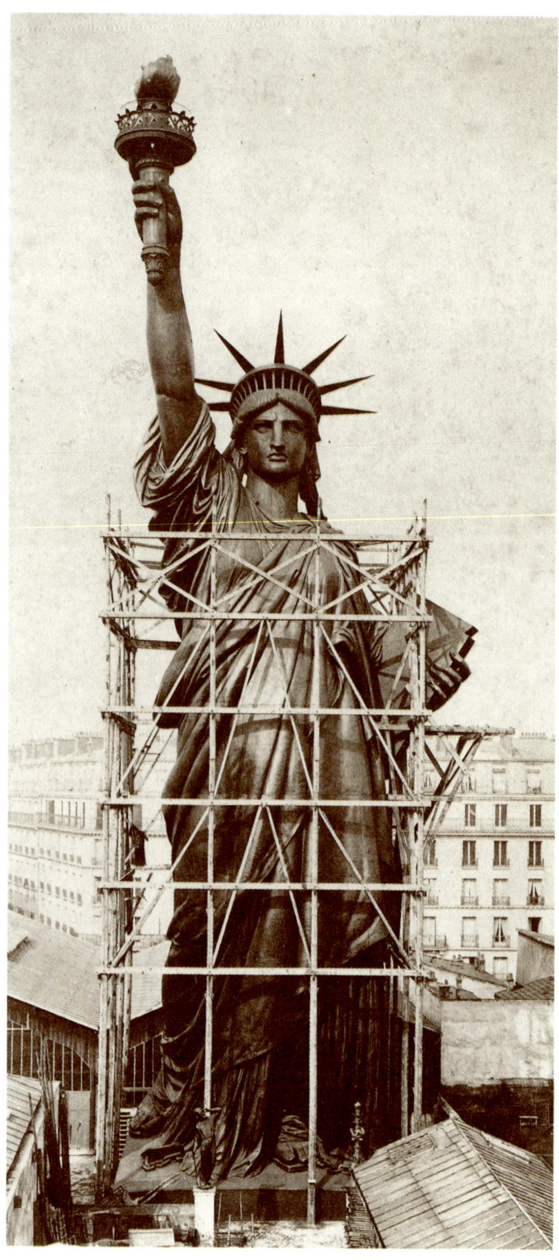

PIERRE PETIT, *Statue of Liberty under Construction in Paris,* 1876–1881, Bibliothèque Historique de la Ville de Paris.

example of the Crystal Palace paved the way not only to the great galleries, like the Galleria Vittorio Emanuele in Milan, but also to the glass-houses of the botanical gardens, natural history museums, libraries like Labrouste', the first skyscrapers in Chicago, and the pavilions of the great international exhibitions.

The Bisson brothers, pioneers of architectural photography, carried out major documentary projects on the pavilions of the 1855 and 1867 Expositions Universelles in Paris. Bissons' work is interesting in all its multiple facets, because the statement it makes, the themes chosen, seem to overcome that split between thought and sensibility which "paralyzed the magnificent force of the nineteenth century".[19] Justly famous for their pictures of Mont Blanc captured in the course of dangerous climbs (1855–1868) – an extreme form of that excitement preached by Ruskin, who exerted such a deep influence on the romantic aesthetic and sensibility of their generation – the Bisson brothers did not, however, follow Ruskin's command to turn away from the "decadent forms" produced by industry. On the frontier of several disciplines – landscape, architecture, sculpture, engineering – the Bisson brothers broke the conventions of a formalistic tradition.

The Exposition Universelle of 1889 was the final culmination of a long evolution. Engineers like Eiffel gave of their best. The long but simple Galerie des Machines of 1855, the immense oval gallery constructed by Krantz and Eiffel in 1867, and the two great transverse aisles of Dion's 1878 Palais des Machines were different stages of an evolution which reached its apogee in 1889 with the Galerie des Machines and the Eiffel Tower. After seeing them, the novelist Octave Mirbeau argued: "While art is seeking to be intimate, or stuck in old formulae, and so is walking on the spot, embarrassed and timid, its eye still turned towards the past, industry marches forward, explores the unknown, conquers form[...] It is not in the studios of painters and sculptors that the revolution so often predicted and so desired will be found. It is in the factories."[20]

It is well known how radically the arrival of the machine renewed fundamental questions of aesthetics, and how great was the importance accorded by the avant-garde to "mechanistic modernity". Marc Le Bot writes on this subject: "The modernity of the avant-garde is not that of Baudelaire which has to do with changing fashion, but that of a revolution in techniques and the appearance of new practices. Under these conditions, the technical object or the mechanical universe are no longer just one picturesque example among others, and occasion for enthusiasm or pathos; they are the constituents of a new beauty which is everywhere."[21] Some will find the embodiment of this new beauty in the Eiffel Tower, which clearly shows, in its majestic uselessness, how functionalism – at first entirely preoccupied with railway stations, hospitals, bridges, factories, theaters – lost its sense of purpose and found its accomplishment in pure aesthetics and the human will to achieve.

The creation of the spider's web tracery of the Eiffel Tower proved to be a powerful experimental laboratory and contributed to a new aesthetic sensibility. Photographic modernism, which was to culminate in the 1920s in the images of Kertész, Moholy-Nagy, Kollar, Thaleman, and Krull, first gained a foothold in the mid-nineteenth century on the construction site of that massive enterprise.

On the instructions of Gustave Eiffel, the photographer Louis-Émile Durandelle, with his successor Albert Chevojon as his assistant, produced, in the tradition of fine-art photog-

19. S. Giedion, *op. cit.* (see pp. 12, 13, 14).

20. Octave Mirbeau in *Encyclopédie d'Architecture,* 1889–1890, p. 92.

21. M. Le Bot, *Peinture et Machinisme,* Paros, Klincksieck, 1973, pp. 160–161.

raphy in which he excelled, two superb albums entitled *Work on the Construction of the Tower*, a series of pictures showing its progressive erection, from the foundations to the assembly of the beacon. Leafing through the plates, with all the shots taken week after week from January 28, 1887 to March 31, 1889, the day the tower was inaugurated, we can sense today how attentive Durandelle was as a photographer to form and perspective: their spatial relationships and the interplay, disappearance, and reappearance of horizontal or vertical lines.

Day after day, stage after stage, Durandelle really did see, in Léon-Paul Fargue's famous phrase, "the Eiffel Tower growing". However, far from simply recording the inexorable progress of the "scaffold" of the "infundibuliform trellis" (J.-K. Huysmans), germinating like some fantastic plant, the photographer slowly transgressed the classic frontal, functional viewpoint, involving himself with ever increasing audacity in a maze of forms and volumes of great geometric daring, as if taking on the innovatory spirit of the engineer. By the time the tower was finished the photographer had invented a new vision: surfaces, curves, crests, grids and struts, beams and pillars, box-girders, and the details of supports provided the new rhetoric of "an abstract, algebraic beauty" which was indecipherable at first because no grammar of art had yet set out its declensions.

Other metal constructions also attracted the attention of photographers, such as the powerful images taken by the photographer/engineer Albert Fernique of the steel skeleton (also constructed by Eiffel) of the Statue of Liberty designed by Bartholdi, which was erected in Paris in the 1880s before being transplanted to New York, or those taken by the Bordeaux photographer Alphonse Terpereau of Eiffel's most audacious bridge, the Garabit viaduct (1880–1884). There is an emotional charge and wealth of allusion in photographs of bridges which we have yet to fathom completely, as the 1983 exhibition "Photo Génie"[22] made clear. They speak directly to the viewer, who discovers in them forms rendered familiar by modern art.

The bridge in fact effects an unbroken synthesis between the notions of horizontal and vertical. Wooden bridges, stone bridges, iron bridges, suspension bridges: the construction of a bridge is always a major event in the history of a river and its city. The bridge – object of tremendous strategic importance and point of neurosis – which mobilizes so much intelligence, effort, and energy to overcome an obstacle, becomes, in so doing, a symbol of human solidarity.

Built by men in an effort to create something extraordinary, bridges, in their heroic technical achievement, offer an image of perfection and union with the area around. There are bridges

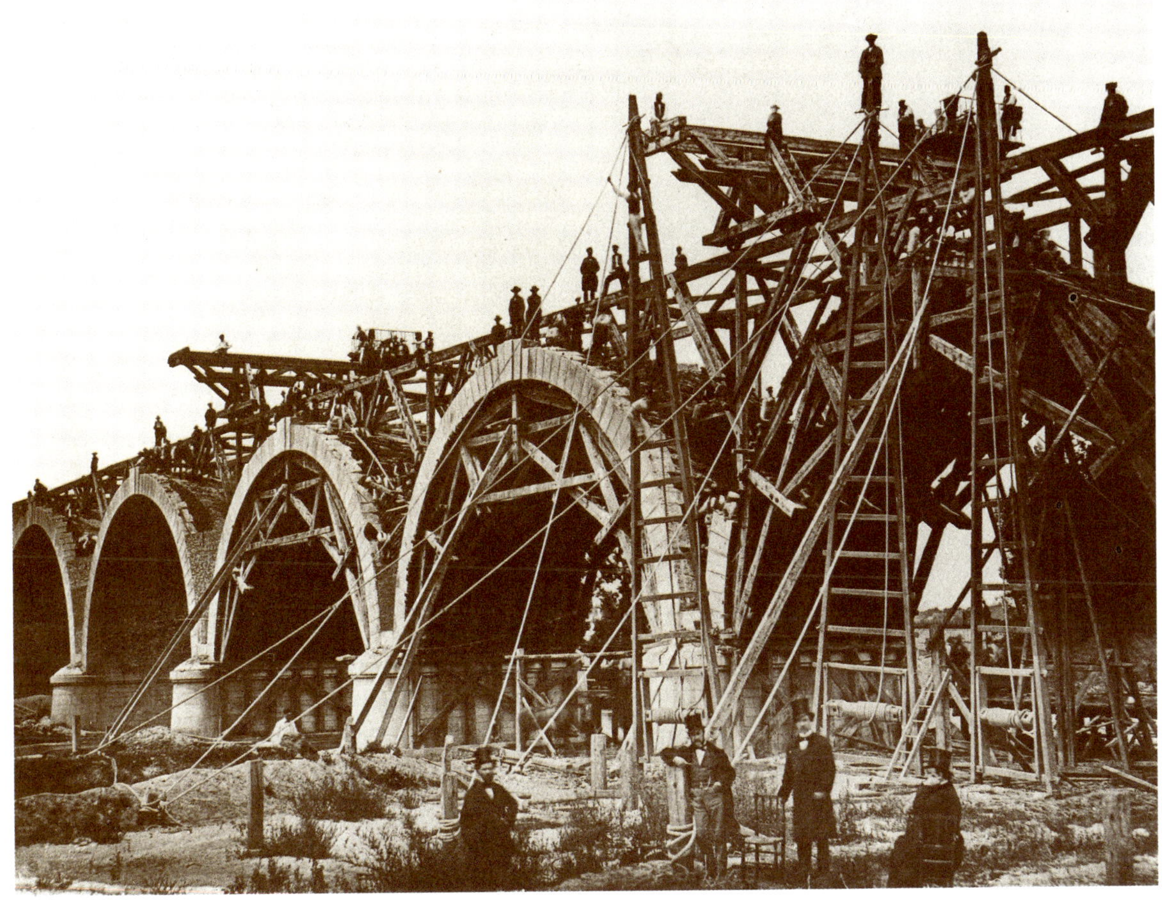

CHARLES CLIFFORD, *Construction of the Puente de Los Franceses on the Northern Railway* circa 1860, Municipal Museum, Madrid.

22. "Photo Génie: Photographies de Génie Civil au dix-neuvième Siècle", an exhibition based on the collection of the École Nationale des Ponts et Chaussées, Paris 14 September–23 October 1983. See also *Le grand Oeuvre: Photographies des grands Travaux: 1860–1900*. Collection: Photo Poche, Centre National de la Photographie, 1983.

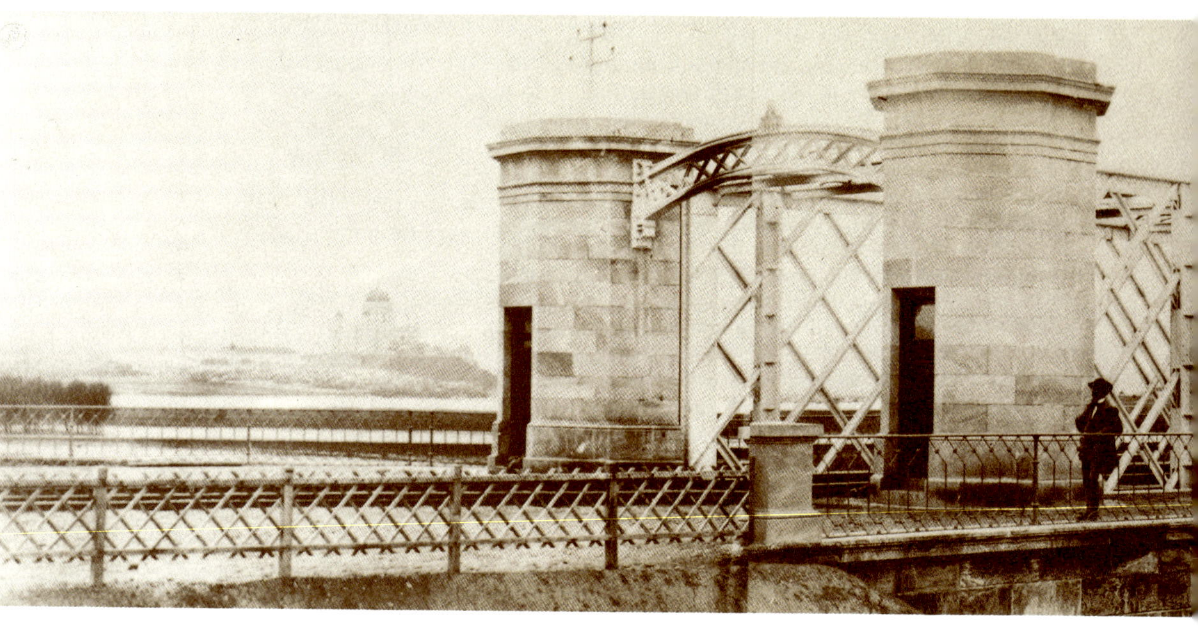

with fantastic spans which reach into landscapes on a cosmic scale and form a superhuman whole with them, like the Brooklyn Bridge, or the Golden Gate Bridge which crosses San Francisco Bay. The bridge motif shows a remarkable poetic density, also metaphorical: the "beyond" of the bridge calls forth the "beyond" in the landscape. It extends its reach by accentuating the feeling of infinity at the edge of the river or the sky, enriching it with effort or ecstasy. Guided by a didactic aim, but taking support from the exalting, sublimating character of photography, the new protagonists of industrial society – engineers, businessmen, administrators, specialist publishers – lent their support, through acquisitions and commissions, to a practical, professional, even corporatist practice in their reports on engineering. The Ministry of Public Works (Ministère des Travaux Publics), in particular the bridges, highways, and mines departments (Services des Ponts et Chaussées et des Mines) which since the eighteenth century had been assembling drawings, lithographs, models, and maps, began, in around 1860, to collect photographic albums and views. These were dominant images of a new type, acting as symbols of the department's ascendancy, its civilizing mission to the country, incontestably registering the state to which the works had advanced, the real topography of what had, until then, been merely abstract projections from plans.

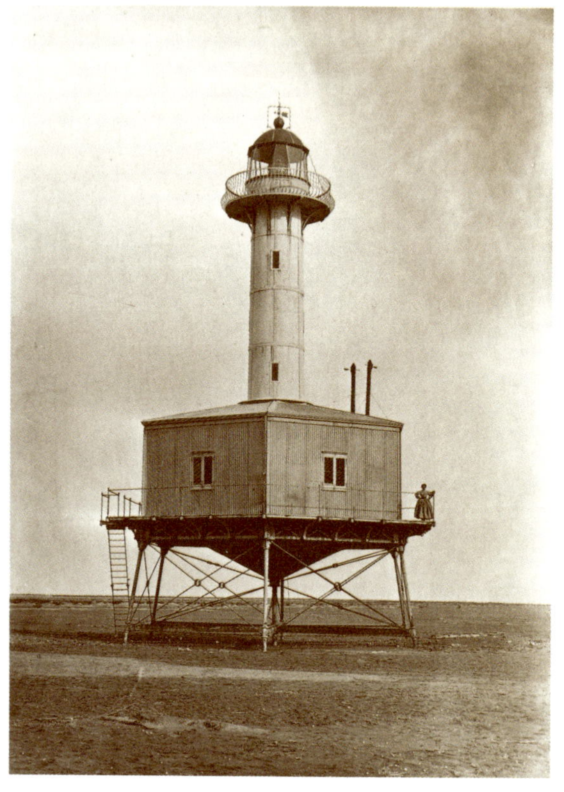

José Martinez Sanchez, *Lighthouse on the Cape of La Bana, Spain,* 1866, Bibliothèque de l'École des Ponts et Chaussées, Paris.

Describing himself as "photographer of bridges and highways", August-Hippolyte Collard started working for the administration in 1857 and carried on the task from his central photographic studio for nearly thirty years.[23] He produced important bodies of documentation on the execution of public works in Paris, among others, the bridges of Saint-Michel (1857), Louis-Philippe (1860–61), Saint-Louis (1862), the bridge at Bercy (1863–4), and the viaduct over the Seine at Point du Jour (1864). His reportage on the diversion of the rivers Dhuis and Vanne towards the capital (1864–1874) is another significant addition to the inventory of civil engineering, a taxonomy of the technical process. Collard, who seems to have had a pronounced sensitivity to, and intuitive understanding of, the forces, movements, and hidden pressures affecting a construction, turns the building-site of a bridge into a privileged panorama which has an immediate impact on the viewer. The framework of a construction and the elements, required to make

23. J.-C. Le Mée, "Collard, Photographe des Ponts et Chaussées", in *Histoire de l'Art*, no. 13/14, 1991, pp. 31–44.

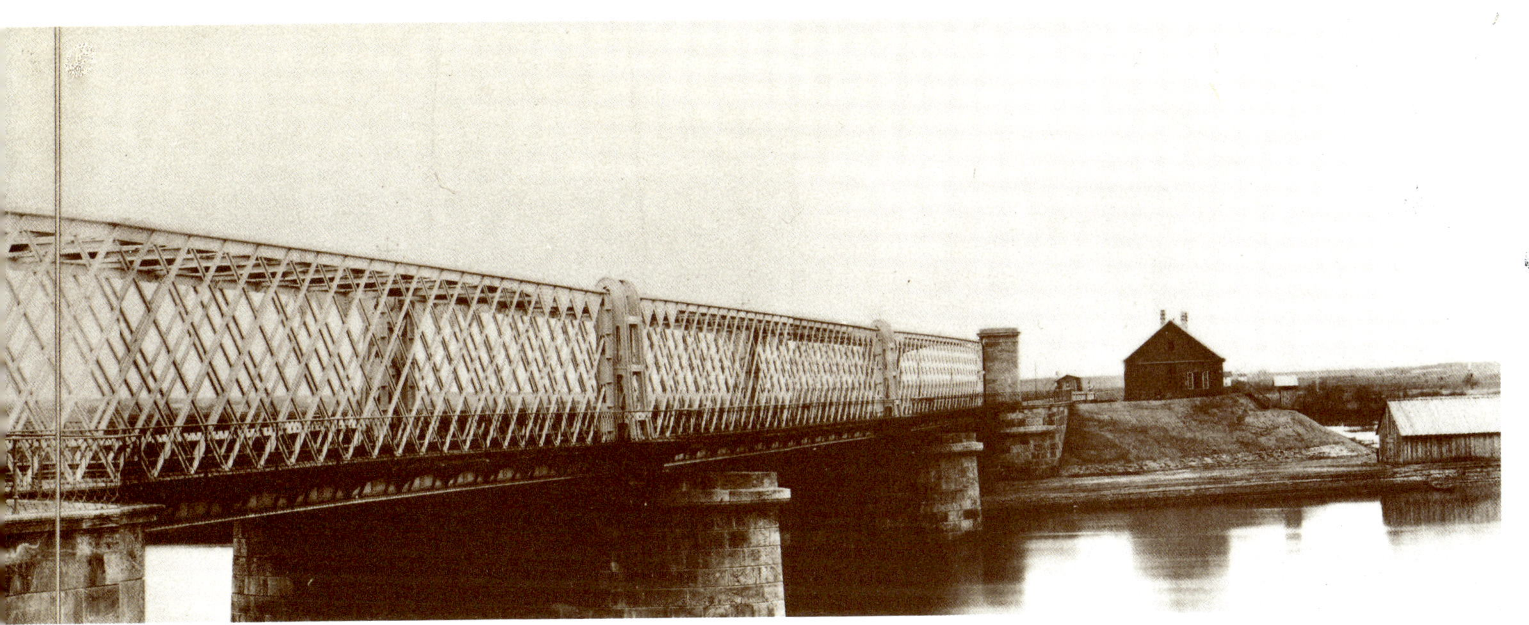

it – scaffolding, arches and key-stones, cranes, pillars – are not inert materials to him. In his images, every element plays an active role: the building site is presented like a sequence of educational tableaux vivants accessible only to those competent in geometry, where the allegorical figure of the engineer in his frock coat is king.

Collard, aiming at a pictorial explanation of the methods and technology of construction, also wanted to add the picturesque quality created by people. In the *Bridges of Paris* series, the differences in people's dress and in the style this imprints upon their bodies and various postures and gestures all add to the animation of the scene. The monumental aspect of the construction is thus juxtaposed to the social hierarchy: laborers and skilled workmen, laborers for the earthworks and specialist carpenters for the heavy woodwork, foremen, technicians. The bridges are all part of the public spectacle, like backdrops. In the positioning of people and materials there is both theatricality and the specific gestures of labor.

The work of Collard is a symbol of pure tension. Unlike the college-trained architects who took an imaginative, even utopian delight in favoring drawings, the "constructor-architects" immediately understood the service that could be rendered by photography in providing a visual record. They immediately adopted this new "at a glance" art which was able, with scrupulous efficiency, to take over the field of linear, graphic or geometric drawing.

Photography is "a stern and faithful brush with which, in a very short time, all the objects of nature can be reproduced with an exactness of detail which an artist could never achieve, however patient, skilled or talented."[24] The code of functionalist aesthetics suited an "objective", unambiguous vision. Far from dreaming of some kind of personal expression, these photographers had a passion for information which gave rise to a particular technique: wide-angle, full-frame, frontal shots, which all combined to make architectural photography absolutely transparent – a pure instrument of representation. Nonetheless, just like drawing, photography has to resolve problems relating to perpendicular and parallel lines, the calculation of angles, and plotting the tangents and secants of circles, polygons, and similar shapes. It has to render a perfect account, from all possible positions, of all the different shapes of an object, its volume, its real dimensions. Drawing on a study of perspective and geometry, it finds the way to represent volume not in its real form but in terms of how it looks

Anton Rohrbach, *Construction of the Bridge over the Gran, Hungary,* 1859, Bibliothèque de l'École des Ponts et Chaussées, Paris.

Auguste Collard, *Arch of the Pont de Grenelle,* Paris, 1874, Bibliothèque de l'École des Ponts et Chaussées, Paris. ▼

24. Dr. É. Loydreau, *De la Photographie appliquée à l'Archéologie*, Batault-Morot, Beaune, 1857, p. 10.

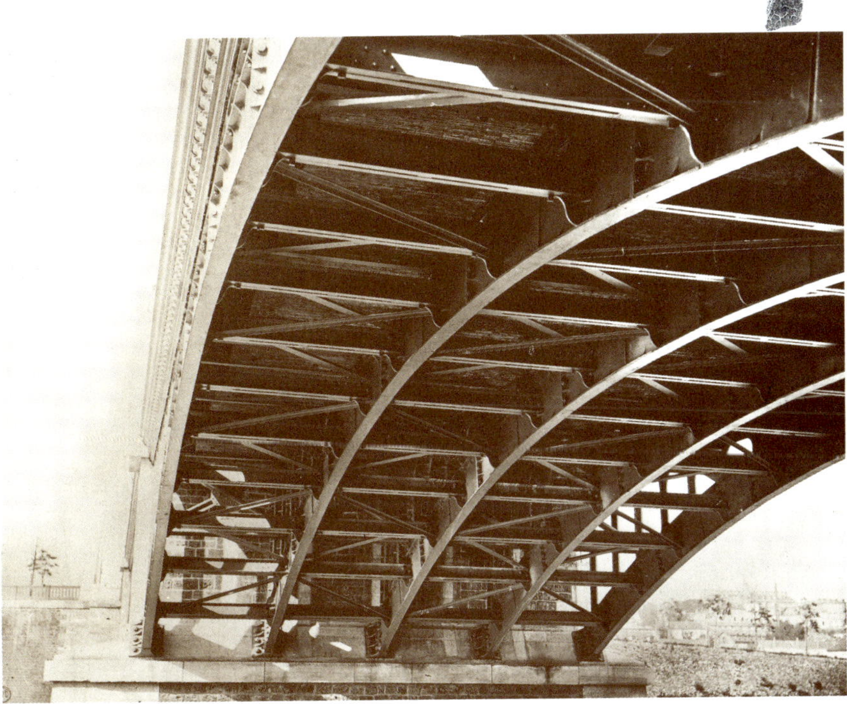

The conquest of knowledge and techniques
Photography at the École des Ponts et Chaussées

The kings of France took an early interest in the building and upkeep of roads and public works, chiefly with the aim of benefiting commerce. In 1747, a School, the École des Ponts et Chaussées, was created, providing specialist training, linked at first to the Administration des Mines (1817) then to the Ministère des Travaux Publics (1839).

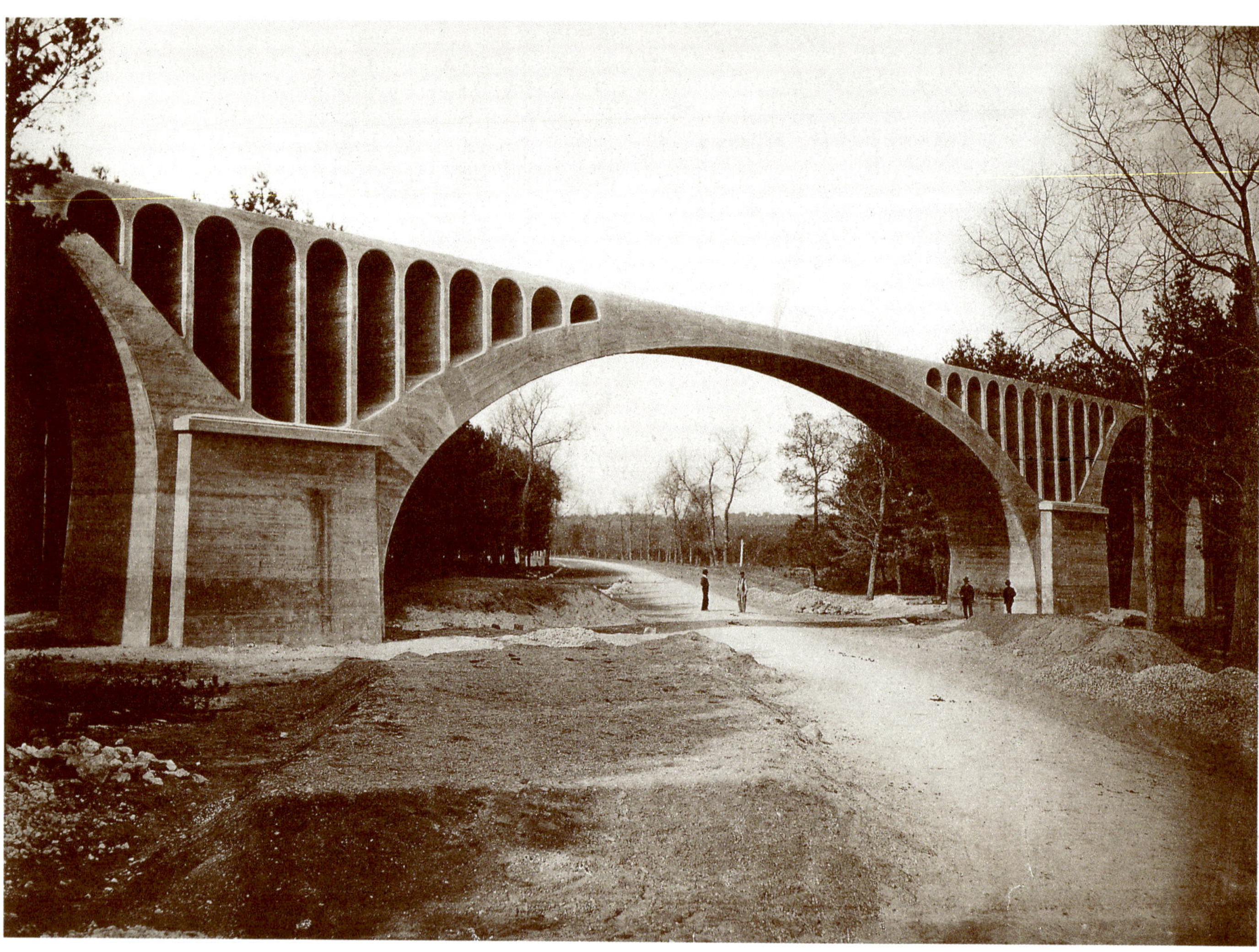

Auguste Collard
Diversion of River Vanne, Great Arch, Road to Orléans, Fontainebleau Forest,
1870, private collection

Engineers examined all aspects of their art in France: design, construction, checking and use of highways, waterways, and railways. It was a particularly intense center of learning and education, and built up important reference collections.

The School took trouble to integrate lessons derived from practical experience into its empirical approach. Photography turned out to be an ideal teaching aid for presenting the art of the engineer. In 1857, following a suggestion by one of the Bisson brothers, the School started lessons in photography for its students, which it was to continue until 1911. The teachers were, in order: from 1858 to 1872 Louis Robert, from 1872 to 1886 Alphonse Davanne – the School published his "Lectures on Photography" in 1883; L. Bordet (from 1886 to 1902), and Colonel Moessard of the engineers corps (from 1902 to 1911).

The collection of photographs (about 10,000 in all) was divided up under various headings. Alongside the work of great pioneers such as Baldus (for the P.L.M. company), Marville (the quarries for Paris at Marcoussis, works done under Haussmann), Collard (bridges of Paris), Delmaet and Durandelle (Paris Opéra, works in metal), we find the products of local photographers: Alphonse Terpereau (Bordeaux), Gabriel Blaise (Tours), Terris (Marseilles), L. Lafon, Lamazouère, Chamoin, and F. de Mauny, Berthaud and Duclos, Broise, Chalois, Cognacq and Godefroy, Pepper, etc. Railway branch-lines laid by the state, various public works under construction, and hydraulic and maritime installations (the ports of Marseilles, Bordeaux, Dunkirk, Calais, Saint-Nazaire etc.), as well as factories, and mechanical devices were all recorded for posterity in this way.

There is considerable material from foreign sources: photographic recording carried out in Poland (bridge over the Vistula in Warsaw in 1865), Russia (the Alexander bridge over the Volga, 1889), Spain, with photographs by Laurent and Martinez-Sanchez (1867), Italy (railways in the south by Mauri 1887), Austria-Hungary (Stern 1890), the United States (public works in Washington – the Capitol, Central Post Office, aqueduct, Ministry of Finance – photographs taken between 1857 and 1860 by Bourmann and Meigt, views of bridges by Crane (1890).

Acquisitions and deposits were numerous from 1857 until the 1890s, but, unfortunately, at the beginning of the twentieth century they began to decline and stopped altogether after 1907.

Elvire Perego

when seen from a given point of view. Just as the artist drawing in three dimensions is preoccupied with the need to light the model correctly so as to be able to draw shadows and half-tones, so the photographer applies himself to finding the correct approach to light and shade. The great exhibition in Bordeaux in 1882 devoted to work relating to the Ponts et Chaussées, gave awards to the finest examples of work in construction: machinery, railways, mechanical devices, and architecture. At this event, text and picture went hand in hand, following the example of Léonce Reynaud's collections on public works in France, illustrated with collotype plates and published by the banker Edmond de Rothschild (who was also the administrator of the French Eastern Railway).

Besides the presentation of reproductions and prints from the photography and photo-zincography workshops of the Ministère des Travaux Publics, there was also considerable publicity for the teaching of photography at the Ponts et Chaussées' own school, which had been started in 1857, at the instigation of one of the Bisson brothers, through displays and lectures given by Professor Davanne, who, in 1881, had just published one of his treatises.[25]

However, perhaps we can get a better idea of how the new techniques for transmitting information were moving through society by looking in a different direction, at those bodies of work which combine documentary record and propaganda, whose aim was to "launch" a product, machine or firm, or to change its image. The classic experiment in this line was made by the Belgian contractor François Hennebique when he embarked on the systematic commercial exploitation of his patents for reinforced concrete between 1892 and 1910. Photographs collected during these years – around 8,000 images produced by little-known photographers of all nationalities – suggest a promotional strategy aimed partially at the media, the purpose of which was commercial success.[26] In 1910, when the headquarters of the now multinational business moved to Rue Danton in Paris, Hennebique and his empire – thirty or so technical offices run by graduates of the state school of civil engineering, 160 concessions scattered round the world – seemed to hold a virtual monopoly in the small world of construction in reinforced concrete.

The work carried out by the Hennebique business was eclectic. The firm responded to all kinds of orders and adapted its system to all programs and all countries: industrial and public edifices, domestic buildings, warehouses, silos, foundations. Everywhere reinforced concrete could, with advantage, replace classic masonry or metal structures. Floors, balconies, water tanks, and workshops were all judged worthy of being photographed and

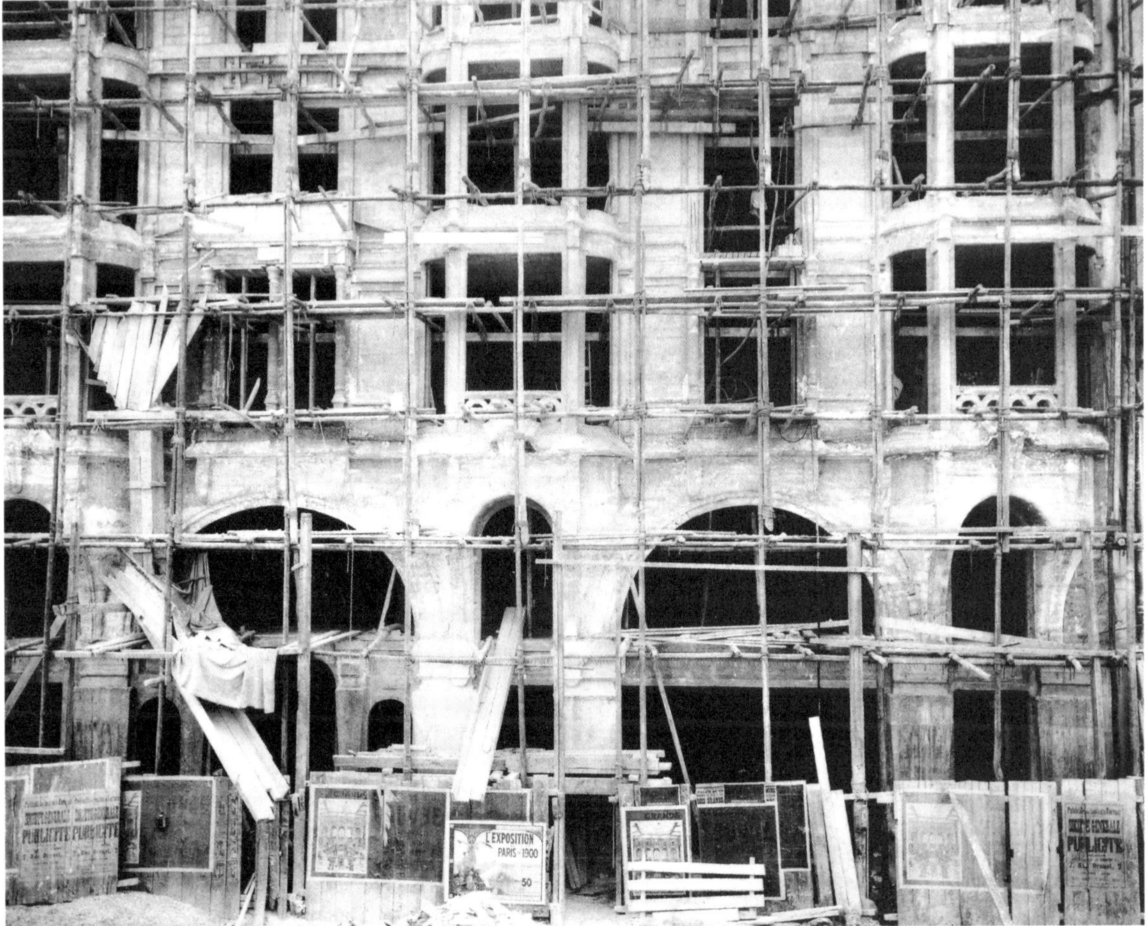

CLÉMENT MAURICE, ***Building owned by the architect Hennebique, facade,*** July 1900, Institut d'Architecture, Archives du Vingtième Siècle, Paris.

25. L.-A. Davanne, *De la Photographie appliquée aux Sciences,* 1881.

26. See on this subject the works by G. Delhumeau: "Hennebique et la Construction en Béton Armé autour des Années 1900", in *Rassegna,* no. 49, March 1992 and "Hennebique, les Architectes et la Concurrence", in *Cahiers de la recherche architecturale,* no. 29, 1992. In the stock of photographs collected by Hennebique, the names of the following studios are to be found, among others: F. Houben (Roubaix), Marmand (Paris), Ybert (Rouen), R. Dal Rio (Turin), J. Branguli Soler (Barcelona), W. Bleuze (Rotterdam), V. Stevani (Venice), A. Volta (Vicenza), G. Brayton (Boston), J. McCracken (Glasgow), J. Timm (Guayaquil), A. Daams (Brussels).

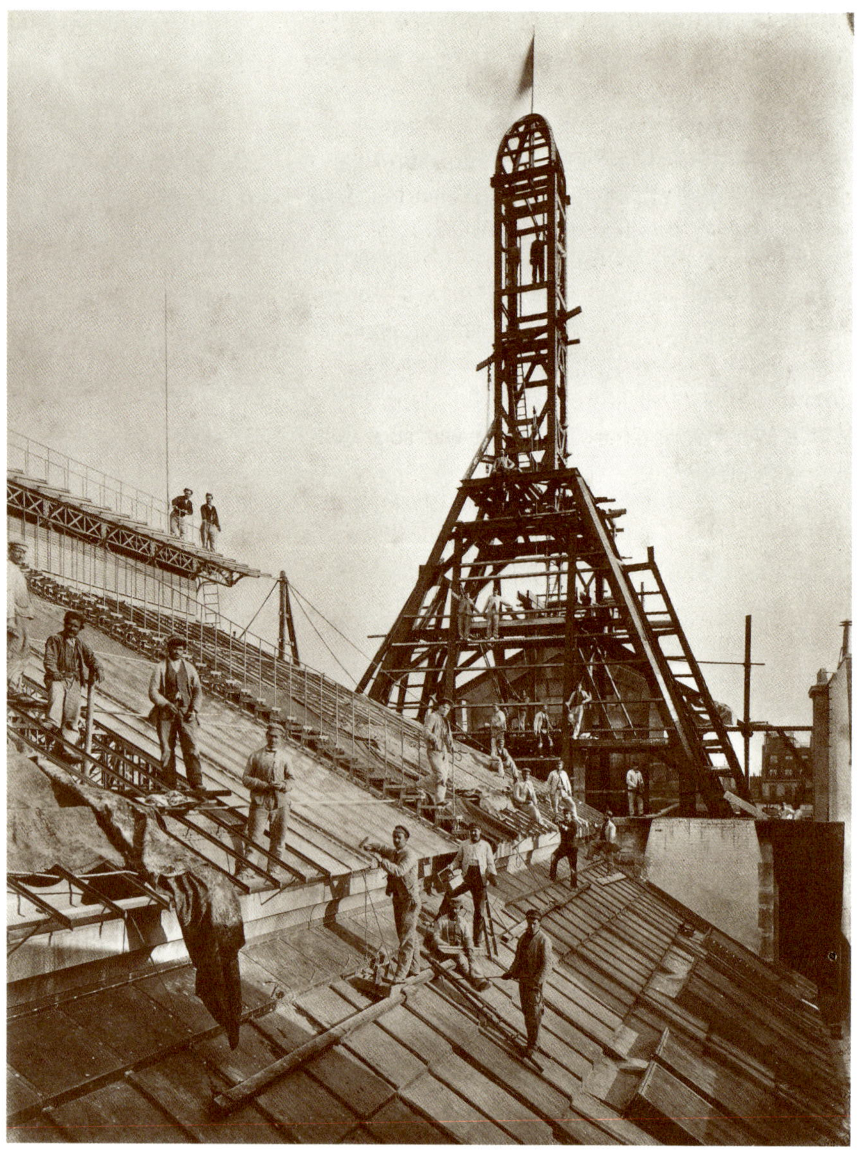

Durandelle, *Construction of the Comptoir d'Escompte (glass roof and scaffolding)*, Paris, 1881, Bibliothèque Historique de la Ville de Paris

published. These images were used in numerous booklets and brochures published by Hennebique as well as in his own review *Béton Armé* a "formidable instrument" which sometimes went into editions of up to 20,000 copies.

Needless to say, the distribution of such architectural literature encouraged success: Hennebique, whose thirst for fame was enormous, won prestigious orders like the Paris refinery of Saint-Ouest (1894), the flour mill for Moulins de Nantes, the famous spinning-mill for Barrois brothers at Fives-Lille (1886), installations for the Exposition Universelle of 1900 and the Ponte del Risorgimento in Rome (1910). The Hennebique archives were deposited with the Institut Français d'Architecture in 1989, and are being made available for use with a grant from the Getty Foundation. They will undoubtedly prove to be one of the most fertile resources for research, leading to a better understanding of the links that grew up between the engineer and the photographer. Though they use different sign-systems, their attention to spatial structure and to shape and mass is the same, and genuine associations and exchanges between visual works and works of civil engineering are brought out by their dogmatic insistence that only photography should be used to express the changing face of architecture.

A new language

Some photographs by Delmaet and Durandelle, in particular those showing the building of the Paris Opéra, can be analyzed as an anticipation of modernism: "These posts, these planks, arranged like the lances in Paolo Uccello's *Battles* to mark perspective, and, playfully perhaps, to make it more complicated, belong to some crazy chess-board under construction [...] It fell to the lot of a photographer, centuries later, on the roof-tops of the half-built Opéra, to interpret it deliriously , in involuntary anticipation of the spatial dream-works of Malevich."[27]

Behind the rigor of these compositions there appears an accumulation of images which show the great construction projects of the second half of the nineteenth century,[28] functional edifices like the Comptoir d'Escompte (1880-1881) or symbolic monuments like the new Opéra (1865–1872), Sacré-Coeur (1887–1890) or the Eiffel Tower (1887–1889). Soaring or subterranean, they mingle beams and relics: scaffolds, frameworks, pillars, but also carcasses, bones, skeletons, and other models for a builder's course in life-drawing. The photographer is the anatomist of architecture.

This Paris photographic workshop, until recently almost unknown, functioned between 1860 and 1890. Today, its output appears as a particularly complete photographic expression of the revolution in industry and of a new language. It had ceased to be the task of the photographer, whether he knew it or not, to simply draw up an inventory of what was there like a bailiff: he had to act like an explorer, and interpret the new objects appearing in the landscape of archeology, architecture, and industry. The Swiss theoretician Siegfried Giedion bore witness to this when he chose to use a photograph by Durandelle, uncredited, in the iconography of his book *Space, Time and Architecture*:[29] (the photograph was *Universal Exhibition of Paris 1889: Base of a Triple Arch)*. So did Lissitzky, who, in 1930, used this same picture of a pillar in the Galerie des Machines as part of a photomontage for the cover of a book on architecture by Roger Ginsburger.[30]

In fact, the evolution of the Delmaet and Durandelle studio's work could be the subject of a purely geometric study, the camera slowly and gradually taking in everything, moving from

27. J. F. Chevrier, in *Photographies*, no. 1, Spring 1983, p. 54.

28. In *Photographies*, no. 5, special number entitled "Photographie, Art moderne et technologie 1850–1950", July 1984, pp. 54–75.

29. S. Giedion, *op.cit.*, p. 161.

30. R. Ginsburger, *Die Entwicklung der neuen Ideen nach Konstruktion und Form* [*The Development of New Ideas of Construction and Form*], Joseph Gautner (ed.), vol. III, Vienna, Anton Schroll, 1930.

decorated areas to extended spaces, from unbroken surface to gap, break, and empty space, from the restrained decorative motifs of the Opéra to the unfurling of metallic forms dreamed up by the engineers.

Charles Garnier, in his reports on the work on the Nouvel Opéra, preserved in the Archives Nationales, noted in 1866: "In order to preserve the memory of different phases in the construction of the Opéra, photographs have been taken every time that changes took place on the site [...] If at some later date one wanted to produce a monograph about the Opéra the photographic material that would be at one's disposition would make it much easier to produce such a publication." The architect had the foresight to entrust this iconographic celebration of his creation to the firm of Delmaet and Durandelle, situated, in 1868, at 4 Rue du Faubourg-Montmartre. Two craftsmen from the north of France founded the studio: Hyacinthe César Delmaet (1828–1862) and Louis-Émile Durandelle (1839–1917). Florence Jacob, Delmaet's wife, was later to marry Durandelle. Essentially they worked to order, and early on specialized in public works. The prestige of the order from Charles Garnier was such that

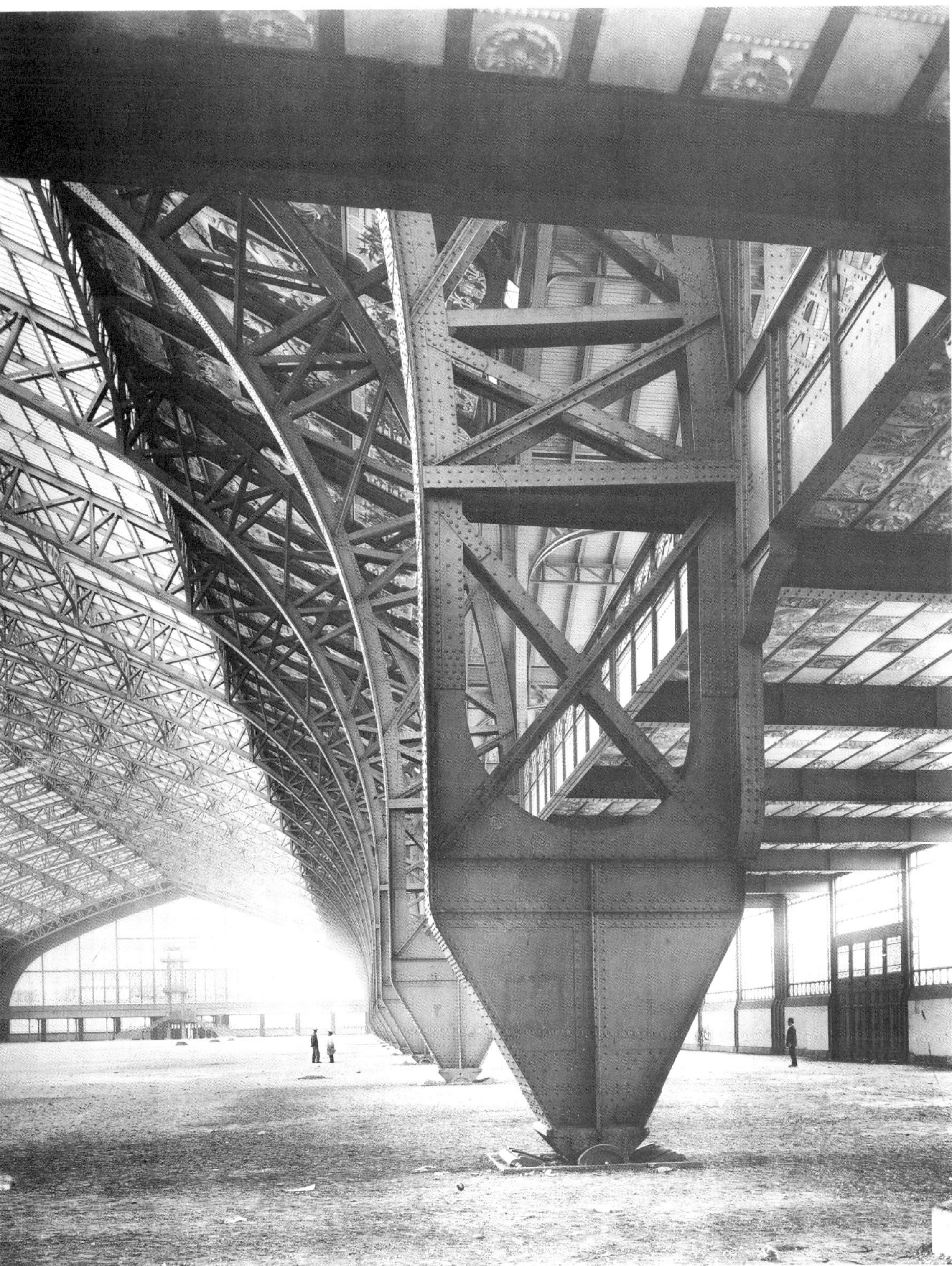

Durandelle and Chevojon, *Gallery of the Machines, International Exhibition of 1889, Paris.*

GEORG BÖTTGER, *"Ostbahn" Station*, Munich, circa 1858, Stadtmuseum, Munich. ▼

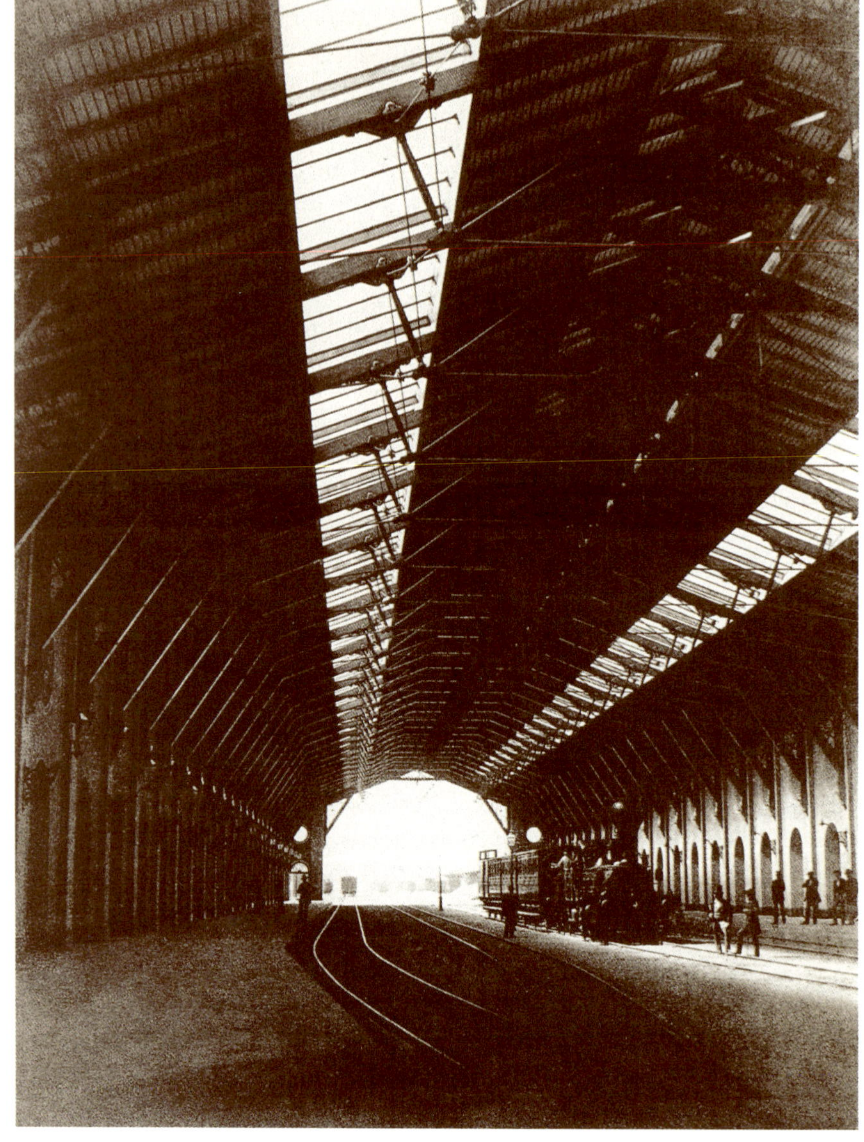

they described themselves in their publicity brochure as "photographers of the Nouvel Opéra and students of the École des Beaux-Arts".

Their best photographs – more than one hundred of them – taken over a period of roughly seven years (1865–1872), were included in various albums published at the time. In particular, four folio albums, *Sculpture ornementale, Statues decoratives, Peintures decoratives,* and *Bronzes* were distributed to numerous architects. These pictures do, of course, fulfil their primary purpose, to record "precisely" and "objectively" the construction of an epoch-making building. Nevertheless, the images of the foundations, metallic structures, neo-Corinthian ornaments, pediments, pilasters, columns, and other architectural details take on an extraordinary artistic power. The project shows a total mastery of all the constraints of photography; it is also a contribution to visual art of "excessive modernity". The interest of seeing how form and the sizes and proportions of things relate to one another is of a subtlety that transcends the factual. Each of the elements is photographed in such a way that a fullness emanates from it, an intrinsic radiance, an autonomous existence. The curtain-walls, windows, planks, objects, and raw materials usually regarded as inconsequential details are here endowed with an enigmatic expressive force. Durandelle was a modernist in the fullest sense of the term. His photographic career developed in conjunction with that of the architectural avant-garde of his day: he was the photographer called upon by the architects Charles Garnier, Edmond Corroyer (the rival of Viollet-le-Duc), Edmond Guillaume, Paul Abadie, Henri Labrouste, and Gustave Eiffel.

When we study these images we can see the photographer passing from reproduction to production. Most of his photographs create the illusion, through the way their elements cross and converge, of unexpected perspectives, previously unknown optical spaces, effects created by lengths of iron, cast-iron or wood, horizontal or vertical, suggesting at the same time both inaccessible distance and palpable proximity. Durandelle established something like a new form of writing or visual language, of which space and chiaroscuro were the main elements. Durandelle thus prefigures some of the most characteristic formal developments of twentieth-century photography. In his images of beams in the Comptoir d'Escompte, he is not rendering its fullness but its emptiness, the space enclosed by the building; instead of creating a play of light upon solid forms, the photographer makes light play with itself in the interior – or rather in the air that circulates round the building – and with a profusion of light, or very little, he creates flashes, reflections, and effects of semi-darkness or transparency. By stressing triangular forms he reinforces the precision of straight lines, and he uses a succession of peaks and diagonals to master the networks, grids and other seams of aerial embroidery. Some photographs that repeat the same object (the ladder, for example) or the same geometrical figure (the triangle) seem to spring from a kind of formal obsession. Another approach, in which the line of sight is off-center, results in an oblique composition, based on asymmetry. Sometimes Durandelle blocks the foreground, using various items such as blocks of stone, pieces of metal or bits of wood, whose function is to act as visual reference points. Or he abandons a frontal point of view and central perspective, stepping off to one side. This question of "open spaces" is too closely related to that of the distribution of light and shade – "chiaroscuro" – to be disassociated from it. Photographs taken during the construction of Sacré-Cœur or of the ancient remains beneath the Louvre, when the architect Edmond

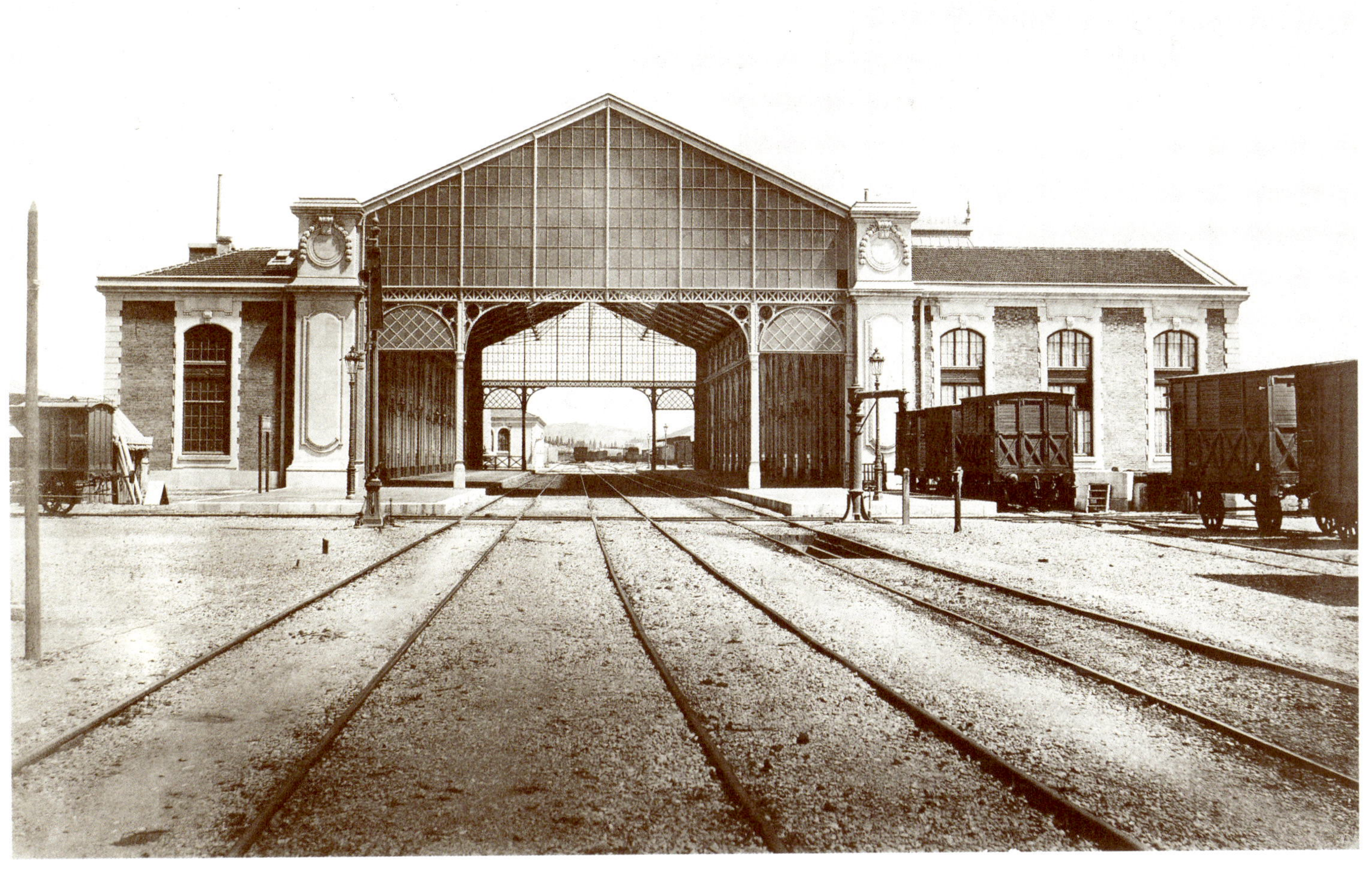

Guillaume was excavating there (1882–1884), display this interplay of light and shade. This fascination with chiaroscuro seems a response to the need for an interior atmosphere, a fascination with the traces left by history. Drowned in a ray of light, walls, partitions, floors, and ceilings seem destabilized, lightened, rendered fragile. These photographs are bathed in a semi-religious atmosphere: the site becomes a vast "cathedral-forest" whose Gothic and medieval connotations are evident. Light, in Durandelle's work, structured by shadows, weighted to a greater or lesser degree by contrast, but always prone to dramatization, is the instrument of a formidable architectural fantasy that evokes the luminosity of Piranesi. Anticipating avant-garde artists of the inter-war years, who tried to resolve the dichotomy of art and technology, Durandelle's art presents only structures at work, as far as the eye can see. There are people, looking like tiny statues, indistinct, akin to effigies or phantoms. The sight of all these elements assembled together induces a state of entranced reverie in the beholder, offering contemporary man a mirror to the labyrinthine, vertiginous underside of things: the mysteries of the body, the unconscious mind.

"The roving railway-men"

"Claude Monet [...] has exhibited some superb interiors of railway stations this year. One can hear the trains thundering into the maw of the station, the smoke billowing out under the vast station canopies. That is the painting of today, framed in these beautifully wide modern settings. Our artists should discover the poetry of stations, as their fathers found it in forests and rivers."[31] When Émile Zola wrote these lines in 1877 photographers had long been aware of the poetic character of the technological "motif" – the hymn to industrial beauty. One such was Édouard-Denis Baldus, who is the subject of a wholesale reinterpretation at present – as one of the great "primitives" of the 1850s, but also as the "most American" of French nineteenth-century photographers and the "first modernist photographer."[32]

His visual innovations ushered in the lyrical aspect of modern sensibility. His favorite subjects – viaducts, stations, railway lines – gave him the themes of a photographic vision that is the quintessence of functional creation. In 1855, he produced, on commission from the banker James

Édouard-Denis Baldus,
Toulon Station, Album of the Railway from Paris to Lyons and the Mediterranean
circa1861,
Musée d'Orsay, Paris.

31. É. Zola, "Notes Parisiennes. Une Exposition: les Peintres Impressionistes, April 19, 1877", in *Écrits sur l'Art*, Gallimard, Coll. Tel, 1991, p. 358.

32. See P. Néagu and F. Heilbrun, "Baldus, Paysages, Architectures", in *Photographies* no. 1, Spring 1983, pp. 57–77.

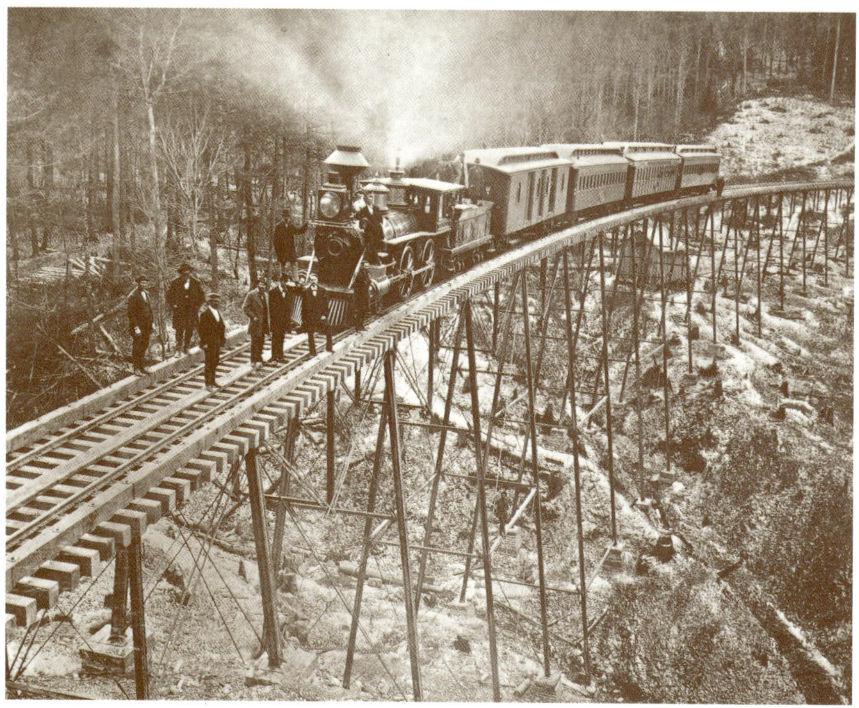

ANONYMOUS,
Block House Viaduct, near Ithaca,
United States, 1873,
Public Archives of Canada.

de Rothschild, a series of albums about the Paris-Boulogne branch of the Chemin de Fer du Nord. A second album was produced on the occasion of the extension to Toulon of the Marseilles-Lyons line. Although recent work has called into question the received opinion that Baldus was the sole author of these images (in particular for the Chemin de Fer du Nord stretch),[33] Baldus's photographs, whether simple or daring in composition, are striking in their sense of space and monumentality, and in their effectiveness as descriptive documents. Rich in latent meaning, these "new landscapes" engender a desire to travel, to explore the land of France. A traveling aesthete, Baldus (who was also a painter) planned his routes alternating architectural subjects and scenery. His modernist train journeys always finish on a superb vista like the seascapes at Bordeaux.

The years 1850–1890 were marked not only by the industrial movement, but by powerful signs indicative of a trend from America. The simplicity, technical precision, and formal rigor of American products – tools and machines – stupefied the visitors at international exhibitions. The sculptor Horatio Greenough considered that "the mechanics of the United States have already outstripped the artists, and have by the results of their bold and unflinching adaptation entered the true track, and hold up the light for all who operate for American wants, be they what they will."[34]

In this era, which witnessed the conquest of the West, from Chicago to the Pacific, the "frontier photographers" introduced Yankee America – recently torn apart by the Civil War – to the beauty of the new territories, symbols of the country's renewed vigor. These men – Timothy H. O'Sullivan, Carleton E. Watkins, Andrew Joseph Russell, Eadweard Muybridge, John K. Hillers, Dr.

TIMOTHY O'SULLIVAN,
The Gould and Curry Mill, Virginia City,
Nevada, 1867,
International Museum of Photography, George Eastman House, Rochester.

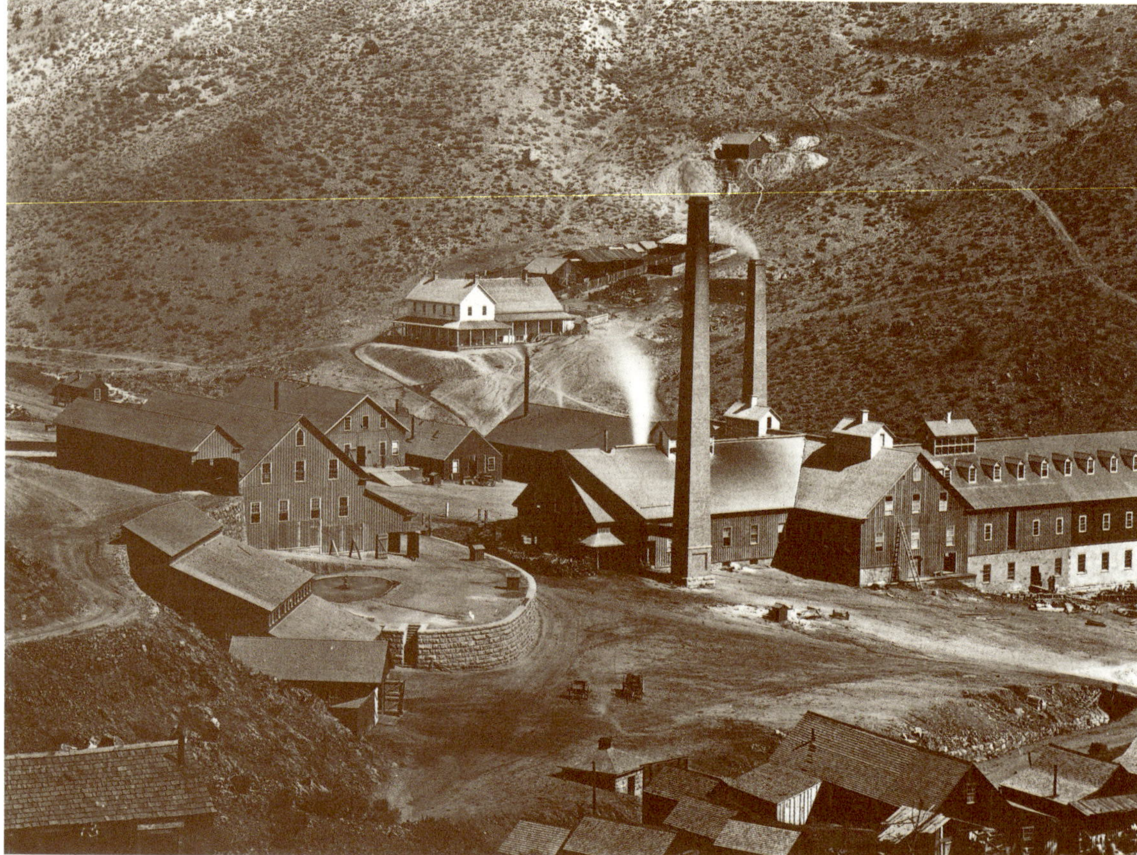

33. See M. Daniel, "Édouard Baldus: les Albums du Chemin de Fer du Nord", in *La Recherche photographique*, no. 8, February 1990, pp. 83–89.

34. H. Greenough in "The Travels, Observations, and Experience of a Yankee Stonecutter", by Horace Bender (pseudonym of Greenough), New York, G. Putnam, 1852.

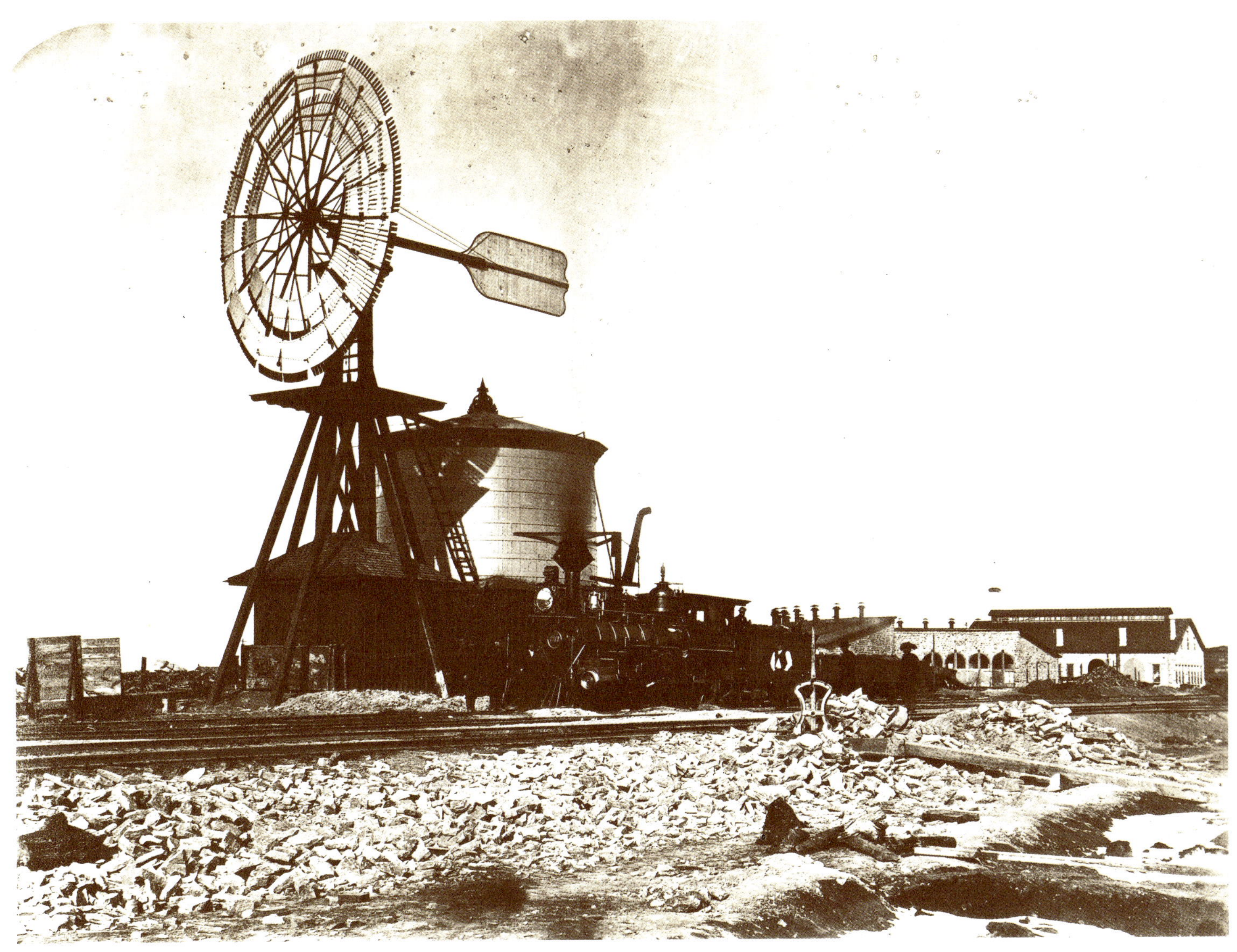

Andrew J. Russell,
Wind Mill at Laramie,
1867–1868,
New York Public Library.

William Abraham Bell, George N. Barnard, William Henry Jackson, William Herman Rau, Adam Clark Vroman – inspired by a passion to know and understand, became photographers in order to render a more truthful account of what they saw.

They were knowledgeable, generous-minded, and turbulent men of action, working with a host of competing railway companies (Pennsylvania Railroad, Lehigh Valley Railroad, U.S. Military Railroad, Union Pacific Railroad, Central Pacific Railroad, Kansas Pacific, Denver and Rio Grande Railroad, etc.) or with government scientific missions (King's Survey, Hayden's Survey, U.S. Geographical Survey, the ethnology department of the Smithsonian Institution). These jack-of-all-trades" lived adventurous lives worthy of a Jack London novel, and collected on their fragile heavy glass plates an extraordinary body of work covering landscapes, natural phenomena, the epic course of the railway. The interest of the land lay in its borders and frontiers: the railway was a line of expansion and peril, the tangible sign of a void that had become dynamic, a space that had become subject to geometry. The "frontier" retreated ever further westward, the new territories attained the rank of states, and those Native Americans who had not been exterminated were pushed down towards Mexico. The wide open spaces of America remained a zone to be crossed by cowboys, Indians, wandering trappers and gold prospectors, hoboes, and steam trains. The triumphalist ethic of political and economic forces gave rise to an image of a natural world waiting to be conquered: man had to use all his strength to force it to yield up its riches. This commitment led photographers to extol the spectacle of these indomitable machines, these locomotives rushing towards communion between men, good relations between States, friendship between peoples. Russell's photograph entitled *East and West Shaking Hands*, May 10, 1869, marking the meeting of the lines, known as Promontory Summit, symbolizes all this. It can be seen as suggesting the dream of a golden age, extended to all humanity: the photographer is inviting us to celebrate victory in a promethean struggle linking the immensity of the land to the

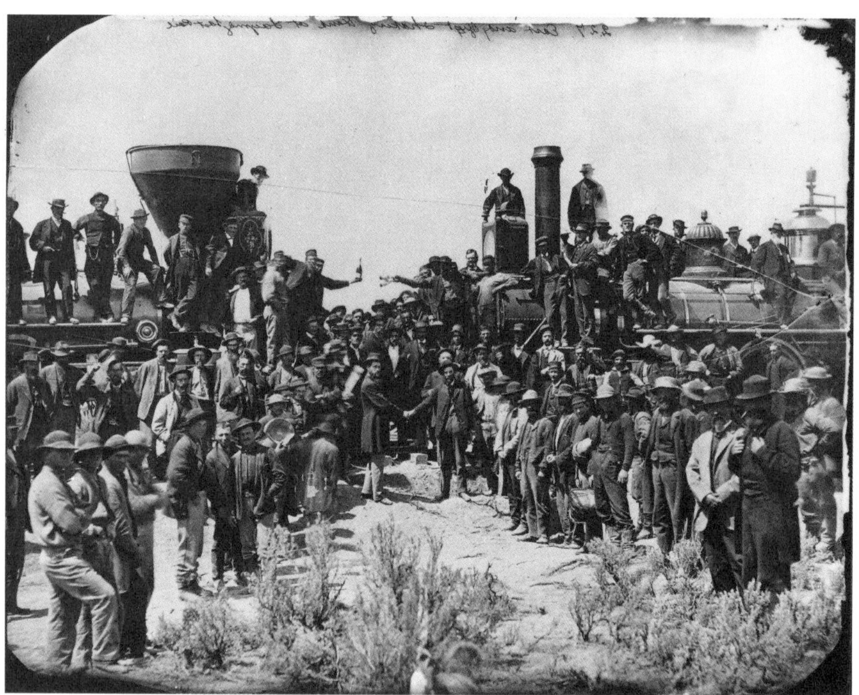

Andrew J. Russell, ***East and West Shaking Hands, Promontory Point, Utah,*** May 10, 1869, Yale University Library, New Haven.

people who live in it. These great pioneers, precursors of classical American photography, who scoured Arizona, Colorado, Utah, Texas, and Sierra Nevada for grand panoramas and dizzying viewpoints, assembled a splendid body of work, a hymn to the deep heart of America advancing towards the conquest of power, liberty, and the elements. In a century split from beginning to end by a deep division between art and technology, the nineteenth-century flowering of photographic images accompanying works of architecture constituted a revolution in itself. A new age of perception and representation opened up, soon to move to other spheres.

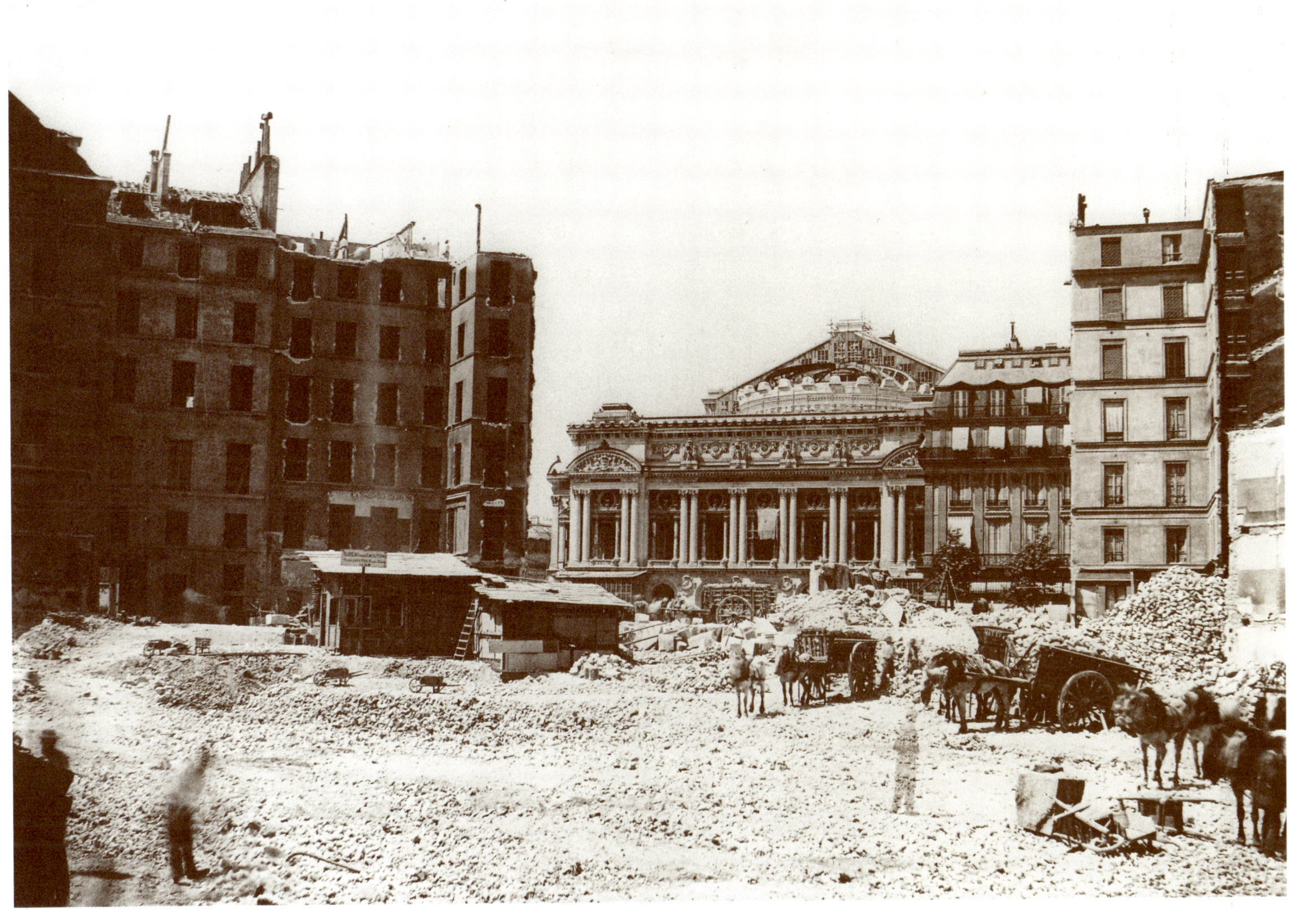

The Paris Opera by Delmaet and Durandelle

The Paris Opera is an essential work for an understanding of theatrical architecture under the Second Empire. It is not just "the temple of pleasure" but also, and above all, the temple of a particular art opera, which speaks to the senses, the heart, and the emotions with a heady all-enveloping magnetism.

This exuberance springs from the architecture itself, the free and slightly adventurous style adopted by a hitherto unknown French architect, Charles Garnier. At the time he carried off the Grand Prix de Rome, unanimously voted the winner out of 171 competitors, Garnier was still only thirty-five.

Begun in 1861, construction took fourteen years, an immense undertaking which was interrupted first by the war of 1870, and then by the Commune. The landmark building, in Napoleon III style, was inaugurated under the Third Republic, on January 5, 1875, by Marshal MacMahon. It hides its copper and iron skeleton under marble partitions luxuriantly decorated in a style breathing new life into forms drawn from a variety of sources.

Charles Garnier's role was not confined to planning the construction of the building. In pursuit of his desire for "story-telling architecture" he supervised the whole iconographic program on the spot, directing workmen, painters, sculptors, mosaic-makers, and photographers. In a publication entitled *Le Nouvel Opéra de Paris* (Ducher et Cie, 1878–1881), in which the architect tells the history of, and describes, his eclectic monument, the list of businesses which took part in the construction work on the new Opera building includes, under "photography", the studio of Delmaet and Durandelle.

The original photographs were gathered into collections of more than 100 prints (with some variants) on the progress of the building works and the different phases of the construction, sculptures, and decorative ornament (1865–1872), which in particular show various stages of construction (which cross-sections and elevations cannot do).

A romantic by nature, Charles Garnier mused: "As for me, when I contemplate the time when the Opera will be no more than a ruin, I do so not simply without regret, but I can truthfully say that I am sorry I shall no longer be in this world when brambles and ivy are climbing over the devastated walls of the edifice."

In order to preserve the memory of the different stages of the construction, photographs were taken every time any important changes occurred on the site. "If, later, one wanted to produce a monograph about the Opera", Charles Garnier added in one of his numerous handwritten reports, "the photographic elements that would then be at one's disposition would make this publication much easier."

With a mathematical, almost clinical, regularity, the photographers Delmaet and Durandelle became, for a while, architectural anatomists – their images of metal girders, trusses, frameworks, rostral columns, classical masks, pilasters, pediments, attics, draped figures, allegories in marble or plaster, and several other types of anatomical models, all combine to create new ways of seeing which anticipate the modernism of the twentieth century.

Over and beyond their documentary interest, these images mark the birth of a genuine photographic language. Today, we recognize that Delmaet and Durandelle, who transcended their status as craftsmen to become artists, figure among the first masters of their craft.

Elvire Perego

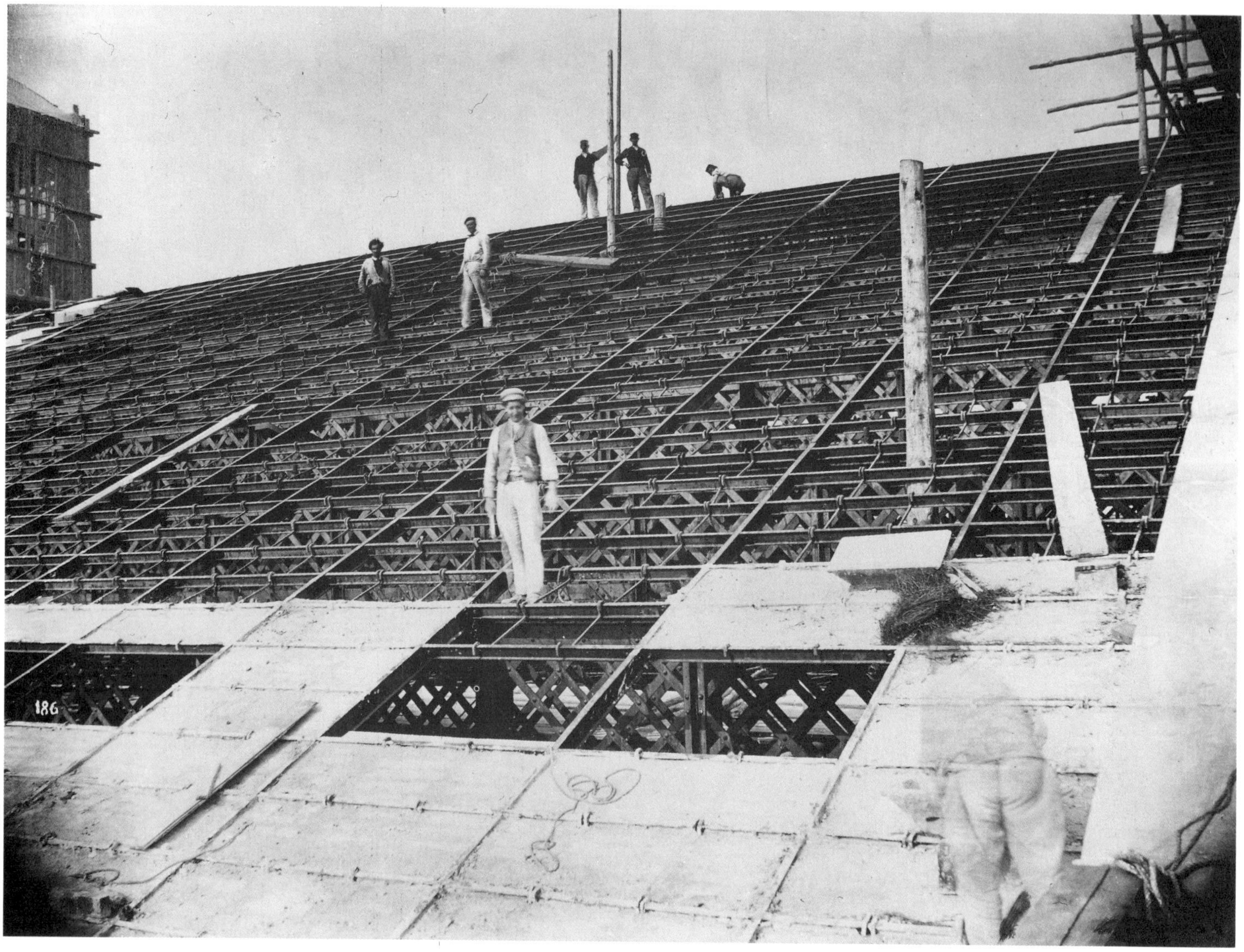

▲
Delmaet and Durandelle,
Opera Roof,
1867–1868,
Bibliothèque Nationale,
Paris.

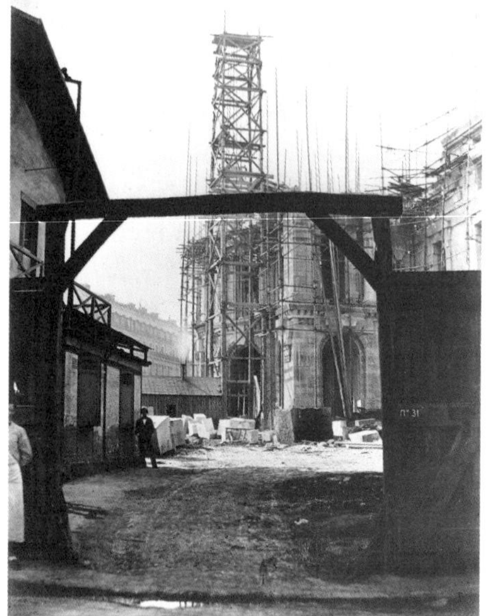

Delmaet and Durandelle,
Scaffolding and Construction of the Season-ticket Holders' Section,
1865,
Bibliothèque Nationale, Paris.

◄◄ On the previous page:
Delmaet and Durandelle,
Opening up Avenue de l'Opéra,
1867–1868,
Bibliothèque de l'École Nationale Supérieure des Beaux-Arts,
Paris.

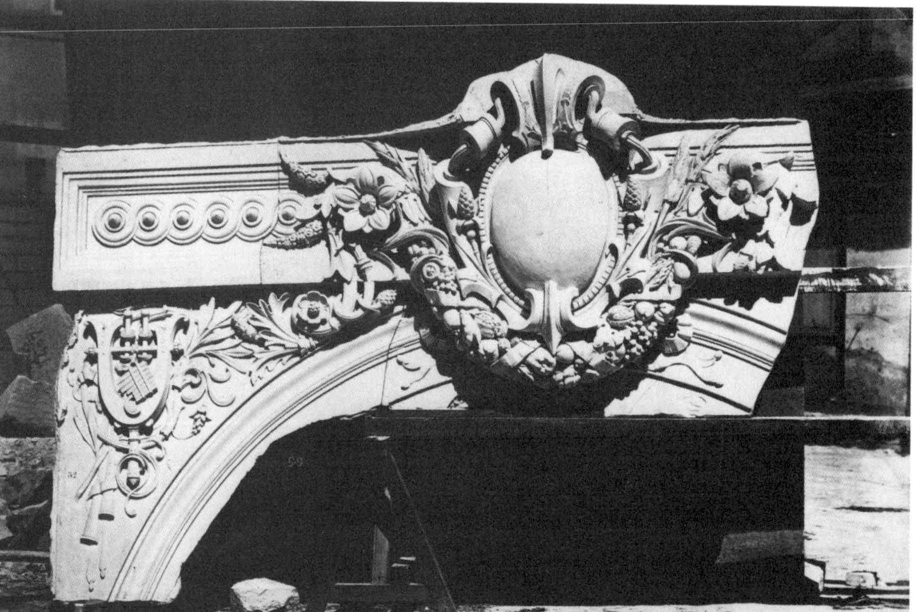

Delmaet and Durandelle
Keystone and Tympanum for the Foyer Archway,
August 1865,
Bibliothèque de l'École Nationale Supérieure des Beaux-Arts.

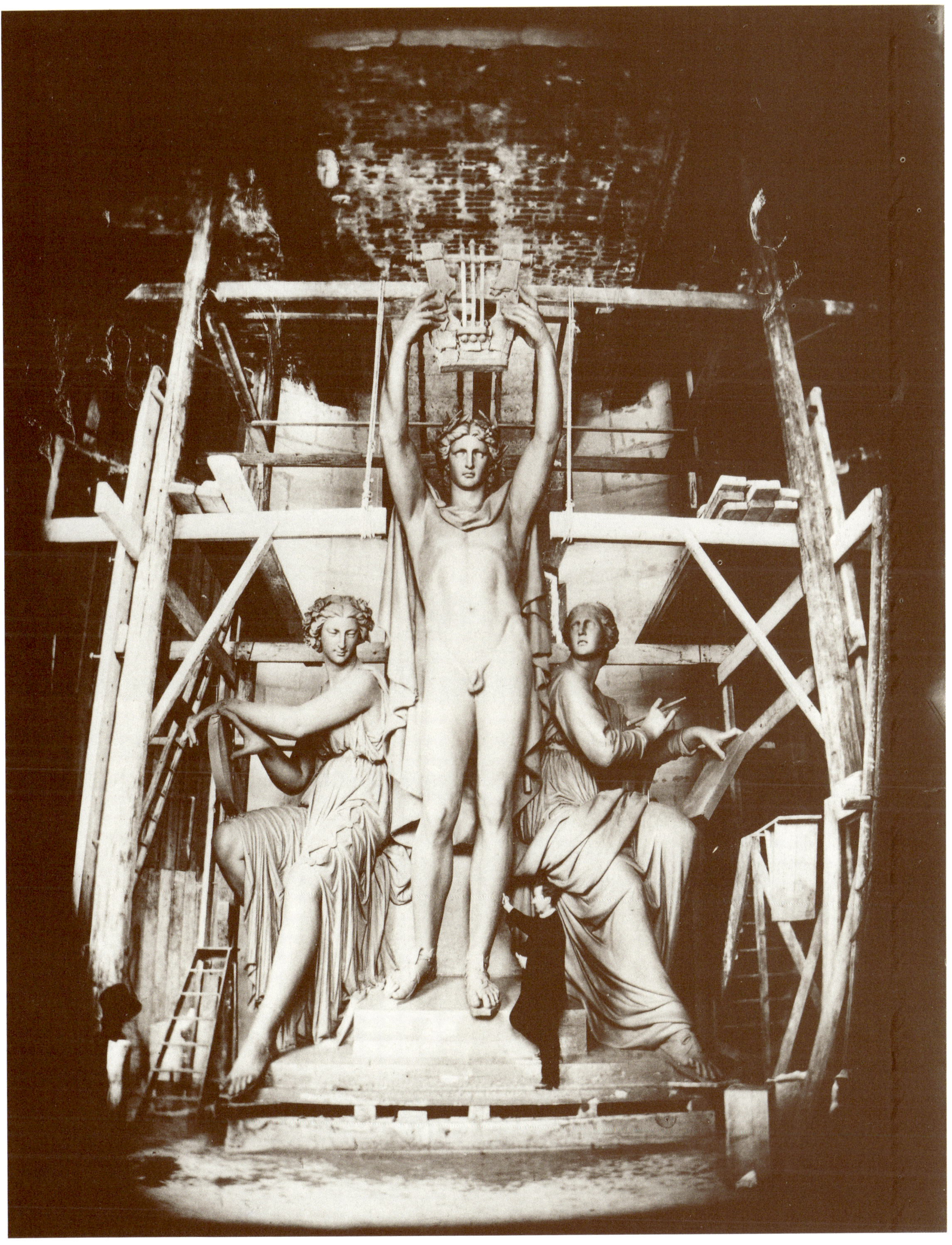

Delmaet and Durandelle,
Apollo Group, with the Sculptor Millet,
1868–1869, Bibliothèque de l'École Nationale Supérieure des Beaux-Arts.

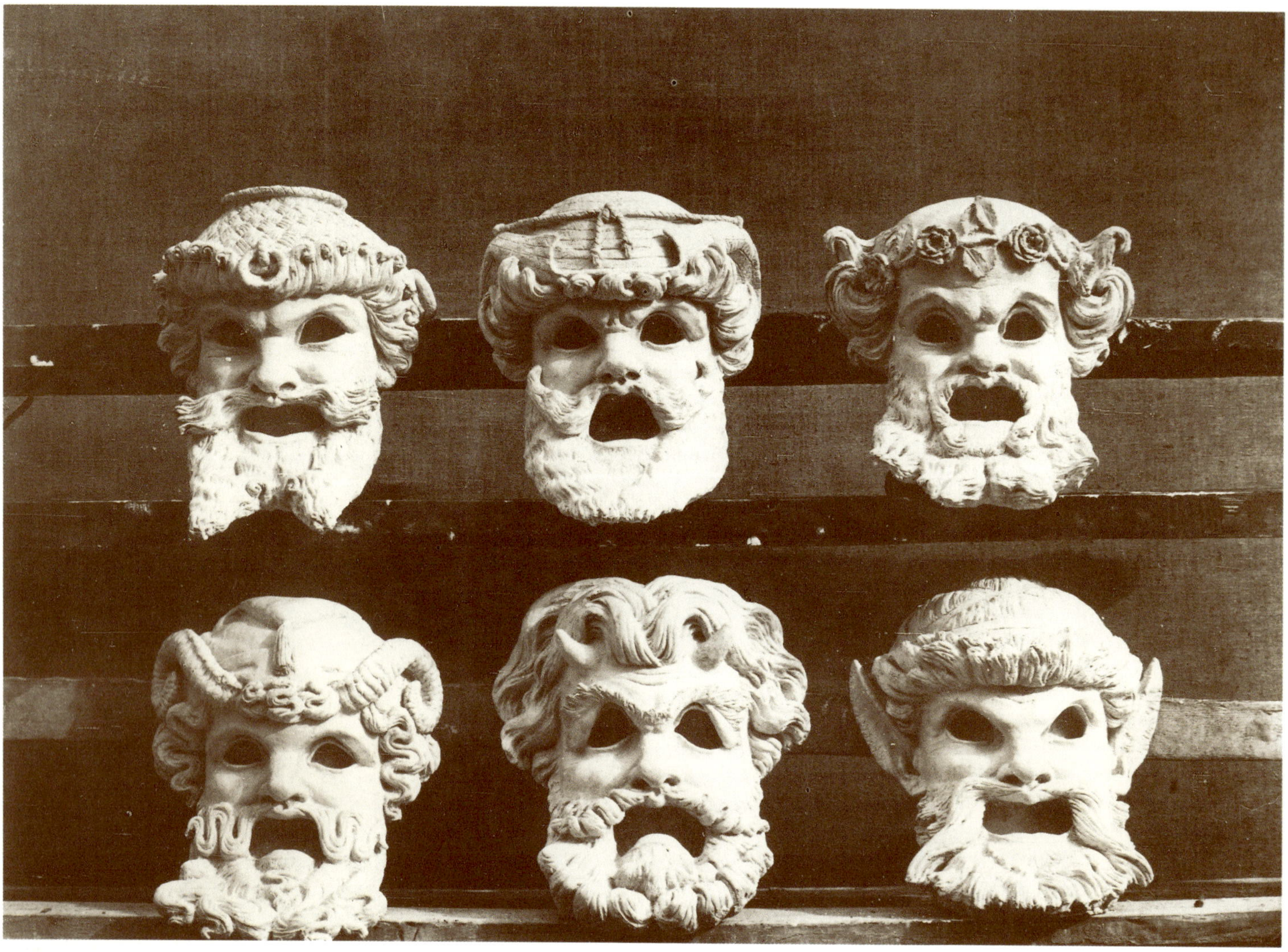

Delmaet and Durandelle,
Masks for the Fireplaces in the Management Area,
September 1865,
Bibliothèque de l'École Nationale Supérieure des Beaux-Arts.

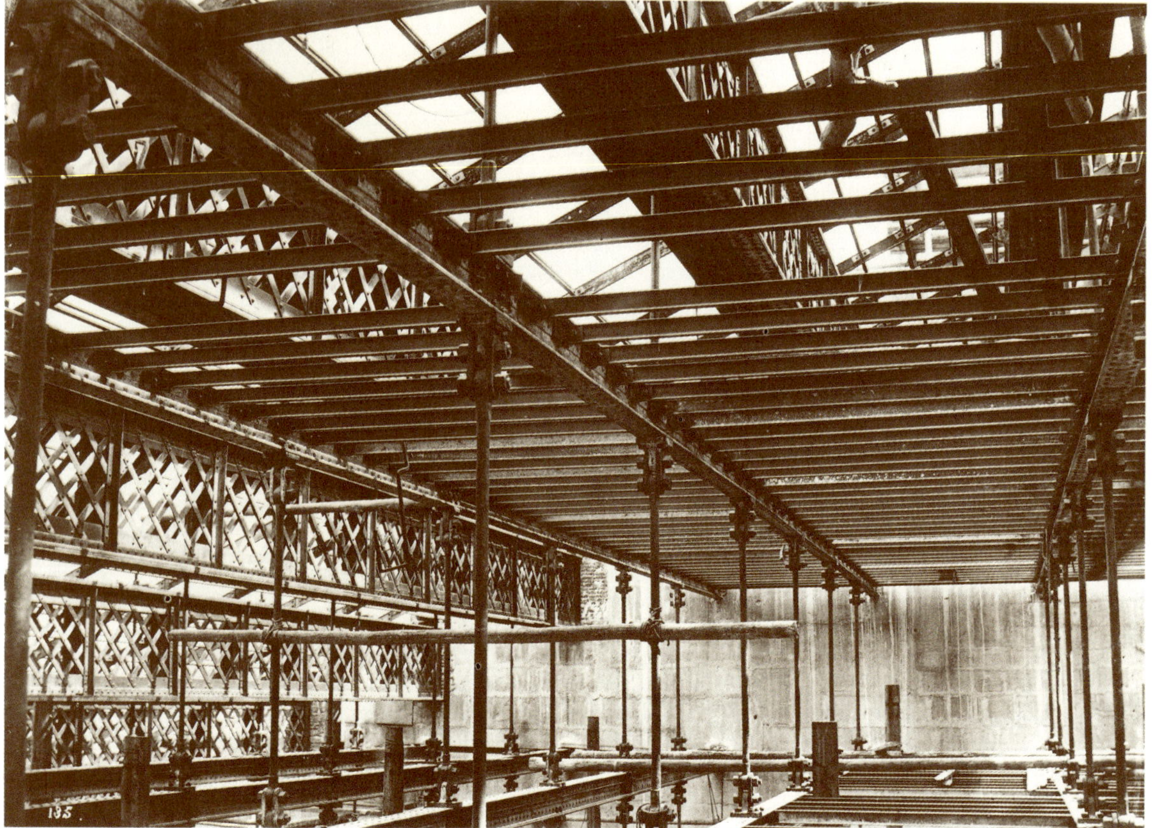

Delmaet and Durandelle,
View of Work at Balcony Level,
Bibliothèque de l'École Nationale Supérieure des Beaux-Arts.

Delmaet and Durandelle, ▶
Decorative Sculpture,
1869–1870,
Bibliothèque Nationale, Paris.

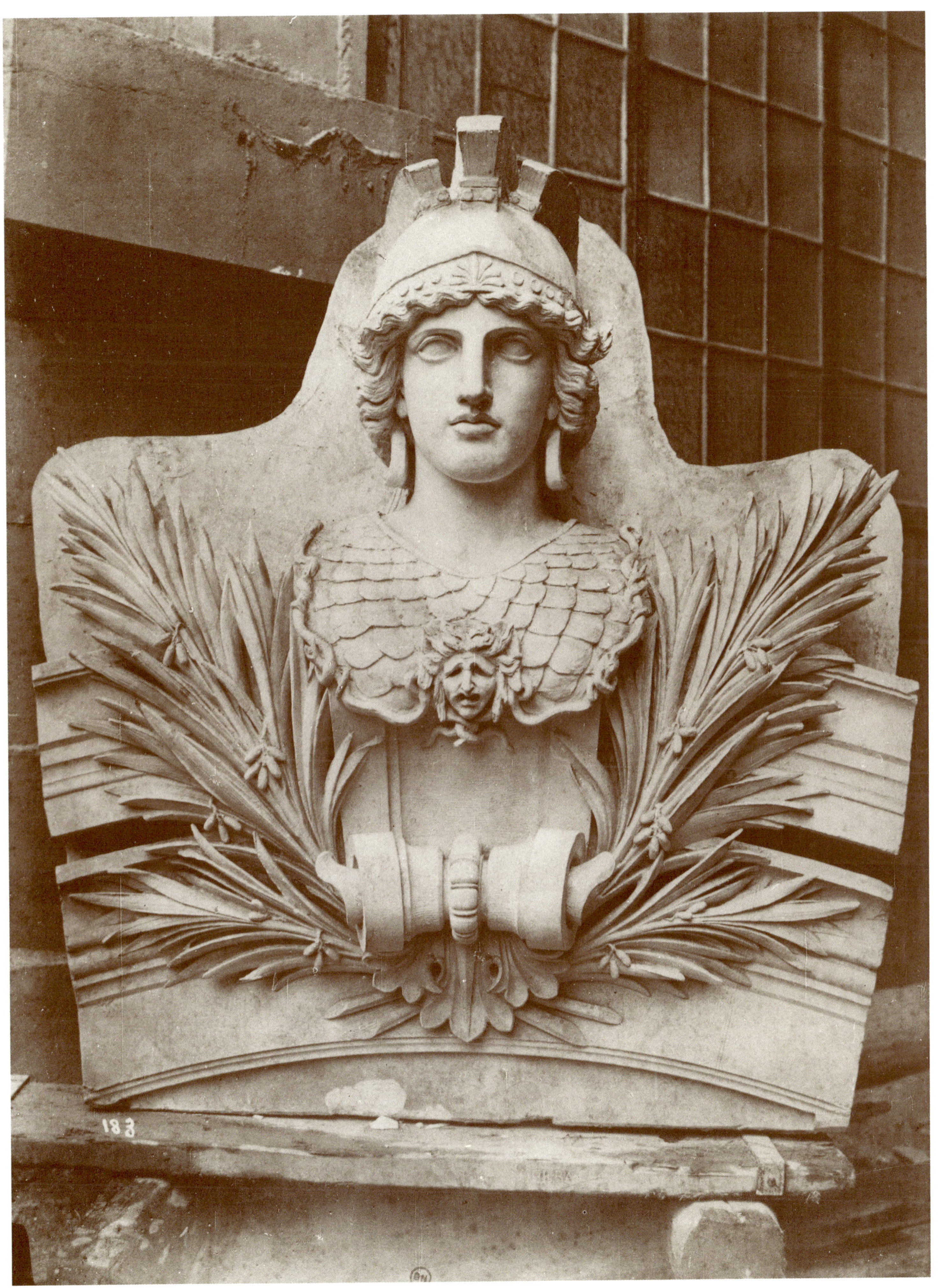
183

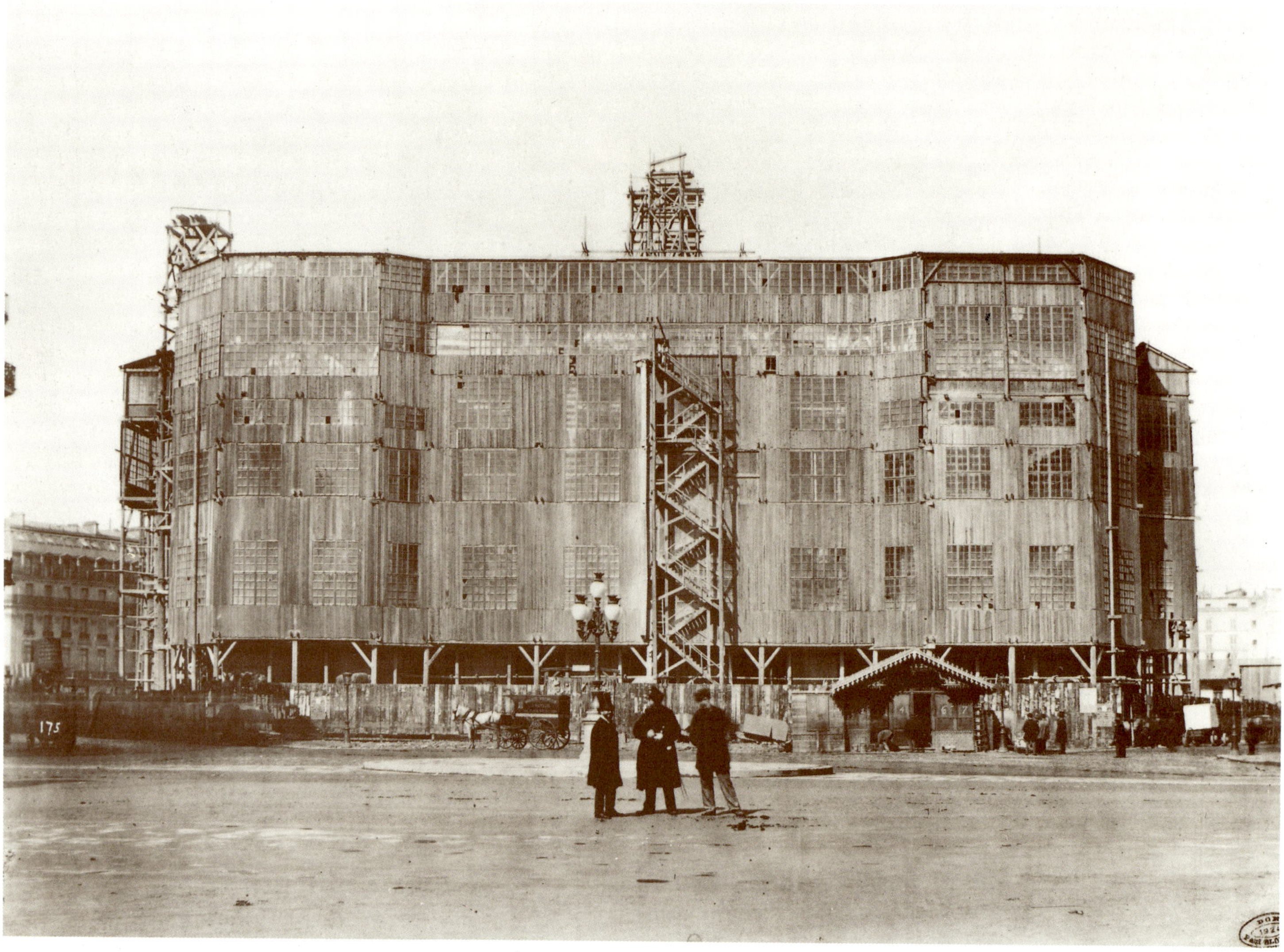

▲
Delmaet and Durandelle,
Glassed-in Scaffolding on Facade,
circa 1865,
Bibliothèque de l'École Nationale Supérieure des Beaux-Arts.

Delmaet and Durandelle, ►
View of Auditorium Floor from Stage,
May 10, 1865,
Bibliothèque Nationale, Paris.

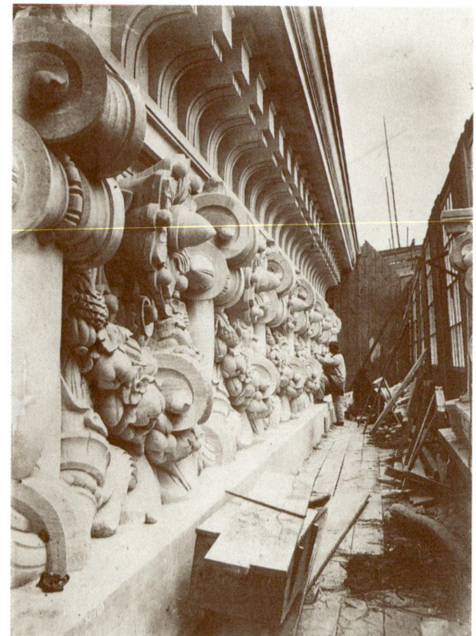

Delmaet and Durandelle,
Sculptors at Work,
circa 1866–1869,
Bibliothèque de l'École Nationale Supérieure des Beaux-Arts.

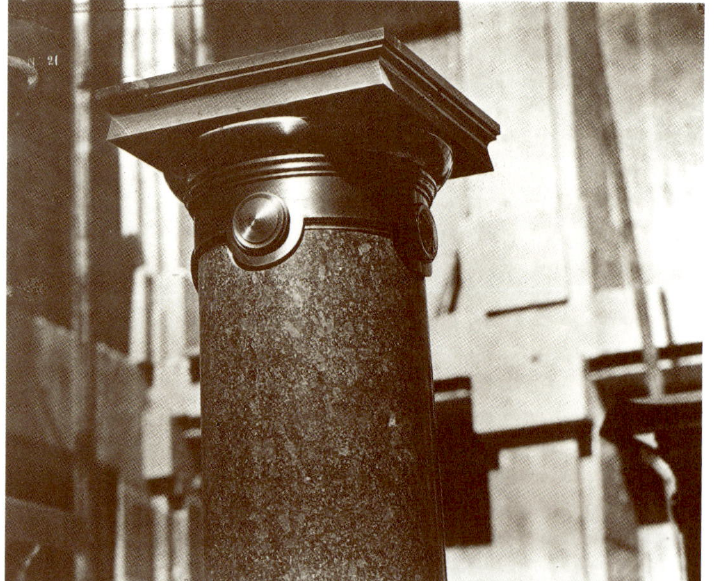

Delmaet and Durandelle,
Rostral Column,
circa 1868,
Bibliothèque Nationale, Paris.

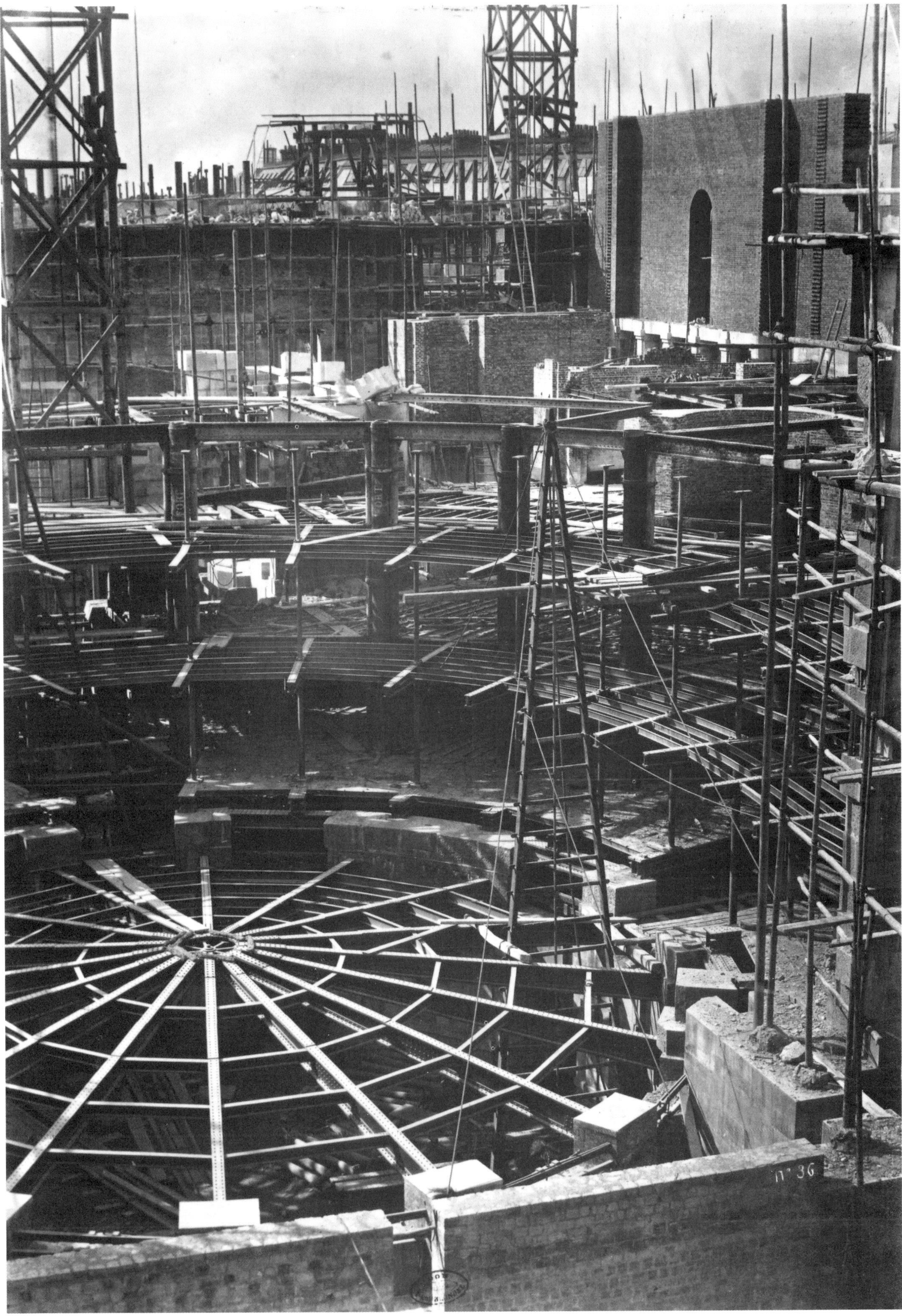
N° 36

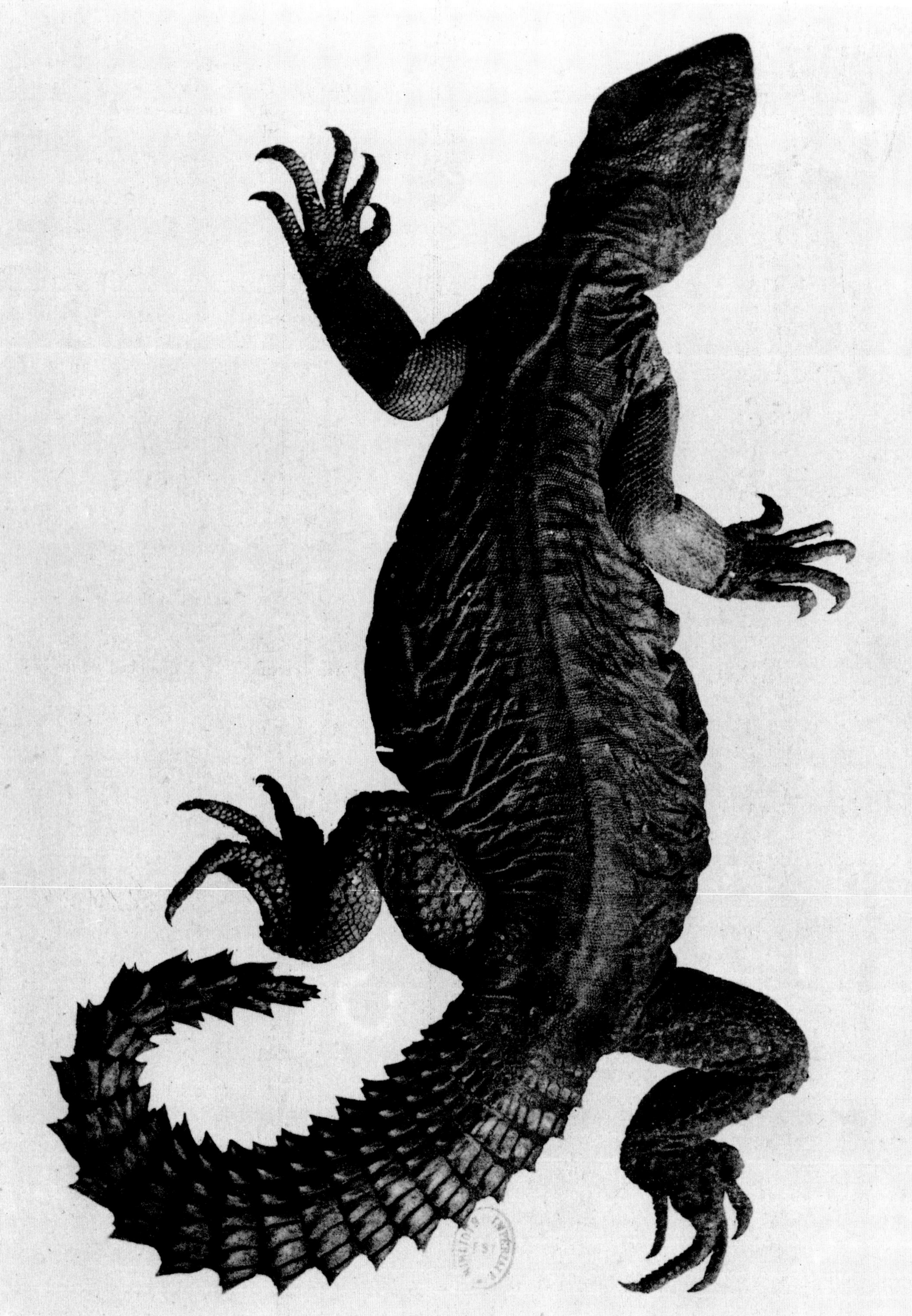

THE PHOTOGRAPH IN PRINT

12

Multiplication and stability of the image

Sylvie Aubenas

Nicéphore Niépce was looking for a way of directly recording images from nature and multiplying them in a form similar to engravings. The invention of photography, however, did not solve the problem of how to obtain images that were stable and permanent. The recording needs of the nineteenth century, associated with the unrivaled accuracy of the photograph, prompted research into ways of transforming photographs into printed images that would be accurate, cheap to produce, and not subject to deterioration. This ambition had been partially achieved by the end of the nineteenth century, but did not reach its full commercial maturity until later.

In August 1839, when Arago presented the daguerreotype process to a combined session of the Académies of Sciences and Beaux-Arts, it was so full of promise that it immediately acquired a unique status. However, if we set aside abstract speculation about photography's potential, and examine the means that existed in 1839 for bringing photography to the attention of the general public, we realize that the daguerreotype image was as fragile as a butterfly's wing, fleeting, and much more difficult to reproduce than an engraving. There was a general consensus that photography would become a force only once it could produce durable, infinitely repeatable images, as Ernest Lacan wrote in 1856: "For us, photography, however complete its results, is only a transitory process; the future lies with heliographic engraving or photolithography."

Each daguerreotype, on its silver-coated copper plate, was a unique image. Talbot's paper negative process (1840) and Niépce de Saint-Victor's glass negative process (1847) opened the way to the multiplication of the image. However, if a negative could, in theory, serve as the original for an unlimited number of prints, in practice technical constraints limited this number. The slowness and high cost of producing a photograph were insurmountable obstacles to the mass distribution of a single image. This was not a barrier to commercial exploitation – especially for portraits – but it did limit the distribution of photographs. Besides the difficulty of multiplication there was another problem – printing onto paper treated with salt or albumen produced an unstable image because silver salts, imperfectly fixed, continued to react to light (depending on the amount of care taken with printing and washing). To palliate this major defect, people tried to find printing methods which did not use silver salts. The work done by Alphonse Poitevin,[1] then Pouncy[2] and Fargier, resulted in a photographic process which used carbon, one of the finest photographic materials. However, this process was too complex to be adopted widely by photographic studios.

Different solutions, some better than others, were proposed throughout the century. Paradoxically, these were characterized from the start by their links with engraving or lithography. These photomechanical processes used a stone (lithography), or a copper, zinc or steel plate as support on which a photographic image was used to produce an inked master which could then be printed off on a press. This is not really a paradox, if one reflects that Niépce's 1826 reproduction of the portrait of Cardinal Georges d'Amboise already combined a metal (pewter) plate with the action of the sun on a sensitized surface, that daguerreotypes are produced on a sheet of silver-plated copper, and that Fizeau had the idea, as early as 1840, of creating photographic etchings by engraving daguerreotypes, using acid.

◀ LOUIS ROUSSEAU, *Lizard*, photolithography by the POITEVIN process, 1856, Bibliothèque Nationale, Paris.

1. L.-A. Poitevin (1819–1882), graduate of the École Centrale, chemist and engineer, became involved in photography as early as 1840, continuing until 1867. He perfected a number of new techniques of which the most remarkable were photolithography and carbon process (using dichromate coated on carbon tissue).

2. The carbon process, inspired by Poitevin's method, enjoyed a certain success in Britain.

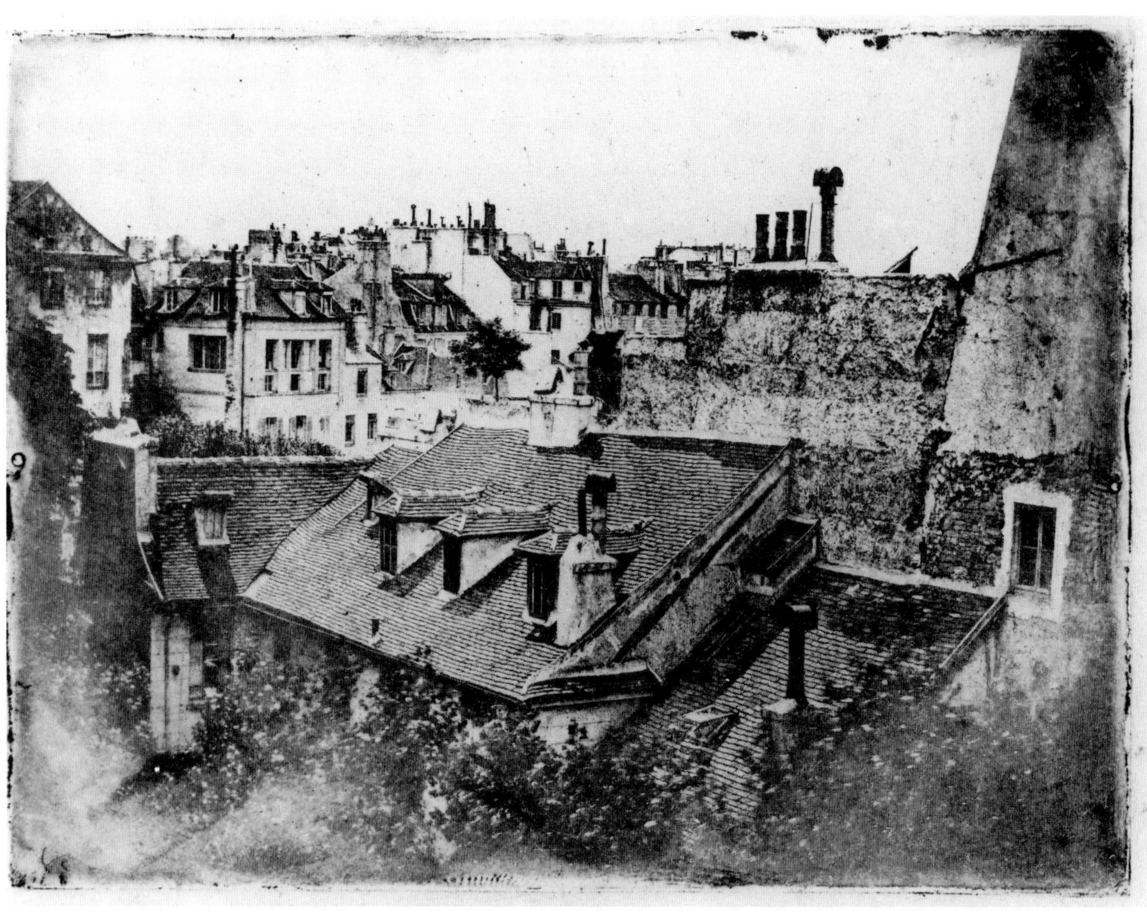

Hippolyte Fizeau,
Rooftops of Paris,
circa 1840,
engraved daguerrotype plate,
Bibliothèque Nationale, Paris.

Pierre Trémaux, ▶
Girl from Dar-Four,
circa 1847–1854,
print from a paper negative,
Bibliothèque Nationale, Paris.

Lithograph from ▶
photograph by
Pierre Trémaux,
Girl from Dar-Four,
circa 1862,
from *Voyage au Soudan oriental*, plate 38,
Bibliothèque Nationale, Paris.

The photomechanical processes used between 1840 and 1880 shared a fairly simple basic principle – their use of a photosensitive[3] substance which had the characteristic of becoming insoluble after exposure to light. This substance was applied to a flat hard surface, stone or metal, and then exposed to sunlight through a photographic negative. Only those areas protected from the light, that is, underneath the black parts of the negative, remained soluble. After washing, the support retained a positive impression of the image, ready to be inked and printed. Alternatively, on metal, a transparent positive image could be used. The photosensitive substance under the dark parts of the image disappeared, leaving those areas to be etched out with acid and inked for printing. The first successful results were those obtained in France by Fizeau, Nègre, Niépce de Saint-Victor, Lemercier,[4] and Poitevin, and in Britain by Fox Talbot.

The first photomechanical processes, grouped under the general term photogravures, were characterized by their use of a metal plates as a support.[5] Just as Nicéphore Niépce had received advice from the engraver Augustin François Lemaître in order to make his 1826 reproduction of the portrait of Cardinal d'Amboise, Hippolyte Fizeau had, as early as 1839, managed to devise, with the help of the engraver Hurlimann, a complex method using the techniques of etching, acquatint, and electroplating to transform daguerreotypes into plates suitable for printing. However, Hurlimann's untimely death discouraged Fizeau from pursuing the work alone. A few years later, Niépce de Saint-Victor continued the work started by his cousin Nicéphore, with the help of Lemaître. It was not until 1856, however, when Charles Nègre patented a photogravure process which he called *damasquinure héliographique*, that the method produced successful results (see box). However, Nègre's method, which was very complicated, and about which he always remained secretive, remained a craft-activity which could not be put to commercial use by anyone else. Research on photogravure was temporarily abandoned by those working on photomechanical processes in favor of techniques of photolithography, which had the advantage of being much simpler to use.

The Duc de Luynes' competition

It is in this context that we should consider the initiative taken in 1856 by Honoré d'Albert, duc de Luynes, an enlightened art-lover, patron, and archeologist, who was himself a photographer. He set up a competition, with the considerable prize of 10,000 francs, to foster the zeal of persons conducting important research, and to

3. Asphalt, or bitumen of Judea, which dissolves only in ether or substances like petroleum, or gelatin bichromate, which is easier to handle because it can be diluted with water.

4. J-R. Lemercier (1803–1887), printer/lithographer, associate of Lerebours, Barreswill and Davanne in the development of a photolithographic process.

5. *De Niépce à Stieglitz: la Photographie en taille-douce*, Lausanne, Musée de l'Elysée, 1982.

6. He gave the Société Française de Photographie the task of organizing the competition, which was announced in its *Bulletin* of July 1856.

reimburse them in part for their necessary outlay.[6] A sum of 8,000 francs would be given to the inventor of the best process for photomechanical reproduction, and 2,000 francs to the person making the most progress in printing from silver-based originals or achieving greater permanence in the results.

The competition created an international stir. Candidates from Britain, Germany, Austria and Holland took part. The jury was composed of scholars (Regnault, Balard, Becquerel), photographers (Aguado, Bayard), engravers, and other personalities. In the competition for the best photomechanical process, the jury eliminated twelve candidates out of fifteen between 1856 and 1859, then proceeded to a new selection between 1859 and 1864 (five candidates). They delayed their verdict yet again, until 1867, in order to choose between three inventors – Alphonse Poitevin, Charles Nègre, and Paul Pretsch – before finally awarding the prize to the method invented and patented by Alphonse Poitevin back in 1855, and already shortlisted in 1856. The competition, which was meant to finish on July 1, 1859, did not close until 1867, eight years later.

This delay calls for an explanation. The jury were not totally satisfied with the methods that had been short-listed, and kept hoping that a new method would appear which would sweep away any doubts. They also eliminated two candidates because they did not see the potential of their work – the Viennese, Charles de Berchtold, who first proposed the half-tone process, and Paul Pretsch, whose system they considered too complicated (though, in fact, it had been in commercial use in London since 1856). The choice was, therefore, between two methods: Charles Nègre's photogravure, which produced magnificent results but was slow and complicated, and Poitevin's photolithography. The jury pronounced the latter "to have completely realized the conditions laid down by the duc de Luynes. That is to say, his process of printing with oily ink, which is that of lithography, will produce easily, without re-touching, and in such a way as to guarantee authenticity, any photographic print in as many copies as may be necessary to make documents useful for the arts and the sciences available to everybody."

The duc de Luynes himself seems to have preferred Charles Nègre's method. In 1856, he commissioned Nègre to print fifty plates illustrating his *Voyage d'Exploration à la Mer morte,* from photographs by Louis Vignes. However, awarding the prize to Poitevin in 1867 for a technique going back to 1855 amounted to an admission that no decisive progress had been made in

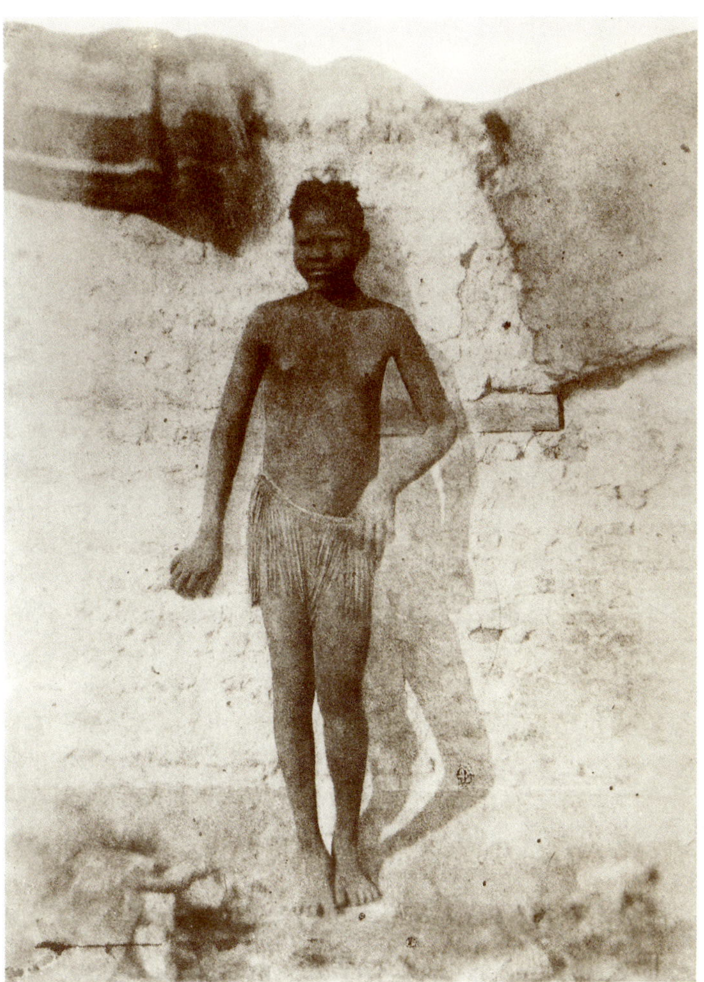

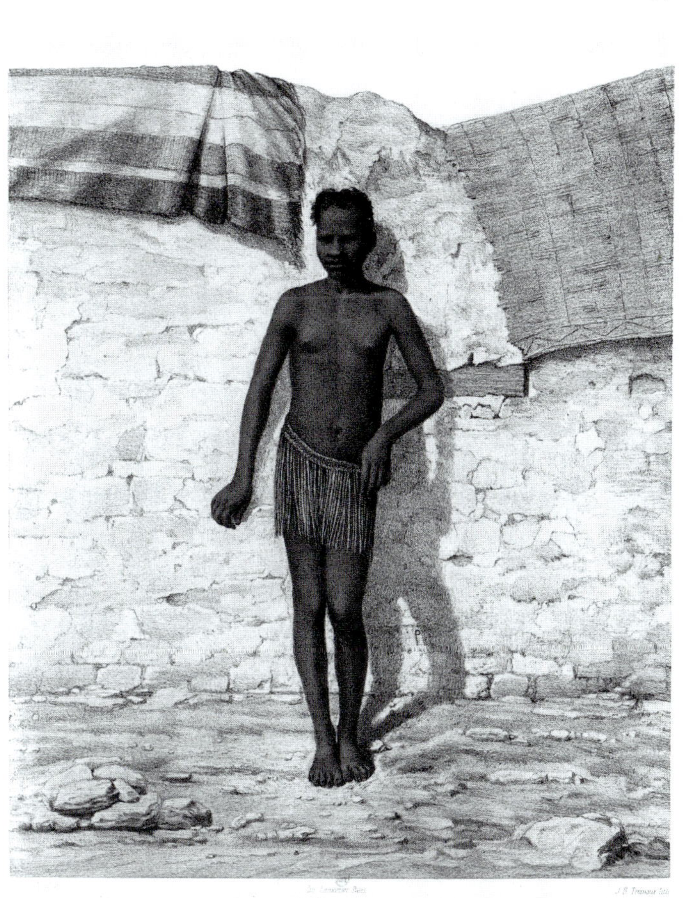

Photogravure

Photogravure[1] is a photomechanical process of reproduction which makes it possible to transfer a photographic image to an inked metal plate, from which one can then print a large number of copies on paper. The traditional processes of engraving – or ink-transfer – are generally divided into engraving in relief (typography, half-tone), incised (etching by hand or with acid) or flat (photolithography or offset), depending on whether the ink goes onto the parts that stand out, into the hollows or into the irregularities on the surface of the plate.

The principles of photogravure, or copperplate engraving (where the ink goes into the hollows), were laid down by Nicéphore Niépce. A metal plate (copper, silver-plated copper or tin) is coated with a photosensitive substance. Light reacts with this substance to produce areas covered with a protective coating, which prevents them from being affected by acid which eats into the unprotected areas of the (Nicéphore Niépce used bitumen of Judea).

The metal plates used for daguerreotypes also seemed to offer a method of rendering shades of gray by the use of acid. Fizeau and Hurlimann worked on this method (three plates in *Excursions daguerriennes*, 1842). However, the great problem that faced all photo-engravers was how to render with precision all the range of half-tones in an image[2] – a problem solved by using black dots to produce different shades of gray.

W. H. F. Talbot used the photosensitive properties of gelatin bichromate to produce a screen (covered with regularly-spaced dots) created by two thicknesses of gauze placed at 45 degrees to each other, or by powdering with resin – a technique known as aquatint (1854–1858). Abel Niépce de Saint-Victor, Nicéphore's cousin, followed his process of using bitumen of Judea, with or without a screen, for Rousseau and Devéria's *Photographie Zoologique* (1853). Working in the same area of research, Charles Nègre took on the challenge of large plates

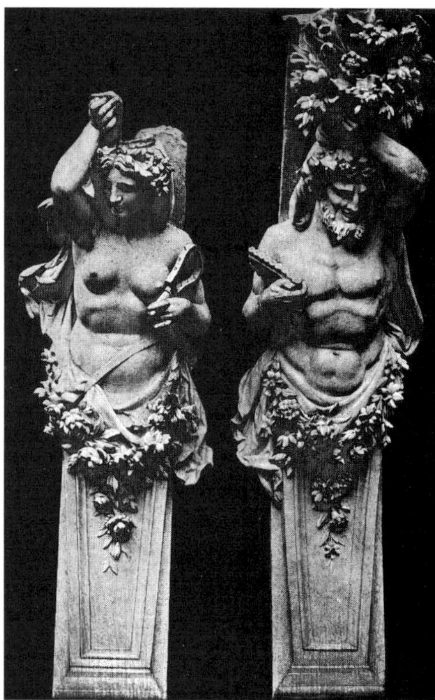

Édouard-Denis Baldus,
Photogravure,
from *Palais du Louvre et des Tuileries*, 1875.

(80 x 59 cm, c. 1857: *Chartres Cathedral*), using successive applications of acid, dusting with resin, and starting with a negative instead of a positive transparency. Nègre was Poitevin's most serious competitor for the duc de Luynes' prize. Édouard-Denis Baldus also used undisclosed photogravure techniques (*Palais du Louvre et des Tuileries*, 1875).

Around 1860, the use of gelatin bichromate as the photo-sensitive layer was fairly general. Some improvements were introduced in the dusting process or the frame by Pretsch (electroplate photo system), Placet, Klič, in Prague (reticulation of the gelatin or resin), and Berchtold (three-lined mechanical screen, 1857).

Klič's method (resin powder, from 1879) was swiftly taken up in Europe and America.[3] The advantage of photogravure is that it produces deep blacks, obtained by the quantity of ink deposited and not by dots clustered together as in half-tone engraving. Consequently the method was highly regarded at the end of the nineteenth century for its faithful reproduction of the tonality of the print. P. H. Emerson considered photogravures of his work to be as good as original prints. He learnt the technique himself in 1890. Alvin Langdon Coburn, after settling in Britain, used the process for printing the images in his books *London* (1909), and *New York* (1910). The review *Camera Work* (1903–1917), created by Stieglitz, had a policy of publishing Pictorial photographs printed by photogravure (416 out of 544 illustrations), considering these reproductions to be like original plates.[4]

Photogravure was (and remains) a perfect process for limited editions. Among those it was used for are *Old Closes and Streets of Glasgow* by Thomas Annan (1900), Curtis's *The North American Indian* (1907–1930), Paul Strand's *Photographs of Mexico*, and the part-works *L'Art photographique* (1899) and *L'Épreuve photographique* (1900).

Photogravure was also the favored process of the inter-war years (Kertész, Krull) and of the 1950s, until it gave way to more rapid methods producing a shiny rather than a matte surface (half-tone, offset).

Michel Frizot

1. In French, the term *héliogravure* is used.

2. *De Niépce à Stieglitz: la Photographie en Taille-douce*, exhibition catalogue, Lausanne, Musée de l'Élysée, 1982.

3. Rotogravure (Klič, 1890) is derived from it. This process uses a squared screen, and the printing is not done flat, but with a cylinder.

4. W. Crawford, *The Keepers of Light: A History and Working Guide to Early Photographic Processes*, Dobbs Ferry, Morgan and Morgan, 1979.

the previous twelve years, and, to all intents and purposes, rendered the patron's generosity useless. It did, however, put the current state of affairs on record, while awaiting the real progress that took place in between the still semi-craft-based procedures of the years 1850–1860, and the industrial processes that grew out of them .

As for the prize of 2,000 francs, familiarly known as the "little competition", which was meant to be awarded in July 1858, that was also awarded to Poitevin in March 1862, after a certain amount of vacillation. Once again, he was preferred to another inventor, Fargier, who, like Nègre, presented more beautiful prints but had simply made practical improvements to Poitevin's work.

Such research, however, were never really to interest the mass of professional photographers, who were satisfied with their silver-salt prints which perfectly fulfilled the desires of their customers.

Photography and publishing

Because photography can faithfully reproduce reality, there was the hope of obtaining images from nature, without relying on the artist or the engraver as intermediary. Growing interest in archeology and the fine arts, as well as the development of the sciences, seemed to offer immense potential for the use of photography within publishing. However, because of its cost, slowness, and the instability of images, photography could not compete with woodcuts and engravings made on steel or lithography – techniques which were perfectly suited to the needs of publishers. Nonetheless, as early as the start of the 1840s, some interesting attempts were made to use photographs for book illustration. We find printers like Lemercier going into research, and researchers like Poitevin going into industry in order to exploit their discoveries.

The optician Lerebours, who sold photographic equipment in Paris, took advantage of the mania for photography by publishing, between 1842 and 1844, his *Excursions daguerriennes*, a hundred or so views engraved from daguerreotypes. Care had been taken to add in people or scenes that had been too fleeting to be captured by the lens. This is the first appearance of the descriptive note after the photograph which recurs throughout the century to give the stamp of authenticity and reality to exotic or picturesque scenes. Another use of photography to illustrate books was to paste original prints into them (as was done by Talbot in his *Pencil of Nature*).

The example of Louis-Désiré Blanquart-Evrard is rather different. He was a Lille printer whose efforts were directed into overcoming the obstacle of slow and costly photographic silver-printing. His answer was to reduce production time by organizing the work along industrial lines. In 1854, it cost him 120 francs to make 100 prints of approximately 25 x 35 cm (at the same period, the average cost of a print sold by a photographic studio was between 6 and 8 francs). All that this achieved, however, was to equal the price of a lithograph, without its permanence. Competition from the photomechanical sector producing non-deteriorating prints proved too strong. In 1855, he had to close down the business which he had started just four years earlier.[7]

In parallel with these experiments, systematic ways of using photomechanical processes in publishing also developed. The first attempt was by Louis Rousseau and Achille Devéria. Their *Photographie zoologique, ou Représentation des Animaux rares des Collections du Museum d'Histoire naturelle*, published in Paris in 1853, is the first scientific work illustrated by photomechanical engraving. Its aim was "to put within the reach of everyone the reproductions obtained by this marvelous method, reproductions so faithful that one can, simply with the use of a magnifying-glass, see letters that cannot be distinguished with the naked eye on the object itself." The photographs, taken by Bisson, were transferred to paper by Niépce de Saint-Victor's photogravure method. Louis-Alphonse Poitevin, after patenting his photolithography process in 1855, took the decision to exploit it himself by turning printer/

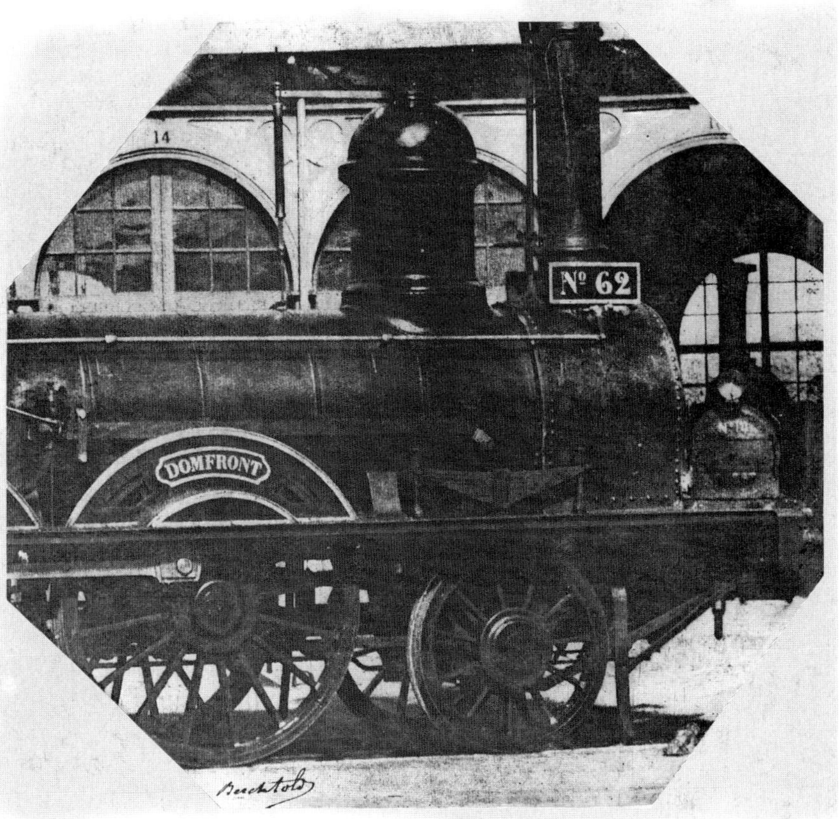

Charles de Berchtold process,
Locomotive,
1859,
Société Française de Photographie, Paris.

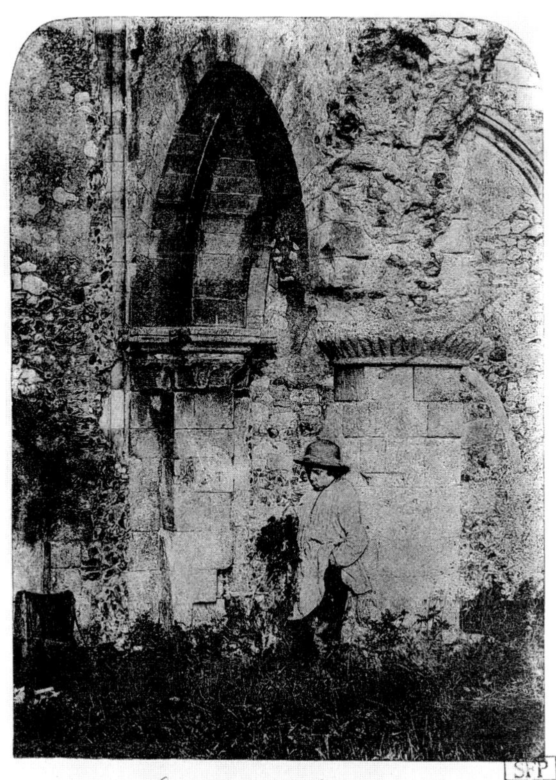

◀ Photoelectrotype by
Paul Pretsch,
Contemplation,
circa 1856,
Société Française de Photographie, Paris.

7. See I. Jammes, *Blanquart-Evrard et les Origines de l'Édition photographique française: catalogue raisonné des albums photographiques edités, 1851–1855*, Paris and Geneva, Droz, 1981.

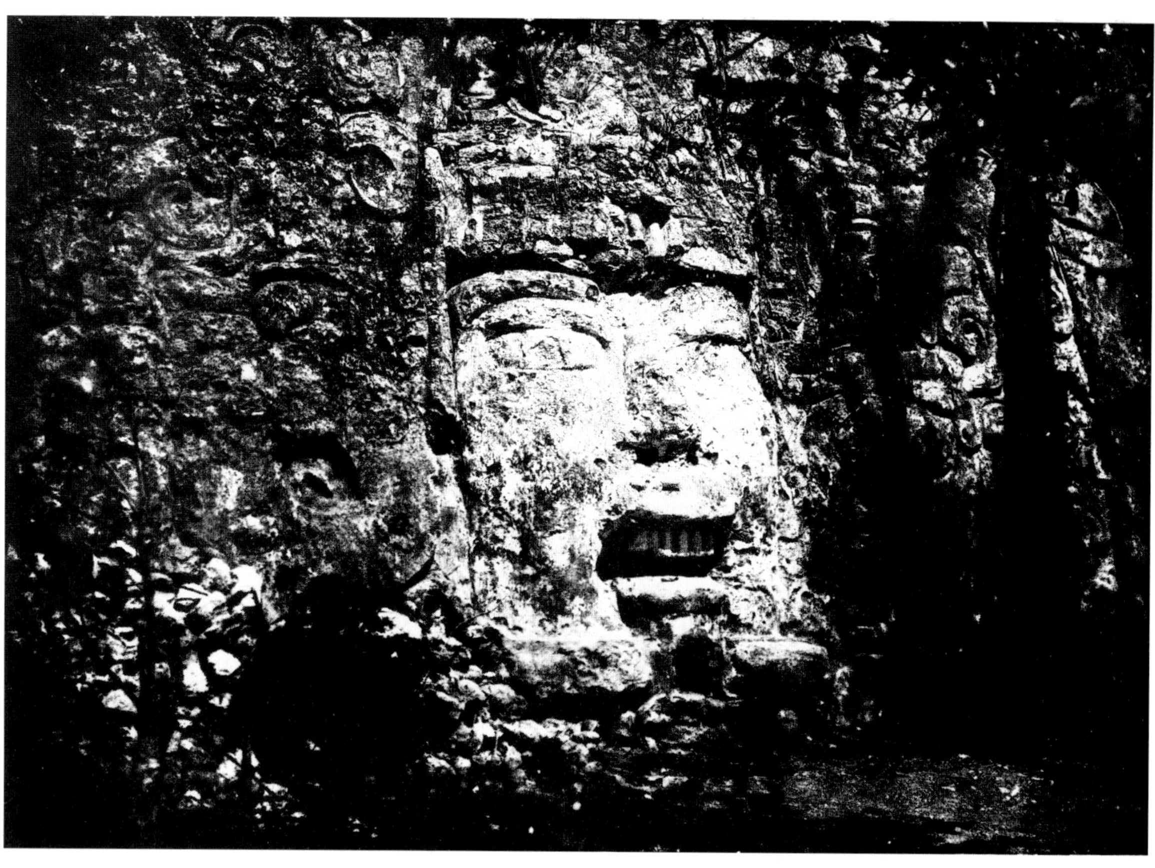

Photolithograph by the **Poitevin** process, from **Désiré Charnay**, ***Izamal, Mexico,*** Mayan sculpture, 1861, Bibliothèque Nationale, Paris.

lithographer. His technique permitted a print-run of 500 to 1,500 prints per stone, averaging eight to ten prints an hour. His workshop produced over 18,000 photolithographs in sixteen months, of which a large number were for use in publishing. Poitevin produced the plates for four works, among them *Recherches expérimentales sur la végétation* by Georges Ville, who was confident that photography would provide irrefutable proof of the influence of certain fertilizers on the growth of plants, and *The Serapeum of Memphis* by

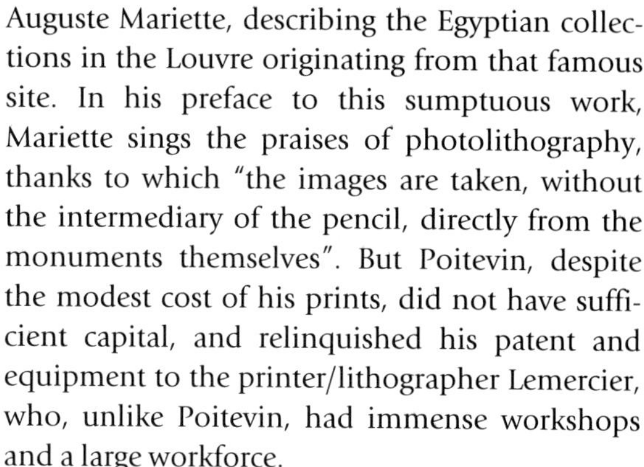

Auguste Mariette, describing the Egyptian collections in the Louvre originating from that famous site. In his preface to this sumptuous work, Mariette sings the praises of photolithography, thanks to which "the images are taken, without the intermediary of the pencil, directly from the monuments themselves". But Poitevin, despite the modest cost of his prints, did not have sufficient capital, and relinquished his patent and equipment to the printer/lithographer Lemercier, who, unlike Poitevin, had immense workshops and a large workforce.

Lemercier took advantage of this transaction to illustrate works on the scientific expeditions to Africa and the Middle East of Lottin, Laval, and Trémaux. However, photolithography remained partially a craft, and did not come up to his financial expectations. In 1871, Lemercier bought the exclusive rights to Eugène Albert's process in France. This process, very similar to Poitevin's, was largely inspired by it. It had the advantage, however, of being twice as productive, with 12 presses producing between 1,400 and 1,800 prints a day.

Another process, also derived from Poitevin's but easier to exploit commercially, was invented in 1865 by an Englishman, Walter Woodbury,[8] and christened by him "Woodburytype". The difference with this process was that the layer of gelatin bichromate exposed to light under the photographic image produced reliefs that were tough enough for a lead mold to be made from them. This was inked and used to print off the

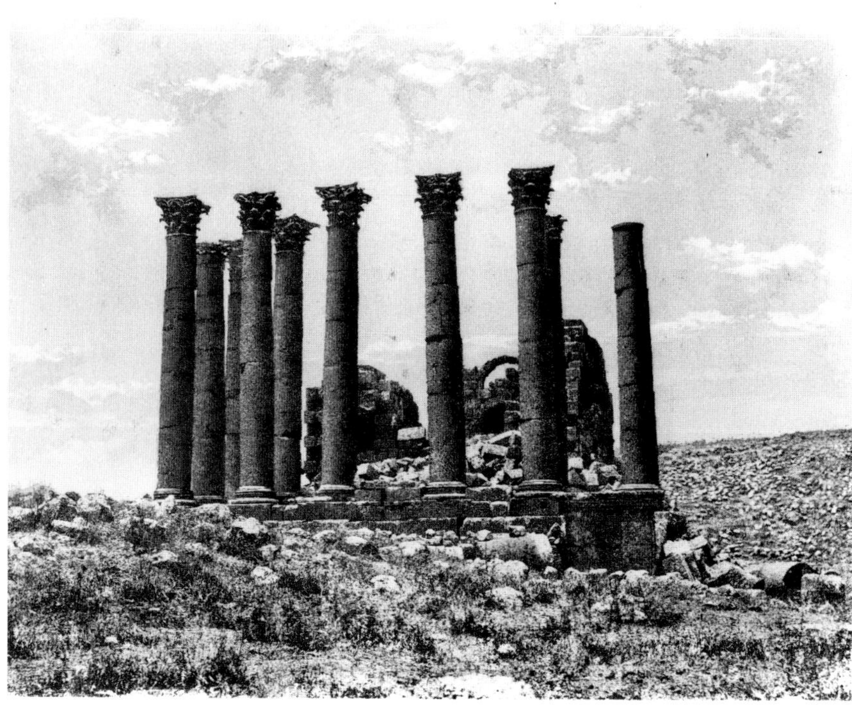

Photogravure on steel by **Charles Nègre**, ***Temple of Jupiter,*** Jerash, photograph by **Louis Vignes**, 1864, from Duc de Luynes *Voyage d'Exploration à la Mer morte*, Bibliothèque Nationale, Paris.

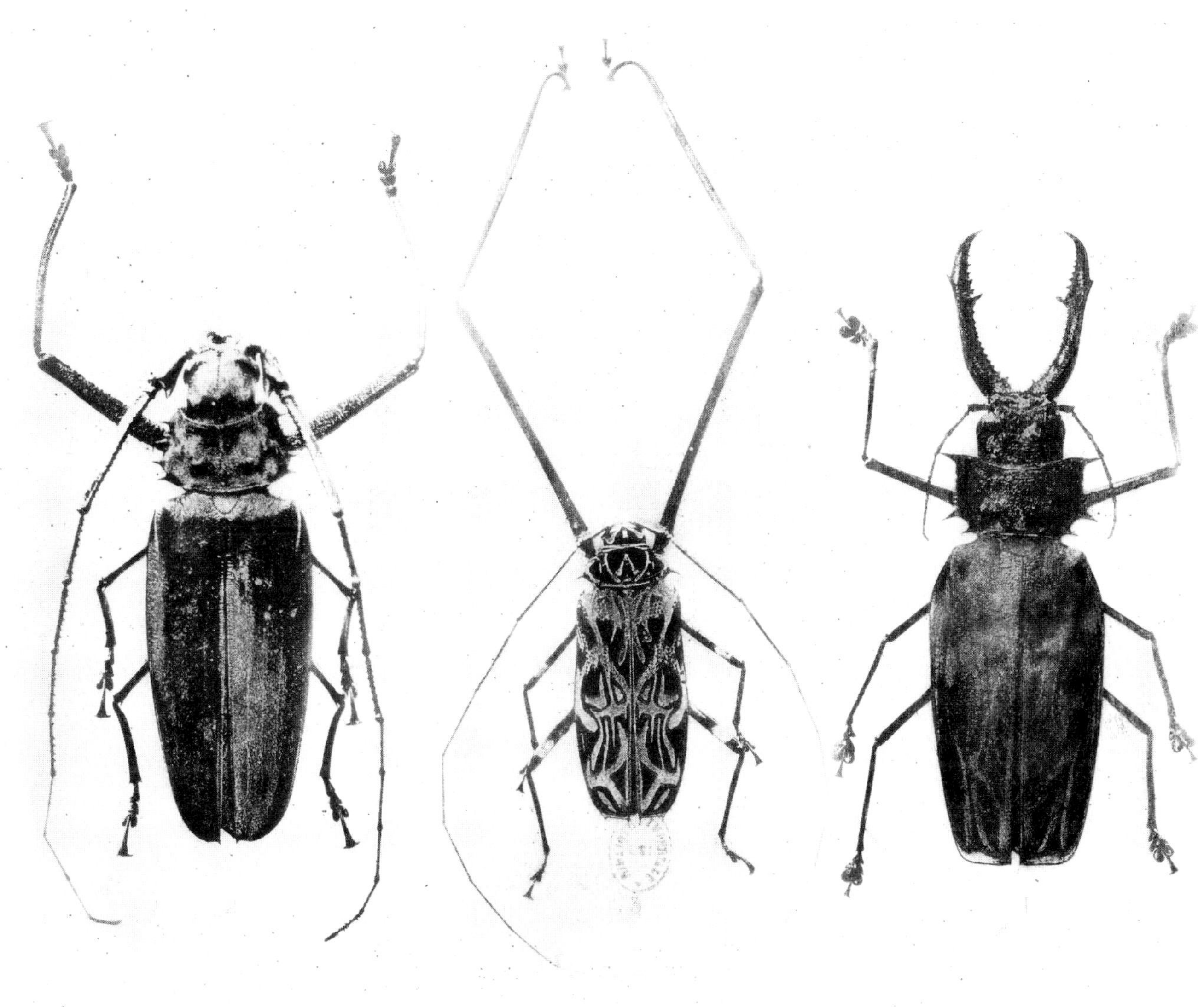

image in the brown tones typical of silver-based printing at that time. Woodbury carried out his first trials in 1864 and took out patents in 1865 and 1866. The process was popular in France, Britain and the United States right up to the end of the century.

The printers Goupil et Cie. gambled successfully on its success when they bought it from the inventor for 150,000 francs in 1867, and then exploited it commercially under the name *photoglyptie*. The quality of prints was entirely comparable to that of the originals. In this way, photography became available to a wider public, notably in Goupil's publication (started in 1876), the *Galerie contemporaine, littéraire et artistique*, a weekly review with a booklet about an artist including a text with inset woodcuts together with one or two photoglyptic prints.

It took until the 1880s before research which had started more than thirty years before began to bear fruit. The jury of the duc de Luynes' competition were not wrong in awarding the prize to Poitevin. His photolithographic process was the basis of all the later techniques, including the half-tone process, perfected in 1878 by Charles-Guillaume Petit and used by all the major daily papers at the beginning of the century.

Nonetheless, the nineteenth century never lost its sense of wonder at the immense illustrative possibilities of photography as they gradually emerged, while at the same time remaining relatively powerless to put them to concrete use. On the other hand, woodcuts, engravings, and lithographs were omnipresent, and fulfilled all the illustrative functions so willingly attributed to photography. If the tide turned quite rapidly at the end of the nineteenth century, and, above all, in the twentieth century, this was unquestionably due to all the preparatory work that had gone before.

Photogravure by **Niépce de Saint-Victor,** ***Longicorn Coleoptera,*** from Rousseau and Devéria, *Photographie zoologique,* 1853, Bibliothèque Nationale, Paris.

8. W. B.Woodbury (1834–1885) was a British photographer who practiced in Australia and Java before settling definitively in Britain in 1864.

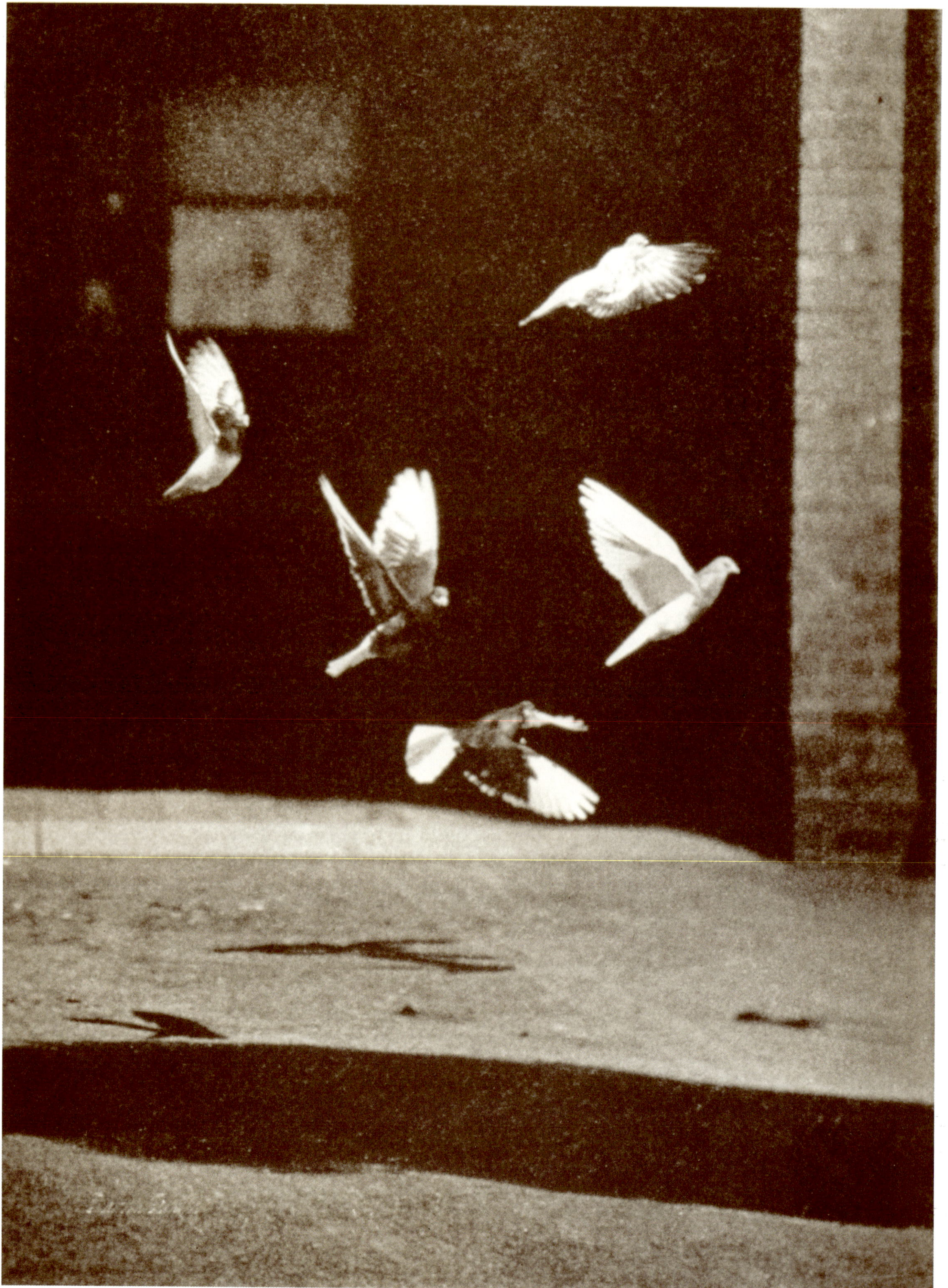

PHOTOGRAPHY ON THE SPUR OF THE MOMENT

13

Instant impressions

Jean-Claude Gautrand

If it is true that, in photography, the content of a picture is determined by, and dependent on, the technology used, then the arrival in around 1880 of plates coated with gelatin-silver bromide brought about a radical change in the photographer's vision. It was not just a question of a mechanical improvement, but an overturning of existing practices, a revolution which came about through cameras, new portability, ease of use, the speed with which they could take pictures, and the photographer's desire for anonymity. To see without being seen, to control time by reducing it to the smallest possible moment, to capture unseen or invisible elements of life on the spur of the moment: for a long time these were to become the specific aims of photography.

For the three decades (1850–1880) in which it was used, the wet collodion process was subject to constant improvement in numerous ways – simplifying it and making it more satisfactory in terms of results.

However, wet-collodion plates still remained as awkward as ever to use, and their sensitivity remained poor: in spite of certain improvements, exposure times in the studio were still several seconds. Photographers sought to find a way of preparing the plates for use when required, and of reducing exposure times down to fractions of a second.

In 1855 J.-N. Taupenot published a method, invented by him, whereby the collodion was covered while still moist with a layer of albumen which was then allowed to dry. This dry collodion plate produced very clear and detailed images, but turned out to be eight times less sensitive than conventional wet-collodion plates.[1] Sayce and Bolton improved this procedure slightly by coating plates with the long-lasting collodion silver-bromide emulsion which the Liverpool Dry Plate and Photography Printing Company started manufacturing in 1867. However, the exposure time still remained longer than with wet collodion, which was an obstacle to capturing images of moving objects. Since public demand was concentrating more and more on subjects that had to be caught rapidly; photographers often felt they were not doing their job properly, despite the increased potential of their medium.

Gelatin-silver bromide

It was an English doctor, Richard L. Maddox, who must be credited with introducing a new, practicable form of dry plates. On September 18, 1871, he announced his method in the *British Journal of Photography*. A warm solution of gelatin was mixed with cadmium bromide and silver nitrate, spread on a glass plate and allowed to dry. However, the sensitivity of these plates was still just as low. The technique was improved by Richard Kennet in 1874, and perfected by Charles Harper Bennett, who, in 1878, had the idea of maturing the emulsion, keeping it for several days at a temperature of 32 degrees centigrade before washing. This new method of preparing the emulsion produced a considerable gain in sensitivity, permitting snapshots of 1/25 of a second, an achievement which astounded the photographic community.

Here, for the first time, was a process of almost childish simplicity. The plate was prepared in advance, retained its light sensitivity for a considerable time, and could be developed in the darkroom a relatively long time after exposure. This increased sensitivity made it possible to take instant pictures (with an exposure time of less than a second) and did away with the need for any kind of tripod or other support, so that the camera could be held in the hand!

It was a discovery that was to have great repercussions and opened up the realms of photog-

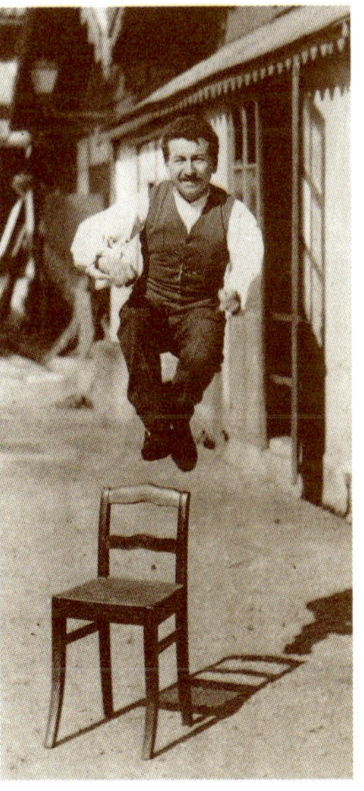

Auguste Lumiere, *Self-portrait*, circa 1900, Fondation Nationale de la Photographie, Lyons.

◀ Francis Blake, *Pigeons in Flight*, circa 1888, George R. Rinhart Collection.

1. In 1872, for his first experiments in photographing horses in motion, Muybridge was still using wet collodion, with less than satisfactory results.

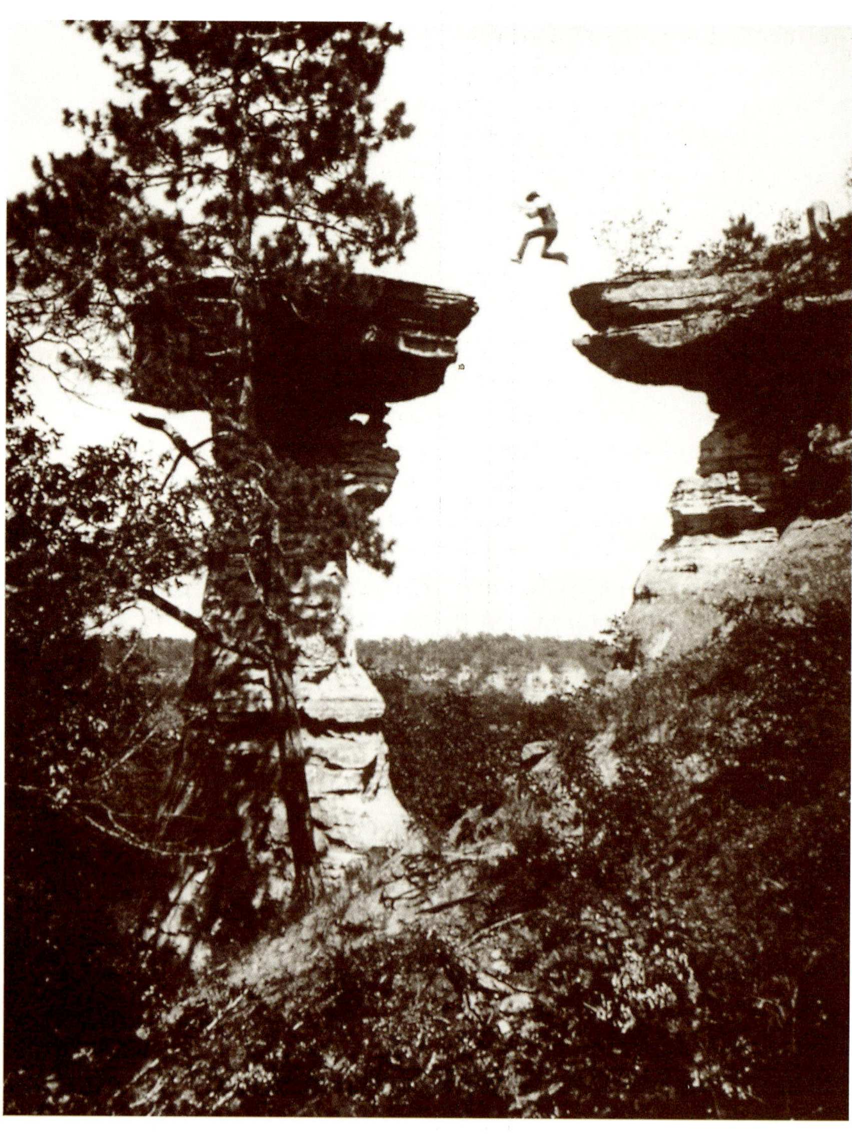

H. H. Bennett, ***Instant Photograph,*** Wisconsin, 1885, H.H. Bennett Studio Collection.

raphy to commercial exploitation on an industrial scale. Gelatin-bromide plates began to be made in a number of locations, and their manufacture became quite general between 1880 and 1882. In France, Antoine Lumière, Braun, and Garcin moved from workshop to commercial production, as did Wratten and Wainright and Samuel Fry in Britain, and George Eastman in the United States (the Eastman Dry Plate Company, founded 1880).

Liébert, a well-known Parisian photographer, wrote about the new technique in 1883: "In the last few years the gelatin-silver bromide method has brought about a veritable revolution in photography, so that one can say that after collodion, which superseded the daguerreotype, it is the greatest step forward in our art, already so fertile in marvelous discoveries."

Sensitivity and effectiveness

The new procedure gave rise to numerous changes, and brought about, among other things, a rationalization in the manufacture of photographic equipment. "To a mind accustomed to methods of scientific precision, it became intolerable to practice an art which – at that time – was so entirely governed by rule-of-thumb, and of which the fundamental principles were so little understood."[3] So wrote, the British scientist Vero Charles Driffield, in 1876, about one of his friends, Ferdinand Hurter. Together, they began a series of experiments in which they tried to establish a consistent relationship between the intensity of light, the sensitivity of the plates, and the length of exposure and of development. The H. and D. (Hurter and Driffield) table for the sensitivity of plates thus became the most practical means of working out exposure times.

Among the various instruments designed to required exposure times, we should mention Decoudin's Photomètre, which indicated the luminosity of the subjects by means of fading light signals; Watkins's exposure meter, Wynne's Infallible meter which calculated exposure time by comparing a piece of sensitized paper against a standard scale, and a sliding calculator called a Posographe – a numerical table giving a light measurement by reference to the height of the sun, the brightness of the day, and the brilliance of the subject. These accessories put an end to the rule-of-thumb methods of the first practitioners and reduced the risk of failure.

Additionally, the sensitivity of plates to all the colors was improved (until then they had been insensitive to the spectral range between yellow and red). In 1873, Vogel discovered that by dipping a plate in a colorant, it became sensitive to the color absorbed. Different kinds of photographic plate began to appear: some sensitive to all colors except red – orthochromatic plates – the others sensitive to all the colors of the spectrum – panchromatic plates. This was to have important repercussions for the image itself.

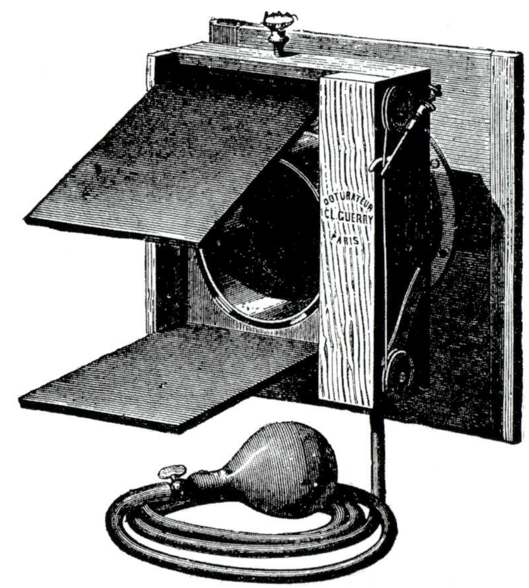

Flap-shutter ▶ after Jacques Ducom, *Les Débuts d'un Amateur Photographe*, 1898.

2. A. Liébert, *La Photographie en Amérique*, Paris, Liébert, 1883 (1st ed. 1864).

3. Quoted by W. B. Ferguson in *Photographic Researches of Ferdinand Hurter and Vero C. Driffield*, London, Royal Photographic Society, 1920.

There were parallel advances in the field of photographic optics. The Aplanat lens had been invented by Steinheil in 1866. Consisting of a pair of convergent, perfectly symmetrical meniscus lenses, it was free of distortion and had already gone into common use. However, this did not prevent makers from trying to improve on it, with Voigtländer's Euryscope, Berthiot's Perigraph, etc. Around 1880, in Jena in Germany, Otto Schott and Dr. Abbe devised a new type of optical glass using barium oxide which made it possible to produce more accurate lenses. Zeiss, an optician, put forward an asymmetric doublet made up of two lenses, one convex, one concave, which provided a better correction of aberrations, a more uniform distribution of light, a larger aperture, and an absolute sharpness. Christened Anastigmat in 1892, this miracle of optics also perceptibly decreased exposure times. The very first anastigmat lens – the famous Protar manufactured by Zeiss – opened up to f/4.5! In 1886 the *Annuaire Général International de la Photographie* wrote: "The progress that has taken place following the work of Dr. Rudolf has been truly revolutionary ... The reign of the Aplanat has been followed by the reign of the Anastigmat." Just as, one could add, gelatin-bromide had supplanted collodion.

Aim, shoot

In the earliest days of photography, an exposure was made by removing a simple lens cap or sliding a metal plate into the lens cylinder. However, the reduction of exposure time to a fraction of a second made it necessary to find a swifter and more reliable mechanism. This was the shutter, which could accurately regulate exposure times by offering the user the required range of speeds.

The simplest form, the flap-shutter, invented by Guerry, opened by means of a spring activated by the pressure of the air contained in a rubber bulb – a mechanism particularly suitable for portraiture. The drop-shutter, invented during the daguerreotype era, consisted of one or two grooved blades which slid by gravity in front of the lens. Also in this category were lateral shutters with a circular movement – uncovering the lens from the side – or central shutters – uncovering the lens from the center. The most highly regarded were those produced by Decaux, the best on the market at the time (1892), and those made by Londe and Dessoudeix (1885) and by Thury and Amey.[4]

In 1887, Dallmeyer and Beauchamp produced a lens with multiple pivoting blades, inspired by the principle of the iris diaphragm. This type of central shutter, activated by a spring and having a pneumatic brake, permitted very fast speeds, which gave it a commanding position on the market for a very long time. Even today, some cameras are still fitted with this type of shutter.

The roller-blind shutter, which was devised up by Humbert de Molard as early as 1855, works on the same principle as domestic roller-blinds: a spring of variable strength activates a mechanism which makes the shutter come down. Examples of this type of shutter are those made by Thornton Pickard – the Time and the Snap Shot, offering speeds between 1/15 of a second and 1/80 of a second – and the Special and the Focal Plane Shutter, a roller-blind shutter which went up to 1/500 of a second or faster (this system was used by Guido Sigriste in 1898 for the binocular camera that bears his name, and achieved an exposure of 1/5000 of a second.)

One of the difficulties of snapshot photography is releasing the shutter at the precise moment when a moving object is in exactly the right place. Viewfinders provide a means of observing and following the scene. They were

HARRISON PUTNEY,
H. Lissik,
Circus Performer,
Twirling Baton,
1886.
Amon Carter Museum
of Western Art,
▼

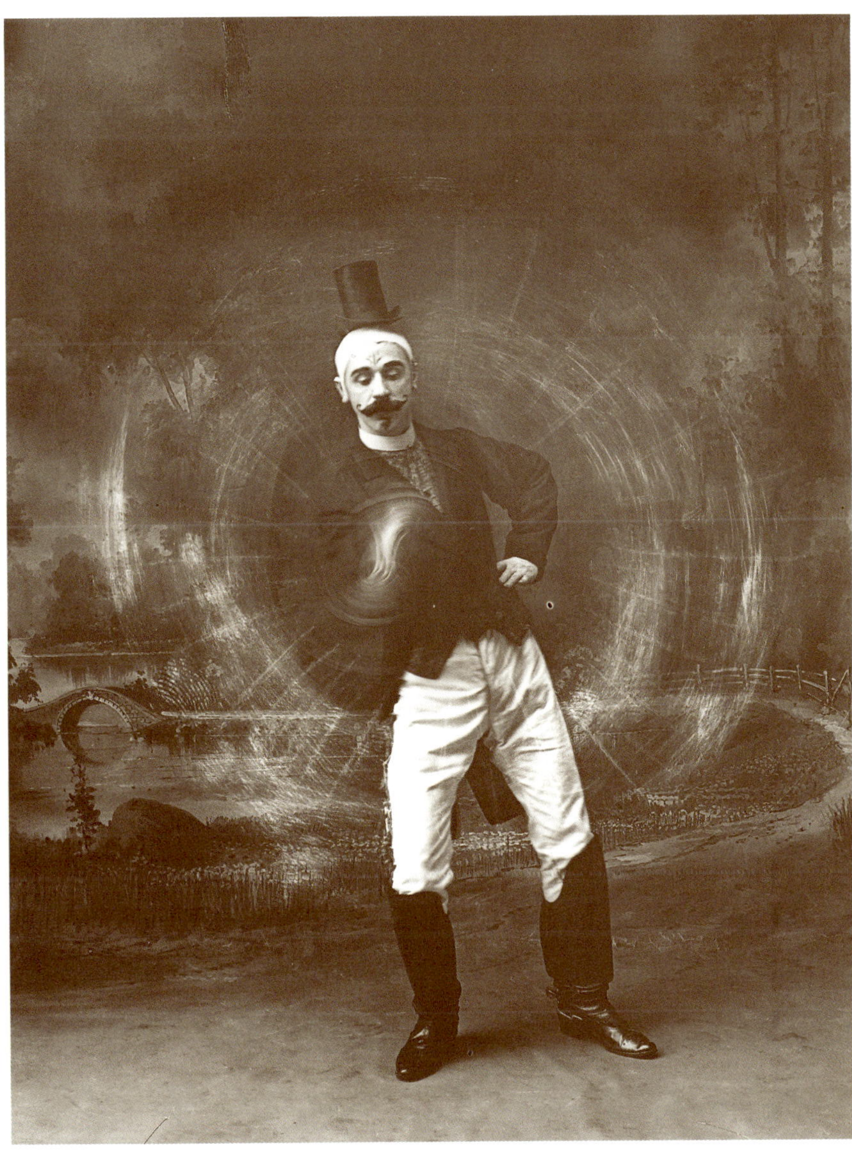

4. Decaux's double-bladed drop shutter; Londe and Dessoudeix's circular-bladed shutter activated by a steel spring, Thury and Amey's central shutter with linear movement, composed of two blades moving in opposite directions.

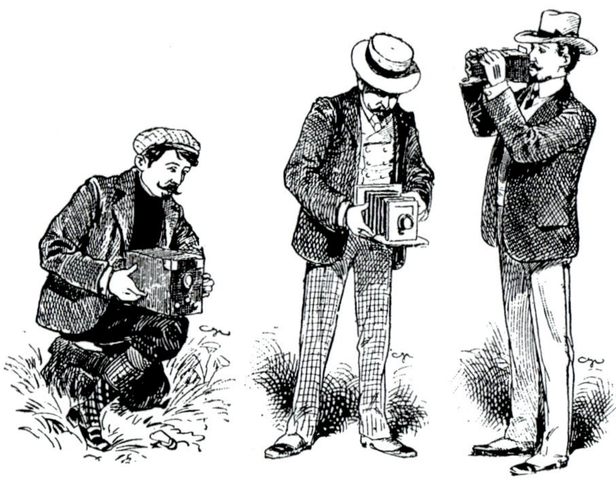

Different ways of looking through the viewfinder of portable cameras, after A. Reyner, *Manuel pratique du Reporter Photographe,* 1903.

composed simply of a double-concave lens, giving an image of the scene the right way up, or of a metal frame placed at the front of the camera in line with an eye-piece at the back of the camera. However, the most commonly found type of viewfinder remained the double effect viewfinder, a miniature *camera obscura* set in such a way as to take in the same view as the lens, and fixed to the side of the camera. It could be used at chest level or eye level, and gave a fairly exact impression of what the effect would be, albeit via an unpolished glass, upside-down and dark: minor defects compared with the advantages.

New types of camera

When Léon Vidal wrote in 1866 in the *Moniteur de la Photographie*: "We want photography, so useful to all branches of knowledge, to become the domain of everyone [...] Industry should aim to make photography for everybody as mechanical as possible in use,"[5] he was suggesting a new route for photography which did not become a reality until the end of the century. From 1880 to 1890, numerous portable cameras entered the market. Most of them contained a magazine loaded with several photographic plates, making it possible to take a dozen or so photographs without having to reload.

The greatest success was enjoyed by hidden or disguised cameras – making candid shots a possibility. Two main categories appeared: cameras that were curious and amusing, designed to make an impression, and cameras that were small and discreet – the miniature or spy cameras,

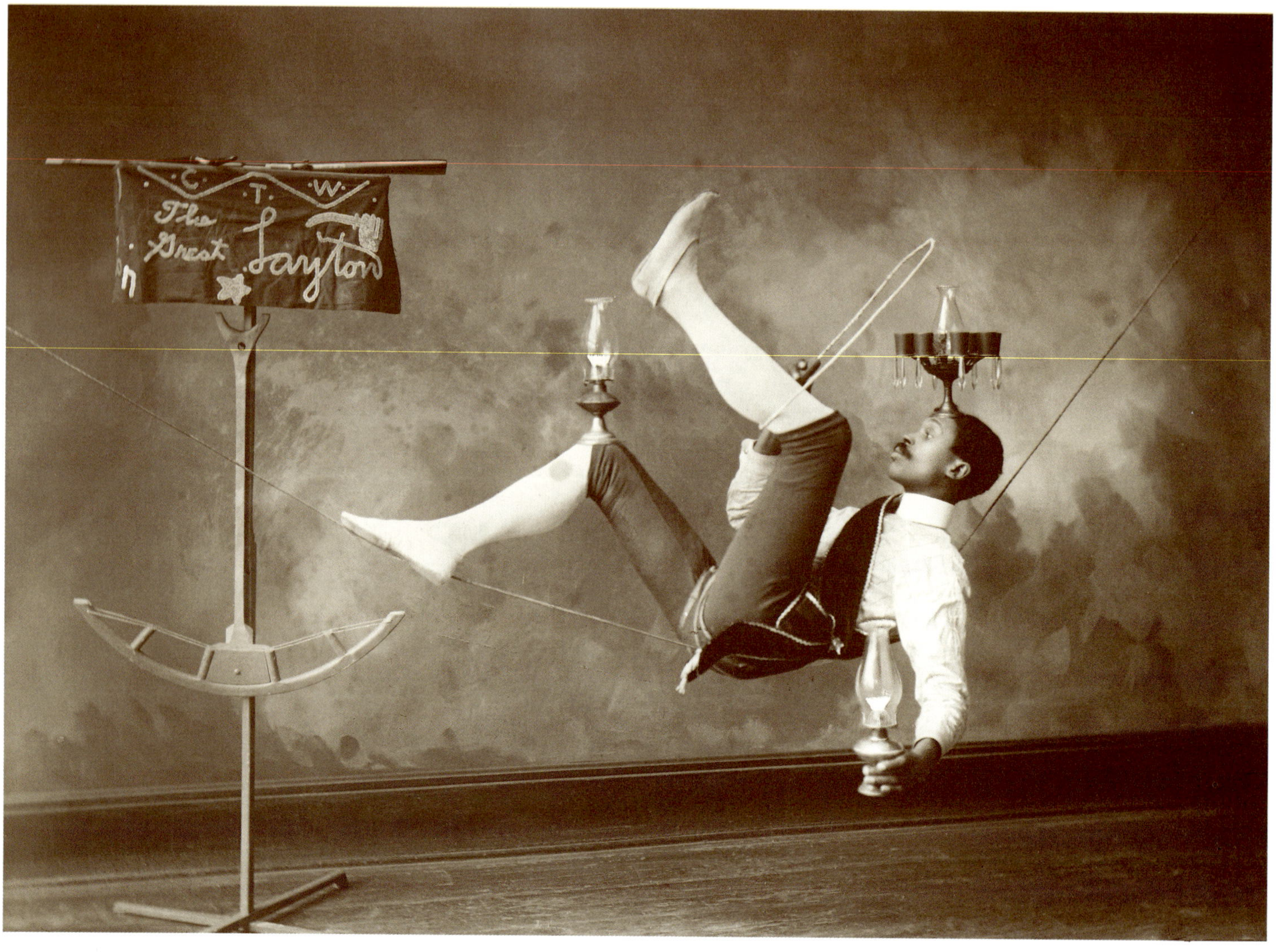

Harrison Putney, ***The Great Layton, Circus Performer*** 1885, Amon Carter Museum of Western Art, Fort Worth.

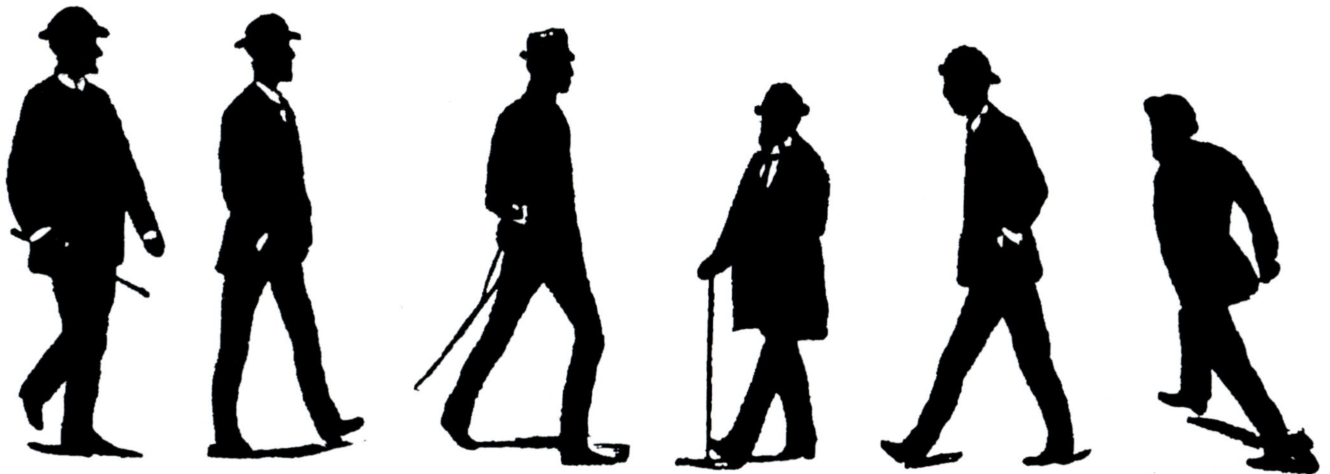

Position of the feet when walking, captured by photography,
after Eder,
La Photographie instantanée, 1886.

the so-called detective cameras. "These little cameras are lightweight, have rapid shutters and do not require any preliminary setting, can be held in the hand and disguised in all sorts of ways to deflect the attention of onlookers, so that one can take any picture, any kind of scene one likes, without their being aware of it."[6]

Under the heading of unusual cameras there was Bloch's "Photo-cravate", a camera hidden under a gentleman's tie (loaded with six 23mm square plates, with the lens in the place of the tie-pin, activated by a rubber bulb concealed in a pocket), and, in the same vein, Fetter's Photo-Éclair (1886) or Gray's Vest camera (1886), circular cameras designed to be hidden under a frock coat, with the lens pointing out of a buttonhole. A camera could take on the appearance of a hat, a lady's handbag (Kauffer, 1895), a lawyer's briefcase or a library-book, like Le Roy's camera (1889), where the lens was inserted in the spine of the book. Some others went so far as to take on the somewhat indiscreet appearance of a revolver, like Enjalbert's Photo Revolver (1882), in which the rotation of the cylinder controlled the changing of the plate and the readying of the shutter, or Darier's Escopette (1889). Most of these cameras, with their excessively small plates, did not give very good results. They were really more like adult toys – what we would today call gadgets – rather than real cameras. Consequently their popularity remained relatively limited.

Cameras included in the detective family were very different. Most of them were equipped with a magazine which held several plates. They were totally discreet, thanks to their plain shape, like a box or a package, and the position of the view-finder, which made it appear as though the photographer was not even looking at the scene he was shooting. The Facile camera, invented by F. Miall (1887), enjoyed immense success, despite its rudimentary construction. It was with a camera of this type (a Facile detective made by Fallowfield) disguised as a package, that Paul Martin took the first really spontaneous photographs, a form of photography that became known as "candid". In France, the most successful makes were the Express Detective Nadar, the work of Félix Nadar's son Paul (1888), which had several shutter speeds, set by friction, the Vélocigraph, one of the most compact detectives, with a plate-loading mechanism linked to the setting of the multi-speed shutter, and the Lumière brothers' Automatique (1890).

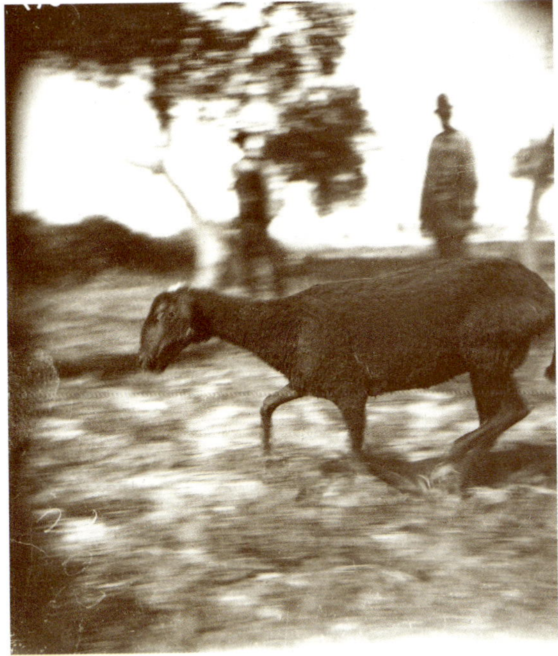

F. P. Michetti,
Running Goat,
circa 1895–1900,
Alinari Archives,
Florence.
▼

George Eastman and the Kodak

However, the glass plates that were then in general use still had their drawbacks: they were heavy, fragile, cumbersome, and expensive. Léon Vidal's dream – which we have already quoted – of being able to practice photography "as one speaks prose, without knowing it still remained just that – a

5. L. Vidal, "La Voie nouvelle en Photographie", in *Le Moniteur de la Photographie*, no. 23, February 15, 1866, pp. 178–180, and no. 24, March 1, 1866, pp. 186–188.

6. H. Fourtier, *La Photographie à l'Exposition Universelle de 1889*, Paris, Bernard et Cie. 1893. See also J. Ducom, *Les Débuts d'un Amateur Photographe*, Paris, Carré et Naud, 1898.

The Kodak family

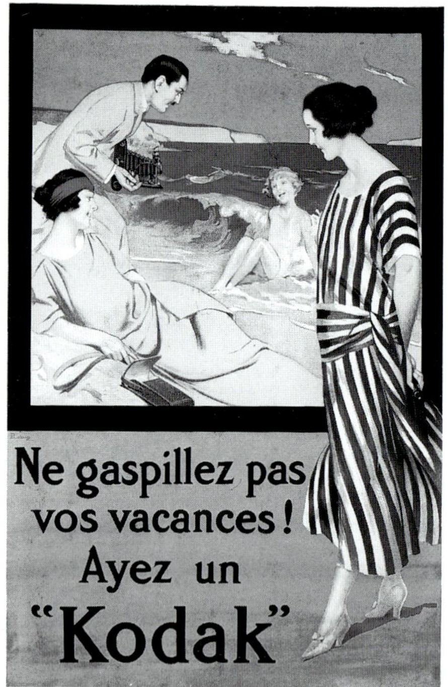

French Kodak poster
circa 1925, private collection.

How to use the Kodak in three motions,
1889.

The Kodak appealed to the mass market because it was so simple. It went on sale in 1888 when it used paper roll film (stripping film) which had to be processed in the factory. Celluloid, invented in 1861, was produced in thin sheets for the first time by J. Carbutt and W. Hyatt. In 1889 Eastman and his chemist Reichenbach coated long strips of celluloid with a photographic emulsion. These strips were then rolled onto a spool. Celluloid roll film was first sold for use in the Kodak later that year. The No. 1 Kodak (1889) had an improved shutter, and the No. 2 Kodak used roll film, which produced bigger, (90mm diameter) pictures. The No. 3 Kodak (1890) was the first Kodak to take rectangular photographs. In 1891, three models of Daylight Kodak cameras appeared (these could be loaded in daylight as the film was protected by a black band). In 1895 another novelty appeared, cartridge roll film, which, from 1913, was numbered according to its format starting from 101 size, the system still in use today. It went with the Pocket Kodak camera, which also appeared in 1895. The Brownie followed in 1900, for people of more modest means, costing one dollar. It took its name from characters made popular in a cartoon series. All these models were box-shaped and usually black. Folding

PHOTOGRAPHY REDUCED TO THREE MOTIONS.

1. Pull the Cord. 2. Turn the Key. 3. Press the Button. And so on for 100 Pictures.

cameras had appeared as early as 1890, but the flatter Folding Pocket Kodak of 1897 led the way for a proliferation of different models: the Folding Pocket Brownie, the Folding Hawk-Eye.

The Eastman Company (which in 1892 became Eastman Kodak) aimed its products at all classes of society, with more expensive cameras like the Cartridge Kodak (1897) with its three-speed shutter, two viewfinders, and sliding front or the No. 4 Panorama Kodak, for panoramic photographs (10 x 30 cm). The greatest popularity was enjoyed by the Vest Pocket Kodak (1912) the soldier's camera, culminating in the Autographic versions (1914), which you could write a caption directly onto the negative after lifting a hinged flap on the back of the camera.

Michel Frizot

dream: [...] That industrialist who intelligent enough, innovative enough, to put the necessary effort into making photography available to all [...] would deserve to be called a public benefactor."

George Eastman was a manufacturer of dry plates at Rochester in the United States, who wanted to simplify photography. In 1884, he manufactured paper negatives, followed by a universal holder for a 24-exposure roll of sensitized paper. In 1886 he launched his American Film, a strip of paper covered with gelatin-bromide emulsion. After developing, the strip was immersed in warm water, and the emulsion separated from its paper backing and was transferred to a glass plate.

But Eastman, like Vidal, remained dissatisfied. The photographer still had to process their own films, and cameras – apart from a few detectives – remained difficult to handle. In 1888, Eastman started manufacturing a plain, box-shaped camera. It was small (16.5 x 9 x 8.3 cm) and fitted with a simple lens opening to f/9, and a shutter which was set by pulling a string. You took the shot by pressing a button. There was a standard exposure time of 1/20 of a second. Christened The Kodak, and having neither a viewfinder or an exposure counter, it sold for 25 dollars, loaded with a roll of paper negative film giving 100 round photographs 65mm in diameter. Once the last picture had been taken, the entire camera had to be returned to the factory, where the film was developed. The prints were sent to the owner and the camera returned, already loaded with

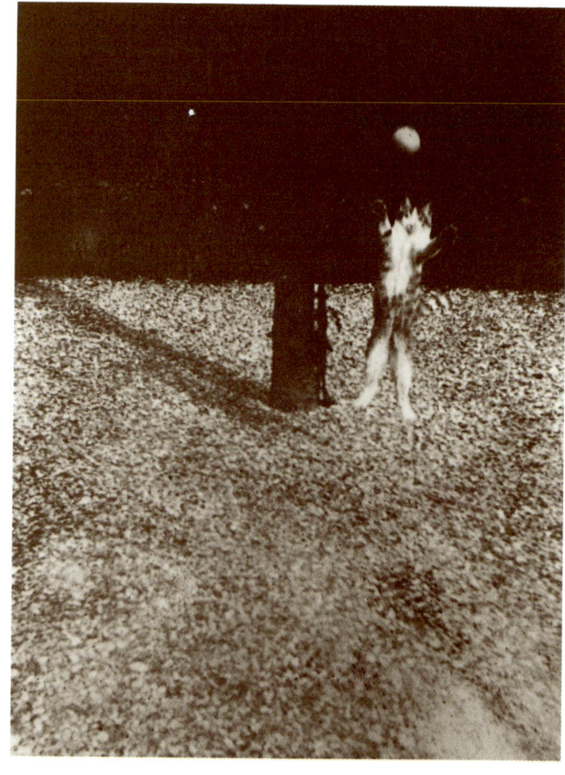

Jacques-Henri Lartigue, ***My Cat Zizi,***
June 1904, Paris.

7. L. Vidal, *op. cit.*

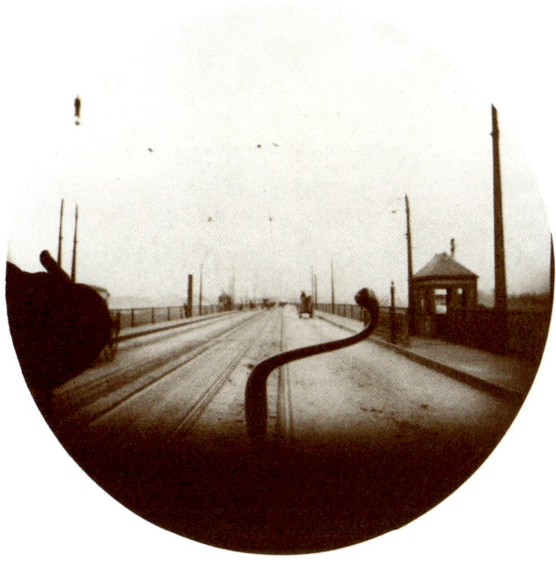

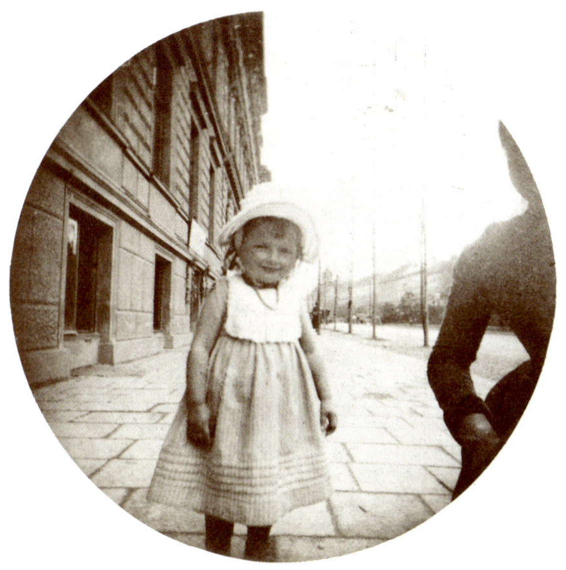

Pictures taken with the Kodak (from left to right):

ANONYMOUS,
circa 1889,
International Museum of Photography, George Eastman
House, Rochester.

URIAH HUNT PAINTER,
Child,
circa 1889,
Library of Congress,
Washington.

fresh film. Kodak's famous slogan "You press the button, we do the rest", accurately summed up the system. George Eastman had thus invented a centralized system of industrial production capable of conquering an important market. The principle of the Kodak system was the separation of the work that any person was capable of doing in a photograph from the work that only an expert could do. "The principle of the Kodak system is the separation of the work that any person whomsoever can do in [making] a photograph, from the work that only an expert can do...We furnish anybody, man, woman or child, who has sufficient intelligence to point a box straight and press a button ... with an instrument which altogether removes from the practice of photography the necessity for exceptional facilities, or, in fact, any special knowledge of the art."[8]

The camera was an immediate success, despite its initial limitations – snapshots were possible only out of doors, negatives were capable of only limited enlargement, and the minimum focusing distance was still excessive. However, the range of cameras produced by Eastman (see box) and other manufacturers really did turn photography into something that anyone could do. Thousands of people all over the world began to take simple, instant, unselfconscious pictures of their leisure pursuits, their families, and their surroundings. Family archives of photographs began to be formed, particularly on the occasion of seaside holidays – at the time available only to the middle class: "What pretty groups of babies and children, and madcap glorious youth forgetting for a short moment the constraints of the town. And the chats under the multicolored tents, the flirtations in the confidential shade of the bathing-huts, the donkey-races, the swimming-feats, the trips out to sea!"[9]

The shoulder-strap camera, photo-binoculars, and folding cameras

It was no doubt for real enthusiasts that certain manufacturers perfected the existing box-cameras by providing them with all the technical improve-

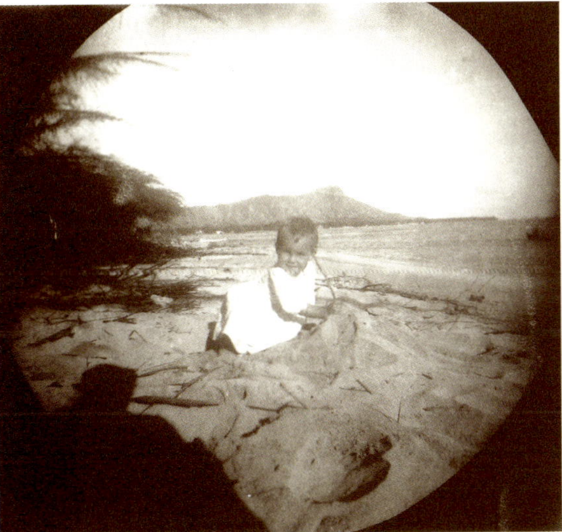

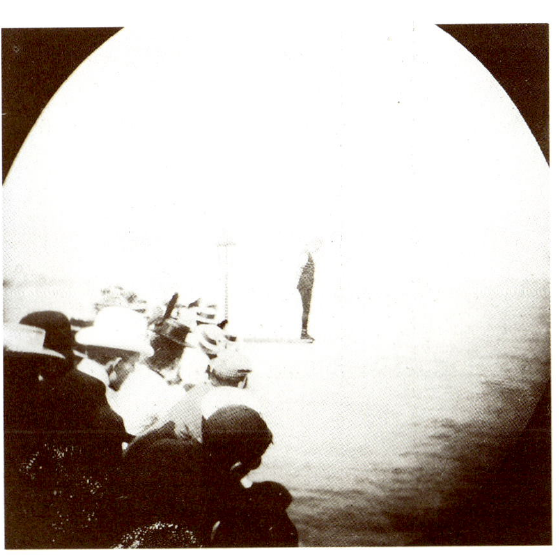

Pictures taken with the Kodak (from left to right):

JOHN S. B. PRATT,
Scott Pratt,
Waikiki, Hawaii,
circa 1890,
Bishop Museum,
Honolulu.

ANONYMOUS,
Jumping Off the Springboard, Tied Hand and Foot,
circa 1890,
private collection.

8. G. Eastman, *The Kodak Primer*, quoted by B. Coe, *George Eastman and the Early Photographers*, London, Priory Press, 1973, p. 67. See also D. Collins, *The Story of Kodak*, Harry N. Abrams, New York, 1990.

9. E. Giard, *Le Livre d'Or de la Photographie*, Paris, C. Mendel, c. 1902, p. 189.

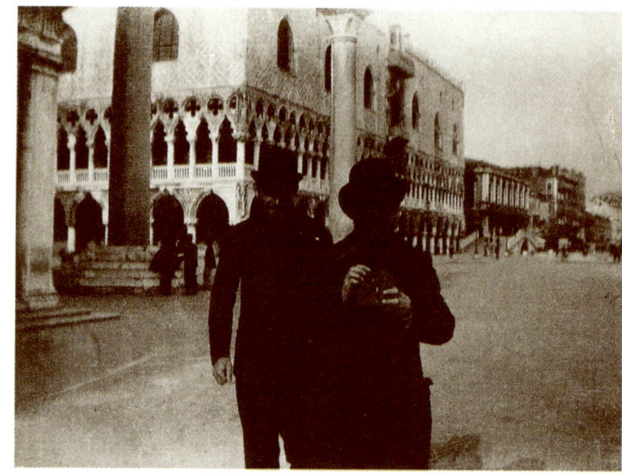

Pierre Bonnard,
Roussel and Vuillard in Venice,
1899,
Musée d'Orsay, Paris.

Paul Martin,
Jersey,
1893,
University of Texas, Austin.
▼

ments already mentioned. Photo-binoculars were the quintessence of the efficient camera: small, light, and easy to conceal. Exactly like ordinary binoculars in appearance, they gave the impression that the user was simply enjoying the view. The most famous, Jules Carpentier's, produced in 1892, had two lenses, one with red glass for the viewfinder, the other for taking the pictures (12 plates in 4.5 x 6 or 6.5 x 9 cm format, fixed focus, drop-shutter giving 1/60 second exposure). The images seen through the viewfinder – which was at eye-level, a natural position – were in a perspective like that of normal vision. Commercial success engendered a whole line of photo-binoculars: Mackenstein's binoculars (1896), Zion's Simili Jumelle (1893), Joux's Stéréo-Jumelle (1894), the Vélo-Jumelle (1895) and the products of Hermagis (1895), Sylvestre (1900), Belliéni (1899), and Spido-Gaumont (1898). Sigriste's photo-binoculars, with a speed of up to 1/5000 seconds made it possible to take startling action-pictures.

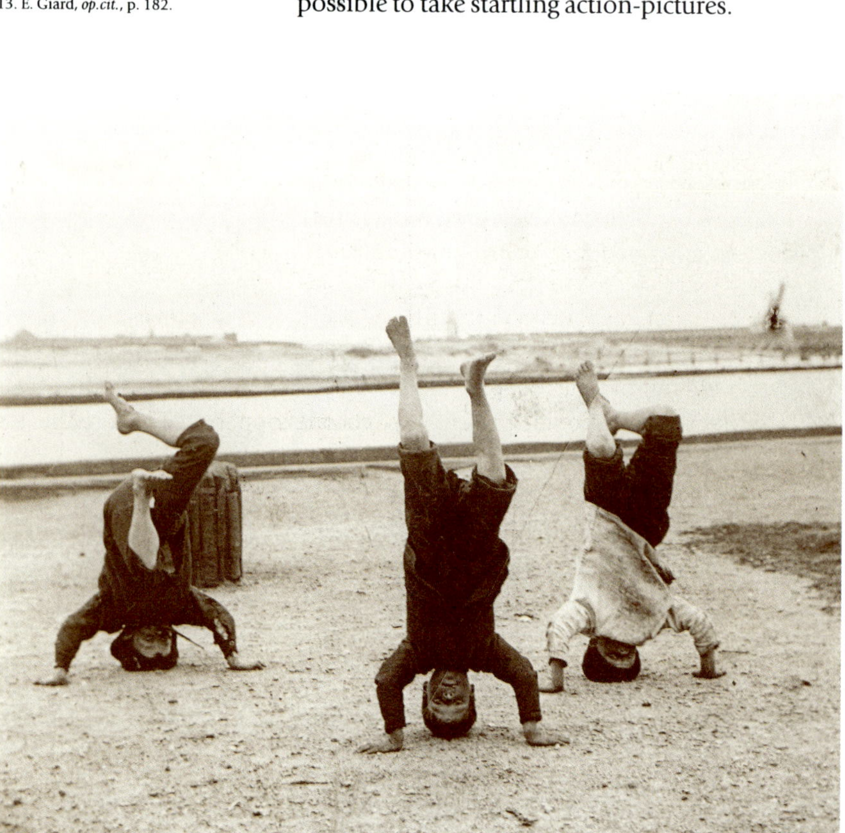

Frédéric Dillaye's enthusiasm was symptomatic: "Here it is, the light, easy to use, easy to hide camera that every photographer should take with him wherever he goes [...] the camera whose size and appearance is bound to make women want to try photography without fear of tiring their pretty shoulders or crumpling their outfits. Setting the camera ready, aiming it at the subject, operating the shutter, replacing the plate with another, all takes only three seconds. With this apparatus and its little prints, we can certainly make trouble-free art."

As photographic optics and emulsions improved, equipment was miniaturized. Since spools of film took up less room than plates, classic box-cameras got smaller, eventually giving way to folding cameras, one side of which folded down, pulling out the inner chamber like an accordion and exposing the lens. The view was generally inspected at chest level, through a horizontal viewfinder on top of the camera. The Folding Kodak of 1890, which used 16.5 x 21.5 cm plates – a typical format for the period – was the first of a series intended for professionals, whereas the Folding Pocket Kodak of 1897, the prototype of the later small formats, was intended essentially for a popular clientele. It was the typical amateur's camera. Folding cameras were to dominate the market up until the end of the 1930s, after which they were supplanted in their turn by the fashion for 35mm cameras such as the Leica.[11] These technical upheavals, following one after another over a period of two decades, effected a profound change in the photographic world and the nature of the images produced.

Among the many cultured, enthusiastic, and sometimes rich amateur photographers could be numbered many for whom photography was only a hobby. Vuillard had a Kodak, Degas took many interior photographs, Zola was fervent about photography: "In my opinion you cannot say that you have seen something in depth unless you have taken a photograph, revealing a mass of detail which would otherwise remain unperceived."[12] No doubt it was photography's aptitude for revealing hidden things, anodyne in themselves but inaccessible to normal sight, which appealed most to the average amateur, even more than their desire to build an archive: "The life of the countryside, the typical postures and groupings are an inexhaustible theme and source of observations and sketches for the artist – the festivals, the gatherings, the country games, the arguments and the affrays."[13] Military preparations were also a subject for photography, sometimes surrounded by a sense of euphoric anticipation: the Vest Pocket Kodak was the particular choice of "the French 'Tommy', photo-

10. F. Dillaye, *La Pratique en Photographie avec le Procédé au Gèlatino-Bromure d'Argent*, Paris, À la Librairie Illustrèe, c. 1900.

11. For the cameras quoted, see M. Auer, *Histoire Illustrée des Appareils photographiques*, Paris, Denoël, 1975; *150 Ans d'Appareils photographiques à travers la Collection de Michel Auer*, Hermance, Camera Obscura, 1989, and E. S.Lothrop Jr., *A Century of Cameras, from the Collection of the International Museum of Photography at George Eastman House*, New York, Morgan and Morgan, 1973.

12. F.-Émile-Zola and Massin, *Zola Photographe*, Paris, Denoël, 1979, p. 11.

13. E. Giard, *op.cit.*, p. 182.

graphing the feverish atmosphere in the railway stations, and on the roads dusty with the passage of battalions and wagons, and the artillery battles, sentries on horseback, improvised bridges, rippling steel across the plain."[14]

At the heart of all these subjects is the question of the spontaneous or posed nature of the photograph – the naturalness or artificiality of the attitudes frozen by the shutter, a position that is only transitory, the one that has been chosen out of innumerable possibilities. For what photography does is to compel our vision to go beyond its usual capacity and see the real in a scientific way – scientific because it is confirmed by a mechanical apparatus which cannot lie. It is, nonetheless, shocking and sometimes impossible to accept until one has become accustomed to it: "The real can sometimes be unreal."[15] The abrupt capture of a simple movement like the way a man walks produces images which are too unusual to be perceived as true, which do not correspond to how they are habitually represented. "Looking more closely we find the most bizarre lines which do not correspond in the least to what is conventionally presented to us in art" wrote J.-M. Eder, with reference to "the strange positions people get into" in "a snapshot taken in the street."[16] In the years when these techniques first came into use, people sometimes condemned the fashion for instantaneous photos – though they were soon to become the norm. "Another type of snobbery which the amateur would do well to guard against, is the too frequent use of snapshots. For the most part the positions of men and animals, captured as one might say on the wing, have nothing attractive about them [...] They look all the more ungracious because our eyes, which perceive things relatively slowly, are not used to capturing them thus."[17]

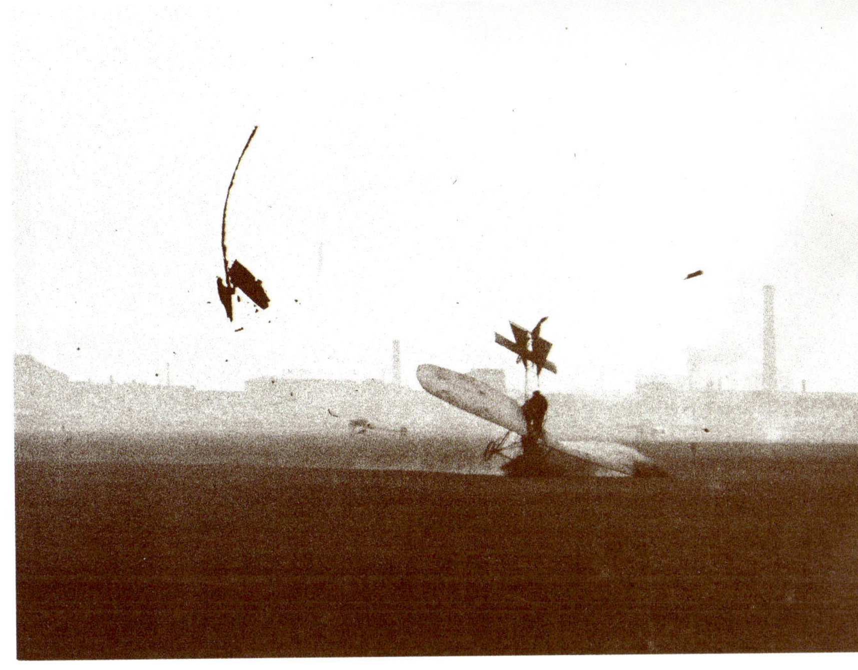

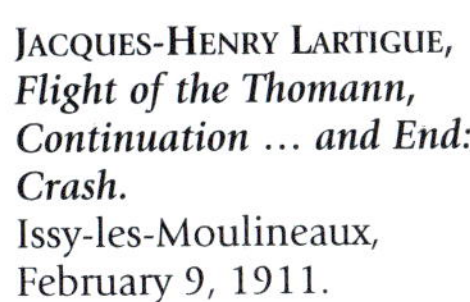

Jacques-Henry Lartigue, *Flight of the Thomann, Continuation ... and End: Crash.* Issy-les-Moulineaux, February 9, 1911.

This proliferation of snapshot images, this "radical upheaval of the figurative norms of photography [...] this questioning of its static nature" (Rune Hassner), was to bring about a profound transformation in the photographer's way of seeing and in their approach to the various realms that photography was preparing to conquer.

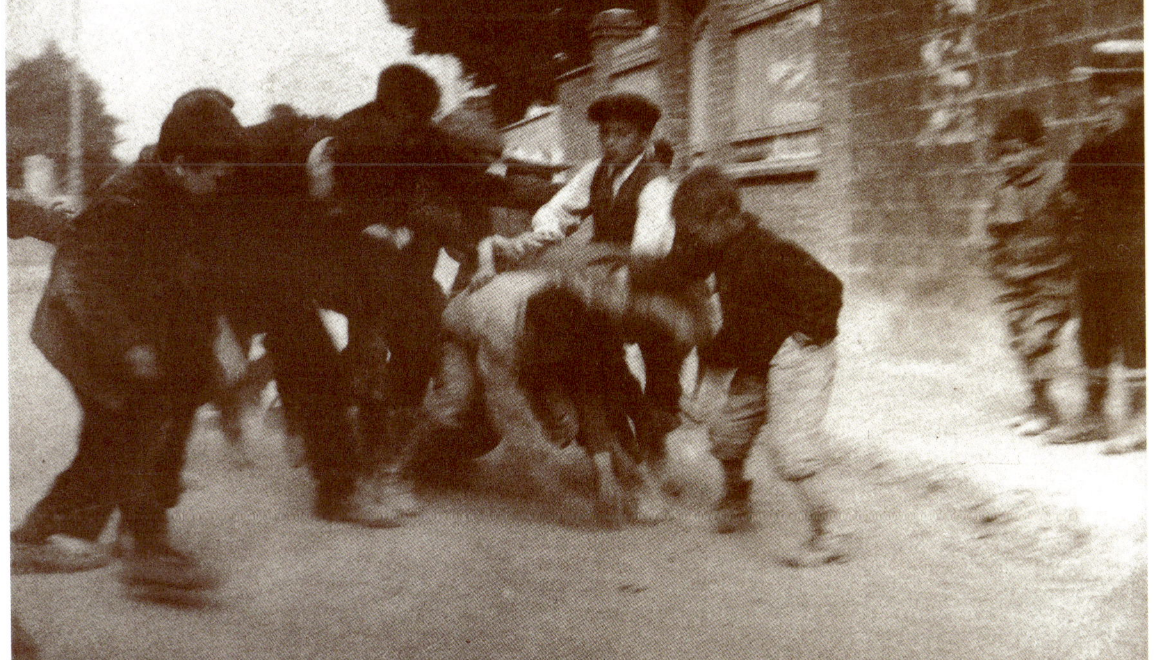

Anonymous Amateur, *Children Playing,* circa 1900, Jean Henry Collection.

14. *Ibid.*, p. 185.

15. *Ibid.*, p. 192.

16. J.-M. Eder, *La Photographie instantanée: Son Application aux Arts et aux Sciences*, Paris, Gauthier Villars, 1888, p. 201; see also T. Starl, *Knipser. Die Bildgeschichte der privaten Fotografie in Deutschland und Österreich von 1880 bis 1980*, Münchner Stadtmuseum, 1995.

17. H. Fourtier, *op. cit.* p.252.

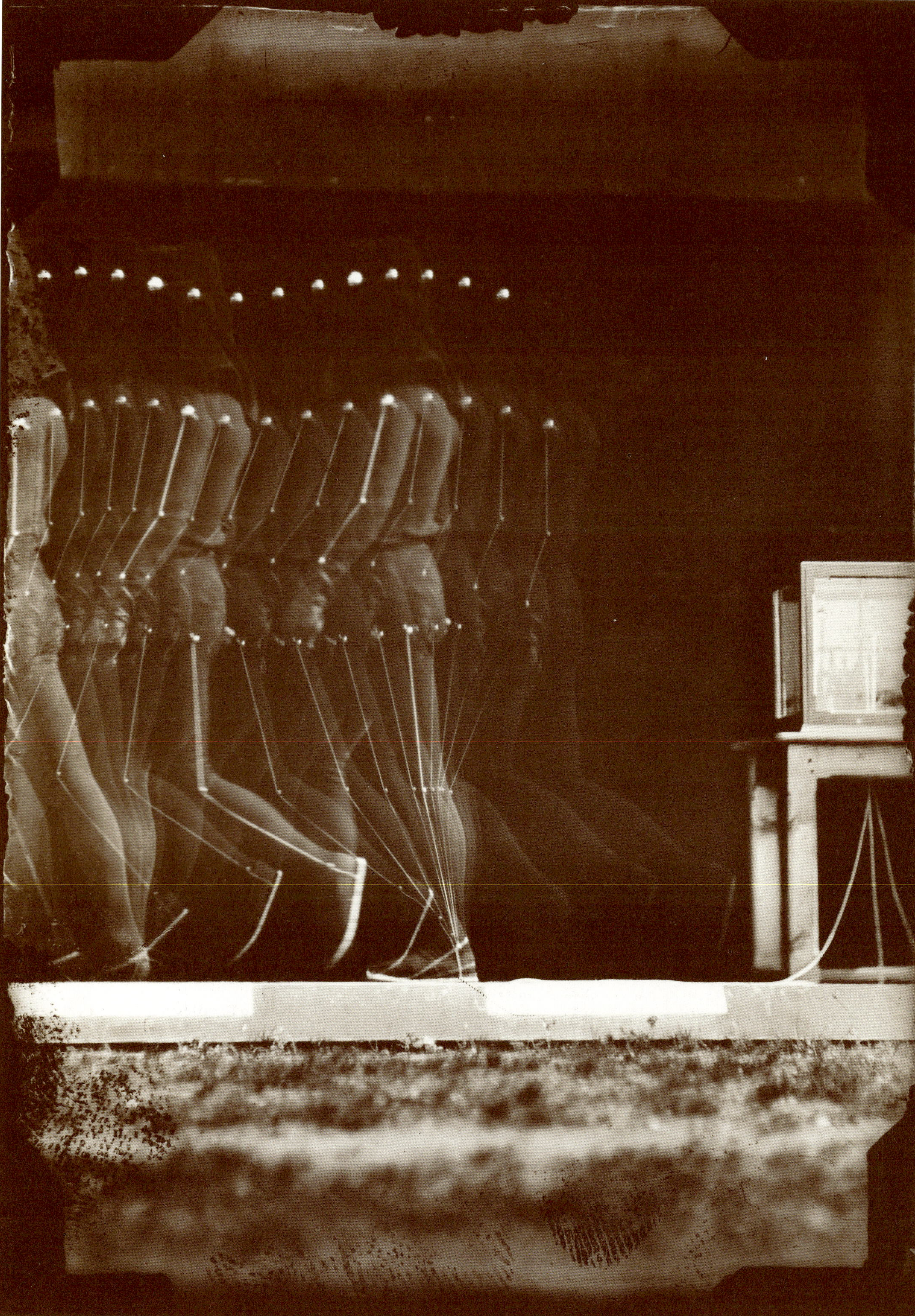

SPEED OF PHOTOGRAPHY 14

Movement and duration

Michel Frizot

Having been tied inescapably to long exposure times for part of the nineteenth century, photographers discovered in about 1880 that with the snapshot a world of unsuspected forms suddenly opened up to them. Things which were imperceptible in the continuum of vision became observable in the photographic image. However, to realize this technical potential also required a mastery, at all levels, of the speed of intervention – a perfect synchronicity in the respective times of subject, photographer, and event, which required an improved technical capability that could respond to variations in timing. Paradoxically, one of these systems resulted – with the cinematograph - in the recomposition of time.

Contrary to what retrospective projections of history tend to affirm, the recording of movement was not a particular aspiration of nineteenth-century photographers or lovers of photography, at least in the form in which it was known at the end of the century. They were quite satisfied with the exposure times necessary to obtain pictures of the major part of the explorable universe, with the exception of (almost) everything that moved.

The representation of a moving object has no absolute definition and does not correspond to fixed criteria because it depends on the relationship between the speed at which the object is moving, and the distance between it and the static camera. The factor which introduces a technical impossibility at a certain moment in photographic practice is therefore the relative speed between object and instrument (it would not be absurd to think of a camera following its object in a linear path, for instance).

Relative speed

The photographic representation of moving objects (human beings among them – very much in the minority, but utterly essential to our eyes) is a problem of relative speed which is translated into optical and graphic terms by what goes on in the *camera obscura*. It can easily be understood, for instance, that an animal running gives a more or less fixed image for half a second when it is at a distance, but not when it is close. On the other hand, in both cases the legs, the movements of which are relative to the body as a whole, remain blurred. Since the invention of photography, people knew that a long exposure produced an image showing traces of movement – blurred, often unintelligible, unidentifiable. It was, in fact, the displacement of the image on the sensitive surface that was being recorded. It was quickly understood that only by reducing the exposure time would it be possible to obtain an image of an object that would be apparently still for the short duration of the exposure.

The speed with which the image was captured became the determining factor – the shorter the time, the greater the chance of capturing an unblurred picture of the object. However, the application of this self-evident remedy was hindered for around four decades (1840–1880) by the inadequate sensitivity of photographic emulsions. We know how photographers used their ingenuity to work their way round this problem – taking advantage of situations where the object's speed appeared less (ships seen from the front), reducing the surface area of the negative (the small format used for stereoscopy, Charles Nègre's studies of people in movement, taken as early as 1852), improving the distribution of light in the optical system, increasing sensitivity by various additives, natural or chemical. To take an opposite example, we also know how Nadar's portrait of Baudelaire (Musée

◄ ÉTIENNE-JULES MAREY
Investigation into Walking,
circa 1884,
geometric chronophotograph (from original negative),
Collège de France Archives, Paris.

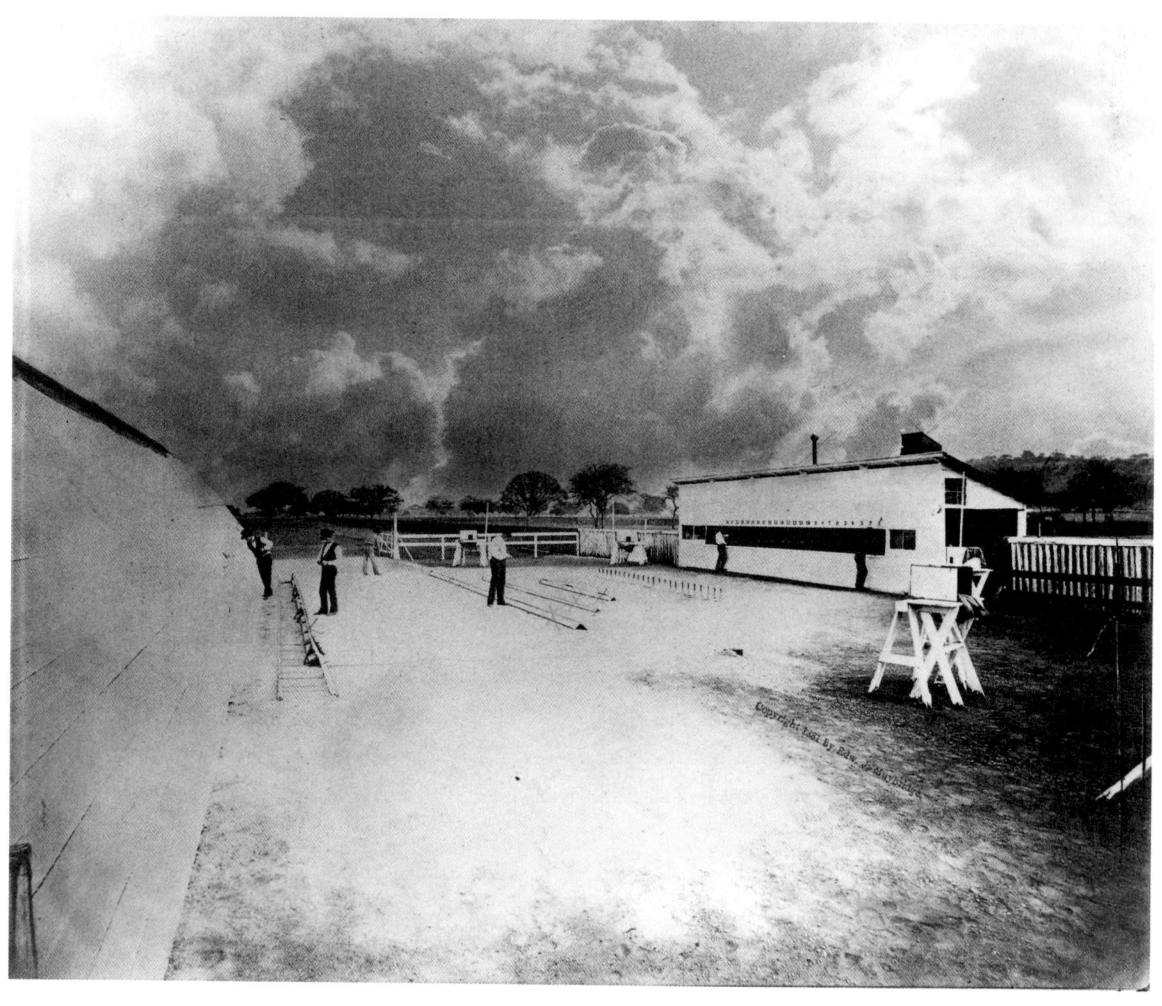

EADWEARD J. MUYBRIDGE
Experimental Area at Palo Alto,
1878–1879,
Musée Marey, Beaune.

d'Orsay) turned out blurred, because, unluckily, it was taken when the poet moved. Judged purely on technical criteria, it ought to be considered a portrait of lesser quality. We have also seen those involuntary ghosts which appear in so many old photographs; from the crowds of idly strolling people in front of the Hôtel de Ville after it had burned down in May 1871, and in front of the Vendôme column after it had been demolished, to the spectral actors in the photographs by Atget taken at the beginning of the next century – due not to his ignorance of instant photography but because he was using a view camera which took 18 x 24 cm plates, necessitating a long exposure. All these vague, involuntary traces seem to us today to be moving witnesses of a living presence, which wrote themselves into the picture by remaining almost motionless for a long time.

The speed of the snapshot

The instantaneous photograph (an exposure of sufficiently short duration for its subject – no fixed definition is possible) has always been a relative concept. For example, it was possible as early as the 1850s (with the calotype process) to stereoscopically depict men marching, at a distance, because their image on a small-format plate (8 x 8 cm) appears immobile, even during a fraction of a second. Instantaneous photography – which is not an end in itself but an element in the evolution of photography – is defined by speed. More precisely, it depends on two different speeds: that of the subject, which can be imagined as going faster and faster, and that of the shutter, that element which determines the brevity of the penetration of light into the camera.[1] Although it was only with the introduction of gelatin-silver bromide emulsions in around 1880 that really instantaneous shots first became possible, notable progress was made by Eadweard Muybridge who, in 1876–1879, captured the movements of a horse using collodion-coated plates (the process in use between 1850 and 1880, still too slow to capture rapid movement).

This type of experiment is generally linked to the invention of the cinema (nearly twenty years later), but that is a pseudo-historical view of events, directed by hindsight, and does not correspond to the real objectives of the protagonists of the decisive years 1875–1885, since none of them had looked for, or even envisaged, that reconstitution of visual reality that we call cinema. On the other hand, other practitioner-theoreticians had taken a real interest in this problem. People such as Louis Ducos du Hauron (1864), Cook and

1. The shutter became indispensable only in the 1880s, when it became necessary to control very short exposures accurately, when very sensitive plates came on the scene. See chapter 13.

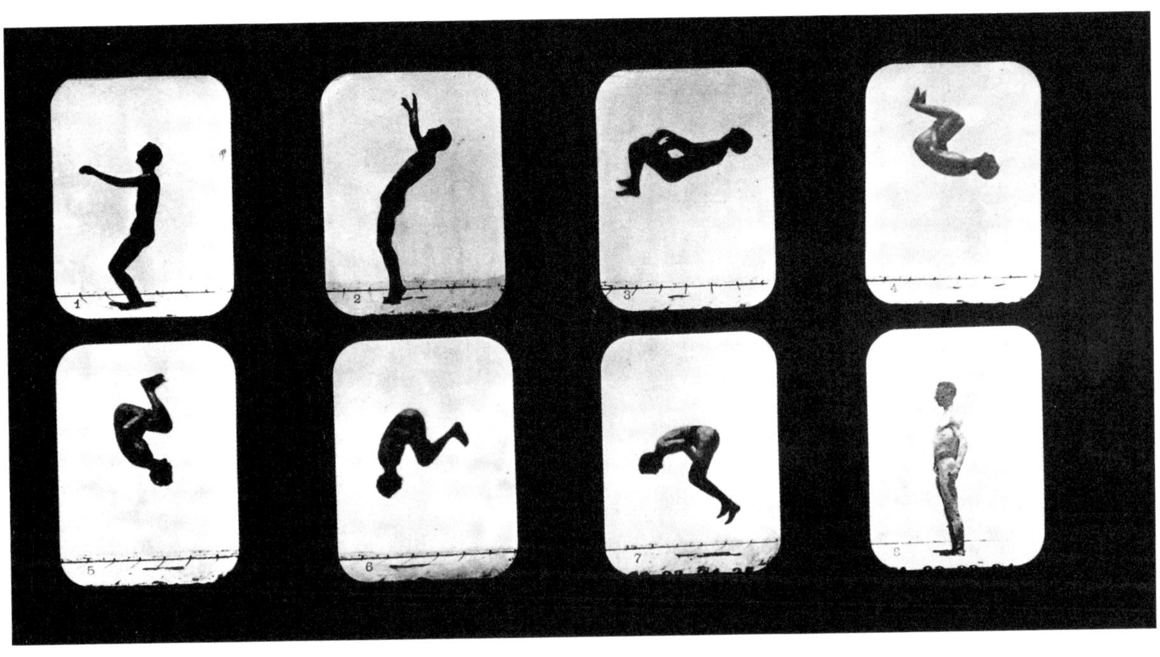

EADWEARD J. MUYBRIDGE
Back Somersault,
sequence of successive positions, taken from *The Attitudes of Animals in Motion,* 1881,
Musée Marey, Beaune.

Bonelli (1863–1865), and Henry Du Mont who wrote in his patent of 1861: "People in motion will be reproduced in all the phases of their movements and with the interval of time which really separated those phases."[2] Because the technology was not yet up to it, all these projects, viable in conception, remained mere theories, awaiting the possibility of the production of real instantaneous pictures of adequate speed.

It was not this sort of research that Eadweard Muybridge had in mind. He was a Californian photographer of British origin, famous for his views of the Yosemite valley and other grandiose sites of the West which were beginning to find favor with the public in the mood of post-romantic lyricism of 1870. It was to Muybridge, a man adept at handling mammoth glass collodion-treated plates, that Leland Stanford, president of the Central Pacific Railroad and ex-governor of California, turned in 1872. Stanford was a great horse-lover, and the owner of a racing stable. He installed Muybridge at Sacramento to take photographs of a horse trotting. This commission was to resolve a semi-scientific problem on which he was at variance with the French physiologist Étienne-Jules Marey – what was the exact position of a horse's limbs during certain phases of the trot?[3] Muybridge's first pictures, taken in 1872 and 1873 in between photographic expeditions to Yosemite Valley, were a failure because of the slowness of the emulsions. The experiments were interrupted in 1874–1876, due to the marital and legal vicissitudes of Muybridge, who had shot and killed his wife's lover. In 1877, a more successful picture, described as an "automatic electric photograph" created a sensation. However it turned out to be merely a photographic copy of a painting which had been produced from the results of a further failure with photography.[4]

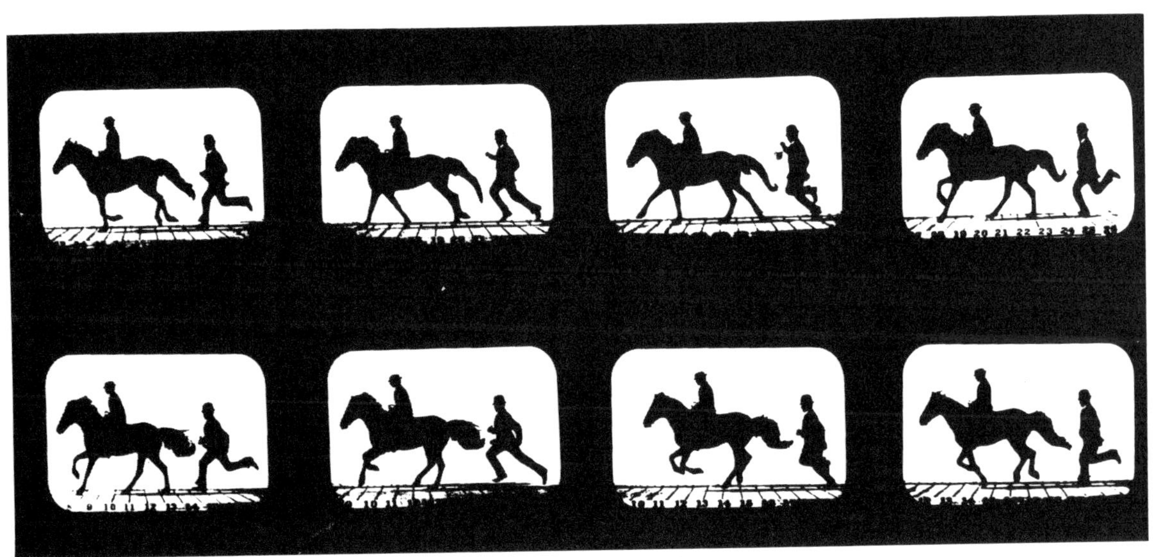

EADWEARD J. MUYBRIDGE,
Leland Stanford Jr. on a Pony,
photographs done with wet collodion, series of eight phases, May 1879.

2. Patent no. 49520 registered in Paris, for a camera suited to reproducing the successive phases of a movement.

3. What precisely was at stake was to verify that, in accordance with Marey's work, there was a particular moment at which none of the horse's hooves was touching the ground, which was difficult to believe.

4. Exhibition catalogue *Eadweard Muybridge: the Stanford Years 1872–1882,* Stanford, Sacramento, Los Angeles, 1972–1973.

E. J. Muybridge's *Animal Locomotion*

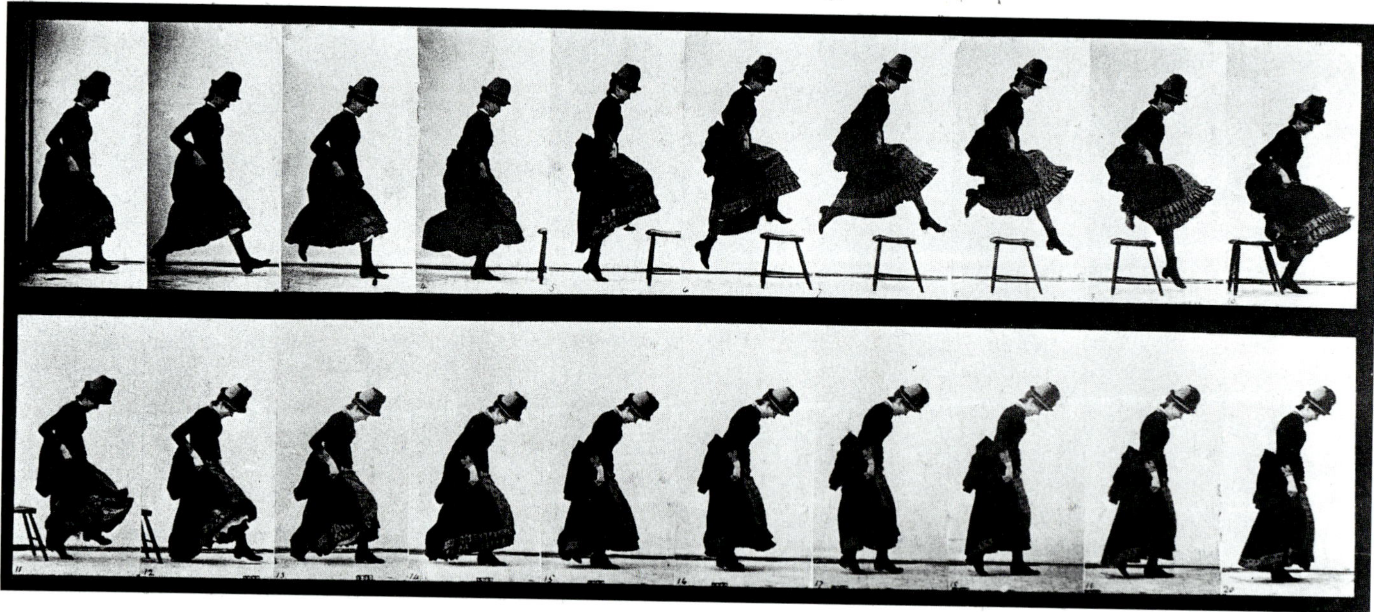

Eadweard J. Muybridge,
extracts from two plates in *Animal Locomotion*, 1887,
Cinémathèque Française, Paris.

The photographic work carried out by Muybridge in 1878–1879 at Palo Alto resulted, first of all, in the distribution in 1881 of several albums of original prints, *The Attitudes of Animals in Motion*. In Paris, while he was on a European tour in the same year, giving demonstrations and projecting his slides, Muybridge formulated a plan with the painter Meissonier and the physiologist Marey for a joint publication on the movements of the horse, combining photography, artistic analysis, and physiological study. In the meantime, the man who had commissioned the photographs at Palo Alto, the ex-governor of California Leland Stanford brought out a book, in 1882, based on Muybridge's research, and signed J. B. D. Stillman. To Muybridge's great disappointment, this was illustrated simply with 91 lithographed drawings *copied* from his original photographs.

After his break with Stanford, Muybridge conceived the project of extending his photographic research to human beings, horses, dogs, cattle, and other domestic and wild animals, making different movements at different speeds. He made an agreement with the university of Philadelphia to carry out the work. The pictures were taken in 1884–1885 in the veterinary department and sometimes the zoo, with the collaboration of the Academy of Fine Arts (particularly the painter Thomas Eakins). Muybridge used a permanent battery of 12 or 24 cameras along the side of the track where the subject was moving about, together with two oblique cameras. These cameras were set off electrically at variable intervals.

Around 20,000 instantaneous negatives were produced, and prints were arranged on 781 plates. These were published in 1887 under the title *Animal Locomotion; an Electro-Photographic Investigation of Consecutive Phases of Animals Movements, 1872–1885*, the plates having been reproduced by the Photogravure Company of New York. The plates were available as a bound volume, in a portfolio or separately (chosen from a catalogue). It was possible to order them by subscription, with a minimum order of 100 plates.

There were 95 plates on the horse, 562 on men, women, and children carrying out various actions, and 124 on animals and birds. Among them we find the typical movements for walking, running, taking part in sports, and other physical acts (sitting, kneeling, jumping, bending over, throwing a stone, picking it up). We also find movements related to work (ironing, washing, gardening, the actions of the stone-mason, the smith, etc.), domestic activities and the movements of handicapped people. The models (male and female) were often presented naked, for both artistic and scientific purposes, which was unusual in view of the puritanism of the times.

Despite a relatively small distribution because of the high cost of the plates, the impact of *Animal Locomotion* was very important at the end of the century (Meissonier corrected the positions of horses' legs in two of his paintings after seeing Muybridge and Marey's results). Among subscribers we find the names of scientists – Edison, Mach, Vogel, Tissandier, and Helmholtz – and of artists such as Tiffany, Meissonier, Bonnat, Bouguereau, Carolus-Duran, Detaille, Gérôme, Puvis de Chavannes, Rodin, Menzel, Kaulbach, Lenbach, Millais, and Watts. However, the real success in terms of the distribution of these images were the two smaller-sized popular editions, *Animals in Motion* and *The Human Figure in Motion*, which were republished many times before Dover's reprints of 1955 and 1957.

Several generations of artists thus acquired a photographic repertory of sequential forms and actions, as well as a generalized picture of a world of everyday experience, unselfconscious, relatively emancipated in its behavior, presented in detail by photography. People were not, perhaps, aware as yet of the changes inherent in these codified representations, which could be taken as accepted norms for imitation. Isadora Duncan appears to have discovered the liberated world of modern dance in them, and Gertrude Stein to have conceived her idea of a space-time full of movement.

Michel Frizot

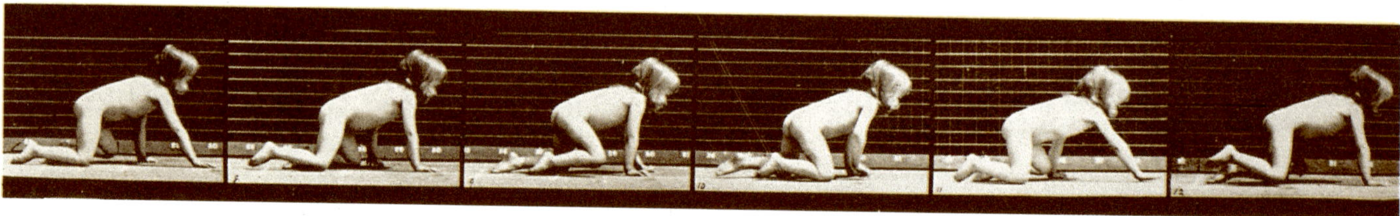

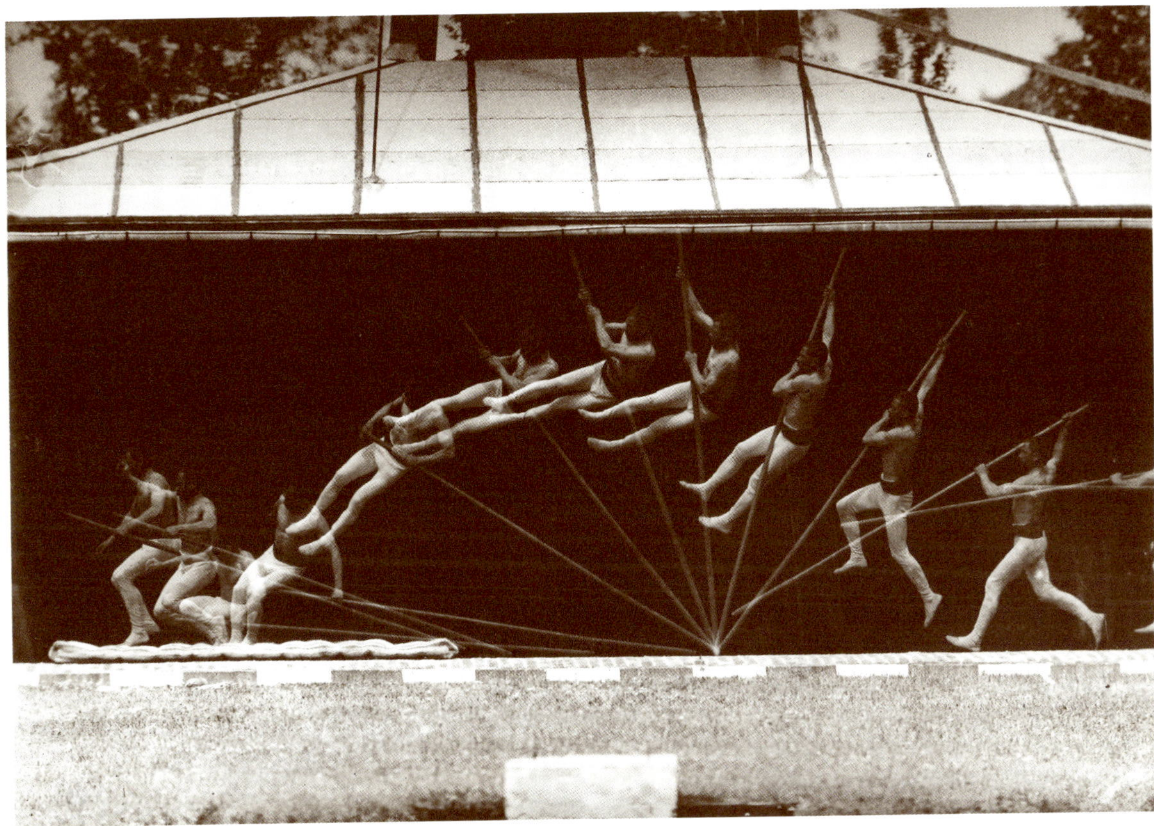

ÉTIENNE-JULES MAREY,
Movements in pole-vaulting,
fixed-plate chronophotograph,
circa 1900,
Collège de France Archives, Paris.

ÉTIENNE-JULES MAREY
Dog Walking,
fixed-plate chronophotograph,
circa 1890,
Musée Marey, Beaune.
▼

It was his photographic session of 1878 at Stanford's stables at Palo Alto which finally solved the problem of instantaneous pictures. Muybridge had installed a battery of 12 cameras with slit-shutters (the drop variety, giving an exposure of 1/25 of a second) which were activated electrically when threads strung across the test-track were abruptly severed. The precision which Muybridge achieved in taking these photographs (at the exact moment when the subject was in front of the camera) and his ingenious multiple-camera system set photography on course for the scientific and systematic study of movement, whereas previously it had been a matter of single, chance results. His system follows on from that suggested by Rejlander in 1873, also for showing the position of horses' legs. The shutter was patented in 1879.

Muybridge's success exceeded the aims of his original project in several ways. In taking twelve pictures simply to be sure of capturing the required moment, Muybridge was opting for a solution which provided him straight off with an exactly timed sequence that captured the evolution in time of a movement or a cycle, for instance, a horse going along at a trot. He thus recorded sufficient data to enable him – at least conceptually – to reconstitute movement.

At this point, Muybridge's studies pass from the domain of the anecdotal to that of systematic research. On December 14, 1878, the French journal *La Nature* published his series of photographs of quite extraordinary interest. These prompted a response from the physiologist Marey who was enthusiastic and suggested that Muybridge apply his method to the flight of birds with the aid of "a sort of photographic gun".[5] Muybridge then started a lecture tour. In 1881, when he was in Paris, he met Marey, and very likely directed the latter's physiological researches towards the use of the camera as a tool (see

5. *La Nature*, December 28, 1878; Muybridge's positive response appeared on March 22, 1879.

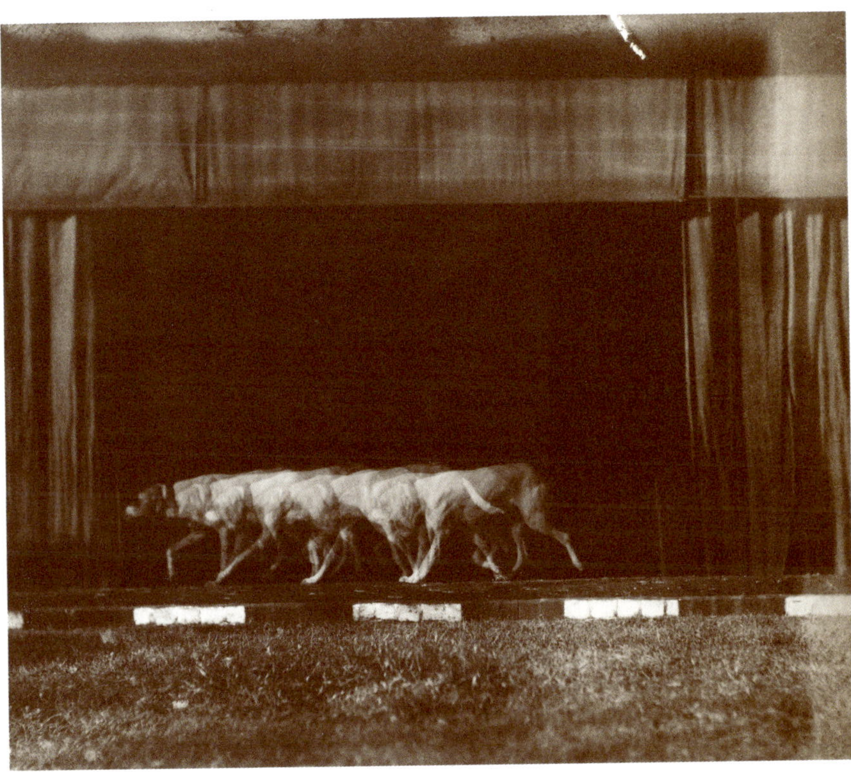

below). Following a disagreement with Stanford, the man who commissioned him, Muybridge abandoned his installation at Palo Alto, but got the University of Philadelphia to finance a much more extensive program of study of animals and human beings. Between 1884 and 1885, Muybridge worked in Philadelphia, stockpiling 20,000 instantaneous pictures which had been made using the new gelatin-silver bromide emulsions.

A selection of these images was published in the form of 781 plates printed by the collotype process and titled *Animal Locomotion* (see box). As well as various sports, there were also genre scenes (a woman throwing a bucket of water or getting into bed) and pathological cases – handicapped people and contortionists. Muybridge himself sometimes appears in the pictures. The work had only limited success because of its cost, but provoked noticeable repercussions in the world of the arts.

What does Muybridge's decomposition of movement consist of? It is actually the unpremeditated juxtaposition of instantaneous exposures of a body in various attitudes, arranged in chronological order. The speed of the photographic process is significant at two levels: the speed of the exposure (1/1000 of a second, if necessary) and the speed at which the photographs follow one another in a very short period of time (a "burst" of exposures). At this time, however, except as a matter of curiosity, there was no idea of recomposing movement which, in any case, lasted only one or two seconds .[6]

Chronophotography

The case of Étienne-Jules Marey was not, perhaps, isolated – he was a major figure at the end of the century – but it was unusual. For he managed to create from his own inspiration, using a logically worked-out photographic system, images that were entirely new – at once scientific and dreamlike. A distinguished physiologist at the Collège de France, he was already renowned for his research into the circulation of the blood, human locomotion, and the movement of horses.[7] A friend of Nadar, he was not, however, tempted to use photography until his correspondence with Muybridge (whose employment by Stanford came about, in fact, because of Marey's work). His successes were due in large part to his scientific rigor and to the wide applicability of his graphic method, which consisted in recording the curves for variations in successive states (impact of feet on the ground, muscle contractions, the beating of wings) on a moving piece of blackened paper. Record, write down, trace: these were the key-words of his approach, the essence of which was to combine visual evidence with a precise registration of the passage of time.

In 1878, when he discovered Muybridge's sequential photographs of horses, Marey realized that photography could become an instrument of exceptional precision for recording. His disappointment when he saw the non-sequential snapshots of birds in flight produced by Muybridge in 1881 stimulated him to carry out his plan to

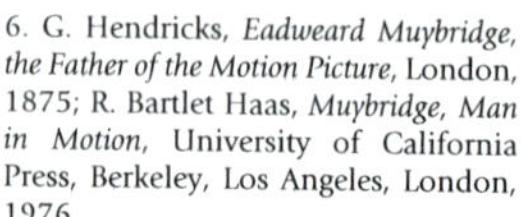

6. G. Hendricks, *Eadweard Muybridge, the Father of the Motion Picture*, London, 1875; R. Bartlet Haas, *Muybridge, Man in Motion*, University of California Press, Berkeley, Los Angeles, London, 1976.

7. *Du mouvement dans les fonctions de la vie*, Paris, B. Baillière, 1868; *La Méthode graphique dans les Sciences expèrimentales*, Paris, Masson, 1878; *La Machine animale*, Paris, G. Baillière, 1873.

8. Letter to his mother of February 3, 1882 in M. Frizot, *E. J. Marey: la Photographie du Mouvement* Paris, Centre Georges-Pompidou, 1977, p.26.

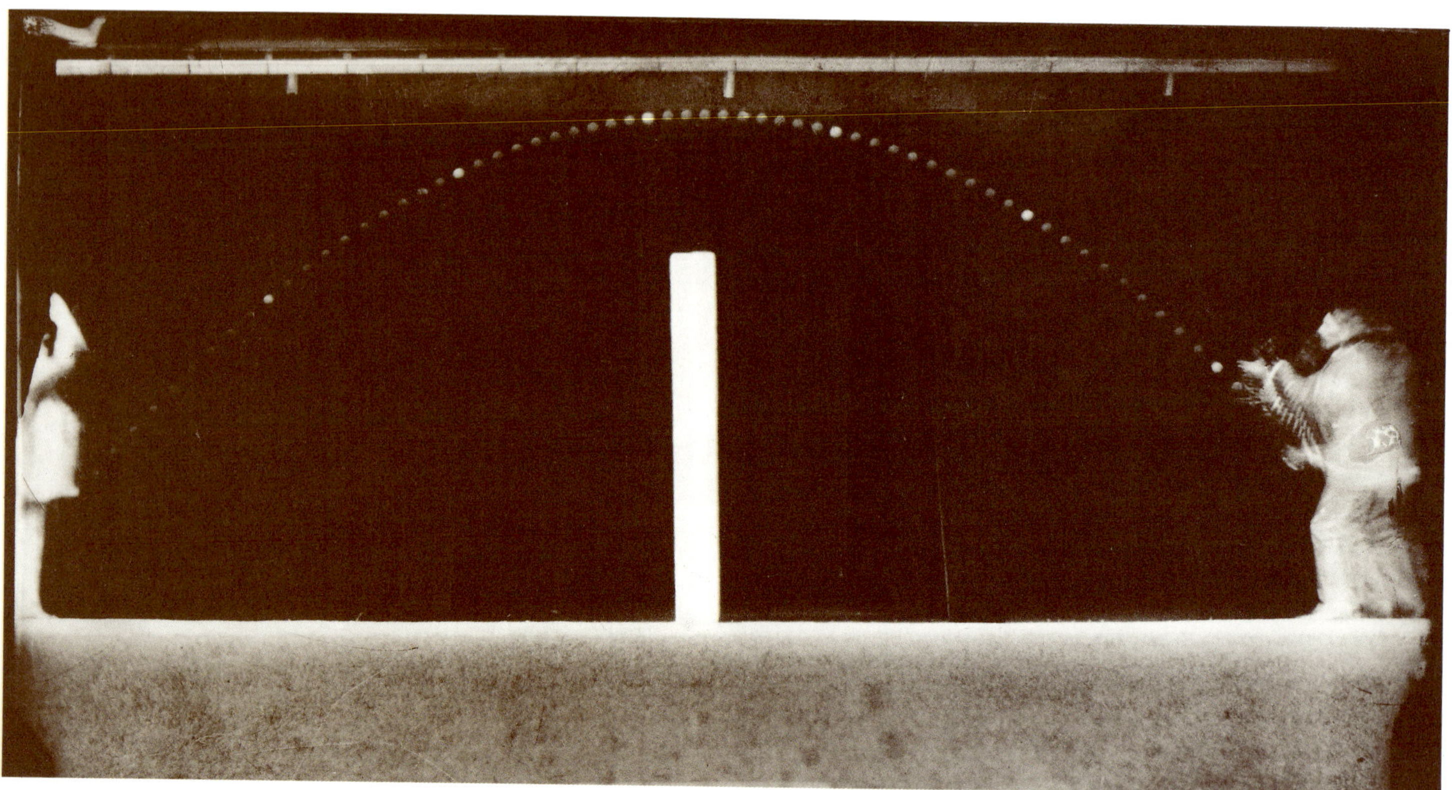

Étienne-Jules Marey, ***Trajectory of a Ball,*** fixed-plate chronophotograph, circa 1886, Collège de France Archives, Paris. ▼

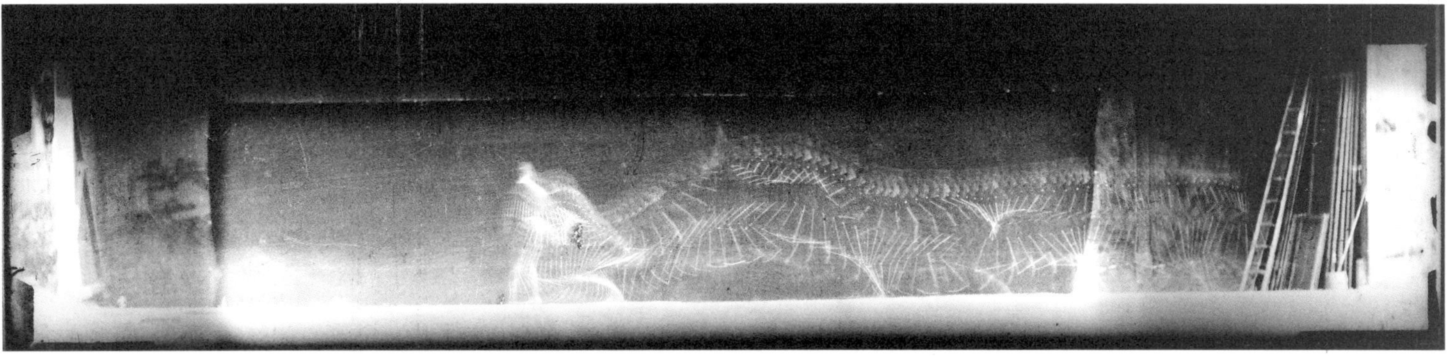

ÉTIENNE-JULES MAREY, *How a Man Runs*, geometric chronophotograph, 1883, (from the original negative on glass), Collège de France Archives, Paris.

make a photographic gun, which he had formulated in 1878.

The gun was constructed at the end of 1881, during his annual stay near Naples, and used in the first months of 1882. He wrote, "I have a photographic gun which has nothing murderous about it, and which takes a picture of a bird flying or an animal running in less than 1/500 of a second. I do not know whether you can really imagine such a speed, but it is something surprising."[8] Apart from the exposure time, the gun had another kinetic feature – it took a series of 12 images a second. Designed like a real gun, with the sight at shoulder-level, the instrument had a lens in the barrel and a cylindrical breech within which was a sensitive plate which revolved when one pressed the trigger. This rotating plate, treated with gelatin-silver bromide emulsion, stopped 12 times behind the lens, while the shutter let in the light for 1/720 of a second.[9]

The importance of the photographic gun in Marey's researches must not, however, be exaggerated. It should be seen as one stage in the development of his ideas since the smallness of the images, the unreliability of the sight, and the absence of a way of recording the passage of time made it unsatisfactory for his scientific needs.

His fixed-plate chronophotograph camera, completed in May-June 1883 fulfilled the physiologist's requirements by "bringing together on the same plate a series of sequential images, representing the different positions that a living being, traveling at a particular pace, occupies in space at a series of given moments".[10] The novelty, by comparison with Muybridge's procedure, consisted in using a single camera as recording instrument, and in superimposing images, taken, one after the other, by the single, fixed lens. This required that the subject, which for preference had to be white or strongly lit, move in front of a black background which would make no impression upon the sensitive surface. This photographic apparatus should be seen as not simply a camera but as the whole experimental area that Marey set up in the Bois de Boulogne – a dark shed to provide the black background, within which there was the area where the subjects moved, a mobile cabin on a rail facing the black background, electric cables transmitting synchronizing signals, and a rapidly-rotating clock placed in the field of vision. The apparatus itself, named the *chronophotographe*, was a camera, taking 13 x 18 cm plates, equipped with a special shutter system – a disc 1 meter in diameter, with several windows which effected the illumination of the plates at intervals regulated by the speed of rotation.[11]

The subjects covered by chronophotography, especially in the period 1883–1887, were of a great variety, combining all Marey's particular interests in the area of physiology: how people walk, run and jump, the different movements of the horse (walk, trot, gallop), a great many birds (a pigeon, a seagull, a pelican, a heron), and kinetics in general (falling bodies, a bouncing ball). After 1890, more specialized studies brought chronophotography to bear on the movement of the jaws, breathing, the stabilizing of a ship, riding a bicycle, etc.

Meanwhile geometrical (or partial) chronophotography had appeared, in which a man moved

Marey's fixed-plate chronophotography machine, with ten slit-disk that acts as a shutter (on the ground is the sensitized-plate holder), 1883 model, and plan of workings of a similar model, 1882.

▼

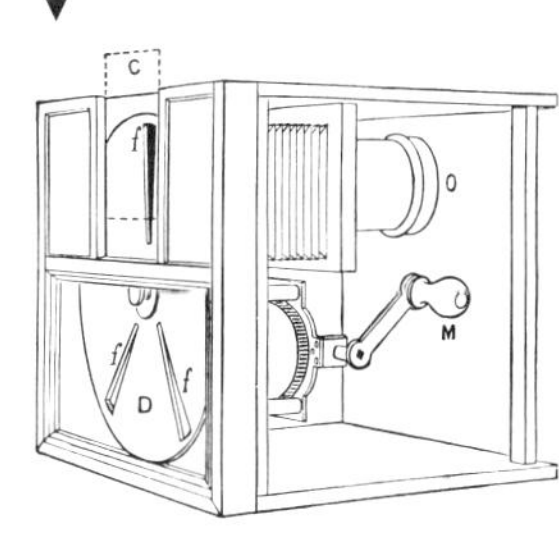

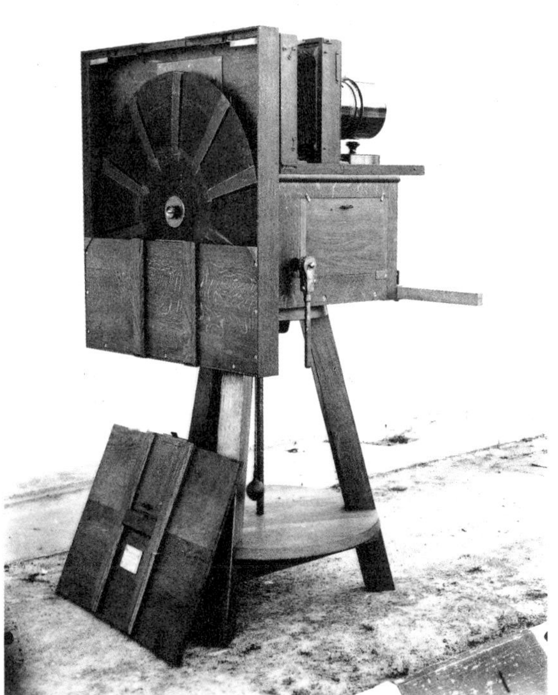

9. *La Nature*, April 22, 1882, pp. 326–330.

10. *Comptes rendus des séances de l'Académie des Sciences*, July 3,1882, p. 15.

11. With a disc having 10 windows, and rotating 10 times a second, 100 images a second could be reached; but a level of 10 to 20 images a second was generally kept to, with an exposure time of 1/100 to 1/900 of a second.

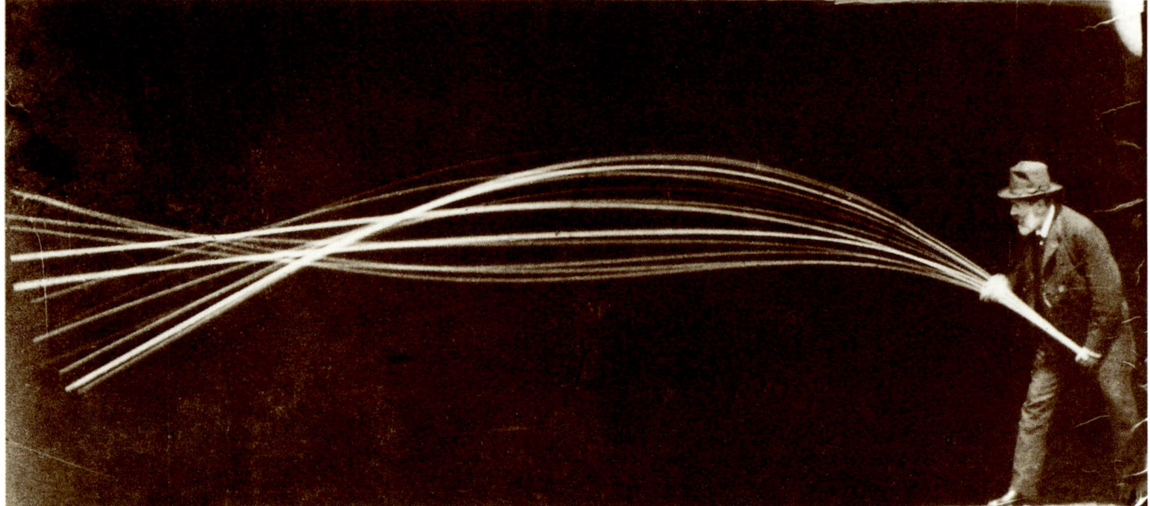

Étienne-Jules Marey, *Vibration of a Flexible Rod*, 1886, Musée Marey, Beaune.

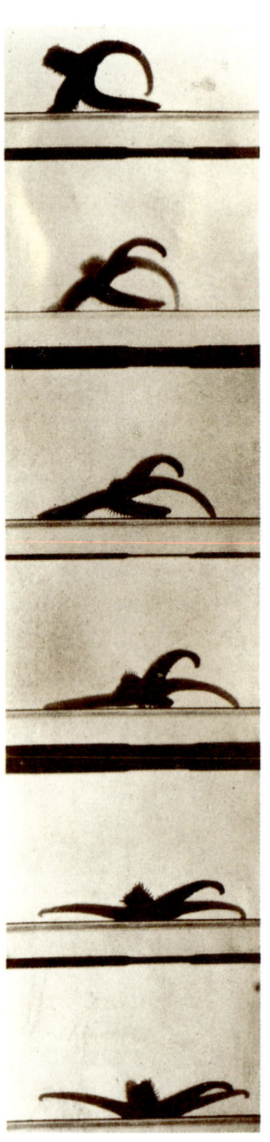

Étienne-Jules Marey, *Movement of Starfish*, **1890**. chronophotograph on moveable film, 1890, Musée Marey, Beaune. ▼

in front of the black background, dressed in black, but with white lines on his limbs and joints. In this way, Marey managed to isolate scientifically useful information which is normally hidden in the general shape of the subject, by reducing that shape to moving lines and dots. These chronophotographs were authentic graphs of movement (but inverted – white lines on black ground) which, since the experiments took place under conditions of almost mathematical accuracy, lent themselves to the measurement of both dimension and time. The applications of these images were more limited but they allowed the experimenter to achieve great precision (*Elephant Walking*).

The novelty of chronophotography as a concept, little remarked upon at the time, lies in three areas: the use of photography to record a phenomenon – of any kind – scientifically; the production of non-realist, even strange pictures of real objects; and, finally, the progressive solution of the problem of recreating movement. Marey, with Albert Londe, who often paid tribute to him, was able, because of his position in the university elite to turn photography at the end of the nineteenth century into a credible, workable laboratory method, freed from the picture-making complexes of artistic representation.

Paradoxically, these scientific photographs show bodies dematerialized by their own speed, in the fleeting way that our eye can perceive them in the fluid current of sight. The magical reunion in a single image of moments that are separate but close, and which together form a unity (a movement), was not to find its philosophical and poetic correlatives until the beginning of the twentieth century, despite Marey's numerous publications, culminating in two key works: *The Flight of Birds*, which was vital for aviation (1890), and *Movement*, 1894.[12]

For a brief period, chronophotography by the Marey method found a reflection in the United States in the work of the painter Thomas Eakins, who had supported Muybridge's application to Philadelphia. In his teaching at the Academy, Eakins was insistent that one should work directly from the nude model (which caused him to be dismissed in 1886) and he often took instantaneous photographs. In the summer of 1884, spurred on by the example of Muybridge, who had begun his photography at Philadelphia, he adopted the rival system, Marey's fixed-plate method, which he continued using until summer, 1885, taking pictures of naked men walking, running and jumping.[13]

From 1888, Marey made further improvements to his system. To prevent even partial superimposition of the images, which could prevent them from being read properly, he opted for a sensitive surface which moved in conjunction with the exposures. First of all he used a glass plate, followed by sensitized paper. In 1890, he was able to take advantage of the recently invented Celluloid film which Eastman had put into the Kodak camera. Marey's first film (a hand which opens and closes) was published in July 1889.[14]

However, despite having performed some crucial work, Marey has not been considered a precursor of cinematography. He intentionally restricted its application to research, and it was used elsewhere (see box). Photography, which had brought forth a flowering of new images once the shutter could be operated with precision and at variable speeds, was to find itself once again reduced to a uniform speed by the regular pace of the cinematograph, though, it is true, with quite different perspectives.

Multiplication of instant exposures

Albert Londe, a photographer appointed by Professor Charcot to head the laboratory at Salpêtrière, quickly adapted Muybridge's sequen-

12. See also M. Frizot, *Avant le Cinématographe, la Chronophotographie*, Beaune, 1984, and *E. J. Marey*, Photo Poche, no. 13, Paris 1983.

13. G. Hendricks, *The Photographs of Thomas Eakins*, New York, Grossman, 1972.

14. *Archives de Physiologie normale et pathologique*, p.516

tial method, using a single camera with multiple lenses. The battery of cameras used at Palo Alto was, in a sense, compressed into a single camera, with nine lenses arranged in a circle (3 x 3 cm on a 13 x 18 cm plate), a single rotating disc with a slit setting off a succession of exposures, regulated by a clockwork mechanism. This piece of apparatus, probably invented in 1883, made it possible to record pathological movements (trembling, epileptic fits, and hysterics) with a picture-frequency that could be modulated at will, but which was limited to nine circular prints.

In 1891 Londe had another camera made which had twelve lenses arranged in three ranks of four (giving twelve pictures measuring 7 x 7 cm on a plate 24 x 30 cm). The successive shots were set off by electromagnets and could be preprogrammed to occur at an interval ranging from several seconds to 1/10 of a second, at variable speeds. Londe was in no way interested in reconstructing the movements that he was recording. His apparatus, which allowed him to make a scientific study of any movement taking place against a white background (outdoors or indoors), was perfectly suited to the goal he had set himself – to obtain an exactly timed succession of instantaneous shots upon which it was possible to make measurements or carry out visual analysis. They could also be used simply as documentary records.[15]

As a sideline to his medical work at Salpêtrière, Londe went in to partnership with Paul Richer to make studies of movement quite similar to Muybridge's. Richer, another ex-pupil of Charcot and a friend of Marey, taught anatomy at the École des Beaux-Arts in Paris. These photographs served as the basis for Richer's sketches for most of his works. One of the outlines adapted by Richer from Londe's plates is none other than a naked man descending a staircase which seems very likely to have influenced Duchamp's concept for his eponymous painting (1911–1912).[16] Two of Londe's publications, the *Atlas of the Movements of the Horse* with Le Bon (1895), and the *Album of Documentary Chronophotographs for the Use of Artists* (1903) stemmed very clearly from the medical applications to which his profession confined him. The second book is, in essence, about the movements of horses and waves – the wave pictures being of an asceticism close to conceptual work of the 1870s (notably Dibbets). However, at the beginning of the twentieth century Londe's ingenious method using glass plates was already archaic. The cinematograph (and, above all, the high-speed cinematograph perfected by Bull, a pupil of Marey's) was an unlimited source of sequential images.

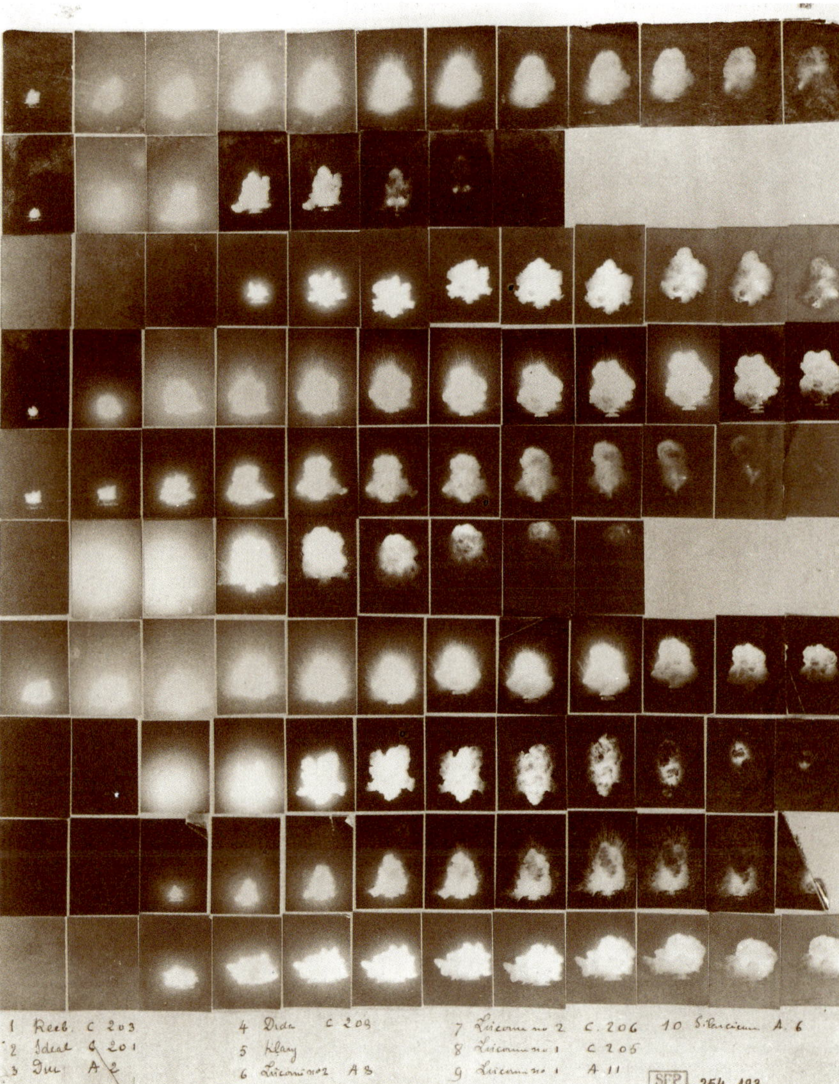

Albert Londe,
Analysis of the flash produced by various magnesium photographic powders,
1905,
Société Française de Photographie, Paris.

The usefulness of photographic speed is not limited to the swiftness of the snapshot. It is part of a totality of practices that can be used in a modular way and adapted to all kinds of situations. The recording of flashes of lightning in darkness, for instance, only requires the lens to be constantly open, whereas the recording of an explosion requires perfect synchronization, with a precise exposure-time. One really ought to talk about a modulation of speed, an idea that is more awkward to put into practice.

Ottomar Anschütz, a Prussian photographer living in Lissa, also worked on the idea of adapting the speed of reaction to the subject. Starting in 1882, he made his name with snapshots using gelatin-silver bromide emulsions (movements of horses and cavalry, artillery maneuvers), which he obtained using a roller-blind shutter of his own invention.[17] From 1885, using batteries of cameras modeled on Muybridge's he took successive series of pictures of horses. He later adapted this technique for other subjects, along the lines of *Animal Locomotion*. Anschütz also played a part in the work which led imperceptibly to the cinema,

15. These pieces of apparatus are described and illustrated by A. Londe in *La Photographie Moderne*, Paris, Masson, 1896, pp. 711–713. See also D. Bernard and A. Gunthert and Albert Londe, *L'instant rêvé*, Nîmes, J. Chambon, 1993.

16. P. Richer, *Physiologie artistique de l'Homme en Mouvement*, Paris, 1895.

17. The very brief moment of light is obtained by means of a slit in the moving blind which passes swiftly in front of the sensitive plate.

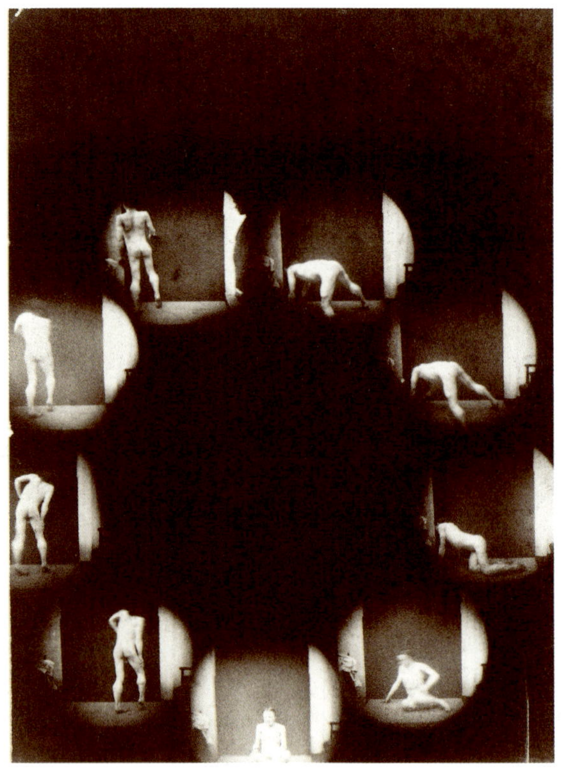

Albert Londe, ***Study of Pathological Locomotion,*** chronophotograph with nine-lens apparatus, circa 1883, École Nationale Supérieure des Beaux-Arts, Paris.

Albert Londe, ***Swinging of the Upper Limb,*** (with twelve-lens apparatus), circa 1893, École Nationale Supérieure des Beaux-Arts, Paris.

▼

using his electrotachyscope (1887) to project real photographic slides on glass. He placed these in a ring around the circumference of a continuously rotating disc, lit by electric sparks synchronized with the passage of each image in front of a window. Here again, the cyclical projection of a score of photographs could show only one or two seconds of movement. However, Anschütz does seem to have been the first to succeed with this sort of projection, a little before Marey. The refinements he made in the system between 1890 and 1894 did not result in a noticeable improvement in its intrinsic limitation as regards time.

An Englishman, A. M. Worthington, had to pinpoint the instant of exposure with great precision in order to capture different images of a very brief phenomenon which he began studying in 1894 – a ball falling into a mixture of water and milk and the ring of turbulence thus produced. To make the moment of photography and the impact coincide, he caused another ball to fall simultaneously. This second ball set off a spark that lit the subject and produced the instantaneous image. By co-ordinating the moment of exposure with the entry of the ball and the formation of the ring, Worthington obtained a number of images that are independent of one another but give the illusion of a continuous series of images of a cinematographic kind (in less than three microseconds).[18] It can be seen that the arrangement of the visual material adopted by all these methods does not always produce an account of scientific reality.

The problem of producing numerous instantaneous photographs in a very short space of time (to capture an object which is moving at high speed) is the same as that of taking a single photograph, at a given moment, of a very fast moving object, like a rifle-bullet. It was in 1886 that Ernst Mach carried out the first experiments in photographing the hyperbolic shock-wave that accompanies a projectile. In 1888, in Prague, he used a spark in a dark environment (the camera

18. A. M. Worthington, *The Splash of a Drop*, London and New York, Young, 1895; *A Study of Splashes*, London, Longman, Green and Co. 1908 (New York, Macmillan, 1963).

19. J. T. Blackmore, *E. Mach: His Work, Life, and Influence*, Berkeley, University of California, 1972; E. Mach, *Popular Scientific Lectures*, Chicago, Open Court, 1910.

20. See *Photographie futuriste italienne, 1911–1939*, Musée d'Art Moderne de la Ville de Paris, 1979, and *Futurismo e Fotografia*, Milan, Multhipla, 1979.

21. G. Lista, in *Photographie futuriste*, op.cit., p.7.

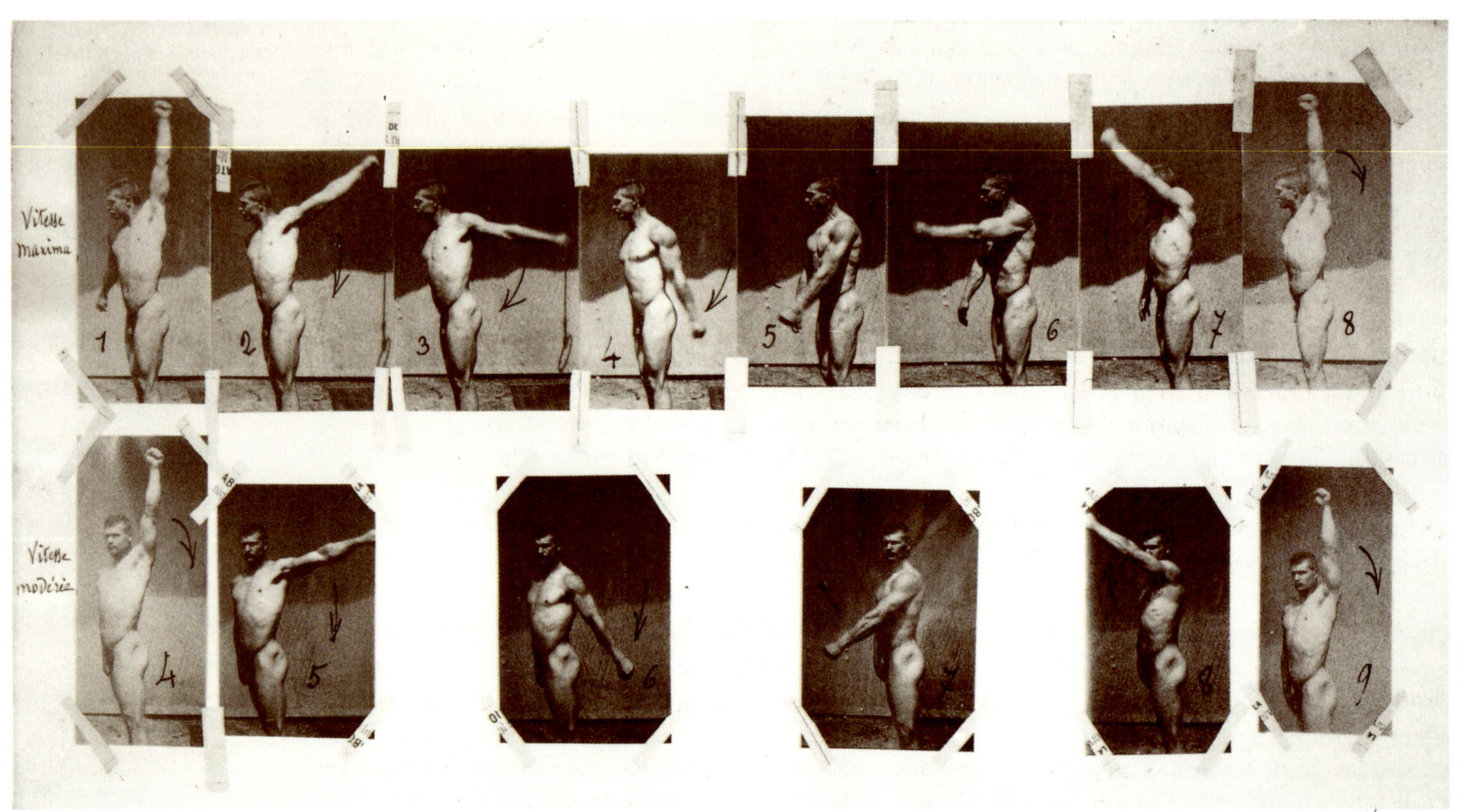

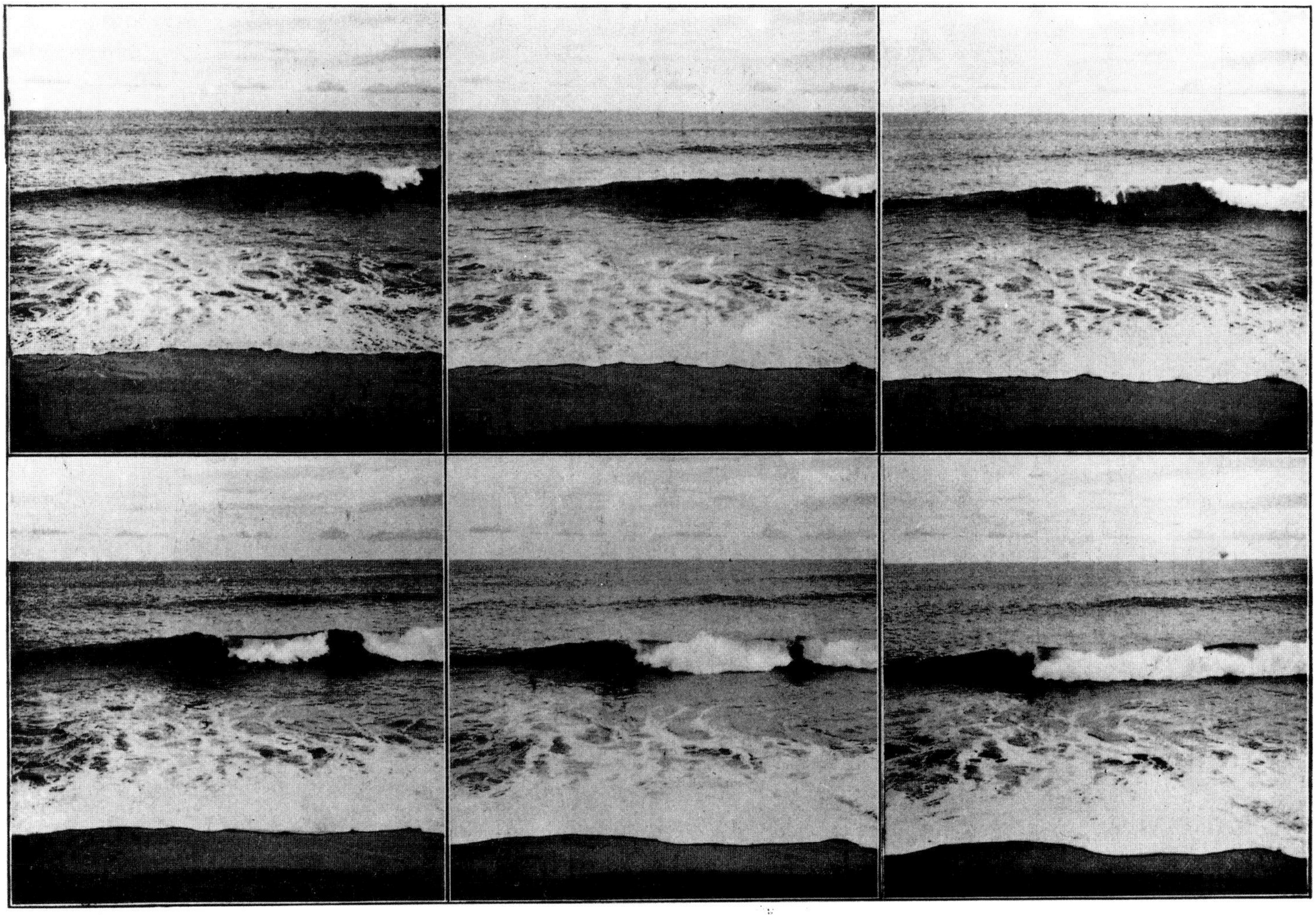

shutter remaining open) to obtain an extremely brief moment of light at the precise instant when the bullet was passing in front of the lens, producing as it does so, a short-circuit between two vertical wires (visible on the photograph). The photographs distributed by Mach show different-shaped bullets, variations in shock-waves, and the following-waves.[19]

Futurist speed

In the strict context of the fixed image, Marey's chronophotography remained a simple curiosity until the double question of the representation of time and energy – the invisible – emerged in the Futurist milieu. As Giovanni Lista[20] has conclusively shown, Marey's example was first perceived by the futurist painters as both a model and a scientific limitation that had to be transcended by personal expressiveness. Only subsequently did it orient them towards a redeployment of photographic practice in conjunction with the idea of speed. Thus, we find that as early as the first manifesto of Futurist painting there is a reference to Marey (April 1910). Boccioni, the principal theoretician of Futurist painting, also knew the work of Bergson, who sometimes supports his arguments by reference to chronophotography, while Marey's writings were published and known in Italy.

But Futurist ideas were not confined to the deconstruction of movement. Rather, they were aiming to activate a vital force within the space of the picture: a modern tremor, the effect of speed. The three *States of Mind* paintings by Boccioni in 1911 mix the optical scanning of movement à la Marey with a vaporizing of the image not unlike the transcendental photographs of the period – the direct transference of the energy of the object onto the plate. However, the dynamism on which Boccioni was working, as with Severini (*Dynamism of a Dancer*, 1912) and Balla (*Dynamism of a Dog on a Leash*, May 1912), was not limited to the chronophotographic model. The reduplication of forms was introduced not so much to give an optical reconstruction of movement as to evoke in the picture the vital intensity of the kinetic phenomenon."[21]

Of all the Futurist pictures which appear to be principally based upon the photographic decomposition of movement, Balla's *Little Girl Running on a Balcony* (1912) is the closest to Marey's geometric chronophotography, as are also the *Plastic Synthesis of the Movements of a Woman* (1912) by

ALBERT LONDE,
Wave, from Infront,
from *Album de chronophotographies documentaires [...]*,
1903,
Bibliothèque Nationale, Paris.

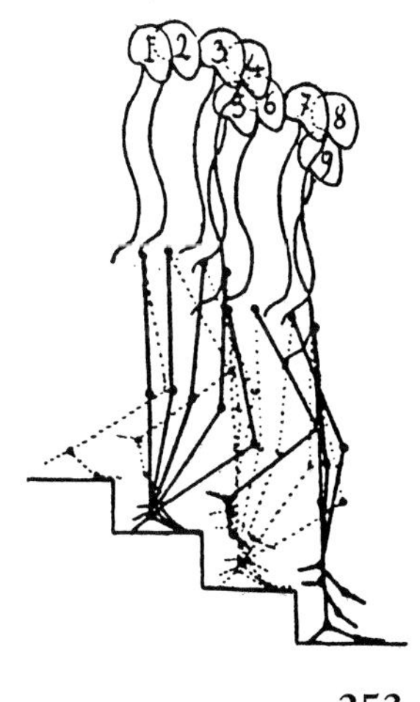

Man Descending a Staircase,
drawing after successive photographs by ALBERT LONDE, from Paul Richer, *Physiologie artistique de l'Homme en Mouvement*, Paris, 1895.

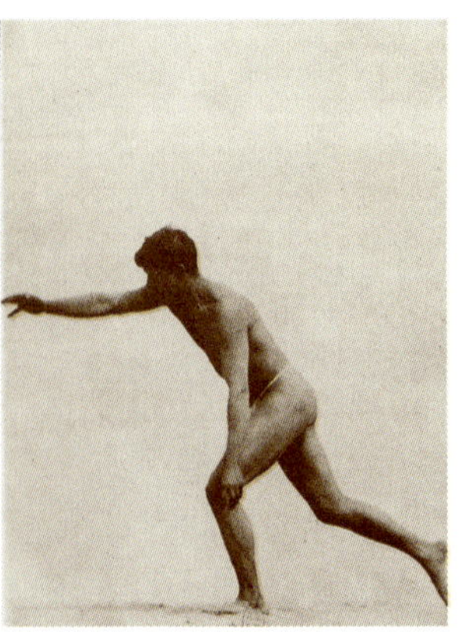
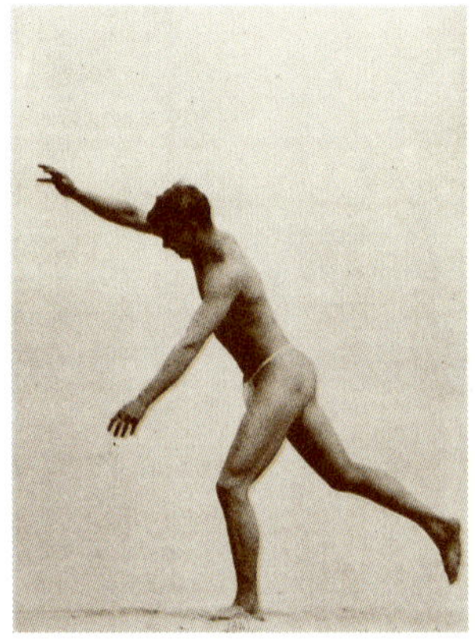
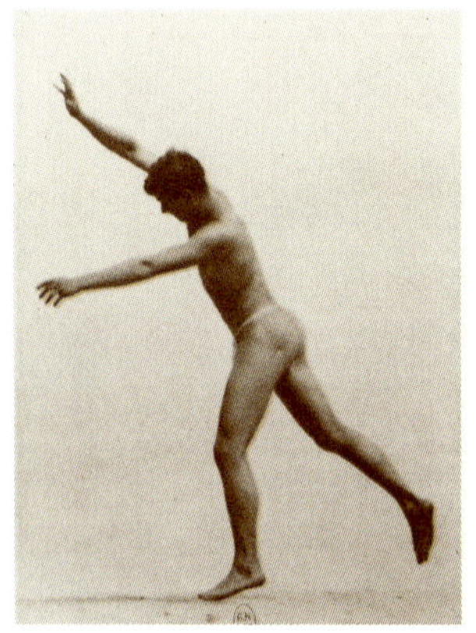
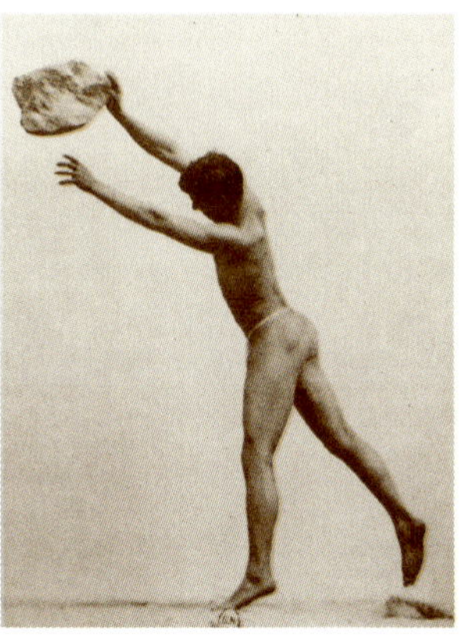
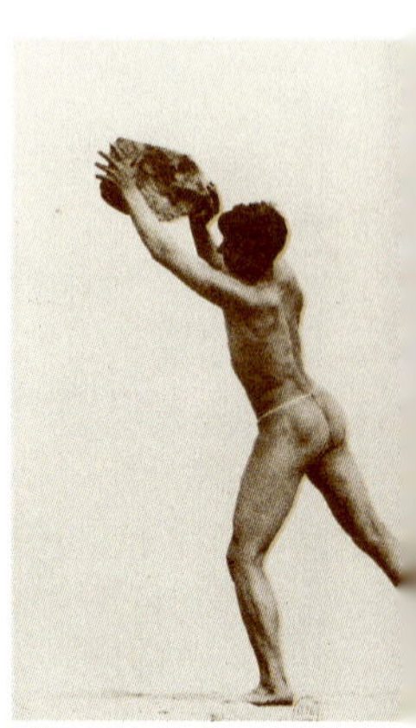

OTTOMAR ANSCHÜTZ, *Instantaneous pictures: throwing a stone, successive photographs on folding card,* Bibliothèque Nationale, Paris.

A. M. WORTHINGTON, ***Instantaneous photographs of splashes in a liquid,*** circa 1908, Science Museum, London. ▼

Russolo and *Elasticity* (1912) by Boccioni, which explicitly refers to the superimposition of pictures of a horse's legs. All these paintings are, in fact, conceived in a Cubist or pointillist style which incorporates a literal chronophotographic decomposition of movement as a language for translating speed. The most chronophotographic (and Futurist) picture of these years is *Nude Descending a Staircase* (1911–1912) by Marcel Duchamp, who belatedly recognized his debt to Marey. Futurist painting was not, therefore, specifically waiting for a photographic model more in accord with its own trends.

It was in May-June 1911 that the brothers Anton Giulio and Arturo Bragaglia began their experiments in photodynamism, producing continuous records of movement in front of a black background (*Salutando*, July 1911), characterized by "the evanescence of the form, which is supposed to render the immediacy of the kinetic event" (G. Lista). These were not chronophotographs, but long exposures covering the whole of a movement which attempted to render dynamism by vaporizing form. It seems not to have been until the beginning of 1913 that the Bragaglia brothers came into contact with the group of Futurist painters, as a result of which they introduced more accentuated phases into their photodynamism. These gave the impression of a jerkier movement, as though a clearer image was being switched on and off when the process slowed down. In February 1913, Boccioni, Balla, and Russolo took part in sessions of photodynamism. *The Photography of Movement* was a manifesto of Futurist photodynamism, written by Anton Giulio Bragaglia, which loudly proclaims its originality and difference in relation to the chronophotography of Marey. Bragaglia attacks what he considers to be the static nature of Marey's images (where every pose, since it is clear, appears immobile), takes up Rodin's arguments against the instantaneous, and preaches a dynamic continuity instead of successive phases. "We abhor and deny the instant photograph or picture, which ridiculously contracts living motions."[22]

In June 1913, after exhibiting his "photodynamics", Anton Giulio Bragaglia published his work *Fotodinamismo Futurista*. After some opening arguments against chronophotography, he states that he gives pride of place to the trajectory rather than the seizing of the moment, "not only at the start and the finish, or even at some intermediate point as chronophotography does, but in a continuous way, from the beginning to the end; [photodynamism] can also render the states in-between-movement of an action".[23]

However, it goes without saying that Bragaglia, with his semi-evanescent images, could not win the support of the painters, who were the large majority in the Futurist movement, and who needed to base

22. Text reproduced in *Photographie futuriste*, p.148.

23. *Fotodinamismo Futurista*, reprinted by Einaudi, Turin, 1970, p. 29.

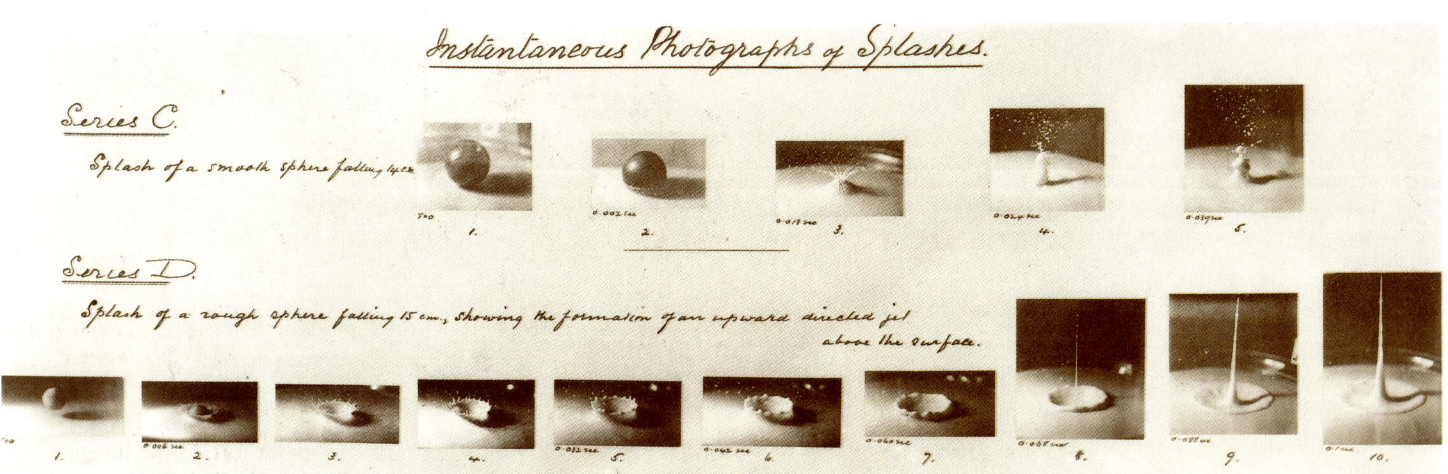

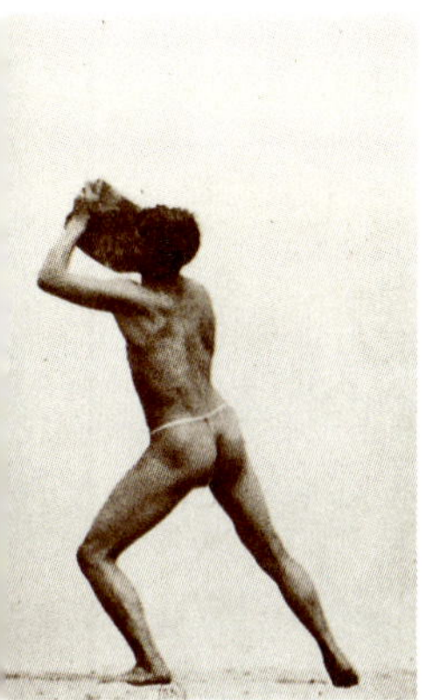
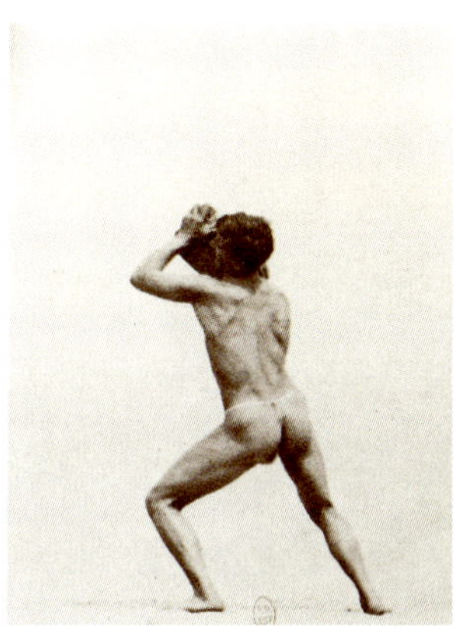
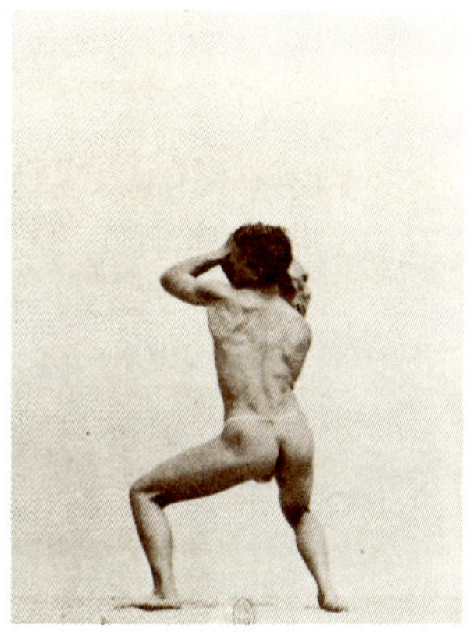
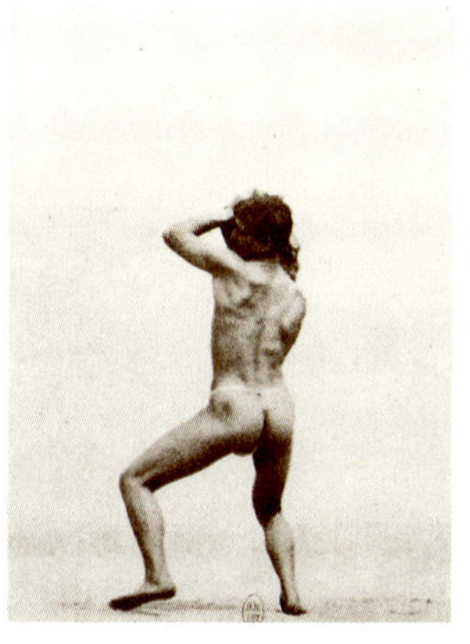
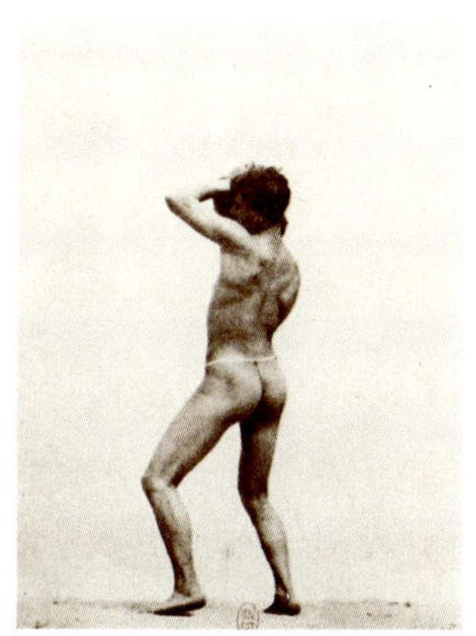

their work on form. Consequently, the Bragaglia brothers were excluded from the Futurist group in mid-1913. In 1914 Boccioni, who was certainly the closest to this immaterial representation of energy, definitely adopted plastic dynamism, which was more Cubist in style, with more clearly-defined masses. The ephemeral research done by Anton Giulio and Arturo Bragaglia, whose combativeness can be seen in pure form in their deliberate disassociation from chronophotography, did not supplant Marey's model of multiple images for use by painters, a model which was, in any case, already being superseded by other, stronger, ideas. Anton Giulio Bragaglia then turned to directing for the stage and cinema.

Futurism, however, stayed faithful to the translation of energy and speed. With the resurgence of the movement after the First World War, many Futurists found in photography a flexible medium which also had avant-garde applications (photomontages, rayograms, superimposition of images, stage-sets). Arturo Bragaglia, who had opened a photographic studio and made Futurist portraits by superimposing images, took up photodynamics again in 1929. In fact, it was not the visual aspect of photodynamics which prevailed, but the idea, which underlies much Futurist work, that there are forces – energy, speed and life – that can be made visual.

The photographic side of the movement was also revived by aerial photography. Masoero, the stunt-pilot, took his camera with him and carried out photography during flight, maintaining that

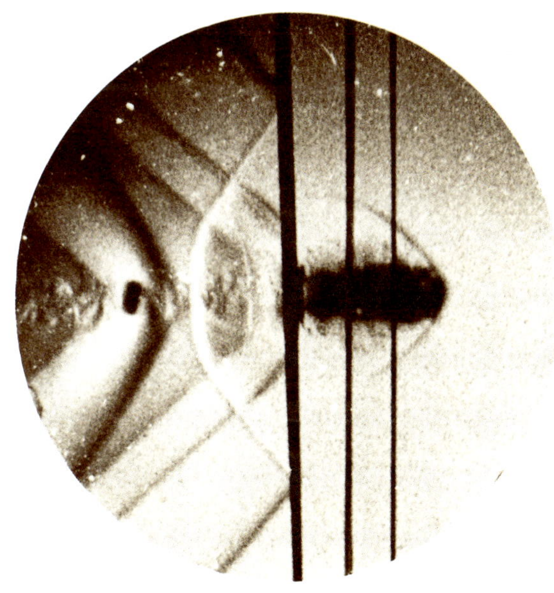

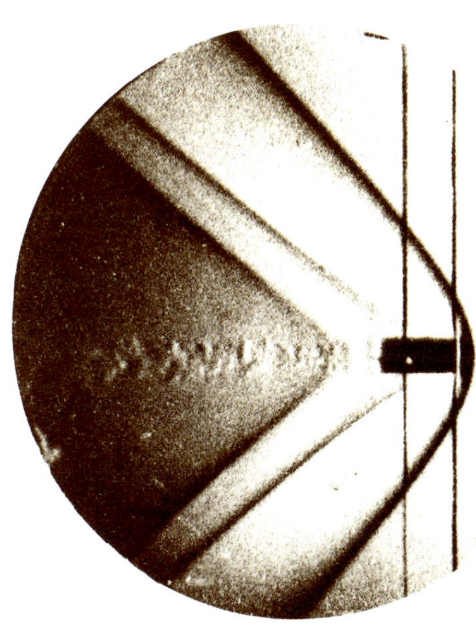

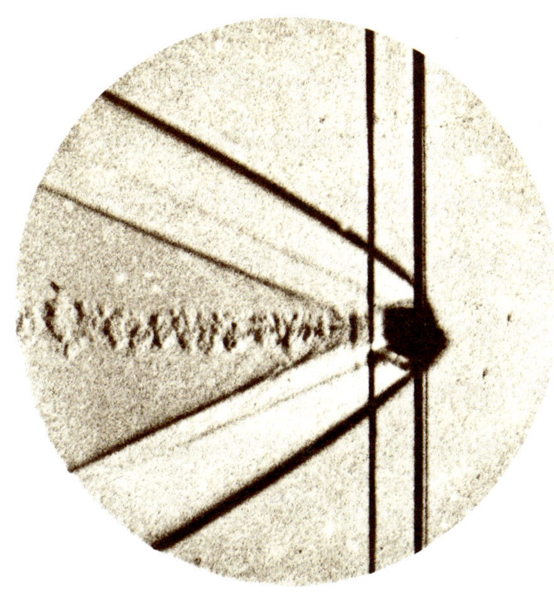

ERNST MACH,
Instantaneous photographs of projectiles meeting an obstacle, and their shock waves,
1888–1889,
Ernst-Mach Institut, Freiburg.

The Cinematograph

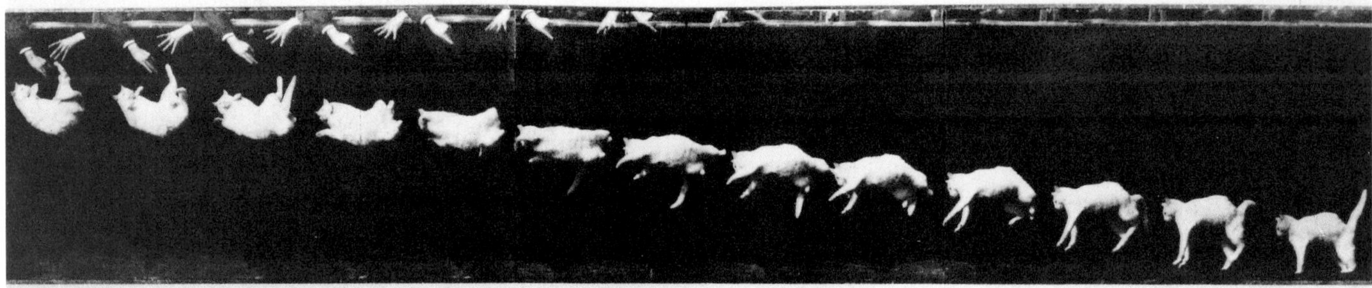

Positions successives du Chat qui sans point d'appui extérieur se retourne en tombant.

ÉTIENNE-JULES MAREY,
How a cat falls, chronophotograph on moving film, 1894, Musée Marey, Beaune.

The transition from instantaneous photography to chronophotography to the cinematograph may be logical. In practice, however, it was not self-evident. The basic principle of the animated image, which we owe to Plateau (1829), rests on the persistence of images on the retina, which brings about an illusory perception of continuity in a series of images being shown at more than ten per second. Numerous nineteenth-century optical toys put this principle into action using drawings – the phenakistiscope, the thaumatrope, and the zoetrope. The next idea was to replace colored drawings with posed photographs showing a sequence of events. Ingenious devices include Henry Dumont's Omniscope, 1859, Cook and Bonelli's Photobioscope, 1863–1865, and Louis Ducos de Hauron's work. However, they all ran up against the impossibility of obtaining instantaneous photographs.

Photographic plates treated with gelatin-silver bromide emulsions (permitting 1/100 of a second exposures in around 1880) opened up the possibility of viewing or projecting scenes recorded in real time, in the form of sequential photographs. Muybridge in 1887 produced the first sequences showing horses in movement, composed of 12 views. In 1881, he gave lectures using projected images of galloping horses, produced by his Zoopraxiscope. With this device, the photographs were redrawn round the edge of a glass disc. Two showings of the same sequence of movement lasted about one second.

The physiological research by the scientist E. J. Marey, who first used photography in 1882, was in no way directed towards a similar goal. However, as a result of the inadequacy of his chronophotographs with superimposed images, obtained on glass plates, for experimental purposes, he adopted the sensitized paper roll film (1888) and then Celluloid film (1m in length) manufactured by Eastman (1890). This technique obliged him to design a camera which would take separate but successive images on a moving strip of film, at a variable rate (up to 60 per second) with an exposure time of between 1/200 and 1/1250 of a second (he used unperforated film, 9cm wide).

The first strips of images were produced in 1888. Marey had an idea for a projector as early as 1892. However, he gave up his attempts at recreating movement because they did not correspond to his scientific needs, which were limited to the analysis of motion. His assistant, Demenÿ, carried on the work with his Phonoscope, a circle of images on a disc. After a quarrel with Marey, he perfected the latter's chronophotograph (patented October 10, 1893) by adding a take-up spool with an eccentric cam. He showed this apparatus to the Lumière brothers (frequent visitors to Marey's laboratory) in November 1894.

Edison had started research in 1888, based on the principle of his phonograph. In 1889, he visited the Universal Exhibition in Paris with Marey, who showed him his chronophotographs made on moving film. A patent of Edison's, of November 2, 1889, proposes the use of a perforated sensitized film of the Eastman type to perfect the Kinetoscope (1890-1891, patented in 1893) – a large box containing a film (several meters long, 35mm wide) designed to be viewed by one person. The Kinetoscope, intended for booths at fairs, offered short filmed scenes – acrobats, mimes, and mini-narratives like *The Interrupted Picnic* or *The Execution of Mary Queen of Scots*. These peep boxes went into commercial manufacture and became available in Paris at the beginning of 1894.

At the same time, the problems of the limited number of shots and the number of scenes that could be projected were being solved by Louis Le Prince (on two alternating strips, 1888), W. Donisthorpe (on one strip, 1889-1890, 6 to 8 images per second), W. Friese-Greene and F. Varley (on one strip, 1889, 3 to 5 images per second), and Léon Bouly (to whom we owe the term *cinematograph*, 1892-1893).

At the end of 1894 the Lumière brothers perfected a camera which used perforated film 35mm wide, dragged along by a claw and held stationary by a pin, using a triangular cam like that on a sewing-machine, with a frequency of 20 images a second. The same apparatus was used for projection. It was patented on February 13, 1895 and christened cinematograph in May. The first projection took place on March 22, 1895 (first performance to a paying audience at the Grand Café, 14 boulevard des Capucines on December 28, 1895). The projection lasted scarcely one minute. Even its creators did not see a big future for this type of entertainment.

Michel Frizot.

the figures described in aviation produce unique visual forms and that aerial photography was an extension of photodynamism, giving a sensation of speed in its pure form. In 1935, he completed his motion effects by superimposing photographs.

One can also see in Schlemmer's photographs, and in those of Lux Feininger, based on the Bauhaus light-shows (1926–1927) – combinations of multiple exposures in darkness and continuous traces – a resurgence of photodynamism. These techniques, however, were no longer limited to the artistic milieu influenced by Futurism.

By the end of the century, photography had incorporated the notion of speed in various ways.

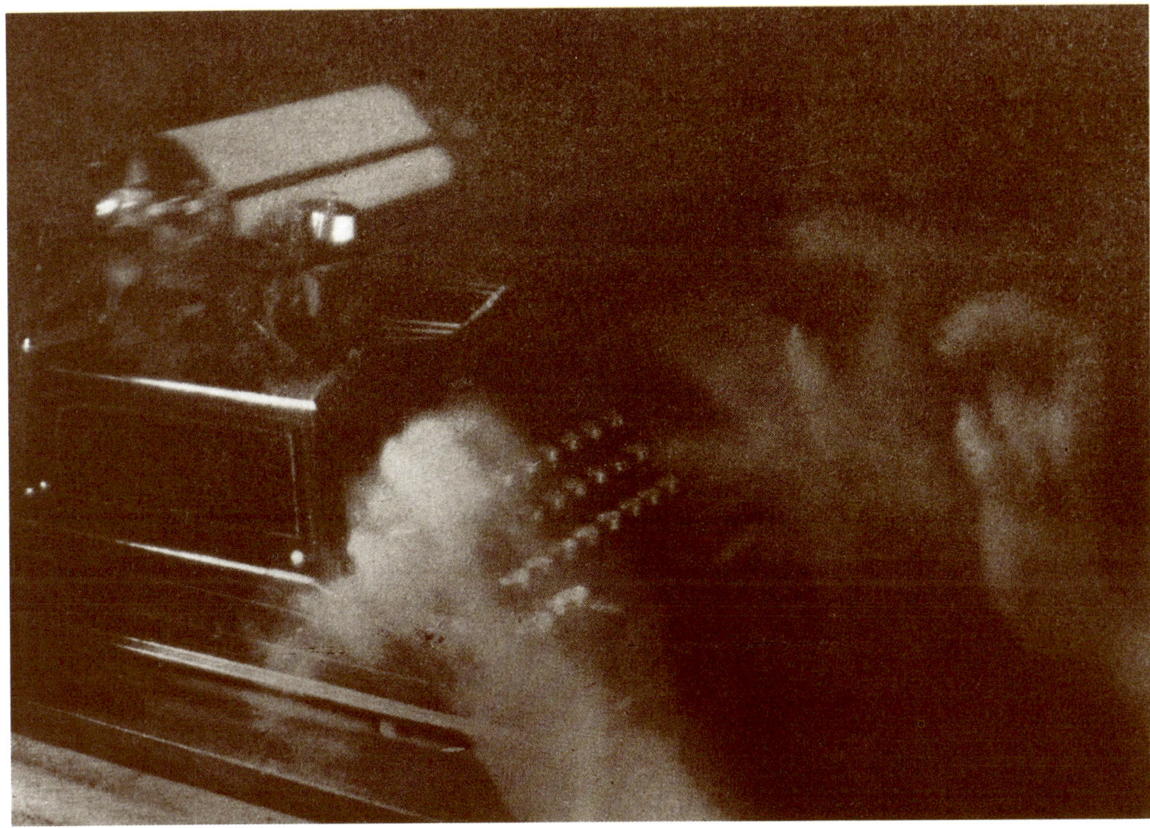

Anton Giulio Bragaglia,
Photodynamic typing,
1911,
Centro Studi
Anton Giulio Bragaglia,
Rome.

These did not favor simply the fastest exposure. Rather, what we have is an adaptation of photographic speed, suited to the subject and the effect required, a process which became possible because of progress in the sensitivity of photographic emulsions. There was shutter-speed, and the speed with which a succession of shots could be taken, then the speed of the cinematograph (16 images per second). However, it was still possible to do long-exposure photography, in darkness, waiting for a flash of lightning.

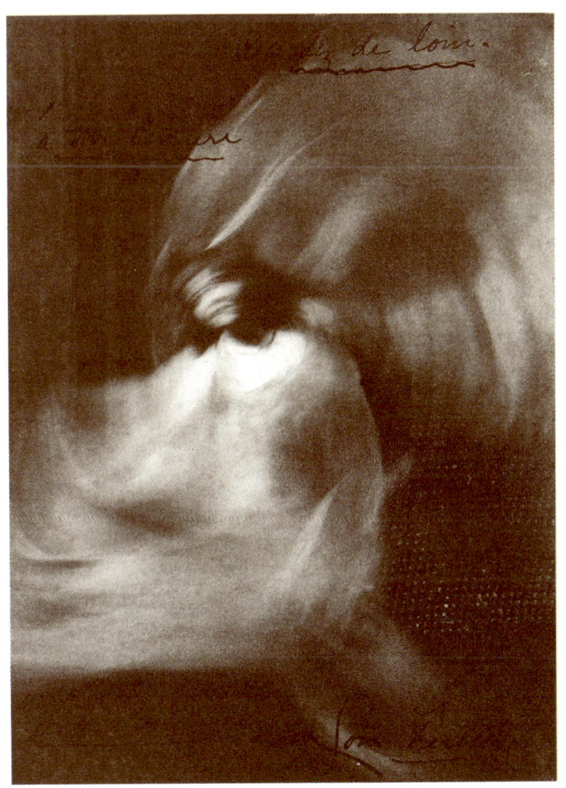

◀ Anonymous,
Loïe Fuller dancing,
circa 1900–1905,
Musée Rodin, Paris.

What unites these systems is the search for synchronicity between opening the lens and the occurrence of the phenomenon (or phase of a phenomenon) which one wishes to photograph – clearly identifiable, or imprecise and allusive. Thus, we find several series of photographs of Loïe Fuller in her dance of the veils dating from around 1893–1900. Some (by Theodore Rivière or Taber) are clear and show a shape produced in a snapshot by the effect of the veil, but in reality imperceptible to the eye (Raoul Larche took up this theme in sculpture). Other (anonymous, Musée Rodin) use a longer exposure time to produce the phantom-like appearance of a constantly metamorphosing form.

The freedom of choice available to the modern photographer of the 1920s opened the way to treating time as a controllable instrument of their will. In the 1930s, Harold Edgerton, at the Massachusetts Institute of Technology, demonstrated anew the value of the method devised by Marey (and perfected by Bull) when he used very rapid sparks to illuminate movement – combining a continuously open shutter with repeated ultra-rapid snapshots. The modernity of photography, subject as it is to the speed of its agent, light, does not necessarily reside therefore in the greatest possible speed, but in the dominance of photographic speed within the parameters of the chosen subject.

24. F. Le Coz, "Le Mouvement: Loïe Fuller", in *Photographies*, no. 7, May 1985, pp. 56–63.

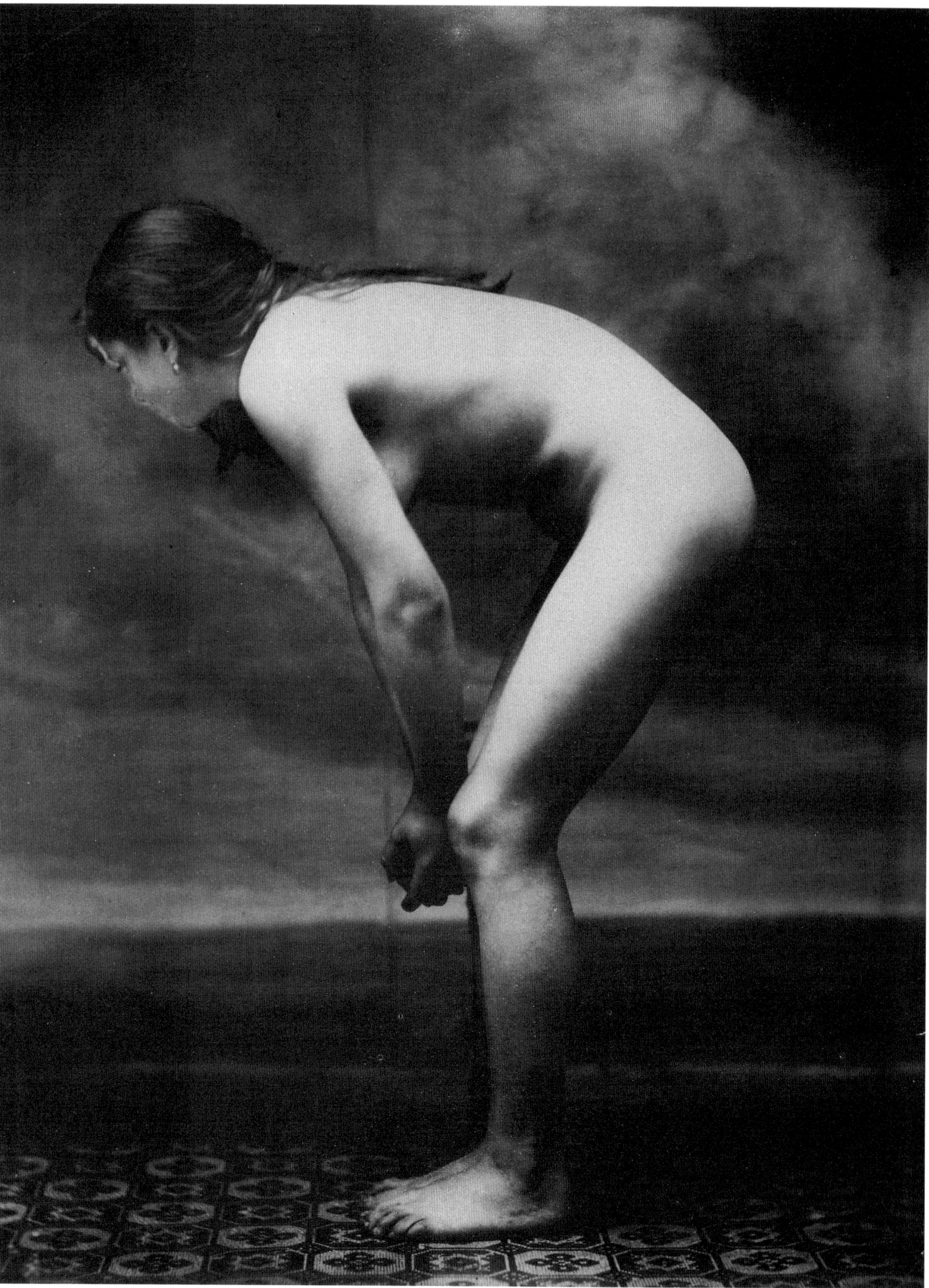

BODY OF EVIDENCE

15

The ethnophotography of difference

Michel Frizot

From the moment it was invented, photography was dedicated to examining the human body. The knowledge which science would thus acquire about our exterior appearance would, it was hoped, result in a greater understanding of the mysteries of the soul. The body was seen as the visible proof of human differences, criminal tendencies, pathology, and delinquency. Anthropometry and ethnology, allied to photography, were the means by which people hoped to reduce innumerable recorded data to a simple human types. In an exaggerated spirit of positivism, many methods were devised to try and define the universal laws by which the human body and soul were, hypothetically, governed.

Even in 1839, it was already clear that the new medium of photography could not be confined to drawing urban views or landscapes. This was because human beings are interested, above all, in each other – in a narcissistic and an altruistic, as well as an individual and a collective, sense. Thus, we find Daguerre already apologizing for not being able to take portraits, a problem that was soon resolved by technical improvements. However, devoted though people were to the representation of themselves as individuals, they found belonging to a hypothetical, larger family of humanity even more significant.

A tendency to regard the body as something anonymous, to see its commonalities rather than its individuality, was everywhere: in the interest in genre scenes – even livelier in photography than in painting – in studies of the outdoors or of occupations. Two general ideas seem to govern the use of photography in certain areas, which turned out to be closer to science than art. First and foremost, the body appeared as the primary symptom, the universal sign of everything that still remained veiled, both in individuals and in the body of society.

By measuring and observing the body, people believed that psychological states could be revealed, that it was through the body's physical appearance that psychological differences manifested themselves. The nineteenth century was the first period in which the individual was submitted to scrutiny by a whole range of agencies (medical, judicial, moral, etc.) which measured their degree of deviation from an undeclared statistical norm.[1] Photography was seen as a future source of authentic historical record. The debate about whether there is such a thing as ethnographic photography came later, as though photography required that name in order to act in that way. Quite clearly, photography is fundamentally ethnographic (including when its sole aim is art or advertising). The habitats, the behavior of human groups, their gestures, their tools, and their possessions are all perfectly visible in the most insignificant photograph, amateur or professional. A whole epoch can be deduced from a minute image. Because a photograph is directly linked to what it signifies, the photographer is also, even if they are unaware of the fact, an ethnologist and an anthropologist.[2]

While it is necessary, for the purpose of this study to concentrate on the scientific intent within photography, we should not forget the innumerable pieces of visual evidence that it has collected quite by chance. The *Chimneysweeps* walking along the bank of the Seine in Paris (Nègre, 1851–1852) are, after all, only the first – admittedly rather picturesque – phase of a concrete analysis of walking, which was to end in publications like the ethnologist E. Regnault's book *How We Walk* (about 1900), based on the physiologist Marey's chronophotographic research.

The individual body will be considered here as the seat of a dual syndrome: an indicator of

◀ ANONYMOUS, *Nude Study*, circa 1880, private collection.

1. A. Rouillé and B. Marbot, *Le Corps et son Image: Photographies du dix-neuvième siècle*, Paris, Contrejour, 1986.

2. *Ethnographie et Photographie*, special issue of *L'Ethnographie*, no. 109, Paris 1991.

psychological stirrings, passions and differences, and an indicator of what is rejected by society, of the deviant and taboo. It was through the body that nineteenth-century society aimed to know, to punish, to exclude and beleaguer, to reduce and to make subject to law. Today, however, a well-organized use of photography in the judicial system seems more important to us as a safeguard for prisoners' rights than as a validation of existing legal records. Photography is also an indicator of these social changes.

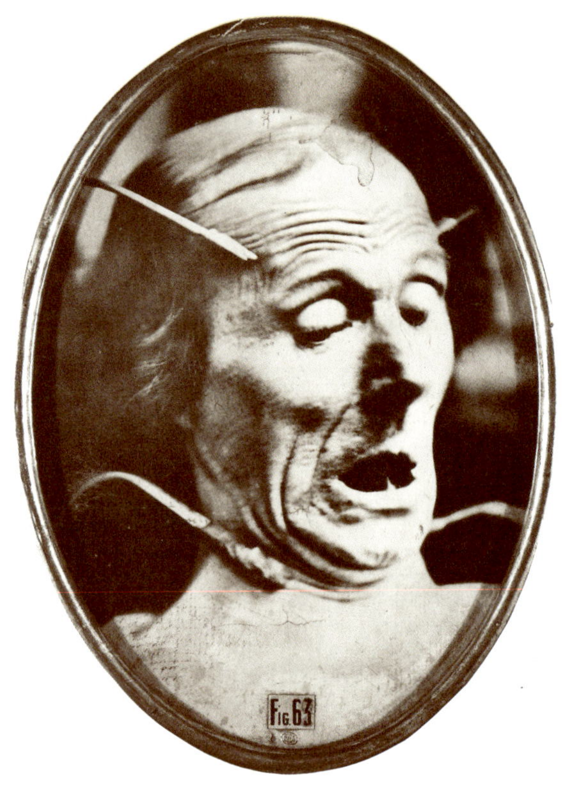

Guillaume ▶ Duchenne de Boulogne, *Study of muscular movements by electrical contraction (Fright)*, 1852–1856, École Nationale Supérieure des Beaux-Arts, Paris.

The expressive body

The photographic experiments of Guillaume Duchenne de Boulogne are symptomatic of an intellectual attitude towards the body which saw it as the place where interior conflicts were made visible. Human physiognomy, in particular, was seen as the visual indicator of the emotions. The thinking of the period had been shaped by a theory about how emotion was represented which had been inherited from classical tragedy and comedy, and the facial characterization in Le Brun. Lavater's physiognomical theory had only an intermittent following, but it lent credence, from the end of the eighteenth century onwards, to the idea that "the exterior diversity of faces and figures must imply particular relations, and present a natural analogy with the diversity of minds and hearts."[3] Duchenne's experiments consisted of applying electrodes (with a weak electric current) to various muscles, causing them to contract, thus showing the un-mysterious mechanisms whereby the typology of expressions could be reduced to a physiology of contractions.

In 1853–1856, Duchenne de Boulogne was helped by the photographer Adrien Tournachon, brother of Nadar and a pupil of Le Gray. It was through the use of photography that Duchenne

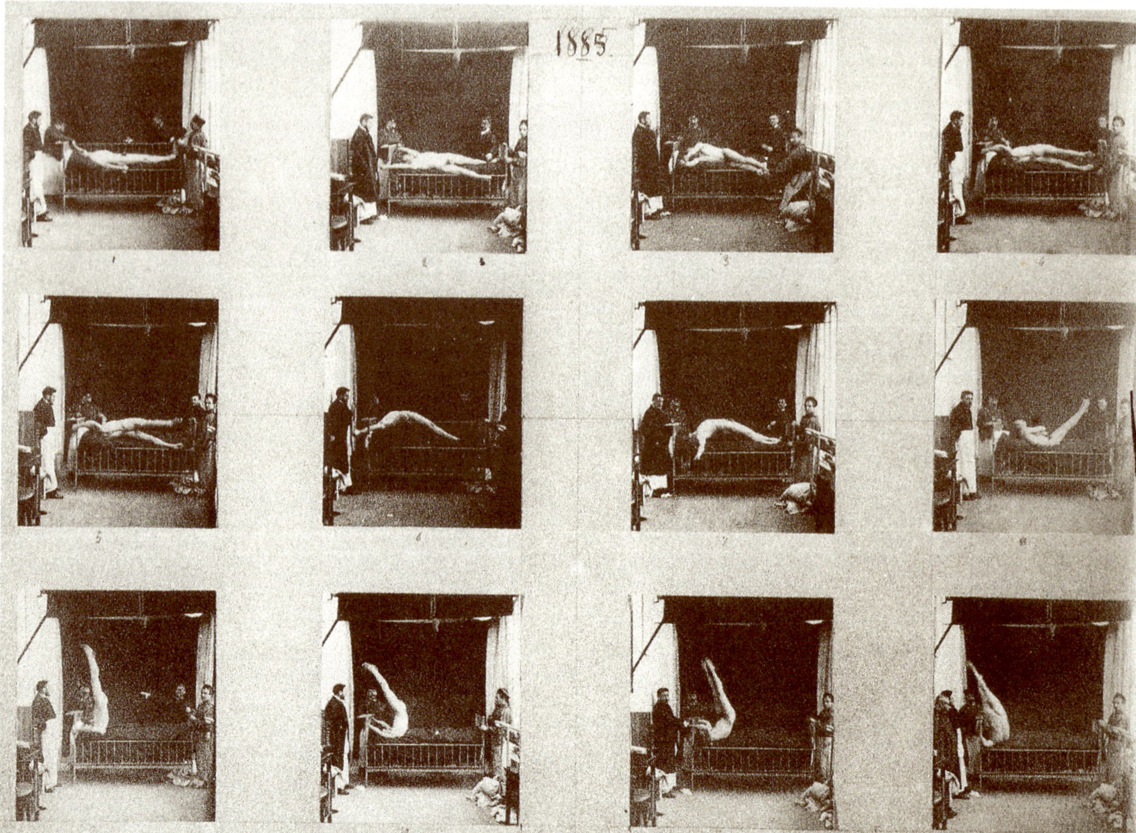

Albert Londe, *Attack of hysteria in a man*, series of chronophotographs, La Salpêtrière laboratory, 1885.

3. Engl. ed. J. K. Lavater, *Essays on Physiognomy, designed to promote the Knowledge and Love of Mankind*, ed. by Thomas Holloway, 3 vols., London 1789–1798.

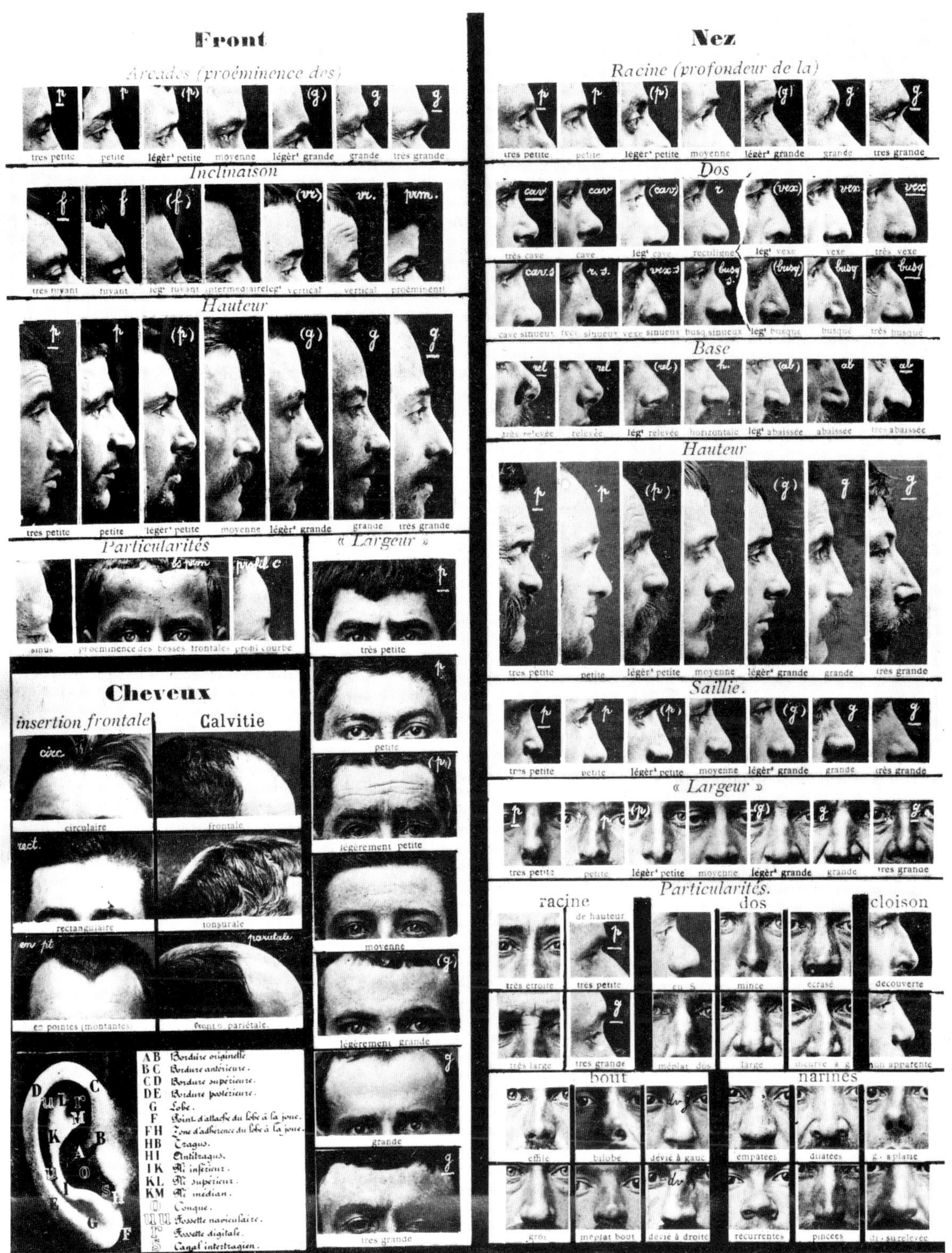

Alphonse Bertillon, *Synoptic table of physiological traits for the study of the portrait "speaking"*, circa 1895.

proved, in his book on physiognomy published in 1862,[4] that the impression of joy, sadness, grief or scorn created by certain facial expressions is mechanically produced. The activation of groups of muscles defines a range of common passions; inversely, they create dominant impressions or expressions. This new iconography of the passions was also taken up by the scientist Charles Darwin,[5] and Adrien Tournachon applied it to a range of typical expressions created by the mime Deburau (1854). It was at this moment that Nadar (Felix Tournachon) began his work as a portraitist.

Differences and identities

Through an excess of compartmentalization, Duchenne's work came to be included under the category of medical photography, "that branch of photography that has not long been in existence", as Londe said in 1893.[6] According to him, the official entry of photography into the service given by hospitals dates from the year 1878, with the creation of the photographic service at Salpêtrière by Charcot. Bourneville and Regnard worked there at that time. Londe took over the direction in 1882 and Bourneville went on to

4. *Mécanisme de la Physionomie humaine, ou Analyse électrophysiologique de l'Expression des Passions*, Paris, Renouard et Baillière Fils, 1862.

5. C. Darwin, *The Expression of the Emotions in Man and Animals*, London, J. Murray, 1872.

6. A. Londe, *La Photographie médicale: Application aux Sciences médicales et physiologiques*, Paris, Gauthier-Villars, 1893.

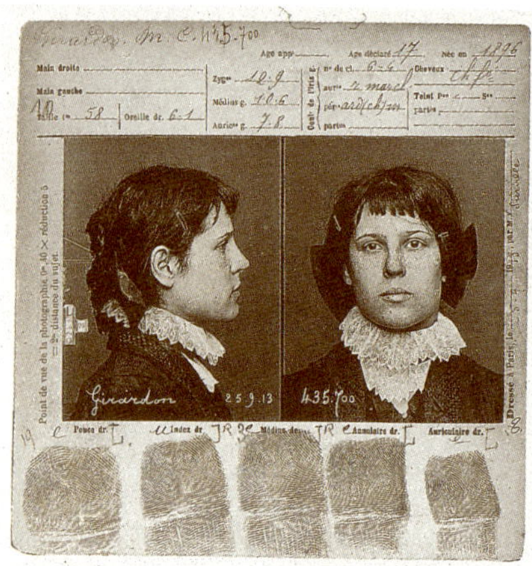
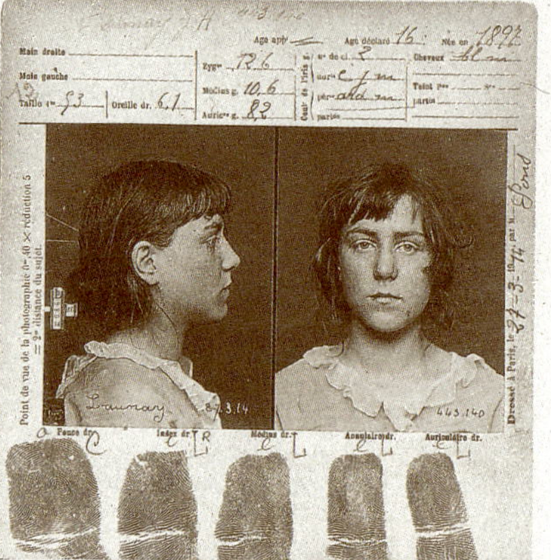
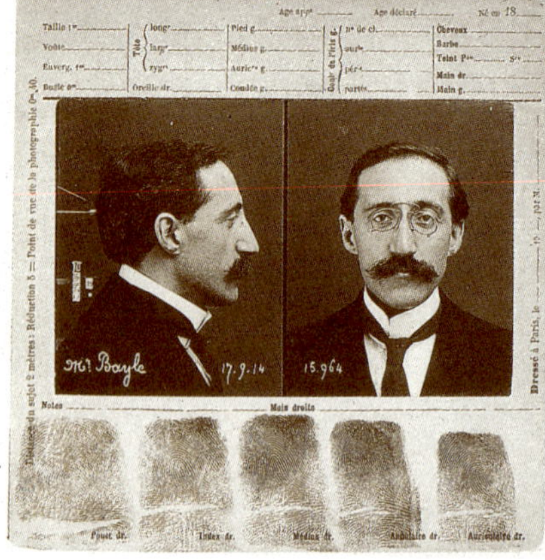
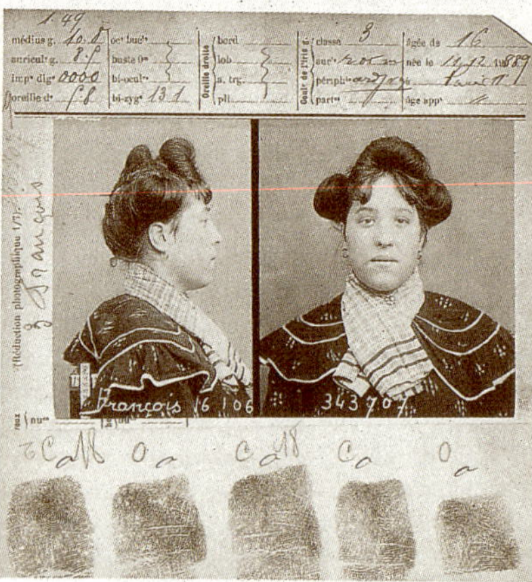

The Bertillon method, ***Four files of the judicial identity service,*** Paris, 1906–1914.

install a similar studio at Bicêtre. It was, in fact, only then that photography became really integrated into the practice of medicine, as an auxiliary in following up on treatment, and to keep a record of the development of individual pathologies. In the introduction to his book, Londe enumerates the contributions of photography to medicine: recording a transitory state, pictures taken before and after treatment, autopsies. With the support of that visual exhibitionism common in medicine, the rarest and most monstrous pathological cases were judged worthy of being photographed – which did not so much advance the progress of science as swell the ranks of the oddities in people's curio collections.[7] The most significant event was the introduction of gelatine-silver bromide emulsions which made possible the perception of excessively rapid movements: epileptic fits, attacks of hysteria, modes of walking in pathological cases.[8] The chronophotographic method was particularly welcome for studying hysterical and epileptic movements, which were one of Londe's particular interests, working beside Charcot. Londe's method was not dissimilar to that used by Muybridge, who also recorded pathological cases in Philadelphia, under the direction of Dr. Dercum, in 1884–1885.

The laboratory at Salpêtrière was certainly one of the best organized of the time, with a developing room, chronophotographic equipment with nine to twelve lenses, a bed placed against a black ground, and a record number (reminiscent of that set up by the police photographic service at the time). As a source of hospital data, the photograph was more of a guarantee to the doctor than the patient, who gained nothing from this piece of technological progress, which was essentially coercive rather than liberating. It was also helpful for making pictures available as lantern-slides, and providing illustrations for lectures (an important activity at the end of the century).

It was, above all, in psychiatric work (if this expression is not too scientific for the incarceration, without treatment, of all categories of mentally ill) that photography had previously found its best justification. In 1868, Montméja and Hardy had created the *Clinique photographique de l'Hôpital Saint-Louis* and, in 1869, Montméja and Rengade published the *Revue photographique des Hôpitaux de Paris*, drawn from the work of the same laboratory, to make available all that was rarest and most interesting in pathology. Henri Dagonet, of the Hôpital Sainte-Anne, also published photographs in his *Nouveau Traité des Maladies mentales*.[9]

The most important project remains the *Iconographie photographique de la Salpêtrière*, by Bourneville and Regnard.[10] In 1879, Bourneville, who was put in charge of the care of mentally handicapped children at Bicêtre, introduced photography there. It continued with *La nouvelle Iconographie de la Salpêtrière*, in which Londe also took part. The study of psychiatry took a new direction under Charcot, who had been a doctor at Salpêtrière since 1862. It became open to hypnosis, to the notion of what may be concealed, of the body as symptom of the soul (one of Charcot's students in 1885–1886 was none other than Sigmund Freud, theorist of the unconscious).

Movements and contractions may be the physical manifestation of psychic disorders that have set in earlier. The iconographies are an iconic index of the experiments and findings of Charcot's department, with photographs or drawings carried out by Paul Richer. The series of attitudes pertaining to the passions (ecstasy, eroticism, mockery) manifested by a patient, Augustine, bear a distinct resemblance to Duchenne's studies. Charcot prolonged these attitudes by hypnotism; the direction of the eyes, the contraction of muscles, the pose, everything is a sign characterizing states that are pathologically inherent or have been provoked, in the subject (lethargy, catalepsy, hysterical epilepsy).[11]

In these experimental series there also appears the notion of the type, which refers to the characteristic reduction of a pathological state to mimicking and points to ways of detecting the

7. S. B. Burns, *Early Medical Photography in America 1839–1883*. The Burns Archive, 1983; *Masterpieces of Medical Photography; Selections from the Burns Archive*, Pasadena, Twelvetrees, 1987; *Photographie et Médecine, 1840–1880*, Lausanne, IUHSMP, 1991.

8. A. Londe, introduction to *La Photographie médicale, cit.*

9. Paris Baillière, 1876, eight plates in Woodburytype.

10. Three volumes (1876–1877, 1878, 1879-1880) Delahaye and Lecrosnier.

11. G. Didi-Huberman, *Invention de l'Hystérie: Charcot et l'Iconographie photographique de la Salpêtrière*, Paris, Macula, 1982, and the catalogue *La Leçon de Charcot*, Paris, Musée de l'Assistance Publique, 1986.

mental via the physiological and behavioral. Since the insane often have faces, attitudes and movements that are entirely characteristic [...] as do idiots and degenerates [...] we have been able to lay down rigorously defined types which correspond to precise afflictions."[12]

Photography's obvious connotations – as evidence, a form of proof, a bearer of visual information, a record – could not fail to inspire the repressive agencies of police and judiciary. As early as 1854, Ernest Lacan[13] formulated a proposal for a police photographic service. Cartes de visite of the 1860s included, among other curiosities, portraits of the most notorious murderers (Troppman by Appert, 1869; Richebourg had photographed his victims). It was the events of the Paris Commune which – like the Civil War in the United States – unleashed photography, previously a scattered phenomenon, on a more systematic basis. Appert took photographs of the Communards in the prisons of Versailles, generally full-face, and from the waist up. The intention was somewhat disingenuous (though the prisoners could buy their portraits). These like-

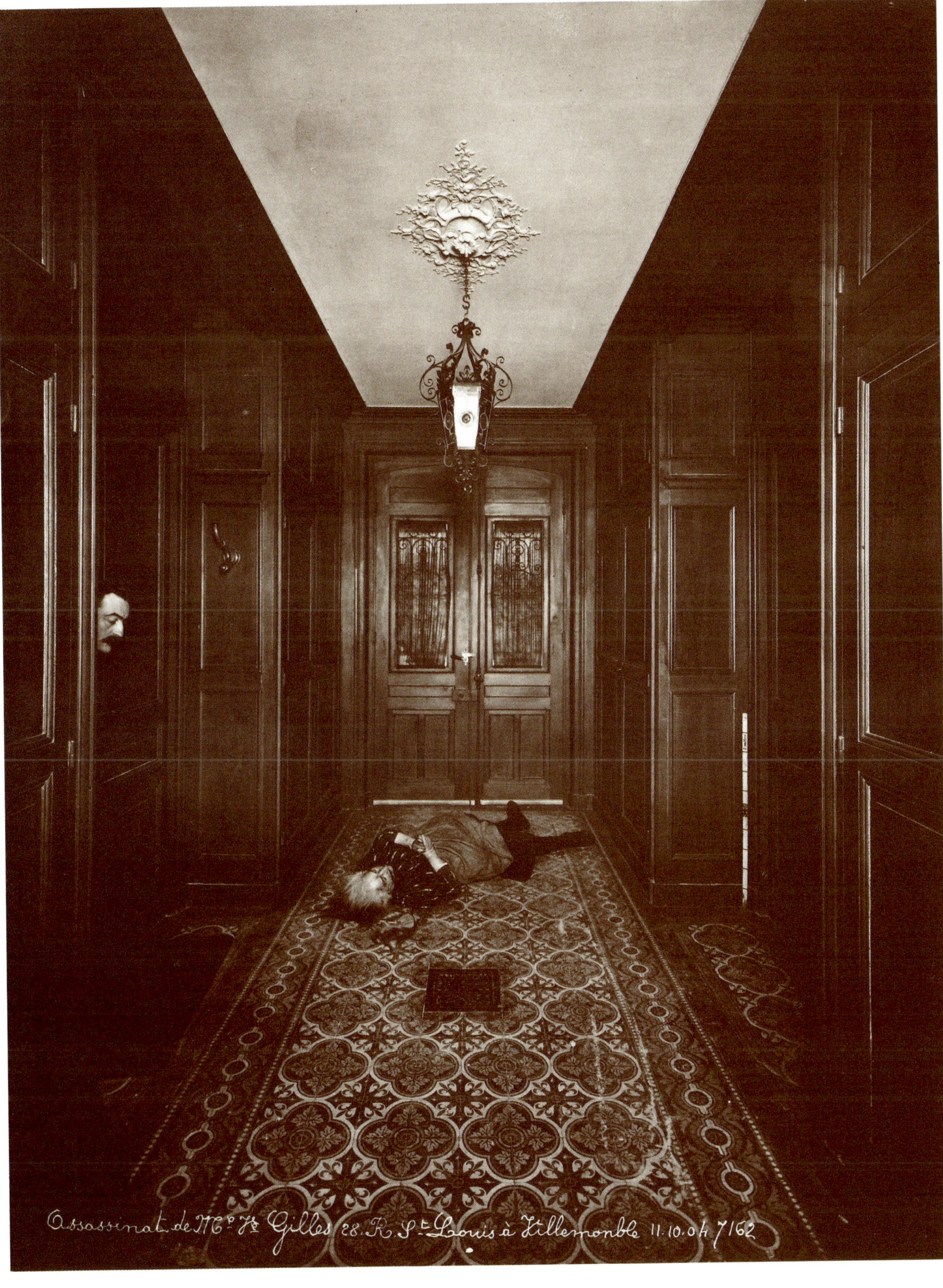

ANONYMOUS,
Murder of Mme Gilles, widow, of Villemonble,
judicial photograph, 1904,
Musée National des Techniques, C.N.A.M., Paris.

12. A. Londe, *cit.*, pp. 4-5.

13. *La Lumière*, July 22, 1854; also in his *Esquisses photographiques*, 1856, pp. 39–40.

Bourneville and Regnard, ▶
Attitudes of the Passions: Ecstasy,
plate 13 of *Iconographie photographique de la Salpêtrière*, vol. 2, 1878.

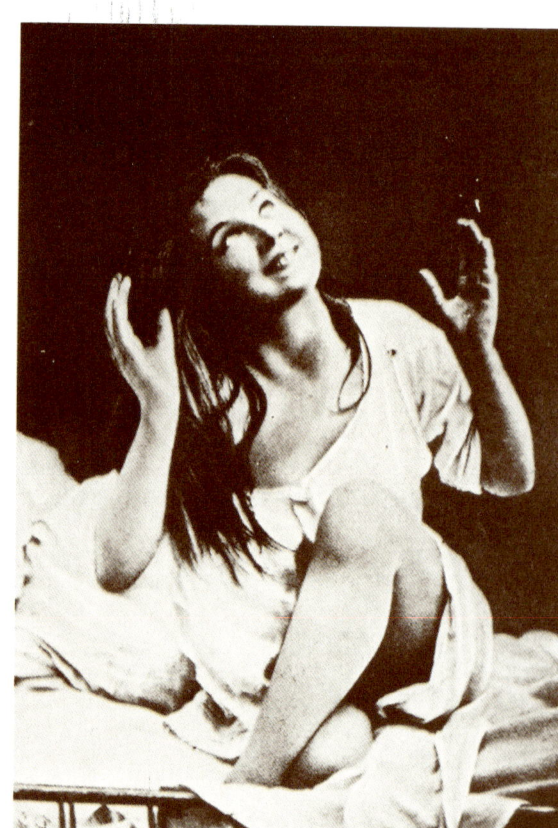

Anonymous,
Tattooed man,
judicial identification photograph, 1920.
▼

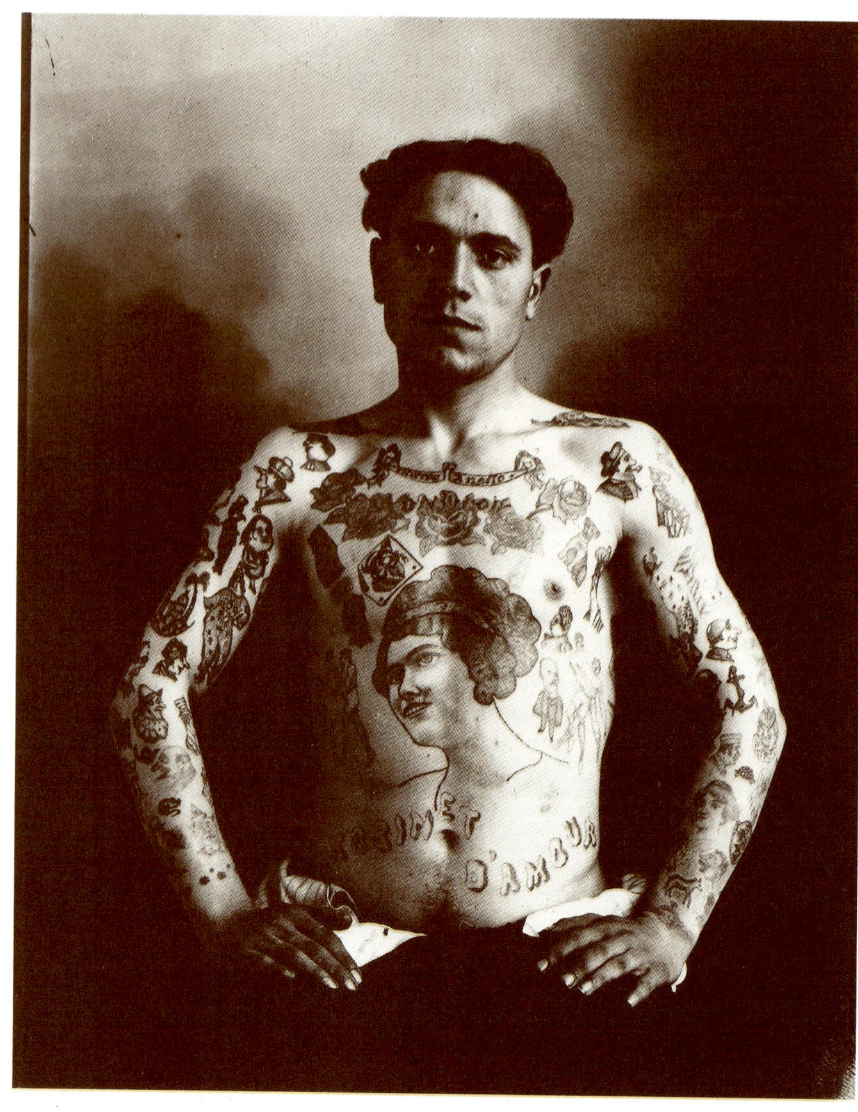

nesses were clearly going into a preventative file, to be consulted if the Communards re-offended.

The first police photographic service derived from this practice was created in 1872. In 1882, the identification service of the Préfecture de Police, under the direction of Alphonse Bertillon, started making use of anthropometric description, and the photographic studio was placed under his authority in 1888. Such a service presupposed the idea of a criminal reoffending, and of "the habitual offender who is forced to recognize himself in this accusing image".[14] Every accused person had their details, of which photographs were only a part, entered on an identification slip.[15] These slips were mounted on card, and had two pictures, one full-face, one in profile (a practice which has, incidentally, remained unchanged to this day), obtained with a fixed lens, at a specified distance, and according to fixed principles whereby the face was reduced to 1/7 life-size, with always the same exposure and lighting. The slip also carried a great number of standard points of information, some numerical (various measurements of the head and limbs), the others a verbal portrait: distinguishing marks (scars, tattoos, deformities), formal description of the features (nose, mouth, hair, eyes). There was a very precise analysis of the ear (an anatomical constant to a certain degree), which had been found "the most important factor from the point of view of identification [...] unvarying in its shape since birth, resistant to the influences of milieu and upbringing".[16] In 1890, Bertillon announced that his index contained 90,000 photographs, far too many by that stage to match against the image of an accused person. Only by noting differences, describing them, classifying them, and, as a last resort quantifying them, would it be possible to attribute to an unknown person an identity stored in the files and shock them with the evidence of their criminality.[17] From this point of view a tattoo was the most reliable distinguishing mark, an image within an image.

Types and differences

Photography claimed for itself the status of a scientific method which would prove not simply that certain anatomical elements resembled each other but that they were the same, and so belonged to a particular individual: "The aim is always identification, and the means is photography."[18] After a rather inglorious deployment in the experts' reports in the Dreyfus file, Bertillon's method gave way, at the beginning of the twentieth century, to the use of fingerprints, which became the general practice, since they are, apart from genes, our only strictly individual and

14. E. Lacan, *Esquisses photographiques[...]*, 1856, p. 39.

15. C. Phéline, *L'Image accusatrice*, Les Cahiers de la Photographie, Paris, 1985.

16. A. Bertillon, *La Photographie judiciaire*, Paris, Gauthier Villars, 1890. pp. 95–96.

17. *Identités: de Disdéri au Photomaton*, Centre National de la Photographie, Paris, 1986.

18. Bertillon, *cit.* p. 3.

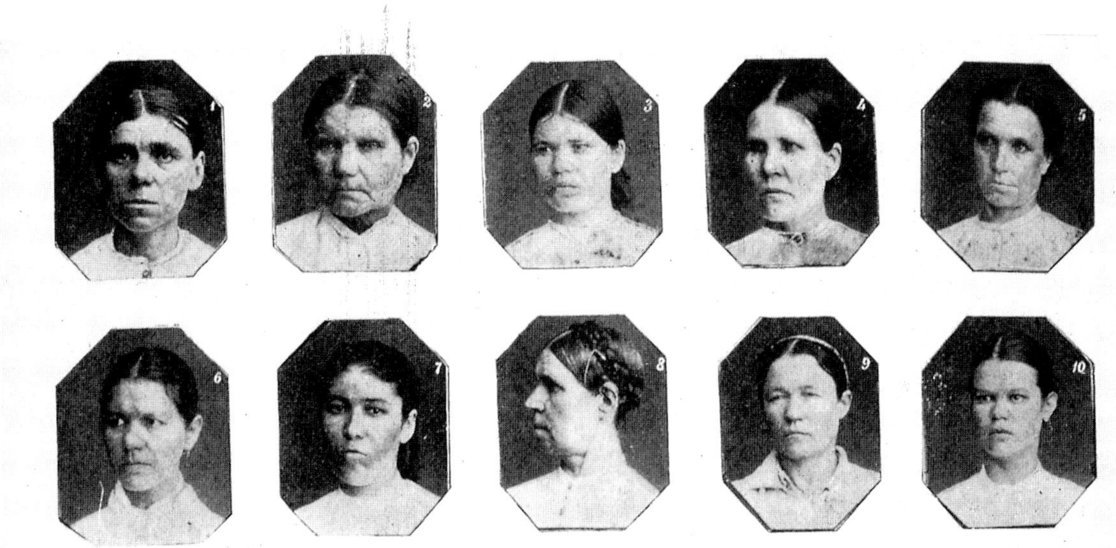

ANONYMOUS,
Types of Russian female criminals,
detail from plate 55,
Cesare Lombroso, *L'Uomo delinquente,*
5th ed., 1897.

permanent characteristics. All these methods were looking to photography to provide a symptom of the invisible, a means whereby that which cannot be seen can still be interpreted through its visible manifestation. After a period during which the boundaries of the visible world and knowledge in general had been greatly extended – with a considerable contribution from photography – many scholars were disoriented, and began to seek some appearance of logic in the disorder they had discovered.

The end of the century abounds in publications which seek to co-ordinate the imaginary with the scientific, and even to use the image to subordinate one to the other. The Bertillon system supposed the existence of a class of individuals, a recurring, classifiable type, who could be controlled simply by registering them in a card-index. In this fluid area identity no longer designates individuality but, on the contrary, a conformity to a type.[19] Such ideas were not very different from those of someone like Lombroso, who, from 1870, was also looking for the criminal type: "The nature of the criminal: an atavistic being who unites in one person the ferocious instincts of primitive humanity and the lesser animals."[20]

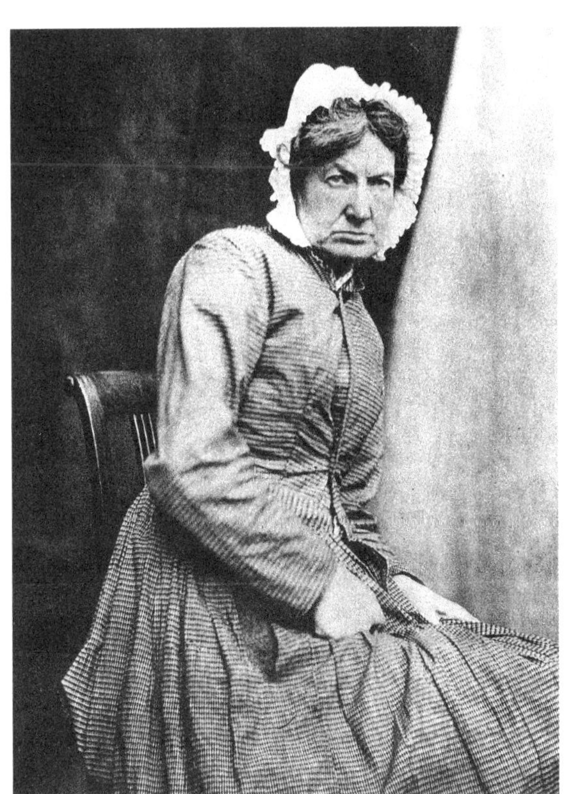

◀ DR. HUGH DIAMOND,
Photograph of a female patient at the Surrey County asylum, Springfield,
1852–1858,
Royal Society of Medicine, London.

Lombroso's extreme theories – which were, fortunately, quickly abandoned – aimed to discover discriminating traits, clinical signs of a disposition to criminality. He started from a supposed anthropometric statistical method: the study of skulls and their anomalies, and the facial characteristics of 4,000 imprisoned criminals, based upon an international collection of photographs. In his book *L'Uomo delinquente*, published in Italy in 1876 and in Paris in 1887,[21] he aimed to distinguish the born criminal from the man who is carried along by habit or yields to momentary passion. Lombroso's indexes were established along similar lines to Bertillon's: measurements, anatomical details, peculiarities. Tattoos, for example, were to be found among the lower classes, and even more among criminals. Lambroso studied left-handedness on the same terms that he studied intelligence and the use of slang; they were all signs which together with physiognomy (where he leaned heavily on Lavater) would produce a portrait of the criminal type. However, these criteria, which had been observed solely from photographs, had been fixed in advance, not deduced through a serious analysis of reality. Lombroso himself admitted that 60 per cent of known criminals were completely lacking in distinctive signs.

His so-called *Atlas* of faces theoretically offered the possibility of comparing the portraits of 424 criminals (mainly Germans) with those of 300

19. C. Phéline, *op. cit.*, p. 113.

20. *Ibid.*, p. 48.

21. *L'Homme criminel, criminel-né, fou moral, épileptique: étude anthropologique et médico-légale*, Paris, Alcan, 1887.

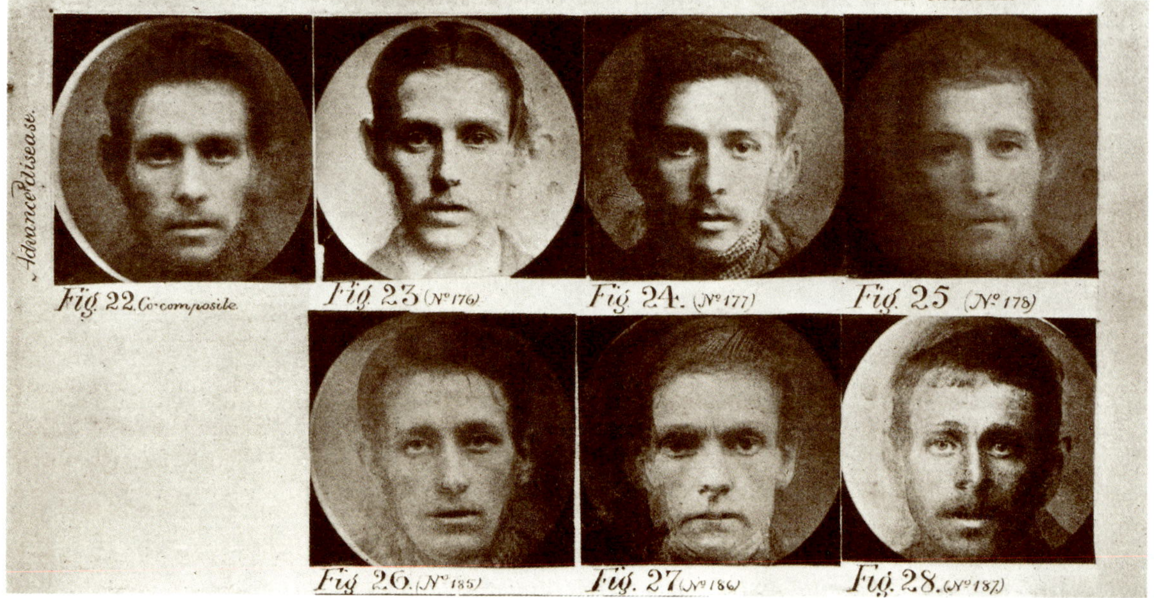

Francis Galton, ***Composite portraits by superimposition of photos seeking a generic portrait of the criminal,*** from *Inquiries into Human Faculty and its Development*, 1883.

students, but the vague definitions (wrinkled eyelids, sinister eyes) led only to a vague presumption based on a plethora of data: "We can now ascertain – with ease, simply by holding up a photograph – that among criminal men the predominant features are a massively developed jaw, sparse beard, hard eyes, thick hair and, secondarily, sticking-out ears, receding brow, a squint, and a misshapen nose."[22]

The apparent objectivity of Lombroso's photographs, with their serried ranks of hundreds of faces, might well impress the reader, all the more so because of their simplifying tendency. Their appeal to natural laws which needed only to be discovered, their reference to individual predestination, might seem to provide an answer to the disarray engendered by modernism. By amalgamating deficiency, delinquency, pauperism, and physiology, Lombroso established an easy link between criminality and madness, the ancient idea that the mental expresses the corporeal pushed beyond the bounds of credibility.

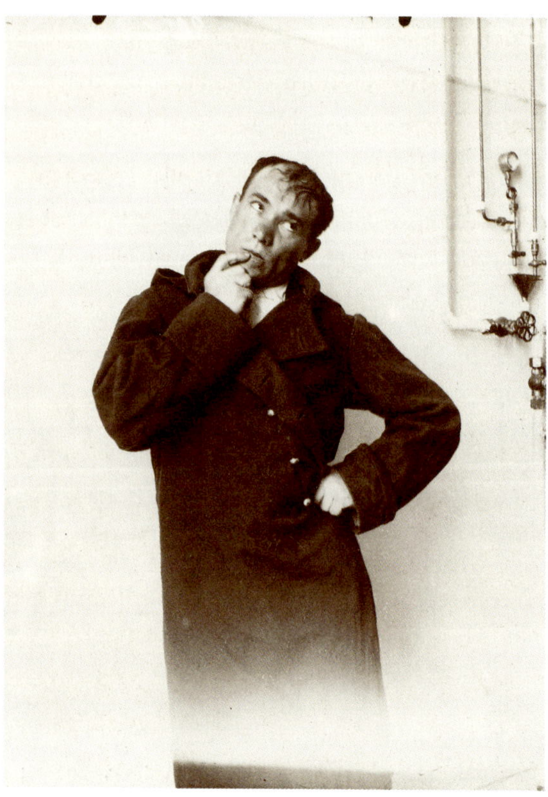

"Passive homosexual", from Lombroso collection, circa 1900.

This approach had already been undertaken by psychiatry: "If we pass from the diseases of the soul to those of the body, we find photography is just as able to play an important role", Lacan emphasized in 1856, before concluding, after having looked at 14 portraits of women by Dr. Diamond: "One word is enough to explain all: these women are mad [...] It is with a painful interest that one follows in these portraits, taken at different periods, the phases of their illness."[23]

The work carried out by Diamond at Springfield asylum, Surrey, is remarkable, above all, for its photographic virtuosity. Diamond was an excellent calotypist. A friend of Scott Archer, and a founder member of the Photographic Society of London, he installed a photographic laboratory in a hospital as early as 1851, and built up an archive of hundreds of portraits of female patients. His *Types of Madness* featured in an exhibition in London as early as 1852. The application of photography to physiognomy and mental derangement was for Diamond an instrument of diagnosis, though it brought some progress to therapy, in that he recommended that patients be shown their pictures in the course of their treatment. His photographs were reproduced as lithographs in John Conolly's *The Physiognomy of Insanity* (1858). This work, however, still assumed an unequivocal relationship between the appearance and the nature of the illness ("nymphomania, madness accompanied by epilepsy, the monomania of suicide", enumer-

22. C. Lombroso, *op. cit.*, p. 233, A. Gilardi, *Storia sociale della Fotografia*, Milan, Feltrinelli, 1976; A. Gilardi, *Wanted*, Milan, Mazotta, 1978; *La Scienza e la Colpa: Crimini, Criminali, Criminologi: un Volto dell'Ottocento*, Milan, Electa, 1985.

23. E. Lacan, *op. cit.*, p. 40.

24. *Nascità della fotografia psichiatrica*, La Biennale di Venezia, 1981; S. L. Gilman, *The Face of Madness: H. W. Diamond and the Origin of Psychiatric Photography*, Secaucus, Citadel, 1977.

ated Lacan), once more creating the illusion of a mental anthropology.[24]

Francis Galton resolved the paradox inherent in Lombroso's comparisons by creating composite types through superimposition whereby all individual characteristics are effaced and only those held in common remain, thus determining the faces proper to one affliction or another (Londe). In this way, differences are dissolved by an optical procedure – the superimposition of photographs – giving birth by subtraction to a type which retains only its dominant, constant traits, seen as the only significant ones: composite portraiture.[25] Galton was not particularly concerned with psychiatry or criminality; he was proposing a photographic method that would be applicable to any subject – with the presupposition that a typology was possible – which derived its rationale from effacing individual deviations: six members of one family, twenty-three army engineers, eight criminals or six consumptives ought, in principle, to deliver "typical" faces.

Galton's method remained influential until the end of the century, Marey often referring to it. Arthur Batut adapted it for *L'Application de la Photographie à la Production du Type d'une Famille, d'une Tribu ou d'une Race* (1887). He took full-face portraits, then re-photographed them one by one, exactly the same size and matching the position of the eyes, putting under-exposed images on top of one another on the same plate. Batut was simply proposing an ingenious method, without proselytizing for any philosophical added-value. He took it as given that physiognomy was personality but without implying any philosophical or social system or the moral ramifications attendant upon one.

The illusory logic of the composite image came into being to deal with the excess of data with which people like Lombroso encumbered themselves and the problems of bringing it together, classifying it, and dealing with the welter of differences. But it was photography that had made possible the elaboration of those lists of data, that normative codifying of differences, which led only to the identification of particular features without any other type of examination. The photographic registers of the San Clemente psychiatric hospital in Venice (which began in 1873, with a card index) were, in fact, clinical records before such things existed, but without a therapeutic role.

Types and races

The first photographers liked to think of forming a universal collection, through photography, of all the significant differences that travelers and ethnologists were beginning to notice: "Portraits taken in India, Africa, America, or Russia, – indeed everywhere – would be adequate to compose an ample collection of all the types of races now extant".[26] Photography was a scientific method in itself: you had to get the subject to pose, usually out of doors, prevent them from moving, put them in a typical attitude, encourage them to make the best of themselves with clothes and accessories. The infant discipline of ethnography, stimulated by travel and colonial conquest, was intimately linked to photography. People noted, researched, recorded, described.[27] There was no traveler armed with a camera who was not already operating as an ethnologist. Experts themselves demanded photography as a necessary aid to their work: "What anthropology lacks is a rich museum of authentic types drawn from the various branches of the human race, and individuals who can be taken as typical of those races. This leads one to understand how useful would be an ethnological collection obtained by photography",[28] wrote Louis Figuier, also the author of *Les Races humaines*, (Paris, Hachette, 1873).

Désiré Charnay,
Madegascans, Creoles from Réunion,
1863,
Musée de l'Homme, Paris.
▼

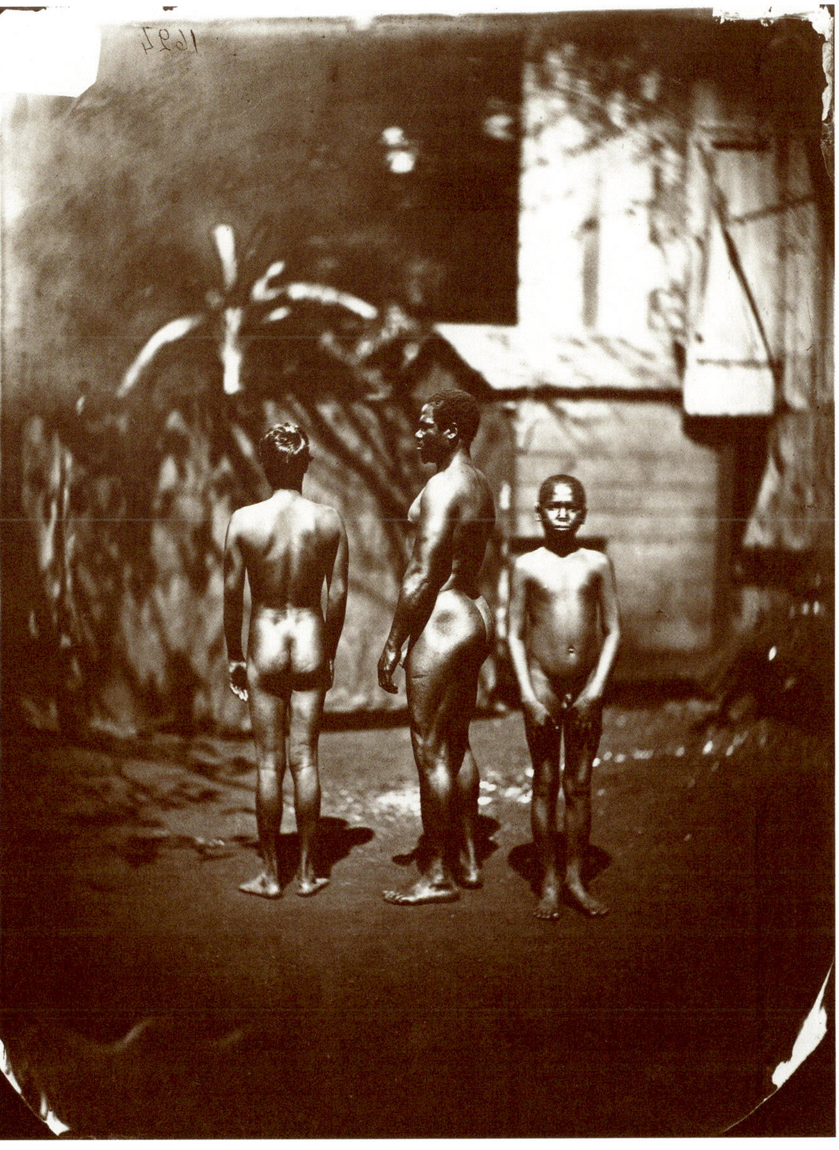

25. F. Galton, *Inquiries into Human Faculty and its Development*, London, Macmillan, 1883.

26. E. Lacan, *op. cit.*, p. 38.

27. G. Le Bon, *L'Homme et les Sociétés: leurs Origines et leur Histoire*, Paris, Rothschild, 1881.

28. *Les Merveilles de la Science*, Paris, Furne, Jouvet et Cie., 1869, vol. 3, p. 170.

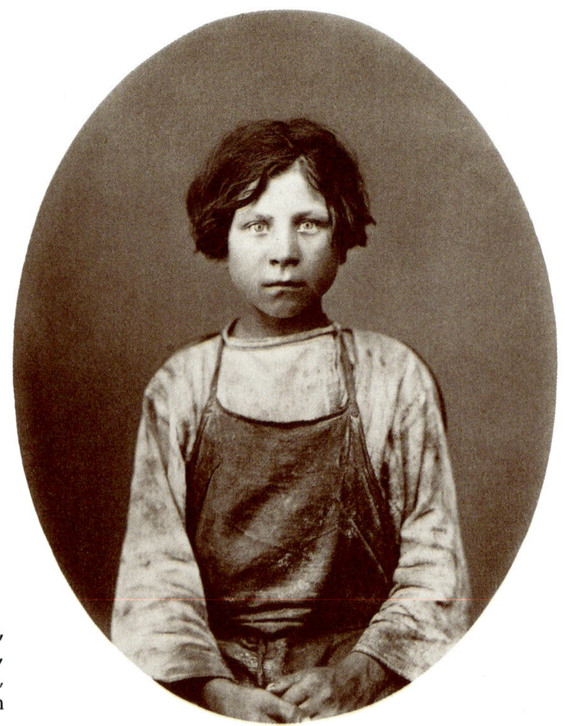

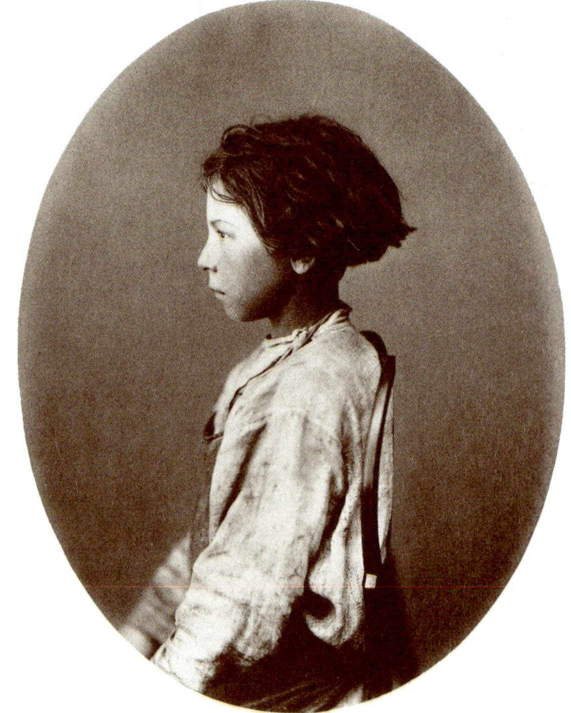

ANATOLE BOGDANOV, *Russian Child,* 1867, Bibliothèque du Museum d'Histoire Naturelle, Paris.

It was ethnographic methods which served as a model for judicial anthropometry, as can be seen from the career of Bertillon, author of *Les Races Sauvages* (Paris, Masson, 1873). Their divergence was due chiefly to lack of confidence on the part of the police: a crook's face generally looks much like that of an honest man, warned the ethnologist Topinard.[29]

The Musée de l'Homme in Paris has a collection of daguerreotypes showing not only living people, full-face and in profile (Botocudos Indians of Brazil, Thiesson expedition, 1844), but also skeletons presented in the same way (*Skeleton of a Negro*, 1844) and skulls: the head of an Arab, given by Horace Vernet, *norma facialis* and *norma lateralis,* with pictures taken from underneath and above (four daguerreotypes). The ethnologist Louis Agassiz, founder of the museum of comparative zoology at Harvard, collected photographs of human types, like the 15 daguerreotypes by J. T. Zealy of slaves in South Carolina, photographed bare-chested (full-face, profile, back). Agassiz' purpose was to show that racial types can continue away from their

E. THIESSON, *Botocudo Indian,* daguerreotype, 1844, Musée de l'Homme, Paris.

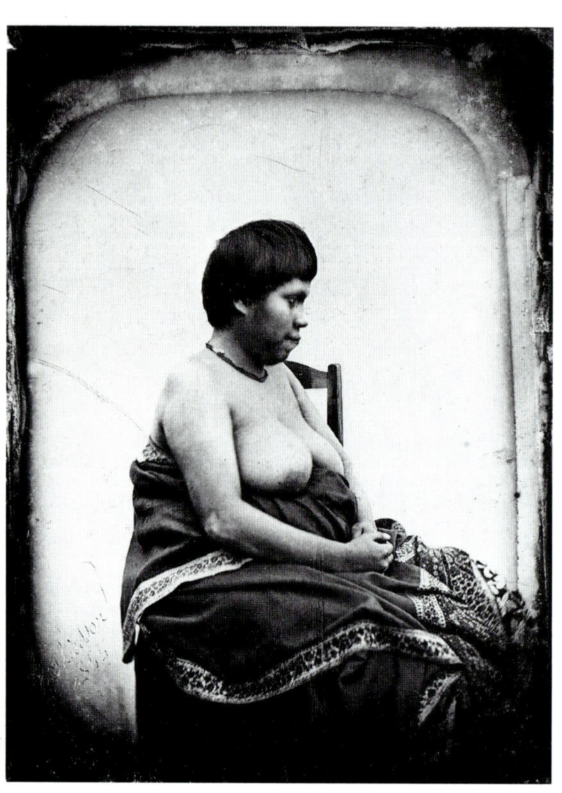

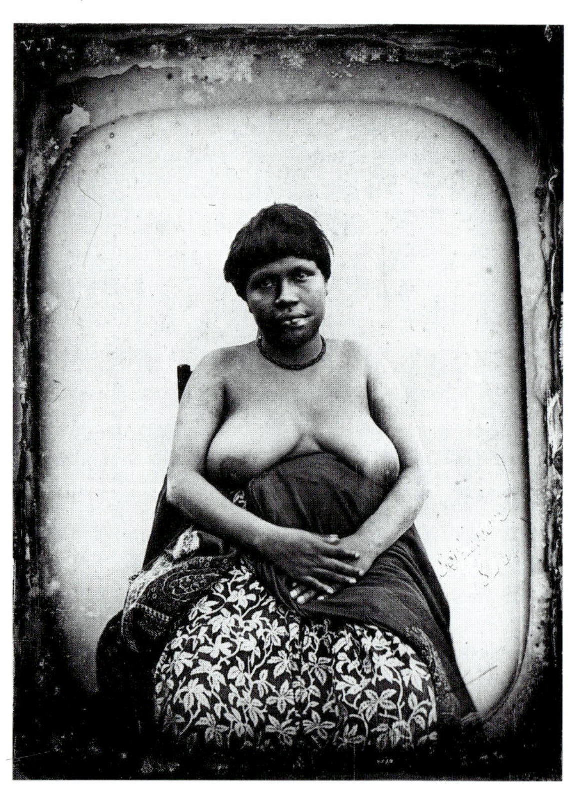

29. Quoted by C. Phéline, *op. cit.*, p. 69.

geographical place of origin. While on an expedition to Brazil in 1865, he and Hunnewell photographed native people partially unclothed or naked, from behind, full-face, and in profile. Others who took part in this scientific activity were Louis Rousseau, of the Musée National d'Histoire Naturelle, who photographed Russians and Hottentots (calotype), Potteau, who studied the people who came on diplomatic missions to Paris (from Siam; 1861, Japan, 1862; Cochin China, 1863), Charnay, who had been in Madagascar (1862–1863), and Bogdanov,[30] who took part in the great ethnographic exhibition in Moscow in 1867 (featuring 600 photographs and 900 objects). On the other hand, the psychiatrist Gaétan de Clerambault, who photographed the veiled women of Morocco between 1917 and 1920, subverted the scientific attitude by his obsession with death and concealment, affording a glimpse of one of the psychological functions of photography: to lift the veil.

This scientific approach was not shared by all photographer-travelers. Most were inclined to react to a multifarious reality by aiming, with whatever means at their disposal, at anything that could be photographed and was worth bringing home, without giving too much thought to the method. A large number of travel-photos was published, in the form of woodcuts, by the illustrated papers of the day (especially *Le Tour du Monde*, first published in 1860, *Le Monde illustré*, and *L'Illustration*). Charnay's types appeared in *Le Monde illustré* on September 24, 1864. In *Le Tour du Monde* one sixth of the pictures were ethnographic portraits, generally accompanied by landscapes and views of buildings by the same artists. Here one uncovers an immense amount of activity by now forgotten photographers: Alary and Geiser (Algeria), Bevan (Réunion), Chambay and Lecorgne (Mauritius), Fournier (Tahiti), Maunoury (Lima), Saint-Priest (Peking), and Szathmari (Wallachia).[31]

Is it possible to describe Moulin (whose photos of Algerian types were published in *L'Illustration* in 1858–1860) as an ethnologist? He was a Paris photographer whose studio produced genre studies, buildings, nudes, etc. He went to Algeria in 1856 under the auspices of the minister of war, and brought back 300 pictures: French troops, personalities, encampments, places of interest, everyday occupations, Jewish women.

What counted as scientific rigor at the time would not be accepted as such today. The universal exhibitions (London, 1851; Paris 1855, 1867, 1878, 1889; Philadelphia, 1876; Chicago 1893) showed photographs but also tableaux scenes recreated with wax figures – and even natives brought from far away. Photographing them under these conditions was not considered inauthentic. Prince Roland Bonaparte published *The Inhabitants of Surinam* with photographs taken in Amsterdam in 1883, whereas his excellent research into the Lapps took place in Finland in 1884.[32]

Now that ethnographic iconography has become an object of study (until recently it had not been collected by photographic societies or institutions), it has become clear that images of this type were produced along with other works. The large archives of photographs that have been discovered at the ethnographic societies (Royal Anthropological Institute of Great Britain, National Anthropological Archives of Washington, the Peabody Museum at Harvard) and their gradual publication[33] leads one to believe that there is copious material. E. H. Man (Sea of Bengal, 1871–1875), Lindt (Australia, 1870s), E. im Thurn (Guyana, 1883–1897), H. B. T. Sommerville (Solomon Islands, 1890–1900) have all reappeared in this way. The Museum of Ethnography in Rotterdam has been publishing a

GAÉTAN GATIAN DE CLÉRAMBAULT, *Study of Draped Figure*, Morocco, 1917–1920, Musée de l'Homme, Paris.
▼

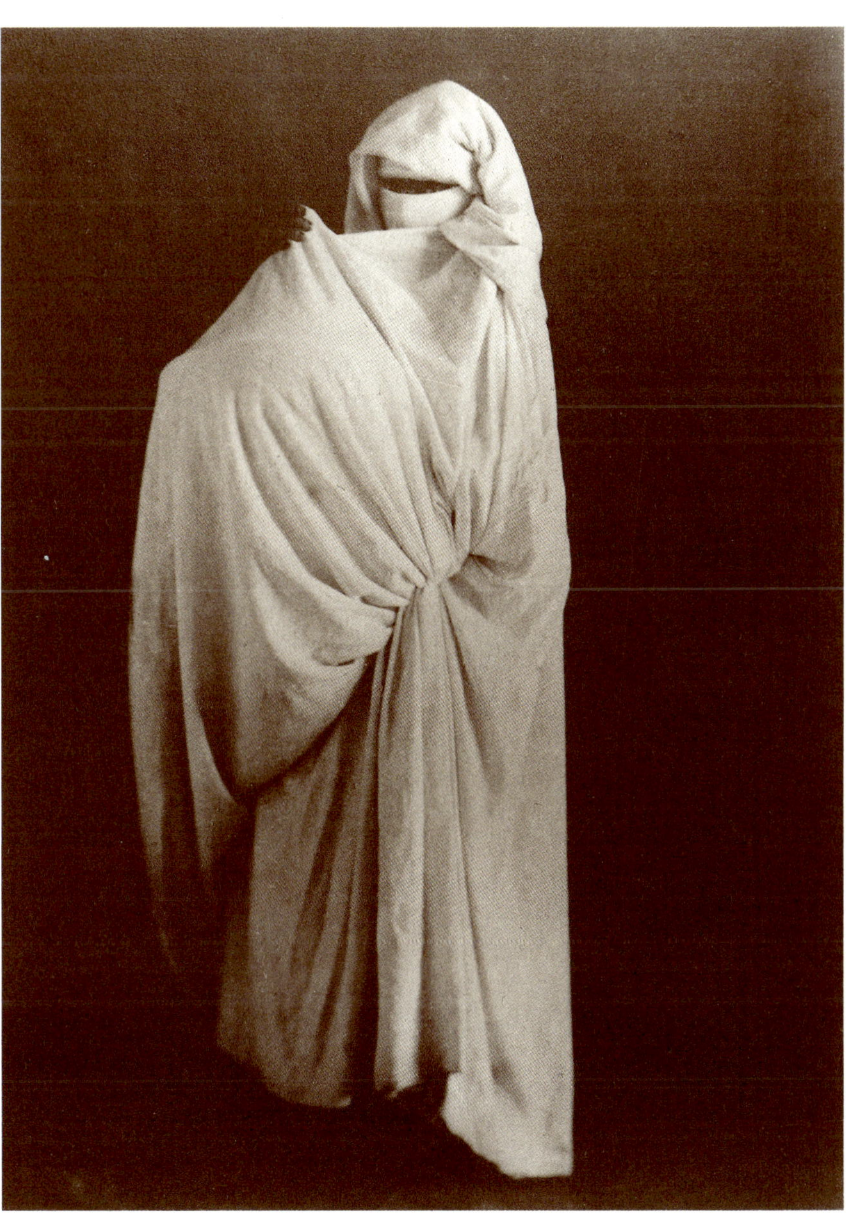

30. *Les Russes*, Moscow, 1867, collection of 56 photographs.

31. S. Rochard, *La Photographie et la Presse Illustrée, 1853-1870*, Master's thesis, University of Paris IV, 1990.

32. "Le Prince Roland Bonaparte en Laponie," special issue of *L'Ethnographie*, no. 104, 1988.

33. *Observers of Man*, London, 1980; *From Site to Sight: Anthropology, Photography, and the Power of Imagery*, Cambridge, 1986; E. Edwards, (ed.), *Anthropology and Photography, 1860–1920*, New Haven and London, Yale Univ., 1992.

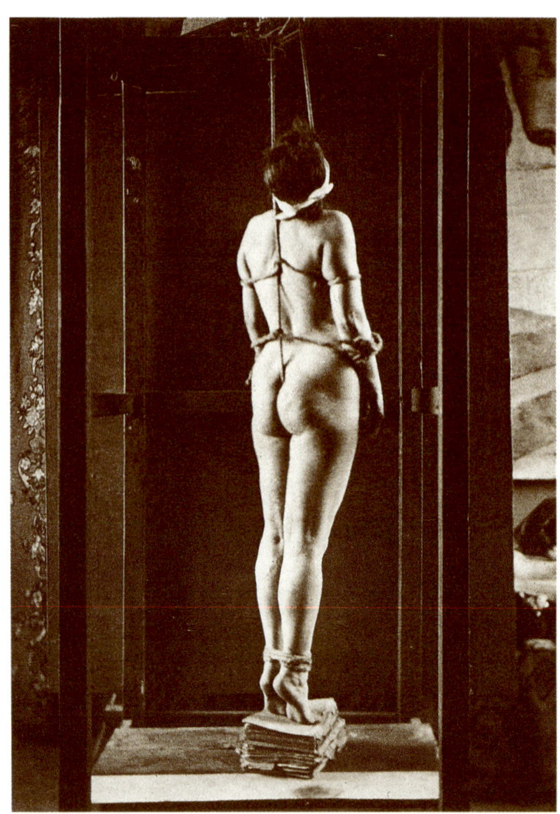

CHARLES-FRANÇOIS JEANDEL, *Female Model Tied Up,* 1890–1900, Musée d'Orsay, Paris.

ANONYMOUS, *Female anatomy,* part of a stereoscopic view, 1861, P.-M. Richard Collection. ▼

series of works based on its collections from which it becomes clear that local studios patiently built up precious collections, like the Burton Brothers in New Zealand.[34]

We must not forget that the material for ethnological studies was often also supplied through the ad hoc activity of professional photographers or was commissioned as part of a wider undertaking. *The People of India: A Series of Photographic Investigations* (eight volumes, 1868–1875) which has many contributors, was launched by Lord Canning in India in 1856; John Thomson brought back the material for his *China and its People* (1873–1874) after his travels in the Far East; J. K. Hillers, photographer for the Bureau of American Ethnology, who studied the Indians of New Mexico, also took part in the Surveys of the 1870s in Utah and Nevada.[35] Hayden's U.S. Geological Survey, which also practiced some rigorous anthropometry, employed W. H. Jackson who took around a thousand pictures of Indian types. The dividing-line between touristic and scientific photography was equally ill-defined in the work of Beato or Stillfried in Japan.

The situation of Vroman (Hopi and Navajo tribes of California, from 1895 to 1904) and Curtis (Alaska, New Mexico, Montana, Arizona, from 1896), who were professional photographers undertaking photographic enquiries about native peoples is not, therefore, a paradoxical one, despite their aestheticizing Pictorialist tendencies. Their work is inscribed in the possibilities of the medium – which is more than just a recording-machine – and in the empirical practice of photography, not in the scientific discipline of ethnography. In these terms, a "local" photographer, like Chambi of Cuzco in Peru, can be counted a genuine ethnologist of his fellow-citizens.

The offending body

In all these coercive attitudes of the photographer towards the individual there appears one constant: the body is under investigation as a place where contradictions may be resolved, and as both theater and symptom of individual renunciations and collective hopes. There is a sense in which the human body eludes photography, makes itself inaccessible, evades it as far as it possibly can. But it is the body, finally, that photography must interrogate if it is to understand deep-lying motivations and provide some explanation of the diversity of the human race, and the perverse spectacle of its behaviour.

It is well known that most of today's photography magazines survive only commercially by publishing erotic images. It seems that, at least in the eyes of the purchasers, photography is the essential medium for satisfying voyeurism. The nude is the point where all photographic subjects converge, whether they suggest it, avoid it or deny it. But the criteria of nudity, eroticism, and pornography, even within European culture, change rapidly from period to period. Prohibition of public sale or display scarcely inhibits the production of pictures and does not define their nature. There are few differences between the era when the lines of Courbet's *Baigneuse* were lashed with scorn by Napoleon III, and the 1930s, when there were abundant collections of female nudes. The visual permissiveness of images has more to do with the mode of distribution of these "objects" than the severity of the law regulating their circulation. Erotic, indeed

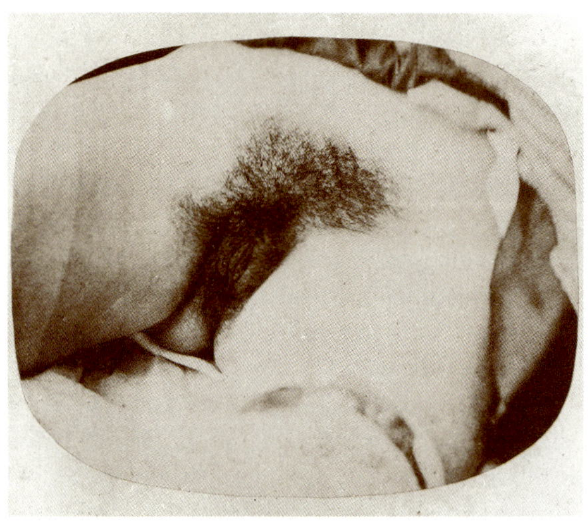

34. *Burton Brothers: Photographers in New Zealand,* 1987; *Images of the Orient,* 1986; *Photography in Surinam,* Amsterdam, Fragment, 1990.

35. D. D. Fowler, *The Western Photographs of J.K. Hillers,* Washington and London, Smithsonian Institution, 1989.

frequently pornographic, daguerreotypes started to be produced in large numbers in the 1840s, and the advent of stereoscopy perfected the system in the 1850s. The precious nature of the materials involved, the illusion of depth, the uniqueness of the image as a work of art, and its high cost meant that the clientele for these images was well-off, but did not make it particularly rare. Moralizing discourses on nudity did nothing to counteract people's realization that the process of "framing" and "taking" a photo was an ideal way of capturing the body.

There are no real taboos in photography. On the contrary, since a photograph is an intermediary which shows the subject without itself being the subject, the only taboo is one of distribution, on being seen by the "other", the knowledge that the other may gain by such insistent sight.[36] The authenticated realism of the photograph opened up an uncharted area of representation. It is a medium – an indirect means of aggression and transgression – an instrument which takes the place of the human eye, makes us forget it, annuls it. However various the inspiration or aesthetic viewpoints behind nude photography, they are all only a question of posture. What the image affirms is the existence of the individual who was photographed, and the certainty that person was seen, rendering visual access to them legitimate. The close-up female genitalia in Courbet's *L'Origine du Monde* (1866), which seemed the height of fantasizing display – though seen only by a few – had equivalents in the photography of the day, more natural ones that are less concerned to make a point. The sadistic obsessions of the artist François Jeandel were not confined to the sufferings endured by his models; photography was a part of the process, and was instrumental in it, by providing it with a raison d'être. The sexually ambiguous male nudes, an Italian speciality (von Gloeden and Pluschow in Sicily, Vincenzo Galdi in Rome), due, it was thought, to the persistence of classical mores and a climate conducive to abandon,[37] were produced for foreign tourists as part of a trade which masqueraded as the supply of artists' models (this is how the purchase of nude photographs, male and female, was justified).

The exhibition *Das Aktfoto*[38] brought together all the occurrences of nudity in photography since the invention of the medium (including a section on the ethnographic nude). No comparison is possible, however, between the sculptural photographs of Mapplethorpe, a Diane Arbus picture of nudists, and a Pictorialist, symbolist nude by Steichen – except outside the typology of the nude. The factor which renders Bellocq's photographs of prostitutes (New Orleans, around 1912) particularly full of meaning is knowing that they are prostitutes, and that taking pictures of them is an act of taking, with all its connotations of taboo and morality. Their bodies feature first as those of prostitutes and only secondly as women. The fact that some of their faces are not seen – rare for erotic photos of the nineteenth century, though they were for sale – shows clearly that they were afraid to be recognized as prostitutes, rather than as women stripped naked. In the same way, the painter Pierre Molinier, in his fetishistic photographs of himself, regards the process as a personal sexual act, not a spectacle for others, which would be simple pornography.

It is not the sight of a naked body that makes a picture erotic, it is the circumstances in which the picture was taken. If there is a close relationship between photography and ethnography (the study of man by man) that is because the body is deemed to reveal something, even in its nakedness. It is the last resort but also the last obstacle, the point where a rupture is always possible in the search for knowledge, the barrier at which looking generally stops. It is, perhaps, the special characteristic of the photographic eye to be able to pierce that screen.

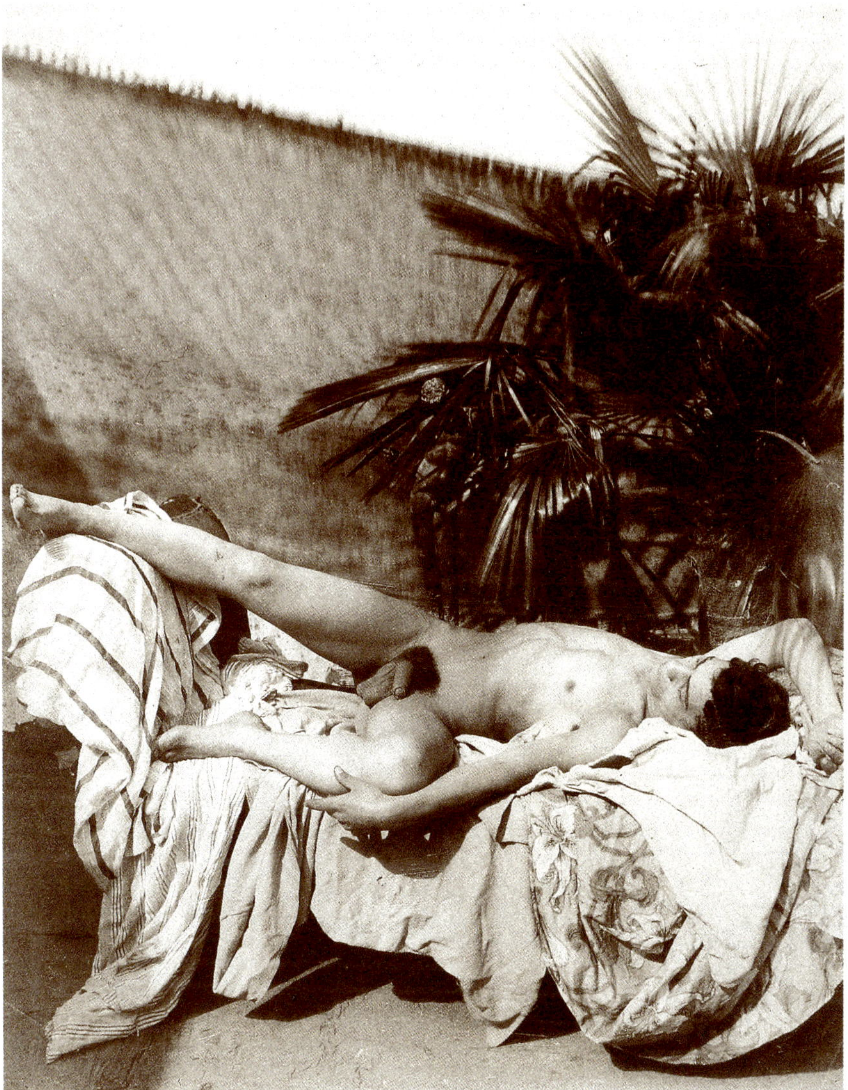

Vincenzo Galdi,
Classisizing Nude,
circa 1890,
private collection.

36. S. de Decker-Heftler, "Le nu photographique: art impur, art réaliste", in *Photographies*, no. 6, December 1984, pp. 50–75.

37. P. Weiermair, *Das verborgene Bild*, Ariadne, 1987; *Taormina Fin de Siècle: Photographies du Baron von Gloeden*, Paris, Chêne, 1975; P. Weiermair, *W. von Gloeden*, Taschen, 1996; G. Plüschow, Taschen, 1994; W. A. Ewing, *The Body: Photoworks of the Human Form*, London, Thames and Hudson, 1994.

38. Kunstverein, Frankfurt, and Museum des Zwanzigsten Jahrhunderts, Vienna, 1985.

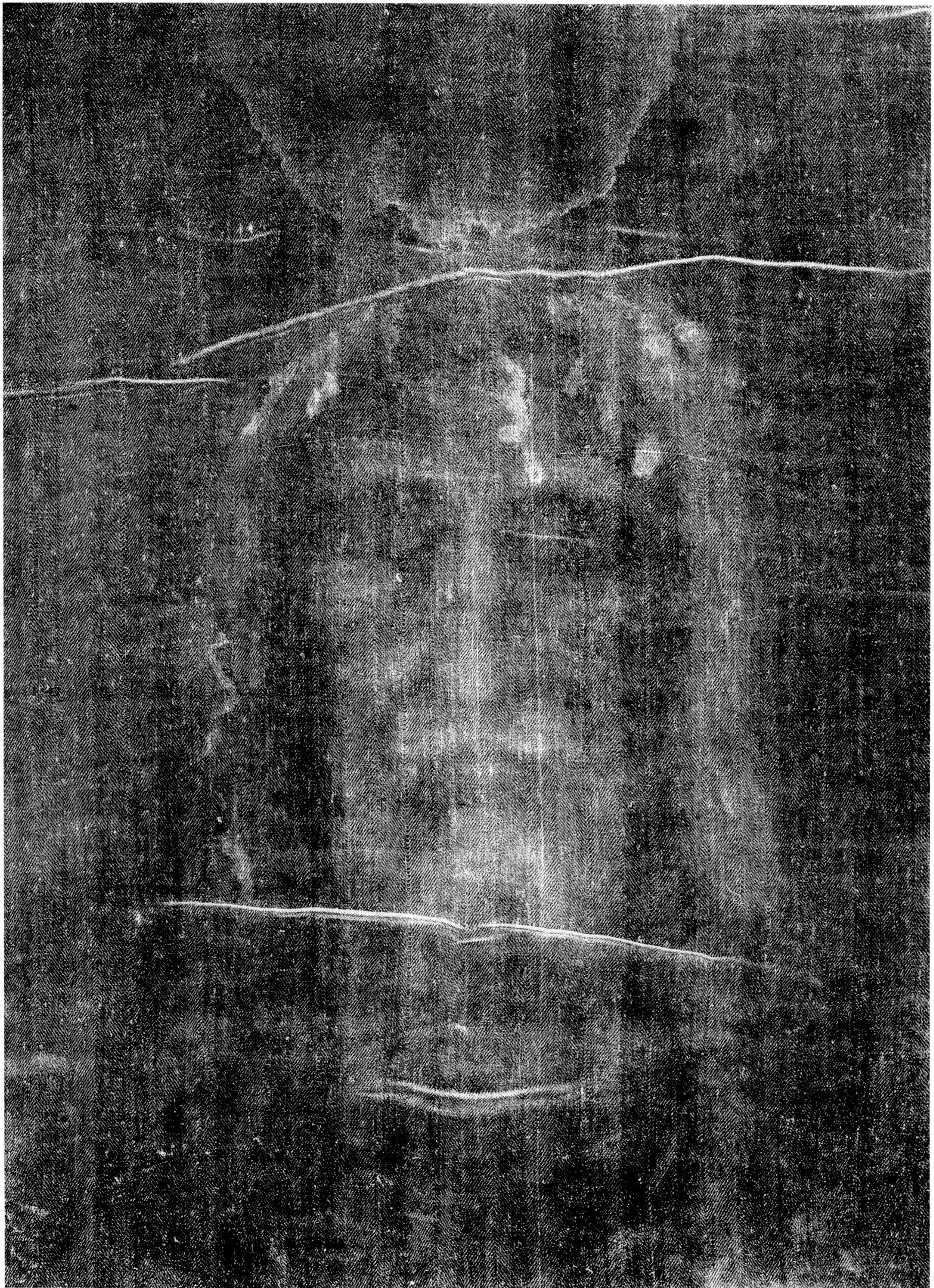

THE ALL-POWERFUL EYE

16

The forms of the invisible

Michel Frizot

Photography only records the effects of light, but it does so indiscriminately. For an object or an event to be captured in a photograph, it must be made into a source of light and instruments must be used which are capable of recording or measuring its radiance. From the very beginning, photography challenged the limits of our visual perception. It mattered little whether the images produced were "beautiful" – it was enough to know that they added in some way to our vision of the world, providing information that was accessible to everyone, everyone, that is, who knew how to interpret it.

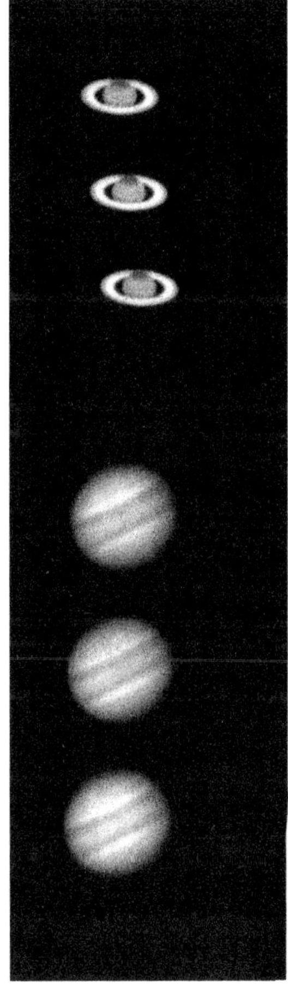

Prosper and Paul Henry, ***Jupiter and Saturn,*** plate by E. Mouchez, *La Photographie astronomique à l'Observatoire de Paris,* 1887.

◀ Giuseppe Enrie, ***The Holy Shroud of Turin,*** detail from a negative, 1931, private collection.

Photography's artistic ambitions have habitually been regarded as more important than its other uses, considered less noble and organized into branches of "application" covering different areas of research and different groups of practitioners. Created in the nineteenth century, "scientific photography" is one of these categories, designed to make it easier to classify work along corporatist lines, in a developing context of craft-activity which permitted few deviations from the norm.

All photographs can *a priori* be considered to be scientific images. They are produced by instruments whose parameters and mechanisms are controlled by the user; they are, first and foremost, a measurement of luminous phenomena, whatever the subjects concerned may be. In addition, photography is perfectly "scientific", in as much as it can be "trusted" more than any other type of image. On condition that certain rules are observed, a photograph is held to be an exact, reliable, and fully imitative record upon which analytical work can be based. A photograph is a record of the number of photons emanating from an object, the graphic witness of an admittedly banal scientific experiment, the conditions of which, however, can be precisely defined, indeed programmed, outside any consideration of the "scientific" validity of the subject. So much so that, at the end of the nineteenth century, "snapshot-fiends" were castigated for an excessively mechanistic attitude, "priding themselves on nothing more than the degree to which they have petrified movement, on the pretext of mechanical perfection. Leave those observation techniques to the physiologists for their abstract studies!"[1] Because they are made "automatically", images obtained using scientific instruments are often held to be less valuable.

Improving vision

In a recent history of photography, purely visual and often formalist aims are ascribed to the medium. However, such aesthetic concerns were not always part of the initial intention of photographers, who were often acting from a more scientific point of view than is obvious at first sight. We now know that Carleton Watkins' trees are not romantic evocations, but were being classified along almost Linnaean lines, and that many of O'Sullivan's views of the American West (*Tufa Domes* for example) were geological studies first and compositions of balanced masses second. Collard's photographs of bridges are comparable to engineers' surveys. The primary function of photography (recording and measuring) was more accepted in the nineteenth century than it is in our day. In any case, it did not have to be set aside in a compartment of its own.

Here, we shall not be considering the "beauty" of the scientific photograph but its *appropriateness,* that is, when and how photography became more than just an elegant accessory, adding a dignified touch to scientific research, but an essential

1. E. Giard, *Le Livre d'Or de la Photographie,* Paris, Mendel, 1902, p. 192.

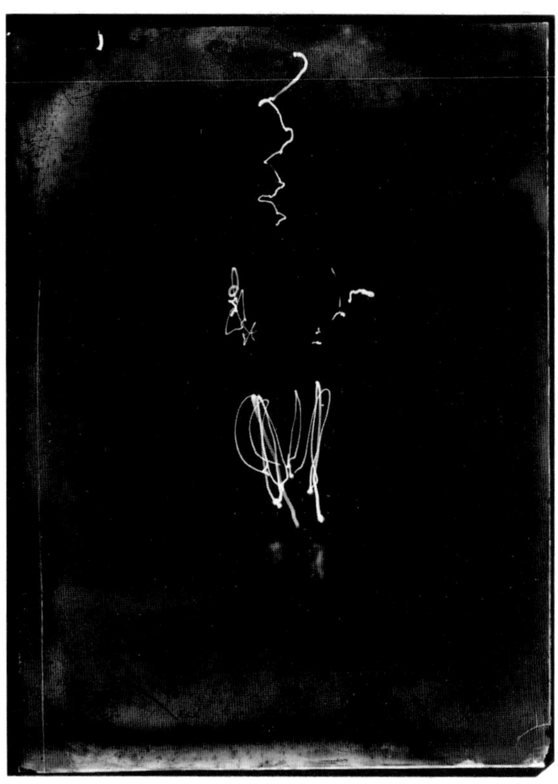

DEMENŸ AND QUÉNU (Marey's laboratory), ***Pathological walk from in front, made visible by incandescent bulbs fixed to the joints,*** circa 1889, Archives of the Collège de France.

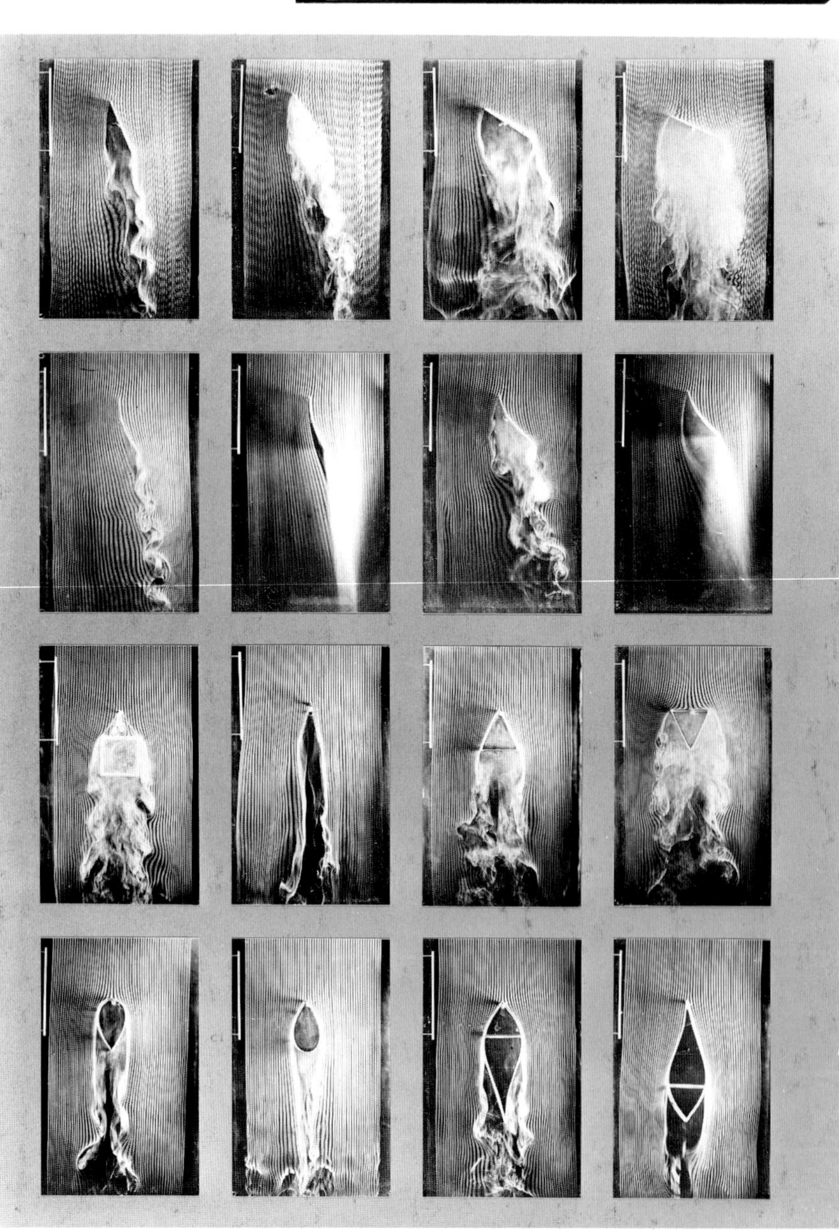

ÉTIENNE-JULES MAREY, ***Study of movement of the air when meeting bodies of different shapes, using wisps of smoke,*** 1900–1901, Musée Marey, Beaune.

2. *Bulletin de la Société française de Photographie*, June 1888

3. L. J. Schaaf, *Sun Gardens: Victorian Photograms by Anna Atkins*, Aperture, 1985.

4. With the help of the practicing photographers Bisson and Mante, work published by L. Rousseau and Devéria in 1853.

5. M. Trutat, *La Photographie appliquée à l'Histoire naturelle*, Paris, Gauthier-Villars, 1884.

element in the process of discovery, an indication of a reality that was impenetrable to ocular vision. Direct knowledge was for a long time confined to what could be seen with the naked eye. Then complementary instruments made it possible to collect data and observations which were translated into measurements and descriptions. From the nineteenth century onwards, science also produced "images", information already coded in its own language. This type of photography brings us face to face with things which we cannot see naturally or correctly. The unifying element in what is known as "scientific" photography might therefore be that it shows us things on a "human scale", mediated by an instrument, which we would not otherwise be able to see, with further data included. The astronomer Janssen liked to define photography as "the real retina of the scientist".[2] The camera can be regarded as the first way of extending human vision.

The natural sciences quickly realized that photography was a relatively trouble-free way of capturing and recording information. Talbot's first photogenic drawings are imprints of leaves, similar to those found in herbals, and, in 1843, Anna Atkins recorded a whole series of types of seaweed using this technique.[3] In the 1850s, the Muséum d'Histoire Naturelle in Paris undertook a program of adapting photography to the needs of research, under the direction of Louis Rousseau, an assistant naturalist, and Philippe Potteau, a laboratory technician. Their work, however, was mainly for the purposes of publication. Rousseau's resulted in *Photographie zoologique,*[4] which did not meet with great success. Potteau, for his part, took photographs of dissections, fossils, and stuffed animals. But it cannot be said that the new medium revolutionized natural history. Was Charnay's photograph of a stuffed fish, taken in Madagascar between 1862 and 1863, a great help to scientists? The naturalist preferred to preserve the original subject and have access to it, possibly also drawing it (in view of the well-known power of drawing to describe structures, explain them, "see" them). Despite exhortations and encouragements,[5] and some fine successes[6], photography could not rest at simply taking account of what the eye could already see. There had to be something additional, whether it was travelling to the scene of an event (the aftermath of the eruption of Mount Etna, photographed by Berthier in 1865), the immersion method proposed by Donnadieu to facilitate observation[7], or the use of small instruments to photograph bodily cavities (larynx, ear).[8]

With the spirit of invention typical of the century, procedures were devised to make visualization easier. The Quénu method (small light-bulbs fixed to a person's limbs) was used by Londe in 1884–85, and by Georges Demenÿ in 1888 in Marey's laboratory[9] to record the involuntary tremors of a sick person. Much of Marey's work has to be understood in this context (see the chapter "Speed of Photography") and he himself returned in his last experiments, around 1900, to using photography in a simple recording role, with instruments of rigorous accuracy. His aerodynamic studies make visible the movement of streams of smoke encountering objects of varying natures.[10]

As a general rule, however, the camera performed little better than the eye. In order to depict photographically what is invisible to the human eye, specialized photographic instruments had to be devised, appropriate to the phenomenon to be observed, whether permanent or ephemeral, repeated or unique. "Photography may be used any time there is any phenomenon to be noted, whether it be momentary or prolonged, or if it has to be recorded continuously over a long period, as in meteorology."[11] Sometimes a photograph will be the only enduring trace of a phenomenon, and all subsequent analysis of the data collected will have to be done on the basis of that photograph alone.

There is often a great difference in scale between the real object being observed and the image of it that one wishes to retain. Photographing what is described as "invisible to the naked eye" supposes that one has the means to enlarge the subject to the dimensions of an image which can be perceived on a light-sensitive surface.

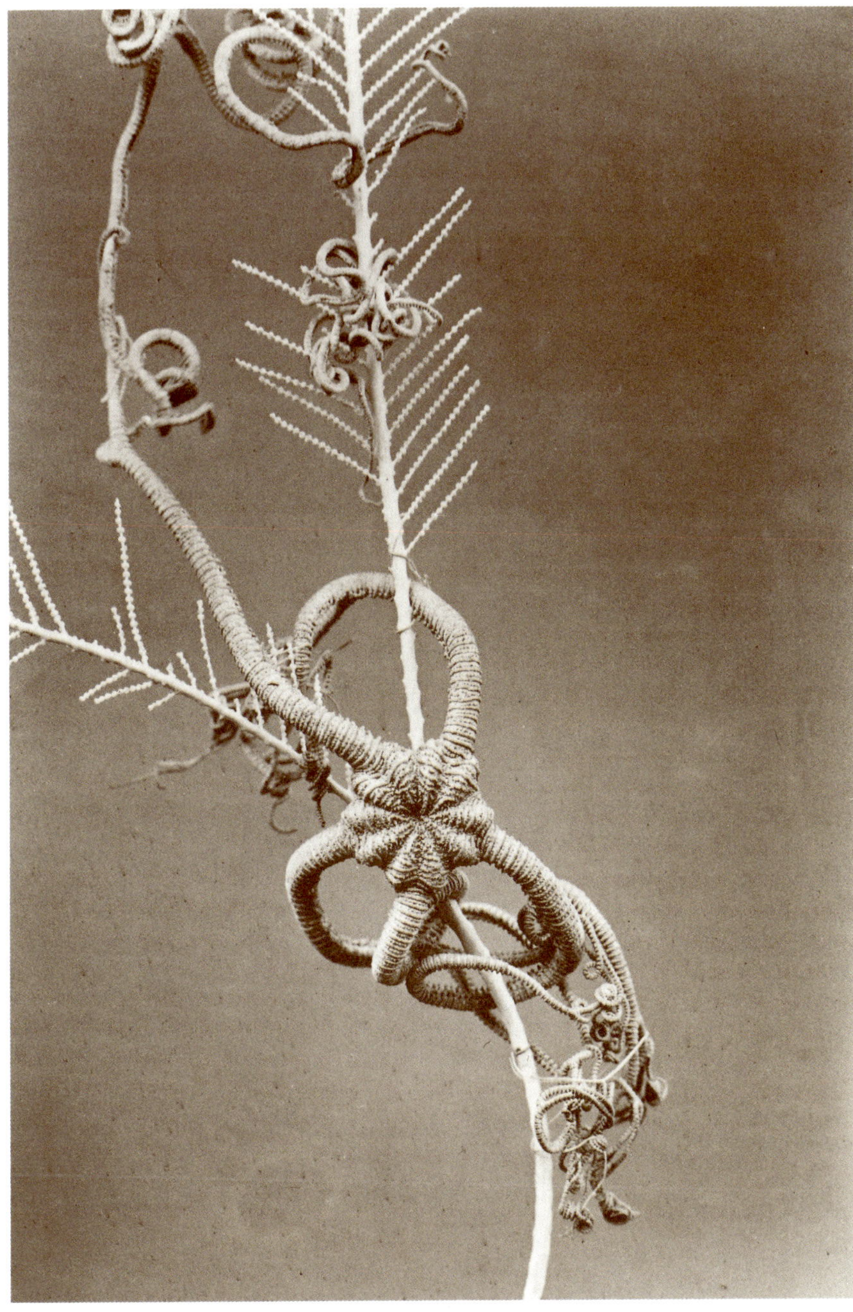

Philippe Potteau,
Trichaster Annulatus,
1868,
Bibliothèque du Muséum d'Histoire Naturelle, Paris.

Photomicrography

It was only natural that Talbot should be the first photographer to show an interest in the scientific implications of the medium, in particular photomicography – taking pictures of images seen through a microscope. Brewster's *Treatise on the Microscope* was dedicated to him in 1837. In 1836, Talbot had conducted research into the luminous effects of crystals. As early as 1837, he adapted the solar microscope to his "photographic" process (the production of photogenic drawings) and obtained pictures of crystals in polarized light and plant sections (1839–1841).[12] His photomicrograph of an insect's wing was shown at the Royal Institution in January 1839, together with other examples of his first successes, in support of the claims he was then putting forward for the use of the medium.

The new element that photography brought to scientific investigation was its power to produce a permanent document that was faithful to what had been observed and which could be easily stored for access at a later date. Line-drawing was replaced by the more realistic image obtained by contrasts in light; the potentially inaccurate hand-drawn schema was replaced by an objective graphic image. The scientific progress achieved depended not only upon access to the invisible, but also upon the transcription of what had been made optically visible – in terms of form, difference of material, the limitations of the substance – and upon the explanation of such differences. These are transcribed in a photograph in a way that retains the indeterminate quality of the original, providing for the possibility of revision and reinterpretation.

The adoption of the glass negative in the 1850s was of primary importance for preserving in the image the nuances of transparency and precision

6. A. L. Donnadieu, *Contribution à l'Histoire du Phylloxéra de la Vigne,* Lyons, Pitrat ainé, 1889.

7. A. L. Donnadieu, *La Photographie des Objets Immergés,* Paris, C. Mendel, c. 1900.

8. R. Koehler, *Les Applications de la Photographie aux Sciences naturelles,* Paris, Masson, 1892.

9. *Comptes rendus de l'Académie des Sciences,* May 28, 1888, pp. 1559–1564.

10. *Ibid.,* July 16, 1900 and June 3, 1901.

11. A. Londe, *La Photographie moderne,* Paris, 1888, p. 185.

12. G. Buckland, *Fox Talbot and the Invention of Photography,* Boston, D. R. Godine, 1980, pp. 18–29.

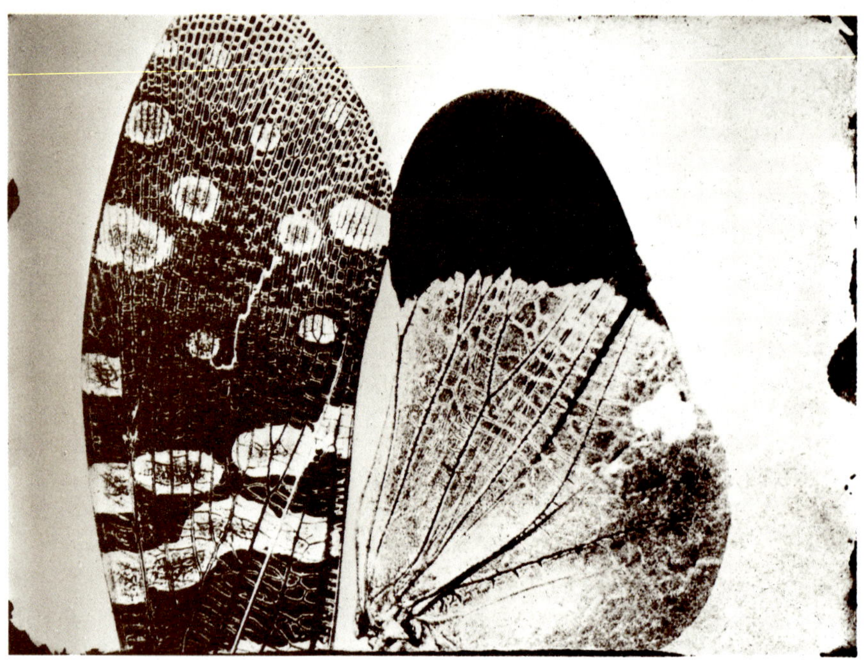

WILLIAM HENRY FOX TALBOT, *Photomicrograph of the wing of a moth*, 1839–1841, Fox Talbot Museum, Lacock Abbey.

seen by the eye. Abel Niépce de Saint-Victor wrote of "the advantage that this new art can bring to natural history [...] I refer to the hosts of subjects that it is difficult for an artist to transcribe faithfully." Following his example, a distinguished botanist, Alphonse de Brébisson, one of the first men to use collodion negatives in France – a process in which he was skilled – built a camera adapted for use with a microscope in 1849. His work on microscopic seaweeds and diatoms stimulated further research, and was still being cited at the end of the century. Using a solar microscope, Edmond Bacot, another native of Normandy, better known for his views of Gothic architecture in Caen, is said to have taken photographs of a flea.[13]

The introduction of photography into the sciences was considered significant enough to be the subject of debate in the Académie des Sciences, centered on the work of Biot and Donné. However, it was book illustration that vindicated photography's use as an aid to scientific research, and, at the same time, revealed its limitations. When Alfred Donné, a professor at the Collège de France who had done research into the structure of daguerreotype plates in 1839, published his *Cours de Micrographie* in 1844, he enlisted the aid of Léon Foucault, a doctor of medicine who also made daguerreotypes, in the production of the plates. They came out in 1845, eighty-six engravings in all. It was not possible, however, to reproduce them in any way other than as drawings *from* the original daguerreotypes, produced with exposures from four to twenty seconds.[14] There are uric acid crystals, photomicrographs of white corpuscles, and sections of blood-vessels (frog's tongue) etc., seen through a solar microscope (magnification 20 to 400 times).

ANDREAS RITTER VON ETTINGSHAUSEN, *Clematis*, microscopic section, daguerreotype, March 4, 1840, Vienna, Ezra Mack Gallery, New York.
▼

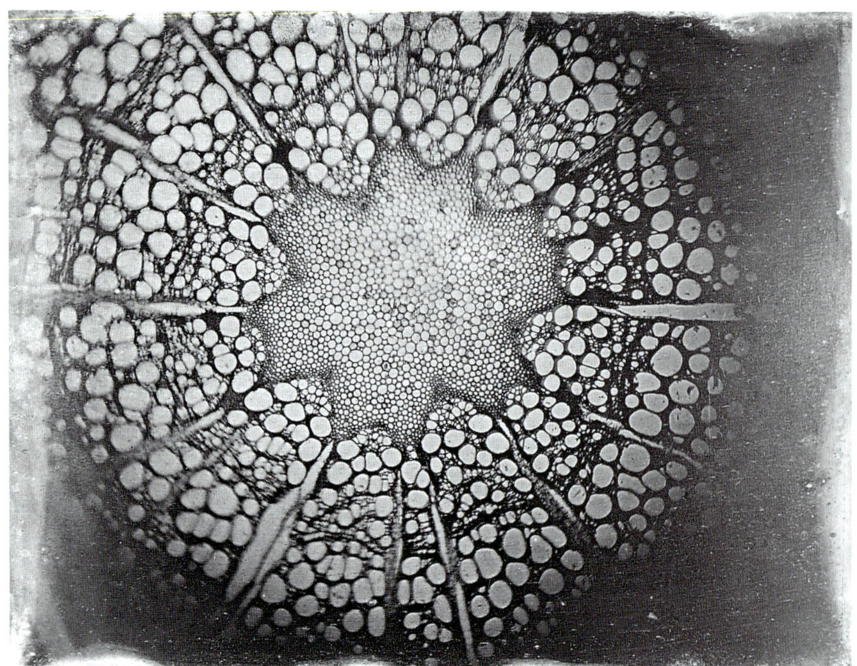

Moitessier, one of the specialists in the area in the 1860s,[15] named "Bertsch and Nachet in France, Mayer in Frankfurt, and Hodgson, Shadbolt and Wenham in Britain" as the people behind significant progress in obtaining the prints on paper which were necessary from a scientific point of view. We also know of some fine prints by Neyt of Brussels, presented at the Exposition Universelle of 1867, and others by Jules Girard, shown in 1868; Gerlach published an album of prints in 1872; and Nachet constructed instruments of great optical and mechanical efficiency, and even a microscope which gave stereoscopic prints. The only interesting feature of Moitessier's book is the three pasted-in albumen prints with which it is illustrated. Duseigneur-Kléber's *Physiologie du Cocon et du Fil de Soie* about the silk-cocoon and thread (Valence, 1855) was one of the first to be illustrated with pasted-in photomicrographs.

Subsequently, prints made on albumen paper – or, better still, Woodburytypes, which retained all the qualities of the original without being liable to fading – ensured the circulation of a bank of scientific references in the form of images. Many of these were subsequently published: works by Viallanes, illustrated with collotypes by Quinsac,[16] by Dr. J. Luys, illustrated with Woodburytypes[17], or by Louis Olivier, with a folio-size volume of 48 Woodburytypes.[18] While prints were useful for publication and building up an archive, in teaching great use was made of projected images.[19] It seems that the first work in this area was done by J. B. Dancer (collodionized glass).

Bertsch was one of the most active practitioners during the 1850s – his *Notice sur l'Emploi du Collodion rapide* was published as early as 1852 in the *Bulletin de la Société française de Photographie* (1857–1863, enlargement by means of the Mégascope) and his photograph of a louse appeared in *La Lumière* on 18 June 1853. Nadar, whose mentor was Camille d'Arnaud, a collaborator of Bertsch, the first man to apply photography to photomicography, described him. "Small and dry and sharp as his temper, Bertsch was the first to apply photography to the very small and the very large, as precise and scrupulous when dealing with a planet as with a microscopic insect".[20] It was his "real" photographs, (not drawn) which really fired the enthusiasm of the scientific community (they were presented at the Exposition Universelle of 1855). His "automatic camera" went on sale in 1861. Among the scientific curiosities that emerged were the Bisson brothers' 1865 photographs of crystals illustrating Marc-Antoine Gaudin's thesis on molecular morphology and crystallography.

Throughout the century, improvements in photomicography were accompanied by the construction of special instruments combining a means of stabilizing the subject and correct lighting. Two rostrum camera set-ups were produced, making it possible to photograph preparations that could only be observed from a horizontal angle: Donnadieu's physiographe, which had a long focal length, and Bézu and Hausser's camera.

Extending vision

It is not surprising that the telescope and the microscope were closely linked to photography in its earliest years – both are optical instruments working on the same enlargement principle, and require only the addition of a *camera obscura* to record an image. Astronomical photographs were attempted as soon as the daguerreotype was invented. J. W. Draper obtained a daguerreotype of the moon in 1840 (30-minute exposure) while Léon Foucault and Hippolyte Fizeau made daguerreotypes of sunspots in 1845 (1/60 of a second, 8 cm image with lens at focal length of 10 m – Fizeau discovered the speeding-up effect of bromide vapor for daguerreotypes and gold toning). In 1850, despite many successes, astronomical photography still suffered from the insufficient sensitivity of the plates whereas microscopic photography was done using sunlight, which is intense, the amount of light emitted by the stars is very weak. The wet-collodion process, with its greater light sensitivity, was exploited by Warren de la Rue in 1852 to obtain photographs of the surface of the moon.

Eclipses have always offered an opportunity for observation. The first eclipse of the sun to be recorded photographically was that of 18 July 1860 (in Spain by Le Verrier and Foucault, Warren de la Rue, in Las Palmas by Secchi, in Algeria by Laussedat). A study of solar prominences was also conducted by Warren de la Rue.

In 1857, an American, Bond, took a picture of the twin stars of the Great Bear and measured their angle and distance. For the scientist, however, the most important objective is to perceive things that are both faint and far away. In 1879, Briton, Common, succeeded in photographing the stars of the constellation Orion

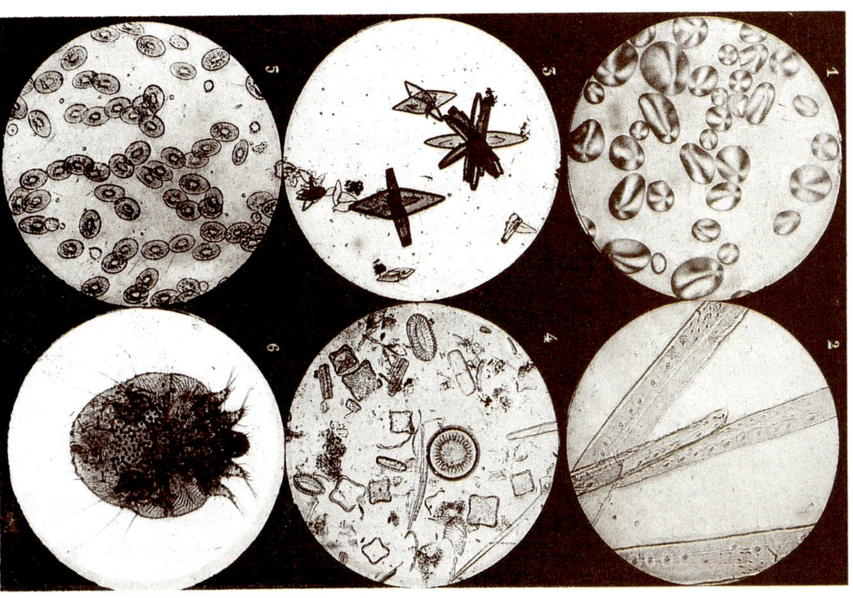

Albert Moitessier, ***Photomicrographs,*** (*starch, vascular tissue of the pine tree, uric acid crystals, diatomea, blood corpuscles, scabies mite*), plate from *La Photographie appliquée aux Recherches micrographiques*, 1866.

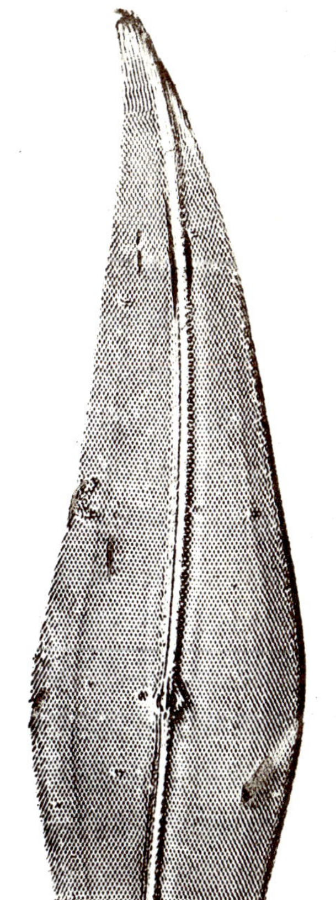

Albert Moitessier, ***Photomicrograph,*** (*Pleurosigma angulatum*), plate from *La Photographie appliquée aux Recherches micrographiques*, 1866.

13. *E. Bacot, A. de Brébisson, A. Humbert de Molard: trois Photographes en Basse-Normandie*, Caen, ARDI, 1989.

14. *Cours de Microscopie[...] Atlas exécuté d'après Nature au Microscope-daguerréotype*, Paris, Baillère, 1866.

15. *La Photographie appliquée aux Recherches micrographiques*, Paris, Baillère, 1866.

16. *La Photographie appliquée aux études d'Anatomie microscopique*, Paris, Gauthier-Villars, 1886.

17. *Traitée clinique et pratique des Maladies mentales*[...], Paris, A. Delahaye and É. Lecrosnier, 1881.

18. *Recherches sur l'Appareil tégumentaire des Racines*, Paris, Masson, 1881.

19. G. Le Bon, *La Photomicrographie en cent tableaux pour Projections*, Paris, Gauthier-Villars, 1872.

AUGUSTE BERTSCH, *Head of larva*, National Museum of Photography, Film and Television, Bradford. ▶

down to the ninth degree. Starting in 1858, Rutherford, an American, began using an equatorial telescope and an achromatic lens to obtain his "Rutherford's moons" – highly detailed pictures of the moon's surface, with highly visible shadows (presented at the Société Française de Photographie in 1865, and at the Académie des Sciences in Paris in 1872). This was a big advance in the study of the geology of the moon, and the images were widely reproduced at the time as "genuine pictures" of the heavenly body that is both the nearest to the earth and the most enigmatic. The moon, an object that exists for man only via the reflected light of the sun, could now be observed with the naked eye, in a book, with the same sharpness and truth to nature as if viewed through a telescope.[21]

JAMES NASMYTH, *Mountains of the Moon, Apennine Range*, plate from C. Flammarion, *Les Terres du Ciel*, 1877. ▼

However, it was not until the appearance of gelatin-silver bromide plates in around 1880, which were much more sensitive to light, that whole programs of astronomical photography were launched, with real scientific rigor and on a scale appropriate to the potential of the photographic medium. Heavenly bodies – stars, galaxies – are visible only by virtue of their emission of light, which can be faithfully recorded on a photographic plate, beyond even the capacity of the human eye. What has been mechanically recorded by the plate unquestionably corresponds to an emission of light, which must then be interpreted. From that moment the "known" universe was no longer defined by limits of human vision, and, since light is only a small part of the totality of electromagnetic radiation, these limits were pushed further and further back as different wavelengths of light were discovered.

21. H. Vogel, *La Photographie et la Chimie de la Lumière*, with a Woodburytype dated 1865, Paris, Baillère, 1878; C. Flammarion, *Les Terres du Ciel* with a photo by Rutherford and one by Nasmyth, Paris, Librairie Académique Didier, 1877.

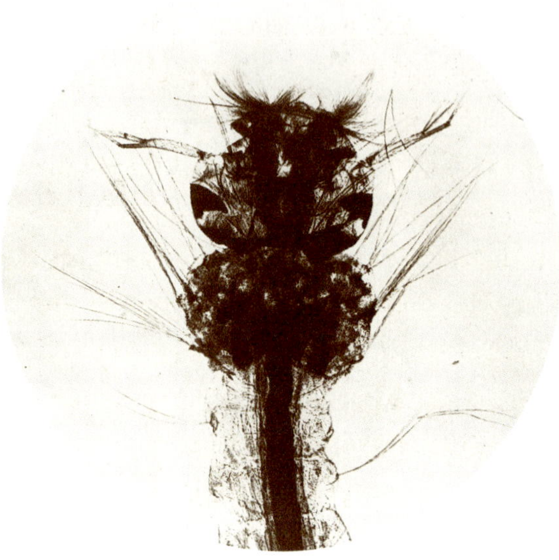

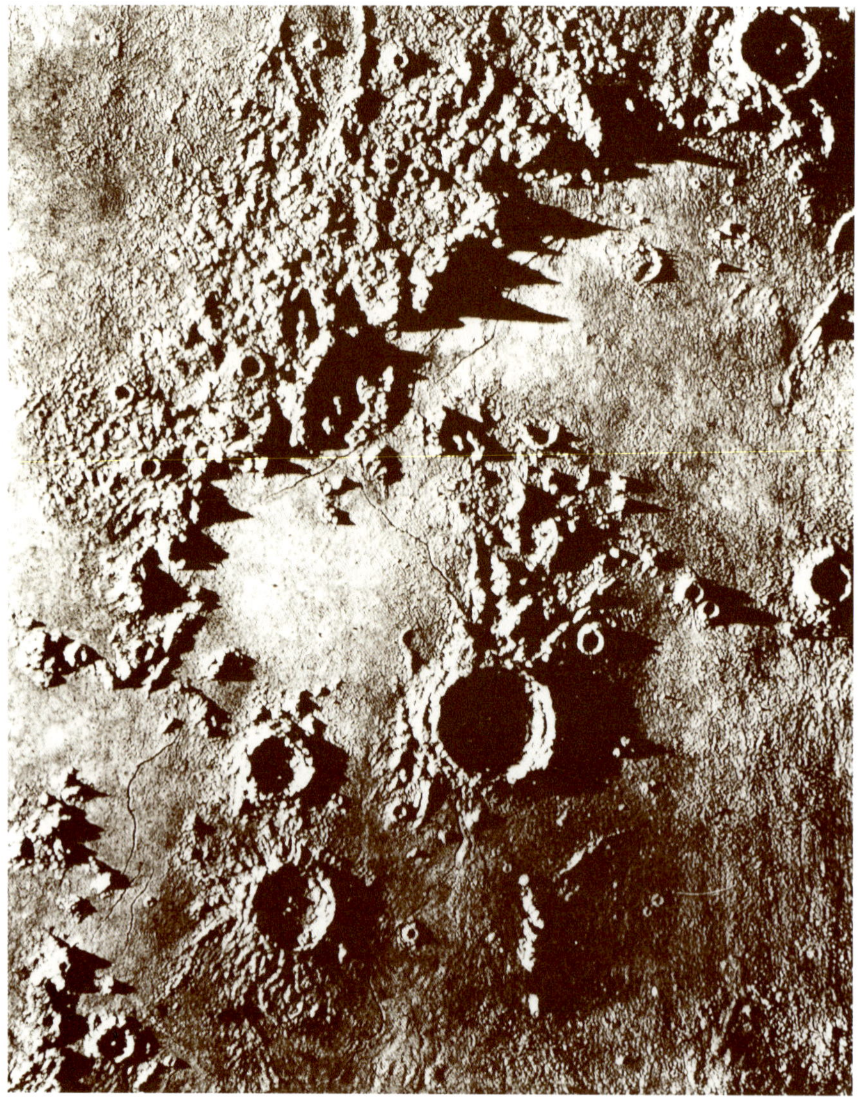

In 1872, Paul and Prosper Henry, astronomers at the Paris Observatory, began adding to the maps of the sky begun by Chacornac, down to the third degree. They soon encountered many difficulties when trying to observe the Milky Way because the stars gave off so little light. They adopted photography in 1884, getting a special lens made for their studies.

The other major difficulty encountered by the astronomer/photographer was in following the apparent movement of the heavens with sufficient precision to avoid any blurring or deformation of the image during the necessarily long exposure times. The answer lay in the use of equatorial reflecting and refracting telescopes, whose movements exactly compensate for the rotation of the Earth. A plan to compile a photographic map of the sky was launched by Mouchez at the International Congress of 1887, with the participation of a score of observatories using the photographic telescope invented by Henry. At the observatory at the Cape of Good Hope they expected that a photographic map of the stars would be produced by 1891. When one realizes that such a catalog is still incomplete, and perhaps impossible, the real question posed by the application of photography to vision through instruments is seen to be that of the utility and

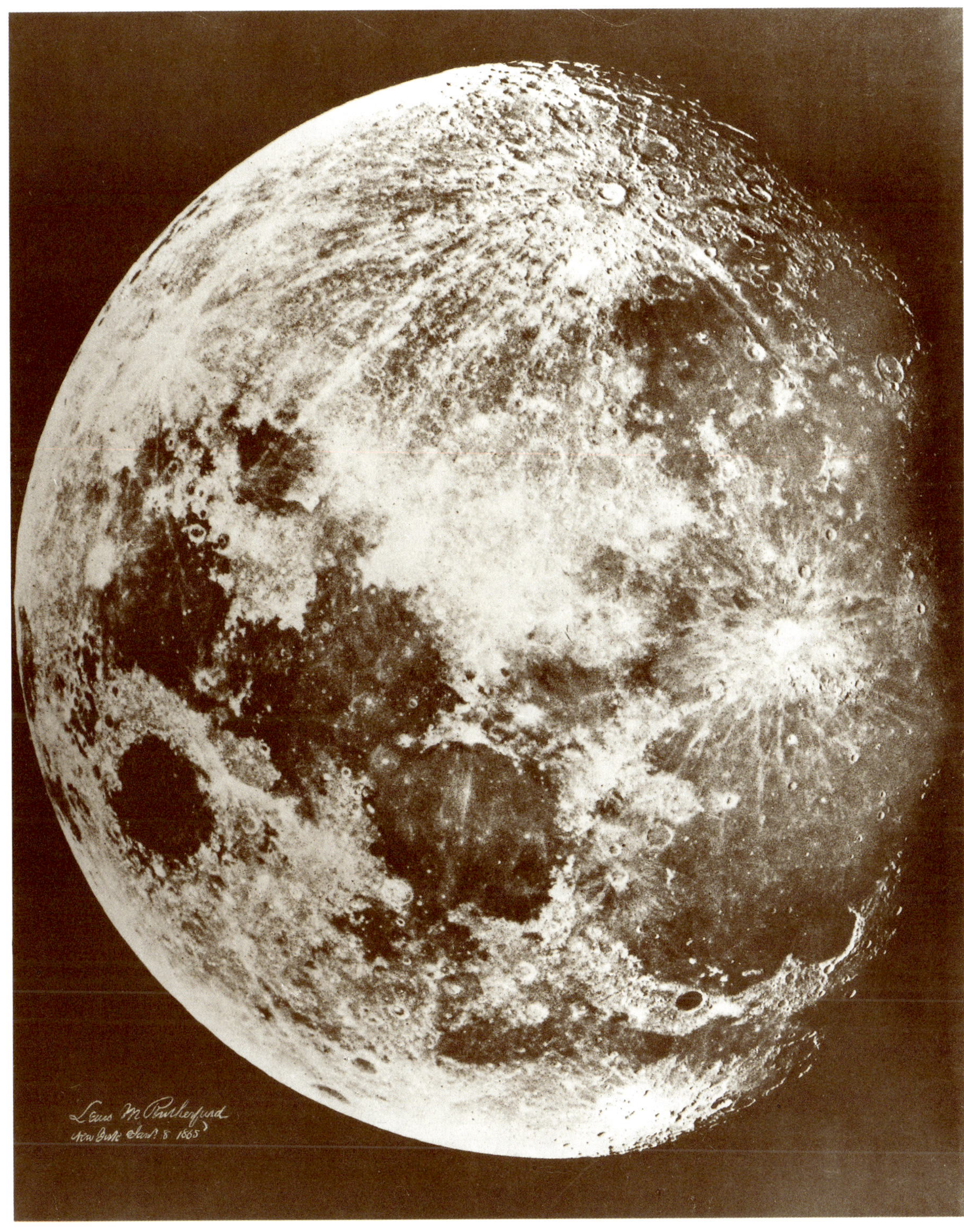

LEWIS M. RUTHERFÖRD,
Photograph of the Moon,
1865,
Société Française de Photographie, Paris.

the capacity of the photographic surface. Does it give us exactly the image that our eye sees via the instrument, or does it permit us to capture and record signals that remain invisible to us?

Special emulsions appeared, adapted to the needs of astronomy, with the result that here and there, in limited areas, photography became a procedure capable of going beyond all the limits of human vision. For the astronomer, the ability to perceive and analyze numerically became more important than seeing an image (in any case it might be asked what sort of image is constituted by a white dot on a black background). "It is photographic photometry, among the most modern branches of astronomy as the century draws to an end. It is the image of the stars fixed upon the surface of a sensitive plate that has become the object of all these endeavors."[22] At the end of the century the moon once again became the focus of detailed attention. By enlarging negative plates, Loewy and Puiseux produced their *Atlas photographique de la Lune* (1896–1910).

Under certain circumstances, the relative insensitivity of the daguerreotype process could actually be an advantage. When the astronomer Jules César Janssen was making his plans to photograph the passage of Venus in front of the sun on

22. A. Cornu, "La Photographie céleste", in *Conférences publiques sur la Photographie organisées en 1891-1892*, CNAM, Paris, Gauthier-Villars, 1893, and J. Janssen, *La Photographie astronomique, ibid.*

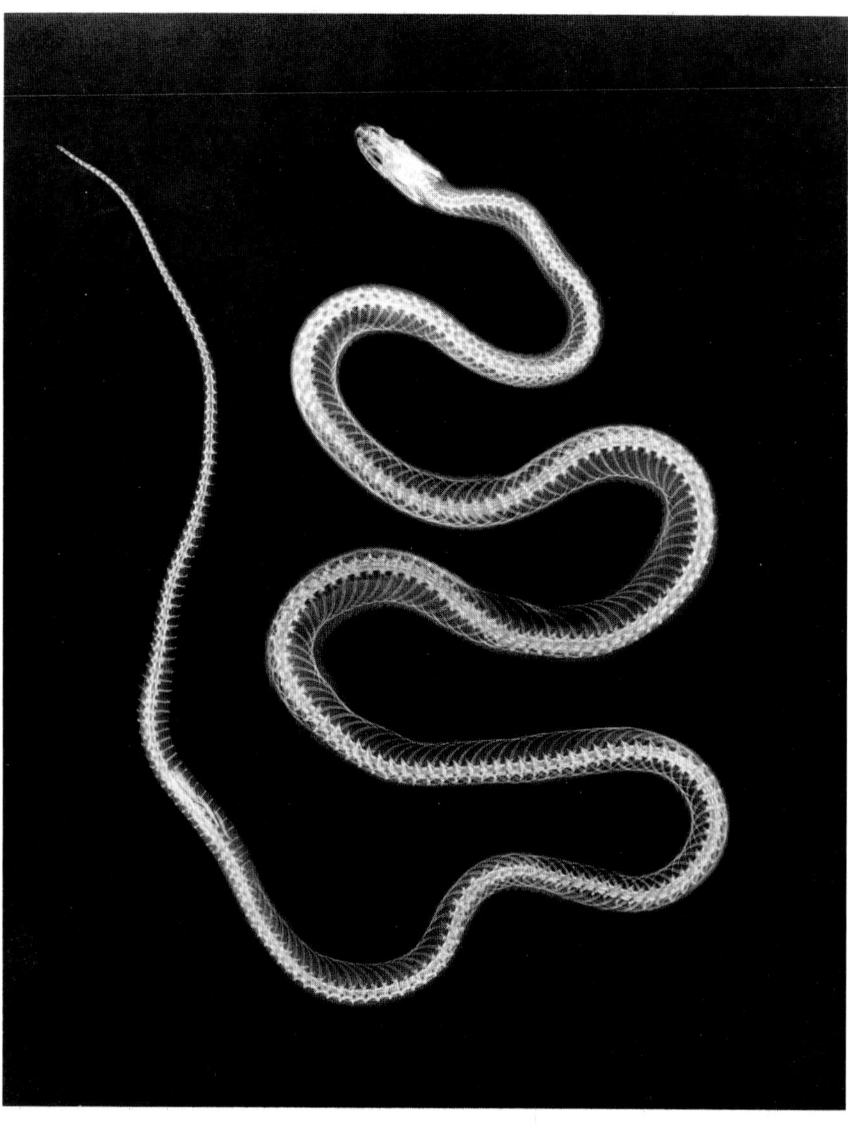

WALTER KÖNIG, *X-Ray photograph of a reptile,* 1896, Deutsches Röntgen Museum, Remscheid.

9 December 1874, using a rotating system that would take a photo a second (the "photographic revolver"), he decided, at the suggestion of his colleague Fizeau, to use the by then obsolete daguerreotype process, which would be more reliable for micrometric procedures. This apparatus was set up on the observation-site in Japan,[23] where it took 48 images in 71 seconds. (Adaptations of Janssen's apparatus were used, with albumenized plates, by the British teams in Egypt.) The experiment was important for its contribution to experimental procedures rather than for the intrinsic validity of its results. The "revolver" is considered, despite the great difference in speed, to have furnished the basic idea for the "photographic gun" suggested by Marey in 1879.

Beyond vision

One of the characteristics of photography in the scientific domain is its ability to go beyond the limits of normal "white" light. As early as 1842, Draper had obtained absorption lines in ultraviolet and infra-red (15-minute exposure), proving that the sensitive plate also reacted to non-visible luminous radiations. Talbot himself had thought very early on (in 1844) of taking photographs using infra-red radiation alone. The same idea was expressed by Niépce de Saint-Victor in 1859.[24] The first examples of an ultraviolet spectrum were obtained by W. A. Miller in 1864. The main drift of this research was therefore to register the existence of radiations invisible to the eye, but recorded by photographic emulsions.

X-rays form part of this invisible radiation. They can, however, be seen by the naked eye when they produce an emission of light (described as "secondary") on impact with certain materials. These rays were discovered by Röntgen at the Institute of Physics at the University of Würzburg in Bavaria in 1895, when he was working in a totally closed room, with a Crookes tube (a cathode-ray tube) surrounded by black cardboard and, consequently, unable to emit by itself any visible light. Röntgen then noticed a faint light, apparently engendered by the functioning of the Crookes tube (in use since 1879) on a panel coated with a fluorescent substance. He also noticed that the shadow of the bones of his hand appeared on the panel when he held it in front of the light-source. This discovery revealed two phenomena of light and shadow: a secondary emission of light evoked by unknown rays (christened "X") and a shadow produced by placing in their path certain substances (bones, metal) that are opaque to X-rays. From there came the idea of photographing the phenomenon, which manifests itself not only by a measur-

WILHELM RÖNTGEN, ▶ *X-Ray photograph of Mrs. Röntgen's hand,* December 22, 1895, Deutsches Museum, Munich.

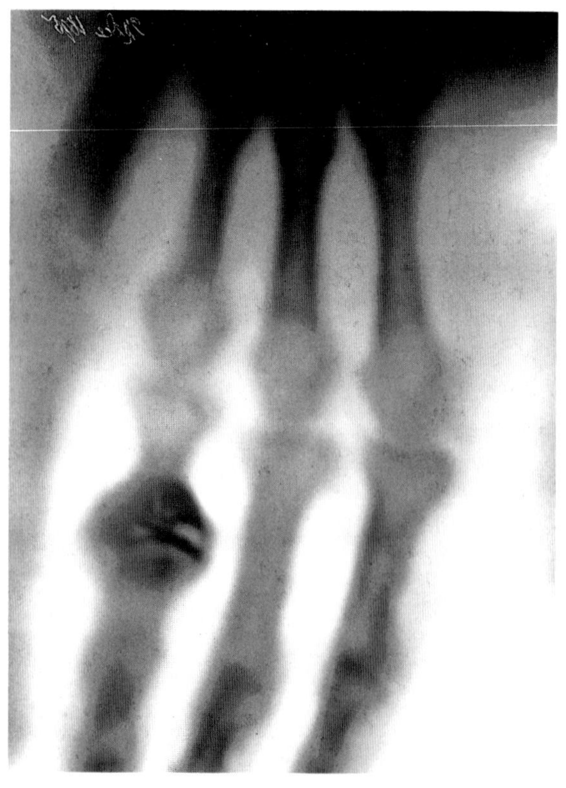

23. Académie des Sciences, March 17, 1873, and *Bulletin de la Société française de Photographie,* April 7, 1876.

24. Emulsions of this type were on general sale in the twentieth century, in black and white and color, sometimes called false color.

able quantity of light, but also by the visible differences it reveals within bodies, due to the heterogeneity of their composition. Röntgen photographed the door of his laboratory in this way, "radiographing" it (shining rays through it), and recording the impact of the rays on a photographic surface (one could see the metal handle and traces of lead paint; the wood was transparent to the rays). Then he photographed the hand of his wife Bertha (December 22, 1895), the definitive image of radiography. Röntgen's X-rays had acquired international renown by the beginning of 1896. Exposure times, between 15 minutes and one hour to start with, rapidly dropped to a few minutes when special emulsions were manufactured by Eastman and Ilford. This type of radiation behaved in the same way as visible light. People were starting to record diffractions of X-rays in 1912, and produce spectrograms of X-rays in 1916.[25]

The discovery of X-rays and their effects had considerable repercussions on modern thought. What had been demonstrated was that a completely invisible emanation could manifest its presence on a photographic plate (the mode of operation and technical intermediaries were soon forgotten), and that this invisible emanation could be used to make visible the internal reality of the body which was also invisible – a kind of "inner life". A popular book by E. N. Santini (editor of *Science en Famille*), published by *Photo Revue*, was called *La Photographie à travers les corps opaques par les Rayons électriques, cathodiques et de Röntgen avec une étude sur les Images photofulgurales* [Photography through Opaque Bodies by means of Electric, Cathod, and Röntgen Rays, with a Study of Photofulgural Images]. The emphatically eclectic title betrays an amalgamation of experimental science with fantasies about apparitions and the unveiling of secrets. From considering X-rays, the text moves onto the effects of lightning, electrical fluids, and "fulgural radiations" supposed to emanate from all bodies, especially in darkness. A "new branch of study" was announced: photographic imprints obtained without any light, by the sole action of mysterious rays, the existence of which was thereby taken as proved.

Hippolyte Baraduc was the "high priest" of this religion based on the supposed existence of a "vital force" similar to X-rays, and capable of forming images on photographic plates. His book *L'Âme humaine* (the human soul) was written, significantly, in 1896 (he discovered "spontaneous iconography" in February 1896, but said he had written the book in 1895, at Mont-St. Michel).[26] A gynecologist, and author of works on the stomach and on hysteria, Baraduc started out from the principle that there is a "subtle force" which manifests itself directly on the sensitive plate. There were imprints of this kind, which could be observed fortuitously on photographic plates. This impact on photographic material from the "field of the invisible" was the sole proof he adduced for his theory. "The invisible fluid

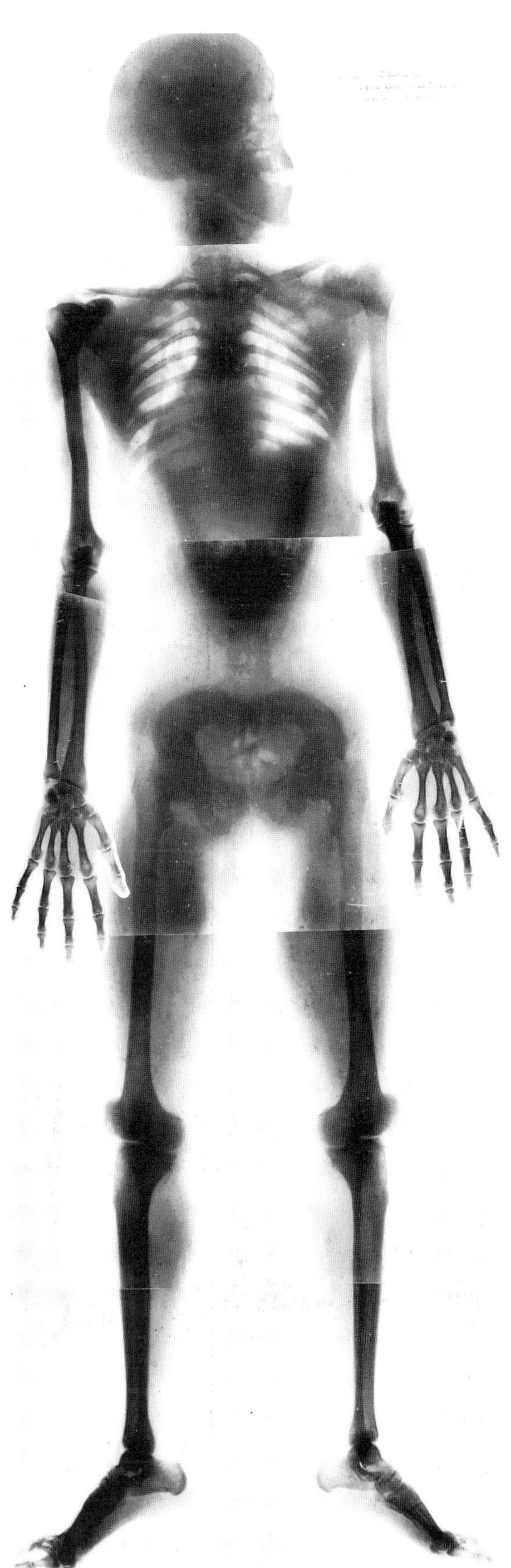

LUDWIG ZEHNDER,
X-Ray photograph of a human body,
(montage of nine films),
August 1896,
Deutsches Museum,
Munich.

25. A. Londe, *La Radiographie et ses diverses Applications*, Paris, Gauthier-Villars, 1889; G. H. Niewenglovski, *La Photographie de l'Invisible au Moyen des Rayons X* [...], Paris, Société des Éditions Scientifiques, 1896.

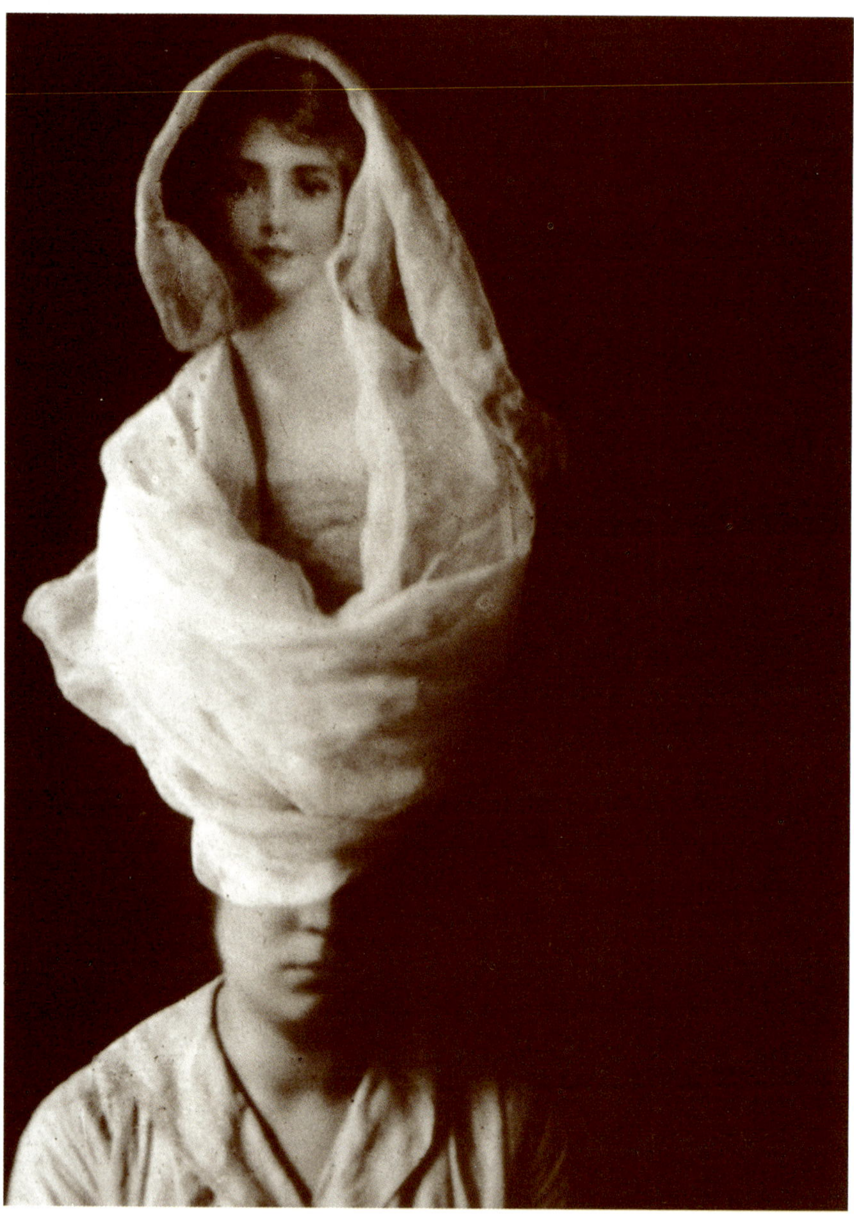

MRS. DEANE, *Ectoplasm and Spirit Image*, about 1920, University of Texas, Austin.

mediums and ectoplasms.[29] For at least a decade there was a general idea that photography "has become an irrefutable witness to the radiation of the human soul".[30] Even a man like Marcel Duchamp was touched by its influence, as can be seen in some of his paintings (*Portrait of Dr. Dumouchel*, 1910), and in his general interest in photography, which he imagined would eventually supplant painting.[31]

At the end of the nineteenth century, science was more changeable and indeterminate than in the more positivist period, the invention and early spread of photography. In 1900, the basic issue seemed to have reversed itself: from being an authentic imprint of what is real (and *a priori* visible), photography had become, in the most scientific way possible, the proof of the reality of the invisible. Was it by chance that this period brought another discovery on the boundary of religion and the irrational? A public exhibition of the holy shroud of Turin – a relic of uncertain origin – which took place over the course of a week in May 1898 attracted a million people. Secondo Pia, a photographer who was also a lawyer, was authorized to make a photographic reproduction of the shroud. He found, when developing his glass negatives, that they gave a "real" picture of Christ, whereas the original was difficult to see. People were inclined to think that the imprint visible on the holy shroud was something like a "negative image", by analogy with the photographic negative. Its reversal to a positive image by photography rendered its contours

manifests itself by its own intimate, luminous, intrinsic force [...] In a word, one must know how to induce the psycho-odo-fluid current which the plate records as it passes by."[27] The luminous vibration of a soul which "draws itself" on a sensitive plate is the "iconography". The images can appear on any photographic plate, whether or not it is in a camera or pointing at a particular subject.

Around 1900, there was a great deal of research into these questions, which were not without interest in relation to how one notoriously invisible entity, the Unconscious, might express itself.[28] For Baraduc, his discoveries were very different from spirit photography, for the photographers "see the apparition that they are photographing"; he himself had "never seen what happened on the plate". The fashion for spirit photography had begun with photography on glass, which lent itself to all kinds of manipulation, particularly superimposition. Albert de Rochas had also just published his research into

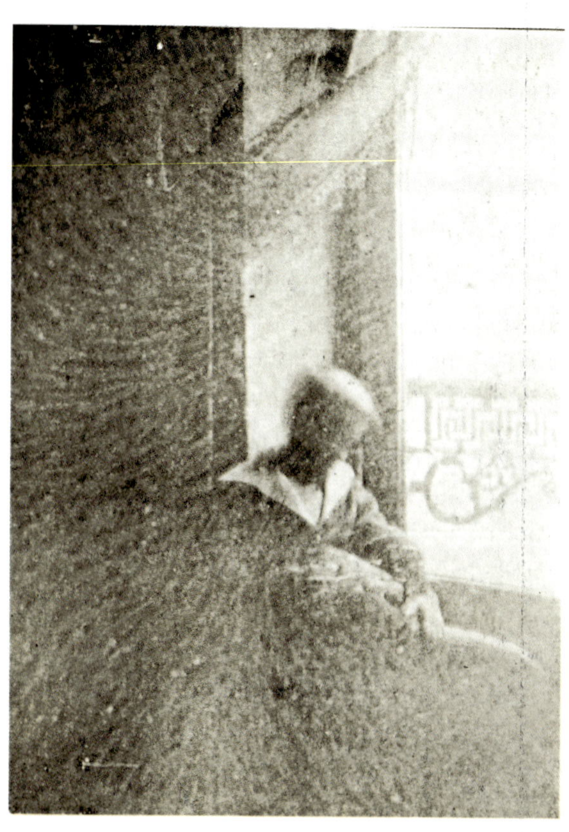

HIPPOLYTE BARADUC, ▶ *Vital Force Attracted by a Child's Feeling of Tenderness*, plate taken from H. Baraduc, *L'Âme humaine*, 1896.

26. *L'Âme humaine, ses Mouvements, ses Lumières, et l'Iconographie de l'Invisible fluidique*, Paris, G. Carré, 1896.

27. H. Baraduc, *op. cit.*, pp. 4 and 5.

28. A. A. Guébhard, *Sur les prétendus Enregistrements photographiques du Fluide vital*, Paris, 1895.

29. *L'Extériorisation de la Sensibilité: étude expérimentale et historique*, Paris, 1895.

perfectly *legible*. This discovery gave a new theological value to the shroud. Its possible authenticity, corroborated by photography, took on a very different resonance. The shroud itself could be considered as a sensitive plate upon which the emanations of a body had left their impression.[32] Pia having been accused of fraud, a new series of photographs were carried out in 1931 on the occasion of King Umberto's wedding. They were more precise (see the beginning of this chapter), but the latest tests to date the cloth (1988) indicate that it is medieval in origin.

The beauty of chance

For a long time, photographic plates were used as *detectors* of radiation within the spectrum of visible light (and a little beyond), while also functioning as a measure of luminosity (photography by telescope, for instance, works by the concentration of photons on the plate). The idea emerged of using the camera as a watching device, patiently awaiting an event, in the same way that flashes of lightning could be caught on camera by leaving the shutter open in darkness. The products of the bombardment by alpha rays (helium nuclei) of other atoms (nuclear disintegration) were first observed as scintillations on a fluorescent screen (E. Rutherford 1918), then in bubble-filled compartments (Wilson's cloud chamber) by P. M. Blackett around 1925. The particles bring about, through ionization, the formation of bubbles of gas which leave a trail of light as they pass which can be photographed. To record a very rare phenomenon, millions of trajectories have to appear on millions of photographs. The sudden appearance of an oblique line in a sheaf of vertical ones represents for someone who knows how to read the image a discovery of particular importance or an observation of great rarity.

One failure to read such an image which has become famous and symbolizes perfectly the difficulty of translating the visible into the legible is that of the French scientists Irène Curie and Frédéric Joliot in the course of their attempts to demonstrate experimentally the existence of the neutron. In 1932, they were using a cloud chamber, bombarding a target of beryllium with alpha rays emitted by polonium. They did not understand the photograph that was obtained, though it was perfectly clear to others who were expecting the effect which showed up on it: a neutron freed in the horizontal white zone, in the upward direction, displaces a proton (nucleus of hydrogen) which produces a trace of ionization (oblique white line). The proof of the existence of the neutron was legible via its effects for James Chadwick of the Cavendish laboratories, who successfully repeated the experiment.[33]

As an instrument of detection and measurement, photography was the ultimate aid to science in the twentieth century, until it was

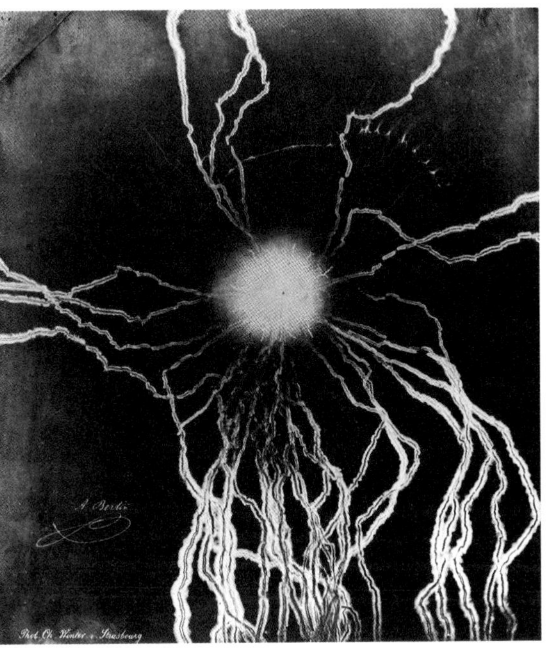

Charles Winter, ***Electrical discharge from a Ruhmkorff machine***, 1850s, Cabinet des Estampes, Strasbourg.

John W. Draper, ***Absorption spectrum of sunlight, obtained with a prism***, daguerreotype, July 27, 1842, Science Museum, London.
▼

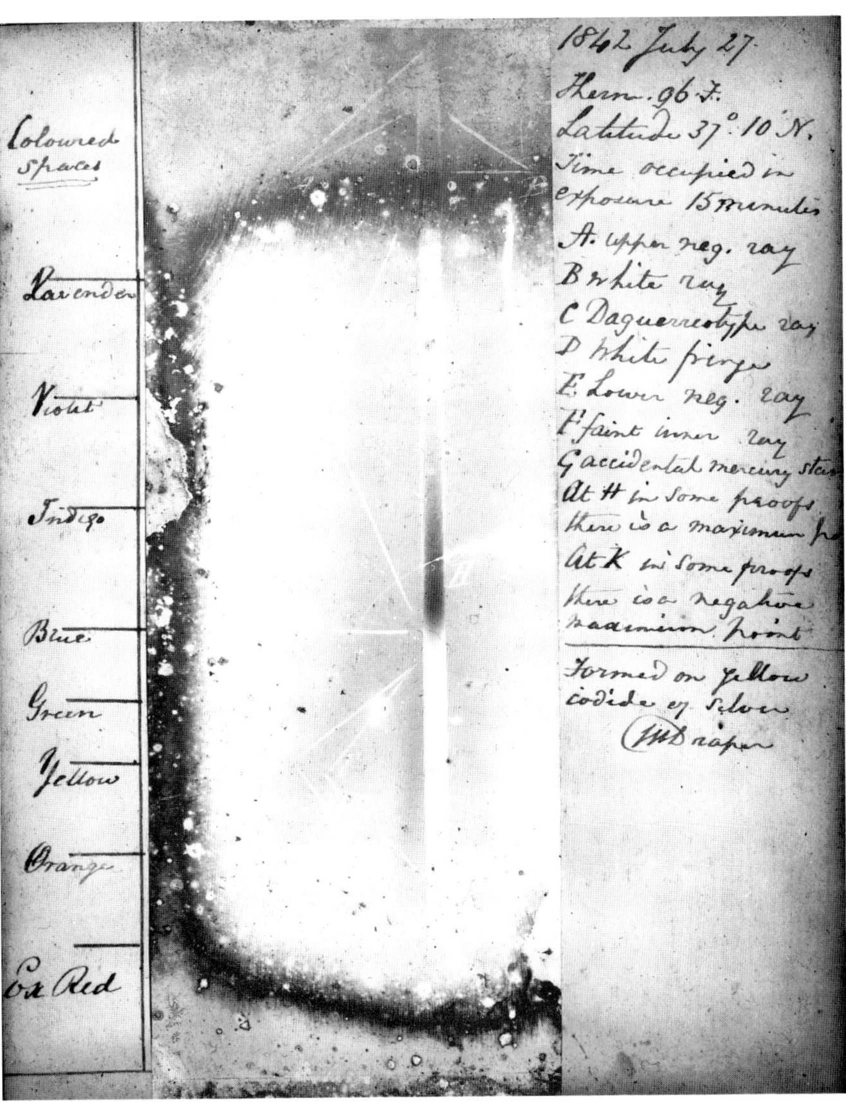

30. Ducasse-Harispe, *La Photographie du Monde invisible*, Paris, Mandélieu, 1909; G. de Fontenay, *La Photographie et l'étude des Phénomènes psychiques*, Paris, Gauthier-Villars, 1912; *La Photographie transcendantale, les êtres et les Radiations de l'Espace*, Paris, Librairie Nationale, 1911.

31. J. Clair, *Duchamp et la Photographie*, Paris, Chêne, 1977.

32. P. Vignon, *Le Linceul du Christ: étude scientifique*, Paris, Masson, 1902.

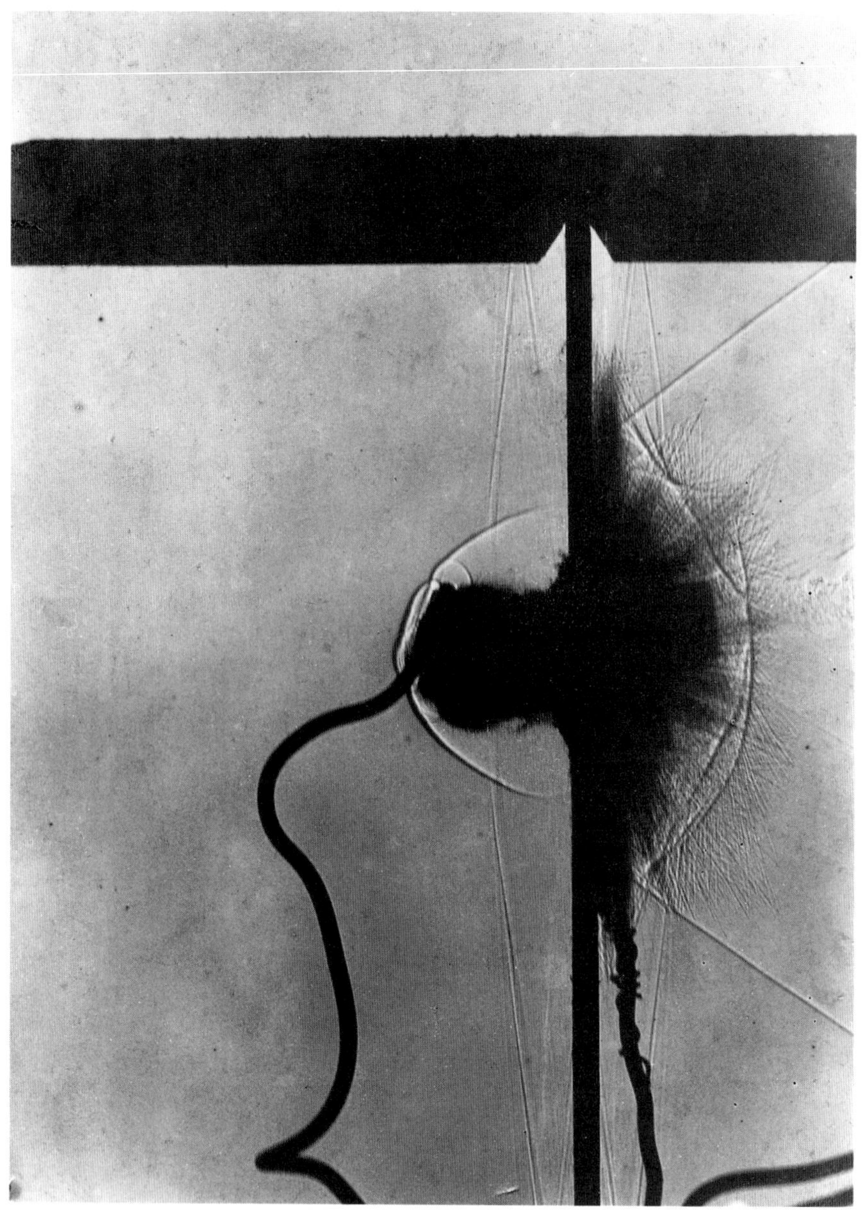

C. V. BOYS,
Shock wave produced by a bullet passing through a pane of glass,
1893,
Science Museum, London.

This was precisely what attracted artists of the 1920s, who saw in the manifestations of scientific photography a constituent element of the New Photography, a new world of images, at once imitative of nature and unexpected, unpredictable. László Moholy-Nagy and Werner Gräff reproduced them in their works,[34] and photomicrographs by Laure Albin-Guillot[35] and Julius Widmayer shared the opening pages of *Photographie* (AGM 1930) with x-ray photographs and spectrograms: "Modern photographers owe it to themselves to use the means that Röntgen put at their disposal."[36] It could be said that the New Photographer scrutinizing matter with his camera turned in all directions was using it now as a microscope, now as a telescope.

replaced by other photosensitive detectors (photoelectric cells), in particular in spectrography, or by cathodic monitoring screens, which can, as a last resort, also be photographed for archive purposes or for the analysis of data.

The physicist, Max Planck, author of the quantum theory, admitted that atomic phenomena were beyond "visualization" (*Anschaulichkeit*), but he also maintained that the unity of physics demanded, in the ultimate instance, the formation of "an image of the world". The issue of visualization was actively debated as soon as photography entered the scientific arena. It even became a dogma: the visibility of something (which can only happen through the intermediary of light) is the proof of its existence. In the course of the twentieth century, while people realized that photography is only the proof of the emission of light, they also realized that the image – flat, fixed, instantaneous – is itself only a means of making intelligible a world made up of instability and uncertainty.

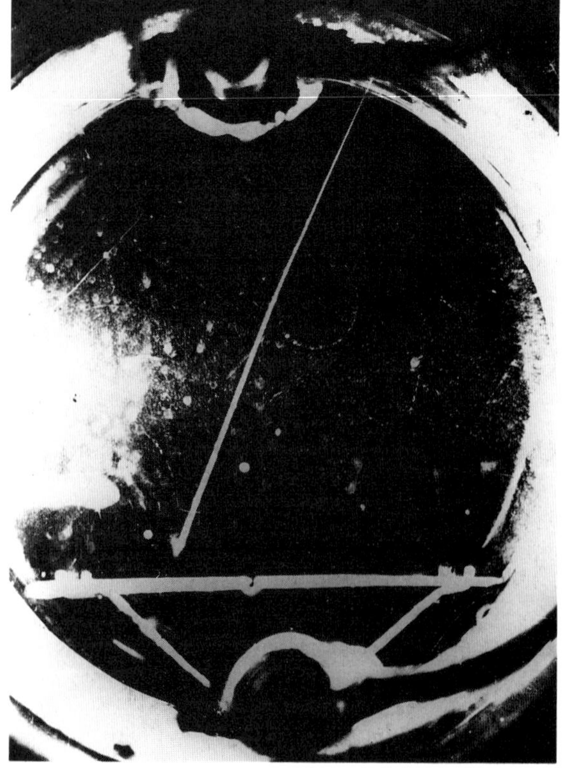

IRENE AND FRÉDÉRIC JOLIOT-CURIE, ▶
Detection of particles in a photograph of a cloud-chamber
(experiments to show the existence of the neutron),
January 1932,
Science Museum, London.

33. J. Darius, *Beyond Vision*, Oxford, Oxford University Press, 1984.

34. L. Moholy-Nagy, *Malerei, Fotografie, Film*, Munich, Lange, 1925; W. Gräff, *Es kommt der neue Fotograf*, Berlin, Reckendorf, 1929.

35. *Micrographie décorative*, Paris, Draeger, 1931.

36. W. George, introduction to *Photographie*, Paris, Arts et Métiers graphiques, 1930, p. 157.

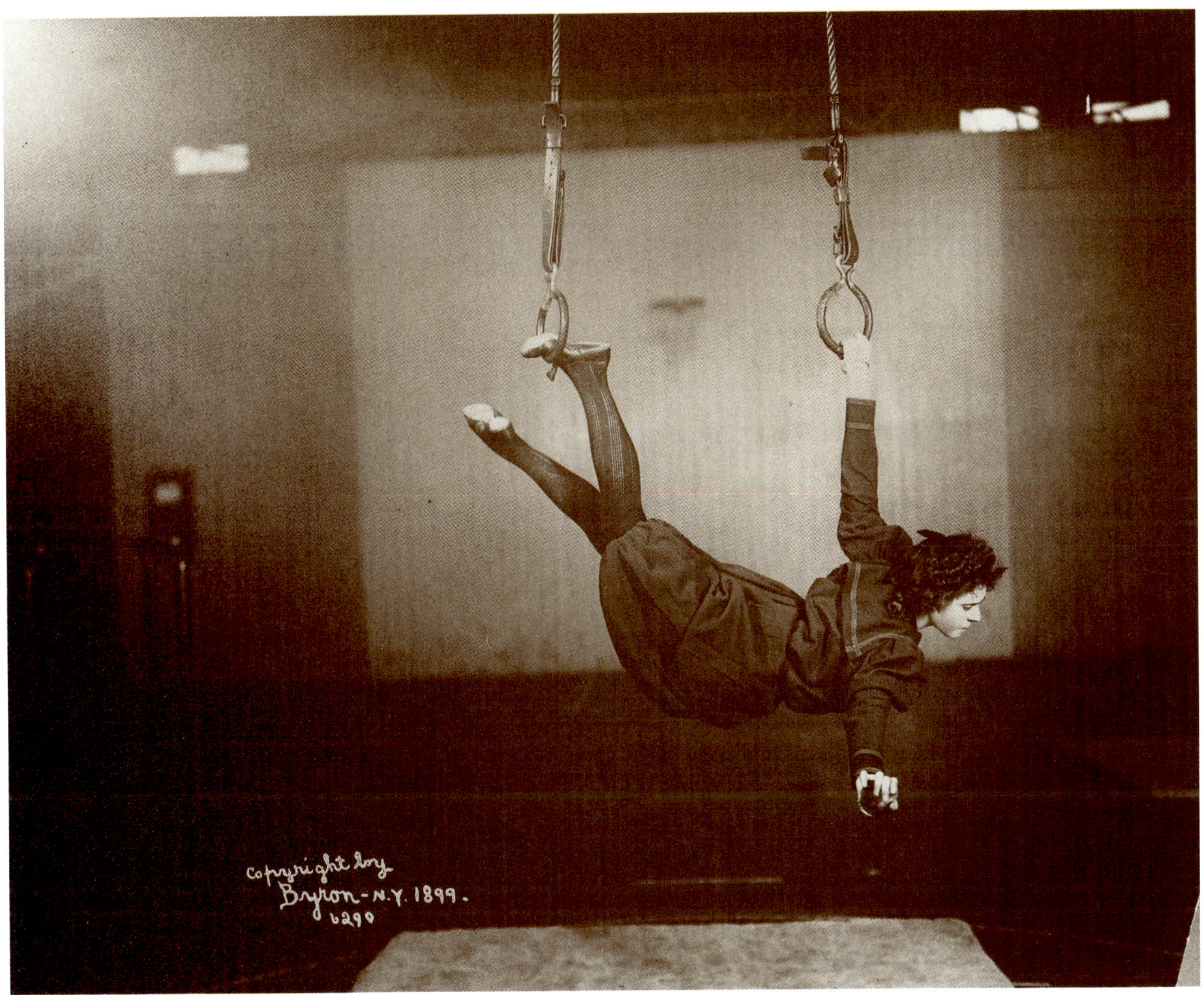

Artificial light

Clearly, there can be no photography unless there is sufficient light. In the absence of sunlight those sources of artificial light which seemed possible in theory turned out, for a long time, to be unsuitable in practice.

It was only from 1857 that "photogenetic substances" (inflammable powders) became available. Such preparations, which were similar to very bright fireworks, consisted of a mixture of charcoal, sulfur, potassium chlorate etc., which burned for several seconds but produced smoke which could spoil the scene. Magnesium, which appeared in 1859, had the same inconvenience, though to a lesser degree, and gave a brighter, sharper light. It could be used in string or ribbon form which burned as it unrolled as in a Salomon and Grant lamp or as a powder which was set alight by a spark or a match. This was how Piazzi Smyth photographed inside the great pyramid of Giza in 1865, and O'Sullivan inside the mines of Nevada in 1867.

In 1860, Nadar, who had just opened his new studio in the Boulevard des Capucines, opted for electric light which, at that time, meant carbon arc lamps powered by Bunsen batteries. After briefly setting up an "electric portrait salon", he undertook a spectacular adaptation of the process, transporting all his equipment into places inaccessible to sunlight: the catacombs and the sewers of Paris. In 1861, Nadar took pictures over a period of three months using collodion plates, exposing them for an average of one or two minutes, sometimes much longer, with one or several arc lights supplied by 50 batteries stored on the pavement above. By the end of the century, the photographic exploration of caves had become commonplace, but Nadar's series remains the most original, because of the strangeness of the location, the meditative atmosphere, and the emotional power of the pictures.

In the 1880s, new, more sensitive, plates could cope with flashes of light, generally produced by magnesium powder (Gaedicke and Miethe's "flashlight" 1/10 second, 1887). Jacob Riis, recognizing this innovation, used it at once, in 1888, for his photographs of the slums of New York. "Flash" quickly became a way of exploring places where there was not much light. Joseph Byron used it for American interiors and shops, Harry Ellis for his travels in Europe, Lewis Hine in factories and in the street, August Strindberg for his self-portraits, Herbert Ponting during the Scott expedition (in the Antarctic, 1910–1912).

Some amateurs, however, enjoyed the effort entailed in making a long exposure. Thus, we find G. B. Shaw sitting under an electric light, and Degas getting his circle to pose for several minutes under the glare of paraffin lamps (1895, portrait of Renoir and Mallarmé; Degas can be seen in the mirror).

In the 1890s, photography celebrated street lighting: Paul Martin in London (1896), Belliéni in Nancy and Paris (before 1900), Alfred Stieglitz, Alvin Langdon Coburn, and numerous Pictorialists took up this always surprising genre which was made popular by magazines, and became one of the favorite subjects for Pictorialism.

The strange sense of inanimate immutability, the impression of a world seen the other way round in reversed shades of light and dark are close to the *fin-de-siècle* preoccupations of the shadow-theatre (Henri Rivière photographed backstage in Montmartre).

Michel Frizot

FURTHER READING:
See R. Martin (ed.), *Floods of Light: Flash Photography*, 1851–1981, text by D. Mellor and G. Badger, London, The Photographer's Gallery, 1982.

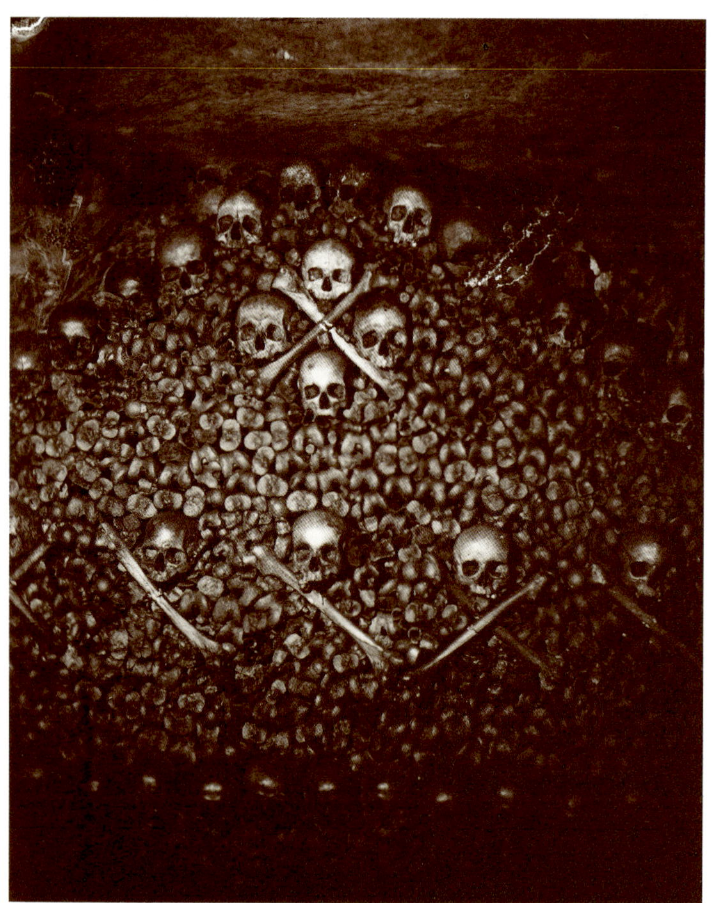

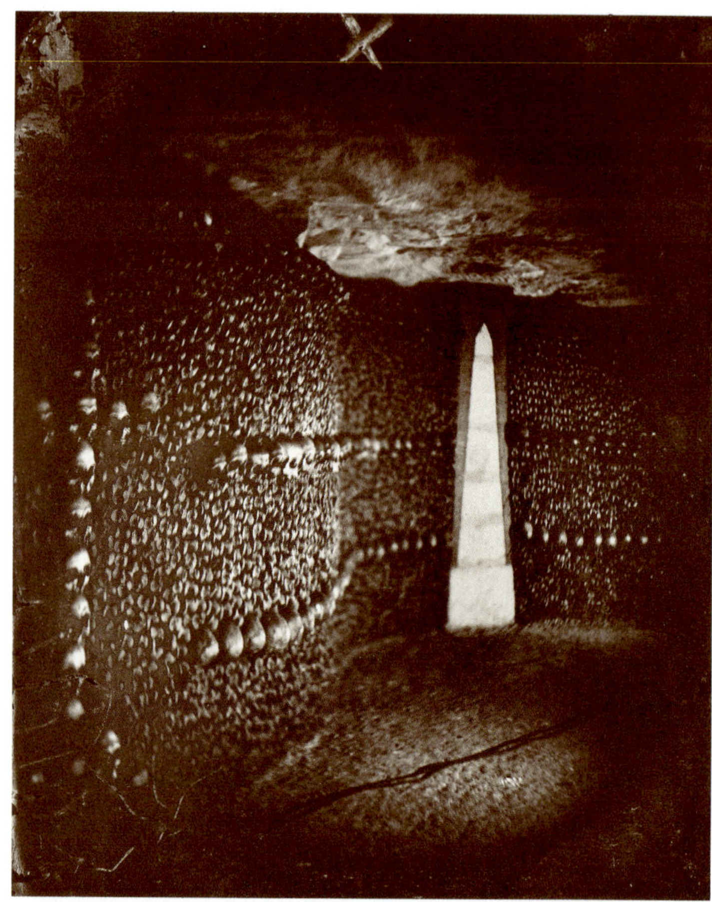

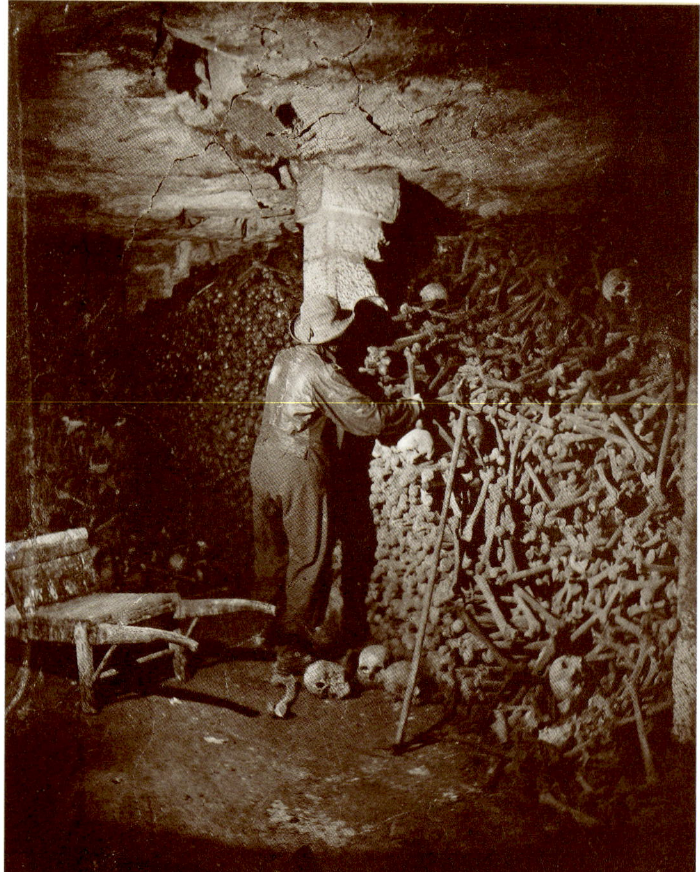

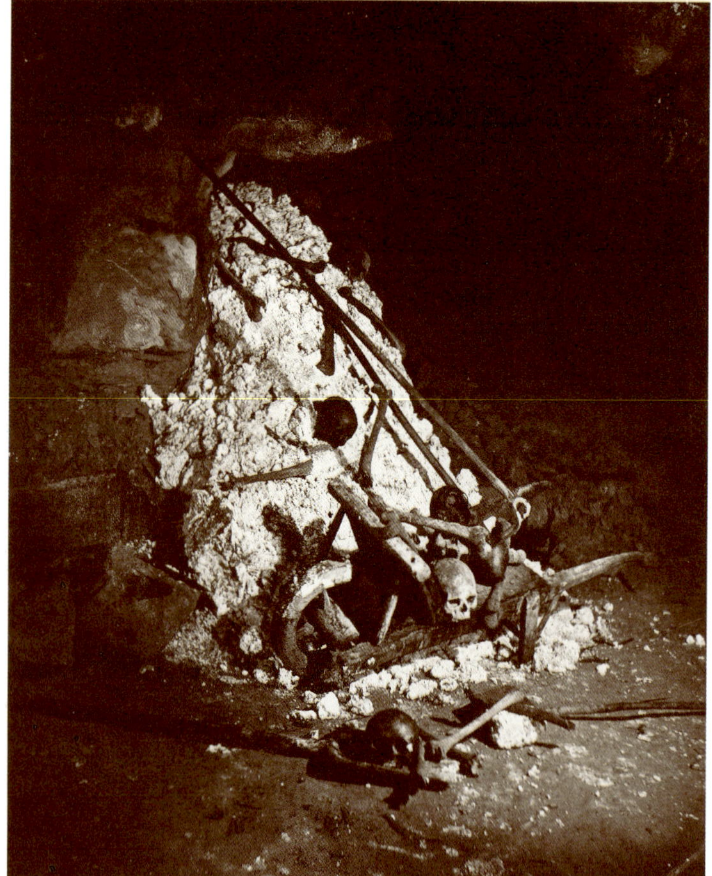

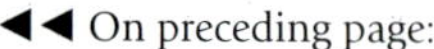

◀◀ On preceding page:

Joseph Byron,
Woman on Rings, Gymnasium, Dr. Savage's School,
New York, 1899,
Museum of the City of New York.

Nadar,
Catacombs of Paris,
1861,
Archives Photographiques,
Paris.

Nadar, ▶
Sewers of Paris, Photographer's Lights, under Notre-Dame Bridge,
1861,
Archives Photographiques, Paris.

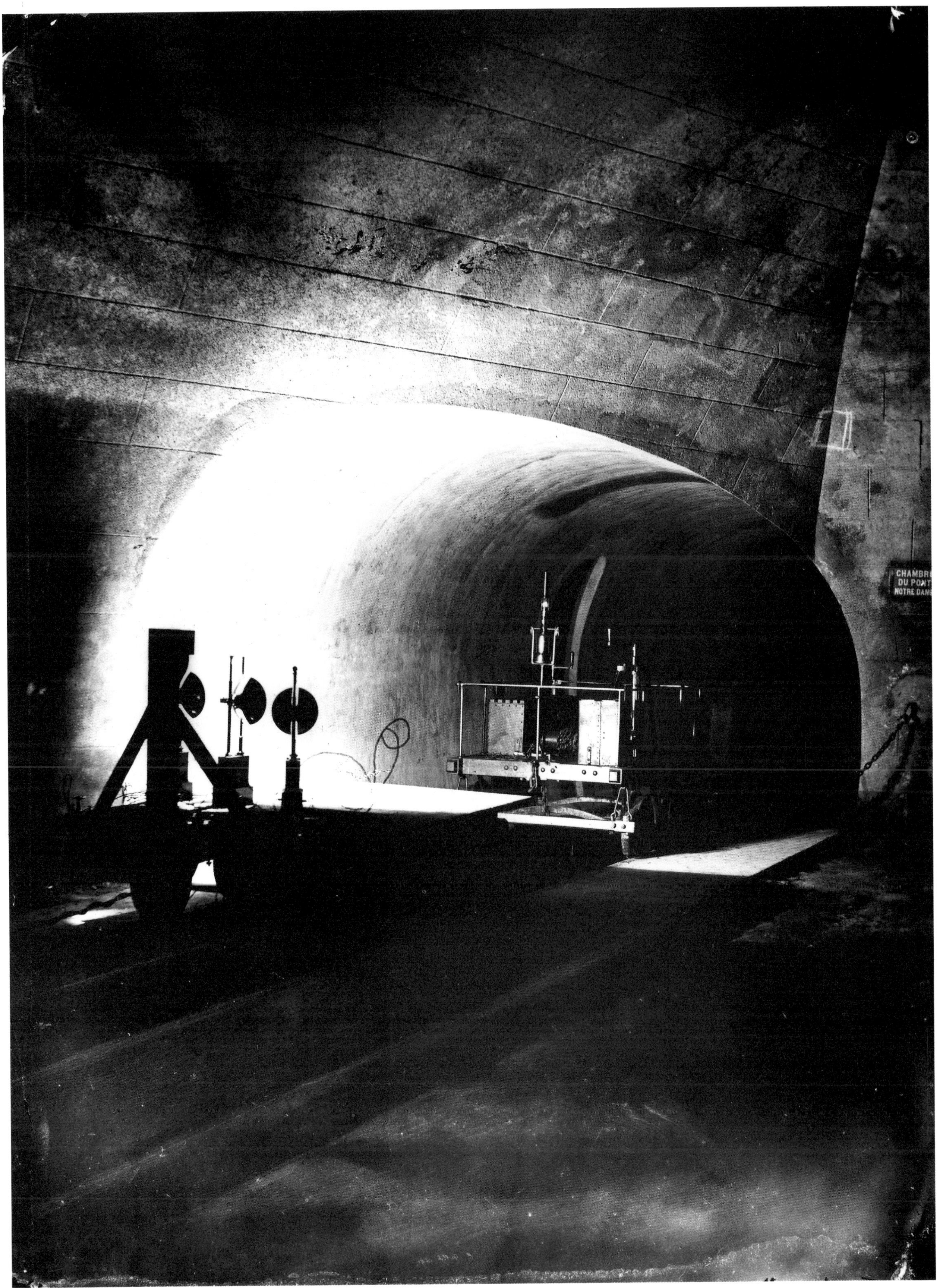
CHAMBR
DU PONT
NOTRE DAM

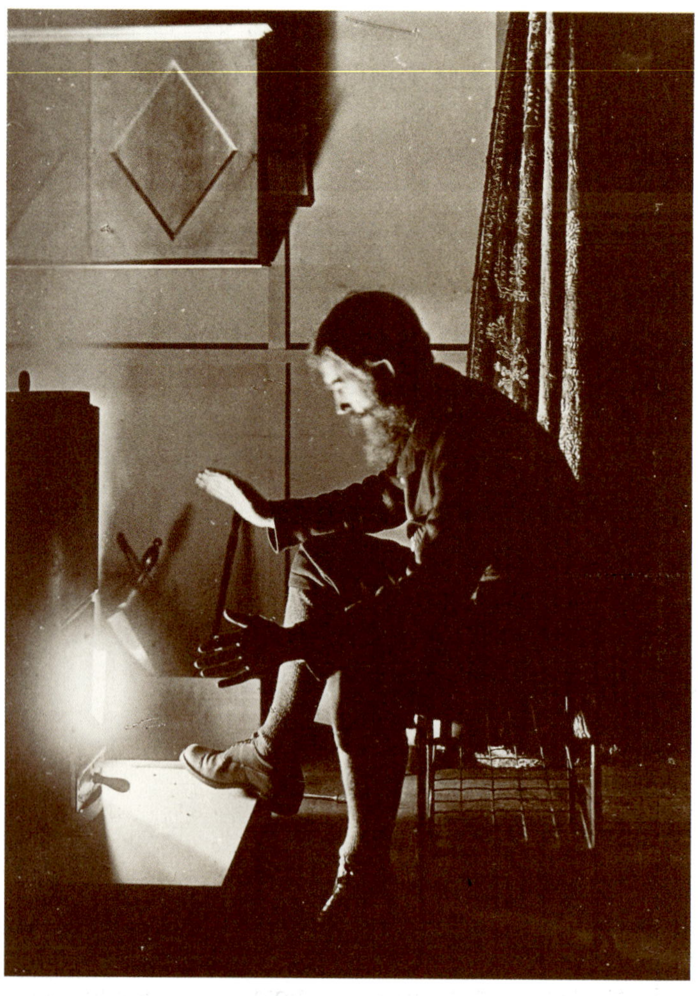

GEORGE BERNARD SHAW,
Self-portrait with Simulated Fire-effect,
circa 1900,
London School of Economics.

▲ AUGUST STRINDBERG,
Self-portrait by Flashlight,
Gersau, 1886,
Strindbergsmuseet, Stockholm.

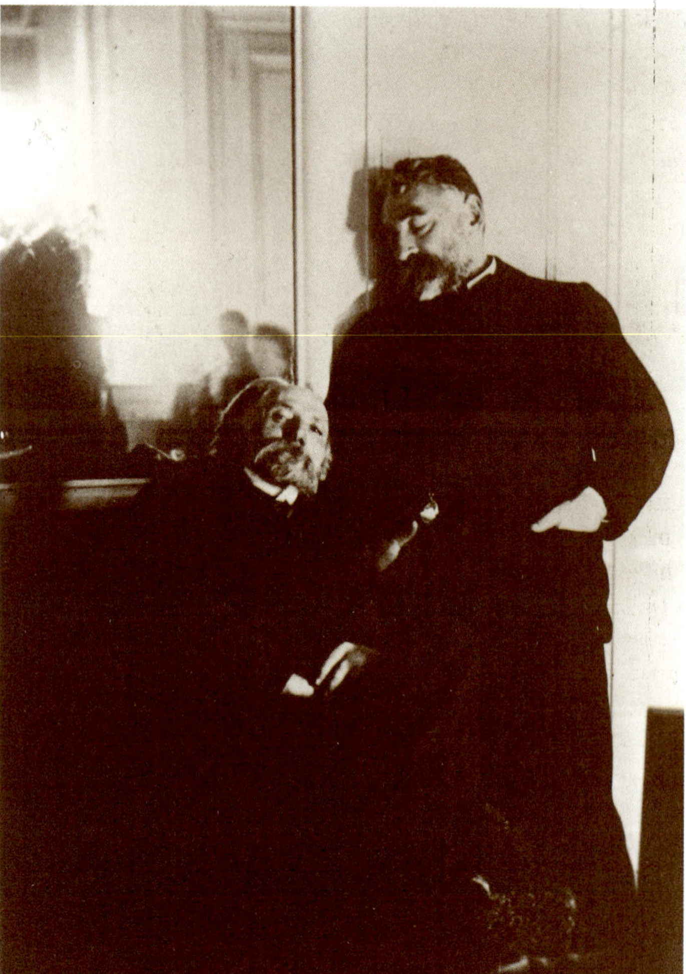

◀ EDGAR DEGAS,
Portrait of Renoir and Mallarmé,
1895.

GEORGE BERNARD SHAW,
Self-portrait Under the Lamp,
1904,
London School of Economics.

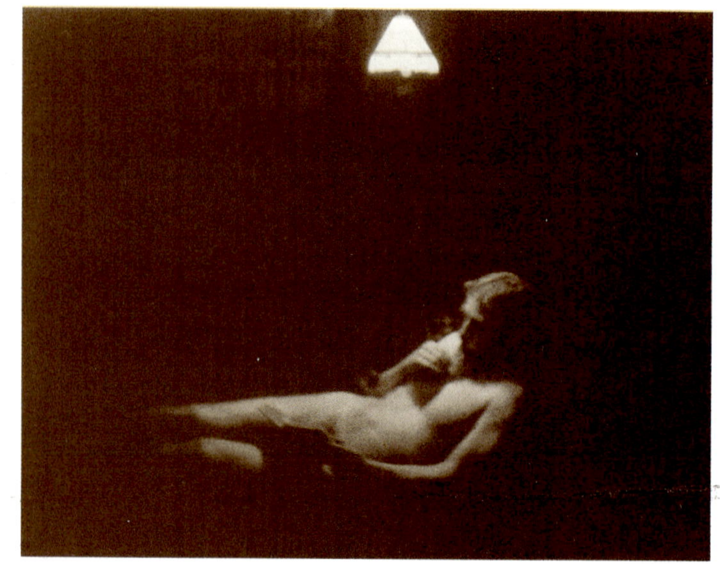

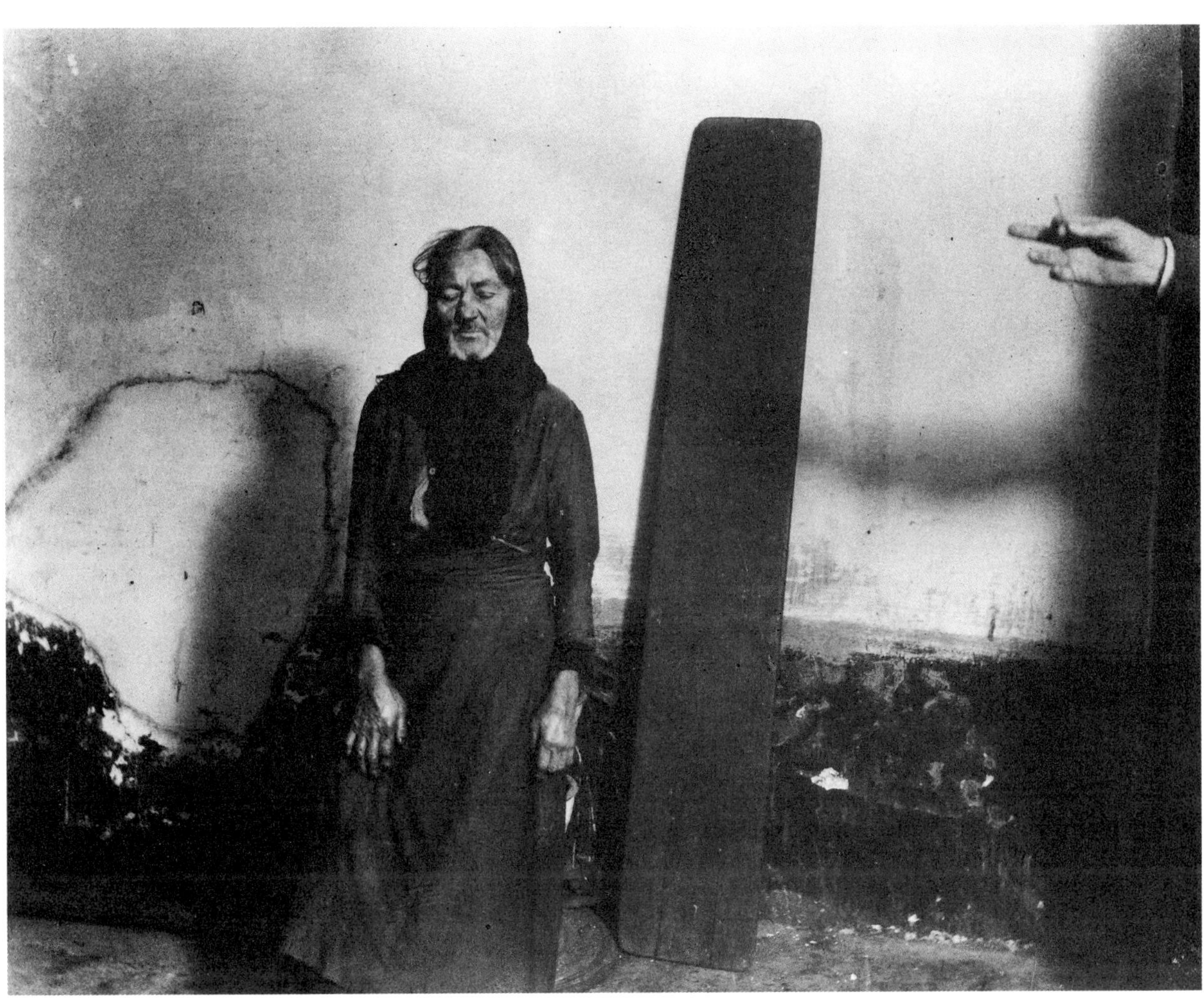

JACOB A. RIIS,
Ancient Lodger at Eldridge Street Police Station,
circa 1890,
Museum of the City of New York.

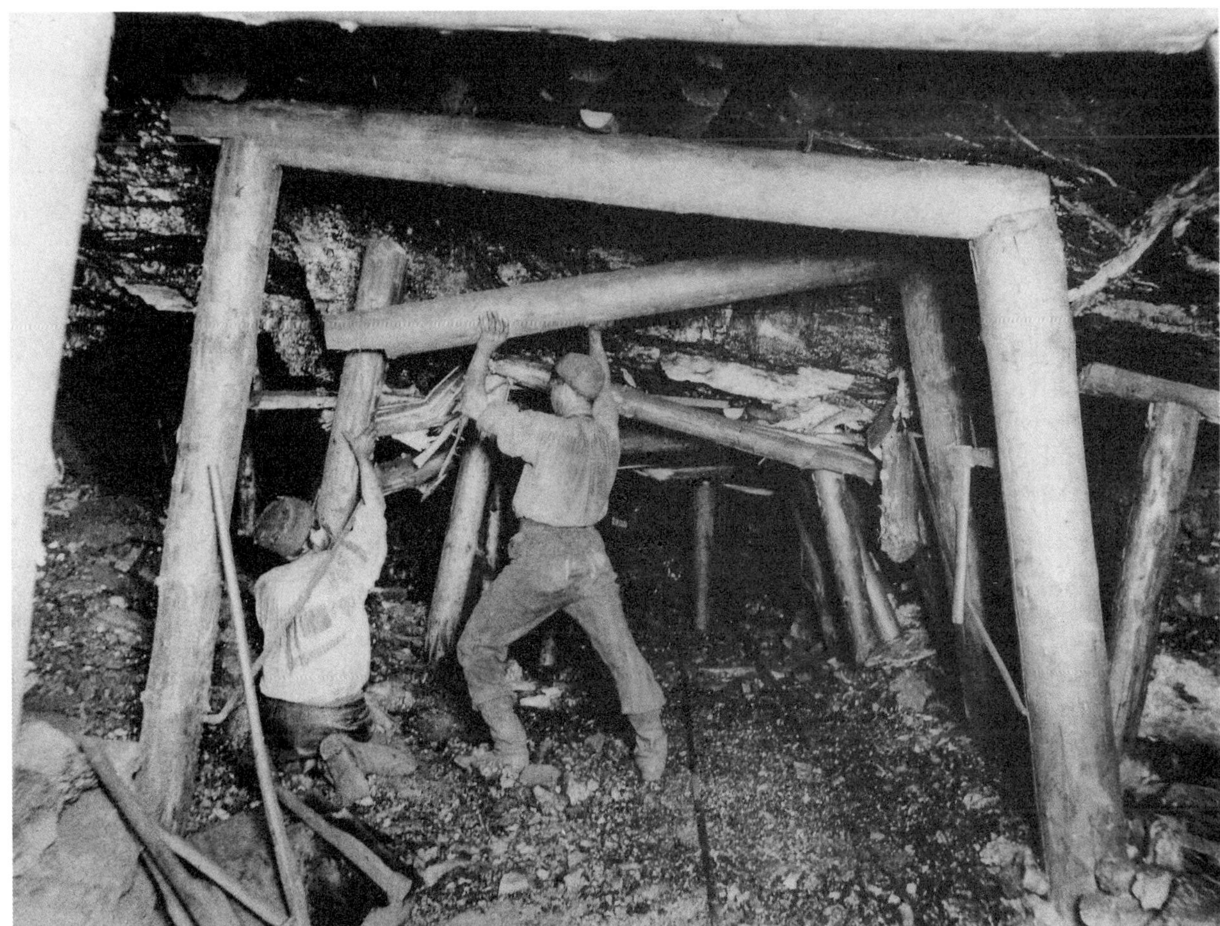

H. BÖRNER,
Propping up a Gallery in a Mine,
1893,
Heimat-und Bergbaumuseum,
Freital.

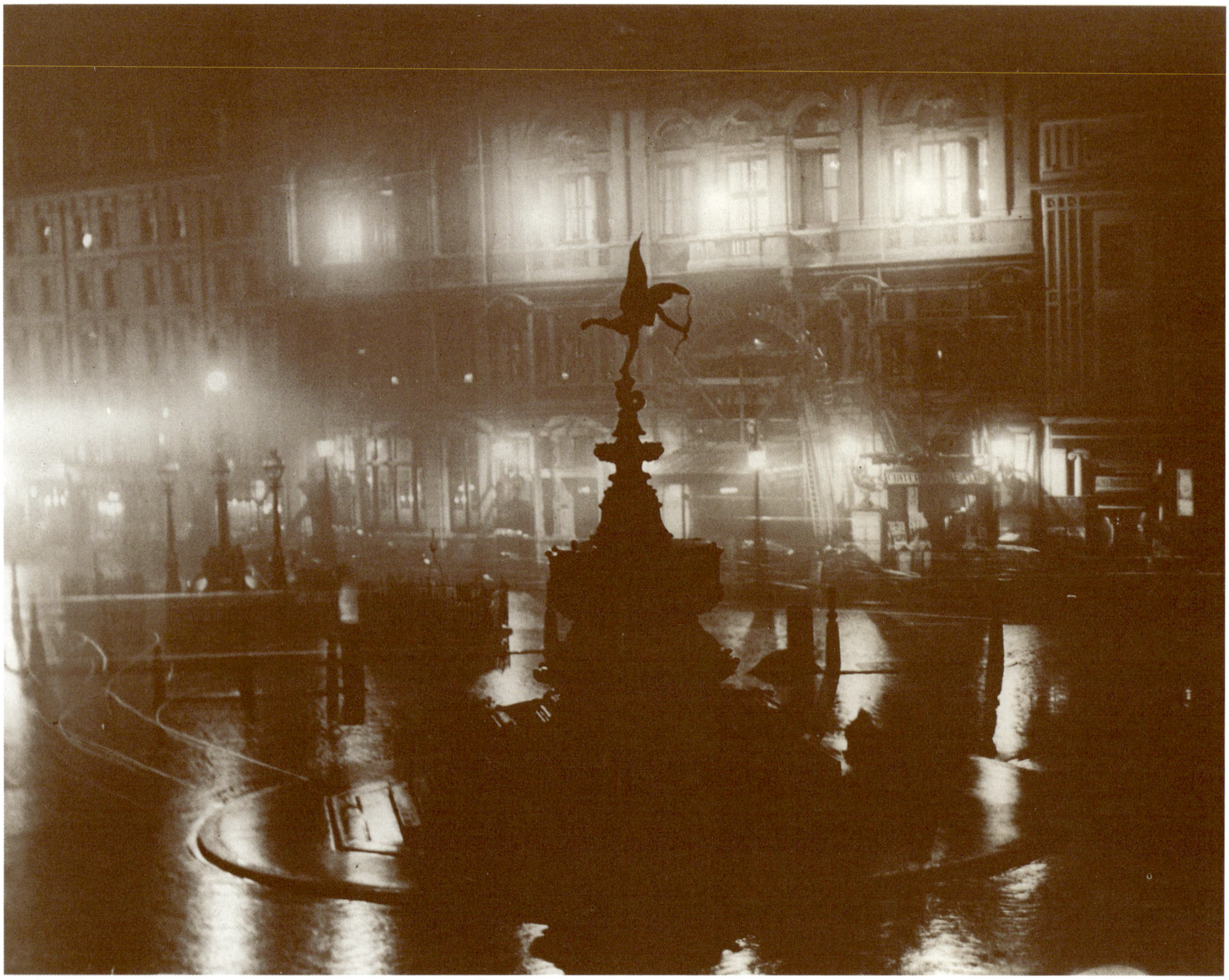

▲
Paul Martin,
Piccadilly Circus at Night, London,
1896,
University of Texas, Austin.

Alvin L. Coburn, ▶
Broadway at Night,
1909, from *New York,* 1910,
Royal Photographic Society, Bath.

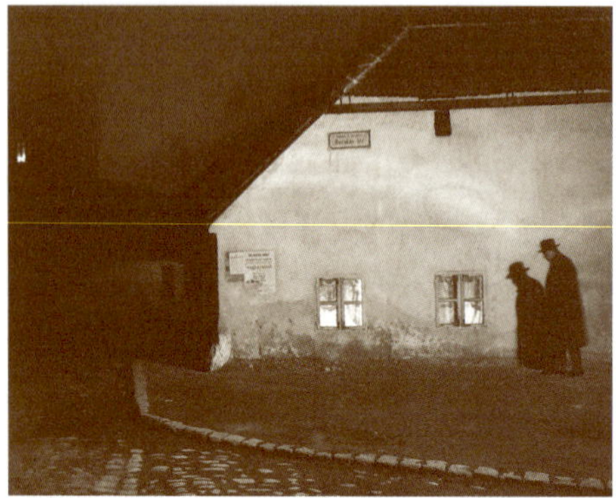

André Kertész,
Boskay ter
[Boskay Square],
Budapest,
1914.

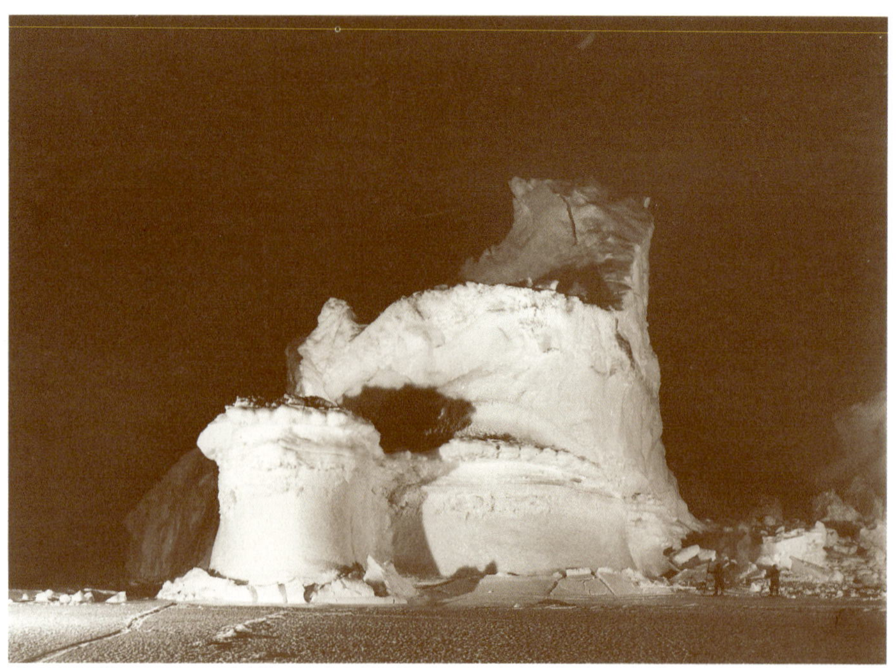

Herbert Ponting,
Iceberg, Antarctica,
Scott Expedition,
1911.

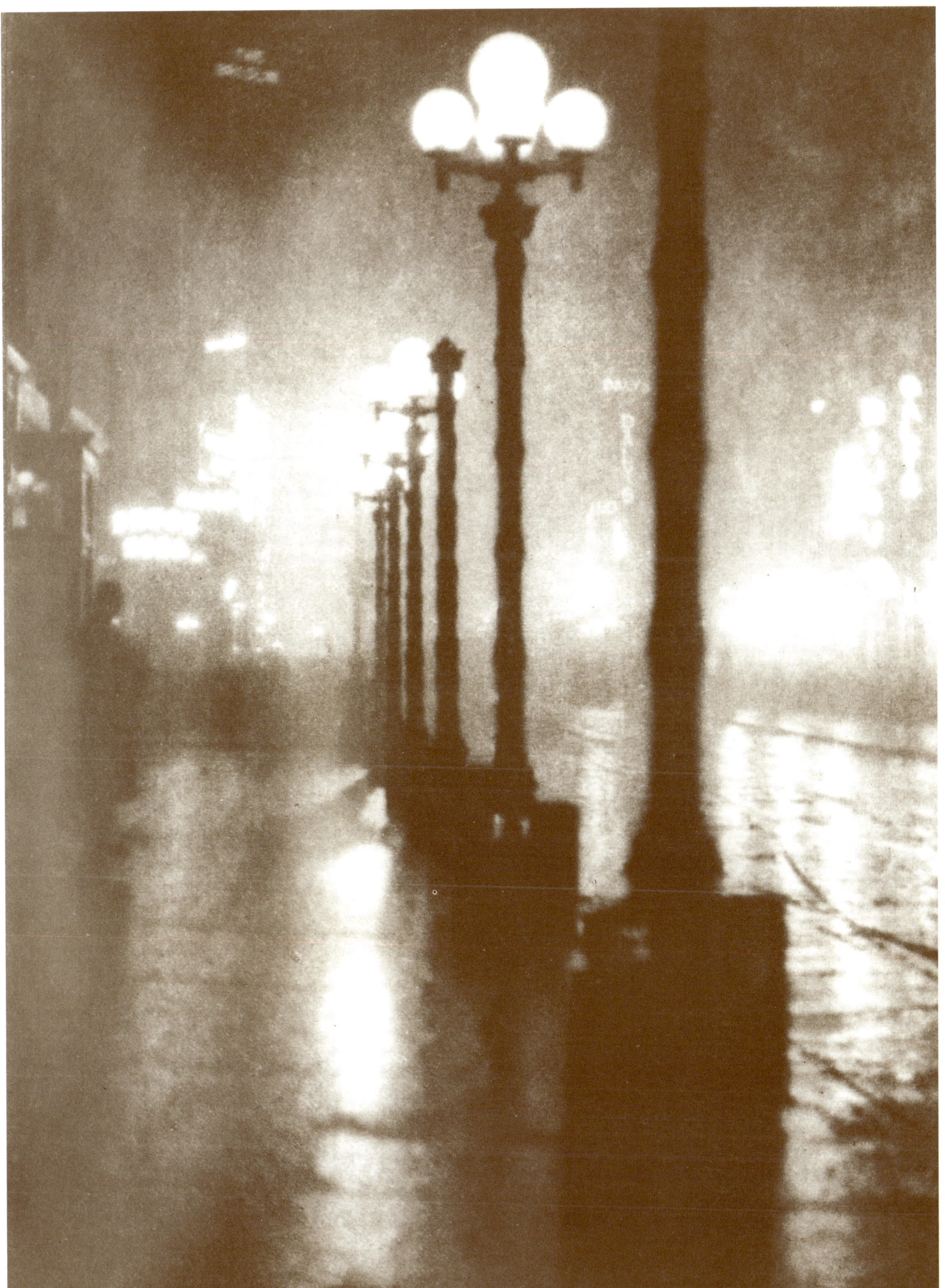

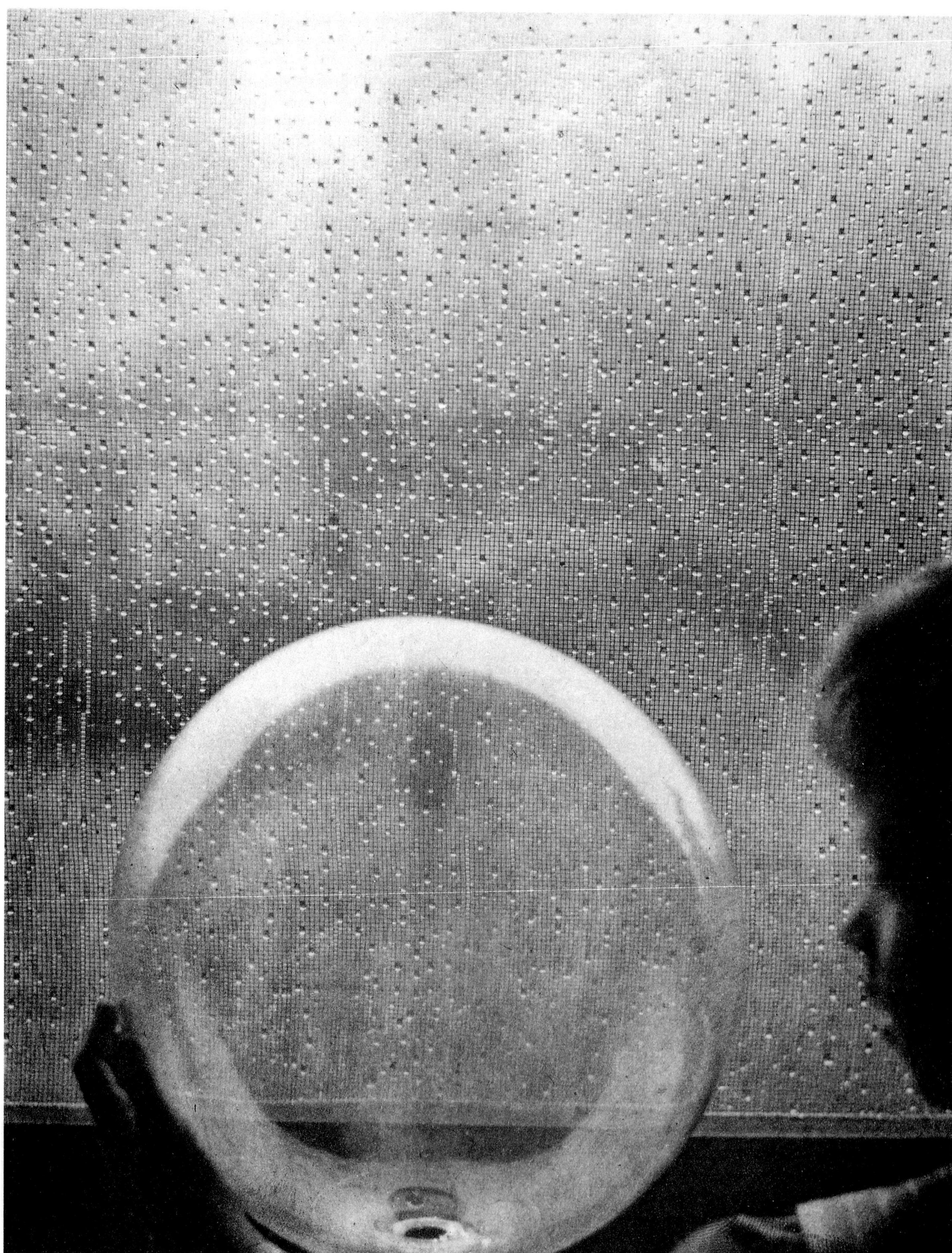

NATURALISTIC VISION AND SYMBOLIST IMAGE

17

The pictorial impulse

Anne Hammond

At the end of the nineteenth century, photography underwent a change: while asking itself questions about the sense of the image, the legitimacy of the representation, and the vocation of the photographer, it sought to take part in the artistic debates of the age. Around Impressionism and Naturalism a style emerged based on optical and pictorial (rather than photographic) considerations, generally known by the name of Pictorialism. In this chapter we analyze some of the initial components of this heterogeneous and convivial movement, tinged with mysticism and naturalist philosophy.

Writing in May 1892, in *Mercure de France*, Remy de Gourmont contrasted two opposing forces in art, Impressionism and Symbolism. The Impressionists desired to convey on canvas the objective impressions of the senses and the Symbolists intended to express not transient effects but "eternal meanings".[1] But although they appeared antithetical, the two tendencies should properly complement each other: Symbolists necessarily drew from a wealth of impressions and Impressionists sought to capture eternal as well as temporal things. The best Naturalist, Impressionist, and Symbolist photographers were those who would achieve this synthesis.

Peter Henry Emerson (1856–1936) turned his full attention to photography in 1885, and co-founded with Captain Abney, George Davison, and other serious amateurs the Camera Club of London. In the same year, he met the landscape painter Thomas Frederick Goodall while cruising on the Norfolk Broads, and a close friendship grew out of their shared interest in art and the countryside. The following year, Emerson published a book illustrated with platinum prints, *Life and Landscape of the Norfolk Broads*, in collaboration with Goodall. Goodall belonged to the New English Art Club, a group of artists who took their inspiration from the French painters of the Barbizon School – Corot, Millet, and Bastien Lepage – whose style was known as Naturalism. English Naturalist painters like Goodall, H. H. La Thangue, and George Clausen were committed to the subjects of rural life and labor and a technique of "selective focus" which rendered only the main point of interest perfectly sharp and all other parts of the picture slightly blurred. An explanation of "The Naturalistic School of Painting" was published in eight parts by Francis Bate in the club's journal *The Artist* during 1886.[2] Here Bate proposed "humanity" to be the proper subject for the modern painter, as it had been for the school of Millet.

The rural ideal

One distinct type of picture Emerson produced was that of people engaged in rural labor. He introduced into this subject a sense of the passage of time by depicting each worker at a different moment in the action of their labor. Emerson held this sequential interest in common with George Clausen, who in his painting *Harvest – Tying the Sheaves*[3] shows four farmworkers, each representing a separate moment in the process of sheaf-tying. In Emerson's version, *During the Sedge Harvest*, a similar sequence of actions is depicted – one laborer cuts the reeds, a woman binds them, and another man loads them into the boat. United in a continuity of work, the harvesters move between a monumental stack of reed bundles and the uncut field of reeds, blown into elusive and indistinct masses by the wind.

Emerson's book *Naturalistic Photography for Students of the Art* (1889) applauded the paintings of Millet and Corot, whose work was shown in

◀ Clarence H. White, ***Raindrops***, from *Camera Work*, July 1908, Musée d'Orsay, Paris.

1. R. de Gourmont, "Les Premiers Salons", *Mercure de France* (May 1892), quoted in R. Delevoy, *Symbolists and Symbolism*, (London, Macmillan, 1978, p. 69).

2. See F. Bate, "The Naturalistic School of Painting", *The Artist*, nos. 8, p. 75 (March 1, 1886) and 82 (October 1, 1886).

3. See C. Wood, *Paradise Lost*, London, Barrie and Jenkins, 1988, p. 89.

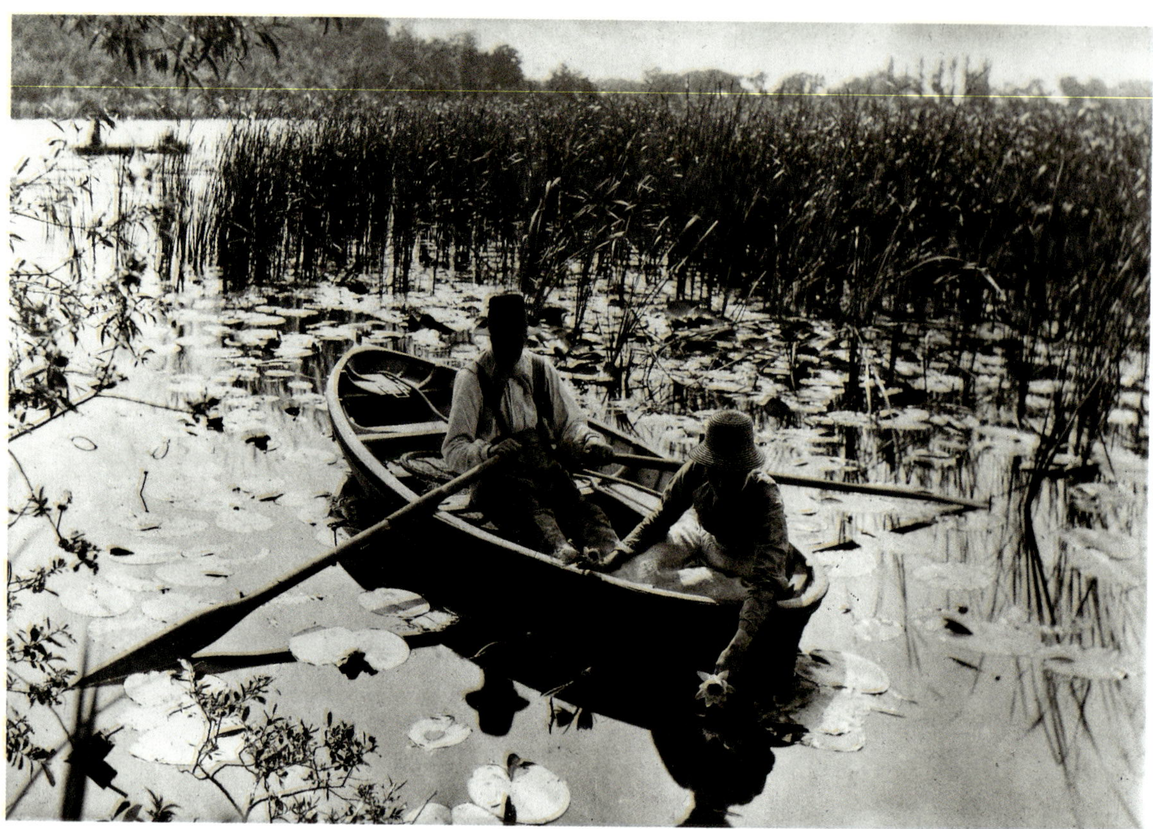

PETER HENRY EMERSON,
Gathering Waterlilies,
1886,
Royal Photographic
Society, Bath.

London at the Deschamps Gallery in the 1870s, and quoted at length from Millet's letters on the importance of impressions received from nature. Emerson's belief in capturing the general effect of landscape modified by local conditions echoed Bate's discussion of "the science of appearances". Bate's explanation of the eye's "center of vision", which determines the focal definition of forms, is picked up again by Emerson in his view that selective focusing is necessary to restore the actual optical effect registered by the imperfect lens of the eye. Both men admitted the power of atmospheric effects (smoke, haze, mist, fog) in mediating tones.

Emerson's public entry into the field of photography, around 1885, coincided with the beginning of James McNeill Whistler's critical acclaim in London. Throughout the 1880s, the club's journal, *The Artist*, carried commentary on Whistler's work. Emerson corresponded with Whistler,[4] sent him copies of his photographic albums, and praised him in *Naturalistic Photography* as the greatest living artist in England. When Emerson suffered a change of heart about the artistic possibilities of photography in *The Death of Naturalistic Photography* (1890), it was probably Whistler to whom Emerson referred as the "great artist" who had convinced him of his mistake in elevating the potential of photography to the highest expression of art. Goodall's paintings and the photographs which he made with Emerson show the compositional influence of Whistler's paintings and etchings in their use of a high horizon line, architectonic arrangements of masts, poles, and other linear objects, and the calligraphic effect of foreground elements such as mooring lines, reeds, and river reflections. These characteristics run through all Emerson's publications, from the soft gradation of the platinum prints in *Life and Landscape* to the "drypoint" effect of his later book of copper engravings by photogravure, *Marsh Leaves* (1895).

However, in *Life and Landscape on the Norfolk Broads,* Emerson's best known photograph, *Gathering Waterlilies,* is an idyllic genre subject, standing out like an exotic flower itself in a book about the dark and difficult life of the Norfolk peasant. Its popularity rested on the public's familiarity with such a motif. In 1873, Luke Fildes painted *The Sweet River*, which appeared as a line engraving in the *Art Journal* (1877). It was later described by the editor: "Two lovers, having found a quiet nook where reeds and trees lend a friendly shadow, and waterlilies deck the water, are holding happy communion together."[5]

While Emerson was photographing life in the fens of East Anglia, Frank Meadow Sutcliffe (1853–1941) was attempting to preserve by photography the simple qualities of life in the port of Whitby where he had settled in 1876, after spending the early 1870s photographing the abbeys and castles of Yorkshire for Francis Frith. Although he was also an enthusiastic photographer of genre scenes, his people of Whitby were

4. N. McWilliam and V. Sekules (eds.), *Life and Landscape: P. H. Emerson*, Norwich, Sainsbury Centre for Visual Arts, 1986, p. 8.

5. D. C. Thomson, "The Life and Work of Luke Fildes, R.A", London, *Art Journal*, 1895, p. 4.

6. N. Newhall, *P. H. Emerson*, Millerton, Aperture, 1975, p. 81.

7. Pinhole photography involves making a tiny hole in the side of a box with a pin. Refraction of light produces an image on the opposite side. Since the image is dim, a long exposure time on a sensitive surface is required. The resulting somewhat hazy image gives the illusion of actually seeing the object.

not arranged as in the photographs of Emerson, in which the peasant is idealized in order to create a type which transcends locality, but in a more documentary style. But his submissions to the annual exhibition of the Photographic Society of Great Britain in 1890 drew praise from Emerson for demonstrating "artistic focusing", and his pictures were offered by Emerson as proof of the "complete triumph of naturalism".[6]

Palpable impressions

The representative of tradition in the photographic clubs was H. P. Robinson, who believed photography could express the complete range of the imagination, and advocated printing from multiple negatives in order to achieve the desired effect. George Davison (1854–1930) came to the defense of the naturalistic style in photography, attacking Robinson for his combination printing, for his use of models costumed as country folk, and for his belief that the characteristic property of the photograph resided in its sharp definition.

Emerson applauded Davison's experiments with the pinhole camera,[7] which he had begun in 1888. In 1891, Davison wrote that the greater the power of the photograph to evoke a direct experience of nature, the more power it would have to affect the aesthetic sensibility.[8] The characteristic quality of seeing was its diffusion and lack of extreme definition, and while some subjects benefited from differential focusing, others required an effect of overall diffusion – one which the pinhole camera could best achieve. In Davison's view, Impressionist and naturalist styles were practically identical. Quoting Emerson at length, he also recommended Francis Bate's *The Naturalistic School of Painting* as essential reading for every photographer.

Davison's pinhole photograph *The Onion Field* (1890) brought certain characteristics of Impressionism to photography: definition of form was sacrificed to a diffused field of tonal values, the idea that the rural landscape itself possessed an essential character or emotion. *The Onion Field* presents a layered landscape: a misty cloudbank hovers over a dark wood behind a modest group of farm buildings, with a smoking chimney and washing on the line. The tiny settlement is isolated in a vast field of flowering onions, the pale dandelion-shaped flower heads merging into a blanket as amorphous as the cloud above. In this tonalist study of transient elements in life, emphasized by the smoke and the clothes drying in the breeze, the shapes of the old farmstead buildings bring a human dimension to an otherwise abstract landscape. Photographs like Davison's pointed away from depiction based on the "science of appearances" and toward a landscape of personal expression.

As a student in Berlin during the 1880s, Alfred Stieglitz (1864–1946) was also interested in pastoral subjects and naturalistic effects. The photographs he submitted to the *Amateur Photographer*'s "Holiday Work" competition in 1887 earned him a silver medal from the judge, P. H. Emerson. He completed his education in Berlin in 1890 and returned to the U.S.A. where he published *Picturesque Bits of New York* (1897) and edited *Camera Notes* for the New York Camera Club. In 1902, he founded the Photo-Secession, an association promoting photography as fine art, modeled on European photographic

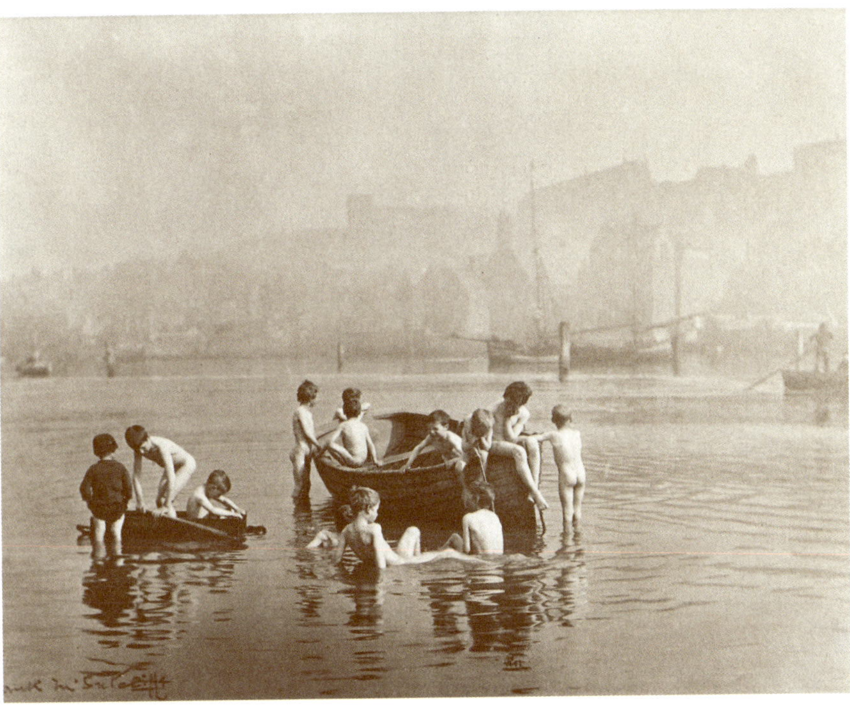

FRANK MEADOW SUTCLIFFE,
Water Rats,
1885,
Royal Photographic Society, Bath.

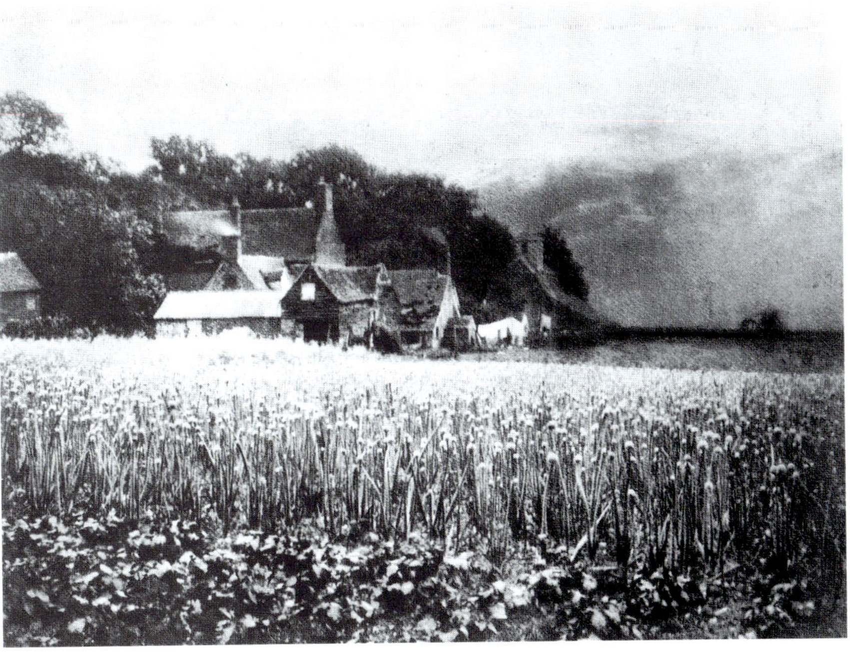

GEORGE DAVISON,
The Onion Field,
1890,
Royal Photographic Society, Bath.
▼

8. G. Davison, "Impressionism in photography", in *Photographic Times*, no. 21, p. 487, January 16, 1891, and p. 491, February 13, 1891.

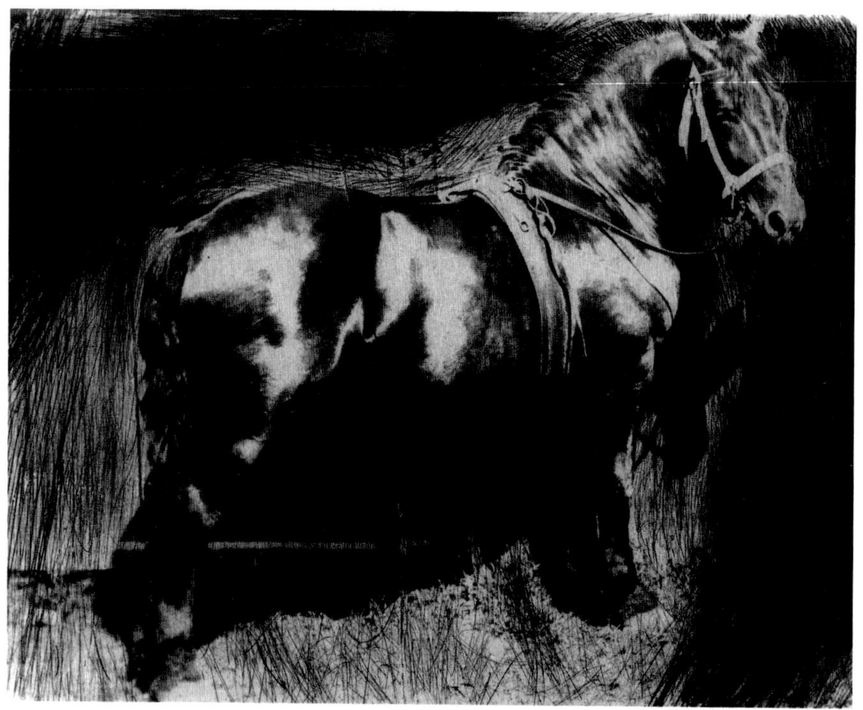

Frank Eugene, ***Horse,*** circa 1901, Royal Photographic Society, Bath.

art societies. He founded and edited the journal *Camera Work* (1903–1917), and in 1905 opened the Little Galleries of the Photo-Secession, later known as "291", exhibiting a wide and important range of visual arts.

In *Spring Showers* (1898) Stieglitz presents a young tree reflected in the rain-washed streets of New York while the hard faces of the city's buildings are dematerialized by mist and rain. This is a picture which is Japanese-influenced in composition and Impressionist in treatment, with a naturalist presence in the streetsweeper.

James Craig Annan (1864–1946) was the son of Thomas Annan, the leading commercial photographer in Scotland from the 1850s to the 1880s. In 1883, father and son traveled to Vienna to learn the new technique of photogravure from its inventor, Karl Klic. Craig Annan began to exhibit his own photographs, printed as photogravures, in 1892. By working toward the photogravure print as his final artistic product, Craig Annan placed himself alongside the Scottish artist-engraver D. Y. Cameron, one of his oldest friends.

During the etching revival of the mid-nineteenth century, a separation was clearly established between those artist-engravers who printed "straight" from the plate as it stood, and those whose interest it was to create a new work of art with each impression by *retroussage.* D. Y. Cameron followed the relatively straightforward procedure. Craig Annan was known on the whole as a purist in his camera work, but he occasionally demonstrated the capacity of the etched photogravure for more expressive printing in images like *Riva Schiavoni, Venice* (1894).[9]

Frank Eugene (1865–1936) was born in New York as Frank Eugene Smith and studied painting at the Royal Bavarian Academy of Fine Arts in Munich from 1886. In 1889, he exhibited photographs at the New York Camera Club which were reviewed as "unphotographic photography". By 1906, he was residing permanently in Germany, and gained recognition as a painter working in the Jugendstil style. In 1907, he began lecturing on Pictorial photography in Munich. The characteristic which most obviously set him apart from other Pictorial photographers was his technique of scratching the negative with an etching needle to suppress unwanted detail and enhance the graphic vitality of the print.

The result was an effect like that achieved in the *Horse* (c. 1901), of which Charles Caffin remarked: "the background and straw have been fearlessly etched in the negative, and brush and point would appear to have been used on the horse. The print, in fact, has the quality and texture of spontaneousness of a fine etching."[10] Eugene's scratched texture makes the glossy body of a carthorse emerge from this background with the photographic sensuousness of a female nude.

Alfred Horsley Hinton (1863–1908) obtained his expressive ends by combination printing, a technique he may have learned from Ralph Robinson, son of H. P. Robinson, when he worked as the manager of Robinson's studio in the early 1890s. Hinton made a transparent positive from two or more negatives, and added his own effects by drawing on it with pencil before making a final negative from it for printing in platinum. His end product was, therefore, printed directly from a laboriously constructed negative. His landscapes were Impressionist in treatment, taking trees, streams, moorland, and storm clouds as material upon which the artist's manual influence could be exercised in order to create an atmospheric effect. In 1893, Hinton became editor of the London journal *Amateur Photographer,* championing Pictorial photography until his death in 1908.

In the mid 1890s the Belgian photographer Léonard Misonne (1870–1943) was well known among the avant-garde in art photography. With an educated background and strong interest in the arts, he gave up a career in the mining industry to pursue his chosen vocation of photography in 1896, and in the following decades his work was exhibited worldwide. As with Hinton, the actual subject before the lens was far less important than the effect of light and atmosphere obtained in the print. He was later referred to as the "Corot of photography". Fog and early-morning mist were the conditions under which he preferred to photograph, not only to obscure

9. *Camera Work,* October 1904.

10. *Ibid.*

the distant view in order in create a sense of intimacy, but often to serve as an atmospheric vehicle for contrejour lighting, which produced a halo around the human form.

Misonne's compatriot and contemporary Gustave Marissiaux (1872–1929) also applied the Impressionist aesthetic to his photographic study of the coal mines in Liège in 1903 for which he received first prize in the photography class at the Liège Universal Exhibition. In 1905, Marissiaux's slide-show to the Société Française de Photographie and the Cercle Volney created a strong impression upon his audience, with its combination of industrial subjects (women hauling sacks of coal, black smoke issuing from chimneys) and delicate Venetian views (quiet waterways and misty silhouettes of bell towers).[11]

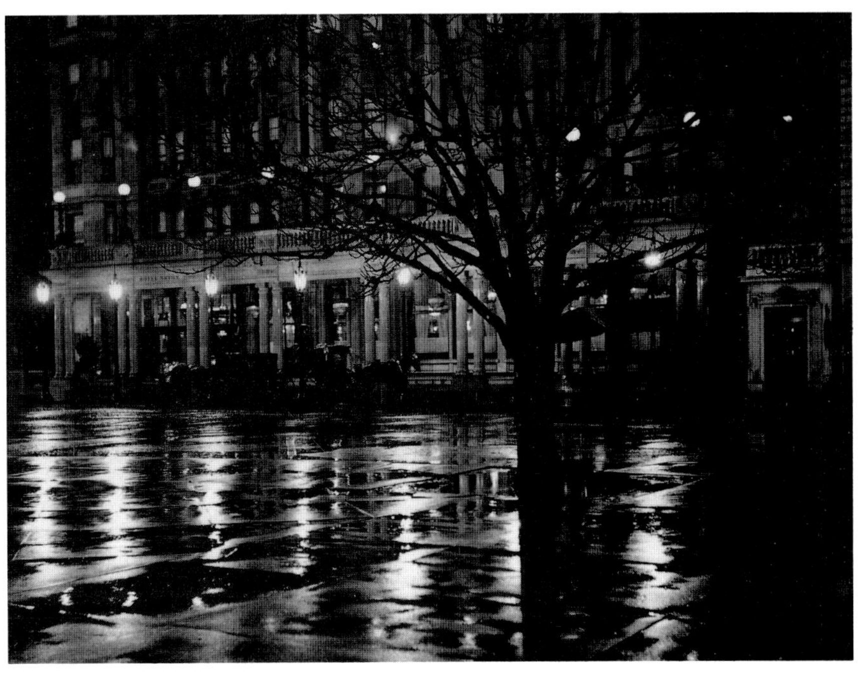

ALFRED STIEGLITZ,
Night Reflections, New York,
circa 1896, Museum of Fine Arts, Boston.

Artistic methods

At the end of the nineteenth century, European culture had reached a peak of capitalism and scientific positivitism. In reaction against this, the artists known as Symbolists set out "to objectivize the subjective (the exteriorization of the Ideal), instead of subjectivizing the objective (nature seen through an individual's temperament)".[12]

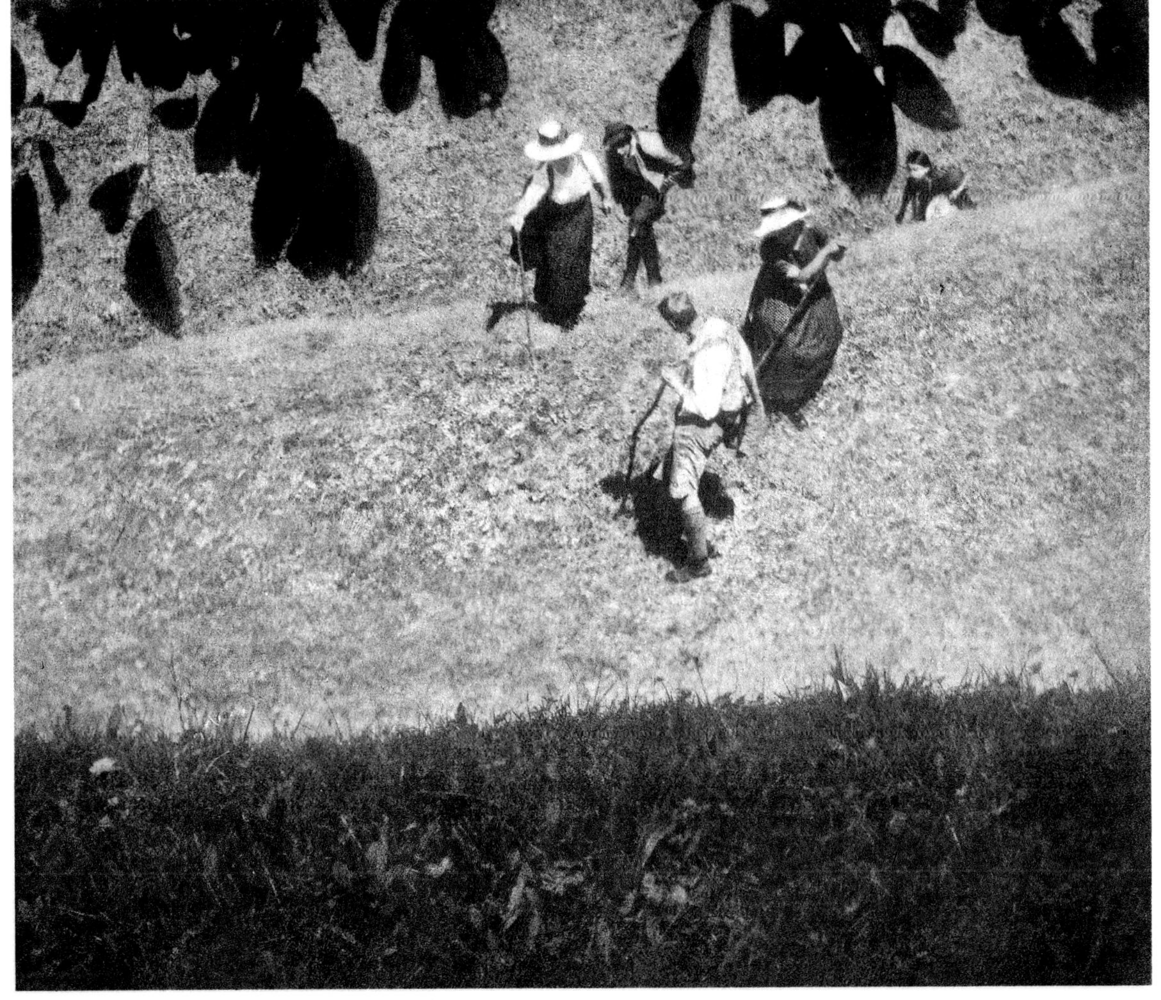

HEINRICH KÜHN,
Country Scene at Burgstall, Tyrol,
circa 1912,
Musée d'Orsay, Paris.

11. Some of these images were published in 1908 as an album of thirty photogravures, *Visions d'artiste.*

12. G. Kahn, *La Vogue*, September 26, 1886.

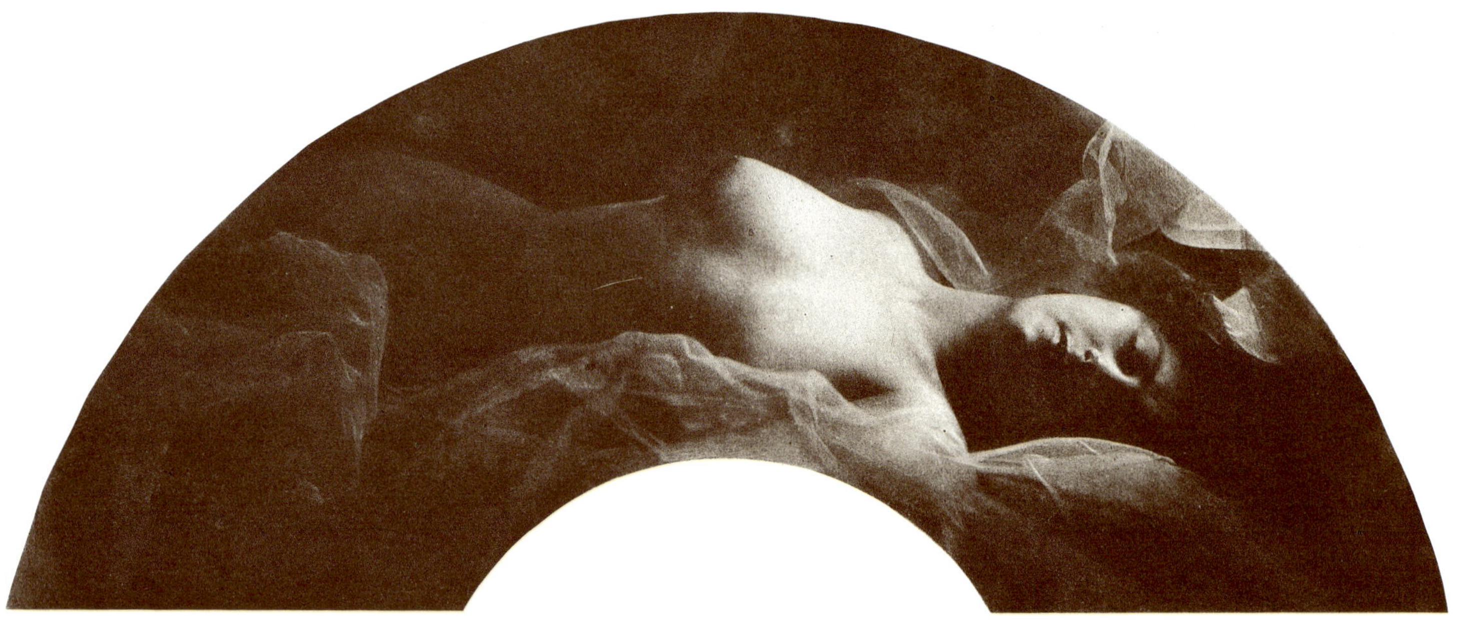

CONSTANT PUYO, *Fan*, circa 1900, Société Française de Photographie, Paris.

RUDOLPH AND MINYA DÜHRKOOP, *Clotilde von Derp*, circa 1908, Royal Photographic Society, Bath.

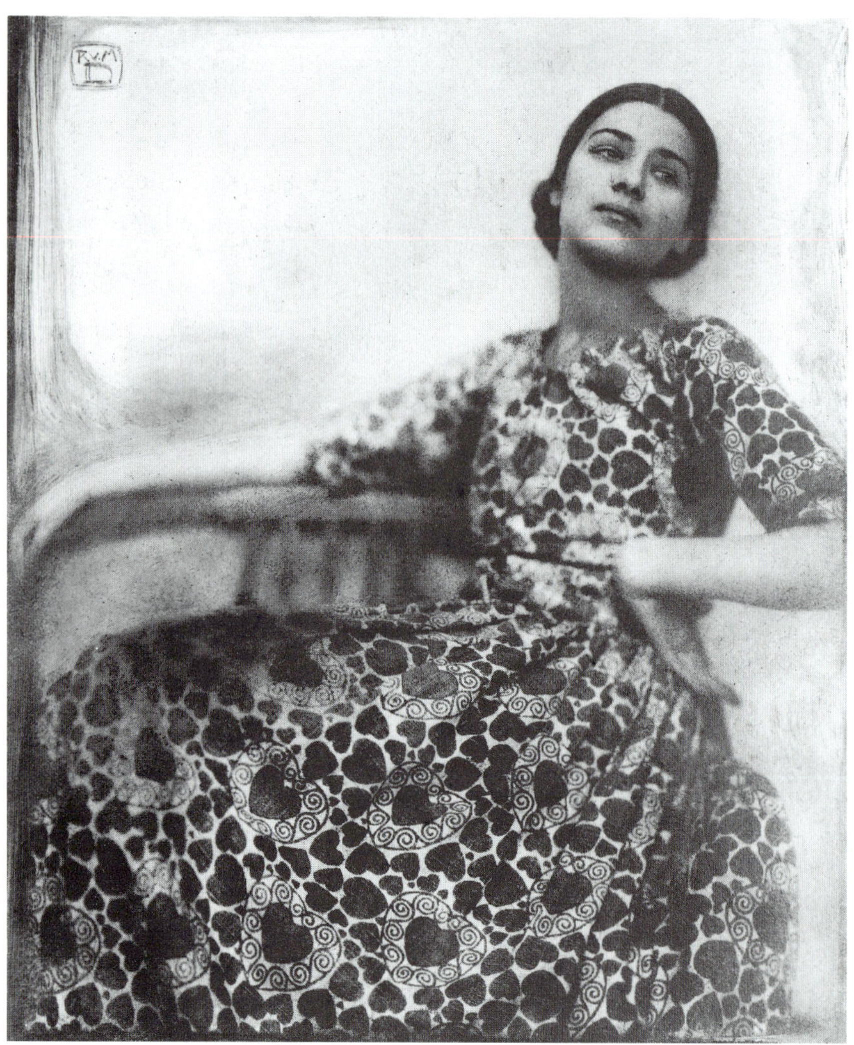

They wished to indicate the existence of a spiritual state rather than describing the material world in terms of sensory perception as the Impressionists had.

During the 1880s and 1890s, Naturalism and Impressionism declined while Symbolism increased in prominence. The internationalist goal of Symbolism, like that of art photography, was advanced by an explosion of new art journals – Steichen's design for Stieglitz's *Camera Work* was modeled on the Symbolist journal *Pan* (Berlin, 1895–1900)[13] while *Ver Sacrum*, the journal of the Vienna Secession, founded in 1898, featured the gum prints of Heinrich Kühn, Hans Watzek, and Hugo Henneberg in its early numbers.

In 1891, at the first international exhibition of photography organized by the Wiener Kamera-Club, Heinrich Kühn (1866–1944) was introduced to the work of George Davison, who was a founder member of the Linked Ring Brotherhood in Britain in 1892. In 1894, Kühn joined the Wiener Kamera-Club, where he met Hugo Henneberg (1863–1918) and Hans Watzek (1848–1903). Henneberg, who had seen gum prints made by Robert Demachy, drew the gum bichromate process to Kühn's attention in 1895, and these three photographers became well known for large gum bichromate prints during the late 1890s.

The idealized pastoral landscapes of Watzek and Henneberg refer most directly to the work of their Symbolist contemporaries, painters like Arnold Böcklin whose *The Island of the Dead* (1880), the most famous painting of the end of the century, evoked deep melancholy with its isolated rocky villa amid funereal cypress trees. Henneberg's *Villa Falconieri, Frascati* (1900) also strikes a tragic chord with its villa as mausoleum flanked by cypresses at the end of a long approach by water, the reflecting surface recalling the river Styx. The critic Muther, writing about Böcklin in 1894, placed him in "the great four-leafed clover of modern Idealism" with Moreau, Puvis de Chavannes, and Burne-Jones.[14] It is interesting that two years later Henneberg, Watzek, and Kühn should name themselves *Das Kleeblatt* [The Clover Leaf].

Theodor Hofmeister (1868–1943) learned the technique of gum printing from Heinrich Kühn in the mid-1890s, and worked collaboratively with his brother Oskar Hofmeister (1871–1937) to produce multiple gum prints of peasant and landscape subjects, often in three colors and to the unprecedented size of 1 x 1.5 meters. The Hofmeisters and the three members of *Das Kleeblatt* were exhibited together by Alfred Stieglitz in his Little Galleries of the Photo-Secession in 1907. Their shared interest in a tonalist aesthetic influenced their choice of the gum bichromate process, which afforded them maximum control over the tonalities within the image. Gable ends of houses, clouds, boat sails, and white summer dresses served as bright foils to a succession of shadows deepening around them, light shapes suggesting life and vitality emerging from the field of grays. Kühn from time to time subtitled his pictures "Study in Values" or "Study in Tones".

Tonalism, as practised by Whistler and the Impressionist painters, implied that a certain level of meaning, independent of narrative content, could be expressed simply by an emotional response to one area of tone or color set against another. The whole spectrum of human feeling stretched between tones of light and dark. In Heinrich Kühn's *In the Dunes* (1905) three women walk away in the high-key landscape of grass and sand. Dressed in black and gray costume and white caps, they represent a tonal progression in themselves, their white heads, seen just beneath the horizon, bright as a peal of bells against the silvery windblown grasses. *The Dark Mountains* (1890) by James Craig Annan is a twilight counterpart to Kühn's noontime study. The melancholy of blackness is somewhat relieved by the light of the setting sun, which partially illuminates the faces of the travelers, but its overall effect is of a dirge, as opposed to Kühn's bright melody.

Rudolph Dührkoop (1848–1918) took up photography around 1880, and in 1883 opened a portrait studio in Hamburg. In 1905, he published a portfolio of photogravures, *Hamburg Men and Women at the Beginning of the Twentieth Century*.[15] In addition to his compositional strength and his interest in the graphic aspect of

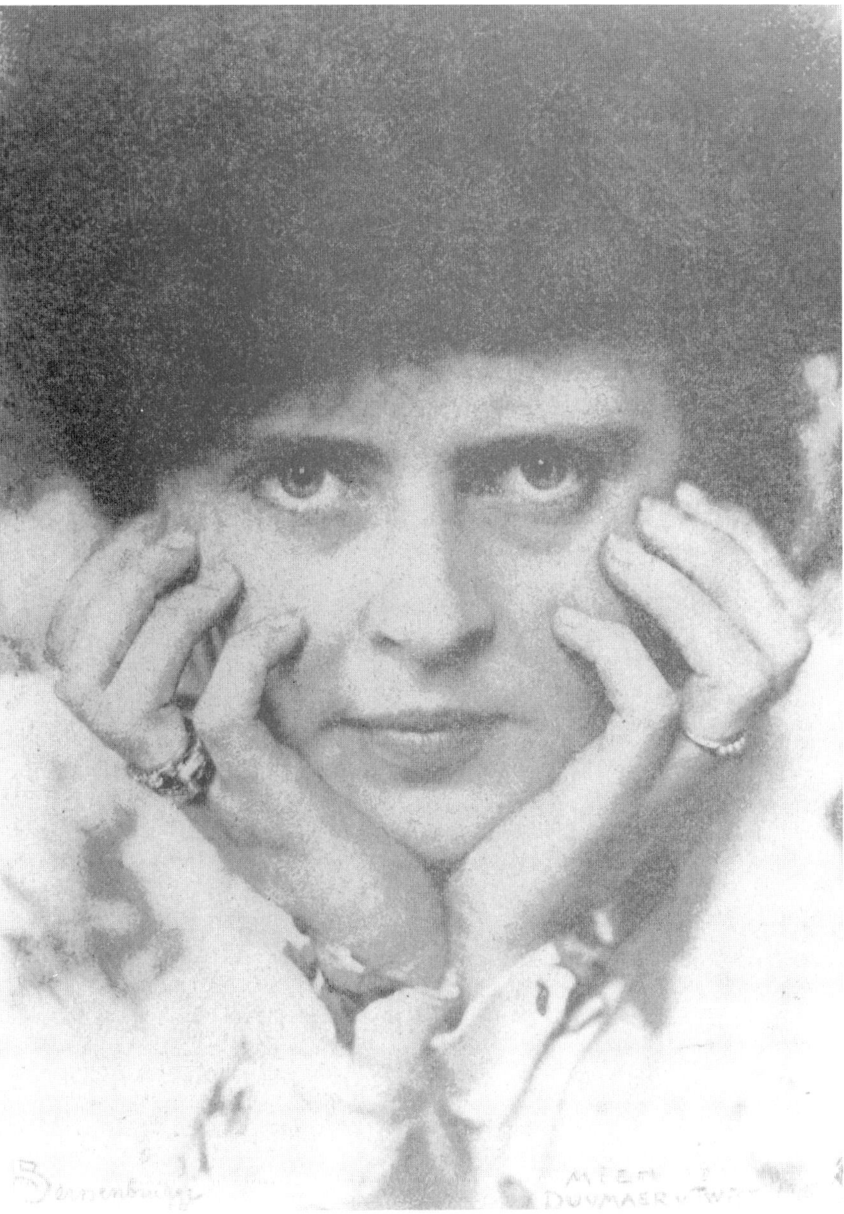

H. BERSSENBRUGGE,
Mien Duijmaer van Twist,
gum-bichromate print,
1915,
print collection,
Rijksuniversiteit, Leyden.

the photograph, shown in his *Clotilde von Derp* (c. 1908), he showed an awareness that fine photography was not dependent upon artistic affectation. He expressed through his work the notion of "truth to materials", one of the motivating ideas behind the new style of "straight" photography.

From 1895, photographers in France were using the gum bichromate process for Symbolist ends. One of its chief promoters was Charles E. J. Constant Puyo (1857–1933), who with Leclerc de Pulligny advocated maximizing the effects of lens aberrations to produce a softer image. In 1894, he was a co-founder of the Photo-Club of Paris. By 1902, when he retired as commandant from the army, he was one of the most famous Pictorial photographers in France. The public was well prepared for the Pictorial photography practiced by Puyo and his colleagues by the painting styles of the 1880s through 1900. The imagery of dream and fantasy is seen in painters like Fernand

13. D. Longwell, *Steichen: The Master Prints, 1895–1914*, New York, Museum of Modern Art, 1978, p. 15.

14. P. Jullian, *Dreamers of Decadence*, London, Pall Mall Press, 1971, p. 164.

15. *Hamburgische Männer und Frauen am Anfang des XX Jahrhunderts*, Hamburg, 1905.

Pictorialist techniques

Reacting against what they perceived as the decadence of photography, a few aesthetes attempted to open up a new way which would move away from reality and give way to interpretation.

To achieve this, the Pictorialists introduced certain optical innovations and, above all, new techniques for development. They rediscovered or invented processes permitting decisive alterations of the print, such as gum-bichromate (whose origins went back to 1858), which gave images the quality of charcoal, ochre or wash.

The emulsion, a paste composed of a colored pigment mixed with gum arabic to which potassium bichromate was subsequently added, was laid on the sheet of paper using a brush. Once dry this mixture was photosensitive and insoluble in proportion to its exposure to light. Having been exposed, sandwiched with a negative, in a printing-frame, the print was developed by a stripping process by being immersed face down in water. The image appeared as the unhardened areas of gum dissolved.

With experience the operator could play a more active role, using paintbrushes and sponges to encourage local stripping of selected areas of the print. Once development was complete (at the end of 60–90 minutes) the print would be dipped in a solution of sodium sulfite, washed, hardened in a formalin bath, rinsed again, and dried. A simple process, but with many hazards, it was used by virtuosi such as Constant Puyo, Robert Demachy, and René Le Bègue.

Patented in 1878 by William Willis, a process comprising the use of platinum salts also achieved some popularity between 1880 and 1914. This allowed images to be obtained which looked like lead-pencil drawings, or pen-and-wash. First immersed in a solution of potassium chloroplatinite to which ferric oxalate

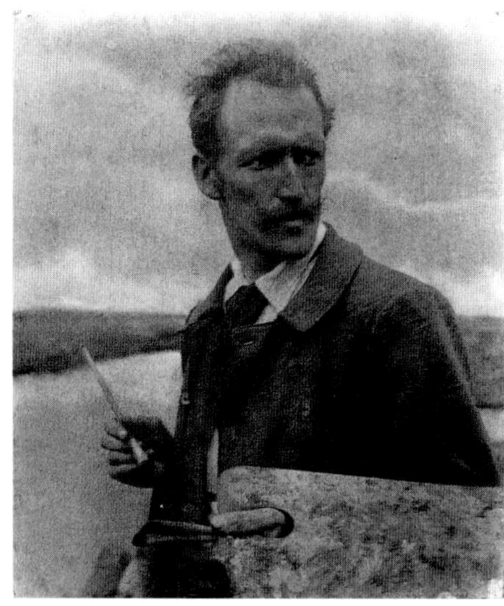

THEODORE AND OSCAR HOFMEISTER,
The Painter Fritz Mackensen,
1898, Museum für Kunst und Gewerbe, Hamburg.

and potassium chloride had been added, the paper was exposed in the usual way (using diffuse light) then developed in a warm bath of oxalic acid and fixed in an acid bath. Alfred Stieglitz and Frederick H. Evans, among others, were keen platinotypists. Although this process, which allowed one to give varied tones to the image and to choose the nuances and the grain of paper, later fell into disuse, a certain number of contemporary photographers (I. Penn, G. Tice) used it to obtain totally archivally stable prints and to give their prints an incomparably smooth texture.

Somewhat later, the Rawlins process (1904) was a development of Poitevin's work on photolithography. Having been exposed by contact with the negative, a paper prepared with bichromated gelatine when immersed in warm water absorbed water in the least exposed areas. A greasy ink could adhere only to the dryest parts of the surface (those that had received the most light through the negative, thus providing the darkest parts of the image). Rawlins's innovation – called the "bromoil" process – was to carry out the inking process using a brush, which allowed him to control local tonal values.

If Puyo became one of the best in this method, it was Demachy who, unsatisfied with the way gelatinized papers lacked substance, had in 1912 the idea of "transfer", that is to say, using these inked prints as printing plates. The inked gelatinized sheet was transferred by printing on a press onto the fine Arche or Japanese papers currently being used by engravers.

However much they sought to manipulate the image, the adherents of Pictorialism thus had at their disposal a large number of processes which could be adapted to suit their individual intentions.

Jean-Claude Gautrand

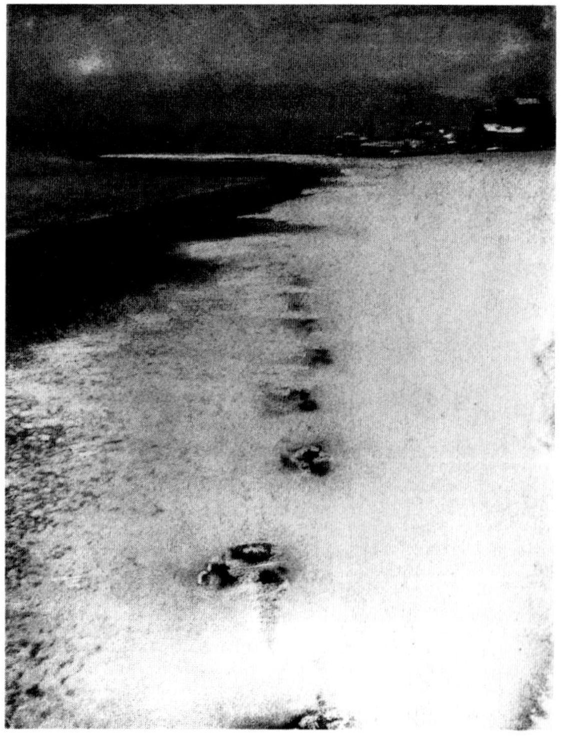

ROBERT DEMACHY, ▶ *Landscape,* gum-bichromate print, circa 1904, Musée d'Orsay, Paris.

Khnopff, whose work, shown in Paris in 1899, offered portraits of sphinx-like women who produce a sense of psychological unease. It is, therefore, not surprising that besides pastoral landscapes, allegorical subjects, and decorative nude studies, Puyo should also present in his *Profil* (1895–1900) such an enigmatic expression.

Robert Demachy (1859–1936) began to work with gum bichromate in 1894. He co-published, with Alfred Maskell, *Photo-aquatint or the Gum Bichromate Process* (1897).[16] With Puyo, he became known as the chief exponent of the process and together they published *Les Procédés d'Art en Photographie* in 1906. He wrote as both critic and technician for European, British, and American journals, and later was converted to the oil and bromoil processes. He was best known for his nudes and landscapes. In *Struggle* (1904), a nude with arms upraised apparently resists a crashing wave which is not real but created by the artist's brush in the gum medium.

16. *Photo-Aquatint or the Gum-Bichromate Process,* London, 1897.

The subject of the nude in a violent sea also appears in *Spleen et Idéal* (1896), an illustration by the Symbolist painter Carlos Schwabe for Baudelaire's *Les Fleurs du Mal*.[17] Schwabe was one of the main exhibitors at the Salon of the Rose-Croix, a group whose aim was to promote the ideal in art through medieval and alchemical revivalism. In Schwabe's image the inherent conflict between the spiritual and the material is resolved in the formula known to alchemists as "the chemical marriage", whereas in Demachy's version the combat is about the eternal resistance of the feminine to the abstract vital power of the male.

International Pictorialism

In 1900, Fred Holland Day (1864–1933) organized an exhibition of the "New School of American Photography" for the Royal Photographic Society in London; it was also shown at the Photo-Club de Paris in 1901. Day was an American aesthete in the English tradition of Keats, Swinburne, and Walter Pater. He and his partner, Herbert Copeland, were publishers in the United States of the *Yellow Book*, a journal of the "decadent" movement. In 1898, he began a series of over 200 photographs on the theme of the Crucifixion, for which he posed as the model. When *The Seven Last Words of Christ* (c. 1898) was first exhibited at the Philadelphia Salon it created a critical uproar. In the summer of 1907, Day produced a series of "pagan" studies, including *Nude Youth with Lyre* (1907). Orpheus with his lyre represented the poet as musician, all art aspiring, in Walter Pater's famous words, to the condition of music. Orpheus was the interpreter between the worlds of the conscious and the unconscious.[18]

Born in America, Alvin Langdon Coburn (1882–1966) was introduced to photography by his distant cousin, Holland Day in Boston. By the age of twenty-one he had been elected a member of both the Photo-Secession (1901) and the Linked Ring (1903), and become associated with the major artistic, literary, and philosophical figures of the day, George Bernard Shaw, Henry James, Arthur Symons, and Edward Carpenter. One of his first publications was a series of four illustrations to Maeterlinck's *The Intelligence of the Flowers* (1907). It was largely through Maeterlinck and Carpenter that Coburn acquired his interest in mysticism.

Coburn's *On the Embankment* (1905) is an urban landscape which combines a stairway, the spiritual idea of ascent to a higher order, and a statue of the Sphinx, a symbol of enigma used by the Symbolist painters to evoke the ultimate meaning of life in the body of a mythical beast.

George Seeley (1880–1955) studied art in Boston, and first gained recognition for his photography at the First American Salon of 1904, when Coburn brought his work to the attention of Stieglitz. He was interested in the motif of the orb or globe, often giving his model a large round bowl to hold, or using the circle of a tambourine to create the flat, decorative effect of a halo behind the model's head.

Clarence White (1871–1925) began to pursue serious amateur photography in 1894 after visiting the Columbian Exposition in Chicago. In 1898, he founded the Camera Club in his hometown, Newark, Ohio, and began to partici-

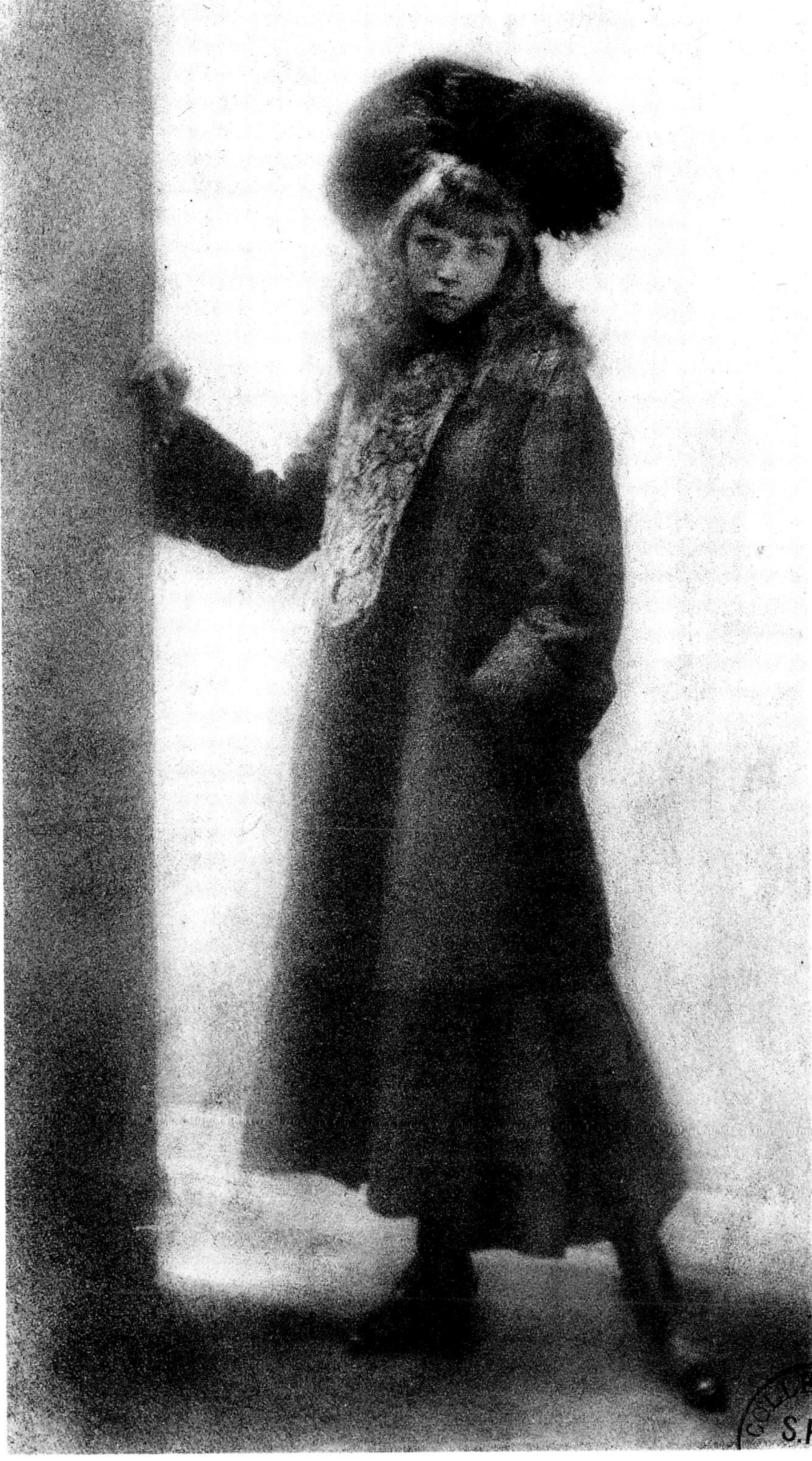

Robert Demachy,
Girl in a Hat,
bromoil print,
circa 1900,
Société Française
de Photographie, Paris.

17. C. Baudelaire, *Les Fleurs du Mal*, Paris, 1897.

18. The Belgian Symbolist author Maurice Maeterlinck wrote of Orpheus as a type of Christ, another martyr in the quest for spiritual knowledge.

19. J. Keiley, "The Buffalo Exhibition", *Camera Work*, no. 33, 1911, p. 23.

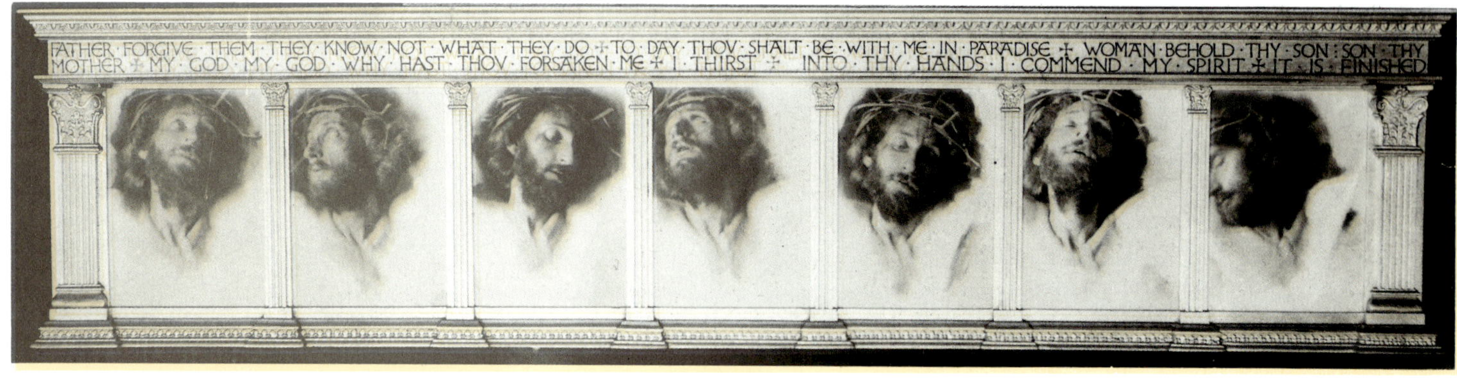

FRED HOLLAND DAY, *The Seven Last Words of Christ*, 1898, Library of Congress, Washington.

pate in exhibitions of Pictorial photography. In 1906, he moved to New York, set up a studio there, and began a lifelong teaching career in photography. Joseph Keiley remarked that his photographs "left the impression of the music of line, and soft singing whisper of tone with only the ghost of a shadow of the personality behind their making".[19]

But besides this decorative tonalism White also had a talent for presenting subjects which could evoke emotional states of hope, melancholy, or meditation. His *Still-life* (1907) presents an arrangement of chrysanthemums in a tall vase next to a square windowpane, both seen through a large glass globe. The two-dimensional compositional style is as Japanese as the chrysanthemums themselves, and the globe superimposed on the square pane of glass alludes to the ancient western philosophical problem of "squaring the circle" – an alchemical proposition based on a spiritual quest for the union of heaven (the circle) with earth (the square). The American philosopher Ralph Waldo Emerson, writing in his famous essay *Nature* (1836) that art is "nature passed through the alembic of man", equated the powers of creative expression with the alchemical process of transmutation. In Emerson, the Platonic symbol of the transparent orb becomes an emblem of spiritual insight: "I become a transparent eyeball. I am nothing. I see all. The currents of the Universal Being circulate through me; I am part or particle of God."[20] The crystal sphere thus symbolizes a condition of spiritual perfection and unity.

In *Waterlilies* (c. 1906) by Adolf de Meyer (1868–1949), the crystal globe is translated into a half-globe, a glass bowl casting its shadowy reflection onto the glass tabletop beneath. Into a composition of great simplicity, de Meyer reintroduces the motif of the waterlily which, lotus-like, rises to unfold its flower on the surface of the still water.

The Czech artist Frantisek Kupka, working in Paris in the 1890s, represented the lotus as the source of human life. Born in Paris, de Meyer entered the world of high society when he married Donna Olga Alberta Caracciolo in 1901. She was goddaughter of Edward, Prince of Wales, and the title of baron was conferred upon de Meyer so that he could attend his coronation as King Edward VII. In 1911, Meyer made a series of photographs of Nijinsky and Diaghilev's other dancers in the Ballets Russes, and published them as *Sur le Prélude à l'Après-midi d'un Faune* (1914).[21]

Annie Brigman (1868–1950), who became a member of the Photo-Secession in 1906, posed as a model for her own Symbolist photographs. In *Soul of the Blasted Pine* (1907) and *The Brook*

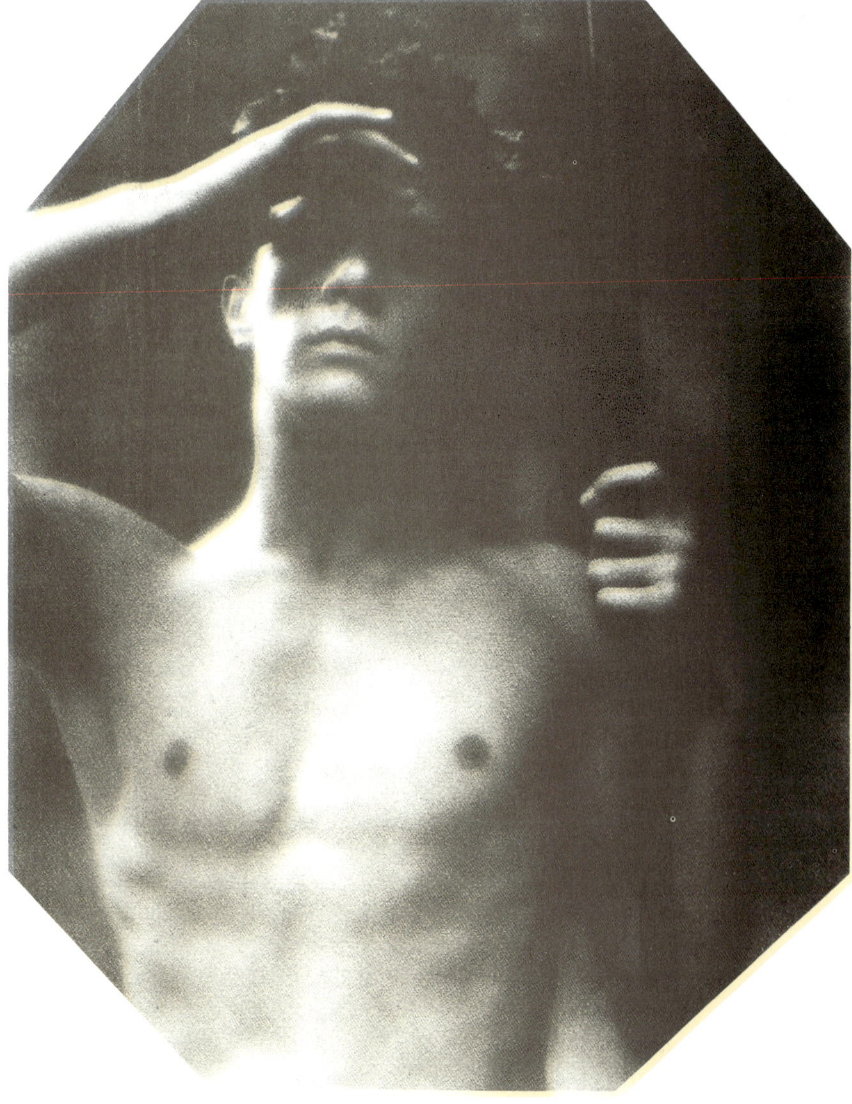

FRED HOLLAND DAY, *Torso*, 1908, Royal Photographic Society, Bath.

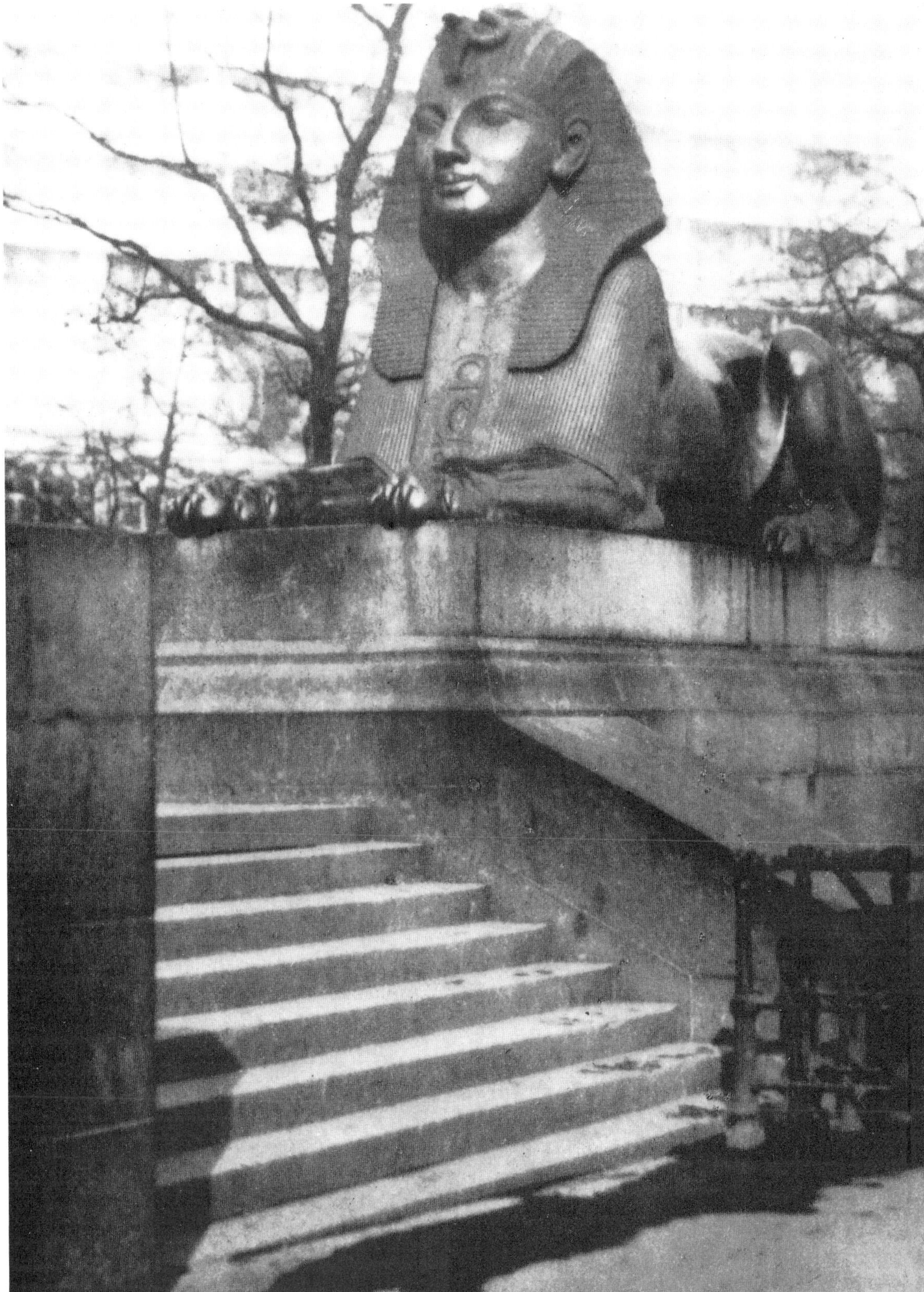

ALVIN LANGDON COBURN,
On the Embankment,
1905,
Royal Photographic Society,
Bath.

(c. 1909; both reproduced in the January 1909 issue of *Camera Work*) she personified these spirits of nature, making a twisted tree stump of her nude torso, and repeating the curves of a shelving brook within the shape of her own body. In another photograph from the same issue of *Camera Work, The Bubble* (c. 1908), the nude figure, kneeling forward in the clear pool of a melting glacier, reaches out to touch a perfect crystal ball as it drifts away.

Symbolist goals

Edward Steichen (1879–1973), born in Luxembourg, studied painting in Milwaukee, Wisconsin in the late 1890s, and learned photography in 1895. Through a letter of introduction from Clarence White he met Alfred Stieglitz in New York before leaving for Paris. In 1901 thirty-five of his photographs were included in Holland Day's "New School of American Photography"

20. R. W. Emerson, "Nature", in N. Foerster and R.P. Falk (ed.), *Eight American Writers*, New York, W. W. Norton, 1963, p. 191.

21. Cecil Beaton in later years described de Meyer as "the Debussy of photography".

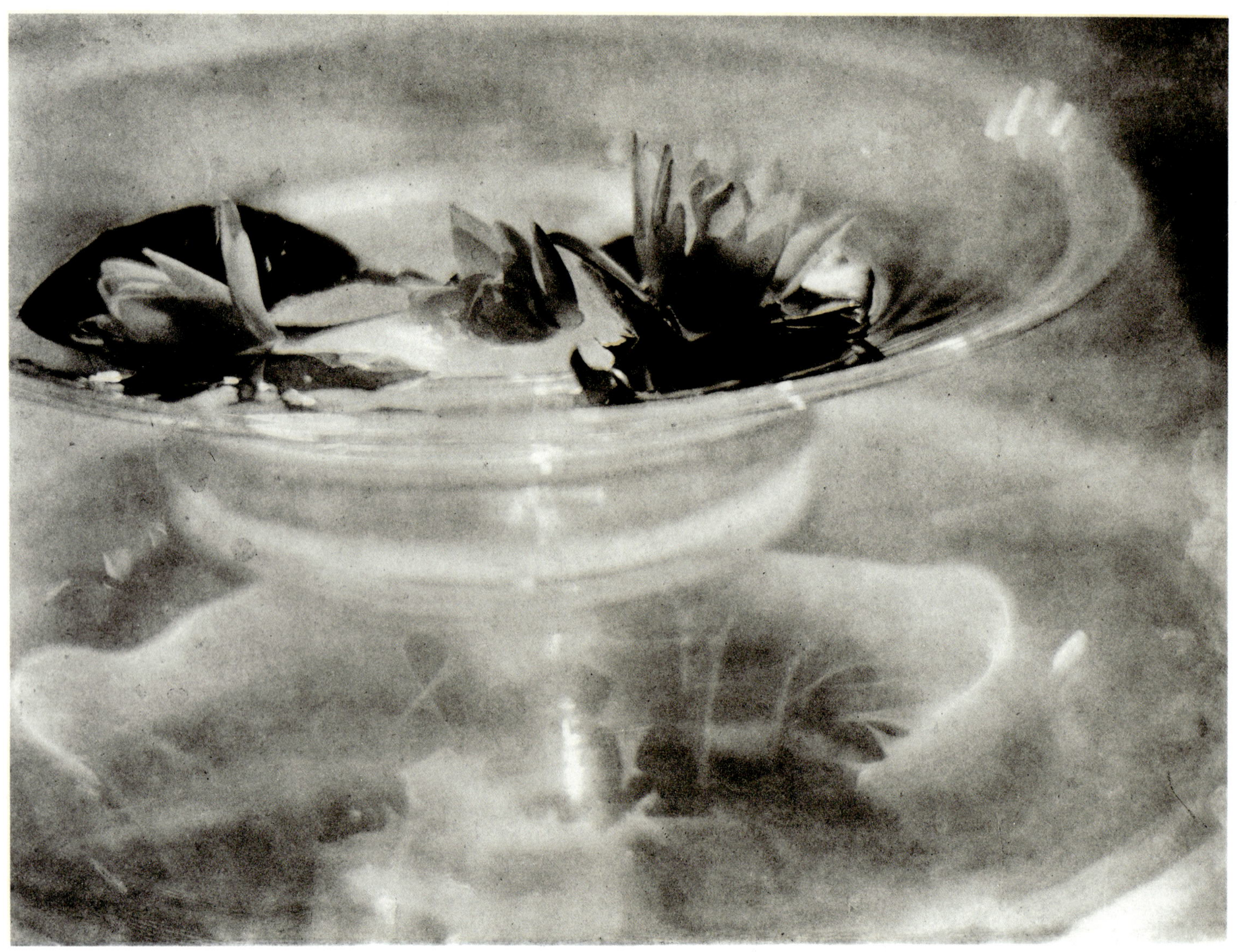

Baron Adolphe De Meyer, *Waterlilies,* circa 1906, Royal Photographic Society, Bath.

Edward Steichen, *The Pond,* ▶ 1898, Royal Photographic Society, Bath.

exhibition at the Photo-Club de Paris, where Steichen became acquainted with Demachy. He also met Rodin.

In Eugène Carrière's lithograph *Rodin Sculpting* (c. 1900), the sculpted form seems to billow out of the artist's hands like a volatile cloud. Writing in *The Photogram* (1901), Steichen admired Carrière's elusive effect: "blending his tones, he secures an exquisite feeling of atmosphere and shrouds that in a lovely sentiment." Carrière obtained the remarkable depth of tone and richness of shadows of his lithographs by a method of successive impressions, a method also employed by gum printers like Steichen and Demachy. In this way, forms emerged from a deep background which, in the words of Claude Roger-Marx, "is itself a living thing, a link between matter and spirit, the sole source of energy and movement".[22]

Also in 1901, Steichen traveled to Munich to photograph the artist Franz von Lenbach. He struck up a friendship with Kühn while he was there. Lenbach, then the most popular portrait-painter in Germany if not in all of Europe, having painted Bismarck, Pope Leo XIII, Schopenhauer, Helmholtz, Liszt, Wagner, and Böcklin, combined an impressionistic technique with photographic accuracy. He is said to have enlarged photographic images directly onto the canvas as a basis for his paintings.[23]

The photographs Steichen made of him were studies after a series of self-portraits Lenbach had made of himself. In one of the paintings, Lenbach portrays himself scowling over palette and gleaming palette-knife, a menacing effect which Steichen remembered, perhaps, when he photographed the American millionaire J. P. Morgan two years later.

In 1902, Steichen had his first one-man show, consisting of both paintings and photographs, at La Maison des Artistes in Paris, and on his return to New York became a co-founder of the Photo-Secession. His ten photographs reproduced in the second issue of *Camera Work* were introduced by Sadakichi Hartmann who likened Steichen's power of expression to that of Maeterlinck. Steichen was especially influenced by Maeterlinck's *Treasures of the Humble* (1897) and *Wisdom*

22. C. Roger Marx, *Graphic Art of the Nineteenth Century,* New York, MacGraw Hill, p. 196.

23. A. Scharf, *Art and Photography,* London, Penguin Books, 1983, p. 57; Erika Billeter, *Malerei und Photographie im Dialog von 1840 bis Heute,* Berne, Benteli-Verlag, 1977, pp. 55–58.

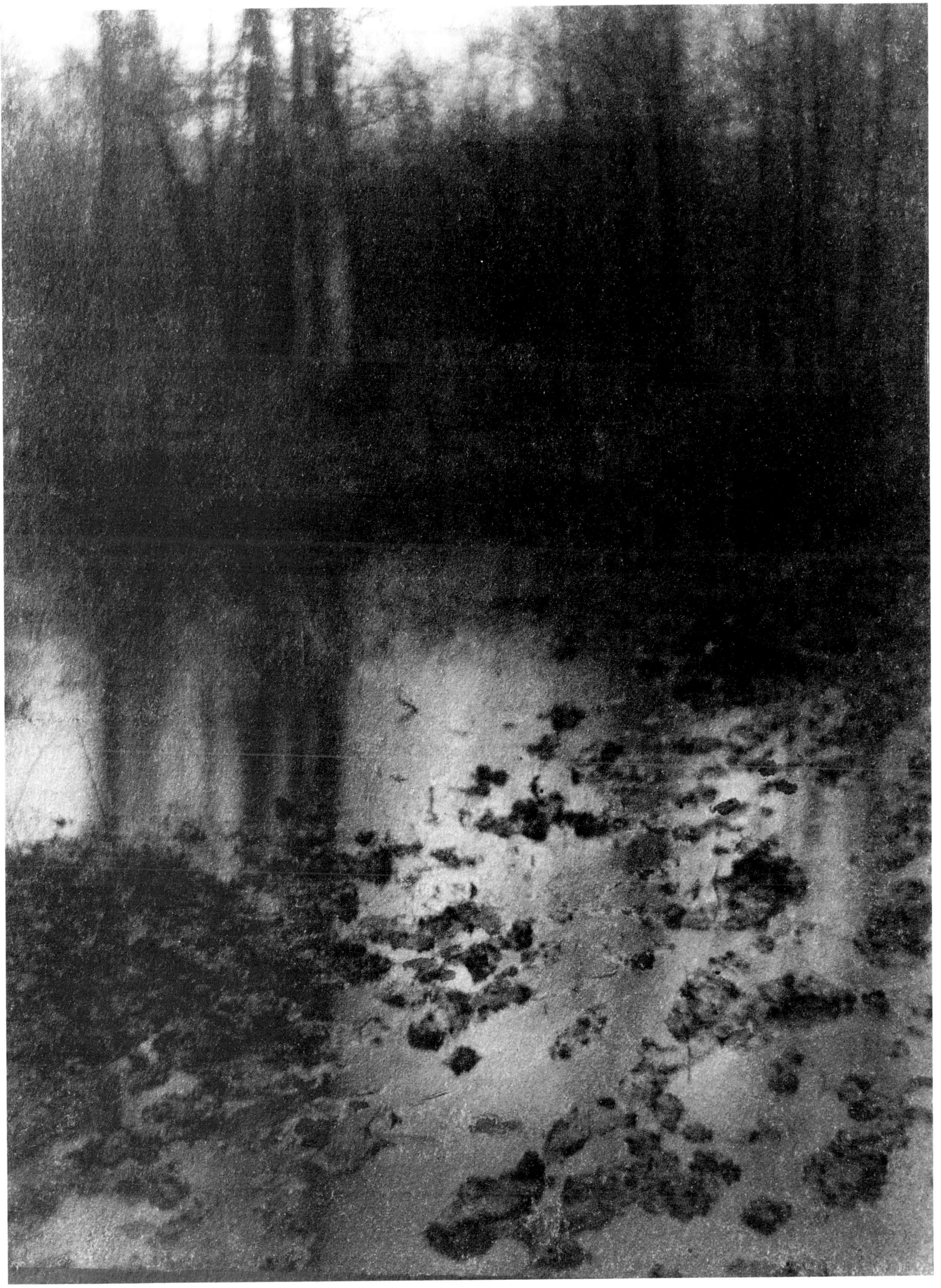

The Linked Ring

In 1891, the first international exhibition of art photography was organized by the Vienna Camera Club. Alfred Maskell, whose work was exhibited there, conceived the idea of an association of photographers in Britain which, through a series of such exhibitions, could promote photography as art. Serious amateurs who considered the Royal Photographic Society unsympathetic to their artistic interests gathered around him. The initial founding group – Alfred Maskell, H. P. Robinson, Lyonel Clark, George Davison, Henry Hay Cameron, and Alfred Horsley Hinton – met at the Restaurant d'Italie in London, on May 9, 1892, and discussed possible names for the club. The first suggestion, "having regard to the mysticism and symbolism implied", was the Gimmal Ring, a hinged double ring of betrothal which could be worn by two persons at once, with hands linked together. This name was changed to the Parabola, which implied in its origin the idea of the "parable" or metaphor, an indication of the pictorial aims of the club members – to produce works of poetic beauty through photography. At the second meeting, the name *The Linked Ring* was agreed on, and the number of founding members had grown to fifteen.

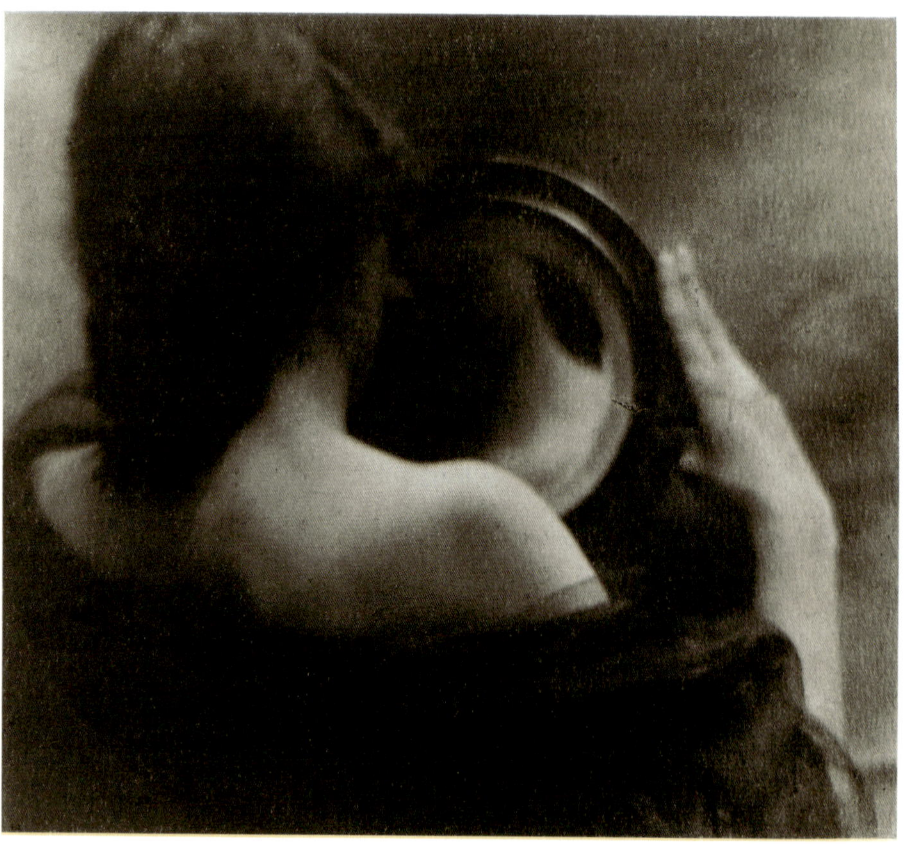

Edward Steichen,
The Mirror,
1902, Royal Photographic Society, Bath

New members were proposed from within, and the photographer would be invited to join only upon unanimous approval of all "Links". In the early years, some of the member Links assumed pseudonyms by which they were known within the group: Horsley Hinton, as "Comptroller of the Exchequer", was Treasurer; F. H. Evans took the name "Hangman" as the one who "hung" the exhibitions; Demachy was "The Parisian", Craig Annan "The Selector", Bucquet "The Grand Huntsman", Coburn "The Hustler", Holland Day "The Psychologist", Keiley "The Attorney", de Meyer "The Baron", and Puyo "The Lamplighter".

The Linked Ring held an annual international Photographic Salon in London, from 1893 to 1904 at the Dudley Gallery and from 1905 to 1909 at the gallery of the Royal Society of Painters in Watercolours. Within the Linked Ring itself a wide range of aesthetic approaches was encouraged. At one extreme, the Purists held that the image must be purely and completely photographic (not permitting any retouching or manipulation), while the Impressionists advocated any graphic means available to achieve their artistic goal.

In 1908, the exhibited works at the Photographic Salon were dominated by a group of photographers associated with Stieglitz's Photo-Secession. In angry response, a Photographic Salon des Refusés was organized by F. J. Mortimer. Arguments about the powers of selection which should be afforded to the Linked Ring eventually brought about its formal dissolution in November 1909.

Anne Hammond

and Destiny (1898), and he photographed him in Paris for the frontispiece of his next book, *The Buried Temple* (1902).

The Symbolists sought to represent the unknowable, that which could not be grasped. The purpose of Symbolist art was to evoke by means of objects a particular state of mind. Sadakichi Hartmann had known Mallarmé and joined his Tuesday evening gatherings in Paris in the 1890s. When he wrote, under the name of Sidney Allan, of one of Steichen's pictures as "a vague vista of some nocturnal landscape seen through […] a group of beech and birch trees, whose bark forms a quaint mosaic of horizontal color suggestions",[25] it was in terms of poetic allusion as set out in the Symbolist manifestos.

The Pond – Moonrise (1903) is one of many variations Steichen made on the theme of "the pool". In earlier versions such as *Inside a Wood* (1898), *The Pool, Evening* (1899), and *Le Mystère du Printemps* (1900), the treatment is naturalistic and tonalist. But in *Moonrise* the forms are posterized into a flattened frieze like that of Khnopff in his painting *The Pool at Ménil* (1890),[25] where the reflections receive even greater compositional weight than the trees on the bank. The elements of the pond, silhouetted trees, and rising moon are also found in Alphonse Osbert's *Song of the Night* (1896). As Symbolists, Khnopff and Osbert would have been well aware of the significance of the pool as the psychic boundary between worlds of reality and dream.

24. S. Allan (S. Hartmann) "A Visit to Steichen's studio", *Camera Work*, no. 2, 1903, p. 25.

25. See P. Jullian, *The Symbolists*, London, Phaidon, 1973, pl. 56.

The young female nude in Steichen's *La Cigale* (1901) is remarkably close to *Writing on the Wall* (1890–1902) by Whistler.[26] With her unselfconscious attitude, absorbed attention, and youthfulness, the nude model expresses a type of beauty which epitomizes a blithe innocence. Steichen's choice of title for his photograph is a witty, lightly self-mocking recognition of the Whistlerian-Impressionist origin of his group of nudes which includes *The Little Round Mirror* (1901) and *The Little Model* (c. 1901).

In 1899, Whistler painted his *Rose and Brown: La Cigale* in order to commemorate the subject of a French burlesque play *La Cigale*.[27] It satirized the Impressionists, caricaturing famous canvases by Monet, Degas, Renoir, and Pissarro, and offering a comic portrait of Whistler himself. The painter-protagonist declares at one point, "We are no longer Impressionists now, we are Intentionists, we have intentions". Thus Whistler, the hero of P. H. Emerson in 1890, left his mark on the whole period from Impressionism to Symbolism in photography.

Gertrude Käsebier (1852–1934) employed Christian motifs in her photographs. Käsebier had studied painting in the early 1890s. After being apprenticed at a commercial photographer's, she opened her own studio in New York in 1897 and, two years later, was given a solo exhibition at the New York Camera Club. In 1902, she was a founding member of the Photo-Secession, and her work was featured in the first number of *Camera Work*.

Sadakichi Hartmann reproached her for being not sufficiently interested in rules of composition and too reliant on Pictorial motifs.[28] The popularity of *The Manger* (c. 1898), which sold in 1899 for 100 dollars, lay in the ethereal treatment of the Virgin with a white gown and veil within the naturalistic context of a stable.

Joseph Keiley (1869–1914) was a contemporary of Käsebier. In 1898, they shared as models Sioux Indians who were visiting New York. He was a spokesman and historian for the Photo-Secession. A New York lawyer who became involved in photography when he joined the Camera Club in 1899, he was associate editor under Stieglitz first of *Camera Notes* and then of *Camera Work*, in which he published a dozen articles between 1903 and 1911. Of his photographs Sadakichi Hartmann wrote: "His work conveys an effect like the ringing of an old church bell. A deep, mysterious sound in the bass and above it a very light ethereal one, so fugitive that it seems to vanish at every moment."[29]

Pierre Dubreuil (1872–1944) embodied each step in the transition from Naturalism to Symbolism (and even to Modernism). His style evolved from spontaneous naturalistic photographs and hand-worked gum portraits to decorative poster-like pictures and Symbolist studies. *Le Coquillage* (1903) presents a relatively straightforward treatment of a subject with a Symbolist undercurrent – a young woman in white walks out onto the exposed seabed at low tide and reflects upon a seashell, at the edge of an immense ocean indicated by the misty horizon line.

Soon after its introduction in 1904, he began to use the Rawlins oil process. After moving to Brussels in 1918, he eventually became president of the Belgian Association of Photography and a committed Modernist, strongly opposing the conservative faction led by Misonne.

Frederick H. Evans (1853–1943) was a bookseller in London who retired in 1898 to devote his time to photographic art. A keen student of religious philosophy, Henry James Senior, father of the novelist and author of *Christianity, the Logic of Creation* (1857), was his favourite philosopher. Evans also knew the theosophical treatises of Jacob Boehme and the works of Emanuel

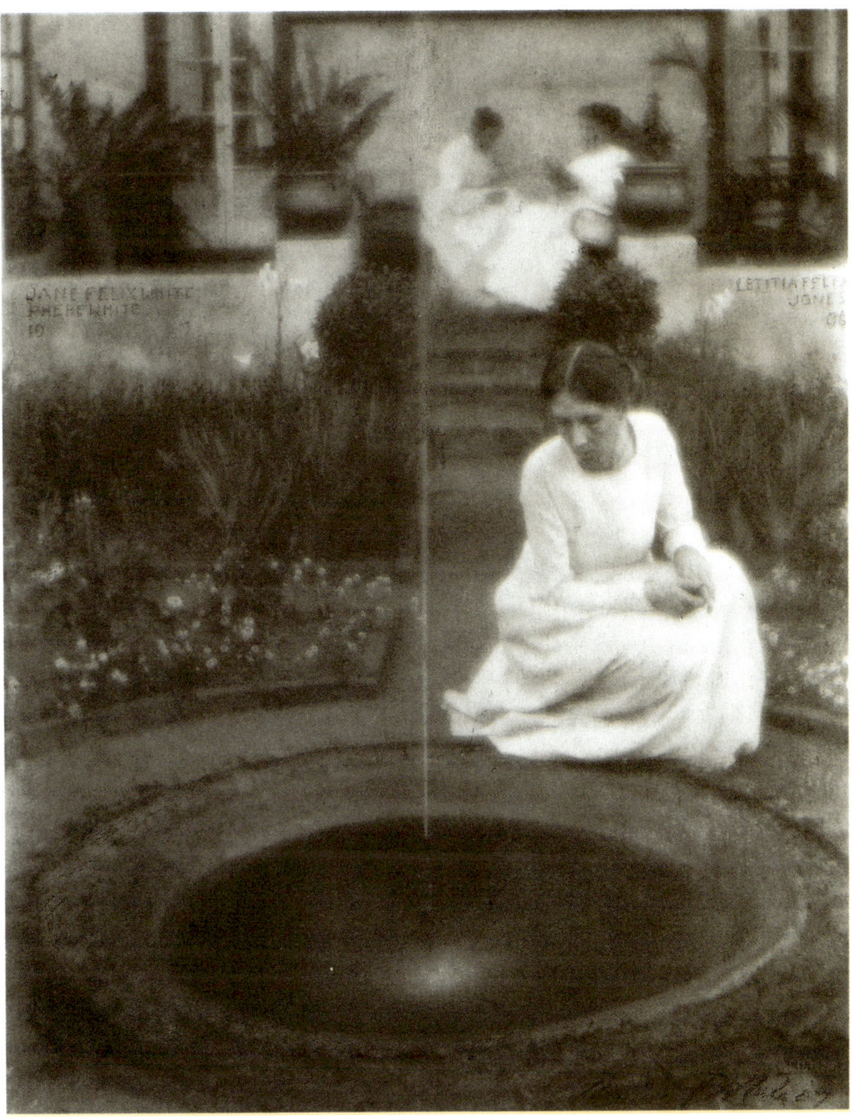

Clarence H. White, *Fountain*,
circa 1906–1907,
Royal Photographic Society, Bath.

26. D. P. Curry, *James McNeill Whistler at the Freer Gallery of Art*, London, W. W. Norton, 1984, p. 271.

27. The play, by Ludovic Halévy and based on the imaginary career of an "Intentionist" painter, was first put on in Paris on October 6, 1877. It was performed in London in the same year and in 1883.

28. S. Hartmann, *The Valiant Knights of Daguerre*, London, University of California Press, 1978, p. 198.

29. S. Hartmann, "The Photo-Secession Exhibition at the Carnegie Art Galleries, Pittsburgh, Pa.", *Camera Work*, no. 6, 1904, p. 49.

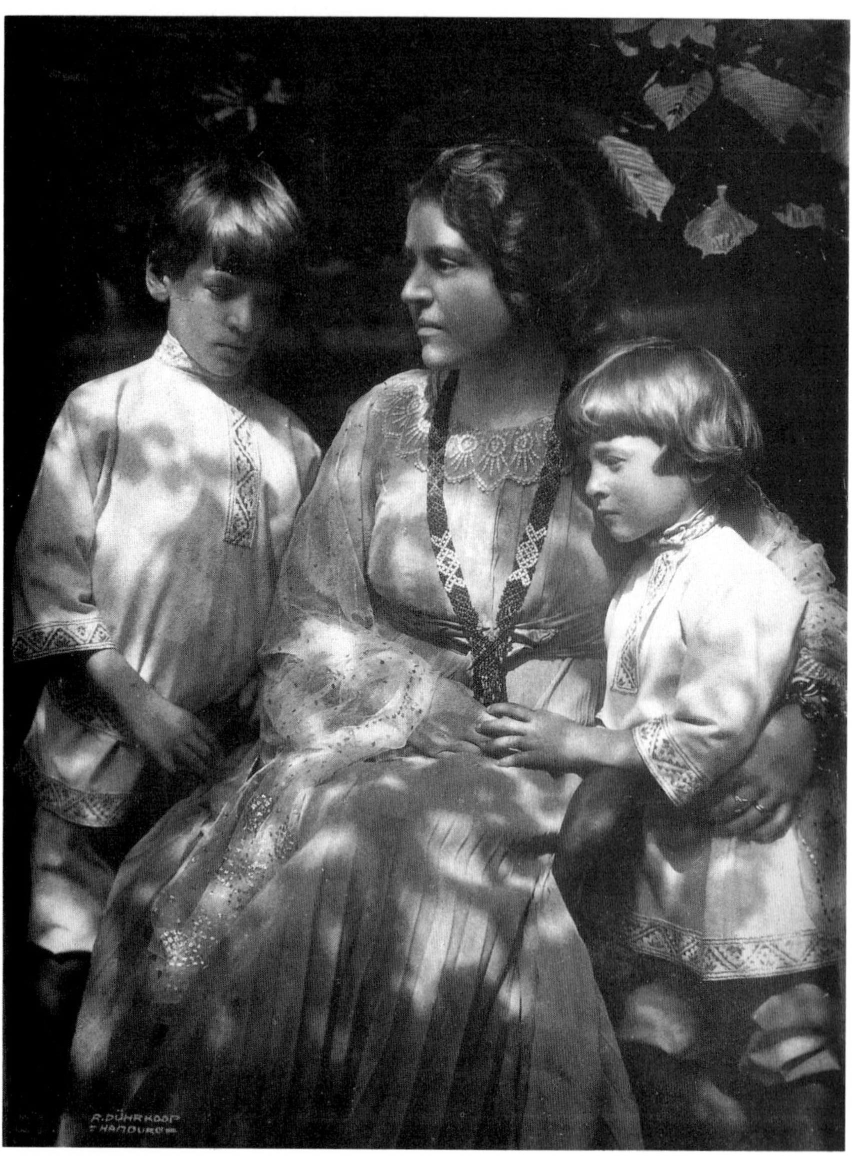

Rudolph Dührkoop, ***Elena Luksch-Makovsky and Her Children***, circa 1900, Museum für Kunst und Gewerbe, Hamburg.

Swedenborg, whose ideas were held in high regard by Symbolist writers. Swedenborg saw in every object in nature a corresponding spiritual quality, and all spiritual life as clothed in the garments of nature.

Evans was especially interested in the geometry of the spiral, partly as a result of his collaboration with Theodore Andrea Cook, in whose book *The Curves of Life* (1914) Evans's picture of Lincoln cathedral stairs was reproduced. In *Lincoln, Stairs in S. W. Turret* (1898) the gothic arch branches out from the trunk of the newel post with the keystone supporting a spiral stair and a corresponding series of arched ribs of the turret ceiling, a movement which is both generative and aspiring.[30]

An ardent admirer of Japanese prints, Evans was also a connoisseur of the European tradition of graphic arts. He owned a collection of lithographs by Odilon Redon. Both Evans and Redon found artistic stimulation early in their careers in their experiments with the microscope, Evans through his friendship with George Smith of the Sciopticon Company, and Redon by his association with the botanist Clavand. The microscopic view may have provided Redon with evidence of a nightmarish, unreal world within the real, but to Evans it was proof of the perfect structure of creation, the logical expression of Neo-Platonist and Swedenborgian ideas of the microcosm.

The decadent Symbolism of Redon, obsessed with the morbid fantasy and the fearful dream, was not that of Evans. His was a symbolism of a restrained variety, excluding the exoticism and excesses of Decadence, but drawing on the Symbolist preference for evocation and poetic suggestion. For Evans a potent psychological system of motifs was already to be found in traditional Christian typology.

Evans's treatment of cathedral interiors in the 1890s was a relatively new departure in photography. Unlike earlier topographical photographers, he framed his interior views for those architectural elements which suggested passage, ascent, and transformation.

In his famous photograph of 1903, *A Sea of Steps; Wells Cathedral: Stairs to the Chapter House and Bridge to the Cathedral Close*, the viewer is confronted with a flight of stairs which leads up to a radiant archway, a safe anchorage in the crests and troughs of this agitated and uneven sea of steps. But the traveler must face on their right the almost insurmountable wall of spiraling stairs which, in its geometric progression, is "like the surge of a great wave", as Evans described it. By transforming stone into sea, relating architecture to wave-motion, Evans expressed the traditional idea of the *sancta scala* [holy stairs] in a Symbolist manner.

Following on from the artistic ambitions of Rejlander and the spiritual aims of Cameron, naturalist photographers continued down the road toward fine printing by means of platinum, gum bichromate, and photogravure. In the context of various international groups of photographers with Symbolist inclinations, the artist-photographer shifted the emphasis from the object drawn directly from nature, and at the turn of the century turned the medium of photography in the direction of the expression of esoteric ideas.

30. A. Hammond, "Frederick H. Evans: The Spiritual Harmonies of Architecture", in M. Weaver (ed.), *British Photography in the Nineteenth Century*, Cambridge, Cambridge University Press, 1989.

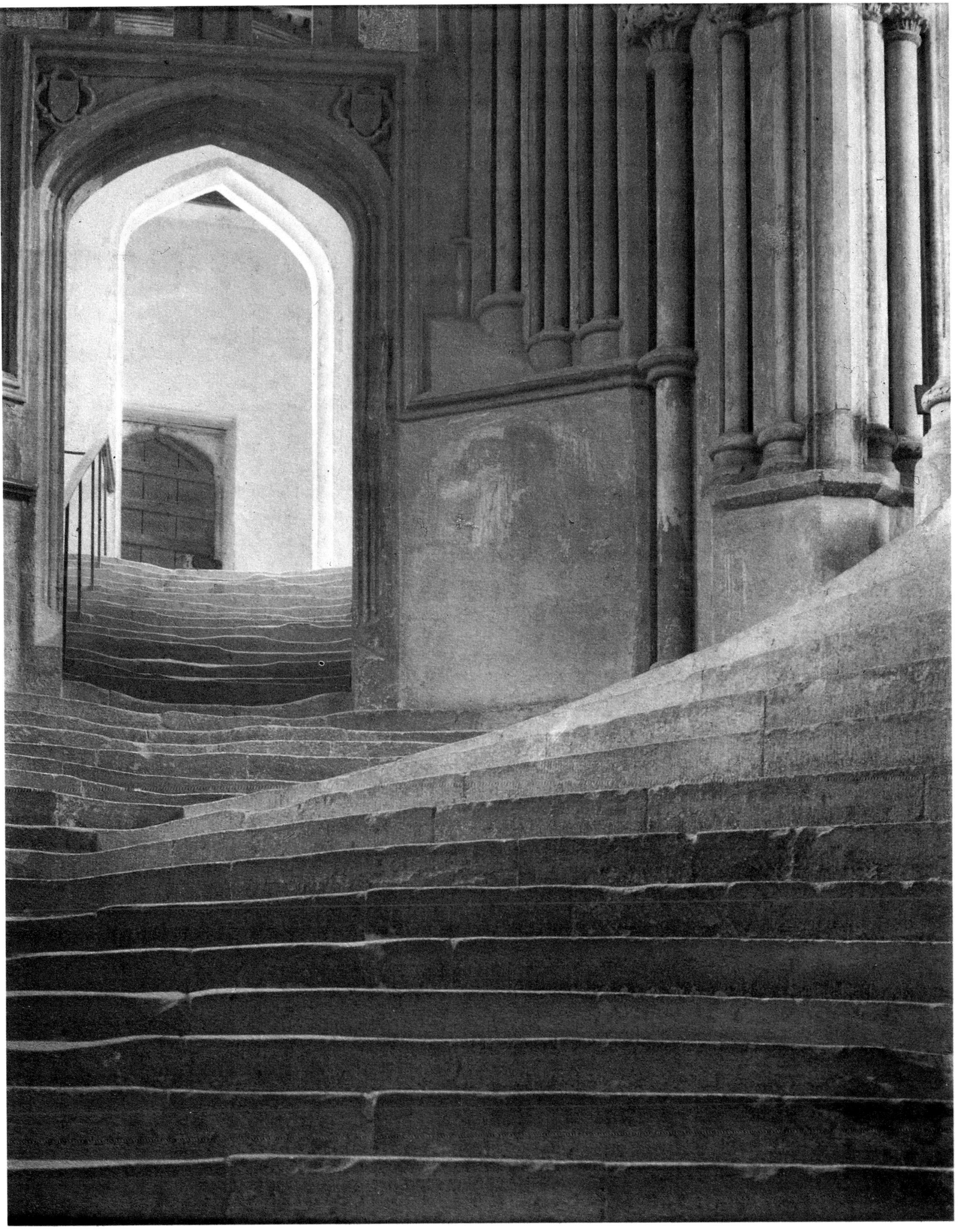

FREDERICK H. EVANS,
A Sea of Steps,
Wells Cathedral,
1903.

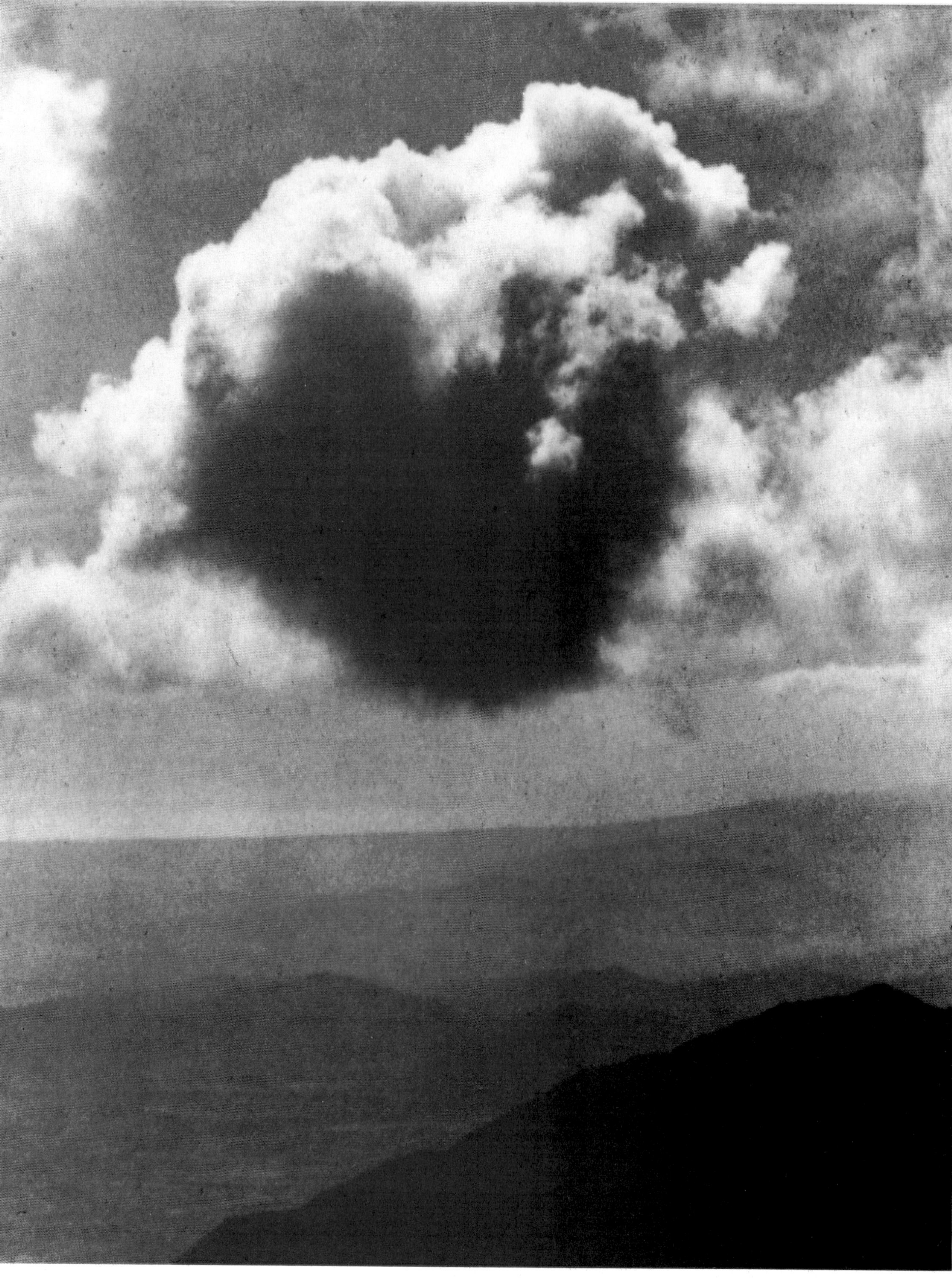

TOWARDS NEW PHOTOGRAPHY

18

Renewals of Pictorialism

Peter C. Bunnell

It was in the United States, in the heart of the Photo-Secession group and the magazine *Camera Work* – that is to say, under Stieglitz's direction – that certain contradictions inherent in Pictorialism were resolved. The movement which sought to adhere to the pictorial qualities of photography, produced where necessary by a series of manipulations, could not ignore the innovations affecting painting at the start of the twentieth century: Cubism, Fauvism, Futurism, the first appearance of Abstract art. So photographic practice was brought back to its special preoccupations, its particular ability, both technical and circumstantial, to capture an image. One option of "pure (that is, unmanipulated) photography was then defined, which abandoned the Pictorial aspect of texture and returned to visual precision and urban themes, while at the same time borrowing new ways of constructing an image from "modern art".

By the first decade of the twentieth century, Pictorial photography had achieved recognition as an international fine arts movement. With its culminating achievements reaching full expression in the United States by 1905, the attention of the serious artist photographer worldwide was now directed to the tenets of Pictorial photography. Two concepts were foremost. Firstly, that making meaningful, expressive photographs required discipline, considerable intentness, and knowledge of the traditional arts. Secondly, that in matters of craft and artistry, producing a fine photographic print was an act analogous to the creative endeavor in any medium. The foundation of these two ideas lay in the now clearly evident division in the practice of photography between the professional or applied commercial photographer at the one extreme, and the aesthetically motivated artist-amateur at the other. There developed a type of practitioner who was educated, knowledgeable, and able to afford expensive materials and equipment, and who, most importantly, was interested in the kind of intellectual and emotional interaction between people that is at the heart of artistic expression. Indeed, expression and not depiction is the key concept in understanding the substance and meaning of Pictorial photographs made by these artist-amateurs.

Between photography and painting

Photography as a means of expression was understood to be a reflection of personal values of conduct and experience, based on the notion of aesthetic significance and tradition. There were acclaimed examples of the first picture of this, the only picture of that. While these feats satisfied the general public's taste for interesting photographic curiosities, those interested in a more serious endeavor in making photographs recognized a fundamental fact about art – it cannot be about nothing. By being concerned with substantial and lasting values, the artist photographer was partaking in a dialogue between people at a level that placed them, and their chosen medium, in proximity to the magnificent store of historical masterworks from the ancients to the present. Indeed, this sense of an historical continuum played a significant role in the creation of photographs as the Pictorialist period initially evolved. Those photographers who became leading Pictorialists encouraged the notion of themselves as links not to the contemporaneity of experience and observation – termed "the impressionism of life" – but to eternal values and essential truths. In this way, much of the first wave of Pictorialist photography was Symbolist oriented. Meaning was frequently rooted in the context of literature

◀ ALVIN LANGDON COBURN, *plate from P. B. Shelley's* The Cloud, 1912, private collection.

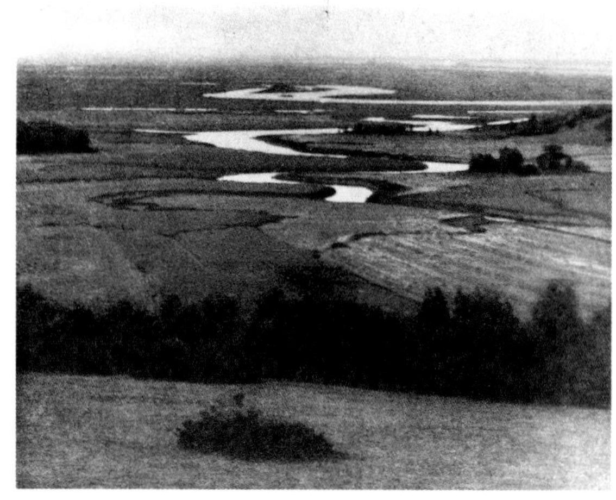

Alvin Langdon Coburn,
The Dragon
(*Camera Work*, April 1904).
Musée d'Orsay, Paris.

which, perhaps more than any other of the Symbolist storehouses, provided the most significant corpus of the collective memory.

As has been suggested, one of the critical components of the Pictorial photographic movement was an insistence on what might be termed the "objecthood" of the work of art. Given that an ordinary photograph is a multiple, that its creation lies in the realm of applied science and technology, and that by 1900 the ability to photomechanically reproduce a photograph had become common, the notion that there was something special and critically significant about the originality of the unique Pictorialist print was a bold, but necessary, conceptual step for the artist photographer to take. Arising from this keystone of Pictorialist aesthetics is the acceptance of the originality of the crafted picture, the understanding that technique is pliable, and that to recognize the subtlety of interpretation in a photograph requires a knowledge and appreciation of its physical beauty; these are the truly modernist notions added to the aesthetics of the photographic medium through Pictorialist theory. Indeed, it is important to remind ourselves that the term Pictorialism itself derives from a conception based on the primacy of making a *picture*: not merely depicting something, not merely stopping an action or event, but taking the fact of observable reality and reconstituting it in a form that is unique – unique to the realm of two-dimensional art.

For instance, landscape has an instructive history in Pictorialism. Basically, the understanding of the time was set forth by A. H. Wall in his book *Artistic Landscape Photography*, published in London in 1896. "In the early days of photography a photographer never thought it worth his while to point his camera to any object that had not some particular interest connected with it [...] Whereas in former times the photographer's aim was to produce a representation or a portrait of a particular scene, that of the modern photographer is to produce a picture."[1]

Edward Steichen,
***Rodin*, The Thinker,**
(*Camera Work*,
July 1905 and April 1906),
Musée d'Orsay, Paris.

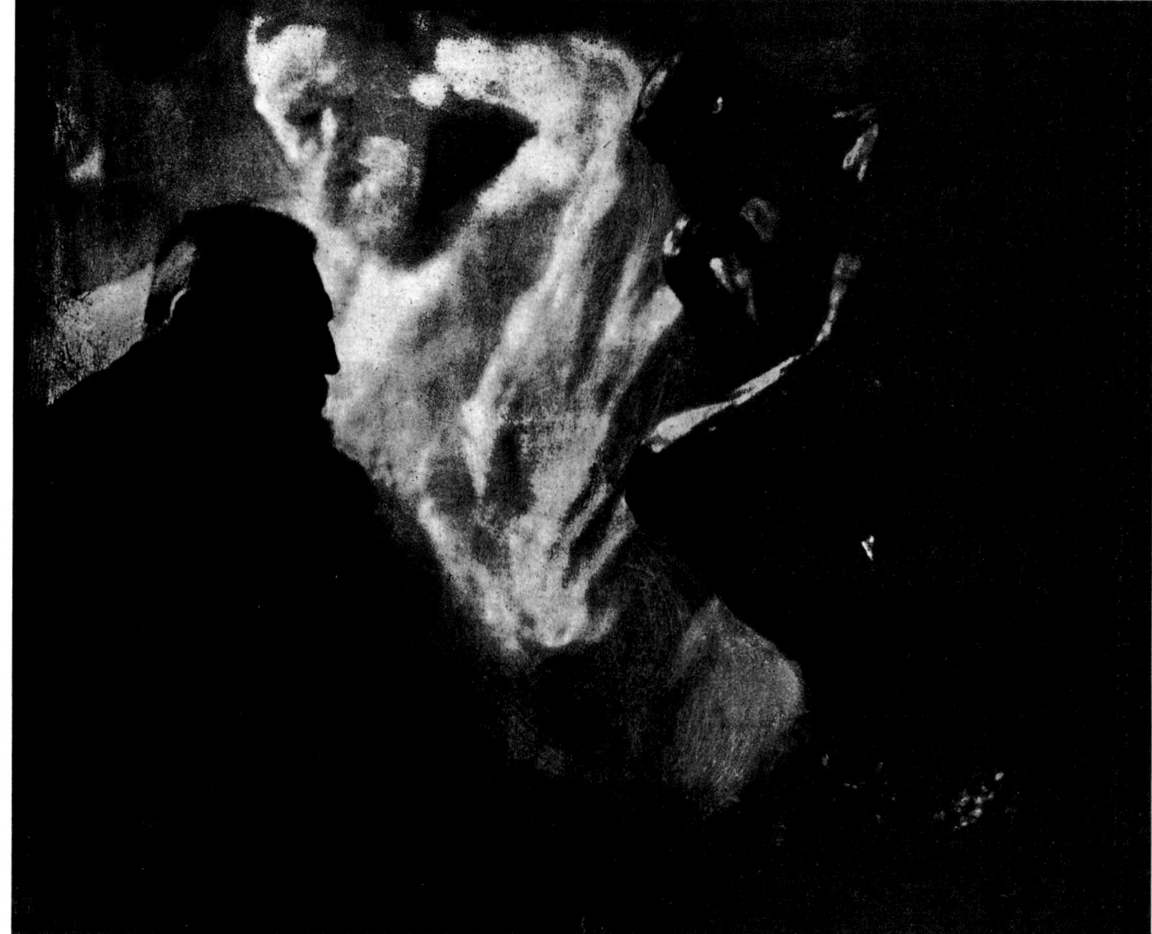

1. A. H. Wall, *Artistic Landscape Photography*, London, Percy Lunn and Company Ltd., 1896, pp. 26–27.

2. C. Caffin, "Some Prints by Alvin Langdon Coburn", *Camera Work*, no. 6, 1904, p. 18.

3. M. Weber, "Tradition and Now", *Photo-Graphic Art*, no. 3, 1916, p. 11.

4. D. Longwell, *Steichen: The Master Prints, 1895–1914*, New York, Museum of Modern Art, 1978.

This is as able a statement about early Pictorialist aesthetics as one can find. However, to recognize the complication that such an idea presented to both the photographer and the contemporary critic (and, assuredly, the audience), one has only to quote the widely read Charles Caffin who, writing in *Camera Work* in 1904, said of Alvin Langdon Coburn's landscape photograph *The Dragon*: "A view [...] with a curious effect of serpentine lines of water winding through the flat-lands. In the fascination of the patterning of the composition it would have been easy to lose sight of the substantial realities of the ground plan. But in this case they are naturally, though unobtrusively, enforced; with the result, I think, that the bizarrerie of the lines receives increased interest [...] I doubt, however, if the treatment of the band of foliage across the foreground is satisfactory. It appears rather formless, leaving one uncertain as to whether it is a hedge or the tops of trees growing lower down the bank; a necessary point to be cleared up, since, if the latter is intended, it would indicate a deeper fall in the ground than is now evident."[2]

Caffin's obvious inability to recognize that Coburn was not aiming to render a topographical landscape is to sense the difficulty many had in coming to terms with this avant-garde photography. As the period unfolded, and more radical expressions became commonplace, even more serious confusions occurred. It was Max Weber, a young European-trained painter and teacher at Clarence H. White's school of photography who, in a statement in *Photographic Art* in 1916, articulated the critical position of the later period. In an effort to differentiate between the observer and the artist, and to position the photographer with the artist, he wrote: "Modernity has closed our eyes and blotted our vision. [...] To see a thing is to *see* its inherent spirit, as the X-ray sees the physical internal structure of matter. To see an art work casually or en passant is a very pleasant experience; but to come in touch with the vision, the spirit of its maker, is seeing in participation, and then it is not only a gratification but an exaltation."[3]

In another area, a virtuoso demonstration of the interrelationship that the Pictorialist photographers first drew between photography and painting may be seen in the work of Edward Steichen. His youthful sensibility was expansive, gestural, and romantic, and only through the use of highly manipulative processes such as gum-bichromate, oil pigment, and other combinations could his vitality be contained and expressed. Twenty-one years old in 1900 when he first went to Europe, Steichen arranged an introduction to the sculptor Rodin and proceeded to photograph the artist and his works. By linking himself to the spiritual gravity of one of the greatest artists of the time, Steichen revealed his deliberate strategy to obtain for himself and for photography a place in the artistic hierarchy, if only by appropriation. His *Self-Portrait with Brush and Palette, Paris* of 1901 is a *tour de force* of process and self-projection, and is executed in the spirit of his renderings of Rodin's own works. Loosely based on a portrait by Titian, the photograph shows Steichen as a painter, a narcissist unafraid to mark his sympathies with the traditional arts but also proud, even eager, to reveal his talents in a work of aggressive pictorial photography.[4]

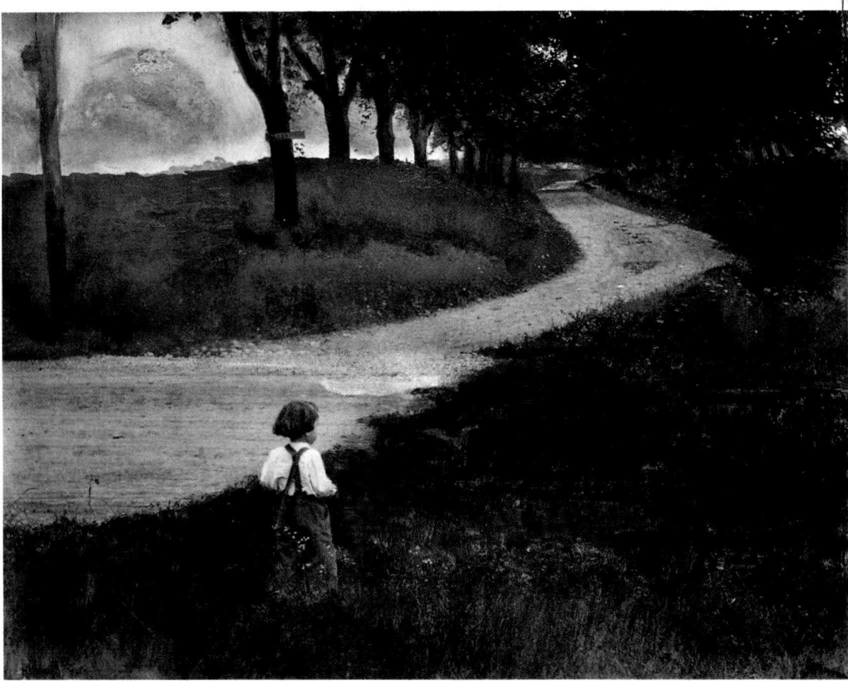

Gertrude Käsebier,
The Road to Rome,
1903,
Art Museum, Princeton University.

A strategy for economic value

By 1905, Pictorialist photography had progressed to a position where this belief in the primacy of the created picture was foremost in the minds of everyone involved. The capitalist concept of the art work as a singularly rare object, with a measure of its importance provided by the extent of its economic value meant that Pictorialist photography was a particularly contemporary form of artistic expression. Understandably, the first country to truly exploit this notion of capitalist enterprise with regard to art photography was the United States. It should come as no surprise that while Pictorialist works in the annual exhibitions or salons in Europe had been for sale, the development of the private gallery, of organized marketing activity replete with regular exhibitions and published criticism, was an American contribution. Largely an urban phenomenon, it was orchestrated out of New

Logo of the Photo-Secession group, 1902.

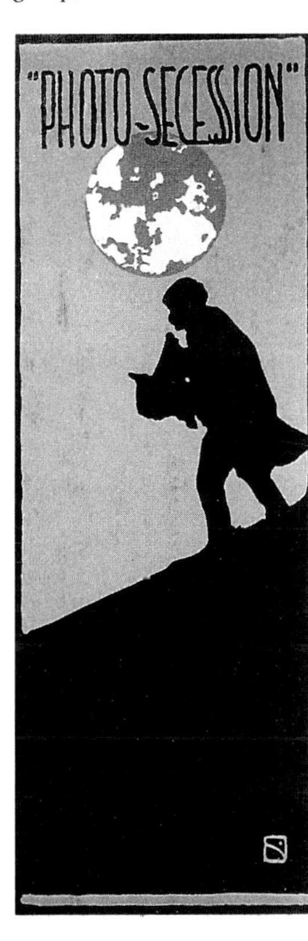

The "291" Gallery

On November 25, 1905, the "Little Galleries" of the Photo-Secession opened on the fourth floor of a building at 291 Fifth Avenue in New York. Showing a 100 print exhibition of members' work, the gallery was to be the showplace for the Photo-Secession under the direction of Alfred Stieglitz.

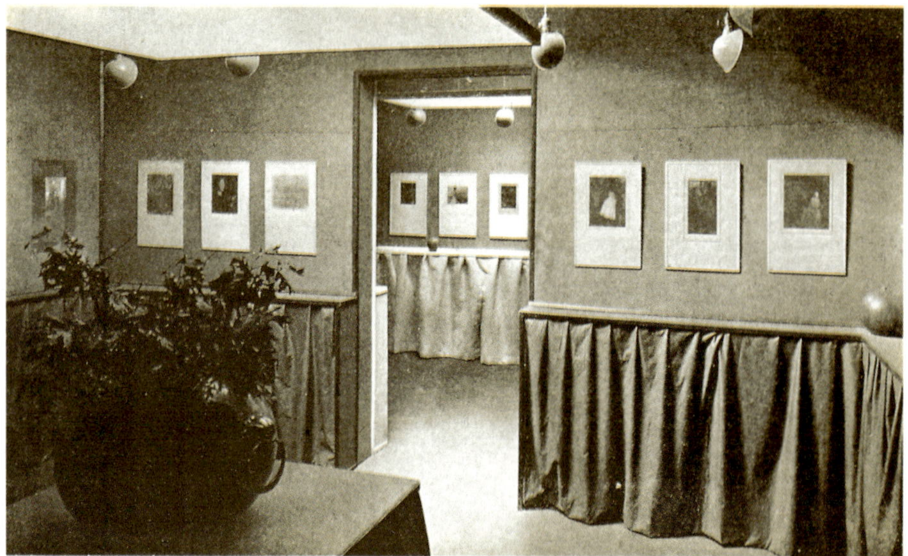

Alfred Stieglitz
View of Little Galleries of the Photo-Secession,
(*Camera Work*, April 1906), Musée d'Orsay, Paris

Like *Camera Work*, which had begun publication in 1902, the gallery was to provide a focus for the efforts to gain recognition for Pictorial photography as a contemporary art form. Noting that, even with its sumptuous reproductions, *Camera Work* was still a publication, Stieglitz recognized that the key to the understanding of the originality of Pictorial photography lay in its crafting of a unique object. To give a forceful demonstration of this idea he had to have exhibitions of these originals in order to bring the public to this understanding – exhibitions more regularized and controlled than the salons that hitherto had been the norm. In addition, and as a further component to his efforts to gain recognition, the pictures had to be available for purchase in an environment customarily understood for such a function – the commercial gallery. While very discreet, with only a notice in the exhibition stating "Prices Upon Inquiry", Stieglitz moved the tangible acceptance of photography to the domain of art patrons and other buyers.

Group- and one-person exhibitions of photographs were the main focus of the gallery for only a short time. In January 1907, the first works in another medium were shown: drawings by Pamela Coleman Smith. Beginning in 1908, under the influence of Edward Steichen advising Stieglitz from Europe, the exhibition program dramatically shifted to works by such masters as Rodin, Matisse, Braque, and Picasso. This shift was made, in part, as an effort by Stieglitz to alter the direction of Pictorial photography from its roots in Symbolism towards formalism and the more realist vision of a straightforward representation of contemporary subjects. Stieglitz sensed that he could show in these exhibitions where modern painting was moving so that photographers and the audience alike would gain an understanding of the unique character of the medium that should be accentuated. While the public remained fascinated with "291", as it came to be known, the photographic community gradually drew away and, by 1912, there were no exhibitions of photographs at all. Stieglitz showed his own work in 1913 and then only the work of Paul Strand in 1916 before the gallery closed in the spring of the next year.

291 should be seen as an educational forum; a place where Stieglitz could hold forth in public, where artists and the public could come together and where original works could be studied and debated. The gallery, like all of his endeavors, was energized by Stieglitz and so controversy was always a part of it.

Without the gallery the development of Pictorial photography would have been very different, but this should not diminish the gallery's importance also for the introduction of avant-garde European and American art to a New York audience.

Peter C. Bunnell

York by the country's leading practitioner and spokesman for photography, Alfred Stieglitz.

The development of a strategy for the promulgation and acceptance of the new photography was almost single-handedly left to him. Club or society activity had been the hallmark of the Pictorialist movement in Britain, where it mostly began, and also in France, Austria, Germany (where Stieglitz first trained), and elsewhere. What Stieglitz did in his effort to promote photography was to transfer the arena of discourse to the more aggressive domain of a single sponsor – the gallery director and the leader of an informal organization. In 1902, he named his group the Photo-Secession[5] and signaled a withdrawal from the usual practices of amateur and professional conduct. He set about defining the boundaries of photographic expertise and character. Through publication and then exhibition he showed a broad spectrum of images from the more or less straightforward but elegantly crafted platinum prints of Clarence H. White or Joseph T. Keiley to the highly articulated exercises in hand-made, multiple gum prints by Gertrude Käsebier or, of course, those by Edward Steichen. Not distracted by the underlying debate over whether photography should or should not be straightforward as opposed to manipulated, Stieglitz dealt instead with the notion of significant content, significant expression, and superior craft in whatever mode was selected as the vehicle of presentation. Sumptuous almost beyond belief for a photography journal, or even an art periodical, his magazine *Camera Work* was a forum for the display of quality illustrations. Significantly, stressed in most of the magazine's issues was the

5. W. I. Homer, *Alfred Stieglitz and Photo-Secession*, Boston, Little, Brown and Co. 1983; R. Doty, *Photo-Secession, Stieglitz and the Fine-Art Movement in Photography*, New York, Dover, 1978.

fact that each reproduction was made from the original negative, and that it was printed to the highest standards available. With but few exceptions, the images published in the magazine, which extended over some fifty numbers from 1903 to 1917, while not being original photographs, were perceived as a unique form of graphic reproduction.[6]

The audience for serious photography had seen the original pictures in the salons held in the United States and abroad, and at a very few selective exhibitions in museums – notably in Paris, Turin, Glasgow, Düsseldorf, and Chicago. In 1905, Stieglitz took the unprecedented step of opening a private exhibition gallery in New York as a showcase for works by members of his Photo-Secession group. This step, like so much of what Stieglitz did, resulted from a sophisticated knowledge of the past combined with a contemporary strategy of applying capitalist economics to the appreciation and acceptance of art. Stieglitz clearly positioned himself at the center of power and he was the major spokesperson for Pictorial photography. To some, he was also the major American practitioner. It was this that gave his views added authority.

The gallery, located at 291 Fifth Avenue in New York, had no real counterpart in Europe for several decades. While there were other exhibition spaces established in a somewhat similar commercial context, none existed with the primary purpose of sponsoring a specific medium and promoting the view that photography was an art form. This, of course, was a necessary concept in order to maintain the differentiation between those who were artists and those who sought only commissions. Most photographers around Stieglitz were unable to derive enough income from their art to be free of portrait work, for instance, to assure their livelihood.

Another byproduct of the Pictorialist movement was the development of schools of photography and the profession of teaching at the same time as making fine art photographs. Clarence H. White began his classes in 1910 and by 1914 had established his own school in New York.

The language of photo-manipulation

Gertrude Käsebier's is revealing for what might be termed the "typical" Pictorialist photographer. A Fifth Avenue portraitist by profession, she also achieved fame as a fine-art photographer, one of the first to be given a solo exhibition by Stieglitz at 291. Her 1905 *Path to Rome* is a paradigm of Symbolist representation and high Pictorial photography. The innocent boy is depicted in a pastoral glade about to embark down the pathway of life. In this rare example where we have the initial gelatin silver work print, the straight camera image is apparent underneath the over-painting and retouching that Käsebier used to obliterate the wealth of detail and the tonal structure of the basic photographic rendering, all in preparation for re-photographing *this* print in order to obtain a new, non-camera negative used in making the final gum-bichromate print. In the final version the tonal massing has been unified in an idealization of dark, undetailed blacks, making an evocative composition, a splendid example of creative expression.

The main issue here was the disharmony in tonal contrast and of sharpness which, as a quality of the lens/optical character of the camera medium, was the delimiting feature Käsebier had to alter to make a new aestheticized object. The key issue is that the manipulation occurs after the act of taking the photograph. A study of almost all Pictorialist works reveals that the camera negatives made by Käsebier or White, Stieglitz or

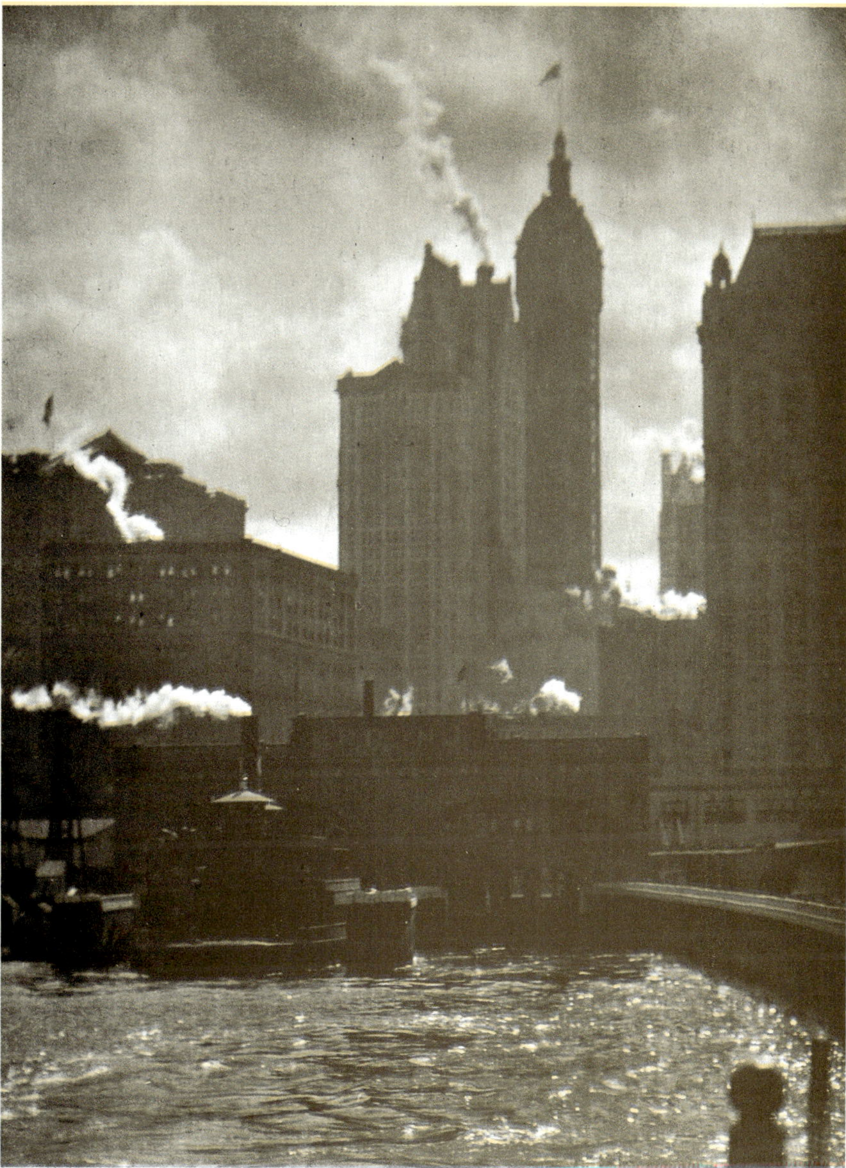

ALFRED STIEGLITZ,
The City of Ambition,
1910,
(*Camera Work*, October 1911),
Musée d'Orsay, Paris.

6. *Camera Work: A Critical Anthology*, J. Green (ed.), Millerton, Aperture, 1973; *Camera Work: A Pictorial Guide*, F. Margolis (ed.), New York, Dover, 1978.

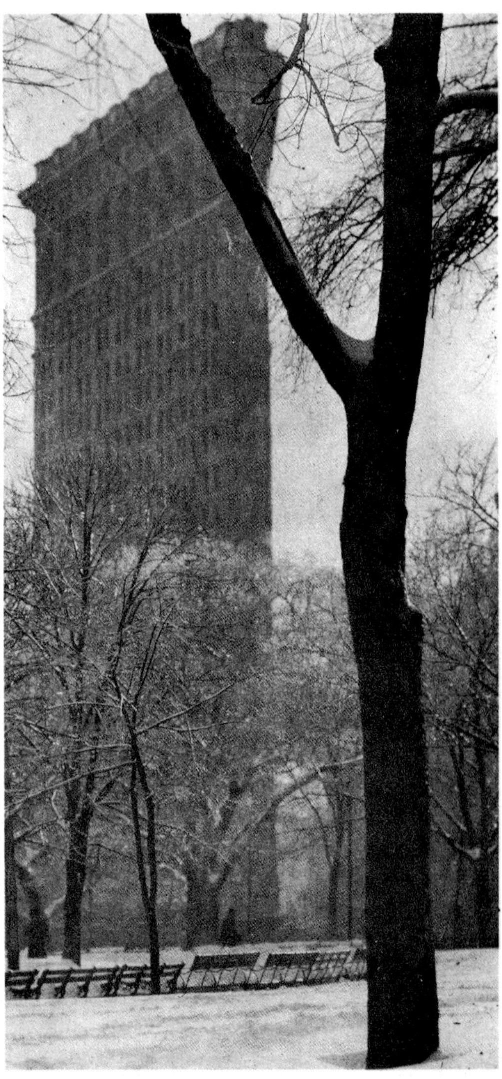

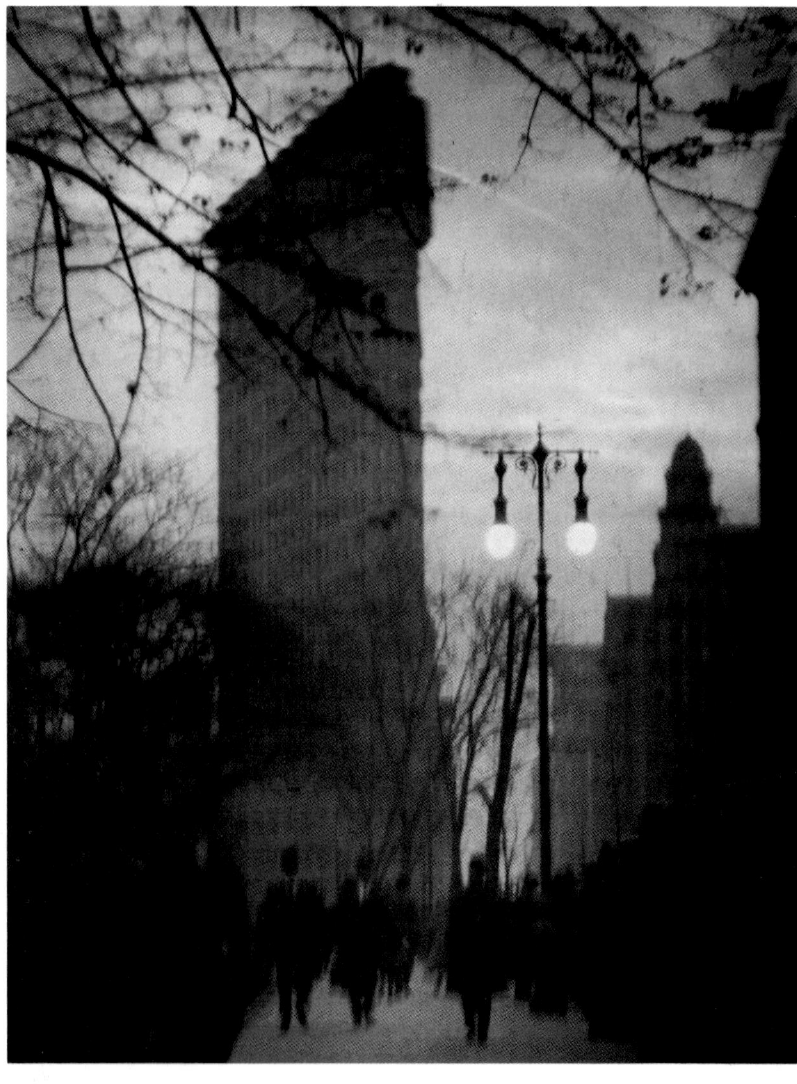

Left:
Alfred Stieglitz,
The Flatiron,
(*Camera Work*, October 1903),
Musée d'Orsay, Paris.

Right:
Alvin Langdon Coburn,
The Flatiron,
New York, 1912,
International Museum of Photography, George Eastman House, Rochester.

Coburn, were essentially straightforward, optically sharp and tonally rich negatives. It was in the transformation of this raw photographic data in the making of the print that their expressive achievement and artistry was made manifest. Their original engagement with the world did not differentiate them significantly from other photographers, regardless of persuasion. This fact, not well understood or recognized, makes it clear that, for these individuals, the ultimate creativity in the photographic process was not in the seeing – the taking of the photograph – but in the rethinking, the transformation of the camera image without regard to, or apart from, the reality of the world itself. By the early 1910s, several manufacturers, and even the practicing photographer Karl Struss had perfected a lens which was termed the "Pictorial Lens". This dramatically affected the character of the camera negative as described above. The 1915 advertisement for Struss's lens that appeared in the magazine for Pictorial photographers, *Platinum Print*, read: "In the advancement of photography there have come to be two distinct fields which cover the activities of the photographer. One is simply the making of records, and the other the making of pictures. In the former, as a scientific result is desired, a scientific instrument such as the anastigmat is used. The chief quality of this lens is to focus sharply on a single plane [...] but in the making of real pictures is this desirable? In photographing all sorts of objects, when is the picture ever seen in one plane? [...] The Struss Pictorial Lens [...] is not a lens for scientific work, but one for interpretative picture making."[7]

The use of such lenses was emblematic of the conflict that had developed by the end of the first decade of the twentieth century – the struggle between the so-called straight or pure image and the Pictorial, or soft-focused, rendering. An articulate statement of this conflict, as prophetic as it was obvious, may be found in Sadakichi Hartmann's article written after the 1910 international exhibition at the Albright Gallery in Buffalo: "Now, as heretofore, the Pictorial army is divided in two camps, the Demachy-Eugene-Steichen camp who favor painter-like subjects and treatment, and the Stieglitz-White-Craig-Annan class who flock around the standard of true *photographic themes and texture*. The camp of

7. "An Advertisement Pictured with the Struss Pictorial Lens", *Platinum Print*, no. 2, 1915, p. 16.

the former, true evidently, becomes more and more deserted, the old flag hangs limp and the fires burn low – only the dense and indifferent public, which is always behind the time, begins to patronize what was popular ten years ago."[8]

A new Pictorialist wave

Interestingly, in a brief comment by Henry McBride, in a review of Stieglitz's 1913 one-man exhibition at 291 one can read the indications that a change had occurred again after 1910: "[The lesson is clearly] enforced that photography, even without the aid of any manipulation of plates or special arrangement of compositions, can represent actualities with something positive and undeniable in the way of expression."[9] This position came to characterize what may be called the second phase of modern Pictorialism, between 1910 and 1920.

While the lay person who did not know the subtle manipulations of the photographic material involved in making a so-called straight image believed that the photographer accomplished little more than the replication of subject matter, the second-phase Pictorial photographer knew the many choices in every step of the process. This becomes the other legacy of the Pictorialist movement whether or not one characterizes the early period only in terms of the elaborate Käsebier-like visual articulation in the gum-bichromate process.

The complex evolution of photographic Pictorialism before the First World War is difficult to summarize. However, those qualities that were singled out as important in Pictorial aesthetics and method – intentful and meaningful expression, the uniqueness of the pictorial object with its creative merit reflected in its monetary worth – were all brought together under one very large and simple concept. In matters of form, such as technical manipulation, composition, and design, Pictorial photographs were to be seen to mirror the analogous development in painting, sculpture or even to a degree poetry during the period 1890 to 1920. It is pointless merely to chart the interrelations or interdependencies between one medium and another. What is more interesting is to reveal the broader linkages as all art moved from avoiding science and technology to embracing them, moved from an ideal, conceptual realm to one of tangible temporality and urbanistic realism.

No doubt, the play of social and economic forces had a good deal to do with these changes. The progressive alteration in the content of Pictorialism was profound, and Stieglitz, as an artist, may be seen to play a large role in these changes. Another, who interestingly gave up life in the United States for an expatriate existence in Britain, was Alvin Langdon Coburn. On the other hand, Clarence H. White, whose pictures from the first decade of his career, beginning in 1897, epitomize the sentiment encouraged by the rituals of everyday ideal life in rural America could not change after his move from Ohio to New York City. By the end of the second decade of the twentieth century, the entire focus of Pictorial work was on the great metropolis as an equivalent of modernist technology and politics, and White was left behind. The work of Coburn, Stieglitz, Karl Struss, and, finally, of Paul Strand all reflect the new avant-garde. However, one must not assume too quickly that because of its radical nature, particularly in form and design, the message these artists articulated was a positive one, or blindly affirmative in the context of the ever moving boundaries of modernity. Indeed, close observation suggests that, as with the subtleties in selection and representation of ancient myth and literature, the experience and interpretation of the city was a matter of equally judicious personal perspective and choice.[10]

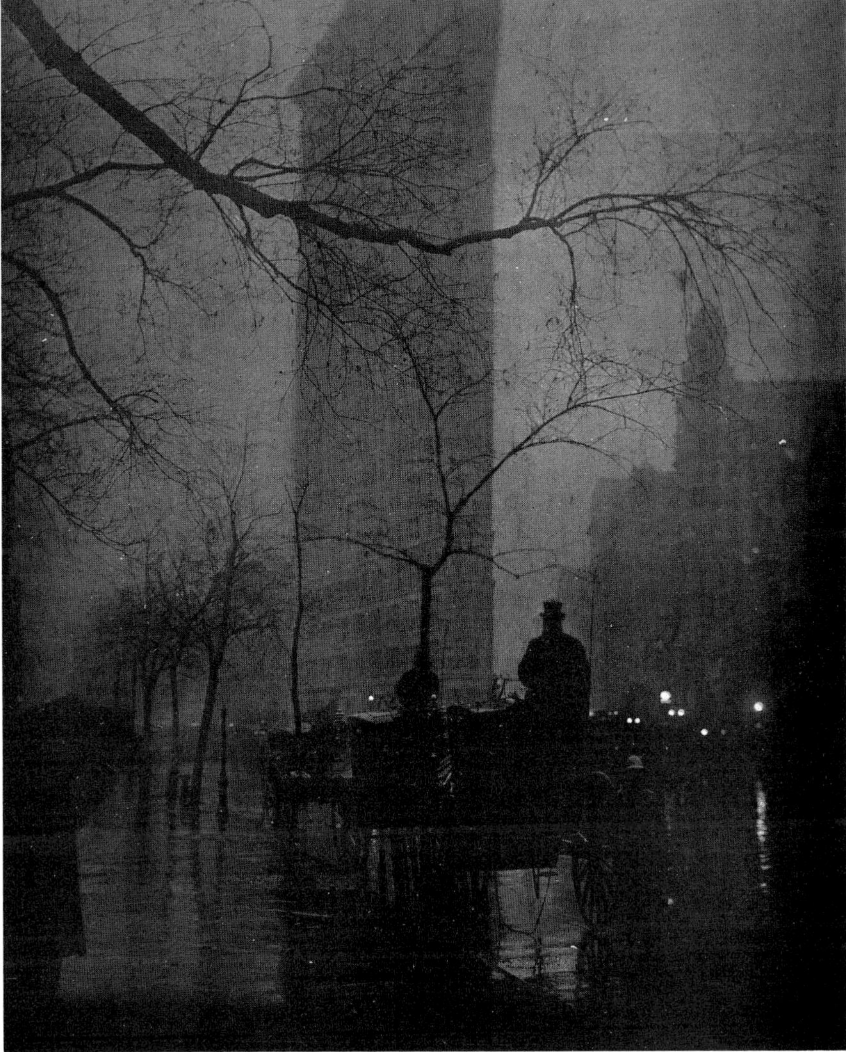

EDWARD STEICHEN,
The Flatiron, Evening,
1905,
(*Camera Work*, April 1906),
Musée d'Orsay, Paris.

8. S. Hartmann, "What Remains", *Camera Work*, no. 33, 1911, pp. 30–32.

9. H. McBride, "Art Photographs and Cubist Painting", *New York Sun*, March 3, 1913.

10. P. C. Bunnell, (ed.), *A Photographic Vision: Pictorial Photography, 1889–1923*, Salt Lake City, Peregrine Smith, 1980.

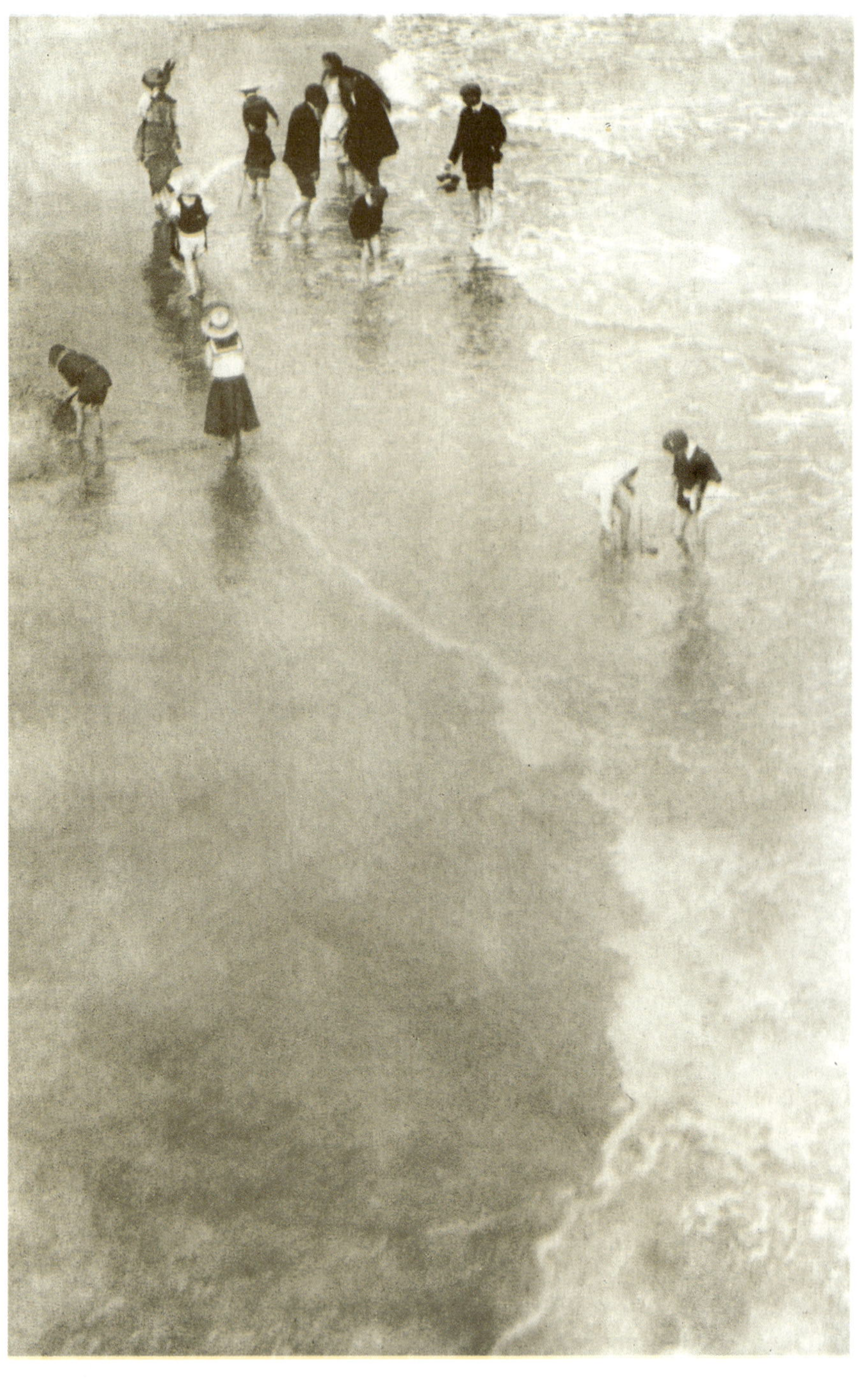

MALCOLM ARBUTHNOT, *By the Sea*, 1910, Royal Photographic Society, Bath.

An illustration of this individual choice and the change in perception over time may be seen in a comparative study of works by three photographers who each addressed the same piece of architecture, the so-called Flatiron Building in New York. Made over a period of a decade, the three pictures are by Alfred Stieglitz (1903), Edward Steichen (1905), and Alvin Langdon Coburn (1912). The Fuller Building, opened in 1902 at the crossing of Broadway and Fifth Avenue in New York, was located at the social and commercial hub of the city at that time. A looming structure, described at the time as "quite the most notorious thing in New York", attracting "more attention than all the other buildings now going up put together", it became one of the most famous and symbolic buildings in the city.[11]

Stieglitz photographed it shortly after it was completed and, typically for him at the time, during a snowfall. He depicted the building as a great ship, seemingly come around to face the land. It is a detail of the city seen as a kind of mirage, mysterious behind its overlay of whiteness, a questioning of a emblem of commerce and industry made by turning the scene into one of introspection and meditation, not in terms of the building's power, but in its relation to the experience of human beings and the fabric of the city itself.

When Edward Steichen photographed the building in 1905, another sensibility was clearly at work, one that revealed an interest in the decorative Japanese composition which had influenced so many Pictorialists. Steichen's photograph is a multiple gum and platinum print that was once in Stieglitz's own collection. Based on the qualities of the American impressionistic renderings called Tonalism, Steichen's photograph is a dramatic representation of that moment at dusk when the sky turns a leaden blue-green and highlights glow in the half-light. Carriages and pedestrians are silhouetted against the rain-spattered street that has created the dynamic foreground. Steichen depicts the building rising up majestically, but in his composition it is also reflected in the lower portion of the image. To heighten the drama of the scene, as well as firmly to anchor the depiction within a two-dimensional picture plane, the top of the building is truncated and the reflection, too, is chopped. There is no clearer example of an early modernist photographic composition, one that combines contemporary Pictorial expression in art, utilizing a device of spatial representation from a new influence such as the Japanese, with a subject at a point in time that is alive with the gestures of living in New York just as it becomes a vital, international metropolis.

Alvin Langdon Coburn photographed the building in 1912, giving the scene a further push into later modernist Pictorialism as he again shows it like a kind of ship, only this time in greater motion, echoing the figures that scurry beneath it and the branches that flutter in the wind. The jumbled mass of people and the blur of their movement all evoke a feeling of urban life that, unlike Steichen's affirmation, is invigorating but also cautioning in its instability. Not long after making this picture Coburn moved to Britain, and, in spite of making some of the ultimately triumphant expressions of modernist Pictorialism, the Vortographs of 1917, he was to remain unimpressed by the increasingly chaotic manifestations of twentieth-century life.

11. *The Architectural Record* (1902), quoted in by G. M. Mayer, *Once Upon A City*, New York, Macmillan Company, 1958, p. 1.

Form and vision

In images of the city viewed from above one can again see how a motif can reflect both the times and the changing attitudes to them of Pictorial photographers. This is, perhaps, the most typical early modernist Pictorial motif in photography, and, while originating out of the simple architectural fact of the increasing number of tall buildings, its influence was enormous. The airplane and balloon, the popularization of which coincided with the skyscraper, also contributed to this new, elevated view of the urban landscape and gave rise to a language of dynamic experience that finds its way into every avant-garde utterance. It is not surprising that the photographer seeking increasingly progressive modernist expression carried his camera higher and higher off the ground. However, it is only those like Coburn, Karl Struss, Strand or Stieglitz who fully utilized the challenge at hand. Struss made a view looking down at the intersection of Fifth Avenue and 42nd Street in New York that may be seen as a link in the progression from such simple views as those from the Eiffel Tower in the late 1880, to those of someone like Paul Strand, with his planar abstractions of New York backyards made at the same time as Stieglitz's more complicated renderings in the 1910s. In all these pictures we see the formal configuration not in terms of a realistic layout, but rather in terms of its architecture within a picture, like the landscape forms analyzed earlier.

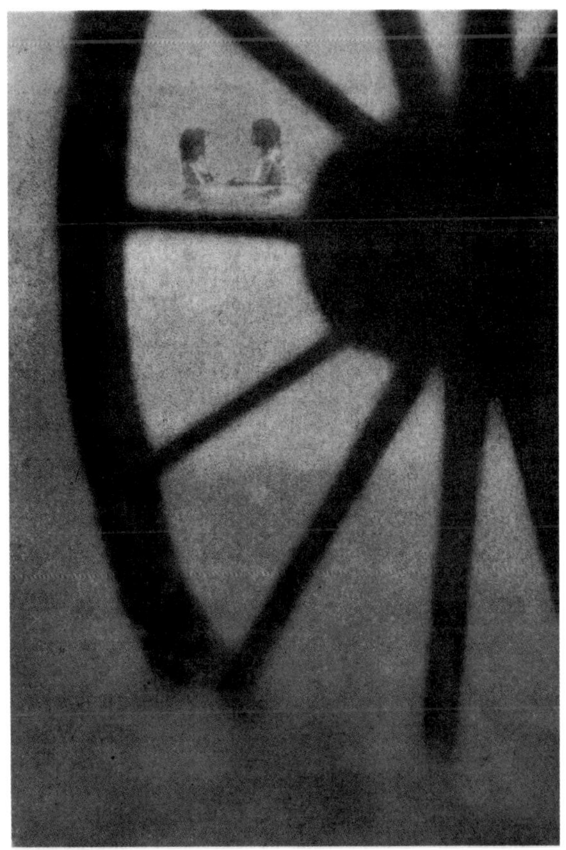

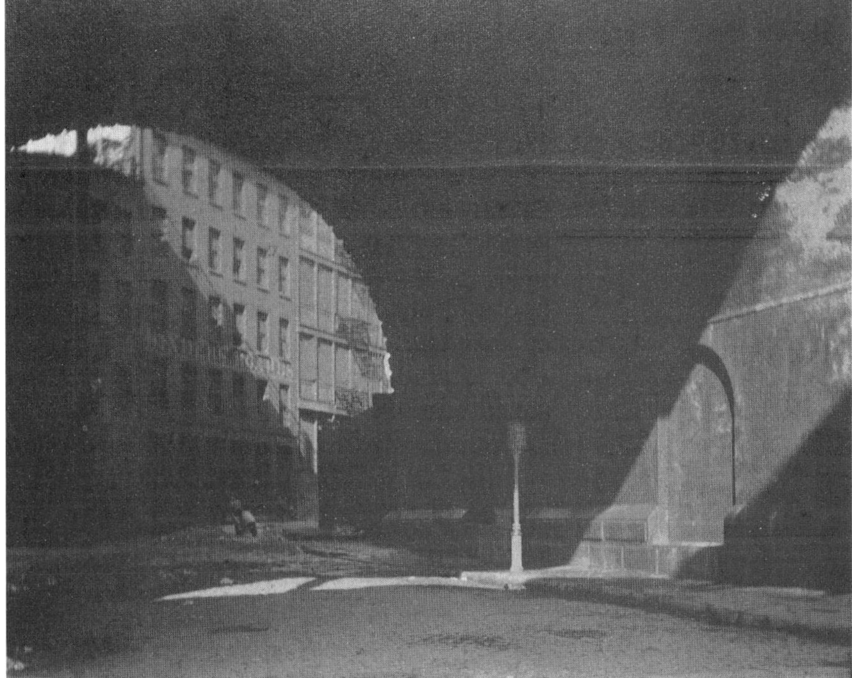

Paul L. Anderson, ***Under Brooklyn Bridge,*** circa 1917, Art Museum, Princeton University.

It is difficult to recognize this today, but at that time everything was being seen in a new way. Newness of experience was the hallmark of the avant-garde. Writing in *Camera Work* in 1913 Marius de Zayas, the artist and friend of Stieglitz, wrote: "The difference between Photography and Artistic-Photography is that [...] the first is the fixing of an actual state of Form, the other is the representation of the objectivity of Form, subordinated to a system of representation. The first is a process of incorporation, the second a means of expression. In the first, man tries to represent something that is outside of himself; in the second he tries to represent something that is in himself."[12]

◀ Malcolm Arbuthnot, ***The Bathers,*** (from *Amateur Photographer*) September 29, 1908, Royal Photographic Society, Bath.

It is the same old Pictorialist argument expressed in another way. De Zayas was one of several foreign artists who encouraged Stieglitz in his evolving critical thinking in the period after 1910. With regard to the notion of abstraction, Stieglitz himself understood its significance for the future. In 1912, he wrote to his artist colleague in Austria, the photographer Heinrich Kühn: "Now I find that contemporary art consists of the abstract (without subject) like Picasso, etc., and the photographic. The so-called photographic art whether attempted with a camera or brush is not the highest art. Just as we stand before the door of a new social era, so we stand in art too before a new medium of expression – the true medium (Abstraction)."[13] Stieglitz was wrong in asserting that abstract art had no subject, but in so far as he was relating to the previous notions of subject identification as being the key element in traditional image-making, he was right. What he sees correctly is the link between the new formal vision and the new international social order.

12. M. de Zayas, "Photography and Artistic Photography", *Camera Work*, no. 42/43, 1913, p. 13.

13. Letter to Heinrich Kühn, October 1, 1912.

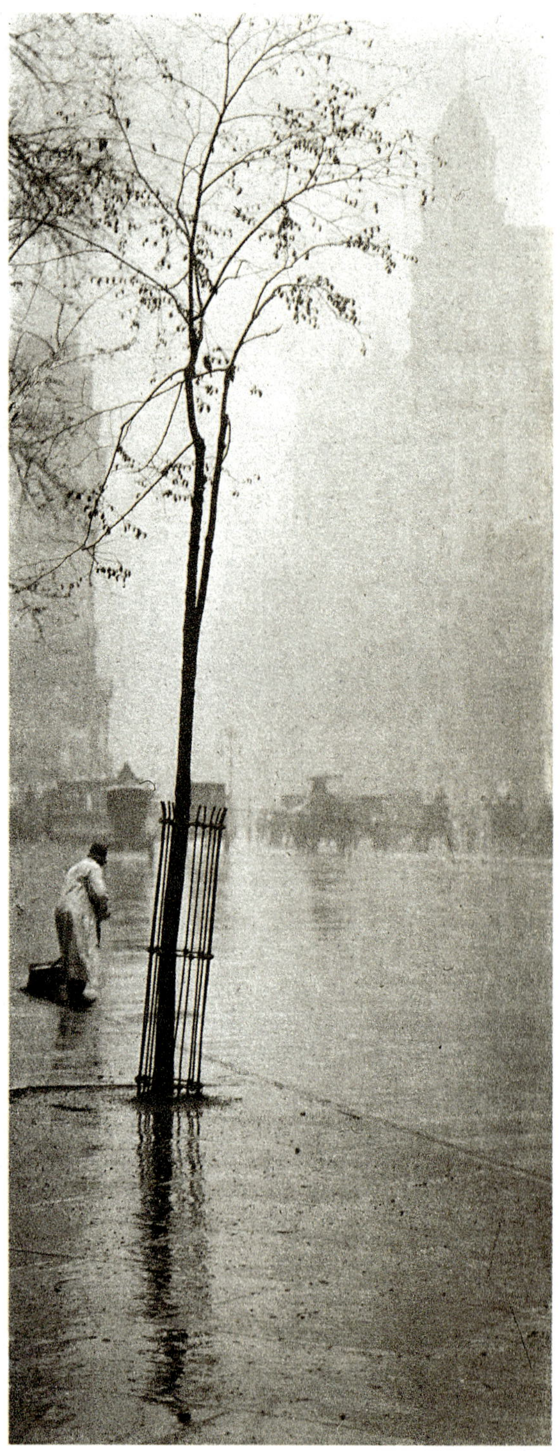

Alfred Stieglitz, ***Spring Showers,*** New York, 1900, (*Camera Work*, October 1911), Musée d'Orsay, Paris.

Japanese influence

As mentioned earlier in conjunction with Steichen's *Flatiron*, Japanese compositional designs played a role in the creation of more abstract arrangements in Pictorialist images. One can recognize Japanese decorative schemes in the early work of White and Coburn, in the elongated formatting of such pictures as Stieglitz's *Spring Showers* of 1900, and also in Steichen's work. Such devices as extreme foreshortening, strong diagonals, planal cropping, exaggerated foregrounds, and silhouetted shapes juxtaposed with deep recessional spaces all became hallmarks of international Pictorialist works and may be seen later in, for instance, Malcolm Arbuthnot's *Bathers* of about 1908, Karl Struss's, *Low Tide* of 1911 or 1912 or Paul L. Anderson's *Under Brooklyn Bridge* of about 1917. Anderson's picture is a particularly good example of the late modernist phase of Pictorialism where an older stylistic influence like the Japanese merges with the architectonic and cubist forms found in the contemporary urban landscape. This Japanese influence was transmitted in various ways, from original prints that were collected by several photographers, the work of Whistler (particularly important in Europe), and the teaching and publications of Arthur Wesley Dow who was close to numerous photographers in the United States. Clearly, it was the sense that the Japanese were so concerned with formalist problems that invigorated the interest in this work and, as the decade evolved, made it seem all the more modernist. It should not be overlooked, however, that such increasing formalist concerns were only a further manifestation of the objecthood of the picture – an idea that had been a tenet of Pictorialism from the beginning.

Throughout the second decade of the twentieth century, the focus on urbanism progressively replaced photographers' concern for the pastoral, for landscape, and for genre. Certainly, as the progressive influence of new painterly forms such as Cubism and Futurism became more a part of the general consciousness, photographers who had been explicitly linked to literary symbolism and historical content became less prominent. It is difficult, for instance, to find any comparative example in this period of the highly sophisticated landscapes that Coburn made in 1903, such as *The Dragon*. In Coburn's own later work the analogous subject would be his *Octopus* of 1912. Notably, in spite of the shift in locale, from rural to urban, he gave both these images anthropomorphic titles.

Choosing the subject

Clarence H. White provides another example in three of his pictures made between 1898 and 1912. *Miss Grace*, a wonderfully characteristic subject of his early years in Ohio, shows a young girl whose youth and sexuality is suggested by the pose and the daring configuration of the dress, each of which is echoed by the sinuous curving lines of the sofa.

This depiction of sexuality played a larger and larger role in such photographic works over the period before the First World War. Not the simple expression of a pseudo-classical arrangement, as might be previously seen in the work of Von

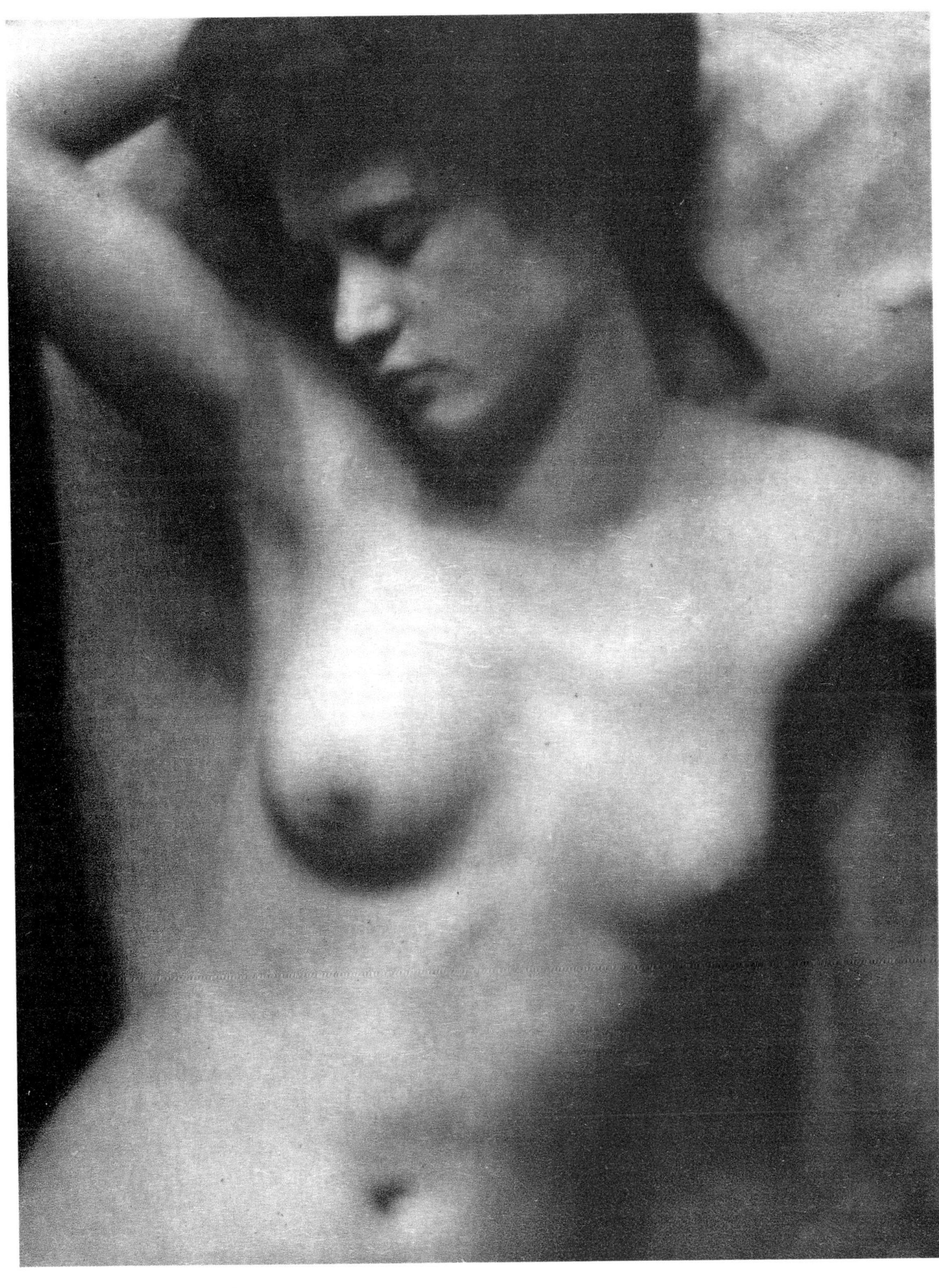

CLARENCE H. WHITE AND
ALFRED STIEGLITZ,
Torso,
1907
(*Camera Work*, July 1909),
Musée d'Orsay, Paris.

Gloeden and others, but a more lyrical and spirited style of work, again drawn from classical sources, as seen, for instance, in Clarence H. White's *Pipes of Pan* of 1905 or in F. Holland Day's *The Prodigal* of 1909. There were elaborate codes of propriety, well understood at the time, that allowed the depiction of male nudity in adolescent boys and children, but not men. In the case of expressions of mixed sex, elaborate precautions were taken to conceal the particularity of the female, as well as to suggest her elevation to the canon of idealized beauty. Males were never shown frontally. Frank Eugene's noted *Adam and Eve* of 1900 is a case in point, where the elaborately worked-over negative allowed a straightforward print made from it to appear highly synthetic and, therefore, evocative, but of suitably idealized propriety. Gertrude Käsebier's use of the gum-bichromate process to render her image *The Bat* was a more aggressive expression of daring sexuality some ten or twelve years later, but still well contained within *fin-de-siècle* rhetoric and attitudes of depicting the female nude.

The Albright Exhibition

In 1910, an International Exhibition of Pictorial Photography opened at the Albright Art Gallery in Buffalo, New York. This unprecedented exhibition contained approximately 600 prints, organized into two categories. The larger of the two, the Invitational Section, accounted for 80 per cent of the works shown. Here, the Photo-Secession, the designated organizer of the exhibition, selected 37 photographers whose work was described in the catalogue as having been "the chief factor in bringing photography to the position to which it has now attained." The smaller group was the Open Section – 28 Americans who, as defined in an earlier 1910 announcement, "hitherto have not had the opportunity of being adequately represented in an important exhibition".

In retrospect, the exhibition may be seen to be the seminal event in the development of American Pictorial photography. Even then, it encountered a strong mixture of praise and condemnation, reflecting not simply the content of the exhibition but the inherent political importance of the show. It was not – if indeed any important modern exhibition could be – simply an artistic event. As one of the last, and probably the greatest, public expressions of the work of Alfred Stieglitz and the Photo-Secession, it became for his supporters the ultimate vindication of his struggle on behalf of Pictorial photography. For his critics it seemed the most obvious demonstration of his arrogant efforts to dominate and direct the photography community. All this was to be expected.

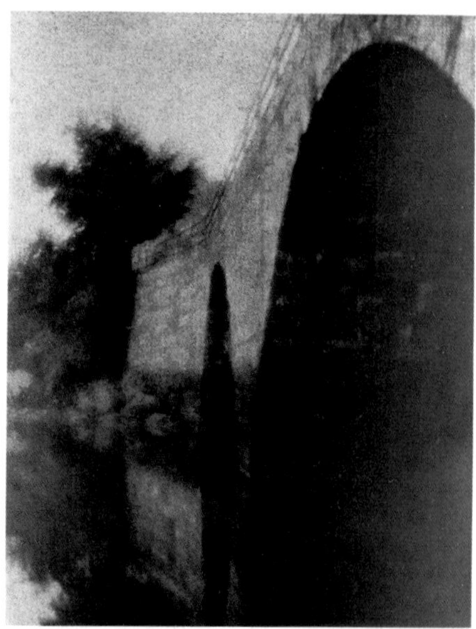

Alvin Langdon Coburn
The Bridge, Ipswich,
(*Camera Work*, April 1904), Musée d'Orsay, Paris.

The exhibition filled the entire museum. The hanging was conceived by the painter Max Weber and the installation was accomplished by Paul Haviland, Stieglitz, and Clarence H. White. The photographs were hung "on line", and were grouped by artist, placed so that their relative tonalities complemented each other, both between and within the smaller groupings. The historical aspect of Pictorialism's development was represented by a room devoted to works by D. O. Hill. Foreign photographers, British, French, and Austrian-German, each occupied a room. The remaining galleries were taken up by the Americans where, in the central room – and seen surely as the keystone – were prints by Edward Steichen, George Seeley, Alvin Langdon Coburn, and Baron De Meyer.

Over 15,000 people visited the exhibition in its month-long run, breaking all attendance records for the gallery. This was viewed as confirmation that photography had reached equality with the other arts. Twelve prints were acquired by the Museum and 65 photographs were sold to the public.

Following the political tensions the exhibition generated, it seems the Photo-Secession began to collapse after reaching this significant height. Several leading photographers, including White, Coburn, and Gertrude Käsebier, left, and Stieglitz turned more of his attention to modern painting. Photography, like so many endeavors, was changing and the Albright exhibition represented not only the apogee of a trajectory but the beginning of a new photography that would appear in the next decade.

Peter C. Bunnell

By 1907, White, who was now residing in New York, found himself collaborating with Alfred Stieglitz in photographing a young female model recommended to them by Francis Bruguiere of San Francisco. The collaboration was rare for each artist and the resulting picture, one of several in a series and called *Torso,* is a richly revealing expression of female sexuality in a still cautious age. The truncated torso and upraised arms are seen to accentuate the ripeness of the breasts. The image exists in two printings and in one, that by Clarence White, the woman's lower trunk is complete, giving a certain anatomical precision to the body though the explicitness is reduced. In another, a print attributed to Stieglitz or certainly made under his direction, the figure is cropped above the navel. This causes a much greater focus on the upper body and the breasts become highlighted. Again, in White's 1909 composition *Nude with Mirror,* while the figure is nude, White has very carefully posed her to preserve her modesty, and, in so doing, he has also created an elaborate composition of reflections, ovals, and design conceits.

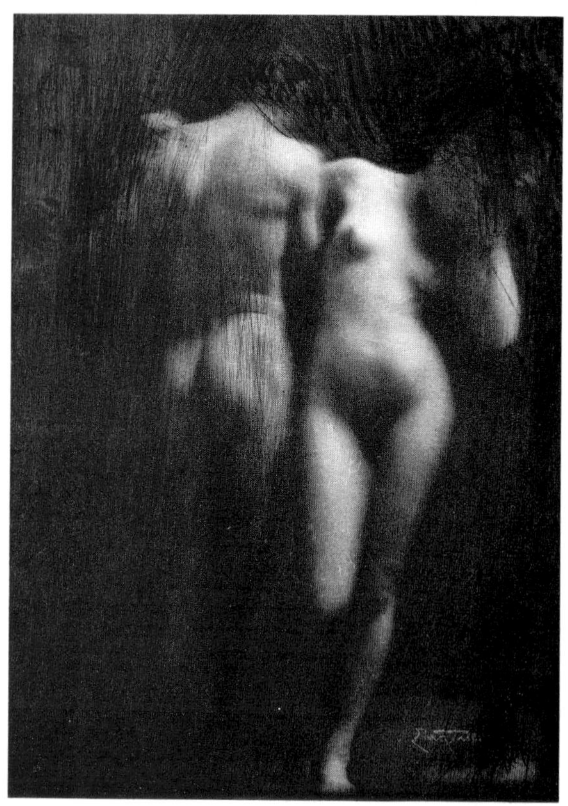

Frank Eugene,
Adam and Eve,
(*Camera Work,* April 1910), Musée d'Orsay, Paris.

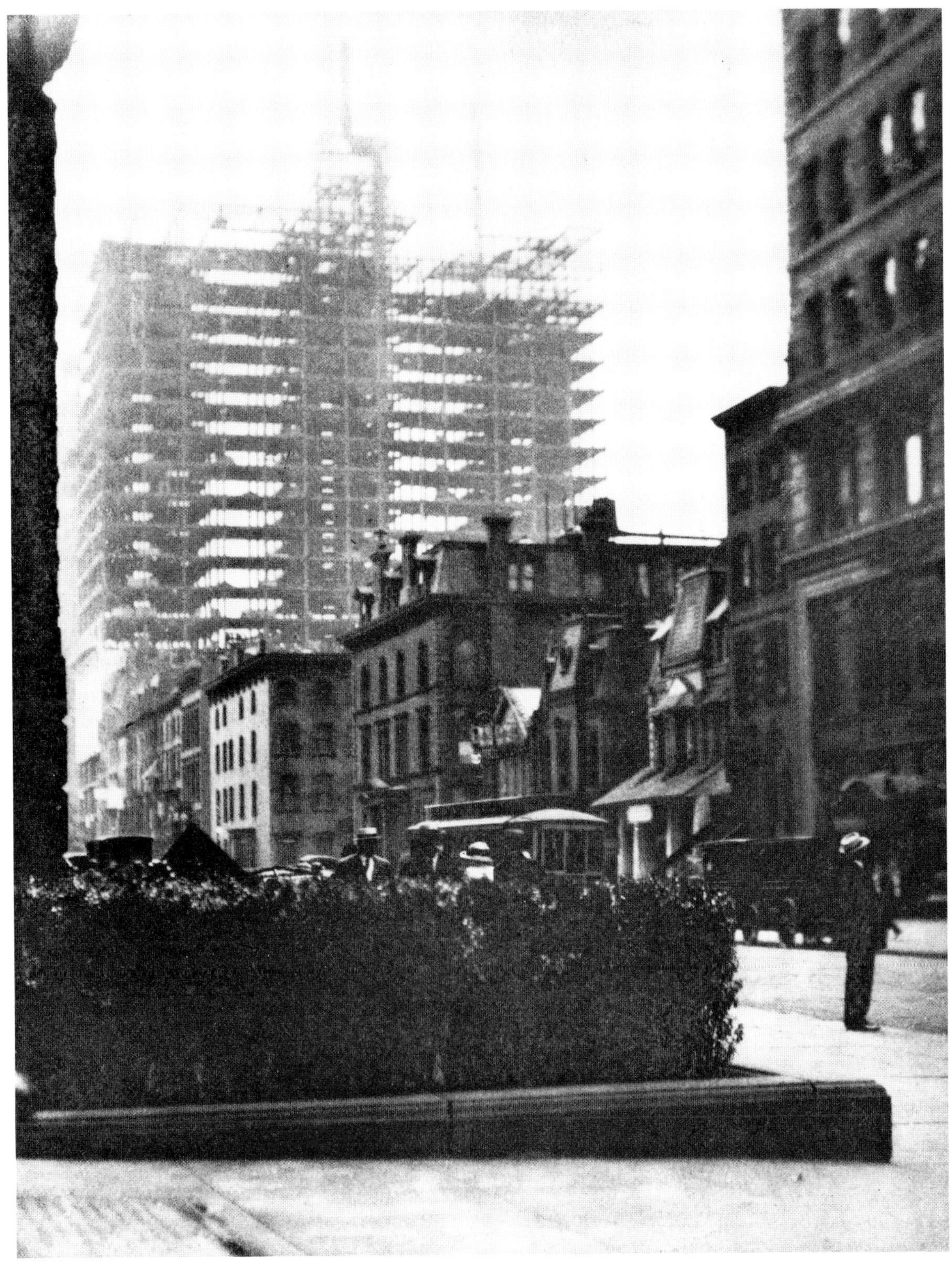

ALFRED STIEGLITZ,
Old and New New York,
1910,
(*Camera Work*, October 1911),
Musée d'Orsay, Paris.

Stieglitz and White are perfect foils for one another in images of such subjects. Stieglitz moved more and more to confront his subject; White, like certain other Pictorialists in America and abroad, withdrew within a hierarchy of design concepts that became successively more and more decorative. White's *Larson Dancers* of 1924 could very well be the archetypal example of what Pictorialism became in its post-First World War phase, a type of expression which would not be taken seriously again until our embrace of a post-modernist sensibility today.

That Stieglitz also struggled in his own work is clear, but he was fascinated with the notion of confrontation – confrontation not only in personal relationships, but in engaging those subjects that he felt he must address to remain vital and contemporary. Another of his urban images is *Old and New New York* of 1910, where a figure stands beneath the rising skeleton of a newly emerging skyscraper in marked juxtaposition to the elegant, human-scale, nineteenth-century houses. As already noted, Stieglitz had clear feelings of ambivalence about the American metrop-

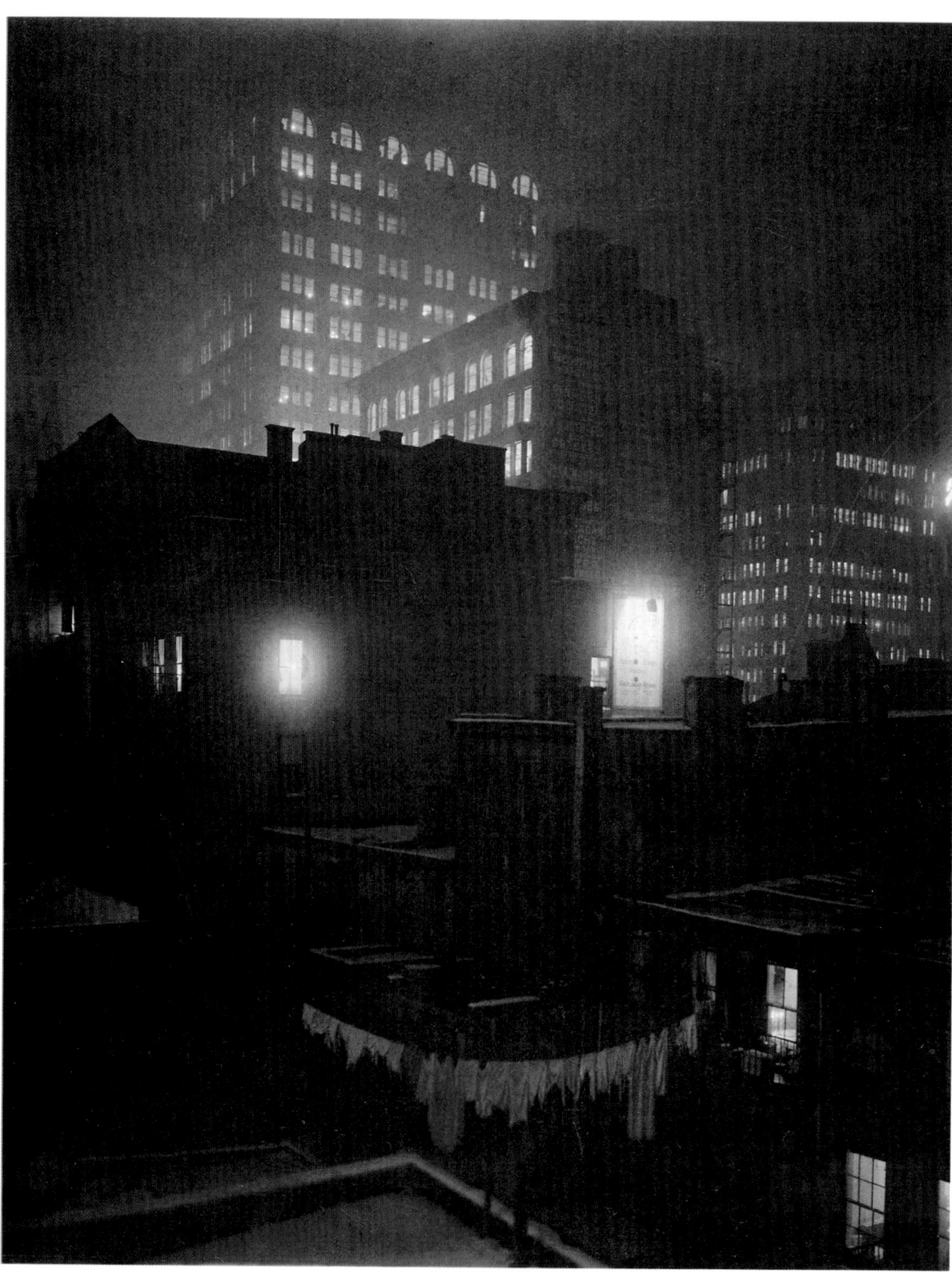

ALFRED STIEGLITZ,
From the Back Window, 291,
1915,
Museum of Fine Arts,
Boston.

olis. Those artists whose birth coincided with the new-won freedom for photography, together with the rise of the cities at the beginning of the century, would now take command and show the way.

Criteria for renewal

Clear evidence of an evolving Pictorial aesthetic was the emergence of a certain radicalism on the part of some photographers. This becomes more pronounced after the time Stieglitz himself recognized that the surest way to invigorate the medium was to reveal its uniqueness by comparing it to what it is not, abstract painting in which recognizability is suppressed. Understood this way, his exhibiting of the newest art becomes a necessity.

In the area of abstraction Stieglitz found exactly the arena in which to demonstrate his point. Taking as his example the remarkable formalist breakdowns that the Cubists were creating, Stieglitz sought to do a similar yet different thing through the sophisticated manipulation of optical, compositional, and tonal devices in straightforward photography. In so doing, however, he left the fully painterly devices – drawing and color – to artists like Braque and Picasso, both of whom he exhibited at 291.

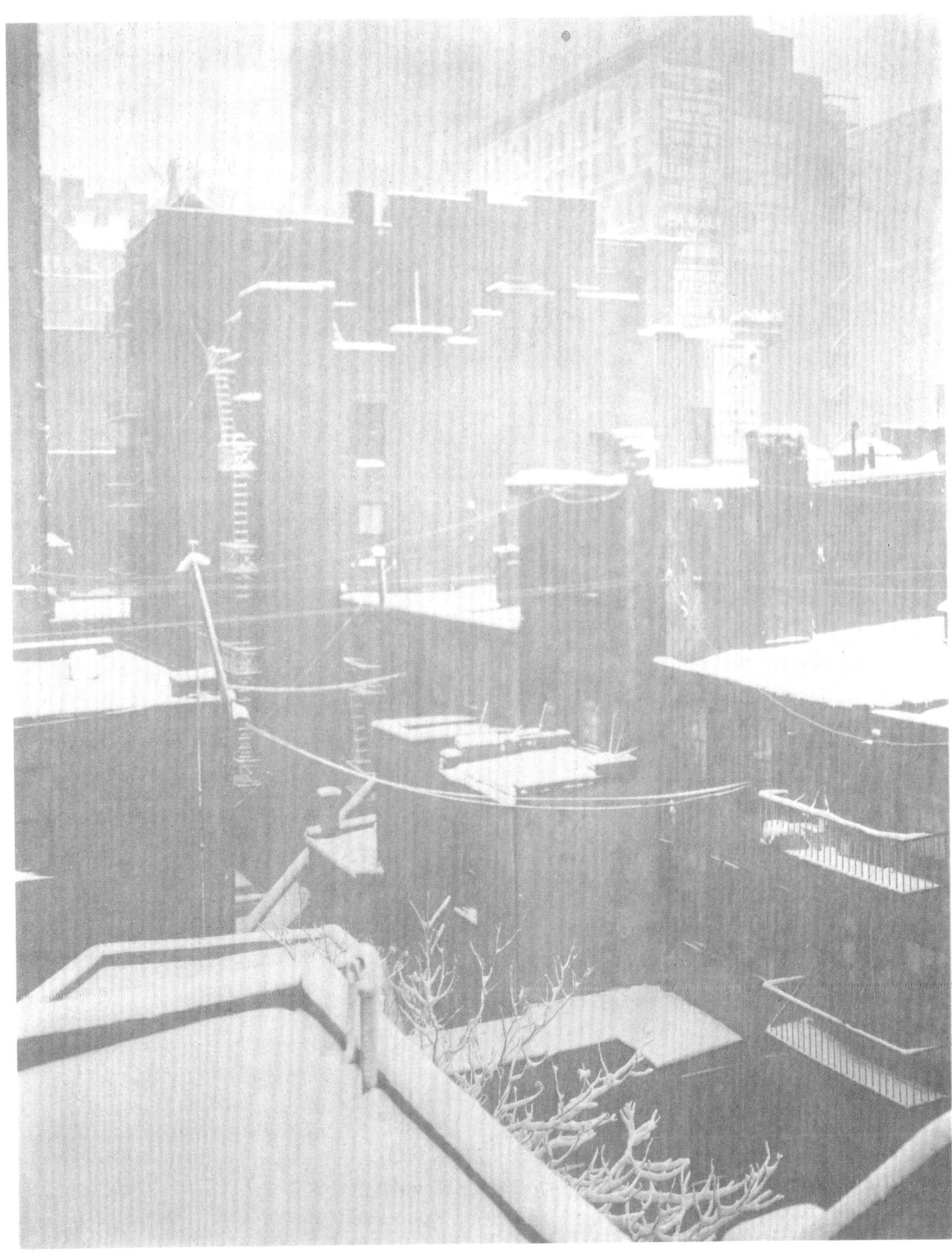

Alfred Stieglitz,
From the Back Window, 291 (2),
1915,
Museum of Fine Arts, Boston.

A demonstration of Stieglitz's approach in his own work may be seen if one compares another significant modernist expression to a Stieglitz photograph. Alvin Langdon Coburn's *Vortographs*, perhaps the only true expressions of synthetic abstraction in photography, were produced in 1917, using a device similar to a kaleidoscope. They are representative of a kind of photograph that should be seen as synthetic form, the late straightforward Pictorialist equivalent to gum-bichromate work of an earlier era. On the other hand, Stieglitz himself demonstrated the remarkable potential of a different type of abstraction, one rooted in the illusionist control of the realist subject itself. This can be seen in one particularly sophisticated example drawn from an important cycle of views taken from the window of 291 in 1915. Simply titled *From the Back Window, 291,* it shows a dense, Cubist-like inner-city architectural space that one found behind the elegant facades of Fifth Avenue where his gallery was located. What is important to note is the cropping and the basic use of decontextualized forms. The tree in the foreground is seen to have no rational stability in relation to the ground below, and the triangular pattern of the snow-covered roof

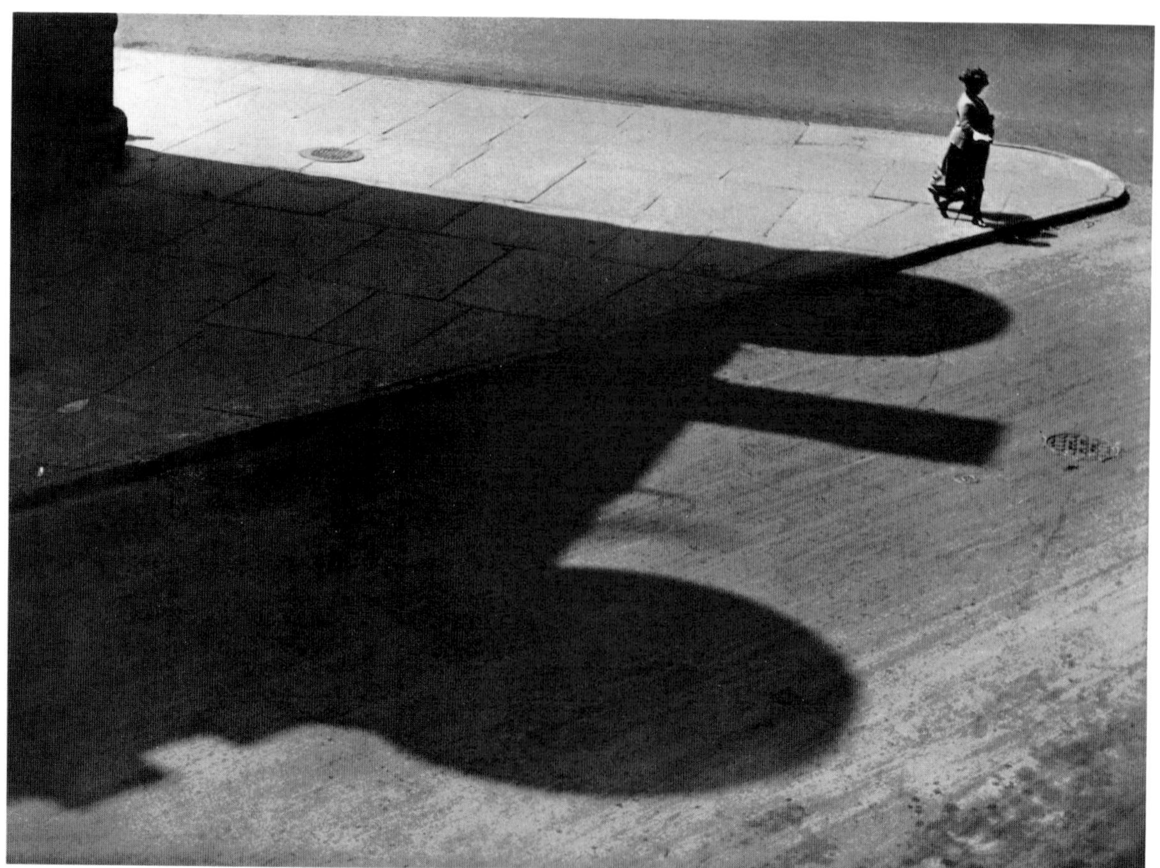

PAUL STRAND,
People, Streets of New York, 83rd Street and West End Avenue,
1915,
National Gallery of Art, Washington.

begins to read both as a design on the surface of the image as well as one that projects illusionistically into the space. The snow on the branches of the tree, also, because of Stieglitz's treatment in the printing, appears both as white shapes and as tufts on the stark black branches. The cropped edges of the picture and its tonality serve to render what, to some, is simply a straightforward photograph of a contemporary urban environment into a highly conceptualized expression of modernist abstraction. Again, however, it is an image that reveals Stieglitz's ambivalent feelings about the urban scene; it is both real and imaginary, both affirmative and negative.[14]

In this comparison between Coburn and Stieglitz one has an example of what was to become the difference between American photographic preoccupations after the First World War and those of Europe. Put simply, it is precisionist versus synthetic. Precisionist, in the sense of moving toward an articulation of what is in the world, as contrasted with the European interest in manipulation and abstracted reordering. It is not surprising that a critical phrase in Ezra Pound's catalogue essay on Coburn's *Vortographs* is that "the camera is freed from reality".[15] He could say no more. Stieglitz, perhaps in spite of himself and his affection for European ways, believed in a modern American achievement that should be rooted in realism. Mainstream photography in Europe in the 1920s would be dominated by the painter-photographers interested in synthetics. In America, however, it would be marked by the emergence of a group of realist artists epitomized if not by Stieglitz himself, then by Edward Weston, whose work would astound Europeans at the 1929 "Film und Foto" exhibition in Stuttgart.[16]

As a movement with a defined beginning in the 1890s, Pictorialism more or less concluded with the catastrophe of the First World War. After this period, photography would no longer be regarded as an insignificant form of pictorial expression. No longer would the medium be seen as merely a mechanical exercise in applied technology. No longer would the idea that striking photographs were mere accidents be accepted. No longer would the common denominator of photography be the populist understanding of mass reportage, documentary, commercial portraiture or advertising. Pointedly, Stieglitz used the phrase "camera work" as the title of his publication. Later, these words came to be synonymous with notions of personally expressive photography and they were employed by Minor White in his philosophical and aesthetic texts in the 1950s. The idea they signify is alive today as we see more clearly than ever that post-modernist photographic artists are returning to the early tenets of Pictorialism. With its revival of the pre-modernist subjects from myth and literature, contemporary work of the 1980s and 1990s should rightly be called Neo-pictorialism.

14. J. Pultz and C. B. Scallen, *Cubism and American Photography, 1910–1930*, Williamstown, Clark Art Institute, 1981.

15. Ezra Pound, *Vortographs and Paintings by Alvin Langdon Coburn*, London, Camera Club, 1917, pp. 2–6.

16. *Photography Rediscovered: American Photographs, 1900–1930*, New York, Whitney Museum of American Art, 1979.

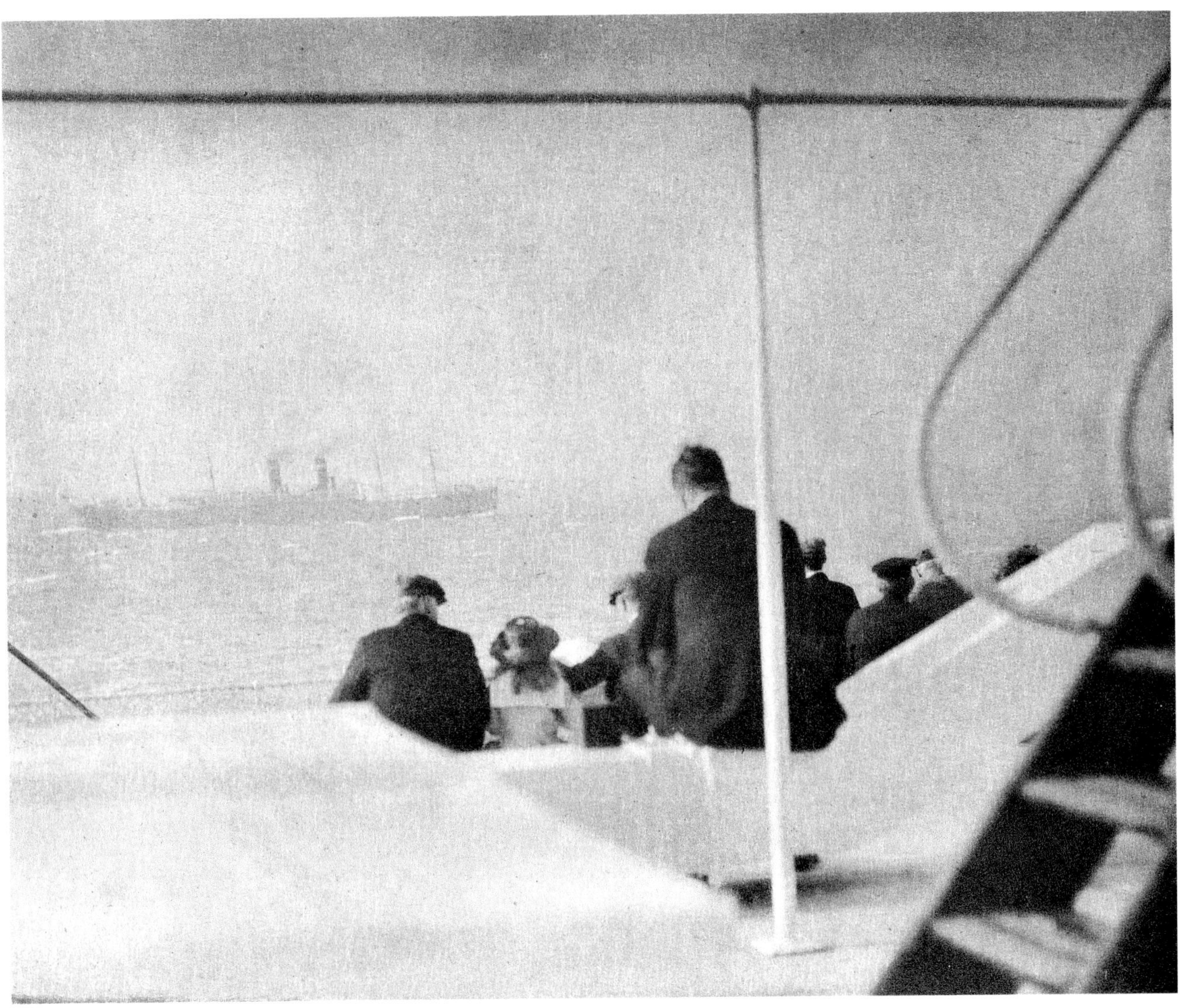

Camera Work magazine 1903–1917

The magazine *Camera Work* was founded under Alfred Stieglitz's inspiration in order to support and promote the work of the new Photo-Secession group (inaugurated in 1901); it was in a sense the group's official organ. The magazine followed on from *Camera Notes*, which Stieglitz had run previously, and would become the voice of American Pictorialism as conceived and guided by Stieglitz. Fifty issues appeared quarterly from 1903 to 1917.

It was the most lavish of all the photo magazines so popular at the time, which included *Amateur Photographer* in Britain, *Photographische Rundschau* in Germany, and the *Revue de photographie* for French Pictorialists.

Stieglitz wanted to create a high-quality publication which would feature only outstanding works, fully accomplished individual creations. Great care was taken over the hand printing of the illustrations (the actual method used was always specified), usually by photogravure from the original negative or from an original print (gum-bichromate, platinum print, etc.). The printing was done on Japanese paper mounted on colored card, and each number contained around ten photographs of this type.

Every issue of *Camera Work* contained in-depth articles, information about the photographs published or exhibition reviews, by authors as varied as Charles Caffin, George Bernard Shaw, Robert Demachy, Sadakichi Hartmann, and Edward Steichen. The views of inveterate "retouchers" like Demachy – whose work was above all Pictorial – were to be found, just as much as Shaw's opinion that "the photographic art should be respected" or Steichen's, who considered that no negative was perfect and that every photograph resulted from manipulation at one stage or other.

The entire theoretical evolution of photography may be followed in the pages of *Camera Work* over a period of some fifteen years, including the growing importance of artistic exemplars from Europe, which Stieglitz would promote in his 291 Gallery (Little Galleries of the Photo-Secession, opened in 1905) and which he included in the actual magazine. Thus Auguste Rodin's *Balzac* was published by Steichen, together with watercolors by Rodin (1911) and John Marin, paintings by Matisse and Picasso (with critical text by Gertrude Stein, 1912), and images from the 1914 exhibition by Brancusi, Braque, and Picasso. European work that tended towards the traditional artistic mainstream was, however, completely excluded.

Changes in photographic aesthetics were also represented by the inclusion of Stieglitz's *The Steerage* (1907, published 1911) and *Pool-Deal* (1910), works which were proclaimed as expressing "pure" photographic qualities, without further intervention: "My photos look like photographs and so in the eyes of Pictorialist photographers they cannot count as art." (Stieglitz, 1923). In the whole of *Camera Work* Steichen featured the most, then Stieglitz, Craig Annan, Coburn, White, Eugene, De Meyer, Demachy, Kühn, and Seeley: all progressive workers who sought status through references to art.

Michel Frizot

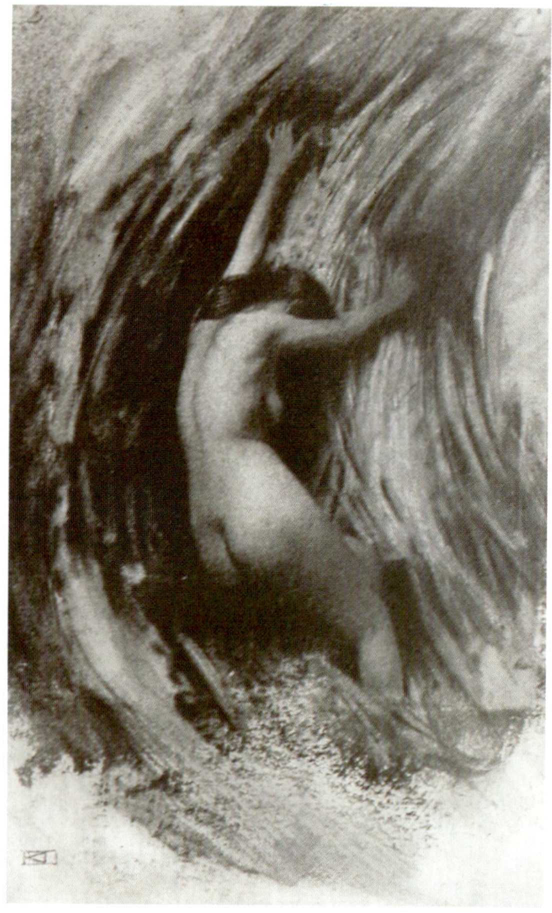

ROBERT DEMACHY,
Struggle,
published in
Camera Work,
January 1904.

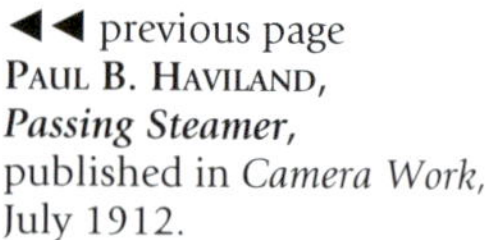

◄◄ previous page
PAUL B. HAVILAND,
Passing Steamer,
published in *Camera Work,*
July 1912.

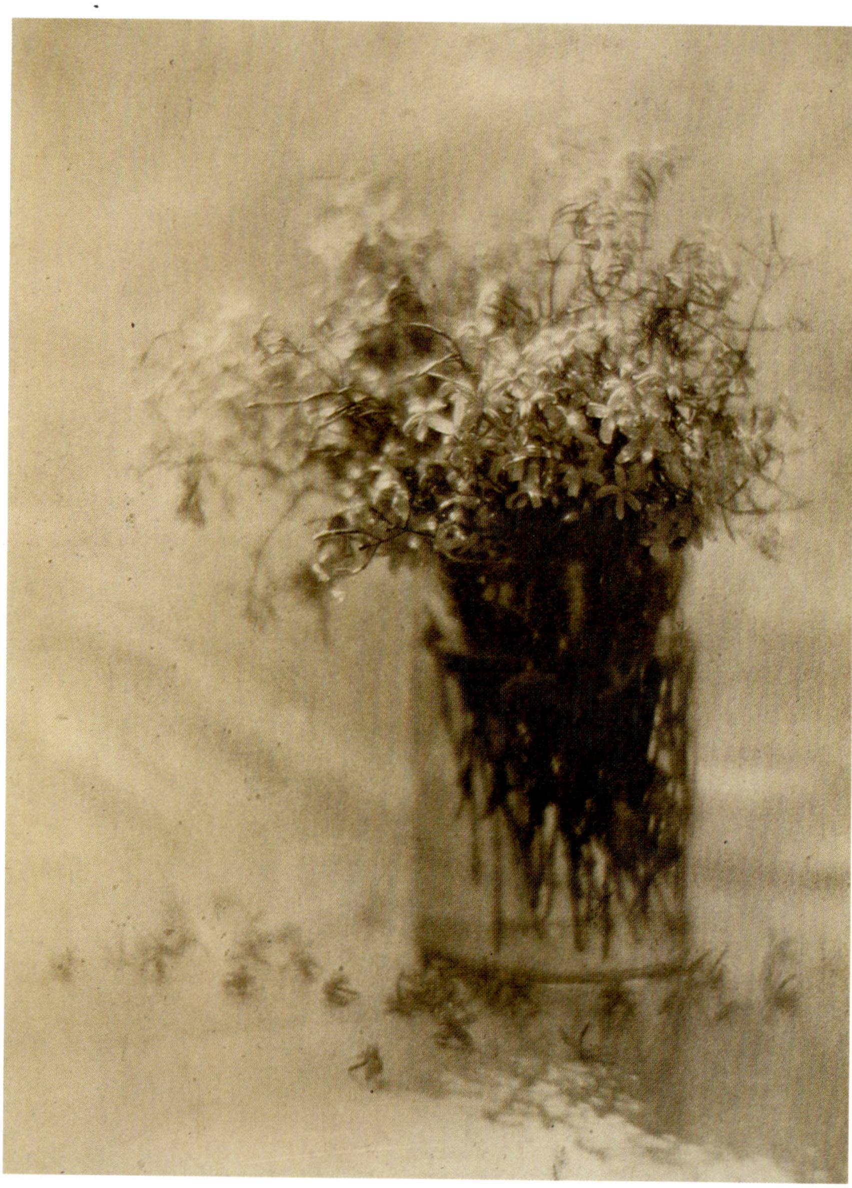

ADOLPHE DE MEYER,
Still-life,
published in *Camera Work,*
October 1908.

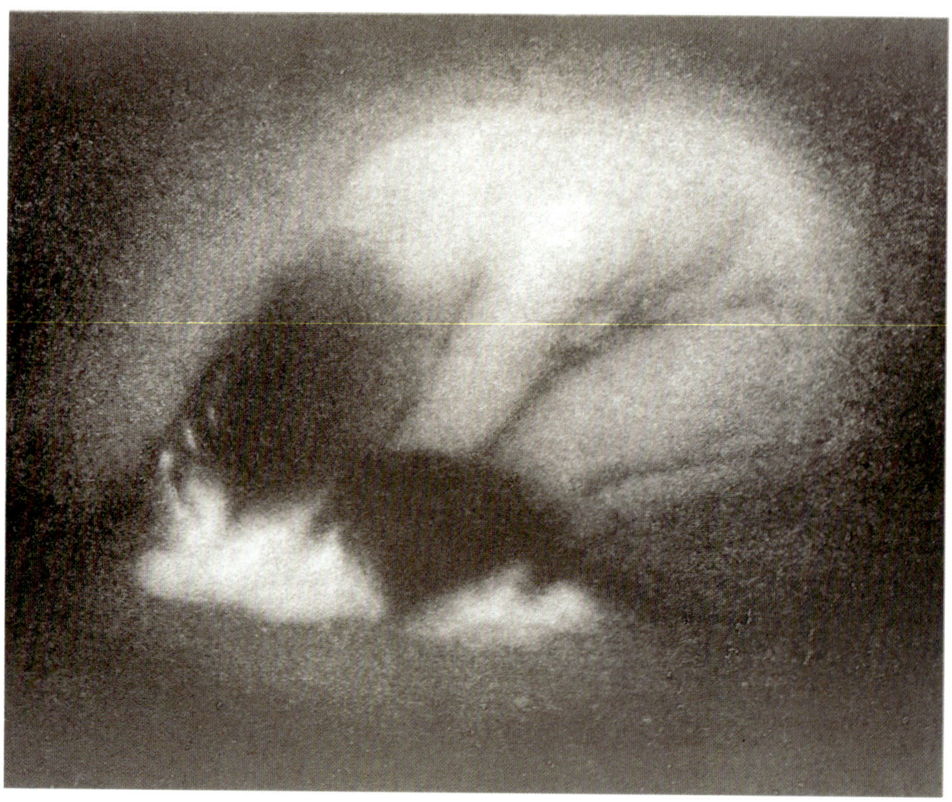

EDWARD STEICHEN,
Nude with Cat,
published in *Camera Work,*
April 1903.

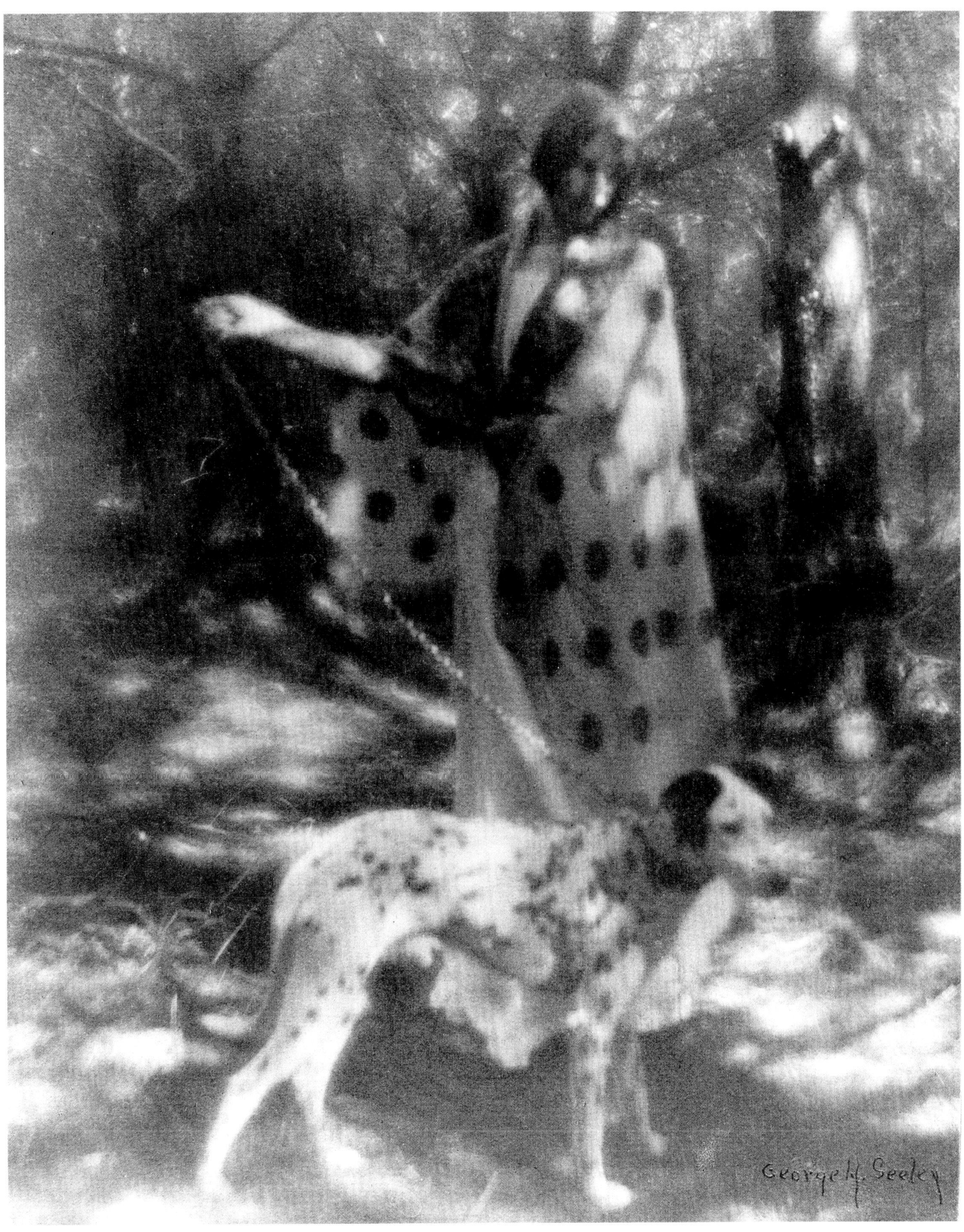

GEORGE H. SEELEY,
Blotches of Sunlight and Spots of Ink,
published in *Camera Work,*
October 1907.

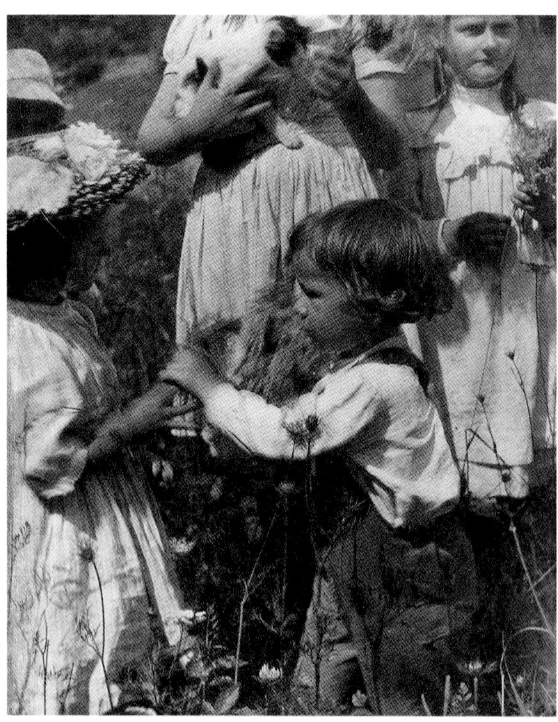

GERTRUDE KÄSEBIER,
Happy Days,
published in *Camera Work,*
April 1905.

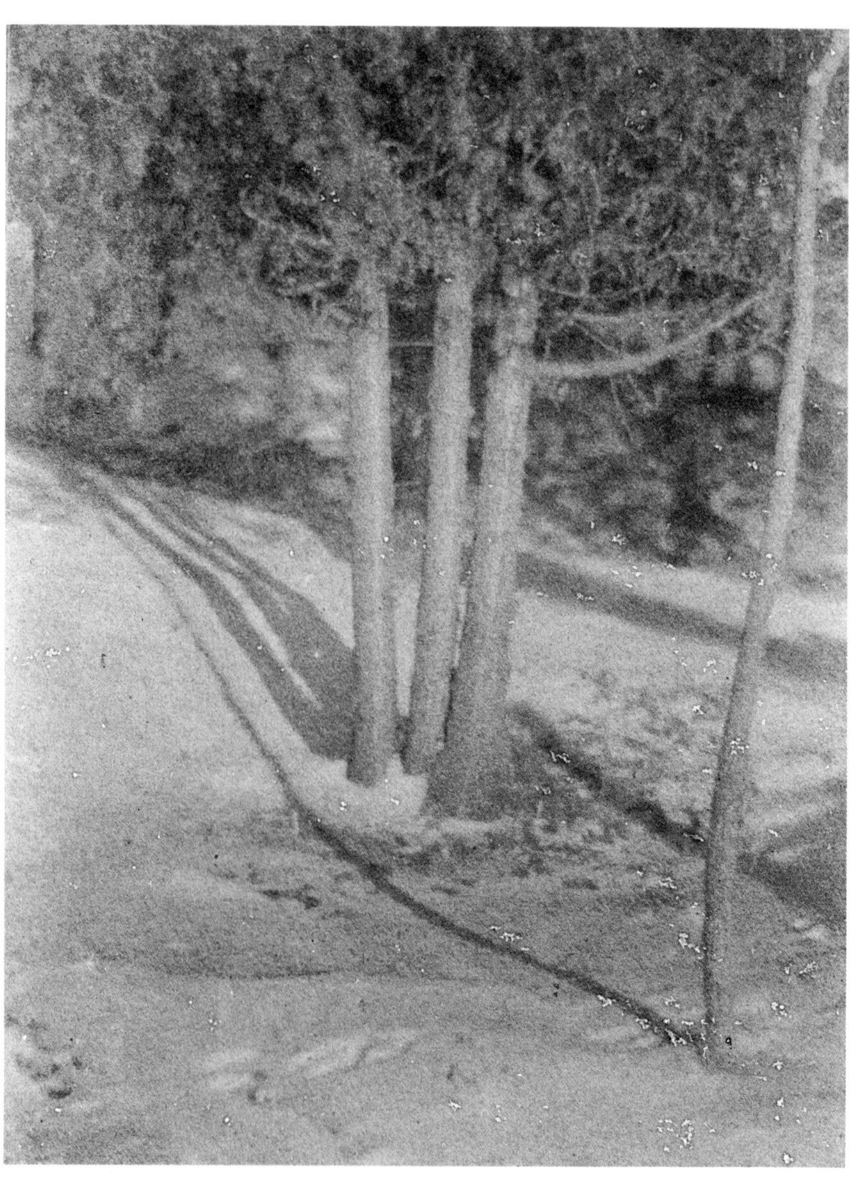

EDWARD STEICHEN,
Judgment of Paris
– A Landscape Arrangement,
published in *Camera Work,*
April 1903.

HEINRICH KÜHN,
On the Shore,
published in *Camera Work,*
January 1911.

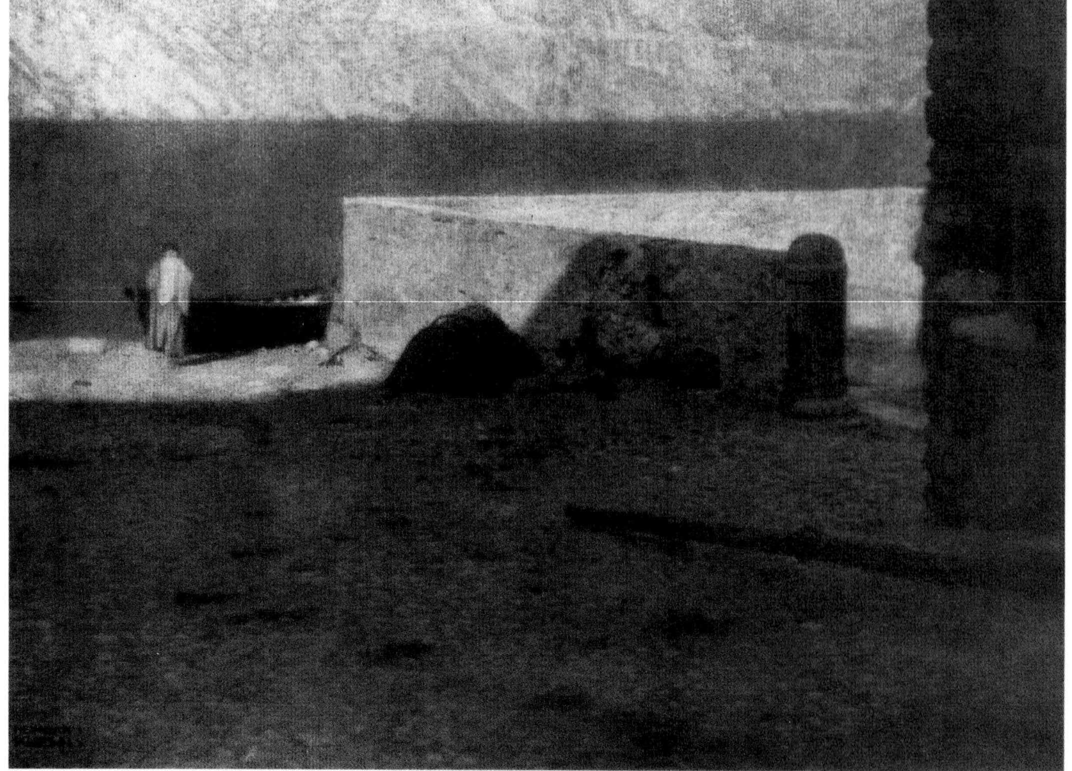

ALFRED STIEGLITZ, ▶
Snapshot – From My Window, New York,
published in *Camera Work,*
October 1907.

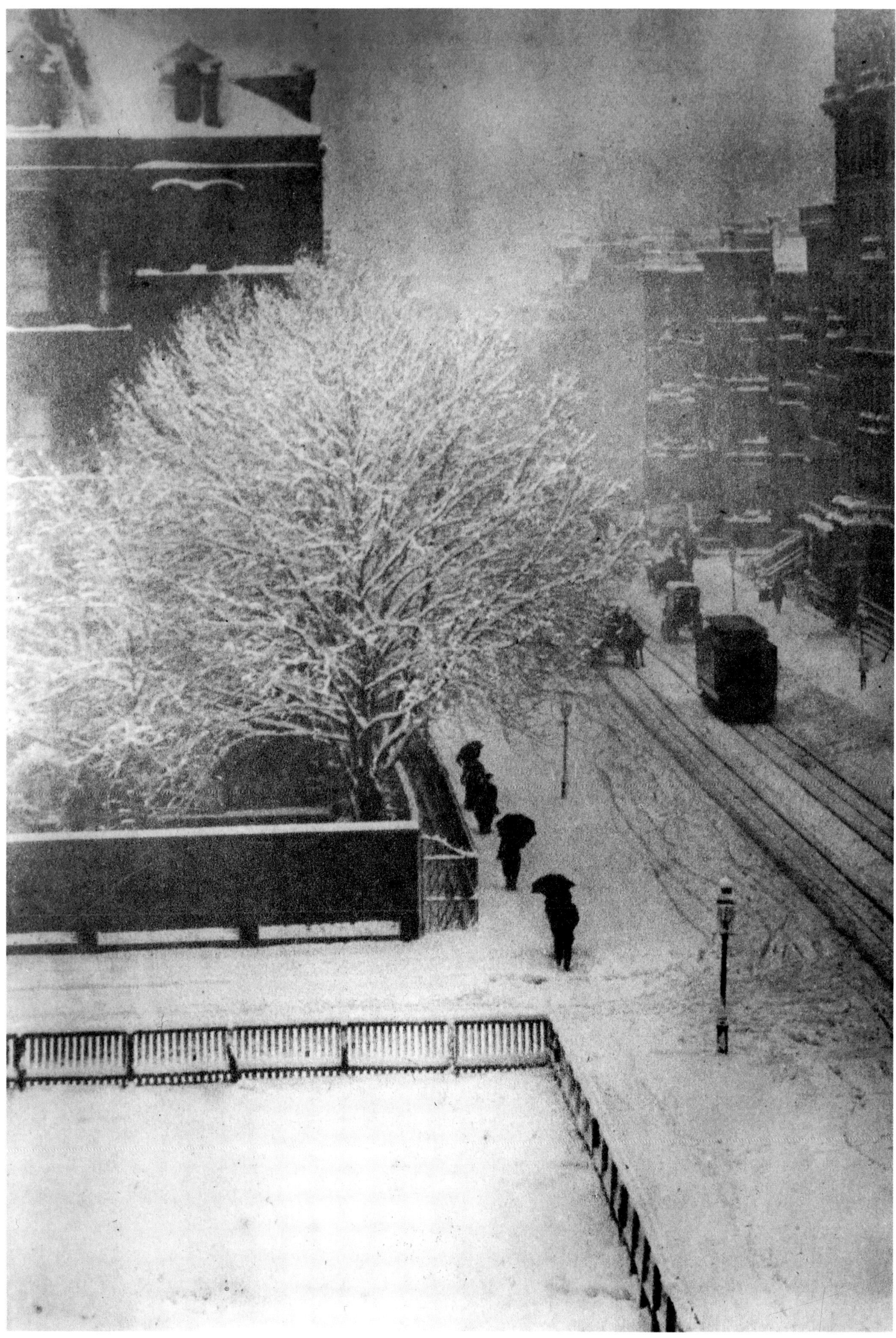

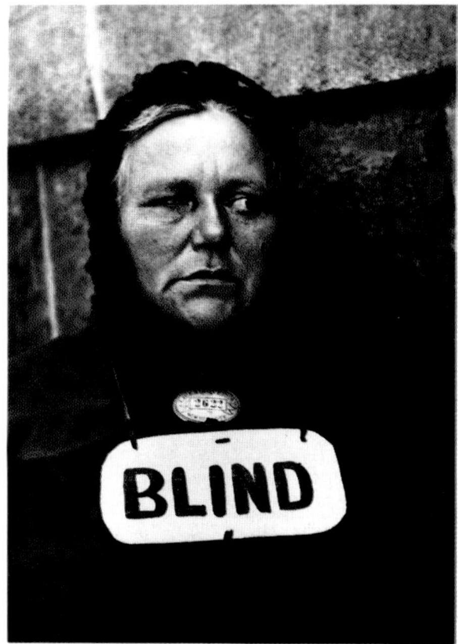

PAUL STRAND,
Photograph – New York,
published in *Camera Work,*
June 1917.

PAUL STRAND,
New York,
published in *Camera Work,*
October 1916.

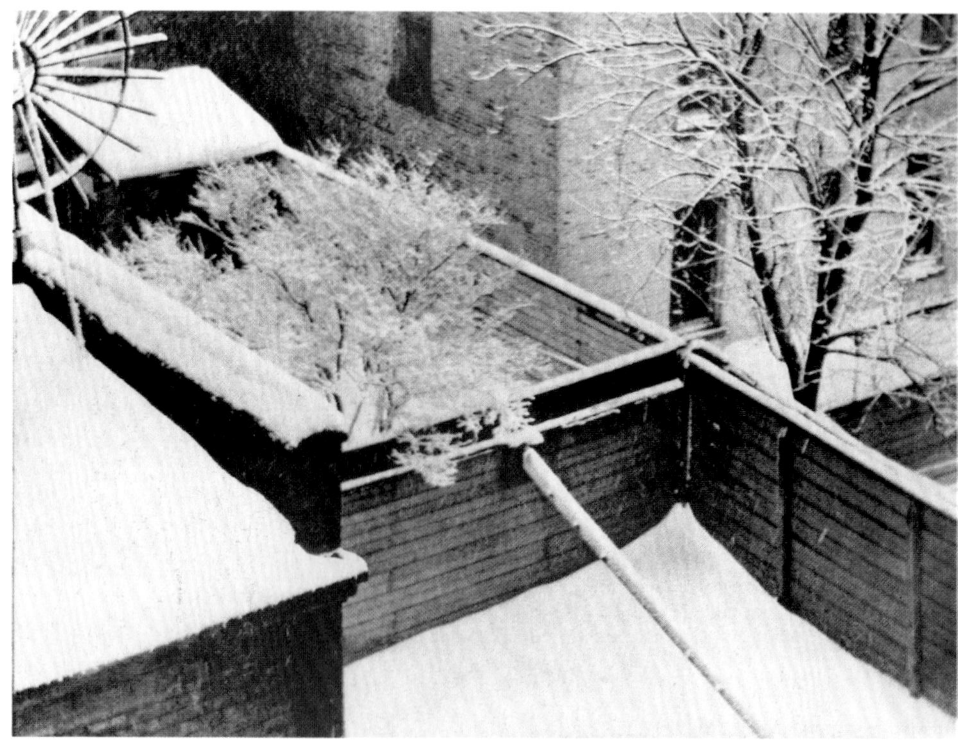

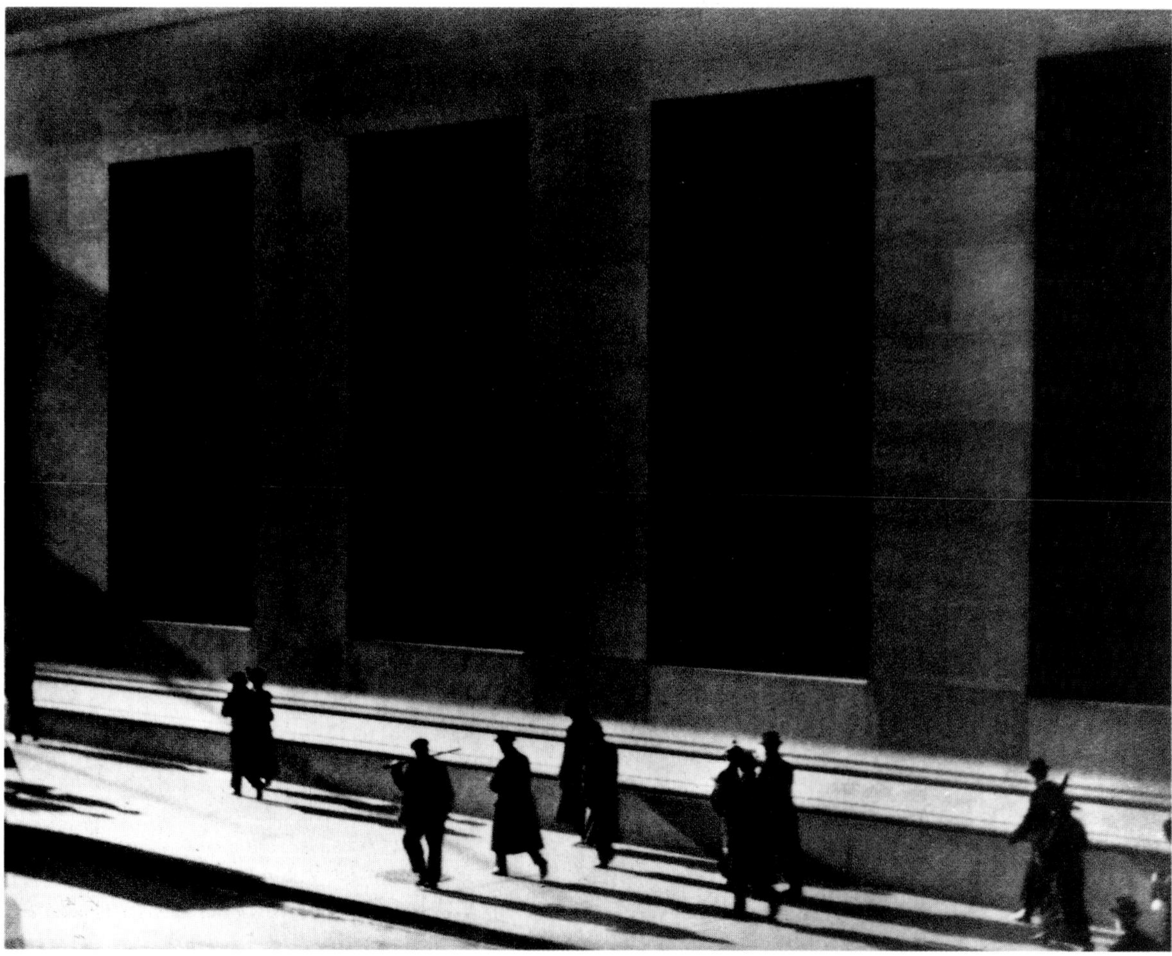

PAUL STRAND,
New York,
published in *Camera Work,*
June 1917.

PAUL STRAND, ▶
Photograph – New York,
published in *Camera Work,*
June 1917.

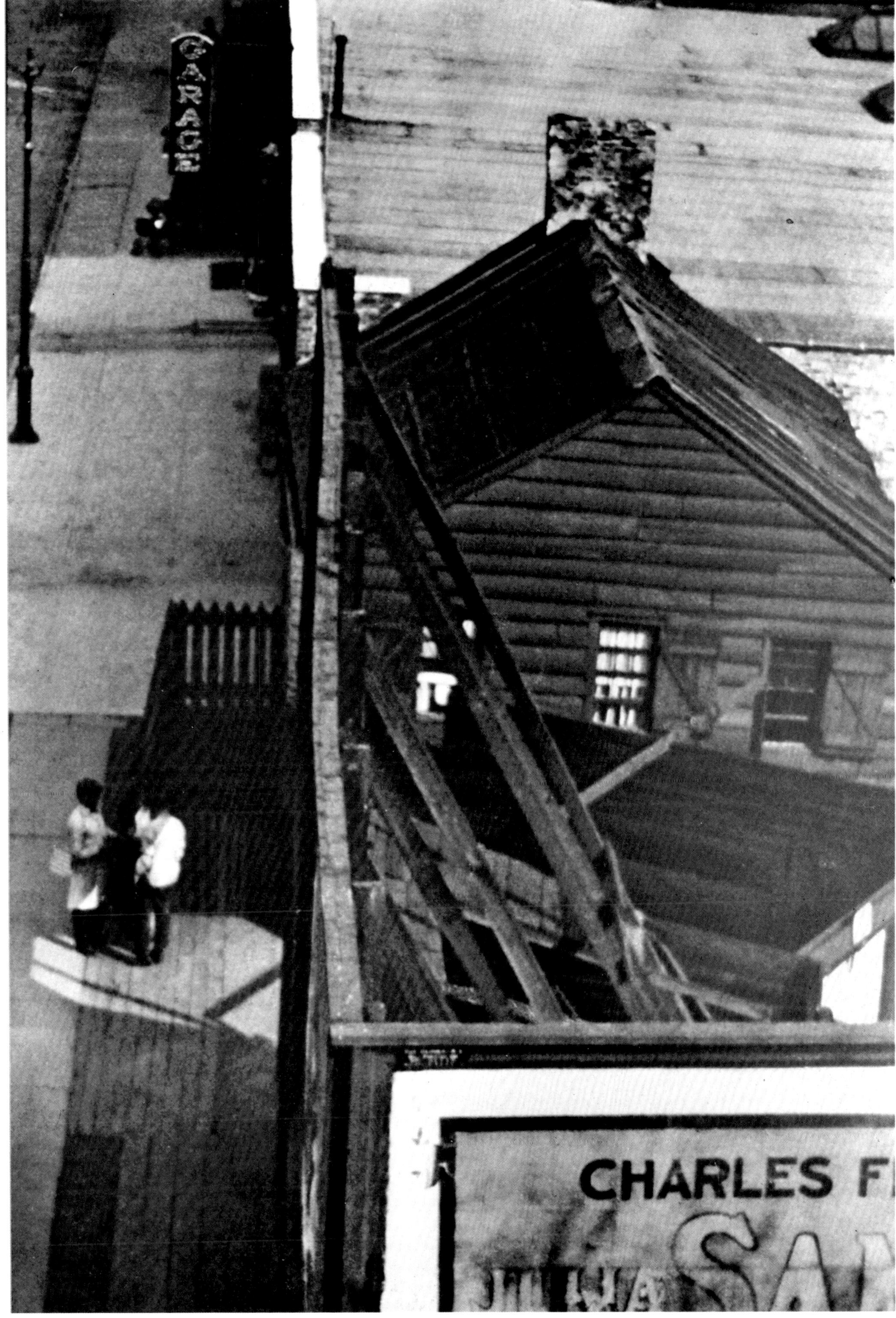
GARAGE
CHARLES F

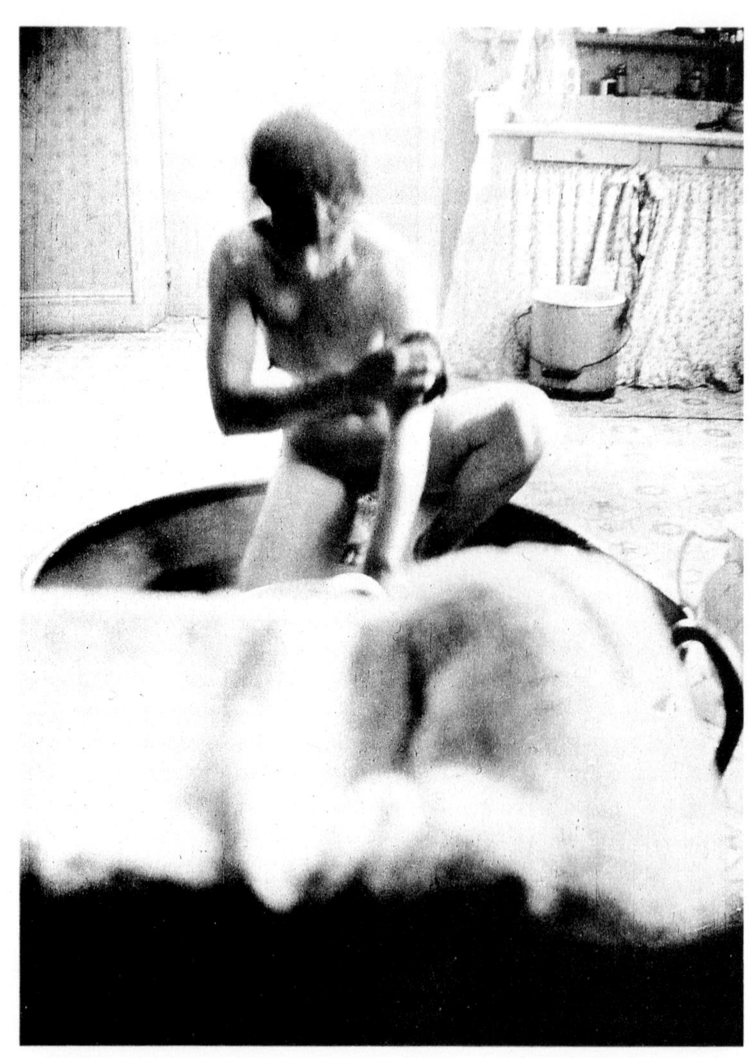

INTIMATE MOMENTS AND SECRET GARDENS

19

The artist as amateur photographer

Elvire Perego

In the field of writings about the self, critics seem to be interested mainly in certain forms of expression: autobiographies, private diaries, letters, interviews. There are others forms of expression, however, which have, until now, been neglected – the teeming reservoir of archives of snapshots and family albums, linking together photographs of "parents, lovers, friends, children",[1] familiar places, travels. In photography, writers, painters, and artists have seen a creative tool which prolongs the fiction of time, outlines the presence of the other, and bears witness to the fragility of perceptions. For amateurs like Zola, Bonnard, Fortuny, Munch, Strindberg, Loti, and Degas, photography became part of a "world of sensations" (Matisse), a sort of objective recognition of emotional states and the spirit of place.

Since the end of the last century, photography has expanded considerably. No longer just a hobby for wealthy dilettantes, it has now become an automatic ritual of "laying down a record" from which no one escapes. A multitude of individuals from every kind of cultural background have set about recording their lives, camera in hand; unknown people and public figures, intellectuals, writers, and painters of genius. Their pictures are vectors of humanity and lived experience, with the common aim of revealing the human being in their emotional life. As they interweave, they give a picture of a universal subject, (the notion of self) in the private life that they have chosen. Apart from seminal texts by Pierre Bourdieu and Roland Barthes,[2] little attention has been paid to examining, in itself and for itself, this unique mode of expression, even though, with its stereotypes, its interchangeable figures and its masterpieces, it has all the characteristics of a specific genre.

Paradoxically, photography – a prime mode of representation in the media – also inaugurated and made available a new space for intimacy and secrecy, of being one to one in an improbable but constantly sought encounter with oneself. For these bodies of personal work, though hallmarked in ways that point to very different aspirations and structures, were not made to be exhibited or published. The documents, words, intentions,

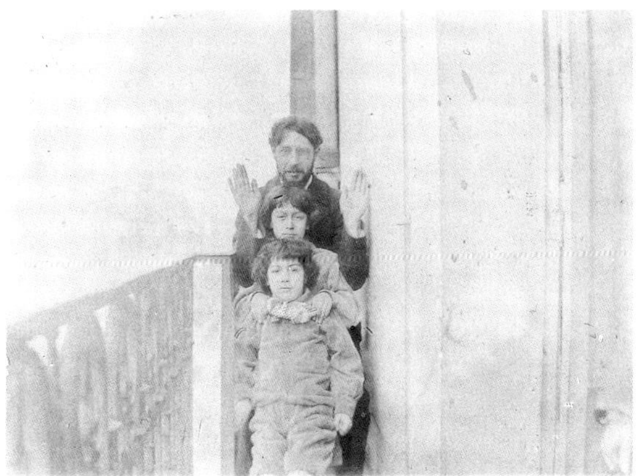

Pierre Bonnard,
On the Studio Balcony, Charles, Jean, and Pierre Bonnard,
1902–1903,
private collection.

and desires that frequently accompanied them have either been voluntarily obscured or are not accessible because they have not been handed down. Bearers of family secrets, or creative secrets – interpolated images in the background of an artist's work – these pictures are like a family without a history. Which means, of course, that photography (just like psychoanalysis) is full of histories and that it is, above all, a family story, a love story.

Of this immeasurably large mass of images, there are, today, a very few which because of their historic interest or aesthetic value have been singled out for attention through exhibition or publication. Research into this area very often chooses to look only at collections emanating from famous people, artists or writers. The French

◄ Pierre Bonnard,
Nude in the Tub (Marthe),
circa 1908,
private collection.

1. G. Gusdorf, *Les Écritures du Moi*, Paris, Odile Jacob, 1991.

2. P. Bourdieu *et al.*, *Photography: A Middle-brow Art*, trans. by Shaun Whiteside, Stanford, CA, Stanford University Press, 1990; R. Barthes, *Camera Lucida: Reflections on Photography*, trans. by Richard Howard, New York, Hill and Wang, 1981.

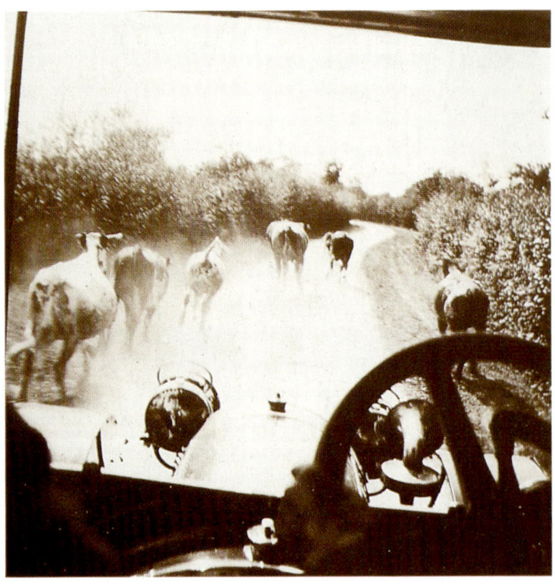

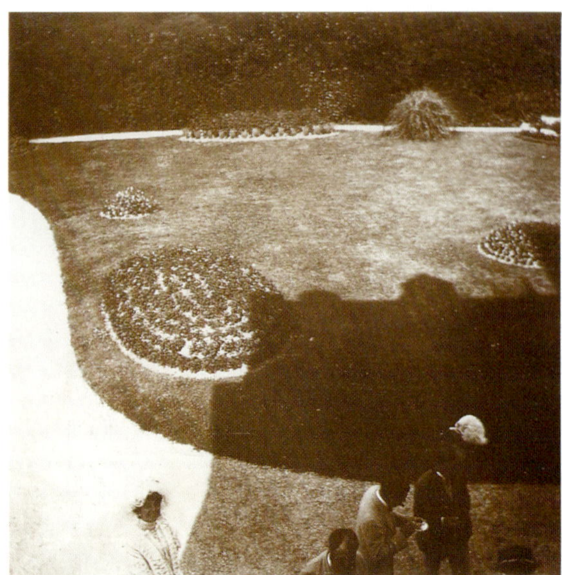

Left:
Édouard Vuillard, ***Travels in Brittany,*** 1906, Antoine Salomon Collection.

Right:
Édouard Vuillard, ***Amfreville,*** 1905, Antoine Salomon Collection.

point of view celebrates the testimony of writers (Émile Zola, Pierre Loti, Pierre Louÿs) and painters (Bonnard, Vuillard, Toulouse-Lautrec, Degas, Matisse, Magritte). Elsewhere, interest has been shown in Mucha, Khnopff, Primoli, Fortuny, Breitner, Munch, and Strindberg. Among the individual names emerging from the modernism of recent times we find Klee, Brancusi, Pierre-Henri Roché, and Claude Levi-Strauss.[3] Even with the addition of some Anglo-Saxon names (Lewis Carroll, Bernard Shaw, etc), this list does not take account of the majority of producers. Amateur photography is in a latent state, like a collective unconscious, and constitutes a fluid, unexplored vulnerable territory in which the personal bodies of work created by individuals stand out like relays or screens in the memory.

The family novel

An unvarying feature of this work, the "secret garden" is more than a metaphor; it is a place of retreat for the psyche, for the imagination, a geographical feature of inner space, the realm of privacy, sheltered and safe from the intrusion of others, the hiding-place to which we are magnetically drawn, the nostalgic Eden – the green paradise of our childhood loves. "To my beloved Jeanne, I dedicate this album of photographs which I have taken of our dear children, Denise and Jacques, in their garden at Verneuil, from June to September 1897." This message, sent by the writer Émile Zola to his "other woman" Jeanne Rozerot, the mother of his children, who lived as a recluse in daily expectation of a visit from the man she loved, not far from the estate at Médan where his wife Alexandrine held regal sway, is discreetly, sensitively symbolic of a double life. In the way Zola slips subtly from one possessive adjective to another ("my", "our", "their"), the author of *The Rougon-Macquarts* gives a delicate sense of a territory that is theirs without being entirely his. A self that is at a distance, a few steps back (as one often steps back to take a photograph), is suggested, implicitly admitted. A private self, but here in the sense of a lack, the self deprived. The photograph, as a means of access to the Other, strangely "does not fill the distance" but confirms it, just as it does not conjure away absence. "One languishes for something that is very near."[4] The album, sumptuously bound, has the style of a book, a literary work. The title and author's name are embossed on the cover: "Denise and Jacques, a true story by Émile Zola". The formulation is striking. While the first person takes the initiative in telling the story ("the photographs I have taken", as the dedication says), it is the third person, the literary man ("by

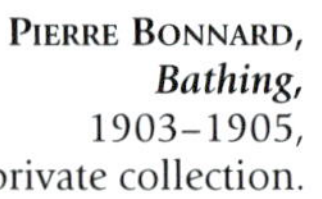

Pierre Bonnard, ***Bathing,*** 1903–1905, private collection. ▼

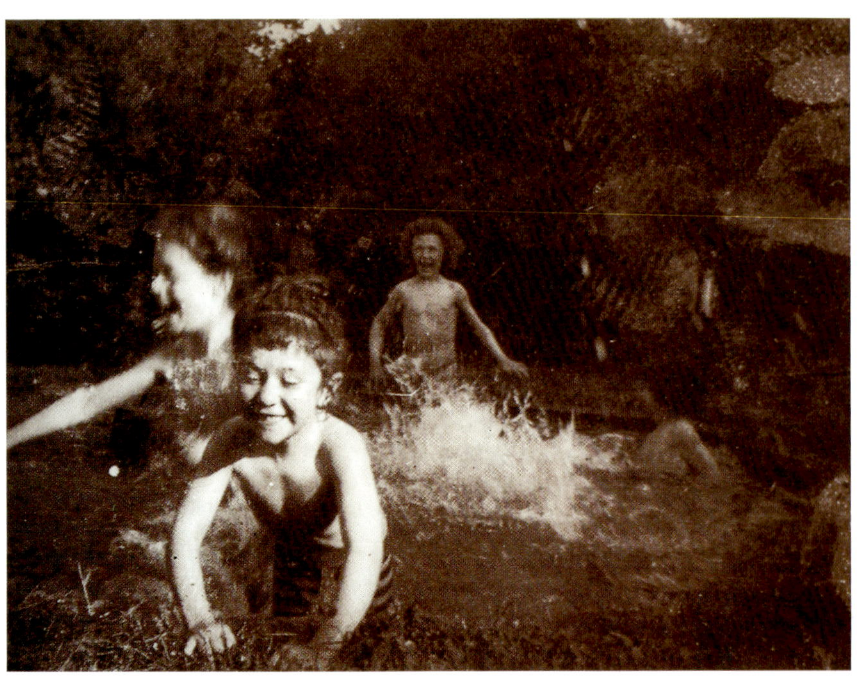

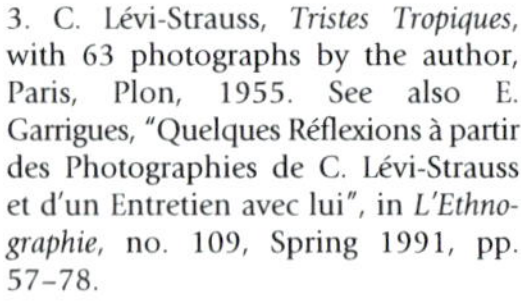

3. C. Lévi-Strauss, *Tristes Tropiques*, with 63 photographs by the author, Paris, Plon, 1955. See also E. Garrigues, "Quelques Réflexions à partir des Photographies de C. Lévi-Strauss et d'un Entretien avec lui", in *L'Ethnographie*, no. 109, Spring 1991, pp. 57–78.

4. E. Levinas, *Totalité et Infini*, Paris, Livre de Poche, p. 271.

Émile Zola") who takes charge of production. The children, designated by their first names, are really his master-work, "his flesh and blood" as the popular expression goes. The album exposes the work of his life and the life of his work as consubstantial with his existence. Is not a child an act of procreation like "a work of art, an individual work, in which you find yourself reproduced with all your joys and all your griefs?"[5] Zola understands perfectly that photography is a manner of speaking which speaks by its manner – a story – just as he affirms that there is a sense, a content, in form: a first-hand utterance that can be felt, that is direct, fundamentally innocent, true. The writer's mission is thus seen as one of making his intimate experience reverberate. As Starobinsky writes, "the law of authenticity does not demand that an utterance *reproduces* a given reality, but that it *produces its truth* in a free and uninterrupted development".[6]

In this respect, photographs possess a wordless form of eloquence. However intimate it may be, the album, just like a book, announces that it belongs to the category of things destined for someone else (Zola's album was dedicated to his beloved). It is a well known feature of dedications – whether on photographs or books – that they link depth of feeling and form of expression in so fundamental a way that the two resonate together. Photographs play the role of talismans, mnemonic substitutes, fetishes in the exact sense of the term, which incarnate beloved faces – love-objects – give them flesh or petrify them, according to what kind of feeling one brings to looking at them. It was in 1888 that Zola, falling passionately in love with Jeanne, also fell in love with photography. His undertaking outlines a sort of prototypical family romance, in which the plot, the episodes, and the protagonists permit one to recapture and reread the past tense of life. There was no shortage of material as the days went by, with the different events of everyday life: the children's amusements – dolls, bubble-blowing, bicycles, the swing, running, the parakeet from Senegal – or Jeanne sewing, putting together a bunch of flowers, reading, playing the mandolin, partially-undressed, reclining languidly, and walking in the country. Even during Zola's period of exile in England he noted "the fine weather there has been, the days spent in the garden, in such bright, mild sunshine", and the photographs he took "here, there and everywhere".[7] The life-story whose composition was spread out over fourteen years between 1888 and his death in 1902 was created in the manner of a personal diary: the sporadic nature of his photographic commemoration of life reflects the way that life itself evolves.

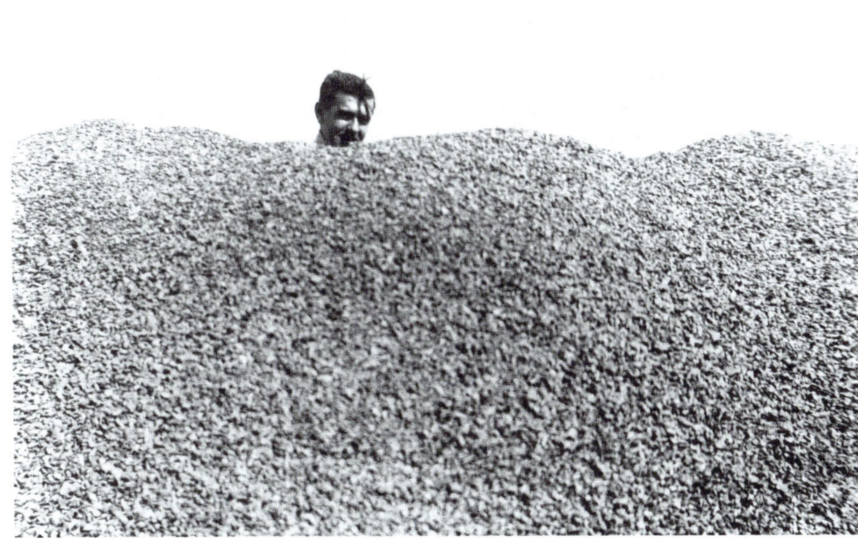

René Magritte,
Lessines,
August 1935.

Though photography has affinities with many other documentary practices relating to science and the visual arts, its affinities with love-relationships, family intrigue, and jubilation of childhood, and the acute awareness of the passing of time, of things remembered, make it almost organic to the understanding we can have of the individual's relationship to the other.

Photography is a form of expression of communal life where the "hearth" (in both the literal and the metaphorical sense) is the radiating center, the paradigm where the memory of emotions is stored, a constellation of shared tenderness and heartbreak which overflows from the center in all directions, outside the boundaries of the sealed metaphorical garden.

A work of art is a corner of creation seen through a temperament.[8] Pierre Bonnard, for

Paul Klee,
Ida Klee,
October 5, 1902,
Felix Klee Collection.
▼

5. É. Zola, *Écrits sur L'Art*, Paris, Gallimard, p. 44.

6. J. Starobinsky, "Le Style de l'Autobiographie", in *L'Oeil vivant, II: la Relation critique*, Paris, Gallimard, 1970.

7. É. Zola, *Pages d'Exil*, quoted by F.-Émile-Zola and Massin, *Zola Photographe: 480 Documents*, Paris, Délégation à l'Action Artistique and Hoëbecke, 1990.

8. É. Zola, *Écrits sur l'Art*, Paris, Gallimard, p. 81.

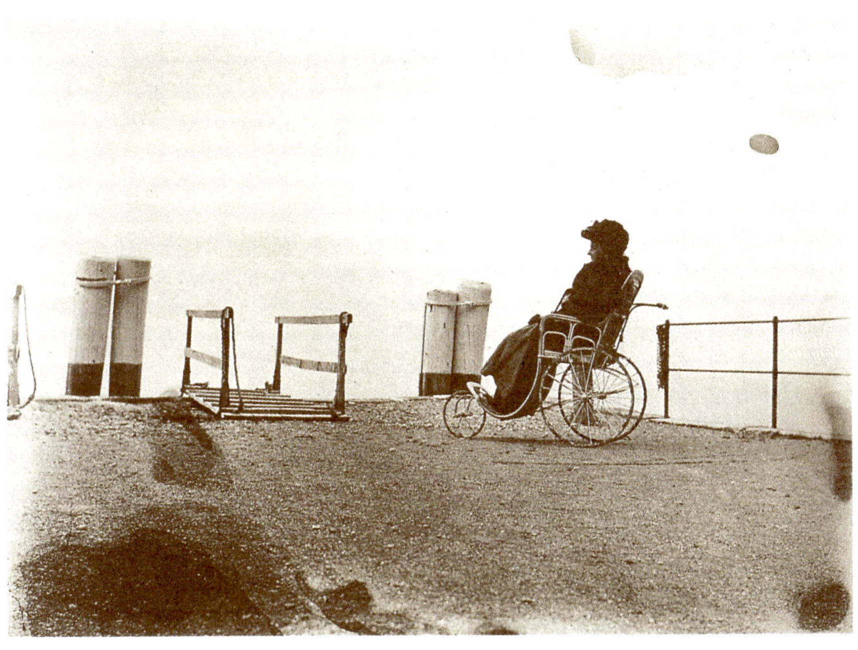

JACQUES-HENRI LARTIGUE, *My Speedboat with Propeller,* 1904. ▶

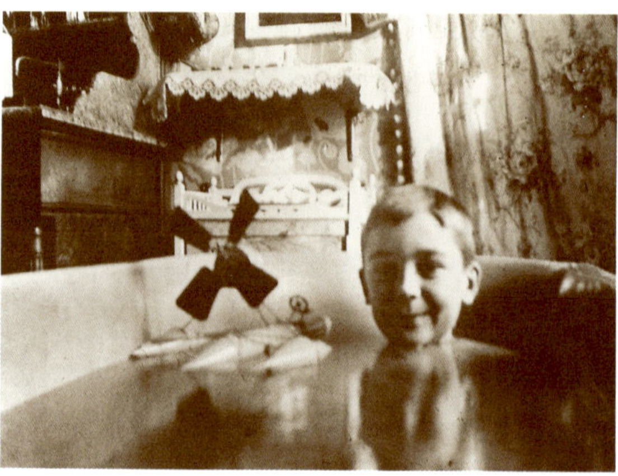

JACQUES-HENRI LARTIGUE, *Picking up the Pilot of the Thomann,* Issy-les-Moulineaux, February 9, 1911. ▼

JACQUES-HENRI LARTIGUE, *Sketches of photos taken at Issy-les-Moulineaux* 1911.

his part, carried out Émile Zola's definition completely. In the Dauphiné, starting in the 1890s, at Grand-Lemps, on the family estate of Clos where he passed his summer holidays, but also at other houses in the country (Noisy-le-Grand, Montval, Vernouillet, and Vernon), Bonnard, armed with a Pocket Kodak camera, devoted himself to photography. His photos, which are in a very small format, are cinematic in essence: pictures taken from a distance, sequences (the children bathing; Marthe, his lover, naked), exteriors and interiors, shots blurred by movement or missing part of the picture, which seem the result of accident or chance.[9] Although Bonnard's photographs are usually only of secondary interest as pictures in the aesthetic sense, except by chance like the *Nude in the Tub (Marthe)* of 1908, the originality of his talent and his temperament shines out of them. We do not know what kind of experimental part Bonnard allotted to them in the totality of his research. But we certainly sense that these fragments have their own particular place in the interstices between life and art, between Bonnard living and Bonnard painting.

The first thing that attracts one to them is the naturalness and fullness running through them. There is, in these photographs – which capture the transitions or movements between one gesture and another – an intermittent, dazzled quality that coincides with the artist's consciousness or the central project of that consciousness. The images of the body, in particular, enclosed as in the garden of Eden – the idyllic garden of Adam and Eve (variations on reciprocal nudity) – or in the space of the bedroom, the space of conjugal fusion, sensuality, and desire (nude pictures of Marthe in the Paris flat in Rue de Douai), together compose a symbolic revelation of Eros. The painter's amorous look takes in, as if by stealth or inadvertence, Marthe's typical movements: awkward, bewildered, ingenuous. "If gestures happen without awareness of what they are aiming for, that is because the appearance of a face and a body is always surprising. Appearance, really, is an apparition. It is not given; one encounters it."[10] The mysterious opening into the essence of intimacy which is at the heart of Bonnard's work is, finally, always on the point of passing from reality through into the space of imagination. It is as if the painter has reached the borderline where the ebullience of life as it happens meets the periphery of memory, the borders of the imaginary, the birth of the creative impulse itself.

His friend the painter Edouard Vuillard – also a photographer in his spare time – noted in his diary "Bonnard's horror of photo-deception-art-artifice in construction [...] harmony, laziness of trusting to observation for observation, as a motive for action, sensation of surprise, study from nature, etc.; observation by surprise – real nourishment for the organizing faculty of imagining [...] Bonnard and repulsion for photography as writing with light without the intervention of consciousness [...]"[11] It is surely possible that the photographic act is ultimately one of pure mental elaboration, the cerebral invention (discovery and recreation) of this interior world.

This interior of the self – at once subject and object – and of consciousness is like a womb of the sight and the senses, which recalls the funda-

9. See J.-F. Chevrier; "Bonnard Photographe", in *Bonnard, Classique du vingtième Siècle,* Paris, Centre Georges-Pompidou, 1984, and F. Heilbrun and P. Néagu, *Pierre Bonnard: Photographs and Paintings,* New York, Aperture, 1988.

10. M. Le Bot, *L'Œil du Peintre,* Paris, Gallimard, 1982, p. 25.

11. Quoted by Émilie Daniel, "L'Objectif du Subjectif: Vuillard Photographe", in *Les Cahiers du Musée National d'Art Moderne,* no. 23, pp. 83–93.

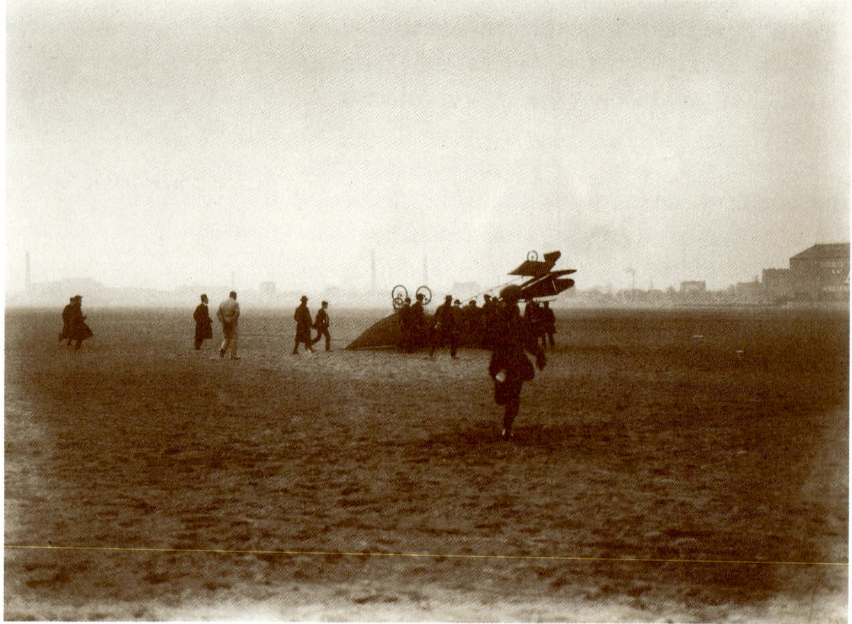

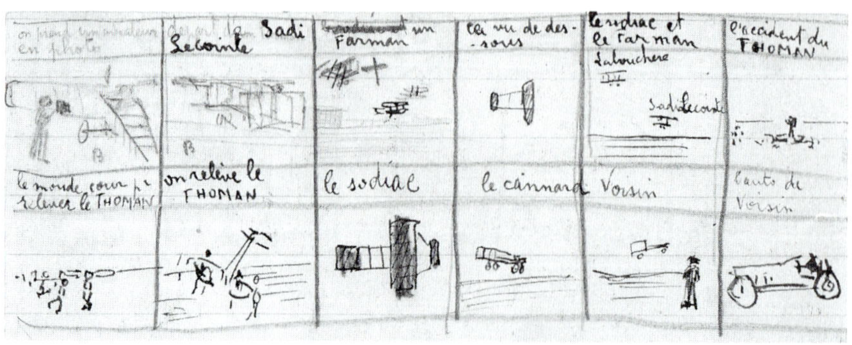

mental maternal image, the "shadow of the mother". In this respect, Vuillard's experience as a photographer is a particularly relevant example. He recorded in his notebook: "Saturday 27. Putting things in order, looked at photos of our mothers with J. Roussel, A. Fontaine". Vuillard's mother, whom he adored, had just died, on November 17, 1928. He had shared a life of perfect symbiosis with her. He began assembling all the photos he had taken of her. "Saturday 2. Melancholy for Mama."[12] The photographs became venerated images – relics – marking the painful, fatal (and fetal) separation. It is within the experience of birth and death, or rather the elements of loss, absence, and mystery within life and death (linked to the theme of symbolic representation), that we have to look for the conceptual framework of photography, at least of this selective kind: "The Rule of Appearances and Disappearances".[13] The work of mourning withdraws into this magnetic distance, into the aura which envelops the physical being of the mother. As D. W. Winnicott has written in this context, *"the precursor of the mirror is the mother's face"*.[14]

Figure of what has been before, center of gravity, submerged, imprinted surface (the photographic image can be conceived as the projection of an indefinitely extended surface), the imprint of the mother, her sweet memory, is surely that of an immense face, at once seen and not seen, both transparent and opaque, disturbing and ravishing, familiar and intangible, directly present and yet foreign, always just about to come, to grasp, to attain. No one can get away from the fascinating image of the mother, who remains obstinately "on the other side of the mirror". Edouard Vuillard's notebooks contain arresting intuitions and fragments of thought: "October 24, 1890. As for objective expression , it is clearly necessary, but its whole importance comes down to: I take this motif, and not that one; it is designation pure and simple. As for the distinction that I wanted to make with regard to subjective expression, the expression which is common to all the works of the same individual, the expression that is peculiar to a single work, there is no such thing. That is objective expression (What I was aiming for was *the objectivity of subjectivity*. I was forced to it.)"[15]

Vuillard's photography is the existential instrument of investigation and field of observation of an intermediary zone, in the double sense of being located and mediating between psychic internal reality (the mother-son relationship in all its mysteries and complications) and external reality: existence that can be touched. Just like his painting, it originates and develops within its own sealed chamber between objective and subjective, reality and perception, the outside and the inside – the founding duality.

The places of the body

The geography of exterior space, seen from this point of view, relates only to the obsession with returning, to the instinct for one's origins. The perception of a place – home, the town, the earth or the distant port of call – can be explored like a body, with its openings, its orifices, its veins, its mass, the volume of its parts, its softness, its skin – the frontier, the envelope, the grain, the *film*. "On my first escape I threw myself onto Italy as though it was a woman's body", recalls Paul Morand.[16] Places can be like cradles evoked by reflexive and erotic desire, invested with meaning, where the eye desirously seeks a forbidden receptacle at once lost and found.

The photographic reveries of Mario Fortuny, the Venetian hidalgo whose finery entered into legend with Proust, are fixated on the *morbidezza* [softness] of the waterlily city, whose essence is entirely liquid, situated in the middle of the void, between the waters of the womb and the Styx.[17] In the ancient palace of Pesaro-Orfei, workshops specializing in engraving, painting, pleated silk, and photography formed a laboratory-library, museum, and aquarium where the Master, "attired, doge-like, in an embossed-velvet robe", orchestrated his innumerable gatherings. Around the

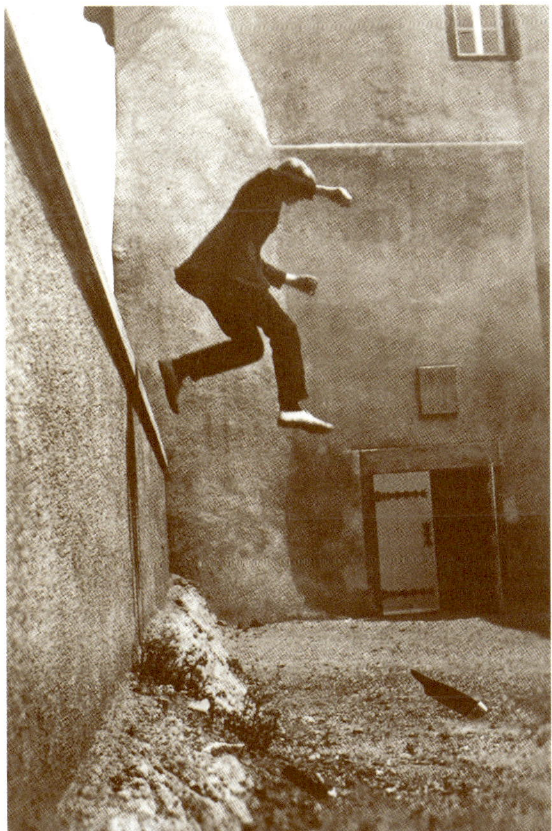

JACQUES-HENRI LARTIGUE, *Oléo*, 1908.

12. *Ibid.*

13. J. Baudrillard, *Fatal Strategies*, trans. by P. Bleitchman and W. G. J. Niesluchowski, ed. by J. Fleming, London, Pluto Press, 1990, p. 174.

14. D. W. Winnicott, *Playing and Reality*, London, Penguin Education, 1980, p. 130.

15. Émilie Daniel, *op. cit.*

16. P. Morand, *Venises*, Paris, Gallimard, p. 26.

17. *Ibid.*, p. 45.

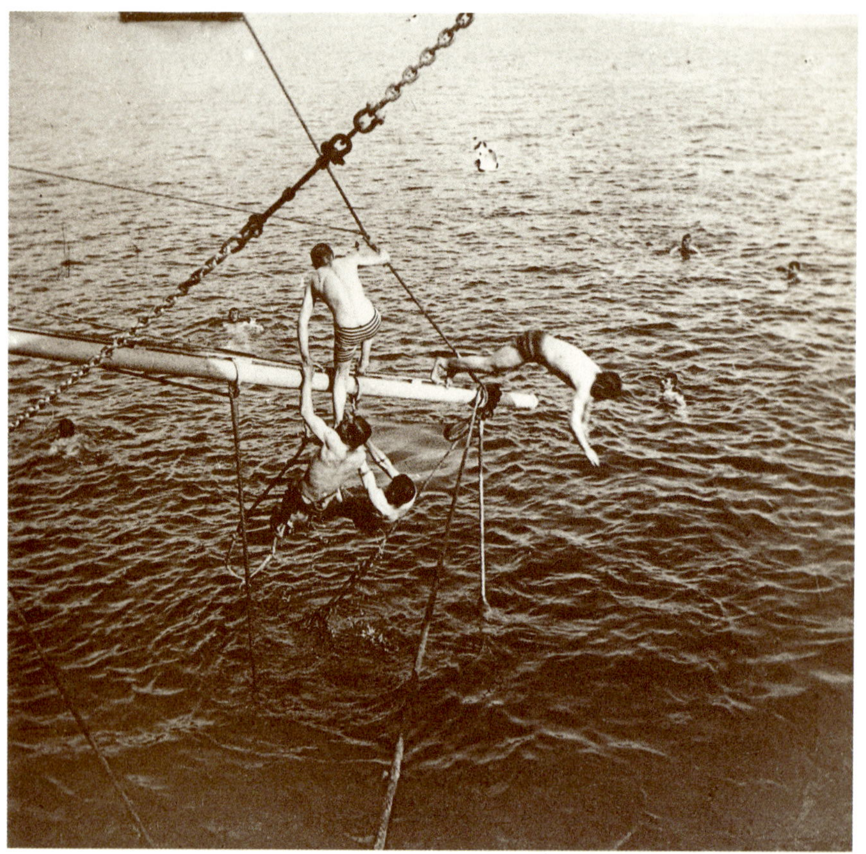

Pierre Loti, ***Sailors of the Vautour Bathing in the Bosporus,*** 1903–1905, Pierre Loti-Viaud Collection.

a rhythm, an ebullience, a quiver of life. Without doubt, his work as a painter owes a great deal to his photographic practice, It was the way he constructed a notebook for himself, a precipitate of things he had seen, animated elliptical scraps, through which he brought into manageable form the restless, boiling, convulsive experience of incubating works of visual art, in short, the living center of the subject.

All this forms a network of analogical correspondences which have the value of a self-portrait, a tormented form of representation if only because of the multiplicity of egos (Anaïs Nin). As Amiel, the classic case here, writes, "I feel chameleon-like, kaleidoscopic, protean, mutable and polarisable in every way, fluid, virtual and by consequence latent, absent even in the representation of myself. I am a spectator, so to speak, of the molecular whirlwind that people call one's life as an individual." Lines that make one understand how "the self-portrait can be both everywhere and nowhere".[20]

In this Chinese-puzzle situation of looker and looked-at, photography – a fundamentally narcissistic medium – comes to terms with the phenomenon of inversion. It offers a world of reversal and duplications where the modulations of the prism never stop exchanging their multiple interpretations – hence its enlargement, displacement, and fragmentation of the horizons of the interior perspective, of identity. "I is another", the celebrated formulation of Rimbaud, opened the way. In this *fin-de-siècle* period, lovers of photography (who were often aesthetes) undertook the construction of their own image and gave themselves up to the pleasure and fantasy of staging a show, a pantomime, a game of disguises. They came up against the dividing-line where the playful childlike world of amusement met the irrepressible anxiety of depression, aging, and death. It was in this way that the photographic self-portraiture of the painter Edward Munch and the writer August Strindberg reinforced "the hallucination of the double". The figure of the double symbolizes this unquiet otherness, distance of the self from the self, and detachment, linked to solitude, interior wounds, and grief.

In his quest for "nostalgic" references, the figure of the novelist-navigator Pierre Loti runs the gamut of incarnations and rebirths, by turn "a Greek, an Albanian, a sailor, a circus acrobat, a Breton, an Emir, the god Osiris, a member of the Academy, a Sheikh, a Chinese mandarin, wearing a fez or a Basque beret, a naked man (or rather one dressed in his muscles), and even as Loti, in his everyday clothes".[21]

For Toulouse-Lautrec, who considered himself "a horribly abject being", the succession of masks

reversible *Venetian Mirror,* Fortuny's panoramic vision, with its aesthetic of circumference, the gyrating circle – a vision both flat and profiled, full of meanderings and undulations, slipping and floating lines – takes the viewer on a walk across treacherous ground, immersed in something that naturally suggests the primal architecture of the abyss within the female body.

Space offers memory less imprecise material than time. An art-lover like Fortuny, who wanted to collect a series of stocks of image/icons constructing – through the play of poetic mimesis and reflected identification – the place for a *memoria sui,*[18] appears like a "mnemotechnician", an archeologist, an anatomist with a psyche of a type that has yet to come to light and be explored and defined: a "being who is a building, a labyrinth, a town" who has behind his head an architectural configuration, a curtain wall, a clandestine nurturing source of new signs.

Another who experimented with snapshots was George Hendrik Breitner, the leader of the Dutch Impressionists. Attracted by the dynamism, the welcoming energy, and the activism of Amsterdam, he had settled there in 1886. With his sketchbook, his paintbox, and his camera, Breitner wandered along the roads and the canals of Amsterdam looking for an incisive visual theme: the man on the street, laborers hard at work, female passers-by, horses, "the muddy hammering of people in a hurry and the heavy rolling of laden carts"[19] all create an atmosphere,

18. See M. Beaujour's analyses on memory, *Miroirs d'Encre*, Paris, Le Seuil, 1980.

19. Written by J. Hofker (Delang), a Dutch author belonging to the literary movement called the "Tachtigers", for whom painting was a primary source of inspiration. Quoted by P. Hefting, *De fotos van Breitner*, S'Gravenhage, SDU, 1989.

20. Quoted by B. Didier, "Autoportrait et Journal Intime", in *Corps écrit*, no. 5, on the self-portrait, Paris, P.U.F., February 1983, pp. 167–182.

21. A. Buisine, "L'Impossible Cliché", in *Revue Pierre Loti*, no. 22 (*Pierre Loti et la Photographie*), April–June 1985.

is touching to observe. His photographer friends recorded a great many: Gauzi, Maurice Guibert, Maxime Dethomas, Paul Sescau, Maurice Joyant, even Bonnard, and he seemed to expect some kind of therapeutic effect from them. When he was surprised on his boat, dressed in the simplest garb, by someone with a folding camera, he was happy, stretched his arms to heaven and cried to the photographer "I'll be a lion".[22] Loti and Toulouse-Lautrec, like many of their contemporaries, practiced the fantasy-cult of exoticism. Primitive peoples, archaic civilizations, Eastern influences, and the fascination with Japan all helped to feed their inclination for eccentricity and disguise.

This passion for the other, the unknown is like a desire for difference, an aesthetic of the diverse where the exiled, maladjusted, suffering, recognizing itself made strange in these contrived self-portraits, at last finds a likeness, feels reunited, like itself.

It was this new emotional approach which inspired travel – or rather pilgrimage, the tour of initiation. To be able to enjoy the pleasure of recognition, stimulated by the proximity of the imaginary, perhaps one needs to be out of one's usual environment with the desire, ambivalence, and excitement that brings. Every departure, every escape may be a return to a hidden self, a pursuit of that self, running after traces, vanished shadows. Even more, it may be the experience of time. Victor Segalen (who later, in 1923–1924, went to China with his traveling companion and photographer Gilbert de Voisins) noted in 1908: "Exoticism in Time. Back into history. Flight from the mean despicable present. The elsewhere and the bygone." In this light, space-time oscillations take on all the seduction of digression-regression, reinforced by what has been called the *libido sciendi* [thirst for knowledge]. Egypt, Palestine, the Orient, Italy and Greece, then Asia are the destinations and extraordinary terrains of instinctual pleasure.

The "souvenir-photo" where relatives and people one loves line up in front of a tourist sight has the value of a trophy, proof that one has been somewhere. It is also, to use a sociological term, an attempt at appropriation. It is even more a rite of passage into another time, a grave experience which confronts human fragility and the time of a monument – ancient, historic – which in the collective sensibility is equivalent to a sort of eternity. The defining quality of holiday photography no doubt lies in the ability of the place as privileged bearer of that eternity to mix the two times, to weave a thread that can be broken, then tied again at every visit to a place of interest where history joins the life after death, where the photograph pins down eternity, where the "forever" of the person taking the pictures seeks to join the "forever" of the place.

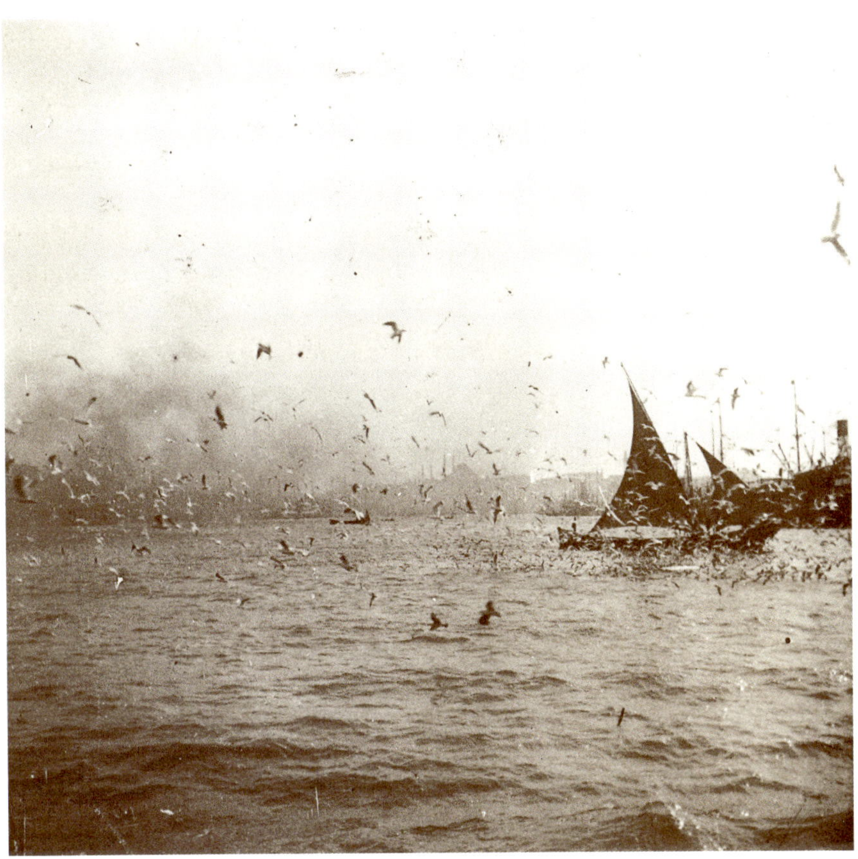

Pierre Loti, ***Flight of Birds on the Bosporus***, 1903–1905, Pierre Loti-Viaud Collection.

Recording sights photographically is analogous to noting down the story of one's travels, which soon became a genre, the *Impressions of a Journey*. Following the example set in 1851 by Maxime Du Camp and Gustave Flaubert with their *Voyage en Orient*, there is a great increase in travel photography. Forgetting all about the aspirations to historical objectivity and scientific seriousness with which it began, travel photography turned into an authentic mode of autobiographical expression. Loti's travels cast a vivid light upon the movement.

After 1894, Loti seems to have resorted to photography to note down the elements of his memories in the margin of his *Journal intime*: more than 600 shots, stereoscopic views, positives on glass or little rectangular images stuck onto sheets of strong cardboard, in series corresponding to their subject: Turkey, principally Istanbul, where he stayed on his boat *Le Vautour* (1903–1905), Persia, India (1899–1900), Korea (1901), China, the Bay of Along (1901–1902), and Egypt (1907).[23] These photographs – "pages from a journey" – mingle ethnological inquiry, picturesque observations on a town or a culture, landscapes, contrasts, shorelines, crossings, and glittering horizons.

Matisse combined the pleasures of life as a Robinson Crusoe or one of the wanderers of the

22. See J. Sagne, *Toulouse-Lautrec*, Paris, Fayard, 1988.

23. J. Sagne, "A propos de l'exotisme dans le portrait photographique au dix-neuvième siècle", *Revue de la Bibliothèque Nationale*, no. 1, September 1981; J.-F. Chevrier and J. Sagne, "L'Autoportrait comme Mise en Scène: Essai sur l'Identité, l'Exotisme et les Excès photographiques, *Photographies*, no. 4, April 1984; *Pierre Loti Photographe, 1850–1923*, exhibition catalogue, Poitiers, 1985.

Iliad with the bliss of rocking in a cradle. He wrote to Bonnard: "A good stay, and a good rest. Have seen all sorts of things. Will tell you all. Lived for twenty days on a coral island; pure light, pure air, pure color: diamond, sapphire, emerald, turquoise. Have done absolutely nothing, except take some bad photos."

Sixty snaps which the painter took during his stay in Tahiti have been recently discovered.[24] Matisse had acquired what he called "an extremely advanced camera". Only as an amateur, but never forgetting his painterly preoccupations with space and light, Matisse tried his hand at simple photographic studies. Noting what was in a place, doing research, and furnishing his mind, he isolates motifs – trees, atolls, lagoons – chooses a frame – often his window – and takes the same picture twice, sometimes three times.

Matisse considered that: "Photography can furnish the most precious of information and no one can contest its interest from this point of view. Done by a man of taste, a photograph appears like a work of art. But I believe that style is unimportant in photographs: they will always be striking, because they show nature, and all artists will find a world of sensations there. Consequently the photographer ought to intervene as little as possible, in order not to deprive the photograph of the objective charm it naturally possesses, despite its imperfections. All the photographer will do, if he tries to add to it, is to make the result look like the echo of a different procedure. Photography ought to record, furnish us with documents."[25]

For Matisse photography is a nascent presence in the world, which gushes into being like a spring, a magical trace, where the virtues of style are not necessary.

24. J.-F. Chevrier, "Matisse et la Photo", in *Matisse Photographies*, Cahiers H. Matisse, 1986.

25. In *Camera Work*, no. 24, October 1908, pp. 13–23.

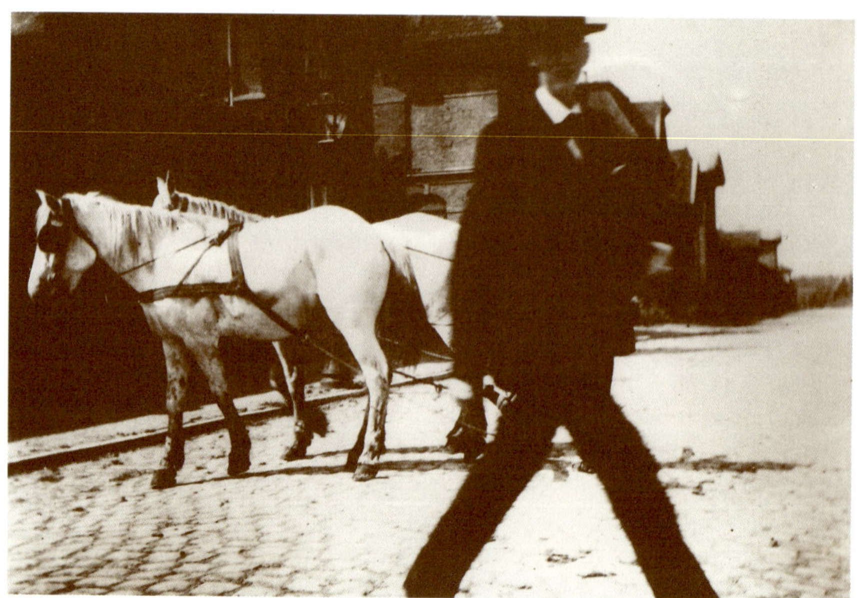

GEORGE HENDRIK BREITNER, *Amsterdam*, circa 1885, Prentenkabinet, Rijksuniversiteit, Leyden. ▼

The mirror of Amiel

An artist who seems to make a success of everything or an amateur touched by the grace of creativity and a genius with form? Jacques-Henri Lartigue is less easy to define than Matisse. What can be said is that his practice was always that of a dilettante, a flaneur with a camera, away from the grand theories or anxieties of creation, as skilled at seizing the small events of daily life within his own circle as the tone of the times and the mutations of the century. With Lartigue, the subject is never the excuse for research into form, and yet most of his images are dazzlingly beautiful: the pleasures of water are inseparable from the graphic lines of the swimming pool, the design of a portrait never veils the sensuality of a face, the gleaming lines of a racing car extol the passion for speed. The graphic line, the design, and the shimmering contours seem to have sprung from the subject to express it better. Form and content, emotion and research, are inseparable. Lartigue constructed a vision, but also an ethic: beauty is an experience of life. Every subject is seized without any premeditation, with a new eye, with the self-evidence and the formal sense of a child's particular vision.

In fact, the whole of Lartigue's art, just like Picasso's, is rooted in the spontaneity of childhood. For it was, in fact, at a very young age that he discovered photography. Born on June 13, 1894 at Courbevoie, he was introduced to photography by his businessman father, who was an enlightened amateur photographer. He was six years old when he became aware of his "eye trap". "I was looking around, enjoying myself. Suddenly an idea began dancing in my head, an invention straight from fairyland, as a result of which I thought I could never be sad or bored again. I open my eyes, then shut them, then open them again, then open them wide and Whoosh! I catch the picture with everything in it: light shadow, fullness and emptiness. And what I get is something alive which moves, palpitates, smells. Even the noise and the silence which are in things. Everything which makes me exist."

His father gave the little boy his first camera (made by Carpentier, with 13 x 18 cm plates) and he decided to photograph everything that intrigued him: outdoor games, experiments with airplanes, sophisticated inventions by his brother Zissou, motorcycles, cars, elegant women in the Bois de Boulogne, family events and pastimes, and summer holidays at Pont-de-l'Arche and the chateau at Rouzat. In 1902, when he was only eight years old, he began compiling hefty albums combining pictures and hand-written notes. He never stopped filling them until his death in 1986

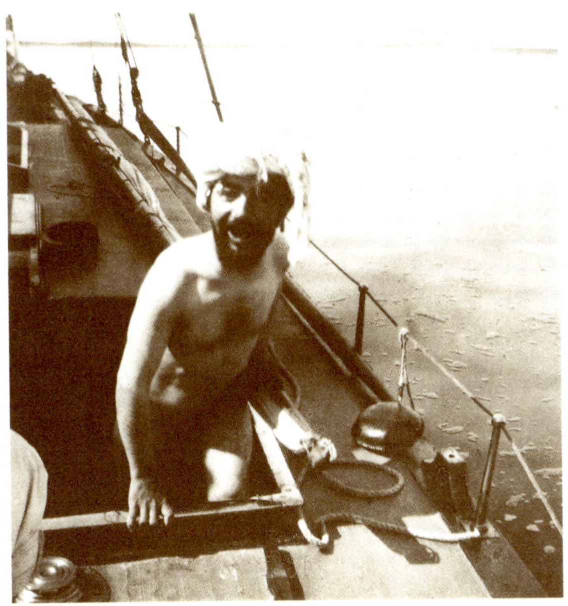

◀ ANONYMOUS, *Henri de Toulouse-Lautrec*, circa 1890, Bibliothèque Nationale, Paris.

– a prodigious saga and an irreplaceable witness to an age when everything was in a state of flux.

A sense of pleasure clings to the man as well as the work. Belatedly hailed by the media at the age of sixty-nine, honored with a first exhibition at the Museum of Modern Art in New York, Lartigue himself did much to reinforce his own legend of an eternally young man, carefree, laughing, indefatigable, describing himself, in the title of one of his works, as "a marveler". In some respects however, the man disrupts the stories that have settled about him, and defies the game of labeling: deeply religious but a great charmer, apparently well off but without real property, worldly, friend of numerous artists (Gance, Guitry, Cocteau, Picasso, Bresson, Fellini) but seemingly haunted by a lonely project of his own, Lartigue cannot be easily defined. In the same way, despite espousing a philosophy of happiness and optimism to the point of incarnating it, he managed to avoid ever falling into the anodyne or the systematic. Finally, his work upsets both the status of the artist as photographer and the definition of photography itself.

There is the additional point that Lartigue's fame as a photographer and as an ultra-elegant dandy should not be allowed to put the rest of his work in the shade: Lartigue was not simply a photographer: born into a "good" family, he was a professional painter all his life, particularly sought after in the interwar period. Although his importance and his talent have to be evaluated with care, nonetheless he lived off the sale of his canvasses (floral motifs, sporting themes, portraits of high society and celebrities, etc).

Lartigue was also a writer. He kept a private diary all his life, of which the few volumes that have been published are only selected extracts. The gift to France of the whole of his work will yield an astonishing 250,000 photographs, thousands of pages of writing, and hundreds of paintings. When one considers the scale of the project, it is clear that it will go down as one of the autobiographical monuments of the twentieth century, the first multimedia autobiography, the work of an Amiel who understood the essential importance of the image next to the text. How is it possible to conceive that such an endeavor, which took several routes without privileging any of them, such an obsession with narration, such a furious desire for self-expression, should not be based upon a mortal wound, a never-surmounted panic at the flight of time? Beneath every pursuit of happiness, there is an undercurrent of sadness. Perhaps, one day, when the work of which we now know only the glittering public face has been seen in its entirety, we shall finally discover its dark side. "To write, to paint, to photograph", wrote Lartigue "these things console me almost wholly".

At the heart of the work

Many painters have used, or practiced, photography. But of all the artists of his time, the "bourgeois" Degas is perhaps the one who has the strongest awareness of his own modernity. Inclined by temperament to speculation, obsessed all his life by technical and aesthetic questions, he was vividly impressed by this new way of transcribing reality. Antoine Terrasse[26] describes how Degas set up a continuous game of to-and-fro in experimental and formal terms between his painting and photography, an art in which he foresaw the revolutionary potential.

In 1895, at the height of the painter's passion for the sensitive plate, Julie Manet, the daughter

PAUL MARTIN, *Boulogne*, 1897 (woman using a Kodak), University of Texas, Austin. ▼

26. A. Terrasse, *Degas et la Photographie*, Paris, Denöel, 1983.

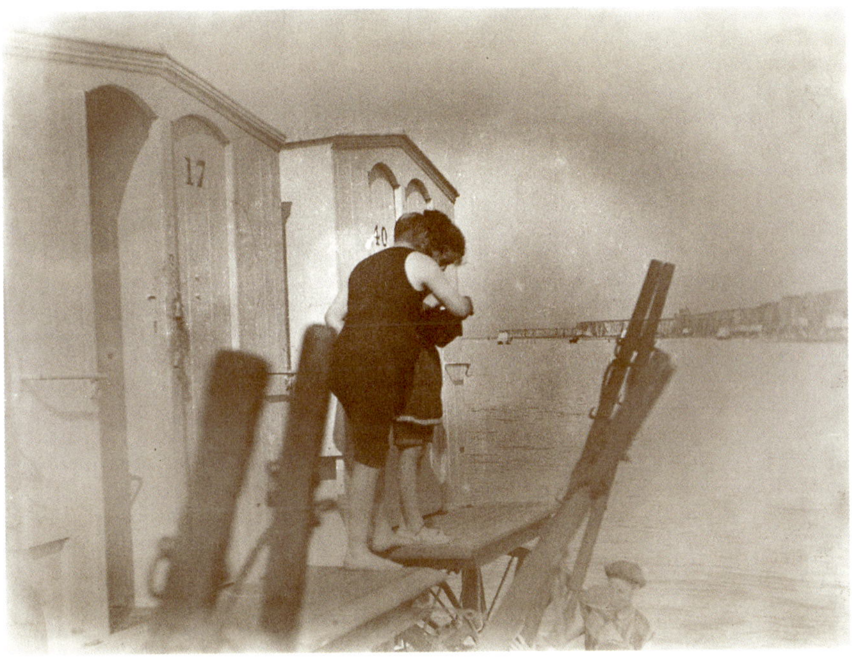

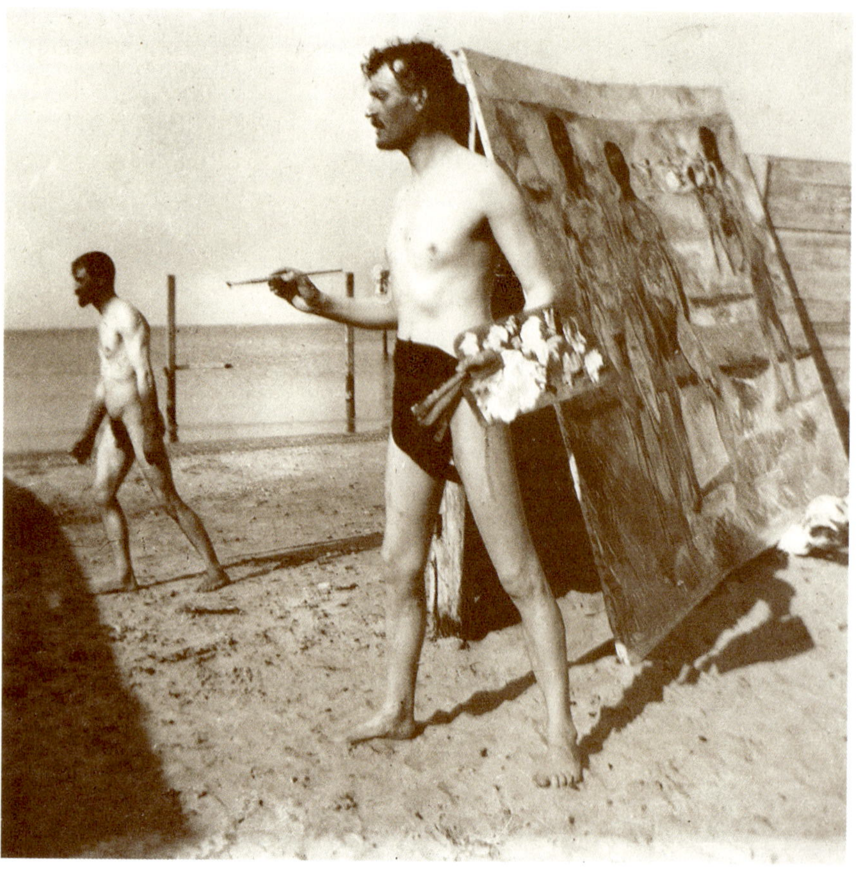

EDVARD MUNCH, *Self-portrait on the Beach at Warnemünde,* 1907, Munch Museum, Oslo.

ÉMILE ZOLA, *Italy,* 1894, Dr. François Émile-Zola Collection.
▼

of Eugène Manet and Berthe Morisot, noted in her diary: "M. Degas thinks of nothing but photography, he has invited us all to dine with him next week, and he will take our photograph in the light; only you have to pose for three minutes; he wanted to see if we were good models, and he got M. Renoir to pose, but he started to laugh".[27] Daniel Halévy also noted: "This morning at Degas' house. We went out; he talked about France, about photography, about photography, then about France, he mixed it all together in the same excited state. He took me to Tasset, his photographer, and showed me his latest prints – Mallarmé, Renoir, the Manet family, a Mme Howland."[28] As these lines suggest, Degas' feverish interest in the new medium was well known to those around him. And indeed the majority of his photographs are portraits – and self-portraits – sometimes skillfully staged: the sculptor Bartholomé, Jacques-Émile Blanche, the Halévys, Christine and Yvonne Lerolle, his faithful servant Zoé, M. and Mme Fourchy, M. and Mme Mallarmé, and Renoir themselves suffer interminable poses. Faces, expressions, attitudes – indolent bodies, soft sofas, dreamy appearance – all are captured without affectation, in the same tempo as conversation, in homely surroundings, on holiday. These photographs constitute a moving kind of family album, where one notes a preference for interiors, for artificial light – "the atmosphere of lamps or moonlight" – and large mirrors which, according to the dazzled memory of Valéry, reflect "Degas with the camera" [...] in a ghost-like state".

Following a twofold dream of ever greater exactness and ever more daring invention, Degas had already expressed his photographic preoccupations in his paintings and his writing. "The snapshot is photography and nothing more", he declared in lapidary style as early as 1872, in a letter sent from New Orleans to the Danish painter Lorentz Frölich. Later, advising Camille Pissarro on the delicate task of making an engraving, he resorted, with the aid of sketches, to a comparison with the technical knowledge of photographers when using collodion. He also collected photographs as a source of documentation. After his death, pictures were found which he used in the composition of certain of his canvases: photos for the portrait of Mme Hertel – *La Femme aux Chrysanthèmes* – or a carte de visite of Disdéri, a fashionable portrait photographer during the Second Empire, which gave him the inspiration for the pose taken up in *Princesse de Metternich*. Most of the landscapes – which he named, poetically, "states of the eyes" – were executed after the event in his studio, using photographs that he had taken himself during his walks at dusk. We know that after the revelations of Muybridge's famous sequences of snapshots, he did dozens of drawings and sketches which variously analyze, from life, the different movements of the horse.

Degas' photography went beyond his practice as an amateur. It was an important part of his working methods and research, and helped him, in particular, to reflect upon the new ways of seeing, to express in his painting what are eminently Baudelarian themes, "the transitory, the fleeting, the contingent". A painter of modern life – ballerinas, singers, laundrywomen, dressmakers, women in a natural state of nudity –

27. J. Manet, *Journal, 1893–1899*, Paris, Klincksieck, 1979.

28. D. Halévy, *Degas parle*, Paris, Geneva, La Palatine, 1960.

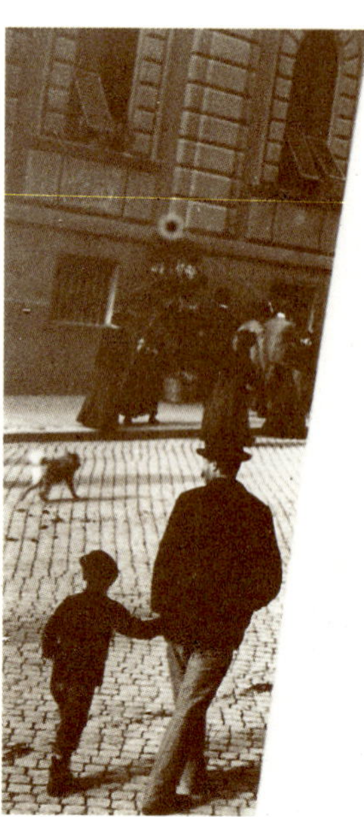

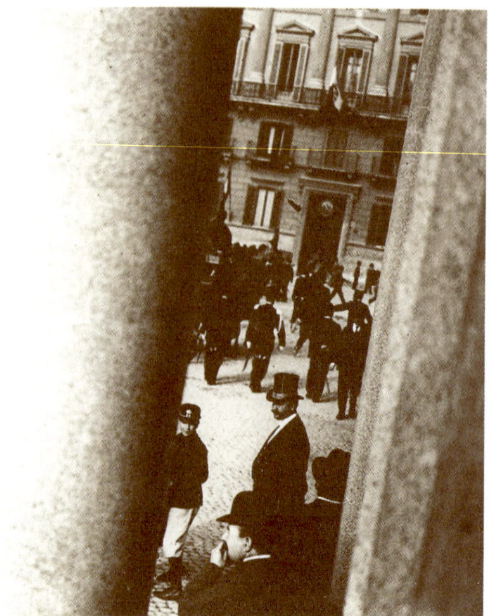

haunted by the recreation of movement through form, Degas untiringly pursued sensation "on the wing" – pulsation and vibration – and tracks the intensity of learned and instinctive gesture, half-seen, quivering with life.

Art historians agree that Degas' "photographic" or "objective" eye can be seen in his painting – to the point where malicious criticism accused him of plagiarizing the "style" of photographers. *La Famille Bellelli, Le Bureau de Coton, La Voiture aux Courses, Musiciens à l'Orchestre, Femmes se Peignant, Le Tub* and many other paintings, without counting the pastels and the monotypes[29] – which, just like photographs, are steeped in chiaroscuro and backlighting – come one after the other like so many snapshots, Impressionist "flashlight pictures". The painter espoused the detached curiosity of the photographer, who subordinates vision to the handing-on of memory.

However, this vision of Degas as influenced by photography is curiously short of dialectic. If his painting was influenced by photography, it was, in its turn, a contributor – to a greater degree perhaps – to the revelation of a way of seeing which was going to overturn all the laws of perception. Degas invents more than photographic painting – he invents photography in his painting. For instance, he anticipates the unfolding vision of the cinema, the wide screen. He shows movement by being himself in movement: framing a view, creating breakdowns of scenes and low-angle shots, filling the picture, emptying it. It was Degas who thought up many of those off-center, oblique compositions, where the image seems as though it has been "knocked sideways". He has a virtuoso way with dissolves and close-ups. There is sometimes a certain brutality about the emphatic way he isolates silhouettes and spaces, sometimes cropping across the arms or legs of a figure or the nape of a neck.

Most of these innovations were not to be practiced by photography, in any conscious, visually exploratory way, until two or three decades later. Thanks to photography, Degas introduced a great deal of innovation into painting. All his work – which constitutes a rare and excellent example of the impact of a technical invention on the fine arts – seems to follow, contain, and anticipate the visual developments of photography.

These bodies of photographs, all to a greater or lesser degree obscure, if only because of their origin in an elite, cast a flickering light upon their original mission: one of making an authenticating record of the movements of life in time, for memory. It is also an experiment of limits; this form of "writing about the self", so dear to Michel Foucault,[30] is related even more closely to these "arts of oneself", an ontological aesthetic of existence.

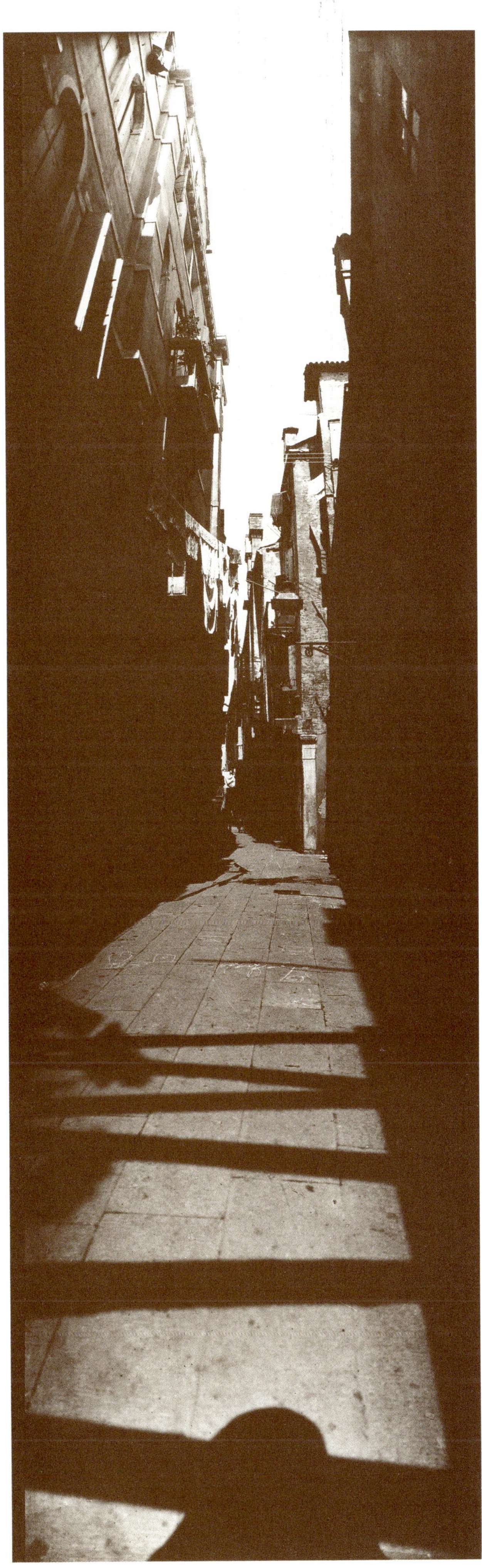

Mariano Fortuny, *Venetian Alley,* circa 1900, Museo Fortuny, Venice.

29. E. Parry-Janis, *Degas Monotypes*, Cambridge, Fogg Art Museum, 1968.

30. Writing about *La Vita Antonii* by Athanasius, "L'Écriture du Soi", in *Corps Écrit*, no. 5, on the self-portrait, pp. 3–23, Paris, P.U.F., February 1983.

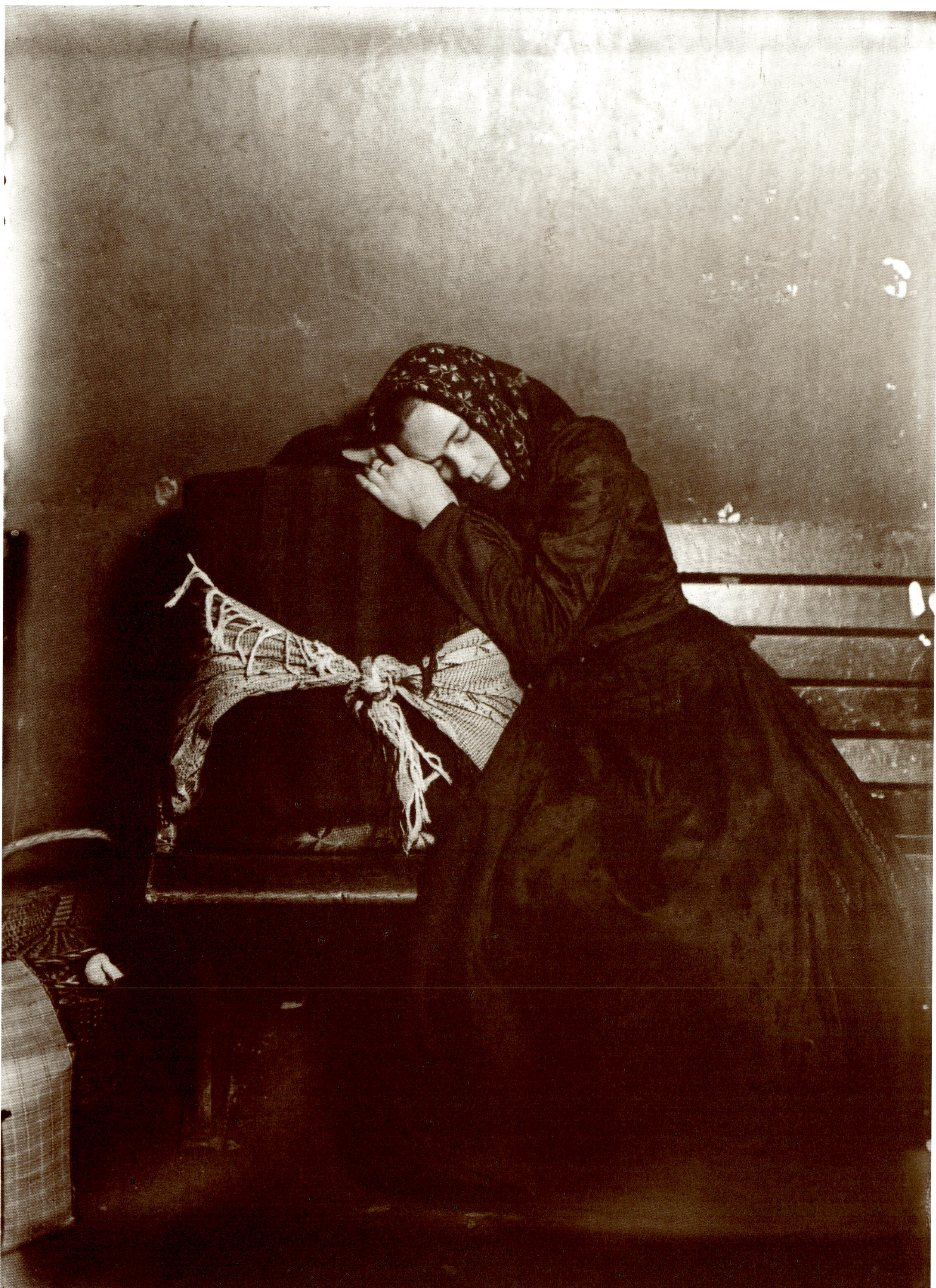

THE OTHER HALF 20

The investigation of society

Thilo Koenig

During the 1880s the intervention of photography became discreet, almost invisible. Photography became a means of investigation, capable of bursting into places where social inequalities were apparent, or where men, women or children were exploited in a scandalous way. Journalism and the emerging science of sociology, both related to ethnology, served to co-ordinate text and image in the denunciation process. In this way research into the health of slums occurred alongside the recording of the ancient customs of the Indian peoples and the contemporary way of life of New York society.

People's living and working conditions were among the earliest subjects for photography. For example, William Henry Fox Talbot took pictures of the workers on his country estate, and the Scottish photographers David Octavius Hill and Robert Adamson photographed the fishermen of Newhaven.

However, there was no photography that could truly be called "social" or "social documentary" until much later in the nineteenth century, even though Hill and Adamson had a charitable motive in photographing the fishermen. In the 1850s, for example, it was hardly a critical investigation of social reality when Charles Nègre induced chimney sweeps to pose for the camera, or when tradespeople and workers were photographed out of context as "types", following an established tradition of pictures of street vendors and craftsmen. Such pictures were inspired too much by the picturesqueness of their subjects.

Christian iconography, too, remained influential for a long time, with mothers being posed so as to resemble Madonnas, or beggars being portrayed as Christ. Nevertheless, there were some nineteenth-century photographers who, though social criticism was not their explicit purpose, did photograph living and working conditions in the town and countryside.

At first, photographic technology was insufficiently advanced to allow subjects to be taken directly from life without some staging of the picture. The wet-plate process and the use of large-format cameras mounted on tripods ruled out rapid – let alone candid – photography until dry plates and hand cameras became available in the 1870s and 1880s. Moreover, printing processes such as photolithography (from 1855) or the Woodburytype (1866) did not allow photographs to be published in sufficient quantity for them to be used to influence public opinion, while the usual wood engravings made from photographs totally lacked authenticity. It was only with the use of half-tone printing, from the 1880s onwards, that photographs entered the printed media.

Furthermore, the different interests which motivated nineteenth-century photographers led to widely differing approaches. Photography itself did not have the same status for all those who practiced it. Thus, an interest in social themes might be shared by both amateurs with artistic aspirations and professional studio photographers. Because of the increase in social problems, such as those of the overcrowded cities of Europe and North America, together with the fact that the social sciences were now becoming recognized disciplines, a further group arose consisting of journalists and sociologists who learned photography only as an aid to their campaigns for reform and who used photographs merely as a secondary medium in conjunction with their writings. Thus, in the nineteenth century three very different approaches may be observed.

First, some photographers with an interest in anthropology or regional history wanted to

◀ Lewis Hine, *Slav Immigrant, Ellis Island,* circa 1905, International Museum of Photography, George Eastman House, Rochester.

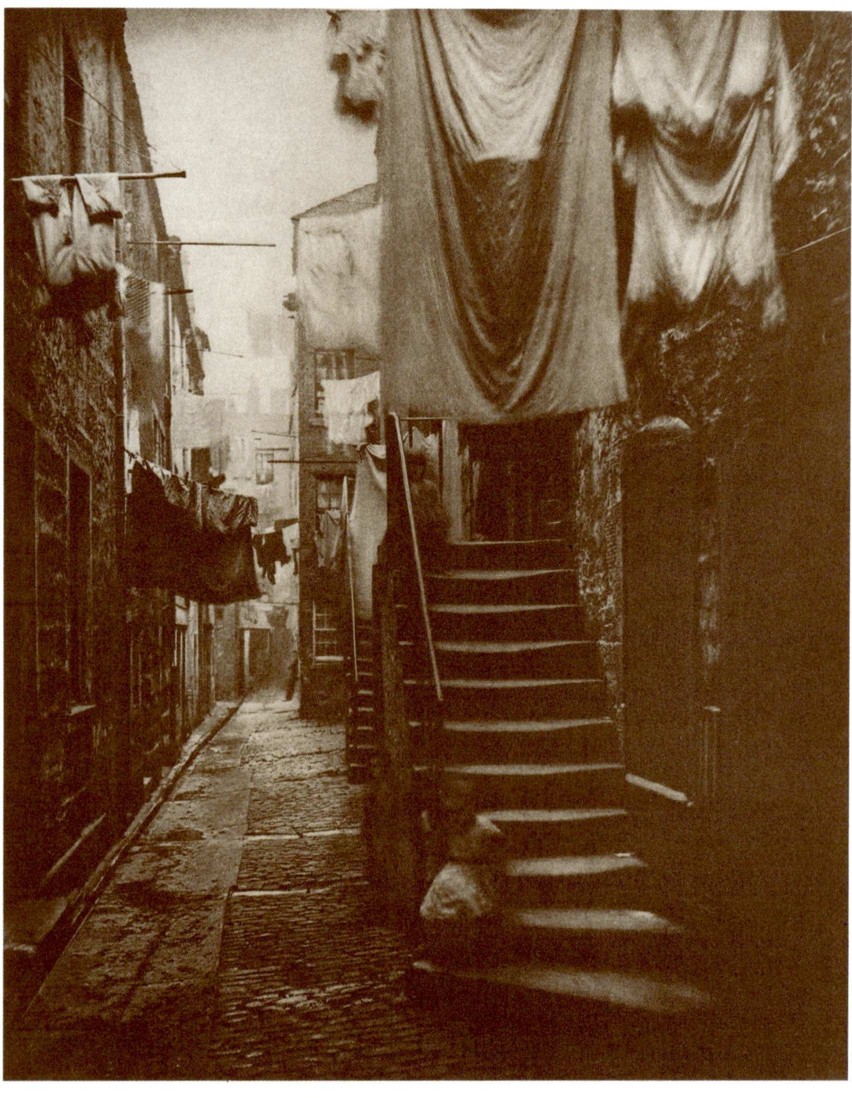

THOMAS ANNAN, *Close No. 193, High Street, Glasgow,* 1868, Victoria and Albert Museum, London.

JOHN THOMSON, ▶ *The Independent Shoe-black,* circa 1876, Victoria and Albert Museum, London.

produce systematic documentary photographic records of social conditions before they vanished forever. For this kind of photography, which as a rule had no political aims, large-format cameras and the wet-plate process were quite adequate.

The second approach, "candid" photography in which pictures were taken using a hand-held or "detective" camera, was not merely a response to technical innovations. The closing years of the nineteenth century saw the period of naturalism in art – a real desire to produce unposed pictures documenting everyday urban life. "Candid" photography occupied a place somewhere between genre photography and "committed" photojournalism, which had begun with travel and war reports.

Last, what we may call "social documentary" photography, used to denounce social evils or call for reform, dates only from the 1880s. Even in this field, however, photographers were quite often prepared to interfere with reality by rearranging their subject matter, or to reinforce the message of their pictures by their choice of perspective or by cropping.

Documentary photography

In 1868, the Glasgow City Improvement Trust, a society for urban renewal, commissioned the Scottish professional photographer Thomas Annan (1829–1887) to photograph the city's slums before they were demolished. In the years up to 1877, Annan, known for his pictures of architecture and works of art, created the first visual documentation of an inner-city slum.[1] He concentrated mainly on the streets, which still had open sewers running through them, and on the unimaginable density of the buildings with only the narrowest of passageways ("closes") between them.

Given the extraordinary population growth in Glasgow at the time, these scenes, taken using long exposure times, appear curiously deserted. In a number of pictures, however, Annan did include individual figures or groups of children – vulnerable human beings set against those bleak, inhospitable surroundings.

John Thomson (1837–1921) was another photographer who worked on social themes only at certain times in his career; he spent his later years as a portrait photographer to London's upper classes. Beforehand, he had spent ten years traveling and photographing in the Far East and had published numerous volumes of his pictures taken there. There, for instance in his scenes of everyday life in China, his subject matter had already included the everyday conditions in which people lived.

At the beginning of the 1870s, having returned to London, Thomson began to photograph life in

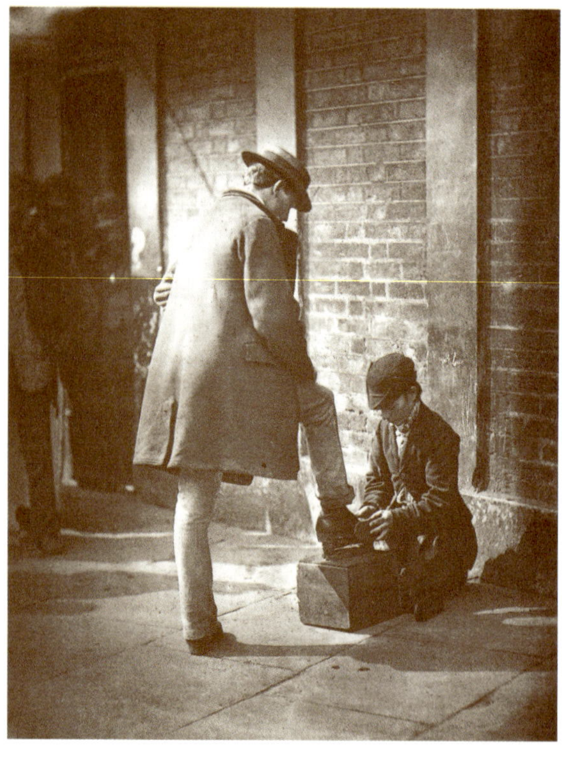

1. See T. Annan, *Photographs of the Old Closes and Streets of Glasgow 1868/1877,* Glasgow 1878–1879, reprinted New York, Dover, 1977.

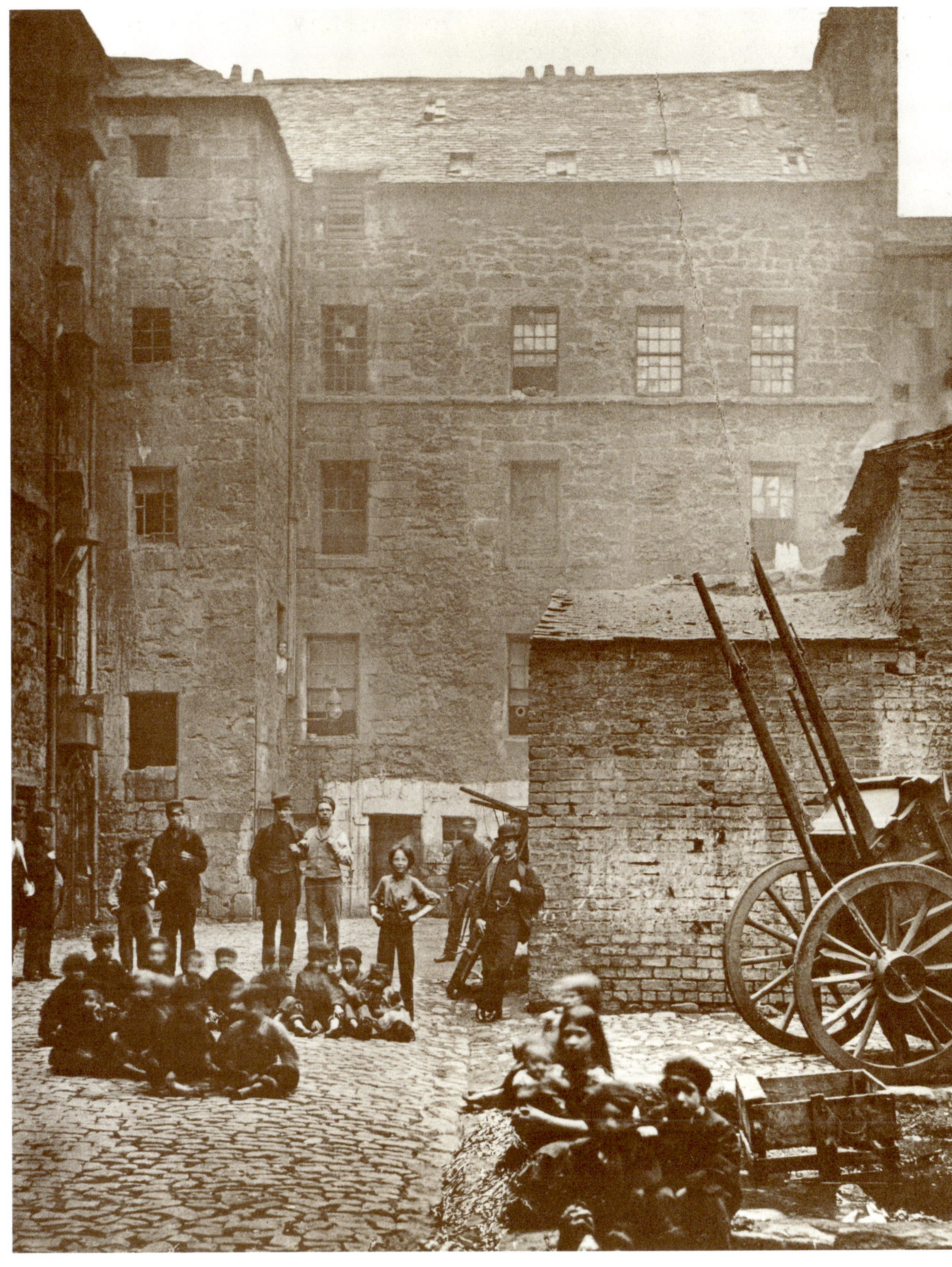

THOMAS ANNAN,
Close No. 46,
Saltmarket, Glasgow,
1868,
Mitchell Library, Glasgow.

the city's streets – tradespeople, workers, and the poor. In 1877–1878, he and Adolphe Smith, a journalist who had reported on social conditions, published *Street Life in London*, initially in twelve installments and then, abridged, in book form. Such a project was not particularly unusual. Thomson himself referred back to the sociological studies which Henry Mayhew had published from 1851 onwards under the title *London Labour and the London Poor*. These had been illustrated with engravings, made from daguerreotypes by Richard Beard and other photographers. In 1870, a series of pictures by Gustave Doré, *London: A Pilgrimage*, was dedicated to the city's poor.

What was original about Thomson's publication was not so much what Thomson called "the true types of the London Poor" themselves, presented in carefully composed photographs, as the extremely good reproductions of these pictures made using the Woodburytype process, and the fact that the background was included so that people were shown in their authentic surroundings. The pictures were accompanied by detailed commentaries on the individual subjects,

2. J. Lehr, *John Thomson (1837–1821)*, in *History of Photography*, no. 4, 1980, pp. 67 ff; Stephen White, *John Thomson: Life and Photographs*, London, 1985.

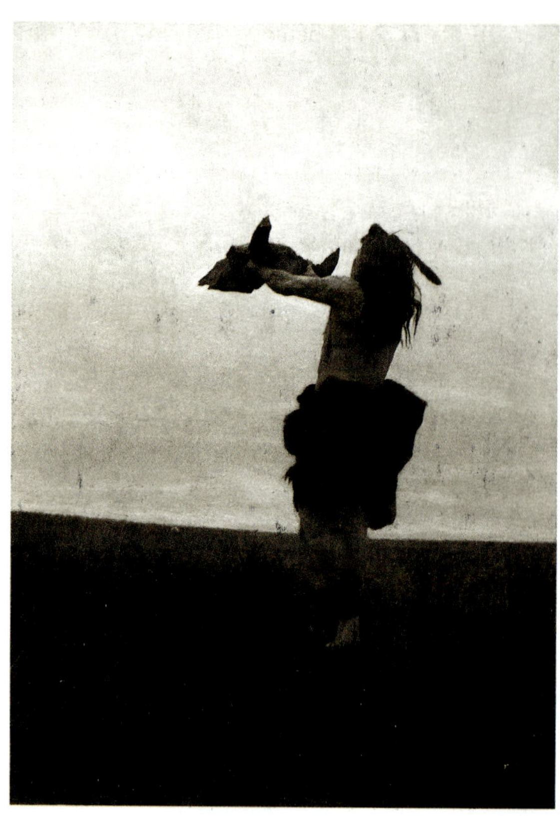

EDWARD S. CURTIS, *Offering Up the Bison's Skull, Mandan Tribe,* 1908, private collection.

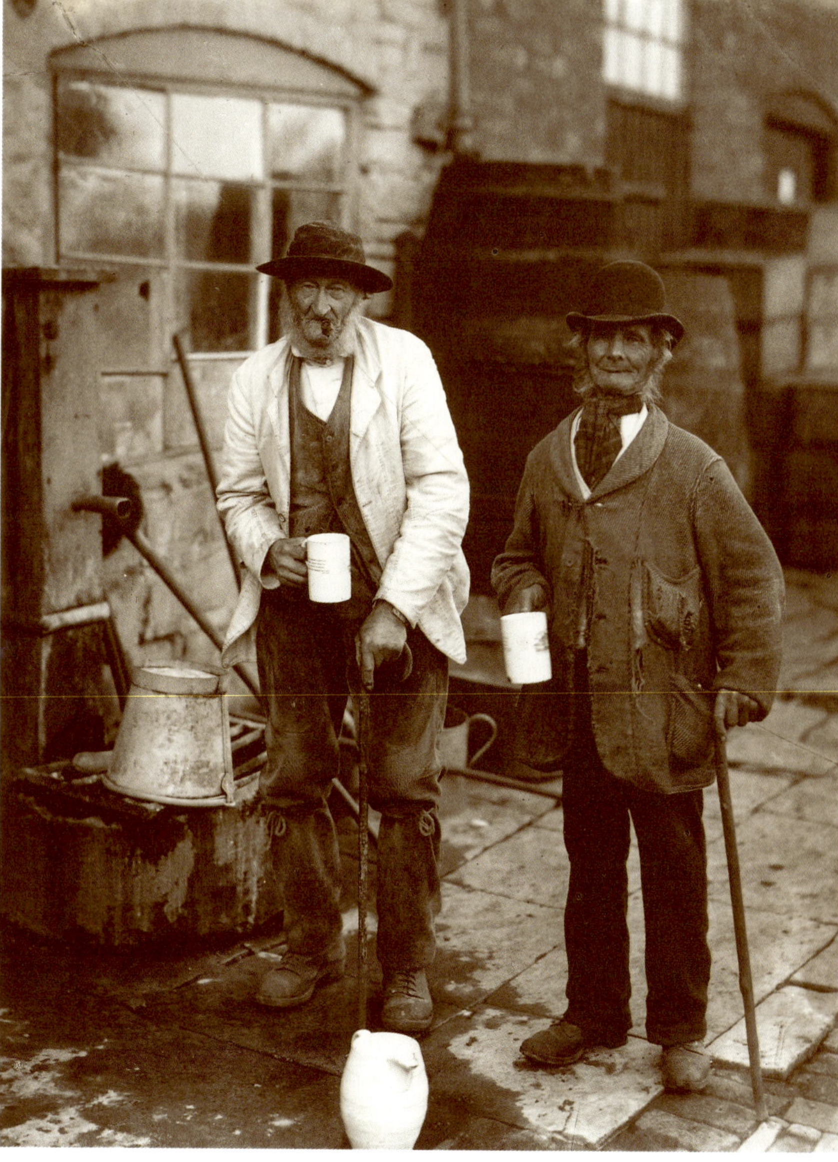

BENJAMIN STONE, *Sippers and Topers at Bidford Mop,* circa 1900, Birmingham Reference Library Collection. ▼

signifying an important development from the mere identification of picturesque "types" to a more analytical approach.[2]

The documentary photography of Sir John Benjamin Stone and Edward Sheriff Curtis, also devoted to specific themes, was far more extensive. Stone (1836–1914), a prosperous entrepreneur and Member of Parliament, had begun to take and to collect photographs in 1868. In 1897, in order to document systematically everyday life of the time, manners and customs, and towns and landscapes, he instigated the foundation of the National Photographic Record Association. By 1910, it had collected and deposited in the British Museum several thousand pictures by many different photographers.[3] This initiative by Stone is linked to the conservation movements of the time as well as to the activities of amateur photographers.

Curtis (1868–1952) was similarly interested in encyclopedic documentation for the purpose of conservation and recording. From 1899 onwards, he dedicated himself to the task of photographing North American Indians. Other photographers had preceded him, starting in the 1840s when Native Americans still had a genuine living culture.[4]

Compared with their work, the photographs taken by Curtis in the course of 30 years spent researching the daily life, ceremonies, and crafts of the Indians on the reservations are really a record of a bygone age.[5] Sometimes he actually had to stage a re-enactment of the old traditions. Many Indians had long since taken to having short haircuts and wearing suits, so Curtis had a stock of wigs and Indian clothing ready to hand. Despite their impressive intensity, his photographs convey more of his romantic, white man's vision than the – already lost – culture of the Indians.

By contrast, Thomas John Barnardo (1845–1905), who, in 1871, had opened the first of the many orphanages known as "Dr. Barnardo's Homes", used photographs in a wholly functional way for public relations and as a source of income for his charitable work. He had the "street Arabs", children who had been picked up from the streets of the city, photographed in their neglected state; from 1874, there was a studio set up for this specific purpose. Barnardo was able to juxtapose these pictures with later photographs of the children, neatly dressed and engaged in work. These "before and after" portraits were stuck onto the children's personal record or sold as picture postcards.[6]

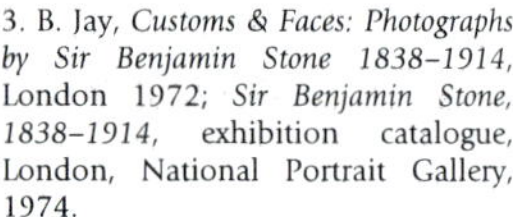

3. B. Jay, *Customs & Faces: Photographs by Sir Benjamin Stone 1838–1914,* London 1972; *Sir Benjamin Stone, 1838–1914,* exhibition catalogue, London, National Portrait Gallery, 1974.

4. W. E. McRae, "Images of Native Americans in Still Photography", *History of Photography,* no. 13, 1989, pp. 321 ff.

5. Curtis, *The North American Indian,* Seattle, 1907–1930; 20 volumes of this documentary work were published. See C. M. Lyman and V. Delona, *The Vanishing Races and Other Illusions: Photographs of Indians by E. S. Curtis,* New York, Pantheon Books, 1982.

"Candid" photography

Unlike such systematic documentation, spontaneous "candid" photography, of which there was a tremendous upsurge around the turn of the century, was usually carried out alongside professional studio work.[7] It was not inspired to any great extent by an interest in history, conservation or social reform. Its attraction lay simply in the pleasure of using the camera to explore and record life as it happened. Joseph Byron (1846–1922) came from a British family of photographers and had come to the USA only in 1888. Together with his son Percy, he photographed life in New York, mainly between 1890 and 1910. His subject matter covered the entire social spectrum, from the elegant life of Fifth Avenue through theaters, hotels and restaurants, parades, and winter pastimes, to markets, factories, and immigrants.[8]

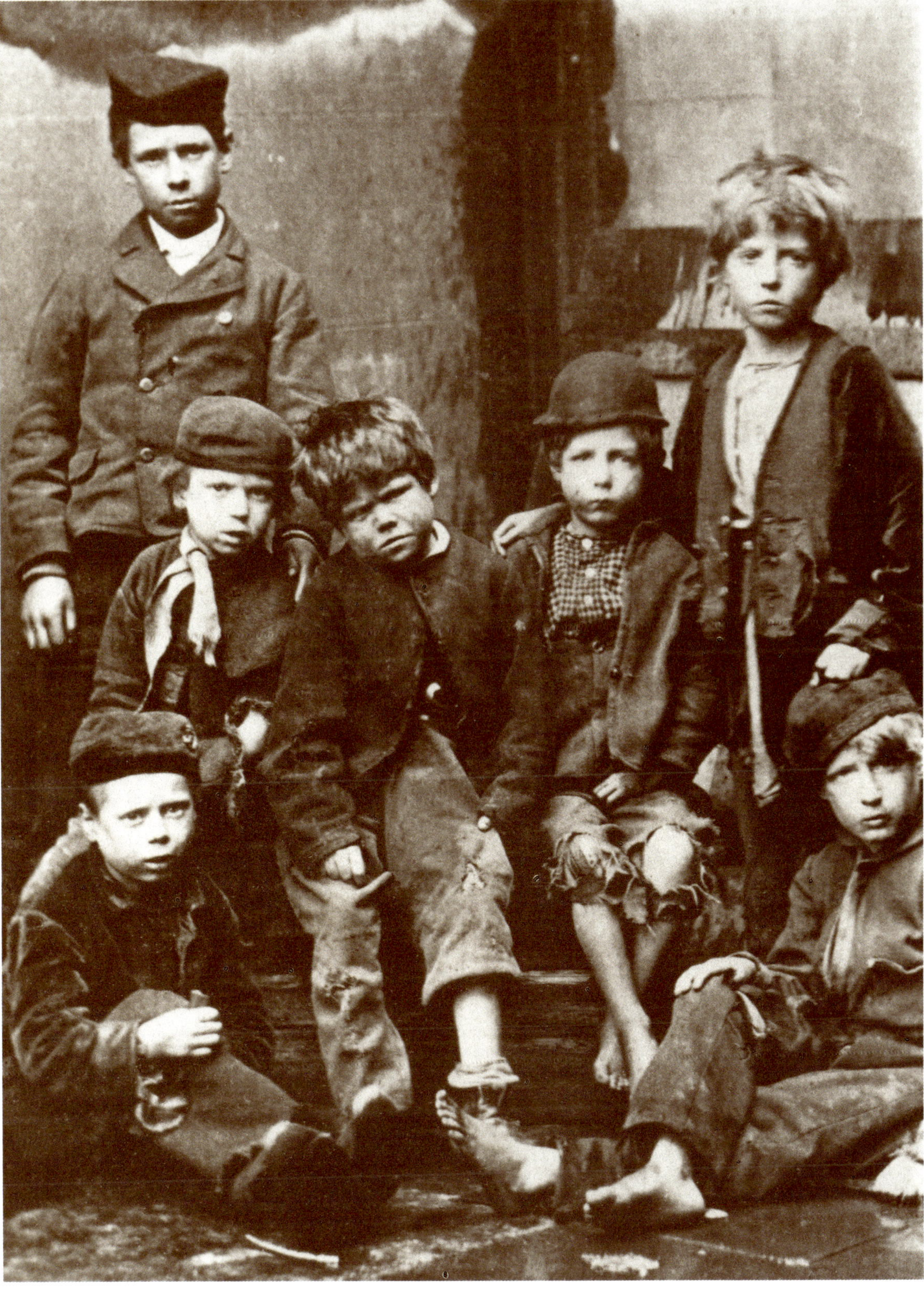

ANONYMOUS,
The Scorrie, King, Brown, and Woodruff Children,
Barnardo's Homes,
1875,
Victoria and Albert Museum, London.

6. *The Camera and Dr. Barnardo*, exhibition catalogue, London, National Portrait Gallery, 1974.

7. See P. B. Hales, *Silver Cities: The Photography of American Urbanization, 1839–1915*, Philadelphia 1984, pp. 221 ff.

8. *New York Life at the Turn of the Century in Photographs by Joseph Byron*, New York, Dover, 1985.

Jacob A. Riis: *How the Other Half Lives*

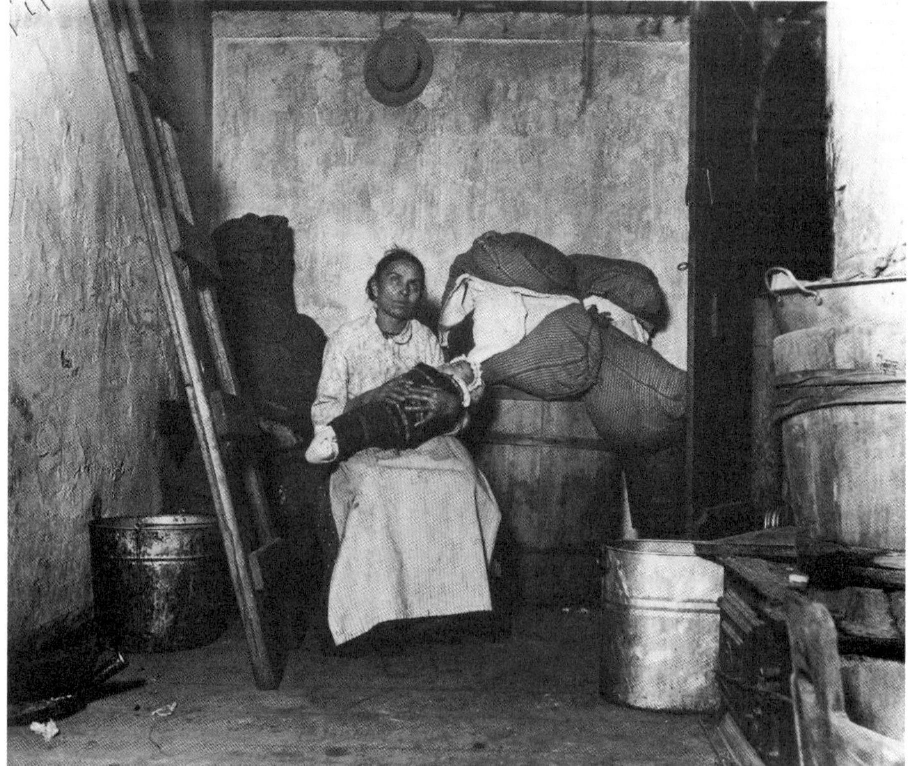

Jacob August Riis,
Home of an Italian Ragpicker,
circa 1890, Museum of the City of New York

This book by Jacob A. Riis, published in New York, is regarded as the first significant work of social documentary photography. Unlike illustrations in earlier publications showing "types", these photographs presented the world of the poor and of the immigrant with almost unprecedented directness. In 304 pages, Riis describes life in the tenements of Manhattan's Lower East Side, covering everything from the original building of the tenements to crime among the children there, and adding statistics and plans of buildings and apartments. The text was accompanied by 43 illustrations, which included 17 half-tone prints, based on photographs taken by Riis and his collaborators, Dr Nagle, Henry G. Piffard, and Richard Hoe Lawrence.

With the support of members of the church, Riis gave slide talks in the Broadway Tabernacle. He was then commissioned to publish an article, illustrated with 19 engravings based on photographs, in *Scribner's* magazine. The title of this article, *How the Other Half Lives: Studies among the Tenements of New York,* was also used when the book was published the following year, as were the printing plates. For this reason, some of the best-known pictures, among them *Home of an Italian Ragpicker* and *An All Night Two Cent Restaurant in 'The Bend'*, appear in the book only as engravings and not as photographic prints.

Two years earlier, Riis had already copyrighted the book title, *The Other Half, how it Lives and Dies in New York, with 100 Illustrations, Photographs from Real Life, of the Haunts of Poverty and Vice in a Great City.*

The book was an immediate success. Theodore Roosevelt, at that time Chief of Police, then Governor of New York and, later, President, was greatly impressed by it and offered his help.

As a result, a whole range of evils were rectified. Measures taken included the demolition of the area around Mulberry Bend, where a park was created, the closing down of sweatshops, and the closure of the emergency shelters which had hitherto been run by the police. The care of the poor was taken out of the hands of the police.

Following this book, Riis published *Children of the Poor* in 1892, and, in 1901, his autobiography, *The Making of an American.*

Thilo Koenig

Arnold Genthe (1869–1942), a philologist educated in Germany who subsequently worked as a private tutor in San Francisco, was first drawn to his later profession of photography in the late 1890s, through his interest in Eastern culture. From 1911 he had a portrait and fashion studio. Around the turn of the century, Genthe took photographs in San Francisco's Chinatown, using a concealed camera. His aim was to capture characteristic actions and behavior, the gestures of those in particular occupations or simply decorations – a kind of photography which falls somewhere between ethnology and reportage.[9] In 1906, Genthe took uncharacteristically journalistic photographs of the San Francisco earthquake and the ensuing fires.

"Candid" photography, however, was also useful to artists as a visual "sketchbook" with which they could record from everyday life motifs and ideas for their pictures. Paul Martin and Heinrich Zille photographed London and Berlin life in this way. Martin (1864–1944), who exhibited, as an amateur, in art photography exhibitions and became a member of the prestigious "Linked Ring", was a wood engraver before establishing himself as a freelance press photographer. From 1890 onwards, using a concealed camera, he took snapshots of passers-by, street urchins or lovers on the beach – quirky and often amusing pictures which he also used as the basis for his work in other graphic media or for lantern slide shows. For this type of use he sometimes painted out the background, detaching the human figures and so once again making them into isolated "types", just as in early graphic adaptations of photographs.[10]

9. A. Genthe, *Pictures of Old Chinatown,* New York 1913; J. Kno Wei Tchen, *Genthe's Photographs of San Francisco's Old Chinatown,* New York 1984.

10. R. Flukinger and L. Schaaf, *Paul Martin, Victorian Photographer,* London 1978, p. 35; B. Jay, *Victorian Candid Camera: Paul Martin 1864–1944,* Newton Abbot, 1973.

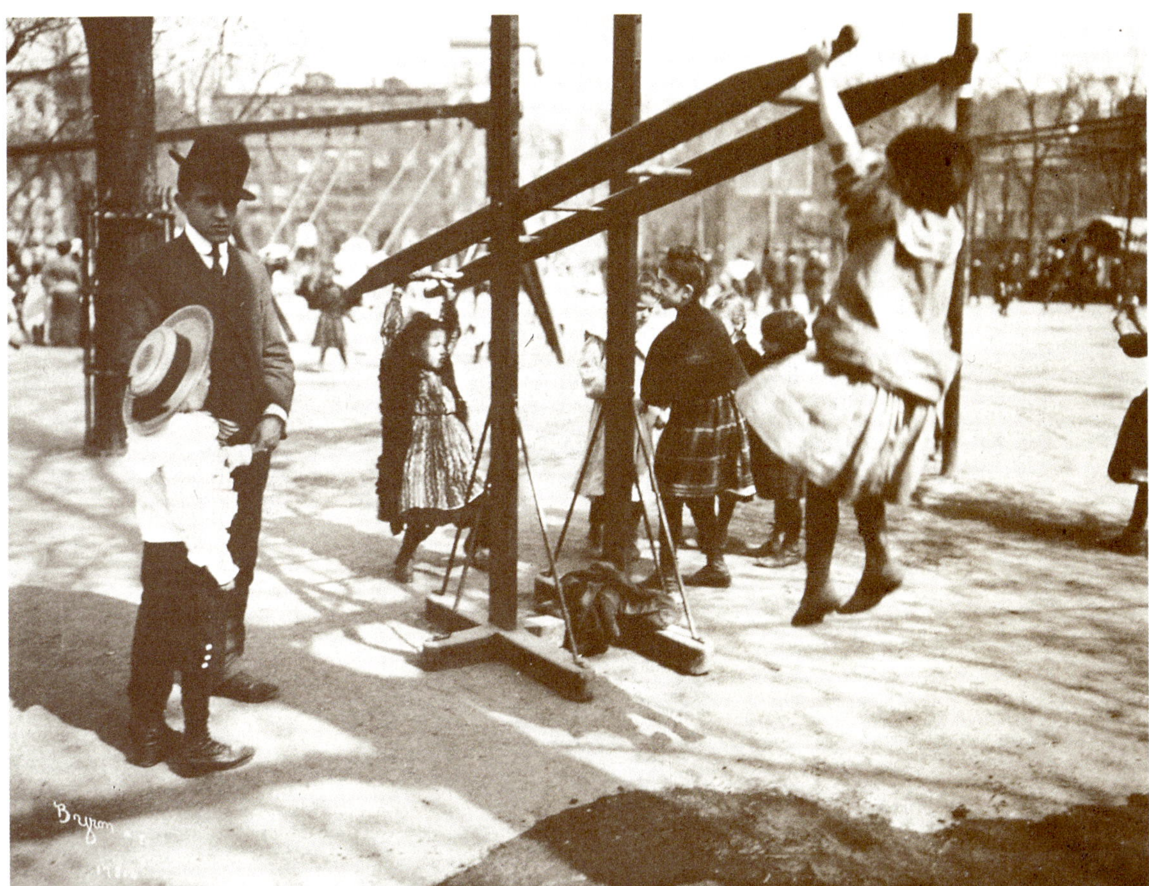

Joseph Byron,
Tompkins Square Park, New York,
1904,
Museum of the City of New York.

Paul Martin,
Yarmouth, "A Loving Couple" on the Sands,
1892,
University of Texas, Austin.
▼

A different use was made of such snapshots by Zille (1858–1929). Apart from using motifs from them for his drawings, he was also, from 1890 onwards, conducting a very subtle visual exploration of the environment in which he lived. Influenced, no doubt, by the preoccupation of naturalism with life in the cities, he took unspectacular views of the streets of old Berlin – back courtyards, artisans, women shopping or gathering wood. These photographs were not a call to action, and did not demand to be interpreted in a particular way. They "show his subjects just as he found them" – "candid" images which constitute "analytical documentary photography".[11] Not content with the side of things that was on public view, Zille also took his camera into courtyards and stairwells. He was also already taking series of pictures in which one could trace a sequence of events.

Denunciation of social evils

While such concern with social and living conditions arose, in part, from mere curiosity or personal interest, for journalists and social reformers the camera performed a very different function. Their task did not end with the photography itself – it also included research into the details of what they photographed, with facts and figures about working conditions or economic circumstances which they could use in support of their calls for reform. This was the method adopted, for instance, by Frances Benjamin Johnston, one of the first female photojournalists, or by Lewis Wickes Hine. They also wrote the captions or articles themselves, unless, like Thomson, they were working in conjunction with a writer from the outset.

11. W. Ranke (ed.), *Heinrich Zille: Photographien Berlin 1890–1910*, Munich, 1985.

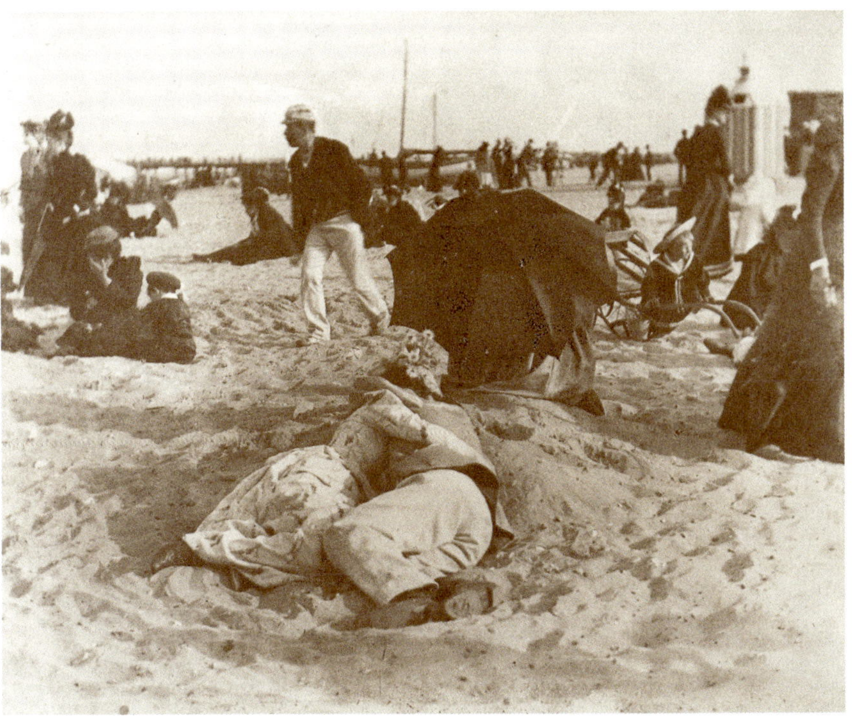

The Archivo Casasola

During the Mexican Revolution of 1910–1920, Agustin Victor Casasola (1874–1938), one of the first photojournalists in Mexico, began to form a collection of photographs documenting contemporary history. This Archivo Casasola contains photographs not only by Casasola and his sons, but also by countless other photographers. It therefore provides the most extensive photographic record not only of the Mexican struggle for liberation but also of the social and political life of the country from the time of the dictator Porfirio Diaz onwards. As well as the life of the people in town and countryside during the Revolution, the collection also documents battles and the military, conferences, demonstrations, prisons, and executions. After 1920, it records chiefly urban life, with its politics, work, and recreation. There is also a large number of portraits.[1]

From the 1890s onwards, A. V. Casasola, a trained typographer, worked as a journalist for Mexican daily newspapers. Alongside his writing, he soon took up photography and, from the turn of the century, worked as a photographic reporter for, among others, the most important daily newspapers of the time, *El Imperial* (one of the first periodicals in the country to print photographs) and *El Tiempo*, and later also *El Mundo Ilustrado*. In 1903, Casasola, an active trade-unionist, joined the Mexican Association of Journalists. In 1911, he founded the Asociación de Fotógrafos de Prensa, an association of press photographers, and, soon afterwards, the first Mexican picture agency, the Agencia de Información Gráfica The work of this agency laid the foundations for his photographic archive. In 1921, he published an *Album Histórico-biográfico*, a first selection of the photographs in the archive.

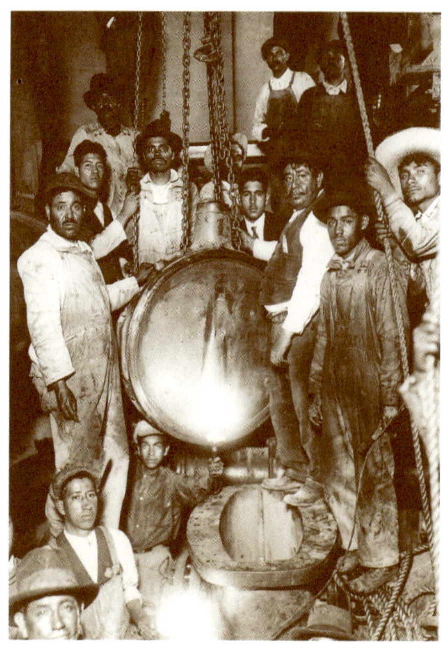

CASASOLA ARCHIVE,
Boiler-makers in the Condesa Factory,
Mexico, circa 1930.

The extensive archive, with its own publishing house, was later carried on by his sons, especially Gustavo Casasola Zapata (1900–1982), who edited the material to produce several large volumes of photographs.[2] Bought by the state in 1976, the archive today forms the basis of the Fototeca del Instituto Nacional de Antropología e Historia (INAH) in Mexico City.

Thilo Koenig

1. P. O. Monasterio (ed.), *Jefes, Héroes y Caudillos, Archivo Casasola, Fototeca del INAH*, Mexico 1986. *¡Tierra y Libertad! Photographs of Mexico 1900–1935*, exhibition catalogue, Oxford, Museum of Modern Art, 1985.
2. Notably the *Historia Gráfica de la Revolución Mexicana* published between 1960 and 1971, 2nd ed. in 10 volumes, 1973.

MISS FRANCES B. JOHNSTON,
Dwelling of a Black Family in Virginia,
1899, Library of Congress, Washington.

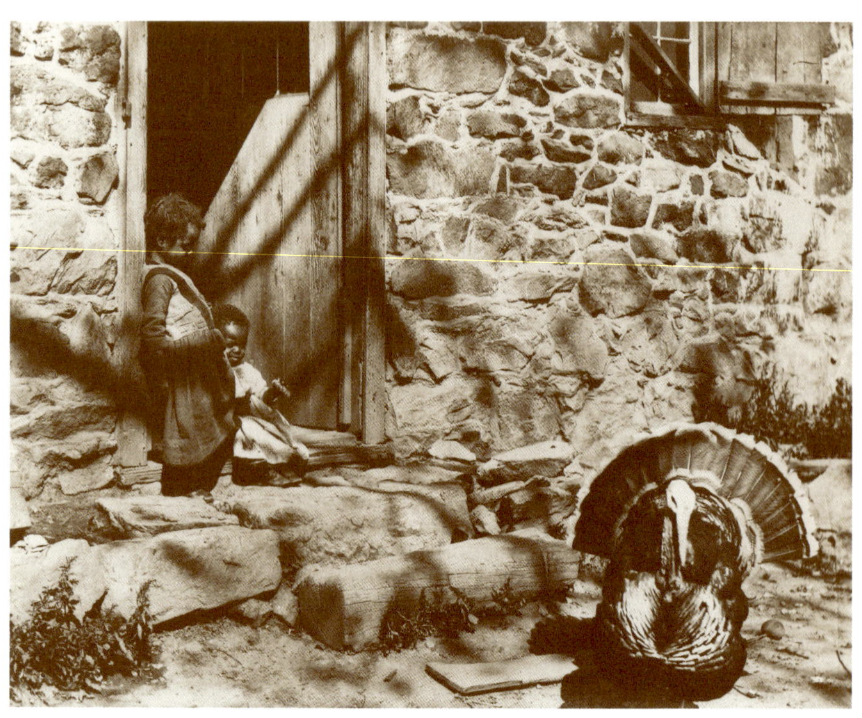

From the late 1880s onwards, Frances B. Johnston (1864–1952), who had studied art in Paris and in Washington, worked for periodicals such as *Demorest's Family Magazine*, writing articles which she illustrated herself. Soon, however, she began to use her own photographs, some of them taken with the Kodak camera. As well as working for greater recognition of women in American photography, promoting their work herself at the World Exhibition in Paris in 1900, Frances B. Johnston wrote articles on the United States mint, mining in Pennsylvania, and women's work in the shoe industry. In her series of pictures of model schools for black people, such as the Hampton Institute, Virginia, the carefully arranged and lit scenes of pupils learning manual skills gave a vivid impression of the reforming work that was being done. She contrasted this with photographs of the living conditions of black people working on the land.[12]

A parallel may be drawn between the work of Jacob August Riis in New York and Hermann Drawe in Vienna. Both had experience of the legal system, Riis, from 1877 onwards, as a police reporter for daily newspapers, Drawe, from 1897, as a court legal assistant and judge. Both were concerned about the desperate housing shortage resulting from rapid urban growth. Riis and

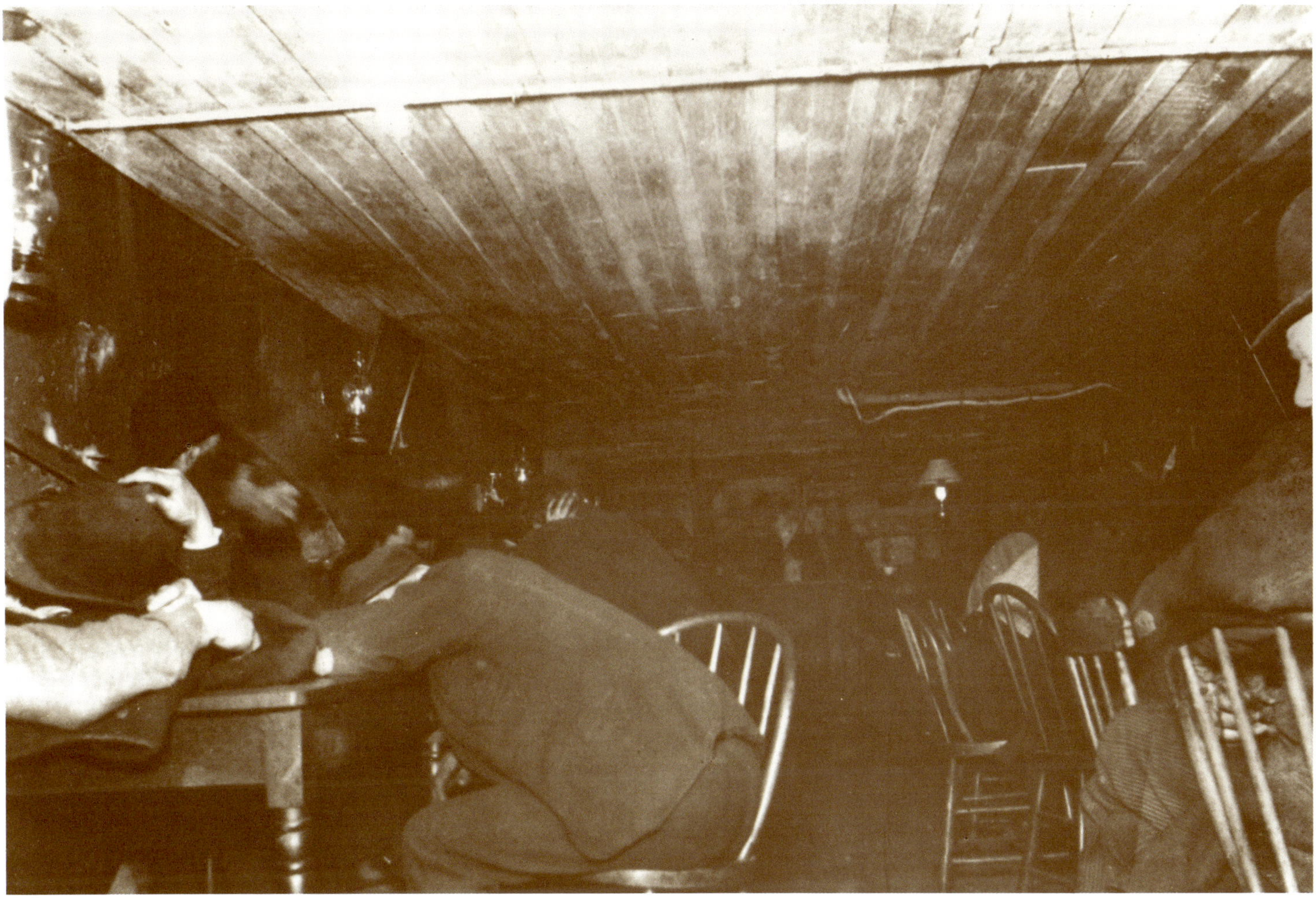

Drawe were not revolutionaries – nor was the somewhat younger Lewis Hine – but they appealed to the social conscience of their fellow-citizens, demanding that humanity be shown even towards the inhabitants of the worst slums.

Riis (1849–1914), who, as an immigrant from Denmark, had experienced social problems at first hand, regularly visited the slums of the Lower East Side in the course of his journalistic work. Soon, however, merely writing about what he saw there no longer seemed adequate. From 1888 onwards, he persuaded friends to go with him on nocturnal photographic expeditions, and then tried in vain to involve professional photographers. Finally, in order to make his appeals more effective and so improve the inhuman conditions which prevailed in tenement blocks, sweatshops, and police-run hostels for the homeless, he learned photography himself.

Using magnesium flash powder (invented in 1887) and the "flash and run" method, he succeeded in taking, virtually without any prior concept or thought for composition, spontaneous photographs which were extremely direct in their impact. He presented these as lantern slides, adding an impassioned commentary. Soon, these pictures, copied as engravings, accompanied his

Jacob August Riis,
Basement of a Pub in Mulberry-Bend at 3.00 am,
circa 1890, Museum of the City of New York.

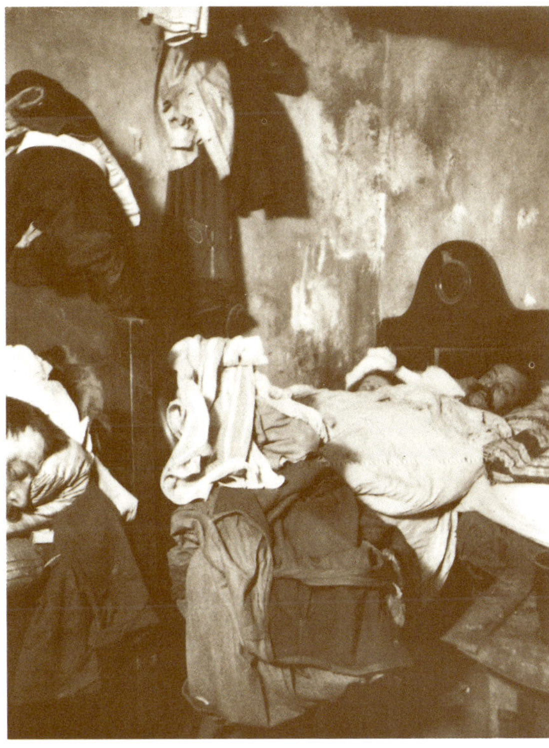

Hermann Drawe,
Communal Lodgings,
1904,
Christian Brandstätter Collection.

12. P. Daniel and R. Smock, *A Talent for Detail: The Photographs of Miss Frances B. Johnston 1889–1910*, New York 1974.

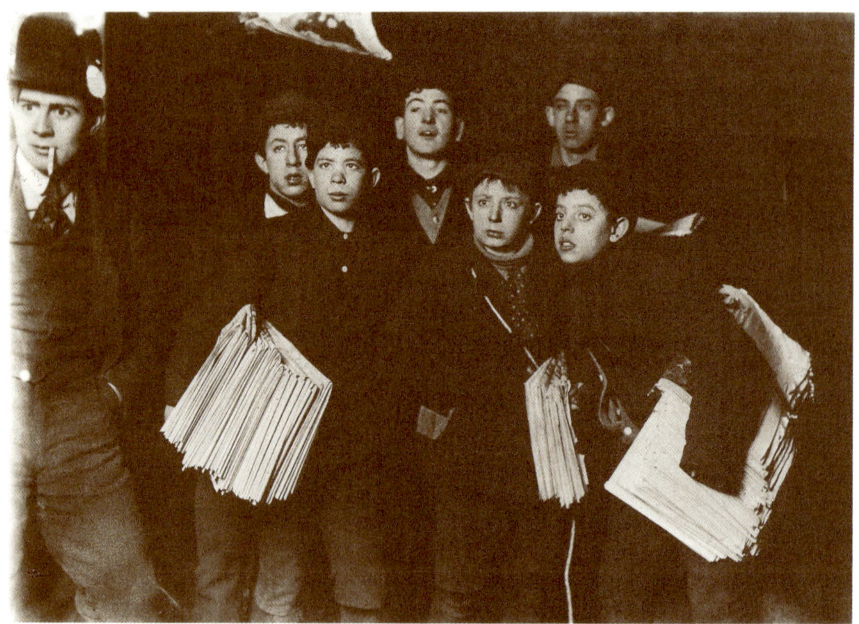

Lewis Hine, *Newspaper Sellers on Brooklyn Bridge at Midnight,* 1906, International Museum of Photography, George Eastman House, Rochester.

articles, starting with "Flashes from the Slum" in the *New York Sun*. In 1890, his book "How the Other Half Lives" and the photographs illustrating it opened a new chapter in photographic social criticism and in the history of the publication of such photographs.

Riis was not a lone pioneer in the social field: his work is linked with the professionalization of social work and town planning which was taking place during those years, and in which he took an active part. He sometimes took up ideas suggested to him by other journalists' reports, and occasionally borrowed from iconographic traditions or used posed models.[13] Yet, unlike Thomson, for example, Riis and the photographers working for him deliberately abandoned the public arena of the street and took their cameras right into the tenements, the basements, and the hostels. Riis's commitment to this cause and his friendship with the later President of the United States, Theodore Roosevelt, led to a whole series of reforms.

Drawe (1867–1925) used methods similar to those of Riis. In 1904, he accompanied the writer Emil Kläger into the slums, and visited the homeless, sleeping rough in the Vienna sewers. He too took photographs using flash powder, and gave slide talks which stirred the conscience of his audiences. His pictures were also used to illustrate Kläger's newspaper articles, which were published, in 1908, as a book entitled *Durch die Wiener Quartiere des Elends und Verbrechens. Ein Wanderbuch aus dem Jenseits.*[14]

On the other hand, the work of Lewis Hine (1874–1940) already showed, both in range and concept, features which only began to be more fully exploited in modern photojournalism following the First World War, notably in the work of the F.S.A. (Farm Security Administration). Paradoxically, Hine himself later went over to an affirmative, heroic style in the photographic portrayal of industrial work. He was a trained sociologist, who early in his career made contact with groups concerned with social reform. He took up photography in 1903, while holding a teaching post at the Ethical Culture School in New York. Two years later, he took a series of photographs of immigrants. These portraits, taken with a large-format camera, still treated their subjects as "types", as is revealed by titles such as *Madonna of Ellis Island*.

Following a documentary record of conditions in the steel town of Pittsburgh, Hine's work for the National Child Labor Committee (N.C.L.C.) showed a more direct approach. For years, from 1908 to 1918, he traveled around the United States taking photographs of illegal child labor in mines, glassworks, and textile factories, against which the N.C.L.C. campaigned tirelessly, making numerous proposals for child protection legisla-

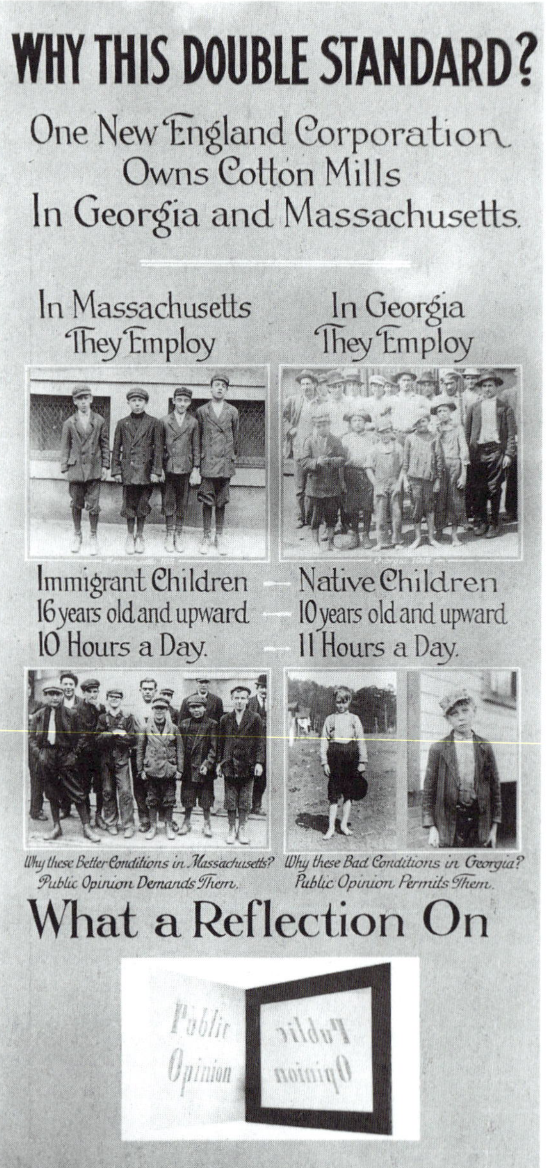

Lewis Hine, ▶ *Why This Double Standard?,* poster comparing the employment of children, circa 1913, Milwaukee Art Museum.

13. S. Stein, "Making Connections with the Camera: Photography and Social Mobility in the Career of Jacob Riis", in *Afterimage*, no. 10, 1983, pp. 9 ff; Hales, *op. cit.*, pp. 162 ff; A. Alland, *Jacob A. Riis, Photographer & Citizen*, Millerton 1974; B. Jung. *Jacob A. Riis: Sozialreformer und Fotograf: Über Fotografie und soziales Elend*, in *Fotogeschichte*, no. 4, 1984, pp. 45 ff.

14. C. Brandstätter, "Durch die Wiener Quartiere des Elends und Verbrechens: Anmerkungen zum Werk des Wiener Amateurfotografen Hermann Drawe", in *Fotogeschichte*, no. 2, 1982, pp. 23 ff.

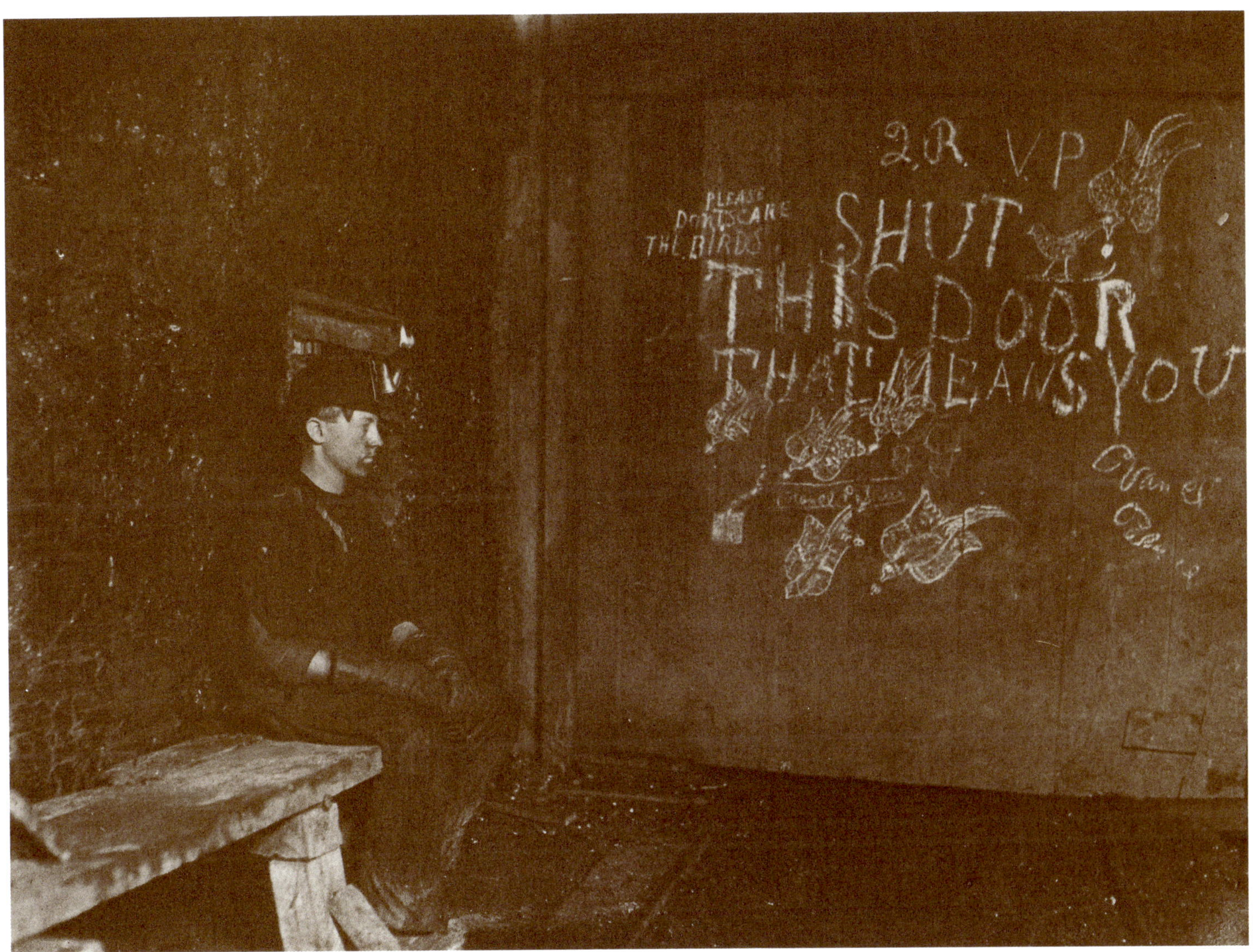

Lewis Hine,
Vance, Aged 15, a Virginia Miner,
September 1908,
International Museum of Photography,
George Eastman House,
Rochester.

tion. In 1906, it had been decided that photographs should be used to provide evidence of the conditions which were being criticized so as to reinforce the credibility of the campaign. Hine often had to enter factories under a false pretext in order to photograph children at their work. He used camera angles which emphasized still further the pitiful contrast between the small employees, whom he often photographed looking straight into the camera, and the huge machines. There was, therefore, also a symbolic element in his technique. He noted the place and time at which each picture was taken and found out the names, ages, and origins of the children, their conditions of work, and any diseases they had. Montages made by Hine for the N.C.L.C. showed comparative pictures of child labor in various states, gave different perspectives on a topic or used "before and after" pictures which were intended to show how industry turned the children into "human junk".[15]

Hine also anticipated the magazine photographers of the 1920s in his use of the "photo story" with a combination of pictures and text. He used montage in a great variety of ways – with text, as a mosaic of photographs, as a photographic essay or in the form of illustrated folders. In 1918–1919, working in Europe during the First World War for the American Red Cross and using a smaller-format camera, Hine developed a more dynamic, less spectacular style for reporting "human interest" stories – a style which was less detached than "candid" photography but did not overtly strive for emotional impact.[16]

During the war, the conditions of photographic practice and its very sense had changed considerably. The somewhat brutal, improvised style, which was that of these visual "predators" who worked like detectives had become the accepted style of photographic societies and magazines. The denunciation of social inequalities would gain support in other media.

15. J. M. Gutman, *Lewis W. Hine, 1874–1940: Two perspectives*, New York 1974; W. and N. Rosenblum and A. Trachtenberg, *America & Lewis Hine: Photographs, 1904–1940*, New York 1977; V. Posener and S. Mallach, *Photography and Reform: Lewis Hine and the National Child Labor Committee*, Milwaukee 1984.

16. D. Kaplan, *Lewis Hine in Europe: The Lost Photographs*, New York, 1988.

29. Septbr. 1929
Nummer 39
38. Jahrgang

Berliner Illustrirte Zeitung

Preis des Heftes 20 Pfennig

Verlag Ullstein Berlin SW 68

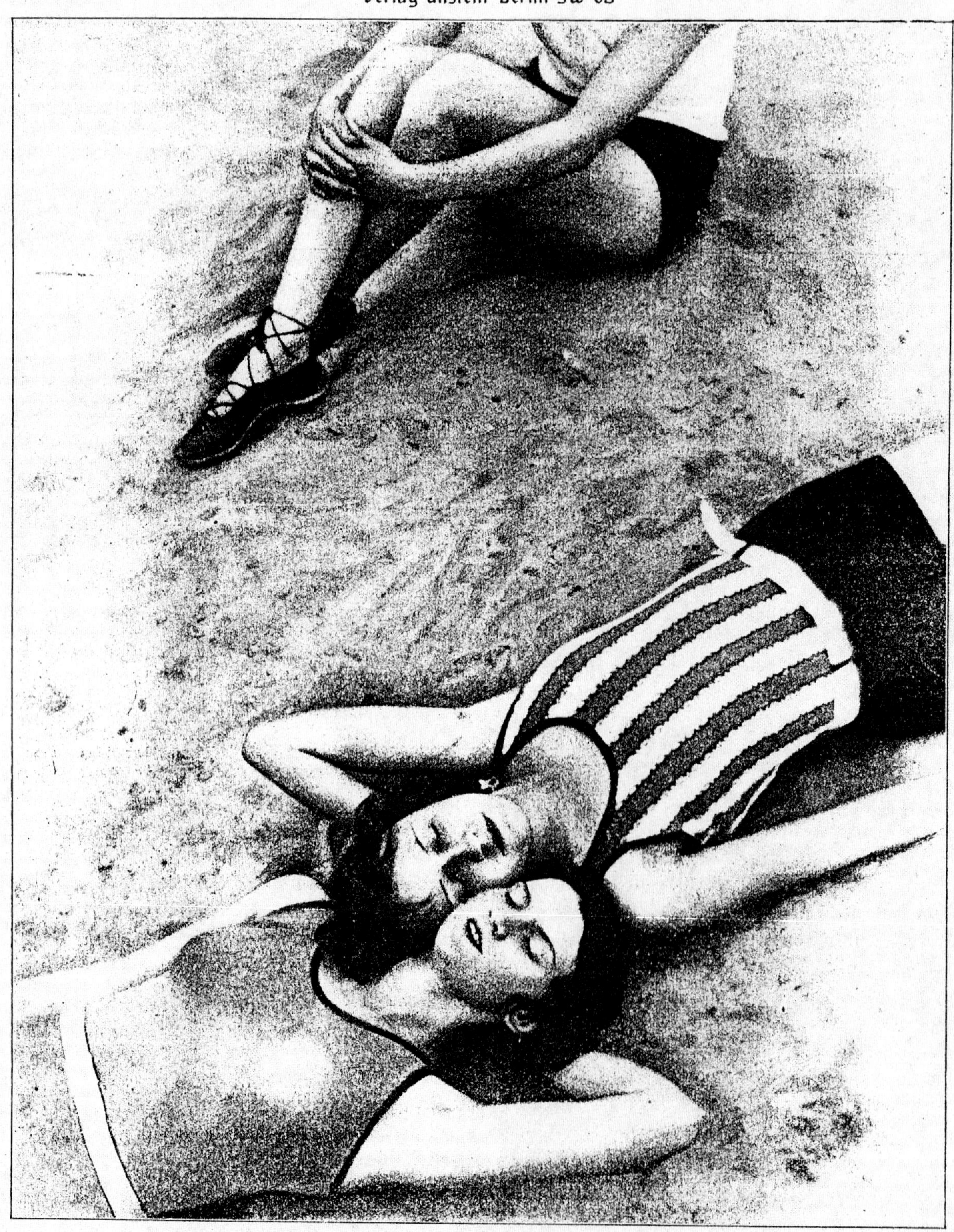

Der schöne Herbst: Die letzten warmen Sonnenstrahlen.

Aufnahme von Martin Munkácsi.

PHOTOGRAPHY AND THE MEDIA

21

Changes in the illustrated press

Pierre Albert and Gilles Feyel

Unlike print-making, where photomechanical processes were rapidly absorbed into workshop practice, the press was unable to adapt photography for use with columns of type before the end of the nineteenth century. At the beginning of the twentieth century, the manufacture of virtually wear-proof printing plates on metal by half-tone engraving, followed by the transmission of photographs by wire, provoked a rapid increase in the use of photography in newspapers and magazines – mainly, at first, to illustrate news stories. The publication of an attested picture of an event within a few hours of it happening had a considerable impact on society and relations between groups.

From the earliest days of photography, printers and practitioners of the new art made great efforts to perfect methods for printing photographs. They had three techniques to work with: typography (in relief), lithography (without relief), from which offset litho (1910) was derived, and etching or copperplate, which worked by hollowing out the plate, and from which photogravure evolved.

These innovations were first applied to book illustration before being used by magazines and newspapers, where problems were encountered, not only from trades unions and former illustrators, draughtsmen, and engravers, but also because of the speed of printing and the mediocre quality of the paper used. There may also have been some reservations on the part of the public, particularly in France, where newspapers traditionally had fewer pages than in the Germanic and Anglo-Saxon countries. For a long time, readers were of the opinion that illustrations, like large headlines, took up valuable space in their newspapers that should have been given over to text. Readers of magazines whose original purpose was to amuse or educate in a popular way took more easily to pictures, but photography's realism remained incompatible with the illustration of highly colored fiction. Since weekly or monthly periodicals had a longer publishing-schedule than daily newspapers they were also better able to accommodate the long delays involved in making phototypes.

The story of how photographic illustration gradually replaced drawing is still very unclear. It is regrettable that so few newspaper publishers' archives have survived, and even those that have are full of gaps.

Before photogravure

The famous ornamental banner heading on Renaudot's *Gazette* (1631) established a tradition that was followed by most newspapers under the ancien régime, who embellished their titles with strips of decoration consisting, for example, of palm-leaf designs or assorted flower-motifs. All these ornaments vanished with the Revolution, and did not reappear in the newspapers of the Empire. While side-grain woodcuts had been used to illustrate occasional publications since the fifteenth century (lampoons, broadsheets, public announcements), it was not until the very end of the eighteenth century that the first real illustrated periodicals appeared, fashion magazines like *Le Cabinet des Modes*(1785–1792), then *Le Journal des Dames et des Modes* (1797–1839), where each number was accompanied by two or three colored copper-plate engravings.

From the 1830s, new techniques made possible the development of a satirical press illustrated with caricatures and cartoons – *Le Charivari* (Paris, 1832), *Punch* (London, 1841), popular magazines dealing in useful knowledge such as *Le Journal des Connaissances utiles* (Paris, 1831),

◀ Martin Munkacsi. *Titlepage of the* **Berliner Illustrirte Zeitung,** September 29, 1929.

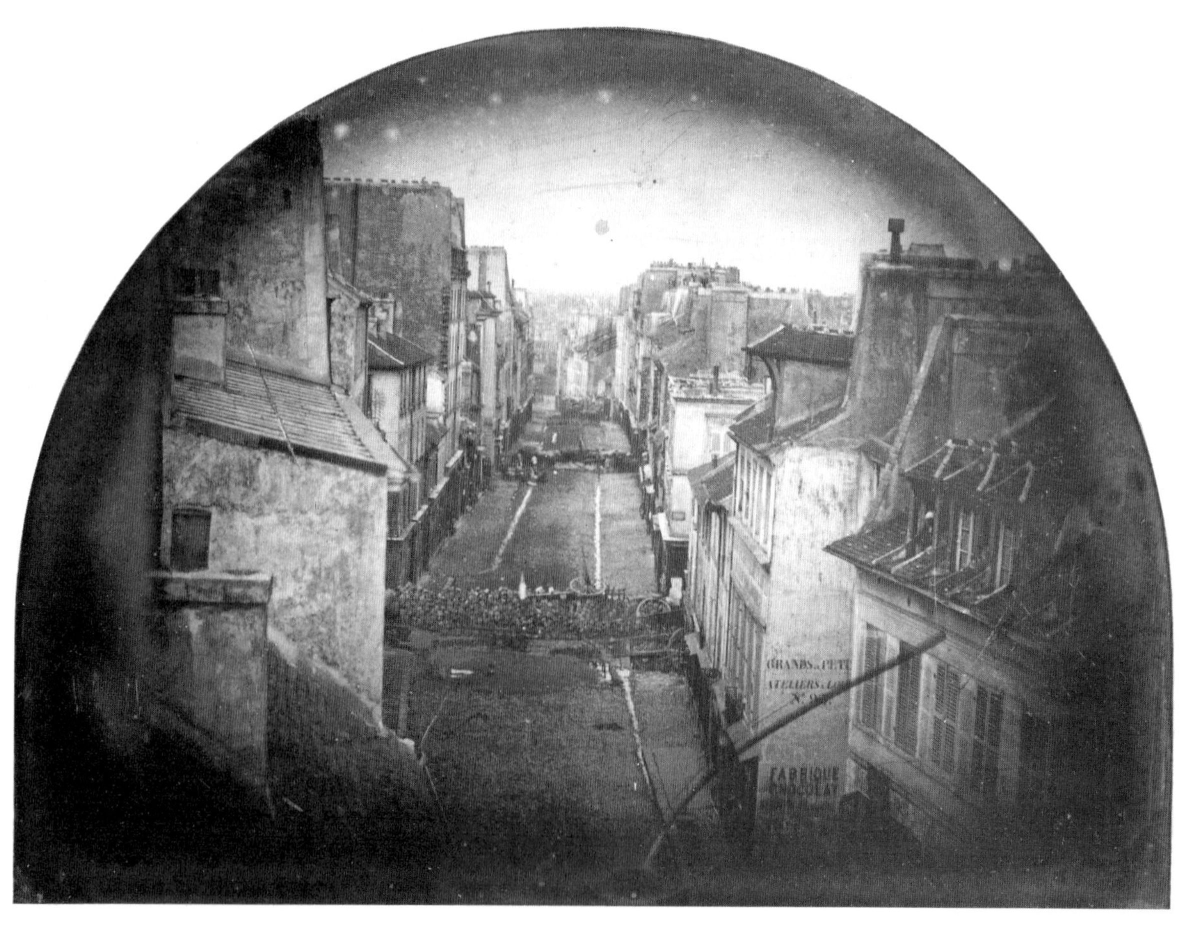

THIBAULT, *Barricades on Rue Saint-Maur,* June 25, 1848, daguerreotype, Musée Carnavalet, Paris.

Penny Magazine (London 1832), *Chamber's Edinburgh Journal* (1832), *Magasin pittoresque* (Paris, 1833), *Musée des Familles* (Paris 1833), and illustrated news magazines such as *The Illustrated London News* (1842), *L'Illustration* (Paris, 1843), *Illustrierte Zeitung* (Leipzig, 1843), *La Illustración* (Madrid, 1849), *Frank Leslie's Illustrated Newspaper* (New York, 1855), *Le Monde illustré* (Paris 1857), *Harper's Weekly* (New York, 1857), and *Vsemirnaya Illyustratziya* (St. Petersburg, 1869). *Le Charivari* published a caricature every day, at first of a political, then, after 1835, of a social character, drawn by artists of the highest calibre such as Daumier and Gavarni. These were full-page illustrations, reproduced by lithography.[1] First the pages of text were printed typographically, then the third page received its illustration via the lithographic press. At the end of the century the lithographic process was further improved by zincography.

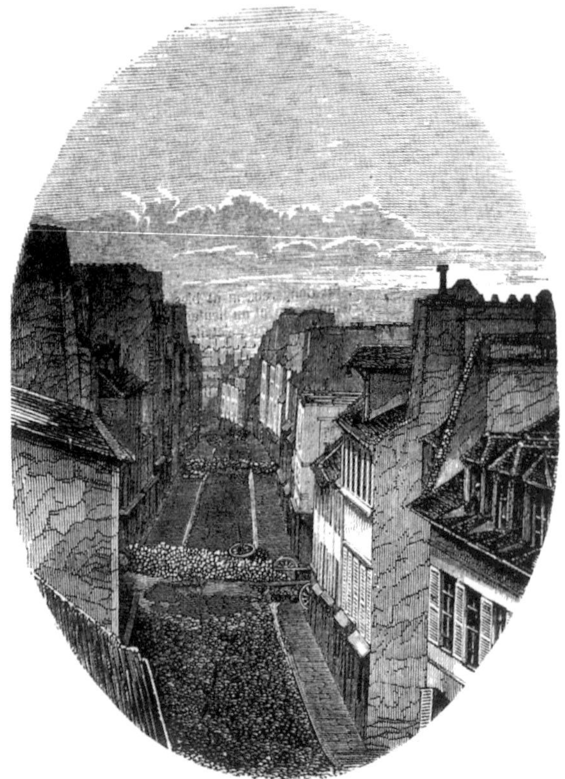

Barricades on Rue Saint-Maur, woodcut from the daguerreotype by THIBAULT, published by *L'Illustration,* July 1, 1848.

Magazines were illustrated by end-grain woodcuts, also known as wood engravings, a technique perfected by an Englishman, Thomas Bewick (1775–1804), which the Paris engravers Best, Andrew, and Lenoir used to illustrate the *Magasin pittoresque* and *L'Illustration.*[2] A very hard wood (boxwood) was sawn across the grain, and assembled in little blocks. The drawing was traced onto the polished surface, the wrong way round, and then swiftly hand-engraved by several workers, each engraving a single block, all doing separate sections which were then reassembled. Work done by Firmin Gillot (1850) led to the drawing being transferred onto a zinc plate; the use of oily ink protected the plate from being eaten away by the acid, producing an engraving in relief. This process, zincography, made possible the publication of a range of new magazines – *Le Tour du*

1. A printing process without visible engraving or relief, using porous limestone, based on the principle of the antipathy of water and oily substances, discovered by A. Senefelder in 1796.

2. J.-N. Marchandiau, *L'Illustration, 1843–1944: Vie et Mort d'un Journal,* Toulouse, Privat, 1987.

Monde (1860), *La Vie parisienne* (1863), and *The Graphic* (1869, London), and gave new life to older titles like *Le Charivari* and *Le Journal amusant*. Papers specializing in caricatures took on a new impetus with *La Lune* (1865), followed by *L'Éclipse*. Adapted to the rotary press, the process had its final flowering with the arrival, in 1889, of the "illustrated supplements" of the major papers: *Le Petit Journal* (printed in three colors from November 1890), *Le Petit Parisien*, *Le Figaro*, etc. These magazines went into decline after 1900, when they began to face competition from photographic magazines.

The Illustrated London News, *L'Illustration*, and other news magazines were illustrated by artists who either witnessed events at first hand, like Guys, Gavarni, and Chandelier in the February 1848 revolution in Paris, or – which was more usual – worked in a studio using eye-witness accounts, press-cuttings, and photographs, like John Gilbert in England and Gustave Doré in France. "Special artists"[3] were sent to the battle-fields in time of war: the Crimean War (1853–1856), the American Civil War (1861–1865), the Franco-Prussian War (1870–1871), and the Boer War (1898–1902). Their job was to record notable military achievements. The Crimean War was covered by Durand-Brager for *L'Illustration*, and by Constantin Guys and others for *The Illustrated London News*.

The acceptance of photography

In the second half of the nineteenth century, progress in lithography, and then zincography, did not affect magazine publishing to any great extent. The illustrated press did not take an interest in engraving techniques until the technique of photogravure was introduced.

Typography was still king. As in book illustration, photographs were first used as models for artists and engravers to work from. In France, the first appearance in the press of an engraving copied from a daguerreotype was a picture in *L'Illustration* on July 1, 1848 of a barricade in Rue Saint-Maur-Popincourt; the first copy of a paper photograph was on May 7, 1853. The same magazine subsequently developed the technique of film on wood, starting in 1877. The support for the photograph was the same piece of wood that was to be used for the engraving, coated with a photosensitive emulsion. The engraver was therefore able to copy the image directly, without the intermediary of a drawing. This new technique was subject to further improvement. In 1891, prior retouching of the photograph was introduced.[4] *L'Illustration* and its long-standing counterparts abroad were thus able to remain faithful to the woodcut, despite the improvement in zincography brought about by Charles Gillot's invention of photographic transfer (1872).

By the end of the Second Empire, photography on paper had become big business. From 1870, for example, theater papers were illustrated with photographs pasted into spaces reserved for them in the printed text. In their own way, these publications played a similar role to the souvenir programs sold in theaters today.

With the advent of half-tone engraving, the press set out definitively on the direct (that is, mechanized) reproduction of photographs. In France *Le Monde illustré* published the first photomechanical reproduction in half-tone ruled-screen zincogravure, a portrait of the polar explorer Nordenskjöld (March 10, 1877). In the middle of the 1880s, the half-tone ruled-screen

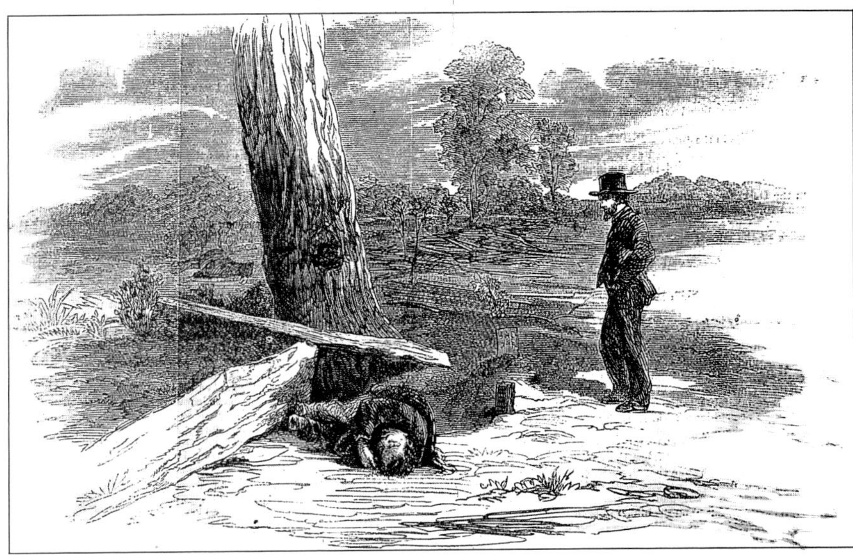

Woodcut after Gardner's photograph, from *Harper's Weekly*, October 18, 1862.

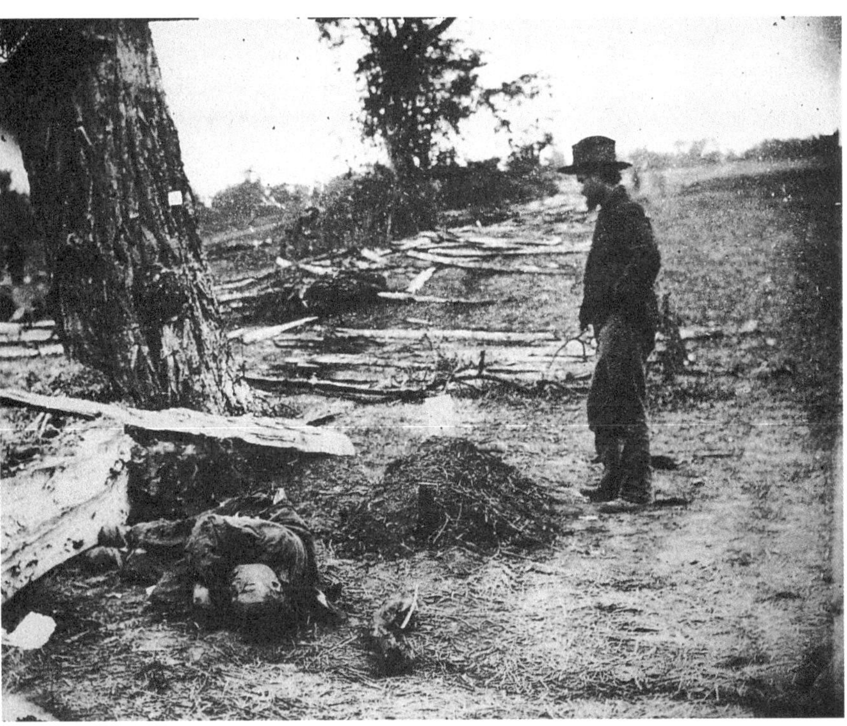

Alexander Gardner, ***The Battlefield of Antietam,*** 1862, Library of Congress, Washington.

3. P. Hogarth, *Artistes reporters*, Paris, Casterman, 1986.

4. The first woodcut where this was used (of a level-crossing keeper) was published on July 25, 1891.

The interview with Chevreul

At the end of August 1886, the chemist and physicist Chevreul celebrated his hundredth birthday. The photographer Félix Nadar, pushed by his son Paul who had taken over his Parisian studio, obtained a "photographic interview" with him. Chevreul had invented the stearin candle and had contributed to the theory of color and simultaneous contrast. He was also a highly regarded figure in the Republic, which made a point of honoring its great men: poets (Victor Hugo) and scientists (Pasteur).

Paul Nadar was also the representative in France of George Eastman, the American who was soon to put the Kodak camera on the market (1888), and who wanted to promote his new system of photography. The Nadars, father and son, had the idea of creating the "journalism of tomorrow" by combining photography, to capture gestures and postures, with the recording of sound, using Ader's phonophone. Finally, the text was to be taken down in shorthand, and kept on file, constituting what Nadar called "the first attempts at photostenography". Paul Nadar took the pictures (which, we may be fairly certain, took three sessions), while his father interviewed the scientist (in his slippers) at home, sitting at a table. The novelty was that no pose was required, and the subject took no notice of the photographer. The link between images and words – which is often present by implication in a photograph – was espoused as a principle for understanding the whole.

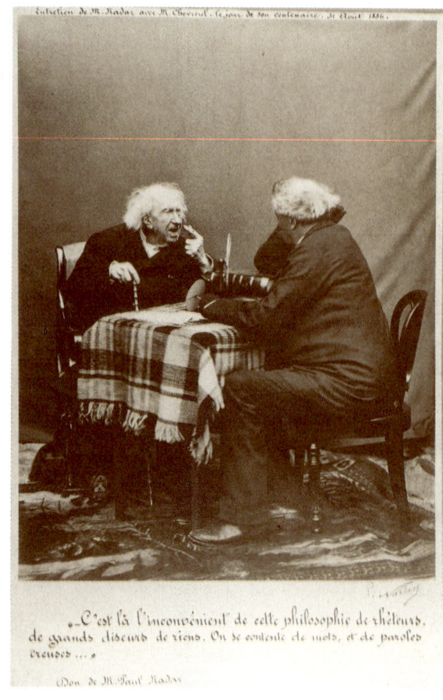

Paul Nadar,
Interview with Chevreul on His Hundredth Birthday,
August 31, 1886,
by Felix Nadar,
private collection.

The published interview consists of photographs accompanied by extracts from what Chevreul said, sometimes reworked to form a sort of "caption" for a photograph, or put next to images to which they did not exactly correspond.

Despite these touches, which do not fit in with modern practice, the interview with Chevreul is a first attempt at complete truth and transparency, the precursor of live reportage. The result was rejected by *Le Figaro* for technical reasons, and published by *Le Journal illustré* on September 5, 1886 with twelve photogravures. It was not until twenty years later that newspapers and magazines adopted this type of illustration, with its acceptance of less stereotypical postures and a naturalness better suited to illuminating the text. Nadar, the all-round man of communications, who had built his career on advertising, humorous drawings, and writing, proved in this interview that photography was suited to recording something other than material reality, and could be fully assimilated into linguistic communication.

Michel Frizot

processes invented by Charles-Guillaume Petit, Georg Meisenbach, and Frederic Ives made the chemical engraving of zinc plates even easier, so that the engraver did not need to intervene except to make the final corrections. On September 5, 1886, *Le Journal illustré,* a weekly magazine belonging to the *Petit Journal* group, celebrated the hundredth birthday of the chemist Chevreul by publishing an interview with him carried out by Nadar and illustrated with twelve photographs. At the end of the 1890s, half-tone techniques became quicker and more reliable. This made possible the launch of the first photographically illustrated magazines: *La Vie illustrée* and *Lecture pour tous* (1898). The big press houses equipped themselves with half-tone studios. Smaller magazines and newspapers had their half-tones made by independent studios. The photographs were supplied by specialist businesses or were taken (in larger publications) by reporter-photographers. Half-tones could now bear comparison with woodcuts or zincographs, and began to appear in the daily papers.

At the same time, it finally became possible to adapt photogravure to the rotary press. The work of Godchaux in Paris (1867), Karl Klič (Lancaster, 1895), Mertens in Freiburg (Breisgau, Germany 1904), and the Comoy brothers in Paris (1910) improved the process, step by step. The press quickly found applications for it, first of all in supplements illustrated with photogravures. The first seem to have been those of the *Freiburger Zeitung* (Easter number 1910), then the *Frankfurter Zeitung* (February 1911). *L'Illustration* had already offered a Corot landscape as an inset, (done in photogravure but described as a copperplate engraving) in its Christmas number of 1908. The paper installed a photogravure studio in 1910. On the eve of the First World War rotogravure, or rotating photogravure, was developing rapidly and gave birth to a second generation of photographic magazines, inaugurated by *Le Miroir* (1913). Offset, which was perfected between 1904 and 1910, was not really used by the press before 1914, except for a few insets in luxury magazines.

In 1902, the discovery by a German, Arthur Korn, of the principles of photo-telegraphy resulted in 1907 in a whole series of transmissions of photographs by electrical signals between Berlin and Paris, and Paris and Lyons (there and back). Édouard Belin improved the

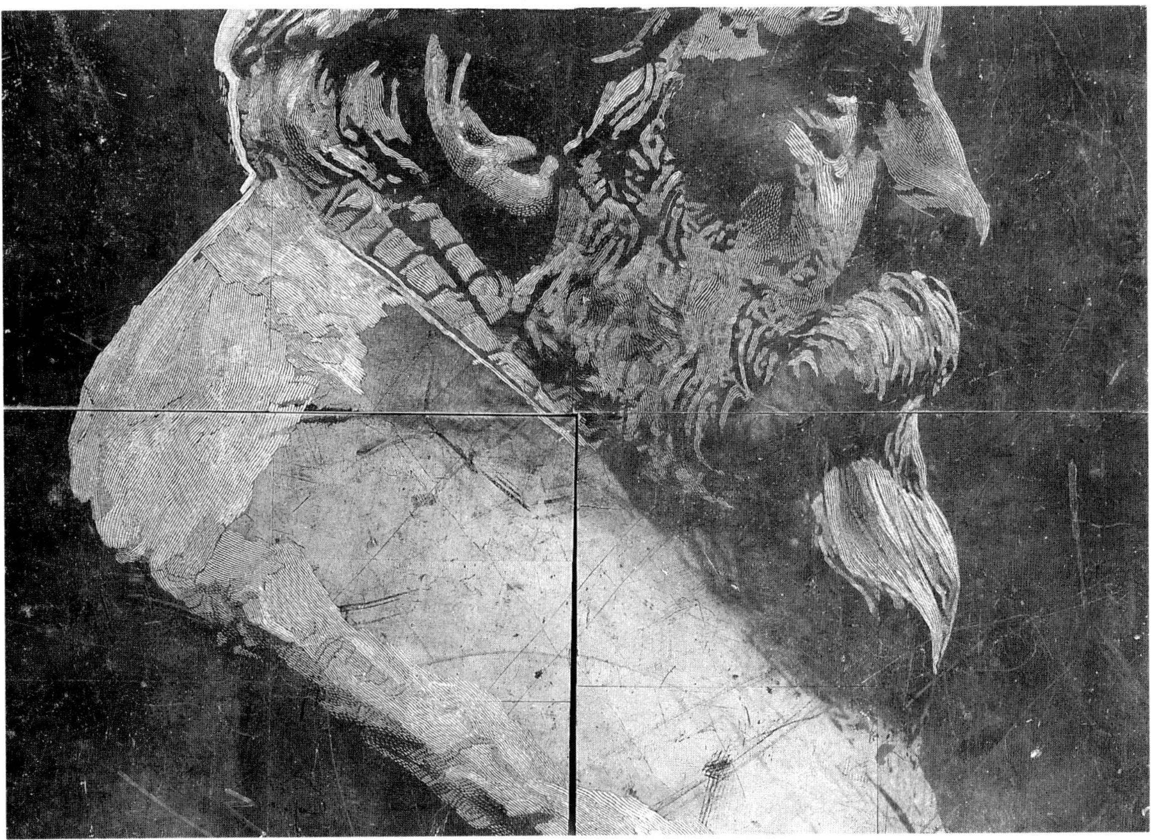

Detail from a boxwood block, with an image in gelatin silver-bromide transferred onto it, in the course of being hand-engraved for printing,
circa 1900,
private collection

system, and, in 1912, demonstrated his famous "suitcase" which made it possible to transmit a photograph in a few minutes, simply by linking it to a telephone or telegraph wire (see box). *Le Journal* published the first picture obtained using this method on May 12, 1914, transmitted in four minutes, showing the opening of the Lyons fair by President Poincaré, but phototelegraphy did not take really off until after the First World War.

The increasing use of photographic illustration created a new sort of journalist, the reporter-photographer.[5] Already, in the nineteenth century, there had been photographic coverage of the Crimean War and the American Civil War. Colonial campaigns, major events, and the discovery of exotic places then gave the spur to the reporters of the illustrated magazines. From now on, with the new, more portable cameras, reporters became photographers too, and were keen to reinforce the authenticity of their text by accompanying it with photographs.

The era of the half-tone

While, at the beginning of the twentieth century, there were no more technical barriers to photographic illustration, other obstacles remained, notably that of distance. At a time when the telegraph and the telephone made it possible to transmit news very quickly from even the most distant parts of the globe, images – drawings as well as photographs – could not reach the editors by any way other than by boat or train, arriving, inevitably, a long time after the event. Illustration, at that time, necessarily lagged behind, and so it was often timeless – hence those innumerable head-and-shoulders portraits, some with the background cut out, that were always available in editors' offices, making it amazingly easy to conjure up the major figures of any event (monarchs, ministers, diplomats, and generals, but also the perpetrators or victims of the most minor crime).

When the *Excelsior* reported Leo Tolstoy's flight from his home and his death,[6] the text was illustrated with photographs of the daily life of the writer and his immediate circle, undated images, often with the background cut out, and thus having the impression of being timeless. The only really contemporary photograph, that of his funeral, was published six days later (November 28, 1919). At the time of the Russo-Japanese war (1904–1905), head-and-shoulder portraits of the major figures and photographs of Port-Arthur and of warships led up to the first news pictures. On March 9, 1904, *Le Matin* published "a snapshot taken three weeks ago" of the recruiting office in Vladivostok, then on March 14 a "snapshot taken six weeks ago, on the eve of the war", and finally, on March 24, "the entry of the first Japanese detachment into Seoul" dating from February 12! In order for an event to have some

5. A. Barret, *Les premiers Reporters-Photographes, 1848–1914,* Paris, A. Barret, 1977.

6. A. Daix, *Au commencement était la photographie:* Excelsior, *premier Illustré quotidien français, 1910–1940,* Mémoire de DEA, Institut Français de Presse, Université Panthéon-Assas-Paris II, 1990.

Half-tone

The processes of photogravure, photolithography, and Woodburytype, despite their respective qualities, all had one major inconvenience – they could not be used in conjunction with typesetting.

The usual procedure in printing was to ink a raised lead typeface. In order to bring together text and photography, a procedure needed to be found whereby the black parts of the image would be represented by raised elements (in the form of raised dots clustered more or less thickly) and the white parts by hollows. That procedure was invented in 1880, and became known as "half-tone". It finally gave photography the opportunity of being disseminated widely, through books and the illustrated press.

An Englishman, William Henry Fox Talbot, had already discovered that in order to reproduce a photographic image by a mechanical printing-process, it was first essential to divide it up into a multitude of closely grouped but distinct elements. To achieve this, he had the idea of superimposing two lengths of thin gauze, in such a way that the meshes crossed diagonally.

Other researchers, in their turn, produced different printing methods: Charles de Berchtold (1857), Baret (1868), and above all Walter B. Woodbury, the inventor of the Woodburytype, 1873), who propounded the idea of pressing a ruled screen down upon a gelatin image in relief, thereby producing a grain and in this way making it suitable for typographic processing. Favorable results were then obtained by Charles Petit, Frédéric E. Ives, and George Meisenbach.

In these later processes (Ives' improvements of 1886, above all) the crossed meshes formed a sort of grid across the image, within which the dots are imprinted lightly or more heavily. The grids are measured in lines per centimeter:

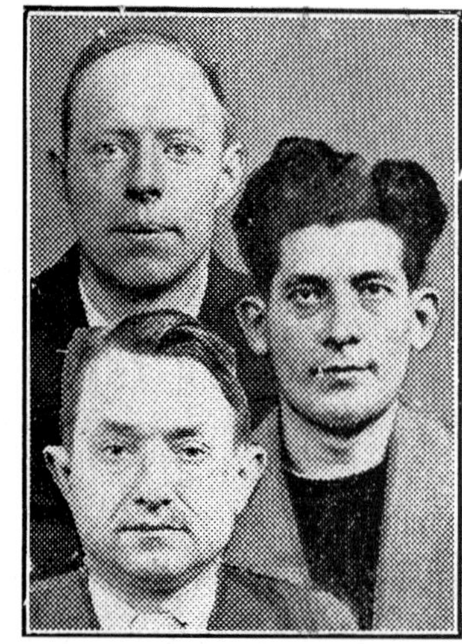

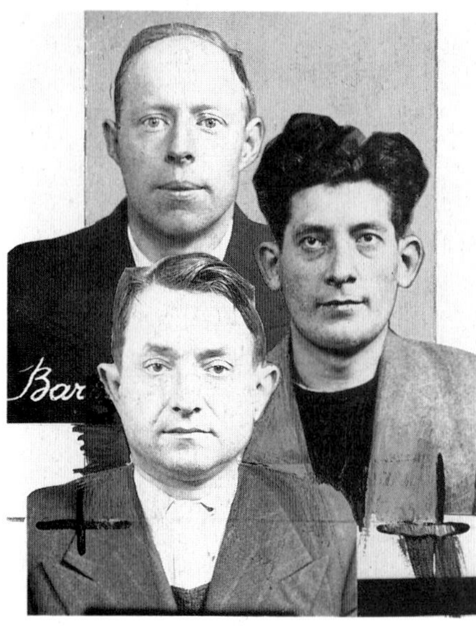

***Photomontage of three portraits ("dangerous housebreakers arrested in Paris") and half-tone print for* Le Petit Parisien,**
December 15, 1938, private collection.

they go from 32 lines for posters to as many as 150 or even 200 lines per centimeter for images which require great precision. The grid is then placed on a frame inside the body of the camera next to the sensitized plate. In a sense, the original picture itself is re-photographed through this grid.

In this way, a negative is obtained where the squares of the grid are variously shaded according to the intensity of the light on the corresponding area of the original: the bright parts are reproduced by transparent dots spread over an opaque area while the dark parts are reproduced by fine, thickly clustered dots. The transposition of this negative gives a positive where the transparent parts become the blacks, and vice versa.

The image is engraved onto a metal plate (copper or zinc) covered with a solution of gum and potassium bichromate. The ruled negative is applied to this layer after it has been dried, and the plate is exposed to light. Washing with water dissolves the gum together with the unexposed bichromate underneath the black parts of the negative which has not being hardened by the light. After drying, the plate is hardened in an oven.

All that now remains is for the metal to be eaten away with nitric acid at the places where the surface has been bared by washing, that is, those areas corresponding to the light areas of the original. The operation is stopped when it is decided that enough of the plate has been eaten away. The picture is washed and mounted on wood, and is then ready for printing.

This method of printing in relief (half-tone) was used for the first time by a daily newspaper in the United States on March 4, 1880, in the *New York Daily Graphic.*

Jean-Claude Gautrand

chance of being well illustrated, it had to stay in the news long enough – for instance the revolutionary disturbances in Russia in 1905, the Boer war or the Russo-Japanese war, the Balkan war of 1912, or else it had to have happened near the editorial office – like the death of Pope Leo XIII, in July 1903.

An artist's reconstruction was often the only way of illustrating an event which had occurred suddenly. This was not always the case, however, as two examples show. On August 7, 1903, *La Vie illustrée* published an account of the hostile interruption of the service in memory of Leo XIII by an anti-clericalist. The accompanying photograph shows him from behind, rushing on to the square in front of Notre Dame cathedral, shouting "Down with the Clergy!" Another snapshot "reproduced without retouching" by the *Excelsior* (November 21, 1910) showed the arrest of Lucien Lacour, who had attacked the President of the Council, Aristide Briand (a snapshot for which both police and attacker seem, rather obligingly, to have posed). Descriptions and reports on the countryside, or any continuing situation were, on the other hand, quite easy to illustrate. The image, whether a drawing or a photograph, was planned in advance to complement the text. Thus *Le Matin* gave a long account, between January 6 and 22, 1904, of the adventures of Nordenskjöld's Antarctic expedition, on the front page, illustrated throughout by photographs taken by members of the expedition.

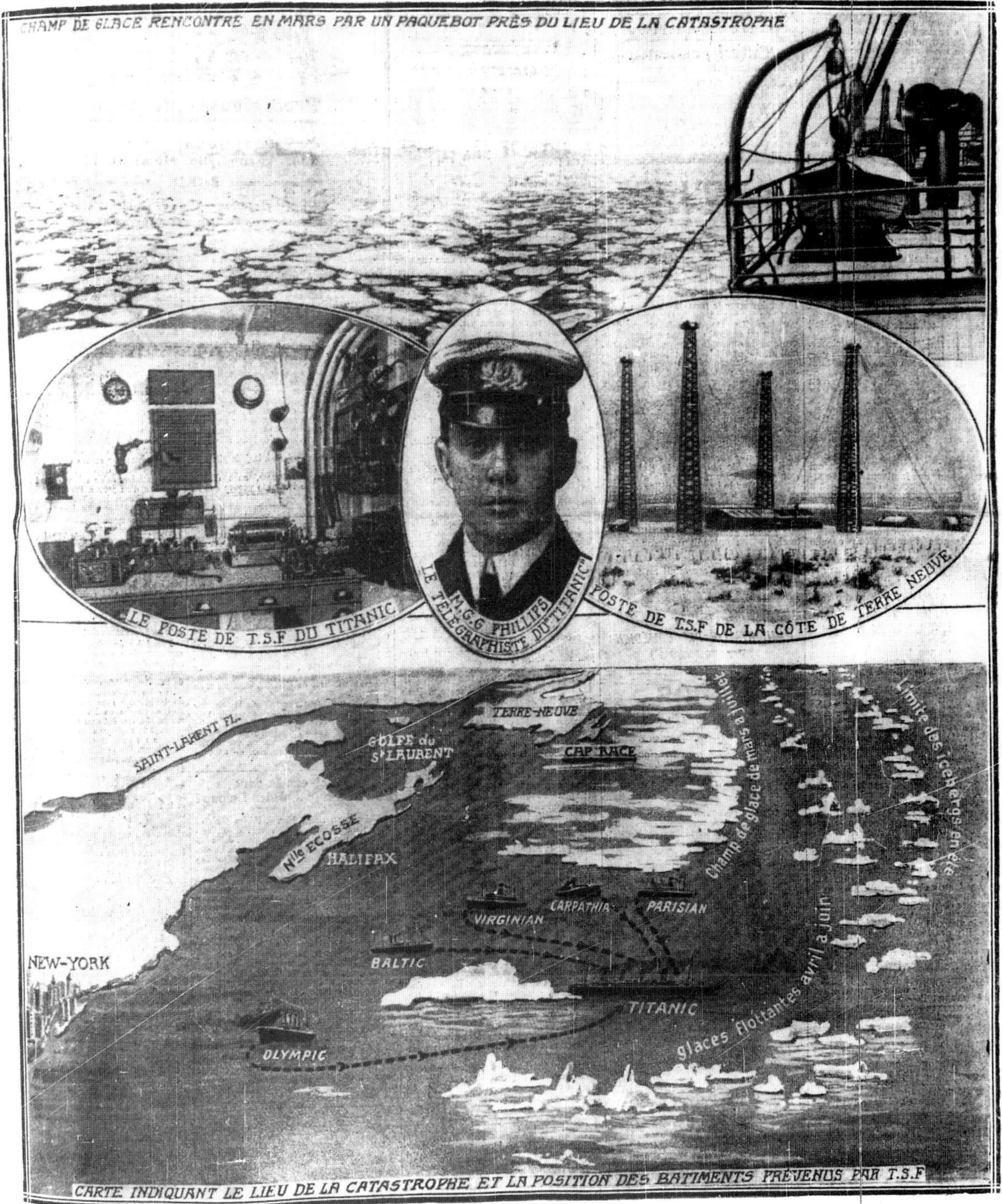

LA CATASTROPHE DU « TITANIC »

CHAMP DE GLACE RENCONTRE EN MARS PAR UN PAQUEBOT PRÈS DU LIEU DE LA CATASTROPHE

LE POSTE DE T.S.F DU TITANIC

M. G. G. PHILLIPS LE TÉLÉGRAPHISTE DU TITANIC

POSTE DE T.S.F DE LA CÔTE DE TERRE NEUVE

CARTE INDIQUANT LE LIEU DE LA CATASTROPHE ET LA POSITION DES BATIMENTS PRÉVENUS PAR T.S.F

LA BANQUISE FAIT PERIR 1,465 PERSONNES, LA T. S. F. EN SAUVE 715

Dans la matinée d'hier se confirmait l'effroyable nouvelle que signalaient nos dépêches de la deuxième édition : l'accident du *Titanic* devenait une catastrophe sans précédent. Dans le choc de l'immense paquebot avec la banquise irrésistible, environ 1,500 passagers ont trouvé la mort; plus de 700 ont été sauvés par la T. S. F., qui permit au navire *Carpathia* d'arriver sur les lieux du désastre assez à temps pour secourir ceux qu'avaient pu contenir les chaloupes. La conduite de l'opérateur du sans fil à bord du *Titanic*, M. Phillips, a été admirable. C'est grâce à lui que la catastrophe ne fut pas absolument générale. Rien ne saurait d'ailleurs donner une idée plus émouvante de ce qu'accomplit cet homme sur le paquebot géant que cette simple dépêche de son collègue à la station Marconi de Cape-Race : « Il (M. Phillips) paraissait absolument de sang-froid; ses signaux ont constamment été très nets, et il a agi du mieux possible. »

The Titanic Disaster, on the front page of **Excelsior**, April 17, 1912, Bibliothèque Nationale, Paris.

At the end of the 1890s, those daily papers which published photographs were still few in number. On January 21, 1897, the *New York Tribune* published the first half-tone picture on newsprint paper, and in 1900 the *Chicago Tribune* devoted several whole pages to a photographic reportage on the slums of New York. Numerous American dailies subsequently followed their example between 1900 and 1914. The British press did not lag far behind. As early as 1892, two provincial papers published half-tone reproductions of photographs. The *Daily Graphic* started printing half-tones from 1895, followed by the *Daily Chronicle* in 1898. In 1904, the *Daily Mirror*, another illustrated daily, began to publish several pages of half-tone pictures every day.[7] In Paris, naturally enough, those papers which concentrated on information – of which the three biggest titles between them sold more than 3.7 million copies in 1910, that is, three quarters of all the daily newspapers printed in Paris – were the first to commit themselves.

7. There were also daily papers in St. Petersburg (1887), in Austria (1893), and in Belgium (1897).

Phototelegraphy

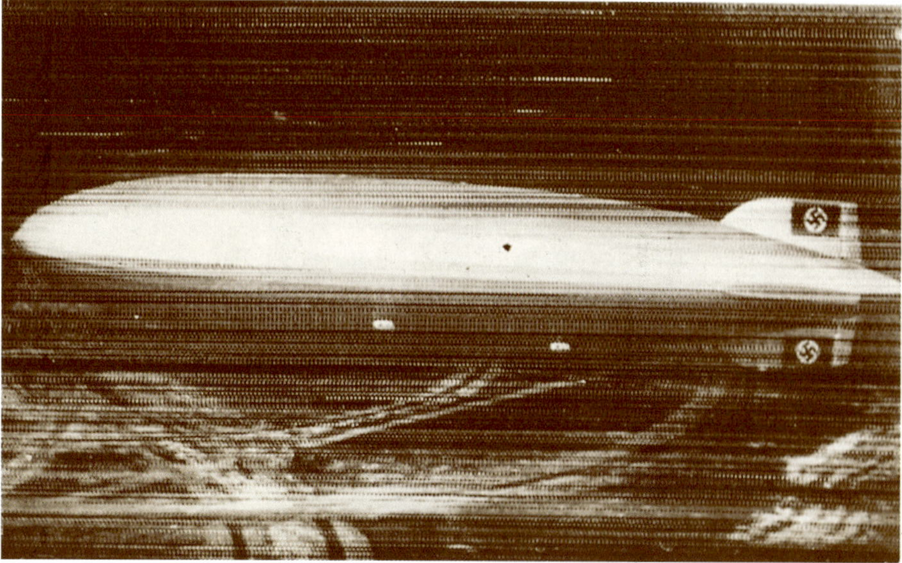

Photo transmitted by radio from New York to London on 11 May 1936, announcing the arrival of the dirigible Hindenburg at Lakehurst (USA), private collection.

Phototelegraphy is the transmission by telegraphic means, that is, by electric wire, of a photograph which has been converted into a series of electrical signals.

Professor Arthur Korn made conclusive experiments between 1902 and 1907, based on the properties of selenium which modifies its electrical resistance according to the amount of light which it receives. The image to be transmitted is wrapped around a cylinder and traversed by a narrow pencil of rays which then strikes a selenium cell. This transmits a current of an intensity proportional to the transparent and opaque sections of the original image. On the arrival of this electrical signal, the intensity of the light is restored by a cathode ray tube which produces an impression on a light-sensitive film, thus reproducing the original image in negative. In 1904, Korn effected the first telegraphic transmission between Munich and Nuremberg and back in 40 minutes, then, on February 1, invited by *L'Illustration*, he repeated the experiment in public, transmitting a portrait of President Fallières from Paris to Lyons and back, a distance of 1,024 km.

In his laboratory, installed in the cellars of the Société Française de Photographie, Édouard Belin set about resolving the problems still inherent in phototelegraphy by mechanical means. His first apparatus was based on the utilization of relief (proportional to the light received) which resulted, after development, in a gelatin bichromate print. This print, mounted on a cylinder, caused a scanning needle linked to a rheostat to move up and down in varying degrees. The intensity of the current passing down the wire thus varied proportionately to the relief. As a receiver, Belin used an oscillograph fitted with a mirror, which oscillated in harmony with the changes in the current being emitted. This oscillograph was placed in front of a camera within which a cylinder was turning, covered in paper coated with gelatin silver-bromide. The rays of light entering the camera thus restored, in tones and half-tones, the "reliefs" (i.e. the intensity) of the original image.

On January 22, 1908, during a lecture at the Fémina Theatre, Belin laid out the nature of the problem, and by way of an experiment, successfully transmitted a portrait of the Queen of Holland from Paris to Bordeaux and back (a round trip of 1,700 km). A year later, Belin replaced the rheostat with a microphone specially constructed in order to have a fixed resistance and translate reliefs into electrical intensity. It was with this system that the first news photograph was transmitted in 1914, the telegraphic reproduction obtained being published in *Le Journal*.

In 1926, Belin replaced the gelatin bichromate print with a photo-electric bulb which read the photographic document directly and transformed the variations in the intensity of the light into electrical variations. The appearance on the market of portable belinographs, weighing about 20 kilograms, gave reporters the possibility of sending back photos taken only a moment ago from the four corners of the world. The whole press corps soon equipped themselves with this apparatus.

In 1983, the Japanese firm Sakaki put on the market a portable belinograph (telecopier) which fitted into a suitcase and weighed just five kilograms – the Fax 2000 – which had simply to be connected to a telephone.

Jean-Claude Gautrand

Always innovatory, *Le Matin* got there before its rivals. On November 2, 7, 8, 10, and 11, 1902, there appeared the first half-tones, advertising its latest serialized novel *Les Rois du Monde*, by Pierre Sales – a photographic portrait of the author along with watercolors of his characters. On November 15, 19, and 22 the front page carried a photographic portrait (Professor Poirier, elected to the Faculty of Medicine, the German Crown Prince, a woman who had been murdered at Passy); on November 24 the first photo-article appeared, dedicated to a German submarine, surrounded by explanatory captions. From then on, *Le Matin* was illustrated with photographs – portraits and group photos with the background cut out in order to make them more legible.

Three other titles rapidly followed. *Le Journal*, the eternal competitor of *Le Matin*, produced half-tones with the background cut out of the monument to Hégésippe Moreau, then of the Villa Medici, on April 5 and 19 respectively. On May 24, there appeared, on the fifth page, the naked torso of a dead woman, murdered by having her throat cut. After several trial runs, *Le Journal* indulged in a veritable orgy of photography when Pope Leo XIII died. The front page on July 21 presented the event with a long photograph, trimmed of its background, of the Pope making a gesture of blessing and wearing the papal crown and another, also trimmed, of the Pope walking. The conclave and the election of Pius X, and the Italian royal visit to Paris were copiously illustrated.

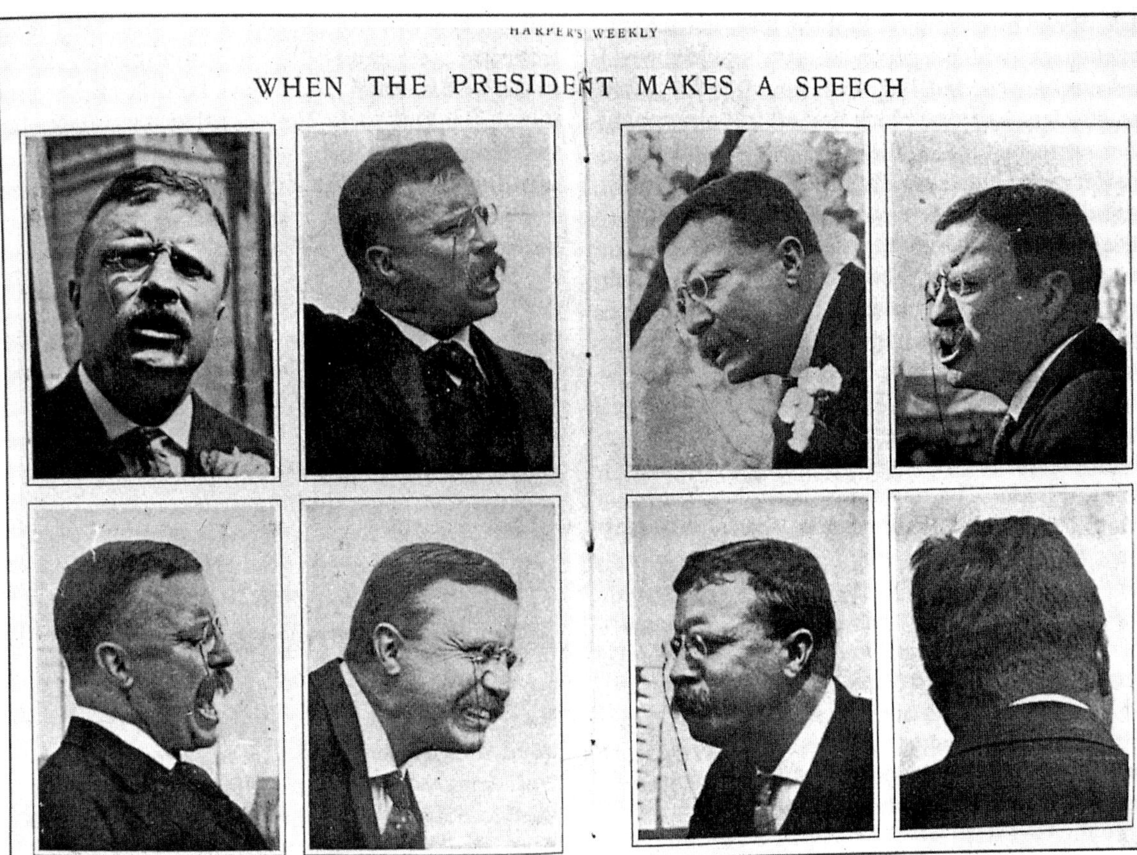
HARPER'S WEEKLY

WHEN THE PRESIDENT MAKES A SPEECH

Underwood and Underwood, ***President T. Roosevelt making a speech,*** from *Harper's Weekly*, January 26, 1907.

A Movie Rescue, *Le Miroir*, May 24, 1914, Bibliothèque Nationale, Paris.
▼

Le Journal took pains to enhance all royal or presidential photos, even the most insignificant, with frames in "modern style". Next to such a luxuriance of photographs *Le Petit Parisien* looks poor. It was only with the visit of the Italian royal family of October 15, 1903 that the paper came round to regularly publishing photographs on its front page. The last of the four big Paris papers, *Le Petit Journal*, inaugurated a regular rogues' gallery of murderers (October 22), specializing in reproducing the photographic portraits of the identification service of the judiciary.

The Russo-Japanese war confirmed the advance that *Le Matin* and *Le Journal* had gained on their rivals. The former sent Pierre Giffard to the Far East, the latter sent Ludovic Naudeau. *Le Journal* published reports about Korea, accompanied by photographs. *Le Petit Parisien* found its opportunity in the revolutionary state of affairs in Russia, publishing a picture of a cavalry charge against the strikers of St. Petersburg (January 27, 1905) – "an instant photograph taken on the Nevsky Prospect, on Sunday January 22".

The influence of photography on page layout can be quantified – the whole front page being taken over by current news; the beginning of a horizontal layout of columns, and so on. Right up until 1914, the use of photography was still evolving in the Paris and provincial daily papers.

SAUVETAGE POUR CINÉMA AU-DESSUS DE LA TAMISE

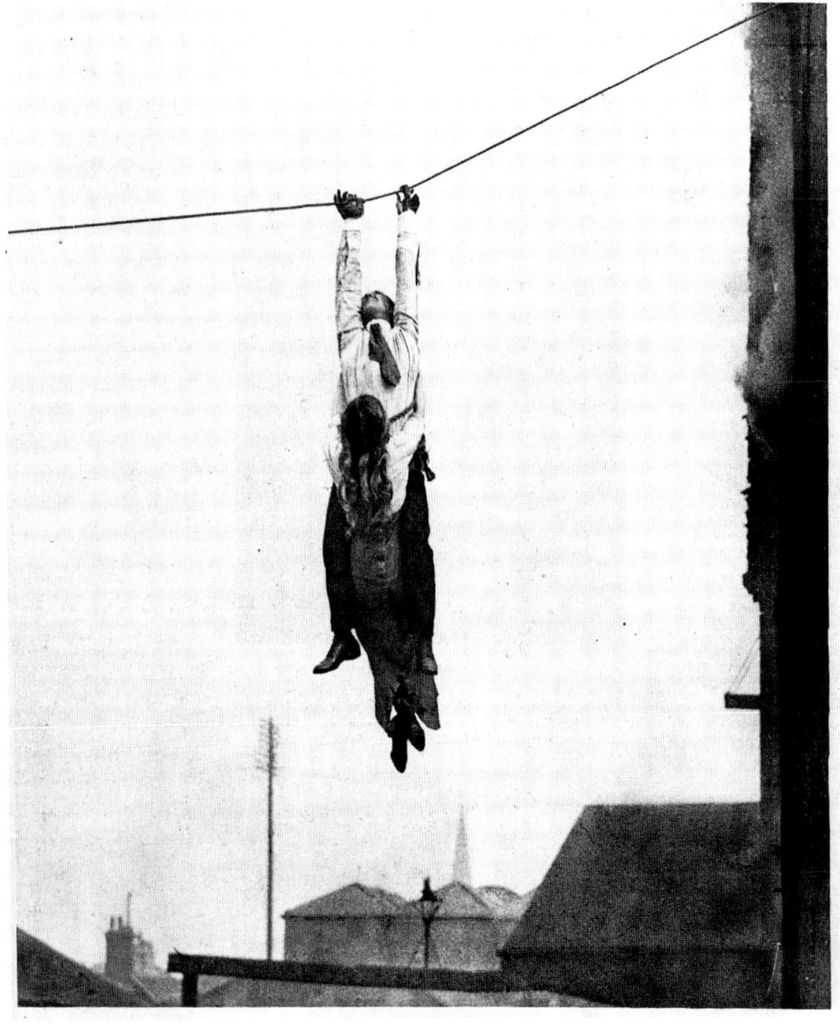

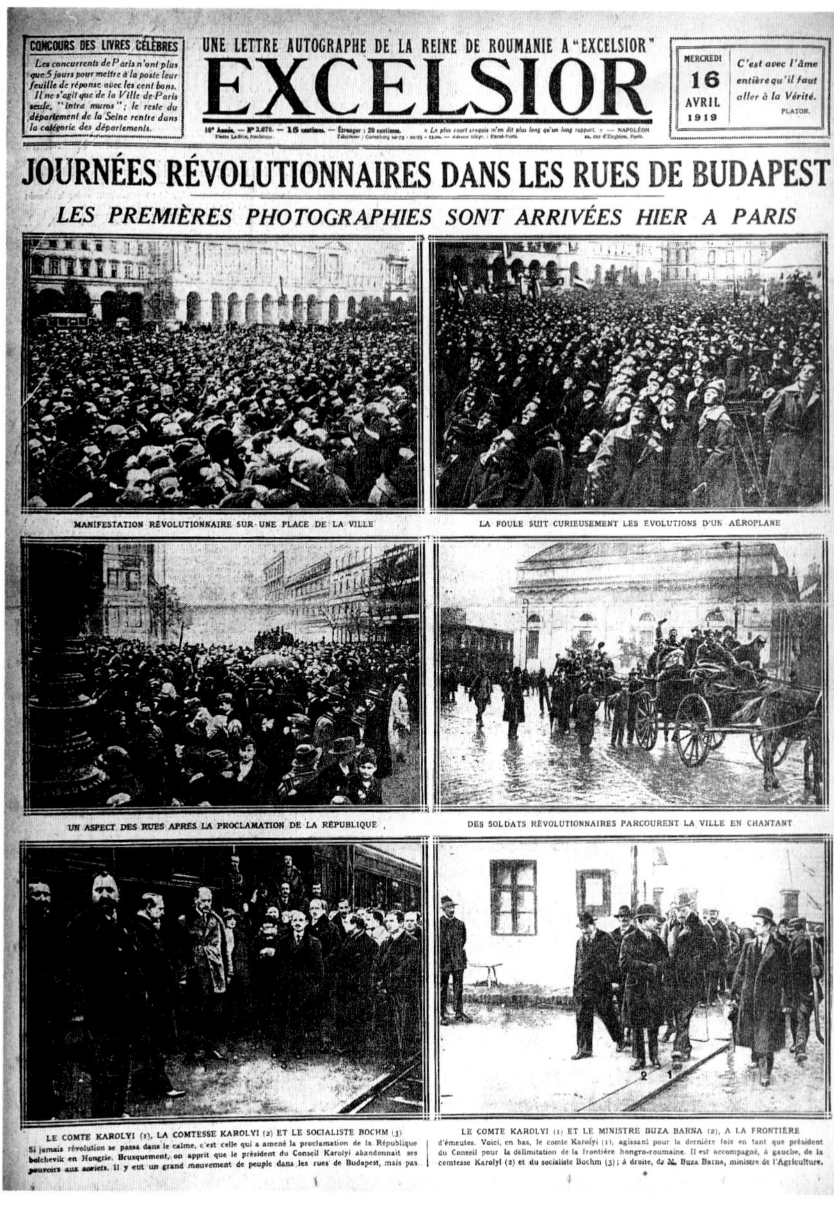

CONCOURS DES LIVRES CÉLÈBRES
Les concurrents de Paris n'ont plus que 5 jours pour mettre à la poste leur feuille de réponse avec les cent bons. Il ne s'agit que de la Ville de Paris seule, "intra muros"; le reste du département de la Seine rentre dans la catégorie des départements.

UNE LETTRE AUTOGRAPHE DE LA REINE DE ROUMANIE A "EXCELSIOR"

EXCELSIOR

10e Année. — No 3.070. — 15 centimes. — Étranger : 20 centimes.

« Le plus court croquis m'en dit plus long qu'un long rapport. » — NAPOLÉON

MERCREDI 16 AVRIL 1919

C'est avec l'âme entière qu'il faut aller à la Vérité. PLATON.

JOURNÉES RÉVOLUTIONNAIRES DANS LES RUES DE BUDAPEST

LES PREMIÈRES PHOTOGRAPHIES SONT ARRIVÉES HIER A PARIS

MANIFESTATION RÉVOLUTIONNAIRE SUR UNE PLACE DE LA VILLE

LA FOULE SUIT CURIEUSEMENT LES ÉVOLUTIONS D'UN AÉROPLANE

UN ASPECT DES RUES APRÈS LA PROCLAMATION DE LA RÉPUBLIQUE

DES SOLDATS RÉVOLUTIONNAIRES PARCOURENT LA VILLE EN CHANTANT

LE COMTE KAROLYI (1), LA COMTESSE KAROLYI (2) ET LE SOCIALISTE BOCHM (3)
Si jamais révolution se passa dans le calme, c'est celle qui a amené la proclamation de la République bolchevik en Hongrie. Brusquement, on apprit que le président du Conseil Karolyi abandonnait ses pouvoirs aux soviets. Il y eut un grand mouvement de peuple dans les rues de Budapest, mais pas

LE COMTE KAROLYI (1) ET LE MINISTRE BUZA BARNA (2), A LA FRONTIÈRE
d'émeutes. Voici, en bas, le comte Karolyi (1), agissant pour la dernière fois en tant que président du Conseil pour la délimitation de la frontière hongro-roumaine. Il est accompagné, à gauche, de la comtesse Karolyi (2) et du socialiste Bochm (3); à droite, de M. Buza Barna, ministre de l'Agriculture.

Revolution in the streets of Budapest, front page of *Excelsior*, April 16,1919, Édimedia, Paris.

Photographed news

Magazines coming out less frequently had, in theory, less difficulty with using photogravures. During the course of the 1880s, *Harper's Weekly* (New York), *The Illustrated London News*, the *Illustrierte Zeitung* (Leipzig), and *Le Monde illustré* (Paris) all published photographs, indeed photo-reportages.

That venerable institution *L'Illustration* evidently had some reservations, preferring to continue with its use of woodcuts, which it pushed to the highest degree of perfection by the use of film-on-wood techniques. It sometimes published half-tones, but had a conception of the image which was too artistic to adopt them permanently. It finally did so in 1903, under pressure from the public and its competitors, in a period of financial difficulties, under the leadership of its new editors Victor Depaëpe, then René Baschet. With the Russo-Japanese war and events in Russia and Morocco (1904–1905) *L'Illustration* became a major organ of news, printing between 50,000 and 70,000 copies, using photogravures from 1911. Like its competitors in France and abroad, the magazine arrived enclosed in pages of advertisements and announcements, bound in a cover. Apart from its long-time competitors – *Le Magasin pittoresque*, the *Tour du Monde*, *La France illustrée*, *L'Illustré national*, and *Le Monde illustré* – *L'Illustration* now had new photographic magazines to contend with, inspired by American magazines, like *La Vie illustrée* (1898 by Félix Juven and Henri de Weindel) and Paul Dupuy's *Le Miroir*.[8]

La Vie illustrée also made a great effort to create a variety of page-layouts, cutting round pictures and frequently superimposing them. The death of the president Félix Faure (covered on February 23 and March 2, 1889) and the retrial of Captain Dreyfus (May 25, 1899) prompted a great many "special numbers" with a wealth of complete illustrated sequences composed of both photographs and drawings. Proclaiming a naive faith in the virtues of the photographic document – de Weindel claimed that the three photographs of Dreyfus showed "all aspects of the man" (October 6, 1899), a man who had "become pitiable" (October 6, 1899).

La Vie illustrée discovered to its cost the propaganda function of certain political photographs. Concerning "the Turkish atrocities in Macedonia", Weindel declared categorically: "We are not publishing stories or anecdotes or literary descriptions, but photographs. [...] The Sublime Porte cannot contest their veracity, because a photographic plate cannot lie." The photographs of the atrocities had been taken between September and December 1902, and as soon as the Ottoman police heard about them, they began taking steps to get them destroyed. Not soon enough, however, as several prints escaped destruction.[9]

One magazine which inherited the traditions of both the daily papers and magazines was *Excelsior*, founded on November 16, 1910, edited along the lines of the British illustrated newspapers (*Daily Graphic, Daily Mirror, Daily Sketch*) by Pierre Laffite, who also published *La Vie au grand Air* (1897), the first French sports magazine with its beautiful photographic montages, *Musica* (1902) and *Femina* (1903), luxury magazines aimed at society women, *Je sais tout 1905),* and *Fermes et Châteaux* (1906).

Excelsior was published in a smaller format than the other dailies (37.5 x 54 cm), at first twelve, then ten pages long, with at least three pages of photographs, under the "artistic direction" of Henri de Weindel. Knowing that it was difficult to illustrate diplomatic news, Lafitte stated that his paper would "accord only secon-

8. Started on newsprint paper in 1910, then in 1913 printed on glossy paper and bound into a colored cover.

9. These appeared on January 16, February 27, and March 6 and 13, 1903.

dary importance to politics" and "reduce to summary proportions the description of bloodthirsty or scandalous events, in order to follow "all the brilliance and the excitement of the ever-changing contemporary scene". What was envisaged was journalism of a high-society sort, giving pride of place to literature, the arts, the sciences, sport, grand social events, and fashion. On the front page there was generally a photomontage with oval, round, square, and circular photographs artistically assembled (the assassination of the Spanish President of the Council, November 13, 1912) or else fashioned into a photo-story (the theft of the Mona Lisa, December 14, 1913). Taking a sample of 25 numbers in 1912, it appears that, despite the declared intentions, nearly one third (44) of the 140 photographs published illustrate politics and international relations.[10]

Many of these documents are like "little films". For example, four photographs illustrate rising tension in Serbia, with captions such as "In Belgrade, distribution of clothes and equipment to the reservists", "Serbian reservists, having just received their arms", "In Belgrade, reservists are outfitted on one of the town squares", "Roll-call of Serbian reservists on the old race-track of Belgrade" (October 14, 1912). However, the fact that the front page, and two other pages are given over entirely to illustrations has the end result of more or less completely separating the information that is read from the information that is seen.

News can often be difficult to illustrate: when the *Titanic* sank (April 14–15, 1912), *Excelsior* published 99 photographs and about ten drawings between April 16 and May 24 (the catastrophe took up the whole front page seven times). The paper was reduced to filling in the wait for photographs of people who had been saved with a long series of archive photos presenting the *Titanic* and its interior, portraits of personalities who were on board, and icebergs. On April 22, drawings appeared reconstructing the catastrophe, and, finally, on April 30, the first photographs of the survivors at last appeared.

It should be noted that the drawings have a much greater dramatic intensity than the photographs, which are, on the whole, fairly insignificant. *Excelsior* deals with the sinking of the *Titanic* in the same way as it treats all events, with an excessive number of redundant photos, where one would have been enough. Here, as happened so frequently at this time, it is the number of images and not the intensity of their content that is used to mark the importance of an event.[11]

The First World War marked a clear break. The reduction in the number of pages in the newspapers almost drove out photographs, whereas both the new and well-established magazines (*Le Pays de France, Sur le Vif, La Guerre aérienne, Le Flambeau*) gave preponderance to them – under close supervision from the censor. After the War, press illustration became essentially photographic, with the exception of caricatures, cartoons, and comic-strips.

Then came the flowering of the third generation of photographic magazines with the founding of *Arbeiter Illustrierte Zeitung* (1925), *Vu* (1928), *Life* (1936), and *Match* (1938), the content of which was entirely dependent on illustration by photogravure.

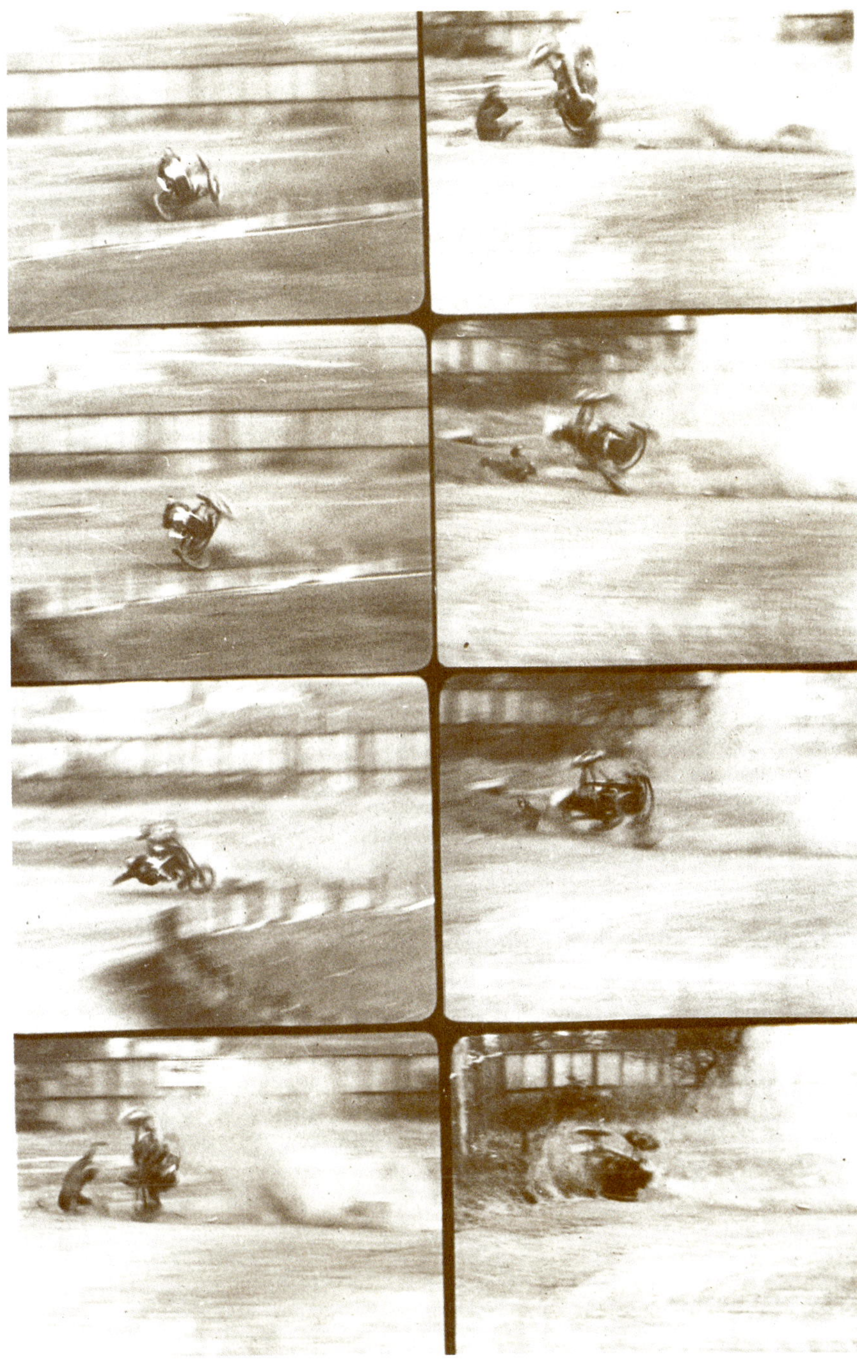

Accident on the motor-racing circuit at Staten Island, October 14, 1927, M.G.M. News Photo, private collection.

10. The other photographs are divided between incidental news (29 items of which only 4 are crimes), society (17 ceremonies, 9 examples of social conflict), aviation (16), sport (16), the weather (6), high society (2), and science and technology (1).

11. P. Albert *et al., Histoire générale de la Presse française*, vol. 3, *De 1871 à 1940*, Paris, P.U.F., 1972.

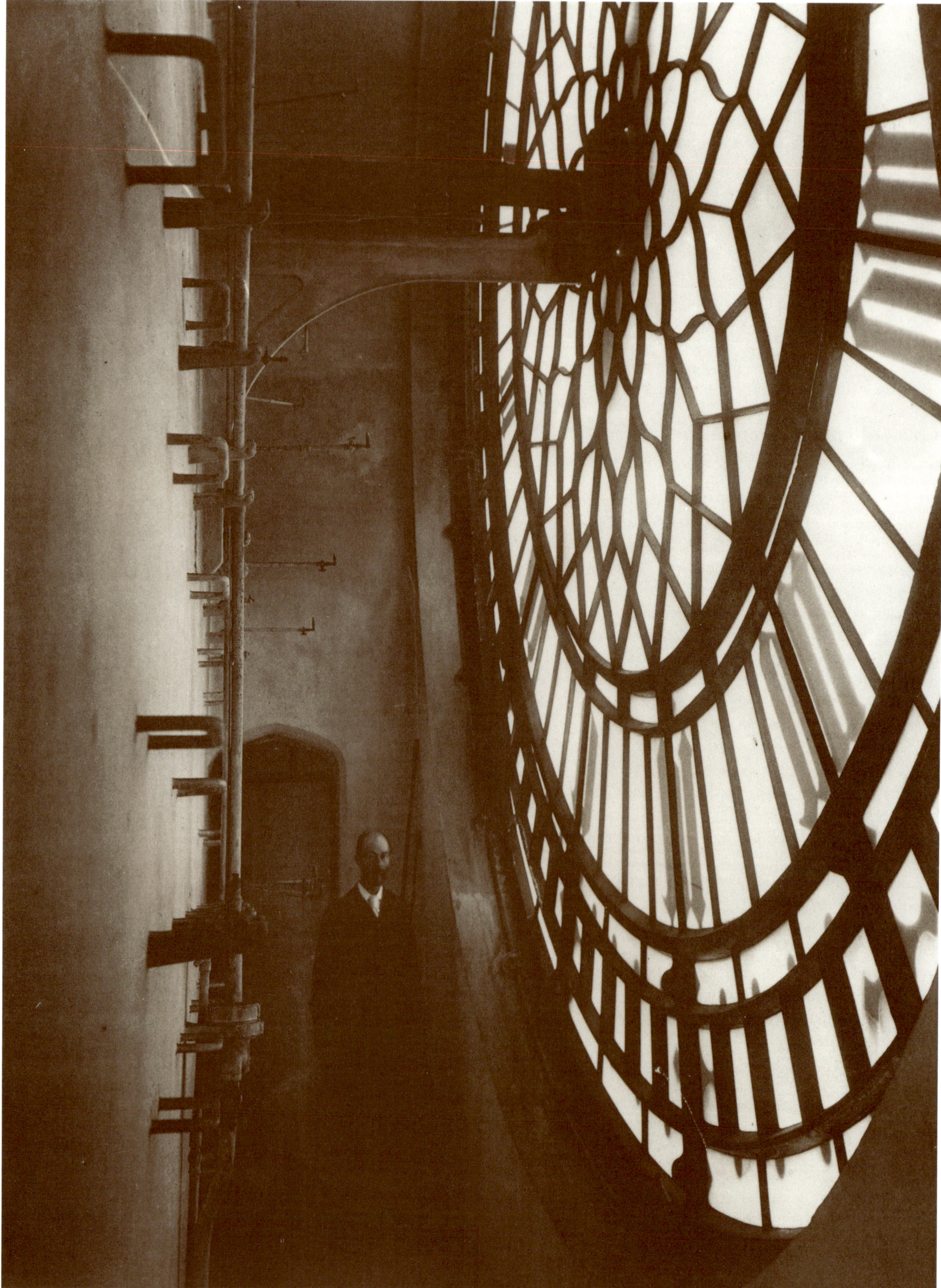

STATES OF THINGS

22

Image and aura

Michel Frizot

Photography captures reality as a series of fragments, as if viewed through a window. It endows each photographed thing with the status of a unique object emerging from the shadows of time, with the authenticity of a typological model. Taking a photograph is like making an archeological discovery, where the object-relic is materially isolated and the most insignificant artifact is transformed into a potential treasure. In the same way, photography idealizes the world around us, communicating it to us through truthful images of lost objects that have taken on an aura unconnected with any sacred origin except its solemnization by photography. Rather than attempting to define photography through hypothetical comparisons with painting, the question is to establish photography's special vocation to be a "new image", and its capacity to establish a new relationship with the world, with time, and with History.

To write a history of photography is also to speculate about the impact of photography on History, on the formation of ideas, and on the way we perceive the world. It has been clearly demonstrated on many occasions – particularly in the press – that photography is not only a source of information "from life", but also an explanation of how things appear at a particular moment, a way of thinking.

Photography is not only a passive observer of History, it plays a leading part – for example, to the extent of giving life and legitimacy to works of art previously appreciated by only a restricted few. "It is often said that Rembrandt has never been better understood nor more appreciated than since the advent of photography", wrote Paul Périer about the passion for photography in 1855.[1]

Photographic fragmentation

At first, it was as a result of the peculiarities of the photographic apparatus itself that a distinct photographic vision emerged. The field of vision of the *camera obscura* or the photographic camera, strictly limited by the parameters of the lens, cuts through the ocular continuum of reality as it unfolds before the spectator's eyes. Photographs – rectangular, flat, illusionist images – present us with a simulacrum of nature that we are asked to recognize as having an authentic reality. This "reality", however, is situated somewhere other than on the paper or glass surface. The pioneers of photography were not disconcerted by these

◄ Sir Benjamin Stone, *Inside the Clock of Big Ben,* 1897, National Portrait Gallery, London

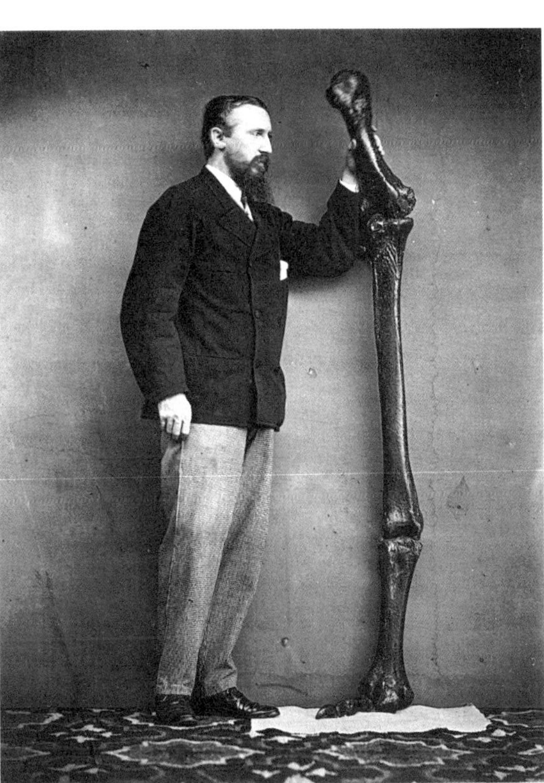

Anonymous, *Colonel Michael with the Leg Bone of an Australian Dinornis,* circa 1872, International Museum of Photography, George Eastman House, Rochester.

1. *Bulletin de la Société Française de Photographie,* 1855, p. 319.

new characteristics of the photographic image (between the realism of the object and its absence); they submitted to its rules with a certain pleasure and, in this way, distanced their art from that of the established tradition of painting, which consisted of carefully balanced shapes, lines, and blocks of color, of the sum of disparate elements brought together by the artist's imagination.

A Second Empire painter, for example, working on an allegorical scene, a still-life or even a landscape, would assemble on a pre-existing surface representations of various fragments which would not naturally necessarily belong together: nymphs, cherubs, plants, and flowers, perhaps, or a vase, statuette or shield, or, maybe, rocks, a bridge, people, animals, and different kinds of trees. Of course, photographers could also arrange the things they wanted to photograph along similar lines. They could place their sitters in a certain pose or carefully arrange a still-life before capturing it with the camera. Indeed, a good number of them were able to build their reputations or their livelihoods on just such an imitation of painting. But the essence of photography did not lie in such work. True photography confines itself to the extreme rigor of the medium, without succumbing to the temptations of an

CHARLES AUBRY,
Long-leafed Hogweed,
circa 1864,
Bibliothèque Nationale,
Paris.

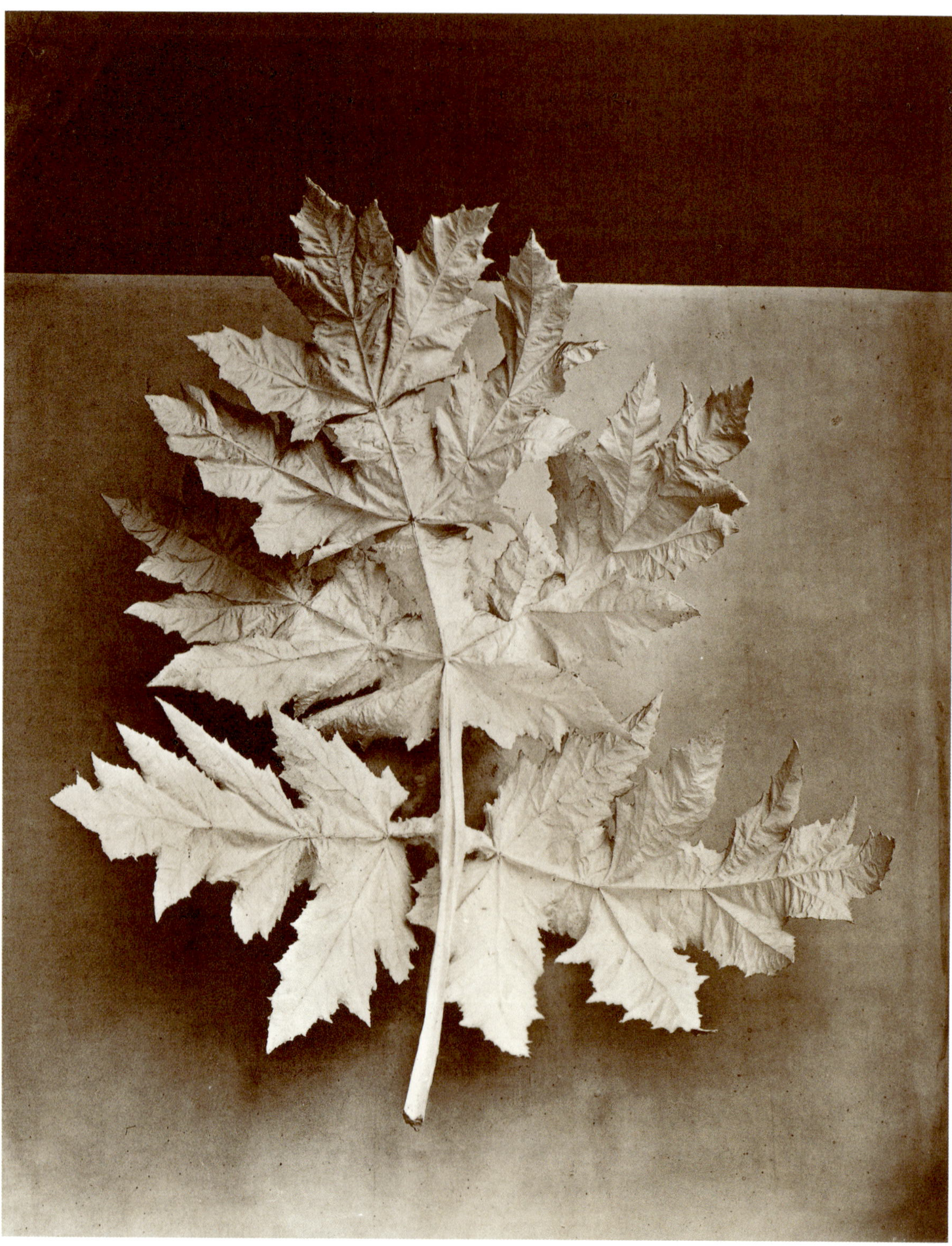

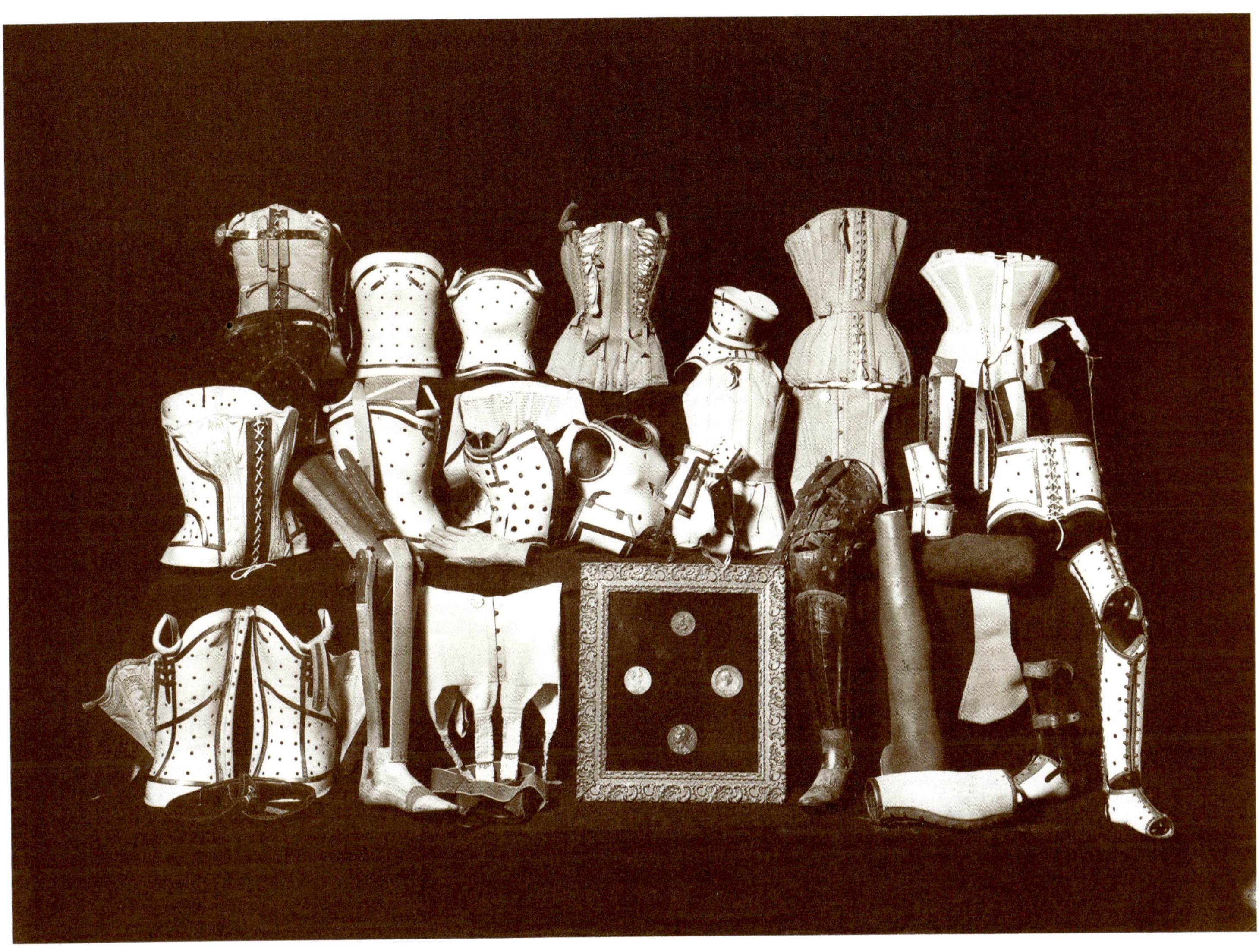

ALINARI,
Advertisement for Dr. Gabbrieli's orthopedic supplies store,
1905,
Museo Alinari, Florence.

older, already established, tradition. A photographic image is created first and foremost by cutting into reality, by slicing through discursive space (in which events, meetings, and dialogues between objects occur). Photography isolates things by removing them from their context, fixing artificial boundaries dictated by a black box with a lens. What goes into the box and is trapped there is dependent only on its technical limitations and on the position of the box in relation to the "subject" in question.

It follows from these pragmatic principles that all photography, of whatever kind, is manifestly answerable for both a presence and an absence: the presence of what was there at a given moment, the absence of everything which found itself excluded from the negative. The painter, by contrast, *includes* in the canvas a space that can be moulded, extended or even merely imagined, with no guarantee of truth or hypothetical presence. The photographer decides what will be included in the image, insofar as it is they who govern the parameters of the instrument. The edges of the frame, slicing through the object, force the photographer either to go nearer, or else to separate the object they wish to photograph from all other objects within the field of view. They are free to point the camera in another direction, to move slightly, to remove certain elements, or to add new ones, found nearby.

Photography is often criticized for tolerating the presence of unwanted objects or figures. However, the photographer is, in fact, constantly choosing between several different versions of reality, by modifying the viewpoint, for example, the better to embrace the presence of a *total* reality, without which they would have to consider the photograph a failure.

It follows from these criteria that within a specific framework photography works by singling out an object, by leading the spectator's eye towards a specific point, and that it must make its objectives clear by managing to curb its ambitions.

In the nineteenth century, photography unhesitatingly assumed this role of fragmentation and isolation (a role that was to be taken up again in quite a different way by advertising), following the tradition, much loved by painters, of studies of drapery, hands, faces, and other details. It

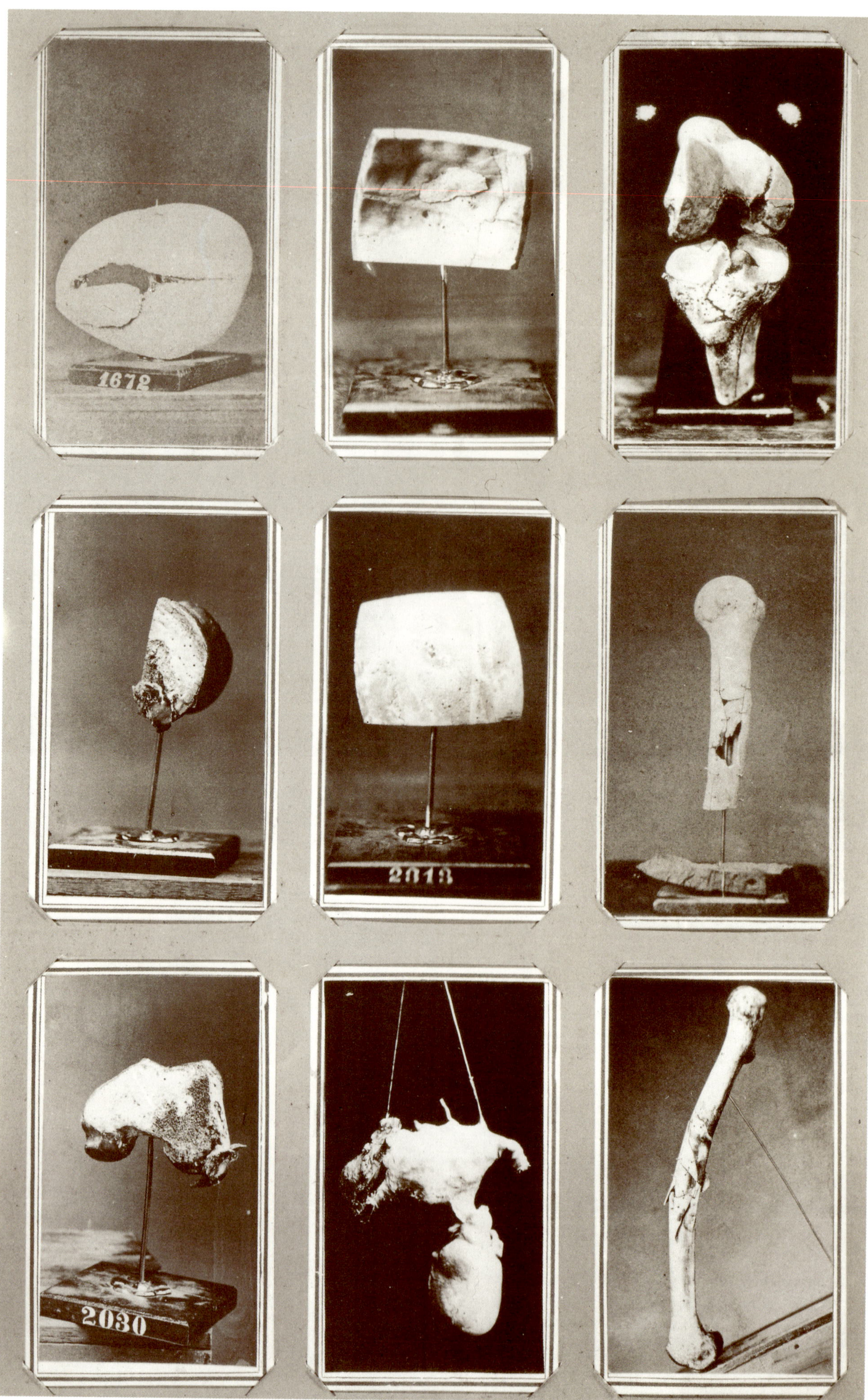
1672
2013
2030

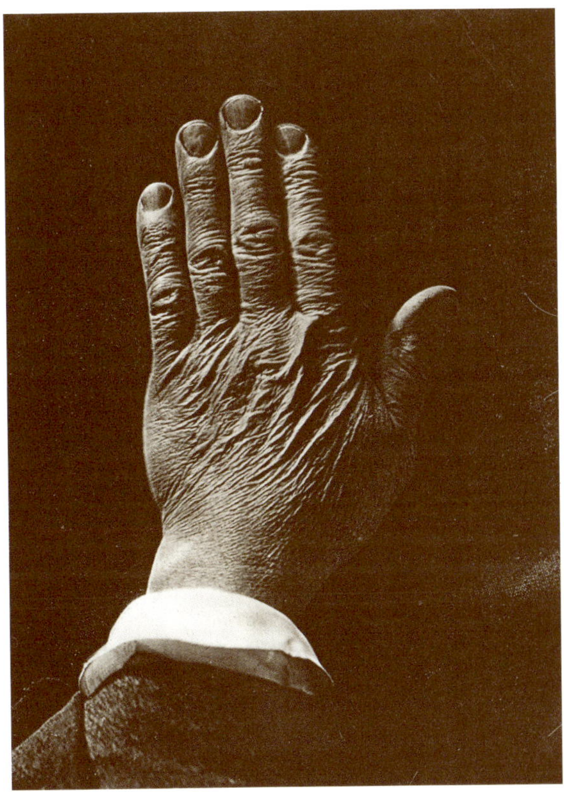

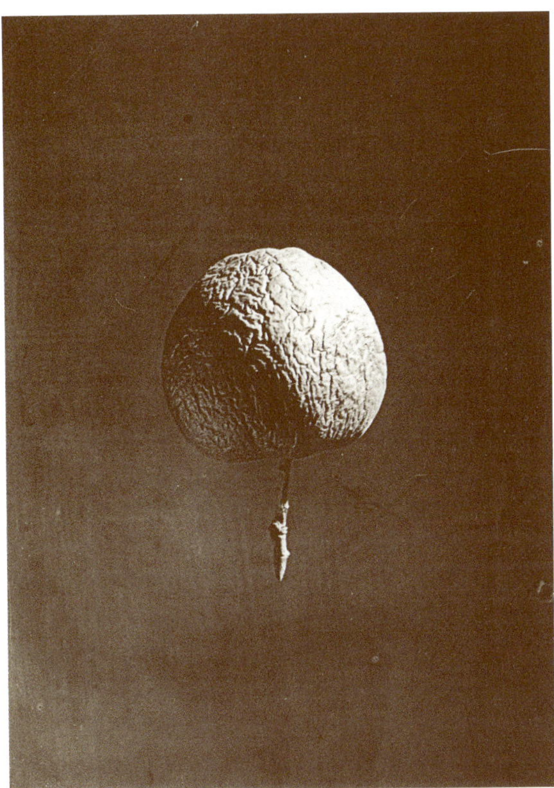

James Nasmyth,
Back of a Hand; Wrinkled Apple,
circa 1874,
University of Texas,
Austin.

2. See the catalogue *L'Invention d'un regard, 1839–1918*, Paris, Musée d'Orsay, 1989, and *Regards sur la photographie en France au XIXe siècle*, Paris, Berger-Levrault, 1980.

became the photographer's task to present or gather up the world in isolated fragments: the Countess of Castiglione's legs, photographed by Pierson, the new Paris street furniture, recorded by Marville, the trees and rocks of the Forest of Fontainebleau, Talbot's broom or Durandelle's picture of a capital on the newly built Opéra.[2] All these constitute a series of catalogues of subjects with poetic virtues, where each selected element is imbued with a life of its own, an autonomy, an *identity* not dissimilar to that which is enjoyed by human beings.

A little later in the century, avant-garde painting was not too proud to adopt – through a process of osmosis – the style of composition that today we call "photographic". To see this, we have only to look at Manet's asparagus (1880) or bunch of violets (1872), or Van Gogh's shoes (1886), piles of books (1887) or chair (1888). The tradition of the "motif", begun with the calotype, is inherent in the nature of the photographic process. This abrupt manner of plucking an object out of real life, isolating it, and singling it out by recording it in minute detail is already typical of the style of the first photographers: Hippolyte Bayard's study of a cart in the middle of the road, Talbot's shelves of books or his haystack, Le Secq's cut-up tree, Louis Robert's ox head on a table, Regnault's ladder.

This style is sometimes described as recording, documentary, but this is to misunderstand the photographer's intention. A "document" must serve a cause, a use, an archive, a case study. Payard's tipcart was not photographed to be of

◄◄ R. B. Bontecou,
Bone Fragments,
1864, Burns Archive,
Washington.

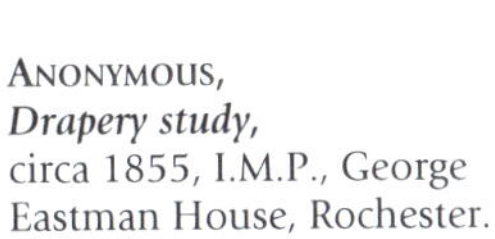

Anonymous,
Drapery study,
circa 1855, I.M.P., George
Eastman House, Rochester.
▼

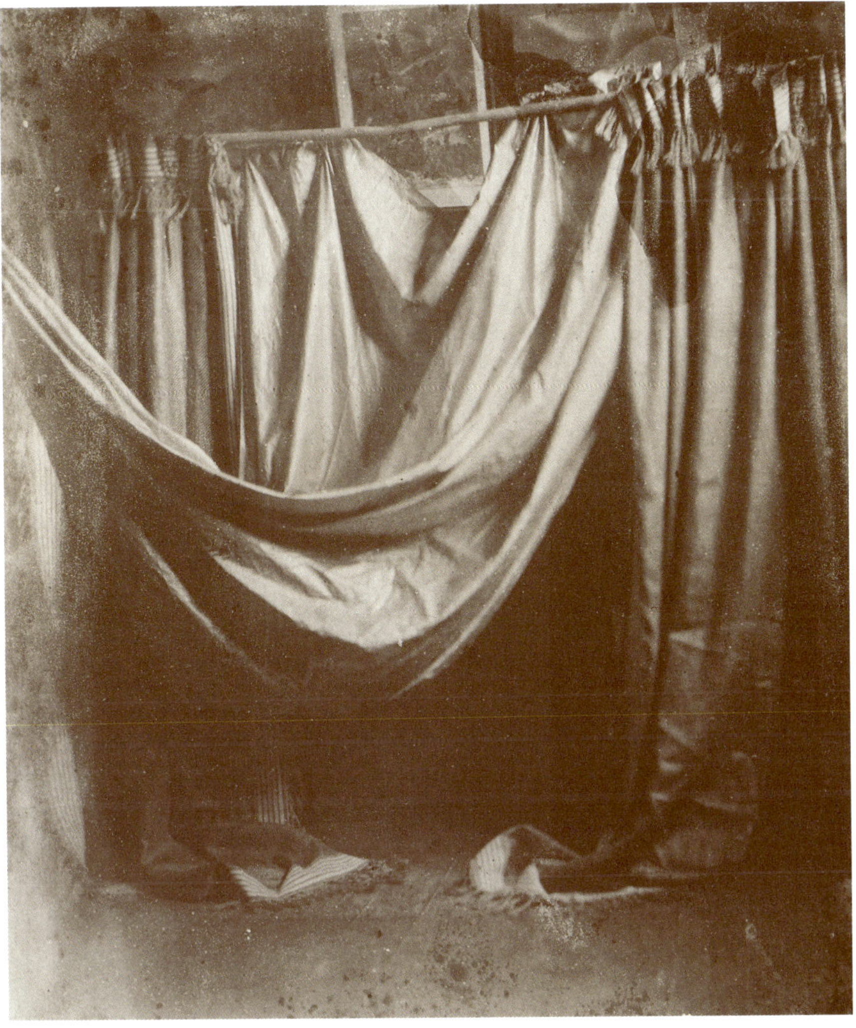

Photography and archeology

Archeology turned itself into a scientific discipline by gathering together what was known – by its very nature scattered – within the covers of books, which, following the example of the great eighteenth-century *Encyclopédie*, embraced two types of information: text and illustrations, with a way of cross-referencing between the two. From the nineteenth century onwards, photography has been consistently involved in the recording of archeological finds, as well as the environment and the circumstances of their discovery. This visual information has always been destined for use in the documentary records of the excavations themselves or for additional specialized reference files (architecture, pottery, sculpture, jewelry, burials). Such files contributed to the "publication" of the excavation in its entirety, or of individual finds, and were the logical outcome of the efforts to restore and reconstruct that motivate the archeologist.

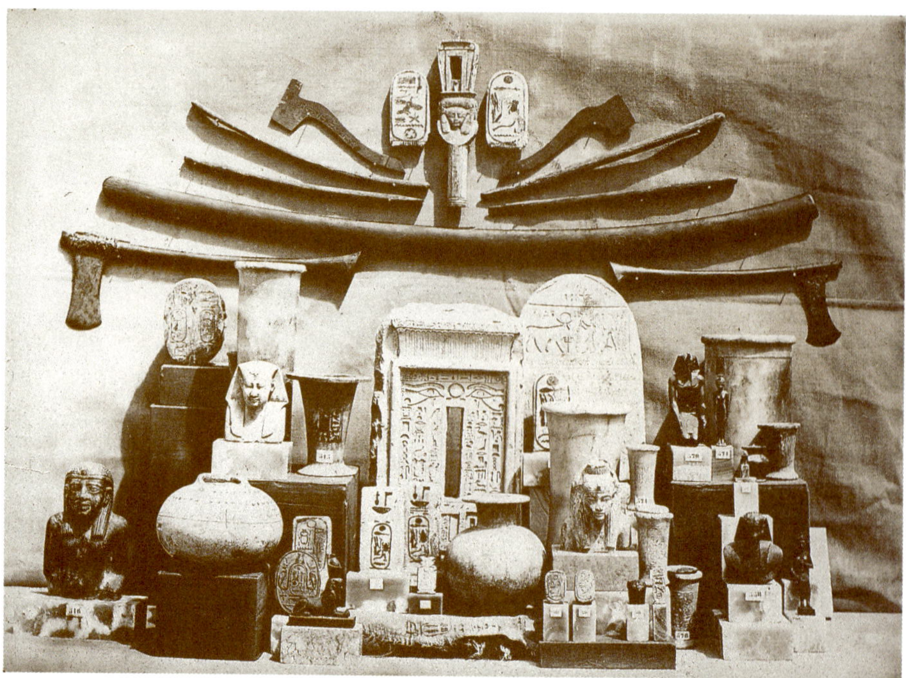

Délié and Béchard,
from *Album du musée de Boulaq,*
1872, private collection.

After it became possible for photographs to be made on paper, archeologists and their patrons were keen to adopt this new medium (one of the first examples of such photographs taken during an excavation is *Le serapeum de Memphis découvert et décrit par Auguste Mariette*, Paris, Gide, 1857). However, as is well known, the instability of photographic prints and the high cost of reproducing them meant that the popularisation of photography was slow to develop. Instead, a "transcription" was often made, drawn either by hand or by a photomechanical process (particularly heliogravure and photolithography). More rarely, the text was accompanied by original photographs, pasted into the volume. Nevertheless, however produced, the illustrations in the majority of archeological works were based on photographic originals. Examples are works such as Espérandieu's *Recueil général des bas-reliefs de la Gaule romaine* (1907–), the *Corpus Vitrearum* or the *Inventaire des richesses d'art de la France*.

Good examples of the use of photography in archeology from the mid-nineteenth century (in addition to the early works mentioned elsewhere of Du Camp, Salzmann, Greene, and others) are the 165 photographs taken by Banville for the *Album photographique de la mission remplie en Egypte par le vicomte Emmanuel de Rougé*, Paris, L. Samson, 1865, *Exploration archéologique de la Galatie et de la Bithynie [...] exécutée en 1861*, text by G. Perrot, photographs by J. Delbet, Paris, Firmin-Didot, 1872 (using Lemercier lithophotographs, Poitevin process), De Luynes, *Voyage d'exploration à la mer Morte*, Paris, Arthus Bertrand, 1877, photographs by L. Vignes engraved by Nègre, P. Trémaux, *Exploration archéologique en Asie Mineure*, 1862–1868; W. J. Stillman, *The Acropolis of Athens*, London, F. S. Ellis, 1870.

However, a much more straightforward use of photography was to make a record of a collection of objects. Photographs were published showing either artistically arranged assemblages of disparate objects or collections displayed as in a museum. This category includes the beautiful photographic work of Richebourg in *Trésors d'art de la Russie ancienne et moderne*, text by T. Gautier, 1859 (particularly armor from the palace of Tsarsko-Selo). Another example of the genre shows Egyptian antiquities: *Album du Musée de Boulaq*, 40 photographic plates by Délié and Béchard, with an explanatory text written by Mariette Bey, Cairo, Mourés et Cie, 1872; we can also mention J. S. Robles, *Tesoro artistico del Palacio Real de Madrid*, Madrid, 1871, G. Demay, *Des pierres gravées employées dans les sceaux du Moyen Âge*, Paris, 1877, and the beautiful series by Clifford and Laurent on the artistic treasures of Spain. An important contribution is that of Schliemann with his *Atlas trojanischer Altertümer*, Leipzig, Brockhaus, 1874 (photographs by Zaphyropoulos).

When, eventually, retrospective works were possible which brought together the sum of combined knowledge on a subject, photography became the indispensable proof of the assertions made in the text; for example, in M. Dieulafoy, *L'Art antique de la Perse, Achéménides, Parthes, Sassanides*, Paris, 1884–1885 (heliogravures by Dujardin) or G. Le Bon, *La civilisation des Arabes*, Paris, Firmin-Didot, 1884, illustrated with engravings and photogravures taken from photographs (in the preface, the author even envisages substituting the truth of photographs for a redundant text), E. Curtius, F. Adler, and G. Hirschfeld, *Die Ausgrabungen zu Olympia*, 1876–1880, and Alice and Augustus Le Plongeon, *Sacred Mysteries among the Mayas and the Quiches 11,500 Years ago*, New York, 1886. In 1904, in *Methods and Aims of Archeology*, London, Macmillan, the archeologist W. M. Flinders Petrie includes a chapter on photography.

Michel Frizot

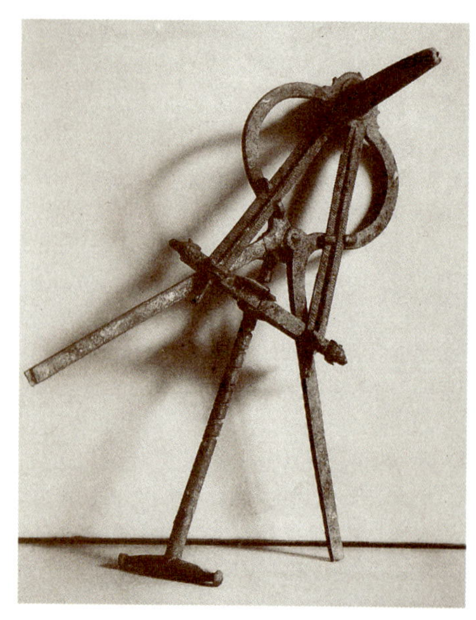

Giorgio Sommer,
Antique surgical instrument,
Naples Museum, circa 1870, private collection.

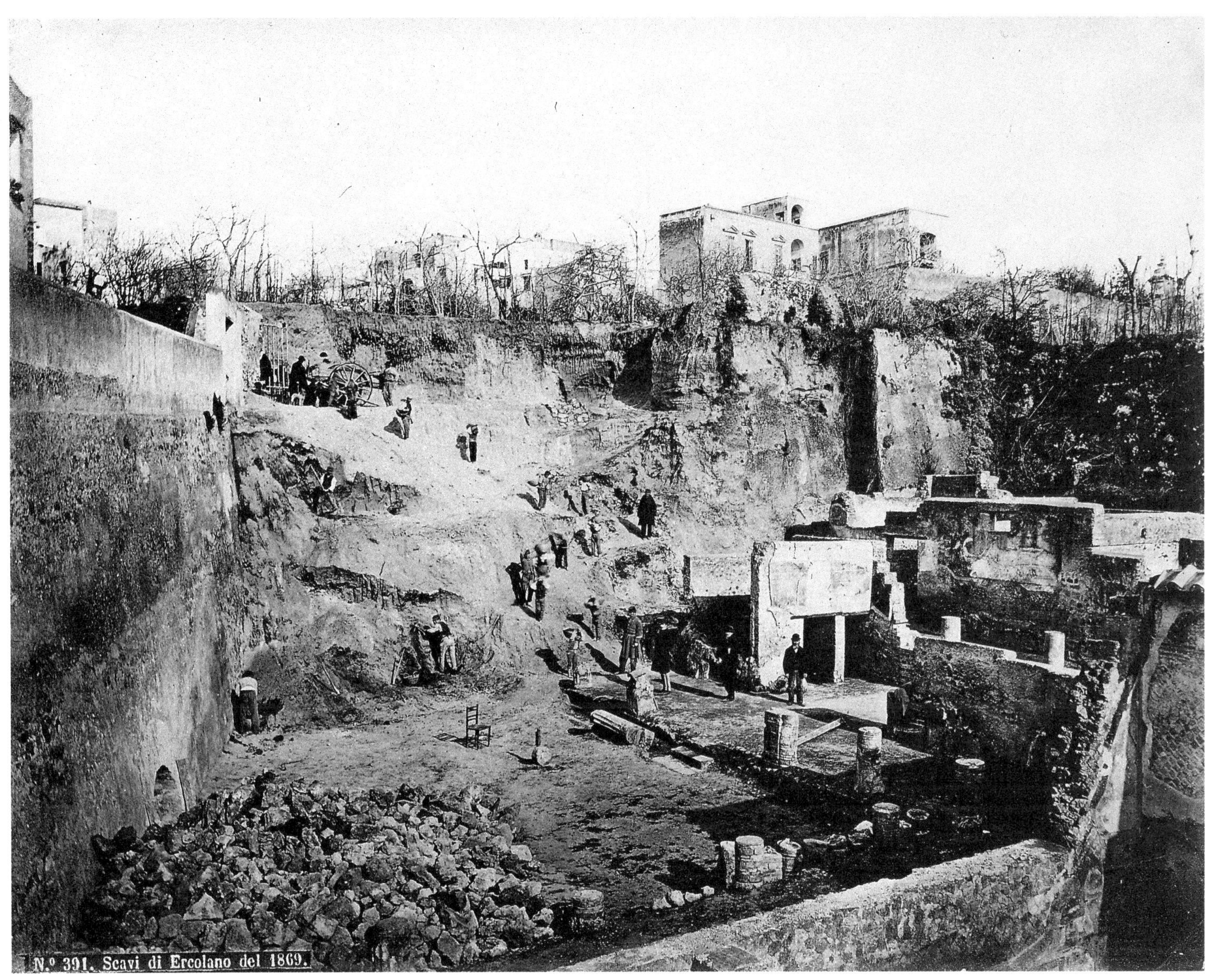

Giorgio Sommer, *Excavations at Herculaneum in 1869*, private collection.

use to cart builders or for the history of transport; it is a willed work of art, with purely photographic intentions and constraints, manifesting an entirely personal interest in the object for its own sake, following criteria that are hard for us to imagine but impossible to refute.

This "tradition" can be traced right through to the work of Atget, whose "documents", far from depriving the fragment of meaning, find, through surrealism, an enhanced subjective value: "each element appears to know something about a hidden presence while preferring not to speak about it; it is in this application of silence that the object itself acquires a particular intensity".[3] In this there is something of contemplation, of fascination for the unknown detail.

The more that photographic technique was able to aim at extreme precision, the more the photographer tended to be satisfied with the information potential of a single object whose image, in the lack of actual possession, increases our pleasure in discovery.

A vocation for archeology

Ernest Lacan, the art critic who sang the praises of the new art of photography at the Paris Universal Exposition of 1855, clearly saw the way in which it could decontextualise and isolate, paralleling the dislocation of the archelogical ruin: "the admirable figures of the Propylaea in Athens, the bas-reliefs, the capitals, the broken columns of the Parthenon, the inscriptions half-obscured by the hand of time", or, at Baalbek, "the piece of granite fallen only yesterday from the collapsed vault". This photographic fragmentation of the physical environment was extended to human beings and domestic objects: "Indian huts, tents of banana leaves, groups of Mexicans standing in their strange costumes on some marketplace" (referring to Tiffereau's photographs of Mexico).[4]

There is no doubt that parallels can be drawn between the historical development of archeology and photography. In both, the process of investigation developed in a context that valued

3. B. Marbot, in *L'Invention d'un regard*, *cit.*, p. 156

4. E. Lacan, *Esquisses photographiques à propos de l'Exposition universelle et de la guerre d'Orient*, Paris, 1856, pp. 19–20.

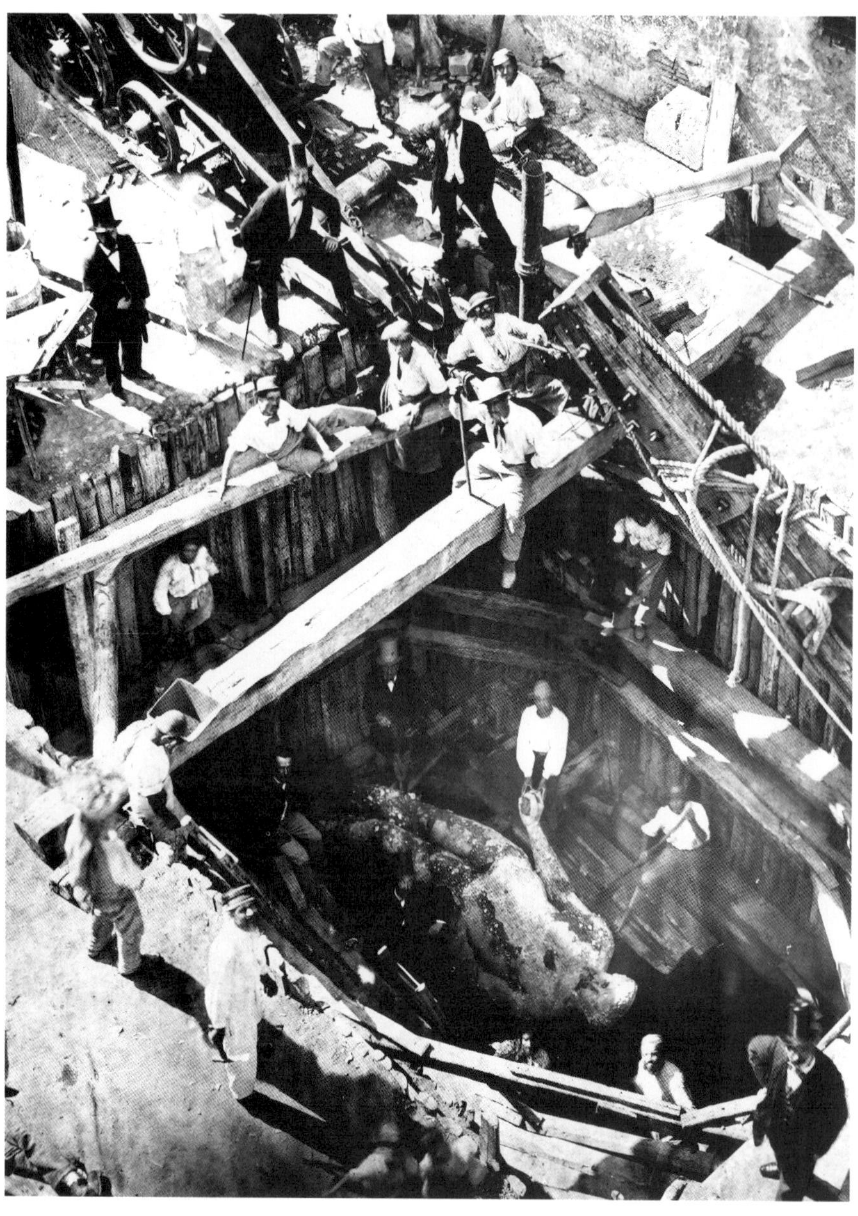

ANONYMOUS, *Excavation of the Mastai Hercules*, 1864, Archivo Fotografico Comunale, Rome.

exactitude, proof – what semiology has called the "index". Archeology and photography both work through extraction, dichotomy, the separation of the fragment from the disparate whole in which it is found (be it a geological layer or a layer from the surrounding visual world). They understand one another; one reveals the object to the light of day, the other uses light to record the object.

They share, too, a significant relationship with time. Archeology actualizes the dated specimen, the "state of the thing" at the moment of taking the photograph, a unique unrepeatable instant. When we look at an old, original photograph, this inscription of the date of production of the image itself is clearly attached to all its parameters: process, support, color, appearance, manner of taking, framing – everything that makes an image appear "of its time". If photography is sometimes perceived as an accessory of archeology, it is also, at the same time, a tautology or a paradigm. By isolating things, photography, regardless of its aim, "archeologizes" in its turn everything that it isolates, fragments or separates. It "transforms the object into a statue" – on a pedestal or in some place which becomes, despite itself, a setting to show it off – exposing it like a work of art, like a recently excavated discovery. That which photography presents – within its strict framework, in the rigor of its viewpoint – is like the resurrection of the archeological artifact, the exhibition of a thing that has lost its essential context of development and use, and now finds itself endowed with a new identity, a new role, made concrete in the instant of the taking of the photograph.

As early as August 1839, in his speech announcing the invention of the Daguerreotype, Arago had emphasized the power of the fledgling art of photography to focus on a fragment or a detail. The photographic lens would make it possible to reach "the highest and most inaccessible parts of buildings". Arago saw archeology (another new science, seeking to understand the past, rather than merely piling up collections) as being the principal beneficiary of the new possibilities for recording – at least so long as the art of portraiture remained inaccessible – allowing the completion with total verisimilitude of Champollion's *Description de l'Égypte* (1804-1826) and *Monuments de l'Égypte et de la Nubie* (Didot, 1845).

In place of the indiscriminate collecting of archeological objects that initially took place at Herculaneum and Pompeii (at the end of the eighteenth century and for a good part of the nineteenth) came the practice of creating a photographic archive of the objects themselves, of the circumstances of their discovery, of their context (walls, archeological layers, coins) – the only true indications for the date and for an understanding of the production and use of the object in its own time. Like John B. Greene, who had worked in Egypt and Algeria in 1854, and Théodule Devéria, who worked in Egypt (1858) with Mariette Bey (finds from excavations, including the Greek sculptures of the Memphis serapeum), so now John H. Parker (1806–1884) set up a project in 1866 to photographically record the remains in Rome, from antiquity to the Renaissance, using local professional photographers. From the 1870s, archeological excavations in the modern sense of the term were undertaken, where the concern to understand and to record (sometimes with photography) that which had been irretrievably damaged in digging was uppermost. By 1869, Parker had already amassed a collection of 1,500 photographs. The complete collection which, by 1879, amounted to 3,300 photographs, was destroyed in a fire in 1893.[5] A Roman photographer, Romualdo Moscioni, active from

5. *Historical Photographs: A Catalogue of 3,300 Photographs of Antiquities in Rome and Italy, Prepared under the Direction of J. H. Parker*, London, 1879; 220 surviving negatives are today in the American Academy of Rome. Parker published *The Archaeology of Rome*, Oxford and London, 1874–1876. See also B. Brizzi, *Roma, cento anni fa nelle fotografie della raccolta Parker*, Quasar, 1975.

6. *Raccolta delle fotografie esistenti nello stabilimento commerciale di Romualdo Moscioni*, Rome, 1921 (24,700 pictures). See *Fotografia Archaeologica 1865–1914*, American Academy of Rome, De Luca, 1979.

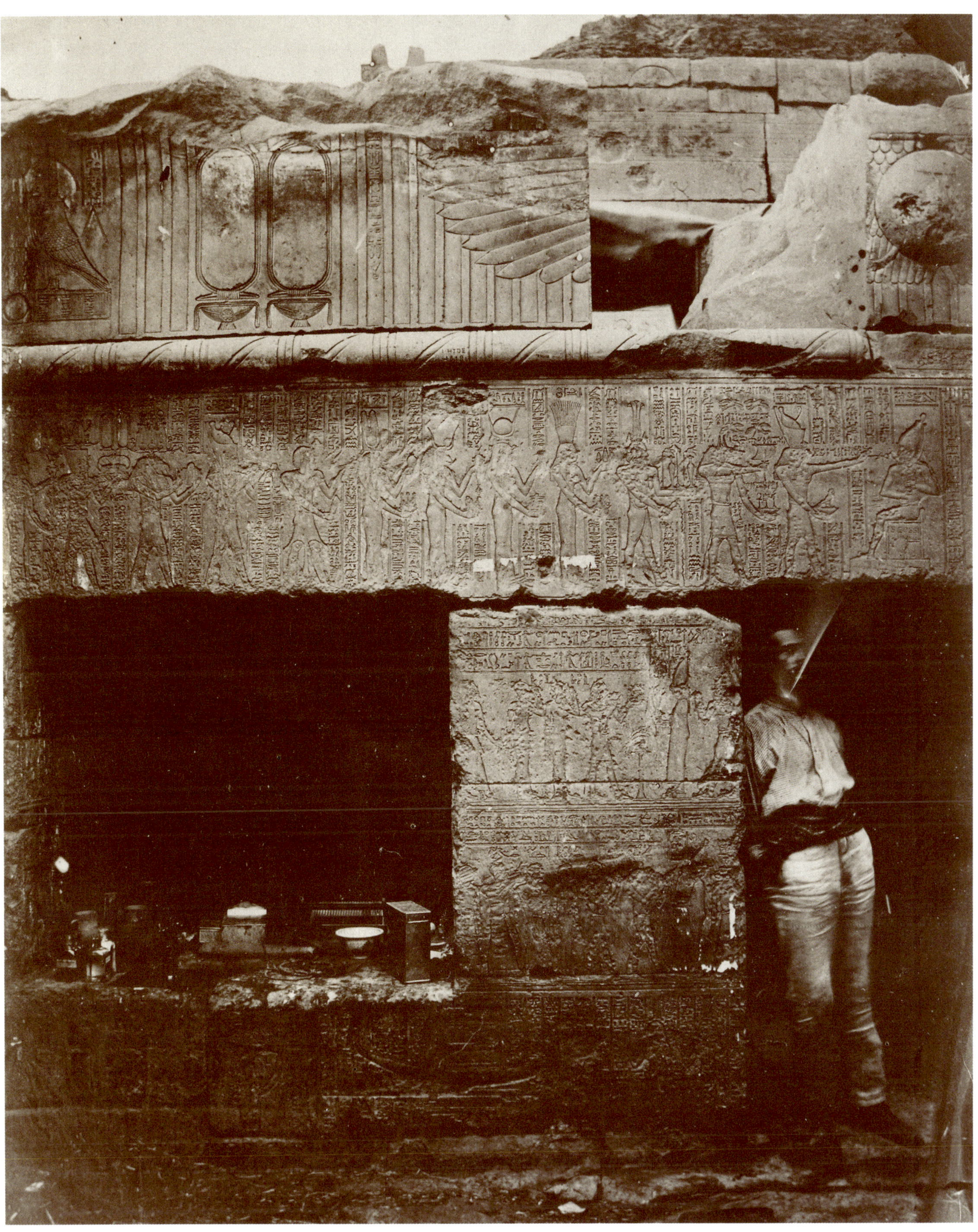

ANONYMOUS,
Photographic equipment, placed in the opening of an Egyptian temple,
circa 1870, Agfa Foto-Historama, Cologne.

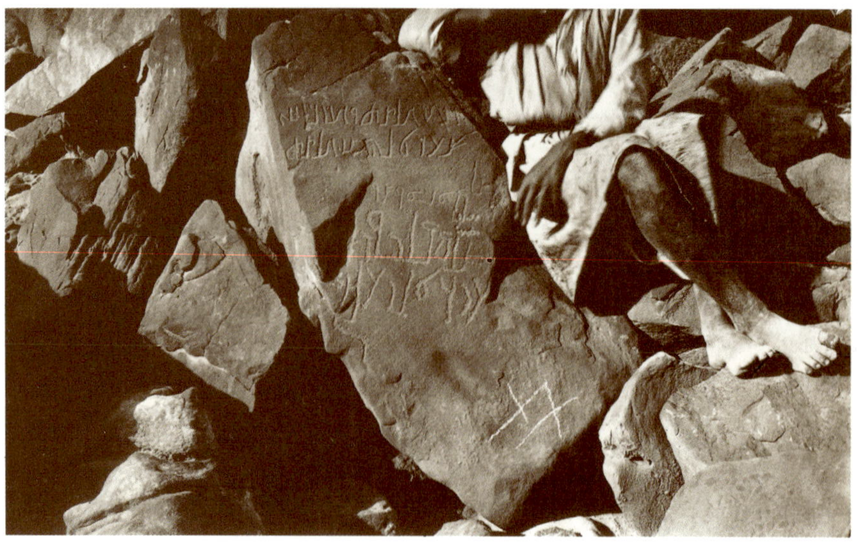

JAMES MCDONALD,
Inscription at Sinai,
1869,
University of Texas,
Austin.

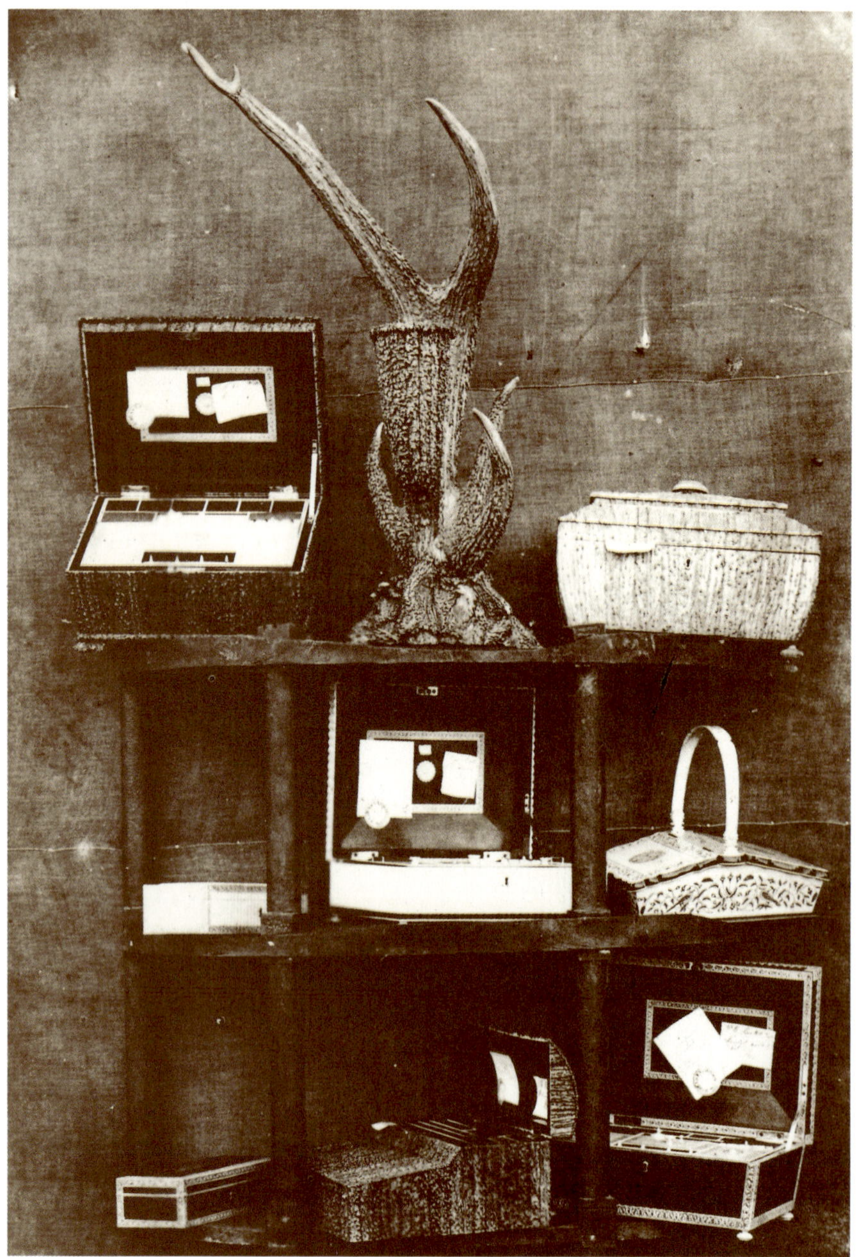

LINNAEUS TRIPE,
Ivory and horn objects from Vizagapatam, India,
1857,
private collection.

1868, put together a collection devoted to Christian excavations and antiquities (24,700 subjects).[6] A passionate archeologist like Esther Boise Van Deman, involved from 1901 in the excavations of the Roman Forum, made considerable use of photographs of stone and brickwork. In addition there were also photographic collections devoted only partly to archeological documentation. These interpreted the notion of *monument* more broadly, with forays into "views" and street scenes such as those in the Alinari and Anderson collections.[7]

Collection, book, monument

From 1860, with the increasing ease of photographic duplication and then with the possibilities opened up by photomechanical processes, the books dedicated to archeology which used photographic illustrations become too numerous to list in entirety (see box). The two volumes of *Egypt and Palestine Photographed and Described by Francis Frith* (1858 and 1859) had print runs of 2,000 copies. Félix Teynard and Louis De Clercq, who both worked with paper negatives, also published collections of 160 and 222 photographs respectively on Egypt and the Middle East.[8]

The album, or portfolio, was the first substitute for a classified reality in which photography found its justification as archeological data. On the other hand, the amassing of records, outside the closed structure of a book, began to constitute what were real files of visual material. The first application of photography had been to record hieroglyphs, then its use was extended to the totality of the survivals of the past. But now, in these archeological volumes, photography was no longer simply "illustration", it was a bearer of truth. The text constantly asks us to refer to the photograph, using expressions like "on the page facing" and "see below", as if it were the object itself – as if the single viewpoint of a photograph contained within it all the useful information needed. Photography had turned quasi-archeological, in so far as it was a scientific operation creating its own neutral language suitable for any subject,[9] while the volume containing photographs (whether original photographs pasted in by hand or photomechanical reproductions) became an archival entity.[10] The book or its substitutes – collections, portfolios, atlases – became places in which to present documentary evidence operating around units of language, and categories of reference such as pottery, weapons, coins or sculpture. The result was that photographed objects could be described or catalogued, thus becoming identifiable, distinct, and sepa-

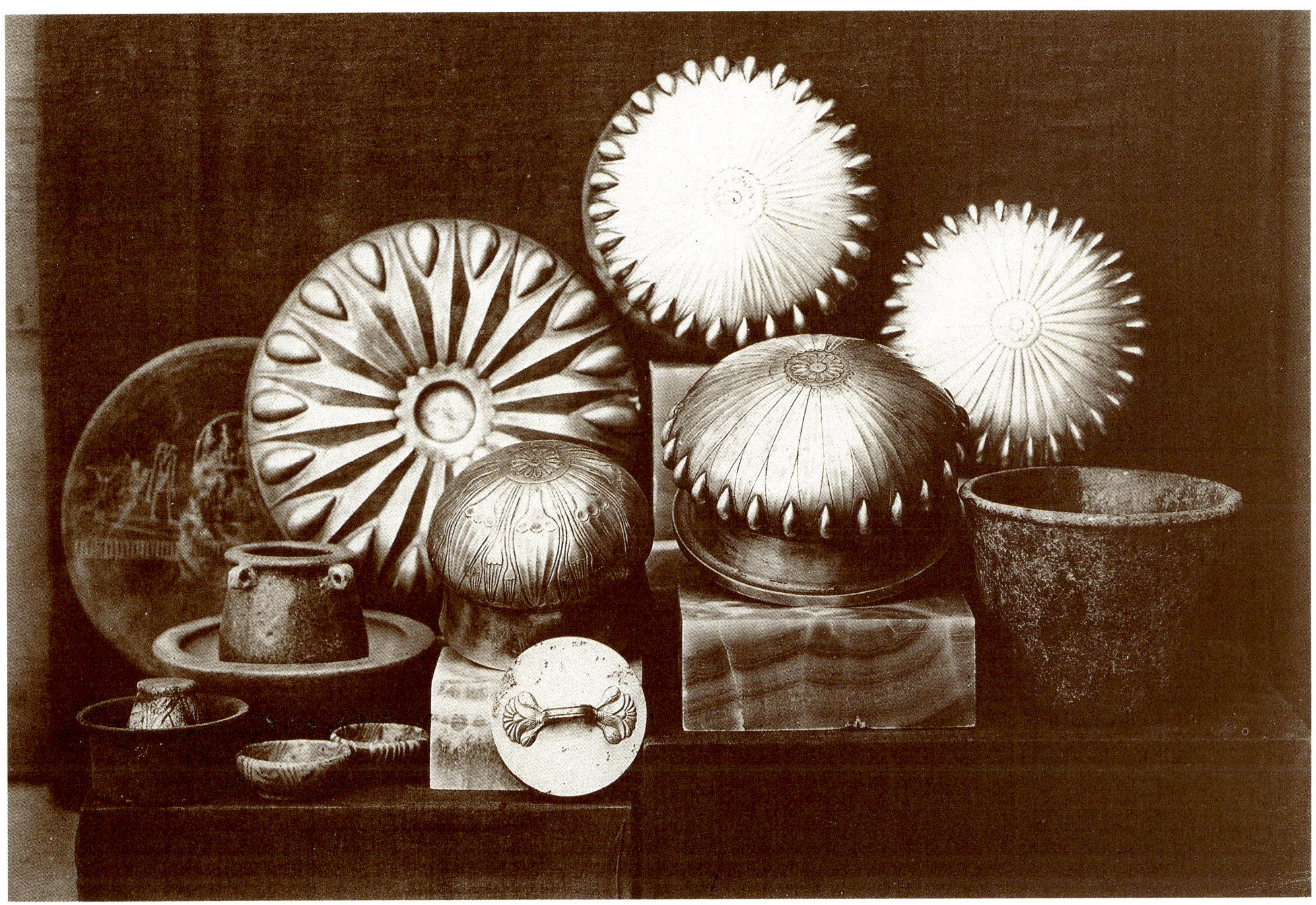

Délié and Béchard,
from *Album du Musée de Boulaq*,
1872,
private collection.

rable one from the other, ready to be categorized. The photographic image endows the three-dimensional object with a recognizable form (*Gestalt*) making it part of a classified type, just as the formal characteristics of a plant place it in its botanical family. Photography merely makes operative this imaginary translation of the real object into a generic type: "photography and casts bring us for the first time documents that are indisputable; the originals are before our eyes."[11] From the 1870s, the photographic collection became the modern equivalent of the cabinet of curiosities, where all things lost their disparity within a system of unified vision. What one lost in the real diversity of material, one gained in the possibilities for the comparison of forms.

Photography's ability to conserve and perpetuate gives it a role with regard to a modern concept, that of the "monument" – one that was symptomatic of the preoccupations of the nineteenth century. It is perhaps possible to see a similarity between the monument, seen as a witness of and ghost from ancient times, and the photographic document which perpetuates its memory, even allowing us, in a sense, to revisit it.

Baudelaire recognized this positive side of photography, saying: "Let it save crumbling ruins from oblivion, books, engravings, and manuscripts, the prey of time, all those precious things, vowed to dissolution, which crave a place in the archives of our memories".[12] Thus archeology, a science and a technology whose birth and development were attendant on those of photography, can be seen as the model which established, in the real field of "application", the nature of photography as a footprint, a cast of a lost object, forgotten then rediscovered, duplicated, exposed. In this field of application, to represent is not to symbolize, but to reproduce "identically" by producing a two-dimensional replica which is a photograph.

To place photography at the service of archeology in this manner is a way of replacing the *object* with its photographic *image*, which refers back, whatever object it is, to the idea of the archeological or museum label. We know that several early photographers (Talbot, Llewelyn, Humbert de Molard, Brébisson) had scholarly interests in the sciences of classification, in botany, biology, archeology, geology, and anthropology. For them, photography represented an indexing system. Whether botanical images, compositions with stuffed animals by Llewelyn, monkeys' skeletons in the British Museum by Fenton (about 1857) – part of a collection that included busts of Roman emperors, examples of

7. Anderson Collection of 40,000 photographs, today housed, along with the Brogi collection, at the Museo Alinari, Florence.

8. F. Teynard, *L'Egypte et la Nubie: sites et monuments les plus intéressants pour l'étude de l'art de de l'histoire*, Paris, Goupil, 1853–1858; L. De Clercq, *Voyage en Orient, 1859–1860: villes, monuments, et vues pittoresques*, 6 volumes.

9. E. Trutat, *La photographie appliquée à l'archéologie*, Paris, Gauthier Villars, 1879.

10. *The Treasury of Ornamental Art: Illustrations of Objects of Art and Vertu; Photographed from the Original and Drawn on Stone by F. Bedford*, London, Day and Son, 1856.

11. D. Charnay, *Les Anciennes Villes du Nouveau Monde: voyage d'exploration au Mexique et dans l'Amérique centrale 1857–1882*, Paris, Hachette, 1885, p. 8.

12. The Salon of 1859, in *Baudelaire: Selected Writings on Art and Literature*, trans. with an introduction by P. E. Charvet, London, Penguin Books, 1992, p. 297.

goldsmiths' work, and shells and fossils – the imperial armor in the Madrid museum by Clifford and Laurent (about 1860), all these images come within a unified catalogue of nature and of History.

We could cite numerous examples – initially from nineteenth-century photography but extending logically and increasingly into the twentieth century – of "things" that have become subjects for photographs that, most frequently under the guise of "documentation", are presented as archeological remains, even when they make no such claims. Originally, this style of solemn presentation came in two variants: either in situ, in the place of discovery (and sometimes still half-buried in the ground) or else on a plinth, often draped, before a neutral background, generally a sheet of cloth.[13] The aim of such a background was to avoid detracting from, or breaking the unity of time attached to, the excavated object.

This insistence on exhibiting artifacts out of their geographical and temporal context derives from the tradition of re-erecting antique sculpture in our towns and museums that began in the Renaissance. In the same way, the "monument", extracted from time and its historical context, is venerated, a symbol of both the continuity of history and the enduring nature of art. For Auguste Salzmann, who undertook what could be described as a "visual" excavation in Jerusalem and the Holy Land in 1854, "photographs are no longer mere accounts, but facts, and facts of a conclusive force".[14] Photography offers us an image which is certainly unique, chosen from an infinity of possible viewpoints, but without unnecessary commentary, definitive in its one-way logic and its peremptory affirmation. Recording by photographic means rapidly became the normal conclusion of an archeological discovery. "Every important piece of art or architecture has been consecrated by photography", wrote Victor Place on the publication of *Ninive et l'Assyrie*, with its considerable use of photographic documentation.[15]

13. This neutral background was the sole accessory used by Nadar and other early portrait photographers.

14. Preface to *Jérusalem: étude et reproduction photographique de la Ville sainte, depuis l'époque judaïque jusqu'à nos jours [...]*, 1856, quoted in *Félix de Saulcy et la Terre sainte*, Paris, RMN, 1982, p. 118.

15. *Ninive et l'Assyrie*, Paris, Imprimerie Impériale, 1867–1870.

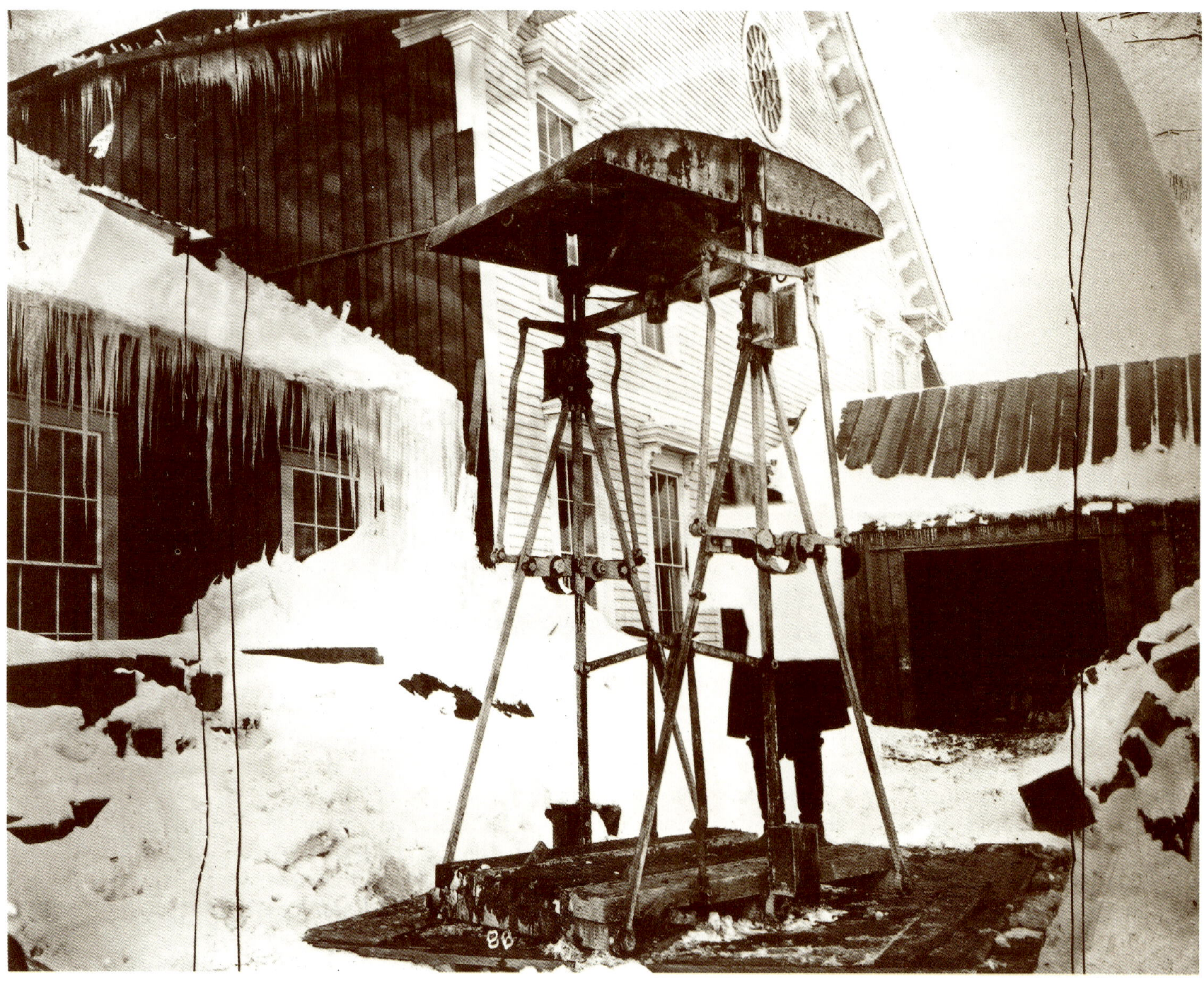

TIMOTHY O'SULLIVAN, *Savage-Cage, Virginia City,* 1867, International Museum of Photography, George Eastman House, Rochester.

Nostalgia and aura

The stylistic and chronological identity of an ancient monument can be perceived only through representative fragments, through the systematic and analytical dismantling of all its elements (capitals, inscriptions, decoration). This dichotomy is very natural for photography. In return, all photography, whether involving a building, a plant, some ruin, an ancient or a recent artifact or even an animal (particularly when it is placed in the center of the picture, framed, with a plinth and a neutral background), is perceived as offering the spectator a timeless "monument" which is worthy of interest and trust.

In the subjects chosen by one of the first users of the calotype process, Alfred Normand (awarded the Prix de Rome for architecture), there exists a sort of memorial equivalence between an aloe at Pompeii, the Aeropagus in Athens, and an antique in the Villa Medici.[16] The same is true of the work of Talbot, between views of the bust of Patroclus and a tree in winter, a coach, a facsimile of an ancient text, and the statue of Sir Walter Scott's dog.[17] The generic image of these photographs is that of the Egyptian mummy or, perhaps, the casts left by bodies submerged by lava at Pompeii, exhibited in situ like a vase, a sculpture or an artifact.

The object is "monumentalized" by the photograph. The fashion for documentary and souvenir photography aimed at the tourists of the Middle East (Bonfils, Frith, Béchard, Zangaki, Hammerschmidt) served only to increase this idealisation of the object. Photography is a work of signaling, of locating. It makes a model of the genre out of each thing it captures, a fragment of civilization that one can almost carry away. The monument (reality) and the document (image) are both the bearers of a message – a message that one has all the time in the world to decipher in the photograph because its truthfulness is no longer in question: "very often one discovers in a print something that one had not noticed at the time", wrote Eugène Viollet-Le-Duc.

To photograph something amounts to *exposing* it, to showing it in one of the great universal exhibitions so characteristic of the second half of the nineteenth century, for which the model was the Great Exhibition of the products of industry from all nations that took place in the Crystal Palace in London in 1851. On this occasion, the prize-winning exhibits were illustrated by photographs (salt prints made by Henneman, one-time assistant to Talbot, from negatives by Owen and Ferrier) of subjects as disparate as a Jacquard weaving loom, a column of granite, a collection of pens, domesticated animals, a locomotive, a vacuum machine, an ivory throne, telescopes, and a monumental clock. The things at the exhibition, of which a selection were preserved in photographs, are contemporary monuments that photography has "archeologized", turning them into finds from an excavation, to jewels from the modern period worthy of resurrection in a future age. Photography "pre-archeologizes" the contemporary object, predestining it to a future excavation.

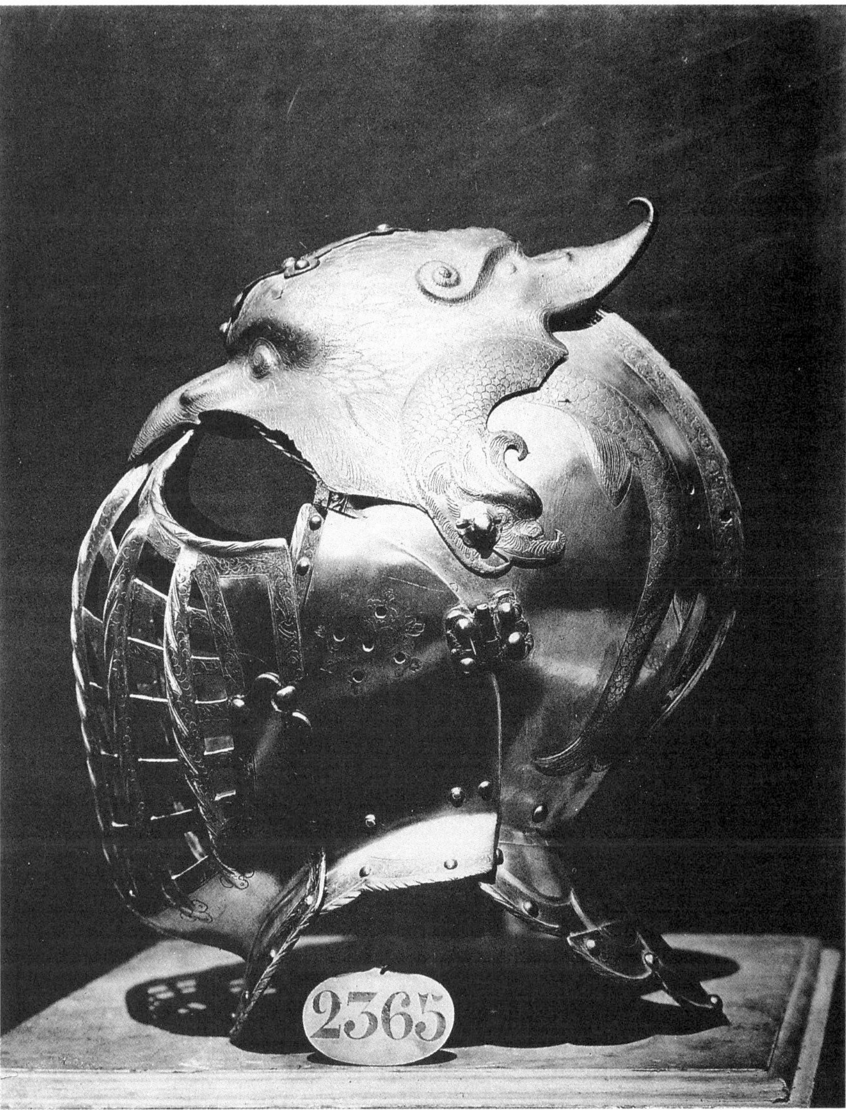

CHARLES CLIFFORD, ***Helmet from the Royal Armory,*** Madrid, circa 1861, Fraenkel Gallery, San Francisco.

In any case, the border between the ancient object and the product of industry was not clearly defined in the nineteenth-century exhibitions, and the fashion on every continent (Philadelphia, 1876; Chicago, 1893) for thematic exhibitions (historical, ethnographic, agricultural, bovine) reinforced an ambiguity that culminated in the retrospective displays (including one of photography itself) at the Paris Exposition of 1900.

Whether the subject is a Lebanon cedar, an obelisk from Karnak or a Chinese junk, any photograph of an object that has been singled out will have an indirect or unconscious reference to

16. *Alfred Normand: calotypes 1851–1852: photographes d'Italie, de Grèce et de Constantinople*, Gorle and Bergamo, Grafica Gutenberg, 1978.

17. See H. von Amelunxen, *Die aufgehobene Zeit*, Berlin, Nishen, 1988.

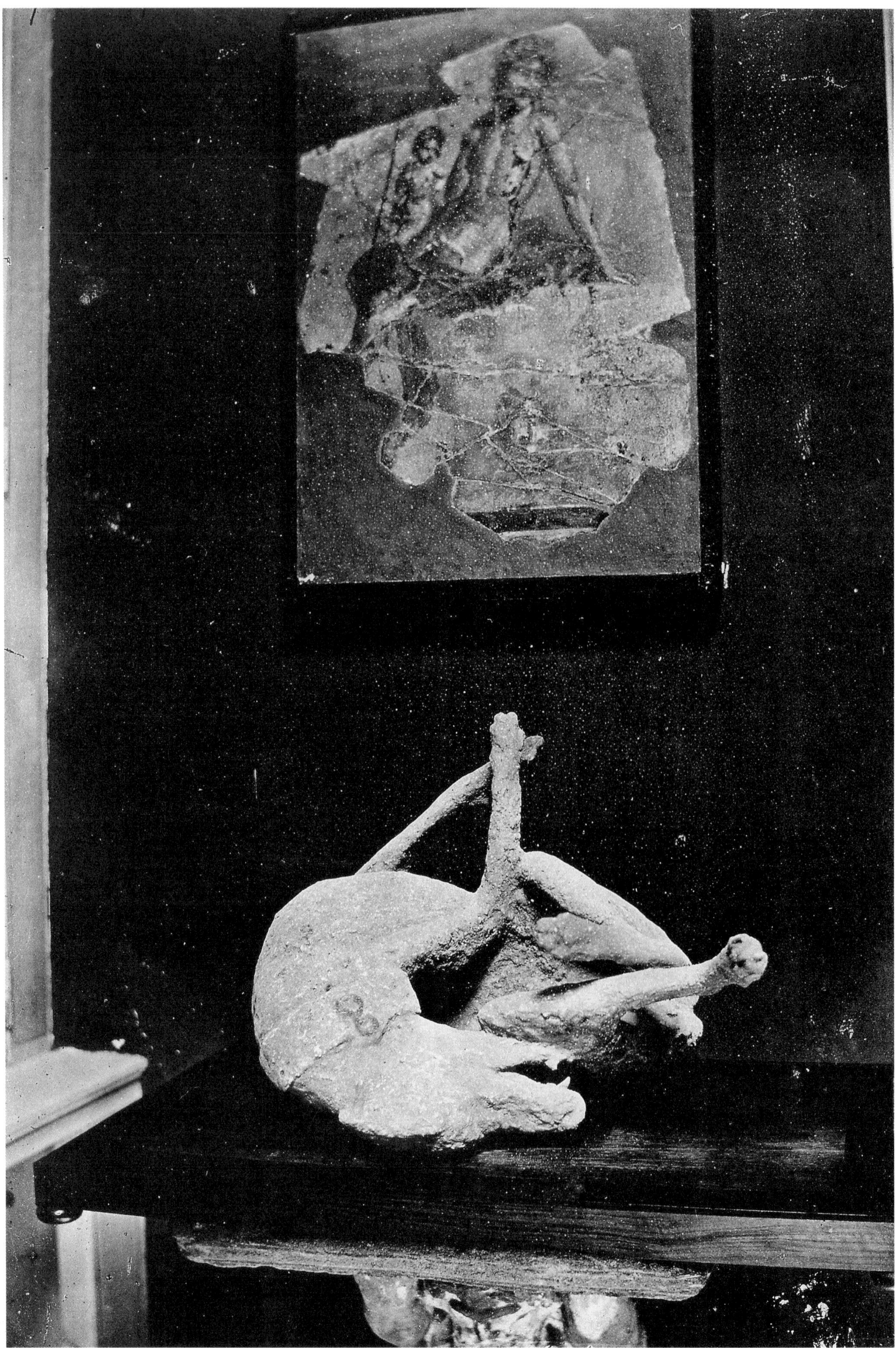

a double "scene of origin": firstly, the archeological discovery, when the antique statue is brought back to life and secondly, when the sacred object (the statue of the god) is exhibited in its new setting.

This, later, exhibiting of the photographs themselves has the function of intensifying the statement and increasing the symbolic value of the object, this time for a wider audience. To photograph a wicker basket, a breastplate or even a man on a bicycle in the neutral surroundings of the studio is to give these objects the appearance of idols, fallen but rehabilitated, set up again outside any modern, and hence disturbing, context, removed, above all, from any kind of comparison with another "fragment" from a particular period. In any image, the mind of the onlooker expects to find a unity of time that intuitively symbolizes that of the photograph but which also refers to a mythical time when the thing which is now seen removed from its geological layers appeared in situ, with its own unique aura and sacred meaning.

It is significant that for most of the nineteenth century photography was unable to do more than capture the image of immobile objects. The consequence was felt in the "Apollo complex" (the statue discovered and exposed) that attaches itself to the photographed object.[18] The photographic act confers a presence on things, a corporeality that is almost tangible, the appearance of a relic, of a fragment saved through good fortune and chance from being entirely lost, the fragment of a lost body whose aura – the sacred fluid – through the photographic image, still leaves an authentic *footprint*.

In a famous passage, all too frequently cited on the slightest of excuses, Walter Benjamin attributes to a work of art an authenticity that is linked in his opinion to "the presence in time and space" of the original work, "its unique existence at the place where it happened to be". Benjamin goes on to regret that photography, a modern means of "reproduction" of a work, causes it to lose, as a result of this ontological displacement, the authenticity that anchors it in a given, precise, certain time, in a "material duration" from which it derives its value as historical evidence.

According to Benjamin, the result of the upsurge of photography (like that of the cinema and the phonograph), by multiplying the copied exemplars and by disconnecting the object from its tradition and from its origins, is the loss of the object's ritual value, the relationship between human beings and things in a concomitant time – what he calls its aura. "That which withers in the age of mechanical reproduction is the aura of the work of art."[19]

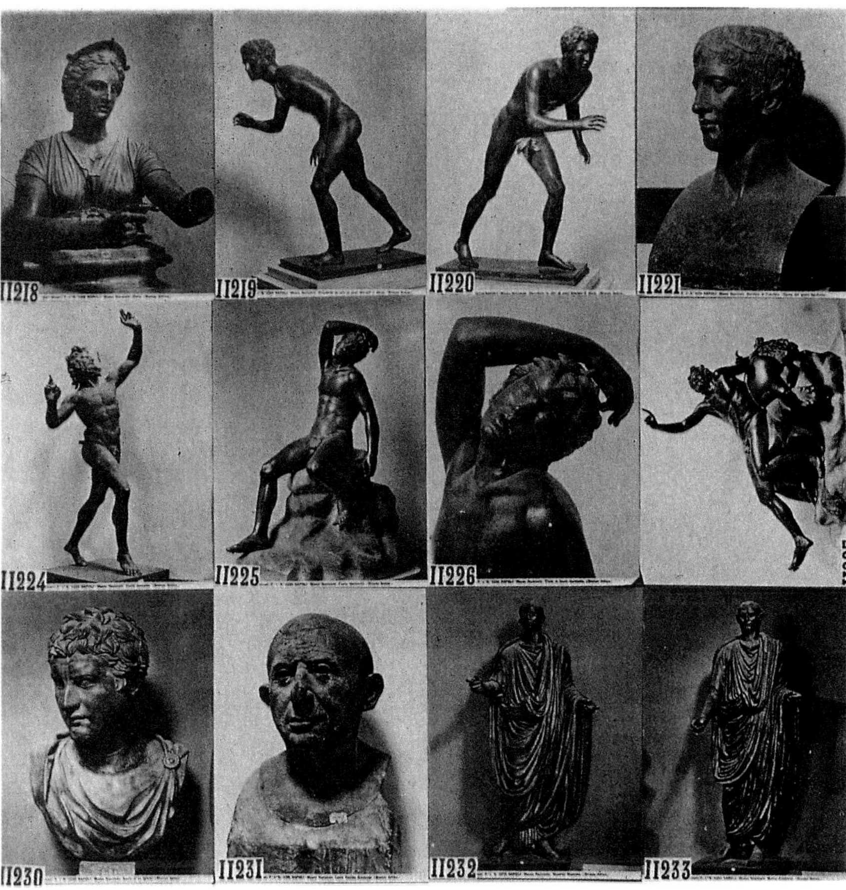

ALINARI,
Sheet catalogue of archeological photographs available,
(detail),
circa 1870,
private collection.

◄ MICHELE AMODIO,
Mould of cast left by a dog,
Naples Museum
(Pompeii excavations, 1878),
circa 1880,
private collection.

But perhaps, following on from all the older forms of representation, and certainly present in painting, there is an aura special to the photographic image, to its particular way of presenting things, to its imaginative version of the truth. This is why, when we look at – or rather, when we exhibit – these photographs, we are re-exposing the true object not any longer in its authentic state, but in its translation into a relic, inevitably with a date and more surely archeological than any real object.

This aura is not only an intrinsic property of the object; it also comes from the eyes and the imagination of the onlooker. If it is true that the photographic image causes the art object, unique in its splendor, to lose a little of its aura, at the same time, photography's extraordinary power of mimicry imbues all things photographed with the aura of the original, the aura of a generic type, of a timeless apparition which has been long awaited.

18. *Pygmalion photographe: la sculpture devant la caméra, 1844–1936*, Geneva, Muséed'Art et d'Histoire, 1985, and *Photographie/Sculpture*, exhibition catalogue, Paris, Centre National de la Photographie et RMN, 1991.

19. W. Benjamin, *Illuminations*, in *Walter Benjamin: Essays and Reflections*, ed. H. Arendt, New York, 1968.

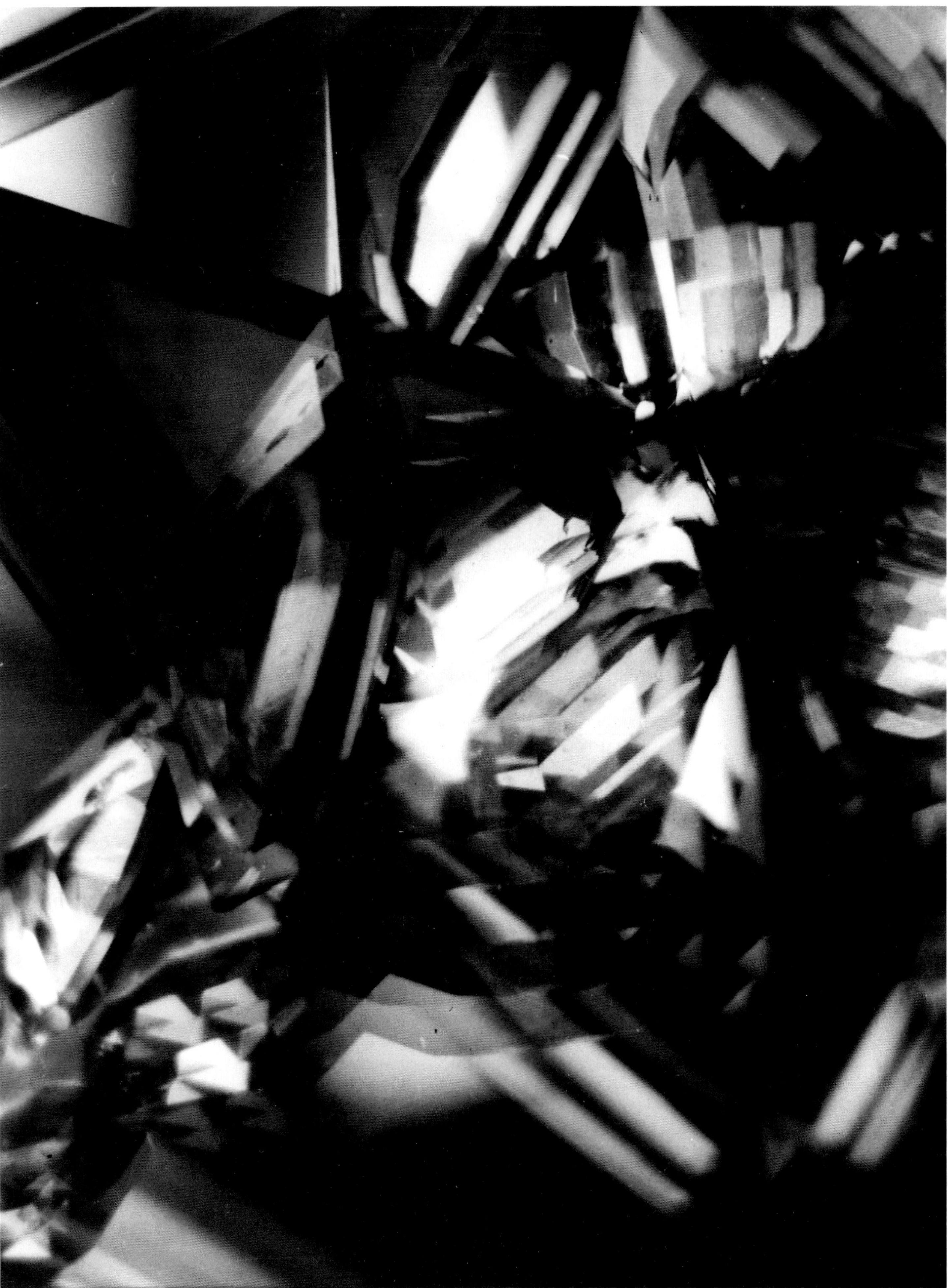

ANOTHER KIND OF PHOTOGRAPHY

23

New points of view

Michel Frizot

At the beginning of this century, a new approach to photography emerged, initially in the Pictorialist milieu in America, centered on Stieglitz, and then strengthened by the European avant-garde. Unbridled urbanization, the acceptance of mechanization, the architecture of skyscrapers, and the innovations made in photography during the First World War revealed a world of unexpected images, very different from the formal ideals of Pictorialism. The photographer-artist reclaimed his origins as an amateur with all of the associations that went with that – spontaneity, free choice, and immediate personal involvement, devoting himself to the search for something which lay beyond the optical surface.

The new century did not mark any comparable turning point for photography. Ruptures were to occur later, triggered by the new types of camera that began to appear at the end of the nineteenth century. Photographers were to experience a change in status, while the images they produced had a greater candor and less social restraint, opening up new perspectives influenced by the artistic tendencies of those involved. More than ever, the question of "art" in photography was becoming crucial, and recognition of the photographer as an artist was increasingly sought, if not granted.

The changes that took place at the beginning of this century reached a point of no return at the time of the First World War. It is generally accepted that the appearance of the last issue of the American magazine *Camera Work*, in 1917, in which all the photographs reproduced were by Paul Strand, marks the arrival of a style that provided the foundation for the essentially international aesthetic of the 1920s. To regard this as a rupture is relevant, however, only to the "artistic" branch of photography, fostered by the powerful photo-clubs of the late nineteenth century.

Other more general factors contributed to this change of mood in photography. In a major article which was published in the same issue of *Camera Work*, Paul Strand invoked the "objectivity" of photography, which defines its limits, but also constitutes its "inherent qualities". "This means [having] a real respect for the thing in front of him, expressed in terms of chiaroscuro (color and photography having nothing in common) through a range of almost infinite tonal values [...] The objects may be organized to express the causes of which they are the effects or they may be used as abstract forms, to create an emotion unrelated to the objectivity as such [...] The existence of a medium, after all, is its absolute justification."[1]

Strand, whilst proposing a new relationship between photographer and subject through the intermediary of an "objective" camera, also insisted on an aesthetic born of "real life" and drawn from the American experience, "without the outside influence of Paris art-schools". This need for independence had been demonstrated by the example of Stieglitz, who, since 1911–1912, had publicised the innovative work of artists such as Rodin, Picasso, and Matisse through the pages of *Camera Work*. It is perhaps significant that *Camera Work* ceased publication at the moment when the United States entered the war against Germany.

Growth of the city

This split had not been a natural result of Pictorialism, even if many of the protagonists of that movement were, together with Paul Strand, to make the step towards the "New Photography". It was the very psychology of the photographer that had changed; he had become freer, now carrying

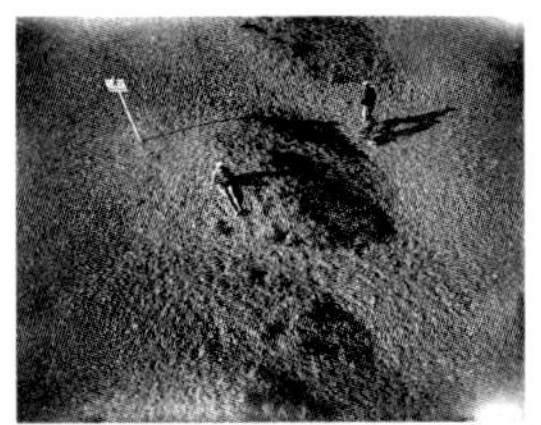

ANONYMOUS,
Cliché taken from a photographic kite,
circa 1910,
private collection.

◀ ALVIN LANGDON COBURN,
Vortograph,
1917,
University of Texas, Austin.

1. *Camera Work*, no. 49/50, June 1917, pp. 3–4, in *Camera Work: A Critical Anthology*, ed. Jonathan Green, Aperture, 1973, pp. 326–327.

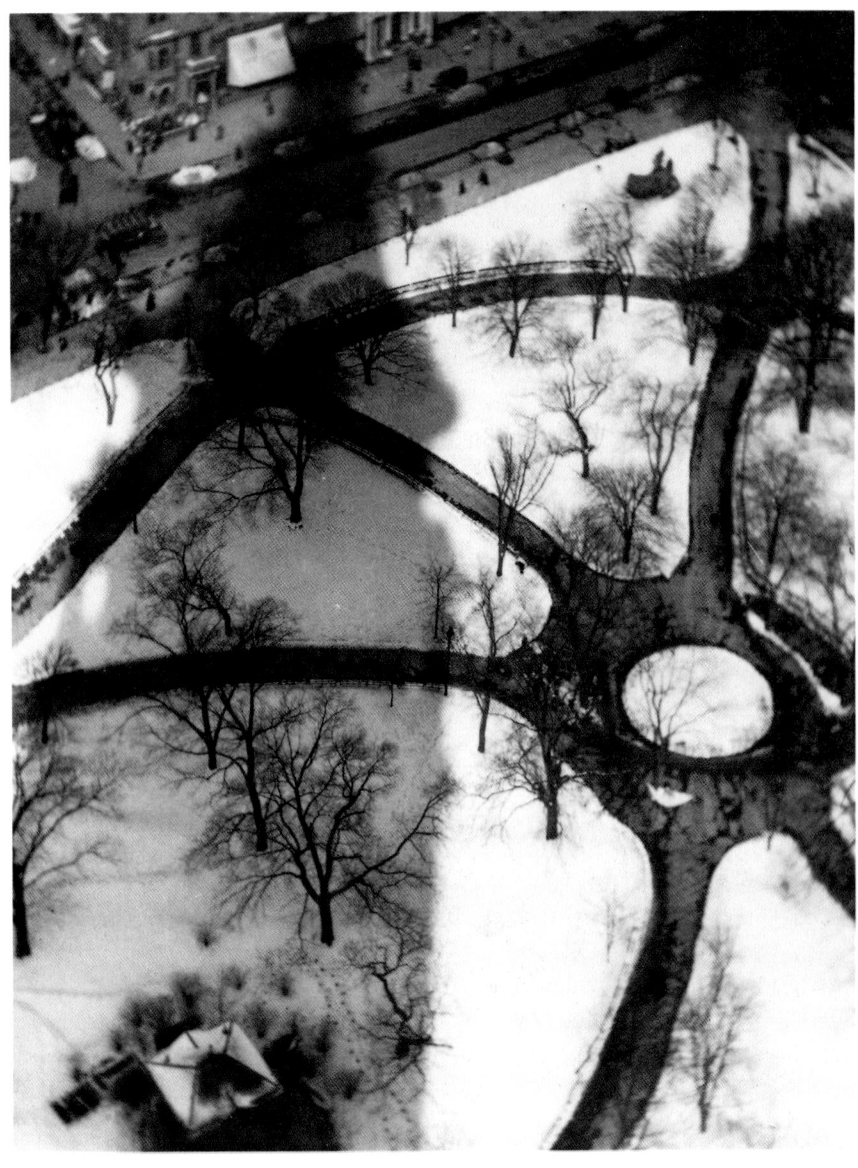

ALVIN LANGDON COBURN, *The Octopus, New York,* 1912, International Museum of Photography, George Eastman House, Rochester.

ALVIN LANGDON COBURN, ▶ *Vortograph,* 1917, International Museum of Photography, George Eastman House, Rochester

a portable camera and able to move around the town whose changing face he so admired. "The age of the skyscraper" had been celebrated since the end of the nineteenth century and was no longer a novelty in the public's imagination. What was certainly unexpected, however, was that photographs of skyscrapers should become the symbol of modernism and progress, as recorded by Stieglitz. In New York, the first skyscraper to have an iron framework was built in 1889. Around 1900, skyscrapers became symbols of the city's growth and commercial power (Singer Building, 1908, Woolworth Building, 1913). Stieglitz recorded them in *The City of Ambition* and *Old and New New York* (1910). The surprising thing was that this celebration of the city arrived in the wake of Pictorialism, created out of a form of Impressionism, with its atmosphere, its rendering of the effects of climate and light. This new photography now came to celebrate stability, geometry, and the gleam of metal as the criterion of urban beauty, and, consequently, of the photographic image.

The effects of this change of direction in favor of modernism, very evident in the pages of *Camera Work*, was felt mainly by photographers in America, its impact, not surprisingly, being weaker in Europe. The "new" photographer in the first decade of this century (as represented by a figure like Stieglitz or the younger Coburn) was concerned with real life and the everyday urban scene, instead of retreating into the representation of a fleeting moment (which was to remain a favorite subject for a number of Pictorialists for a long time). Certain ductile subjects, such as the movement of a crowd, smoke or cloud effects, persisted in the new style of photography, but this time allied to a more realistic depiction of social and urban life or to the creation of "abstract" images, rather than pastoral scenes. Cars, trams, telephones, electric lighting, every kind of machine, elevators, and the subway make up the natural landscape of modern man, a landscape that could not be ignored by any art wishing to be "modern".

Meanwhile, in Europe, a movement appeared in 1909 – Futurism – which praised the mechanical energy and brutal beauty of the city, but did not find an echo in photography for another two years.[2] The Futurists, poets and painters for the most part, invented a city of light densely inhabited by militant individuals, ferocious in their defense of machinism and their hostility towards the past – as symbolized by Venice, whose canals they proposed to fill in. *La città che sale* (1910–1911) and *The Street Enters the House* (1911), by Boccioni, as well as *What the Tram Told Me* (1910–1911), by Carrà, are structured around the vibrant tumult of the street. An architecture capable of producing new sensations was soon proposed: "bright underground areas, large stores, layers of tunnels for subway trains, the erection of gigantic American skyscrapers".[3] An architect, Sant'Elia, proposed an aesthetic of the "Futurist city, resembling an immense and tumultuous construction site, agile, mobile, and dynamic in

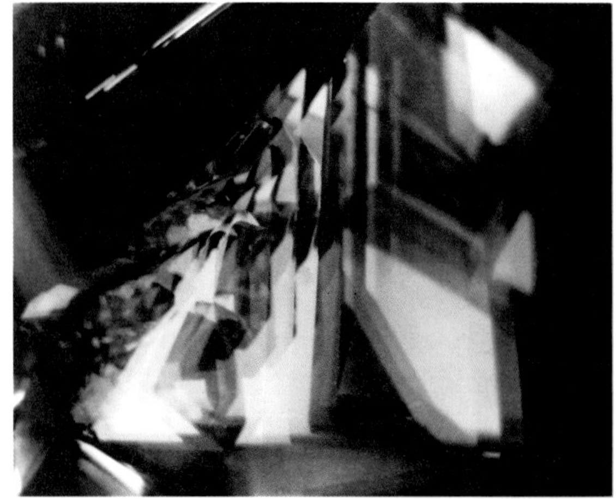

2. *Futurist Manifesto,* published by Marinetti on February 20, 1909.

3. *Manifesto of Futurist Architecture,* 1914.

every detail". However, Boccioni and Sant'Elia both died in the First World War, a war whose violence they had accepted, engendered as it was by mechanical monsters of steel and speed and considered by Futurism as "the world's only way of cleansing itself" (Manifesto of 1909).[4]

For a time (between 1905 and 1917), the photographer Alvin Langdon Coburn found himself at the crossroads of all these influences: Symbolism, Pictorialism, Modernism, Avant-gardism. After an initial training with his cousin, Frederick Holland Day (with whom, aged 17, he toured Europe in 1899), from 1905, when he was staying in London, Coburn forged links with Britain and the intelligentsia. Forming friendships with writers sympathetic to socialism, Coburn found in the city a transitional theme between symbolism and real life. He became interested in modernist subjects such as dockers, miners, and industrial scenes rendered unreal by smoke and *contre-jour* shots. A friend of Henry James, Coburn became interested in illustrating books with photographs. The first result was *London* (1909, with an introduction by Hilaire Belloc), followed by *New York* (1910, introduction by H. G. Wells), and H. G. Wells's *The Door in the Wall, and Other Stories* (1912).

Coburn had an idea for a series of books, *The Adventures of Cities* (London, Birmingham, Liverpool, Edinburgh, Paris, Pittsburgh, New York, and Boston), following the model of *Cities* by his friend Arthur Symons.[5] Henry James suggested a city like a theatre, populated with mental images, "always recognizing themselves as optical symbols or echoes, expressions of no particular thing in the text".[6] The model for an illustrated book celebrating the city is *The New New York* of John C. Van Dyke, (illustrations by Pennell, 1909), echoed by Stieglitz's similarly named photograph. The positive image of the tentacles of the city, constantly reaching upwards and outwards, was perfectly acceptable at the start of the century. This vision, one which ignored social deprivation (photographed by Hine at this time), was taken up by newspapers and magazines, finding an echo in Europe.[7]

Coburn developed an analogy between the bridge-builder and the photographer: "The one uses his brain to fashion a thing of steel girders, a spider's web of beauty to glisten in the sun, the other blends chemistry and optics with personality in such a way as to produce a lasting impression of a beautiful fragment. The work of both – builder or photographer – owes its existence to man's hold over nature."[8] However, the attractions of the city and technology did not replace those of nature. Coburn went to the Grand Canyon in the autumn of 1911. Greatly impressed, he returned to photograph New York from all its highest vantage points. One photograph resulting from this project was *The Octopus* (1912), taken from the Metropolitan Tower, over Madison Square: "A composition or exercise in filling a rectangular space with curves and masses. Depending as it does more upon pattern than upon subject matter, this photograph was revolutionary in 1912."[9]

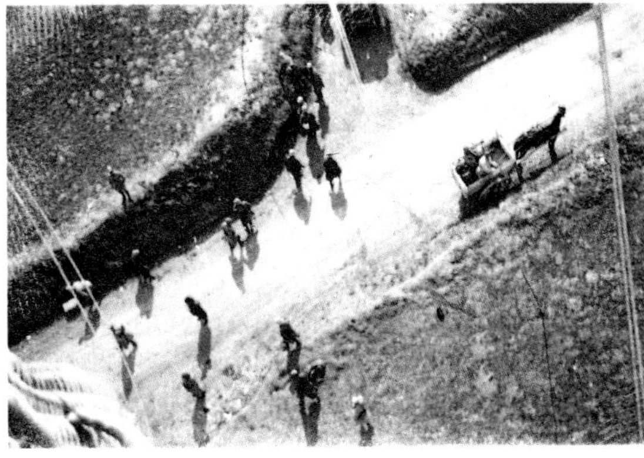

Anonymous,
"High angle" Shot,
First World War,
March 1916,
private collection.

Anonymous,
Aerial View, Tracks in the Fields (Oise),
First World War,
June 16, 1918,
Musée d'Histoire Contemporaine, Paris.

Thus a modern vision of the environment evolved from a merging of the ideas of nature, city, and power (Van Dyke also published *The Grand Canyon of the Colorado*, in 1920). The poetry of the metropolis stimulated the *New Vision* of the 1920s. Younger photographers such as Strand and Sheeler, inspired by this offshoot of Pictorialism, built their aesthetic on a justification of urbanism. The film they conceived together, *Manhattan*, was originally intended to be called *New York the Magnificent* (1920).

The vortex of the avant-garde

July 1914 saw the publication of the first issue of the magazine *Blast*, with contributions by

4. *Futurisme et Futurismes*, exhibition catalogue (Palazzo Grassi, Venice, 1986), Paris.

5. M. Weaver, *Alvin Langdon Coburn, Symbolist Photographer*, Aperture, 1986, p. 33.

6. *Ibid.*

7. Blaise Cendrars' great poem, *Les Pâques à New York*, dating from 1912, was influenced by the Futurist aesthetic, as was his *Prose du transsibérien* with S. Delaunay, of 1913.

8. A. L. Coburn, 1910, on the Pictorialist retrospective in Buffalo, quoted in M. Weaver, *op. cit.*, p.38.

9. *Alvin Langdon Coburn, Photographer: An Autobiography*, H. and A. Gernsheim (eds.), New York, Dover, 1978, p. 84.

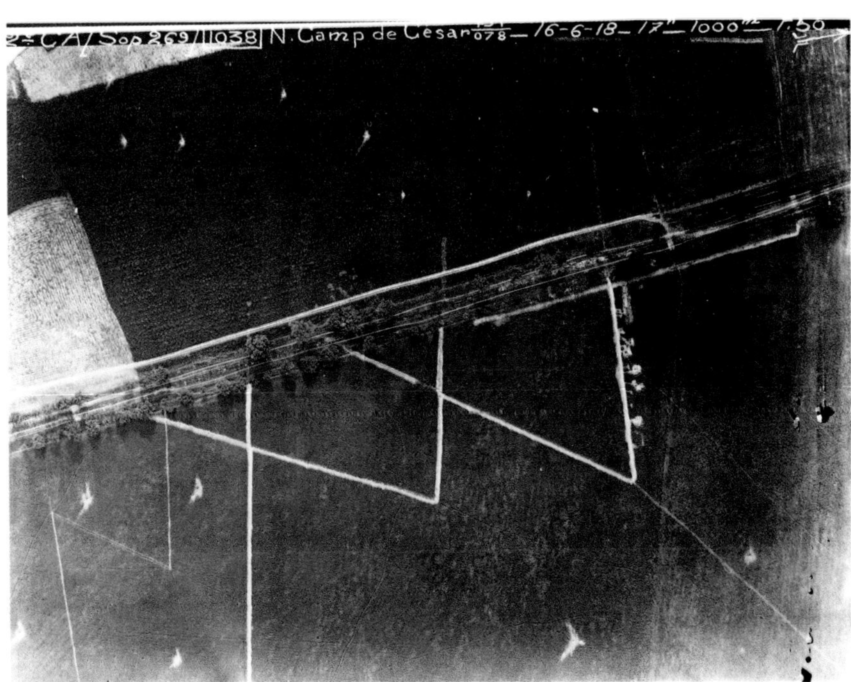

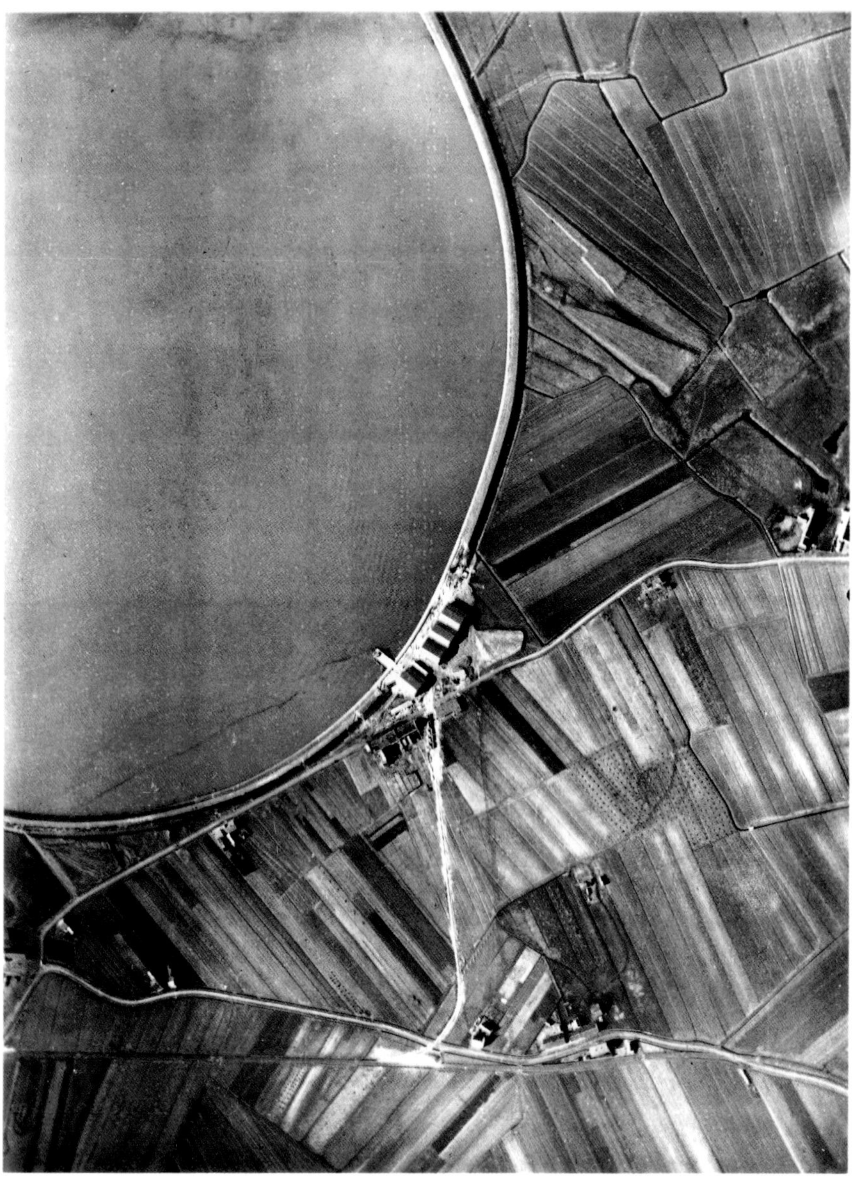

SECOND-LIEUTENANT BELTS, *Aerial View,* Belgium, March 1, 1917, Musée d'Histoire Contemporaine, Paris.

Wyndham Lewis, Ezra Pound, and Gaudier-Brzeska. *Blast* was the mouthpiece of the Vortex group and the Vorticists. The group manifesto explained the meaning of the word: "The vortex is the point of maximum energy [...] We use the words 'greatest efficiency' in the precise sense – as they would be used in a textbook of mechanics." Vorticism can be seen as a specifically British movement, with close affinities to Futurism, fuelled by a reaction to the oppressiveness of Victorian England, and an absolute passion for "the forms of machinery, factories, new and vaster buildings, bridges, and works".

In British Pictorialist circles, tightly grouped around the Linked Ring since 1892, splits had taken place in 1908 on aesthetic grounds. The American presence, deemed too innovative and too disturbing, had been denounced at the Salon, bringing about the formation of a Salon des Refusés led by the rather conservative Francis J. Mortimer – editor of *Amateur Photographer* magazine – who opposed the modernist and pro-American faction led by Malcolm Arbuthnot. The modernists then in turn founded the London Secession, in 1911.[10]

Without exaggerating the impact of the Vortex group, whose activities were quite limited, it is important to stress its "abstracting" tendency, the influence of which was felt, for the first time, by a number of photographers, in particular, Arbuthnot, one of the signatories of the *Blast* manifesto, and Coburn. In the same way, at precisely this time Picasso was also moving towards abstraction, although it was not yet a fully formed aesthetic objective.

The question of links with European avant-garde movements (Fauvism, Cubism, Futurism), now openly supported by Stieglitz, had been raised. Until this time, people had been content to talk about nobility, harmony or tonality. Now the question was the intrinsic significance of art and the meaning of representation, beyond a purely imitative or decorative system. In 1916, Coburn exhibited his views of the Grand Canyon, considered to be very modernist, and his Vorticist portraits of Ezra Pound and de Zayas. Coburn spoke in ironic terms about his convincing break with the usual "nice pastoral landscape with plenty of woolly sheep" Pictorialist images. Henceforth, every photograph was an "experiment". In 1916 [11] Coburn published *The Future of Pictorial Photography,* echoing the iconoclastic texts of *Blast,* in which he proposed the development of the use of shutter speeds, multiple exposures on the same plate, "neglected" perspectives, microscopic views, the use of prisms, and time-lapse exposures: "Do something outrageously bad if you like, but let it be freshly seen [...] If it is not possible to be 'modern' with the newest of all the arts, we had better bury our black boxes."

In a brief but radical experiment (late 1916 to early 1917), which called into question the very concept of the photograph and the traditional, representative, role of photography, Coburn created his vortographs, photographs obtained independently of any "natural" subject by means of a kind of rudimentary optical machine, a simple kaleidoscope with mirrors.[12]

It was clear that Coburn wished to integrate photography into modern art, and, by stripping bare the object photographed, reducing it to effects of light, and cutting it off from any reference to Pictorial symbolism, he found a means of reaching a willed, mechanical abstraction. While it would be a mistake to exaggerate the impact and influence of Coburn's experiment,[13] it nevertheless had the advantage of establishing a space for "free creation" which had been considerably extended (see below) since Stieglitz had asserted that the art of photography was a personal expression and a distancing from reality.

10. J. Taylor, *Pictorial Photography in Britain, 1900–1920,* London, Arts Council of Great Britain, 1978.

11. In *Photograms of the Year,* 1916, pp. 23–24.

12. "The Vortoscope, he [Pound] said, freed photography from the material limitations of depicting recognizable natural objects", *A. L. Coburn, Photographer, op. cit.,* p. 104.

13. An exhibition of paintings and vortographs was mounted at the London Camera Club in February 1917, and a vortograph was published in *Photograms of the Year* for 1917.

A bird's eye view

The "view from above" or high-angle shot, which was to become one of the trademarks of the new photography at the end of the 1920s, was also, in certain respects, a necessity of the period – or at least a natural result. The reasons for the popularity of this viewpoint, so unexpected for the spectator, were, not surprisingly, linked to the new-found mobility of the camera (which no longer needed a tripod), the movements of the operator's body, and the natural direction of his gaze. The high-angle shot also resulted from the new possibilities for access to the top of tall urban buildings in order to admire the "panoramic view". (Interestingly, the Eiffel Tower did not so obviously inspire such photographs as did the skyscrapers of New York.) Ruins in the countryside were also transformed into observation posts for the surrounding area. The American photographer and film-maker Karl Struss took views from high buildings from 1911, as did Coburn, who had already gained experience in "views from above" on his trip to Colorado. In London, in 1913, he exhibited his series *New York from its Pinnacles*, which included *The Octopus* and *The House with a Thousand Windows*, described by its author as "almost as fantastic as a Cubist fantasy".

Other factors had also helped to form the taste for images taken from a great height. The photographer Nadar, who was also involved in experiments in "heavier than air" flight, had taken the very first photographs from a balloon in 1858. Balloons were also used to take photographs in the Franco-Piedmontese war against Austria of 1859. Nadar has left us a long description of what can be seen from a balloon, of the inverted and seemingly abstract perception of the world where ordinary things took on new, unrecognizable forms: "The fields, like irregular chessboards, look like quilts made of multicolored but harmonizing patches stitched by the patient needle of the seamstress [...] Everything appears to us with the exquisite impression of a marvelous, ravishing cleanliness! No squalor or blots on the landscape. There is nothing like distance to remove us from all ugliness."[14] The photographer's evidence is particularly pertinent here. Gaston Tissandier, another keen balloonist – and photographer – obtained the first image of Paris directly overhead in 1885, and Arthur Batut developed the technique of taking photographs using a camera attached to a kite.[15]

Soon the advantages of balloon photography began to be applied to cartographic surveys and to strategic observation in times of war. The high-angle shot was not simply an "idea" dreamed up by artists to challenge normal perspective; it was

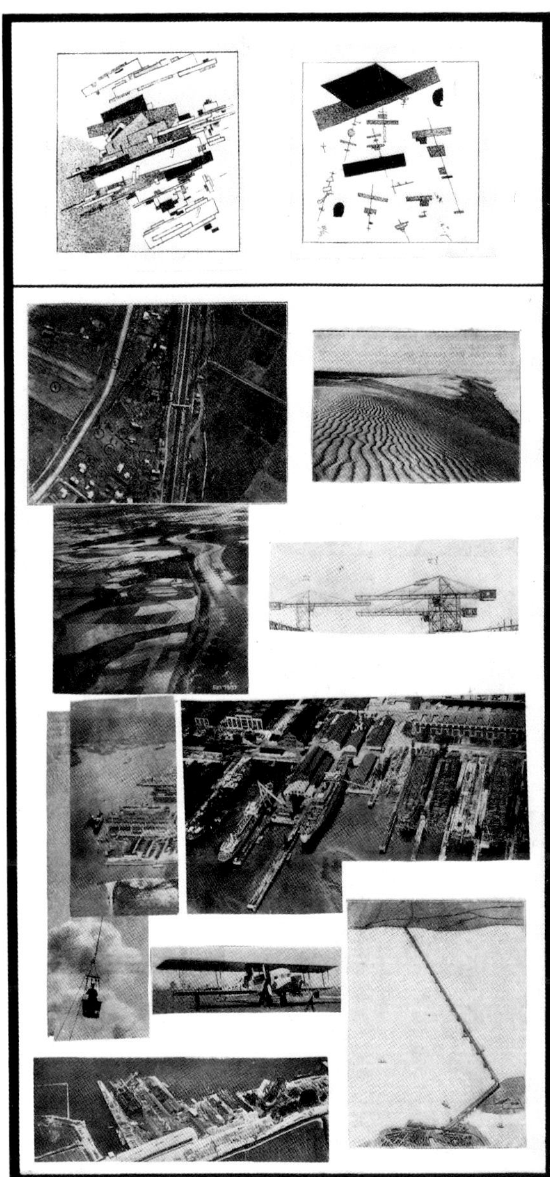

KASIMIR MALEVICH,
Educational poster,
detail, *Suprematism*,
1925–1926.
Museum of Modern Art,
New York.

14. Nadar, *Quand j'étais photographe*, Paris, Flammarion, 1900, pp. 77–78.

15. G. Tissandier, *La Photographie en ballon*, Paris, Gauthier-Villars, 1886; Arthur Batut, *La Photographie aérienne par cerf-volant*, Paris, Gauthier-Villars, 1890.

LE CORBUSIER,
Rome, Interior of the Pantheon,
October, 1911,
Foundation Le Corbusier, Paris.

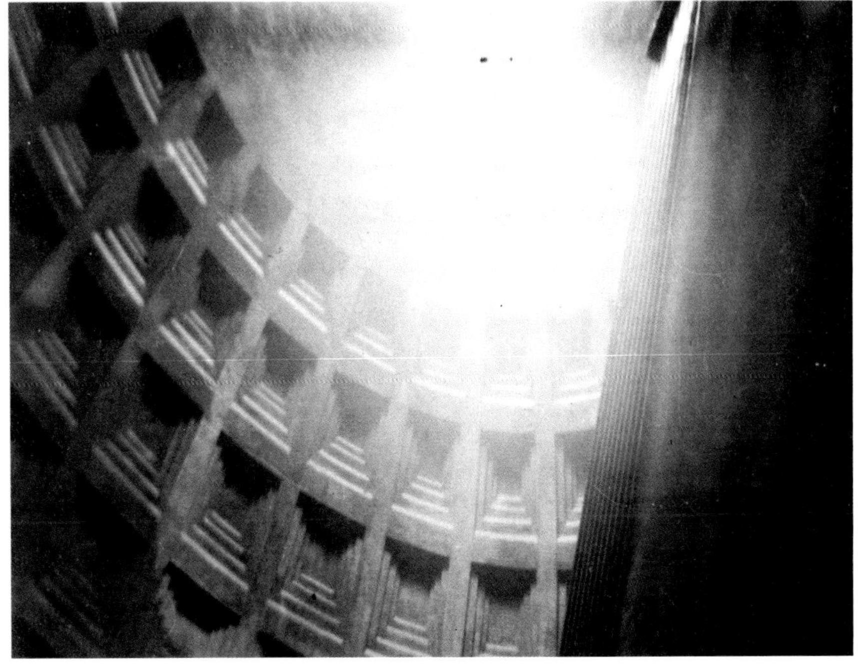

Camera Work, no. 49/50, 1917

The significance of the final edition of *Camera Work*, which appeared in June 1917, has often been recognized. Because of the war, the double issue appeared after several delays in the regular publication of the magazine. But it was not only external events that made this collection of photographs an indication of the important changes that had taken place during those years, often unknown to the photographers themselves. The illustrations (11 photographs) for the June edition were devoted entirely to a newcomer who had already published six photographs in the previous edition of October 1916.

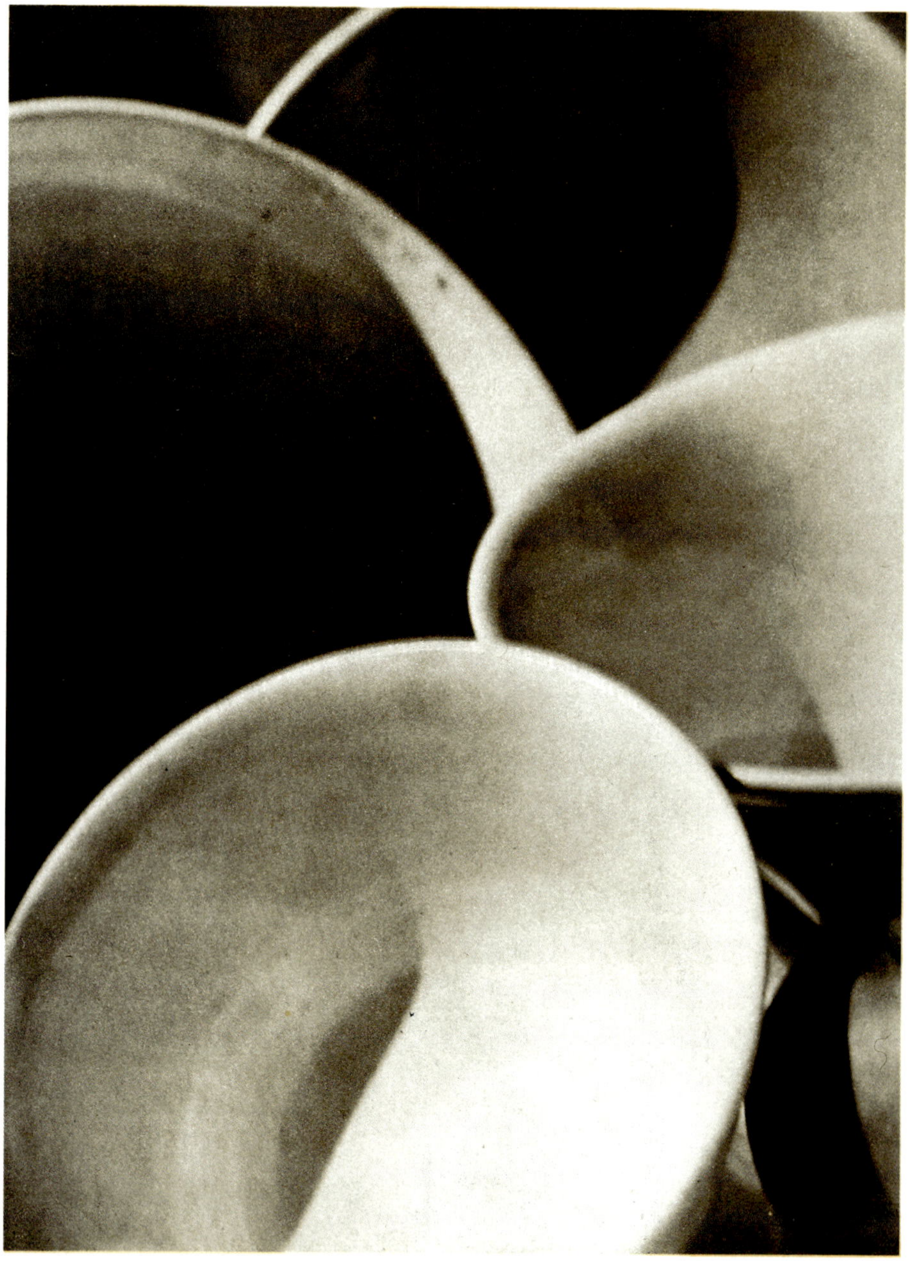

Paul Strand, photograph,
from *Camera Work*, June, 1917,
Musée d'Orsay, Paris.

Born in 1890, Paul Strand joined the Camera Club of New York in 1908. Although he was a pupil of Hine, and met Stieglitz in 1917, he was originally influenced by Pictorialism, beginning to take more personal photographs in 1914. A first series (from which the illustrations of the October 1916 edition were taken) was concerned with "movement in New York, movement in the streets, the movement of traffic, the movement of people walking in the parks", themes which had already been explored by Stieglitz, Coburn, and Struss.

Two following series provided the selection published in the last number of *Camera Work* and went as far as it was possible to go in a "hard" definition of a photographic point of view. The work consists of, on the one hand, studies of light and shade in natural subjects that become "non-figurative" insofar as the object photographed is not always recognizable (summer, 1916), and, on the other hand, close-up portraits of ordinary people taken in the street (end of 1916).

Of his "abstract" studies, Strand said that it was a matter of clarifying "for me what I now refer to as the abstract method, which was first revealed in the paintings of Picasso, Braque, Léger, and others (...) things that were – as [Stieglitz] used the word – 'anti-photographic'". The "social documents" in turn were produced with the intention of "photographing people without their knowing", by using a prism which made it possible for Strand to take photographs at right angles from the direction in which the camera was apparently pointing.

Thus Strand produced a variety of work: wide-angle shots which were not dissimilar to journalistic, documentary images on urban reality (under the title of *New York*), destructuring compositions that produced images without identifiable subjects, together were close-ups, bordering on social documentary (these two collections appeared under the single title of *Photography*).

Exhibited in the 291 Gallery at the same time as they were published in *Camera Work*, his photographs of a blind woman, a woman yawning, a sandwich-man, and a man in a hat are the most artistically anachronistic, representing as they do a return to naturalism and realism. However, what is most important here is, rather, the nature of the photographic act: the break with academic art and the affirmation of the freedom that was to found a new photography.

In an article published in the same number of the magazine (also intended to promote a specifically American art), Strand justified his *total* use of the camera. "The photographer must see clearly the limitations and, at the same time, the potential qualities of his medium [...] This means a real respect for the thing in front of him, expressed in terms of chiaroscuro (color and photography having nothing in common) [...] The fullest realization of this is accomplished without tricks of process or manipulation, through the use of straight photographic methods."

Stieglitz added a short article in support of this new aesthetic on which the revival of American photography was, temporarily, to close: "The work is brutally direct; devoid of all flim-flam; devoid of trickery and of any 'ism'; devoid of any attempt to mystify an ignorant public, including the photographers themselves." *Camera Work*, which, for fourteen years, had assiduously promoted "photography as art", thus concluded with a few portraits and two studies in chiaroscuro, difficult to read as figurative studies: these were "photographs".

Michel Frizot

also a type of photography which was naturally associated with a visit to a building or monument, with technical advances in observation and, soon, with the coming of the First World War, with strategies for defense and survival.[16] Thus, it could equally well be found in the work of amateurs and semi-professionals (for example, landscapes photographed from balloons or views from the Arc de Triomphe taken in around 1900–1910, by Léon Gimpel, who worked for the magazine *L'Illustration*), as in that of technicians who took aerial views in order to shed new light on unknown aspects of geography. Such views, taken over the sea or the land and sometimes including views of clouds and newly developed machines (balloons, airships or airplanes), had begun to be popularized even before 1914, thanks to reproductions published in the media.[17] *Paris vu en ballon* [Paris Seen from a Balloon], 1913, was to feature on the cover of Le Corbusier's *L'Art décoratif d'aujourd'hui* [Modern Decorative Art], and was then used again by Rodchenko for *Paris*, by Mayakovsky, in 1925.

Above all, it was the development of military aviation, with the resulting profusion of aerial photographs, that had the effect on some people of changing the very basis of their photographic vision. The first photographs taken from an airplane probably date from 1909 (the year of Blériot's crossing from Calais to Dover). At the beginning of the war, in November 1914, photographic units were formed in France, which used Vest Pocket Kodak cameras and then 18 x 24 cm cameras (with 12-plate magazines). Trench warfare encouraged effective and systematic photographic documentation for the information it provided about the movements of the enemy. Several thousand photographs were taken before the battle of Verdun in August 1917.[18] Already gaining a reputation at this time, Edward Steichen, an American photographer and modernist Pictorialist, joined the Signal Corps Photographic Service as an aerial photographer after the sinking of the Lusitania and was subsequently appointed to organize the American aerial photographic service in France.[19]

Observation procedures set up during the First World War (aerial photography or photographs taken from any high vantage point such as a tower or steeple) had enormous repercussions on the manner in which images were viewed, on the mental link between what is seen and what really exists. Looking at the interweaving geometric forms, which are defined not in terms of criteria of beauty but of function, one could not help but question the legitimacy of traditional forms of representation and their chances of survival in a world that had discovered other rules, other

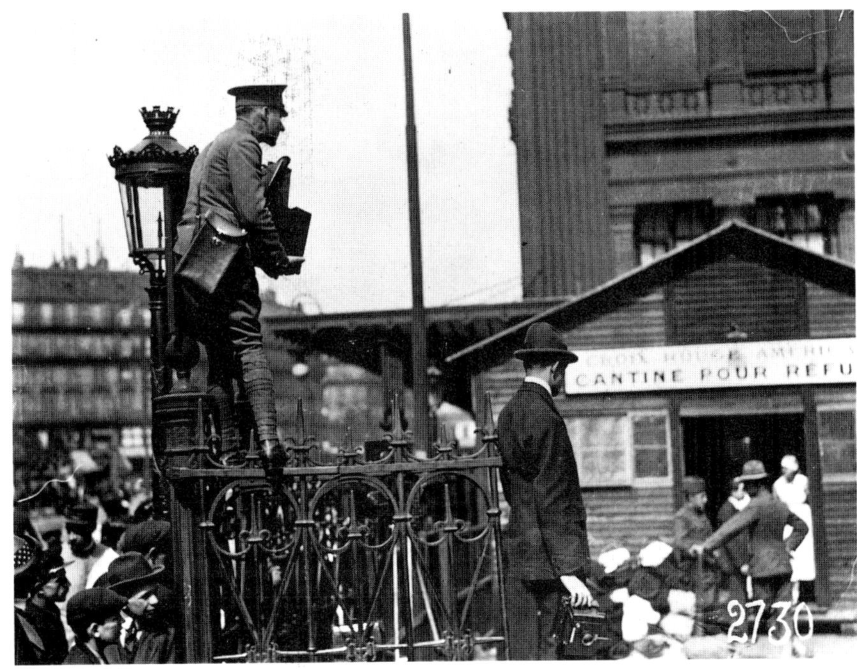

▲
Lewis Hine photographing refugees, Gare du Nord, Paris, June 1918, International Museum of Photography, George Eastman House, Rochester.

Alfred Stieglitz,
The Steerage, 1907, (from *Camera Work*, October 1911), Museum of Fine Arts, Boston.
▼

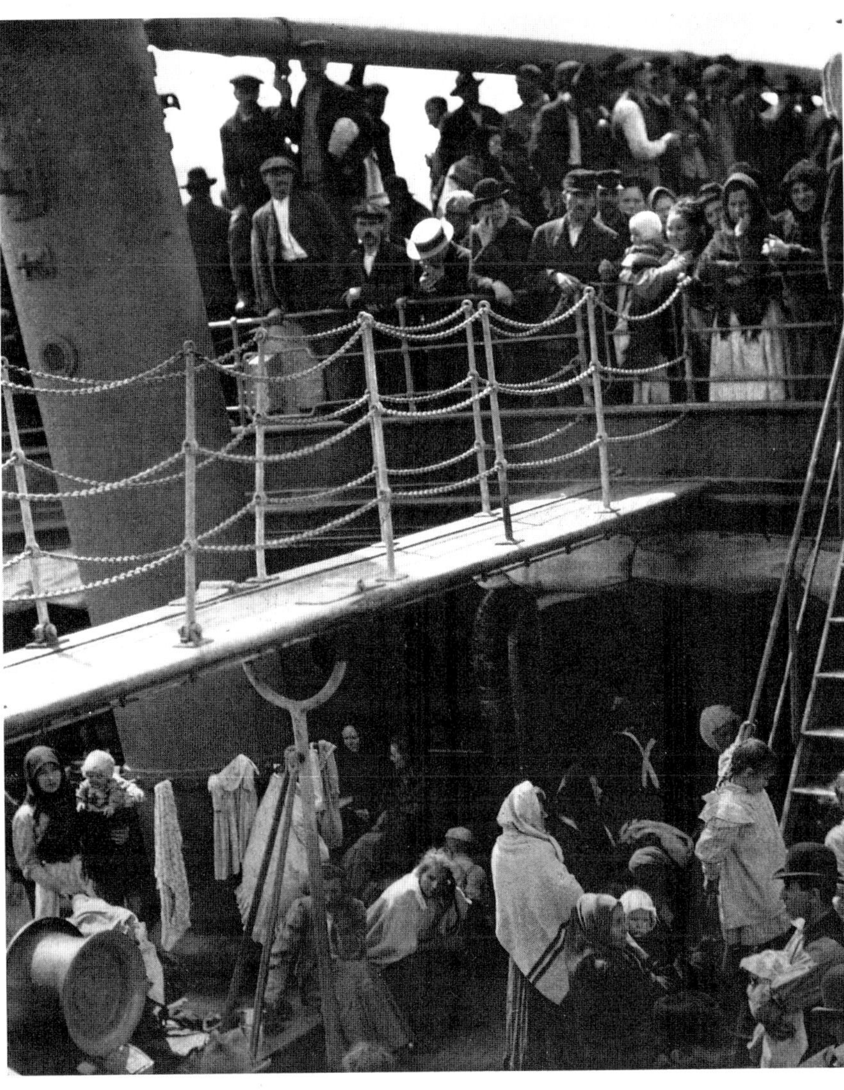

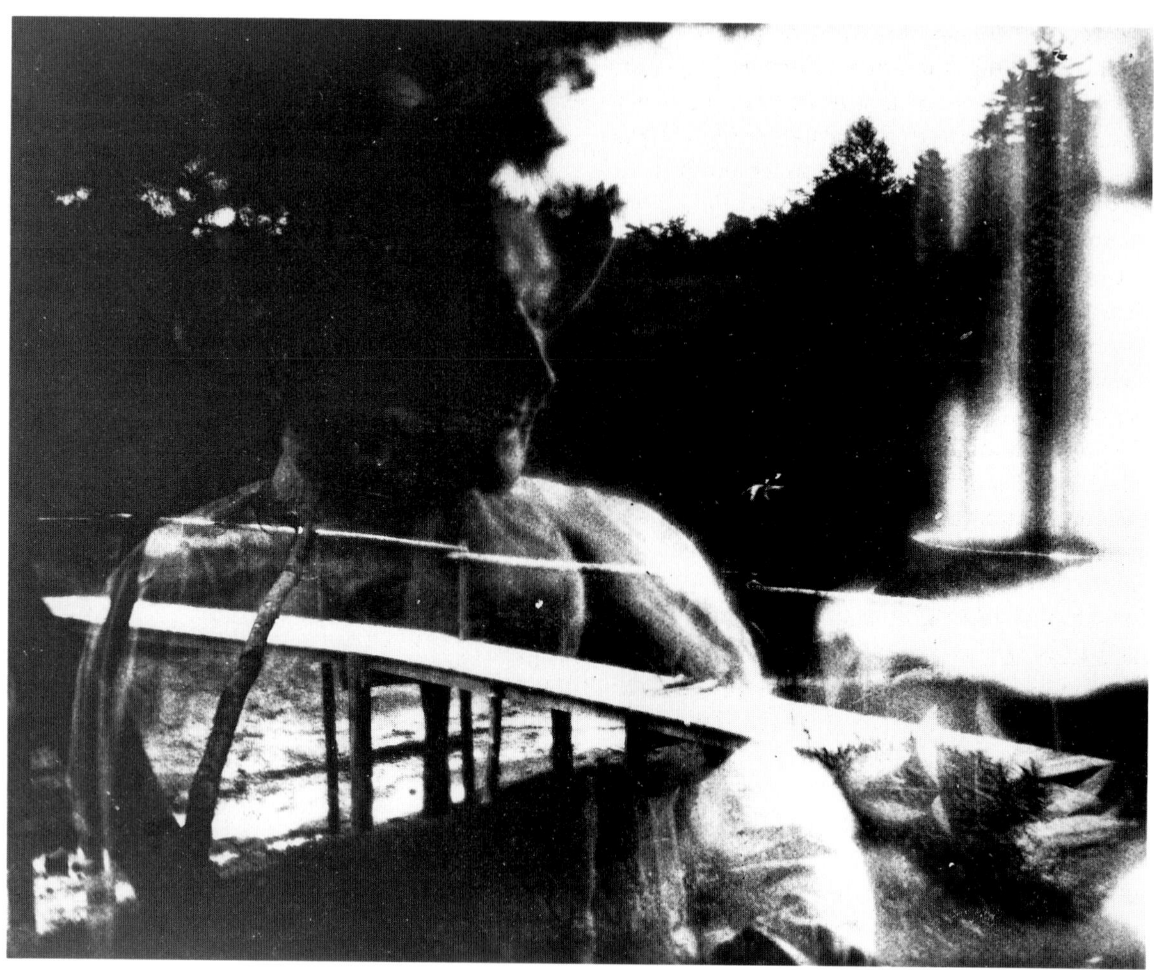

FRED HOLLAND DAY, [*Self-portrait with double exposure*], bichromated gelatin print, before 1917, Library of Congress, Washington.

forms of violence done both to the body and to the eyes.

These influences are apparent in the area of the plastic arts, and particularly that of the Russian avant-garde. As early as 1915, Malevich gave one of his Suprematist paintings the title *Airplane in Flight*, and another *Sensation of Flight*, in 1920.[20] The visual world constructed by Malevich after 1913, made of simple, graphic "bodies" floating in white space, thus finds its visual reference in a high-angle shot that destabilizes the conventional horizontal pictorial viewpoint of the Renaissance. This dependence is well illustrated in *Die Gegenstandlose Welt* [The Anti-Objective World] (1927), Malevich's theoretical book published by the Bauhaus, which is illustrated with examples of aerial views of towns and pictures of airplanes and machines. Similarly, in an explanatory photomontage (1925–1926), Suprematism is interpreted in photographs: seven aerial views, an airplane on the ground, cranes on a building site. The text evokes "Suprematism with an aerial aspect". Malevich's interest in an art without limits, without identifiable figuration, gains support from the uncertainty of aerial pictures. This "New Vision" stimulated both the development of Constructivism (Lissitzky, Rodchenko, Moholy-Nagy) and debate about the real meaning of the photographic image. The "view from above" was, in the 1920s, to become so common that it became one of the clichés of the New Vision. Moholy-Nagy, painter, graphic artist, and photographer, was to make it one of the elements of the dynamic of the image, of the perceptive deconstruction of space, of new relationships between objects.[21] In the 1920s, as the public learned to read these images, photographs taken from airplanes or zeppelins by Robert Petschow began to be accepted as real representations of the land (a large number of them appearing in Eugen Diesel's *Das Land der Deutschen* [Land of the German People] of 1931).

Thus, people learned to see in images other things besides the usual forms, to find several possible interpretations in one photograph. As long as some imagination is used, an image can open itself up to other meanings, and reveal its mysteries. Duchamp's photograph of the *Grand Verre*, later called *Élevage de poussière*, was published in 1922 under the title of *View Taken from an Airplane*.

Free creation

Around 1900, in American Secessionist circles around Stieglitz there emerged the notion of "free creation" which was to replace the general tendency of Pictorialist photography, the latter

16. R. Martin (ed.), *The View from Above*, London, The Photographer's Gallery, 1983; Beaumont Newhall, *Airborne Camera: The World from the Air and Outer Space*, New York, Hastings House, 1969.

17. G. F. Leberecht, *Luftfahrten im Frieden und im Kriege*, Berlin, Leonhard Gimion, 1913.

18. L. Dumarche and M. Bacchus, *Vues d'en haut: la photographie aérienne pendant la guerre 1914–1918*, Musée de l'Armée, Paris, 1988.

19. See C. Phillips, *Steichen at War*, New York, H. N. Abrams, 1981.

20. Museum of Modern Art, New York.

21. *Malerei, Fotografie, Film* (Bauhausbücher no. 8), 1925. English translation, MIT Press, 1969, 1973.

being guided by an imitation of painting, the senior art, and therefore *a priori* superior. Photographers were conscious of having to obey rules and limitations that were determined by the possibilities of their photographic equipment (both in taking the picture and in printing it). Perhaps influenced by certain British purists hostile to modifications made to the image (George Davison, Frederick H. Evans), the autonomy of photography increasingly asserted itself, without conforming to some other, foreign, aesthetic. In other words, there could be a specifically photographic aesthetic.

During the same period (the early years of this century), important new scientific discoveries were being made: relativity (Einstein, 1905), Rutherford's and Bohr's models of the atom (1911, 1913), and the challenging of basic beliefs after the announcement that physics had finally been "completed" (Lord Kelvin), culminating in the discovery of X-rays (1895) and radioactivity (1896). The general impression for the non-specialist was that of a new scientific order (implying the abandonment of the old mechanistic references). The unimaginable potential of invisible resources gave new force to everything connected with the imagination.

In a seminal article published in *Camera Work*, "On the Possibility of New Composition",[22] the art critic Sadakichi Hartmann claimed that photography was the foremost medium for the "faithful representation of life", accessible to all and popularized through illustrations in magazines. Artists, he said, were about to feel the effects of this change, produced by the activities of amateur photographers. The impossibility of recreating the "initial impulse" of the image, as caught by the camera, encouraged continual experimentation: snapshots, night photography, candid street photography – all of these calling for an "accidental" approach. Photography had to adapt to its own methods, exteriorizing nothing but that which allowed it to be an image (light, the fleeting glimpse, spontaneity), conforming to purely photographic criteria: detail, depth of shadow, gradations of tone. Photography was to lend itself to a new expressiveness "like the unresolved chords of Debussy". Hartmann preached a photography whose "composition" should be governed by its subject, made of "reciprocal relationships of space", which would find its motivation in the innocent and curious vision of the photographic "amateur".

This article echoes a feeling for photographic immediacy that was strongly felt by photographers like Clarence White, Gertrude Käsebier, Coburn, and, particularly, Stieglitz. The key work of this apparent reversal of aesthetics – one that can nevertheless find its place in the natural logic of Pictorialism – is Stieglitz's *The Steerage*. Taken in 1907, it was published in *Camera Work* in 1911 and in *291* in 1915. In a later article,[23] Stieglitz explained how this picture, telling in terms of the personal involvement of the photographer, had come about. In June 1907 he had been on his way to Europe, on a steamer, travelling first class. As he was strolling on deck, he was struck by the sight of the steerage deck and a white gangway bridge, gleaming and freshly painted: "On the upper deck, looking over the railing, there was a young man with a straw hat. The shape of the hat was round. He was watching the men and women and children on the lower steerage deck [...] The whole scene fascinated me [...] I saw a picture of shapes and underlying that the feeling I had about life [...] I had but one plate holder with one unexposed plate. Would I get what I saw, what I felt? Finally I released the shutter."

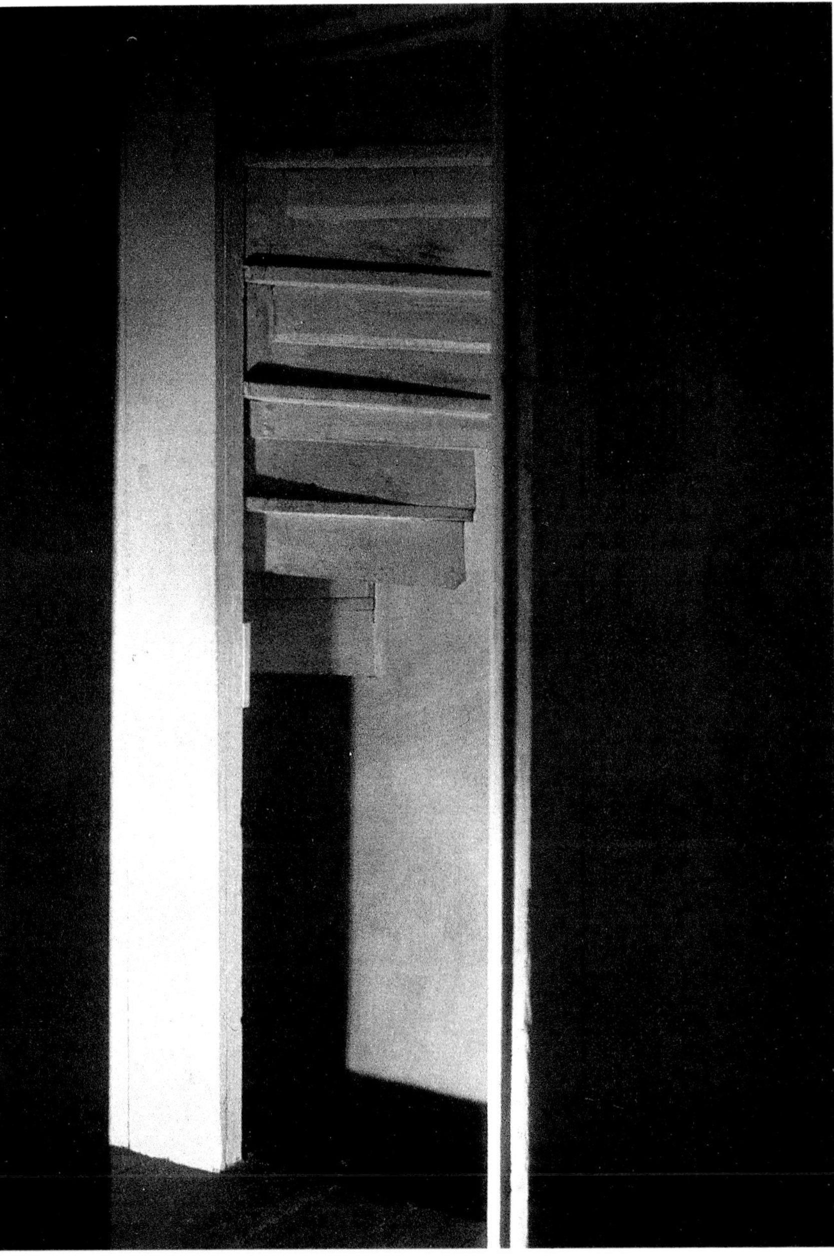

CHARLES SHEELER,
Doylestown House; Stairwell,
1917,
Museum of Fine Arts, Boston.

22. "On the Possibility of New Composition", in *Camera Work* no. 30 April 1910, pp. 24–25, published in *Camera Work: A Critical Anthology*, J. Green (ed.), Aperture, 1973, pp. 199–202.

23. Extract from his *Memoirs* (1942), "How *The Streerage* happened", in "Alfred Stieglitz: Four Happenings", in N. Lyons (ed.), *Photographers on Photography*, Englewood Cliffs, 1966, pp. 129–130.

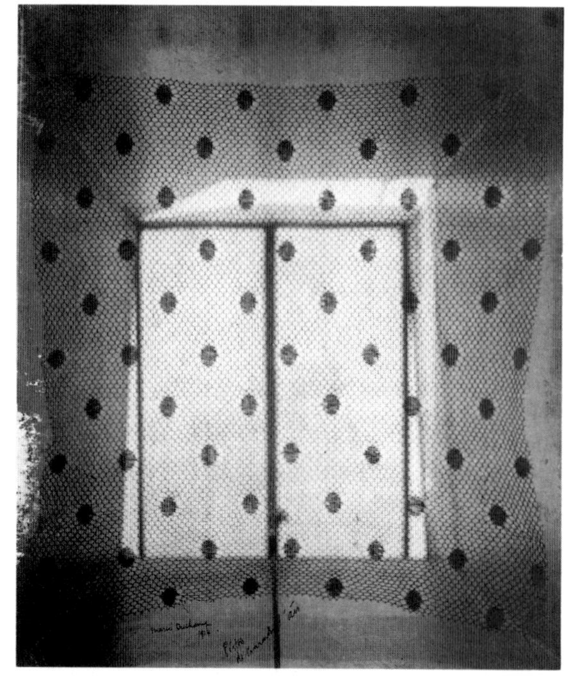

MARCEL DUCHAMP, 1914, Madame Marcel Duchamp Collection.

CHARLES SHEELER, *Doylestown House; Stove, Horizontal* 1917, Museum of Fine Arts, Boston. ▼

In this experience of real life, the photograph symbolizes the discovery of a "third world" – that of the steerage deck, of a primary emotion at the sight of the moving details, correctly lit and placed. This part of instinctive personal creation, expressible only within the circumstances experienced, but made external without Pictorial constraints, was to be developed by Paul Strand with the street photographs published in *Camera Work* in 1916 and 1917. It is significant that issue 36, of October 1911, which contains *The Steerage*, also gives an account of the exhibitions at the 291 Gallery, including one devoted to Picasso, and Coburn's important article, "The Relation of Time to Art". Stieglitz had discovered (and was to promote) the new forms of "modern" art, so much more threatening than tasteful academicism.

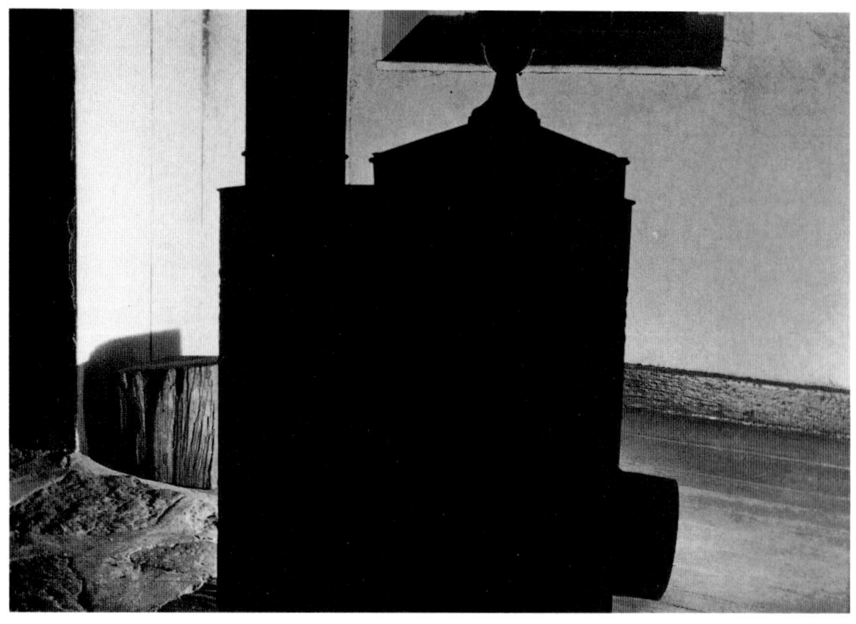

The Steerage appeared as a taste of things to come, an advance guard, as it were, into a world open and receptive to photography as to no other art form. The influence of this liberation could be felt in the work of Paul L. Anderson, Karl Struss, and Coburn, among others. "Free creation", more respectful of photographic criteria (instantaneity, spontaneity), can be seen as leading to straight photography, which, as early as 1910, was characterized by the absence of manipulation and a suspicion of Pictorialism.

The credo "all photographic and only photographic", that of an operator subjugating himself entirely to the possibilities of his equipment, is even more significant in the personal experience of Steichen, brought about by the horror of the First World War and his work as an aerial photographer. When he retired to Voulangis in France (1920–1922) he burned his paintings, saying that he did not want them to be "sold in a gold frame and end up as wallpaper". "I would learn how to take photographs that could go on the printed page, for now I was determined to reach a large audience instead of the few people I had reached as a painter."[24]

In a single summer, Steichen took more than a thousand photographs of a white cup and saucer. He also photographed an apple using long exposures, discovering the opacity of the symbolist message (*Time-Space Continuum*, circa 1920, an investigation of the theory of relativity). Beyond Steichen's personal experience and his attachment to a certain formal elegance, this reversal of the situation revealed the changes that had taken place in "creative" photography between 1910 and 1920.

Sheeler is one of these links leading towards the new photography, particularly in his collection of photographs (which can be described as anticipating the "purist" approach) meticulously produced during a stay in his Shaker house in Doylestown. A friend of De Zayas (who showed these photographs in his Modern Gallery in December 1917), Sheeler considered these works as "drawings", "something personal", transmitted through the supposedly impersonal camera, the aim of which was to show that the basics of modern art can just as well be found in nature, up to the very limits of abstraction itself.

It was necessary to find a way of going beyond the rigor and supposed automaticity of the photographic apparatus, by, for example, accepting the results of a superimposition of images (double-exposure), a frequent "accident" that could be turned to aesthetic advantage, as F. H. Day – a one-time rival of Stieglitz – had done by deliberately causing, rather than accidentally experiencing, these spontaneous meetings of

24. E. Steichen, *A Life in Photography*, Doubleday & Co., New York, 1963.

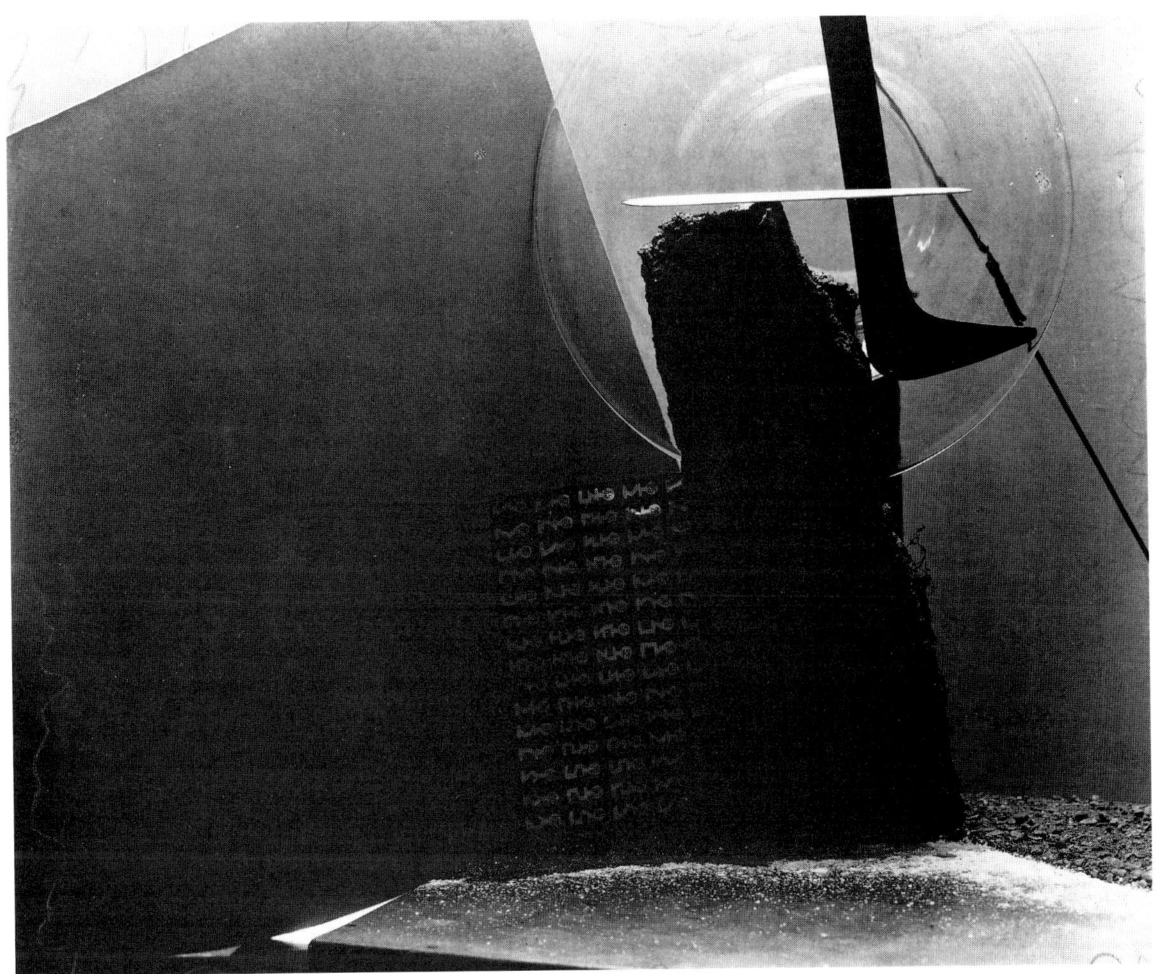

Edward Steichen,
Time-space Continuum,
circa 1920,
Metropolitan
Museum of Art,
New York.

autonomous images, very much in the main tradition of symbolism (see for example his *Self-portrait with Double Exposure*).

Miniature cameras were increasingly used for the experimentation that was taking place in photography. The photographic image was no longer the preserve of "high society" who came to the openings of the Salons; it could now reach a much wider audience through the "printed page" of the press.

Above all, the subjects chosen to be photographed were to be found no longer in the suspended effects of symbolist equilibrium, but in brief effects of light, flashes of emotion, mechanistic experiments or purely human encounters, the fleeting look already captured by the exercise of the amateur's free choice.

This aspect of photography, of lying in wait like some predatory animal, thus found itself linked to the logic of Marcel Duchamp's ready-mades: an industrial object, picked up almost at random but with a conscious act of will, individualized for its qualities of association and for its possibilities for semantic twisting: the *Sèche-bouteilles* (1914) that can take on quite another meaning and quite another function, the upside-down urinal that is transformed into a fountain (*Fountain*, 1917).

Duchamp did the same kind of thing with the camera, generator of the "beauty of indifference" through the precision of photographic recording and through its infallible flattening of perspective. His photograph *Piston de courant d'air* (1914) can be considered not only as preparation for the *Grand Verre* (1915–23), where three forms of a similar type appear, but also as a metaphor of the new photography, this material surface which was capable of filtering light.

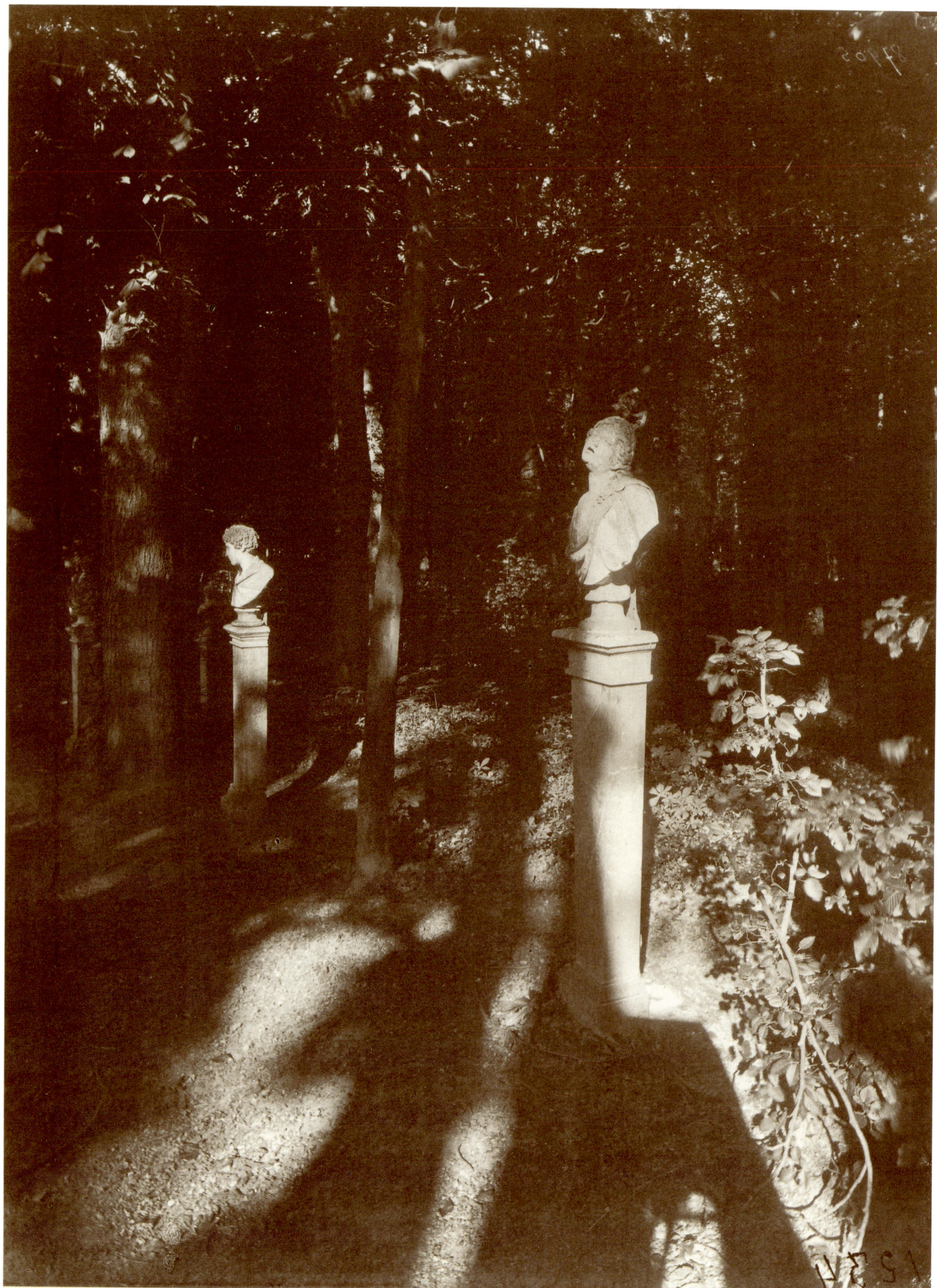

PHOTOGRAPHY AND HISTORY

24

Eugène Atget

Molly Nesbit

One photographer, Eugène Atget, forms a link between two quite separate worlds: nineteenth-century in his technique and ambition to record events, he belongs to the twentieth century when defined by the chronology of his works and the way in which some young artists looked up to his work during the mid-1920s. Thus it comes about that he speaks of the place of photography in knowledge, in history, and in the image market, and of the function of the document in society. Atget also reveals the double language of the photograph: the sense which its taker gives it, and the interpretation given by those who examine it subsequently.

◀ EUGÈNE ATGET, *Versailles, Trianon: a Verdant Amphitheatre*, 1923-1924, Archives Photographiques, Paris.

"There are moments when I detest Photographs: what have I got to do with Atget's old tree trunks?"[1] Eugène Atget (1857–1927) is the photographer that almost everyone admires – everyone, that is, except Roland Barthes – who knew that these remarks about Atget's work would scandalize. He might as well have said that he found Shakespeare boring. For Atget is the sacred forefather in the history of photography, the incarnation of the "great photographer", having displaced Alfred Stieglitz, Nadar, Ansel Adams, and Cartier-Bresson. We must recognize this fact, even if it means that this book must break its rule against monographic chapters to devote a chapter to him alone. However, we shall use this as an opportunity to examine both the general concept of the photographer's role and the history of this particular photographer's practice. For Atget's identity as the great photographer is a complete paradox.

A deserved place in history

Eugène Atget makes his presence felt twice in the history of photography. The first time, in around 1890, he made himself known to his clients in Paris. The second time, his work was presented, after his death, to the entire world. The second time around there was some uncertainty over how to present Atget, how to see his photographs, and how to assess their significance. Nowadays, this uncertainty has become a part of Atget's historical identity. He occupies much the same place in the history of photography as Cézanne does in the history of painting – at the turning point between nineteenth- and twentieth-century pictorial standards. A photographic tradition has been established, originating with Atget and running through the new documentary work of the 1920s and 1930s: Berenice Abbott, Brassaï, André Kertész, Henri Cartier-Bresson, and Walker Evans. The line of descent continues and spreads across America. Atget's heirs include Robert Frank, Garry Winogrand, and Lee Friedlander, as well as countless others. As a lineage it has been legitimized and elaborated by John Szarkowski, Director of the Department of Photography of the Museum of Modern Art in New York, which now houses what remains of Atget's own archive of prints and glass negatives. As a line of descent, it gives photography a destiny as a medium in a state of constant self-perfection and refinement, a medium that behaves like the painting of Cézanne. This tradition is now entrenched and is itself an historical phenomenon, a counterpart to the formalist tradition set up for painting by the American critic Clement Greenberg.[2] The great photographer is the same as the great artist.

It is misleading, however, to compare Atget with Cézanne. Atget was hardly a pure art photographer: impurity was his specialty and the aesthetic was not his field. Ordinarily, he used photography to make beautiful, but deeply practical images. They represent a turning point in the history of photography, it is true, but if one wants an analogy from the history of art, it is better to

1. R. Barthes, *Camera Lucida*, trans. by R. Howard, London, Flamingo, 1984, p. 16.

2. See John Szarkowski's many catalogues for the Museum of Modern Art, especially the series of four books he did in collaboration with Maria Morris Hambourg, *The Work of Atget*, New York, Museum of Modern Art, 1981–1984. See Clement Greenberg, *Art and Culture* Paris, Macula, 1989, and "Four Photographers", *New York Review of Books*, January 23, 1964), pp. 8–9.

consider Duchamp, the man who during the First World War tried to make a work that was not a work of art. Like Duchamp's, Atget's eloquence was designed to speak from outside art. Like Duchamp, that would be the sign of his strength and of his greatness.

Atget did not plan his entry onto the world stage. In fact, he did not live long enough to see it for himself. That entrance was largely the work of another, younger, American photographer, Berenice Abbott. Abbott had met Atget in the course of her work as Man Ray's studio assistant in the mid-1920s. It was a simple meeting: Atget lived down the street from Man Ray and had a business selling photographic documents to artists, which entailed making visits to their studios. In the course of his regular business, he met Man Ray, and became known to the other Surrealists who frequented Montparnasse. The encounter with Abbott followed. She visited Atget's studio a few times, with a friend, another American, Julien Levy, and bought some of his work. Atget was some fifty years older than them. He told them, despite their less than perfect French, that his pictures were documents – documents for artists. The Americans took the phrase back with them, treating it, like the photographs, as something of an enigma. Meanwhile, in 1926, the Surrealists published a few of Atget's pictures in their magazine, *La Révolution surréaliste*. The Surrealists did not see Atget as Cézanne. On the contrary, they embraced his documents into their infatuation with Paris popular culture. They saw the difference in his work; they did not see Atget as one of them. Unlike the Americans, the Surrealists knew how important it was that Atget's work belonged to another category.

Atget died the following year. Berenice Abbott undertook to buy his studio effects (now the Museum of Modern Art Atget archive), and to promote his work. She arranged for Atget's work to be included in the Salon Indépendant de la Photographie in May 1928. She also arranged for the publication of a book in 1930, *Atget, photographe de Paris*, with a preface written by Pierre Mac Orlan. This book was perhaps the best of all possible vehicles for the wider dissemination of Atget's photographs. In California, Edward Weston saw it and was disappointed: "I had expected a flame, and found but a warm glow."[3] In Germany, Walter Benjamin wrote a review of it and then, a few years later, an extrapolation which became the famous essay *The Work of Art in the Age of Mechanical Reproduction* (1936).[4] He too saw Atget as the great transitional figure in the history of photography but his reasoning proceeded along somewhat different lines. He saw Atget's work as marking a shift from an image

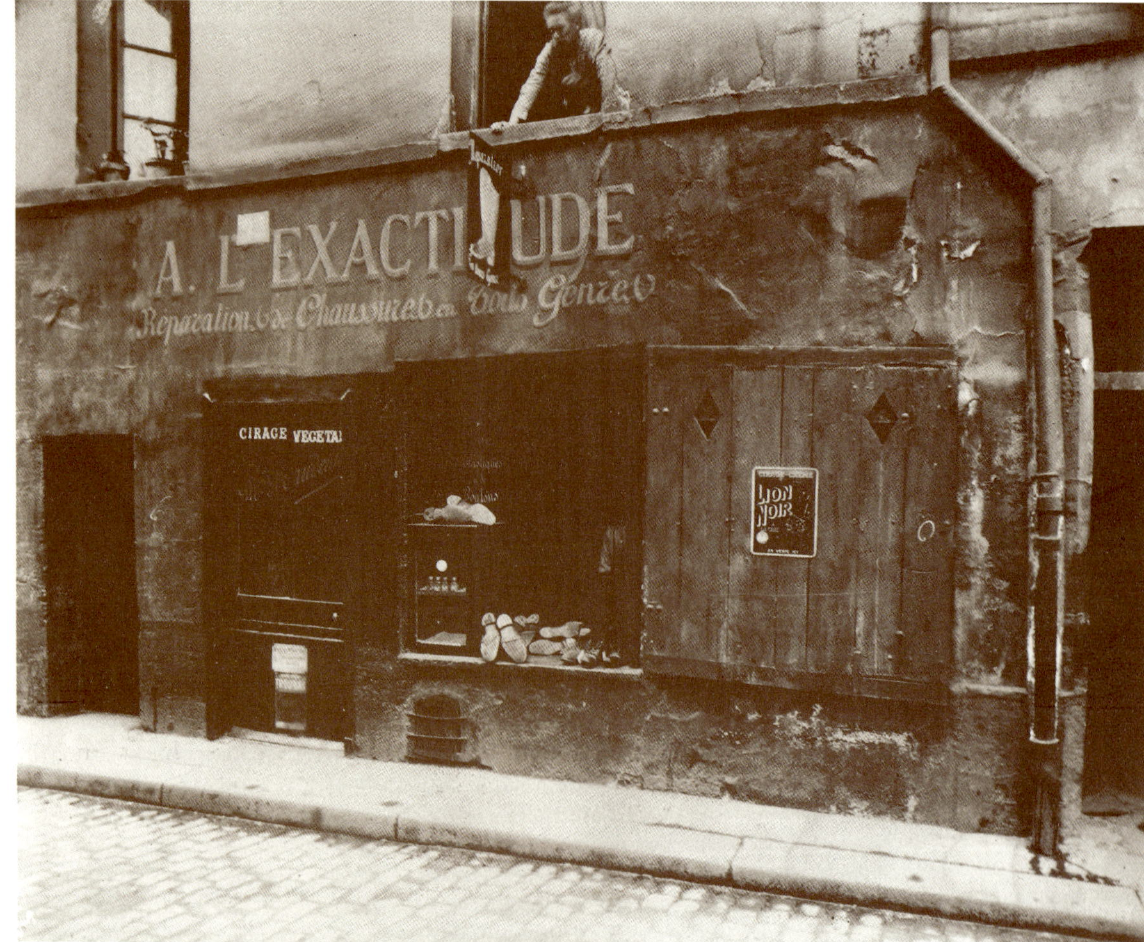

EUGÈNE ATGET,
Shop, 93 Rue Broca,
1912,
Museum of Modern Art,
New York.

3. E. Weston, *The Daybooks of Edward Weston*, vol. 2, *California*, ed. Nancy Newhall, Millerton, Aperture, n.d., p. 202, December 27, 1930.

4. W. Benjamin, "The Work of Art in the Age of Mechanical Reproduction", in *Illuminations*, ed. Hannah Arendt, trans. Harry Zohn, London, Fontana Press, 1973, and "The Short History of Photography", French translation in *Essais 2, 1935–1940*, Paris, Denöel and Gonthier, 1983.

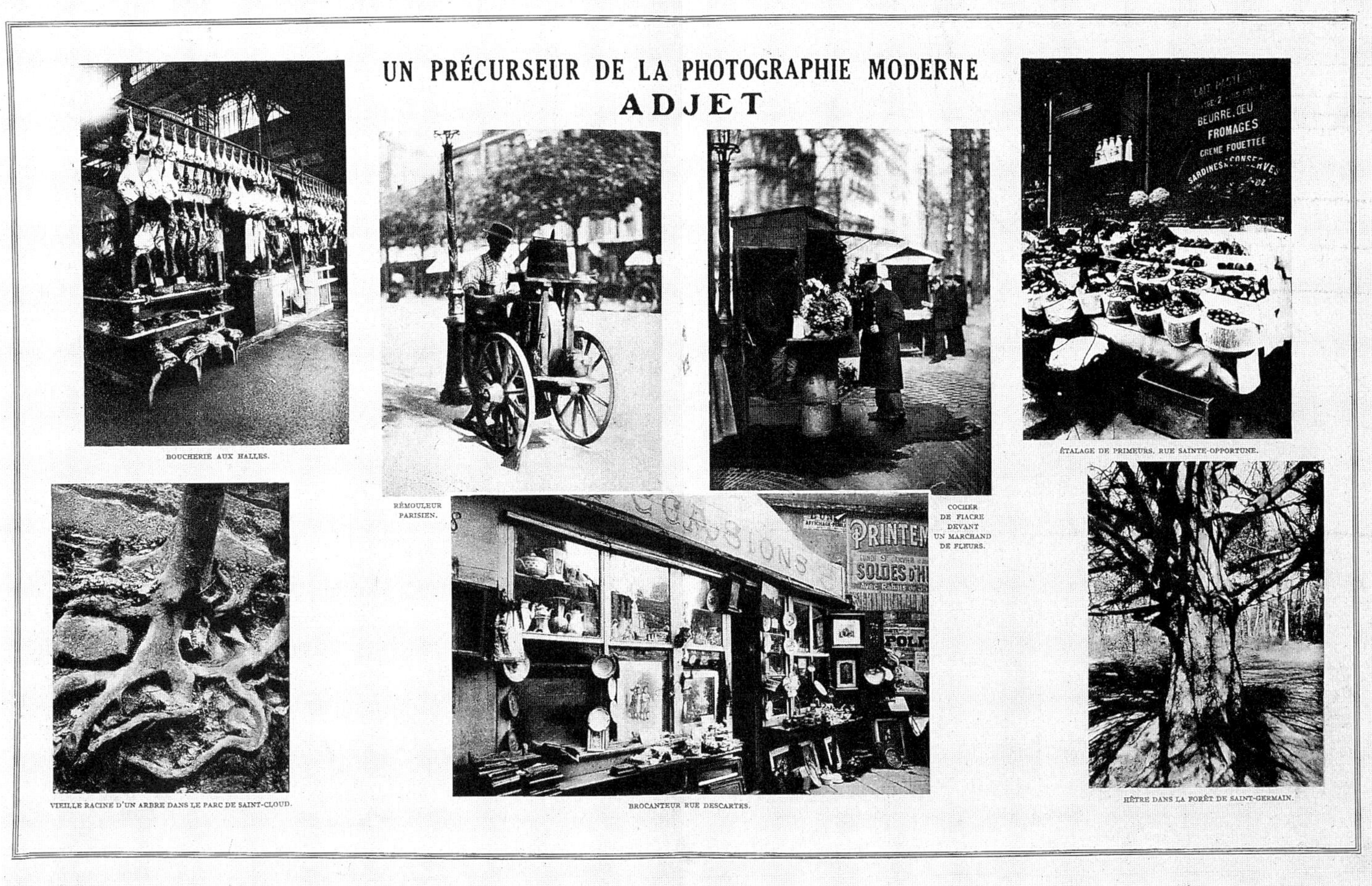

UN PRÉCURSEUR DE LA PHOTOGRAPHIE MODERNE
ADJET

BOUCHERIE AUX HALLES.

RÉMOULEUR PARISIEN.

COCHER DE FIACRE DEVANT UN MARCHAND DE FLEURS.

ÉTALAGE DE PRIMEURS, RUE SAINTE-OPPORTUNE.

VIEILLE RACINE D'UN ARBRE DANS LE PARC DE SAINT-CLOUD.

BROCANTEUR RUE DESCARTES.

HÊTRE DANS LA FORÊT DE SAINT-GERMAIN.

ARTICLE ON "ADJET", double-page spread from *L'Art Vivant*, no. 97, January 1, 1929.

culture based on ritual and cult value to one based on exhibition value and an appeal to the masses. Benjamin saw the expository value of Atget's photographs; when he understood that free floating contemplation was not appropriate to them, he spoke to their status as documents.

Nature of the document

First, we must understand what kind of picture a document was. It was not necessarily a photograph. A document was a picture which had a job to perform. Not a style, it was an entire class of images and a supremely practical image. Before the First World War it was understood to be poles apart from the aesthetic. After the War, the proliferation of news photographs and half-tone reproductions led to another conception of the photographic document, as a supremely modern form, ripe for exploitation by modern artists. That new concept of the document attracted Walter Benjamin, László Moholy-Nagy, André Kertész, Henri Cartier-Bresson, and Berenice Abbott, and the Surrealists, to cite just a few examples. But while Atget worked, the document was perhaps the lowest order of image imaginable. Artists who looked at documents did so to use them, not to emulate them.

The document is difficult to consider as a general case. It becomes unbelievably open-ended, lacking in intellectual rigor, flexible to the point of vagueness. Yet the document was in large part defined by this very openness. The best definition of the document, given on the occasion of the Fifth International Congress of Photography held in Brussels in 1910, speaks of nothing but neutral, rubbery options: "A document must be used for studies of a varied nature, hence the necessity to include as much detail as possible in the given subject area. Any image may, at a particular moment, be used for research. Nothing should be scorned. The beauty of the photograph is of secondary importance; all that is required is for the image to be clear, rich in detail, and treated with care in order to survive undamaged for as long as possible."[5]

To put a somewhat finer point on it, a document was a study sheet. Its beauty was secondary; use came first. This meant that the document had no prescribed form; in absolute terms we could say that it was a detailed blank – and, by extension, that it was an impersonal, expository picture, the zero degree of the image, taking shape as its job became clear. As Albert Londe, the photographer who worked with Dr. Charcot, explained, the photograph was a good document

5. A. Reyner, *Camera obscura*, quoted in *Ve Congrès International de photographie*, Brussels, 1910, ed. C. Puttemenas, L. P. Clerc, and E. Wallon Brussels, Bruylant, 1912, p. 72. Fréderic Dillaye, in his book, *Principes et pratique d'art en photographie: Le paysage*, Paris, Gauthier-Villars, 1899, p. 2, gave a similar defintion in order to distinguish the document from the artistic photograph.

Eugène Atget

Born at Libourne, in the Gironde *département* in 1857, and brought up as an orphan by his grandparents, becoming a sailor, it was not Atget's intention to become a photographer. He wanted to be an actor and entered the Paris Conservatoire, but with very little success; at the age of 30 he abandoned the idea.

It was in around 1890 that he became a photographer, specializing in "documents for artists" – landscapes, animals, flowers, monuments – for "collecting was not a mere tradesman's activity". He undertook systematic "campaigns" on various subjects presumably chosen with particular ends in mind and because they were likely to be in demand. He offered his photographs to professionals wanting to build up a historical corpus (for example, of decorative elements in ironwork or bas-reliefs).

He started in 1897 with a series on minor trades in Paris (some images would be published as postcards), then tended to emphasize "art in old Paris" (from 1901) and the architectural details of large private houses mantelpieces, balconies, carriage entrances, staircases), and the inner courtyards of buildings, stalls, and storefronts, in an attempt to assemble a documentation of things which would be obliterated by renovation works. He photographed the statues of the Tuileries, the park at Versailles, and later the park at Sceaux (1925). His architectural shots, which provide a record of elevations of building which, though characterless, were destined to disappear, were offered to institutions, which still preserve huge numbers of them (more than 5,000 at the Musée Carnavalet; about 1,600 in the library of the École des Beaux-Arts; more than 5,000 in the Bibliothèque Historique de la Ville de Paris; more than 4,000 in the Bibliothèque Nationale; around 1,600 in the Bibliothèque des Arts Décoratifs; a similar number in the Bibliothèque Doucet; and many in the Victoria and Albert Museum) Atget used a large-format camera with 10 x 8 inch bromo-gelatine plates, and produced his own contact prints using direct darkening albumen paper which was gold toned. All his negatives were numbered and catalogued in classified series, allowing him to locate and print each image on demand.

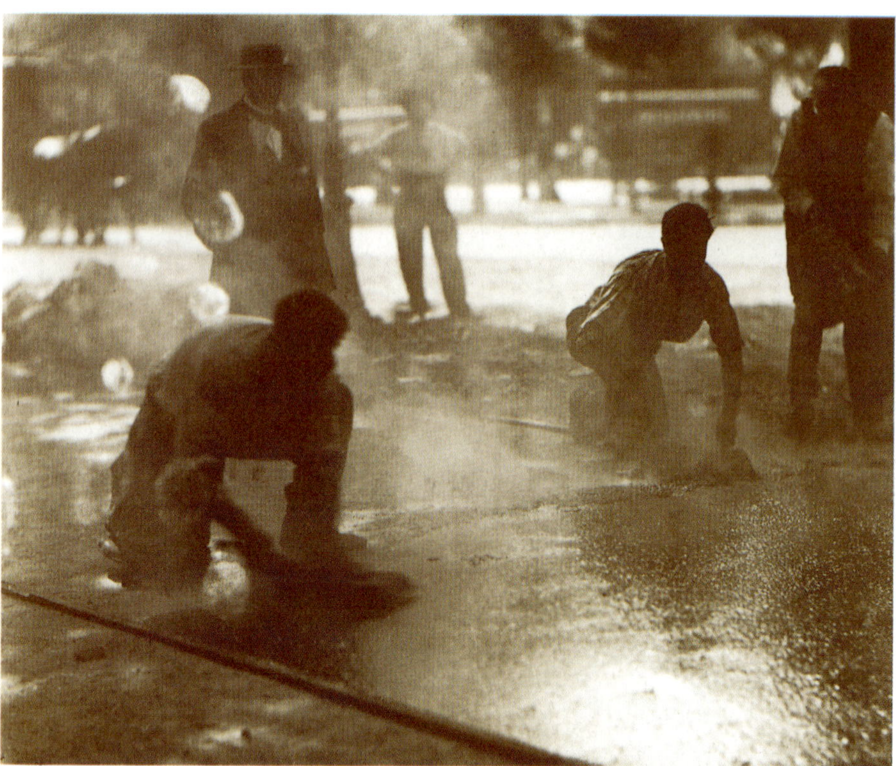

Eugène Atget, *Men laying tar,* 1899–1900, Museum of Modern Art, New York.

Atget also pursued political activities as a lecturer at local workers' schools and a reader of the Socialist press. He collected a large dossier of press cuttings on the notorious Dreyfus case.

Atget must have taken around 7,000 photographs. Contrary to popular belief, his work was not entirely neglected during his lifetime. He was known by Man Ray, who lived in the same street (Rue Campagne-Première). The Surrealists of 1926 regarded him as a photographer of odd things. At that time he was a tradesman using outdated techniques, yet his discipline and devotion to his art still provided an example to others. In 1920 the administration of the École des Beaux-Arts took up his offer to sell 2,600 of his negatives. Another 2,000, showing old Paris, bought at his death in 1927 are now in the photographic archives of the Direction du Patrimoine, at Saint-Cyr. Around 4,000 prints and 1,300 negatives were acquired shortly after his death by Julien Levy, an American collector and gallery director, at the suggestion of Berenice Abbott, Man Ray's assistant (now in the Museum of Modern Art, New York).

Atget was undoubtedly not a naive artist or a premature Surrealist. If towards the end of his life his documents became more inspired and stranger – shop mannequins, for example – thus attaining the sense of weirdness in everyday life preached by Man Ray or Breton, this was also because even the most methodical and austere photographic practice may lead, when out of its temporal and spatial context, to mysteries of interpretation – an outcome which the images are powerless to prevent.

Michel Frizot

because it was true, exact, rigorous. It could be applied to art as well as to science, providing a "document vu" to accompany the "document écrit".[6] It would tell the truth about, say, a doorway, an animal in motion, an earlobe or a hysteric. So an architectural photograph would be called a document, as would a chronophotograph, a police identity card or an x-ray. They had one thing in common: all of them were pictures that went to work.

The document's relation to knowledge was neither natural nor trivial. These photographs did not trade on the simple physical relation between motif and referent: the document was not to be a guileless mirror. Rather, the document was full of conventional relations not only between itself and its motif but between itself and an ulterior product.

Here, the photograph becomes more than a mirror of nature: it participates in the higher orders of communication. Very simply, the

6. A. Londe, *La photographie moderne: pratique et applications* (2nd ed., Paris, Masson, 1896, p. 570. See chapter XI, "Photographie Documentaire", pp. 545–571.

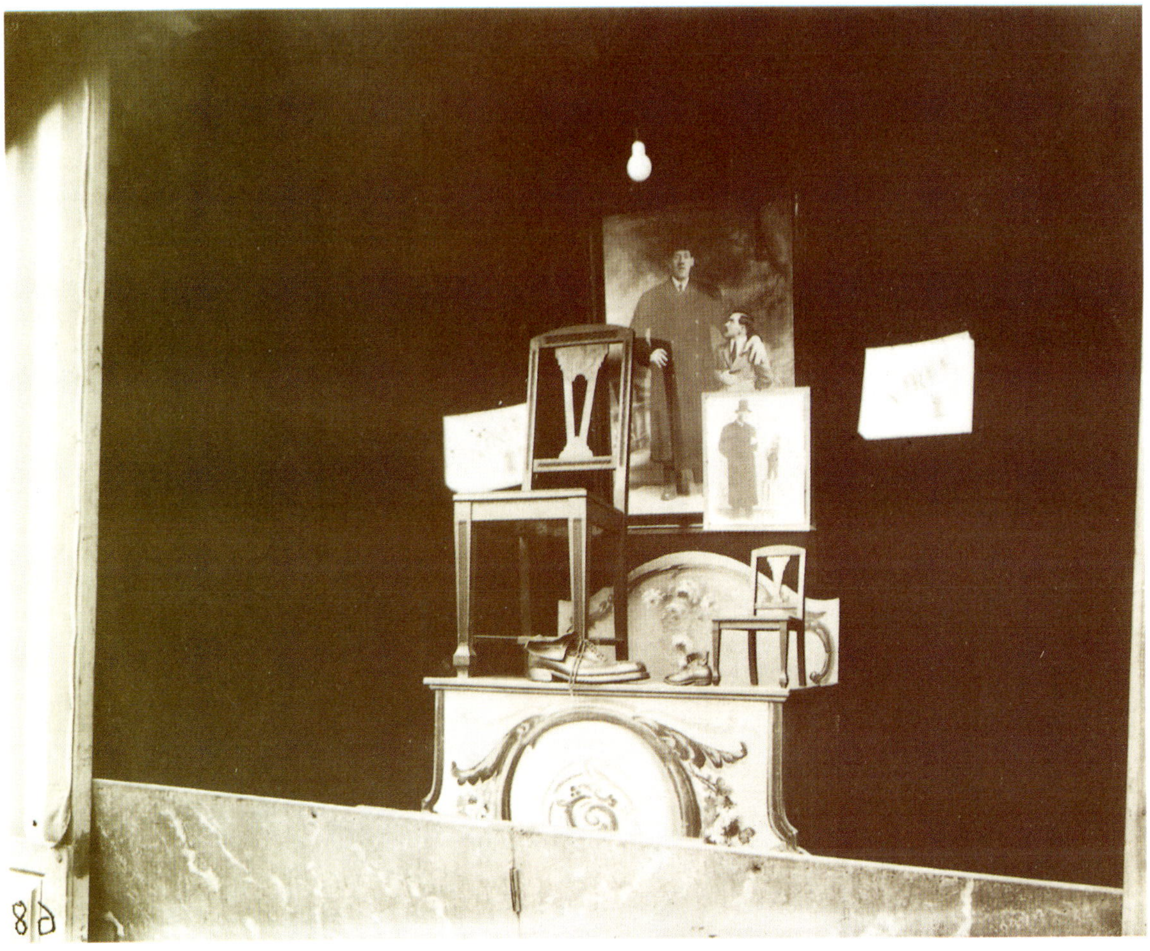

Eugène Atget,
Shop Window, Fête du Trône, (the Giant and the Dwarf),
1925,
Art Institute of Chicago.

photograph enters language. The document became such an important *kind* of picture because it set up new, modern models for the relationship between pictorial form and knowledge.

The document was, therefore, not an end but a beginning. The document held grains of knowledge that would, in turn, be used to produce more advanced knowledge, usually in another form. So, a document of old Paris would inform an antiquarian's account of a seventeenth-century political event; a document from a lampshade salesman's catalogue might inform a genre painting meant for exhibition at the Salon. The document was not itself, however, a source of power. Rather, it spoke from the position of a worker producing for an employer, a worker helping to produce certain areas of bourgeois knowledge. Documents fed a reservoir of such knowledge. The relationship of these bits of knowledge to one another was not mapped out, nor were they set out in some hierarchical order. Rather, they jostled one another, overlapped each other, started and stopped wherever. Any supplier of documents knew this automatically. Knowledge exists not as a distinct body but as a confused jumble of *connaissances*.

Obviously, a document could not function very well at the general level of its definition. Its details acquired their full significance only when given a sense of purpose. A document could not exist alone – it needed a viewer and a task. For a document was actually defined dialectically, that is, by a viewer extracting a certain kind of technical information from the picture and by the picture's ability to display just that technical sign. Both were needed for the document to become a document. In fact, the many possible different technical uses for pictures produced different, discontinuous families of documents, each of which had their own characteristics. Even so, all documents contained technical signs which were lodged in the very appearance of the picture.

Atget's pictures, complete with their technical signs, moved back and forth in a crowd of what must be understood as professional references. They worked behind the scenes, and then, duty done, could expect to be buried in a file. When Atget called his pictures documents he was explaining that they circulated in the closed channels of painter's cartoons, decorators' folios, and libraries' files, where individual pictures counted for little and the quality of the file was measured by its quantity and breadth of coverage. Unlike Baudelaire, he saw a inherent dignity in this kind of picture. This puts Atget's ideas against the grain of so many others that it bears stopping to

7. M. Foucault, *L'Archéologie du savoir*, p. 171. Some of the best analyses of the photographic archive work directly with Foucault's propositions. See especially R. Krauss, "Photography's Discursive Spaces: Landscape/View", *Art Journal*, 41, winter 1982, pp. 311–319, A Sekula, "The Body and the Archive", no. 39, winter 1986, pp. 3–64, and "Photography between Labour and Capital", in *Mining Photographs and Other Pictures 1948–1968: A Selection from the Negative Archives of Shedden Studio, Clace Bay, Cape Breton*, ed. B. H. D. Buchloh and R. Wilkie, Halifax, NASCAD, 1983, pp. 193–268. For more on the archive itself see the issue of *Traverses* devoted to the subject, no. 36 (January 1986).

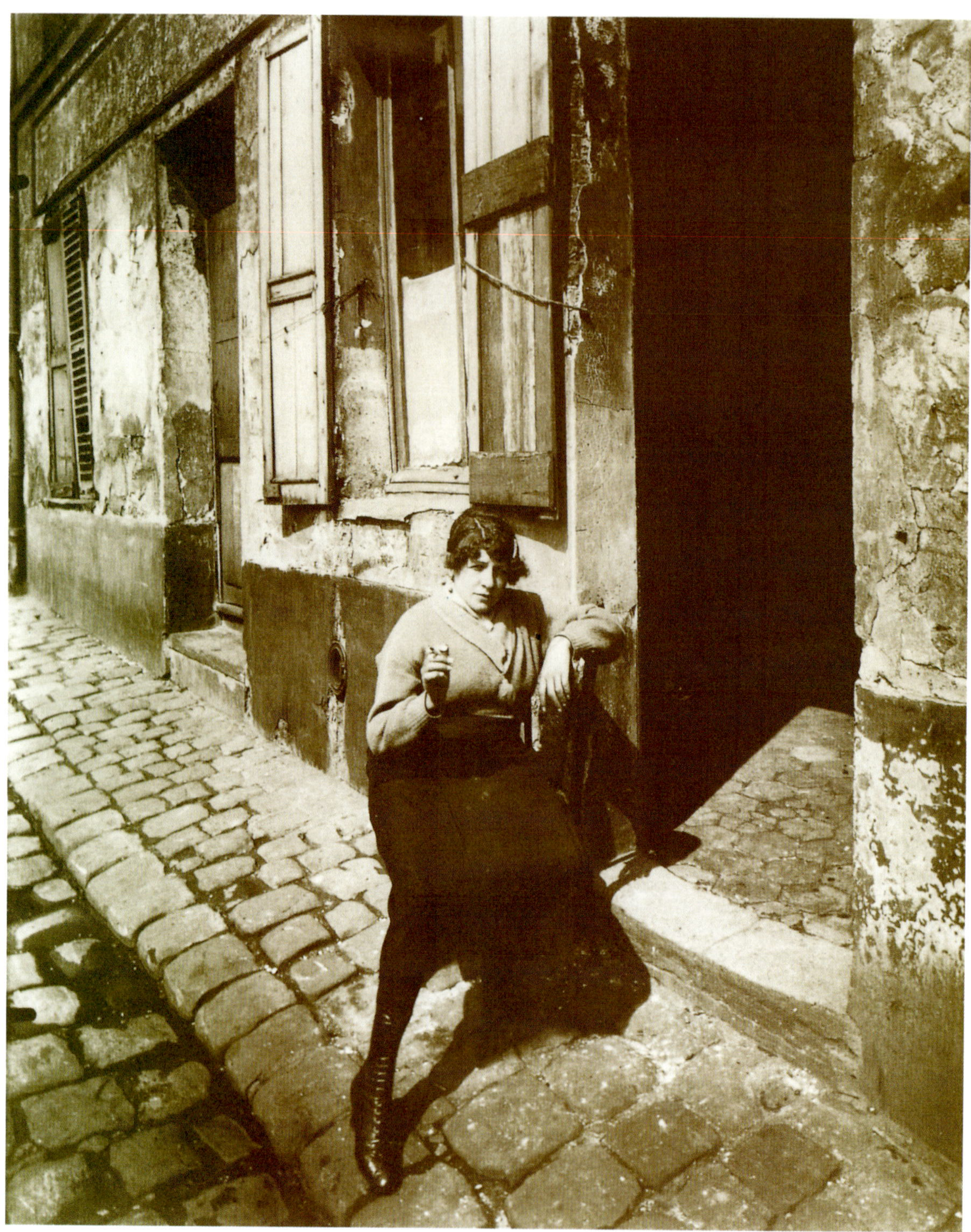

EUGÈNE ATGET, *Prostitute Touting for Trade at Villette,* 1921, Museum of Modern Art, New York.

consider how to reconcile this with our preconceptions about culture. We might first try calling the entire complex of documents and references an archive, though not exactly following Foucault, who used the term abstractly to describe "the general system of the formation and transformation of statements", the general order of words and things.[7] A philosophical notion of the archive will not do as a defining concept when discussing knowledge after it has entered history, if only because it ignores specific archives, from Atget's own personal archive to the files kept by his clients, like the Bibliothèque Nationale or the painter Édouard Detaille.

A general definition of the archive, like the general definition of the document, deflects us from considering the qualitative differences between specific archives. It also discourages an examination of their essential incompatibility. For each of these archives hoped to establish its own special relation to a kind of knowledge, and sometimes to more than one kind. Each exercised its own power over its own strand of knowledge. In practice, the same documents could take on different roles in different archives. Indeed, the way in which archives were organized varied a great deal. Specific, small archives did not come together like the French state, centralized, indexed, under the control

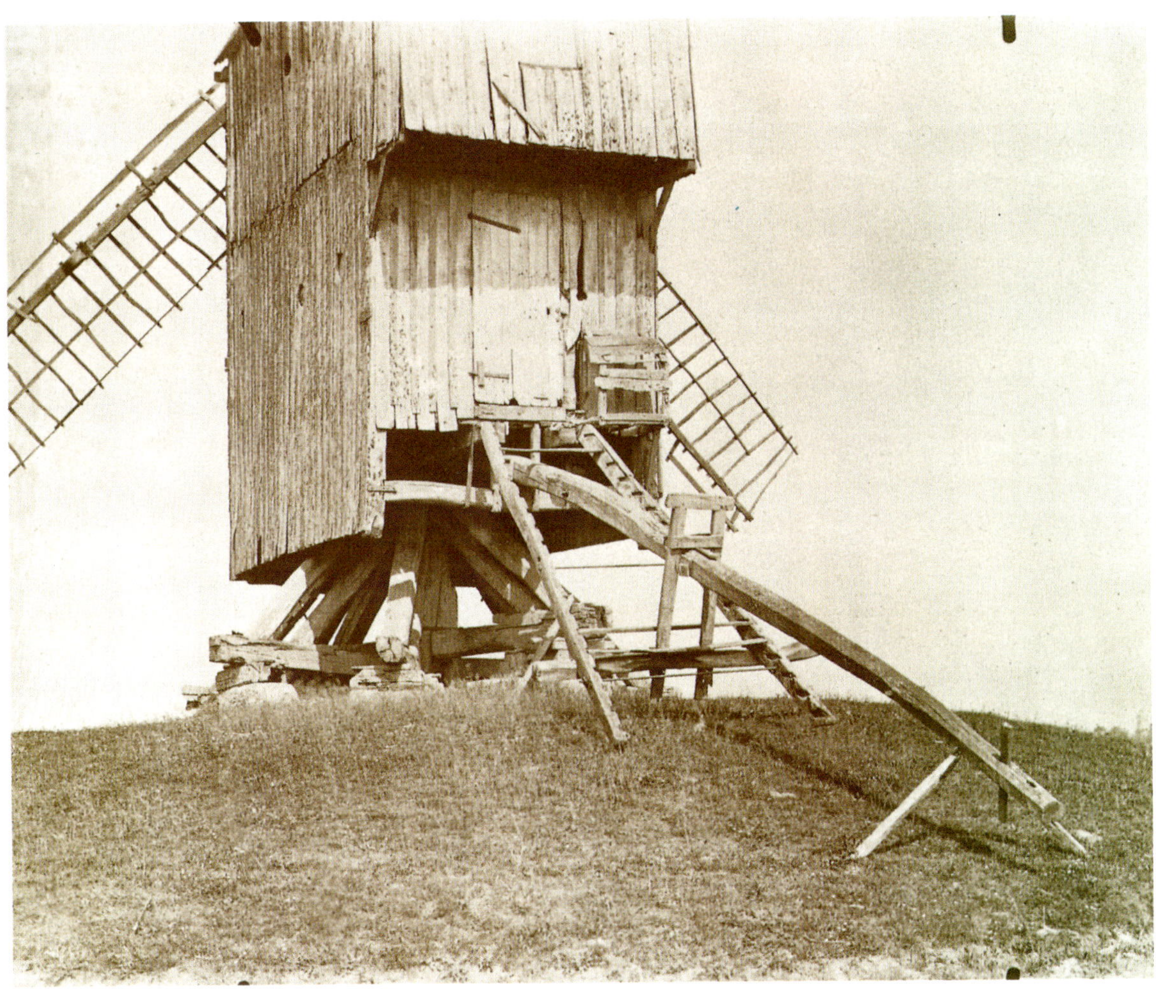

EUGÈNE ATGET,
Windmill in the Somme Département,
circa 1890,
John Paul Getty Museum,
Malibu.

of a single authority. It would have been impossible for Atget to have developed a general, let alone a monolithic, idea of "The Archive", just as it would have been impossible for him to have developed a single idea of his own œuvre or his own style. Those were ideas for philosophers. The diversity of this culture of documents overrode such abstractions and rendered them obsolete.

A market culture

Technical rather than aesthetic considerations prevailed. Documents were dissected and the required information extracted from them. Any pleasure was practical; this culture was a culture of work. Let us consider a few examples – "document-types". Atget supplied certain markets and produced documents tailored specifically for their use. The bulk of his energy was directed towards producing documents for artists, builders, set designers or historians. Each of these professions had their own visual criteria for documents and their own conventions for seeing their particular kind of knowledge. It was up to Atget to master those conventions – and he did.

Embedded in each kind of document were sets of conventions that depended upon the existence of technical signs. For painters like Édouard Detaille, for example, it was necessary to have a file of motifs on hand – drawn, painted or photographed, it did not matter much. These motifs were used and combined when assembling a painting.

When Detaille began to paint he would turn to his stock of documents, which included photographs by Atget. For two paintings, for example, he referred to Atget's picture of an old windmill in the Somme département. Perhaps Detaille liked the way its stairs elevated the action above the troops and projected it beyond the frame. In both paintings we are shown the sentry looking out. In both,

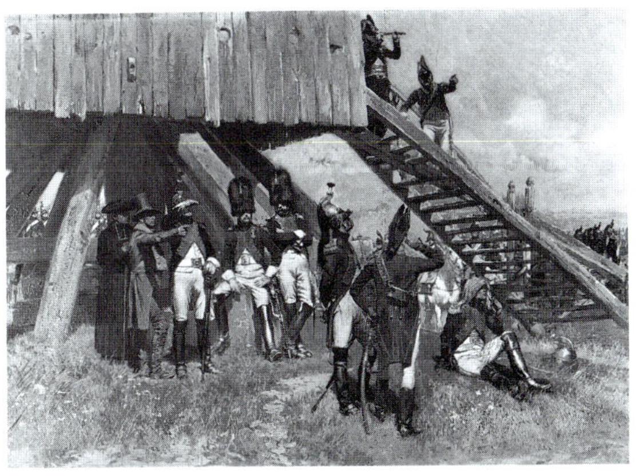

ÉDOUARD DETAILLE,
Reporting to Headquarters,
oil on canvas,
1903,
Musée de l'Armée, Paris.

8. J. Humbert kindly pointed me toward this material. See his book, *Édouard Detaille: l'héroïsme d'un siècle*, Paris, Copernic, 1979.

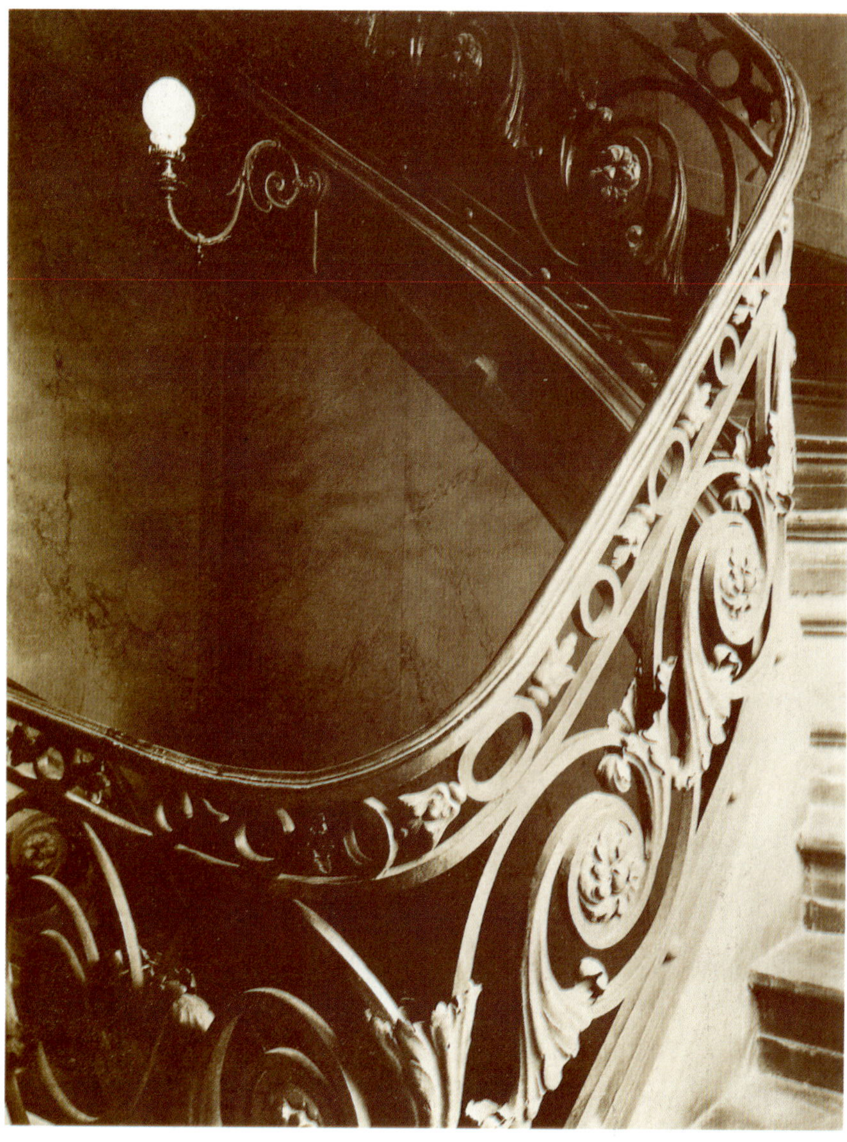

Eugène Atget, *Hôtel Sully-Charost, Rue du Cherche-Midi,* circa 1904–1905, Museum of Modern Art, New York.

Eugène Atget, ▶ *Nasturtiums,* circa 1921–1902, Museum of Modern Art, New York.

the mill has been converted to the business of war.

The first painting, *En observation dans un moulin* [On Watch in a Windmill], was an undated study for another project and, like any good study, it narrowed its focus to work on one aspect of the composition – here, the integration of the troops with the mill. Much the same process happened in the second painting, *Renseignements à l'État major* [Reporting to Headquarters], 1903. Detaille took battle seriously.

Atget's mill, of course, did not suggest battle. It was a willfully incomplete composition that demanded a more complete realization. It could only set the scene, suggest an appropriate starting point, a backdrop. This could lie anywhere in the document: the surfaces of buildings, the play of light across wood or stone. These details would be caught by the painter's eye, considered, and, if accepted, be transformed in the course of painting, in much the same way that cotton can be spun into cloth. The role of this background was not to predict action, but to lie waiting for it, a blank sheet and nothing more. Detaille painted his mill in two different wars. He exploited Atget's photograph, extracted the information he needed from it, and converted that information to paint.[8]

Those involved in the construction industry looked at documents in other ways and for other reasons. Much of the building industry was devoted to the business of reproducing the architectural styles of the ancien régime. Its craftsmen looked to images of historic buildings for stylistic references and for help in designing typical decorative motifs. Here, the photographic document was doing the job of the architectural drawing – not the thing itself but an image of the thing. Photographs also served the needs of the interior designer and decorator, like the photograph of a panel from the Hôtel Roquelaure. From such a detail a whole room could materialize.

Historians seeking to preserve "old" Paris from redevelopment compiled large and important collections of documents during the period in which Atget worked. Oddly, their visual criteria were minimal. In their eyes, the most important things were the detail and clarity of the images. In addition, however, they also wanted historical purity in the document, which meant that, ideally, no trace of modern times should be seen. In 1909, when Fernand Bournon used Atget's document of the Fontaine Bouchardon to illustrate his book *La voie publique et son décor* he made sure that a cart in the foreground of the picture was retouched into oblivion. An antiquarian would ignore such an anachronism: the cart was not part of the technical sign, it was nothing but an imperfection.

Atget would come to understand that his documents were supposed to come "cleansed" of the present. However, he would also understand that as long as the basic requirements of documentary convention were met, as long as the document remained useful, he could still sell less than perfect documents to archives. Atget's practice as a documentary photographer is characterized by series of wilful, but slight, imperfections.

Atget learned fairly quickly that different kinds of documents could be combined into a single picture. In other words, that a photograph could contain several kinds of technical sign at the same time. Sometimes, the presence of more than one technical sign would barely trouble the form of the photograph. A close-up of nasturtiums, for example, which revealed the outlines of the leaves and flowers, was also useful to decorators like Eugène Grasset, who looked to nature when developing the *art nouveau* style. The same detail could also serve a painter of landscapes or still-lifes, who would consider the form of the plant differently, seizing on some other visual quality. The form of the plant was being scrutinized differently, but the photograph remained the same.

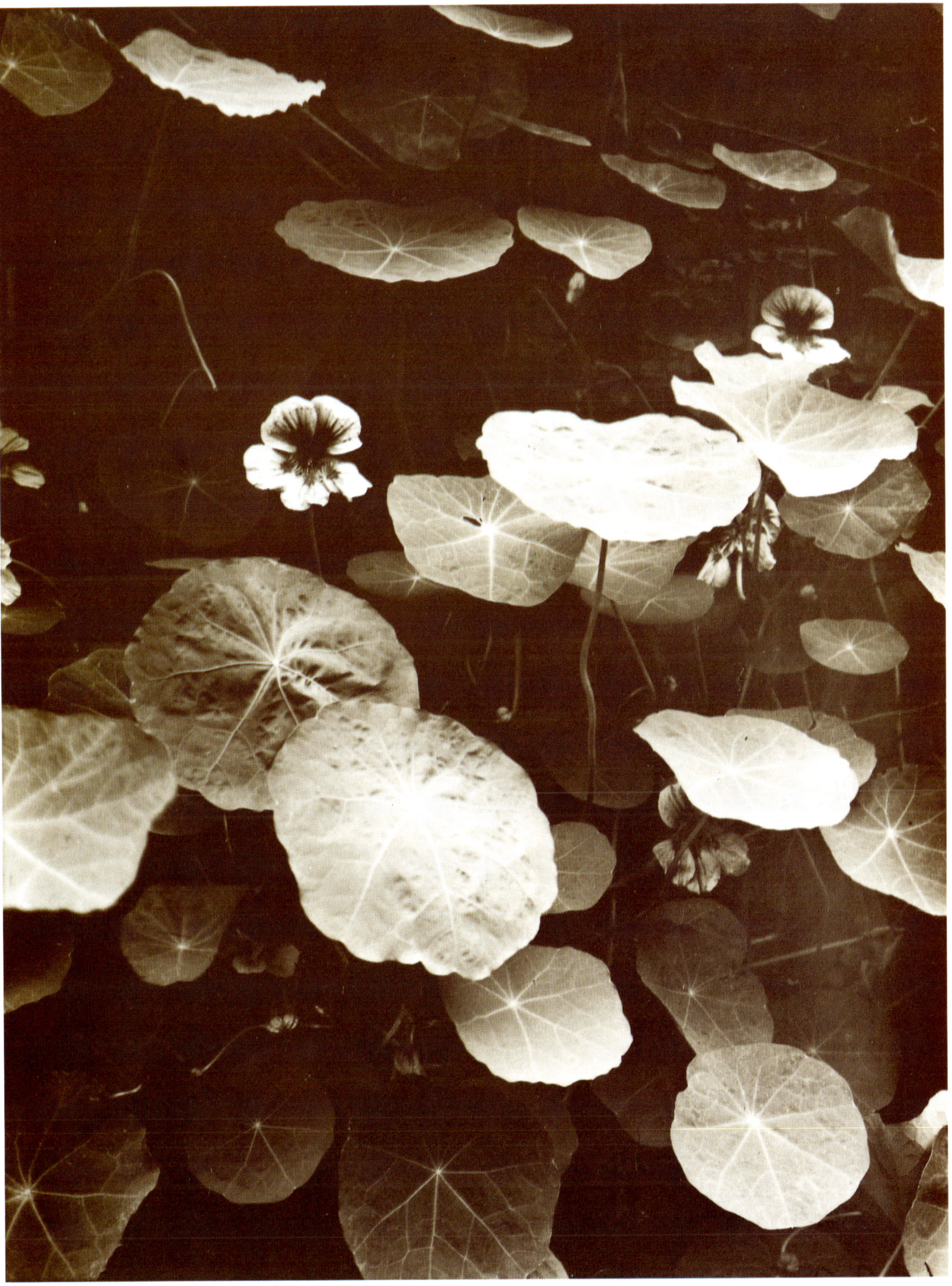

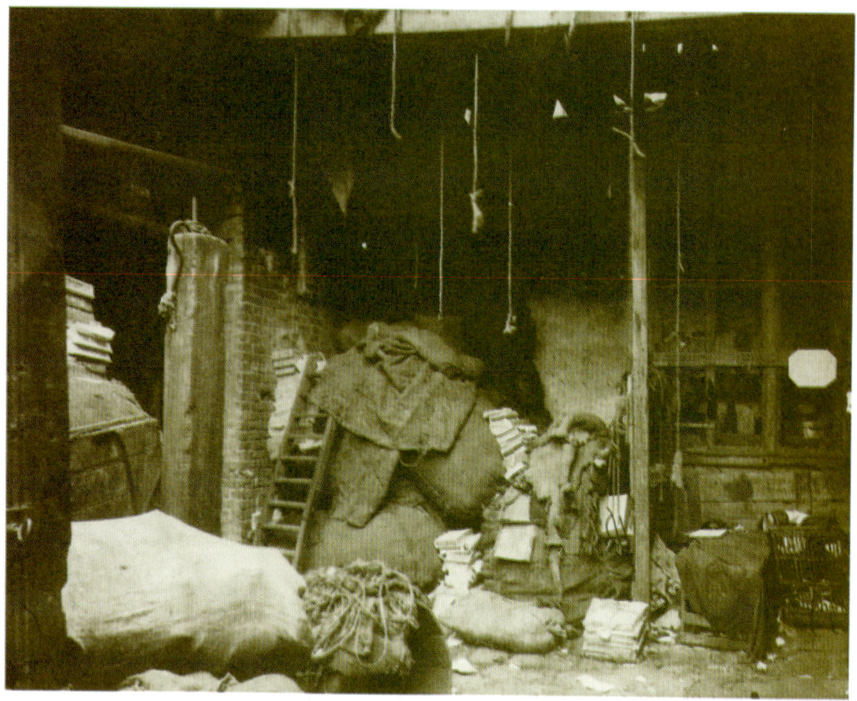

Eugène Atget, ***Ragpicker's Store, Porte d'Asnières, Cité Trébert,*** 1913, Museum of Modern Art, New York.

Other pictures, *Café "Au Tambour"*, for example, actually told of this differential scrutiny. There, the technical signs existed in different parts of the picture. There were signs for historians of Paris, who were interested only in the drum (*tambour*); there were signs for metalworkers, looking to see just how the grille and sign had been made; and there were signs of modern life – the distorted figures in the doorway.

In *Café "Au Tambour"*, these multiple uses were revealed in Atget's usual way. A cafe was shown on a bright winter's day, the light reflecting a view of the city in the glass window. The technical signs bumped against one another but plenty of intermediate space was left open. Into one such space, the windowpane, Atget captured his reflection, attaching it, together with that of his camera, to another man's head. The window was not crucial to any of the technical signs. In order to preserve the pictorial integrity of the facade, it should really have been kept free of any reflections. However, what transpired on or behind this pane of glass was immaterial to the professional viewer.

By working his reflection into the free space between the technical signs, Atget compromised the technical perfection of his document without undermining its usefulness. This allowed him to insert himself among the signs. He did not identify himself with the technical signs of the image; the document was fetishized in the intermediate spaces that bound the signs together and held the functional ambiguity in place. It was in the binding and grafting of the signs that Atget emerged as an author or, as he called himself, *auteur-éditeur*.

However, this document not only had more than one function, it also had more than one ontology. Atget included the image in an album, *Enseignes et vieilles boutiques de Paris*, one of a group of albums dealing with aspects of modern life that he eventually sold to the Bibliothèque Nationale between 1910 and 1915. These albums did not go into the library's files; they were catalogued under Atget's name as if they were published books.

With this shift from archive to book, the document entered the new century. The professional viewer became a general viewer. At this juncture – the aforementioned turning-point in the history of photography – the old hierarchy of technical signs was upset. The windowpane now became the critical space.

The album posed a different problem for the document, namely the photography of modern life, which in the case of the cabaret was assumed to be the low life of the lower classes. But the life of *Café "Au Tambour"* does not bear the usual signs of objectivity. This document proposed other forms for its truth. The truth of the cabaret is shown not so much through form as through obscurity. The men do not speak, they stare out with faint interest; the door has closed off any sense of drink and jest; outside there is but a chalked menu and cold stone.

If one can say anything about knowledge here, it is that knowledge is not given as a transparency but as a block. Modern life is shown through interrupted bodies, shadows, and glare. Any single truth has been occluded.

And yet the photograph has not turned its back on truth to reach an aesthetic alternative: it has turned toward more prosaic philosophical ground. It offers a conclusion: popular culture is not to be comprehended as an object or a form; it is unthinkable and hard to see. Atget brought the document to the *impensé*. His successors would work to transform the document into something else.

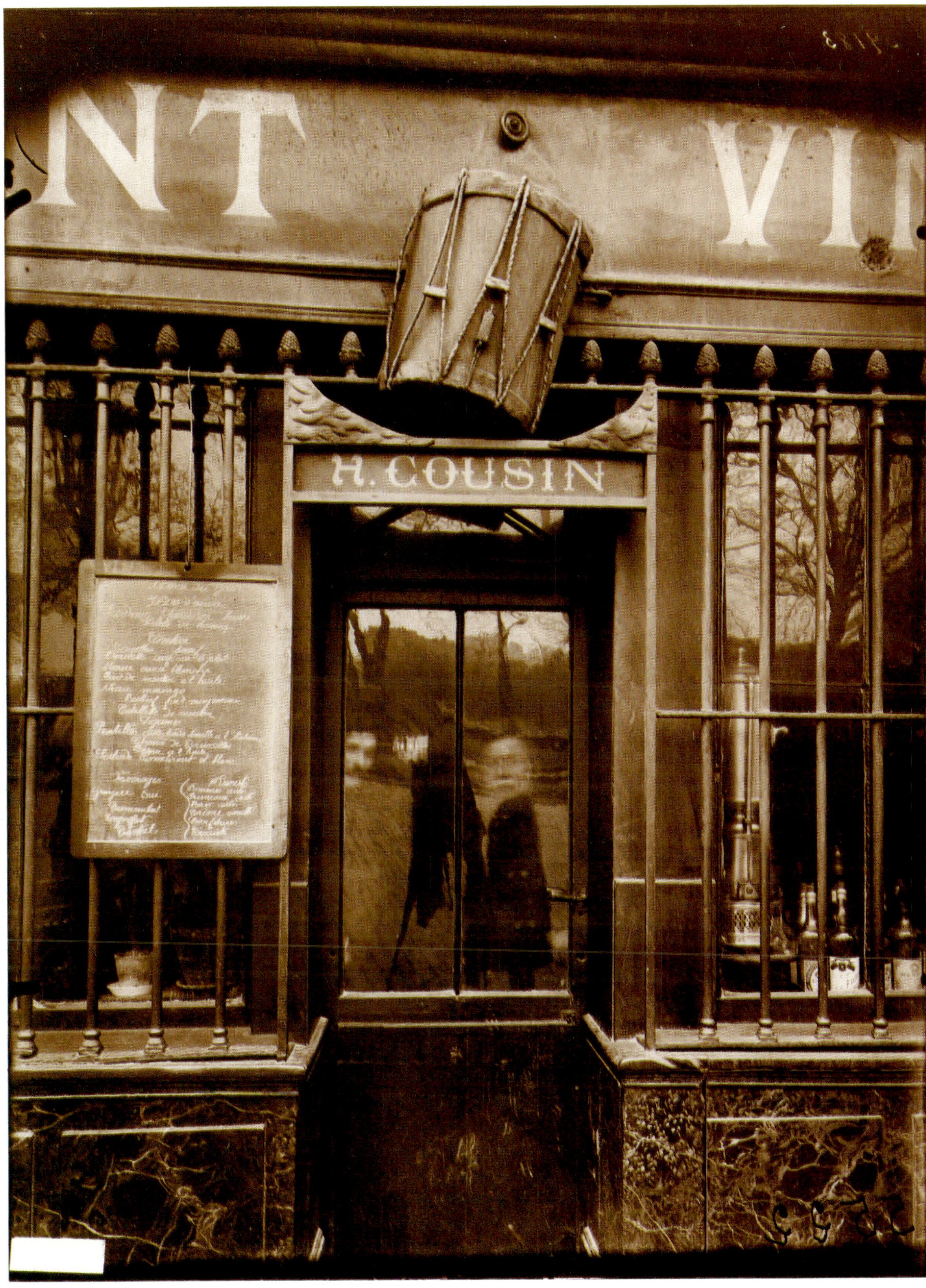

EUGÈNE ATGET,
Café "Au Tambour",
Quai de la Tournelle,
1908,
Archives Photographiques,
Paris.

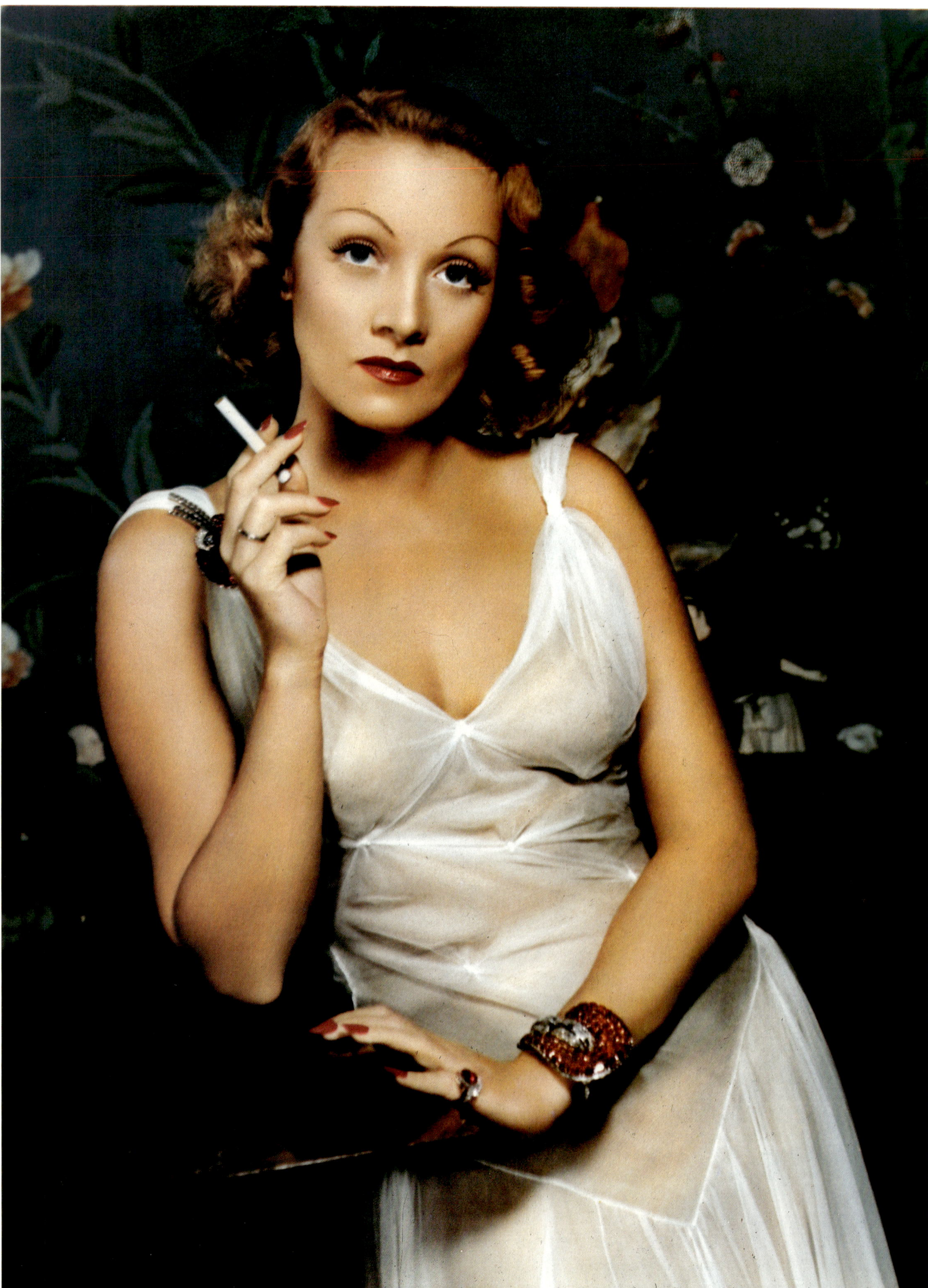

A NATURAL STRANGENESS

The hypothesis of color

Michel Frizot

By the middle of the nineteenth century, photography possessed the ability to reproduce exactly the forms of nature. Even several decades later, however, it was still incapable of capturing and preserving impressions of color. As the twentieth century progressed, a succession of complicated methods were tried, in an attempt to solve "the problem of color". These, however, gave results that were very different from the natural appearance of things. As techniques progressed, this discrepancy became more obvious and color photography, paradoxically, acquired an artificiality – an uncontrollable "strangeness" which a number of contemporary photographers learned to make use of in creating their pictures

People had dreamed of "colored" photography ever since the early work of Niépce who in his writings seems, at times, surprised that he obtained only images reproducing tonal values of light and shade. Like it or not, photography would have to make monochrome imagery the basis of its aesthetic. A black and white photograph, however, is totally unrealistic in terms of human perception, since our eyes do not naturally disassociate the intensity of light from the color of that light. Although light-sensitive emulsions recognized the wavelength of light received (and, therefore, its color) – nineteenth-century photographic emulsions were not sensitive to red light – the black and white negative left aside this notion of color. There was a real difficulty with incorporating color into the photographic process, since it is personal and subjective, perceived in different ways by different people. When it became clear that it was not going to be possible to reproduce color fully and exactly by photographic means, attention turned towards techniques that split the color into its composite elements and then recomposed it. The challenge of representing color and of recreating a colored view of reality was undertaken by these very varied processes.

But it is clear to everyone, looking at examples produced over a period of several decades, that this view of "reality" varied considerably depending on the process used. The period in which a particular process was used therefore came to represent the color of the time. There is a distinctive quality of color in an autochrome, just as there is for Technicolor film, that defines, simultaneously, both a style, and a particular historical period. Each process proclaims its color, each period proclaims its own dominant tones.

◀ Nickolas Muray, *Marlene Dietrich*, Carbro print, 1930, International Museum of Photography, George Eastman House, Rochester.

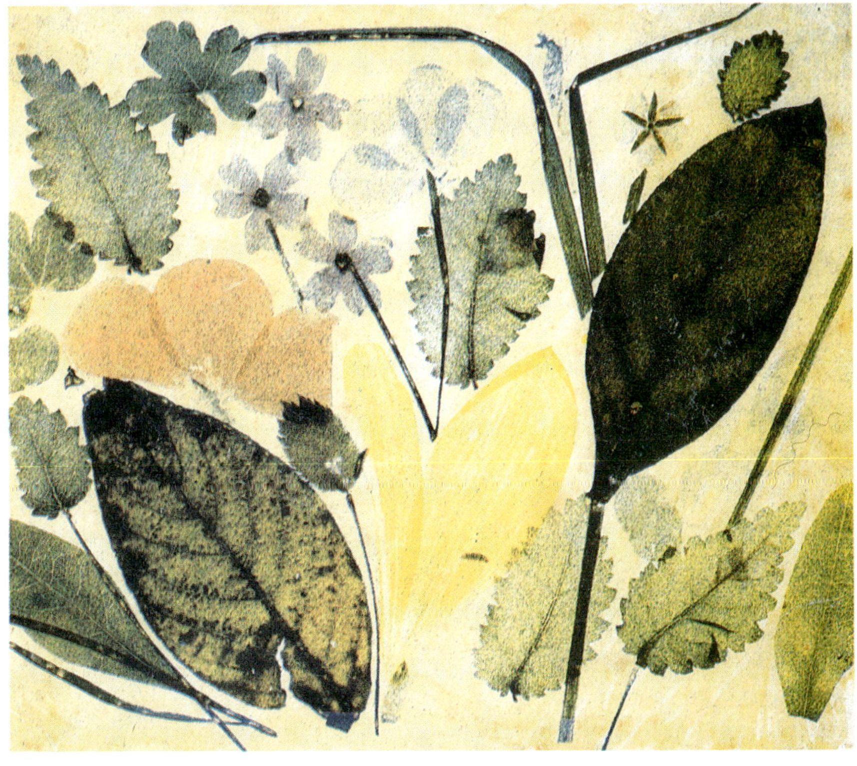

Louis Ducos du Hauron, *Trichrome, early experiments*, 1869, Société Française de Photographie, Paris.

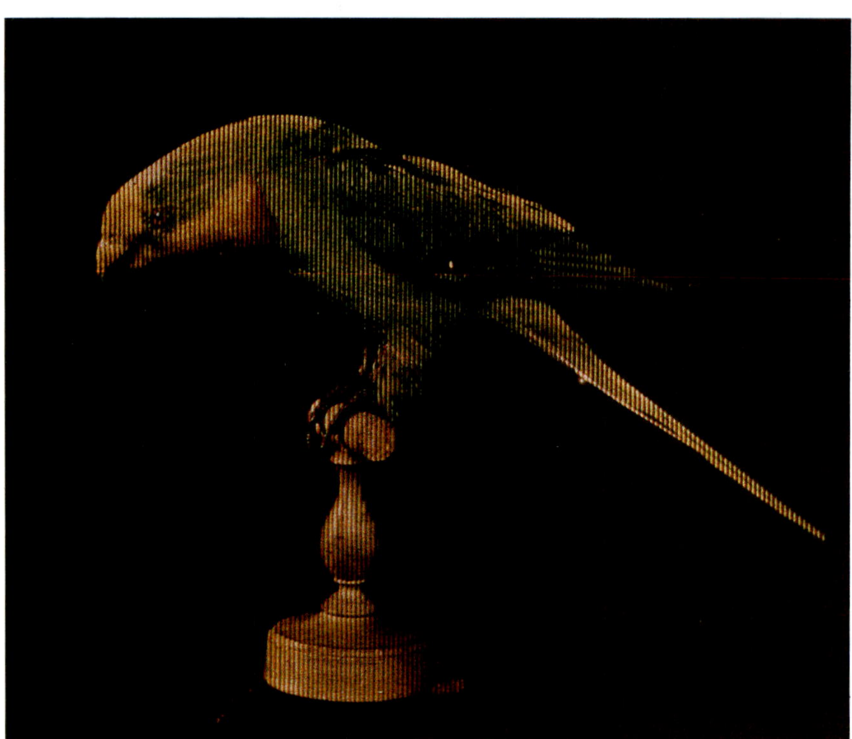

JOHN JOLY,
Parrot,
circa 1897,
Société Française
de Photographie, Paris.

There were other drawbacks, too. Just as great difficulties were encountered in transferring photographs to the printed page, there were also a number of problems associated with the photomechanical reproduction of color (half-tone engraving, heliochrome, three-color, four-color), which was governed by different optical laws from those of photography. The challenge of color was to make the transition from a colored object (a vase of flowers, for example) to a (transparent) slide, viewable only by transmitted light, or to a color negative, a color print made on paper or a color image printed in a magazine, without "betraying" the color of the original object and whilst retaining the impression of viewing the same thing.

To this should be added commercial considerations: Four-color reproduction, for books and the press, was significantly more expensive than black and white. This has obscured the possibility of a proper assessment of "color" material produced in the past. The colors were very unstable and the materials used to produce these images (apart from paper) have resulted in difficulties with storage and conservation. Whilst color photography represents the major part of present-day output, early color photography is still relatively unknown because it was not popularized in the mass media. Prohibitive reproduction rights, particularly in the field of fashion photography, have been an obstacle and private amateur photography is a neglected area for scholarly research. Thus, we cannot really know today what impact color photography, beginning in the 1930s, has had on the aesthetic of photography.

Colored illusion

Color is, in a way, an optical illusion. It is the most visible but, at the same time, most immaterial of natural phenomena. The discovery in the nineteenth century of a way of reproducing the illusion of color required an understanding of the physiological and optical laws that govern the way that we perceive color. Although Descartes had studied the laws of refraction, it was Newton, a century later, who discovered the "splitting" of sunlight ("white" light) by passing it through a prism, thus forming the seven colors of the spectrum (the experiment took place in a darkened room similar to a *camera obscura*).

The entire theory of color derives from this experiment and from the possibility of producing any color through mixing the colors of the spectrum. Two factors were at play here: luminance (the quantity of light) and chrominance (the nature and intensity of the various components of the light). Color synthesis could be achieved in two ways: through the combination of light of different colors (additive synthesis) or by viewing light from which certain colors have been filtered out (subtractive synthesis). We see the "natural" color of an object, for example, through a process of subtraction – the object absorbs part of the sunlight which shines on it and reflects the rest. One would see a different color if the object were viewed using a light with different wavelengths.

From these complex principles, practical discoveries at last made it possible to break out of the impasse facing Niépce de Saint-Victor around 1860 when he wished to capture all the colors of nature in a single sensitized layer (heliochrome), or Becquerel, with his non-permanent results with daguerreotypes. As a result of noticing that adding one color to another resulted in a third, different, color, it soon became clear that all colors could be synthesized through a combination of just three colors – known as primary colors. In about 1722, for example, Le Blon had invented a technique for printing colored engravings by combining blue, red, and yellow images. Additive color synthesis, originating in the theories of Young and Helmholtz, completed by Maxwell in 1857 and first demonstrated by him in 1861, made possible the creation of colored images through the superimposition on a screen of three separate black and white images, projected through filters of the primary colors – red, green, and blue. These observations were to have an important influence on painters, particularly the Impressionists and Post-Impressionists, through the work of Rood and with the republication of the work of Chevreul.[1]

1. O. N. Rood, *Modern Chromatics; Students' Text-book of Color with Applications to Art and Industry*, incl. a facsimile of the 1st American ed. of 1879 by D. Appleton and Co., notes by F. Birren, New York, Van Nostrand Reinhold Co., 1973; E. Chevreul, *De la loi du contraste simultané des couleurs*, 2nd ed., 1889.

Color and photography[2]

By coincidence, both Charles Cros and Louis Ducos du Hauron presented two very similar methods of color synthesis, using the same three-color principle, at the same meeting of the French Photographic Society on May 7, 1869. Cros, a poet, offered a method that was somewhat theoretical; that of Ducos was actually put into practice and used by many other researchers. Cros had, in fact, been pre-empted by the patent taken out by Ducos on November 23, 1868. However, their suggestions did not lead to any real practical success for a couple of decades. Frederick Ives, encouraged by the discovery of dry plates, which were more sensitive, made colored images in 1888, using three superimposed colors. He marketed his Kromscop camera commercially in 1895.[3] Ducos du Hauron went on to perfect a Chromographoscope (1897) and a Mélano-chromoscope (1899), which used mirrors and lenses to superimpose three images in blue, yellow, and red. Ducos used "coloring preparations of a transparent nature" in a variant of the carbon process, using three color-separation negatives obtained through orange-red, violet-blue, and green filters.

Becquerel had already criticized the results achieved with three-color processes at the Académie des Sciences on June 26, 1876, saying that "the positive images, tinted according to the whim of the operator [...] lead to touches of fantasy". However, the Lumière brothers presented similar images at the Universal Exhibition of 1900, as did Nachet with his Chromoscope.

At the same time, a very different method was put forward, less rudimentary but one whose scientific precision made dissemination difficult. This was Gabriel Lippman's interference method, based on the creation of interference patterns between light waves. A layer of mercury forming a mirror in contact with the sensitized surface created, at the moment of taking the photograph, interference patterns between the incident ray and the reflected ray. These registered in the gelatin-bromide emulsion layer. "The deposit of silver formed at the moment of developing is like a mold of the colored ray that produced it." These

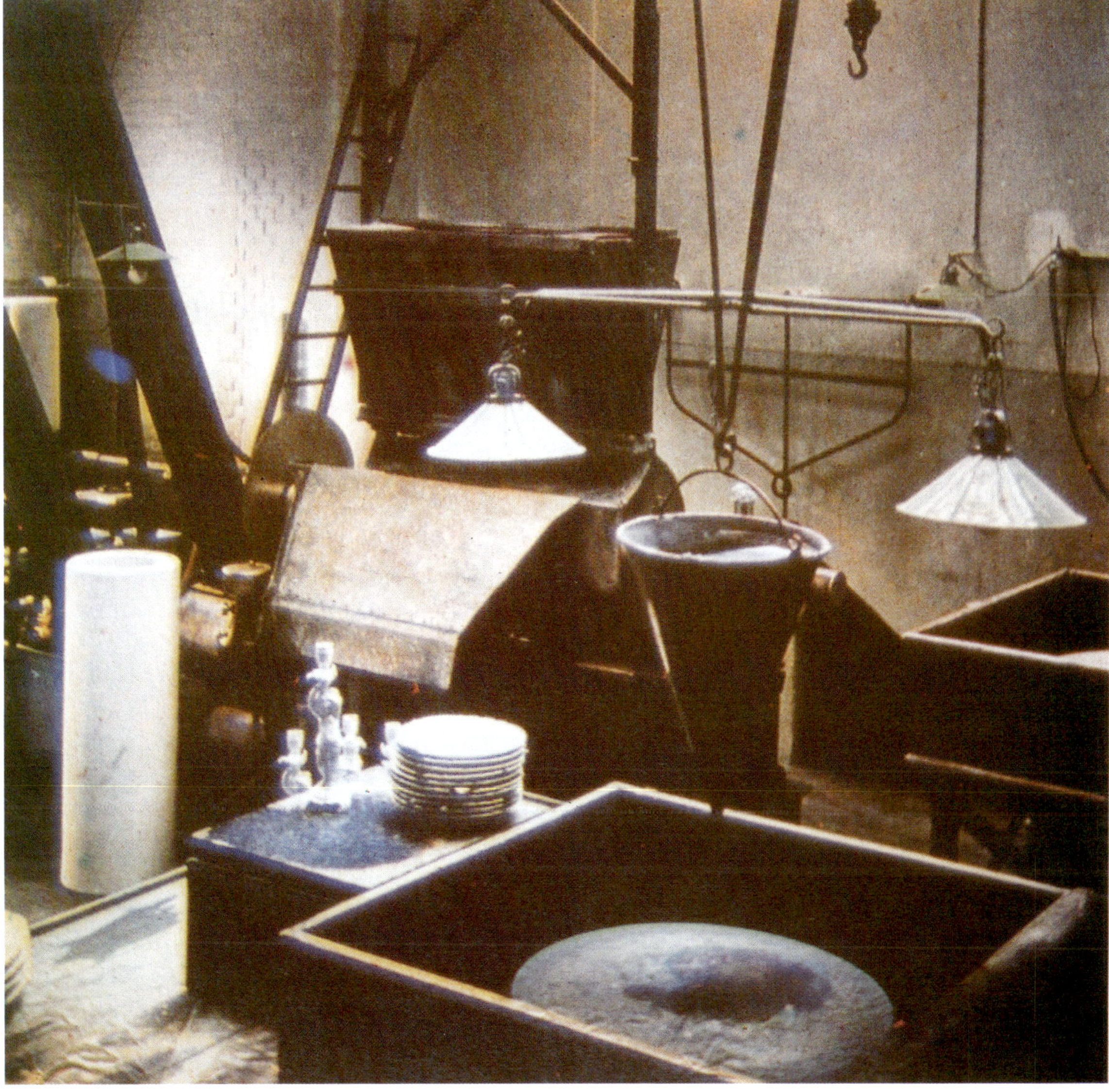

ADOLF MIETHE, ***Trichrome,*** circa 1903, Fachhochschule, Cologne.

2. J. H. Coote, *The Illustrated History of Colour Photography*, Surbiton, Fountain Press, 1993.

3. B. Coe, *Colour Photography*, London, Ash & Grant, 1978, pp. 34–42.

interference patterns were a function of the wave length of the light and, therefore, of its color. Viewing the plate in natural light recreated the original colors. The exposure time required, however, was several minutes. For this elegant discovery,[4] with its delicate precision, Lippman was to be awarded the Nobel prize in 1908.

Ducos had also attempted to produce colored images on paper. Taking advantage of the properties of photosensitive bichromated gelatin (Poitevin's "carbon process") and adapting it for use with three colors for "heliochromes", he obtained three negatives filtered through complementary colors. These were then printed to produce positive images on three separate layers of colored bichromated gelatin (red, yellow, and blue), which he then positioned on a paper support, superimposing them exactly. The "bichromated gum images" produced by the Lumière brothers were similar to this, and Léon Vidal applied the process for his "photochromes" (1877).[5] From such work was to come Manley's Ozotype and Ozobrome (1905), whose colored layers were the direct result of sensitized gelatin-bromide emulsions. Methods such as these were used to "reproduce" color photographs obtained by other processes.

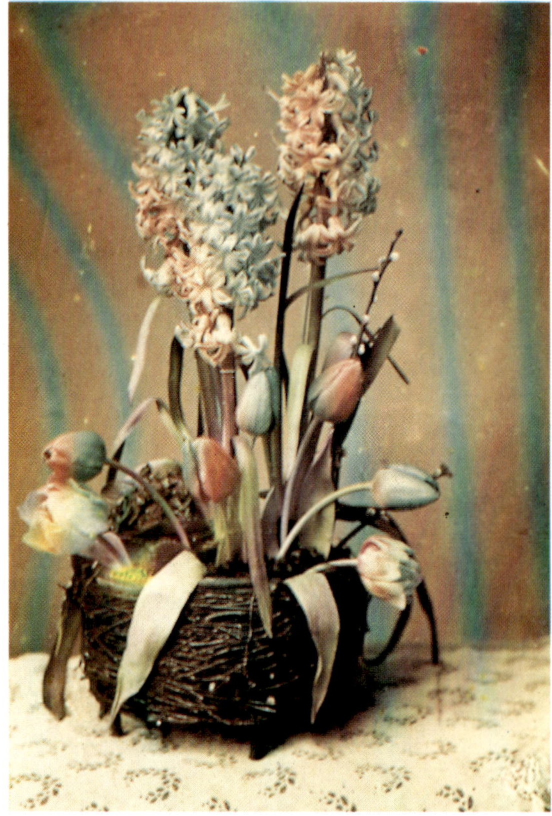

KRAYN PROCESS, *Vase of Flowers*, circa 1910, National Museum of Photography, Film and Television, Bradford.

Single plates

In his article of May 7, 1869, Ducos du Hauron also imagined "a paper whose surface is simply covered with alternating lines of red, yellow, and blue [...] At a distance these lines merge into a single color." This lined paper, when placed in front of a sensitized plate, would act like a filter, selecting out the three primary colors. This was a basic description of the concept of the filter screen, to be used in printing.

This principle was first used by John Joly in Dublin (1897). He placed a screen of colored lines on glass (10 lines per millimeter) in front of the photographic plate. This screen filtered the colors (red, green, and violet) and produced a negative, and then a positive on glass which "presents an exact reproduction of the properties of the colors of the desired tints". Viewing a similar screen, bearing the same colored pattern through this positive transparency serving as a mesh, restored the original colors.

It was the "Autochrome" process, however, that dominated color photography during the early years of the century. Its success was due to the ingenuity of the process, the comparative perfection of the results obtained, and the commercial strategies of the Lumière brothers. The plates invented by the brothers went on sale in June 1907.[6] Another additive process, Autochrome plates consisted of a screen made up of very fine grains (the idea of "grains" can also be found in Ducos' notes of 1869) of potato starch. These grains, colored orange, green, and violet, formed a three-color filter. The screen was coated with a gelatin silver-bromide emulsion, as for a "normal" photographic plate (the Lumière factories in Lyons were among the most important manufacturers of these at this period). The plate was exposed "so that the light rays coming from the lens pass through the colored particles before reaching the sensitized layer" (exposure time in sunlight was about one second). After developing and reversal processing, a positive black and white image was produced in the emulsion. It is the colored starch grains, when viewed by transmitted light and through the positive mask of the emulsion, that create the colored image. The Autochrome process was to enjoy some popularity with wealthy amateurs, the procedure being relatively easy to use but also comparatively expensive.

Louis Ducos du Hauron, a tireless inventor and the inspiration for many color processes, had in the meantime conceived a process which used a screen printed (in oil-based ink) green, violet, and red. These "Omnicolor" plates by Jougla first went on sale in 1909, but his invention was to suffer from competition from the Lumière business that

4. Presented on February 2, 1891, at the Académie des Sciences (*Comptes rendus*, CXII, p. 274) and in 1892 at the Exposition Internationale de Photographie.

5. *Traité pratique de photographie au charbon [...] impressions inaltérables, photochromie et tirages photomécaniques*, Paris, Gautier Villars, 1877.

6. Presented at the Académie des Sciences on May 30, 1904; public demonstration at *L'Illustration* on June 10, 1907.

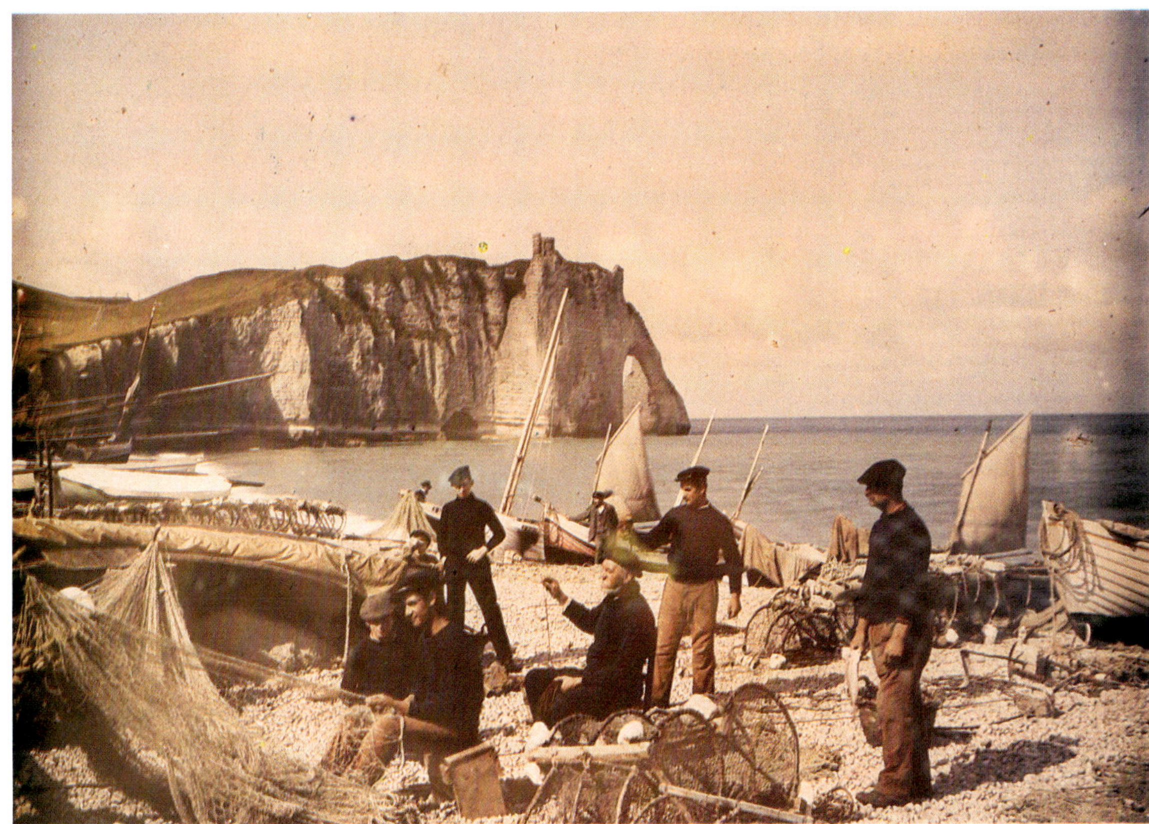

ANONYMOUS,
***Étretat*,**
autochrome,
circa 1910,
private collection.

took over Jougla in 1911. Another screen process was perfected by Louis Dufay in 1907[7] using red-orange parallel lines overlaid at right angles with alternating blue-violet and green lines – the Dufay Dioptichrome process. In 1909, Dufay added a fourth, complementary, color, so that "the screen is made up exclusively of spots" formed by overlapping pairs of lines (red/blue and yellow/violet). Although not particularly successful commercially, the process continued in use for two decades.

A large number of screen processes appeared in around 1910, including the Krayn process and the Finlay process, which consisted of a screen of bichromated gelatin – a technique derived from the gauze used in the half-tone process. Christensen's process, bought by I. G. Farbenindustrie (Agfa), became known as Agfacolor (1932), and was manufactured using emulsified shellac in turpentine.

Technicolor

From the 1930s, photographic processes responded to the demands of the cinema, for which they were hastily perfected. It was primarily for the needs of the cinema that new photographic emulsions were put on the market. This was a general phenomenon, since the Leica camera had been designed in the 1920s to use 35mm cine film stock. At the beginning of the twentieth century, several companies that produced movie films quickly made considerable profits compared to those producing conventional "still" photographic materials: Eastman Kodak, Lumière, Pathé Brothers, and Agfa. In 1914, Pathé began manufacturing film in Vincennes (the factory was soon to be taken over by Kodak).

The processes used for early color motion pictures had to satisfy new requirements, particularly for the multiplication of images projected in a short space of time. The additive principle was still used, several separate colored images being

ANONYMOUS,
Paget process,
circa 1914,
National Museum
of Photography,
Film and Television,
Bradford.
▼

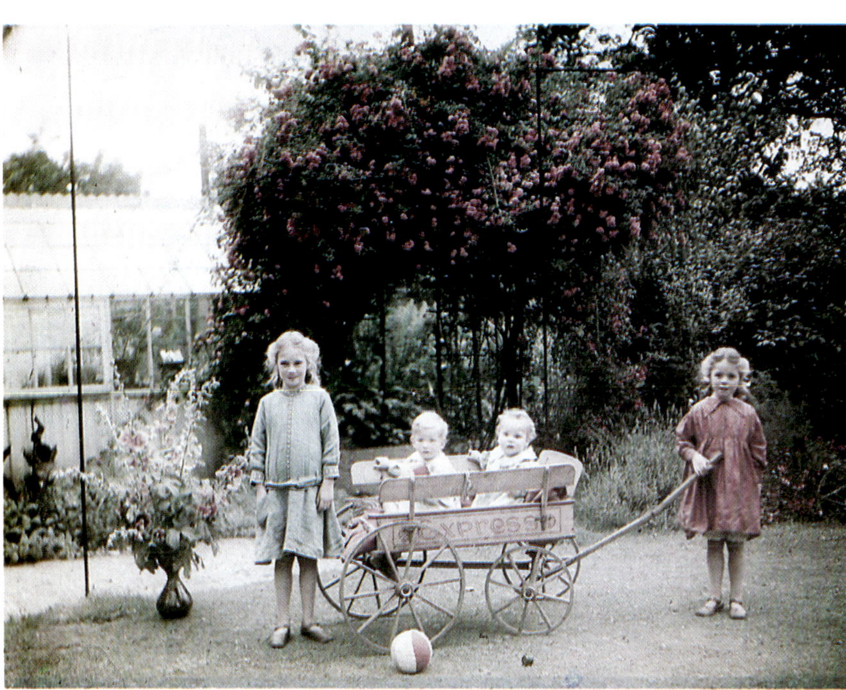

7. Letter, June 4, 1907.

WILLY ZIELKE, *Still-life,* circa 1933, Carbro print, Galerie Michèle Chomette, Paris.
▼

superimposed on the cinema screen (two-color Kinemacolor, 1909; three-color Gaumontcolor, 1913) or onto embossed film, the embossing making up the filter screen. In the 1920s, Dufaycolor, now called Versicolor, opted first for embossed film, and then for the more simple screen system.

Technicolor, which appeared at this time, represented a return to the ideas unselfishly made public by Ducos du Hauron, who never personally benefited financially from them. The technique of using three separate emulsion layers (sensitive to blue, green, and red) which were then superimposed was reduced to two colors (blue and red) by Comstock for the Technicolor Motion Picture Co., run by Herbert Kalmus, who later returned to a three-color process in 1931. After passing through the lens, the light was split up, by mirrors, and three films were exposed simultaneously, through colored filters. Technicolor began trading in 1935 (Walt Disney's *Snow White and the Seven Dwarfs* appeared in 1937). It was superseded, after the Second World War, by subtractive processes such as Kodachrome and Eastmancolor.

8. W. Heering, *Im Zauber der Farbe*, Harzburg, Heering, 1943.

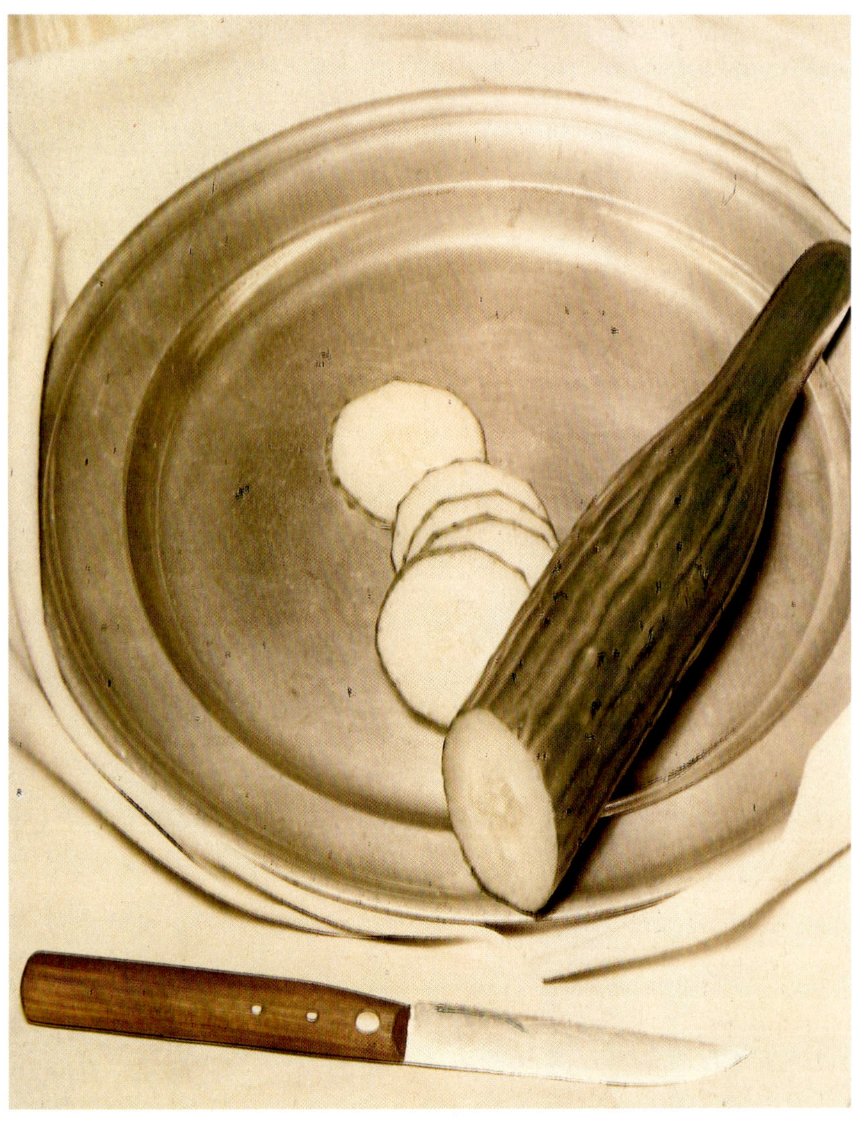

It was the revival of industry after the two world wars that determined the nature and development of color processes. As a result of the technical problems posed by additive techniques, the idea was revived of a single emulsion which would be made up of the three separate color-sensitive layers, inside which the colors could be produced through chemical processing (another of Ducos du Hauron's ideas). Subtractive synthesis was used, since white light has to pass through layers within which certain colors are absorbed (or subtracted). Color is seen by projection onto a screen or as transparencies on a "slide", the blue, green, and red filters producing the complementary colors of yellow, magenta, and cyan. At first, in order to produce these complementary colors within each layer, bleaching was used (Gasparcolor, 1934). Subsequently, Rudolf Fischer discovered chromogenic development, which takes place separately in each layer. During development, chemicals free colored dyes by combining with other molecules (hence the term chromogenic). These colored dyes are produced in direct proportion to how much silver is present and, therefore, how much light has reached the film. Metallic silver is then bleached out, leaving behind only the complementary color attached to it in that particular layer. Reversible Agfacolor film, invented by Schneider, first became available in 1936.

However, by the time that Agfacolor appeared, Kodachrome, made by Eastman Kodak, had already been available since 1935. Leopold Mannes and Leo Godowsky, two independent researchers, perfected another chromogenic process for the Rochester-based company. In this case, the color couplers were included in the developing chemicals rather than in the sensitized emulsion layers (as they were in Agfacolor). Kodachrome, a five-layer film and initially very complicated to process, was modified in 1938 and soon went on to overtake all of its competitors. On the eve of the Second World War, the American version of the German Agfacolor, Anscocolor, was available both in America and in France, while Lumière was producing Autochromes on celluloid, under the brandnames Filmcolor and Lumicolor.[8]

During the war, Agfacolor color negative film was put on the market, promoted by the U.F.A. film studio (*Die goldene Stadt*, by Veit Harlan, 1942; *Münchhausen*, by Josef von Baky, 1943) in direct competition with Kodacolor (color negative film) and Kodachrome Prints (color enlargements on paper). The end of the war, with the more or less official takeover of patents, witnessed a decline in Agfa's fortunes, along with the emergence of other products based on the same principles – Sovcolor in the U.S.S.R.,

Fujicolor in Japan, Ferraniacolor in Italy, and Gévacolor in Belgium. At the end of the war, Kodak launched a reversible color film with color couplers in the emulsion, very similar to Agfacolor. Called Ektachrome (1946), it was sold in various sensitivities during the 1950s. During this period, Agfacolor and Ektachrome shared the market, trading under a variety of different names.

As for printing color images, since the beginning of the century processes had been used that were somewhat laborious, requiring the preparation of separate colored layers for each "primary" color which then had to be carefully superimposed. Howard Farmer had discovered how bichromated gelatin could be hardened in the presence of silver – a technique which made Ozobrome, sold under the tradename of Raydex, possible (1905). It then became the Carbro process (1919) of the Autotype Company. Carbro (carbon and silver bromide) prints are made up of three separate images, colored with pigments and then superimposed (for example, the Carbro prints made by Outerbridge). The French process Pinatype (Léon Didier, 1903) was also based on the same principle. Vivex (1928), used by, among others, Moholy-Nagy, was another variation of the Carbro process. Eastman's Wash Off Relief process (1935) was an adaptation of the Technicolor additive three-color process (three separate layers). This led, in 1945, to the Kodak Dye Transfer process, a faster process. The Fresson process derived from Ducos du Hauron's Heliochromes. All of these processes were much admired for the faithfulness of their colors and their permanence, due to the fact that the colors came from stable mineral-based pigments.

Kodacolor paper prints first appeared in 1942, at the same time as Kodacolor color negative roll film (perfected in 1954 with the Type III). Agfacolor paper prints followed in 1943. Since the 1960s, the proportion of prints in color has gone on increasing, made from color negative film or from slides. Cibachrome (1963), a process using bleaching, without color couplers, is renowned for the richness of its colors, and has earned a reputation amongst professional photographers. A modification of this process was produced for use in photo booths in 1976. Polacolor (1963) was an "instant" process, giving an eight-layer negative which produced, by adherence, a three-layer positive print to be pealed off. These two stages were rendered unnecessary by the introduction of the SX-70 camera in 1972. The instant film used in this camera had 16 layers, and produced a 8 x 8 cm color print in less than a minute.

These improvements in color processes were not always necessarily made as a response to a demand from photographers, whether professional or amateur. They were, rather, the result of the prevailing industrial interests and the restructuring of businesses: Agfa and Gevaert amalgamated in 1964, Ciba took over Lumière in 1963 and Ilford in 1967. From this time, the rapid disappearance of black and white photography was predicted, and, particularly after rises in the price of silver in the 1970s, larger firms began to reduce the range of black and white products. In the last decade – thanks partly to the action of photographers themselves – there has been no further change.

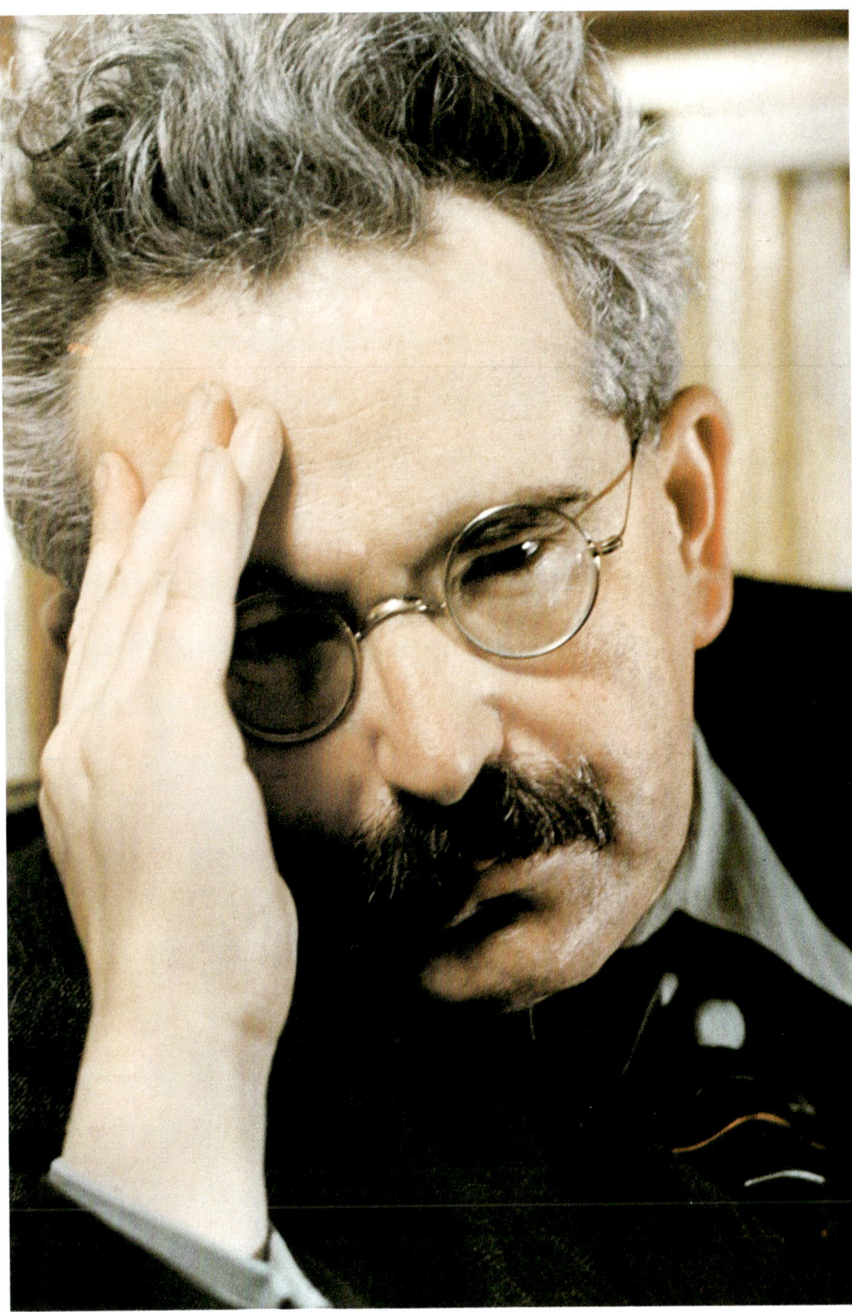

Gisèle Freund, *Walter Benjamin*, 1936.

An aesthetic of color?

The aesthetic history of color photography since the 1930s is still not well known. The books that have appeared on the subject have confined them-

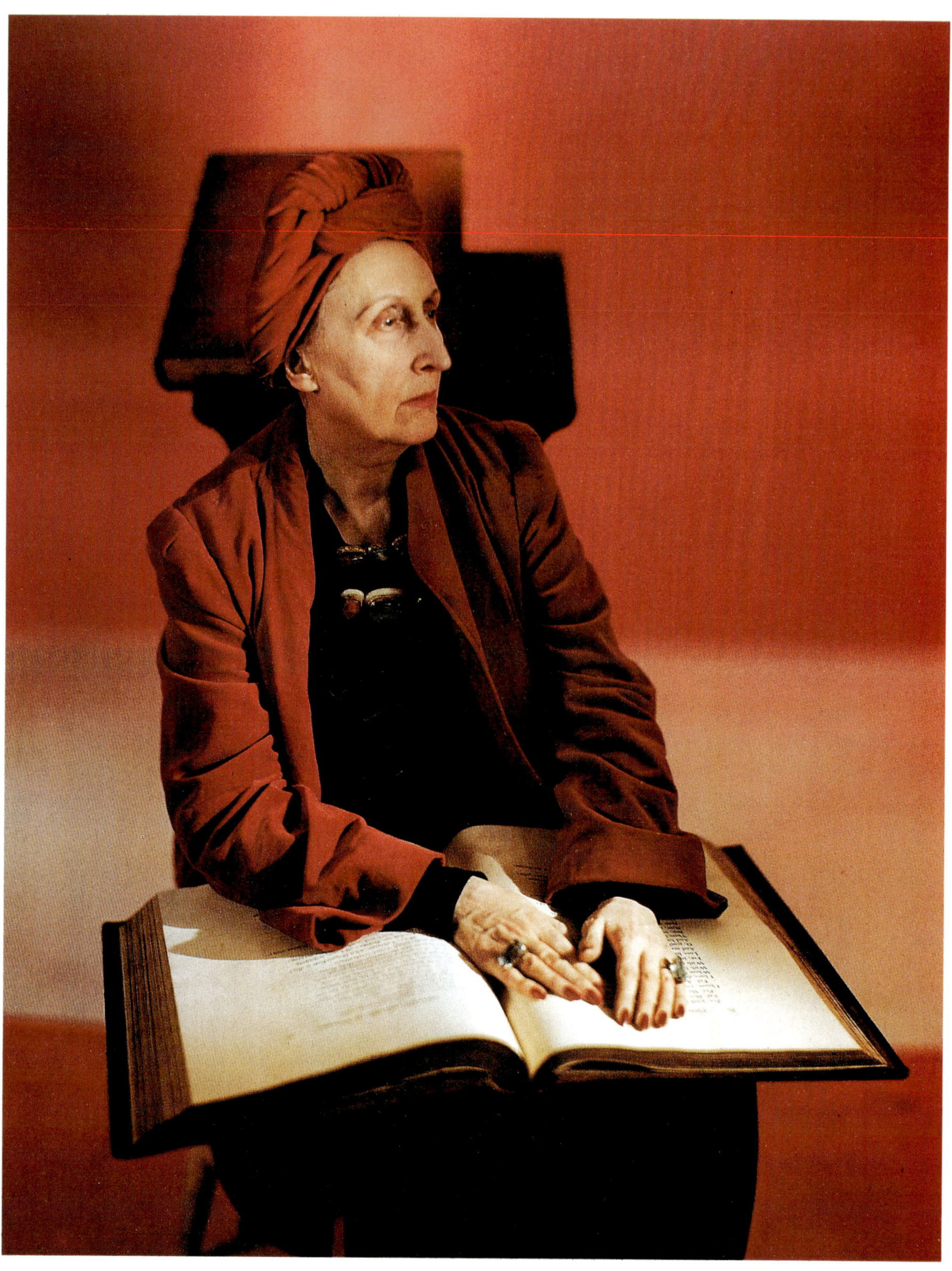

Horst P. Horst,
Edith Sitwell,
circa 1935.

selves largely to a listing of processes or of photographs.[9] It must be admitted that a clear expression of the criteria for any evaluation linked specifically to color remains fraught with difficulty. To put it briefly, color is not "thought".[10] The long history of black and white photography, and its resistance to the introduction of color have not helped. Furthermore, there are only two areas in which color has really taken root: amateur photography, which has not been overly concerned to exploit the qualities of the medium, being satisfied with a mimesis of reality; and so-called applied photography (fashion, advertising, industry), which became, through magazines, the chief outlet for color photography. However, if we look at what has happened in photojournalism and art photography, it is apparent that the black and white/color divide does not follow aesthetic considerations. Since 1970, the growing significance of photography as art has not been accompanied by any particular enthusiasm for the more recent technical innovations in color photography. It is as though black and white photography still best represents the concept of "art".

9. R. Bellone and L. Fellot, *Histoire mondiale de la photographie en couleurs, des origines à nos jours*, Paris, Hachette, "Realités", 1981.

10. G. Koshofer, *Farbfotografie*, vol. 1, *Alte Verfahren*, Munich, Laterna Magica, 1981; *Farbe im Photo: Die Geschichte der Farbphotographie von 1861 bis 1981*, Cologne, Josef-Haubrich-Kunsthalle, 1981.

Color photography was introduced in the 1930s to serve the needs of advertising. This was soon joined by fashion photography, distributed through the medium of magazines. Louise Dahl-Wolfe, Cecil Beaton, and Egidio Scaïoni were among the first to use color. However, the gradual process of taking over from black and white photography was somewhat chaotic, since this was determined by the possibilities of printing only certain pages in color, at a considerably higher price. Color photography was also used in photojournalism by a number of the participants in the F.S.A. project in the United States. These pictures were never widely known, however, because of a lack of interest from the press. After 1945, color quickly became established in the areas of "applied" photography which became more clearly separated from "art" photography – advertising, fashion, and photojournalism.[11]

In his book of 1951, Alexandre Liberman[12] (artistic director of Condé-Nast Publications, publishers of *Vogue*, *House and Garden*, and *Glamour*) commented on the introduction of color photography in magazines, underlining the difficulty of handling the medium: "the photographer must physically place an object of the desired color and form before his lens". He stressed, furthermore, the importance of the photo-engraver, whose job it was to transpose colors that had already been once modified by the photographic emulsion. We see models photographed in front of a background made out of cut paper by Cecil Beaton, still-lifes and compositions by Penn, three landscapes by Kertész, the famous *Picasso Drawing with Light* by Gjon Mili, a composition with birds by Matter, another with flowers by Rawlings, and Blumenfeld's *Times Square*.

Blumenfeld was certainly one of the most active in promoting the new medium. Like his colleagues, he stressed the advantages, risks, and contradictory results of color photography, demanding for the future faster film ("as fast as black and white") and new printing methods that would lose nothing of the vibrant color of the original. It will be noted that in the concept of color photography, only photo engraving (in three or four colors) had a selective role. Beaton attempted to modify colors by the use of colored filters. Blumenfeld described how the famous *Face* (a close-up of an eye and a mouth) was originally in black and white: "[Graphic artists and photo-engravers] transform a black and white photograph into a wonderful cover." It was to become increasingly difficult to see color as a photographic entity; it seemed rather to lead to a disassociation of functions.[13]

In the United States, following Moholy-Nagy in Chicago, Callahan became interested in color in 1941, Arthur Siegel in 1946 (Kodachrome 35 mm film), and Eliot Porter began to work in color in 1940. It was not until the 1970s, however, that color was truly "recognized", thanks to its entry into museums. John Szarkowski staged the exhibition *William Eggleston's Guide* at the Museum of Modern Art (MoMA) in 1976. At the time, Eggleston was considered the inventor of color photography, in the sense of someone who controlled it, played with it, and negotiated with it, without allowing the limitations that imposed themselves on the colors of photojournalism and photo magazines to be imposed on him. Unfortunately, this point of view, which rested on the ideas of progress, and the "coming of age" of the colored medium (Max Kozloff), made earlier work seem incomprehensible, when in reality its only crime was to have been produced with technically "insufficient" means. To be preferred is Moholy-Nagy's fairer assessment. He believed he was witnessing, with color, a return to the technical conditions of the Renaissance, when

LÁSZLÓ MOHOLY-NAGY, ***Study with Pins and Ribbons,*** Vivex print, 1937, International Museum of Photography, George Eastman House, Rochester.
▼

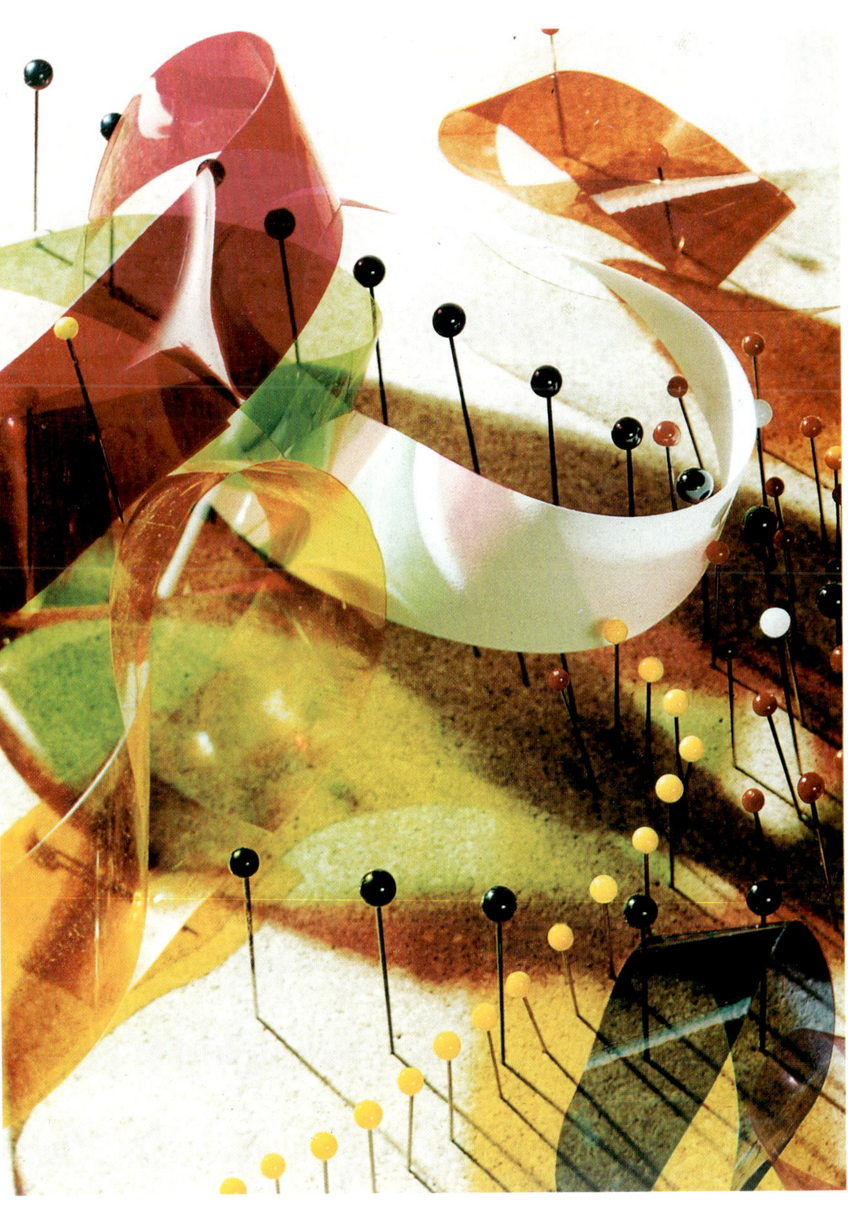

11. A. D. Weinberg, *On the Line: The New Color Photojournalism*, Minneapolis, Walker Art Center, 1986.

12. *The Art and Technique of Color Photography*, New York, Simon and Schuster, 1951.

13. A good approach has been initiated in *Color as Form: A History of Color Photography*, Rochester, International Museum of Photography, George Eastman House, 1982.

Polaroid

Many inventors had dreamed of a camera that could produce a print automatically. A number of cameras were proposed that offered the same solution. Usually, the developing process took place adjacent to the camera and the plates were processed immediately.

Only the Dubroni camera (1860) seems to have given good results. In this, the usual camera bellows were replaced by a tank, made of red "safe" glass. The operator could sensitize his plate, then develop and fix it in daylight by introducing chemicals into this tank.

It was not until 1947 that the American Edwin H. Land launched a camera that could "take and print a photo in one minute". Twenty years later, 14 million such cameras had been sold.

The first, folding, version was loaded with two different reels of paper, one the negative support, the other the printing paper, both attached to the same strip. When the exposure had been made, the operator, by pulling the strip, drew the two – the negative and the printing paper – together between two wheels. The positive and the negative were now tightly pressed together in a sandwich, and the pressure exercised by the wheels having meanwhile emitted a jelly contained in a capsule, the process of developing could take place. The positive image was formed thanks to the unexposed silver bromide crystals of the negative which, under the action of a reagent consisting of the developer and a solvent, were transferred (in the form of soluble salts) from the surface of the negative to the positive surface (from which it was separated by a very tiny distance) and, from there, reduced to silver.

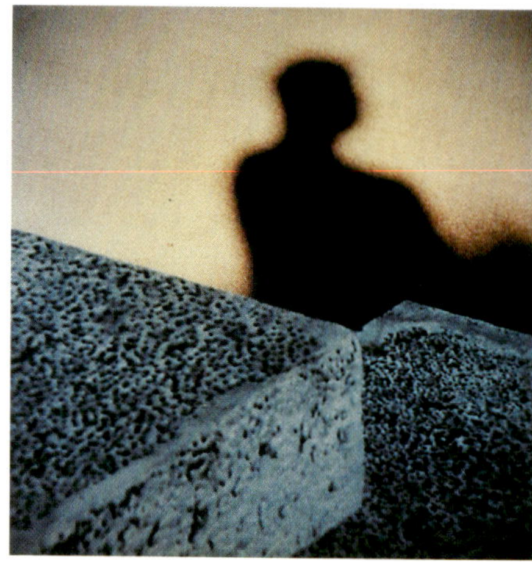

Franco Fontana,
Shadow,
Polaroid, circa 1977, Polaroid Collection, France.

The silvered image thus produced was positive and could be seen directly. Detached from the film negative, it was then varnished to help preservation.

New ideas for films and cameras led, in 1963, to the use of films in packs and, particularly, to the adaptation of the process to color photography. The Polacolor process formed colored images by subtractive synthesis – by the transfer of color couplers from the unexposed areas of the negative to the overlaid layers towards a receiving layer on the positive that ensured the permanence and stability of the positive colored image.

In 1972, with the launch of the SX–70 system, using a film claiming an "integrated structure" consisting of 16 layers of a thickness of a few microns and bringing together into a single whole, and permanently, the print and the negative, Land had entirely achieved his aim: a completely automatic camera. In less than two seconds, the photograph is automatically ejected from the camera and, protected by an opaque layer, gradually develops in the light, without any risk of deterioration. This ease of use instantly endeared the Polaroid to amateur photographers.

Jean-Claude Gautrand

artists attempted "to imitate nature with inadequate means". These means might remain inadequate for ever.

Besides that of Eggleston, the most successful work of the 1970s was that of Callahan and Meyerowitz. Callahan[14] had made a radical decision to change to color in 1977, after his exhibition of black and white prints at the Museum of Modern Art He worked as he traveled (Egypt, 1978; Morocco, 1981; Portugal, 1982), experimenting with reflections and double exposures, deconstructing perspective through the use of a wide-angle lens, superimposing chance shots (streets and television screens in the series *Providence*, 1984; streets, New York, 1985). Meyerowitz had first used black and white, in the style of Frank, but then undertook some color work with a 20 x 25 cm camera at Cape Cod in 1976–1977.[15] With Eggleston, Callahan and Meyerowitz, color has certainly given another meaning to photography as a whole – to the point where no one is now surprised at the use of either color or black and white.[16]

It remains to define criteria for the reading of color photography, that are more than just naive historicism, so that old techniques and new techniques can be considered on an equal footing.

14. Harry Callahan, *Color 1941–1980*, Providence, Matrix Publications, 1980; S. Stein, *Harry Callahan: Photographs in Color, The Years 1946–1978*, Tucson, Center for Creative Photography, 1980.

Nickolas Muray,
1943,
Carbro print,
International Museum of Photograpy, George Eastman House, Rochester.

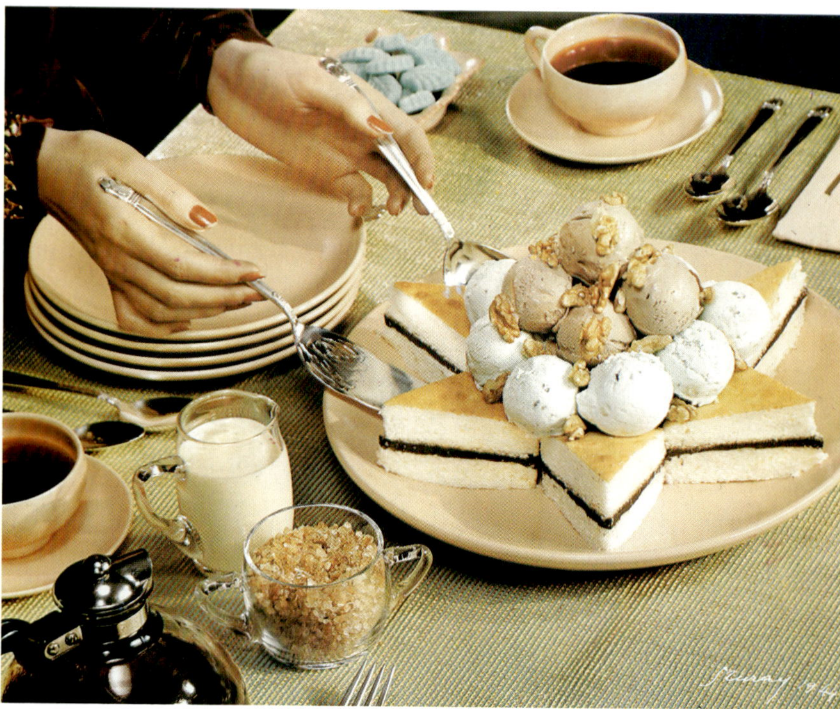

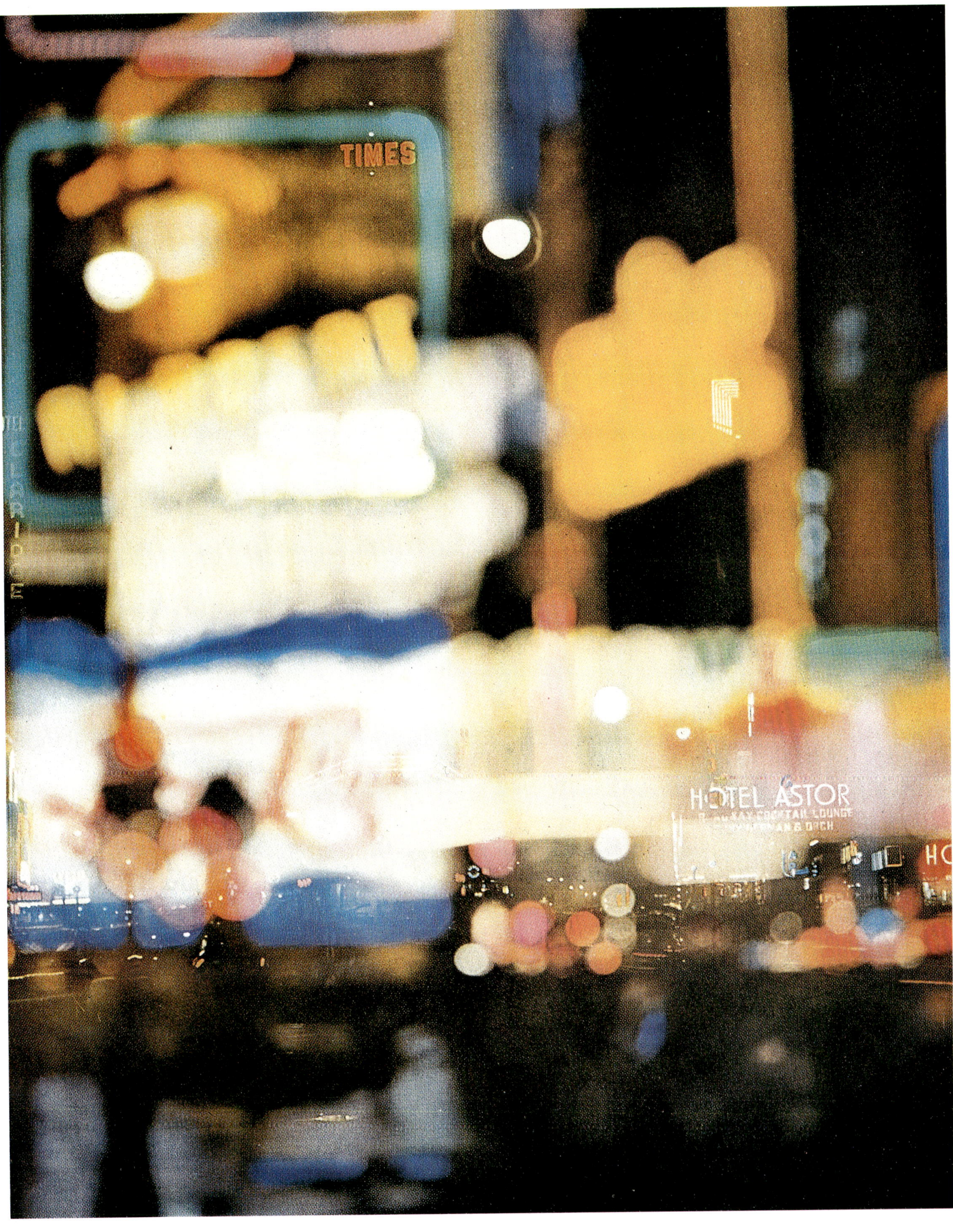

ERWIN BLUMENFELD,
Times Square,
Ektachrome,
1951.

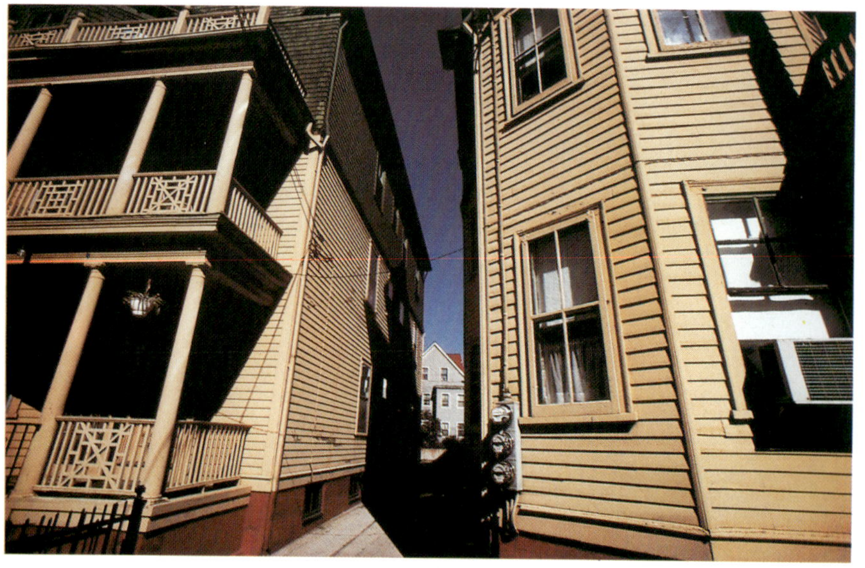

HARRY CALLAHAN, *Providence*, 1977.

Taking a color photograph is not the same as painting a picture (and a painted picture no more reproduces exactly the colors of nature than does a photograph). While color in painting is judged according to a internal sense of harmony, and not in relation to how exactly it relates to nature, color photography is first perceived by reference to reality, a manifest but subjective reference. It is supposed to correspond to what existed at the moment the photograph was taken (even if it is allowed that this colored reality is sometimes created to suit the needs of the shot), when we know perfectly well that it is a sensitized surface recording the colors according to methods for which it is specifically manufactured. This surface clearly does not "see" in the same way as the human eye sees.

The freedom of action of the photographer working "in color" might seem to be limited by the need to reproduce color accurately. However, he is also free to rework these colors, particularly in the laboratory. The famous (formal) truth that runs through the history of photography disappeared with the intangible mirage of color. The work of Harry Gruyaert at the Olympic Games of 1972, subsequently transmitted by television and doubly distorted by the cathode ray tube and the photographic process, also revealed, in essence, the only reality of color, that of the photographic print, such as was possible at a given date.

Any critique of Harry Callahan's color photographs of painted houses involves many factors which have to be considered simultaneously – the relationships of the original colors, the choices made by the inhabitants themselves, the contrasts created within the photographic frame, and the transformations that took place during the chemical process. The reading of a color photograph is the same as for a black and white image, but with the addition of the imagination of color, and its intrinsic vagueness.

The culture of color photography in which we have, nevertheless, been submerged in the last few decades would appear to conform to rules, to psycho-formal relationships that remain concealed from us by the double polarity of our judgment of painting and of photographic truth. The colored photograph has been considered as a technical object, no less answerable to criteria of usage, appropriation, consumption, manipulation, and subjectivity than any industrial object.

15. *Cape Light: Color Photographs by Joel Meyerowitz*, Boston, Museum of Fine Arts/Bullfinch Press, 1978; *Wild Flowers*, Boston, Little, Brown & Co., 1983.

16. S. Eauclaire, *The New Color Photography*, New York, Abbeville, 1981.

PIERRE BÉRENGER, ▶ *Toucans*, 1978.

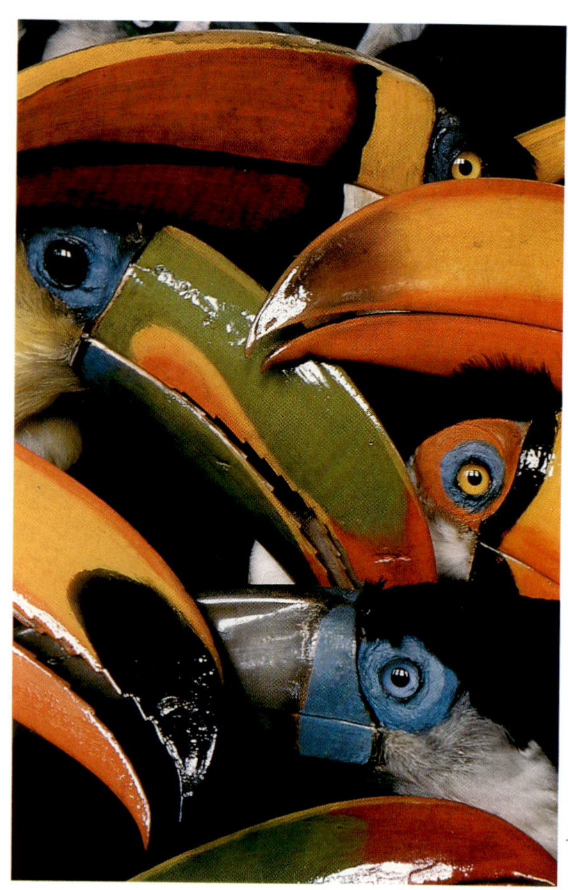

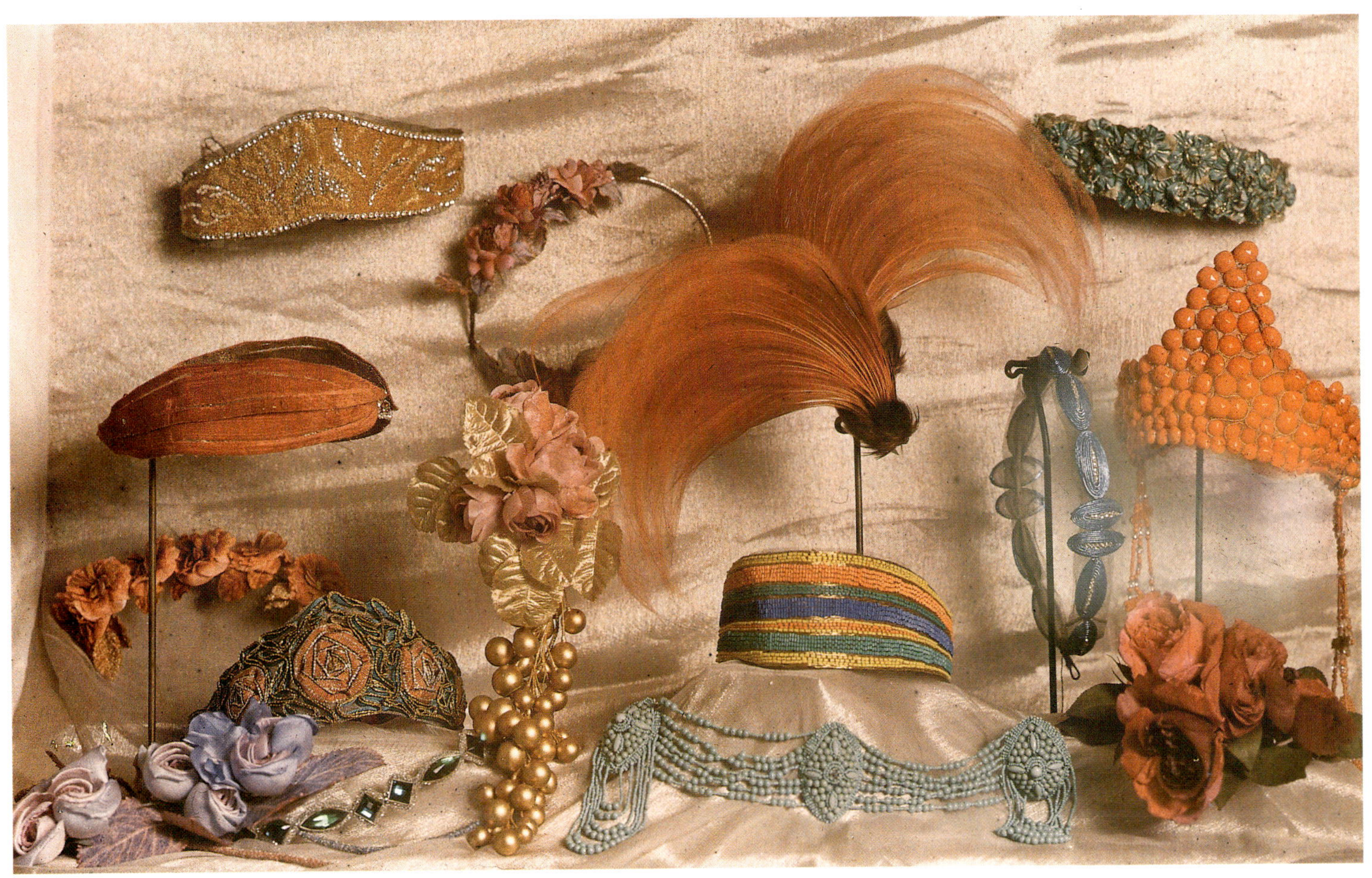

Autochromes

The appearance, in 1907, of the Autochrome process caused great excitement in photographic circles. The Lumière brothers, in introducing "color", saw themselves as the worthy successors of Daguerre who had provided "form". The French magazine *L'Illustration* announced that "the old and cold interpretation of black and white will soon be of only secondary interest" (June 15, 1907).

Interest was immediate from the best artist-photographers of the day: Stieglitz was in Paris in June 1907 when the Autochrome process was presented at the Photo-Club. He, Steichen, Kühn, and Eugene met up soon afterwards and together tried it out, at Tutzing in Bavaria, in the summer of 1907. In September, Stieglitz exhibited his own Autochromes in his gallery in New York, together with those of Steichen and Eugene. Coburn, the youngest of these American modernists, also discovered Autochromes in 1907, in Paris at Steichen's house. A special supplement to *Camera Work* was planned - though it never appeared - and 40 Autochromes were exhibited in 1909 at the International Exhibition of Pictorial Photography in New York.

The appearance of the Autochrome in Pictorialist circles can perhaps be seen as an interruption of modernism. Although these photographers did not persevere long in the exploitation of this novelty, it caused a split and raised questions that might, in part, account for the revived interest in Pictorialism around 1909.

The process raised crucial questions about the relationship between photography and painting, but it also excluded the possibility of any manipulation of the final image – techniques that had been used in the early days of Pictorialism.

A number of photographers used the Autochrome process in the early years. The special edition "Colour Photography" of the magazine *The Studio* (1908), which was prepared by Charles Holme and assisted by Coburn, reproduced Autochromes by Craig Annan, Coburn, Kühn, De Meyer, and Shaw.

However, the process remained more or less confined to Europe and, subsequently, to France in particular. The cost was high, and the process risky compared with black and white photography. Personnaz complained of having to expose the plate, for a single picture, for fifteen seconds for the ground, and two seconds for the sky.

A famous amateur like Jacques-Henri Lartigue used the Autochrome process often, between 1912 and 1927, sometimes for stereoscopic pictures. There must certainly be many other amateur collections waiting to be discovered, such as, recently, that of Julien Girardin in Nancy (1907–1916).

The French Photographic Society preserves the work of Antonin Personnaz and of Gimpel, photographer for the magazine *L'Illustration* (night views); the Royal Photographic Society in Bath has collections by Warburg, Knowles, Paneth, Coburn, and De Meyer, among others.

The most important collection is probably that of the financier Albert Kahn (Boulogne-sur-Seine), who, from 1909, amassed a collection of 72,000 Autochromes, taking photographs himself and sending collaborators all over the world to take pictures for scientific and educational use.

The Autochrome process was prized for views which were intended for publication in color in magazines (furniture, architecture, and interior decoration in *L'Illustration*, for example) or to illustrate exhibitions. In 1927, the *National Geographical Magazine* published the first underwater Autochromes, taken by Charles Martin. However, Autochromes were unique images, and could be viewed only as a transparency. Their true and subtle colors were difficult to transfer to paper, particularly given the limitations of the printing techniques of the time (three-color processing).

The examples which have been reproduced here from the pages of the magazine *The Studio* (1908) make this insurmountable gap between the luminous quality of the original photograph (the Autochrome) and the photo-mechanical printing of the day only too evident.

Michel Frizot

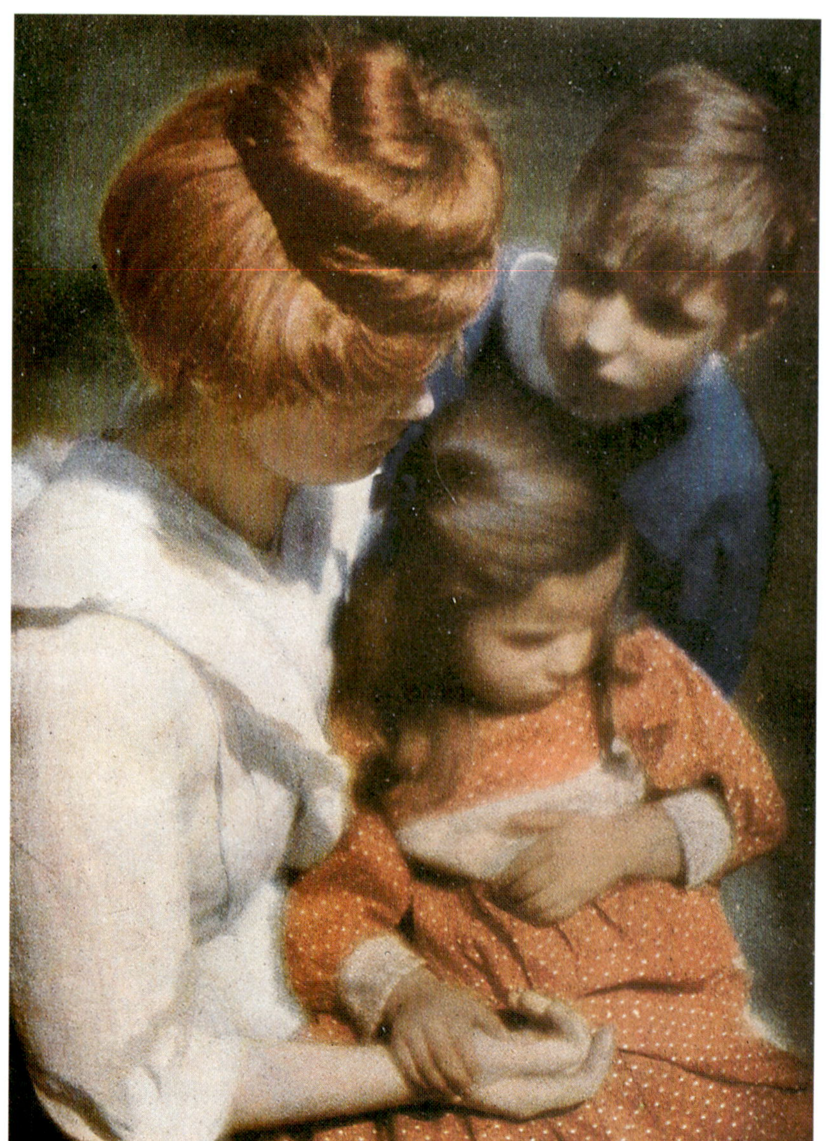

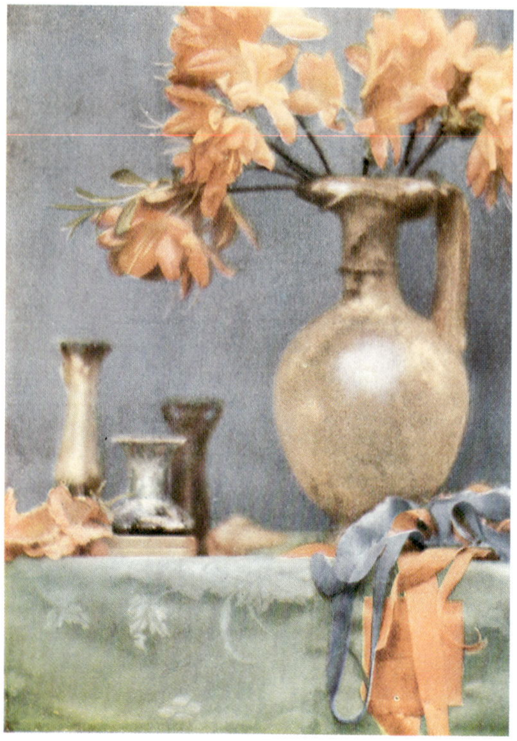

Heinrich Kühn,
Group,
reproduction of
an autochrome
from *The Studio,* 1908.

Adolphe de Meyer,
Still-life,
reproduction of an autochrome
from *The Studio,* 1908.

Heinrich Kühn,
The Painter's Table,
autochrome,
circa 1910.

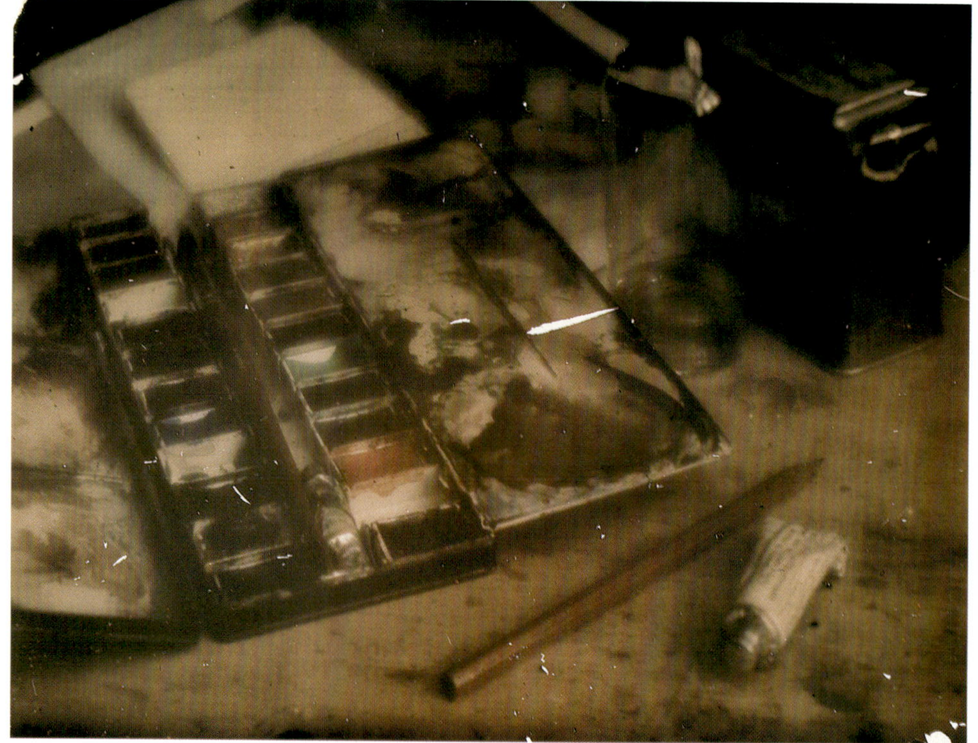

(On the previous page:)
Anonymous,
Tiaras and headdresses by Charles Aîné, fashion designer, Paris,
circa 1925,
Musée des Arts et des Métiers, Paris.

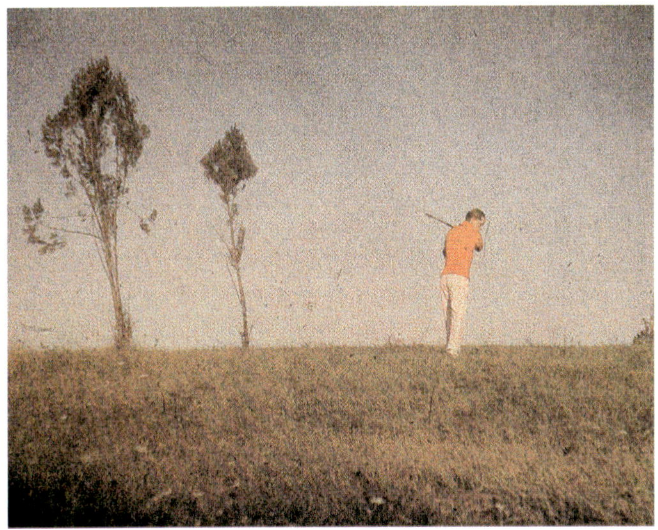

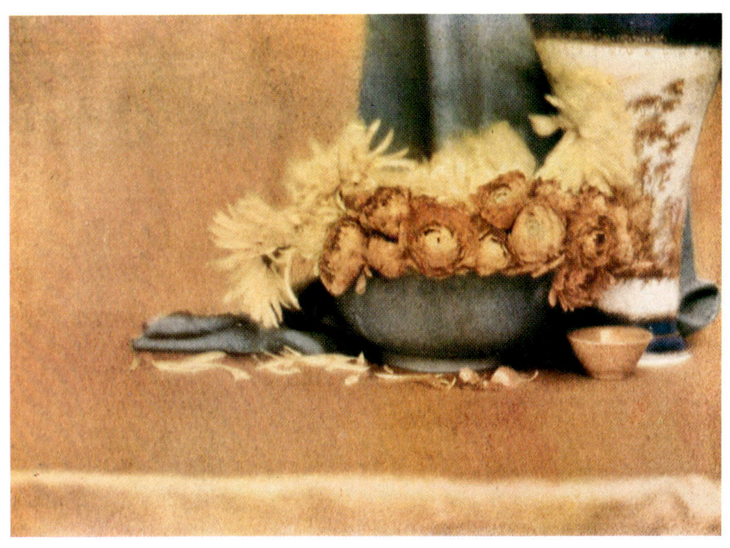

ADOLPHE DE MEYER,
Still-life,
reproduction of an autochrome
from *The Studio*, 1908.

▲
JACQUES-HENRI LARTIGUE,
The Golfer,
Rouzat, 1913.

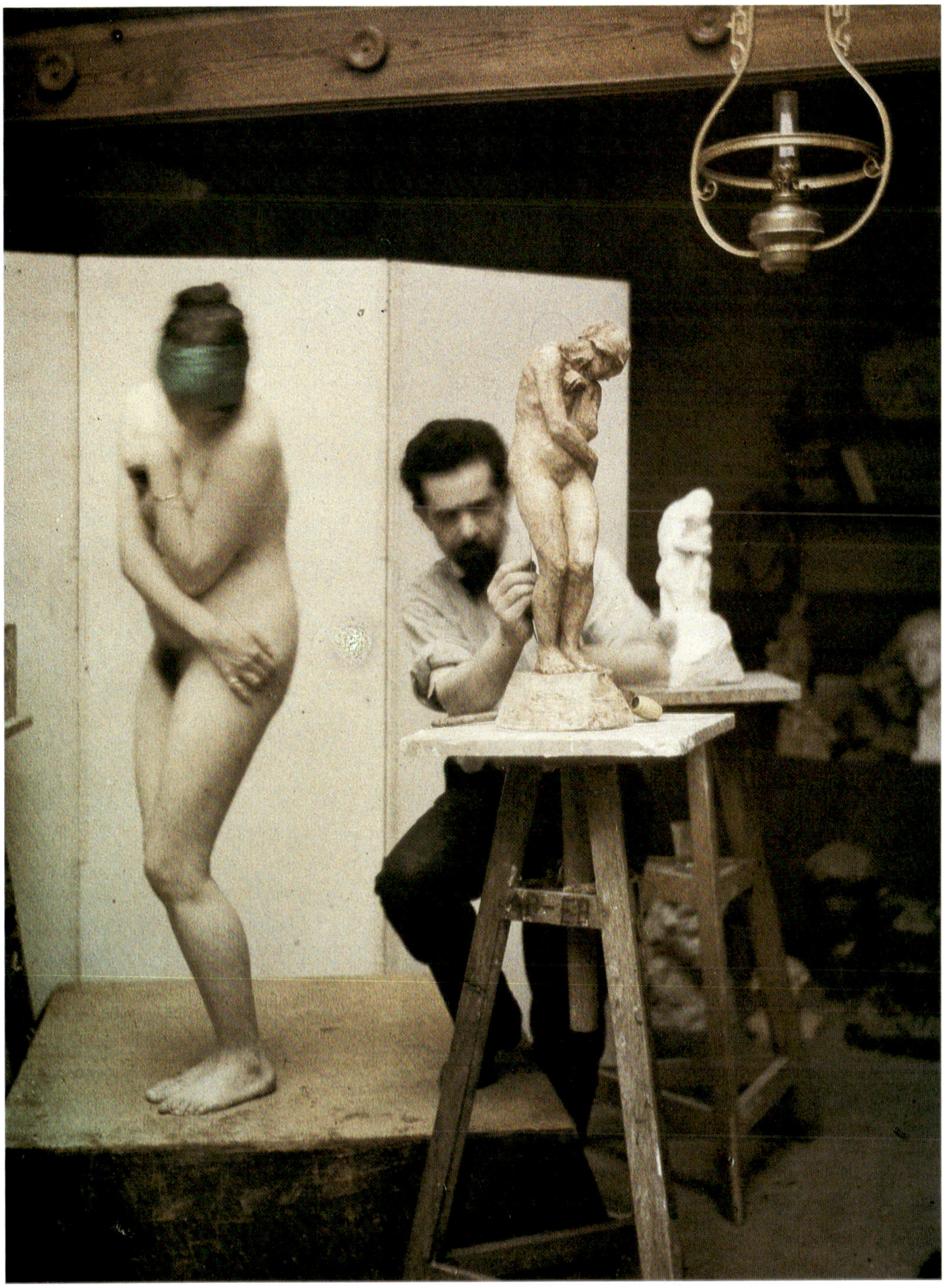

LÉON GIMPEL,
Sculptor's Studio,
circa 1911,
Société Française de Photographie,
Paris.

LÉON GIMPEL, ▶
Departure of the Dirigible Zodiac III,
August 28, 1909,
Société Française de Photographie,
Paris.

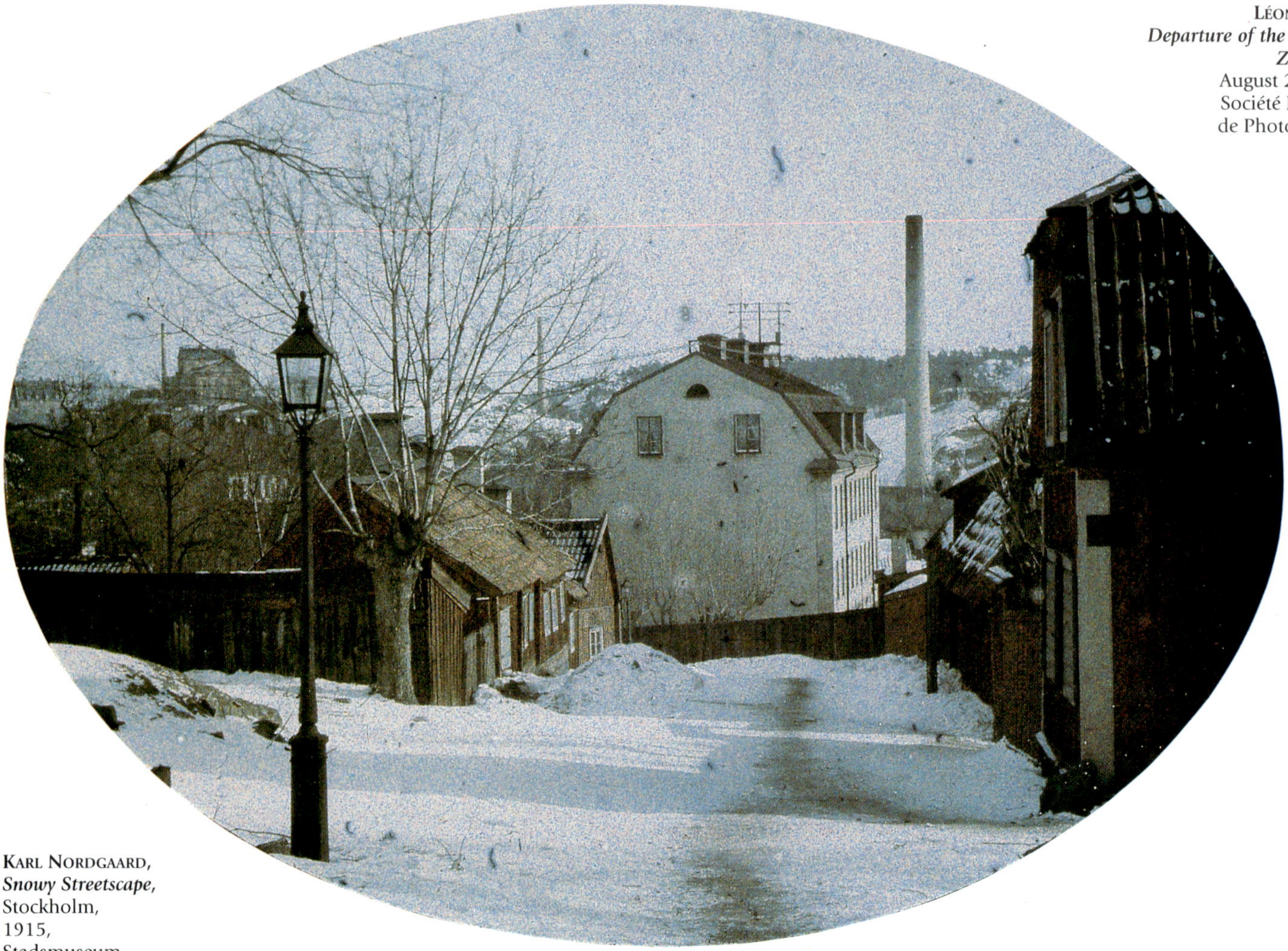

KARL NORDGAARD,
Snowy Streetscape,
Stockholm,
1915,
Stadsmuseum,
Stockholm.

AUGUSTE LÉON, ▶
Venice,
Albert Kahn Collection,
Boulogne-sur-Seine.

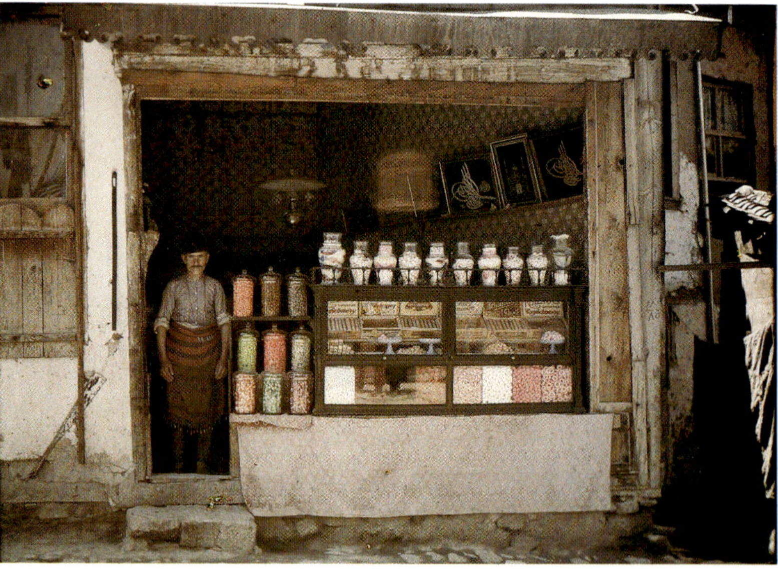

AUGUSTE LÉON,
Sweetshop in Bursa,
Turkey, June 1913,
Albert Kahn Collection
Boulogne-sur-Seine.

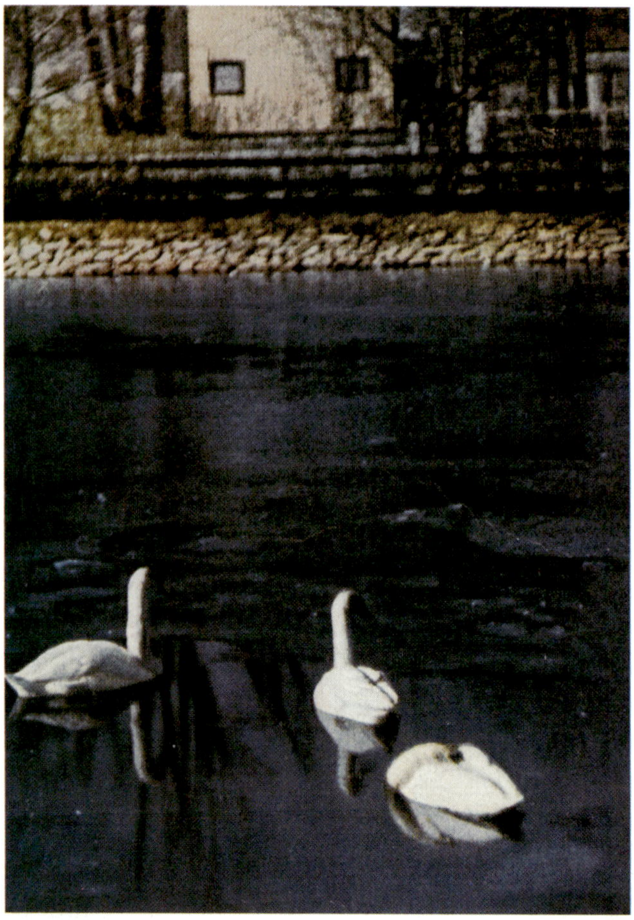

ARTHER C. ELDREDGE
In the American Countryside,
May 1909,
New York Public Library

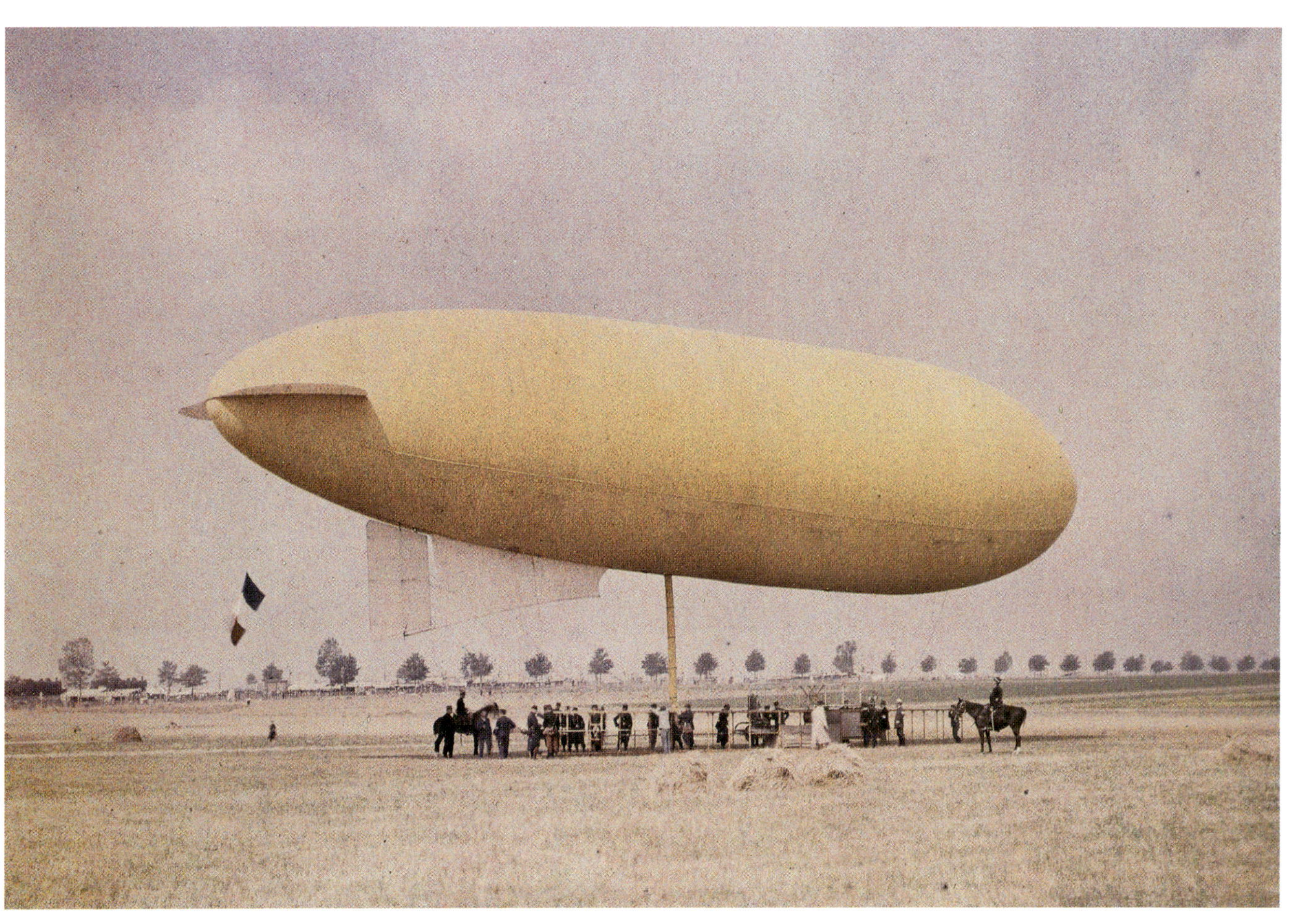

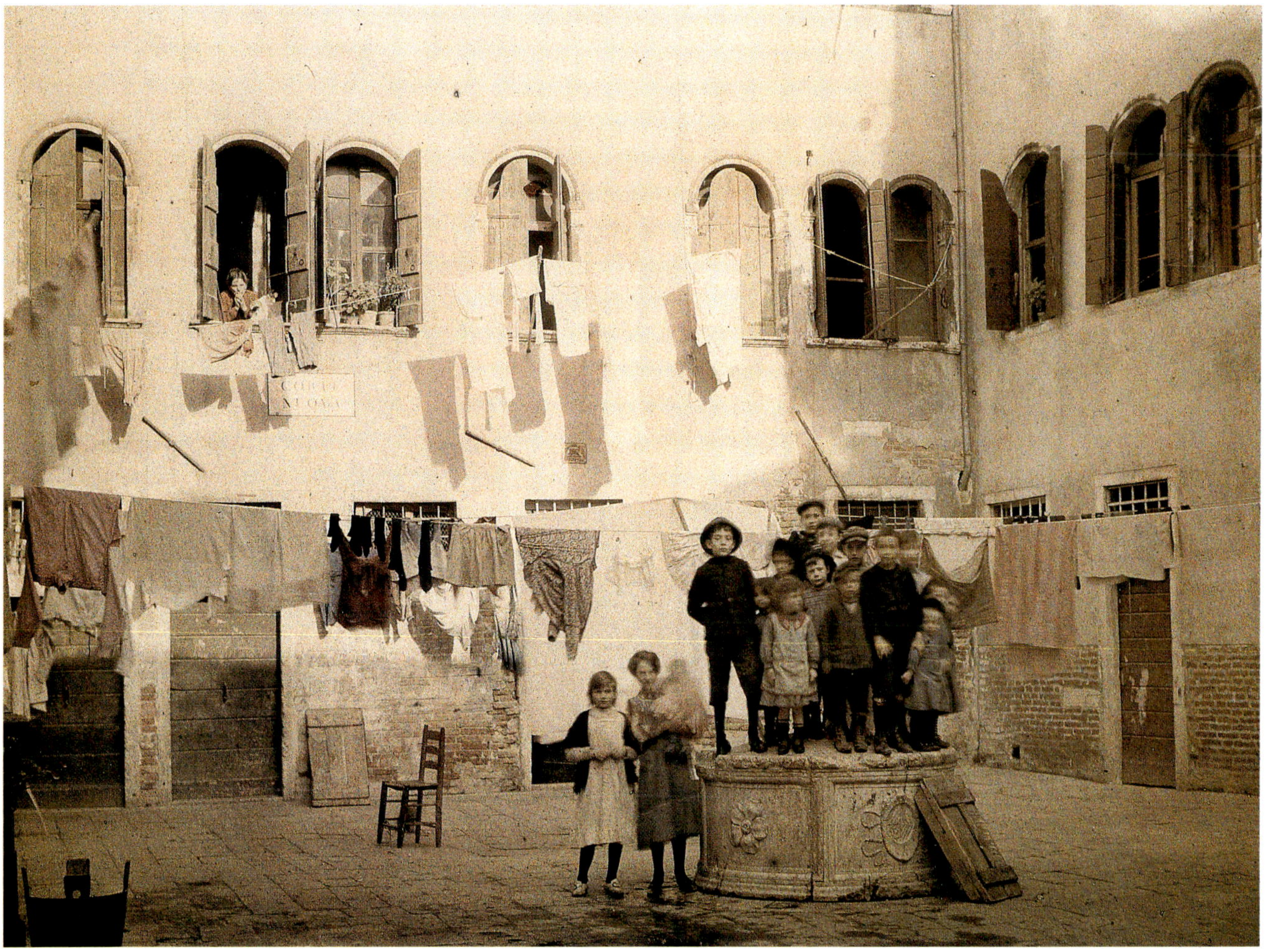

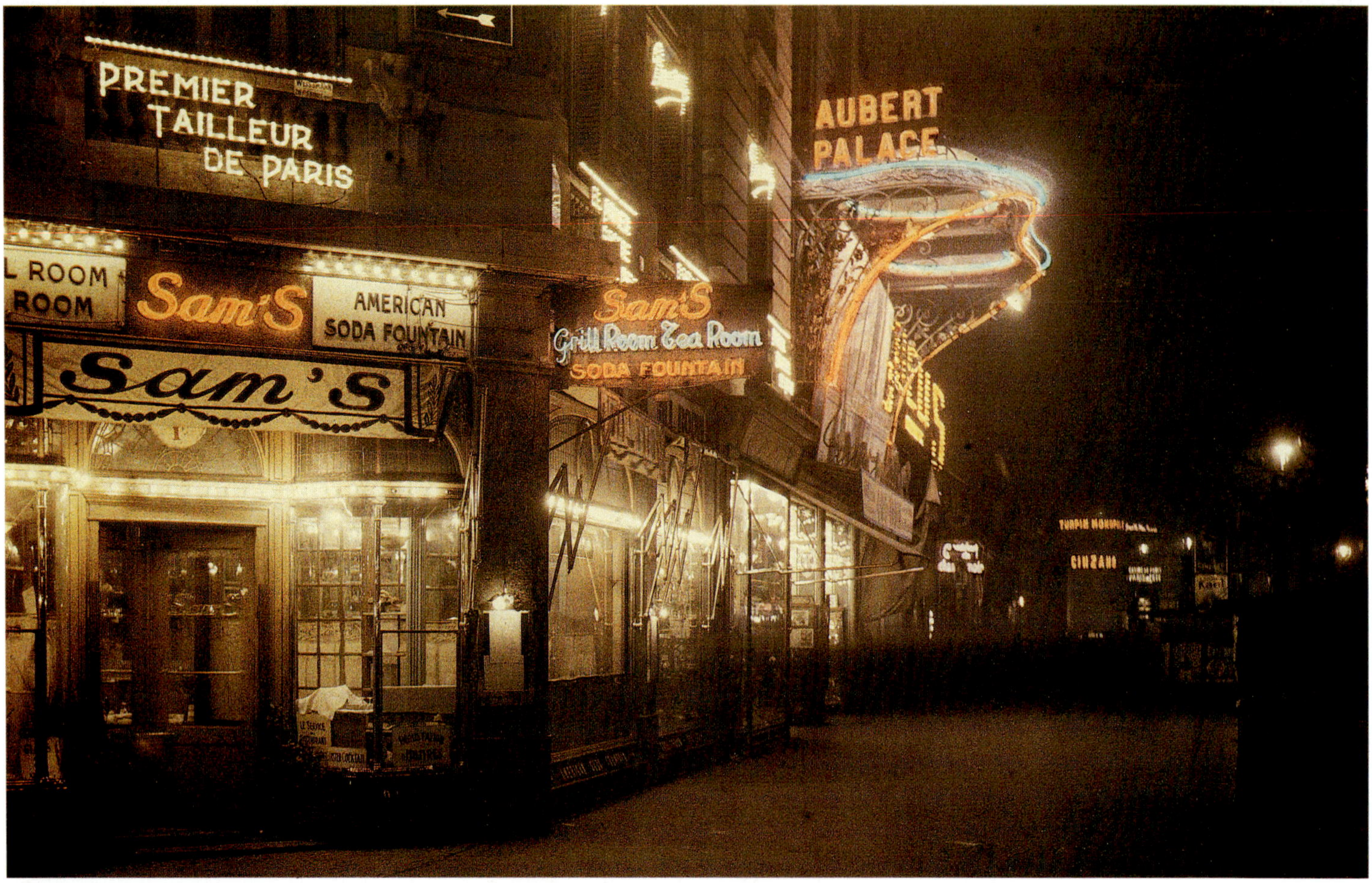
PREMIER
TAILLEUR
DE PARIS
L ROOM
ROOM
Sam'S
AMERICAN
SODA FOUNTAIN
Sam's
Sam'S
Grill Room Tea Room
SODA FOUNTAIN
AUBERT
PALACE
CINZANO

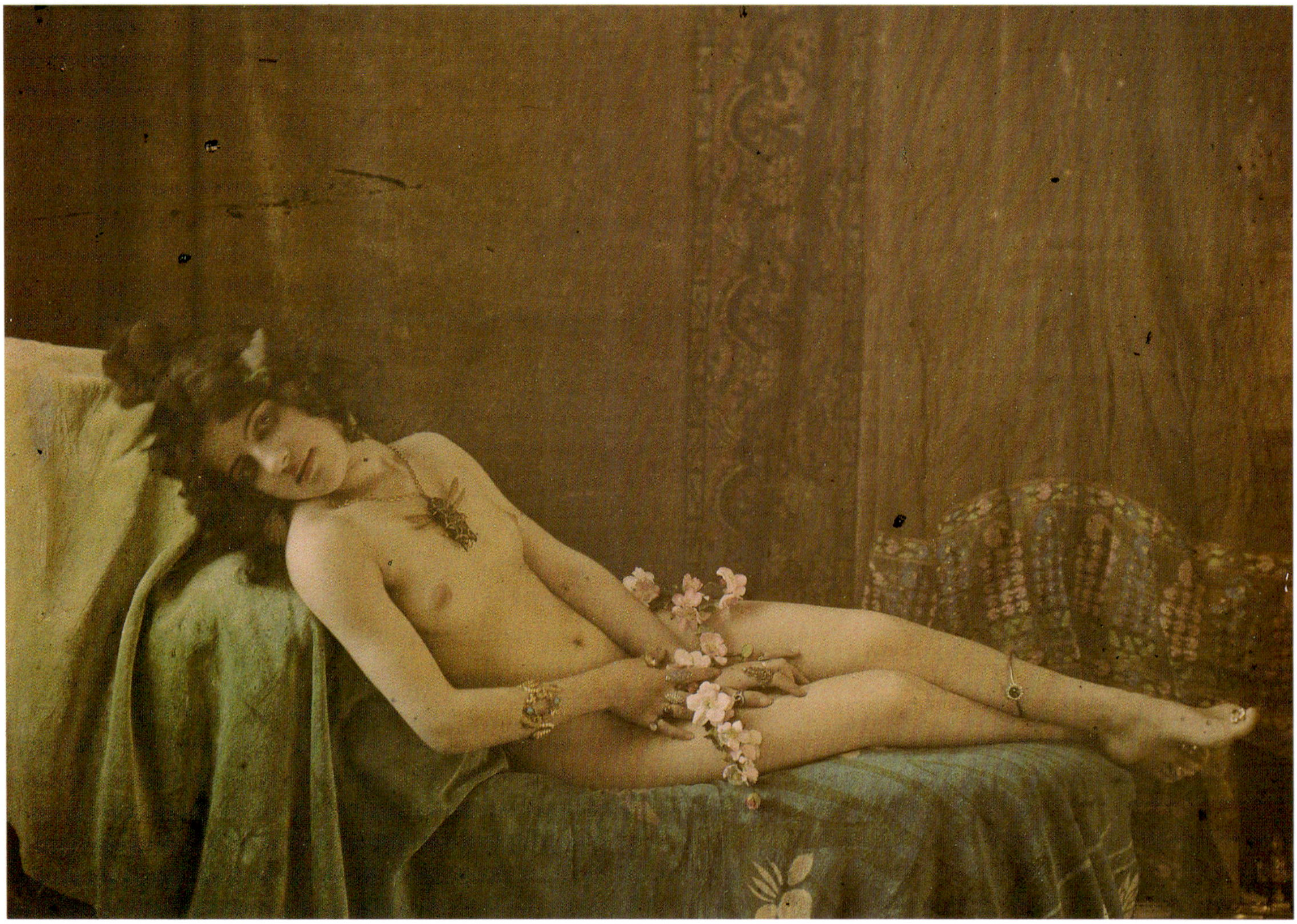

◀ LÉON GIMPEL,
Neon Signs on the Boulevards,
from the corner of Rue des Italiens
in Paris,
December 3, 1925,
Société Française de Photographie,
Paris.

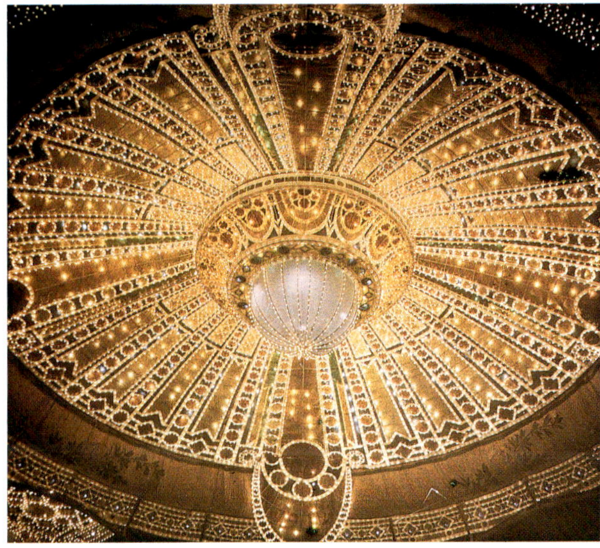

ANONYMOUS,
Large ceiling light,
circa 1920,
private collection.

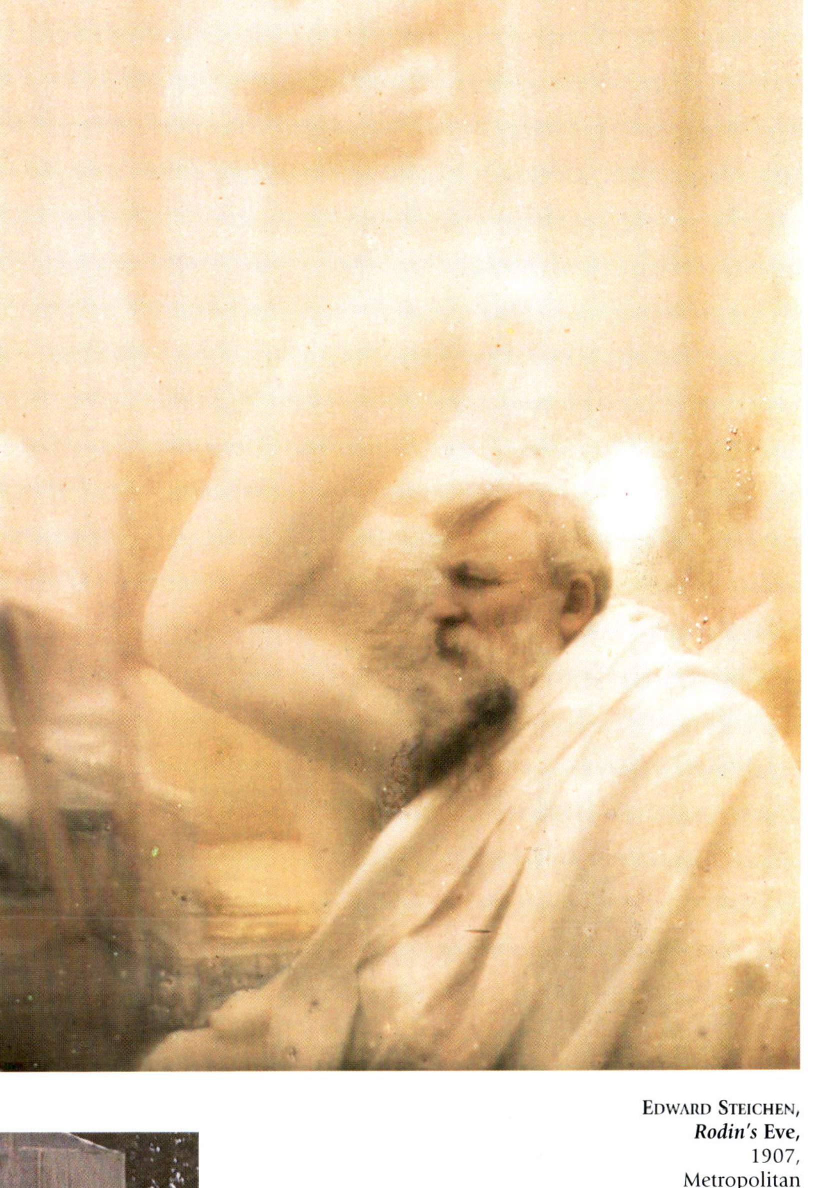

◀ PAUL BERGON,
Female Nude,
undated,
Société Française de
Photographie, Paris.

EDWARD STEICHEN,
Rodin's Eve,
1907,
Metropolitan
Museum of Art,
New York.

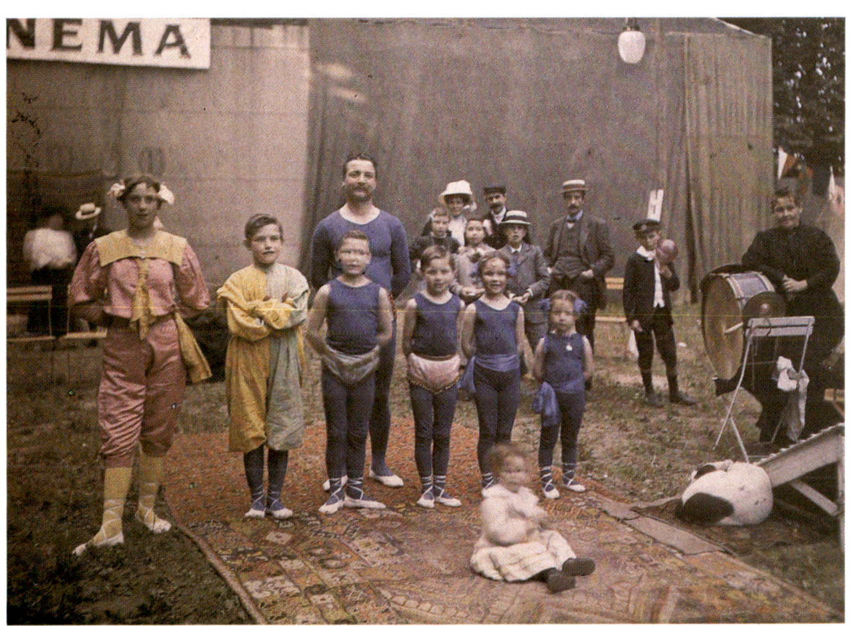

LÉON GIMPEL,
*Family of Acrobats
at the Saint-Cloud Fair,*
September 19, 1909,
Société Française de Photographie,
Paris.

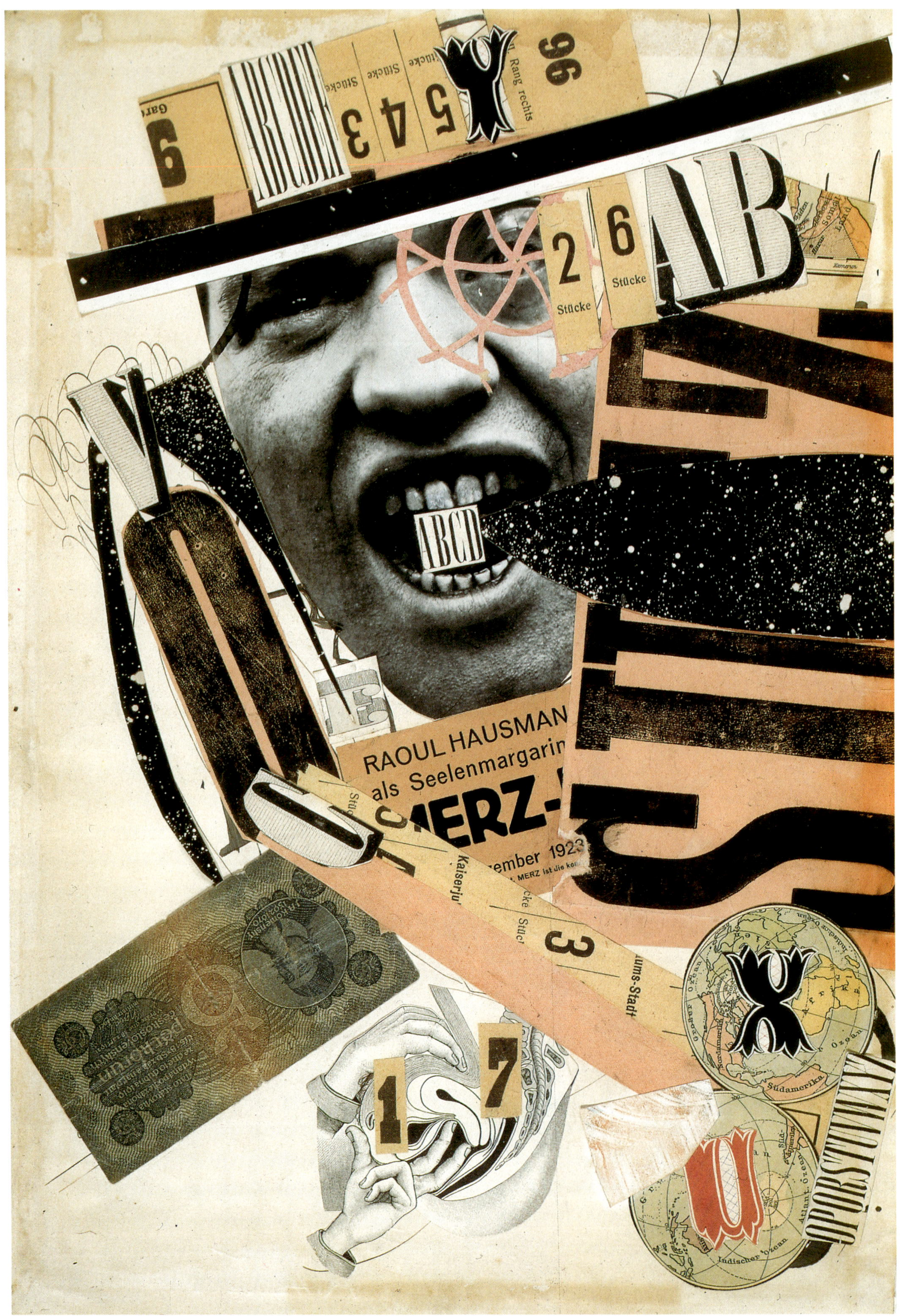

Rang rechs
Stücke
AB
2
6
Stücke
ABCD
RAOUL HAUSMAN
als Seelenmargarin
MERZ-
ember 1923
MERZ ist die ko
Kaiserju
3
Südamerika
Indischer Ozean
17

METAMORPHOSES OF THE IMAGE

26

Photo-graphics and the alienation of meaning

Michel Frizot

In about 1918, with the emergence of Dada, the destructured image became a visual language of protest, a reaction against the art of the Salons. Photomontage and photograms, first developed in Dada and Constructivist circles, led to an entirely new use of photography in the illustrated press, propaganda, and posters. At the same time, photography was being forced to acquire a greater flexibility in its relationship with reality. Surrealism in the 1920s and 1930s was able to extend its forays into the world of the imagination by using photographic procedures that could invent fantastic figures or give strange meanings to images of familiar objects. The repercussions of these developments were to have a profound effect on photography in the media, and on photography as a source of information and a means of communicating ideas.

In the 1920s, photography experienced a period of destructuring of the image, a result of the upheavals of the First World War, and the avant-garde artistic developments that had preceded it. In the fields of art and literature photography was seen as a significant element, a way of bringing order (or disorder) to meaning.

Photomontage

Among these developments, photomontage can be seen as a branch of the early years of Cubism, between 1906 and 1911, and then more directly as being related to Braque's *trompe-l'œil* collages (of wallpaper, imitation wood, chair cane) of 1912 or Picasso's paintings that incorporate pasted-on papers and fragments of typography (1911–1912), as well as sharing the outlook of the Dadaist movement, founded in Zurich in 1916. It was to be within these Dadaist circles that this technique of manipulating the photographic image was born. Randomly selected photographic fragments – taken from the artist's personal photographs, from newspapers or from reproductions in magazines – were cut out and reassembled following a new logic that ignored the usual unities of space, texture, style or origin. It is not entirely certain when the first photomontages were made. Their invention has been claimed, retrospectively, as being by Georg Grosz and John Heartfield in 1916 or by Raoul Hausmann, Hannah Höch, and Johannes Bader in 1918.

Whatever the case in these early years (pure coincidence, a failure to realize the future importance of a simple game of cutting-out or chronological confusion), photomontage began to be more widely practiced after 1920, describing itself as "assemblage and combination of expressive elements taken from photographs" (Stepanova, 1928) and showing the influence of the polemical and sometimes destructive spirit of Dadaism towards the entire pre-war visual heritage that had sought to perpetuate a society of illusory order – photographs, paintings, popular iconography, and press illustrations. Photomontage stemmed from a desire to mix these genres, to destructure through the abolition of "bourgeois" typologies, to create an objectively disparate synthesis, "a new unity which can create out of the chaos of war and revolution the reflection of a vision that is optically and conceptually new" (Raoul Hausmann).[1] To this can be added a successful attempt to link the image and the word, as the Futurists had tried to do with their "free words" and Balla's "interventionist manifestation" (an arrangement of pieces of cut-out text forming a "picture", 1914). Applying collage techniques, as used by the Cubists, photomontage presents, through the juxtaposition of real and independent photographic elements (as objective as Braque or Picasso's wallpaper, scraps

◀ Raoul Hausmann, *ABCD (Portrait of the Artist)*, photomontage, 1923–1924, Musée National d'Art Moderne, Paris.

1. "Fotomontage", in *a bis z*, May 1931, published in *Raoul Hausmann: Je ne suis pas un photographe*, Paris, Chêne, 1975.

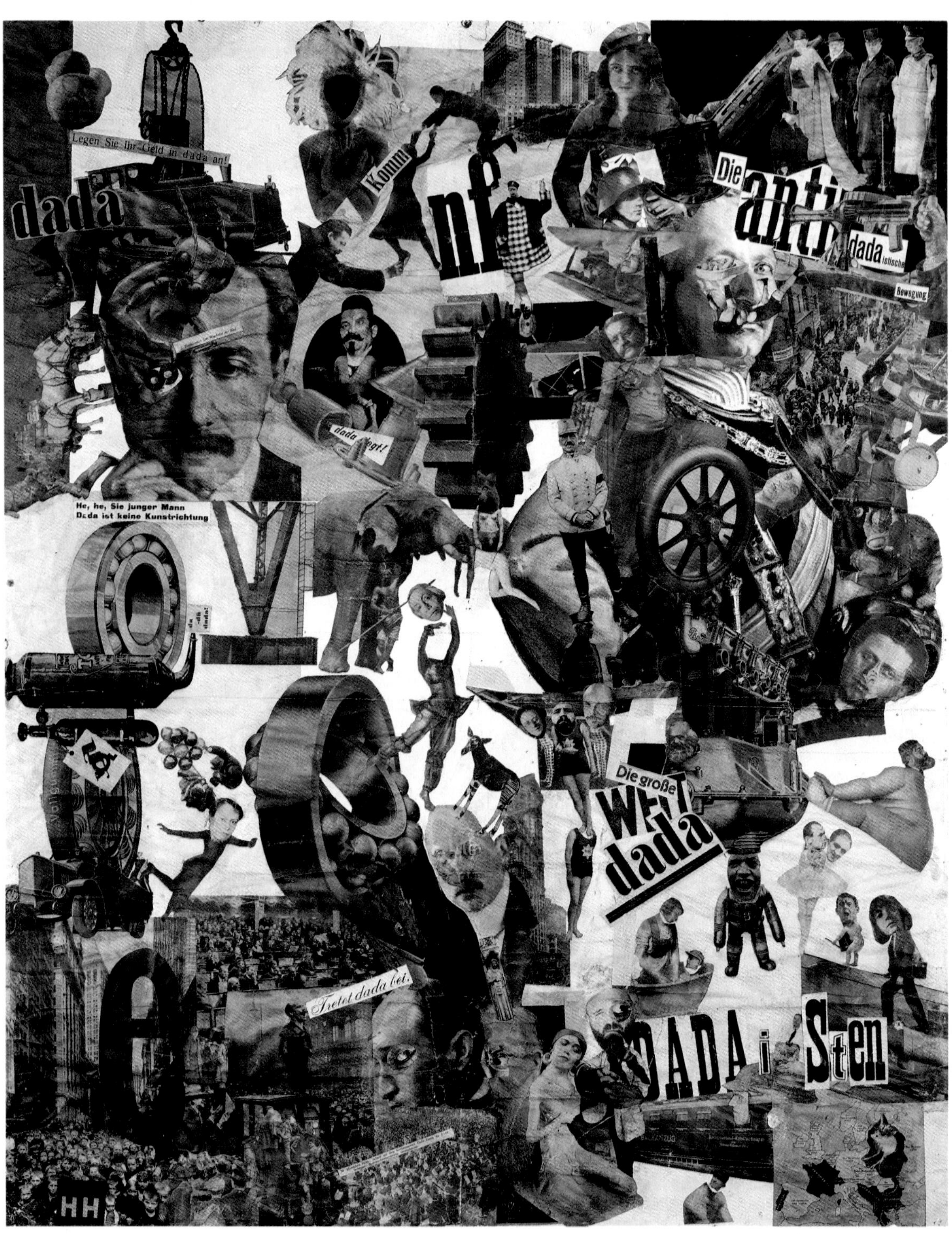

HANNAH HÖCH, *Cut-out with Kitchen Knife,* 1919, Staatliche Museen Preussischer Kulturbesitz, Nationalgalerie, Berlin.

of newspaper, tobacco packets), a quasi-literary expression of anti-realist agitation, of Dadaist denunciation, "so that it was possible to say in the picture what, if spoken, would immediately have been censured" (G. Grosz).

Because of its origins, photomontage was initially characterized by ideas (essentially Futurist and Dadaist) of visual anarchy, of the shattering of the image's traditional references (and, in particular, its unity of style). It was not long, however, before this new medium developed along more positive lines, towards "constructing" or assembling images, in the mechanical sense of the word (not so distant from the machinist and energetic fantasies of the Futurists). For Raoul Hausmann, the word photomontage (*Fotomontage*) "translated our hate for the artist; seeing ourselves more as engineers, we wanted to construct, assemble our works, and set them going (*montieren*)". Gustav Klutsis, a Soviet photomonteur of the 1930s, went so far as to say that "the very word photomontage grew out of industrial culture: the montage of machines, the montage of turbines".[2] Individual pieces are assembled and a visual message is produced that cannot be translated into words. Diverted early away from its more negative tendencies, by Max Ernst, who adapted photomontage to "painting"

2. 1932, quoted in C. Lodder, *Russian Constructivism*, New Haven and London, Yale University Press, 1983, p. 296.

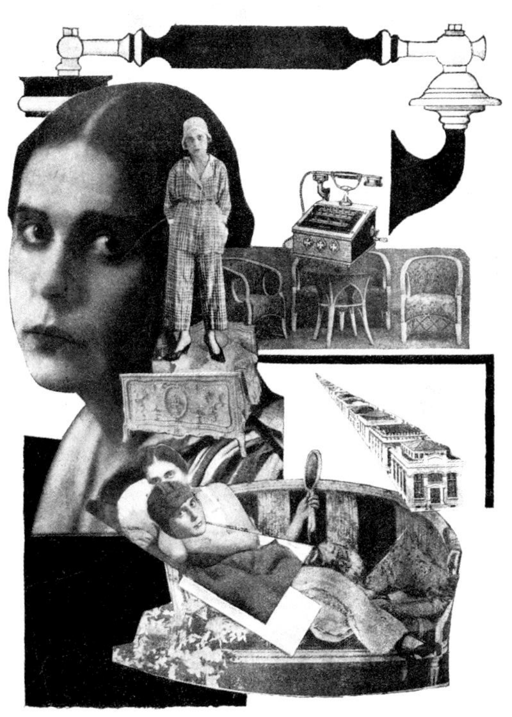

В постели она, она лежит, —
Он.
На столе телефон.

image and by its color. Photomontage is a technique that cuts across stylistic boundaries, uniting the different aesthetic movements in Europe in the 1920s and 1930s, when ideas were circulating very rapidly as a result of exhibitions, meetings, and publications. Some places became a focus for this dynamism: Berlin, Paris, Moscow, Weimar and then Dessau with the Bauhaus, while individual artists made their presence felt in the Netherlands and Italy.

Three events in particular, which took place some ten years after it first appeared, provide evidence of the fashion for photomontage – the publication of Roh and Tschichold's book *foto-auge / œil et photo / photo-eye* in 1929, the huge exhibition *Film und Foto* organized that same year in Stuttgart, and the exhibition *Fotomontage*, held at the Kunstgewerbemuseum in Berlin in 1931. In the exhibition catalogue the term "photomontage" appeared under the names of Schwitters, Heartfield, Herbert Bayer, Hannah Höch, and the Folkwangschule of Essen.[4] To these should be added the anonymous works from Soviet artists,

◀ **Alexander Rodchenko,** photomontage from *Pro Eto,* poems by Mayakovsky, 1923, International Museum of Photography, George Eastman House, Rochester.

László Moholy-Nagy, *Mass Psychosis,* photomontage, 1927, International Museum of Photography, George Eastman House, Rochester.
▼

3. *Dada Photomontagen,* exhibition catalogue, Hannover, Kestner, 1979; D. Ades, *Photomontage,* London, Thames and Hudson; New York, Random House, 1976; *Photomontages,* Photo Poche no. 31, Paris, 1987.

4. Republished Stuttgart, DVA, 1974 and New York, Arno, 1979.

by including in his tranquil painted surfaces the frank realism of a cut-out photograph, the unifying principles of photomontage developed in a variety of different ways according to the artistic movements that adopted it, in view of the possibilities for reform, protest or style that it offered to all. It is possible to trace a typology of photomontage that follows (and reveals) the course of the evolution of inter-war artistic movements, the contours of the chief trends, merging into the field of "isms in art" (*Kunst-ismen*) that proliferated in the 1920s.[3]

Like many of the dazzling contributions of Dada, photomontage found a less provocative application in the work of those artistic circles more closely attached to "construction" and "production", works of a more craft-based, personal or popular character. Although it had the texture of collage, photomontage was not interested in the creation of unique works. The photomontage was, in its turn, photographed, in this way becoming a work of photography, produced in several copies (Citroën, Moholy-Nagy, Domela). A collage of objects, some of which might be photographic, such as those produced by Schwitters, printed in multiple photographic copies, could be manipulated in a variety of ways, from re-coloring to pictorial or typographic additions. There is always, at whatever level of interpretation, a stage where painting, object, and photograph are mixed, the differences being marked by the surface of the

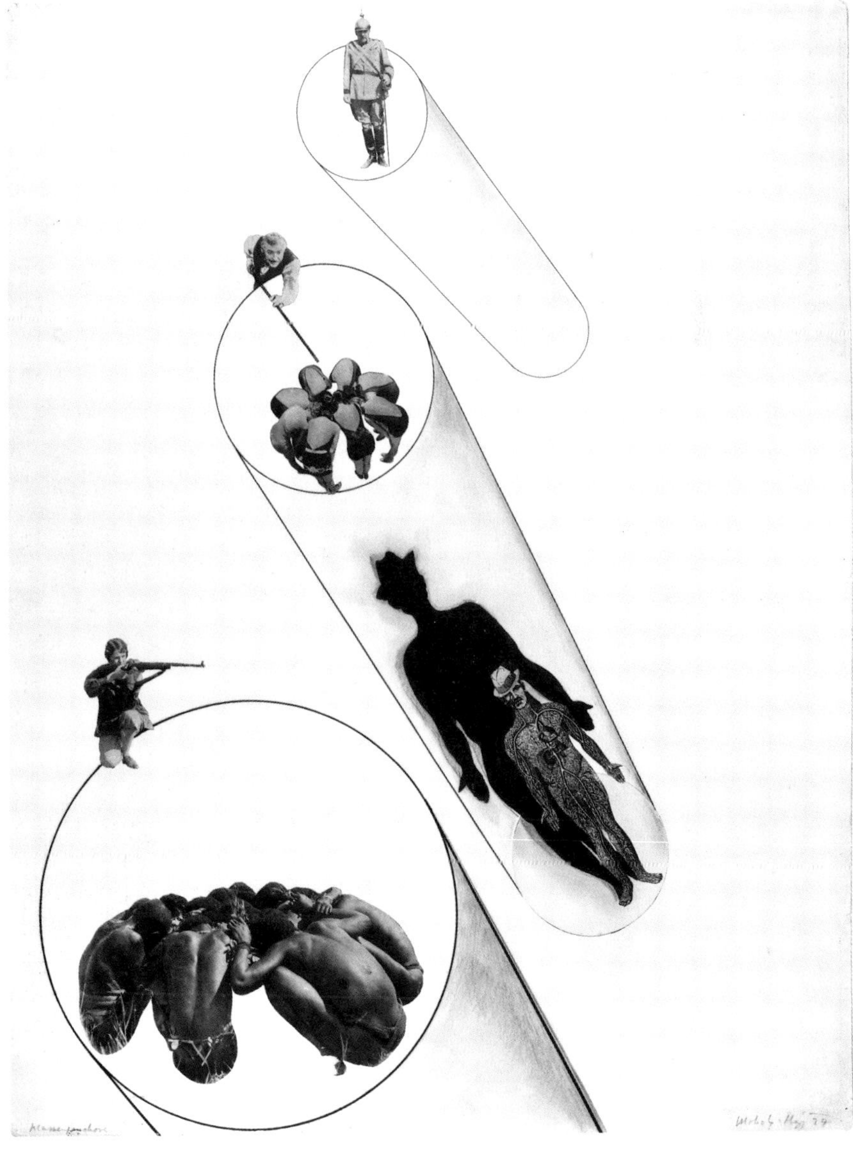

presented as a group. The term was also applied, under the heading "photoplastique", to Moholy-Nagy and, under the category of phototypographies (that is, mock-ups for posters, books, prospectuses), to the Dutch artists Schuitema, Zwart, and Tschichold, and to those from the Kunstgewerbeschule of Stuttgart.

It is clear that photographs used for publicity or advertising developed directly out of photomontage, in which typography is integrated into and complements the image. Particularly well-known are works by Moholy-Nagy, Tschichold, and Rodchenko. The schools of applied arts (Essen, Munich, Stuttgart, the Bauhaus) made an important contribution, as did the Soviet group, led by Lissitzky. The medium known as graphics was not separated from "pure" photography produced with a camera. In this respect those from east-central Europe differed from the other participants (with the exception of Maximilien Vox), since it appears that photomontage was non-existent among the French and the American participants (or at least among those selected for *Film und Foto* – Kertész, Tabard, Henri, Stieglitz, and Steichen). The multitude of terms used to describe these works is indicative of the diversity of approaches of the photomonteurs. At this time, John Heartfield, who is particularly known for his later anti-Nazi imagery, used no fewer than five different names for his work which involved photography (*Foto-Montage, Foto-Graphik, Foto-Satire, Foto-Plakat, Foto-Einbände*).

László Moholy-Nagy was certainly the most active photomonteur in avant-garde Germany. A Constructivist painter and teacher at the Bauhaus in Weimar, he turned to photomontage in 1922, soon using it to make a less "abstract" version of the geometric compositions he was producing at that time (quite similar to Lissitzky's *Prouns*). Moholy-Nagy simplified the accumulation of cut-out pieces and the multiplication of perspectives, textures, and scales on a single surface, concerning himself with a more sober and pure exploitation of these elements. Some of his

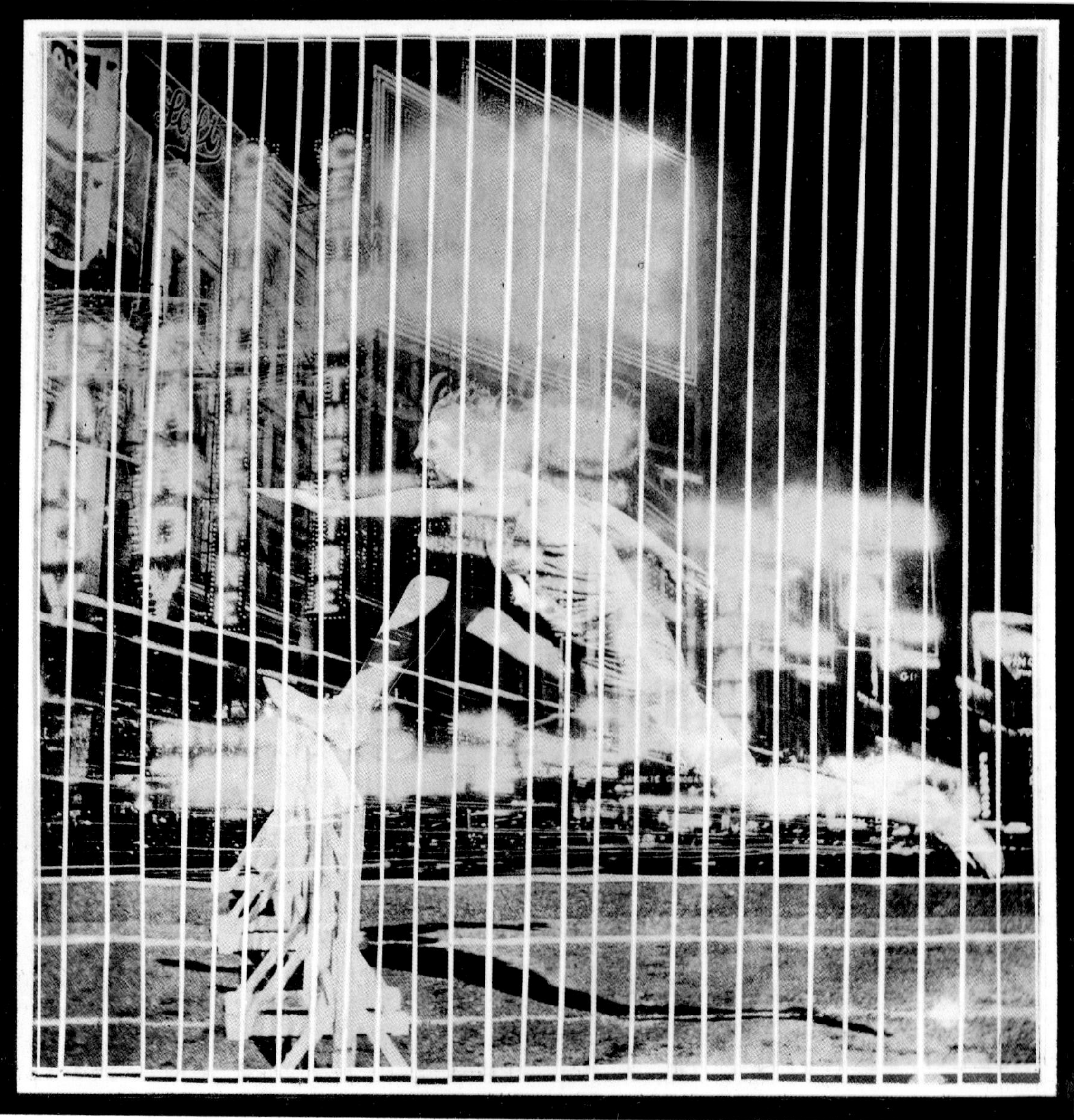

El Lissitzky, *Runner in the City*, photomontage, circa 1926, Metropolitan Museum of Art, New York.

photographic *découpages* are joined by straight or curved lines, or by a colored plane, while perspectives are created by variations in the scale of the figures (human or animal), all perfectly realistic in treatment and having reference to a three-dimensional universe. "Linear elements, structural patterns, close-up, and isolated figures are here the elements for a space articulation. Pasted on a white surface, these elements seem to be embedded in infinite space, with clear articulation of nearness and distance. The best description of their effect would be perhaps to say that each element is pasted on vertical panes, which are set up in an endless series each behind the other."[5]

Thus, Moholy-Nagy's intentions in photomontage reflect the economy of his pictorial means: an intensely poetic simplicity, allusive rather than demonstrative, and without aggression. In Moholy-Nagy's key work *Malerei, Fotografie, Film*, published by the Bauhaus in 1925, and in Werner Gräff's *Es kommt der neue Fotograf* (1929), photomontage is given an important place. It was accepted as one of the distinctive elements of the New Vision and the New Photography.

Not surprisingly, in the U.S.S.R. photomontage was one of the techniques used by revolutionary art in the service of ideology. If Suprematism and Constructivism had seemed elitist, impenetrable, and poorly adapted to the socialist objectives of the day, now avant-garde artists – who were recognized as such in a Europe as yet still very open in the early 1920s – including Lissitzky, Klutsis, the Stenberg brothers, and Rodchenko, co-operated with the party's injunctions that the reading of the aesthetic message should be made more widely accessible. Applied photography should make up for the "imperfect methods of painting" in order to depict the "mechanical complexity of the external forms of objects and of our industrial culture". Photomontage came to be seen as a way of continuing to "paint" at the same time as being understood by everyone. In the same poetic vein as Moholy-Nagy, Rodchenko worked in 1923 on a series of photomontages as illustrations for a collection of poetry, *Pro Eto* [About This], by Mayakovsky. Here, the scattered photographic fragments are the visual equivalent of the words in the poems, including photographic "quotations" – a kind of realist inlay – of objects mentioned in the text together with a portrait of the poet.

The principles of propaganda also helped to form the vision of Klutsis, one of the first producers of photomontage. "Not only an assemblage of photographs, [it] must be accompanied by political slogans, colors and graphics."[6] From 1920, he began to include figures of workers

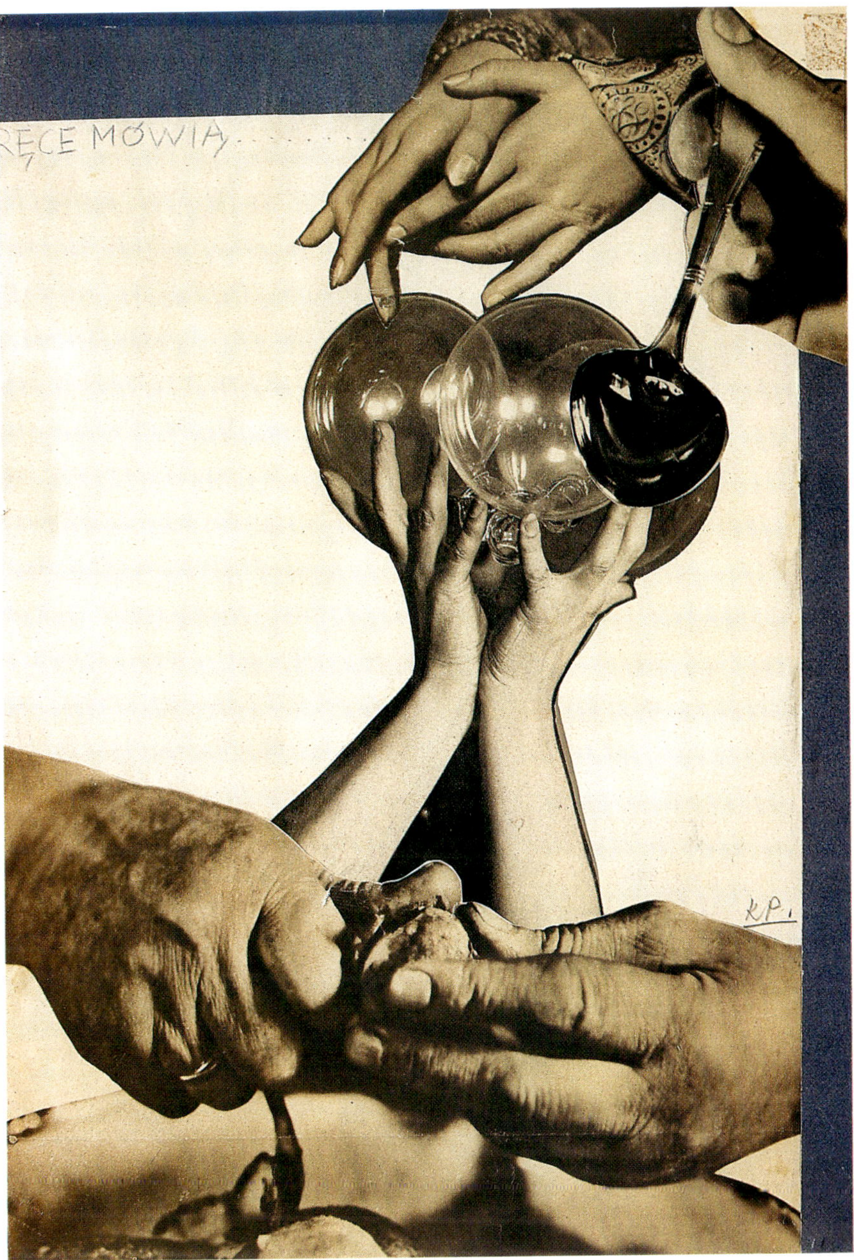

KASIMIERZ POSADECKI,
Hands Speaking,
photomontage,
1933,
Museum Sztuki, Lodz.

(pasted-on photographs) in his Suprematist paintings, and it was he who produced the photomontage postcards for the Moscow Spartakiades (Games) in 1928 and the posters for the first five-year plan (1930). Photography, through photomontage, was becoming a force for change in graphic art.

Photo-graphics

Photomontage was to find its public fulfillment in graphics and the art of communication. In Russia, after the Revolution, graphic art held pride of place, being taught in the Vkhutemas [Higher Technical Institutes], along similar lines to the teaching in the Bauhaus. Following the ideas of Constructivism, students were taught to study volume, and how to treat it effectively in two dimensions. From 1922, after the relative incomprehensibility of the language of Constructivism, a return to an aggressive pictorial realism favored

5. "Space-Time and the Photographer" (1942), reprinted in R. Kostelanetz (ed.), *Moholy-Nagy*, New York, Praeger, 1970, pp. 57–66.

6. Quoted in C. Leclanche-Boulé, *Typographies et photomontages constructivistes en U.R.S.S.*, Paris, Papyrus, 1984.

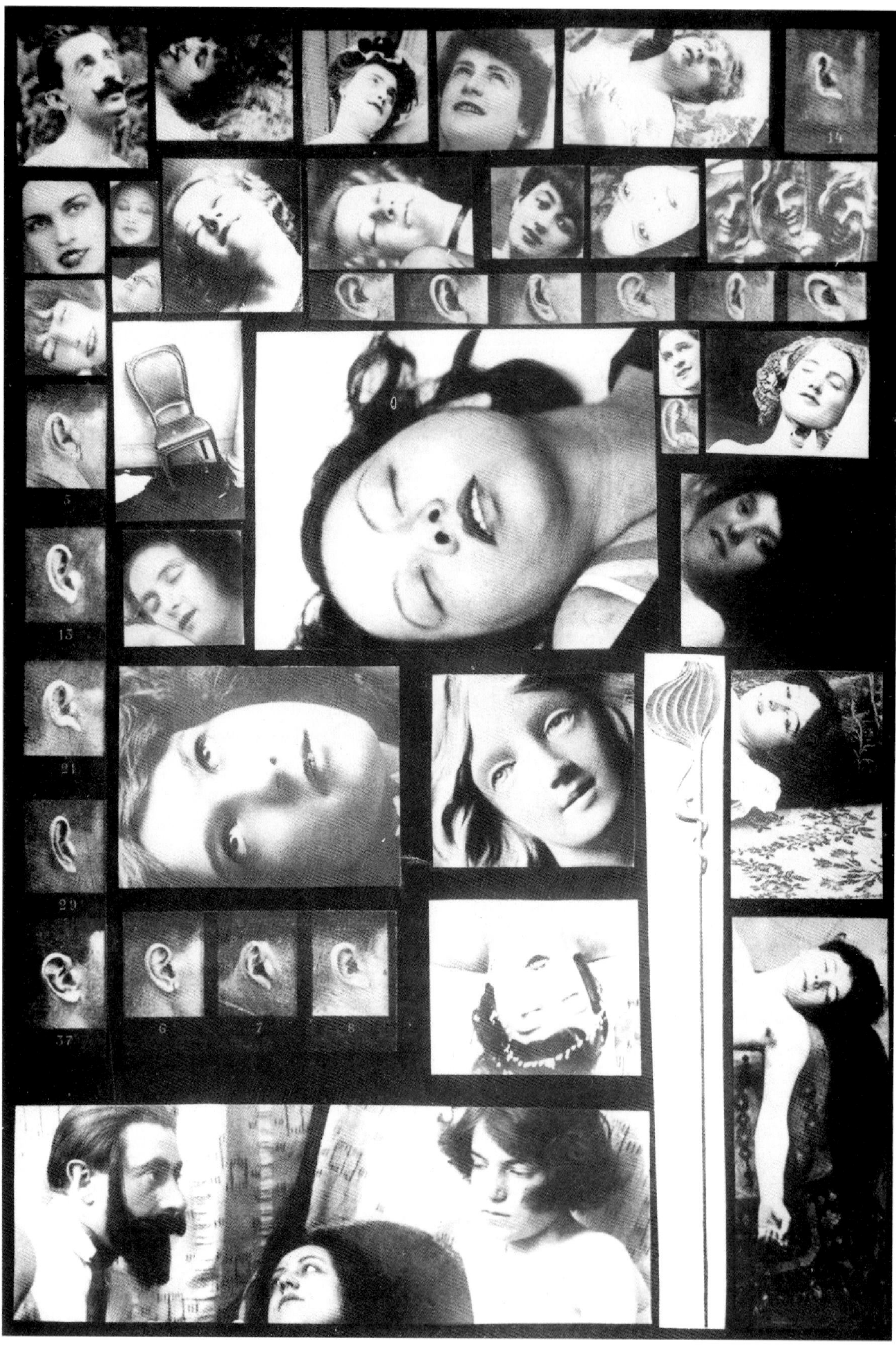

SALVADOR DALÍ, *Phenomenon of Ecstasy*, from *Le Minotaure*, no. 3/4, December 1933.

the use of photography. It contributed to a dynamic art that was pre-established but restructured and fragmented. This use of photography implied an immediate reference to the practice of photomontage that Lissitzky had discovered in Germany, for example, in 1921: "The combination of photographs changes the composition of graphic images. The meaning of this change is that the photograph is not the drawing of a visual fact, but the exact fixation of it. This precision and documentary quality gives the photograph a power to influence the viewer that the graphic image is never able to attain."[7]

7. "Foto-montazh", in *LEF*, no. 4, 1924, p. 41, quoted in C. Lodder, *op. cit.*

Klutsis, known particularly for his designs for exhibition stands, claimed that he had been the first to combine photography with painting (1919). His poster for the *Total Electrification of the Country* (1920) does indeed include a photograph of Lenin marching. However, it was only from 1922 that this usage became more widespread. *Sport* (1922) is a purely graphic photomontage, without the poetry of Rodchenko's creations for *Pro Eto*. In the diagonal compositions inspired by Lissitzky's *Prouns*, the photographs accompany planes of pure color and strict typographical elements (clearly distancing themselves from commercial usage), giving a prominent position to machinism (for example in the repetition of the locomotives in Klutsis' poster *Transport*, 1929). This artist's later work – such as his posters the *Election of the Soviets* (1930), the *World Proletariat Brigade* (1931), and the *Anti-Imperialist Exhibition* (1931) – are excellent examples of this paradoxical linking of antithetical styles, bringing together the apparent depth of the photograph with the flatness of painting and typography.

The graphic art used on products intended for public consumption (book covers, leaflets, tracts, posters, magazines, newspapers, even the sweet wrappers designed by Rodchenko and Mayakovsky) followed the new party line of productivism which governed the relationship between art and revolution, and which favored photography as being more comprehensible to the masses than "abstract" art. Other Constructivists adopted it: Popova, Stepanova, Lavinsky (poster for *Battleship Potemkin*, 1925). Lissitzky's exploration of ways of linking typography and expressed ideas led him to design magazine covers (*Architecture*, for the Vkhutemas, Moscow 1927, and *U.S.S.R. in Construction* which he edited from 1931 to 1933), posters (the Russian Exhibition in Zurich, 1929, with the portraits of two Young Pioneers), and, above all, to be the "constructor" (the title of his self-portrait of 1924) of exhibitions. In the Russian pavilion of the World Press Exhibition (*Pressa*) held in Cologne, the walls were covered with gigantic photomontages of press photographs. The same technique was used in Dresden in 1930. From early on in his career, Rodchenko also designed book covers – that of *Pro Eto*, with a full-face portrait of Lili Brik – and posters – three designs for *Kino Glaz*, a film by Dziga Vertov, 1924. The New Economic Policy demanded propaganda material for industry and agriculture, provided by Rodchenko and the Vkhutemas:

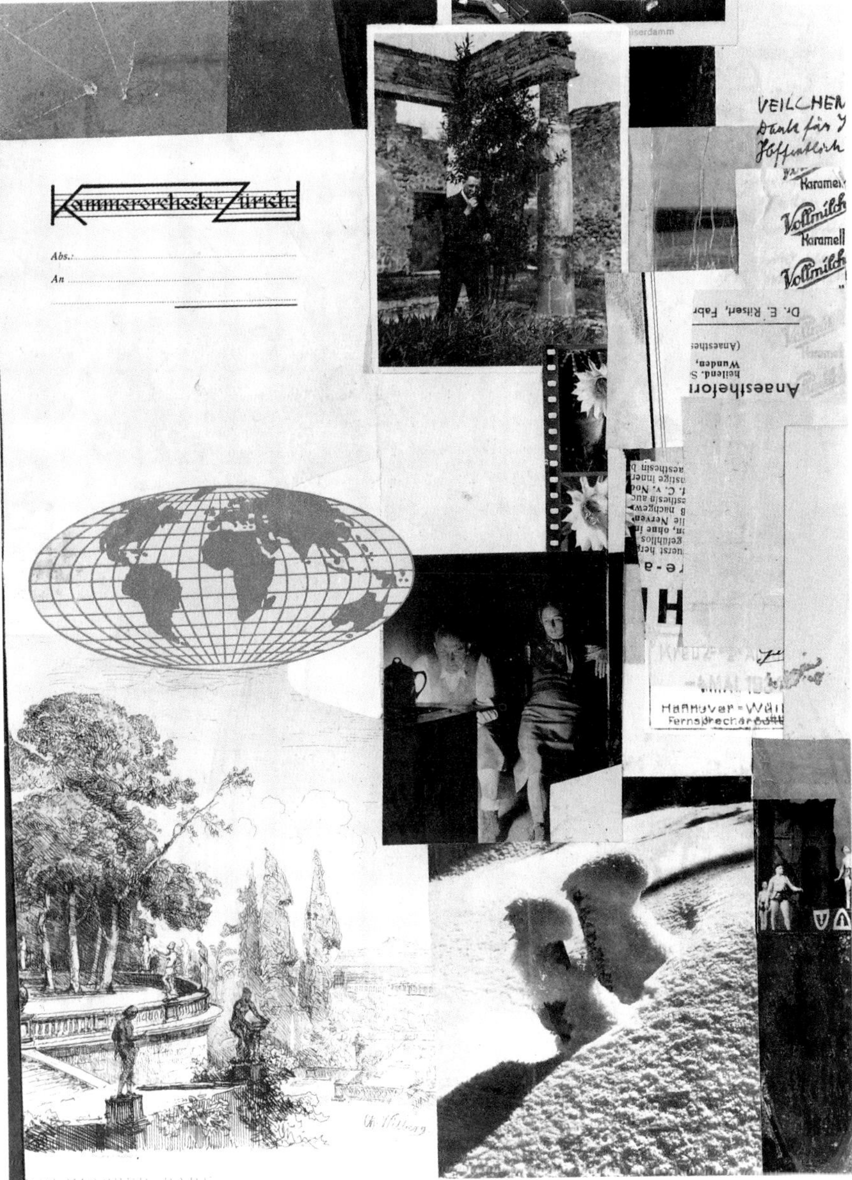

Kurt Schwitters, *Roman Park*, collage, 1934, Rheinisches Bildarchiv, Cologne.

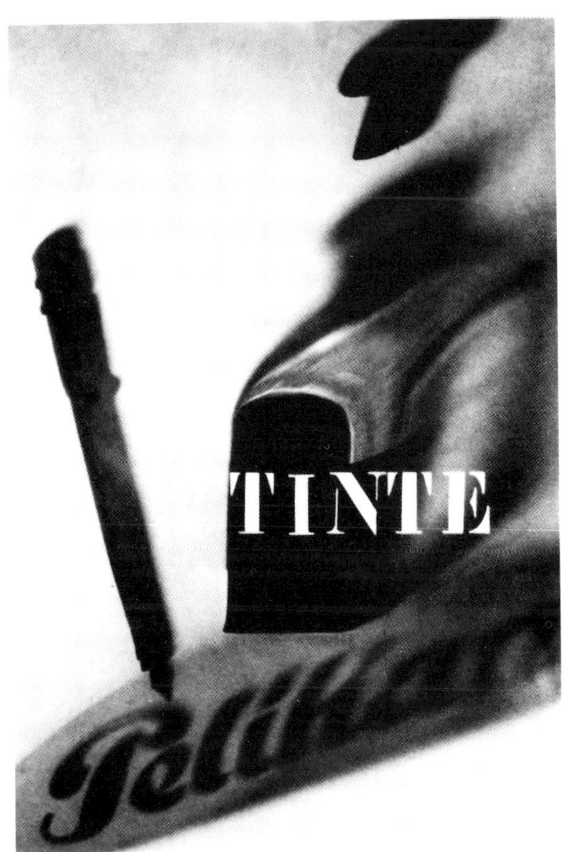

◀ **El Lissitzky,** advertisement for Pelikan inks, with photogram, 1924.

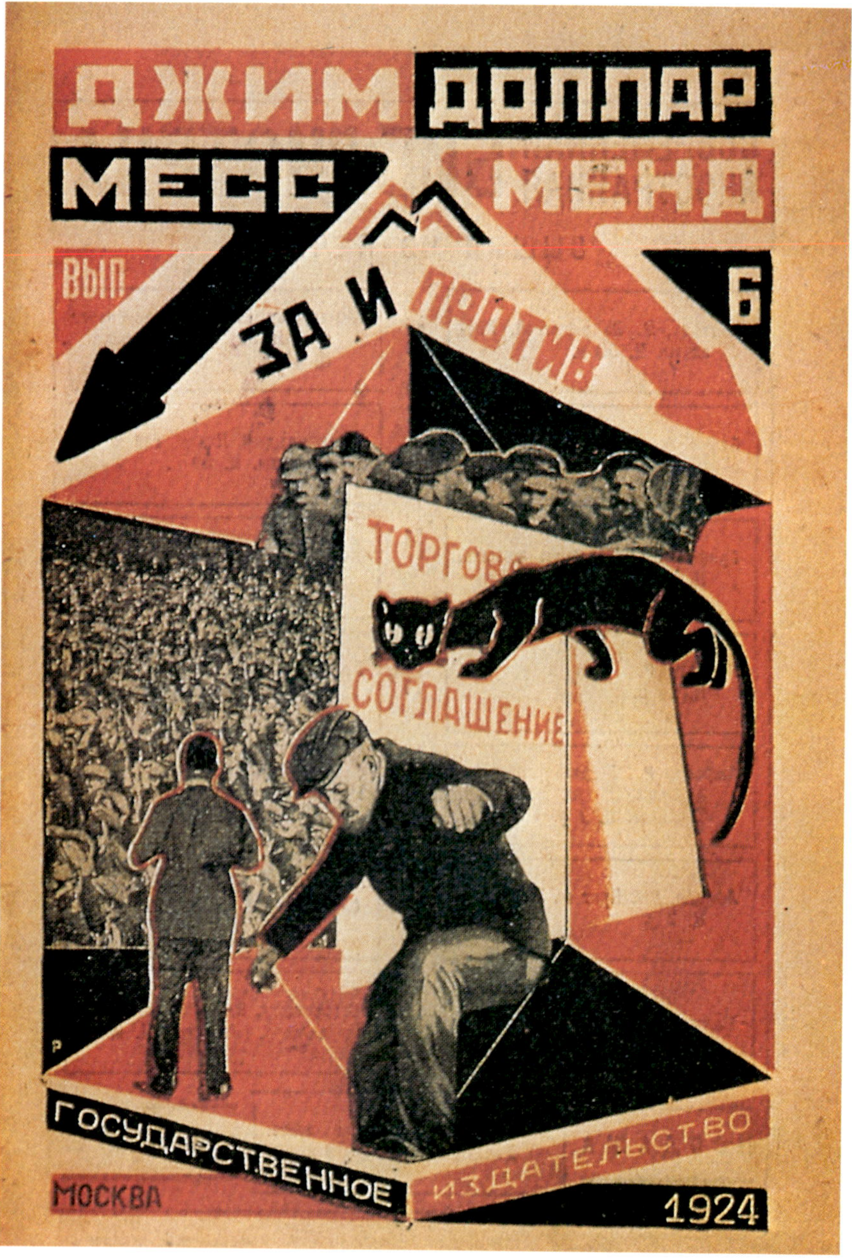

Alexander Rodchenko, wrapping paper for the magazine *Miss Mend*, 1924.

László Moholy-Nagy, ▶ cover of *die neue linie*, June 1930.

posters, banners, packaging, press publicity or murals. Photomontage found its place within this general activity, as a realistic and convincing graphic language. From 1922, Rodchenko did the page lay-outs for the magazine *Kino-Fot* and designed the covers of *LEF* (later *Novyi LEF*) between 1923 and 1928, as well as the paste-ups for *Miss Mend*, a serial novel (1924). No doubt it was partly in order to obtain the raw materials for these montages that Rodchenko himself became a photographer in 1924, and one of the inventors of the New Photography, which had a strong impact on press photography, propaganda, and the celebration of the proletariat. Moholy-Nagy, on the other hand, represented a more purely aesthetic tendency, though similarly drawing inspiration from the same principles of construction.[8]

From 1923, film production in the U.S.S.R. was centralized (Sovkino). Former pupils of the Vkhutemas and Constructivist artists promoted Soviet films through their poster designs. Notable among these were the Stenberg brothers, who drew from photographic originals for their posters for Vertov's *The Man with a Movie Camera*, *The Three-Million Dollar Case* (1926), and *A Screw from Another Machine* (1927), Anatoly Belsky, who worked in a similar way for *Five Minutes*, Prusakov for *Law of the Mountains* (1927) and *Khaz-Push* (1927), Rodchenko for *Battleship Potemkin* (1925), and Vertov's *One Sixth of the World* (1926).[9]

The art of the poster was an important meeting-point between the Communist East and western Europe. The young typographer Jan Tschichold played an important role: "Photography is also part of the primary resources of the new typography in the modern world, organized around the lens" (1925). His posters for the Phoebus Palast cinema – *Die Hose, Lasten der Menscheit, Die Kameliendame, Die Frau ohne Namen* (1927) – are among the purest products of Constructivism, made in the refined style of Moholy-Nagy's photomontages.

In this field – the meeting-point between typography and photography – influenced by the typographic work of Schwitters, the Bauhaus played an important role. Due to the suggestion of the Bauhaus, a non-Gothic typeface was used, further revolutionised by the abandonment of capital letters – as in *foto-auge* – another body-blow to German syntax. This mixture of techniques was described by Moholy-Nagy in 1925 as "typo-photo: visual communication represented with maximum accuracy". His cover for *Malerei, Fotografie, Film*, consisting of a photogram, directly supported this modern outlook (the first photogram integrated into a graphic work is that by Lissitzky for Pelikan ink, 1924). Advertising leaflets, posters, and magazine covers were all part of the applied studies of the students and teachers of the Bauhaus and the German schools of graphic art, where photography was being progressively assimilated.

The "New Advertising" advocated by Hartlaub in 1927 aimed at precision, effectiveness, and clarity in the description of the product. Based in Berlin, the centre for this form of communication, and particularly active in the late 1920s, were Herbert Bayer (project for a newspaper kiosk, 1924), Walter Dexel, Cesar Domela, Max Burchartz (poster for the *Festival of Dance*, Essen, 1928, and the Werbung exhibition, Essen, 1931), Joost Schmidt, Leistikow, and Stankovski. Peterhans was running not only the photography school but also the advertising studio at the new Bauhaus in Berlin in 1932–1933. Moholy designed the covers for Piscator's *Das politische Theater* and for the magazine *die neue linie* (1929–1930). The cover of the magazine *Qualität*

8. C. Leclanche-Boulé, *op. cit.*

9. M. Friedman (ed.), *Posters: The 20th-Century Poster: Design of the Avant-Garde*, New York, Abbeville, 1984.

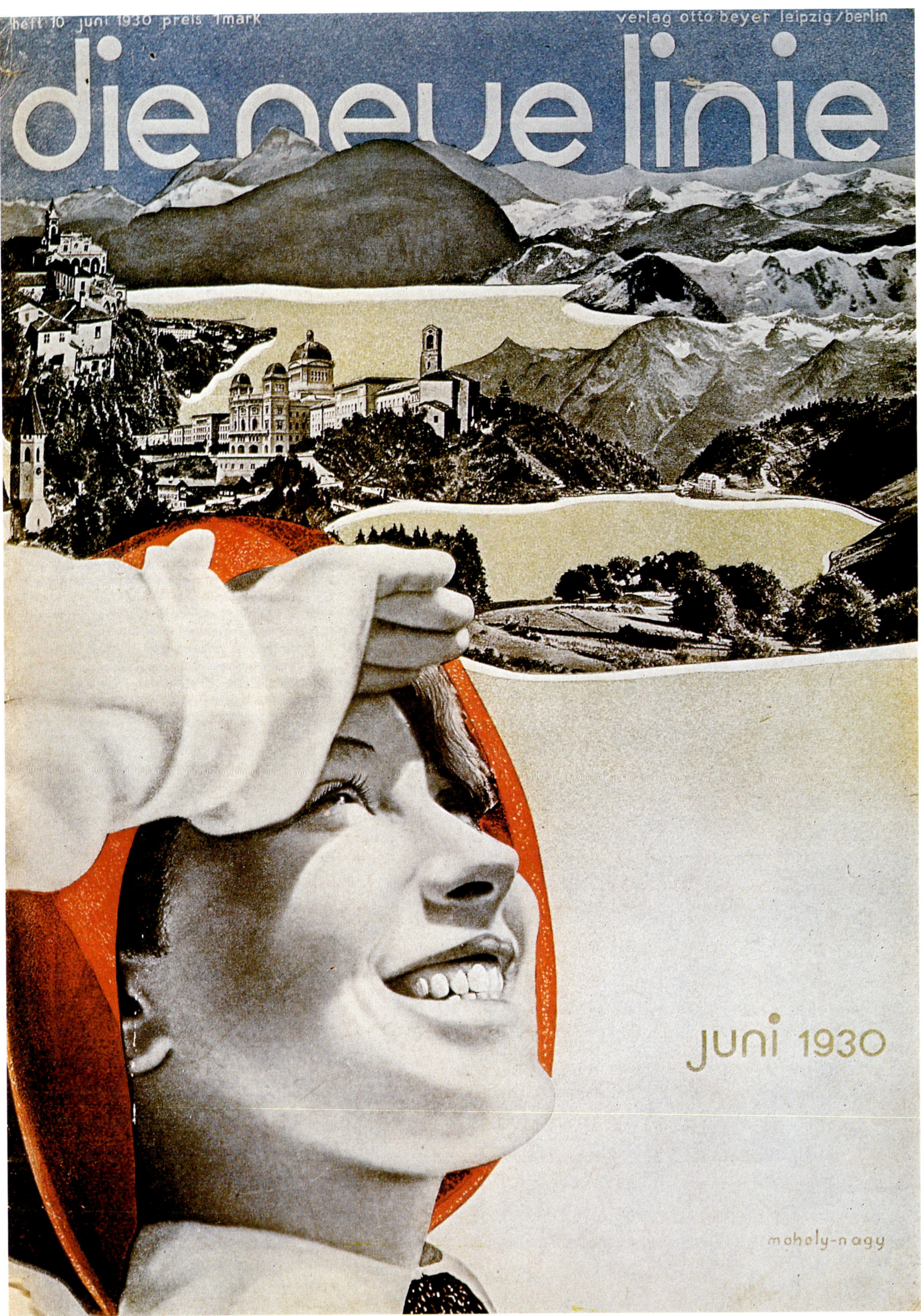
heft 10 juni 1930 preis 1mark
verlag otto beyer leipzig/berlin
die neue linie
juni 1930
moholy-nagy

Gustav Klutsis, ▶ *Postcard for the Moscow Spartakiades,* 1928.

Jan Tschichold, poster for the film *Die Frau ohne Namen,* 1927, Graphische Sammlung, Kunstgewerbemuseum, Zurich. ▼

10. For other examples, see the exhibition catalogue *Moholy-Nagy,* Musées de Marseille, pp. 317 ff., and K. Passuth, *Moholy-Nagy,* Budapest, Corvina, 1982.

11. *J. Heartfield: Photomontages of the Nazi Period,* New York, Universe Books, 1977; P. Pachnicke and K. Honnef, *John Heartfield,* New York, Harry Abrams, 1992.

12. In Tretjakov and Telingater, *John Heartfield,* Moscow, 1936; quoted in *Paris-Berlin,* exhibition at Centre Georges-Pompidou, Paris, 1978, p. 304.

reused an earlier photogram, reversed, with a picture of a camera superimposed on it; the advertisement launching the Schocken stores re-used the 1925 photomontage *The Law of Series.*[10] Heartfield's polemical pieces [11] were inspired by both "art" photomontage, conceived as a work of evocation, and by propaganda.

Heartfield – or Helmut Herzfelde as he was originally called – was a militant revolutionary, a member of the Dadaist group in 1918, and secretary of the Association of Communist Artists. He turned photomontage into the equivalent of political caricature. The precision of his collages, combined with his technical skill, made them into a powerful weapon, rendered more striking by the realism of the images in which the observer is forced to "believe". "The clever and intelligent juxtaposition of pre-assembled photographic documents was to have an enormous influence as propaganda and agitation on the masses."[12]

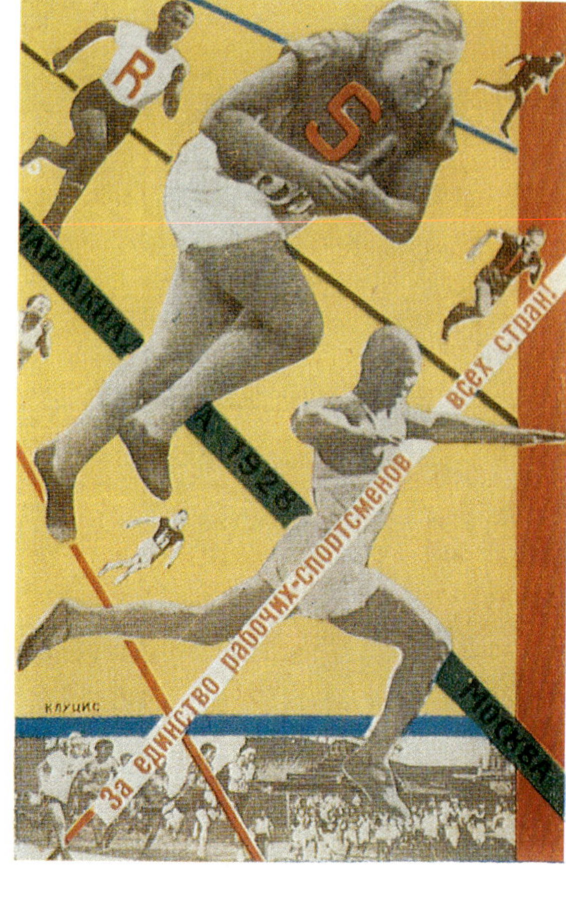

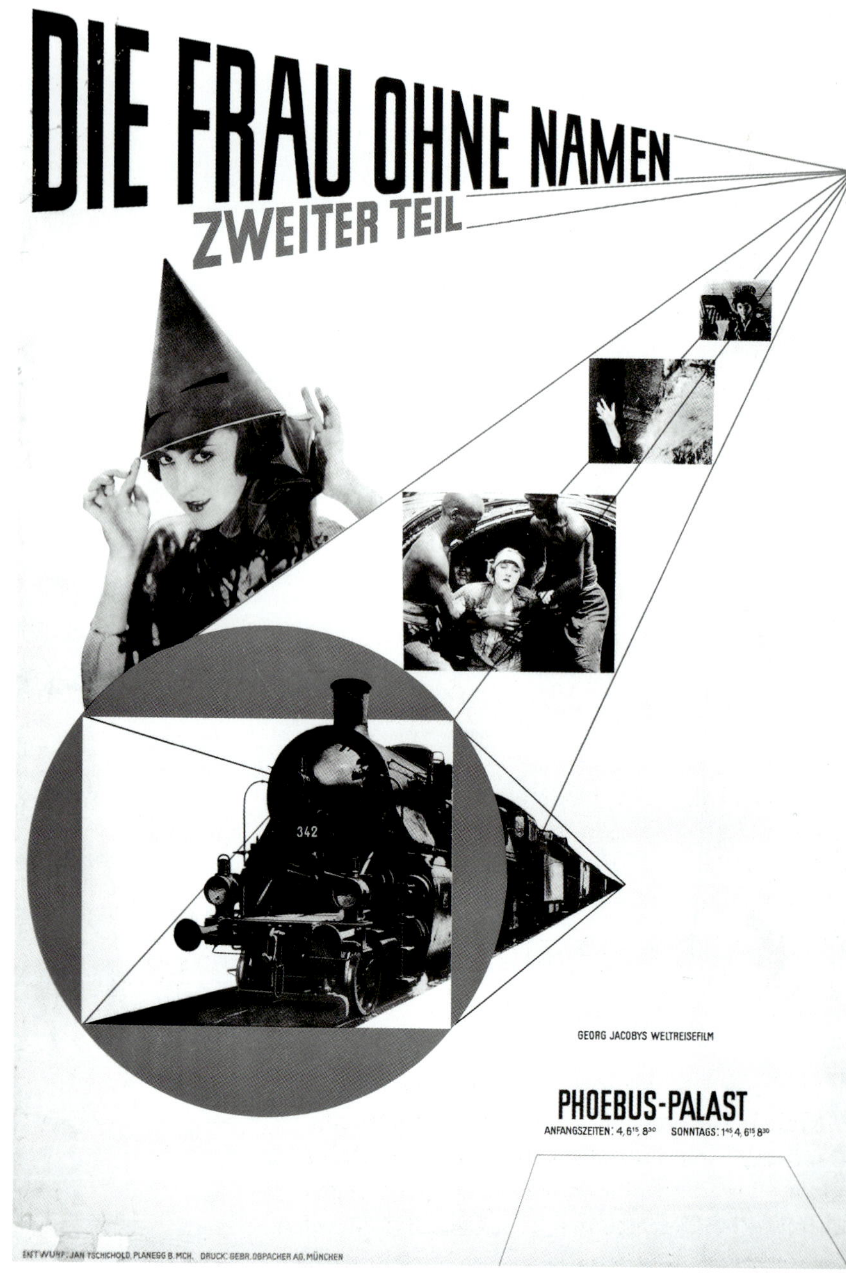

Heartfield's photomontages were designed to be "read" in conjunction with their titles, which brought them into the context of politics, where they were a way of fighting Fascism. They were published every week on the front page of the *Arbeiter Illustrierte Zeitung* (more than 200 between 1930 and 1935). Heartfield also produced advertisements (calling on voters to vote Communist for Thälmann, and for the KPD, 1932).

Piet Zwart was, together with Paul Schuitema, the main representative of the New Photography in the Netherlands, where he introduced, with all the rigor of the De Stijl group, the mechanist typography inspired by Lissitzky, made less uncompromising in 1924 by the introduction of photograms and then of photomontage, producing flyers and leaflets for the firms of NKF (1927–1929) and Delft Kabels (1929) and for Scheveningen Radio (1929).[13]

At the end of the 1920s, the growth of the illustrated press and its increasing use of photographs meant that novelty of presentation was the only way to reach a new public. The graphic arts brought a greater flexibility in the relationships between the page, the text, and the image. A large variety of fonts and typographic styles led to many designs for page layouts. Thus it was that a weekly magazine like *VU,* started in 1928 by Lucien Vogel, could be, at the same time, both popular and artistic: a logo by Cassandre, unusual page layouts, text framed in vignettes, overlap-

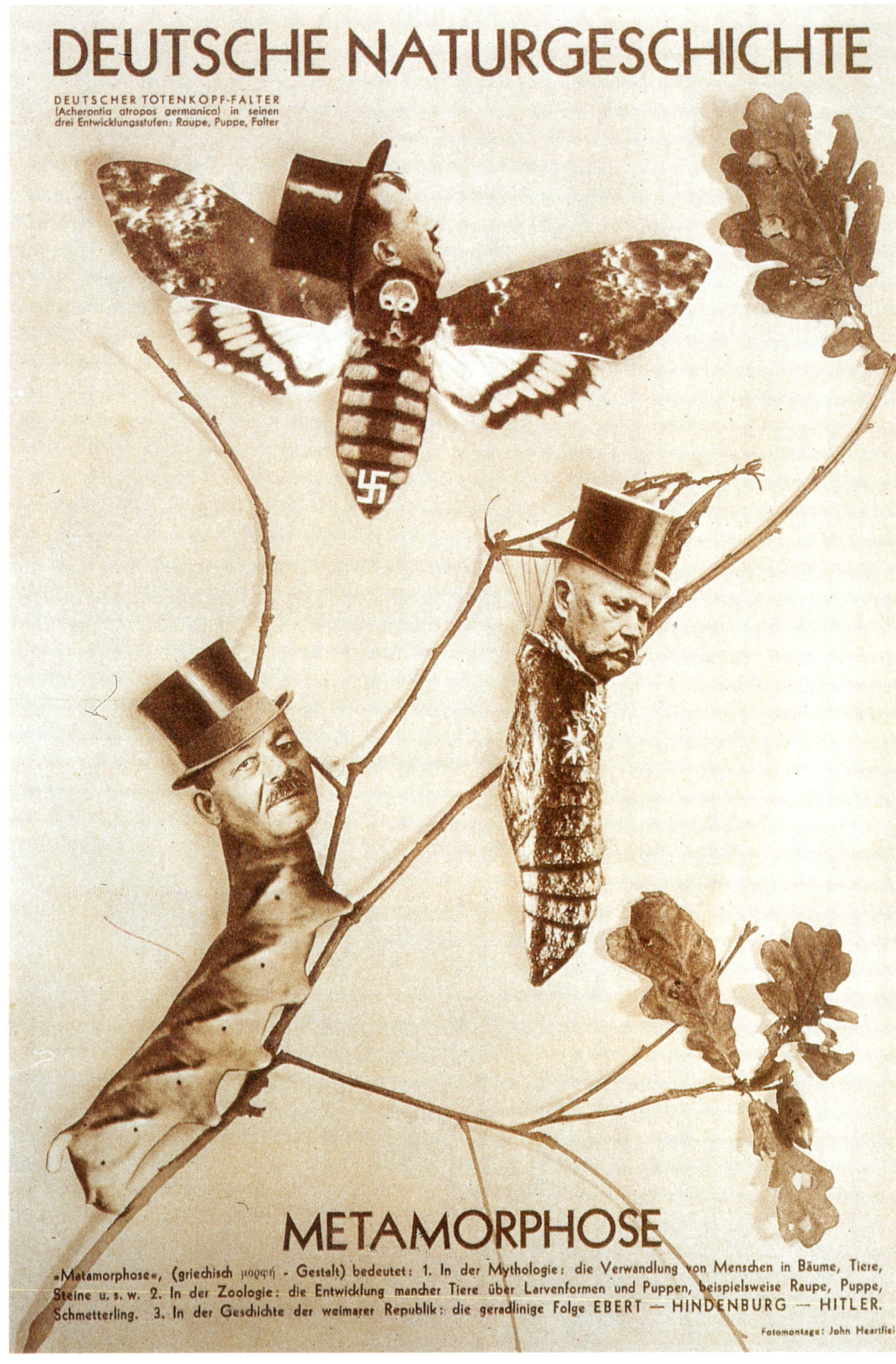
DEUTSCHE NATURGESCHICHTE

DEUTSCHER TOTENKOPF-FALTER
(Acherontia atropos germanica) in seinen
drei Entwicklungsstufen: Raupe, Puppe, Falter

METAMORPHOSE

»Metamorphose«, (griechisch μορφή - Gestalt) bedeutet: 1. In der Mythologie: die Verwandlung von Menschen in Bäume, Tiere, Steine u. s. w. 2. In der Zoologie: die Entwicklung mancher Tiere über Larvenformen und Puppen, beispielsweise Raupe, Puppe, Schmetterling. 3. In der Geschichte der weimarer Republik: die geradlinige Folge EBERT — HINDENBURG — HITLER.

Fotomontage: John Heartfiel

John Heartfield, photomontage, front page of *Arbeiter-Illustrierte-Zeitung*, August 16, 1934.

ping illustrations, rules and boxes, the graphics of the text rearranged around the illustrations. Some of the covers with photomontages by Liberman (signed Alexandre) represent, along with the satires published in *Marianne*, the purest examples of political photomontage.

In the 1930s, this apparent disorder became the rule in the press: the center-spread of *Détective* was treated as a single decorative picture. Oblique angles, superimpositions, and découpage began to appear in illustrated magazines (*Regards, Miroir du monde*) before being adopted by the senti-

13. K. Bros, *Piet Zwart, 1885–1977*, Amsterdam, Van Gennep, 1982.

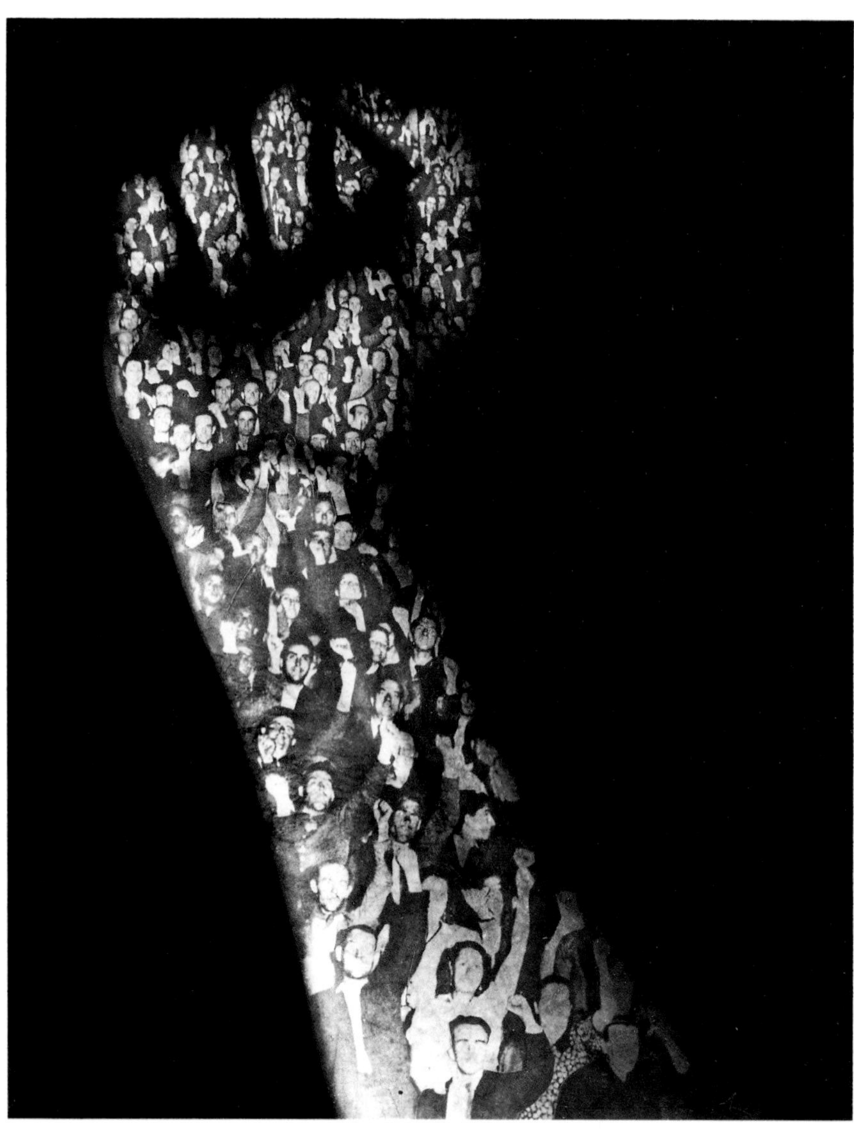

JOHN HEARTFIELD, photomontage for the "Unity of anti-fascist action" number of *Arbeiter-Illustrierte-Zeitung*, October 4, 1934, Akademie der Künste, Berlin.

mental press. Book covers looked to both photography and photomontage for inspiration (Roger Parry, for *La Condition humaine* by Malraux, 1933). In 1931, Germaine Krull produced two "phototexts" in collaboration with Simenon (*La Folle d'Itteville* and *L'Affaire des 7*, published by Firmin-Didot), which marked the beginning of the photo-novel. More unusual was the cover of Simenon's *Le Chien jaune* (1931) by Robert Doisneau (at the time André Vigneau's assistant).

During the 1920s, photomontage enjoyed a dual role: it was both a medium for polemic in the tradition of Dada and a poetic form of expression in the style of Moholy-Nagy, with adaptations depending on individual or group objectives. Polish photomonteurs (Berman, Brzeski, Podsadecki) were clearly influenced by De Stijl and Polish unism, while the Italian Futurists (Pannaggi, Boccardi, Demanins, Fillia, Pacetti, Vottero, Paladini) emphasized modernity. In France, Surrealism was not insensitive to the evocative powers of photomontage, but did not limit it strictly to photography. While Claude Cahun created montages from her own photographs, Max Ernst (after 1920), Georges Hugnet (around 1935), and Léo Malet combined cut-out engravings, drawings, photographic fragments, and every kind of popular illustration to create dreamlike images and unexpected juxtapositions called *histoires montées*. *Le Phénomène de l'extase*, by Dalí (1933), on a theme used by Maurice Heine, brings together "ecstatic" female faces and details of ears taken from photographs by Bertillon. André Breton, and Albert Valentin around 1930 left us some allusive photomontages that share the atmosphere of incongruity of Max Ernst and from which there generally emerge naked young women.[14] Thus, one branch of surrealist painting, which also used collages consisting of figurative elements and associations, developed through the transposition of photomontage to Surrealism.

Art by subtraction

In the 1920s, following on from photomontage, other techniques that departed from the "pure" photographic image appeared, adopting the philosophy typical of the New Photography, as anticipated by Moholy-Nagy and Gräff. It was natural that photography, having re-established itself in the field of artistic practice but without having returned to the ideals of the Pictorialists, was, in a certain way, obliged to revert to those things which distinguish the artist from the technician: manipulation, dexterity, the imprint of the individual.

It was with Man Ray's arrival in Paris in the summer of 1921, when Dada was at its height, that photographic experimentation, temporarily leaderless after the disastrous war, took a decisive new direction. Born in Philadelphia in 1890, the painter Emmanuel Radnitsky – known as Man Ray – had, from 1913, after visiting the Armory Show, frequented the avant-garde circles of New York, in particular Stieglitz's 291 Gallery, the chief meeting-place of modern art (at this period Stieglitz was showing mostly painting and sculpture, with very little photography). Man Ray's painting was influenced by Picasso and Braque, and by two French artists exhibited in New York, Picabia and Duchamp. He produced pictures in a colored, Cubist style. It was after he had taken some photographs of his own pictures that he became interested in photography, encouraged by Duchamp who saw in photography the ideal route for a "secession" from all the traditional notions of art. When he arrived in Paris, Man Ray, who had been preceded shortly before by Duchamp, was already known to the small circle of Dadaists for his *New York Dada* that had appeared in April 1921, and for the two photo-

14. E. Jaguer, *Les Mystères de la chambre noire: Le Surréalisme et la Photographie*, Paris, Flammarion, 1982.

graphs he had sent to the Dada Salon of 1921, *L'Homme* and *La Femme* (1918). It was, quite simply, a shortage of money that brought about Man Ray's future as a photographer within the group (Breton, Aragon, Eluard, Tzara, Picabia). Through Picabia's wife he met the fashion designer Poiret, for whom he produced some fashion photographs. Thanks to Cocteau he became the favorite portraitist of Paris intellectuals and artists (Gertrude Stein, Braque, Brancusi, Proust on his deathbed in 1922). It was after he had moved to a studio in Rue Campagne-Première – where Atget also lived – that Man Ray discovered a form of photographic "ready-mades", a way of producing, or subtracting, images starting from reality and operated directly

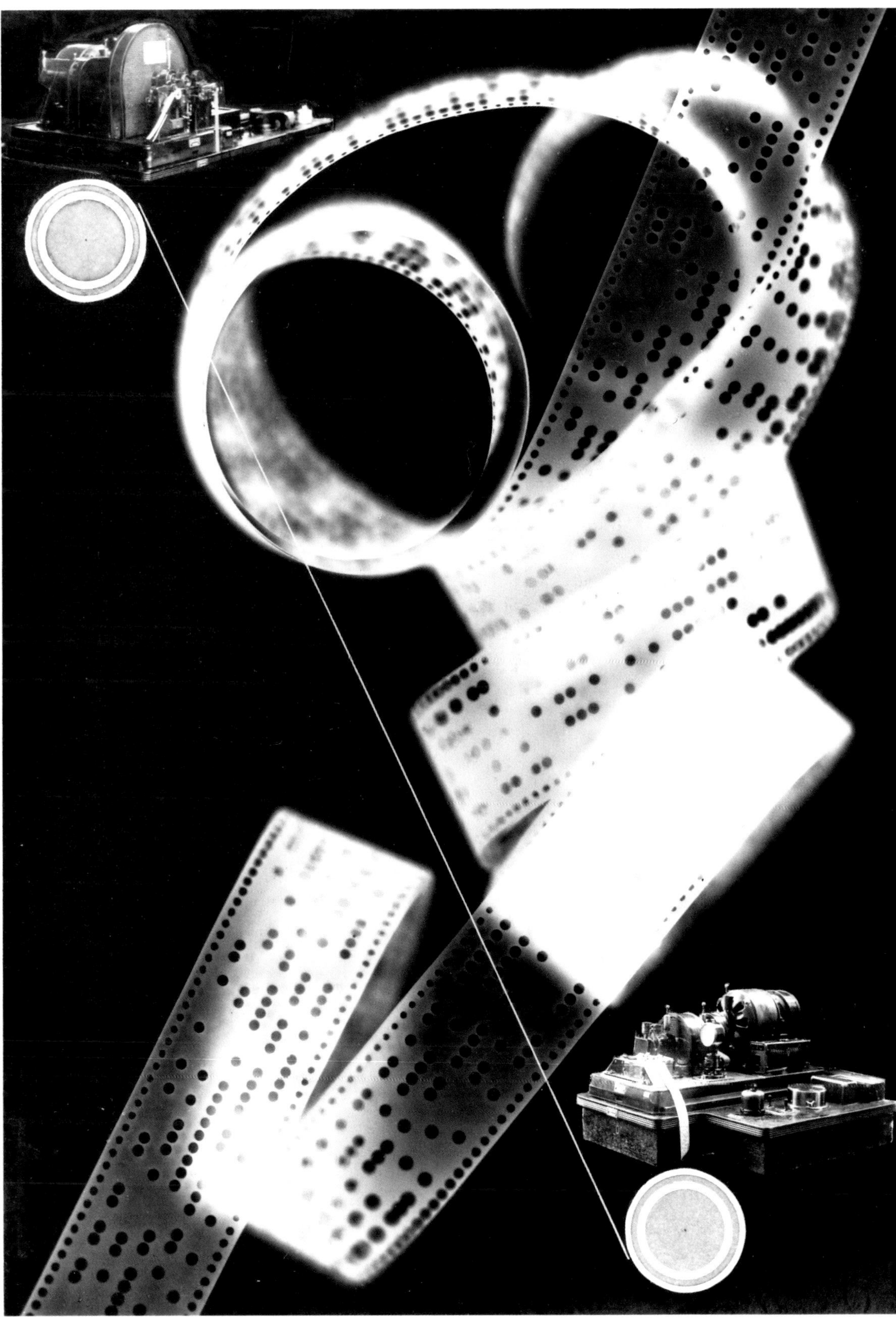

Piet Zwart, advertisement for "Via Scheveningen Radio PCH", 1929, Municipal Museum, The Hague.

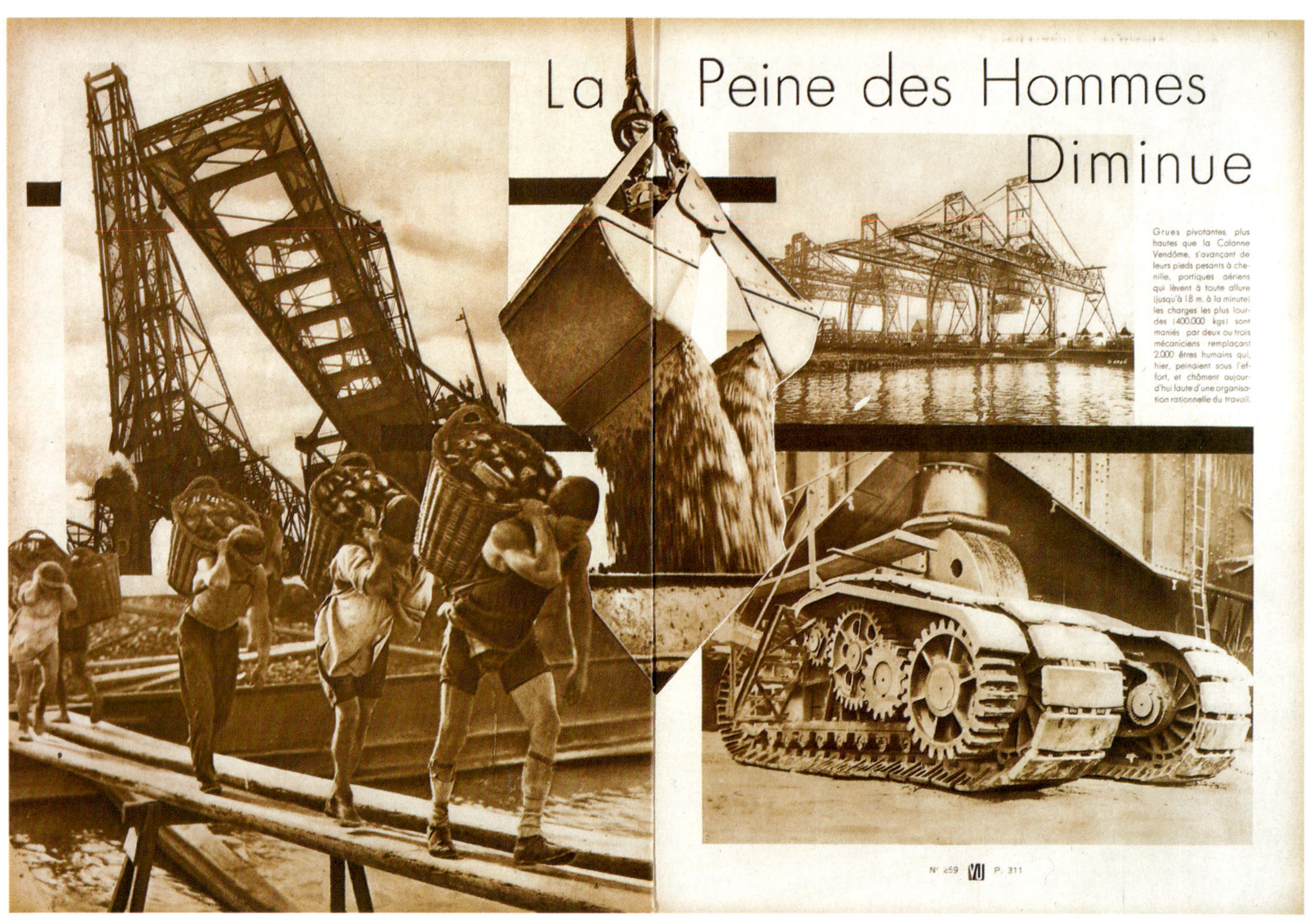

La Peine des Hommes Diminue

Grues pivotantes, plus hautes que la Colonne Vendôme, s'avançant de leurs pieds pesants à chenille, portiques aériens qui lèvent à toute allure (jusqu'à 18 m. à la minute) les charges les plus lourdes (400.000 kgs) sont maniés par deux ou trois mécaniciens remplaçant 2.000 êtres humains qui, hier, peinaient sous l'effort, et chôment aujourd'hui faute d'une organisation rationnelle du travail.

Nº 259 VU P. 311

ANONYMOUS, *Montage of a double spread from "VU"*, no. 259, March 1, 1933.

ALEXANDRE, ▶ *Cover of VU, Vive le Cinéma!*, photomontage, December 15, 1934.

by the objects themselves, without manipulation and even without a camera. These were the "rayographs" that began to appear in the spring of 1922, made by placing objects on a sheet of light-sensitive paper and exposing them to light. The rayograph was, in fact, the shadow of the object, a negative image, a subtraction of light.[15]

An unidentifiable object, or one that does not ask to be identified – subtracted from the image and remaining there as nothing more than an impression – the rayograph was self-sufficient in that it was a work of light, a work of pseudo-uncertainty. It was self-created, an *objet trouvé*, without a legitimate existence and suitable in every way as a work to change the direction of art, and hence, in the words of Tzara, "pure Dada". Some rayographs were published in *Vanity Fair* in November 1922 ("New method for the realization of the artistic possibilities of photography"), and a portfolio of twelve pictures appeared in December, with a text by Tzara, *Les Champs délicieux*.

In fact, the rayograph was not an entirely new idea. The concept being akin to radiography, it was known as lensless photography in scientific circles. This was the name under which it had been used on a smaller scale by Christian Schad, another Dadaist, since 1918. Curiously – as with photomontage – there is considerable uncertainty about this "discovery", since László Moholy-Nagy and his wife Lucia were producing what they called, more impersonally, "photograms", in the same year (1922). At this time, Moholy had not yet started to use photography to any great extent, and hence these experiments were purely artistic, outside the field of photography, allowing the construction of images with transparent planes and the effects of light. As a Constructivist painter, Moholy-Nagy, here influenced by Schwitters – the advocate of collages made out of rubbish – saw in the photogram a pictorial automatism, a rule for abstract and mechanized composition, the suppression of subjectivity. The choice of the word "photogram" came from the word "telegram" and formed part of the search for a "telephone picture" that Moholy-Nagy was engaged on at this time. If Man Ray alienated objects from their real function and image, Moholy-Nagy created luminous objects without reference to anything but their pictorial function, not unlike Coburn and his vortographs of 1917. The photogram or rayograph immediately became part of the program and artistic language of the New Photography, which Moholy-Nagy publicised in *Malerei, Fotografie, Film* of 1925.[16]

15. *Perpetual Motif: The Art of Man Ray*, National Museum of American Art, Washington, Abbeville Press, New York, 1988.

16. F. M. Neusüss, *Das Fotogramm in der Kunst des 20. Jahrhunderts*, Cologne, DuMont, 1990.

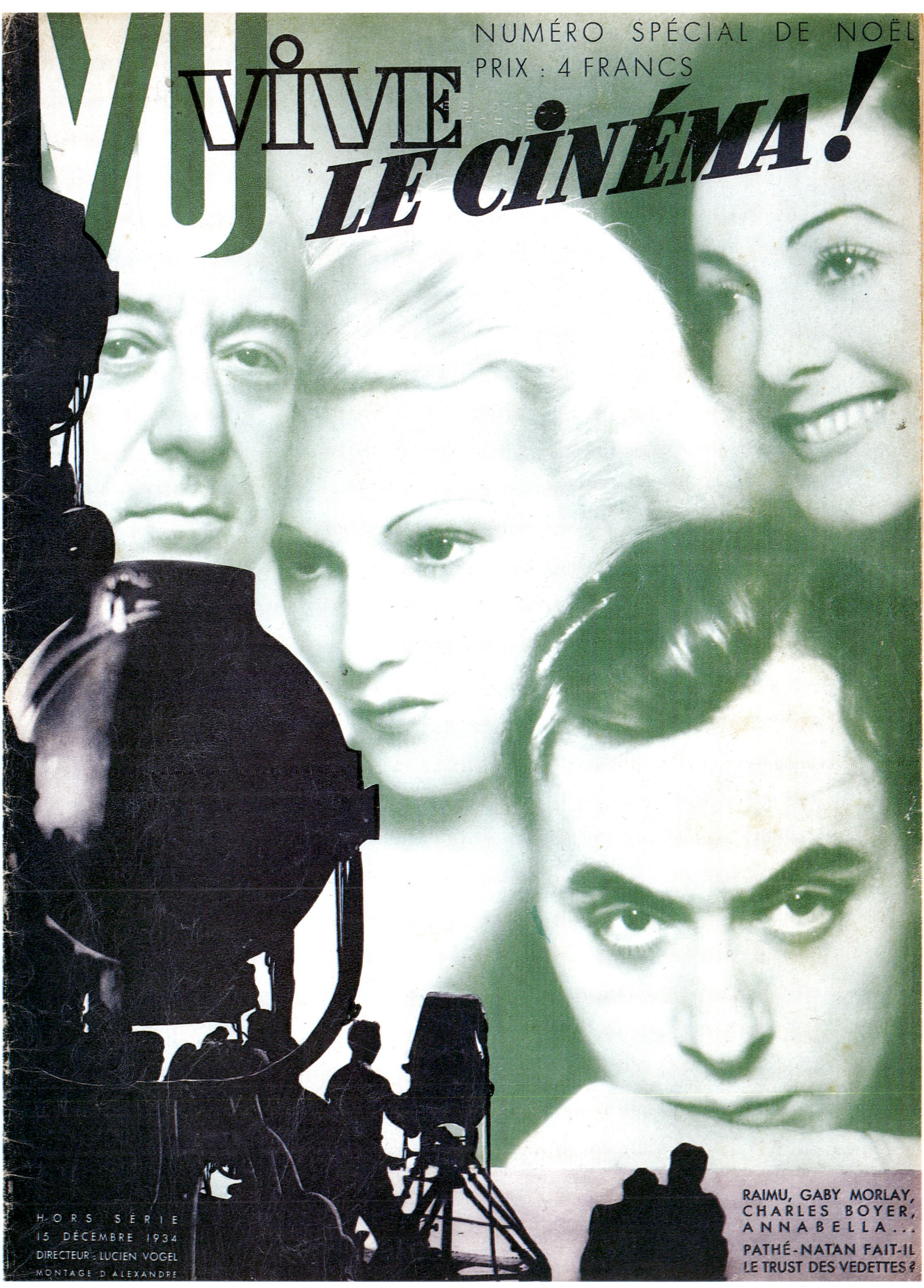
VU
NUMÉRO SPÉCIAL DE NOËL
PRIX : 4 FRANCS
VIVE LE CINÉMA!
RAIMU, GABY MORLAY, CHARLES BOYER, ANNABELLA...
PATHÉ-NATAN FAIT-IL LE TRUST DES VEDETTES?
HORS SÉRIE
15 DÉCEMBRE 1934
DIRECTEUR: LUCIEN VOGEL
MONTAGE D'ALEXANDRE

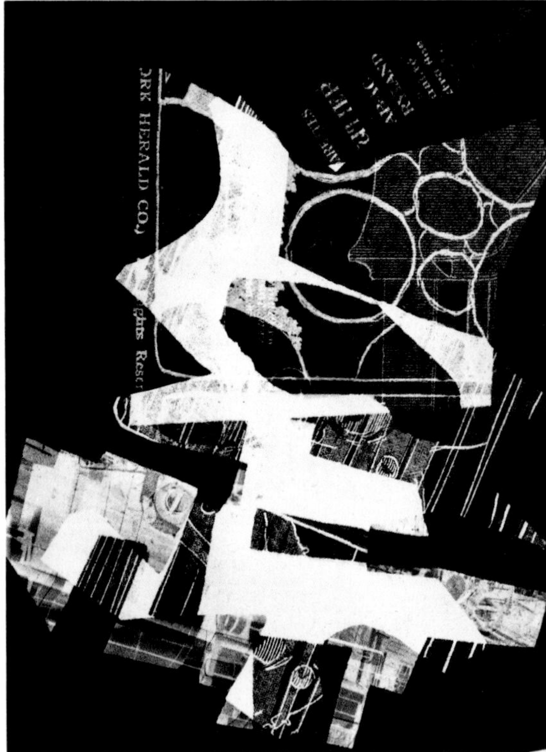

CHRISTIAN SCHAD, *Schadograph*, 1919, Museum of Modern Art, New York.

MAN RAY, ▶ *Rayograph*, from *Les Champs délicieux*, 1922, Musée Nationale d'Art Moderne, Paris.

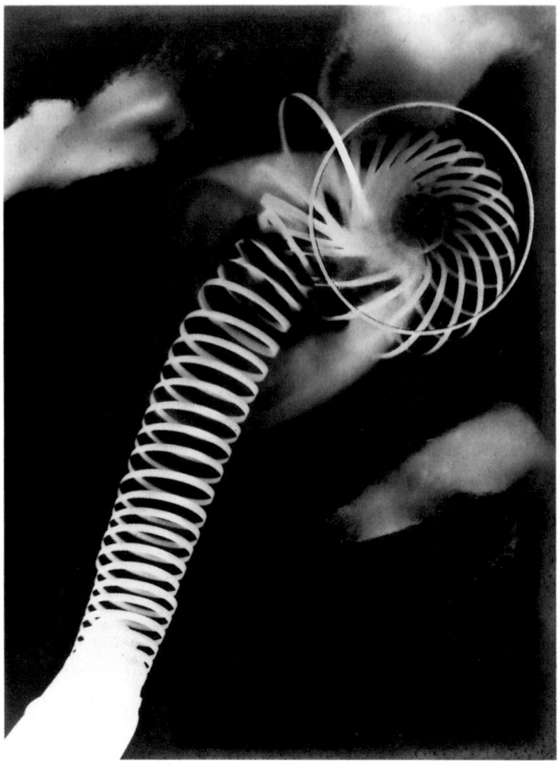

Spectacular as it was, the introduction of the photogram, along with photomontage, into the panoply of the New Photography, was not the only new element. It formed part of a wider strategy, enunciated by Moholy-Nagy, that consisted of promoting both "cameraless photography", as was the case here, and unusual, even incorrect, uses of the camera. Examples cited by Moholy-Nagy are views from above or below or at an angle, "which show distortion, deformation or foreshortening as they really are", hence objectively. The camera does not give things their meaning as we do conceptually; it allows us to see with "new eyes".

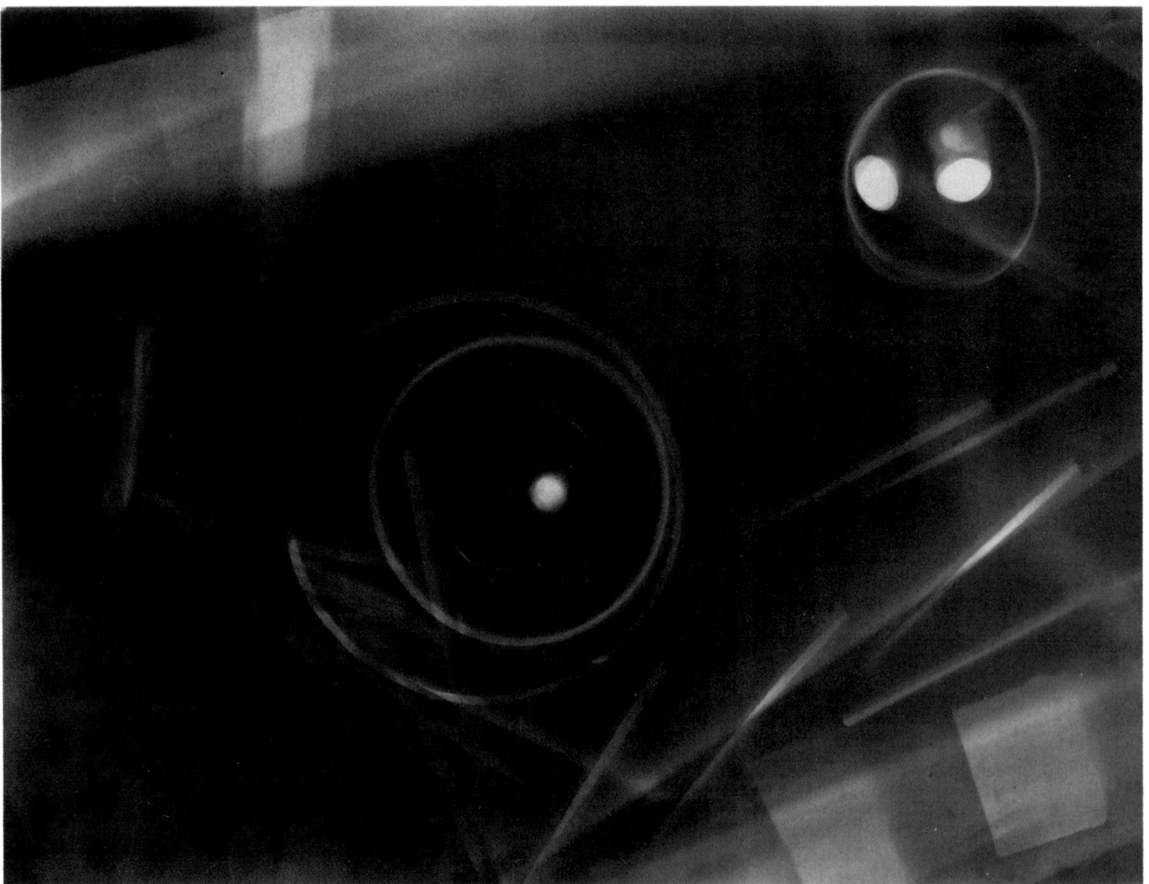

LÁSZLÓ MOHOLY-NAGY, *Photogram*, 1925.

It followed that other deficiencies or mistakes could also be revealing. They were often to be found in the work of amateurs. Double exposures (what Moholy calls a "simultaneous portrait") became very popular. Some artists did it deliberately and systematically (cameras had no security device to prevent a double exposure) or created the same effect in the darkroom by superimposing two negatives during printing, adjusting their relative positions until a satisfying composition was obtained. The double exposure became more than a mere game: it became a method for evoking dreams, apparitions or unexpected encounters that were impossible to effect in real life.

Franz Roh was one of the masters of the genre in the late 1920s (often with two images head to tail, giving a picture that could be inverted) but there were others: Lissitzky, Heinz Loew, Oscar Schlemmer, and Lux Feininger at the Bauhaus, as well as Edmund Kesting, Lucia Moholy, and Xanti Schawinsky. Other examples were produced by Florence Henri (whose use of mirrors can be considered a version of the same duplication of perspective), Moï Ver (*Paris*, 1930), and Walker Evans, who took a "simultaneous" portrait of Berenice Abbott on his return from Paris in 1927. Man Ray, always in the vanguard of such techniques for new points of view, put it to good use in 1921 for his portraits of Tzara with an axe and of the marquise Casati (1922, a double portrait made by moving the camera).

Things that were usually considered to be mistakes became sought-after for their novelty. This was, however, an artistic technique which had its origins in the earliest days of photography. Like photomontage, which had been used since the 1850s, manipulation of negatives was already common in the 1860s, for instance by Robinson and Rejlander. In the 1920s, the technique was widespread in Europe and became a rallying point for the New Photography, which had expanded well beyond the criteria for graphics of the German photographers. Here, the bringing together of two objects of different origin created possibilities for literary interpretation and poetic evocation in which Surrealism could see one of the logical developments of automatic writing. Lissitzky (double portraits of Arp and Schwitters, 1924; *Le Constructeur*, of the same year) and Rodchenko were among those who first used this technique. In France, Roger Parry used it for his publication *Banalité* (1930), and Maurice Tabard made superimposition very much his own around 1930 with his subtle manipulation of subjects, placing, and associations; portraits of women, nudes, and hands, in dramatic settings that smacked of crime novels and erotic literature. He also used the superimposition of several negatives in combination with the use of masking.[17] Some second-generation Futurists (in the 1930s) adopted it: Tato, Castagneri, Demanins, Wanda Wulz, with her beautiful *Me + Cat*, and Bragaglia, with an extended series of multiple images.

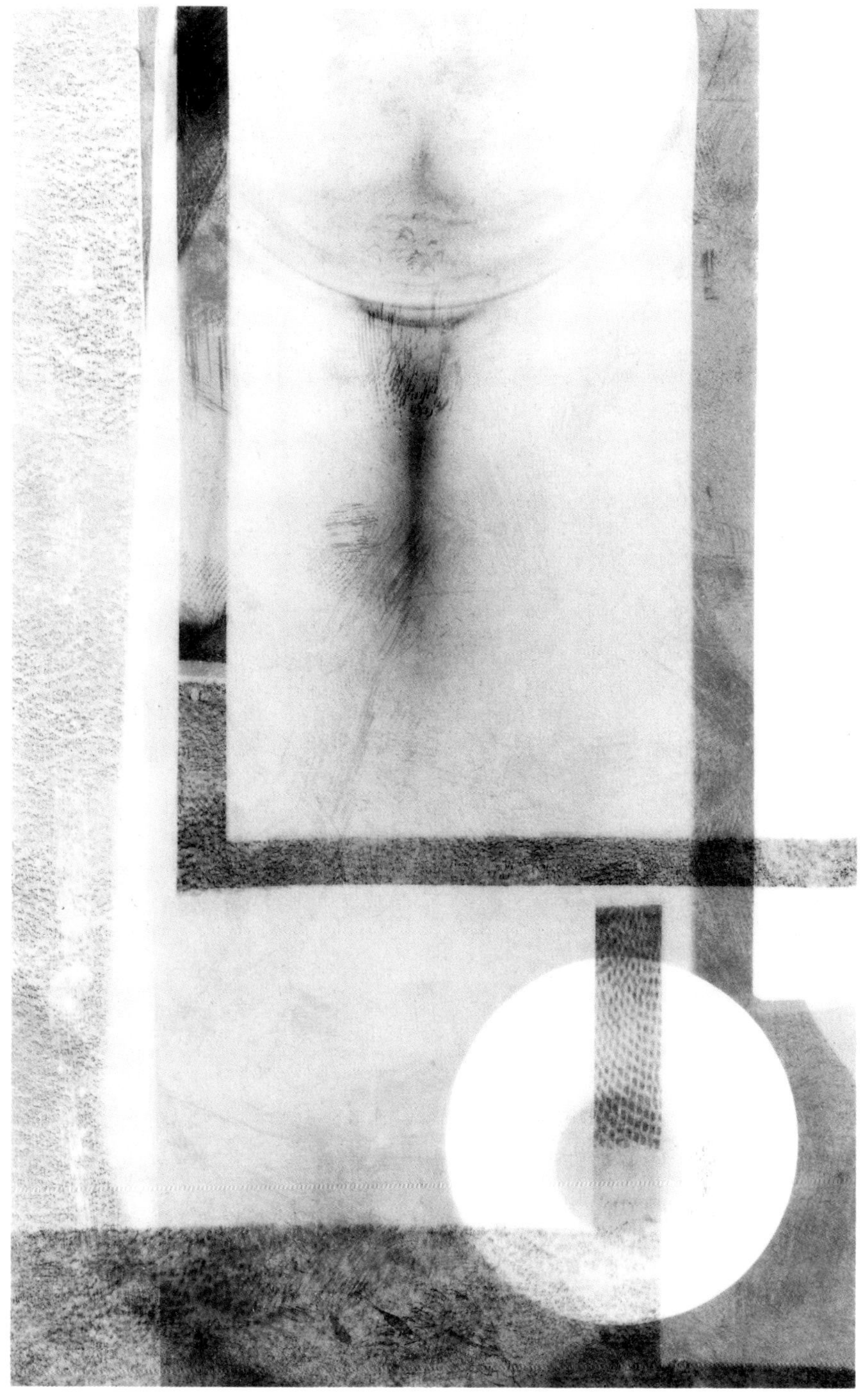

Lászlo Moholy-Nagy,
Photogram,
1922,
Art Institute of Chicago.

Highly regarded in the 1920s, superimpositions and multiple exposures continued to be used for a long time, even outside the artistic movements that had brought them into being, becoming one of the criteria of Subjective Photography. Heinz Hajek-Halke carried the practice over into the 1950s, as did Denise Colomb (*Les Ponts de Paris*, 1951); some, like Man Ray, Clarence John Laughlin or George Platt-Lynes experimented with ways of adapting

17. D. Baqué, *Maurice Tabard*, Paris, Belfond, 1991.

El Lissitzky, *In the Studio,* 1923. ▼

photography to surrealist fantasies, as did Jerry Uelsmann in the 1960s. There was little fundamental difference between photomontage and superimposition, as can be seen in the works of Heartfield or the portrait of Paul Citroën by Umbo, based on the latter's photomontage *Metropolis*. The "montage" was carried out either by placing one image on top of the other or by including it within the photograph. Either way, an addition or a subtraction of elements, information, light, and shadows was being effected.

This was a period rich in ideas for ways of subverting the image. In the 1930s, when Surrealism had replaced Dadaism – producing work that was more civilized, more pictorial, more directly readable, and less aggressive – photographers rediscovered the "Sabatier effect", the inversion of tones known today as "solarization". Man Ray and his assistant Lee Miller, around 1930, and Tabard "in about 1932", according to his own estimation, seem to have been the rediscoverers of this technique – unveiled by Tabard in *Arts et Métiers graphiques* (November 1933). Solarization was suited to fashion photography and portraiture. Without obliterating recognizable forms, it introduced a quality of strangeness, an uncertainty in the identification of areas of light and shade. The graphic aspect of solarization, which accentuates the contrasts in some places and blurs them in others, brought photography closer to painting at a moment when the "graphic arts" were juggling with the two styles of representation.

18. *André Kertész, distortions*, Paris, Chêne, 1976. *André Kertész: Ma France*, Paris, La Manufacture, 1990.

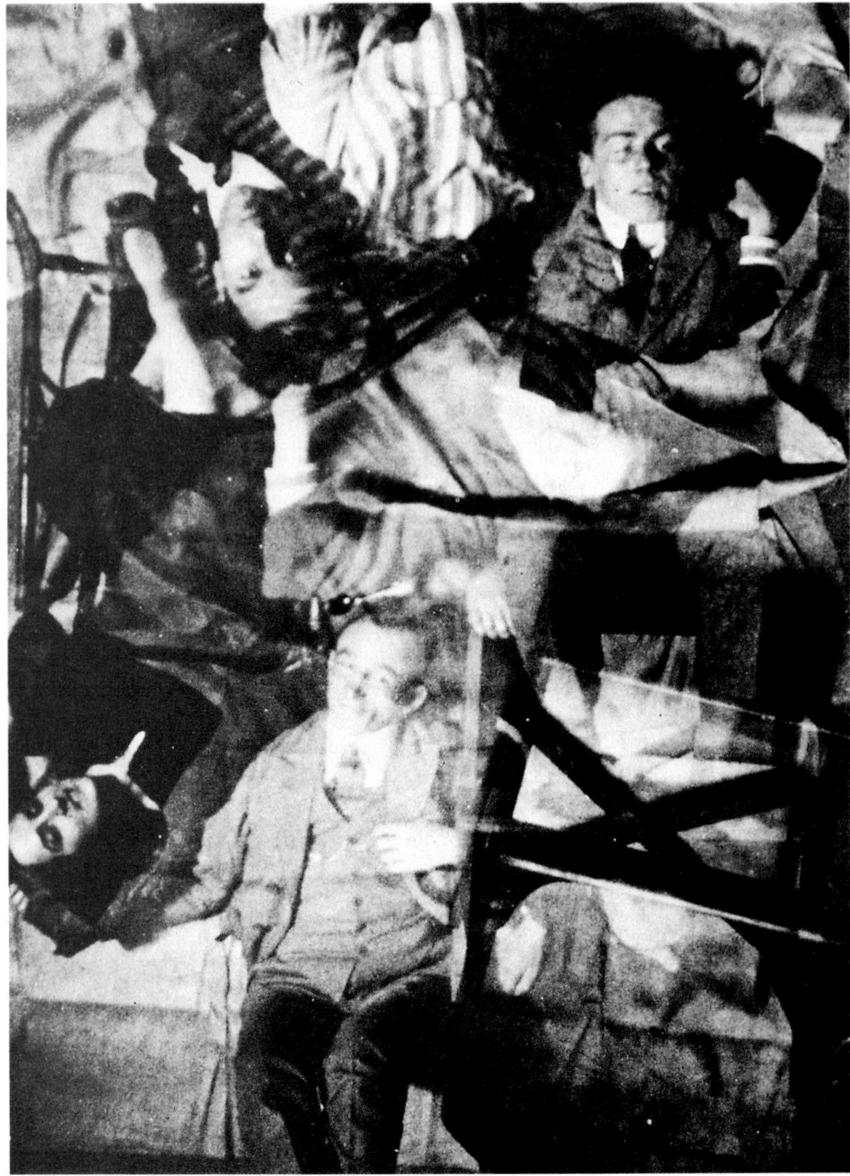

In the photogram, as with superimposition, it was the plastic qualities of the negative that were under scrutiny. Moholy, in particular, realized around 1926 that the negative contained the same "image" as the positive print, the same variations of light, and allowed the subject to be recognized in just the same way; "The inversion of tones also brings about that of the relations between the tones. The small amount of white is emphasized: it becomes a determinant for the whole picture", he wrote in *Malerei, Fotografie, Film* about a figure printed in reversed tones. His famous *Cat (Negative)*, of c. 1926 lets the animal be seen while, at the same time, producing a completely new plastic effect with its fur. Moholy also juxtaposed – in the style of a collage – positive and negative prints so as to accentuate this paradox of asymmetrical duplication (*Nude [Positive and Negative]*, 1931). For him, the photogram functioned equally well as a negative.

Other ways of approaching reality emerged from these highly active artistic circles. These could be multiplied according to the accessories used. Distortions were the result of the use of an intermediary between the camera and the subject, so that the sensitive plate perceived the image as though reflected by a distorting mirror. These experiments, or ways of seeing (the aim of which was to extend the field of vision starting from a fragment of an image), began in about 1927 and were popularized in several publications: self-portrait in the reflector of a headlamp by Renger-Patzsch, which appeared in *Uhu* in 1929, the portrait with distortions of Carlo Rim by Kertész (*VU*, August 6, 1930) and his *Diseuse de bonne aventure* (*VU*, September 30, 1930). The leaflet for *Film und Foto* designed by Moholy-Nagy consists of four repetitions of the same scene, viewed in a reflecting ball (photograph by Georg Muche). Kertész was then commissioned to take a series of female nudes with distortions for the journal *Le Sourire*. He was provided with two nude models and some metal sheets that served as distorting mirrors and spent several weeks working on the photographs. Twelve of the 200 pictures were published in March 1933.[18] With this collection, Kertész showed how close he was to the Surrealism then fashionable in Paris, to Dalí's

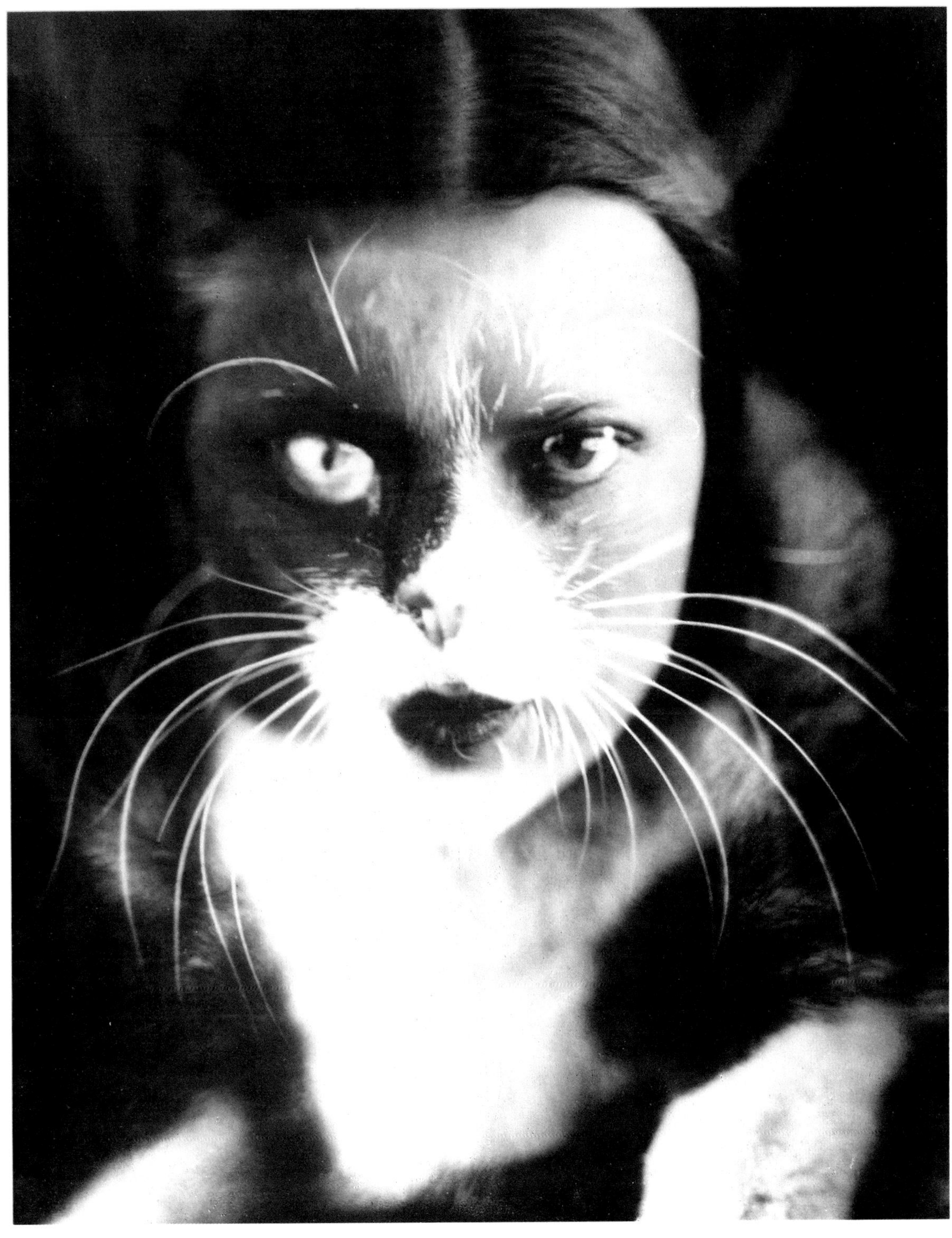

WANDA WULZ,
Me + Cat,
1932,
Museo Alinari / Zannier Collection, Florence.

soft watches, to Picasso's deformed nudes, and to other unsettling metamorphoses.

Diversions of images

During the 1920s and into the 1930s, photographers experimented with ways of distancing the photographic image from its inevitable referent. The link with real life had become more elastic, increasing the discursive space within the image, between what is shown and what can be understood. Surrealism – following on from the theories of Dada – was able to take advantage of this freedom, using photographs for imaginative extrapolations. "I am sorry that I have been unable to provide, to complete the illustration of this text, the photograph of a high-speed locomotive, abandoned for many years to the ravages of the virgin forest", wrote André Breton (the founder of Surrealism with his *Manifesto* of 1924), in the introduction to *L'Amour fou* (1937). An image actually glimpsed or a dream image, this example of "convulsive beauty" (of movement and repose), this photograph (which was to be published in *Minotaure*) can serve as a metaphor, representing all photographs planned from a Surrealist point of view. Those who rediscovered for their own times Lautréamont's

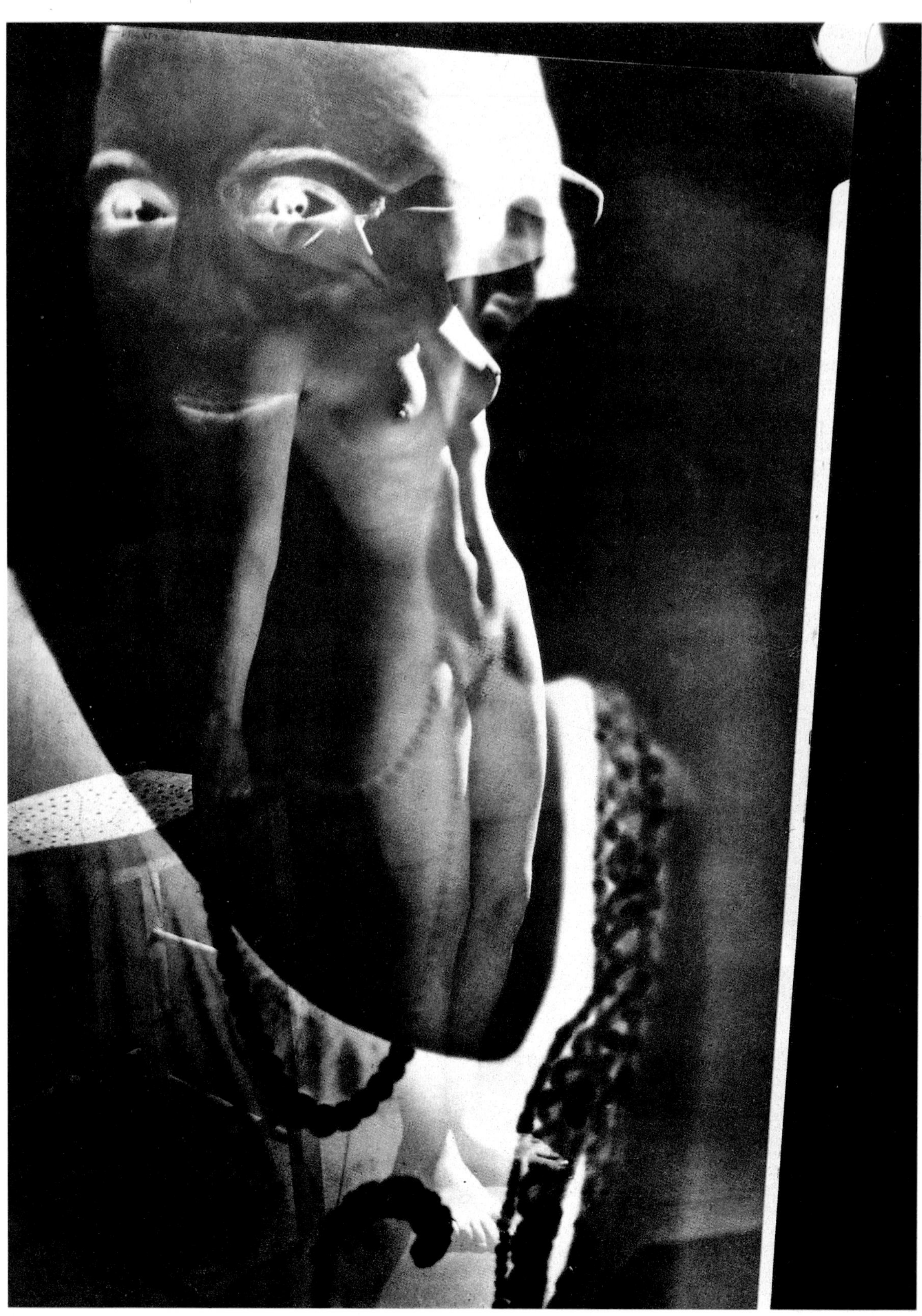

MAURICE TABARD, *Composition,* 1930.

"beauty like the encounter between an umbrella and a sewing machine on a dissecting table" in the *Chants de Maldoror* (1869) recognized here the syntactical power of the image and its ability to make a contribution to the literary revolution then raging. A photograph is able to draw on "the image, such as it appears in automatic writing".[19]

The Surrealists, or those close to them, used collage extensively (made up of engravings, texts, drawings – the "exquisite corpses"), as well as its photographic equivalent, photomontage. Practitioners include Georges Hugnet, Max Ernst, Nusch Eluard, Claude Cahun for his *Aveux non avenus* (1930), and Raoul Ubac, with his montages of solarized female nudes, of about 1939. The association of ideas, the automatic meeting of words are another form of collage capable of "creating images". But there were also other ways

19. A. Breton, *L'Amour fou*, p. 21.

of subverting the logical language of the image: by acting on what it showed, or by modifying the title. There are techniques for alienation in photography (and photography is itself a way of alienating the object); it is, furthermore, itself an *objet trouvé*, an object constructed from a fortuitous reality, a meeting of signs. "I have wanted to see the construction of a very special object, answering to some poetic fantasy [...] Well, it has come about that I have discovered it, probably unique among other fabricated objects."[20] In the eyes of the Surrealists, the photograph was to become a constructed, malleable object; a maze in which to become reoriented, the "forest of signs" sought by Breton. Strange associations can also arise naturally, photography recording the discordant signs upon demand; the decoding mind seeks the image's internal logic, its reason for existence, even if it is forced to attribute it to a departure from common sense.[21]

These upheavals had been introduced around 1918, particularly by Man Ray, who arrived in Paris in 1921 with some strange works – or, to be more exact, with works that appeared objective but which bore titles that referred, through a Dadaist negation, to other subjects entirely: a photograph of white sheets drying (*Moving Sculpture*, 1920), a close-up of Duchamp's "Great Glass" taken when the latter was moving out of his studio (1920). Man Ray was interested in creating objects like *L'Énigme d'Isidore Ducasse* (1920), a mysterious object wrapped in a sheet, later turned into a photograph and reproduced in the first edition of *La Révolution surréaliste*. Influenced by Duchamp, to whom he supplied photographs of his *Tonsure* (1919) and *Eau de voilette* (1921), Man Ray had already photographed two Dada objects in 1918: an eggbeater entitled *L'Homme*, and a montage of a car reflector and clothes pegs, called *La Femme*. Object and image, photography could be charged with those powers that Breton recognized in literary collage and automatic writing.

In particular, Surrealism relied on printed photography in relation to – or in conflict with –

André Kertész, ***Distortion***, 1933.

20. *Ibid.*

21. R. Krauss, J. Livingstone, D. Ades, *L'Amour Fou: Photography and Surrealism*, New York, Abbeville Press, 1985.

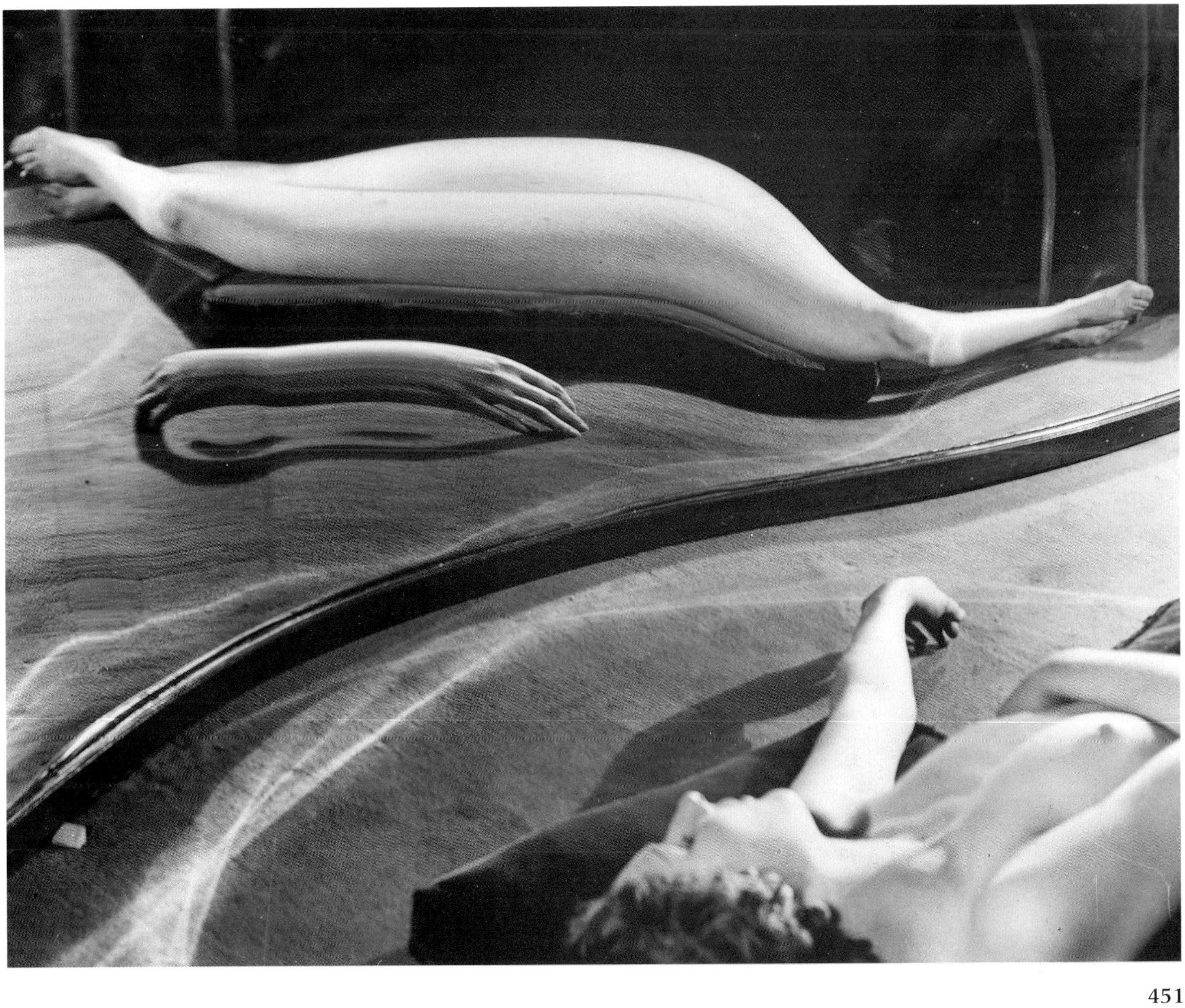

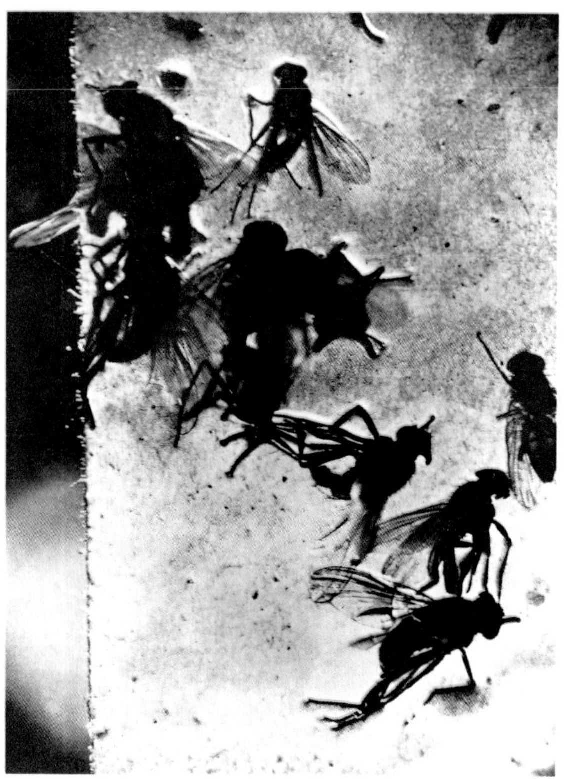

Jacques-André Boiffard, ▶ photograph published in *Documents*, 1930.

a piece of text: "Any discovery changing nature, the destination of an object or a phenomenon represents a surrealist act".[22] *La Révolution surréaliste* published photographs, particularly on the cover: *Moving Sculpture* by Man Ray appeared on March 1, 1926 with the title *La France*; Atget's picture of people observing an eclipse appeared, retitled *Les dernières conversions* (June 15, 1926).

Such alienation of meaning by means of the choice of title was continued in *Bifur*, a review edited by Georges Ribemont-Dessaignes (May 1929 – June 1931), with contributions particularly from those who opposed Breton (Tzara, Soupault, Michaux). Photographs without text were published, particularly in the first issues: Moholy-Nagy, Krull, Tabard (his *Jeu* is a view from above of men playing dice on the reclining body of a woman). In May 1929 (no. 1), three photographs by Kertész were also detached from their objective subject, as from their normal use: *Sources* (wine barrels), *Le baiser qui tue* (a corner of the road with a cinema poster), *Garage* (a hearse).

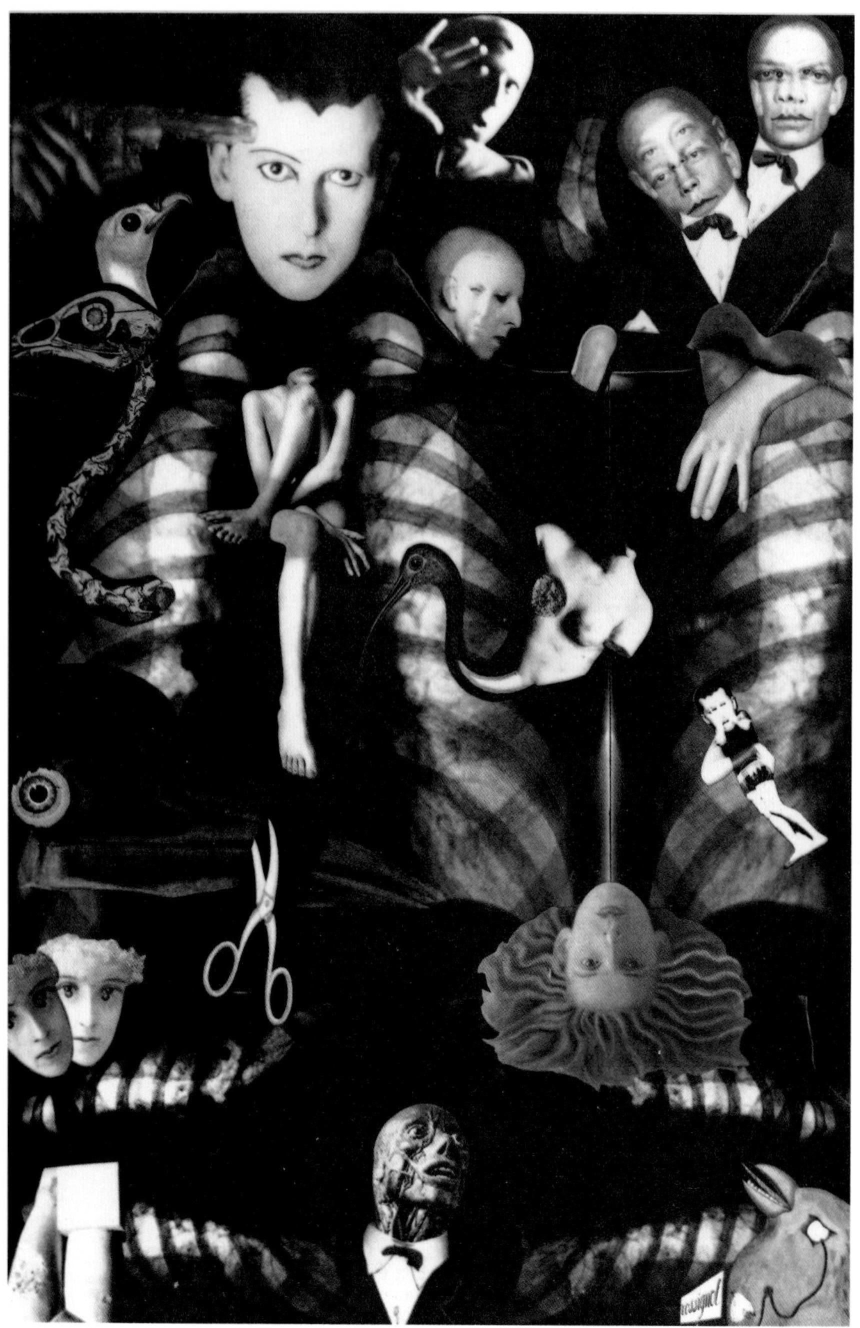

Claude Cahun, *"H.U.M."*, photomontage, plate VIII in *Aveux non avenus*, 1929–1930, Galerie Zabriskie, Paris. ▼

This interest in the objective alienation of images – which extended further, of course, well beyond the field of photography – is a constant theme in the work of Man Ray (*Violon d'Ingres*, 1924; *La prière*, 1930). It was reinforced in around 1929, at the time of the Second Surrealist Manifesto, by the arrival on the scene of Dalí and the appearance of *Documents* (1929-1930), the magazine edited by Georges Bataille, another member of the Surrealist opposition. In 1928, Breton had published *Nadja*, a kind of detective novel about an unsuccessful love affair, illustrated with photographs of Paris (facades, streets, shops) by Jacques-André Boiffard, assistant to Man Ray, that punctuate the narrative with the authority of reality, thereby revealing with an image what is hidden in the text. *Documents* often published other photographs by Boiffard as illustrations – or rather as a contrasting counterpoint – to the texts. In Bataille's dictionary, the word *Abattoir* is illustrated by three photographs by Eli Lotar taken in the abattoirs at La Villette, one showing calf trotters cut off and lined up against a wall (*Documents*, 2, no. 6, June 1930). Typical of the modern spirit and the use of transpositions is a text by Bataille (*Documents*, 2, no. 8, August 1930, pp. 49–52) illustrated with photographs of chapels of the Capuchin monks of Rome (decorated with fragments of skeletons) and photographs by Boiffard of flies stuck to a fly-paper.

Other "natural" pictures, requiring the detailed preparation of what will appear to be an *objet trouvé* include a pile of sand by Parry (in *Banalité*, 1930), an abandoned piece of ground by Man Ray (earth bank, tree, old iron bedstead), and constructions by Claude Cahun for *Le cœur de pic* (1937).

When the image does not, through an unexpected juxtaposition of signs, result in an internal paradox – an associative surrealism within its own confines – the same desire to destabilize forms can be seen in the use of extreme close-up which creates a "special object" – mouth, eye, tongue, foot, neck sometimes distorted by an unaccustomed viewpoint, as we see in Man Ray, Roger Parry or Boiffard, whose *Gros orteil* [Big Toe] accompanies a text of the same name by Bataille in *Documents*. Such details, made monstrous by enlargement, were a way of subverting modern objectivity, as illustrated by Blossfeldt's plants (also in *Documents*). Brassaï also made extreme close-ups: photographs of crystals in *L'Amour fou*, or of a germinating potato, entitled *Magique circonstancielle* in *Minotaure* (1933); *Sculptures involontaires*, using, in particular, crumpled Metro tickets (in the same magazine). In all of these cases it is the notion of the object that is called into question. Hans Bellmer "played" with an articulated doll, imposing on it bodily metamorphoses of an erotico-sadistic nature in order to make it into a "provocative object" (*Les Jeux de la Poupée*, 1939). Slicing through reality like this, or isolating details, allows the signs to be transformed,

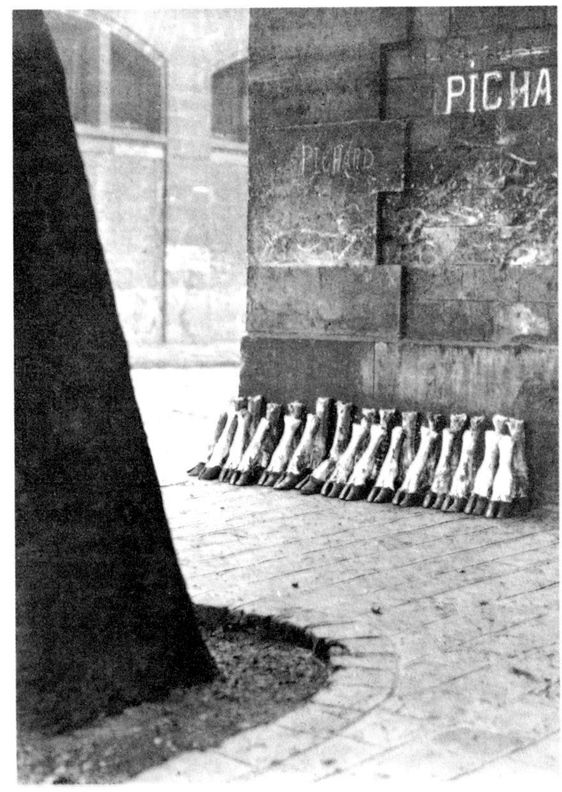

Eli Lotar, *Abattoir*, photograph published in *Documents*, 1929.

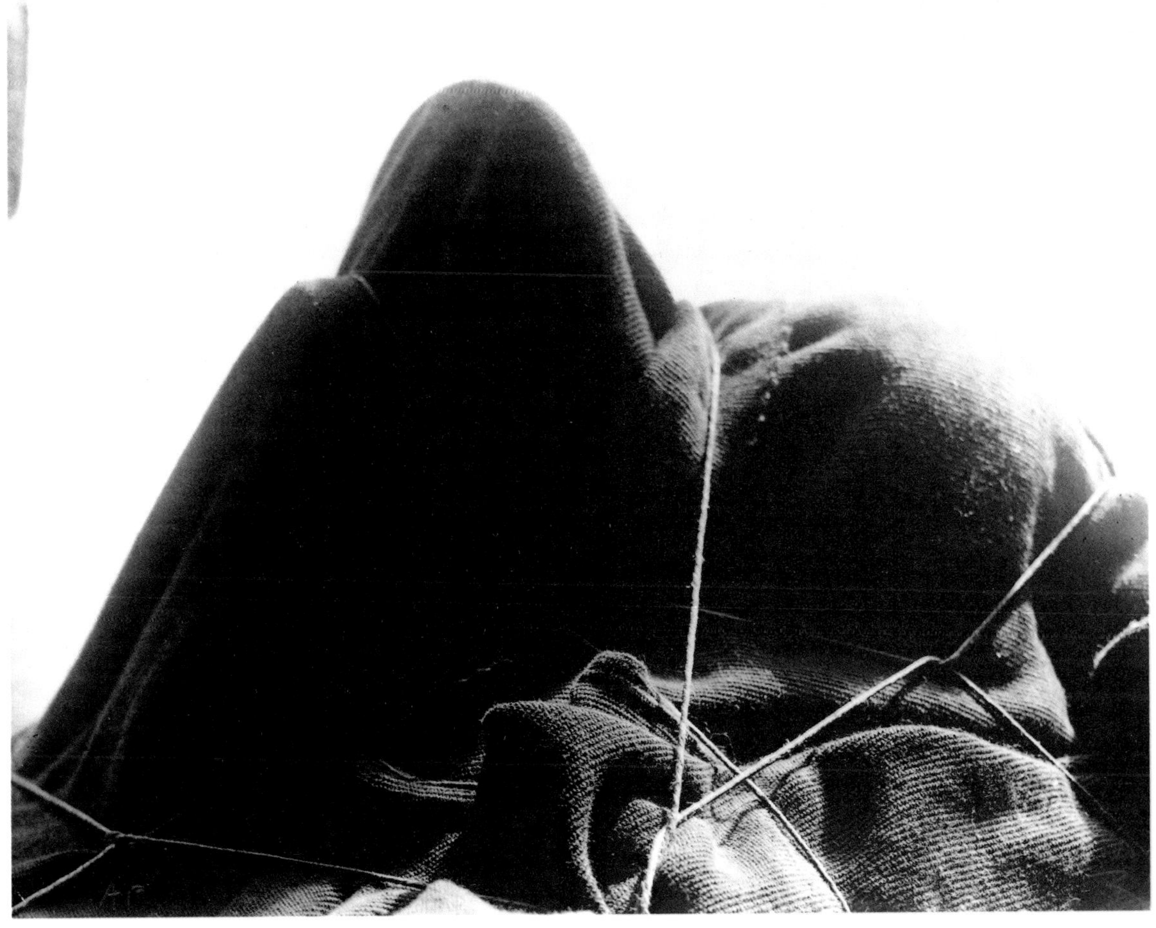

Man Ray, *The Enigma of Isidore Ducasse*, photograph of an object constructed by Man Ray, 1920.

22. *La Révolution surréaliste*, December 1, 1924.

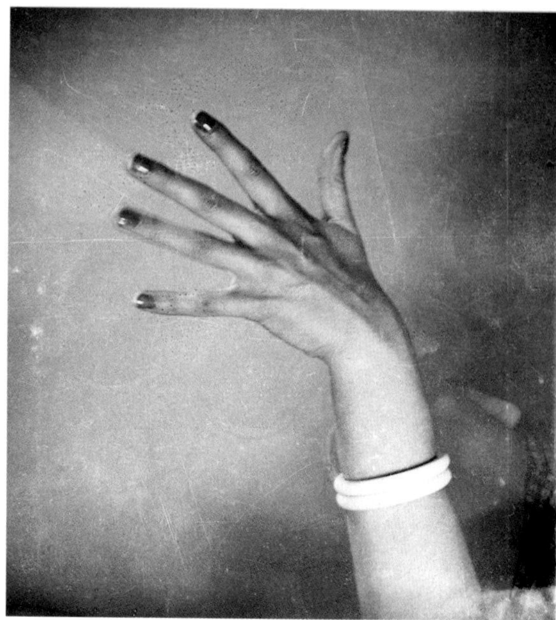

Wols ▶
(Wolfgang Schultze),
circa 1932.

making it possible to attain an automatic photographic handwriting, to bring to the text those symbols that are lacking in the imagination or which, possibly, disorientate it under the pretext of coming to its aid. Breton accompanied his editions of *L'Amour fou* with photographic plates by Brassaï, Man Ray, Dora Maar, Rogi-André, and Henri Cartier-Bresson. A similar strangeness emanates from the extreme banality of the subjects chosen by Wols, while Ubac causes the contours of his photographs to contort. Both these photographers, who were subsequently to become abstract painters, had already glimpsed through photography the distortions that can be imposed on reality and on the human figure.

The magazine *Minotaure* (1933–1939) tended to present photographs as works having a language of their own rather than as merely illustrations or foils. Bill Brandt and Alvarez Bravo appear as "photographers", pursuing a poetry of symbols. Brassaï is particularly evident, with his Graffiti, his night views of gargoyles (1933), and his night shots of Paris (*Minotaure*, no. 7, 1935), all derived from a less fragmentary reality where camouflage has replaced distortion. The strangeness of the 1930s is a result of the use of light, of effects that are formal or which involve difficulties of identification, but at a distance, without literary waverings. In the work of people like Roger Caillois, the idea of mimicking the biological and mineral kingdoms replaces the brutal confrontation of signs.

In the period between the two world wars, the reassessment of formal methods brought about by Dadaism and Constructivism led to a reworking of the photographic image and its meaning in relation to text. The photograph had become a literary language in itself, with its own syntax, associations, and changes in meaning. The poetry of chance encounters inspired the *fantastique social* of Pierre Mac Orlan: "A mixture of inherited innocence and baseness acquired patiently through contact with human beings gives the photographic lens, this inconvenient witness, such a choice of experiences and conclusions that a family photograph album becomes something more moving than nature itself".[23] Young photographers like Kertész, Brassaï, Krull, and Cartier-Bresson were to find that the path of modern photography lay in the direction of a search for particular transitory minute signs, in the concretisation of the unexpected, in the strangeness of the moment.

Raoul Ubac,
The Nebula,
1939,
Musée Nationale
d'Art Moderne, Paris.
▼

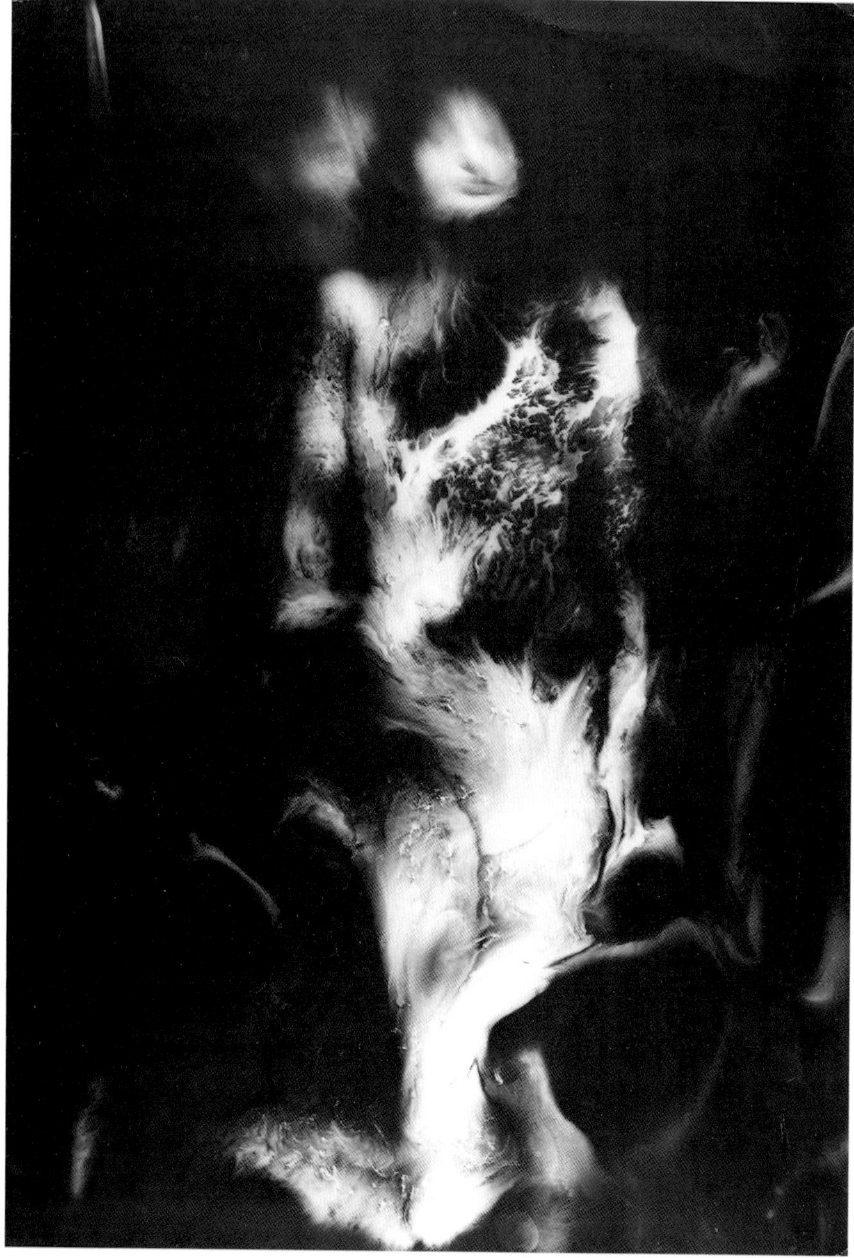

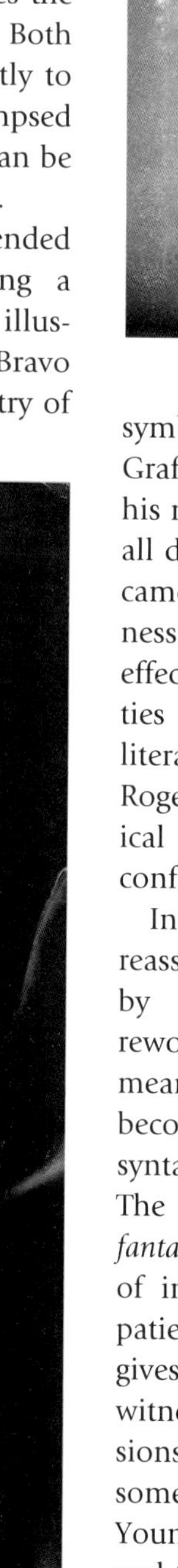

23. Introduction to *Germaine Krull* in the *Photographes Nouveaux* series, Paris, NRF, 1931.

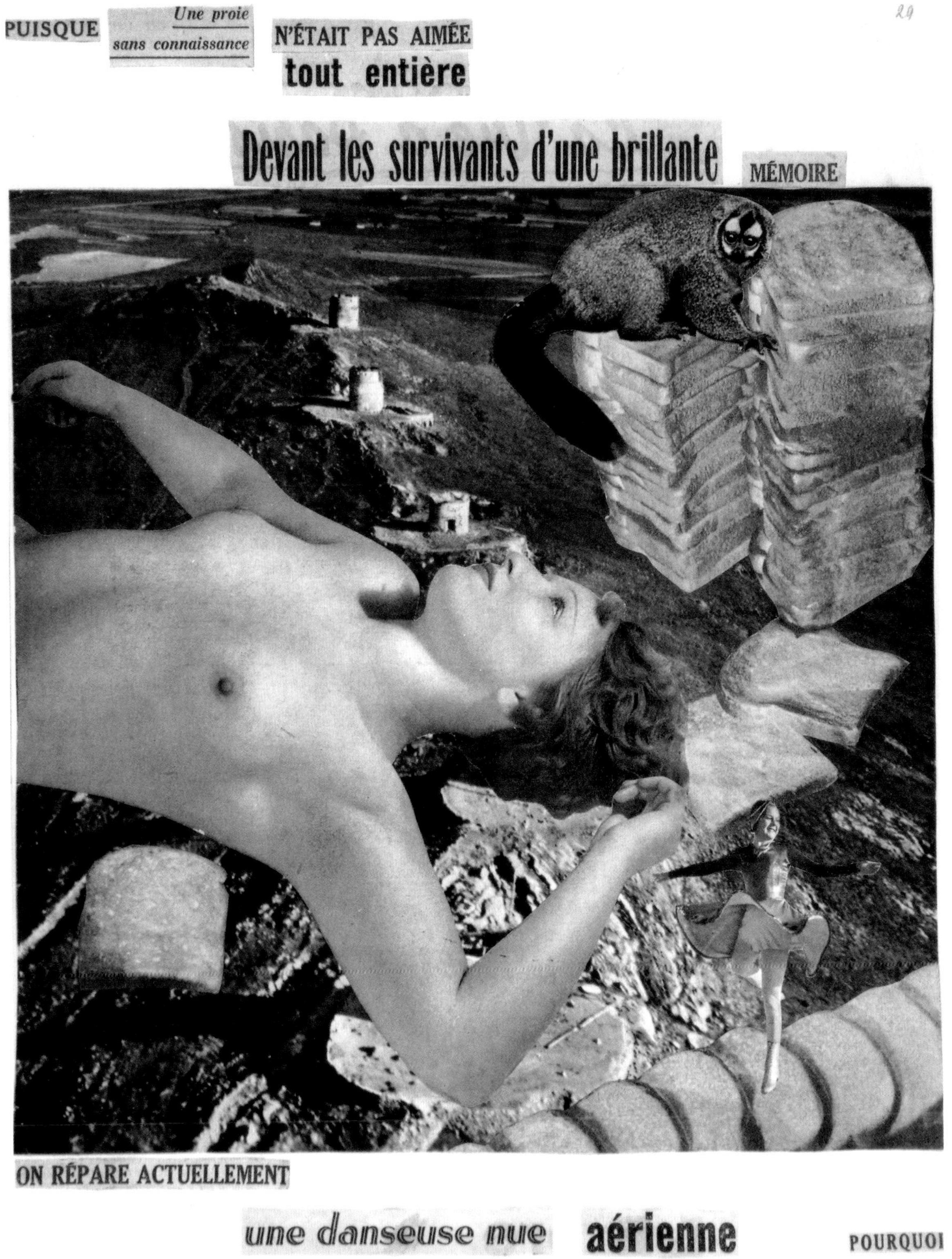

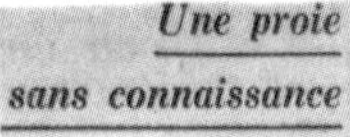

GEORGES HUGNET, photomontage from the series *The Seventh Face of the Dice*, 1935.

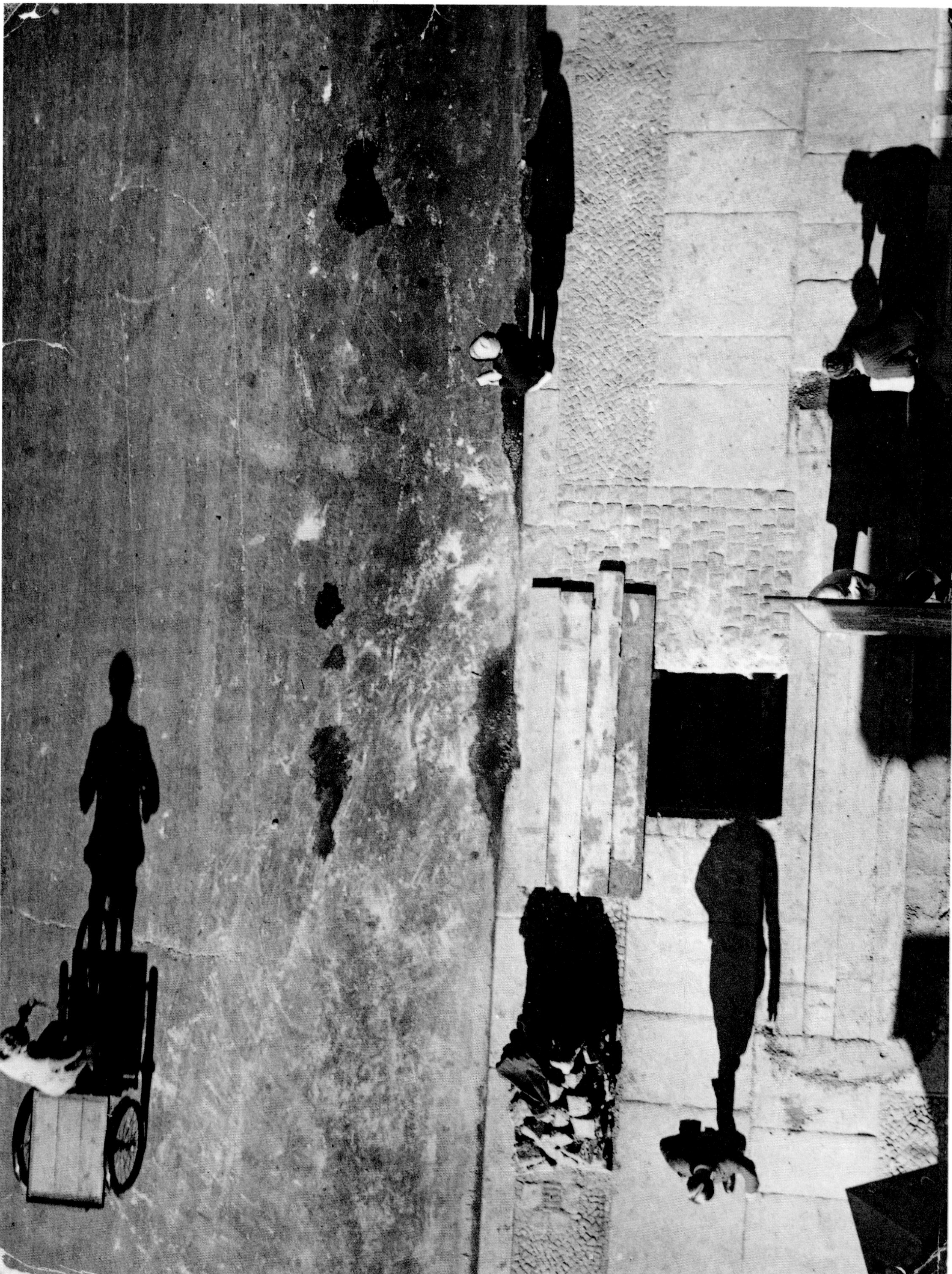

FIGURES OF STYLE

27

New vision, new photography

Andreas Haus and Michel Frizot

It was not until after the First World War, when the traditional hierarchy of art came under attack from Futurism and Dadaism, that photography was able to take its place as a branch of the plastic arts, chiefly in the Soviet Union and in Germany in the context of Constructivism. The aim of the New Vision was to teach people to see the modern world in ways different from the old concepts of representation; the New Objectivity wished to impose a flawless technical image – one, however, that was uniform and depersonalized. The New Photography was to export these ideas, adapted to the needs of the different media and different national tendencies, in the form of recurring stylistic motifs: high- and low-angle shots, oblique views, close-ups, and the fragmentation of objects.

The First World War of 1914–1918 and the Russian Revolution of 1917 represented, in the words of Bertolt Brecht, "a great lesson for a new vision of the world". The spectacle of socio-economic upheaval and widespread devastation called for a new conception of art, which would no longer serve the abstract and timeless ideals of beauty. The nineteenth-century philosopher Nietzsche's famous concept of the "inversion of values" acquired, for many, a conscious significance and gave rise, in progressive artistic and intellectual circles, to hopes for a realist art that was closer to real life. The realities of the modern world – industrial work, megalopolises, mass political movements, and urban traffic – were henceforward to be seen as important factors of society.

Traditional art had played no role in these developments – apart from that of disguise – just as it had been unable to represent war. Photographers, on the other hand, who had (almost) never been thought of as artists, had covered all these aspects of real life with documentary and press photography.

Many artists saw in such works a point of departure for a new approach to their own work, either by becoming photographers themselves, or by using the particular characteristics of the photographic image for their own creations. From this was to be born a new photography and a new graphic art.

Promotion and objectives of photography

Photography during the 1920s gave rise to many changes and new meanings in plastic representation. The most important element in these changes was the "functionalization" of the "photo-image", determined by its quantitative development. In the media (daily papers, illustrated magazines, advertising), photography played an increasingly important role. Books and publications of all sorts – science, leisure, politics or ideological propaganda – were likely to contain photographs that were no longer simply illustrations but were central to conveying some message or piece of information.

A rapid increase in knowledge altered people's awareness of their place within the world. Alongside reporter-photographers producing a new type of "news", cinema in the 1920s represented a particular form of inducement to the understanding of society through images. Photography was a socially determining dimension of artistic reality that no other form of art had previously achieved. Furthermore, photography had become a mass leisure activity. From the 1920s, anyone could afford to use a camera. This strengthened the idea that the reality of the world of photographic images was immediate, close at hand. This quantitative

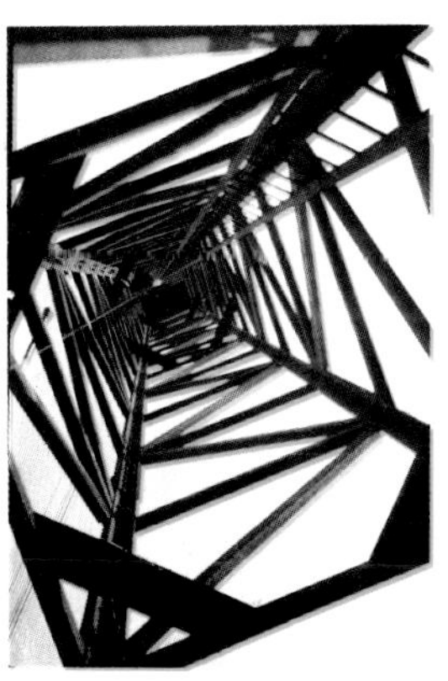

ANONYMOUS AMATEUR, *Rakovitza Radio Tower*, 1930, private collection.

◀ UMBO, *Untitled*, 1928, Rudolf Kicken Gallery, Cologne.

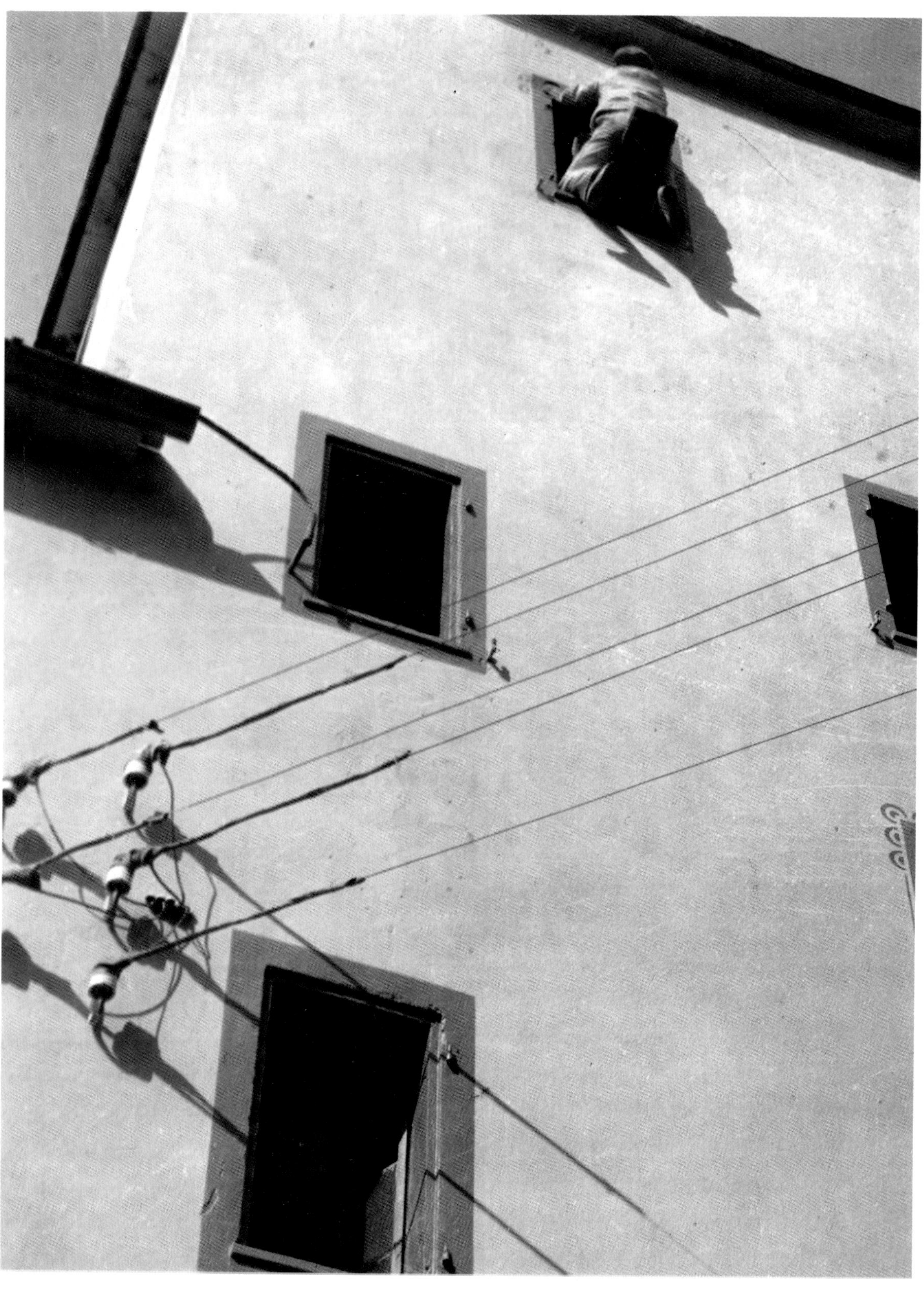

László Moholy-Nagy, *House-painting*, 1925, Museum of Fine Arts, Boston.

increase reinforced the social significance of photography.

Such considerations help to explain why those artistic movements that sought to become involved in activities with social implications turned to photography in such large numbers. In some cases it was for pedagogical motives (László Moholy-Nagy and New Vision), in order to obtain a new objective relationship with the world (Albert Renger-Patzsch and New Objectivity) to use its strength as a form of public protest (John Heartfield and his political photomontages) or, perhaps, to inform others of the power of photographic images (the writer Walter Benjamin).

It was in Germany that the new direction taken by photography in the 1920s was most discussed. German Expressionism, with its search for a "new man", had opened the way to the social and human aspirations of art. From this arose basic – and sometimes pretentious – theories about the educational "aims" and "value" of photography.

The art historian Franz Roh, a great believer in the New Photography and its extension to the greatest number of people, described the situation in the following terms: "For a mechanical device to find such wide acceptance, three factors usually must be present: the apparatus has to be relatively inexpensive, it has to be technically easy to use, and the pleasure it offers (in this case, visual pleasure) must be in tune with the mood and direction of contemporary life."[1]

Franz Roh hoped that from the age would arise a new "feeling of style", the aesthetic elements of which he foresaw in the new visual possibilities of sensation and representation, which he defined by the "actual aspect, tighter and more constructive" and the "real force of lived experience" of photography. He saw the New Vision as being characterized by a number of elements and stylistic motifs: "New ways to isolate details: this allows us to experience the inner form of a thing, by removing the usual, and distracting, context that connects one thing to the whole or to other, adjoining things [...] Large overviews (aerial shots) that put a piece of the world back into a more inclusive context than we can perceive in everyday life, and also views from above (from a chimney, for instance) that have the magical effect of showing the verticals at a slant, so that they take on the astronomical meaning of radia pointing to an imaginary center of the earth – which, in a higher sense, they actually are. Finally we capture the world of the microscope, not just for scientific reasons, but also with elemental amazement at the wondrous forms of the microcosm. Above all, of course, we record and preserve the movements of everyday life [...] This is the source of photo reportage, a genre that represents the quintessence of photography."[2]

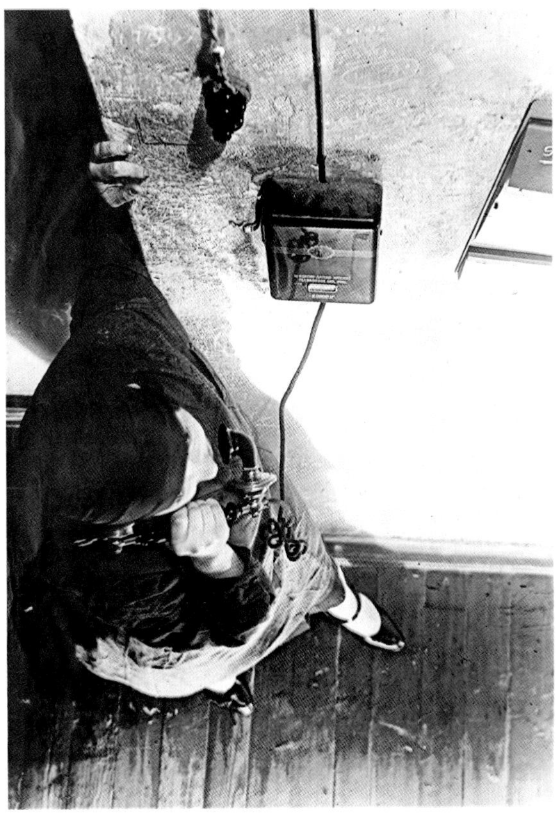

Alexander Rodchenko, *At the Telephone,* 1928, Museum of Modern Art New York.

Franz Roh saw photography as possessing an essential duality: "On the one hand the joy of reality, of the most exact possible 'recognition' of a piece of reality; on the other hand, the subtle pleasure in what is strange, hidden, unusual in this same surrounding world."

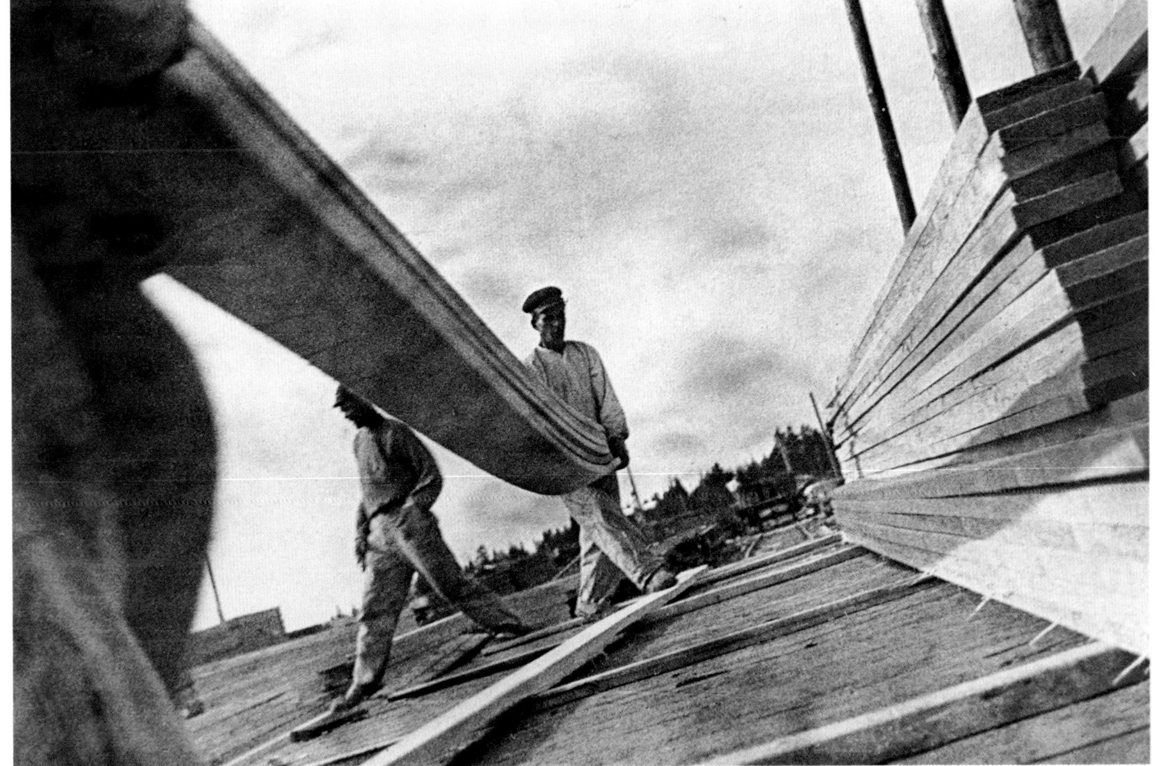

Alexander Rodchenko, *Sawmill, Piles of Wood,* 1931, Musée Niépce, Chalon-sur-Saône.

1. F. Roh, "Der Wert der Photographie", in *Hand und Maschine*, February 1930, quoted in C. Phillips (ed.), *Photography in the Modern Era: European Documents and Critical Writings, 1913–1940*, New York Metropolitan Museum of Art, 1989, pp. 160–163.

2. *Ibid.*

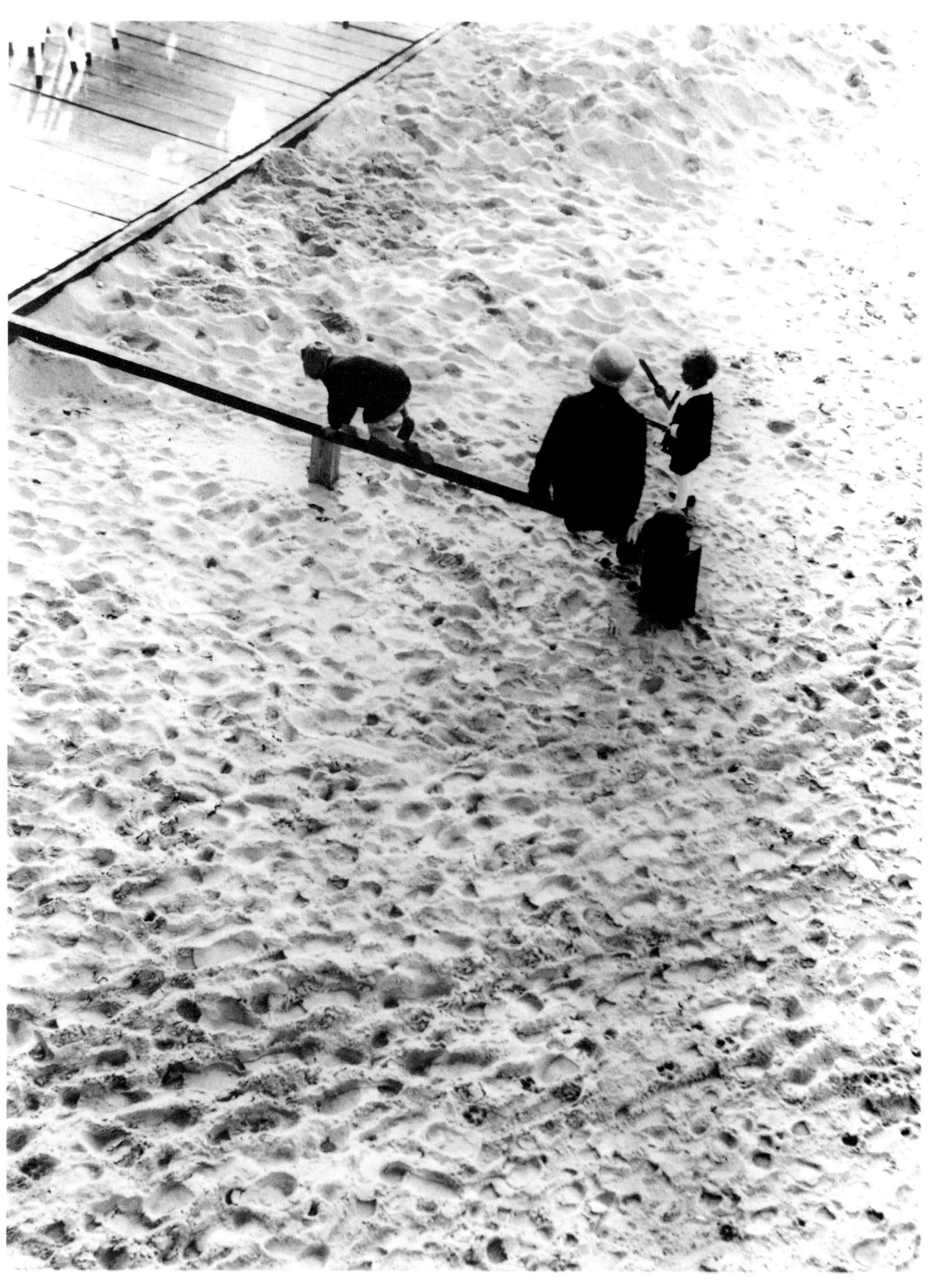

LÁSZLÓ MOHOLY-NAGY, *Untitled,* circa 1931, Staatliche Museen Preussischer Kulturbesitz, Berlin.

Photographic techniques and processes contributed to this synthesis of idealistic hopes for "humanity" with materials and methods that were already uncompromisingly modern in nature, characteristic of many avant-garde artistic programs: "The techniques of photography (macrophotography, photograms, photomontage, negative printing, photocomposition) must be practiced together. It is precisely this proximity that fosters modern creativity."

László Moholy-Nagy, artist and teacher at the Bauhaus, was not originally a photographer, but a Constructivist painter in search of socially responsible aesthetic activities. He collected photographs taken from newspapers, magazines, and other printed material, writing in 1928: "For years I have been collecting the best photographs of the period, because I have always been moved and intrigued by their existence. I have published 100 of these photographs in my book [*Malerei, Fotografie, Film*] so that others can share the same immense joy."[3]

3. In *Der Photograph,* no. 2, 1928, p. 5, quoted in Eskildsen and Horak, Film und Foto der zwanziger Jahre, Stuttgart 1979, p. 68.

The New Vision in Germany

As we have seen elsewhere, American Pictorialism had begun, even before the First World War, to move towards "straight" photography, without any manipulation. Such new developments were, however, as yet little known in Europe. Around 1920, the traditional perfectionism of "art" photography was to undergo a drastic upheaval with the arrival of a young Soviet Constructivist. With the famous slogan "Easel painting is dead!" (1921) Alexander Rodchenko not only turned his back on conventional bourgeois art but also, at the same time, established a new program of creative expression. According to this program, all of the basic methods of artistic production – with pride of place going to technical elements – were to be employed for the construction of a "new world". What was needed was not the old "image" but a "realization" of life and of society itself. This new art form was to use both photomontage (Hausmann, Höch, 1918; Rodchenko, 1923) and photograms – techniques that were to be strongly recommended by the New Photography.

Painting and sculpture were the areas favored for technical production and experimentation in architectural and "machine" constructions. By contrast, photography – practiced by Rodchenko from 1924 – was used, in close connection with film, for the stirring depiction of the new human and social perspectives opened up by the October Revolution. Daring visual angles were used to suggest, with their perspective and exaggerated foreshortening, the invincible strength of the "new man", the revolutionary worker, and his domination over his environment. Through the use of high- and low-angle shots, this art, placed in the service of the technical revolution, was able to encompass all space and make it its own.

These criteria of the "New Vision" also drew on the discoveries made by Cubism and Surrealism to overcome all feelings of earthly weightiness: "We are spiraling out into space", declared Lissitzky, in an expression of the exalted optimism of the revolutionary artists. The "inward-looking perspective" of traditional photography, seen as "bourgeois", became the object of derision. In Berlin, which had responded with enormous hope to ideas of revolution and where Russian artists like Lissitzky stayed frequently from 1919, Russian films and photography became models for a generation of young artists. To this was added the theory formulated in Russia of "production art", according to which the artist's activity should be inspired by technical productivity, exploiting the "elemental" properties of matter and machines.

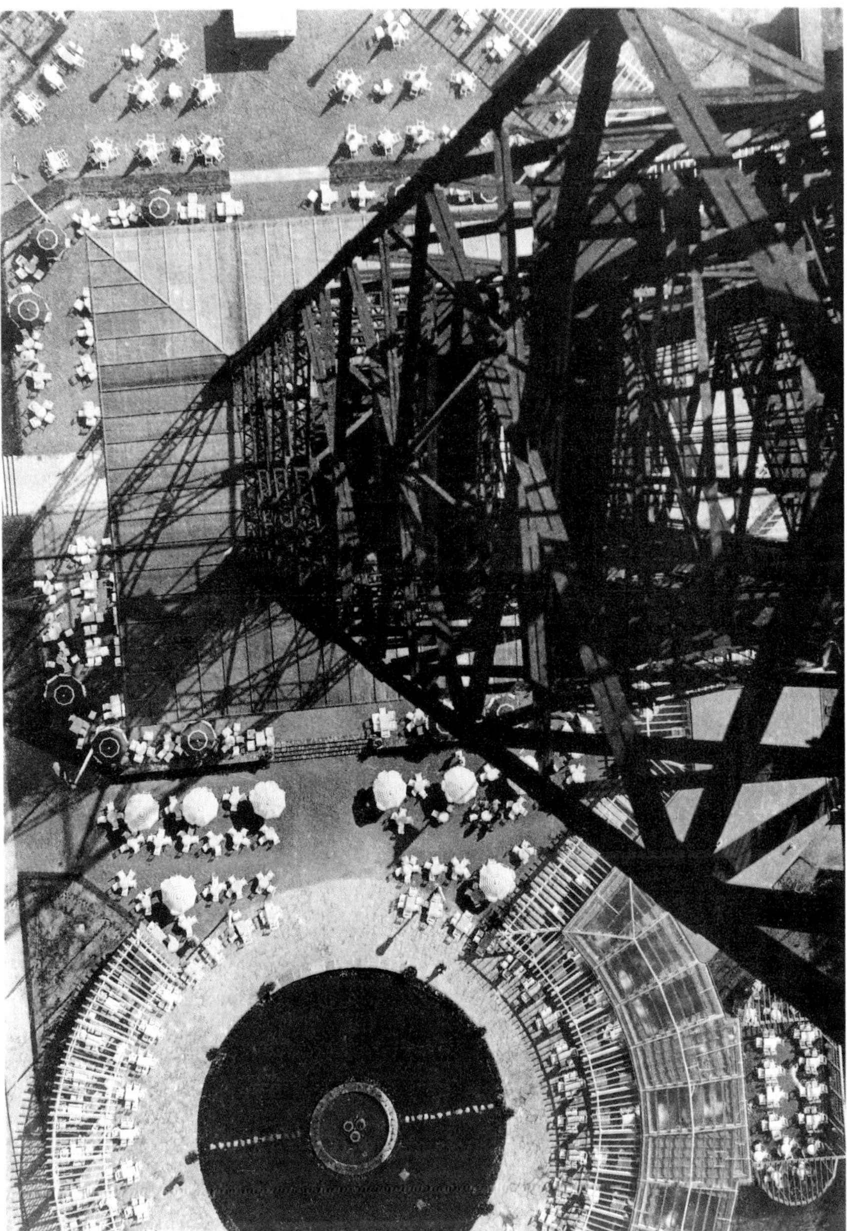

László Moholy-Nagy, *Berlin Radio Tower*, circa 1928, Art Institute of Chicago.

Profoundly influenced by these ideas, the Hungarian Constructivist László Moholy-Nagy was invited to the Weimar Bauhaus by Walter Gropius in 1923. In collaboration with his wife, the art historian and photographer Lucia Moholy, he had "invented", following the dictates of "production art", the "photogram" or cameraless photograph. In all these experiments his true calling as a painter is always in evidence. The same can be said of the photographs he took from 1925. In the spirit of the Russian Constructivists, he used oblique shots and structural abstractions resulting from the use of close-ups and unusual angles (from above or below). These pictures remained, nevertheless, much closer to the values of painting than when they were used, as by the Russians, purely to suggest experiments with space and movement in the world of production. In a search for the constant renewal of their "production", Moholy and the many representatives of the New Photography,

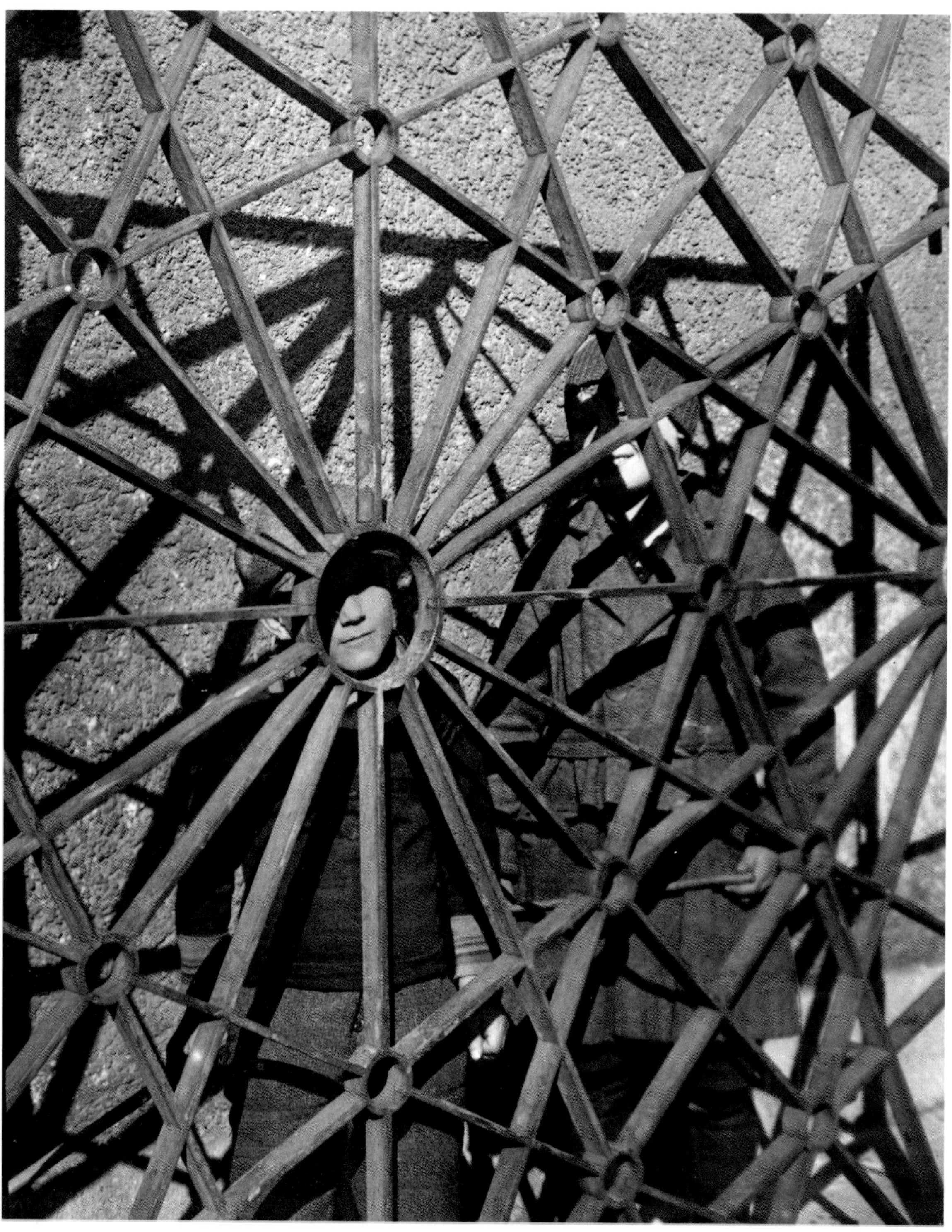

LÁSZLÓ MOHOLY-NAGY, *Boys Behind Iron Fence,* International Museum of Photography, George Eastman House, Rochester.

on whom he had a considerable influence, always made uninhibited use of that unique characteristic of the camera which is to record "everything", without differentiating "between a chimney sweep and the Apollo *Belvedere*", as Talbot had written in 1844. It was precisely this "soulless" equality in recording – for which photography had long been criticized – that Moholy used as the basis of the New Vision, that was to give the world new values of perception.

Moholy-Nagy's New Photography and the trend known as the New Vision embraced what was essentially a pedagogical aesthetic for the sensory understanding of the modern environment. In living conditions that had become abstract as a result of industry and technology, human awareness could keep abreast of events thanks to a "new way of seeing", one that was active and dynamic, and supported by photography. It was a highly subjective program – and one that was to bring the wrath of numerous critics down on his head.

It was Moholy-Nagy's belief, radical at the time, that photography should replace the old arts of painting and become the visual means of communication of the future (he taught the introductory course at the Bauhaus from 1923 to 1928 and ran the metalwork studio, leaving in

1928). He developed this point of view in his book, published by the Bauhaus in 1925, entitled *Malerei, Fotografie, Film*.[4] His argument ran as follows: painting is a craft while photography is a technique; the latter is therefore better suited to a technical modern age than is painting. Grafted onto these ideas was an enthusiasm for the "immaterial" aspects of glass façades and chrome furniture, the lights of the big city, airplanes, and the daring of modern buildings – the new "dynamism", "lightness", and "weightlessness" of the conditions of modern life. For Moholy, who was attempting to dematerialize reality, representation was no longer to be achieved with matter, but with "pure light". For him, photography, which uses nothing but light, was the ideal "medium" – one that entirely satisfied his demand for "pigment in light". He saw man's salvation lying in the "crystalline symbol of a new faith still to come", as Walter Gropius put it in 1919, on the opening of the Bauhaus.

This institution had embarked on a program for human co-operation achieved through the social ethic of a collective craft industry – something that entirely suited Moholy. In 1923, Gropius formulated his new theory: "Art and technology; a new unity". "Craft" production was replaced by "technology", and the range of expression shifted towards modern means of technical production, in the Constructivist sense of the word, or was even, in some cases, entirely "handed over" to technology. A "new vision" would take hold of the new reality in a living and active way and in this way guide every aspect of man's path. Moholy's pedagogical program was based on this training in the "new" way of seeing, and, for him, photography was the ideal instrument for such an education. He devoted himself to the study and understanding of photography, and recommended the use of all types of photographic techniques, both formal and plastic, even those considered hitherto to be "errors" – exaggerated perspective, hard shadows – and called for the creation of new forms through the use of unusual angles.

In *Malerei, Fotografie, Film*, Moholy wrote with a certain optimism: "We have hitherto used the capacities of the camera in a secondary sense only [...] This is apparent too in the so-called 'faulty' photographs: the view from above, from below, the oblique view, which today often disconcert people who take them to be accidental shots [...] Whereas the eye, together with our intellectual experience, supplements perceived optical phenomena by means of association and formally and spatially creates a *conceptual image*. Thus in the photographic camera we have the most reliable aid to a beginning of objective vision."[5]

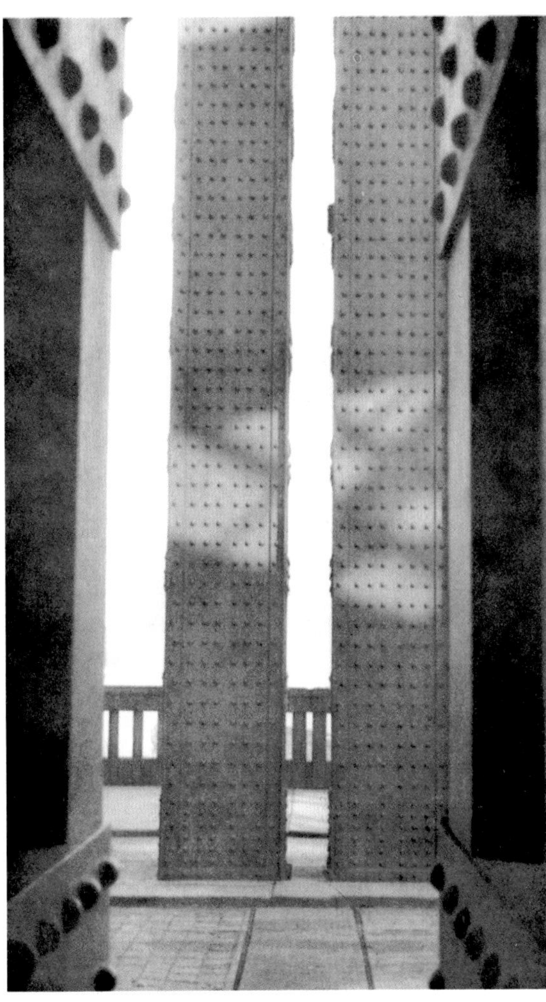

ARVID GUTSCHOW,
Piles of the New Bridge Over the Elbe at Hamburg,
circa 1928,
Museum Moderner Kunst,
Vienna.

The "textures" and the "structures" of the real world were sought out for their ability to translate the photographic interaction of light and shade. The concept of "making", indicating the artistic style of an individual painter, was adapted to this dematerialization through photography. Now, the innate value of the optical representation was determined by the apparition of fine gradations of light on rhythmical and worked surfaces, together with their effect on the light-sensitive plate. Thus, it was the duty of photography to keep modern man's way of seeing "active" and "productive" when surrounded by the city, advertising, and the media. Photography should help to create a new "aesthetic" territory for the structures of a technical civilization, that was too abstract for conventional perception.

The fact that Moholy-Nagy, the most ardent proponent of this school of the New Vision, was himself not a photographer but a painter explains the extremely subjective aspects of the tasks prescribed. In his handling of a camera he remained an amateur whose images are interesting not for their technical prowess but for their absence of prejudice and their creative imagination. They are not so much "photographs" in the traditional meaning of the word as documents about the "reorganization of vision". Further-

4. L. Moholy-Nagy, *Malerei, Fotografie, Film*, Bauhaus-Buch, no. 8, Munich, 1925 (expanded edition 1927); English translation: *Painting, Photography, Film*, MIT Press, 1969, 1973.

5. *Ibid.* (English translation), p. 8.

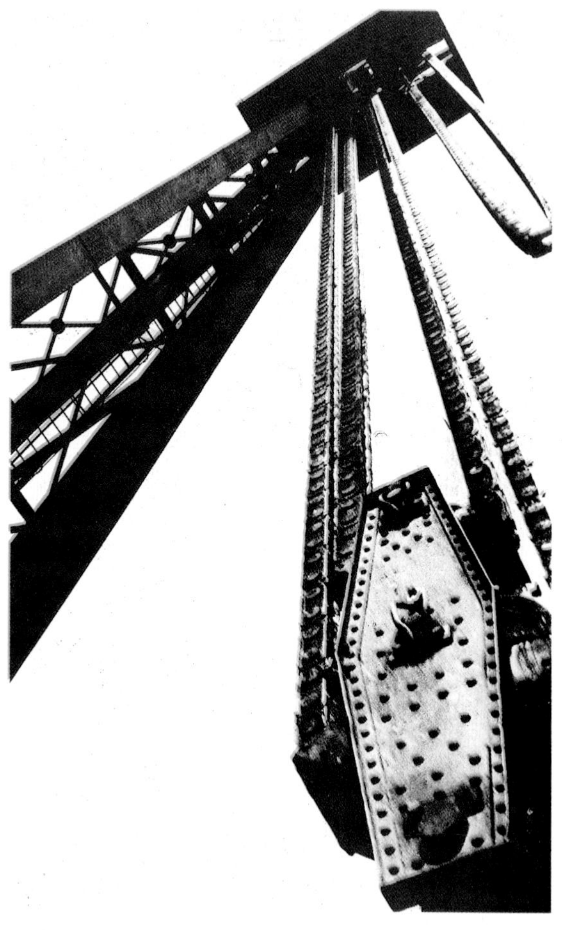

Albert Renger-Patzsch, *Giant Crane,* from *Hamburg,* 1930.

more, the effect of Moholy's numerous publications, lectures, and exhibitions was that his aspirations were adopted by magazines and advertising, thereby gaining in popularity.[6]

The New Objectivity

Albert Renger-Patzsch, ▶ *Brazilian Tree,* from *Die Welt ist schön,* 1928.

It was not long before, among professional photographers, a reaction to these tendencies began, slowly but surely, to show itself. Those who had mastered the technique of using large-format plate cameras were not prepared to be driven out by amateurs with their snapshot cameras. They emphasized instead the strengths of their methods: scrupulous faithfulness to the subject, correct lighting, irreproachable truth in the rendering of detail, and total mastery of optical and chemical procedures.

Albert Renger-Patzsch, one of the most prominent figures of the German *Neue Sachlichkeit* ("New Objectivity"),[7] explained the aims of his conception of photography in a text written in 1927: "The secret of a good photograph, which can possess artistic qualities just as a work of visual art can, resides in its realism. For rendering our impressions of nature, of plants, animals, the works of architects and sculptors, and the creations of engineers, photography offers us a most reliable tool. We still don't sufficiently appreciate the opportunities to capture the magic of material things [...] To do justice to modern technology's rigid linear structure, to the lofty gridwork of cranes and bridges, to the dynamism of machines operating at one thousand horsepower – only photography is capable of that [...] The absolutely correct rendering of form, from the brightest highlight to the darkest shadow, imparts to a technically expert photograph the magic of experience. Let us therefore leave art to the artists, and let us try to use the medium of photography to create photographs that can endure because of their *photographic* qualities – without borrowing from art."[8]

This principle is not so different from that underlying Moholy's statement of the necessity to develop "the autonomy of the photographic medium". However, Moholy would never have agreed that the aim should be to restore "our impressions of nature". His belief – that nature should be used in whatever way the photographer wished – went further: what was needed was to see the world with totally new eyes.

Professional photographers sneered at what they regarded as Moholy's amateurish experiments and their technical inadequacies, and responded instead to another cultural question: how to record in images the perception of the objective reality of the world as modified by industry and science?

In an almost logical way, the New Vision implied the need for a "new objectivity", the concept of which was borrowed from painting.

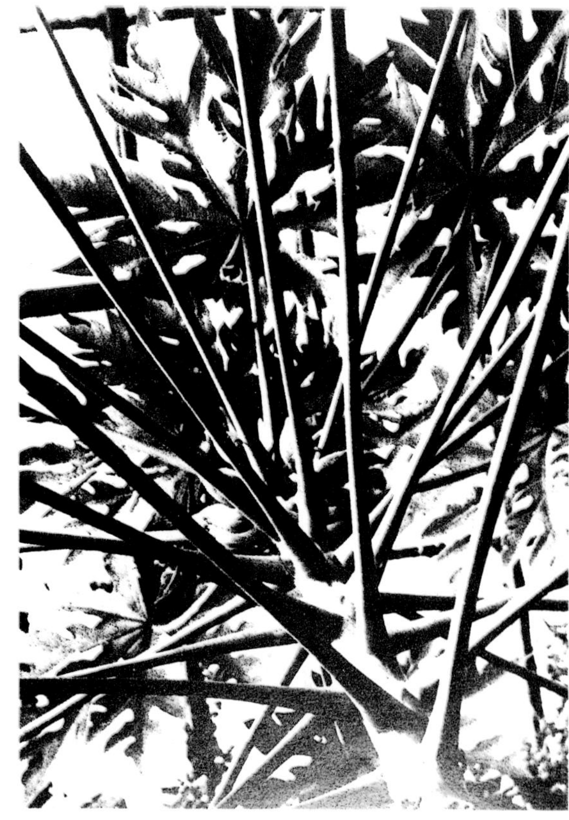

6. A. Haus, *Moholy-Nagy, photographies, photogrammes,* Paris, Chêne, 1979; exhibition catalogue "Moholy-Nagy", Valence and Marseilles, 1991; *Moholy-Nagy; Fotoplastiks: The Bauhaus Years,* New York, Bronx Museum of the Arts, 1983.

7. "Neue Sachlichkeit" was the title of an exhibition of "realist" painting put on in 1925 in the Kunsthalle in Mannheim.

8. "Ziele", in *Das Deutsche Lichtbild,* 1927, quoted in Eskildsen and Horak, C. Phillips (ed.), *op. cit.,* p. 105.

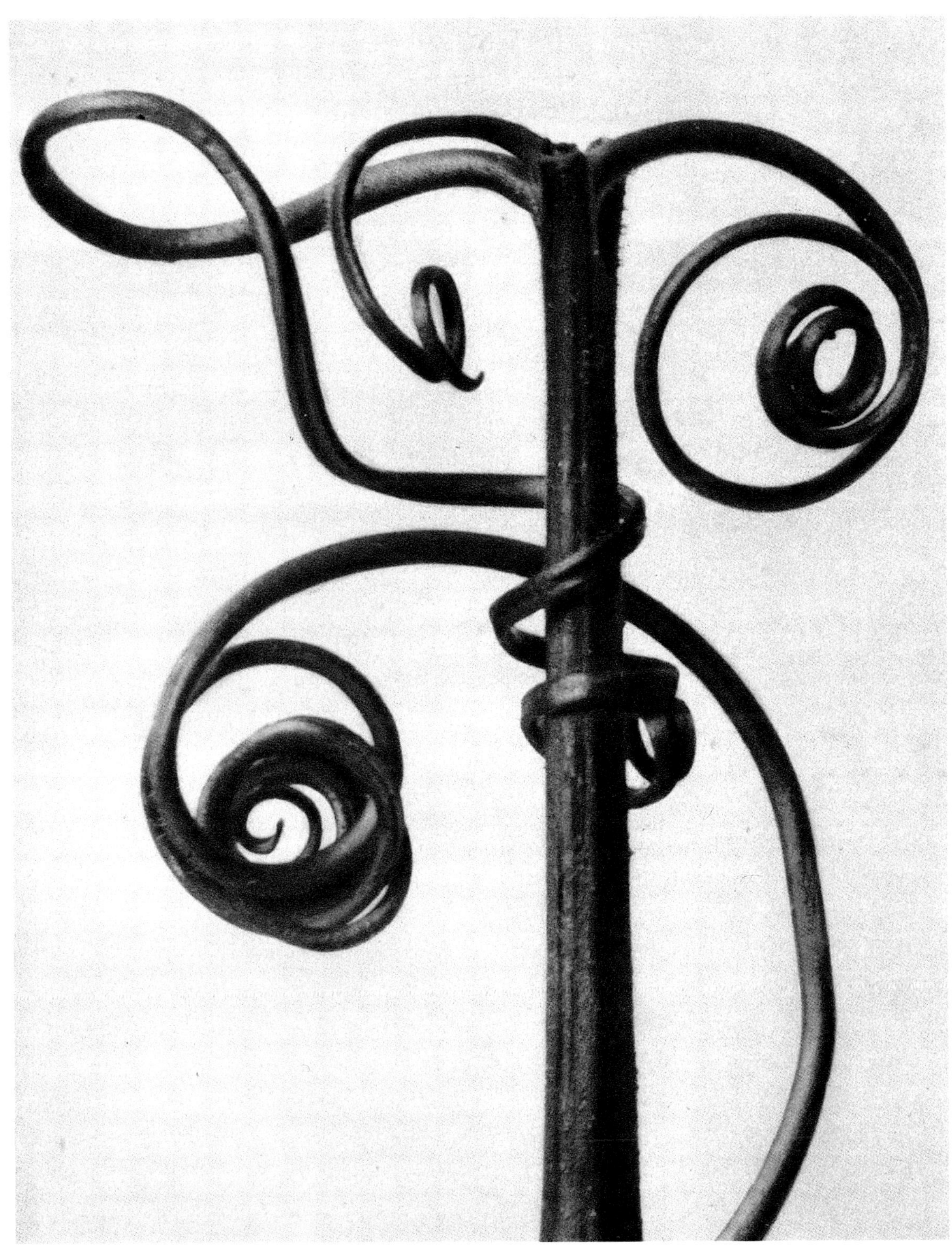

KARL BLOSSFELDT,
Cucurbita,
from *Urformen der Kunst,*
1928.

New Objectivity – a new and formal realism – had started to appear around 1920. In their pictures, the many painters exemplifying this tendency (Grosz, Schrimpf, Hubbuch, Schad, Dix) turned to a prosaic and emotionless realism that aimed at presenting the world of the senses not through the expression of a soul experiencing the world, but through the cold objectivity of things themselves. This tendency was particularly marked in Germany, as a response to the subjective emotionalism developed by the Expressionist school. Inevitably, it took on a somewhat hermetic character, that was sometimes mysterious and tormented. To some extent, the "new objective painting" took as its model the silent precision of photography. "One could even go so far as to say that the painting of the *Neue Sachlichkeit* is defined by a two-way exchange between the traditional craft of painting and photography."[9]

What was being produced linked up, to some extent, with a technical culture already re-established by the American school ("pure photography") but built this time on a different, spiritual approach. In the United States, there existed a philosophy of old-fashioned romanti-

9. G. Metken, in *Les Réalismes, 1919–1939,* Paris, Centre Georges-Pompidou, 1980, p. 112.

Film und Foto, Stuttgart, 1929

New Photography made its mark at the great exhibition held from May 18 to July 7, 1929 at the Schlossgarten in Stuttgart by the Deutscher Werkbund under the title *Film und Foto* (FiFo), at the same time as the famous Weissenhof architecture exhibition. The poster for FiFo, a photograph taken using a daring low-angle viewpoint, came to stand as the program and symbol of a number of formal and creative theories on which the New Photography was founded. The camera, placed in the centre of the poster, appears to form part of the body of the photographer, the dynamic of the typography supporting the oblique perspective of the low-angle shot.

A text by Gustav Stotz announcing the exhibition in the magazine *Das Kunstblatt* in 1929 gives a manifesto of the New Photography:

"1. New instruments of creation are available to us, with cameras, lenses, and new, more light-sensitive, faster plates.

"2. An optical epoch has developed. We see the things around us differently from before, without pictorial aims in the Impressionist sense. Some things have become important for us, when formerly they were scarcely noticed: clogs, a gutter, cotton reels, cloth, machines, etc. They interest us in their material existence, in their simple essence; they interest us as means of structuring space on a flat surface, as supports for light and shade.

"3. Fixing time. Faster plates and better lenses allow us to seize even the briefest movement and fix it in time (a photograph of a bullet!). Photography has once more become, in the true sense of the word, "actual".

"The areas affected are numerous and important: photographic reportage, sport, war, street views, night photography, forensic photography [...] zoology, botany, medicine (X-ray photographs), physics (microphotography), aerial views, macrophotography [...] photograms, solarizations, over-exposures, etc. [...] photomontage – and photocomposition.

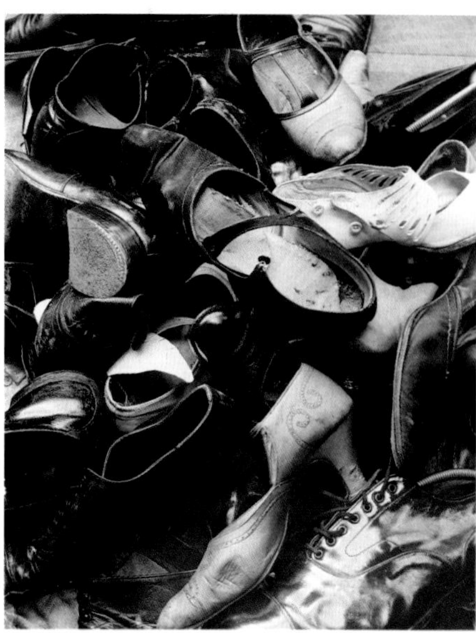

Sasha Stone,
Expressive Shoes,
circa 1925, Berlinische Galerie, Berlin.

"Alongside works by anonymous photo-reporters, there will be exhibited works by pioneers in the field of modern photography, with examples by Man Ray (Paris), Lissitzky (Moscow), and Steichen (New York). Germany will be represented by Lerski, Heartfield, Moholy-Nagy, Stone, Umbo and others. Piet Zwart (The Hague) has put together images from the Netherlands. Works from Russia, Britain, France, Switzerland, and America will complete the exhibition."

The exhibition was not concerned with what was "artistic" in photography; it covered instead all aspects of the new "medium" of communication, including film. These were individual photographers, sometimes arranged according to nationality, and groups formed around schools of applied arts. The general conception related most closely to the views of Moholy-Nagy, while the graphics were overseen by Tschichold. Lissitzky was in charge of the exhibits from the Soviet group. The first room was devoted to historical photographs, including those of Atget, and to general categories, such as radiography, astronomy, and enlargements. Two weeks in June were dedicated to film screenings, organized by Hans Richter. The American group, represented by Edward Weston and Steichen, included Abbott, Bruehl, Cunningham, Outerbridge, Sheeler, and Brett Weston. The French contribution (probably put together by Man Ray and Christian Zervos) included F. Henri, Hoyningen-Huene, Kertész, Krull, Lotar, Man Ray, Maximilien Vox, and Tabard. From the Netherlands were shown works by Schuitema and Zwart, and from the U.S.S.R., Alpert, Klutsis, Ignatovich, Rodchenko, Schaichet, and Lissitzky.

However, not surprisingly, the largest number of contributors were German: Baumeister, Bayer, Biermann, Burchartz, Erfurth, Andreas Feininger, Finsler, Grosz, Heartfield, Höch, Lerski, Lucia Moholy, László Moholy-Nagy, Peterhans, Alice and Oscar Nerlinger, Renger-Patzsch, Schwitters, Stone, Umbo, Paul Wolff, Zielke, the Bauhaus group – including Marianne Brandt and Lux Feininger – and other schools. Cecil Beaton was also represented.

The FiFo exhibition was subsequently mounted in Munich, Vienna, Berlin, and Zurich, in a reduced version, and then, in 1931, in Tokyo and Osaka.

The exhibition marked the end of the period of "daring experiments", and the work became acceptable and categorized under the title of "style" – a style that had, what is more, become international.

Andreas Haus

Bibliography: In addition to the reprinted catalogue (Stuttgart, DVA, 1979, and New York, Arno Press, 1979), see also U. Eskildsen and J.C. Horak (eds.) *Film und Foto der zwanziger Jahre*, Stuttgart, Hatje, 1979.

cism, tinged with a vein of religious naiveté. European thought, in contrast, brought up on a diet of dialectic philosophy, was able to accept real life with a calm certitude. In 1926, Paul Westheim presented for the first time in the avant-garde journal *Das Kunstblatt* photographs of American "objects", with an accompanying commentary; they were greeted in Germany as models of aesthetic perfection. In its uncomplicated professionalism and its commercial-like precision, American photography, with its rigor and its emotionalism, opened up in the German spirit the perspective of an as yet unknown form of aesthetic serenity, giving hope for a modern "beauty" in the world.

It was in this context that the most famous photographic collection of the New Objectivity, Albert Renger-Patzsch's *Die Welt ist schön* [The World is Beautiful] appeared, in 1928.[10] The background was the industrial culture of the pre-war years of Emperor Wilhelm, characterized by an enthusiasm for the power of machines and the Prussian philosophy of rationality – very different from the aesthetic of the photographed object found in America. The title originally chosen by the author was, in fact, *Die Dinge* [Things]. The

10. *Die Welt ist schön: einhundert photographische Aufnahmen von Albert Renger-Patzsch*, Munich, K. Wolff, 1928; republished in slightly different form, Paris, Créatis, and Cologne, Boston, Schürmann and Kicken, 1979.

book depicts a world united by the eye of the photographer, illustrated with 100 photographs of nature, industry and apparently disparate objects such as factory chimneys, the head and neck of an ostrich, piles of objects, plants in the style of Blossfeldt, a crane viewed from below, and motifs multiplied or repeated (trees, barrels, electric insulators, logs). Albert Renger-Patzsch's *Locomotive* is typical, with the strong oblique lines of the connecting rods that seem to be part of a living thing, made of steel. At the same time, Renger-Patzsch was producing many views of industrial sites (factories, stations, furnaces) with a similar dehumanized calmness.

In some respects, the New Objectivity represented a revival of some of the criteria of professional scientific photography. A good example is provided by Blossfeldt. The close-ups and macrophotographs of plants published in his book *Urformen der Kunst* (1928) associated him, somewhat against his will, with the vision of Renger-Patzsch. In fact, his œuvre derived from a scientific approach applied to art. These documentary images, while certainly corresponding in technique to the demands of the New Objectivity, were the product of thirty years' teaching at the Berlin School of Applied Arts, which saw in such natural structures the archetypes of industrial blueprints, in a context that was an extension of Art Nouveau. Blossfeldt's "pure" photographs were thus subjected to the interpretation of others, as would be those of Atget, or those of contemporary American photographers (Weston, Cunningham) – though the "objective" world of the latter was sometimes more sentimental and intuitive than that of the Europeans.[11] Similarly, the sociological portraits taken by August Sander, while conforming to the aesthetic criteria of the New Photography, and related to the New Objectivity both in their social realism (derived from painting) and in their professionalism, are nevertheless very different from the machinist excitement of a Renger-Patzsch image.

Moholy had a naive confidence in the "imaging" ability of the camera. The photographers of the New Objectivity – and their figurehead, Albert Renger-Patzsch – worked in a different way. They used the medium of photography to seize the "realities" of the world in its reflections. In this, they were looking back to the old nineteenth-century concept of the photographic image. But the photographers of the New Objectivity also adopted, in part, the daring Constructivist ideas of the New Vision, while, at the same time, giving physical expression to the real existence of the thing represented rather than to the individual's experience of looking at the thing. The world of things often appears in their work, therefore, as possessing an extraordinary impersonality. The New Vision attempted to enable man, as a sentient individual, to master the world. The New Objectivity, by contrast, gave rise to the idea that man was dominated by things. Thus, it was possible to talk of the "link with things". "[Photography] in a very particular way links the man of today – with today's special technical means – to things that had threatened to escape him in the incessant whirlwind of movement. In this way it backs up a deeply and naturally metaphysical force in man: perception."[12]

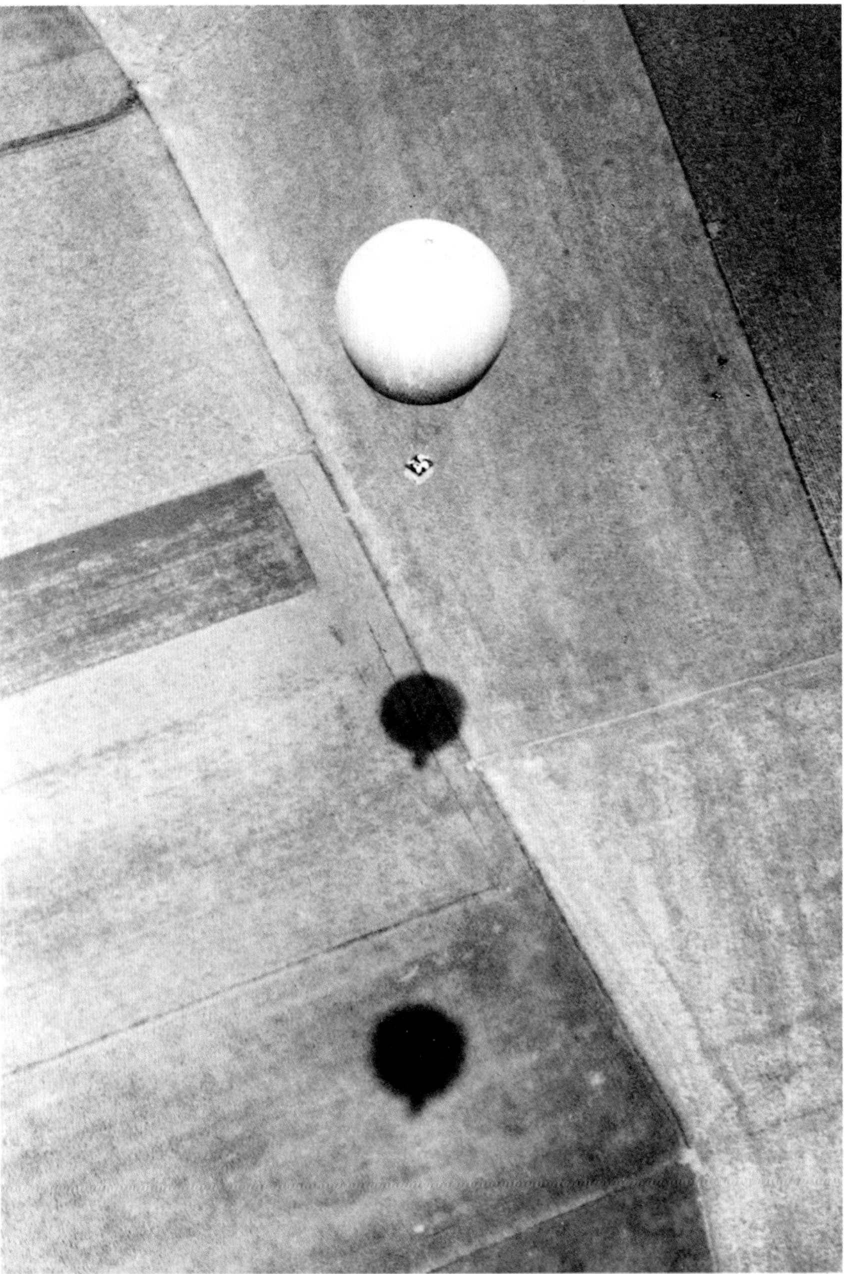

Robert Petschow,
How Many Balloons in the Air?,
1926,
Metropolitan Museum of Art, New York.

Diffusion of a style

In the wake of the publication of *Malerei, Fotografie, Film*, which popularized the principles of the new photography, a movement of photographers, emerging from an artistic background

11. Texts by Renger-Patzsch, Gräff, and Roh, collected in D. Mellor (ed.), *Germany, the New Photography, 1927–1933*, London, Arts Council, 1978.

12. W. Petry, "Bindung an die Dinge", in *Das Kunstblatt*, no. 13, 1929, p. 246.

ANONYMOUS, *International Exhibition, "Das Lichtbild"*, Essen, 1931, Museum Folkwang, Essen.

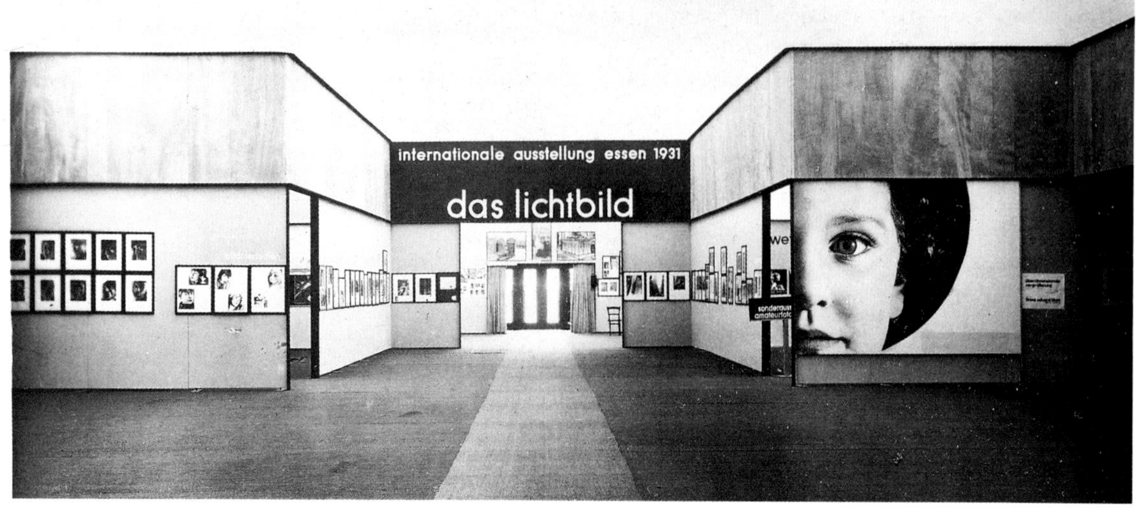

PAUL SCHUITEMA, *Gramophone*, 1929, Municipal Museum, The Hague. ▼

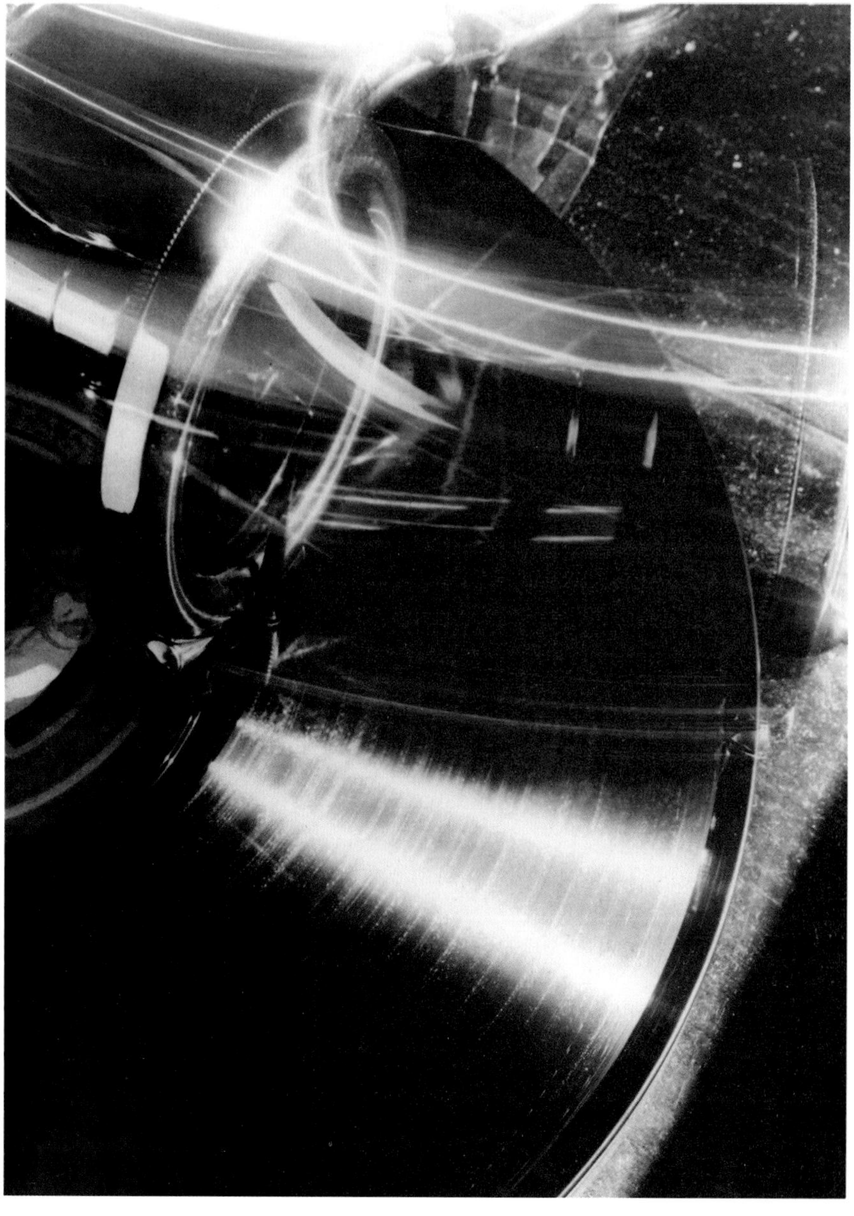

but operating more as amateurs (with techniques and equipment condemned by the professionals), became involved in a trend that was encouraged, year after year, by a large number of exhibitions and publications. They showed their work in exhibitions such as *Pressa* in Cologne and *Neue Wege der Photographie* [New Paths in Photography], mounted in 1928 in Jena, shortly before *Film und Foto*. Their work appeared in Werner Gräff's book *Es kommt der neue Fotograf* [Presenting the New Photographer] of 1929,[13] and in another work following on from FiFo, Franz Roh and Jan Tschichold's *foto-auge / œil et photo / photo-eye*. Gräff also published work ranging from aerial views and press photographs to film stills, photomontages, and phototypography by Umbo, Sasha Stone, Oscar and Alice Nerlinger, Lux and Andreas Feininger, Renger-Patzsch, Herbert Bayer, and Willi Baumeister. *foto-auge*, with its avant-garde typography without capital letters, page layout by the graphic artist Tschichold, cover by Lissitzky of his famous photomontage self-portrait *The Constructor*, and theoretical text by Roh in three languages (German, French, and English), was more an "art book" than an exhibition catalogue.

Roh claimed for supporters of the New Photography the status of "amateur", "dilettante", "outsider", thus escaping from the "conventional mannerism" of the profession. He stated that a good photograph should not be a mere copy of nature but must "depend on principles of organization and individualization". Following Moholy-Nagy, he advocated the use of new viewpoints, new perspectives, mixed-media, photograms, and photomontage. The first photograph reproduced is the window of a corset shop, by Atget. There follow, as examples of diversity, works by Gutschow, Florence Henri, Max Burchartz, Petschow (aerial views), Hans Finsler, Piet Zwart, Peterhans, Man Ray, Max Ernst,

13. *Unter Mitarbeit von Hans Richter*, Berlin, Reckendorf, 1929; reprinted Cologne, König, 1979.

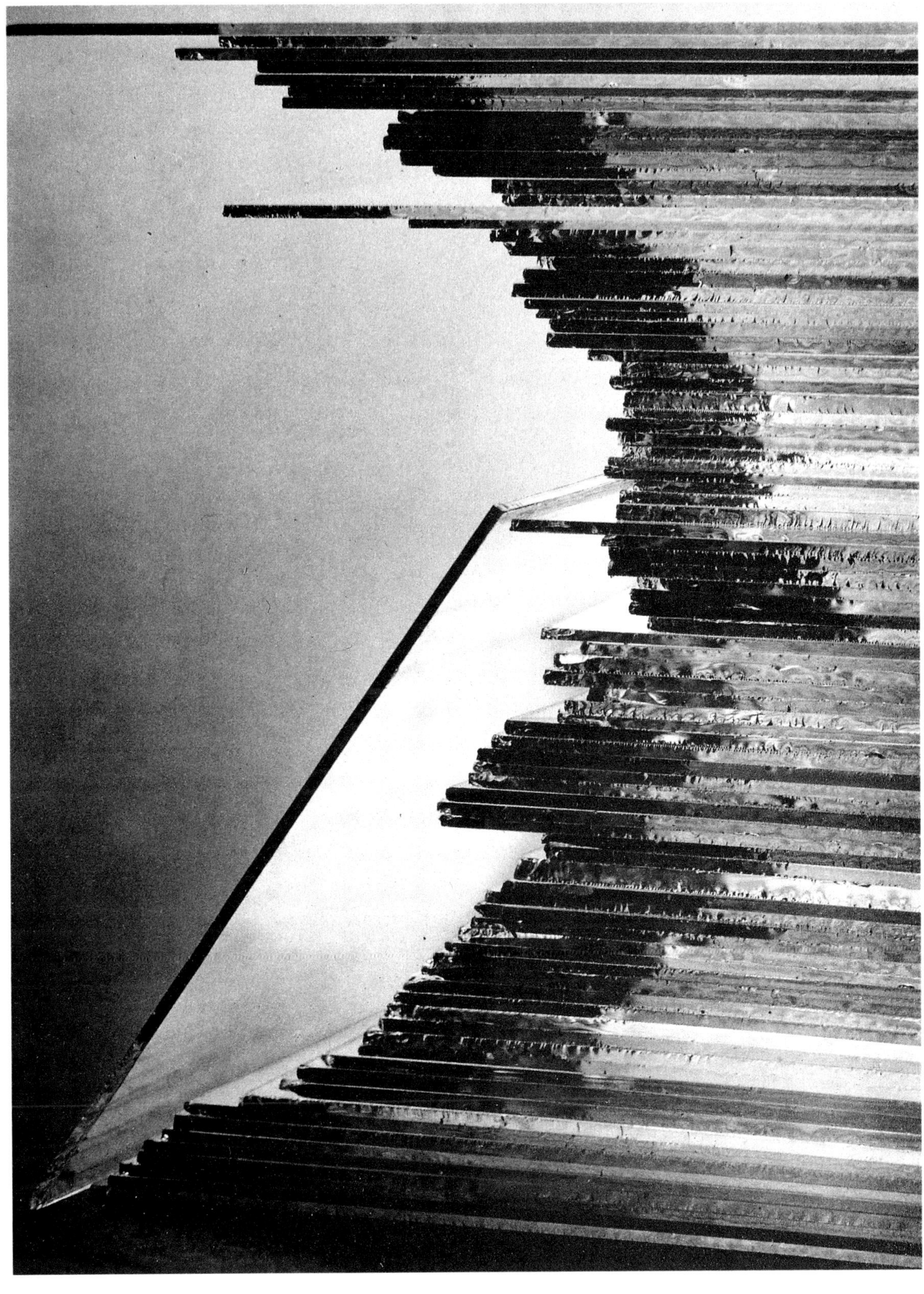

WILLY ZIELKE,
Staking of Glass Plates I,
1929,
Galerie Michèle Chomette,
Paris.

Schuitema, Moholy-Nagy, Tabard, Umbo, Mesens, Dziga Vertov, Höch, and even Edward Weston and his son Brett. The general unity of the modern style was unable, however, to conceal the difference in the aims of these photographs. There were photographs intended for the press advertising, studies in graphics and beautiful formalist images, all unified by the newness of their way of seeing the world, their departure from an earlier norm. At the same time, modernist magazines like *Der Querschnitt* were also reproducing these same photographs.

In fact, the avant-garde nature of these images was not only the result of an "artistic need". It was also a response to a demand for originality and modernity. In 1930, the exhibition "Das Lichtbild", organized by Burchartz in Munich (also shown in Essen, in 1931), introduced other practitioners of the new vision, including Kesting, Hein Gorny, Lotte Jacobi, and August Sander,

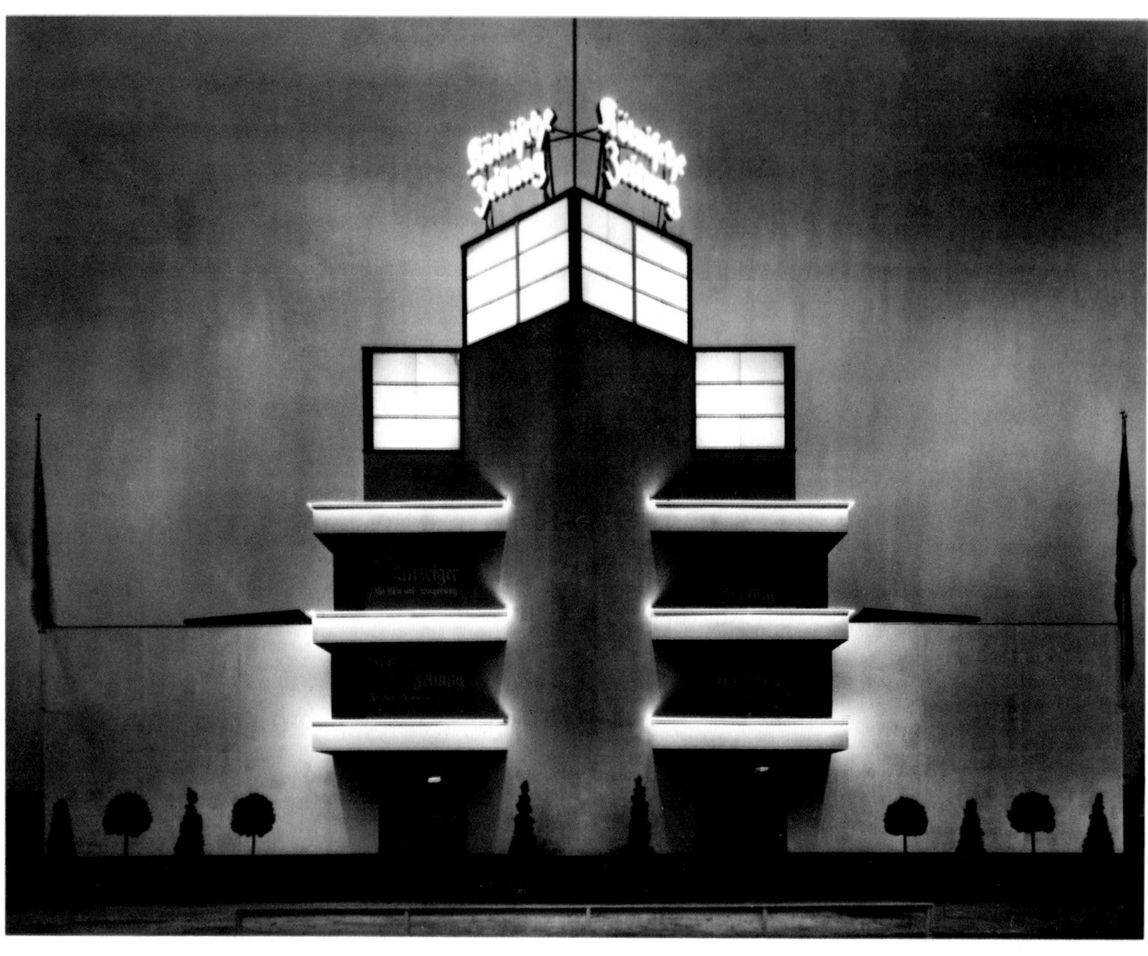

Werner Mantz, ***Kölnische Zeitung Building,*** Cologne, 1928, Museum of Modern Art, San Francisco.

Albert Braun, ***Schlemmer's "Rings Dance",*** 1928–1929, Bauhaus Archive, Berlin.
▼

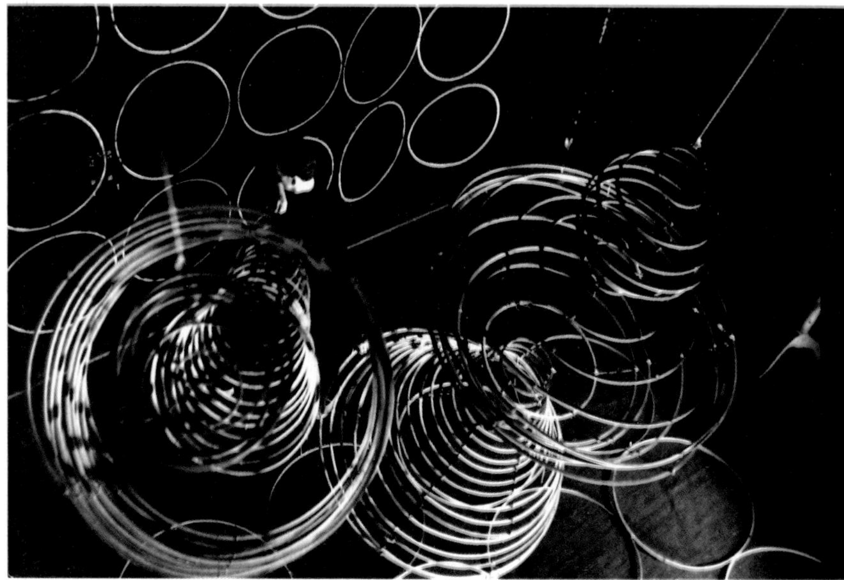

though what affinity he felt with someone like Moholy-Nagy is hard to understand. The claims of modernity were also extended to a variety of categories of "photographers" or "people practicing photography" for a variety of reasons, whose objectives would turn out in the long run to be scarcely compatible. The New Photography can be seen as a collection of stylistic elements, an assemblage of criteria that could be adapted both to the photographer as an individual, and to the aims (commercial, media, artistic) of photography as a whole. Photographers' need to make a living – something that is often referred to in their autobiographies – was a significant motive for a unity of style in a period of economic upheaval, when photographers sought to make a name for themselves, and attempted to establish the use of locations other than the portrait photographer's studio.[14] Each photographer, consciously or unconsciously, tended to specialize: Werner Mantz became one of the greatest photographers of architecture; Lucia Moholy acquired a reputation not only for portraiture but also for photograms and architecture (starting with views of the Bauhaus buildings); Arvid Gutshow took landscapes, adding "magic realism", and publishing *See, Sand, Sonne* in 1930; Heinz Hajek-Halke made montages using multiple negatives, or negative prints, including female nudes. Hajek-Halke had taken up photography in about 1930 and was to be the link with the *Subjektive Fotografie* movement after the Second World War. Willy Zielke became known for his carefully constructed still-lifes and his luminous studies (plants, glass plates), and for the use of New Vision perspective and composition. All that was needed to ensure that such semi-professional work could be continued – often as a sideline to other more lucrative employment – was to have a picture published in a magazine or a retrospective

14. Van Deren Coke, *1919–1939, avant-garde photographique en Allemagne,* Paris, Sers, 1982; K. Steinorth, *Photographen der 20er Jahre,* Munich, Laterna Magica, 1987. See also M. M. Hambourg, and C. Phillips, *The New Vision: Photography between the World Wars: The Ford Motor Collection,* New York, Metropolitan Museum of Art, 1989.

15. *Bauhausfotografie,* Stuttgart, Institut für Auslandsbeziehungen, 1983; *Photography at the Bauhaus, 1919– 1933,* London, Nishen, 1990.

where the personal style of this or that photographer could be clearly identifiable.

In the early years, the spread of the influence of the new aesthetic was assisted by others who worked as teachers (in the schools of applied arts that flourished most notably in Germany). One such teacher was Max Burchartz, who taught at the Folkwang Schule in Essen and who played an important role in the field of graphic art, poster and exhibition design (following Lissitzky). He trained, among others, Anton Stankovsky, who later went to work in Zurich and then Stuttgart. Another teacher was Hans Finsler, first at the Kunstgewerbeschule in Halle, where one of his pupils was Werner Rohde, and then in Zurich where he taught Werner Bischof and Emile Schulthess. Herbert Bayer, close to Moholy-Nagy, was a pupil and then a teacher at the Bauhaus, before becoming one of the most important graphic artists in America.

The Bauhaus, the model for other schools, offering the most complete and most modern training, was obviously particularly effective as a training ground for the New Photography. It should be remembered, however, that photography was not included in the curriculum until the arrival of Walter Peterhans, whose aesthetic was, in any case, rather different from that of Moholy-Nagy (who had just left the Bauhaus). Students practiced photography as "amateurs" – at parties, to record their work, or when preparing preliminary studies for graphic work – but rarely as the final aim of their art.[15] It would be a mistake to see the New Photography as being the same thing as the Bauhaus aesthetic, or to confuse the activities of the teachers (Moholy and Bayer) with the teaching in the school.

In this interwoven network of pedagogical, personal and professional relationships, photography in the inter-war period was able to mediate and act as a channel for communication, at the same time itself evolving under these multiple influences.

The New Photography can be defined and followed in its development through individual careers. Aenne Biermann, the wife of a businessman, is an example of someone who discovered photography through Franz Roh and became an excellent professional photographer, applying modern principles to her portraits, close-ups, architectural studies, still-lifes, montages, geological photographs, etc.[16] Sasha Stone was an industrial designer who, having worked in New York and Paris, opened a studio in Berlin in 1930, taking industrial pictures. He also worked with the director Piscator, and published a beautiful portfolio of nudes (*Femmes*, 20 photogravures, Paris, 1933).[17] Lotte Jacobi, on the other hand, profiting from the teaching of her father, a professional

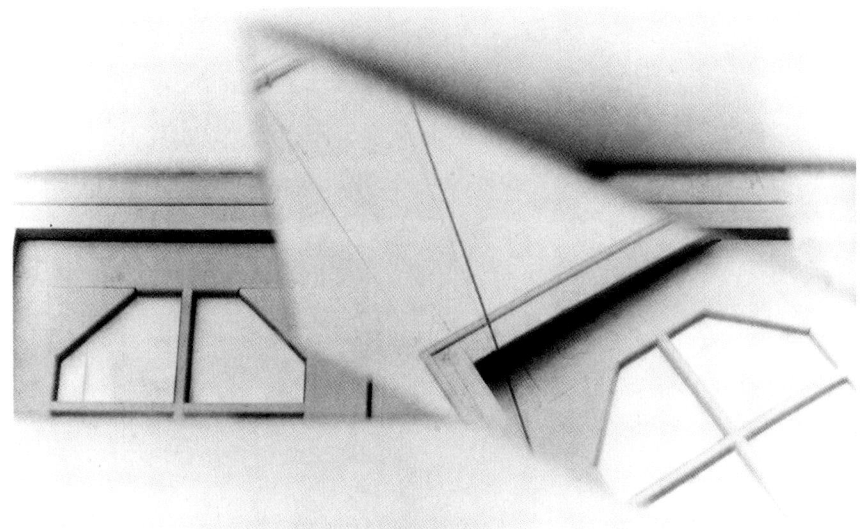

FLORENCE HENRI,
Abstract Composition No. 12,
circa 1929,
International Museum of Photography, George Eastman House, Rochester.

SASHA STONE,
from *Femmes*,
Paris, 1933.

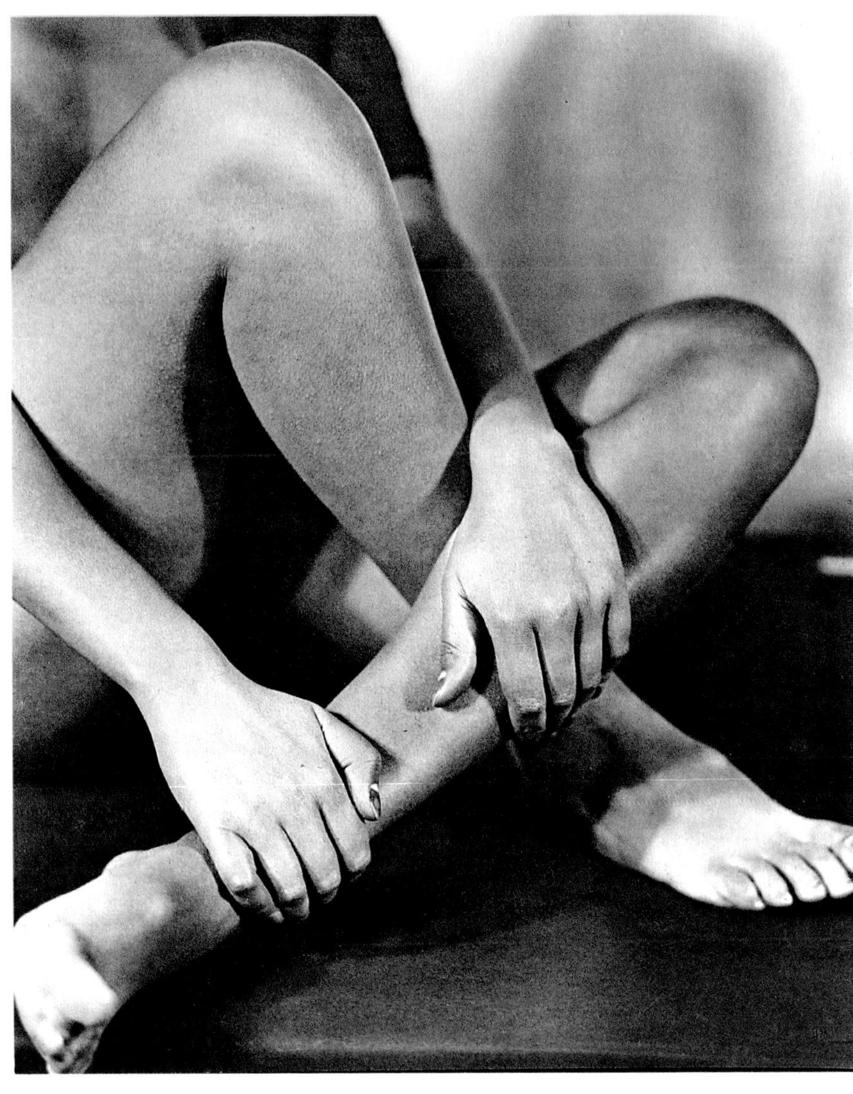

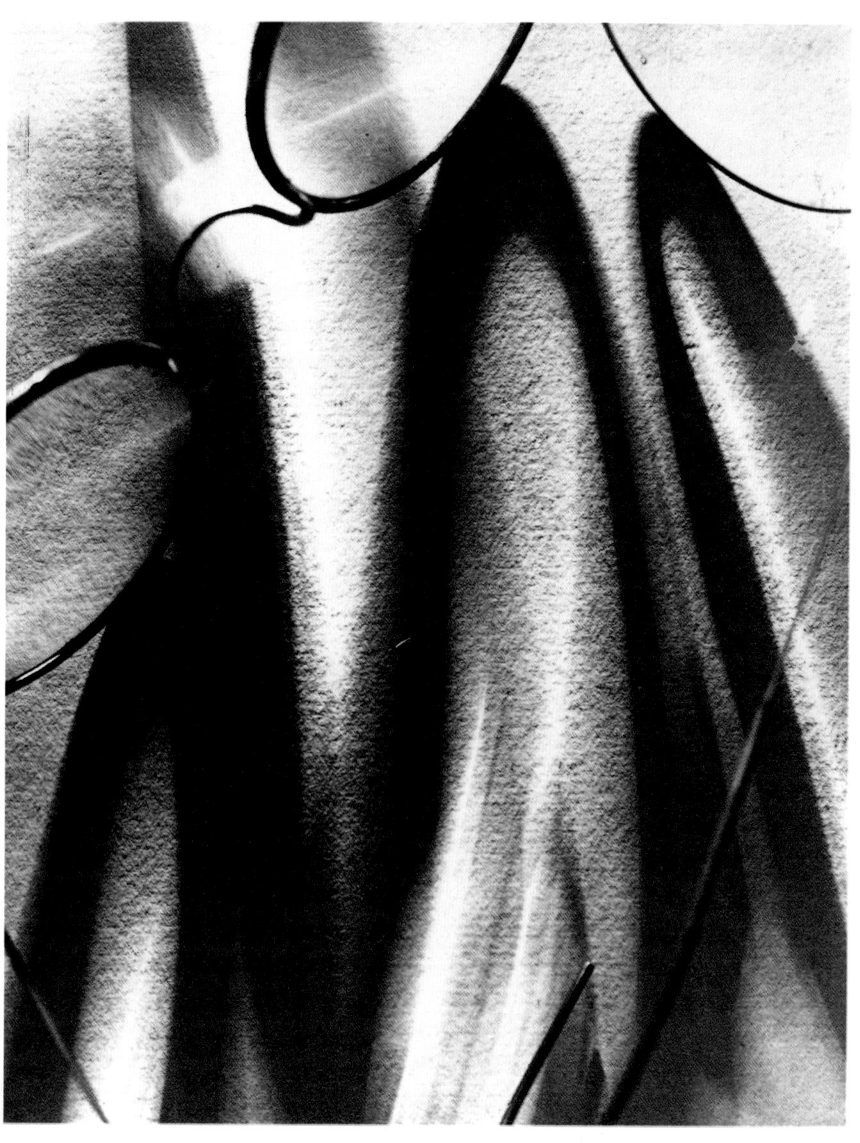

Pierre Dubreuil, *Pair of Spectacles*, circa 1928–1933, Museum voor Fotografie, Antwerp.

photographer, took the logical step of setting up in Berlin in 1927 (and in New York from 1935). She is remembered particularly for her portraits of figures from the art world.[18]

A European style

European followers of German New Photography sometimes produced work that followed closely the German model and, at other times, work tinged with a Mediterranean non-conformism. With Florence Henri the link between the two was more specifically established. Born in New York, and trained as a pianist, she studied in Berlin, and as a painter was close to a variety of avant-garde movements (Dadaism, Futurism, Constructivism, De Stijl, and Léger and Ozenfant's Purism). Living mainly in Paris, she attended the summer school at the Bauhaus, where she got to know Lucia and László Moholy-Nagy, Klee, and Kandinsky. Thus, it was as an artist that she approached photography in 1928, while continuing to paint in a style close to that of the abstract geometric group *Cercle et Carré* (founded in 1929). From 1930, her abstract compositions, using windows and mirrors moved towards advertising images which she was obliged to produce because of financial difficulties caused by the Depression. Like many of her colleagues, she then became interested in the neo-classicism of the 1930s (particularly antique sculpture) and rococo (shells, pearls) before returning to concentrate on painting.[19]

The influence of the New Vision is strikingly apparent if one looks through the pages of the annual volume of *Photographie* published by the magazine *Arts et Métiers graphiques (AMG)* which appeared from 1930[20] – particularly the first issue, coming in the wake of *Film und Foto*. The publisher, Deberny-Peignot, had set up a publicity studio, run, in 1929, by Maurice Tabard with the collaboration of Roger Parry, Émeric Feher, Rémy Duval, and Pierre Boucher. François Kollar, "new photographer" of the Draeger Studio, then became Vigneau's assistant at the Lecram studio.[21] Thus, it was partly in the world of advertising that the New Photography found an echo, in parallel with the world of arts, the review of which, *L'Art vivant*, became its chief supporter by publishing work not only by Man Ray and Germaine Krull, but also by Kertész. More generally, in France this was the publication that offered the best opportunities for photographers and produced a demand for illustrations.

Encouraged by its position as leader in this professional field, *AMG* (1927-1939) actively supported the adherents of the New Photography in its monthly issues, also publicizing recent books such as Roger Parry's *Banalité* (text by Léon-Paul Fargue, Gallimard, 1930), Man Ray's *Electricité* (1931), *Paris* by Moï Ver (J. Walter, 1931), and *Paris de nuit* by Brassaï (Arts et Métiers graphiques, 1933). In *AMG* circles the establishment of a strict style, strongly influenced by the graphic arts of northern Europe (the Netherlands and Germany), was due to the joint activities of Sougez (also in charge of the photographic side of *L'Illustration*), Lucien Vogel, and Carlo Rim (respectively founder and editor of *VU*), Alexei Brodovitch (who worked for the shop *Les Trois Quartiers*) and the graphic artists Maximilien Vox and Henri Jonquières. Nevertheless, despite the success of the new typography, and the influence of photomontage, the New Vision encountered some resistance in France, where Pictorialism and tradition were still alive and well (particularly in the work of Laure Albin-Guillot), and where reportage was creating more direct routes of access to the world, that Sougez described in 1935 as "impressions received no one knows how, when, where, by any old means".

16. *Aenne Biermann: Photographs 1925–1933*, London, Nishen, 1987.

17. *Sasha Stone: Fotografien 1925–1939*, Berlin, Nishen, 1990.

18. K. Wise (ed.), *Lotte Jacobi*, Danbury, Addison House, 1978.

19. D. C. du Pont, *Florence Henri: Artist-Photographer of the Avant-Garde*, San Francisco Museum of Art, 1990.

20. 1931, 1932, 1933–1934, 1935, 1936, 1938, 1939, 1940, and 1947.

21. *25 Photographies de François Kollar*, Paris, 1934.

In his preface to the first volume of *Photographie* (*AMG*, 1930), Waldemar George, under the title *Photography, Vision of the World,* returned to the Moholy-Nagy concept of photography as the "putting into practice of an idea, a conception of the world", "a creative impulse", "modern magic" which "captures the world of appearances" with the photogram, the abstract photograph, the discovery of the object, tactile understanding, close-ups, views from above, rising perspectives, the conquered might of the machine (terms used by W. George), "objects seen as *trompe l'œil,* more exact, more precise, and concrete than real objects, distorted objects, broken by light and by perspective", night photography and negatives ("spectral images of the world"), not forgetting scientific photographs, radiography, and micrography, to which a considerable part of the volume is devoted. While the series of reproductions starts with crystals, algae, sunspots, dispersion spectra, photograms, and macrophotographs, there are also contributions from Biermann, Burchartz, Moholy-Nagy, Stankovsky, Renger-Patzsch, and Munkacsi, as well as the major Paris "new photographers", Germaine Krull, Eli Lotar, Florence Henri, Roger Parry, Maurice Tabard, Sougez, Zuber, Vigneau, and Kertész, alongside Steichen and Sheeler. Waldemar George was careful, however, to place this modern photography within the context of the French photographic tradition which, in an extended section of the text, he traces back to Niépce, Daguerre, Nadar, and, particularly, Atget, who had died in 1927 and whose photographic eye, he says, "reveals a world that is more than real" thanks to a "frank, crude, and direct style".[22]

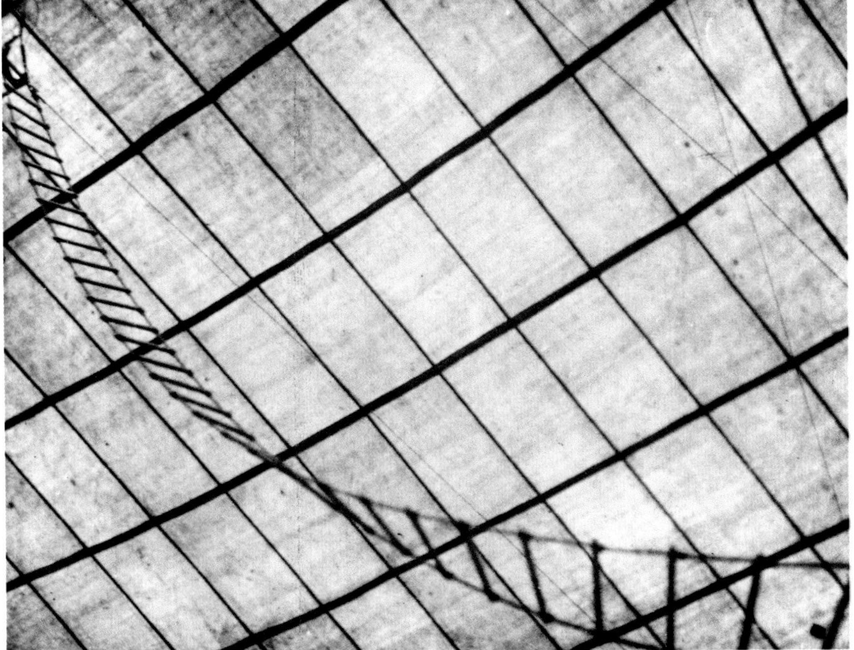

Eli Lotar,
Untitled,
circa 1930,
Art Institute of Chicago.

The impact of the New Photography is probably best represented by Germaine Krull, whose German origins, taste for travel, and cosmopolitan background contributed to her European stature. After studying photography in Munich, she set up a portrait studio for a short time in Berlin (1920) and lived in Holland from 1921–1924 (marrying the movie-maker Joris Ivens), before moving to France in 1924. She provided pictures for many European newspapers and was put in charge of photography for the Free French in 1940. A typical product of the New Vision, she applied its principles in a career as a journalist which allowed her to make a living from her art. In 1927, she published *Métal*, a portfolio devoted to iron architecture (Paris, Calavas), and then *100 x Paris* (Berlin, Verlag der Reihe, 1929), which abounds with bird's-eye views of roads or large stores. As with Moholy, Bayer, and others, one of her favorite themes is the famous transporter bridge in Marseilles, a fruitful source of new and disconcerting viewpoints (*Marseille*, Paris, Plon, 1935).[23]

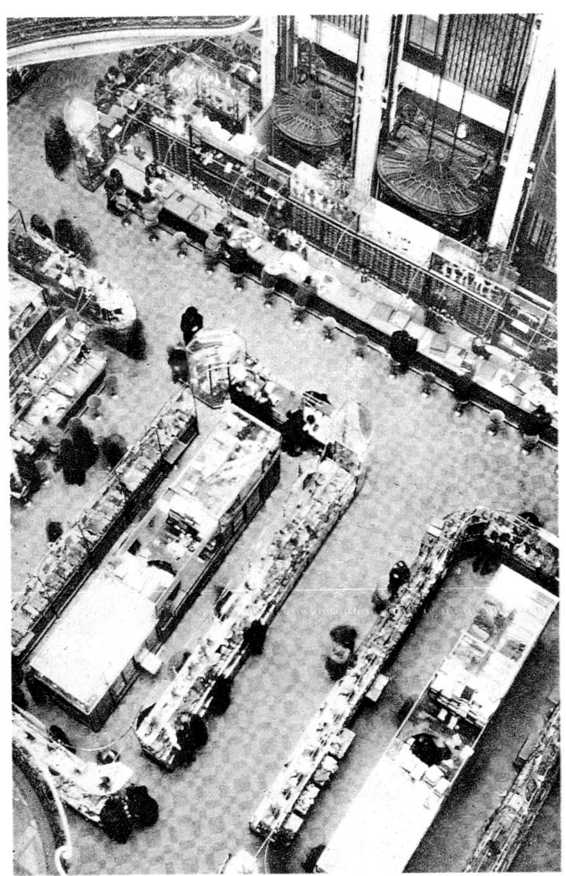

◀ Germaine Krull,
Printemps Department Store,
from *100 x Paris*,
Berlin, 1929.

Ilse Bing is another notable example. Born in Frankfurt in 1899, she taught herself photography in 1928, and emigrated to Paris in 1930.[24] The Eiffel Tower (the fortieth anniversary of which had been celebrated in 1929, particularly in *VU* with views by Kertész, see p. 566), shop signs, night views, the world of work, and the Seine embankments were her subjects. Her work also reveals the inevitable influence of Paris Surrealism.

22. Republished in facsimile, Paris, Arts et Métiers Graphiques, 1980, p.136.

23. *Germaine Krull; photographie 1924–1936,* Arles, Musée Réattu, 1988; *Le pont transbordeur et la vision moderniste,* Musée de Marseille, 1991.

24. *Ilse Bing: Three Decades of Photography,* New Orleans Museum of Art, 1985.

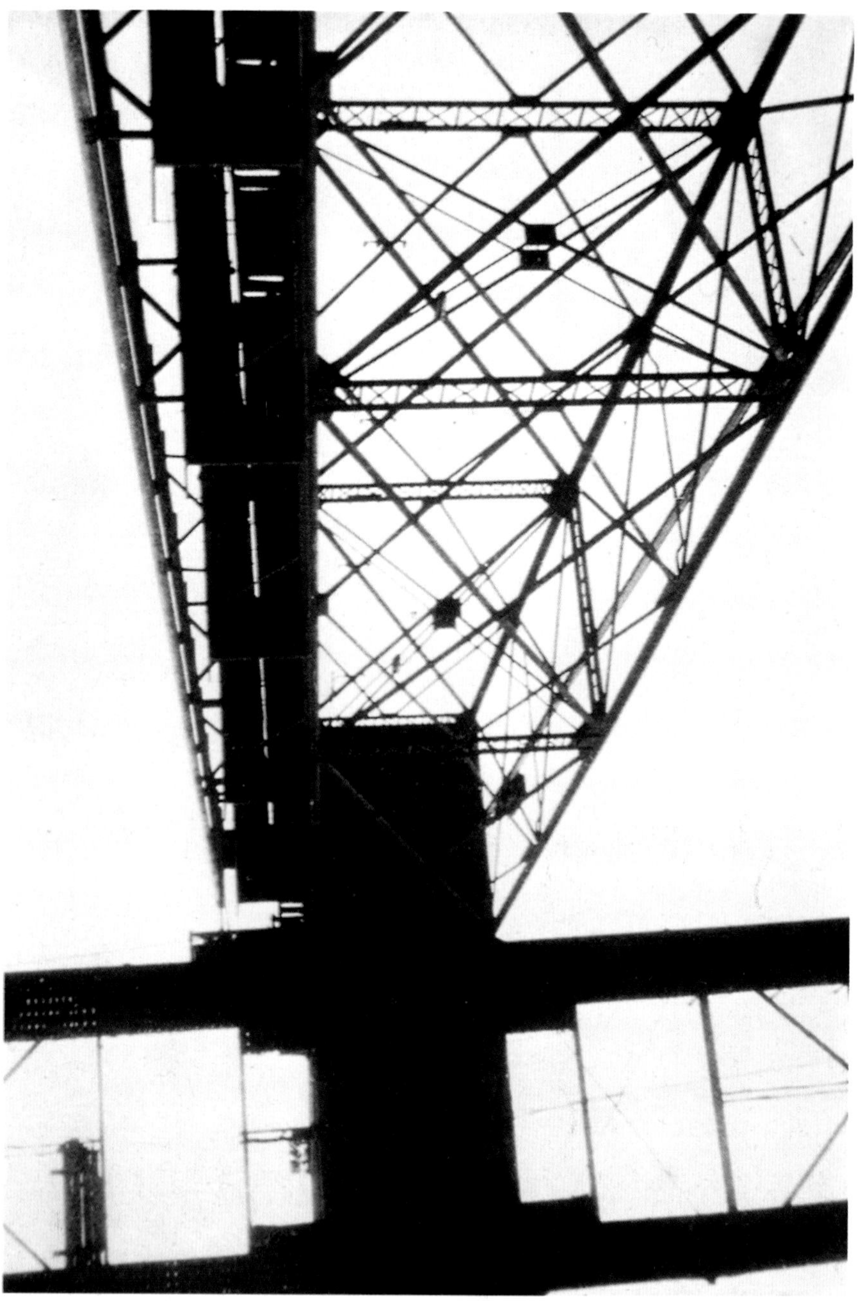

Germaine Krull, ***Rotterdam Suspension Bridge,*** circa 1926, private collection.

Piet Zwart, ▶ ***Floorboards with Wood Shavings,*** 1930, Municipal Museum, The Hague.

The same was true for Eli Lotar, an underrated Hungarian emigré.

The numerous applications to which the New Photography was put in France occurred, for the main part, after the publication of *Photographie* (1930). If photographers such as Kertész or Brassaï kept their distance from this sometimes systematic style of construction-deconstruction, it became very popular among those who had recently arrived in Paris and set up as photographers – Ergy Landau, André Steiner, Nora Dumas, François Kollar, Eli Lotar, Émeric Feher, and Ylla – or among young photographers who were beginning to make a living from press commissions and from advertising: Rémy Duval, Jean Moral, Pierre Boucher, René Zuber, Roger Parry, and Roger Schall.[25] Outside France, the Netherlands were very receptive to the message of the New Vision, which there benefited from an environment that favored its rigor of graphics and architecture. Piet Zwart, close to the De Stijl group, and Mondrian and Van Doesburg, a collaborator of Berlage, and in contact with Lissitzky, had, since 1924, adapted the photogram for use in advertising, working for the Dutch Post Office, radio, various industries, and publishing. Together with Paul Schuitema and Paul Citroën, Zwart is, perhaps, the best representative of the new trends, both in his typographical work and in his photography.

New Photography, whose origins should be sought in media and graphic publications in central and eastern Europe, is thus characterized by its instantly recognizable style. Popularized by specialist publications and exhibitions, from the beginning of the 1930s it could be seen – particularly in the illustrated press – all over Europe (or at least in those countries where the need was felt to give the world a new way of seeing more suited to the innovations being made in science and technology).

25. C. Bouqueret, *La Nouvelle Photographie en France, 1919–1939*, Musée de Poitiers, 1986.

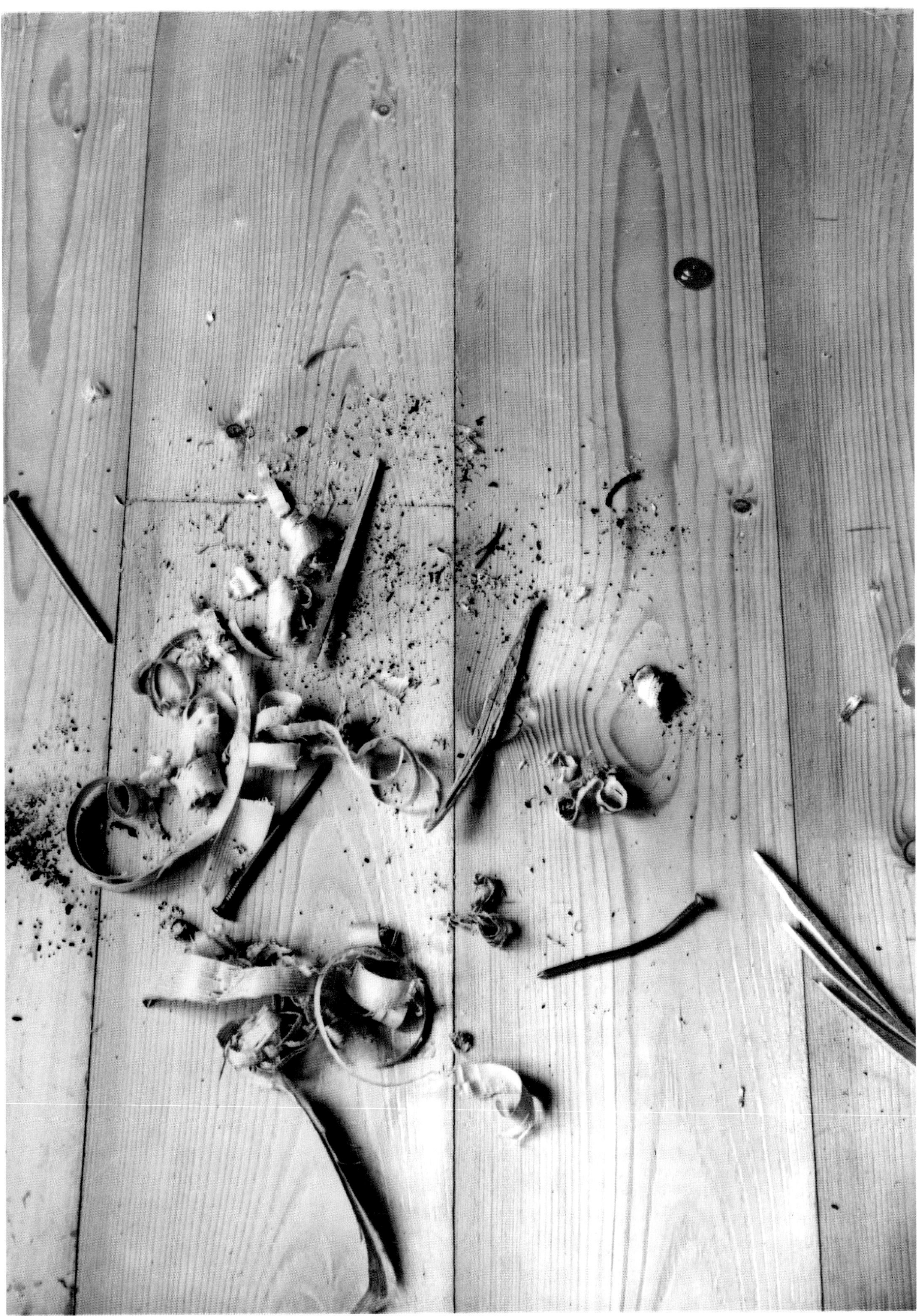

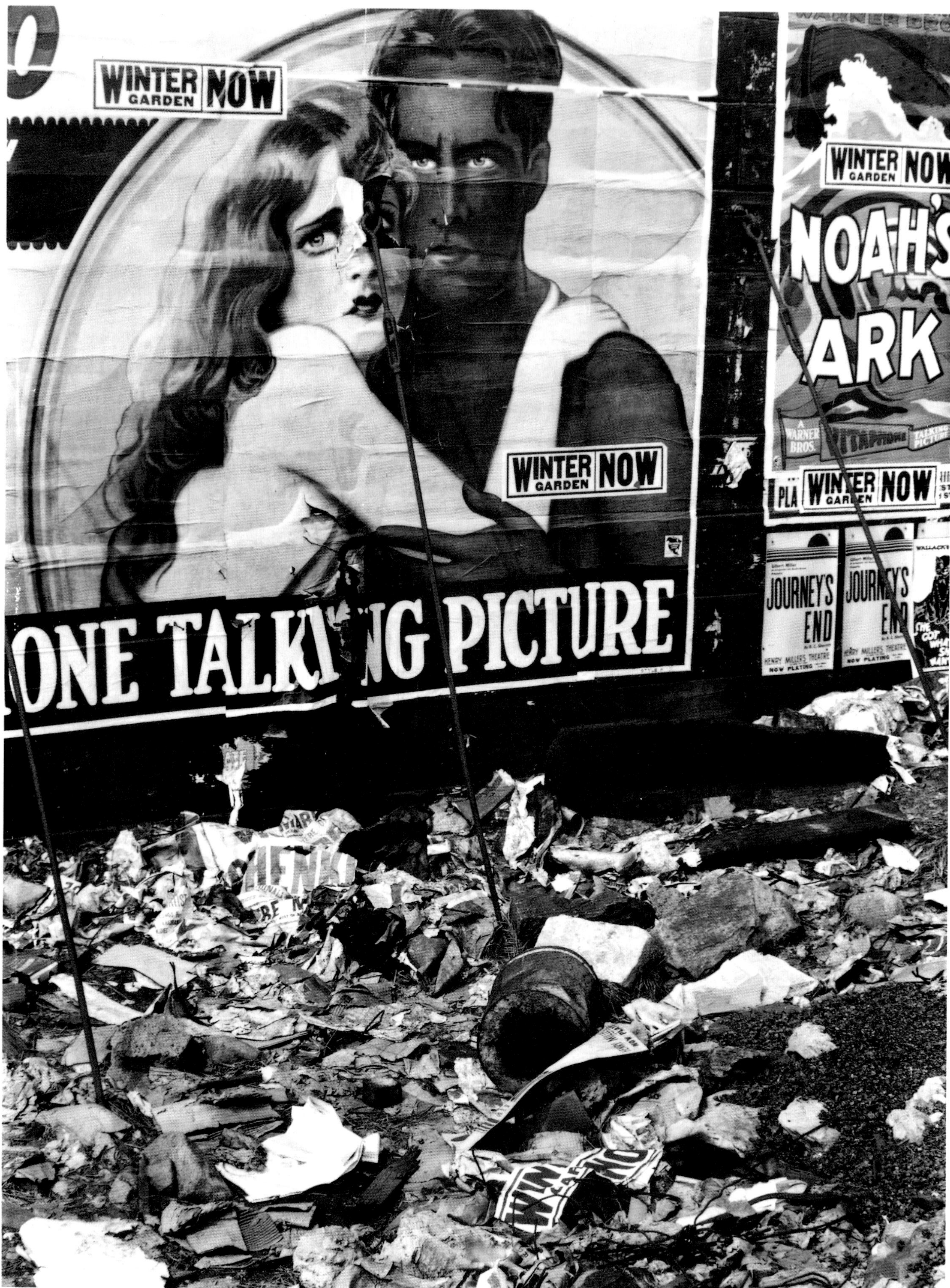

WINTER GARDEN NOW
WINTER GARDEN NOW
ONE TALKING PICTURE
WINTER GARDEN NOW
NOAH'S ARK
A WARNER BROS.
WINTER GARDEN NOW
JOURNEY'S END
HENRY MILLER'S THEATRE
NOW PLAYING
JOURNEY'S END

AUSTERITY AND CLARITY

28

New photography in the United States, 1920–1940

John Pultz

The First World War did not form a decisive cut-off point for American photography, which was emerging from Pictorialism and recovering its specifically photographic qualities (sharpness, precision, framing) with the advantages of the instantaneous photograph and less bulky cameras. Furthermore, the professional engagements demanded by imperatives of publicity and the country's emerging industrial power, together with individual aspirations towards a certain spiritual quality in the image and the social usage of photography in the media – coupled with changes in viewers' perceptions – introduced new norms which found in "pure photography" a response to those ideals of clarity, objectivity, and realism which were also emerging in post-war Europe.

Between 1920 and 1940, artistic photography in the United States saw the emergence of a radically new aesthetic. In direct opposition to Pictorialism, this new, "straight" aesthetic accepted and celebrated photographic qualities previously considered appropriate only for utilitarian images. But despite attempts to describe the emergence of straight photography as an autogenous process by which photographers abandoned Pictorialism's artiness to reveal their medium's "essential" qualities, the truth is otherwise. The straight photographic aesthetic derived its validity and power from the emerging modernist aesthetic, which esteemed the documentary, the mechanical, and the technological, as well as the highly formal. Straight photographs emphatically disclose their mechanical origins; formed as segments cut from the visual field, they are printed without manipulation from sharply focused negatives, often on glossy paper in order best to exploit the full range of photographic tones, from the richest blacks to the brightest whites. Furthermore, they have in common subjects taken from everyday modern life, especially the means and products of modern industrial life, including factories, machines, skyscrapers, automobiles, and mass-market consumer goods.

The Pictorialist aesthetic that defined artistic photography between 1895 and 1910 had held that photography was a fine art only to the extent that a creator's intentions could defy the medium's seemingly intractable mechanical realism and transform a subject from the realm of the ordinary and contemporary to an idealized one, be it historical, symbolic or mythological. Even though this Pictorialist stance had won artistic acceptance for American photography by 1910, the victory was short-lived. Exposure to European modern art ranging from Cézanne to Picasso, gained first through travel abroad and then from exhibitions at Alfred Stieglitz's 291 gallery, forced advanced American photographers to realize that the art styles on which pictorialism was grounded were academic and hopelessly out-of-date.[1]

Photographic realism

Based on the American understanding of contemporary European art, especially analytical Cubism's philosophical search for knowledge, there emerged a new definition of the aesthetic potential of photography's realism, stated most clearly by the Mexican artist Marius de Zayas, a close friend of Stieglitz and director of the Modern Gallery in New York. In *Camera Work* in 1913, de Zayas argued that photography was not expressive but truthful.[2] In a second essay that year, he further distinguished between artistic photography and pure photography.[3] According to de Zayas, artistic photography, represented by the Pictorialist work of Edward Steichen, sought

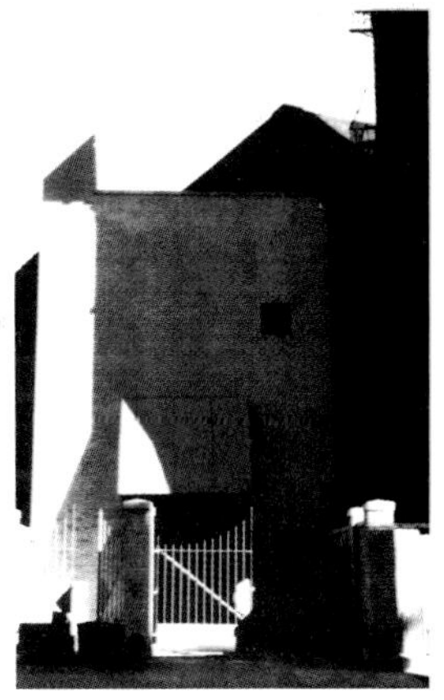

WALKER EVANS, ***Untitled,*** 1928–1929, Museum of Modern Art, New York.

◄ RALPH STEINER, ***1925 Movies,*** circa 1930, Museum of Modern Art, New York.

1. See J. Pultz and C. B. Scallen, *Cubism and American Photography, 1910-1930*, Sterling and Francine Clark Art Institute, Williamstown, Massachusetts, 1981, and J. Pultz, "L'interprétation américaine du cubisme", *Photographies*, no. 7, May 1985, pp. 18–20.

2. M. de Zayas, "Photography," *Camera Work*, no. 41, January 1913, p. 17.

3. M. de Zayas, "Photography and Artistic-Photography", *Camera Work*, no. 42-43, April-July 1913, pp. 13–14.

PAUL OUTERBRIDGE, *Marmon Crankshaft,* 1923, Metropolitan Museum of Art, New York.

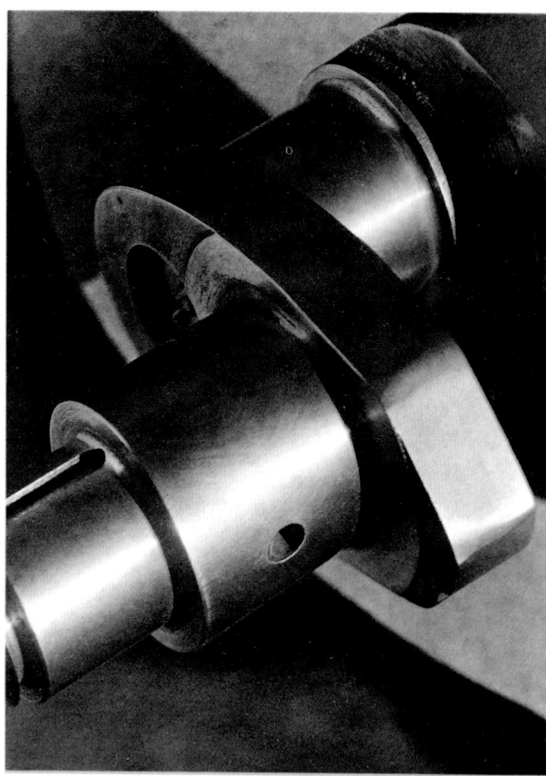

PAUL STRAND, *Wire Wheel,* 1917, Museum of Art, Philadelphia.
▼

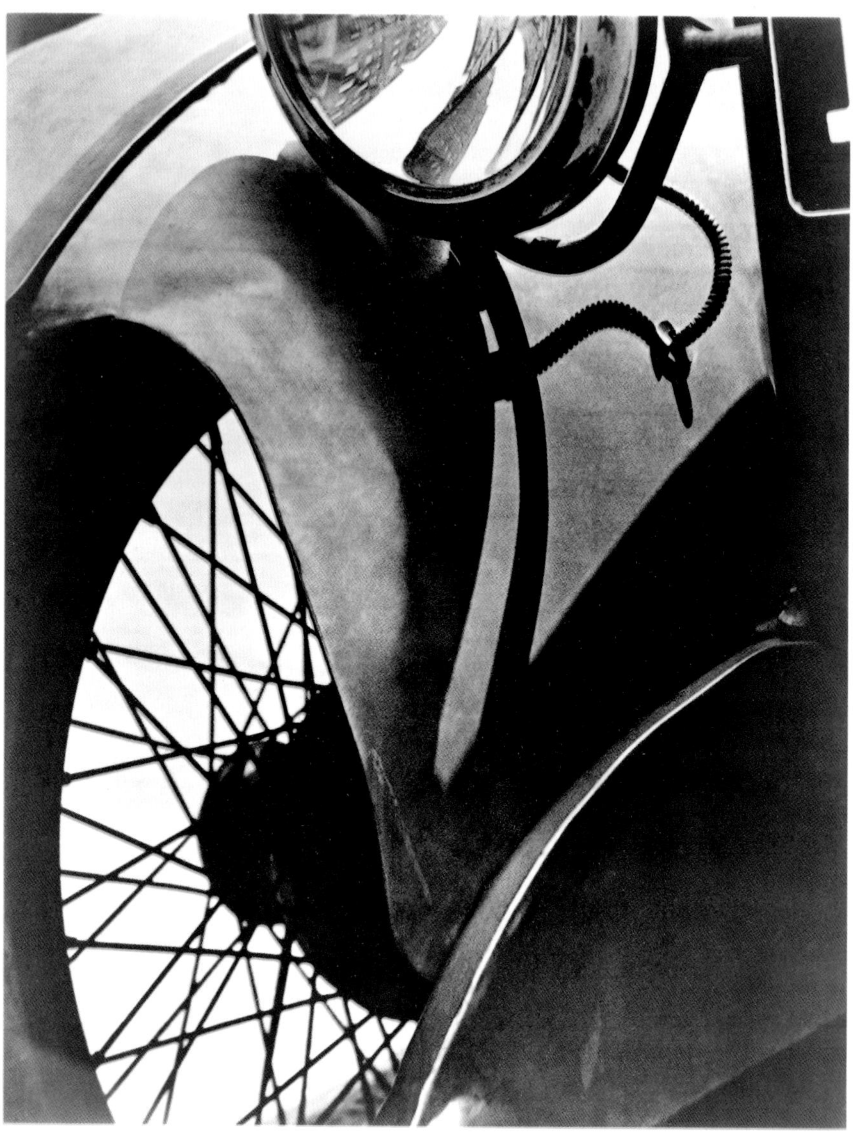

4. On the connection of Stieglitz, Strand and other American photographers to these efforts, see S. Greenough, "An American Vision", in *Paul Strand: An American Vision,* National Gallery of Art, Washington, 1990.

to give pleasure and convey emotion; pure photography, as practised by Stieglitz, eliminated both the subject and representational system and instead used "free and impersonal research" to arrive at the "comprehension of the object". Photography's power to record faithfully the everyday and the ordinary was given further meaning by the proto-Dadaist activity of Marcel Duchamp and Francis Picabia in New York during 1915 and by contemporary European art's attention to the local, the vernacular, and the primitive, which also sparked concurrent attempts to develop a uniquely American artistic culture.[4]

Influenced by de Zayas, Stieglitz by 1915 no longer cared whether photography was art or not; instead he valued it as a means to externalize truth through the close examination of surfaces and the meanings behind them. In photographs he made that year of New York buildings seen from the rear window of 291, Stieglitz used rigorous geometry and radical cropping in an effort to eliminate the kind of expressiveness found in his romantic city views of 1910, which extolled New York's vitality. Despite Stieglitz's advocacy of pure photography, in his own work he achieved pristine objectivity only in the early 1930s, photographing New York's changing skyline with rigorous attention to the interplay of buildings' shadows and forms.

Stieglitz did develop an ever more sober directness in the portraits he made between 1915 and 1923, most notably those of Georgia O'Keeffe, but the breakthrough to pure photography emerged from the Cubist experimentation undertaken between 1914 and 1917 by three younger photographers: Paul Strand, Charles Sheeler, and Morton Schamberg. Of the three, Strand most closely achieved the purity Stieglitz (and de Zayas) sought. Working in Connecticut during the summer of 1916, Strand made close-up still-lifes of cups and saucers and near-abstractions from shadows of porch balustrades. Through tight cropping and, in one case, actual reorientation of the photograph by ninety degrees, Strand flattened pictorial space and defamiliarized subjects to create intensely seen presentations of pure form. Similarly, in 1917, Sheeler used lessons learned from Cubism to recreate, in a series of rigorously objective photographs, the austere simplicity of his Shaker country house, which he valued for its vernacular primitivism. Schamberg, a close friend of Sheeler's who was to face an early death in 1919, adapted in a few, now rare, urban views of 1916 the abstract machine-style of his paintings to present the city as if it too were a machine constituted of interlocking parts.

These initial experiments led in a variety of directions. Strand applied the abstraction and

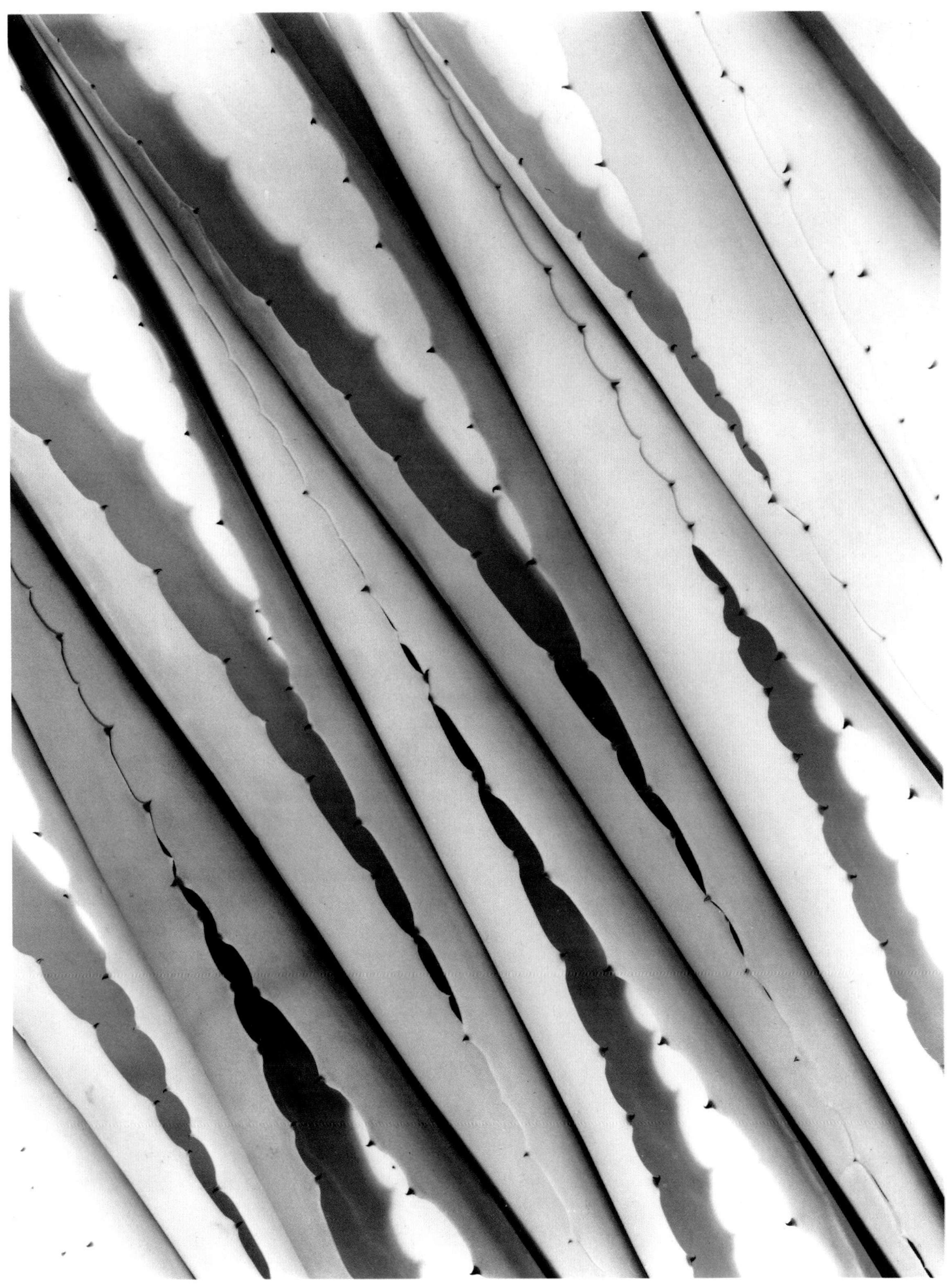

IMOGEN CUNNINGHAM,
Agave Design 2,
circa 1920, Berkeley.

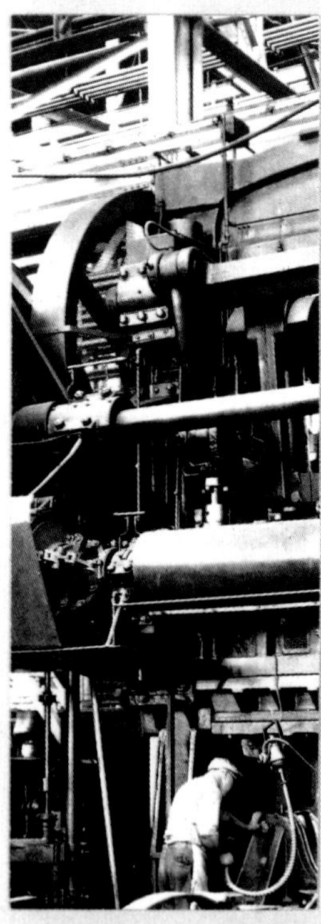
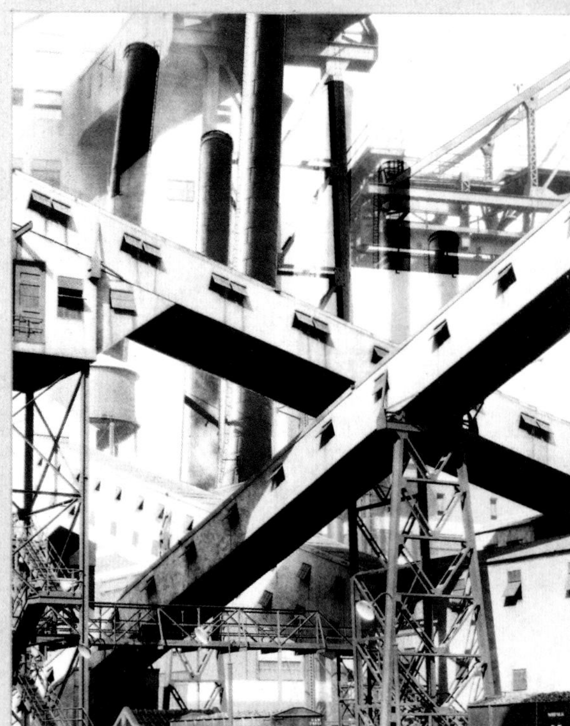
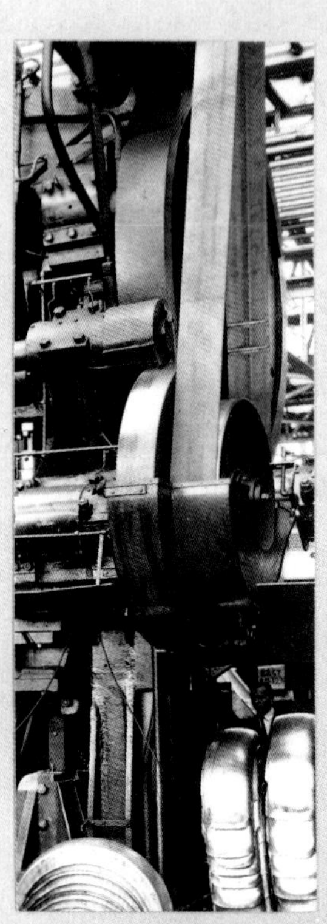

CHARLES SHEELER, *Industry*, triptych, 1932, Art Institute of Chicago.

flatness of his Connecticut work to more varied subject matter. In the fall of 1916, he made a series of portraits of anonymous people on the street which are strikingly direct, at once formally powerful and richly descriptive. In his *Wheel Organization* of the following year, close cropping accentuates the brute force and repetitive forms of the still novel modern automobile. With this photograph, the connection that the new photography was to have with America's Machine Age faith in machines and corporate power to bring a better life was made manifest.[5] As one machine documented another with mechanical reliability, the seemingly automatic nature of the medium no longer impeached a photograph's value but, to the contrary, ensured its absolute truthfulness.

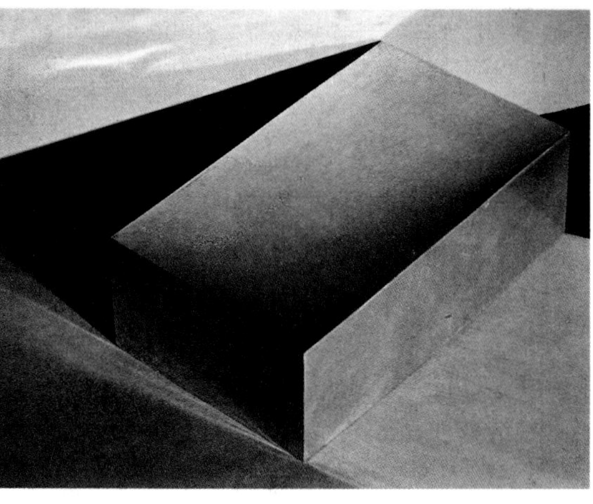

PAUL OUTERBRIDGE, *Saltine Box*, 1922, Museum of Art, Laguna Bridge.

In 1920, Sheeler and Strand collaborated on the six-and-a-half-minute documentary film *Manhattan*, which was composed of a series of still shots showing the skyscrapers and ferries of lower Manhattan's financial district and was captioned with lines from Walt Whitman's poetry. The film's detached view of the city's architecture became the basis for subsequent photographs both men made of New York buildings. As in their work of 1910s, Sheeler's photographs such as *New York, Temple Court* of 1920 present broader and more recognizable forms, while Strand's pictures, such as *The Court* of 1924, are abstractly expressive tight arrangements.

Professional realities

Several events of 1923 affected the direction of the new photography. Abandoning the objectivity of pure photography, Stieglitz began that year to photograph clouds as abstract symbols, "equivalents", of his inner feelings. In contrast to his previous position, which opposed expressive art to truthful photography, Stieglitz now sought to achieve in photography the kind of self-expression that post-war cultural nationalists saw as crucial to the emergence of a collective American soul.[6] Also in 1923, Sheeler split with the Stieglitz circle, leaving Strand to pursue pure photography alone. Sheeler came to align himself with Edward

5. R. G. Wilson, D. H. Pilgrim and D. Tashjian, *The Machine Age in America, 1918–1941* New York, Abrams, 1986.

6. See S. Greenough, "Les nuages d'Alfred Stieglitz, forme et sentiments", *Photographies*, no. 7, May 1985, pp. 37–39.

7. T. E. Stebbins and N. Keyes, *Charles Sheeler: The Photographs*, Boston, Little, Brown and Company, 1987.

8. Ibid., p. 27.

Steichen and Clarence White, photographers who were less rigidly aesthetic than Stieglitz and whose broad tolerance for a commercial as well as artistic use of modern photography suited Sheeler's parallel career as a commercially successful photographer of architecture and fine art.

Beginning work in 1923 for a New York advertising agency and for Condé Nast, the publishers of *Vanity Fair* and *Vogue*, Steichen abandoned Pictorialism for a style that fused the appreciation of sharp-focused detail that he had gained as an aerial reconnaissance photographer during the First World War with the chic angularity of Art Deco. Steichen's move into advertising and magazine photography marked a shift in the position of straight photography. No longer a purely aesthetic style, the new photography proved a perfect means to promote consumer products. Unlike Pictorialist views, whose narrow tonal range reproduced poorly, the fullness of photographic tones encouraged by the new aesthetic made pictures that reproduced well, with clearly defined highlights and shadows and clean lines at the interstices of light and dark. Likewise, close-up views were not only stylish but clearly presented the product.

Sheeler, too, expanded his commercial work, joining a Philadelphia advertising agency in 1924 and taking assignments under Steichen at Condé Nast between 1926 and 1929. Sheeler's most striking commercial work publicized the 1927 debut of the Ford Model A, illustrating the car's manufacturing plant at River Rouge rather than the car itself.[7] Beneath the objective presentation of the plant's sheer might, Sheeler evoked the enormous financial resources and complex organizational power that made the plant a monument to the expansionist capitalism of the 1920s. In 1929, Sheeler, who believed that "our factories are our substitute for religious expression",[8] made a series of photographs of Chartres Cathedral in which he avoided the picturesque by focusing on the powerful form of the building's underlying structure. That the River Rouge and Chartres series are less abstract and more grounded in locale than the Doylestown and New York photographs is due to the influence the American objectivist poet William Carlos Williams had over Sheeler beginning around 1923; Williams called for American artists to abandon the machine aesthetic, which he saw as too tied to materialistic values, and to replace the abstraction of reality with a realism based in a closely observed sense of place.[9]

Before the arrival of Steichen and Sheeler, American advertising photography had already been modernized by students from the Clarence H. White School of Photography. In opposition

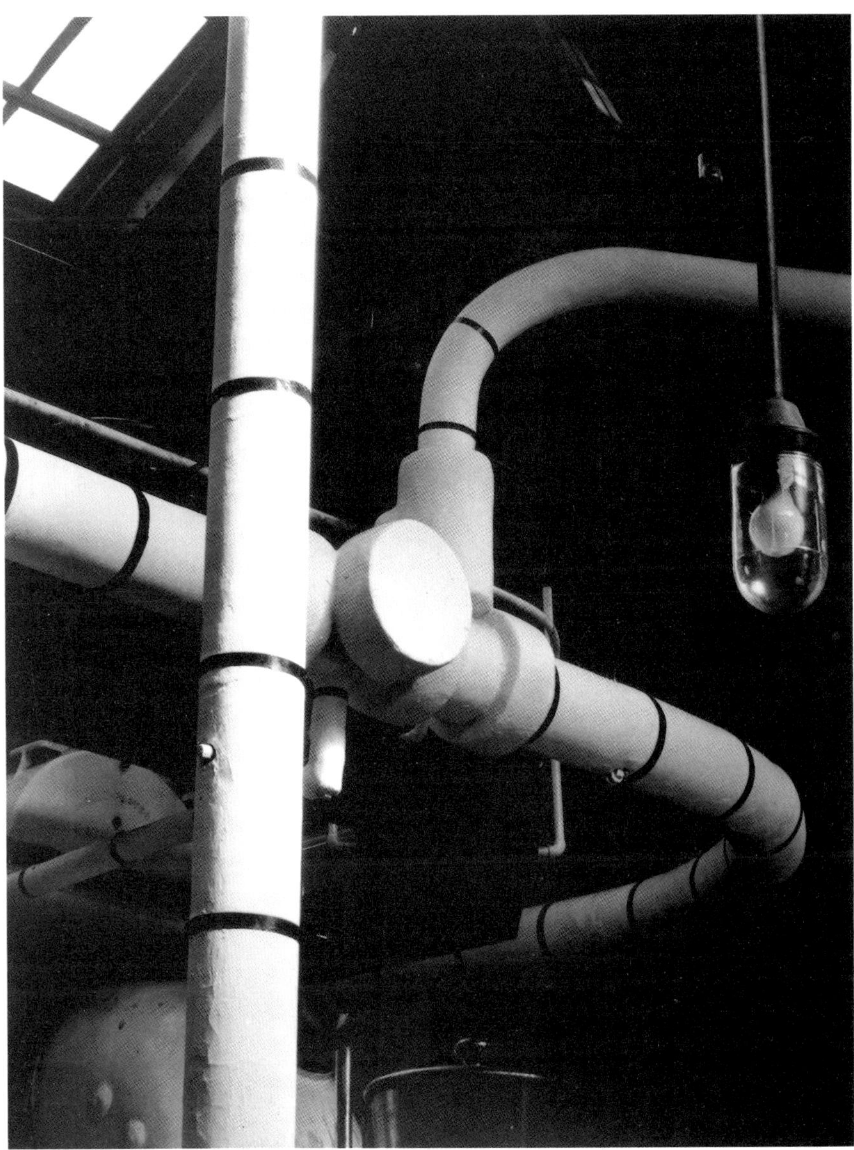

Anton Bruehl,
Gasworks,
Stamford, 1927,
Center for Creative Photography, Tucson.

to Stieglitz's elitist pursuit of pure objectivity, White's school advocated a decorative straight approach predicated on the teachings of Arthur Wesley Dow.[10] Dow's teachings, presented in his book *Compositions* (1899), offered White's students not only the aesthetic basic of a graphically bold style, but also the justification for applying the style to advertising. In the tradition of the reformist Arts and Crafts movement in Britain, Dow saw no insurmountable barrier between fine and commercial art and sought instead to reinvigorate the latter through the aesthetic he proffered.

White's early students kept the soft Pictorialism of their teacher even as they turned to potentially modern subjects.[11] Karl Struss's pictures from 1910 to 1913 of lower Manhattan skyscrapers and waterfront are softly atmospheric platinum prints, but their flat space, high vantage points, and industrial content, like the contemporary New York photographs of Alvin Langdon Coburn, point to the later city pictures by Strand and Sheeler. Similarly combining in platinum prints the indefinite space of earlier

9. See R. Stewart, "Charles Sheeler, William Carlos Williams, and Precisionism: A Redefinition", in *Arts Magazine*, no. 58 November1983, pp. 100–114. Arguing that "Precisionism" properly refers only to the work of Sheeler and a few other artists after they came under Williams's influence, Stewart takes issue with the broad application of the term by Karen Tsujimoto, in *Images of America: Precisionist Painting and Modern Photography* (Seattle, University of Washington Press, 1982), to include most of the photography discussed in this present essay.

10. B. Yochelson, "Clarence H. White Reconsidered: An Alternative to the Modernist Aesthetic of Straight Photography", in *Studies in Visual Communication*, no. 9, Fall 1983, pp. 24–44.

11. See *A Collective Vision: Clarence H. White and His Students*, University Art Museum, California State University, Long Beach, 1986, as well as Chapter 4 ("Cubism and Pictorialism in the Twenties: The Clarence H. White School and Commercial Photography"), in Pultz and Scallen, *Cubism and American Photography*.

Margaret Bourke-White, *Detail of a La Salle*, circa 1933.
▼

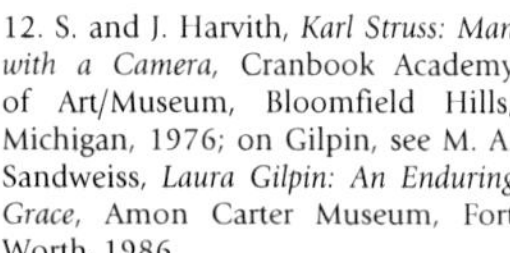

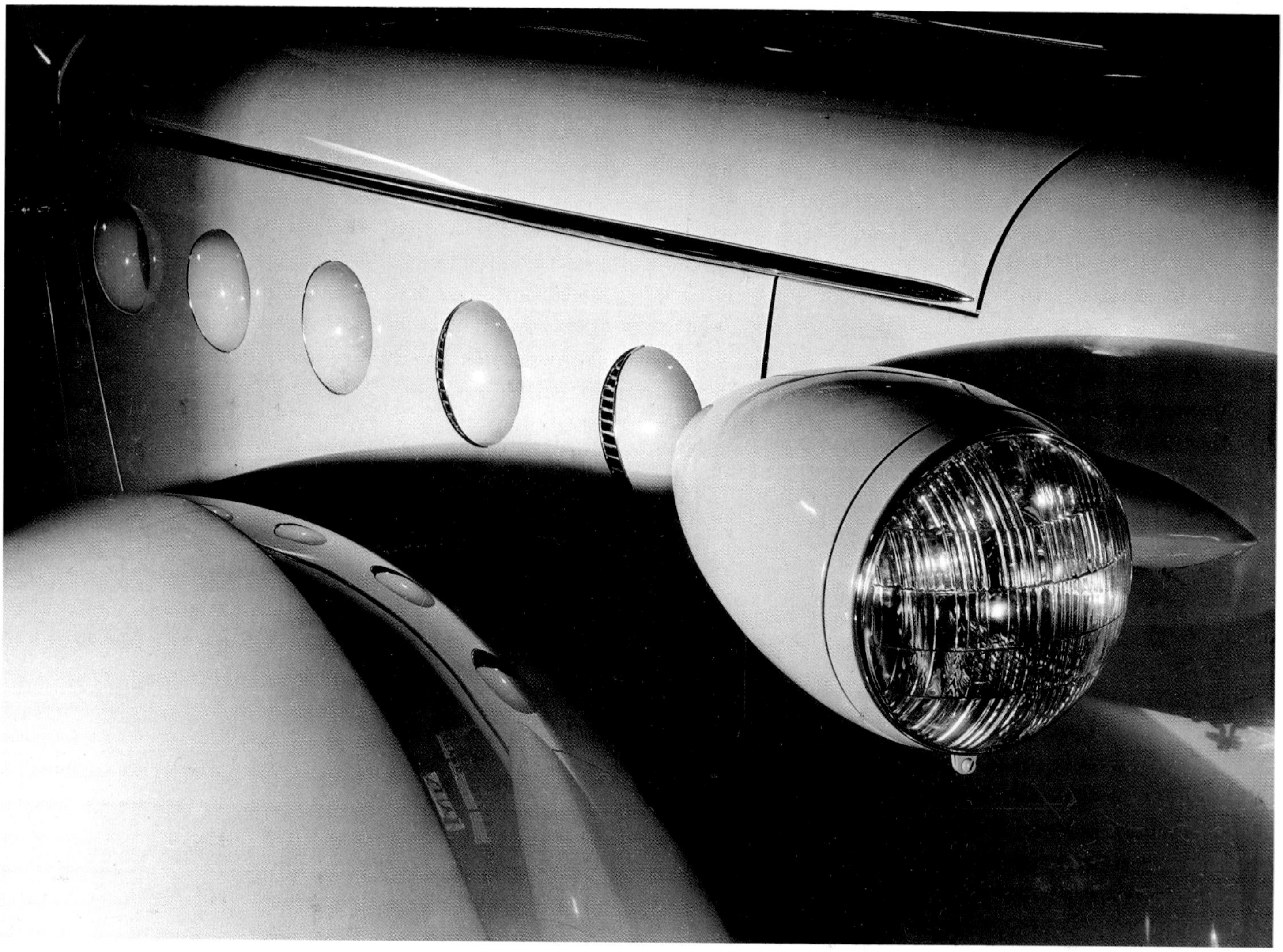

Pictorialism with bold geometric forms, Laura Gilpin documented the lives and habitats of native Americans in the American West.[12] Ira Martin made photographs that, like San Francisco Pictorialist Francis Bruguière's *Light Abstractions* of the late 1920s, were Cubist-derived abstractions of light and shadow which were presented in muted gray tones.

White's students who achieved the greatest success in the realm of commercial photography were Paul Outerbridge, Anton Bruehl, Margaret Bourke-White, and Ralph Steiner.[13] Outerbridge and Bruehl, who studied at the school in the early 1920s, quickly grasped the commercial value of Cubist form and graphic clarity. While Outerbridge's 1922 advertisement for Ide shirt collars boldly contrasts a sweeping curve and checkerboard grid, his *Saltine Box*, also of 1922, reveals even more complex spatial contradictions, creating a convincingly straight picture of a seemingly impossible situation. Bruehl followed Outerbridge into advertising and magazine photography, making in the first half of the 1920s bold black and white photographs, many of which were based on the modern industrial landscape. Bourke-White, who took only one course with White, translated what she learned into pictures that, like Sheeler's River Rouge work, served to show the power of reigning American industrialism. Working first for *Fortune*, and then its sister publication *Life*, she made icons of the industrial age, like *Niagara Falls Generators* of 1928, which shows sleekly silent electrical dynamos, and *Fort Peck Dam, Montana*, which graced the cover of *Life*'s first issue, on November 23, 1936. During the 1920s, Steiner worked in public relations, photographing eye-catching formal arrangements that he found or made, before turning away from the school's design emphasis, which he later called "a strait-jacket".

Social documentary

Not all photographers joined the burgeoning advertising and magazine industries. Like other American artists and writers who were alienated from their native land by the ascendancy during the 1920s of materialistic commercial values, some photographers fled to Europe, especially France, where they found greater intellectual and

12. S. and J. Harvith, *Karl Struss: Man with a Camera*, Cranbook Academy of Art/Museum, Bloomfield Hills, Michigan, 1976; on Gilpin, see M. A. Sandweiss, *Laura Gilpin: An Enduring Grace*, Amon Carter Museum, Fort Worth, 1986.

13. F. Dines, *Paul Outerbridge: A Singular Aesthetic*, Laguna Beach Museum of Art, Laguna Beach, California, 1981; on Bourke-White, see V. Goldberg, *Margaret Bourke-White: A Biography*, New York, Harper and Row, 1986; on Steiner, see R. Steiner, *A Point of View*, Middletown, Connecticut, Wesleyan University Press, 1978.

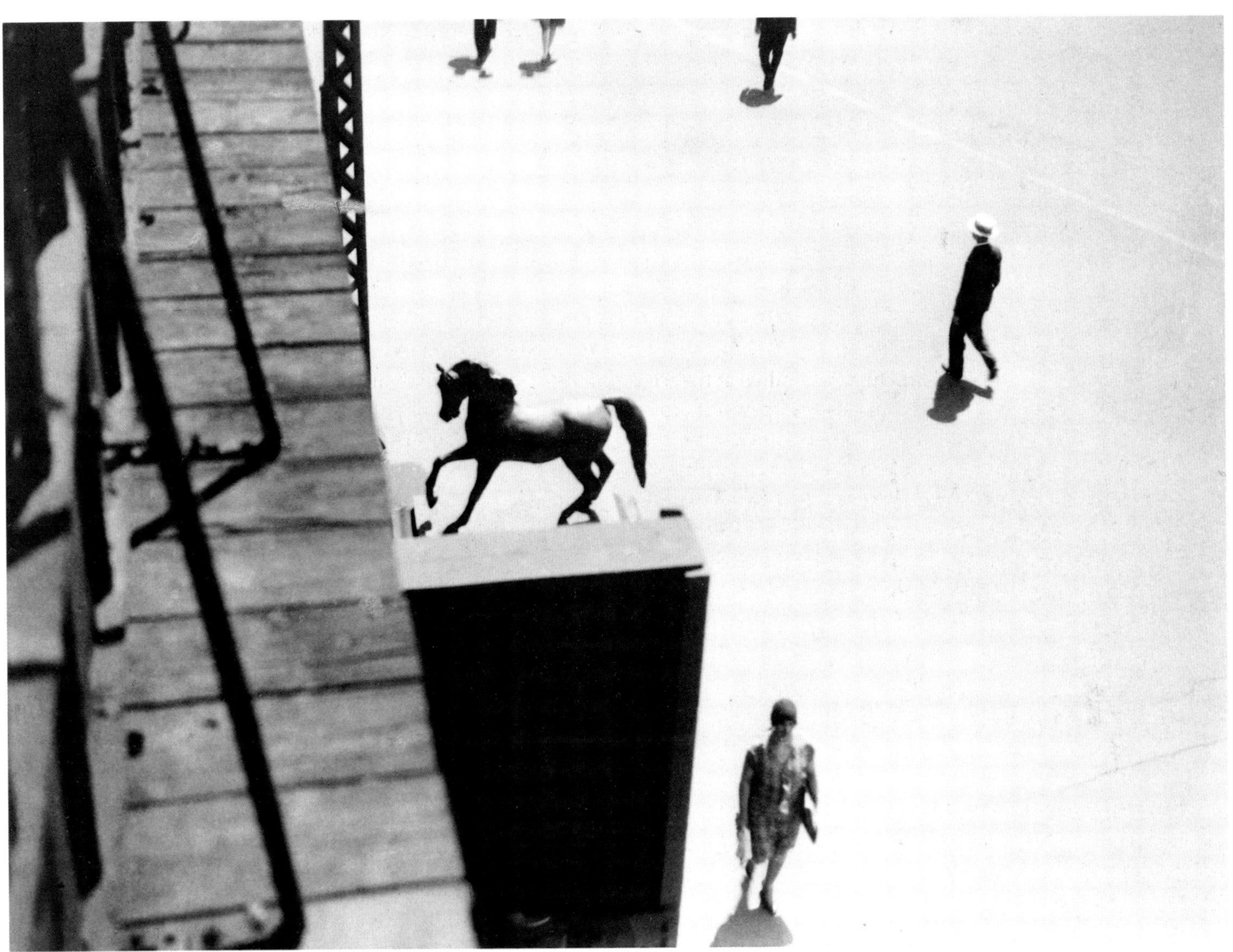

artistic freedom. At the end of the decade, on the eve of the Great Depression, many of these expatriots returned to the United States.

Two such Americans were the photographers Berenice Abbott and Walker Evans. Upon their arrival home, both Abbott and Evans set about making small snapshots of New York in a Cubo-Constructivist style that used high-angle shots to produce dominant geometric forms. Unlike American-based straight photography, which maintained objects' wholeness despite close cropping and emphatic geometries, the European style Abbott and Evans practiced fragmented what they saw. Evans's *Untitled* (building with metal gate) of 1928 or 1929, one of a series of pictures made with a vest-pocket camera, reads overwhelmingly as a study in two-dimensional design, with no sense of solidity.[14] The deeper truthfulness attributed to photography by de Zayas is gone; what remains is contingent on the momentary alignment of form and shadow. Similarly, Abbott's *Subway Station on the Corner of Broadway and Columbus* of 1929 emphasizes not eternal truths but temporary aspects of a scene.[15] Abbott's and Evans's work in this style was short-lived. By the early 1930s, both photographers had abandoned this modernistic style, adopting instead subtly transparent documentary styles that did not impede the viewer's recognition of the pictures' motifs. Such social documentary photography quickly came to dominate the 1930s.

Berenice Abbott,
El at Columbus and Broadway,
1929,
Art Institute of Chicago.

Precision and depth of field

Stieglitz's elitist modernism was matched on the West Coast by the Californian photographer Edward Weston.[16] Throughout the 1910s, Weston made commercial portraits using a soft-focused, Japan-influenced style, while exhibiting nationally in Pictorialist salons. By 1920, Weston was exploring a hybrid modernistic Pictorialism, introducing angular forms rendered in subtle gray tones into his portraits and nudes. In 1922, en route to New York to introduce himself to Stieglitz, Weston made his first sharply focused photographs; these presented a modern, industrial subject, the Armco Steel Works, in Ohio, in a

14. For other Evans photographs from this early New York period, see *Walker Evans at Work*, New York, Harper and Row, 1982, pp. 22–47.

15. Abbott's New York City photographs were part of a project she called "Changing New York". These pictures were first published in a 1939 book of that title, which has been reprinted as *New York in the Thirties*, New York, Dover Publications, 1973.

16. T. E. Stebbins, Jr., *Weston's Westons: Portraits and Nudes*, Boston, Museum of Fine Arts, 1989, and A. Conger, *Edward Weston in Mexico, 1923–1926*, Albuquerque, New Mexico, University of New Mexico Press, 1983.

Ansel Adams: An American Place, 1936

In 1936, two of the most powerful individuals in twentieth-century American photography came together when Alfred Stieglitz exhibited photographs by Ansel Adams at his New York gallery, An American Place.

Stieglitz had been the major force in avant-garde American photography for over forty years. He had exerted his will, and would continue to do so, not only through his own photography but also through the three photography periodicals he had edited between 1893 and 1917 and the three New York galleries he was to run between 1905 and his death in 1946. Consistent with the preference for non-photographic art that he had first expressed around 1910 at his earliest exhibition space, The Little Galleries of the Photo-Secession ("291"), and in his journal *Camera Work*, Stieglitz had exhibited at his later galleries, The Intimate Gallery and An American Place, only two photographers prior to 1936: Paul Strand and himself. Nevertheless, over the years, young American photographers, from Edward Weston to Walker Evans and Harry Callahan, journeyed to New York to show their photographs to Stieglitz, in the hope that his blessing would grace their careers.

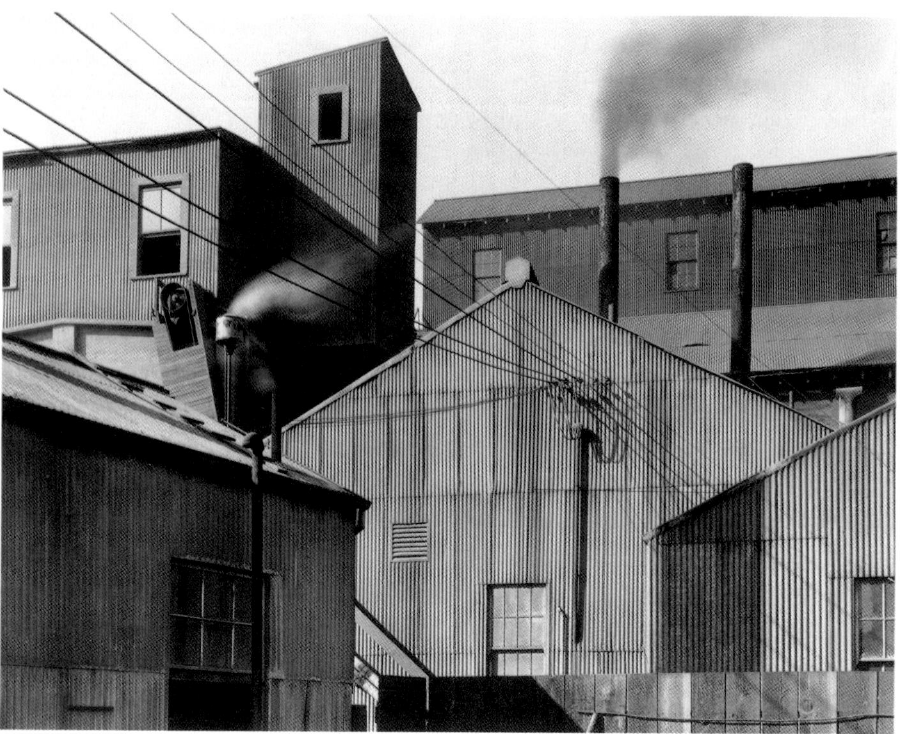

ANSEL ADAMS,
Factory, San Francisco,
1932, Center for Creative Photography, Tucson.

Thirty-one-year-old Adams made his pilgrimage in 1933. At first, Stieglitz sent Adams away, but upon seeing Adam's photographs on a second visit Stieglitz declared them to be "among the finest prints I have ever seen". Adams wrote to Stieglitz that their meeting "touched and clarified many deep elements within me", and, in emulation of Stieglitz, he opened a photography gallery of his own in San Francisco. Stieglitz and Adams continued to correspond and when they met again, in January 1936, Stieglitz agreed to exhibit this younger photographer's work the following fall.

The forty-five photographs that Adams exhibited at An American Place from October 27 to November 25, 1936 were printed from negatives made between 1931 and 1936. The pictures summed up his photography of those five years, showing a movement from the flat patterned work made under the influence of Group f/64 to later, more sculptural work. The pictures included landscapes and nature scenes, but none resembled the heroic landscapes to come in the late 1940s. Rather, these early works were quiet ("tenderness" is the quality Stieglitz saw in them) and included commercial portraits, tombstones, a white wood-framed church, a poster-covered wall, and a factory. The realism of this early work is apparent in *Factory, San Francisco* of 1932. A Cubist arrangement of walls and roofs, the image never yields to total abstraction but remains firmly rooted in reality, showing power lines and, under strong sunlight, the texture of corrugated steel.

Adams made the prints for the exhibition carefully, knowing the high standards to which Stieglitz held photographers. Unlike the large-size photographs then in vogue at pictorial salons, the prints in the exhibition were contact prints from negatives, mostly 8 x 10 inches, with a few being 4 x 5. In the gallery Adam's photographs, in white mounts and passe-partout frames, were hung on atypically gray walls and lit with a mixture of natural light diffused through window blinds and indirect artificial light. According to Adams, Stieglitz's careful sequencing of the work served to critique it and penetrate Adam's own artistic personality. After seeing the exhibition, Adams wrote Stieglitz (November 27, 1936) "My own work has suddenly become something new to me – new, and existing as never before".

John Pultz

strikingly architectonic manner. Weston subsequently developed an intense fascination with the forms of everyday objects and expressed it through the exquisite tonal nuance and sharpness of his prints. Working in Mexico from 1923 to 1926, he photographed children's toys, local pottery, wall posters, and a toilet. Afterwards, in California, he first photographed objects isolated in his studio, such as peppers, halved cabbages, and fungi, revealing less their forms than found designs; beginning around 1930, he made close-up photographs of seaweed and stones on beaches. Subsequently, he came to describe the environments in which the objects and people he photographed existed, and by 1937, the year he received a Guggenheim Fellowship to support his photography, his work clearly documented broad but specific spaces and places.

In addition to the stylistic precociousness of his photographs, Weston was central to the development of modern photography in California through his personal relationships with Johan Hagemeyer, Margrethe Mather, and Tina Modotti. A Dutch-born amateur Pictorialist and professional portrait photographer who had met Stieglitz in 1916, Hagemeyer may have brought to Weston and the West Coast an admiration for Stieglitz and modern art, but his own photography of the 1920s, even when concerned with modern subjects, retained Pictorialism's tonal and optical softness. In the 1920s, Mather abandoned the orientalist aesthetic of spare, asymmetrical composition she had shared in the 1910s with Weston but retained a decorative interest in surface pattern and form. While Hagemeyer and Mather hung on to the preciousness of Pictorialism, even into the 1920s, only the Mexican artist Modotti made photographs as radically unarty as Weston's. While Weston was in Mexico, she made tightly composed, sharp-focused pictures, some of which are very close to his. As in Weston's *Desde la Azotea* of 1924, an untitled view of housetops Modotti made between 1924 and 1926 uses interlocking forms to collapse near and far objects in an unsentimental presentation of vernacular architecture.[17]

The effects of the Depression were felt later and less intensely in the still largely agrarian West Coast than in the industrial cities in the eastern United States. Perhaps for that reason interest in straight photography endured there later than in the East. After the East Coast high modernist movement had become diffuse, a group of northern California photographers who advocated the sharp-focused presentation of texture and detail as an alternative to Pictorialism banded together informally and exhibited in San Francisco, first, in 1932, at the M. H. de Young Memorial Museum and the following year at the Ansel Adams Gallery. These photographers took the name Group f/64, in reference to an extremely small aperture setting which would produce sharp focus and great depth of field. The founders of the group, in addition to Weston, were Ansel Adams, Imogen Cunningham, Willard Van Dyke, Sonya Noskowiak, John Paul Edwards, and Henry Swift. Peter Stackpole and Dorothea Lange were later invited to join. The 1932 exhibition included the founders as well as Alma Lavenson, Brett Weston, Preston Holder, and Consuelo Kanaga.

Of these photographers, Cunningham perhaps best followed Weston in the presentation of pure

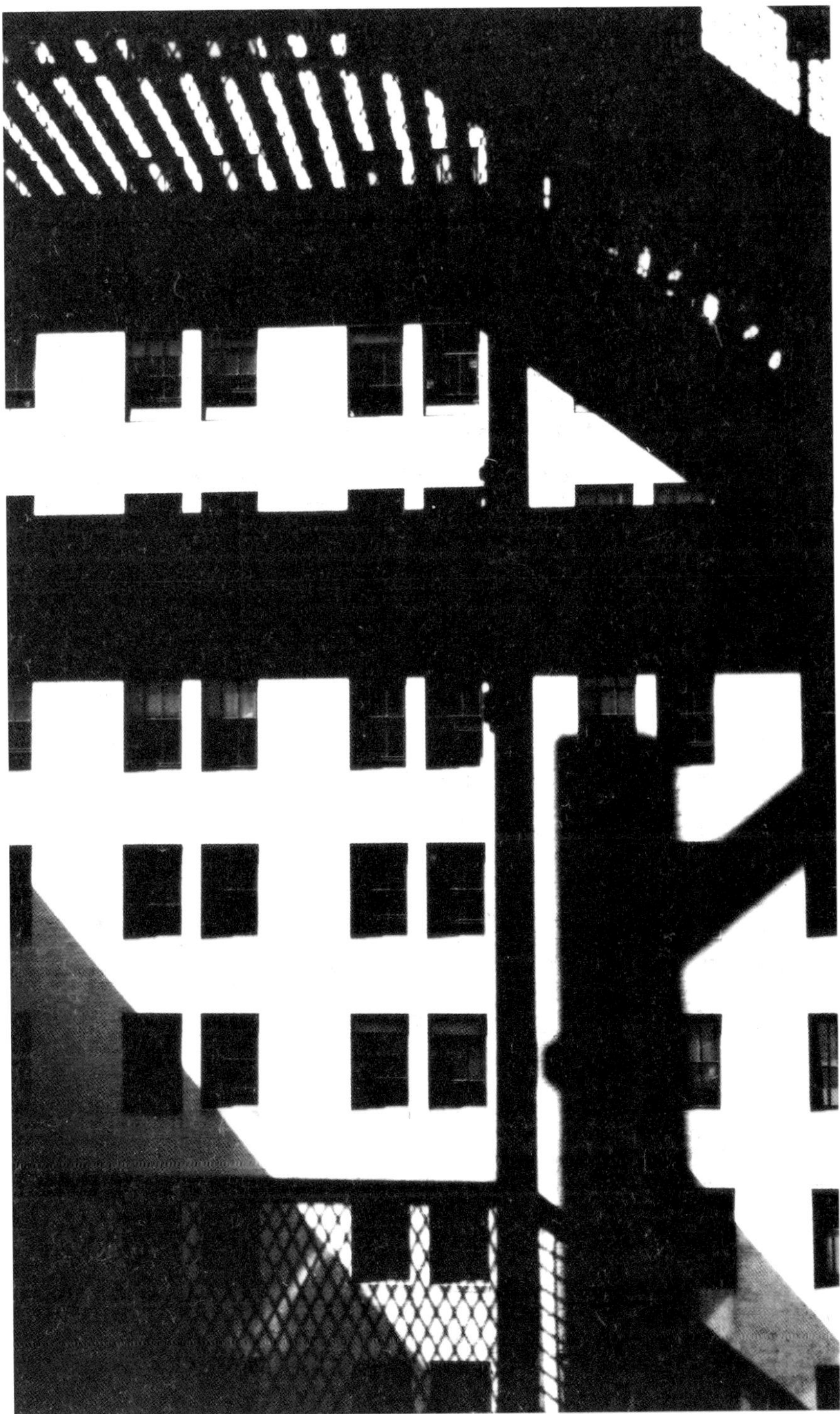

WALKER EVANS, ***Untitled***, circa 1929, Art Institute of Chicago.

17. M. Constantine, *Tina Modotti: A Fragile Life*, New York, Paddington Press, 1975.

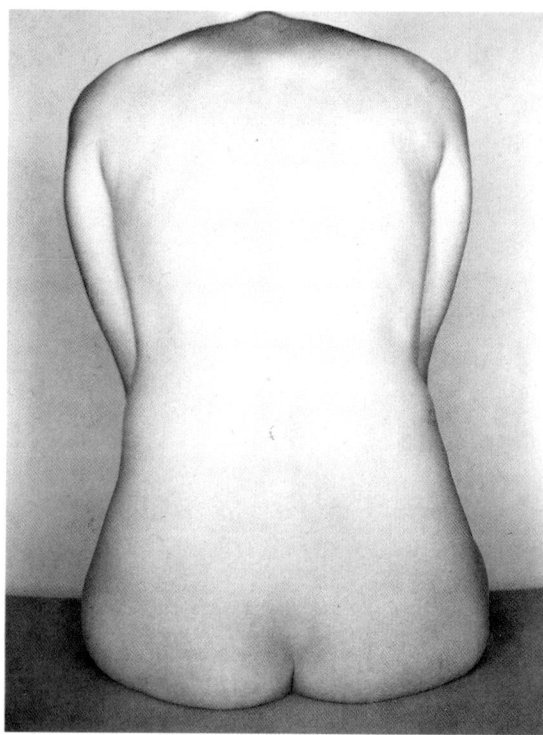

Edward Weston, ***Nude,*** 1927, John Paul Getty Museum, Malibu.

form. Limited during the 1920s by her role as mother and wife, she frequently photographed plants and flowers that grew in, or could be brought into, her home. The resulting photographs have straight photography's bold graphicness and dramatic contrasts of dark and light even though some of them are printed on platinum paper.

Although Adams brought to Group f/64 a respect for craft and technique that he had acquired during years of piano study, by 1935 he considered the group's emphasis on texture and detail too restrictive of his need to develop his individual aesthetic expression.[18] Unlike his work of the 1940s and 1950s, which was almost exclusively devoted to the heroic presentation of majestic mountains and open parklands in the Western United States, his photography of the 1930s was more varied (see box). In these photographs Adams matched the crisp perfection Strand and Weston had established in the 1920s but, as in their work of the 1930s, documented the world itself.

Adams, Strand, and Weston were hardly alone in their preference in the 1930s for facts over pure form. The Great Depression made irrelevant the high modernist style and the luxury goods whose consumption it supported. During the 1930s, as the United States turned its attention to the plight of the unemployed and the battle for economic recovery, documentary-style photography came to dominate. But even as high modernism, like Pictorialism, became out of date, it left as its legacy the possibility that photographers could use their medium's mechanical realism, as Walker Evans would do, to make documentary equivalents of reality that were expressive through formal rather than sentimental means.

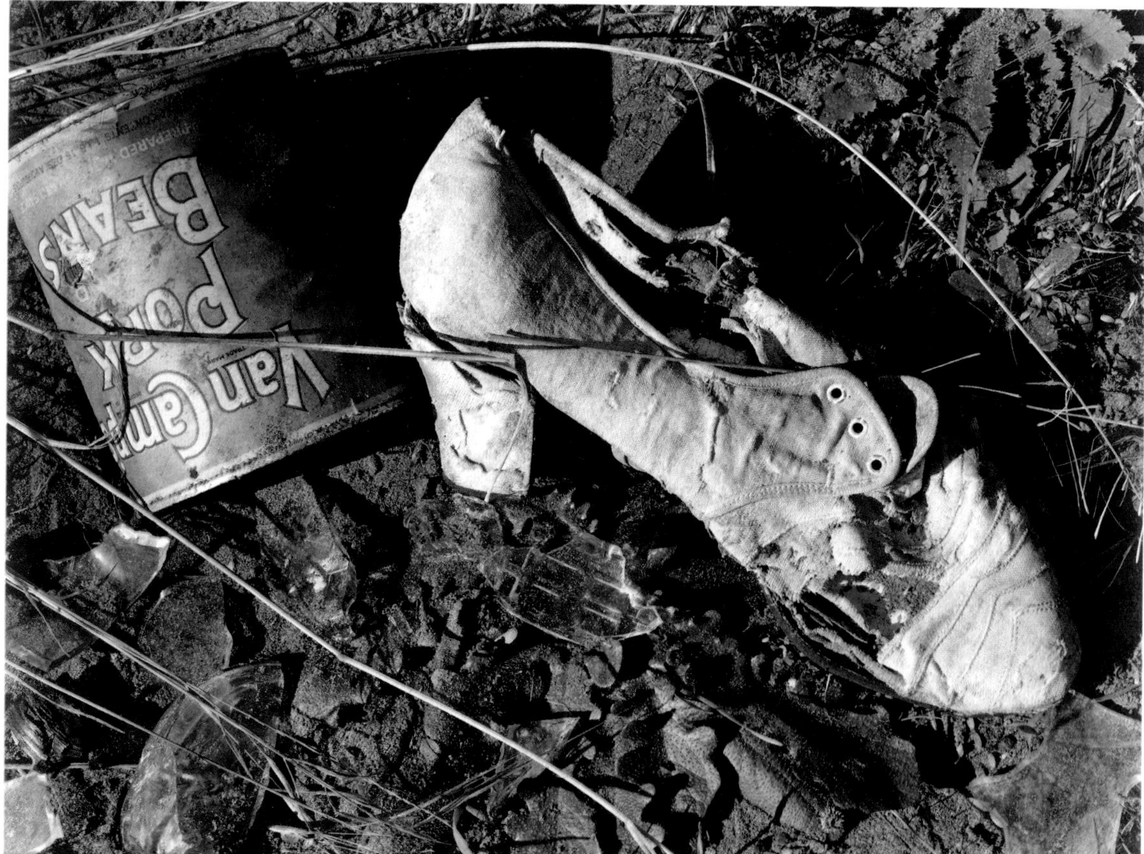

Edward Weston, ***Moonstone Beach,*** 1937, Huntington Library and Art Gallery, San Marino.

18. M. S. Alinder, *Ansel Adams: An Autobiography,* Boston, Little, Brown and Company, 1985. For Group f.64, see *Seeing Straight. The f.64 Revolution in Photography,* The Oakland Museum, 1993.

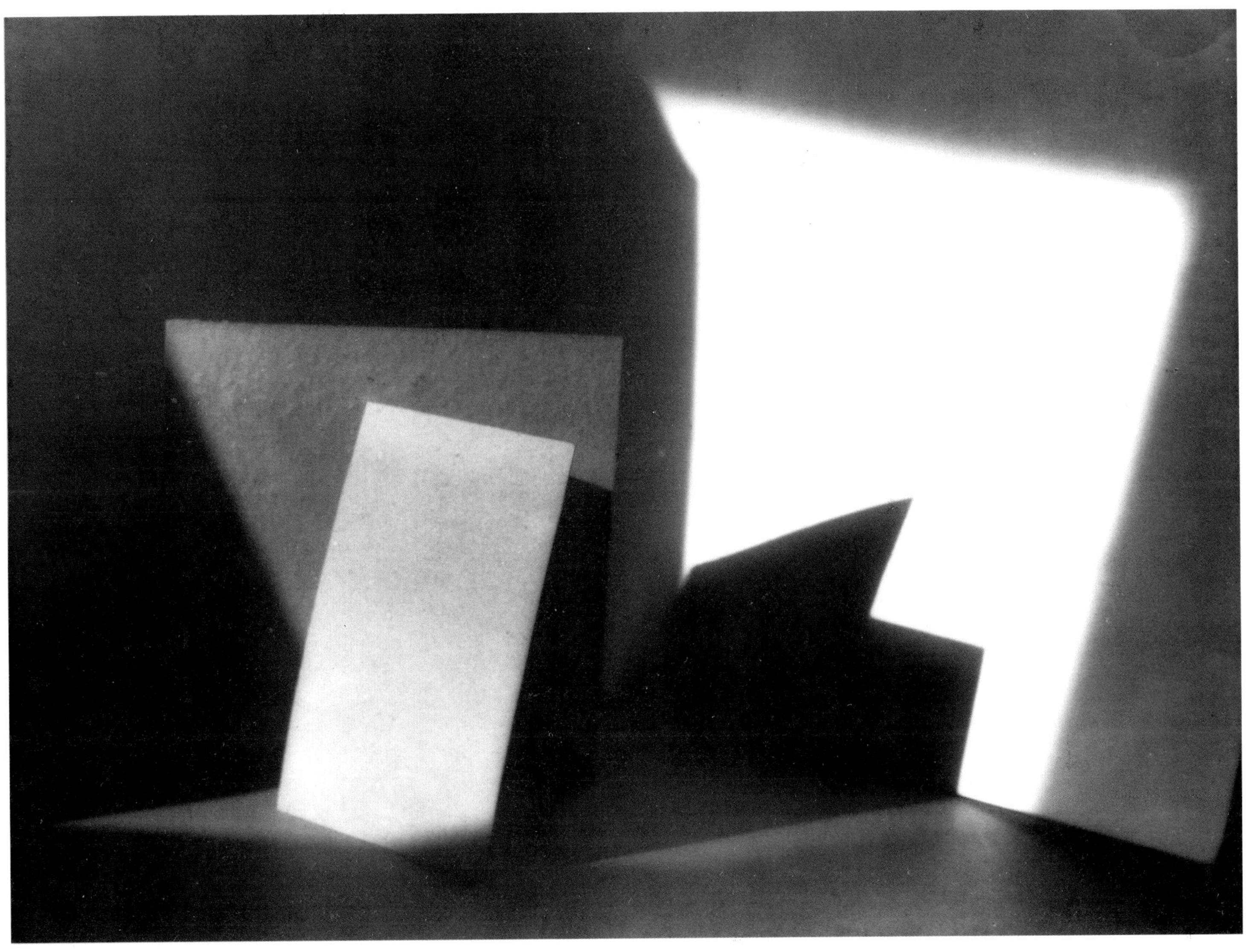

The spirit of Czechoslovakia

A valid question regarding the spread of photographic practice is, do national "schools" exist in the sense which is accepted in the history of painting, or at least trends characterizing the evolution of photography in a particular country, related to specific cultural features? While such criteria are now scarcely applicable to the history of photography, it is clear that temporary influences have from time to time been apparent in particular situations and countries.

Such was the case in Czechoslovakia between the two World Wars. In the stable world of the new republic born in 1918, the intelligentsia was closely in touch with what was going on in Russia and western Europe. Cubism had made its way into painting, architecture, and interior design. At that time the avant-garde movement was attracting followers, and exciting experiments were being made in cinema: in 1922 Karel Teige published *Foto-Kino-Film*, propagating ideas close to those of the Weimar Bauhaus, which shortly afterwards would be given photographic expression by László Moholy-Nagy.

Czech artistic activity, which was based mainly in Prague and Brno, was in tune with German and Russian Constructivism, but with a sweetening of its ideological resonances. The aim was to reach out to a certain popular spirit and to create a link between Modernism and the general public through the media, particularly photography, and via a mechanistic and functional aesthetic.

To these preoccupations were joined a poetic tendency which in some ways prefigured Surrealism (in which it would find an echo in 1924). The Devetsil groups of artists and the Poetism movement organized around Karel Teige laid down lines of thought which revalorized the object, the machine, and Modernism, by giving them a lyrical component, emphasizing mental associations rather than advances in artistic form.

Frantisek Drtikol was the most "classical" of these Czech photographers (he opened a studio in Prague in 1910). Under the influence of the Pictorialism of his fellow-countryman Josef Ruzicka, his artistic vocabulary employed both soft-focus and Art Nouveau forms, but in a Symbolist vein. A mystic, who was fascinated by the occult, he retired from the world in 1935.

His assistant Jaroslav Rössler (who lived in Paris from 1928 to 1935), as well as Jaromir Funke, a professor of photography at Bratislava, then at Prague, more obviously followed the Bauhaus school, publishing their work in avant-garde magazines and working for publicity firms, opting for photograms and photomontage.

Josef Sudek (who founded the Czech Photographic Society with Funke in 1924) also undertook publicity work (for the graphic artist Sutnar), before turning to Surrealism and a poetry of object and light (views from his window through the seasons, shots of glasses of water).

Jindrich Styrsky, who with Karel Teige translated the *Chants de Maldoror*, and worked in Paris from 1925 to 1928, produced photographic series between 1932 and 1935 which transposed Eugène Atget's nostalgic world and which condemned the subjectivity of the view of "realities possessing, paradoxically, a dream-like character" (Teige, 1948).

With Vilem Reichmann, and Frantisek Vobecky, and continuing to the present day with Jan Saudek and Tom Drahos, Czech photography seems like a poetical, lyrical activity which tries to look beyond the object photographed.

Michel Frizot

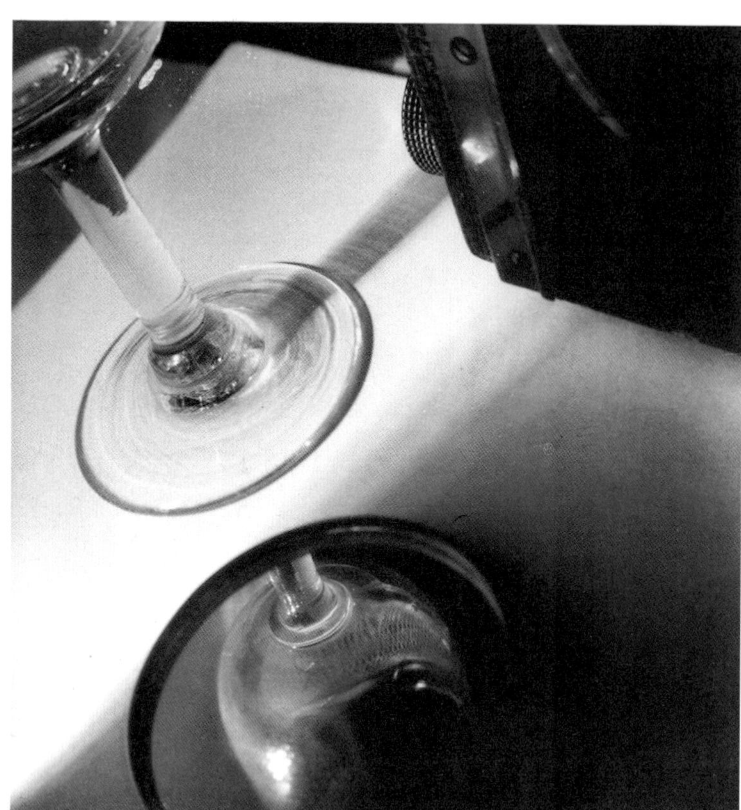

JAROSLAV RÖSSLER,
Paris, Glasses,
circa 1926,
Rudolf Kicken Gallery,
Cologne.

JOSEF SUDEK, ▶
Portrait of the Painter Vaclav Sivko,
1955,
F.R.A.C. Collection,
Aquitaine

◀◀ previous page:
JAROMIR FUNKE,
Abstract Photograph,
1927–1928
Morave Gallery, Brno.

JAROMIR FUNKE,
from the series
Glass and Reflections,
1929,
Morave Gallery, Brno.

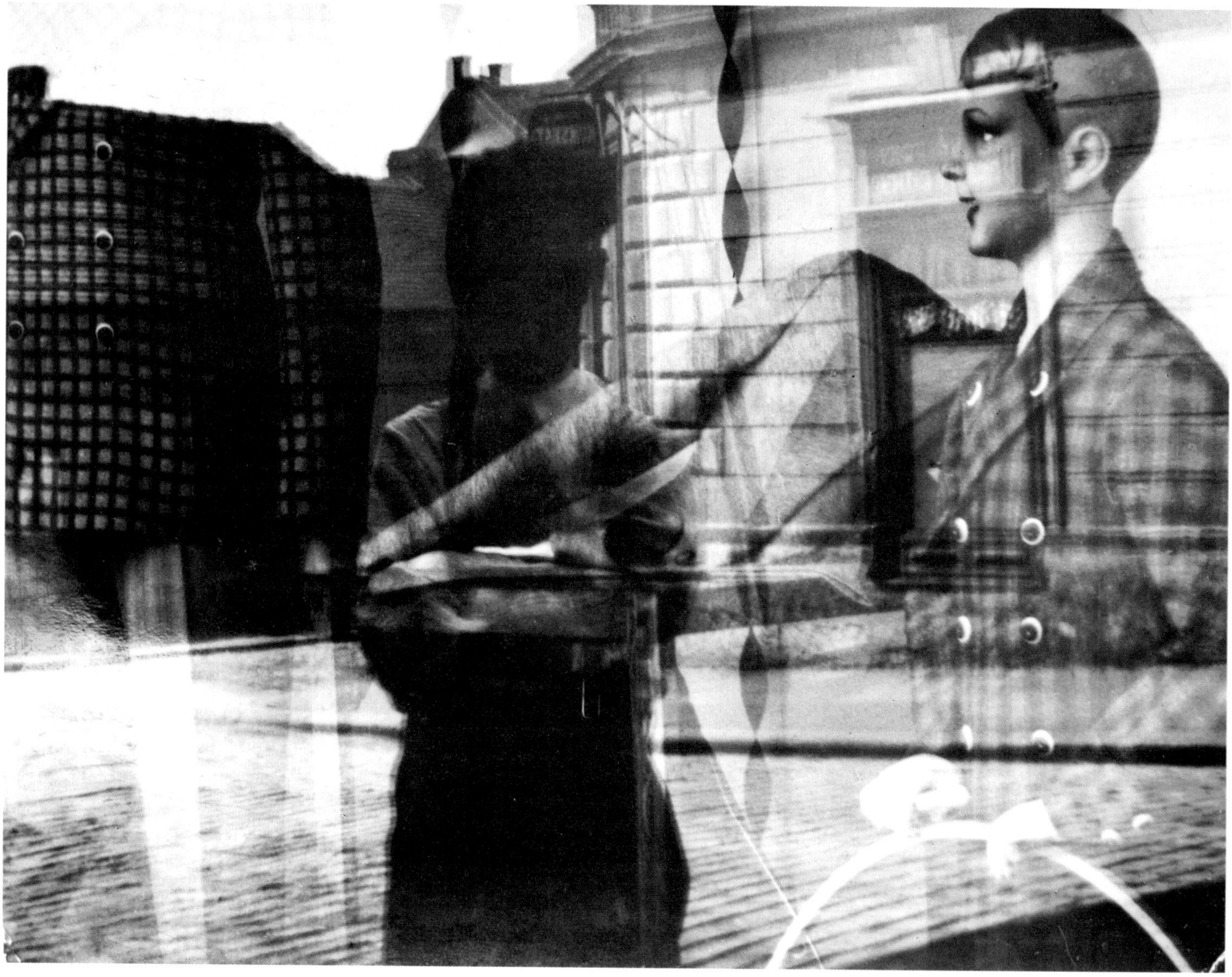

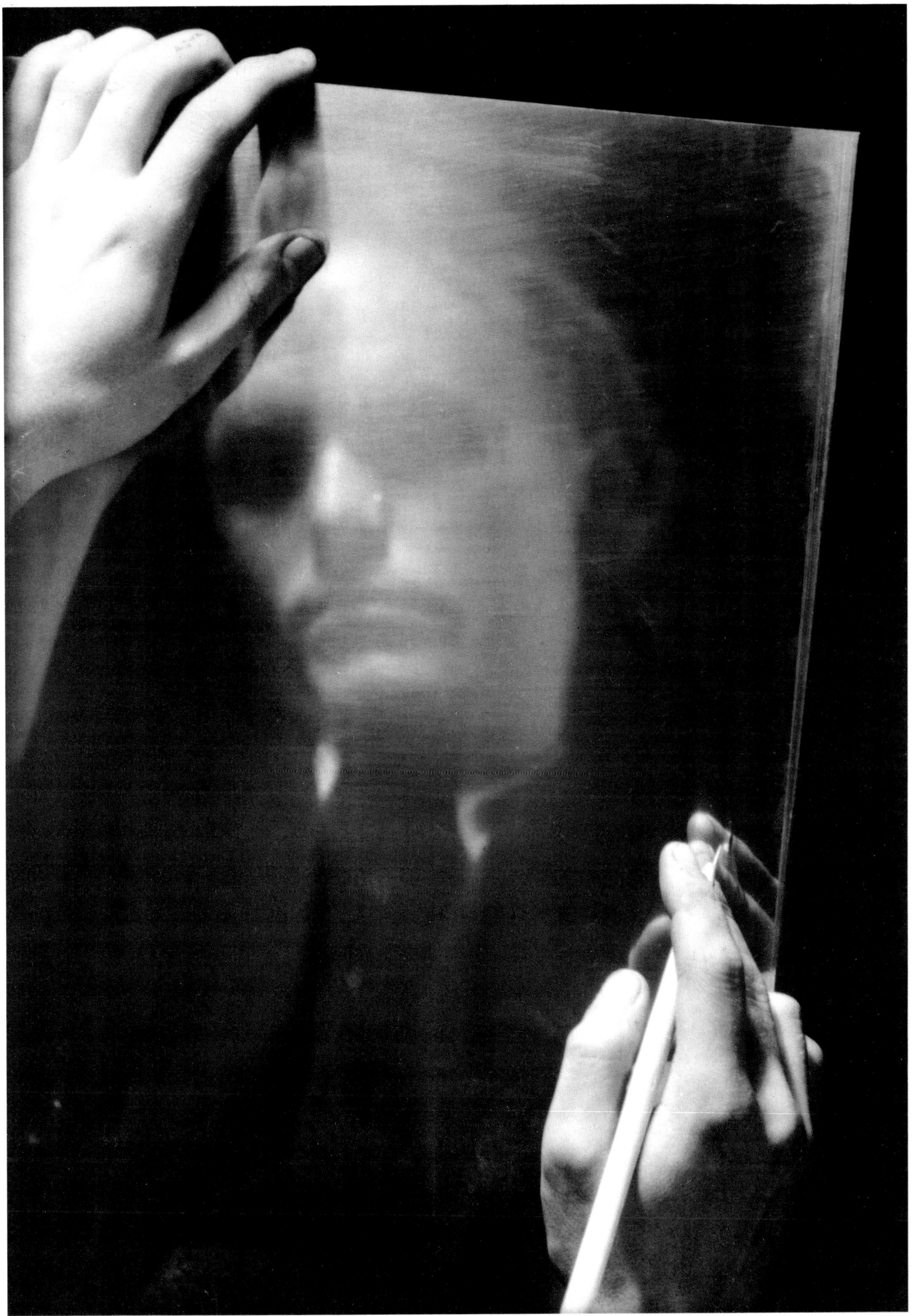

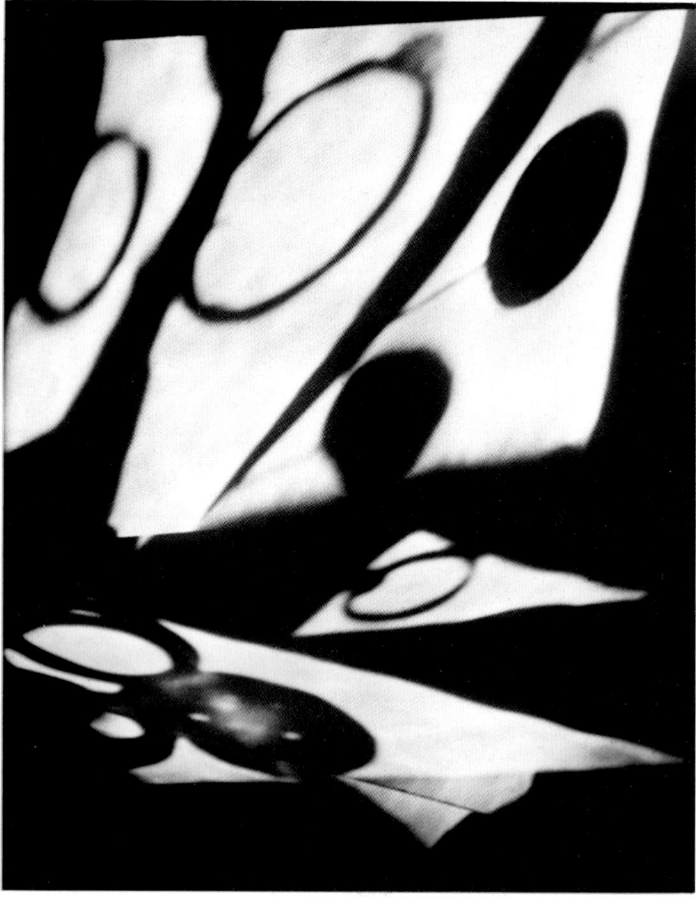

JAROMIR FUNKE,
Abstract Photograph,
1928–1929,
Rudolf Kicken Gallery, Cologne.

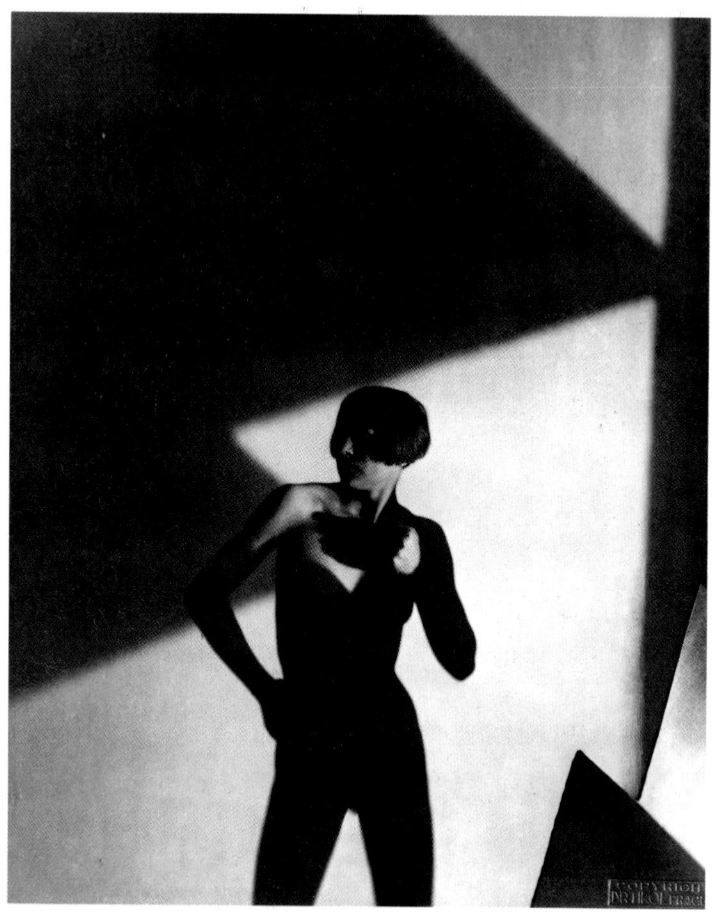

FRANTISEK DRTIKOL,
Study,
1927,
Museum of Decorative Arts,
Prague.

BOHUMIL NEMEC, ▶
Publicity photograph,
circa 1938,
Morave Gallery, Brno.

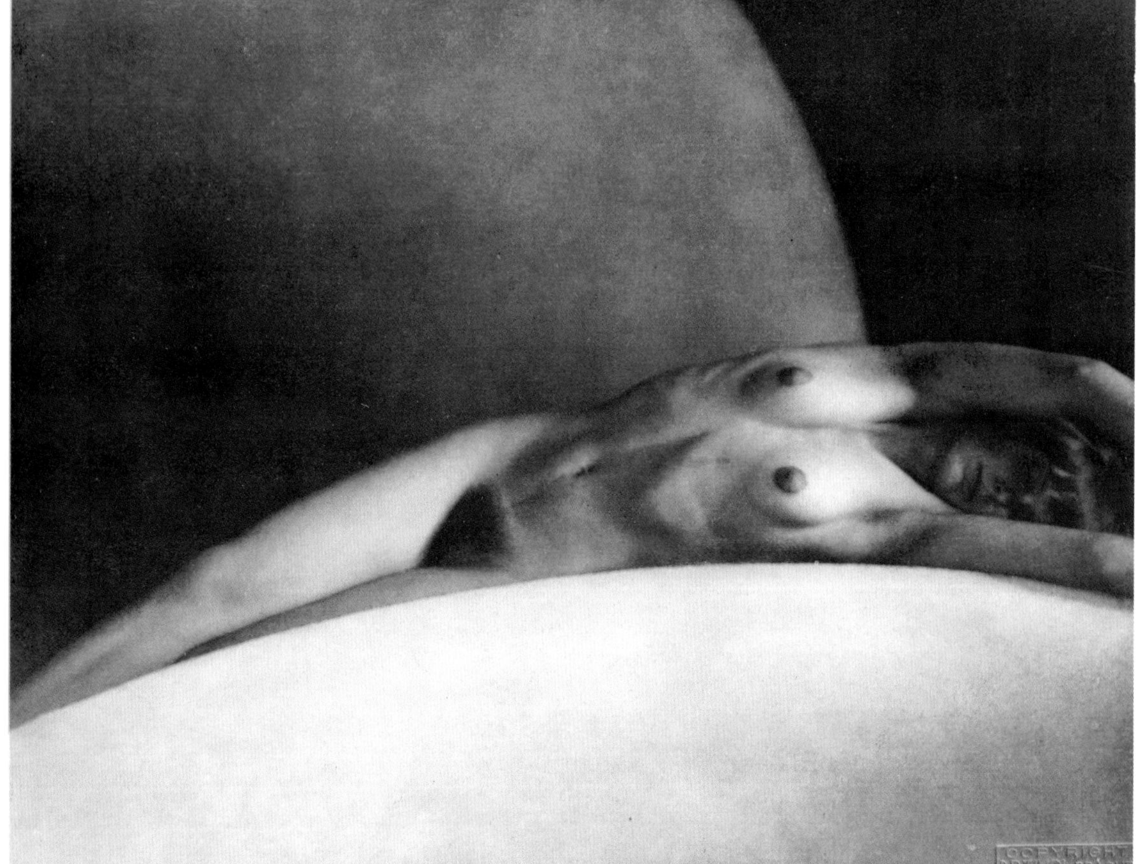

FRANTISEK DRTIKOL,
The Arch,
1928,
Museum of Decorative Arts,
Prague.

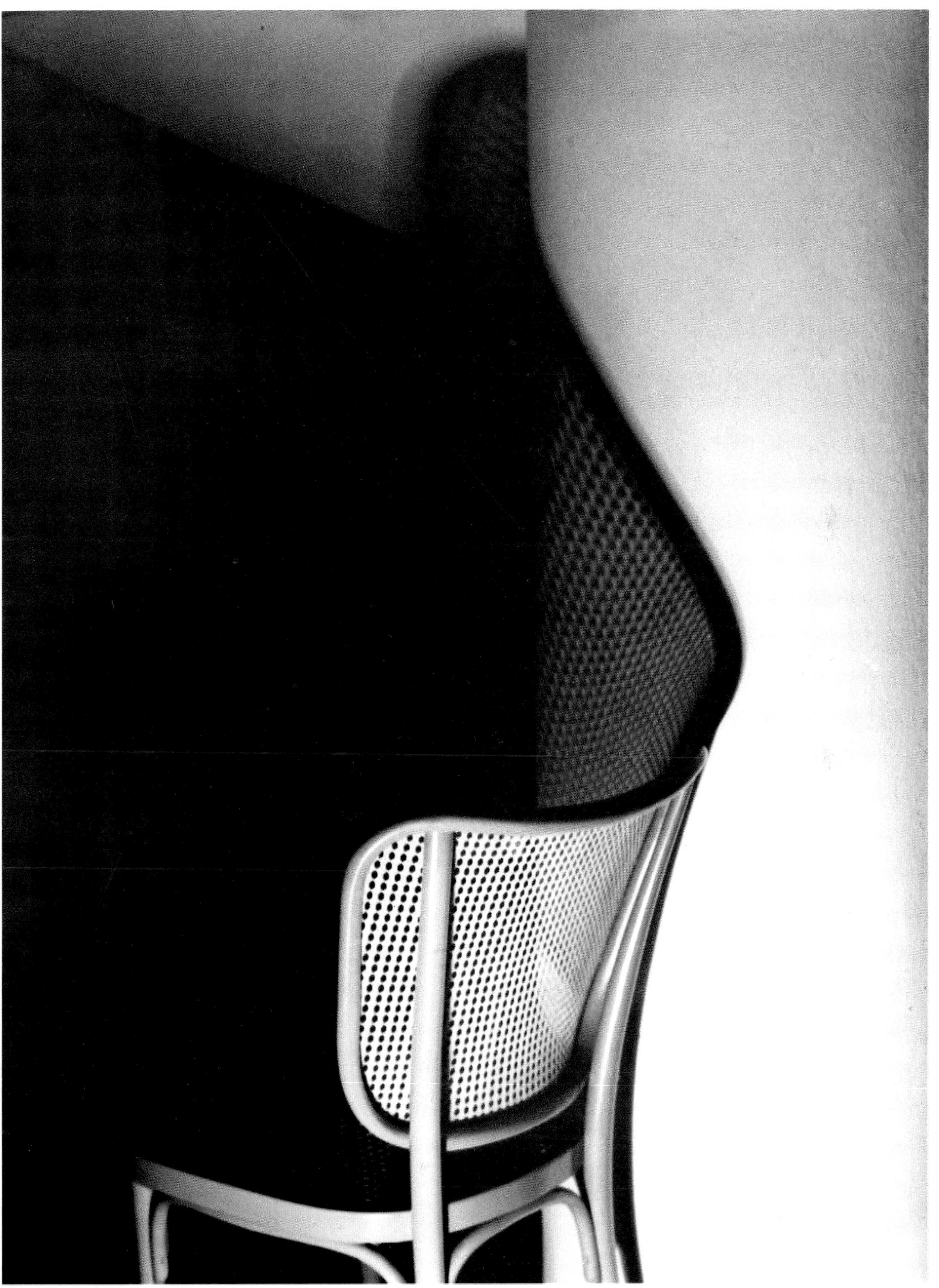

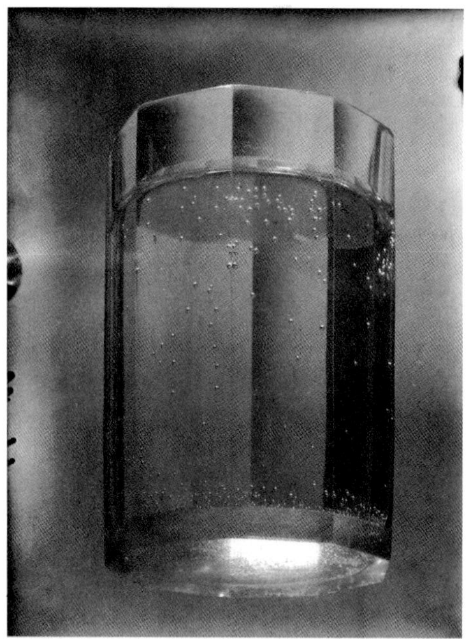

Josef Sudek,
Simple Still-life,
1950–1954,
Cabinet des Estampes,
Musée de Strasbourg.

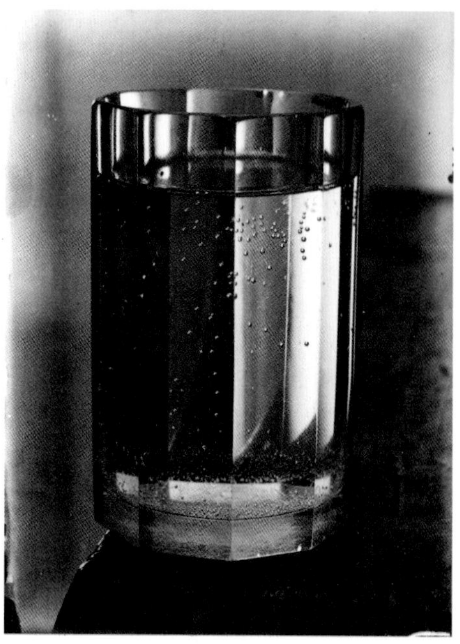

Josef Sudek,
Simple Still-life,
1950,
Museum of Decorative Arts,
Prague.

Josef Sudek, ▶
First Frost,
from the series
From the Window of my Atelier,
1950,
Museum of Decorative Arts,
Prague.

Josef Sudek,
from the series
From the Window of my Atelier,
1940–1954,
Museum of Decorative Arts,
Prague.

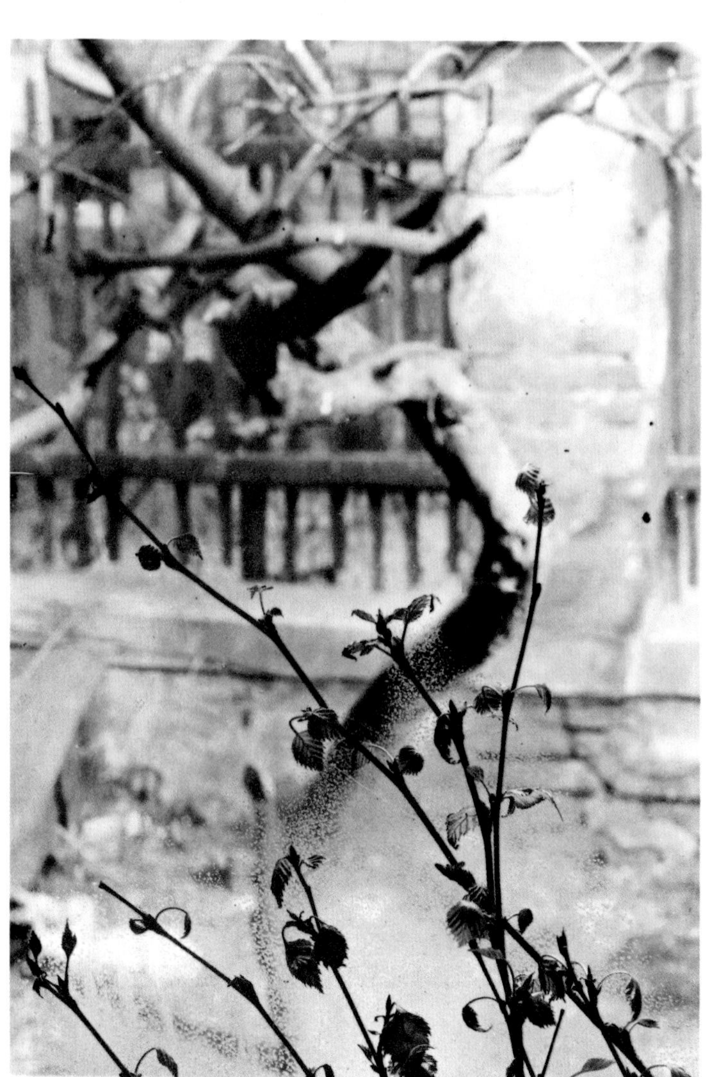

Josef Sudek,
from the series
From the Window of my Atelier,
1940–1954,
Museum of Decorative Arts,
Prague.

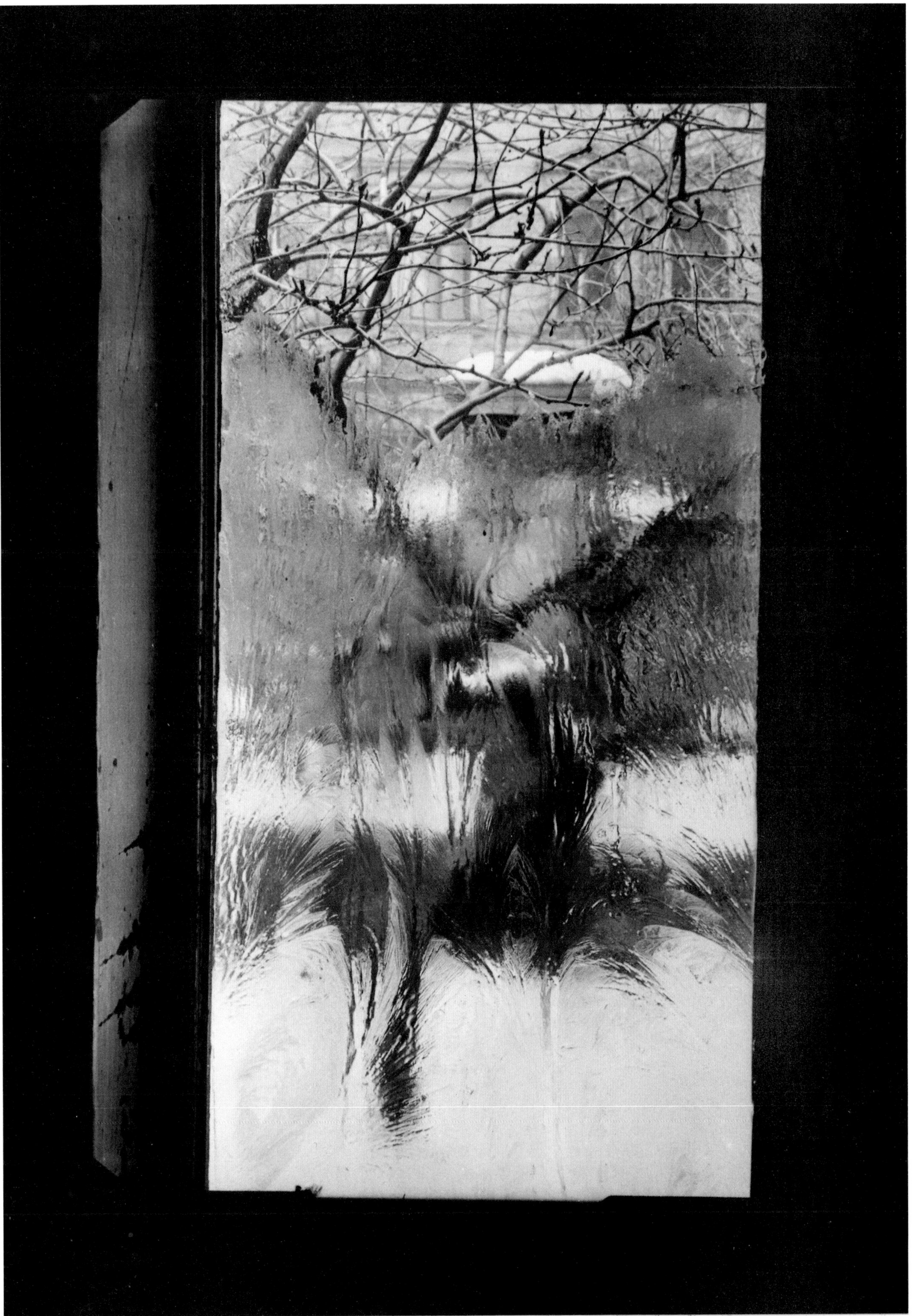

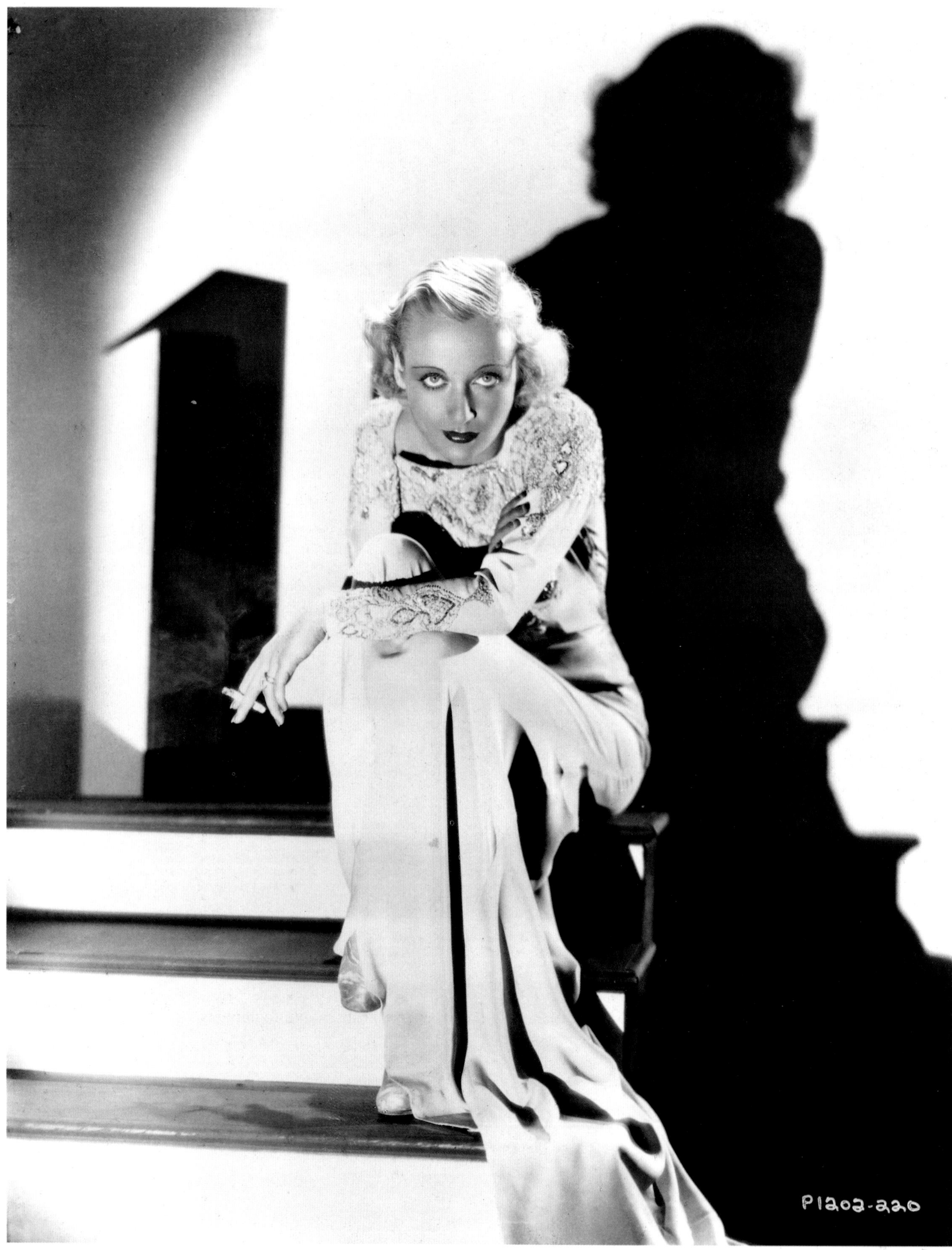
P1202-220

PORTRAIT OF SOCIETY

29

The anonymous and the famous

Pierre Vaisse

At the beginning of the twentieth century, following on from the standard studio portrait of the nineteenth century, a freer approach to portraiture began to emerge in the work of both professional and artist photographers. By using different camera angles or originality of pose, attempts were made to give each subject a unique, personal identity, within a limited and much circumscribed social group. The uniformity of the carte de visite was to be replaced with portraits of micro-societies – artists, writers, celebrities, model workers. These portraits were often used to satisfy the growing demand for images from the media, to the extent that became something of a press cliché.

From the moment it first became possible to capture an image on a light-sensitive surface, the camera lens was turned on the human face.[1] As time went on, portraiture was to become the main application for the daguerreotype process. However, despite their value as souvenirs, the precision of their delineation, and the delicacy and brilliance of their silvery tones, these images brought little to the art of photography. Usually half-portraits, photographed from close up, subjects posed before a plain background or next to some conventional accessory. Any invention or imagination that the professional photographer might have added did not fit in with the expectations of the client who wanted a stereotypical portrait, the only function of which was to make them look good. Nevertheless, the majority of professional photographers at the end of the last century were portraitists who made their living from an occupation that was becoming increasingly accessible to an ever wider public. A painting by Dagnan-Bouveret, *A Wedding at the Photographer's*, exhibited at the 1879 Salon, gives an amusing picture of this social phenomenon – which would later diminish in importance with the advent of the fashion for portable cameras and the development of amateur photography. By the middle of the twentieth century, most portraits were taken by a friend or relative. In practice, only "identity" photographs now require the services of a professional photographer, and even these can now be taken in an automatic photo booth. In the ground lying between popular amateur photography and the identity photograph there is an area where portraits are taken by professionals, but professionals who try to vary the poses and ways of taking the picture to give each image a specific "identity" reflecting and interpreting the characteristics of the individual.

Studio portraits

In some countries, particularly in small towns, the visit to the photographer's studio is a tradition that continues, to this day, to be an obligatory accompaniment to certain solemn acts and moments in life, in particular – if not exclusively – marriage. It is difficult to pick out just one example from this immense and repetitive genre, the only aim of which is to please the client. While the names of certain studio photographers have been recorded, it is not so much the quality of their product as chance that has allowed their work to be preserved and rediscovered. One such photographer was Norbert Ghisoland (1878–1939), son of a Belgian miner in a small town in Le Borinage;[2] another was Michael Disfarmer, whose real name was Michael Meyer (1884–1959) who, between 1930 and 1946, took a thousand portraits of the people of his native Arkansas. The example of Martin Jiménez Chambi (1891–1973), a Peruvian photographer working in Cuzco, is rather different, in that during his life he enjoyed a national reputation

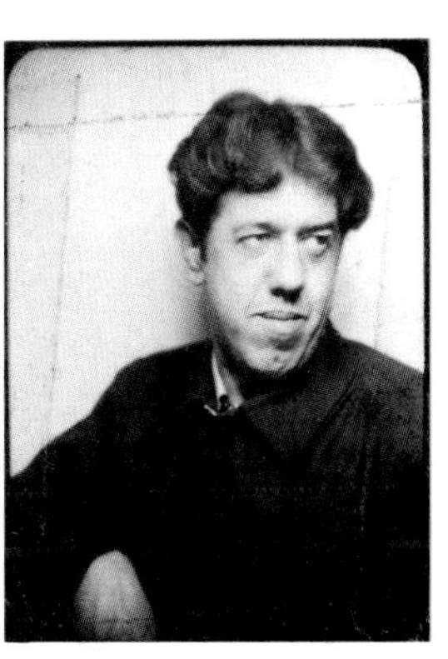

Photomaton of Michel Simon, circa 1930, Photomaton Collection.

◄ Otto Dyar, *Carole Lombard*, 1932 (for Paramount), Kobal Collection, London.

1. This chapter owes much to the catalogue of the Gruber Collection of the Ludwig Museum in Cologne: *Sammlung Gruber: Photographie des 20. Jahrhunderts*, Cologne, Ludwig Museum, 2nd ed., s. d. See too (for photographic documentation) *Lichtbildnisse: Das Porträt in der Fotografie*, Cologne, Rheinland-Verlag, 1982, published on the occasion of an exhibition at the Rheinisches Landesmuseum in Bonn.

2. On Ghisoland, see *Norbert Ghisoland: photographies 1910–1930*, Brussels, Damase, 1977.

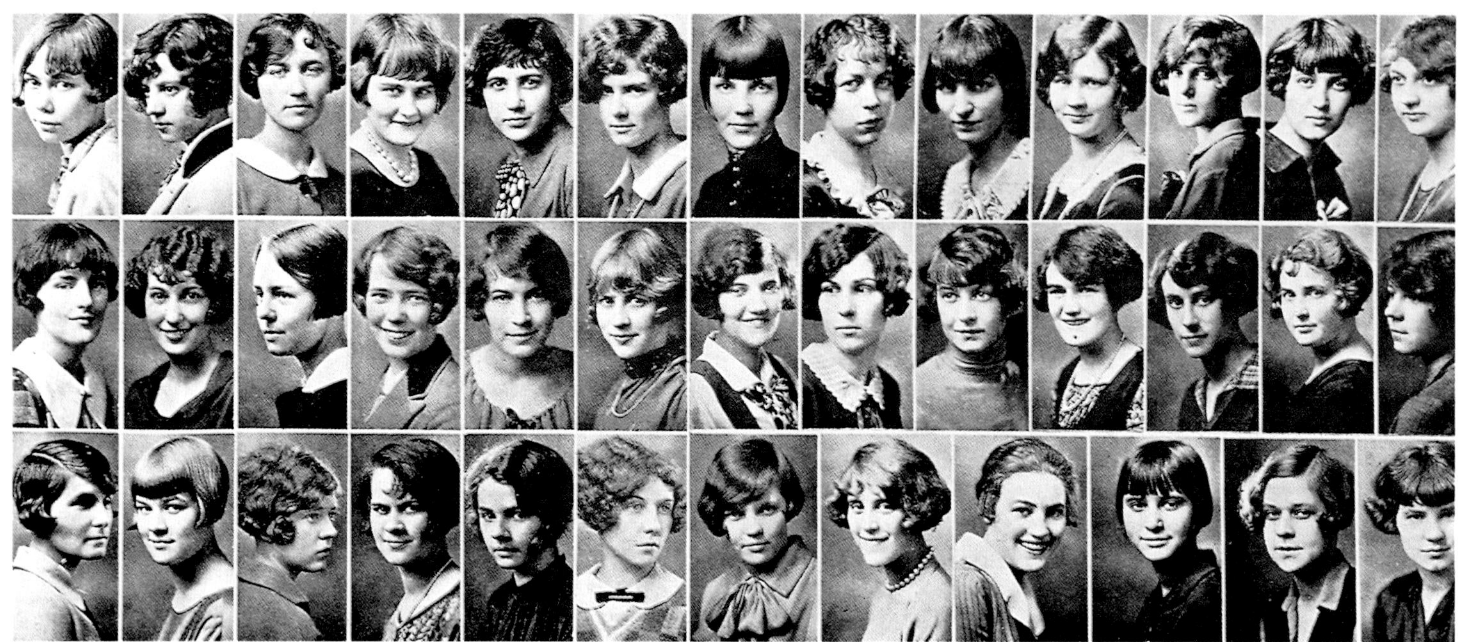

Caufield and Shook Studio, *Portrait Collection,* 1920s, Photographic Archives, University of Louisville.

rewarded with medals and titles. Another famous name is that of August Sander (1876–1964) but, as we shall see below, his portraits of peasants in their Sunday best would probably not have achieved their present reputation had it not been for their author's wider ambitions.

From an aesthetic point of view, this mass production of portraits has undergone a number of developments. In the last twenty or thirty years, the use of color has become general. Another development of no lesser importance occurred at the time of the First World War. Paradoxically, it was the result of a reaction against the lowering in standards of the art of photography that had been brought about by the success of the professional portrait. The Second Empire had been the golden age of the photographic studio. In an attempt to attract clients, photographers rivaled one another in the luxurious surroundings they offered. An increase in both the demand for and supply of portraits was to be accompanied by an increasing banalization of the product and its aesthetic value. Rightly or wrongly, it is to this expansion that the general drop in the quality of photography detectable between 1870 and 1890 was attributed. It was this deterioration in quality, and the abuses of professionalism and industrialization, that led a number of photographers, particularly amateurs, to attempt to revive photography, considered by them to be an art form, from its decadence.

Art portraits

In order to to do this, they followed the model of contemporary painting – hence the name given to their movement, Pictorialism – increasing the number of manual interventions carried out between exposing the negative and producing the final print. For a long time, and from early on, these photographers have been criticized for what seemed like a betrayal of the medium, without sufficient credit being given to their successes and the revival that they brought about. Yet, as amateurs, the majority of them were no more interested in portraiture than in landscapes, still-lifes or nudes. Neither the studies of women in a

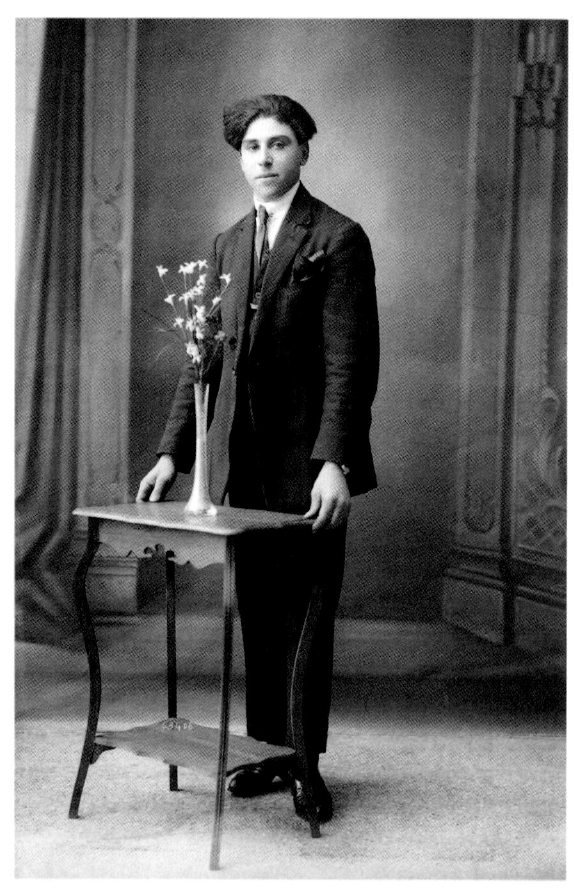

Norbert Ghisoland, ▶ *Studio Portrait,* 1930s.

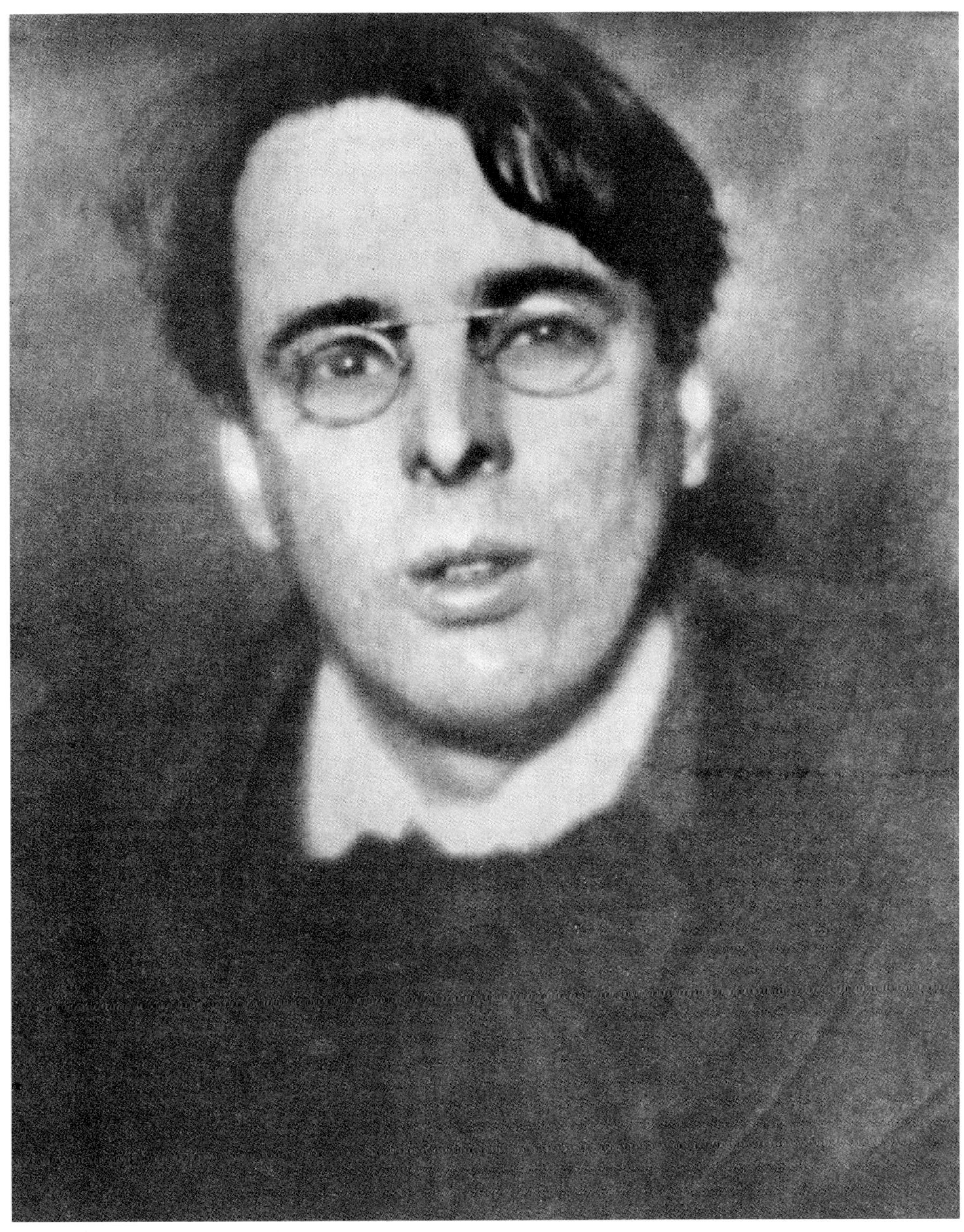

ALVIN LANGDON COBURN,
W. B. Yeats,
1908,
Royal Photographic Society, Bath.

garden by Puyo, nor Demachy's *Primavera* – by the two most famous French Pictorialists – are, strictly speaking, portraits, but rather compositions that aspire to poetry, taking inspiration from contemporary painting. Renoir would seem to be an obvious source if it were not for the fact that such subjects had become commonplace in fashionable painting at the end of the century. We see the same thing with the women and children at play or walking in the country photographed by Heinrich Kühn (1866–1944), one of the most striking personalities in the Vienna Camera-Club. Despite their intimate character, even his numerous family portraits partake of this aesthetic in that they are reminiscent of certain genre scenes of the period.

Like many nineteenth-century photographers, Kühn had received a scientific and medical training. Originally, he was interested in microphotography in the context of anatomical research. Having given up medicine in order to devote himself to art photography, he was typical of those rich amateurs who originated Pictorialism. This did not prevent him, however, from setting up a professional portrait studio in 1905.[3] In fact, the dividing line between amateurs and

3. Exhibition catalogues *Heinrich Kühn, 1866–1944*, Essen, Folkwang Museum, 1978, and *Heinrich Kühn*, Munich, Zurich, Cologne, etc., 1981–1982, Cologne, Greven Bechtold, 1981.

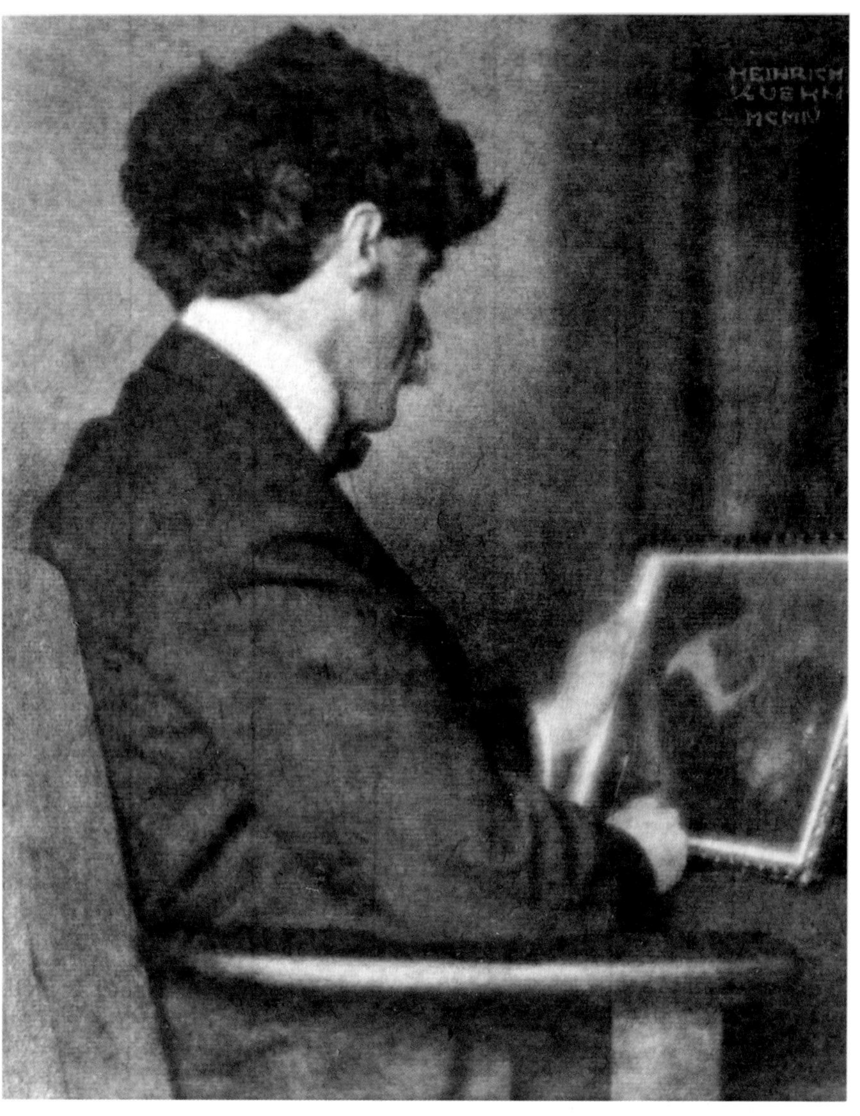

HEINRICH KÜHN, *Alfred Stieglitz*, 1904, Museum für Kunst und Gewerbe, Hamburg.

professionals was not always clearly drawn, particularly with certain American photographers, like Alvin Langdon Coburn (1882–1966). The son of a Boston industrialist, drawn to Pictorialism by his cousin F. Holland Day, Coburn never had a studio, but worked for various publications, sometimes himself acting as editor. Leaving for London in 1904, he asked the editor of the New York *Metropolitan Magazine* to give him a list of artists and writers he would like photographed. The resulting portraits are not, in themselves, distinguished by any particular stylistic originality, unless it is the frequent use of close-up. However, they are good examples of portraits of artists – a genre that was subsequently to see a rapid expansion. Photogravures made from thirty-three of these portraits were collected together in a volume published in 1913 entitled *Men of Mark*. Its publication announced the success of collections of photographic portraits of famous (or unknown) faces in the years between the two World Wars. "If I admired the writings or expressed visions of any person, I was impelled by the desire to meet and photograph him."[4] Among the collection we find H. G. Wells, Hilaire Belloc, W. B. Yeats, Mark Twain, Theodore Roosevelt, Henry James, Rodin, G. B. Shaw, and G. K. Chesterton – giving us not so much a collection of "notables" of the period as a coherent intellectual self-portrait of the photographer.

This publication had been preceded by the series of 120 portraits of men and women of Hamburg published in 1905 by Rudolf Dührkoop (1846–1918), although this consisted not of a book but of photogravures in a slipcase. Self-taught, Dührkoop had opened a professional portrait studio in 1899 in Hamburg, one of the most important centres of Pictorialism, thanks, in particular, to the encouragement of Alfred Lichtwark, the conservator at the Kunsthalle, and one of the first art historians to take an interest in photography. His lectures converted Dührkoop to the new aesthetic. No longer posing his clients in the artificial surroundings of the studio, he captured them in the intimacy of their own homes, or outdoors. This way of working might seem the opposite of the artifice of which Pictorialism was normally accused, but this is not the case; artifice was involved, not in the choice and treatment of the subject, but in the procedures used in processing. The pursuit of intimacy and naturalness corresponded to one of the trends in painting at that time.

Thus, Pictorialism penetrated the professional studios, as Alfred Lichtwark, a born teacher, had hoped it would. His daughter, Minya Diez-Dührkoop (1873–1929), continued in the same vein, as did Nicolas Perscheid (1864–1930), a photographer who had lived in Berlin since 1905[5] who was also the inventor, in 1925, of a lens adapted to the Pictorialist style. This style lasted, in fact, much longer than is sometimes implied in histories of photography, which – like the traditional way of writing histories of painting – tend to describe a succession of supposedly avant-garde movements. It was widely used throughout the inter-war years, and even, in a watered-down form using misty outlines and pencilled shading, much later. Born at the moment when Impressionism was becoming accepted, and when Symbolism was triumphing, Pictorialist photography cultivated soft-focus, atmospheric effects. Paradoxically, this mannerism, born of a desire to lift photography out of the mediocrity into which professional portraiture had, supposedly, plunged it, was to last longer in portraiture than in any other genre. It must have seemed perfectly adapted to portraits – particularly, it must be said, to those of women – bathed in a halo of dreams or mystery. The faces of Anna Pavlova, Isadora Duncan, Eleonora Duse or Greta Garbo are presented in this way in around 1925 by Arnold

4. *Alvin Langdon Coburn: An Autobiography*, H. and A. Gernsheim (eds.), New York, Dover, 1978. Another volume, *More Men of Mark*, was published in 1922.

5. See F. Kempe, *Nicolas Perscheid, Arthur Benda, Madame d'Ora*, Hamburg, Museum für Kunst und Gewerbe, 1980.

Genthe (1868–1942), a photographer who had displayed a very different sense of precision in his reportage on the San Francisco earthquake of 1906. The same can be said of the work of Laure Albin-Guillot, whose female figures – better described as "expressive heads" or nudes rather than portraits – appear with regularly softened contours. Gradually, however, Pictorialism went out of fashion, as we can see from the work of Dora Kalmus, known as Madame d'Ora (1881–1963), who had worked in Perscheid's studio before opening her own studio in Vienna in 1907, and moving to Paris in 1924. Her last portraits, after the Second World War – that of Colette, for example, or of Maurice Chevalier – give no trace of her early training and style.

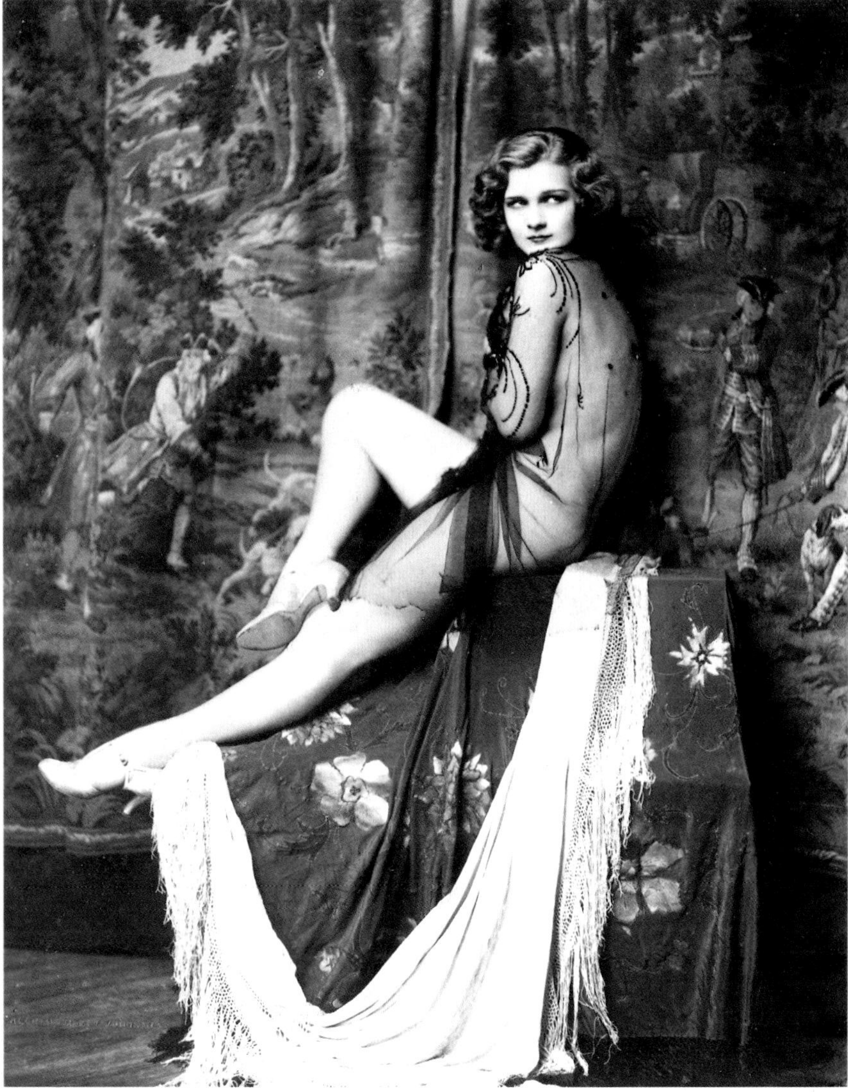

Alfred Cheney Johnston, *Drucilla Straine,* 1924, Rheinisches Bildarchiv, Cologne.

Portraits for publication

Shortly after 1920, a violent reaction occurred against Pictorialism, as can be seen from numerous articles and manifestos. This is generally presented as a decisive moment – the beginning of modern photography. Whether or not this was the case, at first it only involved a small number of photographers, in touch with contemporary developments in painting. In general, the professional portrait was not seriously threatened, partly, as we have said, because of a fondness for the Pictorialist style, but also because its existence depended on technical and social conditions every bit as restrictive as aesthetic fashions.

From the beginning of the century, but especially after the First World War, the most decisive change to affect the practice of professional photography was, without doubt, the discovery of practical photomechanical processes that could at last be used to illustrate books and periodicals, giving rise to a new and huge demand for photographs.

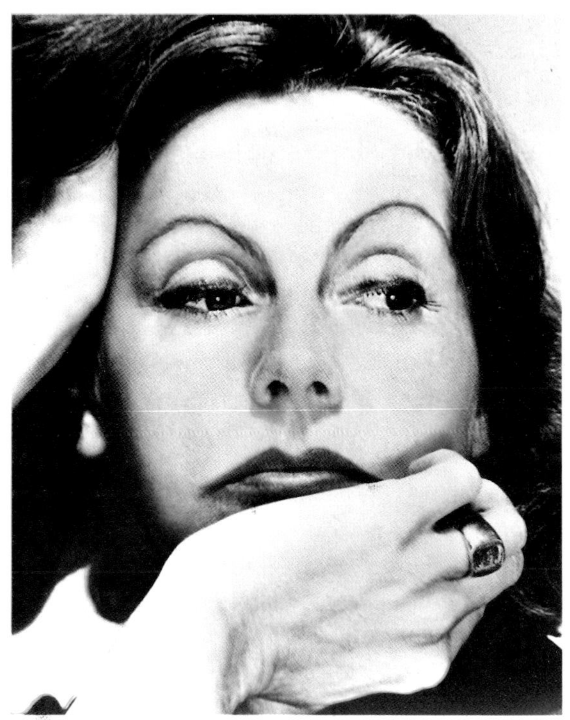

◄ George Hoyningen-Huene, *Greta Garbo,* 1951, Rheinisches Bildarchiv, Cologne.

The effect on portraiture was, perhaps, less marked than on photoreportage, the latter owing, if not its birth, then at least its increasing popularity, to these new techniques. Nevertheless, the portrait was profoundly affected by the advent of magazines which specialized in publishing photographs of society circles, fashion or entertainment – magazines such as *Vogue, Vanity Fair* or *Harper's Bazaar.* Meanwhile, photoreportage was moving closer in style to the portraiture of political personalities. This explains the very different aspects that are well illustrated in the works of Erich Salomon (1886–1944) and Alfred Cheney Johnston (1893–1971).

Erich Salomon first studied law and came late to photography. He worked for the publishing house of Ullstein, of Berlin, and for a number of magazines. He was able to take advantage of his social connections in order to approach celeb-

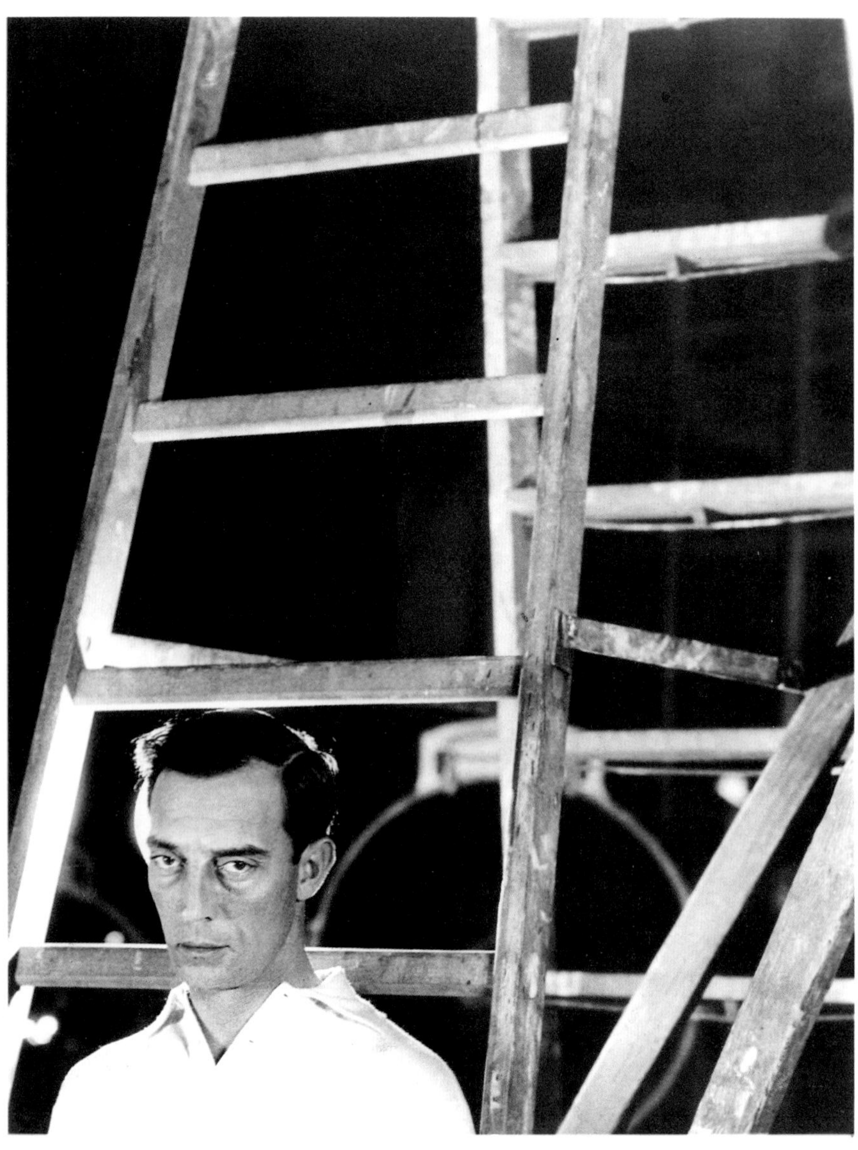

CECIL BEATON, *Buster Keaton,* 1931, Sotheby's Belgravia, London.

rities, particularly politicians. However, his photographs have nothing of the historical document about them. Whether he shows us Hindenburg or Brüning, or Stresemann conferring with Briand and Chamberlain, nothing makes us feel the gravity of the situation nor what was at stake for the fate of the world. What he was interested in capturing was the physiognomy of these official and public figures, at a moment when they were unaware of being observed. He obtained these results by using a miniature camera and film sensitive enough to be used without flash – hence the title he gave to his book published in 1931, *Berühmte Zeitgenossen in unbewahrten Augenblicken* [Famous Contemporaries Captured Unawares]. They are unexpected portraits, amusing, sometimes cruel, but for the most part betraying a real sympathy for his subjects.

The genre was not in itself new, even if technical developments facilitated a freer approach – and we should not exaggerate the naturalness of the portraits of subjects who, in the majority of cases, could hardly be unaware of the photographer. We can look back to the photographs of Chevreul (1886) or General Boulanger (1888), captured by Paul Nadar in mid-conversation. Almost half a century later, in 1931, Felix H. Man published in the *Münchner Illustrierte Presse* a series of photographs of Mussolini at work. Similarly, Erich Salomon, who was almost as interested in the world of the arts as in politics, took a series of photographs showing Marlene Dietrich on the telephone, in informal poses. The viewer was thus drawn into the star's private life, reduced to its humdrum daily level.

This was the exact opposite of the aims of the famous Studio Harcourt, a Paris studio that specialized in the world of entertainment – at least, if one agrees with Roland Barthes in his brilliant analysis of these works, when he says that they aimed to make the actor appear "eternally young, forever fixed at the summit of their beauty [...] ideally silent, which is to say mysterious, pregnant with those deep secrets which we imagine dwell in any beauty that does not speak".[6] It was the opposite too, though in a different way, of the aims of the American Alfred Cheney Johnston, one of the most famous representatives of what is now known as "glamour photography" – a polished, prettified, disembodied style of photography for movie magazines and publicity photographs. Whether the subject is Norma Talmadge, Drucilla Straine or Gloria Swanson, their eyes cast down or looking romantically upwards, the poses and decor, the bouquets of flowers concealing a plunging décolleté, the long fringes and transparent veils against a background of antique tapestry all recall, though with a greater freedom made possible by technical progress, the best products of society photographers of the nineteenth century.

Like that of Erich Salomon, the work of Johnston represents what may be an extreme example of the genre, explained by his career as the official photographer to the variety troupe the Ziegfeld Follies. Nevertheless, not all such portraits followed this pattern, and a measure of contrast can be seen between the works of Alfred Eisenstaedt (1898–1995) and Horst P. Horst (1906–), two photographers of German origin who emigrated to the United States after Hitler came to power. The first was known particularly for his reportage (he worked for *Life*), the second as a former collaborator on *Vogue*, and society portraitist. The first photographed Marlene Dietrich in town clothes, sitting at a restaurant table, smiling at her interlocutor; the second gives her an expression whose distance and mystery are reinforced by the artificial decor and the contrasting interplay of skilful lighting.

6. R. Barthes, "L'acteur d'Harcourt", in *Mythologies*, Paris, Le Seuil, 1957.

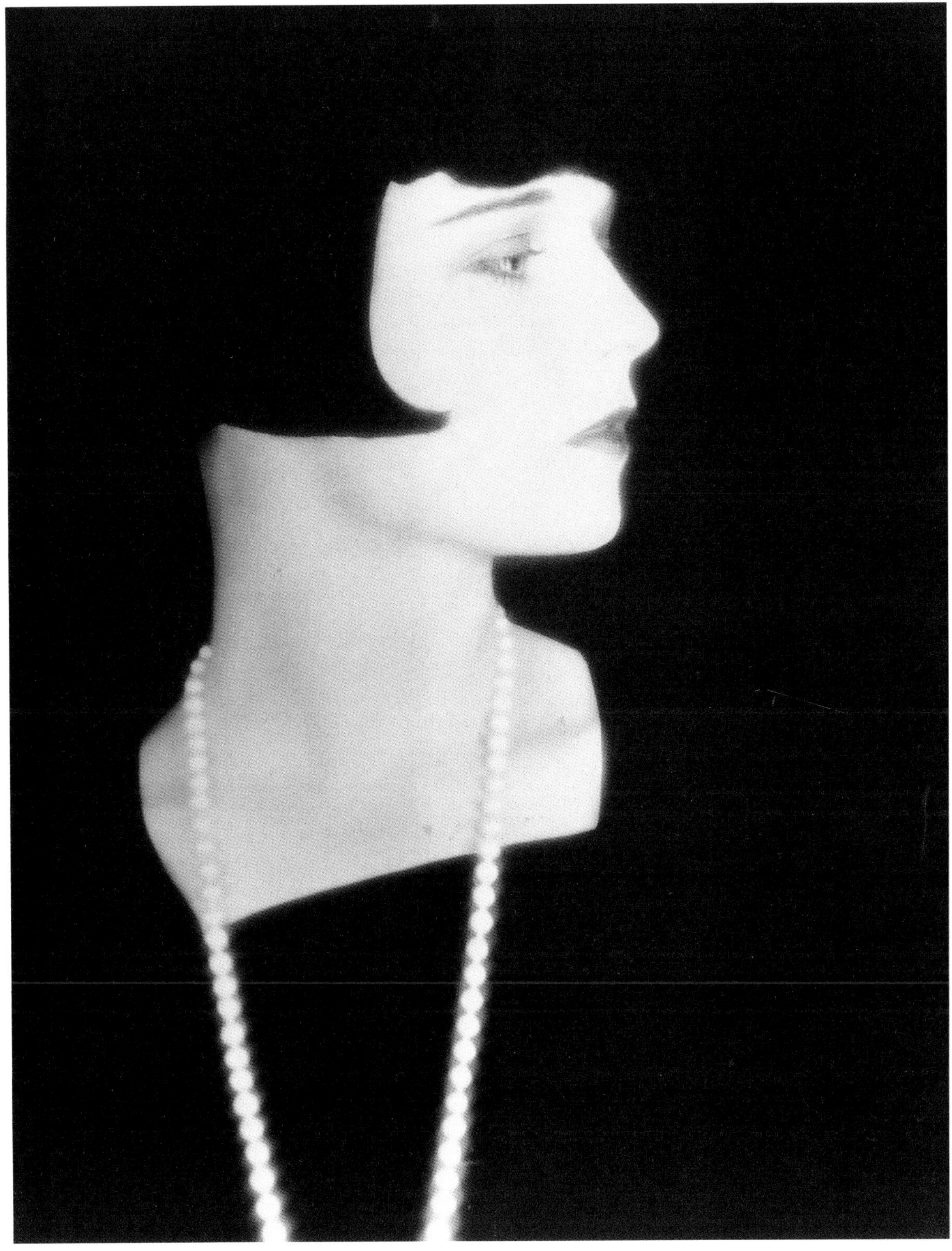

EUGENE R. RICHEE,
Louise Brooks,
1928 (for Paramount),
Kobal Collection, London.

Romantic portraits

But not all differences can be explained in this way. Horst worked for a time with Hoyningen-Huene (1900–1968), a Russian by birth who became chief photographer for *Vogue* before emigrating, like so many others, to the United States, where he worked for *Harper's Bazaar*. In 1946, he moved to Hollywood and devoted himself to portraits of movie stars. Previously, he had concentrated on fashion photography, with all that this requires in originality in order to attract attention. From his training with André Lhote he retained a taste for strict, spare, stripped-down compositions, in line with the return to a sense of order that characterized painting of the period. We are struck by the simple and direct (or so it seems) style of his portraits of the stars – Ava Gardner or Greta Garbo – seen front-on, in close-up, without accessories or decor, as if nothing should come between the spectator and the interior life of these personalities.

Sir Cecil Beaton (1904–1980) also photographed for *Vogue*, after studying art and architec-

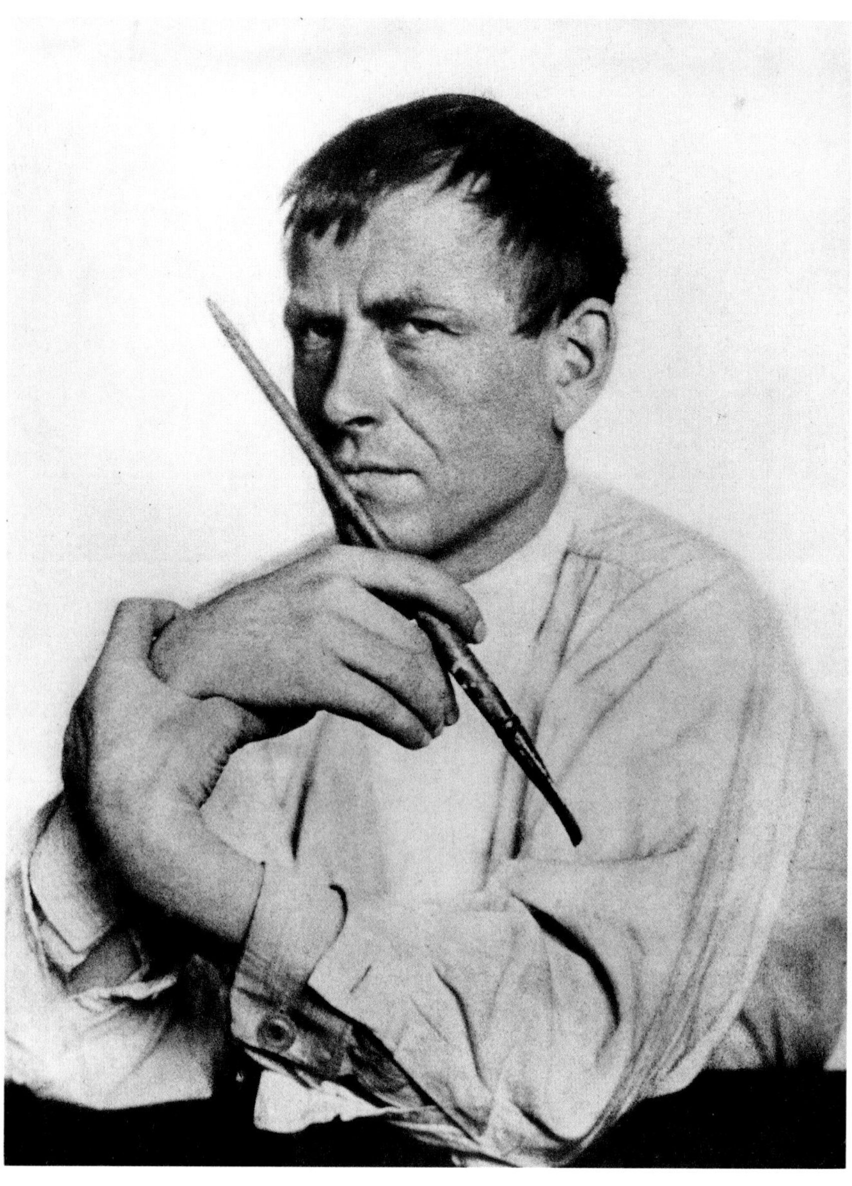

HUGO ERFURTH, *Otto Dix*, Dresden, 1925, Agfa-Foto-Historama, Cologne.

ture. He took fashion photographs as well as society portraits, and yet his vision is totally different from that of Hoyningen-Huene. As a painter and interior decorator, he attempted to interpret the personality of his models through their surroundings. The result is often convincing. His portrait of Picasso in 1933 in his apartment wearing a dinner jacket could not be a better expression of the life of the painter at that period. All too often, however, the artifice is too obvious, or the portrait takes on an official character – as was probably the intention, and only to be expected in a portrait of Her Majesty the Queen Mother, but which reveals an undeniable coldness in other examples. His Churchill, posing at his ministerial desk, lacks the extraordinary presence of the famous photograph by Yousuf Karsh (1908–) where Churchill stands with a decisive hand on his hip, a mixture of concern and strong will reflected in the lines of his face.

Two personalities, however, dominate the art of the professional portrait in the inter-war years. Both belong to the previous generation: the German Hugo Erfurth (1874–1940) and the American, originally from Luxembourg, Edward Steichen (1879–1973). Both had begun their careers at the time of Pictorialism and while Erfurth was influenced by it Steichen embraced it wholeheartedly. It is often said that after the Great War, following the general trend, Steichen adopted a very precise style, a frequently reproduced example of which is his portrait of Gloria Swanson, seen through a lace veil, that appeared in *Vanity Fair* in 1926. Although not incorrect, this assertion, based on a over-simplified schema of stylistic development, is insufficient for a full understanding of his art. As not only a portraitist and fashion photographer, but also the author of advertising and architectural photographs, Steichen practiced all genres and was able, with exceptional flexibility, to change his style to suit the subject. His portraits of men, generally very sober, are chiefly concerned to show contrasts in light values, so that his portrait of Charlie Chaplin, published in *Vanity Fair* in 1925, is not, basically, very different (apart from the subject's expression!) from that of the Secretary of State Cordell Hull taken two years earlier, or from that of Stieglitz, taken fifteen years earlier. Women, on the other hand, are set in surroundings that seem at times to be inspired by fashion photography. A good example is his extravagant portrait of Marlene Dietrich taken for *Vogue* in 1935, with her studiedly insolent pose, her feathered hat, and carnations in the foreground. One would take it for the worst kind of "glamor photography" if it were not for the underlying humour, the virtuosity of the artist in his use of a Japanese style that had been all the rage in painting in his youth, and the dazzling handling of the black silhouette that stands out from the clever range of light tones.

Portraits of artists

The work and career of Erfurth provide a complete contrast to that of Steichen. The owner of a studio in Dresden, he carried on the traditional trade of portrait photographer without ever turning to another genre or working for magazines. He enjoyed a considerable reputation in his own country (he was president of the Society of German Photographers for over twenty years, having been one of the founder members in 1919), and built up a clientele of personalities from the world of politics and the arts. His style underwent no major changes: all his life he remained faithful to prints made with greasy inks, a technique favoured by Pictorialists, but he gradually departed from his initial taste for landscape backgrounds or interiors – used very discreetly

7. Quoted in the exhibition catalogue *Lichtbildnisse, op. cit.*, p. 708.

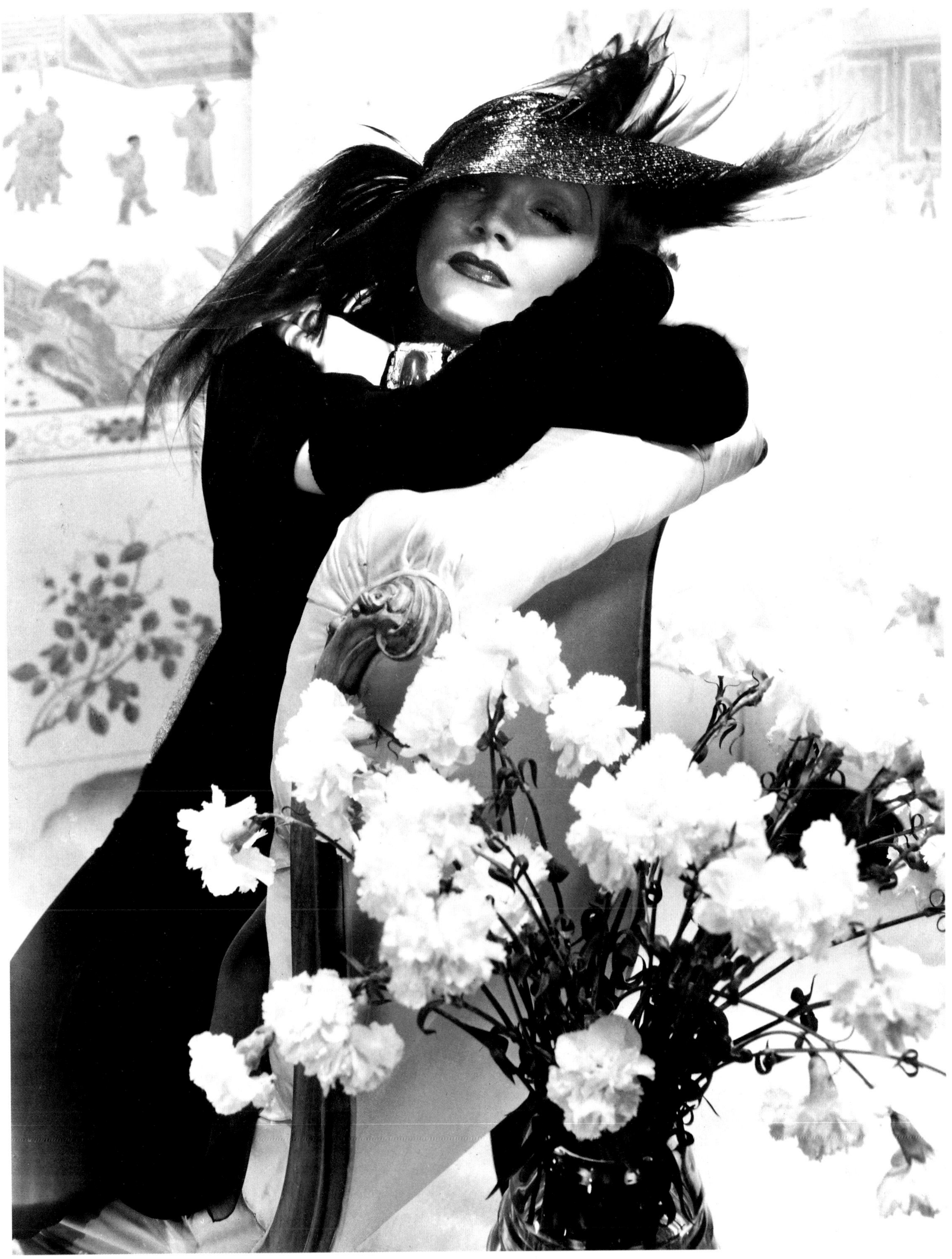

EDWARD STEICHEN, *Marlene Dietrich,*
1935, Rheinisches Bildarchiv, Cologne.

The Photomaton

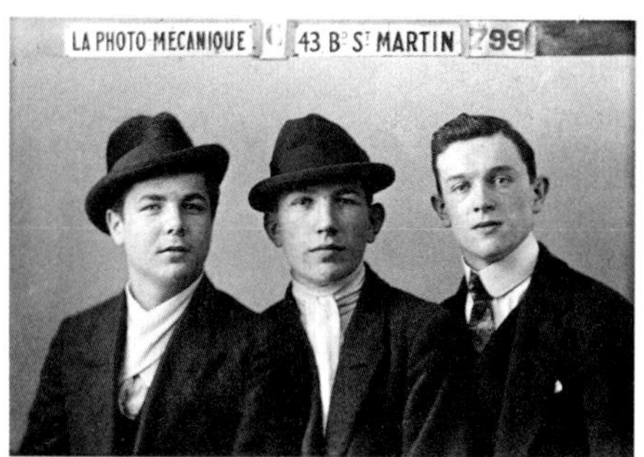

The principle of the automatic photo booth is based on the mechanization of the development of the negative and the almost instantaneous printing of a small-format portrait, needing no enlargement. In 1924, a patent was taken out in New York by Anatol Marco Josepho and the first public machine was installed in December 1926, while the Photomaton business was established in November 1927.

Even if automation was, in itself, new, several earlier processes had offered the almost immediate production of a portrait. Indeed, this was the case for the majority of daguerreotypes, single images requiring little in the way of lengthy processing (at least once the experimental years were over). Similarly, the ambrotypes of the 1850s and then Ferrotypes, or tintypes, were also produced shortly after exposure. However, these were unique images. Multiple copies became possible only with the introduction of the carte de visite on paper. These processes were confined to much frequented public places such as fairs, beaches, markets, and agricultural shows from which people liked to take away a souvenir, albeit of only average quality. In 1894, Conrad Bernitt's Bosco system (for ferrotypes) had simplified the automatic taking and processing of photographs. Automatic machines for printing on paper (allowing several copies to be made) were invented before the First World War. In use until the 1930s, they bore the address of the studio and a number that enabled new prints to be made.

The Photomaton Society first held rights for Britain, France, Germany, Italy, and Canada, but soon "Photomaton studios" were to be found in places as far-flung as China (10), Japan (15), and Latvia (2). In 1933 there were 140 studios in France and 240 in the United States.

The first five booths were installed in Paris in June 1928 (Galeries Lafayette, Sam's, Petit-Journal, Luna Park, and the Jardin d'Acclimatation or Botanical Gardens). Six (different) poses could be delivered in eight minutes. At first an operator was needed, but customers soon learned to operate the machine themselves, using a mirror to check the pose.

Besides the identity-card format, it was also possible to have enlargements in postcard format, 50 x 60 cm. In the 1930s, an operator in Place Blanche collected for Photomaton a series of instant portraits of famous figures from the entertainment world who were passing through. Michel Simon, Foujita, Dranem, Damia, Sacha Guitry were among those who were happy to co-operate in this harmless amusement.

Michel Frizot

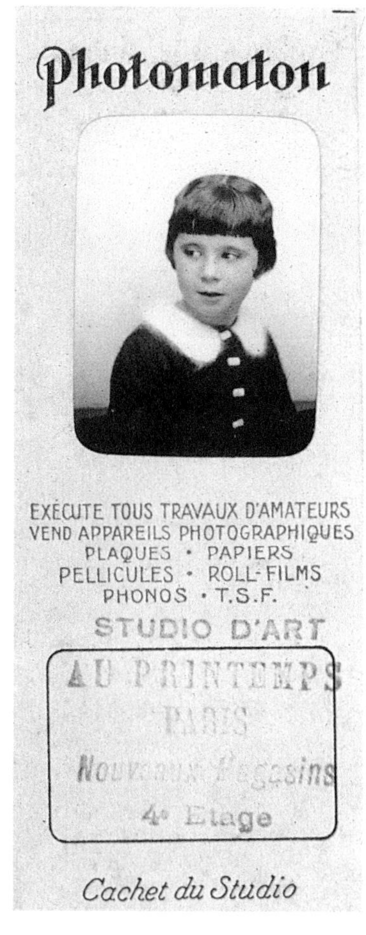

"Photomaton" presentation folder, Paris, circa 1935, private collection.

◀ ***"Photo-Mécanique" group photograph,*** Paris, circa 1920, private collection.

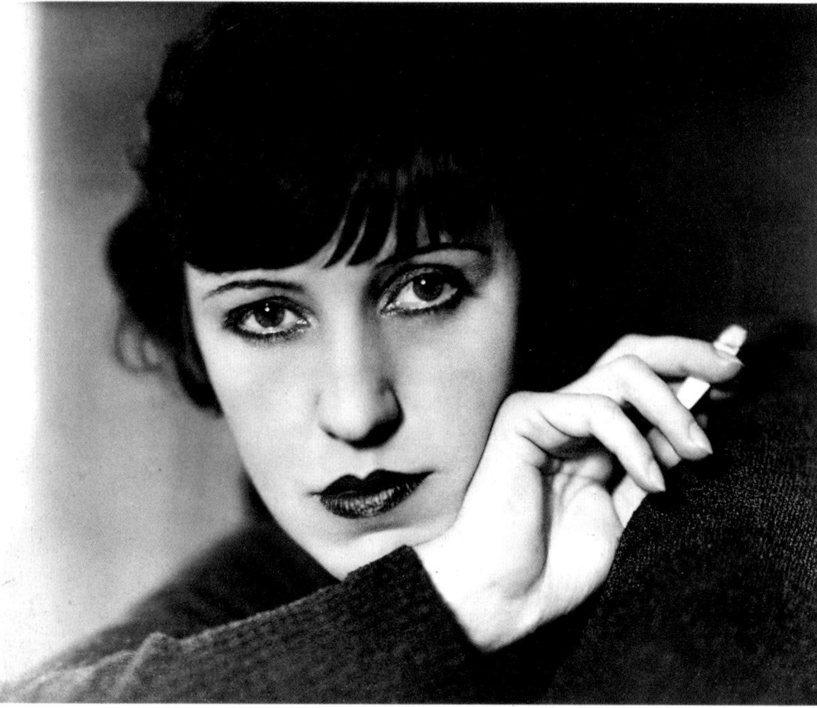

but, nevertheless, rather too reminiscent of late nineteenth-century painting. He soon gave up characterizing his models by photographing them with some kind of prop, such as the portrait of Paul Klee with paintbrushes, coming to concentrate the lens on the face alone, seeking, as he said, faces "marked by destiny or the demon of creativity".[7] We can see this in his portraits of the painter Beckmann, looking straight at the camera with that expression of strong will that Beckmann himself gave to his self-portraits, of Kokoschka, lost in a troubling dream, or of Kandinsky, in the guise of some civil servant.

Between the wars, the portrait of the artist took on an importance that was due, in part at least, to the integration of photographs into literary and artistic circles. The phenomenon was not entirely new – such had been the situation for Nadar in the mid-nineteenth century – but cases like this had become increasingly rare as the profession of photographer developed. Pictorialism contri-

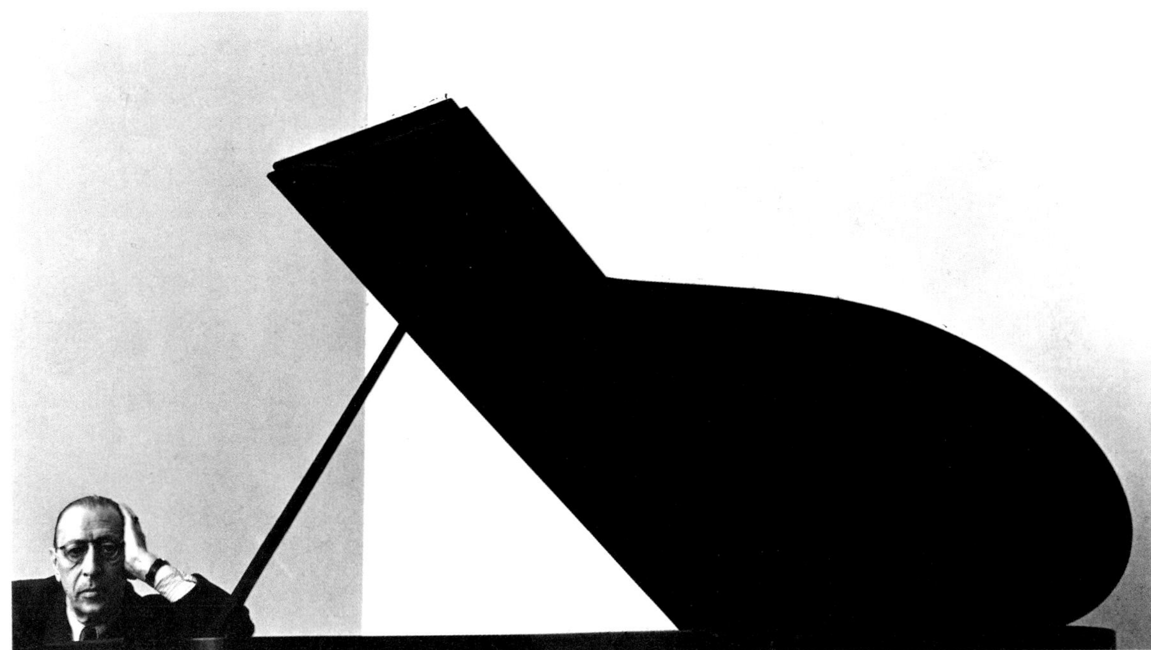

ARNOLD NEWMAN,
Igor Stravinsky,
1946,
Rheinisches Bildarchiv, Cologne.

MAN RAY,
Jean Cocteau,
1924,
Lucien Treillard Collection.
▼

◀◀ Opposite:
LOTTE JACOBI,
Lotte Lenya,
circa 1928,
Museum Folkwang, Essen.

buted, outside France at least, to the re-establishment of these links, as the remarkable career of Stieglitz so compellingly shows. It was, however, two other Americans who opened the way to the portrait of the artist or the writer as a particular genre, based on an empathy between subject and photographer: Edward Steichen, whose portraits of Rodin are still justly famous, and, above all, Alvin Langdon Coburn. Coburn took many portraits of George Bernard Shaw, with whom he had formed a close friendship – in 1912 Shaw wrote "Steichen and Coburn are the two greatest photographers in the world"[8] – but he also photographed Maeterlinck, Mark Twain, Rodin, Matisse, Gertrude Stein, and the American painter Brangwyn, as well as many others.

Coburn's early portraits are notable for their quality rather than for any great originality of style; in general the upper half of the figure is seen, or sometimes just the face. If he painted Matisse and Brangwyn at work, a palette or paintbrush in hand, he was merely reviving a formula that had already been current for a long time in the history of portraiture. But when he wished to capture Ezra Pound, the inventor of Vorticism, he used the device of three superimposed negatives (1916) or a camera which he had designed himself that could provide pictures suitable for the Vorticist aesthetic (1917). Thus he did not characterize his subject by using the conventional props of a palette and brush for an artist or a pen for a writer, but, rather, by making an analogy between the subject's art and the appearance of the image. This new way of conceiving the portrait of the artist – although the path had already been opened by painting – was to be used frequently in future years.

Demanins (1903–1944), in his *Marinetti à la radio* (1932), or Tato (1896–1974), in his *Portrait mécanique de Remo Chitti* (1930), were both directly inspired by the principles of Futurism in their characterization of their subject. Rodchenko (1891–1956) used a similar Futurist effect to

8. Quoted by Coburn (*op. cit.*, p. 14), who recalls having read this remark on the back of E. Steichen's book, *A Life in Photography*.

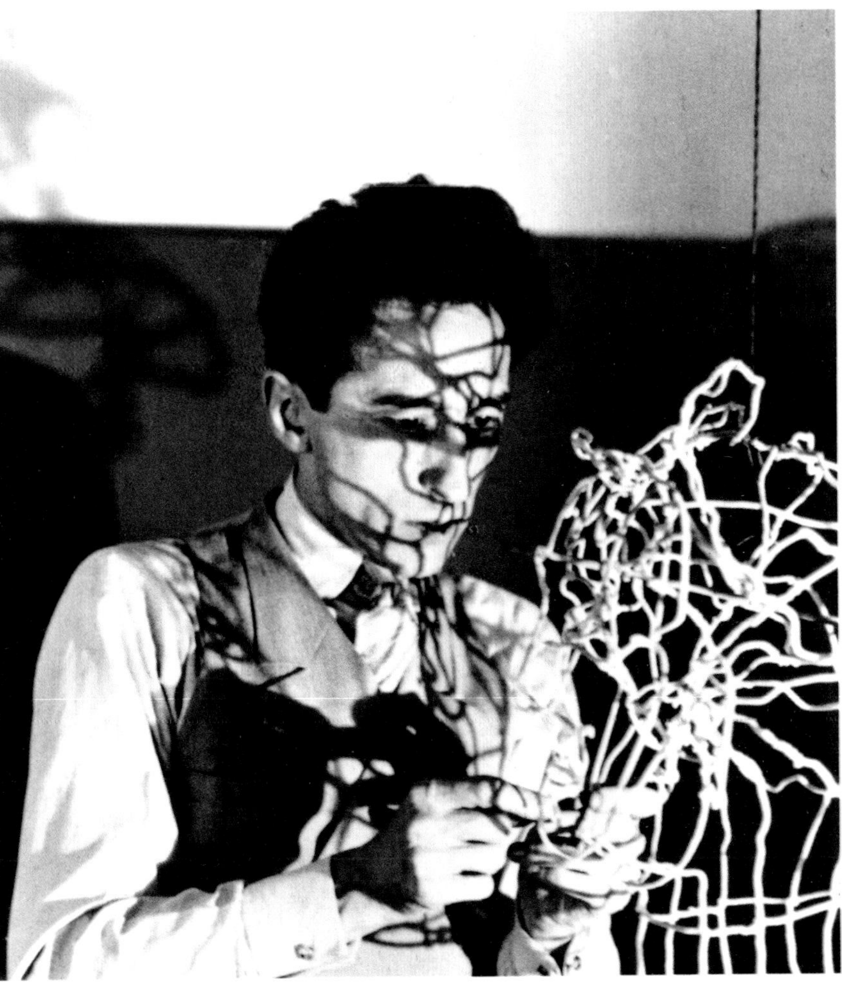

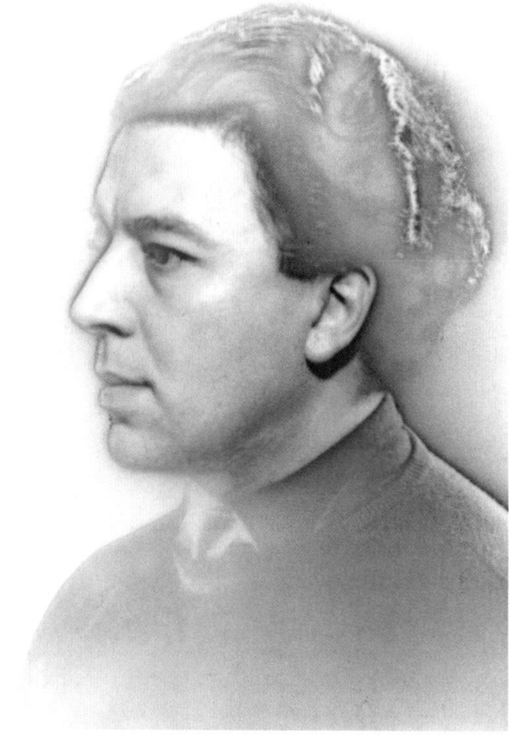

MAN RAY, *André Breton*, 1929, Lucien Treillard Collection.

LOTTE JACOBI, *Franz Lederer*, circa 1929. ▼

characterize the art of the painter Tchevchenko, in 1924. The hand shown *contre-jour*, without an arm, in George Platt Lynes's *Cocteau* (1930) is an allusion to the latter's Surrealism, just as the fragmenting of shapes in Arnold Newman's *Stravinsky* (1946), recalling the paintings of Ozenfant, is supposed to refer to the composer's aesthetic, even if it is easy enough to recognize that the black shape standing out from the background is the lid of a grand piano.

In this genre of portrait photography, there can be no more famous or typical examples than those by André Kertész (1894–1985), as in his treatment of Mondrian's studio, with its geometric divisions of dark and light tones, and the enigmatic single flower in a vase, perhaps representing the painter's extreme rigor, or maybe the opposite, a secret concession to the beauties of nature. These are portraits made at one remove, of interposed objects (such as Mondrian's spectacles and pipe, 1926). But when he photographs artists, his friends, Kertész generally prefers to show them, with an apparent simplicity, in their daily context, whether it is Chagall having lunch in the garden with his family, Colette at home, Vlaminck having a break, a cigarette in his hand, or Eisenstein, sitting on the floor near a rug with a geometric design (1929).

9. Man Ray, *Self-portrait*, 1963.

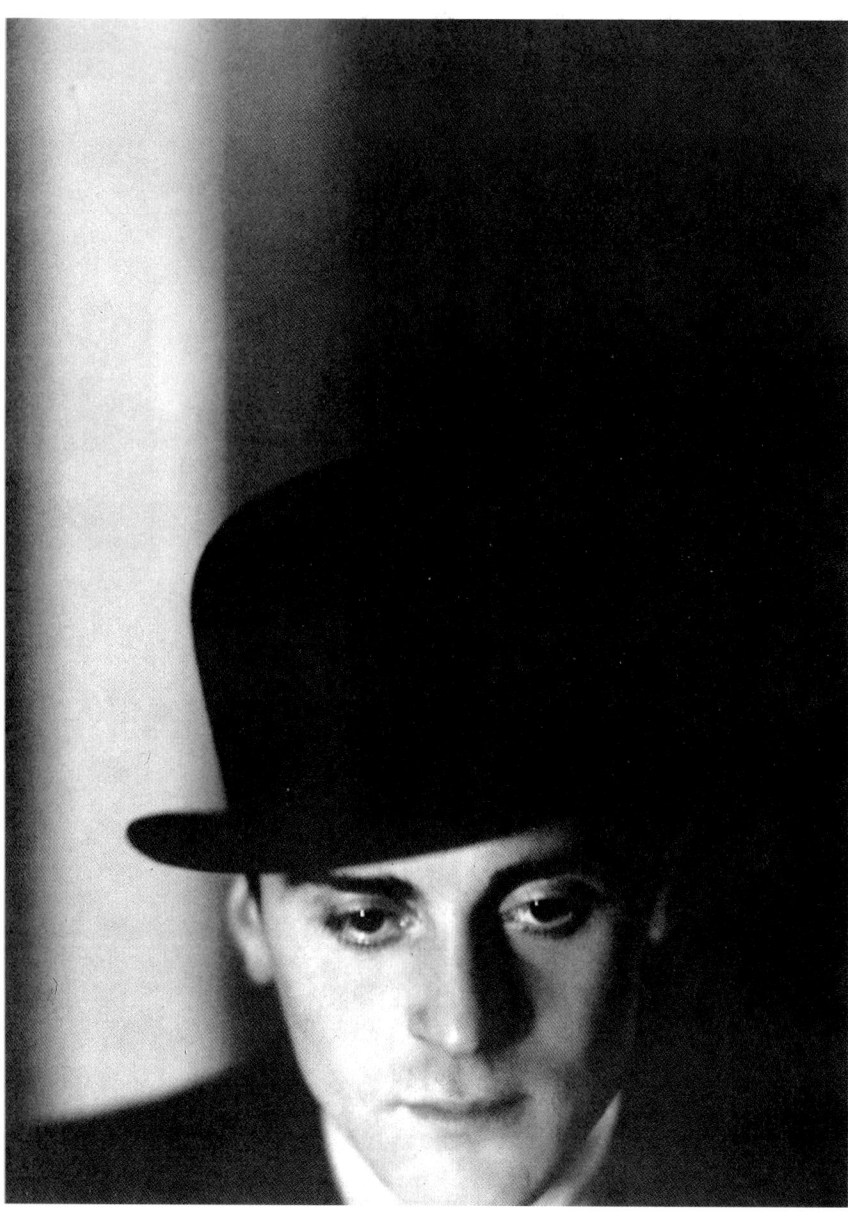

This last portrait can be compared with one taken by another immigrant, Man Ray (1890–1976), of Picasso, sitting with his elbows on a café table, in front of an ashtray full of cigarette butts – a Picasso whose pose and hands recall, in 1933, the figures he was painting some ten years earlier. The neutral white background is derived from an aesthetic very different from that of Kertész, but one that is difficult to define. A painter by training, Man Ray was one of the founders of the Dada movement in the United States before moving to Paris where he joined the Surrealist movement. As a photographer of portraits of artists, he was himself an artist, photographing his peers or his friends.[9] More than in any other, he excelled in this genre which he practiced with complete freedom, never submitting to the constraints of any formula. If he occasionally used evocative props, he could also confine himself to the face alone, as in his famous portrait – probably the best we have – of the architect Le Corbusier with his round glasses and expression of a clergyman. Sometimes, as in the case of his nudes, he uses the technique of solarization – which detaches the face from the background, giving it an unreal, surreal quality, as is the case with his portrait of Max Ernst – but he can also be simple and direct,

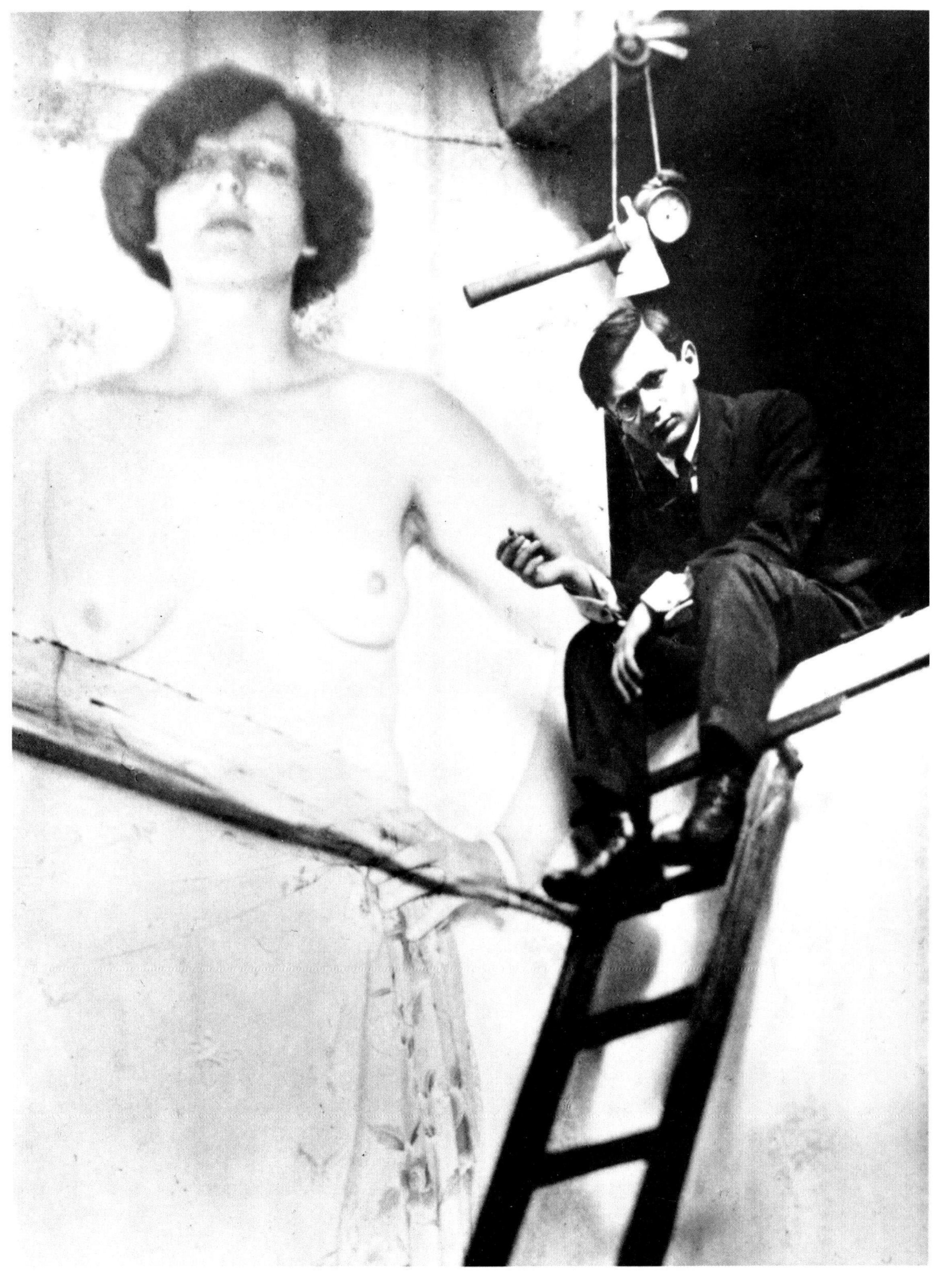

MAN RAY,
Tristan Tzara,
1921,
Lucien Treillard Collection.

or at least appear so, as in the aforementioned portrait of Picasso.

Among Man Ray's portraits, one of the most famous is the one showing himself in profile next to the camera. While the self-portrait is closely related to the portrait of the artist, a certain romantic propensity and a taste for speculation about self-awareness have tended to make it, both in painting and in photography, something of a genre in its own right.[10] This is, in fact, illusory, since neither the image of a painter before his canvas nor a photographer by his camera are necessarily "self-portraits". The frontal shot, in front of a mirror, deriving from an entirely traditional conception of the representation of the artist, was to enjoy great success in the inter-war period, particularly in Germany in so-called "experimental" circles, to the extent that its revival in 1974 by Ralph Gibson (born in 1939) can be seen as a homage to the masters and an affir-

10. The exhibition catalogue *Self-Portrait in the Age of Photography: Photographers Reflecting Their Own Image*, published by E. Billeter, Lausanne, 1985, provides the most important documentation for this subject.

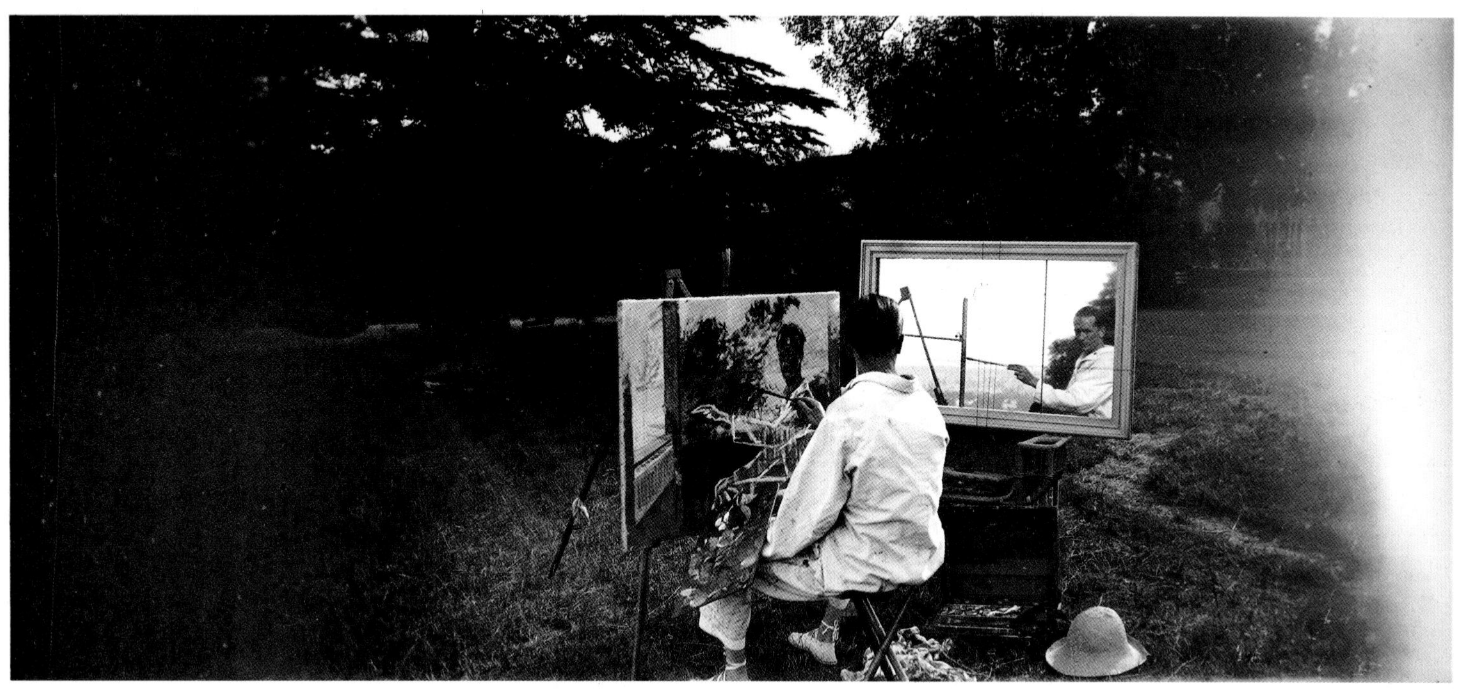

JACQUES-HENRI LARTIGUE, *Self-portrait*, Rouzat, 1923.

ANDRÉ KERTÉSZ, *Self-portrait*, Paris, 1927.

mation of his membership of the tradition they had created.

Outside this clearly defined group, the self-portrait, once again, differed little from the portrait of the artist, with which it shared a freedom not available in the taking of portraits of ordinary clients or personalities. This freedom manifested itself in different ways. Because of it, the portrait of the artist became, if not the favorite area for new aesthetic research, then at least one of the genres where experiments first conducted in the field of painting found their application in photography. The reaction against Pictorialism that took place after 1920 had, in fact, been prompted by a fallacious argument. By claiming to be breaking their subservience to painting in order to establish an art that was specifically photographic, photographers were affirming a principle that had long been accepted in other forms of art. However, what they were, in fact, breaking with was an old-fashioned style (that of Impressionism and Symbolism), in order to take inspiration partly from Surrealism, partly from Cubism, and, sometimes, from the beginnings of Abstraction. Coburn's use of Vorticism is such an obvious example that the point does not need to be labored, but there were many other photographers who followed a similar path, although often less obviously, and perhaps less consciously.

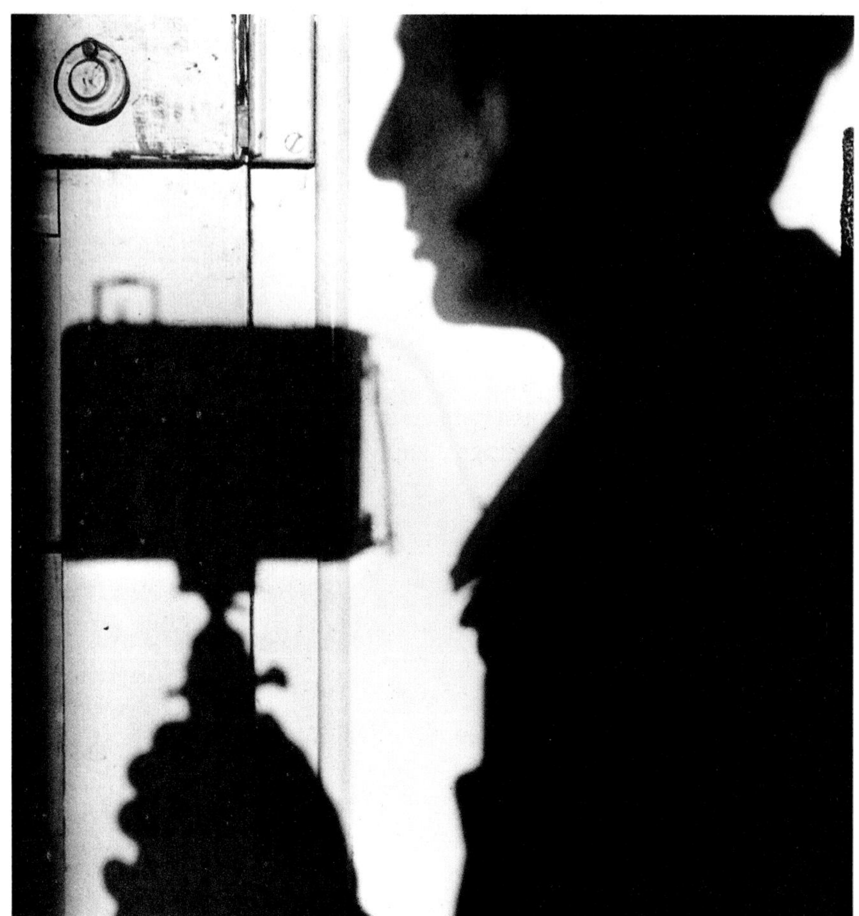

Out of such developments came – particularly in Germany, thanks to the reform movement in the art schools, of which the Bauhaus is the most famous example – a style of photography known as "experimental", in which the human face was often relegated to the rank of a mere object in a stylistic experiment, devoid of all meaning – even when the picture is ostensibly a portrait and not an image of an anonymous face. The New Vision and the New Objectivity lent themselves to considering a face, or an individual, as just another object to which the same objective criteria could be applied as to a machine. The German school (Lotte Jacobi, Lucia Moholy, Max Burchartz, Lux Feininger, Edmund Kesting) and

Russian photographers (especially Rodchenko) favored particularly the use of close-ups, high- and low-angle shots, and vertical or horizontal movement of the lens, the latter being an integral part of the new photography. If, in the portraits of the artists mentioned above, allusions to the style of the artistic work of the subjects represented a way of qualifying them as creators (a more subtle and personalized equivalent of the conventional prop), Lucia Moholy's (1899–) experiments in page layouts and the use of light that dominate her portraits of the critic Franz Roh or the painter Georg Muche taken in 1926 and 1927 seem to have no objective other than themselves. The tradition of the portrait of the artist was to be carried on by, among others, Willy Maywald, another fashion photographer who worked for magazines (*Artistes chez eux*, 1949).

Despite their apparent gratuitousness, these formal experiments contributed to the creation of a period style, and opened the way to new possibilities for expressiveness in portraiture. High- or low-angle shots, unexpected framing, close-ups, faces cut off by the edge of the picture, and violent contrasts of light all became common currency, as exemplified by the portraits of Salvador Dalí by Philippe Halsman (1906–1979), Audrey Hepburn by Angus McBean (1904–), Belmondo by Chargesheimer (Carl Hargesheimer, 1924–1971) or Henri Barbusse by Lotte Jacobi (1896–1990). Although in many ways working close to experimental photography, Lotte Jacobi used these stylistic techniques with great discretion, making them subservient without prejudicing the expressive intention. While a low-angle shot brings out the energetic determination of Barbusse, she turns to an entirely Pictorialist softness to express the melancholy of Käthe Kollwitz, and her Chagall seen *contre-jour* in front of the studio window resembles one of the fantastical floating figures which appear in his paintings.[11]

Yousuf Karsh offers a very different example, in that he developed his own personal style through the systematic use of strong lighting, bringing into relief the smallest irregularities of the face, thus giving an unusual intensity to his portraits of George Bernard Shaw, Sibelius or Thomas Mann. However, the true master of dramatic lighting, pushing the technique to its extreme limits, was, without doubt, Helmar Lerski (1871–1956).[12] The origins of his style should not be sought, however, in the formal experiments conducted after 1920 by younger photographers, but, rather, in the Pictorialism of his early years as a professional photographer (in the United States, around 1910), and in the two other careers he led: that of actor, in his youth, and then, after the war, a movie cameraman. These influences help to explain his grandiose, mad – and often misunderstood – enterprise of the *Verwandlung durch Licht* [Metamorphosis through Light], which brought together some 200 photographs of the same model, transformed into a similar number of different people. Just as a stage director can make an actor enter into the role of another person, so the photographer (or cameraman) can, by controlling the light, impose any character they like on any face.

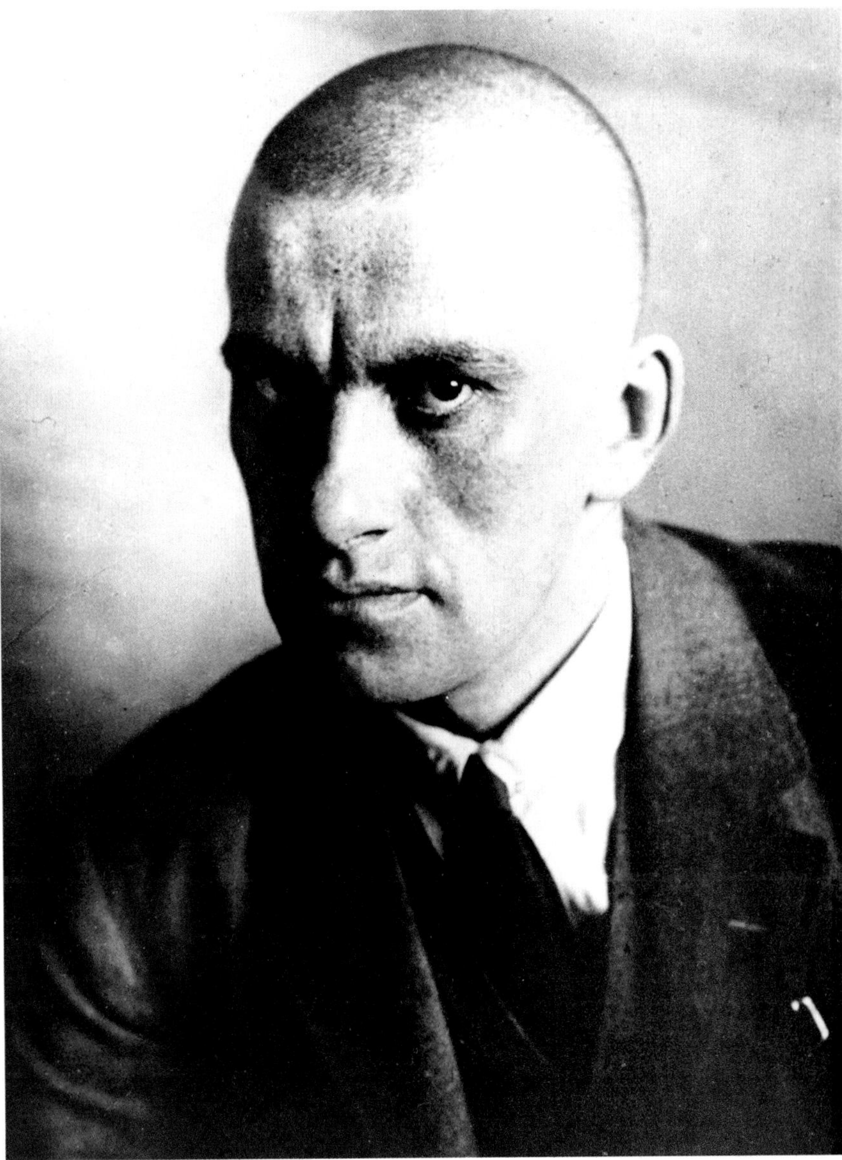

ALEXANDER RODTCHENKO, *Vladimir Mayakovsky*, 1924, Musée Niépce, Chalon-sur-Saône.

Portrait of society

Lerski's work was, in a sense, a radical negation of the portrait, in asserting that the individual is nothing in themselves, and can become anything through the power of the photographer. Yet the same aesthetic of close-ups and complex lighting that he had used for portraits of celebrities, particularly from the world of entertainment, he now put at the service of a very different aim when, in 1931, he published his *Köpfe des Alltags* [Everyday

11. K. Wise (ed.), *Lotte Jacobi*, Danbury, Addison House, 1978.

12. Exhibition catalogue, *Helmar Lerski, Lichtbildner, Fotografien und Filme, 1910–1947*, Essen, Volkwang Museum, 1982.

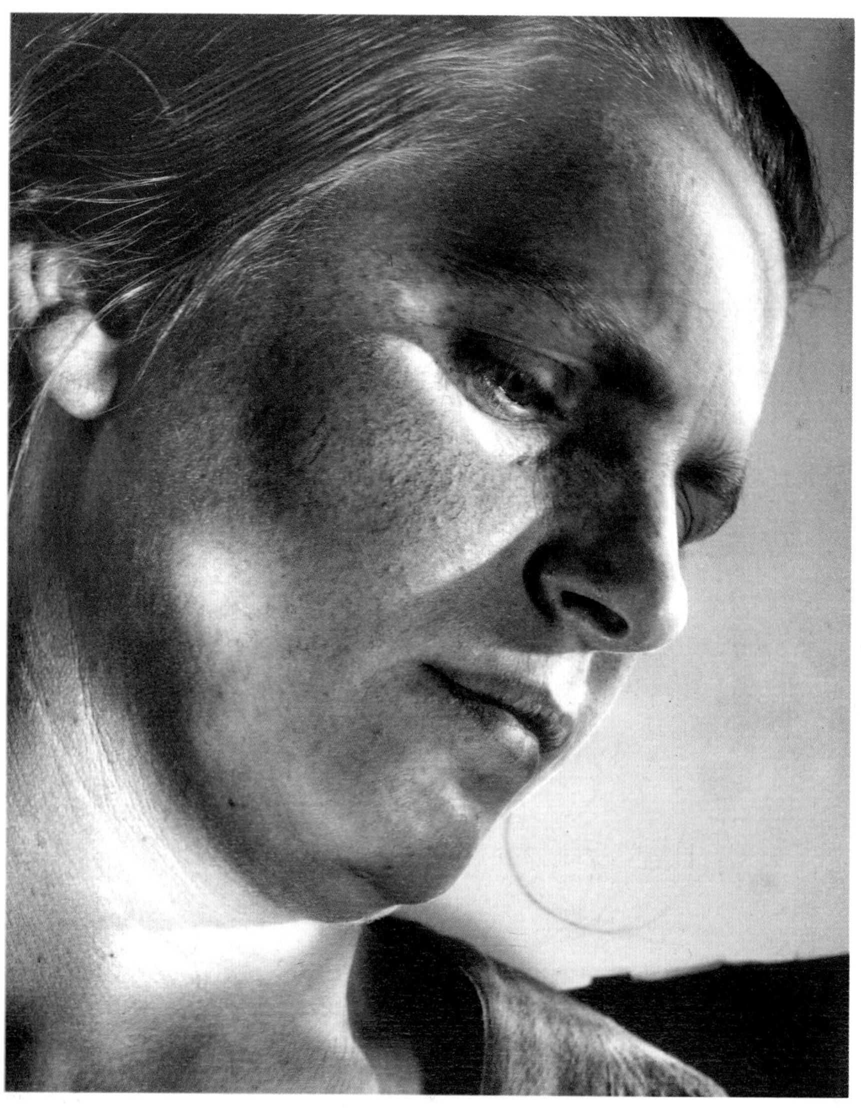

Helmar Lerski, ***Tailor,*** from *Köpfe des Alltags*, Berlin, 1928–1931, Museum Folkwang, Essen.

Faces], a series of anonymous faces illustrating working-class figures to whom he was drawn by his political sympathies. This was not the only such scheme, nor was it new in the Germany of the time, where other photographers, with a variety of intentions and ideological viewpoints, fostered the ambition of portraying an image of society – at least as they saw it.

The progress made in photomechanical printing processes had not resulted simply in the appearance of more illustrated magazines. It also made possible the publication of books, often commissioned by a publisher, but sometimes proposed by photographers, allowing their work and their name to become better known. As we have seen, Coburn was quick to take advantage of such a possibility.

In Germany, anonymous images of ethnic or social types came to be more popular than collections of portraits of famous people, with titles like August Sander's *Antlitz der Zeit* [Face of the Times, 1929], Erich Retzlaff's *Antlitz des Alters* [Face of the Age, 1930], and Erna Lendvai-Dirksen's (1883–1962) *Das Deutsche Volksgesicht* [Faces of the German People, 1932], and *Unsere deutschen Kinder* [Our German Children, 1932], as well as other volumes. While fashion certainly played a role in this phenomenon, it does not, on its own, explain the success of this genre. With a belief in a sort of mysticism of the forces of nature, Erna Lendvai-Dirksen devoted herself to photographing the peasant types of the different provinces; one can understand the success of her books under the Third Reich. Similarly, August Sander has been praised by some photographic historians for having classified his subjects according to their place in society, even though the categories he used, of condition rather than social class, were derived from an extremely traditional point of view.[13]

Despite profound ideological differences, a common trait remained: a preference for the anonymous subject. This can be seen as reflecting the ideological conflict – which played an important role in German ideas of the period, whether on the left or the right – between the collective (the people) and the individual. On the other hand, it may be no more than the traditional tension, running through academic art criticism in the nineteenth century, between the individual and the "type".

Another difference that has often been stressed was the way in which Lendvai-Dirksen, like Retzlaff, photographed her subjects in close-up, beneath a light that sculptured the features of the face, while Sander presents them full-length or in close-medium shots dressed in their workclothes, in surroundings that categorize them socially. From this, it was but a short step to the attribution of an ideological intent in these formal choices – a step, unfortunately, too often taken. The example of Lerski, Jewish and a Communist sympathizer (leaving Germany in 1932), ought to have inspired prudence, and is a reminder that a period style can take on very different meanings.

The photographs collected by Sander for his *opus magnum*, for which *Antlitz der Zeit* was only a sketch, or rather a foretaste, were of two types. The first group consisted of portraits of individuals seen as types and portraits of well-known personalities in the intelligentsia and politics, as well as portraits of unknown people, from the town or the countryside, these last portraits dating, for the most part, from before the War. These were to fall victim to a retrospective attempt to try to detect the author's critical intentions, which would have driven away his clientele. The other photographs, taken as part of this vast scheme of socio-economic documentation, belong to the style of genre photography as practiced in the mid-nineteenth century, an example of which is Rejlander's 1870 picture of a little coal porter.

13. Studies of Sander are particularly numerous, but not all equally good. Useful are *August Sander: Photographs of an Epoch, 1904–1959*, preface by B. Newhall, text by R. Kramer, New York, Aperture, 1980; review by W. Kemp in *Kunstchronik*, December 1982, pp. 481–488 of G. Sander and U. Keller. *August Sander: Citizens of the Twentieth Century*, Cambridge, Mass., MIT Press, 1986.

Irving Penn, the fashion photographer, revived this tradition around 1950 with his portraits of plumbers or chimney sweeps. The deliberate artifice and archaism of these images leaves the impression of a parody of a genre which, even in Sander's time, was already part of the past.[14]

The face of our times – the anonymous face – is to be found not only in these vast systematic enterprises, with their basis in pseudo-science, that promote the individual to the rank of an abstract type. It can also be found in some reportage, a branch of photography that has flourished in recent times. Among the most influential pictures were those resulting from the photographic survey commissioned in the United States by the Farm Security Administration (F.S.A.) to document those regions most affected by the poverty of the Depression years, shortly before the Second World War, or those from the early reportage work of Cartier-Bresson.

These represent very different masterpieces, lying at either extremity of the genre of reportage. The F.S.A. commission came in response to a dual concern: the need to document, and the need to gain support for the New Deal. Although given complete freedom in what they recorded, the photographers responded to this dual requirement in that their images are framed in a style that transfigures the reality that it documents, a style whose rigor recalls the work of that great master of American photography, Paul Strand (1890–1976). Thus, Walker Evans (1903–1975), Ben Shahn (1898–1969, better known as a painter), Jack Delano (1914–), and Dorothea Lange (1895–1965) position their subjects, often facing the camera, in such a way that their photographs are true portraits, even if the names of these poverty-stricken people have not been recorded for posterity – portraits elevated to the status of symbols. Such is the case with what is probably the most famous of all these photographs: Dorothea Lange's *Mother*, who, with her ragged clothes, anxious gaze, and nervous gesture, seems to be a dethroned Madonna in a world abandoned by divine grace.

Henri Cartier-Bresson (born in 1908), first studied painting with André Lhote and cinematography with Paul Strand before becoming a pure reporter. Armed with his Leica, he was happy merely to release the shutter, thus recording the scene offered by chance, refusing to interfere with the developing or printing of the film. But things

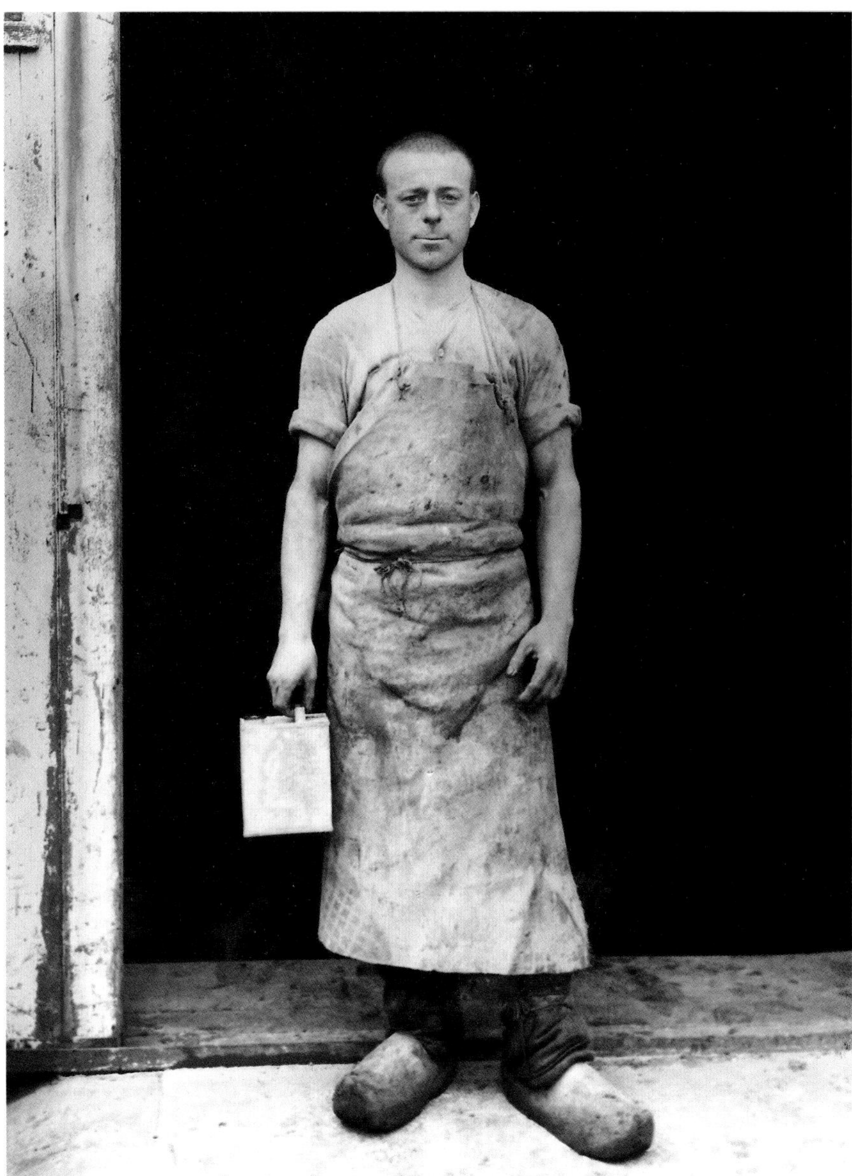

AUGUST SANDER,
Varnisher,
Cologne, 1932,
Sander Archive, Cologne.

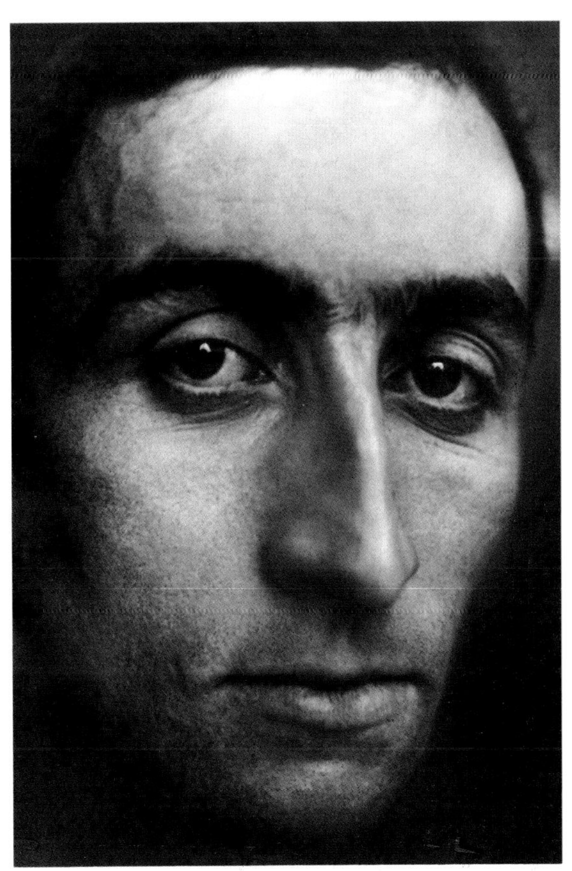

◄ ERNA LENDVAI-DIRKSEN,
Miner from Upper Silesia,
Agfa Foto-Historama,
Cologne.

14. I. Penn's photographs were published by *Photo Magazin*, Munich, September 1952.

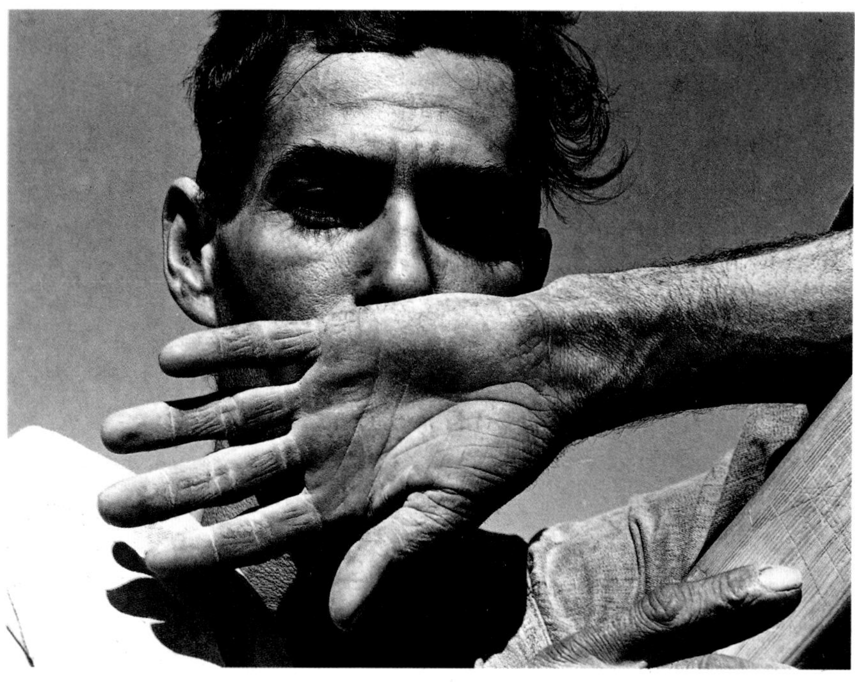

Dorothea Lange, ***Cotton-picker,*** Eloy, 1940, Metropolitan Museum of Art, New York.

cannot be left to chance alone, and photographs taken by amateurs according to this method usually show scenes that lack interest because they lack life. Cartier-Bresson possesses, to a superior degree, the dual gift necessary to the reporter: that of knowing when to seize the moment, and that of knowing, at that moment, how to frame the image in such a way that it possesses both the indispensable rigor of composition and the original, unusual character, that seems to be the guarantee of life. These qualities, on which the fame of some of his photographs relies (such as that of children playing in a street in Madrid or that of workers on holiday picnicking on the banks of the Marne), can also be found in his more personal portraits: Steichen sitting on his bed and unfolding a handkerchief, Sartre in conversation with someone turned away from us, cut off by the edge of the picture, in the foggy atmosphere of a Paris winter, the writer huddled in a leather coat sucking on his pipe and looking away as if to seek the answer to the question he has just been asked in the surrounding fog, Giacometti crossing the road on a rainy day or Matisse, who seems to be being observed by his doves.

This last photograph dates from just after the war, and evokes the intellectual atmosphere of the time. During the same period, Steichen, now director of the department of photography at the Museum of Modern Art in New York, organized the huge exhibition *The Family of Man* (1955), devoted entirely to human beings, alone or in groups, with their joys and their sorrows, their daily life, and their work. After the apocalypse, this represented an act of faith in humanity. Today, the images assembled by Steichen amaze us, so profoundly old-fashioned and of another age do they seem.

And yet the 1939–1945 war did not mark a break, any more for photography than for any other form of art. However attractive, the portraits of actors taken by Liselotte Strelow (1908–1981), like those of Thérèse Le Prat (1895–1966), collected in volumes from 1950, remain in their composition and in their use of light faithful to the aesthetic developed in the period between the wars.[15] This same aesthetic was, as we have said, carried on by portraitists like Yousuf Karsh, Philippe Halsman, and Chargesheimer. In this way they also preserved the tradition and the unity of the genre.

It is not that the portrait no longer exists – far from it, any more than fashion photography or reportage – but insofar as it is not subject to the commercial constraints that influence fashion or architectural photography, making these into clearly defined specialisms, the portrait seems (but perhaps merely an illusion, due to the fact that we are still too close to events) to show us its own face, one that seems indecisive, punctured, a reflection perhaps of the weakening of our traditional conception of humanity.

No other conception has emerged to take its place, thus leaving the field open to the despairing images of Richard Avedon (born in 1923) – probing the marks of old age in the face of his father or the weariness in the face of Marilyn Monroe – to the cruel irony of Diane Arbus (1923–1971) or, much more recently, the total unreality of Italian aristocrats photographed by Patrick Faigenbaum, posing, like ghosts, in their palaces.[16]

August Sander, ***Dwarfs,*** Westerwald, circa 1906, Sander Archiv, Cologne. ▼

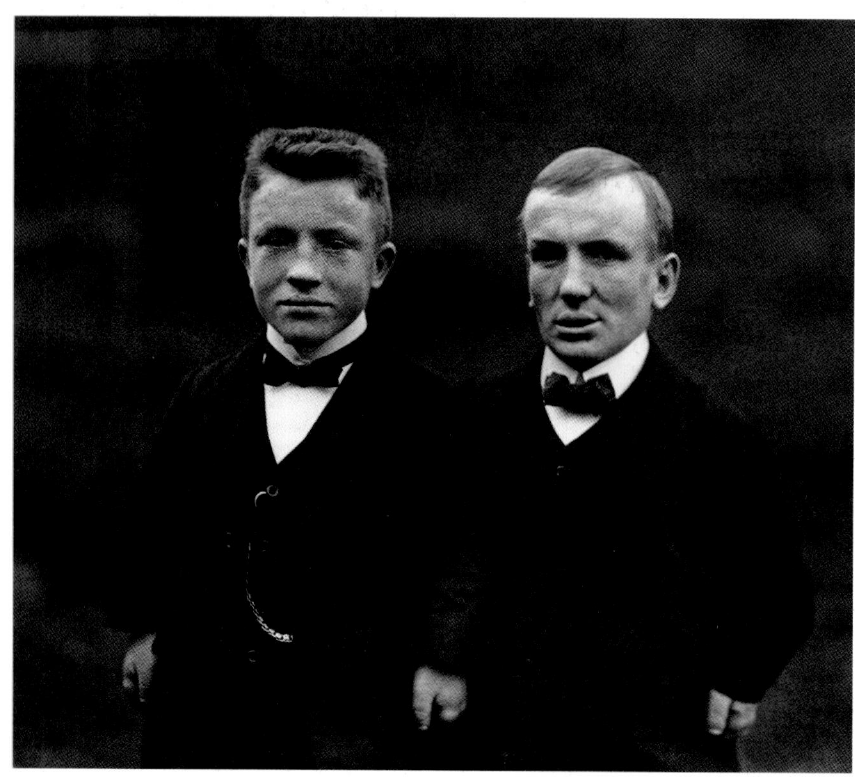

15. The best-known work by T. Le Prat, *Visages d'acteurs* (1950), was followed by *Autres visages d'acteurs* (1952).

16. Exhibition catalogue, *Patrick Faigenbaum*, Paris, Musée d'Art Moderne de la Ville de Paris, 1991.

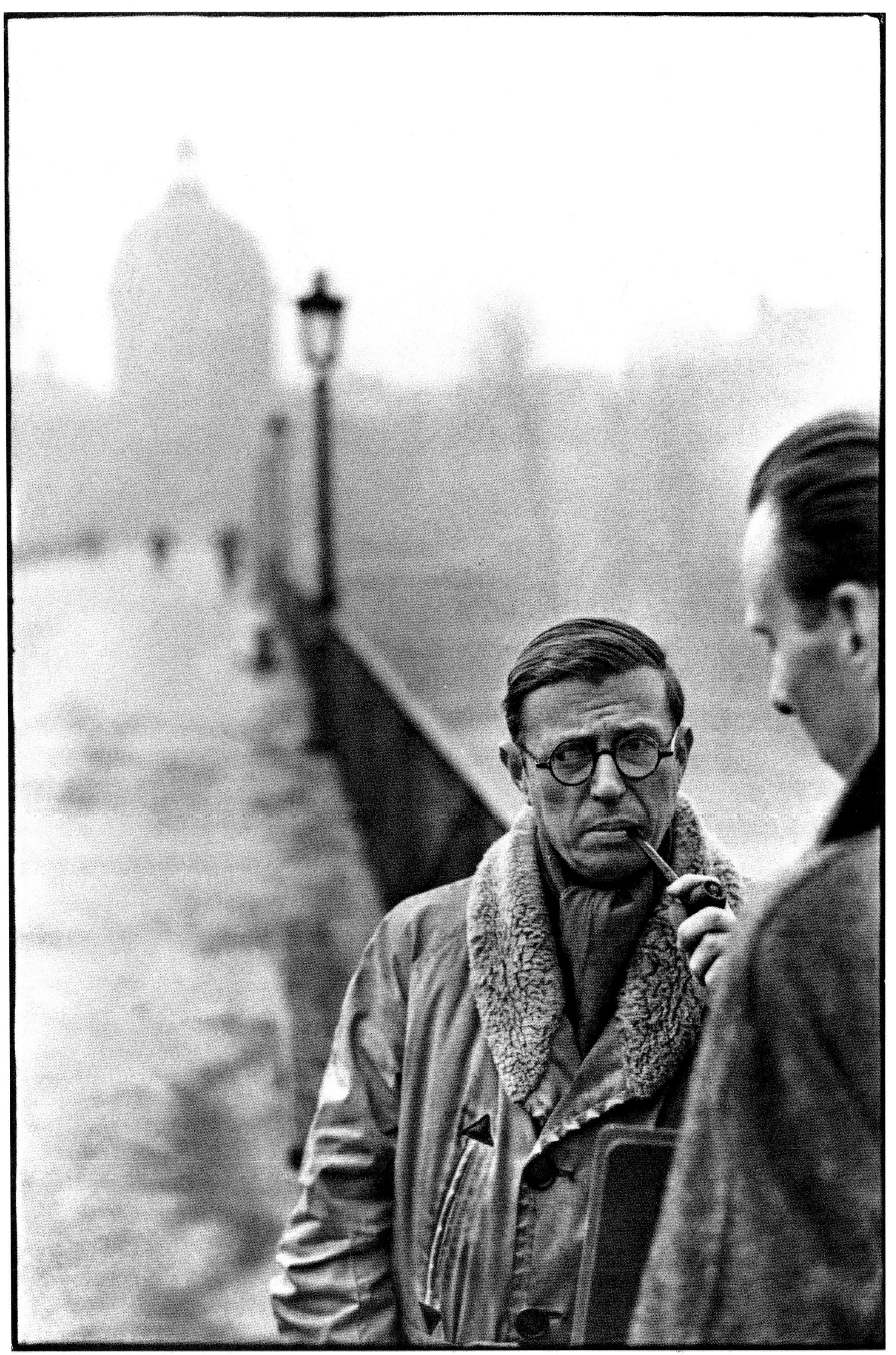

HENRI CARTIER-BRESSON, *Jean-Paul Sartre*, 1946.

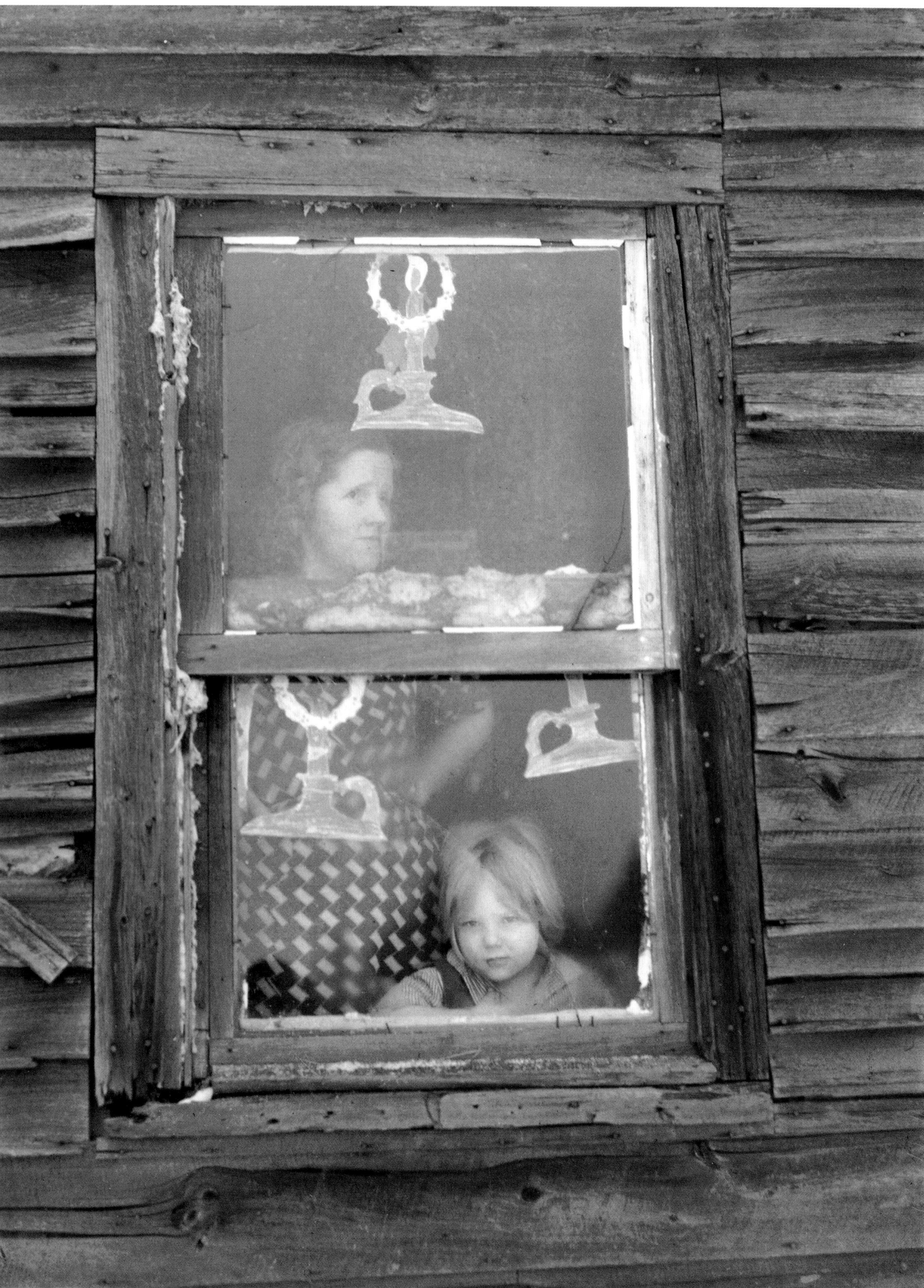

THE WAY LIFE GOES 30

Suffering and hope

Ian Jeffrey

Human activity, the hopes and fears of men and women, was a core preoccupation for many photographers during the 1930s. A kind of creative euphoria gave way to concern for humanity in the face of economic difficulties. In press photography the Soviet model predominated. A type of photography which told a story by means of images evolved to meet the needs of the media, in which the subject was directly apprehended, as though caught in a stage role. Photographic genres emerged in Europe and the United States which were determined by underlying ideologies, all of which nevertheless tended to exalt labor and defend enslaved humanity.

There was a prevailing hieratic manner, which was both complemented and challenged by a more informal, conversational photography. The hieratic style dignified labor and humanity, whereas the informalists stressed and valued inventiveness, vivacity, and individualism in response to the various collectivisms which were in the ascendant during the 1930s. Between these two poles there were a number of middle ways in which photographers and their editors tried to compromise between the monumental and the informal.

The Soviet style

Documentary in the 1930s, one of the great eras of reportage, was determined in both style and substance by the Soviet manner of about 1930. The Russians themselves concentrated on heavy industry, collective farming, and education. Their pictures, whether of workers or of sites, were unambiguous. In a culture oriented towards the future, allowances were not made for tradition and for anomalies. Representative workers of about 1930 were either young or in their prime, and unreconstructed tribesfolk scarce and shy.

The lucid Russian style, with its intact objects and scenes, was a refutation of earlier (and foreign) manners. The German was the dominant photographic culture of the 1920s, and its tendencies were both modern and romantic. *Die Blauen Bücher* presented a shadowy land of ancient buildings inhabited by soulful geniuses of the kind put on show in *Menschen der Zeit* (1930).[1]

By contrast, the Soviet was a collective, daylit, active world. Secondly, German modernism, as exemplified by Werner Gräff's *Es kommt der neue Fotograf* of 1929, rephrased the world in fragments drawn from the city, cinema, and fashion.[2] Soviet candor opposed this vision of the place in kit form, as constituted of alienated engine parts, windows, shoes, and microbes magnified. American radicals of the Photo League, founded in 1936 and centered on New York, also disliked the "German manner" with its cult of red filters and confusing angles, and opted instead for something more "honest".[3]

Alexander Rodchenko, the outstanding Russian modernist, who published pictures in and wrote for *Sovjetskoje Foto,* argued for agitated, active, modernist formats, as being analogous to the real state of things. Rodchenko was criticised in the Soviet Union on the grounds that his modernism, with its disconcerting angles, made the tower of the Moscow radio station, for example, look like a collapsible breadbasket.[4]

Rodchenko's collapsed radio tower did, nevertheless, appear in a major conspectus of 1931, Ernst Glaeser and F. C. Weiskopf's photographic survey of the first three years of Russia's five-year plan, *The Land Without Unemployment.* Published in Berlin, its pictures were uncredited but came from the agencies Ogonjok in Moscow and

◄ Arthur Rothstein, *Christmas Window, Oswego County,* 1937, Library of Congress, Washington.

1. *Menschen der Zeit: Hundert und ein Bildnisse aus deutscher Gegenwart,* Leipzig, Karl Robert Langewiesche, 1930, with a large proportion of pictures by Hugo Erfurth

2. Republished by Walter König, Cologne, 1978.

3. See special issue of *Ovo Magazine,* vol. 10, no. 40/41, 1981, Montreal, with a detailed article by Anne Tucker, pp. 3–8.

4. S. Morosow, *et. al., Sowjetische Fotografen, 1917–1940,* Berlin, Elefanten Press, 1980; A. Lavrentiev, *Rodchenko Photography,* Cologne, Könemann, 1995.

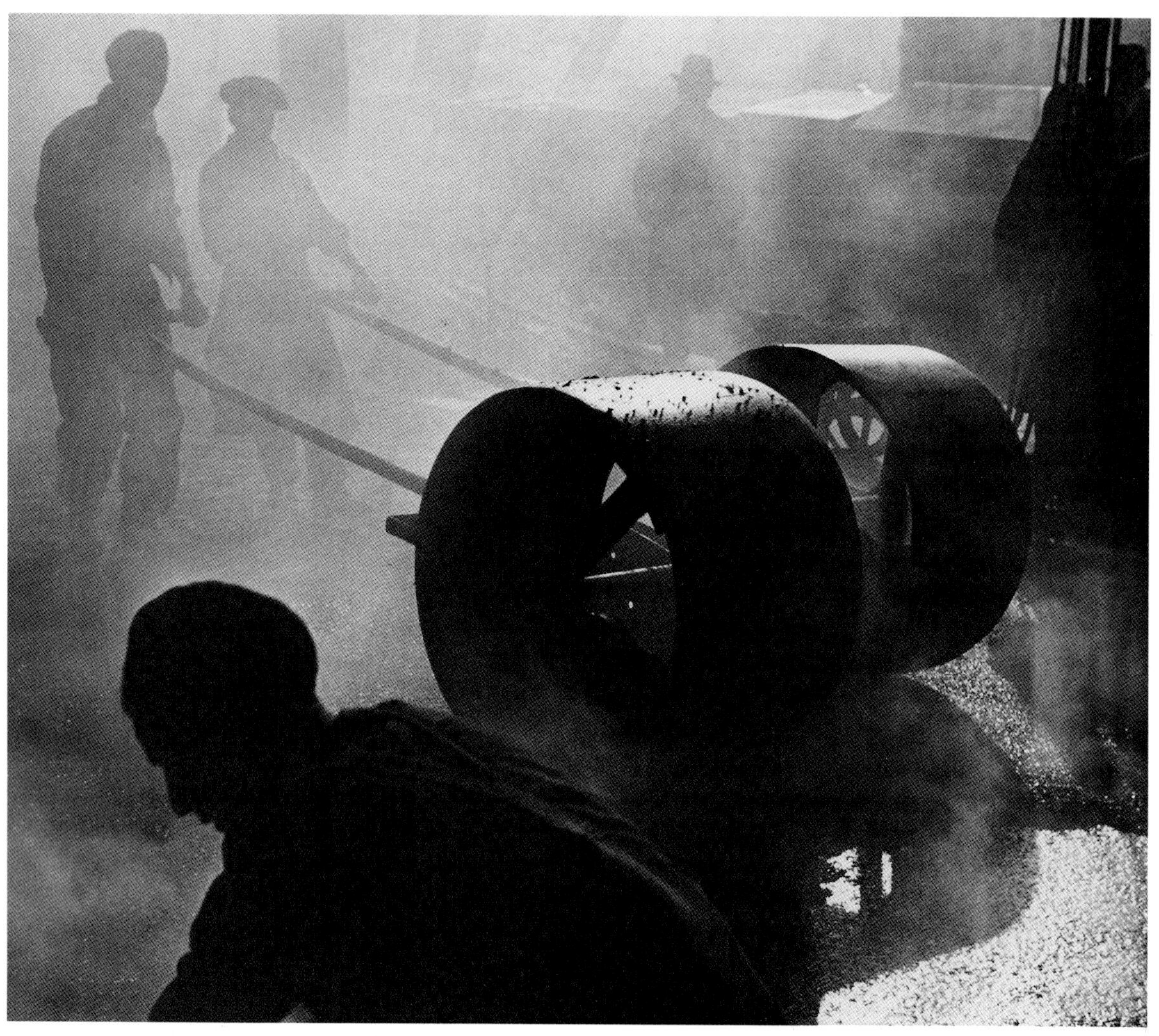

ANDRÉ KERTÉSZ, *Street Work,* 1929

LÁZLÓ MOHOLY-NAGY, ▶ *In the London Flea Market,* from *The Street Markets of London, 1936.*

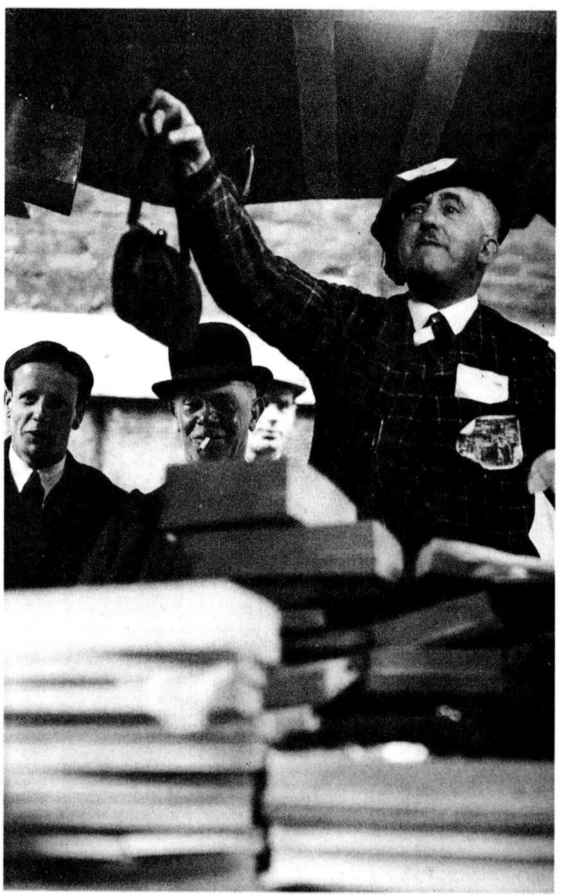

Unionbild in Berlin. Their pictures, arranged under eleven headings, suggested an orderly multiplicity, and were of nurseries, gymnasiums, tractors ("the tank of peace"), Donbass miners, and the handsome leaders of shock brigades. A new world order was foretold in which the races of the earth would be united, if not submerged, in common tasks, willingly and cheerfully undertaken.

Russian photography disclosed nothing less than a future world order. In those circumstances ambiguities of the kind cultivated by Rodchenko were anomalous.

For the first time in its history, photography was placed under a strong teleological sign. The Russian enterprise associated photography with an ideal destiny. In Weimar Germany especially, it had been implicated in current affairs, or in history as contingency, unresolved. Soviet icons and archetypes promised a release from the darkness and confusion of Weimar reportage.[5] It is worth noting in this context that one of the great successes of 1929 was a three-page article by André Kertész in the *Berliner Illustrierte Zeitung* on life in a Trappist monastery – an epitome of order.[6] Secondly, the Soviet example, which had

5. See *Zur Geschichte der Pressefotografie 1930–36*, ed. Diethart Kerbs, Walter Uka, and Brigitte Walz-Richter, Berlin, Frölich & Kaufmann, 1983.

6. Cited by Tim N. Gidal in *Modern Photojournalism: Origin and Evolution, 1910–1933*, New York, 1973, p. 19.

the whole of a society for its subject, helped establish a survey paradigm in Europe as also in the United States.

In North America, the connection was made most notably by the Mexican muralist Diego Rivera, who had returned from Russia to Mexico in 1930, before painting his way across the United States in the early 1930s. He was clear in his own mind: "The social development of our time is a continuous, accelerated march toward collectivization." His *Portrait of America*, taken from the murals, came out in 1934. One of the photographers of the New York murals (New Yorkers' School) was Walker Evans, whose own conspectus, *American Photographs*, would appear in 1938.

America's own exponent of the iconic "Russian" style was Lewis Hine, author of *Men at Work*, a set of fifty "photographic studies of modern men and machines", published in 1932, and meant as a picture book for adolescents. In this book, which centered on the erection of the Empire State Building, Hine intended to correct an impression of an era proceeding independently of its workforce. His new style was Russian in terms of the integrity of its figures, and modernist in its reference to the space frame of the unfinished building.

However, his athletic heroes of labor were out of keeping in a culture which traditionally imagined city life as incoherent and threatening, in contrast to the dignity of the rural areas. *Men at Work* also contrasts with his earlier pictures which included wider, darker, everyday contexts. Hine had been a campaigning documentarist since 1907, intent on disclosure of working conditions rather than on idealization. It was the earlier manner which was admired by the photographers of the Photo League later in the decade.[7]

The Russian idiom was impressive, and univocal. The modernism of the 1920s had meant montage, or analysis and assemblage. The German reporters also disclosed a world in fragments, and, at the same time, garrulous and affecting. European and American photographers in the 1930s acknowledged the authority of the "Russian" lingua franca, but tried always for inflections. In particular, the adapted, hybrid style of the 1930s was compatible with speech. The 1930s was an era of speaking likenesses, after the mute beauty of the Russian icons.

Roles and celebrities

Documentary everywhere was aligned with the people somehow brought to life. Even as radical a modernist as László Moholy-Nagy accommodated the new bias. As author of *Malerei Photographie Film* (1925) and *Von Malerei zu Architektur* (1929), Bauhaus books numbers 8 and 14, he was synonymous with modernism, with all those close-up and eccentric viewpoints expressive of a turning, shifting world and its inventive inhabitants.

On the closure of the Bauhaus in 1933 by the new German government, he went first to Amsterdam and then to London, where he was almost immediately involved in one of the great works of British documentary, *The Street Markets of London* (1936, text by Mary Benedetta). After a decade of manipulative, abstracting photography, unmarked by narrative, he became an *intimiste* and narrator, as if heir to generations of British cartoonists and social observers. He combined British interests in character with modernist dispositions. His market traders dress and act like figures in pantomime, but they work in arranged settings – stacked, piled, and heaped. Although talkative enough for Dickens, they are also artisans and constructors in a modified Bauhaus style.

The importance of the folk speech implied by Moholy-Nagy and reported by Mary Benedetta

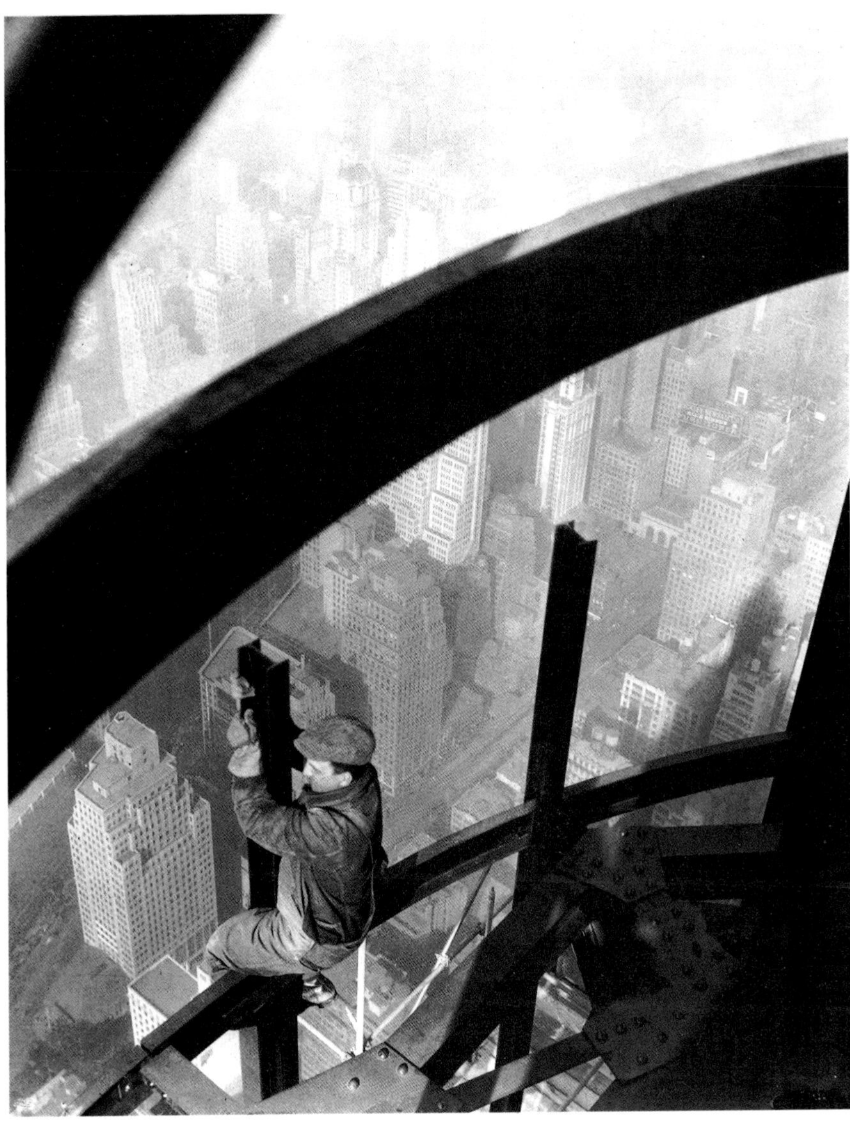

Lewis Hine,
***Construction of the Empire State Building*,**
1931,
International Museum of Photography,
George Eastman House,
Rochester.

7. *Men at Work* was republished, with supplements, by Dover Publications, New York, 1977.

Bill Brandt's Britain

Contrary to legend, Bill Brandt was born not in London, but in Hamburg, Germany, on May 3, 1904. The asthmatic son of a banking family, he came to his own country for the first time in 1931, having lived in a sanatorium in Davos and in Vienna and Paris, where he was Man Ray's assistant.

His ambition was to become an independent professional photographer. His first book, *The English at Home*, appeared in 1936. Based on the portrayal of types and stereotypes, this was a kind of manifesto of British society, through which Brandt undertook to show the British their real faces. The complete opposite of the ideal motherland of his dreams, he discovered a divided people, a stratified society with a well-defined caste system, in the grip of economic crisis. Two years later he published *A Night in London*; in the same way as his friend Brassaï, Brandt enjoyed the uncertain, magical lighting effects of the night. Prowling around almost invisibly, he recorded London, revealing social inequality. He did not hesitate to ask his close friends to pose for him for certain situations.

In 1937 Bill Brandt traveled north, where he undertook at his own expense a photo-reportage on the economic and social situation in the great cities of the Midlands and Tyneside. There he took his most memorable instantaneous photographs, such as the one of the emblematic figure of a scavenger for coal returning home, a modern myth of Sisyphus.

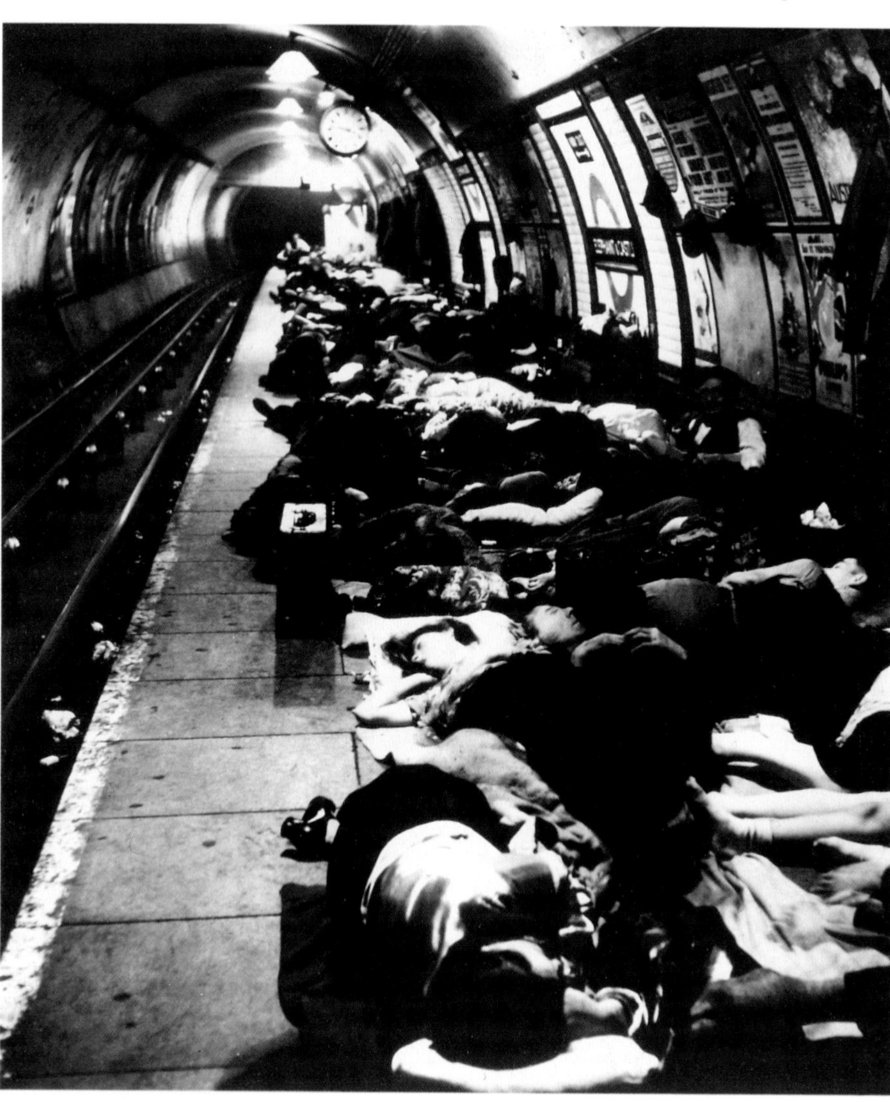

Bill Brandt
The London Underground during the Blitz, 1940

During the war Brandt was employed by the Home Office to show how well Londoners taking refuge in air-raid shelters were coping with air raids. He was also commissioned to produce a major photographic inventory of the capital's important buildings. The work was carried out during the black-out, without flash, rather in the style of Atget. This reportage, notable for its use of light and shade, was published in *Picture Post* and emphasized Brandt's interest in social documentation.

During the second half of his career Bill Brandt devoted himself to portraiture, landscapes, and nude photography. It was his revolutionary treatment of the last category which brought him notoriety. His first nudes were photographed with an old wooden plate camera which the police had formerly used, lacking a shutter and equipped with a wide-angle lens. These photos seemed inspired by Balthus, Hitchcock, and Orson Wells. Their dramatic atmosphere is enhanced by the unusual viewpoints of the architectural backgrounds, imbuing them with a menacing atmosphere of murder or suffocation, perhaps connected with the asthma from which Brandt suffered all his life. These unnatural perspectives, which shocked people at the time, based on the enlargement of volumes and close-up treatment of details, may be compared with the experiments of Picasso, the forms of Henry Moore, and, of course, the distorted work of André Kertész. Increasingly turning to abstract photography, from 1951 to 1960, when he gave up nude work, Brandt undertook exterior views (on the beaches of East Sussex, Normandy, and the south of France), in which he brought together the eternal themes of women and the sea, birthplace and symbol of creation.

At the same time, Brandt was taking portraits for *Lilliput*, *Picture Post*, and *Harper's Bazaar* of the artists, intellectuals, and writers whom he admired. He detested naturalism. Rather he sought to decipher enigmas, and in his work portraiture is combined with a quasi-judicial chronicle of events. Going beyond external appearances, he tried to decode the mysteries concealed behind a face, as in his intriguing portrait of Francis Bacon (1963), far from a straightforward rendering of the subject.

His passion for literature led him to illustrate *Literary Britain* (1951), which unfurls naturally with romantic, tortured scenes evoking *Wuthering Heights*. At Stonehenge, or on Skye, Brandt demonstrated his fascination for untamed sites, those providing a sense of majesty, the sublime, the infinite. The cult of nature fostered the attraction that open spaces had for him, allowing him to bring out the emotional appeal of the landscape. This aspect of his work reached its high point when he chose 200 twentieth-century photographs for "The Land", a project completed shortly before his death in London on December 20, 1983.

In the context of the art of his time, whose aesthetic experiments are reflected in his work, Bill Brandt was one of the first photographers to have created an individual style. While allowing the vocabulary of his art to evolve, he consciously worked at creating a personal photographic language. Based on the alliance between form and content, the fruit of experiment, exploration of the imaginary and an ever deeper investigation of the same themes, his work is notable for its splendid use of strong contrasts and densely printed images.

Patrick Roegiers

was that it situated its photographed subjects within the discursive, everyday milieux in which they were scanned and received. Icons in the Russian style, by contrast, stood handsomely apart. The photography of the 1930s was as anxious to be heard as it was to be seen; it declared on behalf of argot and idiom, it was conversational, articulate, and sometimes histrionic, intent on familiarity one way or another. If the Russian drama of blast-furnaces and shock workers was enacted on behalf of destiny and all the people of the world, succeeding and superseding dramas were to have national audiences in mind.

The style of the Russian documentarists was transparent and sincere. By comparison, what follows looks as if it involved a knowing enactment of national costume dramas. In Britain, for example, the Russian style was parodied by James Jarché working from 1931 for the *Daily Herald*, a market leader on the Left. A photoreporter of long standing with the *Daily Sketch*, Jarché had concentrated on sportsmen, criminals, royalty, and other actors in the British drama.[8] When the people moved to center stage in the 1930s he accorded them celebrity status, and they responded as exuberantly and characteristically as any of Moholy's marketeers.

In 1936, Bill Brandt in *The English at Home* allowed for an abiding British interest in class differences in juxtapositions of, say, a workmen's restaurant with a clubman's sanctuary. He introduced a range of toffs, bookies, and skivvies, a conspectus readily spoken into place in the argot of the day. It was an identifiable but, at the same time, an inauthentic Britain, for the artist himself and his relatives starred in what were, in effect, dramatisations. Costume documentary asserted role-playing and appearance, leaving the question of the real to one side.

In the collectivist context of the 1930s, Britain and France looked increasingly like sites of last resort – France especially. In these ominous conditions there could be no disinterested photography. In a special issue of the photomagazine *VU* in June 1932, headed *La France Pays de la Mesure*, Lucien Vogel – editor and founder of the magazine in 1928 – wrote in an editorial of an "Occident individualiste" in the process of losing Germany to burgeoning, violent, collectivist forces.

In earlier special issues on the Soviet Union, the United States, and Germany, the American masses – in Vogel's terms – had seemed resigned, hoping without hope, and the Germans in a state of moral and material deprivation, but waiting for a leader to give shape and direction to their desperate hopes. Vogel then admitted to wanting

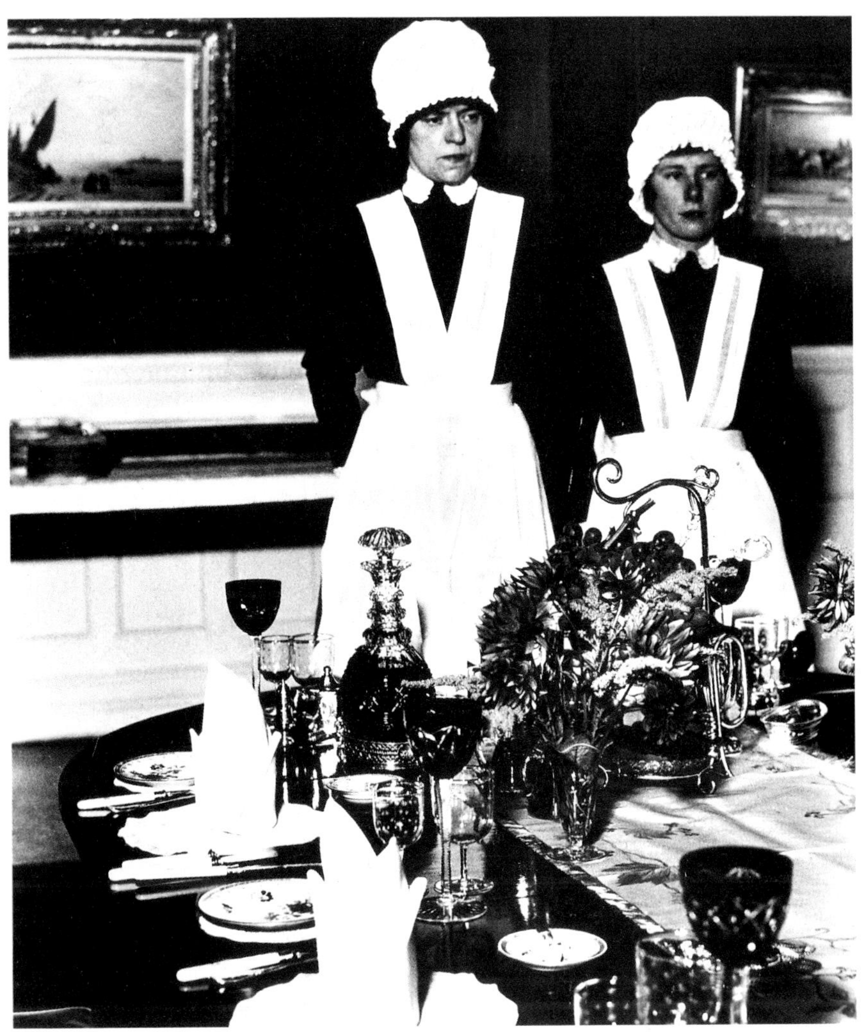

Bill Brandt,
Parlour Maids Waiting to Serve Dinner,
London, 1934.

James Jarché,
Gutting Herrings,
1931,
National Portrait Gallery, London.

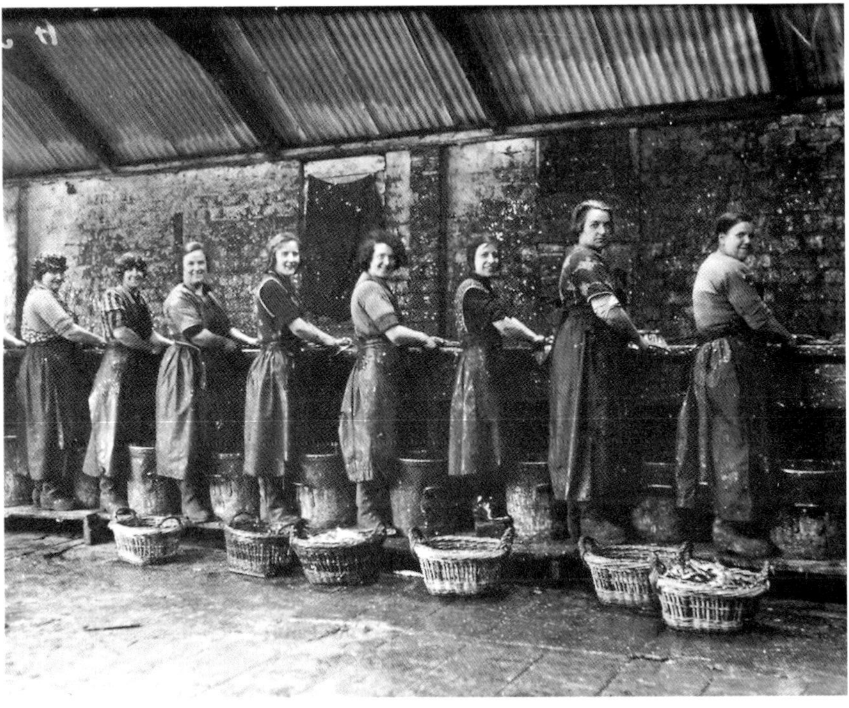

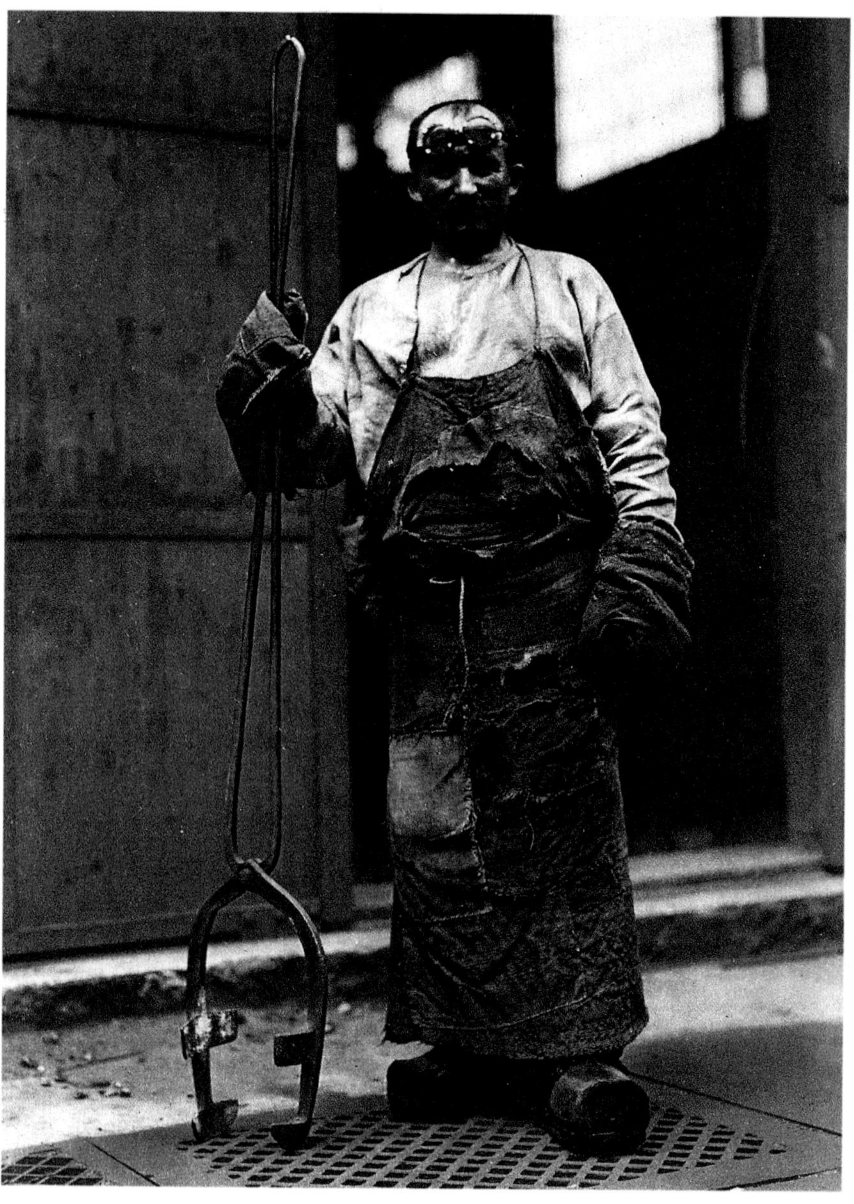

François Kollar, ***Steelworker***, from *La France travaille*, 1932.

to correct an external emphasis on France as a land of luxuries and pleasure, an artificial, cosmopolitan misrepresentation, having nothing to do with the true face and work of the nation.

Although Vogel's invocation of "aspects of labor in cultivation and the nation" sounds resonantly nationalistic, the "France" which emerged was differentiated. A hieratic "Russian" France was represented by François Kollar, whose massive two-volume survey *La France travaille* was in process of publication. Meant to run to 880 pages with 1,200 illustrations, it too was published in sections of which the first two, *Miners* and *Ironworkers*, were advertised in the June issue of *VU*. Kollar's mariners, steelworkers, and gardeners act, like their contemporaries in Jarché's story, in a costume drama of national life.[9] Kollar's personnel, in contrast to the unblemished shock workers of the five-year plan, look like old hands comfortable in familiar parts.

Their German equivalents eventually emerged in the shape of the men who built the motorways, smiling and smoking, old and young, in what might be family snapshots, taken by Erny Lendvai-Dircksen for *Reichsautobahn Mensch und Werk*, published in 1937 by the Volk und Reich Verlag, Berlin.

Street life

Kollar's genial portraits, printed to a monumental ratio, were complemented by much smaller pictures of interiors and provincial streets taken by André Kertész. Where Kollar narrated on an epic scale, Kertész recounted rooms, tabletops, street corners, and alleyways, as if engrossed by whatever *petit bonheur* was to be found in everyday life.

Kertész's was one of the determining ideologies of "French" documentary, which tended towards the private and conversational – a style of reverie. The style, compatible with the "Occident individualiste" savored by Vogel, was a symptom with several sources. In 1930, for instance, a set of Germaine Krull's pictures illustrated a concluding chapter, *Charmes de Paris 1930*, in André Warnod's *Visages de Paris*, in which the life of the city was told in terms of a rich tradition. Several night pictures appear, suggestive of noctambulism, mystery, and solitude.

In 1931, Krull's assistant and partner, the Rumanian Eli Lotar, illustrated Émile Chautard's huge study of the underworld and street slang of Paris, *La Vie étrange de l'argot*, a book which was owned and used by the British photographer Bill Brandt, then at work in the city.

Krull's noctambulists and Lotar's street traders and cardsharps were an advance guard for one of photography's outstanding books, Brassaï's *Paris de Nuit*, published with 62 pictures and a text by Paul Morand in 1933. Brassaï had been introduced to photography by Kertész in 1929, and had then applied Kertész's *intimisme* to that world in which Chautard's argot was spoken. Although Morand and Brassaï acknowledged responsible, social tendencies in the shape of drains, boilers, and milk deliveries, their emphasis was on nightlife and on a threat inherent in the dark. With its bar-going personalities, production-line dancers, and supporting cast of itinerants, *Paris de Nuit* was a counterversion of the *bien pensant* "Russian" style, but its other topics were exclusion and private pleasures. Its captions, spoken familiarly, offer help with the small print of posters, and with other meanings half hidden in the darkness.[10]

Kertész's achievement was to naturalize "new vision" modernism. He used the kind of significant fragments identified in that analytical mode, but now assembled and complemented: a bourgeois in the frame with street people, for example,

8. Jarché's story appears in James Jarché, *People I Have Shot*, London, 1934.

9. P. Roegiers, D. Baqué, *François Kollar*, exhibition catalogue, Paris, 1989.

10. Other, more explicit, imagery from that time appears in *Brassaï: Le Paris secret des années 30*, Gallimard, Paris, 1976.

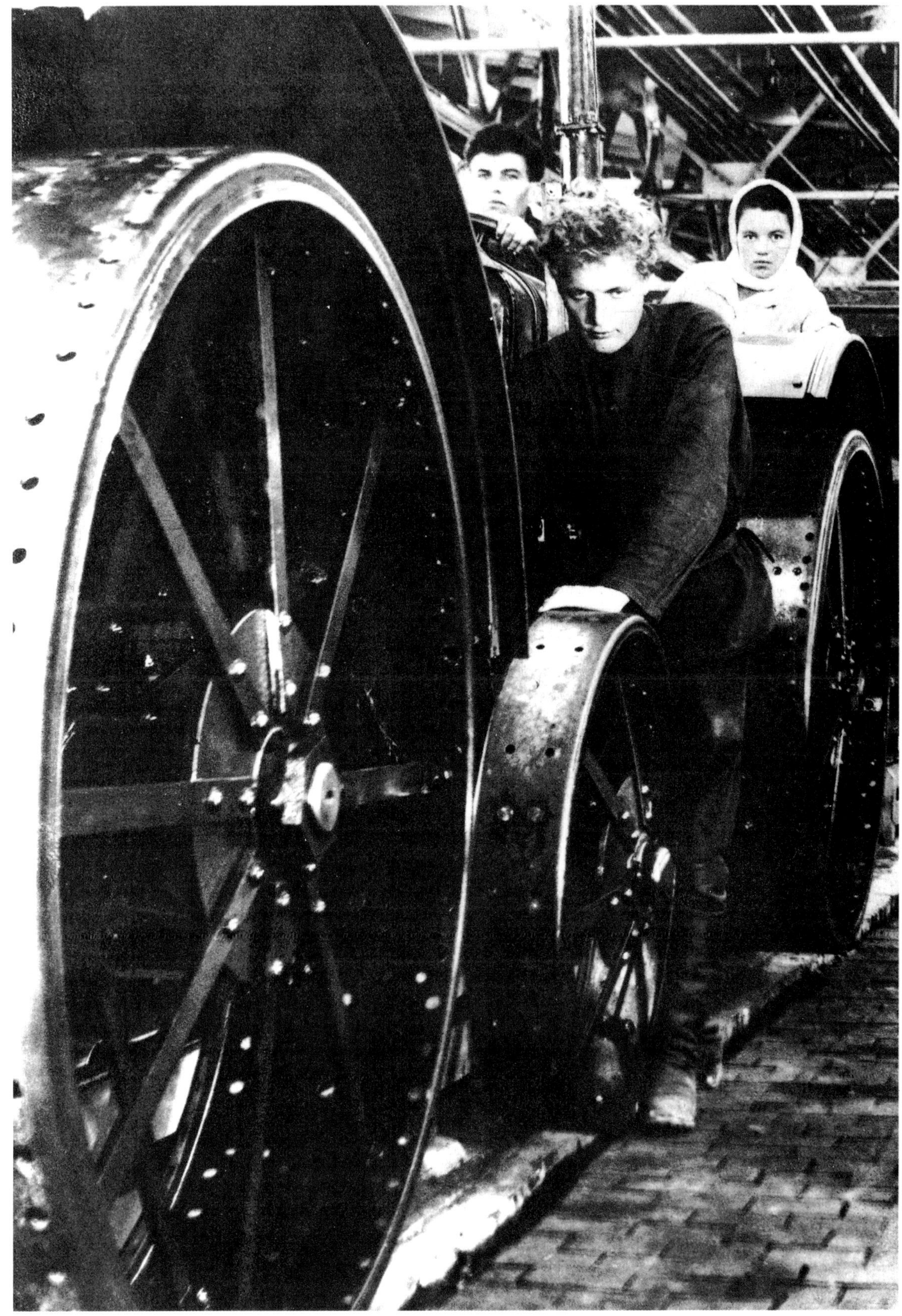

MARGARET BOURKE-WHITE, *Tractor Factory, Stalingrad,* 1931.

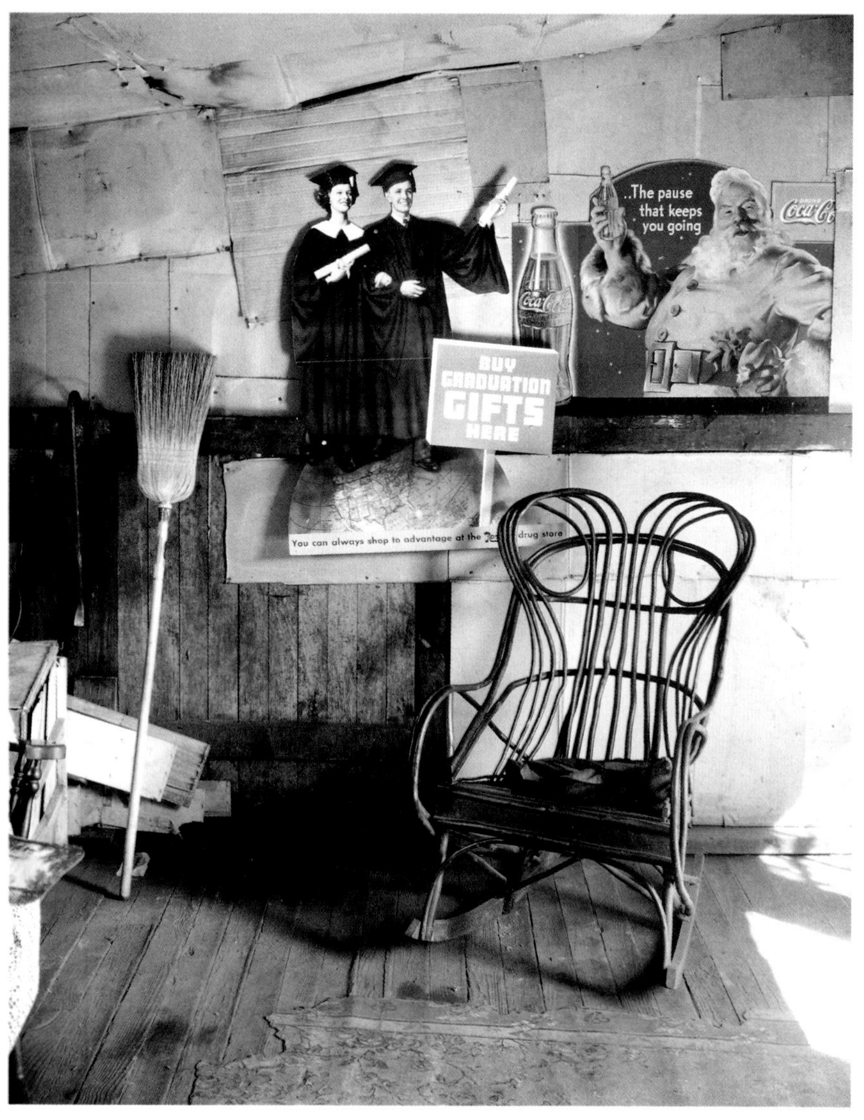

WALKER EVANS, *West Virginia Coal Miner's House,* 1935, Museum of Modern Art, New York.

or a solitary watcher in a crowd of onlookers. His miniatures, as published in *VU*, allowed for enlargement and isolation, for they formed structured, comprehensible wholes.

In 1934, the Librairie Plon published *Paris vu par André Kertész,* which marked the recognition in Europe of the documentarist as author. *Marseille par Germaine Krull* followed in that series in 1935, although without any trace of that closure which was the Kertész hallmark.[11]

The problem with the "closed" style was that it reduced readily to aphorism and to anecdote. By contrast, the photography of disclosure, as practiced by Krull, reported on conditions in being, and its purposes were best served by an unstructured manner faithful to the chaos of the streets. In Britain, that informal, originally German, manner helped shape Humphrey Spender's account of Bolton, made in 1937–1938 for the Mass Observation organization, itself founded in 1937.[12]

The "closed" manner, as perfected by Kertész, endured in European documentary alongside Krull's kind of informality. In addition there was a poetic, metaphoric, third strand, inaugurated to some degree by *Paris de Nuit*: startling shadows and ragged natural phenomena translated in monochrome photography into a subjective graphics, disturbing and sometimes thrilling. In Paris during the 1930s, reportage was associated with Surrealism. In 1933, for instance, the annual photography show at the Galerie de la Pléiade included Kertész and Cartier-Bresson, as well as Kollar and Krull.

Photographers who survived and flourished in post-war France and Switzerland especially were fluent in all three idioms. In *Belleville-Menilmontant*, Willy Ronis's celebrated report of 1954 published by Arthaud, there is a prevailing "German" sense of everyday life unsupervised, punctuated by paradox in the shape of a workman carrying a sunlit window – epitome of sight and light – up a rising street, as well as revelations and vivid gestures from the subconscious of the city.

American photographers responded more abruptly to problems which were skirted by their European contemporaries. In the experienced Margaret Bourke-White, for example, they had one of the most adept photographers of the decade. She had worked for the business magazine *Fortune* from its inception in 1930, and from 1936 for the newly established picture magazine *Life*. In 1930, 1931, and 1932, she visited Russia for *Fortune* where she took pictures which were entirely in the iconic "Russian" style. In 1936, she collaborated with Erskine Caldwell, author of Tobacco Road, to produce *You Have Seen Their Faces,* a book on Southern share-croppers, a grossly exploited and abandoned stratum of small farmer-renters. Her portraits are speaking likenesses, supported by their own words taken down by Caldwell – and a far remove from her seamless Russian pictures.[13]

The F.S.A.'s United States

At the same time, a government agency founded in 1935 and known from 1937 as the Farm Security Administration was setting about a photographic survey of rural deprivation. Although never involved in its work, Bourke-White had a determining influence in that her share-cropper pictures were read as condescending dramatizations.

The F.S.A. reporters, under the direction of Roy Stryker, were careful to avoid accusations of overdetermination. Initially, his group included Arthur Rothstein, who was a scientific photographer, the photojournalist Carl Mydans, Walker Evans, who had also worked for *Fortune*, the painter and illustrator Ben Shahn, and, from the autumn of 1935, Dorothea Lange, a Californian documentarist. Their problem was ideological, for in recording

11. *Germaine Krull: Fotografen 1922–1966,* Bonn, Rheinisches Landesmuseum, 1977.

12. For the photographs of Humphrey Spender see *Worktown People: Photographs from Northern England 1937–38,* ed. Jeremy Mulford, Bristol, Falling Wall Press, 1982. For British documentary in action see Wal Hannington, *The Problem of the Distressed Areas,* London, Gollancz, 1937.

13. S. Callahan (ed.), *The Photographs of Margaret Bourke-White,* New York, 1972; V. Goldberg, *Bourke-White,* exhibition catalogue, New York, ICP and United Technologies Corporation, 1989.

farm life they were recording a class and an activity fundamental to the idea of American civilization. But, to complicate matters, the distress in questions was at its greatest amongst the generally despised blacks and poor whites of the South. In the beginning they concentrated on hardship, but by 1938 began to take a more affirmative view of the rural scene. Russell Lee, Marion Post Wolcott, Jack Delano, John Vachon, and John Collier joined the group, and Walker Evans quit.

The F.S.A. reporters established a picture file to be used as a resource by publishers. Their images were used, sometimes six or more to a page, in Herman C. Nixon's *Forty Acres and Steel Mules*, an "integrated interpretation of the rural South", put out by the University of North Carolina Press in 1938. The 150 pictures in Nixon's book amount to another conspectus, although this time ragged and anecdotal. Though an academic study, its pictures are completed by reported speech.

In Richard Wright's *Twelve Million Black Voices of 1941*, subtitled "A Folk History of the Negro in the United States of America", another 82, mainly F.S.A., pictures appear again in relation to a text rich in speech, to which the pictures give support, as they adduce evidence of ploughing, cropping, and picking, of living conditions and black servitude.

Reported speech and adjacent texts limited the extension of F.S.A. pictures. Speech situated them in an everyday time of encounters, observations, and asides. In the 87 photographs included in *American Photographs* published by the Museum of Modern Art, New York, in 1938, Walker Evans countered that reductivist tendency by showing his series of pictures one to a page spread, with minimal captions listed at the back. On the original dust-jacket, viewers were instructed to view the series in sequence, as they would a film.

Thus Evans courted ambiguity and complexity in what purported to be another conspectus. Speech was implicit in many frames, but there are modernist "German" details and angles in evidence too. It amounts simultaneously to an elaborated version of what Moholy-Nagy had attempted in *Street Markets* and a purified and silenced vision of that American both spoken and staged by Bourke-White and by many of Evans's contemporaries in the F.S.A.

Around the Photo League

Some of Evans's Americans were speaking likenesses, and some were artificer-modernists. *American Photographs* is a culmination rather than a beginning. The American future, by contrast, took its cue from such photographers as Jacob Riis and Lewis Hine working in the slums and

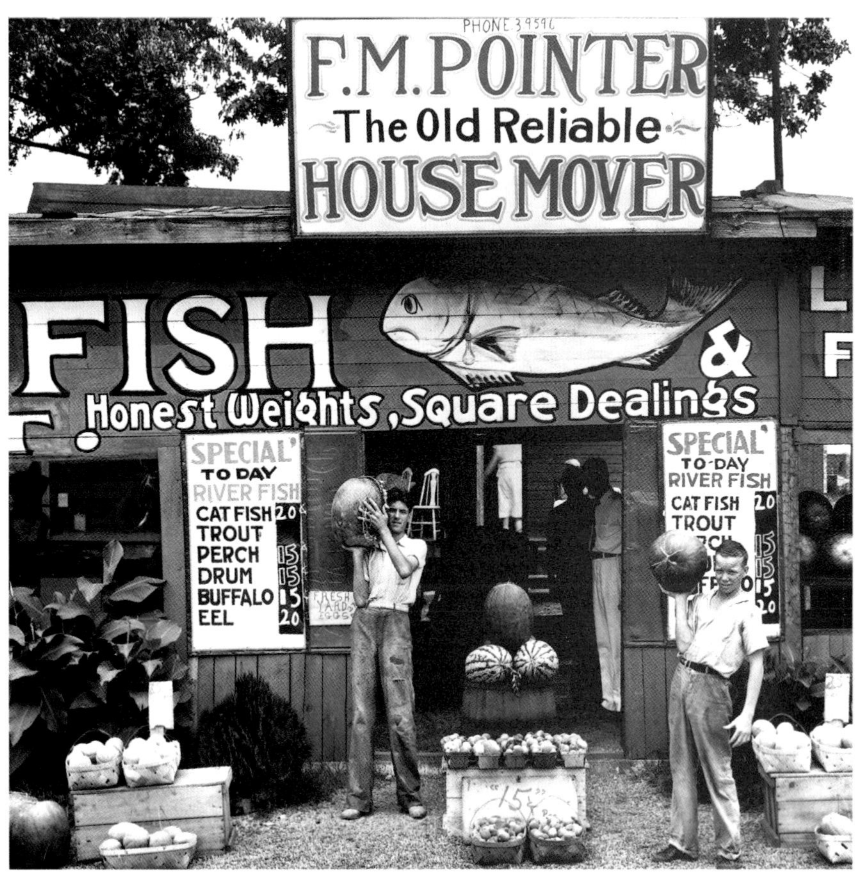

WALKER EVANS,
Roadside Stand near Birmingham, Alabama,
1936,
Museum of Modern Art, New York.

WALKER EVANS,
Church of the Nazarene, Tennessee,
1936,
Museum of Modern Art, New York.

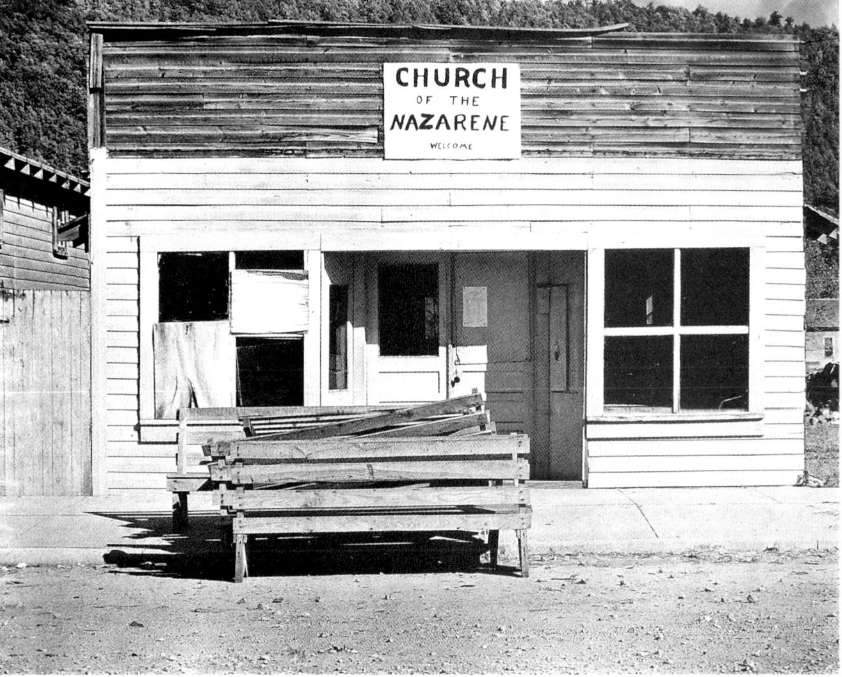

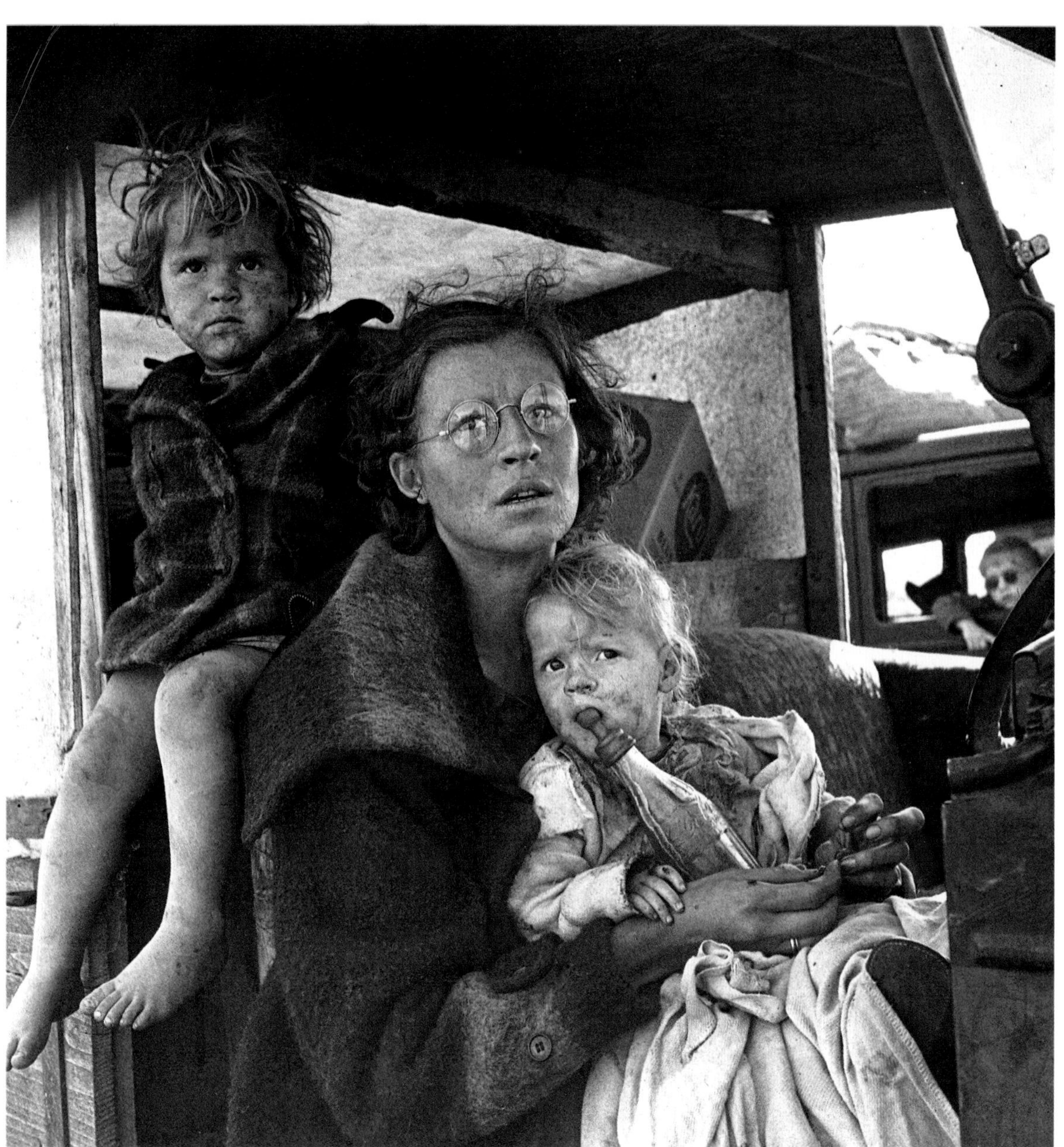

Dorothea Lange, *Mother and Children, Tuletecke, California,* 1939, Library of Congress, Washington.

streets of New York around the turn of the century.

While the F.S.A. was in action a number of more radical photographers combined to form the Photo League in New York in 1936. The League held meetings, staged exhibitions, and organized workshops until it disbanded in 1951. Paul Strand was associated with it, and Aaron Siskind, who in 1936 began work on a Harlem project,[14] which he resumed in 1940 with Max Yavno. It exhibited the work of Henri Cartier-Bresson, Helen Levitt, Lisette Model, and the great Mexican artist Manuel Alvarez Bravo, and seems to have helped clarify a metaphoric tendency in photography – a tendency which culminated in Robert Frank's *The Americans* of 1959.

Photo League pictures were made in the street, and in workplaces and living spaces, in line with the art of the great generation. But the new mode allowed for a greater degree of spontaneity than before, and its call-sign was the human figure in vivid action, often against a dark ground. Such League photographers as Sol Libsohn, Walter Rosenblum, and Sid Grossman rephrased humanity in organic, expressive terms, whereas the F.S.A. artists registered static tableaux. Even if they meant to document folk life, they achieved a new expressionism, one which was often acknowledged in the shape of graffiti and nervous, unsteady hand lettering.

Nevertheless, the F.S.A. tableau manner, with all its speaking likenesses. and household appliances, predominated in the documentary of the 1940s. In 1943, many F.S.A. personnel, along with Sol Libsohn and Harold Corsini of the Photo League, moved with Roy Stryker to work on a documentary project for Standard Oil, which amounted to a continuation of F.S.A. work.[15]

The metaphoric tendency in the U.S.A. was important, even if marginal. Its principal artwork,

14. Aaron Siskind, *Harlem Document: Photographs, 1932–1940,* with a text collected and edited by A. Banks, Providence, Rhode Island, Matrix, 1981.

15. S.W. Plattner, *Roy Stryker: U.S.A. 1943–1950: The Standard Oil (New Jersey) Photography Project,* Austin, University of Texas Press, 1983.

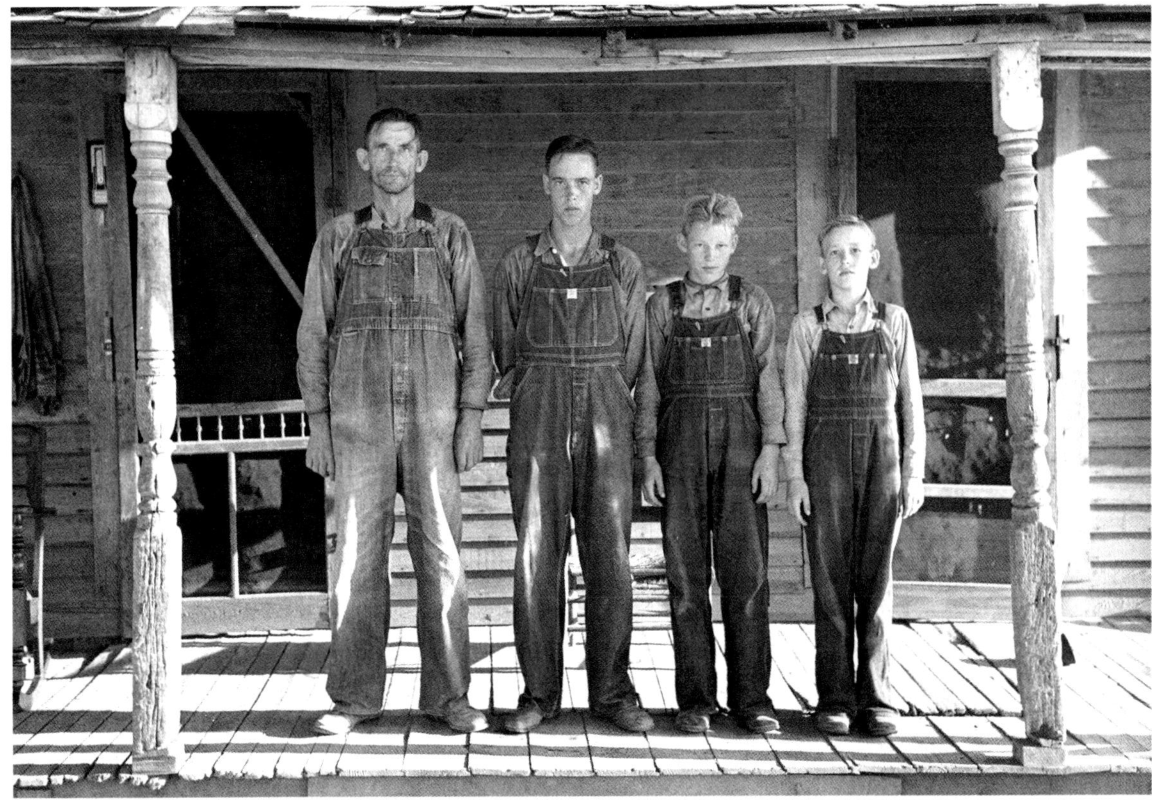

RUSSELL LEE,
Beneficiary of the Farm Security Administration and his Sons, Missouri,
1938,
Library of Congress, Washington.

RUSSELL LEE,
Young Farmworker Coming back from the Fields, Oklahoma,
1939,
Library of Congress, Washington.

Helen Levitt's *A Way of Seeing*, was put together in 1946, but published only in 1965;[16] and Aaron Siskind's vivacious Harlem pictures of 1936 and 1940 emerged in ensemble only in *Harlem Document* in 1981. James Agee's introduction of 1946 to Levitt's series interprets her street children as actors in a *reprise* of the creation myth among "the satanic incongruities of a twentieth-century metropolis" (New York).

Metaphoric documentary was always more suggestive than explicit. Its isolated motifs were of a cryptic significance, and required a poetic apprehension; they were primitive inscriptions, and a witness to a deep-lying creative impulse. Paul Strand's collection of inscriptions, folk portraits, and closely observed natural phenomena, *Time in New England*, published in 1950, with texts selected by Nancy Newhall, is metaphoric through and through. Adjoining texts served to associate the images with historic voices.[17]

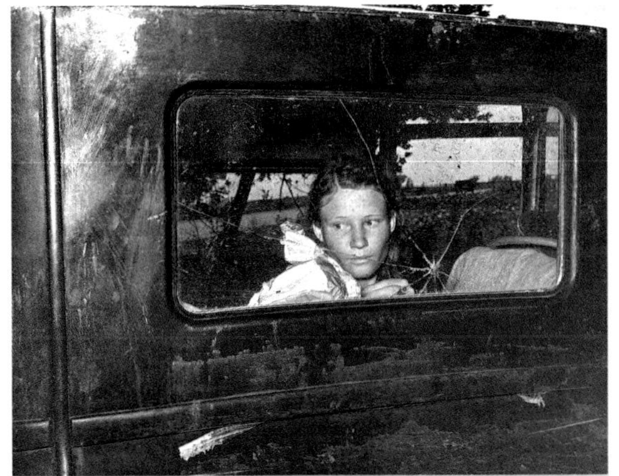

In Europe in the same year, Izis Bidermanas' *Paris des Rêves* confronted images and autograph texts from Audiberti to Virel. In 1951, a text by Jacques Prévert accompanied another 59 of Izis's pictures in *Grand Bal de Printemps*.

Under the metaphoric rubric an isolated figure might symbolise humanity, but only as a mystery incarnate. Wols's (Wolfgang Schulze) photographs of the destitute in Paris (1932–1933) were of that order,[18] as were Lisette Model's Riviera portraits of 1937, and subsequent figure studies in New York, after 1941.[19]

One consequence of this mode was that it restored an idea of genius to photography. In the United States in particular, F.S.A. practices had promoted a persuasive common style. In France, respect for the documentary author produced Henri Cartier-Bresson's majestic *Images à la Sauvette* of 1952, which was published by Verve under a cover by Matisse, and was in the style of such publications as the Mourlot *Cahiers* of Braque (1948).

A second consequence was that documentary, which the Russians and then the F.S.A. had autonomised, ceased to be narrowly considered. In Edward Steichen's conspectus of 1955 of "503 pictures from 68 countries", assembled for the Museum of Modern Art in New York and entitled *The Family of Man*, metaphoric documentary is related to landscape and astronomy.

The universalism of *The Family of Man* established an impossible agenda. Moreover, it

16. Supplemented and republished by the Horizon Press, New York, 1981.

17. Republished by Aperture, New York, in 1977.

18. See L. Glozer, *Wols, Photograph*, Schirmer/Mosel, Munich, 1978.

19. See Ann Thomas, *Lisette Model*, Ottawa, National Gallery of Canada, 1990.

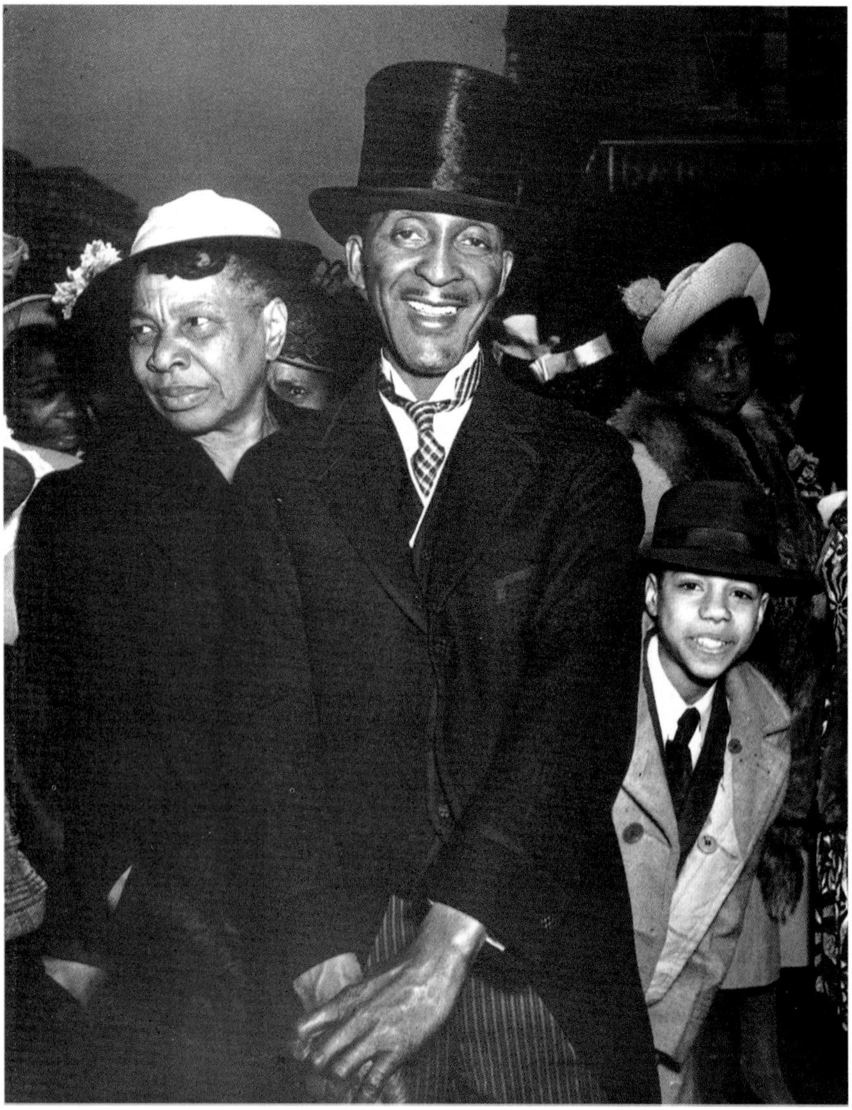

WEEGEE, *Easter Day, Harlem,* 1940.

showed its family in country conditions, unaffected by automobiles, advertising, and crime. Post-war French photoreportage, which dominated in Europe, had a similar pastoral to small-town bias, as if still deeply affected by Vogel's regret for the passing "Occident individualiste" of around 1932.

More traumatized and less consoling aspects of American culture had been aired in 1945 in Weegee's *Naked City*. Weegee (Arthur Fellig), absent from *The Family of Man*, was a "rather portly, cigar-smoking, irregularly shaven" man who worked for *PM Picture News* in a vertiginous night-time mode involving death and joking. Weegee had been first shown by the Photo League. In 1950, Max Yavno, another artist implicated in the Photo League and absent from Steichen's exhibition, was responsible for *The Los Angeles Book*: 113 pages of urbanism, oil installation, automobiles, hoardings, and unflattered citizens.

Europe's own naked city was Paris, taken in narrative close-up by the Dutch photographer Ed Van Der Elsken and published as *Love on the Left Bank* (undated, but circa 1956). Like Weegee, Van der Elsken was a night-time photographer of marginal and threatened life.

Despite Van Der Elsken, the documentary drift was towards the United States. European post-traumatic pastoralism was entrenched, and America answered better to the kind of metropolitan nightmare which had been invoked by James Agee in 1946.

Europe's artist was the Swiss Robert Frank, author of *Les Américains*, published by Robert Delpire in Paris in 1958. In 1956 Delpire had published, *From Incas to Indians*, with pictures by Frank, Werner Bischof, and Pierre Verger. Frank's Andeans, anonymous wearers of hats, look like fearful actors in a drama by Kafka, and the bulk of his North Americans, too, look over-determined by a constraining cultural framework. Although both Van Der Elsken and Frank were represented in *The Family of Man*, both in their own work were sceptics.

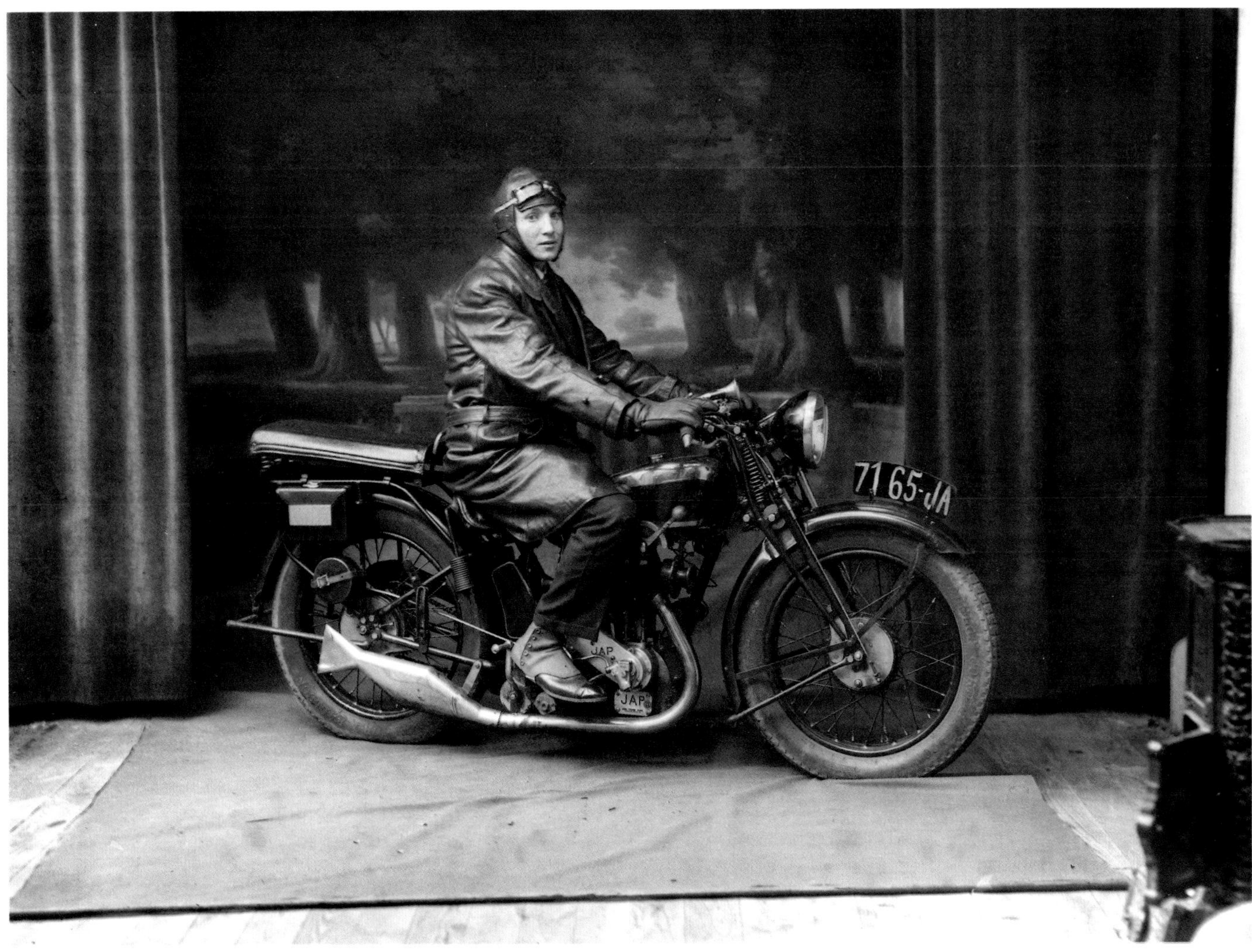

The anonymous studio

A strictly photographic environment where one of the major rituals of modern society has evolved is the photographer's studio. While the basic concept goes back to the Second Empire (Nadar, Mayall), studios subsequently evolved into a large number of different types, depending on time and place, the extent to which they have modernized, and the photographer's personal charisma. The quality of a studio depends above all on the presence of the operator and the relationship that they form (or not, as the case may be) with their client. Their personality – confidence, meekness, anxiety, restraint – is all too apparent in the way people appear in photographs.

The studio is not neutral territory but a completely artificial environment, to the point of being decorated with fake painted foliage or recreating a false drawing-room. This imposes itself on the action so that portraiture is a three-way struggle between parties armed in different ways: the client, the photographer, and the place itself which, when all is said and done, must be invested with a real sense of the self.

Some photographers work in the open air, in front of a door, a wall, a pile of wood; others attend an event, wedding, deathbed or banquet; others have several possible backgrounds, chosen at random or according to the type of photograph involved, even equipped with papier-mâché accessories to suit the natural aspects of the pose; others use only a plain black or white backcloth in order to avoid the distraction of objects scattered here and there. Everything conspires to isolate the most willing victim in an environment where they are denied the usual landmarks of daily life, retaining only a few special symbols of their identity, ones which will not betray but will give a personal meaning.

Dogs, umbrellas, chairs, benches, tables, bicycles – even motorbikes – musical instruments, flowers, sporting costumes (tennis or boxing, for example) are not mere indications of the sitter's hobbies, but also indicate why the person is being photographed, the reason for capturing this particular occasion: coming out of church, for example, as a way of emphasizing the subject's friendships.

For a long time people looked down on the photography carried out in those local studios set up by the thousand in every country, but during the past twenty years they have increasingly been re-evaluated for their ethnographic, naive, historical, and vernacular characteristics. All these elements feature simultaneously; it is an anonymous, collective portrait of social groups and communities. Whether the photographer's name is known or not is immaterial, because he is only a more or less inspired figure in a process akin to intercession. If up until now people have perceived only uniformity, this was a reflection of shortcomings in our own vision.

Typical studios include those of the "Photographe des Ponts" at Saint-Étienne (operating from 1910–1969), Norbert Ghisoland in Frameries, Belgium (1900–1935), Martin Chambi in Cuzco, Peru (1920–1970), Tomás Montserrat, a Majorcan priest (1900–1925), Léon Aymonier, a chemist in Châtelard-en-Bauges (1892–1934), Germain Eblé in Beaune, France, Romualdo Garcia in Guanajuato, Mexico, James Van der Zee in Harlem, the Deriaz dynasty at Baulmes (Switzerland), and numerous producers of postcards.

Michel Frizot

FURTHER READING:
- Maurice Müller and Pierre-Yves Perrier, *Le photographe des Ponts: cérémonies du portrait*, Saint-Étienne, Maison de la Culture et Le Hénaf, 1983.
- *Le Photographe et le Pharmacien: autopsie du Châtelard*, Champ Vallon, Seyssel, 1981.
- *Norbert Ghisoland*, Paris, Centre National de la Photographie, 1991.
- Toni Catany, *Tomás Montserrat, retratista de un poble*, Palma, 1983.
- Claudia Canales, *Romualdo Garcia, un fotografo, una ciudad, una época*, Guanajuato, 1980.
- *Germain Eblé*, Chalon-sur-Saône, 1993.
- *La Famille Deriaz*, Schaffhausen, Stemmle, 1988.

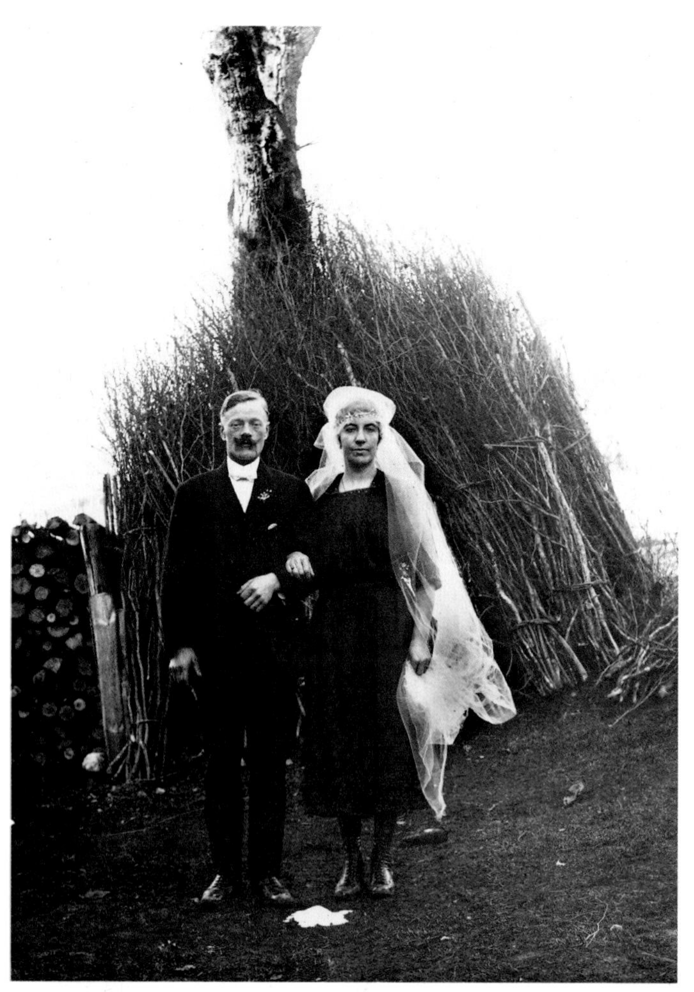

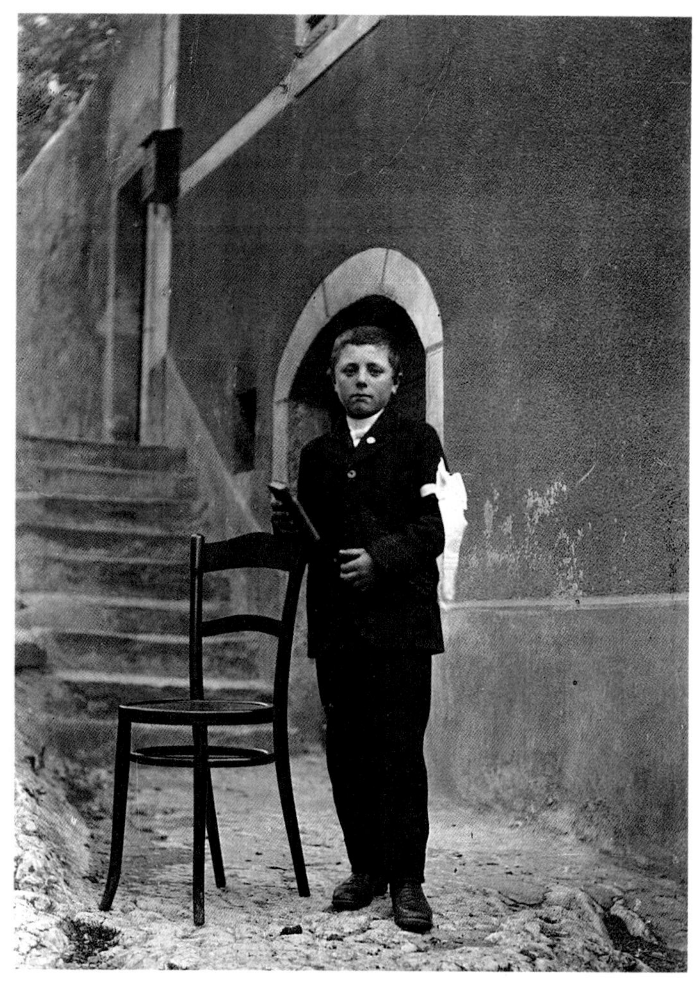

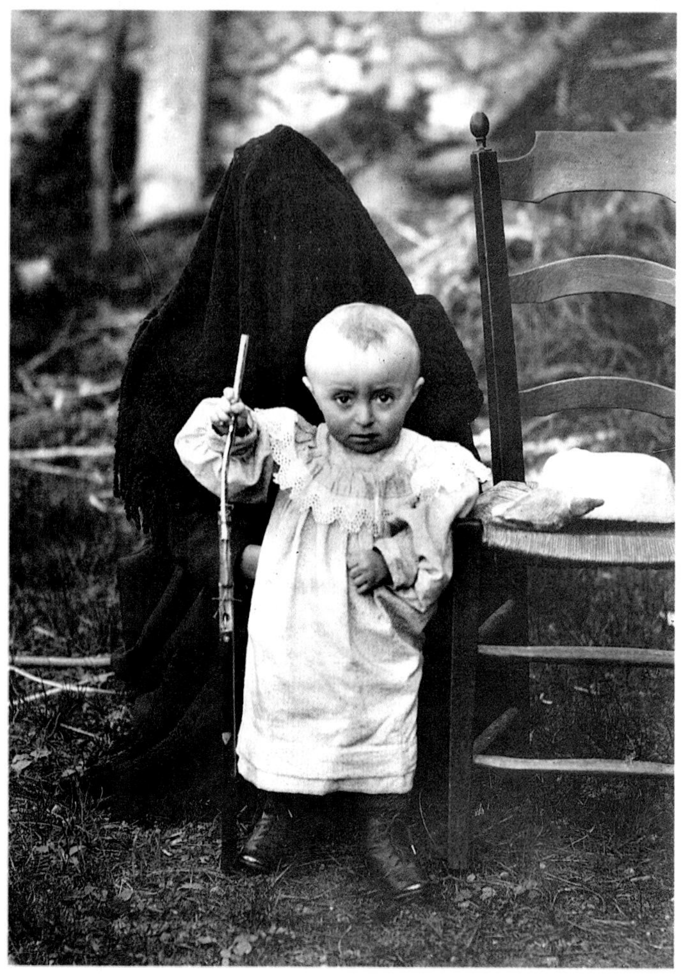

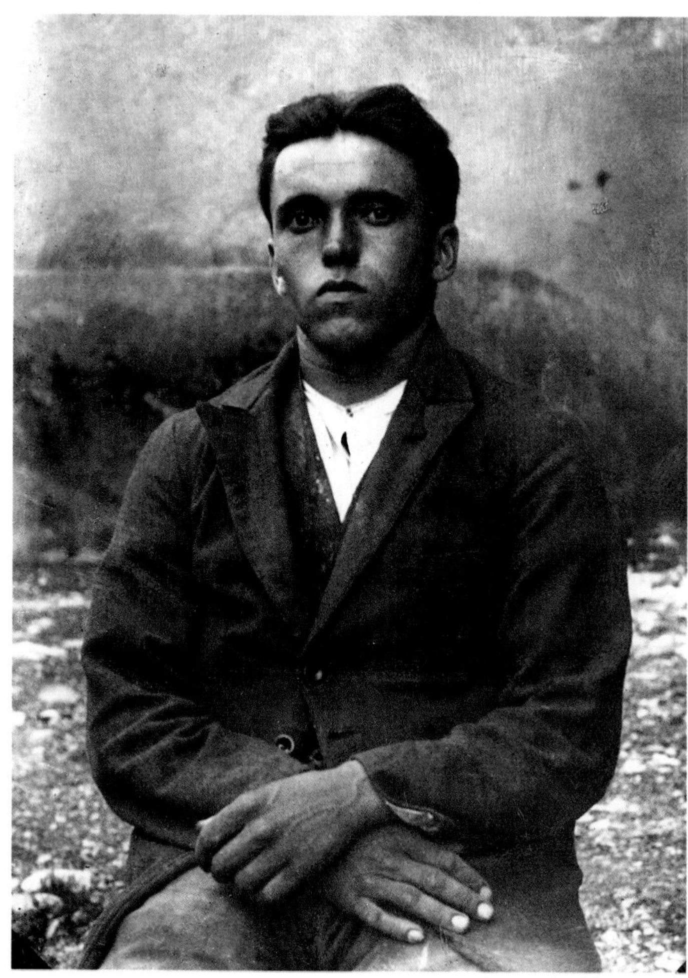

◀◀ page 527:
"Le photographe des Ponts",
Saint-Étienne, 1930s.

◀ page 528:
Léon Aymonier,
Le Châtelard-en-Bauges,
between 1892 and 1934,
Musée Savoisien, Chambéry.

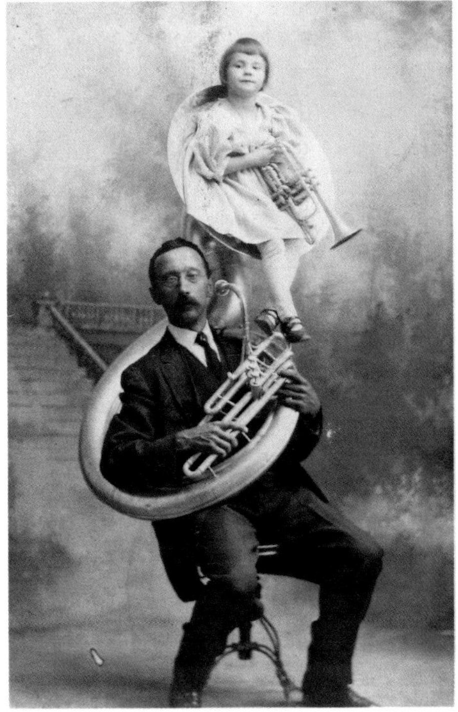

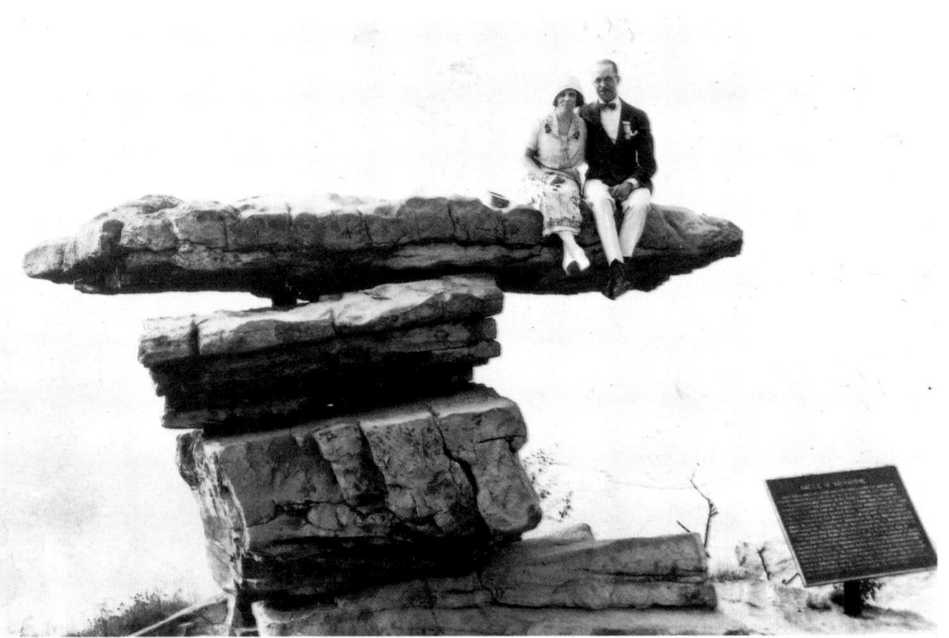

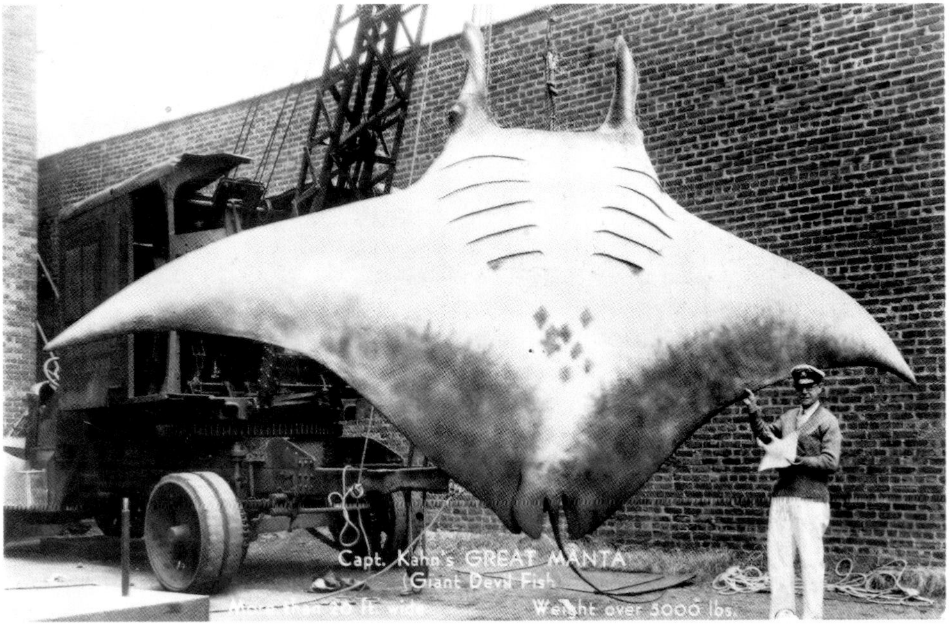

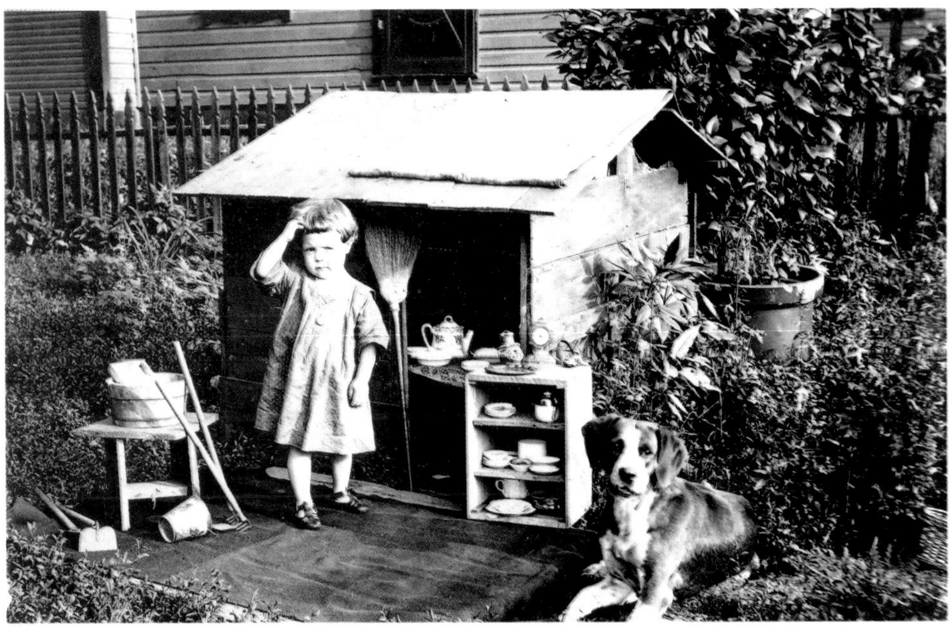

American photographic postcards:
Andreas Brown Collection,
John Paul Getty Museum, Malibu.

above:
Anonymous,
1910.

top right:
Anonymous,
1920s.

middle:
Garraway Co., Rutherford,
New Jersey, Captain Kahn's Great Manta,
1933.

below:
Anonymous,
Lizzie Brown,
circa 1910.

page 530 ▶▶
"Le photographe des Ponts",
Saint-Étienne, 1930s.

page 531 ▶▶
Norbert Ghisoland,
Frameries, Belgium, between 1900 and 1935.

page 532 ▶▶
Tomás Montserrat,
Llucmajor, Majorca, between 1900 and 1925.

page 533 ▶▶
Martin Chambi,
The Giant of Paruro,
Cuzco, Peru, 1929.

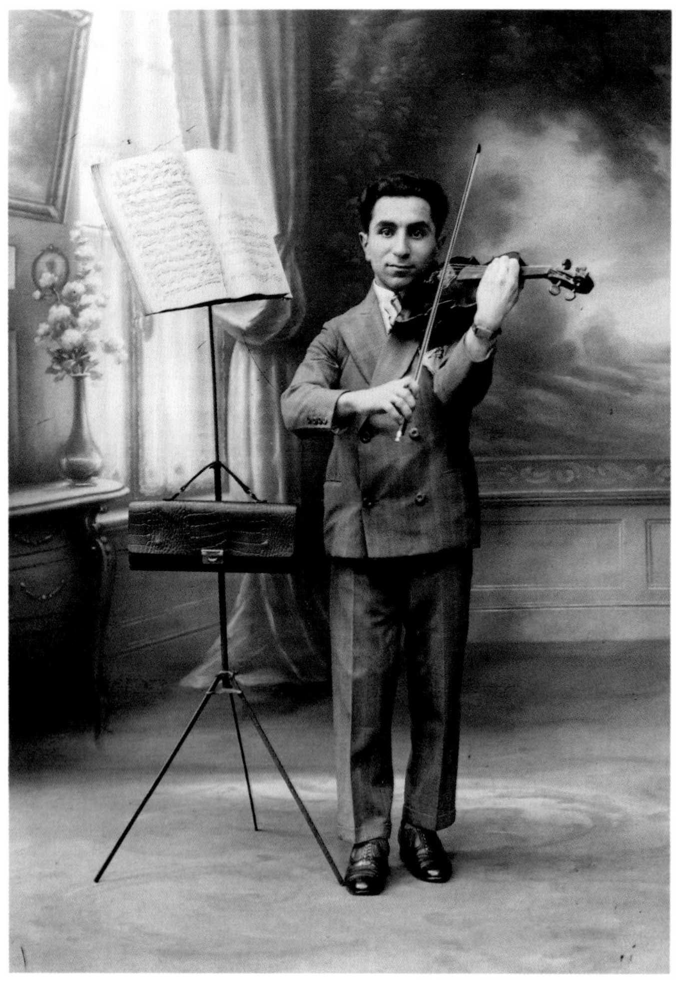

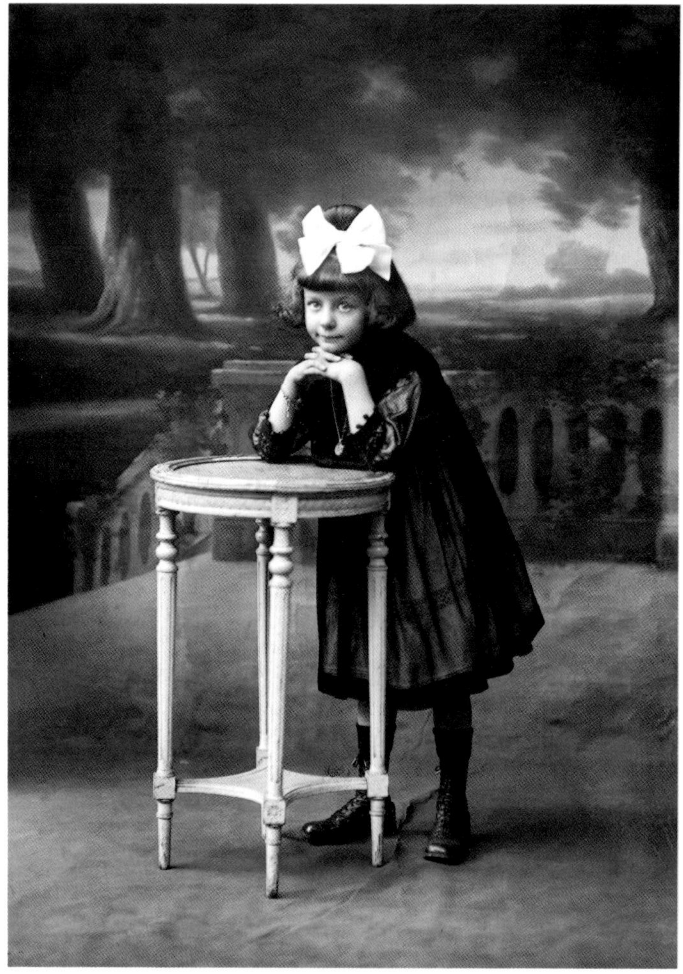

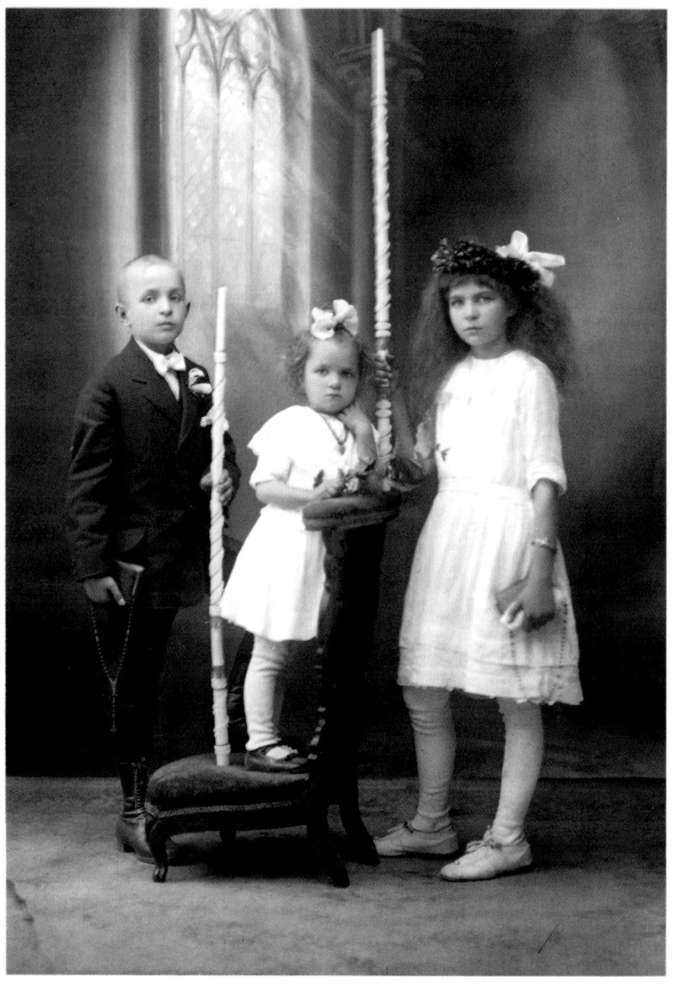

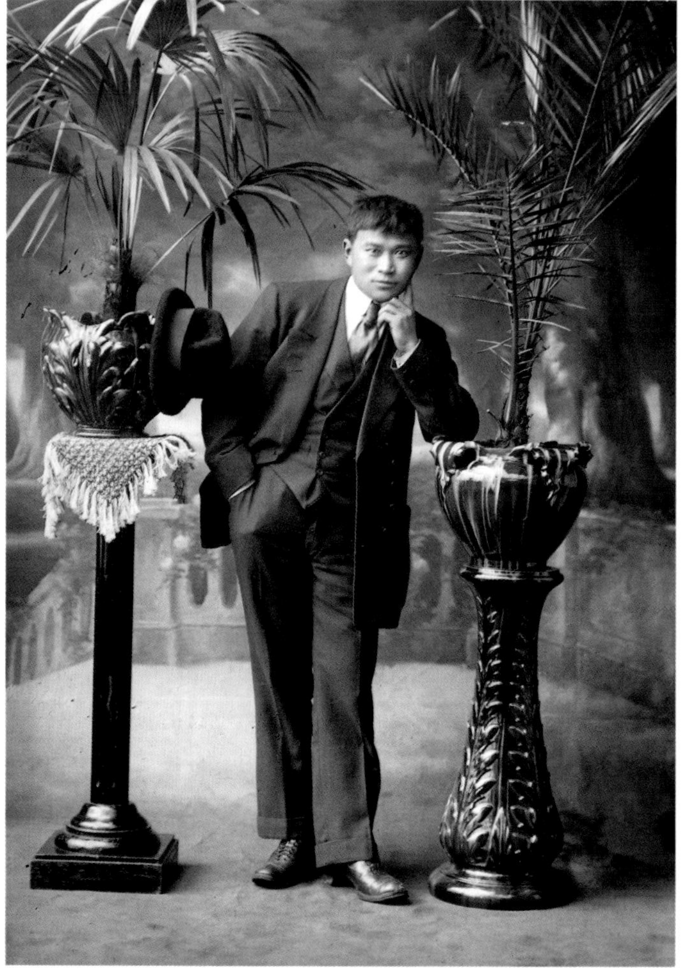

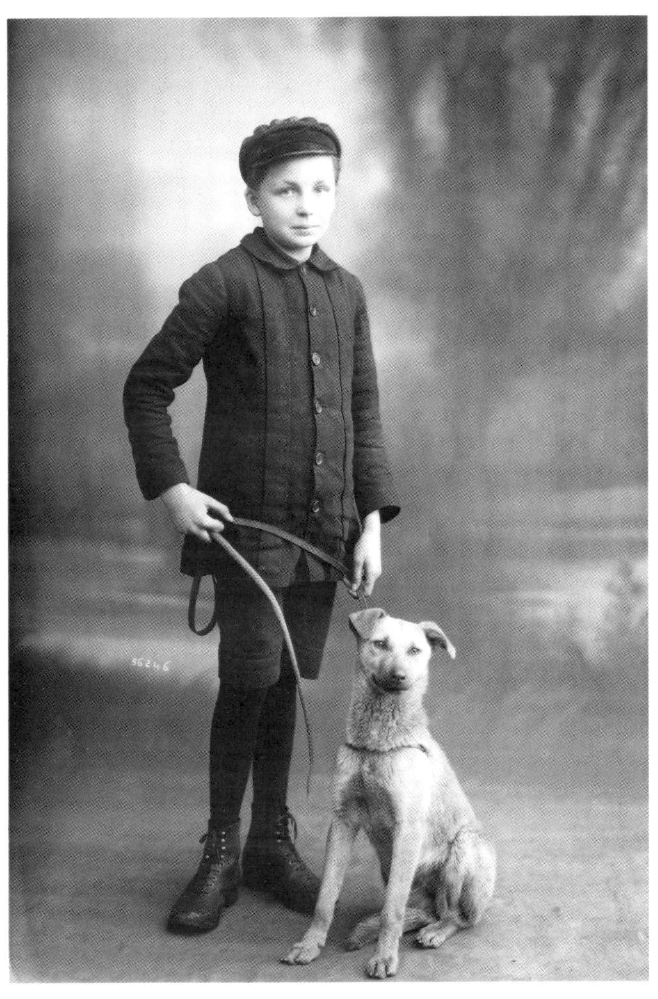

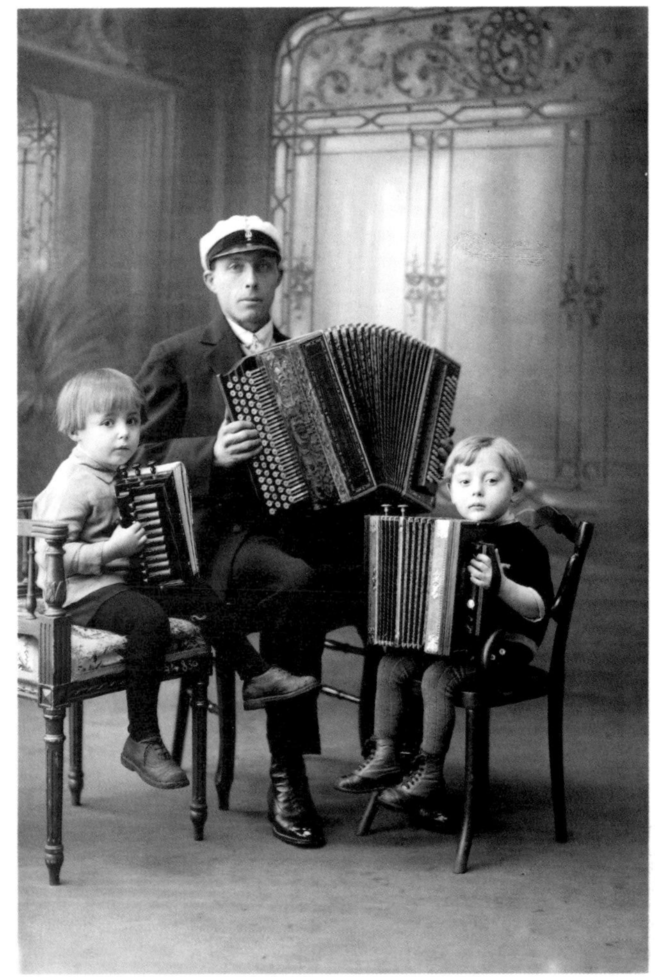

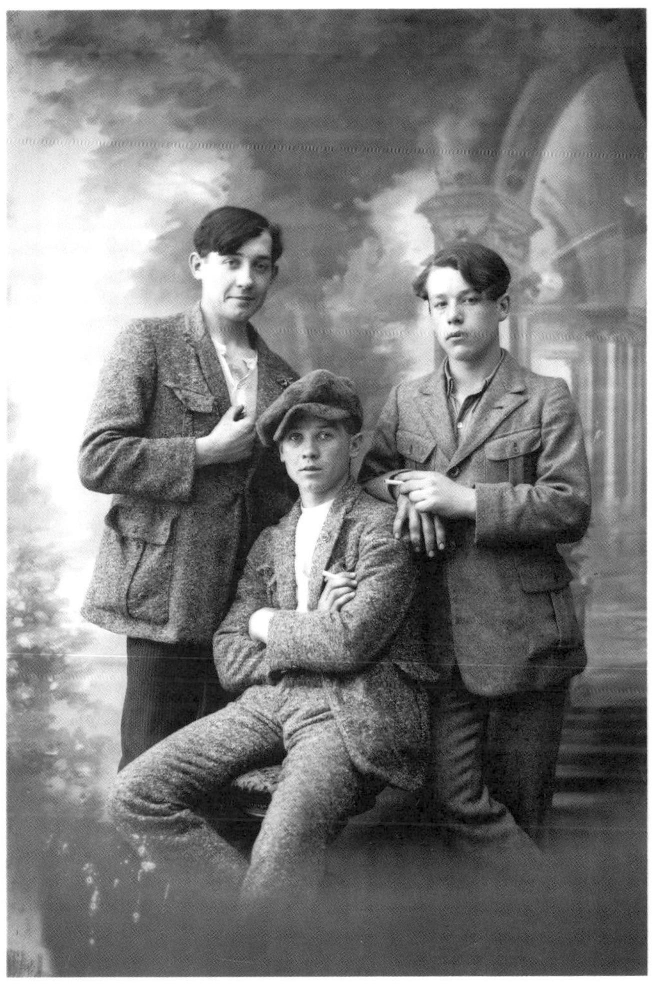

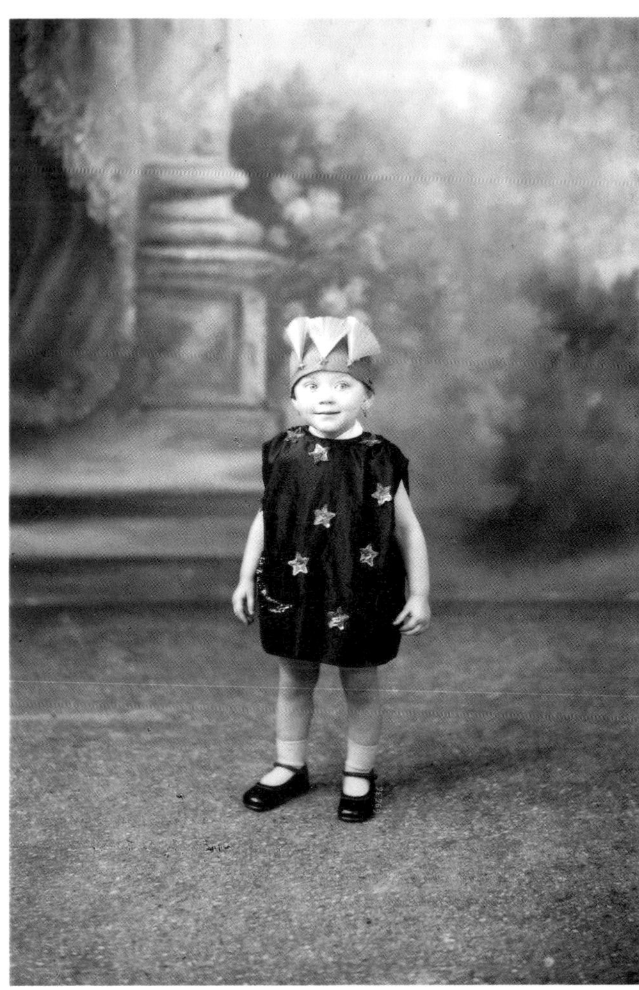

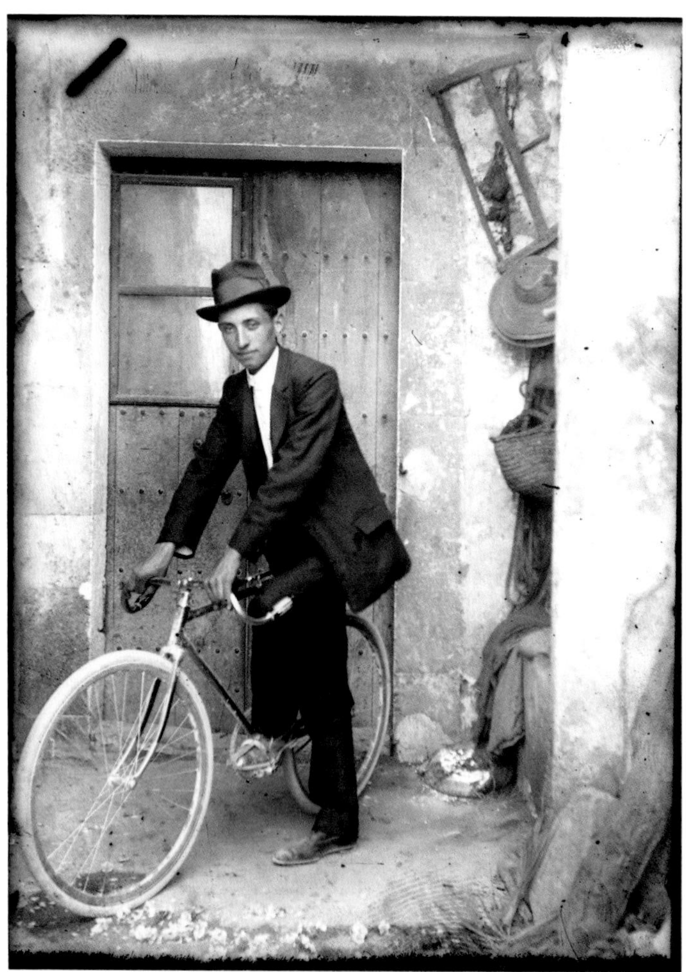

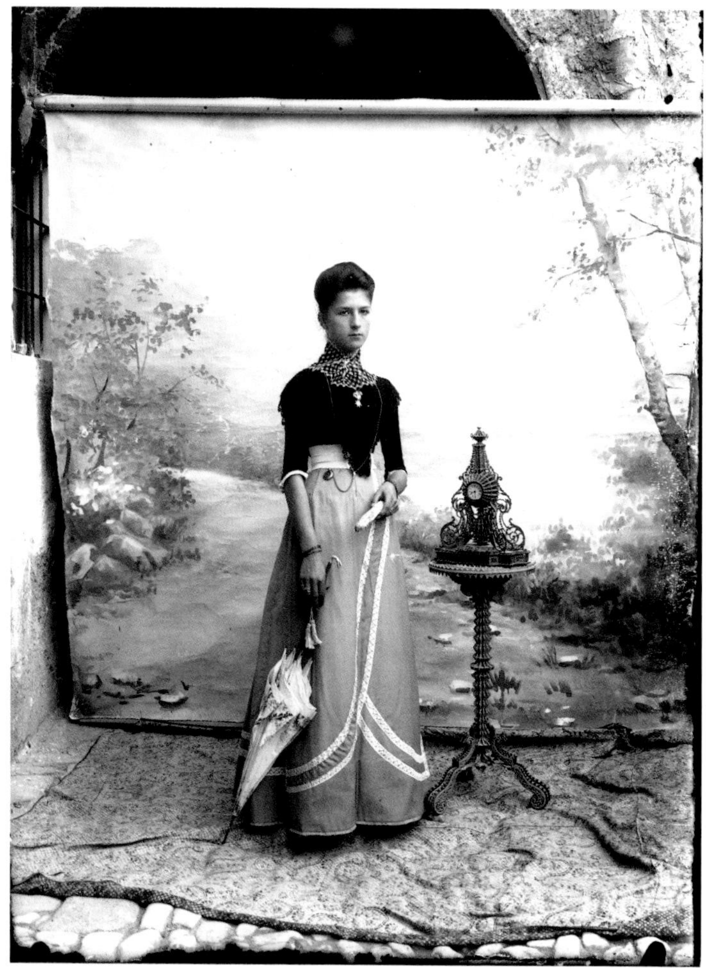

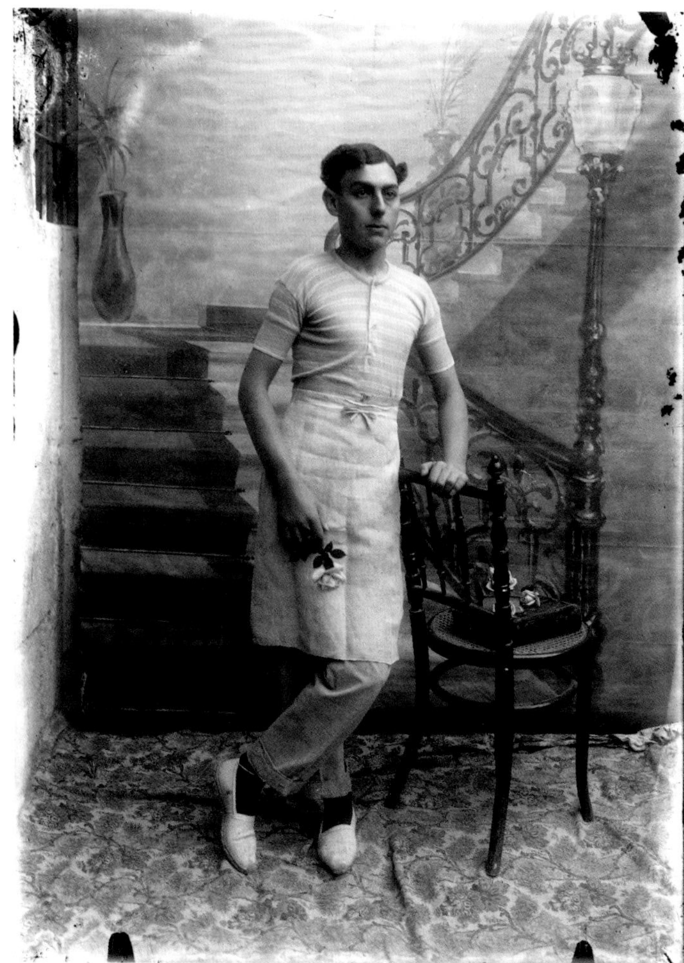

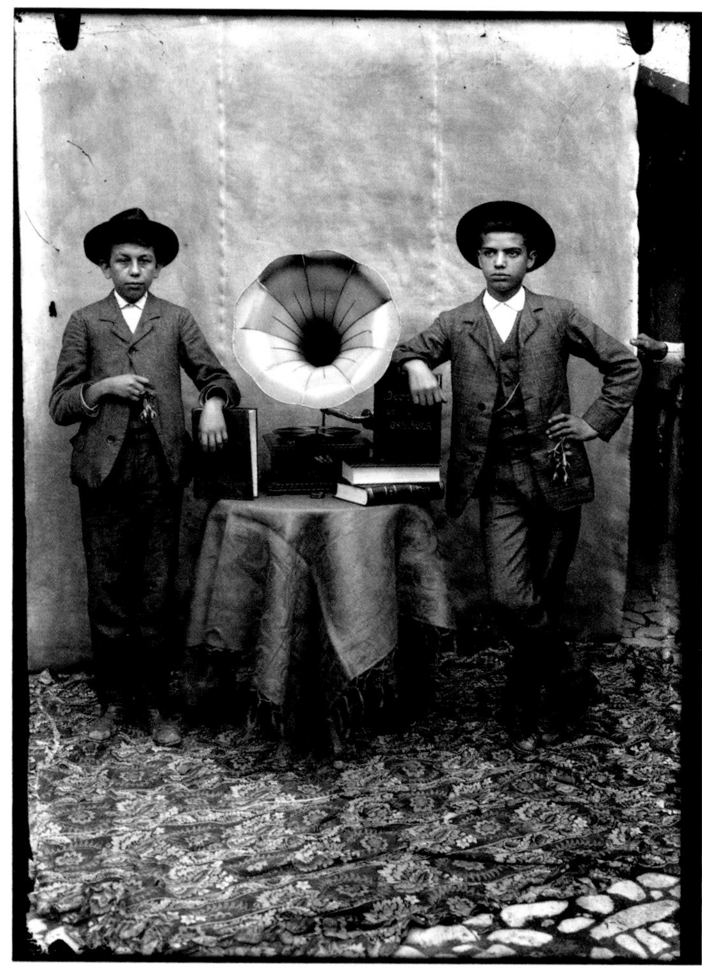

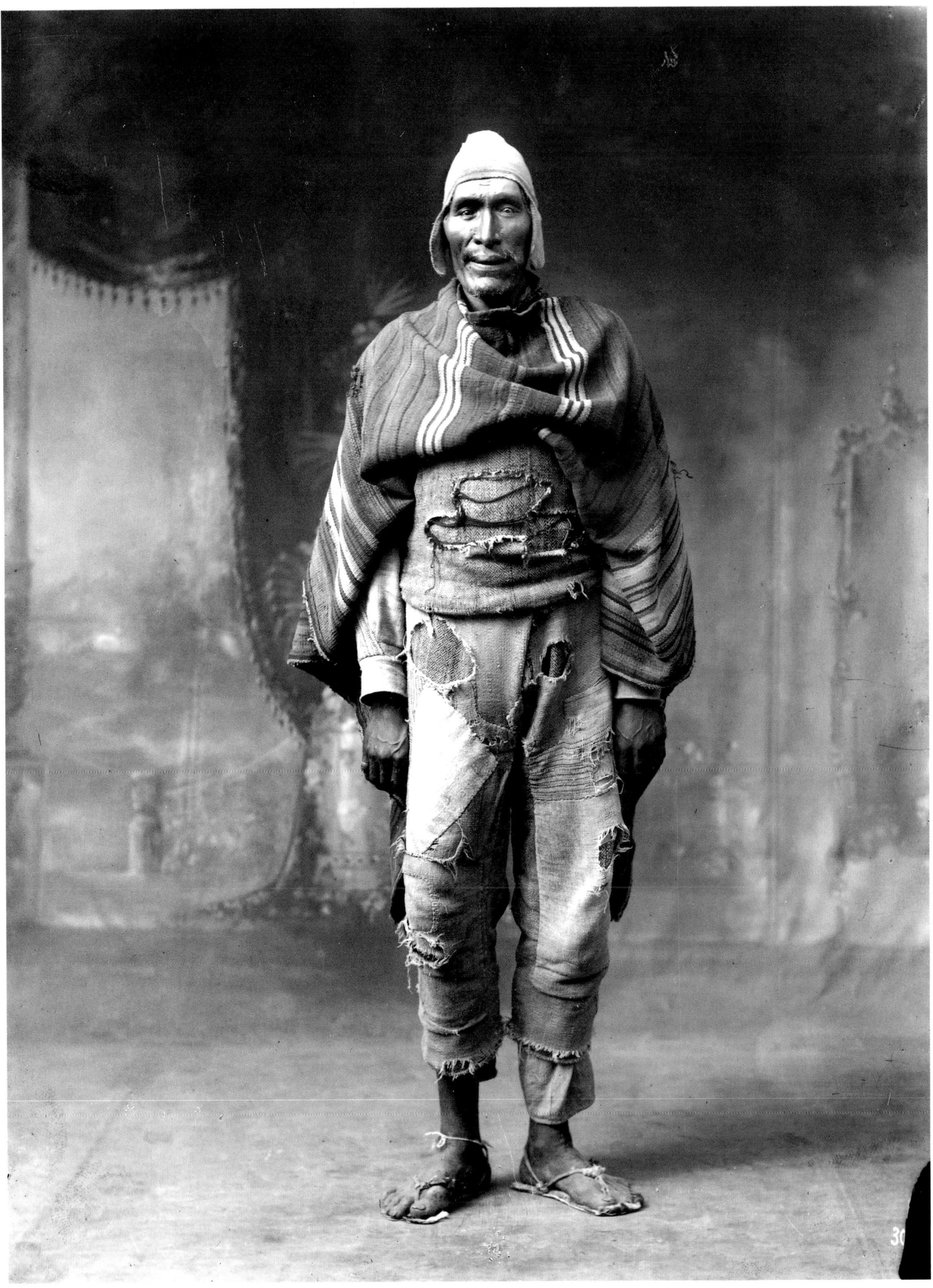

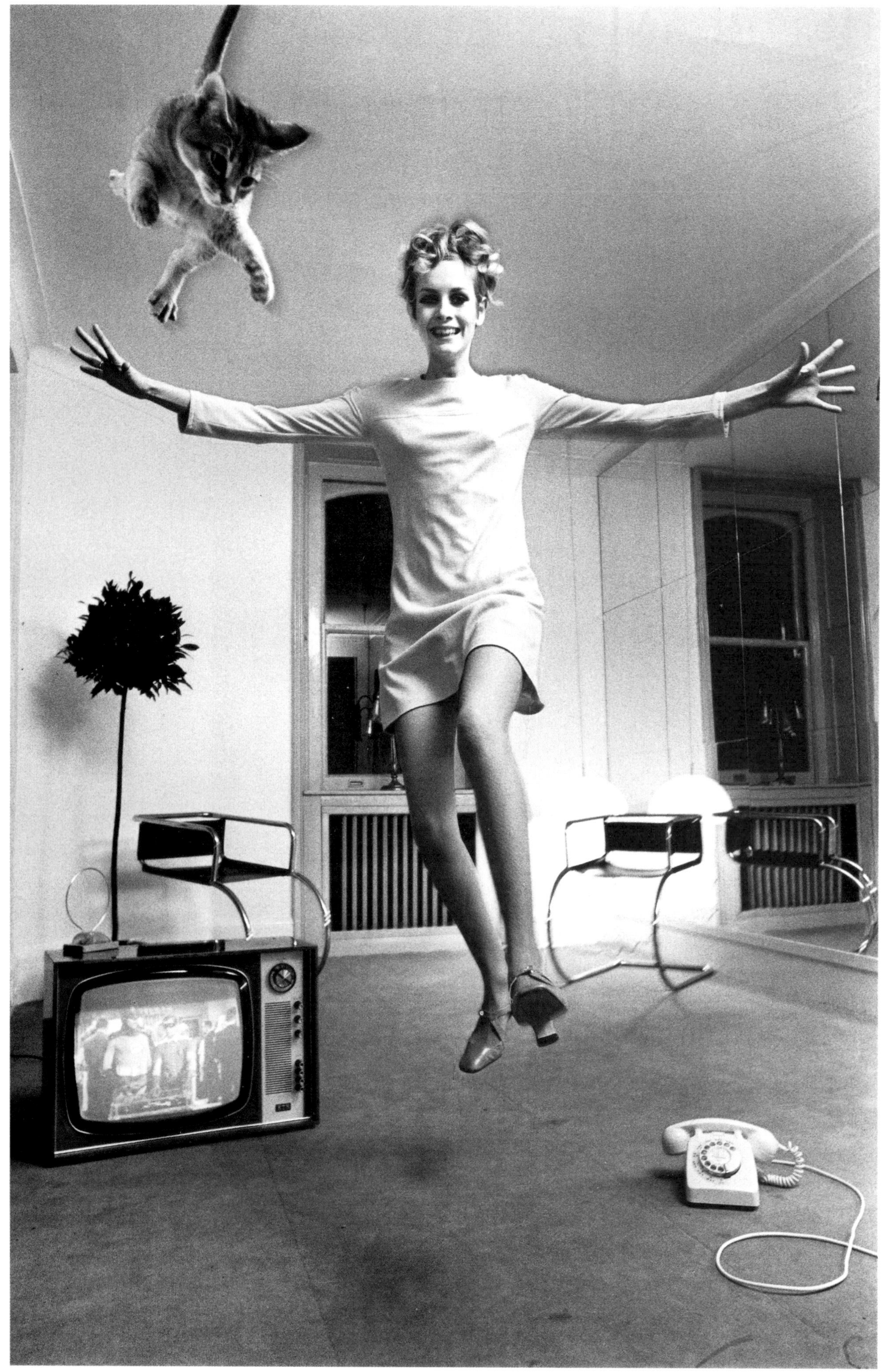

THE DREAM OF BEAUTY 31

Fashion and fantasy

Françoise Ducros

At the beginning of the twentieth century, clothing began to feature in photographs. The intention was to sell it more effectively by displaying it in an idealized world, created by photography. So-called "fashion" photography created a collective fantasy which depended essentially on the way society at large viewed the role of women. This imaginary world of allurement and beauty was carried along by aesthetic novelties and passing photographic trends; it made use of optical tricks and stylistic references borrowed from reportage, realism, and Surrealism.

When considered in the context of photography in general, fashion photography is, first and foremost, a response to the commissioning of a particular image rather than an act of free choice on the part of the photographer. The photographer's aim is to create an image which will sell a piece of clothing by showing it off in its best light. To achieve this, fashion photography has had to create its own visual language and grammar, that of image-clothing to use Roland Barthes' terminology. In his analytical study of the "fashion system" he claimed that "it is the woman who is featured, not the garment".[1] The whole history of fashion photography is marked by this question of how clothing should be presented, and around the notion itself hovers a vision of the ephemeral, abstract, and imaginary body of Woman. Male bodies, on the other hand, have, until very recently, remained constrained by the uniformity of men's clothing.

During the Second Empire, dress codes became less rigid and new types of social behavior evolved. It was at this time that the phenomenon of the great fashion designer appeared. When he opened his own fashion house in Paris in 1857-1858, Charles Worth conferred on the couturier a status comparable to that of an artist. In order to display his creations he made use not only of mannequins, as he had done previously, but also of living human beings. Fashion photography, affected by social and cultural distinctions, and dependent on the first products of a mass media, became a subject with popular appeal – just like sports and the cinema. Indeed, these have often provided a social setting for fashion photography as well as a framework for its development.

As a visible manifestation of individuality, photography displays an image of femininity which is both physical and symbolic. While magazines ensure wide public distribution, fashion photography has had a huge influence on the imaginary world, to such an extent that the commercial and technical realities of the clothing industry have almost been overwhelmed by pure fantasy.[2]

The tradition of portraiture

From 1886, technical improvements introduced by the American Frederick Eugene Ives allowed text and photographs to be printed on the page simultaneously. Half-tones then replaced wood engravings "taken from a photograph". The process was used in 1892 in *La Mode pratique*, then became gradually more widespread. At the beginning of the century, the magazine *Les Modes* specialized in photographic illustrations which were color-enhanced. Fashion photography had not yet achieved its independence. It still adhered to illustrative conventions comparable to those of the carte de visite, borrowing their props and painted backdrops for example. By identifying itself with the established genre of portraiture, fashion photography initiated a tendency for the

◀ Helmut Newton, ***Vogue,*** 1967, London, Tuffin and Foale.

1. R. Barthes, *The Fashion System*, trans. M. Ward and R. Howard, London, Jonathan Cape, 1985, p. 302, note 22.

2. For an overview of this subject, see Nancy Hall-Duncan, *The History of Fashion Photography*, New York, Alpine Book Co. 1979 and Martin Harrison, *Appearances: Fashion Photography since 1945*, London, Jonathan Cape, 1991.

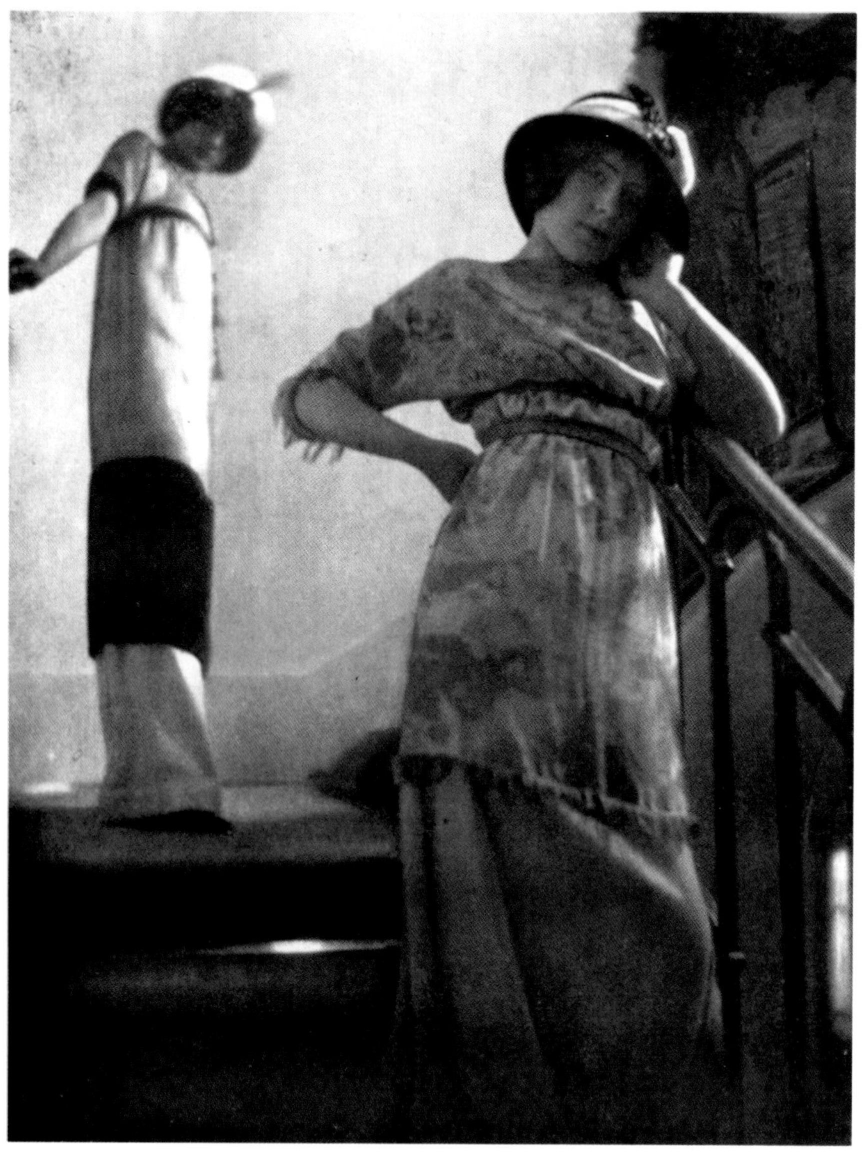

EDWARD STEICHEN, *"Bakou" and "Shepherdess", by Poiret,* from *Art et décoration,* April 1911.

visual lexicon of elegant dressing to symbolize, even more intensely than in the portrait, the quest for a social and psychological identity.

Although the Reutlinger studio had, from the outset, been involved mainly with the world of theatre and music, the way in which it began to interest itself in fashion photography illustrates the equivocal role of the visual setting created in the studio.[3] At that time, fashion photography required both space and lighting identical to those needed for portraiture. Indeed, initially, there was little difference between taking photographs of people in costume and photographing a model showing off the creations of a couturier. The two genres were so similar that actresses from the world of theatre or variety were often asked to pose in a designer's gowns. In 1911, for example, Mistinguett presented examples from different designers in the periodical *Les Modes*. From the very beginning, fashion photography was subject to an interplay of several factors: commercial considerations and fantasy, the quest for publicity, and the repetition of visual clichés. The album of the Countess of Castiglione, which includes both portraits and costume studies (details of feet, knees, backs, etc.) is indicative of the element of narcissism that photography encouraged. The album was assembled by Louis Pierson for private use, and it demonstrates how photography could serve to create and change identities at will, depending on how the wardrobe and the accessories were put together.

Fashion photography as an art form

Fashion photography first became subject to aesthetic considerations in New York in around 1914, when Adolphe De Meyer was taken on by *Vogue* magazine, which Condé Nast had recently acquired. The first period of his work, notable for its Pictorialist slant, lasted until 1925. It was a style adopted by numerous photographers, such as Émile Otto Hoppé and Paul O'Doye.

In this way, fashion photography continued a trend which had developed between 1885 and 1910, both in Europe and the United States. In photography, Pictorialism corresponded to the artistic movements of Impressionism, Symbolism, and Art Nouveau. The portraits of the American painter Whistler and the development of the decorative arts provided a model for the treatment of space and the use of background which would serve as a model for the photography of garments.

Adolphe De Meyer's fame came from his membership of the Linked Ring, a dissident British group of Pictorialist photographers. Alfred Stieglitz exhibited his work at his 291 Gallery in New York. Taking his inspiration from the Pictorialists' sensitivity to light and atmosphere, De Meyer created a delicate, elegant world, recalling the way of life at the beginning of the century. He increasingly liked to employ gestures and body language (such as a hand-on-hip pose) which embodied a sense of well-being and seemed to enhance the social status of the wearer. The career of Baron De Meyer reveals the ambiguity of the new social status of the fashion photographer, illustrating that the success of a photographer's career depended increasingly on cultivating acquaintances in society, as well as knowing his way about the equally closed world of the artistic fraternity.[4]

De Meyer developed an image of misty femininity, whose sophistication derived as much from the loose-fitting cut of the model's garment as from the background into which she appeared to dissolve. In his work, a bouquet of flowers became an accessory suggesting social privilege, a subtle link between nature and the inner world. The suggestion of this intimate relation between clothing and the domestic environment is

3. J.-P. Bourgeron, *Les Reutlinger, photographes à Paris, 1850–1937*, Paris, J.-P. Bourgeron, 1979.

4. The title of "Baron" De Meyer was in itself a fabrication indicative of the ambiguous nature of his personality.

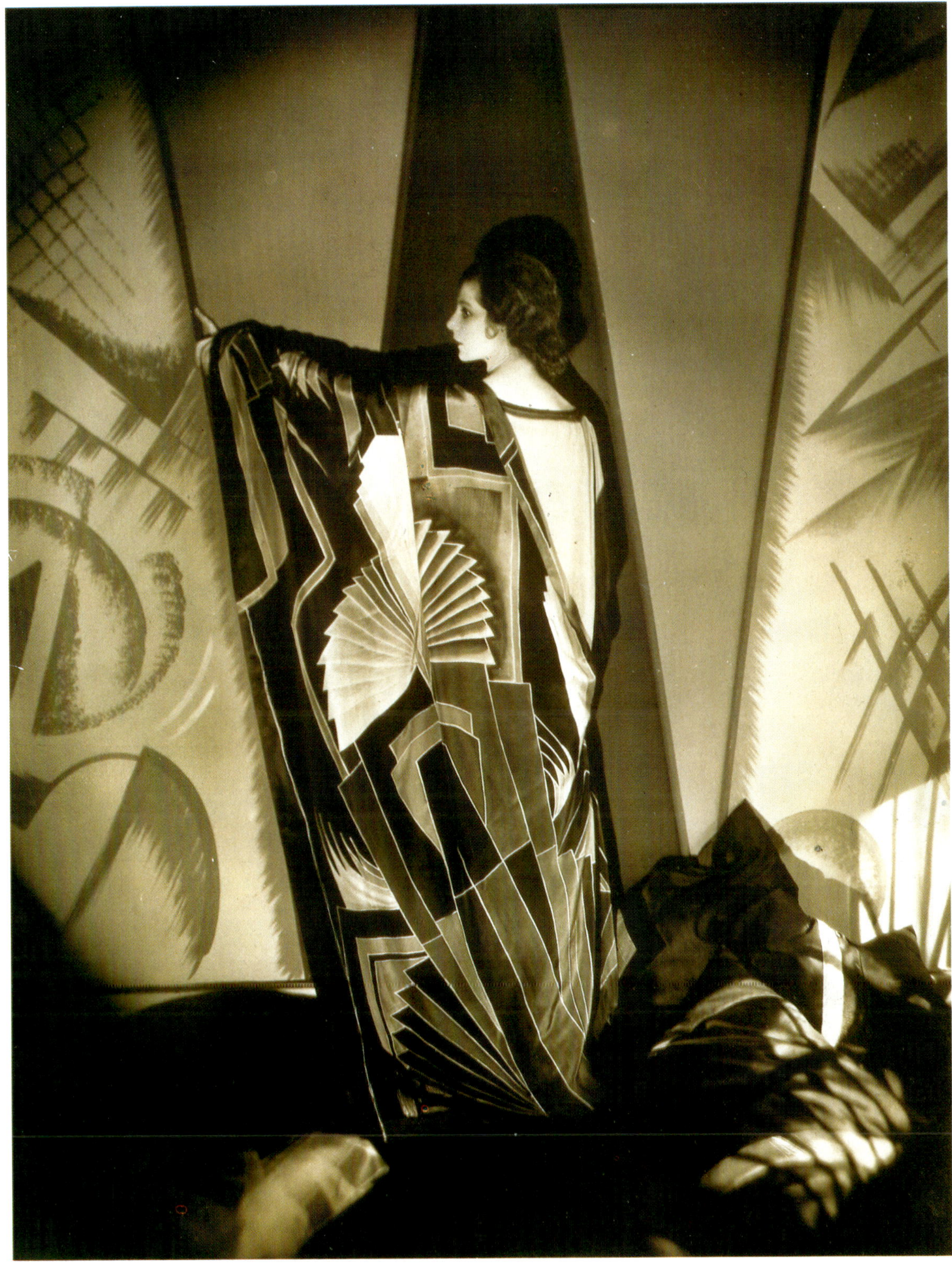

EDWARD STEICHEN,
Modernist garments,
1925.

perhaps explained by the fact that De Meyer was also an interior decorator. Thus, these photographs allowed him to obtain commissions to decorate private town houses. Furthermore, he pioneered another essential element in the language of fashion photography: the use of soft-focus produced by special lenses or by covering the lens with silk gauze, a trick which served to tone down the reality of garments and obscure their more obvious manufactured qualities.

The enigmatic effect created by the use of artificial back-lighting gives images a particular radiancy. It envelops the subject while dematerializing it; the garment is assimilated into the immaterial space of dreams. The nebulous quality of clothing, its transparency, the glitter of lamé have the effect of suggesting exotic surroundings and evoking a graceful life-style; this effect is created by the brilliance of light on a face or a piece of cloth. The photographer has achieved the metamorphosis of objective reality.

During the inter-war years, photography was inspired largely by the innovations of the avant-garde school. The poetic haziness of the previous

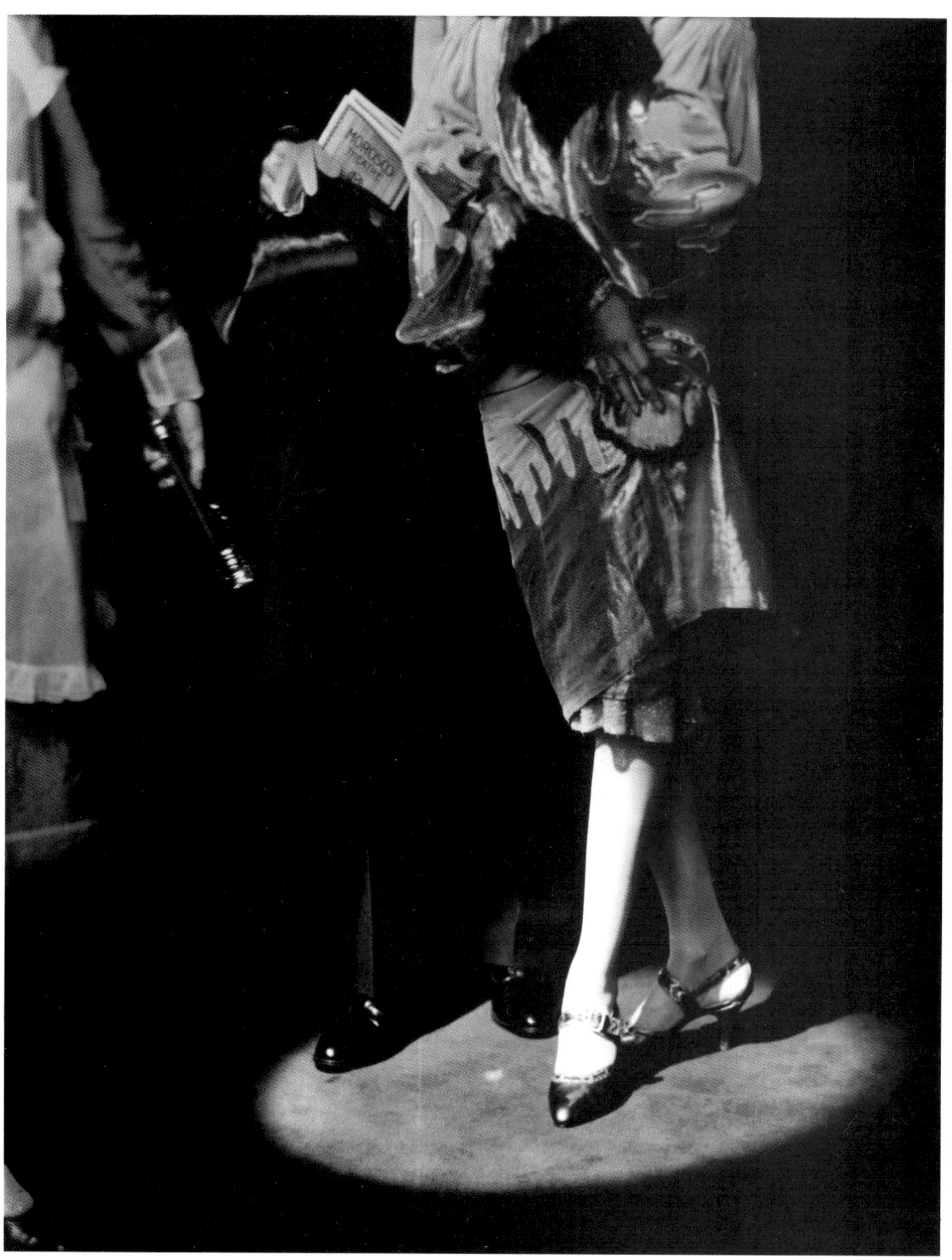

EDWARD STEICHEN,
Golden sandals and patent-leather shoes,
New York Vogue,
December 15, 1926.

generation disappeared. While women's bodies became more slender and their hair shorter, their clothes now revealed square shoulders and wasp waists, emphasizing their bust and their flat hips. This style was illustrated in various ways by Alix, Vionnet, and Elsa Schiaparelli. It implied a new perception both of the female body and of garments.

The evolution of Steichen's photographic style is marked by a development from misty outlines to sharp-focus. He had illustrated the intangible style of Pictorialism in a series of fashion shots for the couturier Paul Poiret which appeared in 1911 in the magazine *Art et Décoration*.[5] He had obtained this commission through the intermediary of the Paris avant-garde group which had formed around Paul Poiret and which had developed mainly from the Cubist movement. His later evolution took place in the context of the fundamental relationship between Modernism and fashion. New visual schemes derived from Cubism were introduced into the background, the cloth, the cut of the garment, and also the photographic composition. Sometimes posing

5. This series appeared in *Art et décoration: Revue mensuelle d'art moderne,* January-June 1911. See also E. Steichen, *A Life in Photography,* New York, Doubleday & Co., 1963.

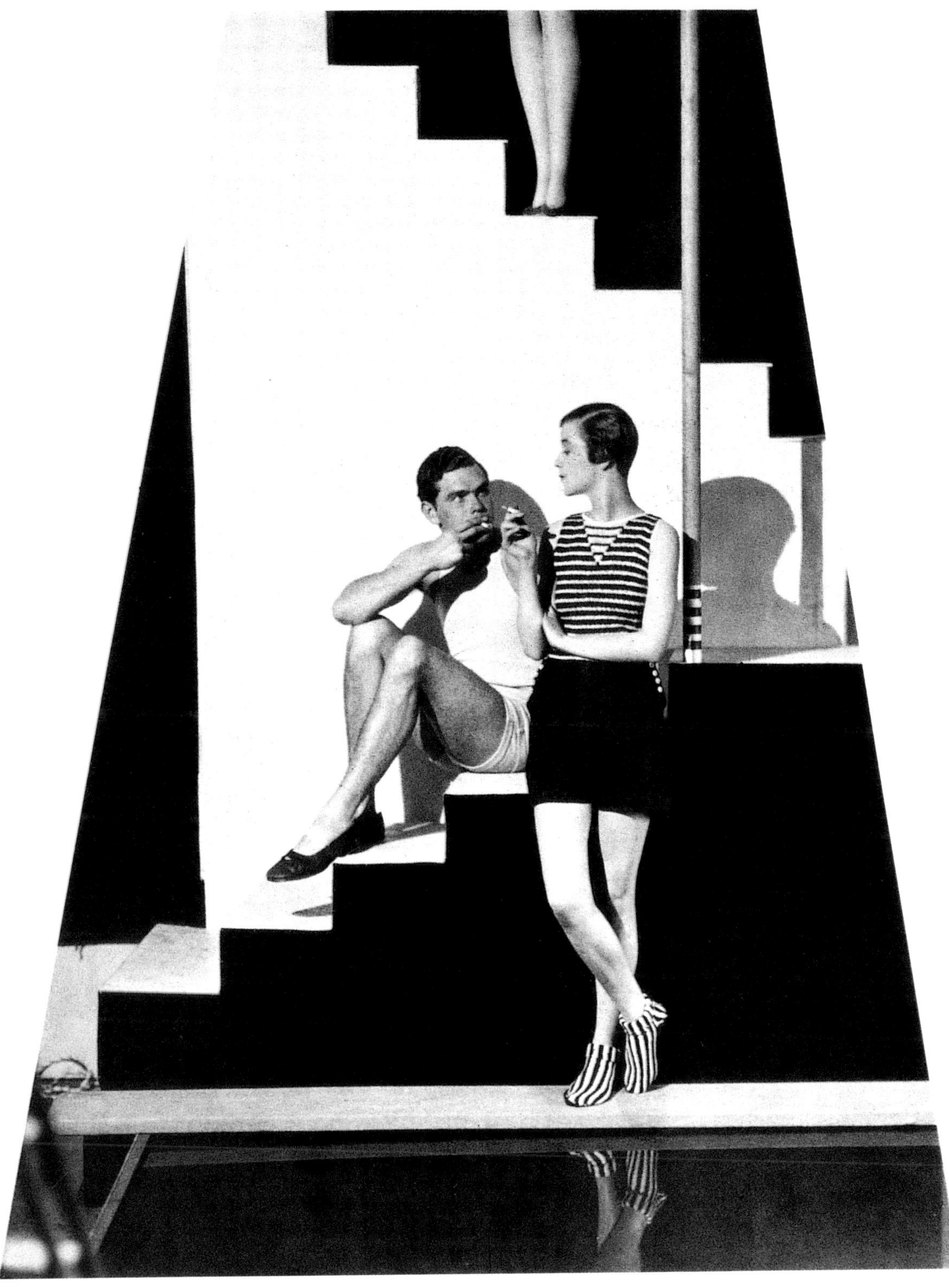

George Hoyningen-Huene, *Bettina Jones, beachwear for Schiaparelli,* 1928.

with her back to the camera and her face in profile, the model appears to be embedded in the receding image planes and in the interplay of light and shade. As for the body image, it derived from the graphic and cultural models which surrounded the enlightened bourgeoisie in the 1920s and 1930s.

In this way, fashion photography took part in the dissemination and the secondary accomplishments of the avant-garde movement. Standing motionless as a statue in a decorative setting, the human figure silhouetted against a background participated actively in the composition of the image. The model might, for example, be shown in a doorway, her back and her profile enlivening the composition in a play of lines and light. In a paradoxical way, fashion suspends time and, one might add, stops it in order to create purely formal and abstract relationships.

The "garment/body" combination has perhaps never played as important a part in forming an image as in Steichen's photograph *Black,* which appeared in 1935. The all-important element in this image is that the model presents the

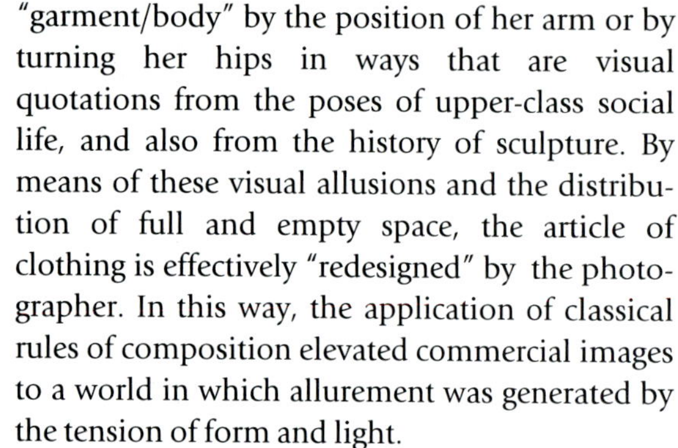

MARTIN MUNKACSI, ▶
for *Harper's Bazaar*,
1939.

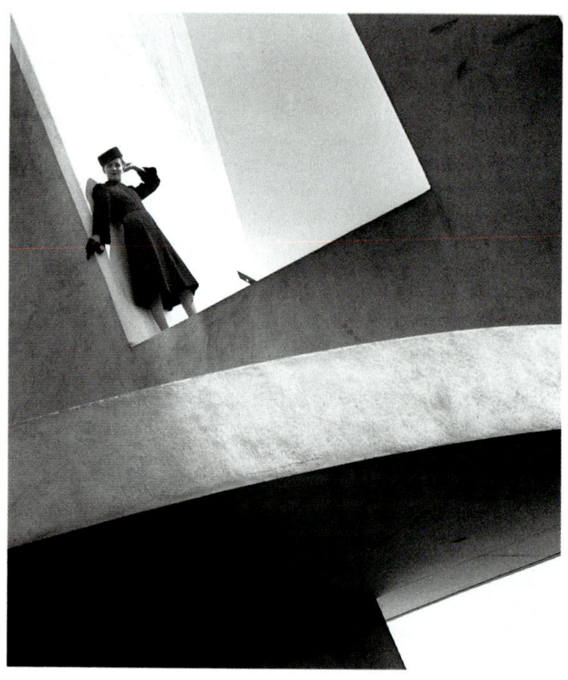

"garment/body" by the position of her arm or by turning her hips in ways that are visual quotations from the poses of upper-class social life, and also from the history of sculpture. By means of these visual allusions and the distribution of full and empty space, the article of clothing is effectively "redesigned" by the photographer. In this way, the application of classical rules of composition elevated commercial images to a world in which allurement was generated by the tension of form and light.

Aesthetic sublimation

George Hoyningen-Huene, who was recruited by *Vogue* in 1925, was the most significant representative of a style of fashion photography whose principle was devoted entirely to the imaginary cult of beauty. His photographs rank amongst the most important of the 1920s and 1930s.[6] They embody that quest for "distinction, elegance, and chic" which was so characteristic of the aristocratic modernism of a generation which had discovered foreign travel and sport.

Hoyningen-Huene's style resulted from a synthesis of qualities derived from the world of cinema as well as from the plastic arts. He had learned how to light actors and stage sets in the Épinay studios, and his visits to the studio of the painter André Lhote allowed him to study living models as well as the formal rules by which Cubists broke down a subject into its constituent parts. Furthermore, his "purist" fashion illustrations are closely allied to those of Douglas Pollard or the posters of Cassandre.[7] His work was published in art magazines such as *Le Minotaure* and *Verve*, and in *Photographie*, directed by Charles Peignot from 1930 to 1940, and he took part in numerous avant-garde exhibitions.

Hoyningen-Huene's "neo-Grecian" inspiration can be seen in the context of a reinterpretation of antiquity pursued by various members of the avant-garde movement at that time. This reference to the ancient world was an important element in contemporary artistic thought. For many artists it formed part of what has been called "a return to order". In particular, it favored the creation of an ideal of feminine beauty deriving from a perception of antique statuary. In a book on Hoyningen-Huene that Frenzel published in Berlin in 1932, the author placed the face of a Hellenistic statue next to that of one of the photographer's female models. The faces of Miss Dolores Wilkinson or Lee Miller (who was herself a photographer, and Hoyningen-Huene's model) are characterized by their harmony, radiance, and fine modeling, but also by their facial expressions and by their sexual ambiguity, inspired by Greek art. This new approach to the

MAN RAY,
Black silk taffeta enriched with lavender, turquoise, pink, and green
(printed as a color tinted negative),
Harper's Bazaar,
February 1937.
▼

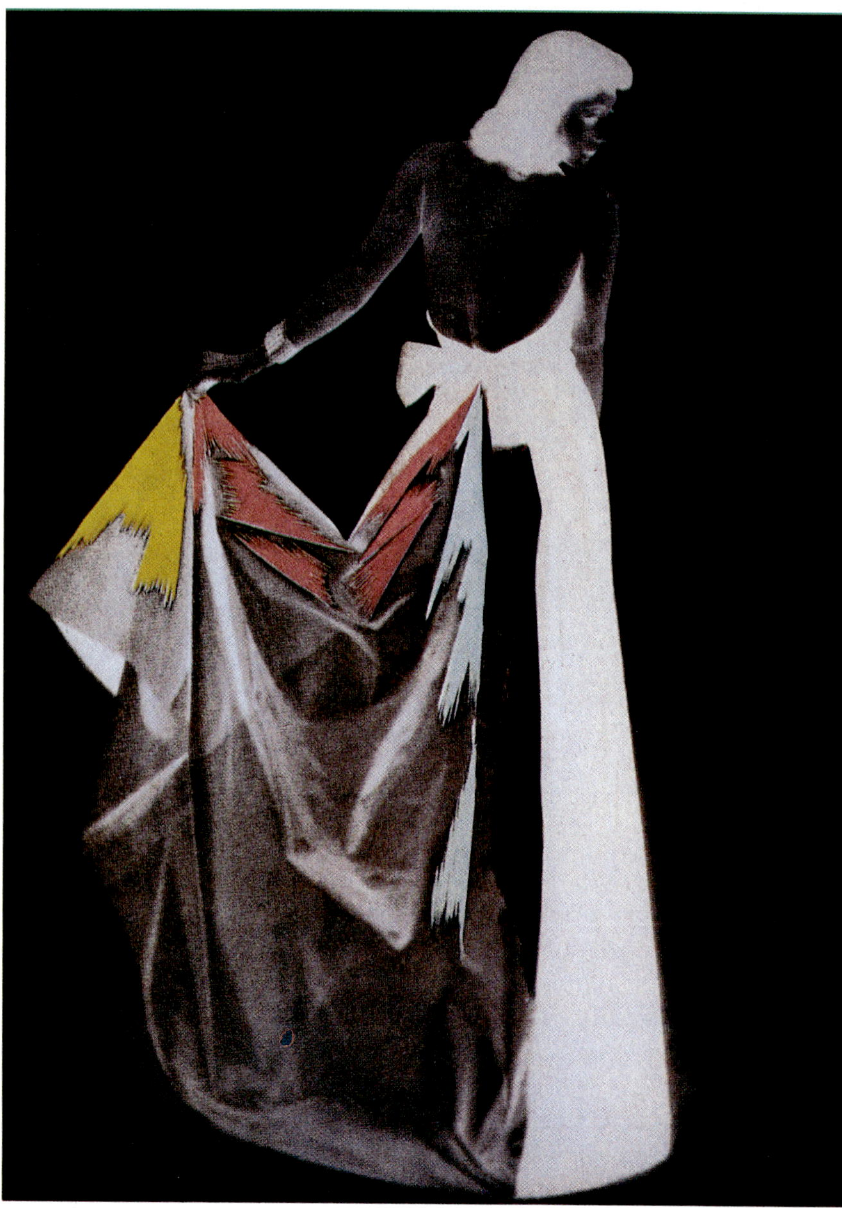

6. W. E. Ewing, *Eye for Elegance: George Hoyningen-Huene*, ICP, New York, 1980 and W. E. Ewing, *The Photographic Art of Hoyningen-Huene*, London, Thames and Hudson, 1986.

7. The term "purism" is used here in the sense of a stylistic movement tending to make forms more geometrical, of which the work of Léger is a particularly good example.

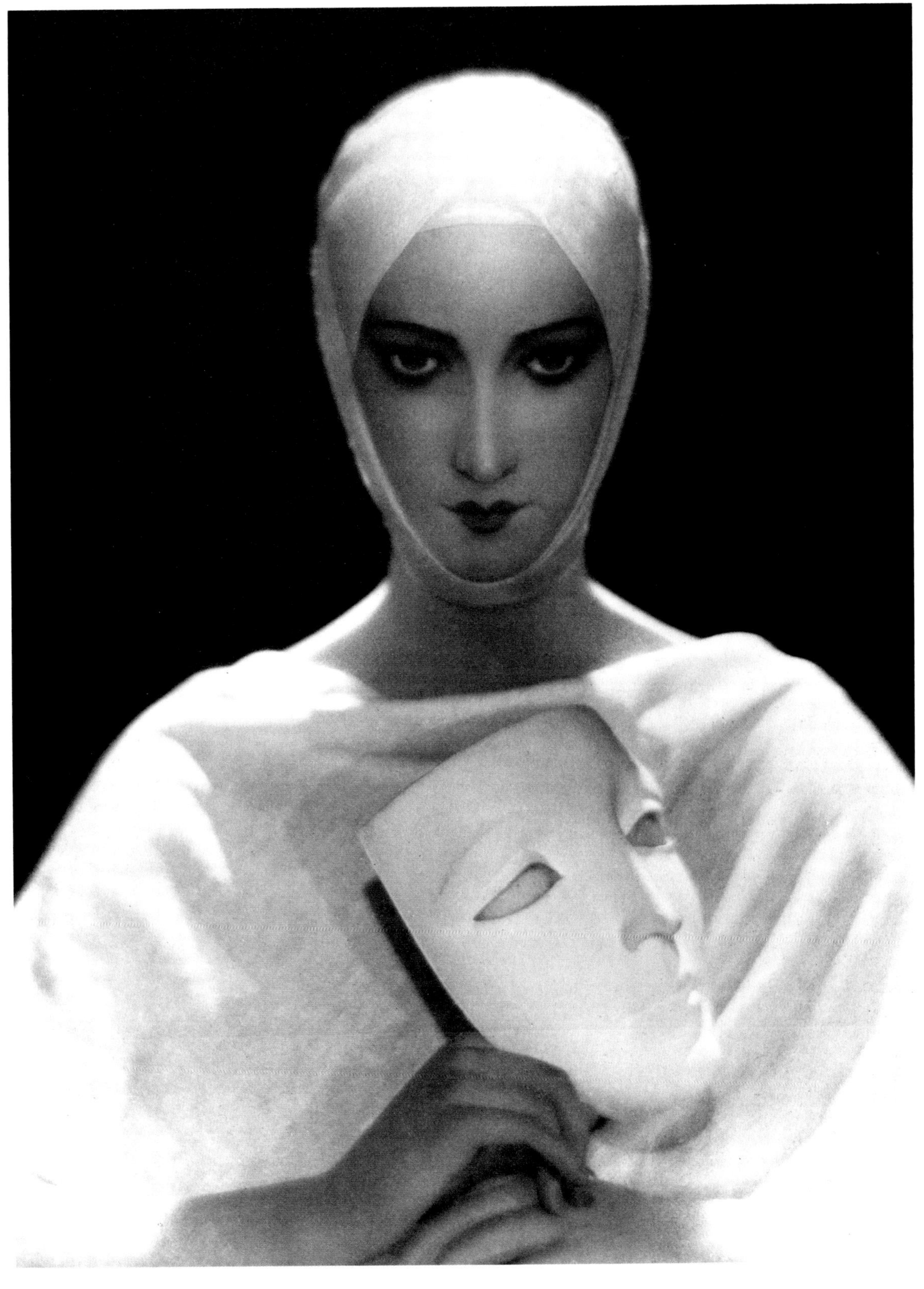

Adolphe De Meyer, publicity photograph for Elizabeth Arden, 1935.

model, who wore dresses with pleated folds in imitation of classical sculpture, was also the result of more prosaic technical constraints. Heavy plate cameras, using plates with slow emulsions, were still being used in the studio. Under the glare of spotlights, the photographer would guide his model in a search for that magic moment when the perfect pose occurred. "Each time I worked with him", recalled Lisa Fonssagrives, "I had the feeling that our studio was like a temple, and that our work resembled a religious rite." This fascination with the aura surrounding the model implies the denial of the commercial and material reality of the garment. As if in a mirage, a woman wearing no more than a simple bathing costume is transformed into a metaphysical dream. From now on, all fashion photography would operate on the level of subterfuge. Reality gave way to the world of dreams. The camera's field of vision would be used as though it no longer obeyed the laws of gravity.

Horst P. Horst, *Electric Beauty*, New York, circa 1938.
▼

In 1934, after Condé Nast had invited Hoyningen-Huene to Hollywood, where he worked for *Vanity Fair* magazine, Horst P. Horst replaced him as the head of the Paris studio of *Vogue*.[8] While his style was broadly inspired by that of his predecessor, who had introduced him to fashion photography, he accentuated certain of his techniques, particularly the use of high-contrast back-lighting and three-quarter profiles. Horst brought into his backgrounds elements that were more complex than the moldings of antique statuary. From now on, shells and cave-like effects were a reaction to the purist spirit of the 1920s, to which he had been introduced by the Hamburg Kunstgewerbeschule and by the architect Le Corbusier whose studio he had frequented. In Horst's photographs, the presentation of femininity relies less on the depiction of the model herself than on the stage properties used.

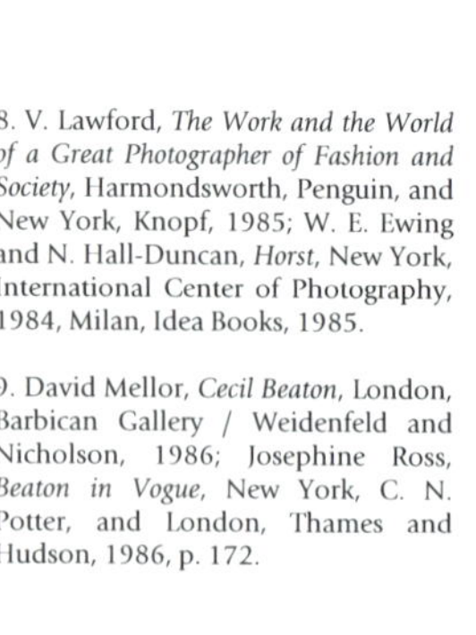

Horst's photographs possess the witty character of visual entertainment, and through this wit they identify themselves with the luxurious world which they are intended to promote. In one of Horst's most original series of works, however, which uses the technique of *trompe-l'œil*, the use of accessories (such as gloves, jewelry, and hats) to link the consumer to the object is completely rejected. Thanks to photo-montage and trickery, fashion photography, adopting the tricks of the illusionist, gives a strange, surreal character to the symbols of allurement. Not only does it send fashion into free-fall, but it also brings it closer to another type of image-making: the world of vanity. This form of fashion photography even goes as far as using its own symbols, such as that of a watch-face replaced by a tiny portrait of the model herself. By appropriating techniques of photomontage Horst brings to the fore the symbolism linking the consumer and the fashion photographer. Objects seem to be coming out of the very photograph. On several occasions, his use of mirrors takes fashion photography into the world of narcissism. It merges into the world of magic, although, in the end, it reveals itself as a will o' the wisp, rather than a true passport into the world of dreams.

8. V. Lawford, *The Work and the World of a Great Photographer of Fashion and Society*, Harmondsworth, Penguin, and New York, Knopf, 1985; W. E. Ewing and N. Hall-Duncan, *Horst*, New York, International Center of Photography, 1984, Milan, Idea Books, 1985.

9. David Mellor, *Cecil Beaton*, London, Barbican Gallery / Weidenfeld and Nicholson, 1986; Josephine Ross, *Beaton in Vogue*, New York, C. N. Potter, and London, Thames and Hudson, 1986, p. 172.

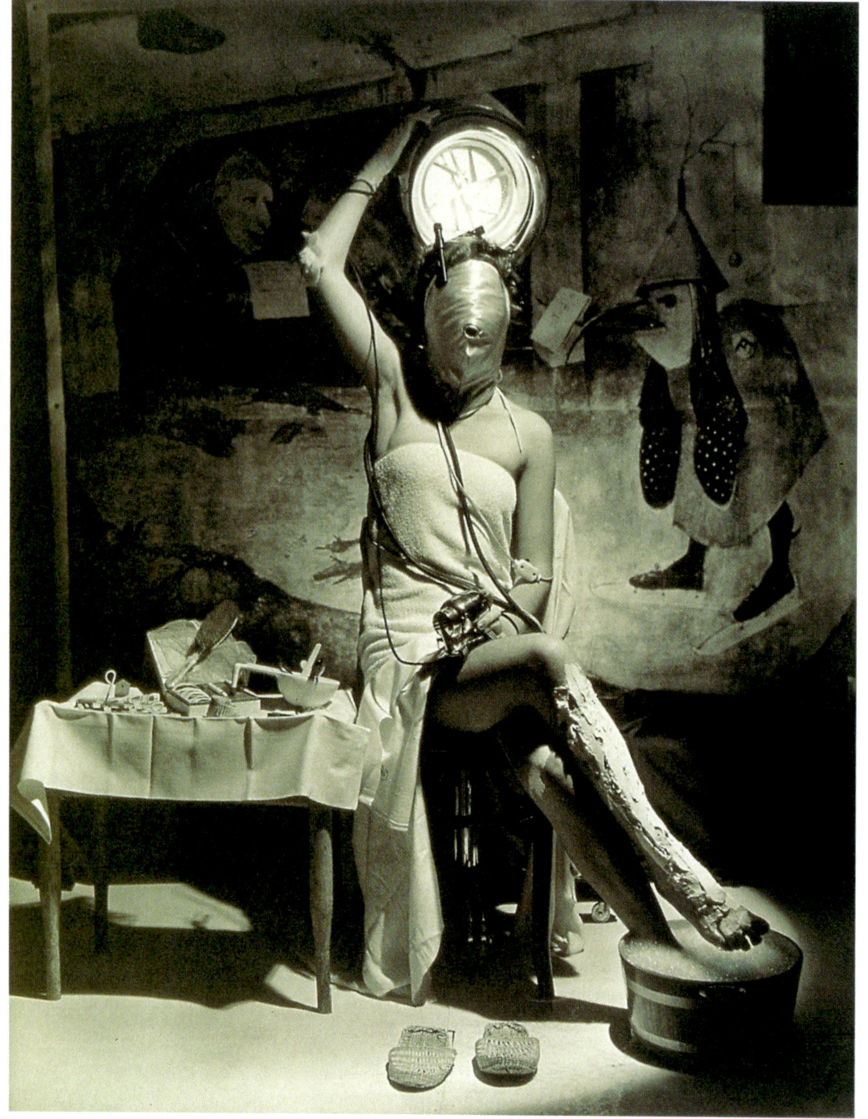

Surrealism and *trompe-l'œil*

Surrealism was an essential reference point in the development of fashion photography. The fashion world of Elsa Schiaparelli closely replicated that of Salvador Dalí, and the mannequin or dress-maker's dummy, borrowed from the world of fashion, was one of the fetish objects of Surrealist painting. The ambivalent dividing line between reality and fantasy challenged the way in which the objective universe could be grasped.

In the 1930s and 1940s, Horst, André Durst, George Platt Lynes, Man Ray, Clifford Coffin, and Peter Ross-Pulham – to mention only the best-known names – were strongly influenced by Surrealism. Some of Man Ray's photographs were published in *La Révolution surréaliste*, while fashion magazines like *Vogue* and *Harper's Bazaar* played a role in popularizing Surrealism. Three repainted photographs by Salvador Dalí, Giorgio de Chirico, and Paul Tchelitchev were published in *Vogue* in 1937. Cecil Beaton photographed his homage to Dalí, showing Schiaparelli's suits with "bureau-drawer pockets" (themselves inspired by Dalí), in an dream landscape recalling Dalí's Surrealist paintings.[9]

As a consequence, Surrealism formed a "modern" backdrop, replacing Hoyningen-Huene's idealized neo-classical landscapes. It was able to bring to life the imaginative process involved in images of allurement. Horst's appropriation of Dalí's pictures allowed him to create backgrounds for his models against which their poses and mechanical attitudes recalled those of a

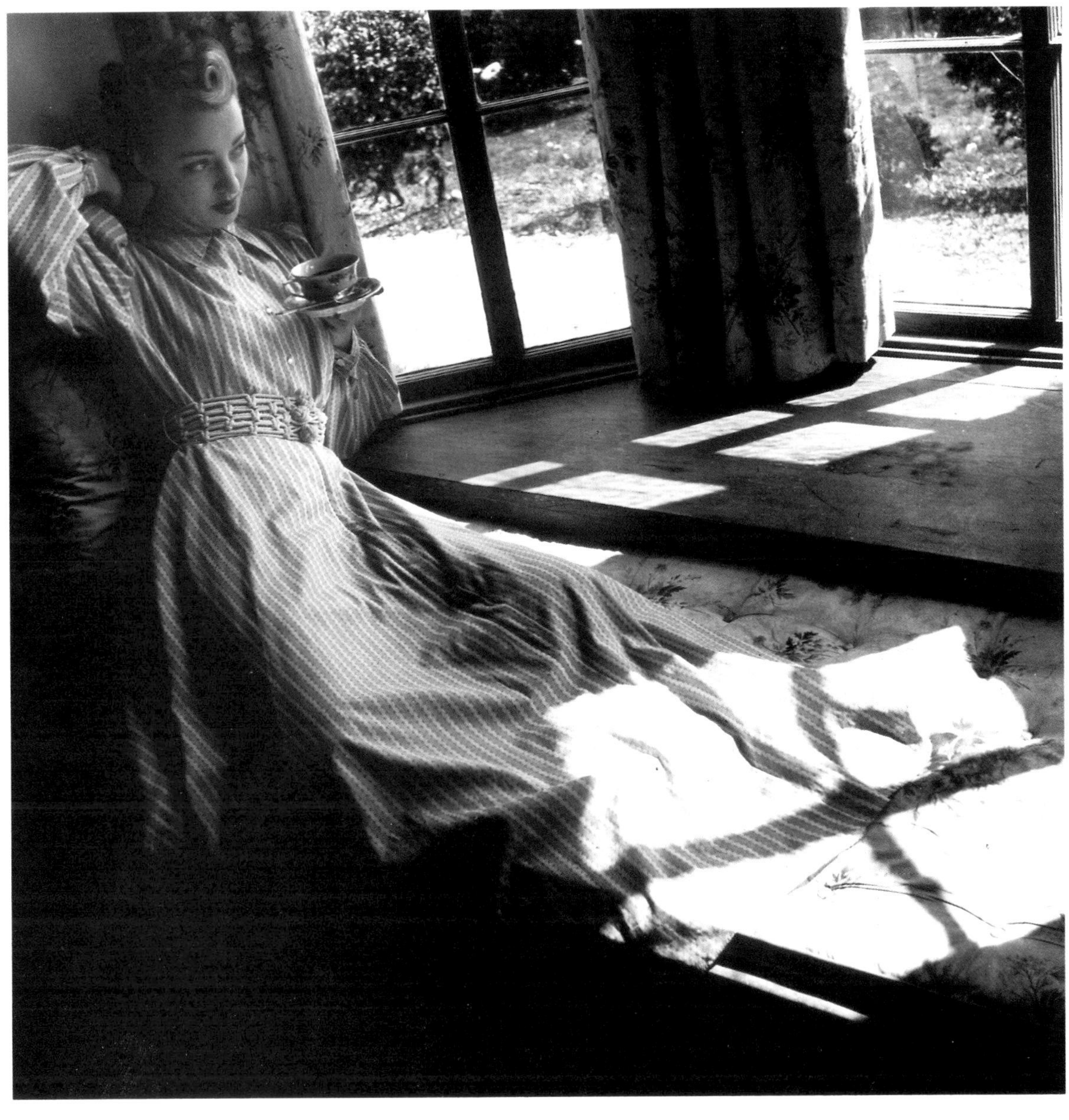

TONI FRISSELL
A pink and grey striped housecoat,
New York Vogue,
June 1, 1939.

puppet theatre. Thus, the "garment/body" combination must be considered in the world of fantasy, tending to create a desire for the body rather than for the clothes. In many photographs of the 1930s, women appear like sleep-walkers, with blank, staring expressions.

In the middle of a notably eclectic career, involving other interests, such as cinema sets, Cecil Beaton introduced Surrealism in a particularly significant way into Hollywood studios, being fully aware of its potential. He described how "The vast sound stages, with the festoons of ropes, chains, and the haphazard impedimenta, were as lofty and awe-inspiring as cathedrals; the element of paradox and surprise was never-ending, and the juxtaposition of objects and people gave me my first glimpse of surrealism."[10]

This encounter was the inspiration for a curious series overladen with antiquities, followed by his use of fantastic background settings, with a clutter of diverse objects, creating an uncomfortable feeling that social conventions had been broken. In another series, the projected silhouette of three male figures is one of the first attempts at bringing men onto a stage where women reigned supreme.

The artistic output of George Platt Lynes, who, between 1946 and 1948, directed the *Vogue* studio in New York, testifies to a deeper and, perhaps, more literary understanding of Surrealism. During the 1930s he often traveled between New York and Paris, where he photographed personalities such as Gertrude Stein and Jean Cocteau. In 1936, he took part in the exhibition *Fantastic Art, Dada, and Surrealism* which was organized by Alfred Barr at the Museum of Modern Art in New York.

His work spills over into varied fields, such as the nude or the evocation of Greek mythology. However, unlike George Hoyningen-Huene he used several different ways of introducing imaginary elements into a fashion setting: models in unusual poses, light and shade provoking a feeling of unease, unusual groupings of stage props, the use of veils or mirrors to introduce a

10. Cecil Beaton, *Photography*, London, Oldhams Press, no date, p. 61, quoted in N. Hall-Duncan, *op. cit.* p. 111.

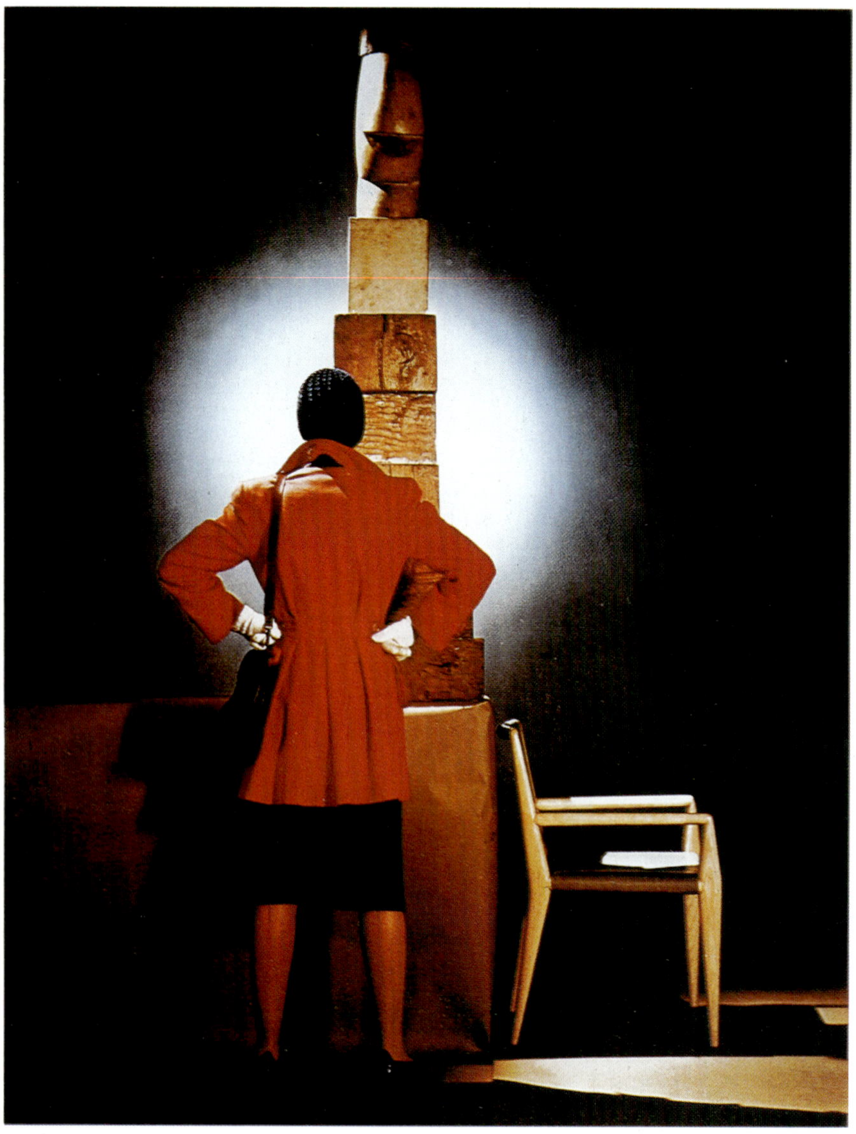

At the heart of the image

Man Ray, Maurice Tabard, and Erwin Blumenfeld accorded less importance to the projection of the inner fantasy world. On the other hand, their work showed an evident interest in the methods by which images were created.

In this respect, Man Ray occupies a privileged position. He expressed the possibility of a transition from pure to commercial photography, and he transposed his technical experiments into the latter, even though he viewed fashion photography primarily as a way of earning a living. In around 1921-1922, he began to work for the couturier Paul Poiret. His recruitment to *Harper's Bazaar* by Carmel Snow and Alexey Brodovitch[11] provided him with the opportunity of developing an original approach to fashion photography. His flair for experimentation allowed him to enlarge the repertoire of stock conventions used in producing graphic illusions. He introduced new darkroom techniques, with the result that fashion photography was, in a sense, linked with a design process similar to that of a fashion designer working out the new lines of their creation on a drawing board. This gave an abstract quality to the garment, allowing free reign to the imagination, which particularly suited the medium of photography. Having pioneered the "rayograph" (photogram) in 1922, Man Ray exploited at the same time the possibilities of solarization, which allowed certain parts of a positive image to revert to the appearance of a negative.[12]

JOHN RAWLINGS, Cover photograph for *Vogue*, January 1, 1944.

CECIL BEATON, ▶ *Pre-bombing Fashion Sitting*, circa 1940.

spatial discontinuity in the composition of the photographic image.

The best photographs by André Durst, who discovered Surrealism through Jean Cocteau and René Crevel and who worked for the French edition of *Vogue* from 1934 until about 1940, made use of similar techniques while producing more conventional images which still allow the garment to be "read".

The American photographer Clifford Coffin also employed techniques which recall the world of dreams, while achieving extreme precision in the realization of the image. By simulating an imaginary world in which narcissism is a powerful component, his photographs introduce quite a different relationship between the private world and public space. They mark the start of a trend whose descendants can be discerned long after this period. The display of emotions discernible in these photographs provide a model for cultural attitudes which can easily be adopted by the individual viewer.

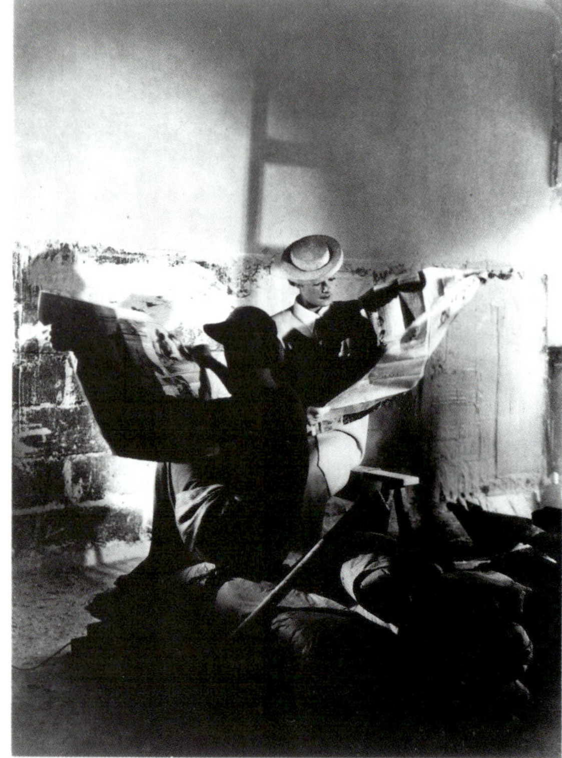

11. For the role played by this photographer, see *Alexei Brodovitch*, catalogue of an exhibition at the Grand Palais, Paris, Ministère de la Culture, 1982.

12. J. Esten, *Man Ray, Bazaar Years*, New York, Rizzoli, 1988.

This superimposition of positive and negative images produces an alluring sense of plasticity while allowing other possibilities to emerge. After his meeting with Philippe Soupault and René Magritte, Maurice Tabard[13] was influenced by Surrealism. He participated with Man Ray in an exhibition called *Film und Foto*, and collaborated on the magazine *VU*. Solarization and the use of negative effects create an enigmatic beauty resulting from the dematerialization of the body which, losing its substance and gaining in transparency, leads to an entirely new way of seeing. This imaging concept enhances photography and its specific language. Allurement is bound up with the visual magic of the object photographed: the image of the "garment/body" is absorbed by a complex operation on the medium which clothes it, in a kind of re-creation.

Although Erwin Blumenfeld claimed to be the heir of the Dadaist movement of which he had been a contemporary and exponent, his exploratory work, carried out first for *Vogue*, then, from 1939, for *Harper's Bazaar*, depended on an experimental concept of photography derived from conservatism and Surrealism.[14] From the late 1920s onwards, these two currents tended to merge. A new approach to advertising brought psychological considerations into play. The new discipline allowed an already established visual language to be used in an even more precise manner. Blumenfeld's photographic world resembled that of a conjurer. Exploiting every single possibility, he falsified the way things appear in nature in order to create a particularly brilliant universe. Nancy Hall-Duncan recalled that "he would go to any extreme to achieve the result: solarization, overprinting, combination of negative and positive images, sandwiching of color transparencies, and even drying his wet negative in the refrigerator to achieve crystallization."[15]

Like Man Ray's fashion photographs, those of Blumenfeld were the result of manipulation in the darkroom. Through its audacious cutting of the silhouette over the urban background, his photograph of Lisa Fonssagrives hanging precariously on a ledge of the Eiffel Tower gives the impression of a photomontage (which it is not), thereby putting the vestment on display spectacularly and efficiently.[16]

During the 1930s and 1940s, make-up developed a previously unknown degree of sophistication. Artificial eye-lashes, plucked eyebrows, talcum powder, and lipstick transformed facial features into an abstract composition of lines and colors. A new sensuality emerged. It seemed that the human face had never been so strongly desired. Close-up work and photographic enlargement concentrated on the face alone.

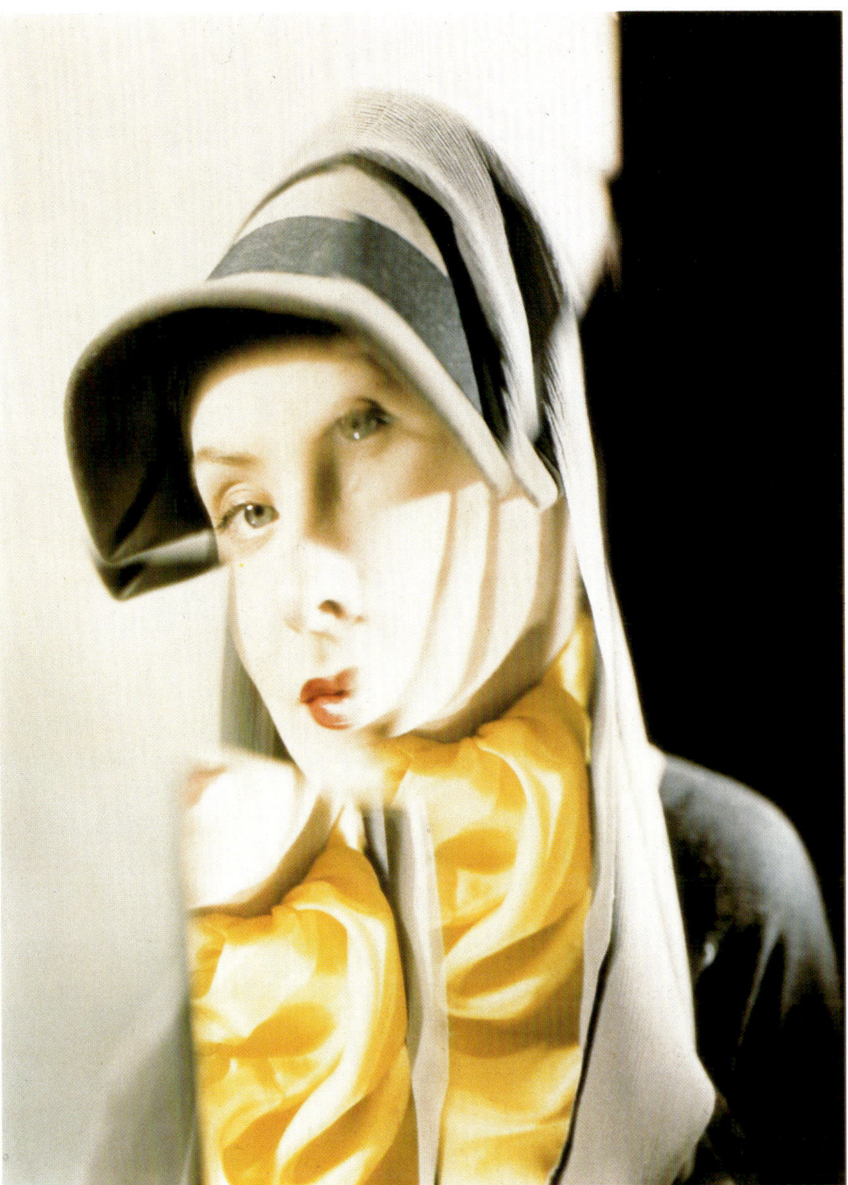

Erwin Blumenfeld, *What Looks New*, 1947.

Fashion photography, now being used to promote beauty products, was, at the same time, subject to the rhetoric of science and technology. Beauty went hand in hand with an approach often cruelly resembling that of a surgical operation, as some of Horst's photographs show: he did not shrink from evoking the fantastic world of Hieronymous Bosch, often with a degree of humor. Such beauty also resulted from a fragmentation of the human body.

From the time of Steichen and his famous photographs of the great film stars – Greta Garbo and Gloria Swanson – the face became a separate artistic entity. Thus, the photograph was "made up" in just the way that cosmetics are used: solarization and bleaching-out effects accentuated the symmetry of the outline or eliminated the ridge of the nose in order to bring out the eyes or the lips.

At the same time, Blumenfeld was at work, developing the language of the photographic image. In one series of advertising photographs devoted to a range of lipsticks, fragmentation

13. *Maurice Tabard*, Paris, Contrejour, 1987.

14. E. Blumenfeld and H. Teicher (ed.), *My 100 Best Photos*, New York, Rizzoli, 1980.

15. N. Hall-Duncan, *op. cit.*, p. 90.

16. Reproduced in Hall-Duncan, *op. cit.*, p. 93.

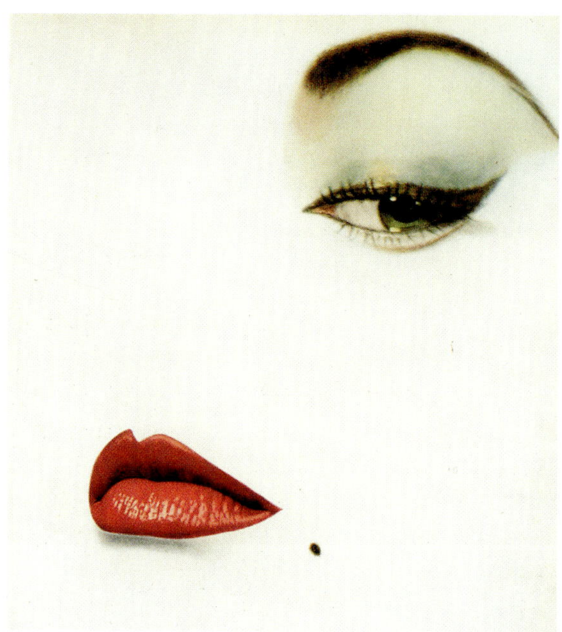

Erwin Blumenfeld, ▶ Cover for *New York Vogue*, January 1, 1950.

effects produced using a mirror gave the face the effect of a Cubist composition.

A cinematographic interpretation of the face seems to have taken over from an expressive or psychological approach. This may have been inspired by experimental cinema, notably by Fernand Léger's *Ballet-Mécanique* of 1924, in which eyelids, lips, and legs were used for their cinematographic autonomy. Fashion photography followed a similar path. In this respect, Erwin Blumenfeld was the first to consider the physicality of the model as a plastic component. He was also the first to explore the use of color in his images, by using saturation techniques and techniques of decomposition allowed by the new color films and filters.

Blumenfeld's style exercised a consistent fascination. Its influence continued to be found, for example, in Paolo Roversi's photographs. Roversi created a fresh approach to advertising photography, while creating an element of sophistication in his pictures of women. The depiction of the natural look was passé. Now, beauty had to be assembled artificially. The game of seduction is based on the manipulation of signs, and photography tells us more about the fetishistic nature of its workings than any spoken language can do.

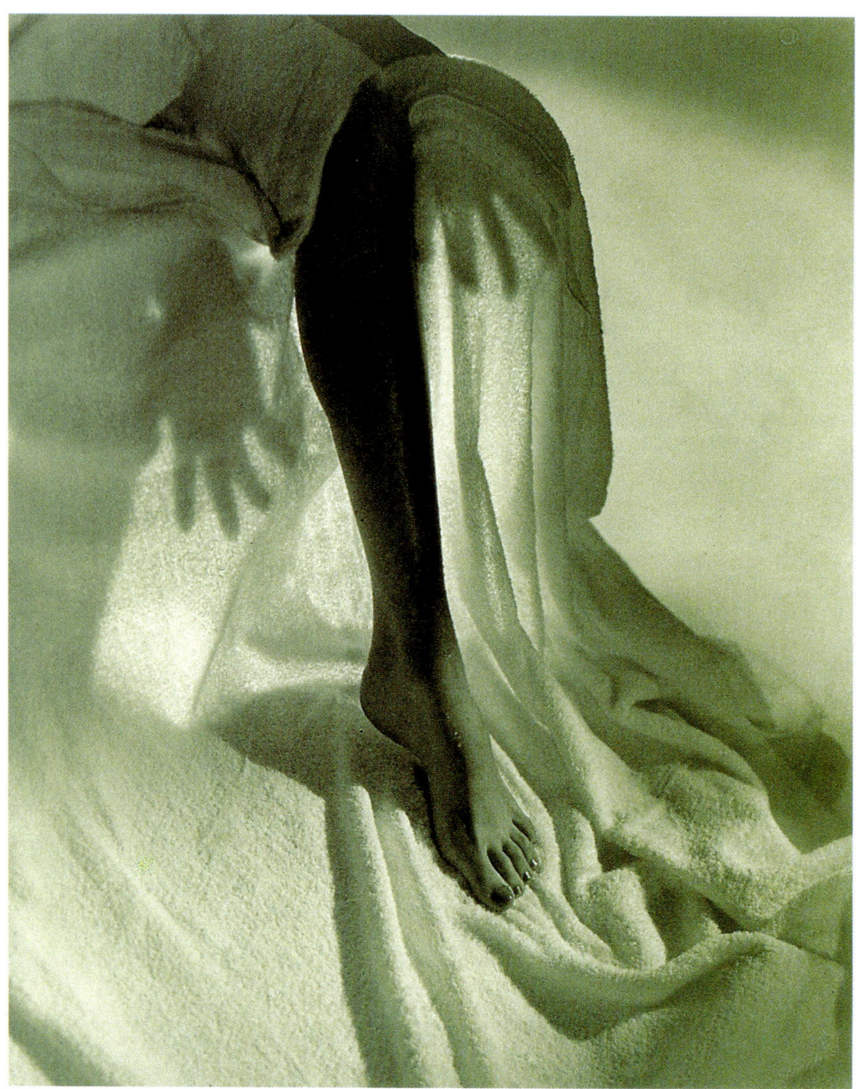

Horst P. Horst, *The New American Foot*, *New York Vogue*, 1948.

The contemporary nature of fashion

A new impetus was given to fashion photography by photoreportage. The drawing together of these two strands first became apparent in 1934, when Martin Munkacsi was taken on by *Harper's Bazaar* in place of Baron De Meyer, whose photographic style was becoming outdated. Munkacsi had started his career with a sporting daily newspaper and then become a photographic reporter in Hungary, where he worked for various European magazines before emigrating to the United States. His characteristic style, which consisted of photographing the model in action, in sporting, even acrobatic, poses, created a new image of the American woman, one closer to her new lifestyle. Thus, he inaugurated a new stylistic trend which is still current. Munkacsi brought to American photography technical innovations which had previously developed mainly in central Europe and Germany around the Bauhaus School. While it is true that they evolved from the new "instantaneous photography", they could not have developed without a new approach to the human body, now liberated from heaviness and immobility.

For the first time, the "real" bodies of women, freed from inactivity, would also be photographed. From now on, female bodies would be shown in action, as when Munkacsi photographed Lucille Brokaw at the seaside using natural light. The model runs energetically, swirling around the photographer. Her clothes, too, display all the movement of real life, faithfully captured by the fast shutter speed. This

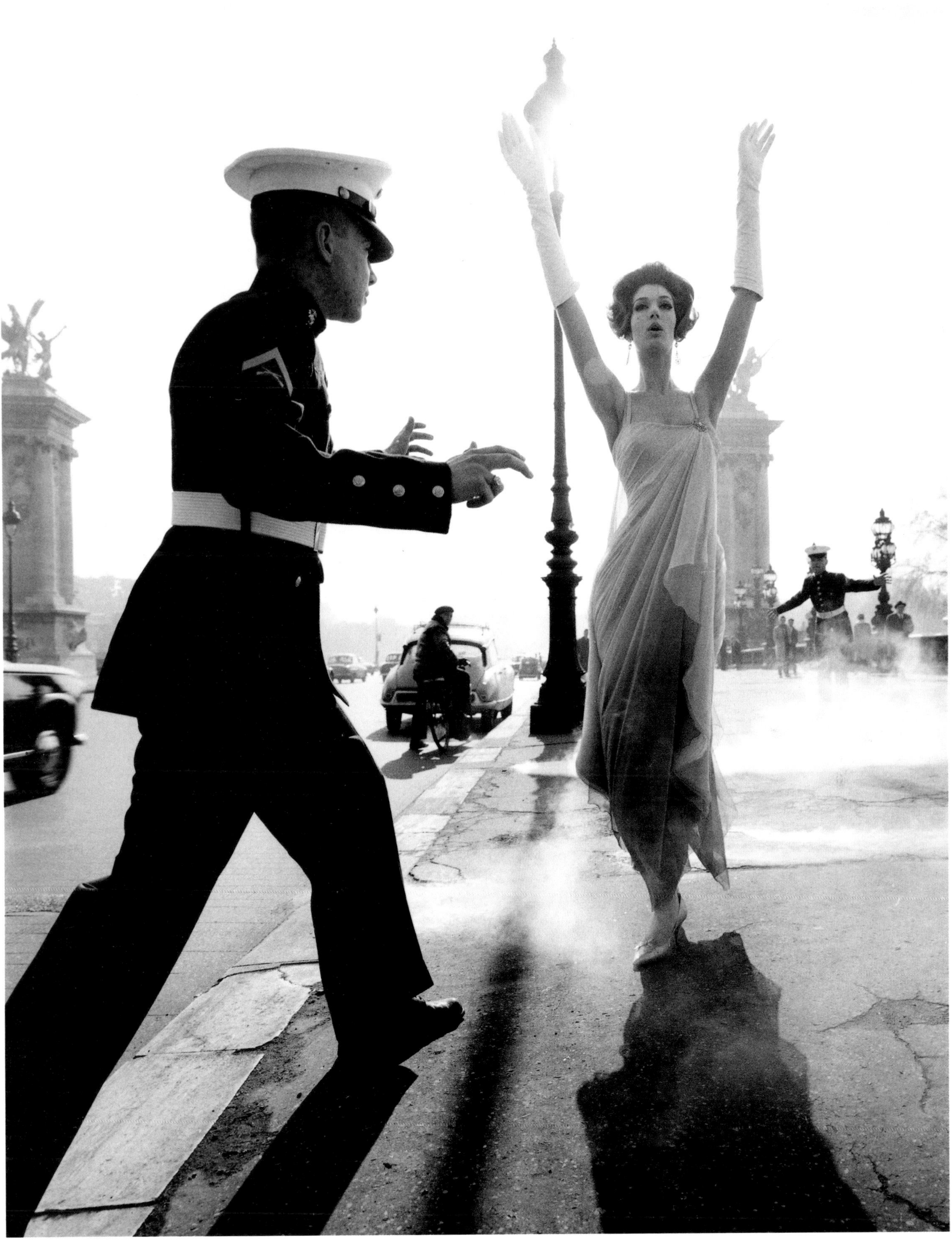

William Klein,
Paris *Vogue*,
1957.

transformation in fashion photography corresponded to a change in the social status of women, just as it resulted from a change in the economics of the clothing industry. It took place against the background of the rationalist or functionalist movement, one of the progressive approaches to modern times. Female emancipation went hand in hand with a wide-ranging changes in society, one of the symptoms of which was the development of a new architectural environment. This evolution was admirably represented in a famous photograph by Munkacsi showing a model posing inside a modernist building at the New York World's Fair in 1939. The way the entire image is slanted, the natural lighting, and the friendly gesture of the model's hand bear witness to the development that has occurred. The change tightly links a new way of

HIRO,
The Power of the Print,
Harper's Bazaar,
February 1967.

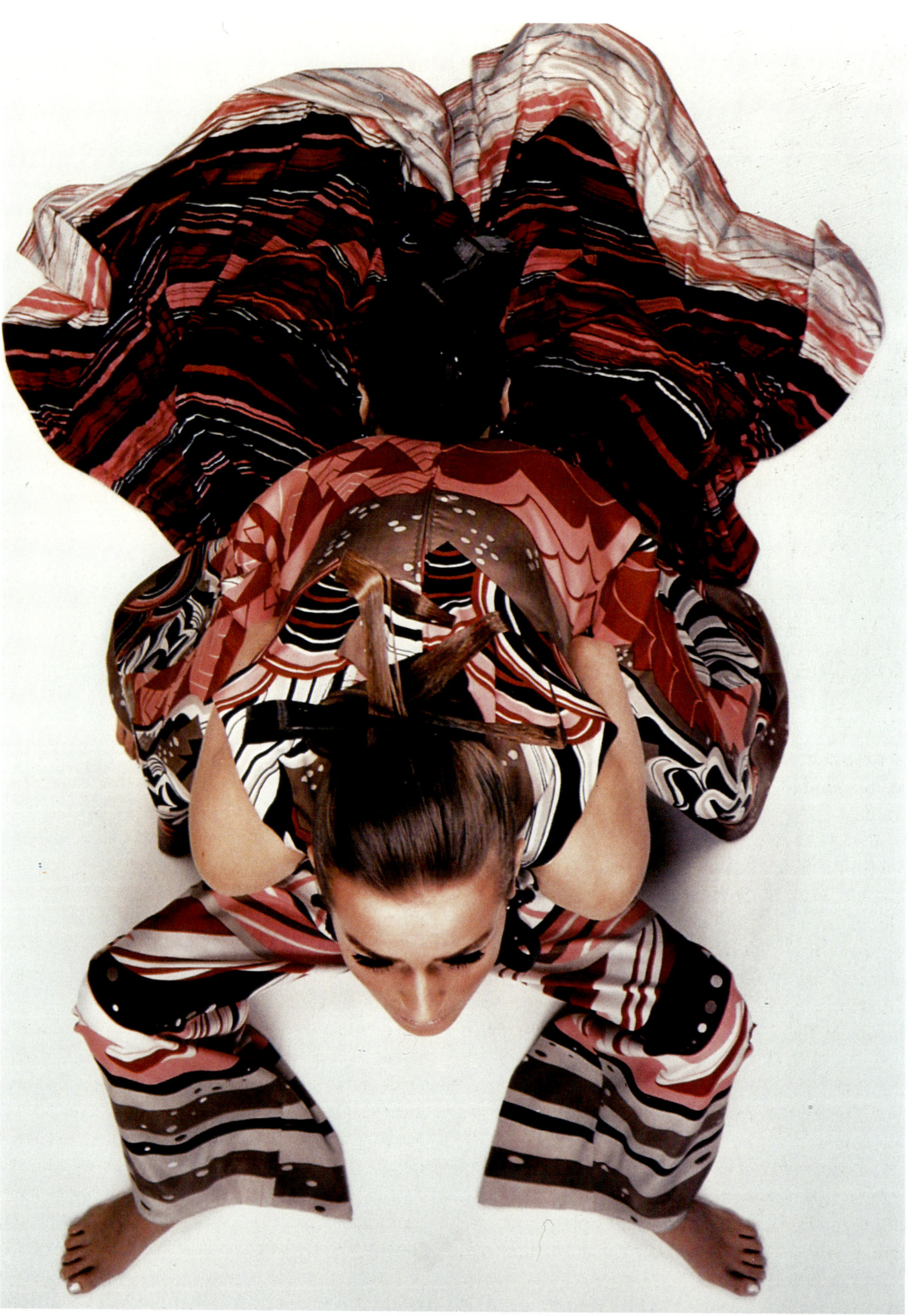

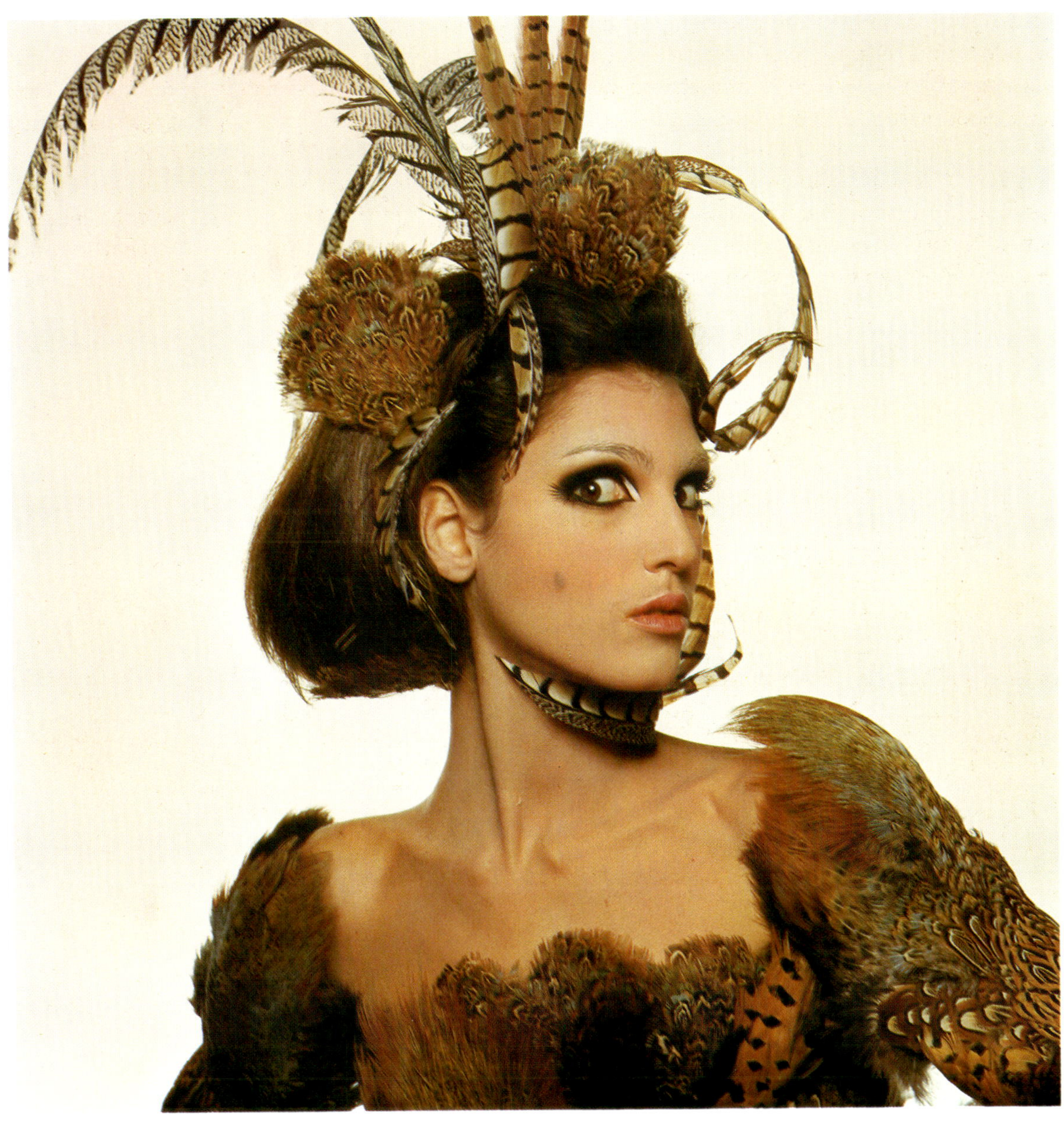

Bert Stern,
for New York Vogue,
January 1965.

seeing and a representation of the world which corresponded with a new vision of democratic values.

Toni Frissel created a style which was influenced by that of Munkacsi, characterized by the use of close-ups, centered on and looking slightly down on the model. The freshness of his fast shutter images comes from their spontaneity and informality. In Europe, this artistic current found its exponents in Jean Moral and Remie Lohse, while in the United States Hermann Landshoff forms the link between photographs taken in natural surroundings and the work of Richard Avedon, of whom he was, in many respects, the precursor.

During the Second World War, fashion photography had to adapt to new historical realities. Photographers were compelled to play down the glitzy world that they had helped to promote. They turned their attention instead to the dramatic scenes of war. The fashion photographs which Lee Miller took during this period, published in *Vogue,* have something of the character of a social and historical document. They show women facing up to wartime conditions, even down to the clothes they wore. This renunciation of the triumphant imaginary world of yesterday's avant-garde made way for harsh reality. Photography recorded the necessary adaptation of clothing which had become austere, functional, indeed, purely utilitarian.

Yet the United States maintained a tradition of fashion photography which sought to affirm a sense of luxury. No aesthetic upheaval took place, and developments in photography were limited to technical improvements in color film – a trend neatly illustrated by Louise Dahl-Wolfe,[17] who concerned herself with the accurate depiction and graduated lighting of intimate scenes. John Rawlings's use of color is also illustrative of this withdrawal from a purely imaginative style in favor of a more formal interpretation of clothing,

17. *Louise Dalh-Wolfe: Photographer's Scrapbook,* New York, New York University, 1983.

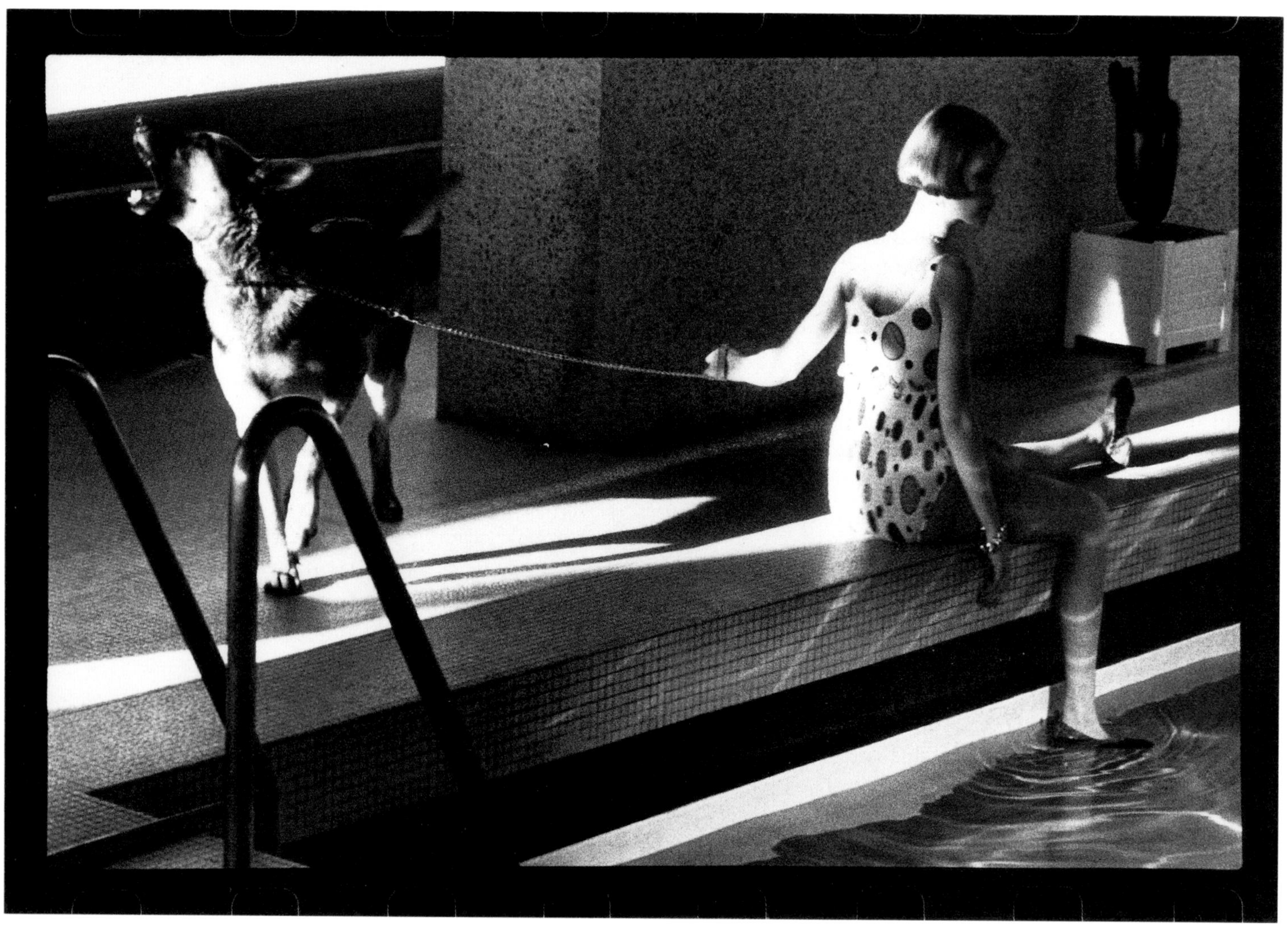

SARAH MOON, *Vogue*, London, 1976.

working within the discipline of a tightly articulated composition.

The rare image

A consequence of the exile of photographers of German origin, such as Blumenfeld, Horst, and Landshoff, was that during the post-war period, the United States was the main center for developments in fashion photography. After 1945, shawls, sheath dresses, and corsets conjured up a stable and reassuringly stereotypical image of womanhood, until the women's liberation movement of the 1960s changed everything. The line that Christian Dior launched in 1947 brought back a concept of female clothing which accentuated the curves of the body.

Irving Penn was the last exponent of the aristocratic concept of fashion photography. He was sent to Paris by *Vogue* in 1950 to photograph the latest collection.[18] The images seemed simple enough, but the representation of fashion was subordinate to the expression of the photographer's personal viewpoint. Irving Penn, like Richard Avedon, operated simultaneously in another branch of commercial photography – advertising – and in his published albums he mixed commissioned images with others produced as part of more personal projects.[19] The result was that his approach to fashion photography was shot through by that ambiguity which turns a commercial snapshot into a creative moment.

The apparent simplicity of Irving Penn's compositions conceals a formal complexity. It is the result of the particular elegance of the model's outline, of the abstract interplay of lines and shapes, of empty and filled space. Irving Penn's deliberate aim was to reinstate fashion photography into the history of painting. "It has been helpful, in orientation," he wrote, "to think of myself, a contemporary fashion photographer, as stemming directly from painters of fashion back through the centuries."[20] If Irving Penn's idea of the existence of a pictorial category involving "fashion painters" was somewhat inexact, it did at least allow him to treat his own commercial activity with the free and disinterested attitude of the painter.

This evolution of fashion photography into a means of artistic self-expression would become particularly obvious in the 1970s. Greatly assisted

18. B. Holme, K. Tweed, J. Davis, and A. Libermann, *The World in "Vogue"*, New York, Viking Press, 1963.

19. J. Szarkowski, *Irving Penn*, New York, Museum of Modern Art, 1984.

20. Portfolio I, Winter 1950, in N. Hall-Duncan, *op. cit.* in note 2, p. 147.

by the unusual physique of his favorite model (Lisa Fonssagrives, who was also his wife), Irving Penn seemed to consider each photograph to be like a portrait which interpreted freely the conventions of pictorial photography – to such an extent that he made little distinction between work in the studio and the more experimental craft of darkroom and printing techniques. Stage props are usually absent from his photographs. They are posed against a plain paper backdrop and translate his perception of a unique moment. In his work, a simple photograph constitutes a personal vision, in which the outline, the gradation of tones, and contrasts, become the trademark of a way of looking which gives form to the world.

The romance of life

In the 1950s, the distinction between *haute couture* and social fashion wear was finally brought to an end by the growth of off-the-peg garments. Henceforth, developments in the clothing industry were the product of values that were at once democratic and individualistic. The growing importance of women's magazines ensured that photography had a promotional and psychological role to play. They also had considerable budgets, which had a great impact on the way photography was carried out.

Richard Avedon's work is symptomatic of this trend, in which social events played a large part.[21] His famous photograph of Dovima wearing an evening dress by Dior, posed amongst the elephants of the Cirque d'Hiver exploited the contrast between the delicacy of the model and the bulk of the animals. The photograph recalls the way Steichen or Landshoff's work alluded to the animal kingdom. In 1956, his ten-part series parodying Elizabeth Taylor and Richard Burton, which caused such a public stir, took the form of a photo-essay featuring Suzi Parker and the actor/director Mike Nichols. This attack on convention brought together the world of the photo-romance, personal history, and pseudo-reportage, and it gave the impression that a closed world had been blown apart. Fashion photography was no longer a separate world – henceforth, it would be on the lookout for other frameworks allowing the clothes to be staged in the context of a narrative. William Klein demonstrated this evolution in a similar way in Paris in the Sixties.[22]

The role of the model was a strange one, midway between a tradition deriving from life

DEBORAH TURBEVILLE, ***Old Bath House, New York City,*** New York Vogue, 1975.

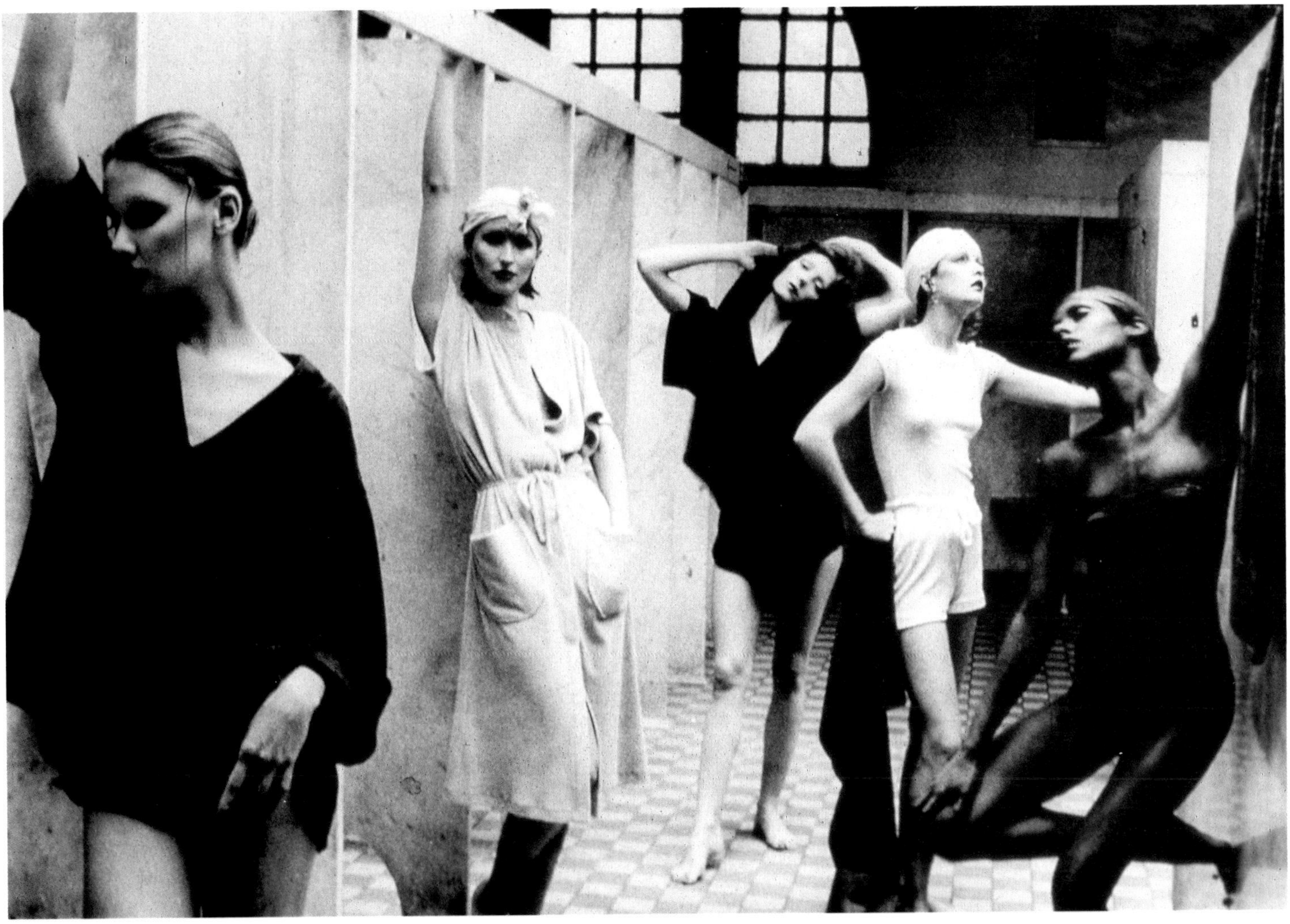

21. *Richard Avedon – Photographs, 1947–1977*, New York, 1978; London (Thames and Hudson) 1978.

22. *William Klein, Photographe etc.*, Paris, Centre Georges-Pompidou, Herscher, 1983.

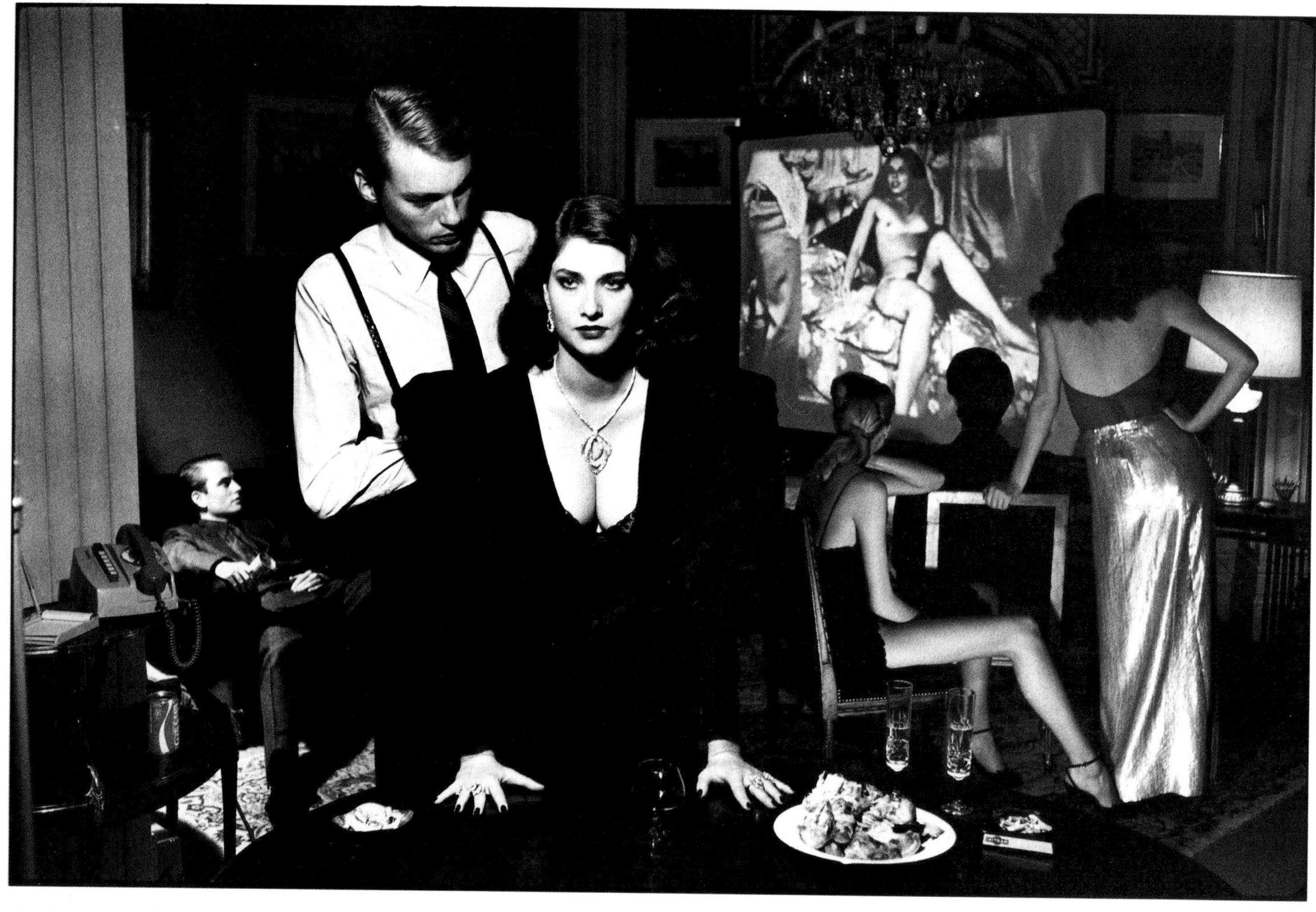

HELMUT NEWTON, *Ungaro and Chanel*, Vogue, 1980.

studies by painters and sculptors on the one hand, and the theater and cinema on the other. Furthermore, having brought their physical and psychological qualities into the fashion world, models suddenly broke with the accepted canons of beauty. The model Donyale Luna was the first black mannequin to pose for fashion photographs. She wore a futuristic dress by Courrèges, and her elongated silhouette and the movement of her hips expressed the new self-awareness and independence of racial minorities. Fashion photography had rarely been so close to sculpture.

The avant-garde artistic movements were less frequently brought into play, even though pop art and op art exercised a great influence. The Japanese photographer, Hiro, who had settled in New York and who reinstated photography using stage props, sought the elements of his style in these two artistic movements. Fashion continued the process of democratization and encouraged a diversity of contemporary styles, by revealing new physical types, such as Penelope Tree with her plucked eyelashes or the cat-like body of Veruschka. Images of cover-girls joined those of rock stars and pop singers to form a gigantic collective portrait with which everyone could identify.

This realignment of the fashion scene with that of mass media also favored the disintegration of previously accepted social and psychological conventions. It expressed a "lifestyle" which broke the established rules. It was one of the formative influences on the sexual liberation of the 1960s. The photographs of David Bailey, a member of the Terrible Three, are a model of the genre. The main subject of fashion photography was now – in appearance at least – the relationship between the photographer and his model. This tendency was equally apparent in Jeanloup Sieff's work. No distance separates photographer and model. Their directly physical relationship comprises a complete transformation of social and sexual roles.

The object of desire

Just as fashion distinguished itself from *haute couture* in order to display the democratic values of off-the-peg clothes, fashion photography in the 1970s broke with the conventions which had maintained it as a specific part of the advertising business. The fashion photographers who left a particular mark on this decade, Guy Bourdin, Helmut Newton, William Klein, Deborah Turbeville, and Sarah Moon, in effect form two groups (masculine and feminine) for whom fashion photography was a recycling process which drew inspiration from so-called "minor" (and thus considered unsound) art forms. Richardson's photographs which appeared in *Harper's Bazaar* had already prepared the way for this evolution by their sensitivity and fragility. Just like the photographs of Diane Arbus, they mark an attempt at revealing the existence of a subjectivity based on an introspective view of personal identity, emotion, the intimate psychology of the subject.

This evolution favored both self-development and the integration of the individual into society. It reflected the expansion of the consumer society in the 1970s, and the way in which self-realization was increasingly felt to be the product of the viewpoint of the Other. Fashion photography in the 1970s was dependent on a process of reversal. The garment or the accessories, such as Charles Jourdan's shoes, lose all functional value. They exercise a specific fascination and express new relationships. For Guy Bourdin, as for Helmut Newton, the desires which go with clothing revolve around sexual fantasies. Fetishism and perversion haunt the images as the field of tension is liberated by the black magic of symbols. Their photographs seem to address the unconscious mind, but the latter turns out to be entirely motivated by elements of the mass media – news items for Guy Bourdin, and pornography for Helmut Newton.

Guy Bourdin often introduces a vein of mystery and, occasionally, even of murderous violence into his work. His aesthetic creed seems to aspire to a kind of cool perfection, in which make-up is one of the essential components. While Bourdin's photographs exploit the visual shock of symbols, those of Helmut Newton,[23] and Chris von Wangenheim, are rather more marked by their sado-masochistic character, one which evokes regimes of terror. But the inspiration of each of these photographers seems to be less an expression of his own inner world than the analysis of the behavior of the jet-set society in which he lived.

In parallel with these excesses, Deborah Turbeville and Sarah Moon brought their specific vision to fashion photography. A feeling of strangeness emanates from their images. Although, in a way, this strangeness renews contact with the legacy of Surrealism, it mainly appears as the expression of an inner vision of one seeking to escape from a female stereotype. Both of these photographers are creators of a world where the image of a woman is no longer imposed on the viewer: the body-language, their quasi-ritual treatment of the female body, and the appearance of the face all answer to considerations of allurement which carry the mark of their difference. Clothing gives free reign to an expressivity revealing their mental state: torpor and depression in the case of Deborah Turbeville,[24] who also likes to work on the framing of the image and on the negative, sensitive perceptions and sharpened emotions of extreme refinement for Sarah Moon,[25] whose work links up with the imprecise images of Pictorialism.

It is certain that both are interpreting a time of crisis in the representation of the sexes, whose roles are "deconstructing", but they also demonstrate in a deliberate way that the photography of clothing has become a personal art form.

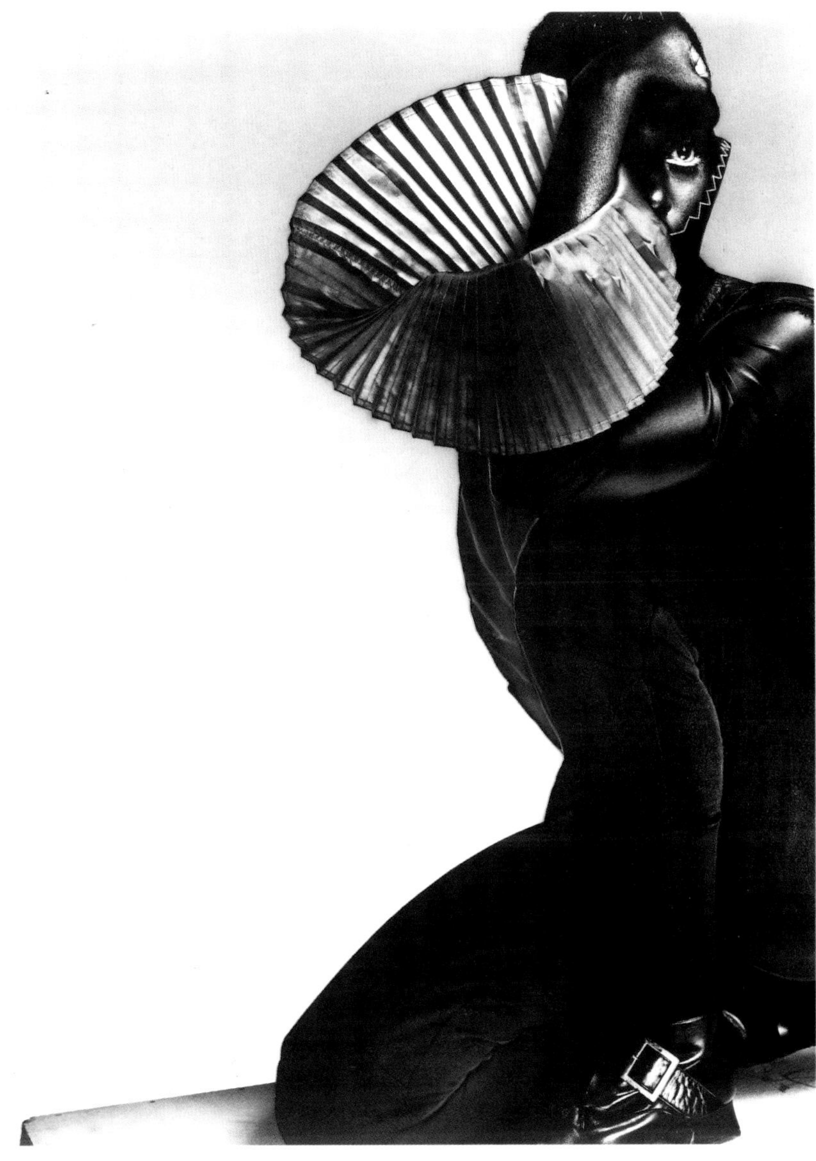

Nick Knight,
model by Martine Sitbon,
1990.

23. *Helmut Newton*, Paris, Éditions du Regard, New York, Congreve; London, Quartet Books; Munich, Schirmer/Mosel, 1981.

24. Deborah Turbeville, *Les amoureux du temps passé*, Tokyo, 1985.

25. S. Moon, *Souvenirs improbables*, Paris, Delpire, 1981.

VU

SALON DE L'AUTOMOBILE ET RADIO

PRIX SIX FRANCS
NUMÉRO SPÉCIAL
HORS SÉRIE
1er OCTOBRE 1933
Directeur : LUCIEN VOGEL

PHOTO MAN RAY
PROCÉDÉ GORSKY FRÈRES
ROBE DE CHANEL

La plus moderne des voitures
LA 10 CV SUPERTRACTION
L. ROSENGART

THE SPREAD OF PHOTOGRAPHY

32

Commissions, advertising, publishing

Thomas Michael Gunther

After the First World War, with the emergence of modern marketing techniques, a huge demand for advertising photographs became apparent. Furthermore, the ease of reproducing photographs in print – soon to be extended to color photographs – created a demand for magazines dealing with current affairs or specialized subjects; these flourished in the 1930s. This expansion of commercial photography would soon be managed by agencies, intermediaries in the distribution process between the photographer and the consumer. Next, photography found a more suitable forum for its aesthetic ambitions with the growth in the number of photographic books on a huge variety of subjects – from animals to sport, from tourism to current affairs – before the complete works of particular photographers themselves became the subject, avowed or implicit, of the photographic press.

Commissioned photography constitutes a huge area of activity, with a multiplicity of links between the image and its commercial use. Such photography implies the production of images intended to sell a product, document an event or illustrate a book. Stock photographs may also be used to satisfy the demands of manufacturers, television producers, artistic directors, copywriters, and editors. Although commissioned photography is often poorly regarded, relegated to the status of a mere wage-earning activity, it is of primary importance for the history of photography as applied photography has always encouraged practitioners to develop new techniques and widen the scope of their art.

Ever since its invention, photography has been used for a wide range of applications: personal self-expression, art, literature, science, ethnology, religion, law, sociology, military matters, industry, commerce, and leisure. While conforming with the requirements of those who commission it and the aesthetic conventions of the day, it fulfils an essential social and commercial role. At the same time, however, as a form of personal exploration and pure creation, it has claimed its place among the plastic arts and played its part in their evolution. A paradigm of the reproductive arts, it is now ubiquitous.

The development of photography, closely linked with its various applications, must also be considered in its political and socio-economic context. The First World War shook Western society to its foundations and introduced a new way of life. Progress in science, technical innovations, and discoveries in the world of psychology all played their part. The creators of political regimes dipped into these for their propaganda. People argued about the ideal political system and about racial and sexual equality. Taylorism was supposed to provide a response to the growing needs of consumer societies, while people were demanding the right to work and to go on strike. Improvements in transport and communication opened up the world to the more frequent exchange of ideas and information, encouraging the increasingly international character of pre-war artistic currents.

In this turbulent context, in which tradition and modernity came face to face, photography proved to be the indispensable vehicle for the spread of ideas and lifestyles. From the 1920s onwards, an explosion in the production of photographic images was apparent. True, the subjects seen through the viewfinder remained the same – children, celebrities, nudes, genre scenes, animals, everyday objects, architecture, technology, landscapes, marine scenes, clouds – but the range of possible treatments of these subjects had broadened. Improvements in the quality of film and photographic paper, together

◄ *Cover of VU,* special number, October 1933, (Chanel dress) photograph by MAN RAY.

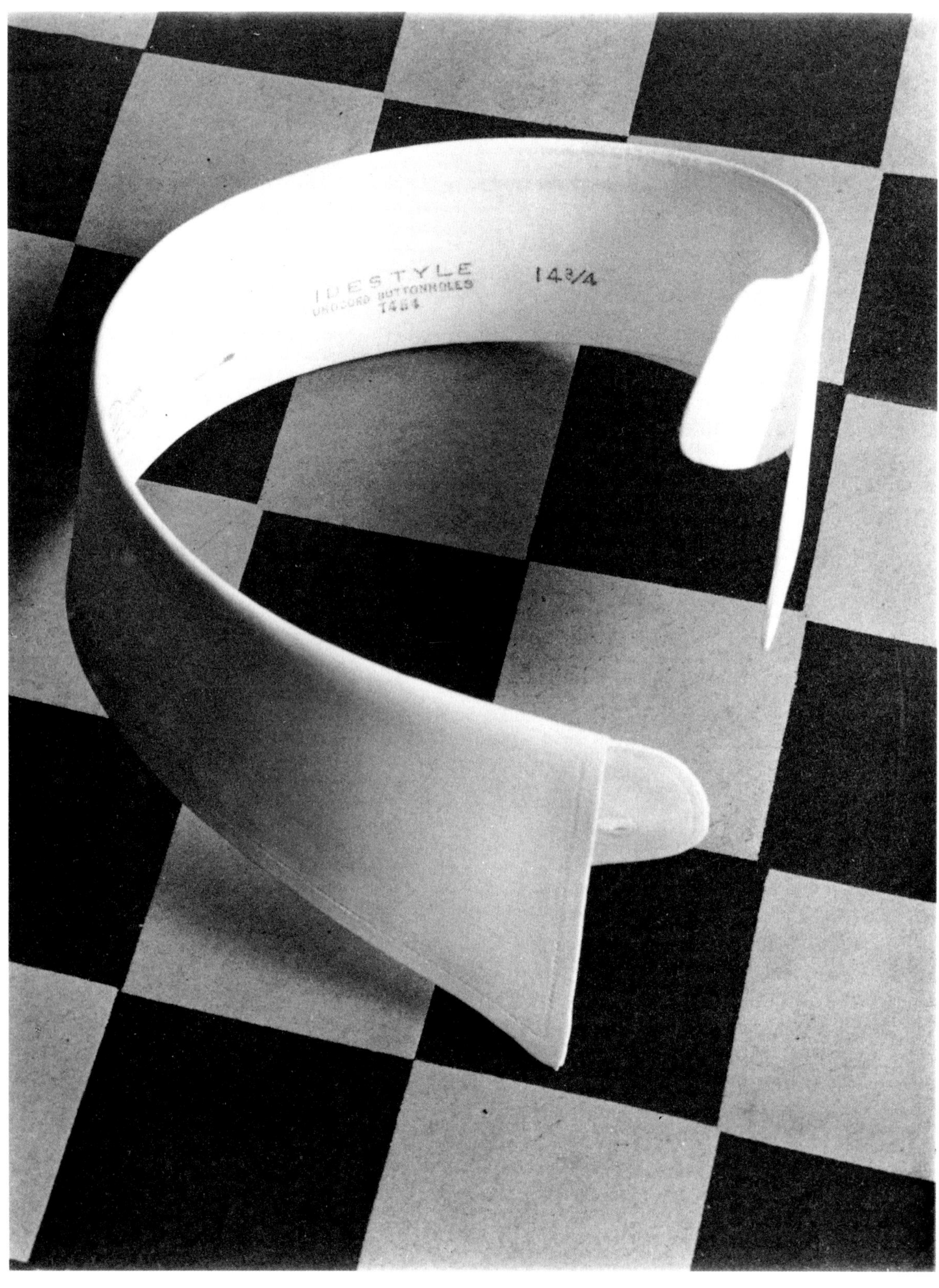

PAUL OUTERBRIDGE,
Ide Collar,
1922,
Museum of Fine Arts,
Houston.

with the introduction of cameras which were more sophisticated and easier to handle, encouraged photographers to try out all the technical possibilities as they were championed by various schools, Constructivism, Bauhaus or Surrealism. Nevertheless, the real driving force behind this development was the spread of images through advertising, the press, and publishing. The extensive use of photographs – whether commissioned or stock shots – in posters, newspapers, journals, magazines, and books, remains one of the main reasons for the success of photography.

From advertisement to publicity

One of most notable social phenomena of the twentieth century is the evolution of the simple advertisement into the publicity industry. While both terms refer to the art of selling, the fundamental difference lies in the choice of the means

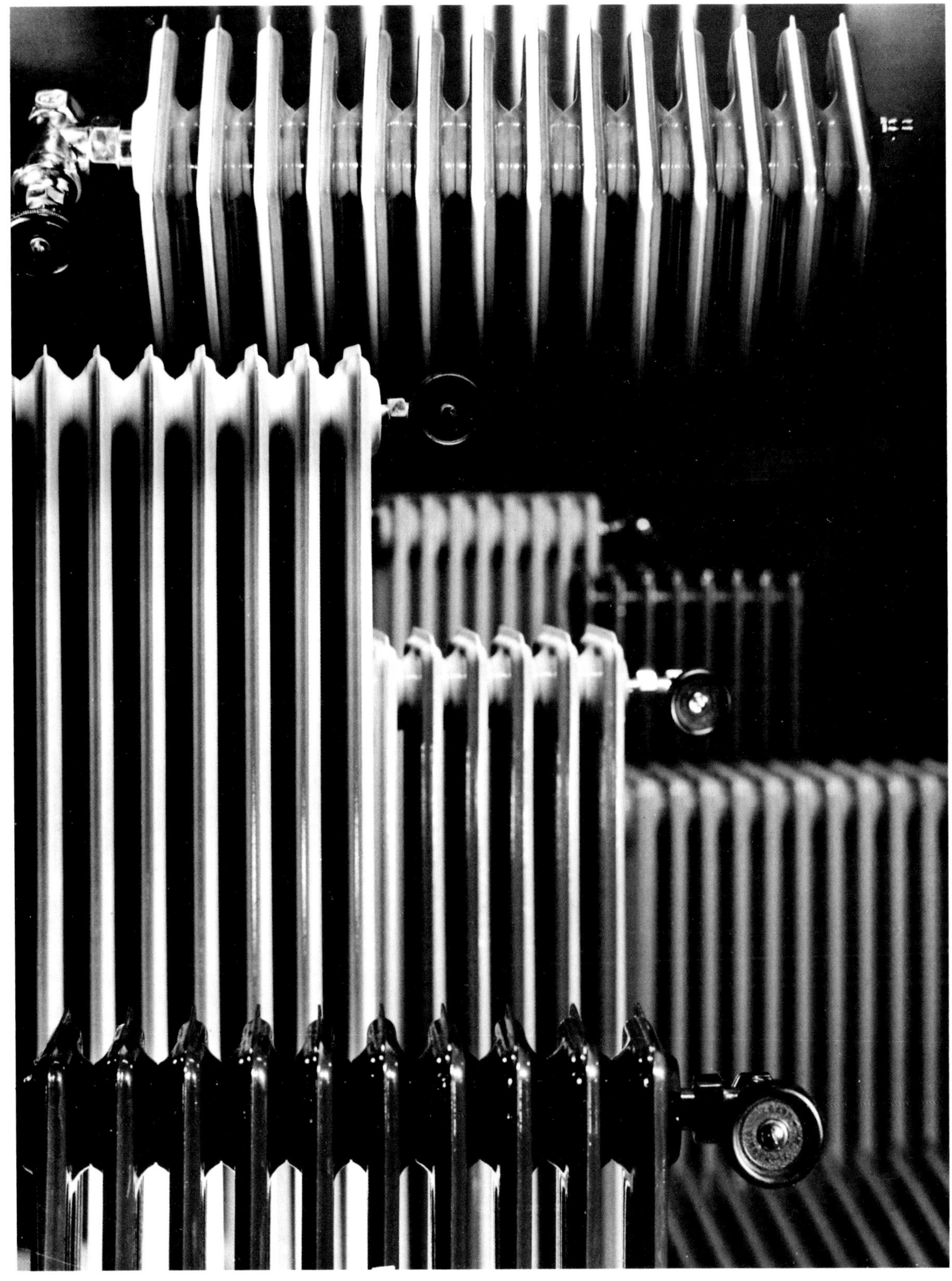

JOSEP MASANA,
Advertising Photomontage,
circa 1927.

of persuasion. An advertisement puts forward its arguments by means of carefully written texts, while publicity recognizes the communicative force of images in general, and photography in particular. Until the First World War, sales techniques relied on glowing descriptive texts and verbal arguments which were distributed by means of posters, leaflets, and newspapers, accompanied by drawings, either in black and white or in color. With the introduction of the latter, especially in lithographs, poster design became an independent art form, even though it remained closely linked to painting.

The introduction of photography into the arsenal of sales techniques coincided with the arrival of the "machine age",[1] which revolutionized production and sales methods throughout the world. This new era was originally considered as a specifically American development. However, American mass-production and industrial

1. See R. G. Wilson, D. H. Pilgrims, and D. Tashjian, *The Machine Age in America 1918-1941,* New York, Brooklyn Museum/Harry N. Abrams, 1986.

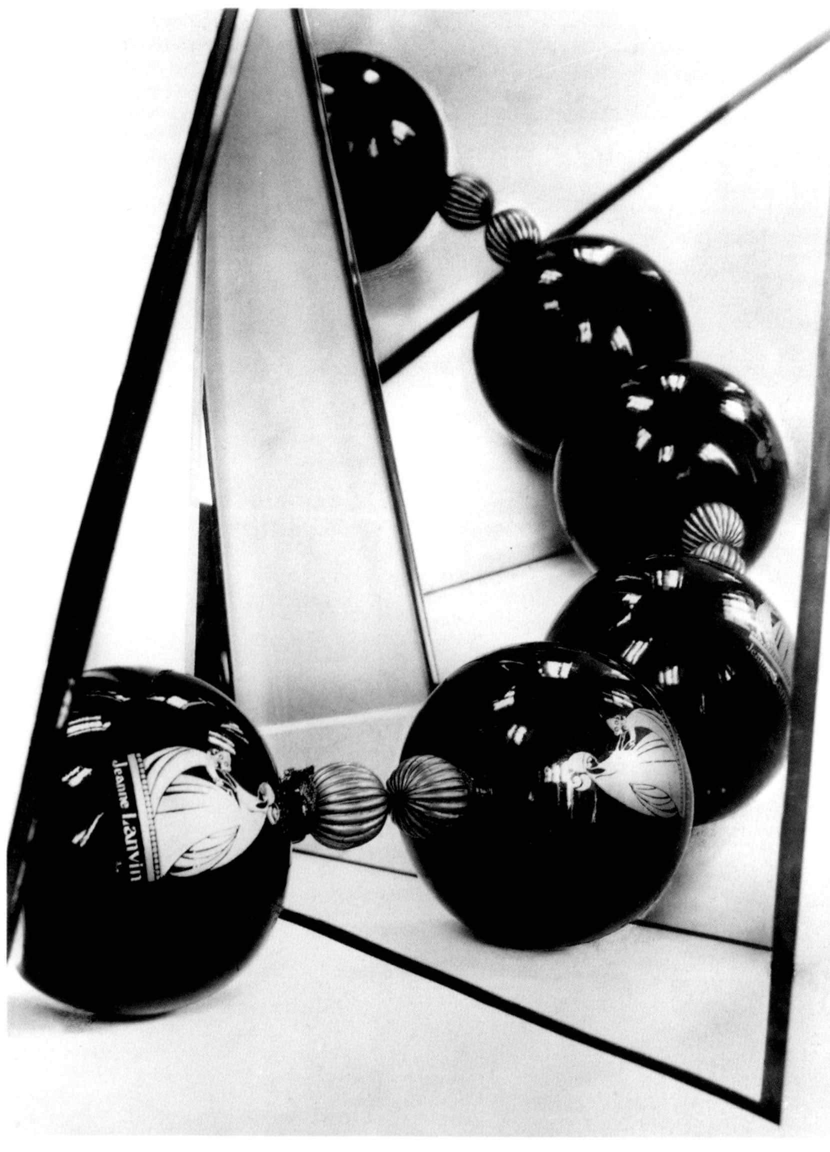

FLORENCE HENRI,
Publicity Photograph for Jeanne Lanvin Perfumes, 1929.
Martini and Ronchetti Gallery, Genoa.

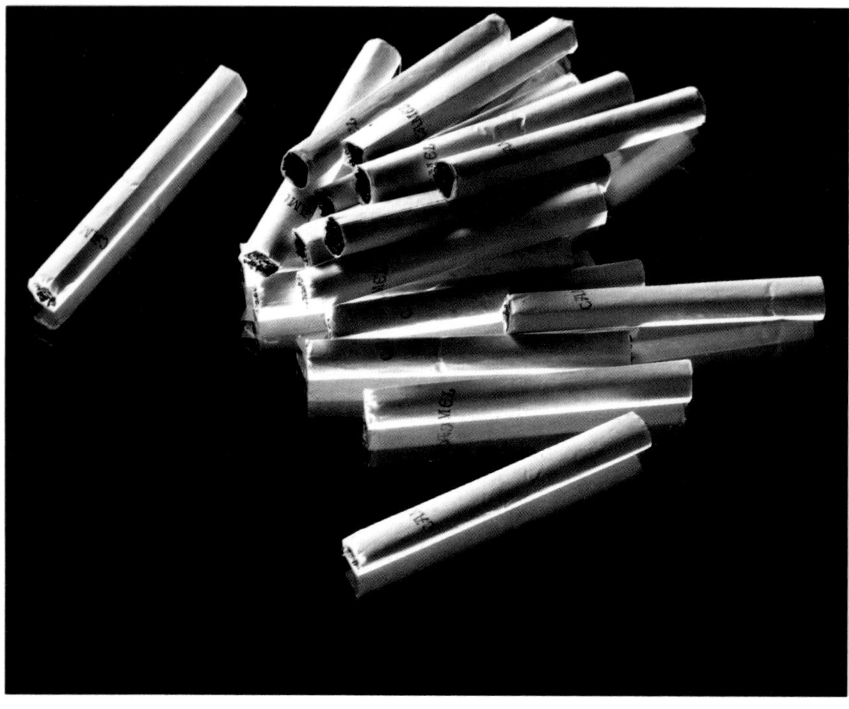

EDWARD STEICHEN,
Camel Cigarettes, circa 1927,
International Museum of Photography,
George Eastman House, Rochester.

standardization soon spread to Europe and Japan. Mass-production would bring about a huge increase in consumption. Psychology began to govern the organization of work. But writers, from Paul Morand to Sinclair Lewis, criticized the adverse effects of growing speed and opportunism, while philosophers such as George Santayana and Ernst Bloch strove to warn humanity against the superficial character of contemporary trends.[2] Members of the artistic avant-garde, however, rallied in support of resolutely modern forms and compositions.

Thus, in the first issue of *L'Esprit nouveau* (October 1920), Ozenfant and Jeanneret (Le Corbusier) issued their manifesto for a "mechanical" aesthetic, addressing "the students of aesthetics who are carrying out laboratory experiments on the psycho-physiological effects of shapes and colors, engineers, and industrialists". Furthermore, in 1925 Fernand Léger insisted on the fact that "all these new values must be employed in the plastic arts", for "there are no longer any values that can be ignored." [3]

Modern advertising, which incorporated all these trends, was born after the First World War. Before 1918, advertising agencies concentrated essentially on selling spaces for posters and intervened very little as regards the advertising concept, illustration or presentation. From the 1920s, they assumed new responsibilities, thus forming a more significant link between companies and the public. The same pattern of development is found in all industrialized countries. Advertising agencies prospered: N. W. Ayer, J. Walter Thompson, Calkins and Holden, Lord and Thomas, Erwin, Wasey and Jefferson, Young and Rubicam, McCann Erikson. They formed part of the American Association of Advertising Agencies, created in 1917. In 1920, an Art Directors' Club was formed, on the initiative of Ernest Elmo Calkins. In Germany, from 1919, the *Bund Deutscher Gebrauchgraphiker* brought together designers and photographers. National and international agencies rubbed shoulders in Berlin in the 1920s and early 1930s, but the reorganization, started at the end of 1933, by the German Council for Economic Publicity (*Werberat*) hampered the development of this sector.

In France, in 1920, Havas, which had merged with the Société Générale des Annonces, created an agency to co-ordinate the influence which the Société exercised on advertising in the major French daily newspapers. Inspired by the principles set out by Octave-Jacques Gérin in his *Précis intégral de la publicité* (Paris, 1918), Étienne Damour and Francis Elvinger each founded an advertising agency. These two men played an important role in the development of the adver-

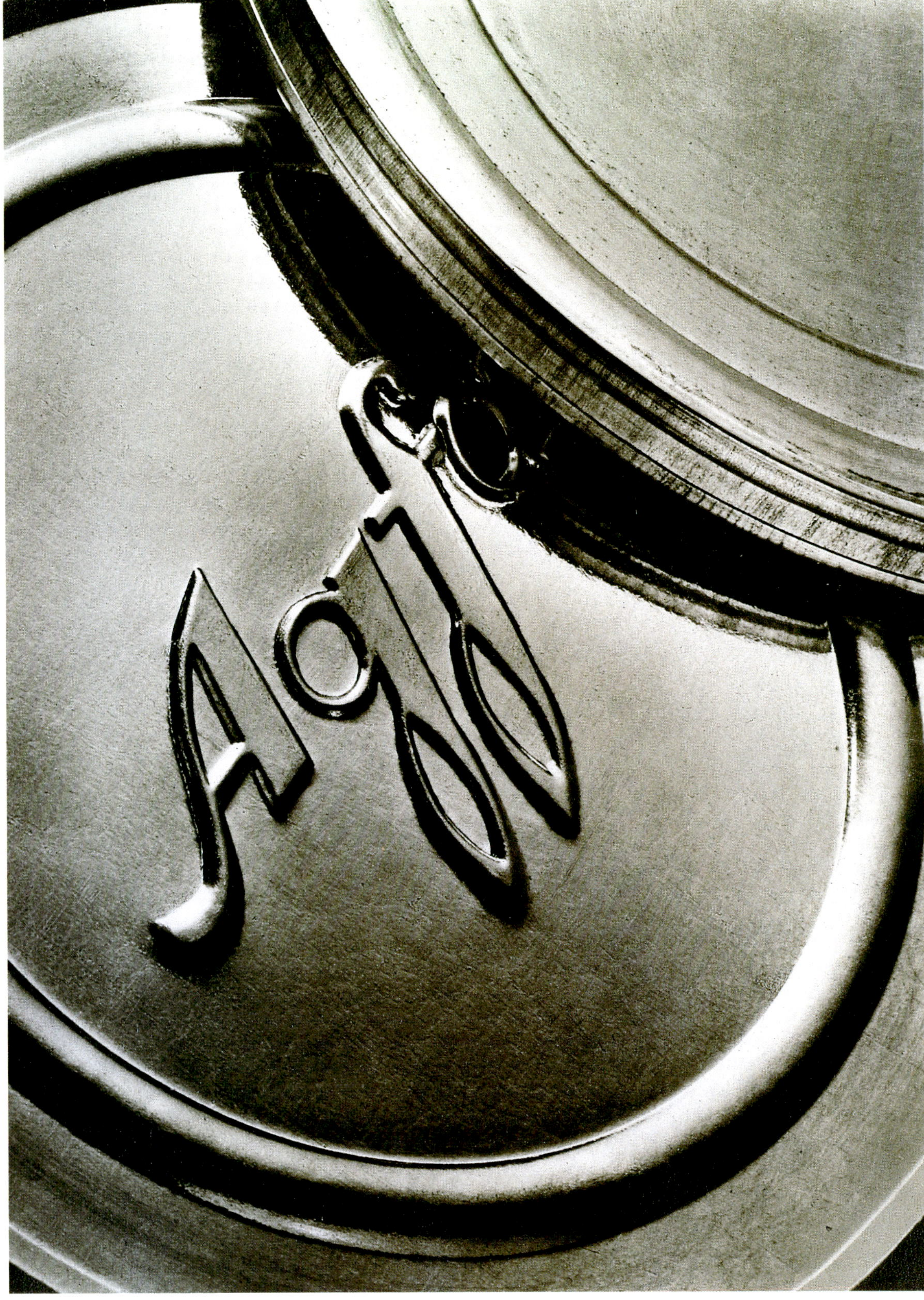

Willy Zielke,
Agfa-variation I,
circa 1930,
Michèle Chomette Gallery,
Paris.

tising industry in Europe: Damour was elected first president of the Continental Advertising Union at its first congress in Berlin in 1929, and Elvinger held the first professorial chair of distribution and publicity at the University of Louvain, from 1931. There was, however, no lack of competition in France. At the end of the 1920s, new agencies were created: Dupuy, in 1927, Printel by Pierre Rophé, André Fortain, and the decorator Chantloup, in 1929, Lecram, thanks to the help of André Vigneau, in the same year, Synergie by Henri Hénault, in 1934. Dorland Paris was directed by Walter Seymour Maas, author of a study on advertising in France.[4] Several American agencies had subsidiaries in Paris, for example J. Walter Thompson and Erwin Wassy.[5]

In around 1930, advertising was considered as an "applied art [...] which should be considered

2. See, for example, P. Morand, *De la vitesse,* Paris, Kra, 1929 and G. Santayana, *Santayana on America,* with introduction by R. C. Lyon, New York, Harcourt, Brace and World, 1968.

3. F. Léger, "L'esthétique de la machine: l'ordre géométrique et le vrai" in *Propos d'artistes,* Paris, 1925, quoted in *Fonctions de la peinture,* Paris, Denoël, 1965, pp. 65–66.

4. W. S. Maas, "Contemporary Advertising in France", in V. Burnham, *Modern Advertising: An Authoritative and Practical Guide to the Use of Every Form of Present-Day Publicity,* London, New Era Publishing Co., 1926, vol. 2, pp. 549 ff.

5. See P. Shuwer, *Histoire de la publicité,* Geneva, Rencontre, 1965.

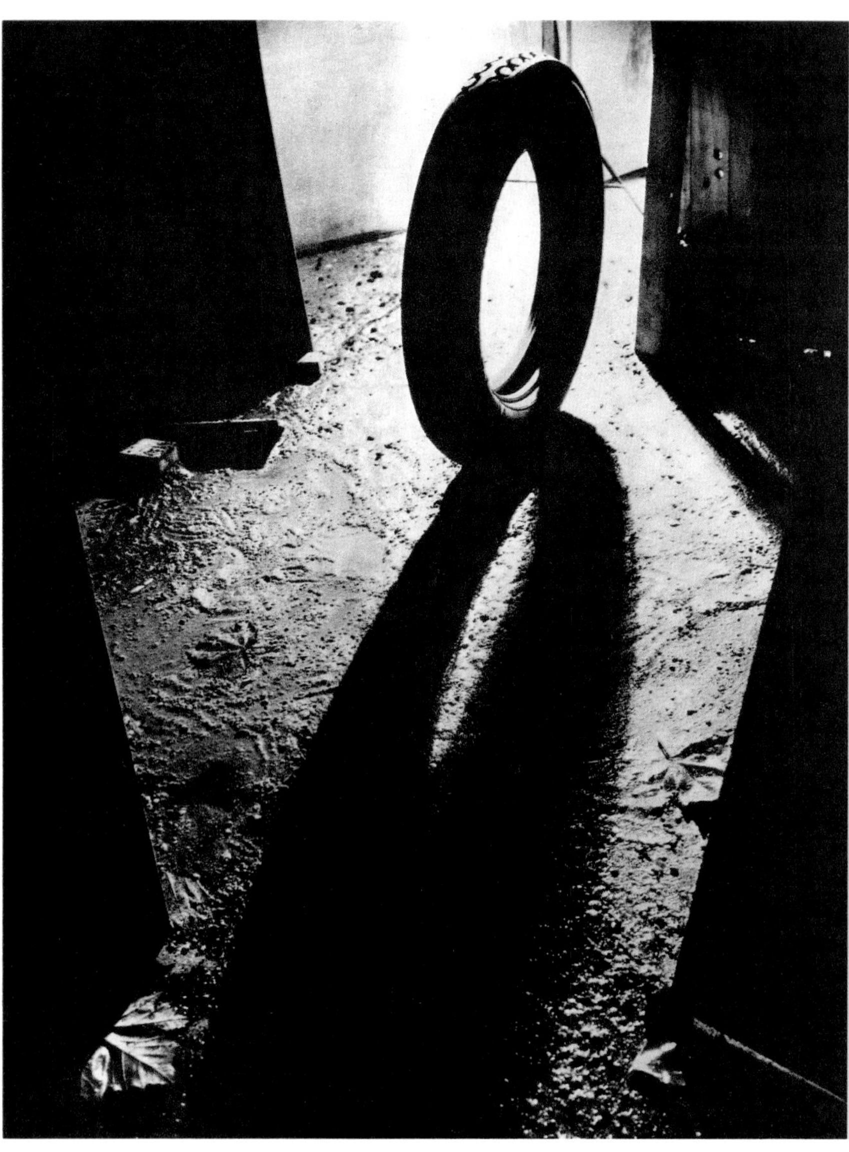

MAURICE TABARD, *Advertisement for Michelin*, 1928–1929.

as one of the plastic arts".[6] Christian Zervos presented it as a "concentrated and intense force through which are manifested the presence and action of a modern mythology and of new visual symbols. It even contains an affective power which touches the emotions and thus attracts the attention which today is solicited by thousands and thousands of events" (*Cahiers d'Art*, 1937). A whole generation of copy-writers and advertising artists labored away at finding slogans and images which would suit the new demands. They used the latest technology – "Magic Electricity", which had arrived to light up the facades and the awnings of shops, illuminated signs, bill-boards mounted on cars, radio advertising.

However, the great innovation, and that which marked the start of the modern publicity industry, was the use of photography to show off the usefulness, the comfort, the luxury or the benefits of a particular product. A growing number of photographers – Edward Steichen (who was working in New York for J. Walter Thompson), Paul Outerbridge Jr. (who opened a Paris studio in 1927), René Zuber, and André Vigneau – began to specialize in publicity photography. Steichen was responsible for advertising photographs of Douglas cigarette lighters (1928) and Camel cigarettes, Outerbridge for the Idestyle detachable collar on a chess-board (*Vanity Fair*, 1922), which Duchamp admired, Grete Stern for the image for the hair oil Pétrole Hahn, Tabard for publicity shots for Christofle, Anton Bruehl for those for Cadillac. Steichen demonstrated his mastery of lighting techniques, and Lejaren à Hiller composed *trompe-l'œil* images influenced by cinema sets. Nickolas Muray, Grancel Fitz, Alfred Cheney Johnston, and John Havinden also made their names through their advertising photography. Much more remains to be learned about this aspect of the art which is so often scorned because it was produced as a response to commissions. A number of unexpected photographers have occasionally worked in advertising. It was in this way that Kertész's famous image of a fork (1928), published by *Uhu* and displayed in *Film und Foto*, was used by Bruckmann to promote their silverware.

Indeed, the photographic image introduced a new element. Even if "illustration is a universal language", it is photography, especially, which "permits the presentation of a faithful reproduction of the article for sale, thus faithfully taking the place of the article itself [...] The photograph itself says more than several pages of description; its incorporation into publicity material increases the value of the text and ensures that the advertisement will remain impressed upon the memory longer" (*Le Professionnel Photographe*, 1929). Thus, the force of photography resides in its capacity to reproduce the product faithfully and to vouch for the truthfulness of the written claims.

Quite soon, however, the experimental work of photographers of the avant-garde movement and their interest in abstract images introduced a note of doubt: photography does not represent *the* reality, but frames *a* reality, unique to the moment of exposure. From then on, publicity photographers concentrated on creating a mood associated with an object rather than recording the object itself, by using the principles promoted by the Bauhaus school and the Surrealists – tilted camera angles or ones looking steeply up or down, lining up rows of objects, photomontage, trick photography, photograms, superimposition, solarization, altering images made in the camera or the darkroom, even using X-ray plates (such as Sougez's publicity for Urodonal, a treatment for arthritis, which showed an X-ray of a hand).[7] The introduction of photography into manufacturers' brochures and the seasonal catalogues of big department stores revolutionized sales tech-

6. V. Huszar, "De reclame als beeldende kunst", *i 10*, no. 1/5, Amsterdam, 1927, p. 161.

7. L. Albin-Guillot, *Photographie publicitaire*, Paris, Gauthiers-Villars, 1933.

niques, whether it was selling automobiles, jewelry, fashion (such as the photographs of Siégel's models taken by George Hoyningen-Huene, in 1927), industry (Margaret Bourke-White's photoreportage on Otis Steel, in 1928) or electricity (Man Ray's "rayographs" for the Paris electricity company, in 1931).

In this way, the photographer's trade was altered dramatically. For a time, however, the photographer remained in control of options such as the type of apparatus used, the studio, the lighting, movements, and locations. In the absence of real specialization, he could carry out commercial commissions with whom or where he liked. Soon, however, a degree of control was imposed, by various people whose influence was to grow continuously throughout the century. Photographic agents, artistic directors, copy-writers, and editors became more and more involved in the production of images – commissioning and organizing photo sessions, making use of increasing amounts of stock images, which had either been commissioned or resulted from a photographer's personal work, and, finally, defining the contents of the photograph and its setting.

Throughout the world, specialized magazines encouraged the use of photography, the gradual abandonment of line-drawings, and the importance of graphic design, typology, and page layout. From 1922, *Commercial Art*, published by *The Studio*, produced a special number devoted to advertising. From 1930, it was called *Modern Publicity*. In *Advertising Arts*, M. F. Agha, Condé Nast's artistic director, concentrated on promoting a specifically American approach. *Printer's Ink*, founded in New York in 1888, discussed major developments arising in the advertising world. In France, Roger-Louis Dupuis founded *Vendre* in 1923, while Charles Peignot launched *Arts et*

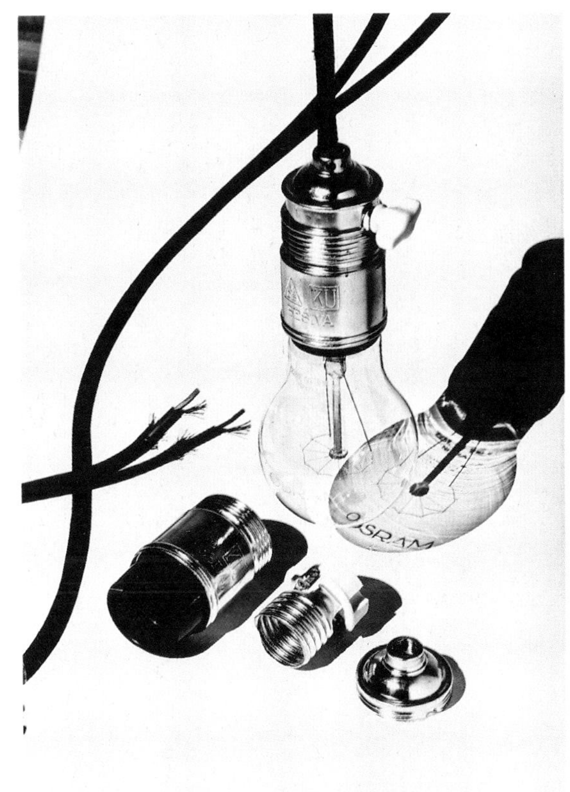

HANS FINSLER,
Electric light bulbs,
1925.
Christian Bouqueret Collection.

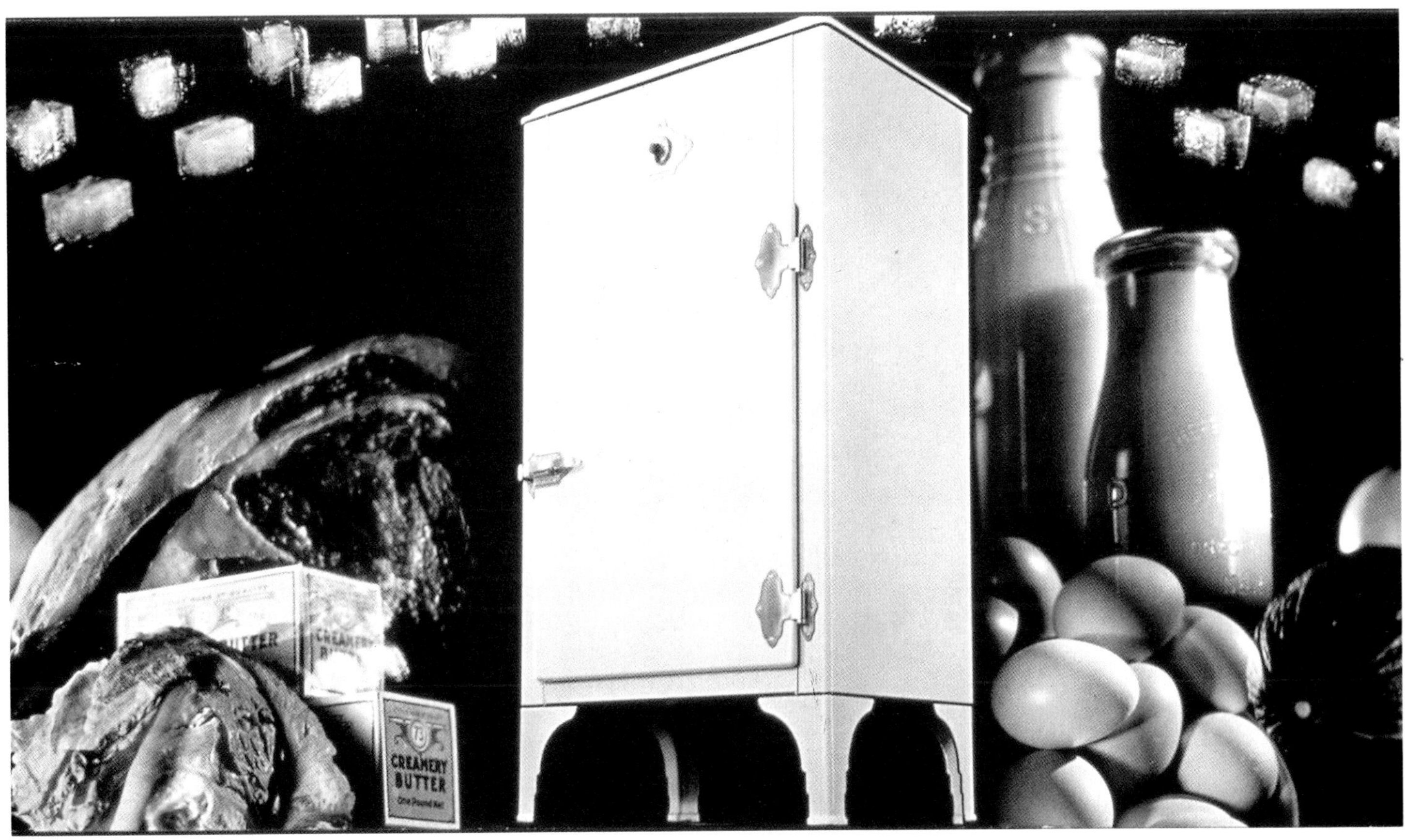

GRANCEL FITZ,
The Ice Box,
circa 1928,
George R. Rinhart Collection.

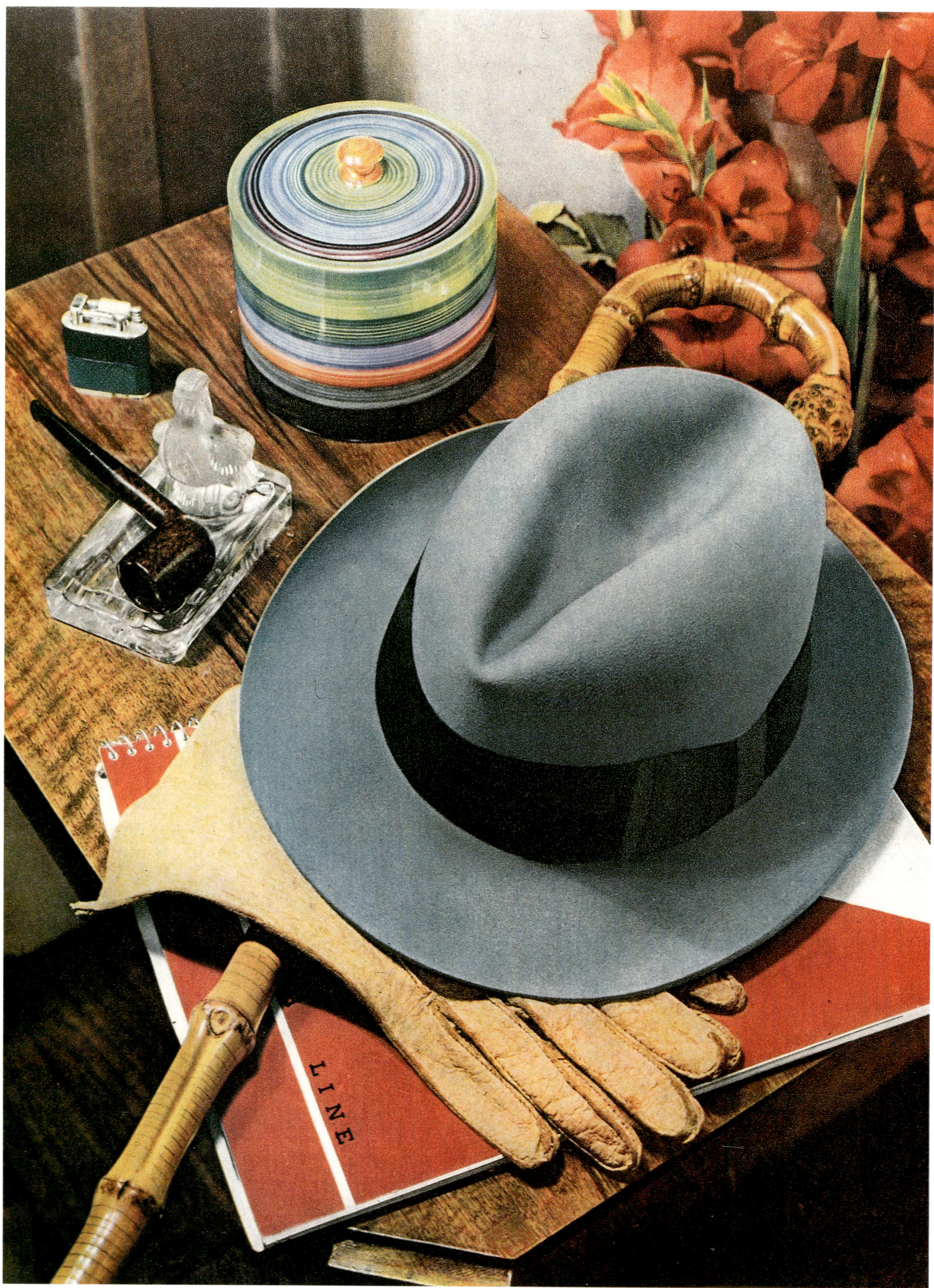
LINE

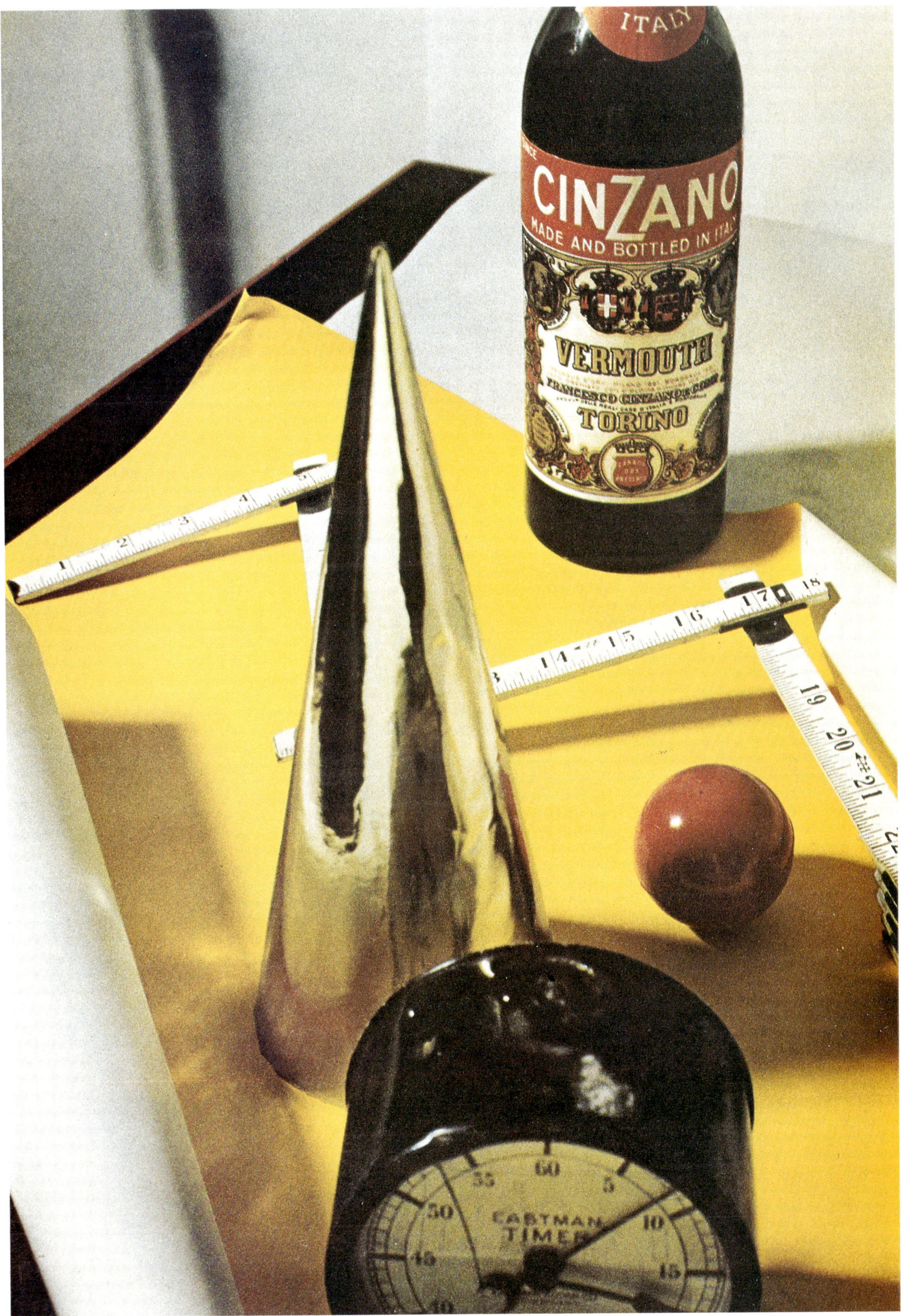
CINZANO
VERMOUTH
TORINO

EDWARD STEICHEN,
Shoes,
1927.

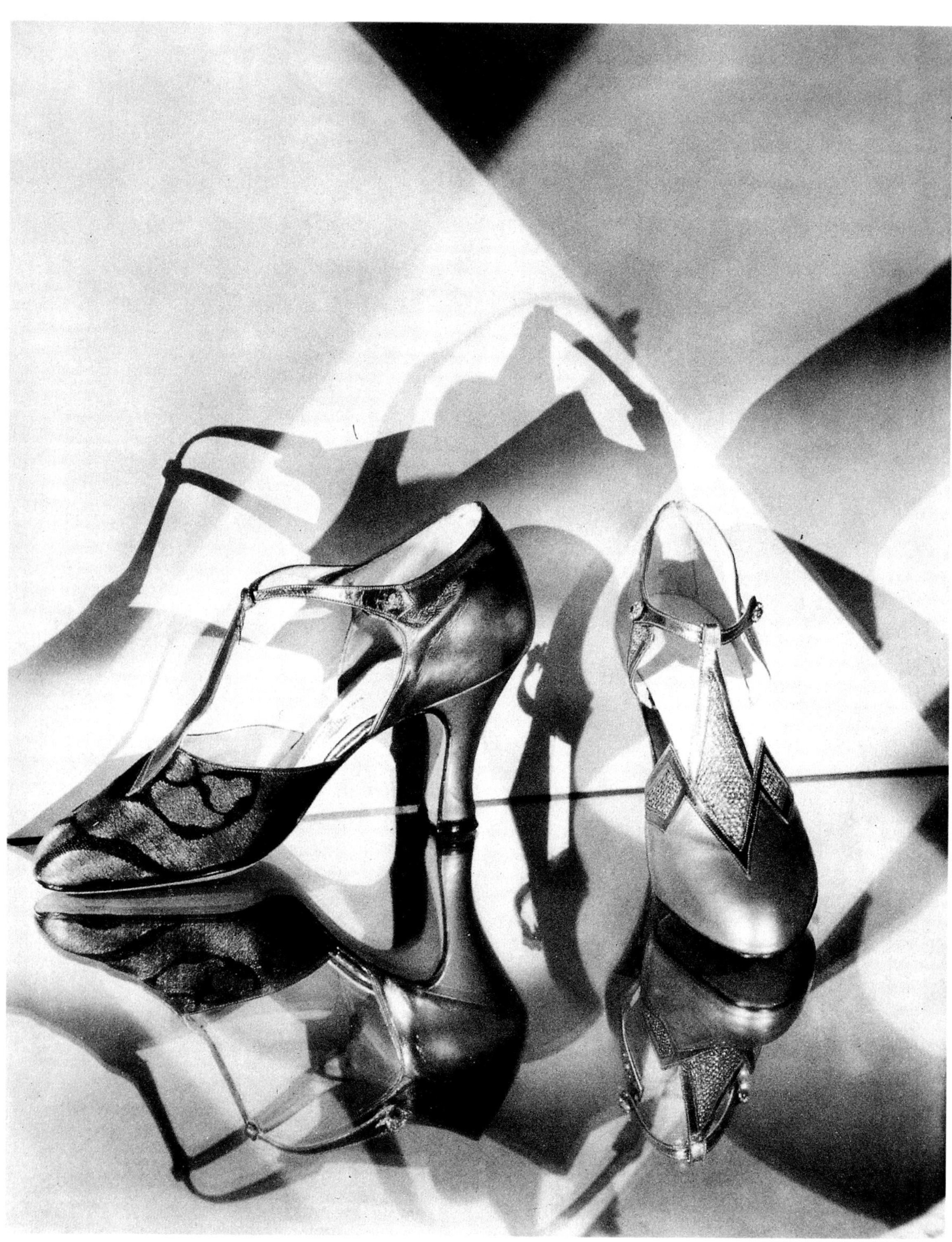

◀◀ Previous pages,
left to right:
FRANÇOIS KOLLAR,
Advertisement for Dunhill,
reproduced by the
Fidhélio-Sadag process,
1934.

PAUL OUTERBRIDGE,
Kandinsky,
1937,
G. Ray Hawkins Gallery.

métiers graphiques in 1927. *Gebrauchsgraphik*, the largest German professional magazine, appeared for the first time in 1924. In Czechoslovakia, the group *Druzstevni Prace* [Collective Labor] published the magazine *Panorama*.

Moreover, photography and the cinema were bound closely by links of partnership and creative inspiration. For example, Jean Mineur, whose company, founded in Paris in 1925, first specialized in illuminated billboards, soon turned his attention to cinema advertising. Encouraged by his experience with Lecram, André Vigneau turned towards advertising films and formed *Caméra*, in 1933. Two years later, Nicolas produced his first promotional film, *L'Âme du vin*.

During the Second World War, advertising photography found its main inspiration in patriotic themes. While manufacturers had to continue selling their goods, they employed sales messages which were those of the public and military powers. Buying in reasonably modest quantities was seen as a way of helping the war effort. At the same time, the war itself had to be "sold". For each nation involved in the conflict, photography was used to reassure civilians, boost the morale of soldiers, preserve national security, denigrate the enemy, and put people on their guard against spies and saboteurs.[8]

In the immediate post-war years, American industry expanded rapidly, while in Europe the industrial and commercial infrastructures were only gradually being rebuilt. On both continents, advertising specialists were ready to intervene, armed with motivation studies based on sociological and psychological research. Cendrars himself regarded advertising as "one of the seven wonders of the modern world and the flower of contemporary life".[9] In 1949, Waldemar George described this stage of development as the "heroic period", predicting a great future for it.

The next step was the universal adoption of color photography; before the war, both in the United States and Europe, color photography was costly and the results were not always convincing.[10] Improvements both in printing techniques and the quality and reliability of color film after the end of the war increased the attraction of images which dramatized domestic scenes – both capturing and playing a part in creating the social trends of the age.

Although, today, color is predominant, there is a renewed interest in black and white photography (for example, the work of Bruce Weber and Herb Ritts), which is often used by advertisers to evoke a sense of the privileged life of the past (for example, Ralph Lauren and Calvin Klein). The taste for "old" photographs exploits well-known portraits, such as those of Einstein or Marilyn Monroe, or easily recognized images (for example, Doisneau or Ansel Adams).

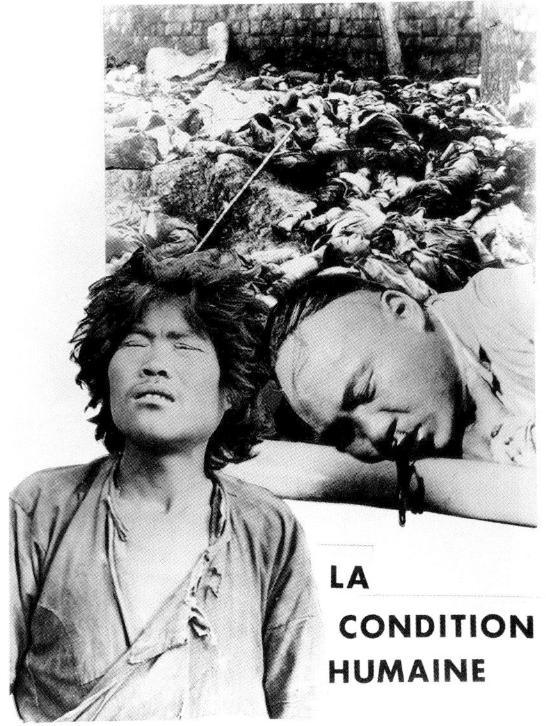

Roger Parry, *Photographic montage for the cover of Malraux's* **La Condition Humaine,** 1933. Christian Bouqueret Collection.

El Lissitzsky, *Part of a mural photographic montage for* **Pressa** *exhibition, Cologne,* 1928, Rheinisches Bildarchiv, Cologne. ▼

Photographic illustrations

During the twentieth century, the press developed in parallel with advertising. At first, these two sectors evolved in the same political, economic, and social context. Later, they became increasingly liberated from their dependence on the written word, so that their communicative power became based on visual representation. This change was essentially due to photography,

8. See Z. Zeman, *Vendre la guerre: art et propagande durant la Seconde Guerre mondiale*, Paris, Albin Michel, 1980.

9. B. Cendrars, "Poésie – Publicité", in E. Schuller, *Art présent*, no. 4/5, 1945.

10. See R. A. Sobieszek, *The Art of Persuasion: A History of Advertising Photography*, New York, H. N. Abrams, 1988, pp. 67–71.

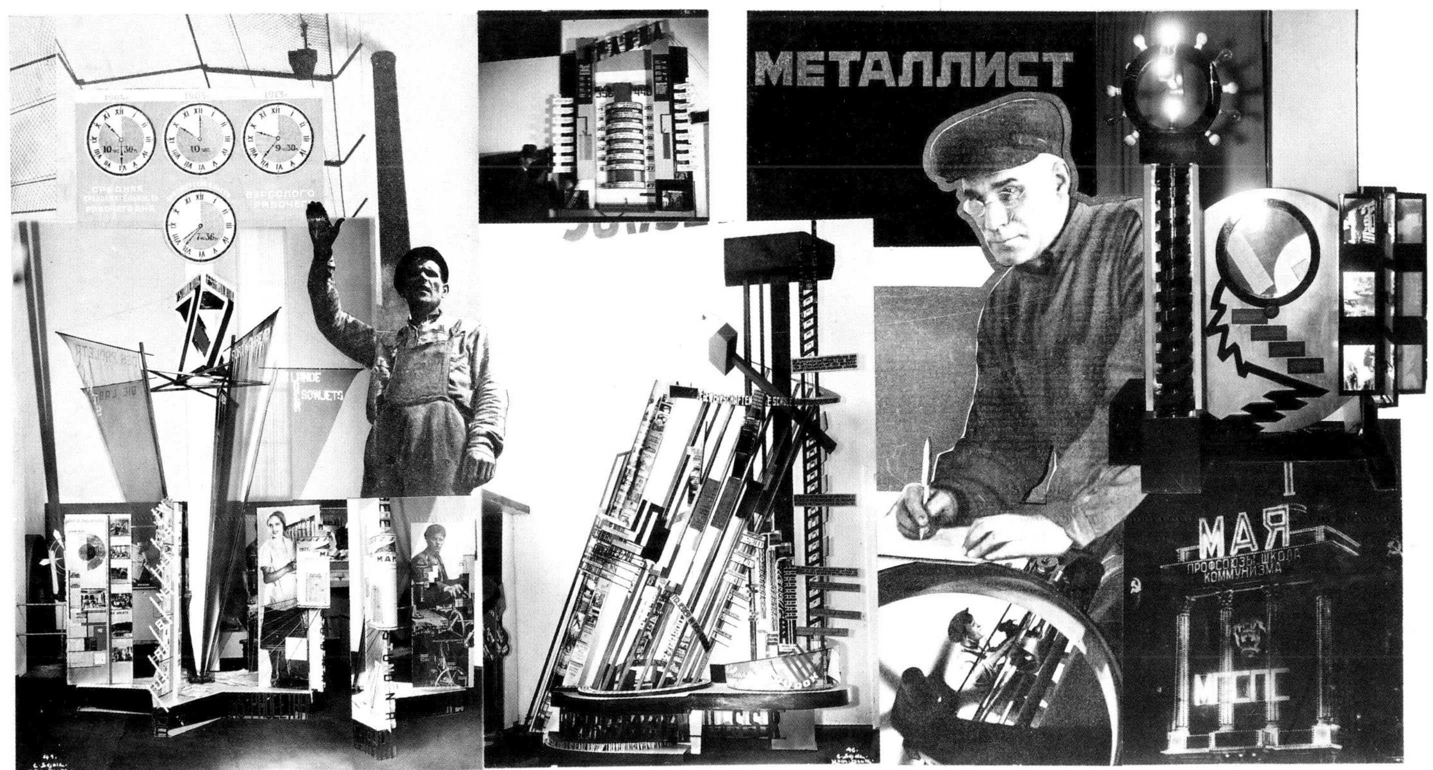

From photographer to publication

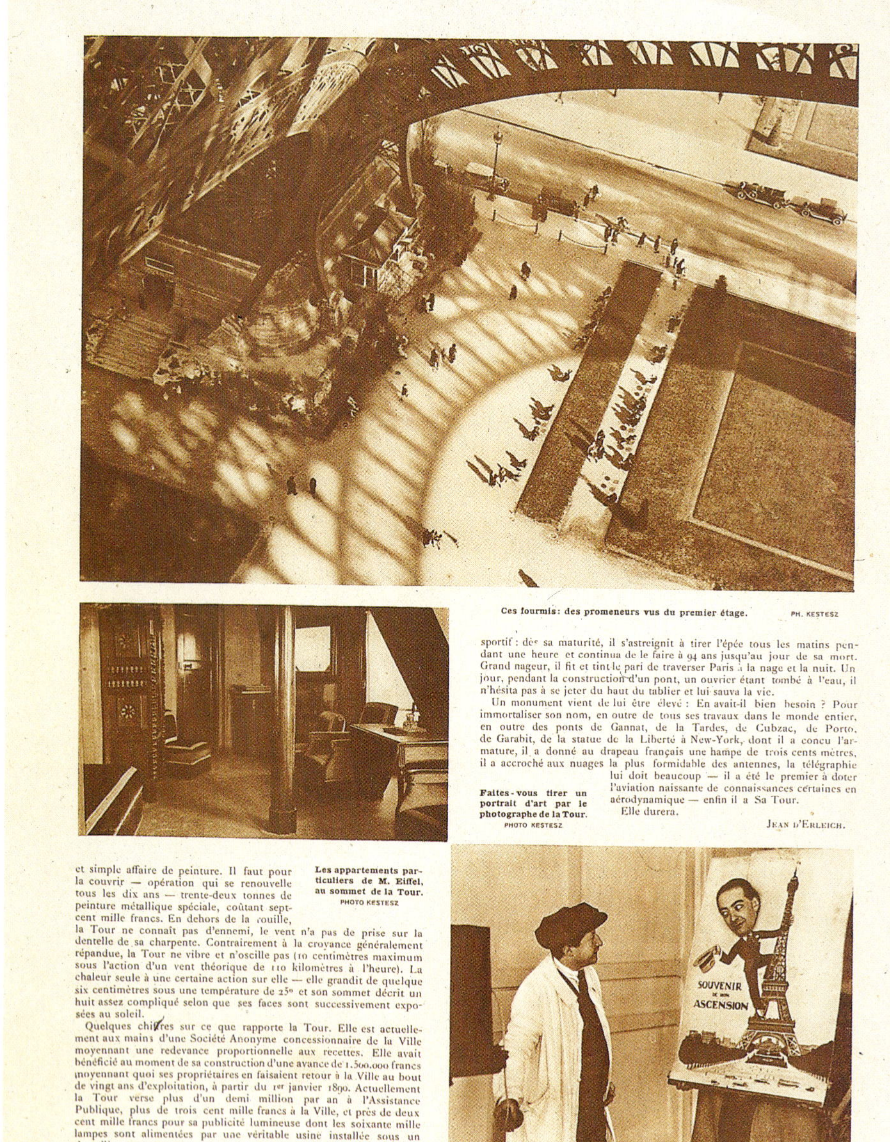

Ces fourmis: des promeneurs vus du premier étage. PH. KESTESZ

Les appartements particuliers de M. Eiffel, au sommet de la Tour. PHOTO KESTESZ

et simple affaire de peinture. Il faut pour la couvrir — opération qui se renouvelle tous les dix ans — trente-deux tonnes de peinture métallique spéciale, coûtant sept-cent mille francs. En dehors de la rouille, la Tour ne connaît pas d'ennemi, le vent n'a pas de prise sur la dentelle de sa charpente. Contrairement à la croyance généralement répandue, la Tour ne vibre et n'oscille pas (10 centimètres maximum sous l'action d'un vent théorique de 110 kilomètres à l'heure). La chaleur seule à une certaine action sur elle — elle grandit de quelque six centimètres sous une température de 25° et son sommet décrit un huit assez compliqué selon que ses faces sont successivement exposées au soleil.

Quelques chiffres sur ce que rapporte la Tour. Elle est actuellement aux mains d'une Société Anonyme concessionnaire de la Ville moyennant une redevance proportionnelle aux recettes. Elle avait bénéficié au moment de sa construction d'une avance de 1.500.000 francs moyennant quoi ses propriétaires en faisaient retour à la Ville au bout de vingt ans d'exploitation, à partir du 1er janvier 1890. Actuellement la Tour verse plus d'un demi million par an à l'Assistance Publique, plus de trois cent mille francs à la Ville, et près de deux cent mille francs pour sa publicité lumineuse dont les soixante mille lampes sont alimentées par une véritable usine installée sous un des piliers.

Terminons par quelques mots sur la personualité étonnante de M. Eiffel. Cet homme, dans toute la force du terme, fut un grand sportif : dès sa maturité, il s'astreignit à tirer l'épée tous les matins pendant une heure et continua de le faire à 94 ans jusqu'au jour de sa mort. Grand nageur, il fit et tint le pari de traverser Paris à la nage et la nuit. Un jour, pendant la construction d'un pont, un ouvrier étant tombé à l'eau, il n'hésita pas à se jeter du haut du tablier et lui sauva la vie.

Un monument vient de lui être élevé : En avait-il bien besoin ? Pour immortaliser son nom, en outre de tous ses travaux dans le monde entier, en outre des ponts de Gannat, de la Tardes, de Cubzac, de Porto, de Garabit, de la statue de la Liberté à New-York, dont il a concu l'armature, il a donné au drapeau français une hampe de trois cents mètres, il a accroché aux nuages la plus formidable des antennes, la télégraphie lui doit beaucoup — il a été le premier à doter l'aviation naissante de connaissances certaines en aérodynamique — enfin il a Sa Tour.

Elle durera.

JEAN D'ERLEICH.

Faites-vous tirer un portrait d'art par le photographe de la Tour. PHOTO KESTESZ

N° 63 VU P. 433

Page from VU, no. 63, May 29, 1929 (40th anniversary of the Eiffel Tower, photographs by **André Kertész**).

From the 1920s, the use of photography in the press confirmed its essential role in communication. The great weekly magazines created by the pioneers of the contemporary press such as Henry Luce (*Time, Life*) and Jean Prouvost (*Paris-Soir, Match*) all broadened the influence of photography significantly.

In these publications, the work of the photographer was the key element. A permanent team provided the pictures demanded by the editor or journalists. The first staff photographers of *Life*, founded in 1936, were Margaret Bourke-White, Alfred Eisenstaedt, Thomas D. McAvoy, and Peter Stackpole; the picture editor was Kurt Korff, the former editor of the *Berliner Illustrierte Zeitung*. In Paris, Jean Provost was able to call on Michel Brodsky, Isaac Kitrosser, Jean Manzon, Jean Moral, and Pierre Vals to ensure the success of *Match*, which first appeared in 1937.

Before the Second World War the contribution of freelance photographers was equally important. Thus, the combined photo-archive of the publications *Paris-Soir* and *Match* at the Bibliothèque Historique de la Ville de Paris contains a large number of striking images by Ilse Bing, Brassaï, Robert Capa, François Kollar, Germaine Krull, Émile Savitry, Sasha Stone, and so on, which were commissioned or bought from these photographers.

The third source from which the main journals and periodicals have always obtained photographs has been by agreement with photographic agencies, such as Dephot, Weltrundschau, World Wide, Associated Press, Keystone, Black Star, L.A.P.I., Rol, and Mondial. Under the terms of their contract, agencies would regularly send for consideration entire packets of prints featuring the very latest events.

Then, just as today, the choice of images made by editors, artistic directors, and, sometimes, journalists, was a response to several criteria: the political orientation of the publication, the documentary value of the photograph, the formal and technical quality of the illustration, and – the most subjective consideration, and the one in which the editor-in-chief's judgement was usually final – the beauty of the image.

Precise instructions as to the order, the cropping, and the size of the photographs were then sent to the layout office, who were expected to follow the orders laid down by the editor or the artistic director. Graphic artists and retouching specialists enhanced the presentation with accompanying drawings or by, more or less discreet, retouching. The photographs were then forwarded to the photogravure (called "heliogravure" on the Continent) or half-tone department who created the plates needed for printing.

Quite rapidly, photography invaded the pages of newspapers and magazines, reducing the space devoted to text, which was sometimes relegated to mere captions. In addition, photography also found a use in creating advertising images, and thus has become at times the principal means of communication in certain media.

Thomas Michael Gunther

which, since the First World War, has become an indispensable component in the propagation of ideas in newspapers and magazines.

From the 1920s, in a feverish burst of competition, copywriters, editors, and advertisers rapidly came to understand the effectiveness of the photographic image. Though, at first, these were mere illustrations, they ended up by replacing written text which was relegated to captions. Photographs became the main reference source, both in news-

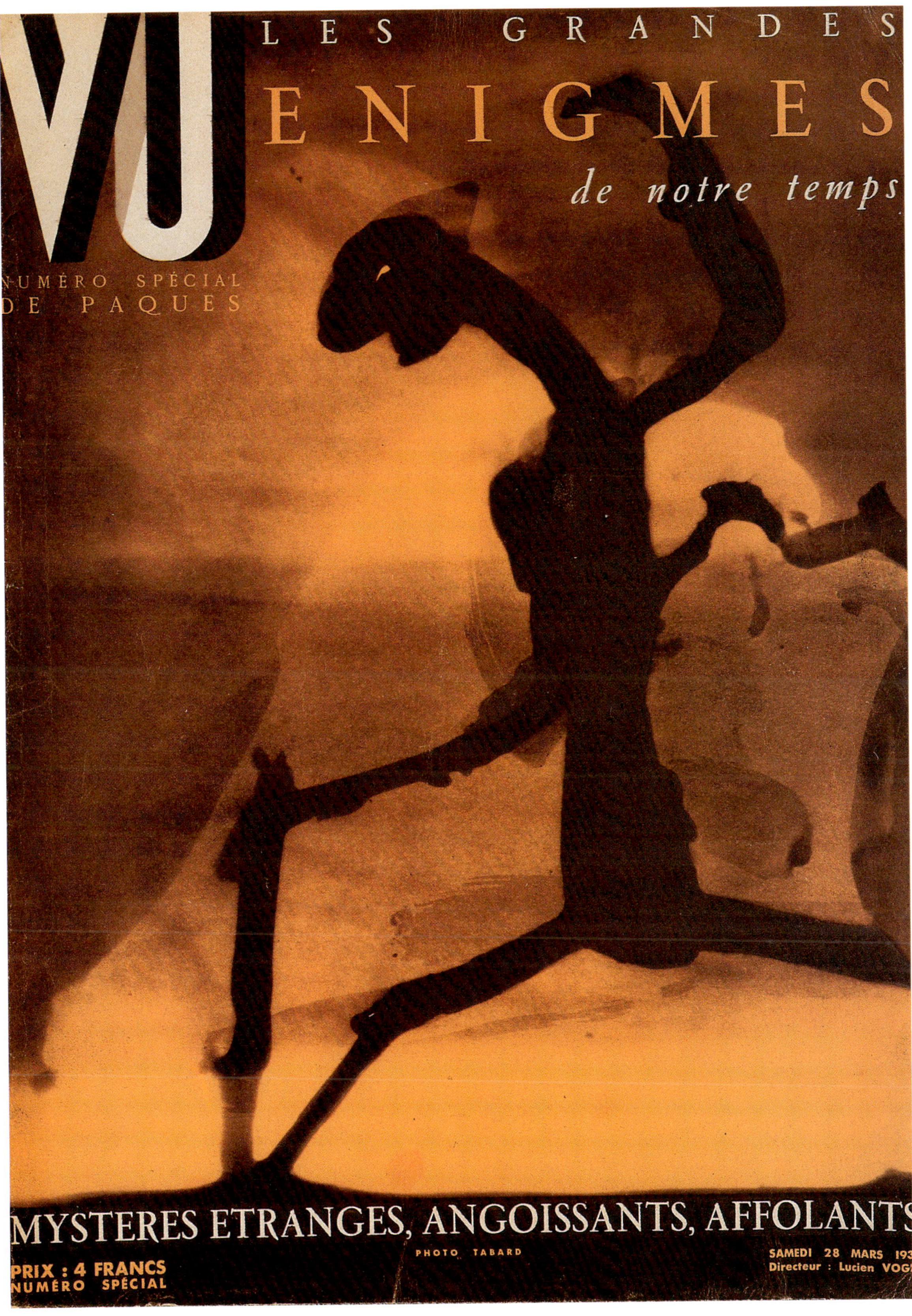

Cover of VU, March 28, 1936, photograph by MAURICE TABARD.

paper coverage of current affairs and in specialized publications. At the same time, thanks to avant-garde magazines, it was finally recognized as a form of artistic expression: *Bifur*, *La Révolution surréaliste*, and *Le Minotaure* in France, *Der Querschnitt* in Germany, *Variétés* in Belgium, *Novyi Lef* in the Soviet Union, *Panorama* in Czechoslovakia, and *Panorama* in the United States. Both as works of art and documentary images, photographs stood for modernity.

At the same time, the number of current affairs magazines increased considerably from the mid-1920s onwards. Encouraged by the success of illustrated daily newspapers, weekly general interest magazines such as *VU* and *Match* in France, *Life* and *Look* in the United States, and

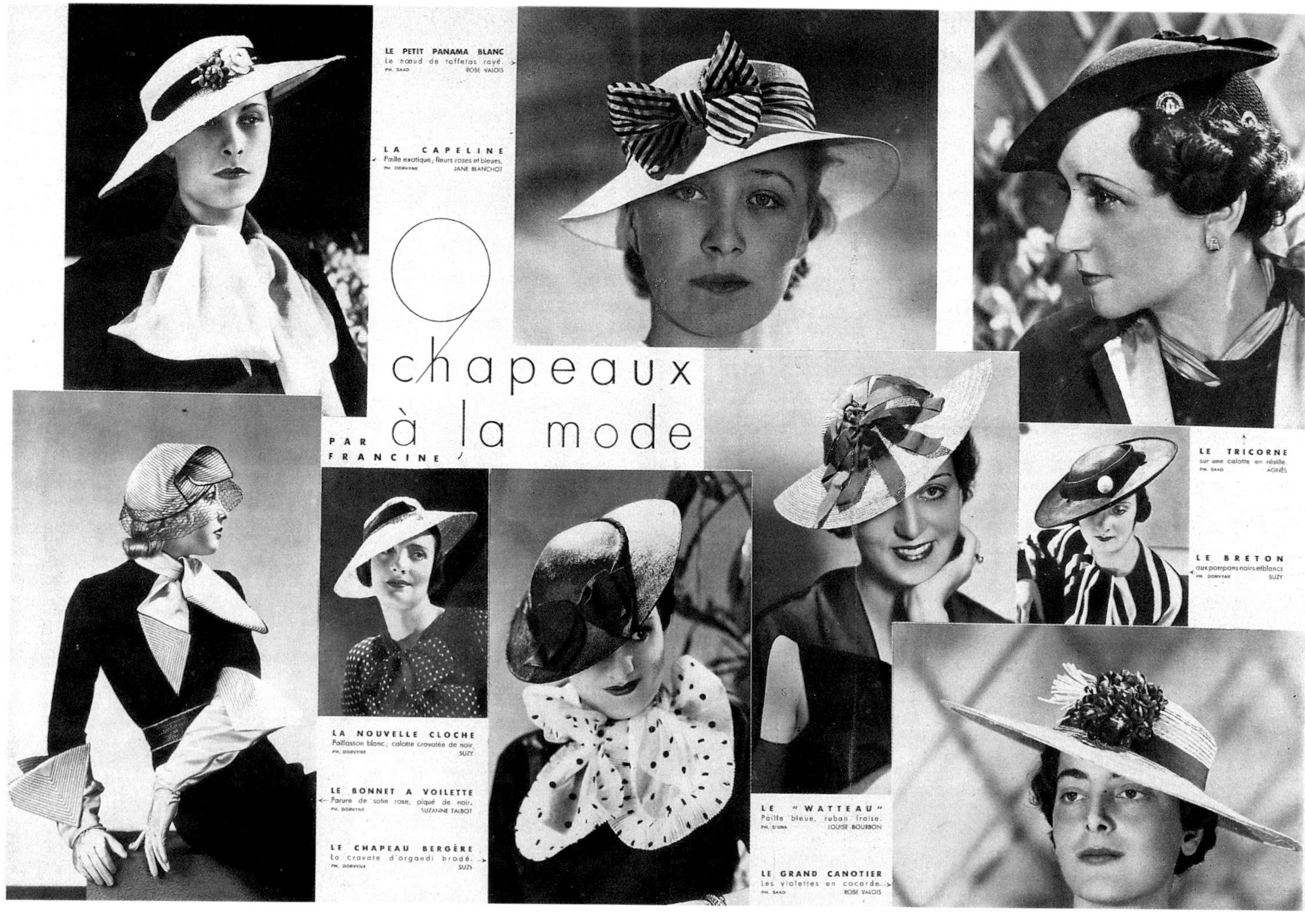
9 chapeaux à la mode

PAR FRANCINE

LE PETIT PANAMA BLANC
le nœud de taffetas rayé.
PH. SAAD ROSE VALOIS

LA CAPELINE
Paille exotique; fleurs roses et bleues.
PH. DORVYNE JANE BLANCHOT

LE TRICORNE
sur une calotte en résille.
PH. SAAD AGNÈS

LE BRETON
aux pompons noirs et blancs
PH. DORVYNE SUZY

LA NOUVELLE CLOCHE
Paillasson blanc; calotte cravatée de noir.
PH. DORVYNE SUZY

LE BONNET A VOILETTE
Parure de satin rose, piqué de noir.
PH. DORVYNE SUZANNE TALBOT

LE CHAPEAU BERGÈRE
La cravate d'organdi brodé.
PH. DORVYNE SUZY

LE "WATTEAU"
Paille bleue, ruban fraise.
PH. D'ORA LOUISE BOURBON

LE GRAND CANOTIER
les violettes en cocarde.
PH. SAAD ROSE VALOIS

Double page spread from VU,
no. 324, May 30, 1934,
photographs by
DORVYNE, SAAD, AND D'ORA.

Weekly Illustrated and *Picture Post* in Britain soon attracted a faithful readership, won over by a style which gave priority to photographs. "Specialist publications devoted to women's interests, sport or material for children, and illustrated daily newspapers, as well as radio, cinema, novels, and popularizing books on technical and scientific subjects, undoubtedly had a decisive influence on the social and cultural behavior of the masses, and perhaps also on their political attitudes."[11]

Various professional, cultural, and leisure sectors benefited hugely from photographic illustrations: machinery, manufacturing equipment, do-it-yourself, tourism, folklore and ethnography, interior decoration, architecture, fine arts, cinema, sport, politics, and propaganda – such as *S.S.S.R. na stroïke* [USSR in Construction], to which Alexander Rodchenko contributed between 1933 and 1941.

The change in women's lifestyle and their growing independence was reflected in a large number of specialized magazines. *Vogue, Harper's Bazaar, Excelsior, Femina, Die Dame*, etc. featured the latest works by fashion designers, while other periodicals gave women advice on how to stay young, beautiful, and healthy. Licentious and erotic magazines also flourished, benefiting from the quality of photographic reproduction, for example, *Paris-Magazine* in France, which published the work of a number of now famous photographers: Man Ray, André Kertész, Germaine Krull, Harry Meerson, Jean Moral, and Brassaï, to name but a few. The private and professional lives of film stars were covered in cinema magazines, which publicized new films with the help of publicity stills. News items, both true and false, were revealed in the sensational press (such as *Détective*), and a certain kind of literary talent found expression in photo-romances.

Also benefiting from the huge popularity of the illustrated press, a number of large companies launched general interest magazines with an eye on the advertising possibilities they offered. These dealt, for example, with painting, architecture, hunting and shooting, travel, books and gramophone records, motoring (*Gazette Dunlop, Revue Ford*), aviation (*Air France Revue*), medicine and pharmaceuticals (*Art et Médecine*, published by Dr. Debat's laboratory, *Mieux-Vivre* and *Ciels et Sourires de France*, published by the Fluxine laboratories, and *Synthèse*, a magazine "reserved for the medical profession", which benefited from the advice of Laure Albin-Guillot).

11. P. Albert, "La presse française de 1871 à 1940", in *Histoire générale de la presse française*", vol. 2, Paris, Presses Universitaires de France, 1972, p. 460.

Photography itself was the subject of a vast number of publications, aimed at amateurs as well as professionals, such as *Photographie*, *Le Photographe*, and *Photo-Illustration* in France, *American Photography* and *Modern Photography* in the United States, *Das Deutsche Lichtbild* in Germany, *Luci ed ombri* in Italy, *Kainourgia Techné* in Greece, *Art de llun* and *Arte Fotographico* in Spain, *Fotograficky obzor* in Czechoslovakia, and *Photo Times* and *Kôga* in Japan.

Photography had attained a position of supremacy. It still remained necessary, however, to discover the most powerful and eloquent images. In theory, newspapers relied on their own staff photographers to record an event or a news item. Soon, however, freelance photographers appeared, offering pictures that they had taken by chance, or looking for commissions. Newspapers and magazines formed libraries of photographs (for example, *L'Illustration*, *Paris-Soir*, *Match*,[12] *New York Times* – who used World Wide Photos to market and distribute them – *Life*[13]) at the same time as photographers accumulated stock images. Often, freelance photographers tired of looking after the commercial side of their collections and entrusted them to intermediaries who could organize their archives and respond to requests from editors and artistic directors. These photographic agents, such as Hug Block, Pawel Barchan, Fritz Goro and Maria Eisner, among others, rapidly proved to be indispensable to the development of the press. Subsequently, several of them set up photographic agencies, such as Dephot, Weltrundschau, Alliance Photo, Rapho, Keystone, Black Star, and Associated Press.[14]

By the end of the 1930s, a basic network had been established for the production and dissemination of photographs intended for the press. During the Second World War, things changed greatly as a result of the forced emigration of photographers and their agents. The main Paris newspapers came under the control of the occupying power. The Germans themselves published propaganda magazines such as *Signal*. In the

BRASSAÏ,
Graffiti of Lutèce,
circa 1950.
▼

12. For the archives of *Paris-Soir* and *Match* (which passed to *France-Soir* after the war), see T. M. Gunther and M. de Thézy, *50 Ans de photographie de presse*, Paris, Bibliothèque Historique, 1990.

13. See L. Wainwright, *The Great American Magazine: An Inside History of Life*, New York, A. A. Knopf, 1986.

14. See the catalogue *Alliance Photo*, Paris, Bibliothèque Historique, 1988, notably the chapter on photo-journalism.

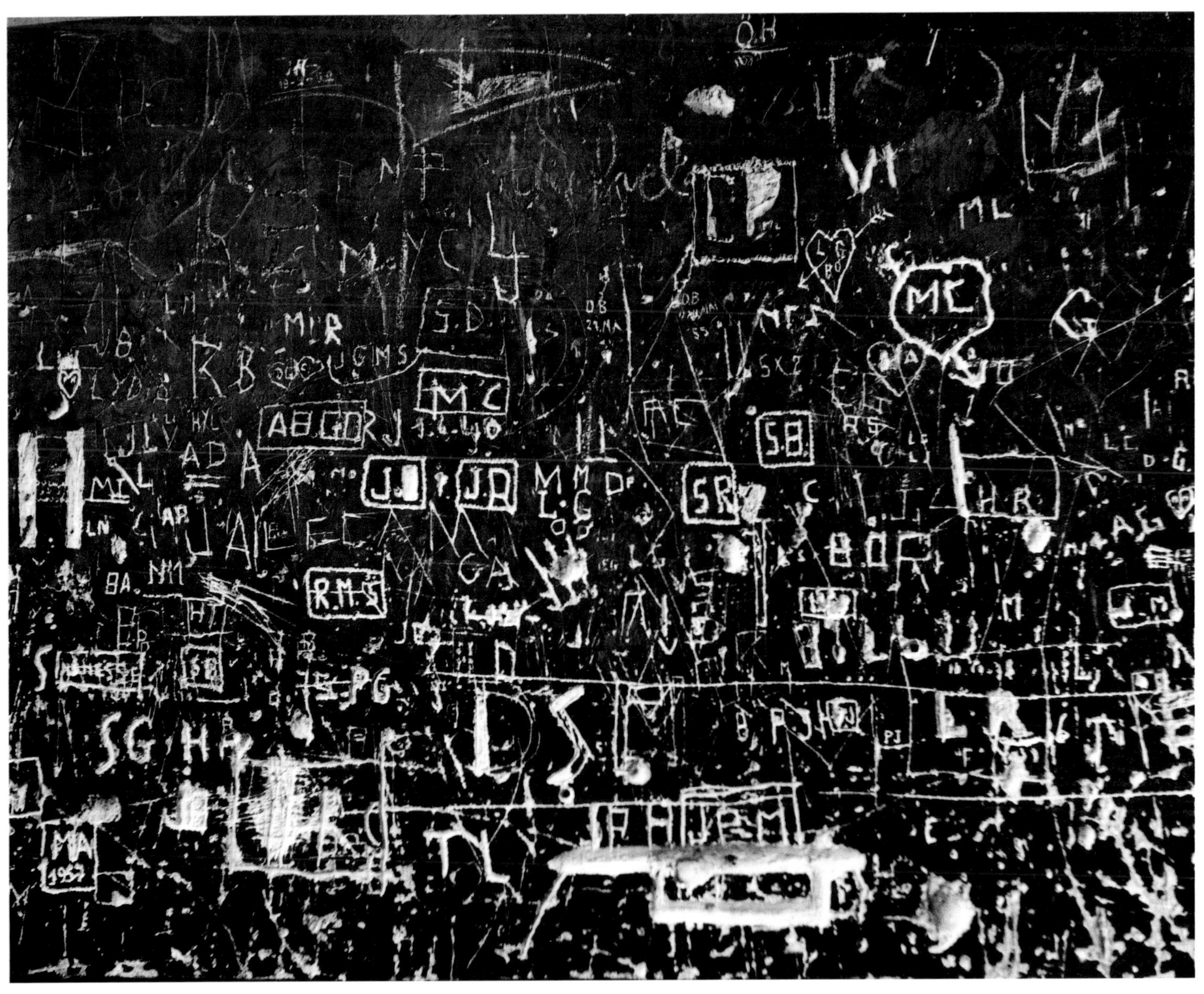

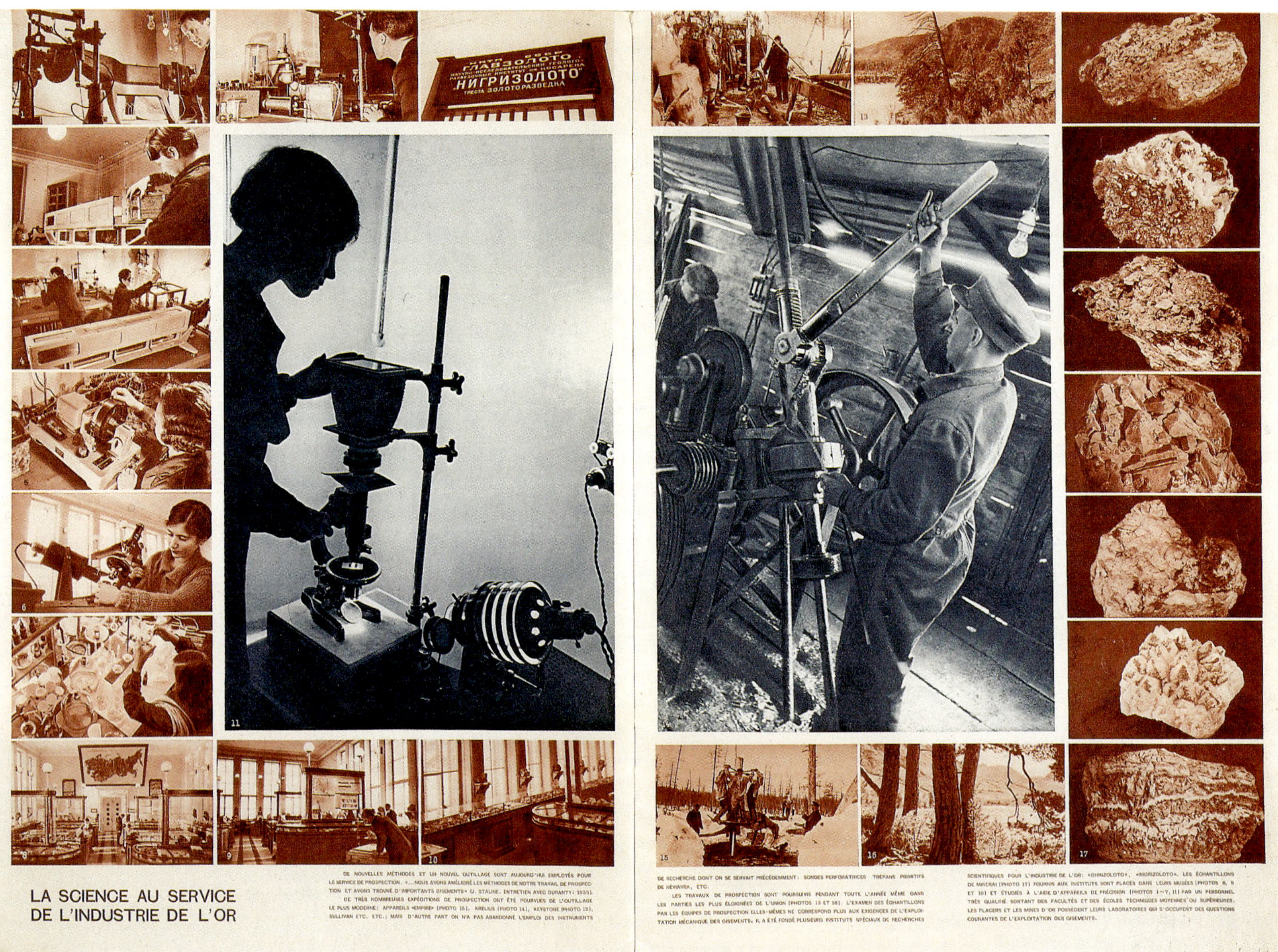

A. Rodtchenko and B. Stepanova, *Gold-diggers;* from *L'U.R.S.S. en construction,* 1937, no. 5.

United States and Britain, as well as in the occupied countries, photographic illustrations were closer in style to the "photoreportage" which had already been a feature of the great magazines of the 1930s, such as *VU*, *Regards*, *Match*, *Picture Post*, and *Life*. The lack of space here permits only a brief mention of the importance of photojournalism, and the impetus which it received after the war from the development of agencies such as Magnum, founded in 1947.

Since the 1950s, the illustrated press has been in competition with television. Cinema newsreels date from the 1930s: in 1935, for example, one year before he founded *Life*, Henry Luce launched a film version of current events entitled *The March of Time*. Television is the heir to this tradition, although monthly or weekly news reports have now been transformed into daily ones.

Photo-books

There is scarcely any need to emphasize the attraction of photographically illustrated books, nor the role which photography played – both as complementary to the text and in its own right – from the moment when photomechanical printing processes (especially rotary photogravure presses) allowed both the accurate reproduction of images and the printing of image and text by the same firm or, better still, using the same press.

Photographers soon showed that they could be ingenious and skilful collaborators in this enterprise. A number of them, such as Louis Caillaud, had already provided sketches to illustrate books. Others, such as René-Jacques, were attracted by the literary aspect of the work. Others still simply saw it as a good way of exercising their trade as photographers. Profiting from the artistic experiments of the avant-garde, from the Bauhaus to Surrealism, they all exploited the technical possibilities of the camera, and of darkroom work. Enjoying considerable creative freedom, they used dramatic lighting and imaginative settings, unusual viewpoints, solarization and photomontage. Photographers worked on commission or drew from their personal photographic libraries. In this field, there was a closer relationship between the photographer and the author or editor; thus, the role of agents or agen-

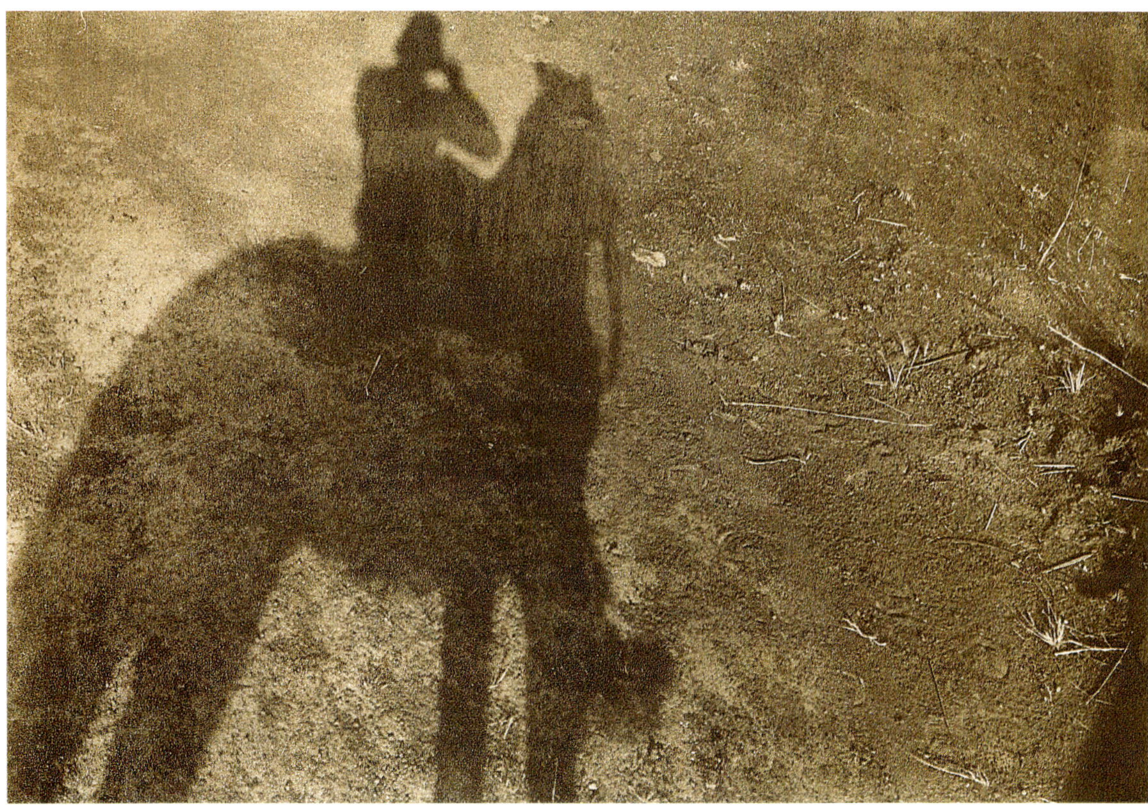

MARC ALLÉGRET, Illustration for André Gide, *Retour du Tchad*, 1929.

cies was more constrained than in advertising or press work.

Soon, subjects such as natural history, archeology or ethnology gave birth to a wide range of themes requiring faithful documentation, such as Wilhelm Uhde's book on Douanier Rousseau, published in Paris in 1911 and illustrated with a portrait of the painter and twenty-seven reproductions of his paintings. Albert Renger-Patzsch's first book, published in Berlin in 1925, dealt with the medieval choirstalls of the church at Kappenberg. During the 1920s, the German

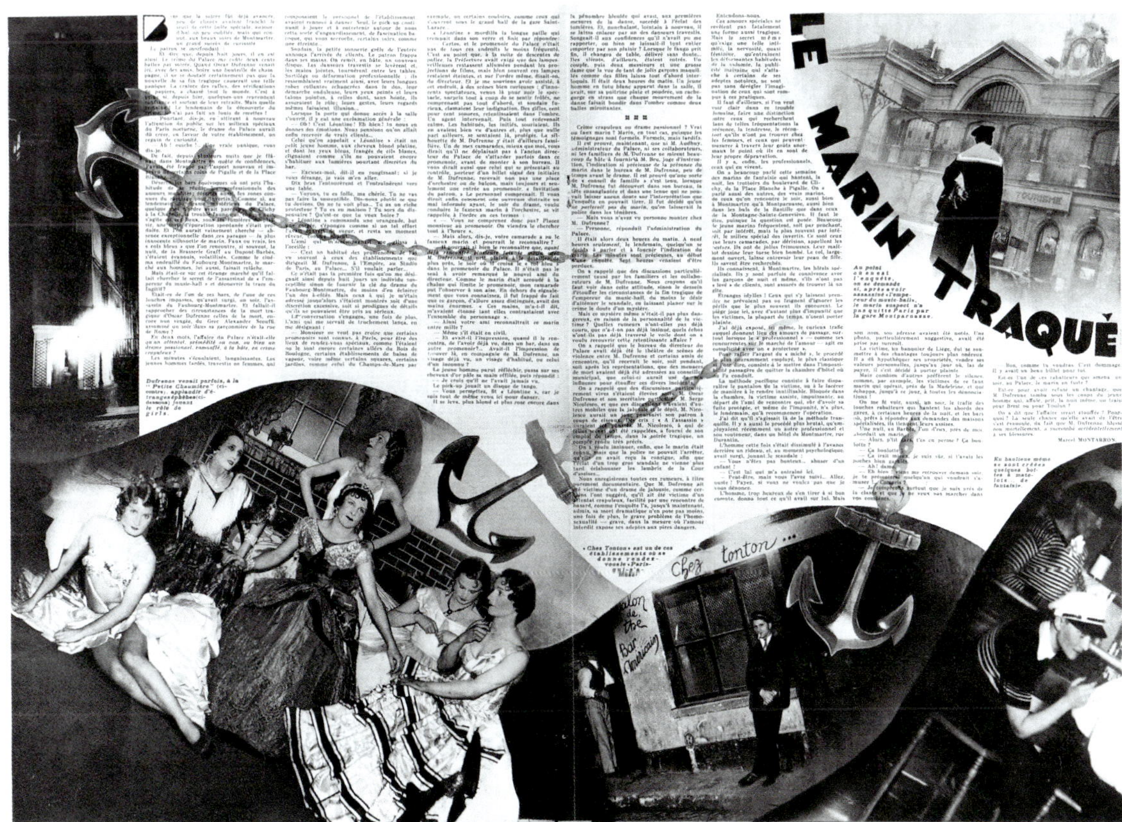

LE MARIN TRAQUÉ

Le marin traqué, double-page spread from *Détective*, no. 258, October 5, 1933.

André Kertész

Born in 1894, André Kertész became a photographer in 1912, when he bought his first 4.5 x 6 cm. Ica camera, which he took to war in 1914. He soon made a name for himself, and won a prize for his photographs in 1917; some of them were published several times by the magazine *Érdekes Újság*. Originally a bank worker, Kertész the photographer was formed by the independent press, which laid particular emphasis on images. However, his career only really started when he arrived in Paris in 1925. As an immigrant, not speaking much French, he sought the company of his compatriots and the artists at the Café du Dôme. Through them he was able to publish a few photographs in German magazines, then at the forefront of the popular press. It was as a result of the growth of the photographic press that Kertész was able to earn a living from his photographs, inventing a style that was both personal and universal. In 1928, the weekly magazine *VU* was launched in Paris under Lucien Vogel, who published a large number of Kertész's photographs, as well as those by Man Ray, Krull, Brassaï, and Tabard.

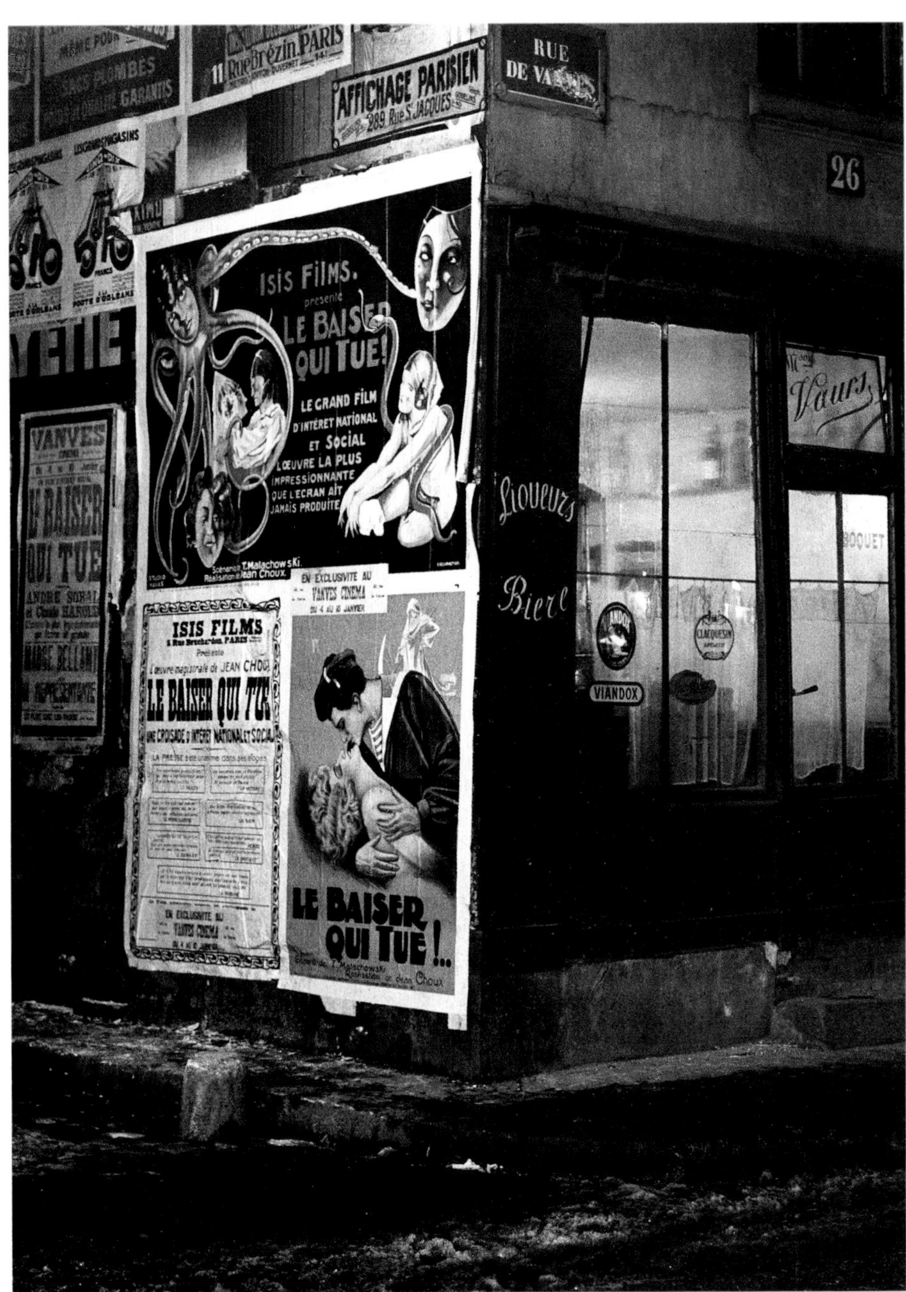

André Kertész,
Rue de Vanves, Montparnasse,
1929.

Photographs were to be found in every part of *VU*: on the front and rear covers and illustrating all the articles inside. The editors had two ways of working: by providing the photographer with a particular subject a few weeks in advance of publication, which allowed him to go out on location, or by choosing a less closely defined subject which might, nevertheless, be suitable for a particular theme – such images might already exist in the files which freelance photographers were slowly beginning to build up (at the same time, agencies were starting to amass photo archives which could provide material without the photographer being involved).

Kertész's photographs appeared in *Variétés, Das Illustrierte Blatt, Das Kunstblatt, Uhu, Der Querschnitt, Die Dame* (which published his *Danseuse satirique* in October 1927). His famous *Fork*, which featured in the exhibition *Film und Foto*, was reproduced in 1929 in *Die Forme, Uhu*, and *Die Dame*.

Kertész was also commissioned by *Art et Médecine*, a high-quality monthly aimed at the medical profession and published by the Debat laboratories between 1930 and 1936. Thus, he travelled in Savoy, Brittany, and Lyons, where he also worked on the theme of marionettes, published in *L'Art Vivant* and elsewhere, and where he visited Maeterlinck and Mac Orlan. It was for *VU* that he photographed (as did Brassaï) the Eiffel Tower in 1929, its fortieth anniversary. For the same magazine he took a photograph of the editor, Carlo Rim, in a deforming mirror (1930), which earned him a commission from a light-hearted magazine, *Le Sourire*, for a series called *Distortions*, published in 1933. Kertész's photographs also appeared in *Voilà, La France à Table, Regards*, etc. At the time political events were causing newspapers to take up more pronounced political stances. In 1936, André Kertész left Paris for New York, where he hoped to find employment in current affairs, leisure or fashion magazines.

Kertész's Paris period was a particular time when he developed a particularly fertile style – very different from the German New Vision – which was to influence other photographers, including Brassaï and Cartier-Bresson. Kertész captured transitory signs, the arrangement of shapes, the repetition of visual indicators, happy juxtapositions of settings, whose subtlety was his particular forte. He brought together a humanist approach and a poetic quality characteristic of his photography in the 1950s. Apart from his private contributions to exhibitions (including *Le Salon de l'Escalier* in 1928 and *Le Salon de l'Araignée* in 1930), Kertész could bring some of his photographs to public attention only through books: *Paris vu par André Kertész* (1934), and *Day of Paris* (1945).

His complete photographic archive, which he left to the Mission du Patrimoine Photographique in France, allows us to consider the nature of voluntary artistic decisions resulting from the diffusion of contemporary media, all within the context of the work of an inspired photographer.

Michel Frizot

editor Karl Robert Langewiesche, published the well-known series of *Blauen Bücher*. In the 1930s, Pierre Jahan photographed the *Dévot Christ* from Perpignan for Raymond Gid's book (Paris, 1934), while André Vigneau undertook the illustration of the *Encyclopédie photographique de l'art* for the works published by Éditions Tel: Egyptian antiquities in 1936, Mesopotamia, Canaan, and Cyprus in 1936, Greece and Rome in 1938.[15]

During the inter-war period, publishers in various countries specialized in works on tourism and ethnography. This was one of the most popular themes, encouraged by the missions of colonial powers; André Gide's *Voyage au Congo* and *Retour du Tchad* appeared in 1929 with photographs by Marc Allégret, though this was mainly due to chance rather than planning. Paul Hartmann is a good example of the editorial system that was establishing itself. During the 1930s and after the Second World War, he published illustrated books on Greece, Spain, Mexico, India, Turkey, Egypt, Tunisia, and Brazil, and Walter Hege's striking photographs of the Acropolis, taken in 1936. More rarely, the great literary publishing houses involved themselves: Gallimard published *Tahiti*, with 106 photographs by Roger Parry (1934), Flammarion placed a photograph on the cover of *New York*, by Paul Morand (1930), and illustrated the popular edition of 1934, entitled *New York le jour et la nuit*, with nine photogravures. Margaret Bourke-White's *Eyes on Russia*, published in 1931, gives a very precise idea of the living and working conditions in the young Soviet republic.

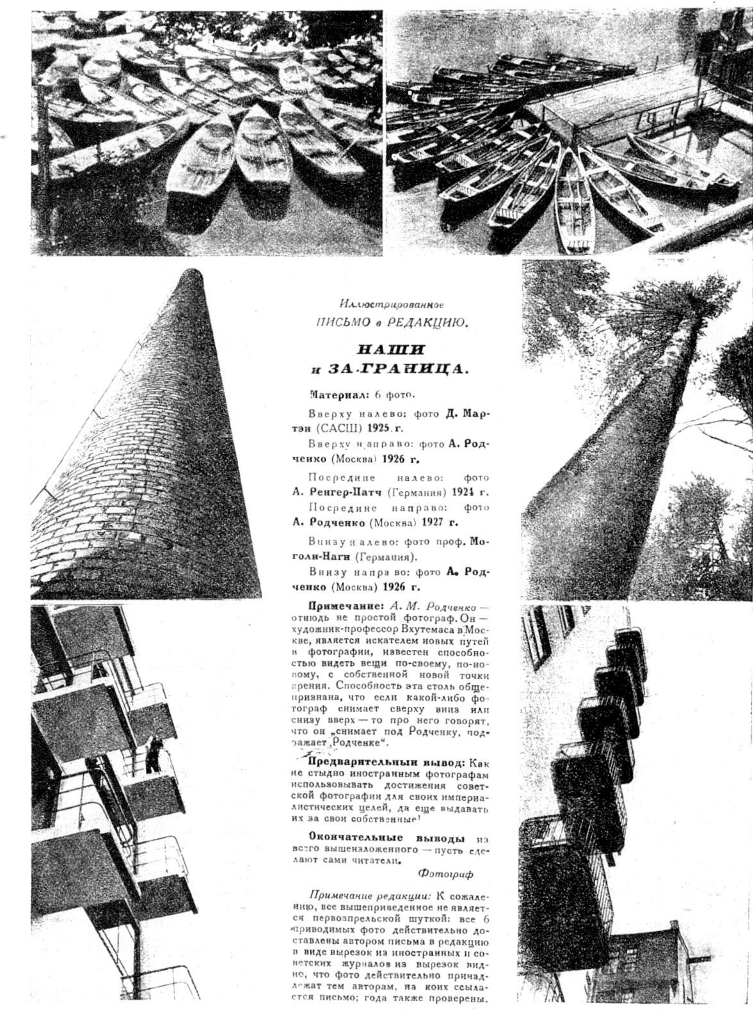

Иллюстрированное
ПИСЬМО в РЕДАКЦИЮ.

НАШИ
и ЗА-ГРАНИЦА.

Материал: 6 фото.

Вверху налево: фото **Д. Мартэн** (САСШ) **1925 г.**

Вверху направо: фото **А. Родченко** (Москва) **1926 г.**

Посредине налево: фото **А. Ренгер-Патч** (Германия) **1924 г.**

Посредине направо: фото **А. Родченко** (Москва) **1927 г.**

Внизу налево: фото проф. **Моголи-Наги** (Германия).

Внизу направо: фото **А. Родченко** (Москва) **1926 г.**

Примечание: *А. М. Родченко* — отнюдь не простой фотограф. Он — художник-профессор Вхутемаса в Москве, является искателем новых путей в фотографии, известен способностью видеть вещи по-своему, по-новому, с собственной новой точки зрения. Способность эта столь общепризнана, что если какой-либо фотограф снимает сверху вниз или снизу вверх — то про него говорят, что он „снимает под Родченку, подражает Родченке“.

Предварительный вывод: Как не стыдно иностранным фотографам использовывать достижения советской фотографии для своих империалистических целей, да еще выдавать их за свои собственные!

Окончательные выводы из всего вышеизложенного — пусть сделают сами читатели.

Фотограф

Примечание редакции: К сожалению, все вышеприведенное не является первоапрельской шуткой: все 6 приводимых фото действительно доставлены автором письма в редакцию в виде вырезок из иностранных и советских журналов из вырезок видно, что фото действительно принадлежат тем авторам, на коих ссылается письмо; года также проверены.

Sovietskoe Foto,
no. 4, 1928, p. 176.
Top to bottom:
left: MARTIN (U.S.A.), RENGER-PATZSCH, MOHOLY-NAGY;
right: RODTCHENKO.

Later, in 1953, Arthaud published François Cali's *France aux visages* including photographs by Brassaï, Lucien Hervé, and René-Jacques. The editor, M. J. Challamel, launched the collection *Charme de la France*, with photographs by Jean Roubier. Mercure de France published Georges Duhamel's *Le Japon entre la tradition et l'avenir* with 60 photographs by Werner Bischof, Gilles Boisrobert, and Pierre Verger. In Switzerland, Clairefontaine published *La Grèce à ciel ouvert* (1953) and *Îles grecques* (1956), illustrated by the Greek photographer, Voula Papaioannou. These are just a few examples of the quality work that was being produced, soon to be found in abundance in every country. Cities, whose importance was increasing, became a favorite subject: among many titles one might single out *Rome* by Émile Mâle (Paul Hartmann, 1936), *A Night in London* by Bill Brandt (1938), *Aspects de Lyon* by Blanc and Demilly (1933) and *Charme de Lyon* by Antoine Demilly (1942), *Praha ve fotografii* by Karel Plicka (1940), *New York* by D. Wronecki, illustrated in the main by Henri Cartier-Bresson (1949), and William Klein's *New York* (1956), *Rome* (1960), *Moscow* (1964), and *Tokyo* (1964).

Paris, in particular, fascinated photographers and publishers, as well as lovers of illustrated books: Germaine Krull's *100 x Paris*, with text by Florent Fels (1929); *Paris vu par André Kertész*, with preface and captions by Pierre Mac Orlan (1930), Francis Carco's *Envoûtement de Paris*, illustrated with 112 photographs by René-Jacques (1938), *Paris*, by Emmanuel Boudot-Lamotte (1939), *Paris*, photographed by Marc Foucault (1942), *Voyage dans Paris*, presented by Pierre Mac Orlan and illustrated with images by Arthaud, Bovis, Durand, Grono, Jahan, René-Jacques, and Roubier (1945), *Paris*, a set of 100 photographs collected by Emmanuel Sougez, reprinted by the publishers Gründ (1947), *La Banlieue de Paris*, by Blaise Cendrars and Robert Doisneau (Seghers, 1949), *Paris*, by André Maurois (1951), *Belleville-Ménilmontant*, by Pierre Mac Orlan and Willy Ronis (Arthaud, 1954). Until the end of the 1940s, new books and reprinted editions often re-used older photographs. It was only in the 1950s

15. See T. M. Gunther, *André Vigneau: l'essor de la photographie dans l'entre-deux-guerres*, Paris, Bibliothèque Historique, 1986.

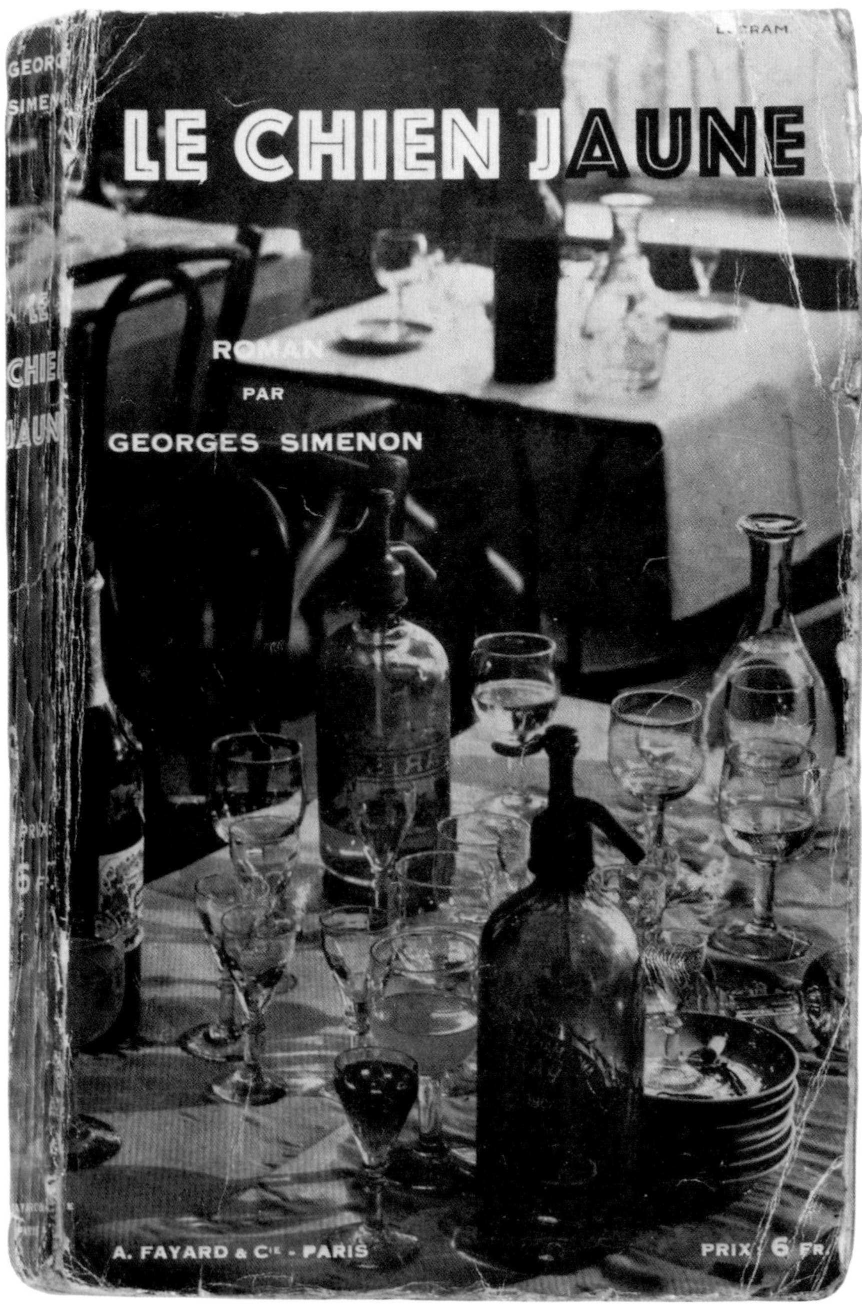

Cover of Simenon's **Le Chien Jaune**, 1931, Studio Lecram, photograph by ROBERT DOISNEAU.

Cover of **Life**, ▶ vol. 7, no. 2, July 10, 1939, photograph by PAUL DORSEY.

that published images became more up-to-date, as in Elsa Triolet's book *Pour que Paris soit*, illustrated by Robert Doisneau (Cercle d'art, 1956).

Similarly, in the Low Countries photographers and publishers showed an interest in the French capital: *Bonjour Paris*, by Cas Oorthuys (1951), *Vrouwen van Parijs*, by Nico Jesse (1954), *Een liefdegeschiedenis in Saint-Germain-des-Prés*, by Ed Van der Elsken (1956), and *Paris mortel*, by Johan Van der Keuken (1963), influenced by William Klein's book on New York.

With a new page layout and format, Robert Delpire's collection *Huit* comprised a "photobook" as an autonomous object, considered as a work of art, even though there was little public interest in such "pocket editions", for example Robert Doisneau's *Les Parisiens tels qu'ils sont* (1954), Cartier-Bresson's *Danses à Bali* (1954), and George Rodger's *Le Village des Noubas* (1955). Delpire was then Paris's most innovative publisher, as much in his choice of photographs and his design as in his pioneering use of images: *D'une Chine à l'autre* (1954) and *Moscou* (1955), by Cartier-Bresson, *Séville en Fête*, by Brassaï (1954), *Guerre à la tristesse*, by Inge Morath, *Afrique* (1958), *Antartica* (1960), and *Amazonie* (1962), by Emile Schulthess, *Indiens pas morts*, by Bischof, Frank, and Verger (1956), and *Japon* (1954) and *Carnet de route* (1957), by Bishof, as well as the complete collection of the *Encyclopédie essentielle*. Also to be taken into account is the innovative activity of the Guilde du Livre at Lausanne, during these years when high-quality printing was not too costly.

Little by little, text had been replaced by images which, much more than mere illustrations to the text, demonstrated an active presence, a kind of encyclopedic inventory of vision, page after page. The model of this genre remains Cartier-Bresson's *Images à la sauvette*, designed by Teriade, with a jacket design by Matisse (Verve, 1952).

In *Urformen der Kunst* (1928), Karl Blossfeldt sought to demonstrate the extent to which art imitates nature. In *Die Welt ist schön* (1928), Albert Renger-Patzsch pursued the analogies between natural formations and manufactured objects. August Sander created an impressive pictorial survey of the German people in *Antlitz der Zeit* (1929). Germaine Krull celebrated the modern world in *Métal* (1927). The powerful and unchanging attraction of the sea provided the subject of *Ports*, by Charles Koechlin, Daniel Biot, and Jean de Morène (1933), as well as *Mer, marines, marins*, with an introduction by Paul Valéry. In the same Firmin Didot series, Jean Brunhès illustrated the diversity of the human race in *Races* (1931), and, in the same year, Jean Giraudoux explored both the tender and savage aspects of animals in *Bêtes*. Animals turned out to be a very popular subject, as demonstrated by the publication of the *Livre des Chiens* (1934, with photographs by S. Henchoz), André Kertész's *Nos amies les bêtes* (1936), and the studies of cats, dogs, and other animals made by Ylla during the thirties. *Enfants*, by André Kertész, appeared in 1933. Portraits regularly took centre-stage, as in *Visages, théâtre*, illustrated by Laure Albin-Guillot (1947).[16] In Paris, Calavas published *Les Nus de Drtikol* in 1929; Daniel Masclet, *Nus* in 1934, and Marcel Natkin, *Le Nu en photographie* in 1937. In London, Francis Jay put together forty-eight nude studies by the best European photographers in *My Best Nude Study* (George Routledge, 1937). In the United States, Nell Dorr persuaded the New York publisher G. P. Putman to publish photographs of naked adolescent girls, taken in Florida in 1929, in a work entitled *In a Blue Moon* (1939).

16. *Études psychomorphologiques de visages, théâtre 1947*, with prefaces by Jean Anouilh, Dussane, and G. Neveux, Paris, Calliope, 1947.

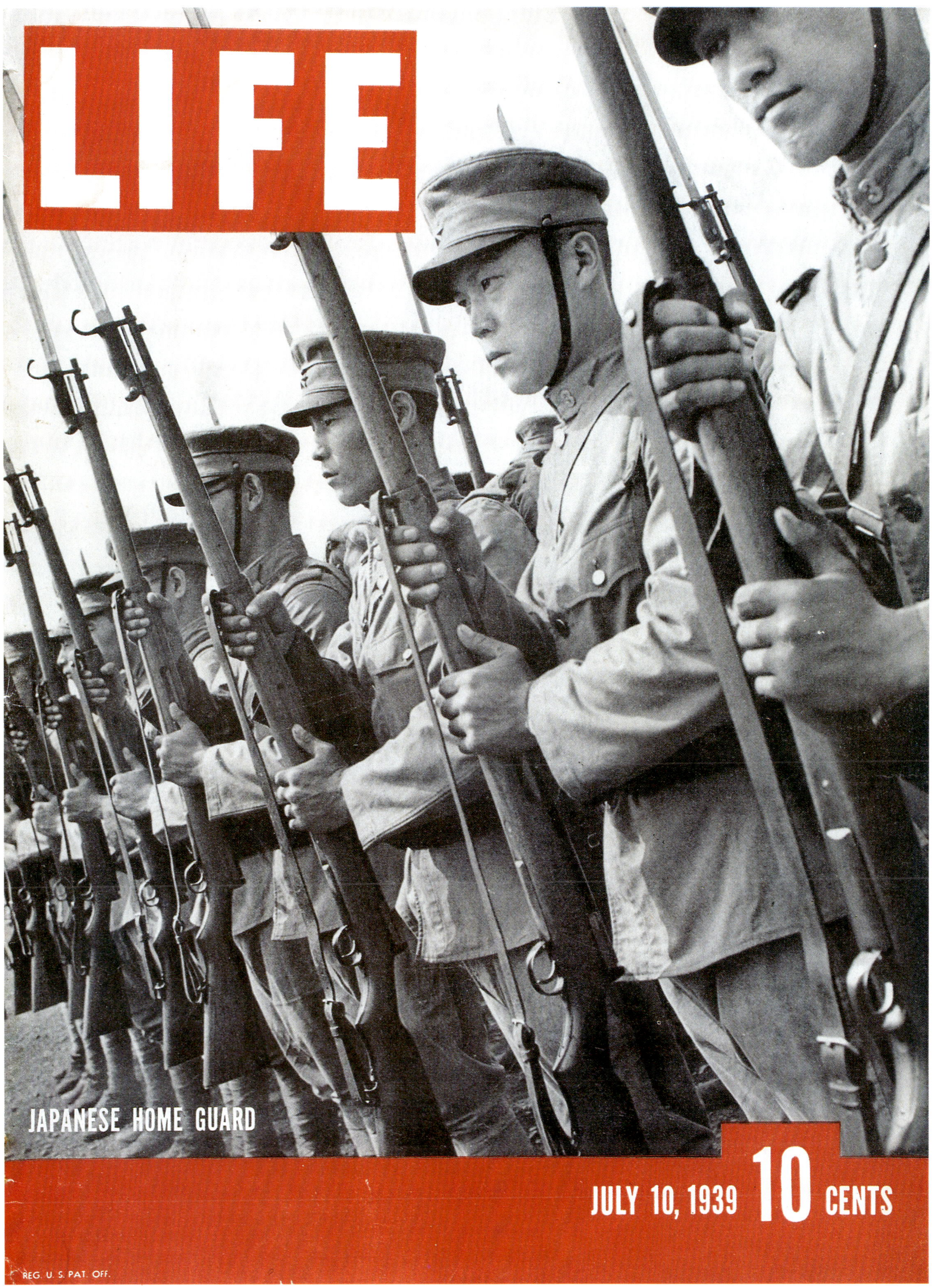
LIFE
JAPANESE HOME GUARD
JULY 10, 1939
10 CENTS
REG. U. S. PAT. OFF.

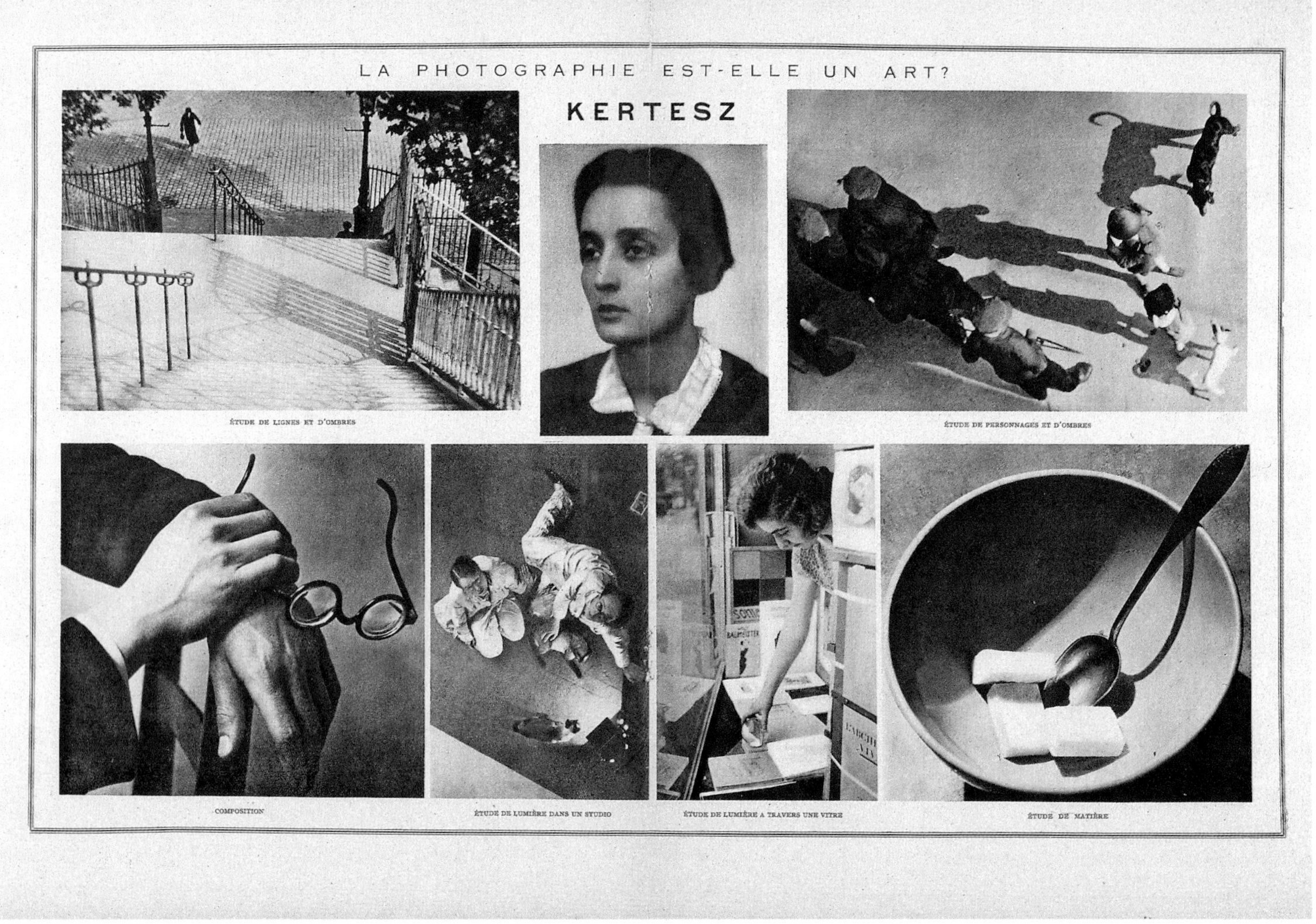
LA PHOTOGRAPHIE EST-ELLE UN ART?

KERTESZ

ÉTUDE DE LIGNES ET D'OMBRES

ÉTUDE DE PERSONNAGES ET D'OMBRES

COMPOSITION

ÉTUDE DE LUMIÈRE DANS UN STUDIO

ÉTUDE DE LUMIÈRE A TRAVERS UNE VITRE

ÉTUDE DE MATIÈRE

Double page spread from **L'Art Vivant,** no. 101, March 1, 1929, photographs by André Kertész.

The world of work was also a popular subject. A large number of books paid homage to workers, peasants, employees, and tradesmen, underlining the dignity with which they carried out their daily tasks. In *La France travaille* (1932), with introductory text by Paul Valéry, François Kollar experimented with new camera angles. His work typified the current fascination with machines and large-scale works. In the United States, the Farm Security Administration, directed by Roy Stryker, allowed several talented photographers to record the difficult economic conditions resulting from the great Depression in the southern states: Dorothea Lange and Paul Taylor collaborated on *An American Exodus: A Record of Human Erosion* (1939). Two years later, Walker Evans and James Agee worked on a joint project, *Let Us Now Praise Famous Men*, a classic documentary study of American rural life. This humanist approach found, perhaps, its most powerful expression in *The Family of Man*, published in 1955, which accompanied the exhibition which Edward Steichen curated at the Museum of Modern Art in New York. This display set the seal on the international character of photography (it included 503 images from 68 countries), and affirmed those common features of human experience, contrasting them with the multiplicity of cultures and races.

Publishing had been affected greatly by the war and, in France, by the Occupation. Photographers fell back on the portrayal of traditional trades and non-industrialized landscapes, as in *Reflets de France*, published in 1942 by Roger Schall. At the end of the war they settled the score. The Schall brothers published *À Paris sous la botte des Nazis* (1944), while the publishers Occident asked André Papillon to put together a photoreportage on the liberation of Paris, published under the title *Barricades*.[17] Pierre Jahan took a distressed but poetic look at wartime damage to Paris in *La Mort et les Statues*, a project which he undertook with Jean Cocteau (1946). In Germany, Hermann Claasen denounced the Allied bombing of Cologne in *Gesang im Feuerofen* (1947), and in Hungary the new rulers stigmatized the old regime by screening, with American help, moving images of the ruins of Budapest in *The Decline and Rise of Budapest* (1946).[18]

During the 1930s and 1950s, practical 'how-to' books began to appear in great numbers, teaching cookery, interior decorating, sport[19] or even photography. In this last field, numerous publications, often financed by manufacturers of

17. *Barricades*, text by L. Gratias, photography by Doisneau, Him, Monneins, Picoche, Papillon, H. Manuel-Sylvestre, Seeberger, and the Presse Libération photographic agency, Paris, Occident, undated.

18. *The Decline and Rise of Budapest*, with preface by P. Vajda, Budapest, Dr M. Miklos Printing Office, 1946.

19. *Méthode française de ski: technique Émile Allais*, with photographs by P. Boucher, Paris, Flèche, 1947, *Le ski*, illustrated by P. Boucher, R. Doisneau, E. Landau, W. Ronis, etc., Éditions de Varenne, 1951.

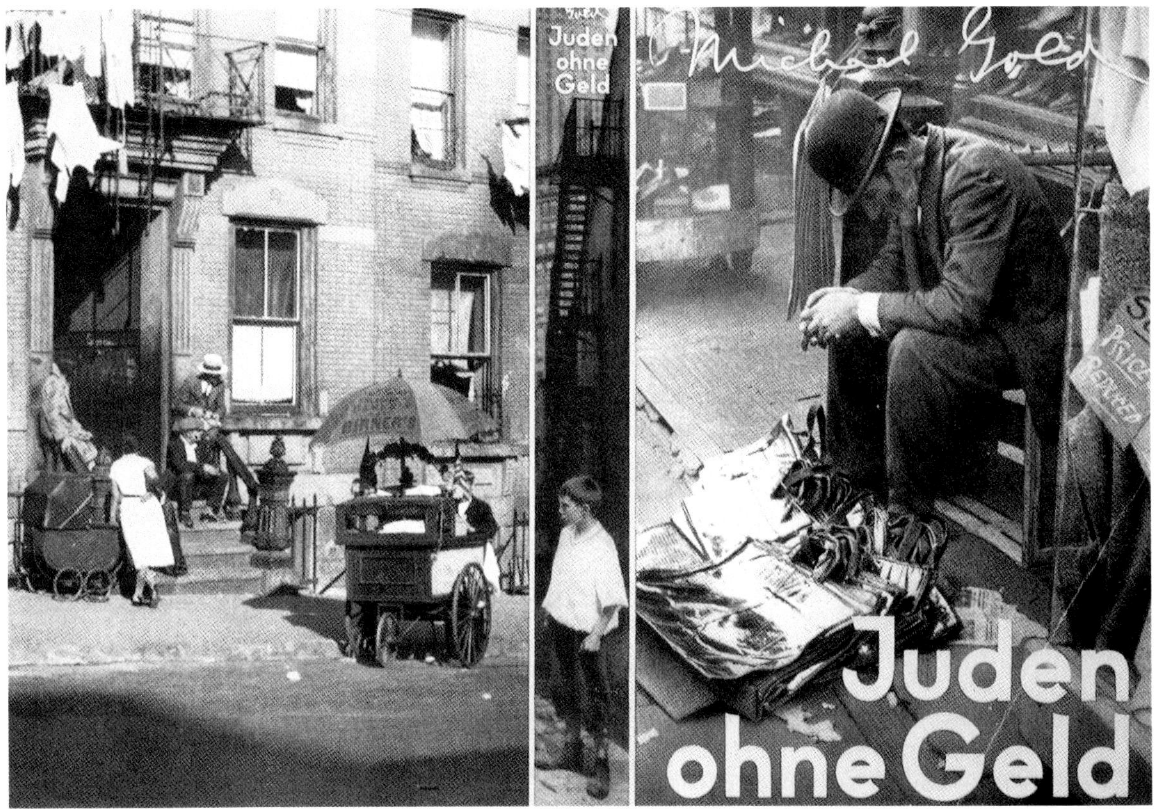

John Heartfield, *montage for the jacket of Michael Gold's* **Juden ohne Geld**, 1931.

cameras, film or photographic paper, offered "advice and useful tips". In every country, the best photographers were invited to reveal good practice and the tricks of the trade.

A number of illustrated books covered the new way of looking that photography provided from the first decades of the twentieth century. In Germany, László Moholy-Nagy published *Malerei, Fotografie, Film* in 1925, Werner Gräff, *Es kommt der neue Fotograf* in 1929, Franz Roh and Jan Tschichold, *Foto-Auge* in 1930. In France, during the late 1930s, Marcel Natkin brought out two important books: *Art de voir en photographie* (1937) and *Truquages en photographie* (1938). There were also unusual books which pushed back the frontiers of practical photography, such

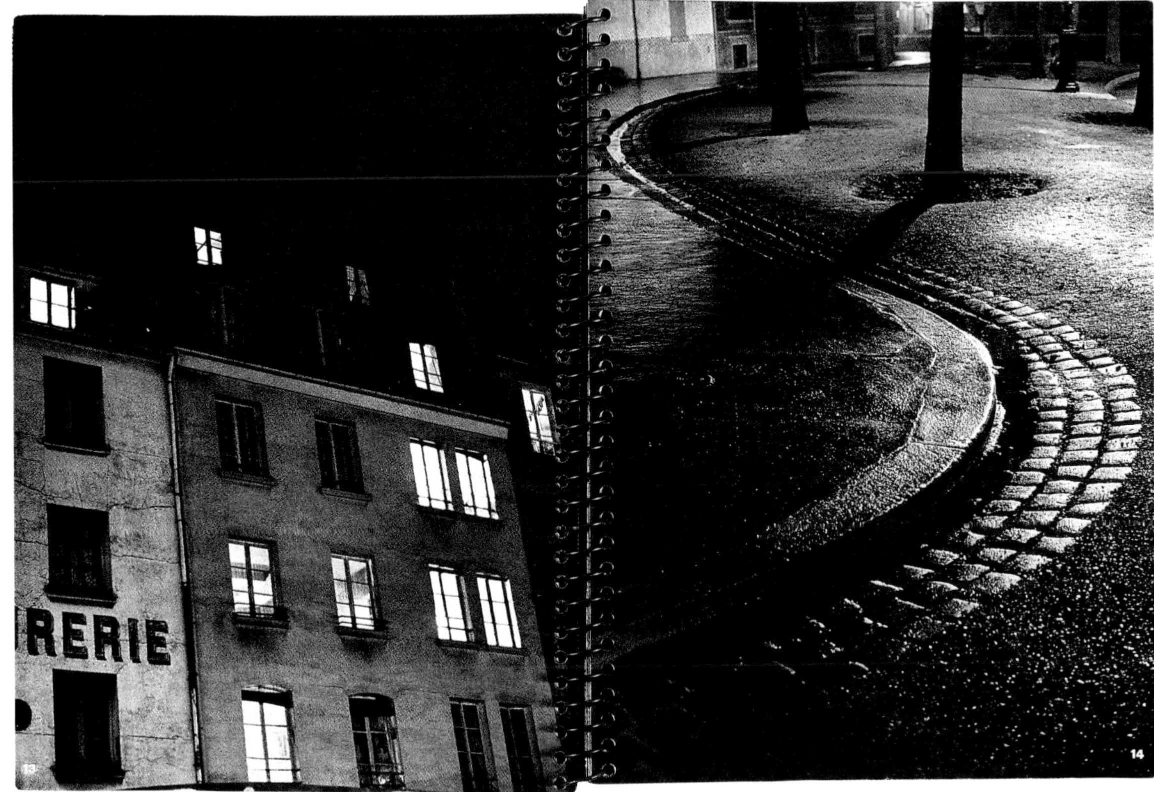

Brassaï, *double page spread from* **Paris de nuit**, 1933.

Double page spread from **U.S. Camera,** 1945, **The U.S.A. at War,** photographs by **U.S. Navy.**

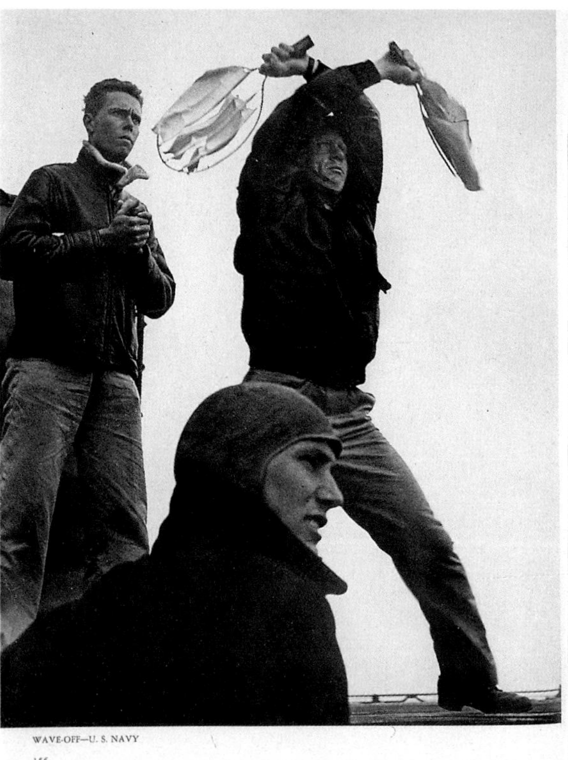

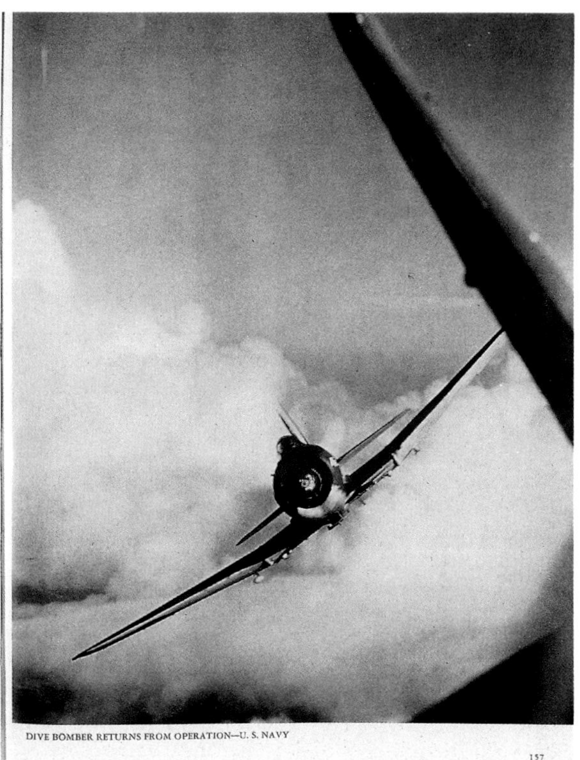

as Roger Parry's *Banalité* (1930), and Laure Albin-Guillot's *Micrographie décorative* (1931).

From an early date, some books were devoted to the work of the photographers themselves: *Steichen the Photographer,* with text by Carl Sandburg (New York, 1929), *Atget* by Pierre Mac Orlan (Paris, 1930), and *Zeme a Lide, Kniha fotografii,* a collection of Jan Lukas's best photographs (Prague, 1946). Since the Second World War, photographic monographs have proliferated, providing an opportunity for historians and writers to interpret images, and sometimes giving the actual photographers the chance of explaining their artistic creed, such as Ralph Steiner in *A Point of View* (1978).

Double page spread from **Marcel Natkin Collection. Le nu en photographie,** 1937, photographs by **Man Ray.**

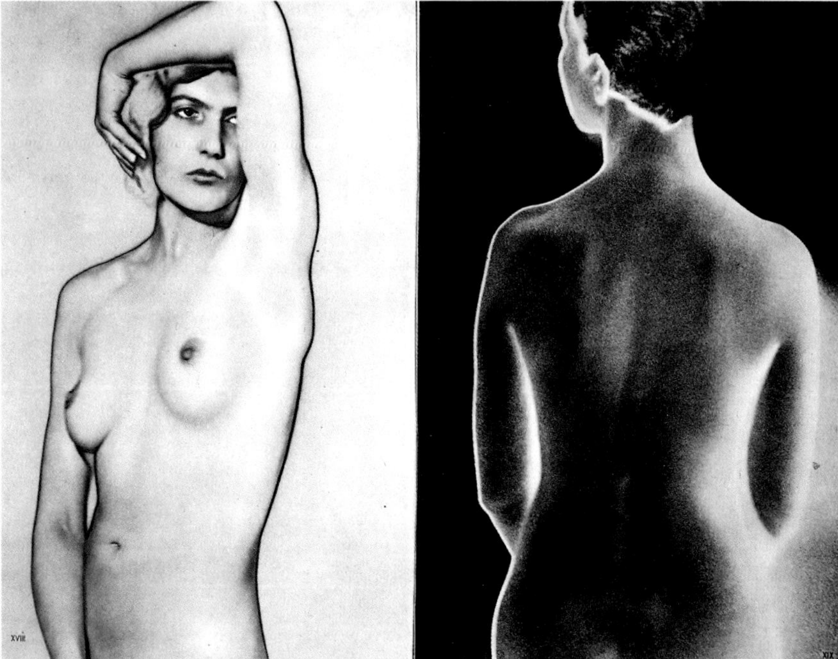

At the same time, various magazines and specialist societies produced annual publications which brought together the best images of the previous twelve months: *Photographie, The Year's Best Pictures, Photography Year Book, The Year's Photography,* not forgetting "Photographie", an annual special number of *Arts et Métiers graphiques.*

It was during the inter-war period that a real interest began to appear in the history of photography and in early photographers. Thus, at the beginning of the 1930s, having published Mac Orlan's *Atget,* the publisher, Henri Jonquières brought together a number of historic photographs in an album entitled *La Vieille Photographie depuis Daguerre jusqu'à 1870.* Gisèle Freund's sociological study, *La photographie en France au dix-neuvième siècle,* appeared in 1936. The celebration of the centenary of the invention of photography allowed its origins and applications to be examined. Beaumont Newhall published the first version of his *History of Photography* for the exhibition "Photography 1839–1937" at the Museum of Modern Art in New York, a book which ran to several revised editions.

Since the 1950s, while the press has shown a decided preference for photoreportage, the photo-book has discovered a new vocation. Abandoning traditional subjects such as flowers and townscapes, it has addressed more theoret-

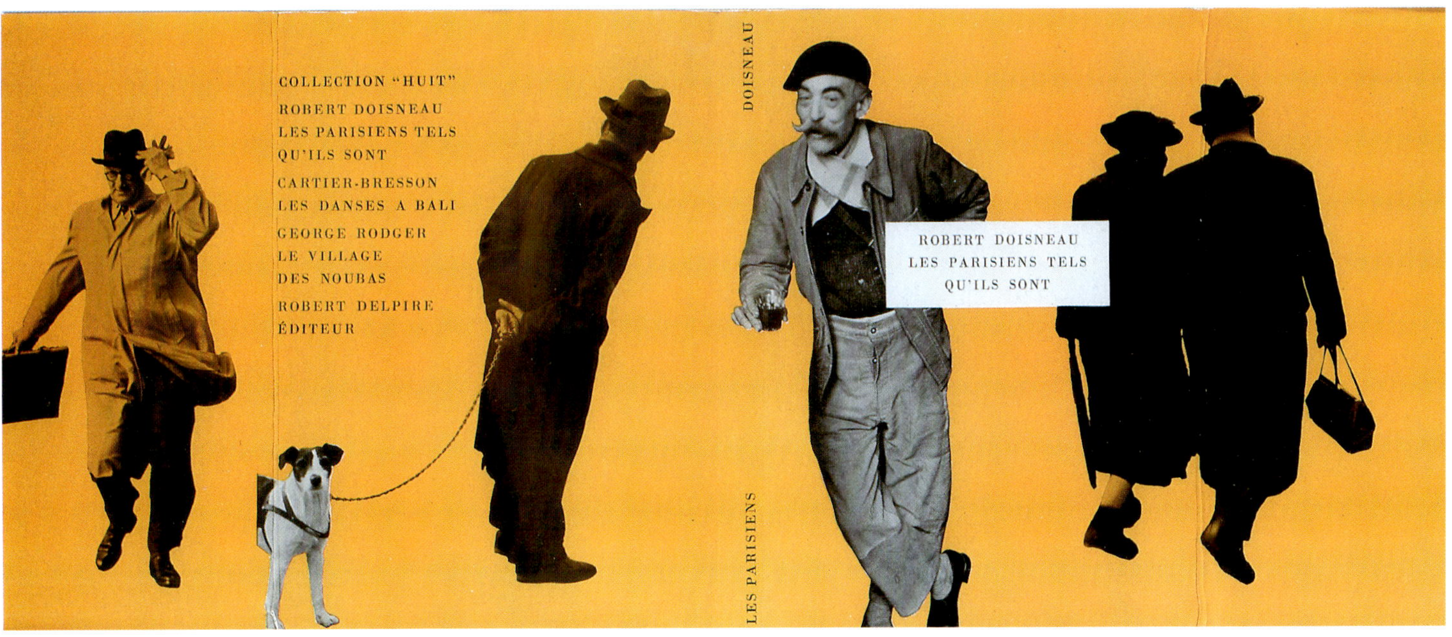

Dust-jacket from **Robert Doisneau, Les Parisiens tels qu'ils sont,** Delpire, 1954.

ical themes, asking questions about personal and social reality and pondering the nature of photography itself. In these works, while drawing on everyday and often apparently banal themes, certain photographers have shown their subjects out of context in a way which has the force of social criticism. Henri Cartier-Bresson's *Images à la sauvette*, published in New York as *The Decisive Moment* (1952), manifested the photographer's wish "to take spontaneous photographs as if catching someone in the act".[20] Robert Frank's *The Americans* (1958) was first published in France, as though the photographer's gaze contradicted the self-image of those people. In this same way, in *Suburbia* (1973) and *Our Kind of People* (1975), Bill Owens displayed a skeptical view of family happiness and the social success of the American dream. At the same time, different authors set about creating collections of anonymous portraits (*American Snapshots*, 1977, by Ken Graves and Mitchell Payne) and scientific or police photographs (*Evidence*, 1977, by Larry Sultan and Mike Mandel), as well as pictures by local professional photographers, such as Michael Lesy's *Wisconsin Death Trip* (1972) and *Real Life* (1976) or Barbara P. Norfleet's *Champion Pig* and *Great Moments in Everyday Life*. These books were intended to demonstrate the inherent

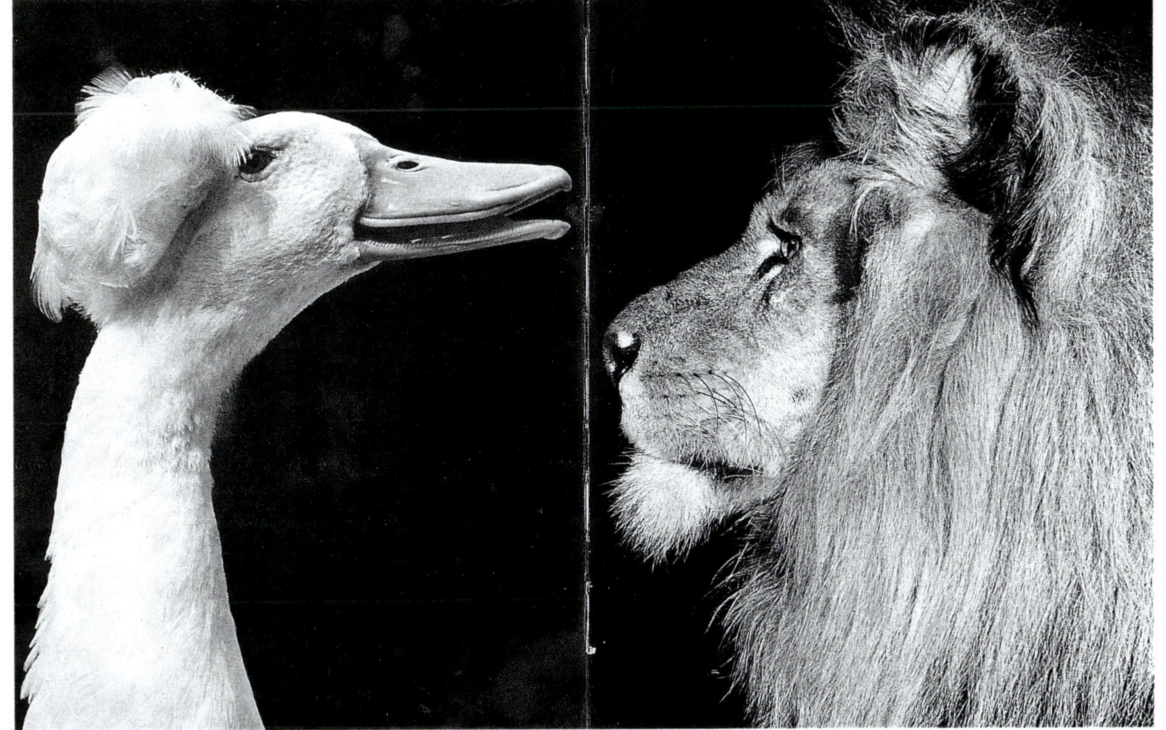

Double page spread from **Animals,** by Ylla, 1950.

20. H. Cartier-Bresson, *Images à la sauvette*, Paris, Verve, 1952, p. 2.

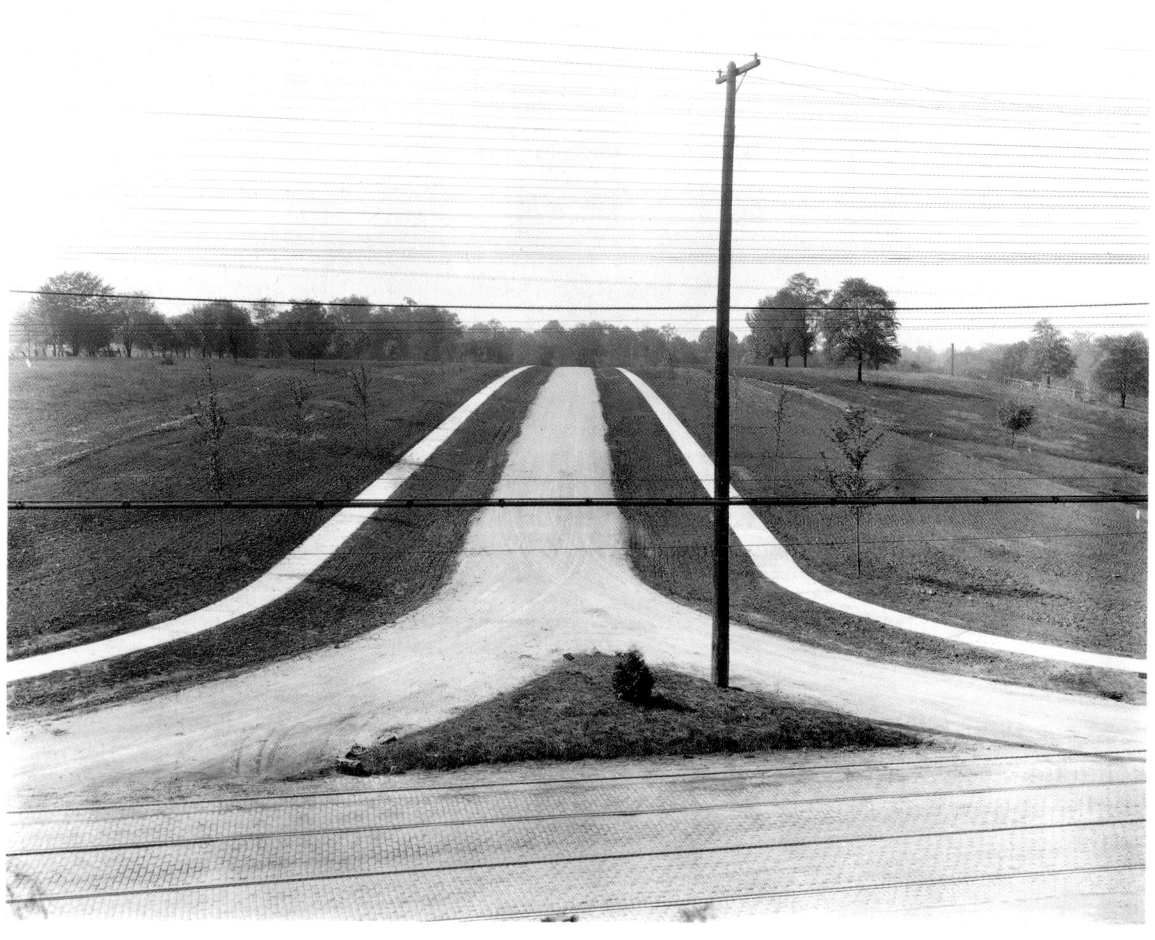

CAUFIELD AND SHOOK STUDIO, ***Near Louisville, Wisconsin,*** 1920s, from M. Lesy, *Real Life: Louisville in the Twenties*, 1976.

force of photographic images, independent of their subject, and they tried to grasp the history of the way people represented themselves.

The books published during the 1950s by Cartier-Bresson, Frank, and Klein inaugurated another category of "photo-books", more specifically "photographers' books" devoted to a single, often retrospective project; photographs were often conceived from the moment the subject was chosen, in order to suit the design of the book, balanced by text and blank pages, a carefully thought-out layout (Frank went even further along this path, even going so far as including his own life in the photo-sequences, with *The Lines of my Hand* in 1972). A guiding theme might then form the main thrust of the book, as in Garry Winogrand's *The Animals* (1969) or Lee Friedlander's *The American Monument* (1976). For many of today's photographers, the photo-book (which may never appear) has (too often) become the reason for following a particular photographic line, particularly since the 1960s when a new twist made photography not only an illustration in the middle of a book, like a piece of documentary evidence, but a work of art which played with its internal relations with the totality of the book-object, an object of reflection on the biographical and social function of images.

In the combined concepts of "advertising" and "publishing", photography had discovered a raison d'être which it never possessed in the nineteenth century, limited, as it then was, to a social elite. Now it had a daily impact on everyone's lives.

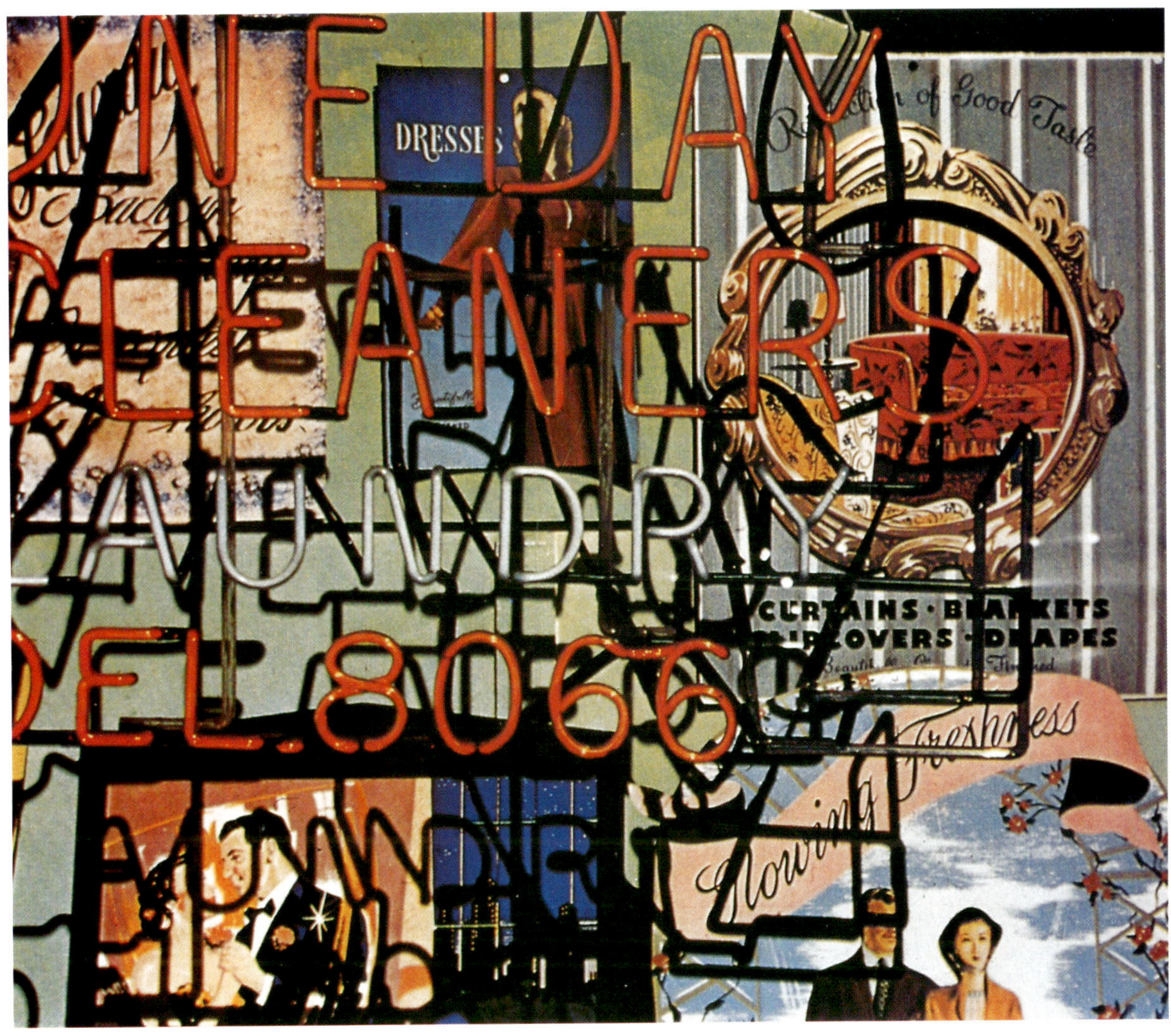

Colors of the age

Even more than black and white photography, color photography can undergo a number of transformational stages which may alter its general tonality and shift the color relationship - the change from negative to positive, the transfer of a positive transparency to photographic paper or to the printed image. While monochrome photogravures or half-tones reproduce the gray scale without changing them too much, color photomechanical printing, unless tightly controlled, can irreversibly distort the color balance of the original photograph. In color work, the concept of reproduction is dominant, accompanied by a quality of relativity which results from both subjective taste and technical imprecision.

Color photography had a real impact in the press only after the development of color photomechanical processes - first in three colors, then four. It was during the 1930s that magazines began to print in color, which created a demand for color images, for example, in *Fortune, Life, L'Illustration, Sunday Mirror.* Because technical processes were changing rapidly (both in the capture of the original and in its printing), a printed color photograph may be defined as the product of a particular period, resulting from all the phases in the process - the technical choices and conditions, the printing method used – not to mention changing fashions in image manipulation and retouching. Each period had its strengths and its weaknesses, and its disasters, and its bold features, which allow a photograph to be dated by its texture. It is possible, from its color balance, to recognize an Ektachrome transparency, a Cibachrome print, a magazine image from the 1940s, or a Technicolor print at the cinema.

The arrival of color photography demonstrates that photographic mimicry is merely an illusion, denuded of any kind of automatic nature. While black and white photography possessed too many connotations of truthfulness, the advent of color photography had, paradoxically, the effect of distancing the image from real life, which it cannot grasp with scientific precision. Color is something in itself, a variable material which must be treated as such, quite independent of the real, changing object behind it. "In the image, color is never, absolutely never, coded from without [...] On the contrary, always from within, with relation to the document which takes it over and the physical support which makes it known to us" (M. Pastoureau). Colors do not exist – except through our eyes.

Thus, we have at least two sorts of color photography: an original, on a photographic base, and its printed version, which has its own demands which are themselves variable. The appreciation of the accuracy of tones and the judgment of color balance depend, among other things, on the contemporary conditions which brought about and surround the image. The examples reproduced in this section provide a rapid history of taste, of truth, of good taste in color, as a function of objectives which are effectively defined by the media in which they appeared: advertising photography (the Draeger 301 process, Alfred Cheney Johnston), press and illustrative photography (Marcel Bovis and the anonymous workers of the 1930s and 1950s), photojournalism (Ernst Haas, Werner Bischof), art photography (Arthur Siegel, William Eggleston, John Batho). Though even here the disparities between these examples will be leveled out to a certain extent by the printing process used in this book!

Michel Frizot

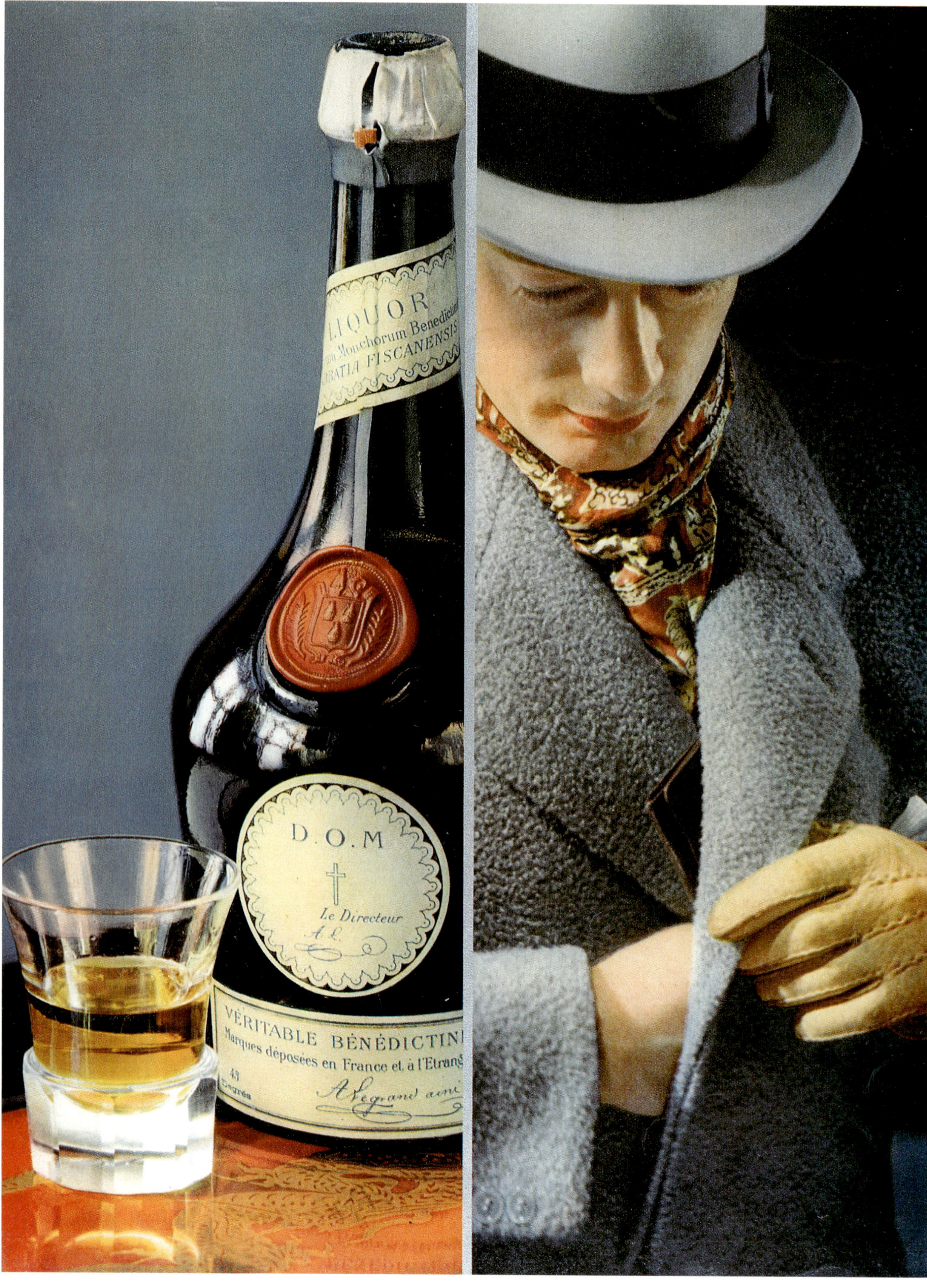

◀◀ preceding page:
ARTHUR SIEGEL,
Dry Cleaning, 1946.

DRAEGER BROTHERS,
Publicity photo for the 301 process,
color photogravure, 1930s.

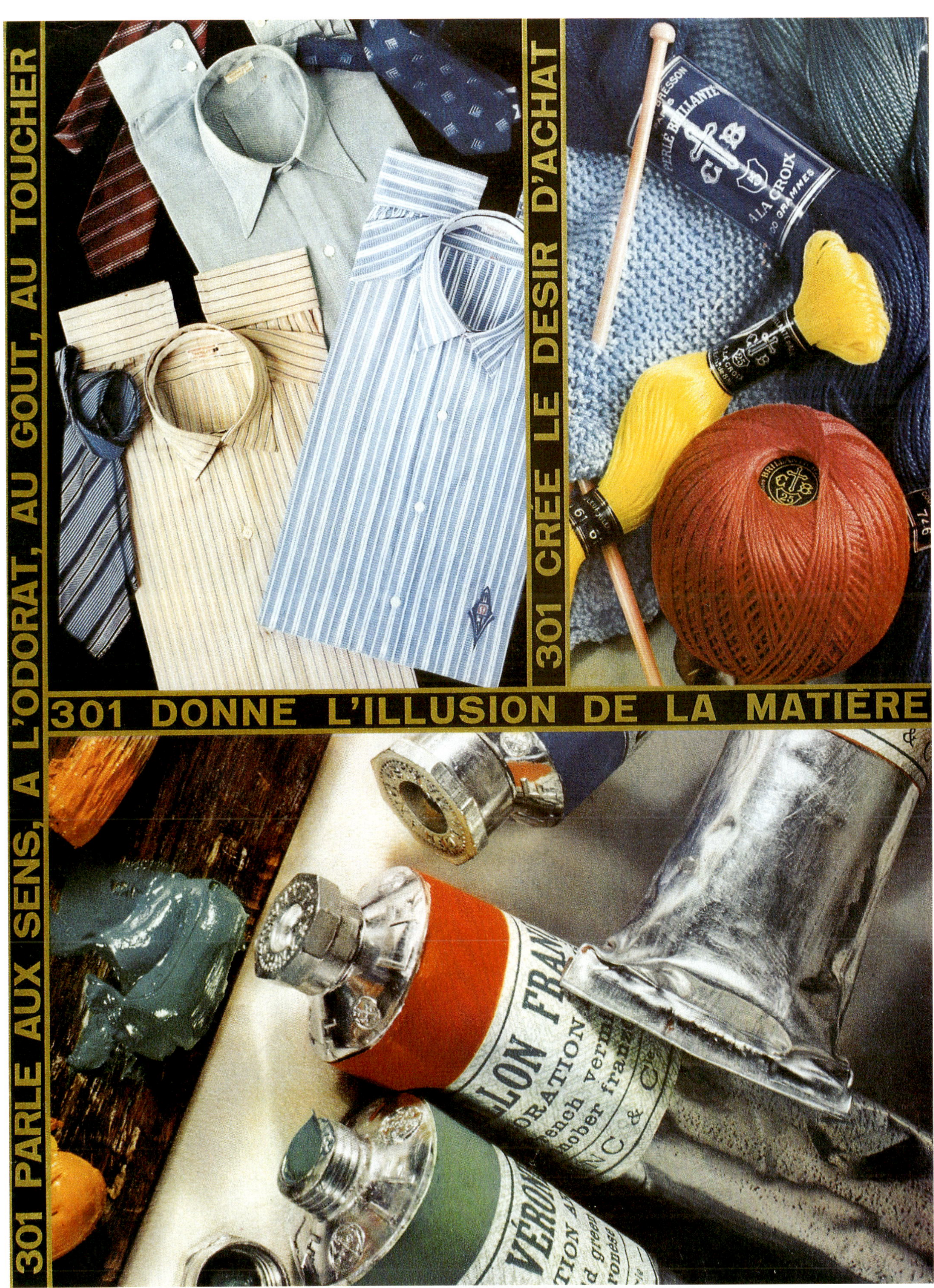

DRAEGER BROTHERS,
Advertisement for the 301 process,
color photogravure, 1930s.

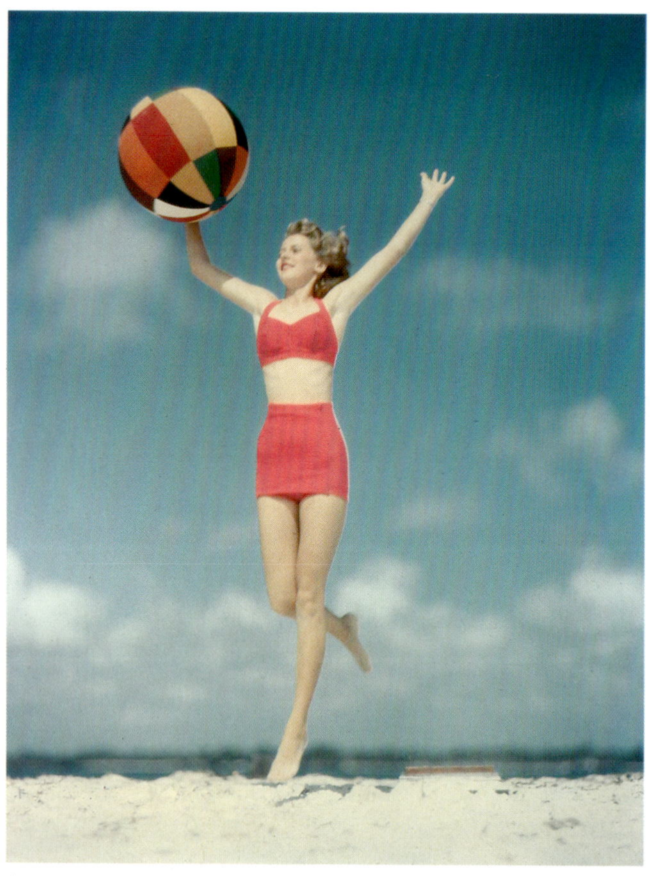

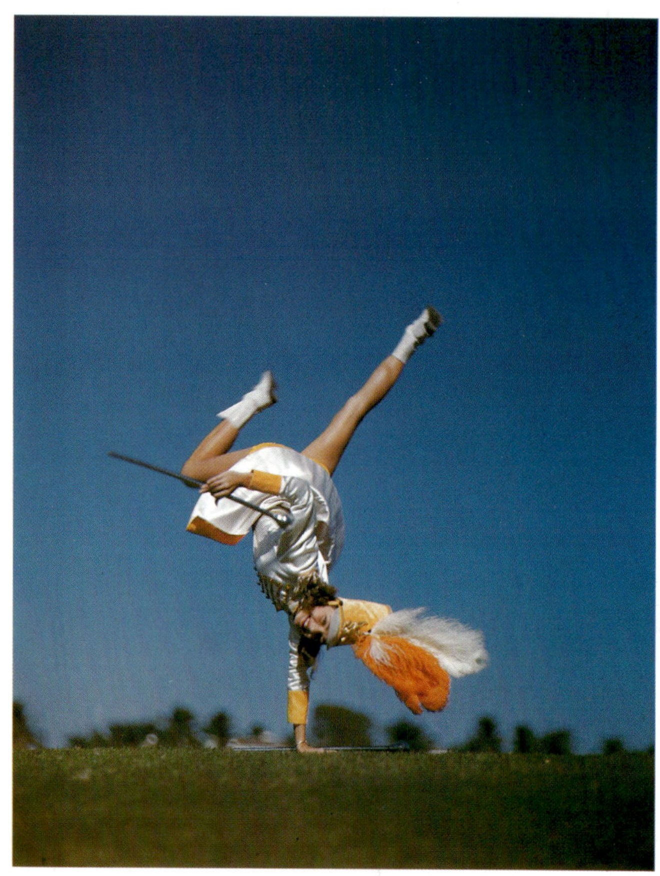

▲ ▶
ANONYMOUS,
photographs for American magazines,
Ektachrome process,
circa 1950,
private collection.

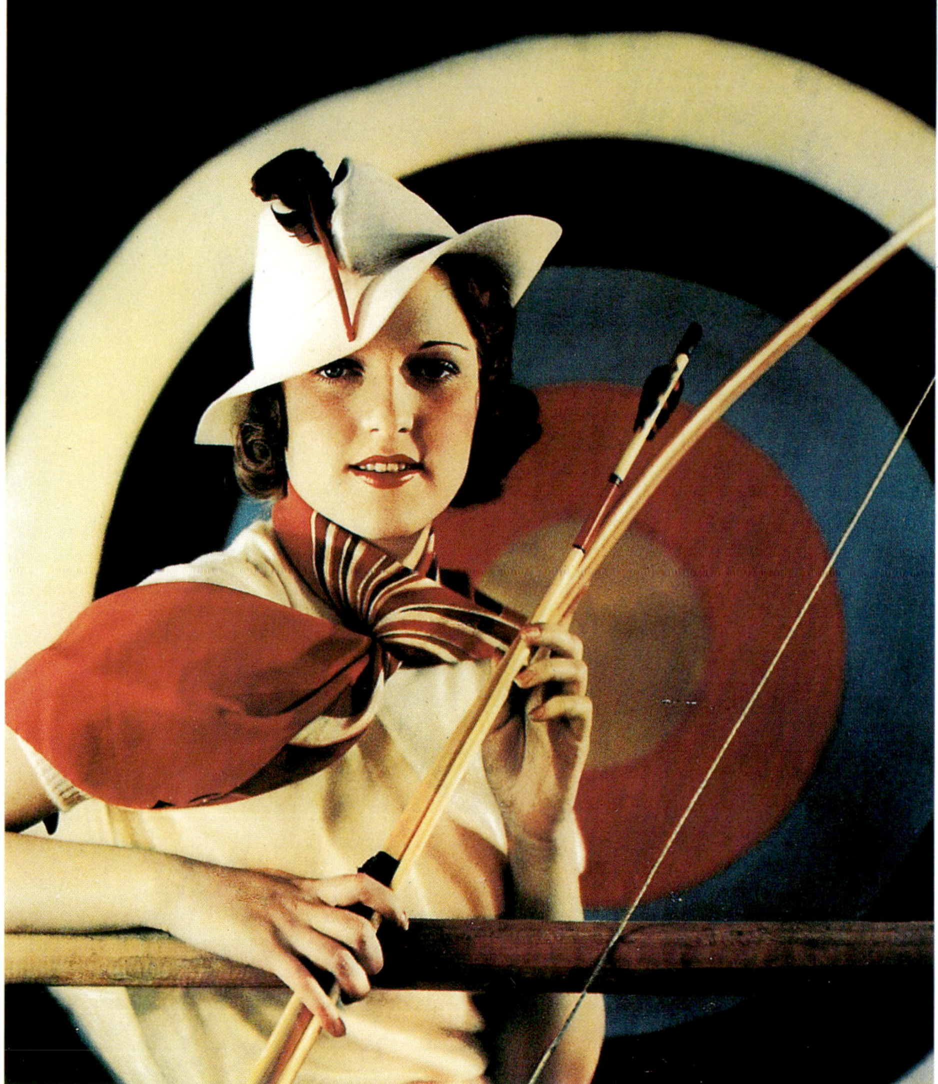

ALFRED C. JOHNSTON,
The Target,
Carbro print,
circa 1938,
George C. Rinhart Collection.

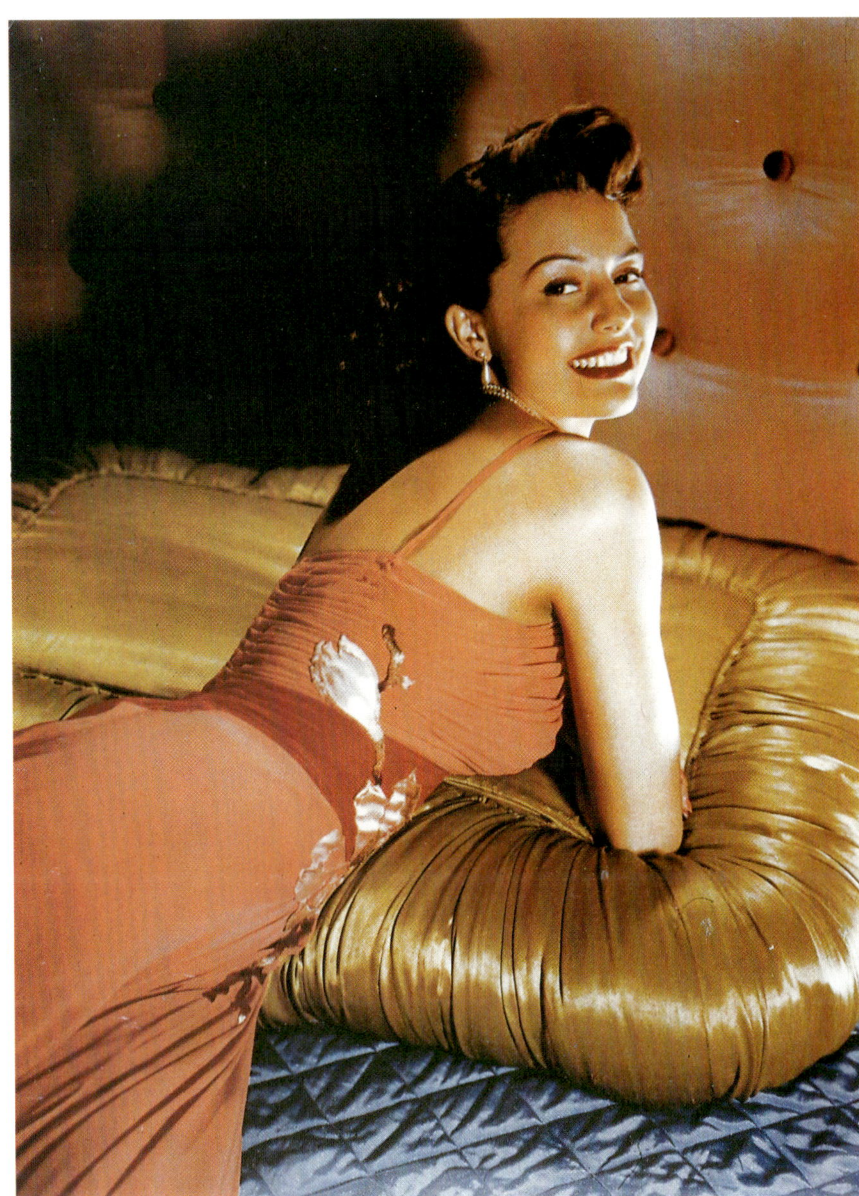

Clarence Sinclair Bull, *Cyd Charisse,* 1947, Kobal Collection, London.

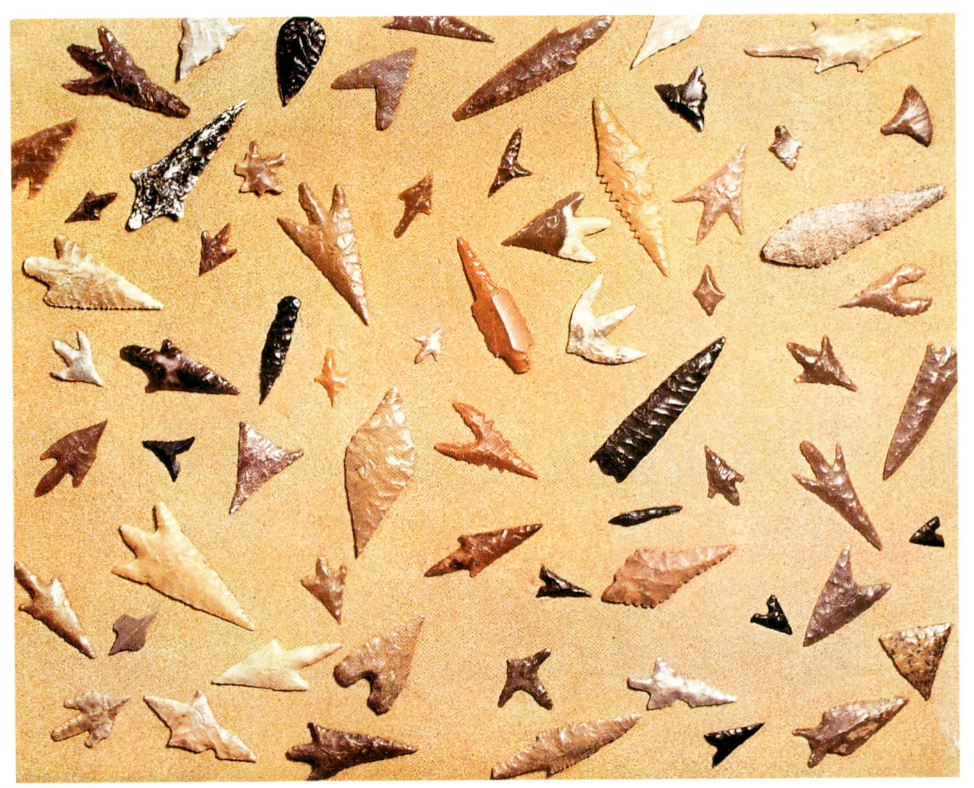

Marcel Bovis, *Stone-Age arrow-heads from the Sahara,* cover photograph for *Algérie préhistorique,* 1958.

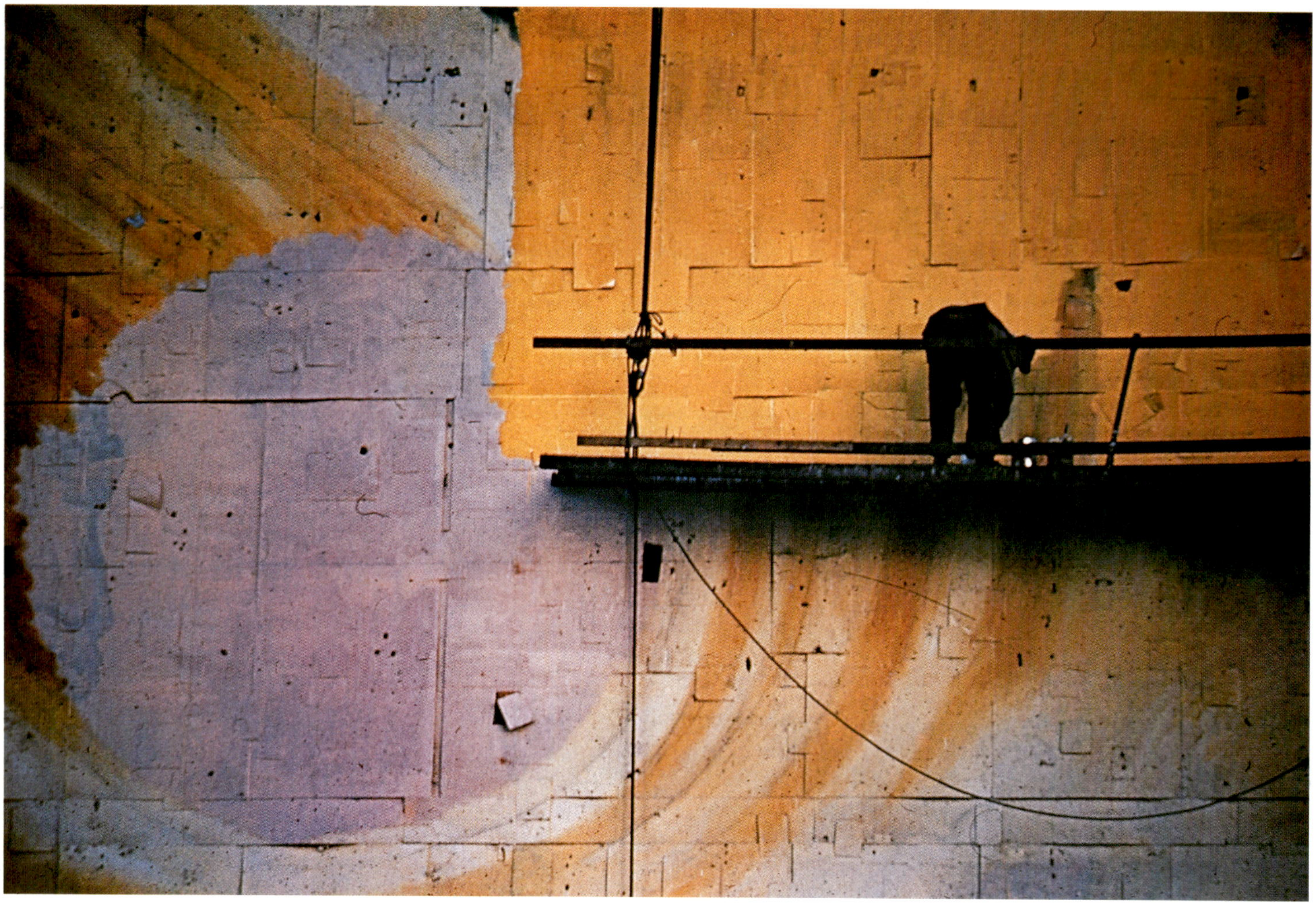

ERNST HAAS,
Sign-painter on Broadway,
1958.

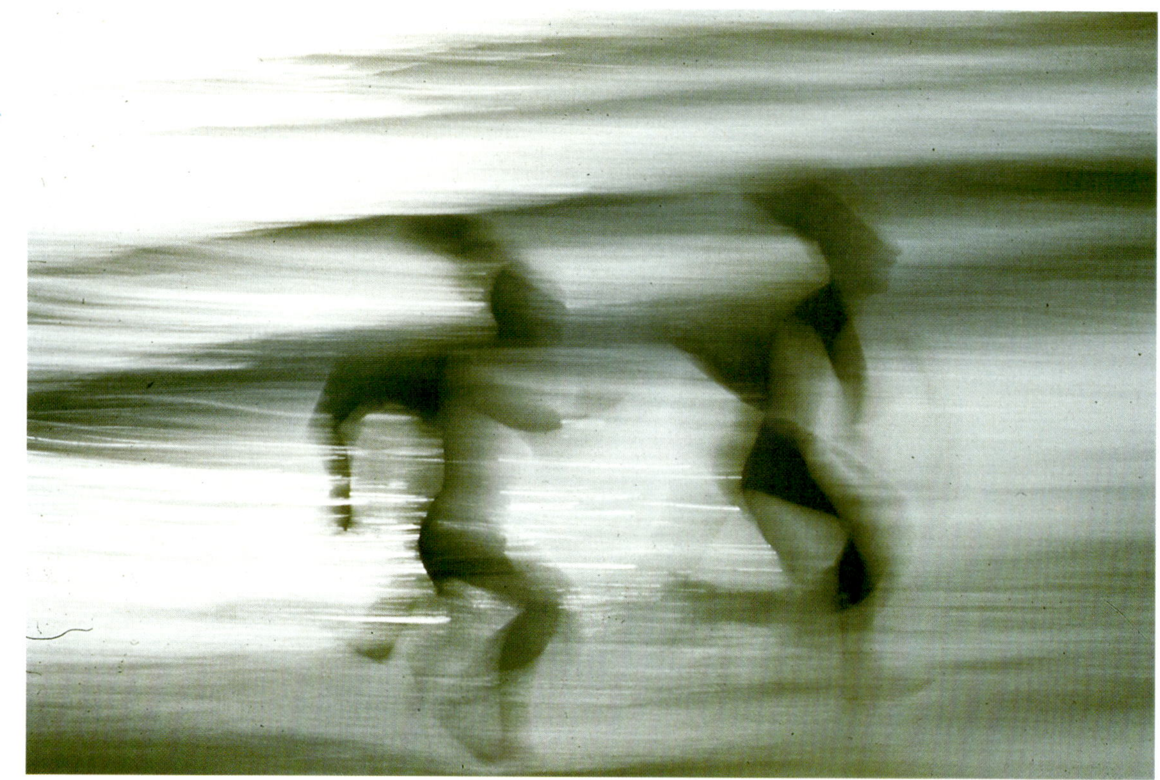

ERNST HAAS,
Race on the Beach,
circa 1960.

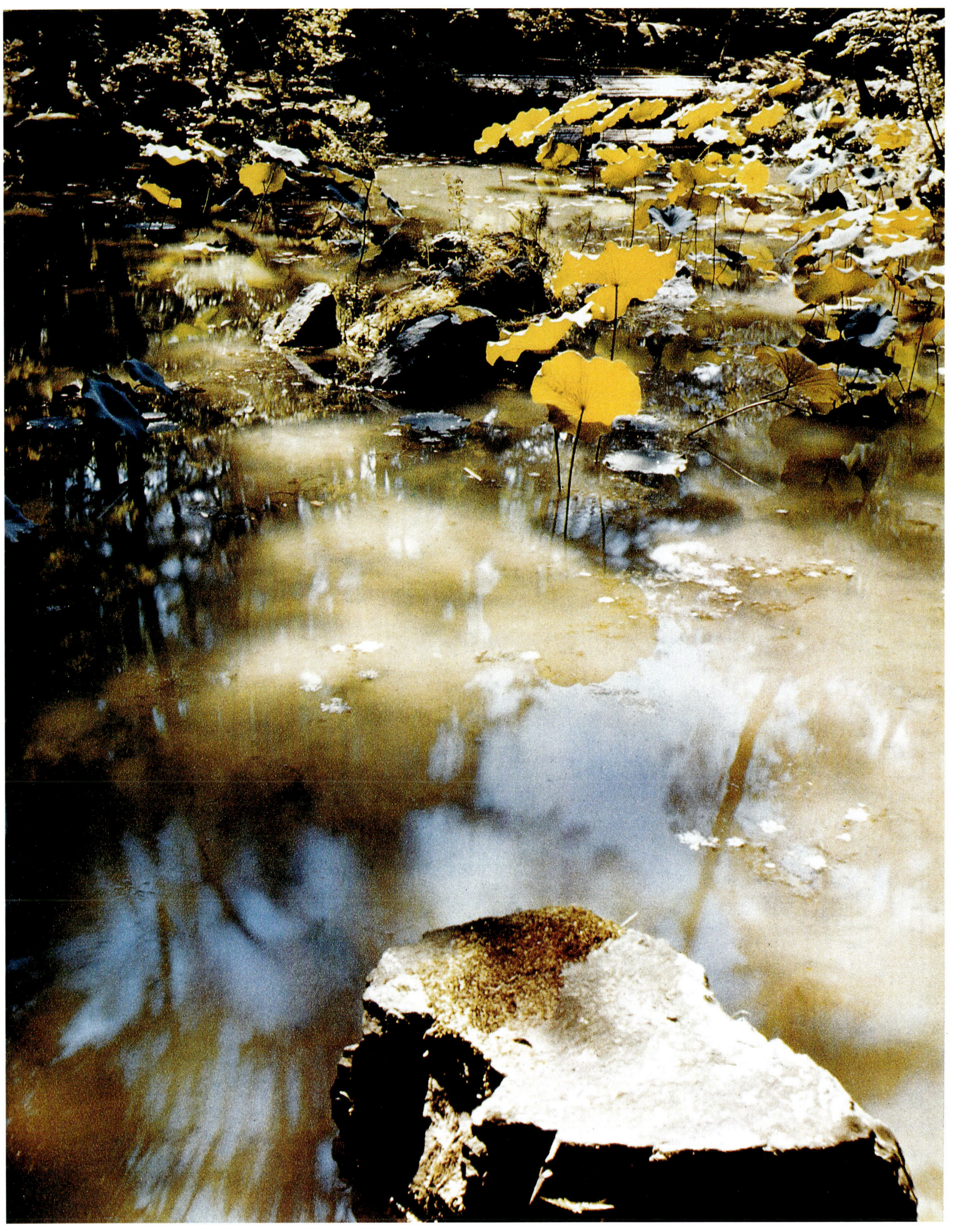

Werner Bischof,
Garden in Kyoto,
from *Japon,* Delpire, 1954.

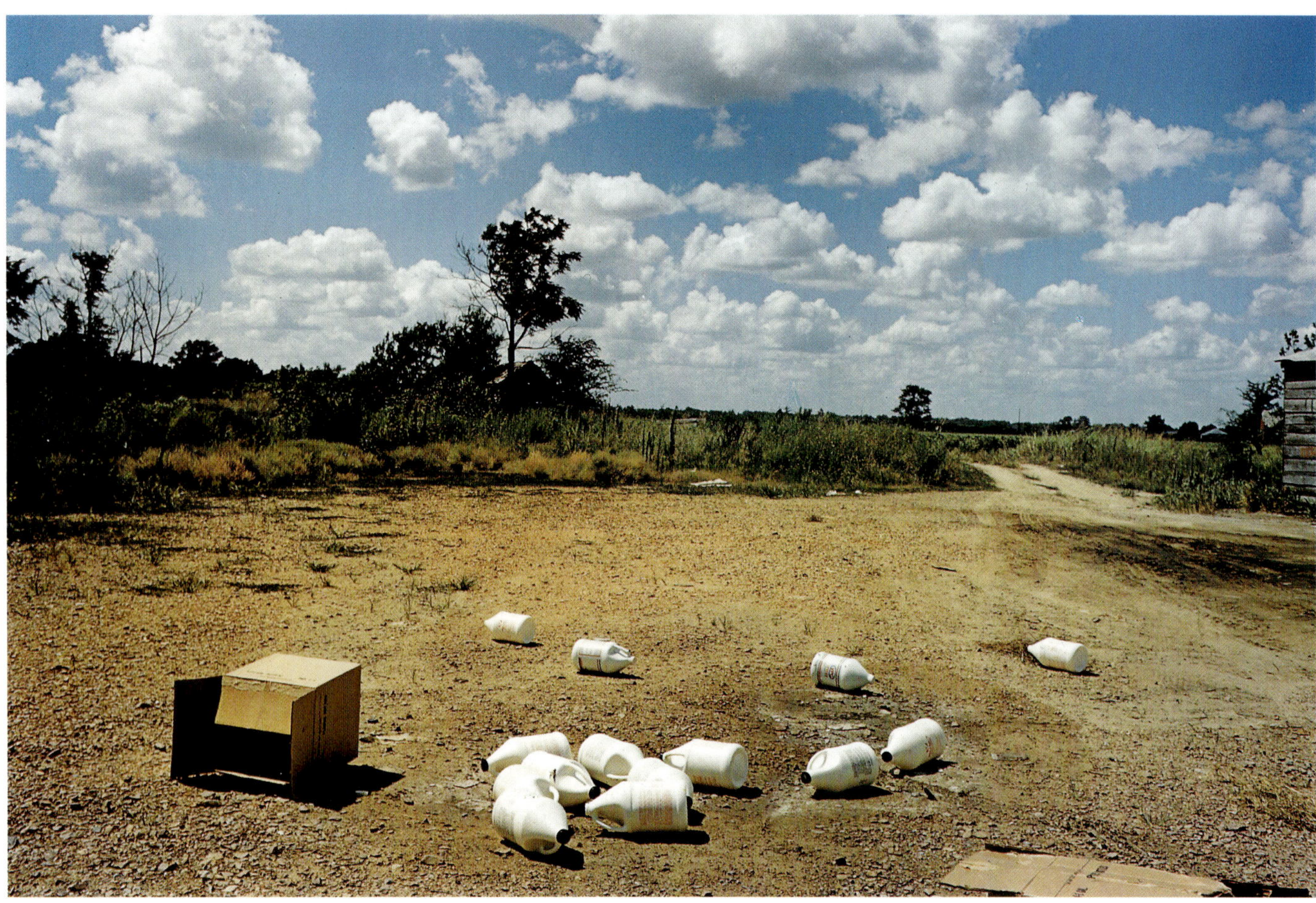

▲
William Eggleston,
Black Bayou Plantation, near Glendore, Missisipi,
1971, Marie Martin Gallery.

William Eggleston,
Tallahatchic County, Missisipi,
1971,
Marie Martin Gallery.
▼

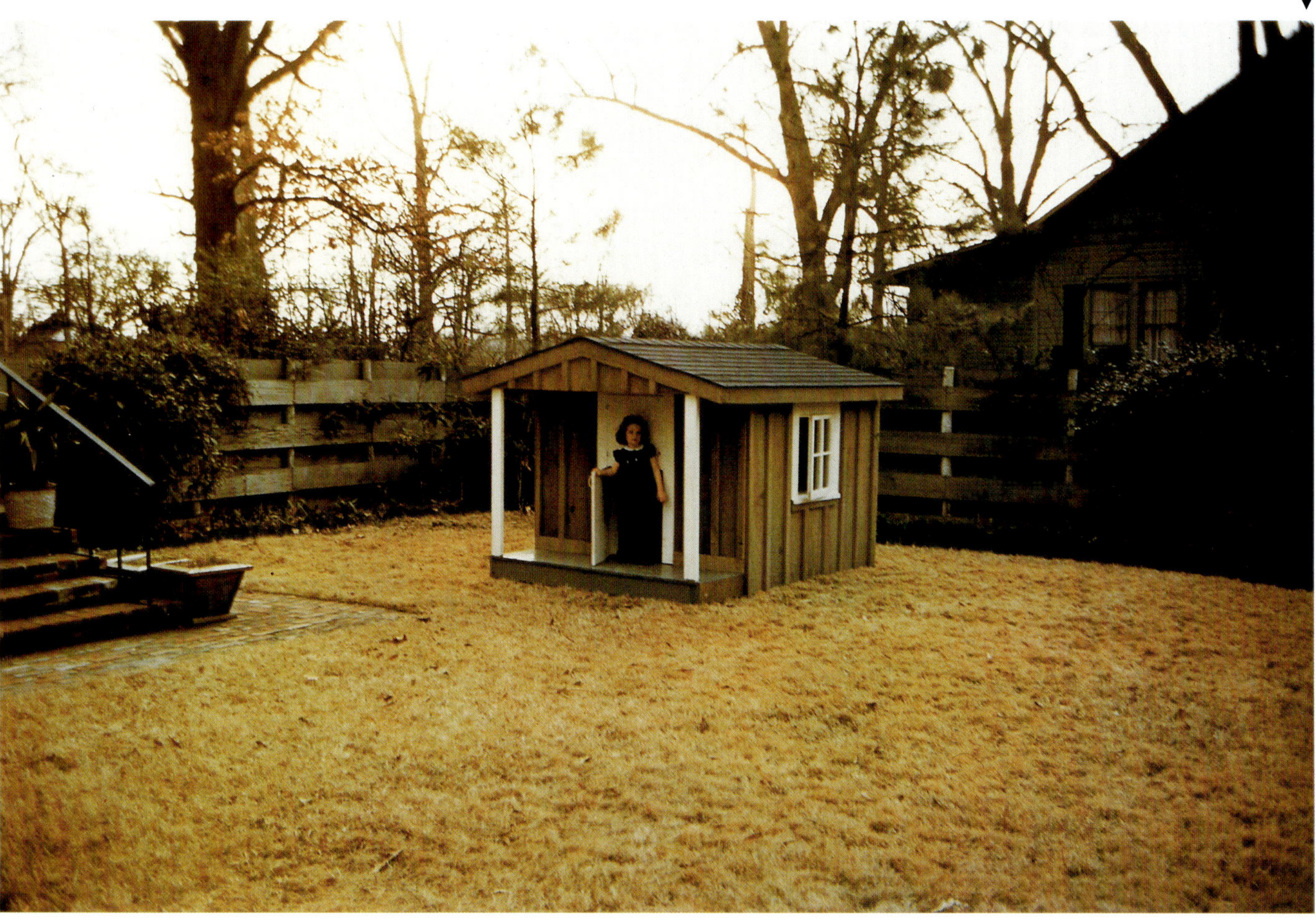

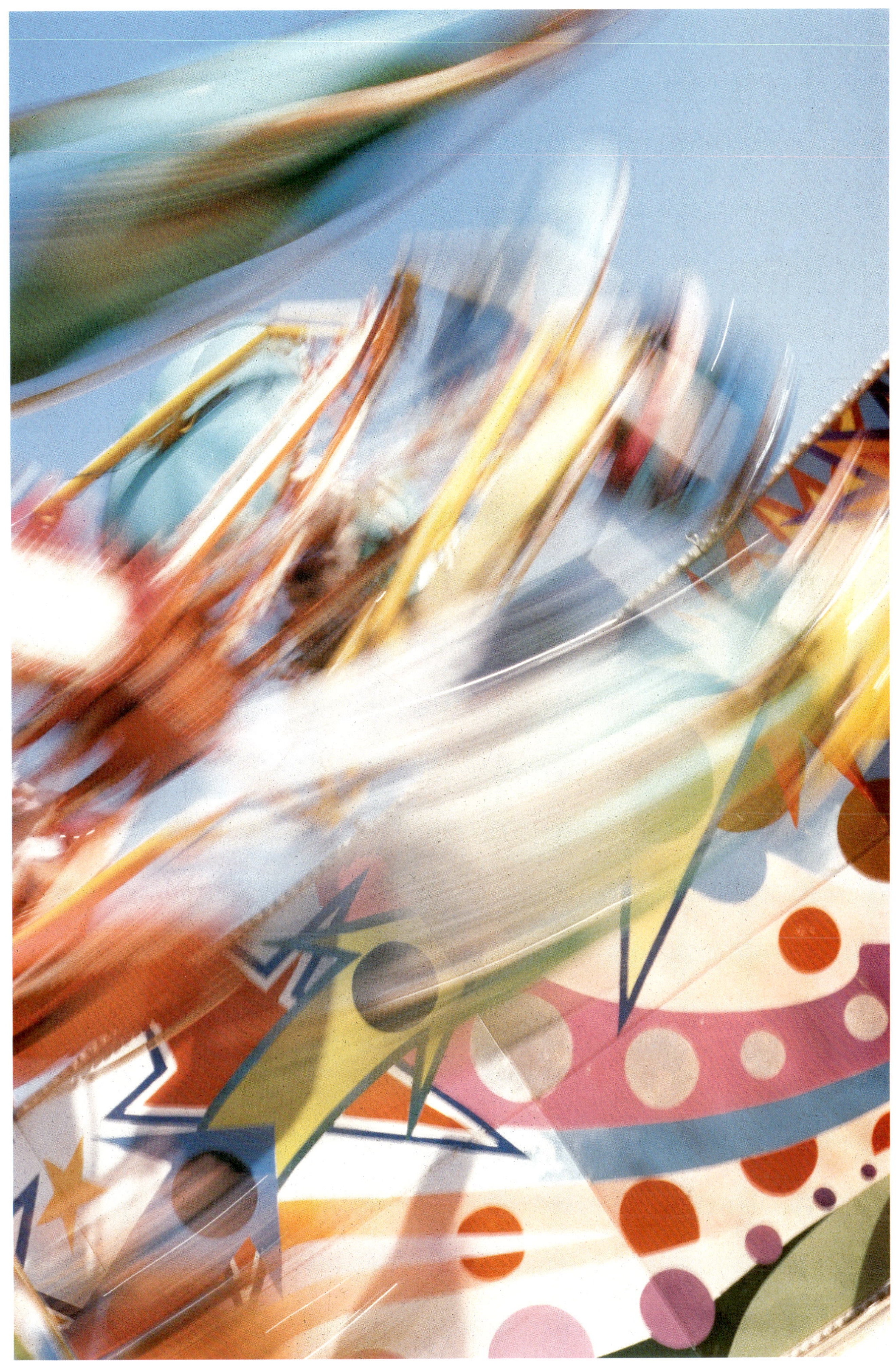

JOHN BATHO, *Carousel in Paris,* 1980.

LIFE

Vol. 3, No. 2

JULY 12, 1937

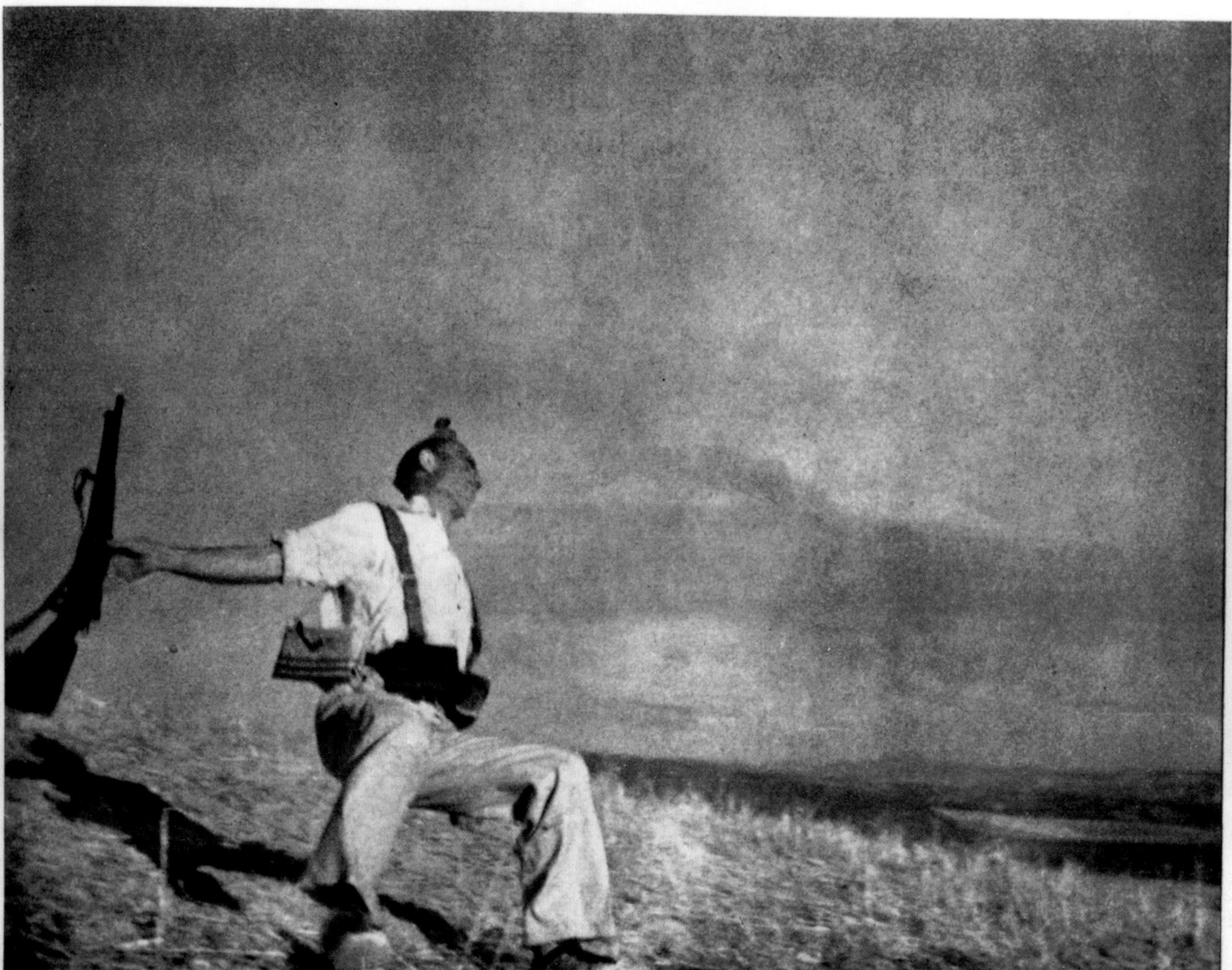

ROBERT CAPA'S CAMERA CATCHES A SPANISH SOLDIER THE INSTANT HE IS DROPPED BY A BULLET THROUGH THE HEAD IN FRONT OF CORDOBA

DEATH IN SPAIN: THE CIVIL WAR HAS TAKEN 500,000 LIVES IN ONE YEAR

On July 17 the Spanish Civil War will be one year old. In that time it has brought Death to 500,000 Spaniards, has shattered such ancient cities as Madrid, Toledo, Bilbao, Irun and Durango, has kept Europe in a state of jitters.

When the war started, most U. S. citizens looked on the Loyalists as a half-crazy, irresponsible, murderous scum that had turned on its honorable betters. A year of war has taught the U. S. more of Spain.

The ruling classes of Spain were probably the world's worst bosses—irresponsible, arrogant, vain, ignorant, shiftless and incompetent. Some 20,000 landlords owned 50% of the land. They did not give their field hands modern machinery or their land modern irrigation. They refused to rent unused land to landless peasants for fear of giving the peasants dangerous ideas of ownership. The land was only about 25% efficient and much of it was idle. And Spain's mineral resources, among the greatest in Europe, lay almost entirely unexploited. The aristocracy of Spain was still living on the interest on wealth brought home from the Americas by the gold fleets in the 16th Century.

To the 20,000 landlords, add 21,000 Army officers, more than twice the total of British Army officers. There was one officer for every six privates, one general for every 150 men. For every $3 spent on soldiers' pay, food, barracks, ammunition, officers got $10 in pay—25% of the national budget. The national law made officers semisacred. Just for pushing a policeman of the swank Civil Guard, six Americans got six months in jail in 1935.

Add to the 41,000 landlords and officers, 100,000 clergy, the most top-heavy Church hierarchy in the world, next to Tibet. These also were paid by the State. The Church, with its enormous wealth, naturally took a capitalist's position. It was up to its neck in politics. Peasants were told that to vote against the Conservatives was usually a mortal sin. The Church was in charge of Spanish education. Result: the Spanish people were 45% illiterate. The reason for the civil war was simply that the people of Spain had fired their bosses for flagrant incompetence and the bosses had refused to be fired.

For a new movie of the Spanish war from the Government side, turn page.

CLOSE WITNESSES

The involvement of the photojournalist

Fred Ritchin

Intrinsically linked with the public world of printed media and with the maneuverability of cameras, photojournalism, which was born at the start of the twentieth century, appeared as a means of showing to the world the evidence for crimes against humanity, to display through images proof of the unbelievable. A language was forged in adversity – a tragic history related through photography – until a crisis of loyalty occurred. The contradictions of the Vietnam war would arouse the protests of the politically committed photographer, who henceforth denounced the hypocrisy of the cause of the conflict and its gratuitous violence. But does photographic clarity still have a role to play in struggles between the media?

There had already been many important photographs of that most apocalyptic of human events, war – Roger Fenton's work in the Crimea, the images of the American Civil War by Mathew Brady and Alexander Gardner, Agustin Casasola's photographs of the Mexican Revolution. However, there had not been the sophisticated printing and photographic technology, nor the enthusiastic audience, which would have allowed these photographs to be widely reproduced and distributed.

By 1938, however, when twenty-five-year-old Robert Capa was called "the Greatest War-Photographer in the World" by the British magazine *Picture Post*, the technology had improved vastly and the audience had become enormous.[1] Photographically illustrated magazines, as well as newspapers, had become a fundamental part of people's lives on both sides of the Atlantic, and war, courtesy of photography, had just begun to enter people's living rooms in a timely and visually forceful way.

"This is War!"

War photography requires, first of all, a war. This it had found two years earlier when Loyalists and Fascists began to do battle in the Spanish Civil War, which would become the prelude to the Second World War. Wars are, because of and in spite of their destructiveness, highly photogenic. They are an example of what Wilson Hicks, *Life* magazine's early picture editor, called "a self-contained and well-paced drama" whose "crises come put up in handy packages".[2]

There were, of course, many wars between the invention of photography and the outbreak of the Spanish Civil War. It was, however, the first conflict in which small portable cameras such as the Leica or the Ermanox, and faster, more light-sensitive films were available. These two technological achievements allowed photographers to depict, for the first time, the battle as it was unfolding. Rather than bringing large heavy cameras on tripods and horse-drawn darkrooms onto the field after the battle was finished – as was done in war photography's early days – a photographer could go into the trenches with the troops, and follow them as they moved on. As Capa himself put it in his most famous statement, "If your pictures aren't good enough, you aren't close enough". This statement, like Capa himself, was a mixture of bravado and compassion – one was now expected to risk one's life in the line of fire while trying to empathize with those on the other side of the lens.[3]

This combination of action and empathy proved very attractive for both the publishers and readers of Western picture magazines. Germany, France, the United States, and Britain all boasted sophisticated mass-circulation publications that had appeared since 1928. The *Berliner Illustrierte*

◄ Robert Capa, *Spanish soldier, page from* **Life**, vol. 3, no. 2, July 12, 1937.

1. *Picture Post*, December 3, 1938.

2. W. Hicks, *Words and Pictures: An Introduction to Photojournalism*, New York, Harper and Brothers, 1952.

3. See R. Whelan, *Robert Capa*, New York, Knopf, 1985.

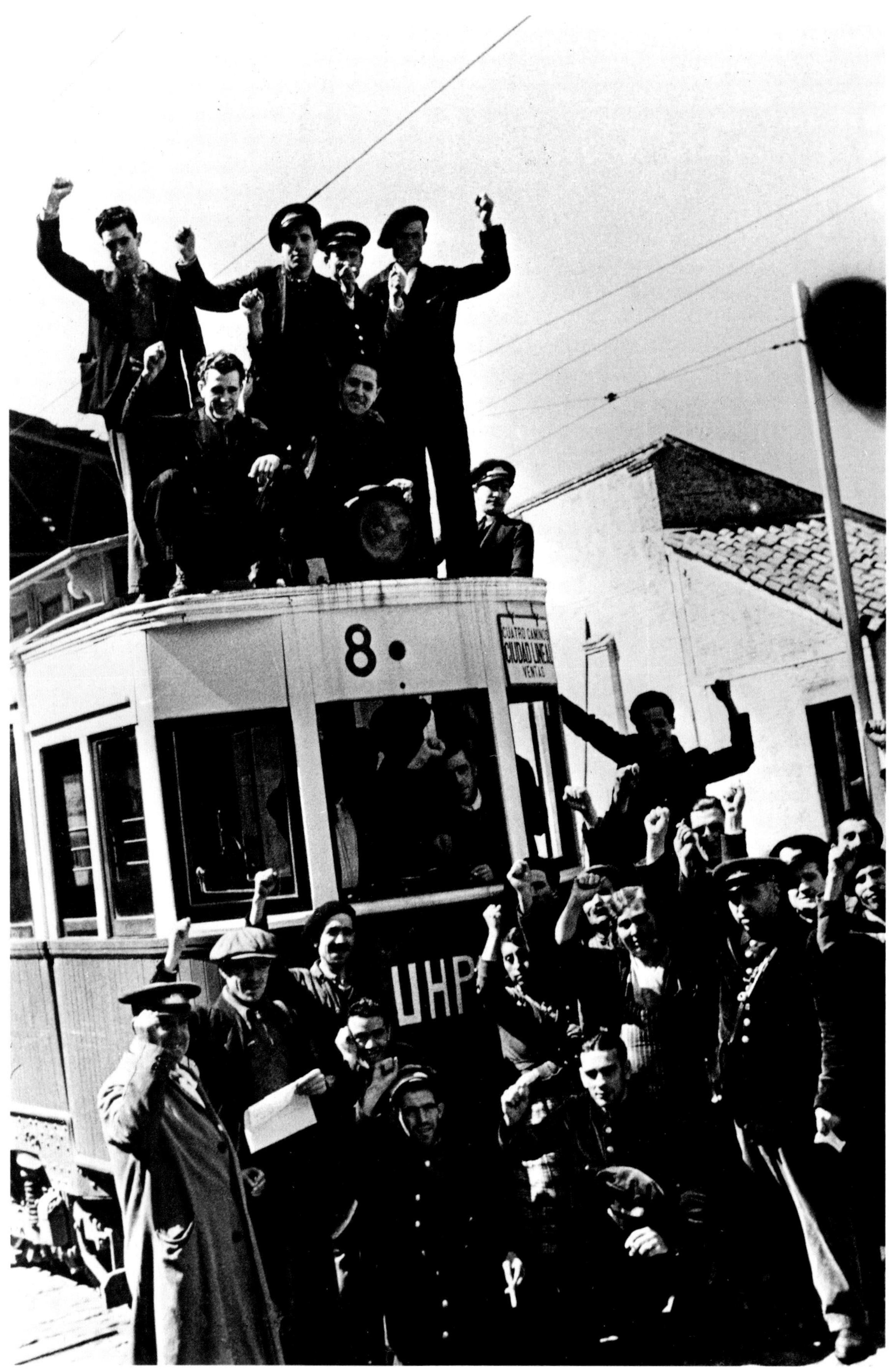

Robert Capa,
Madrid,
1936.

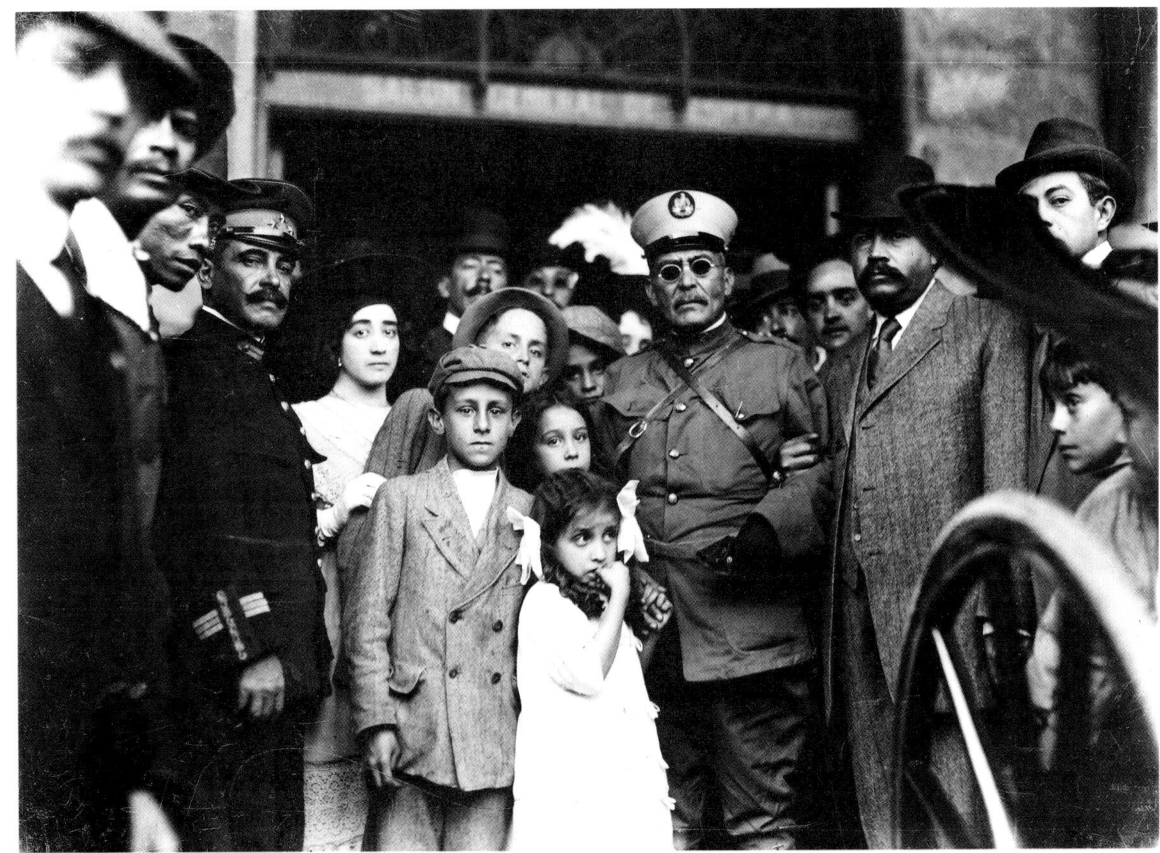

CASASOLA Collection,
The Victorious General Huerta,
Mexico, 1912,
Casasola Archives,
Mexico.

Zeitung would reach a weekly circulation of some 2 million copies; *Life* magazine sold all 466,000 copies of its first issue in 1936. Photography, so similar to human sight, allowed people vicariously to experience what was going on beyond their circumscribed routines.

For the reader, the experience of being exposed to such lifelike representations of events one had never seen could be intense. In this context, the words written about Capa's photographs that were published on eleven pages following the "Greatest War-Photographer" accolade in *Picture Post* are revealing. Headlined "This is War!" – as if one were seeing war for the very first time – twenty-six images from one battle were shown as "the finest pictures of front-line action ever taken".[4] One caption boasted that "you can almost smell the powder in this picture".

Another, next to a photograph of soldiers sitting under an overhanging rock with thin smoke hanging in the almost empty background, is particularly telling. Entitled "In the Heart of the Battle: The Most Amazing War Picture Ever Taken", the caption reads: "This is not practice. This is war. These men crouching beneath the ledge feel the shock of every shell-burst. They know that a better aim will bring their own piece of rock down on top of them. They know that in a minute's time they may be ordered forward over the shell-swept ground. They are not worrying. This is war, and they are used to it."

ERICH SALOMON,
Diplomats
(including Aristide Briand and Pierre Laval),
from *Berliner Illustrierte Zeitung,*
July 31, 1931,
Rheinisches Bildarchiv,
Cologne.
▼

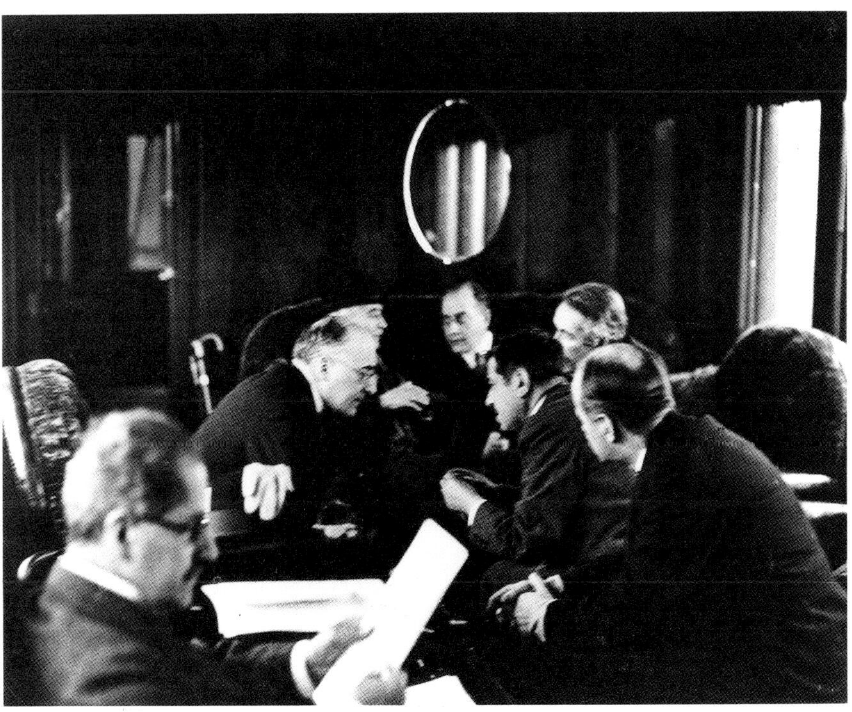

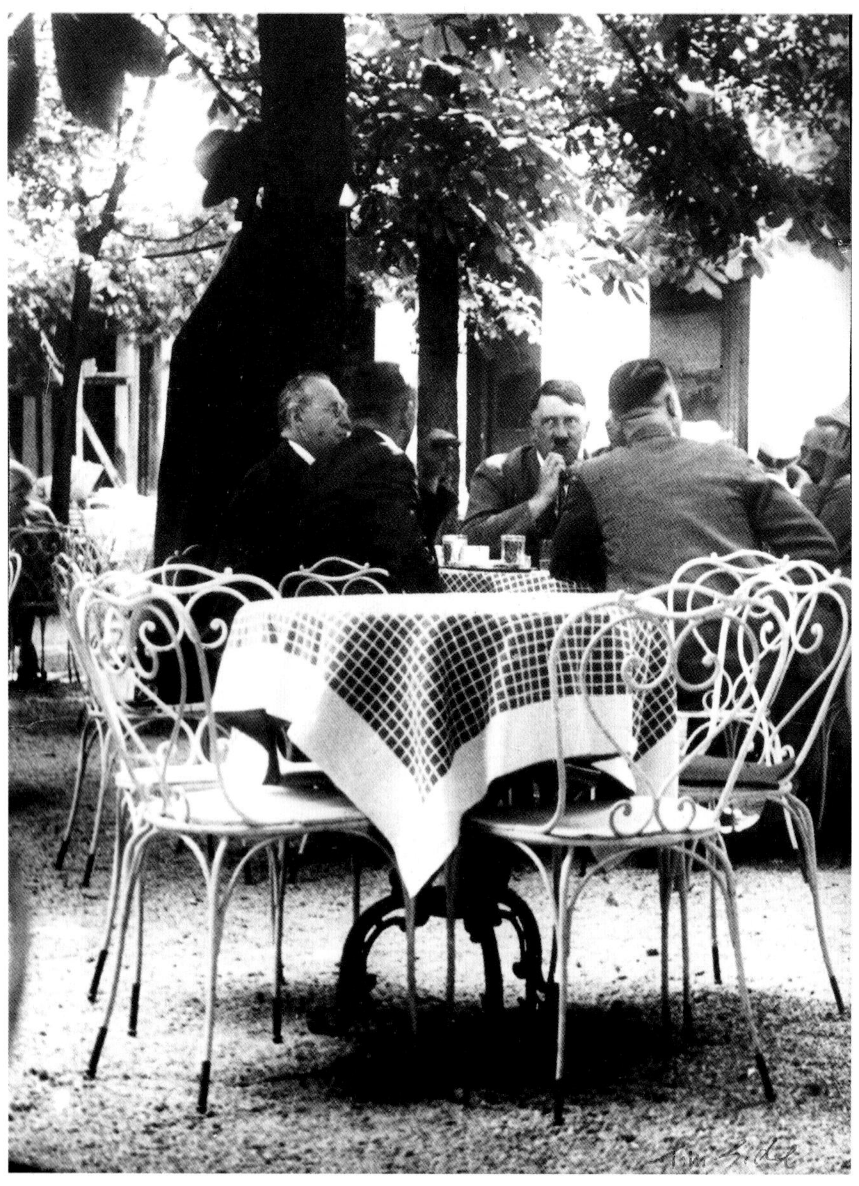

TIM GIDAL,
In the Biergarten, Munich,
1929.

uncrossable boundary, death, while remaining physically unscathed – even, perhaps, while drinking a coffee.

However, photography involved much more than experiencing the heights of human drama – something which painting had long allowed the viewer. The key component of photography was its apparent mechanical "objectivity", the sense that had anyone else been there they would have seen basically the same scene. The image, it was thought, did not come from its creator's imagination, but primarily from reality itself.

Photoreportage and the media

The success of photoreportage in the mass media would have been impossible before the Scientific Revolution (with its belief that external, concrete, verifiable forces were at work, molding the world) and before the Industrial Revolution (with its faith in machinery's virtues). Photography gave a sense of heightened reality. Looking at a photograph of a scene or an event could, and would, be viewed as equivalent to actually being there. So that, as Susan Sontag pointed out in her book *On Photography*, tourists quickly visit a scene in order to photograph it and thereby possess it, rather than experience it personally.[5]

Picture magazines capitalized on this thirst. *Life* magazine, for example, promised to allow the reader "To see life; to see the world; to eyewitness great events; to watch the faces of the poor and the gestures of the proud; to see strange things – machines, armies, multitudes, shadows in the jungle and on the moon [...] to see and to take pleasure in seeing; to see and be amazed; to see and be instructed."[6] Eight years earlier, in 1928, *VU* magazine trumpeted its *raison d'être* in its first issue somewhat similarly: "There is no picture magazine here [in France] which expresses the speeded-up rhythm of present-day life, a magazine that informs and documents all the manifestations of contemporary life: political events, scientific discoveries, disasters, exploration, sports exploits, theater, film, art and fashion. *VU* has taken upon itself to fill this gap [...] Animated like a fine film, *VU* will be awaited each week by all its readers."[7]

There are similarities between each statement, as well as divergences that begin to suggest certain cultural differences. Whereas *VU* magazine was seen in part as depicting the rhythm of life while being "animated like a fine film" in order to inform, *Life* was about seeing things, places, events, people. This difference between the two statements is essentially that which exists between photojournalism and reportage, two terms which are generally used interchangeably.

As a measure of how far we have come, and the multitude of photographic images we have been exposed to in the half-century since "The Most Amazing War Picture Ever Taken" was published, it can be noted that today this photograph would almost certainly be discarded. As a photograph of battle it lacks dynamism, action, and involvement – the very elements for which it was praised over half a century ago.

In 1938, however, before the advent of television, before movies became omnipresent and foreign travel *de rigueur*, the photographic image on the page was fascination itself. While sitting in relative comfort in their homes, people could entertain the illusion that the battlefield had entered their living room. It was possible to identify, or at least empathize, with someone else's perils, power, and adventure. The much more famous photograph taken by Capa two years earlier, showing a Loyalist soldier falling at the instant of his death, allowed the reader to come close to the most powerful unknown, the one

4. "This is War!", *Picture Post*, December 3, 1938.

5. See S. Sontag, *On Photography*, New York, Farrar, Straus and Giroux, 1977.

6. Quoted in P. B. Kunhardt, Jr. (ed.), *Life: The First 50 Years 1936–86* Boston, Little, Brown and Company, 1986, p. 5.

7. *VU*, March 21, 1928, p. 11.

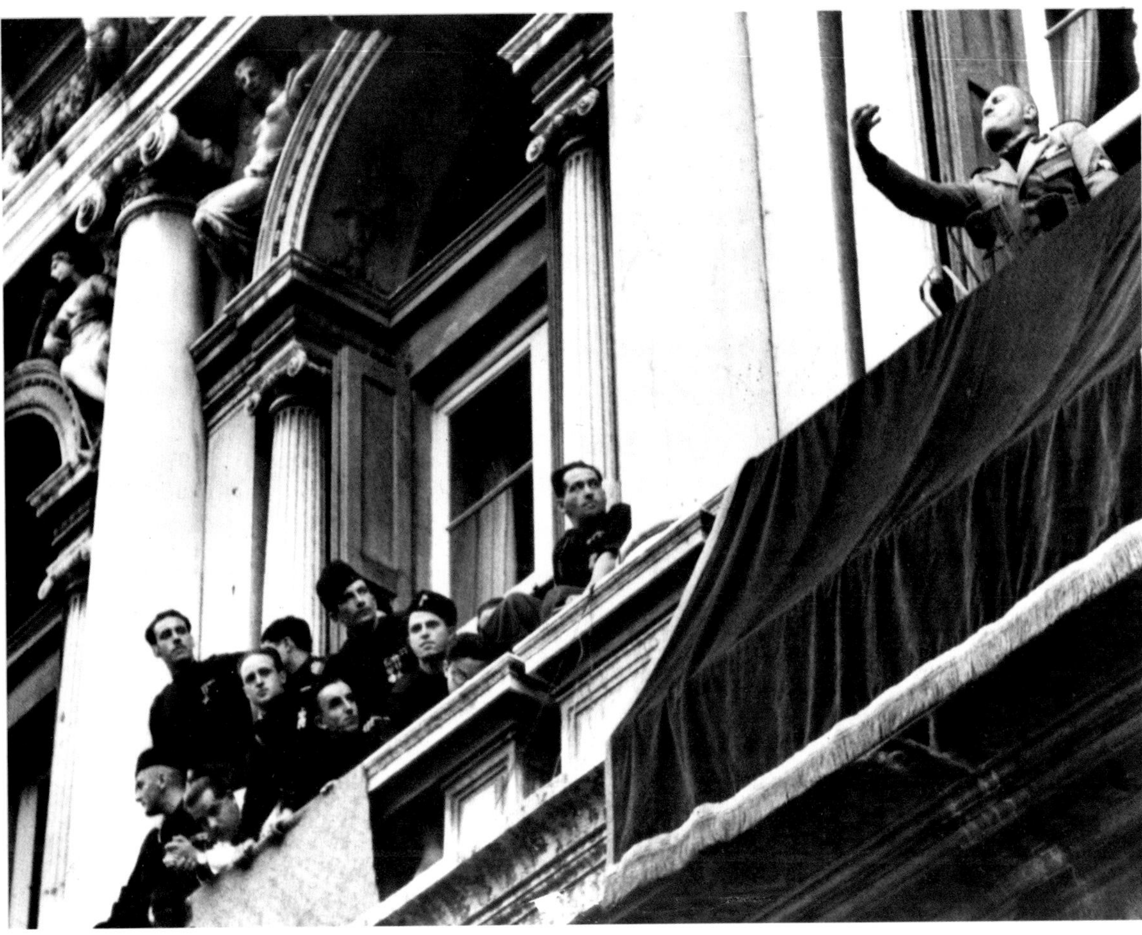

ALFRED EISENSTAEDT,
Mussolini,
Piazza San Marco,
1934.

A. PORRY-PASTOREL,
Mussolini Arrested during a Demonstration,
1914,
Zannier Collection,
Museo Alinari
Florence.

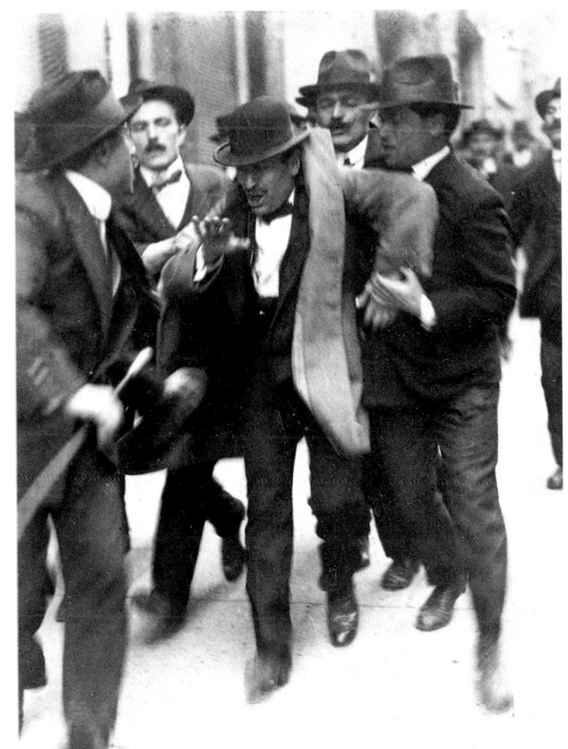

The French concept of reportage, which involves the articulation of the rhythm of events (one thinks of the work of Henri Cartier-Bresson, for example), is in fact different from the American concept of photojournalism, which targets key players in a manner that is more direct and with less visual nuance. It also reflects differences between the two languages – French adopting an approach that is more indirect than American-English which is generally quite concrete. Like language, photography can also be articulated differently.

An amusing and telling anecdote about Cartier-Bresson concerns how he went about covering the coronation of King George VI in 1937, when on assignment for *Ce Soir* newspaper. Despite having a much coveted entry pass to the coronation, he preferred to concentrate on those spectators who were less well-connected and, from distant view-points, craned to see what was going on, even sitting on each other's shoulders. It was in their body language, their straining credulity at the periphery, that he found the rhythm and essence of the event – not in its purported center according to photojournalistic convention.

It is interesting, then, to look at the publicity brochure for an illustrated magazine in the Soviet Union, *U.S.S.R in Construction*. In its first editorial it conceived a use for photography quite different

8. See S. Morozov and V. Lloyd, *Soviet Photography: An Age of Realism*, New York, 1984; S. Morozoc *et al.*(eds.), *Russian Photographs, 1917–1940*, New York, 1983.

The Leica

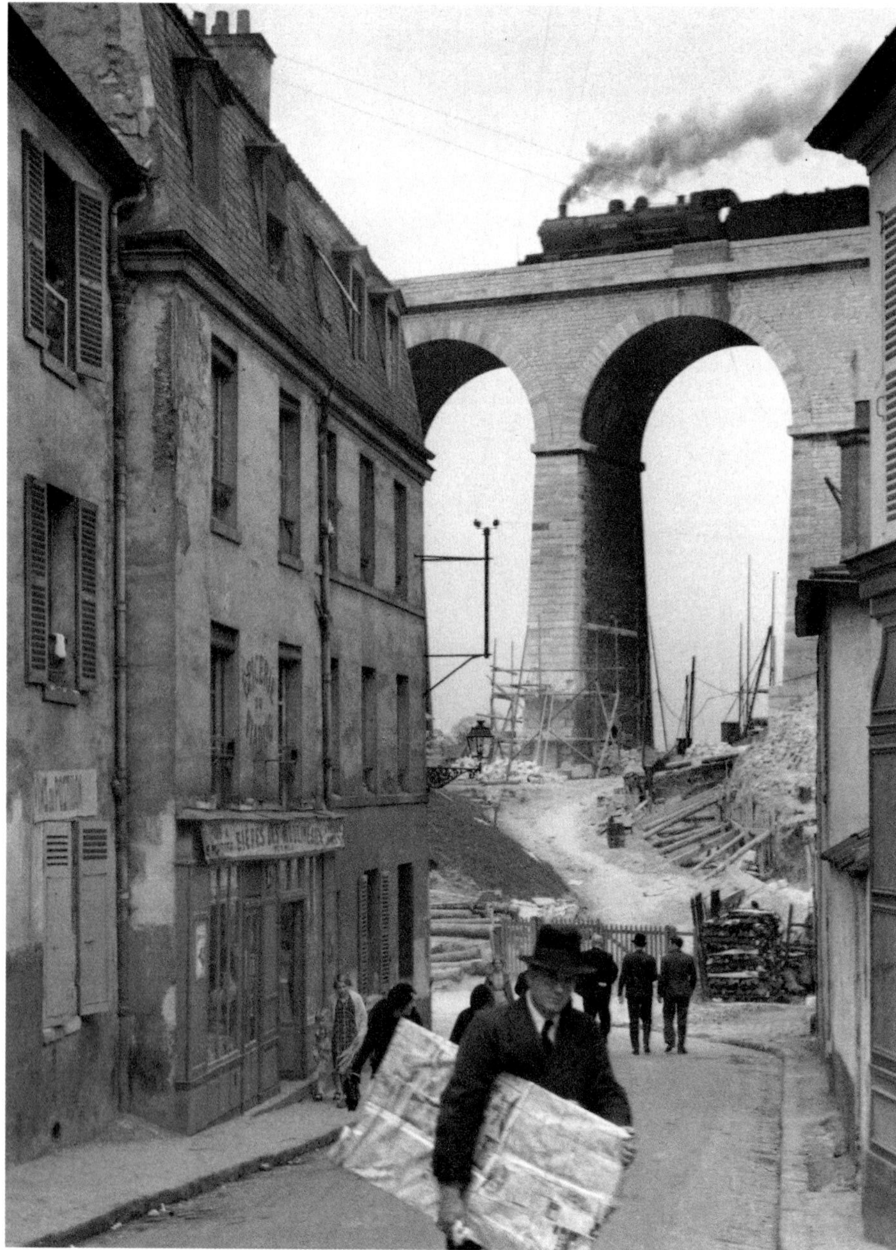

André Kertész,
Meudon,
1928, Ministère de la Culture, Paris.

Taken on by Ernst Leitz in 1911 as head of research into microscopy, Oscar Barnack first built a movie camera. Unfortunately, cinematographic emulsions at that time were of uneven sensitivity. Unsatisfied with the results obtained, Barnack invented a small metal still camera in order to test the development time of cinema films. Its characteristics were identical to that of the movie camera (same way of altering the shutter speed, same film, same lens, a 50mm f/3.5 Kino-Tessar). This allowed him to take a few frames every time a movie was being shot, to develop them immediately, and thus to work out the correct average time for this operation.

In order to be able to see the test shots better, Barnack created in 1913 a new camera which linked up two normal-sized film images, thus inventing the 24 x 36 mm format. First called "U.R.", this camera, equipped with a retractable 42mm f/4.5 Milar lens, took 2 meters of 35mm cine film and possessed a knurled knob which allowed the film to be wound on while setting the focal-plane shutter, as well as a rotating screen which closed the lens during this operation. This synchronization speeded up the shooting process and avoided double exposures. Henceforth this invention would go everywhere in its inventor's pocket. He was a keen traveler – and the photos taken were of astonishing quality.

Research was interrupted for a time by the war. As soon as hostilities were over, Barnack took the work up again, asking the chief optician at the factory, Max Berek, to design a new, faster lens which was specially adapted to the 24 x 36 format, the Elmax, a 50mm opening to f/3.5, soon to be replaced in turn by the famous Elmar.

Up until then small cameras had always been basically equipped with a frame-type of viewfinder lacking any optical system – thus being subject to parallax and unexact in their framing of the picture area. Finally Barnack fitted a Newton-type viewer to his camera, an eyepiece with a diverging lens, giving an exact, aligned, and reduced version of the field of vision.

The first 31 handmade Leicas were given to professionals with the job of testing them. Their opinion was somewhat unfavorable: the format was too small. Yet production went ahead in 1924, and the first Leica (an abbreviation of Leitz Camera) appeared at the Leipzig trade fair the following year. It had a fixed lens, was loaded with metal film magazines containing 40 shots, and had a curtain-type shutter and an adjustable distance meter. 1,000 cameras were sold in the first year, as many as 15,000 in 1929.

Success had arrived, the more so as Paul Wolff, the "Leica wizard", would display at numerous exhibitions and lectures on instantaneous photography landscapes or still-lifes which were of perfect technical quality.

The Leica produced a large offspring, and improvements followed year by year. In 1932 the Leitz company launched the first camera with an integral focusing mechanism, coupled with a complete range of interchangeable lenses, removable backs, and a shutter speed range increased both in the slow and the fast range (up to 1/1,000 second in 1933).

This discreet instrument, being solid, quick to use, and capable of producing good images in all circumstances, with its cheap films (ranging from a fine-grain 4 ASA to the "ultra-rapid" 50 ASA) would, despite the reservations of press photographers and printers (who referred to the "postage-stamp" format), become the favorite tool of numerous photojournalists.

Masters such as Henri Cartier-Bresson and André Kertész would use the Leica to create dynamic images that were full of life. Increases in the Leica range and of accessories, together with the appearance of color, meant that the Leica would triumph and be copied throughout the world.

Jean-Claude Gautrand

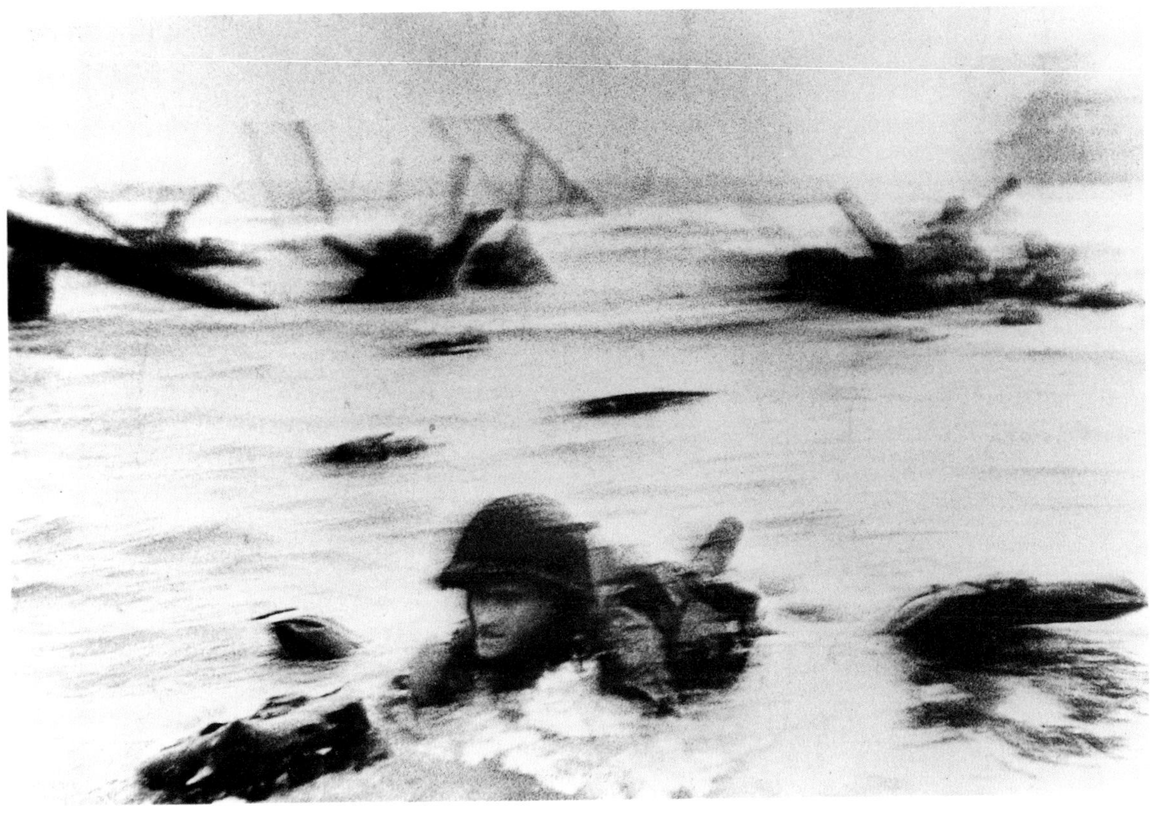

ROBERT CAPA,
Omaha Beach,
June 6, 1944.

from that of most of the Western press: "Photography must serve the country, not in a haphazard, unsystematic way but constantly and according to plan." Many Soviet press photographers concentrated on themes such as the advancement of the worker through education or training or the country's increasing mechanization and productivity.[8] For example, Max Alpert, a member of the Union of Russian Proletarian Photographers, worked on a series of photographs of a young volunteer worker who went from illiterate laborer to first-class builder during the first five-year plan in a town where massive steel factories were being built. Similarly, three photographers including Alpert (the others were A. Shaikhet and S. Tules) who were members of the Soyuzfoto agency that had been founded in 1926, produced an early photo-story about the life of a typical Russian worker's family. It attracted international attention, traveling abroad in 1931 to several venues as an exhibition of some 80 photographs and appearing in the popular and influential German weekly, the *Berliner Illustrierte Zeitung*.

Their style, however, was quite different from that of some other Soviet photographers, a difference which would have ideological repercussions. Those photographers working in the "October" group, the best-known among them being Alexander Rodchenko, took a more visually experimental, at times iconic, and less traditional approach to depicting the regime's achievements. When the approved strategy was to reach the masses and not the elite, aesthetic innovation could be a problem – Rodchenko was thrown out of "October" for being too formalist.

Germany, which boasted an extraordinarily lively photojournalistic press led by the *Berliner Illustrierte Zeitung* and the *Münchner Illustrierte Presse*, also supported a workers' illustrated press, most notably the popular weekly *AIZ* which reached a circulation of some half-million.[9] It featured, among other notable work, the extraordinary political photomontages of John Heartfield and contributions by worker-photographers who formed groups in cities

9. Special issue of *Creative Camera*, no. 197/198, May/June 1981, entitled "Der Arbeiter-Fotograf and the British Worker in Photographs, 1839–1939".

DMITRI BALDERMANTS
Attack,
1941,
Scott Hyde Collection.
▼

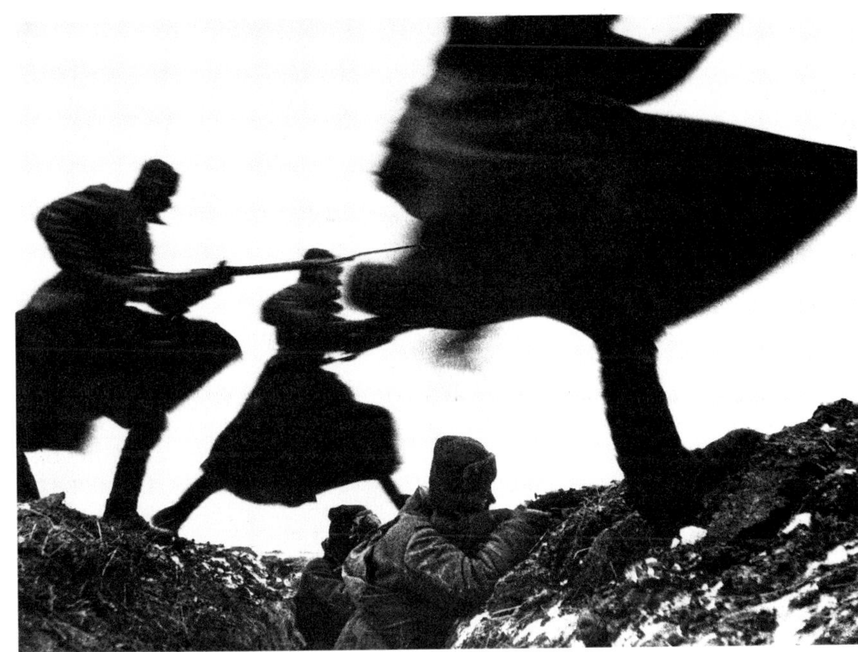

Magnum Photos

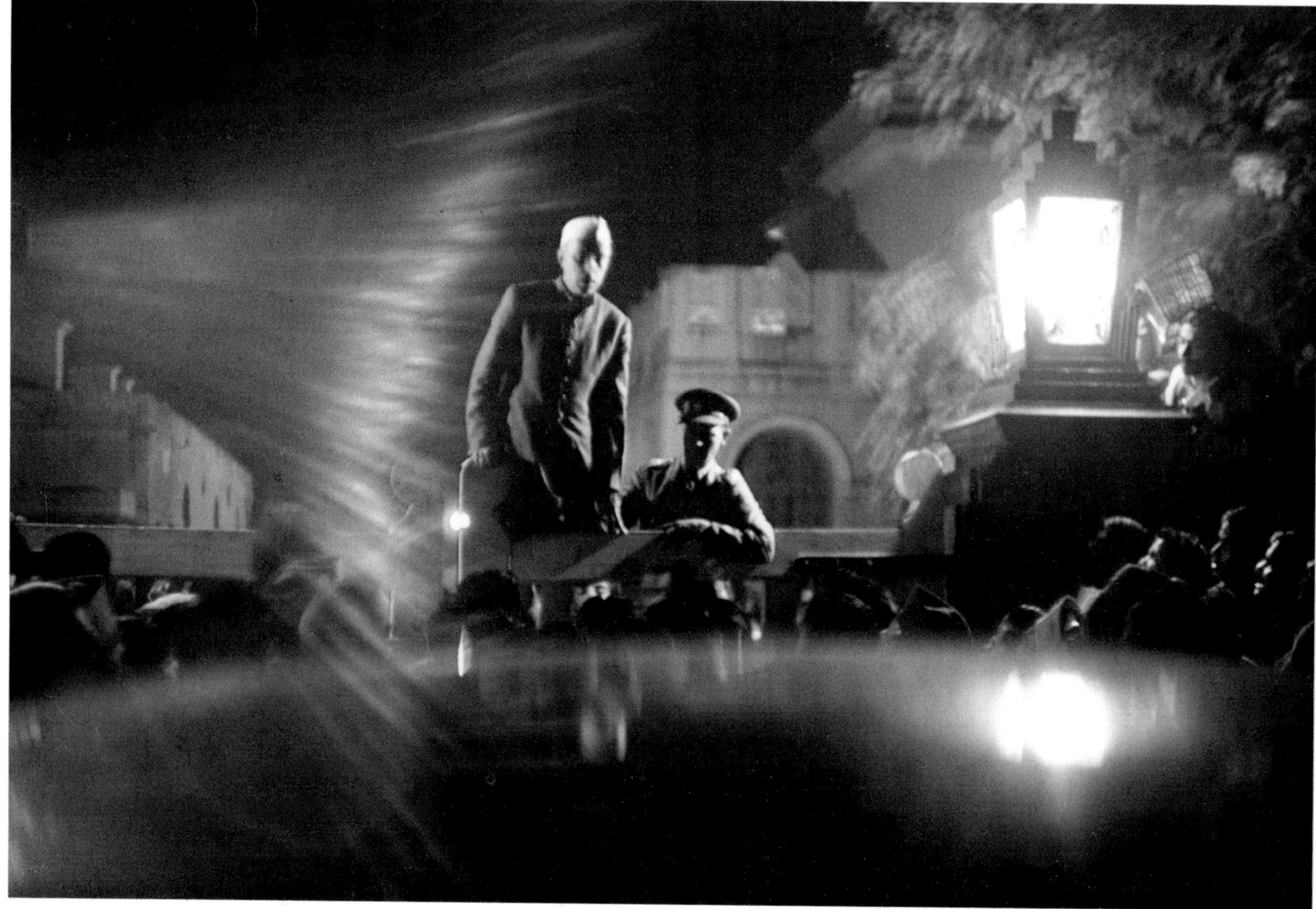

Henri Cartier-Bresson,
Nehru Announcing Gandhi's Death at the Gate of Birla House
1948.

Two years after the end of the Second World War, fueled by the sense of hope and optimism of the post-war years, a new kind of co-operative photographic agency, Magnum Photos, was founded by five photographers from as many countries: Robert Capa, a courageous, empathetic Hungarian, widely known for his coverage of war; Henri Cartier-Bresson, a peripatetic Frenchman and former painter inspired by Surrealism; George Rodger, a freelance photographer who, like Capa, had covered the war extensively but would concentrate for years on tribal Africa; David "Chim" Seymour, a gentle Pole who made sensitive images of children ravaged by war and portraits of intellectuals; and another war photographer who, like Capa and Rodger, had worked for *Life* magazine, William Vandivert from the United States (Vandivert left Magnum after only a year to concentrate on industrial photography). The two other original shareholders were Maria Eisner, who had previously run Alliance Photo, a Paris-based agency, and Rita Vandivert, who worked in London on the influential newsreels *March of Time*.

Capa's early guidance and his charismatic personality were critical to the agency's success. As fellow-founder George Rodger wrote about him: "He recognized the unique quality of miniature cameras, so quick and so quiet to use, and also the unique qualities that we ourselves had acquired during several years of contact with all the emotional excesses that go hand in hand with war. He saw a future for us in this combination of mini cameras and maxi minds."

Magnum Photos was special in several ways. Unlike a conventional agency in which photographers worked under the direction of others, it was co-operatively owned by the photographers themselves, who hired others to administer it but set their own goals. Also diverging from contemporary practice, Magnum's members insisted that they, and not the publications, retained the rights to their photographs. The point of the agency was to safeguard its members' freedom to photograph as they wanted without always having to respond to the dictates of the marketplace.

In its early years, Magnum suffered some terrible setbacks. In 1954, Robert Capa was killed by a landmine in Indo-China, and Werner Bischof, an early member (he had joined in 1949, a year before Ernst Haas), died in a jeep accident in Peru the same month. Chim, who took over the leadership from Capa, died two years later, accidentally, from gunfire at the Suez Canal. However, the remaining membership pulled together, the Magnum concept prevailed, and now, remarkably, over four decades later, Magnum's photographers continue to produce some of the most provocative reportage anywhere.

Photographic landmarks in the history of the agency include Henri Cartier-Bresson's *Decisive Moment*, Bruce Davidson's *East 100th Street*, Elliott Erwitt's *Photographs and Anti-Photographs*, Leonard Freed's *Black in White America*, Philip Jones Griffith's *Vietnam Inc.*, Josef Koudelka's *Gypsies*, and Susan Meiselas's *Nicaragua*. More recent achievements include *Exploding Into Life* by Eugene Richards and writer Dorothea Lynch, Sebastião Salgado's *Other Americas*, and Alex Webb's *Hot Light/Half-Made Worlds*. There are many more photographers – Magnum now has some three dozen members, as well as stringers, associates, and trainees, and offices in London, New York, Paris, and Tokyo – whose work is widely seen in magazines, books, and museums, changing our notion of the world and expanding our sense of photography itself.

Fred Ritchin

throughout the country (25 groups met in 1927 to form the *Vereinigung der Arbeiter-Fotografen Deutschlands* [Federation of German Worker-Photographers]).

German publications were at the forefront of the development of the illustrated press, particularly the picture story, in terms of both conception and lay-out. Freelance photographers and their agents had relatively easy access to top publishers, and would often show up with independently conceived and completed stories. As in other countries, photo agencies, particularly two founded in Berlin at the end of the 1920s, *Weltrundschau* [Worldview], directed by Rudolph Birnback, and *Dephot* (*Deutscher Photodienst*), directed by Simon Guttmann, did much to come up with ideas and images for German publications. Germany was rife with photographic talent, including photographers such as Felix Man and Kurt Hutton (Dephot), Alfred Eisenstaedt (Associated Press), Erich Salomon, the great pioneer of candid political photography, and

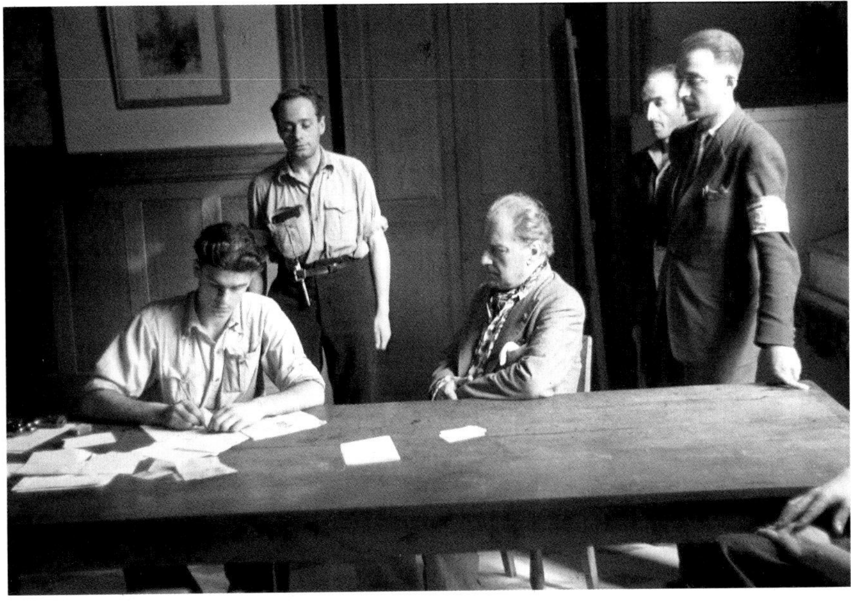

HENRI CARTIER-BRESSON,
Sacha Guitry at the Town Hall of the Seventh Arrondissement, Paris, 1944.

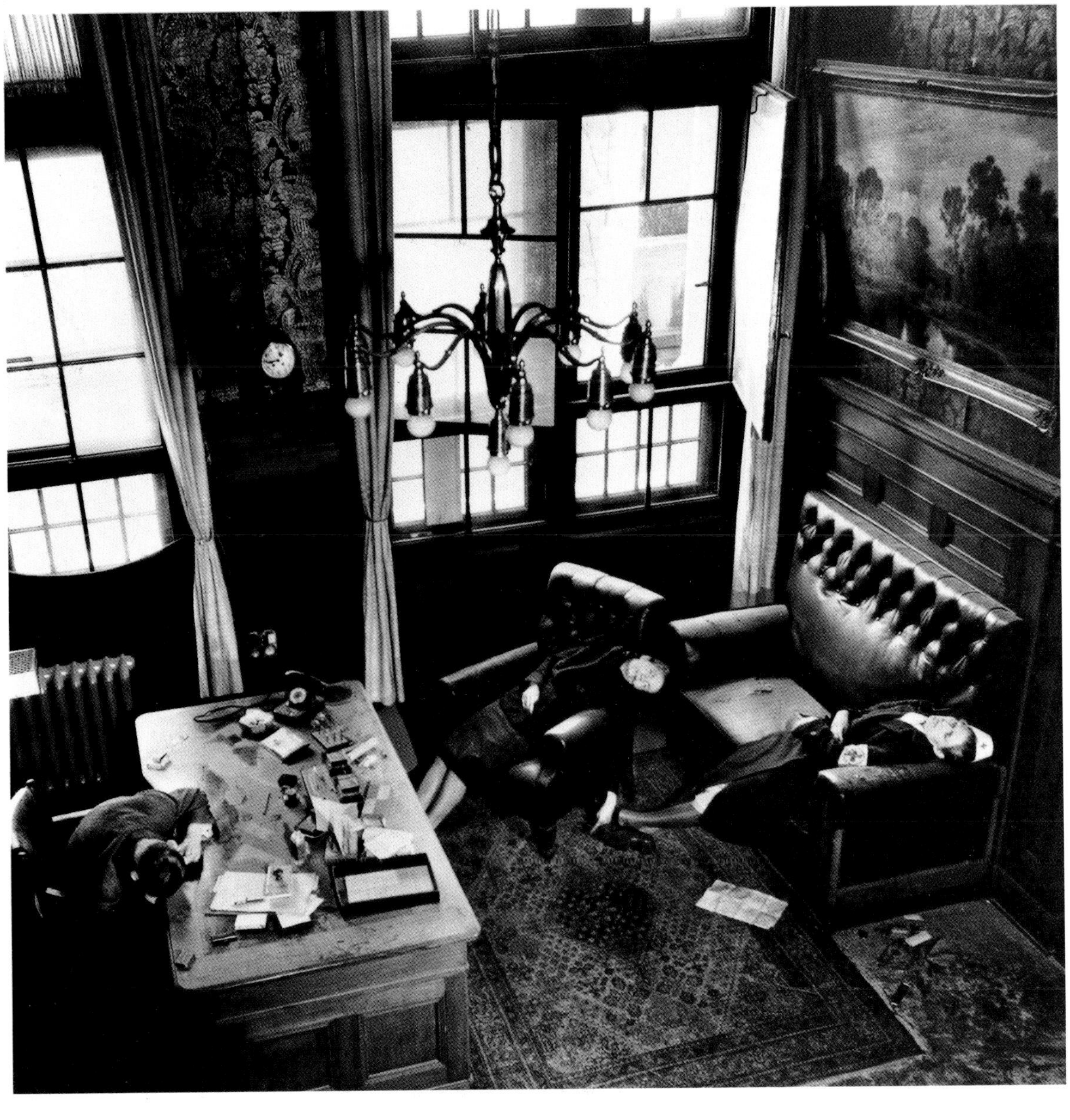

MARGARET BOURKE-WHITE,
German Suicides at Leipzig City Hall, April 1945,
H. F. Johnson Museum of Art, Cornell University, Ithaca.

10. See Tim Gidal's article, "Modern Photojournalism – The First Years", in *Creative Camera* no. 211, July–August 1982. Not only does he provide an excellent overall explanation of the origins of photojournalism in Germany, but as one of its important pioneering photographers, he does so with the added insight of eyewitness and participant. For further reference, see Gidal, *Origin and Evolution of Modern Photojournalism*, Macmillan-Colliers, 1973.

The "Final Solution"

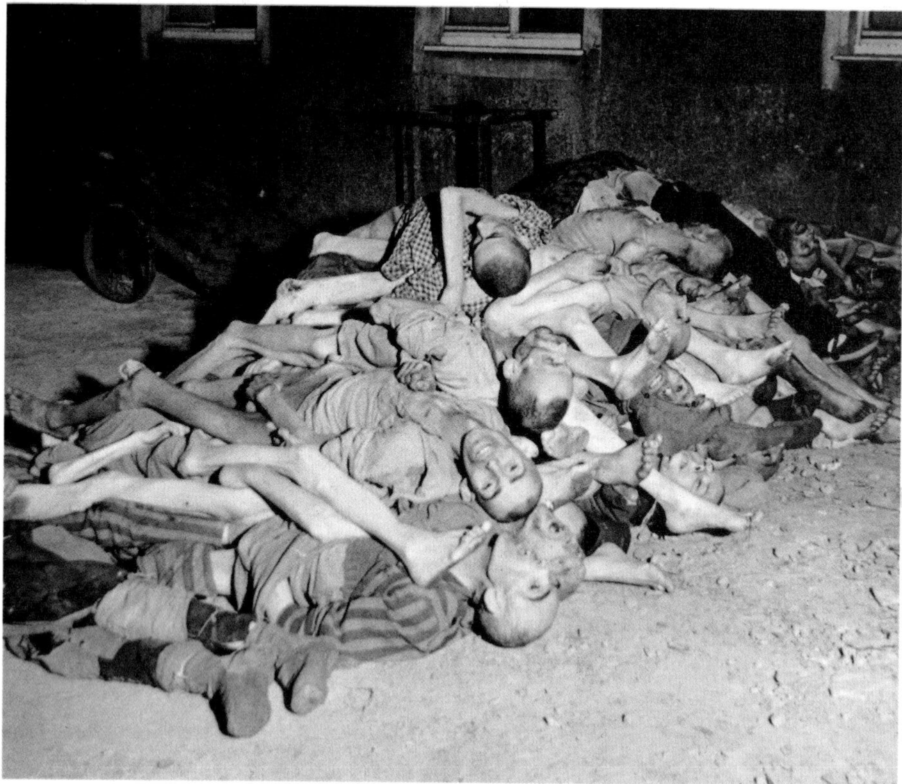

Lee Miller, ***Buchenwald,*** 1945.

From 1933 to 1945 the world saw the virtual annihilation of the Jewish community of central Europe. Key stages in the process included Hitler's coming to power, the "Crystal Night" in 1938, and the Wannsee Conference, when the "Final Solution" was decided. German Jews, the inhabitants of the Warsaw ghetto, and those who had been able to go into exile in France were brought together for their final journey to "another planet", Auschwitz.

Testimonies of this murderous madness have been brought to us by numerous acts of witness: oral, written, and, above all, photographic. Thus photography is the tangible proof of one of the greatest tragedies of contemporary history.

Paradoxically, the greatest proportion of photographic documentation comes from Nazi archives. The extermination had to be recorded, at every stage, and this systematic control involved a photographic archive.

Most of the photos of the Warsaw ghetto were taken by the request of or with the authorization of the political hierarchy in Berlin. Those of the census of Soviet Jews in Odessa come from the services of German "propaganda firms".

Amateur photos recording a mass execution in Latvia were discovered in an office abandoned by the Gestapo after the war. Finally, with the huge arrival of Hungarian Jews in 1944, deportees were methodically photographed by the camp authorities before they were exterminated in the gas chambers. These pictures are the last testimony of the Jewish community of Budapest.

These different examples show the prominent role accorded to photography by the Nazis, underlining the authorities' wish to control each stage of the annihalation of the "old world". Photography used in this way was proof of the way old Europe was being transformed into a Reich which, according to the propaganda machine, was intended to last for a thousand years.

As for the Jewish victims, they quickly understood the need to retain a memory of their own history. Each photograph taken resulted from a struggle with pressing danger, even risking imminent death for the photographer. Roman Vishniac traveled 5,000 miles across Poland, Latvia, Lithuania, Hungary, and Czechoslovakia before the war. Out of his 16,000 photographs, 2,000 have been preserved, a unique witness of Jewish life in the towns and villages of central Europe.[1] Edmund Engelman, foreseeing the enforced exile of Sigmund Freud, photographed his apartment.

Mendel Grossman, an amateur photographer since February 1940 from the Lodz ghetto in Poland, whose inhabitants were transported 50 miles away, thousands of whose photographs were discovered after the war, died after being deported to Germany. Conscious of the imminent death of his fellow Jews he spent all his energy in recording, day by day, the way living conditions deteriorated in the ghetto.

These images formed the only link with the outside and with the future: that future was the discovery of the intolerable reality of the extermination camps. From the moment of the Russian and Allied advance and the liberation of the camps, President Eisenhower ordered a dozen American politicians and major newspaper editors to come to carry out a news report. To the product of these official missions were joined numerous images taken by the press photographers of Allied troops.

Thus the documentation covers a period of 15 years, from the exclusion of a race to its extermination.[2] It constituted crucial evidence for the Nuremberg trials, harrowing, irrefutable acts of witness, which contributed towards the invention at this exceptional court of the notion of crimes against humanity.

Anne Lilensztein

1. R. Abramovitch, (ed.), *The Vanished World*, photograph by Roman Vishniac, New York, 1947.
2. G. Schoenberner, *The Yellow Star: Persecution of Jews in Europe, 1939–1945*, trans. from the German by Susan Sweet, revised and enlarged edition, London, Corgi, 1969.

Records of an Inmate at Auschwitz, circa 1943, Auschwitz Museum.

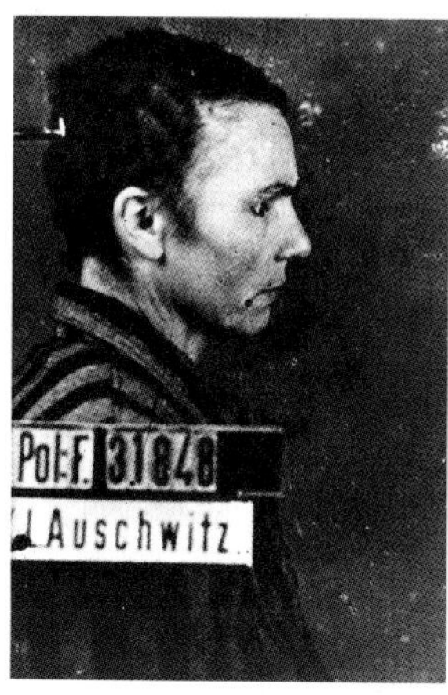

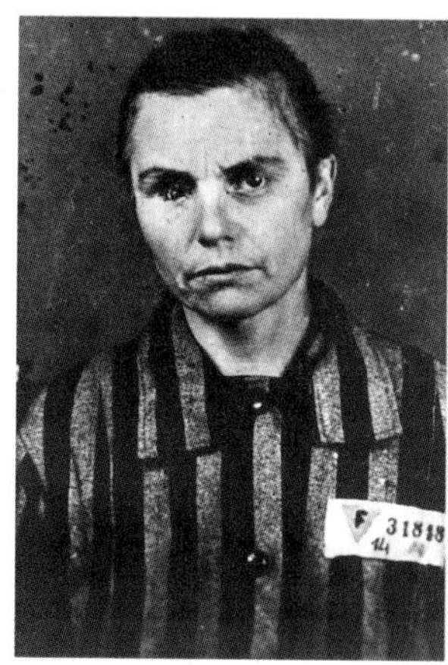

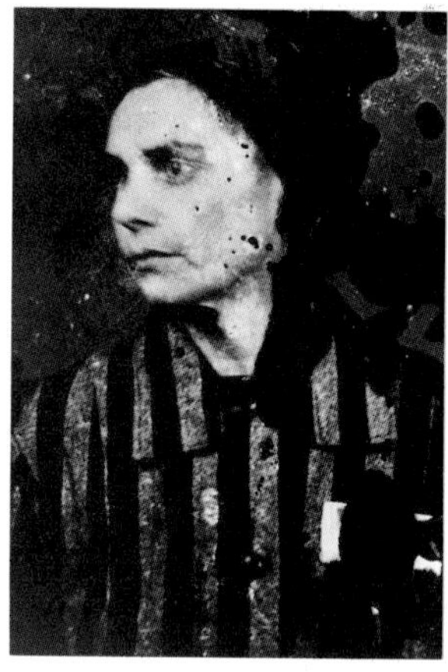

Martin Munkacsi, who served for a while as a staff photographer for the *Berliner Illustrierte Zeitung* and was a highly influential formalist innovator.[10]

Unfortunately, with the coming to power of the Nazis, publications were taken over and modified in line with the government's ambitions. The resulting emigration of photographers and editors advanced photojournalism in other countries dramatically. Many settled in Britain and the United States (Salomon was gassed in a concentration camp). Kurt Korff and Kurt Szafranski of the *Berliner Illustrierte Zeitung* would go on to become founders of the Black Star agency in New York, where the young W. Eugene Smith found a home, and Stefan Lorant of the *Münchner Illustrierte Presse* would become picture editor of Britain's *Weekly Illustrated* (which featured as its three principal photographers Felix Man, Kurt Hutton, and James Jarché) and then editor-in-chief of *Picture Post*.

Alliance Photo, the French photographic agency that lasted from 1934 t0 1940, also benefited from emigration from the east.[11] Maria Eisner, its director, came from Germany in 1933 due to the changing political situation. Two emigrés from eastern Europe, Capa and Chim, a Hungarian and Pole, worked with Eisner at Alliance Photo before all three of them went on to become founders of Magnum. Other photographers at Alliance Photo included Denise Bellon, Pierre Boucher, Pierre Verger, and René Zuber.

At this time, Paris was the innovative centre for photojournalism, with *Regards* and *VU*, two weeklies, coming up with dynamic lay-outs, and using the work of a wide variety of photographers including André Kertész, one of photojournalism's pioneers, who would later achieve great fame for his nudes, distortions and still-lifes (in this diversity of interest Britain's Bill Brandt would resemble him). *VU*, which benefited from the editorial direction of Lucien Vogel and the artistic direction of Alexander Liberman, in particular, used photomontage, tilted images, and odd cut-outs to strong effect.

With the conflagration of war enveloping Europe and with many publications out of business or in Fascist hands, *Life* magazine took the lead in its coverage on the Allied side, employing twenty-one photographers from many countries to cover the war. The photographers, covering everything from the soldier's life in the trenches to bombing raids, the massive allied landing and casualties on D-Day, and the liberation of the concentration camps, remained, for the most part, in the mould that Robert Capa had fashioned during the Spanish Civil War, several years earlier. Compared to coverage of the Vietnam War, a quarter-century later, atrocities were downplayed, shown as an inevitable part of war, while the courage of the combatants was stressed. The work of Soviet photographers such as Dmitri Baltermants was also of very high quality, showing the tragedy and drama of battle with great compassion. However, due to official censorship, much of their work was not seen until well after the war had ended.

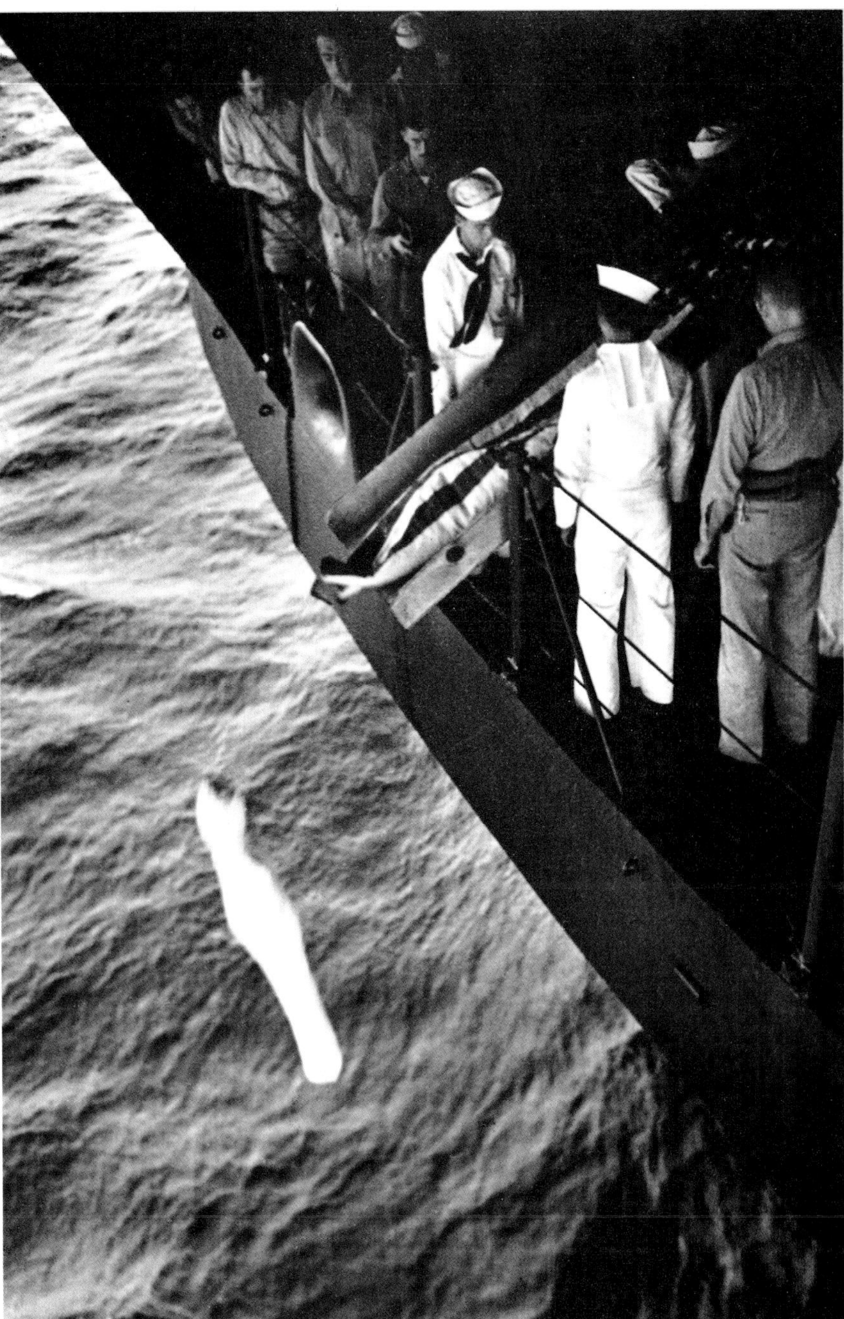

W. EUGENE SMITH, ***Burial at Sea***, 1944.

A precarious peace

In the post-war era, with the renewed optimism and curiosity that came from peace, a variety of publications recommenced publication, and new ones started. Photographers took advantage of newly reopened borders to travel and report on

11. See *Alliance Photo: Agence photographique 1934–40*, Paris, 1988, with texts by T. M. Gunther.

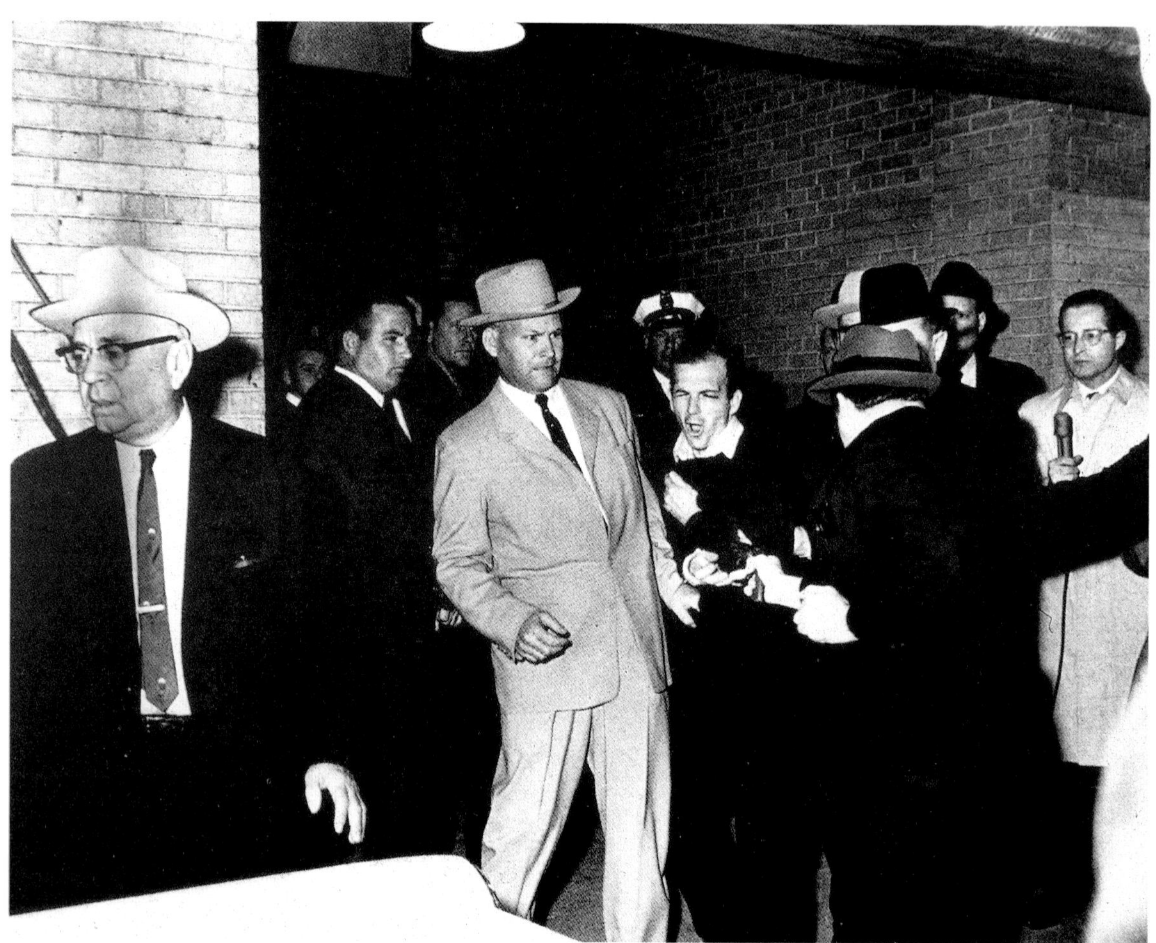

BOB JACKSON,
Jack Ruby Shoots Lee Harvey Oswald, Dallas,
November 24, 1963,
Associated Press.

other ways of life. British photographer George Rodger, a veteran chronicler of the war, went to Africa, where he spent two years traveling and reporting on the tribes untouched by the devastation he had just experienced.[12] Both Robert Capa and Henri Cartier-Bresson crossed into the land of the new enemy, the Soviet Union, behind the Iron Curtain. Cartier-Bresson also traveled extensively in Asia, where he documented the end of colonialism. All three photographers, along with David Seymour and William Vandivert, were involved in the founding of Magnum Photos in 1947, an agency which would in future provide a launch-pad for many of the finest freelance photographers.

There were, of course, still wars to cover, along with celebrities, exotic climes, and everyday events. For the French, the hotly debated Algerian War was covered cautiously. The Korean War was depicted, particularly in the images of David Douglas Duncan, largely as a reprise of the Second World War. Capa died in 1954, having stepped on a landmine while photographing French soldiers in Indo-China; his colleague, David Seymour, would die two years later, covering the Suez crisis.

However, in these last days before television would begin to dominate images, there were many possibilities for photographers, apart from war. One could still find parts of the world where no photographer had been before, or photograph celebrities and political leaders, for whom the public had an insatiable curiosity. For the freelance photographer, there was a variety of publications in different countries eager to buy pictures that explored the newly opened world.

In the United States, the photo essay – a grouping of photographs, usually published with text, that, like its written equivalent, attempts to get at the essence of a person, place or event – reached new heights, especially those by W. Eugene Smith. The essay became both more psychologically astute (*Country Doctor,*1948) and more lyrical (*Spanish Village,* 1951). Many of the most memorable essays and narrative picture stories published in *Life* magazine appeared between the late 1940s and the 1950s. It was a period when the photograph was still relatively fresh, when television was still in its infancy and had not yet become the dominant visual form of communication.[13]

It was also a time of curiosity and of optimism, when memorable heroes could be created in photographs. Eugene Smith alone, for example, produced several essays on heroic healers for the battered post-war world – the great humanitarian doctor Albert Schweitzer, a hardworking, heroic nurse-midwife, and the dedicated country doctor –

12. See C. Naggar, *George Rodger en Afrique*, Paris, Herscher, 1984.

13. See M. Edey, *Great Photographic Essays from Life*, Boston, New York Graphic Society, 1978, for an interesting compilation of essays by W. Eugene Smith and others.

as well as essays on the age-old rhythms of a Spanish village and a romantic look at the great industrial city of Pittsburgh.[14]

It is clear, not only from Smith's essays, but also from the history of reportage generally, that it has been much easier for photoreporters to sympathize with their subjects than to criticize them. Critical photographs, particularly of people, appear to be much more malicious than more flattering images which are equally subjective. This is, in part, because the photographer is generally seen as performing an illustrative function, to entice the reader without providing a specific point of view. Photographs usually respect the hierarchy of power (heads of state, for example, continue generally to be depicted more regally than they actually are), and replicate popular mythologies (the starlet made to look sexy). If there is criticism to be made, it is often the writer (who unlike the photographer does not require physical proximity to their subject) who is asked to do it, while the photographer is more responsible for allure and excitement.[15]

In retrospect, *The Americans*, an essay by Swiss photographer Robert Frank, photographed 1955–1956 and published as a book both in France and the United States, opened up a new strategy for photoreportage. Unlike the 1955 New York Museum of Modern Art exhibition, *The Family of Man*, which used photoreportage to posit the commonality (and sentimentality) of human existence, Frank used photographs to ask questions, to raise ambiguities, to dispute visual icons rather than adorn them. Frank was able to remain the cool, intense outsider in his imagery, engaging in a dialectic with the society around him rather than an overt sympathizer.

Frank's work served as a bridge between the empathetic social documentarians who preceded him in the United States, working for the Farm Security Administration, and the caustic, at times alienating, street photography of practitioners such as Diane Arbus and Garry Winogrand who were fascinated by the socially bizarre and outrageous and who, in Winogrand's case, used photography "to see what things look like photographed". In photojournalism, Frank's work also served as a bridge between the generally supportive imagery of the Second World War and the wars which followed it, and the much more sardonic, upsetting imagery of the Vietnam War. His work predicted the social revolutions in Europe and the United States in the following decade which challenged institutional truths and cultural mythologies.

W. Eugene Smith, *Tomoko and His Mother, Minamata,* Japan, 1972.
▼

14. See W. S. Johnson, (ed.), *W. Eugene Smith: Master of the Photographic Essay*, New York, Harper and Row, 1981, and Jim Hughes, *W. Eugene Smith: Shadow & Substance: The Life and Work of an American Photographer*, McGraw Hill, 1989.

15. This is exemplified by the well-known Paris Match slogan, "The weight of the words, the shock of the photos".

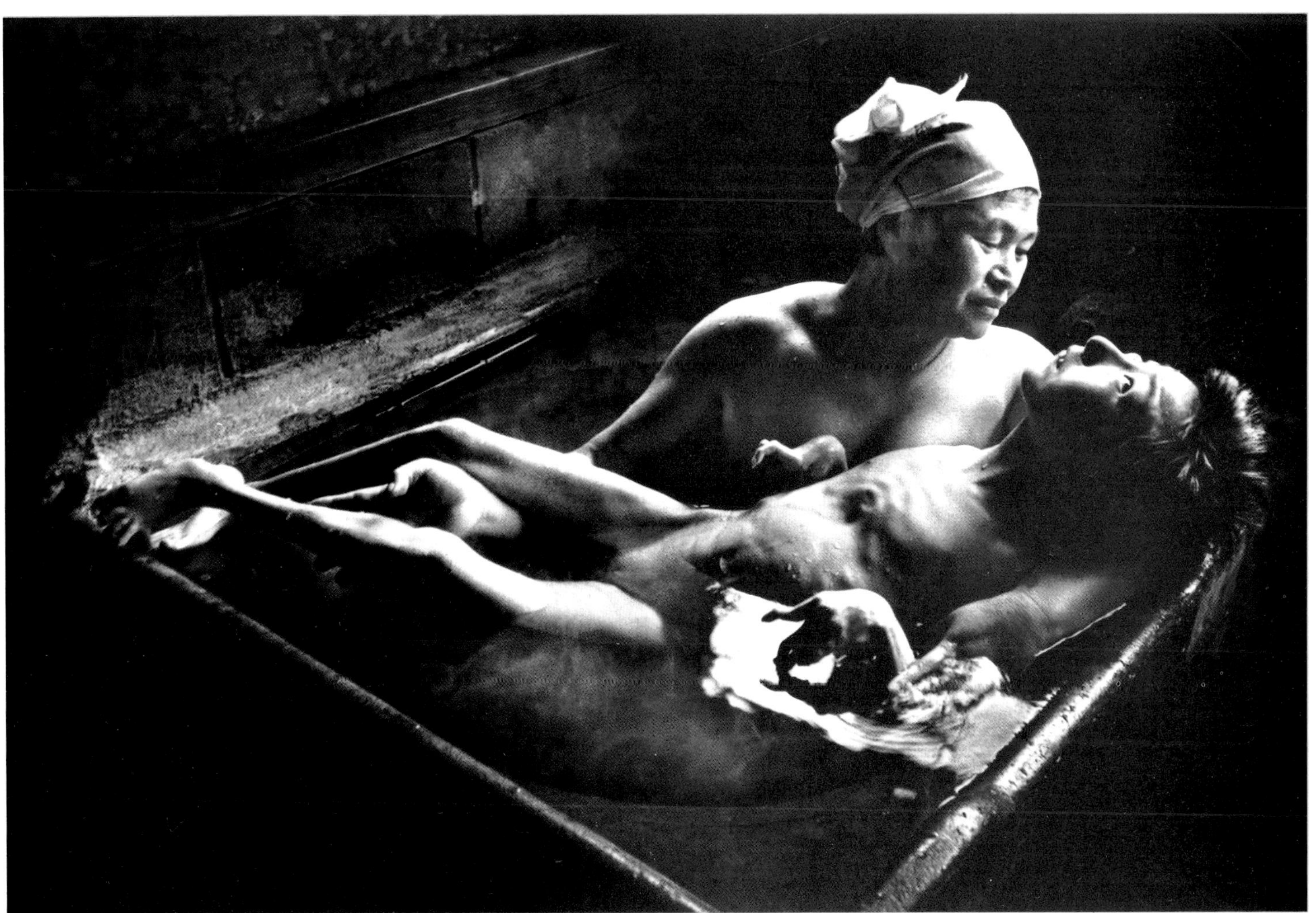

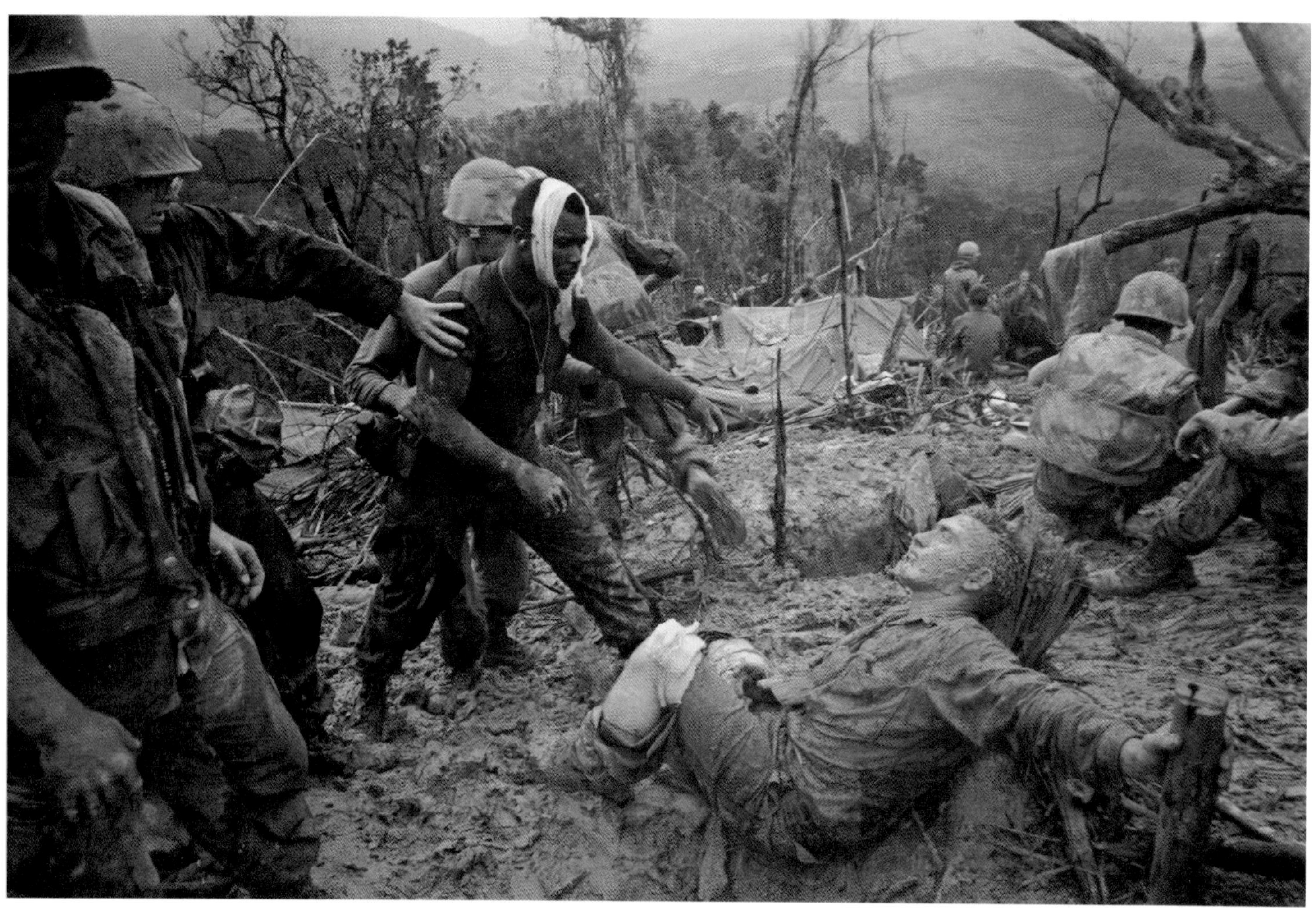

LARRY BURROWS, *Reaching Out, Battle of Hill 484, South Vietnam,* 1966, (original in color).

Vietnam: contradictions and protest

The Vietnam War was fought during an era of great expansion in the press. Paris-based photo agencies such as Gamma, Sygma, and Sipa opened, providing more in-depth, magazine-style coverage than did large international agencies such as Agence France-Presse, Associated Press, and United Press International, which primarily served newspapers. In the United States, while great picture magazines such as *Life* and *Look* were closing (the weekly *Life* would later return as a monthly publication), a variety of specialty magazines were founded, requiring, in sum, many more photographs. In this new market, there were not many staff photographer positions outside newspapers – instead, publications relied on the great diversity of material made by agency photographers and other freelancers. In Europe, due in part to the lack of advertising on television, magazines were more healthy financially and photographers were able to sell their work to major non-competing publications in a variety of countries. Much of the market for magazine photojournalists moved, during the 1970s and 1980s, from the United States to Europe, with magazines such as *Bunte, Epoca, Geo, Paris Match,* and *Stern.*

The Vietnam War, like the Spanish Civil War, provided a conflict with global implications for publications to report upon. It also had – at first – a willing host. In the early days of the war, the United States government was interested in as much coverage as possible. Two letters certifying that publications awaited one's pictures could assure almost any freelancer of credentials entitling them to free rides into battle on a helicopter and various other press privileges.[16] The Associated Press office in Saigon offered nearly everyone who turned up the use of a camera, film, and light meter, and a brief lesson on their use, and would write a letter helping the photographer to obtain credentials. The American government was so eager for publicity that at one point it even paid for some journalists' airplane tickets to Vietnam. With official controls relaxed, journalists were free to roam the land, exploring, sharpening their skills, and perhaps, over the length of their stay, developing their own deeper interpretations of what was going on.

In fact, this is exactly what happened. Just as journalists were providing the public with large numbers of photographs, their points of view were diverging from the institutional truths that were being offered by government spokesper-

16. See P. Knightley, *The First Casualty*, New York, Harcourt Brave Jovanovich, 1975.

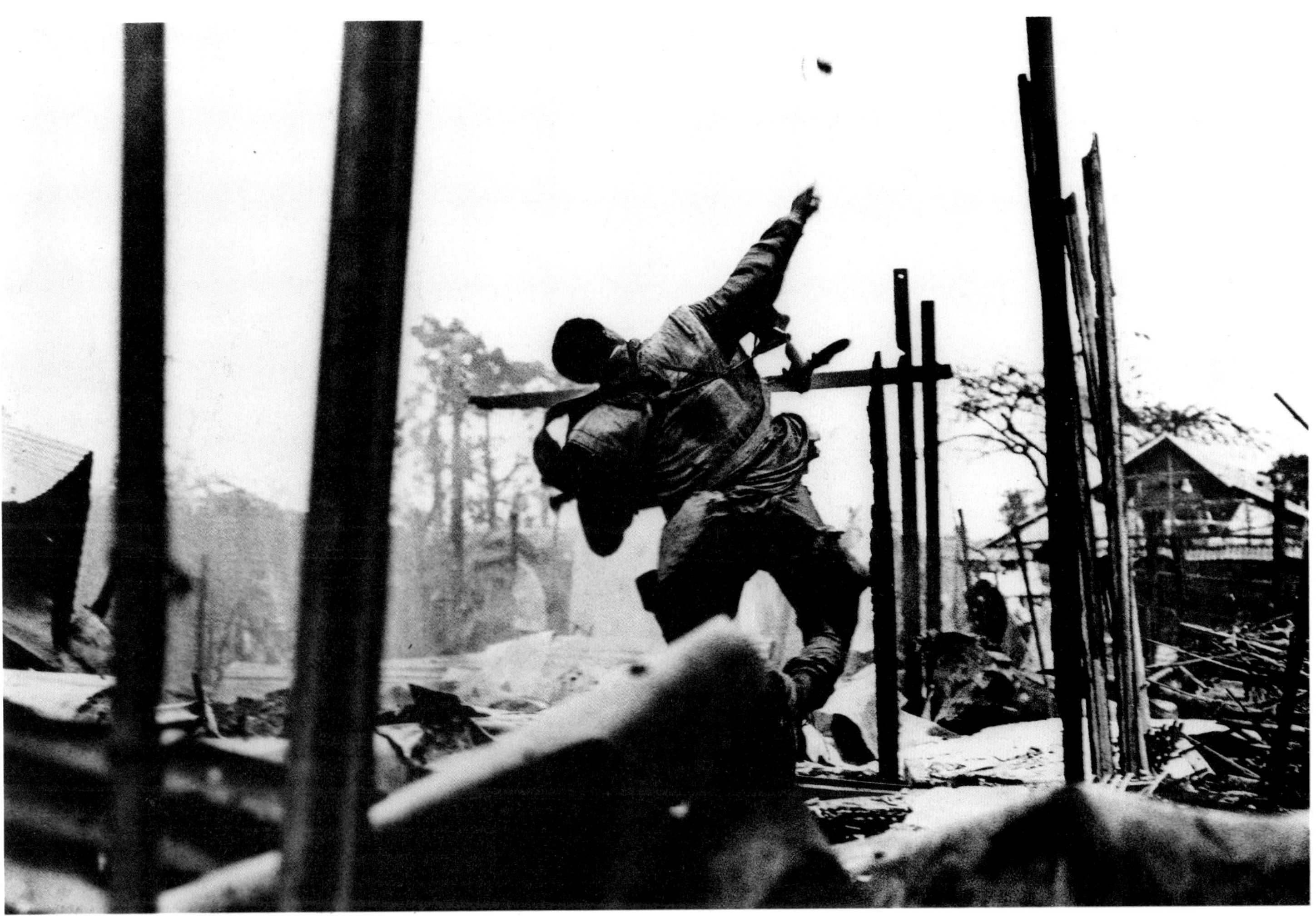

DON MCCULLIN,
Soldier Throwing a Grenade,
Hué, Vietnam, 1968.

sons. While the American government was suggesting that the war was being won and offering body counts of the enemy dead to prove it, the images of the war in Vietnam that were published in the media were contradicting these statements.

This divergence changed society's easy relationship with photoreportage. In a general sense, never again could photoreporters be trusted to confirm the point of view of others, because through their photographs they began effectively to challenge the legitimacy of the war that their society, whether directly or indirectly, and many major publications, were sponsoring. Using their supposedly objective cameras they made images that contradicted official thinking – a Buddhist monk self-immolating, a little girl fleeing napalm, a member of the Viet Cong being summarily executed, a grieving widow crying over an anonymous body bag, dignified North Vietnamese peasants working in the countryside. Rather than authenticating idealized images of Americans – like the photographs taken of heroic soldiers on D-Day or the flag-raising at Iwo Jima – many of the photographs arriving from Vietnam were now, when viewed in the context of information provided by other media, providing a disturbing, even a somewhat radical, point of view.

The individual photojournalist's point of view was now, at times, being asserted as a strong opinion. Two famous war photographers, David Douglas Duncan, an ex-U.S. Marine, and Larry Burrows, publicly expressed disillusionment and anger about the war. In 1968, Duncan, well known for his heroic coverage of American soldiers in the Second World War and the Korean War, published a small book entitled *I Protest!*, showing the sufferings of Marines over an eight-day period during the siege at Khe Sanh, and expressing his outrage at the conduct of the war.[17] His text began: "For more than the last quarter century I've been shot at by any number of extremely unattractive men, the bulk of them Communists. I'm no peacenik, Vietnik, Pinkie, Commie, liberal, conservative, kook, hippie, hawk or dove. I'm just a veteran combat photographer and foreign correspondent who cares intensely about my country and the role we are playing – and assigning to ourselves – in the world of today. And I want to shout a loud and clear protest at what has happened at Khe Sanh, and in all of Vietnam."

Larry Burrows had been working in Vietnam for much of the previous seven years when in

17. D. D. Duncan, *I Protest!*, New York, Signet Broadside, 1968.

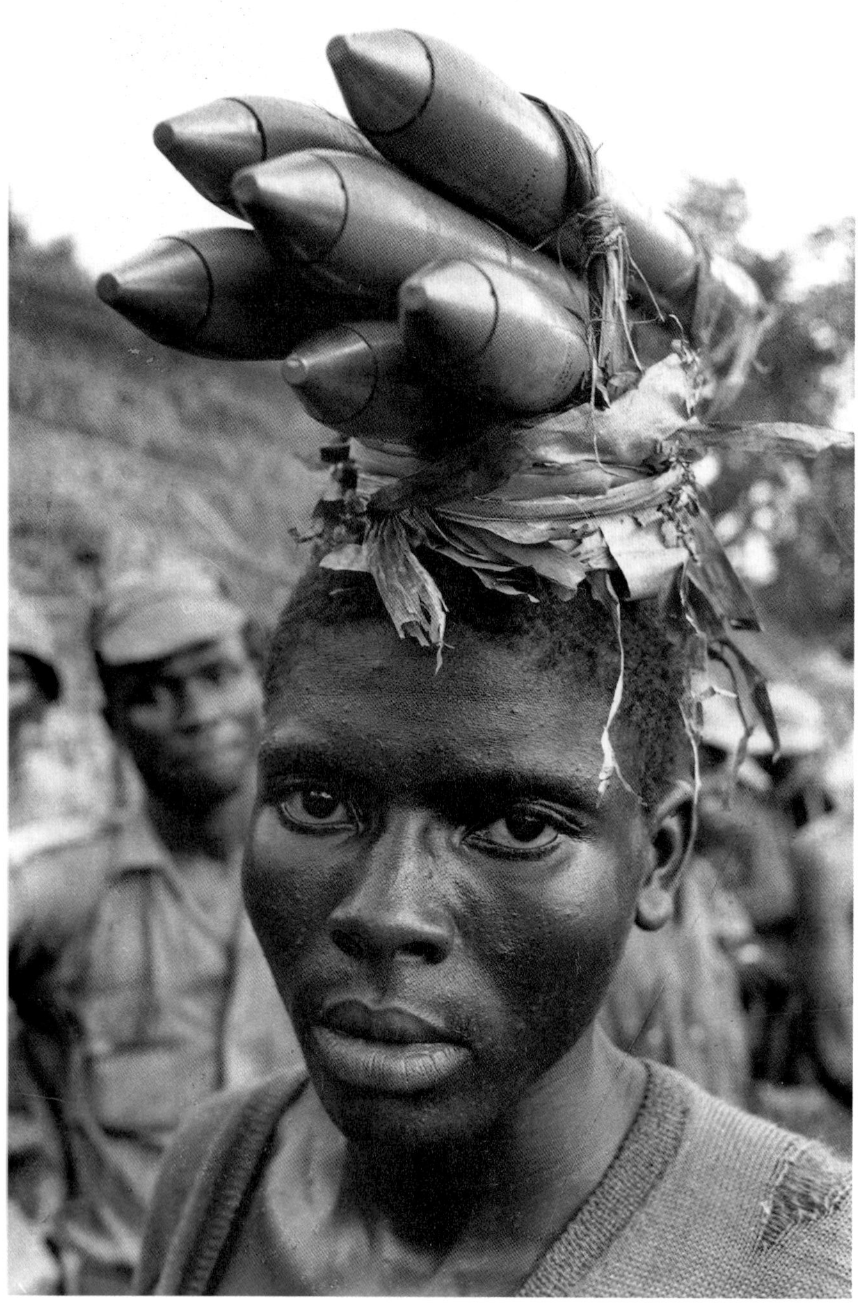

GILLES CARON, *Biafra*, 1968.

1969 *Life* published ten pages of his color pictures under the headline "Vietnam: A Degree of Disillusion". His accompanying text began: "All over Vietnam you see the faces – more inscrutable and more tired now than I have ever known them to be [...] I have been rather a hawk. As a British subject I could perhaps be more objective than Americans, but I generally accepted the aims of the U.S. and Saigon, and the official version of how things were going." He goes on to describe his trip to Vietnam as having been prompted by government statistics which asserted that things were better, and expresses in his photographs and text growing doubts as to whether this was so.

A French photographer, Marc Riboud, an early member of the Magnum agency, also went to Vietnam to photograph, but to the North.[18] His coverage of the "enemy", a rare foray by a member of the Western press, and the quiet, dignified images of the North Vietnamese people that he brought back, served as a counterpoint to some of the typical demonization of the enemy that is almost an inevitable product of war. Don McCullin is another angry, eloquent witness of the Vietnam War, as he was of major conflicts before and after (the Congo, Biafra, Cyprus, Lebanon, Northern Ireland). Obstinately determined to reveal the truth, in his 1970 book *Beirut: A City in Crisis*, he contributed to the notion of "history in the making" with his photographic sequences.

However, the most angry attack on U.S. policy was probably a book by a Welsh photographer, Philip Jones Griffiths, entitled *Vietnam Inc.*[19] Griffiths himself wrote the text and did the layout while providing photographs that avoid the depiction of the war as high drama. There are, to be sure, dramatic large photographs – for example, a child lost in grief over a body in the back of a truck, the head of a corpse lying near a gun, two American soldiers crawling towards a Vietnamese prostitute on the floor, a Vietnamese soldier crouched in amazement and distress over a dead woman on the road.

But there are many other images as well, often of civilians, which are generally less visually striking and which are used to explore particular facets of the war – a picture of napalm next to pictures of napalm victims, frightened people on the street, military personnel with the computer that "proves" the war is being won. There is a photograph of men on an aircraft carrier with the caption, "They have never seen the faces of their victims, the Vietnamese people", and a photograph of children captioned "Orphans visit a United States Army hospital to sing and dance for the wounded men whose predecessors were responsible for robbing these children of their parents."

In *Vietnam Inc.*, Griffiths is unwilling only to make universal, eloquent pictures of yet another photogenic conflict. Instead, through careful juxtaposition and sequencing of direct, unadorned, and sharply observed images, and through his informative, terse, and sardonic text, he authors a comprehensively detailed and relentless work that explodes much of the rhetoric surrounding the war in Vietnam.

Griffiths' book, now considered by many a classic, is one of the earliest subject-oriented books in which the photographer, in a complete, decisive way, becomes the author of their own imagery rather than a producer of photographs for others to choose from and to recontextualize by caption, headline, and lay-out, as is the case in much of the mass media.

18. See M. Riboud, *Face of North Vietnam*, New York, Holt, Rinehart and Winston, 1970.

19. P. J. Griffiths, *Vietnam, Inc.*, New York: Macmillan, 1971.

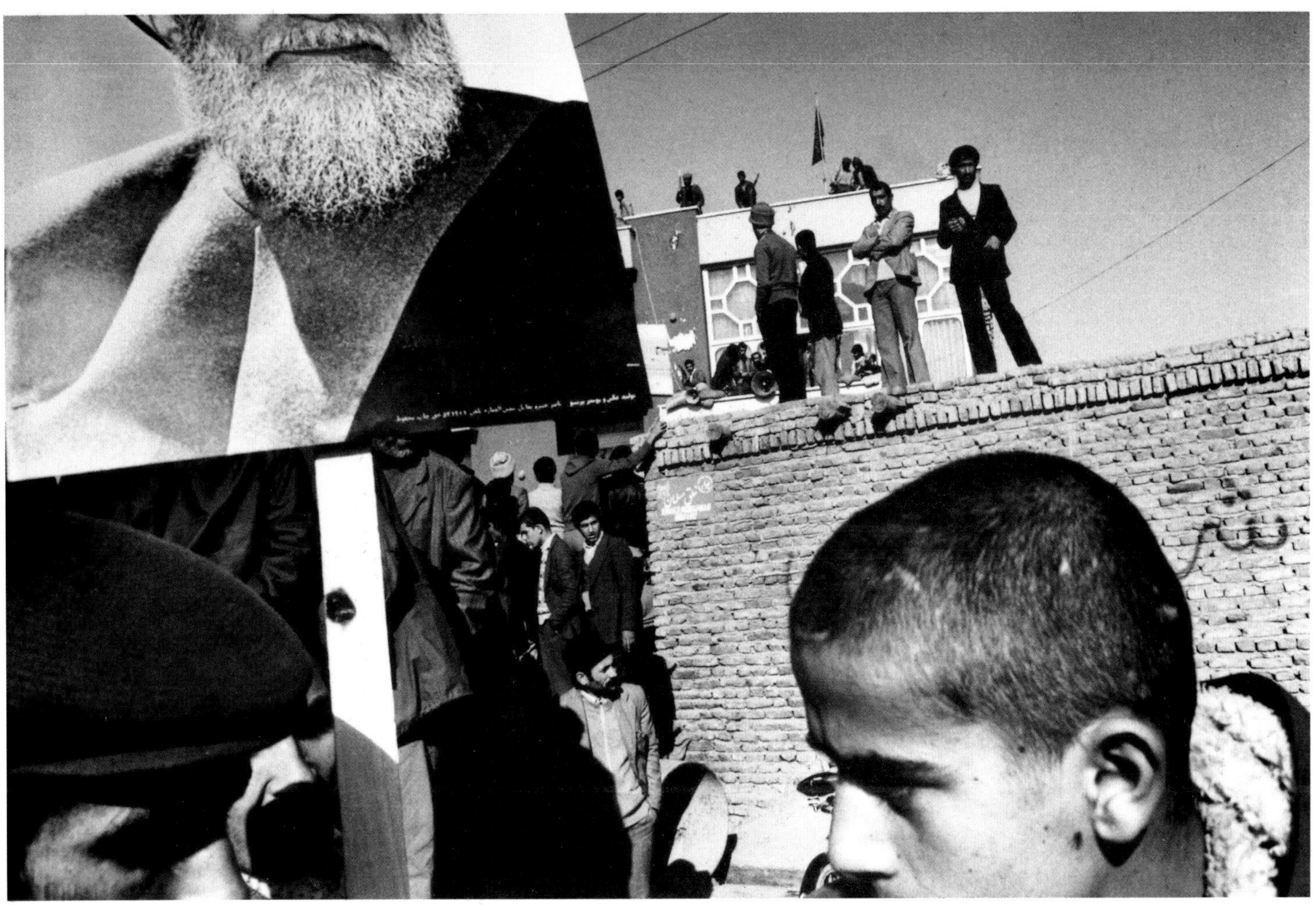

Gilles Peress, *Demonstrations at Tabriz, Iran,* 1979–1980, from *Telex: Iran.*

The photographic inquiry

During the last two decades, there have been many other books dealing with a host of issues, including the photography of conflict. For the book *El Salvador*, for example, thirty photographers pooled their work, largely out of a feeling that their point of view was not being adequately reflected in the mass media which simplified and sensationalized the violence there. Although the images in the book, edited by photographers Harry Mattison and Susan Meiselas, with Fae Rubenstein, are largely the by-products of assignments for the mass media, the volume as a whole transcends the more superficial coverage in news weeklies by providing the reader with a sense of the history of El Salvador, a taste of the daily life of the various kinds of people living there, and an understanding of the diversity of the issues surrounding the conflict.[20]

As photographers looked for other ways of presenting their work, and as galleries and museums began to open their doors much more frequently to the work of photojournalists, the 1970s and the 1980s became an era when one no longer necessarily looked to the mass media for the most in-depth coverage of world events. For example, the Brazilian photographer Sebastião Salgado's work on Latin America and the famine in the Sahel in Ethiopia has been widely seen in magazines, books, and exhibitions. The American photographer Eugene Richards has produced a series of books on poverty and medical care while continuing to work for magazines.

The diversity of the media has contributed to the development of new strategies of reportage. Paris-based reporter Sophie Ristelhueber, for example, published a small book, *Beirut*, which looked at the devastation wrought upon that city by utilizing quiet cityscapes rather than more traditional journalistic images of the dead and wounded.[21] Gilles Peress, in his book *Telex: Iran*, looked at the effect of the revolution upon the country in impressionistic, overtly subjective imagery, using telexes to reinforce the reader's sense of his foreignness, posing photographs as intriguing questions rather than authoritative answers.[22] French photographer Raymond Depardon worked for the foreign affairs page of the Paris daily *Libération*, sending back an image from New York each day, with his own diary-like jottings entered underneath.[23]

Also, as photographic technology has spread to other countries around the world, international

20. H. Mattison, S. Meiselas and F. Rubenstein (eds.), *El Salvador: Work of Thirty Photographers*, New York, Writers and Readers, 1983.

21. S. Ristelhueber, *Beirut*, London, Thames and Hudson, 1984.

22. G. Peress, *Telex: Iran/In The Name of Revolution*, New York, Aperture, 1983.

23. See R. Depardon, *Correspondance New-Yorkaise*, Paris, Libération/Éd. de l'Étoile, 1981. Photographed for *Libération*, Paris, France, between July 2 and August 7, 1981.

Picture-editing

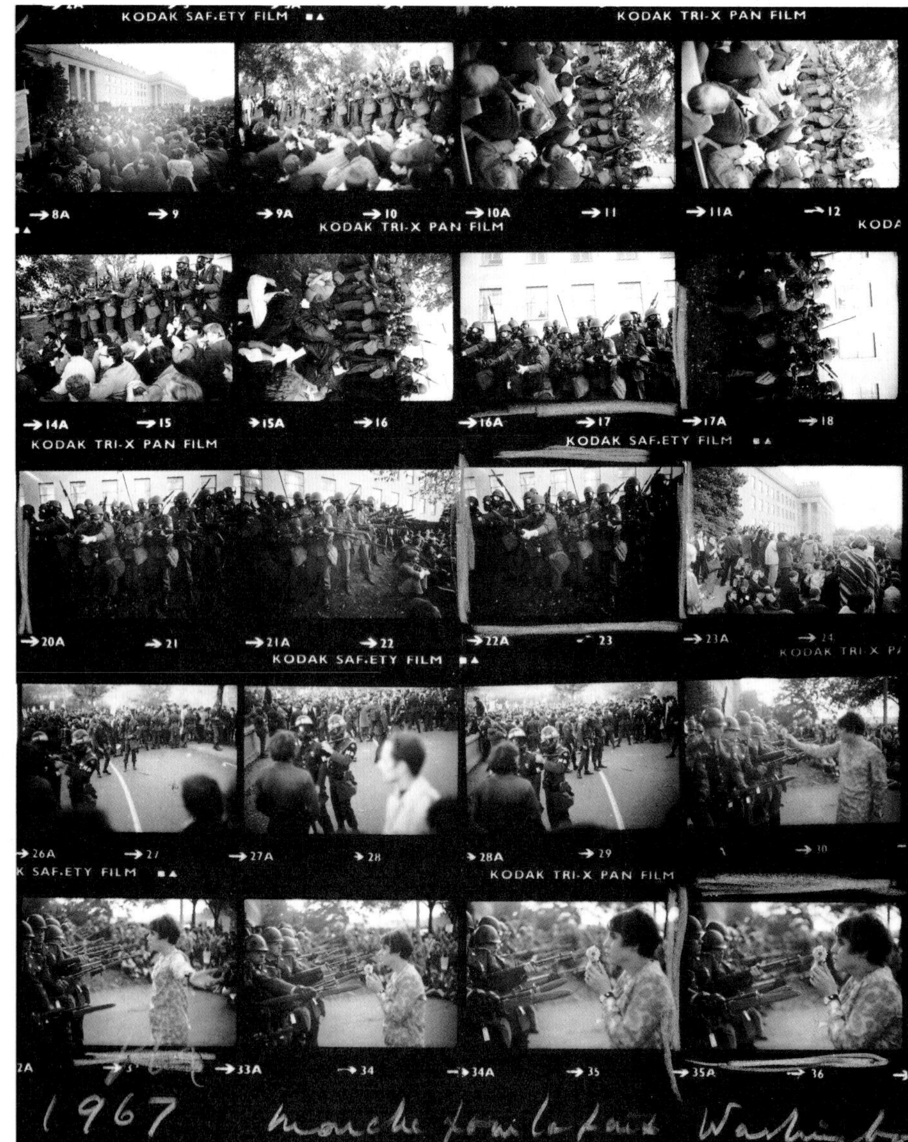

Marc Riboud,
Contact plate, Vietnam peace march,
Washington, 1967

The selection of photographs is critical. Unlike a writer's text, which is considered a synthesis of various possibilities, a photographer's contact sheet offers very different and sometimes mutually exclusive points of view on the same subject. A person can be shown in one image as ebullient and then, in another photograph from the same roll of film, quietly serious – which one best captures the real character of the person?

There may be little time to make the choice, as in a newspaper where the photograph must often go to press almost immediately after the film is developed. Because of the urgency of the deadline and the cost, many newspaper images are selected directly from the film itself without waiting for a contact sheet to be made. It is a more difficult way to edit since one can miss certain details and nuances and there is a greater danger of damaging the negative with more handling. However, since a newspaper photograph is generally more simply composed and reproduced with less detail than, for example, photographs which appear in magazines, editing from a negative is considered permissible.

The general preference, however, is to edit from contact sheets, and, even better, to make enough work prints so that the final choices can be made from larger images. This helps one to see the smallest details and sense the *gestalt* of the image more than is possible on a standard contact sheet, where each image is only 24 x 36 mm.

The extensive use of 35mm color slides in magazine photography in recent years also allows the projection of enlarged images directly from the slide. Nowadays, new technology makes possible even the instant enlargement of an image onto a video screen from a black and white or color negative without requiring a print.

It is generally preferable for the photographer, who knows what they intended to say, to edit their own photographs. But an editor can provide another point of view which, because of their comparative distance from the scene depicted, may help to address what an image actually says rather than what it was intended to say.

An effective editor will carefully read a contact sheet and attempt to understand what the photographer was trying to achieve in the images. This allows the editor to understand, as in the example given above, whether a person is more characteristically ebullient or quietly serious before deciding which image to select.

Even after extensively evaluating their own contact sheets, photographers generally preserve them and are later able to go back and re-evaluate their work from another perspective and, perhaps, select other images. Many photographers find that the way they really get to know the work of another photographer is by reading their contact sheets, not just by looking at the few images that have been selected for publication or exhibition.

Henri Cartier-Bresson's contact sheets, for example, exemplify a methodical, intelligent, analytical attempt to coax visual subtleties from a scene, while William Klein's approach, on the other hand, (a film was made about his contact sheets) is more confrontational and gestural. Some photographers arrive at what they are after in one or two frames while others at times seem to approach a situation from a variety of perspectives until they are satisfied.

One begins to see the photographer's approach, the risks taken, the clarity of thought and vision, the emotional impact of the scene on the photographer. Unfortunately, contact sheets are generally ignored in any consideration of a photographer's work. They can, however, give an enormous insight into the photographer's methodology and, by providing a context, into the image itself.

It should also be pointed out that in some poorer countries a photographer may be required to complete three assignments on one roll of film, whereas some photographers from rich countries have been known to expose 100 rolls of film in a single day. Obviously any judgement of a photographer's approach which relies upon their contact sheets must be tempered by a sense of what is economically possible with the particular situation.

Fred Ritchin

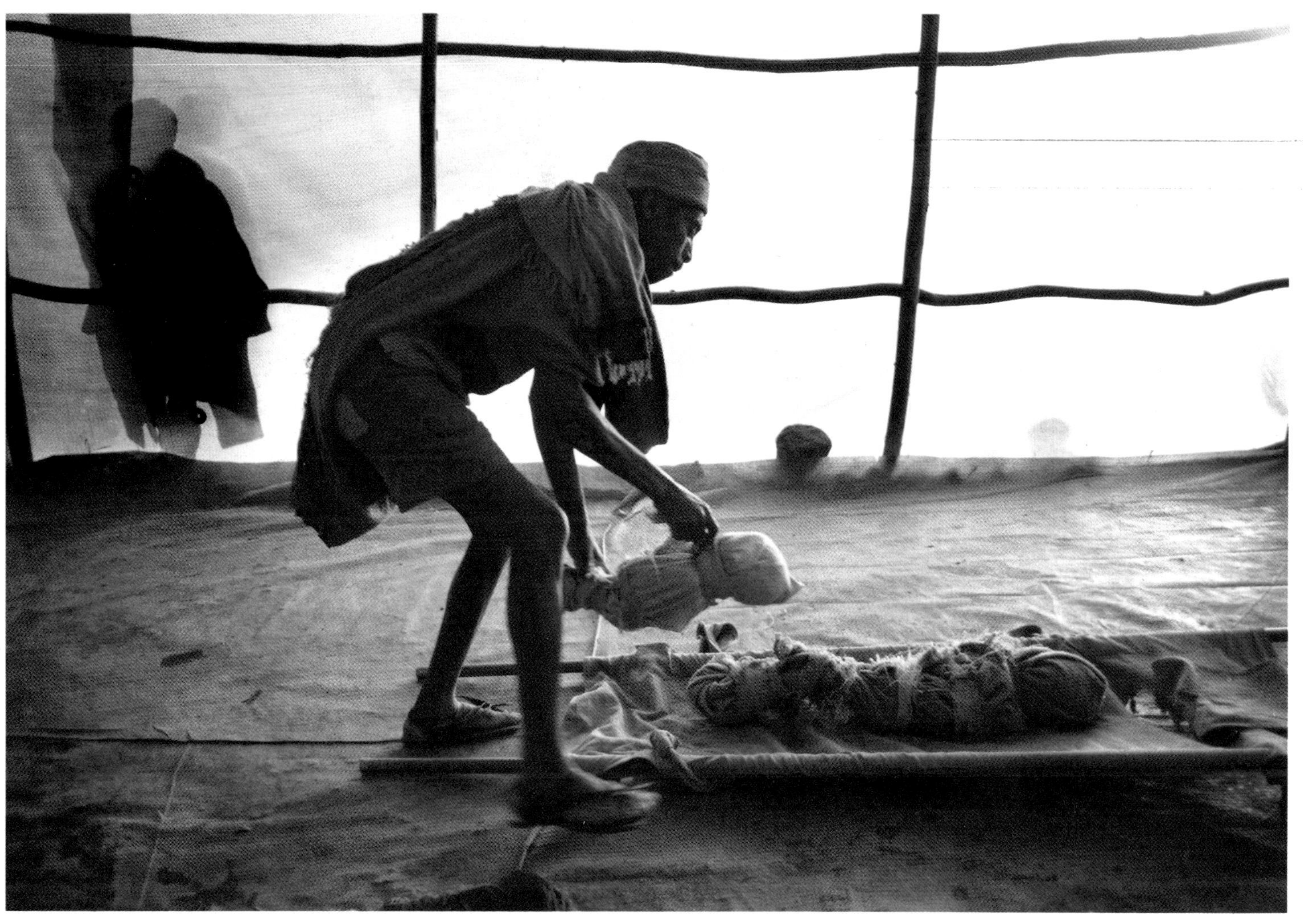

MARY ELLEN MARK, *Inside "Die Place"* (Famine in Ethopia), 1985, (original in color).

journalistic coverage has extended beyond the control of photographers from Europe and the United States. Beginning, perhaps, with the Iranian revolution, which was very well-covered by Iranian photographers whose work has been widely seen abroad, a number of other conflicts have been reported upon with much greater depth by indigenous photographers. More recently, Afrapix, a multi-racial group of South African photographers, has been distributing images worldwide. Many Filipino photographers worked with great international success, covering the ascension of Cory Aquino.

Increasingly, documentary photographers everywhere are working on long-term projects that find their way into books, exhibitions, and the foreign press. A notable success story is in Mexico, where the work of many professionals, including Pablo Cabado, Graciela Iturbide, Eniac Martinez, and Pedro Meyer, is enjoying international recognition and changing the world's view of that country. In Peru, villagers are producing photographs which document their own difficult situation, under assault by guerillas and government forces in the Shining Path. Foundations such as the W. Eugene Smith Grant in Humanistic Photography and the Mother Jones Fund for Documentary Photography are providing sizeable grants for photographers to avoid the dictates of the mass media to work on their own – the original motive of Magnum's founders.

Truthful immediacy

There have also been technical developments. New high-speed color and black and white films and automatic cameras have made the photoreporter's job easier. There is also an unfortunate tendency in some of the press to ask photographers to light their subjects using strobes, a requirement that can result in more attractive, but static, conventional images.

Recent advances in digital technology have an extraordinary potential for news photography. Recently introduced still video cameras, which capture images using a small magnetic disc rather than film, allow photographers to transmit photographs to a picture agency or publication over a telephone wire, without processing and printing, giving them more time to stay at an event. Furthermore, computer systems in use by publishers now allow images to go directly to press without ever appearing as a print.

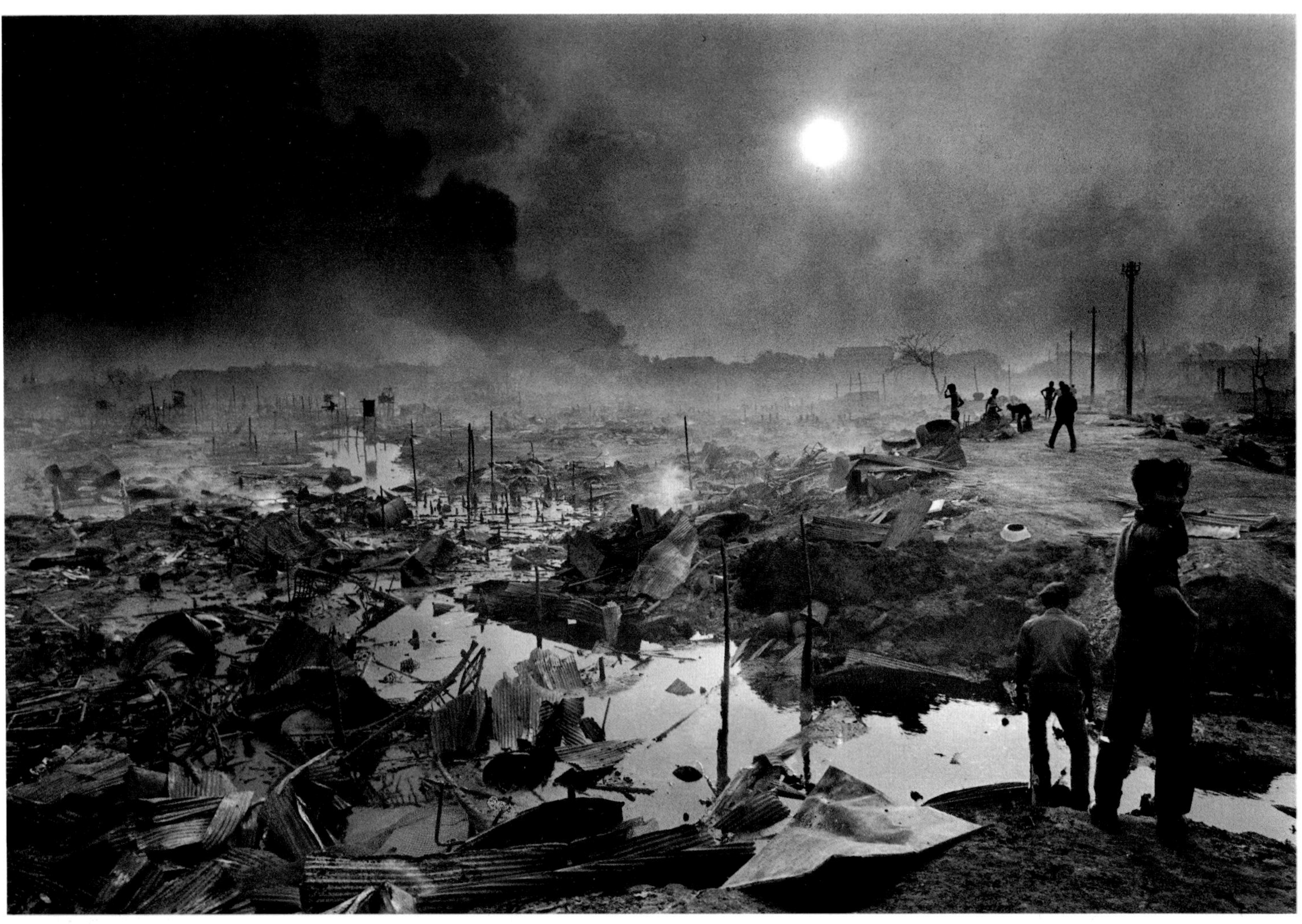

CHRISTINE SPENGLER, *The Bombing of Phnom-Penh,* 1974.

However, with this new efficiency also come some real and potential problems. Since the discs are made to be reused, and there is no negative or print, how can one prove that a photograph has not been manipulated or retouched if its subject denies that the event depicted ever happened? With the addition of computer systems that help to do lay-outs, placing text and photos and then transmitting them to press over telephone wires, it becomes very easy to manipulate a photograph once it has been entered in an digital form. Adding or subtracting elements can take seconds; one can see immediately what the changed image looks like, and it is virtually impossible to detect the modification.

As a result of this new technological sophistication and the growing tendency of editors to want to control photographic imagery in every detail, publications in Europe and the United States have printed "news" photographs of two people who were not in the same place, but made to look as if they were, two people combined into one, scenes in which elements have been pushed closer together, others in which unwanted elements have been simply removed (in one case, a gun), and even one in which no photographer was present – the "photograph" was made using file material assembled according to eyewitness reports.[24] One partial solution that has been proposed in Scandinavia is to use the letter "M" or the word "montage" to indicate computer manipulation. Another trend is to use what is called "frame-grabbing" – technology that allows the editor in the newsroom to select still images from television broadcasts. This allows the editor to become, in a sense, the "photographer". Cartier-Bresson's "decisive moment" becomes a televised event.

In the six decades that modern photojournalism has existed, since the introduction of portable cameras and more light-sensitive film and the emergence of the picture magazine, much has changed. Nowadays, neither film nor print are always necessary, and even the necessity for a camera can be circumvented through "frame-grabbing". We have gone from the photographer being increasingly implicated in the events of the day by proximity and empathy to photographers employing new strategies and new media to analyze and question what is going on. In the process, many photoreporters are increasingly becoming the "authors" of their own work, contextualizing its presentation themselves in books, audio-visual presentations, films or exhi-

24. See F. Ritchin, *In Our Own Image: The Coming Revolution in Photography* (New York: Aperture, 1990), and, for a historical discussion of photo fakery, G. Le Marec, *Les Photos Truquées: Un siècle de propagande par l'image* (Paris: Editions Atlas, 1985) and A. Jaubert, *Le Commissariat aux archives: Les photos qui falsifient l'histoire,* Paris, B. Barrault, 1986.

bitions, or demanding a greater say in a publication's ultimate use of their material.

The future of reportage is not clear. As societies become more and more submerged by great numbers of images, will readers still be able to, or want to, react? As publications continue to become more formulaic, what will the photo reporter be allowed to say? Will the new digital technologies be used in a way which will call into doubt the integrity of photographs to the point where the public no longer believes them?

What becomes clear in any consideration of the evolution of photojournalism and reportage is its extraordinary vitality, its potential for increasing sophistication, and the large number of men and women in countries around the world who are engaged in documenting their own societies. In many ways, it is a form that has been considered so self-evident, so automatic, that few in the mainstream have tried to plumb its possibilities. In an increasingly complex and troubled world, strong and reliable photographic reporting seems more necessary than ever.

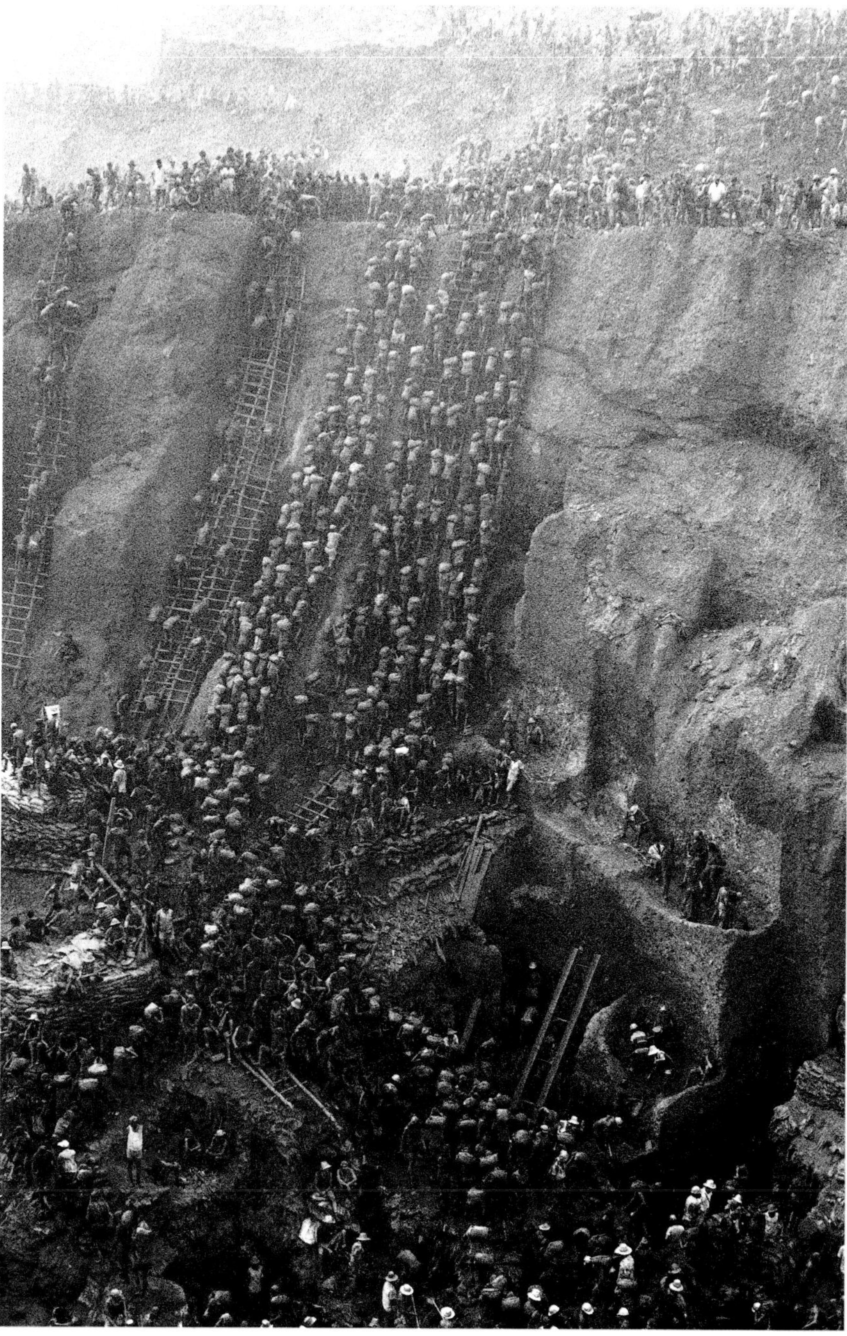

SEBASTIÃO SALGADO, *Gold-miners in the Serra Pelada Mine,* Brazil, 1986.

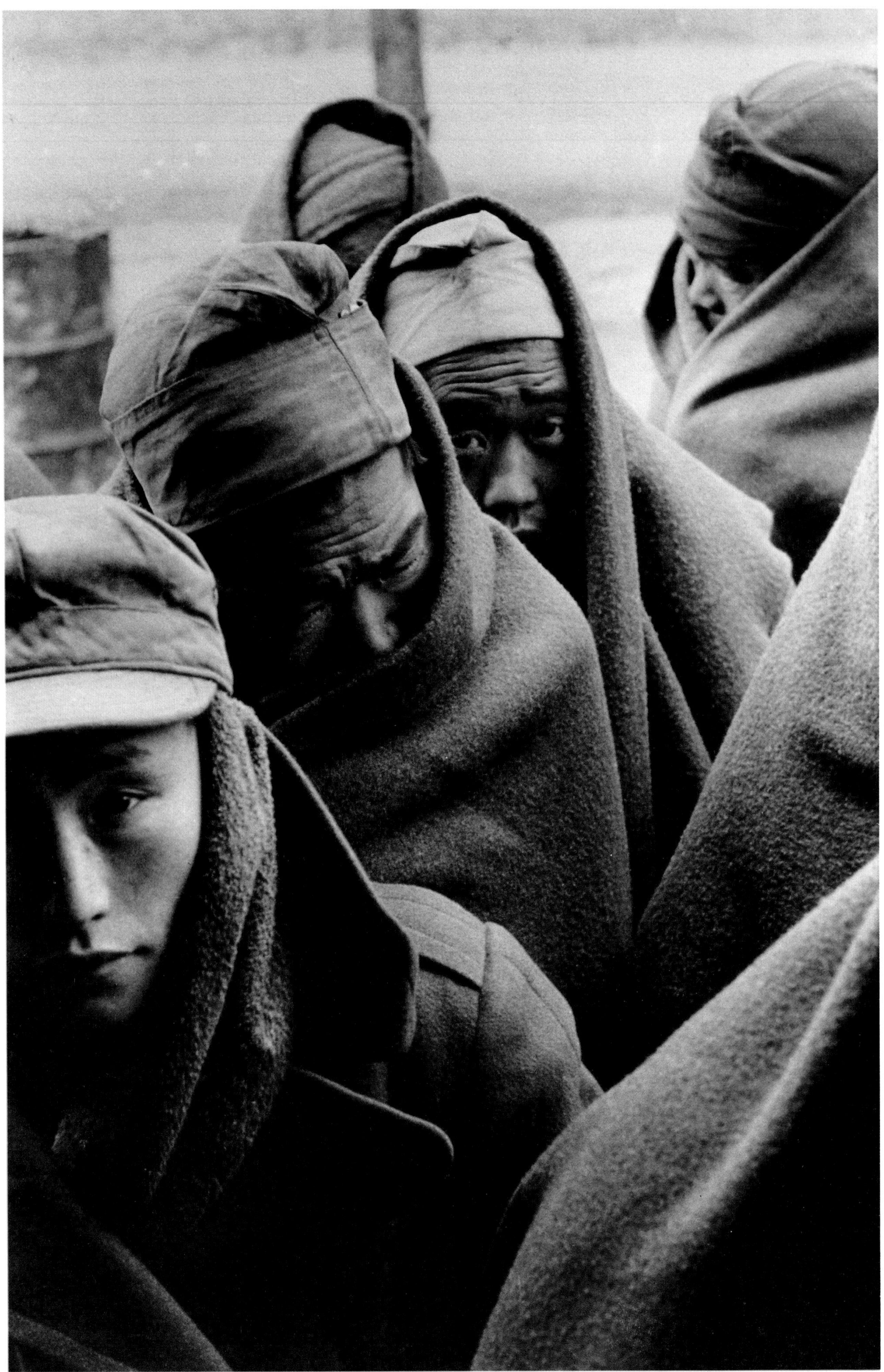

LOOKING AT OTHERS

34

Humanism and neo-realism

Jean-Claude Gautrand

Already discernible during the 1930s, but forged by the flames of the Second World War, a lyrical trend, warm, fervent, and responsive to the sufferings of humanity began to assert itself during the 1950s in Europe, particularly in France. Sympathetic to neo-realist cinema or the poetry of Jacques Prévert, photographers often dreamed of a world of mutual succor and compassion, encapsulated ideally in a solicitous vision. The exhibition *The Family of Man*, organized by Steichen in New York in 1955, marked the culmination of this humanistic universalism, which sought to understand rather than pass judgment.

If we accept that photography can, among other things, provide an account of human existence, it was able to do this from the moment when, at the end of the nineteenth century, the photographer became an irrefutable witness to life in the world at large. Several trends arose from this. Some photographers plunged into the drama of current events that were often violent. Others opted for a more scientific or sociological approach which calmly explored daily life. That was the task which Stryker entrusted to the Farm Security Administration's photographic program, as opposed to the mere reporting of events. "News photos treat events as a single entity; ours are episodic. The news photo is dramatic; in every subject is action whereas our photograph shows what lies outside the action. It covers things more broadly."[1]

The photographer and his time

Other photographers, however, distanced themselves from these two approaches. They preferred to wander as their fancy took them, looking at people tenderly, ironically, humorously or sympathetically, producing images which, cumulatively, bear witness to a veritable personal creation. Preferring to work for books and magazines, they were less interested in particular events than in the places which they traversed and explored and in the exchange of looks, the implicit yet fleeting relationship between them and the subject photographed. For them, the primary motive of an artistic project involved the routine and the banal, recorded with tenderness and, above all, with a great faith in humanity.

Already Baudelaire had characterized the painter of modern life as seeking "the transitory, the fleeting, the conditional half of art" but ignoring the other half – "the eternal and the unchanging". Here there is a clear analogy between, on the one hand, those who ceaselessly pursue the newsworthy, the exceptional, that which sets people apart, and, on the other hand, those who are concerned with those things which bring people together. As Jean Clair wrote, "poets of the identical [and] not of the different", these photographers wandered the streets, seeking a ray of light or a slice of life, suddenly magnified by a smile or a look.

This "humanist" photography, which reached its peak in the 1950s, would follow various paths, sometimes parallel but always maintaining, whoever the people concerned or whatever their behavior, obvious characteristics in common: a certain generosity, optimism, sensitivity to the simple joys of life, an empathy for people in the street, caught in action, and for the symbolism of scenes which suggest a common sense of the wonderful. This "photographic humanism", a fairly specific aspect of French photography in the immediate post-war years, did not simply appear unexpectedly, without warning. It is deeply rooted much further back in time.

◀ Werner Bischof, *Chinese Prisoners of War, South Korea*, 1951.

1. R. E. Stryker, "The F.S.A. Collection of Photographs", in R. E. Stryker and N. Wood, *In this Proud Land*, Boston, Little, Brown and Co, 1973.

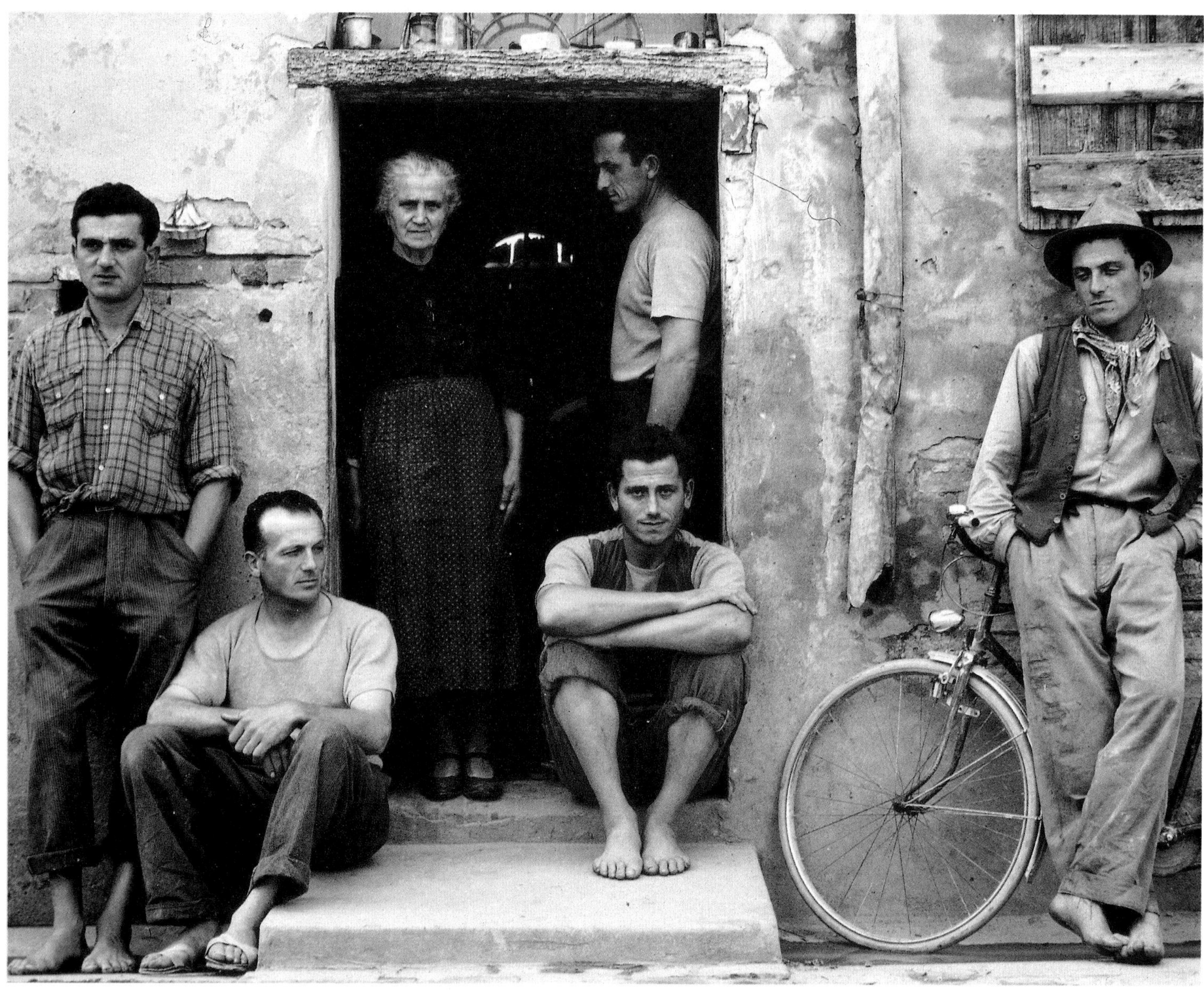

PAUL STRAND, *The Lusetti family, Luzzara, Italy,* 1953.

Without going as far as back as the Middle Ages, like Blaise Cendrars, for whom "every artist who stoops towards the people returns to tradition,"[2] we have to go back to the end of the nineteenth century to find a few photographers who, thanks to technical innovations, widened their field of vision by concerning themselves with street life and human activities. The "candid" photography of Paul Martin, the minor tradespeople of Atget, the portraits of "typical Parisians" by Paul Géniaux or Louis Vert, both of whom scoured the French capital in search of daily rituals – far removed from contemporary aesthetic tastes – these were, without doubt, the first examples of that poetico-social predisposition which would reach its zenith half a century later. This picturesque, tender world was already the essential preoccupation of *Paris Moderne*, a review launched in 1896 which sought to be "an original and lively collection of inestimable documentary value, for it is the infallible and truthful interpreter of Life in all its aspects".[3] Indeed, several of the photographs published in it display an astonishing artistic realism, undoubtedly heralding that kind of slightly sentimental and anecdotal photography which paints a real picture of the human condition. "If those actual street characters who so much amused our forefathers have disappeared, like actors going back into the wings when their part is finished, others have replaced them, so the stage is never empty. It is a theatre which never lets up. The play isn't the same, the scenery and costumes have changed, but the show goes on."[4]

This idea was shared by some postcard publishers – a form of photographic distribution which was extraordinarily popular at the beginning of the twentieth century. Millions of postcards flooded the market, pandering to the popular taste for these simple, lively images. Postcards, whose important role is still undervalued, are evidence of what *Paris Moderne* had already realized: the existence of a need for social documentation. These cards, which Yvan Christ

2. B. Cendrars, in R. Doisneau, *La Banlieue de Paris*, Paris, Seghers, 1949; revised edition, Paris, Denoël, 1983, p. 17.

3. A. Delinières, in *Paris Moderne*, no. 1, October 1896.

4. *Ibid.*

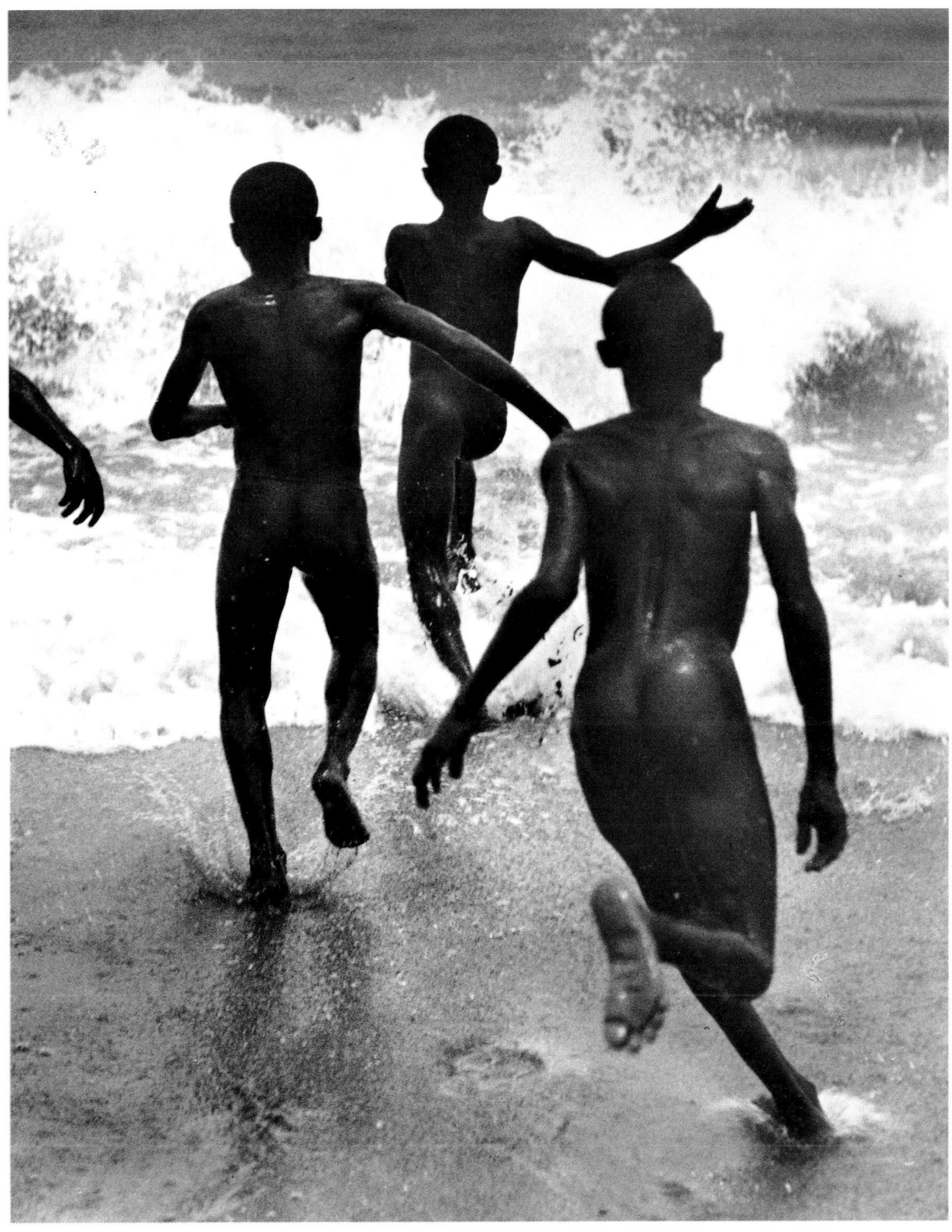

MARTIN MUNKACSI,
Liberia,
1931.

aptly called "the perfect mirror of everyday life" – reflecting, so well, habits and traditions, holidays and work, a contemporary tastes in decor – mark the birth of a human kind of new photographic documentation.

This trend was international, often resulting from the spread of photographic studios to even the smallest towns and villages or the role of traveling photographers.

Life through the media

The press, now expanding rapidly, also created a demand for more and more images. Some photographers favored, above all, spontaneity and an implicit relationship between the photographer and the photographed – an attitude more usually found in amateurs than professionals. As early as 1912, in Budapest, one of the main centers of culture at the beginning of the century, André Kertész, an amateur, took photographs which followed this trend. In his images of military life at the front or of peasant life in the Hungarian countryside, Kertész did not work like a "reporter", but adopted a sympathetic approach to his subjects. Without any artistic preconceptions, he photographed ordinary things, magnified by his poetic vision, conferring a new

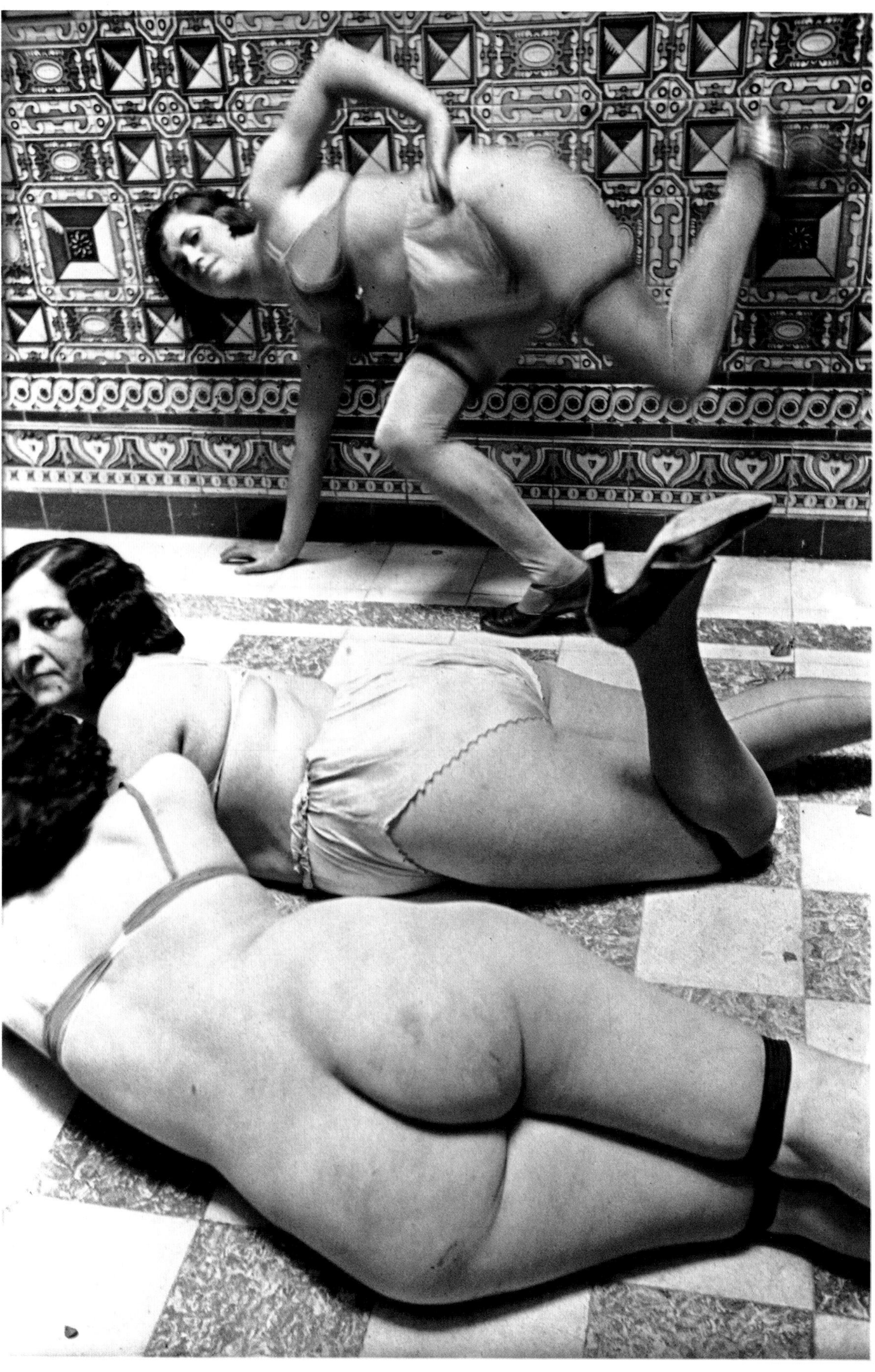

Henri Cartier-Bresson, *Prostitutes at Alicante, Spain,* 1933.

dignity on anonymous people – passers-by, peasants, tramps, children – all captured tenderly and modestly, without any ambiguity. The first Hungarian photographs by his friend Munkacsi, recently rediscovered, reveal the interest which this eclectic artist had in the same subject matter. Both of them would later change their approach. Kertész, however, always remained attached to this humanistic approach, at the point where realism meets poetry.

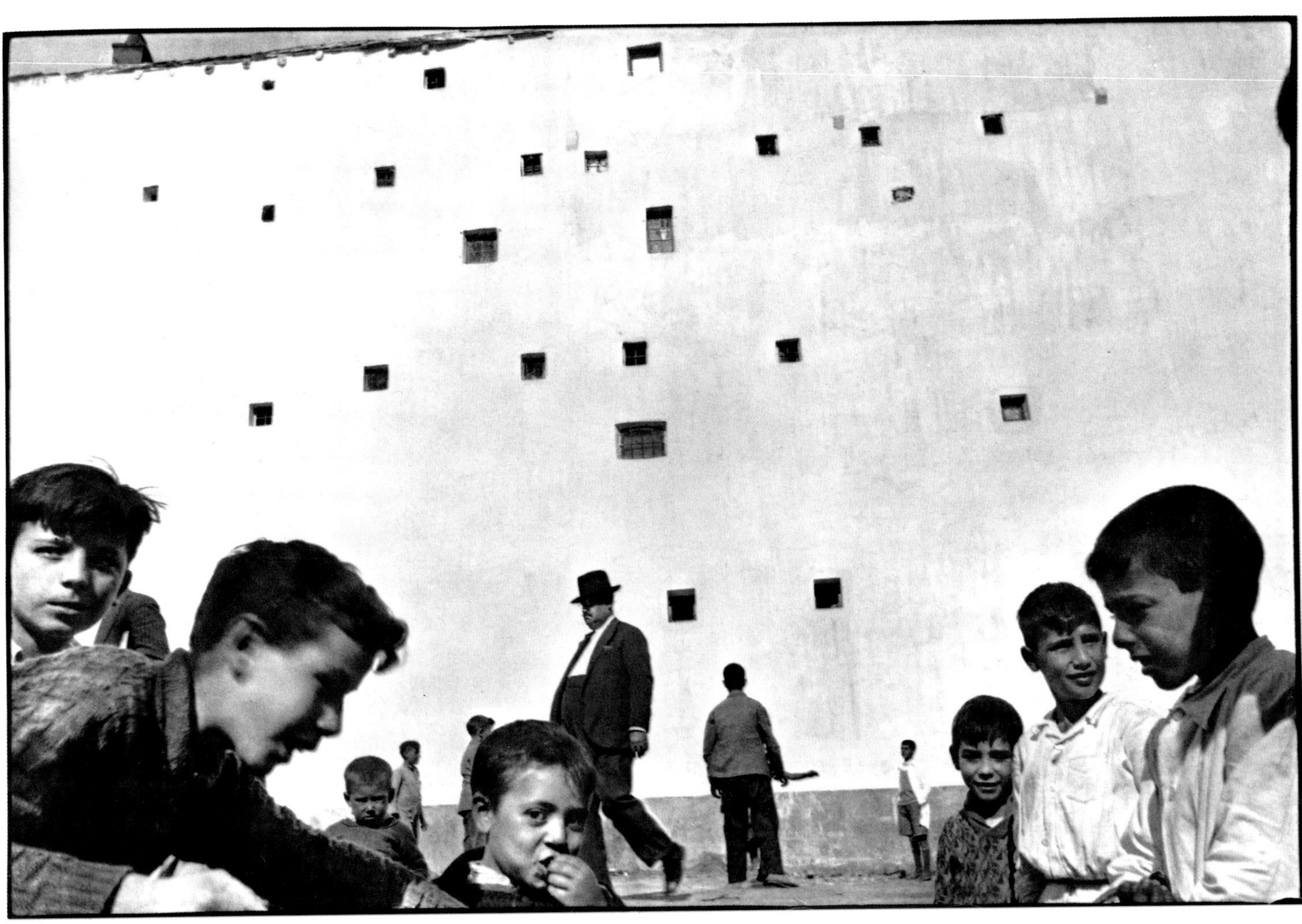

HENRI CARTIER-BRESSON, *Madrid*, 1933.

In the United States, in 1916–1917, the magazine *Camera Work* published a series of instantaneous street photographs by the young Paul Strand. Stieglitz described his images as "brutally direct". They too affirm a profoundly humanistic point of view, which Strand confirmed throughout his later work, from *Mexican Portfolio* (1933) to *Un Paese* (1955), including *La France de Profil* (1952). Like Kertész, but perhaps more vigorously, Strand captures the dignity and nobility of these simple people, and their lives.

In the early 1930s, during the long period of experimentation which characterized the start of his work, Henri Cartier-Bresson (who recognized his debt to, among others, Kertész and Munkacsi) was influenced by this new spirit, which, in his case, coexisted quite happily with the influence of Surrealism. He explored the world of humble people and those on the fringes of society in Mexican slums or on the streets of Marseilles. "His attitude is sympathetic, but devoid of compassion", noted Peter Galassi, adding "his subjects are often aware of the photographer's presence, and it is clear that he has obtained their cooperation".[5] This co-operation, implicit at the very least, would prove to be one of the primary characteristics of humanist photography.[6]

Thus, during the same period, Kertész, Cartier-Bresson, and also the latter's Mexican friend Alvarez-Bravo, who was rooted in the very depths of his country's culture and traditions, looked on social conditions with a compassionate eye. Likewise, in the early 1930s Brassaï photographed with generous candor the people he met by chance while walking in the street. His book *Paris de nuit* (1933), which illustrates the night-time denizens of bars and dance-halls, reveals some extraordinary individuals. This "living eye" which, as Miller says, is all-seeing, created an astonishing, yet unknown, world by concentrating on humble people as much as great artists. Believing that one must start with everyday life to attain the surreal, Brassaï rejoined his compatriot Kertész on the shores of a Surrealist world that was already very influential, together with Bill Brandt, for whom the most banal aspects of everyday life remained worthy of consideration.

Whatever path they were to follow later, it is undeniable that through the eyes of these creative artists, the 1930s saw the appearance of that inspiration which later would be called "humanist". For Strand, it was social, for Kertész, it was based on the unusual, for Cartier-Bresson, the formal and surreal, for Brassaï, set in fantasy,

5. P. Galassi, *Henri Cartier-Bresson: The Early Work*, Museum of Modern Art, New York, 1987.

6. M. de Thézy, *La photographie humaniste, 1930–1960: histoire d'un mouvement en France*, Paris, Contrejour, 1992.

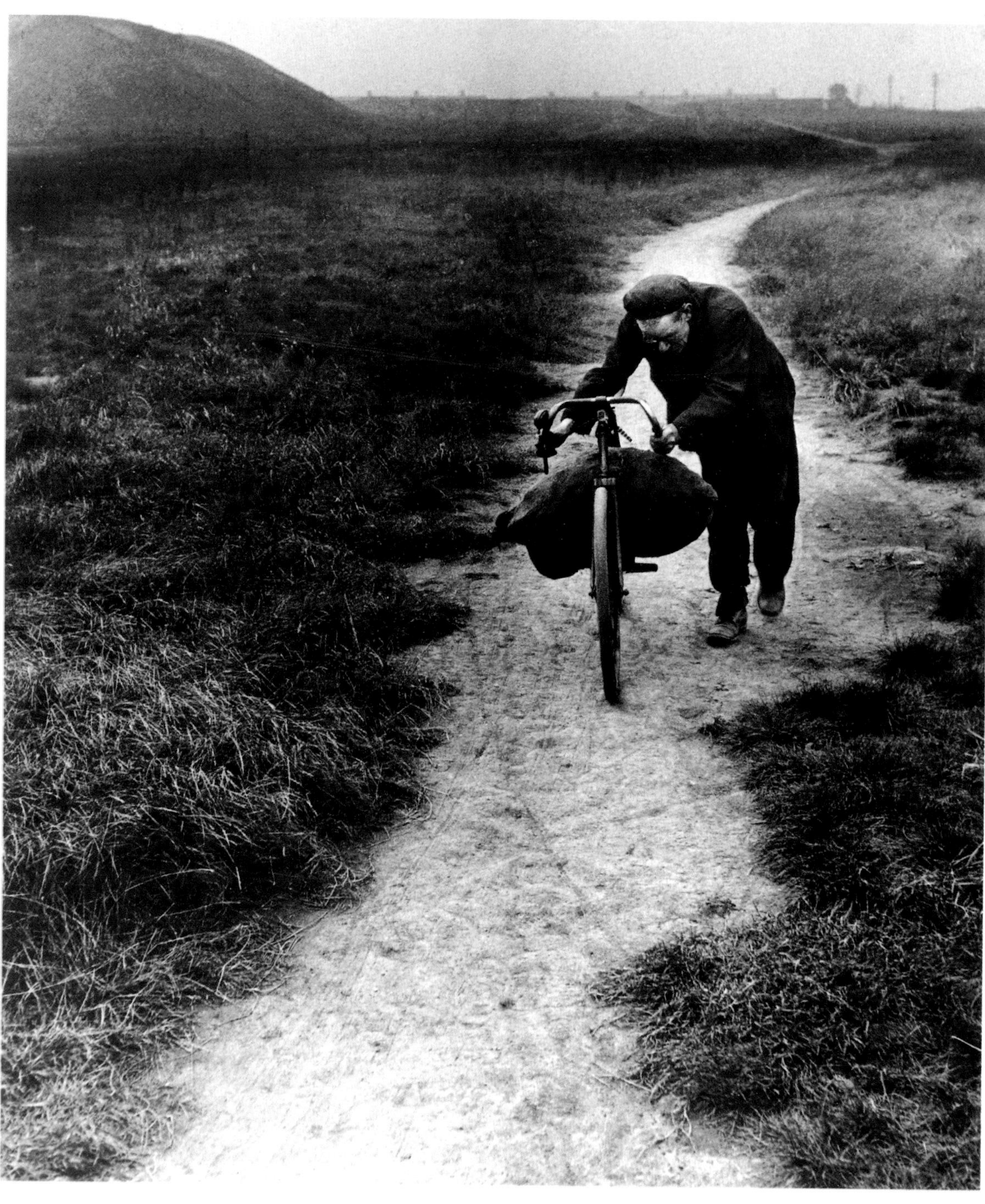

BILL BRANDT,
Coal Searcher Going Home to Jarrow,
1937.
Art Institute of Chicago.

for Alvarez-Bravo, in magic. Their influence would be even greater because of the number of illustrated magazines at this time (*Regards, VU,* etc.), particularly those linked to the socialist or communist movements. The exhibition mounted in 1936 by the A.E.A.R. (Association of Revolutionary Writers and Artists) at the Pléiade Gallery in Paris was devoted to *Documents de la Vie Sociale* [Documents of Social Life]. This trend was also reinforced by the emergence in the mid-1930s of the great realist current in poetry, literature, and, above all, cinema, which accompanied the social upheavals of the Popular Front in 1936.

This poetic realism, which was so much a feature of contemporary cinema, was completely saturated with the bitter-sweet poetry and the popular voice of Jacques Prévert. The poetry of the banks of the Marne, which would inspire a famous photograph by Cartier-Bresson, was already present in Carné's film *Nogent, Eldorado du dimanche* (1929), just as the tender, humorous, and popular spirit of Paris appeared in René Clair's film *Sous les toits de Paris* (1930). This concern for the well-being of workers, for their joys and sorrows, found its finest expression in two famous films: Carné's *Quai des brumes* (1938), and Duvivier's *La Belle Époque* (1936).

New photographers were emerging at the time: Doisneau, Willy Ronis, René-Jacques, Émile Savitry, Pierre Jahan, Papillon. Some of them joined ranks in the association of revolutionary writers and artists which staged *Documents de la Vie Sociale* in June 1936. Others such as René Zuber, Pierre Boucher, Émeric Feher, Denise

Bellon, and Pierre Verger founded the photographic agency Alliance Photo in 1934, which Cartier-Bresson, Robert Capa, and David Seymour joined at an early date. Linked in friendship, these photographers, whose preoccupations were still journalistic and documentary, paid particular attention to the glances and smiles they received from people they met and the new cults of leisure and athletic activities, and the exaltation of the body.

The Second World War, however, interrupted this process of evolution by hindering photographic activity. Film and cameras were hard to obtain and the Nazis controlled the press. Widely dispersed photographers had few opportunities for work, and humanism was a long way from their current preoccupations. Wartime iconography consisted mainly of photoreportage work signed by Roger Schall or Zucca. Even if among their many images devoted to the pleasures of the occupying powers discovering Paris a few photographs show streetside soup kitchens, people wearing yellow stars or queues in front of food stores – images which are emotive in a special way – we are a long way away from the poetic-realistic intentions of pre-war years. Only with the Liberation would they flourish again, thanks – among others – to a few images by Robert Doisneau, who immortalized the people of Paris erecting their barricades.

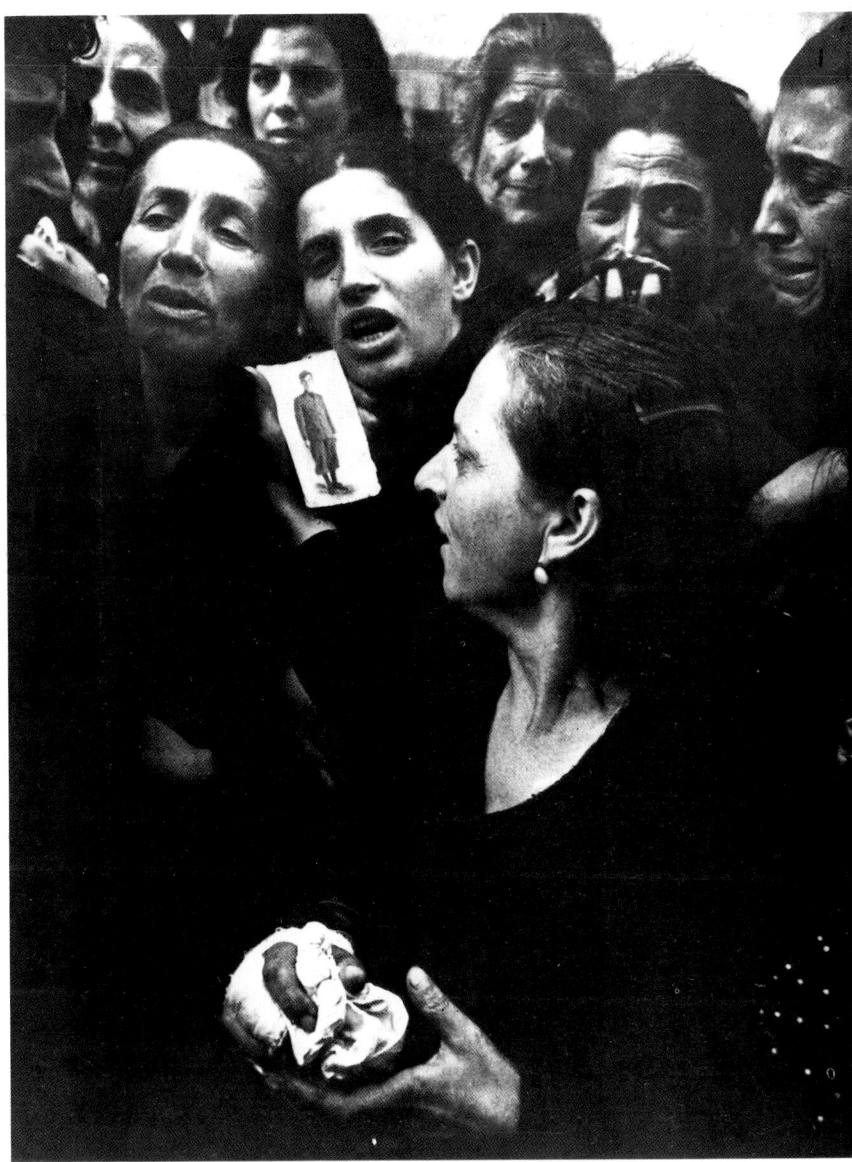

Robert Capa, *Mothers of Naples,* 1943.

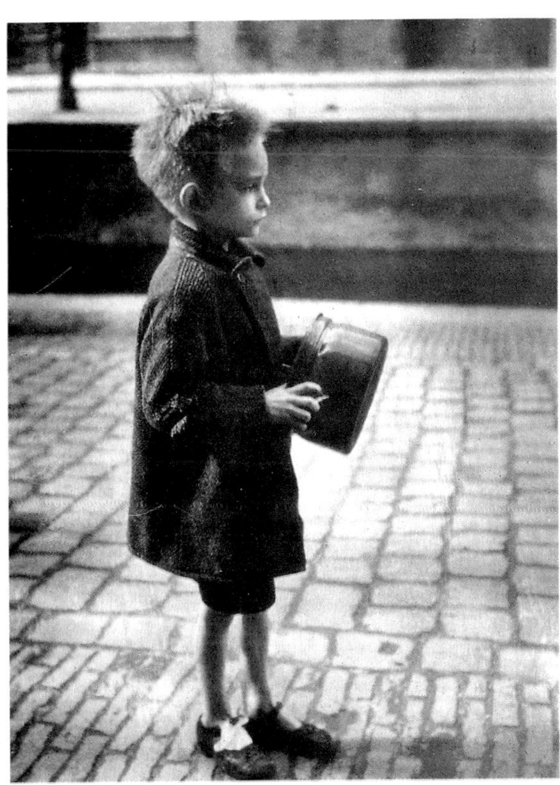

◄ Emmy Andriesse, *The Famine Winter, Amsterdam,* 1944–1945, print collection, Rijksuniversiteit, Leyden.

The humanism of the media

Immediately after the war, more than ever, reporters had the main say. The illustrated press started up again with new vigor, reflecting the public's thirst for news stories. Already, however, the very notion of reporting was changing. If for some it involved primarily the traditional recording of burning topical issues, others attempted to promote hope and encourage dialogue in order to prevent tragic events happening again.

W. Eugene Smith is the perfect example of this type of humanistic journalist which sprang up immediately after the cataclysm. An idealist, often an optimist, a passionate, sensitive, and demanding man ("I try to understand before I photograph, then I shoot with passion what I want to photograph"),[7] Smith, who was taken on by *Life* magazine in 1939, undertook a number of important commissions on specific subjects such as *Country Doctor* (1948), *Spanish Village,* and *Nurse Midwife* (1951). His photographs bear wit-ness to his

7. Quoted by C. Osman in *Histoire de la photographie,* Paris, Bordas, 1986, p. 169.

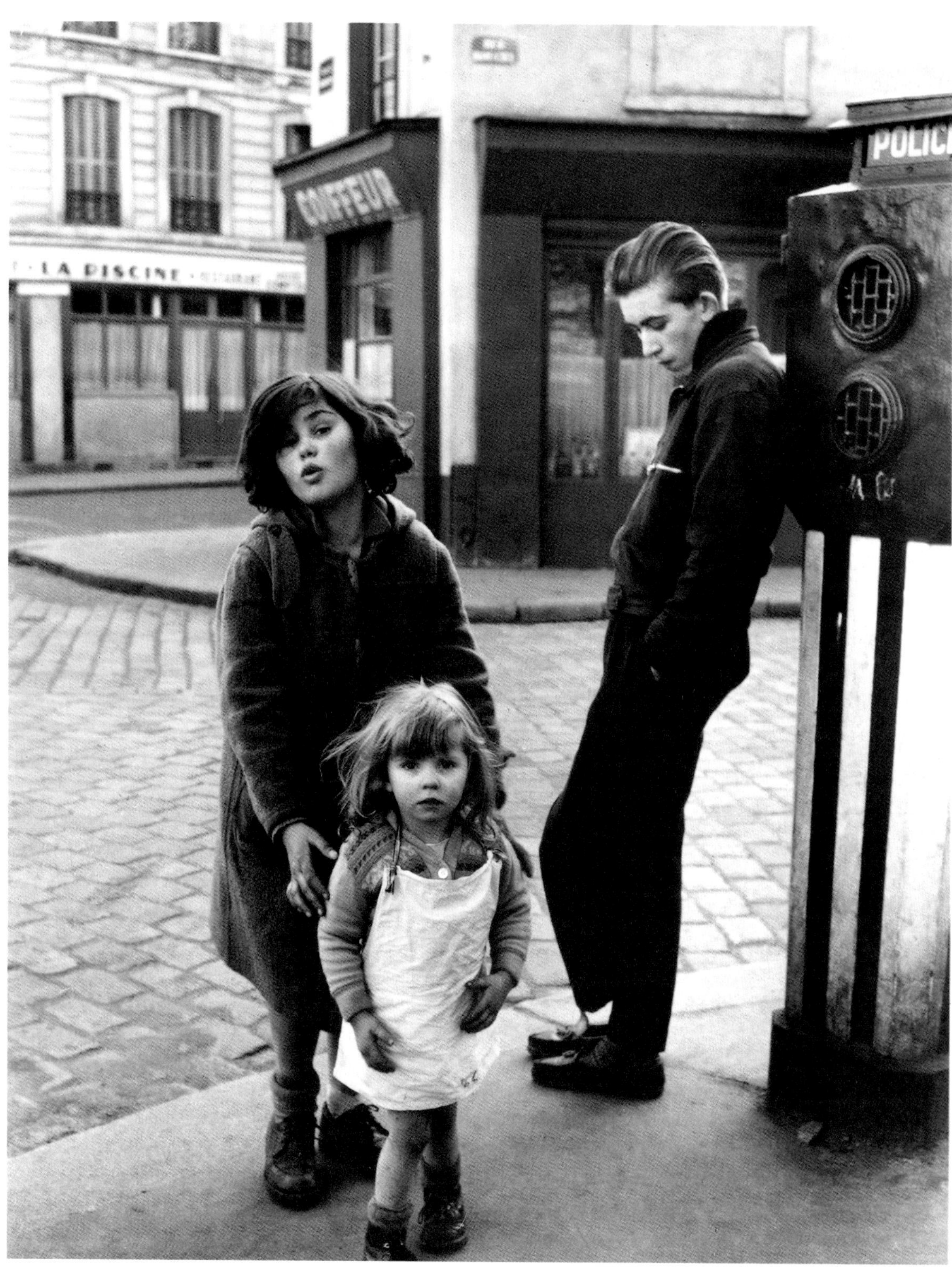

ROBERT DOISNEAU, *The Children of Place Hébert,* 1957.

commitment and his certainty that he could create a better world by giving his readers "the experience of life". His powerful photographic output is characterized by its emotional content and commitment, its realism and its aesthetic quality. As demanding about form as about substance, Smith confessed to being "constantly torn between the attitude of the conscientious journalist who reports facts and that of the creative artist who knows that poetry and literal truth seldom go together".

At the center of the photo agency Magnum, founded in 1947, Werner Bischof modified his approach, which until then had been directed towards formal research, and adopted a similar viewpoint to Smith. "I think I have now transferred to a human dimension the importance that I formerly accorded to form and matter [...] the face of suffering humanity has moved into the foreground."[8] He went to Indo-China in 1952, where he photographed the sufferings of the civilian population: "There are still human souls without uniforms". Werner Bischof corresponds to the model of a humanist for whom "photography is a philanthropic message whose signs must move people in a calm way, evoke with discre-

8. *Werner Bischof, 1916–1954,* Paris, Arthaud, 1960.

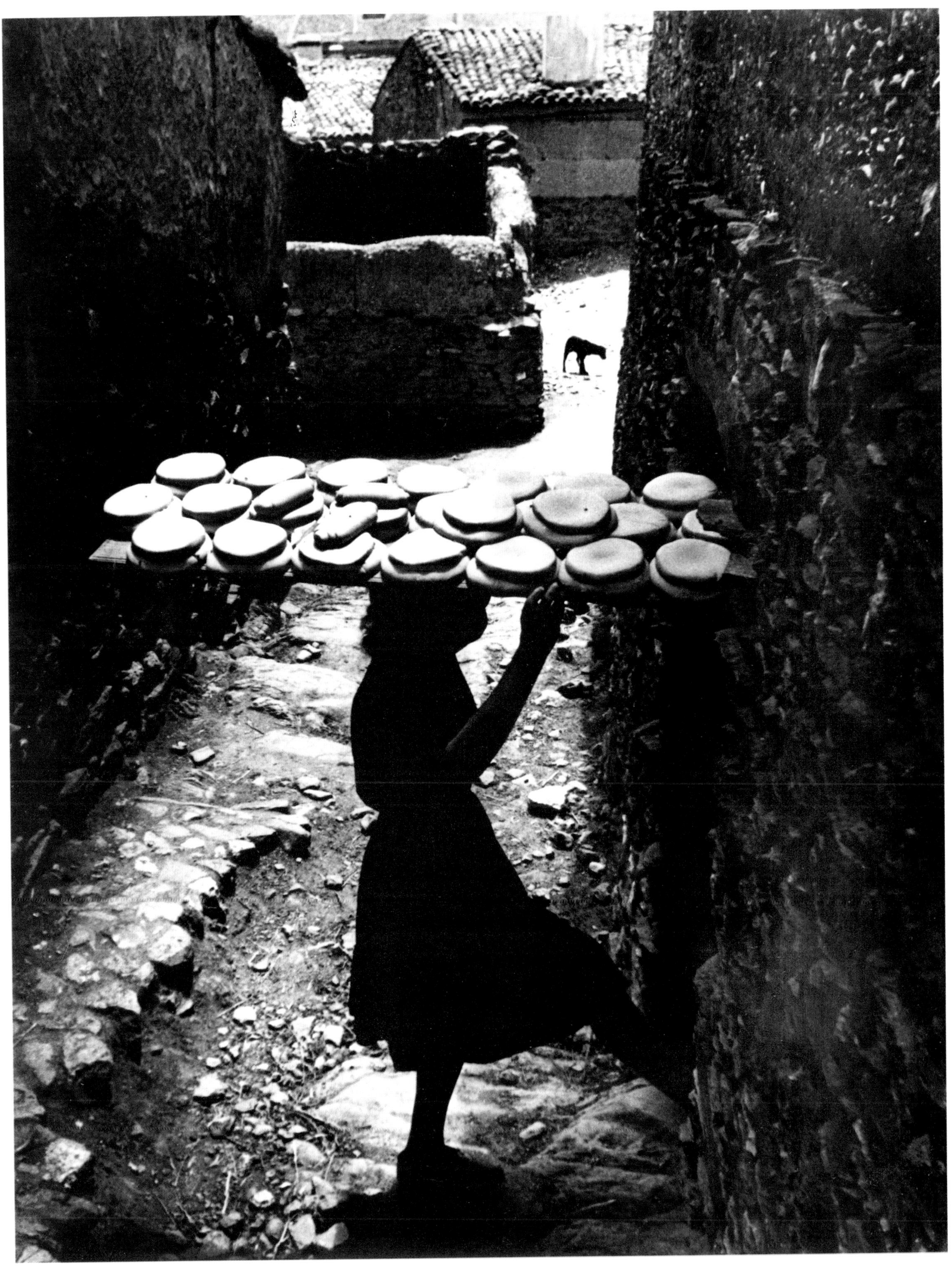

W. EUGENE SMITH,
Delivering the Bread, from "Spanish Village", 1951.

ROBERT DOISNEAU, *Strict Intimacy, Montrouge,* 1945.

ROBERT MAYNE, *Children in Southam Street,* 1956.
▼

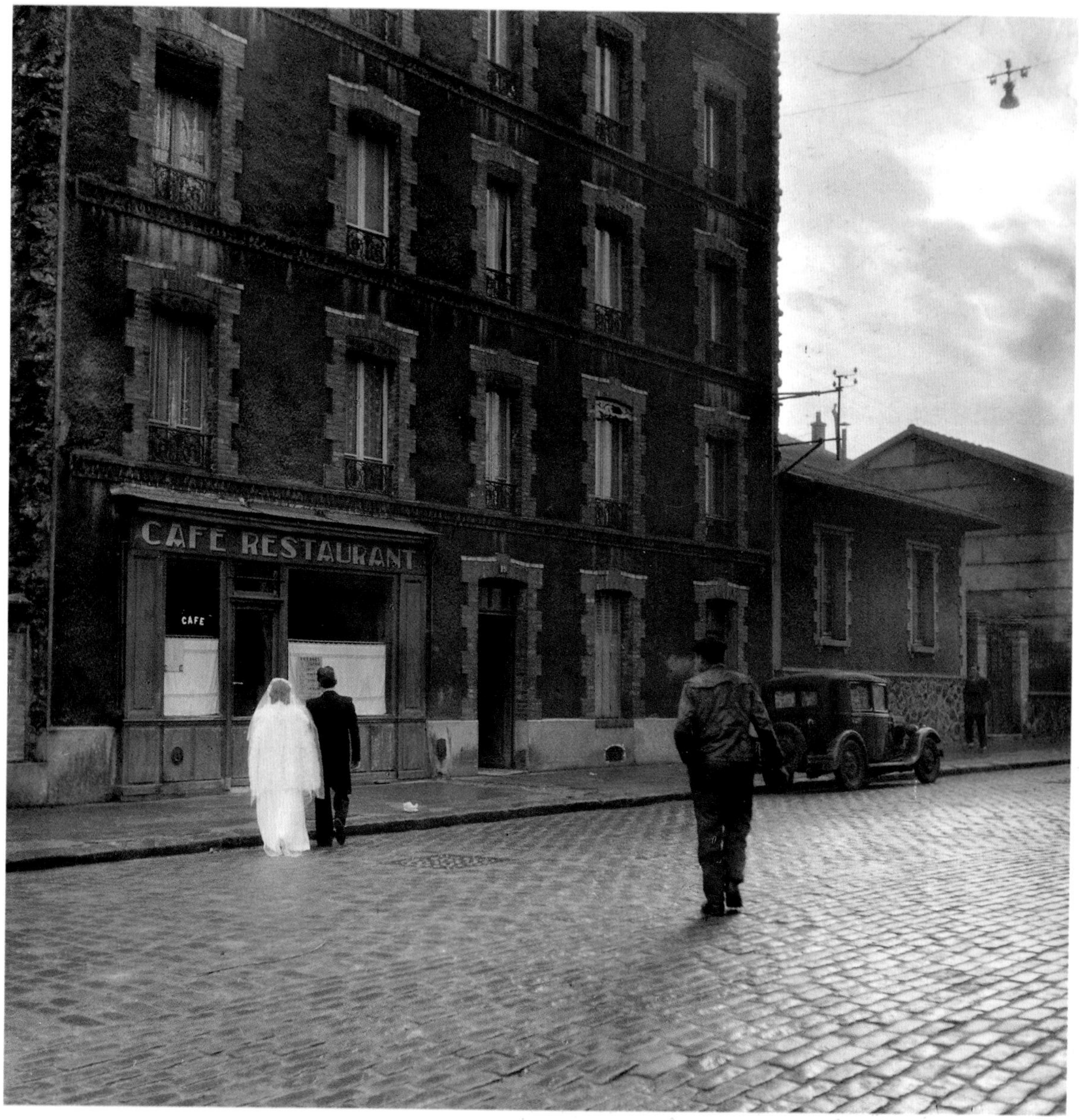

tion, express without insisting".[9] Trained artistically (with Emil Schulthess) through contact with the hard humanitarian realities of the immediate post-war period, by his charity work for the organization Don Suisse, and by his reporting of the famine in India (1951–1952), he revealed in Japan in 1952 a more peaceful and serene style than his approach in Chile and Peru, in 1954, where he died in an accident.

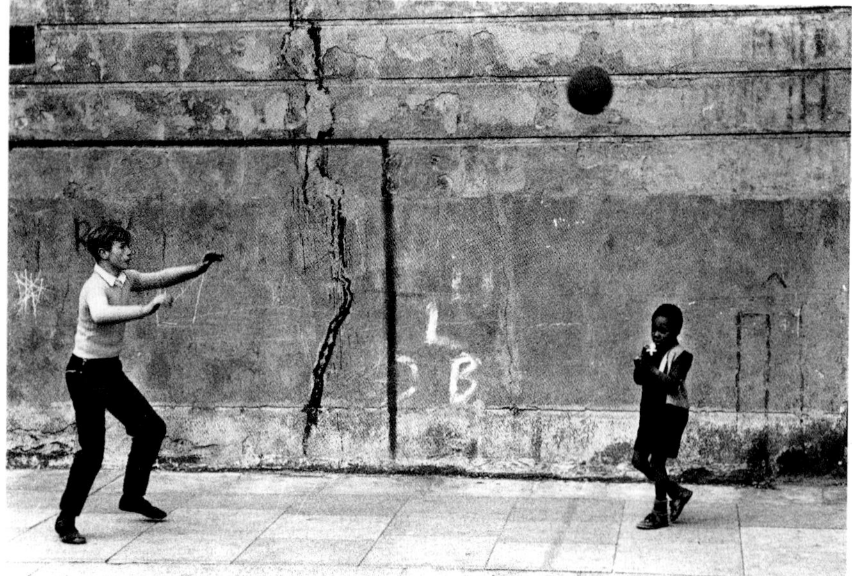

Other photographers also became involved with their subjects in a similar way. Bruce Davidson sought "not only to arouse emotion but also to do something for mankind".[10] It was Smith's pictures, he said, "which showed me the way I wanted to go". His series on Mme Fauchet taken in Montparnasse (1955), all displaying a nostalgic tenderness, illustrates the way he sought sensitive expression in the most banal situations. In this series, as in his work *East 100th Street* on the black people of Harlem, he does not attempt to downgrade them or insist on their misery, but succeeds, rather, in photographing them as if he were holding out his hand to them. Even more deeply engaged, Marc Riboud considered photography as a means of communicating and sharing his love for others and of involving himself in

9. *Histoire de voir: de l'instant à l'imaginaire,* Photo Poche no. 42, Paris, 1989, p. 28.

10. *Bruce Davidson,* Photo Poche no. 14, Paris, 1984.

their troubles. "A look", he wrote, "is the sign or at least a hint of an exchange [...] I like that visual tenderness which makes Doisneau's brief glances so successful."[11]

During the 1950s, Robert Doisneau does, indeed, seems to have been the model of that artistic trend which was imposing itself in France and elsewhere, encouraged, once again, by the revival of the cinema which immediately after the Liberation renewed its links with pre-war traditions. The Carné-Prévert partnership was still active (*Les portes de la nuit*), joined by Jacques Becker (*Antoine et Antoinette*), René Clément (*La bataille du rail*), and Rouquier. This phenomenon, however, remained most powerful in Italy where neo-realism took over the market and spawned films which were inspired by the street, the Resistance, and socio-economic problems. Rossellini (*Rome, Open City*), V. de Sica (*Sciuscià* and *The Bicycle Thieves*), and Visconti produced films which in turn inspired photographers such as Ferdinando Scianna or members of the active avant-garde group La Bussola [The Compass], including Finazzi, Cavalli, Fulvio Roiter, and, above all, Mario Giacomelli, who concealed his humanism beneath an expressionist visual style. Somewhat isolated in Britain, Roger Mayne, the direct heir of Brandt, portrayed life in the street, while Dutch photographers oscillated between urban landscapes and sociological images.

This style was, however, appreciated above all in France, where a photograph was considered as a judgment on human values and attitudes, a witness to unexpected encounters. Furthermore, this type of image benefited from the resurgence of the illustrated press – *Cavalcade, Réalités, Ambiance, Paris Match, Noir et Blanc, Point de Vue – Images du monde, Plaisirs de France* – all of which were heavily illustrated – and also from the publishing industry, which produced many works, abundantly illustrated by the principal photographers of the day.[12]

Many of them, furthermore, were involved with the agency Rapho, refounded in 1945. The old team of Savitry, Landau, and Brassaï was soon joined by Doisneau, Boubat, Ronis, Janine Niépce, and Sabine Weiss – a group which was particularly representative of the humanist trend. This trend was also represented by photographers such as Lucien Clergue (who portrayed acrobats and gypsies from 1955) or Jean Dieuzaide, whose *Voyage en Ibérie* (1951) is a model of empathy with and attention to the simple gestures of the artisan and the peasant. Like him, Sabine Weiss expressed faith in mankind: "Light, gesture, look, movement, silence, tension, repose, rigor, relaxation. I would like to incorporate all these things in the creative instant in order to express, with a minimum of means, the essential part of humankind."[13]

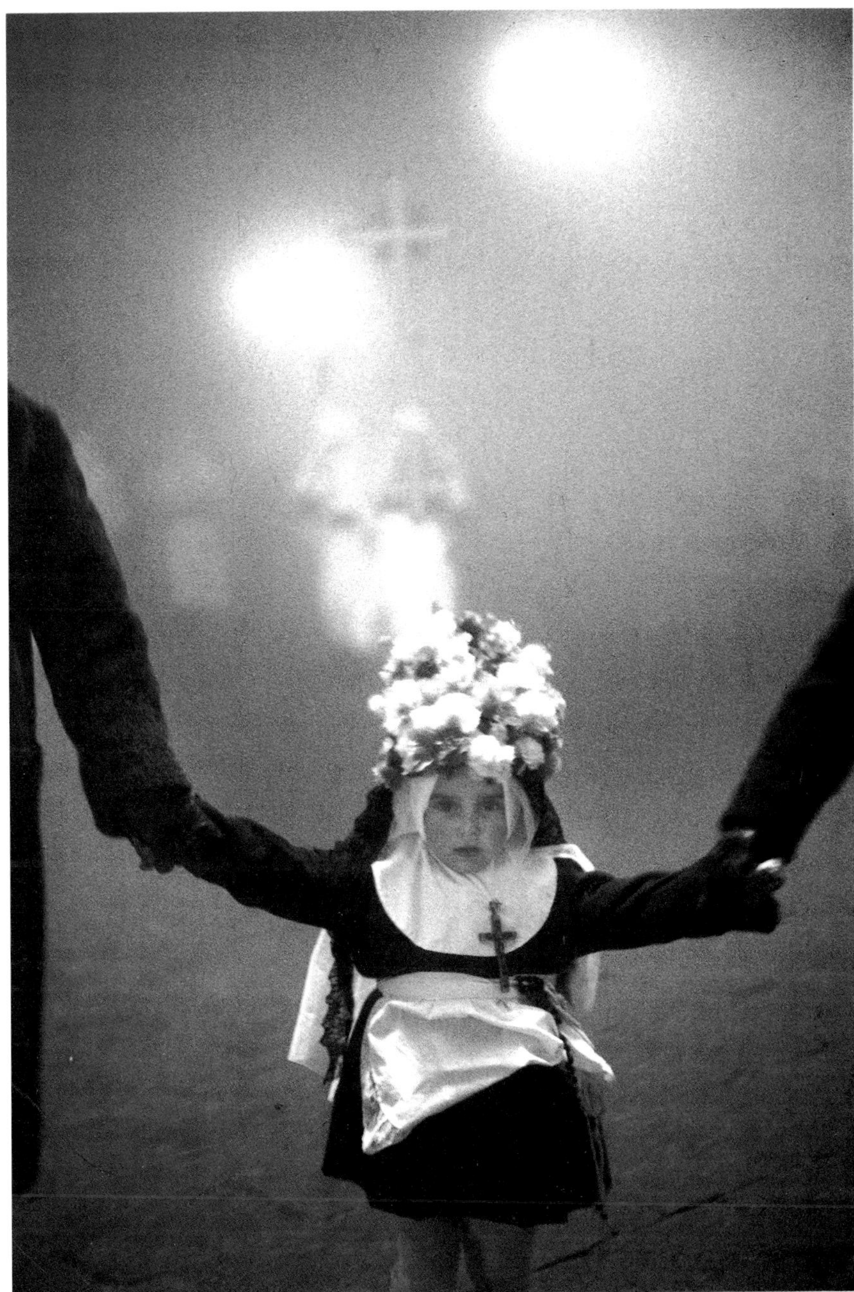

Ferdinando Scianna,
Religious Festival in Sicily,
1963.

"My country and Paris"

In written accounts of this period, the name *Group des XV* [Group of Fifteen] often crops up. While this group, founded in 1946 by André Garban, certainly included Willy Ronis and Robert Doisneau among its members, as well as Marcel Bovis and René-Jacques, other members displayed quite different preoccupations. It was really in the National Salon, also created in 1946 and subsequently organized each year at the Bibliothèque Nationale, that the real nature of this trend emerged. Describing the National Salon of 1948, Waldemar George wrote, "The repertory of photographs is huge. Their sources of inspiration are numerous and varied. While they

11. *Marc Riboud*, Photo Poche no. 37, Paris, 1989.

12. F. Cali, *France aux visages*, Paris, Arthaud, 1953; *La France à livre ouvert*, Paris, Seghers, 1954; F. Cali, *Dictionnaire pittoresque de la France*, Paris, Arthaud, 1955.

13. *Sabine Weiss: intimes convictions*, Paris, Contrejour, 1989, p. 17.

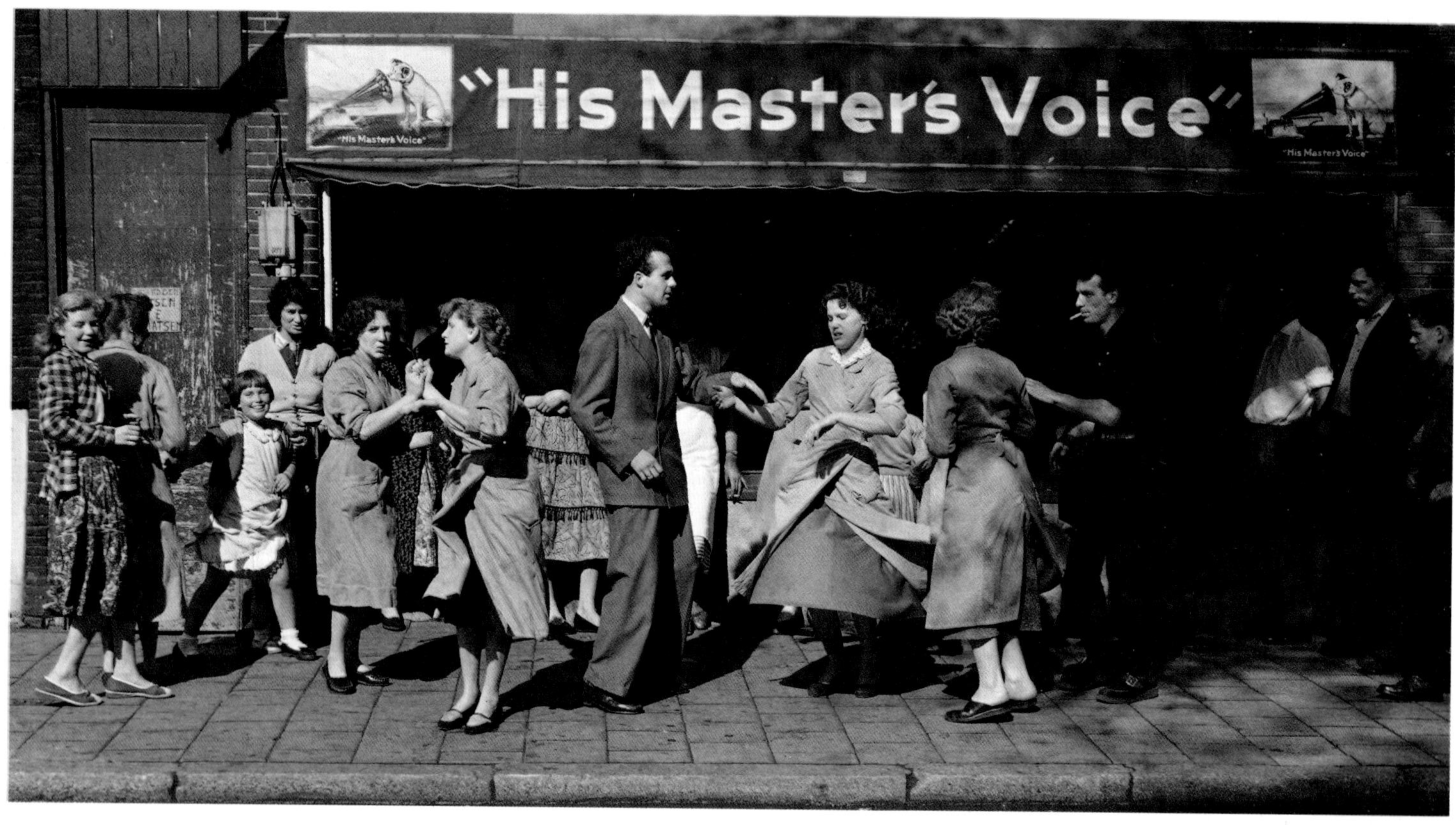

E. VAN MOERKERKEN, *Lunchtime on the Lindengracht, Amsterdam,* 1956.

have not been influenced by any painter, unless it be Utrillo, they listen to the voices of poets. The imprint of Jacques Prévert may be discerned in a large number of pages." So, also, might the influence of Pierre Mac Orlan, Francis Carco, Marcel Carné, and Kurt Weill. He added: "Ménilmontant and la Porte de Clignancourt are the sites portrayed by the majority of our image chasers. This liking for the vermin-ridden suburbs might perhaps be interpreted as a fashion, but above all as a fervent quest for a truth which can scarcely be touched in the fine districts of Paris."[14] Among the exhibitors, Waldemar George mentions Brassaï, Boubat, Ronis, Papillon, and Doisneau. When these same images were exhibited by the Photo League in New York, they drew an enthusiastic response from the *New York Times*'s critic: "Their French origin is unmistakable, marked by a subtlety, tolerance, and understanding which are often lacking in American photography! [...] These are images which have something to say, and which say it successfully." Barrett Bildersee, writing in *Camera Eye*, perceived "the way a Frenchman's camera reflects the people and the times in which he lives" as the deep motivation of this trend, the raison d'être of these "simple, human, often somewhat melancholy images, because life is often gray in France these days, and French photographers do not represent only the image of a subject, but also the emotion which comes from it, its spirit."[15]

These were photographs which were concerned as much with content as with form, and which attached an extreme importance to the emotions. This was a form of poetry – an exchange of knowing looks which, in France, found their favorite location in the characteristic setting of the old streets and gleaming cobblestone streets of working-class Paris. Chief among those who celebrated this place was, of course, Robert Doisneau. His benevolent, somewhat ironic approach allowed him to capture "the ordinary gestures of ordinary people" thanks to the privileged relationships he established with those he met. "Exotic settings and distant travel are often a confession of failure. When I am stressed I simply go to Paris or to the suburbs [...] In this everyday setting I am finally able to take my time, and to enjoy wasting it. In watching things and people whom you might well think devoid of interest but which, if one pays more attention, have buried within them their weight of emotion, feelings of pity, idiosyncrasies." There were days, he added, when "the simple fact of seeing felt like real happiness".[16] Doisneau was to share this happiness in *La Banlieue de Paris* (1949), *Instantanés de Paris* (1955), and *Trois secondes d'éternité* (1979). Doisneau's settings – bistros, streets, the embankments of the Seine, the old districts which were vanishing, a world balancing precariously between yesterday and today – was precisely the background chosen, each in a different way, by two other visual poets of Paris, Izis and Willy Ronis.

Willy Ronis, who like his friend Doisneau belonged to the Groupe des XV, was more inclined towards reportage, social problems, and working-class struggle. *Belleville Ménilmontant*

14. *Le Photographe*, no. 684, November 1948, p. 347.

15. *Le Photographe*, 1949, p. 233.

16. *Trois secondes d'éternité*, Paris, Contrejour, 1979, p. 27.

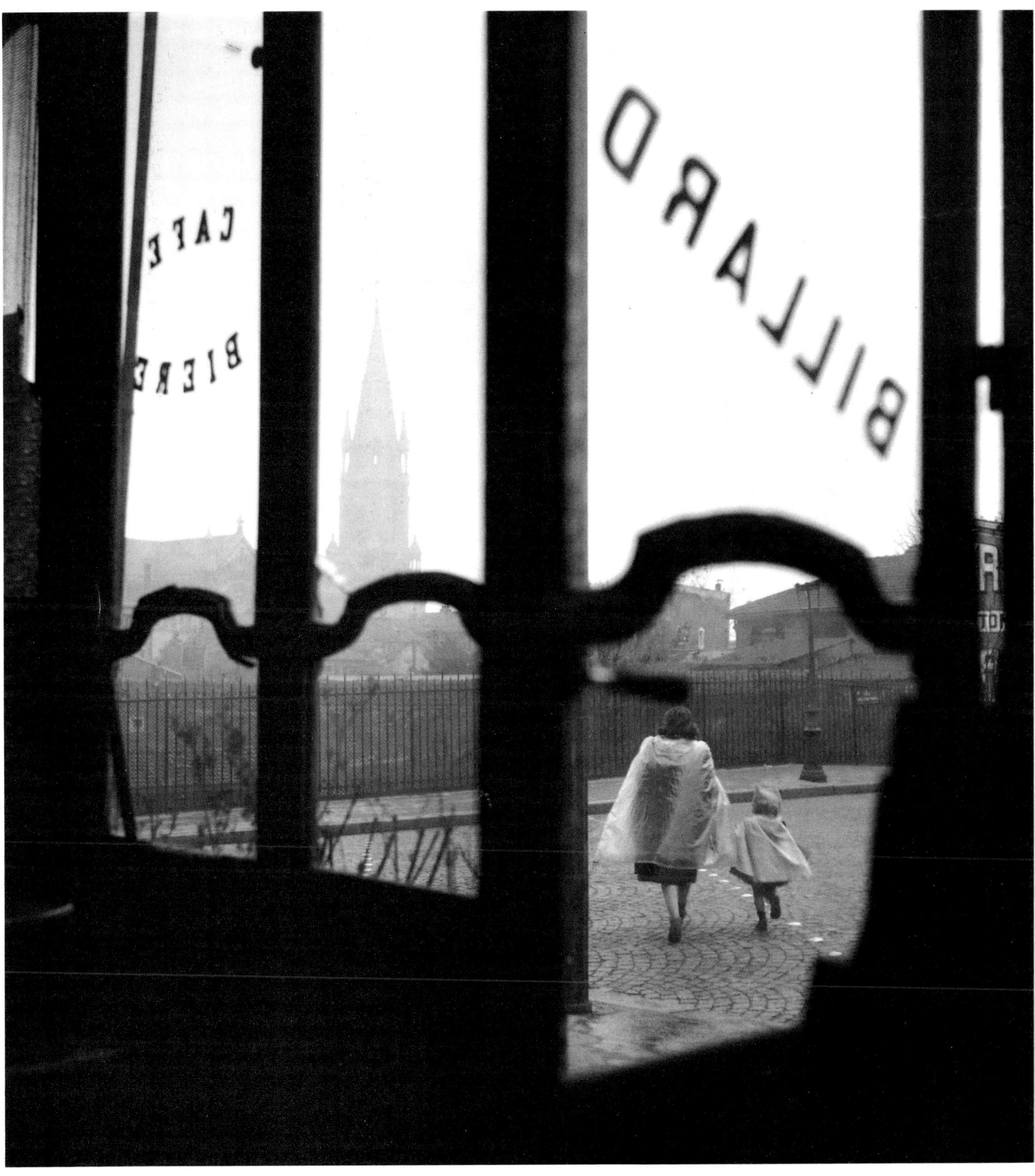

WILLY RONIS,
Rue des Couronnes, Paris 20e,
1948.

(1954) was his favorite haunt. He dealt with the daily life of Parisians with great modesty and with great respect for the feelings of other people. Less humorous than Doisneau, more concerned with form, he excelled in capturing people in their urban environment, photographing them in a way which let his kindheartedness and his profound sense of brotherhood show through.

Izis, much more nostalgic and solitary, was a dreamy wanderer, "a marveling passer-by", as Prévert called him. His work, *Paris des rêves* (1950), *Grand bal du printemps* (1951), and *Paris des poètes,* among others, clearly illustrates the steady, somewhat surreal approach of a photographer who paid no attention to current events, but photographed what intrigued him moved him or left him dreaming: "The people I photograph don't notice me, because most of the time they are in their own inner world, in their own dreams."[17] Izis's wanderings unceasingly led him

17. Catalogue, *Izis,* interview conducted by M. Voyeux, Paris, Caisse Nationale des Monuments Historiques, 1988, p. 135.

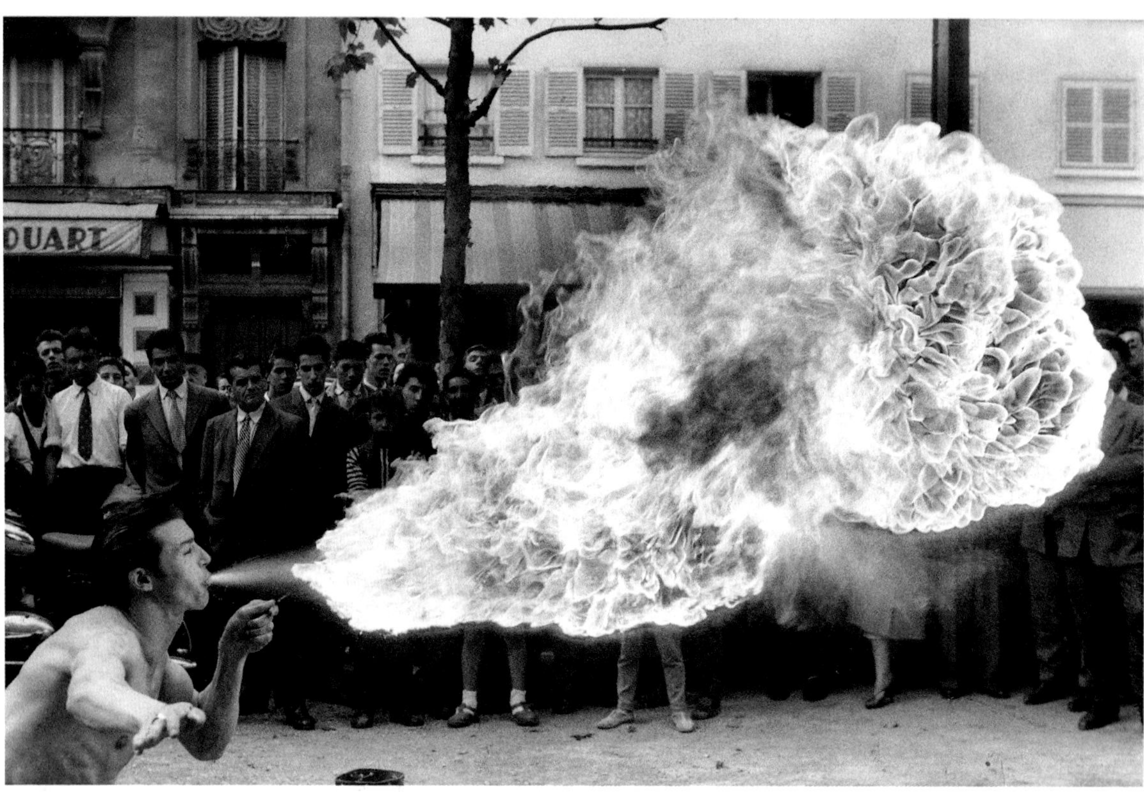

IZIS, *Fire-eater*, 1959.

JOHAN VAN DER KEUKEN, *Place de la République, Paris, Christmas 1957*, from *Paris mortel*, 1963. ▼

towards "people in the working-class districts, because they are visibly marked by life". He photographs them with discreet melancholy, paying attention to the often amazing relationships between people and things.

A love of the lyricism of the city and a compassion for its inhabitants was not restricted to Parisians. A number of Dutch photographers, close to Doisneau in their approach, were also responsive to such subjects. They benefited from a fine tradition of photographic publishing in Holland. After the war, Cas Oorthuys published a book on Rotterdam, as well as other books on women and on children. Emmy Andriesse published her reportage on the "winter of famine" in 1947. Johan van der Keuken, who had produced a book on young people (*Wij zijn 17* [We are Seventeen], 1955), studied cinema in Paris and systematically photographed its inhabitants. *Paris mortel* (1963) came out of this – a critical and poetic study of people in the city. In 1956, Ed van der Elsken published a book on Saint-Germain-des-Prés, and E. van Moerkerken published *Amsterdam* the following year.

Édouard Boubat traveled all over the world. For him, photography was a way of approaching people and speaking to them. Boubat possessed, to the highest level, that great skill – the art of meeting people. He tried to go beyond mere anecdote and, calmly and serenely, sought, above all, to treat his subjects with enough respect and sympathy for all of their inherent nobility to emerge. "One must see, not look! […] learn to contemplate life in every village."[18]

18. *Édouard Boubat*, Photo Poche, no. 32, Paris, 1988.

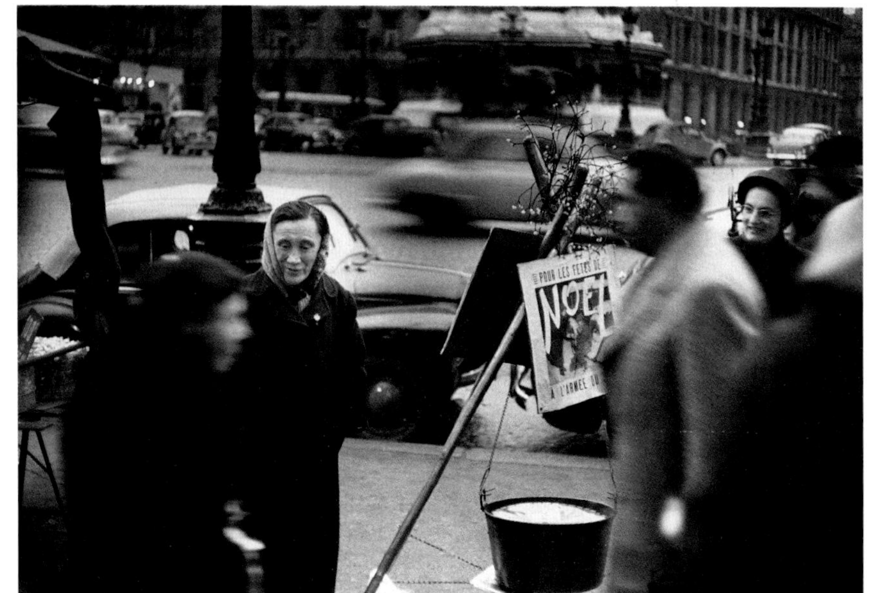

The great family of man

Édouard Boubat was on the staff of *Réalités*, an important magazine of the 1950s, which, leaving to *Paris Match* their (as their slogan went) "photo shock" and sensational news events, preferred to deal with discovering the world and its inhabitants. From Burma to the banks of the Seine, Jean-Philippe Charbonnier, one of the magazine's great photoreporters, undertook a feverish quest to bring together unknown aspects of human behavior. *Réalités* ceased publication in 1976, having played an important role in allowing photographers to choose their subject matter and

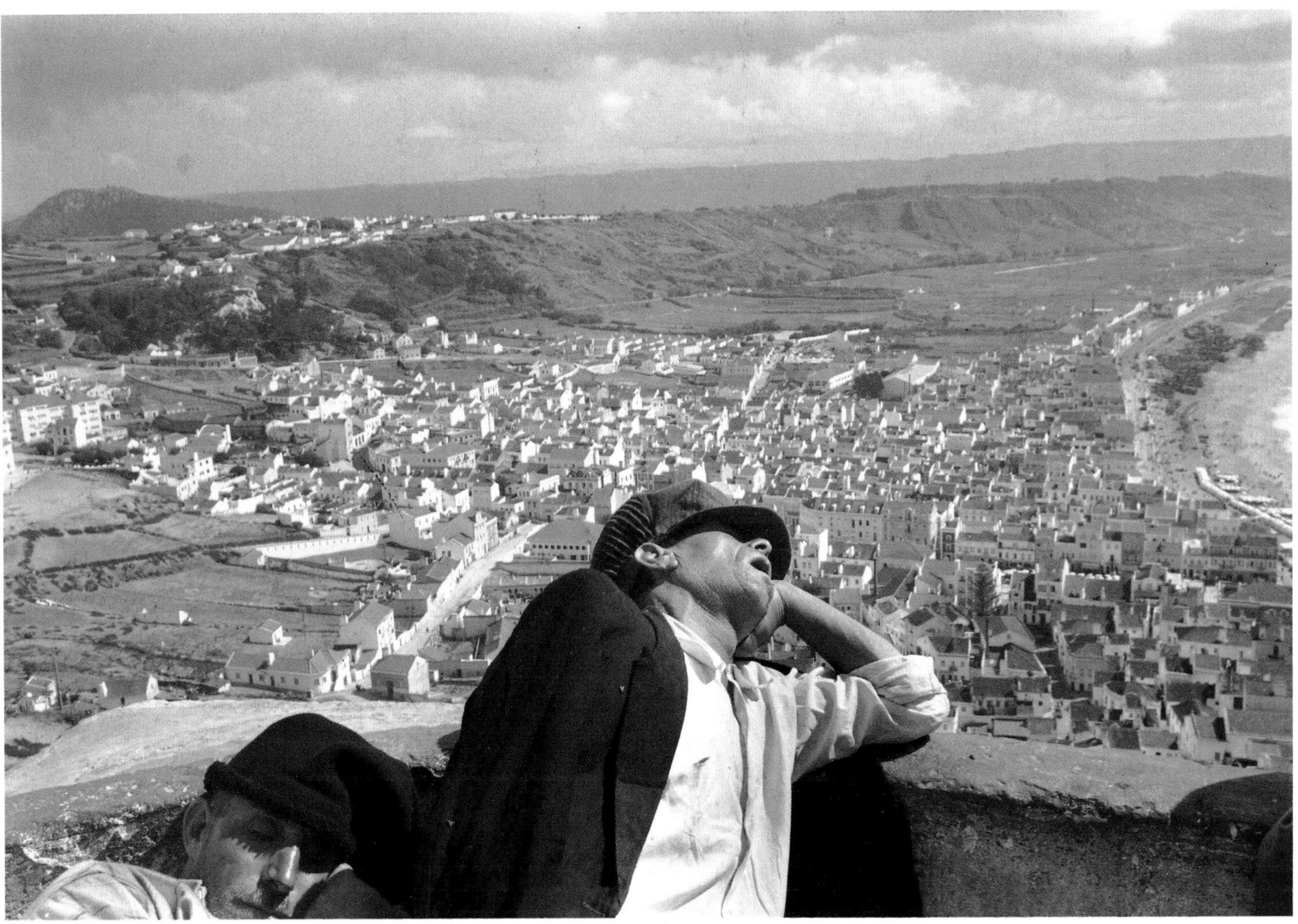

Édouard Boubat,
Nazaré, Portugal,
1956.

also respecting their aesthetic sensibilities. Jean-Louis Swiners was also part of the original team, joined, from time to time, by Gilles Ehrmann and Frank Horvat.

Without a doubt, the climax of this great idealistic trend was the huge exhibition which Edward Steichen organized at the Museum of Modern Art, New York, in 1955, entitled *The Family of Man*. Based on the idea that "the art of photography is a dynamic process of giving form to ideas and of explaining man to man",[19] benefiting from a sophisticated use of display space, accompanied by a magnificent catalogue, and arranged around great moments of human existence (birth, love, work, death), this exhibition enjoyed huge success all over the world. Seen as a message of hope and brotherhood, it marked the triumph of humanism. Skillfully mixing reportage and "humanist" photography, *The Family of Man* was full of optimism. In Paris, however, a few critical voices were raised (notably Barthes) against its "caution of wisdom and lyricism".[20] In viewing reality quite differently, Barthes seems to argue in favor of a new type of photography. This type of photography did, in fact, appear, in embryonic form, in the exhibition, in work by Robert Frank, Diane Arbus, Garry Winogrand, Wayne Miller, Elliott Erwitt, Lisette Model, Roman Vishniac, Vito Fiorenza, Roy DeCarava, Gotthard Schuh, and Gordon Parks.

The culmination of humanist photography, albeit somewhat overflowing with optimism and warmth, *The Family of Man* also admirably summed up this trend which had spread, with significant modifications, far beyond its epicenter in France.

Reality without frills

The direct heir of Italian neo-realism, Mario Giacomelli remained attached to the traditional village way of life, to work on the land, to the old and the sick. His somber images capture characters sunk in solitude. Here, optimism has given way to a certain pessimism, just as a classical photographic style is, in his case, combined with a graphic quality, enhanced by the contrast of his prints, which seek a heightened sense of reality.

The visits to Paris, in around 1950, by the Swiss-born Robert Frank had left little impression on the Paris photographic scene. However, his book *The Americans*, first published in Paris in 1958, was to spark off a reaction in the United States, where people refused to accept this sinister

19. E. Steichen, *The Family of Man*, New York, Museum of Modern Art, 1955.

20. R. Barthes, "The Great Family of Man", in R. Barthes, *Mythologies*, selected and translated from the French by A. Lavers, New York, Hill and Wang, 1972, pp. 101–102.

"The Family of Man"

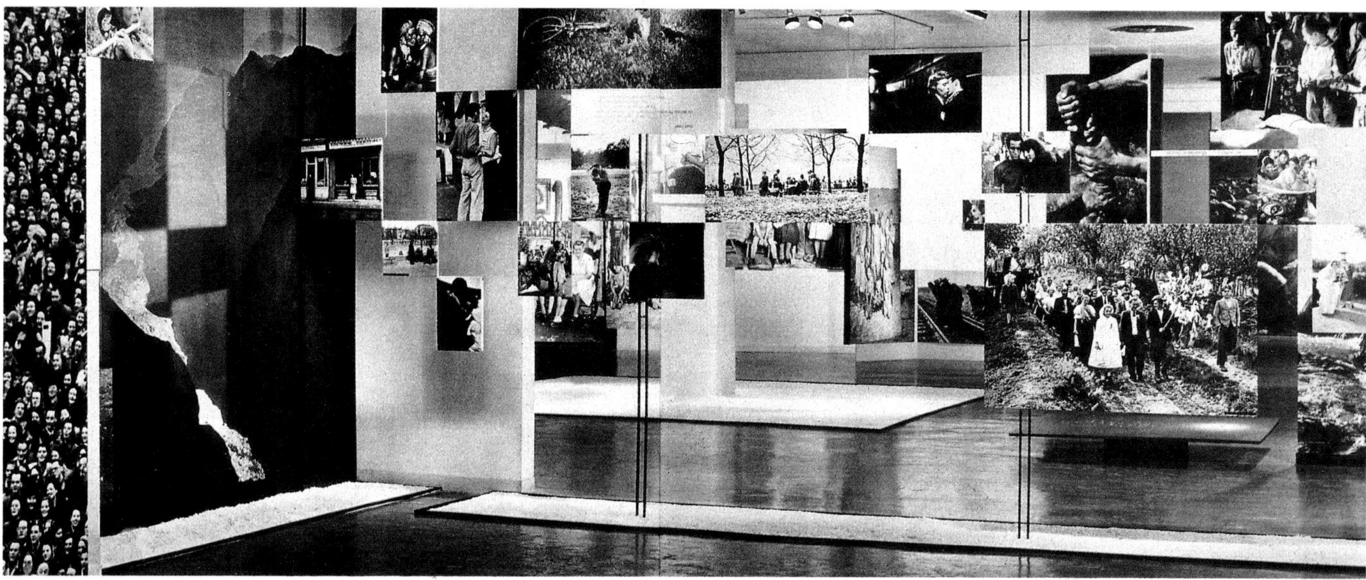

Ezra Stoller,
View of the exhibition "The Family of Man",
New York, 1955.

"*The Family of Man* is, I feel, the most ambitious and challenging project photography has ever attempted. The exhibition demonstrates that the art of photography is a dynamic process of giving form to ideas and of explaining man to man. It was conceived as a mirror of the universal elements and emotions of the every-dayness of life – as the mirror of the essential oneness of mankind throughout the world", as Edward Steichen concluded in his introduction to the exhibition which he characterized as having been "created in a passionate spirit of devoted love and faith in man".

Three years' work, 2 million photographs from every corner of the world, 10,000 images chosen and classified into themes, 503 works exhibited by 273 photographers, both famous and unknown: such are the statistics of this visual description of "moments of existence, from birth to death" through which Steichen intended to transmit his profound belief in the importance of community.

In 1947, after a long career in photography, which had originally started with Stieglitz's entourage and with *Camera Work*, Steichen became the director of the photographic department of the Museum of Modern Art, New York. It was there that this huge exhibition was staged in 1955.

To visualize the position of each work and to define their format (from 5 x 7 inches to the size of a whole wall), a model of the exhibition had been made, showing the way spectators would move about and the layout of the various sections, each of which had its own unity and told a story which formed part of the whole narrative.

The presentation of the photographs, mounted on plain board without any frame, ignored the fame of their creators, responding only to the strength of the images, and to their place within the chosen theme. As for the way in which they were displayed, it demanded the skill of a stage manager: works were placed on circular display columns or articulated panels; huge enlargements were suspended on wires or rods. The careful work of mounting was complemented by the choice of quotations from literature or folk sayings from the various cultures.

Inaugurated in January 1955, *The Family of Man* met with resounding success throughout its travels in America, and from 1959, in numerous other countries. From New York to Paris and Moscow, ten million visitors passed before these images, which sought to demonstrate "to what degree men are all the same all around the world".

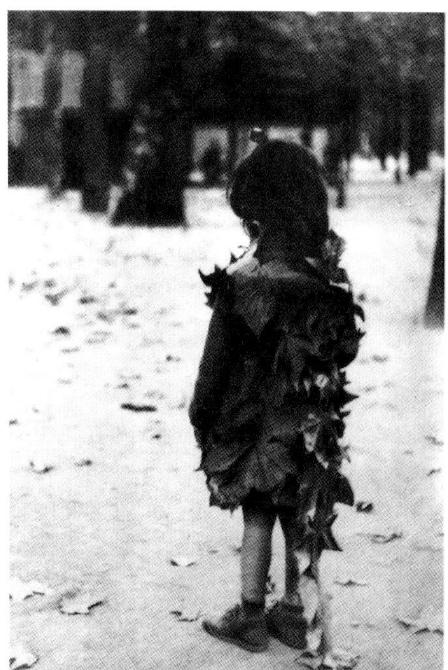

Édouard Boubat,
Jardin du Luxembourg, Paris, 1946,
from "The Family of Man".

In France, it received a warm welcome, despite a few voices raised in protest, such as that of André Chamson, who criticized Steichen's concept as containing "too much tenderness and optimism", and above all, that of Roland Barthes, whose severe judgment was published first in the *Lettres Nouvelles*, then reprinted in *Mythologies*: "The failure of photography seems to me to be flagrant in this connection: to reproduce death or birth tells us, literally, nothing. [...] So that I rather fear that the final justification of all this Adamism is to give to the immobility of the world the aliby of a 'wisdom' and a 'lyricism' which only make the gestures of man look eternal the better to defuse them."

The idealism displayed by *The Family of Man*, coming, as it did, a few years after the Marshall Plan, marks the culmination of humanist photo-reportage. The exhibition sought its coherence in the universal figure of humanity. It should be noted, however, that a few artists appeared in it (Diane Arbus, Robert Frank, Garry Winogrand) who no longer subscribed to this simplistic and reductive point of view. It was also quite clear that, despite similarities in subject matter, Robert Doisneau, Louis Faurer, Robert Capa, Manuel Alvarez Bravo, Irving Penn, Alfred Eisenstaedt, Bill Brandt, Russell Lee, Gotthard Schuh, Jakob Tuggener, and Gjon Mili each displayed very different aesthetic intentions and styles.

Jean-Claude Gautrand

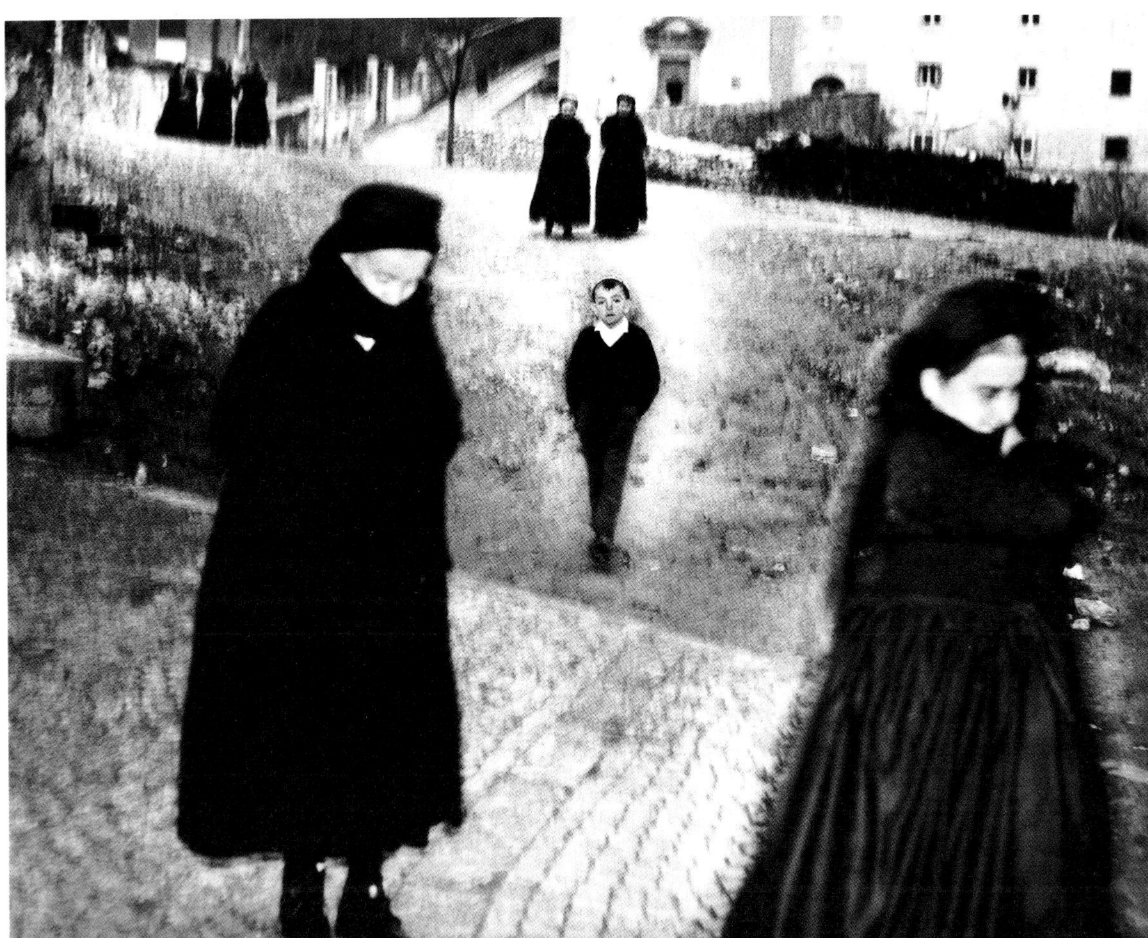

MARIO GIACOMELLI, *Scanno*, 1957–1959.

vision of their country. He also met with serious reservations in France, where people were disconcerted by images which challenged the current optimistic and lyrical view of life. Robert Frank, a "solitary observer", reveals, above all, the loneliness and banality of individuals who seem to rub shoulders without noticing each other. These disillusioned images are charged with tension and with a sense of mystery: "It is a far cry from all the woolly, successful 'photo sentiments' about human familyhood", wrote Walker Evans.[21] William Klein too tried "to liberate photography from its fetters", breaking taboos, producing aggressive, rough, "unframed" images which display the meeting between the unseen photographer and the crowd in which he immerses himself and which ignores him. Frank and Klein dissect reality with a scalpel, analytically, with an apparent detachment which breaks with the spirit of their predecessors.

Neither reportage (for it ignores current events), nor pure documentary photography (for it is carried out without any preconceived plan), the photography of Frank and Klein is certainly an extreme variation on the theme of photographic humanism. It led the way to the work of photographers such as Garry Winogrand, Lee Friedlander, Joël Meyerowitz, Burk Uzzle, and Charles Harbutt, whose style is rather more iconoclastic and critical.

In 1972, determined to make a return to the values of traditional press photography, Claude Raymond Dityvon, Guy Le Querrec, Hervé Gloaguen, Martine Franck, and François Hers founded the agency Viva in Paris, with the aim of distributing news photographs which would

CHRIS KILLIP, *Boy on a Wall, Jarrow,* 1976.

21. W. Evans, "Robert Frank", in *US Camera 1958*, ed. Tom Maloney., New York, U.S. Camera, 1957, p. 90.

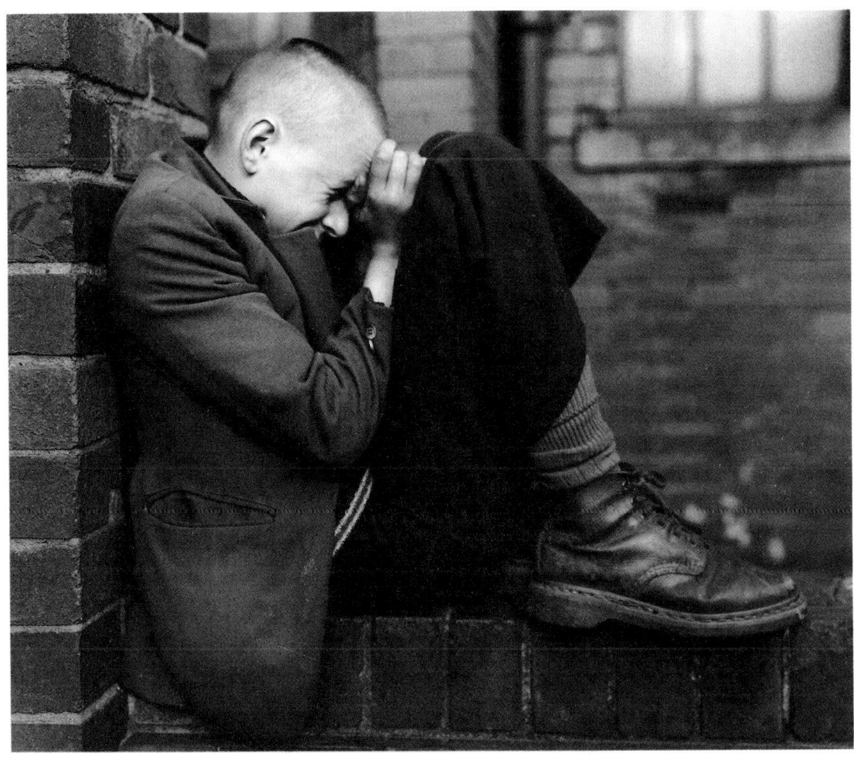

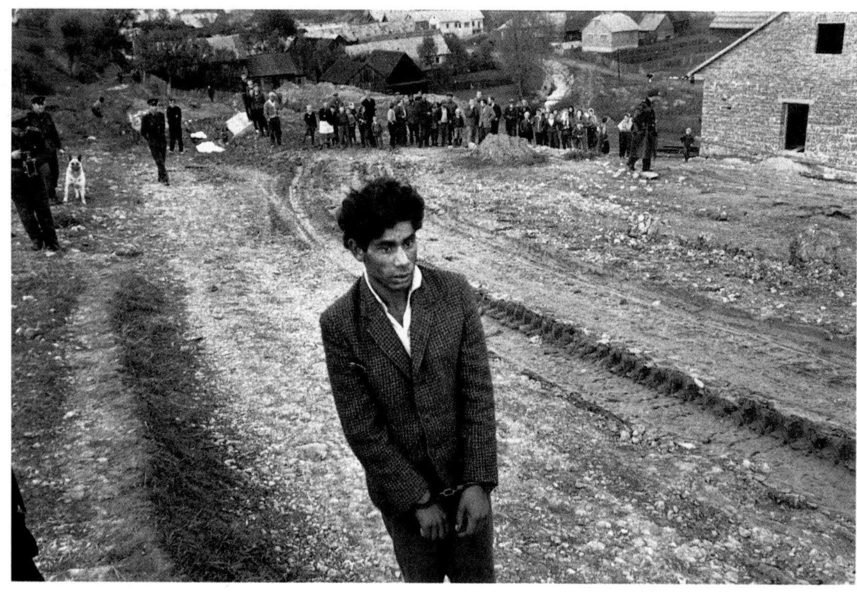

JOSEF KOUDELKA, *A Man Suspected of Murder, Czechoslovakia,* 1963.

JOSEF KOUDELKA, *Gypsies, Czechoslovakia,* 1965.

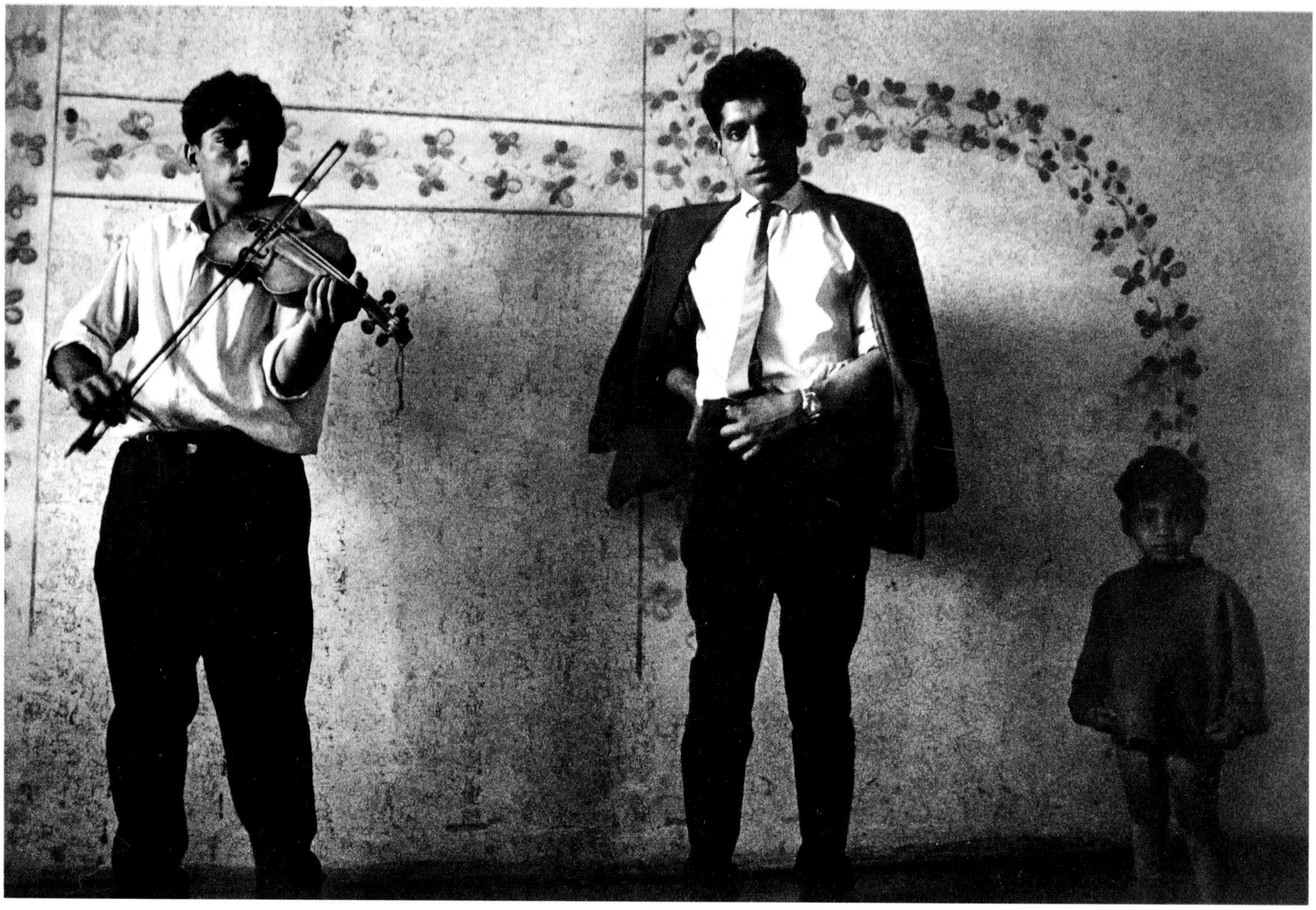

avoid sensationalism, and concentrate, instead, on daily problems and everyday actions. An exhibition entitled *Famille en France* (1973) gave concrete expression to their work before the agency disappeared. This change of direction also occurred in other countries. In Britain David Hurn and Tony Ray-Jones (who published *A Day Off*) took a fresh look at the world through images displaying a powerful inner vision, where imagination and observation were mingled. Martin Parr, with his photographs of the British seaside, pushed this trend to the point of caricature, while Chris Killip, whose photographs reached a formal perfection approaching that of Eugene Smith, continued his realization of a vast portrait of everyday life in Britain. In Lithuania, during the 1980s a powerful humanist current which is represented by Rakauskas Straukas, and Macijauskas, photographed large groups using wide-angle lenses, with the obvious co-operation of the subjects, who were treated with much sympathy and idealism.

In Mexico, the influence of Manuel Alvarez-Bravo remained strong. Graciela Iturbide, who had been his assistant, sought, without any sense of the exotic, the poetic realism of the strange and the transitory, in full complicity with her models. Cristina Garcia Rodero, concerned with form, observed Mexican society in order to recover "magic realism". This approach is pushed to the limits in the photographs of Sebastião Salgado, a faithful disciple of Eugene Smith, who seems to have made it his mission to become a photographic witness of humanity's state in the world. His reporting missions have led him to discover mysticism in South America, the tragedy of the Sahel, and the gold-miners of Brazil, while still striving to celebrate human dignity.

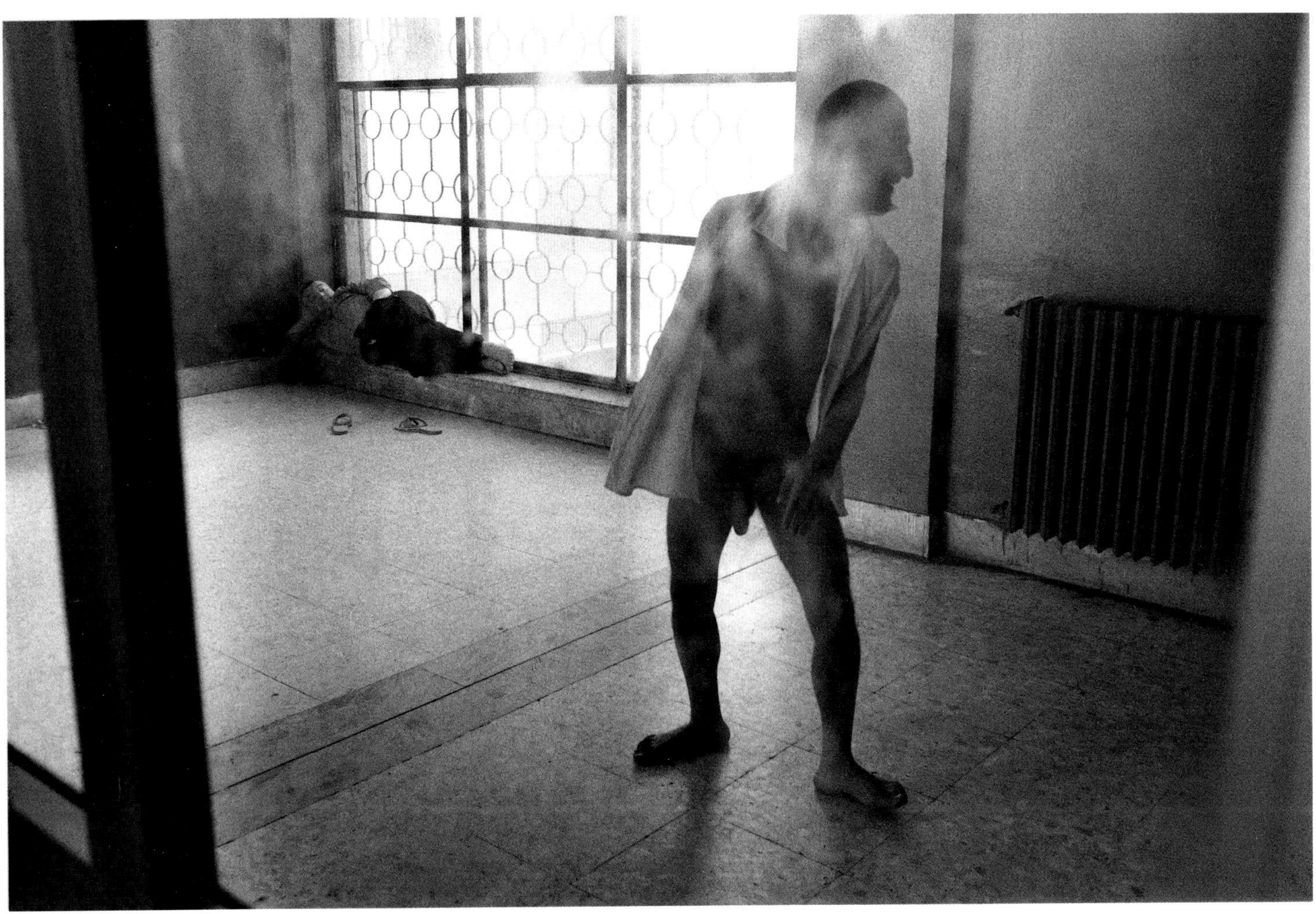

RAYMOND DEPARDON, *San Clemente Psychiatric Hospital, Venice,* 1979–1980.

Another indefatigable traveler, Josef Koudelka, following in the footsteps of Cartier-Bresson and Frank, was a powerfully original photographer, possessed by a frenzied desire to see. In images which sometimes seem theatrical and expressionist, he captured on film the world of the gypsies, whose lifestyle he often shared. Also the author of more "journalistic" types of reporting, such as the events in Prague in 1968, and for a long time lacking any nationality, he endowed his photography with timeless human values and experiences, like a nomad who finds a temporary stopping-place merely by the tension of his gaze.

This was a way of working which was often adopted by humanist photographers, allowing them to exchange subliminal signs of friendship and to blend into the communities they photographed. "Though they are often violent in themselves, his photographs commit no violence. A kind of sad gentleness emanates from them, determined to understand that which has no sense and can be understood."[22]

Two photographers who were Koudelka's companions in Magnum, René Burri and Raymond Depardon, were also travelers possessed by a desire to enter into and to understand the world of others. In Depardon's case, this desire manifested itself in photographs which are almost personal memories (his family, the places of his childhood) or states of mind, like his moving series on the San Clemente psychiatric hospital in Venice – a hard and somber photo-essay, and an attempt to communicate with the patients which well illustrates the often difficult relationship between the photographer and the photographed. In the case of other photographers, such as Bernard Plossu, their work has evolved into a more autobiographical intimacy, by means of places, objects, and looks. His are photographs without a message, intuitive images which are detached from the usual formal rules, like sketches fixing the fleeting nature of visual impressions.

During the 1950s, the need to rediscover and celebrate human dignity was even more acute after five horrific years of war. Added to this was the need to forget recent events and to recapture the bitter-sweet visual poetry of the 1930s. These photographers, who were, above all, sensitive to a given situation in a given framework, are not, therefore, witnesses to the world's upheavals. The importance of the photographer's gaze, the existence of a real collusion between "looking at" and "being looked at", a generally optimistic vision, the populist poetry of these images goes hand in hand with an extreme attention to the patterns of

22. B. Cuau, in *Josef Koudelka*, Photo Poche, no. 15, Paris, CNP, 1984.

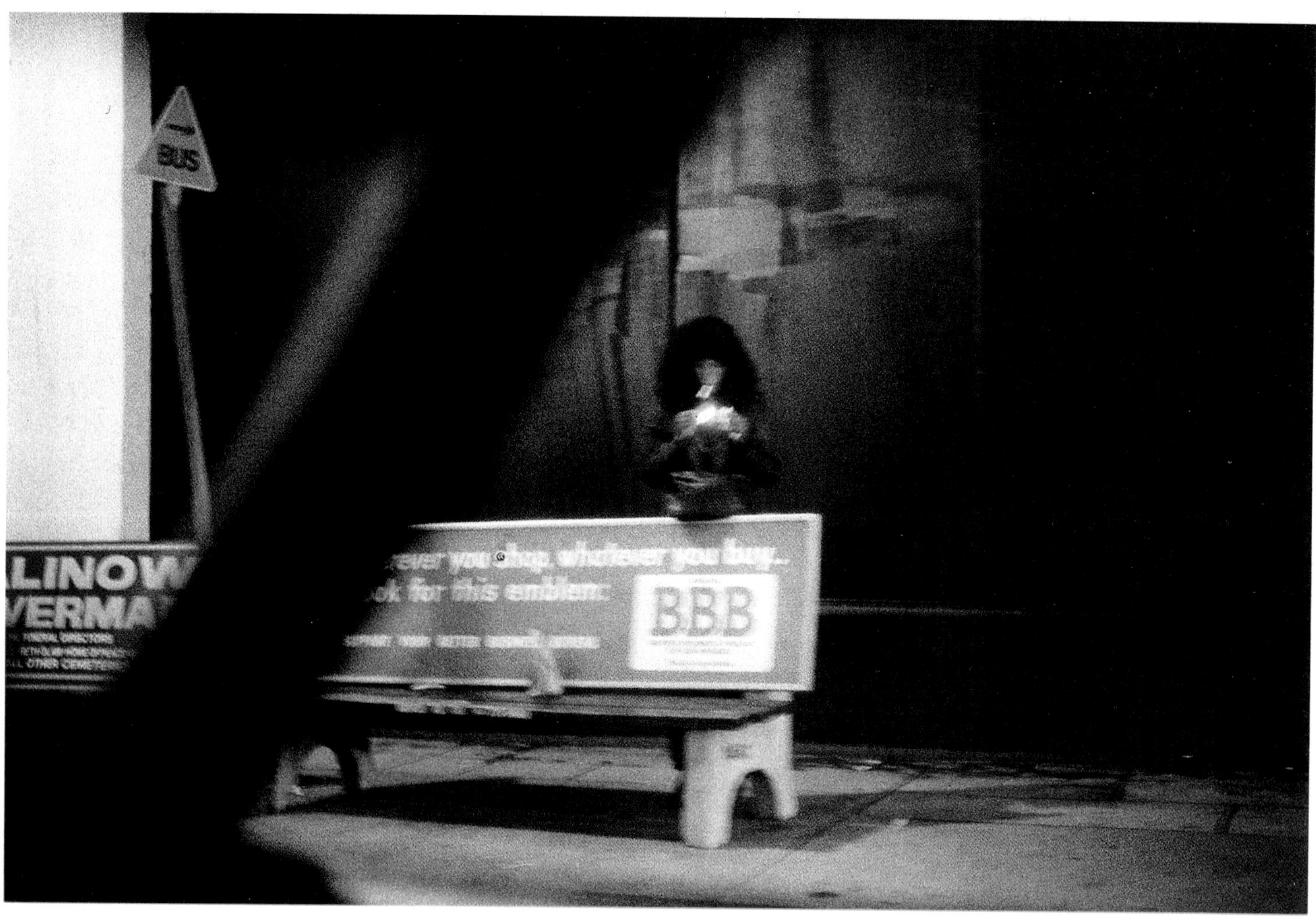

BERNARD PLOSSU, *Los Angeles*, 1980.

life, the symbolism of settings. Time vanishes in favor of a timelessness which encourages contemplation and the transformation of reality into poetry. These photographers are not witnesses but actors, the *alter ego* of their haphazard subjects, set against recurring backgrounds: park benches, the banks of the Seine, old gardens, and bistros, inviting the viewer to engage with the popular themes of the family, friendship, love, public holidays.

Today, this poeticized reality is sometimes decried as "garrulous", "populist", "sentimental", "petit-bourgeois", "the poetry of an aging and reactionary world".[23] Such a judgment is scarcely fair. By restricting the trend, in an almost Manichean way, to just a few names, by neglecting to spot that this kind of photography announces its own mutations within itself, these critics misunderstand a real quest for symbolic and universal truths.

One of these actor-witnesses, Sabine Weiss, has responded to this charge: "If present-day photographers find us a bit sentimental, I think it's because at that time people were pretty optimistic. They had emerged from a great trial and thought they could get on with things. They were fine times." She added that in those days the aim of photographers was "to arrive at that simplicity of vision by means of which you could take in a situation at a glance: the tiny detail which expresses the whole, the gesture which explains movement, the bending of a finger which expresses a state of mind, the expression on an individual face which represents the crowd, the infinitely small which recounts the large, the look of the other who tells of his anguish or his joy."[24] To this vision, which wanted to be reassuring and benevolent, perhaps Utopian, would succeed questioning and anxiety.

23. *Les Cahiers de la photographie*, no. 9, p. 30.

24. S. Weiss, *op. cit.*, p. 16.

Through its signs, to know a city?

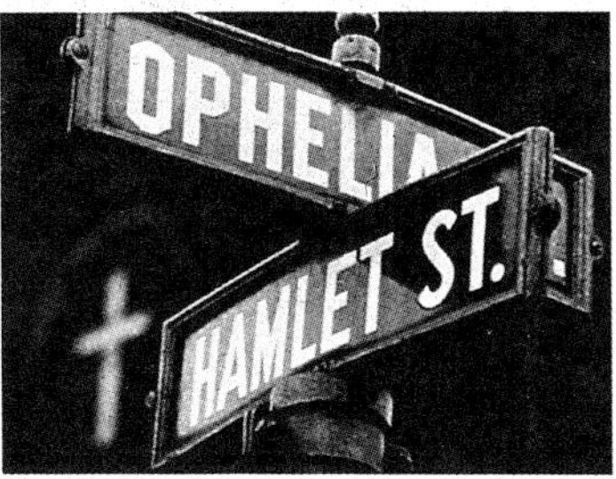

Romeo and Juliet approach each other, then swerve apart. Virgin Way vanishes before Oliver. And from the intersections such speeches can be conjured: *Orphan Basic Race Obey Judicial Breed Plow Forward Venture Divinity Blessing Abstract Refuge Superior Diamond Flush Freeland Rescue Liberty.*

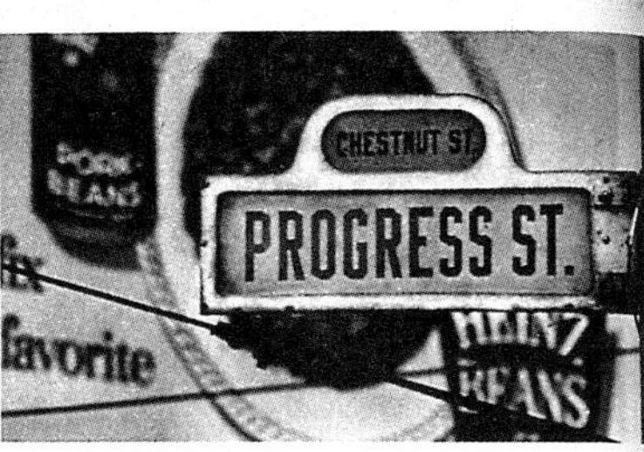

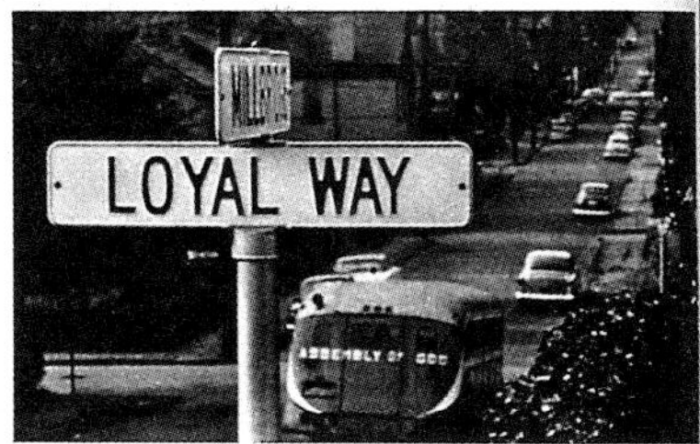

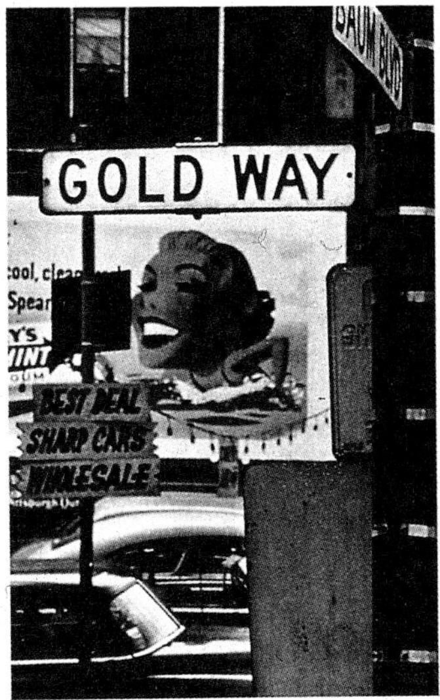

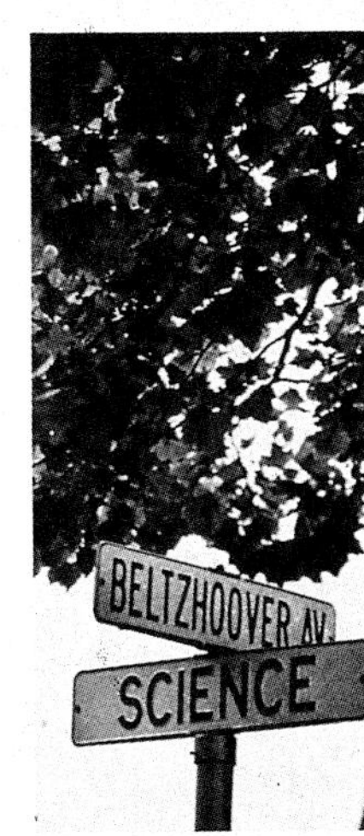

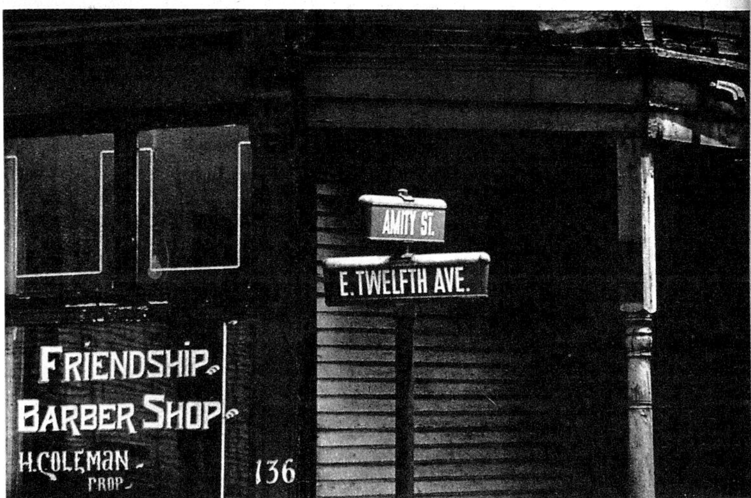

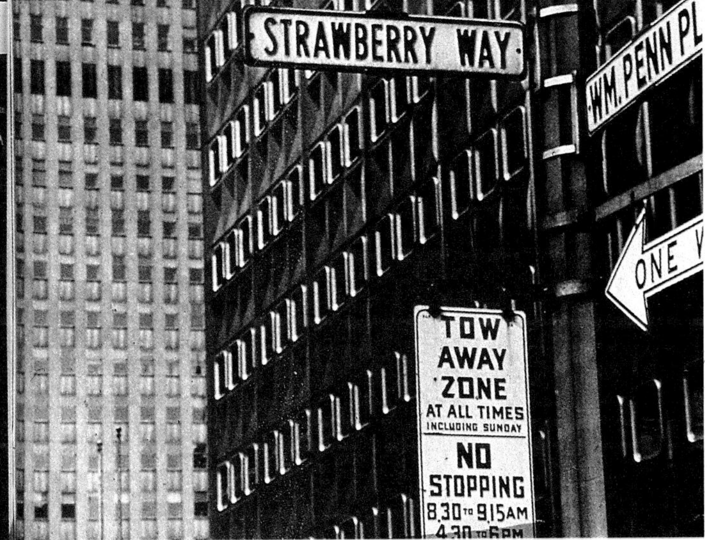

Pittsburgh, a "photographic essay" by W. Eugene Smith

An assignment which normally would have taken two to three-and-a-half weeks to complete was turned into a tortuous three-year ordeal by W. Eugene Smith that resulted in his essentially unfinished masterpiece, the "Pittsburgh" story. He made 11,000 negatives over five months in 1955 and a few weeks in 1957. During this time, Smith's marriage was breaking up, his health deteriorated, he was threatened with a lawsuit, he ran up huge debts with the agency Magnum Photos, and he went bankrupt himself, leaving his family near destitution, despite the two successive Guggenheim Fellowships he received.

Born in 1918 and raised in Kansas, Smith began his professional career in his teens supplying pictures to the local newspaper. Advancing to national magazines, he rapidly acquired an international reputation for his bold photographs of the Second World War in the Pacific. While on the staff of *Life* magazine, Smith produced the classic photographic essays "Country Doctor", "Spanish Village", and "Nurse Midwife" in the late 1940s and early 1950s. With these three features he set a new standard for evocative picture stories.

Increasingly frustrated with the restrictions of working for the magazine, he resigned at the end of 1954 over an essay he had done on Dr. Albert Schweitzer. Smith soon joined Magnum where he obtained the Pittsburgh commission. Noted picture editor Stefan Lorant needed some photographs for a pictorial history of Pittsburgh, a book intended to support an urban renewal program in one of the most polluted cities in the United States. Smith received an advance of $500 on a guaranteed final fee of $1,200.

He saw in this commission the opportunity to expand the form of the photographic essay to the dimension of "an epic in the tradition of Walt Whitman's *Leaves of Grass*" (W. S. Johnson). Smith moved to Pittsburgh where he improvised a darkroom in his apartment and hired an assistant and a local guide. Working with relentless intensity, he invested all of his financial resources in the project. This project was hampered not only by Smith's often self-destructive personality and stubborness, but also by bad luck and legal complications. Lorant's book finally appeared only in 1964 (with 64 of Smith's images).

Attempting to salvage the work, Magnum arranged for publishing agreements with *Look* and *Life*, but they collapsed because Smith, dissatisfied with the page layouts, kept modifying them in an attempt to weave a complex fabric of themes and metaphors with multiple connotations and resonance. The Pittsburgh story has never been published in any form approaching his book-length intentions. The most complete version, in his own layout, comprising 88 photographs covering 37 pages, was published in *1959 Photography Annual*. Smith considered it a failure.

The Pittsburgh project is a remarkable milestone of his noble effort to push the photographic essay into a larger dimension. Smith finally achieved that goal with *Minamata* in 1975.

Stuart Alexander

FURTHER READING:
- S. Lorant, *Pittsburgh: The Story of an American City*, Garden City, Doubleday, 1964.
- W. S. Johnson, *W. Eugene Smith, Master of the Photographic Essay*, New York, Aperture, 1981.

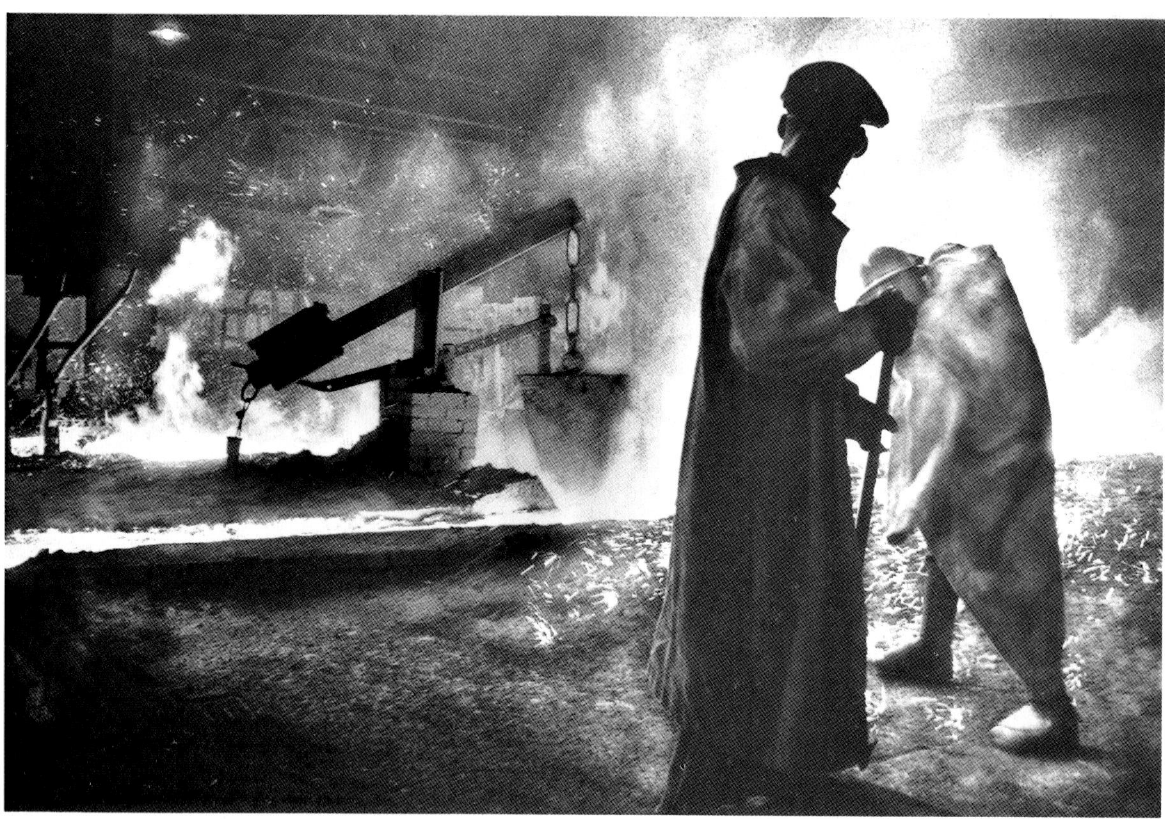

All the photographs in this dossier are by **W. Eugene Smith,** ***Pittsburgh,*** 1955–1956.

◀◀ previous page:
double-page spread from **Photography Annual,** 1959,
page layout and presentation by W. Eugene Smith.

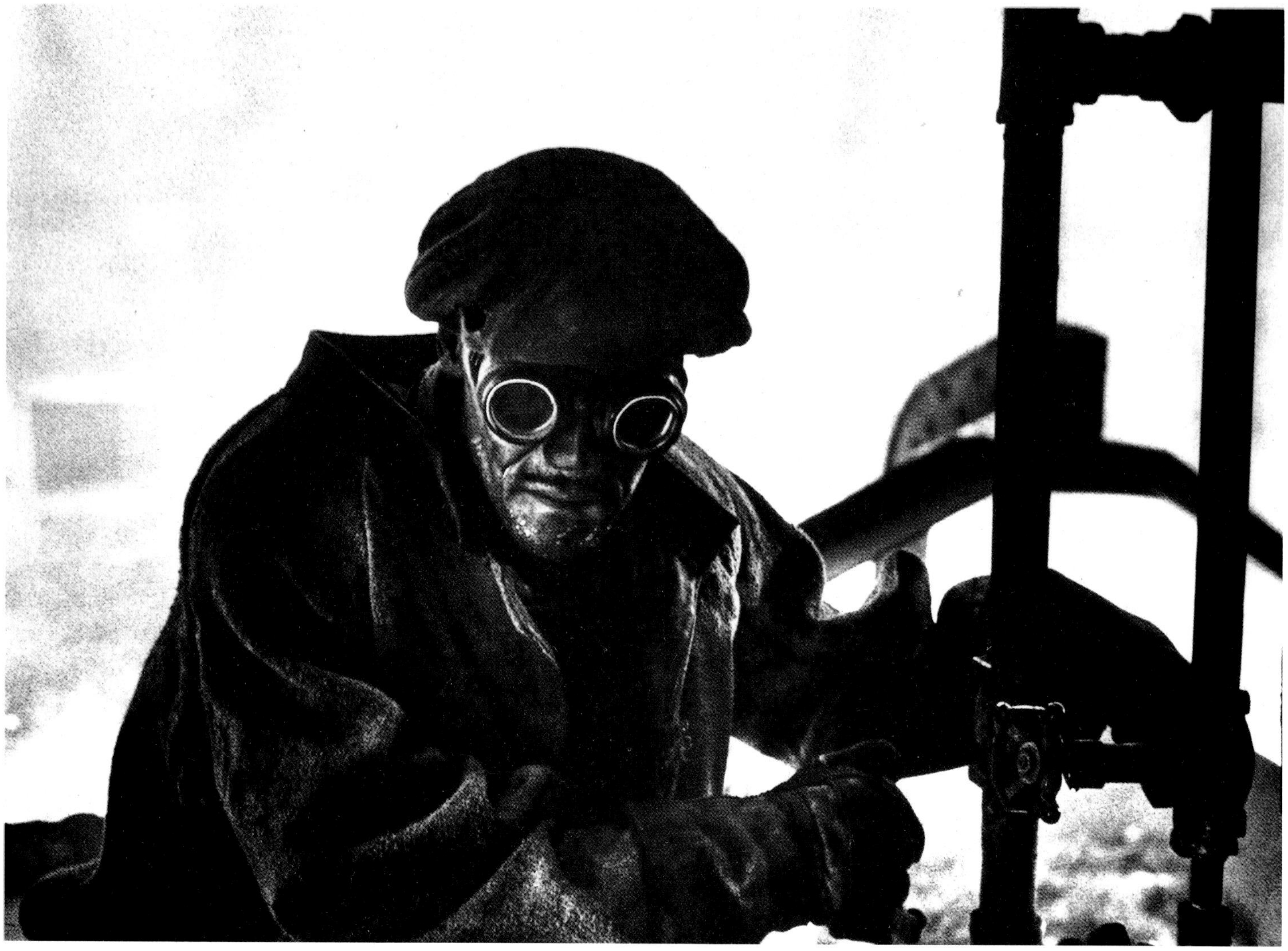

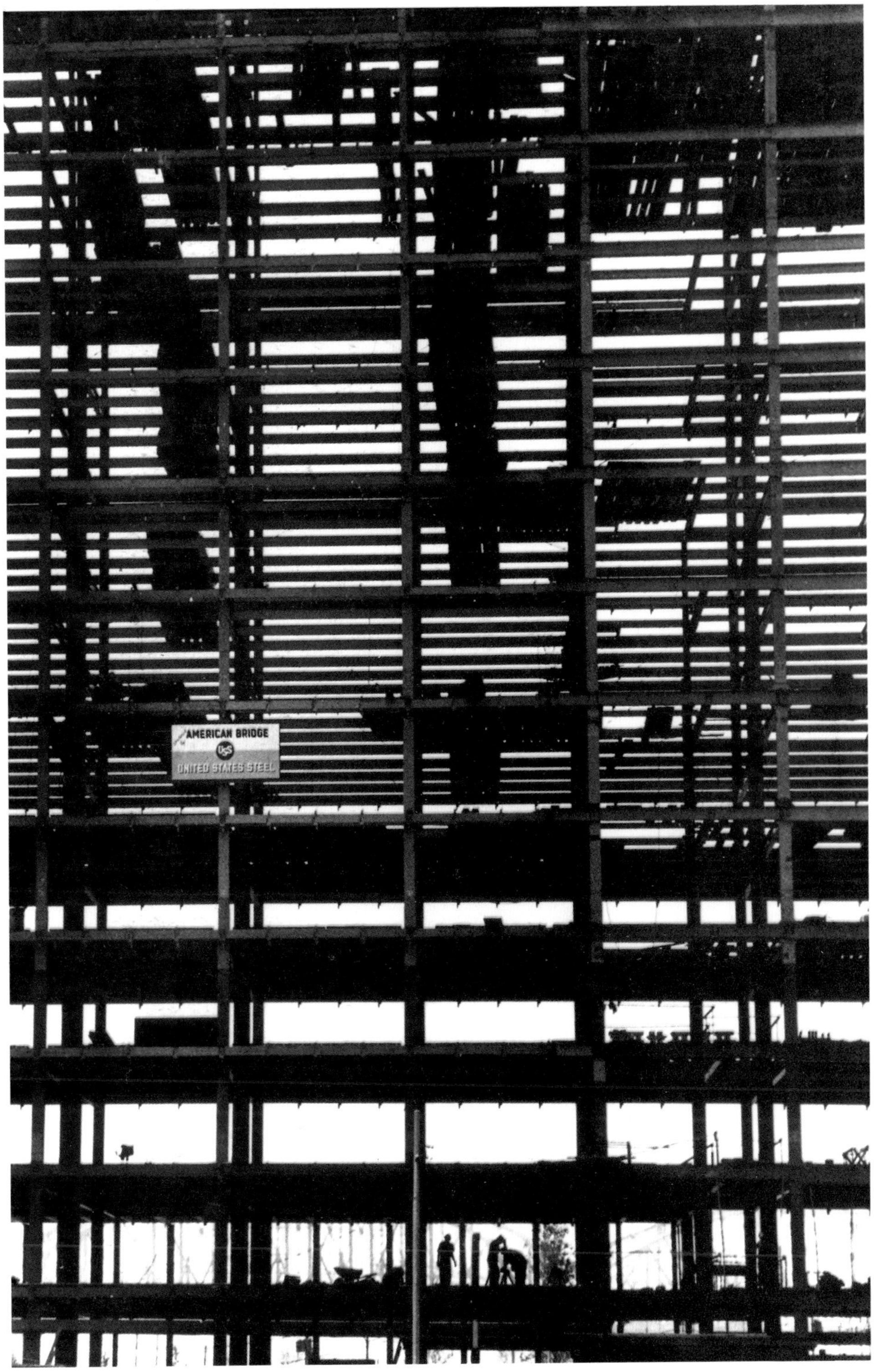

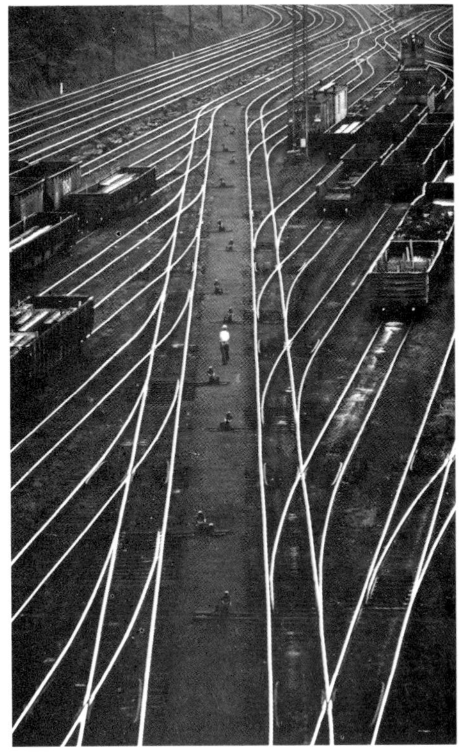

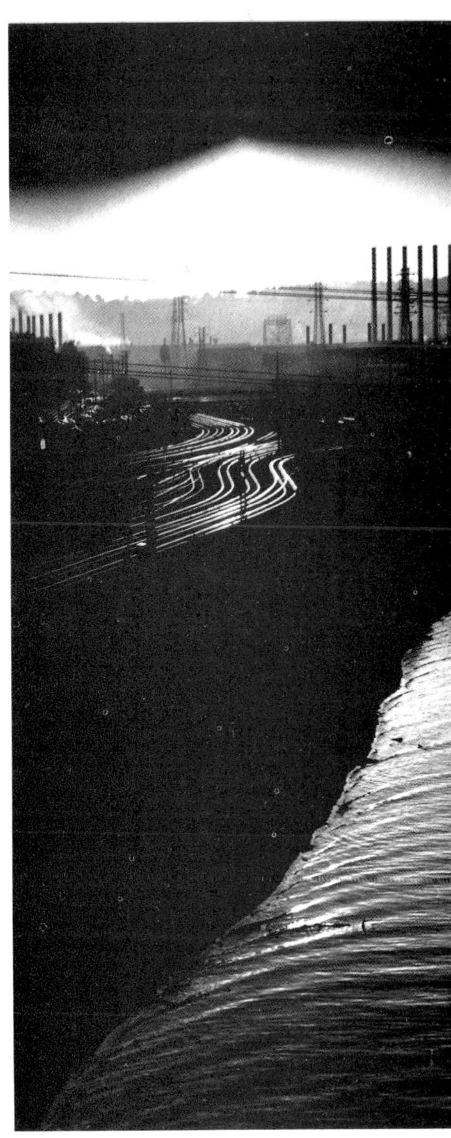

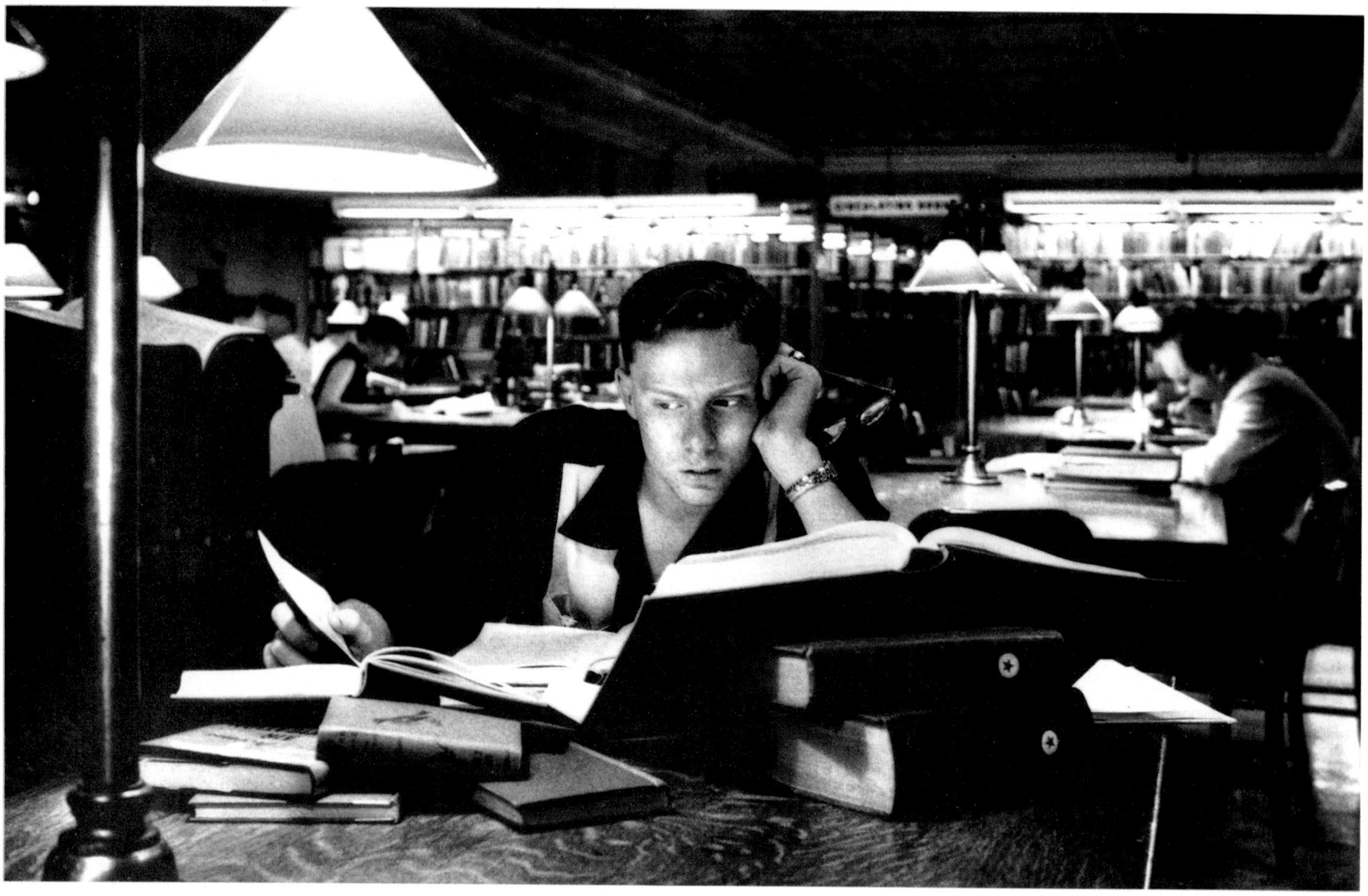

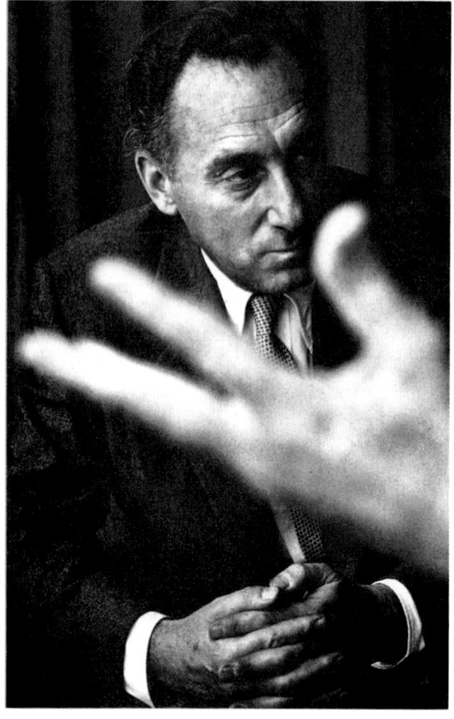

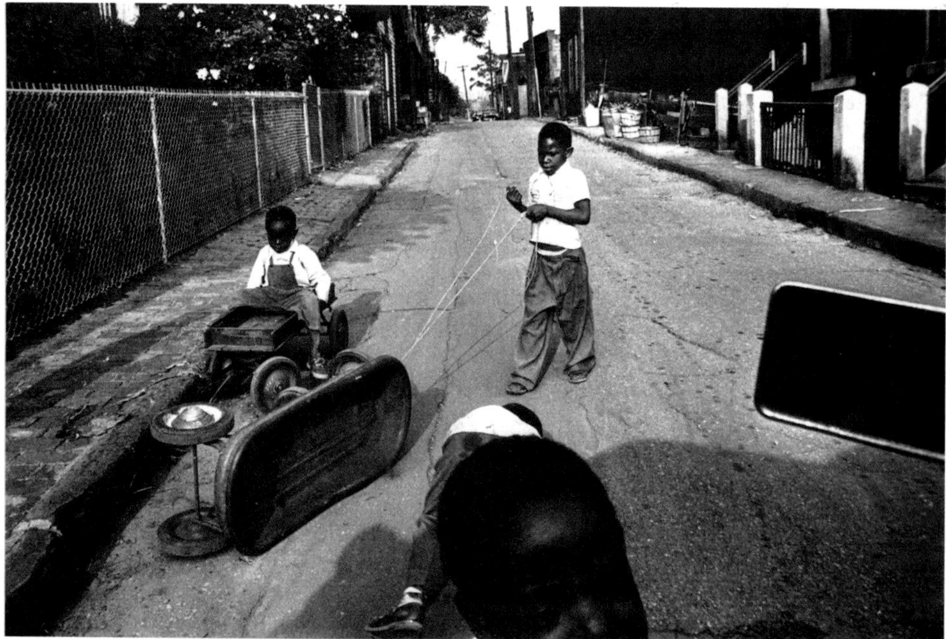

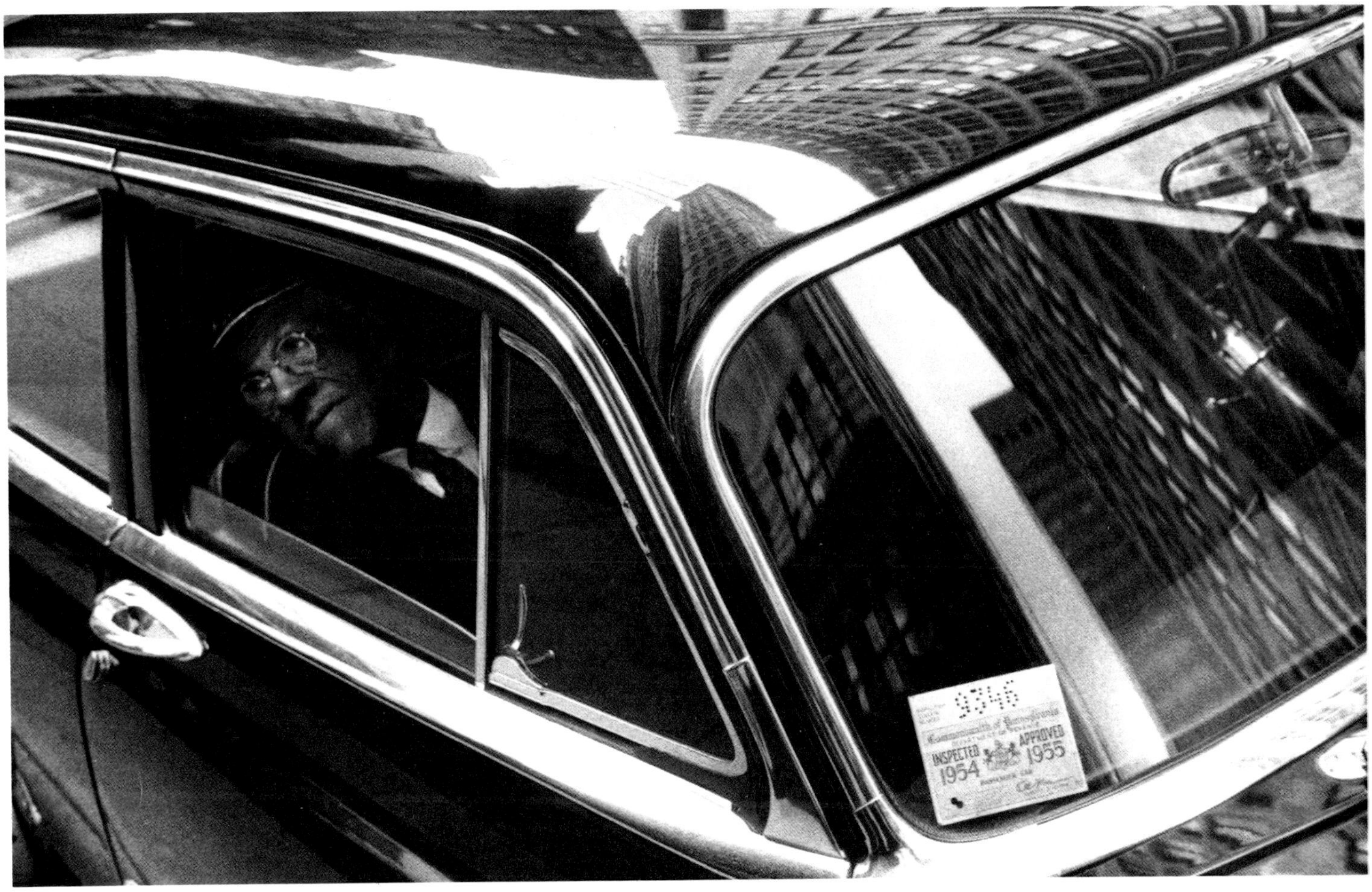
INSPECTED
1954
APPROVED
1955

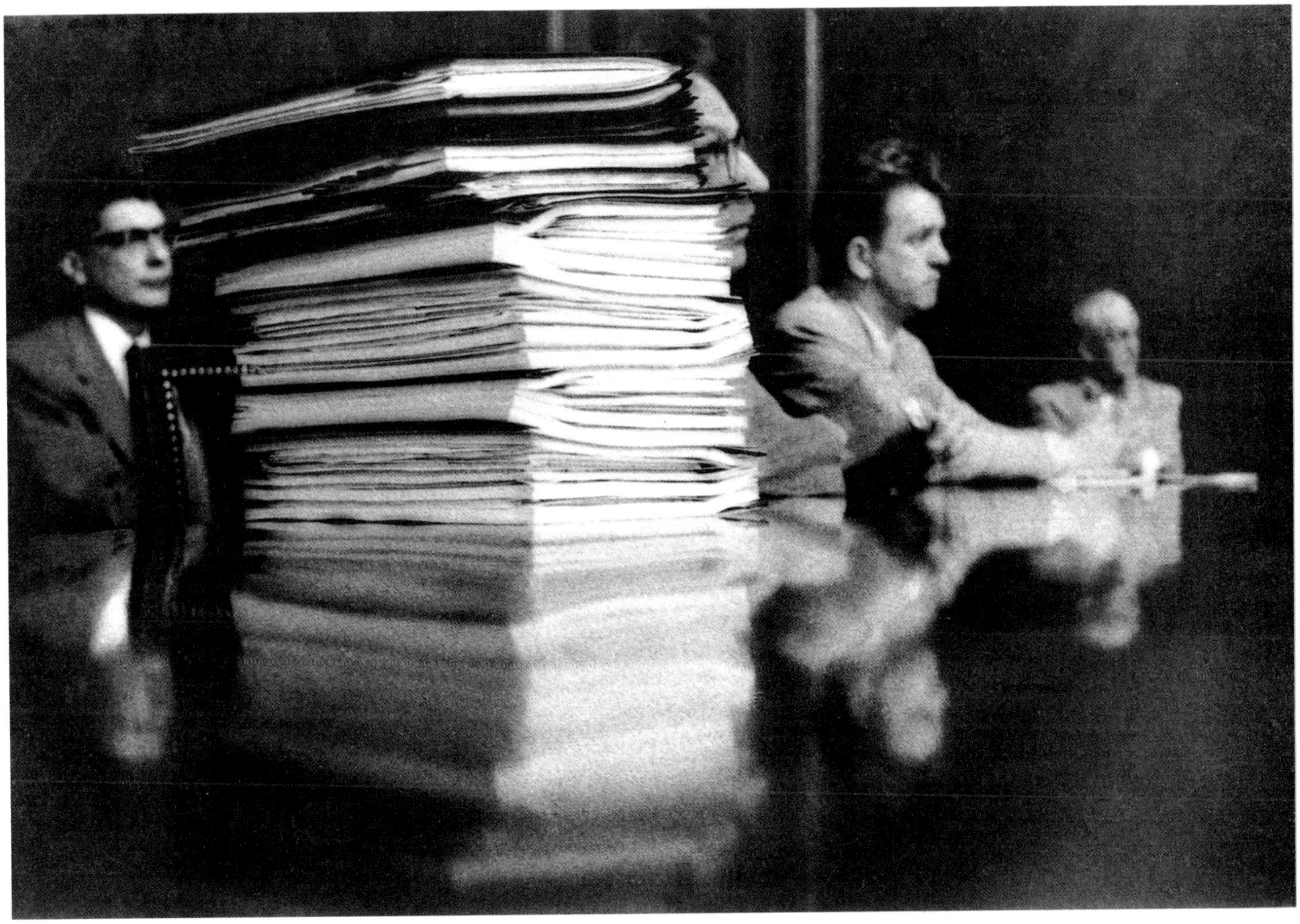

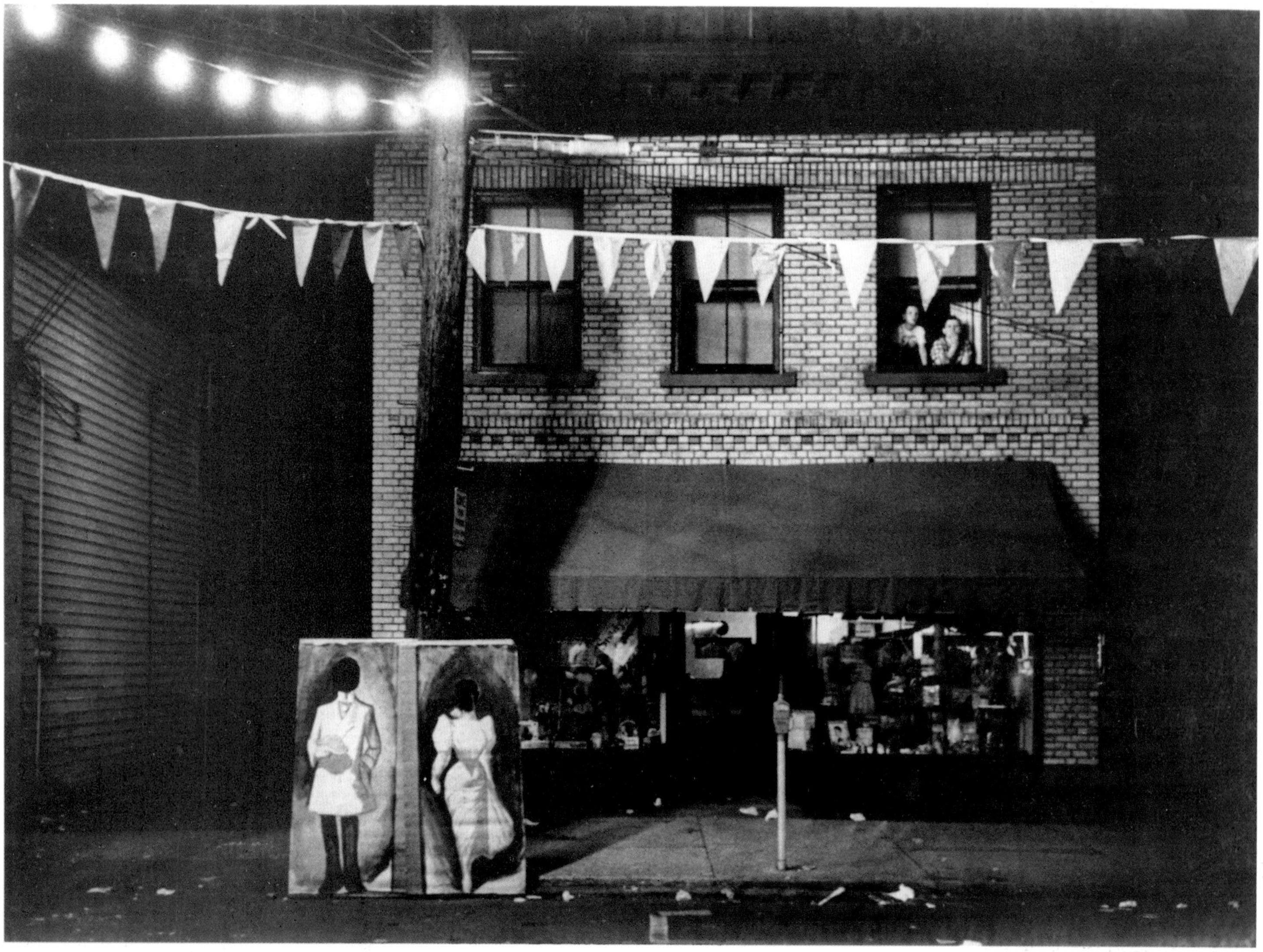

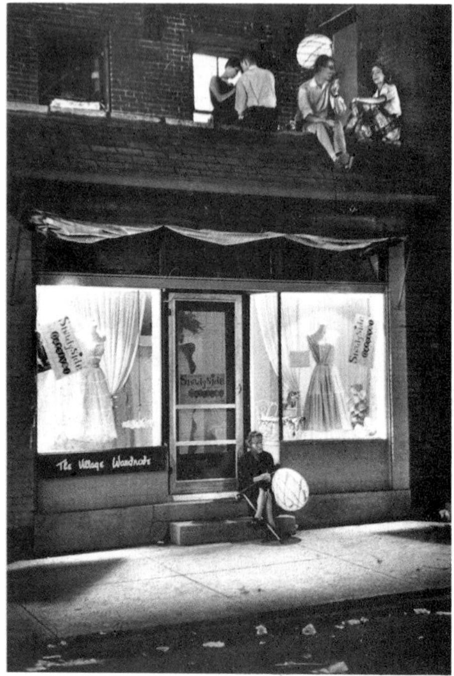

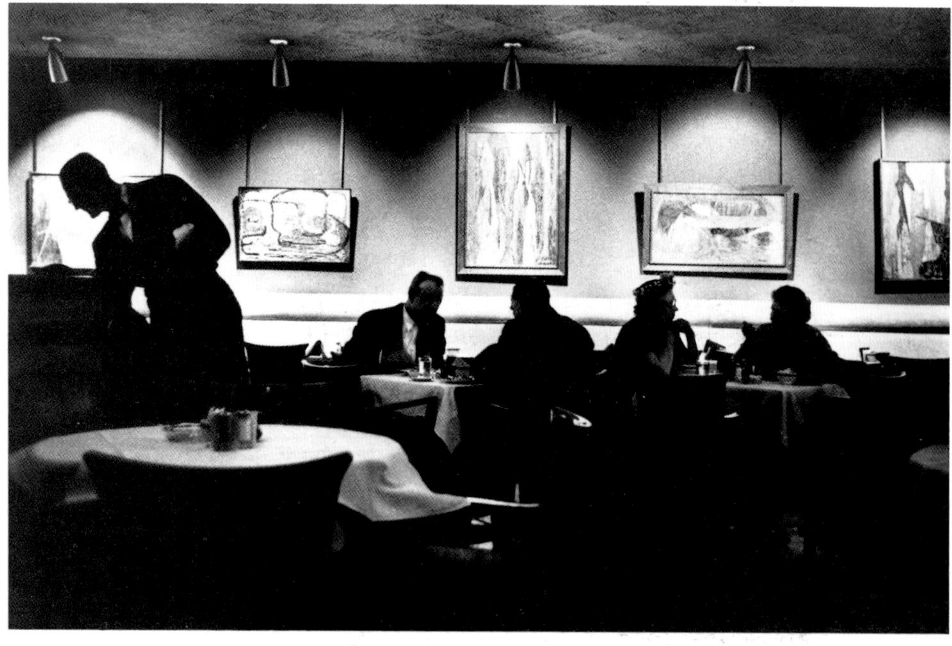

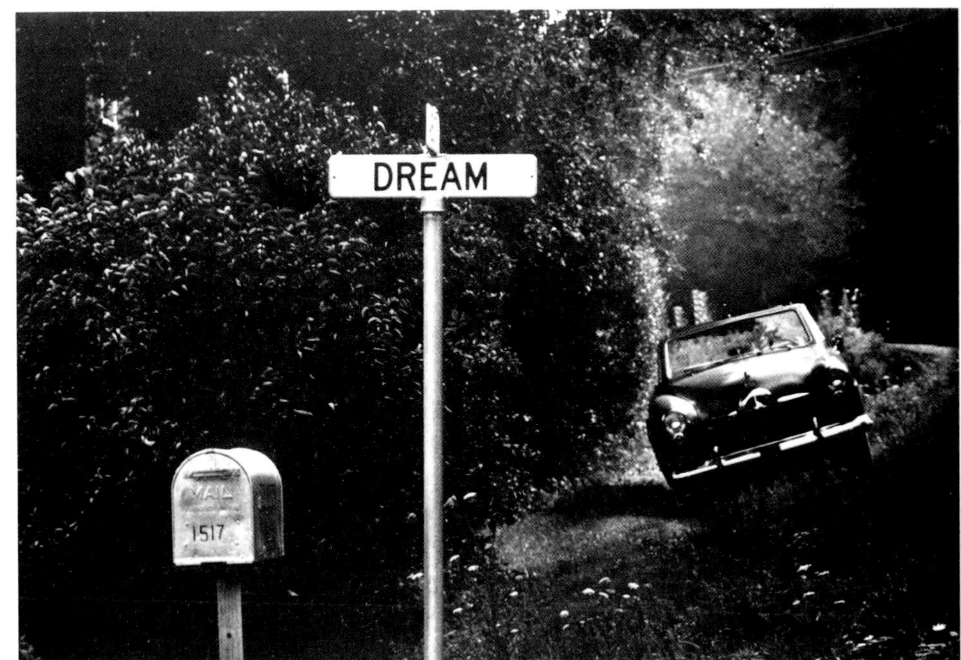
DREAM
MAIL
1517

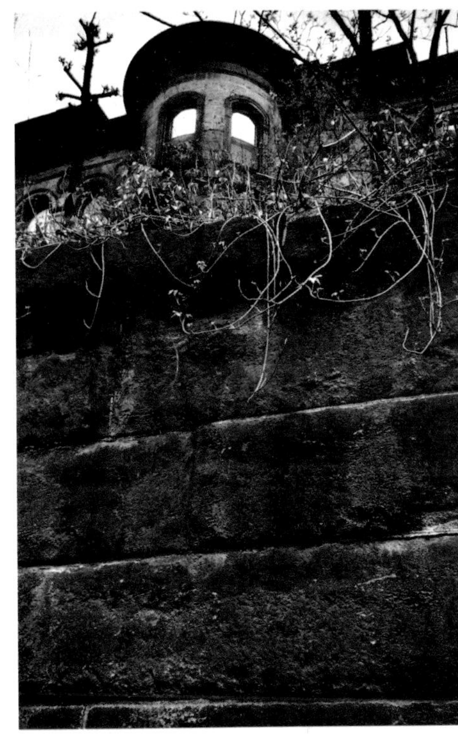

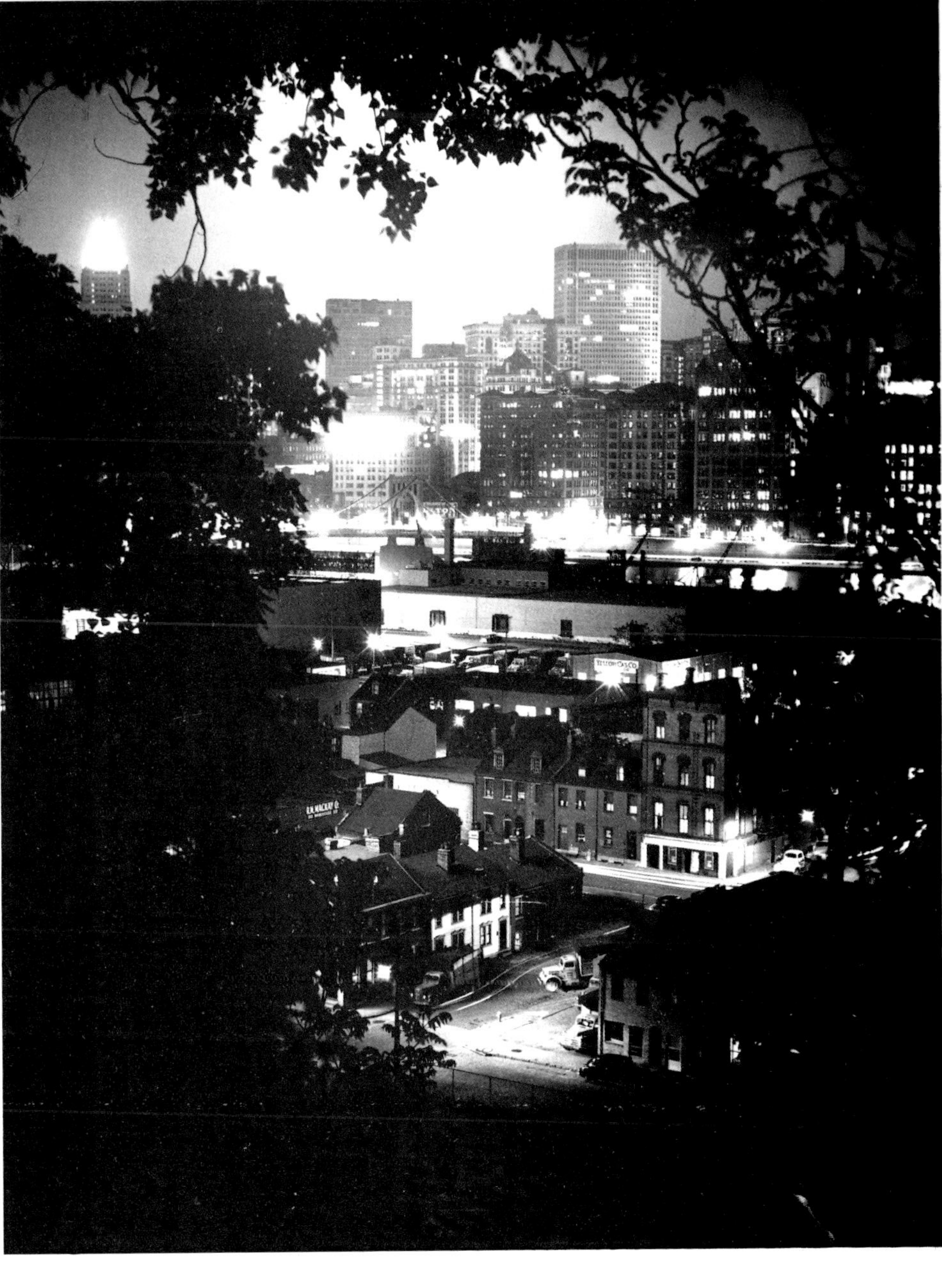

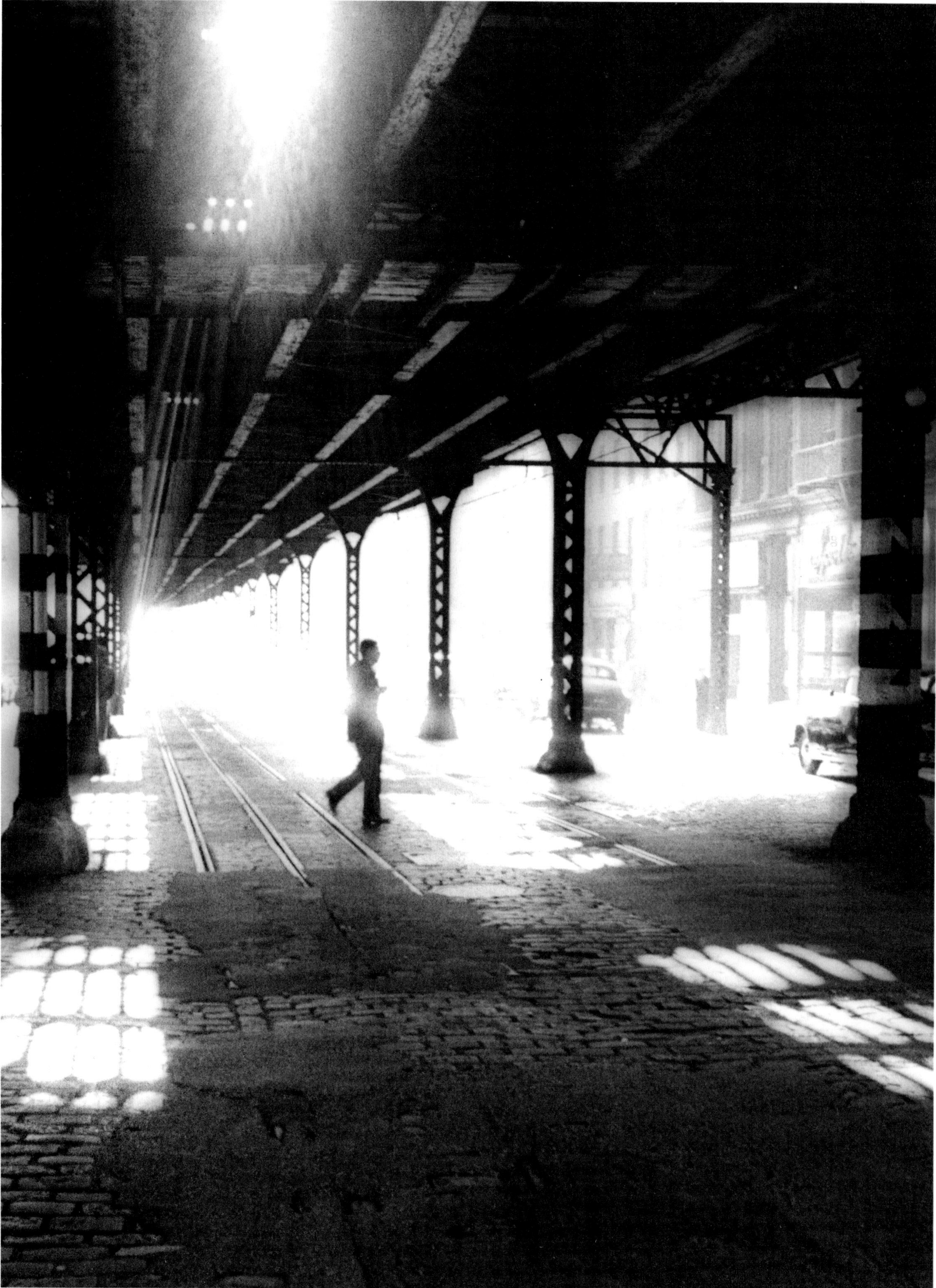

ON THE ROAD AND IN THE STREET

35

The post-war period in the United States

Colin Westerbeck

After the Second World War, American photography was marked by disillusionment and by a quest for the poetic – transcending the insignificance of the subject and random clicking of the shutter – which replaced formalism and professional norms. Following the example of Walker Evans and his carefully considered procedures (though sometimes in opposition to them), it is in the street that "new photographers" encounter that America whose transient clues they wish to capture. It is also in the roads of the hinterlands, in a wandering quest for the signs left by an ill-considered civilization – a quest akin to the vacuous state of mind of the beat generation, which forges an image which yields nothing to American topography – places which still harbor declining activities, spaces resounding with disappointment or simply echoing nature.

In the late 1930s, Andre Kertész left his beloved Paris for New York for what he thought would be a brief stay. But, first the failure of the picture agency he had come to work for, then a shortage of funds for his passage back, and finally, the outbreak of war delayed his return. When the war was at last over, the decimation of the European economy, which made the prospect of work there less likely, caused him to postpone his return yet again. In the end, he resigned himself to remaining in the United States, even though he felt that doing so cut him off from both the way of life and the kind of photography he loved.

His predicament had already become clear to him in 1939, before the war had even started, when he had been turned down by two New York editors to whom he had gone with proposals. The first, at a publishing house, told him that the photographic book he wanted to do on New York would never sell because, "You are too human, Kertész, sorry [...] Make it brutal." The second editor, at *Life*, explained bluntly, "You are talking too much in your pictures."

Kertész had been among the most influential photographers in Paris in the 1920s. "My poetic source", Henri Cartier-Bresson has called him, thus acknowledging the importance of the lead Kertész took in creating modern photography. And ironically, in his isolation and decline after the Second World War, he remained, as it were, avant-garde. He was one of the first to realize, to his chagrin, that the kind of lyrical humanism he had pioneered in Europe was now to be eclipsed by a new post-war style of photography which was both less joyous in its nature and more American in its origins.

It was not particularly the subject matter that changed, but rather the style of photography. Aesthetics were at issue, more than content. An angry, grainy, gestural look that developed early in street photography later gave way to an impassive blankness, a factuality that was almost perversely even-handed and non-committal, in landscape photography. But the stoniness of the one was just a continuation, in a different form, of the roughness of the other. Each was an attempt, if not to de-humanize the image, then at least to de-personalize it. Both were true to that editor's dictum to "make it brutal".

◀ William Klein, *Beneath the High-level Subway, 3rd Avenue,* New York, 1955.

Post-war disenchantment

In the United States the period from 1950 until 1980 can be divided right in the middle. 1965 was a watershed in which the documentary tradition, so dramatically transformed after the war, was modified once again, though in a less radical way. The impetus shifted from "New Documents" to the "New Topographics", from the street photography of the 1950s and early 1960s

Regarding this chapter, see also C. Westerbeck and J. Meyerowitz, *Bystander: A History of Street Photography*, New York, Little, Brown and Co., 1994; J. Livingstone, *The New York School: Photographs 1936–1963*, New York, Stewart, Tabori and Chang, 1992.

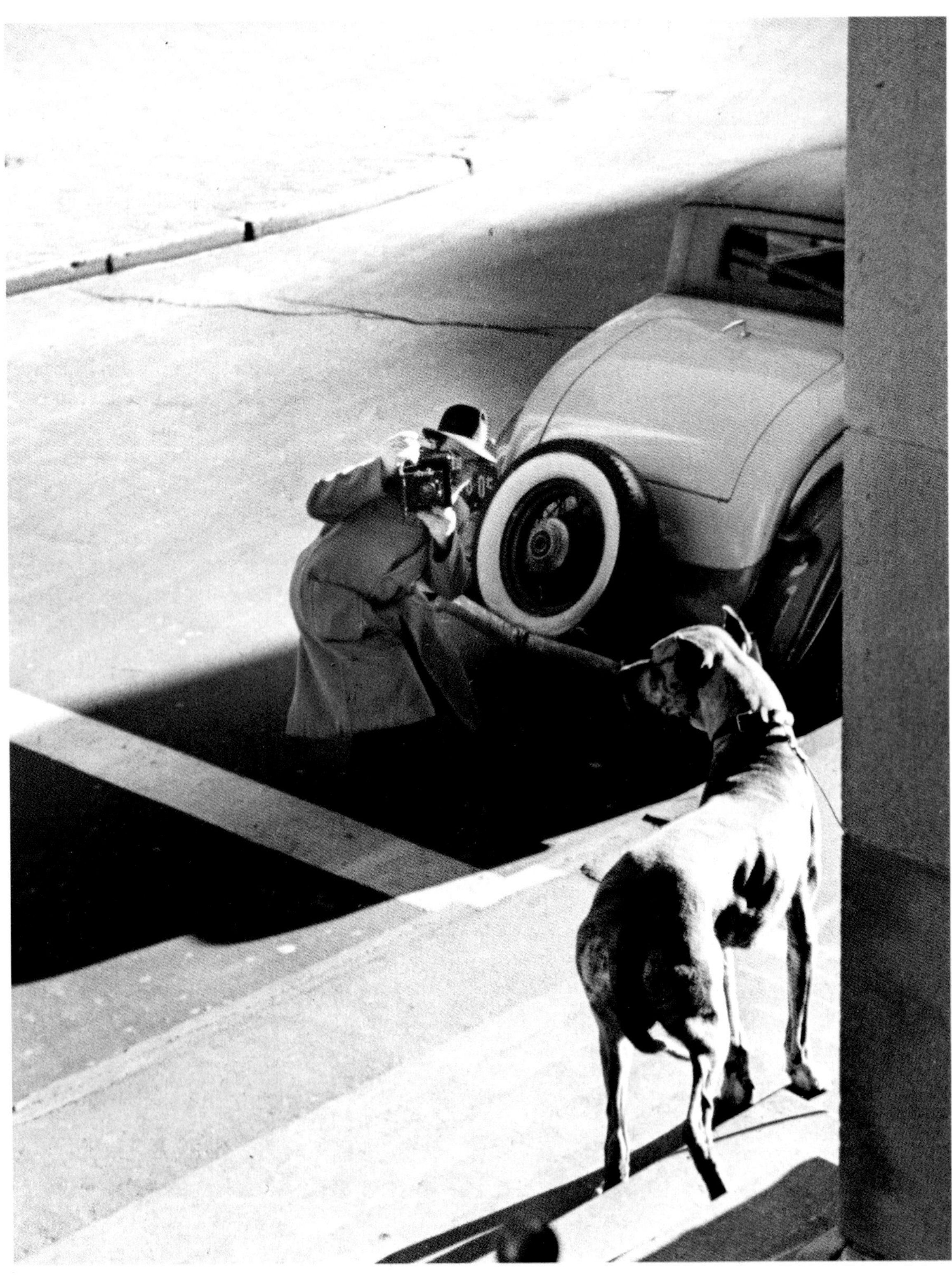

André Kertész,
At the Metropolitan Museum of Art,
New York, 1936.

centered in New York to the landscape photography of the late 1960s and the 1970s done primarily in the West.

The historical dialectic apparent here existed in parallel with the one working itself out in American painting, where Abstract Expressionism was gradually replaced by Minimalism as the dominant style. Just as these two movements in painting both perpetuated the same tradition – abstraction – so the two successive stages of post-war photography both recast a figurative vision, an imagery of humanity and nature, damaged in the aftermath of the war.

Moreover, the new documentary and the new topography were also alike in their determination not to "talk too much". The pre-war photography of Kertész, Cartier-Bresson, and the other great European modernists has an elegance that is, at times, a kind of literary eloquence based on formal control. In the most influential post-war work in America, photography is struck dumb. It falls mute when photographers begin rejecting formalism in order to avoid poetic symbolism, when they become disillusioned with the metaphorical meanings that analogous shapes paired in the frame create. If they believe that photographs ought to have any poetry in them at all, it is only the type that has a relentless existential monotony to it. Living in reduced artistic circumstances, like the characters in a Beckett play, these photographers insist on making dumb pictures.

Admittedly, the photographic tradition of which Kertész had been a founder did not just stop dead at the war's close. On the contrary, it institutionalized itself in photo-cooperatives like Magnum where Cartier-Bresson and a great many protégés were to have long prosperous careers. Because of this overlap of past and future or, rather, the overlay of the one on the other, the singularity of what was happening in America was not immediately apparent. Nor was the separation between the European and the American neatly distinct. Both people and ideas did a great deal of travelling back and forth across the Atlantic.

Though born in Paris, Elliott Erwitt, for instance, grew up in Hollywood, California. This product of the American Dream Factory went on to become the archetypal Magnum photographer, capable of composing, with all the grace and wit of a metaphysical poet, the sort of Bressonian conceit whose surprising juxtaposition of subjects in the frame generates a little shock of recognition in us.[1]

Cartier-Bresson's own renown came primarily after the war,[2] and even Kertész, lost in New York, continued to work, to have shows, and to publish books.[3] Yet it is clear, in retrospect, that these men had done their greatest work in Europe before the war. No matter how deserved the post-war honors earned by them – or by a newcomer like Erwitt – may have been, the work they were doing then was, at its best, a consolidation of earlier ideas. The innovation lay elsewhere.

The book as witness

Among the comings and goings from Europe in this period, two were crucial to the emergence of the new photography: New Yorker William Klein's move to Paris and Swiss photographer Robert Frank's from Paris to New York. These reciprocal journeys occurred within a year of each other – Frank's in 1947, Klein's during 1948 – and led each photographer to publish in the following decade a seminal book of American photographs. The one great difference in the two men's experiences was that while Frank had to live in America to see it clearly as a subject, Klein had to leave in order to do so.

In 1956, Klein published his book under the improbable title *Life Is Good and Good for You in*

Elliott Erwitt, *New York*, 1950.

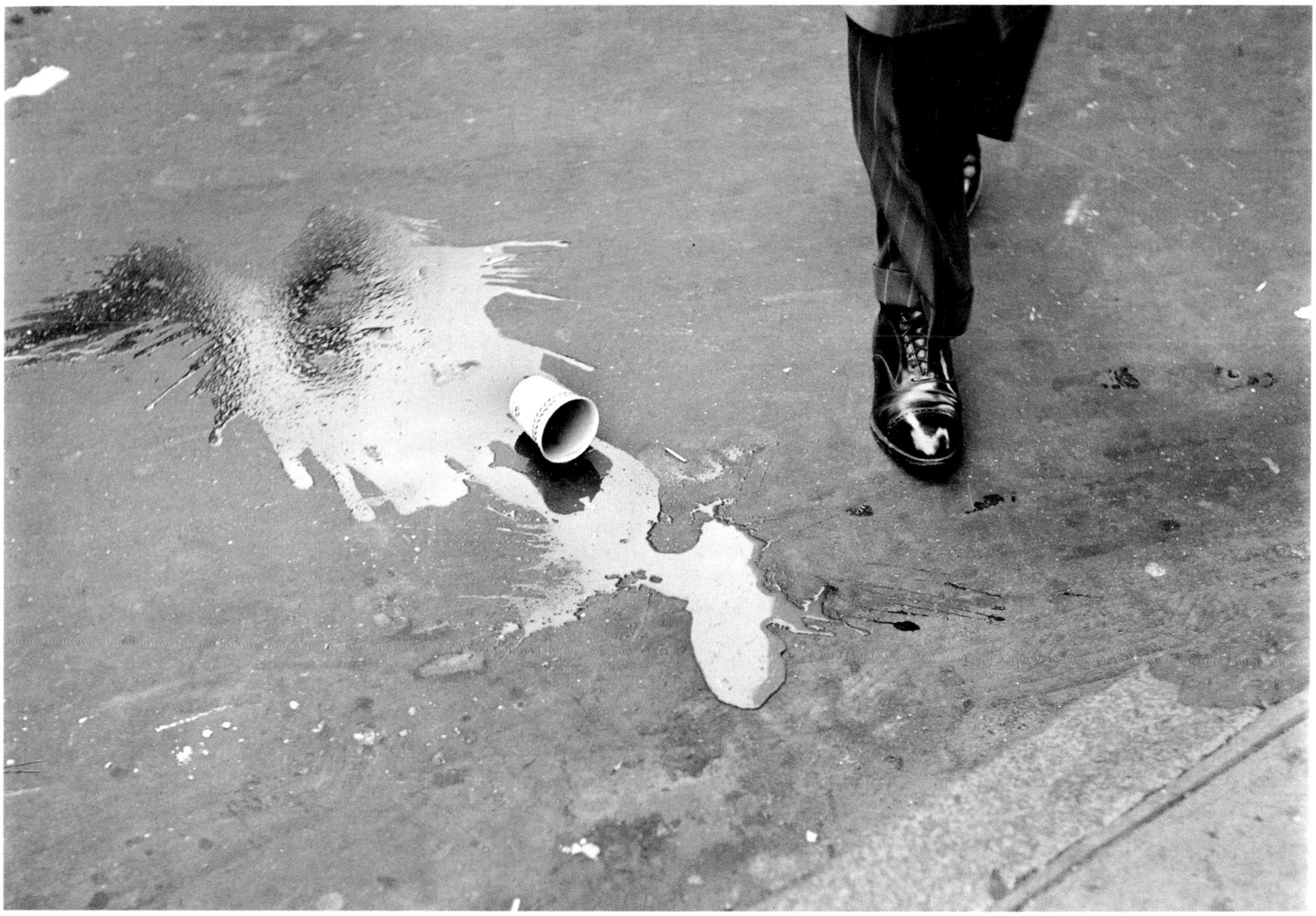

1. See especially Erwitt's three monographs: *Son of Bitch*, New York, 1974, *Recent Developments*, New York, 1978, and *Personal Exposures*, New York, 1988.

2. Cartier-Bresson's influence in the United States was established by his exhibition at the Museum of Modern Art, New York, 1947, with its catalogue entitled *The Photographs of Henri Cartier-Bresson*, as well as by the publication of *The Decisive Moment*, New York, 1952.

3. Kertész's recognition in the United States began with the publication of *Day of Paris* (New York, 1945) and his first American one-man exhibition at the Art Institute of Chicago in 1947.

WILLIAM KLEIN, *Charity Ball at the Waldorf, New York,* 1954–1955.
▼

New York: Trance Witness Revels.[4] Just as "Life is good and good for you" is a parody of an American advertising slogan of the 1950s, "chance witness reveals" is a stock phrase used by the tabloid press. This sentence sums up perfectly, like a motto, or an advertising slogan, Klein's whole attitude towards photography.

Klein took the medium up by chance in 1952 when, in the process of documenting some revolving panels on which he had done paintings, he bumped one so that it became motion-blurred in the photograph. Although he had come to Paris to study painting, he was finding the traditions of modernism already in place there oppressive. Photography was appealing not only because he discovered its powers by accident, but because that power lay in having accidents with the medium. Proposing itself to him as an art from in which recklessness could be creative, photography was, he realized, exactly what he was looking for. He would do his utmost (as he admitted later) to "brutalize" the equipment and "break all the rules".

Being an iconoclast by nature, Klein also liked photography because it was not considered high art. It offered an opportunity to attack the expectation of viewers who regarded refinement and sensibility as the key to aesthetic experience. He wanted the photographs themselves to have the energy and effrontery of a tabloid newspaper, imagery "as vulgar and brutal as the *News*", by which he meant New York's *Daily News*, the scandal-sheet newspaper he had grown up with.

He had needed to escape from New York because, as a poor Jewish child in a tough Irish-Italian neighborhood, he had spent his youth being terrorized by street gangs. By the time he went back, in the early 1950s, photography was for him, he has confessed, a "weapon" with which to "get even". He wanted his photographs to reveal the harshness of life on the New York streets, and he realized that the way to do so was to cultivate in himself a killer instinct for pictures as ferocious as the primal emotions he wanted to betray in his subjects. This is why the "chance witness" also had to be a "trance witness". He needed to let his photographs well up from the unconscious, to tap into the kind of libidinal instincts in human nature that would provoke a like response in his subjects.

The picture in Klein's book that is the nastiest stylistically (that is, the blurriest and least readable) happens to have been taken at a society ball

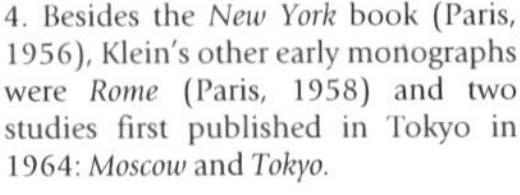

4. Besides the *New York* book (Paris, 1956), Klein's other early monographs were *Rome* (Paris, 1958) and two studies first published in Tokyo in 1964: *Moscow* and *Tokyo*.

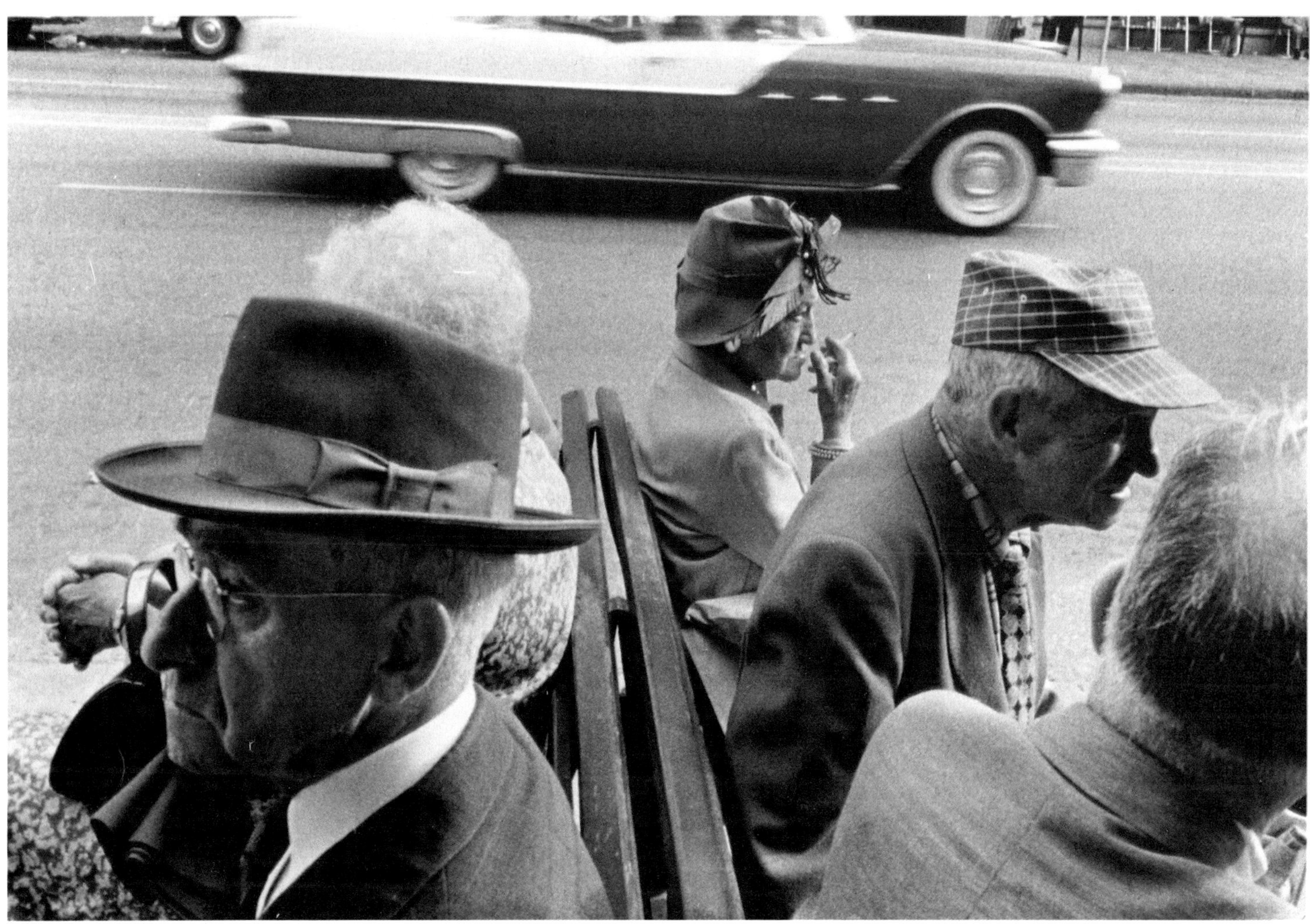

ROBERT FRANK,
Saint Petersburg, Florida,
1955–1956,
from *The Americans.*

where Robert Frank was also present, shooting pictures for his own book, *The Americans.*[5] The two men were only remotely aware of each other. Like Klein, Frank was working out for himself an aesthetic based on loose, anti-formal, open-ended pictures – pictures of America that had a profound ambiguity, growing out of the photographer's deep ambivalence toward his subject. Yet the amount of mutual influence the two men had was almost negligible.

If there was ever a photographer whose work is *sui generis,* it is Frank. This is not to say that he did not have influences; he did – more than Klein, in fact – for both his career and his vision were shaped crucially by Walker Evans. But his photography is so much the product of his own, unique temperament that it is ultimately fruitless to look for its origins anywhere except in Frank himself. Where Klein is capable of turning a certain cynicism he has about life into an extraordinarily powerful imagery, Frank is a tragedian, a man in whom a more capacious emotion – pessimism, rather than mere cynicism – has turned ambivalence towards paradox.

Klein's photographs may not "speak too much", in the manner of Kertész, but they are noisy in a sense: they are raucous. Frank's are truly quiet. According to Frank himself, the experience that matured his vision more than any other was one in which he was almost completely mute for many weeks. This was on a trip to Peru that he made in 1948, travelling by native transport in the Andes, where he was often unable to communicate with anyone because he could not understand local dialects. His feelings of incomprehension, of the absolute otherness of his subjects, was what he wanted his photography to capture from then on.

Frank had taken off for Peru, like an naturalized Huck Finn in Mark Twain's novel, because he wanted to escape the commercial success he was beginning to have in New York shooting for fashion magazines. He has always felt that failing at something is more stimulating than succeeding (that is why he would leave photography altogether for a while to become a filmmaker after *The Americans*). Nevertheless, the Peru trip did result in one concrete achievement: a hand-made book of the photographs that he put together after his return.

This was actually the second in a series of maquettes he created that were like milestones marking the route by which he got from Paris to *The Americans.* He had gone to Paris at the war's end and loved it there. Indeed, he had left for

5. Frank's key publications are G. Arnaud, *Indiens pas morts,* Paris, 1956, *The Americans,* Paris, 1958, New York, 1959, and *The Lines of My Hand,* Tokyo, 1971.

The Americans, a model

The first thing Robert Frank said to Wright Morris when they met in the early 1950s was "Are you the guy who did that book?" It is significant that the question was not "Are you the guy who took those pictures?" The implicit admiration was for *The Inhabitants* as a book rather than just for the photography. At a time when there was no art market in photography, few departments devoted to the medium in American museums, and only infrequent exhibitions, to many photographers, books seemed to be their only chance to gain either money or recognition for their work.

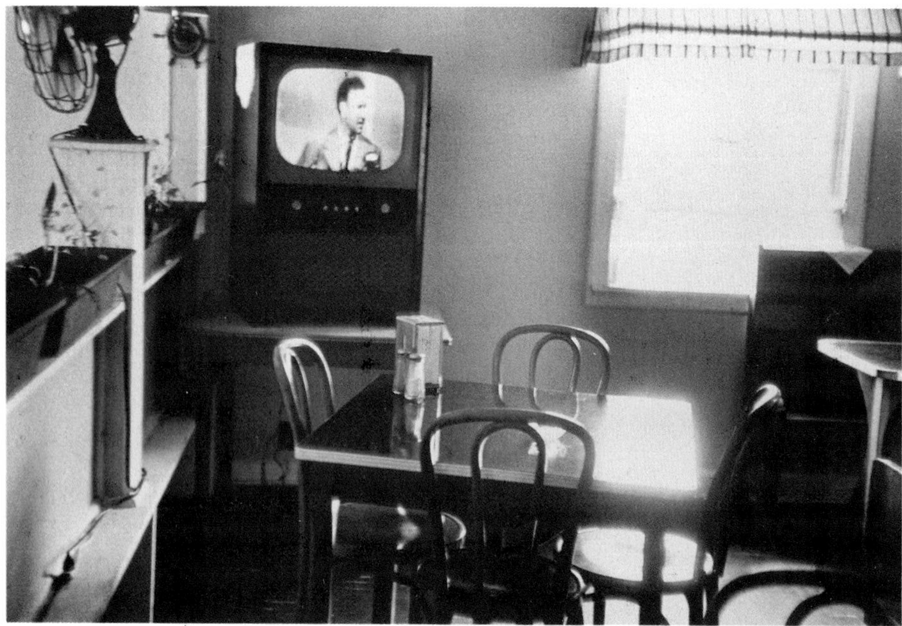

ROBERT FRANK,
Restaurant, Columbia, South Carolina,
1955–1956, from *The Americans.*

It was Frank's *The Americans* (Paris, Delpire, 1958; New York, Grove Press, 1959) that made the photographic book into an art form in its own right. Frank was following the lead set by Morris's book and, especially, by Evans's *American Photographs*, both of which are designed to let pictures play off each other in a way that controls and reinforces their effect on the viewer. Even Klein's New York book displays this tendency. But Frank's goes much further, creating a denser, richer, deeper structure of images than any book before it.

Perhaps because he was already on his way to being a filmmaker, Frank was able to apply the principles of cinematic montage to still photographs in an innovative fashion. The pictures follow on from each other by a kind of metamorphosis: a flag becomes bunting on the next page, a highway stripe turns into stripes on yet another flag, or the stars on a third flag are transformed into little star-shaped lights over a bar. A half-dozen motifs such as these – flags, cars, hats, cemeteries and other signs of death – are melded into a structure for the entire book. Because they have behind them the momentum of earlier carefully placed pictures, certain images in this way acquire an impact that they could never have had by themselves.

However tentative the lead Frank was following from earlier books, his own book had enormous appeal among contemporary photographers in the same genre. Among the photographers of the 1960s, 1970s, and 1980s discussed here, getting a monograph published was as important, if not more urgent, than an exhibition. Although the two often went together, it was the publication of a book which mattered more.

Books both established the careers of individual photographers and – as in the collections edited by Sally Eauclaire, *The New Color Photography* (New York, 1981) and *New Color/New York* (New York, 1984) – surveyed recent developments whose existence and importance might not otherwise have been recognized.

Colin Westerbeck

New York (it is ironic to note) only for the same reason Kertész had stayed there – because he could not make a living in Paris. Once in America, he made a little booklet of sentimental Paris pictures to give to his future wife, Mary.

When you trace a line from this maquette through the one from Peru and then one other he was to do entitled *Black, White and Things*, you see projected forward onto *The Americans* something not quite apparent at first. It is the degree to which Frank's photography expresses a kind of yearning for his subjects, a longing for them and a tenderness towards them that give his vision a fullness and complication which Klein's work never quite achieves. What makes *The Americans* a great book is not just Frank's alienation from America, but rather that alienation mixed with the unassuagable compassion he felt for the people of his adopted nation.

The significance of *The Americans* lies in the way in which, while eschewing Cartier-Bresson's finished, self-sufficient type of picture, it uses the more unresolved sort Frank preferred to build up dense, meaningful groups of images. By playing off each picture against many others within the totality of the book, rather than one subject against another within the single frame, *The Americans* achieves, in spite of the reticence of the photographs in it, the complexity demanded by Frank's two-mindedness about his subject.

Klein's book hints at this sort of structure, but only in Frank's are the possibilities fully realized. If there was any decisive precedent from which Frank drew inspiration, it was Walker Evans's book of 1938, *American Photographs*. Nobody else, besides perhaps the editor-publisher Robert Delpire, played the role of mentor with Frank and his book that Evans did. Evans helped his young colleague by getting him a crucial assignment from *Fortune* magazine as well as the

Guggenheim grant on which he traveled throughout the country.

More important still, Evans was a patriot who could love America without being blind to its flaws and its narrowness. In the New York subway portraits of 1939 and the street portraits from Chicago and Detroit right after the war, Evans wrenched from both his subjects and himself one of those simplifications of his medium so severe, so reductive, that it stands as a tremendous clarification as well.[6] Here was a tragic vision of the common man, of "ourselves made worthy in our anonymity", as the poet William Carlos Williams said of the pictures in *American Photographs* when he reviewed the book for the magazine the *New Republic*. In the subway pictures that followed from that 1938 book – those unblinking, somber portraits that reveal, nonetheless, the photographer's enormous sympathy and esteem for his subjects – Frank found a potent example for his own work.

The art of pointing the camera

Only in the way he shot his pictures did Frank depart from the reflective, deliberate methods of Evans and draw closer to Klein and to that spirit with which the post-war period alone was imbued. When taking pictures, Frank depended on unpremeditated, unmediated instinct to such an extent that at times he did not even put the camera to his eye. Holding it down at his side or cradled in the crook of his arm, he relied on the third eye of our inner vision to guide him to the picture.

At such moments, Frank was wielding his camera in the same way that the Abstract Expressionists, some of whom were his friends, wielded their brushes.[7] In both himself and his subjects, he was probing for different emotions from Klein, yet working intuitively in a similar manner to him.

Just as the earlier tradition of Kertész and Cartier-Bresson did not end abruptly simply because something new emerged in the work of Klein and Frank, so, too, was the new work not altogether without antecedents and predecessors. Evans was not the only native photographer who played Virgil to Frank's Dante by serving as a guide to the American nether worlds Frank wished to explore. The eye for Americans and the sympathy for Americans Frank developed were also inspired by the photographer and novelist Wright Morris, whose series of late 1940s phototexts – especially *The Inhabitants* – depict life in the Midwestern state of Nebraska where Morris grew up. Had Morris not given up photography to return to the writing of fiction after the brief period when he published these monographs, he might have become an influence on post-war American photography second only to Evans.

If Evans's and Morris's work provided a precedent for one side of Frank's – the side that had a kind of stolid tenderness to it – other photographers from the pre-war era anticipated the side that could be more pitiless and harsh. A brutalist approach to both the medium and the subjects can be found earlier in the photography of Weegee, Lisette Model, and even Jacob Riis, who got recognition as a photographer only after the war despite having published his work a half century earlier.[8]

The career that Weegee (Arthur Fellig) had as a news hawk for the New York papers began forty years after that of Riis, but his recognition in the art world came at the same time. In 1944, he was

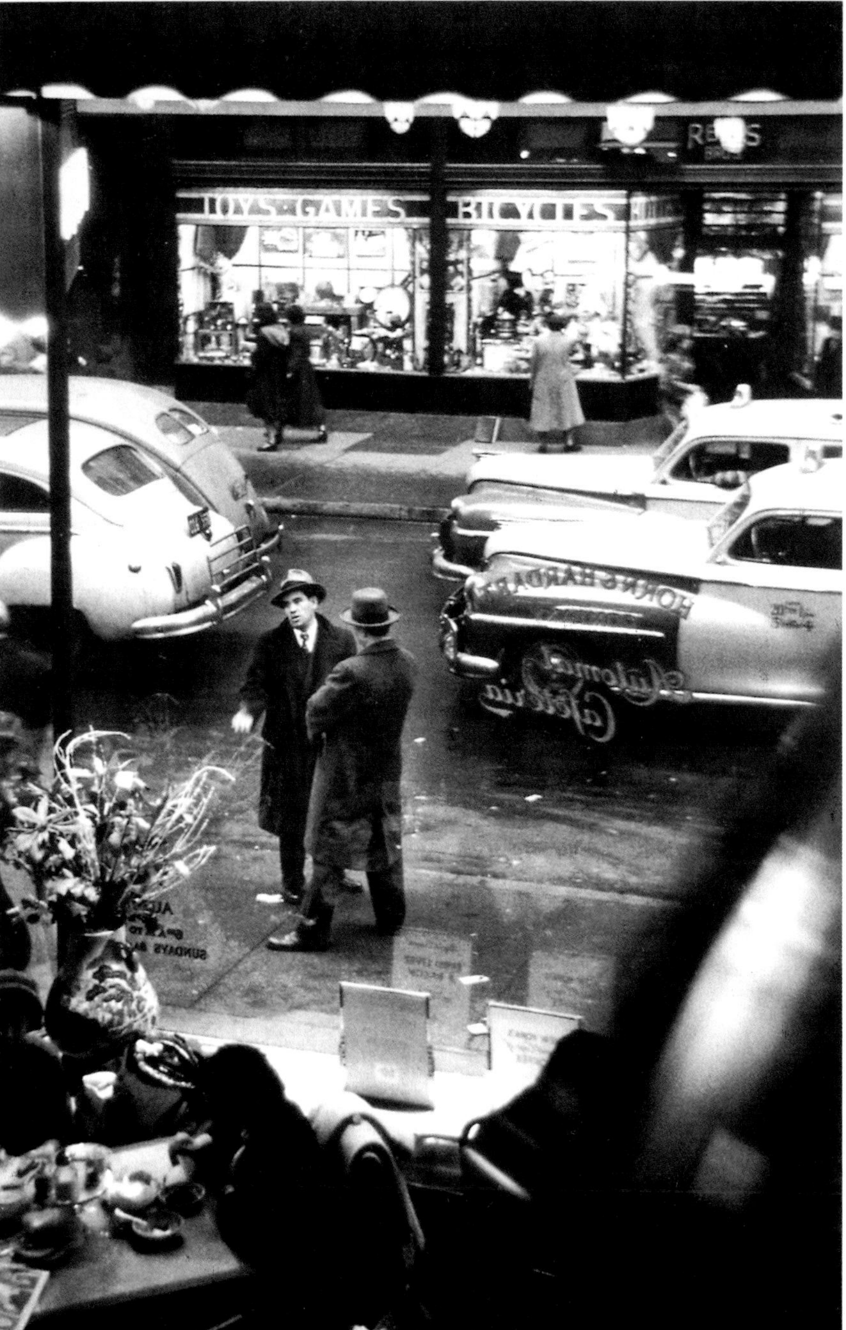

David Vestal,
From the Automat, East 59th Street,
New York, 1950.

6. *Many Are Called*, Boston, 1966; *Message from the Interior*, New York, 1966, *Walker Evans*, New York, 1971; *First and Last*, New York, 1978.

7 Frank had a studio across a courtyard from Willem De Kooning, whom he would watch for hours pacing as he painted. Jackson Pollock's darting, probing approach to a canvas laid on the floor is also analogous to Frank's movements with his camera on the street.

8. Only after an amateur recovered Riis's long-lost negatives in the early 1940s did Riis get his first New York exhibition. In 1949 Beaumont Newhall included Riis in the new edition of his *History of Photography*.

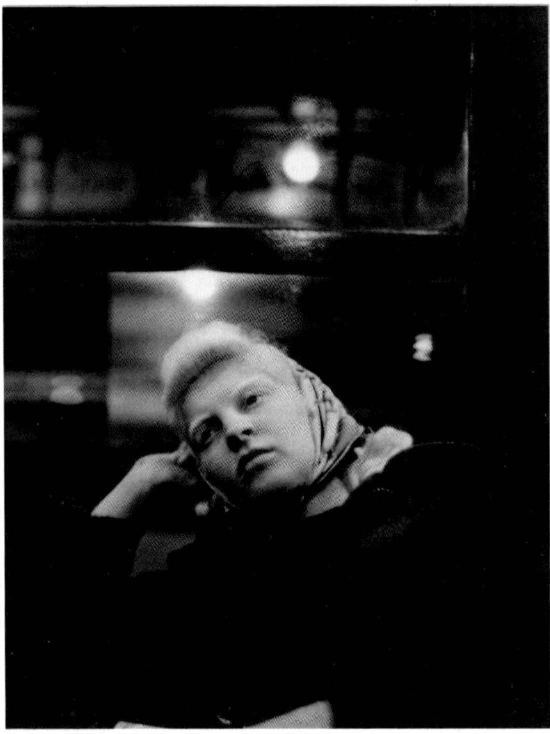
WALKER EVANS, *Subway Portrait,* 1941.

invited to give a talk on his work at the Museum of Modern Art, and a suggestion someone made during the question-and-answer that evening prompted him to put together, in the following year, a book of his photographs entitled *The Naked City.*[9] After that, his work appeared in a number of exhibitions, and he became rather an art-world celebrity. Like Riis's grim images of slumdwellers, Weegee's of both victims and bystanders at automobile smash-ups or gangland slayings appealed to the mood of the age.

Weegee had been making this imagery since 1935, using a Speed Graphic, the standard press camera of the day, fitted with the new flashbulbs that had replaced Riis's flash powder. In Weegee's pictures, as in Riis's, the flash had a levelling effect on everything it touched, as if all of human experience were the same. The flash flattened every scene exposed to it, turning the victims of violence, disaster, and poverty into victims of its harsh glare. All Weegee's subjects look like people who have been shot with stun guns.

Lisette Model was not only a contemporary of Weegee's in New York in the 1940s, but a cohort who used to hang out with him at a dive called Sammy's on the Bowery. The two photographers also shared a steady outlet for their work at *PM* magazine, whose editor, Ralph Steiner, had published, under the title *Why France Fell,* a portfolio of Model street portraits done in Europe shortly before her 1940 departure.

Many of these pictures were from a few test rolls Model had shot on the Riviera to see whether she could put into practice the brief instruction she had received from Kertész's wife. In other words, at the very moment that Kertész himself was being rejected by New York editors, Model was enjoying great success by showing a few, first, tentative experiments as inept as Riis's had been. Like Riis, she saw at once that she should not improve her technique. On the

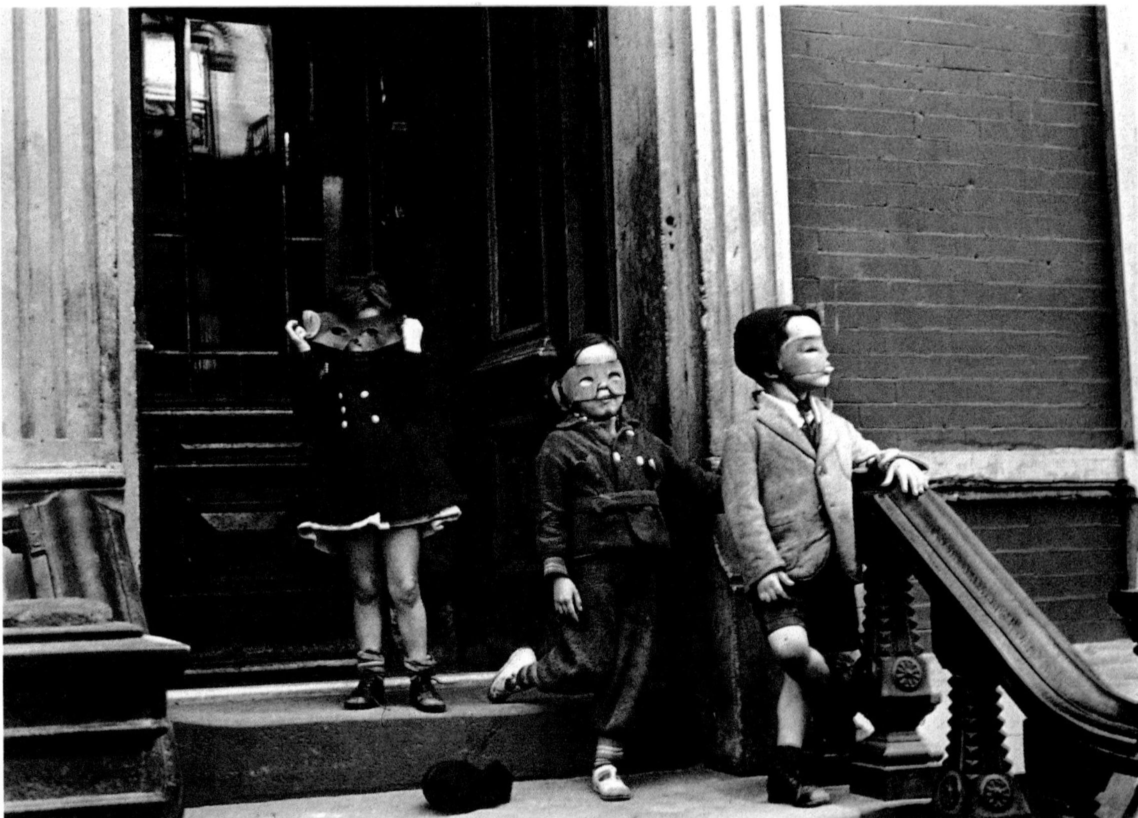
HELEN LEVITT, New York, 1939.

9. In addition to *The Naked City,* New York, 1945, Weegee's key publications are *Weegee's People,* New York, 1946, *Naked Hollywood,* New York, 1953, and *Weegee by Weegee,* New York, 1961.

contrary, she made over-sized prints in which the images became even grainier and coarser. When Edward Weston, recognizing the raw power of such work, once asked her how she managed to achieved it, she answered contemptuously that she just sent her negatives out to the corner drugstore to be processed.

Although such easy, unearned acceptance made her as cynical about the photography world as she was about the one in which her subjects lived, Model continued to work in the same vein in America.[10] In New York, she photographed Wall Street capitalists from below, with a camera held down at the level of the pavement and the tangle of passing feet in the crowd. Both sorts of pictures looked as if they were taken from the point of view of somebody being trampled in a panic in the streets.

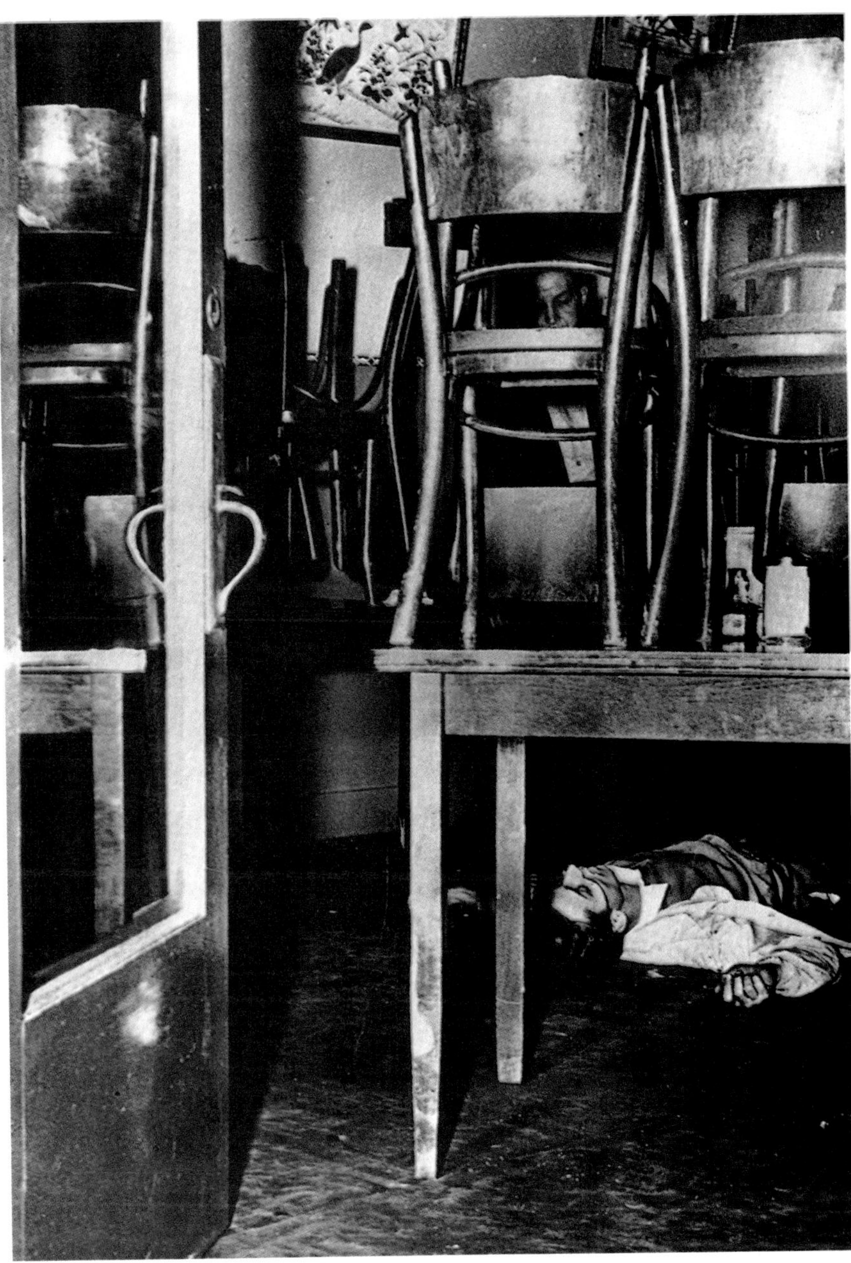

Weegee,
Murder in a Restaurant,
New York,
1940s.

Street school

While Model's vision may have benefited from her having had almost no training in photography, later in life she herself became a teacher of others. This was a sign of the change of times, an indication of the extent to which what was once exciting because it was so unconventional had now become the convention. A whole new school of New York street photography grew up in the early 1960s, and one of the two photographers around whom it formed was Model's star pupil, Diane Arbus. Arbus's work projected the grimness of Model's onto the turbulent America of the Vietnam era.

Shooting most of the time, it seems, in overcast weather, Arbus gave her imagery a grayed-out, ennervated look that causes everyday people caught at parades or in the park to blend, in the end, with the dwarfs, the midgets, and the carnies, the flabby nudists in their colonies and the retarded and schizophrenic in institutions. She printed down her pictures, creating a vapid sameness for all her subjects to live in, and leaving strangely wavy, unfocussed edges on her prints as if, once you went beyond what was in them, you fell into the void.

The freaks, geeks, and grotesques in her pictures are, like the subjects of Model, being made to stand in for the rest of us. They are a fun-house mirror that the photographer holds up to society. It is, therefore significant, perhaps, that the posthumous show John Szarkowski, the curator at the Museum of Modern Art, did of these pictures in 1972 should have been enormously popular.[11] It was the best attended photography exhibition since *The Family of Man*, curated by Szarkowski's predecessor, Steichen, in 1955.

That two shows so contradictory in nature should have rivaled one another in appeal seems strange, until one considers the difference in the times at which the two were done. Steichen's, with its editorial and sentimental message, came in the middle of a complacent decade – the middle decade of what *Life*'s founder, Henry Luce, had called "the American century" – while Szarkowski's Arbus show, which was monographic and disturbing, came towards the end of the Vietnam era.

When you consider that Model's European pictures found a ready market in America, while both Klein's book and Frank's had to be first published in Europe in order to be published at all, you might be tempted to think that an American audience is willing to entertain a negative view only of foreigners, never themselves. Frank and Klein were creating an image of America for which Americans were not yet ready (though Frank's book did come out in the United

10. The first monograph exclusively of her work was not published until four years before her death (Millerton, New York, 1979).

11. The only monograph on Arbus since the one that served as catalogue for this exhibition (Millerton, New York, 1972) is *Diane Arbus: The Magazine Work* (Millerton, New York, 1984).

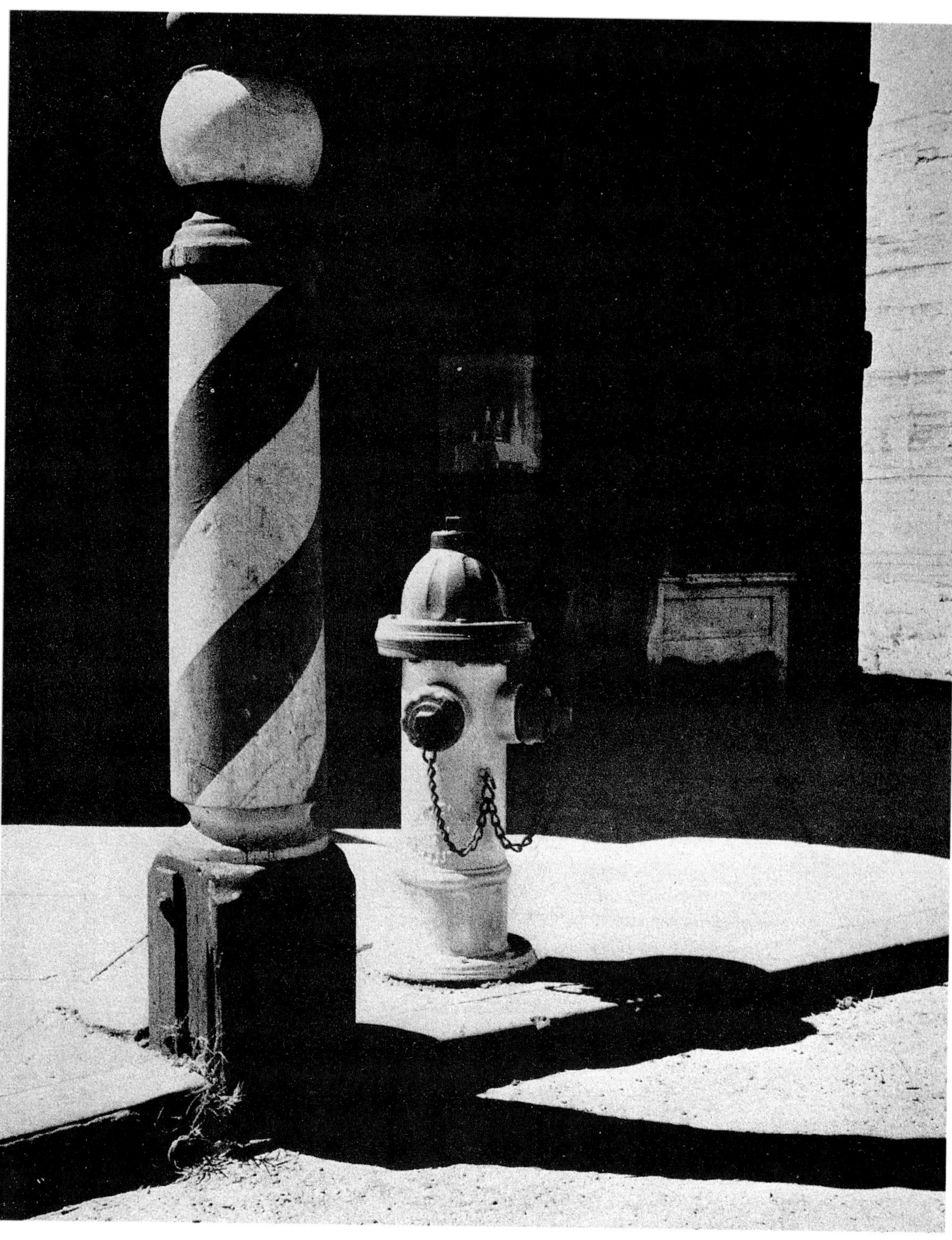

WRIGHT MORRIS, *Barber Pole and Hydrant,* California, 1938, from *The Inhabitants,* 1946.

States in 1959, a year after the French edition). By the early 1970s, the same people were almost too eager for Arbus's view of them.

According to Joel Meyerowitz, Arbus was always somewhat of a loner. Her pictures were known to other street photographers working in New York in those days, but she herself remained somewhat aloof, mysterious – "a wraith," as he recalls her. For Meyerowitz, whose own involvement with photography dates from that period in the early 1960s, the photographer who was setting the pace and leading the way for everybody else was Garry Winogrand. Meyerowitz and Winogrand would meet most mornings at a coffee shop on the Upper West Side of Manhattan, then go out and hit the streets to shoot. They would go to Central Park, to the Village, to Fifth Avenue (especially if there was a parade) – wherever they thought the action might be.

Meyerowitz remembers Winogrand as incredibly restless, energetic, and keyed-up; his approach to the streets was a kind of tender assault. Certainly there is in Winogrand's photographs in New York and on later trips around the country an element of aggressiveness comparable to Klein's. There is a raw, sometimes slashing edge to the work. But there is also a vulnerability, not unlike Frank's.

The knee-jerk quality of Winogrand's reactions is evident from the tilted frame of pictures whose horizon lines veer this way and that in utter disregard for the niceties, the neatness, of a squared-up composition. This indication of the gestural nature of his habits as a picture-maker practically became his trademark, and, in his later work, perhaps a bit too much of an affectation still to be effective. Yet lunging, confrontational, and abrasive as his pictures can be, there is never anything cold or vicious about them. They are warm-blooded. They express a capacity to wonder at life: "Wow! Look at that!" is what they keep saying.

Winogrand identified with the New Yorkers whose pictures he took, as the title of his first book, *The Animals,*[12] suggests. For he always referred to himself as an animal, too, and frequently seemed to Meyerowitz to be, of all the creatures that they visited at the zoo, most like the bear. Trapped in his cage, the bear paces up and down constantly in front of the bars; his hug is an all-encompassing embrace, a bone-crushing kind of affection. That is what Winogrand's embrace of America was in his photographs.

Meyerowitz's own street photography was always in a more agile, classical, even Bressonian vein. He was lighter in spirit by temperament, less brooding and brutish than Winogrand, and his photographs show it. Yet they too have their sarcastic, sardonic side, their element of incredulity at life in the United States. What his early street pictures share most with Winogrand's is an unassuming energy. They are work done on a hot streak, images that seem, at times, superheated, almost out of control, like a run-away power plant.

His sheer unadulterated enthusiasm for life was such that in order to achieve his greatest originality as a photographer, he ultimately needed the added expressiveness of the color view camera and the counterpoint that taking on a traditionally pretty, potentially clichéd subject like Cape Cod provided. In the pictures that he has made in this New England resort area since the mid-1970s, the street smarts of the New Yorker have remained intact, implicit. These bayscapes retain – and draw their power from – the city-slicker's smart-assed eye for errant details.[13]

There were, of course, street photographers working in New York independently of this group. From the 1950s on, Roy DeCarava was living and working in Harlem, a black man documenting the life of his own community.[14] Perhaps because he was completely at home in the world he depicted, DeCarava's work has always been less edgy and alienated than that of the street shooters downtown. His compositions have tended to be more contemplative and centered, though that may also be because he

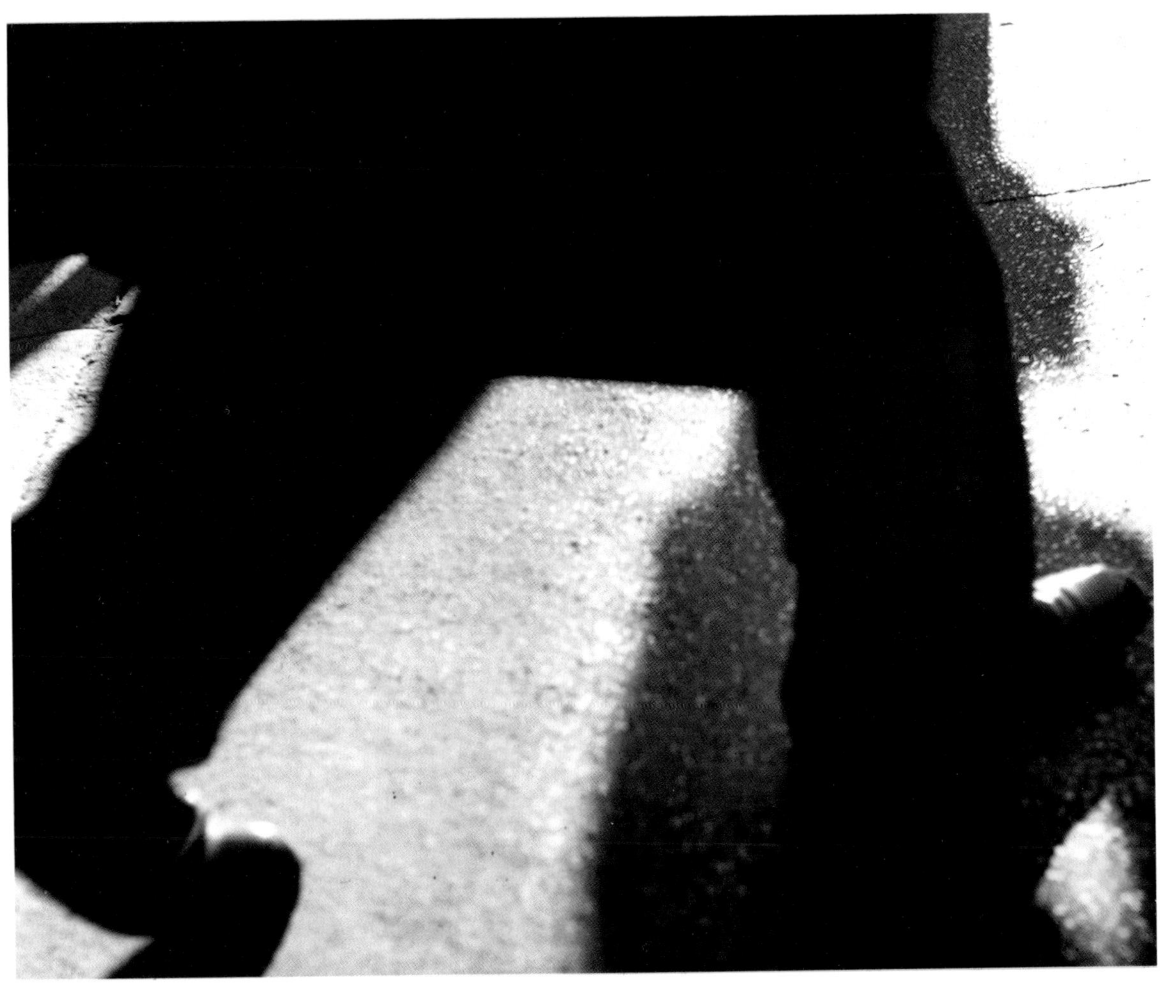

LISETTE MODEL, ***Running Legs,*** New York, 1940–1941.

12. After *The Animals* (New York, 1969), which accompanied an exhibition at the Museum of Modern Art, Winogrand published *Women Are Beautiful* (New York, 1975), *Public Relations* (New York, 1977, which was also a Museum of Modern Art catalogue, and *Stock Photographs* (Austin, Texas, 1980).

13. *Cape Light,* Boston, 1978, *St. Louis and the Arch,* Boston, 1980; *Wild Flowers,* Boston, 1983, *A Summer's Day,* New York, 1985; *Redheads,* New York, 1991.

14. De Carava's first publication was *The Sweet Flypaper of Life* (New York, 1955; reprinted Washington, 1984). A retrospective monograph of his career was published by the Friends of Photography (Carmel, California, 1981).

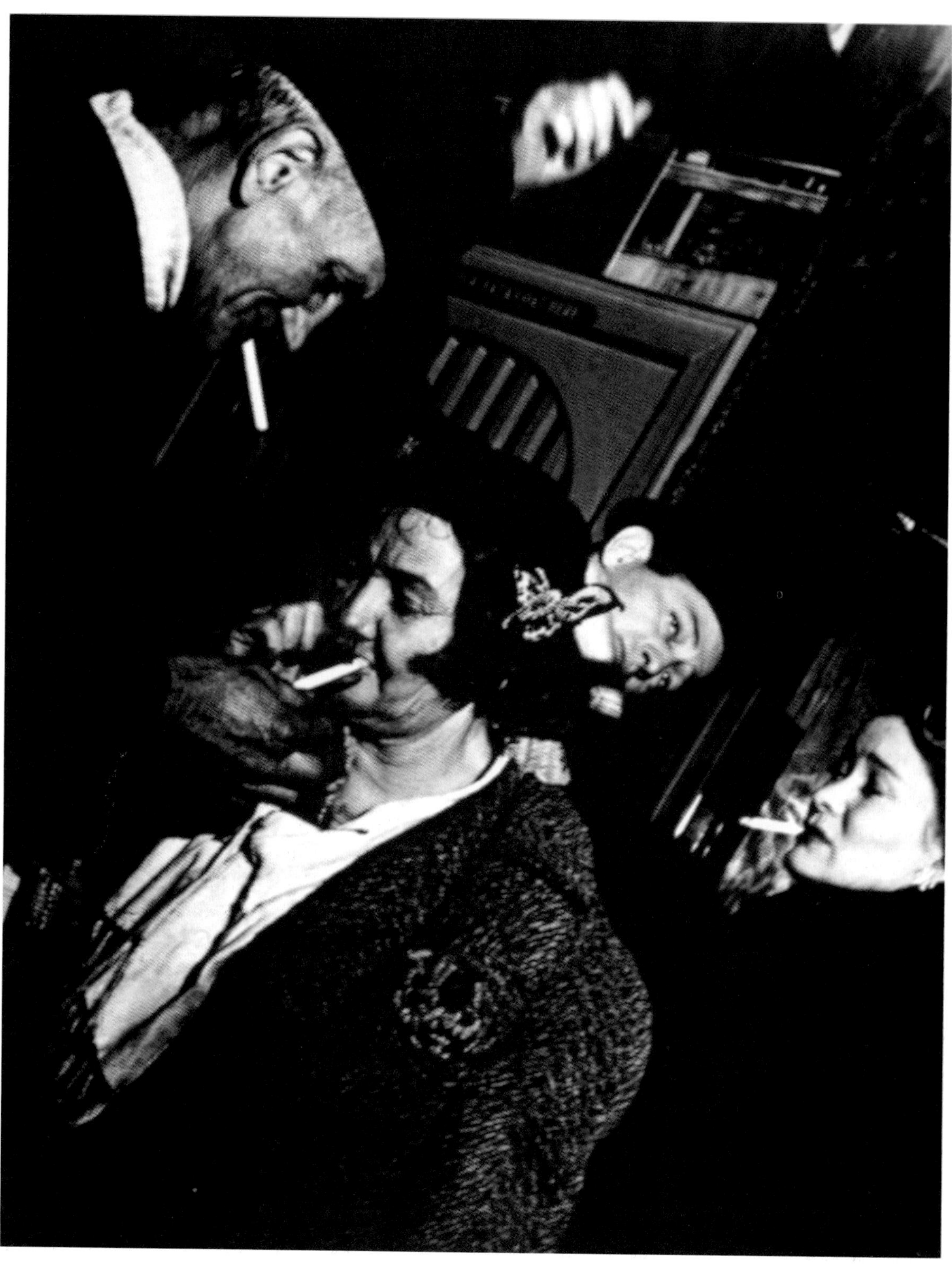

LISETTE MODEL, *At Sammy's*, New York, 1940–1944.

needed to shoot at slower speeds with a steadier hand to capture the activities of a black people living in a dim place. Even to his work there has been, quite literally, a dark side.

Though he lived on Upper Broadway, near Meyerowitz and Winogrand, Bruce Davidson went his own way too, particularly when he ventured up into DeCarava's turf to do a study of life on East 100th Street.[15] A member of Magnum who has repeatedly taken time off from his career to do personal work like this, he has remained, nonetheless, essentially photojournalistic in his approach.

From the East 100th Street material shot in black and white to the color work done riding the New York subways, Davidson has poked his camera into more squalid corners of the city than many of his colleagues were willing to dwell upon. What he was looking for though, as the pictures have always showed, was a kind of awkward human beauty, visible in even the most unforgiving of settings.

There were still more photographers working in New York in the 1960s and 1970s who might deserve mention – the Englishman Tony Ray-Jones,[16] and Tod Papageorge, who was as close a companion of Winogrand's as Meyerowitz – but

15. After *East 100th Street* (Millerton, New York, 1970), Davidson's most notable publications have been *Bruce Davidson Photographs* (New York, 1978) and *Subway* (Millerton, New York, 1986).

16. Ray-Jones's only monograph, published posthumously, is *A Day Off* (London, 1974).

the other truly major figure, Lee Friedlander, is the hardest to classify. On the one hand, he was a street shooter who ran into, and occasionally ran with, Winogrand, Meyerowitz, etc. On the other hand, he always lived outside New York and made images that have a different attitude and look – a different temperature, one might say – from those of his contemporaries in the city.

Friedlander's pictures in New York occasionally have the stacked-up, multi-layered density, the busy-ness, that Winogrand's or Meyerowitz's display, but more characteristic of his work is an imagery that is less frenetic than theirs. Like the photographer himself as he appeared in picture after picture in his 1970 book *Self-Portrait*[17] the photographs he has made are essentially dead-pan. Where Meyerowitz in person fixes you with a gaze that is Rasputin-like in its intensity, Friedlander's eyes are heavy-lidded and unblinking. In contrast with the expressionism of the gestural imagery of Frank or Winogrand, Friedlander's is, like his own self-portraits, expressionless. His is a laconic, flat-footed, nearly non-committal style.

Although most of the photographers discussed so far established their visions with work done in the streets of New York, that imagery blended in later with work done on the road travelling around America. Frank's book was not just about one city, nor was the body of work done by Winogrand or Meyerowitz, who had a Guggenheim grant on which to go see the whole country. And the books for which Danny Lyon is best known, *The Bikeriders* (1968) and *Conversations with the Dead* (1971),[18] are not about New York either. In fact, they contain no New York pictures at all.

In these studies of an outlaw motorcycle gang from Chicago and life inside a Texas prison, we again get the sort of fleeting, furtive glimpse at life that New York street photography gives us. Yet

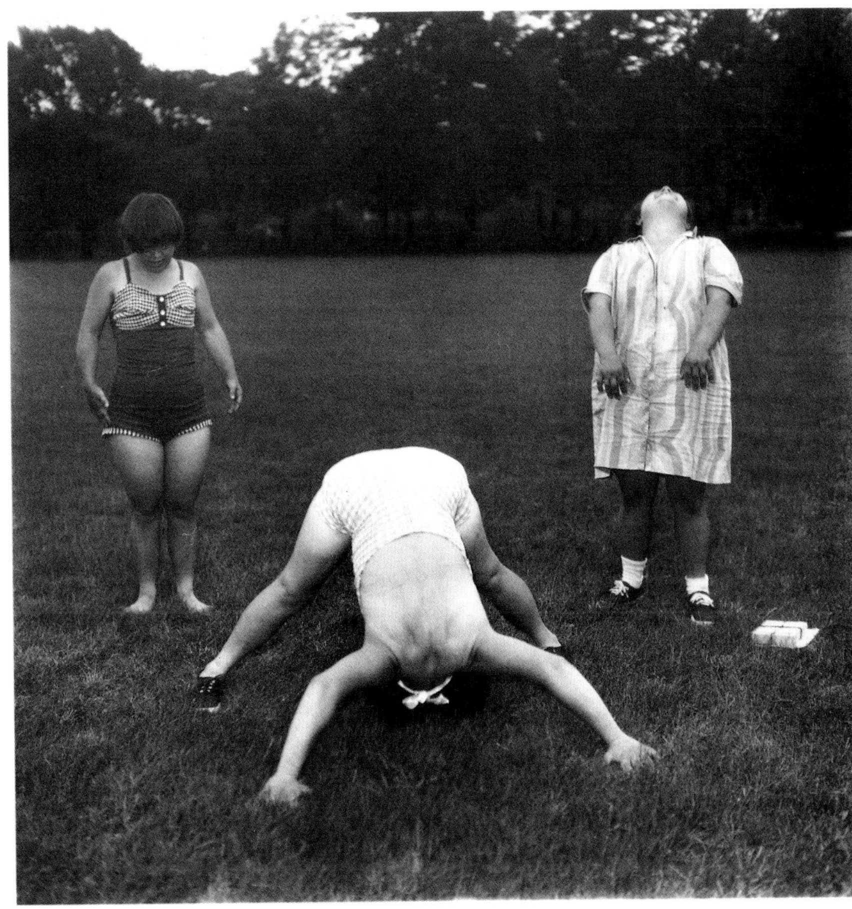

DIANE ARBUS,
Untitled (6),
1970–1971,
Robert Miller Gallery,
New York.

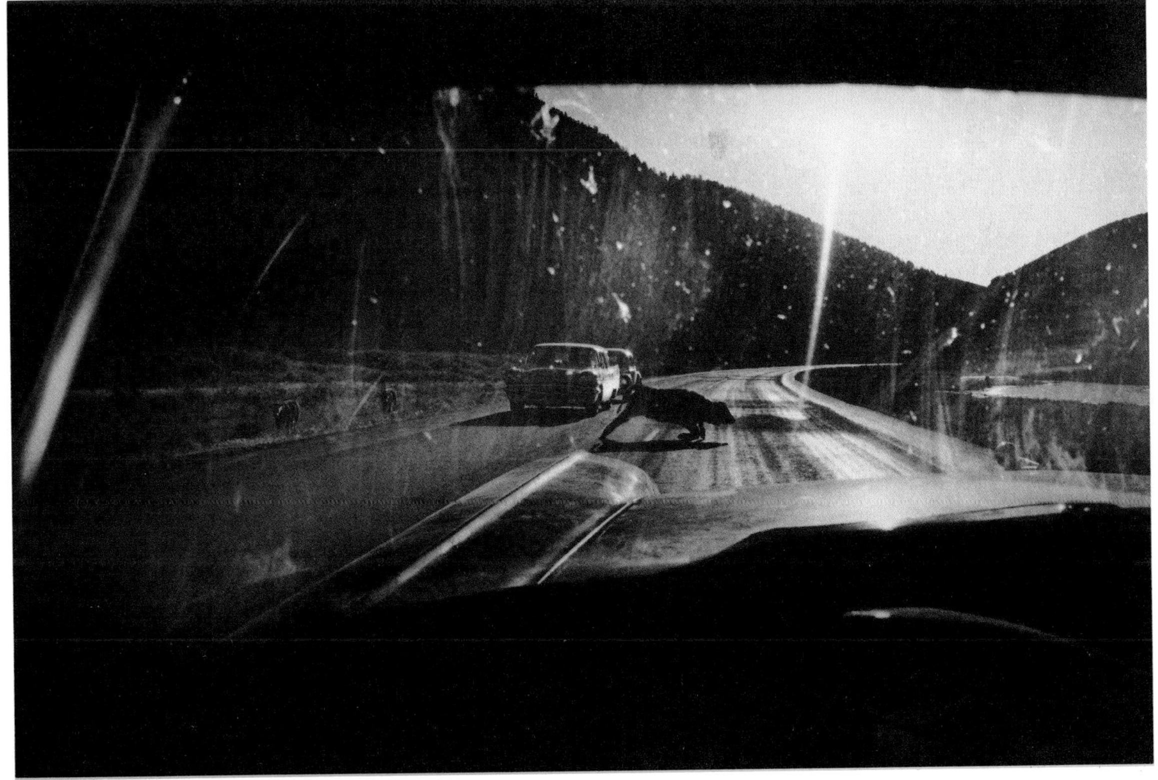

GARRY WINOGRAND,
Utah,
1964,
Center for Creative Photography, Tucson.

17. Since *Self-Portrait* (New York, 1970), he has come out with *The American Monument* (New York, 1976), *Factory Valleys* (New York, 1982), and *Like a One Cat* (New York, 1989), among others.

18. *The Bikeriders* (New York, 1968) and *Conversations with the Dead* (New York, 1971). Lyon published *Pictures from the New World* (Miller, New York, 1981).

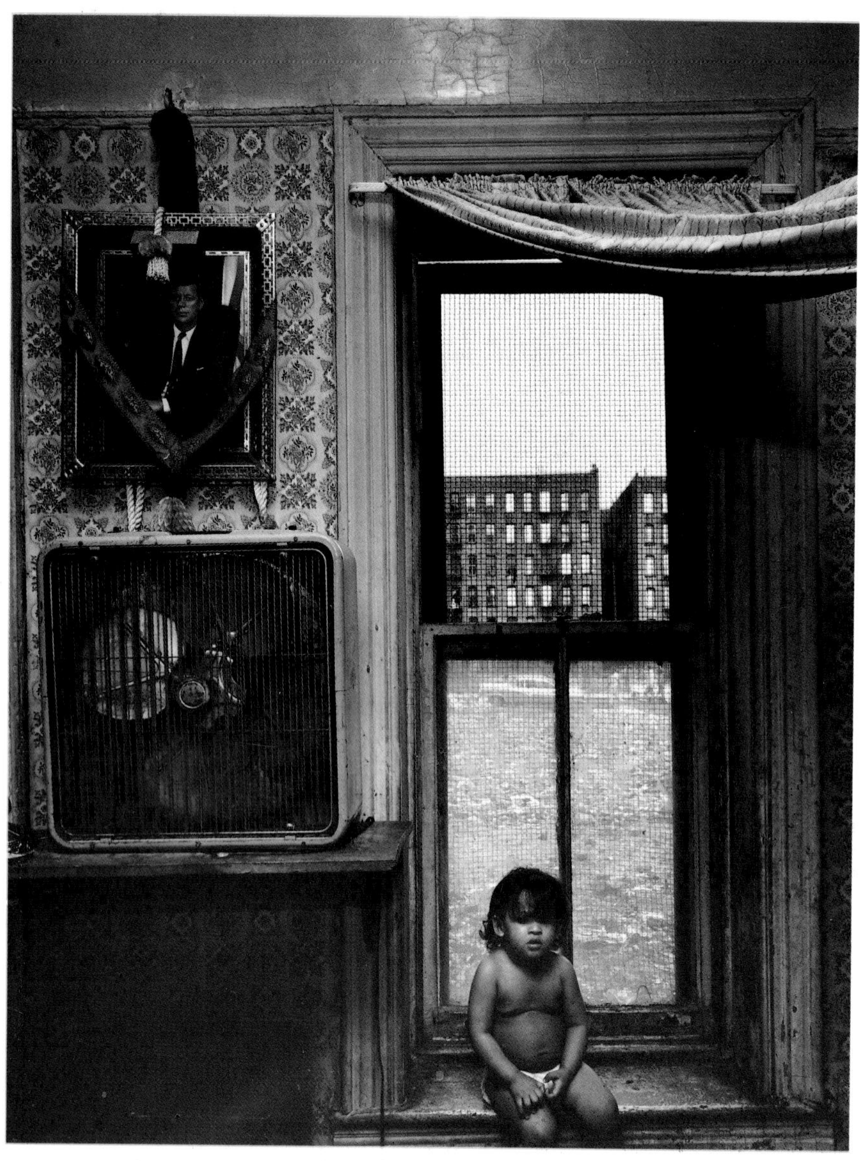

Lyon's career in the 1960s and 1970s, despite his having worked in New York at one point and having formed a film company with Frank, was much more like a road movie in nature.

The point is that during this period, on the cusp between the 1960s and 1970s, and in the work of certain photographers like Lyon, or, even more, Friedlander, one photographic tradition was feathering out into another. Just as there was an overlap between pre-war conventions dominated by European influences and post-war innovations made in America, so too was there within that American work a certain merging at the edges where street photography met landscape. In Friedlander's career especially, the two historical phases of post-war documentary in America seem to have come together. Country and city, a hot aesthetic and a cool one, the New Documentary and the New Topographics all met.

New Topographics

Again, one cannot help being struck by how central Frank was, how both his photography and his sensibility remained the common denominator, the one constant in the equation, by which everyone else appears to have been touched. Where Winogrand's photographs combine the gruff vulgarity of Weegee with the dour vulnerability of Frank, Friedlander's pair that same Frank-like dourness with a very opposite emotion, a more stoical response to life of the sort found in Robert Adam's photography. Friedlander's 1976

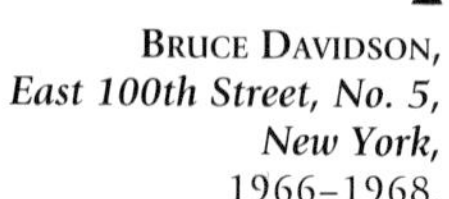

▲
BRUCE DAVIDSON, *East 100th Street, No. 5, New York,* 1966–1968.

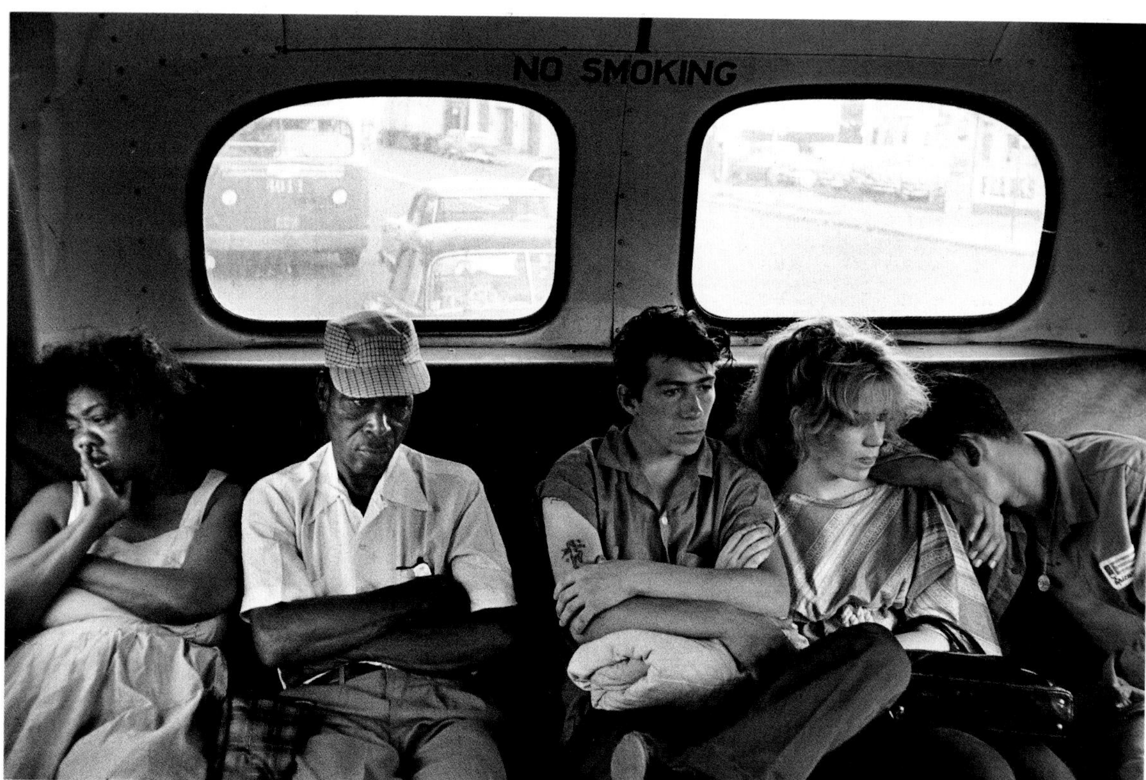

BRUCE DAVIDSON, *The Brooklyn Gang,* 1965.

book *The American Monument*, done after a photographic pilgrimage to visit all the small-town war memorials he could find, contains pictures whose compacted, complex compositions look back to New York street photography of the 1960s inspired by Frank, while their subject matter and their calm, reflective mood look forward to Adam's *From the Missouri West* (1980).

Like the unvarying expression on his face in those self-portraits, the pictures Friedlander has taken are intentionally dumb (not in the metaphorical sense of stupid, but in the literal sense of unspeaking). This is a trait that the work of Robert Adams, Lewis Baltz, and many of the other New Topographers share. They, too, have made pictures that reserve judgement in some way, speak only in a monotone, and have about them a feeling of the monolithic.

Not the least of the reasons that Robert Adam's prints are monolithic, as a visual surface, is that he has tended to shoot his landscapes in either the grayness of overcast weather or under a full Western sun whose effect, equally leveling, is to give a blasted-out appearance to the terrain.[19] In both instances, a toneless uniformity results in the 8 x 10 inch view-camera negative that Adam's darkroom technique meticulously preserves in the print.

His is a highly unified vision. His work gives the impression that his subject matter and his way of seeing it are of a piece; it is as if the dull, featureless scene had taken a picture of itself. This is photography from which individual human personality is as scrupulously absent as possible – indeed, pictures that at times appear to have been made without any human intervention.

Adam's point of view is as devoid of emphasis as the diffused, almost dissipated light is of highlights. The placement of the camera does nothing to direct our attention to the beer can on the river bank, the tracks of dirt-bike tires swirling across the top of the mesa or the other tell-tale, despoiling signs of man in the landscape. We stumble upon these traces in the photograph as unexpectedly as we might upon those left long ago in nature itself by some primordial beast. And since we are as unprepared for what we find, our astonishment at it is as great.

Adams apparently sees the human race as just another phase of history, like dinosaurs. His view suggest that, in the end, human nature might well sink back into the larger, primeval one from which it arose, and disappear without trace.

The vision of the West that this Adams has had is intentionally, methodically, almost programmatically the opposite of that made popular by the other Adams – Ansel Adams – earlier in the post-war period. In place of Ansel's mountain gloom and mountain glory, Robert has given us a landscape ground down to a ubiquitous sameness by the glacial eons of its history. In Robert's photographs, the easy, nostalgic pantheism of Ansel has been supplanted by a rigorous agnosticism. This is a West in which the numbing brightness at high noon and the enveloping darkness of *Summer Nights*, as Adams called his most recently published series, simply balance, or maybe even cancel each other out. Here the vacant, vacuous terrain runs uninterrupted into both the forlorn little towns of yesteryear and the equally nondescript suburbs of today.

This last venue in which Adams has worked is also the one where Lewis Baltz, whose pictures appeared in the New Topographics exhibition along with Adams's, has done his most prominent photography. In Baltz's photographs of a

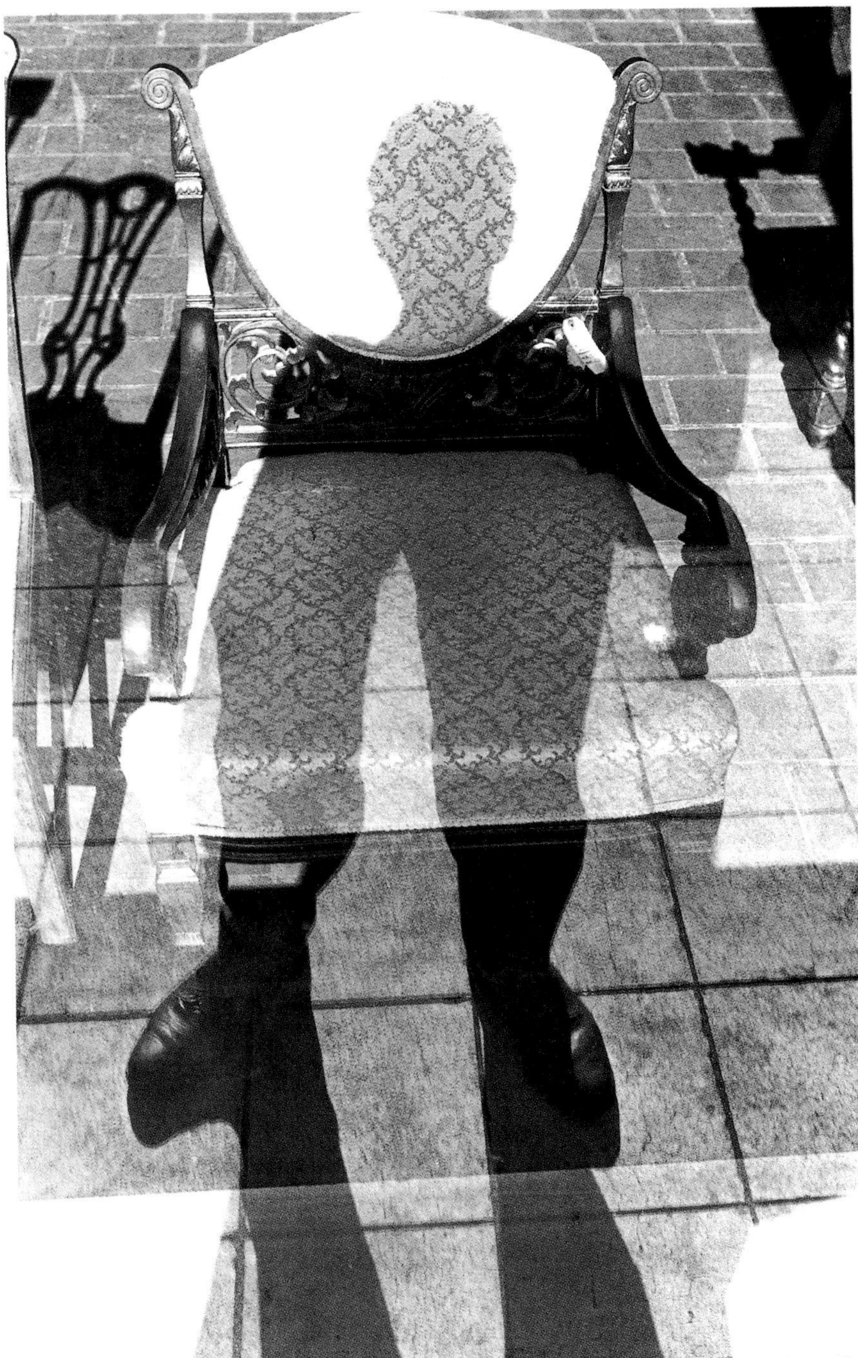

LEE FRIEDLANDER,
Wilmington, Delaware,
1965,
from *Self-Portrait* series.

19. See catalogue for Adams's 1989 retrospective at the Philadelphia Museum of Art, *To Make It Home: Photographs from the American West*.

The role of exhibitions

In the years from the mid-1950s to the mid-1970s, both of the important new trends in photography, "New Documents" and "New Topographics", acquired their names from the landmark exhibition in which they were first identified as movements.

The former, which was curated at the Museum of Modern Art by John Szarkowski in 1967 and intended as a summary of the most significant developments in American photography over the last dozen years, included work by Garry Winogrand, Lee Friedlander, and Diane Arbus.

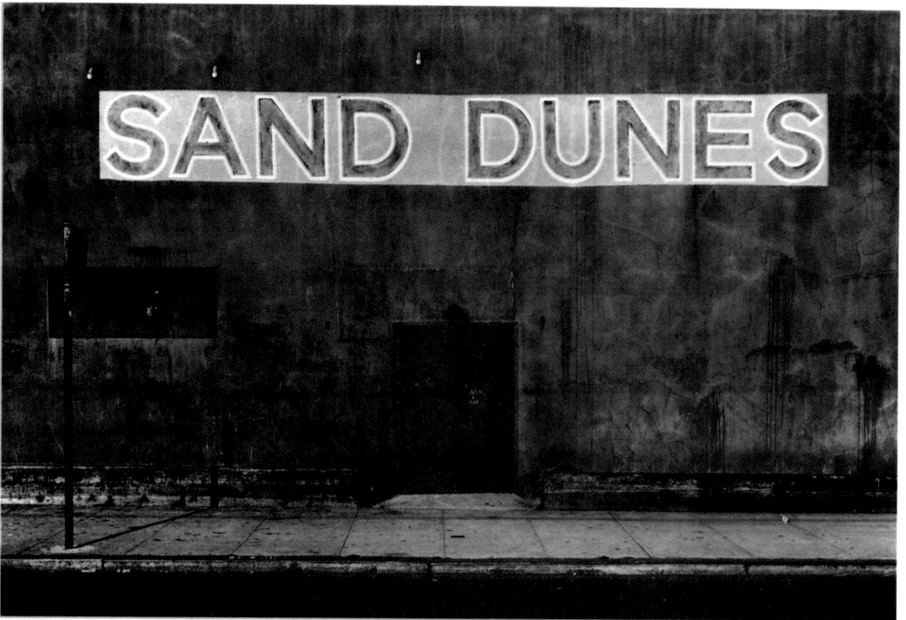

Lewis Baltz,
San Francisco,
1973, International Museum of Photography, George Eastman House, Rochester.

The second exhibition, whose full title was *New Topographics: Photographs of a Man-Altered Landscape,* was curated eight years later at the International Museum of Photography at George Eastman House in Rochester, New York, by the then Assistant Curator of Twentieth-Century Photography, William Jenkins, with work by the photographers Robert Adams, Lewis Baltz, Bernhard and Hilla Becher, Joe Deal, Frank Gohlke, Nicholas Nixon, John Schott, Stephen Shore, and Henry Wessel, Jr.

Although exhibitions were, perhaps, not as influential as books, key ones attracted attention. Szarkowski's Diane Arbus retrospective, a year after her death in 1971, was the most popular photographic show the Modern had staged since Edward Steichen's *The Family of Man,* in 1955. Each suited the mood of its day, Steichen's sentimentalism as a curator appealing to the smugness of the mid-1950s, while Arbus's merciless vision spoke to shell-shocked Americans just emerging from the Vietnam War and the hippy rebellion of the 1960s.

Szarkowski's impact as a curator can hardly be overestimated. He redefined the medium's aesthetic priorities in a series of exhibitions that extended from *New Documents* through to his 1976 Bill Eggleston show, which legitimized color photography as an art form in the United States, and the Atget sequence of the 1980s, which revised historical perspective on photography's development. Yet also noteworthy were more obscure shows and more transient exhibition spaces than the Museum of Modern Art represents.

The more prosperous photography galleries of the 1970s and 1980s followed in the footsteps of Helen Gee's Limelight, in New York, supported between 1954 and 1961 by a coffee house where photographers could meet and discuss their work.

Crucial nuances of the history in this period would have been lost on anyone who had not sought out the occasional shows available in such venues. Only if you had seen Winogrand's 1960 exhibition at New York's Image Gallery, for instance, would you have realized how heavily influenced he was by Frank and W. Eugene Smith: the prints in that show were all dark in ways that reveal his work to be more like theirs than the later, lighter versions of it we know today would suggest.

Colin Westerbeck

landscape left in heaps by earthmovers, of tract houses under construction and newly built shopping malls, the obduracy of the light in Adams's pictures turns into an actual wall, one made of the dirt, sheet rock or siding that Baltz's camera has confronted head on.[20] Baltz's pictures are monolithic in the sense that they make southern California, where he grew up, literally two-dimensional and abstract. The unbroken surfaces that Baltz has depicted have – in the photograph anyway – a kind of purity as pattern, often quite beautiful. Yet also implicit is a social comment that is less soothing, for the imagery has a closed-off, claustrophobic quality, as if nature itself were being blotted out by man's presence in it. The work derives its power from the tension between its visual attractiveness and, as it compels us to see, the invasive historical reality that these sensuous compositions represent.

Baltz's work has a Minimalism to it that, although less obvious in Adams's work – less visible as a spare from of graphics – is, nonetheless, present there too. In photographers' views, both the subject matter and the emotional response to it have been reduced to the barest essentials necessary to make an image. In order to find a precedent in post-war photography for a vision such as this, one has to search out an alternative to both the moodiness of Frank and the flamboyance of Klein, Winogrand or Meyerorwitz.

In some respects, this New Topographical vision was *sui generis,* especially where Adams was concerned. A professor of English literature at a university in Colorado before he turned to photography full-time, he has developed a visual aesthetic that clearly draws upon the American literary tradition pioneered by Ernest Hemingway. Yet at the time in the 1960s when the New

20. Lewis Baltz, *Park City,* Albuquerque, New Mexico, 1980; *San Quentin Point,* Millerton, New York, 1986; *Candlestick Point,* Tokyo, 1989.

21. *The Multiple Image,* Chicago, 1961, *Callahan,* Millerton, New York, 1976, and *Harry Callahan Color,* Providence, Rhode Island, 1980. He was given a one-man exhibition (with catalogue) at the Museum of Modern Art in 1967.

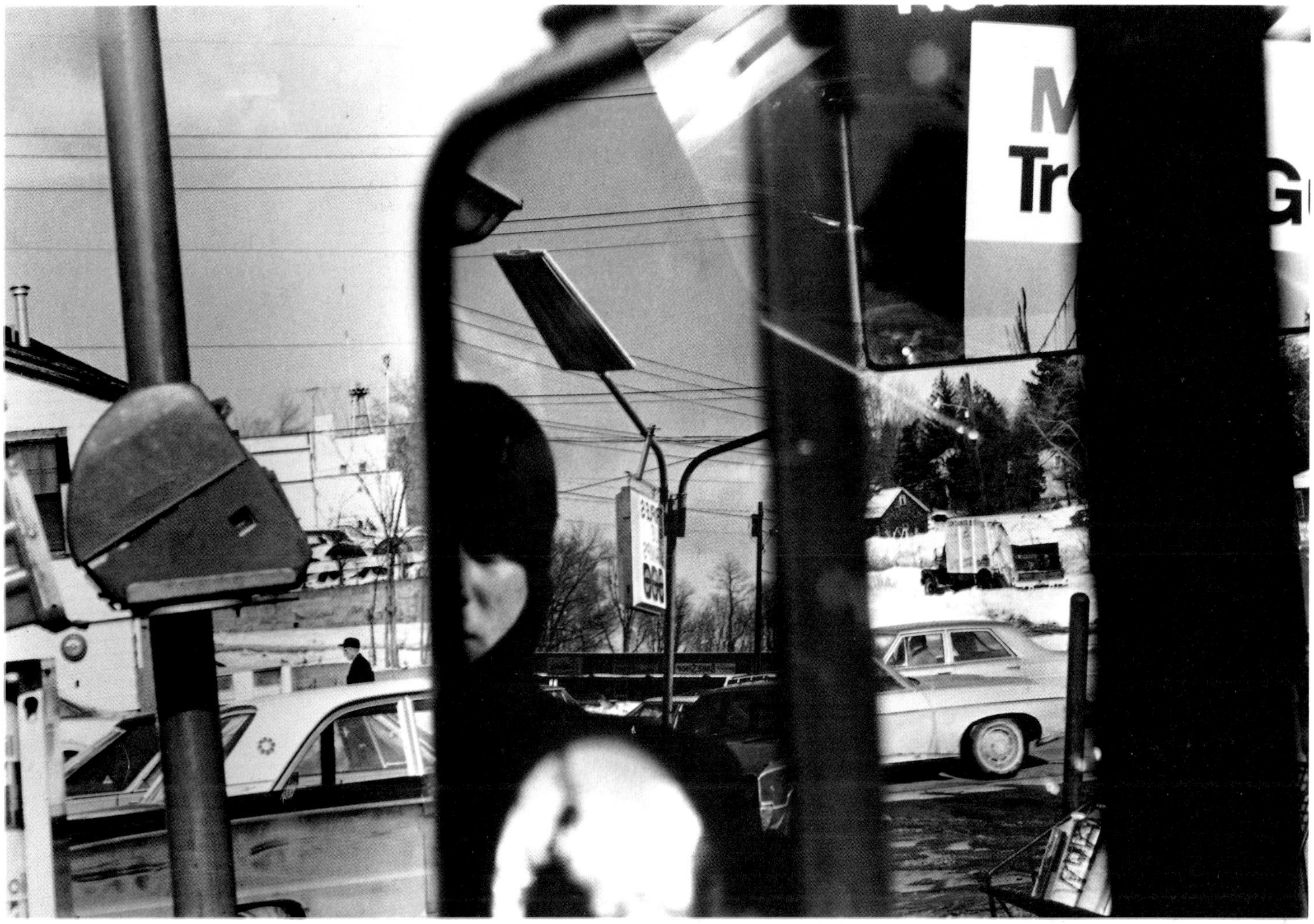

LEE FRIEDLANDER,
Hillcrest, New York,
1970.

Topography of Adams, Baltz, and others was taking shape, there already existed a photographic Minimalism which, whether it was an influence or not, certainly set an example.

This was the imagery created by Harry Callahan and some of his students and colleagues at the Institute of Design, founded in Chicago by László Moholy-Nagy after he fled Nazi Germany. (The photography faculty at the Institute included at one time or another Moholy-Nagy, Gyorgy Kepes, Harry Callahan, and Aaron Siskind. Among the graduates are Nathan Lerner, Arthur Siegel, Ray Metzker, Ken Josephson, Barbara Crane, Art Sinsabaugh, Linda Connor, Eileen Cowin, and many others). In views done along Lake Michigan, in bare rooms where his wife Eleanor posed nude, and later amid the dunes and beaches on Cape Cod, Callahan produced a photography every bit as quiet and economical, if not as dispirited, as the New Topographers would produce in the West.[21]

Even as a street photographer in Chicago's Loop area, Callahan often stayed at a meditative distance from his subjects, trapping lone, isolated figures in slantwise patterns of sunshine and shadows by which they were dwarfed as much as man is by nature in Adams's landscapes. As can

WILLIAM EGGLESTON,
Outskirts of Morton, Mississippi, 1971,
High Museum of Art, Atlanta.

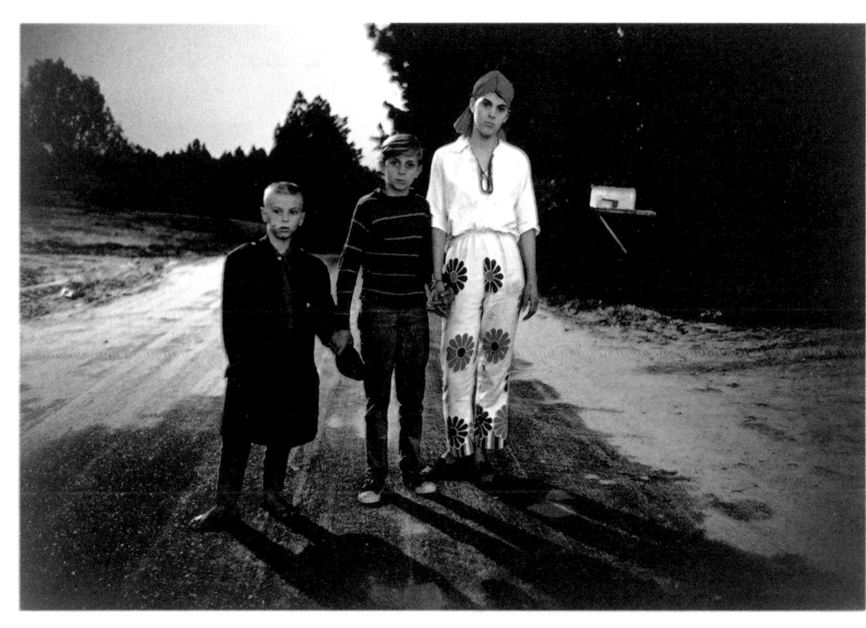

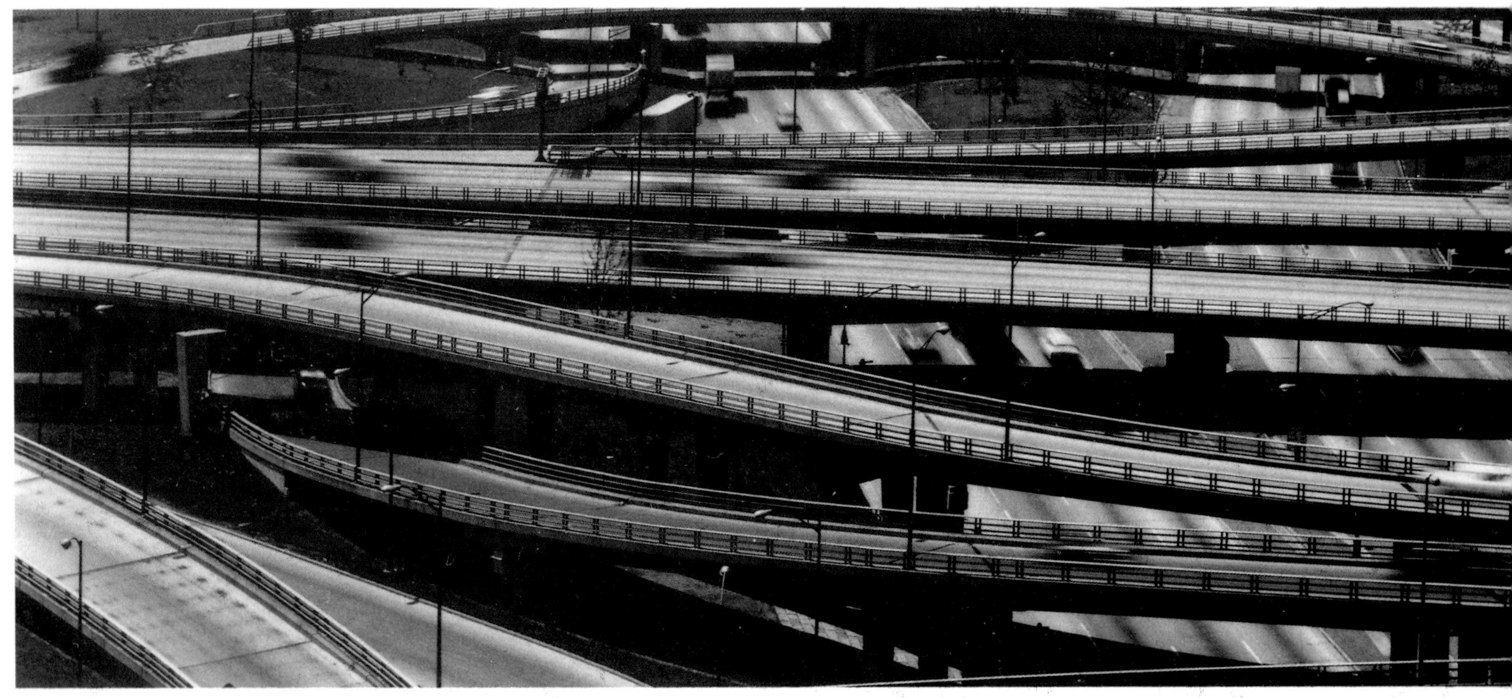

ART SINSABAUGH, *Chicago Landscape No. 117,* 1966.

be seen in studies Callahan did of strands of weed against snow, the stringency of his vision was in some of its aspects even greater than that of Adams or Baltz, driven as it was not by their secularism but by a Zen-like sense of perfection. Callahan's conception of street photography was refined by Ken Josephson,[22] among other notable students he had, and his ideas about photography in general provided, at the very least, a context in which the reticence and abstinence of much New Topographical work could make sense.

If the New Topographers had Midwestern forerunners in Callahan or yet another graduate of the Institute of Design, Art Sinsabaugh, whose panoramas extended flatness to the point where a geological contour became an artistic statement, they have also had a Western successor in someone like Mark Klett.[23] In black and white landscapes of the Southwest that he has done with a view camera using the Polaroid negative/positive process, the ethereal, silvery cast that material gives to its images has been exploited to make the whole of the American desert look like the Ghost Ranch, an ecological mirage fading from view even as we approach it. The result is an eerily New-Age version of the New Topographics.

Besides an entire constellation of photographers who might be mapped around the New Topographics, a couple more who deserve comment were actually in the 1975 exhibition of that title. One was Frank Gohlke, a Texan who went to teach in Minnesota in the 1970s but continued to photograph in his home state. Making workman-like views of houses and marshlands, he created a body of pictures that connects the geography there to that in Adams's Colorado or Baltz's California.[24]

Perhaps the most curious figure to be included in the New Topographics show, however, was color view-camera photographer Stephen Shore. If that exhibition had an odd-man-out, like Friedlander in the New Documents show, it was Shore. When you consider the stripped-down Minimalism inherent in the rest of the work that the show contained, there might be a prima facie case against any color photography. Color, by its very nature, adds a sensuality at odds with the aesthetic that was being explored elsewhere in the show.

Nobody was more aware of this than Shore himself, who had devised ways to tone down the richness built into color materials by the manufacturers to please the commercial market, giving to color photography a bracing thinness, diluting the values of the colors in a way that approximates the monotone of Adams's photographs. For the pictures he was to publish in *Uncommon Places,* moreover, Shore chose as subjects the same type of small town that Adams was portraying.[25] Shore often circled around the back side of the business district, taking the town's measure from across an expanse of parking lots that gave him the distance and the obliqueness to put the buildings into a New Topographical perspective.

In William Eggleston's 35mm color work, too, there is often a washed-out quality. His imagery gives to the New South, where he has photographed, a faded look, more evocative of the fallen culture of the Old South.[26]

At first, work like this seemed to be just an extension in color, or at most a new synthesis, of earlier black-and-white traditions. But the diversity of careers ranging from Shore's and Eggleston's to Meyerowitz's or Joel Sternfeld's,

22. See *Kenneth Josephson* (Chicago, 1983), the catalogue published in conjunction with a retrospective exhibition at Chicago's Museum of Contemporary Art.

23. See *Second View: The Rephotographic Survey Project,* Albuquerque, New Mexico, 1984 and, more recently, *Traces of Eden: Travels in the Southwestern Desert,* Boston, 1986.

24. See Frank Gohlke, *Landscapes from the Middle of the World: Photographs, 1972–1987,* San Francisco, 1988.

25. Shore contributed to John Rewald, *The Gardens at Giverny: A View of Monet's World,* New York, 1983.

26. See *William Eggleston's Guide,* New York, 1976. More recently, Eggleston has published *The Democratic Forest,* New York, 1989.

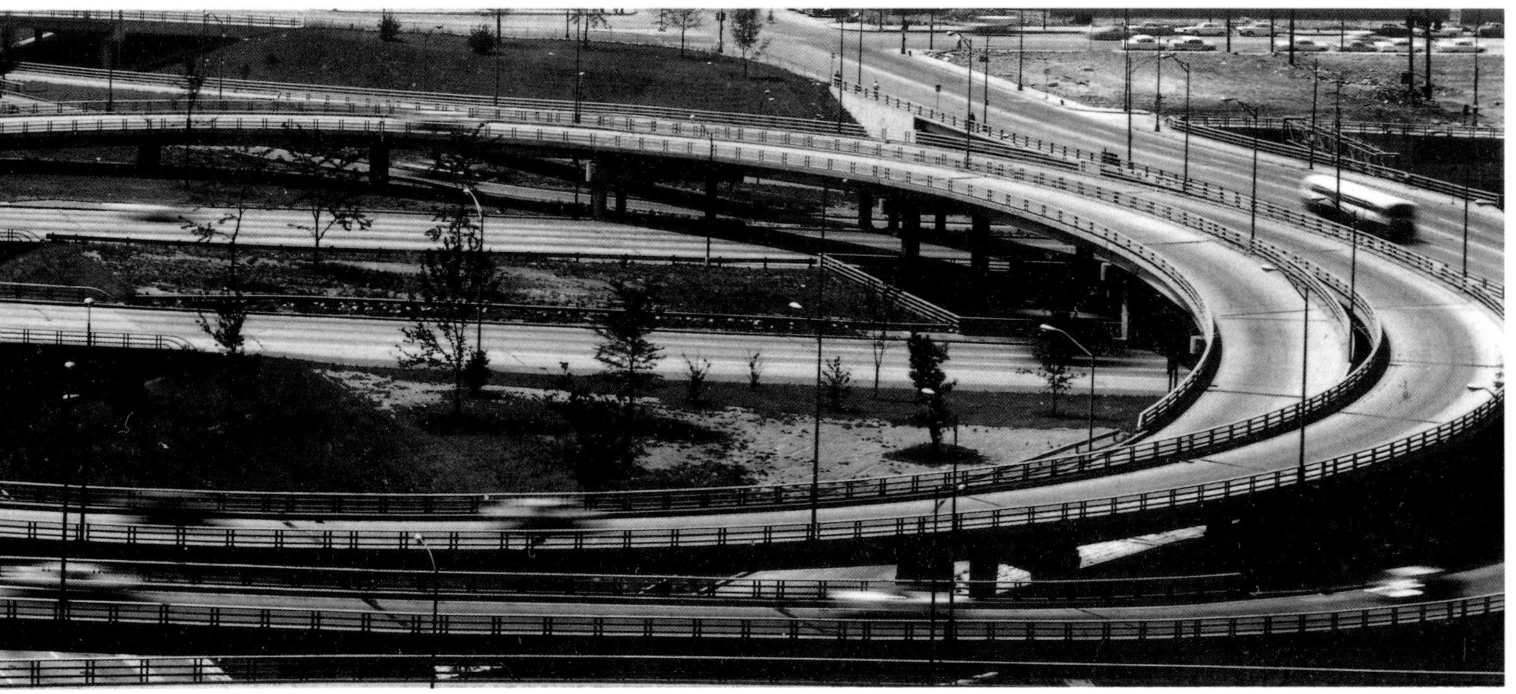

suggests that, in effect, color has become a new tradition in its own right. In it, all of the difficulties already solved, all the options selected and aesthetic choices made, have had to be reviewed, reconsidered, revised.

In Sternfeld's work, for instance, the quirky eye of the New York street-shooter, with his quick take on peripheral incidents and his grasp of fly-away details, gets applied to view-camera work done all around the country.[27] Sternfeld's is a kind of photography in which we seem to be, despite the color and the larger format, right back where we started with Klein or Frank, Winogrand or Meyerowitz. Once the entire gambit of images has been run, it seems, the whole cycle just begins all over again.

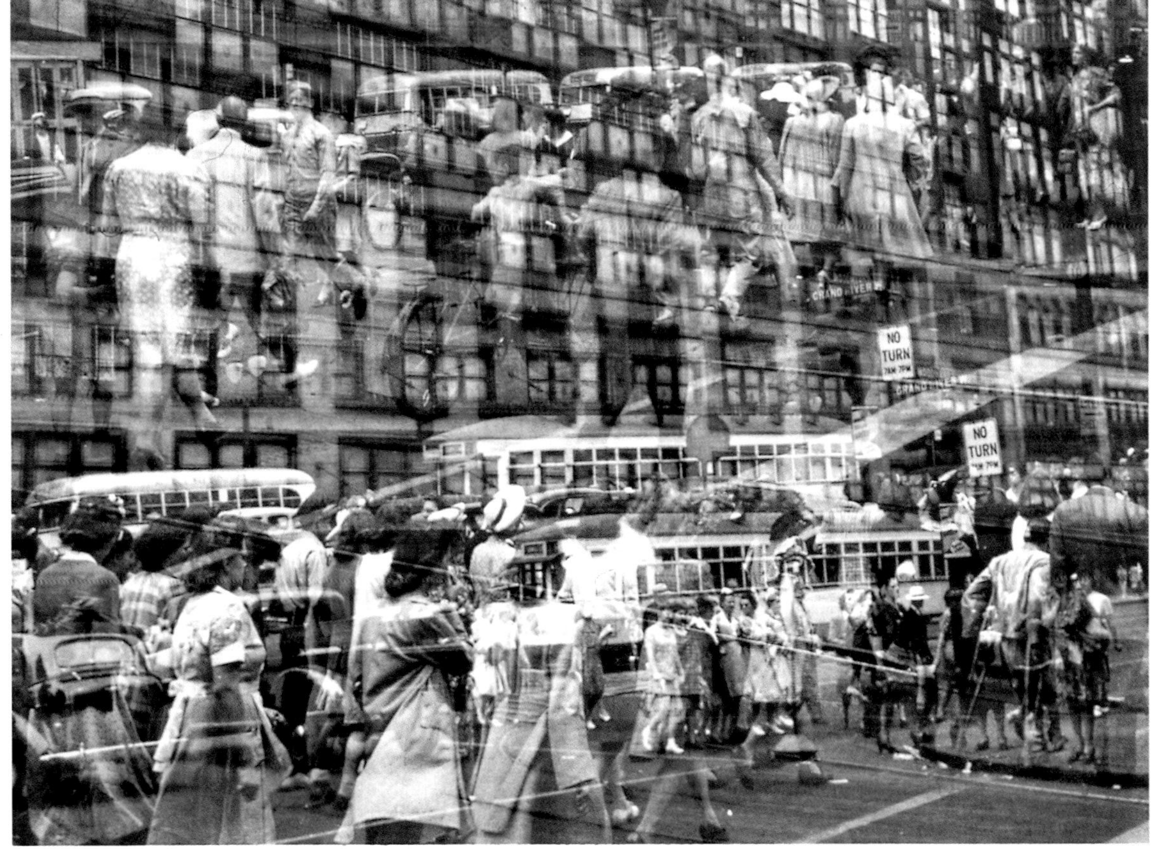

HARRY CALLAHAN, *Street Scene in Detroit,* 1943.

27. See Joel Sternfeld, *American Prospects,* New York, 1987, the monograph published in conjunction with his exhibition at the Museum of Fine Arts in Houston, Texas.

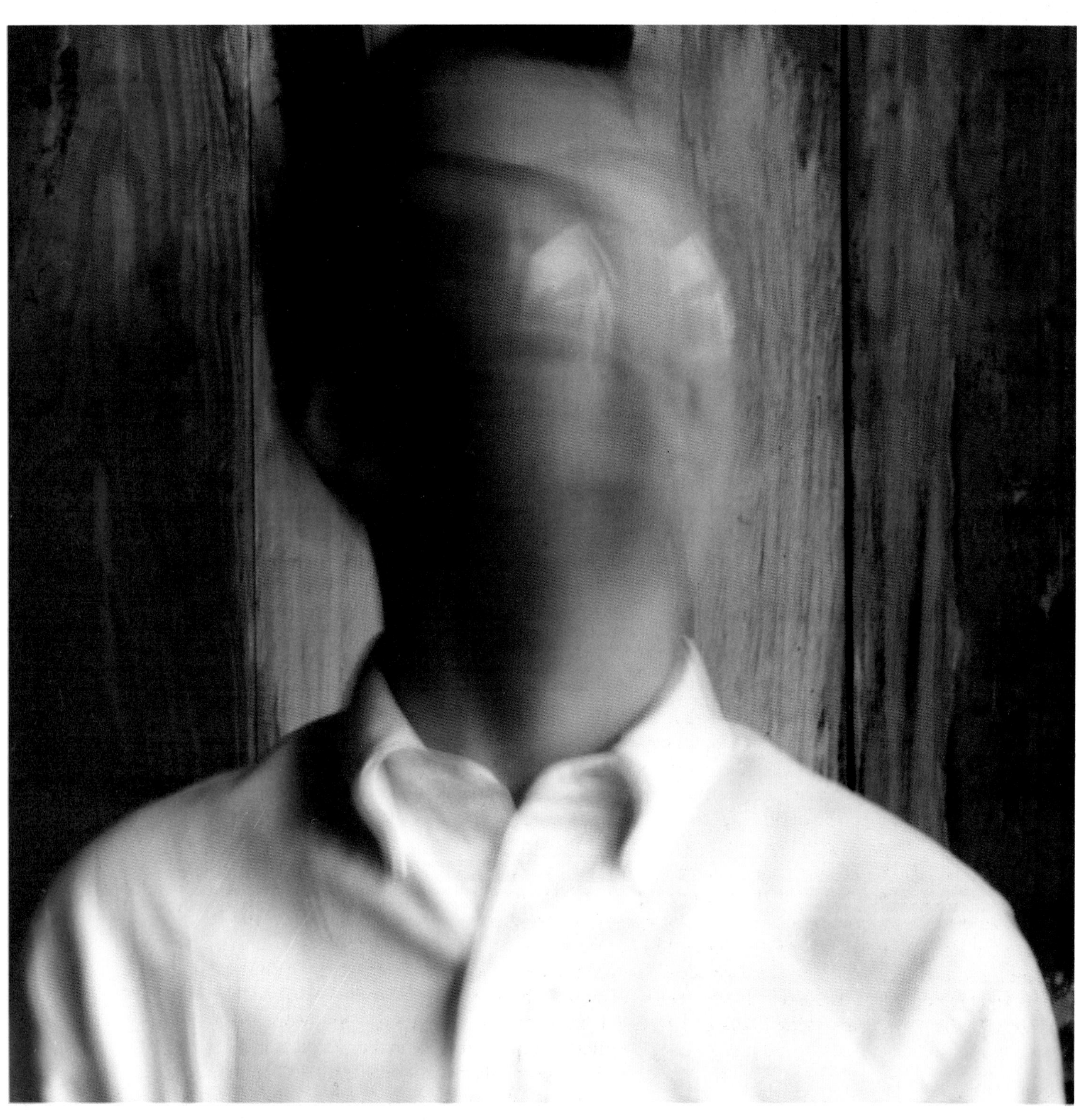

Ralph E. Meatyard,
Untitled,
1960.

BEYOND REALITY

36

The subjective vision

Shelley Rice

The renaissance of photography after the Second World War did not challenge earlier acquisitions, the fruit of its relationship with the avant-garde (photomontage, superimposition of negatives, shooting at an oblique angle), but it cast a dreamier glance on the world. For many photographers the image was an unveiling, an evocation, an irrational construction space, an interiorization of vision removed from the strict documentary snapshot. Europe differed considerably from the United States in the way it followed this tendency, despite continuous dialog; the orientation towards imaginary and subjective themes tended to give it an artistic status which is far from the realism or so-called "objectivity" which had characterized the previous few decades.

The idea that photography can be a subjective medium, capable of creatively expressing individual insights, is not a twentieth-century invention; it was accepted as a truism by photographers as early as Talbot in the 1840s and Gustave Le Gray in the 1850s. However, this notion grew in importance and expanded in relevance around the turn of the century, as self-conscious "art" photographers seceded from the ranks of amateurs, commercial workers, and documentary image-makers to define their own styles and ideologies. The definition of creative or subjective photography developed in different ways in the United States and Europe. On both continents, however, the foundations for ideas that would blossom in the 1950s and 1960s were laid between the World Wars, in the 1920s.

Equivalents

In the United States, it was Alfred Stieglitz who was to define the parameters of American ideas about photography's emotional and expressive potential – ideas that still hold sway over a large segment of the photographic community. Born in Hoboken, New Jersey to a wealthy family, Stieglitz studied in Germany, and was well-known in Europe by the time his family called him back to New York in 1890. Stieglitz's comfortable economic circumstances, and his disdain for American materialism and business practices combined with his experience of European cultural life to shape his ideas about the "purity" of art and artists, untainted by commercial considerations. His own work, his publications like *Camera Work*, and even his galleries, like "291", were influenced greatly by his backlash against American commercialism. His efforts to have photography accepted as a means of creative expression, on a par with painting and sculpture and separate from the mainstream of American social or political life, must be seen within this context.

Stieglitz's respect for the spiritual purity of art was not the only thing he brought home from Europe. Arriving back in New York, he brought with him certain ideas – many of them Symbolist in origin – that provided him with the philosophical basis for his own photographic work. His earliest pictures were done in the context of international Pictorialism; his works after 1907, more formalist in approach, linked him strongly to the modernist revolution of the Cubists and their followers, whose work he exhibited and published in New York. It was not until after the First World War, when he felt himself isolated from the artistic community in New York, that he began to create the "Equivalents" – an ongoing series of small, exquisitely composed and printed, black and white photographs of clouds – that helped him to define, in words as well as pictures, the photographic aesthetic that has so influenced twentieth-century American photography.

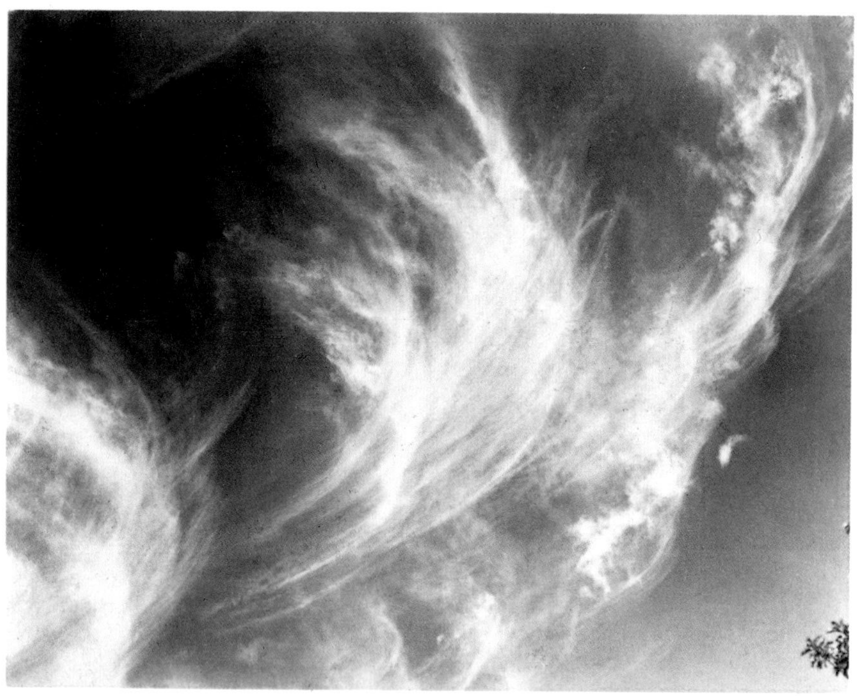

ALFRED STIEGLITZ, *Equivalent*, 1930, Museum of Fine Arts, Boston.

In choosing clouds as his subject matter, Stieglitz chose a neutral, and abstract, non-subject. Constantly changing physical phenomena, his clouds fill the frame, and are seen from the viewpoint of the earth without the horizon lines or tangible objects which could anchor them in everyday experience. His choice of cloud forms (which are usually used in images to create mood) as primary subject matter allowed him to test his theories about the convergence between the plastic arts and music. Searching for visual shapes which could communicate mood directly, as do musical tones, without the intermediary of a sitter or physical subject, Stieglitz placed himself within the mainstream of artistic concerns which were much discussed at the turn of the century in both Europe and New York. The abstract forms of Stieglitz's serial photographs were intended to express the emotional "equivalents of my most profound life experience, my basic philosophy of life".[1]

Stieglitz's work, therefore, equated visual images – photographed directly from nature, but removed from normal contexts – with metaphor. "Shapes, as such, do not interest me unless they happen to be an outer equivalent of something already taking from within me [...] What is of greatest importance is to hold a moment, to record something so completely that those who see it will relive an equivalent of what has been expressed."[2] As he got older, Stieglitz eventually expanded his definition of this "equivalence" to include all of his successful photographs – thereby leaving American photographers with a definition of art photography which emphasized a print's ability to communicate, not documentary reality, but emotional experience, and which, furthermore, focused almost exclusively on the symbolic meaning of form, which ultimately had as its reference not the real world but the artist's inner life.

This definition took on increasing importance in the United States during the 1950s, in the aftermath of the Second World War. In both Europe and America, the 1930s and 1940s – dominated as they were by the social issues raised during the Depression and the War – witnessed the resur-

ALFRED STIEGLITZ, ▶ left: *Equivalent*, Set A, No. 1, 1929, Art Institute of Chicago.

right: *Equivalent*, Set G, 1929, Museum of Fine Arts, Boston.

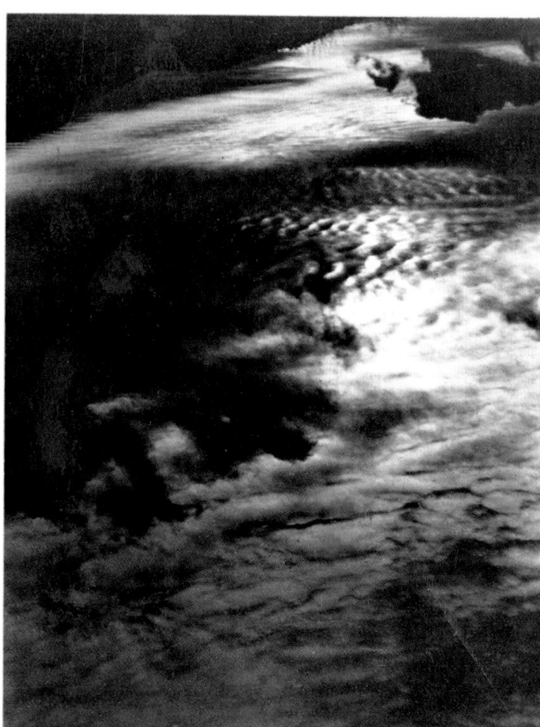

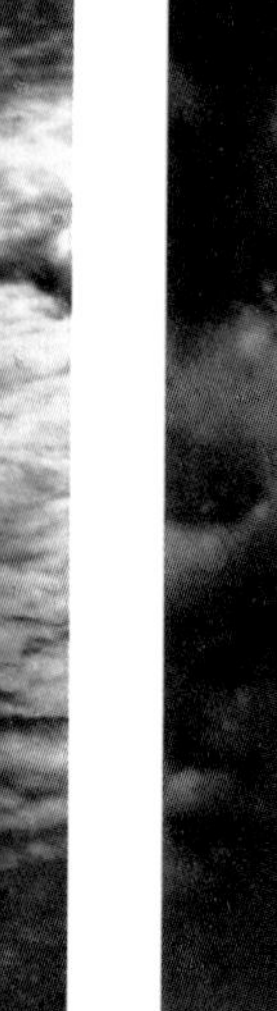

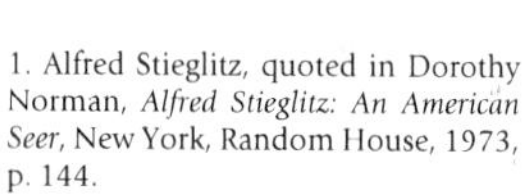

1. Alfred Stieglitz, quoted in Dorothy Norman, *Alfred Stieglitz: An American Seer*, New York, Random House, 1973, p. 144.

2. *Ibid.*, p. 161.

gence, for the first time on a mass scale, of documentary photography. Picture magazines like *Life, Picture Post,* and *VU,* government agencies like the U.S. Farm Securities Administration, and widespread social preoccupation with poverty and war coverage made artistic and/or formal concerns and experimentation a low priority. By the late 1940s and the 1950s, however, these issues were resurfacing. In the United States, artists proceeded to reclaim the aesthetic isolationism that they had lost in the heat of political events.

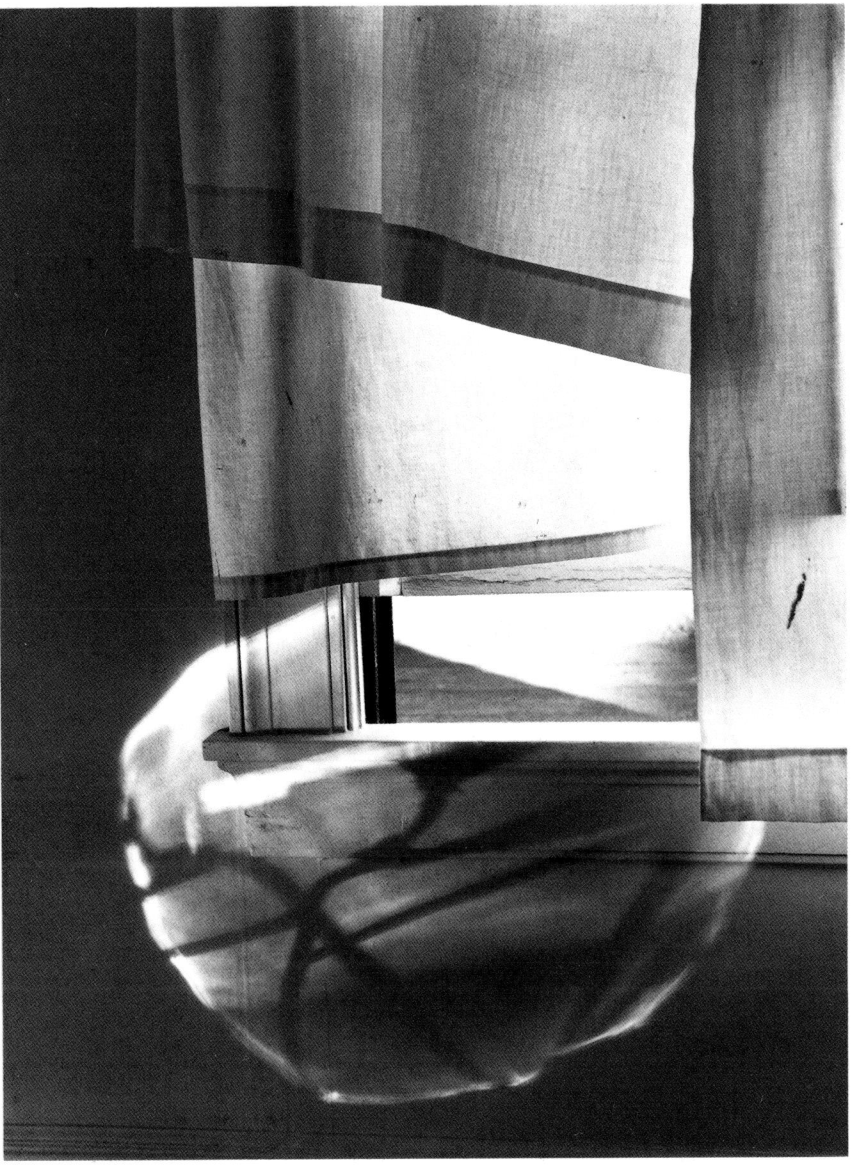

Minor White, *Windowsill Daydreaming,* 1958, Museum of Modern Art, New York.

The emotion of tonalities

The person most responsible for spreading Stieglitz's doctrine (Stieglitz himself died in 1946) was Minor White. Born in 1908, White studied botany at the University of Minnesota, and learned to develop and print photographs as a student of photomicrography. These beginnings made a profound impression on White, who told friends and colleagues that he had first seen modern art forms under the microscope.[3] By the early 1940s, after a stint as a poet, White had become a photographer. From this time on, his impact on photography in the United States was formidable. As an artist, a curator (at the George Eastman House), a teacher (at the California School of Fine Arts, Rochester Institute of Technology, and Massachusetts Institute of Technology),[4] and an important editor (of *Aperture,* which he co-founded in 1952 and edited for over 20 years), he served as an image-maker and a writer, an intellectual and a spiritual guru, for a generation of art photographers in America. His decision to adopt, and to propagate, Stieglitz's concept of Equivalence – the path, as Minor White explained it, of "inner growth through camera work"[5] – had far-reaching consequences.

White adopted not only Stieglitz's theoretical ideas, but also his formal structures. The abstract shapes of Stieglitz's *Equivalents* are defined by the varying relationships between the whiteness of clouds and the blackness of the sky. At times central masses, at other times diagonal lines, at still other times wispy designs on a larger field, the clouds cease to be objects and instead become players in an ongoing, constantly changing drama of black and white, of darkness and light. Shown together in a series (as the *Equivalents* always were during Stieglitz's lifetime), these pictures represented the shifting emotional tones of life, the ongoing dramas of subjective feeling which can find their visual equivalent in the material world.

White's work is based on Stieglitz's idea that darkness and light, objects and spaces, carry spiritual as well as material meanings. Less emotionally oriented than Stieglitz's œuvre, White's varies in its subject matter – his "sequences" of images, with titles like *The Sound of One Hand,* move back and forth between abstraction and documentary realism, emphasizing that both, ultimately, lead to metaphor. White was influenced by Eastern religious ideas: Zen, the I Ching, and the teachings of Gurdjieff provided the mystical framework through which he interpreted the visual world. In his mind, even found forms resembling objects seen under a microscope could create, by their relationships of space and tone, a mirror into the spiritual life of the "inner man", which could find its expression also in a landscape, a portrait or an icy window.

These ideas, though without an Eastern flavor, also influenced one of White's contemporaries, Aaron Siskind. Born and raised in New York City, Siskind's work reflects both the photographic ethos of Stieglitz and the practices of the New York School of Abstract Expressionist painters

3. J. B. Hall, essay in *Minor White: Rites and Passages,* New York, Aperture, 1978, p. 20.

4. Minor White's program, especially at MIT, which involved both living and working with his students, has become legendary in the United States. An unconventional teacher, he insisted that his students practice not only photography but also meditation, in order to more clearly "perceive" the world they were photographing.

5. Minor White, "The Light Sensitive Mirage", *Aperture,* no. 6, 1958.

Minor White and photographic education

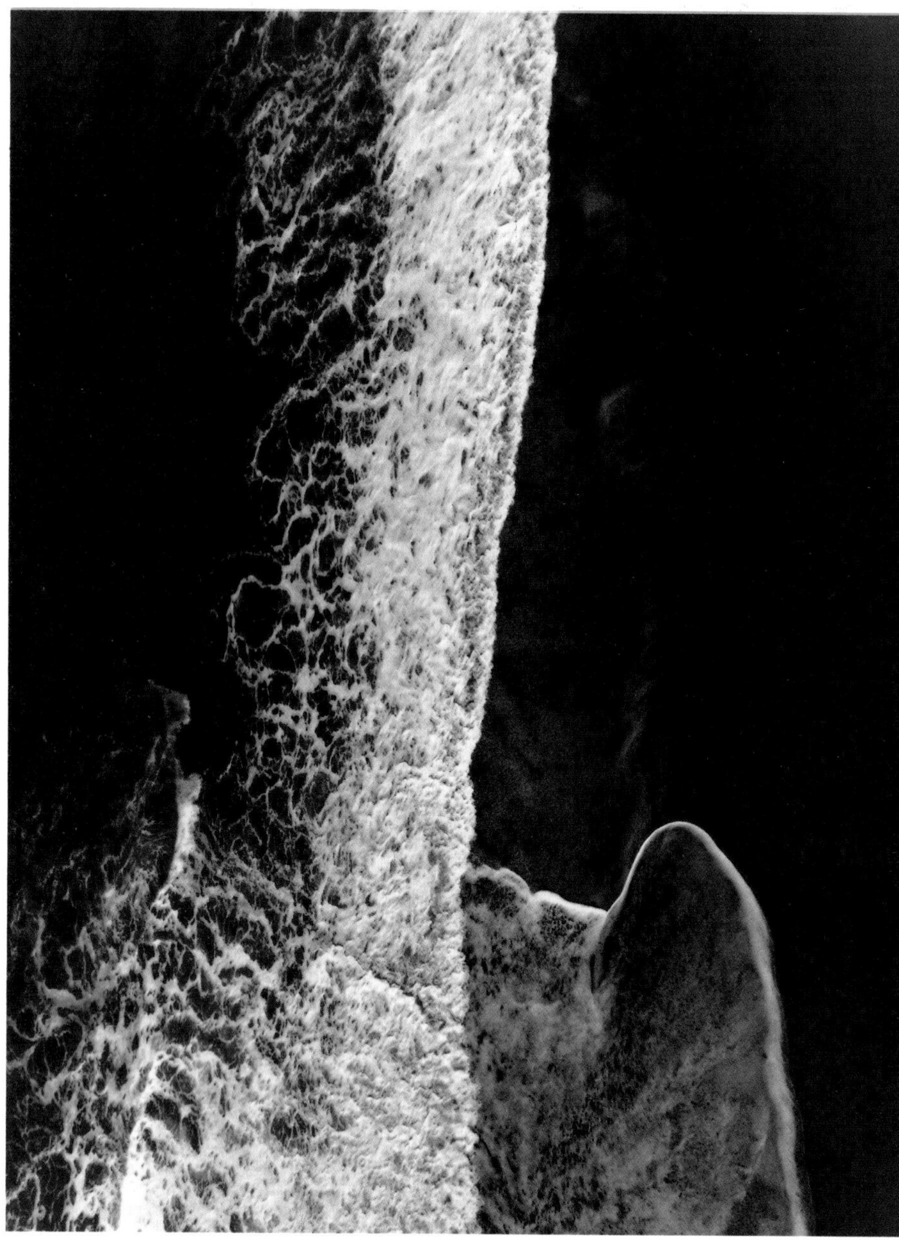

MINOR WHITE,
Surf Vertical, San Mateo County,
1947, Art Museum, Princeton University.

Minor White, who began his career as a teacher in 1946 at the California School of Fine Arts, San Francisco, was one of the most influential professors of photography in the post-war United States. While favoring personal emotions and creativity, Minor White sought to encourage his students to acquire a total mastery of every technical aspect of the subject in question.

Based on ideas resulting from his first contact with the work of Alfred Stieglitz and from his great interest in psychology, White launched the notion of expressive photography and the "reading of photographs". It involved using the camera to reveal one's personal feeling as symbolized by objects in the real world. In Minor White's perspective one does not photograph something simply for "what it is", but "for what else it is".

To really get this idea across to his students, he suggested projects to them which were inspired by various procedures based on the greatest affirmation of the self. These ranged from the study of theatre techniques – a lifelong enthusiasm which White first acquired on reading *Acting: the First Six Lessons* by Richard Boleslavsky – to sessions in Zen meditation, and, later, the application of Gurdjieff's teaching.

From 1952 he completed his teaching work with the publication of the photographic magazine *Aperture*. Over a period of twenty years he published numerous articles such as "The Way through Camerawork" (1959), in which he set forth his concept of photography to the wider public.

In 1953 Minor White left California to teach at the Rochester Institute of Technology. In 1965 he was appointed professor at Massachusetts Institute of Technology (M.I.T.) in Cambridge, where he remained until his death in 1976. His adherence to the new workshop system contributed to consolidating his reputation as much as the posts which he held in these prestigious institutions. These workshops, which fostered deeper relationships between teacher and student and which became celebrated; consisted of work groups which studied given questions in depth. They came about in the 1960s with the quest for new methods of education.

Throughout his whole career Minor White gave courses but once a year he directed intensive summer workshops just about everywhere in the United States. This allowed him to infuence a much greater number of students from a wide variety of backgrounds.

Minor White understood that to ensure expressive photography gained the status of fine art, he must teach the public to appreciate these images. Towards the end of his life he set up a program called "Creative Audience" at M.I.T., with the intention not of creating future artists, but of giving the public the reading tools which would favor better communication and richer exchanges.

Peter C. Bunnell

who were his friends. Beginning his photographic career as a documentary, socially oriented photographer working with the Photo League in Manhattan,[6] Siskind drastically changed course during the Second World War. Less interested in political statements than in the inner workings of his mind, he began photographing rocks, walls, graffiti, and decayed objects from vantage points close enough to abstract these subjects from their normal contexts and forms.

"I'm not interested in nature, I'm interested in my own nature", Siskind has said. "When I make

6. The Photo-League was the organization which provided the backbone of the photographic community in New York during the Depression years of the 1930s. There was an active gallery space, and classes were offered. See also Chapter 30 by Ian Jeffrey.

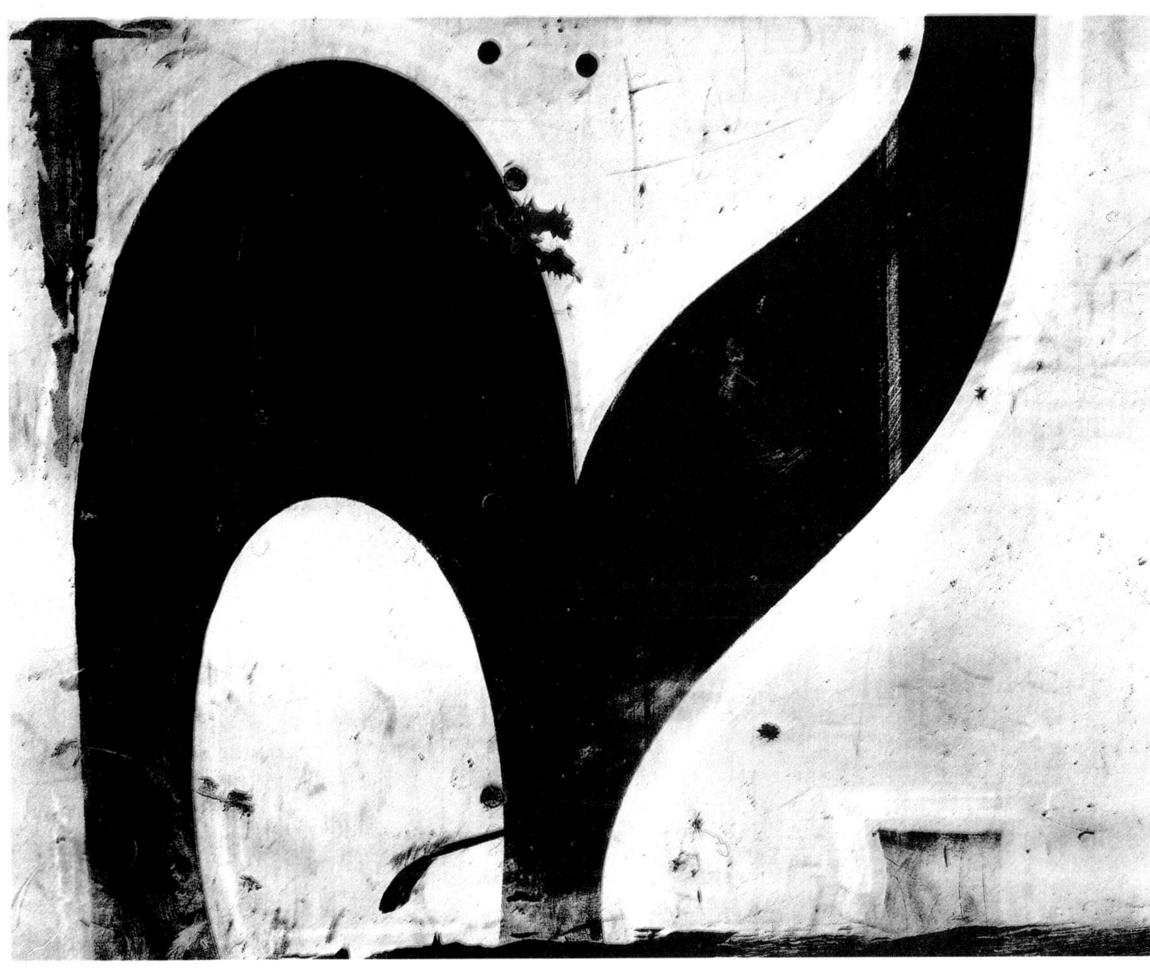

Aaron Siskind, *Chicago,* 1949.

a photograph I want it to be an altogether new object, complete and self-contained, whose basic condition is order (unlike the world of events and actions whose permanent condition is change and disorder)."[7] Like Stieglitz, Siskind sees his pictures as arenas within which the chaos of life can be frozen and, therefore, stilled. In his pictures lightness and darkness confront each other and often struggle, as if these tones themselves embody moral challenges. Spontaneous graffiti scribbles, abstracted from their mundane meanings and everyday contexts, become symbolic forms (or "conversations", as he calls them) whose interrelationships communicate drives for power, bonds of love or the inevitability of loss and decay.

Siskind's work is often juxtaposed with that of Harry Callahan, primarily because both worked together as professors for several decades, first at the Institute of Design in Chicago, and then at the Rhode Island School of Design. There is, in fact, little resemblance between their work. Siskind's, more oriented toward the emotionalism of Stieglitz, is less formal and less detached than that of his friend. Callahan began photographing when he was a clerk with the Chrysler Corporation in Detroit, and at the beginning of his career was influenced significantly by the creative ideas of Ansel Adams and Alfred Stieglitz. However, he became a colleague of László Moholy-Nagy in Chicago,[8] and the importance of the Bauhaus's more experimental and more emotionally detached attitudes is evident in his work.

Formally and technically, Callahan's work encompasses a huge range: black and white and color prints, straight photographs and montages, double exposures and multiple images have subjects as diverse as landscapes, portraits, cityscapes, street photographs, and architectural studies. In this, he contrasts with Siskind, whose work embodies a more limited range of subjects and techniques. Whereas Siskind's work – so often about decay and, therefore, the passage of time – is organic and often expressionist, Callahan's œuvre is usually intensely formal, relying on geometric relationships to create both a classical compositional balance and an aura of isolation and alienation. In this body of work, black and white do not represent moral dramas but contrasting tones in a world of pristine and untouchable beauty – a world in which the alienation of a city can be compared to a deserted beach, and the isolation of the artist's wife is linked in spirit to the closed self-sufficiency of a New England house.

7. Aaron Siskind, quoted in Cecil Beaton and Gail Buckland, *The Magic Image*, London, Weidenfeld and Nicholson Ltd., 1975, p. 176.

8. Moholy-Nagy fled Germany in 1935. After working in London he accepted the directorship of the New Bauhaus (ultimately named the Institute of Design) in Chicago in 1941. Callahan began photographing in 1938, and was hired as professor in 1946, the year of Moholy's untimely death.

HARRY CALLAHAN, *Dearbon Street,* Chicago, 1949.

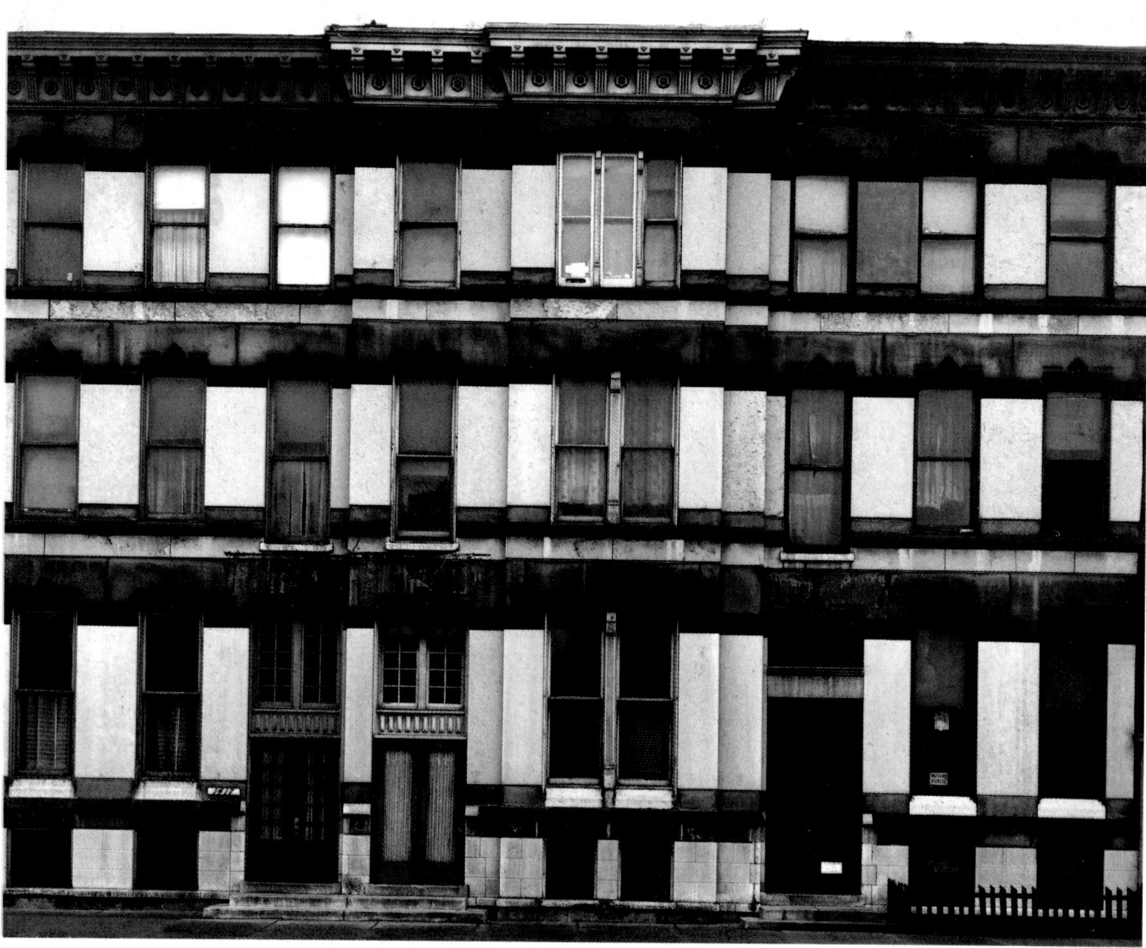

HARRY CALLAHAN, *Providence,* circa 1962.
▼

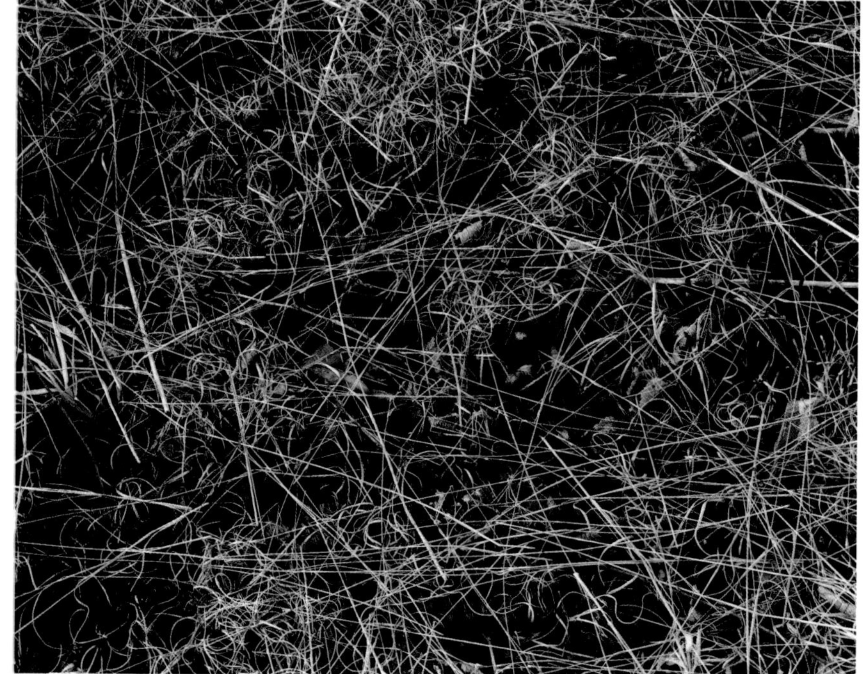

A strange way of seeing

Whereas Siskind's work reflects the milieu of the Abstract Expressionist painters, and Callahan's provides a link with the creative ideas important at the Bauhaus in the 1920s, Frederick Sommer's photographs were directly influenced by Surrealism. However, Sommer's initial interest in the medium also came through Alfred Stieglitz and his ideas about creative art photography. An American citizen, born in Italy in 1905, Sommer studied to be a landscape architect, and practiced this profession in Rio de Janeiro in the 1920s. He began drawing and painting in the early 1930s, but switched to photography after spending a week with Stieglitz in 1935. Drawn to Surrealist ideas and fascinated (like Siskind) by time and decay, Sommer describes himself as a man "walking about the world searching for something we carry within ourselves".[9] In the process, he found amputated human feet, dead animals, and other unsavory objects – which he transmuted into silver prints of extraordinary delicacy and beauty. This emphasis on Surrealist transformation links many of his works, from his multiple-exposure portraits of friends like Max Ernst to his abstract pictures of smoke on cellophane and his montages of images from old and dilapidated books.

Another photographer whose work is related to that of the Surrealist painters is Clarence John Laughlin. Born in Louisiana in 1905, Laughlin discovered the French Symbolist writers in 1925. Turning to photography in 1935, he spent the rest of his long life photographing what Fritz Gruber called "the psychic interior".[10] But he has done this in a manner that links him very strongly with

9. Frederick Sommer, in *Frederick Sommer*, New York, Aperture, 1962.

10. Fritz Gruber, quoted in Cecil Beaton and Gail Buckland, *op. cit.*, p. 201.

an American tradition of both art and literature – represented by artists like Flannery O'Connor, William Faulkner, Ralph Eugene Meatyard, and, more recently, filmmaker, David Lynch – whose emphasis is on the bizarre underpinnings of normal life, and which has historically been a strong and original mode of expression in the Southern part of the United States.

In an essay published in 1982, Laughlin called this type of photography "the third world of photography". Contrasting it with the two dominant forms of the medium in the United States – documentation and artistic purism – Laughlin saw this third world as a type of photography that treats subject matter "in terms of inner perceptions and compulsions, in terms of intuition and symbolism".[11] The 17,000 sheet film negatives Laughlin produced during his long life represent a range of both subject matter and technique, but the fundamental strangeness of his vision never varied, whether he was photographing a Gothic figure in architectural ruins, ghostlike forms involving multiple exposures, landscapes, cemeteries or Southern architecture. Filled with bizarre apparitions, decaying statues, and deteriorated traces of times gone by, his pictures embody the romance of Gothic novels and haunted houses.

Laughlin discusses the "third world of photography", but it should be noted that there are artists from the Third World itself whose works echo some of the concerns discussed here – though, in their case, these concerns grow out of indigenous cultural roots rather than Western aesthetic influences. The best known of these is M. Alvarez Bravo, the Mexican master revered by the Surrealist André Breton. Since the 1930s, this photographer has been creating images, mostly black and white, which are deeply imbued with death, isolation, and the dreams and mysteries that infuse the life of the Mexican people. Often accompanied by poetic titles, Alvarez Bravo's photographs bring to mind the mystical universe described by novelist Gabriel García Márquez rather than the Gothic horrors often associated with the works of Laughlin.

There are few photographers in the history of the medium, however, who have created odder Gothic images than Ralph Eugene Meatyard, another artist of the American South. Born, believe it or not, in Normal, Illinois, Meatyard, an optician by profession, moved to Lexington, Kentucky to take a job in 1950, and, until his early death in 1972, raised his family in this town. Throughout this quiet, family-oriented life, Meatyard exposed close to 18,000 negatives, all of them pictures of commonplace subjects: his wife, his three children, his friends, and the trees, barns, and gorges in his neighborhood. However, when seen through this artist's eyes, these subjects became haunted with the motion of ghosts. He himself said that he aimed to create "uncanny pictures – that is, not surreal, but which give the feeling of being not quite of this world".[12] Shadows have a primordial significance in Meatyard's pictures; it is almost as if darkness, not light or air, is the substantive environment within which his subjects move and breathe. Masks are a

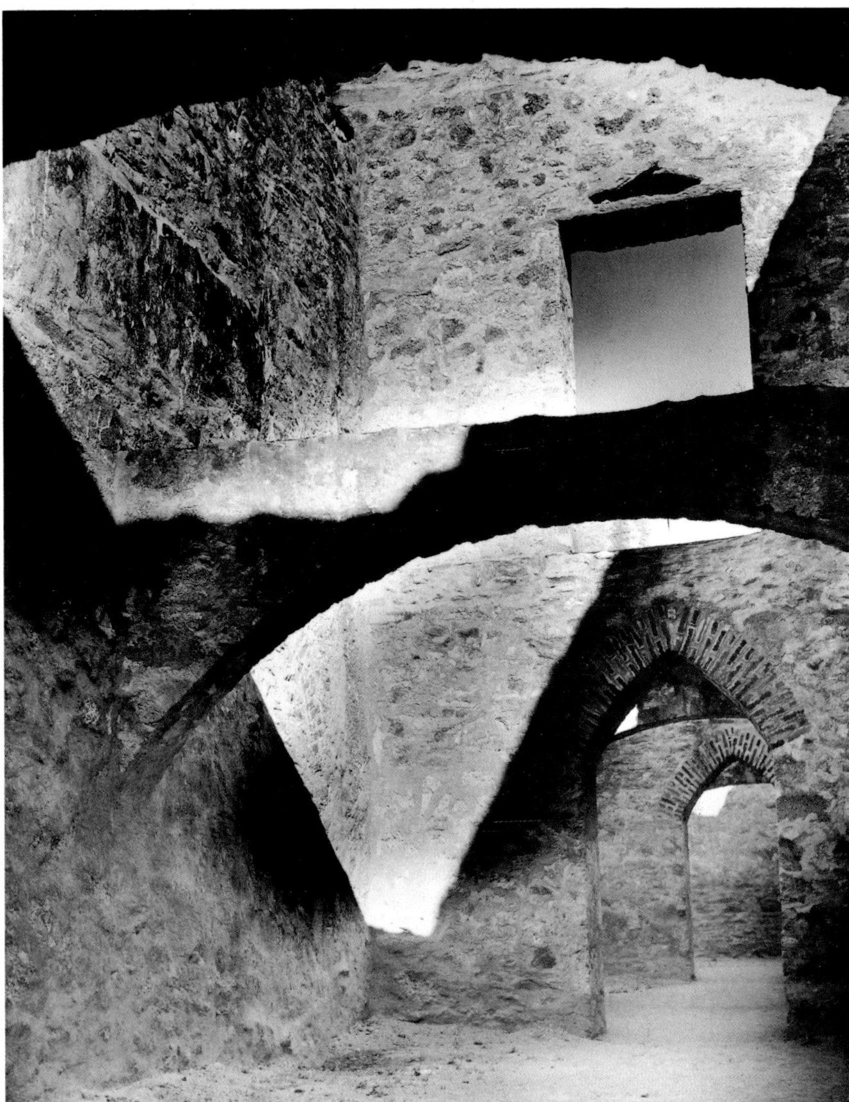

Clarence John Laughlin, *The Space Pendulum, San Antonio,* 1952, Center for Creative Photography, Tucson.

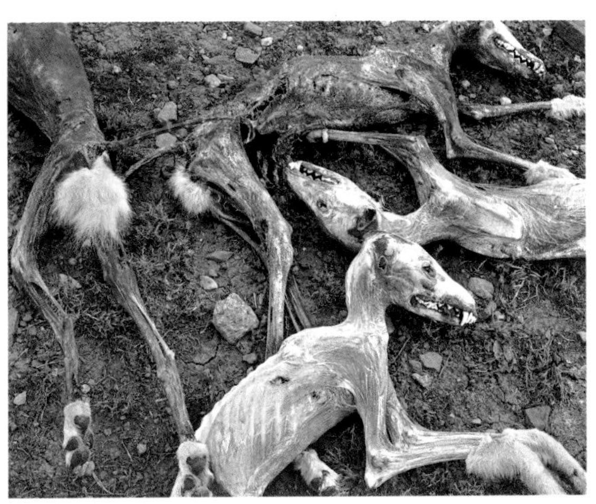

◀ Frederick Sommer, *Coyotes,* 1945, Center for Creative Photography, Tucson.

11. In *Edward Weston and Clarence John Laughlin*, exhibition catalogue, New Orleans Museum of Art, 1982, p. 8.

12. Quoted in Shelley Rice, "Dangling Conversations", in *On Campus*, October 1984, p. 26.

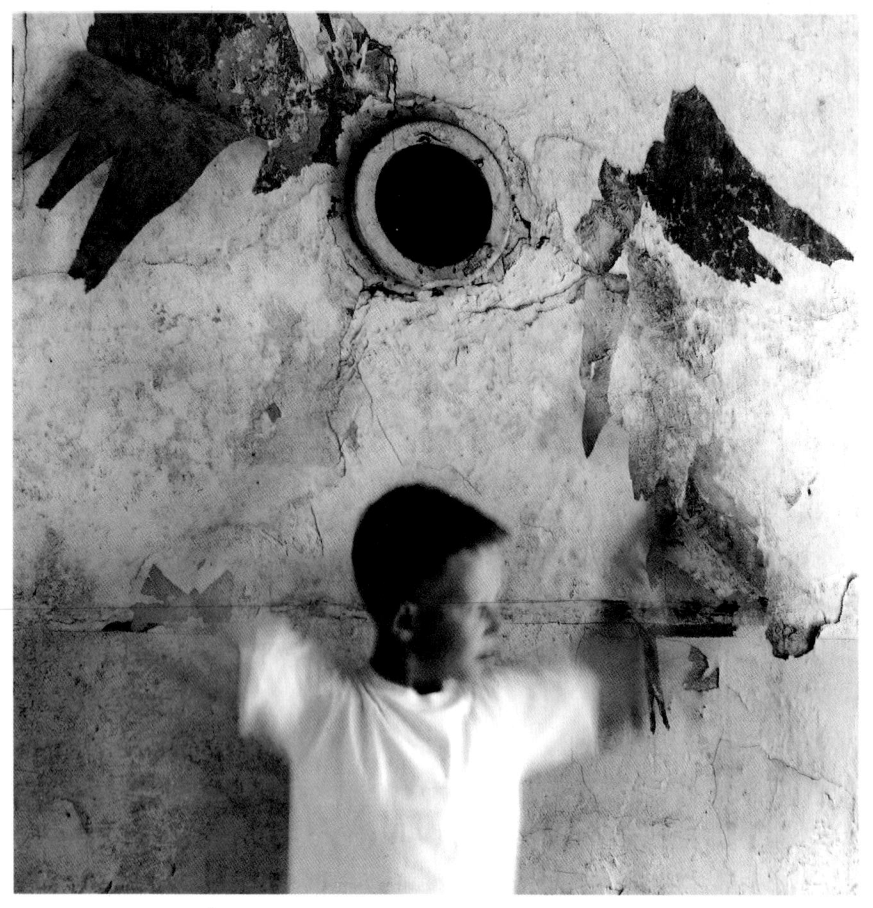

Ralph E. Meatyard, *Untitled*, 1961.

recurrent theme. Children, donning universalized faces of death and decay, are transmuted into strange *memento mori*, echoing, even in their youth, the degradation of old wooden barns, broken windows, and graffitied walls that barely hold their own against the onslaught of time. "Metaphors for a constantly shifting reality",[13] his pictures depict a world in the process of metamorphosis, moving toward imminent disintegration.

Interestingly enough, Meatyard was influenced by, among others, Edward Weston. A Californian artist whose still-life and nature pictures have no trace of the enigmas found in photos like Meatyard's, Weston nevertheless left his mark on this type of photography. Wynn Bullock and Paul Caponigro, both artists who created shimmering nature images filled with the passage of time and mystery embodied in fog and light, were deeply affected by the work of this master. Caponigro, especially, pushed Weston's love of landscape towards the realm of mystery. Seen by this artist, the light in a peaceful forest, diffuse and soft, could suggest nature's most ancient secrets, and rock faces worn and steeped in darkness seemed to hide the wisdom of the ages in their craggy surfaces. Caponigro sought out not only nature's secrets, but also humankind's; his images of Stonehenge, with their slabs of stone looming upward toward the sky, against the paleness of a half moon, suggest the majesty of our hidden histories.

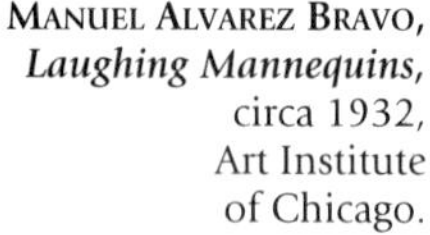

Manuel Alvarez Bravo, *Laughing Mannequins*, circa 1932, Art Institute of Chicago.

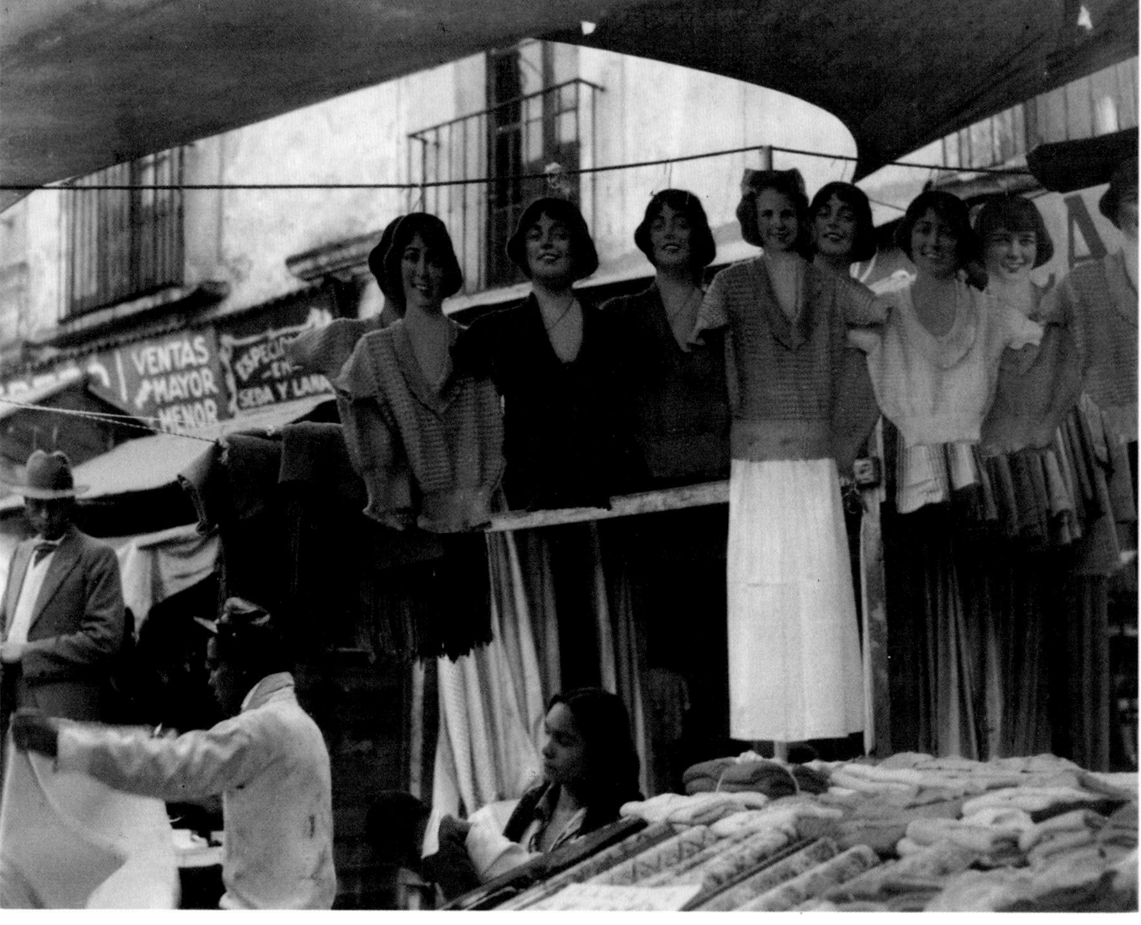

13. A. D. Coleman, *Ibid.*

Works like these are a far cry from the "objectivity" proclaimed by Edward Weston, who aimed to capture the true and timeless "essence" of his subjects, be they cabbage leaves, toilets or rocks on a beach. Weston's still-life photographs of the 1920s, begun at the same moment in international photographic history that Moholy-Nagy became influential in Germany, were parallel to the Neue Sachlichkeit movement that was to transform creative photography in both the United States and Europe.

Subjective photography

This period, one of the most fascinating in the history of the medium, was cut short in Germany, in 1933, by the rise of Hitler and National Socialism. Numerous artists from the Bauhaus, including Moholy-Nagy and Herbert Bayer, fled to the United States to escape persecution. Moholy-Nagy's influence continued strongly in the United States until his early death in 1946, since he spent his last years as the head of the Institute of Design in Chicago. As Europe recovered from the War, German artists tried to recover the energy and richness of the New Vision as practiced by Moholy-Nagy and Man Ray, to pick up where they had left off in the production of creative photography.

The most important person in this movement was Otto Steinert, who left medical practice to teach photography at the Saarbrücken School of Arts and Crafts in Germany. Encouraging his students and his contemporaries to revive the creative spirit of the 1920s, to expand the vocabulary of documentation and illustration that had dominated photographic production during the war years, Steinert first organized the group "Fotoform" in 1950 (including, besides Steinert himself, P. Keetman, S. Lauterwasser, W. Reisewitz, T. Schneiders, L. Windstrosser, and later, H. Hajek-Halke and C. Stromholm). More purist than photographers of the Bauhaus, rejecting expressive techniques which relied on links with drawing, painting, typography or cinema, Steinert's followers nevertheless experimented with montages and photograms. In 1951, dissatisfied with many of the exhibitions like those in Stuttgart, Neustadt-an-der-Haardt, Cologne, and Eindhoven in 1948–1950 taking place in Europe, because they lacked clear themes or organizational concepts, Steinert organized *Subjective Photography: An International Exhibition of Modern Photography* in Saarbrücken.

Opening on July 2, 1951, the exhibition consisted of several sections, and comprised 725 works of which 197 were shown under the title "Subjective Photography". Other sections included exhibitions by groups from Italy (La Bussola, Circolo Fotografico Milanese), Britain, France (Groupe des XV), Switzerland (Kollegium Schweizerischen Fotografen, including Bischof, Schuh, Tuggener), the Netherlands, Sweden, and Austria, as well as Fotoform and other representatives from Germany. To provide historical continuity, there were displays devoted to photography since 1930 and, most importantly, retrospectives of works by Moholy-Nagy, Man Ray, and Herbert Bayer.

In his introduction to the exhibition catalogue, Steinert wrote: "The aim of the exhibition 'Subjective Photography, [...] is to make a contribution towards highlighting the ambitions of contemporary photography [...] 'Subjective Photography' is the title of this exhibition because the phrase underlines its essential character: the creative personality of photography (in contrast with practical photography in illustrations or documentation). So this exhibition is devoted mainly to a type of photography in which the artist has altered the basic material of exterior reality by means of transformations suggested to him by his

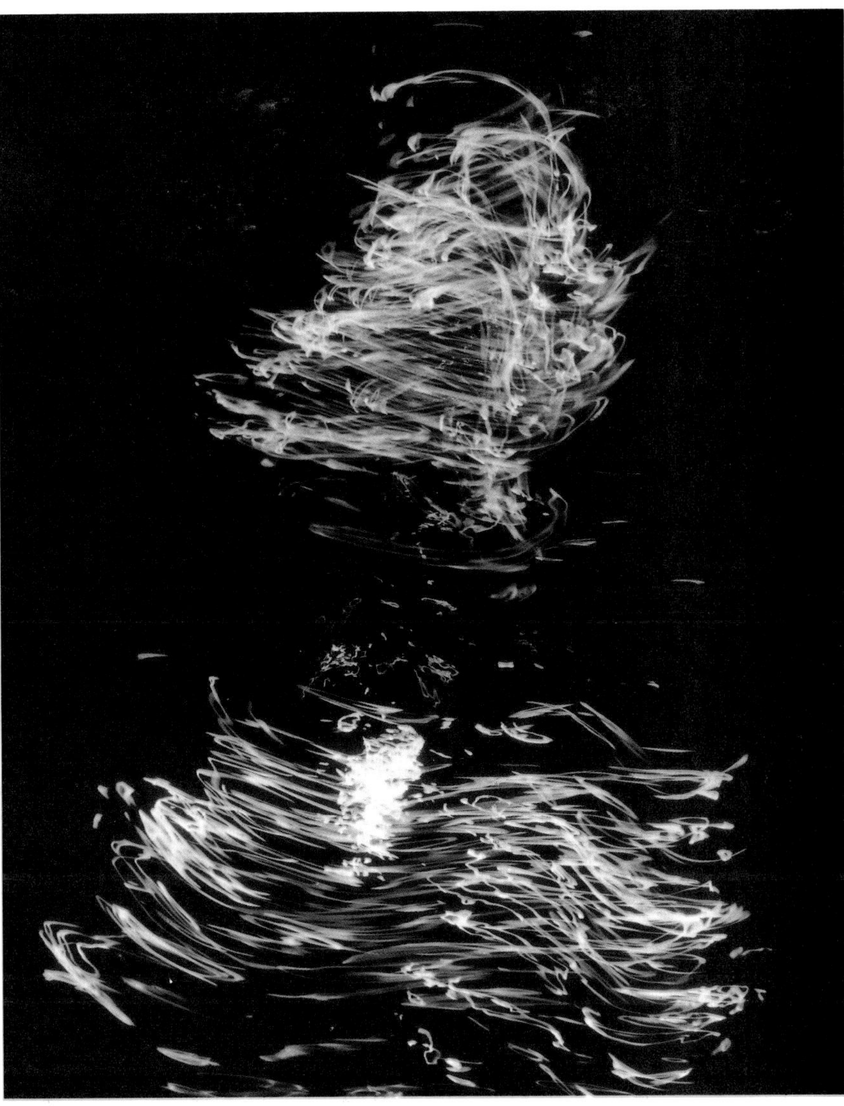

Ralph E. Meatyard, *Untitled*, circa 1967.

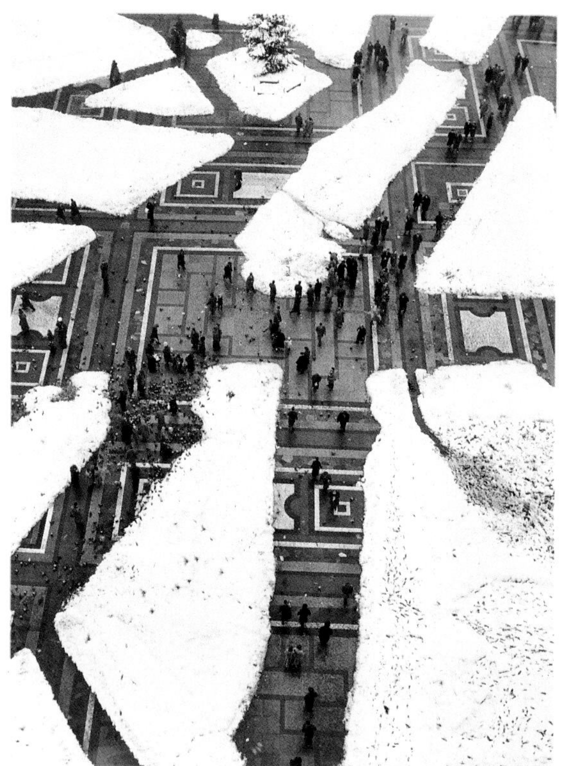

MARIO DE BIASI, *Piazza del Duomo, Milan,* 1951, Museum Folkwang, Essen.

personal vision of the world."[14] To this end, Steinert assembled photographs from Europe, Japan, and the United States, bringing together works from different cultures, different fields (art photographs were mixed with works by fashion photographers like Irving Penn, and photojournalists like Bert Hardy and Henri Cartier-Bresson), and different sensibilities to prove the personal nature of all photographic vision.

The original "Subjective Photography" exhibition was the first of three, organized in 1951, 1954, and 1958. As the years went by, the shows became more focused, less flawed by the general sprawl of unrelated images that characterized the original display. In fact, probably the only thing linking the numerous works in the 1951 exhibition was an overall feeling of darkness, of the somber and almost sinister.[15] In order to gain this effect, certain important photographers were represented by works that now, in hindsight, seem uncharacteristic; Brassaï, for instance, showed an unusual, almost abstract image of shoe leathers rather than the images of Paris at night for which he is best known. Numerous documentary photographers like Bill Brandt, Henri Cartier-Bresson, and Werner Bischof were represented here by works whose formalism or dark tonality allowed them only marginally to be squeezed into a framework which, by definition, stressed creative transformation rather than objective description.

However, seen from the point of view of a war-torn Europe, steeped in Surrealism as an artistic movement, these juxtapositions become more

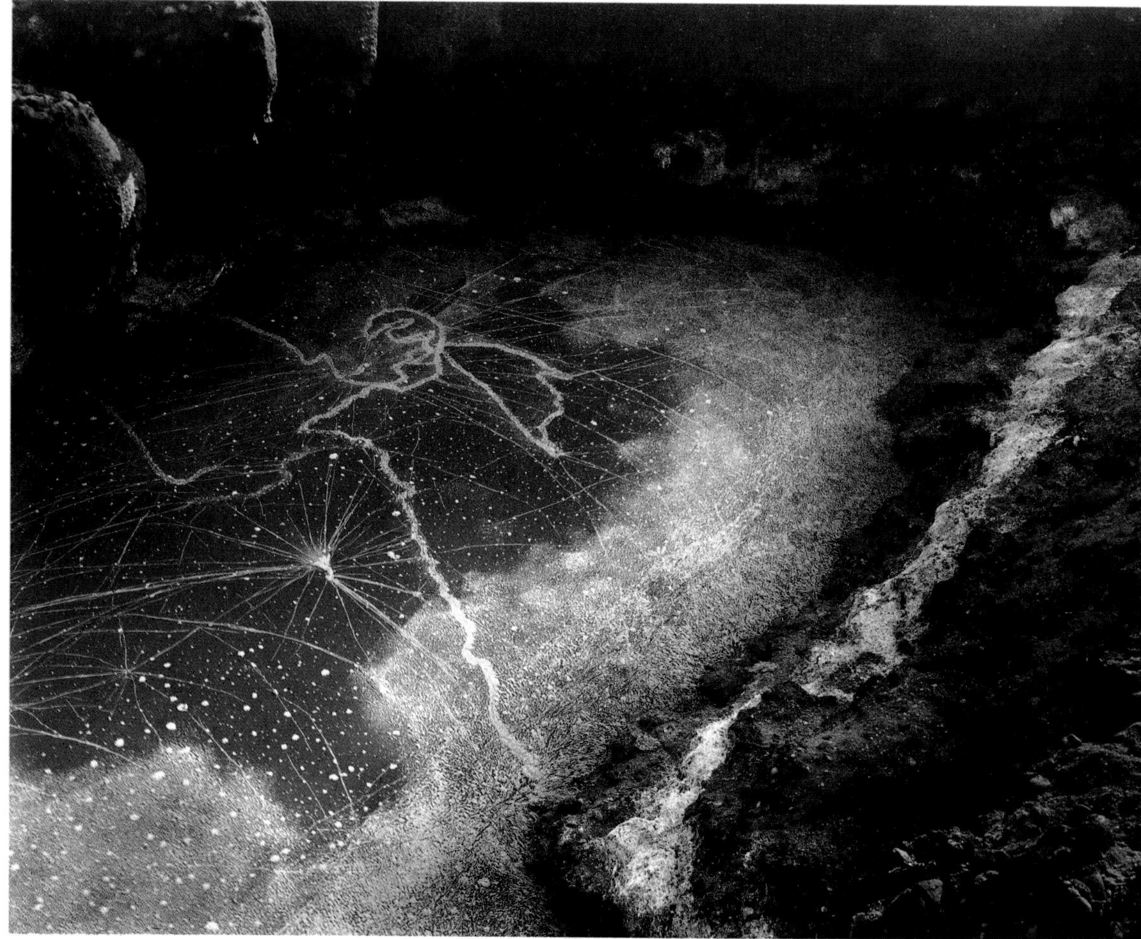

WYNN BULLOCK, *Tide Pool,* 1957, Center for Creative Photography, Tucson.

14. Otto Steinert, exhibition catalogue, *Subjektive Fotografie,* 1951.

15. Three catalogues were published: *Subjektive Fotografie: Internationale Ausstellung moderner Fotografie,* Saarbrücken, 1951; *Subjektive Fotografie 2,* Saarbrücken, 1954; *Subjektive Fotografie 3,* Cologne, 1958 (in Fotokina); and two books, *Subjektive Fotografie: Ein Bildband moderner (europäischer) Fotografie,* Munich, Brüder Auer, 1952 and 1955. The exhibition cataloque *Subjektive Fotografie: Bilder der 50er Jahre,* Essen, Museum Folkwang, 1984, does not clearly indicate the photographs shown in three former exhibitions.

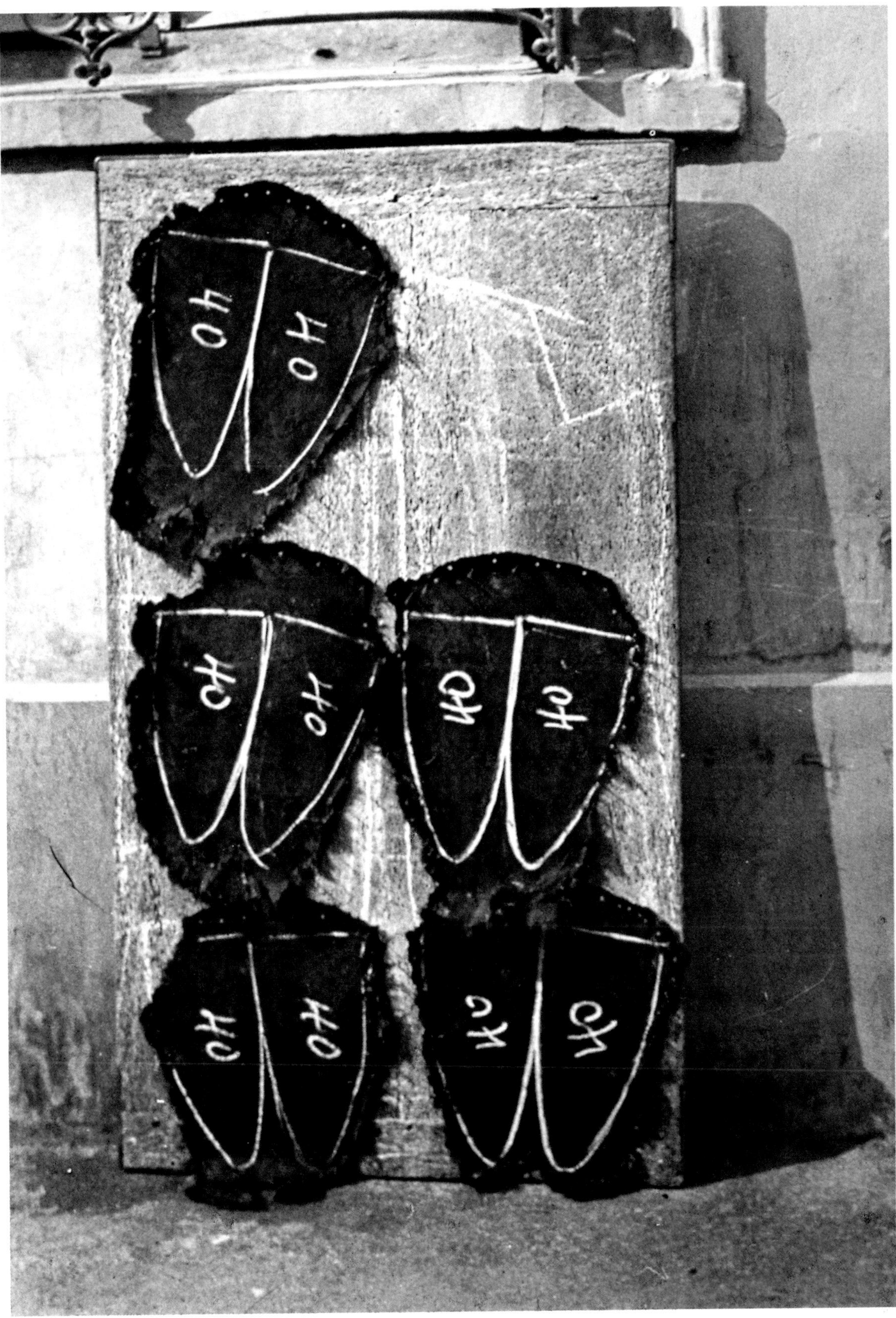

BRASSAÏ,
Shoes Coming into Being,
1933,
from A. Gheerbrant,
Anthologie de la poésie naturelle,
1949.

Subjektive Fotografie

Immediately after the Second World War, in a devastated Europe, the tendency was to forget the horror of the present and, in order to achieve this, to give free rein to individual expression which had been crushed by Nazi ideology. It was in Germany that, renewing links with the fervor of the 1930s and the great lessons of the Bauhaus, a few photographers such as Heinz Hajek-Halke, Peter Keetman, and Wolfgang Reisewitz came together to form the group "Fotoform", soon joined by Otto Steinert. The originality of this group became apparent at the 1950 Photokina in Cologne, displaying an almost austere vision and images that were strongly structured and contrasted.

From that moment on Otto Steinert's influence continued to increase. It was he who, in 1950, prepared an exhibition which would shake the photographic world to its foundations and become the creed of a new way of seeing: "Subjektive Fotografie", a phrase which expresses the personal factor in the creative act (in contrast with photography which is purely documentary) and which embraces "every domain of personal photographic creation, from the abstract photogram to photo-reportage". Steinert, A. Schmoll, and the historian Franz Roh (author of the preface to the catalogue for the "Foto-Auge" exhibition in 1929) were the theoreticians of the movement. The first exhibition opened in Saarbrücken in 1951 and showed a wish to bring together not images but photographers, whose main aim was to prove the existence of a personal vision, an aesthetic *parti pris* evident in both form and content, and to affirm "the creative power of the photographer who, single-handedly, transforms the subject into an image".

The influence of Subjektive Fotografie would be particularly strong in Europe and would serve as a reference point for the whole youthful photographic movement in revolt.

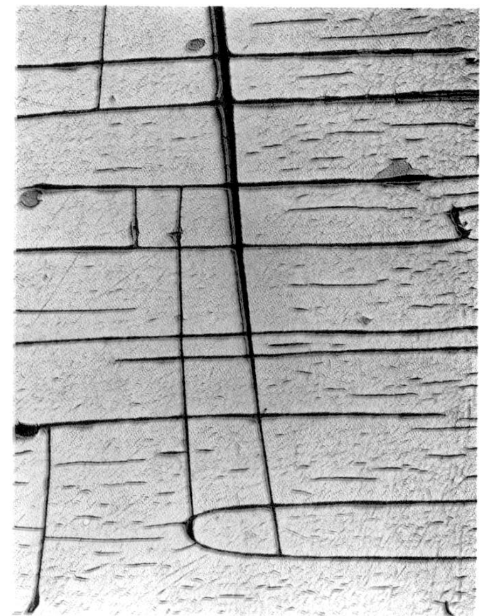

Hans Hammarskjöld,
Untitled,
1949, Museum Folkwang, Essen

Contacts were established with Martiens Coppens and the Nederlandse Fotografische Kunstring (N.F.K.) in the Netherlands, the Italian group La Bussola (Cavalli, Veronesi, Giacomelli, Roiter), founded in 1947, the Swedish group Unga (1949) (Rolph Winquist, L. Olson, H. Hammarskjöld), and the Belgian clubs such as the Cercle Iris Anvers or the Photo-Club de Boitsfort (Coulommier, De Keyser, Dries, Cordier). Most of them met at the second Subjektive Fotografie exhibition in 1954, accompanied by a new catalogue in which Steinert analyzed the photographic world according to four broad categories: photographic reproduction (documents), photography tending towards representation (*belle image*), creative photographic representation (subjective photography), and absolute creation (abstract photography).

While the Subjektive Fotografie group disappeared after its third and final exhibition in 1958, its influence remained potent: in the United States, Bernard Newhall staged the first of these exhibitions at George Eastman House (Rochester) in 1953, while the New York Museum of Modern Art organized in 1958 the exhibition "Abstraction in Photography", followed by "The Sense of Abstraction" in 1960, exhibitions which included a large number of images previously shown in Saarbrücken. In France, directly inspired by this movement, a few photographers, in the ambit of P. Riehl, J. Dieuzaide, and J.-C. Gautrand, tried to react against the routine of salons, founding the group "Libre Expression" (1963) which favored research photography and exhibited photographers such as Jean-Pierre Sudre, Heinz Hajek-Halke, Jerry Uelsman, and Paul Caponigro, the follower of Minor White.

Jean-Claude Gautrand

readily understandable. During the 1920s and 1930s, young artists like Brassaï and Brandt and even photojournalists like Cartier-Bresson, worked within the framework of the Surrealists' transformation of reality. Though the movement itself had disbanded by the postwar years, its influence could still be felt in Europe, and this whole generation of important photographers used it as a reference point for defining their aesthetic. Brassaï, for instance, differentiated himself from the Surrealists in this way: "The surrealism of my images was nothing more than reality rendered fantastic by vision. I sought only to express reality, for nothing is more surreal. If we no longer marvel at it, that's because habit has made it seem banal. My ambition was always to show off some aspect of everyday life as though we were discovering it for the first time. That's what separates me from the Surrealists."[16] However the works may differ, the influence of Surrealism lingered in Brassaï's and other photographers' search for "the real rendered fantastic by vision", for the poetry of the streets and the mystery of daily life. This quest is the conceptual thread that linked the works exhibited in the Subjective Photography exhibitions.

The "Subjective Photography" exhibition was divided into sections, organized by country. Its checklist is, therefore, a good indication of exactly which photographers were considered by the international community to be in the forefront of creative photography in 1951. France was represented by, among others, Brassaï, Cartier-Bresson, Doisneau, Raoul Hausmann, and Daniel Masclet, whose contribution included a dark and formal image of a cracked and stained wall. Doisneau's documentary photograph of a wedding party walking through an empty street took on Surrealist overtones which were amplified by some of Germany's representative photographs. A

16. Brassaï, *Culture et Communication*, 1980, p. 15.

print by Otto Steinert, for instance, depicted a sidewalk scene, sparse and formal, seen from above; a tree to the left became part of an oddly viewed shape reminiscent of the perspectival transformations seen in Moholy-Nagy's works, while the figure off to the right, captured in motion, seems to disappear in a blur, so only their foot is really visible.

Steinert's blurred motion picture also linked him with William Klein, an American artist who contributed a street photograph whose moving subjects became bizarre indeed when frozen by the camera. Other exhibitors from Germany included Heinz Hajek-Halke, a member of Fotoform who contributed a multiple exposure work depicting a nude whose body was superimposed over a scrawled text and whose face was replaced by an empty window, and Herbert List, represented by his well-known photograph of a woman, draped in both fabric and mystery, standing alone in an expanse of desert. Unlike those who sought the fantastic in the quotidian, List, like de Chirico, searched for Surreal overtones in the classical. This feminine apparition in the desert links his work with the fantasms of Clarence John Laughlin.

The British photographer Bill Brandt (who worked as Man Ray's assistant in 1929) contributed a sombre image of a coal miner searching on his bicycle for coal chips in an empty landscape. This resonated with a work by the Italian Mario Giacomelli of a formally beautiful and high-contrast street scene, complete with cattle. Another Italian, Fulvio Roiter, was represented by a documentary image of a black couple during Carnival in Rio de Janeiro. This print, like Werner Bischof's depiction, in the Swiss section, of a tramp in a marketplace in Transylvania, fits into the "artistic" pretensions of the exhibition much less happily than, for instance, a work like the Swiss, Hans Finsler's, a formal study of light on three white eggs floating on a black field. Hans Hammerskiöld from Sweden and Gotthard Schuh from Switzerland added their work to displays by artists from Belgium and Japan, and a large section was also devoted to American creative photography.

The American contingent consisted (in 1954) of many of those already discussed in this essay as the vanguard of creative photography in the United States: Wynn Bullock (*Burned Chair*), Harry Callahan, Clarence John Laughlin, Aaron Siskind, Frederick Sommer, and Minor White. Other contributors included Ansel Adams, Irving Penn, and Brett Weston, the son of Edward and a photographer whose images, which often resemble his father's in terms of their subject matter, have more of a biting emotional edge. It was the bringing together of all of these different image-makers, the naming of Subjective Photography as an international movement that cut across continents, that marks the significance of these shows, which did much to foster a rebirth of creative work in this medium in Europe.

By the term "creative" one should understand an effort ("work") to prepare the perceptions and mind before taking the photograph and during the process, a wish to construct the true meaning of images, which refer to something other than their material subject, and which arouse unexpected emotions. Such features (photography considered as work, intuition, thought as object), difficult to pin down in the strictly formal sense, are present for example in the heart of the Groupe des XV.[17] This group was established in Paris by André Garban from 1946 to 1957 and included, among others, Lucien Lorelle, Emmanuel Sougez, Marcel Bovis, René-Jacques, Daniel Masclet, Robert Doisneau, Willy Ronis, Pierre Jahan, Pierre Ichac, and Thérèse Le Prat. Some of these photographers continued a kind of "pure photography", others looked for "the imaginative conception of the creator" (Lucien Lorelle) or

WILLIAM KLEIN, ***Abstract Photograph for a Wall Panel,*** 1952.

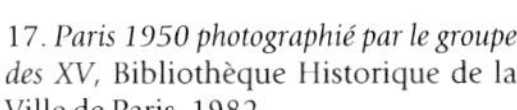

17. *Paris 1950 photographié par le groupe des XV*, Bibliothèque Historique de la Ville de Paris, 1982.

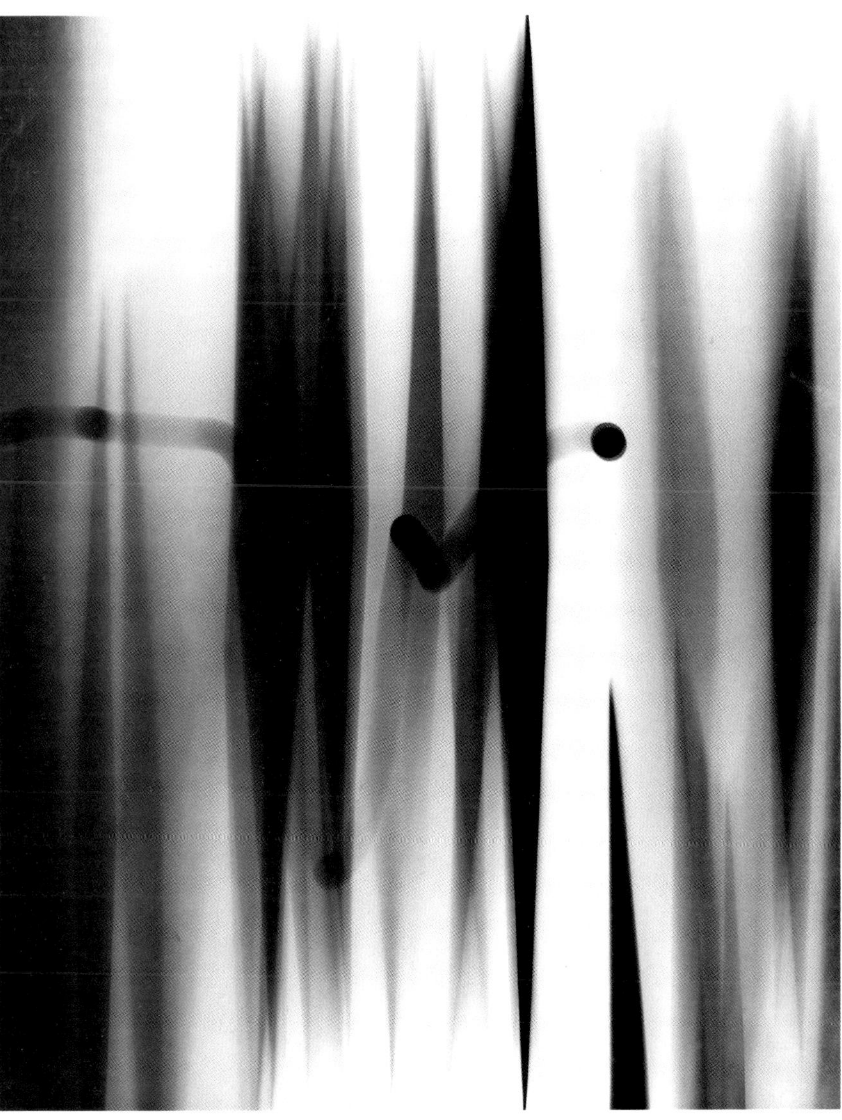

Art, science, and nature

As an experimental tool, photography sheds light on visible or invisible phenomena, new or artificial forms. By bringing infinity closer, by reducing or increasing distances, it plunges into a reality from which astonishing plastic shapes sometimes emerge: the experiments of Muybridge and Marey (which enjoyed a resurgence in 20th-century art) and the micro-photographs of Bertsch already intrigued viewers in the 19th century. In *Malerei, Fotografie, Film* in 1925 Moholy-Nagy showed his interest in scientific photography, which was profoundly integrated with the concepts of the Bauhaus school in Weimar and Dessau and the modernist themes of the avant-garde movement of the 1920s and 1930s.

Photography indeed allows us to explore time (ultra-rapid photography), space (astro-photography), invisible matter (micro- and macro-photography); it reveals unexpected shapes via X-rays or ultra-violet and infra-red light, "a kind of beauty which is often born by chance" (Moholy-Nagy), which join up with the pictorial preoccupations of the time. Huge graphic designs produced by aerial photography, the elementary shapes of single-cell animals, the fascinating beauty of molecular or crystalline structures, the exulting, dream-like images of space: these are so many means of scientific investigation which open up to the photographer's imagination previously unsuspected pictorial repertoires which they try to capture without the aid of laboratory equipment. These are domains in which, as Brassaï wrote, "photography breaks down time and space, searching physical, chemical, and biological structures in order to bring unexpected images to us. The strange beauty of a reality beyond the visible, in which we feel totally estranged, lacking reference points. But curiously it is precisely those photos, mostly scientific ones, a thousand miles away from aesthetic aims, which bring us back to art". The great exhibition "Art and Nature" at the Basle Kunsthalle in 1958 demonstrated the convergence of contemporary photographic and pictorial treatment (the work published by Georg Schmidt and Robert Schenk was also widely distributed).

After Karl Blossfeldt's *Urformen der Kunst* (Berlin, 1928), Laure Albin-Guillot's *Micrographies décoratives* (Paris, Draeger Frères, 1931), and the publication of scientific photographs in books by Moholy-Nagy and Werner Gräff, and in numerous annuals entitled *Photographie* published by *Arts et Métiers graphiques*, certain works emphasized in a more particular way these ideas of a link between art forms and natural forms captured by optical means (micro- or macro-photography): in particular, Horst P.Horst's *Patterns from Nature* (New York, J. J. Augustus, 1946), Carl Strüwe's *Formen des Mikrokosmos* (Munich, Prestel, 1955), V. J. Stanek's *Die Schönheit der Natur* (Prague, Artis, 1955), or even, in a more restricted milieu, Moholy-Nagy's *Vision in Motion* (Chicago, Paul Theobald, 1947).

These widespread examples supplement the information of magazines (or annual publications, such as *Photo Almanach Prisma*, which, for example, published in 1952 the photographic work of Raymond Hains, as well as an article by György Kepes of the M.I.T) and which notably allowed subjective photography, which took up again the experimental work of the 1930s, to find a justification in natural forms, while still preaching an escape from visible reality.

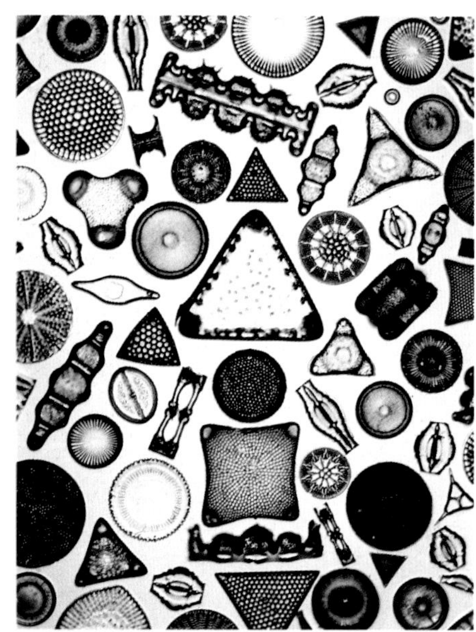

▲ **Carl Strüwe,**
Original Image of Individuality: Single-celled Algae, 1933

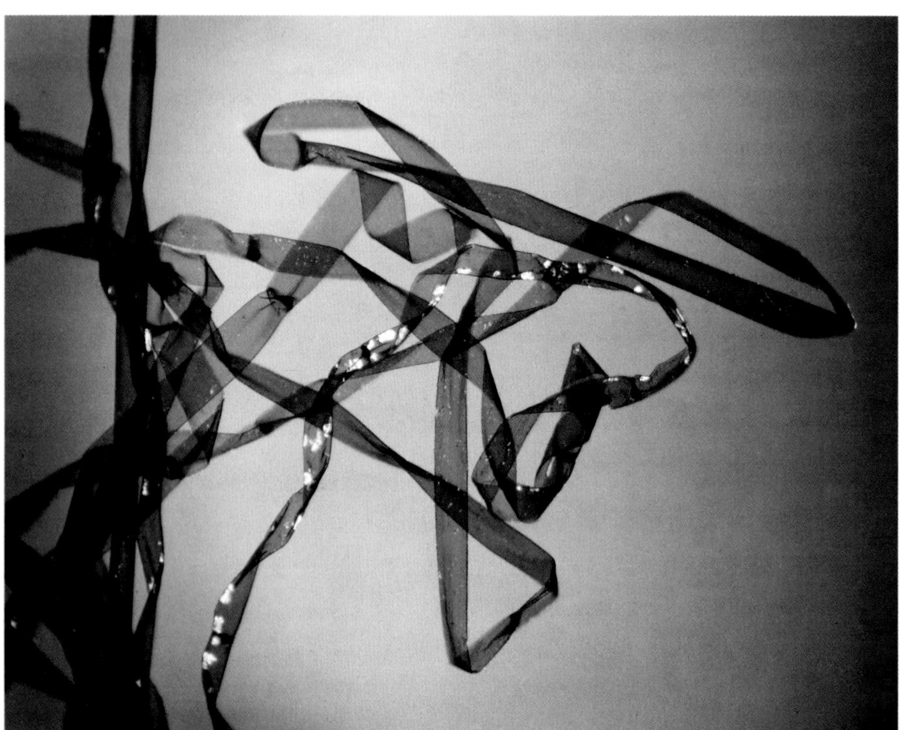

◄ ***Filamentary Silhouette with Dance Movement: Cibotium, 1952,***
(micro-photographs from *Formen des Mikrokosmos*, 1955), Kunsthalle, Bielefeld.

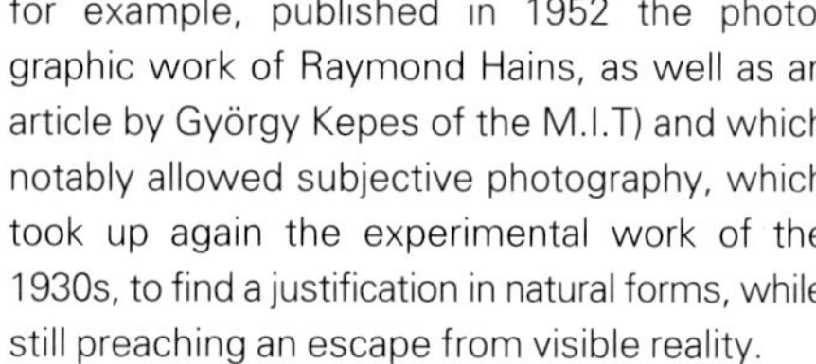

A large number of photographers who had grouped around the "Subjektive Fotografie" movement were inspired by these techniques and adopted its formal language. A keen enthusiast for the natural sciences, Heinz Hajek-Halke used every possibility that experimental photography could provide in order to transform objects into Surrealist visions. Chargesheimer discovered astonishing graphic effects in the swelling of the sensitive layers of the film. Manfred Kage photographed crystals under a polarizing microscope, while Jean-Pierre Sudre grew them on a glass plate in order to transform them into "materiographic landscapes". Pierre Cordier invented the "chimigramme" (1956), which combined the physics of painting with the chemistry of photography, without using a camera, sometimes using existing images (by Muybridge and Marey, for example) as a departure-point. On a completely different scale, William Garnett created "abstract" works by aerial photography while Lennart Nilson discovered unexpected artistic forms within the human body.

Michel Frizot
Jean-Claude Gautrand

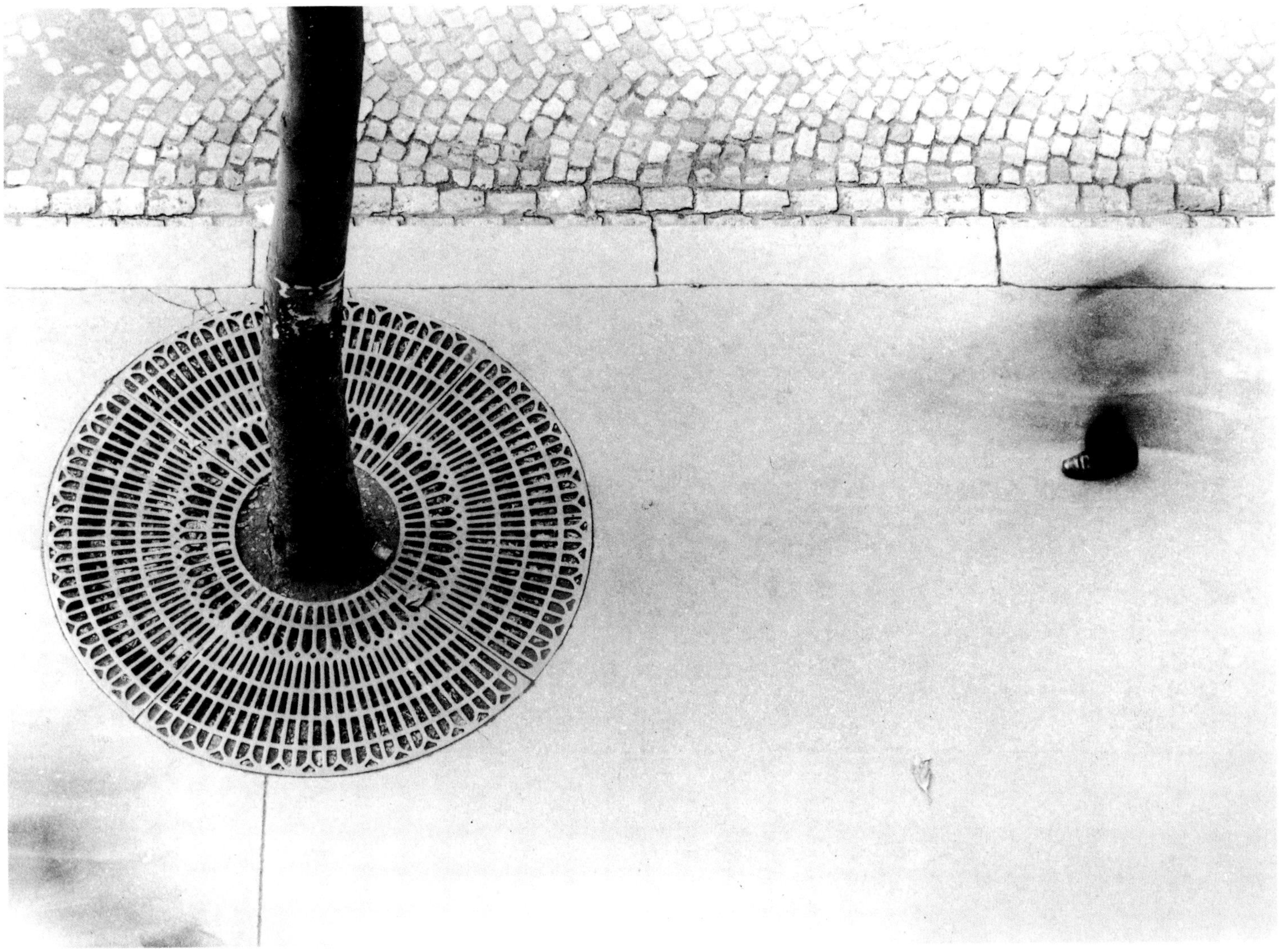

Otto Steinert,
One-legged Pedestrian,
1950,
Museum Folkwang,
Essen.

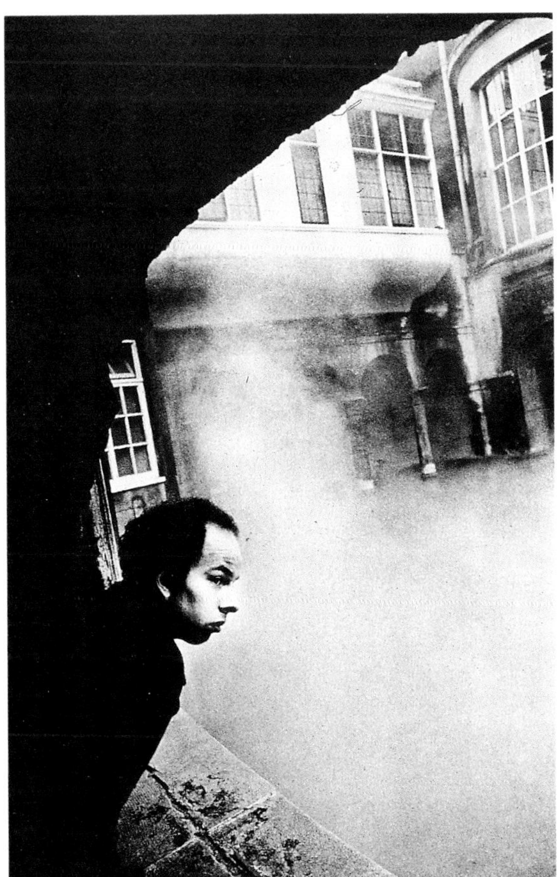

◀ Ralph Gibson,
Untitled,
from *Déjà vu*, 1973.

"the poetry of time and place" (Robert Doisneau). The "Subjektive Fotografie" movement had repercussions in the whole of Europe, notably on Belgian groups (Serge Vandercam, Pierre Cordier, Gilbert de Keyser) and through the intermediary of the exhibition *Images inventées* (Brussels and The Hague, 1957, Leverkusen, 1958),[18] which also presented Minor White, Wynn Bullock, etc. Henceforth photography appeared to be set in a perspective which it had itself defined, reflecting itself and asking itself questions in the mirror of a recent past, giving a boost to its technical aspects through certain spiritual values.

The meaning of the mystery

While the impact of the exhibitions was not as strong in the United States, the strength of subjective photography in America during the 1940s and 1950s influenced greatly a generation of artists who came of age in the 1960s. Representing a range of styles and of techniques, these photographers began to explore the mystery lurking beneath the veneer of objective reality as seen by the camera. Some of them, for instance

18. *Images inventées, la photographie créative belge dans les années 50*, Musée d'Art Moderne de la Ville de Paris, 1990.

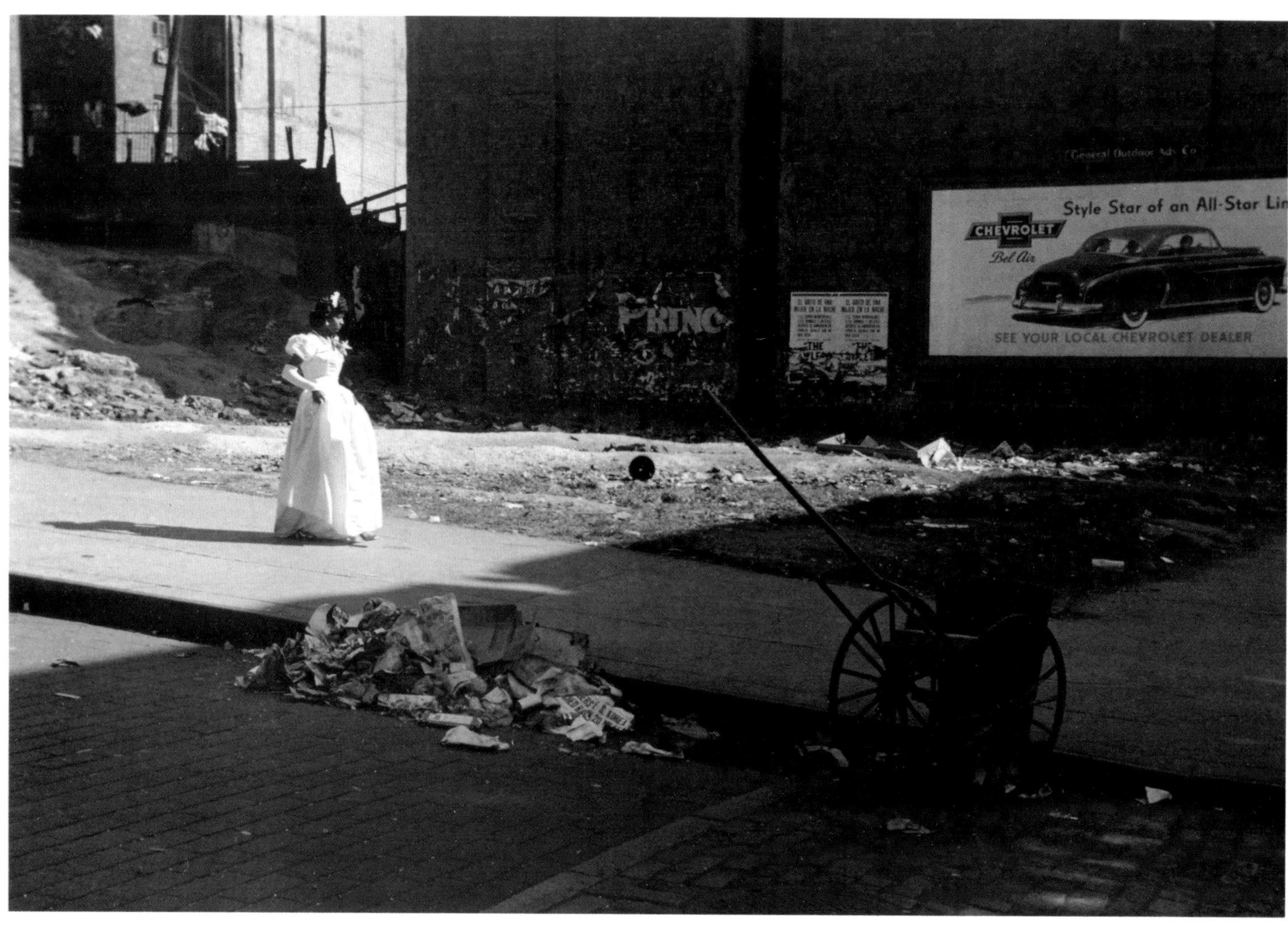

ROY DECARAVA,
Graduation,
New York,
1952,
Center for Creative
Photography, Tucson.

Ralph Gibson, who became important not only for his own works but also as a book publisher, were straight photographers. Gibson's dark images, surreal in tone, focused on eroticism, empty spaces, and the strange vagaries of light to create a world charged with unanswered mysteries. Their debt to Surrealism is, perhaps, more evident than the debt of Lee Friedlander's *Self-Portrait*, a series of black and white pictures by this artist which highlight the photographer's reflected or shadowed images cast as he traveled through the American urban and suburban landscape making pictures. Straightforward documentary images, usually classified within the context of the numerous social landscapes created in the United States during the 1960s, these photographs nevertheless raise questions about the photographer's role in creating the reality he perceives. In Friedlander's self-portraits, the artist himself is the apparition.

Another straight photographer who began exploring the enigmas of daily life was Emmet Gowin. First known for his pictures of his wife Edith and his family in Danville, Virginia, Gowin started experimenting, about 1970, with a circular lens, whose strange perspectives transformed everyday portraits into romantic, almost ritual images. Seen in this way, fish, his wife's necklace, and even a child's dance costume became mysteries steeped in blackness or bathed in light. Deeply influenced by Frederick Sommer, Gowin, at his best, uses the transforming properties of the camera to, as James Agee said, "perceive simply the cruel radiance of what is".[19]

The same can be said of Roy DeCarava, a black American artist whose works, like Friedlander's, are often perceived as purely documentary images – in this case of inner-city neighborhoods. However, DeCarava's photographs, which won him major awards in the United States as early as the mid-1950s, use black and white to make powerful statements about the spiritual meanings inherent in urban life. Sunlight and shadow, striking litter-strewn streets, seem to embody moral forces in the lives of black people coping with the pressures of New York City. And the pleasures too: one of DeCarava's best-known works is a series of portraits, steeped in darkness, of jazz musicans lost in their own private world of creative mystery.

More obviously indebted to the pictorial style of the Surrealist movement is Jerry Uelsmann,

19. James Agee in *Emmet Gowin Photographs*, New York, Knopf, 1976, frontispiece.

who rejected straight photography for a multiple image technique, harking back to the nineteenth-century innovations of Robinson and Rejlander. On photographic expeditions, Uelsmann "collects" images, which become part of his personal archive. When beginning a new picture, the artist chooses from these "found" motifs, and prints unrelated pictures together in strange montages. Unexpected juxtapositions and spatial relationships and settings allow his camera works to approximate the bizarre worlds created by a painter like Magritte.

Perhaps more original are the complex works of Duane Michals, who uses his camera to explore those spiritual areas of human experience which are in fact intangible. Often working with narrative sequences, multiple exposures or single black and white images juxtaposed with handwritten texts, Michals has consistently chosen themes about death, eroticism, chance occurrences, dreams, the spirit world, and the cosmos. Nude figures, often in ordinary interiors, enact scenes which describe the most fundamental aspects of the human condition. *A Young Girl's Dream*, for instance, photographically depicts, in a sequence of black and white images without words, a woman's erotic fantasy. *Death Comes to the Old Lady*, another sequence, uses blurred motion techniques to visualize the "disappearance" death entails. *Self-portrait with My Guardian Angel* is a black and white image juxtaposed with a handwritten caption that describes a man, long since dead yet depicted in the photograph, whose spirit guides the artist. Michals has readily accepted the challenge of making visible the intangible aspects of life that can be felt by all but never seen – and he has chosen to do this by means of photography, the quintessential "documentary" medium best-known for its faithful description of the tangible world.

Michal's work was widely influential in the United States during the 1970s because it suggested that the camera could be used to create "conceptual" images, rather than simply to document what already existed. "None of my photographs would have had any life or any reality without my mind – without my imagination," he has said.[20] His works are set up in his studio, and are, literally, "stage-managed" by him – a fact that has led them to become known as "directorial photographs".[21]

Another master of the "directorial photograph" during this period was Les Krims, whose taste for the bizarre – deerslayers, dwarfs, murdered women, and naked Jewish mothers making chicken soup – made him one of the more controversial artists of the 1970s. His series *The Incredible Case of the Stack o' Wheat Murder*, for instance, a take-off on police photographs of

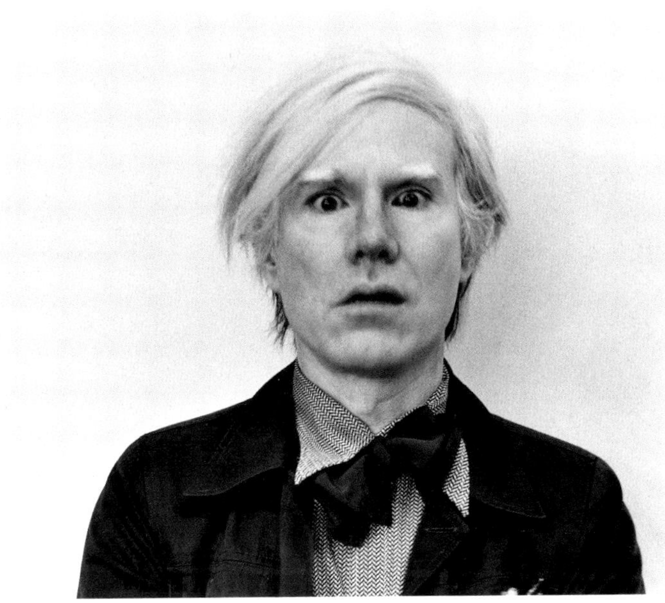

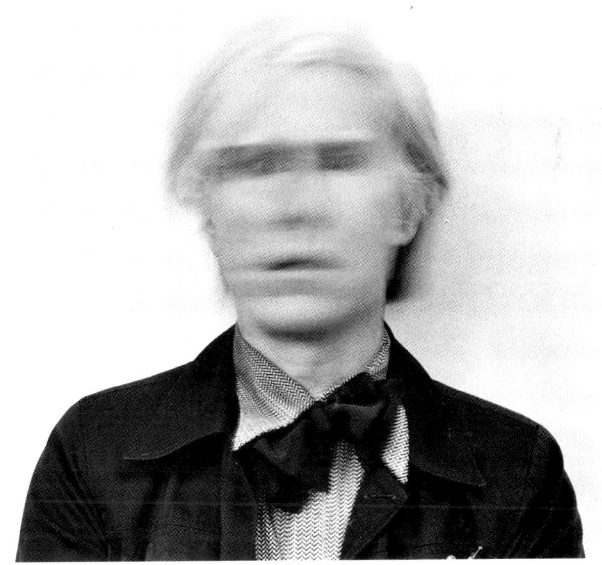

Duane Michals,
Andy Warhol,
1973.

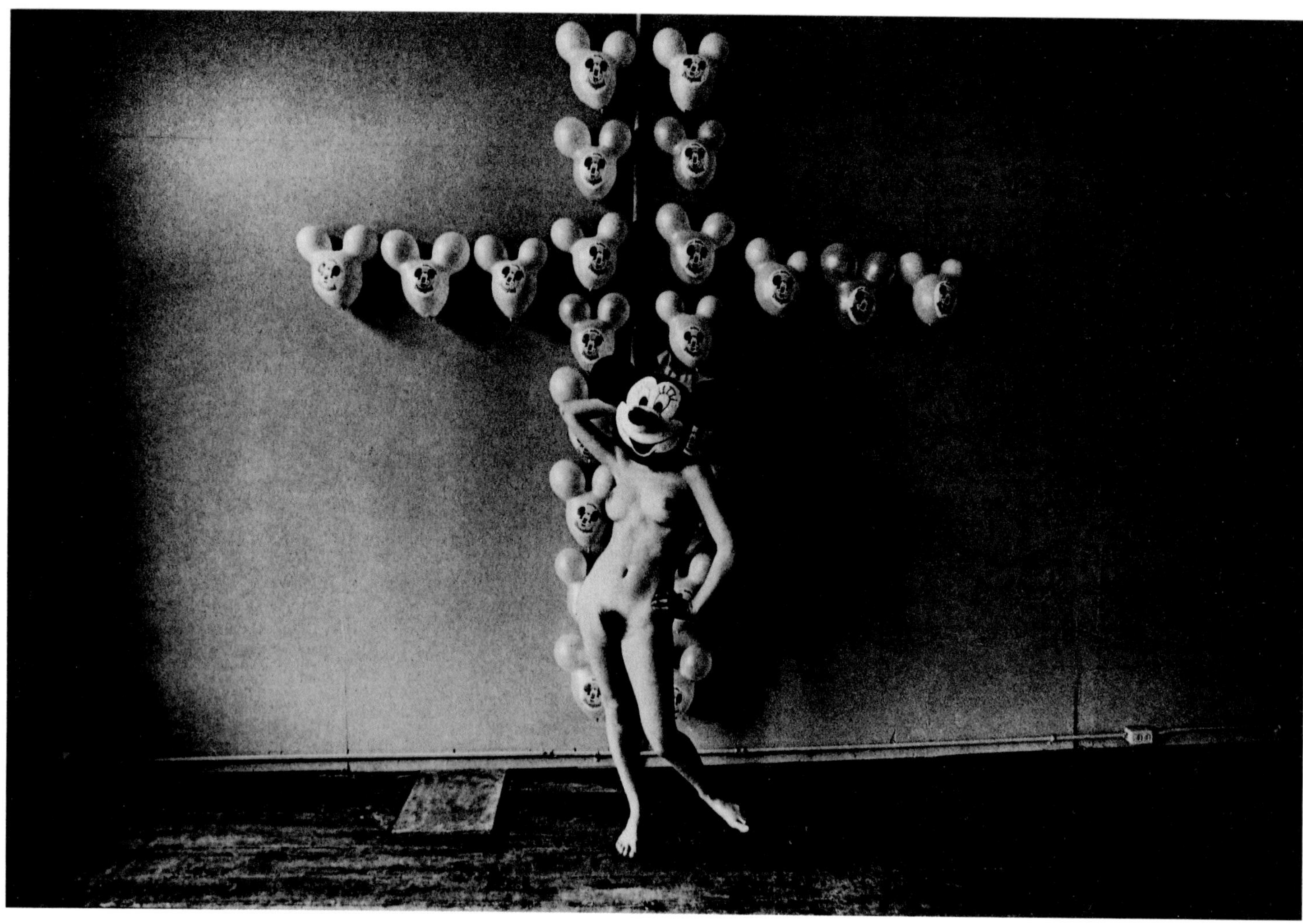

LES KRIMS,
The Electrostatic Effect,
1969,
Musée National
d'Art Moderne, Paris.

20. Duane Michals, in "This is a Real Dream", an interview by W. Jenkins. Published in *Photographers' Choice*, ed. K. Wise, New Hampshire, Addison House, 1975, p. 35.

21. A. D. Coleman, "The Directorial Mode: Notes toward a Definition", in *Light Readings*, New York, Oxford University Press, 1979, p. 246. This article, originally published in *Artforum* in 1976, was influential in defining this important but controversial type of photography in the United States.

crime sites, portrayed a series of naked women, "dead" in pools of blood next to a stack of pancakes. Selenium-toned, Krims's set-up images took on an air of unreality, almost of nostalgia. This tension between fact and fiction, between popular culture and the look of Old Master photographs, would, in the 1980s, become one of the strategies of the postmodern movement.

It would also be seminal to the works of Joel-Peter Witkin, a young photographer who is continuing, in the 1990s, to explore the domain of the mysterious. Attracted to the bizarre, like Krims and, before him, Diane Arbus, Witkin photographs transvestites, deformed people, dead fetuses, and other strange phenomena. Often placed within a religious context, surrounded by icons and reinforced by Biblical titles, the images are manipulated – in printing or on the negative – to give the look and feel of old processes, and to suggest their inherent decay. The temporal distance created by this technique, coupled with the sheer beauty of these often horrifying, pictures is one of the strengths of this body of work – and a testament that the pursuit of the mysterious continues to the present day, with the certitude that photography is qualified to express not only the tangible but also the intangible aspects of modern life.

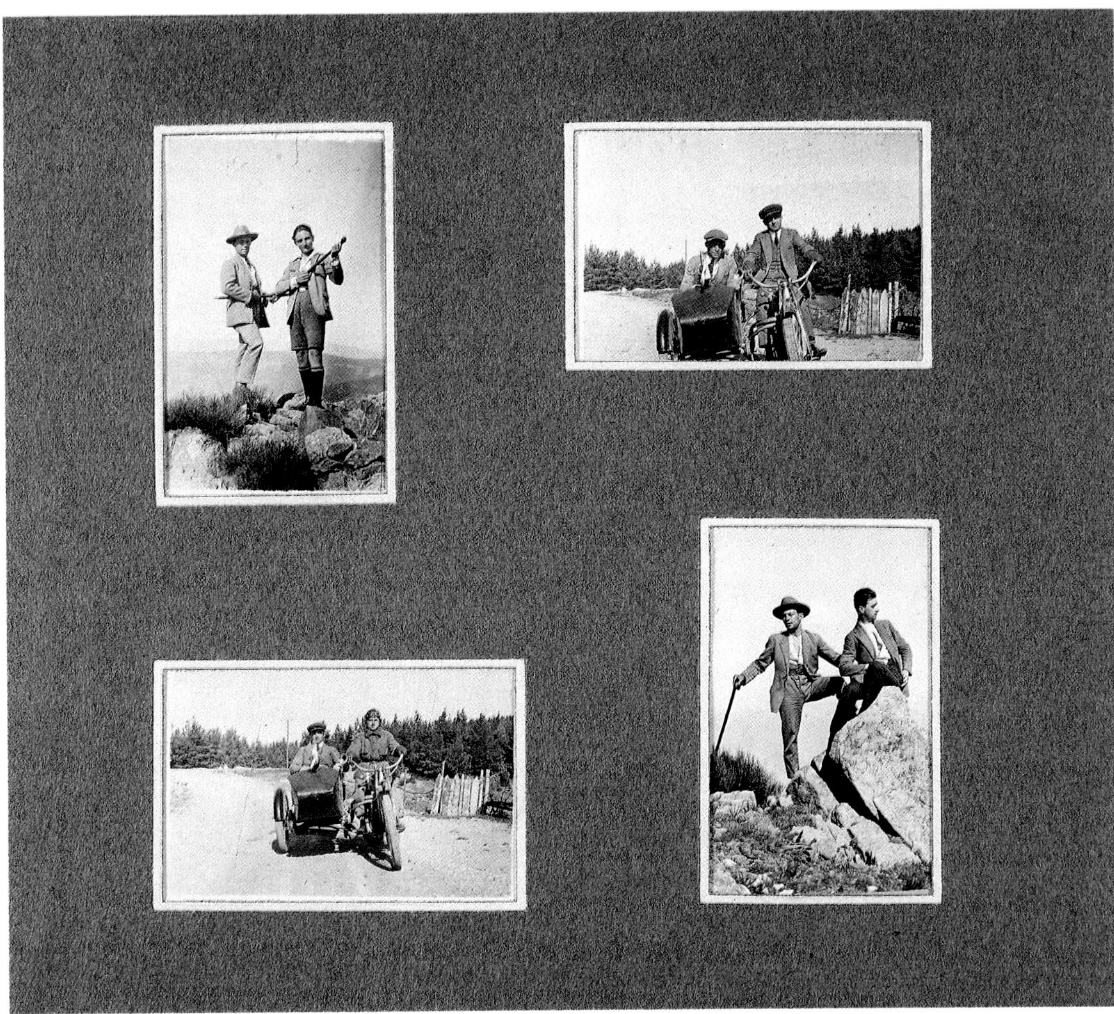

The universal album

The participation by amateurs in the practice of photography from the 1890s onwards brought about not only a new kind of photographic image but a special means of communication, the family photograph album.

It is undoubtedly wrong to see in this a continuity of the album of portrait-cards of the Second Empire, a genre which lingered on until the First World War years and which brought together portraits taken in the studio. The new album, on the other hand, was intended to present, arrange, and preserve photographs which people had taken themselves.

The vast majority of amateur photographic snapshots were destined for this kind of presentation and archiving. The notion of an organized album which was to be used in every case for the more or less systematic bringing together of private pictures was scarcely to survive the appearance of color or Polaroid photography, or the popularizing of personal photography in the 1960s.

Between 1890 and 1950, however, the amateur took photographs with their ideal final destination in mind; they would be quite standardized, the images lined up side by side to form a more or less coherent ensemble.

For this reason, amateur photographs – and the album - are not to be looked at merely for the success or beauty of individual images, but rather as a fragment of history which has rarely developed to the full, but which is left in the state of a visual sketch.

Running over a number of pages, a statement is apparent which is composed of sentimental, social or topographical elements; a story is told, more or less explicitly, more or less clearly. Layout, graphic work, the use of pages into which windows are cut to display prints or the way the photos are stuck in (usually contact prints taken directly from the negative, rather than enlargements); all these are part of a choice, an atmosphere, the very spirit of albums, some of which are laid out according to strict formal rules. Images are often chosen to match each other, without, nevertheless, respecting any sort of expected academic approach.

And even in the holiday photograph album, which takes account of an excursion or the ritual of visits to sites and monuments, ready-made images are added, finally becoming a collage of impressions.

Intended firstly for private communication, the small images from photographic albums do not have to come up to the artistic criteria of other categories of photo. They are a response to the standard working of the camera, including poor focus, errors in composition, and technical failure. It is precisely in the spontaneous surprises of practice that photographic appreciation develops, that permissive approach which allows us to accept a tilted horizon, a cut-off head, a person looking at the ground.

These types of images are obviously not in the pictorial tradition, and are certainly photography in the hands of non-experts, which exonerates them. László Moholy-Nagy, far from laughing at them, tended to regard amateur snapshots as a kind of laboratory for the production of new images.

A better knowledge of these sorts of photographic events, hitherto neglected, will allow us sooner or later to formulate an alternative, less formalized, photographic aesthetic which takes intentions and feelings into account, the working out of a visual language, preconceived associations between images.

The amateur does not have the material means to control the image in advance in the way that a professional could; what they produce above all – with their reduced, uncontrollable means – is movement, spontaneity, concordance between movements. They conjure up attitudes, inventing those highly visible – and in the viewer's eyes quite novel – displays of joy, pleasure, family life, innocence, and love, which are commonly called snapshots.

Michel Frizot

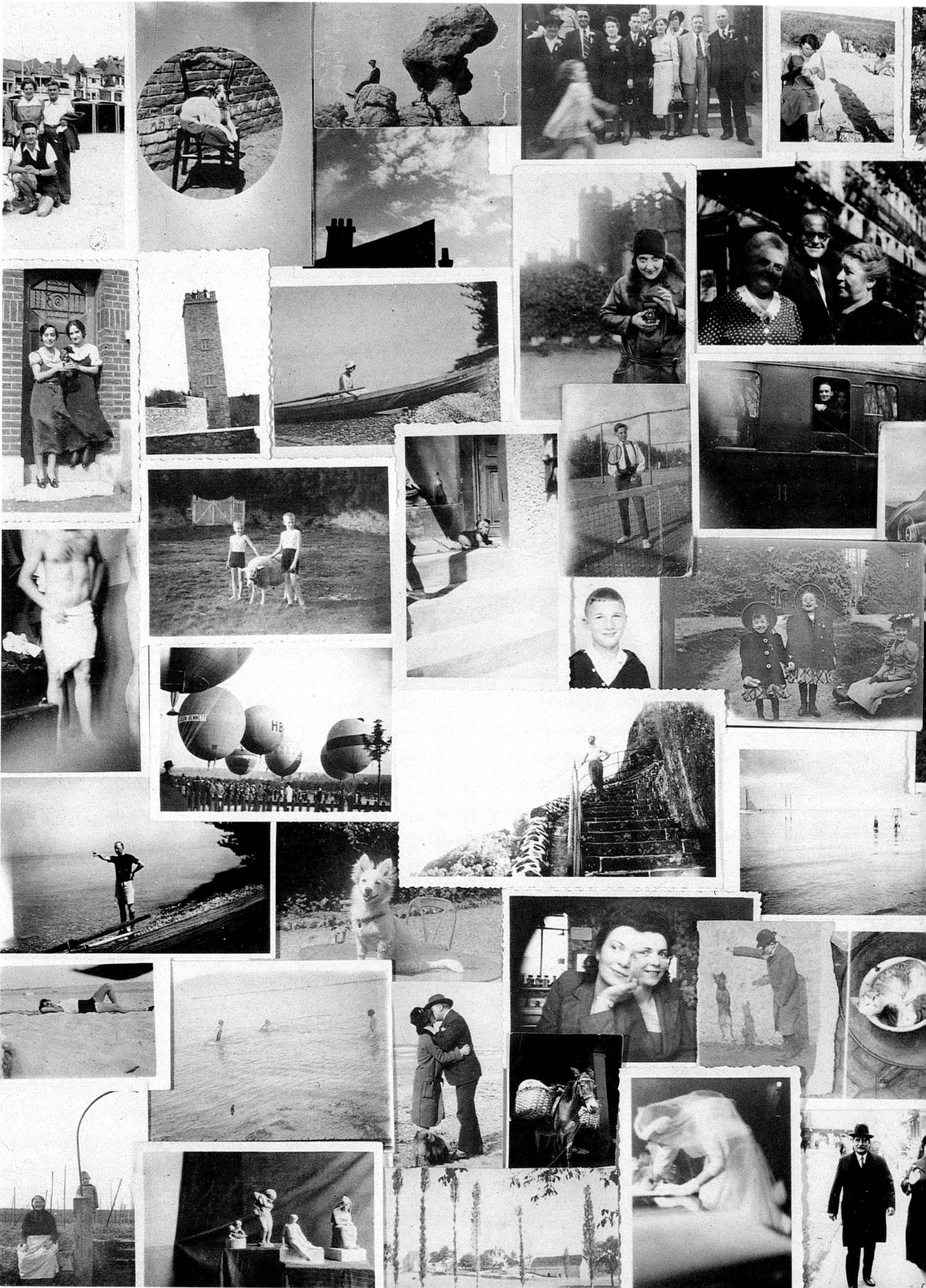
BENNETT
HB

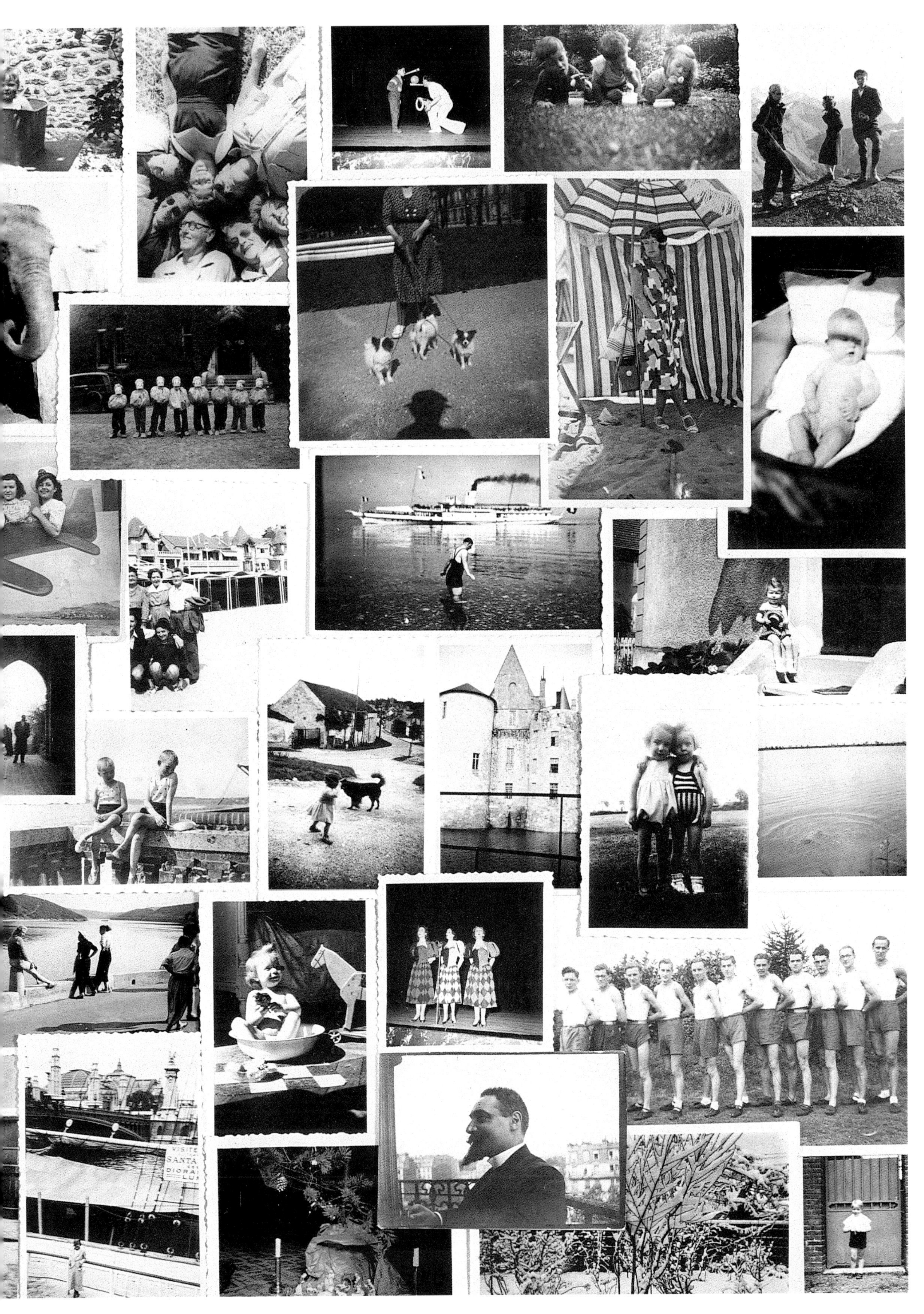
VISITE
SANTA
DIORA
LU

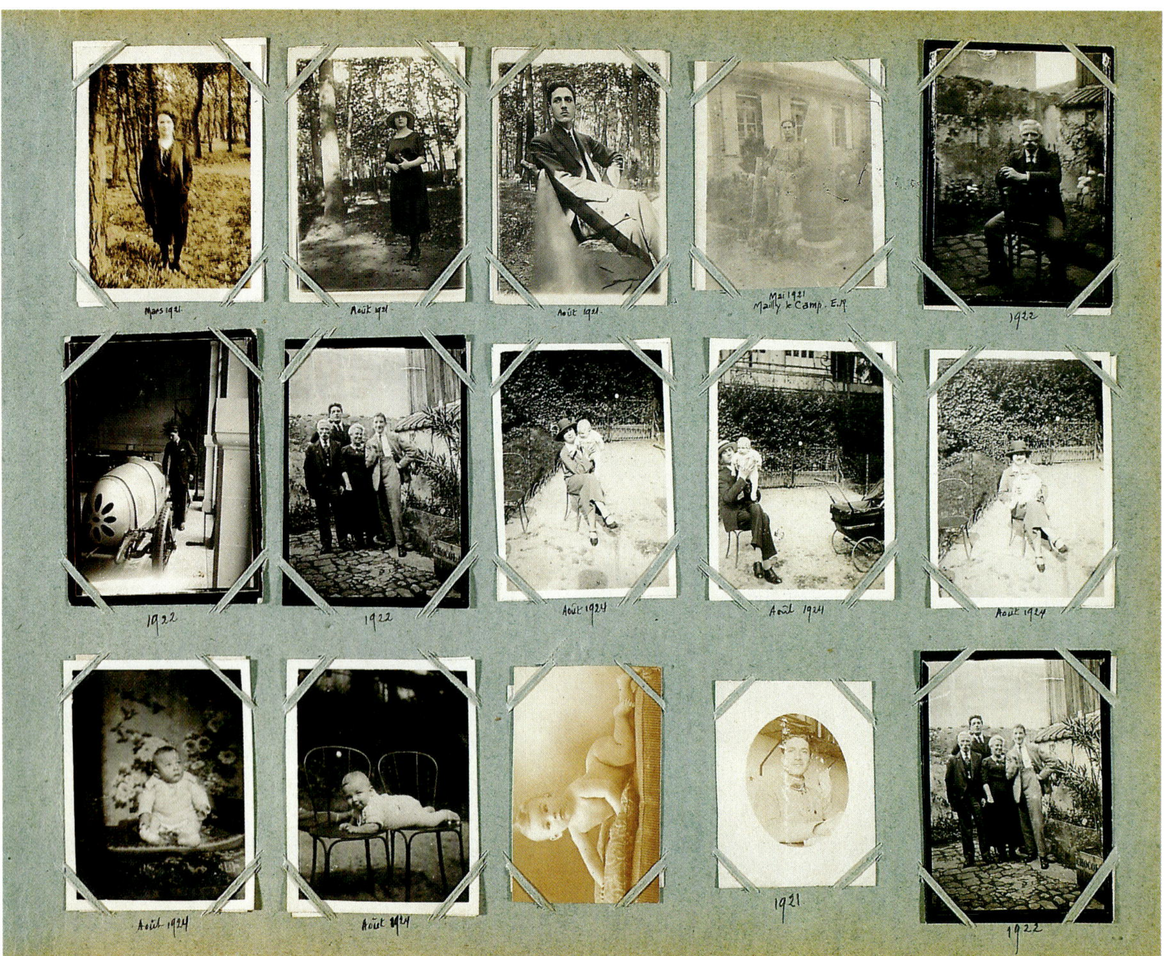

Page from an album,
France,
1921–1924,
private collection.

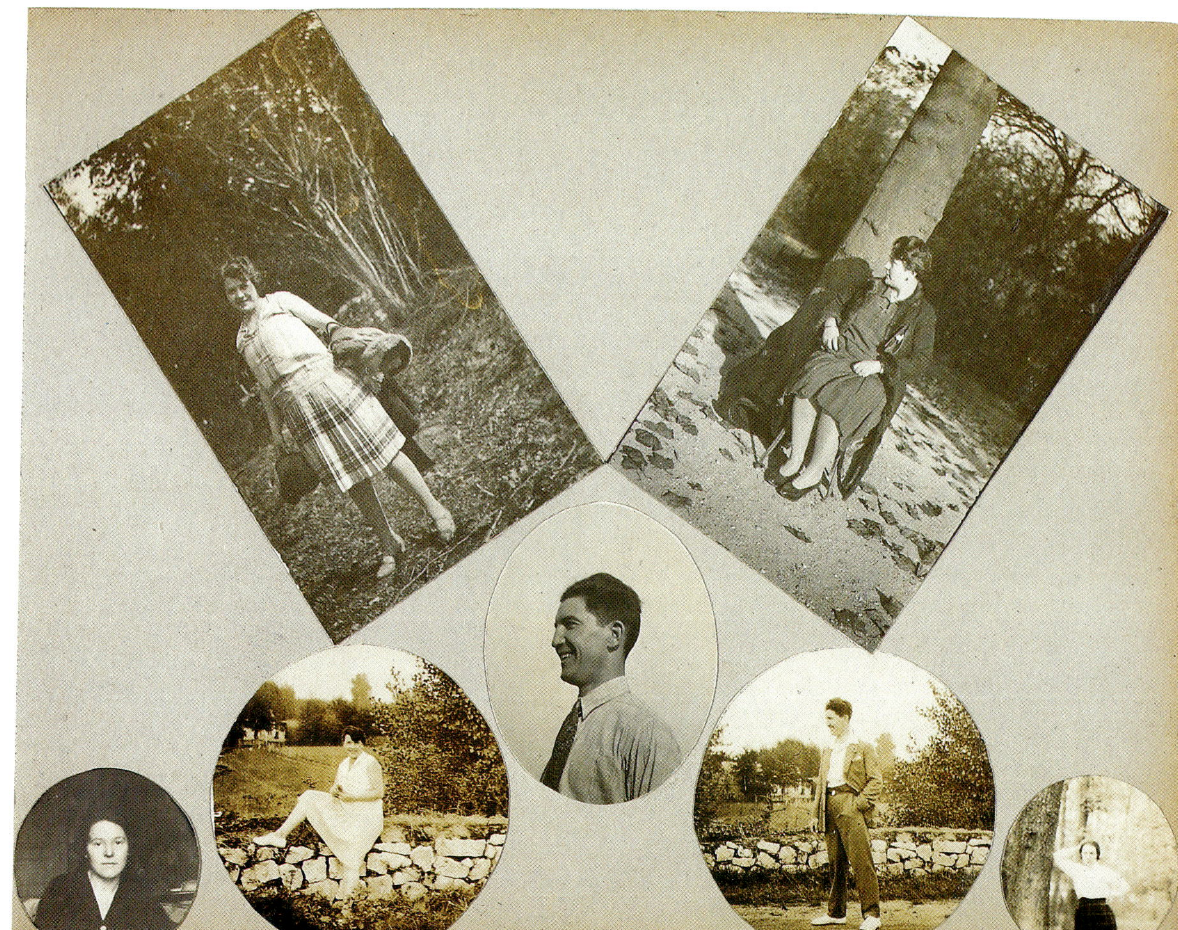

Page from an album,
France,
1930s,
private collection.

◄◄ Previous pages:
Montage of amateur snapshots,
contact prints,
France,
1920–1955,
private collection.

◄◄ Page 679:
Page from an album,
France,
1930s,
private collection.

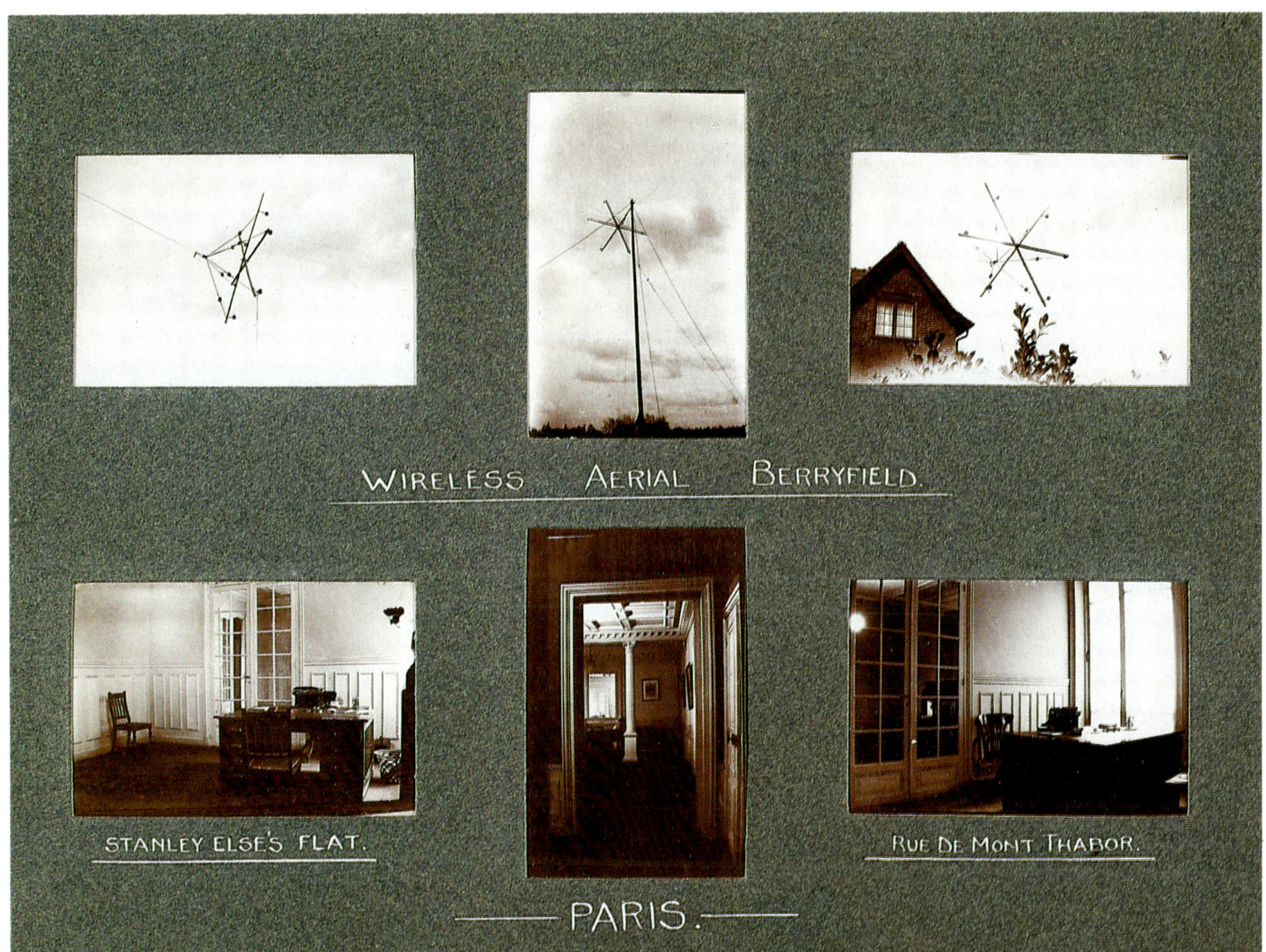

Two pages from an album, France–Britain, 1913–1917, private collection.

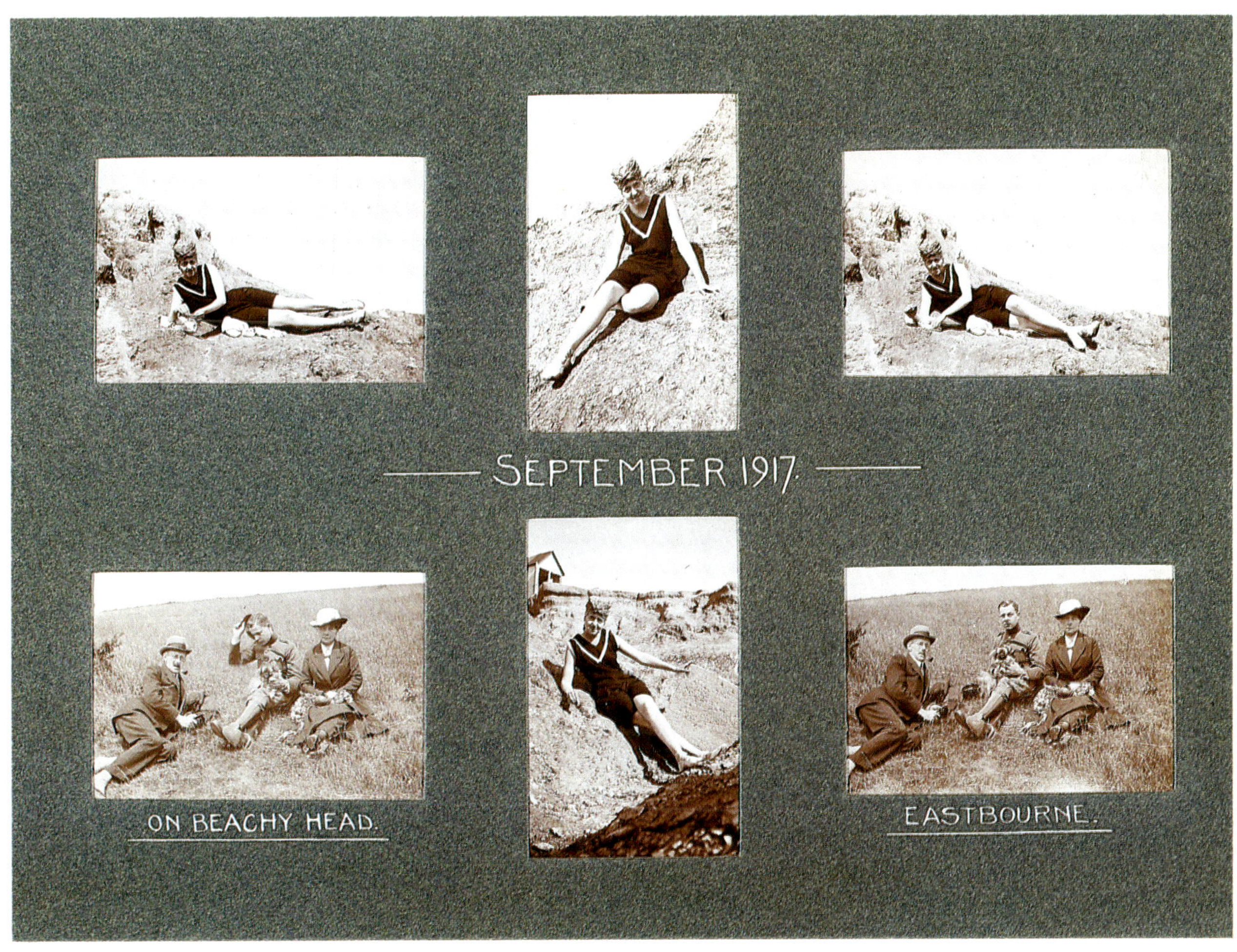

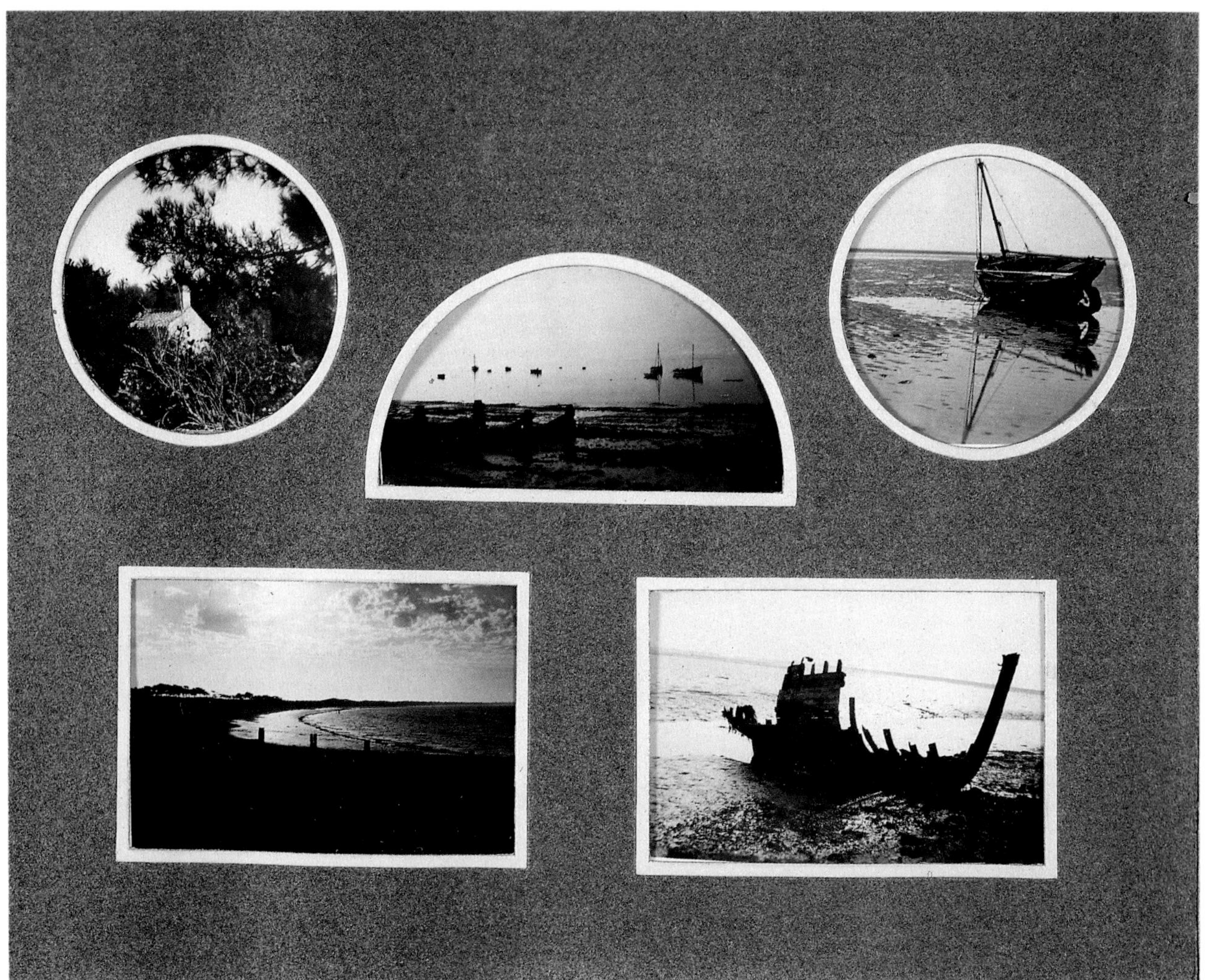

Page from an album,
France,
circa 1950,
private collection.

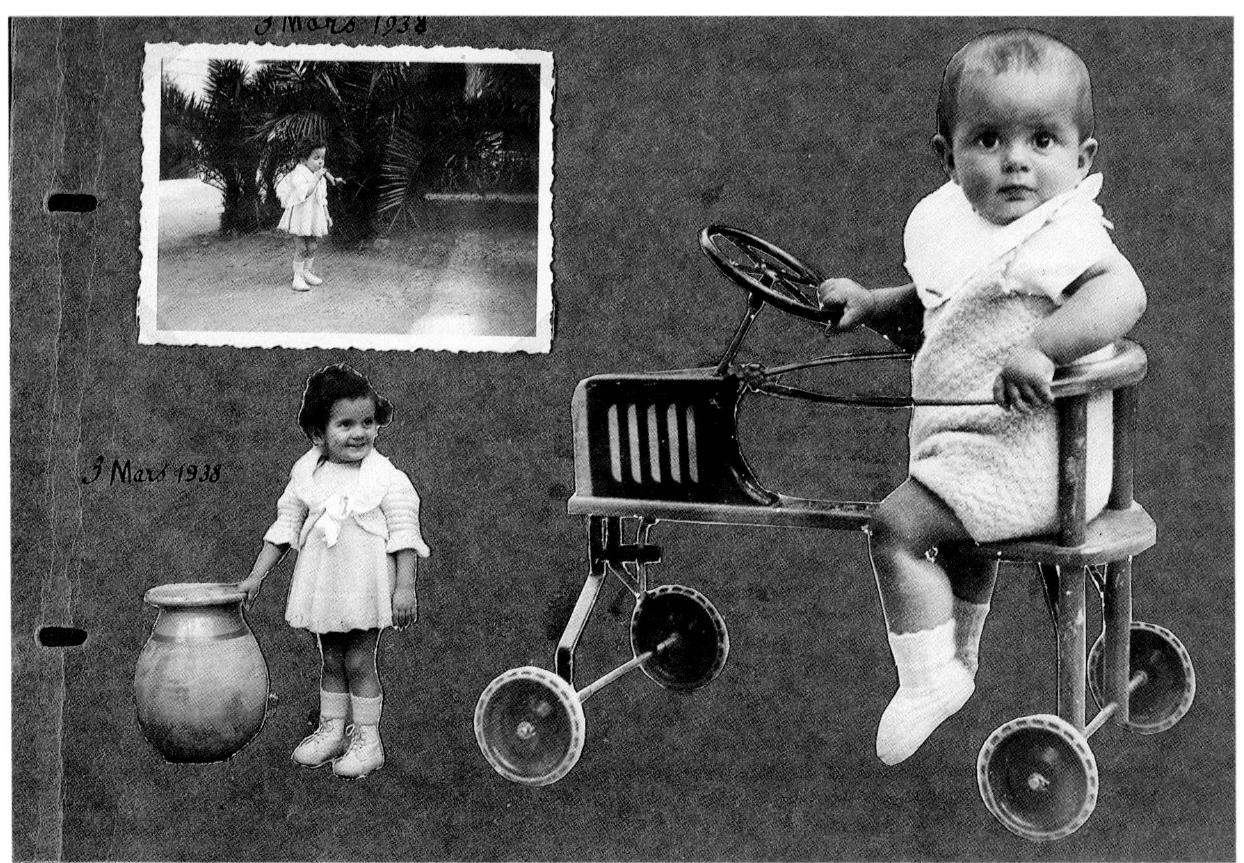

Page from an album,
France,
March 3, 1938.
private collection.

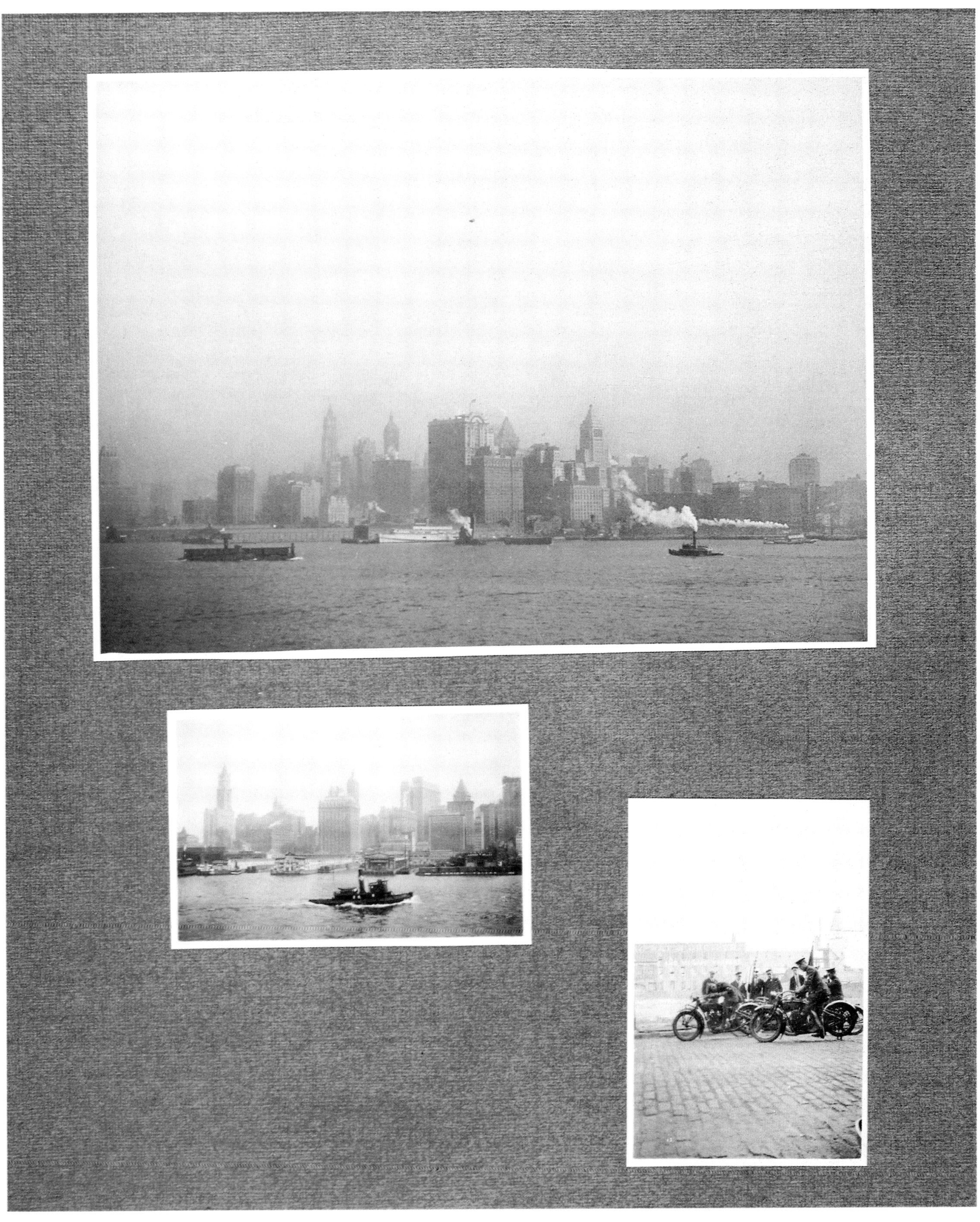

Page from an album,
United States, 1930s,
private collection.

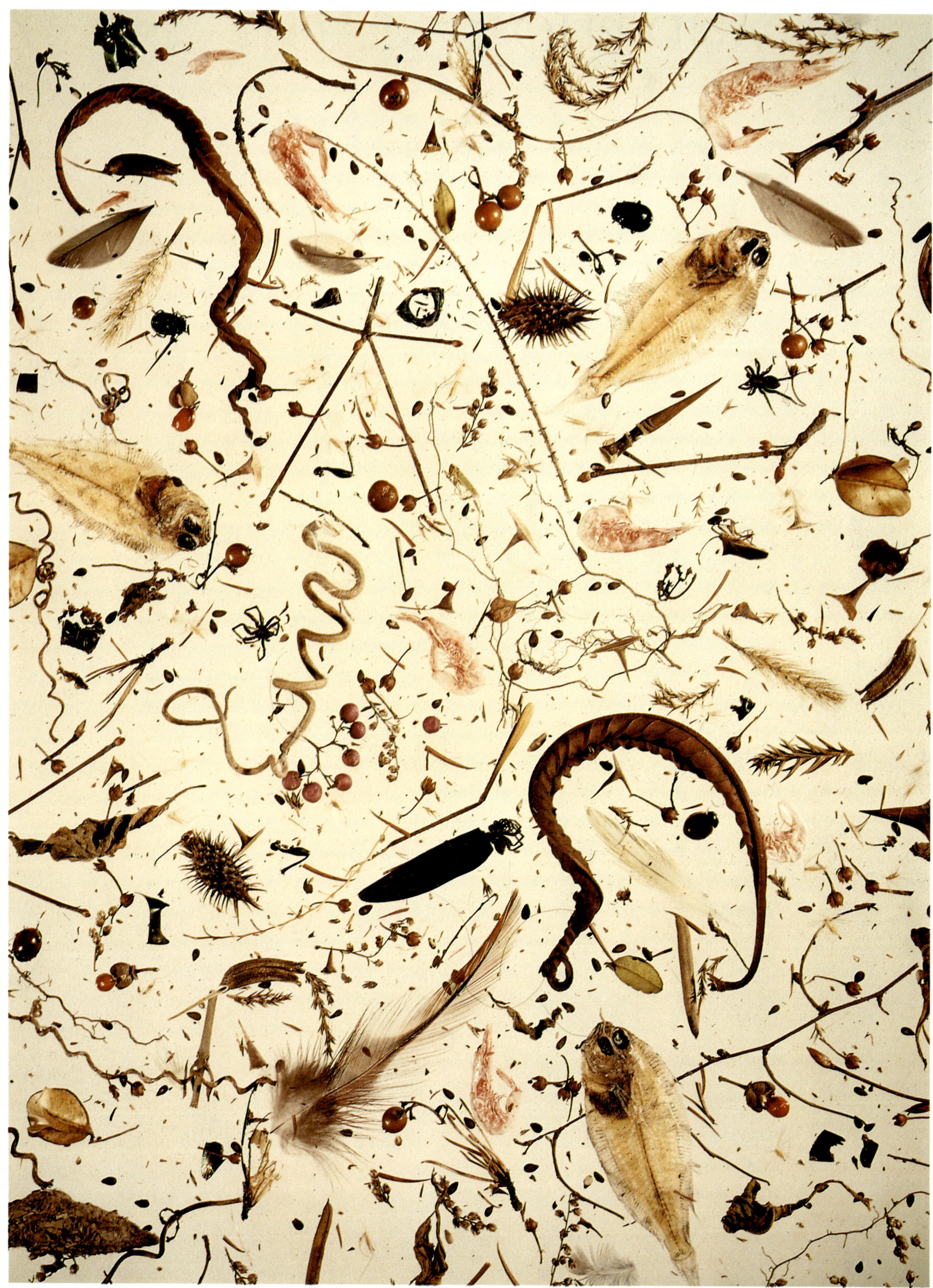

JAPAN AND PHOTOGRAPHY

In quest of the other

Chihiro Minato

Although this book is not concerned with the question of national aesthetics as such, it is, nevertheless, interesting to see how photographic techniques have passed from one country to another and to consider how each society has adapted photography to its own culture. Photography arrived in Japan in the nineteenth century as an exotic art form and an intrusive example of Western imagery, but also as a modern medium with which the country would have to come to terms. Indeed, in certain respects Japan is now "the land of photography". In this chapter we examine this dialectic of acceptance and change, conversion and invention by considering Japanese creativity as symbolic of the disorganized metamorphosis of photography in one particular society and of the issues which modern humanity must consider.

Before examining Japanese photography in the context of the world wide development of the medium, we should place it in its historical context. Everyone knows that photography was a technique imported from Europe in the nineteenth century. However, it is not generally appreciated that European art history was also introduced to Japan at the same time. Since the Renaissance, a tradition of portraiture had existed in Europe, in the light of which photography appeared as a technical and scientific accomplishment. However, the key point is that portraiture and photography were introduced into Japan at the same time.

In a very short space of time Japan had to assimilate four centuries of artistic evolution, at the end of which photography had demolished perspective, that European invention, while integrating it into its own history.

All this must be set in the context of a massive influx of European culture into Japanese society from the end of the nineteenth century. In the case of photography this historical problem became more and more superficial after the period when photographic techniques had been acquired.

Finally, the period when modern photography developed, during the late 1920s and 1930s, was one when Japanese photographers began to become fully conscious of their own specific problems.[1]

The birth of modern photography

From the end of the Meiji period, and during that of Taisho, numerous photographic clubs appeared in Japan. "Artistic photography", usually known as Pictorialism, developed mainly around Shinzo Fukuhara, the theorist and technical photographer, then Yasuzo Nojima, the pioneer of modern photography. From the 1920s, magazines specializing in art photography appeared. However, when one considers that, at the same time, the magazine *Camera Work* had

◄ Shomei Tomatsu, *Untitled,* from the series *Gardens of Ruins,* 1964.

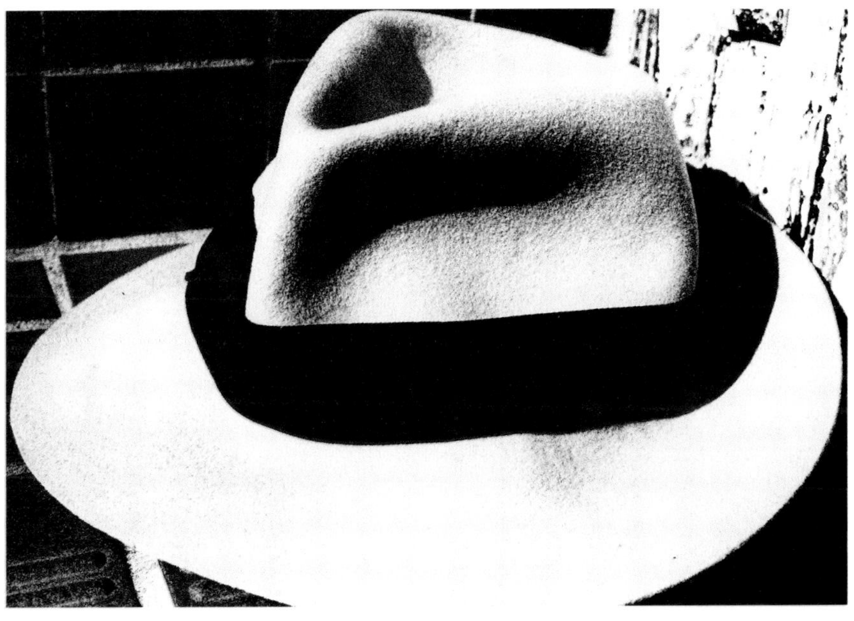

Daido Moriyama, *Light and Shade,* 1982.

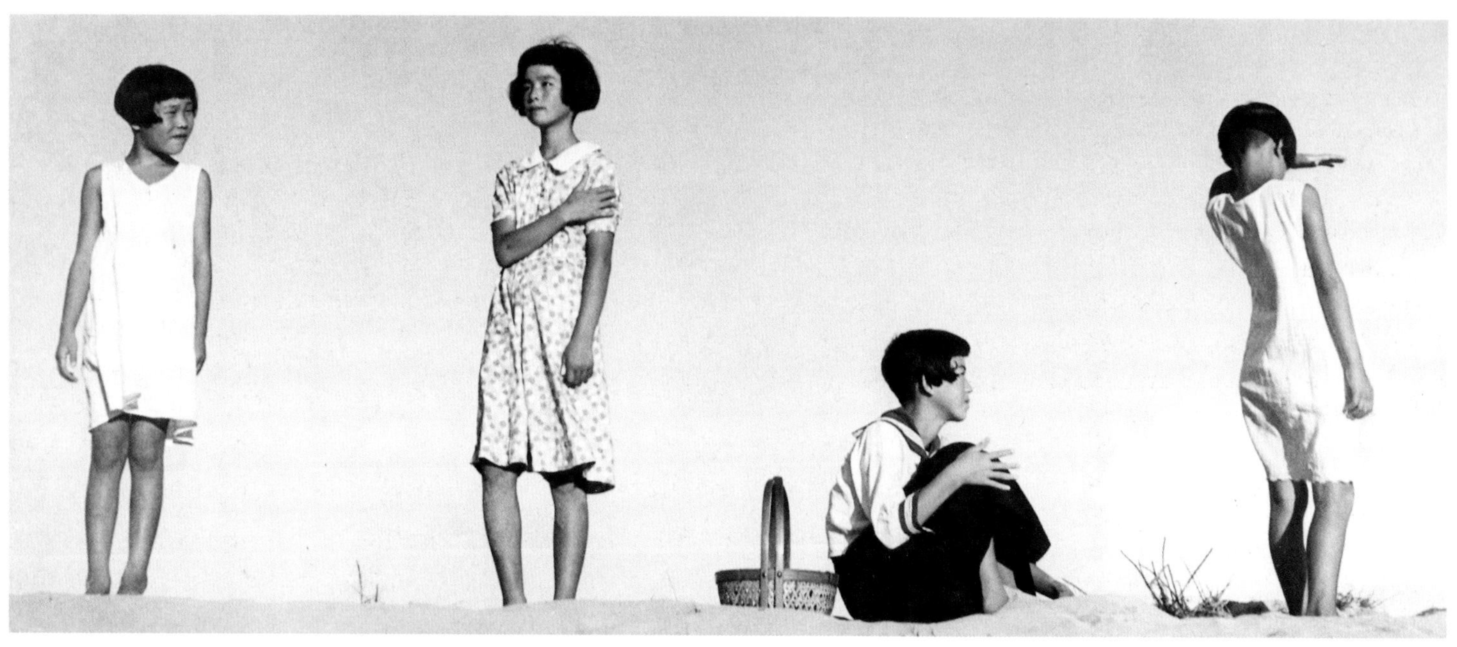

SHOJI UEDA,
Four Figures,
1939,
Kawasaki City Museum.

YASUZO NOJIMA,
1931,
National Museum
of Modern Art, Kyoto.
▼

already ceased to exist, it is obvious that the development of Japanese Pictorialism lagged behind that of Europe and the United States by a good twenty years. Even in Japan, Pictorialism soon lost its influence after 1925, when contemporary fashion encouraged new forms of expression. The turning-point marking this new epoch occurred at the time of the great Kantô earthquake, which struck Tokyo with full force on September 1, 1923.

This earthquake transformed the town into a heap of ruins. It was just about at this time that real Japanese graphic journalism first appeared. Tokyo was born again in the form of an entirely modern town, using new materials such as iron and concrete. Modern forms of popular culture, represented by cinemas and theatres, flooded the capital. Photographers also were keenly aware of this transformation and tried to create an original art form starting in this city which was changing every day.

At that time, the German avant-garde movement was exercising an important artistic influence. The international exhibition "Film und Foto", organized in 1929 in Stuttgart and seen in 1931 in Tokyo and Osaka, opened up new perspectives not only in photography, but also in art, architecture, and design. The photography magazine *Koga* was published in Tokyo the year after the disaster, and was centered around Yasuko Nojima, Iwata Nakayama, Ihei Kiumura, and Nobuo Ina. The magazine not only featured the work of these photographers but also contained a large number of articles and translations of theoretical accounts, notably about the photography of Moholy-Nagy and Franz Roh. In an essay entitled *Let's Get Back to Photography!*, Nobuo Ina denounced "artistic photography" and tried to encourage the setting up of an aesthetic which would be restricted to photography alone, based on the technical characteristics of cameras.

This article may be considered as the manifesto of modern Japanese photography, insofar as the author affirms that the photographer must become a "social man" who records, interprets, and criticizes society and nature, using to this end "real photography" which would bring together all the means of expression of the German avant-garde, such as the "new objectivity" and photomontage.

At first, Nojima was a Pictorialist, but he began to find an original expression from the time he took over the magazine *Koga*. Looking at his nudes, it is immediately obvious that although he was influenced by the avant-garde movement, he differed from it through the erotic element present in his work. His approach was doubly

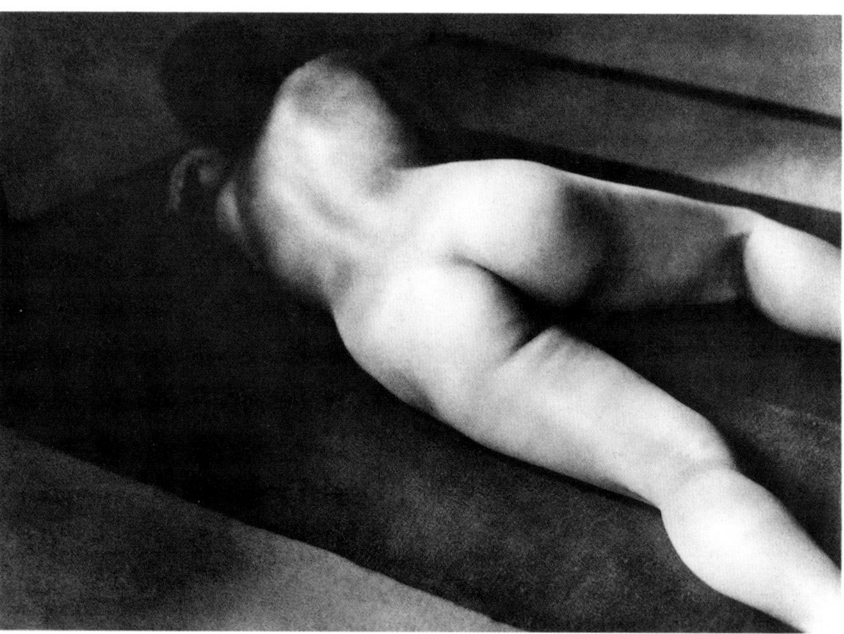

1. For more on this subject, see *New Japanese Photography*, Museum of Modern Art, New York, 1974; *Neue Fotographie aus Japan*, Graz, Kulturhaus, 1977; *History of Japanese Photography*, Tokyo, Heibonsha, 1979; and *The Complete History of Japanese Photography*, 12 vols., Tokyo, Shogakukan, 1986.

2. *Shoka Sinkei*, [Sensitivity at the Beginning of Summer] remains his major work.

innovative because he photographed the naked bodies of women at a time when the European artistic tradition of the nude was unknown to Japanese society. In the center of the modern town, seething with new desires, Nojima succeeded in imposing a woman's body as the symbol of a Japanese society in full evolution.

Unlike the first half of the 1930s, when *Koga* was directly influenced by the German avant-garde, the following years saw the arrival of new forms of expression, thanks to photographers in the Kansai region (Osaka and Hyogo) who were influenced by Surrealism and abstract expressionism. The most important were Nakaji Yasui and Kiyoshi Koishi, whose series *Hansekai* – in which he showed a skilful mastery of all kinds of techniques to liberate his poetic imagination in a radical way – shows the extent to which he had detached himself from the avant-garde in order to enter his own inner world.[2] As for Shoji Ueda, by taking as his theme the dunes of Tottori, he forged a unique style, with an idiosyncratic sense of perspective.

Similarly, Yasui was also strongly influenced by European modernism. He, however, completely assimilated it and stood out from other photographers, especially through his way of using photography's objectivity. His characteristic distinctive style comes from the broad range of his subject matter. Whether it involved nature, a social event or some quite different subject, Yasui always found a personal aesthetic. Most astonishing is his freedom of vision, which is never constrained by the European subject/object or art/nature duality. In this respect, it is significant that Yasui often used to quote Basho's mastery of the haiku verse form. This is because his originality lay in intuitively bringing together the object and his own personality, to bring out its symbolic character.[3]

There can be no doubt that, with Nojima, Yasui contributed to the formation of modern photography in Japan by seeking through the mechanical process of photography a sensitivity peculiar to the Japanese. Even though European photographic techniques were transplanted into Japan without modification, the Japanese were able to adapt them to suit their own "language". Furthermore, Yasui and Nojima's photographs show how both of them used photography as a new tool in order to become conscious of the world, and how they began to use themselves as their subject matter.

Both of them tried to regard themselves as Japanese, as soon as this point of view was made possible through photography. Thus, they came to encapsulate modern human relationships between the self and the other through the intermediary of their photographic subjects. However, their unprecedented work would soon be forcibly interrupted as in this period. The world was rapidly moving towards war. Yasui died at the early age of thirty-seven, and so the golden age of Japanese photography lasted for only a short time.

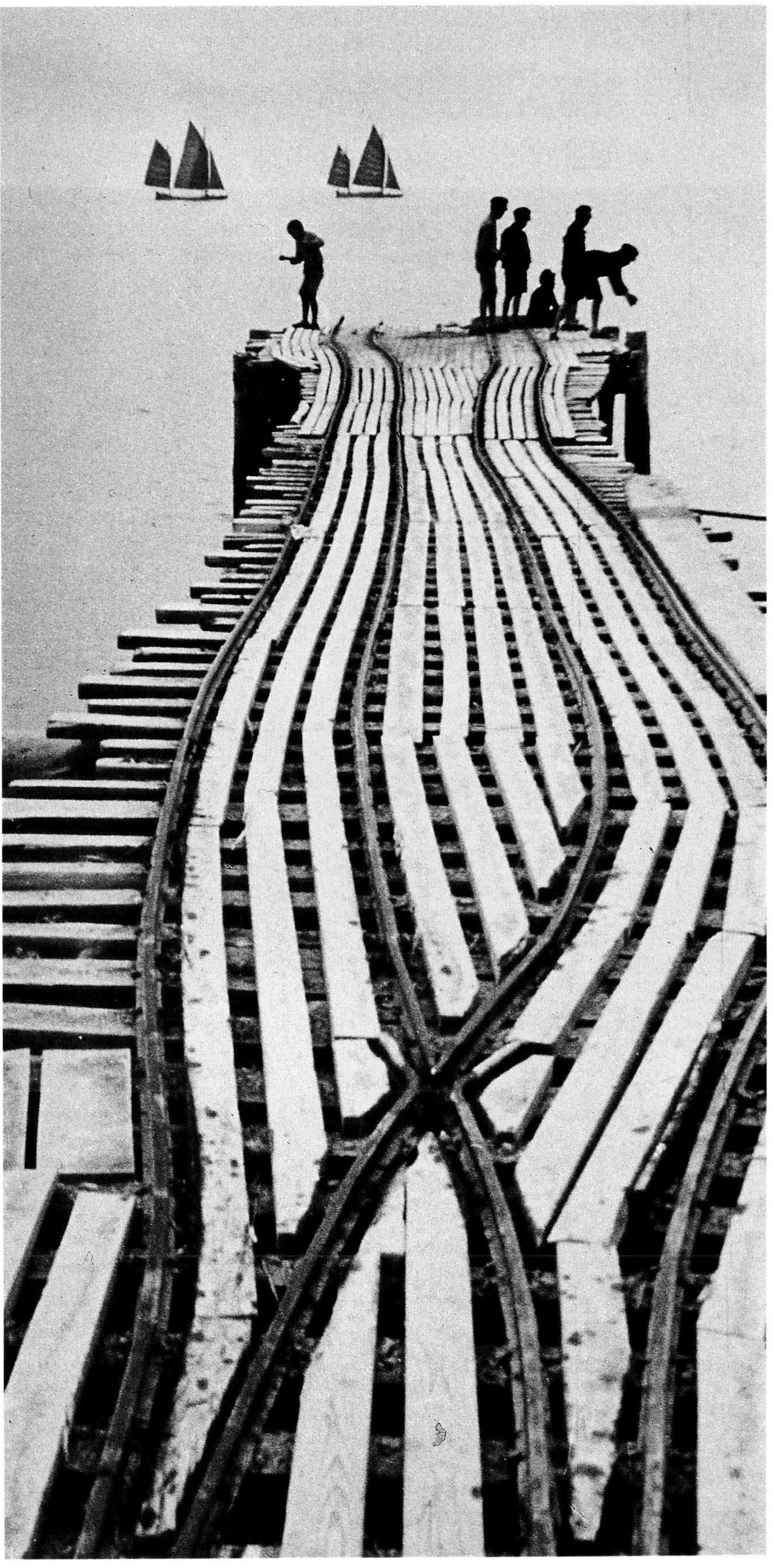

NAKAJI YASUI,
Pier,
1938,
Hyogo Prefectural Museum of Modern Art.

3. "Nakaji Yasui et les années 30", *Déjà-Vu*, no. 12, 1993.

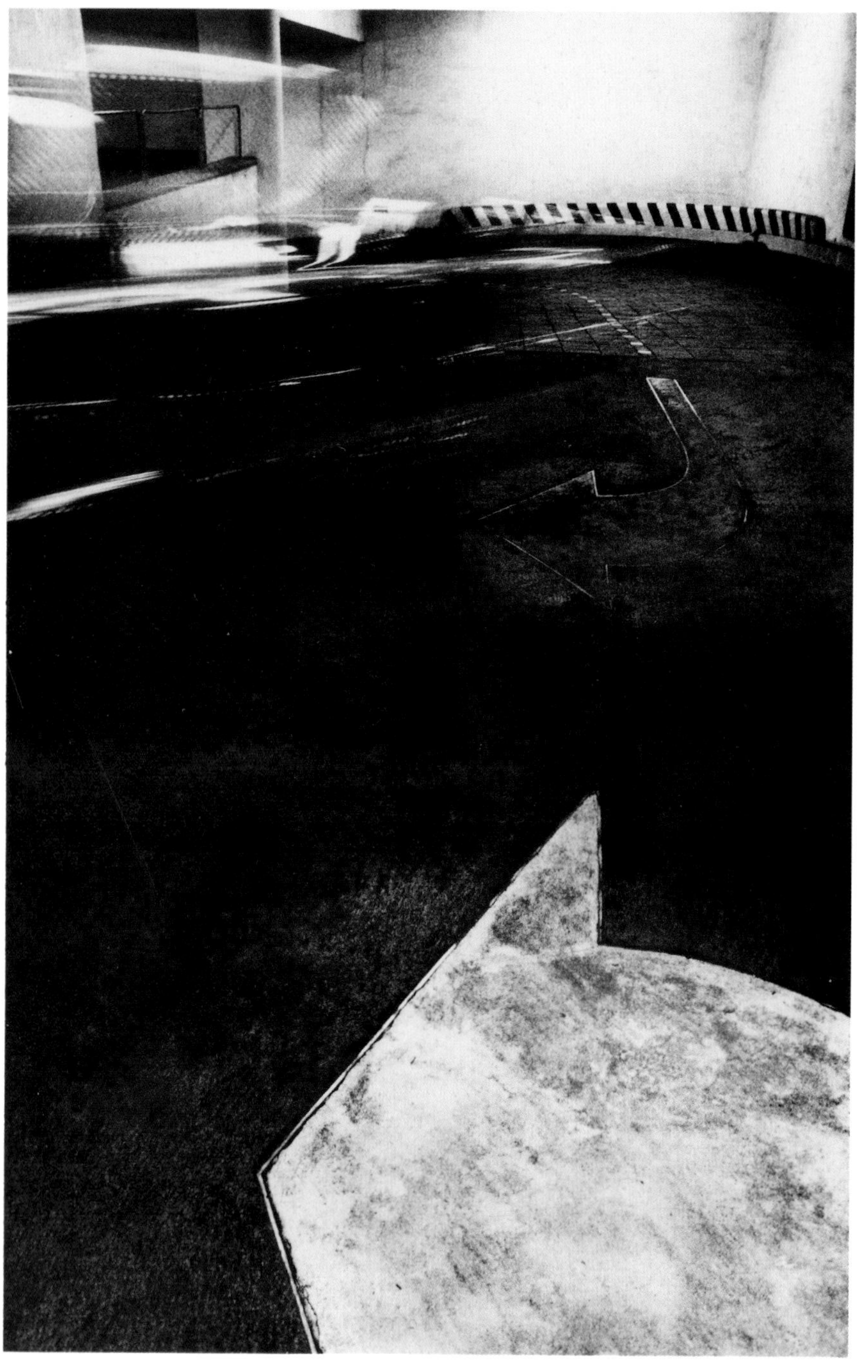

SHOMEI TOMATSU, *Car Park,* 1962, from the series *I am a King,* 1959–1969.

Photojournalism and the Vivo agency

Ihei Kimura, a member of *Koga,* was already taking "instantaneous" photographs from the early 1930s thanks to the Leica camera. However, in around 1935, when photo magazines were first making their appearance, true photographic reporters emerged such as Ken Domon, Hiroshi Hamaya, and, of course, Kimura. Kimura was undoubtedly responsible for inventing a new way of seeing – that of the city-dweller always on the move. However, all those photographers who focused on real life by using a miniature camera as an extension of their bodies fully embodied the "social man" that Ina had proclaimed.

The Second World War transformed Tokyo into a wasteland once again. Photographers, once freed from the censorship, discovered in the homeless people wandering through the ruins as far as the eye could see, a sight which contrasted starkly with pre-war prosperity. Tadahiko Hayashi's series showing the population working to rebuild their lives is typical of the re-emergence of photographers who observed the rebirth of life in the midst of the ruins.

During the 1950s, Ken Domon, inaugurating the "realist movement" in photography magazines, exercised a great influence on amateur photographers. Domon refused to be influenced by ideologists and tried to record social reality by basing his work on the camera's objectivity – a point of view which he undoubtedly developed as a result of his participation in the peasant movement.[4] But post-war Japanese society had already become so complex that it could no longer be captured by such simple methods. The peasants and citydwellers were beginning to confront each other. Hamaya never stopped taking geographical or folklore photographs, but to these were added a "historical" and "climatological" dimension of timeless character. His works are the result of his research into the relationship between man and his environment.[5] Japan had experienced brutal changes since the country opened up to the West, and Hamaya tried to observe what had or had not changed, in the life of peasant villages rather than in that of the citydwellers.

All these photographers had begun their work before the war. However, during the 1950s a new generation who had started photographing after the war became influential. They were characterized particularly by the growing influence of American photography, and by a subjective, if not personal, view of reality. Their leaders were the six members of the independent agency Vivo: Ikho Narahara, Eikoh Hosoe, Shomei Tomatsu, Kikuji Kawada, Akira Tanno, and Akira Sato. Even though each of these photographers possessed an individual personality and a different way of expressing themselves, the fact that they formed an organized group demonstrates clearly that mass journalism and commercial influences had caused an upheaval in the previous self-governing world of photographers.

At this time, the Japanese economy was just entering a phase of rapid growth. With the construction of highways, penetrating right into the heart of towns and cities, the number of private automobiles grew considerably, and the first signs of pollution began to appear. It is significant that *Ningen no tochi,* the work which marks the appearance of Narahara, is a documen-

4. With this engaged realism, Domon also worked on Buddhist and traditional art: *The Complete Works of Ken Domon,* 13 vols., Tokyo, Shogakukan, 1983.

5. Hiroshi Hamaya, *Fifty Years of Photography,* Yokyo, Iwanomishoten, 1981.

tary series on the artificial island of Gunkanjima, which was initially reserved for coal-mining. It is precisely because this island, located in Nagasaki Bay, had become an over-populated town and a symbol of the Japanese economic boom, before becoming rapidly depopulated and reduced to a state of ruin after World War II, that it provided a microcosm of modern Japan. Narahara considered it from a highly individual viewpoint. Rejecting abstract concepts such as history, society or the state, his choice of a simple approach which considered photography as a way of seeing which allowed a degree of personal interpretation directly provided the opportunity for the creation of Vivo.

The confrontation between students and police during the 1960s over the renewal of the Japan-United States defense treaty marked a turning-point in post-war renewal. The period of reconstruction had already ended, and the time had come for a gigantic – even fanatic – program of urban construction, unprecedented in scale. By 1962, with ten million inhabitants, Tokyo had become the most populated city in the world. Land development took place on a vast scale, and the life-style of the Japanese changed radically. Shigeichi Nagano remained heedful of this transformation. His powerful images transmit a strong message, and the documentary activity which he continues to the present day maintains an incomparable intensity, even against the background of dizzying change. As for Yasuhiro Ishimoto, he maintains the tradition of architectural photography in Tokyo at this time.

Such sudden urban and industrial development compelled the Japanese people to pay attention to the immediate present. Everything else was forgotten; yesterday's defeat was never mentioned; there was no time to reflect on the consequences of the war. Among the first to recognize the dangers of this collective amnesia and to attempt to reconsider the real situation of the country were Kawada with *Chizu* and Tomatsu with his *Nagasaki*. They pointed their lenses towards the shadows of forgetfulness, as if searching for the radiation which annihilated Hiroshima and Nagasaki, even though nothing could now be seen because everything was concealed beneath the superficial layers of the new town. Both of them took ruins as their subject, but not with the aim of bringing back the past or in chronicling it. What they saw, while imprinting on it their own feelings in the form of a mark or symbol, were the ruins which exist today – ruins which they sought out in the demolition and reconstruction being carried out by bulldozers working at top speed and, more generally, in the frenzied daily life of the Japanese.

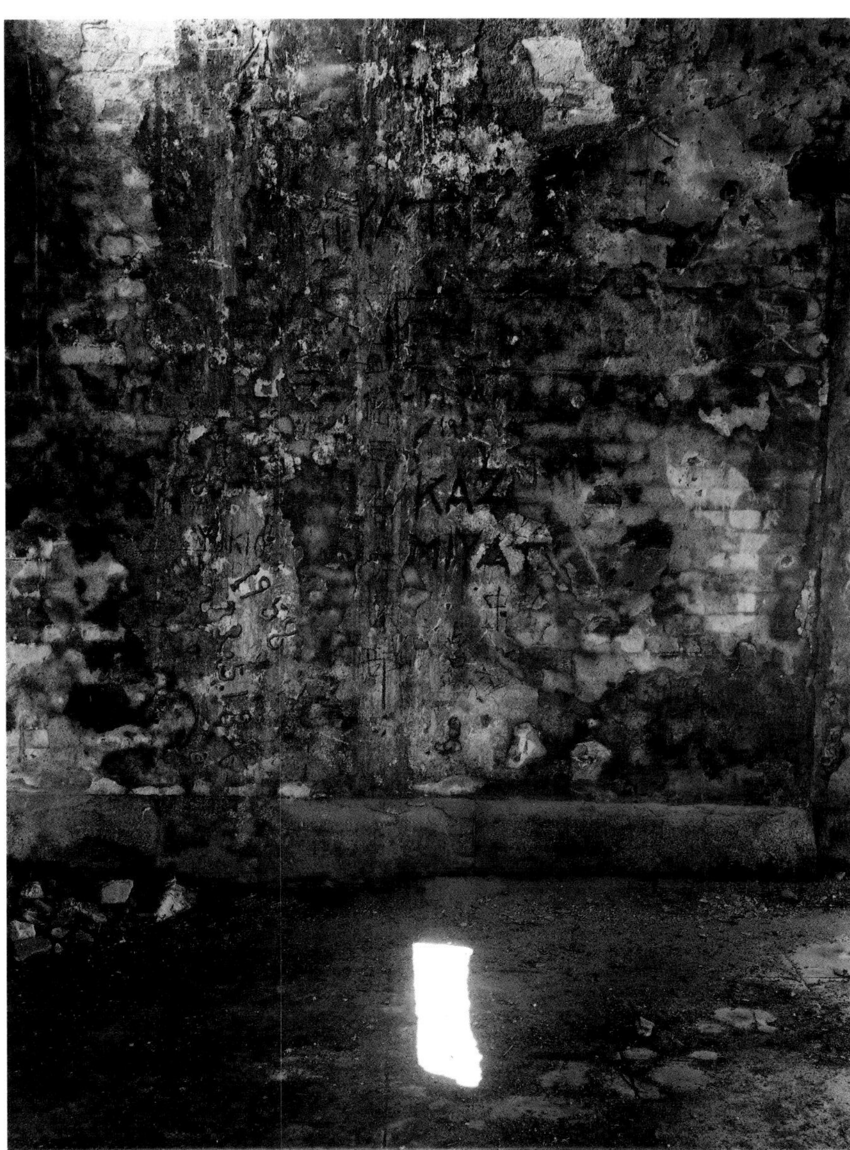

KIKUJI KAWADA,
Graffiti on a Wall of the Atomic Dome, Hiroshima,
Map series, 1960–1965.

These ruins corresponded to those in the Tokyo countryside which William Klein was photographing at the same time. The same thing is apparent in the beauty of the convulsed bodies which Hosoe was photographing.[6] The human body was indeed in danger, as Mishima's suicide demonstrated in 1970, torn between his Japanese ego and a society which was sliding into anonymity and forgetfulness.

This ultra-fine sensitivity towards the subject and the deep sense of detachment which is to be found in these photographs may, perhaps, be considered as the culmination of modern Japanese photography that had first appeared in the 1930s. In particular, an approach which consisted of transforming everyday subjects into powerful symbolic images was brought to perfection by Tomatsu. His photographs provide a powerful incentive to confront social reality, and his consistent openness towards others, through the medium of photography, means that he exercised a great influence on young photographers.[7]

6. Eikoh Hosoe, *Ordeal by Roses* (with Yukio Mishima), Tokyo, Sueisha, 1984; *Universe of Gaudí*, Tokyo, Sueisha, 1984.

7. *The Pencil of the Sun*, Tokyo, Manichi-Shinbunsha, 1975; *Ruins*, Tokyo, Parco Publishing, 1987.

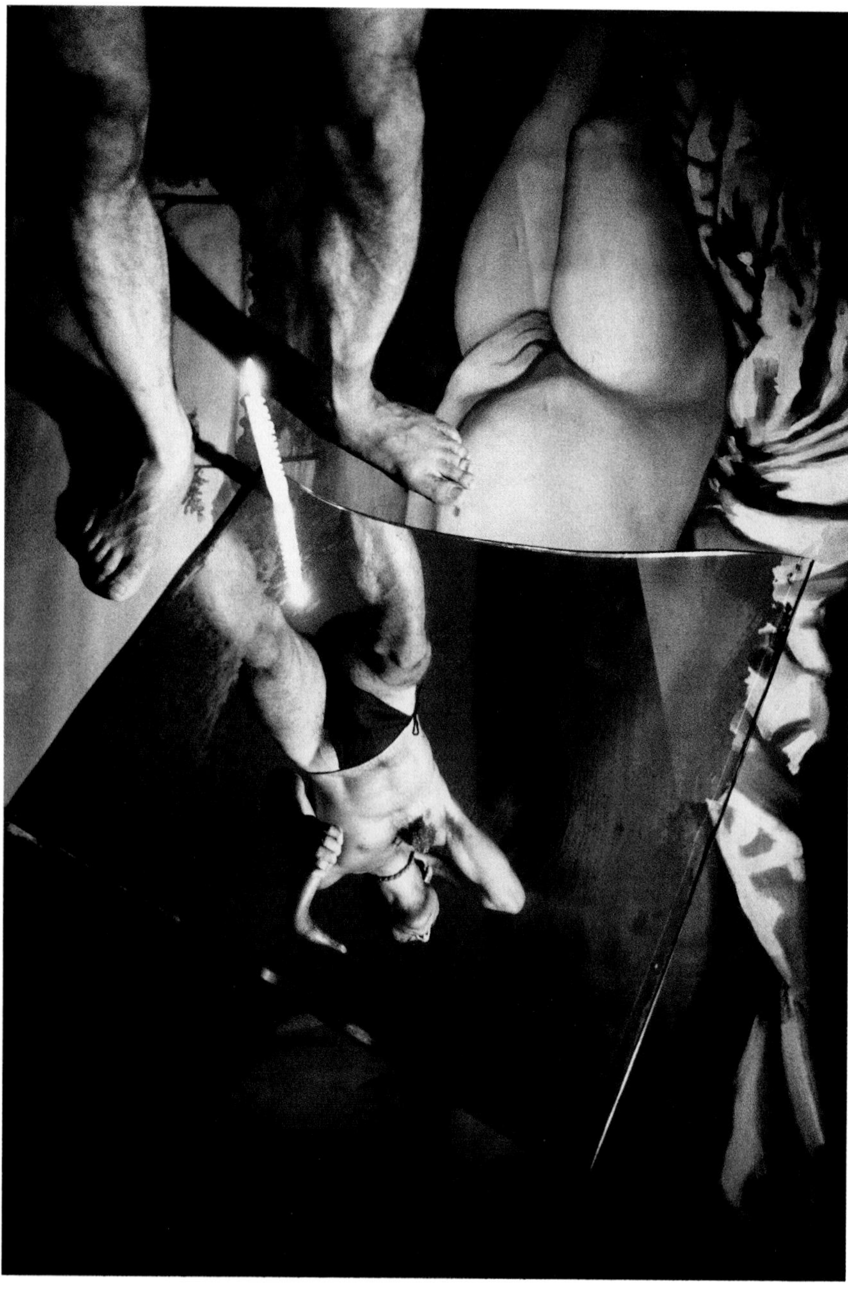

Eikoh Hosoe,
Barakei No. 18,
from the series
Ordeal by Roses,
with Yukio Mishima,
1961–1962.

Assumed diversification

At the beginning of this chapter we mentioned the difficulties which Japan encountered when photography was first introduced – difficulties which appear in the Japanese word for photography, *shashin* [to draw truth]. Because artistic realism and photography arrived in Japan practically simultaneously, many authors felt obliged to reflect on the essential significance of representation by publishing theoretical studies. From *Koga* onwards, photographers wrote their own theses on the subject and, since the late 1960s, some of them have not merely kept to simple theories about photography but have gone as far as forging an epistemological philosophy. Among these, Takuma Nakahira exercised a powerful influence on contemporary photography with his in-depth study of the relations between image and language. In numerous writings Nakahira denied the modern philosophy which consists of placing the world on one side and its observer on the other. He explained that the artist is no longer at the center of the world and that the world is not the exteriorization of the image which artists have made of it. He tried to show through his writings that taking a photograph consists of making the object communicate by placing it in the world and that the role of the photographer is to organize the composition from the starting-point of the world which surrounds the object which is being photographed.

This inverted schema, which consists of saying "I am not looking at the world, but the world is looking at me", goes hand-in-hand with developments at a time when there were no unequivocal relationships. In 1974, the index of Japanese economic growth went into the red, and, just as Japan was entering the post-industrial period, industry moved from a structure based on manufactured goods to one based on information. People were leading increasingly fragmented lives, relationships between individuals were becoming increasingly tense, and phenomena typical of post-industrial society began to make themselves felt. Faced with such a situation, it was no doubt quite natural that photographers should have used their cameras to renew the links within society. Kobo Abe, one of the representative writers of contemporary Japan, aptly wrote *The Box Man* at this time – this strange story of the destruction and reconstruction of human relationships provoked by a man shut up in a box exactly reflects the position in which contemporary photographers found themselves (the book contains photographs taken by the author).

The world which the box-man observes is filled with strange forms of nostalgia. Daido Moriyama, Nakahira's most faithful friend, never stopped producing curious images, as if he were trying to go back in his memory to a time when something had come to an end. With skilful lighting he produced extremely personal memories of a world which he had seen in the past. Furthermore, he wrote idiosyncratic textbooks on photography, and his artistic use of lighting is somewhat reminiscent of Yasui, for whom he had a high regard.[8]

It is, without a doubt, Nobuyoshi Araki who has taken this study of human relationships to its most fundamental level – sexuality. With the compartmentalization of humanity, it is sexual relations which have undergone the most radical change. Araki considers sex as a means of bringing together the world-object and the intimate life of the photographer, and has ended up by identifying himself with photographic exhibition. No doubt, one could interpret this extreme

8. Moriyama was the founder of the group "Provoke" with Takuma Nakahira and the critic Koji Taki. See *Light and Shadow*, Tokyo, Tojusha, 1982, and *Daido Moriyama, 1970–1979*, Tokyo, Sokyusha, 1989.

strategy with reference to the Orpheus myth, hell being the sort of image in which the ego, the world, and the photograph fuse together, and from which Araki tries to extricate lost souls.[9]

From the starting-point, opened up by Nakahira, of this problem of the reorganization of the self and of the world, photographers turned towards different subjects while still considering their own position in respect to the world. In his most typical work, *Hiroshima*,[10] Hiromi Tsuchida starts with documentary images, almost with the character of folklore, before deploying the full force of his vision so as "to make things speak". Just as Eugene Smith is universally recognized thanks to *Minamata*, since the beginning of the 1970s the negative aspects of this time of economic growth are emerging in various parts of the country in the form of pollution. The influential role of American photography continues, and new artistic trends (from "social landscape" to "new topographics") are finding a response among young Japanese. The topographical approach applied to the environment inspires them with a particular empathy, and new photographs of the countryside have appeared during the 1980s. Toshio Shibata, for example, has traveled to the most remote corners of Japanese mountains in order to take detailed photographs of particular sites ruined by the construction of a dam or river works. As for Naoya Hatakeyama, he has captured the subtle nuances of mining which has completely changed the mountainous regions of Japan. For the first time since the beginning of the century, it is being recalled that Pictorialism developed by taking the beauty of nature as a subject. Photographers who have gone to the mountains have discovered that a verdant Japan, so rich in nature as the seasons go by, now belongs to a very distant past. It must, however, be emphasized that their vision of today's hybrid countryside has lost none of its exceptional sensitivity as regards detail.

In less than a century, photographers have stared in the face of numerous catastrophes which have affected this small country. Japan has been an exceptionally privileged place for those armed with a camera, who wonder how to react to earthquakes, nuclear weapons or an economic explosion; all those gigantic things which surpass human scale, comparable to those which Kant qualified as sublime. And yet the dangers which now threaten Japan – with its cultural and environmental problems and fear of losing its national identity in the uniformity of the world economy and globalization – are the same as those which threaten the whole world. If Japan was the first to enter the post-modernist age, and thus serves as a testing-ground, photography in this country may no doubt be considered as the focal point of a conscience in full evolution and with contradictory feelings.

It is the story of a struggle to arrive at the universal by setting off in quest of the other, that unknown person, through the camera lens, while still remaining conscious of the unique character of Japanese culture. And if this aesthetic, breaking the shell of exoticism, inspires a certain sympathy, is this not because it suggests that we all live at the same time and on the same planet, and that henceforth there can no longer be any question of East and West?

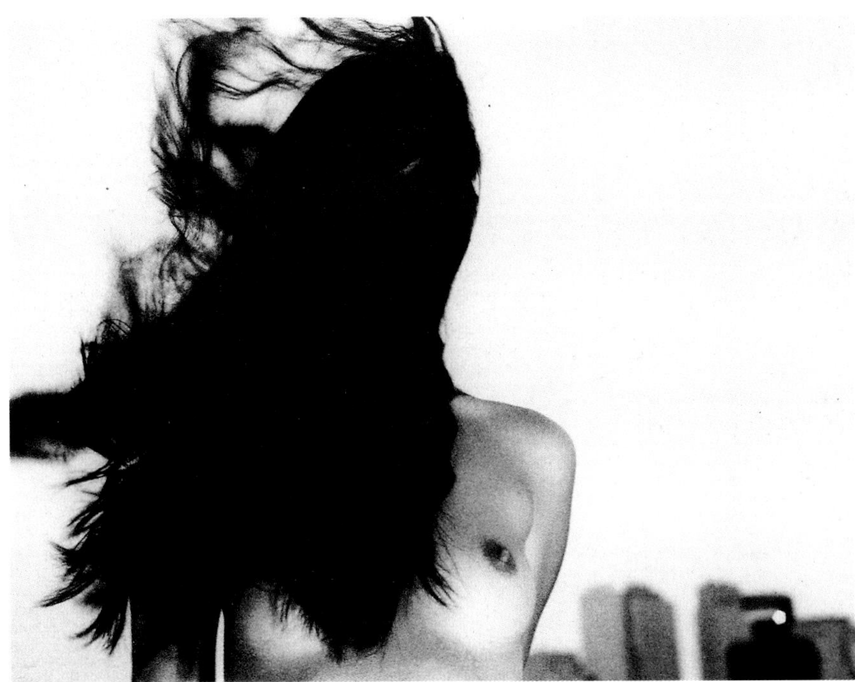

NOBUYOSHI ARAKI, from the series *Tokyo Stories*, 1988.

TOSHIO SHIBATA, ***Kamiso, Tochigi Pref.***, from the series *Quintessence of Japan*, 1988.

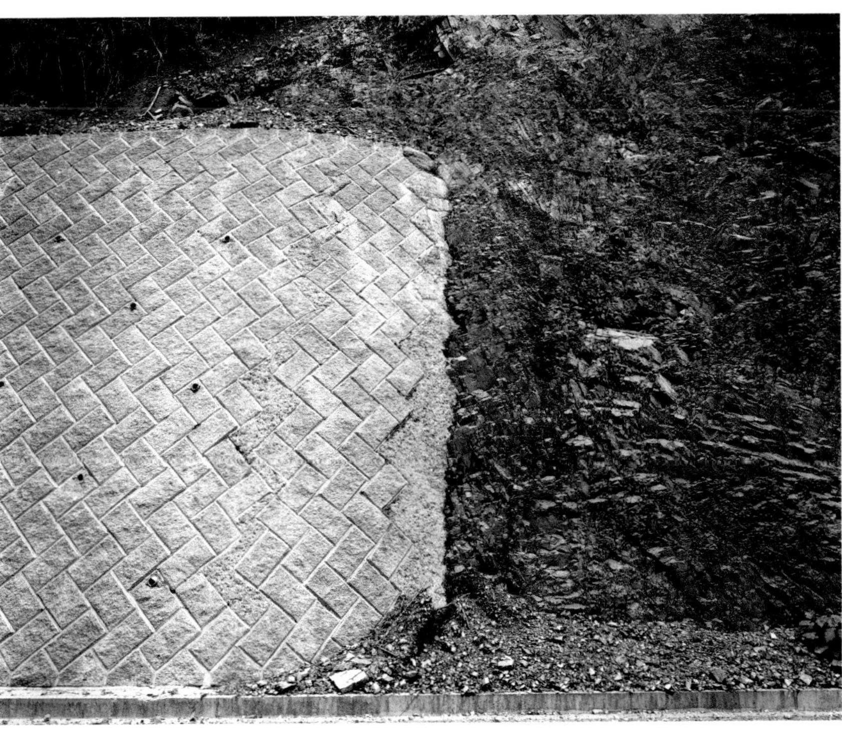

9. Haraki has published more than 80 photographic albums. See *Tokyo Stories*, Tokyo, Heibonsha, 1989, and *After the End of the War*, Tokyo, 1993.

10. Tokyo, Kosei, 1985; see also *Counting Grains of Sand*, Tokyo, Toseisha, 1990.

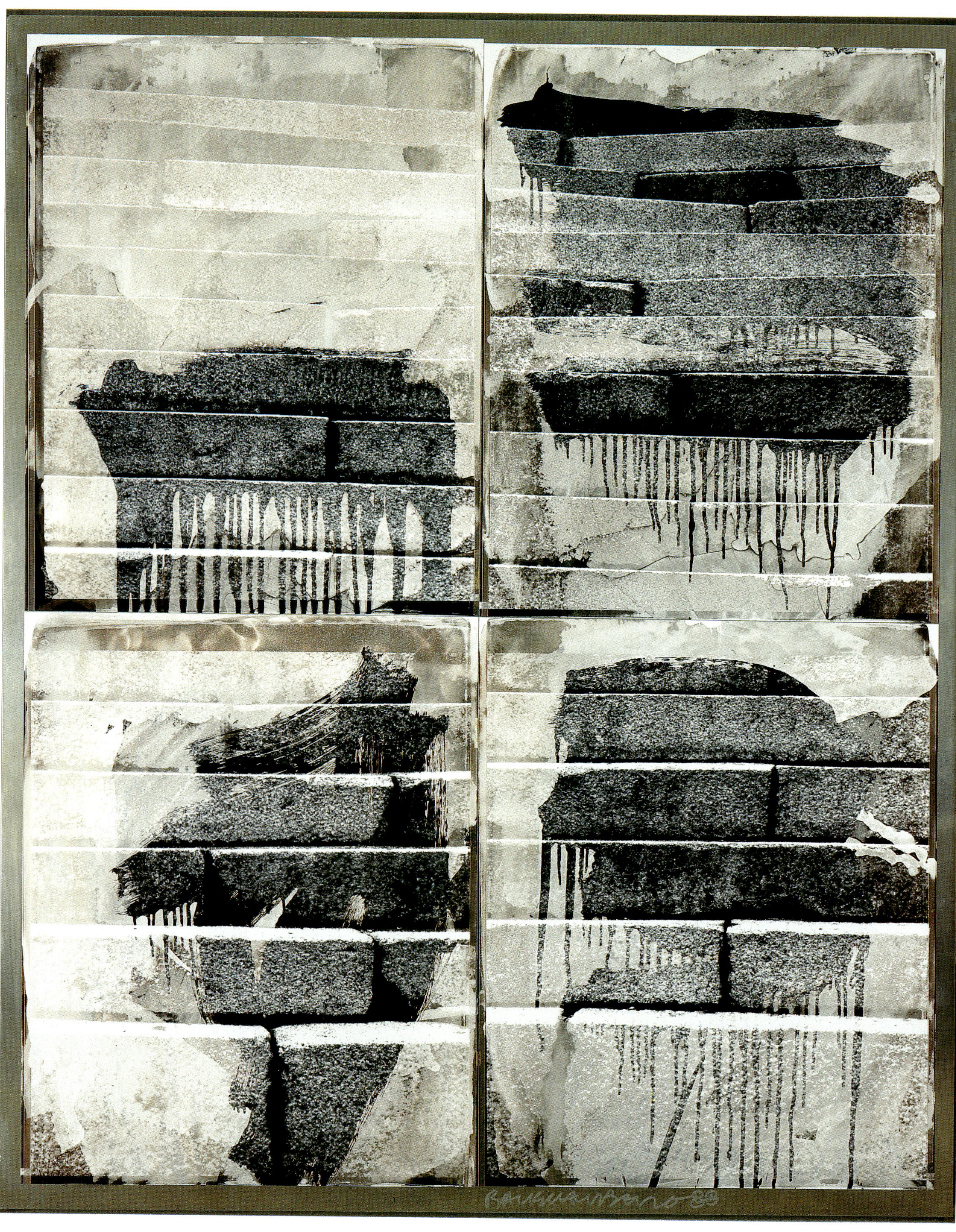

ROBERT RAUSCHENBERG,
Chinese Steps
(Bleacher Series),
1988,
Polaroid on
aluminum panel.

PHOTOGRAPHIC INSTITUTIONS AND PRACTICES

38

Stuart Alexander

The works presented in this chapter are not to be considered in a critical rapport with the text; they form part of a complete collection of illustrations and texts relating to the contemporary period (including the following chapters).

Since the 1970s, "photography" has little by little become an institution, in the sense in which it has become institutionalized and is now a recognized medium with which powers and authorities must come to terms. This involves more than a simple change of status, which alters the output of photographers, orients, and channels it, according to grants, prizes, commissions, and purchases; photographing no longer necessarily responds to the same wagers, to the same risks, to the same pleasures as in the past. By a parallel mutation to that which has occurred in other arts, museums, collections, and contemporary art collections – organizations which vary from one country to another – have created a "politics" of photography. At a moment when the photographic image is capable of passing from analogue to numerical form, it is time to take stock, for the present situation will determine the context of future production.

You won't find a report on "recent trends" here, nor will you find a discussion of the rise of "post-modernism". There are more fundamental and less ephemeral issues to discuss. The most important development in creative[1] photography over the past twenty-five years is the establishment of photographic institutions and the expansion of the infrastructure for photography as a medium of creative expression. What follows is a look at the rise of these support systems and the effect they have on contemporary photographic practice.

For a young photographer with artistic ambitions just beginning their career today, there are many opportunities that simply did not exist twenty-five years ago. This variety of support, from exhibitions, publications, and photo events to print sales, grants and awards, makes it possible for some photographers – albeit a very few – to earn a living from their personal work. In the 1960s, there was little hope that one's personal photography might be exhibited, published or sold. No photographer could earn their living solely from artistic work then.

The institutions

The generation that was coming of age in the 1960s is largely responsible for the institutions that exist at the end of the twentieth century. The "baby boom" generation (born between 1940 and 1955) was more visually sophisticated than its predecessors. Not only was it the first generation to be raised with television but it also grew up during the photographic essay's peak era. The picture magazines such as *Life* and *Paris-Match* were at the height of their success and were a symbol of this vogue for photography.[2] It is natural that as they matured "baby-boomers" would want to learn how to create, use, and understand photographs.

From the end of the Second World War until the late 1960s, photographic institutions developed gradually. The explosion of interest in photography at the end of this period began in the United States and rapidly spread from there. The American university system and a few museums that sponsored travelling exhibitions laid the groundwork for this phenomenal growth. Before the war, photography was taught on a relatively small scale, as a profession and not as an expressive medium. In the post-war period, art photography programs began to appear in university curricula. Subsequently, there appeared not only a burgeoning group of practitioners and teachers but also an expanding audience that was sensitive to creative photography. This development loosely followed a few nodes such as the West Coast (Weston, Adams), the Institute of

1. Photography is often discussed – separately and simultaneously – as a means of recording and as an art form. It appears that it is only in the past 25 years that photography has passed definitively into the realm of art by universal acceptance into art museums and inclusion in standard art history textbooks. For lack of a better term, we speak of creative photography or art photography, in order to distinguish photographs intended for an expressive purpose from those intended for a simple recording purpose.

2. The rest of the world lagged behind the United States in this respect.

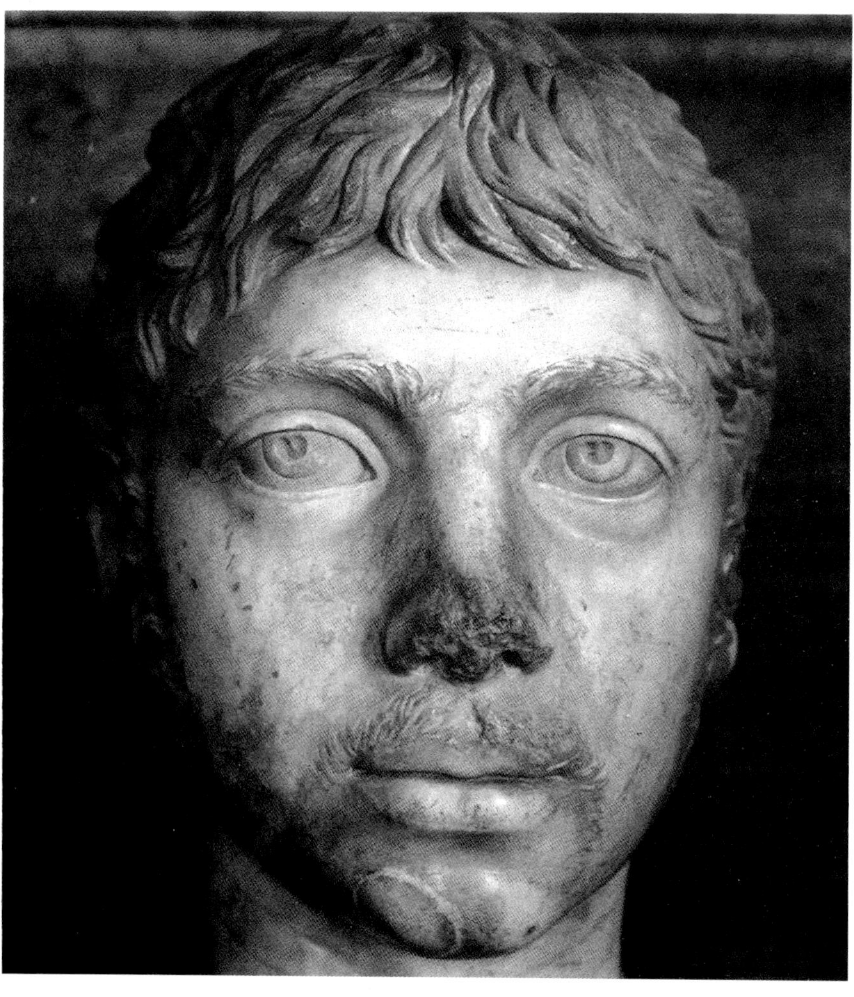

PATRICK FAIGENBAUM, *Heliogabalus*, from the series *Parallel Lives*, Rome, 1987.

Design, Chicago (Moholy-Nagy, Callahan, Siskind) and Minor White.

The New York Museum of Modern Art was effectively the only museum in America that regularly exhibited photography in the 1930s. Beaumont Newhall presented his landmark history of photography exhibition there in 1937, *Photography 1839–1937*. The accompanying catalogue was virtually the first draft for his well-known history of the medium. Following the Second World War, the number of photography exhibitions at the museum increased under the curatorship of Edward Steichen. Meanwhile, Newhall became the first curator of the International Museum of Photography at George Eastman House in Rochester in 1949, where he initiated an active collecting, exhibiting, and publishing program.

Elsewhere in the world, institutions were beginning to stir as well. Otto Steinert began collecting photographs for the Museum Folkwang in Essen. Under the editorship of Romeo Martinez from 1953, *Camera* magazine became ever more responsive to the needs of an international audience. In France, Robert Delpire published his first photographic books in 1952. Back in America, the deluxe quarterly *Aperture* was founded in the same year. This growth continued through the 1950s.

The pace quickened at the start of the 1960s. Both Nathan Lyons at the George Eastman House and John Szarkowksi at the Museum of Modern Art organized numerous photographic exhibitions that traveled extensively all over the world – from the furthest capital cities in Asia to the smallest college towns in the American Midwest. These exhibitions, along with the university programs, helped to create a larger and better informed audience for photography.

In the mid-1960s, the "baby boom" generation did not find openings available to it, so, as in nearly everything else, its constituents seized what power they could and created new opportunities for themselves. Contemporaneous with the broad social changes erupting around the world, photography experienced an enormous wave of popular interest, especially among the younger generation. At the phenomenal Woodstock music festival in 1969 (and a few months later on the Isle of Wight in Britain), hundreds of thousands of youths openly violated social conventions. They flaunted their nakedness and drug use before television cameras. All across the United States protests against the war in Vietnam escalated. Students burned their draft cards and the American flag. The events of May 1968 in Paris and of August that year in Prague (in which youths were often in positions of leadership), were widely reported by the international mass media.

Photography found itself in a position of rivalry with the slick and increasingly efficient television. Photography was so readily adopted it seemed almost as though it was the new language of the youth movement. Today's establishment magazines such as *Rolling Stone* grew out of the underground press.

Parallel to this, young people published their own photography books and magazines. They began to organize exhibitions and symposia devoted to the medium. This mushrooming activity became known as the "Photo Boom". It was the beginning of the proliferation of photographic institutions.

What is significant about the "photo boom" is that there was a void that was rapidly filled by young people. The youths who created the new institutions were also the very ones whom they are intended to help. Thus, a strong symbiotic relationship was formed. This generation had grown up and gone to school together. They generally shared similar goals and tastes. They began to create their own support system.

Today, the same people are at the helm. As they are moving into later middle-age, their institutions are stabilizing and present only a limited number of new opportunities yearly. The boom years are long over. Maturity has settled in and a certain stasis along with it.

Institutions are conservative by nature and tend to reflect the character of the individuals that they are composed of. There lurks the danger of academicism. What sometimes occurs is that work that is chosen for exhibition or publication often looks alike. Another pitfall is that people who are caught up in a closed world such as this often end up caring only about what concerns them and their circle. As a result, their photography is more about photography than about anything else. Formalism and Post-modernism could have developed only in this kind of an environment.

The best of institutions continually, or at least periodically, renew themselves. To survive the changing times they must evolve. Defiance of the status quo, on whatever relative scale, is what saves them from stagnation and death. These institutions owe their origins to that.

The market

Around 1969, several young turks ignored what their elders had told them and forged ahead. For example, and in no special order, Ralph Gibson and Lee Friedlander published their own books, Jean-Claude Lemagny began to build a collection of contemporary photography at the Bibliothèque Nationale, Nathan Lyons left the George Eastman House to found the Visual Studies Workshop, and Lee Witkin opened a photography gallery. The list could go on and on but let's begin to look at how the "photoboom" has led us to where we are now.

Against the advice of many, Lee Witkin launched his Witkin Gallery in 1969. He stocked many classic and popular photographers' works, such as Ansel Adams and Edward Weston, with prices ranging from $25 to a high of around $200. His venture experienced great success and became the first commercially viable gallery devoted entirely to photography. Several enter-

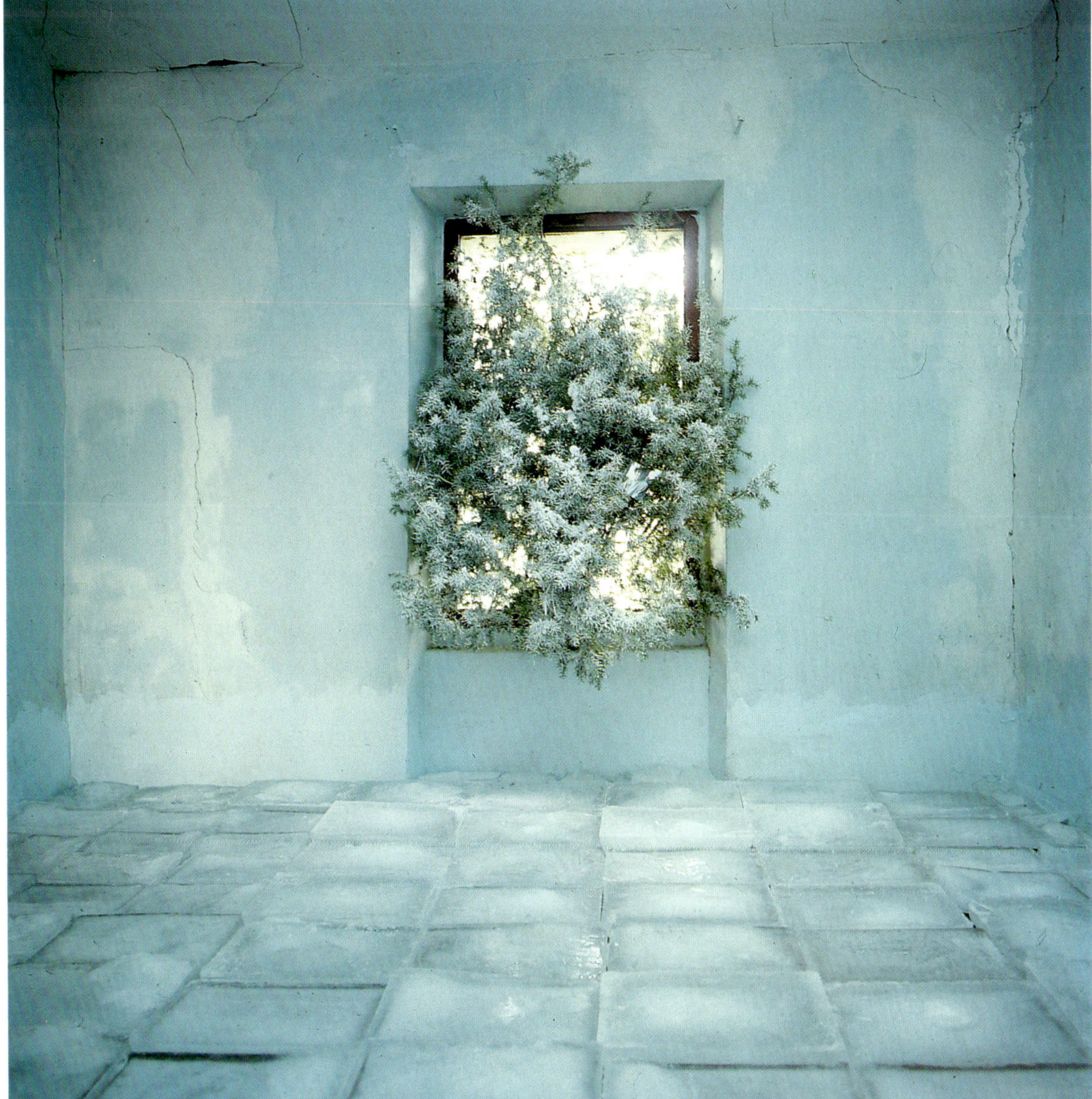

BERNARD FAUCON, *The Room in Winter*, 1986.

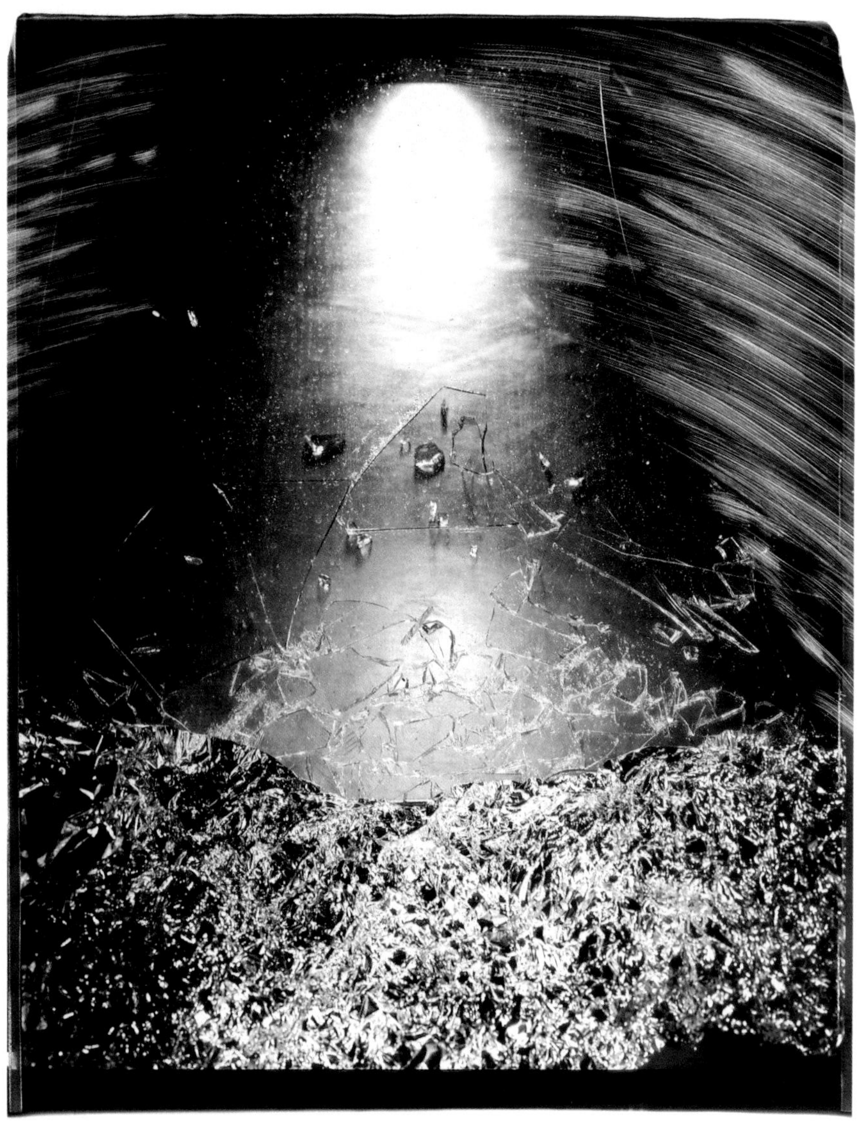

KEICHI TAHARA, *Polaroid,* 1985.

of galleries closed. In recent years, the market has come back stronger, although it has climbed much more slowly than in the boom years.[4] Both dealers and collectors are more knowledgeable and there is a much higher level of connoisseurship.

Beginning in the early 1970s, photography auctions experienced a development similar to the galleries. Today, photography auctions do a fair share of business at the world's major auction houses in New York (Sotheby's, Christie's, Swann), London (Sotheby's, Christie's, and Phillip's), and Cologne, among others.

The photography market is relatively stable now. Dealers know what they can and cannot sell and roughly how long it will take them to turn a profit. This alone helps predetermine what will be shown in galleries. Risk-taking, innovation, and originality are reduced. Photographers today know that if they want to exhibit in a particular gallery they must present work that is similar to what that gallery already handles.

There is a curious hierarchy in the gallery system. Any photography dealer will admit that it takes the same amount of effort to sell a photograph as it does to sell a painting. On the average, paintings bring a significantly higher price than do photographs. If a photograph purports to have a certain level of conceptual content and is made by someone who rejects the title of "photographer" it can be sold as an artist's piece in the range of prices for canvases. Many a young photographer is careful to call themselves an "artist" instead of a "photographer". They understand that they may be taken more seriously and could sell their work for much more money than a "lowly photographer".

Some photographers make large prints often without any regard to whether or not the image really justifies a larger size. Sometimes they are framed like paintings and may even be printed on canvas. The dealers like them because they produce a greater profit than do smaller prints.

prising people followed his lead. Tennyson Schad opened Light Gallery in New York in 1971. It was oriented to contemporary photography and lasted just over ten years. Soon afterward, Marlborough Gallery, also in New York, began to handle photographs. Prices escalated rapidly. Elsewhere, the Photographers' Gallery started in London while in Paris Agathe Gaillard opened her gallery, the first in France, in 1976. The pioneering photography galleries were as much an affair of love and devotion as they were a commercial business.

In the mid-1970s, a shift occurred among some dealers. Following the lead of Harry Lunn, they introduced modern business practices to the field. They bought work in bulk and sold it later at a considerable profit. Some indulged in tax write-off schemes and manipulated the market to their advantage. In the period from 1975 to 1991 prices increased 680 per cent.[3] The market for photographs climbed so rapidly that it gained the attention of the *Wall Street Journal*.

This high did not last. At the beginning of the 1980s there was a severe setback when a number

Conservation and distribution

At the same time that photography began to be sold in galleries, some art museums were willing to accept the medium into the fold. Young men and women leaving graduate photography programs, mostly with M.F.A. degrees in the practice of the medium, found work as assistant or associate curators in print departments. They rapidly assembled significant photography collections and in some cases created separate photography departments (David Travis, Art Institute of Chicago, 1974; Anne W. Tucker, Museum of Fine Arts, Houston, 1975; Mark Haworth-Booth, Victoria & Albert Museum,

3. R. Duthy, "Surprises in the Photography Market", *Journal of Art* no. 4, 1991, p. 81.

4. This phenomenon was much less dramatic in Europe than in the United States.

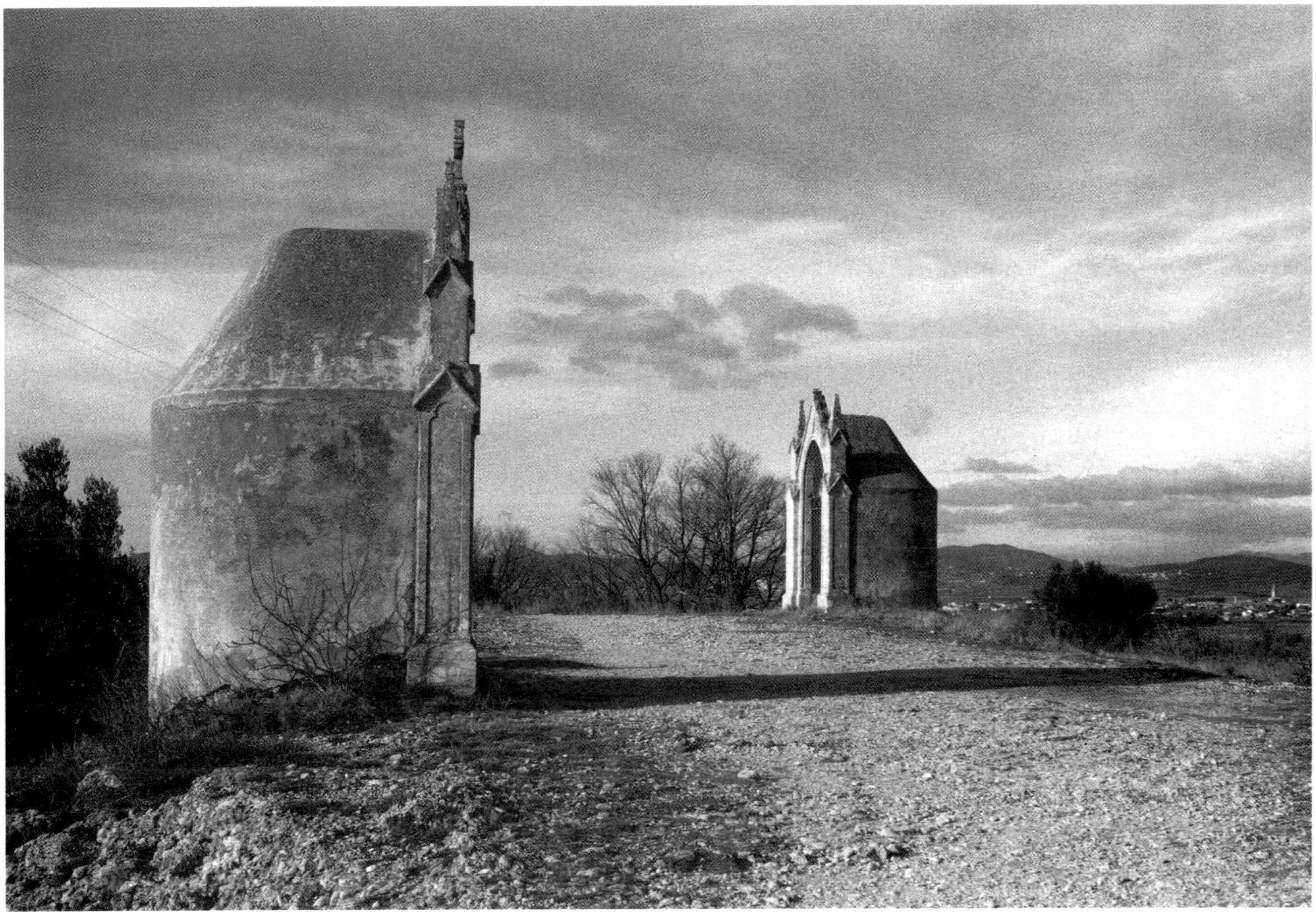

Pierre de Fenoÿl,
21/9/84, 19h,
D.A.T.A.R.
Photographic Mission.

London, 1975). Other large museums added photography departments or expanded their mandates to include significant collections of photography (Metropolitan Museum of Art, New York, Minneapolis Institute of Arts, J. Paul Getty Museum, Los Angeles, Musée National d'Art Moderne, Paris, Museum Folkwang, Essen, Museum Ludwig, Cologne, Museum of Decorative Arts, Prague, Stedelijk Museum, Amsterdam, National Gallery of Canada, Ottawa, Musée d'Orsay, Paris).

Several new museums devoted exclusively to photography, including archival research centers, were founded in various countries around the world in the 1970s and continue to flourish (Musée Nicéphore Niépce, Chalon-sur-Saône, 1972; California Museum of Photography, Riverside, 1973; International Center of Photography, New York, 1974; Center for Creative Photography, Tucson, 1975; Centre National de la Photographie, Paris, 1982; National Museum of Photography, Film and Television, Bradford, 1983; Museum voor Fotografie, Antwerp; Fotografiska Museet, Stockholm; Museet for Fotokunst, Odense; Tokyo Metropolitan Museum of Photography; Musée de l'Elysée, Lausanne).[5]

Museum administrators and trustees found that photography was inexpensive and exciting. Rela-

Tom Drahos,
from the series
Robois Metamorphoses, 1976.
▼

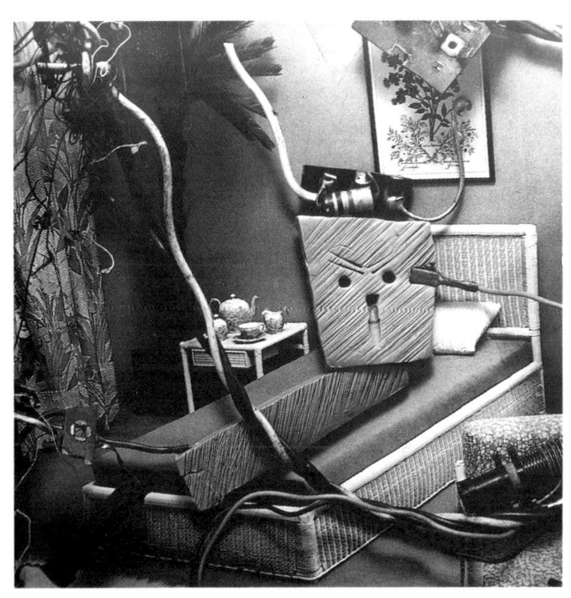

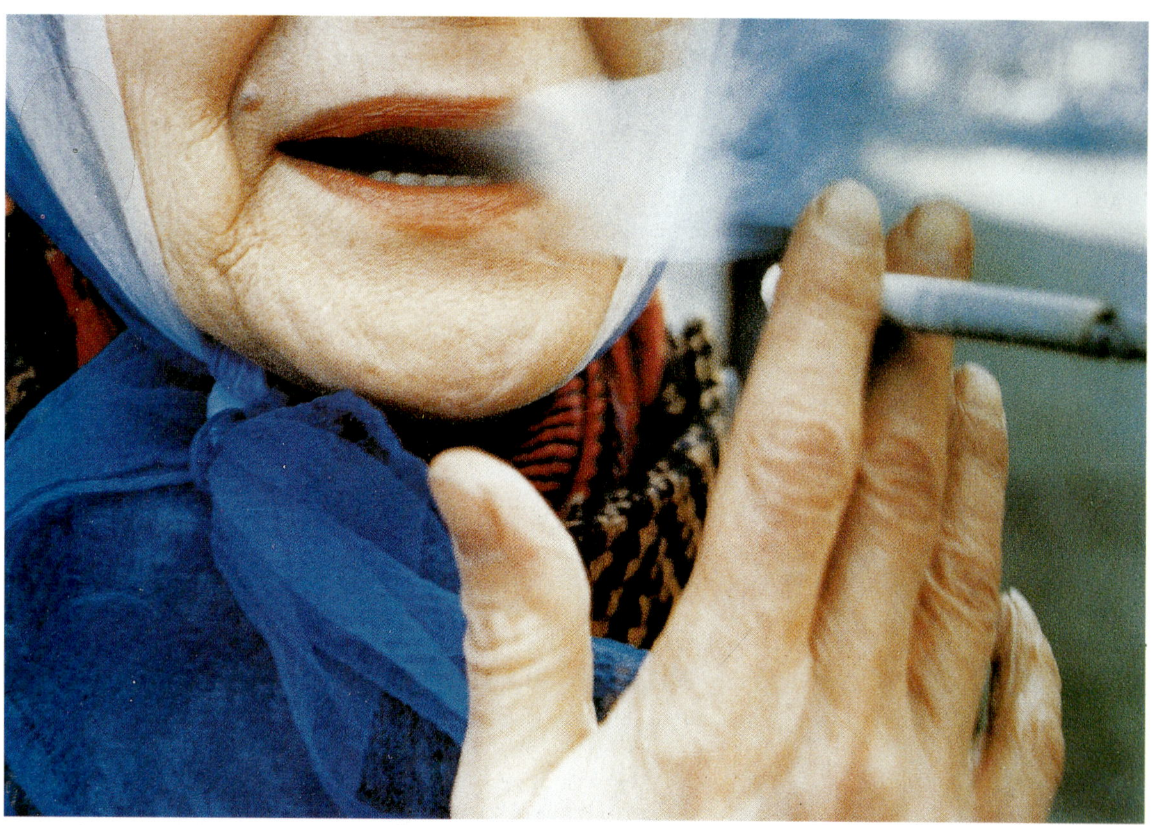

MARK COHEN, *Untitled*, March 31, 1975.

tive to other media, it was easy to build an excellent collection for a small amount of money. Often plagued by declining attendance figures, they discovered to their pleasure that photography exhibitions brought crowds back into their museums. Photography collections and exhibitions were a good investment.

Today, it is increasingly more expensive to produce exhibitions. Curators have to work harder to procure enough money to simply keep their regular exhibition and acquisition programs alive. The openness and excitement of the early days are gone because it requires so much more effort to raise the money to mount an exhibition that only sure-fire projects are proposed.

Alternative co-operative photography galleries and regional photographic centers spread throughout the 1970s and 1980s (The Friends of Photography, Carmel, then San Francisco; Lightwork, Syracuse; Los Angeles Center for Photographic Studies; Houston Center for Photography; Galerie du Chateau d'Eau, Toulouse; Centre Régional de la Photographie Nord-Pas-de-Calais, Douchy-les-Mines; Impressions Gallery, York; Perspektief, Rotterdam; Ffotogallery, Cardiff; Il Diaframma, Milan; Photography Center, Athens; Fotogaleria Forum, Tarragona; Fotogalerie Forum Stadtpark, Graz).

Naturally, because of their smaller size they are able to take more chances with the kind of work they present. There have been some casualties of economic hard times but a number of these institutions have securely established themselves. Abundant opportunities for photographers to share their work with the public do remain.

The fact that a photographer has a much greater chance to exhibit today than twenty years ago has made an impact on practice. Some works, including installations, are made expressly to be shown in a museum or gallery environment. This simply could not exist before because the chance to exhibit did not exist.

Recognition

The story of photographic publishing follows a similar course. At the beginning of the 1970s a number of photographers published their own books. Some, such as Ralph Gibson and his partners (Lustrum Press, New York) and Claude Nori (Contrejour, Paris), began ventures that lasted for several years through the publication of other artists' books as well. These products of the counterculture rapidly became the establishment.

The situation appears to be changing again. There are a number of new smaller publishers and some artists are turning again to self-publication. In the early 1970s, one could keep up with all of the new photography publications. Today, there is a flood of monographs, histories, and collections of theory and criticism from all over the world. There are over a hundred different titles of photography periodicals alone. This steady stream of literature fulfills the function of keeping the system moving. It provides many more outlets for photographers' work, historical,

5. More recently, in 1992, the Whitney Museum of American Art (New York), the Solomon R. Guggenheim Museum (New York), and the Castello di Rivoli (near Turin) have announced their intention to accelerate activity in collecting and exhibiting.

theoretical, and critical foundation, and exposure to, and the education of, a broader public.

By 1963, the teaching of photography at the university level had become such a significant force in the United States that, under the instigation of Nathan Lyons, the Society for Photographic Education was founded as a forum to discuss educational issues. That first year there were fewer than one hundred members. Today, numbering about 1,500 members, it is one of the largest groups in America oriented to supporting creative photography.[6] It has its own internal hierarchy and exerts a great influence on American photography.

When the younger generation reached college-age, at the end of the 1960s and the early 1970s, university photography programs could not expand fast enough to satisfy the demand. Later, in the 1980s as the college-age population shrank, enrolments declined as well. In these times of economic hardship for universities, professors are being offered early retirement, fewer new positions are created, and teachers are struggling to hang on to their jobs.

In the 1970s, the history of photography became a regular feature in university curricula at undergraduate and graduate levels. This system had become so self-referential that by the end of 1991, a graduate seminar at an American university produced an exhibition and symposium on "Teacher/Student Relationships Since 1945 in American Photography" as part of their course work. Ironically, or perhaps, significantly, this narcissistic exercise was designed to give the students "real-world" practical experience in the study of photographic history.

Several photographers' work began to reflect their training in the history of the medium. For example, the photography of Mark Klett and Joel-Peter Witkin, both graduates of the academically highest-rated studio program at the University of New Mexico, is directly influenced by examples in the history of the medium.[7] Others, such as Patrick Bailly-Maître-Grand, Joan Fontcuberta, and Lewis Baltz are just a few of the many artists who make explicit reference to historical antecedents.

Of course, from the very beginnings, the most cultivated photographers learned from and paid homage to their predecessors. For example, every generation since the 1840s revered the work of Hill and Adamson, most notably featured in *Camera Work* at the beginning of the twentieth century. But over the past three decades, university education and numerous publications and exhibitions of earlier photography presented in the context of art museums and galleries exerted a great influence on contemporary photography. Postmodernism, veiled in its conceptual dignity, theorized about these "reversions" and made it its duty to recycle the past and to condemn the frantic originality of the previous decades.

The number of photography grants and awards has steadily increased since the end of the 1960s when the number of Guggenheim Fellowships awarded to photographers grew dramatically.[8] The National Endowment for the Arts (USA) began in 1965 to support photography through

6. Nathan Lyons "Afterword", in *Decade by Decade: Twentieth-Century American Photography from the Collection of the Center for Creative Photography*, ed. James Enyeart, Boston, Bulfinch Press in association with Center for Creative Photography, University of Arizona, Tucson, 1989, p. 105.

7. *Revealing Territory: Photographs of the Southwest*. Albuquerque, University of New Mexico Press,1992; *Second View: The Rephotographic Survey Project*. Albuquerque, University of New Mexico Press,1984.

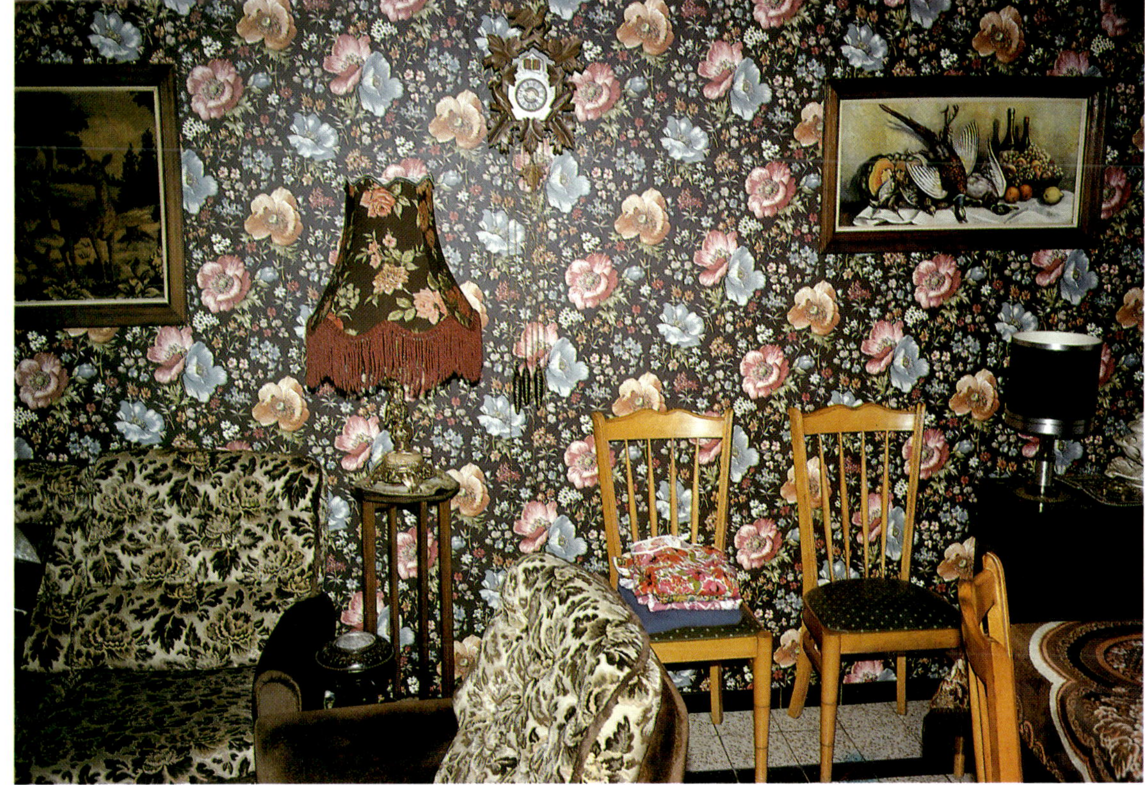

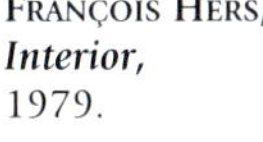

François Hers, ***Interior***, 1979.

grants but the rate did not accelerate significantly until the early 1970s.

Elsewhere in the world, a vast array of awards and grants is available and many more are created nearly every year.[9] Many cultural exchange organizations sponsor photographic projects. This is an inexpensive way to get publicity for the goals of the organization. Cultural prestige is the result. Usually an exhibition and catalogue are the product.

One of the drawbacks of this system is that it is often the same people who win all of the awards and contracts. There seems to be a lack of daring on the part of the juries and commissioners. In some cases the juries are from a very small world and even include former awardwinners. This assures a certain continuity. The photographer supposedly has free rein to produce whatever they want. But they never would have been selected for the award or the commission, in the first place, if their work did not already satisfy certain criteria. Artists who are likely to produce unacceptable surprises are rarely selected.

Following the example of the Farm Security Administration (1935–1942), the Mission Photographique de la D.A.T.A.R. (Délégation à l' aménagement du territoire et à l'action régionale) [Regional Regeneration Delegation] was launched in France in 1983 by Bernard Attali.[10] Each artist's project was devoted to activities or places that revealed sociological changes in the country. Often coastlines, industrial sectors, and construction sites were selected.

The choice of photographers, often young and little-known, and their concerted interest in carefully delimited themes, showed a true renewal in photographic practice, the public commission, and the social role of the photographer. Notably, Gabriele Basilico, Tom Drahos, Gilbert Fastenaekens, Jean-Louis Garnell, Werner Hannapel, Suzanne Lafont, and Sophie Ristelhueber found confirmation of their former orientation without the institutional valorization of their images inciting them to deviate from their own esthetic.[11] The Mission Photographique du Transmanche (Channel Tunnel Project) in France, the Central Arizona Project in the United States (Mark Klett, Lawrence McFarland, Ruthe Morand, and Anne Simmons-Myers), and the Beirut City Center project[12] take on the same redefinition of the uses of photography and its social and media impact as opposed to its private valorization.

One of the new avenues for young photographers to draw attention to themselves and their work is through participation in another institution introduced in the past 25 years, the international photographic event. The original is the Encounters Internationals de la Photographie that was first held in Arles, France in 1970. This

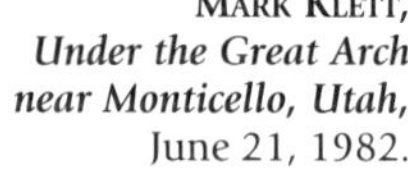

MARK KLETT, *Under the Great Arch near Monticello, Utah,* June 21, 1982.

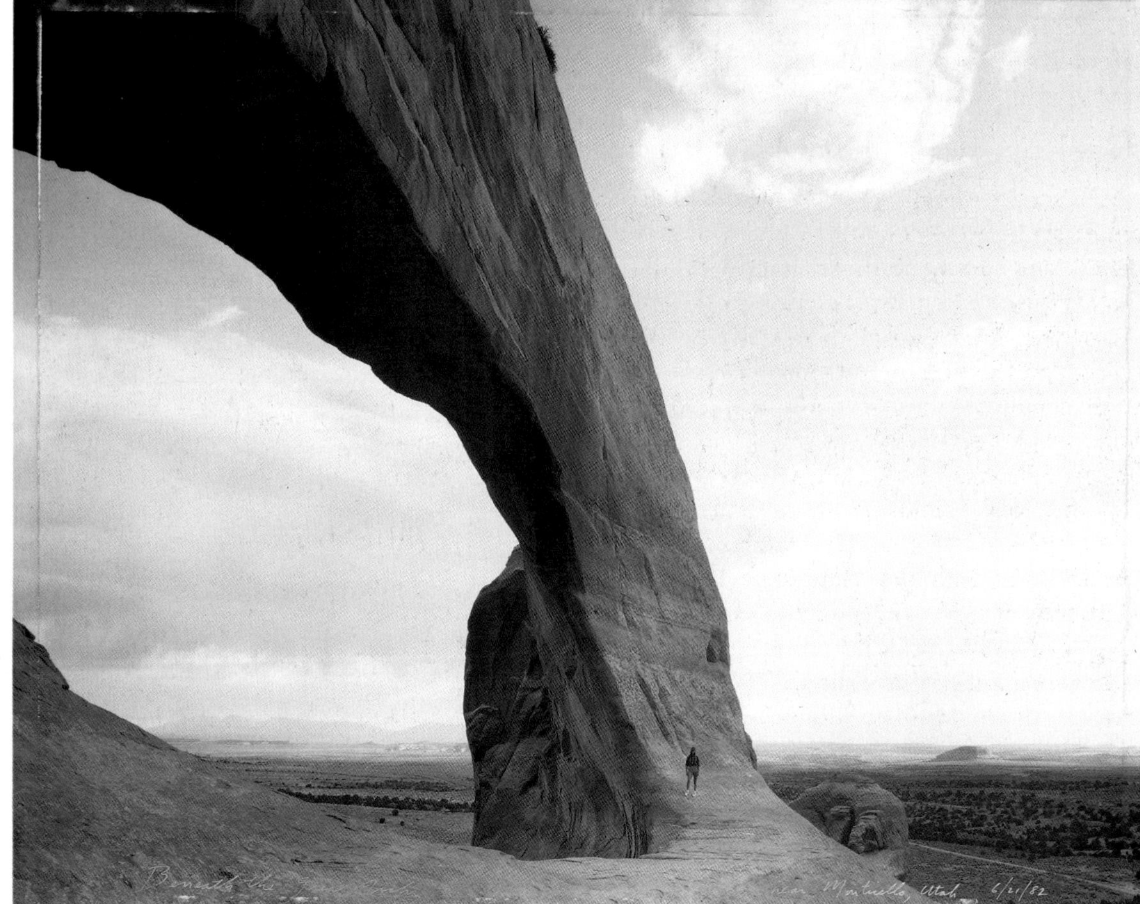

8. The first photographer awarded a Guggenheim Fellowship was Edward Weston in 1937.

9. Among others are Grand Prix National de la Photographie, Ministry of Culture, Paris, Infinity Awards, International Center of Photography, New York, and Erna and Victor Hasselblad Award, Stockholm.

10. Subsequently directed by Jacques Sallois, it was managed by Bernard Latarjet and François Hers.

11. Also included were Raymond Depardon, Robert Doisneau, Despatin et Gobeli, François Hers, Christian Milovanoff, Holger Trülzsch, Josef Koudelka, Richard Pare, Dominique Auerbacher, Pierre de Fenoÿl, Frank Gohlke, Lewis Baltz, and Hervé Rabot.

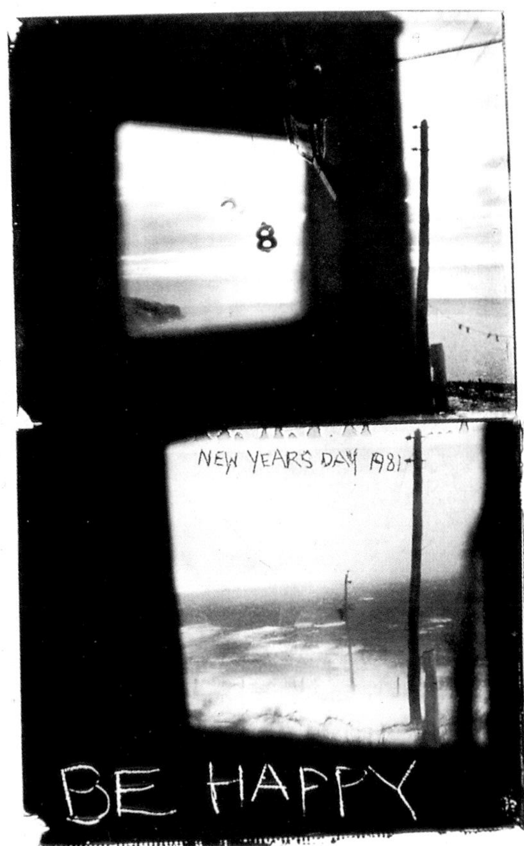

◄ ROBERT FRANK, *Mabou, Nova Scotia,* 1981.

annual international meeting was founded by Lucien Clergue, Jean-Maurice Rouquette, and Michel Tournier who were encouraged by a handful of enthusiastic supporters, now eminent figures in the French photographic scene. The Rencontres d'Arles with its projections, workshops, and exhibitions is where American photography of the 1960s and 1970s began to influence European photography.

A decade later, in the 1980s, European photographers started to pay more attention to their own identity and became less interested in American photography. A renewed vitality in European photography developed – thanks largely to the multitude of indigenous support systems – and subsequently began to interest and influence American photographers.

One of the major points of contact between the Old and New Worlds is at the international photographic event. The "Film und Foto" exhibition in 1929, and the "Subjektive Fotografie" exhibitions in 1951, 1954, and 1958 served this purpose in earlier decades.

The new urbane form of such an event began in Paris. In 1980, Jean-Luc Monterosso, head of Paris Audiovisuel since 1977, initiated the bi-annual city-wide event called the Mois de la Photo [Month of Photography], held in November. Aside from supporting local talent, it also exposes Parisians and visitors to a broad array of work from all over the world, further sensitizing them to photographic art. This multi-exhibition celebration of photography has been copied in cities around the world.

In America, the Foto Fest in Houston, Texas, is modeled on Paris's pioneering extravaganza but with a decidedly more commercial twist. Founded in 1986 by Fred Baldwin, Wendy Watriss, and Petra Benteler, the Foto Fest combines the workshops and portfolio reviews that take place at Arles with the plethora of exhibitions common to the Mois de la Photo.

The unabashedly commercial aspect of the American festival risks turning it into something which is more like a traditional trade fair. Copy from a brochure for the 1992 Foto Fest reads: "Foto Fest '92 is your chance to participate [...] in personal encounters with world-class experts who can advance your career. Maybe even change your life."[13] The brochure is covered with the logos of large corporations who sponsor the event.

A "Month of Photography" was also created in Montreal. Rotterdam started a biennial (1988) oriented to the avant-garde, and the Primavera Fotográfica of Barcelona offers a proliferation of exhibitions. The latter event developed hand-in-hand with the rebirth of the city and artistic activity in post-Franco Spain.

The stakes

The problem of sponsorship is a question of liberty. Can one create freely while having to worry about a corporate image? Is it possible to portray in photographs the fact that the Eastman Kodak Company is the largest effluent polluter in America[14] and still have that work shown or published in the institutions or publications that depend increasingly on such corporate sponsorship for their survival?

12. Gabriele Basilico, Raymond Depardon, Robert Frank, Josef Koudelka, Fouad El Koury, and René Burri.

13. Foto Fest brochure, Houston, Texas, 1992.

ANDY WARHOL, *Untitled* (tesselated photographs), circa 1980. ▼

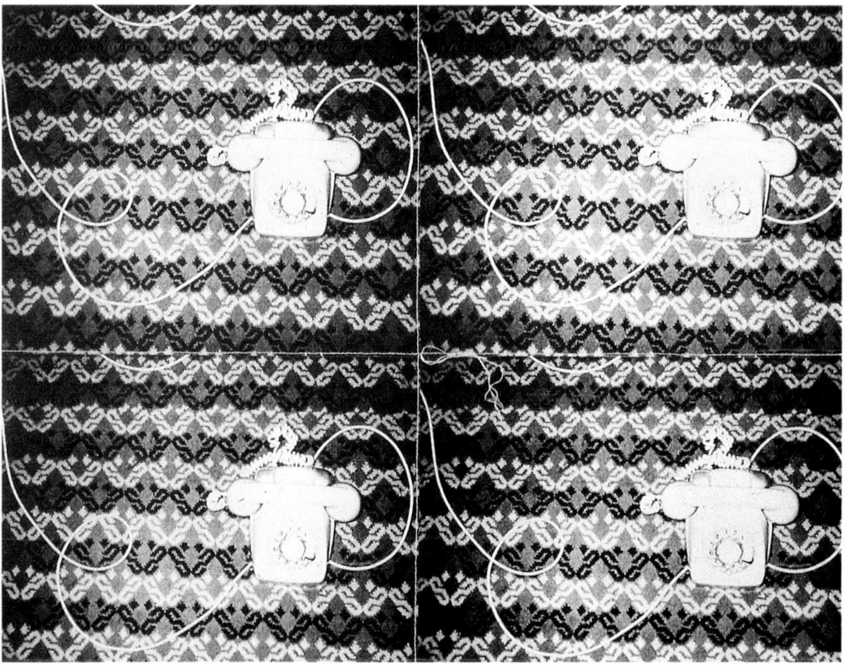

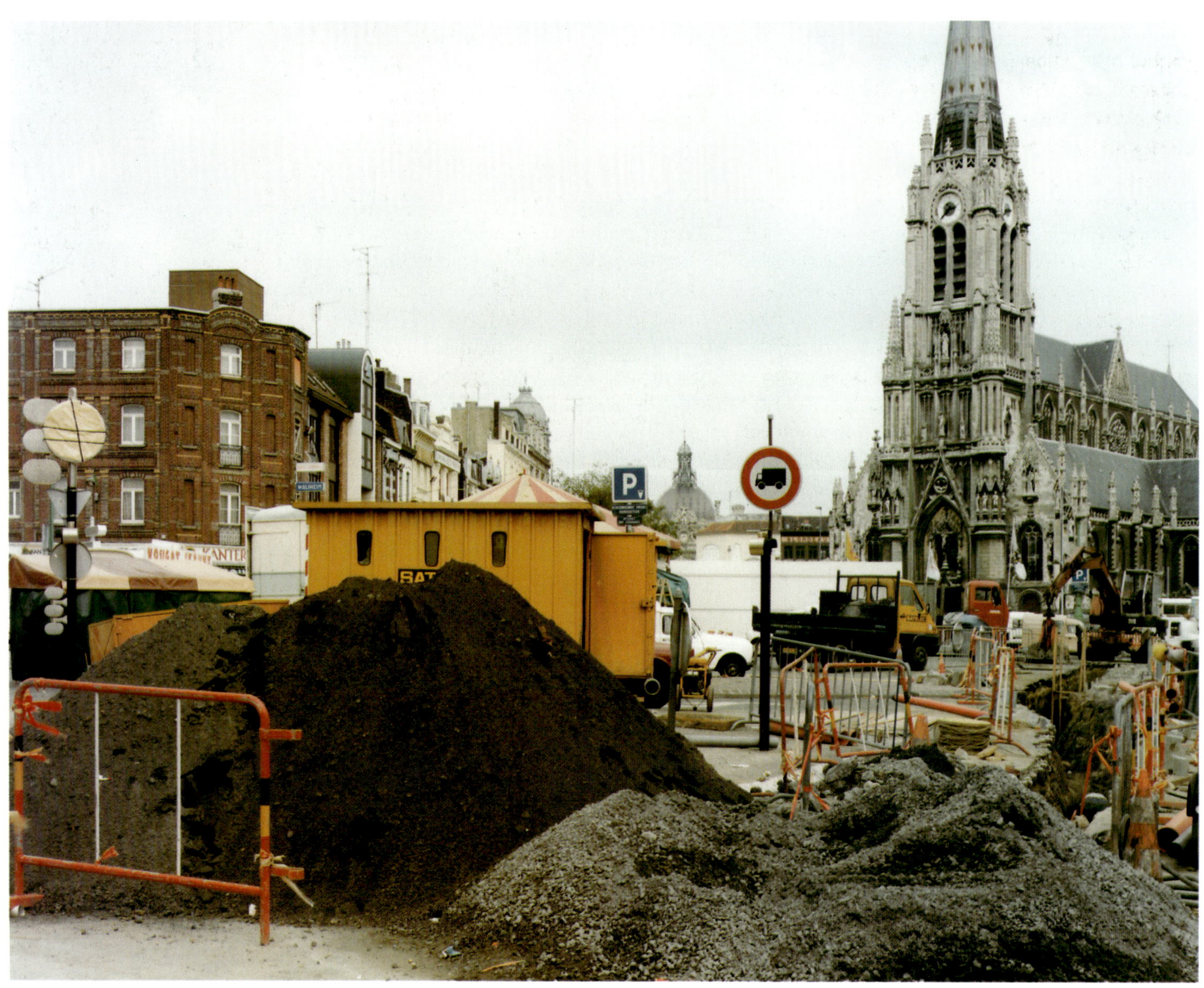

JEAN-LOUIS GARNELL, *Landscape,* 1986, (D.A.T.A.R. Photographic Mission).

Ideally, one could do so freely, but the current climate of the photographic infrastructure makes it seem less and less likely. In 1993, Kodak reduced by one-half its support of the Rencontres d'Arles because of the "insufficient international implications" of the annual meeting. It chose instead to devote its cultural sponsorship to only two photographers, Richard Avedon and Sebastião Salgado.[15]

This grave matter of censorship through funding – or lack of funding – for the arts arose in the United States in 1990 over the National Endowment for the Arts' support of artists Andres Serrano, Jock Sturges, and Robert Mapplethorpe. A morality debate was foisted on the issue of federal support for the arts and used as a political tool by conservatives. It was a nasty battle but the result included a healthy re-examination of the censorship/arts support issue. Unfortunately, it also engendered a certain paranoia among artists and arts institutions.

Economic, social, and cultural pressures may not have as great an impact on the future of creative photography as the advances of technology. The rapid development of practical methods of electronic imaging may be the greatest challenge of all. Negative-positive photography based on light-sensitive silver chemistry may soon be practiced only by a small group of traditionalists such as daguerreotype revivalists working today. The possibilities for creating, reproducing, transmitting, and manipulating photographic imagery will be so great, and the diffusion of these images will be based on such a variety of different networks, that the traditional institutions will have to evolve rapidly to catch up, or fall by the wayside. Certainly, new institutions will arise as well. Already, Nathan Lyons – seemingly always one step ahead – hosted Montage '93, the first international event devoted to creative uses of the new electronic media in Rochester, New York in 1993. Meanwhile, Eastman Kodak Company, referred to by many as "The Great Yellow Father", opened the Center for Creative Imaging, a workshop facility in Camden, Maine to initiate interested people to the new electronic media.

14. Reported on "CBS Evening News with Dan Rather", Columbia Broadcasting Service, New York, 1991.

15. *Le Monde* (April 29, 1993).

If it is, perhaps, unfair to say that all photographic production is under institutional control (the institution can take on many different forms), it is legitimate to question more often the nature of the control by those institutions which retain nearly all power over the dissemination, exhibition, and publication of photographs while managing major commissions, effecting stylistic choices, and directing the sponsorship of big corporations.

If the art and practice of photography have become more international, the notion of the medium has become concurrently more globally historic, that is to say, it has integrated with all photographic production since its origins around 1839. There is not a photographer today who is not aware of belonging to a great social body in evolution for a century and a half, a member of a noble "guild" that has shaped, at least in some small way, the civilization of the image.

It was at the end of the 1970s that serious exhibitions such as *Une Invention du XIXème siècle: La Photographie*, Paris, 1976,[16] *Photography Rediscovered*, Whitney Museum of American Art and the Art Institute of Chicago, 1979–80 and *Regards sur la photographie en France au XIXème siècle*, Paris, 1980 and Metropolitan Museum of Art, New York, 1981,[17] presented the entirety of early photographic production, freed from hagiography (the great figures to glorify) and from being

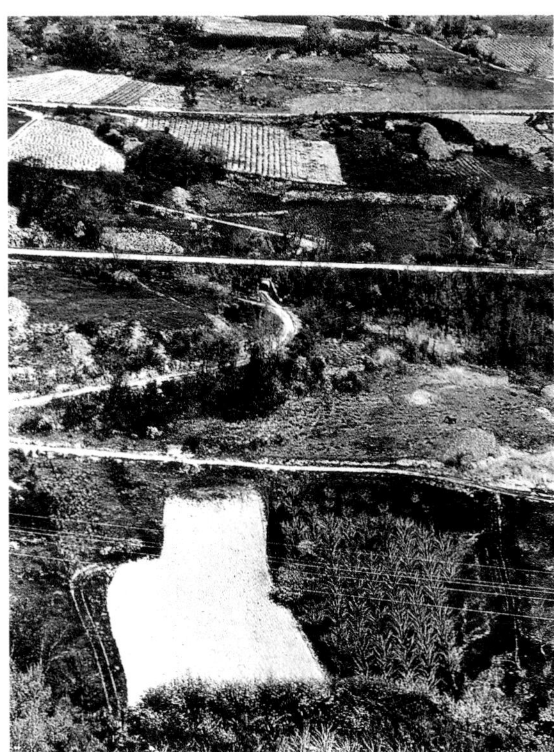

SOPHIE RISTELHUEBER, *Near Saint-Clément (Hautes-Alpes)*, 1984–1985, D.A.T.A.R. Photographic Mission.

GABRIELE BASILICO, *Merlimont Plage*, 1985, D.A.T.A.R. Photographic Mission.

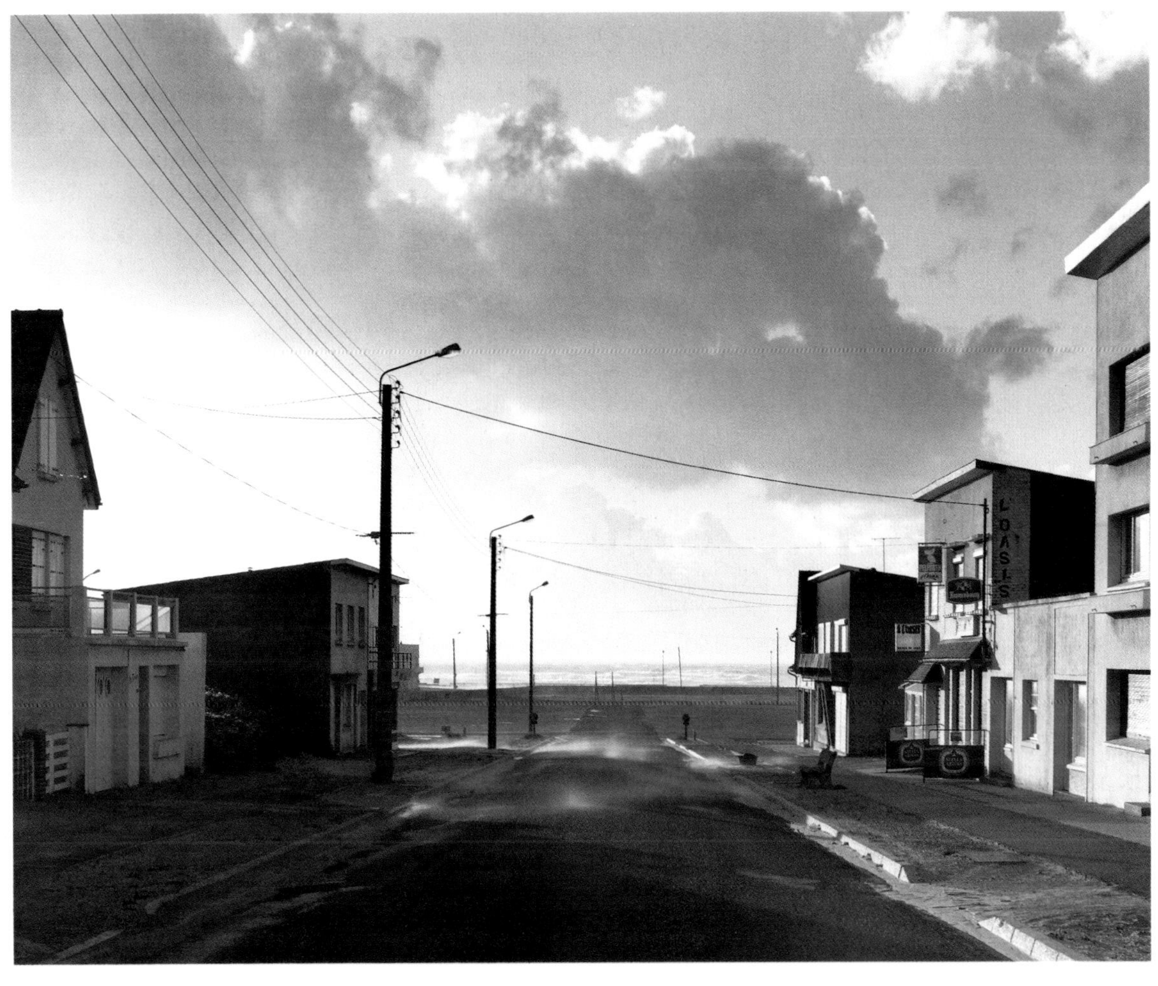

16. Collections of the Société Française de Photographie, exhibited at the Bibliothèque Nationale, Paris; *Les Trésors de la Société Française de Photographie*, Trianon de Bagatelle, Paris, 1979.

17. Catalogue published by Berger-Levrault, Paris.

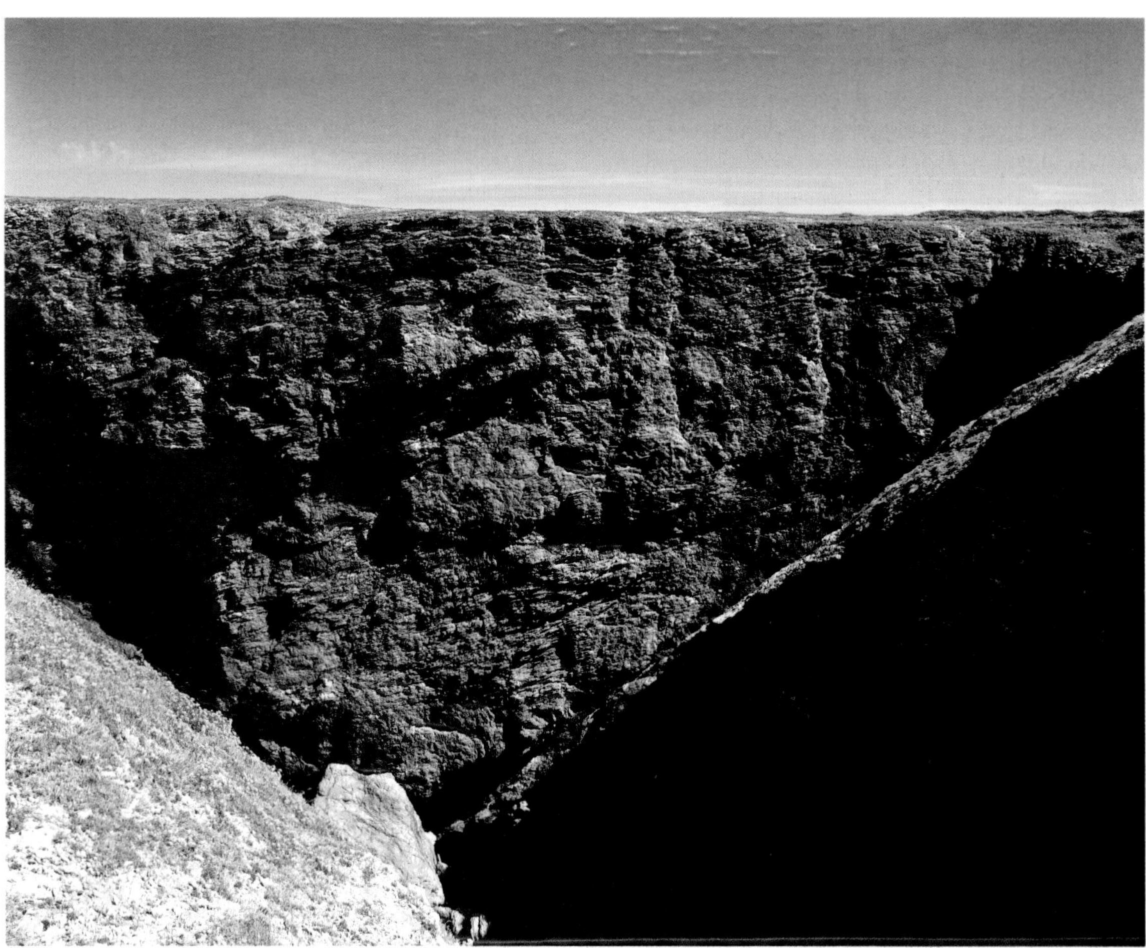

Werner Hannapel, *Belle-Île*, 1986, D.A.T.A.R. Photographic Mission.

18. In 1942, Ansel Adams shared with Beaumont Newhall his discovery of the geological photographs of Timothy O'Sullivan, then known only for his photographs of the Civil War. This rediscovery by Adams is not surprising given his taste for grand landscapes. It has been a relatively common occurrence that photographers have brought the work of excellent earlier practitioners to the attention of historians and curators.

19. The Wagstaff Collection, along with the Arnold Crane collection and several others, was later acquired by the Getty Museum.

20. *Niépce to Atget: The First Century of Photography*, exhibition catalogue.

21. Publications of Michael Lesy, *Wisconsin Death Trip*, New York, Pantheon Books, 1973, and *Real Life: Louisville in the Twenties*, New York, Pantheon Books, 1976; Pierre de Fenoÿl, *Chefs-d'œuvres des photographes anonymes au XIXe siècle*, Paris, Hachette, 1982; Ken Graves and Mitchell Payne, *American Snapshots*, Oakland, Scrimshaw Press, 1977.

Lewis Baltz, *Nevada Series, 1978, No. 4*, Michèle Chomette Gallery, Paris.

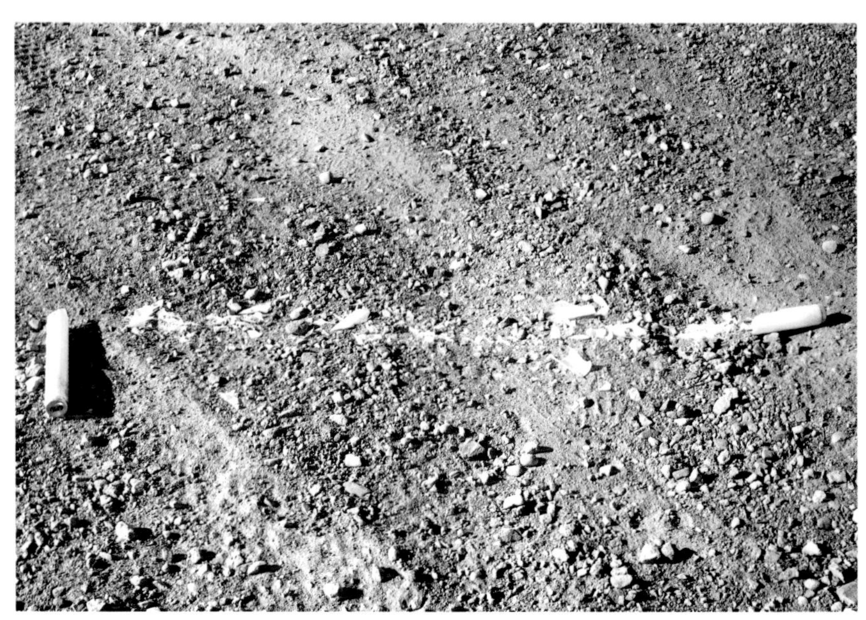

too closely linked to photographic material, cameras, equipment, and technology.

In an intellectual environment marked by conceptual art as well as by the antagonism between the readability of photojournalism and the occult signification of modern creations, photographic images reclaimed a life they had lost while resting in boxes and drawers at museums and libraries. They were appreciated again for what they were at their origins, with their own tonality, their special cropping, modeling, and contrast which certainly go well beyond the sole function of "documents" to which they had been relegated.[18] Postmodernism was about to nourish itself upon these rediscoveries.

The activities of private collectors have served both the private (galleries, auction houses) and the public (exhibitions, museums) sectors. Between the wars, the relationship of collection to institution was marked by the French government's rejection of the Gabriel Cromer collection. It was finally bought by the George Eastman House in Rochester, New York, thus forming the core of its collections. The Sam Wagstaff collection, created in the 1970s, was exhibited in 1982 (*A Book of Photographs from the Collection of Sam Wagstaff*)[19] and the Jammes' collection was also exhibited at the Art Institute of

Chicago (1977).[20] Well illustrated books and catalogues published at this time did much to further the rediscovery of nineteenth- and early twentieth-century photography. Even among the enlightened, few suspected the richness in quality and quantity.[21]

In one century, modern photography (the birth of which could be established with the invention of silver gelatin bromide) itself has become an institution defining its fields of application and defending its specific domain against other arts or other technologies. The threat of video and digital imagery and the technical modifications under way should, by themselves, bring significant disruptions. It will, without a doubt, be the occasion to remedy the control of the photographic institution and to recover a certain virginity of the medium.

There will be an accompanying shake-up of institutions but it appears that as long as photography – be it chemical or digital – is valued as an art in our culture, there will continue to be photographic institutions. As long as there are photographic institutions, there will continue to be institutional photography.

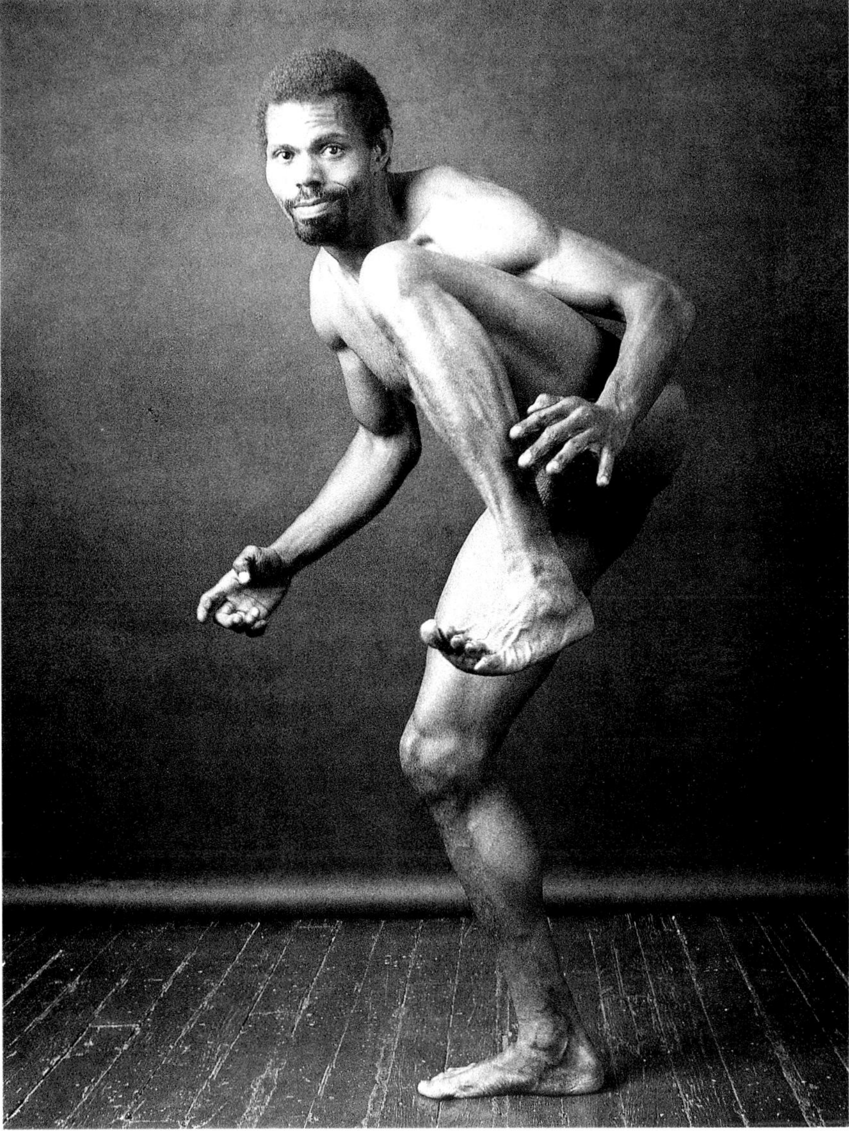

ROBERT MAPPLETHORPE, *Raymond*, 1984.

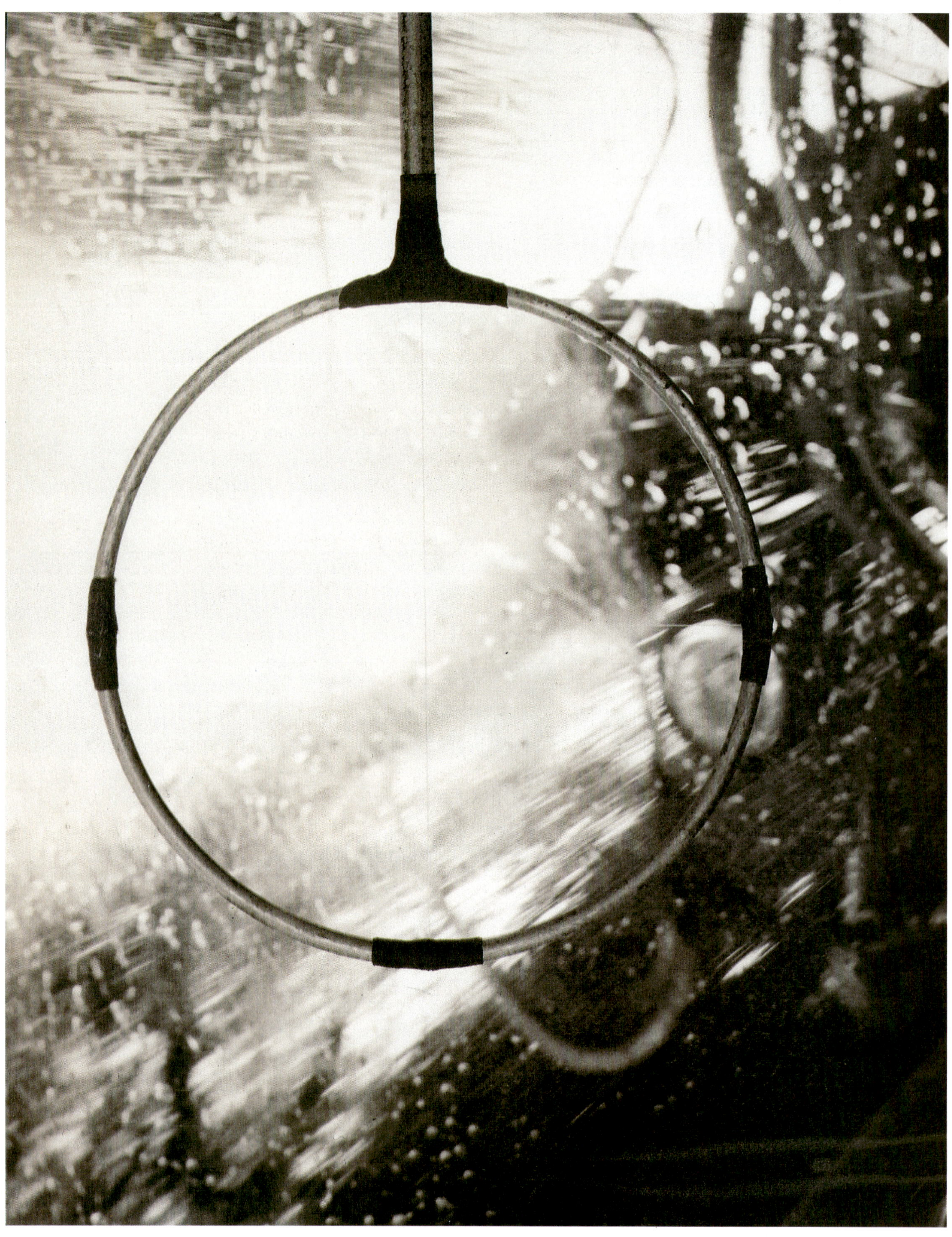

Dieter Appelt,
San Giacomo,
1986.

THE SENSITIVE SURFACE

Photographic substrate, imprint, memory

Michel Frizot

The works discussed in this chapter form part of a complete collection of illustrations and texts relating to the contemporary period; additional images are found in the preceding and following chapters.

During the 1960s, photography entered the art world, not by adopting the aims or the appearance of painting, but by replacing the traditional canvas – already rejected by numerous artists – with a photographic base material or "substrate". As well as being a vehicle for pop art and a medium which was universally accessible via the media, photography also proved to be highly versatile, with its possibilities of cut-outs, collages, color tints, overlays, and integration with letterpress. Moreover, it was easily produced and had popular connotations, while conforming with modernist standards. The closeness of photography and language quickly made it the favorite medium of conceptual art: a way of giving substance to an idea or recording an effect on the environment – defined as a sculptural process – the visualization of a mental process or simply achieving an artistic objective. Furthermore, the automatic compression of visual space and the opening up to multiple interpretations and ambiguity of perception, made photography, midway between the real and the imaginary, a form of communication which went beyond the senses.

In an interview by Alfred Stieglitz in 1922 entitled "Can a photograph have the significance of art?" Marcel Duchamp said: "I would like it to make people lose interest in painting, until something else makes photography unbearable".[1] We might now wonder if, at the end of a century when painting has been pushed to its absolute limits, photography will not also undergo the crisis of artistic renewal which Duchamp predicted, to be replaced, in turn, by an as yet undefined "something else". The loss of interest in painting predicted by Duchamp occurred during the 1960s. Would photography be the replacement medium, more up to date than any other, that artists longed for so much?

THE BLIND MAN

The Richard Mutt Case

They say any artist paying six dollars may exhibit.

Mr. Richard Mutt sent in a fountain. Without discussion this article disappeared and never was exhibited.

What were the grounds for refusing Mr. Mutt's fountain:—

1. *Some contended it was immoral, vulgar.*
2. *Others, it was plagiarism, a plain piece of plumbing.*

Now Mr. Mutt's fountain is not immoral, that is absurd, no more than a bath tub is immoral. It is a fixture that you see every day in plumbers' show windows.

Whether Mr. Mutt with his own hands made the fountain or not has no importance. He CHOSE it. He took an ordinary article of life, placed it so that its useful significance disappeared under the new title and point of view—created a new thought for that object.

As for plumbing, that is absurd. The only works of art America has given are her plumbing and her bridges.

"Buddha of the Bathroom"

Marcel Duchamp, Fountain (signed R. Mutt), double page spread from *The Blind Man*, no. 2, May 1917, photograph by Alfred Stieglitz.

Photography on the side of art

The rivalry between photography and painting no longer revolved around the question of imitation, as it had done in the past. Rather, it involved an exchange of terminology and procedure. In general, people no longer sought to integrate photography into art but, on the contrary, began to consider every art form, irrespective of the medium, as possible and legitimate from a photographic starting-point. The question of "photography as art", complicated by the diversity of photographic practice, goes back to the origins of the medium, when the only socio-artistic categories into which its inventors could place photography were *arts, artist*, and *fine arts*. While Gustave Le Gray and Julia Margaret Cameron loudly proclaimed their right to belong to a small world of artistic creativity, the majority of portraitists devoted themselves to the immediate satisfaction of their customers' desire to have their picture

1. *Manuscripts*, no. 4, December 1922.

taken, which, in Baudelaire's view, could only harm photography's prestige. Today, "photography" is no more a unified concept than it was then. It is composed of hugely diversified practices and aims. There were no grounds, therefore, for forcing the whole of photography into alien categories. It would have been quite possible to agree that a photograph could only be defined as "art" or "modern art" when it was produced in that particular context.

From around 1900, Stieglitz had already confronted the same problem. The concept of *Camera Work* and of his 291 Gallery implied that the representational content of the work was far less important than the way it was presented and perceived. In other words, it was up to photography, in order to be considered an art form, to proclaim clear artistic intentions and to conform with "nobler" methods of circulation. At the time, around 1900, amateur photography and photojournalism were growing in importance, to the dismay of professional photographers. A group of strong personalities who wanted to have their work recognized as something more than a trade or leisure activity defined a "photographic art", emphasized by a desire to break with plebeian practices. This wish became reality through a link with Impressionism and Symbolism. However, this association was soon rejected in favor of urban modernism and, as far as distribution was concerned, by the extreme care taken with the reproduction of the photographic prints in *Camera Work*, attention to display conditions, and the cost of the works themselves.

During the 1960s, the same question of "photographic art", which came up in quite similar circumstances and contexts, could not, therefore, have been resolved by allowing the whole of photography to enter the global field of "art" (as defined by a historiography which had survived until the post-war period). Affiliation to contemporary art, in around 1970, emerged around the same common ground, along the same fault lines as at the beginning of the century.

JOEL-PETER WITKIN, *Woman on a Table*, 1987.

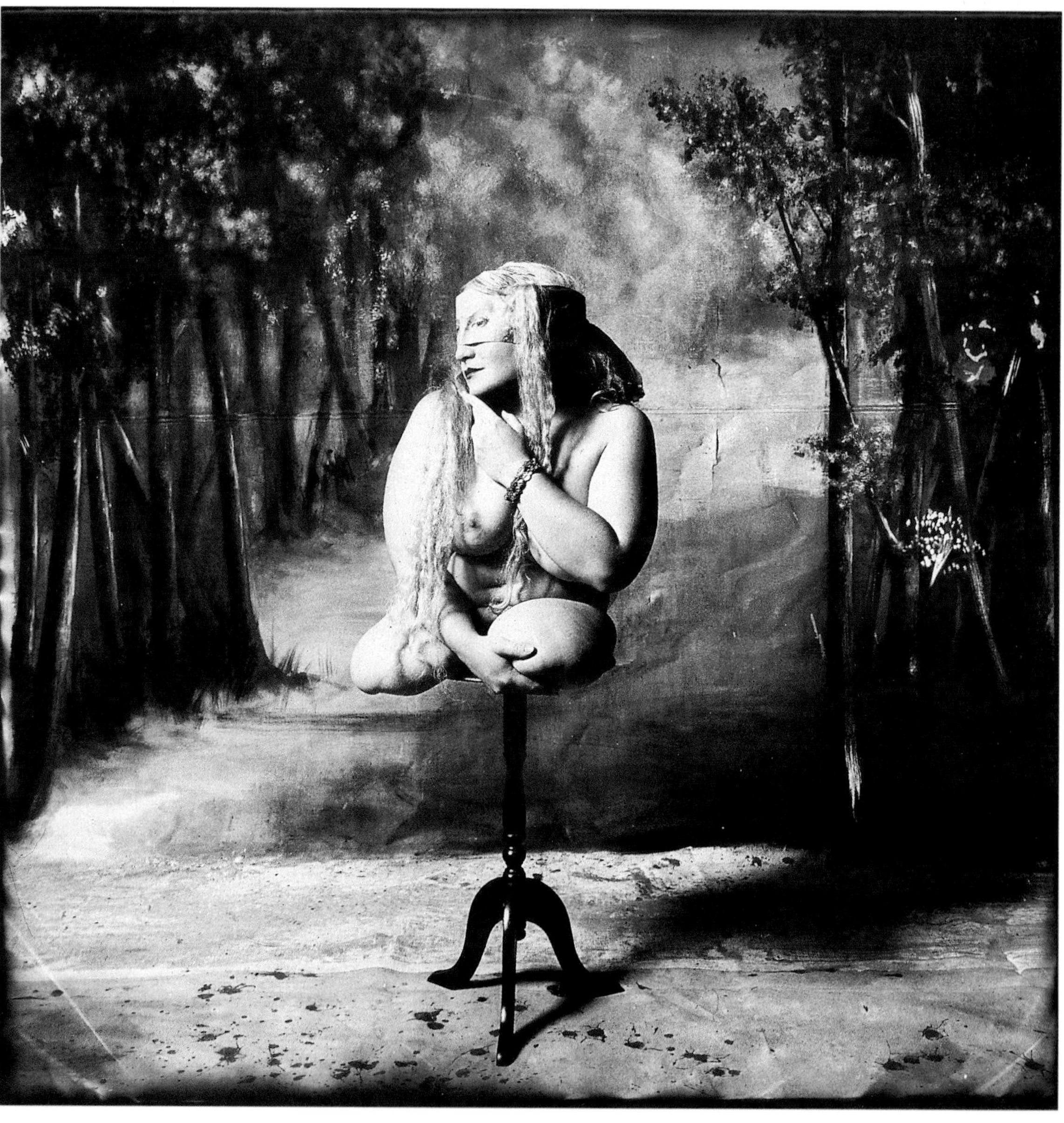

These were ideas which Duchamp had already followed with his "ready-made" art of 1910–1920. Duchamp brought to the gallery space manufactured objects, whose primary purpose was not artistic (such as the urinal or the winerack), but whose qualities as created objects could not be questioned. In the same way, photography could find respect on the contemporary art scene only if museums or institutions accepted it. The linguistic pair "gallery/museum", with its operator (the exhibition) would define what is an "art object". Duchamp's *Fontaine,* which he had been tempted to display in an exhibition, would be passed on to future generations thanks to Stieglitz's studio photograph of it, which was published in an avant-garde magazine, *The Blind Man* (1917).

Thus it was that, shortly before 1970, photography became a part of the contemporary art scene, not through deliberate acceptance by everyone but as a result of progressive infiltration resulting from the use of photography by a number of young artists.[2] This acceptance had a double consequence, with paradoxical effects – the splitting-off of photography of events, of photojournalism, from an "art photography" that was, above all, the preserve of photo clubs, and also a renewal of the strategies of those who, nevertheless, wished to adhere to the accepted criteria of photography. Galleries dedicated to photography appeared, exhibitions were mounted in the great museums of modern art, and photographic collections were formed by institutions. Even more than the photographic substrate, the way in which the medium was used and artistic intentions became the trademark of a few groups who were, at first, considered marginal and rebellious, both in photography and politics (in France these were the post-1968 years; in the United States, the time of the Vietnam War).[3]

Today, the word "photography" means very different things to different people. Photography really appeared on the contemporary art scene in 1969, with the exhibition *Live in Your Head: When Attitudes become Form,* which Harald Szeemann put on at the Berne Kunsthalle. Here, photography found its unity both in the material used (the "sensitive surface") and in the production process (exposure, development, printing). The subtitle, *Works-Concepts-Processes-Situations-Information,* emphasized the absence of painting or sculpture *qua* techniques and the dilution of traditional methods of artistic production in favor of attitudes which found material expression in unsettling works, which were sometimes displayed merely at the concept stage. The exhibition promoted an art-form that was based on ideas, that scorned the objet-d'art, that recovered three-dimensional space and time, and had vital implications for "self-creating art".

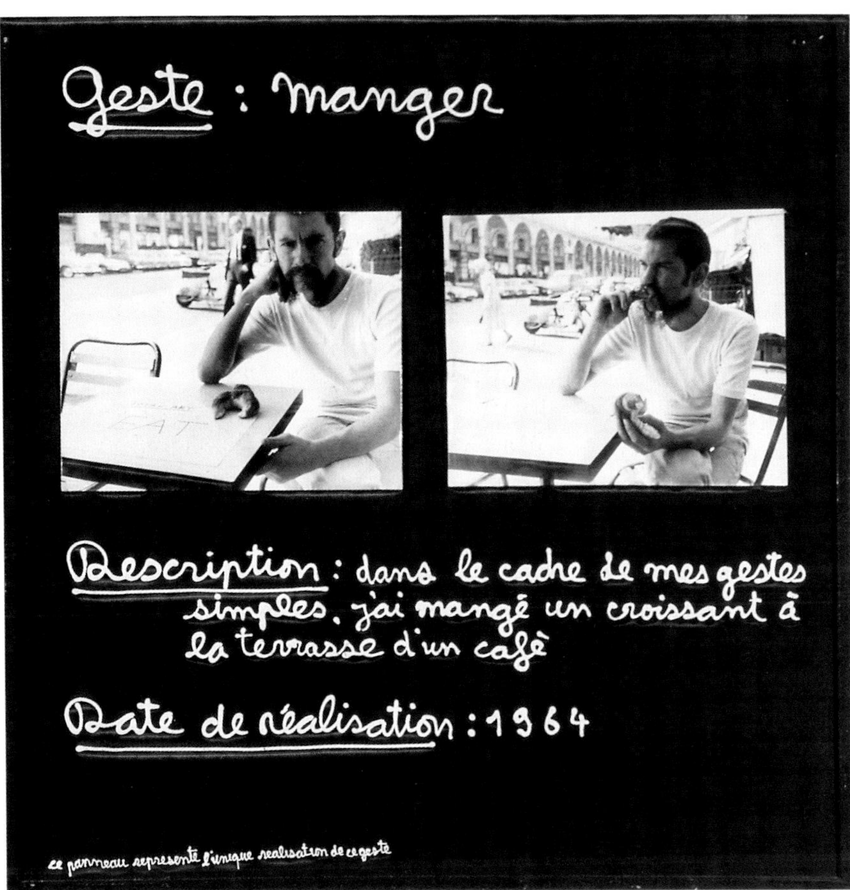

BEN,
Gesture: Eating,
1964,
painting and photography on panel.
F.R.A.C. Rhône-Alpes Collection.

During the following years, this movement, at first vague and defined by the breadth of that which it rejected, expressed itself in a more defined way, both in actions and words: conceptual art, *Arte Povera,* land art, body art, happenings, performances, etc. These artists, who wanted to create art without painting – and often by direct intervention on reality – are in many respects the heirs of pop art, of the New Realists, and especially of the artist Yves Klein (d. 1962), whose catalogue symbolically reproduced the photograph *Saut dans le Vide* (A Jump into the Void, 1960).

Although it was still fairly marginal, photography already appeared in this exhibition as a distinct aesthetic entity, on the same basis as language (Robert Barry, Hanne Darboven), art by telephone (Walter De Maria), contrasting materials (felt by Robert Morris, neon tubes by Merz and by Nauman, coal by Kounellis, metals by Carl André) or anti-painting (Robert Ryman). Indeed, a few artists presented photographs or incorporated photographs into their work, especially to accompany their biographical notes in the catalogue – Jan Dibbets, with *Perspective Correction* (1968), Michael Heizer, Hans Haacke, Richard Long, Walter De Maria, Bruce Nauman, Dennis Oppenheim, Robert Smithson. These were, in fact,

2. M. Vaizey, *The Artist as Photographer,* New York, Holt, Rinehart and Winston, 1982.

3. A. Grundberg and K. McCarthy Gauss, *Photography and Art: Interactions since 1946,* New York, Abbeville, 1987.

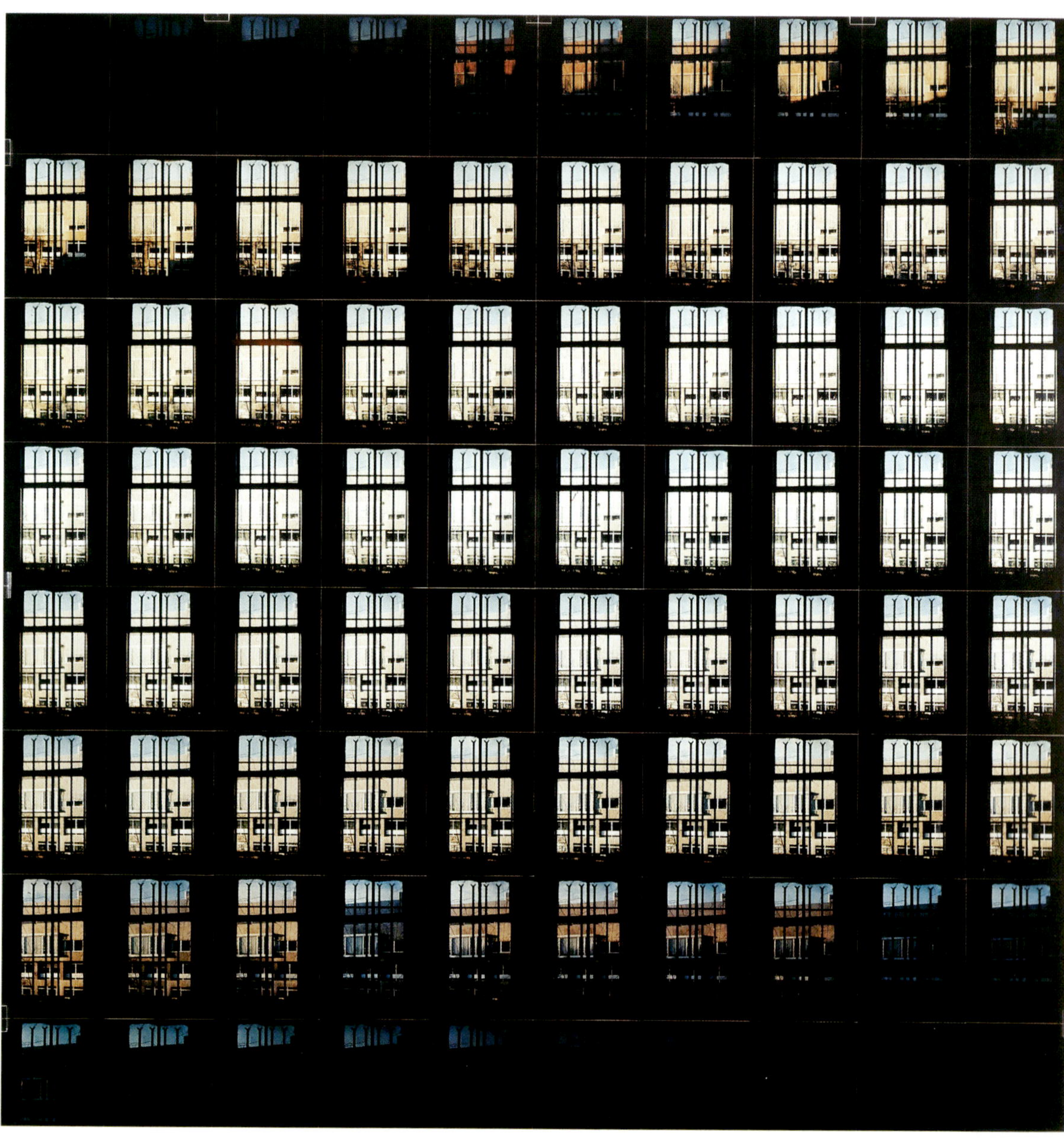

JAN DIBBETS, *The Shortest Day at the Van Abbemuseum,* Eindhoven, 1970.

the main representatives of this first generation of so-called "artists using photography".

Ten years later, another exhibition summed up the evolution of this question (see box). Its very title, *Photographie als Kunst/Kunst als Photographie* [Photography as Art/Art as Photography], demonstrated how, in the field of contemporary art, photographic genres had become polarized and established attitudes more entrenched (this was a schism which lasted through the 1980s). On the one hand, there was a photographic tradition which accorded most importance to the primacy of the actual taking of the image as an "operator" on the senses (represented by Duane Michals or Lee Friedlander, for example). On the other hand, there was the tendency for the medium to be taken over by artists from a different creative sphere and another tradition of displaying their works. To a certain extent, this line of development forms part of the tradition of painting. This second trend is represented, among others, by Christian Boltanski, who works mostly *with* photography while claiming that he is a "painter" who does not use a brush. It is the cerebral nature of art which is in question here rather than its faculty for creating images – what the works themselves refer to, not what the actual images show us, however figurative they may be.

These two worlds, which often ignore each other, nevertheless cooperate, observe each other, are jealous of each other, and learn from each other. The result of this split is that photography over the past ten years has shown paranoid tendencies, a conflict of definition, as though the word "photography" must avoid duplicity at all costs. The ambiguous status of the photographic medium, and its quarrels with "art" have even formed the subject of recent exhibitions,[4] in which exponents take sides (see box). In more concrete terms, in response to this ambivalence, institutions have had to adopt two approaches – either to favor the "print room" formula (as at the Bibliothèque Nationale in Paris, for example) or to provide facilities for the display of "pieces"

4. *Ils se disent peintres, ils se disent photographes,* Paris, ARC, Musée d'Art Moderne de la Ville de Paris, 1981.

several meters long, conceived as objects, in an unusual frame or on very fragile supports (as at any museum of modern art). Such decisions depend on established practice in the institutions concerned, who have to pronounce on the category of works received – unless they make a conscious decision to devise a totally new way of displaying the work. The unambiguous presence and acceptance of the "photographic" in contemporary art has not yet been totally achieved, now that painting, which had been rejected in the 1970s, has made a comeback.

In the face of these often arbitrary stances, resulting from complex historical circumstances, our aim is to demonstrate the homogeneity of these practices centered on the notion of the "sensitive substrate": a vector of a particular meaning within varying forms of photography and often contradictory situations within museums.

The inner theater

During the 1950s and 1960s, the prevailing model was that of a photography of actions or feelings, in the service of mankind, whose creed could be summed up as the "painful necessity of putting one's eye, head, and heart on the same line of sight", as Henri Cartier-Bresson described it.[5] In other words, the nature of the work is based on one's attitude when shooting and on the physical act of taking the photograph. But the photographer is, at the same time, both a spectator and an actor in a theater which escapes them and yet with which they are well acquainted, for they already carry it inside. "If the photographer manages to reflect a world which is as much outside as inside, it is because people have 'got into the part' as they say in the theater."[6]

The poetic quality of the "decisive moment" resulted from spontaneity, from the use of miniature cameras, from confrontations with serious situations, from a humanistic approach to journalism which could flourish in newspapers which were eager for the truth. When defining the new trends of the 1970s, the "decisive moment" option, which was the universal watchword of a great number of photographers, need not be totally denied. However, a split had certainly occurred between the spirit and the method. The new generation offered its photographs for exhibitions rather than as illustrations or reproductions. Books had become the motive force behind photography, following the example of Cartier-Bresson, Friedlander, Koudelka, and, especially, Frank's *The Lines of my Hand*.[7] "Photo-books" also introduced a discursive style for the presentation (and understanding) of photography which was very different from what the press had offered. Linguistic units confront each other, visual links and associations are created in the sequences of images, implying another story. It is, therefore, patently obvious that there exists a photographic language (a question which Barthes considered at the time).[8] Photography is not content with portraying an event and bringing it to us; it provokes a multiple discourse, first within the image, then in relation to other images (in a series of images, in successive images in an exhibition or a book).

The notion of a unified and retrospective œuvre, when applied to photographers as it had formerly been to painters, was the result of such publications. Images were no longer seen as isolated successes, which had occurred more or less at random, but as elements in a carefully formulated personal language – while remaining within the specific field of photography.

This evolution helps us to view the practices of certain photographers in the 1970s and 1980s as a narrative concept (rather than mere passive observation) – a narrative whose working-out is more or less visible, more or less assumed. For example, while Friedlander remained faithful to his quest for disorder in composition and blurring of perspectives, Larry Clark showed the difficulties (drugs, sex, etc) inherent in a society into which he had to merge completely in order not to appear as a predator.[9]

But in both cases the exterior that is photographed has become a mini-theater, a microcosm

Abramovic and Ulay,
Modus vivendi,
1984,
Stedelijk Museum,
Amsterdam.
▼

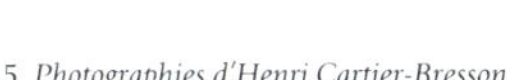

5. *Photographies d'Henri Cartier-Bresson*, Paris, Delpire, 1963.

6. H. Cartier-Bresson, *The Decisive Moment*, New York, Simon and Schuster, 1952.

7. R. Frank, *The Lines of My Hand*, Tokyo, Yugensha, Motomura, 1972; 3rd edn., London, Secker and Warburg, 1989.

8. "Le message photographique", 1961, "Rhétorique de l'image", 1964, printed together in *L'Obvie et l'Obtus*, Paris, Le Seuil, 1982.

9. *Tulsa*, New York, Lustrum, 1971; *Teenage Lust*, New York, Lustrum, 1982.

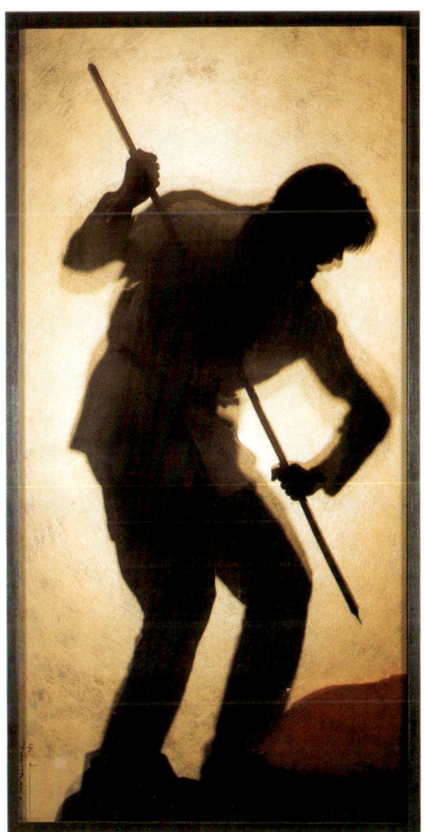

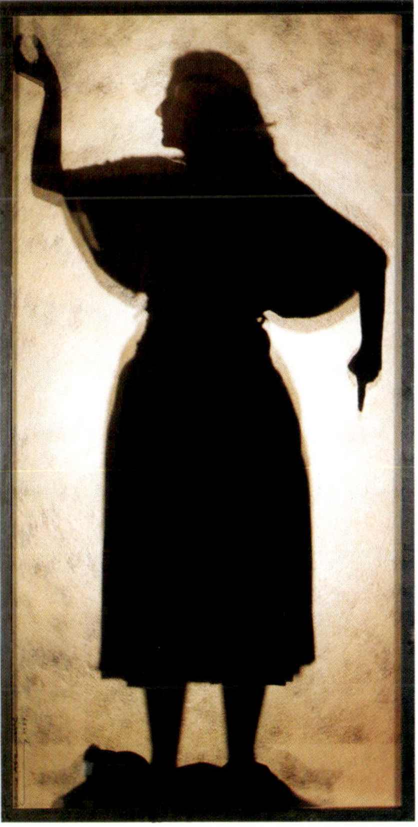

Exposure value

If photography has, since the 1970s, imposed itself as a supporting medium and a material of contemporary art, it is through its capacity to "expose itself". The "exposure value" of photography (Walter Benjamin) is relevant to all attempts to integrate it (alone or in combination techniques) into contemporary art. It is logical that the focus of the aesthetic debate should be exhibitions, where the reality of dissent is exacerbated.

The first exhibition to accord an important place to photography was *When Attitudes Become Form* (Berne, 1969), which confirmed a conceptual practice that was already a few years old. In the same way, in 1972 *The New Art* (Hayward Gallery, London) offered works on a photographic substrate without displaying any aggression towards the pictorial tradition that they superseded. This conciliatory attitude was also found in *Un certain art anglais* [A Certain English Art, Musée d'Art Moderne de la Ville de Paris, 1979], staged by Burgin, Gilbert and George, Hilliard, etc., which made photography the innovative material.

However, other exhibitions in the 1970s brought the controversy back to life, insisting on the episodic and fluctuating relationships between photography and painting. Even so, their antagonism was more like the arguments of critics than those of artists.

These various manifestations sometimes raised the question of "reflecting the model" (photography as the model of painting and vice versa), which was treated by Van Deren Coke (*The Painter and the Photograph*, Albuquerque, 1964), Otto Stelzner (*Kunst und Photographie*, Munich, 1966), and Aaron Scharf (*Art and Photography*, London, 1969) as one of the symptoms of the development of modern art. *Combattimento per un immagine, Fotografie e Pittori*, Galleria Civica d'Arte Moderna, Turin, 1973 presented itself as a battle for photographic objectivity and the space conquest of communication ("The Museum without Walls"); hyper-realism rubbed shoulders there with Huebler, Penone, Wegman, and Mulas (*Omaggio a Niépce*, 1968). In 1977, *Malerei und Fotografie im Dialog* (Zurich) established a more confident relationship between the different media: amateur photographic practice (Bonnard, Vuillard, Mucha, Munch), models of pictorial composition for the nineteenth-century photographers, attempts to come closer to Pictorialism, the annexation of photography to the arts of the avant-garde movement, going as far as recent works by Baldessari, Acconci, Rinke, Gerz, Michals, Krims, and Long, brought together in *Konzept-Art*. The "sequence" appears as one of the specific expressions of photography in this context, which favors the "picture".

The dichotomy which underlined the exhibition *Photographie als Kunst 1879-1979; Kunst als Photographie, 1949-1979* (Innsbruck, Linz, Graz, Vienna) in 1979 provided materials for the two volumes of the catalogue, which dealt with the art of photography and art with photography. In the first, a broad notion of innovative photography brought together Diane Arbus, Franco Fontana, and Ralph Gibson, which went beyond the idea of a document. In the second, which dealt with the integration of photography into contemporary art, the distinction intervened through a particular method of presentation (format, mounting, display of sequences of images, the location of the display), which then marked off the modern "work of art".

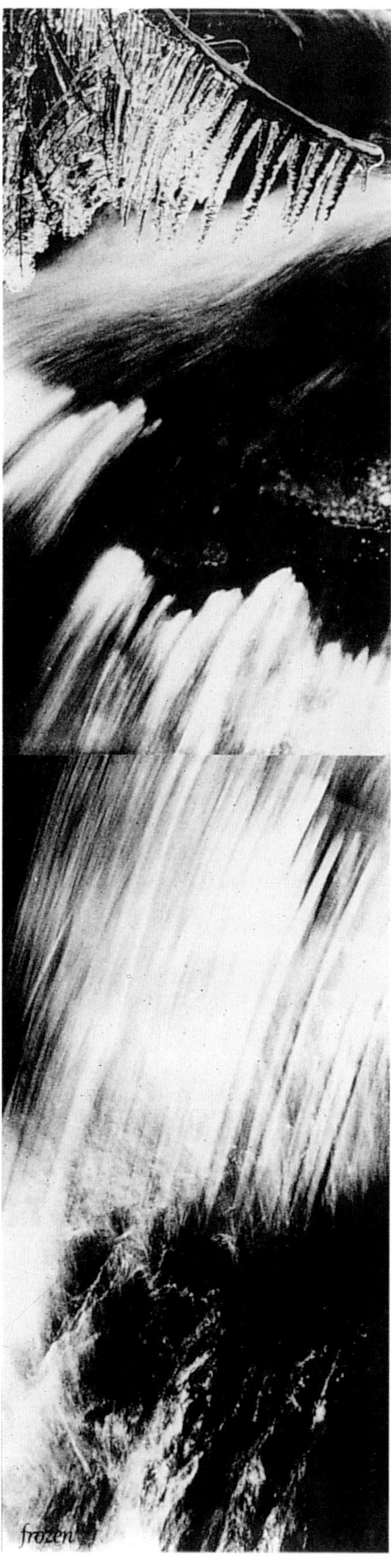

John Hilliard
Frozen,
1979.

Ils se disent peintres, ils se disent photographes (Musée d'Art Moderne de la Ville de Paris, 1981) was the statement of individual attitudes and intentions, no longer distinguished from each other by the photographic substrate or the way they were displayed. Undoubtedly, though, the catalogue gives too great an impression of a unity of practices.

By limiting its analysis to the idea of a stage set, the exhibition *Théâtre des réalités* (Metz, Paris, 1986) brought together the worlds of photographers such as Meatyard, Saudek, Gibson, Turbeville, and Esclusa with a more conceptual approach (Baldessari, Lüthi, Cowin). *Kunst mit Fotografie* (Berlin, Cologne, Munich, 1983-1984) was the first time the Krauss collection had been shown, defined as a collection of contemporary art on a photographic substrate.

The photo/painting debate was taken up again, with respect to the continuity of American art, in *Photography and Art: Interactions since 1946* (Los Angeles, 1987), which locates post-war photographic strategy: photographic reproductions in pop art, the impact of conceptual art on documentary work, considered as a sculptural process, creation of fiction in the studio.

Postmodernism was particularly credited with the arrival of a "photographic culture" (Allan MacCollum, Barbara Kruger, Sherri Levine) which recycled reproductive and repetitive schemes. It may be noted that particular problems existed in American art, not overly keen to regulate the so-called internationalism of art (regulated as it was by market forces).

The 150th anniversary of photography in 1989 provided an occasion for the debate to be revived. None of the retrospective exhibitions organized for the occasion avoided it, despite a wide diversity: *Photography Now* (London), *Photography Until Now* (New York), *L'invention d'un art* (Paris), *On the Art of Fixing a Shadow* (Washington, Chicago, Los Angeles), *The Art of Photography* (Houston, Canberra, London), and *Foto-Kunst* (Stuttgart), all organized by museums, suggested, to varying extents, that photography was not totally accepted as an artistic medium, but that the differences had become notably ironed out since its entry into museums.

Michel Frizot

in which the tensions existing between groups or individuals are revealed. The photographer can be a spectator, actor, producer or script-writer. The theatrical character of the photographed space is analyzed in *Théâtre des réalités*.[10] The way it has distanced itself from the traditional position of the profession may be assessed from the way the subject has had to be prepared, and the way reality is more or less dressed up. In this way, Marc Trivier,[11] always concerned with the constant elements of the photographic set-up as well as with the content, seems to photograph with an anguished sense of expectation, as in Beckett's *Waiting for Godot*, whether he is dealing with a poet, a psychopath, a tree or a slaughterhouse. Mark Cohen, too, provides this sense of a personal theater in the context of everyday news snapshots. William Eggleston, a color photographer who seems very much the heir of the F.S.A. program of the 1930s, could also be considered as sharing this theatricalizing tendency, as could Les Krims, who also came to color after working with sepia-toned prints. However, unlike Eggleston, Krims has a more and more complex conception of the space within which he works, bringing together in a haphazard way all the standard objects of American kitsch, with its fantasies and excesses, its gadgets and naivety, and participating himself (often in the nude) in these orgies of the consumer society. R. E. Meatyard (who died in 1972) appears as the ancestor of this photographic practice – often deriving from amateur amusements – when he tried to capture fleeting moments, embodied by his children (appearance, disappearance, dissolution, death) by a creative use of camera-shake and shadows produced by long or multiple exposures. In this

UN HOMME DANS L'ESPACE !

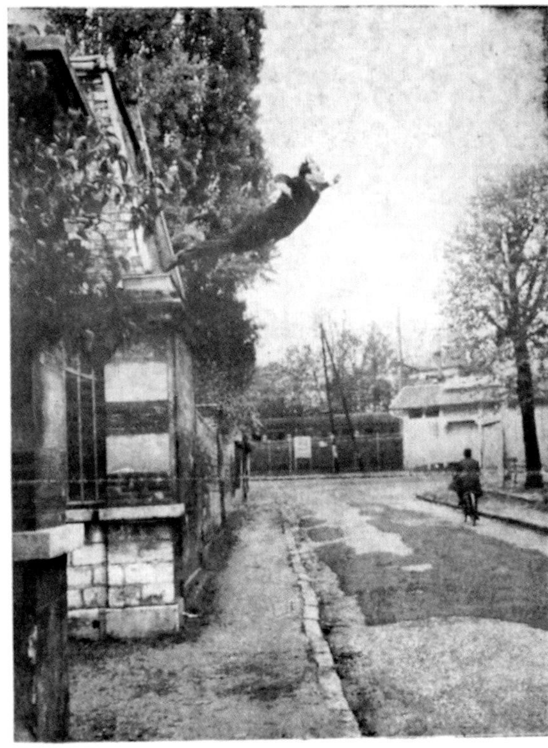

Le peintre de l'espace se jette dans le vide !

Yves Klein,
"A Man in Space!"
(A Jump into the Void),
titlepage of *Dimanche*,
November 27, 1960,
unique edition
(photo Shunk-Kender).

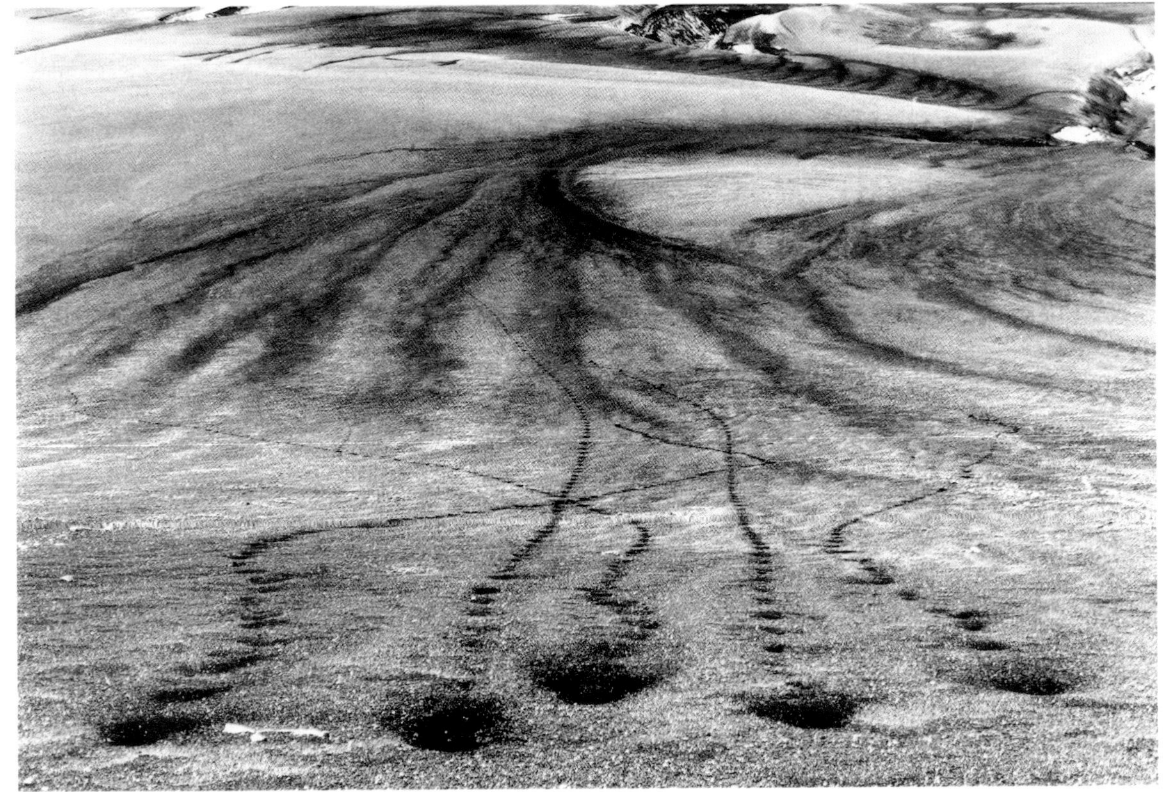

Richard Long,
Five Stones,
Iceland, 1974,
Leeds City Galleries.

10. "Théâtre des réalités", Metz pour la Photographie, 1986.

11. *Marc Trivier: Photographies*, Denain, Lausanne, Centre Régional de la Photographie/Musée de l'Elysée, 1988.

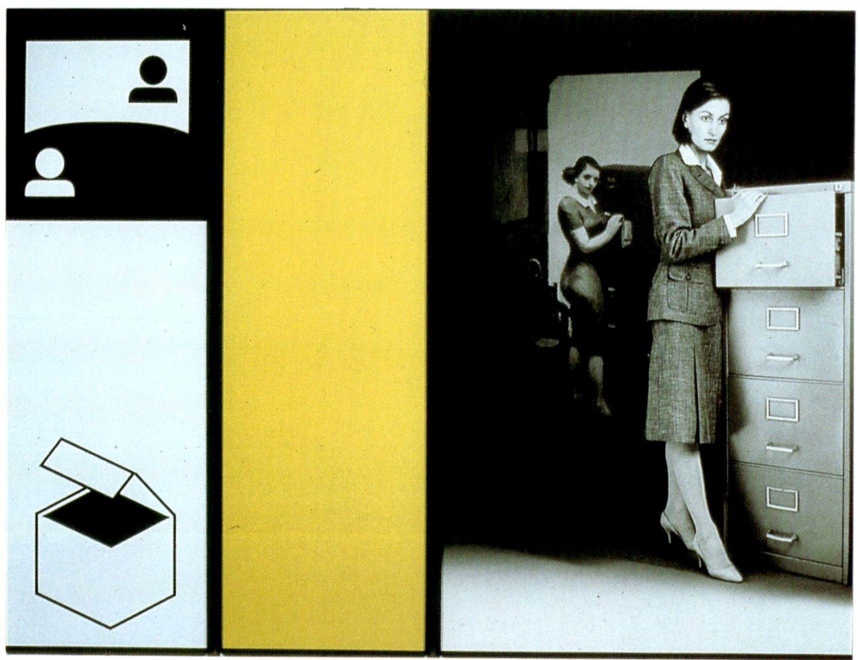

VICTOR BURGIN, *Office at Night*, 1984–1985.

way, these photographers personalized their work of evocation by the aggressiveness of their denunciation, by irony, by distance, by the use of the third party.

Some photographers meticulously constructed a theater of perverse imitation of nature, submitting the viewer to the ambiguity of a reality which seemed guaranteed as authentic through the photographic act, as in the fake plants made out of odds and ends but registered with as much objectivity as Blossfeldt, which Joan Fontcuberta included in his *Herbarium*, and, more recently, his false animal species, said to have been discovered in hypothetical museums of natural history, which eloquently evoke the mutation of species.

Through this theatricalization of the photographic framework, many photographers have finally come back to the studio – perhaps an echo of the phobic spaces painted by Francis Bacon, who himself obtained them from photography! The cube-shaped space of the viewpoint demands to be totally filled (as in the case of Les Krims) with objects, bodies or even with subjective tensions, as in the love chambers of Bernard Faucon, each organized like a poem – colors, fictions or natural elements (air, fire, ice).

Thus, photographic compositions derive, at least in spirit, from the theater of behavior – happenings and actions – which, by providing, to a certain extent, concrete expression to Antonin Artaud's theater of cruelty, had transformed the art of pictorial considerations of the 1970s into the exteriorization of the social unconscious (*Anthropométries* by Yves Klein, 1960; the happenings of Fluxus). From 1962, Hermann Nitsch had photographed, filmed, and recounted the expiatory *Aktion* of his Orgien-Mysterien-Theater: a denunciation of war, a catharsis of fear, with its rituals of blood and violence. These sessions were open to the public and formed his personal work, but now survive only through the photographic record which eventually became the way the accomplished work was exhibited and thus made public.

Art was capable of transforming life, awakening political conscience, creating new, sensitive relationships. The actions of Beuys (*Twenty-Four Hours*, 1965; *Coyote*, 1974) were quickly changed to images (particularly photographic ones) which represented situations which were ephemeral rather than a lived-through continuity, just like the *tableaux vivants* which also comprised the performances of Iannis Kounellis, Gilbert and George (*Living Sculpture*, 1969), Luigi Ontani, Klaus Rinke, and Dan Graham.

As modernist versions of the theater of the absurd, these scenic creations had no small effect on the intentions of a whole generation during the 1970s, who saw in the internal organization of the studio and in the composition of subjects a way of visualizing the collective unconscious. That is what Joel-Peter Witkin seems to have wanted to demonstrate.[12] For Witkin, the unlikely could actually happen, since he photographed it. The fantastic can be realized behind the closed doors of the workshop. However, Witkin multiplies the perversity of his constructions – often employing deformed models or handicapped people – by constant references to painting and to the history of representation, to its myths, to the "pose" which endows his fantastic invention with a pictorial sense which is sometimes too glibly organized. Something of the performance remains also in the case of Ulay and Abramovic, whose behavior as a couple is scrutinized by photography, in Urs Lüthi and his exploration of random body movements, or even in the case of Ger Van Elk (*Missing Persons*, 1976). Everything happens as if, after having studied the privileged way in which photography could render works of land art, body art, etc., certain artists had recreated the circum-

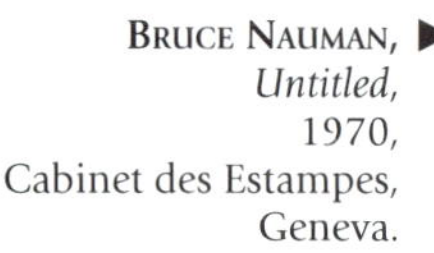

BRUCE NAUMAN, ▶ *Untitled*, 1970, Cabinet des Estampes, Geneva.

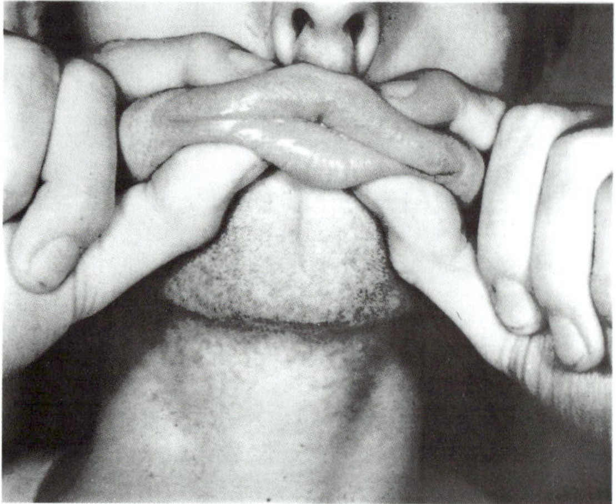

12. *Joel-Peter Witkin*, Twelvetrees Press, 1985; J. Yau and G. Blaisdale, *Gods of Earth and Heaven*, Twelvetrees Press, 1989.

stances, the intentions, the motivations, in the more private area of personal space which could be transferred to the sensitive surface. Neurotic scene-painting, displayed to a passive audience, mutated into an inner scene which was flat and dumb, and which could be fixed to a photographic mount.

Logically, other artist photographers had to interrogate another parameter of this "instantaneous" theatrical stage witnessed by the photographer, the scene designer, and even the actor: the narrative, in the form of scenario or text. The photographic sequences of Duane Michals, which for a long time were taken as his personal stamp, have for around ten years been condensed into single photographs, sometimes painted, accompanied by (often long) texts of an autobiographical character. These fables, which are presented by means of photographs like a film synopsis made with frame enlargements, are also an echo of the photo-romance, with their sometimes outmoded morality.

Eileen Cowin portrays family situations in an similarly quasi-biographical style by imagining short scenes depicting personal relationships controlled by common laws, acted out by the people around her, in which each viewer can interpret the states of mind evoked by the poses displayed. Karen Knorr, who had photographed middle-class interiors displaying disturbing monotony, worked more concretely during the 1980s on the relationship between language and visual and verbal reality, performing a critical analysis of society by means of the differences born out of the contrast of decoration, attitudes, and legends, in the style of a nineteenth-century illustration.

A similar expectation of revelation guides Patrick Faigenbaum in his restricted "social investigations" into the great Italian families and their history (including what remains visible in their actual bodies), or Sophie Calle, in her quest for every person's story, her desire to verbalize difficult issues through her images. Photography corroborates a narrative, or replaces it, or even authenticates an inner image (as in the series *Les Aveugles*).

Indeed, a certain type of photographic creation calls for theatrical analysis: the scenic space is an interior in which inexpressible entities will reveal themselves and display tensions which will be captured on film. Often, this quest for an ancient presence is characterized by a tendency to produce very dark prints (as with most of the photographers mentioned above). The image seems submerged in the luminous wake which is left by the haunted place where the scene is recorded, itself similar to a gigantic darkroom. The phantom ships of Manuel Esclusa or the disturbing settings of an accursed industrial civilization by Gilbert Fastenaekens are the gloomy witnesses of a tragicomedy, though it was through such clues that the photographers of the 1930s praised the technological impossibility of progress or working-class achievements, won at such cost.

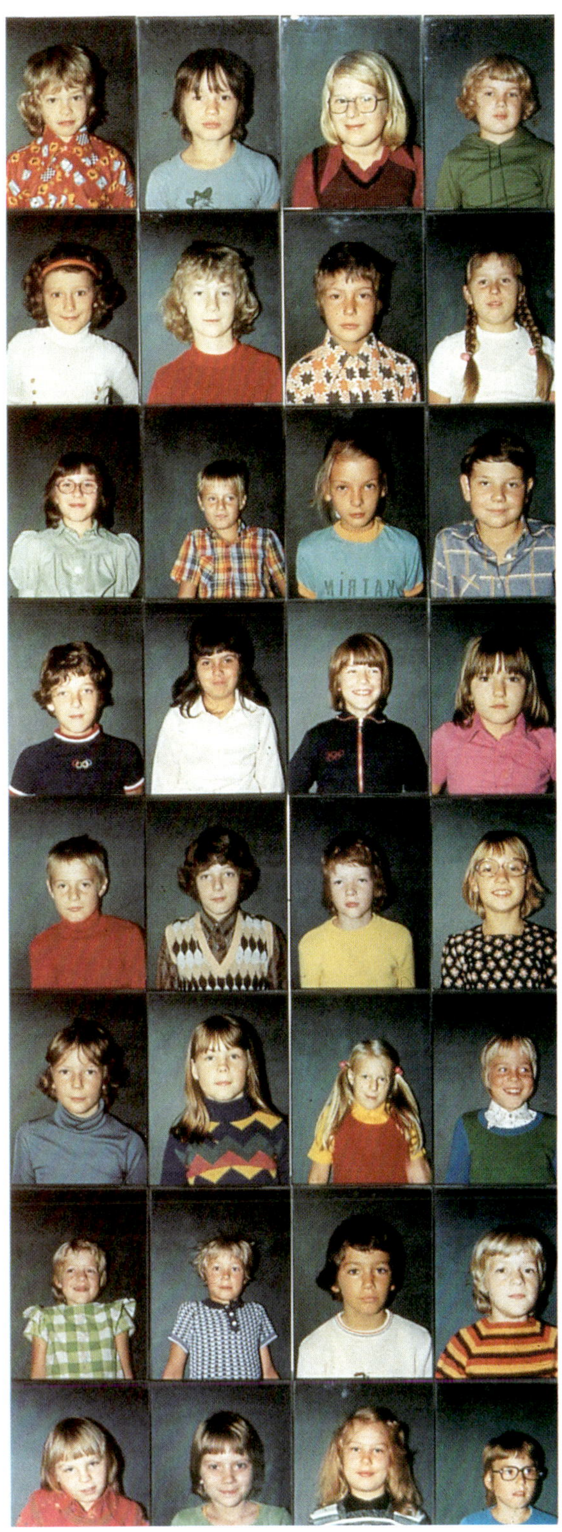

Christian Boltanski, *The Children of Berlin*, 1975, F.R.A.C. Aquitaine.

Photography and language

At the end of the 1960s, at the same time that the photography which had evolved from the photojournalism or humanism of the 1950s became an accepted way of expressing a rebellious nature, it also appeared to others to be an operator of the

Robert Smithson, ***Two photographs of*** **Spiral Jetty,** Salt Lake, Utah, 1970, Ludwig Forum für internationale Kunst, Aachen.
▼

senses. Structuralism, and especially the studies of Roland Barthes, tried to consider photography globally, as a linguistic fact. That is, they took into account the specific nature of photographic apparatus, with all its inherent automaticity, immediacy and fidelity: a means of creating an imprint of reality, captured the moment the shutter is pressed. This is the character of photography as indicator, which has frequently been stressed by philosophers for at least twenty years.[13] However, this awareness of a certain instrumental bias brings us to the observation that photography cannot be completely assimilated to reality in terms of simple substitution; it recreates only partial, that is, schematic signs: exact shapes, the illusion of volume, the identification of objects. It was necessary to put an end to the naive belief in a "photographic whole" which could explain the world through the medium. Faith in the positivist authenticity of photography was a consequence of photojournalism and a result of the realist objectivity of the 1930s. In the area of images in general (illustrations, paintings, advertisements), photography is first perceived *qua* photography, that is to say, comprising all the characteristics (as indicators) inherent in its disposition as imprint, with the result that, rightly or wrongly, what is shown in a photograph passes for having really happened at a given moment and place, in the presence of a privileged and active witness – the photographer – whose image proves the pertinency of their vision.

13. R. Krauss, "Notes on the index: Seventies Art in America", part 1 in *October*, spring 1977, pp. 65–81, part 2 in *October*, fall 1977, pp. 58–67; Charles S. Peirce, *The Art of Reasoning*, chap. 2, 1895.

14. J. Kosuth, quoted by Catherine Millet, *Textes sur l'art conceptuel*, Paris, Templon, 1972, p. 16.

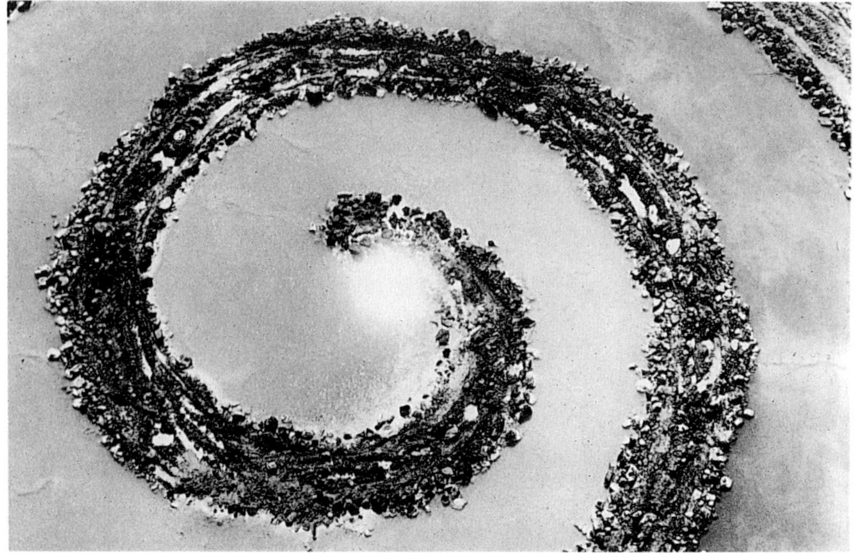

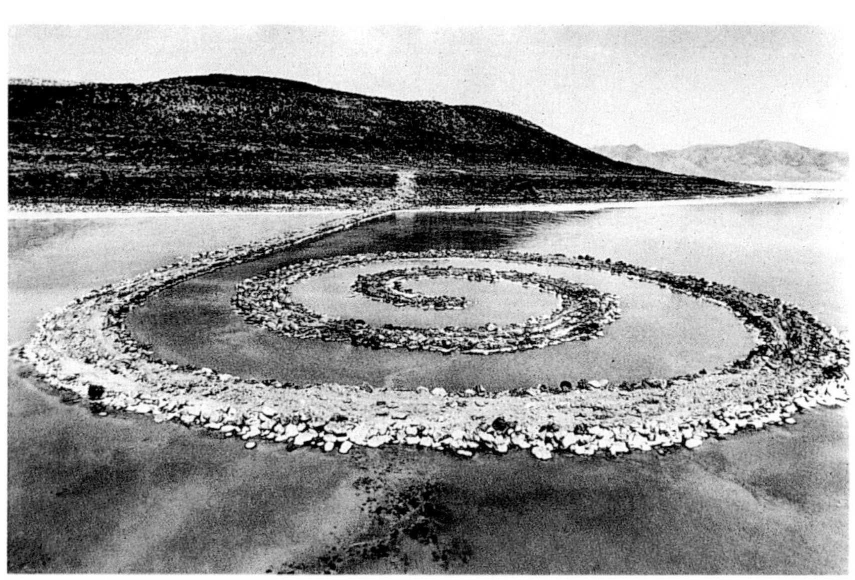

It is this almost unconscious awareness of *an image perceived as photographic* which determined photography's use in the "new" works of art of the late 1960s, especially in the broad area of conceptual art. It is also what, in artists' eyes, constituted the greatest asset of photography as compared with painting, which was now rejected as subject to lyricism and the sentimentality of color. As for conceptual art, it accorded primacy to the linguistic nature of all art. "Fundamental to this conception of art was the understanding of the linguistic nature of every artistic statement, whether past or present, without taking into account the elements used in their construction."[14] From this comes a structuring and creative function first recognized as language, which could stop there in certain cases (the Art Language group recognized only art as a linguistic fact). It soon turned out, however, that certain texts – in order to escape definition as "literary" – had to be organized as demonstrations, supported where necessary by a visual commentary. That is where photography came in, being itself capable of assimilation to a form of language, to syntax or to a commentary.

Already in behavioral arts (deriving from Fluxus and taking in body art), photography was needed as a witness of the event. In his work *Gesture: Eating* (1964), Ben toyed with the verbal announcement and the supporting photographic proof. Gina Pane, as well as Abramovic and Ulay, worked in this same register of the previously defined "action", where the photographic image could suffice as a representation of a mental act, with a parallel video recording if the event took longer. Yves Klein, with his *A Jump into the Void* (1960), was, perhaps, the first to borrow this "new realism" from amateur photography.

All those artists who "used" photography for one end or another, in such and such a conceptual system, were little concerned with photographic qualities (such as sharpness, lighting, formalism, quality of the print). On the contrary, they underlined the popular, workaday character to deny any return to a "Pictorial" stance or the "artist's hand" – a schism in which their special character as non-painters was firmly anchored.

By bringing together language and photography, Victor Burgin explored the unexpected

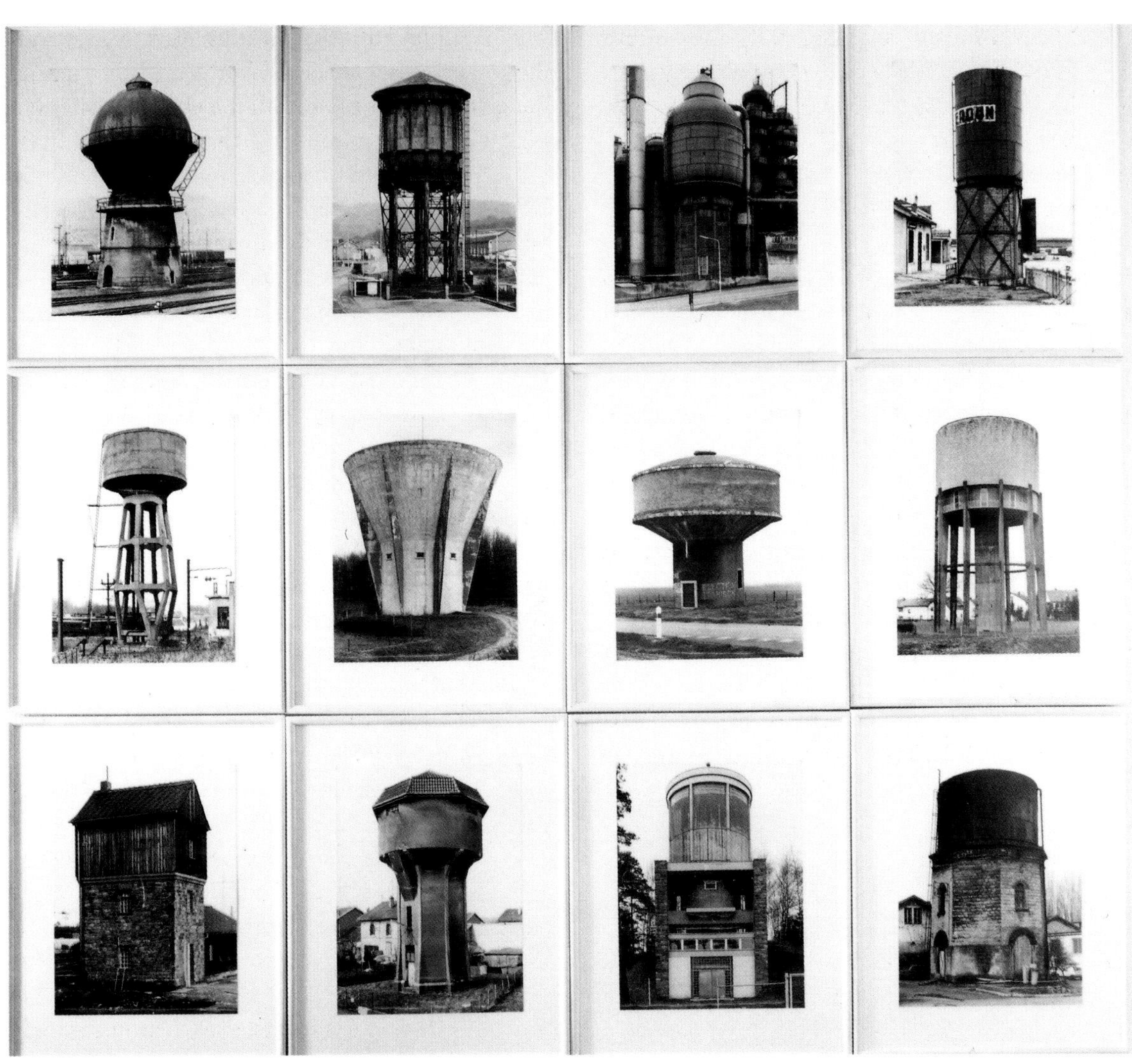

BERNDT AND HILLA BECHER,
Twelve Water-towers,
1978–1985,
F.R.A.C. Lorraine

relationships between a text and a photograph – that interface in which an imaginary world is created (as in *Performative-Narrative Pieces*, 1971), defined by "the criteria according to which you can decide that the aspects of 1 (the narrative) are analogous, correlative, or capable of being placed in a common context to aspects of 2 (the photograph)". Several levels of meaning come in, like strings linking the text and the photograph, along which travel what Burgin called "the voices of others". Joseph Kosuth, on the other hand, sought to eliminate any interpretation which might arise from this confrontation of two disjointed and heterogeneous languages (text and photography). In his works, a lexical definition of an object is juxtaposed with a photograph and the object itself. Text and image are relegated simply to their symbolic and indicative function with respect to the object. More recently, Barbara Kruger and Hans Haacke have joined this category of artists – the former, with works of the proportions of advertising posters whose peremptory caption is without apparent echo in the image, the latter, with his political slogans.

Most of the typical works of this period were less rigorously defined. In any case, rigor of definition could scarcely have survived intact during the period. For certain artists, photography was more loosely linked with language. In around 1970, Le Gac, who had often replaced photography by drawing, produced narrative to which photography provided the asides (rather than the other way around). In these, he displayed his unchanging role as an anonymous painter in difficulties (particularly with language). During this period, Christian Boltanski also raised the status of the amateur photographer to that of the modern painter (see below).

The introduction of photography as an *art moyen* (in the double sense of both "average art" and "art-medium", to use Pierre Bourdieu's expression, who studied its sociological implications) sought to stimulate painting, to throw into doubt its system of values. Douglas Huebler[15] (*Variable Pieces*, dating from the 1970s) mounted amateur color photographs on a single panel with text and a drawing, in order to analyze a particular situation in each country or place visited. Dennis

15. *Douglas Huebler*, text by R. J. Onorato, La Jolla, Ca., La Jolla Museum of Contemporary Art, 1988.

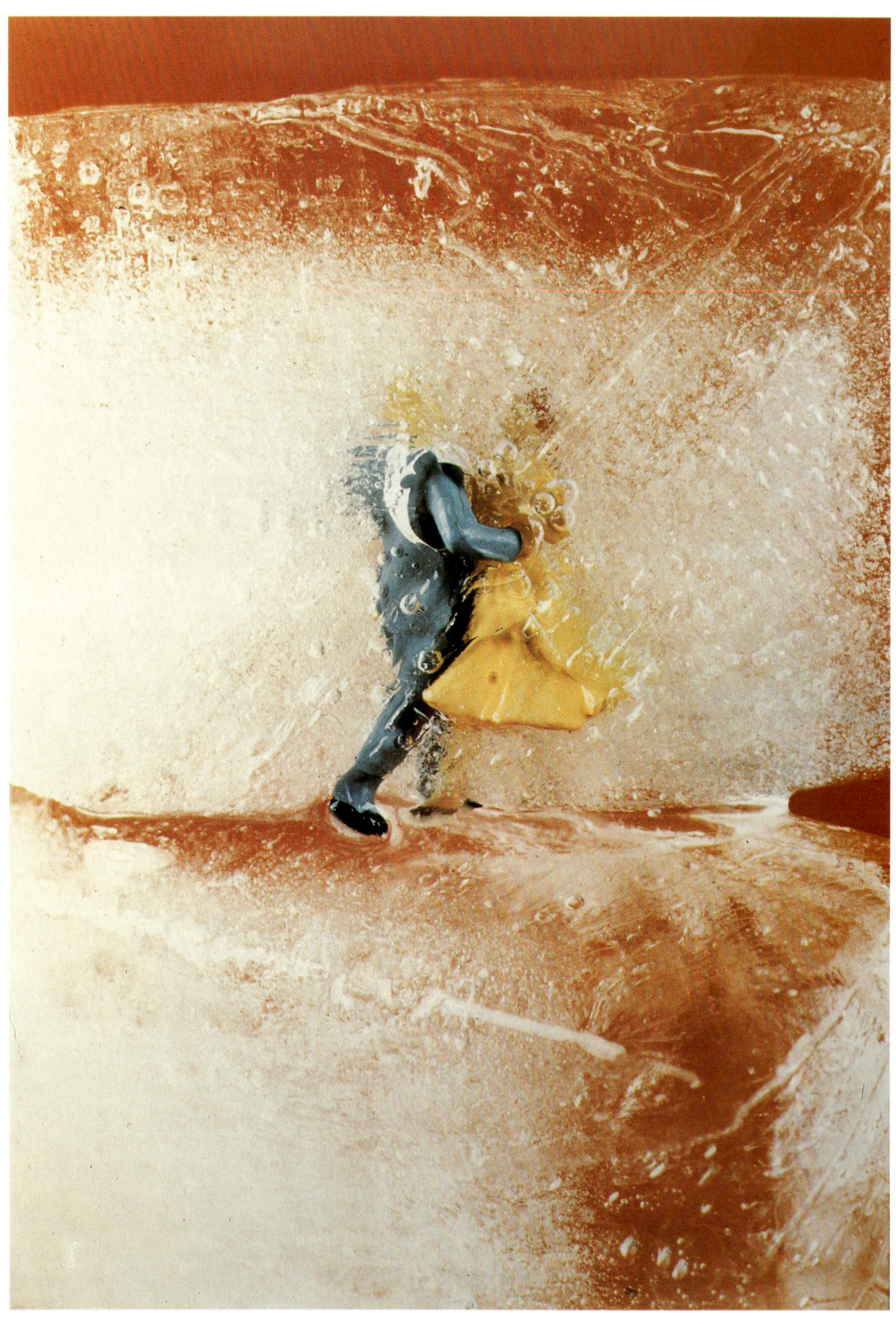

PATRICK TOSANI,
Waltz,
1983,
F.R.A.C. Lorraine.

Oppenheim,[16] preoccupied with "earth art" and body art, displayed a montage of "witness photographs" and topographical maps as indications of an arbitrary modification of the countryside (*Land Slide,* 1968). Works which willingly relied on industrial vulgarization of photography were also opposed to the commercialism which was then affecting "art" photography, to which, as Susan Sontag noted, people willingly accord the unique value of the object depicted (her book[17] may be considered as reflecting "average" ideas that were current on photography in the 1970s, following which artists tried to create works which could be directly assimilated).

16. A. Heiss, *Dennis Oppenheim: Selected Works, 1967–90, And the Mind Grew Fingers* , with an essay by Thomas McEvilley, New York, The Institute for Contemporary Art, P.S.1 Museum, New York, in assoc. with Harry N. Abrams, Inc., New York, 1988.

17. S. Sontag, *On Photography,* New York, Farrar, Straus and Giroux, 1977.

Conceptual or assimilated works held that photography was the visual medium that was closest to language, juxtaposing the one with the other.[18] Large panels were produced which mixed the two, or carefully titled prints in which the title permitted a particular interpretation to be assigned to the image (perceived as embodying all the parameters of photoreproduction of a type mimicking reality), without ever achieving the finality of "fine" photography. Such text and presentation underline the distance from "average" photographic procedure.

The two principal representatives of land art in Britain were then very close to each other. At first, Richard Long was the better known, giving more emphasis to the titles of his works, though they subsequently become increasingly rare. Long's method of working was to walk across the countryside, punctuating this walk with impersonal views of the environment. From this, he came to create "natural" sculptures in situ and to photograph them, before displaying them in a gallery or museum where he exploited the displacement of the photographed subject, contrasted with the visible, created work. On the other hand, Hamish Fulton's "new landscape art" sought to bring out the specific character of a landscape, for example by identifying the stereotypical symbols of travel and perambulation (a path, waterfall or rock formation) or the elemental, mineral or vegetable characteristics of the place. At this time, David Tremlett also created short texts associated with photographs. In the exhibition *Un certain art anglais* [A Certain English Art, Paris, 1989], the majority of the 26 artists featured used photographs, at least in part.[19]

After a few years, the use of photography had become common in contemporary art. It had become an artist's material, like gouache or lead pencil. It took part in the general conception of the work, as for Christo, who drew his wrappings or giant installations on photographs of the intended site. It formed an integral part of the original language of every work of art, completed by using other media for the methodical and poetical work of Jochen Gerz on the gestural quality and instability of forms or Bernard Borgeaud on light, natural elements, and photographic improvisation. Broodthaers himself, in his vast enterprise to "recuperate" the work of art, met up with photography – an *objet trouvé* at least in the method – and did not disdain its popular realism (*La Soupe de Daguerre*, 1975).

It is undoubtedly with the works of Christian Boltanski[20] that the standards of a civilization polarized by the photographic image have really been unfurled in an analytical way: family memories, post-mortem inventories, childhood gestures, mug-shots, class photographs, personal creations (his photographs of Japanese gardens, marionettes, Christmas decorations), the derisory memories of the post-Holocaust period. The medium has turned its back on itself, on its everyday history, on the stereotypes of mass culture, in the direct lineage of pop art. Annette Messager explores the world of the media (crime thriller, romantic fiction) and, more recently, relying alternately on words and on photographs, explores the standards of passion and expression.

Sculpting space

Other artists – or, rather, other works by these same artists, for none of them can be restricted to a single genre – sometimes considered photographic materials as sufficient for their needs, which, by definition, called for minimalist means. When the work of art comprises an action in natural space, the enlarged, mounted, exhibited photograph then *constitutes* the work and is its sole visible expression. The photographic arrangement which accompanies the artist in

JAN GROOVER, ***Untitled***, 1978.

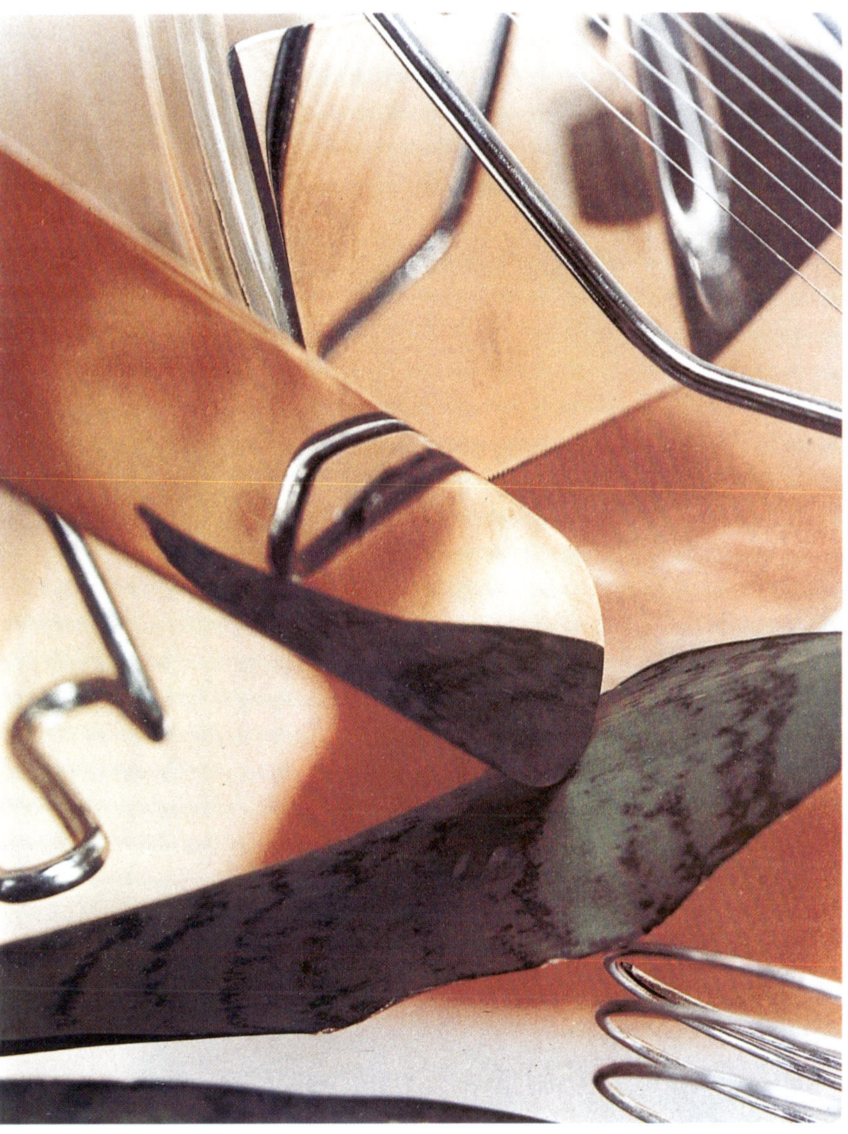

18. *Une scène parisienne, 1968–1972*, Rennes, Centre d'Histoire de l'Art Contemporain, 1991.

19. ARC, Musée d'Art Moderne de la Ville de Paris.

20. *Christian Boltanski: Lessons of Darkness*, texts by M.J. Jacob and L. Gumpert, Chicago, Los Angeles, The Museum of Contemporary Art, Chicago, The Museum of Contemporary Art, Los Angeles, The New Museum of Contemporary Art, New York, 1988.

The artist's book

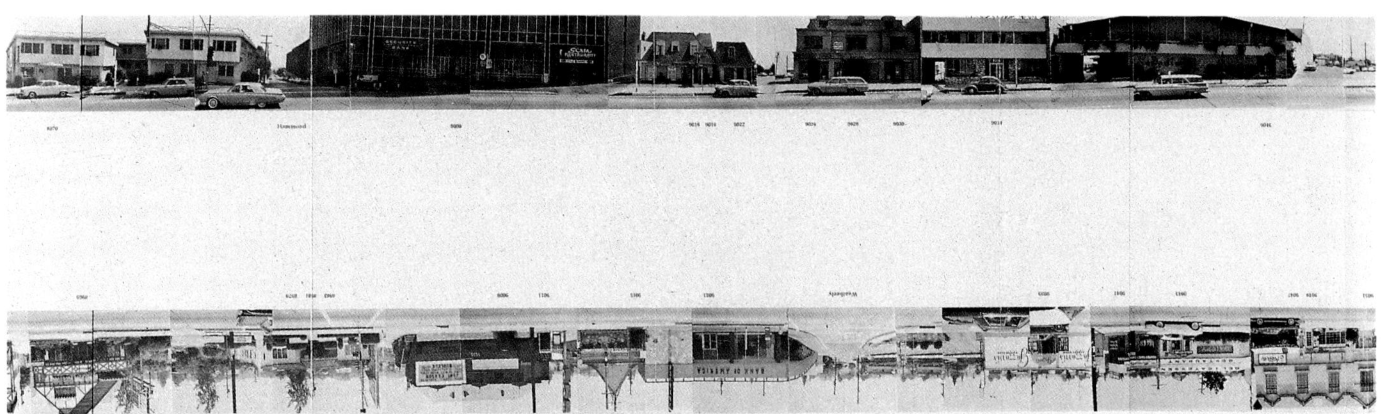

Detail of ***Every Building on the Sunset Strip***, by **Ed Ruscha**, 1966

Following pop art, and set in the context of conceptual art, photography was considered as the ultimate popular art of the image. In around 1970, the revival of craft processes such as lithography and, silk-screen printing, then the appearance of offset techniques and photocopying, which fully transmitted the values of photography and could be carried out in small "alternative" workshops or even at home, encouraged the publication of booklets or brochures.

The typical "artist's book" of this period, which made a come-back in the 1980s, forms one part of the work of an artist and often constitutes an œuvre in itself.

From 1963, Ed Ruscha had worked on the problem of the dissemination of art with *Twenty-six Gasoline Stations*, then *Some Los Angeles Apartments* (1965). His small unpretentious photobooks showing subjects borrowed from mass culture (*Nine Swimming Pools and A Broken Glass*, 1968, *Babycakes*, 1970, *A Few Palm Trees*, 1971, *Colored People*, 1972, and especially the fold-out book *Every Building on the Sunset Strip*, 1966), formed a model for artists' books in the 1970s.

From Carl André (*144 Blocks and Stones*, 1973) to Sol LeWitt (*Autobiography*, 1980), many artists who did not favor photography nevertheless gave in to this possibility of establishing a continuous overview of a work in the process of becoming or operating an accumulation of indicators by means of photos taken from several viewpoints. Although a number of artists' books are equally created by means of texts or drawings, "amateur" style photographs formed the basic vocabulary. Some photographers regressed to a child-like type of practice, such as Ilse Bing (*Numbers in Images*, 1970) and Nancy Rexroth (*Iowa*, 1977, whose photographs were taken with a two-dollar "Diana" camera).

Most of these artists, whether American or European, are located between conceptual art, performance art, and postmodernism, and often reached a wide public by means of the book in the first instance.

During the 1970s, the coherence of the book developed around a concept or an action rather than an inventory, to the point of becoming an art form in itself: John Baldessari (*Brutus Killed Caesar*, 1976), Dieter Appelt (*Monte Isola*, 1976), Peter Downsbrough, Robert Cumming (*A Discourse in Domestic Disorder*, 1975), Dan Graham, Hans Haacke, Jenny Holzer, Douglas Huebler, Ken Josephson (*The Bread Book*, 1973), Allan Kaprow, Mel Bochner (*Misunderstanding: A Theory of Photography*), Les Levine, Barbara Kruger (*Picture/Readings*, 1978), Robert Smithson (*Torn Photographs*, 1970), Urs Lüthi (*The Personal Dissolves So Easily in the Typical*, 1977), Richard Long, John Hilliard, Dennis Oppenheim, Richard Prince (*War Pictures*, 1980), Michael Snow (*Cover to Cover*, 1975), Bernar Venet, Lawrence Weiner (*Pertaining to a Structure*, 1977), and Gerhard Richter (*128 Details from a Picture*, 1980). Anselm Kiefer perpetuated the form if not the spirit with his photo/object/book assemblages.

The book (often as a fold-out) was used as a way of interpreting and for initiating work as much as for work in progress. Jan Dibbets's *Domaine d'un rouge-gorge* [Domain of a Robin, 1969] is one of the most attractive. It describes in photographs accompanied by text and sketches the "sculpture" which is formed by the movements of a bird which is enticed on to perches which have been set up in an Amsterdam park.

Michel Frizot

their reflection (for the work is for the greater part a mental process) forms a report, an inventory, which restores the work – immovable because it is worked out in situ – to a dimension which is suitable for the museum or the gallery.

Their work is therefore offered in the single, visible form of a photograph. The intrinsic ambiguity of this method must be underlined. What distinctive trait separates a conceptual work presented in the form of a photograph (for example, a work by Hamish Fulton) from a classic photograph? This is a point of contention which constitutes the stumbling-block (and also, sometimes, a reason for suspicion) of all art "using photography" (this expression, common during the past few years, expresses quite directly the critical malaise created by this "use".)

In "classic" photographic images the minimal medium of a representation did appear, because one had to do without it by means of a product and, under the circumstances, an image: especially Jan Dibbets with his "all-over" pictures of foliage and automobile bodywork, Bruce Nauman, with the series *Eleven Color Photographs* (Castelli, 1970), which includes *Bound to Fail* (1966), *Self-Portrait as a Fountain* (1966), assorted concepts, snapshots of artistic thoughts. Photography authorizes a minimal amount of *doing*, while

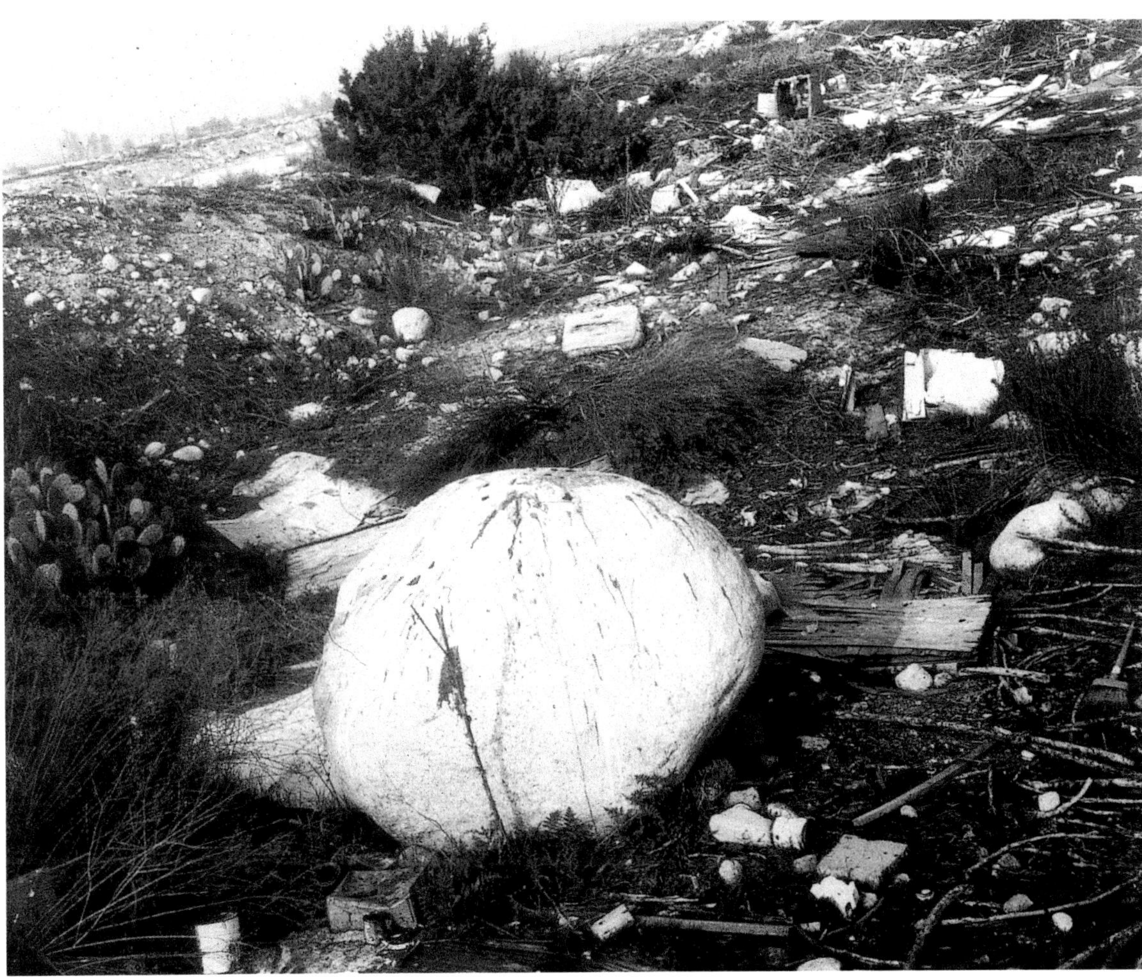

ROBERT ADAMS,
Santa Ana Wash, 1982.

taking notice of a movement, a situation, a reflection provoked by the artist.

Thus, certain works are envisaged as the production of mental sculptures created through the medium of photography. Robert Smithson, who photographed and filmed his *Spiral Jetty* (1970), did not consider that photography constituted the work in its entirety, but that it took account of it *a minima*; it was the visual link, its setting as a shape and an image. It was an index, a statement of the developmental stages of the work, on the same plane as his writings.[21] One could say the same of Gordon Matta-Clark, whose empty spaces in derelict buildings could be retained only by transposing them on to a reference medium. The premature deaths of Smithson (1973) and of Matta-Clark (1978) accentuated the value of the ocular and photographic witness which they had succeeded in establishing. Thus, photography regained its popular function as a "souvenir" of the vanished action and vanished object – which also amounted to providing them with an attestation of existence, a form of proof, which can be all that exists of some works of conceptual art in its strictest sense. The mobility of photographic apparatus now allows several different viewpoints. This is essential for any consideration of sculpture. Giulio Paolini often evokes in his installations the process by which the sculpture is returned to the photograph by means of a mirror.

Bernd and Hilla Becher, active since the 1960s, have attained the highest level of "sculpturization" through "pure" photography with their series of monuments to modern times (their "anonymous sculptures")[22] – photographs of furnaces, water-towers or suburban houses. Their strict composition and multiplication of similar images constitute the vocabulary of an imaginary ordering of volumes – a form of mental sculpture. Furthermore, they won first prize for sculpture at the 1990 Venice Biennale, specifically for their work in the medium of photography.

A number of purely photographic works may thus be considered as sculptural achievements,[23] understood in the sense of taking a space or a form and modeling it. The busts of Roman emperors by Patrick Faigenbaum speak simultaneously of identity, of biography, of the history of sculpture, and of the photographic capturing of volume.[24] William Wegman sets up and photographs scenes with his dog-like visual puns. Boyd Webb constructs imaginary situations in the studio based on the opposites high/low and inside/outside, in which the paradoxes of a bad dream are compressed like a telescope.

The recent work of Pascal Kern, who has explored the possibilities of molding and the

21. *The Writings of Robert Smithson*, New York University Press, 1979.

22. B. and H. Becher, *Framework Houses of the Siegen Industrial Region*, Munich, Schirmer/Mosel, 1977; *Watch Towers*, Cambridge, MIT, 1988; *Blast Furnaces*, Cambridge, MIT, 1990.

23. *Photographie/Sculpture*, Centre National de la Photographie, Paris 1991; *Sculpter/Photographier*, Actes du Colloque, Musée du Louvre, Paris, Marval, 1993.

24. P. Faigenbaum, *Roman Portraits*, intr. by L. Barkan, biographical essay by J.-F. Chevrier, Chicago, Art Institute of Chicago, 1988.

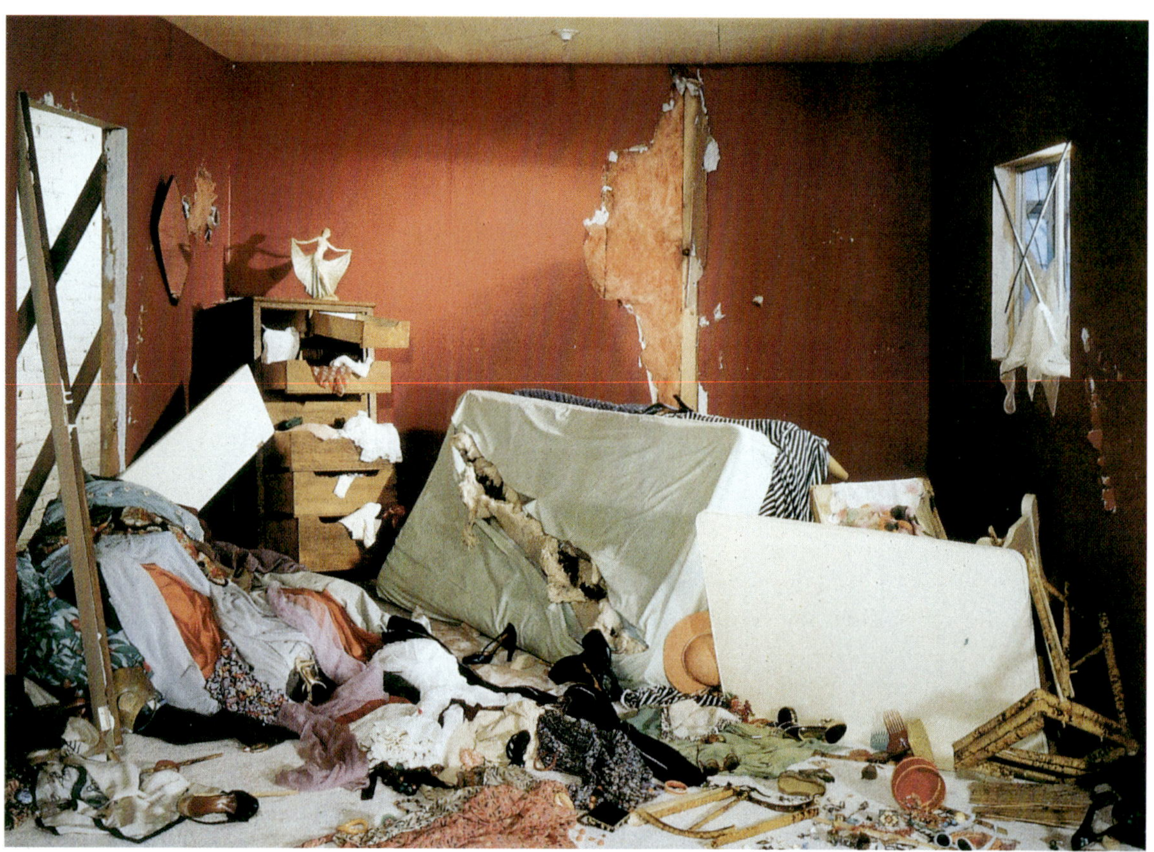

JEFF WALL,
The Destroyed Room,
1978.

JOHN COPLANS,
Foot, Dark Sole,
1989.
▼

alternatives of negative and positive, of Patrick Tosani, who develops the ambiguity of scale and enlargement, or of some of Bernd and Hilla Becher's pupils, such as Thomas Ruff and Thomas Struth, may be considered in the same perspective. Photography organizes states of volume, transforms them, organizes them, working out the relationship of spaces (which is the definition of a work of sculpture) which are limited by the photographic camera without any need to work on the substance itself. The photograph is a medium for molding "after nature", whether this nature is already there, reorganized or created from bits and pieces. But all these artists also participate (especially Thomas Ruff with his large-format color portraits and his reproductions of press photographs) in another process which reinvests photography in the process of its own creation, as if the very medium were asking itself questions about its function and its raison d'être.

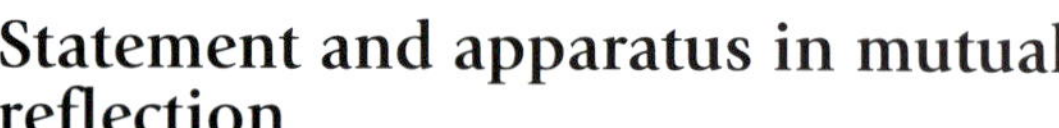

Statement and apparatus in mutual reflection

Outside the false opposition of photography versus art, there exist, above all, photographic practices. Some make fuller use of the technical apparatus while others seek to become part of a greater artistic domain or one that is socially more promising. What most frequently distinguished the actions of photographic artists is the way their works are distributed – being simultaneously unique by nature and multiple in essence – the attention paid to printing and the size of the print, and the refusal to allow any "reproduction" of the original other than when permitted by the photographer.

A particular kind (somewhat specific to the United States) of photographic procedure could be defined which was rooted in the double tradition of "straight photography" and of an objective appreciation of the everyday, banal in appearance and compelled to be realistic.

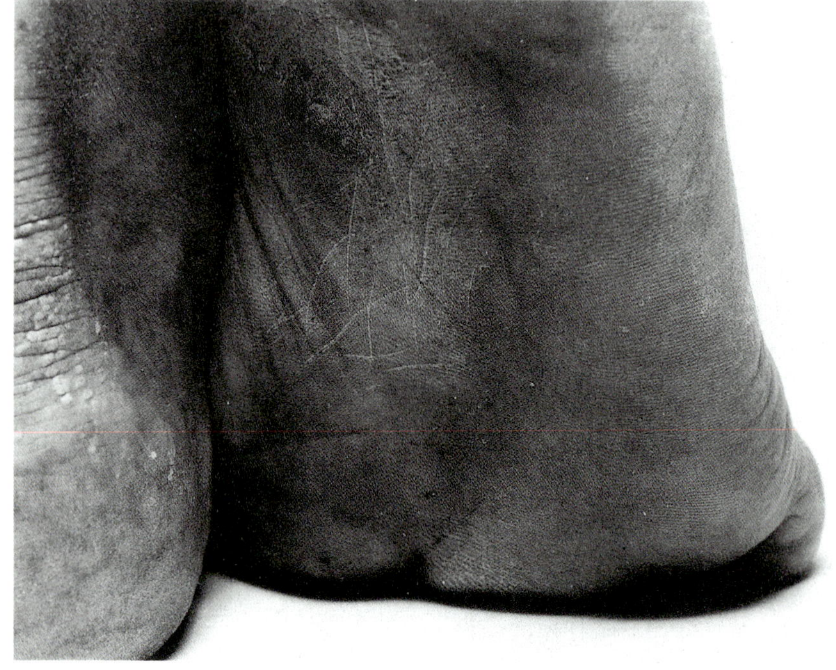

Several generations have coexisted in this double tradition, even though they have entered the new field of land or environmental art, which is particularly vigorous in the United States. This involves returning to earlier professional practice, with large-format cameras, using color, which implies the principle that photography is a registration, a recording carried out by the camera, which captures entities which are slightly different from those perceived by the human eye (in details of lighting, movement, contrast, depth of field). If Harry Callahan, whose outlook was shaped in the school of Moholy-Nagy at the Chicago Institute of Design, seems to appear as a master of this purist manner, Robert Adams, Joel Meyerowitz, and Stephen Shore are also proceeding, with a certain cohesive spirit, towards working out the perceptible changes of the countryside in its shapes and colors.

It is always the presence of the human race which is at stake and our ability to destroy the original purity of nature: Richard Misrach, who photographed cacti in the Saguaro desert under artificial light; Lewis Baltz, who was interested in architectural photographs, then in industrial waste; John Pfahl, who intervened willingly on the geometry of nature. Jan Groover,[25] after working on movement and color, is now more concerned with a relationship with sculpture via photography, which serves to give order to volumes and matter in space.

This option for allowing the photographic set-up to reflect itself, as if the camera undertook to register its own qualities and parameters, was possible only in the tradition of conceptual art, and thanks to a re-evaluation – which derives in part from post-modernism – of the underlying mechanical aspects of photography. The apparatus, in fact, only "expresses" what it is: an arrangement which suffices to decode the world in a certain, unequivocal direction. This procedure might be defined by the title of an important series which Ugo Mulas undertook in the 1970s, the *Verifiche* [Verifications], which tended to

Georges Rousse, ***Untitled***, 1988
Farideh Cadot Gallery, Paris.
▼

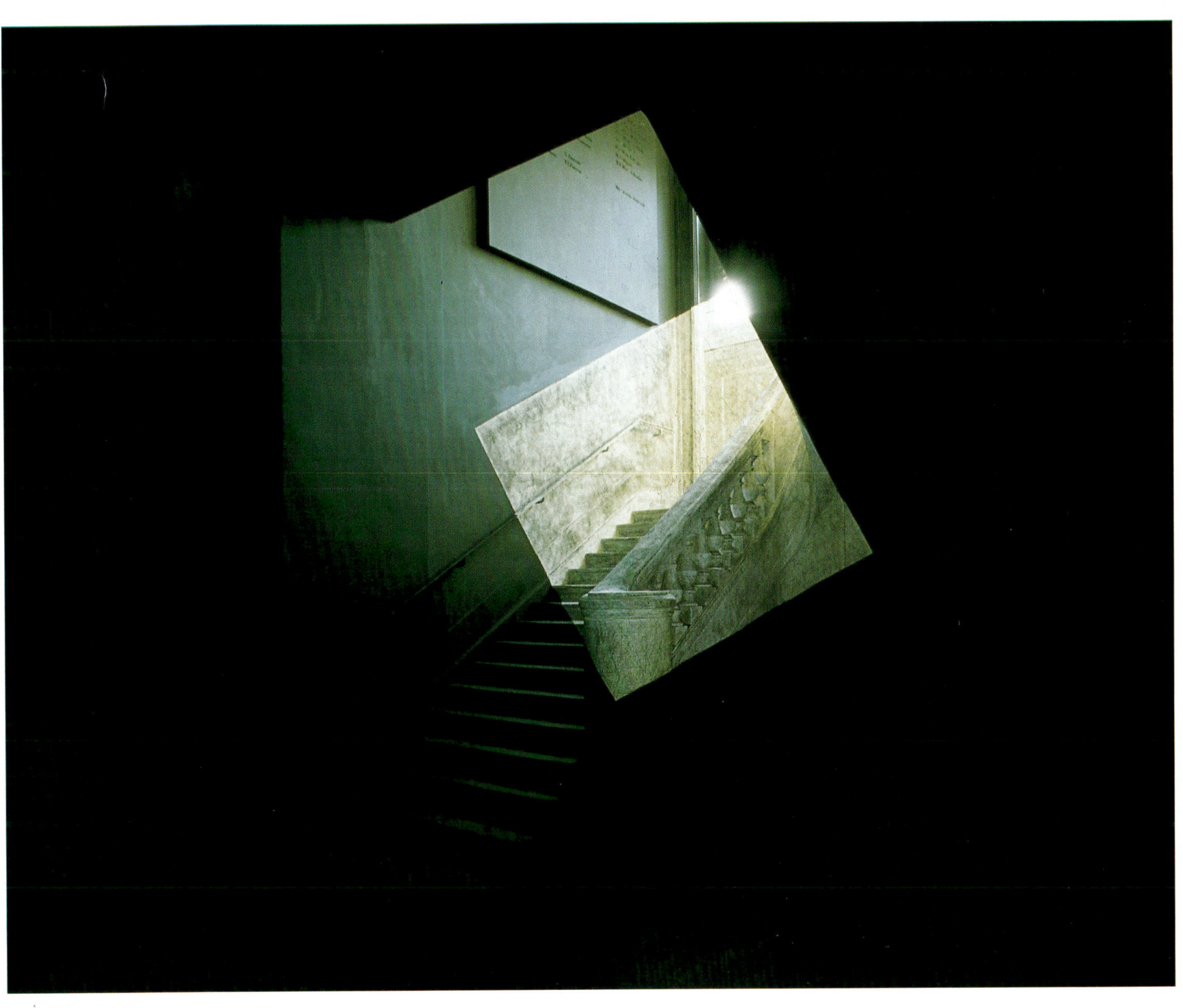

25. S. Kismaric, *Jan Groover*, New York, Museum of Modern Art, 1987.

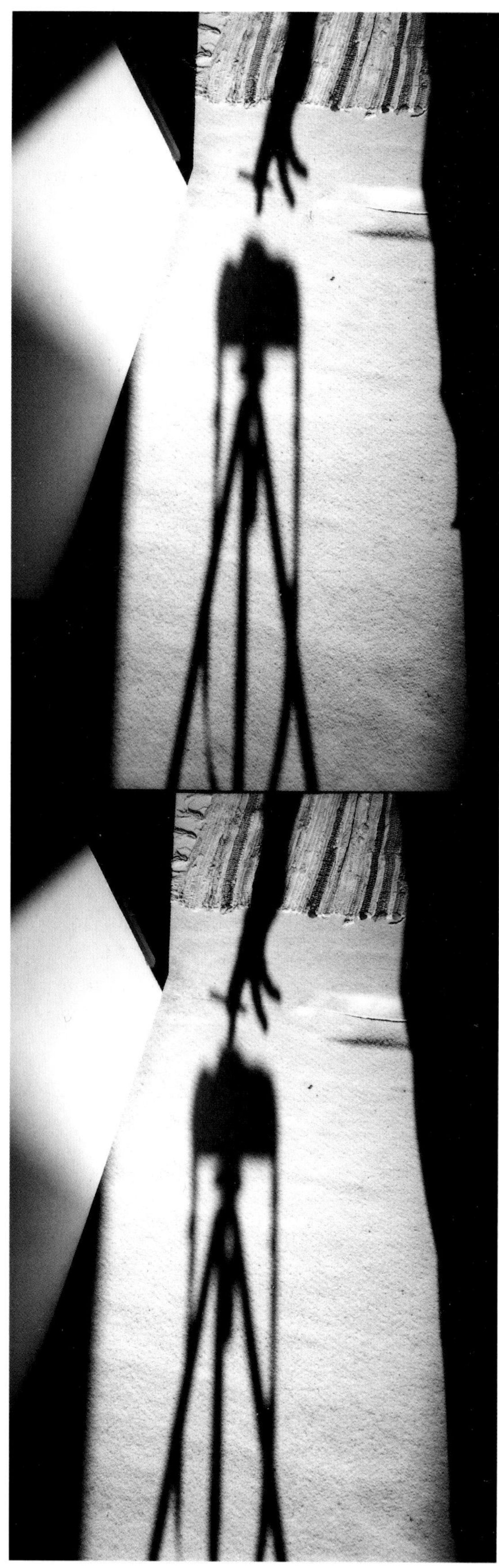

Denis Roche,
October 11, 1987, Paris,
(two successive shots).

include in the image the criteria by which the photographic apparatus was actually used.

In 1968, Jan Dibbets explored the two-dimensionality of photography with his *Perspective Correction* which was produced by the camera automatically. He then analyzed exposure times as a function of the lighting, the production of shapes by the mount, and the optical deformation of photography, which formed the basis for his "reconstitutions" using collage techniques in the 1980s.

John Hilliard also worked on variations in the depth of field, the exposure time, the sharpness and the nature of the subject, and the difference between ocular and photographic perception. The works of Georges Rousse, produced by actually drawing on architecture, can be visualized in their finished geometric state only from a single viewpoint, which the photographic lens can capture perfectly.

John Coplans,[26] whose work belongs simultaneously to the categories of body art and sculpture, features the iconic faculties of framing by fragmentation of his own body. The reflection of the mechanical aspect of the instrument can be considered in its historical perspective, leading back to the *camera obscura* or drawing aids (Patrick Bailly-Maître-Grand) or to the Polaroid, and, at the same time, to techniques of inventors (Paolo Gioli) and archaic printing techniques (Nancy Wilson-Pajic) – without any suspicion of anti-modernism. This boils down to admitting photography, at whatever stage of production, only as a process subject to its own physico-chemical rules, without any transfer of the "subject". Thus, Riwan Tromeur produces completely concrete images in his darkroom, without any apparent "subject", by the action of light alone – that is, by photographic images.

In this case the image really constitutes a tautology of the photographic process, or even a form of writing. Denis Roche[27] has carried out an exemplary and systematic investigation on the two fronts of textual analysis and mechanical practice. Photography and text make explicit the dialectic of the workings of the camera and the meaning of images, which are at once unique in time, evocative, fortuitous, foreseen, unrepeatable. In its domestic simplicity, photography can be lived like an act of mourning for the gesture.

Multiple meaning

In all these forms of contemporary art, recourse to photography was evidently based on an underlying idea of multiple reproduction. This reconsideration of the medium and the resurgence of the photo-book (see box) were the rallying signs of post-modernism in the "Gutenberg galaxy",[28] which was proclaimed above all in the United States. It proposed that one should reflect on the aims of art, the systems of production and representation in a historical perspective. Despite certain appearances, it was not a question of a

26. B. Lifson and R. Roos, *John Coplans*, Brussels, Liverpool Gallery, 1992.

27. D. Roche, *Ellipse et Laps*, Paris, Maeght, 1991.

28. A. Grundberg, "The Crisis of the Real: Photography and Post-modernism", in *Multiple Views*, ed. D. P. Younger, Albuquerque, University of New Mexico, 1991.

"return to", but of a somewhat resigned acceptance of the way modern art and the media were developing, in contrast with conceptual isolationism. Furthermore, the critical thinking of postmodernism encouraged people to explore the world of popular photography, recognizing (as did conceptual art) that photography, in all its previous forms, had been responsible for modifying our vision of the world: the story-images close to photo-romances, borrowed from advertising by Richard Prince; the recreation of stereotypical images of pop stars, rock magazines or photo-thrillers by Cindy Sherman (first in black and white, then in color).

Postmodernism has taken the influence of photography (and cinema and television) into account, and asked questions of the place of the image in culture, as well as the responsibility of those who create those images – and above all those who reproduce them.[29] Sherrie Levine has reappropriated paintings or photographs by other people thanks to "reproduction", Allan MacCollum shows the emulsion, repetition, the photographic substrate, the texture, Laurie Simmons the omnipresent miniaturized world of the dolls' house and the television screen, which is coming so close to "replacing" reality.

Depending on the place and the mental and material environment in which it is examined, photography is open to several "virtualities" of reading. By naturally allying itself with certain processes now employed in modern art, the medium has escaped the strait-jacket of mimetic interpretation. It has gained a multiplicity of meanings. If photography lends itself to verbalized interpretation, it also demands it – hence its closeness to acts of language and its interpretative openness,[30] in spite of its link, through all kinds of indicators, with the time when the "statement" was formulated. Thus, Boltanski could imitate amateur holiday snaps by playing himself as a child, twenty years later. Everything in the picture seemed to come from the period, and confirmed the authenticity of its value as a memory.

One can imagine the work of one of those major actors on this modern photographic stage appearing under the banner of a plurality of senses – always unstable and never fixed. Dieter Appelt[31] has conceived a multiform work, which, by turns, belongs to conceptual art, body art, art as a language, the interrogation of primitivism and original myths. But from *Erinnerungspur* (1979) to *Double Take* (1984), from *Ezra Pound* to *Komplementäre Raum* (1986), it is the set-up for acquiring photographic images which has been modified to take account of the creative process. In these works, the photographic image is conceived as a deposit of successive layers (if necessary, of images created by the play of light) on a photographic substrate, an act of recording impalpable data which has to accumulate to be perceived, even though this means accepting the unforeseen chaos. From the recording of nearby physical situations, practiced by Beuys or the Viennese "actionists" to the construction of illusions of lighting, the camera is the witness of primal stirrings, whether of a

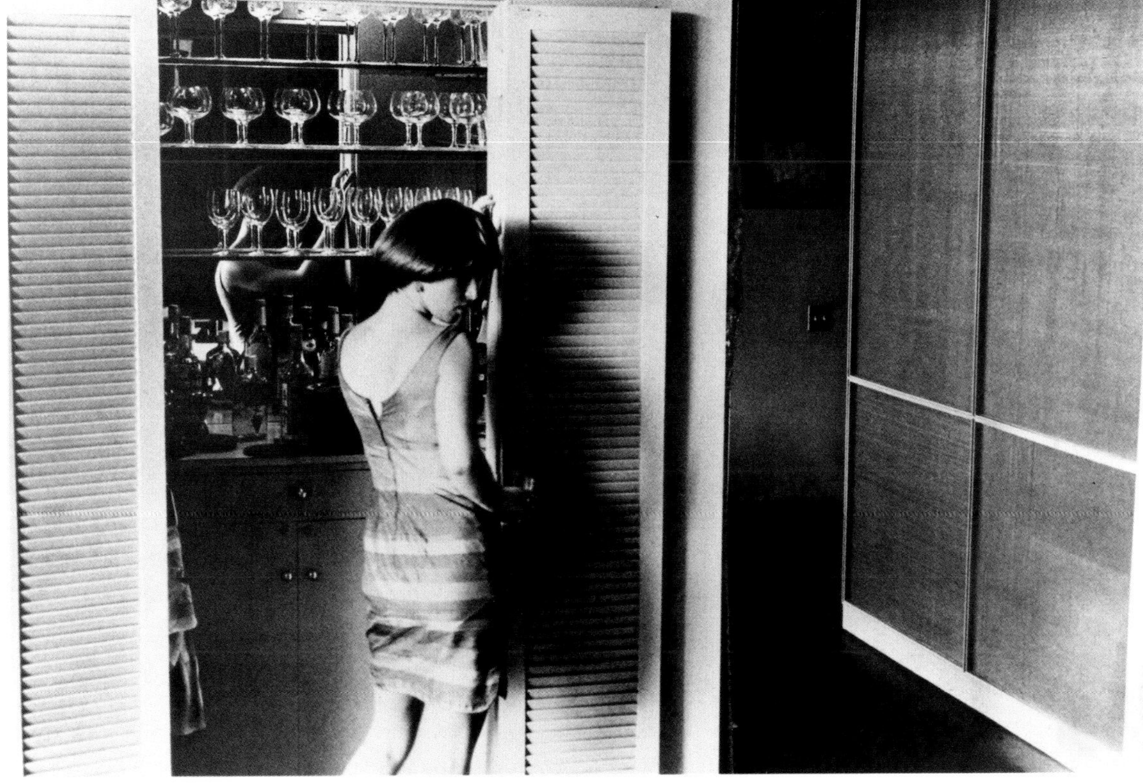

CINDY SHERMAN,
Untitled Film Still,
1979,
High Museum of Art,
Atlanta.

29. A Grundberg and K. McCarthy Gauss, *op. cit.*.

30. Photography is an open form of art, a concept that was particularly prevelant in the art of the 1970s.

31. S. Wolf, *Dieter Appelt*, with an essay by W. Schmied, Chicago and Berlin, 1994.

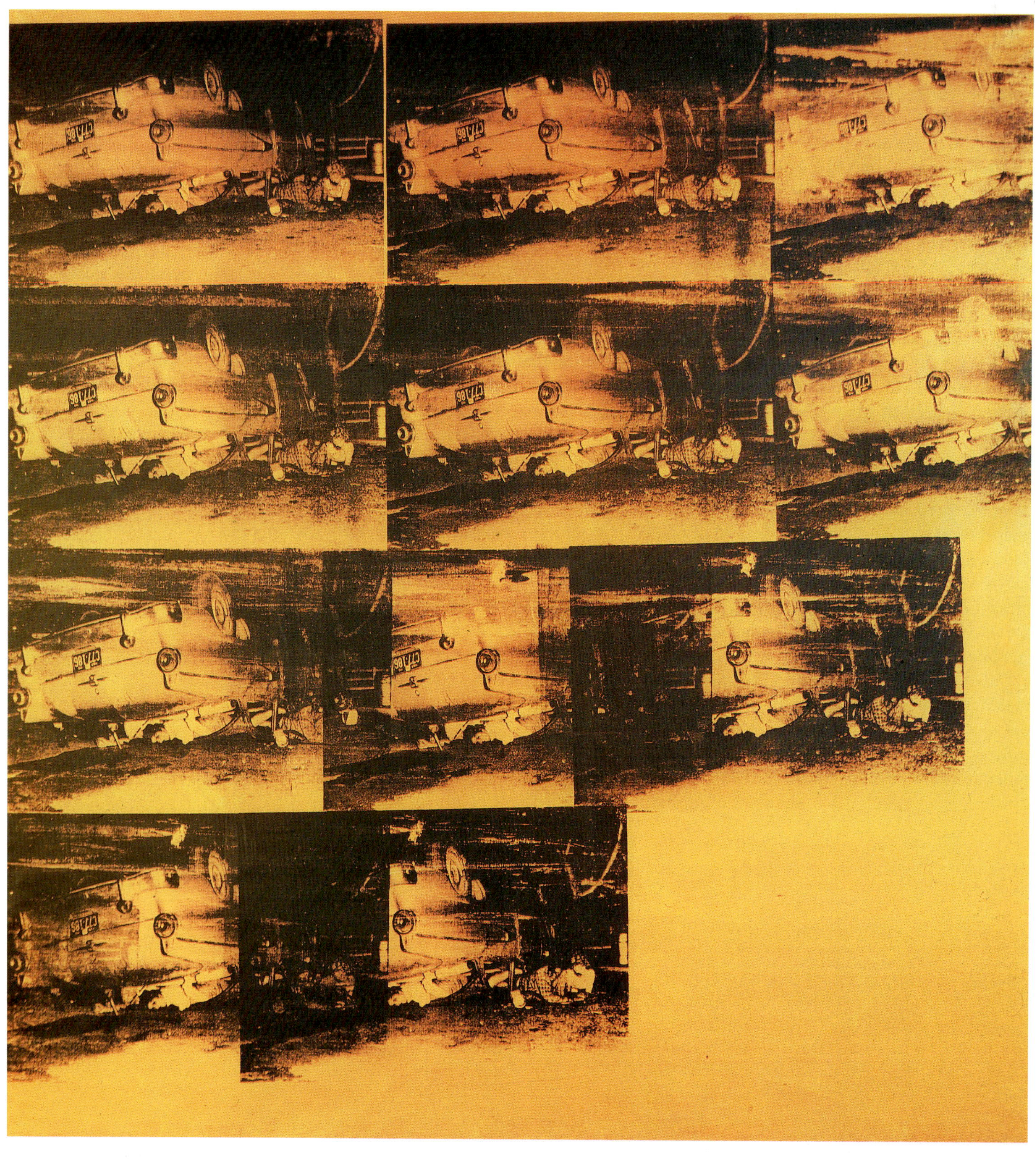

Andy Warhol,
Orange Car Crash,
silk-screen print on canvas,
1964,
Galleria Civica d'Arte
Moderna, Turin.

suffering body, of life relegated to matter or of the pulsation of lights. Other Germanic artists, such as Gerd Bonfert or Anna and Bernhard Blume, thus followed the calculated subjectivity of Beuys and the concrete imaginary world of Hajek-Halke or Chargesheimer.[32]

Photography today is in irremediable opposition to painting. The debate which has been active for some 150 years has no raison d'être. The categories created arbitrarily to satisfy market needs have no transcendental significance. In other words, a photograph is not more significant because it has been classified as "contemporary art". Photography remains a fluid and precarious medium, both promising and derisory, on a level of meaning which has not been predefined: at once image, illustration, work of art, document, trace and imprint.[33]

In the field of pop art, photography had been the popular medium *par excellence*, and, at the

32. *Photography in Contemporary German Art: 1960 to the Present*, Minneapolis, Walker Art Center, 1992.

33. J.-M. Schaefer, *L'image précaire: du dispositif photographique*, Paris, Le Seuil, 1987.

same time, a total imprint of the coveted reality. Like other 1960s artists, Robert Rauschenberg and Andy Warhol had exploited the pigmentary multiplication of photography,[34] often in the form of silk-screen prints, as the basis of their language of borrowings and linguistic deviation, like other 1960s artists. Both of them continued further along this route, taking their own photographs instead of merely using pre-existing material. Rauschenberg not only worked as a photographer but also produced images directly on photographic material, by controlling the chemistry of the developer. These large prints formed part of his collages and constructions. Warhol, on the margin of his works, whose photographic element derived from the media (*Disaster Series, Marilyn,* etc.) dreamed up pieces made of four or nine separate identical prints which were joined edge to edge, and thus brought together the repetition of multiple images, the creation of an object by a process of accumulation. Warhol also brought together photobooth pictures[35] and Polaroids.

For twenty years, photography has appeared, above all, as a supporting witness. On the first level, it can serve simply as a support, in all senses of the word, to certain types of painting, by appearing behind the pigments like an image of reality. Thus it constitutes the material and pictorial support of Arnulf Rainer's brutal acts of negation and deletion or of Anselm Kiefer's imaginary world, covering all or part of the photographic image by blots or effects of blotting out, or as the support for a change of media in the transfer of an ancient engraving or photogravure for Sigmar Polke[36] (*Bunnies,* 1966; *Der Traum des Menelaes,* 1982; *Hochsitz* series, 1984–1985).

For Gerhard Richter, who founded his output as a painter on a relation with the photographic image, the "substrate" or photographic base material is the starting point for a work on vision and representation, in pictorial terms, of a reality which passes directly via the photographic medium in order to be apprehended in its sensorial truthfulness.

If photography can serve in this way as a basis for a pictorial statement, it is really because it also responds to a choice and an intentionality which painting is not alone in creating (see the following dossier showing a collection of contemporary art on photographic materials).[37]

An index of time, space, form, identity: photography's capacity to substitute itself for various forms of reality has allowed it to emerge from simple imitation and to escape the simple recording of events – a role to which some people tried to confine it. Photography does not bear witness only to its own time, as is said; it assumed the impact of all the forces of sensitivity and vision.[38] In any case, contemporary art will no longer be able to be defined in terms of a past "anti-photography", but rather by its photo-sensitive affinity.

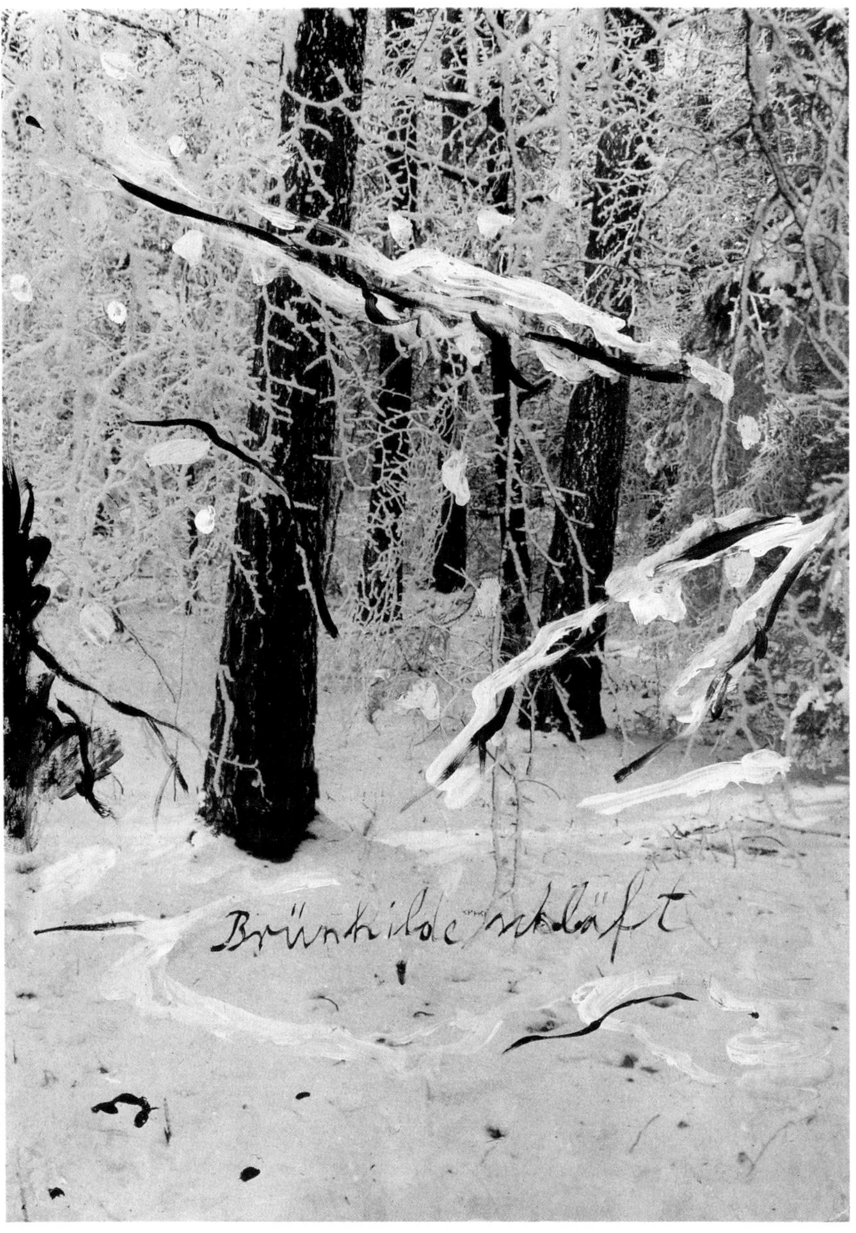

ANSELM KIEFER,
***Cover of the book*
Brünhilde schläft,**
1980, oil painting on photograph,
Museum of Art, Toledo.

34. *R. Rauschenberg: photographs,* New York, Pantheon Books, 1981; M. L. Kotz, *Rauschenberg: Art and Life,* New York, R. Miller Gallery, 1989.

35. *Andy Warhol, Photographs,* New York, R. Miller Gallery, undated; *Andy Warhol: Photobooth Pictures,* New York, R. Miller Gallery, 1989.

36. *Sigmar Polke,* San Francisco Museum of Art, 1990.

37. R. H. Krauss *et al., Kunst mit Photographie,* Fröhlich und Kaufmann, 1983; *Photo-Kunst,* Stuttgart, Cantz, 1989.

38. Other elements will be found in J.-F. Chevrier and J. Lingwood, *Another Objectivity,* Milan, Idea Books, 1989, and in *Roots and Turns: Photography in the Netherlands: 20th Century,* The Hague, SDU Publishers, 1988.

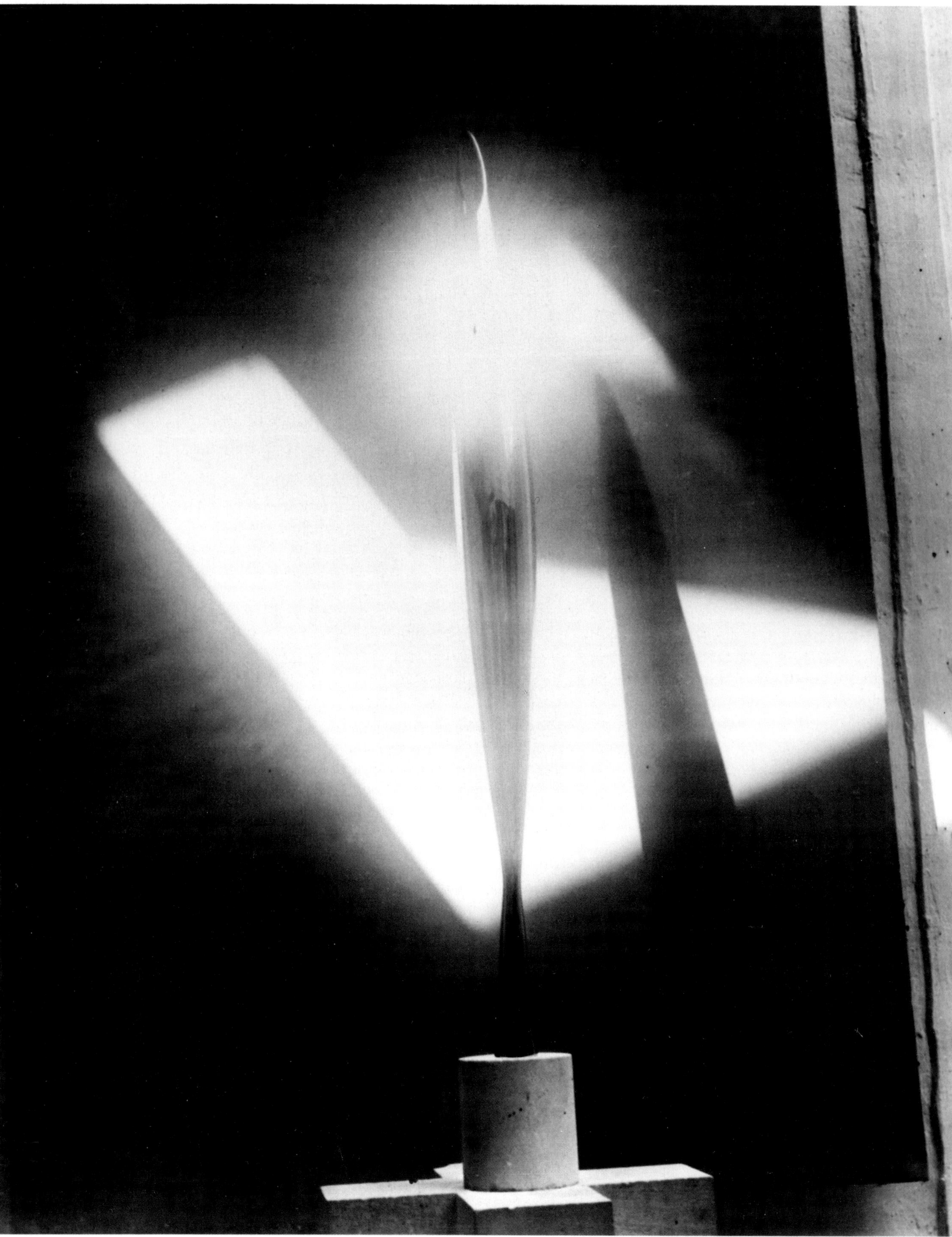

FORMS OF LOOKING 40

Philosophy and photography

Yves Michaud

The works presented in this chapter are not to be considered in a critical rapport with the text; they form part of a complete collection of illustrations and texts relating to the contemporary period (including the preceding chapters 38 and 39).

There can be no doubt that philosophy can deliberately examine photography. In return, however, photography places philosophy in an false position in connection with discussions on the nature of reality, which is increasingly perceived *through* images. Mental images and the imaginary, which share with philosophy the visual – immediate – registering of information, occupy a fundamental position in contemporary thought, notably through psychoanalysis and semiology. The photograph, apparently "transparent" but returning the interpreting gaze both towards the viewer and towards the object viewed, has become, despite itself, the pivotal point in the dilemma between image and thought.

Philosophy does not invariably have something to say about everything. It is not charged with interpreting everything that happens in the world, and it has not been regarded as a scientific discipline for a long time. It may be thought surprising, therefore, that a history of photography should include thoughts on philosophy and photography. Our justification is that the invention of photography has created the conditions for a new kind of looking and new ways of seeing, and that philosophy is concerned, above all, with analyzing our ways of seeing – the conditions of representation, to use the Kantian expression. This appearance of new types of images and new ways of seeing was not immediately clear to philosophers. When one reviews philosophical literature from the time photography was invented it is surprising to note how little attention philosophers paid to photography, even though it was affecting artists, essayists, poets, and, of course, photographers themselves – and though philosophers never stopped discussing images.

This delay in "reflection", in the true sense of the term, does not invalidate subsequent examination of the subject. It is no more scandalous than the tardiness of art historians and critics in realizing the importance of the changes that photography was introducing into the art world. Artists broke down the hierarchy and compartmentalization of the arts well before art specialists realized what was going on. In my opinion, a meaningful approach involves three stages. First, an overview of the ways in which philosophers have approached photography – this will be as brief as it is sparse. From this starting-point, we can study in conceptual terms the characteristics of the photographic image and way of looking. It will emerge that most approaches are marked by a kind of permanent dilemma between analogon and artifice. If we stopped there, we would be left with an idealist conception in which philosophy was immune from being affected by the time, the technique, and the conditions of its own speech. That, in short, is why it is important to try to evaluate the effects of photography on philosophical thought. Every attempt must give way to circularity. What we say about things, if we are attentive to them, must, in return, be affected by those things themselves and, *pace* Foucault, the order of speech always unwittingly bears the marks of the changing order of things. The least the philosopher can do is to try to take this into account, albeit belatedly.

◄ Constantin Brancusi, *Bird in Space*, 1930, Musée National d'Art Moderne, Paris.

On photography

When one studies the way philosophers, or those reputed as such, dealt with photography, one is disappointed. Such discussion as took place when photography first appeared was restricted to scientists, photographers themselves, journalists, and engravers – but not philosophers.[1] At the already

1. A. Rouillé, *La Photographie en France, textes et controverses, une anthologie: 1815–1871*, Paris, Macula, 1989.

late date when Pictorialism was in full swing William James mentioned photography only in order to make the traditional comparison between the workings of the human eye and the camera.[2]

Almost at the same time, a few subtle comments by Peirce, in his composite text *Logic as Semiotics: The Theory of Signs*, in around 1895-1902, clearly demonstrate that for him photographs were just one set of signs among others, which, in order to be understood, formed part of the same complexity of function and production, the same pragmatic determinants: "Photographs, and, especially, instantaneous photographs, are very instructive, because we know that in certain respects they exactly resemble the objects which they represent. But this resemblance is due to photographs which were produced in circumstances such that they were physically forced to correspond with nature in every respect. From this point of view, therefore, they belong to the second class of signs: signs by physical connection."[3]

It is Bergson who mentions photographic images most frequently, notably in *Matter and Memory*, 1896. It might, however, have been expected that his idiosyncratic concept of the notion of the image would lead him to consider the photography as something other than a simple means of comparison. This is not the case. He indicates in an important passage, however, that the photographic view of things is not perception, that the image of an object becomes pure representation when one suddenly suppresses "all that follows it, precedes it, and that which fills it", when all that is retained is "the external crust, the superficial film".[4]

The totality of the world's images, argued Bergson, when they strike the film of consciousness, produce images which are at once fixed and impoverished – as fixed and as poor as photographic images.[5] Photography operates by sampling life. It destroys the unity of nature, which survives only in splinters and fragments.

PAUL DEN HOLLANDER, *Untitled*, 1985.

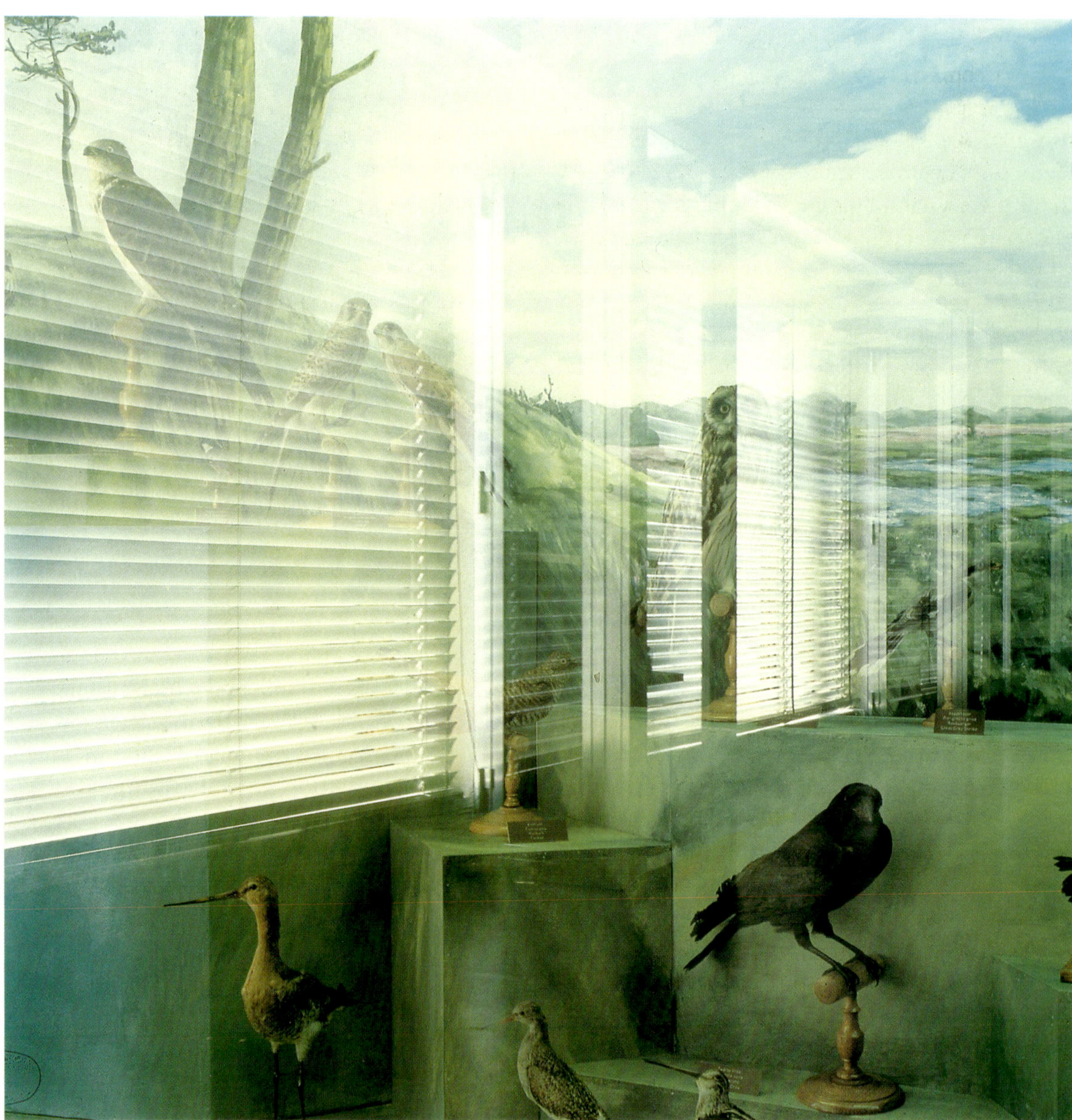

2. W. James, *The Principles of Psychology*, New York, H. Holt and Company, 1890.

3. C. S. Peirce, "Logic as Semiotic", in *Philosophical Writings of Peirce*, New York, Dover, 1955, p. 106.

4. H. Bergson, *Matter and Memory*, London, 1962.

5. *Ibid.*

6. Both texts in: W. Benjamin: *Das Kunstwerk im Zeitalter seiner technischen Reproduzierbarkeit. Drei Studien zur Kunstsoziologie*, Frankfurt am Main, 1977.

The 1930s, following the astonishing explosion of creativity which took place in the 1920s, when photography enjoyed a favored status, saw the appearance of two decisive contributions by authors on the margins of philosophy: by Walter Benjamin in *The Short History of Photography* (1931) and *The Work of Art in the Age of Mechanical Reproduction* (1936),[6] and by Rudolf Arnheim in *Film als Kunst* (1932).[7] Arnheim developed an analysis of photography's formal contribution and the kind of attention to which it calls. Benjamin, split as always between a piercing sense of the present, with its promising yet ravaged destiny, and nostalgia for a past which he fundamentally detests, mingles comments on the presence, in the heart of the photographic image, of a reality which has vanished, with a presentiment of the effects of novelty and banality which engenders the very "authenticity" of photography, its ability to show us another nature "where man works unconsciously",[8] a "free field where all intimacy gives way to the illumination of details",[9] in the element of technical reproducibility.

I do not pretend in these remarks to do justice to these important contributions. However, by comparison, the analytical writings of Sartre which appeared in *L'Imaginaire* (not to mention those of Alain) seem even more impoverished. Here, once again, the unfortunate "photo" serves to argue for the intentional character of the chosen photographic image: "If I am suddenly shown a photo of Pierre, the situation is functionally the same as when an image suddenly appears without any conscious desire for it on my part. Now this photograph, if it is simply perceived, appears to me as a paper rectangle, with special qualities and colors, with shadows and light patches distributed in a certain way. If I perceive this photograph as "a photo of a man standing on the front steps", the mental phenomenon is inevitably already of a different order, animated by a different intention. And if this photo appears to me as the photo 'of Pierre', if, behind it, I see Pierre in a certain way, a certain involvement on my part is necessary in order to give life to this bit of card, providing it with a sense that it hitherto lacked. If I perceive Pierre in the photo, *it's because I put him there.*"[10] A few lines further on, however, Sartre observes: "Occasionally the photo doesn't function as an object and presents itself immediately as an image" (a question with which he might have begun).

Perhaps the only analytical writer to cut through the miasma of phenomenological analysis fashionable since the 1940s was André Bazin in his *Ontologie de l'image photographique* (1947), in which he defended an admittedly simplistic theory of imprint and analogon.[11]

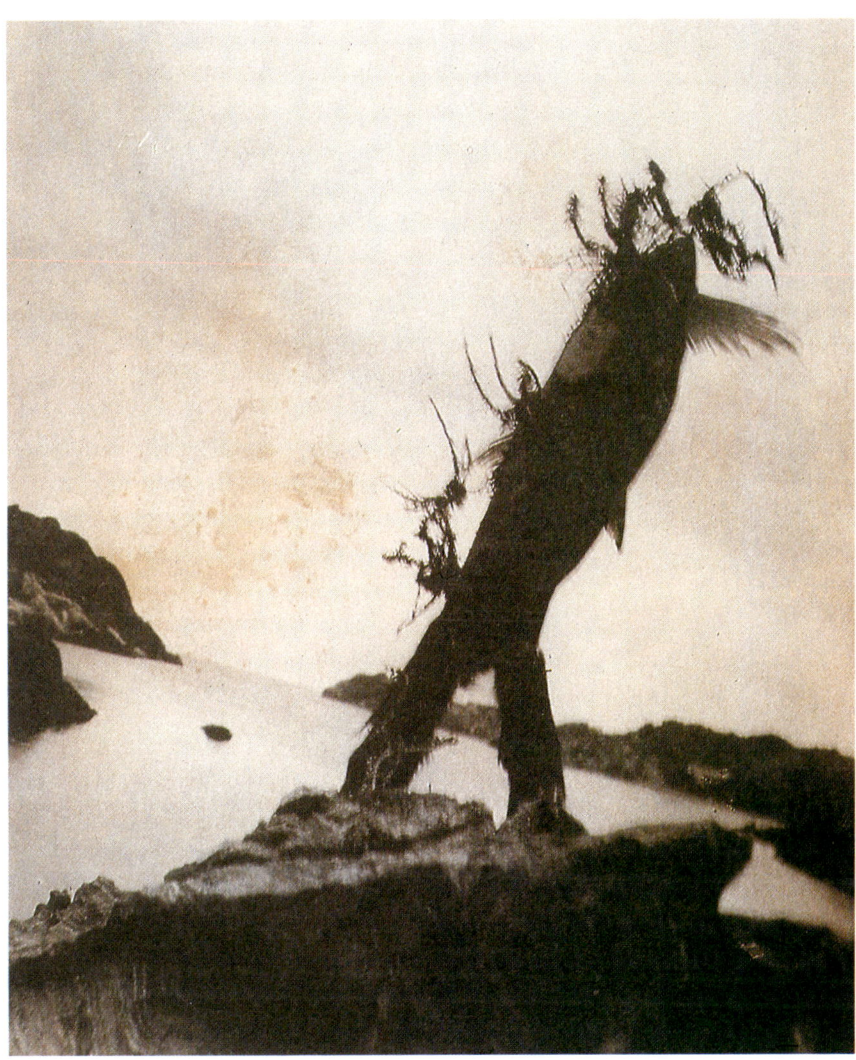

JOAN FONTCUBERTA,
Ictiocapra Erecta,
1987,
Galerie Zabriskie,
Paris.

Reflection on the nature of photography and the photographic image started up again, and in a more profound way, only in the 1970s, with a flood of images, the triumph of photoreportage and advertising, and the arrival of photography as art and artistic merchandise. Contributions were made by R. Arnheim,[12] Susan Sontag,[13] Roland Barthes,[14] Kendall T. Walton,[15] Yves Michaud,[16] and Jean-Marie Schaeffer.[17]

Dilemmas of the image

If we no longer consider the history of thought (or of the absence of thought) but the conceptual position, a consistent dilemma is noticeable throughout the history of photography. The photograph is understood either in terms of the magical presence of that which is far away or vanished, or, on the other hand, as an image which is as artificial and fabricated as any other sort of sign.

The spontaneous and, one might add, naive tendency is to consider photographs as the result of a purely mechanical process of reproduction. Once the laws of optics and chemistry are taken into account, things print themselves by themselves on the plate or the film. The mechanical

7. R. Arnheim, *Film als Kunst*, Berlin, Rowohlt, 1932.

8. W. Benjamin, *Kleine Geschichte der Photographie*, in *op. cit.* p. 50.

9. *Ibid.*, p. 58.

10. J.-P. Sartre, *L'Imaginaire*, Paris, Gallimard, 1940, pp. 40–45.

11. A. Bazin, "Ontologie de l'image photographique", in *Qu'est-ce que le cinéma?*, Paris, Cerf, 1961.

12. R. Arnheim, "On the Nature of Photography", in *Critical Enquiry*, September 1974.

13. S. Sontag, *On Photography*, New York, Farrar, Straus and Giroux, 1977.

14. R. Barthes, *Camera Lucida: Reflections on Photography*, trans. by R. Howard, New York, Hill and Wang, 1981.

15. K. T. Walton, "Transparent Pictures: on the Nature of Photography", in *Critical Inquiry*, December 1984.

16. Y. Michaud, "Les photographies: reliques, images ou vrais semblants?" in *Critique*, no. 459/460, August/September 1985, pp. 761–780.

17. J.-M. Schaeffer, *L'Image précaire: du dispositif photographique*, Paris, Le Seuil, 1987.

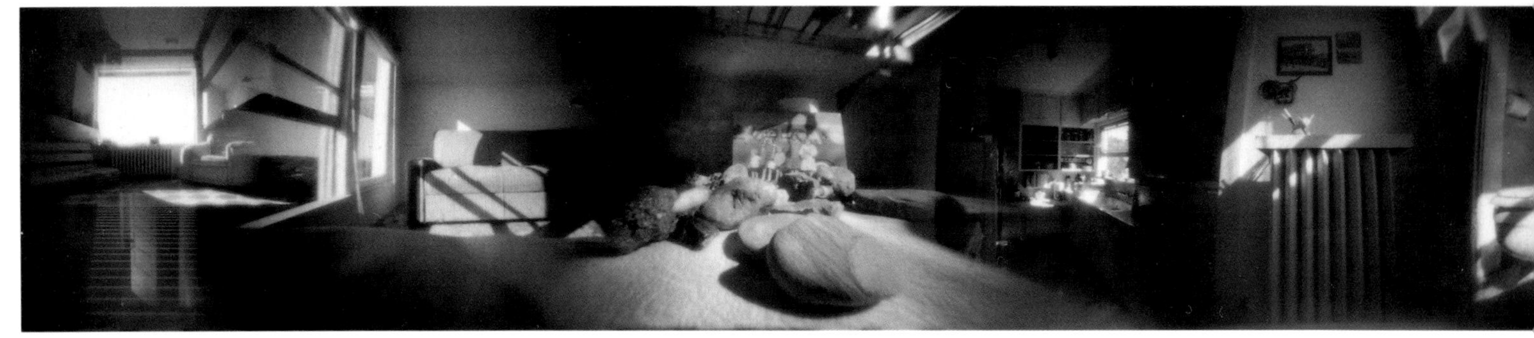

nature of the process guarantees the resemblance of images which are, by their nature, truer than paintings or drawings – which depend on the freedom and the invention of the artist. A photographic image is the analogon of the object, its natural trace and its double. The scientific and careful practice of the first photographers, or the entirely mechanized approach of present-day amateurs with their fully automated autofocus cameras or Polaroids, could only reinforce this judgment. Photographs are not "made", they "make themselves".

This photographic hyper-realism was at the heart of the language used by the pioneers of photography: from the sun artists to the mirror with a memory, via the pencil of nature, the consensus is complete. Two parallels are evoked time and time again – the engraving as a means of mass reproduction, and optics as a guarantee of the exactness of the resemblance. Photography plagiarizes nature by means of optics, as Lamartine opined in 1858. The true image is the image of things taken by themselves, and this image can be reproduced indefinitely, or nearly so. Whether this concept is formulated with an existentialist pathos or with good scientific sense, it is based on the consideration of photographic causality: the particular presence of the photographed object in the photograph is guaranteed by an automatic, mechanical process. The causal

URS LÜTHI, *Two images from "Just Another Story About Leaving"*, 1974, Stadler Gallery

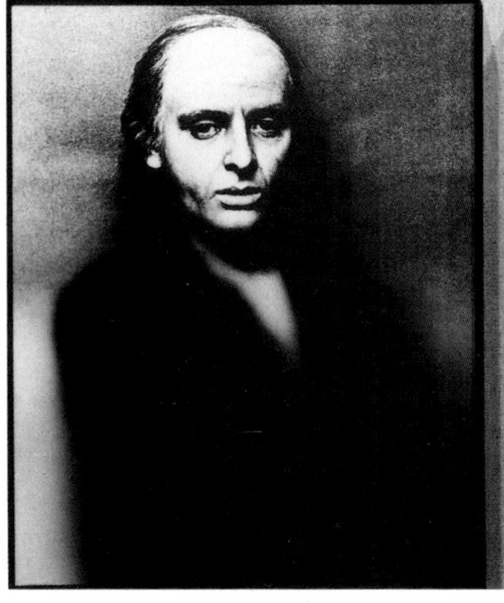

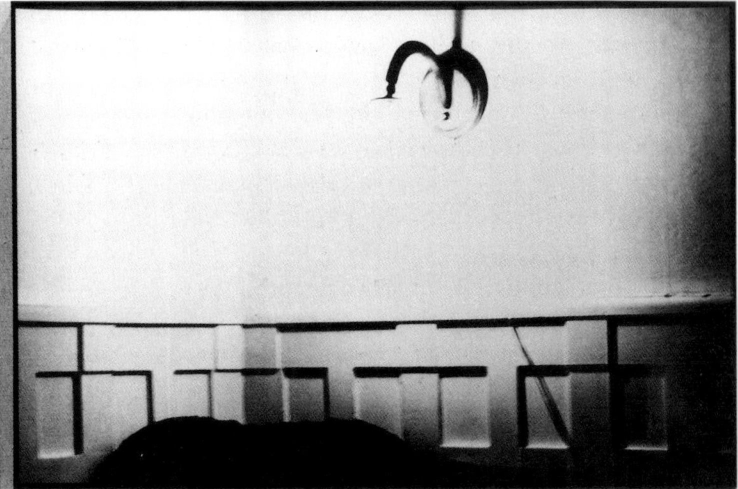

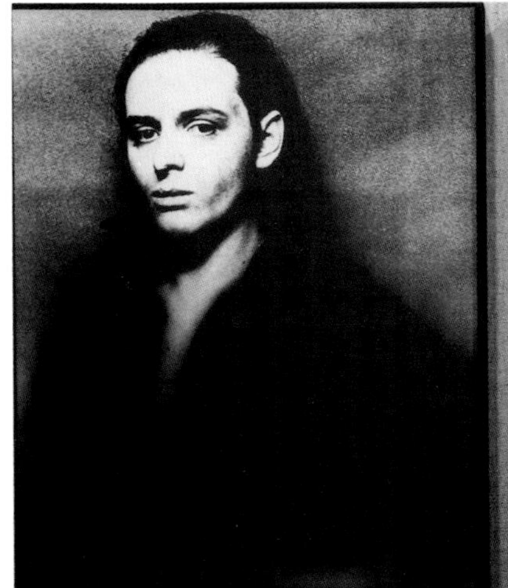

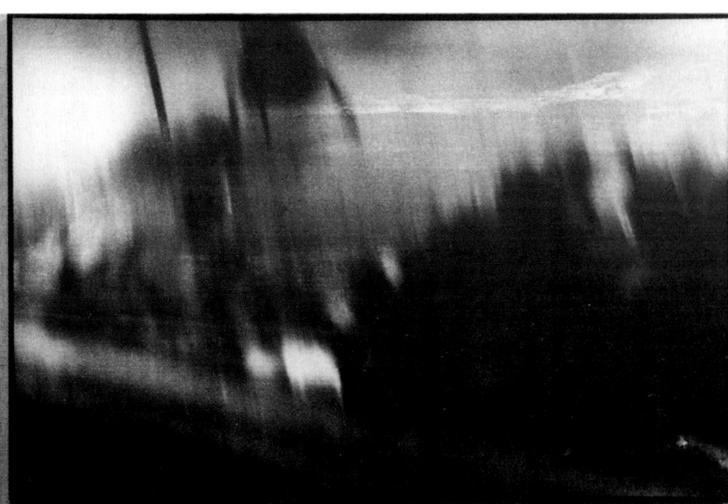

18. W. Benjamin, *op. cit.*, p. 50.

19. A. Bazin, *op. cit.*.

20. R. Barthes, *op. cit.*.

21. *Ibid.*, p. 120.

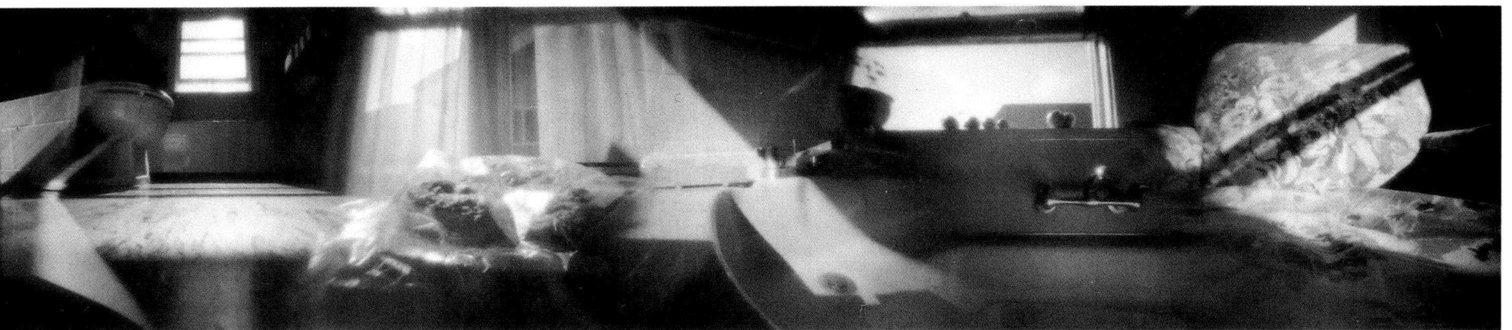

conditions of the representation make the presence special. Few thinkers, of whatever epoch, have escaped from this sentiment of magic.

Thus, Walter Benjamin wrote: "The most exact technique could provide its products with a magical value which no painted image would ever have for us again. Despite the photographer's technical mastery, despite the concerted character of the attitude imposed on the model, the spectator is despite himself compelled to seek, in such an image, the tiny spark of chance, of here and now, thanks to which reality has, as one might say, destroyed the image character."[18]

Fifteen years later, André Bazin spoke of "man's primitive need to have the last word in his dispute with death by means of a form which will endure".[19] Roland Barthes, for his part, defined photography as the perfect analogon, which incorporated its own referent, to the point that the photograph as an object, "the photographic thing", becomes almost invisible, so powerful is the presence of the eidolon, the simulacrum transmitted by the photographed object.[20] As always, it was a question of causality: "I call a 'photographic referent' not the optionally real thing to which an image or a sign refers, but the obligatorily real thing which has been placed in front of the lens, and without which there would be no photographs."[21] While the painter can invent a reality which he has not seen, in photography "a double, conjoined position exists: of reality or of the past."[22] Even as demanding an analyst as Jean-Marie Schaeffer in *L'Image Précaire* was unable to break away from this naive ontology of the photograph as an imprint: "The identity of the image may only be captured by starting with its genesis."[23] The rest of his analysis, however, is a more subtle and watered-down version of this affirmation, now favoring a pragmatic analysis of the "photographic apparatus".

It was probably Kendall T. Walton who offered the most radical and, at the same time, the most coherent, version of this theory of "the transparent image".[24] He maintained that photographs are not more exact images than others: they are different images, "transparent images" through which we see that which was photographed. Photography is an aid to vision, just like the microscope or the telescope. It helps us to see things which no longer exist or which are absent from us or are no longer present. In a photograph of my mother, I do not see an image of my mother, but I see her just as she was when the photograph was taken. Photographs are carriers of natural meanings because they depend entirely on the photographed scene, and not on the beliefs of the photographer.

This "analogic" theory, which is still maintained by Rosalind Krauss in her article on the "index",[25] cannot resist a reflection on causality which, if properly pursued, should lead us back to Hume. Peirce underlined that photographs are icons (images which themselves carry the terms of resemblance), because in certain cases, as in

Jeff Guess,
Seattle,
1989
(successive views taken by a pinhole camera on 35mm film).

Richard Misrach,
Cactus,
undated,
Musée National d'Art Moderne, Paris.
▼

22. *Ibid.*

23. J.-M. Schaeffer, *op. cit.*, p. 13.

24. K. T. Walton, *op. cit.*

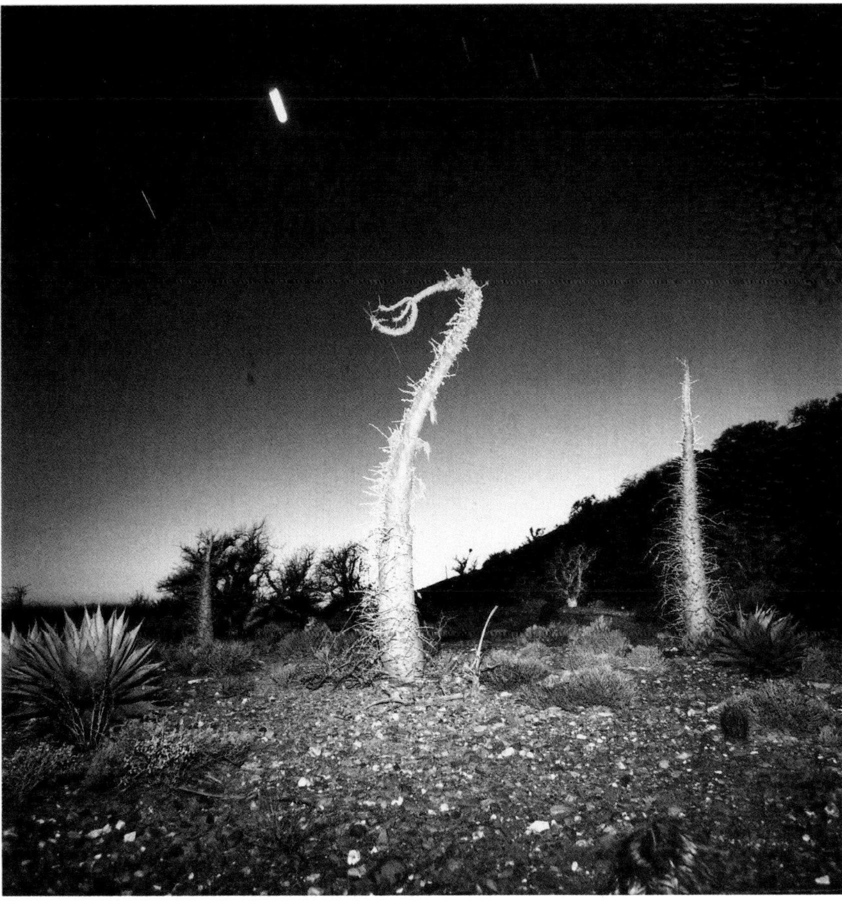

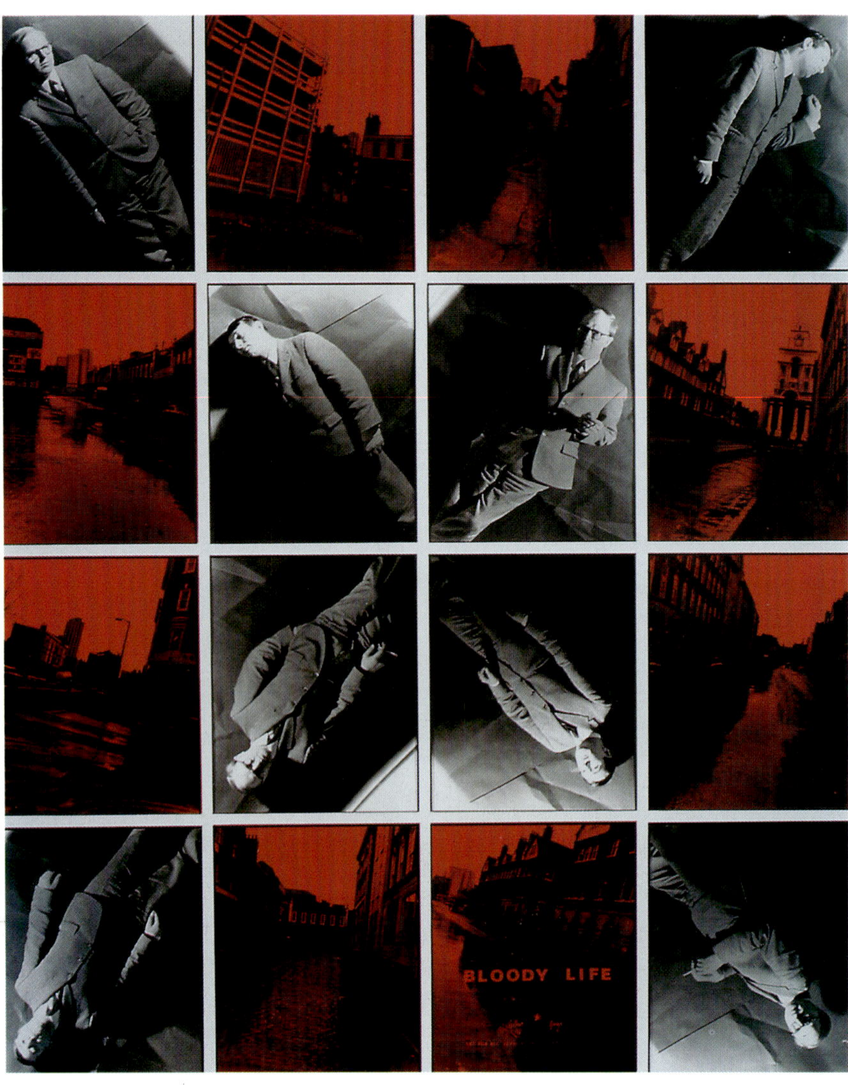

Gilbert & George, *Bloody Life, No. 16,* 1975.

neutrality, in principle, of the photographic image. It is, by its very nature, detached from what is photographed. For reasons which may be easily understood, connected with the mechanical character of the medium, the photographic image possesses a certain coldness. As Bergson already glimpsed, this image is abstracted from the continuity of life and events; and this is something which limits investigation to the information contained within the image, while opening up a proliferating space to interpretation by association.

Photographic vision is instantaneous and artificial. It make things visible which otherwise would have remained invisible; other things visible which would never have existed. As Walter Benjamin said: "Yes, of course, another nature speaks to the camera insofar as it speaks face to face; and about all in another mode, because instead of a space consciously elaborated by man, we have a space in which he works unconsciously. In general one is aware, for example, even in a crude way, of human behavior, but it is clear that one knows nothing of their attitude during that fraction of a second in which their behavior changes."[26]

A camera does not see as we see, and the image obtained is the result of a production process which can be modified. "Correct exposure" and "a good print" inevitably give an "average result" which itself depends on current conventions as to what constitutes an acceptable image. The history of photography bears ample witness to the continual modification of such conventions. Cameras do not produce images of anything real, if by "real" we mean "what we can see ourselves". Indeed, a serious study of photographic causality ends up in by routing "analogic" concepts. The mechanical nature of the camera/photographer system is no more evident than the subjective

that of the instantaneous photograph, they are actually indicators, signs produced causally by that of which they are the sign.

It remains, however, as in every pragmatic situation, to evaluate the causal circumstances. Resemblance is what it is and is worth what it is worth – that is, not much. A photographic image is manufactured, produced with the help of instruments. All we can say about it is that something has left a trace there – but the causes cannot be read in their effects; the former are limited to causing them. A photograph is the imprint of something – of what is another matter. Something which realizes not its truth but simply its value as a trace or a relic. A photograph is not a "true image", it is the trace of something which has disappeared.

It is at this point that we should turn things upside down. Photographic causality should no longer be considered in the abstract, but as a production process in which, at every stage, it is possible to intervene. The position which comes out of this is at least as strong and as constant as the analogical position. It is going to be necessary, for example, to take account of the

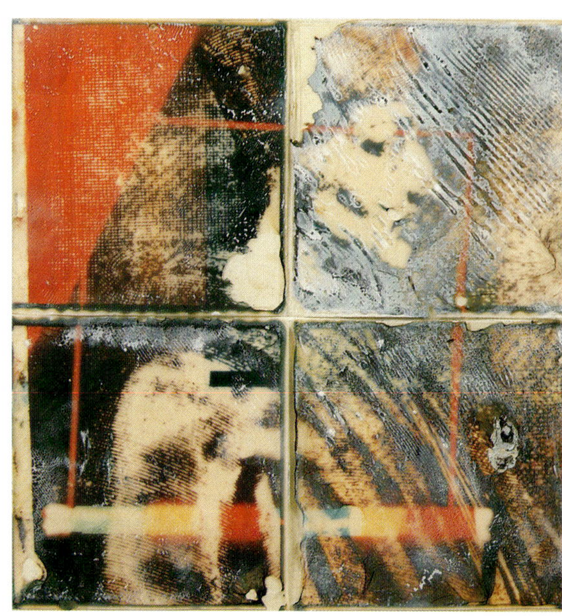

Paolo Gioli, ▶ *Homage to Niépce,* 1983, Galerie Michèle Chomette, Paris.

25. R. Krauss, "Notes sur l'index", in *Macula,* no. 5–6, pp. 165–175.

26. W. Benjamin, *op. cit.,* p. 50.

freedom which exists at the heart of the paintbrush/painter system.

Pictorial recipes exist just as do photographic inventions – except if we take as our model of the act of photography the practice of the amateur. Photography is more complex and less predetermined than we spontaneously believe it. One photographs what is technically possible with the camera in the time available. There are innumerable possibilities for manipulating the medium. Even photographers like Strand and Weston and their friends in the f64 school who claimed the absolute objectivity of the medium also recognized its formal conventions: "It is in the organization of this objectivity that the photographer's viewpoint with regard to life comes in; and a formal conception born of the emotions or the intellect, or both, is as much required of him before he takes the photo as it is required of the painter before he touches the canvas with his brush."[27]

This is why the aesthetic values which play their part in photography are the same as those of contemporary art in general: a conscious and exacerbated exploration of the formal possibilities of the medium, reference to the framework of a living tradition, an unceasing quest for innovation with, as a counterpoint, a very small content of reality which is continuously trying to conceal itself.

Fundamentally, the whole problem of the photographic image is that it "seems" to be transparent. It "seems" to provide us with the actual things, while really giving us only a relic. Objects seem to push their way through the image, but we only ever see, to use Garry Winogrand's words, "what they look like when they are photographed".[28] The specific experience of looking at a photograph consists of this rapid, incessant, even brutal change of reference. It is a bit like banging one's head against a pane of glass which one hasn't noticed, as in the photographs of Lee Friedlander. Our eye is constrained to move from the thing itself to what it looks like when it is photographed, then to the actual photograph, and finally to itself as a looking eye. The content is an image, this image itself is a thing, and finally our way of looking at the image and the thing. The invention of an art form is in fact that of a new type of object and of an unstable form of looking.

In the order of speech

Classical philosophy, from Descartes to Wolff, by way of Locke and Leibnitz, was a philosophy of ideas whose central model was that of the painting, or rather the engraving, with all that this implies for key notions such as clarity, sharpness, and mathematical precision in the representation of perspective and in the application of optical theory. When the emphasis changed from a content centered on ideation to synthetic dynamism, this philosophy of ideas suddenly faded into the background. The first edition of Kant's *Critique of Pure Reason* appeared in 1781, then, in 1786, Reid's *Essays on the Intellectual Powers of Man*. The Kantian critique heralded the age of the concept, and Reid mercilessly attacked the notion of knowledge via idea/image.

Curiously, the age of the invention of photography was also that of a return to the language of ideas and images, notably in the associationist psychology of the second half of the nineteenth century. It is symptomatic that in the last years of the century Bergson tried to ponder, against this associationist psychology, the continuity of psychical life by having recourse, once again, to the idea of the image, and simultaneously trying to separate the images from their inherently static and instantaneous – that is photographic – element.

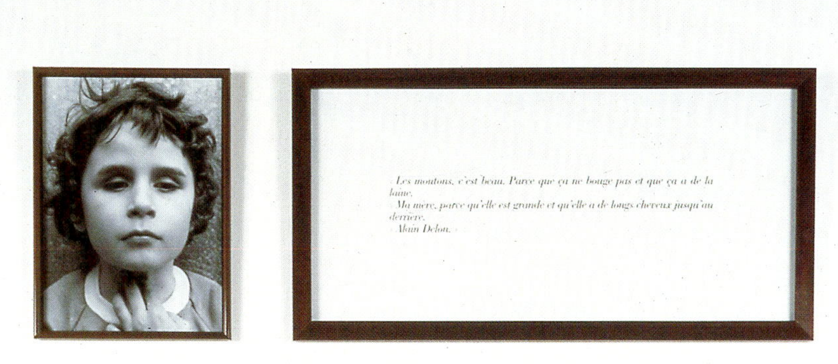

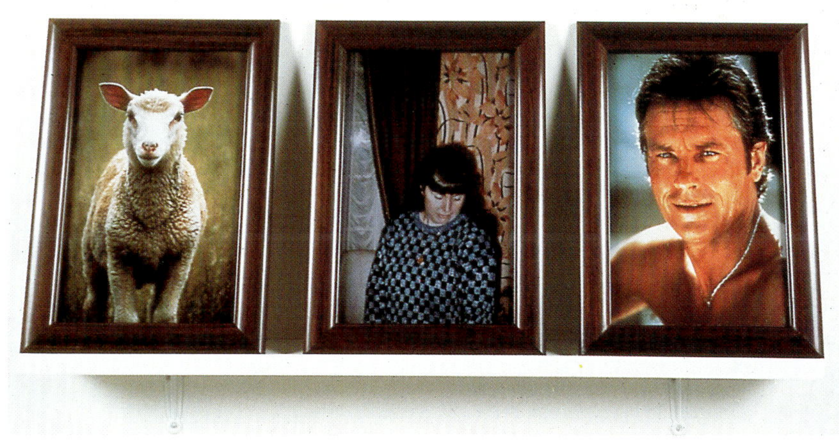

Sophie Calle, from the series ***The Blind, No. 6,*** 1986.

27. P. Strand, "Photography", in B. Newhall (ed.), *Photography, Essays and Images*, New York, Museum of Modern Art, 1980, p. 219.

28. G. Winogrand, "Interview", in P. R. Petruck (ed.), *The Camera Viewed: Writings on XXth Century Photography*, New York, E. P. Dutton, 1979, vol. 2, p. 127.

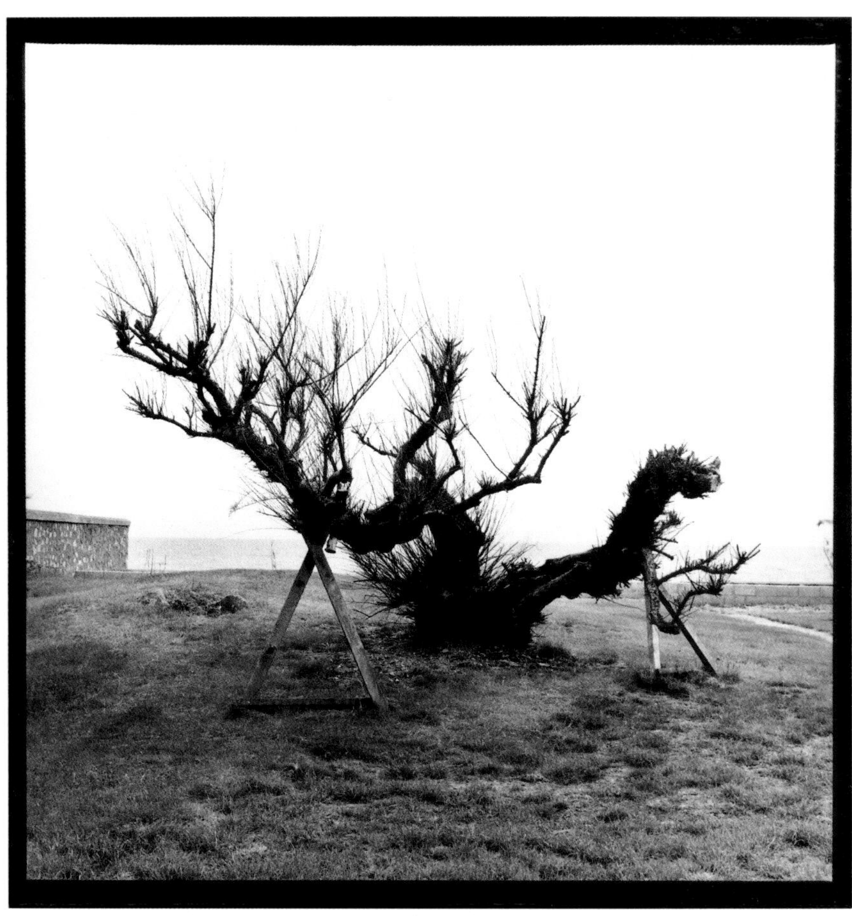

MARC TRIVIER,
Tree I,
Folkestone, 1986.

Even Husserls's phenomenology, at least in its static and descriptive phase, was a captive of the notion of the image; it describes our mental states in the way one describes a photograph – while adding the intentionality and the abstract actions which constitute the sense of these states.

It is curious that philosophy, which achieved at the turn of the twentieth century a double revolution of signification and intentionality, should have continued to work with such a static notion as that of the image, and should have progressively reached the limits which such a notion could bring.

It would be the subject of another essay to sustain this hypothesis of the influence of the photographic model at the centre of philosophical analysis – an influence which is found in literary description, especially in Zola.

This is not surprising when one considers that philosophers carry out their activities with the instruments available to them. Among these are the conceptual resources of tradition and the contributions of science, but there are also the metaphors provided by the state of technology and of culture. Today, computers play no small part in the new wave of cognitive approaches. Photography has played its role in, once again, enticing philosophers back to the charms of the image.

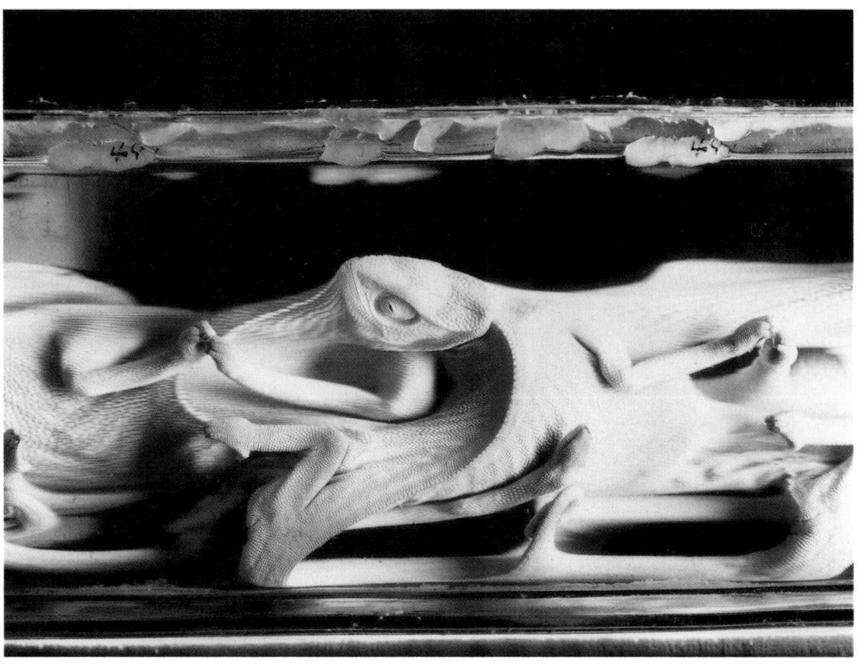

PATRICK
BAILLY-MAÎTRE-GRAND,
The Frieze,
extract from *Formol's Band,*
1986–1987.

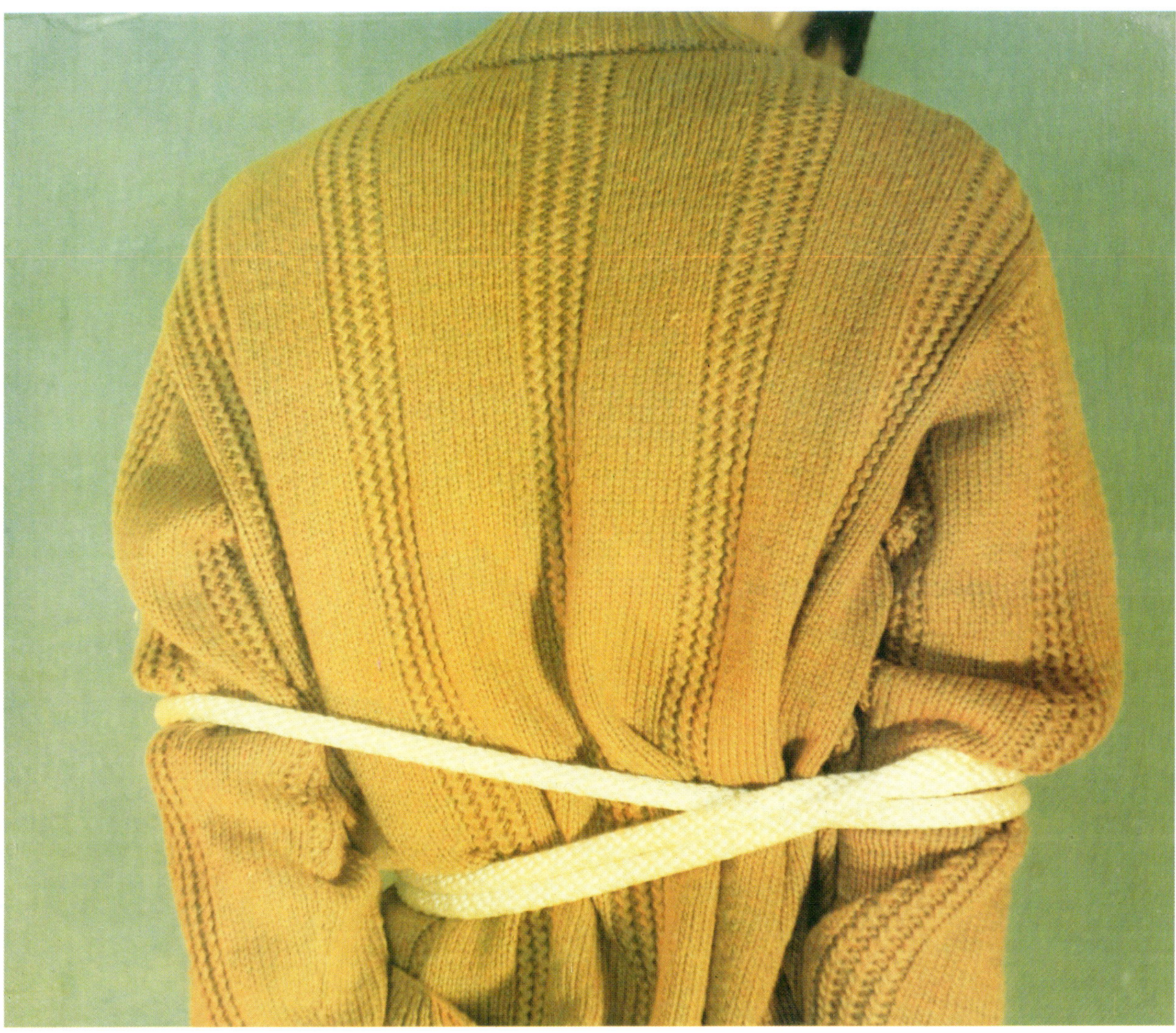

A collection of contemporary art

It might be regarded as symptomatic of the end of the twentieth century that it is possible to assemble a coherent collection of contemporary art which includes only items – dating from the 1960s onwards – which have been created on a photographic base material or directly referring to the medium. The private collection made by Rolf H. Krauss was acquired by the Stuttgart Staatsgalerie, continuing a collection of earlier photographic prints (the Rolf Mayer collection, from Fox Talbot to Man Ray).

This museum situation (bringing together ancient photos and contemporary photographic art) objectively illustrates a historical evolution of the medium and the various functions which it has fulfilled since the beginning of the twentieth century, in turn documentary or artistic, unified or conflicting.

Considered in the homogeneous context of the Krauss collection in Stuttgart, the photograph is no longer an image captured in a brief moment or a longer pose and arranged graphically to conform with so-called "expressive" rules or models; it is, rather, a vehicle for communication, a workable and ductile operator between the artist and reality. It is in addition what legitimately provides the spectator with an almost direct access to the primary concept (this is "the transparency of photography").

In images such as Bruce Nauman's *Bound to Fail* or Gordon Matta-Clark's *Conical Intersect*, photography illuminates a process, exteriorizing it and making it present, away from all manipulation, dissemblance or grinding down of the material; it is the place where an artistic process takes place – assumed by the artist – a system for recording a phenomenon which affirms through visual rhetoric its temporal and mental aspects and its discursive elaboration.

No longer is an event furtively seized by the photographer; rather he constructs an imaginary space, a conception of something impossible in nature, which would have had no existence without the willing intervention of an artist.

Having emerged from Pop Art and the mass media during the 1960s, photography has become assimilated to a "taking of an impression" of art during the process of its creation. Connected with, or resulting from, a number of factors – the lessening of interest in painting, the staging of "personal myths", Land Art, Body Art, narration, sequences, and accumulation – the use of photography makes manifest the passage from the sensorial to the cerebral.

Quite clearly, the works in this collection offer a tremendous variety of approaches to the analysis of the medium: closeness of language and photography (Marcel Broodthaers, John Hilliard, Joseph Kosuth, Ugo Mulas), visual experience of real space (Vito Acconci, Bernhard and Anna Blume, Jan Dibbets, Gilbert and George, Richard Long, Klaus Rinke) or built space (Joseph Beuys, Gordon Matta-Clark, Dennis Oppenheim's *Land Slide*, Michael Snow, Boyd Webb), links with cinema and its conventions (John Baldessari, Cindy Sherman), impact of photography in the media (Victor Burgin, Barbara Kruger), the possibility of inflecting an account or questioning its truth (Jean Le Gac, Jochen Gerz's *Lived Not Lived*, Sigmar Polke's *Gilbert and George in Willich*) or bringing it back to the memory (Christian Boltanski's *Visit to the Zoo*), the system of accumulation and photographic repetition (Berndt and Hilla Becher, Ugo Mulas, Klaus Rinke), and identity between a body and an inscribed surface (Arnulf Rainer, Urs Lüthi, Bruce Nauman).

The historical pertinence of numerous items ensures that this collection has an exemplary value in summing up the artistic phenomena of the last decades.

Michel Frizot

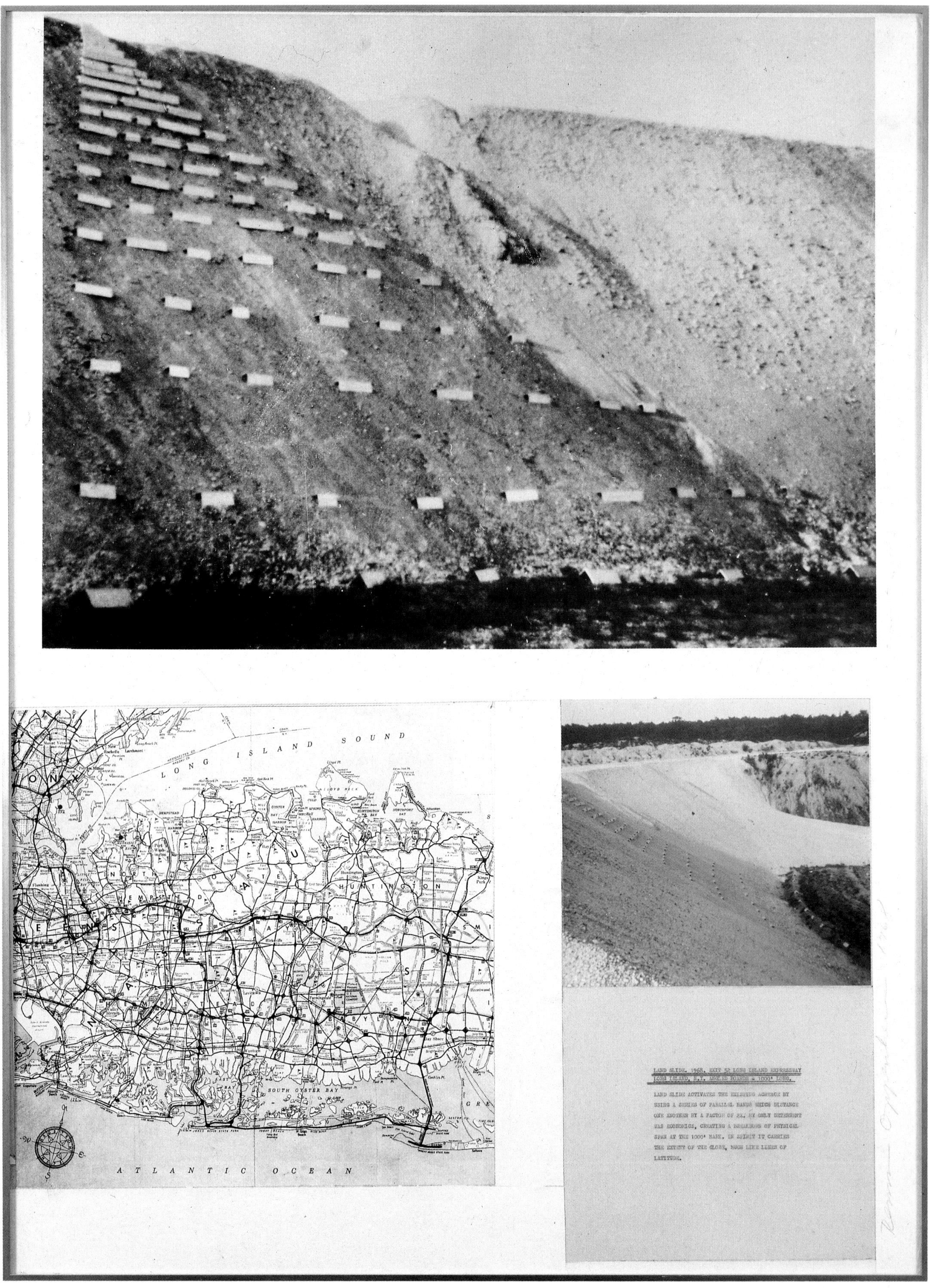

◀◀ preceding page:
BRUCE NAUMAN, *Bound to Fail,* 1966.

All the works in this dossier come from the print collection of the Stuttgart Staatsgalerie (Dr. Rolf H. Krauss Collection).

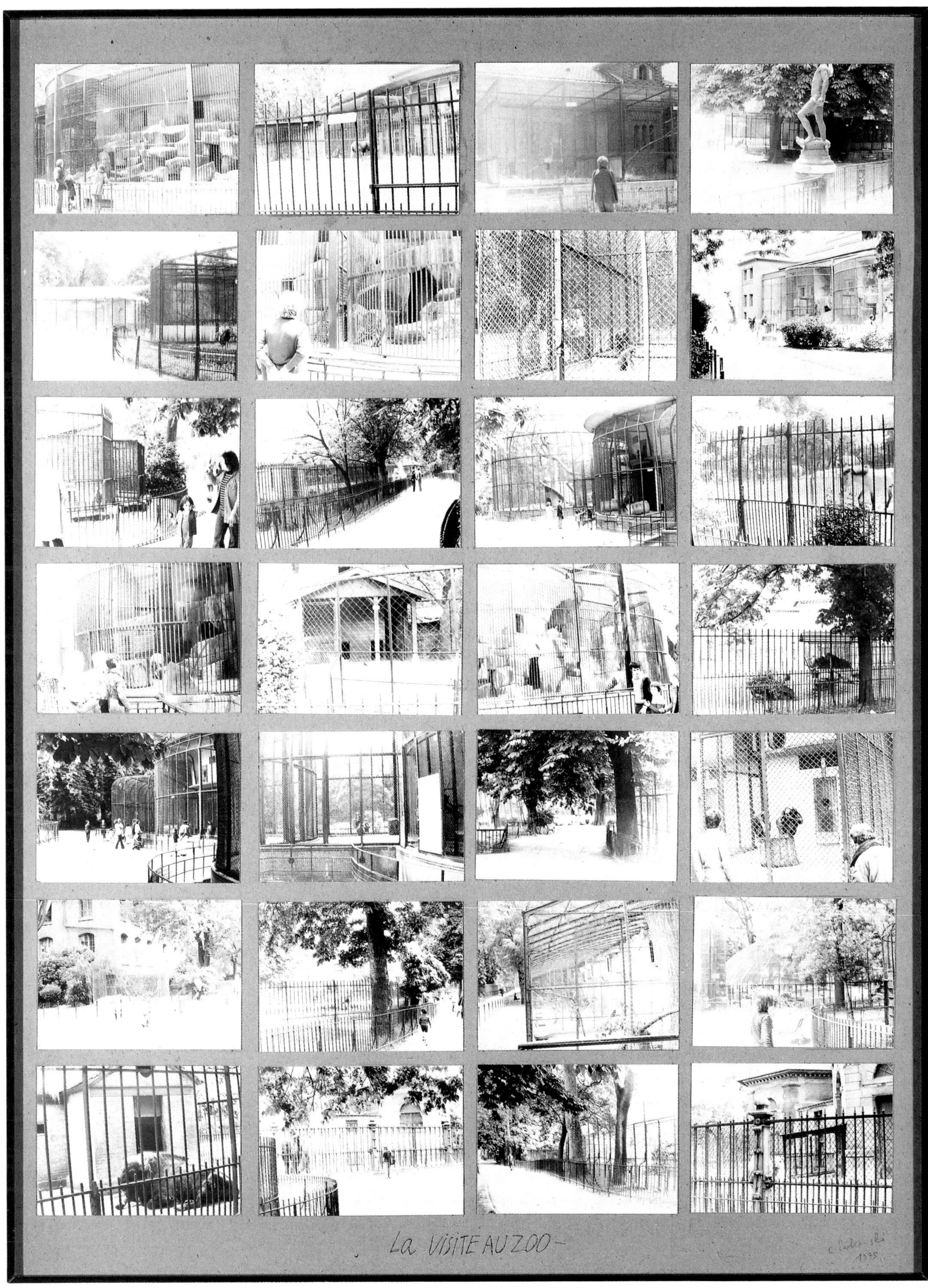

◀ Dennis Oppenheim, *Land Slide*, 1968.

Christian Boltanski, *The Visit to the Zoo*, 1975.

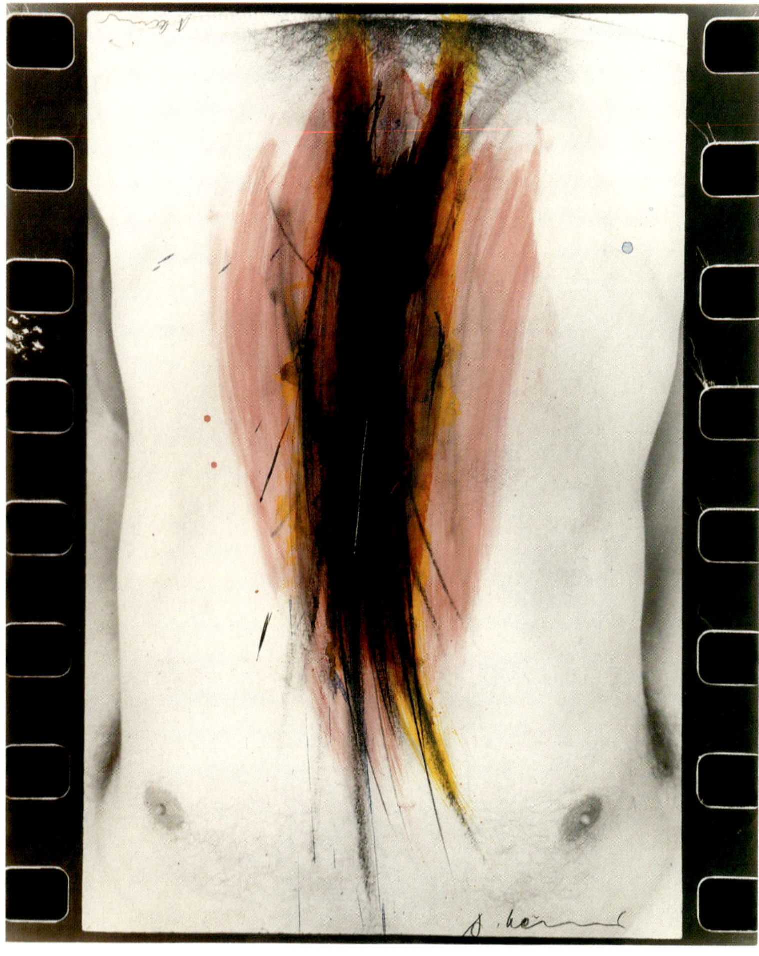

ARNULF RAINER,
Bauchmalerei,
1970–1973.

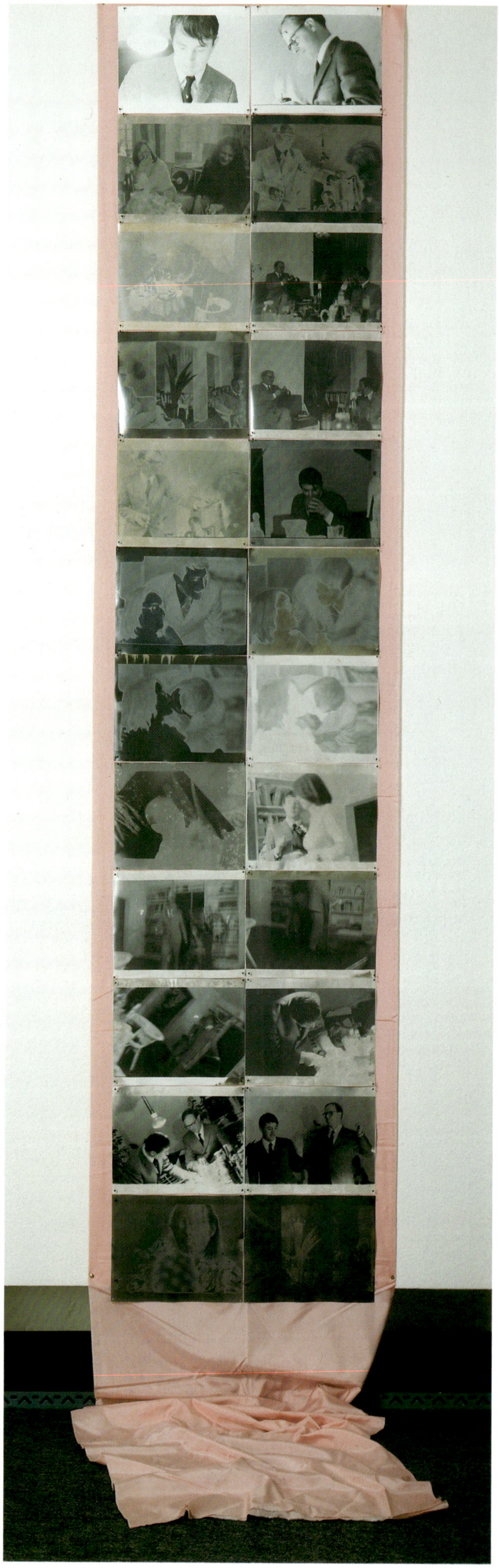

SIGMAR POLKE,
Gilbert and George in Willich,
1974.

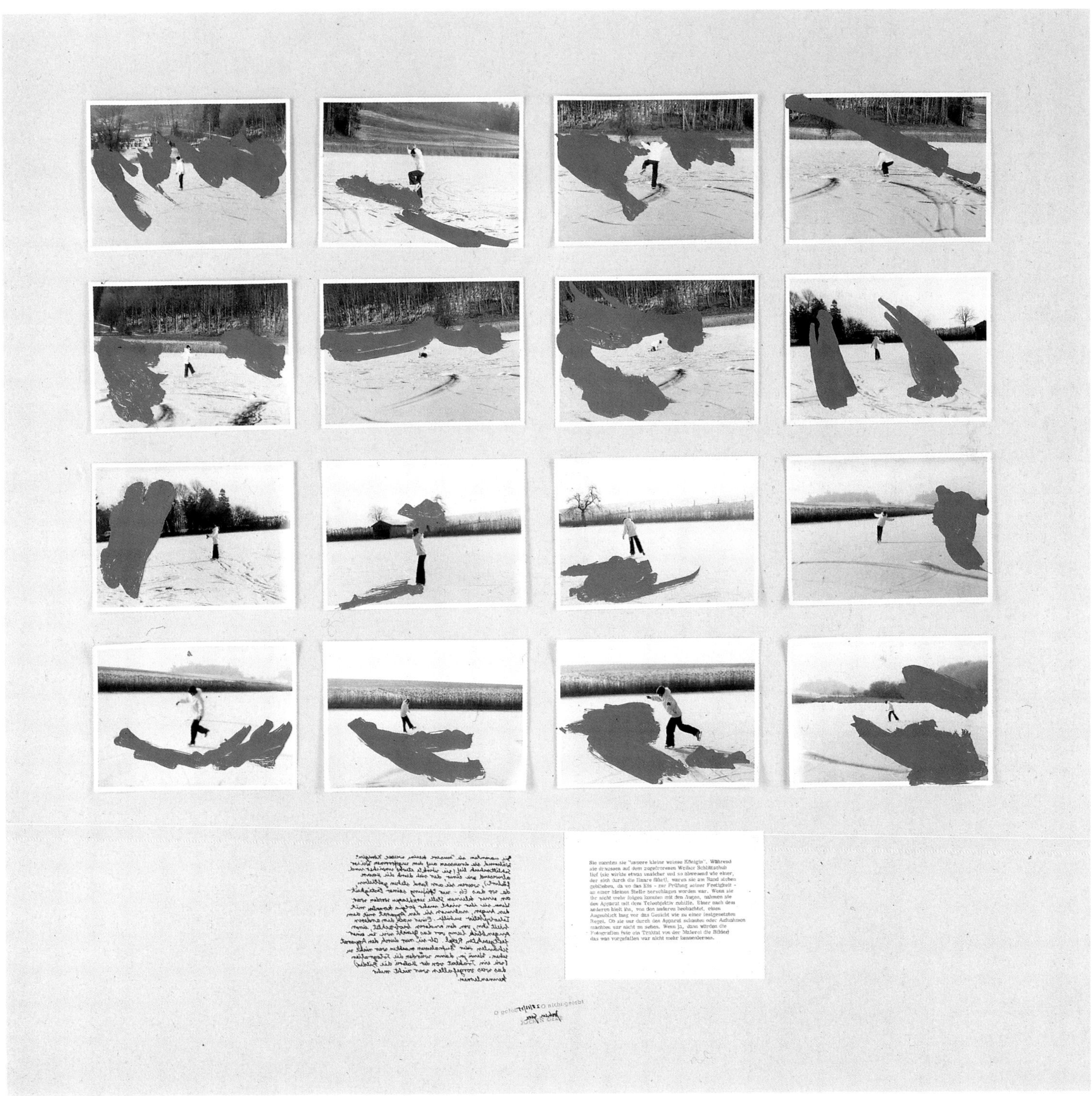

Jochen Gerz,
O gelebt o nicht gelebt
[Lived Not Lived], 1975.

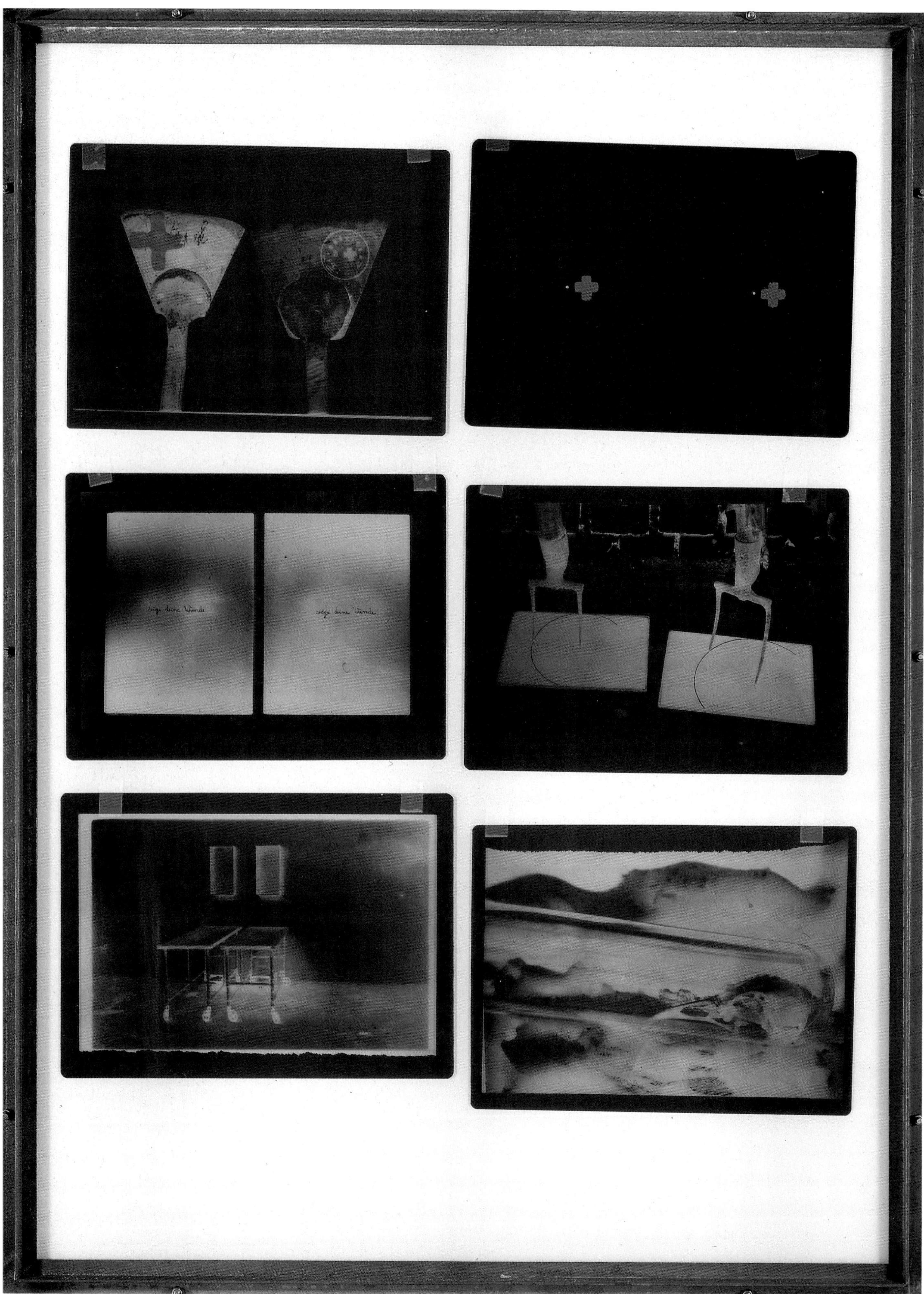
zeige deine Wunde
zeige deine Wunde

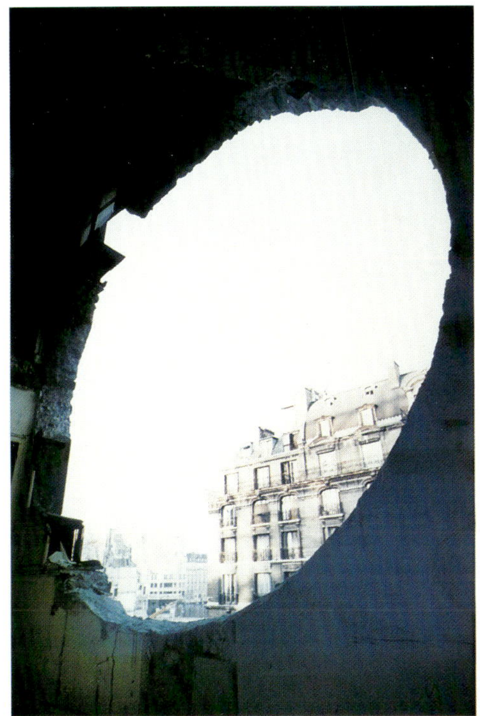

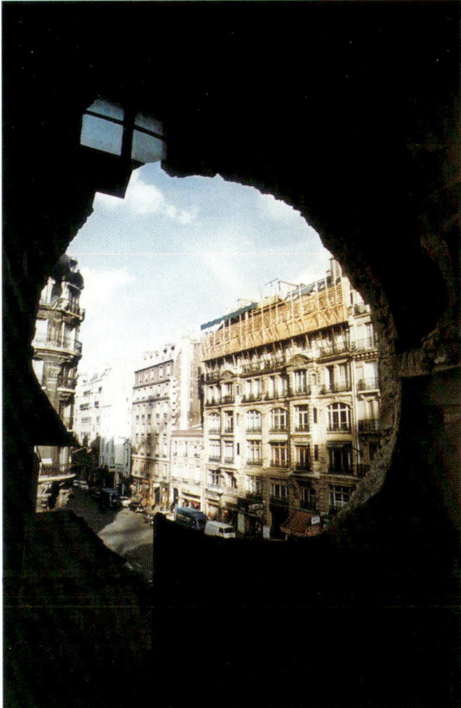

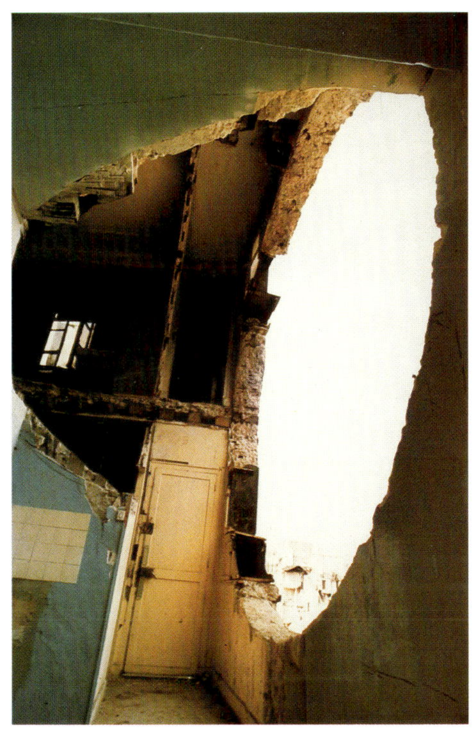

▲
GORDON MATTA-CLARK,
Conical Intersect,
1975.

◀ JOSEPH BEUYS,
Zeige deine Wunde,
("Show Your Wound"),
1976.

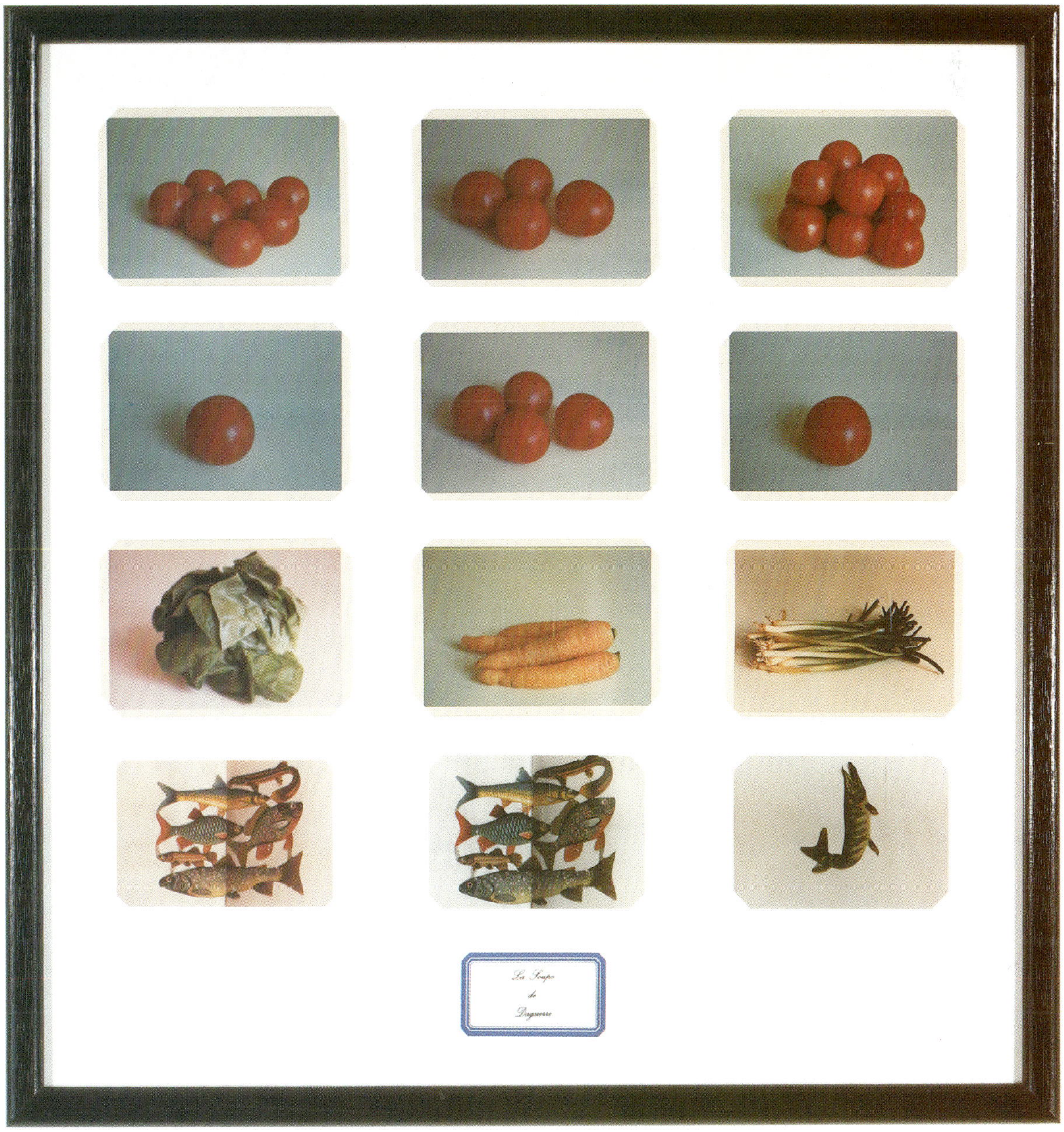

MARCEL BROODTHAERS,
Daguerre's Soup,
1975.

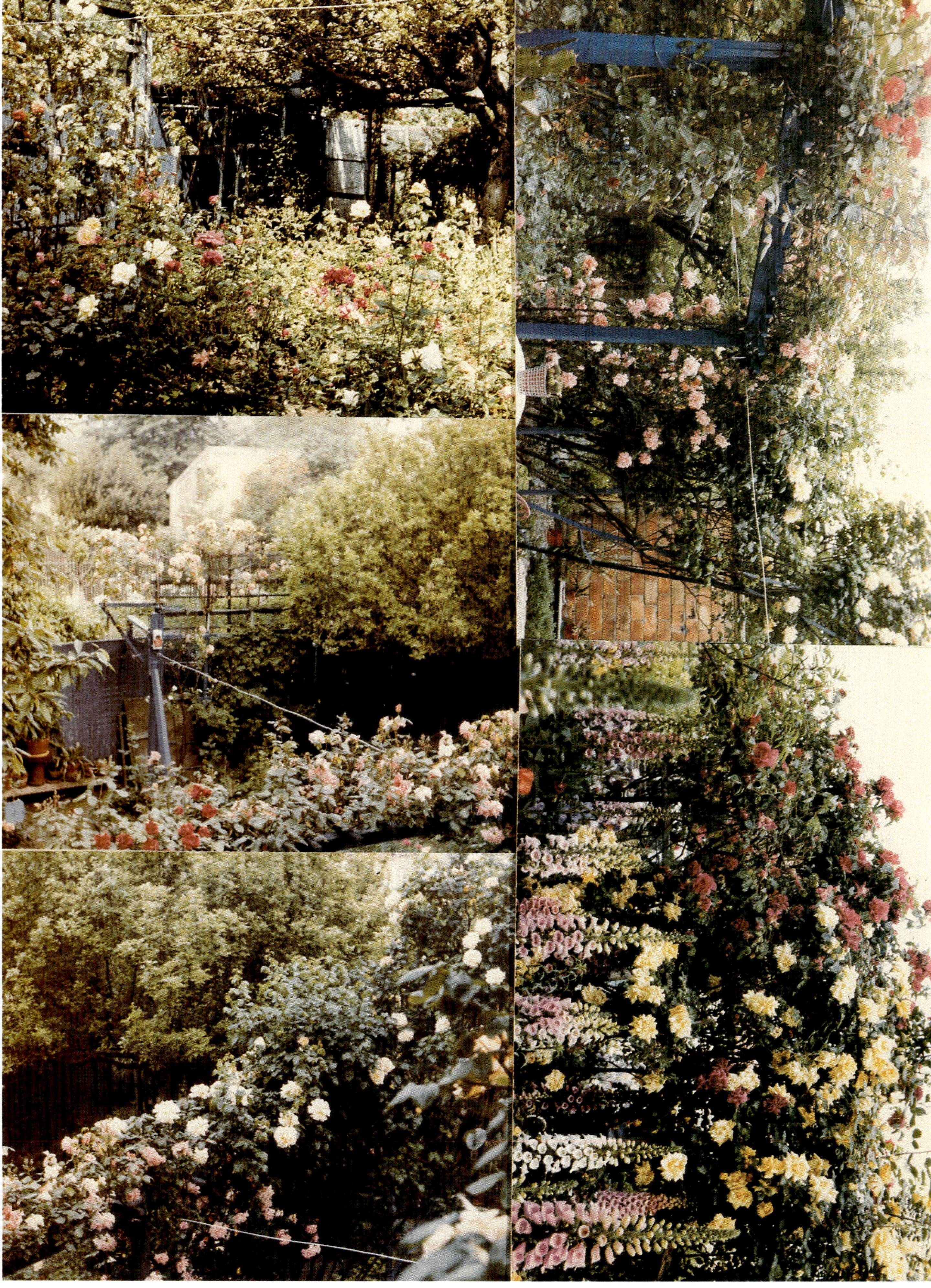

RITUALS AND CUSTOMS

Photographs as memories

Michel Frizot

Many photographs fall into a category of images, now obsolete, which was produced by photographers who labored, almost anonymously, in small towns and in the countryside to produce "photographic craft objects" rather than images which adhered to artistic doctrines. However, those qualities and specific traits which we immediately recognize as "photographic" were perpetuated and even exaggerated in such work – retouching, additions, and framing, along with embellishments such as tinting, painting, collage, photomontage or arrangements of images. In these departures from photographic convention, fragments of human life tell their story, and are still able to trigger an emotional response despite their veneer of ritual and custom.

The history of photography is special because, during the 150 years of its existence, the development of the medium has embraced an ever broadening social spectrum. Individuals have become ever more intimately involved with photography, even to the extent of sometimes being deprived of freedom of choice while within this "rite of passage" because it is subject to its own social rules and popular ritual. While the notion of "culture" imposed by the media has been shown to be as arbitrary as it is fickle, we must now demonstrate that the slow penetration of photography into people's homes and the social fabric also has its own history – that it was not programmed in advance so as to arrive at that commercial golden age revered by magazines. We have to understand how photography has been accepted, taken over by certain groups with varying degrees of success, developed by "vernacular" usage which passed from village to village rather than being imposed, as one might believe, by the example of Paris. Indeed, current more or less international popular practice is not the direct result of the invention of photography; it preserves quirks, cultural influences, and strange photographic artifacts which still have their place in people's homes and which each country has adapted to its own traditions or religious beliefs. Everyone must have seen in country cottages those photographic enlargements of the husband and wife, each in an oval frame, or the wedding photograph given pride of place on the chest of drawers. Even during the 1950s, images of those killed during the First World War were still displayed in French homes, decorated with those tarnished medals that subsequent history had rendered somewhat derisory.

The present undeniable resurgence of photography – to which this book also bears witness – has led people to become interested first in works, then in photographic artists who have gradually

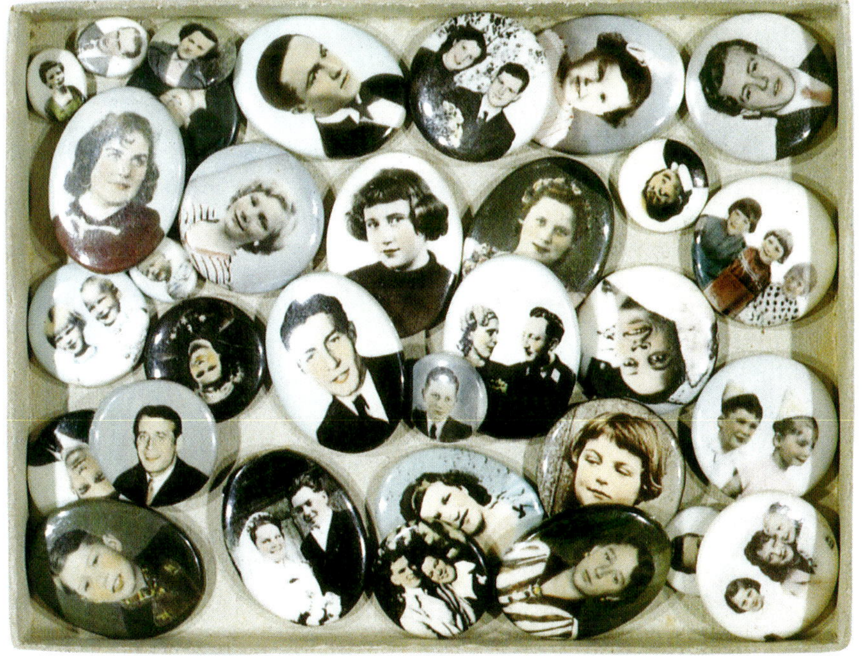

Miniature colored portraits for buttons or badges,
circa 1950,
private collection.

◀ Anonymous,
The Garden,
five prints mounted in an album.
1978,
private collection.

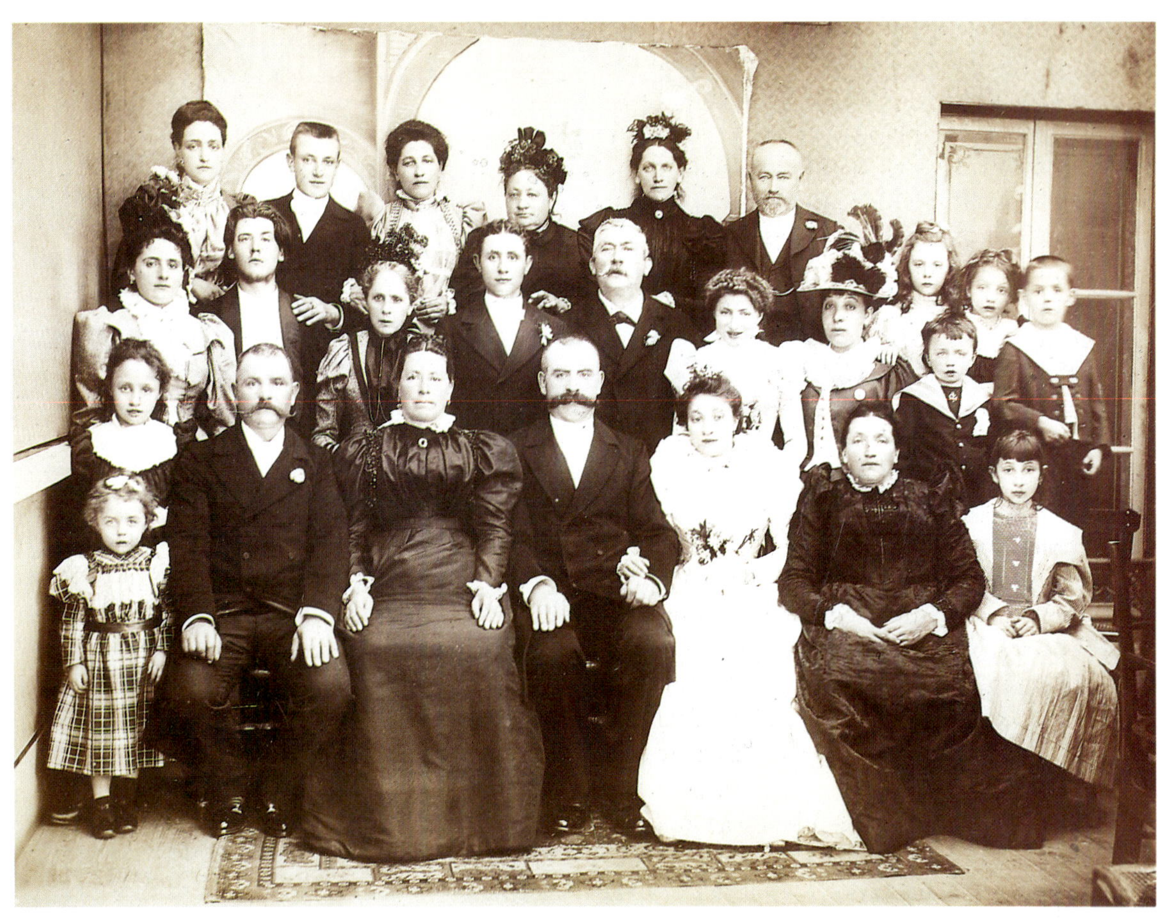

STUDIO J. CHARRIÈRE, *Wedding Picture*, France, circa 1900, private collection.

recovered their former glory. However, although some workers have been lucky enough to have been rediscovered, others have been consigned to obscurity. How should we judge rural photographers, amateurs whose names have been lost, all those enthusiasts who did not risk signing their work because in the milieu in which they lived photography was not regarded as a "proper" trade?

The historian has a duty to go further than simply resuscitate the great figures from the past to create a hall of fame. The most modest photography carried out at a country fair or the smallest snapshot brought back from an outing teaches us more about social behavior with regard to photography than any detailed description of the ritual of the photographic pose as practiced by Disdéri or Nadar. It is not just the price of a print or the eminent quality of the subject photographed which determines the interest people might have in a photograph. Abandoned sources of photographic material exist, still willingly consigned to the rubbish tip for lack of artistic "taste", that museums will, sooner or later, have to make an effort to collect and preserve. There are many categories of photographs to which nobody devoted a single line in the specialist magazines of the period. Yet these photographs, evolving, adapting, disappearing as they did, marked the rhythm of individual human lives.

Among ordinary people illustrative material deriving from photography is regarded in the same way as were earlier domestic prints but, at the same time, criteria of "readability" which are peculiar to photography are applied to it. This means that its quality as an "imprint", as a truthful record, as an objective version of reality (all qualities attributed to it without question), is also subject to other laws of communication, which sometimes contradict each other. Various ways of treating the image – such as retouching, massive enlargement, or miniaturization – modifications which are supposed to improve it,

STUDIO J. DAVID AND E. VALLOIS, *Paris, Top Form in a Lycée*, 1932, private collection.

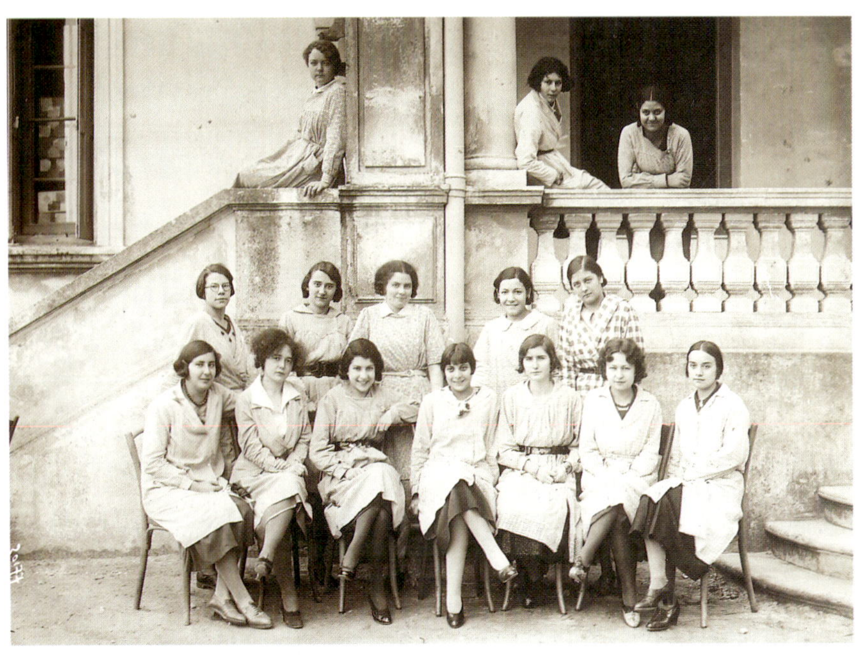

in fact give it a status quite different from that of the raw, unaltered photograph. At the same time, these treatments bring photographs such as these closer to popular imagery, from which they borrow certain criteria of simplification and visual evidence. The photograph which has been altered for domestic consumption speaks another language; it is a commentary on the affinities in force between social groups, making manifest their relationship with art (by bringing it closer to painting techniques), and their capacity for imposing objects controlled by artistic norms.

Objective memories

The physical appearance of a photograph is defined primarily by its function. As soon as the daguerreotype was invented, images could be presented in a variety of ways. As well as being placed in traditional frames hanging from a nail (replacing painted miniatures and silhouettes) they could be inserted into silver lockets, which allowed people to carry photographic portraits around with them on necklaces or as brooches. For these particular uses the photographer had to provide smaller prints. Cases with fabric linings were devised to hold portraits. These cases were usually decorated in repoussé leather. However, in the United States there developed a long-lasting fashion for cases molded in black resin. This fashion became so widespread that these cases have now become collectors' items in their own right, quite independent of the photographs inside them, which are often less interesting or valuable than their cases. Among people attached to mementos, photographs had replaced personal relics such as locks of hair or ribbons.

After the decline of the daguerreotype from the 1850s, cheaper ferrotypes were inserted into photographic jewelry, to be followed by cut-out paper prints in which only the face appeared. Such portraits, mounted in brooches decorated with floral motifs or art nouveau volutes, continued to be popular until the Second World War. They could also be found on hatpins, hairpins, and buttons. From 1860, a technique for transferring photographic prints onto copper allowed the production of photographic enamels, often hand-colored, which could also be inserted into jewelry. In Paris, Lafon de Camarsac made this his specialty, but other manufacturers were to be found everywhere. From the end of the century other enamel portraits, both miniatures and larger, framed images, were produced on porcelain. These were often placed on gravestones.

Such photographic mementos were not limited to sweethearts or the dearly departed. These discreet and sentimental images stemmed from a much more widespread involvement of photography in social rituals and ceremonies. A visit to the photographer's studio became a substitute for other initiatory rituals marking one's passage through life and regulating the duration of one's relationships with other people. Such rituals punctuated the phases of life, from birth to death from the cradle to the grave. The life of an

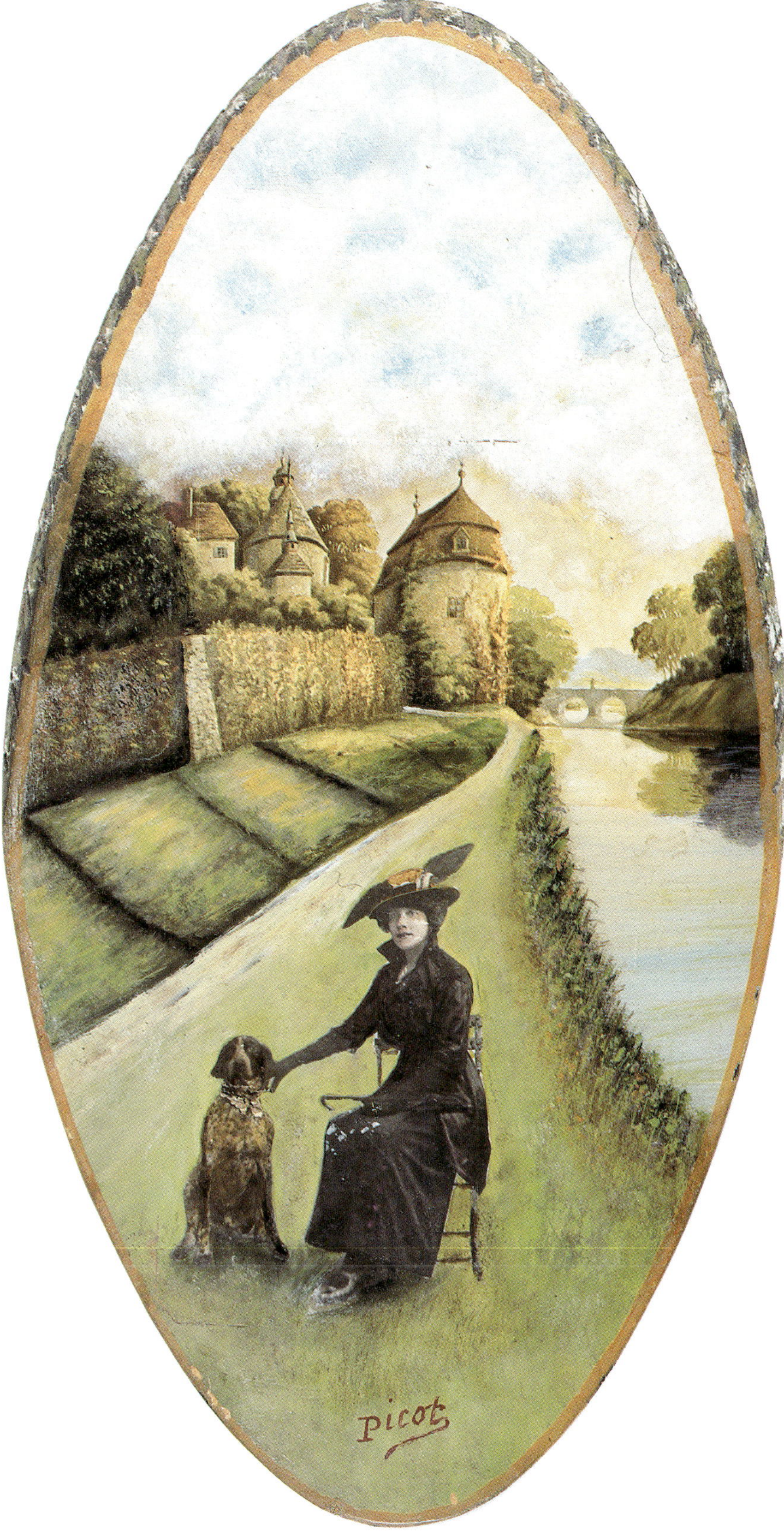

PICOT,
Montage of a postcard and a photographic portrait on wood, highlighted in gouache,
circa 1910,
private collection.

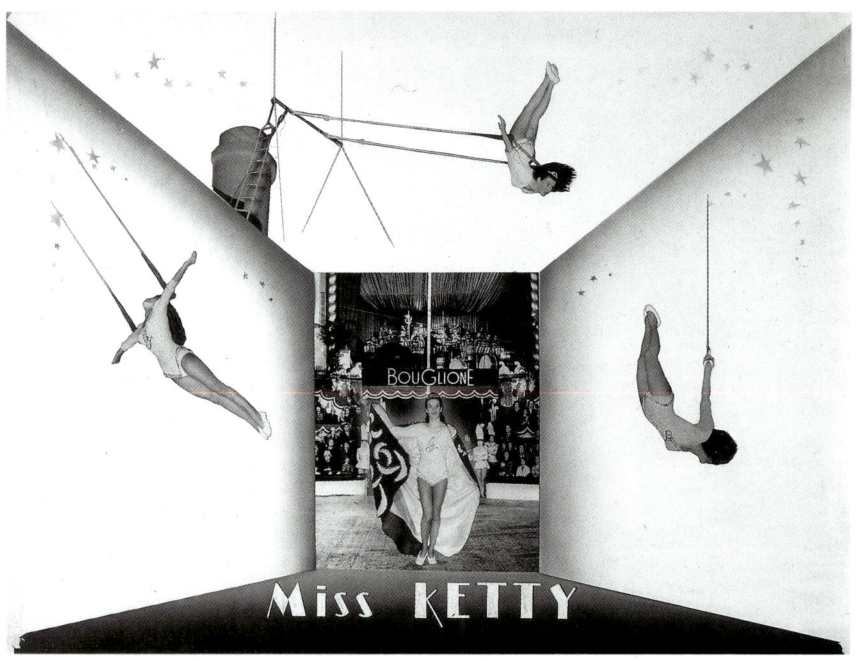

ANONYMOUS, *Miss Ketty (from the Bouglione circus)*, photomontage enhanced with airbrush and gouache, circa 1950, private collection.

individual, especially in closed micro-societies such as an isolated village, seemed to be punctuated by a certain number of photographic events. While the rite of baptism did not necessarily correspond with its secular equivalent, that is, the portrait of the baby (a genre which first appeared in the 1880s), the photograph of the first communion was no more than a duplication and confirmation of the religious ceremony. Then came military service, which also produced events which needed to be commemorated photographically. From the Second Empire onwards, when photographs of generals had become popular, photography gradually worked its way down through the ranks until every soldier felt obliged to send his family his portrait taken in uniform. In every garrison town several studios undertook this work, and photographers also visited the barracks to take group photos on the spot (in the 1920s these were printed onto postcards). New conscripts sometimes took part in more informal ceremonies before the military rituals took place. They would go to the photographer in small groups before attending the recruiting board. Next, marriage was a great photographic event. Wedding photographs take various combinations – head-and-shoulder portraits of the couple, full-length portraits, studio portraits with the bride carrying flowers, photographed against a painted backdrop, a group photograph of all the wedding guests, etc. Even the seating plan followed certain conventions and a precise symbolism, reflecting the social hierarchy of the time.

On several occasions an individual might be required to sit for a group photograph – among his family, when the children had reached a certain age, to proclaim the stability of the family unit, or in family reunions (especially among the bourgeoisie), an opportunity for family relationships to be permanently recorded by means of the camera. In this case, too, the local

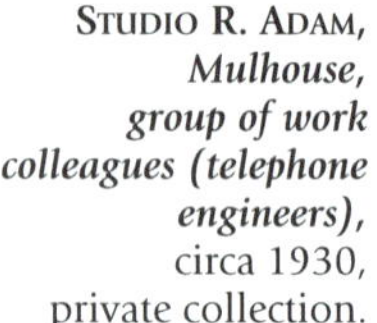
STUDIO R. ADAM, *Mulhouse, group of work colleagues (telephone engineers)*, circa 1930, private collection.

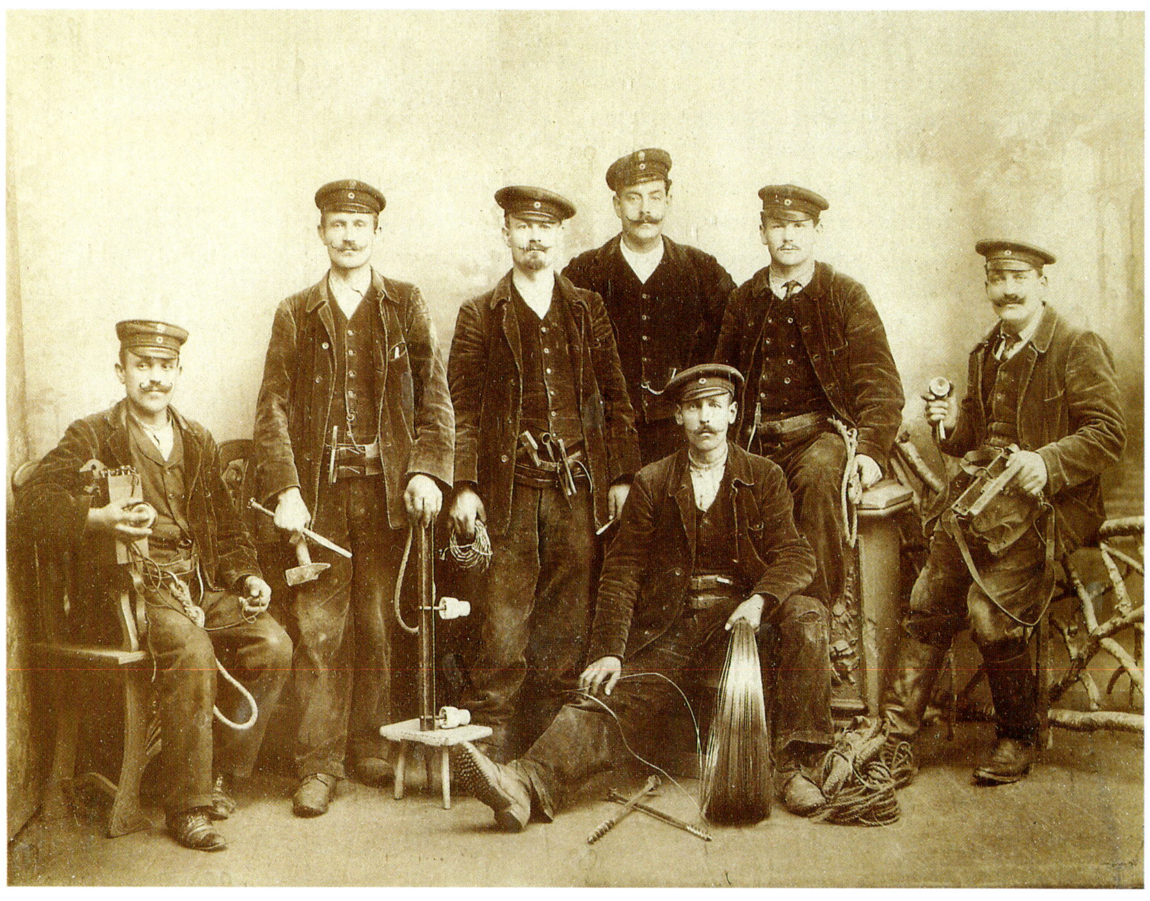

photographer came out and worked in the open air. Two other, fairly similar, types of group portraiture were popularized by photography – work- or profession-related and class (school or college) photographs. While the professional group portrait goes back in spirit to the portraits of guilds and corporations well-known in Holland in the seventeenth century, few examples occur until the end of the nineteenth. It is, therefore, a creation peculiar to photography, resulting from the possibility of an objective view provided by the camera (the same thing happened in Germany with the appearance of the daguerreotype). It would be fascinating to study the circumstances of such practices, the reasons why a particular group decided on a photograph and whose idea it was – particularly as such images contain clues, provided by the sitters, which clearly indicate their trades (the place and date is usually added on a slate or board). Photographers themselves used to take each other in group photographs during the numerous photographic outings organized by amateur clubs, particularly between 1890 and 1914. As for class photographs, these were most probably initiated by the academic establishment, both as a display of solidarity and as a memento: a statement, to be reflected on in the future, that one belonged to a group which had now split up. The individual could read the photograph in several different ways: who was in the class, what had happened to each of them? What relationships had developed between the sitters, and what was their outcome? The photograph was often completed by an individual portrait, mounted on card, which could be given to friends.

Finally, there remain various kinds of photographic novelties which do not need to be categorized – the group in front of a shop (friends and relations of the shopkeeper, and customers), groups on the beach by itinerant photographers from the 1920s – enlarged as photographic postcards and produced in multiple copies. Certain cases are spectacular – the pilgrimage groups at Lourdes, photographed with a panoramic camera in front of the basilica or a more widespread use of the panoramic view in the United States, above all in the military (the panoramic groups of E. O. Goldbeck or Arthur Mole).

Retouching history

All photography intended for popular consumption, even more so than that produced for the press or for books, is based on the unfolding of a plot, the recounting of a story which, though lacking the vivid colors of an epic, is nevertheless an essential one in the eyes of its subjects and viewers. It is the relatively restrained nature of these deeds and actions of any and everybody, the smothering of individuality in conventions from which little deviation is allowed, which prevents these individual creations from falling into mere banality in our eyes. Each school, wedding or military photograph tells – within a fairly rigid framework – the story of a personal adventure lived as if unique, and, what is more, as exemplary, confirmed as it is in everyone's sight through true images. To each of these images the individual brings their own contribution, through their pose, the use of "props" or their expression. The composition may be modified in a number of ways: in the photographer's studio (see the dossier *The anonymous studio*) the painted backdrop may be altered, flowers or bottles may be arranged, one can sit or stand, look in a particular direction, pose on a bicycle, etc. There are a thousand ways of modifying an interpretation which *a priori* appears immutable. It is, therefore, possible to read these images as montages of available elements rather than as pleonastic artifacts produced in the same mold.

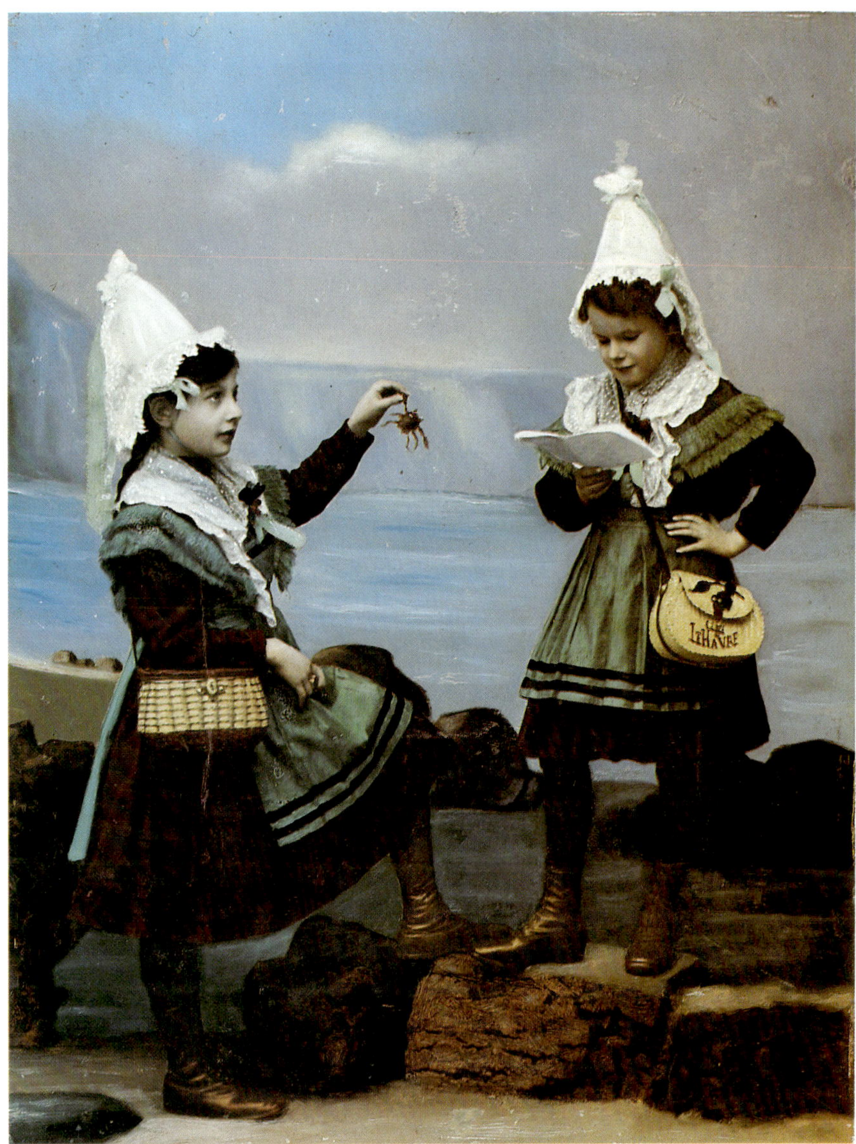

Anonymous,
Girls in Local Costume,
photographic print
enhanced in gouache,
Le Havre,
circa 1920,
private collection.

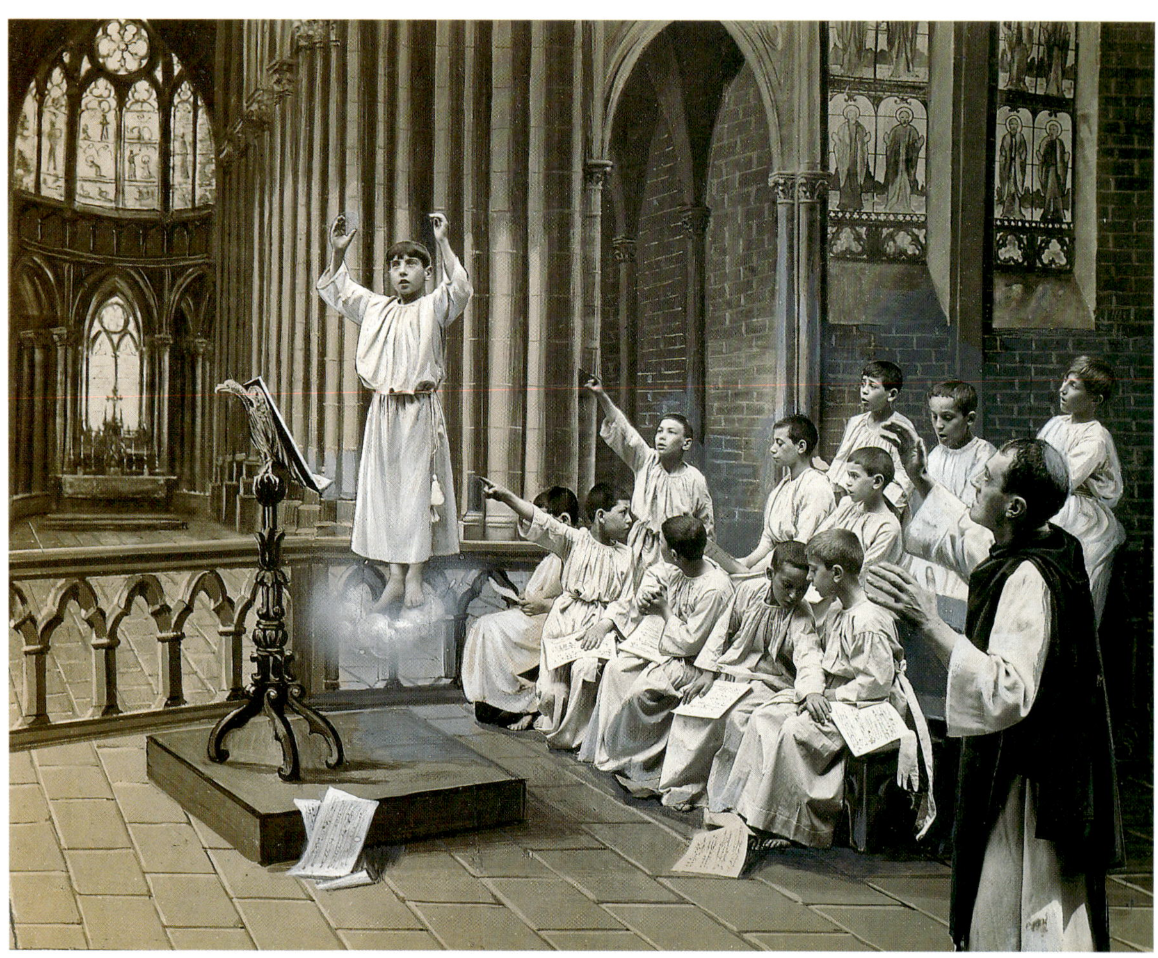

Photomontage for educational transparencies, from series *The Little Chorister of Notre-Dame,* Paris, circa 1930, private collection.

This potential for transforming images is used a good deal in popular photography, which lacks the prejudices of the urban classes as far as artistic rules are concerned. Photomontage, an essential element of the vocabulary of the avant-garde movement in the 1920s, was, according to Hannah Höch, "invented" by Raoul Hausmann by imitating a military image in a rented holiday room on the Baltic. "Opposite their bed a large color print hung in its frame. In the centre stood the young Kaiser Wilhelm II surrounded by his ancestors and descendents, oak trees, and German military decorations and, a little higher up and also in the center, the figure of a young bombardier under whose cap the portrait of our host had been pasted. Thus the young pioneer stood proudly, surrounded by his superiors, in the middle of the glories of this world. The paradox of this situation aroused Hausmann's ever-hidden aggressive spirit."[1] A tiny photographic fragment (a face), glued into this color print which displayed such careful, hierarchical organization, was enough to turn it into a true display of a slice of life: photomontage, with all its possibilities of distorting an account, existed well before artists began using it in a more critical, aggressive way.

Together with this technique, all forms of collage and retouching should be included, from the simple removal of facial blemishes to the entire color tinting of the photographic print. All these techniques combine to modify the account, to transform slightly what is shown, to elevate the image towards a symbolic function. Many variations of those military color prints mentioned by Hausmann are known, adapted to suit the customer (infantry, cavalry, etc.) The central part of the frame, into which the portrait of the individual was inserted, could be printed or painted (sometimes on a pale photographic background). In resorts (seaside, spas) a whole industry churned out artificial paintings, reproduced photographically, on demand. Color accentuated the realism of the scene, already underlined by the truthfulness of the pose (two little girls on a Normandy beach, for example). Hand-coloring, introduced with the daguerreotype, was popular throughout the nineteenth century until the arrival of color photography; it was via this bias that photomontage defined itself when photography was only a cut-out part of the image. Around 1900, portraits painted on wood made their appearance (the edges of the photograph disguised by a layer of paint), with variations in which painted landscapes on oval slices of wood replaced the traditional studio background, often displaying real virtuosity of perspective. Tourist postcards, mounted on wood

1. Quoted in Michel Giroud, *Raoul Hausmann: "Je ne suis pas un photographe"*, Paris, Chêne, 1975, p. 23.

and reworked, provided one of the most common items of interior decoration in the 1930s.

It must be stressed, however, that photomontage is not just a simple way of transforming quiet or shabby lives; it transposes, to use the proper term, reality into another setting. Circus and music-hall artists had recourse to specialist studios which prepared posters and publicity postcards on this principle. The performer seemed to float in an idealized space, devoid of obstructions, as if waiting both for the public and for success. It was a publicity technique which allowed an unreal adventure to be recounted or to suggest that it was possible: thus the story of a levitating choirboy could be presented at parochial church meetings or confirmation classes; and pets which disliked being photographed could be shown off to better advantage.

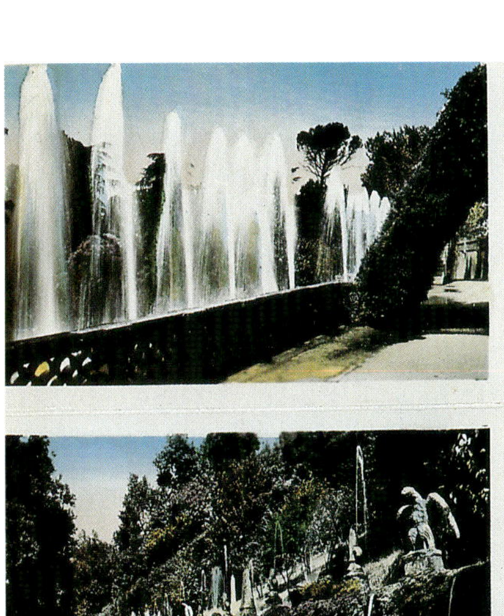
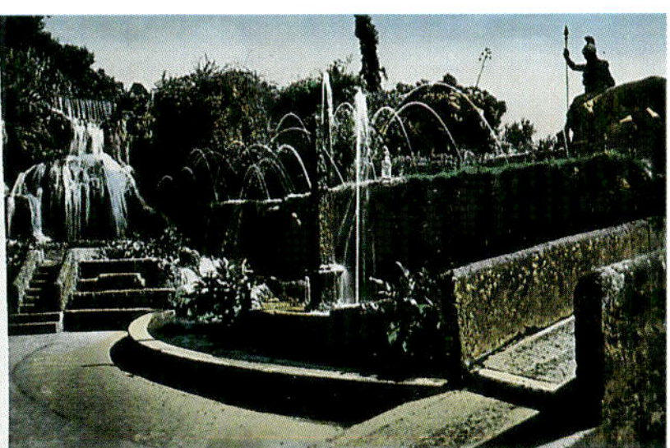
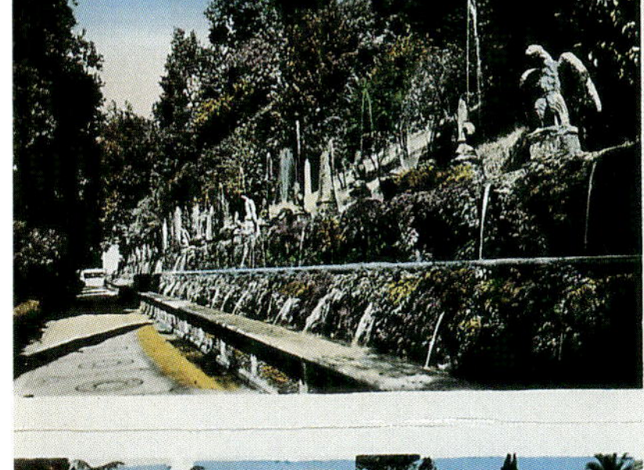
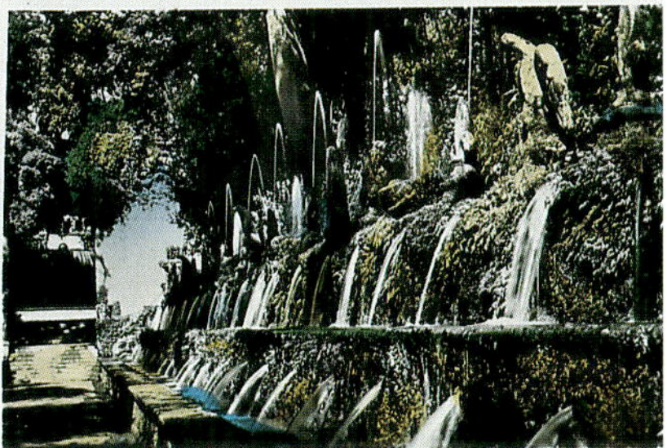
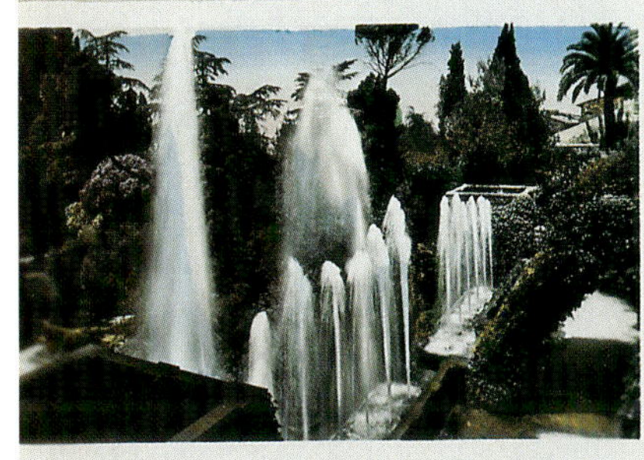
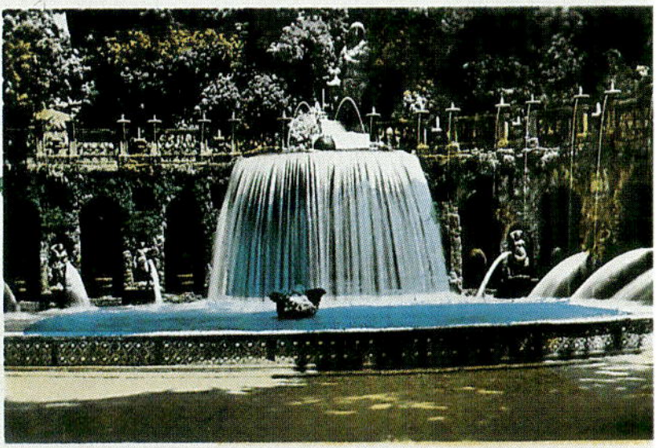
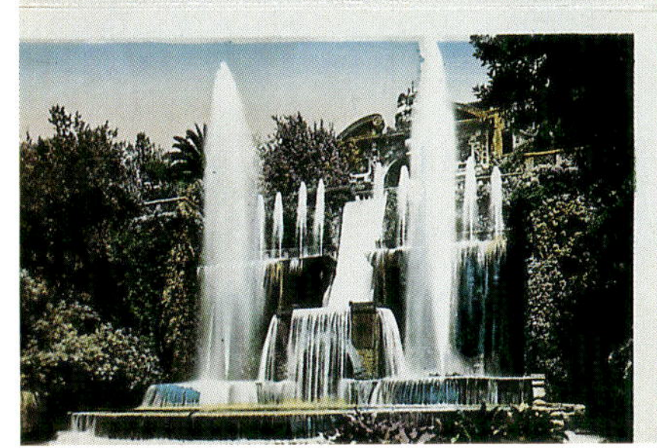
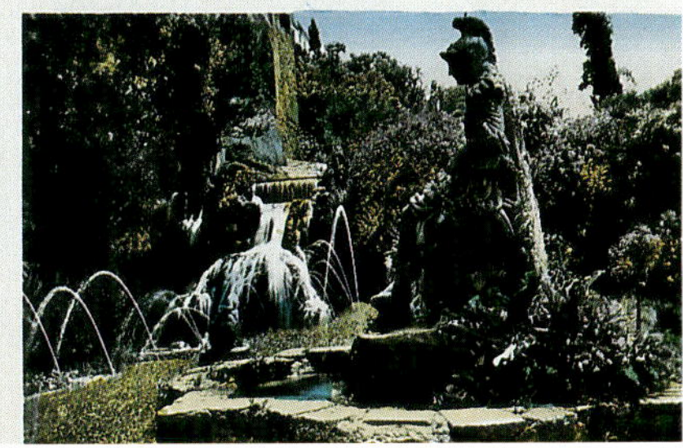

Scenes of life

The unavowable and unavowed aim of a retouched or remounted photograph is, ultimately, to give a new meaning to people's existence by hinting at the air of success represented by those symbols of achievement that are portrait painting and the media. The individual willingly escapes from the prosaic definition of their social setting to which photography bears public witness by modifying this setting. Although this work of metamorphosis is entrusted to a professional, the customer follows examples and models which they regard as the norm, and the result, though a long way from photographic realism, responds to a deliberate intention: "The reading of a photograph is always the perception of a conscious intention, even if this is not always consciously suspected."[2]

While travel is a form of open appreciation of the world, tourist photographs which people bring back from that world (postcards, concertina-folded multiple views) are already a formal reduction of it, a sequential account. In the 1930s or 1950s, the tourist back from holiday usually ran through the account of their imaginary adventures in a codified world by sticking these images into their holiday scrapbook. Restaurant menus, entry tickets, postcards, and letters, were interspersed with notes, dates, and comments. Such albums are not only a formalized image of family life; they are also the subjective account of an individual unity obvious only to the eyes of the person who has created the album. But these small photographs are themselves montages on various levels: black and white snaps, hastily hand-colored, put in to give the impression of "doing" a place. Even the amateur is familiar with

Anonymous,
Fountains at Villa d'Este,
photomontage of views for tourists (produced as tinted photographs in a fold-out wallet),
travel souvenir album,
1957,
private collection.

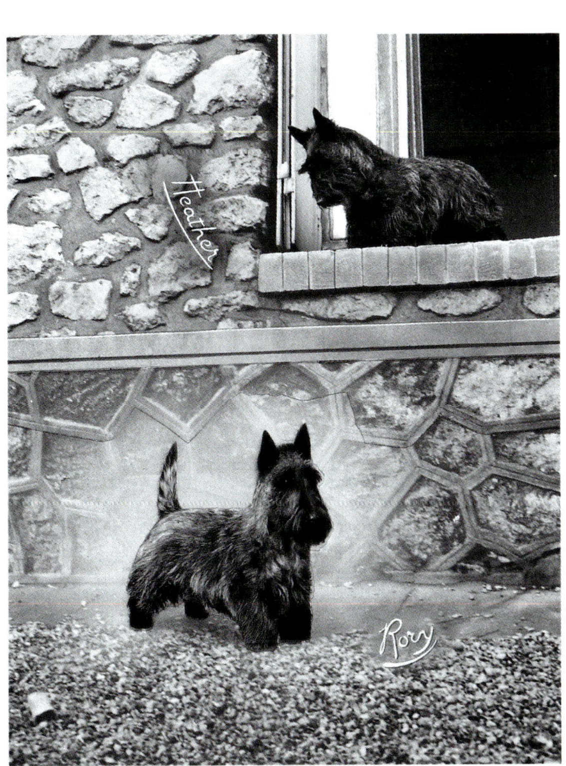

◀ **Henri Dimont,**
Rory and Heather,
retouched photomontage,
circa 1960,
private collection.

2. P. Bourdieu *et al.*, *Photography: A Middle-brow Art*, trans. by Shaun Whiteside, Stanford, CA, Stanford University Press, 1990.

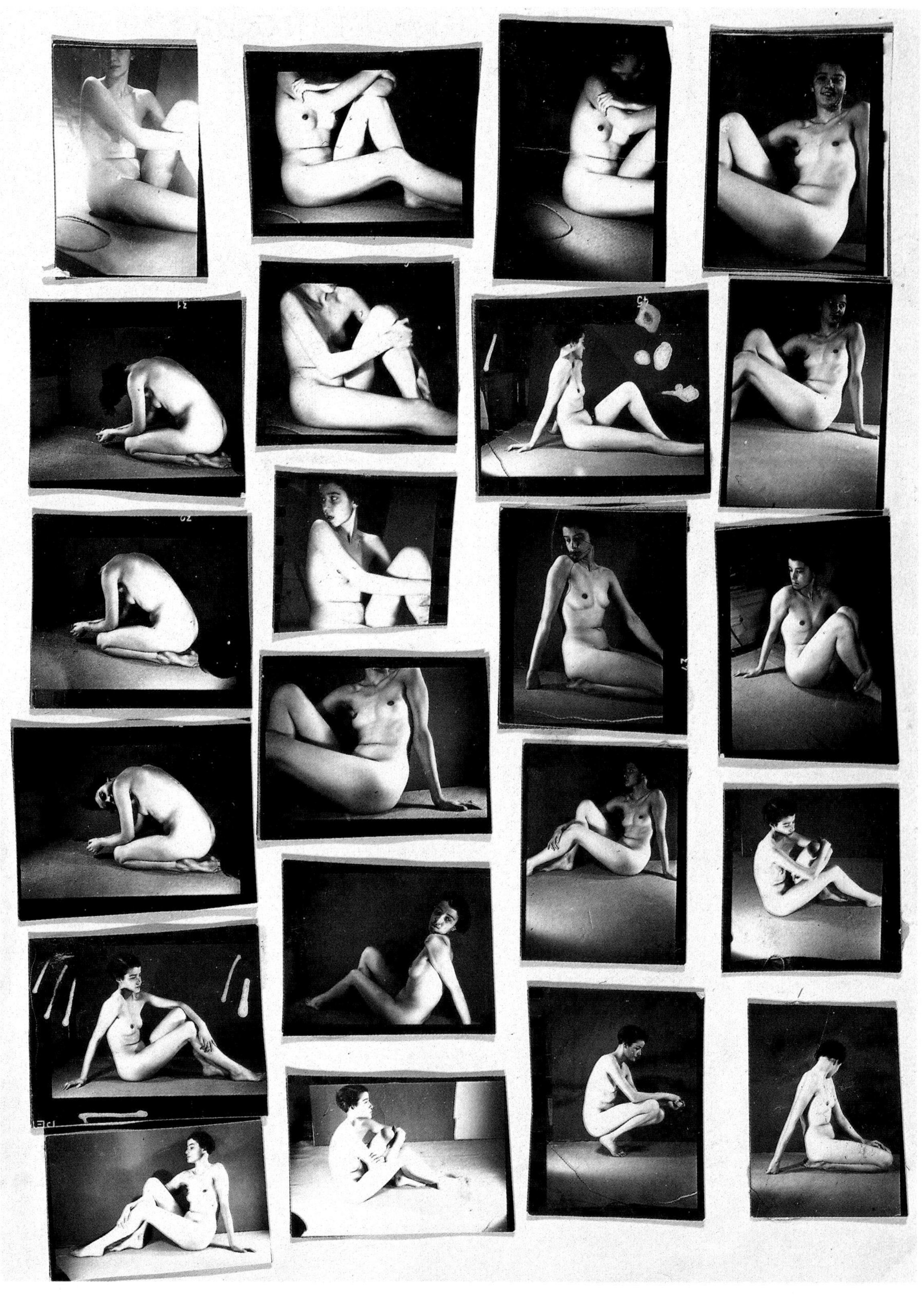

ANONYMOUS,
Nude studies,
collage of contact prints,
circa 1935,
private collection.

this fragmented vision, for they know that all they can do is wander around their subjects in order to show different aspects without exhausting its attractions, just like the painter who revolves around the nude model until all viewpoints have been used up.

The example at the beginning of this chapter from an amateur photo album reconstitutes the colored luxuriance of the garden by literally decorating the pages of the album with floral pictures, without the least regard to the unity of space or the position of the viewer. Only popular photography could accept to such a degree being merely a packaged form of reality wrapped up in fantasy, staking its success on the emulation of the inherent profundity of all photographs – those cut-out viewpoints in human vision: constrained within frames and highlights which never cease toning down its obsessive presence.

Methods of producing photographic prints

Anne Cartier-Bresson

I. Salted paper prints

Salted paper prints (1839–1860) were produced by direct contact with the negative (printing-out process). The paper was prepared by soaking in common salt solution, then sensitized with silver nitrate. The structure was simple, comprising just one layer, and the silver grains were in direct contact with the fibers of the paper, which were therefore visible. Salted paper prints were more or less matt depending on the use of an additional glaze introduced during the salting process (dilute gelatine or egg albumen, starch, etc.).

From the 1840s the prints could be toned in gold chloride solution. Thus their originally brownish tone became colder, depending on the make-up of the solution and the duration of the toning process. Salted paper prints were used once again at the end of the century for their aesthetic character.

II. Albumen prints

Introduced in 1850, this was the commonest printing method in the nineteenth century. Although the technique was similar to that of salted paper prints, it differed from them in one important respect. Albumen, used as a binding material for the silver salts, provided an image structure in two layers. It gave a shiny surface to the paper and allowed an improved contrast. Less shiny prints could be obtained by diluting the albumen (salted albumen papers) or by adding starch to the sensitive layer (matt albumen prints).

Albumen papers were not replaced by other, more stable printing methods until after the First World War. As with salted paper prints, albumen prints were obtained by a printing-out process, by contact with the negative.

III. Gelatino-chloride or collodio-chloride prints

Also known as "aristotypes", these were the first emulsions on paper to be commercially produced at the end of the nineteenth century and to be widely used by amateurs and professionals. These printing-out emulsions were either of gelatine or collodion type. They are of low sensitivity, but by contact with the negative they provided very fine-grained images of a brownish color, varying according to the toning process. As with the other emulsion processes, an intermediary layer of barium sulfate could be used to increase the whiteness and brilliance of the images (structure in three layers). In the case of matt aristotypes, this intermediary layer was thinner, with the possibility of allowing the paper fibers to appear on the surface. This was particularly used for matte collodion prints, very popular at the start of the twentieth century, which were a neutral black color due to gold or platinum toning.

These gold chloride papers were abandoned during the early 1920s in favor of silver bromide emulsions which, being more sensitive, allowed printing to be done by enlargement from small-format negatives.

IV. Gelatino-bromide process

As a result of research published by Richard Leach Maddox in 1871, gelatino-bromide gradually replaced most of the previous techniques from 1880, especially for the negative. The sensitive emulsions were produced in the factory and sold ready for use. Three principal types of substrate (base material) were used:

- glass plates for negative or positive (for projection) images
- flexible substrates for negatives (cellulose nitrate, cellulose diacetate or triacetate, polyester from 1960)
- paper substrates for positive prints, whose tone was a neutral black after development of the latent image, but which could be modified subsequently by a toning process.

The sensitivity of gelatino-bromide papers allowed prints to be made by enlargement of the negative image.

As with aristotypes, the inclusion of an intermediary layer of barium sulfate increased the brilliance and whiteness of the image. This layer was thinner for matte papers, and gelatine starch was added. These emulsions, developed chemically, with their structure of filament-like silver granules, were more stable than printing-out papers, with their very small, photolytic silver grains.

V. Platinum prints

Based on the sensitivity to light of iron salts, platinum prints were greatly appreciated by professional photographers at the turn of the century for their aesthetic quality. The paper, sensitized by a mixture of ferric salts and potassium chloro-platinate, was exposed by direct contact with the negative. The image, treated in potassium oxalate solution, was formed of very fine-grained platinum metal. It usually has a neutral black tone, but warmer tones could be obtained by modifying the development process. These very stable images have, however, the disadvantage of attacking paper with which they come in contact, owing to the acidity of the process. Platinum became too expensive and was replaced by palladium at the beginning of the century.

VI. Woodburytypes

The invention of W. B. Woodbury in 1865 (in French, *photoglyptie*) process, was the only photomechanical process to produce continuous tonal gradation, and was therefore very hard to distinguish from photographic images (notably carbon prints).

This high-quality process was used until the beginning of the century, especially for book illustrations. From a photographic print was produced a relief matrix of gelatine bichromate from which a lead printing plate could be produced by means of a hydraulic press. The final print was made using a hand press; it was formed of pigmented gelatine, and various colors were therefore possible. Usually brownish pigments were used, in order to imitate albumen prints. The prints shown in the *Galerie Contemporaine* (1876–1884), printed by Goupil, are Woodburytypes (*photoglypties*).

VII. Photogravure (known on the Continent as heliogravure)

This was a photomechanical reproduction process derived from engraving methods. Printed on a copper-plate press, photogravure was developed from the work of Niépce, Fox Talbot, Baldus, and Charles Nègre, before its commercial application resulting from the modifications made by Karel Klic in 1880.

As with the aquatint process, a plate is mulled using fine resin powder, then covered with bichromatized gelatine. The photographic image is transferred by direct contact, the degree of hardening of the gelatine depending on the amount of light it receives. The resin granules serve as a resist. Successive treatment with the mordant penetrate the gelatine by different amounts, selectively etching the plate. The most deeply etched parts, holding the most ink, correspond to the darkest areas of the final print, while the light areas of the image correspond to the location of resin granules protected from the etching effect of the mordant.

Photogravures, which showed excellent definition thanks to the fineness of the aquatint granules, were greatly appreciated by Pictorialists such as Emerson, Coburn, and Stieglitz.

VIII. The half-tone process

This photomechanical process transfers all the tonal variations of the original photograph by reproducing it by means of a screen.

The principle of the use of a meshed screen to transpose half-tones was proposed by Talbot, but was employed commercially only as a result of the work of Charles-Guillaume Petit, Georg Meisenbach, and Frederick Ives during the 1880s. The dots of the screen, whose size determines the tones of the image, are easily seen at low magnification. It is the number of dots per inch which determines the quality of the final printed image. Color prints are produced by four-color printing, the paper passing through the press four times.

The photographs reproduced on pages 756 and 757 have been kindly provided by Atelier de Restauration des Photographies de la Ville de Paris.

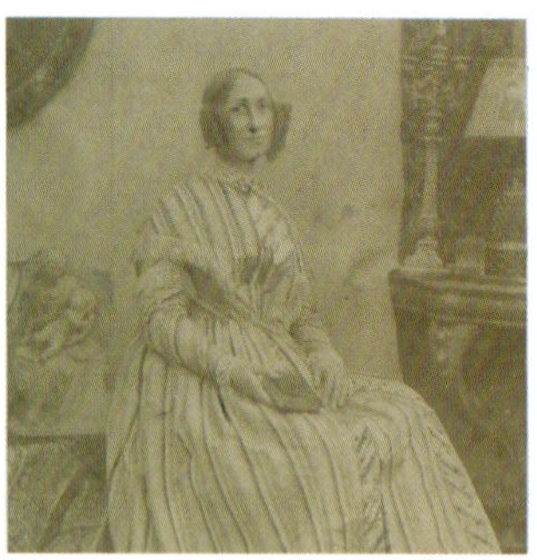

1. Salted-paper print: Blanquart-Evrard, *Female Portrait*; Musée Carnavalet.
a) x 2 magnification. *b*) x 20 magnification

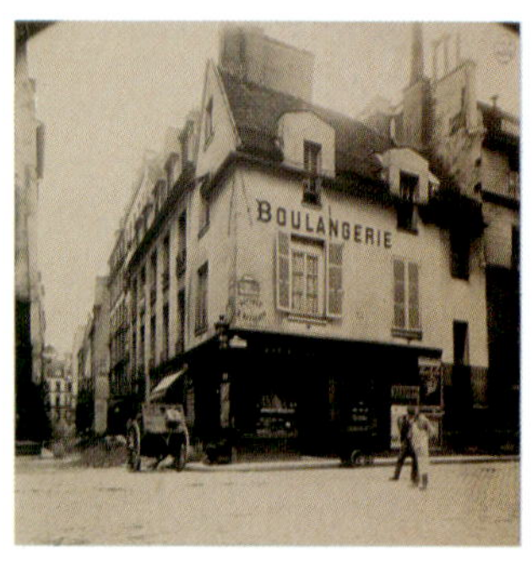

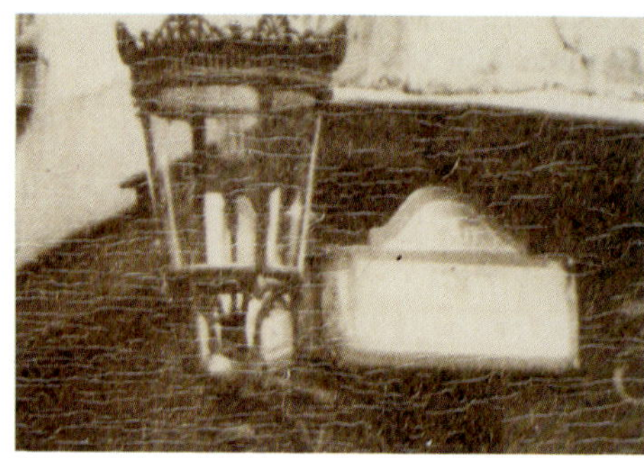

2. Albumen paper print: Atget, *Old House, 2 Rue des Écouffes*; Musée Carnavalet.
a) x 2 magnification. *b*) x 20 magnification

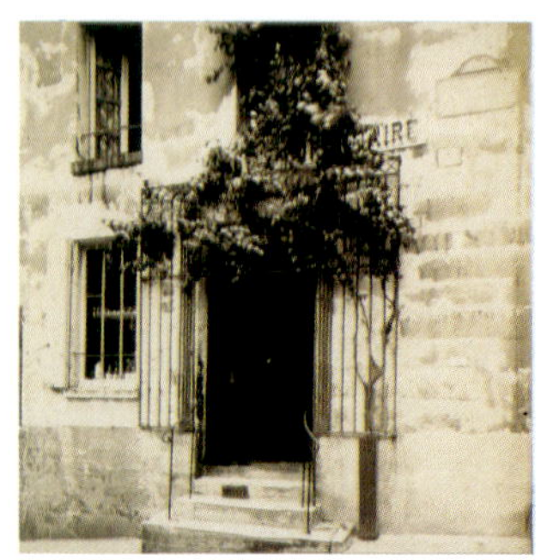
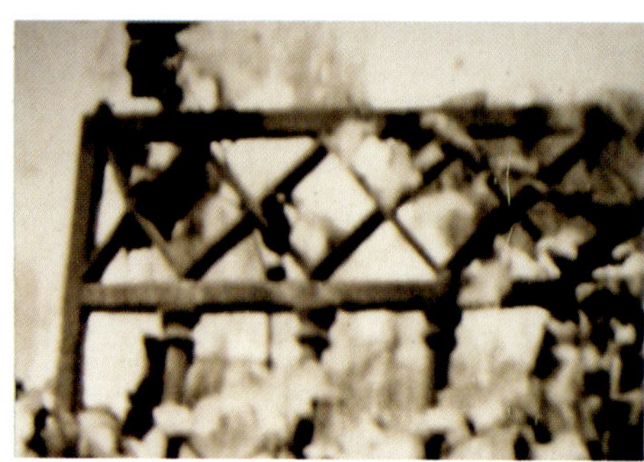

3. Gelatino-silver chloride emulsion: Atget, *Rue de la Montage Sainte-Geneviève*; Musée Carnavalet.
a) x 2 magnification. *b*) x 20 magnification

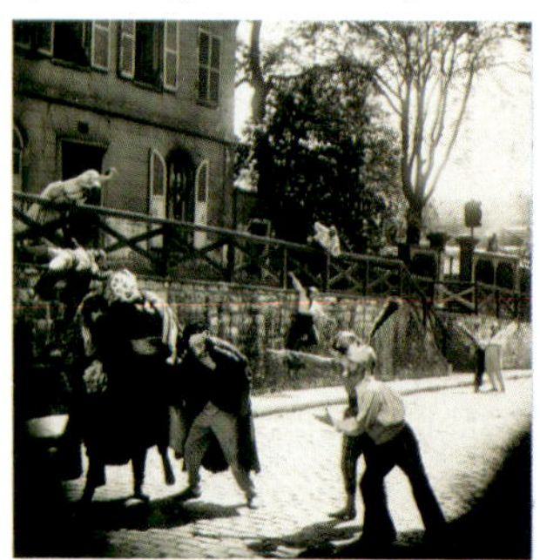
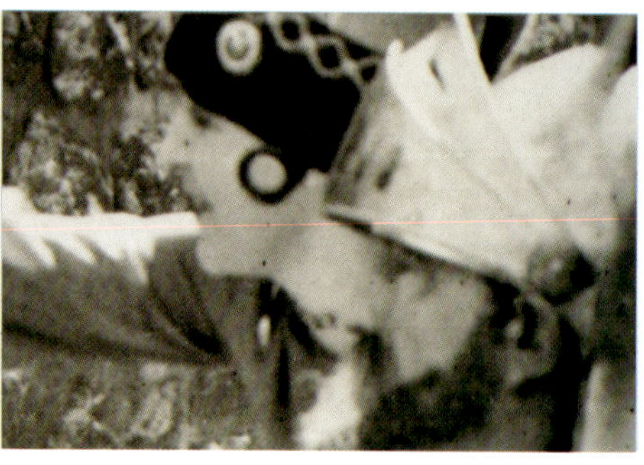
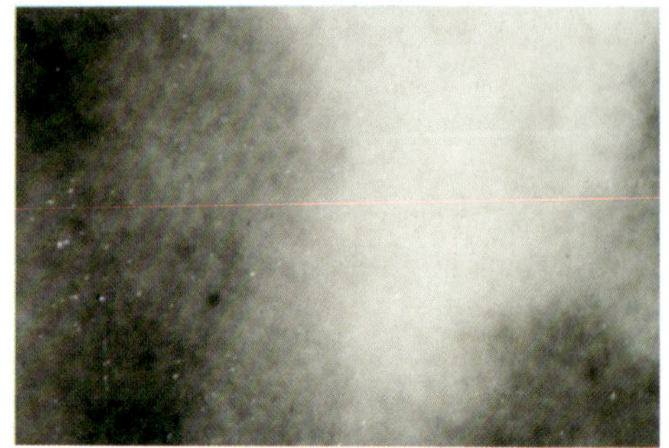

4. Gelatino-silver bromide emulsion: anonymous, *Carnival*; Musée Carnavalet.
a) x 2 magnification. *b*) x 20 magnification

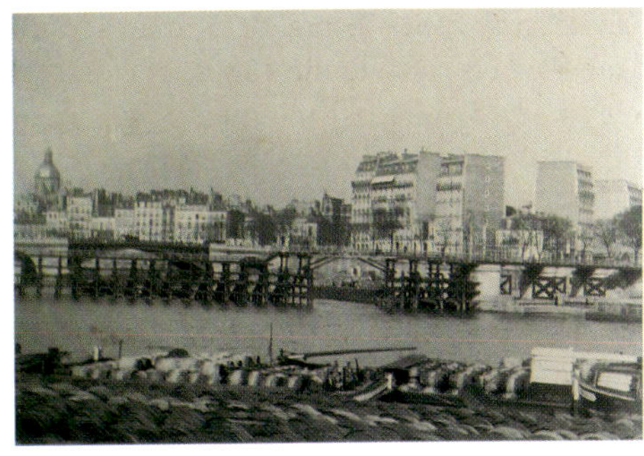
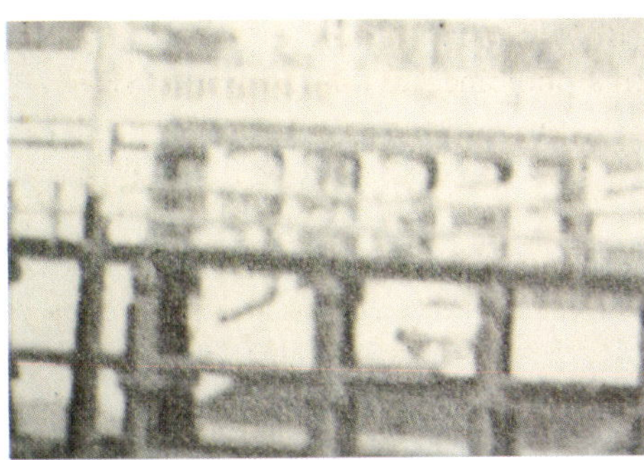
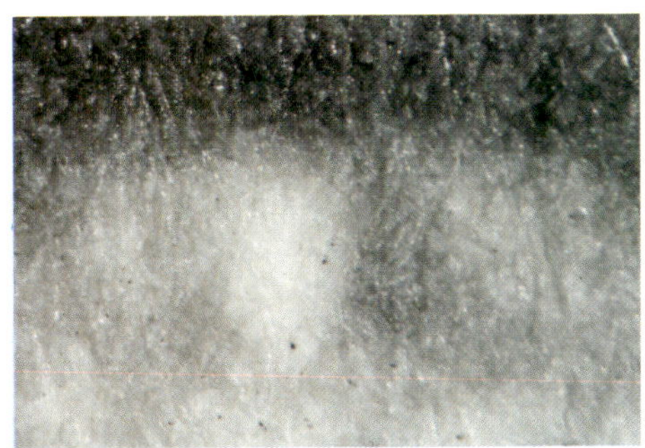

5. Platinum print: H. Blancart, *Wharf, with the Church of Saint-Paul to the Left;* Bibliothèque Historique de la Ville de Paris.
a) x 2 magnification. *b*) x 20 magnification

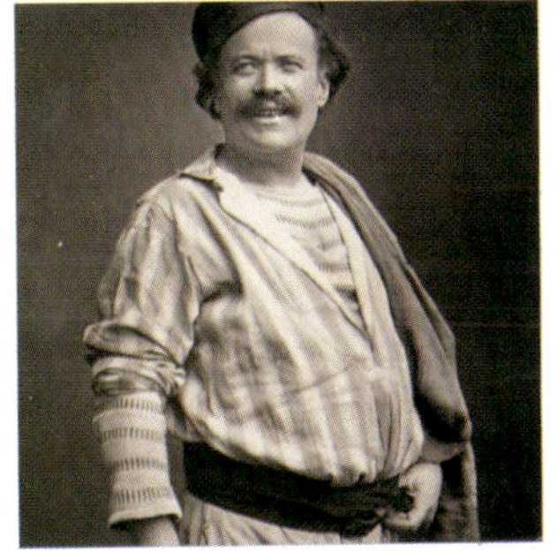
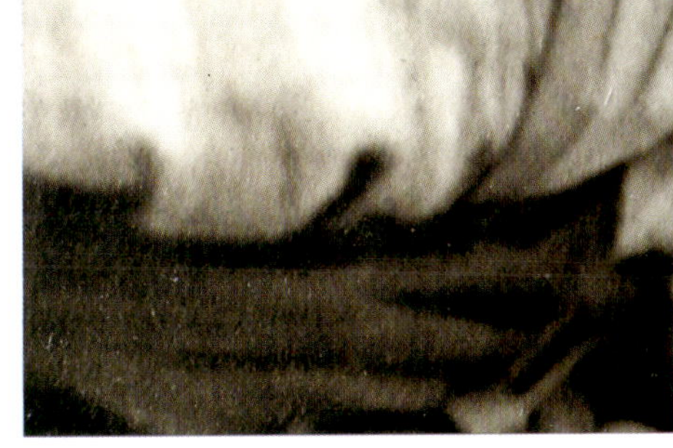
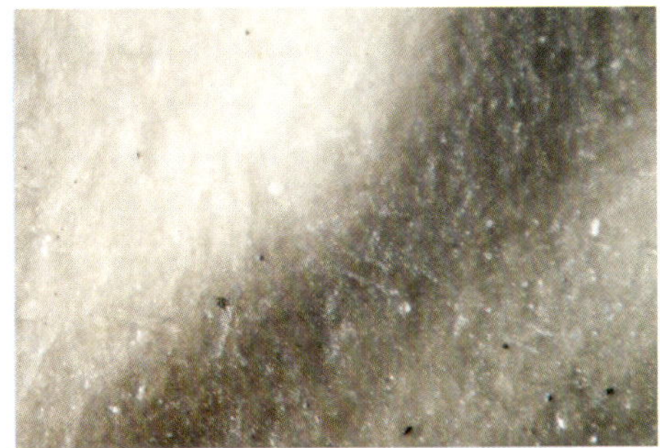

6. Photoglyptic print (Woodburytype): Nadar: *Portrait of the Actor Gil Naza;* Musée Carnavalet.
a) x 2 magnification. *b*) x 20 magnification

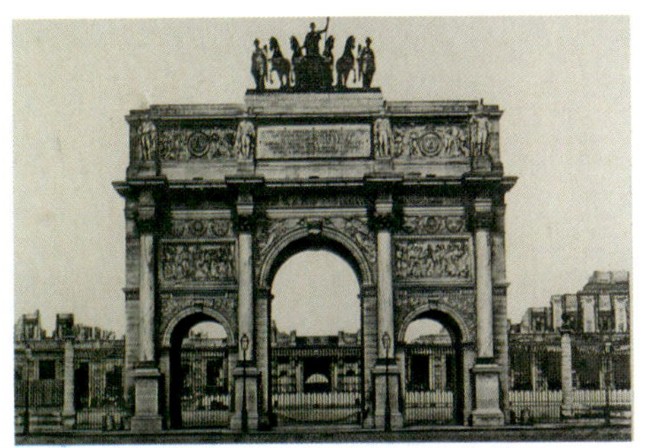
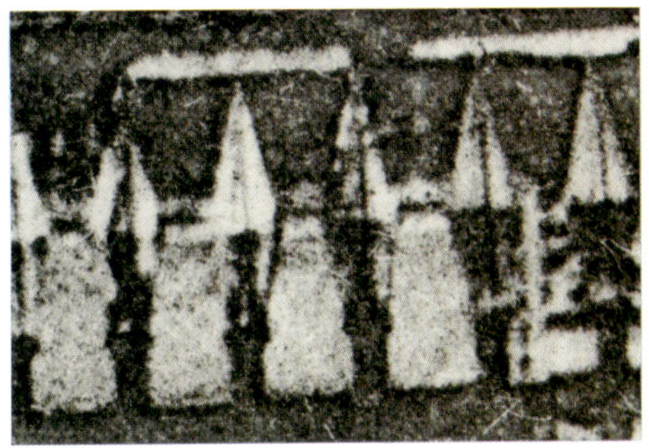
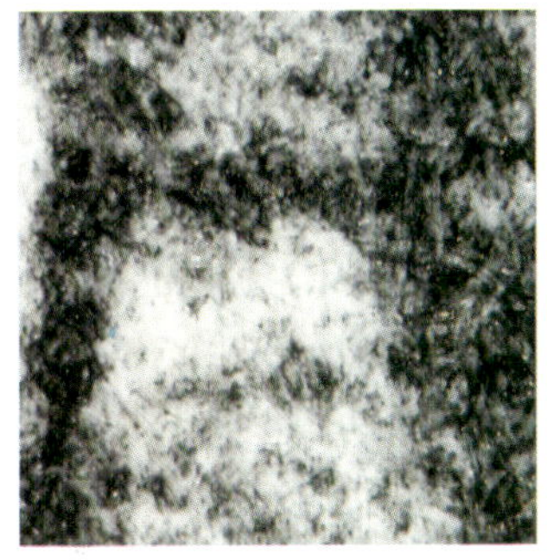

7. Photogravure: Baldus, *Arc de Triomphe du Carrousel;* Musée Carnavalet.
a) x 2 magnification. *b*) x 20 magnification

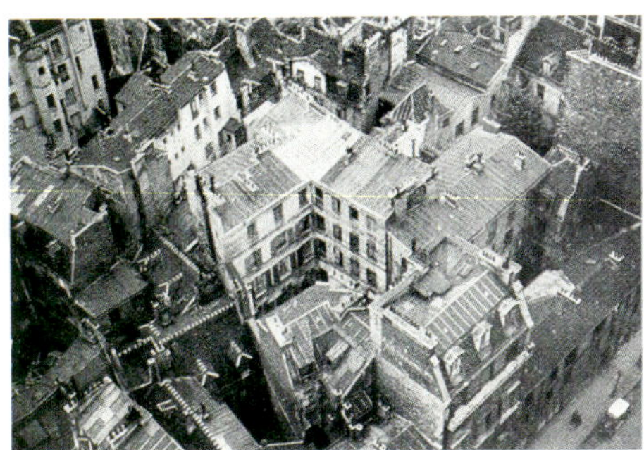
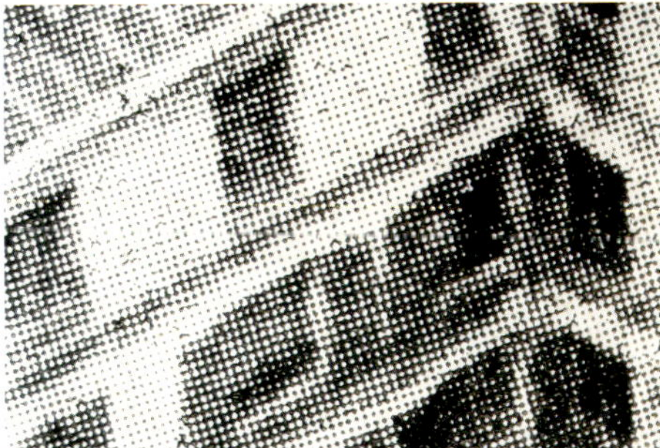
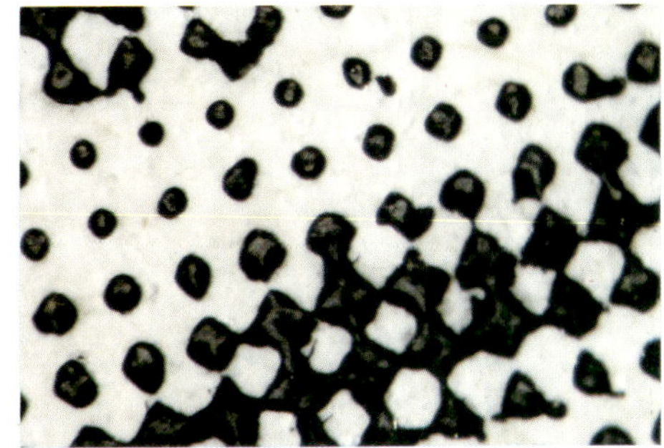

8. Half-tone: E. Sougez, *Paris Roofs in the Notre-Dame District,* from R. Lécuyer, *Histoire de la Photographie,* Paris, Baschet, 1945.
a) x 2 magnification. *b*) x 20 magnification

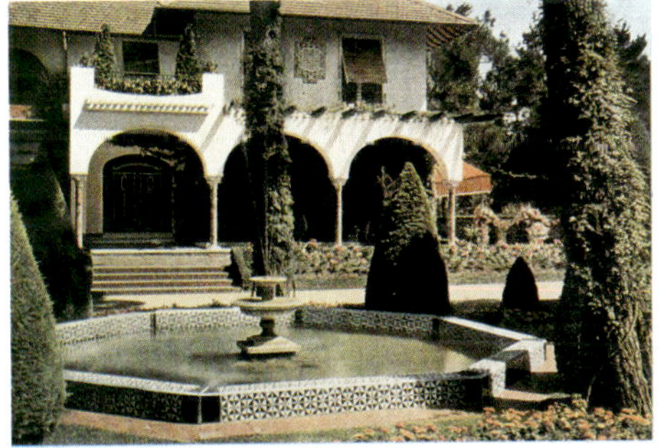
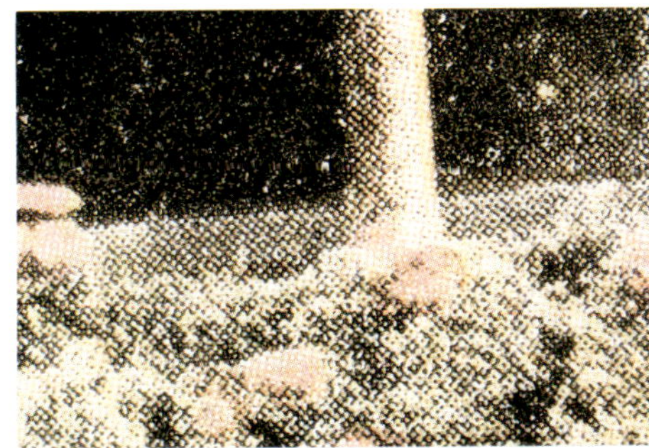
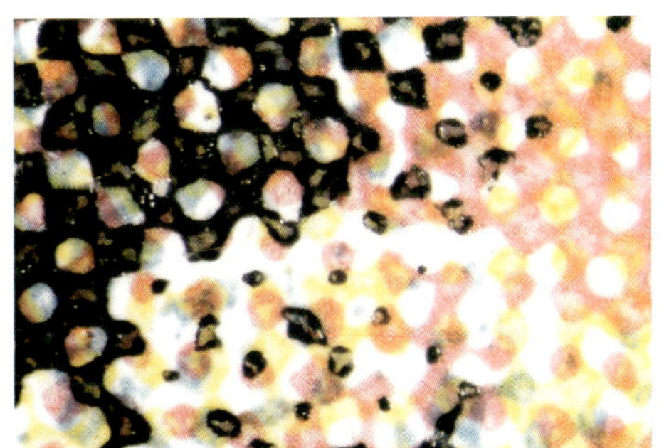

9. Four-color printing: Léon Gimpel, *Ornamental Pond of a Villa in the Basque Country,* from R. Lécuyer, *Histoire de la Photographie,* Paris, Baschet, 1945. *a*) x 2 magnification. *b*) x 20 magnification

BIBLIOGRAPHY

Fred and Elizabeth Pajerski

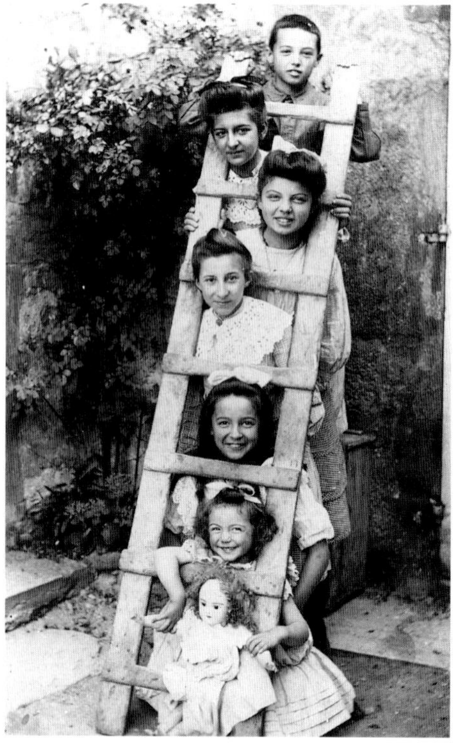

ANONYMOUS AMATEUR, circa 1930, private collection

These suggestions for further reading are intended to assist those seeking further information on a particular topic. The stress is on recent publications and on monographs or books which offer the fullest possible treatment of individual photographers and issues. For ease of reading, only essential bibliographical details are given.

GENERAL HISTORY OF PHOTOGRAPHY

BEATON Cecil and BUCKLAND Gail, *The Magic Image: The Genius of Photography from 1839 to the Present Day,* Boston and Toronto, Little, Brown & Co. and London, Weidenfeld & Nicolson, 1975.

BRAIVE Michel, *The Era of the Photograph,* London, Thames and Hudson, 1966.

CHRIST Yvan, *L'Âge d'or de la photographie,* Paris, 1965.

EDER Josef Maria, *History of Photography,* New York, Columbia Univ., 1945; repr. New York, Dover, 1978.

FRIZOT Michel, *Histoire de voir,* Paris, Centre National de la Photographie, 1989.

GERNSHEIM Helmut and GERNSHEIM Alison, *The History of Photography: From the Earliest Use of the Camera Obscura in the Eleventh Century up to 1914,* London, New York and Toronto, Oxford Univ., 1955; 2nd. ed., New York, McGraw-Hill, 1969; London, Thames & Hudson, 1969; rev. ed., 2 vols., *The Origins of Photography,* New York and London, Thames & Hudson, 1982 and *The Rise of Photography, 1850–1880: The Age of Collodion,* New York and London, Thames & Hudson, 1988.

GILARDI Ando, *Storia sociale della fotografia,* 2nd. ed. Milan, Feltrinelli, 1981.

LÉCUYER Raymond, *Histoire de la photographie,* Paris, SNEP-Illustration, 1945.

LEMAGNY Jean-Claude and ROUILLÉ André (ed.), *A History of Photography: Social and Cultural Perspectives,* New York, Cambridge Univ. Press, 1987.

NEWHALL Beaumont, *The History of Photography: from 1839 to the Present,* 5th ed., New York, New York Graphic Society / Little, Brown, 1982.

POLLACK Peter, *The Picture History of Photography from the Earliest Beginnings to The Present Day,* New York, Harry N. Abrams, 1969.

ROSENBLUM Naomi, *A World History of Photography,* New York, Abbevie, 1989.

SKOPEC Rudolf, *Photographie im Wandel der Zeiten,* Prague, Artia, 1964.

SOUGEZ Emmanuel, *La Photographie: son histoire* and *La Photographie: son univers,* Paris, L'Illustration, 1968–1969.

STENGER Erich, *The History of Photography: Its Relation to Civilization and Practice,* ed. Edward Epstean, New York, Arno Press, 1979.

TILLMANNS Urs, *Geschichte der Photographie: ein Jahrhundert prägt ein Medium,* Frauenfeld, Huber, 1981.

ENCYCLOPEDIAS, BIBLIOGRAPHIES, DICTIONARIES

AUER Michel and AUER Michèle, *Photographers Encyclopedia International,* 2nd. ed., Neuchâtel, Switzerland, Ides et Calendes, 1997, CD-ROM.

BALDWIN Gordon, *Looking at Photographs: A Guide to Technical Terms,* Malibu, J. Paul Getty Museum and British Museum, 1991.

BARGER M. Susan, *Bibliography of Photographic Processes in Use Before 1880: Their Materials, Processing and Conservation,* Rochester, Rochester Institute of Technology, 1980.

BONI Albert (ed.), *Photographic Literature: An International Bibliographic Guide,* New York, Morgan & Morgan, 1962, and *Photographic Literature, 1960–1970,* Hastings-on-Hudson, Morgan & Morgan, 1972.

CANADA, PUBLIC ARCHIVES. *Guide to Canadian Photographic Archives,* Ottawa, Public Archives of Canada, 1984.

EDWARDS Gary, *International Guide to Nineteenth-Century Photographers and Their Works: Based on Catalogues of Photographic Dealers and Auction Houses,* Boston, G. K. Hall & Co., 1988.

EPSTEAN COLLECTION. *A Catalogue of the Epstean Collection on the History and Science of Photography and Its Application Especially to the Graphic Arts,* Pawlet, Helios, 1972.

ESKIND Andrew H. and GREG Drake (ed.), *Index to American Photographic Collections,* 2nd. ed., Boston, G. K. Hall & Co., 1990.

F.S.A. Penelope Dixon, *Photographers of the Farm Security Administration: An Annotated Bibliography, 1930–1980,* New York and London, Garland, 1983.

GERNSHEIM Helmut, *Incunabula of British Photographic Literature: A Bibliography of British Photographic Literature, 1839–1875, and British Books Illustrated with Original Photographs,* London and Berkeley, Scolar Press, 1984.

GOLDSCHMIDT Lucien and NAEF Weston J., *The Truthful Lens: A Survey of the Photographically Illustrated Book, 1844–1914,* New York, Grolier Club, 1980.

HEIDTMANN Frank, *Bibliographie der Photographie. Deutschsprachige Publikationen der Jahre 1839–1984, Technik-Theorie-Bild. Bibliography of German-Language Photographic Publications, 1839–1984: Technology-Theory-Visual,* 2nd. ed. Munich, K. G. Saur, 1989.

INTERNATIONAL CENTER OF PHOTOGRAPHY ENCYCLOPEDIA OF PHOTOGRAPHY, New York, Crown, 1984.

JOHNSON William S., *Nineteenth-Century Photography: An Annotated Bibliography, 1839–1879,* Boston, G. K. Hall & Co., 1990.

KOELZER Walter (ed.), *Bibliography of Photographic and Cinematographic Periodicals, 1840–1940,* Düsseldorf, Edition der Foto Brell, 1992.

JONES Bernard E. (ed.), *Cassell's Cyclopaedia of Photography,* London, Cassell & Co. 1911; New York, 1912; repr. New York, 1974 and London, 1982.

LAMBRECHTS Eric and SALU Luc, *Photography and Literature: An International Bibliography of Monographs,* London and New York, Mansell, 1992.

MACMILLAN BIOGRAPHICAL ENCYCLOPEDIA OF PHOTOGRAPHIC ARTISTS AND INNOVATORS, New York, Macmillan, 1983.

NADEAU Luis, *Encyclopedia of Printing, Photographic and Photomechanical Processes,* 2 vols., Fredericton, Canada, Luis Nadeau, 1989–1990.

PALMQUIST Peter E. (ed.), *Photographers: A Sourcebook for Historical Research,* Brownsville, Carl Mautz, 1991.

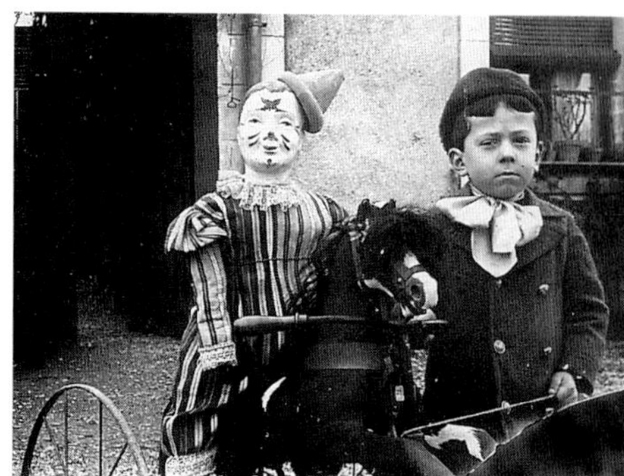

ANONYMOUS AMATEUR, circa 1900, private collection.

ROOSENS Laurent and SALU Luc, *History of Photography: A Bibliography of Books*, 3 vols., London and New York, Mansell, 1989–1996.

SMITHSONIAN INSTITUTION. Diane Vogt O'Connor, *Guide to Photographic Collections at the Smithsonian Institution*, Washington and London, Smithsonian Institution Press, 1989.

VOIGNIER JEAN-MARIE, *Répertoire des photographes de France au dix-neuvième siècle*, Le Pont de Pierre, 1993.

WALL John (ed.), *Directory of British Photographic Collections*, London, 1977.

JOURNALS

APERTURE, San Francisco, 1952–, quarterly.

CAMERA, Lucerne, C. J. Bucher, 1922–1981, monthly, 61 vols., articles in English, German and French.

ETUDES PHOTOGRAPHIQUES, Paris, Société française de photographie, 1996–.

FOTOGESCHICHTE, *Beiträge zur Geschichte und Ästhetik der Fotografie*, Frankfurt, 1981–.

FOTOLOGIA, Studio di storia della fotografia. A cura di Italo Zannier, Florence, Fratelli Alinari, 1985–.

HISTORY OF PHOTOGRAPHY. *An International Quarterly*, London, Taylor & Francfis, 1977–.

IMAGE, Rochester, N.Y., International Museum of Photography at George Eastman House, 1952–.

THE PHOTOGRAPHIC COLLECTOR, London, Bishopsgate Press, 1980–1986.

PHOTOGRAPHIES: Recherches historiques et critiques, Paris, 1983–1985, 9 vols., 1983–1985.

PRESTIGE DE LA PHOTOGRAPHIE, Paris, 10 vols., 1977–1980.

LA RECHERCHE PHOTOGRAPHIQUE, Paris, Paris Audiovisuel et Université Paris VIII, 1986–.

HISTORY OF EARLY PHOTOGRAPHY

DAGUERREOTYPES

BARGER Susan M. and WHITE William B., *The Daguerreotype: Nineteenth-Century Technology and Modern Science*, Washington and London, Smithsonian Institution, 1991.

BECCHETTI Piero and PIETRANGELI Carlo, *Roma in dagherrotipia*, Rome, Quasar, 1979.

BUERGER Janet E., *French Daguerreotypes*, Chicago and London, Univ. of Chicago, 1989.

FORESTA Merry A. and WOOD John, *Secrets of the Dark Chamber: The Art of the American Daguerreotype*, Washington, D.C., Smithsonian Institution Press, 1995.

ISENBURG COLLECTION. *American Daguerreotypes from the Matthew R. Isenburg Collection*, New Haven, Yale Univ. Art Gallery, 1989.

KEMPE Fritz, *Daguerreotypie in Deutschland: Vom Charme der frühen Photographie*, Seebruck am Chiemsee, Heering, 1979.

KEMPE Fritz and DEWITZ Bodo von, *Daguerreotypien, Ambrotypien und Bilder anderer Verfahren aus der Frühzeit der Photographie*, Hamburg, Museum für Kunst und Gewerbe, 1983.

MORAND Sylvain and KEMPF Christian, *Le Temps suspendu: le daguérreotype en Alsace au XIX*[e] *siècle*, Strasbourg, Oberlin, 1989.

MOSSAKOWSKA Wanda, *Dagerotypy w zbiorach polskich: Katalog*, Warsaw, Wydawnictwo Polskiej Akademii Nauk, 1989.

NEWHALL Beaumont, *The Daguerreotype in America*, 3rd. ed., New York, Dover, 1976.

PARIS ET LE DAGUERRÉOTYPE, Paris, Paris Musées, 1989.

PFISTER Harold F., *Facing the Light: Historic American Portrait Daguerreotypes*, Washington, Smithsonian Institution, 1978.

RINHART Floyd and RINHART Marion, *The American Daguerreotype*, Athens, Univ. of Georgia, 1981.

RUDISILL Richard, *Mirror Image: The Influence of the Daguerreotype on American Society*, Albuquerque, Univ. of New Mexico, 1971.

SCHEID COLLECTION. Rainer Wick (ed.), *Die erotische Daguerreotypie: Sammlung Uwe Scheid*, Weingarten, Kunstverlag Weingarten, 1989.

SOBIESZEK Robert A. (ed.), *The Daguerreotype in Germany: Three Accounts, 1854–1872*, anthology of texts, New York, Arno, 1979.

WOOD John, *America and the Daguerreotype*, Iowa City, Univ. of Iowa, 1991.

——(ed.), *The Daguerreotype: A Sesquicentennial Celebration*, Iowa City, Univ. of Iowa, 1989; London, Duckworth, 1989.
——, *The Scenic Daguerreotype: Romanticism and Early Photography*, Iowa City, Univ. of Iowa Press, 1995.

CALOTYPES

BRETTELL Richard R. *et al.*, *Paper and Light: The Calotype in France and Great Britain, 1839–1870*, Boston and London, D. R. Godine, 1984.

BUERGER Janet, *The Era of the French Calotype*, Rochester, International Museum of Photography, 1982.

I CALOTIPI DELLA SOCIETÀ FRANCESE DI FOTOGRAFIA, 1840–1860, Venice, Marsilio, 1981.

JAMMES André and JANIS Eugenia P., *The Art of French Calotype: With a Critical Dictionary of Photographers, 1845–1870*, Princeton, Princeton Univ., 1983.

COLOR

AUTOCHROMES. *Il colore della belle époque: i primi processi fotografici diapositivi*, Venice, Palazzo Fortuny, s.d.

BELLONE Roger and FELLOT Luc, *Histoire mondiale de la photographie en couleurs des origines à nos jours*, Paris, Machette, Réalités, 1981.

COE Brian, *Colour Photography: The First Hundred Years, 1840–1940*, London, Ash & Grant, 1978.

Farbe im Photo: Die Geschichte der Farbphotographie von 1861 bis 1981, Cologne and Leverkusen, Josef-Haubrich-Kunsthalle and Agfa-Gevaert, 1981.

La Couleur sensible: Photographies autochromes (1907–1935), Marseille, n.p., 1997.

LUMIÈRE, *La Couleur inventée, Les Autochromes*, Collection privée de la famille Lumière, Lyon, A. Scheibli, 1995.

SIPLEY Louis Walton, *A Half Century of Color*, New York, Macmillan, 1951.

WOOD John, *The Art of the Autochrome: The Birth of Color Photography*, Iowa City, Univ. of Iowa Press, 1993.

VARIOUS

BURNS Stanley B., *Forgotten Marriage: The Painted Tintype & the Decorative Frame, 1860–1910: A Lost Chapter in American Portraiture*, New York, The Burns Press, The Burns Collection, 1995.

COE Brian and HAWORTH-BOOTH Mark, *A Guide to Early Photographic Processes*, London, Victoria and Albert Museum and Hurtwood Press, 1983.

DARRAH William C., *Cartes de Visite in Nineteenth-Century Photography*, Gettysburg, William C. Darrah, 1981.
——, *The World of Stereographs*, Gettysburg William C. Darrah, 1977.

FELDVEBEL Thomas, *The Ambrotype, Old and New*, Rochester, Graphic Arts Research Centre, 1980.

GLASSMAN Elizabeth and SYMMES Marilyn F., *Cliché-verre: Hand-Drawn, Light-Printed: A Survey of the Medium from 1839 to the Present*, Detroit, Detroit Institute of Arts, 1980.

HANSON David A. and TILLIM Sidney, *Photographs in Ink*, Teaneck, Fairleigh Dickinson Univ., University College Art Gallery, 1996.

HÉLIOGRAVURE. *De Niépce à Stieglitz: la photogravure en taille-douce*, Lausanne, Musée de l'Elysee, 1982.

HENISCH Heinz K. and HENISCH Bridget A., *The Painted Photograph, 1839–1914, Origins, Techniques, Aspirations*, University Park, Penn State Press, 1996.

JUSSIM Estelle, *Visual Communication and the Graphic Arts: Photographic Technologies in the Nineteenth Century*, New York and London, R. R. Bowker, 1983.

LAVÉDRINE Bertrand, *La Conservation des photographies*, Paris, CNRS, 1990.

MATTHEWS Oliver, *The Album of Carte-de-visite and Cabinet Portrait Photographs, 1854–1914*, London, Reedminster, 1974.

NAZARIEFF Serge, *Der Akt in der Photographie / The Stereoscopic Nude / Le Nu stéréoscopique, 1850 1930*, Berlin, TACO, 1987

One of a Kind: Recent Polaroid Photography, Boston, D. R. Godine, 1979.

PAVIOT Alain, *Le Cliché-Verre: Corot, Delacroix, Millet, Rousseau, Daubigny*, Paris, Paris Musées, 1994.

PELLERIN Denis, *La Photographie stéréoscopique sous le second Empire*, Paris, Bibliothèque nationale de France, 1995.

REILLY James M., *Care and Identification of 19th-Century Photographic Prints*, Rochester, Eastman Kodak Co., 1986.

SNELLING Henry, *A Dictionary of the Photographic Art: Forming a Complete Encyclopaedia of all the Terms, Receipts, Processes, Apparatus and Materials in the Art*, New York, 1854; repr. Arno, 1979.

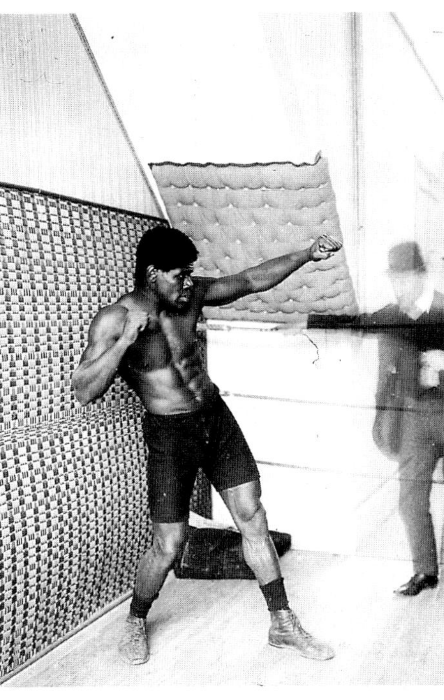

ANONYMOUS, ***Sam Mac Vea***, 1930s, private collection.

WALDSMITH John S., *Stereo Views: An Illustrated History and Price Guide*, Radnor, Wallace-Homestead, 1991.

WEINSTEIN Robert A. and BOOTH Larry, *Collection, Use, and Care of Historical Photographs*, Nashville, American Assoc. for State and Local History, 1977.

WELLING William, *Collectors' Guide to Nineteenth-Century Photographs*, New York and London, Macmillan & Collier Macmillan, 1976.

WITKIN Lee D. and LONDRES Barbara, *The Photograph Collectors' Guide*, Boston, New York Graphic Society, 1979.

ZOETE Johan de, *A Manual of Photogravure: A Comprehensive Working-Guide to the Fox-Talbot/Klic Dustgrain Method*, Haarlem, Joh. Enschedé en Zonen, 1988.

TEXTS, CRITICAL STUDIES, AESTHETICS

BAIER Wolfgang, *Quellendarstellungen zur Geschichte der Fotografie*, Munich, Schirmer/Mosel, 1977.

BAQUÉ Dominique, *Les documents de la modernité: anthologie de textes sur la photographie de 1919 à 1939*, Nimes, Jacqueline Chambon, 1993.

BARTHES Roland, *Camera Lucida*, New York, Hill and Wang, 1981.

BOLTON Richard (ed.), *The Contest of Meaning: Critical Histories of Photography*, MIT, 1989.

BUDDEMEIER Heinz, *Panorama, Diorama, Photographie: Entstehung und Wirkung neuer Medien im 19. Jahrhundert*, Munich, Wilhelm Fink, 1970.

CAMERA WORK. Jonathan Green (ed.), *Camera Work: A Critical Anthology*, Millerton, Aperture, 1973.

DUBOIS Philippe, *L'Acte photographique et autres essais*, Paris, Nathan, 1990.

EDER Josef Maria, *Quellenschriften zu den frühsten Änfangen der Photographie bis zum XVIII. Jahrhundert*, Halle, 1913; repr. New York, Arno, 1979.

FREUND Gisèle, *Photography and Society*, Boston, David R. Godine, 1980.

GOLDBERG Vicky (ed.), *Photography in Print: Writings from 1816 to the Present*, Albuquerque, Univ. of New Mexico, 1988.

GRÄFF Werner, *Es kommnt der neue Fotograf!*, Berlin, 1929; repr. New York, Arno, 1976.

KOPPEN Erwin, *Literatur und Photographie: Über Geschichte und Thematik einer Medienentdeckung*, Stuttgart, J. B. Metzlersche, 1987.

KRAUSS Rosalind, *Le Photographique: pour une théorie des écarts*, Paris, Macula, 1990.

LYONS Nathan (ed.), *Photographers on Photography: A Critical Anthology*, Englewood Cliffs, N. J., Prentice-Hall, 1966.

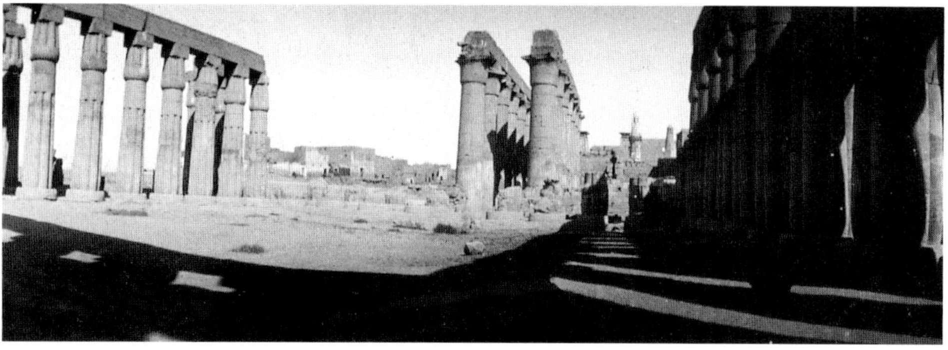

ANONYMOUS AMATEUR, *Great Court, Temple of Luxor*, circa 1900, private collection.

MORA Gilles, *Photospeak: A Guide to the Ideas, Movements, and Techniques of Photography 1839 to the Present,* New York, Abbeville Press, 1998.

NEWHALL Beaumont, *Latent Image: The Discovery of Photography,* Garden City, N.Y., Doubleday & Co., 1967; repr. Albuquerque, Univ. of New Mexico, 1983.

PHILLIPS Christopher (ed.), *Photography in the Modern Era: European Documents and Critical Writings, 1913–1940,* New York, Metropolitan Museum of Art and Aperture, 1989.

Photography: Discovery and Invention, Malibu, J. Paul Getty Museum, 1990.

POHLMANN Ulrich, *Kultur, Technik und Kommerz: Die Photokina Bilderschauen, 1950–1980,* Cologne, Historisches Archiv der Stadt Köln, 1990.

ROUILLÉ André, *L'Empire de la photographie: Photographie et Pouvoir bourgeois, 1839–1870,* Paris, Le Sycomore, 1982
——, *La Photographie en France: textes et controverses: une anthologie, 1816–1871,* Paris, Macula, 1989.

SCHAEFFER Jean-Marie, *L'Image précaire: du dispositif photographique,* Paris, Le Seuil, 1987.

SCHWARZ Heinrich, *Art and Photography: Forerunners and Influences: Selected Essays,* Rochester and Layton, Visual Studies Workshop and Peregrine Smith, 1985.

SHAW Bernard, JAY Bill and MOORE Margaret (ed.), *Bernard Shaw on Photography,* Salt Lake City, Peregrine Smith, 1989.

SNELLING Henry H., *The History and Practice of the Art of Photography,* New York, 1849; repr. Hastings-on-Hudson, Morgan & Morgan, 1970.

SONTAG Susan, *On Photography,* New York, Farrer, Strauss, Giroux, 1977.

YOUNGER Daniel P. (ed.), *Multiple Views: Logan Grant Essays on Photography, 1983–1989,* Albuquerque, Univ. of New Mexico, 1991.

THEMES, PERIODS, MOVEMENTS, SUBJECTS

ANIMALS. Ruth Silverman (ed.), *The Dog Observed: Photographs, 1844–1988,* San Francisco, Chronicle, 1984.
Alexandra Noble (ed.), *The Animal in Photography, 1843–1985,* London, Photographers Gallery, 1986.
Sally Eauclaire, *Le Chat en photographie,* Paris, Adam Biro, 1991.

BANTA Melissa and HINSLEY Curtis M., *From Site to Sight: Anthropology, Photography, and the Power of Imagery,* Cambridge, Peabody Museum, 1986.

BAUHAUS. Carl Haenlein (ed.), *Photographie und Bauhaus,* Hanover, Kestner, 1986.
Jeannine Fiedler (ed.), *Photographie at the Bauhaus,* Cambridge, MIT, 1990.

BILLETER Erika (ed.), *Self-Portrait in the Age of Photography: Photographers Reflecting Their Own Image,* Lausanne, Musée Cantonal des Beaux-Arts, 1985.

BONNEMAISON COLLECTION. *Panoramas, collection Bonnemaison: photographies 1850–1950,* Arles, Actes Sud, 1989.

BOTANY. *Photographies de végétaux aux XIXe et XXe siècles,* Paris, Centre National de la Photographie, 1987.

BOUQUERET Christian and LIVI François, *Le Voyage en Italie: les photographes français en Italie, 1840–1920,* Lyons, La Manufacture, 1989.

BUCKLAND Gail, *First Photographs: People, Places, and Phenomena as Captured for the First Time by the Camera,* New York, Macmillan, 1980.
——, *Reality Recorded: Early Documentary Photography,* Greenwich, New York Graphic Society, 1974.

BURNS ARCHIVE. Joel Peter Witkin (ed.), *Masterpieces of Medical Photography: Selections from the Burns Archive,* Pasadena, Twelvetrees Press, 1987.

BURNS Stanley B., *Sleeping Beauty: Memorial Photography in America,* Altadena, Calif., Twelvetrees Press, 1990.

CARLEBACH Michael L., *American Photojournalism Comes of Age,* Washington and London, Smithsonian Institution Press, 1997.
——, *The Origins of Photojournalism in America,* Washington and London, Smithsonian Institution, 1992.

CASTRO Federica Di, *Nel raggio dell'utopia: l'esperienza fotografica ungherese tra le due guerre,* Venice, Cataloghi Marsilio, 1987.

CHALLE Daniel and MARBOT Bernard, *Les Photographes de Barbizon: la forêt de Fontainebleau,* Paris, Hoëbeke, Bibliothèque Nationale, 1991.

CHEVRIER Jean-François and LINGWOOD James, *Une autre objectivité. Another Objectivity,* Milan, Idea Books, 1989.

COE Brian, *The Birth of Photography: The Story of the Formative Years, 1800–1900,* London, Ash & Grant, 1976.

COKE Van Deren, *Avant-garde photographique en Allemagne, 1919–1939,* Paris, P. Sers, 1982.
——, *The Painter and the Photograph: From Delacroix to Warhol,* Albuquerque, Univ. of New Mexico, 1972.

CRIMÉE, 1854–1856, Premiers Reportages de guerre, Paris, Musée de l'Armée, 1994.

DATAR. *Paysages Photographies en France dans les années quatre-vingt,* Paris, Mission Photographique de la Datar / Hazan, 1989.

EAUCLAIRE Sally, *American Independents: Eighteen Color Photographers,* New York, Abbeville, 1987.
——, *New Color / New Work: Eighteen Photographic Essays,* New York, Abbeville, 1986.

EDWARDS Elizabeth (ed.), *Anthropology and Photography, 1860–1920,* New Haven and London, Yale Univ., 1992.

EWING William M., *Danse: chefs-d'œuvre de la photographie,* Paris, Herscher, 1987.

EXPLORATION, TRAVEL. Weston J. Naef, *Era of Exploration: The Rise of Landscape Photography in the American West, 1860–1885,* Buffalo, Albright-Knox Art Gallery, 1975.
Robert Hershkowitz, *The British Photographer Abroad: The First Thirty Years,* London, Robert Hershkowitz, 1980.
Rainer Fabian and Hans-Christian Adam, *Masters of Early Travel Photography,* New York, Vendome, 1983.
Daniel Wolf (ed.), *The American Space: Meaning in Nineteenth-Century Landscape Photography,* Middletown, Wesleyan Univ., 1983.
Wilson Michael G. and Jane, *Collection. Excursions along the Nile: The Photographic Discovery of Ancient Egypt,* Santa Barbara, Santa Barbara Museum of Art, 1993.
——, *Collection. Revealing the Holy Land: The Photographic Exploration of Palestine,* Santa Barbara, Santa Barbara Museum of Art, 1997.

FABER Monika and KROUTVOR Josef, *Photographie der Moderne in Prag,* Schaffhausen, Stemmle, 1991.

FASHION. Nancy Hall-Duncan, *The History of Fashion Photography,* New York, International Museum of Photography and Alpine Books, 1979.
Martin Harrison, *Apparences: la photographie de mode depuis 1945,* Paris, Chêne, 1991.
Vanités: photographies de mode des XIXe et XXe siècles, Paris, Centre National de la Photographie, 1993.
FOCH Elisabeth, *Montagne des photographes,* Paris, Bordas, 1989.

FONTCUBERTA Joan and ZELICH Cristina, *Photographies catalanes des années trente,* Paris, Dept. de Cultura de la Generalitat de Catalunya, 1982.

FRIZOT Michel *et al., 1839: La Photographie révélée,* Paris, Centre National de la Photographie, 1989.

"From Today Painting is Dead." The Beginnings of Photography, London, Arts Council of Great Britain, 1972.

GALASSI Peter, *Before Photography: Painting and the Invention of Photography,* New York, Museum of Modern Art, 1981.

GAUTRAND Jean-Claude, *Paris des photographes,* vol. 1, *Paris éternel,* Paris, Contrejour and Paris Audiovisuel, 1985.

GIDAL Tim N., *Modern Photojournalism: Origin and Evolution, 1910–1933,* New York, Collier, 1973.

GREENHILL Ralph, *Engineer's Witness,* Toronto and Boston, Coach House and David R. Godine, 1985.

GROUP F.64, Therese Thau Heyman (ed.), *Seeing Straight: The f.64 Revolution in Photography,* Oakland, The Oakland Museum, 1992.

GUERRIN Michel, *Profession photoreporter: vingt ans d'images d'actualité,* Paris, Centre Georges-Pompidou et Gallimard, 1988.

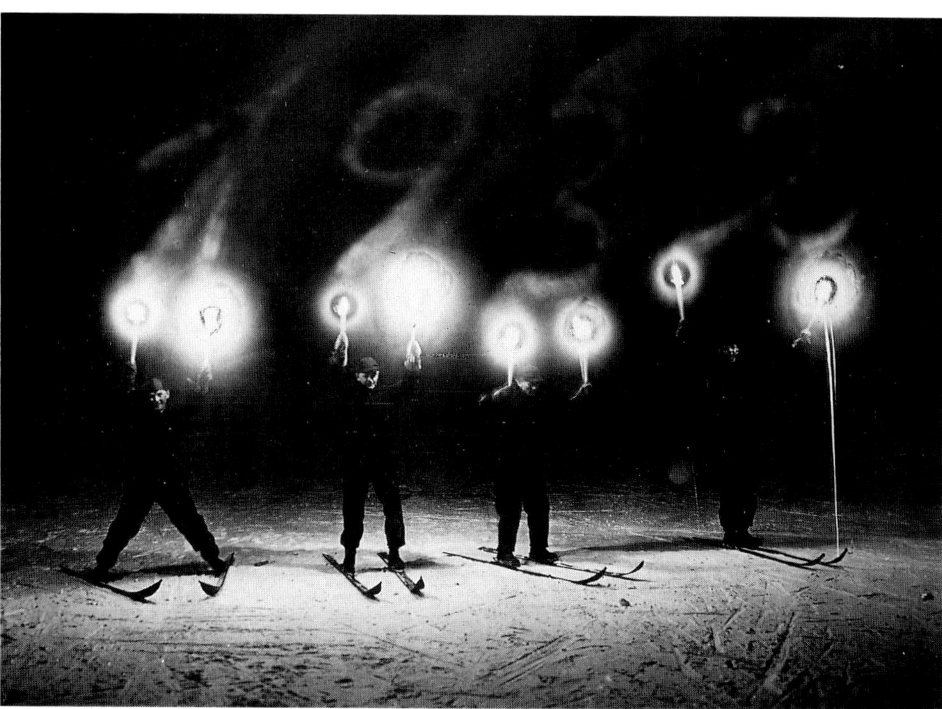

ROBERT SENNECKE, *Skiers with Torches*, New Year 1932, press photograph, private collection.

Haenlein Carl-Albrecht (ed.), *Dada: Photographie und Photocollage*, Hanover, Kestner, 1979.
——, *Künstlerphotographien im XX. Jahrhundert*, Hanover, Kestner, 1977.
——, *Momentbild: Künstlerphotographie*, Hanover, Kestner, 1982.

Hales Peter Bacon, *Silver Cities: The Photography of American Urbanization, 1839–1915*, Philadelphia, Temple Univ., 1984.

Henisch Heinz K. and Henisch Bridget A., *The Photographic Experience, 1839–1914: Images and Attitudes*, University Park, Penn State Press, 1994.

Hight Eleanor M., *Picturing Modernism: Moholy-Nagy and Photography in Weimar Germany*, Cambridge, MIT Press, 1995.

Hochreiter Otto, *Im Zeichen des Janus: Portale, Türen und Tore in der Architekturfotografie, 1840–1980*, Vienna, Ariadne, 1986.

Hurley F. Jack (ed.), *Industry and the Photographic Image: 153 Great Prints from 1850 to the Present*, New York, Dover, 1980.

The Image of War, 1861–1865, Garden City, Doubleday & Co., 1981–1984.

Images inventées: la photographie créative belge dans les années 50, Musée d'Art Moderne de la Ville de Paris, 1990.

Jacobson Ken, *Étude d'après nature: 19th Century Photographs in Relation to Art*, Petches Bridge, Ken & Jenny Jacobson, 1996.

Jaguer Edouard, *Les Mystères de la chambre noire: le surréalisme et la photographie*, Paris, Flammarion, 1982.

Jaubert Alain, *Le Commissariat aux archives*, Paris, Barrault, 1986.

Jenkins Reese V., *Images and Enterprise: Technology and the American Photographic Industry, 1839 to 1925*, Baltimore, Johns Hopkins Univ. Press, 1975.

Klett Mark, Manchester Ellen and Verburg JoAnn, *Second View: The Rephotographic Survey Project*, Albuquerque, Univ. of New Mexico, 1984.

Krauss Rosalind, Livingston Jane and Ades Dawn, *L'Amour Fou: Photography and Surrealism*, New York, Abbeville Press, Inc., 1986.

Lista Giovanni, *Futurismo e Fotografia*, Milan, Multipla, 1979.
——, *Photographie futuriste italienne, 1911–1939*, Paris, Musée d'Art Moderne, 1981.

Livingston Jane, *The New York School: Photographs 1936–1963*, New York, Stewart, Tabori and Chang, 1992.

Manassé Studio. Monika Faber, *Die montierte Frau: Aktphotographien des Atelier Manassé aus den 20er und 30er Jahren*, Vienna, Christian Brandstätter, 1988.

Mc Cauley Elizabeth Anne, *Industrial Madness: Commercial Photography in Paris, 1848–1871*, New Haven and London, Yale Univ. Press, 1994.

Morris Hambourg Maria and Phillips Christopher, *The New Vision: Photography between the World Wars*, New York, Metropolitan Museum of Art, 1989.

Movement. *Vanishing Presence*, Minneapolis, Walker Art Center, 1989.
Sprung in die Zeit: Bewegung und Zeit, Berlin, Ars Nicolai, 1992.

Mrázková Daniela and Remeš Vladimír, *Tschechoslowakische Fotografen, 1900–1940*, Leipzig, VEB Fotokinoverlag, 1983.

Neusüss Floris M., *Das Fotogramm in der Kunst des 20. Jahrhunderts: Die andere Seite der Bilder: Fotografie ohne Kamera*, Cologne, DuMont, 1990.

Nir Yeshayahu, *The Bible and the Image: The History of Photography in the Holy Land, 1839–1899*, Philadelphia, Univ. of Pennsylvania, 1985.

The Nude, Eroticism. Uwe Scheid, *Das erotische Imago*, vol. 1, *Der Akt in frühen Photographien*, Dortmund, Harenberg, 1984, vol. 2, *Das Aktphoto von 1900 bis heute*, Dortmund, Harenberg, 1986.
Jorge Levinski, *The Naked and the Nude*, London, Weidenfeld & Nicolson, 1987.
Peter Weiermair, *The Hidden Image: Photographs of the Male Nude in the Nineteenth and Twentieth Centuries*, Cambridge and London, MIT, 1988.
Bilderlust: erotische Photographien aus der Sammlung Uwe Scheid, Heidelberg, Braus, 1991.
Nazarieff Serge, *Early Erotic Photography*, Cologne, Benedikt Taschen, 1993.
L'Art du nu au XIXe siècle: Le photographe et son modèle, Paris, Hazan / Bibliothèque nationale de France, 1997.
Palazzoli Daniela and Carluccio Luigi, *Combattimento per un immagine: fotografi e pittori*, Turin, Amici Torinesi dell'Arte Contemporanea, 1973.

Pare Richard (ed.), *Court House: A Photographic Document*, New York, Horizon, 1978.
——, *Photography and Architecture: 1839–1939*, Montreal and New York, Canadian Centre for Architecture / Callaway, 1982.

Photomontage. *Idas y caos: Aspectos de las vanguardias fotográficas en España*, Madrid, Ministerio de Cultura, 1984.
Claude Leclanche-Boulé, *Typographies et photomontages constructivistes en URSS*, Paris, Papyrus, 1984.
Dawn Ades, *Photomontage*, New York and London, Thames & Hudson, 1986.

Pictorialism Robert Doty, *Photo Secession: Photography as a Fine Art*, Rochester, International Museum of Photography; repr. New York, Dover, 1978.
Margaret Harker, *The Linked Ring: The Secession Movement in Photography in Britain, 1892–1910*, London, Heinemann, 1979.
Peter C. Bunnell (ed.), *A Photographic Vision: Pictorial Photography, 1889–1923*, Salt Lake City, Peregrine Smith, 1980.
Janet E. Buerger, *The Last Decade: The Emergence of Art Photography in the 1890s*, Rochester, International Museum of Photography, 1984.
Erika Kempe, Fritz Kempe and Heinz Spielmann, *Die Kunst der Camera im Jugendstil*, Frankfurt, Umschau, 1986.
Michel Poivert, *Le pictorialisme en France*, Paris, Hoëbeke, 1992.
Le Salon de photographie: les écoles pictorialistes en Europe et aux États-Unis vers 1900, Paris, Musée Rodin, 1993.

Pittori fotografi a Roma, 1845–1870: Immagini dalla raccolta fotografica comunale, Rome, Multigraficae, 1987.

Rabb Jane M. (ed.), *Literature & Photography: Interactions, 1840–1990*, Albuquerque, Univ. of New Mexico Press, 1995.

Roh Franz and Tschichold Jan (ed.), *foto-auge/œil et photo/photo-eye*, Paris, 1929; repr. New York, Arno, 1972.

Rosenblum Naomi, *A History of Women Photographers*, Paris, Abbeville, 1994.

Scharf Aaron, *Art and Photography*, Baltimore, Allen Lane, Penguin, 1969.

Sculpture. Rainer Michael Mason and Hélène Pinet, *Pygmalion photographe: la sculpture devant la caméra, 1844–1936*, Geneva, Musée d'Art et d'Histoire, 1985.
The Kiss of Apollo: Photography and Sculpture, 1845 to the Present, San Francisco, Fraenkel Gallery and Bedford Arts, 1991.
Photographie / Sculpture, Paris, Centre National de la Photographie, 1991.

Sobieszek Robert A., *The Art of Persuasion: A History of Advertising Photography*, New York, Harry N. Abrams, 1988.
Stotz Gustaf *et al.*, *Film und Foto*, Stuttgart, 1929; repr. New York, Arno, 1978.

Thézy Marie de, *La Photographie humaniste, 1930–1960: histoire d'un mouvement en France*, Paris, Contrejour, 1992.

Thomas Ann, *Beauty of Another Order: Photography in Science*, New Haven and London, Yale Univ. Press, in association with National Gallery of Canada, 1997.

Twelve Photographers of the American Social Landscape, Waltham, Brandeis Univ., 1967.

Victorian Age. Jeremy Maas, *The Victorian Art World in Photographs*, New York, Universe, 1984.
Michael Bartram, *The Pre-Raphaelite Camera: Aspects of Victorian Photography*, Boston, Little, Brown, 1985; London, Weidenfeld & Nicolson, 1985.
Grace Seiberling and Carolyn Bloore, *Amateurs, Photography, and the Mid-Victorian Imagination*, Chicago and London, Univ. of Chicago, 1986.
Frances Dimond and Roger Taylor, *Crown and Camera: The Royal Family and Photography, 1842–1910*, Harmondsworth, Viking, 1987.

A Vision Shared: A Classic Portrait of America and Its People, 1935–1943, New York, St. Martin's, 1976.

Westerbeck Colin and Meyerowitz Joel, *Bystander: A History of Street Photography*, Boston, Little, Brown, 1994.

Zannier Italo, *Neorealismo e fotografia*, Udine, Art&, 1987.

ANTHOLOGIES, CATALOGUES, PHOTOGRAPHIC COLLECTIONS

Isaacs Charles, Collection. Merry A. Foresta, *American Photographs: The First Century*. From the Isaacs Collection in the National Museum of American Art, Washington, D.C., National Museum of American Art and Smithsonian Institution Press, 1996.

Agfa Foto-Historama. *Das Agfa Foto-Historama im Wallraf-Richartz-Museum / Museum Ludwig der Stadt Köln: Eine Auswahl von Photographien des 19. und des frühen 20. Jahrhunderts*, Cologne, 1986.

Alinari Archives. *Italy: One Hundred Years of Photography*, Florence, Alinari, 1988.

Amon Carter Museum. Martha A. Sandweiss, *Masterworks of American Photography: The Amon Carter Museum Collection*, Birmingham, Ala., Oxmoor, 1982.

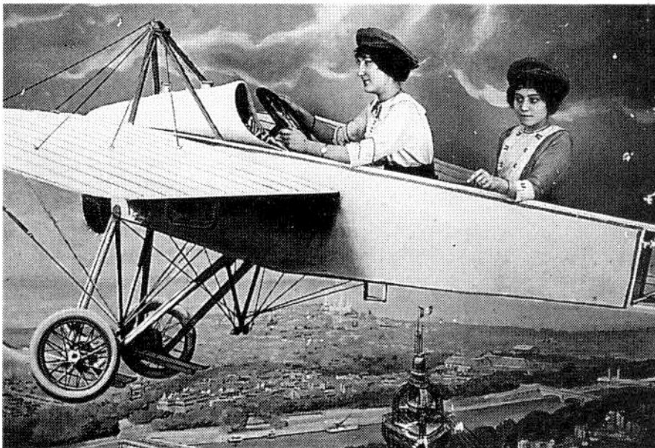

Anonymous, *Souvenir of Our Flight*, May 17, 1912.

Bäckström Collection. Åke Sidwall and Leif Wigh, *Bäckströms Bilder! Prints from the Helmer Bäckström Collection in Fotografiska Museet*, Stockholm, Fotografiska Museet, 1980.

Bernard Bruce, *Photodiscovery: Masterworks of Photography, 1840–1940*, New York, Harry N. Abrams, 1980.

Bertelli Carlo and Bollati Giulio, *L'immagine fotografica, 1845–1945*, Turin, Giulio Einaudi, 1979.

Blanquart-Evrard. Isabelle Jammes, *Blanquart-Evrard et les origines de l'édition photographique française: catalogue raisonné des albums photographiques édités, 1851–1855*, Geneva, Librairie Droz, 1981.

Breitenbach Collection. *Die Sammlung Josef Breitenbach zur Geschichte der Photographie*, Munich, Münchner Stadtmuseum, 1979.

Camera Work. Marianne Fulton Margolis (ed.), *Camera Work, A Pictorial Guide, with Reproductions of all 559 Illustrations and Plates, Fully Indexed*, New York, Dover, 1978.
Camera Work, the Complete Illustrations, 1903–1917, Cologne, Benedikt Taschen, 1997.

Caulfield and Shock Studio. Michael Lesy, *Real Life: Louisville in the Twenties*, New York, Pantheon, 1976.

Center for Creative Photography. James Enyeart (ed.), *Decade by Decade: Twentieth-Century American Photography: from the Collection of the Center for Creative Photography*, Boston, Little, Brown & Co., 1989.

Cincinnati Art Museum. Kristin L. Spanenberg, *Photographic Treasures from the Cincinnati Art Museum*, Cincinnati, Cincinnati Art Museum, 1989.

Dresden. *Photographien aus zehn Ländern in Dresdner Sammlungen*, Dresden, Staatliche Kunstsammlungen Dresden, 1983.

École des Beaux-Arts, Paris. Catherine Mathon and Anne-Marie Garcia, *Les Chefs-d'œuvre de la photographie dans les collections de l'École des beaux-arts*, Paris, ENSB-A, 1991.

George Eastman House. Robert A. Sobieszek, *Masterpieces of Photography from the George Eastman House Collections*, New York, Abbeville, 1986.

Gilman Paper Co. Pierre Apraxine, *Photographs from the Collection of the Gilman Paper Co.*, New York, White Oak, 1985.
Maria Morris Hambourg, et al., *The Waking Dream: Photography's First Century: Selections from the Gilman Paper Company Collection*, New York, The Metropolitan Museum of Art, 1993.

Grégoire Auguste, *Honderd Jaar Fotografie*, Bloemendaal, Focus, 1948.

Grégoire Collection. Ingeborg T. Leijerzapf, *Het Fotografisch Museum van Auguste Grégoire; Een Vroege Nederlandse Fotocollectie*, The Hague, SDU, 1989.

Gruber Collection. *Sammlung Gruber: Photographie des 20. Jahrhunderts*, Cologne, Stadt Köln, 1984.

Gunther Thomas Michael and Thézy Marie de, *50 ans de photographie de presse: archives photographiques de Paris-Soir, Match, France-Soir*, Paris, Bibliothèque Historique de la Ville de Paris, 1990.

Heilbrun Françoise, Marbot Bernard and Néagu Philippe, *L'Invention d'un regard (1839–1918)*, Paris, RMN, 1989.

Henisch Heinz K. and Henisch Bridget A., *The Photographic Experience: Exhibition to Celebrate the 150th Anniversary of the Invention of Photography*, Univ. Park, 1988.

Jammes Collection. *Niépce to Atget: The First Century of Photography from the Collection of André Jammes*, Chicago, Art Institute, 1977.

Lebeck Collection. *Panorama einer Vergangenheit: Die ersten dreissig Jahre, 1840–1870*, Hamburg, Print Verlag für Kunst und Photographie, 1982.
Lebeck Robert, Collection. Bodo von Dewitz and Roland Scotti (ed.), *Alles Wahrheit! Alles Lüge! Photographie und*

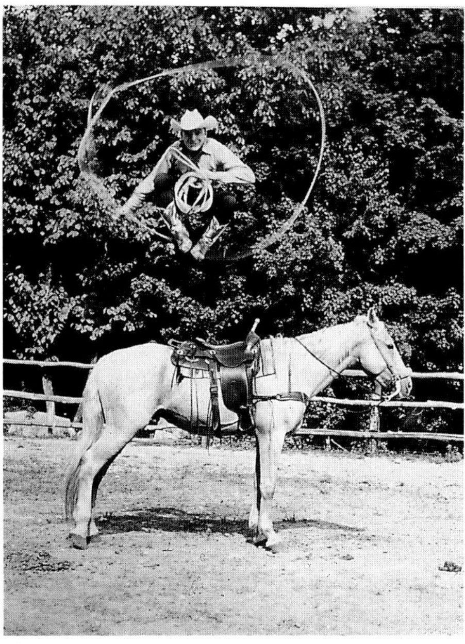

Anonymous, **press photograph**, 1930s, private collection.

Wirklichkeit im 19. Jahrhundert: Die Sammlung Robert Lebeck, Amsterdam and Dresden, Verlag der Kunst, 1996.

Levy Collection. *Photographs from the Julien Levy Collection, Starting with Atget*, Chicago, Art Institute, 1976.

Madrid, Biblioteca Nacional. *150 años de fotografía en la Biblioteca Nacional*, Madrid, El Viso, 1989.

Minneapolis Institute of Arts. Carroll T. Hartwell, *The Making of a Collection: Photographs from the Minneapolis Institute of Arts*, Millerton, Aperture, 1984.

Mission Héliographique. *La Mission héliographique: Photographies de 1851*, Paris, 1980.

Néagu Philippe and Poulet-Allamagny Jean-Jacques, *Anthologie d'un patrimoine photographique, 1847–1926*, Paris, Caisse Nationale des Monuments Historiques et des Sites, 1980.

New Mexico Univ. *Nineteenth-Century Photographs at the University of New Mexico Art Museum*, Albuquerque, Univ. Art Museum, 1989.

Newhall Beaumont and Newhall Nancy (ed.), *Masters of Photography*, 2nd. ed., New York, Park Lane, 1981.

On the Art of Fixing a Shadow: One Hundred and Fifty Years of Photography, National Gallery of Art and The Art Institute of Chicago, 1989.

Paris, Bibliothèque nationale. Jean-Claude Lemagny, *La Photographie créative*, Paris, Contrejour, 1984.
After Daguerre: Masterworks of French Photography (1848–1900) from the Bibliothèque Nationale, New York, Metropolitan Museum of Art, 1980.

Paris, Centre national d'art et de culture Georges Pompidou. Annick Lionel-Marie and Alain Sayag. Collection de photographies du Musée national d'art moderne, 1905–1948, Paris, Editions du Centre Pompidou, 1997.

Photographie, Paris, Arts et Métiers Graphiques, 11 vols., 1930–1947 ; repr. Dortmund, Harenberg, 1983.

Riddell Collection. *Masterpieces of Photography from the Riddell Collection*, Edinburgh, Scottish National Portrait Gallery, 1986.

Royal Photographic Society. Tom Hopkinson, *Treasures of the Royal Photographic Society, 1839–1919*, New York, Focal Press, 1980.

Sandweiss Martha (ed.), *Photography in Nineteenth-Century America*, Fort-Worth and New York, Amon Carter Museum, Harry Abrams, 1991.

Sayag Alain and Lemagny Jean-Claude (ed.), *L'Invention d'un art: cent cinquantième anniversaire de la photographie*, Paris, Centre Georges-Pompidou and Adam Biro, 1989.

Société française de photographie. Bernard Marbot, *Une invention du* XIX*e siècle, expression et technique, la photographie; collections de la Société française de photographie*, Paris, Bibliothèque Nationale, 1976.

Steinert Collection. *Sammlung Otto Steinert, Fotografien: Fotografische Sammlung in Museum Folkwang, Essen*, 2nd. ed., Essen, Museum Folkwang, 1985.

Stieglitz Collection. Weston J. Naef, *The Collection of Alfred Stieglitz: Fifty Pioneers of Modern Photography*, New York, Metropolitan Museum of Art and Viking Press, 1978.

Szarkowski John, *The Photographer's Eye*, New York, Museum of Modern Art (MoMA), 1966.
——, *Looking at Photographs: 100 Pictures from the Collection of the Museum of Modern Art*, New York, MoMA, 1973.
——, *Photography Until Now*, New York, MoMA, 1989.

Van Schaik Collection. Lesy Michael, *Wisconsin Death Trip*, New York, Pantheon, 1973.

Victoria and Albert Museum. Mark Haworth-Booth, *Photography: an Independent Art: Photographs from the Victoria and Albert Museum, 1839–1996*, Princeton, Princeton Univ. Press, 1997.

Wagstaff Collection. *A Book of Photographs from the Collection of Sam Wagstaff*, New York, Gray, 1978.

Weaver Mike (ed.), *The Art of Photography, 1839–1989*, New Haven and London, Yale Univ., 1989.

NATIONAL AND REGIONAL STUDIES

EUROPE

Abeels Gustave, *Les Pionniers de la photographie à Bruxelles*, Zaltbommel, Bibliothèque Européenne, 1977.

Alle origine della Fotografia: un itinerario toscano, 1839–1880, Florence, Alinari, 1989.

Autrefois la Russie: photographies inédites des archives soviétiques de 1839 à la révolution, Paris, Liana Levi, 1990.

Becchetti Piero, *Fotografi e fotografia in Italia, 1839–1880*, Rome, Quasar, 1978.

Bouqueret Christian, *Des Années folles aux années noires: La Nouvelle Vision photographique en France, 1920–1940*, Paris, Marval, 1977.

Coppens Jan, *Een camera vol stilte: Nederland in het begin van de fotografie, 1839–1875*, Amsterdam, Meulenhoff, 1976.

Coppens Jan, Roosens Laurent and Van Deuren Karel, *Introductie en integratie van de Fotografie in België en Nederland, 1839–1869*, Gemmentekrediet, 1989.

Costantini Paolo and Zannier Italo, *Venezia nella fotografia dell'ottocento*, Venice, Arsenale / Böhm, 1986.

Cresens André, *150 jaar fotografie te Leuwen*, Bruges, Marc Van de Wiele, 1989.

Dewitz Bodo von and Matz Reinhard (ed.), *Silber und Salz: Zur Frühzeit der Photographie im deutschen Sprachraum, 1839–1860*, Cologne and Heidelberg, Braus, 1989.

Eskildsen Ute et al., *Fotografieren hieß teilnehmen: Fotografinnen der Weimarer Republik*, Dusseldorf, Richter, 1994.

Elliott David, *Photography in Russia, 1840–1940*, London, Thames & Hudson, 1992.

Flukinger Roy, *The Formative Decades: Photography in Great Britain, 1839–1920*, Austin, Univ. of Texas, 1985.

Fontanella Lee, *La Historia de la fotografía en España: Desde sus orígenes hasta 1900*, Madrid, El Viso, 1981.

Fotografia italiana dell'ottocento, Milan and Florence, Electa and Alinari, 1979.

Fotografie in Nederland, The Hague, Staatsuitgeverij, 1978–1979.

The Frozen Image: Scandinavian Photography, New York, Abbeville, 1982.

Galassi Peter, *American Photography, 1890–1965*, New York, The Museum of Modern Art, 1995.

Gebhardt Heinz, *Königlich bayerische Photographie, 1838–1918*, Munich, Laterna Magica, 1978.

Haworth-Booth Mark (ed.), *The Golden Age of British Photography, 1839–1900: Photographs from the Victoria and Albert Museum, London*, Millerton and Philadelphie, Aperture and Philadelphia Museum of Art, 1984.

Hochreiter Otto and Starl Timm, *Geschichte der Fotografie in Österreich*, Bad Ischl, Verein zur Erarbeitung der *Geschichte*, 1983.

"In unnachahmlicher Treue", Photographie im 19. Jahrundert: Ihre Geschichte in den deutschsprachigen Ländern, Cologne, Museen der Stadt, 1979.
Kunstreich Jan S., *Frühe Photographen in Schleswig-Holstein*, Heide in Holstein, Boyens & Co., 1985.

López Mondéjar Publio, *Crónica de La Luz: Fotografía en Castilla-La Mancha (1855–1936)*, Madrid, El Viso, 1984.
——, *Las Fuentes de la memoria*, vol. 1, *Fotografía y sociedad en la España del siglo XIX*, Barcelona, Lunwerg, 1989.
——, *Las Fuentes de la memoria* vol. 2, *Fotografía y sociedad en España, 1900–1939*, Barcelona, Lunwerg, 1992.
Morozov Serguei and Lloyd Valerie, *Soviet Photography: An Age of Realism*, New York, Greenwich House, 1984.

Nori Claude, *La Photographie française: des origines à nos jours*, Paris, Contrejour, 1988.

Ochsner Bjørn, *Fotografer i og fra Danmark til og med år 1920. Les photographes au et du Danemark jusqu'en 1920 inclus*, Bibliotekscentralens Forlag, 1986.
——, *Fotografiet i Danmark, 1840–1940: En Kulturhistorisk billedbog*, Copenhagen, Forening for Boghaandvaerk, 1974.

Peters Ursula, *Stilgeschichte der Fotografie in Deutschland: 1839–1900*, Cologne, DuMont, 1979.

Rome in Early Photographs: The Age of Pius IX: Photographs, 1846–1878 from Roman and Danish Collections, Copenhagen, Thorvaldsen Museum, 1977.

Sehsucht: das Panorama als Massenunterhaltung des 19. Jdts, Basle, Stroemfeld / Roter Stern, 1993.

Siegert Dietmar, *Venedig in frühen Photographien, 1848–1905*, Ebersberg, Achteinhalb Lothar Just, 1984.
——, *Rom vor hundert Jahren: Photographien 1848–1890*, Ebersberg, Achteinhalb Lothar Just, 1985.

Söderberg Rolf and Rittsel Pär, *Den Svenska Fotografins Historia, 1840–1940*, Stockholm, Bonnier Fakta, 1983.

Szilagyi Gábor and Kardos Sándor, *Leletek: A magyar fotográfia történetéből*, Budapest, Képzömüvészeti Kiadó, 1983.

Tory Clara, *La Photographie hongroise, 1900–1945. Hungarian Photography between 1900 and 1945*, Paris, Bibliothèque Forney, 1984.

Xanthakis Alkis X., *History of Greek Photography, 1839–1960*, Athens, Hellenic Literary and Historical Archives Society, 1988.

Zannier Italo, *70 Anni di fotografia in Italia*, Modena, Punto e Virgola, 1978.
——, *Storia della fotografia italiana*, Rome and Bari, Editori Laterza, 1986.

NORTH AMERICA

Bush Alfred L. and Mitchell Lee Clark, *The Photograph and the American Indian*, Princeton, Princeton Univ. Press, 1994.

Cavell Edward, *Sometimes a Great Nation: A Photo Album of Canada, 1850–1925*, Banff, Altitude Publishing, 1984.

Finkel Kenneth, *Nineteenth-Century Photography in Philadelphia: 250 Historic Prints from The Library Company of Philadelphia*, New York and Philadelphia, Dover, 1980.

Greenhill Ralph and Birrell Andrew, *Canadian Photography: 1839–1920*, Toronto, Coach House Press, 1979.

Koltun Lilly (ed.), *Private Realms of Light: Amateur Photography in Canada, 1839–1940*, Markham, Fitzhenry & Whiteside, 1984.

Livingstone Jane, *The New York School: Photographs, 1936–1963*, New York, Stewart, Tabori & Chang, 1992.

Sandweiss Martha A., *Photography in Nineteenth-Century America*, Fort Worth, Amon Carter Museum; New York, H. N. Abrams, 1991.

Severa Joan L., *Dressed for the Photographer: Ordinary Americans and Fashion, 1840–1900*, Kent, Ohio, and London, Kent State Univ. Press, 1995.
Taft Robert, *Photography and the American Scene*, New York, Macmillan, 1938: repr. New York, 1964.

Welling William B., *Photography in America; The Formative Years, 1839–1900*, New York, Crowell, 1978.

LATIN AMERICA

Billeter Erika, *Canto a la realidad: Fotografía Latinoamericana, 1860–1993*, Barcelona, Lunwerg, 1993.
——, *Fotografie in Lateinamerika von 1860 bis Heute*, Berne, Benteli, 1981.

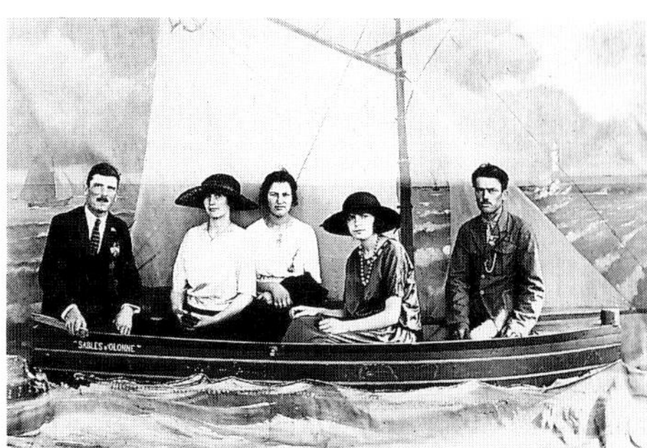

Anonymous, **Les Sables d'Olonne**, circa 1920, private collection.

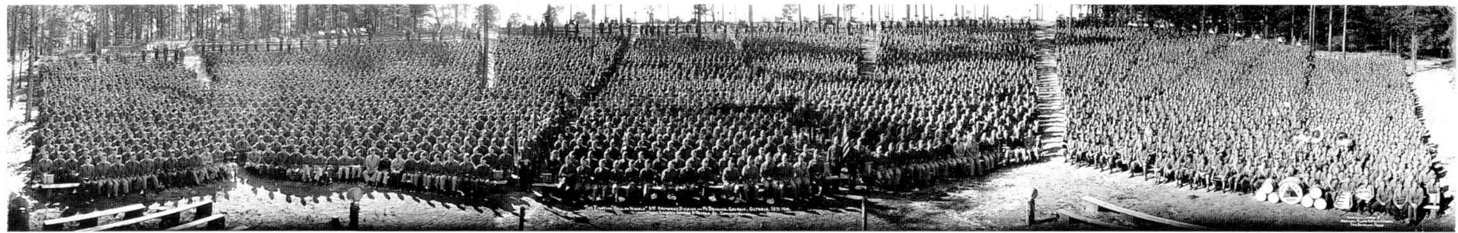

EUGENE O. GOLDBECK, *2nd Armored Division, Fort Benning, Georgia,* October 25, 1941.

CASANOVA Rosa and DEBROISE Olivier, *Sobre la superficie bruñida de un espejo: Fotógrafos del siglo XIX*, Mexico, Fondo de Cultura Económica, 1989.

Documentos gráficos para la Historia de México, vol. 1, *El que usted está leyendo (1848–1911)*, vol. 2, *La reforma y el imperio (1854–1867)*, vol. 3: *Veracruz (1858–1914)*, Mexico, Editora del Sureste, 1985–.

FERREZ Gilberto, *Photography in Brazil, 1840–1900*, Albuquerque, Univ. of New Mexico, 1990.

FERREZ Gilberto and NAEF Weston J., *Pioneer Photographers of Brazil, 1840–1920*, New York, Center for Inter-American Relations, 1976.

GÓMEZ Juan, *La fotografía en la Argentina: Su historia y evolución en el siglo XIX, 1840–1899*, Buenos Aires, Abadía, 1986.

MCELROY Keith, *Early Peruvian Photography: A Critical Case Study*, Ann Arbor, UMI Research, 1985.

MISLE (CAREMIS) Carlos Eduardo, *Venezuela siglo XIX en fotografía*, CANTU, 1981.

SERRANO Eduardo, *Historia de la fotografía en Colombia*, Bogota, Museo de Arte Moderno de Bogotá, 1983.

WATRISS Wendy and ZAMORA Lois Parkinson (ed.), *Image and Memory: Photography from Latin America, 1866–1994*, Austin, Univ. of Texas Press, 1998.

MIDDLE-EAST AND AFRICA

An den süßen Ufern Asiens: Ägypten, Palästina, Osmanisches Reich: Das 19. Jahrhundert in frühen Photographien, Cologne, Agfa Foto-Historama im Wallraf-Richartz-Museum, 1988.

BULL Deborah and LORIMER Donald, *Up the Nile: A Photographic Excursion, Egypt, 1839–1898*, New York, C. N. Potter, 1979.

BULL Marjorie and DENFIELD Joseph, *Secure the Shadow: The Story of Cape Photography from its Beginnings to the End of 1870*, Cape Town, Terence McNally, 1970.

ÇIZGEN Engin, *Photography in the Ottoman Empire, 1839–1919*, Istanbul, Haset Kitabevi, 1987.

MONTI Nicolas (ed.), *Africa Then: Photographs, 1840–1918*, New York, Alfred A. Knopf, 1987.

MUSEUM VOOR VOLKENKUNDE, ROTTERDAM, *Beelden van de Oriënt: Fotografie en Toerisme, 1860–1900 / Images of the Orient: Photography and Tourism, 1860–1900*, Amsterdam and Rotterdam, Fragment, 1986.

PEREZ Nissan, *Focus East: Early Photography in the Near East (1839–1885)*, New York, Harry N. Abrams, 1988.

VACZEK Louis Charles and BUCKLAND Gail, *Travellers in Ancient Lands: A Portrait of the Middle East, 1839–1919*, Boston, New York Graphic Society, 1981.

ASIA

GUTMAN Judith Mara, *Through Indian Eyes: 19th and early 20th Century Photography from India*, New York, Oxford Univ., 1982.

JAPAN PHOTOGRAPHERS ASSOCIATION, *A Century of Japanese Photography*, New York, Pantheon, 1980.

MARBOT Bernard, *Objectif Cipango: photographies anciennes du Japon*, Paris, Bibliothèque Nationale and Paris Audiovisuel, 1990.

RIJKSUNIVERSITEIT LEIDEN, PRENTENKABINET, *Herinneringen aan Japan, 1850–1870: Foto's en Fotoalbums in Nederlands Bezit*, The Hague, Staatsuitgeverij, 1987.

WORSWICK Clark, *Japan: Photographs, 1854–1905*, New York, Knopf, 1979.

——, and EMBREE Ainslie, *The Last Empire: Photography in British India, 1855–1911*, Millerton, Aperture, 1976.
——, and SPENCE Jonathan, *Imperial China: Photographs, 1850–1912*, London, Scolar Press, 1979.

AUSTRALASIA AND PACIFIC

ABRAMSON Joan, *Photographers of Old Hawaii*, 3rd. ed., Honolulu, Island Heritage, 1981.

DAVIES Alan and STANBURY Peter, *The Mechanical Eye in Australia: Photography, 1841–1900*, Melbourne, Oxford Univ., 1985.

KNIGHT Hardwicke, *Photography in New Zealand: A Social and Technical History*, Dunedin, John McIndoe, 1971.

MAIN William, *Maori in Focus*, Wellington, Millwood, 1976.

O'REILLY Patrick, *Les Photographes à Tahiti et leurs œuvres, 1842–1962*, Paris, Société des Océanistes, 1969; repr. Tahiti, 1981.

REED Jane Levy (ed.), *Toward Independence: A Century of Indonesia Photographed*, San Francisco, Friends of Photography, 1991.

PHOTOGRAPHERS

ABBOTT. *Berenice Abbott: Changing New York. The Complete WPA Project*, New York, The New Press, 1997.
Berenice Abbott, Photographs, New York, Horizon, 1970.
Julia Van Haften (ed.), *Berenice Abbott Photographer: A Modern Vision*, New York Public Library, 1989.

ADAMS Ansel. *Images, 1923–1974*, Boston, New York Graphic Society, 1974.
Ansel Adams: An Autobiography, Boston, Little, Brown, 1985.
Ansel Adams: Letters and Images, 1916–1984, Boston, Little, Brown, 1988.

ADAMS Robert. *Robert Adams: To Make it Home: Photography of the American West, 1965–1986*, Millerton, Aperture, 1989.
What We Bought: The New World: Scenes From the Denver Metropolitan Area 1970–1974, Hanover, Stiftung Niedersachsen, 1995.

ALBERS. Marianne Stockebrand (ed.), *Josef Albers: Photographien, 1928–1955*, Munich, Schirmer/Mosel, 1992.

ALBERT. Winfried Ranke, *Joseph Albert: Hofphotograph der bayerischen Könige*, Munich, Schirmer / Mosel, 1977.

ALBIN GUILLOT. Christian Bouqueret, *Laure Albin Guillot, ou la volont, d'art*, Paris, Marval, 1996.

ALINARI. *Gli Alinari: fotografi a Firenze, 1852–1920*, Florence, Alinari, 1977; repr. 1985.

ALVAREZ BRAVO. Jane Livingston, *M. Alvarez Bravo*, Boston, David R. Godine, 1978.
Manuel Alvarez Bravo: 303 photographies 1920–1986, Paris-Musées and Paris Audiovisuel, 1986.
Revelaciones: The Art of Manuel Alvarez Bravo, San Diego, Calif., Museum of Photographic Arts, 1990.

ANDRIESSE. Flip Bool et al., *Emmy Andriesse* [1914–1953], Amsterdam, Focus, 1995?.

ANNAN. *Thomas Annan: Photographs of the Old Closes and Streets of Glasgow, 1868–1877*, New York, Dover, 1977.
Sara Stevenson, *Thomas Annan, 1829–1887*, Edinburgh, National Gallery of Scotland, 1990.

APPELT. *Dieter Appelt, Photographie*, Berlin, Nishen, 1989.
Dieter Appelt: Die Schatten erinnern an nichts, Frankfurt, Springer und Winkler, 1991.

ARAKI. *The Works of Nobuyoshi Araki*, 20 vols., Tokyo, Heibonsha, 1996–1997.

ARBUS. Patricia Bosworth, *Diane Arbus: A Biography*, New York, Knopf, 1984.
Diane Arbus, Paris, Nathan, 1990.

ATGET. *Atget, Paris*, Paris, Hazan, 1992.
John Szarkowski and Maria Morris Hambourg, *The Work of Atget*, vol. 1, *Old France*. vol. 2, *The Art of Old Paris*. vol. 3, *The Ancien Régime*. vol. 4, *Modern Times*, New York, Museum of Modern Art, 1981–1985.
Françoise Reynaud, *Les voitures d'Atget*, Paris, Carré, 1991.
Molly Nesbit and Françoise Reynaud, *Intérieurs parisiens: Eugène Atget*, Paris, Carré, 1992.

ATKINS. Larry Schaaf, *Sun Gardens: Victorian Photograms by Anna Atkins*, Millerton, Aperture, 1985.

AUBRY. *Charles Aubry, photographe*, Paris, Bibliothèque Nationale de France, 1996.

AVEDON. Richard Avedon, *Nothing Personal*, New York, Atheneum, 1964.
Observations, New York and Lucerne, Simon & Schuster and Bucher, 1959.
In the American West, London, Thames & Hudson, 1985.
Une Autobiographie, Schirmer / Mosel, Munich, Paris and London, 1993.

BACOT. *E. Bacot, A. de Brébisson, A. Humbert de Molard: trois photographes en Basse-Normandie au XIXe siècle*, Caen, ARDI, 1989.

BALDUS. Malcolm Daniel, *The Photographs of Édouard Baldus*, New York and Montreal, The Metropolitan Museum of Art and the Canadian Centre for Architecture, 1994.

BALTZ. Lewis Baltz, *The New Industrial Parks near Irvine, California. Das neue Industriegelände in der Nähe von Irvine, Kalifornien*, New York, Leo Castelli Graphics, 1974.
Lewis Baltz: Candlestick Point, Tokyo, Gallery Min, 1989.
Bernard Lamarche-Vadel, *Lewis Baltz*, Paris, La Différence, 1993.

BARNARD. George N. Barnard, *Photographic Views of Sherman's Campaign*, New York, 1866; repr. Dover, 1977.
Keith F. Davis, *George N. Barnard: Photographer of Sherman's Campaign*, Kansas City, Hallmark Cards, 1990.

BASILICO. Gabriele Basilico, *Bords de mer: mission photographique de la Datar, 1984–1985*, Udine, Art&, 1992.

BAYARD. Jean-Claude Gautrand and Michel Frizot, *Hippolyte Bayard: naissance de l'image photographique*, Amiens, Trois Cailloux, 1986.

BAYER. *Herbert Bayer: Photographic Works*, Los Angeles, Arco Center for Visual Art, 1977.

BEARD Peter. Alistair Graham, *Eyelids of Morning: The Mingled Destinies of Crocodiles and Men, Being a Description* [...], Greenwich, New York Graphic Society, 1973; repr. 1990.

BEATO. Italo Zannier, *Verso oriente: Fotografie di Antonio e Felice Beato*, Florence, Alinari, 1986.
Claudia Gabriele Philipp, Dietmar Siegert and Rainer Wock, *Felice Beato in Japan: Photographien zum Ende der Feudalzeit, 1863–1873*, Heidelberg, Braus, 1991.

BEATON. James Danziger (ed.), *Beaton*, London, Secker & Warburg, 1980; New York, Viking, 1980.
Hugo Vickers, *Cecil Beaton: The Authorized Biography*, London, Weidenfeld & Nicolson, 1985.
Philippe Garner and David Alan Mellor, *Cecil Beaton: Photographs, 1920–1970*, New York, Stewart, Tabori & Chang, 1994.

BECHER. Bernd and Hilla Becher, *Blast Furnaces*, Cambridge and London, MIT Press, 1990.
Bernd and Hilla Becher, *Gas Tanks*, Cambridge and London, MIT Press, 1993.
Bernd and Hilla Becher, *Industrial Facades*, Cambridge and London, MIT Press, 1995.

BELLMER. *Hans Bellmer, photographe*, Paris, Filipacchi and Centre Georges-Pompidou, 1983.
Carl Haenlein (ed.), *Hans Bellmer Photographien*, Hanover, Kestner, 1984.

BELLOCQ. John Szarkowski (ed.), *E. J. Bellocq, Storyville Portraits: Photographs from the New Orleans Red-Light District, circa 1912*, New York, Museum of Modern Art, 1970.

BERGGREN. *Photographic Views of the Bosphorus and Constantinople: A Presentation of Swedish Photographer G. Berggren and His Activities in the 19th Century in Ottoman Turkey*, Stockholm, Fotografiska Museet, 1984.
BIERMANN. *Aenne Biermann: Photographs, 1925–1933*, London, Nishen, 1987.

BING. *Ilse Bing: Paris, 1931–1952*, Paris, Paris Musées, 1987.

BISCHOF. Marco Bischof and René Burri, *Werner Bischof, 1916–1954: His Life and Work, A Book*, London, Thames & Hudson, 1990.

BLOSSFELDT. Karl Blossfeldt, *Urformen der Kunst*, Berlin, 1928; repr. Dortmund, Harenberg, 1985.
Gert Mattenklott, *Karl Blossfeldt, 1865–1932: Das fotografische Werk*, Botanische Bearbeitung von Harald Kilias, Munich, Schirmer / Mosel, 1994.

BLUMENFELD. Erwin Blumenfeld, *My One Hundred Best Photos*, London, Zwemmer, 1981.

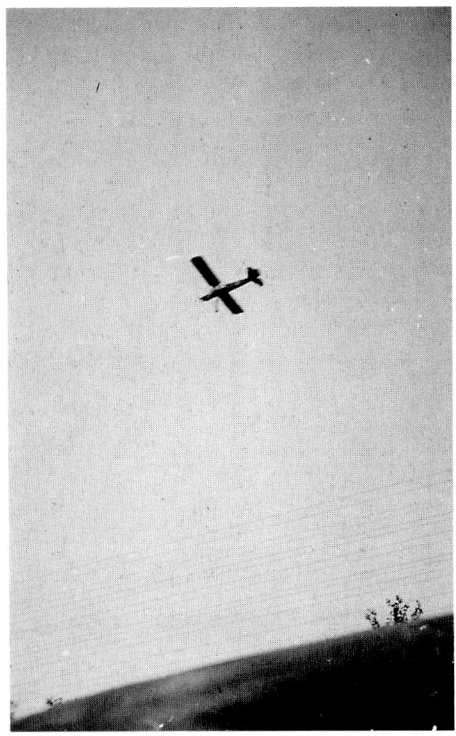

ANONYMOUS AMATEUR, 1930s, private collection.

Erwin Blumenfeld, Dada collages e fotografie 1916–1930 and *Erwin Blumenfeld, fotografie 1933–1968,* Milan, Galleria Milano and Superstudio, 1989.

BOISSONNAS. Nicolas Bouvier, *Boissonnas: une dynastie de photographes, 1864–1983,* Lausanne, Payot, 1983.

BOLTANSKI. Didier Semin, *Christian Boltanski,* Paris, Art Press, 1988.

BONFILS. Carney E. S. Garvin, *The Image of the East: Nineteenth-Century Near Eastern Photographs by Bonfils from the Collections of the Harvard Semitic Museum,* Chicago and London, Univ. of Chicago, 1982.

BONNARD. Françoise Heilbrun and Philippe Néagu, *Pierre Bonnard: Photographs and Paintings,* New York, Aperture 1988.

BOUBAT. *Miroirs, Autoportraits: Photographies d'Édouard Boubat,* Paris, Denoël, 1973.
Le Paris de Boubat, Paris, Paris Musées, 1990.

BOURKE-WHITE. Margaret Bourke-White, *Eyes on Russia,* New York, Simon & Schuster, 1931.
Theodore M. Brown, *Margaret Bourke-White, photo-journalist,* New York, White Museum of Art, Cornell University, 1972.
Vicki Goldberg, *Bourke-White,* Paris, United Technologies Corp., 1988.

BOURNE. Arthur Ollman, *Samuel Bourne: Images of India,* Carmel, Friends of Photography, 1983.

BRADY. Dorothy Meserve Kunhardt and Philip B. Kunhardt, *Mathew Brady and His World,* Alexandria, Time-Life Books, 1977.
Mary Panzer, *Mathew Brady and the Image of History,* Washington and London, Smithsonian Institution Press, 1997.

BRANCUSI. *Brancusi Photographer,* New York, Agrinde, 1979.
Constantin Brancusi: The Sculptor as Photographer, London and Lyme, D. Grob and Callaway, 1979.
Elizabeth A. Brown, *Constantin Brancusi, Photographer,* Paris, Editions Assouline, 1995.

BRANDT. Bill Brandt, *Perspectives of Nudes,* London, Bodley Head, 1961.
Ian Jeffrey, *Bill Brandt: Photographs, 1928–1983,* New York, Thames & Hudson, 1994.
Shadow of Light: Photographs, London, Gordon Fraser, 1977.
London in the Thirties, London, Gordon Fraser, 1983.

BRASSAÏ. *Paris by Night,* New York, Pantheon, 1987.
Brassaï: Paris le jour, Paris la nuit, Paris, Paris Musées, 1988.
Manuel J. Borja-Villel, *Brassaï,* Barcelona, Fundació Antoni Tapies, 1993.

BRAUN. Christian Kempf, *Adolphe Braun et la photographie, 1812–1877,* Valblor, Lucigraphie, 1994.

BRÉBISSON. See Bacot.

BREITENBACH. T. O. Immisch, Ulrich Pohlmann and Klaus E. Gölitz (ed.), *Josef Breitenbach: Photographien zum 100. Geburtstag,* Munich, Schirmer / Mosel, 1996.

BREWSTER. A. D. Morrison-Low and J. R. R. Christie (ed.), *"Martyr of Science": Sir David Brewster, 1781–1868,* Edinburgh, Royal Scottish Museum, 1984.

BRIGMAN. Susan Ehrens, *A Poetic Vision: The Photographs of Anne Brigman,* Santa Barbara, Santa Barbara Museum of Art, 1995.

BRODOVITCH. Andy Grundberg, *Brodovitch,* New York, Abrams and Documents of American Design, 1989.

BRUGUIÈRE. James Enyeart, *Bruguière: His Photographs and His Life: Photographs by Francis Joseph Bruguière, 1879–1945,* New York, Knopf, 1977.

BULL. Terence Popper and John Kobal, *Clarence Sinclair Bull: photographe des stars de la MGM,* Munich, Schirmer / Mosel, 1989.

BULLOCK. Tom Beck, *An American Vision: John G. Bullock and the Photo-Secession,* New York, Aperture, 1989.
Wynn Bullock, San Francisco, Scrimshaw, 1971.

BURRI. René, *Die Deutschen: Auswahl der Texte von Hans Bender,* Zurich, Fretz and Wasmuth, 1962; rev. ed. Munich, Schirmer / Mosel, 1990.

BURROWS. *Larry Burrows: Compassionate Photographer,* New York, Time-Life Books, 1972.

BURTON. Hardwicke Knight, *Burton Brothers: Photographers,* Dunedin, John McIndoe, 1980.
Burton Brothers: Fotografen in Nieuw-Zeeland, 1866–1898 / Burton Brothers: Photographers in New Zealand, 1866–1898, Amsterdam and Rotterdam, Fragment and Museum voor Volkenkunde, 1987.

BYRON. Grace M. Mayer, *Once upon a City: New York from 1890 to 1910,* New York, Macmillan, 1958.

CAHUN. François Leperlier, *Claude Cahun: l'écart and la métamorphose,* Paris, Jean-Michel Place, 1992.

CALLAHAN. *Harry Callahan: Photographs,* Santa Barbara, El Mochuelo Gallery, 1964.
Keith F. Davis, *Harry Callahan: New Color, Photographs 1978–1987,* Kansas City, Hallmark Cards, 1988.

CAMERON. Helmut Gernsheim, *Julia Margaret Cameron: Her Life and Photographic Work,* 2nd. ed., Millerton, Aperture, 1975.
Mike Weaver, *Julia Margaret Cameron, 1815–1879,* London, Herbert Press, 1984.

CANEVA. Piero Becchetti, *Giacomo Caneva e la scuola fotografica romana (1847–1855),* Florence, Alinari, 1989.

CAPA. Richard Whelan, *Robert Capa: A Biography,* New York, Alfred A. Knopf, 1985; London, Faber & Faber, 1985.
Robert Capa Photographs, New York, Alfred A. Knopf, 1985.
Cuadernos de guerra en España (1936–1939), Valencia, Sala Parpallo, 1987.

CAPONIGRO. Paul Caponigro, *The Wise Silence: Photographs,* Boston, New York Graphic Society and International Museum of Photography, 1985.

CARJAT. *Étienne Carjat, 1828–1906, photographe,* Paris, Musée Carnavalet, 1982.
Élizabeth Fallaize, *Étienne Carjat and "Le Boulevard", 1861–1863,* Geneva and Paris, Slatkine, 1987.

CARROLL. Helmut Gernsheim, *Lewis Carroll, Photographer,* London, Parrish, 1949; repr. New York, 1969.
Lewis Carroll photographe victorien, Paris, Chêne, F. M. Ricci, 1976.
Patrick Roegiers, *Le visage regardé ou L. C. dessinateur and photographe,* Paris, Créatis, 1982.
Karl Steinorth (ed.), *Lewis Carroll: Photographien / Lewis Carroll: Photographs,* Schaffhausen, 1991.

CARTIER-BRESSON. Henri Cartier-Bresson, *The Decisive Moment: Photography by Henri Cartier-Bresson,* New York, Simon & Schuster, 1952.
Henri Cartier-Bresson, photographe, Paris, Delpire, 1979.
Henri Cartier-Bresson: The Early Work, New York, Museum of Modern Art, 1987.
Peter Galassi, *Henri Cartier-Bresson: premières photos,* Paris, Arthaud, 1991.

CASASOLA. *Tierra y libertad: Photographs of Mexico 1900–1935 from the Casasola Archive,* Oxford, Museum of Modern Art, 1985.

CHAMBI. *Martín Chambi, 1920–1980,* Barcelona, Madrid, Lunwerg, 1990.
Martín Chambi: Photographs, 1920–1950, Washington and London, Smithsonian Institution Press, 1993.

CHARNAY. Keith F. Davis, *Désiré Charnay, Expeditionary Photographer,* Albuquerque, Univ. of New Mexico, 1981.

CHEVOJON. *Le Studio Chevojon: Une Dynastie de photographes parisiens,* Paris, Créaphis, 1994.

CITROËN. *Paul Citroën,* Bielefeld/Düsseldorf, Marzona, 1978.

CLAINE. Steven F. Joseph and Tristan Schwilden, *À l'aube de la photographie en Belgique: Guillaume Claine (1811–1869) et son cercle,* Brussels, Crédit Communal, 1991.

CLARK. Larry Clark, *Tulsa,* New York, Lustrum, 1971; repr. New York, 1983.

CLERGUE. Lucien Clergue, *Eros and Thanatos,* Boston, Little, Brown and International Museum of Photography, 1985.
Lucien Clergue: 30 ans de photographies 1954–1984, Paris, Musée d'Art Moderne, 1984.

CLIFFORD. Lee Fontanella and Gerardo F. Kurtz, *Charles Clifford: Fotógrafo de la España de Isabel II,* n.p., El Viso, 1996.

COBURN. Helmut Gernsheim and Alison Gernsheim (ed.), *Alvin Langdon Coburn, Photographer: An Autobiography,* London, Faber & Faber, 1966; repr. New York, Dover, 1978.
Mike Weaver, *Alvin Langdon Coburn, Symbolist Photographer (1882–1966),* New York, Aperture, 1986.

COPLANS. John Coplans, *Autoportraits,* Arles and Marseilles, Actes Sud and Musées de Marseilles, 1989.

CORNELIUS. William F. Stapp, *Robert Cornelius: Portraits from the Dawn of Photography,* Washington, Smithsonian Inst., 1983.

CUNNINGHAM. *Imogen! Imogen Cunningham Photographs, 1910–1973,* Seattle and London, Univ. of Washington, 1974.
Judy Dater, *Imogen Cunningham: A Portrait,* Boston, New York Graphic Society, 1979.
Imogen Cunningham: Photographs, Seattle, London, 1988.

CURTIS. Edward S. Curtis, *The North American Indian: Being a Series of Volumes Picturing and Describing the Indians of the United States and Alaska,* Seattle and Cambridge, E. S. Curtis and Cambridge Univ., 1907–1930; repr. New York 1970.
Barbara A. Davis, *Edward S. Curtis: The Life and Times of a Shadow Catcher,* San Francisco, Chronicle Books, 1985.

CUVELIER. Ulrike Gauss (ed.), *Eugène Cuvelier,* Stuttgart, Cantz Verlag, 1996.

DAGUERRE. Helmut Gernsheim and Alison Gernsheim, *L. J. M. Daguerre: The History of the Diorama and the Daguerreotype,* London, Secker & Warburg, 1956; rev. ed. New York, 1968.

DAVIDSON. Bruce Davidson, *East 100th Street,* Cambridge, Harvard Univ., 1970.

DAY. Estelle Jussim, *Slave to Beauty: The Eccentric Life and Controversial Career of F. Holland Day, Photographer, Publisher, Aesthete,* Boston, David R. Godine, 1981.
F. Holland Day: Suffering the Ideal, Santa Fe, Twin Palms Publishers, 1995.

DAYAL. Clark Worswick, *Princely India: Photographs by Raja Deen Dayal, 1884–1910,* New York, Knopf, 1980.

DE CLERCQ. Rolf Mayer (ed.), *Louis De Clercq: Voyage en Orient,* Stuttgart, Cantz, 1989.

DEMACHY. Bill Jay, *Robert Demachy, 1859–1936: Photographs and Essays,* London and New York, Academy and St. Martin's, 1974.

DE MEYER. Adolph de Meyer, *A Singular Elegance: The Photographs of Baron Adolph de Meyer,* San Francisco, Chronicle Books, 1994.
Robert Brandau (ed.), *De Meyer,* New York, Knopf, 1976.

DEPARDON. *San Clemente: photographies de Raymond Depardon,* Paris, Centre National de la Photographie, 1984.

DERIAZ. Charles-Henri Favrod, *La Famille Deriaz,* Schaffhausen, Stemmle, 1988.

DIAMOND. Sander L. Gilman (ed.), *The Face of Madness: Hugh W. Diamond and the Origin of Psychiatric Photography,* New York, Brunner / Mazel, 1976.

DIBBETS. *Jan Dibbets,* Minneapolis and New York, Walker Art Center and Rizzoli, 1987.

DISDÉRI. Elizabeth Anne McCauley, *A. A. E. Disdéri and the*

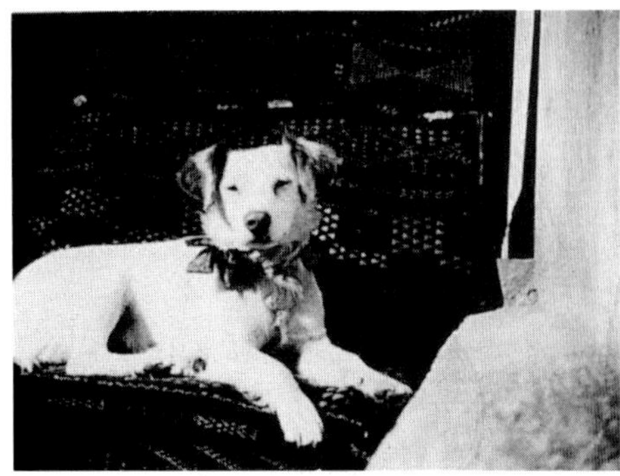

ANONYMOUS AMATEUR, circa 1950, private collection.

Carte-de-Visite Portrait Photograph, New Haven, Yale Univ., 1985.

DOISNEAU. Robert Doisneau, *Three Seconds From Eternity*, Boston, New York Graphic Society, 1980.
Un certain Robert Doisneau: la très véridique histoire d'un photographe racontée par lui-même, Paris, Chêne, 1986.

D'ORA. Monika Faber, *Madame D'Ora, Wien-Paris: Portraits aus Kunst und Gesellschaft, 1907–1957*, Vienna, Christian Brandstätter, 1983.

DRAHOS. Tom Drahos, *Métamorphoses*, Paris, Créatis, 1980.

DRTIKOL. Vladimír Birgus, *Fotograf Frantisek Drtikol*, Prague, Prostor, 1994.
Anna Fárová, *Frantisek Drtikol: Photographe Art déco*, Munich, Schirmer / Mosel, 1986.
Katerina Klaricová (ed.), *Frantisek Drtikol*, Prague, Panorama, 1989.

DUBOIS DE NEHAUT. Steven F. Joseph and Tristan Schwilden, *Le Chevalier L. P. T. Dubois de Nehaut, 1799–1872: sa vie et son œuvre*, Antwerp, Museum voor Fotografie, 1987.

DUBREUIL. *Pierre Dubreuil: Photographs, 1896–1935*, San Diego, Dubroni Press, 1987.

DU CAMP. Bodo von Dewitz and Karin Schuller-Procopovici (ed.), *Die Reise zum Nil, 1849–1850: Maxime Du Camp und Gustave Flaubert in Ägypten, Palästina und Syrien*, Göttingen, Steidl, 1997.

DUNCAN. *This Is War! A Photo-Narrative in Three Parts*, New York, Harper, 1951; repr. New York, 1967.
David Douglas Duncan, *I Protest!*, New York, New American Library, 1968.

EAKINS. Gordon Hendricks, *Thomas Eakins: His Photographic Works*, Philadelphia, Pennsylvania Academy of Fine Arts, 1969.
Susan Danly and Cheryl Leibold, *Eakins and the Photograph: Works by Thomas Eakins and His Circle in the Collection of the Pennsylvania Academy of the Fine Arts*, Washington and London, Smithsonian Institution Press, 1994.

EASTERLY. Dolores A. Kilgo, *Likeness and Landscape: Thomas M. Easterly and the Art of the Daguerreotype*, Saint Louis, Missouri Historical Society, 1994.

EDGERTON. Gus Kayafas (ed.), *Stopping Time: The Photographs of Harold Edgerton*, New York, Abrams, 1987.

EGGLESTON. *William Eggleston: Ancient and Modern*, New York, Random House, 1992.

EISENSTAEDT. Alfred Eisenstaedt, *Witness to Our Time*, New York, Viking, 1966; repr. 1980.

EMERSON. Peter Turner and Richard Wood, *P. H. Emerson, Photographer of Norfolk*, London, Gordon Fraser, 1974.
Nancy Newhall, *P. H. Emerson: The Fight for Photography as a Fine Art*, Millerton, Aperture, 1975.
Neil McWilliam and Veronica Sekules (ed.), *Life and Landscape: P. H. Emerson, Art and Photography in East Anglia, 1885–1900*, Norwich, Sainsbury Centre for Visual Arts, 1986.

ERFURTH. *Hugo Erfurth*, Cologne, Wienand, 1989.

ERWITT. *Elliott Erwitt. Photographs and Anto-Photographs*, Greenwich, New York Graphic Society, 1972.
Elliott Erwitt, *Vies de chiens*, Paris, Arthaud, 1992.

EUGENE. Ulrich Pohlmann (ed.), *Frank Eugene: The Dream of Beauty*, Munich, Nazraeli Press and Fotomuseum im Münchner Stadtmuseum, 1995.

EVANS Frederick. Frederic Beaumont Newhall, *Frederick H. Evans: Photographer of the Majesty, Light and Space of the Medieval Cathedrals of England and France*, Millerton, Aperture, 1973.

EVANS WALKER. Walker Evans, *American Photographs*, New York, Museum of Modern Art, 1938; repr. New York, 1988.
Walker Evans at Work: 745 Photographs together with Documents Selected from Letters, Memoranda, Interviews, Notes, New York, Harper & Row, 1982.
Gilles Mora and John T. Hill, *Walker Evans: The Hungry Eye*, London, Thames and Hudson, 1993.

FAURER. Edith Tonelle and John Gossage (ed.), *Louis Faurer: Photographs from Philadelphia and New York, 1937–1973*, Univ. of Maryland Art Gallery, 1981.
Louis Faurer, Paris, Centre National de la Photographie, 1992.

FEININGER. *Andreas Feininger, Photographer*, New York, Abrams, 1986.

FENOYL, DE. *Chronophotographies*, Lausanne, Pastel and Musée de l'Élysée, 1990.

FENTON. Helmut Gernsheim and Alison Gernsheim, *Roger Fenton, Photographer of the Crimean War: His Photographs and His Letters from the Crimea*, London, Secker & Warburg, 1954; repr. New York, 1973.
Roger Fenton: Photographer of the 1850s, London, South Bank Board, 1988.

FERREZ. Gilberto Ferrez, *O Rio Antigo da fotografo Marc Ferrez: Paisagems e tipos humanos do Rio de Janeiro, 1865–1918*, São Paulo, 1985.

FINSLER. Hans Finsler, *Mein Weg zur Fotografie: 30 Aufnahmen aus den 20er Jahre*, Zurich, Pendo, 1971.

FONTANA. *Franco Fontana: fotografie 1965–1987*, Turin, Umberto Allemandi, 1987.

FONTCUBERTA. Joan Fontcuberta, *Herbarium*, Göttingen, European Photography, 1985.

FRANK. *The Americans: Photographs by Robert Frank*, New York, Grove Press, 1959; reiss. New York, Pantheon, 1986.
The Lines of My Hand, Tokyo, Yugensha, 1972; New York, Lustrum Press, 1972; rev. ed. New York, 1989.
Robert Frank, *Black and White and Things*, Washington, D.C. and Zurich, National Gallery of Art and Scalo, 1994.
Sarah Greenough and Philip Brookman, *Robert Frank*, Washington and Zurich, National Gallery of Art and Scalo, 1994.

FRIEDLANDER. Lee Friedlander, *The American Monument*, New York, Eakins, 1976.
Lee Friedlander: Photographs, New York, Haywire, 1978.
Nudes, New York, Pantheon Books, 1991.

FREUND. Gisèle Freund, *Le Monde et ma caméra*, Paris, Denoël / Gonthier, 1970.

FRITH. *Egypt and the Holy Land in Historic Photographs: 77 Views by Francis Frith*, New York, Dover, 1980.

FUNKE Jaromír, *Jaromír Funke (1896–1945): Prukopník Fotografick, Avantgardy: Pioneering Avant-Garde Photography*, Brno, Grafex, 1996.

GARDNER. *Gardner's Photographic Sketch Book of the Civil War*, Washington, 1866; repr. New York, Dover, 1959.
Brooks Johnson, *An Enduring Interest: The Photographs of Alexander Gardner*, Norfolk, Chrysler Museum, 1991.
D. Mark Katz, *Witness to an Era: The Life and Photographs of Alexander Gardner: The Civil War, Lincoln and the West*, New York, Viking Press, 1991.

GENTHE. Arnold Genthe, *As I Remember: With One Hundred and Twelve Photographic Illustrations by the Author*, New York, Reynal & Hitchcock, 1936.

GHISOLAND. *Norbert Ghisoland: photographies 1910–1930*, Paris, Jacques Damase, 1977.

GIACOMELLI. Angelo Schwarz, *Mario Giacomelli: fotografie*, Turin, Priuli and Verlucca, 1980.
Mario Giacomelli, Carmel, Friends of Photography, 1983.
Mario Giacomelli, *Mario Giacomelli*, Milan and Florence, Charta, 1992.
Mario Giacomelli, Paris, Contrejour, 1993.
Karl Steinorth, *Mario Giacomelli: Fotografien, 1952–1995*, Ostfildern, Cantz, 1995.

GIBSON. Ralph Gibson, *The Somnambulist*, New York, Lustrum, 1970.
Syntax, New York, Lustrum, 1983.
Ralph Gibson, *L'Œil flottant*, Paris, Paris Musées, 1986.
Tropism, Oxford, Phaidon, 1987.

GIDAL. Ute Eskildsen, *Tim Gidal: Bilder der 30er Jahre*, Essen, Museum Folkwang, 1984.

GILPIN. Martha A. Sandweiss, *Laura Gilpin: An Enduring Grace*, Fort Worth, Amon Carter Museum, 1986.

GLOEDEN. *Taormina début de siècle: Photographies du baron de Gloeden*, Paris, Chêne, 1975.
Charles Leslie, *Wilhelm von Gloeden, 1856–1931: Eine Einführung in sein Leben und Werk*, Innsbruck, Allerheiligenpresse, 1980.
Ulrich Pohlmann, *Wilhelm von Gloeden: Sehnsucht nach Arkadien*, Berlin, Nishen, 1987.

GOHLKE. Frank Gohlke, *Measure of Emptiness: Grain Elevators in the American Landscape*, Baltimore and London, Johns Hopkins Univ. Press, 1992.

GOLDBECK. Clyde W. Burleson and E. Jessica Hickman, *The Panoramic Photography of Eugene O. Goldbeck*, Austin, Univ. of Texas, 1986.

GOSSAGE. *John Gossage: Stadt des Schwarz*, Washington, Loosestrife, 1987.

GOWIN. *Emmet Gowin: Photographs*, Boston, Toronto, and London, Philadelphia Museum of Art and Bulfinch Press, 1990.

GRIFFITHS. *Dark Odyssey: Photographs and Commentary by Philip Jones Griffiths*, New York, Aperture, 1996.

GROOVER. Susan Kismaric, *Jan Groover*, New York, Museum of Modern Art, 1987.
Jan Groover Photographs, Boston, Bulfinch, 1993.

HAAS. *Ernst Haas: Colour Retrospective, 1852–1986*, New York, Abrams, 1989.

HAJEK-HALKE. *Abstract Pictures on Film: The Technique of Making Light-Graphics*, New York, Viking, 1965.

HANFSTAENGL. Heinz Gebhardt, *Franz Hanfstaengl: Von der Lithographie zur Photographie*, Munich, C. H. Beck, 1984.

HAUSMANN. Hildegund Amanshauser and Monika Faber (ed.), *Gegen den kalten Blick der Welt: Raoul Hausmann, Fotografien, 1927–1933*, Vienna, Österreichisches Fotoarchiv im Museum Moderner Kunst, 1986.
Raoul Hausmann, Valencia, IVAM Centre Julio Gonzalez, 1994.

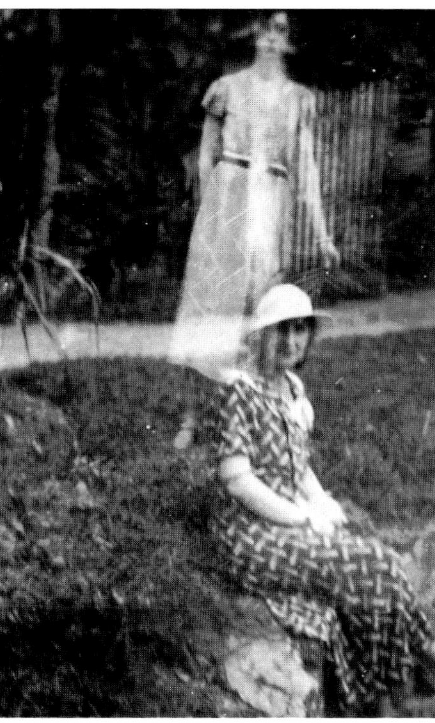

ANONYMOUS AMATEUR, ***Accidental double exposure***, 1934, private collection.

HEARTFIELD. Douglas Kahn, *John Heartfield: Art and Mass Media*, New York, Tanam, 1985.
Peter Pachnicke and Klaus Honnef, *John Heartfield*, New York, Harry Abrams, 1992.
David Evans, *John Heartfield: AIZ, Arbeiter-Illustrierte Zeitung, Volks Illustrierte, 1930–38*, New York, Kent Fine Art, 1992.

HEINECKEN. *Robert Heinecken*, Carmel, Friends of Photography, 1980.

HENRI. Diana C. du Pont, *Florence Henri: Artist-Photographer of the Avant-Garde*, San Francisco, San Francisco Museum of Modern Art, 1990.
Florence Henri, Milan, Electa, 1995.

HERSCHEL. Larry J. Schaaf, *Tracings of Light: Sir John Herschel and the Camera Lucida*, San Francisco, Friends of Photography, 1989.
Larry J. Schaaf, *Out of the Shadows: Herschel, Talbot and the Invention of Photography*, New Haven and London, Yale Univ. 1992.

HILL AND ADAMSON. Sara Stevenson, *David Octavius Hill and Robert Adamson: A Catalogue of Their Calotypes Taken between 1843 and 1847 in the Collection of the Scottish National Portrait Gallery*, Edinburgh, National Galleries of Scotland, 1981.
John Ward and Sara Stevenson, *Printed Light: The Scientific Art of William Henry Fox Talbot and David Octavius Hill with Robert Adamson*, Edinburgh, Scottish National Portrait Gallery and HMSO, 1986.
Sara Stevenson, *Hill and Adamson's The Fishermen and Women of the Firth of Forth*, Edinburgh, Scottish National Portrait Gallery, 1991.

HINE. Judith Mara Gutman, *Lewis W. Hine and the American Social Conscience*, New York, Walker & Co., 1967.
Kaplan Daile, *Lewis Hine in Europe: The Lost Photographs*, New York, Abbeville, 1988.
Karl Steinorth (ed.), *Lewis Hine: Passionate Journey. Photographs 1904–1937*, Schaffhausen, Edition Stemmle, 1997.

HOCKNEY. David Hockney, *Photographs*, London, Petersburg Press, 1982.
David Hockney, *Cameraworks: True to Life*, London, Thames and Hudson, 1984.

HÖCH. Maud Lavin, *Cut with the Kitchen Knife: The Weimar Photomontages of Hannah Höch*, New Haven and London, Yale Univ. Press, 1993.
The Photomontages of Hannah Höch, Minneapolis, Walker Art Center, 1996.

HOLLANDER. *Paul den Hollander: een keuze uit zijn foto's*, Noordbrabants, S'Hertogenbosch, 1991.

HOPPÉ. E. O. Hoppé. *Deutsche Arbeit: Bilder vom Wiederaufstieg Deutschlands: 92 Aufnahmen von E. O. Hoppé*, Berlin, Ullstein, 1930.

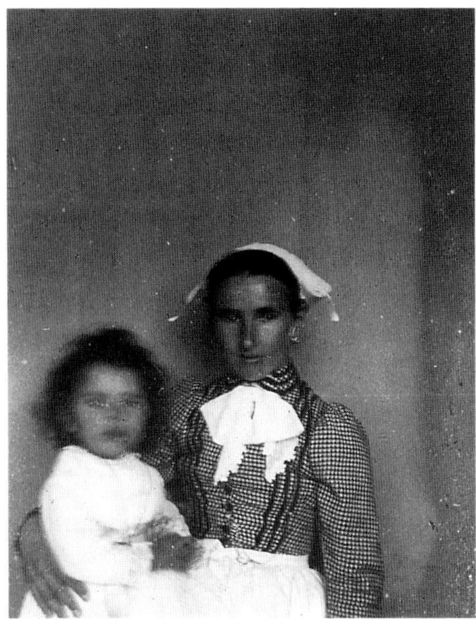

Anonymous Amateur, ***Nurse and Child,*** circa 1900, private collection.

E. O. Hoppé: Hundred Thousand Exposures: The Success of a Photographer, London and New York, Focal, 1946.

Horst. *Horst: Sixty Years of Photography*, London, Thames & Hudson and New York, Rizzoli, 1991.
Form: Horst, Altadena, Twin Palms, 1992.

Horvat. Frank Horvat, *Entre vues*, Paris, Nathan, 1990.

Hosoe. Eikoh Hosoe, *Ba-ra-kei: Ordalie par les Roses: photographies de Yukio Mishima*, Paris, Hologramme, 1986.
Eikoh Hosoe: Meta, Los Angeles, Curatorial Assistance, 1991.

Hoyningen-Huene. William E. Ewing, *Hoyningen-Huene: l'élégance des années 30*, Paris, Denoël, 1986.

Humbert de Molard. See Bacot.

Izis. *Izis: De Paris and d'ailleurs*. text by Pierre Borhan, Paris, Paris Musées, 1988.
Izis: photos 1944–1980, Paris, La Martinière, 1993.

Jackson. William Henry Jackson and Howard R. Driggs, *The Pioneer Photographer: Rocky Mountain Adventures with a Camera*, Yonkers-on-Hudson, World Book Co., 1929.
Beaumont Newhall and Diana E. Edkins, *William H. Jackson*, Dobbs Ferry, Morgan & Morgan, 1974.
Peter B. Hales, *William Henry Jackson and the Transformation of the American Landscape*, Philadelphia, Temple Univ., 1988.

Jacobi. Kelly Wise (ed.), *Lotte Jacobi*, Danbury, Addison House, 1978.

Johnston. Pete Daniel and Raymond Smock, *A Talent for Detail: The Photographs of Miss Frances Benjamin Johnston, 1889–1910*, New York, Harmony Books, 1974.

Jones. Rollin Buckman, *The Photographic Work of Calvert Richard Jones*, London, Science Museum and HMSO, 1990.

Käsebier. Barbara L. Michaels, *Gertrude Käsebier: The Photographer and Her Photographs*, New York, Harry N. Abrams, 1992.

Keita. André Magnin (ed.), *Seydou Keita*, Zurich, Berlin, New York, Scalo, 1997.

Keith. John Hannavy, *Thomas Keith's Scotland, 1852–1857*, Edinburgh, Canongate, 1981.

Kenna. *Michael Kenna: A Twenty Year Retrospective*, Tokyo, Treville, 1994.

Kertész. Nicolas Ducrot, *André Kertész: soixante ans de photographie, 1912–1972*, Paris, Chêne, 1972.
André Kertész, *Of Paris and New York*, Chicago, Art Institute, 1985.
André Kertész, *Ma France*, Paris, La Manufacture and Ministère de la Culture, 1990.

Klein. *William Klein, photographe etc.*, Paris, Centre Georges-Pompidou and Herscher, 1983.
William Klein, *Close Up*, New York, Thames & Hudson, 1990.
William Klein, *New York: 1954.55*, Manchester, Dewi Lewis, 1995.

Klett. *Revealing Territory: Photographs of the Southwest by Mark Klett*, Albuquerque, Univ. of New Mexico, 1992.

Kollar. François Kollar, *La France travaille: regard sur les années 30*, Paris, Bibliothèque Forney, 1985.
Patrick Roegiers and Dominique Baqué, *François Kollar*, Paris, Ministère de la Culture / P. Sers, 1989.

Koppitz. Jo-Ann Conklin and Monika Faber (ed.), *Rudolf Koppitz, 1884–1936*, Vienna, Verlag Christian Brandstatter, 1995.

Kotzsch. *August Kotzsch, 1836–1910: Pionier der deutschen Photographie; Pionnier de la photographie allemande; Pioneer of German Photography*, Stuttgart, Edition Cantz, 1992.

Koudelka. Josef Koudelka, *Exils: photographies*, Paris, Centre National de la Photographie, 1987.
Josef Koudelka, *Cerny trojuhelník: Podkrusnohorí, The Black Triangle: The Foothills of the Ore Mountains. Le triangle noir. La région située au pied des Monts métallifères, fotografie 1990–1994*, Prague, Magnum, 1994.

Krims. Leslie Krims, *Fictcryptokrimsographs: A Book-Work*, Buffalo, Humpy, 1975.

Krull. *Germaine Krull: photographie 1924–1936*, Arles, Musées d'Arles, 1988.
Germaine Krull: Fotografien 1922–1966, Cologne, Rheinland, 1977.

Kühn. *Heinrich Kühn: Photographien*, Salzburg and Vienna, Residenz, 1988.

Lange. Dorothea Lange and Paul Schuster Taylor, *An American Exodus: A Record of Human Erosion*, New York, Reynal & Hitchcock, 1939; repr. New Haven, 1969.
Milton Meltzer, *Dorothea Lange: A Photographer's Life*, New York, Farrar, Straus & Giroux, 1978.

Lartigue. Richard Avedon (ed.), *Diary of a Century: Jacques-Henri Lartigue*, New York, Viking, 1970; repr. Penguin, 1978.
Les Autochromes de J.-H. Lartigue, 1912–1927, Paris, Herscher, 1980.
Le Passé composé: Les 6 × 13 de J.-H. Lartigue, Paris, Centre National de la Photographie, 1984.
Jacques-Henri Lartigue: Le choix du bonheur, Paris, La Manufacture, 1992.

Laughlin. Keith F. Davis, *Clarence John Laughlin: Visionary Photographer*, Kansas City, Hallmark Cards, 1990.

Laurent. *Ciudades del XIX: La España de Laurent*, Barcelona, Fundación La Caixa, 1992.

Le Gray. Eugenia Parry Janis, *The Photography of Gustave Le Gray*, Chicago, Art Institute of Chicago and Univ. of Chicago, 1987.
G. Prévot, et al., *Une Visite au camp de Châlons sous le Second Empire: photographies de Messieurs Le Gray, Prévot ...*, Paris, Musée de l'Armée, 1996.

Lerski. Ute Eskildsen (ed.), *Metamorphosis through Light / Verwandlungen durch Licht*, Freren, Luca, 1982.

Le Secq. Eugenia Parry Janis and Josiane Sartre, *Henri Le Secq, photographe de 1850 à 1860: catalogue raisonné de la collection de la bibliothèque des Arts décoratifs*, Paris, Musée des Arts Décoratifs and Flammarion, 1986.

Levitt. *Helen Levitt*. A *Way of Seeing: Photographs of New York*, New York, Viking Press, 1965; 3rd. ed., Durham, 1989.
Sandra Phillips and Maria Morris Hambourg, *Helen Levitt*, San Francisco Museum of Art, 1991.

Lissitzky. *El Lissitzky: Experiments in Photography*, New York, Houk Friedman, 1991.

List. Günter Metken, *Herbert List: Photographs, 1930–1970*, Munich, Schirmer / Mosel, 1980.

Londe. Denis Bernard and André Gunthert, *L'instant rêvé: Albert Londe*, Nîmes, Jacqueline Chambon, 1993.

Long. Richard Long, *Mountains and Waters*, New York, George Braziller, 1993.

Lorent. *Ägypten, Alhambra, Tlemsen, Algier: Reisebilder aus den Anfängen der Photographie*, Mannheim, 1861; repr. Mainz, Philipp von Zabern, 1985.

Lotar. *Eli Lotar*, Paris, Editions du Centre Pompidou, 1993.

Lumière. Maurice Bessy and Lo Duca, *Louis Lumière, inventeur*, Paris, Prisma, 1948.
Paul Génard and André Barret, *Lumière: les Premières Photographies en couleurs*, Paris, André Barret, 1974.
Bernard Chardère and Guy Borgé, *Les Lumière*, Paris, Payot, 1985.

Lüthi. *Urs Lüthi*, Paris and Zurich, Stähli, 1978.
Urs Lüthi, Zurich, Kunsthaus Glarus, 1991.

Lyon. Danny Lyon, *The Bikeriders*, New York, Macmillan, 1967, 1968.
The Destruction of Lower Manhattan, Toronto, Macmillan, 1969.
Pictures from the New World: Photographs and Text by Danny Lyon, Millerton, Aperture, 1981.

Lyons. *Notations in Passing: Visualized by Nathan Lyons*, Cambridge, MIT, 1974.

Maar. *Dora Maar*, Fotógrafa, n.p., Centre Cultural Bancaixa, 1995.

McCullin. Don McCullin, *Is Anyone Taking Any Notice? A Book of Photographs and Comments*, Cambridge, MIT, 1973.
Images des ténèbres, Paris, Robert Laffont, 1980.
Unreasonable Behaviour: An Autobiography, London, Jonathan Cape, 1990.

MacPherson. Piero Becchetti and Carlo Pietrangeli, *Un inglese fotografo a Roma: Robert MacPherson*, Rome, Quasar, 1987.

Magritte. *Photographies de Magritte*, Paris, Contrejour, 1982.

Man. Felix H. Man, *Man with Camera: Photographs from Seven Decades*, New York, Schocken Books, 1984.

Man Ray. *Man Ray: L'immagine fotografica*, Venice, La Biennale di Venezia, 1977.
Man Ray Photographs, London, Thames and Hudson, 1982.
Merry, Forester, *Perpetual Motive: The Art of Man Ray*, New York, Abbeville Press, 1988.
Man Ray, Paris, Gallimard, 1989.

Mantz. *Werner Mantz: Architekturphotographie in Köln, 1926–1932*, Cologne, Museum Ludwig, 1982.

Marey. Michel Frizot, *E. J. Marey, 1830–1904: la photographie du mouvement*, Paris, Centre Georges-Pompidou, 1977.
Avant le cinématographe: La chronophotographie: temps, photographie et mouvement autour de E.-J. Marey, Beaune, Amis de Marey and Ministère de la Culture, 1984.
Marta Braun, *Picturing Time: The Work of Etienne-Jules Marey (1830–1904)*, Chicago and London, Univ. of Chicago Press, 1992.

Mark. Mary Ellen Mark, *Les prostituées de Bombay: Falkland Road*, Paris, Photo Filipacchi, 1981.
The Photo-Essay: Photographs by Mary Ellen Mark, Washington and London, Smithsonian Institution, 1990.

Martin. Roy Flukinger, Larry Schaaf, and Standish Meacham, *Paul Martin: Victorian Photographer*, Austin, Univ. of Texas, 1977.

Marville. *Charles Marville: Photographs of Paris at the Time of the Second Empire on Loan from the Musée Carnavalet, Paris*, New York, French Institute and Alliance Française, 1981.
Marie de Thézy, *Marville: Paris*, Paris, Hazan, 1994.

Mayne. *The Street Photographs of Roger Mayne*, London, Victoria and Albert Museum, 1986.

Maywald. *Willy Maywald: die Splitter des Spiegels: Eine illustrierte Autobiographie*, Munich, Schirmer / Mosel, 1985.

Meatyard. James Baker Hall (ed.), *Ralph Eugene Meatyard*, Millerton, Aperture, 1974.
Ralph Eugene Meatyard: An American Visionary, New York, Akron Art Museum and Rizzoli, 1991.

Meyerowitz. Joel Meyerowitz, *Cape Light: Color Photographs*, Boston, Boston Museum of Fine Arts, 1978.
Joel Meyerowitz, *Bay/Sky*, Boston, Bulfinch Press, Little, Brown and Company, 1993.

Michals. *Duane Michals: Sequences*, Garden City, Doubleday, 1970.
Duane Michals: photographies de 1958 à 1982, Paris, Musée d'Art Moderne, 1982.
Album: The Portraits of Duane Michals, 1958–1988, Pasadena, Twelvetrees, 1988.

Mili. Gjon Mili, *Photographs and Recollections*, Boston, New York Graphic Society, 1980.

Miller. Antony Penrose, *The Lives of Lee Miller*, New York, Holt, Rinehart & Winston, 1985.
Jane Livingston, *Lee Miller, Photographer*, New York, Thames & Hudson, 1989.

Misonne. Marian Schwabik and Maurice Misonne, *Léonard Misonne: ein Fotograf aus Belgien, 1870–1943: Romantische Landschaft*, Seebruck am Chiemsee, Heering, 1976.
La Couleur du temps: photographies de Léonard Misonne, Paris, Centre National de la Photographie, 1991.

Misrach. *Richard Misrach*, San Francisco, Grapestake Gallery, 1979.
Richard Misrach, *Desert Cantos*, Albuquerque, Univ. of New Mexico, 1987.

Model. *Lisette Model*, Millerton, Aperture, 1979.
Ann Thomas, *Lisette Model*, Ottawa, National Gallery of Canada, 1990.

Modotti. Mildred Constantine, *Tina Modotti: A Fragile Life*, 2nd. ed., New York, Rizzoli, 1983.
Tina Modotti, photographe et révolutionnaire, Paris, Des Femmes, 1981.

Moholy. Rolf Sachsse, *Lucia Moholy*, Düsseldorf, Marzona, 1985.

Moholy-Nagy. Andreas Haus, *Moholy-Nagy: Photographs and Photograms*, New York, Pantheon, 1980.
László Moholy-Nagy: Frühe Photographien, Berlin and Cologne, Nishen, 1989.
László Moholy-Nagy, Marseilles and Paris, Musées de Marseilles and RMN, 1991.
László Moholy-Nagy, Stuttgart, 1991.
László Moholy-Nagy: Compositions lumineuses, 1922–1943, Paris, Centre Georges-Pompidou, 1995.

Moon. Sarah Moon, *Souvenirs improbables*, Paris, Delpire, 1981.

Vrais Semblants: photographies de Sarah Moon, Paris, Delpire, 1991.

MONSERRAT. Toni Catany, *Tomas Monserrat, retratista d'un poble*, Palma, 1983.

MORRIS. *Wright Morris: Origin of a Species*, San Francisco Museum of Modern Art, 1992.

MULAS. *Ugo Mulas: Fotógrafo, 1928–1973*, Geneva, Musée Rath, 1984.
Germano Celant, *Ugo Mulas*, New York, Rizzoli, 1990.

MUNCH. Arne Eggum, *Munch and Photography*, Newhaven and London, Yale University, 1989.

MUNKACSI. *Martin Munkacsi*, Bielefeld and Düsseldorf, Marzona, 1980.
Martin Munkacsi: Biographical Profile by Susan Morgan, New York, Aperture, 1992.

MUYBRIDGE. Gordon Hendricks, *Eadweard Muybridge: The Father of the Motion Picture*, New York, Grossman, 1975.
Robert Bartlett Haas, *Muybridge: Man in Motion*, Berkeley, Univ. of California, 1976.
Muybridge's Complete Human and Animal Locomotion: All 781 Plates from the 1877 Animal Locomotion by Eadweard Muybridge, New York, Dover Publications, 1979.
Eadweard Muybridge in Guatemala, 1875: The Photographer as Social Recorder, Berkeley, Los Angeles and London, Univ. of California Press, 1986.

NADAR. Nigel Gosling, *Nadar*, New York, Alfred A. Knopf, 1976.
Philippe Néagu and Jean-Jacques Poulet-Allamagny, *Nadar*, vol. 1, *Photographies*, vol. 2, *Dessins et écrits*, Paris, A. Hubschmid, 1979.
Maria Morris Hambourg, Françoise Heilbrun, and Paul Néagu, *Nadar*, New York, Metropolitan Museum of Art, 1995.

NASH. Paul Nash, *Fertile Image*, London, Faber & Faber, 1951; 2nd. ed., London, 1975.
NAYA. Italo Zanier, *Venice, the Naya Collection*, Venice, O. Böhm, 1981.

NÈGRE. James Borcoman, *Charles Nègre, 1820–1880*, Ottawa, National Gallery of Canada, 1976.
Françoise Heilbrun, *Charles Nègre, 1820–1880: Das photographische Werk*, Munich, Schirmer/Mosel, 1988.

NEWTON. Helmut Newton, *White Women*, Stonehill, 1976.
Sleepless Nights, New York, Congreve Publishing Co., 1978.

NIÉPCE. Paul Jay, *Niépce: genèse d'une invention*, Chalon-sur-Saône, Musée Nicéphore Niépce, 1988.

NORMAND. *Alfred-Nicolas Normand: photographies d'Italie, de Grèce et de Constantinople, calotypes 1851–1852*, Bergamo, Grafica Gutenberg, 1978.

NOTMAN. Stanley G. Triggs, *William Notman: The Stamp of a Studio*, Toronto, Art Gallery of Ontario and Coach House Press, 1985.
Roger Hall, Gordon Dodds, and Stanley Triggs, *The World of William Notman*, Boston, David R. Godine, 1993.

O'SULLIVAN. Joel Snyder, *American Frontiers: The Photographs of Timothy H. O'Sullivan, 1867–1874*, Millerton, Aperture, 1981.
Rick Dingus, *The Photographic Artifacts of Timothy O'Sullivan*, Albuquerque, Univ. of New Mexico, 1982.

OUTERBRIDGE. Elaine Dines (ed.), *Paul Outerbridge: A Singular Aesthetic: Photographs and Drawings, 1921–1941: A Catalogue Raisonné*, Santa Barbara, Arabesque, 1981.
Jeannine Fiedler, *Paul Outerbridge Jr: photographies*, Munich, Schirmer / Mosel, 1993.

PARR. Martin Parr, *The Cost of Living*, Manchester, Cornerhouse, 1989.
Martin Parr, *Home and Abroad*, London, Jonathan Cape, 1993.

PENN. John Szarkowski, *Irving Penn*, New York, Museum of Modern Art, 1984.
Irving Penn, *En passant*, Paris, Nathan, 1992.
Mary Foresta and William F. Stapp, *Irving Penn Master Images: The Collections of the National Museum of American Art and the National Portrait Gallery*. Washington, Smithsonian Institution, 1990.

PERESS. Gilles Peress, *Telex Iran*, Millerton, Aperture, 1983.

PFAHL. John Pfahl, *Arcadia revisited: Niagara River and Falls from Lake Erie to Lake Ontario*, Albuquerque, University of New Mexico, 1991.

PLOSSU. Bernard Plossu, *Les Paysages intermédiaires*, Paris, Contrejour, 1988.

PLÜSCHOW Guglielmo, Peter Weiermair, *Guglielmo Plüschow*, Cologne, Benedikt Taschen, 1994.

PONTING. H. J. P. Arnold, *Photographer of the World: The Biography of Herbert Ponting*, London, Hutchinson, 1969.

PRIMOLI. Lamberto Vitali, *Un fotografo fin de siècle: Il conte Primoli*, 2nd. ed., Turin, Einaudi, 1981.
Roberta Innamorati and Enrico Valeriani, *Giuseppe Primoli: Fotografo europeo*, Rome, Quasar, 1982.

RAINER. *Arnulf Rainer: Self-Portraits*, Vienne, Ulysses, 1986.

RAUSCHENBERG. *Robert Rauschenberg: Photographs*, New York, Pantheon, 1981.

RAY-JONES. Tony Ray-Jones, *A Day Off*, Boston, New York Graphic Society, 1974.

REJLANDER. Edgar Yoxall Jones, *Father of Art Photography: O. G. Rejlander, 1813–1875*, Newton Abbot, David & Charles, 1973.

RENÉ-JACQUES. *René-Jacques*, Paris, La Manufacture, 1991.

RENGER-PATZSCH. *Albert Renger-Patzsch: Ruhrgebiet-Landschaften 1927–1935*, Cologne, DuMont, 1982.
Ann Wilde (ed.), *Albert Renger-Patzsch: Meisterwerke*, Munich, 1997.

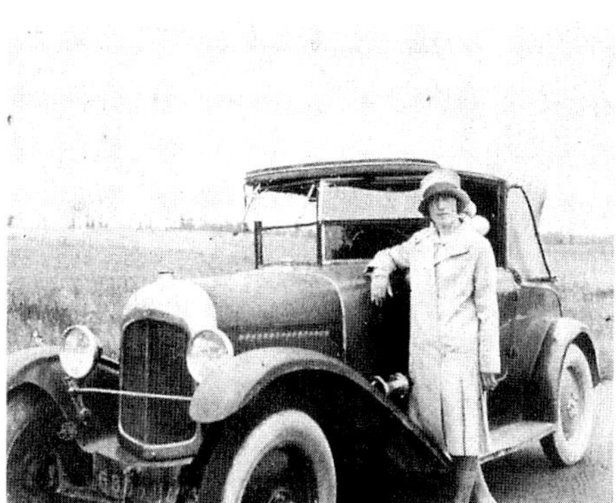

ANONYMOUS AMATEUR, 1920s, private collection.

REUTLINGER. Jean-Pierre Bourgeron, *Les Reutlinger, photographes à Paris, 1850–1937*, Paris, J.-P. Bourgeron, 1979.

RIBOUD. *Marc Riboud: photos choisies, 1953–1985*, Paris, Musée d'Art Moderne, 1985.

RIIS. Alexander Alland, *Jacob A. Riis: Photographer and Citizen*, New York, Aperture, 1974.

RIVIÈRE. *Henri Rivière: Graveur and photographe*, Paris, RMN, 1988.

ROBERTSON. Bahattin Öztuncay, *James Robertson, Pioneer of Photography in the Ottoman Empire*, Istanbul, Eren, 1992.

ROBINSON. Margaret F. Harker, *Henry Peach Robinson: Master of Photographic Art, 1830–1901*, Oxford and New York, Basil Blackwell, 1988.

ROCHE. Denis Roche, *Ellipse and Laps*, Paris, Maeght, 1991.

RODCHENKO. Hubertus Gassner and Alexander Lavrentjev, *Rodcenko Fotografien*, Munich, Schirmer / Mosel, 1982.
Selim O. Khan-Magomedov, *Rodchenko: The complete Work*, Cambridge, MIT, 1986.
Alexander Lavrentiev, *Alexander Rodchenko: Photography, 1924–1954*, Edison, Knickerbocker Press, 1996.

RODGER. *Humanity and Inhumanity: The Photographic Journey of George Rodger*, London, Phaidon, 1994.

ROH. Franz Roh, *Teórico y fotógrafo*, Valencia, IVAM Institut Valenci... d'Art Modern, 1997.

RONIS. *Willy Ronis par Willy Ronis: Donation Willy Ronis*, Paris, Ministère de la Culture, 1985.
Ronis, *Mon Paris*, Paris, Denoël, 1985.

ROSENBLUM. *Walter Rosenblum*, Dresden, Verlag der Kunst, 1990.

ROUSSELET. René Pierre-Lin, *L'Inde: Photographies de Louis Rousselet, 1865–1868*, Bordeaux, Musée Goupil, 1992.

RUSSELL. *Russell's Civil War Photographs: 116 Historic Prints by Andrew J. Russell*, New York, Dover, 1982.

SALGADO. Sebastião Salgado, *Workers: An Archaeology of the Industrial Age*, New York, Aperture, 1993.

SALOMON. *Erich Salomon: Portrait of an Age*, New York, Macmillan, 1967.

SALZMANN. *Félix de Saulcy et la Terre sainte*, Paris, RMN, 1982.

SANDER. August Sander, *Men Without a Mask: Faces of Germany 1910–1938*, Greenwich, New York Graphic Soc., 1973.
Wolfgang Kemp, *August Sander: Rheinlandschaften: Photographien 1929–1946*, Munich, 1975.
August Sander: Photographien 1902–1939, Berlin, 1995.

SARONY. Ben L. Bassham, *The Theatrical Photographs of Napoleon Sarony*, Kent, Kent State Univ., 1978.
SAUDEK. Pierre Borhan, *Jan Saudek: 200 photographies, 1953–1986*, Paris Musées, 1987.

SAVAGE. Bradley W. Richards, *The Savage View: Charles Savage, Pioneer Mormon Photographer*, Nevada City, Carl Mautz, 1995.

SCHUH. *Gotthard Schuh: Frühe Photographien, 1929–1939*, Zurich, Verlag der Arche, 1967.

SCIANNA. *Ferdinando Scianna: le forme del caos*, Udine, Art&, 1989.

SHAHN. Davis Pratt (ed.), *The Photographic Eye of Ben Shahn*, Cambridge and London, Harvard Univ., 1975.

SHEELER. Theodore E. Stebbins Jr. and Norman Keyes Jr., *Charles Sheeler: The Photographs*, Boston, Little, Brown & Co., 1987.

SHERMAN. *Cindy Sherman*, Stuttgart, Cantz, 1991.

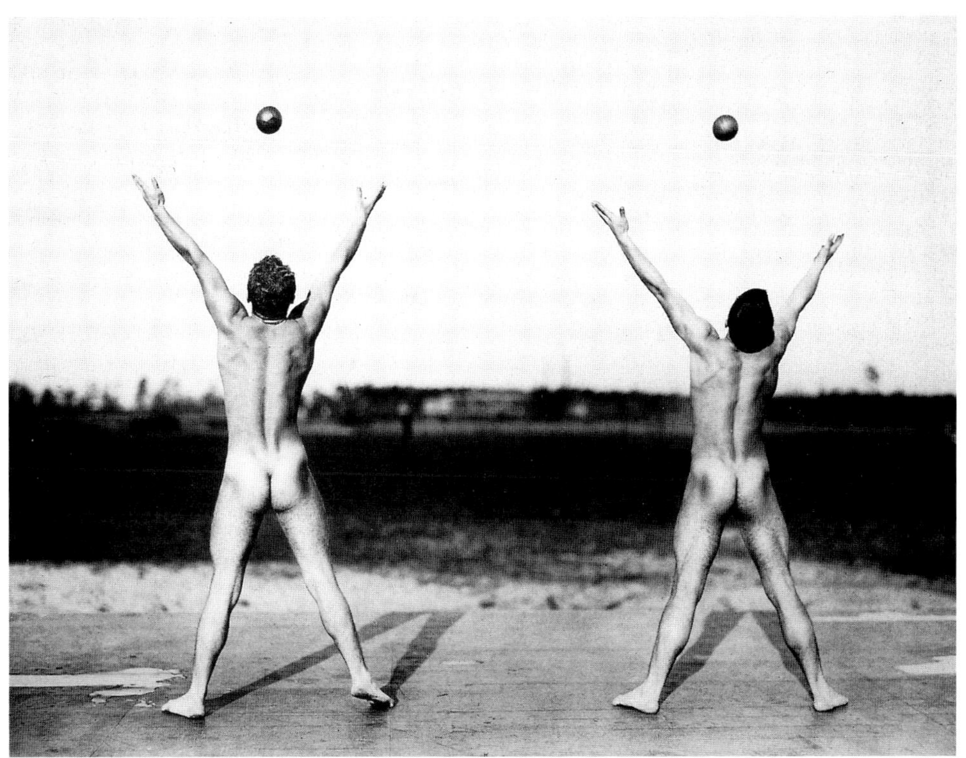

GERHARD RIEBICKE, ***Naturist Exercises***, 1924–1925, private collection.

Rosalind Krauss and Norman Bryson, *Cindy Sherman, 1975–1993*, New York, Rizzoli, 1993.
Zdenek Felix and Martin Schwander (ed.), *Cindy Sherman: Photographic Work, 1975–1995*, Munich and London, Schirmer Art Books, 1995.

SIEFF. Jeanloup Sieff, *Photographies 1953–1986*, Paris, Paris Musées, 1986.

SILVY. Mark Haworth-Booth, *Camille Silvy: River Scene in France*, J. Paul Getty Museum, Malibu, 1992.

SISKIND. *Aaron Siskind, Photographer*, Rochester, George Eastman House, 1965.
Harlem Document: Photographs, 1932–1940, Aaron Siskind, Providence, Matrix Publications, 1981.

SMITH. W. Eugene and Aileen M. Smith, *Minamata*, New York, Holt, Rinehart & Winston, 1975.
Jim Hughes, *W. Eugene Smith: Shadow and Substance: The Life and Work of an American Photographer*, New York, McGraw-Hill, 1989.

SOMMER **Frederick.** John Weiss (ed.), *Venus, Jupiter and Mars: The Photographs of Frederick Sommer*, Wilmington, Delaware Art Museum, 1980.
Frederick Sommer, *The Box*, Munich, Nazraeli Press, 1994.

SOMMER **Giorgio.** Daniela Palazzoli, *Giorgio Sommer, fotografo a Napoli*, Milan, Electa, 1981.
Marina Miraglia *et al.*, *Giorgio Sommer in Italien: Fotografien, 1857–1888*, Heidelberg, Braus, 1992.

SOUGEZ. *Emmanuel Sougez: Photographien, Photographs 1928–1953*, Frankfurt, Bochum, 1982.
Emmanuel Sougez: l'éminence grise, Créaphis and Ministère de la Culture, 1993.

SOUTHWORTH AND HAWES. Robert A. Sobieszek and Odette M. Appel, *The Spirit of Fact: The Daguerreotypes of Southworth and Hawes, 1843–1862*, Boston and Rochester, D. R. Godine and George Eastman House, 1976.

STANKOVSKI. *Anton Stankovski: Das Gesamtwerk 1925–1982*, Stuttgart, Gerd Hatje, 1982.

STEICHEN. Edward Steichen, *A Life in Photography*, Garden City, Doubleday & Co., 1963.
Dennis Longwell, *Steichen: The Master Prints, 1895–1914: The Symbolist Period*, New York, Museum of Modern Art, 1978.

STEINER. *A Point of View*, Middletown, Conn., Wesleyan Univ., 1978.
Ralph and Caroline Steiner (ed.), *In Spite of Everything, Yes*, Albuquerque, Univ. of New Mexico, 1986.

STEINERT. *Otto Steinert and His Students: Photography and Education, 1948 to 1978*, Essen, Museum Folkwang, 1990.

STIEGLITZ. Sarah Greenough and Juan Hamilton, *Alfred Stieglitz: Photographs and Writings*, Washington and New York, National Gallery of Art and Callaway, 1983.
Christian A. Peterson, *Alfred Stieglitz's Camera Notes*, New York and London, W. W. Norton & Co., Ltd., 1993.

STILLMAN. *Poetic Localities: Photographs of Adirondacks, Cambridge, Crete, Italy, Athens by William J. Stillman*, New York, Aperture, 1988.

STONE **Sir Benjamin.** Bill Jay, *Customs and Faces: Photographs by Sir Benjamin Stone, 1838–1914*, New York and London, St. Martin's Press and Academy Editions, 1972.

STONE **Sasha.** *Sasha Stone: Fotografien 1925–1939*, Berlin, Nishen, 1990.

STRAND. Paul Strand, *Time in New England*, New York, Oxford Univ., 1950; repr. 1980.
Claude Roy and Paul Strand, *La France au profil*, Lausanne, Guilde du Livre and Clairefontaine, 1952.
Paul Strand, *Un paese*, Turin, Einaudi, 1955.
Sarah Greenough, *Paul Strand: An American Vision*, Washington, National Gallery of Art and Aperture Foundation, 1990.
Paul Strand, *Un paese: Portrait of an Italian Village*, New York, Aperture, 1996.

STRÜWE. *Carl Strüwe*, Düsseldorf, Marzona, 1982.

STRUSS. Barbara McCandless, Bonnie Yochelson, and Richard Koszarski, *New York to Hollywood: The Photography of Karl Struss*, Fort Worth, Albuquerque, Amon Carter Museum, Univ. of New Mexico Press, 1995.

SUDEK. Sonja Bullaty, *Sudek*, New York, Clarkson N. Potter, 1978.
Anná Farová, *Josef Sudek*, Prague, Torst, 1995.
Manfred Heiting (ed.), *The Pigment Prints, 1947–1954*, Los Angeles, Cinubia, 1994.

SUTCLIFFE. Michael Hiley, *Frank Sutcliffe: Photographer of Whitby*, London, Gordon Fraser, 1974.

TABARD. *Maurice Tabard*, Paris, Contrejour, 1987.

TAHARA. *Keiichi Tahara: exposition*, Paris, Espace Photographique, 1991.

TALBOT. H. J. P. Arnold, *William Henry Fox Talbot: Pioneer of Photography and Man of Science*, London, Hutchinson Benham, 1977.
Gail Buckland, *Fox Talbot and the Invention of Photography*, London, Scolar Press, 1980.
Hubertus von Amelunxen, *Die aufgehobene Zeit: Die Erfindung der Photographie durch William Henry Fox Talbot*, Berlin, Nishen, 1988.
W. H. Fox Talbot: The Pencil of Nature, New York, H. P. Kraus Jr., 1989.

TEIGE. *Karel Teige: Surrealistické koláze: Surrealist Collages, 1935–1951*. From the collections of the Museum of National Literature in Prague, Prague: Vydala Stredoevropska galerie a nakladatelstvi, 1994.

TEYNARD. *Félix Teynard: Calotypes of Egypt*, New York, Kraus, Hershkowitz and Weston, 1992.

THOMSON. John Thomson, *Street-life in London: Eine Fotoreportage aus dem Jahre 1876*, Dortmund, Hartenberg, 1981.
Stephen White, *John Thomson: A Window to the Orient*, New York, Thames & Hudson, 1985.
Richard Ovenden, *John Thomson (1837–1921), Photographer*, Edinburgh, National Library of Scotland, 1997.

TOMATSU. *Ruinous Gardens, Photographed by Shomei Tomatsu*, Tokyo, Parco, 1987.

TRIPE. Janet Dewan and Maia-Mari Sutnik, *Linnaeus Tripe: Photographer of British India, 1854–1870*, Toronto, Art Gallery of Ontaria, 1986.

TRIVIER. *Marc Trivier photographies*, Denain and Lausanne, Centre Régional de la Photographie Nord-Pas-de-Calais and Musée de l'Élysée, 1988.

UELSMANN. James L. Enyeart, *Jerry N. Uelsmann: Twenty-five Years: A Retrospective*, Boston, Little, Brown, 1982.

UMBO. *Umbo: Photographien 1925–1933*, Hanover, Die Photogalerie, 1979.

UZZLE. Burk Uzzle, *All American*, St. David's, 1984.

VAN DER ELSKEN. Ed van der Elsken, *Once upon a Time*, Amsterdam, Fragment, 1991.

VAN DER ZEE. *The Harlem Book of the Dead: James Van Der Zee, Owen Dodson, Camille Billops*, Dobbs Ferry, Morgan & Morgan, 1978.
Once Upon a Time, Amsterdam, Fragment, 1991.

VERGER. Jean Loup Pivin and Pascal Martin Saint Léon (ed.), *Pierre Verger, Le Messager, The Go-Between: Photographies, 1932–1962*, Paris, Editions Revue Noire, 1993.

WALL. Jeff Wall, *Transparencies*, Munich, Schirmer / Mosel, 1986.

WARHOL. *Andy Warhol Photographs*, New York, Robert Miller Gallery, s.d.
Andy Warhol Photobooth Pictures, New York, Robert Miller Gallery, 1989.
Andy Grundberg, *Andy Warhol Polaroids, 1970–1986*, New York, Robert Miller Gallery, 1992.

WATKINS. James Alinder (ed.), *Carleton E. Watkins: Photographs of the Columbia River and Oregon*, Carmel, Friends of Photography, 1979.
Peter E. Palmquist, *Carleton E. Watkins: Photographer of the American West*, Albuquerque, Univ. of New Mexico Press, 1983.
Carleton E. Watkins: Photographs, 1861–1874, San Francisco, Fraenkel Gallery and Bedford Arts, 1989.

WEEGEE. Louis Stettner (ed.), *Weegee*, New York, Alfred A. Knopf, 1977.
Naked City, New York, Essential, 1945; repr. New York, 1985.

WEGMAN. *Man's Best Friend: Photographs and Drawings by William Wegman*: New York, Abrams, 1982.

WESTON. Nancy Newhall (ed.), *The Daybooks of Edward Weston*, vol. 1, *Mexico*, vol. 2, *California*, Rochester and New York, George Eastman House and Horizon Press, 1961–1966; 2nd. ed., 1990.
Ben Maddow, *Edward Weston, Fifty Years: The Definitive Volume of His Photographic Work*, Millerton, Aperture, 1973.
Charis Wilson Weston and Edward Weston, *California and the West*, New York, Duell, Sloan & Pearce, 1940; repr. Millerton, 1978.
Theodore E. Stebbins, *Weston's Westons: Portraits and Nudes*, Boston, Museum of Fine Arts, 1989.
Amy Conger, *Edward Weston: Photographs from the Collection of the Center for Creative Photograph*, Tucson, Center for Creative Photography, 1992.

WHIPPLE AND BLACK. Sally Pierce, *Whipple and Black: Commercial Photographers in Boston*, Boston, Boston Athenaeum, 1987.

WHITE Clarence. *Clarence H. White: The Reverence for Beauty*, Athens, Ohio Univ. Gallery of Fine Art, 1986.

WHITE Minor. Minor White, *Mirrors, Messages, Manifestations*, New York, Aperture, 1969; 2nd. ed., 1982.
Peter C. Bunnell, *Minor White: The Eye That Shapes*, Princeton, Princeton Univ. Art Museum, 1989.

WILSON. Roger Taylor, *George Washington Wilson: Artist and Photographer, 1823–1893*, Aberdeen, Aberdeen Univ., 1981.

WINOGRAND. Gary Winogrand, *Women Are Beautiful*, New York, Farrar, Straus & Giroux, 1975.
Public Relations, New York, Museum of Modern Art, 1977.

WINTER. *Charles Winter, photographe: un pionnier strasbourgeois, 1821–1904*, Strasbourg, Musées de Strasbourg, 1985.

WITKIN. Joel-Peter Witkin, *Gods of Earth and Heaven*, Altadena, Twelvetrees, 1989.
Joel-Peter Witkin, Paris, Centre National de la Photographie, 1989.

WOLS. László Glozer, *Wols photographe*, Paris, Centre Georges-Pompidou, 1980.

WOODBURY **and** PAGE. Steven Wachlin, *Woodbury and Page: Photographers Java*, Leiden, KITLV Press, 1994.

WORTLEY. Katherine DiGiulio, *Natural Variations: Photographs by Colonel Stuart Wortley*, San Marino, Huntington Library, 1994.

ZIELKE. *Willy Zielke, photographies, 1923–1937*, Arles, Rencontres Internationales de la Photographie, 1982.

ZILLE. Winfried Ranke, *Heinrich Zille: Photographien Berlin, 1890–1910*, Munich, Schirmer / Mosel, 1985.

ZOLA. François-Émile Zola and Massin, *Zola, photographe: 480 documents*, Paris, Denoël, 1979.

ZWART. Kees Bros, *Piet Zwart*, 1885–1977, Amsterdam, Van Gennep, 1982.

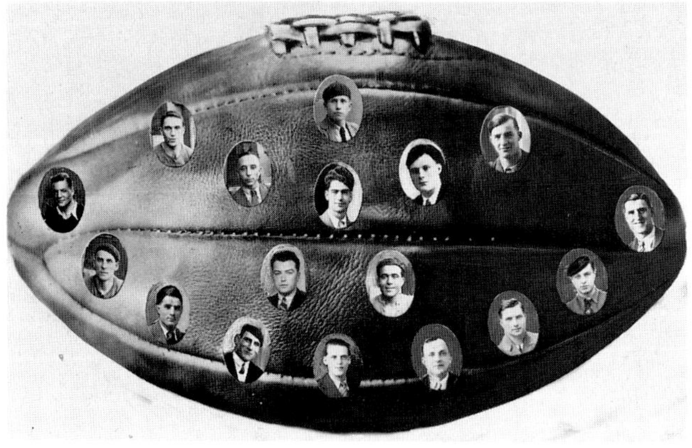

Burgundy team (rugby),
press photomontage,
1935,
private collection

INDEX

Numbers in ***bold italic*** refer to illustrations.

N

O

P

Q

R

S

T

U

V

W

Y

Z

CONTRIBUTORS

Pierre Albert
Emeritus Professor at the Panthéon-Assas University and former director of the Institut Français de Presse there. Author of *Histoire générale de la presse française*, vol. 3, *1870–1914*.

Stuart Alexander
Author of *Robert Frank: A Bibliography, Filmography and Exhibitions Chronology, 1946–1985*, 1986. Curator of exhibitions on photography.

Hubertus von Amelunxen
Director of the Interdisciplinary Forum, Muthesius Hochschüle für Kunst und Gestaltung in Kiel. Curator of international exhibitions. Author of *Die Aufgehobene Zeit: die Erfindung der Photographie durch W. H. Fox Talbot*, Berlin, Nishen, 1988 and *Allegorie und Photographie: Das Vermächtnis der Moderne*, 1997.

Sylvie Aubenas
Curator at the Bibliothèque Nationale in Paris, responsible for the nineteenth-century collections. Author of a thesis on Alphonse Poitevin. Curator of exhibitions including *Le photographe et son modèle: l'art du nu au XIXe siècle*, 1997.

Anne Cartier-Bresson
Conservator of the heritage of the City of Paris, responsible for the photographic restoration workshop of the city of Paris. Author of *Les papiers salés: altération et restauration des premières photographies sur papier*, Paris, Paris Audiovisuel, 1985.

Peter Bunnell
Professor of the history of photography and history of modern art at Princeton University. Author of *Minor White: Mirrors, Messages, Manifestations*, New York, Aperture, 1969, *C. H. White: The Reverence for Beauty*, Athens, Ohio, 1986, *A Photographic Vision: Pictorial Photography, 1889–1923*, Salt Lake City, Peregrine Smith, 1980, *Minor White: The Eye that Shapes*, New York, Museum of Modern Art, 1989, *Degrees of Guidance*, New York, Cambridge University Press, and *Aaron Siskind: Photographs 1944-1963*, New York, Glenn Horowitz, 1997.

Françoise Ducros
Inspector for Artistic Creation at the French Ministry of Culture. Lecturer in history of twentieth-century photography at Université Paris IV. Author of *Gustav Klimt*, Paris, Hazan, and articles on photography and contemporary art.

Gilles Feyel
Lecturer at the Panthéon-Assas University in Paris and lecturer in the history of media at the Institut Français de Presse; articles on magazines from the nineteenth century onwards.

Jean-Claude Gautrand
Journalist and photographer. Author of *L'assassinat de Baltard*, Paris, 1972, *Paris des photographes* (vol. 1, Paris, Contrejour, 1989, vol. 2, Paris, Marval, 1996), *Visions du Sport*, 1989, and *Bercy: la dernière balade*, Paris, Marval, 1993; co-author of *Hippolyte Bayard: Naissance de l'image photographique*, Amiens, 1987.

Thomas Michael Gunther
Lecturer at the Institut d'Etudes Politiques de Paris. Author of *François Tuefferd*, Paris, 1993, and *Images de la Libération de Paris*, Paris Musées, 1994; co-author of *Pierre Jahan; André Vigneau*, Bibliothèque Historique de la Ville de Paris, 1986, Alliance-Photo, 1988, and *50 ans de photographie de presse*, 1990.

Anne Hammond
Co-editor of *History of Photography*. Series editor of *World Photographers Reference Series*, ABC-Clio; author of *Frederick H. Evans: Selected Texts and Bibliography*, Oxford, Clio Press, 1992.

Andreas Haus
Author of *Raoul Hausmann: Kamerafotografien*, Munich, Schirmer/Mosel, 1979 and *Moholy-Nagy: Fotos und Fotogramme*, Munich, Schirmer/Mosel, 1978, Pantheon / Thames & Hudson, 1980; co-author of *Fotografie am Bauhaus*, (J. Fiedler, ed.), Berlin, Nishen, 1989; *Das neue Sehen*, (R. K. Wick, ed.), Munich, Klinkhardt und Biermann, 1991.

Françoise Heilbrun
Head Curator at the Musée d'Orsay, Paris, responsible for the photographic collections. Author of *Charles Nègre*, Munich, Schirmer / Mosel, 1984; co-author of *L'Invention d'un regard*, Paris, Réunion des Musées Nationaux, 1989 and *Nadar: Les années creatrices*, Paris, Réunion des Musées Nationaux, 1994.

Ian Jeffrey
Writer and historian, author of *The British Landscape 1920–1950*, London, Thames & Hudson, 1984. Co-author of *Cityscape, 1910–1939*, Arts Council of Great-Britain, 1978, *Photography: A Concise History*, London, Thames & Hudson, 1981, *The Photography Book*, Phaidon, 1997, and *Timeframes*, Ivy Press, 1998.

Thilo Koenig
Lecturer on history of photography at the Hochschüle fur Gestaltung und Kunst, Zürich, and freelance writer. Publications on photography. Curator of exhibitions on the Steinert School (Museum Folkwang, Essen, 1990) and on photography at the Hochschule für Gestaltung Ulm, HfG-Archiv, Ulm, 1991.

Yves Michaud
Professor of Philosophy at Paris I University. Former director of the École Nationale Supérieure des Beaux-Arts in Paris. Author of *Hume et la fin de la philosophie*, Paris, 1983, *L'artiste et les commissaires*, Nîmes, Jacqueline Chambon, 1989, *Enseigner l'art*, 1993, *Les marges de la vision*, 1995, and *La crise de l'art contemporain*, Paris, PUF, 1997.

Chihiro Minato
Professor in history of art and photography at Tama Art University. Author of *La théorie de la masse: Sur la photographie au XXᵉ siècle*, Tokyo, Libro-Port, 1990, and *L'image: de la lumière à la mémoire*, Tokyo, NHK Books, 1998.

Molly Nesbit
Professor of history of modern art at Vassar College. Author of *E. Atget: Intérieurs parisiens*, Musée Carnavalet, 1982, and *Atget's Seven Albums*, Yale University Press, 1992.

Elvire Perego
Researcher, picture researcher, and historian of photography. Author of studies on *Delmaet and Durandelle* and on photography exhibitions in the nineteenth century. Staff member of the Museo di Storia della Fotografia Fratelli Alinari, Florence.

John Pultz
Author of *Harry Callahan: Early Street Photography 1943–1945*, Tucson, Center for Creative Photography, 1990, and *Photography and the Body*, Weidenfeld and Nicolson, London, 1995; co-author of *Cubism and American Photography 1910–1930*, Williamstown, 1981, and *A Personal View*, New York, 1985.

Shelley Rice
Professor of history of art and photography at New York University and School of the Visual Arts. Author of *Parisian Views*, MIT Press, 1997; co-author of *Paris et le Daguerréotype*, Musée Carnavalet, 1989.

Pierre-Marc Richard
Historian of photography, expert on old photography and editor (index of *La Lumière*, 1989, *Bulletin de la Société Française de Photographie*, 1990); author of *Sur les traces de Paul Emile Miot, 1863–1871*, galerie Michèle Chomette, 1995.

Fred Ritchin
Professor of photography and communications at New York University. Author of *In Our Own Image: The Coming Revolution in Photography*, Aperture, 1990; co-author of *In Our Own Time: The World as seen by Magnum Photographers*, W. W. Norton, 1990, *An Uncertain Grace: The Photographs of Sebastião Salgado*, W. W. Norton, 1990, and *Mexico Through Foreign Eyes: Photographs 1850-1990*, W. W. Norton, 1993.

Jean Sagne
Author of *Delacroix et la photographie*, Paris, Herscher, 1982, and *L'atelier du photographe*, Paris, Presses de la Renaissance, 1984.

Timm Starl
Editor of *Fotogeschichte*. Author of *Knipser: Die Bildgeschichte der privaten Fotographie in Deutschland und Österreich, von 1880 bis 1980*, Münchner Stadtmuseum, 1995; co-author of *Geschichte der Photographie in Österreich*, Bad Ischl, 1983.

Pierre Vaisse
Professor of history of contemporary art at the University of Geneva. Author of a study on Helmar Lerski (*Photographies*, no. 8).

Mike Weaver
Co-editor of *History of Photography*. Author of *Julia Margaret Cameron, 1815–1879*, London, Herbert Press, 1984, *A. L. Coburn: Symbolist Photographer*, Aperture, 1986, *The Photographic Art*, London, Herbert Press, 1986, *Henry Fox-Talbot: Selected Texts and Bibliography*, Oxford, Clio-Press, 1992. Editor of *The Art of Photography, 1839–1989*, London, Royal Academy of Arts, 1989.

Colin Westerbeck
Associate curator of photography at the Art Institute in Chicago. Co-author of *Bystander: A History of Street Photography*, Bulfinch, 1994. Editor and co-author of *Irving Penn: A Career in Photography*, Bulfinch and Schirmer / Mosel, 1997.

The bibliography was compiled by **Fred** and **Elizabeth Pajerski**, specialist dealers in books on photography, New York.

The Editor

Michel Frizot
State researcher at the CNRS (Centre de Recherche sur les Arts et le Language, Ecole des Hautes Etudes en Sciences Sociales, Paris), professor of history of photography at the Ecole du Louvre, Paris. Author of numerous articles on photography from its origins to the present. Curator of expositions and catalogs for the Centre National de la Photographie (1982–1990): *Identitées, Le temps d'un mouvement*, collection Photo Poche; author of *E.J. Marey, La photographie du mouvement*, Centre Georges-Pompidou, 1977; *La chronophotographie*, Musée de Beaune, 1984; *Le passé composé, les 6 x 13 de Jacques-Henri Lartigue*, Centre National de la Photographie, 1984; *Histoire de Voir*, Centre National de la Photographie, 1989; *Dieter Appelt*, 1992; co-author of *Hippolyte Bayard, naissance de l'image photographique*, Amiens, 1987; *André Kertész, Ma France*, Paris, La Manufacture, 1990; *Photographie/Sculpture*, 1991.

PHOTOGRAPHIC CREDITS

Abbreviations: t = top, b = bottom, r = right, l = left.

8, 9, 11t, 13t, 19, 32, 56bl, 72b, 77t, 77b, 101b, 105b, 109t, 110, 111, 114, 115, 117, 120, 125, 135t, 137, 138t, 145, 147, 148, 154t, 157b, 160b, 161, 163, 164b, 170bl, 176b, 179t, 180t, 181, 182t, 200, 202t, 208, 228, 234b, 236t, 238t, 239br, 241b, 258, 260b, 265t, 271, 272, 273, 277t, 277b, 278b, 310, 334, 335, 336b, 362, 363, 364, 369, 376t, 377, 381, 384, 385, 329tl, 457, 504bl, 504tr, 679 to 685, 746 to 754, 759: private collections ◆ 679 to 685, 758 to 762, 764 to 768: private collections / a.r.r. ◆ 10, 66, 94, 124br, 286, 287, 398, 409: © Archives Photographiques, Paris / S.P.A.D.E.M. ◆ 11b: Archivio Böhm, Venice. ◆ 12, 285, 289t, 352, 353t, 355t: Museum of the City of New York. ◆ 13b, 97t, 472t: Museum voor Fotografie, Antwerp. ◆ 14, 17, 26t, 35b, 36, 37, 47b, 56br, 57, 71t, 76, 90, 95, 98, 100, 101, 107, 108, 109b, 118t, 126, 151b, 153, 160t, 178b, 179b, 180b, 202b, 218t, 218bl, 221, 222br, 223, 224, 226, 227t, 227b, 230t, 230b, 231, 253, 254-255, 343t, 365, 367b, 372: Bibliothèque Nationale, Paris. ◆ 16: Institut National de la Propriété Industrielle, Paris. ◆ 18t, 18b, 116: Biblioteca Nacional, Madrid. ◆ 20, 459b, 509: Musée Nicéphore Niépce, Chalon-sur-Saône. ◆ 21t, 21b, 134b, 146, 189, 190, 194, 240b, 375t, 380t, 386: Gernsheim Collection, Harry Ransom Humanities Research Center, University of Texas, Austin. ◆ 22, 27, 54t, 67b, 139, 159t, 162, 173, 176t, 193, 405t: J. Paul Getty Museum, Malibu. ◆ 24t, 29t, 60, 276t: Fox Talbot Museum, Lacock Abbey. ◆ 24b, 30, 31t, 31b, 55t, 67t, 68, 69, 78, 79, 133, 151t, 229t, 229b, 251b, 279, 298t, 301, 411, 412, 425b, 427t, 428t, 428b, 429b: Société Française de Photographie, Paris. ◆ 25, 26b: Musée National des Techniques, C.N.A.M., Paris. ◆ 28, 158, 201, 212: Stadtmuseum, Munich. ◆ 29b: Oxford Museum of the History of Science. ◆ 33, 232, 561b, 584b: George R. Rinhart Collection. ◆ 39, 42, 47t, 49b, 50, 55tr, 55bl, 104, 106, 128br, 136, 140t, 157t, 196, 214b, 239tl, 316tl, 346, 356t, 357, 371, 375b, 382, 388t, 388b, 393t, 410, 419, 420b, 433t, 433b, 471t, 517, 558b, 604: International Museum of Photography at George Eastman House, Rochester. ◆ 34: International Museum of Photography at George Eastman House, Rochester / gift of Z. P. Mackay. ◆ 35t: Musée Historique, Mulhouse, photo C. Kempf. ◆ 41, 52t, 52b: Uwe Scheid Collection. ◆ 40: Museum für Kunst und Gewerbe, Hamburg. ◆ 43t: New York Historical Society. ◆ 43b, 93b, 282t, 290t, 343, 353b, 763: Harry Ransom Humanities Research Center, University of Texas, Austin. ◆ 44: Maison de Balzac, Paris / Photothèque des Musées de la Ville de Paris. ◆ 45t, 55bd: Ruskin Galleries, Isle of Wight. ◆ 45b, 127tr, 171, 235t, 236b: Amon Carter Museum of Western Art, Fort Worth. ◆ 46: American Antiquarian Society, Worcester. ◆ 48, 360t, 756, 757: Musée Carnavalet, Paris. ◆ 49t: Matthew R. Isenburg Collection. ◆ 51: Massachusetts Historical Society, Boston. ◆ 52tr, 53: Collection © Stefan Richter, all rights reserved. ◆ 54b, 144, 199t, 283t, 492hg: Musées de Strasbourg. ◆ 56t, 71b, 74t, 75, 81, 113, 129, 203, 213, 240t, 270t, 292, 297b, 300b, 312t, 312b, 314, 315, 316tr, 317, 320, 321, 322, 322b, 323, 327 to 333, 392: Musée d'Orsay, Paris / R.M.N. ◆ 58, 74b, 164-165: Bibliothèque des Arts Décoratifs, Paris. ◆ 61, 278t, 414, 415b: National Museum of Photography, Film and Television, Bradford. ◆ 62: Monmouth Calotype. ◆ 63, 64, 65b, 195b: Hans P. Kraus Jr. ◆ 65t, 150, 348t, 348b, 351, 437b: Victoria and Albert Museum. ◆ 70: Y. Christ Collection. ◆ 72t: National Gallery of Canada, Ottawa. ◆ 73: Musée Ingres, Montauban. ◆ 80t: Höhere Graphische Bundes-Lehr und Versuchanstalt, Vienna. ◆ 80b: City Libraries, Edinburgh. ◆ 82: Piero Becchetti Collection. ◆ 83 to 89: Bibliothèque Municipale, Lille, assisted by the Centre Régional de la Photographie du Nord Pas-de-Calais. ◆ 97b: Bibliothèque de la Ville de Colmar, reproduction C. Kempf. ◆ 99, 154b, 184, 195t, 309, 518, 519: © Philip de Bay. ◆ 102: France Debuisson Collection. ◆ 105t: Archives Départementales, Haut-Rhin. ◆ 118b: National Library of Wales, Aberystwyth. ◆ 96, 119, 186, 188, 191, 291, 294, 295t, 295b, 296, 298b, 302b, 303, 304, 305, 306, 307, 318, 319b, 497: Royal Photographic Society, Bath. ◆ 121: Musée Toulouse Lautrec, Albi. ◆ 122: New Orleans Museum of Art. ◆ 123: Musée d'Unterlinden, Colmar / Archives Départementales, Haut-Rhin. ◆ 128g: Raymond Gid Collection. ◆ 127bd: Chicago Historical Society. ◆ 127g: Royal Archives, Windsor Castle. ◆ 128hd: Parrish Collection, Princeton University Library. ◆ 130, 134t, 239tr, 302t, 354b, 361b, 394, 514, 524, 525t, 525b: Library of Congress, Washington. ◆ 132: Musée de l'Armée, Paris. ◆ 138b, 174: Roger-Viollet Collection, Paris. ◆ 141, 172t, 215: New York Public Library. ◆ 142: Städtische Kunsthalle, Mannheim. ◆ 143: S. Kakou Collection. ◆ 152: Aberdeen Art Gallery. ◆ 155: Istituto di Fotografia Alpina Vittorio Sella, Biella. ◆ 156, 373: © Alinari-Giraudon. ◆ 166, 267, 268b, 269: Musée de l'Homme, Paris. ◆ 167: University of California, Los Angeles, Department of Special Collections.. ◆ 168t: Centre Canadien d'Architecture, Montreal. ◆ 168b: Denver Art Museum. ◆ 169, 170bl, 172b, 383: Fraenkel Gallery, San Francisco. ◆ 170t: Academy of Natural Sciences, Philadelphia. ◆ 177t, 183, 270t, 366: P. M. Richard Collection. ◆ 177b, 182b: Debuisson Collection. ◆ 192: Musée Victor Hugo, Paris. ◆ 197: Metropolitan Museum, New York. ◆ 198: H. Louvet Collection. ◆ 199b: Bibliothèque Administrative de la Ville de Paris. ◆ 204, 210, 757: Bibliothèque Historique de la Ville de Paris. ◆ 205: Museo Municipal, Madrid. ◆ 206-207, 206b, 207: Bibliothèque de l'École des Ponts et Chaussées, Paris. ◆ 209: Institut d'Architecture, Archives du XXe siècle, Paris. ◆ 211: © Studio Chevojon, Paris. ◆ 214t: Public Archives of Canada. ◆ 216: Yale University Library, Newhaven. ◆ 217, 218br, 219, 220t, 222t, 222bl, 252t, 252b, 260t: Bibliothèque de l'École Nationale Supérieure des Beaux-Arts, Paris. ◆ 233: Fondation Nationale de la Photographie, Lyons. ◆ 234: H. H. Bennett Studio Collection. ◆ 237b: Archives Alinari, Florence. ◆ 238b, 241t, 338t, 338b, 339, 425hg: © Association des Amis de Jacques-Henri Lartigue, Paris. ◆ 239bg: Bishop Museum, Honolulu. ◆ 241b: Jean Henry Collection. ◆ 244, 245t, 247b, 249b, 250, 251, 256, 274b: Musée Marey, Beaune. ◆ 245b, 441, 442, 448, 506b, 578t, 584t, 628t, 665, 722, 757/8 and 9: D.R. ◆ 246: Cinémathèque Française, Paris. ◆ 242, 247t, 248, 249t, 274t: Archives du Collège de France, Paris. ◆ 254b, 283, 284t, 284b: Science Museum, London. ◆ 255: Ernst-Mach Institut, Fribourg. ◆ 257t: Centro Studi Anton Giulio Bragaglia, Rome. ◆ 257b: Musée Rodin, Paris. ◆ 261, 262, 264b: from *Identités*, Paris, 1986 / D.R. ◆ 263: Musée National des Techniques, C.N.A.M. Paris. ◆ 265b: Royal Society of Medicine, London. ◆ 266b: Giorgio Colombo photo from the orginal in the Lombroso Collection. ◆ 268t, 275: Bibliothèque Centrale of the Museum d'Histoire Naturelle, Paris. ◆ 276b: Ezra Mack Gallery, New York. ◆ 280t: Deutsches Röntgen-Museum, Remscheid. ◆ 280b, 281: Deutsches Museum, Munich. ◆ 288hg and 288bd: London School of Economics. ◆ 288bg: with permission of Etude Beaussant Lefèvre, Paris. ◆ 288hd: August Strindbergsmuseet, Stockholm. ◆ 289b: Heimat und Bergbaumuseum, Freital. ◆ 290bl, 451, 508b, 516t, 520, 562, 571, 572, 585b, 596, 642: ©Ministère de la Culture, France. ◆ 290bd: ©Popperfoto. ◆ 297t: Museum of Fine Arts, Boston© gift of Miss Georgia O' Keeffe. ◆ 299, 342b, 619b: Prentenkabinet, Rijksuniversiteit, Leyden. ◆ 300t, 308: Museum für Kunst und Gewerbe, Hamburg. ◆ 313t: Art Museum, Princeton University© gift of Estate of Mina Turner. ◆ 319t: Art Museum, Princeton University© gift of Raymond C. Collins. ◆ 324, 325, 393b: Museum of Fine Arts, Boston. ◆ 326, 614: ©Aperture Foundation Inc., Paul Strand Archive. ◆ 336tl, 336hd: Antoine Salomon Collection / SPADEM. ◆ 337t: Galerie Isy Brachot, Brussels. ◆ 337b, 715t: ©ADAGP. ◆ 340, 341: Pierre Loti-Viaud Collection. ◆ 344t: Munch Museum, Oslo. ◆ 344b: Dr. François Emile-Zola Collection. ◆ 345: Museo Fortuny, Venice. ◆ 349: Mitchell Library, Glasgow. ◆ 350b: Birmingham Reference Library Collection. ◆ 354t, 593t: Archives Casasola. ◆ 355b: Christian Brandstätter Collection, Vienna. ◆ 356b: Milwaukee Art Museum, gift of Robert Mann. ◆ 358, 540t, 541, 615: ©Joan Munkacsi. ◆ 368: Edimedia, Paris. ◆ 370, 519b: National Portrait Gallery, London. ◆ 374: Burns Archives, Washington. ◆ 378: Archivio Fotografico Communale, Rome. ◆ 379, 502, 511b: Agfa Foto-Historama, Cologne. ◆ 380b: Art Gallery of Ontario. ◆ 389b, 390: © Universités de Paris, B.D.I.C., Hôtel National des Invalides, Paris. ◆ 391t, 402, 407, 446tl, 476, 522, 523, 523b, 663: Museum of Modern Art, New York. ◆ 391b: © S.P.A.D.E.M. ◆ 395, 396b: Museum of Fine Arts, Boston, Bill and Sandra Lane Collection. ◆ 396t: Madame Marcel Duchamp Collection. ◆ 397, 434, 467, 478t, 512t: Metropolitan Museum of Art, New York, Ford Motor Company Collection, gift of Ford Motor Co and John C. Waddell. ◆ 400, 404, 406, 408: Museum of Modern Art, New York, Abbott-Levy Collection, gift of Shirley C. Burden. ◆ 403, 447, 472b, 480t, 483, 668b: Art Institute of Chicago, Julien Levy Collection, gift of Jean Levy and Estate Julien Levy. ◆ 405b: Musée de l'Armée, Paris. ◆ 413: Fachhochschule, Cologne. ◆ 416, 469, 559, 736b, 738b: Galerie Michèle Chomette, Paris. ◆ 417: ©Gisèle Freund. ◆ 418: ©Horst P. Horst. ◆ 420: Polaroïd Collection, France. ◆ 421, 545: ©Kathleen Blumenfeld. ◆ 422t, 666t, 666b, 702, 703t: Pace / MacGill Gallery, New York. ◆ 422b: ©Pierre Bérenger. ◆ 423: Musée des Arts et Métiers, Paris, Photo Pascal Faligot. ◆ 424tr, 424tl, 425hd: from *The Studio*, 1908, D.R. ◆ 424b, 456, 488t, 490hg: Galerie Rudolf Kicken, Cologne. ◆ 426br, 427b: Albert Kahn Collections, Département des Hauts de Seine. ◆ 426t: Stadsmuseum, Stockholm. ◆ 426bg: New York Public Library, General Research and Humanities Division, Astor, Lenox and Tilden Foundation. ◆ 429hd: Metropolitan Museum of Art, Alfred Stieglitz Collection, 1955. ◆ 430, 454b, 678, 730, 735: Musée National d'Art Moderne, Paris. ◆ 432: Staatliche Museen Preussischer Kulturbesitz, Nationalgalerie, Berlin. ◆ 435: Museum Sztuki, Lodz. ◆ 436: Bibliothèque Forney, Paris. ◆ 439, 516b: ©Hattula Moholy-Nagy. ◆ 440b: Graphische Sammlung, Kunstgewerbemuseum, Zürich. ◆ 443: Musée Municipal, The Hague. ◆ 446tr, 554: ©TMR-ADAGP. ◆ 446b: ©with permission of Sotheby's, New York. ◆ 449, 595b: Museo Alinari / Zannier Collection, Florence. ◆ 450: ©Association des Amis de Maurice Tabard. ◆ 452t, 453t: Lucien Treillard Collection. ◆ 452b, 455, 733: ©Galerie Zabriskie, Paris. ◆ 453b: Lucien Treillard Collection/ TMR-ADAGP. ◆ 454t: private collection, D.R. ◆ 458: Museum of Fine Arts, Boston, Charles Amos Cummings Fund ©Hattula Moholy-Nagy. ◆ 459t: Museum of Modern Art, New York, M. and Mme John Spencer Collection. ◆ 460: Staatliche Museen Preussischer Kulturbesitz, Berlin. ©Hattula Moholy-Nagy. ◆ 461, 662bl, 709: Art Institute de Chicago, ◆ Julien Levy Coll. ©Hattula Moholy-Nagy. ◆ 462: International Museum of Photography at George Eastman House, Rochester. ©Hattula Moholy-Nagy. ◆ 463: Museum Moderner Kunst, Vienna. ◆ 465: ©Karl Blossfeldt Archiv- Ann und Jürgen Wilde, Zülpich. ◆ 466: Berlinische Galerie, Berlin. ◆ 468t, 504b, 510, 670t, 672, 675t: Museum Folkwang, Essen. ◆ 468b: Musée Municipal, The Hague. ◆ 470t: Museum of Modern Art, San Francisco, Mrs. Ferdinand C. Smith Collection. ◆ 470b: Bauhaus-Archiv, Berlin. ◆ 475: Municipal Museum, The Hague. ◆ 477: Museum of Modern Art, New York, gift of Dr. Iago Gladstone / Walker Evans Estate. ◆ 478b: Museum of Art, Philadelphia, gift of Mr. and Mrs. Robert A. Hauslohrer / Paul Strand Archive, Aperture Foundation. ◆ 479: ©Imogen Cunningham Trust, Berkeley. ◆ 480b: Museum of Art, Laguna Beach. ◆ 481: Center for Creative Photography, Tucson. ◆ 482: with permission of Time-Life. ◆ 484: Center for Creative Photography, Tucson / Trustees of Ansel Adams. ◆ 485: Art Institute of Chicago, gift of Arnold Crane / Walker Evans Estate. ◆ 486t: J. Paul Getty Museum. ©Center for Creative Photography, Arizona Board of Regents. ◆ 486b: Huntington Library and Art Gallery, San Marino. ◆ 487, 488b, 491: Galerie Morave, Brno. ◆ 489: Collection F.R.A.C. Aquitaine. ◆ 490tr, 490b, 492tr, 492bg and 492 br, 493: Museum of Decorative Arts, Prague. ◆ 494, 501, 585b: Kobal Collection, London. ◆ 495: Photomaton Collection. ◆ 496t: Photographic Archives, University of Louisville. ◆ 496b: ©Marc Ghuisoland. ◆ 498: Museum für Kunst und Gewerbe, Hamburg. ◆ 437t, 499t, 499b, 503, 505t, 565b, 593b, 437t: Rheinisches Bildarchiv, Cologne. ◆ 500: Sotheby's Belgravia, London. ◆ 505b, 506t, 507: © Lucien Treillard Collection / TMR-A.D.A.G.P. ◆ 511t, 512b: August Sander Archiv, Cologne. ◆ 513, 598, 599t, 616, 617: Henri Cartier-Bresson / Magnum. ◆ 521: ©Fortune Magazine, 1931, Time Warner Inc./ Cosmos, Paris. ◆ 526, 649: ©Wilma Wilcox. ◆ 527: Maurice Muller. ◆ 528: Musée Savoisien, Chambéry. ◆ 529: Andreas Brown Collection, J. Paul Getty Museum, Malibu. ◆ 534: ©Helmut Newton. ◆ 536, 537: ©Joanna Steichen. ◆ 538: ©1926 (renewed 1954) Condé Nast Publications Inc. ◆ 539: ©1928 (renewed 1956) Condé Nast Publications Inc. ◆ 541: ©Elisabeth Arden Co. ◆ 540b: ©Harper's Bazaar / ADAGP. ◆ 542, 546b: ©Horst P. Horst. ◆ 543: ©1939 (renewed 1967) Condé Nast Publications Inc. ◆ 544b: ©with permission of Sotheby's London. ◆ 544t: ©Condé Nast Publications Inc. ◆ 546t: ©Kathleen Blumenfeld and Condé Nast Publications Inc. ◆ 547: ©William Klein and Condé Nast Publications Inc. ◆ 548: ©Hiro ◆ 549: ©Bert Stern Productions Inc. ◆ 550: ©Sarah Moon. ◆ 551: ©Deborah Turbeville. ◆ 552: ©Helmut Newton. ◆ 553: ©Nick Knight, with the participation of Yannik Morisot. ◆ 556: Museum of Fine Arts, Houston. ◆ 557: ©Rosandra Masana. ◆ 558t: Galleria Martini e Ronchetti, Genoa. ◆ 560: ©Association des Amis de Maurice Tabard. ◆ 561t, 565: Christian Bouqueret Collection, Paris. ◆ 563: G. Ray Hawkins Gallery. ◆ 564: with permission of Vogue ©Condé Nast Publications Inc. ◆ 569, 577b, 671: ©Gilberte Brassaï. ◆ 570b: ©Nouveau Détective. ◆ 575: ©Life Magazine, Time Warner Inc. / Cosmos, Paris. ◆ 577t: ©John Heartfield-Archiv, Akademie der Künste, Berlin. ◆ 580: Photographic Archives, University of Louisville. ◆ 581: ©Edwynn Houk Gallery, Chicago. ◆ 582-583: ©Draeger. ◆ 586t, 586b: ©Ernst Haas / Magnum. ◆ 587, 612: ©Werner Bischof / Magnum. ◆ 588h and 588b: ©Marie Martin. ◆ 589: ©John Batho. ◆ 590: ©Robert Capa, Magnum / Life Magazine 1937, Time Warner Inc. / Cosmos, Paris. ◆ 592, 597t, 619t: © Robert Capa / Magnum. ◆ 594: ©Tim Gidal. ◆ 595: ©Alfred Eisenstaedt, Life Magazine, 1936, Time Warner Inc., Cosmos, Paris. ◆ 597b: Collection. Scott Hyde. ◆ 599b: H. F. Johnson Museum of Art, Cornell Univ., Ithaca / Emil Ghinger. ◆ 600t: ©Lee Miller Archives. ◆ 600b: Auschwitz Museum. ◆ 601, 603, 621, 633 to 639: ©W. Eugene Smith / Magnum. ◆ 602: ©Associated Press. ◆ 605: ©Don Mc Cullin / Magnum. ◆ 606: ©Gilles Caron / Contact Press Images. ◆ 607: ©Gilles Peress / Magnum. ◆ 608: ©Marc Riboud / Magnum. ◆ 609: ©Mary Ellen Mark Library, New York. ◆ 610: ©Christine Spengler. ◆ 611: ©Sebastiao Salgado/ Magnum. ◆ 618: Art Institute of Chicago, gift of Noya Brandt, 1985-850. ◆ 620, 622t: ©Robert Doisneau / Rapho. ◆ 622b: ©Mary Evans / Roger Mayne. ◆ 623: ©Ferdinando Scianna / Magnum. ◆ 624: ©E. van Moerkerken. ◆ 625: ©Willy Ronis / Rapho. ◆ 626t: ©Louise Izis. ◆ 626b: ©Johan van der Keuken. ◆ 627, 628b: ©E. Boubat. ◆ 629t: ©Mario Giacomelli. ◆ 629b: ©Chris Killip. ◆ 630t, 630b: ©Josef Koudelka / Magnum. ◆ 631: ©Raymond Depardon / Magnum. ◆ 632: ©Bernard Plossu ◆ 640, 644: ©William Klein. ◆ 643: ©Elliot Erwitt / Magnum. ◆ 645, 646: ©Pace / MacGill Gallery / Robert Frank. ◆ 647: ©David Vestal. ◆ 648: ©Walker Evans Estate ◆ 648: Laurence Miller Gallery / Helen Levitt. ◆ 650: ©Wright Morris. ◆ 651, 652: ©Sander Gallery / Lisette Model. ◆ 653t: Robert Miller Gallery, New York, ©Estate of Diane Arbus 1972. ◆ 653b: ©Estate of Garry Winogrand. ◆ 654t, 654b: ©Bruce Davidson / Magnum. ◆ 655, 657t: ©Lee Friedlander, with permission of the Zabriskie Gallery. ◆ 656, 706b: ©Lewis Baltz, with the help of Galerie Michèle Chomette. ◆ 657b: High Museum of Art, Atlanta, gift of Lucinda W. Bunnen. ◆ 659: ©Indiana University Art Museum. ◆ 659: ©Pace /MacGill Gallery / H. Callahan. ◆ 660, 668t, 669: ©Christopher Meatyard. ◆ 662t, 662bd: Museum of Fine Arts, Boston; gift of Miss Georgia O'Keeffe. ◆ 664: ©Minor White Archive, Princeton University / 1982 Trustees of Princeton University. ◆ 667t: Center for Creative Photography, Tucson ©1981 Historic New Orleans Collection. ◆ 667b: Center for Creative Photography, Tucson ©1984 Frederick Sommer. ◆ 670b: Center for Creative Photography, Tucson, ©1971, Wynn and Edna Bullock. ◆ 674: Kunsthalle, Bielefeld. ◆ 675b: ©Ralph Gibson; with the help of Galerie Agathe Gaillard, Paris. ◆ 676: Center for Creative Photography, Tucson, ©1981 Roy DeCarava. ◆ 677: ©Duane Michals. ◆ 686, 690: ©Shomei Tomatsu. ◆ 687: ©Daido Moriyama. ◆ 688t: ©Shôji Ueda. ◆ 688b: ©Nojima Collection, on loan to National Museum of Modern Art, Kyoto, with permission of the museum. ◆ 689: Hyogo Prefectural Museum of Modern Art. ◆ 691: ©Kikuji Kawada. ◆ 692: ©Eikoh Hosoe. ◆ 693b: ©Nobuyoshi Araki. ◆ 693b: ©Toshio Shibata. ◆ 694: ©Galerie Samuel Lallouz. ◆ 696: ©Patrick Faigenbaum, with permission of Sylviane de Decker Heftler. ◆ 697: ©Galerie Yvon Lambert. ◆ 698: ©Keichi Tahara. ◆ 699t: ©Véronique de Fenoÿl / Mission Photographique de la Datar. ◆ 699b: ©Tom Drahos. ◆ 700: ©Mark Cohen. ◆ 701: ©François Hers. ◆ 703b: ©Robert Miller Gallery, New York. ◆ 704: ©Jean-Louis Garnell / Mission Photographique de la Datar. ◆ 705t: Sophie Ristelhueber / Mission Photographique de la Datar. ◆ 705b: Gabriele Basilico / Mission Photographique de la Datar. ◆ 706t: ©Werner Hannapel / Mission Photographique de la Datar. ◆ 707: ©Laurence Miller Gallery, New York. ◆ 708: ©Dieter Appelt, with the assistance of Galerie Bouqueret-Lebon. ◆ Mary Reynolds Collection. ◆ 710: ©Joel-Peter Witkin. ◆ 711: F.R.A.C. Rhône-Alpes. ◆ 712: Stedelijk Van Abbemuseum, Eindhoven. ◆ 713: Stedelijk Museum, Amsterdam. ◆ 714, 716t: Galerie Liliane and Michel Durand-Dessert. ◆ 715b: Leeds City Galleries. ◆ 716b: Cabinet des Estampes, Geneva. ◆ 717: Collection F.R.A.C. Aquitaine. ◆ 718: Ludwig Forum für internationale Kunst, Aachen. ◆ 719, 720: Collection F.R.A.C. Lorraine. ◆ 721: ©Jan Groover, with the participation of Sylviane de Decker-Heftler. ◆ 723: ©Robert Adams, with the participation of Sylviane de Decker-Heftler. ◆ 724t: ©Jeff Wall. ◆ 724b: ©John Coplans, with the participation of Sylviane de Decker Heftler. ◆ 725: Galerie Farideh Cadot. ◆ 726: ©Denis Roche. ◆ 727: High Museum of Art, Atlanta; Bunnen Collection. ◆ 728: Galleria Civica d'Arte Moderna, Turin. ◆ 729: Museum of Art, Toledo. ◆ 732: ©Paul den Hollander. ◆ 734: ©Jeff Guess. ◆ 734: Galerie Stadler. ◆ 736t: Galerie Anthony d'Offay, London. ◆ 737: Galerie Crousel-Robelin-Bama. ◆ 738t: ©Marc Trivier. ◆ 739, 740, 741, 742, 743, 744, 745: Graphische Sammlung Staatsgalerie Stuttgart, Sammlung Dr. Rolf H. Krauss.